W9-CKM-453

Rand McNally
CONCISE
WORLD
ATLAS

Rand McNally
CONCISE
WORLD
ATLAS

Rand McNally & Company
Chicago • New York • San Francisco

Title page photo by Michel Tcherevkoff

CONCISE WORLD ATLAS

Copyright © 1987 by Rand McNally & Company
All rights reserved. No part of this publication
may be reproduced, stored in a retrieval system,
or transmitted, in any form or by any means —
electronic, mechanical, photocopying, recording,
or otherwise — without the prior written
permission of Rand McNally & Company.

Printed in the United States of America

Library of Congress Catalog Card Number: 87-42817

ISBN 0-528-83285-9

Contents

Using the Atlas ———————— vi

Reference Maps ——— 1–128

Map Symbols ———————— 1

The World and Special Regions ——— 2–7

The World ———————— 2
Polar Map of the World ——————— 4
Atlantic Ocean ———————— 5
Pacific Ocean ———————— 6
Antarctica ———————— 7

Europe ———————— 8–29

Europe and Western Asia ————— 8
British Isles ———————— 10
Ireland ———————— 11
England and Wales ——————— 12
Scotland and Northern England ——— 13
Norway, Sweden and Finland ——— 14
Denmark and Northern Germany ——— 15
France and the Low Countries ——— 16
Belgium, Netherlands, Luxembourg
   and Western Germany ————— 17
Germany, Austria and Switzerland —— 18
Central Germany ———————— 19
Alpine Regions ———————— 20
Switzerland ———————— 21
Spain and Portugal ——————— 22
Italy ———————— 23
Yugoslavia, Hungary, Romania
   and Bulgaria ———————— 24
Greece, Albania and Western Turkey — 25
Poland and Czechoslovakia ——— 26
Western Soviet Union ——————— 27
South Central Soviet Union ——— 28
Soviet Union ———————— 29

Asia ———————— 30–41

Asia ———————— 30
China, Mongolia, Korea,
   Japan and Taiwan ——————— 31
Northeastern China ——————— 32
Japan and Korea ———————— 33
Indonesia and the Philippines ——— 34
Kampuchea (Cambodia), Laos, Vietnam,
   Thailand and Malaysia ————— 35
India, Pakistan, Bangladesh, Burma
   and Sri Lanka ———————— 36
Central India and Nepal ————— 37
Middle East ———————— 38
Iran and Afghanistan ——————— 39
Turkey, Cyprus, Syria, Jordan,
   Israel and Lebanon ——————— 40
Israel and Northern Egypt ———— 41

Africa ———————— 42–49

Africa ———————— 42
Northeast Africa ———————— 43
Northwest Africa ———————— 44
West Africa ———————— 45
Equatorial Africa ———————— 46
East Africa ———————— 47
Central Africa ———————— 48
Southern Africa ———————— 49

Australia and Oceania ——— 50–52

Australia ———————— 50
Southeastern Australia
   and New Zealand ——————— 51
Pacific Islands ———————— 52

South America ——— 53–60

South America ———————— 53
Central and Southern Argentina
   and Chile ———————— 54
Bolivia, Paraguay, Northern Argentina
   and Chile ———————— 55
Uruguay and Southern Brazil ——— 56
Eastern Brazil ———————— 57
Peru and Ecuador ———————— 58
Guyana, Suriname, French Guiana
   and Northern Brazil ————— 59
Colombia and Venezuela ———— 60

North America ——————— 61–127

North America ———————— 61
Central America ———————— 62
Mexico ———————— 63
West Indies ———————— 64
Caribbean Islands ——————— 65

Canada ———————— 66

Alberta ——— 68   Newfoundland — 72
British   Ontario ——— 73
   Columbia —— 69   Quebec ——— 74
Manitoba —— 70   Saskatchewan — 75
Maritime
   Provinces —— 71

United States of America ——— 76

Alabama ——— 78   Montana ——— 103
Alaska ——— 79   Nebraska ——— 104
Arizona ——— 80   Nevada ——— 105
Arkansas ——— 81   New Hampshire 106
California ——— 82   New Jersey — 107
Colorado ——— 83   New Mexico — 108
Connecticut —— 84   New York ——— 109
Delaware ——— 85   North Carolina 110
Florida ——— 86   North Dakota — 111
Georgia ——— 87   Ohio ——— 112
Hawaii ——— 88   Oklahoma —— 113
Idaho ——— 89   Oregon ——— 114
Illinois ——— 90   Pennsylvania 115
Indiana ——— 91   Rhode Island — 116
Iowa ——— 92   South Carolina 117
Kansas ——— 93   South Dakota — 118
Kentucky ——— 94   Tennessee —— 119
Louisiana ——— 95   Texas ——— 120
Maine ——— 96   Utah ——— 121
Maryland ——— 97   Vermont ——— 122
Massachusetts — 98   Virginia ——— 123
Michigan ——— 99   Washington — 124
Minnesota —— 100   West Virginia — 125
Mississippi — 101   Wisconsin —— 126
Missouri ——— 102   Wyoming ——— 127

North Polar Regions ———————— 128

Index to World Reference Maps — 129–224

Introduction to the Index
   and List of Abbreviations ———— 129
Index to World Reference Maps ——— 130

Using the Atlas

Maps and Atlases

Mapmaking appears to have had its origins in the earliest ages of human history. People of all cultures have needed maps, and artifacts show they possessed the skill to draw them. The ease with which almost anyone can sketch simple directions lends credibility to the assumption that maps have been around a long time. They have always played an important and unique role in presenting information about the world — its routes, territories, and the lay of the land.

Some of the earliest maps are those defining territory and ownership. Dating from the second and first millenia B.C., the rock carving map of the Val Camonica, Italy, in figure 1 shows stepped square fields, paths, rivers, and houses. Elegant as well as useful maps have been produced by many cultures. In figure 2, the Mexican map of the Tepetlaoztoc Valley, drawn in 1583, marks hills with wavy lines and roads with footprints between parallel lines. The methods and materials used to create these maps were dependent upon the technology available, and their accuracy suffered considerably, whereas modern maps are highly accurate, benefiting from our ever-increasing technological knowledge. Satellite imagery, shown in figure 3, now furnishes current, highly precise material from which maps such as that in figure 4 may be created or updated.

In the 1500s Gerardus Mercator, a Flemish cartographer, coined the word *atlas* to describe a collection of maps. The atlas is unique among reference publications because only it, with its maps, actually shows *where* things are located in the world. As a dictionary defines words, as an encyclopedia defines things, an atlas graphically defines the world. Only on a map can the countries, cities, roads, rivers, and lakes covering a vast area be simultaneously viewed in their relative locations. Routes between places can be traced, trips planned, boundaries of neighboring states and countries examined, distances between places measured, the meandering of rivers and streams and the sizes of lakes visualized — and remote places imagined.

figure 1

figure 3

figure 2

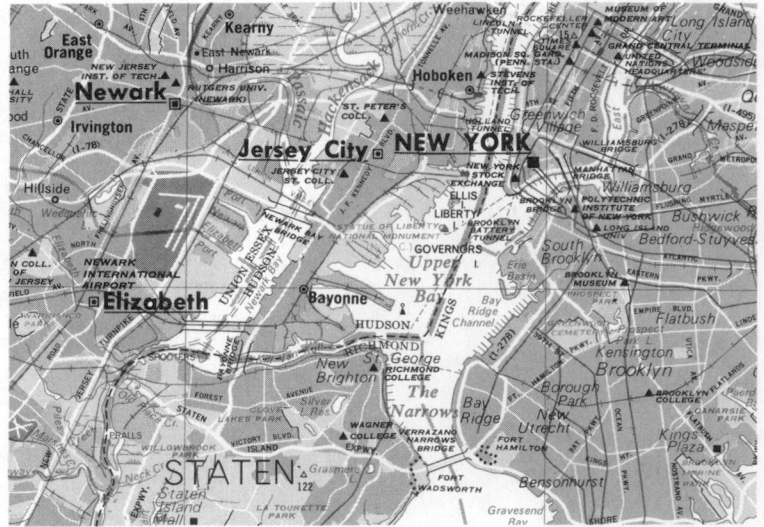
figure 4

Sequence of the Maps

The world is made up of seven major land-masses: the continents of Europe, Asia, Africa, Australia, South America, North America, and Antarctica (figure 5). To allow for the inclusion of detail, each continent is broken down into a series of maps, and this grouping is arranged so that as consecutive pages are turned, a continuous and successive part of the continent is shown. Larger-scale maps are used for regions of greater detail (having many cities, for example) or for areas of global significance.

The continental sequence of the maps is as follows: Europe (traditionally first in atlases), Asia (connected to Europe and forming the Eurasian landmass), Africa, Australia and Oceania, South America, and North America.

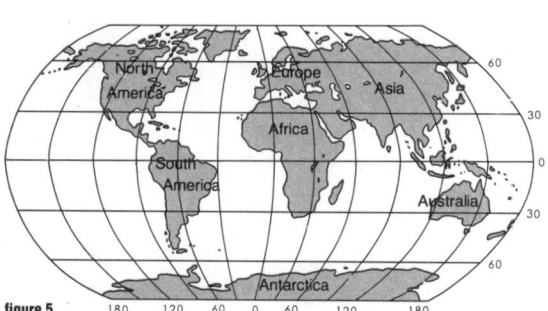

figure 5

Getting the Information

An atlas can be used for many purposes, from planning a trip to finding hot spots in the news and supplementing world knowledge. But to realize the full potential of an atlas, the user must be able to:

1. Find places on the maps
2. Measure distances
3. Determine directions
4. Understand map symbols

Finding Places

One of the most common and important tasks facilitated by an atlas is finding the *location* of a place in the world. A river's name in a book, a city mentioned in the news, or a vacation spot may prompt your need to know where the place is located. The illustrations and text below explain how to find Benguela, Angola.

1. Look up the place-name in the index at the back of the atlas. Benguela, Angola, can be found on the map on page 48, and it can be located on the map by the letter-number key *D1* (figure 6).

Benevento, Italy	D5	23
Benevolence, Ga., U.S.	E2	87
Benewah, co., Id., U.S.	B2	89
Benezett, Pa., U.S.	D5	115
Benfeld, Fr.	A3	20
Bengal, Ok., U.S.	C6	113
Bengal, hist reg., Asia	D8	36
Bengal, Bay of, b., Asia	F8	36
Ben Gardane, Tun.	C7	44
Bengbu, China	E8	31
Benghazi (Banghāzī), Libya	C4	43
Bengkalis, Indon.	E2	34
Bengkalis, i., Indon.	L5	35
Bengkulu, Indon.	F2	34
Bengo, dept., Ang.	C1	48
Bengough, Sk., Can.	H3	75
Benguela, Ang.	D1	48
Benguela, dept., Ang.	D1	48
Benham, Ky., U.S.	D7	94
Ben Hill, co., Ga., U.S.	E3	87
Beni, Nig.	D7	45
Beni, Zaire	A4	48
Beni, dept., Bol.	B2	55
Beni, stm., Bol.	B2	55
Béni Abbas, Alg.	C4	44

Benzonia, Mi., U.S.		
Beo, Indon.		
Béoumi, I.C.		
Beowawe, Nv., U.S.		
Beppu, Japan		
Beqa, i., Fiji		
Beqa Passage, strt., Fiji		
Bequia, i., St. Vin.		
Berach, stm., India		
Berati, Alb.		
Berau, F.R.Ger.		
Berau Bay, b., Indon.		
Berbera, Som.		
Berbérati, Cen. Afr. Rep.		
Berbice, stm., Guy.		
Berceto, Italy		
Bercher, Switz.		
Berchogur, Sov. Un.		
Berchtesgaden, F.R.Ger.		
Berck, Fr.		
Berclair, Tx., U.S.		
Berdichev, Sov. Un.		
Berdsk, Sov. Un.		
Berdyansk, Sov. Un.		
Berea, Ky., U.S.		
Berea, Oh., U.S.		

figure 6

2. Turn to the map of Central Africa on page 48. Note that the letters A through E and the numbers 1 through 7 appear in the margins of the maps.

3. To find Benguela on the map, place your left index finger on D and your right index finger on 1. Move your left finger across the map and your right finger into the map. Your fingers will meet in the area in which Benguela is located (figure 7).

figure 7

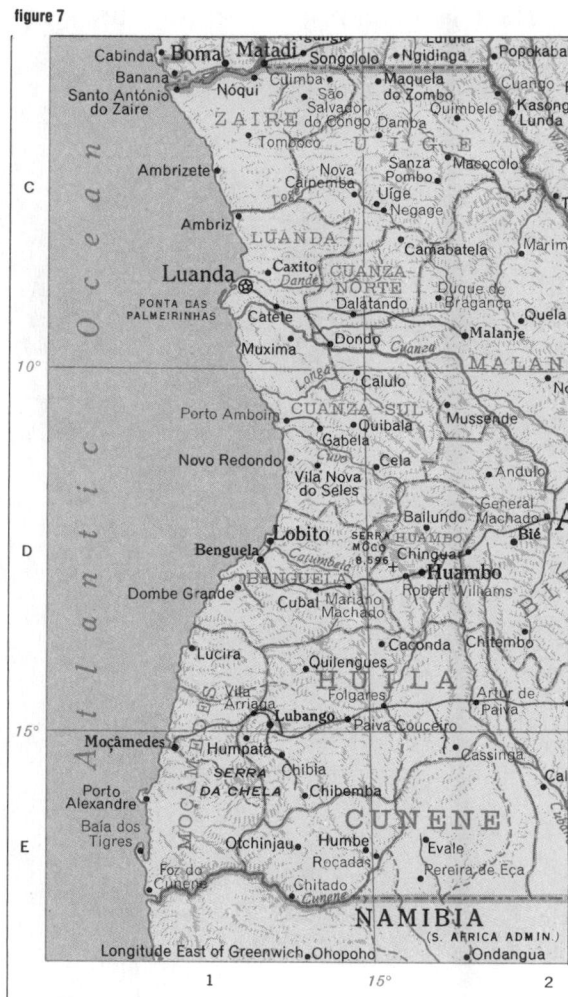

Measuring Distances

In planning trips, determining the distance between two places is essential, and an atlas can help in travel preparation. For instance, to determine the approximate distance between Paris and Rouen, France, follow these three steps:

1. Lay a slip of paper on the map on page 16 so that its edge touches the two cities. Adjust the paper so one corner touches Rouen. Mark the paper directly at the spot where Paris is located (figure 8).

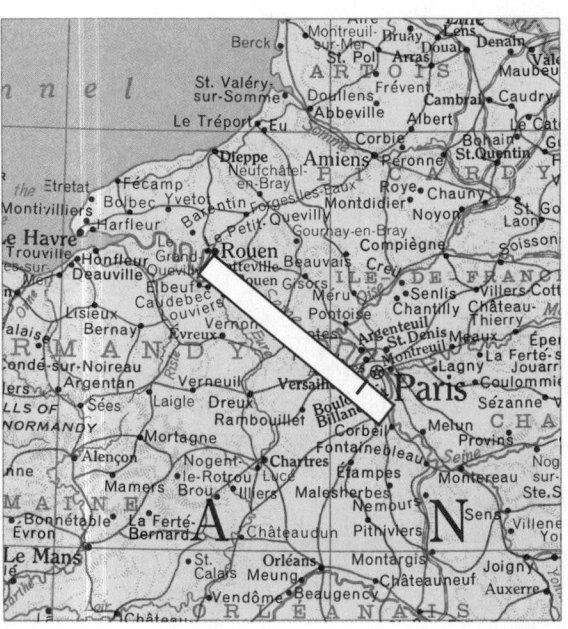

figure 8

2. Place the paper along the scale of statute miles beneath the map. Position the corner at 0 and line up the edge of the paper along the scale. The pencil mark on the paper indicates Rouen is between 50 and 75 miles from Paris (figure 9).

3. To find the exact distance, move the paper to the left so that the pencil mark is at 50 on the scale. The corner of the paper stands in the fourth 5-mile unit on the scale. This means that the two towns are 50 miles plus 15 miles plus 2 miles, or 67 miles, apart (figure 10).

figure 9

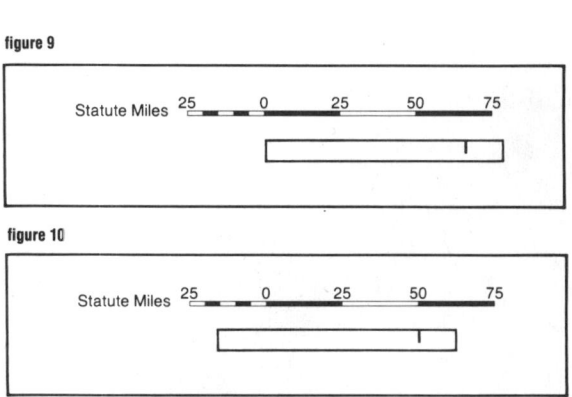

figure 10

Statute Miles 25   0   25   50   75

The scale relationship of the map to the earth may also be expressed as a ratio, for example, 1:1,000,000 (one to one million). The map unit in the ratio is always given as one, and the number of similar units the map unit represents on the earth's surface is written after the colon. Thus for a 1:1,000,000 map, 1 inch on the map represents 1,000,000 inches on the earth's surface. In order to determine how many miles on the earth 1 inch on the map represents, divide 63,360 (the number of inches in one mile) into 1,000,000. This results in the written scale for a 1:1,000,000 map being stated as, 1 inch (on the map) = 16 miles (on the earth).

Determining Directions

Most of the maps in the atlas are drawn so that when oriented for normal reading north is at the top of the map, south is at the bottom, west is at the left, and east is at the right. Most maps have a series of lines drawn across them — the lines of latitude and longitude. Lines of latitude, or parallels of latitude, are drawn east and west. Lines of longitude, or meridians of longitude, are drawn north and south (figure 11).

Parallels and meridians appear as either curved or straight lines. For example, in the section of the map of Europe in figure 12, the parallels of latitude appear as curved lines. The meridians of longitude are straight lines that come together toward the top of the map.

Latitude and longitude lines help locate places on maps. Parallels of latitude are numbered in degrees north and south of the *Equator*. Meridians of longitude are numbered in degrees east and west of a line called the *Prime Meridian*, running through Greenwich, England, near London. Any place on earth can be located by the latitude and longitude lines running through it.

To determine directions or locations on maps, you must use the parallels and meridians. For example, suppose you want to know which city is farther north, Bergen, Norway, or Stockholm, Sweden. The map in figure 12 shows that Stockholm is south of the 60° parallel of latitude and Bergen is north of it. This means that Bergen is farther north than Stockholm. By looking at the meridians of longitude, you can determine which city is farther east. Bergen is approximately 5° east of the 0° meridian (Prime Meridian), and Stockholm is almost 20° east of it. This means that Stockholm is farther east than Bergen.

Understanding Map Symbols

In a very real sense, the whole map is a symbol, representing the world or a part of it. It is a reduced representation of the earth; each of the world's features — cities, rivers, etc. — is represented on the map by a symbol. Map symbols may take the form of points, such as dots or stars (often used for cities, capital cities, or points of interest), or lines (roads, rivers, railroads). Symbols may also occupy an area, showing extent of coverage (states, forests, deserts). They seldom look like the feature they represent and therefore must be identified and interpreted. For instance, the maps in this atlas show and differentiate political units (countries, states) with color. The political units are further defined by a heavy line depicting their boundaries. Neither the colors nor the boundary lines are actually found on the surface of the earth, but because countries and states are such important political components of the world, strong symbols are used to represent them.

The legend on page 1 identifies the symbols used in this atlas.

figure 12

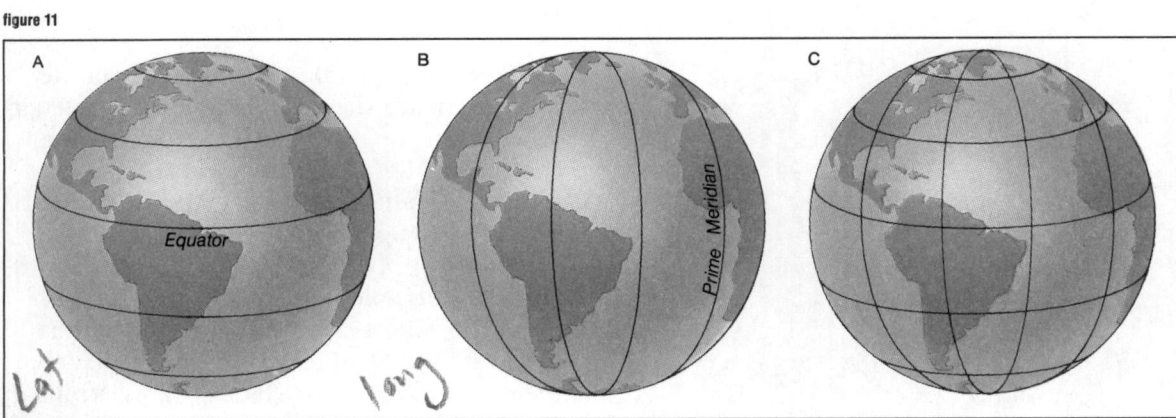

figure 11

Reference Maps

MAP SYMBOLS

CULTURAL FEATURES

Political Boundaries

▬▬▬ International

───── Secondary (State, province, etc.)

───── County

Populated Places

Cities, towns, and villages

·•••●● Symbol size represents population of the place

Chicago
Gary
Racine
Glenview
Edgewood

Type size represents relative importance of the place.

▱ Corporate area of large U.S. and Canadian cities and urban area of other foreign cities

 **Major Urban Area**
Area of continuous commercial, industrial, and residential development in and around a major city

○ Community within a city

⊛ Capital of major political unit

☆ Capital of secondary political unit

◉ Capital of U.S. state or Canadian province

◦ County Seat

▲ Military Installation

☉ Scientific Station

Miscellaneous

▤ National Park

▫ National Monument

▱ Provincial Park

▭ Indian Reservation

△ Point of Interest

∴ Ruins

■ ⛩ Buildings

⬭ Race Track

───── Railroad – International Maps

─┼──┼─ Tunnel

┄┄┄┄ Underground or Subway

⚓ Dam

Bridge

Dike

───── Highway – U.S. and Canadian Maps

───── Railroad – U.S. and Canadian Maps

LAND FEATURES

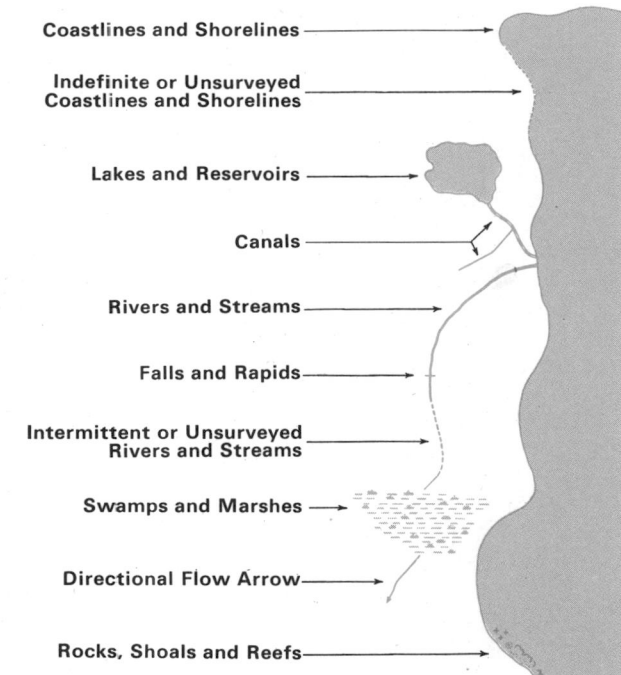

Ranges →

Peaks →

Passes → LITTLE PASS

Point of Elevation above sea level → 8,520 FT.

Escarpments, Bluffs, Cliffs, and Plateaus → PLATEAU

Glaciers →

Volcanoes →

Lava Flows →

Sand Dunes →

Deserts →

WATER FEATURES

Coastlines and Shorelines →

Indefinite or Unsurveyed Coastlines and Shorelines →

Lakes and Reservoirs →

Canals →

Rivers and Streams →

Falls and Rapids →

Intermittent or Unsurveyed Rivers and Streams →

Swamps and Marshes →

Directional Flow Arrow →

Rocks, Shoals and Reefs →

TYPE STYLES USED TO NAME FEATURES

A S I A	Continent	PANTELLERIA (ITALY) Country of which unit is a dependency in parentheses	UINTA DESERT Major Terrain Features
DENMARK CANADA	Country, State, or Province	SRI LANKA (CEYLON) Former or alternate name	MT. MORIAH Individual Mountain
BÉARN	Region, Province, or Historical Region	Rome (Roma) Local or alternate city name	STROMBOLI NUNIVAK Island or Coastal Feature
		Naval Air Station Military Installation	Ocean Lake River Canal Hydrographic Features
CROCKETT	County	MESA VERDE SAN XAVIER National Park or Monument, Provincial Park, Indian Res.,	

Note: Size of type varies according to importance and available space. Letters for names of major features are spread across the extent of the feature.

THE INDEX REFERENCE SYSTEM

Place	Location	Index Key	Page
Cadillac, Que., Can.		*h11	73
Cadillac, Sask., Can.		H2	70
Cadillac, Fr.		E3	14
Cadillac, Wexford, Mich.		B4	90
Cadiz, San Bernardino, Calif.		E6	82
Cadiz, Trigg, Ky.		D2	94
Cadron, creek, Ark.		B3	81
Caen, Fr.		C3	14
Caetité, Braz.		D2	57
Calcutta, India		D8	39
Cambridge, Eng.		B8	12
Catania, It.		F5	21
Ceará, state, Braz.		C3	57
Chamblee, DeKalb, Ga.		h8	87
Chambly, Que., Can.		D4	73
Chambord, Que., Can.		A5	73
Champagne, former prov., Fr.		C5	14
Champaign, Champaign, Ill.		B4	90
Champdore, lake, Que., Can.		g8	75
Champerico, Guat.		C2	62
Champéry, Switz.		D2	19
Champex, Switz.		D3	19
Champigneulles, Fr.		F6	15
Champion, Chase, Nebr.		D4	103
Champlain, co., Que., Can.		B4	73
Champlain, lake, N.Y., Vt.		B2	120
Champotón, Mex.		D6	63
Changchou, China		E8	34
Chanthaburi, Thai.		F5	38
Chaparral, Col.		C2	60
Charleville-Mézières, Fr.		C6	14
Chatham, Eng.		C8	12
Chiapa de Corzo, Mex.		D6	63
Chiapas, state, Mex.		D6	63
Chiba, Jap.		I10, n19	37
Chiba, pref., Jap.		*I10	37
Chibemba, Ang.		E1	48
Chibougamau, Que., Can.		k12	73
Chicago, Cook, Ill.		B4	90
Chichaoua, Mor.		C3	44
Chichen Itzá, ruins, Mex.		C7	63
Chichester, Eng.		D7	12
Chickasaw, co., Iowa		A5	92
Chiclana, Sp.		D2	20
Chiclayo, Peru		C2	58
Columbus, Franklin, Ohio		C3	111

The indexing system used in this atlas is based upon the conventional pattern of parallels and meridians used to indicate latitude and longitude. The index samples beside the map indicate that the cities of *Chicago, Cadillac,* and *Champaign* are all located in *B4.* Each index key letter, *in this case "B,"* is placed between corresponding degree numbers of latitude in the vertical borders of the map. Each index key number, *in this case "4,"* is placed between corresponding degree numbers of longitude in the horizontal borders of the map. Crossing of the parallels above and below the index letter with the meridians on each side of the index number forms a confining "box" in which the given place is certain to be located. It is important to note that location of the place may be anywhere in this confining "box."

Insets on many foreign maps are indexed independently of the main maps by separate index key letters and figures. All places indexed to these insets are identified by the lower case reference letter in the index key. A diamond-shaped symbol in the margin of the map is used to separate the insets from the main map and also to separate key letters and numbers where the spacing of the parallels and meridians is great.

Place-names are indexed to the location of the city symbol. Political divisions and physical features are indexed to the location of their names on the map.

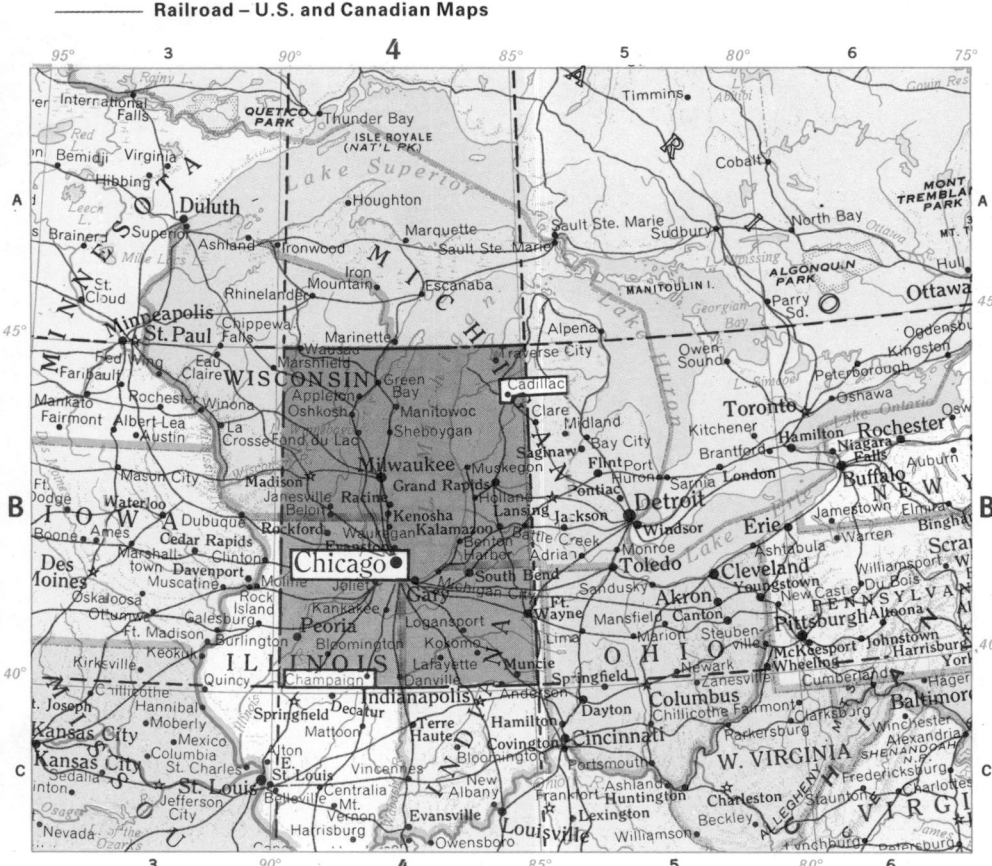

COMPARATIVE WORLD TIME
(Legal Clock Time)

In comparing the time of one zone with another, consider the zone numbers as hours, then by subtracting find the difference in time. The lower zone number represents the earlier hour and the higher zone number the later hour. (If the difference is greater than 12 hours, subtract this difference from 24 hours to find the nearest time difference.)

Antarctica has no legal time.

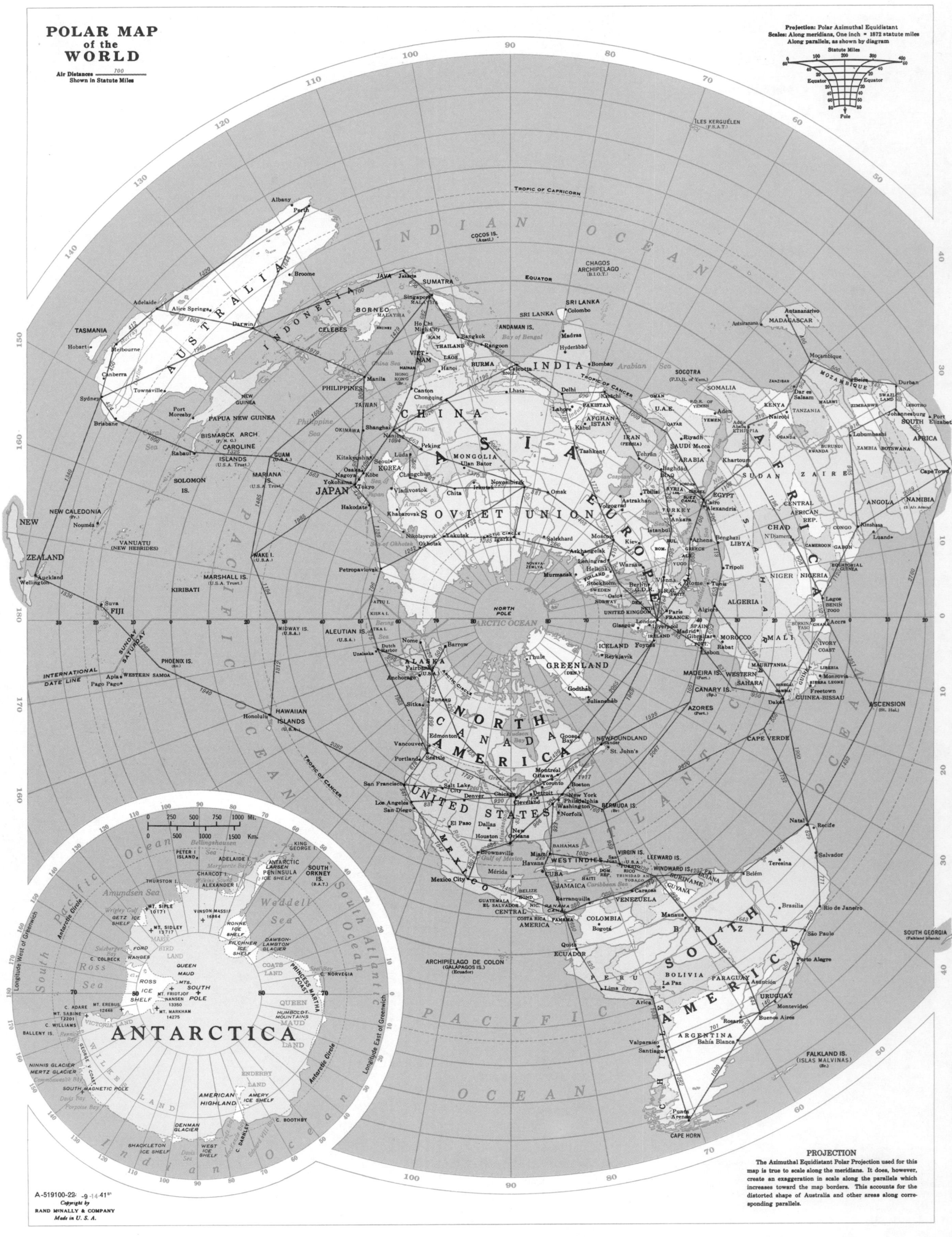

Polar Map of the WORLD

Air Distances — 700 — Shown in Statute Miles

Projection: Polar Azimuthal Equidistant
Scales: Along meridians, One inch = 1872 statute miles
Along parallels, as shown by diagram

ANTARCTICA

PROJECTION

The Azimuthal Equidistant Polar Projection used for this map is true to scale along the meridians. It does, however, create an exaggeration in scale along the parallels which increases toward the map borders. This accounts for the distorted shape of Australia and other areas along corresponding parallels.

A-519100-22· -9 -14 41⁵¹
Copyright by
RAND McNALLY & COMPANY
Made in U. S. A.

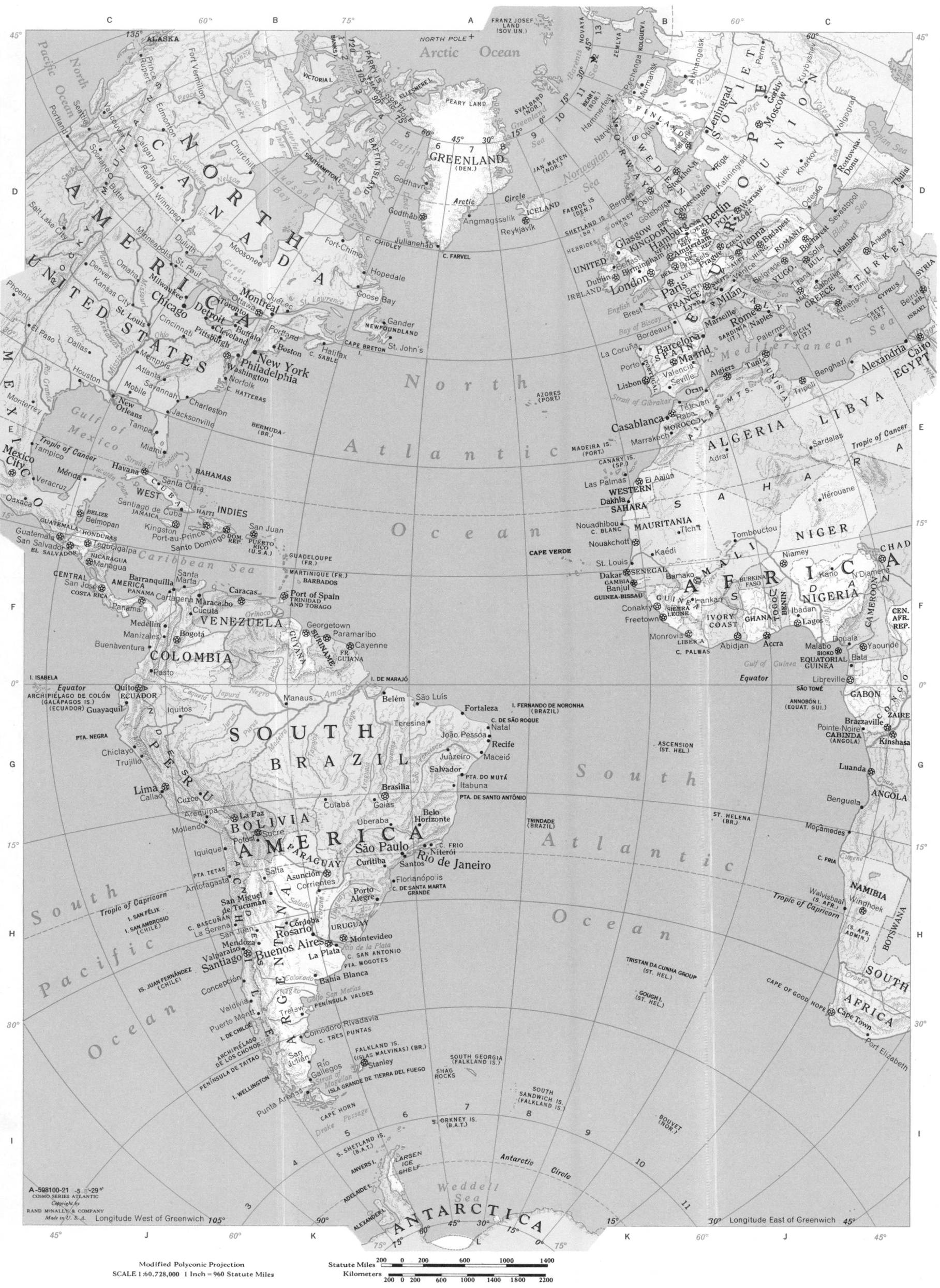

Modified Polyconic Projection
SCALE 1:60,728,000   1 Inch = 960 Statute Miles

Statute Miles
200 0   200   600   1000   1400
Kilometers
200 0   200   600 1000 1400 1800 2200

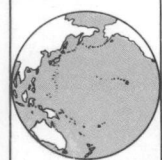

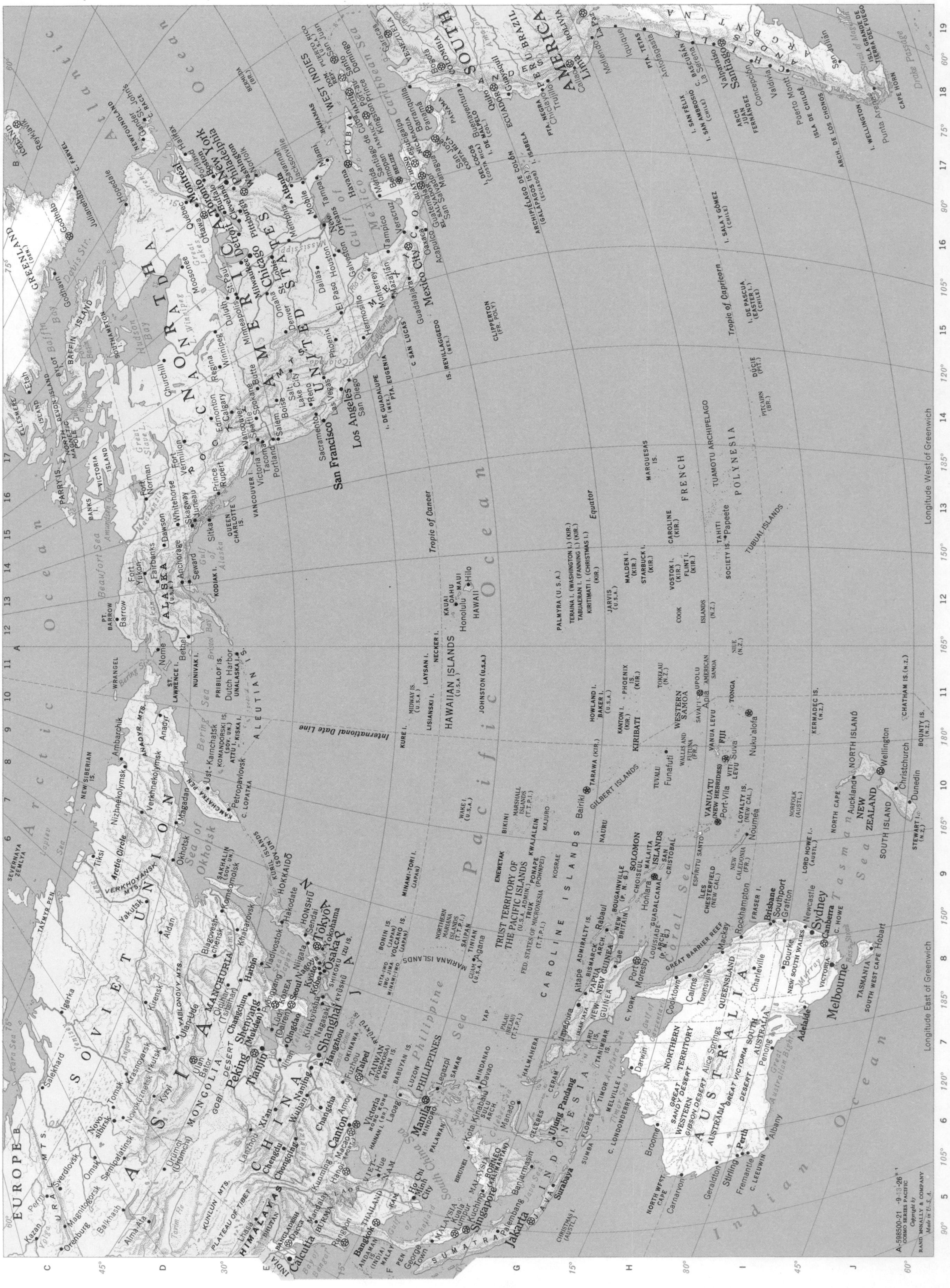

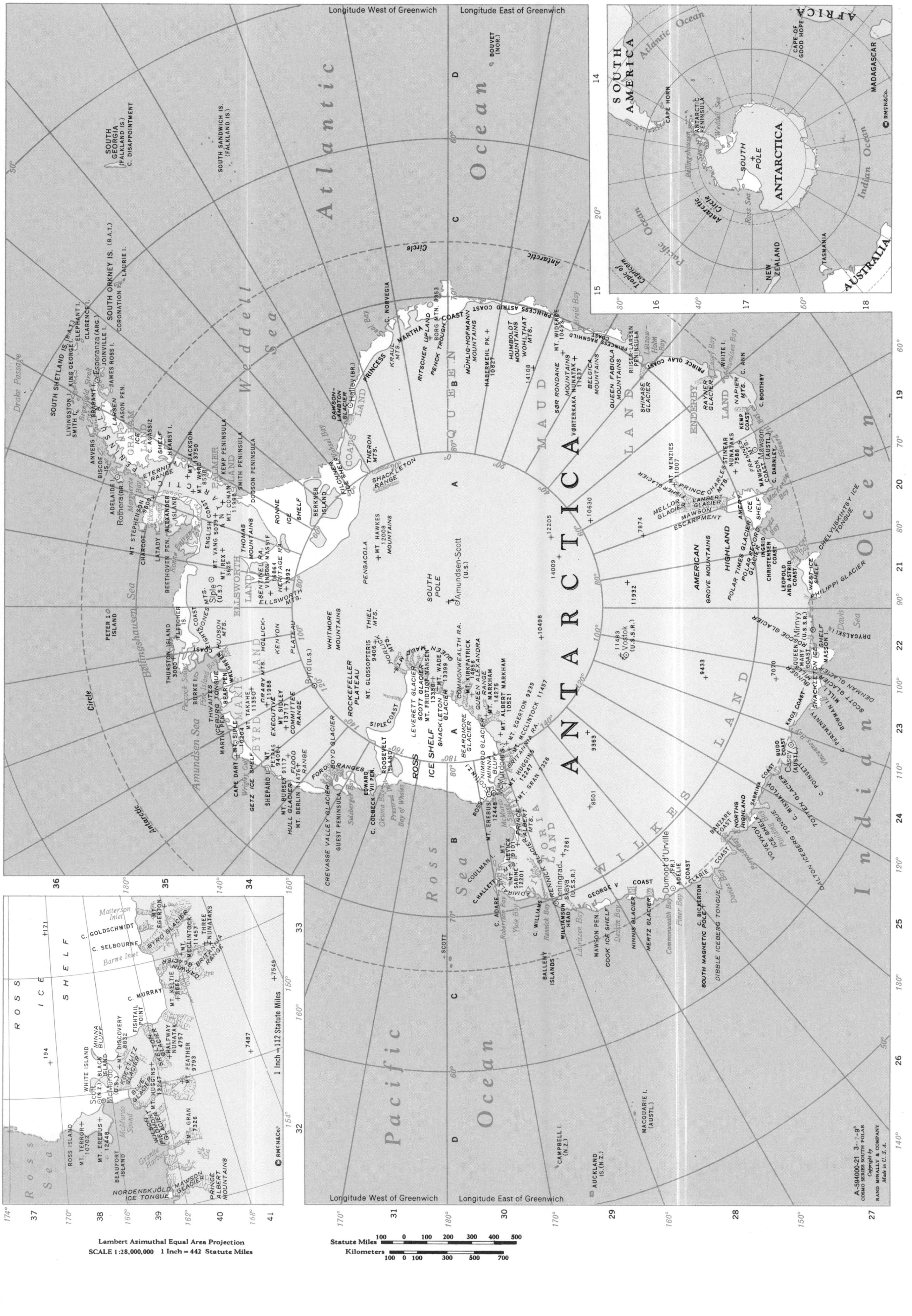

SOVIET UNION

RUSSIAN SOVIET FEDERATIVE SOCIALIST REPUBLIC

WEST SIBERIAN LOWLAND

CENTRAL SIBERIAN UPLANDS

KAZAKSTAN

CHINA

MONGOLIA

IRAN (PERSIA)

AFGHANISTAN

PAKISTAN

TURKEY

SYRIA

IRAQ

SAUDI ARABIA

JORDAN

LEBANON

KUWAIT

TURKMEN S.S.R.

UZBEK

KARA-KUM DESERT

KYZYL-KUM DESERT

DASHT-E KAVIR

DASHT-E LUT

PLATEAU OF IRAN

HINDU KUSH

TIEN SHAN

URAL MOUNTAINS

CAUCASUS MOUNTAINS

ZAGROS MOUNTAINS

ELBURZ MOUNTAINS

Kara Sea

Barents Sea

White Sea

Caspian Sea

Black Sea

Sea of Azov

Aral Sea

Lake Balkhash

Persian Gulf

Arabian Sea

Arctic Ocean

Novaya Zemlya

Moscow (Moskva)

Leningrad

Gorkiy

Kharkov

Volgograd

Rostov-na-Donu

Baku

Tbilisi

Yerevan

Tashkent

Samarkand

Tehran

Baghdad

Damascus (Dimashq)

Beirut (Bayrūt)

Karachi

Kabul

Mashhad

Esfahān (Isfahān)

Shirāz

Mosul (Al Mawşil)

Aleppo (Halab)

Basra (Al Başrah)

Kuwait

Tabrīz

Arkhangelsk

Perm

Sverdlovsk

Chelyabinsk

Omsk

Novosibirsk

Karaganda

Alma-Ata

Frunze

Ashkhabad

Krasnovodsk

Astrakhan

Saratov

Kazan

Ufa

Orenburg

Kustanay

Petropavlovsk

Semipalatinsk

Yenisey (river)

Ob (river)

Volga (river)

Tigris (river)

Euphrates (river)

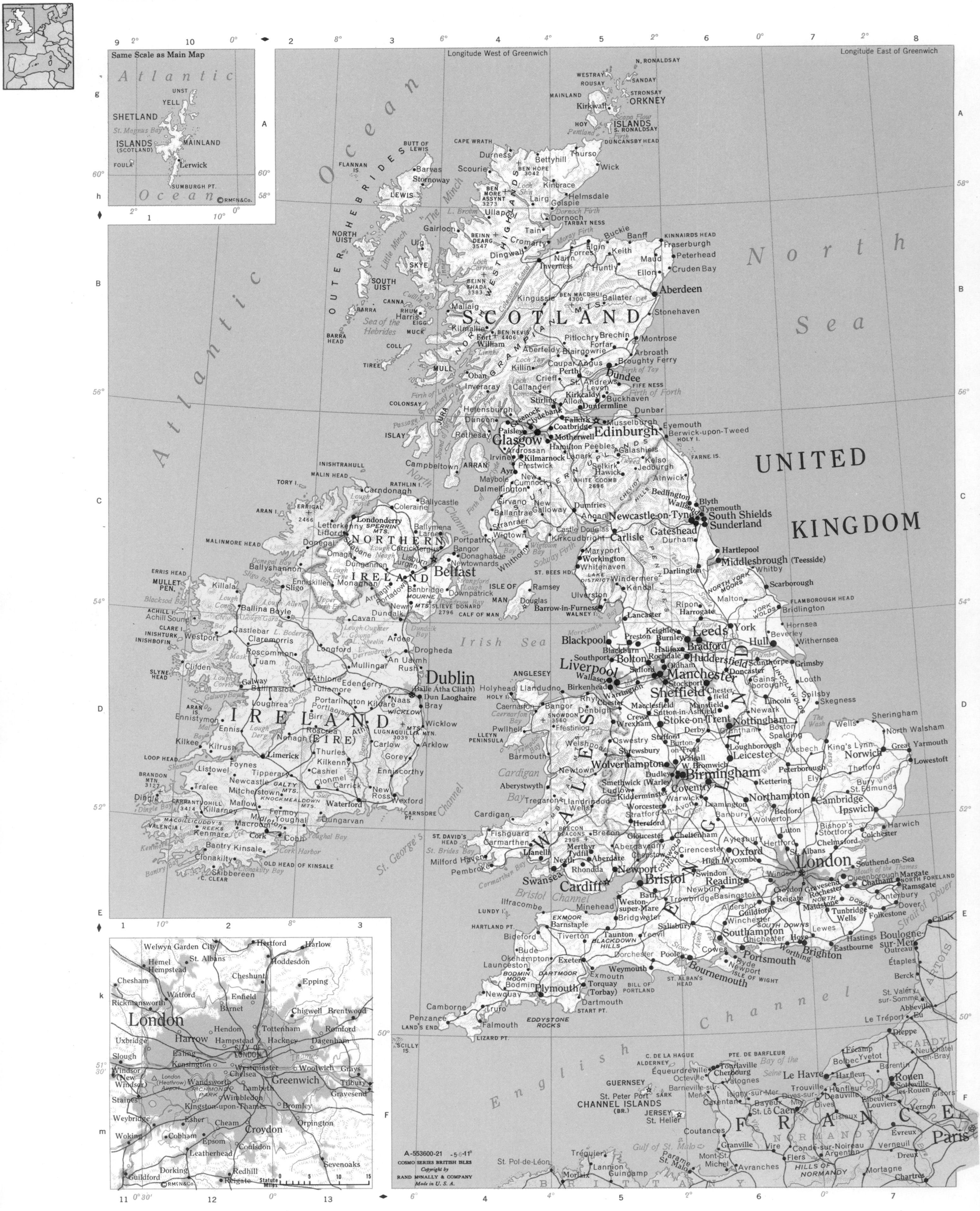

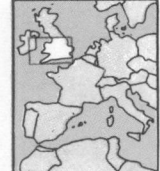

COSMO SERIES SCOTLAND
Copyright by
RAND McNALLY & COMPANY
Made in U.S.A.
A-553500-21--3 8°

Lambert Conformal Conic Projection
SCALE 1 : 2,000,000 1 Inch = 32 Statute Miles

Statute Miles
Kilometers

Longitude West of Greenwich

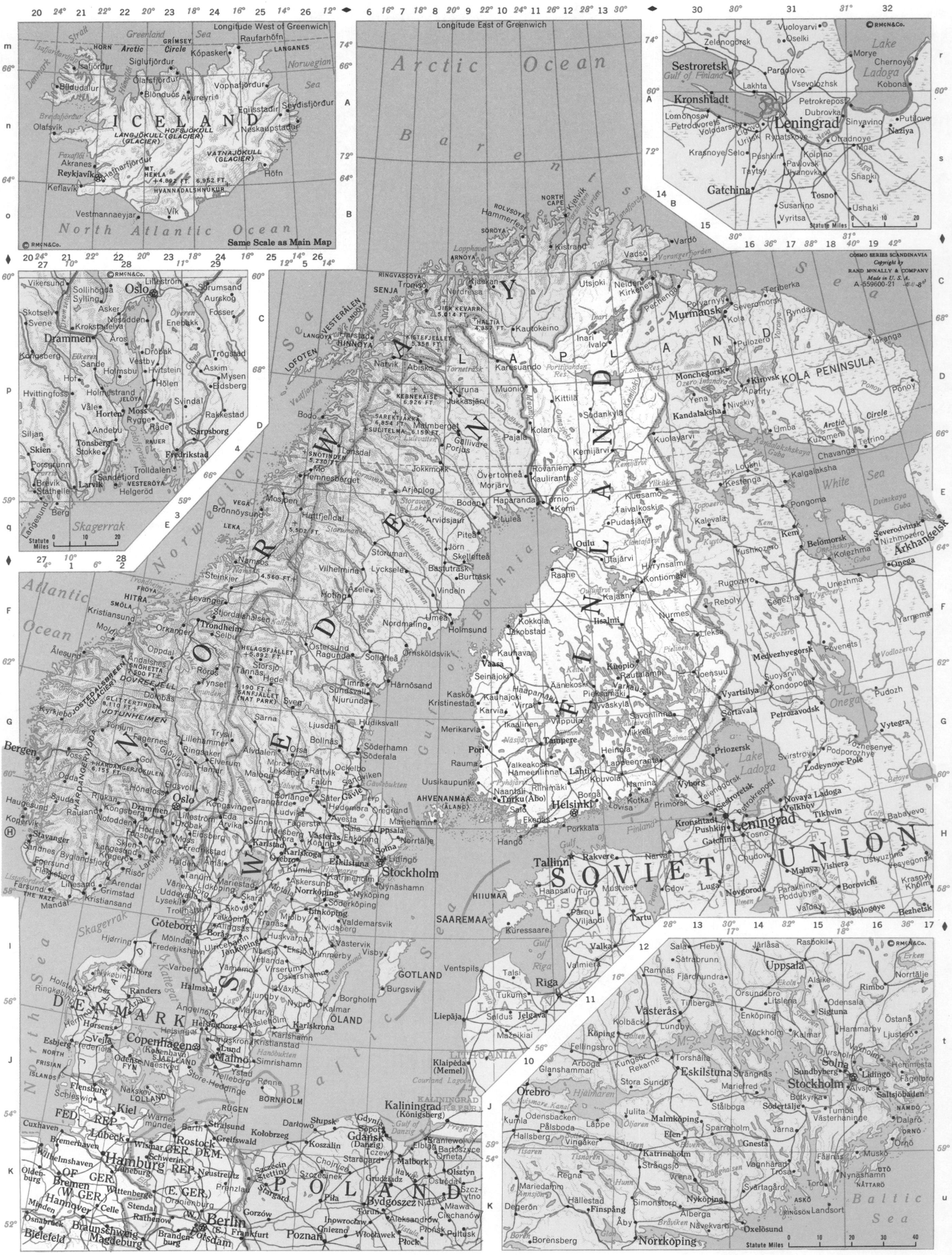

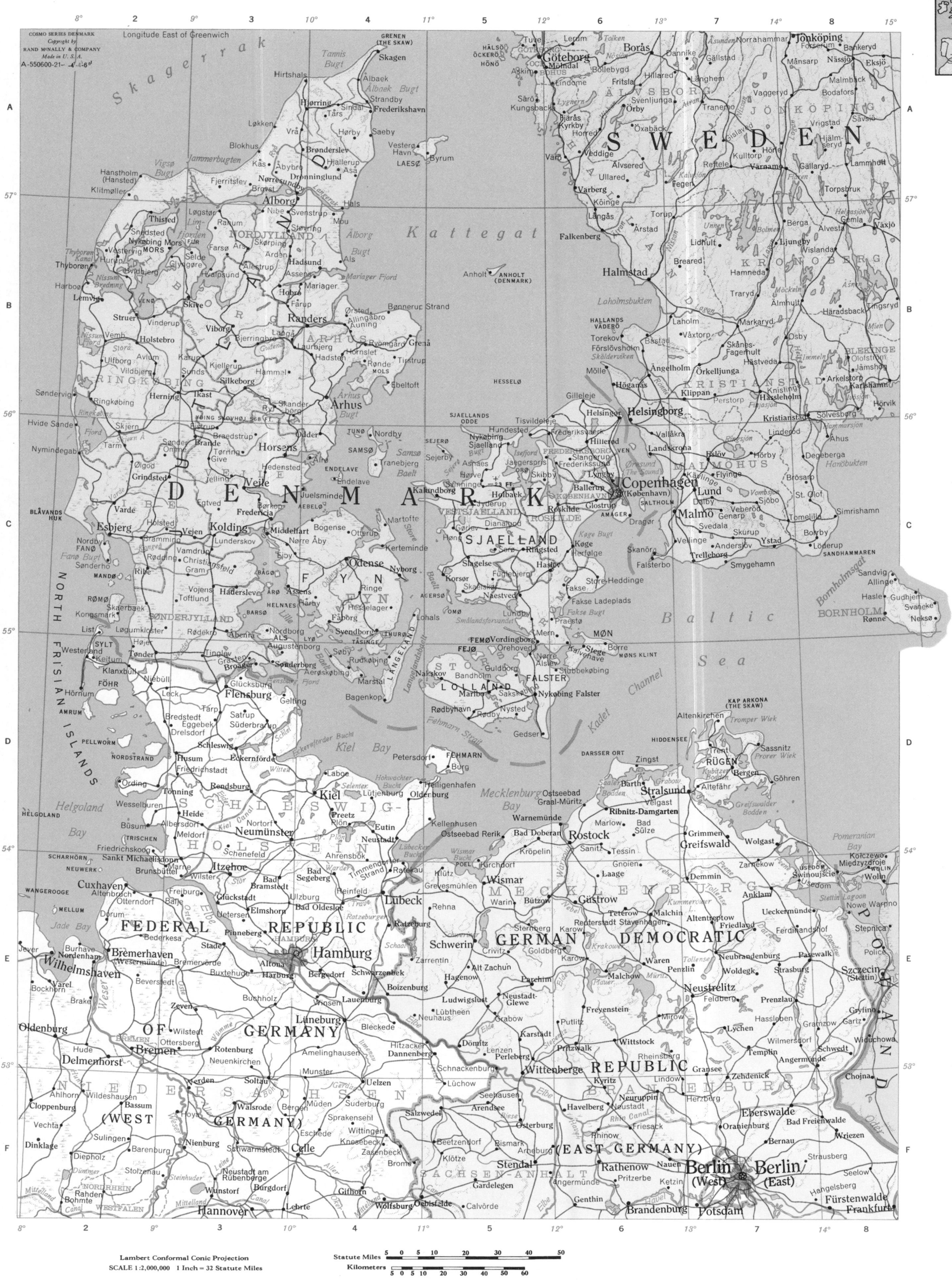

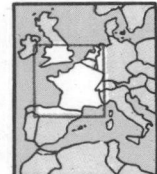

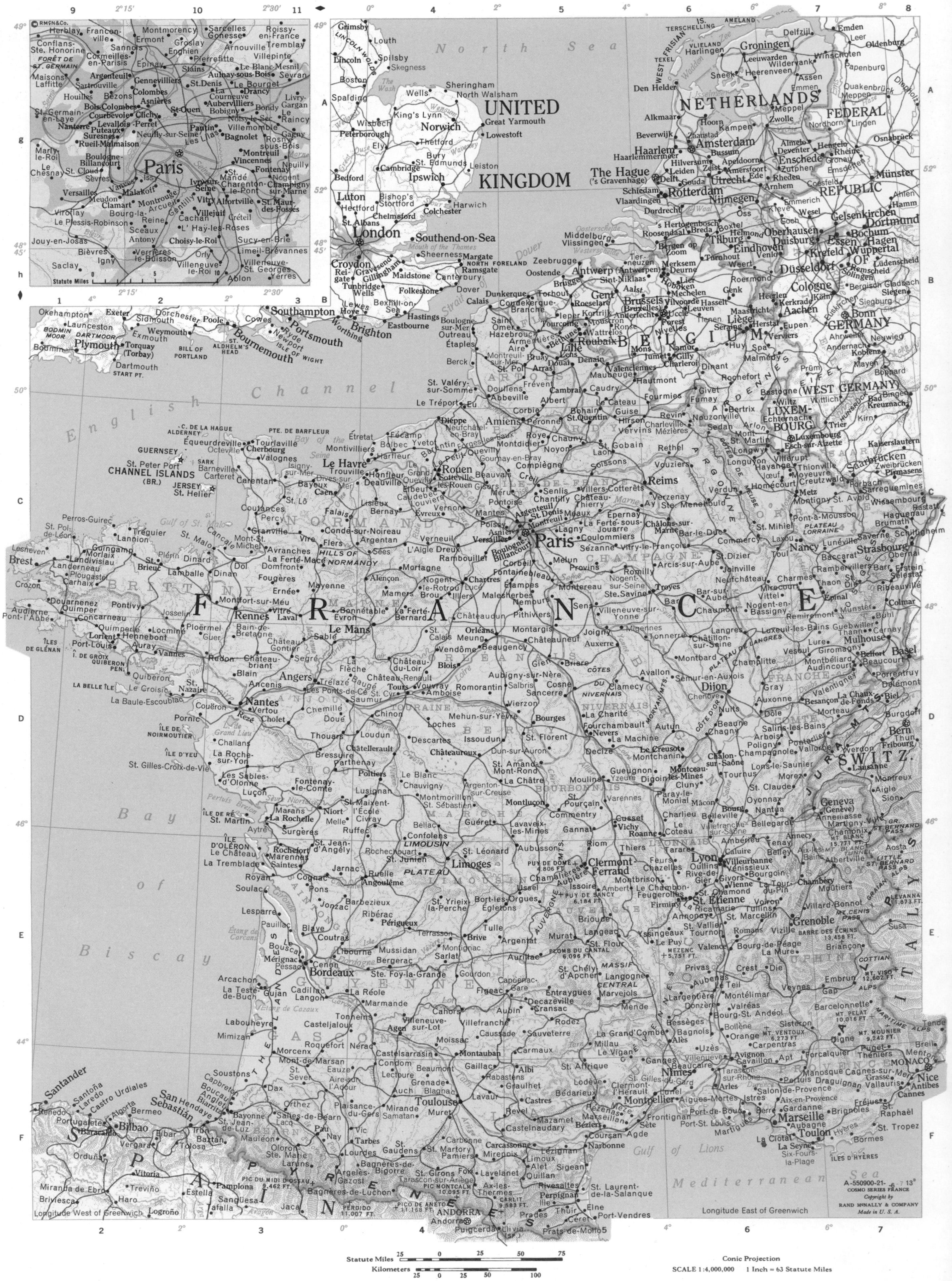

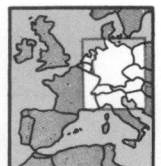

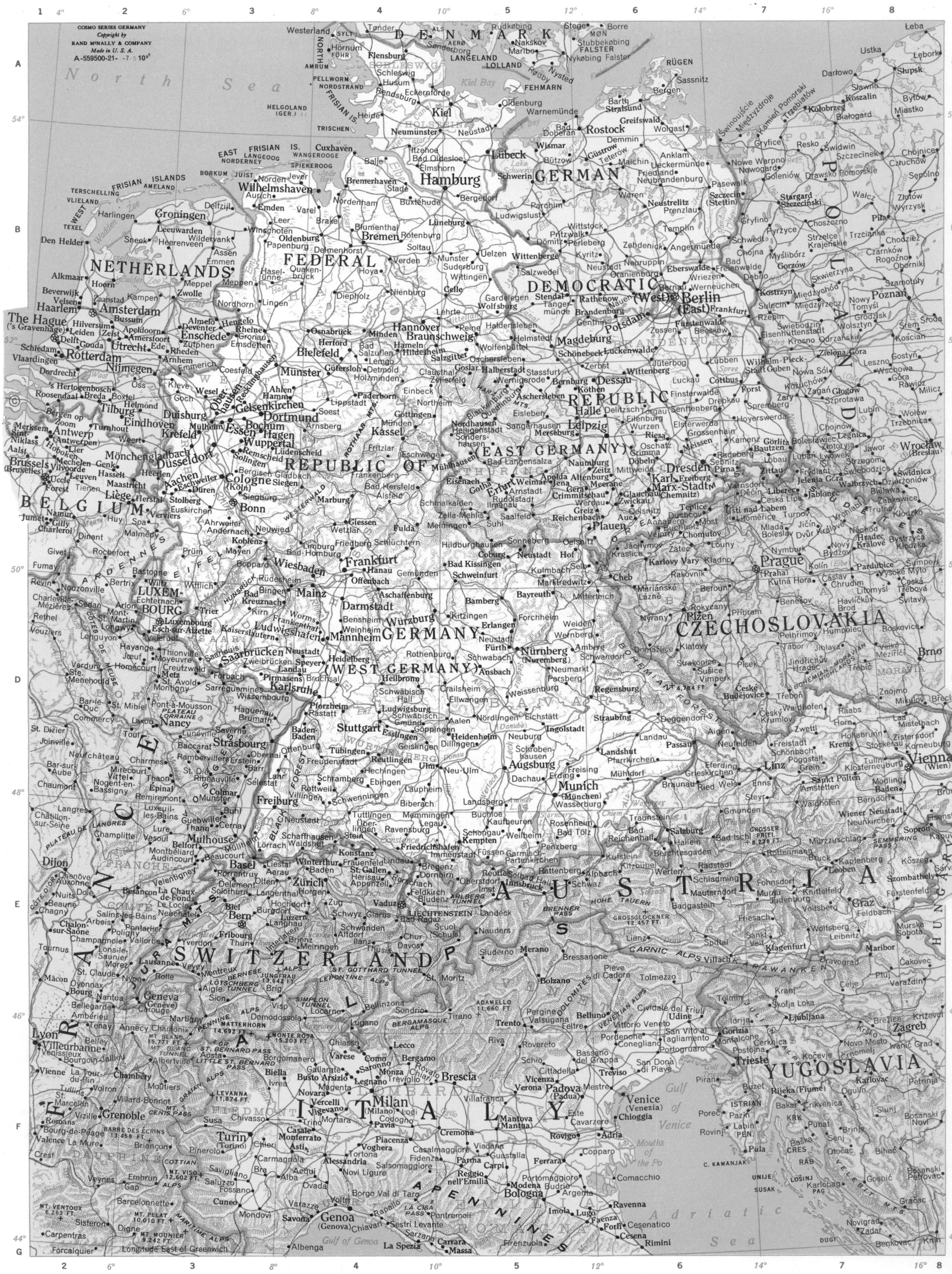

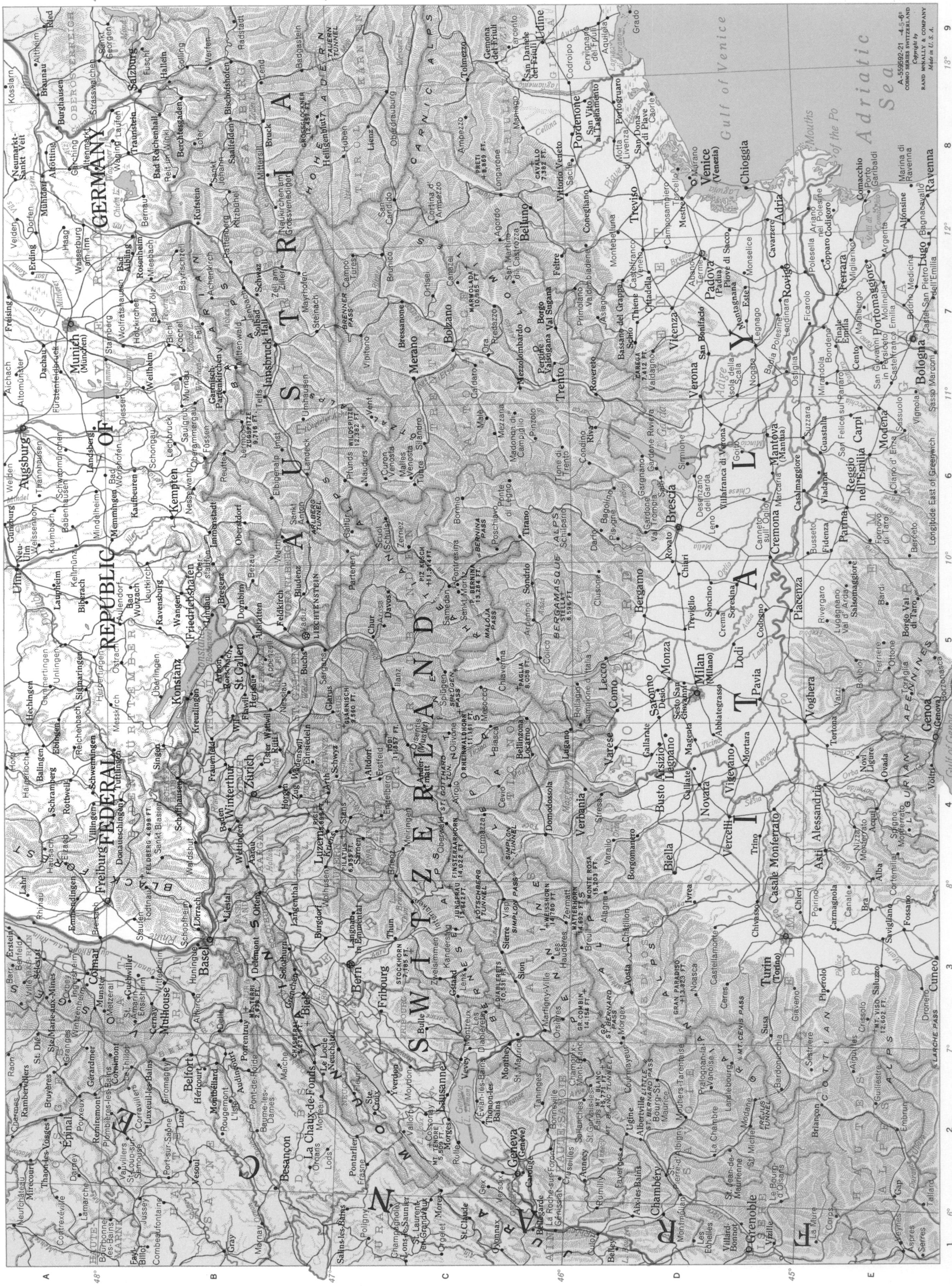

Statute Miles 5 0 5 10 20 30 40 50
Kilometers 5 0 5 10 20 30 40 50 60

Lambert Conformal Conic Projection
SCALE 1:2,000,000   1 Inch = 32 Statute Miles

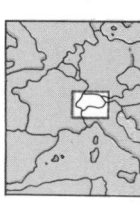

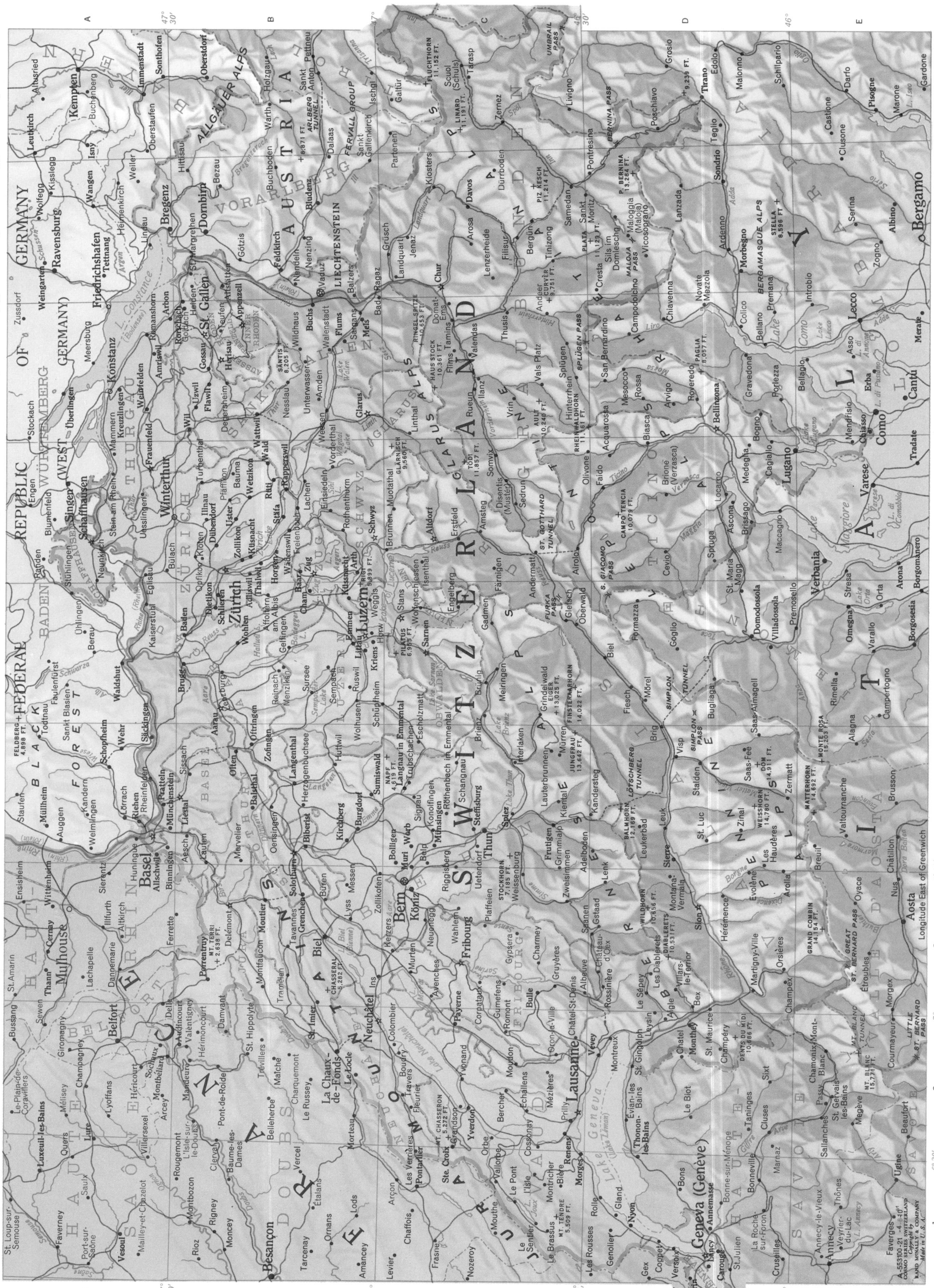

Lambert Conformal Conic Projection
SCALE 1 : 1,100,000 1 Inch = 17 Statute Miles

Statute Miles 5 0 5 10 20 30
Kilometers 5 0 5 10 20 30 40

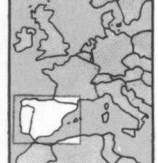

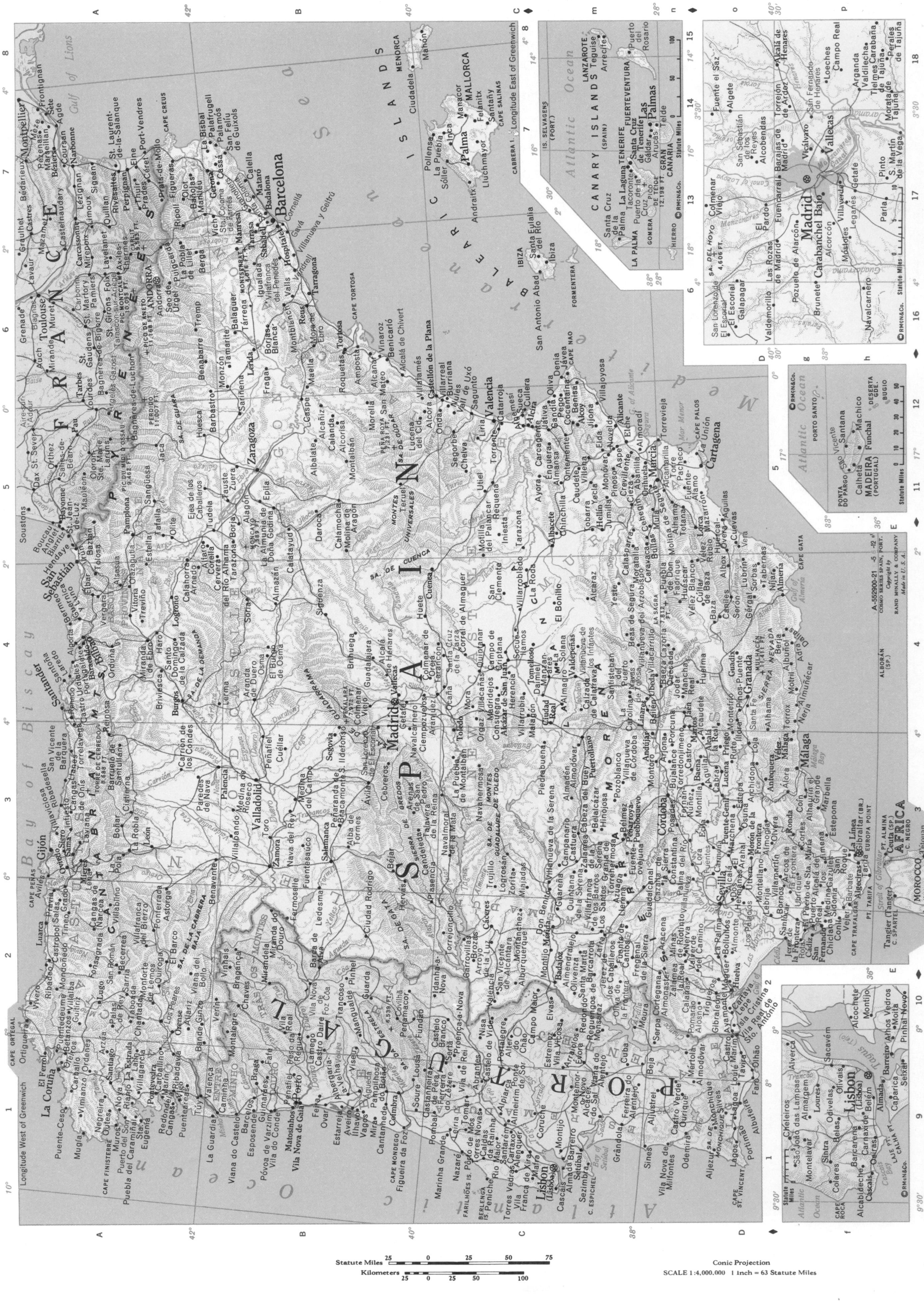

Statute Miles 25 0 25 50 75

Kilometers 25 0 25 50 100

Conic Projection

SCALE 1:4,000,000   1 inch = 63 Statute Miles

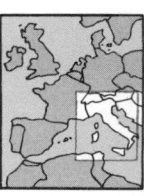

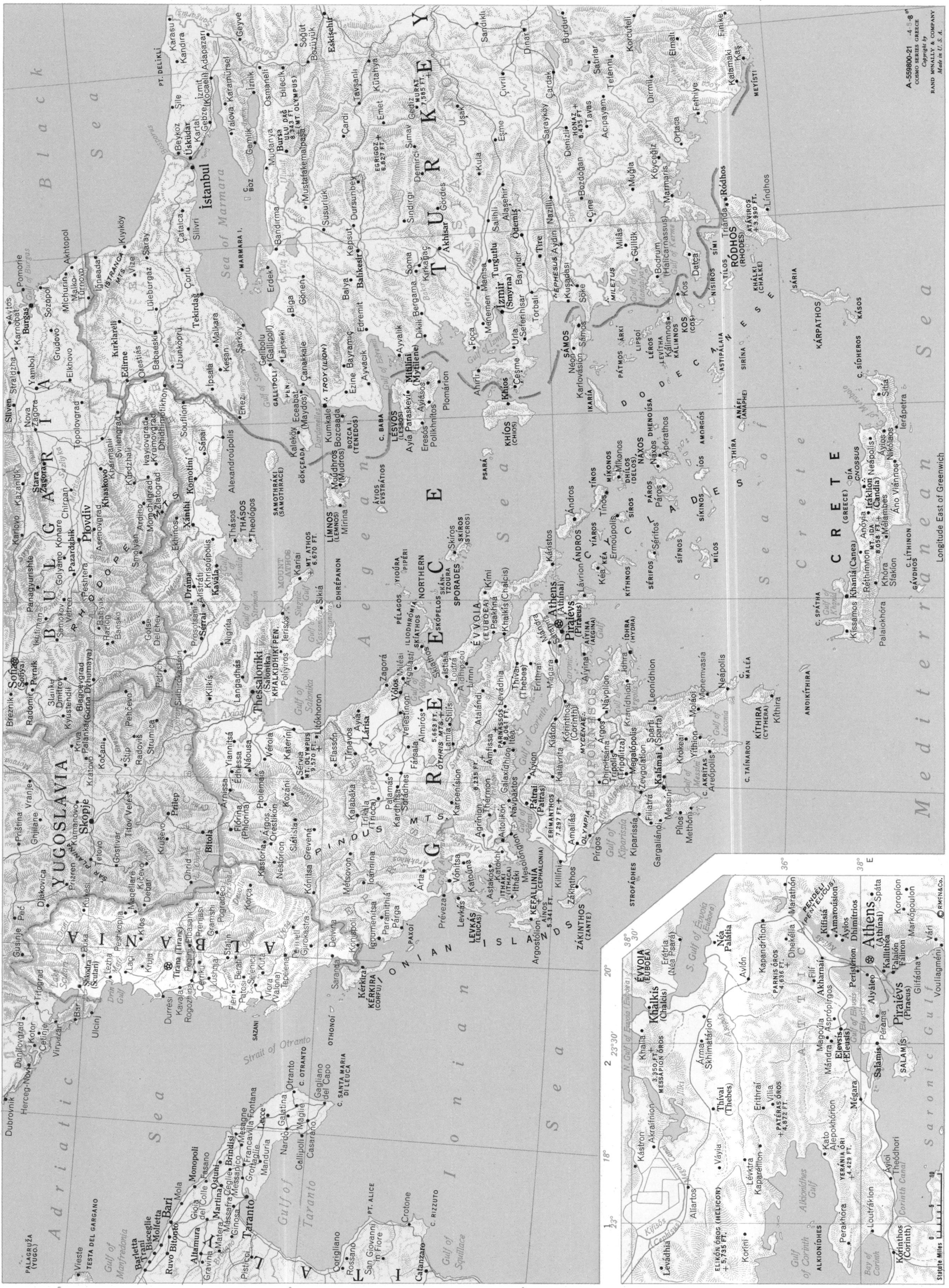

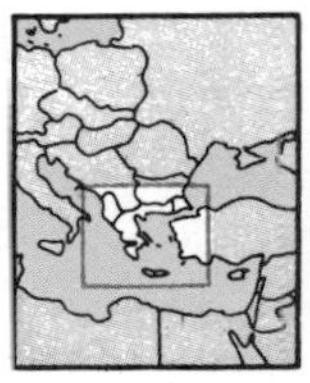

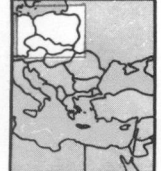

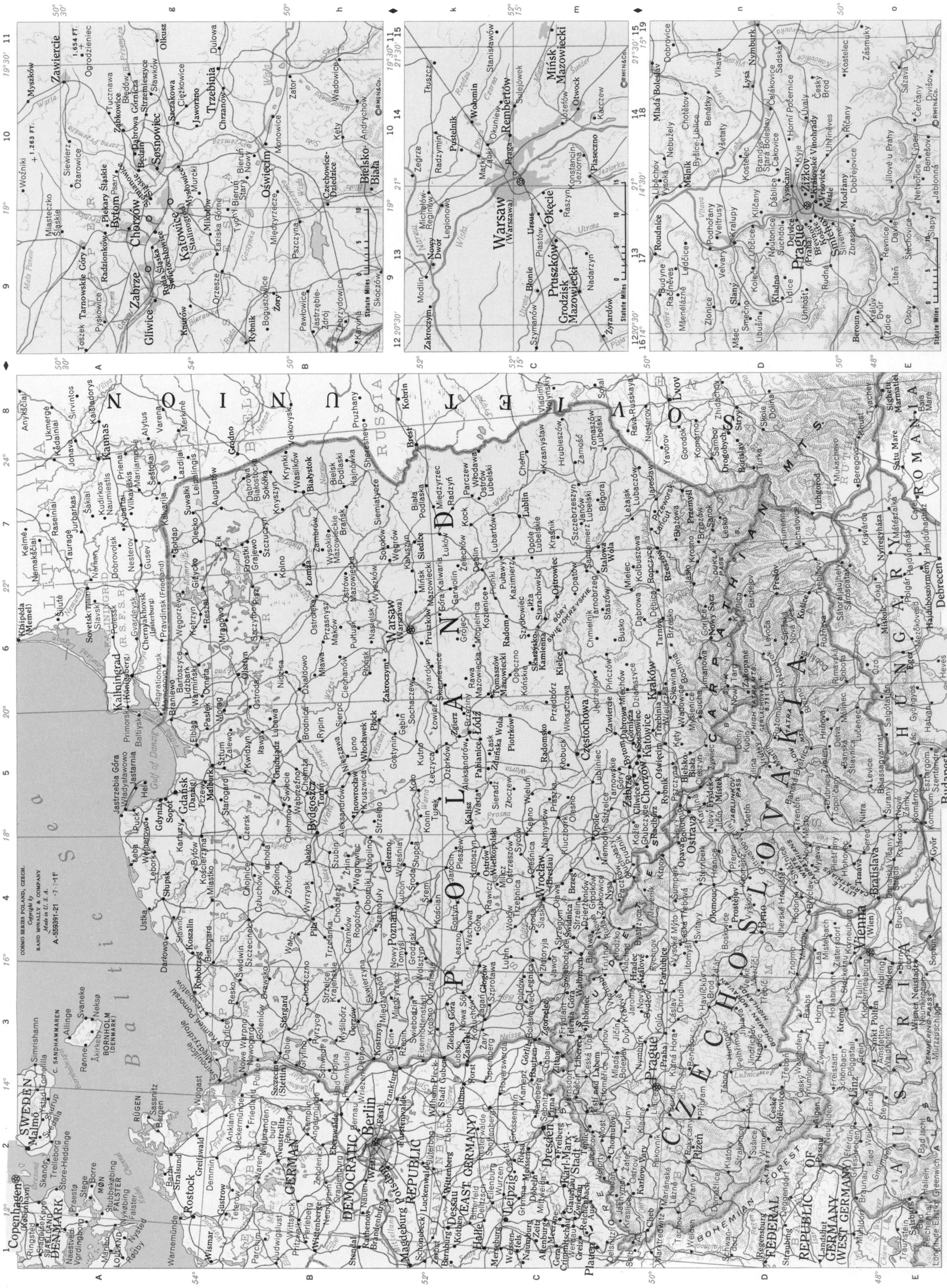

Statute Miles 25 0 25 50 75
Kilometers 25 0 25 50 100

Conic Projection
SCALE 1:4,000,000 1 Inch = 63 Statute Miles

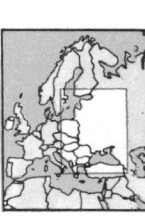

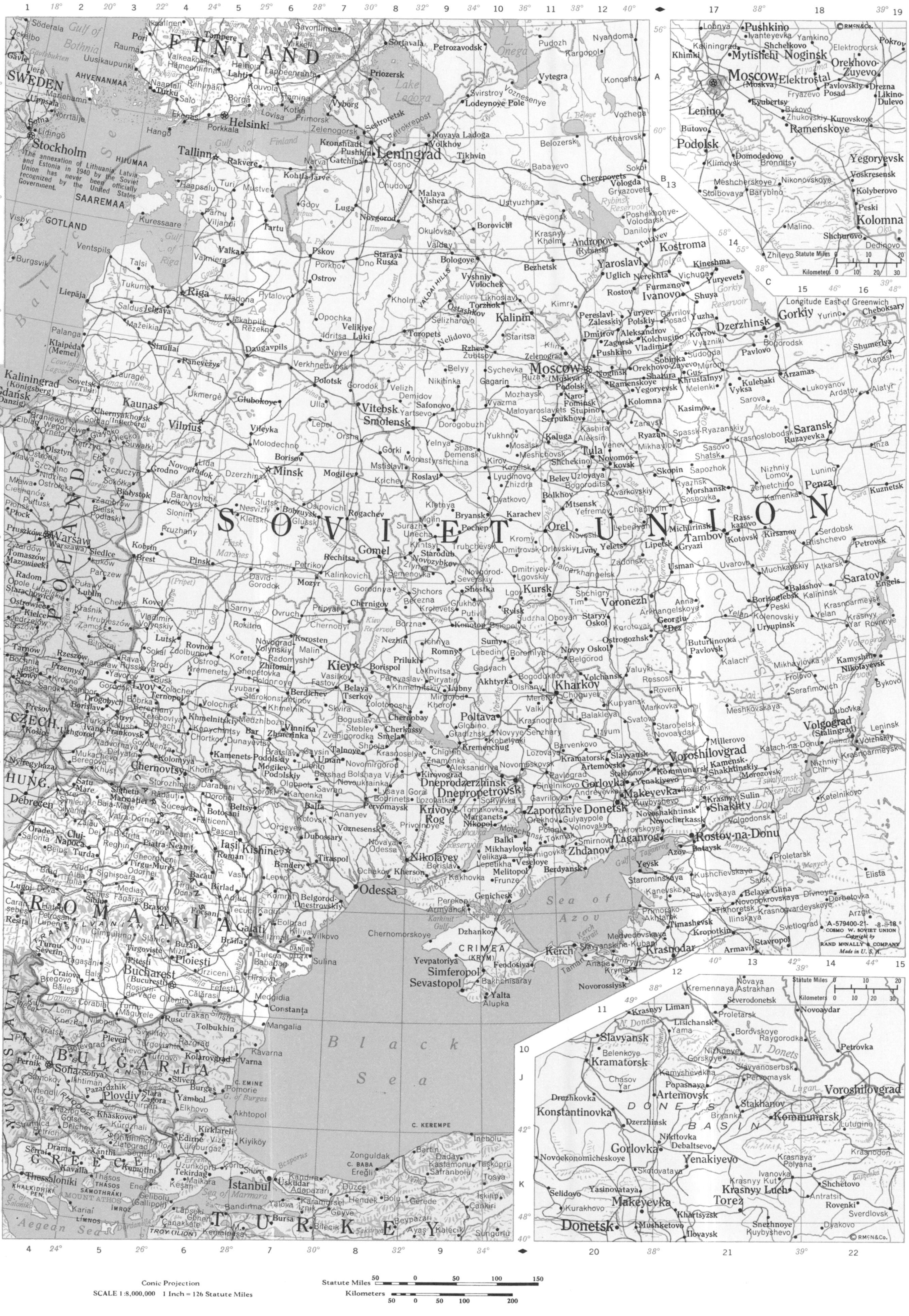

Statute Miles 50 0 50 100 150 200 250

Kilometers 50 0 50 100 150 200 250 300

Sinusoidal Projection

SCALE 1: 11,400,000   1 Inch = 180 Statute Miles

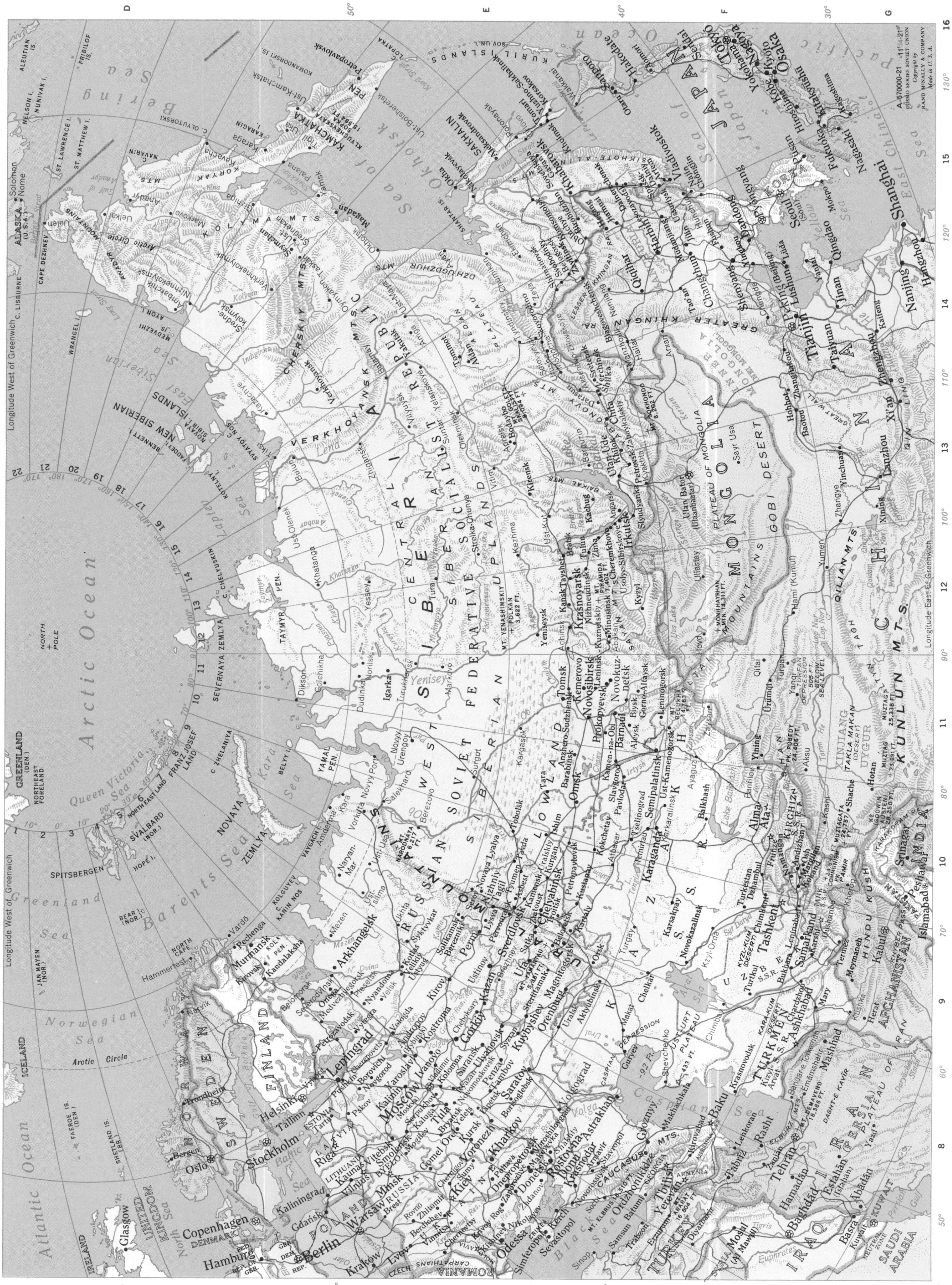

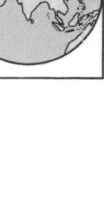

Lambert Azimuthal Equal Area Projection
SCALE 1:28,000,000   1 Inch = 442 Statute Miles

Statute Miles   100 0 100 200 300 400 500
Kilometers   100 0 100   300   500   700

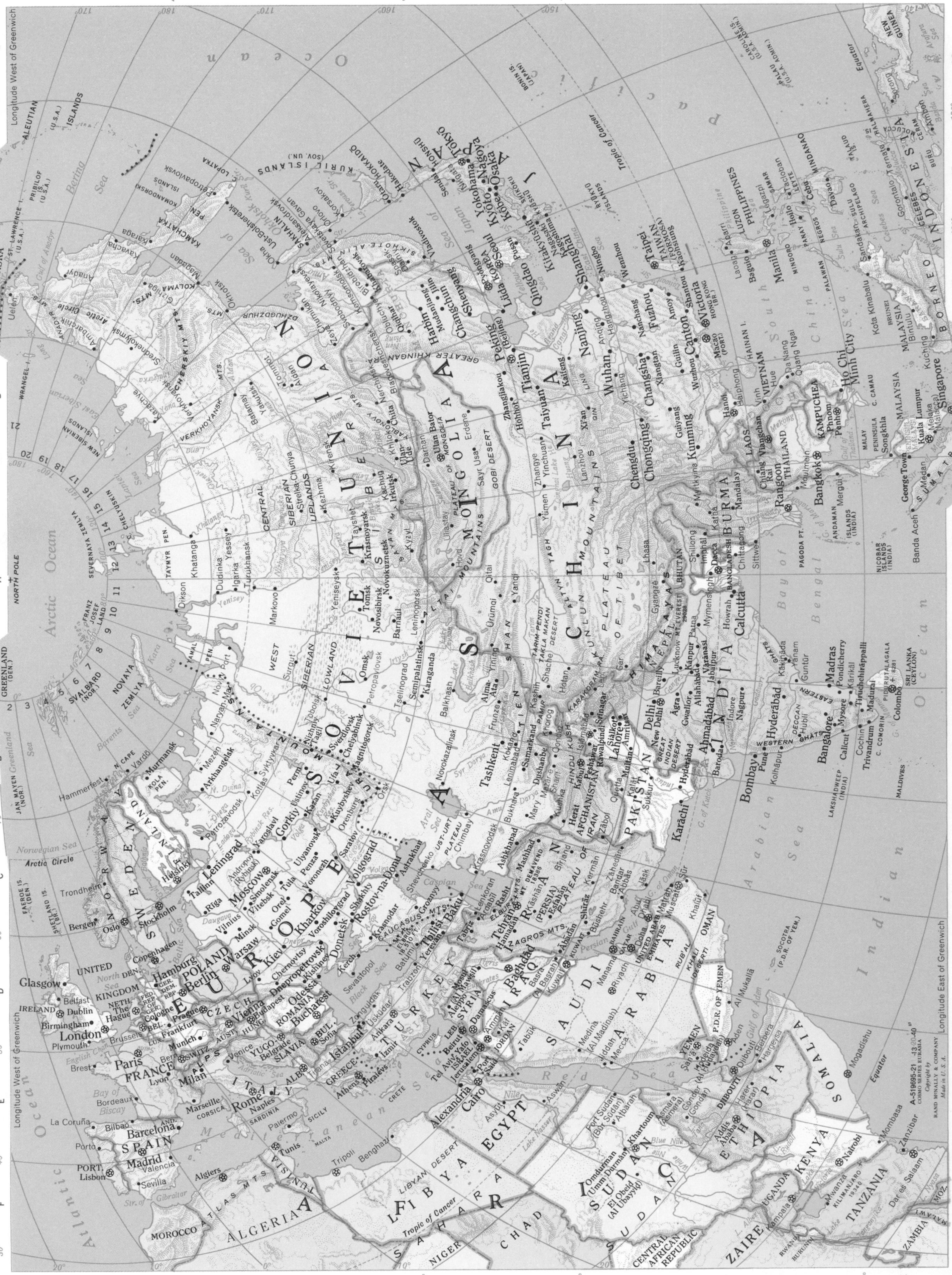

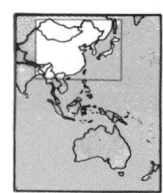

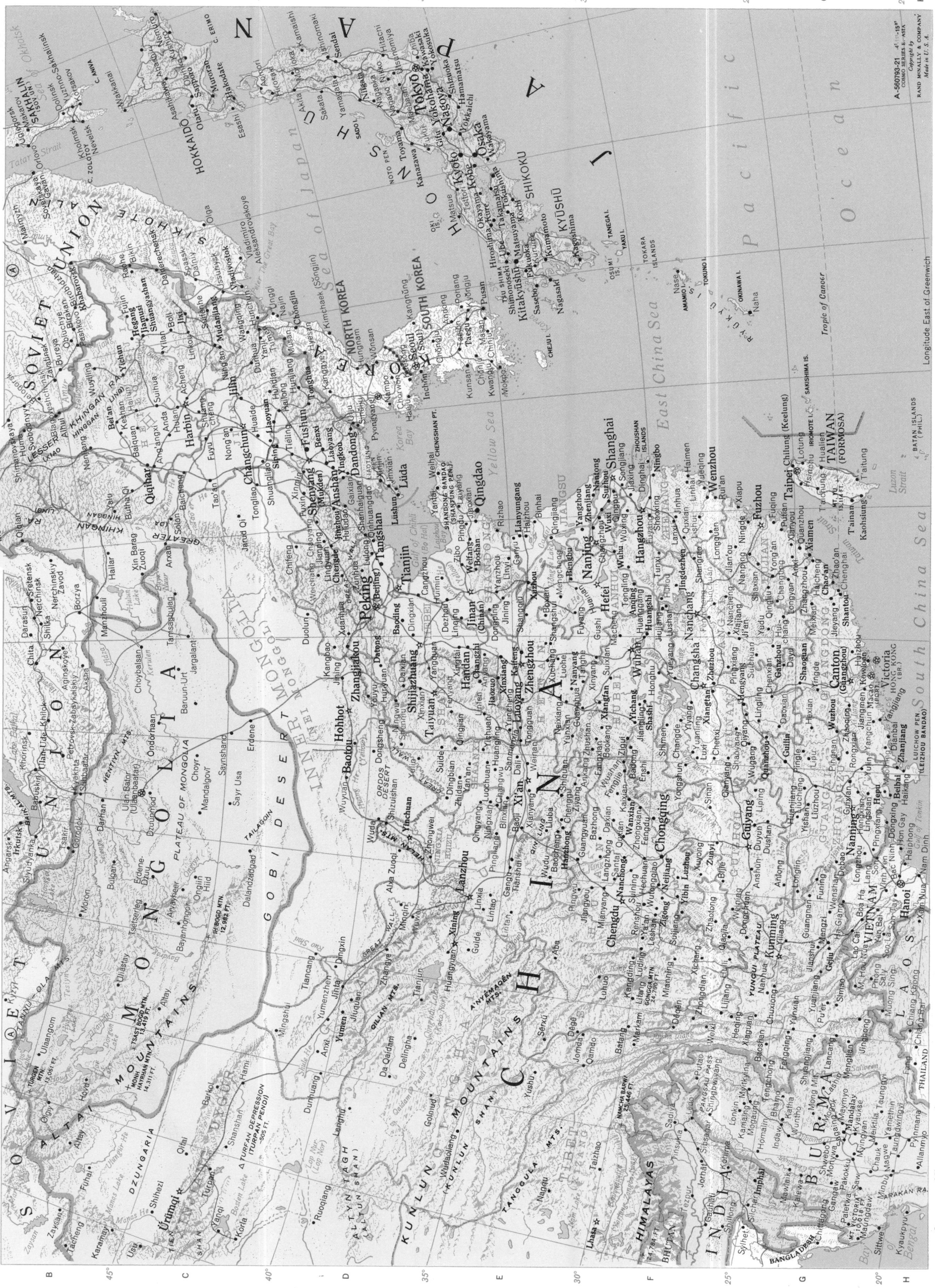

Polyconic Projection

SCALE 1:16,000,000 1 Inch = 252 Statute Miles

Statute Miles 100 0 100 200 300

Kilometers 100 0 100 200 300 400

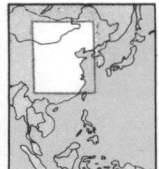

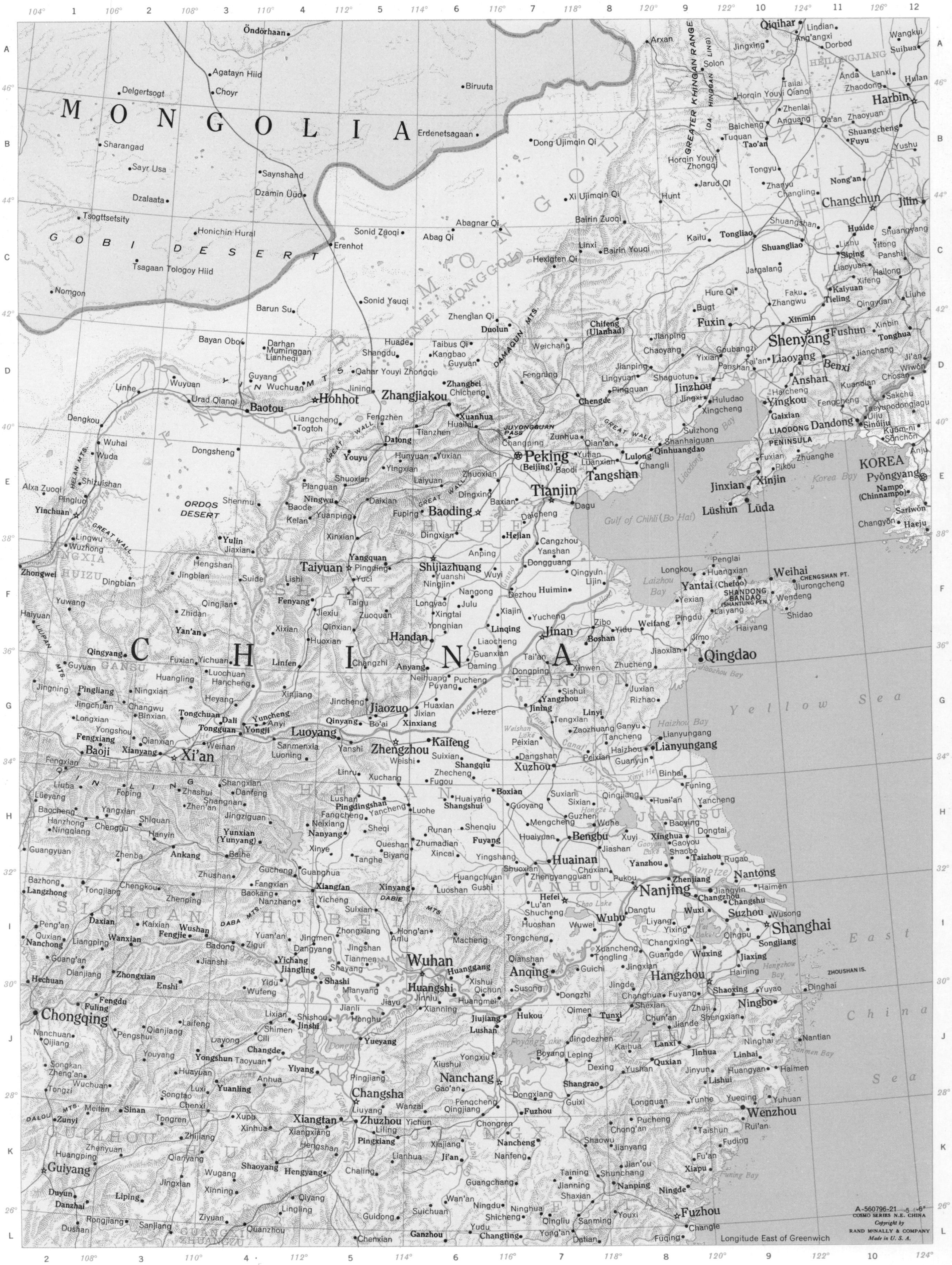

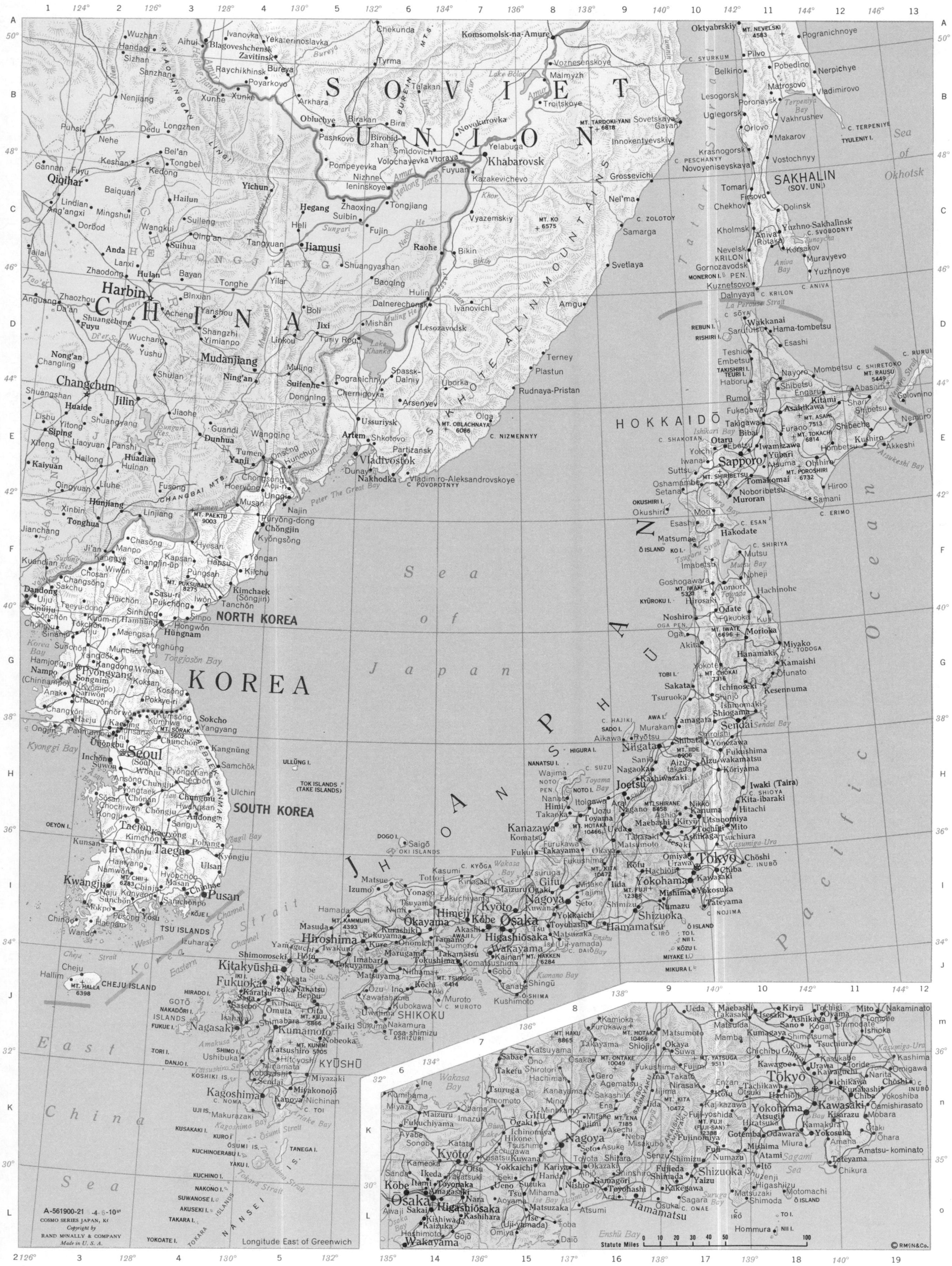

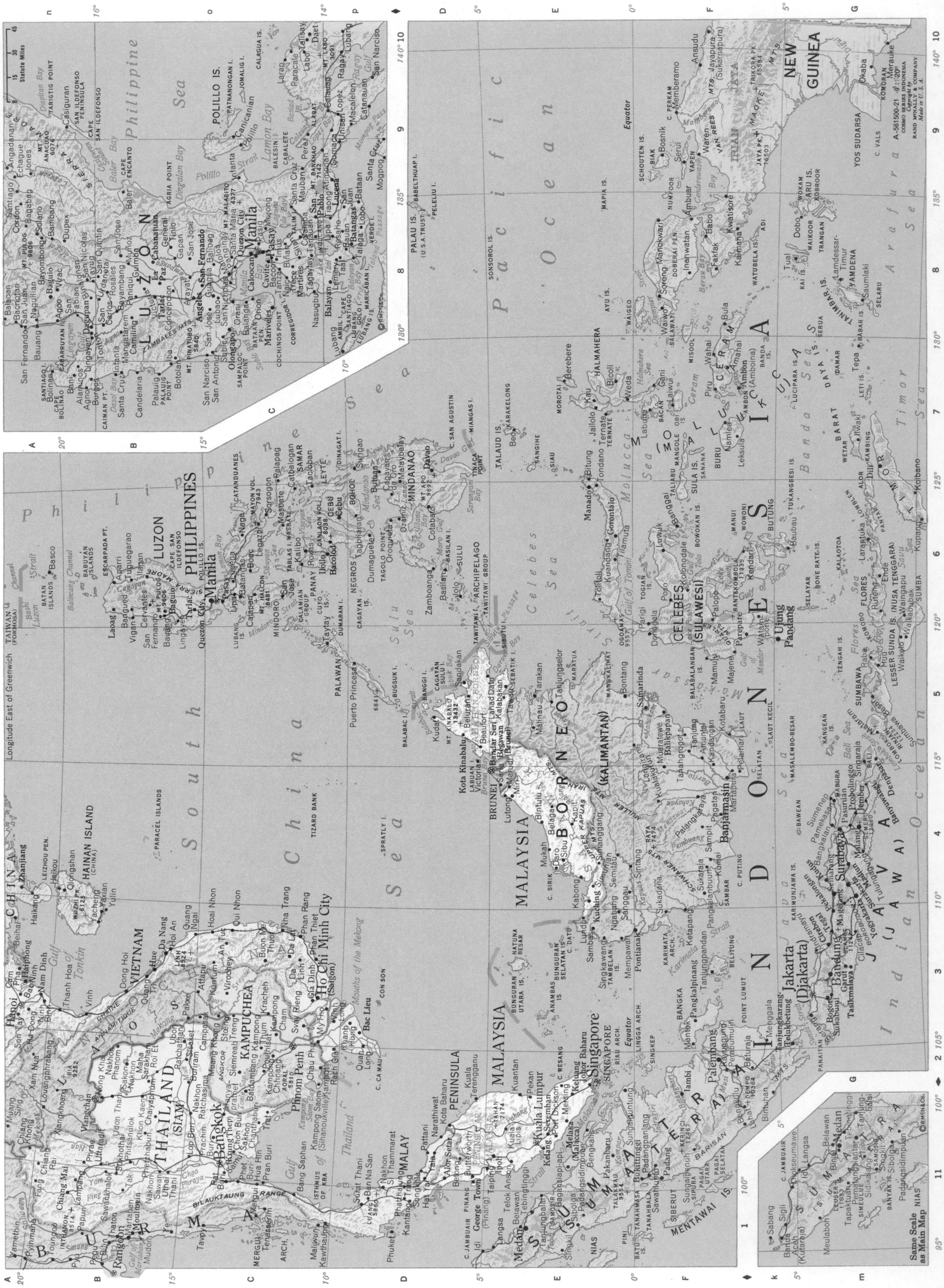

Statute Miles 100 0 100 200 300
Kilometers 100 0 100 200 300 400

Polyconic Projection
SCALE 1:16,000,000 1 Inch = 252 Statute Miles

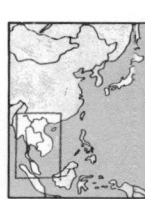

CHINA

BURMA

LAOS

THAILAND (SIAM)

KAMPUCHEA (CAMBODIA)

VIET- NAM

MALAYSIA

SUMATRA

INDONESIA

BORNEO

Andaman Sea

Gulf of Thailand

Gulf of Tonkin

South China Sea

Strait of Malacca

MERGUI ARCHIPELAGO

MALAY PENINSULA

Major cities and places:

Mandalay, Rangoon, Moulmein, Bassein, Prome, Toungoo, Pegu, Henzada, Bangkok, Krung Thep, Chiang Mai, Chiang Rai, Nan, Lampang, Phrae, Uttaradit, Phitsanulok, Sukhothai, Tak, Nakhon Sawan, Uthai Thani, Lop Buri, Sara Buri, Phra Nakhon Si Ayutthaya, Nakhon Ratchasima, Khon Kaen, Udon Thani, Sakon Nakhon, Kalasin, Roi Et, Ubon Ratchathani, Maha Sarakham, Buriram, Sisaket, Surin, Nakhon Pathom, Kanchanaburi, Ratchaburi, Phet Buri, Pran Buri, Prachuap Khiri Khan, Chumphon, Surat Thani, Nakhon Si Thammarat, Phuket, Trang, Phatthalung, Songkhla, Hat Yai, Yala, Pattani, Narathiwat, Satun

Hanoi, Haiphong, Nam Dinh, Ninh Binh, Thanh Hoa, Vinh, Ha Tinh, Dong Hoi, Quang Tri, Hue, Da Nang, Hoi An, Tam Ky, Quang Ngai, Qui Nhon, An Nhon, Tuy Hoa, Nha Trang, Cam Ranh, Phan Rang, Phan Thiet, Da Lat, Bien Hoa, Ho Chi Minh City (Saigon), Vung Tau, My Tho, Can Tho, Rach Gia, Bac Lieu, Quan Long, Pleiku, Kontum, Buon Me Thuot, An Loc, Tay Ninh

Viangchan (Vientiane), Louangphrabang, Louang Namtha, Phongsali, Xam Nua, Savannakhet, Pakxe, Muang Khammouan, Muang Xepon, Attapu

Phnom Penh, Batdambang, Siemreab, Kampong Cham, Kampong Chhnang, Pouthisat, Kampong Thum, Kracheh, Kampong Saom (Sihanoukville), Kampot, Takev, Svay Rieng, Stoeng Treng

Kuala Lumpur, Kelang, George Town (Pinang), Butterworth, Ipoh, Taiping, Seremban, Melaka (Malacca), Muar, Batu Pahat, Johor Baharu, Singapore, Kuala Terengganu, Kuantan, Kota Baharu, Kelang

Medan, Banda Aceh (Kutaraja), Lhokseumawe, Langsa, Tebingtinggi, Pematangsiantar, Padangsidimpuan, Sibolga

China: Nanning, Zhanjiang (Tsamkong), Haikou (Hoihow), Haikou, HAINAN, Beihai (Pakhoi), Qinzhou, Dongxing, Hepu (Lianzhou)

Lambert Conformal Conic Projection
SCALE 1:8,000,000 1 Inch = 126 Statute Miles

Statute Miles 50 0 50 100 150
Kilometers 50 0 50 100 200

A-561100-21
COSMO SERIES INDOCHINA, THAILAND
Copyright by
RAND M·NALLY & COMPANY
Made in U.S.A.

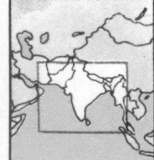

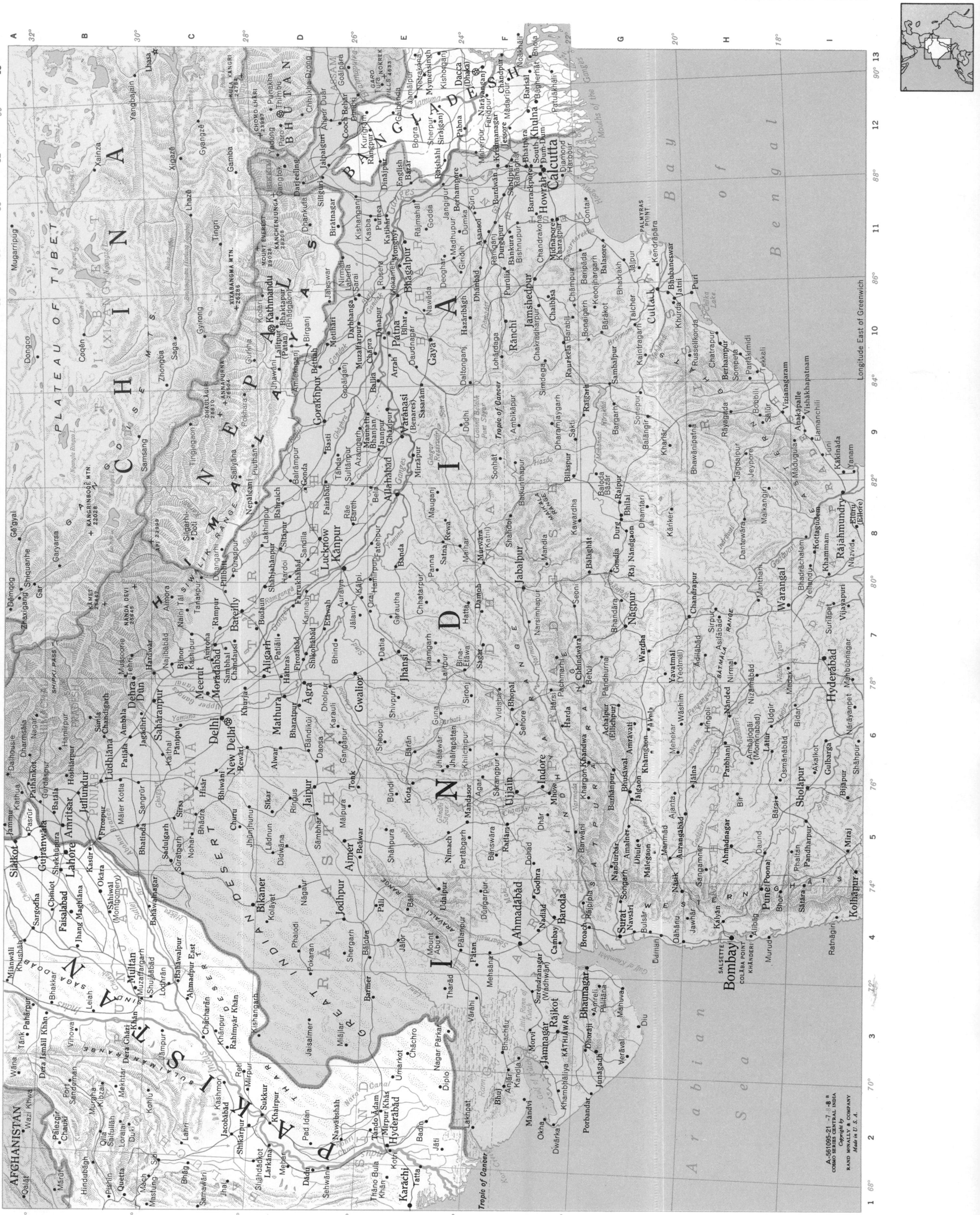

Lambert Conformal Conic Projection
SCALE 1 : 8,000,000   1 Inch = 126 Statute Miles

Statute Miles

Kilometers

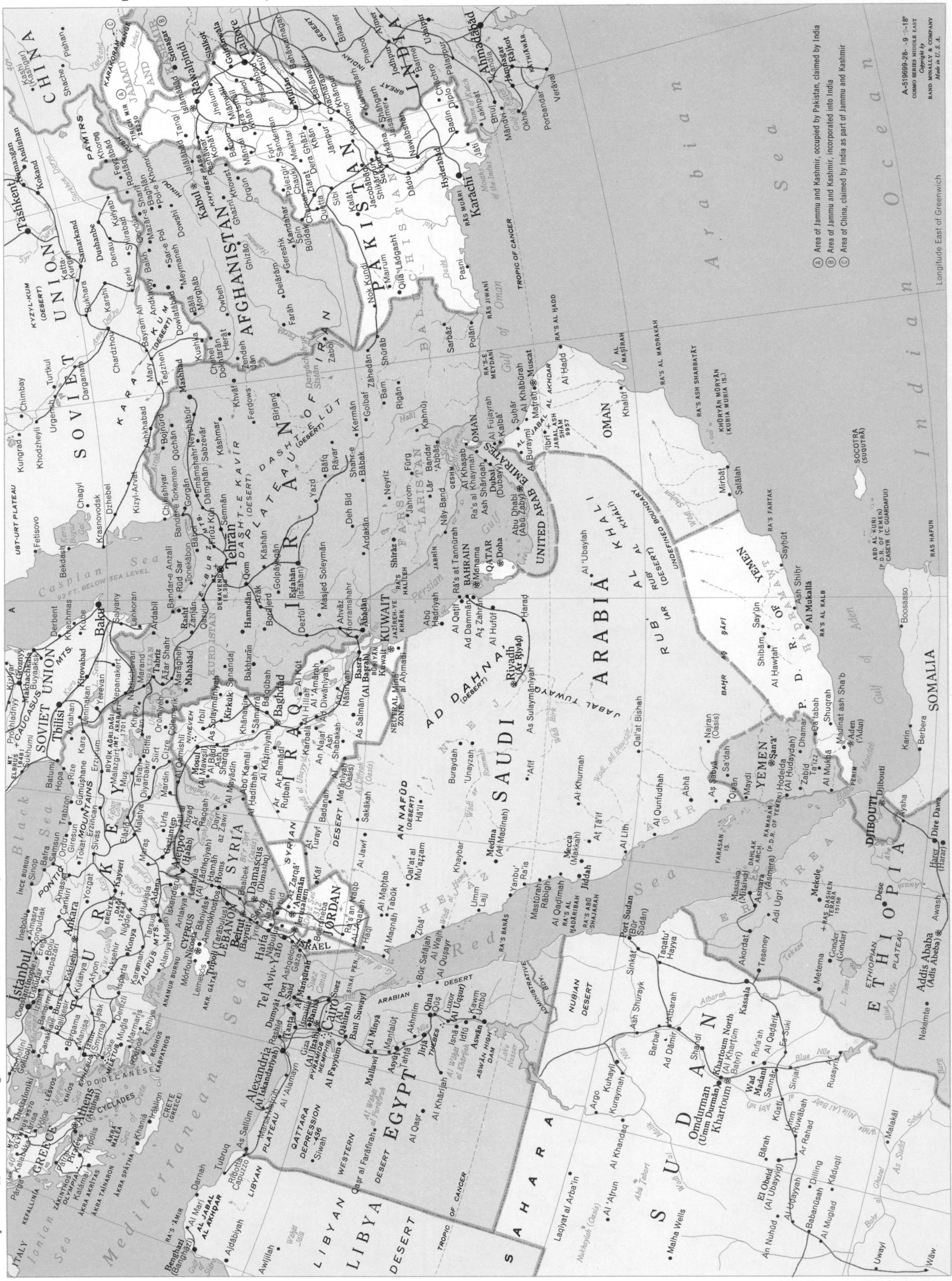

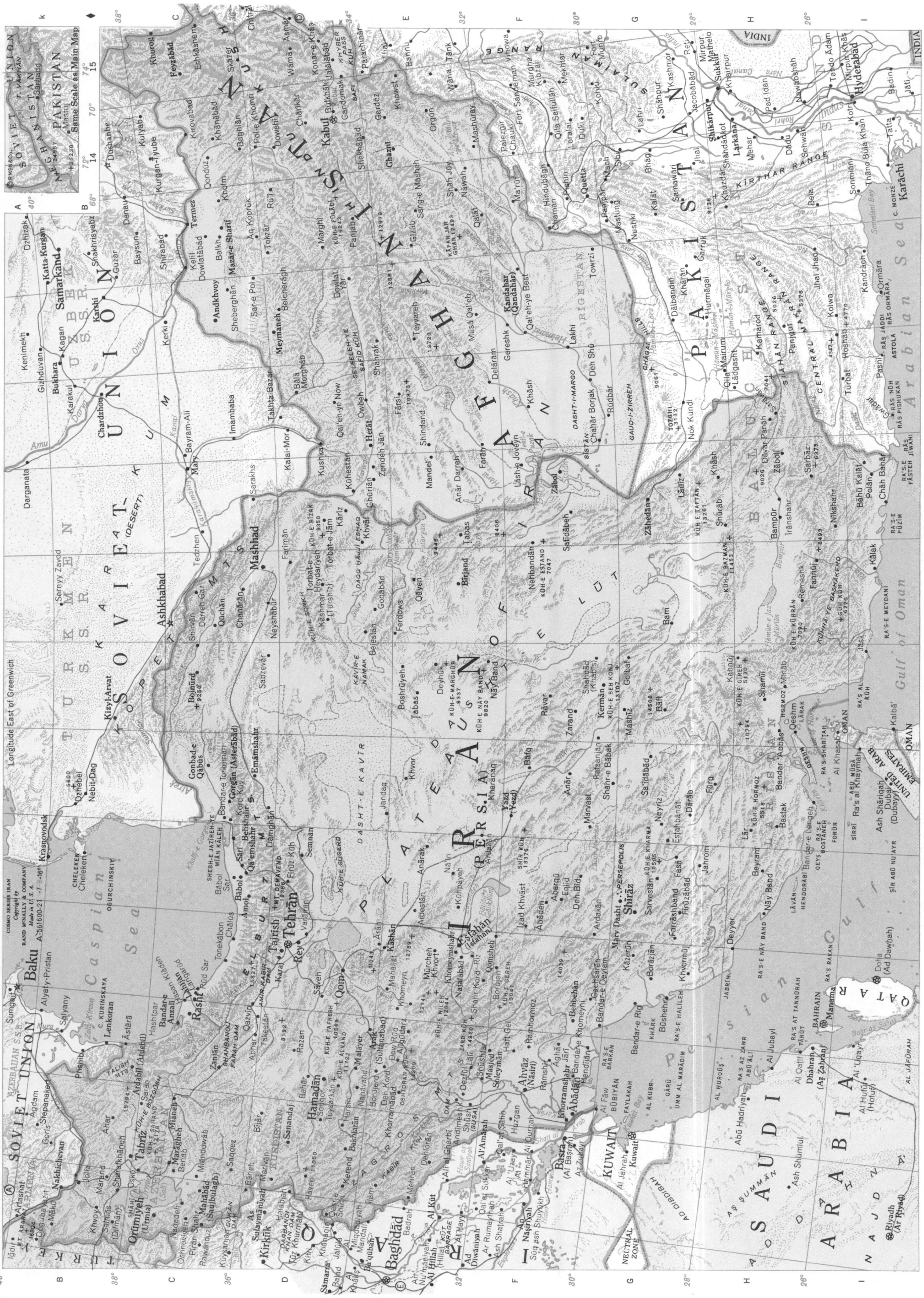

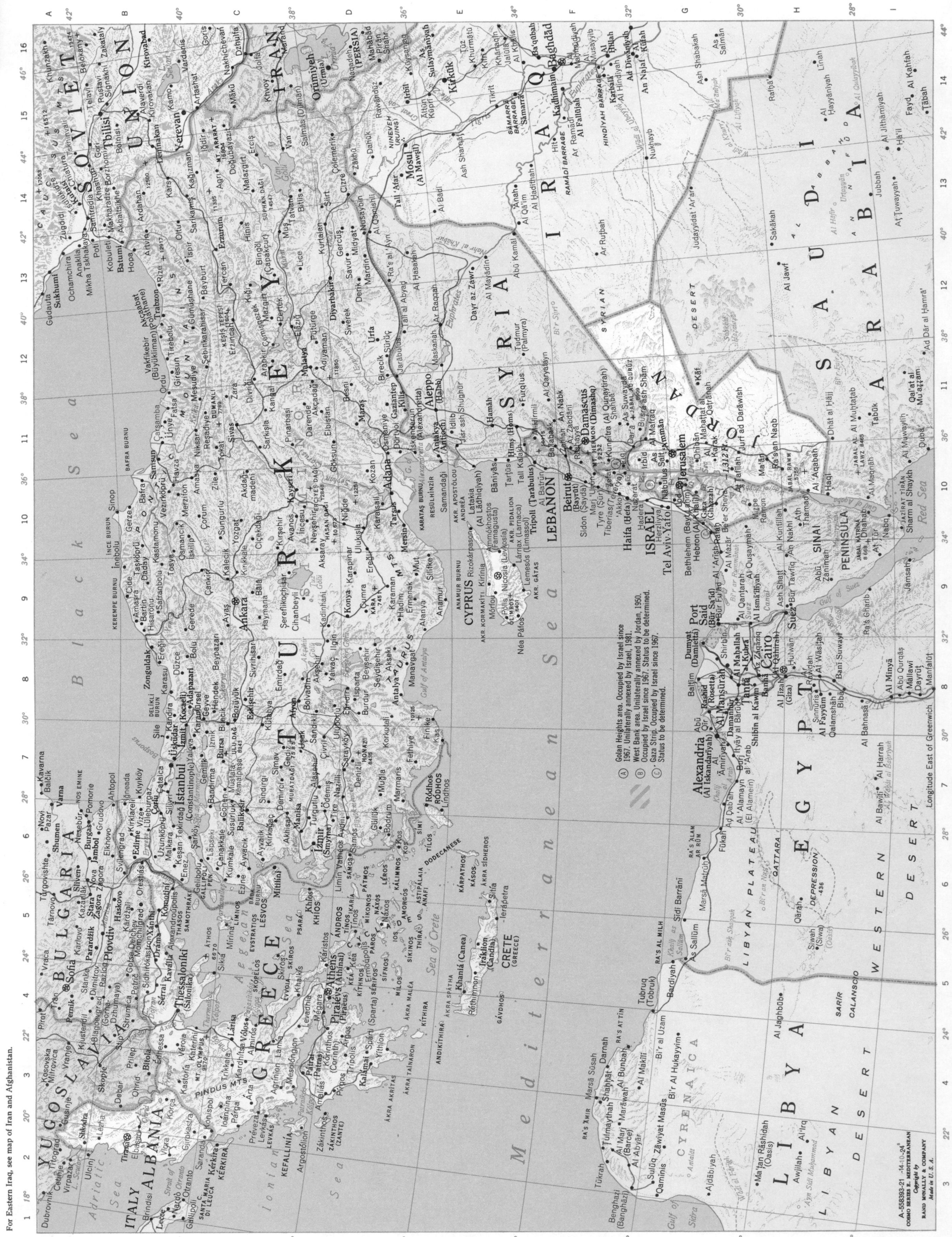

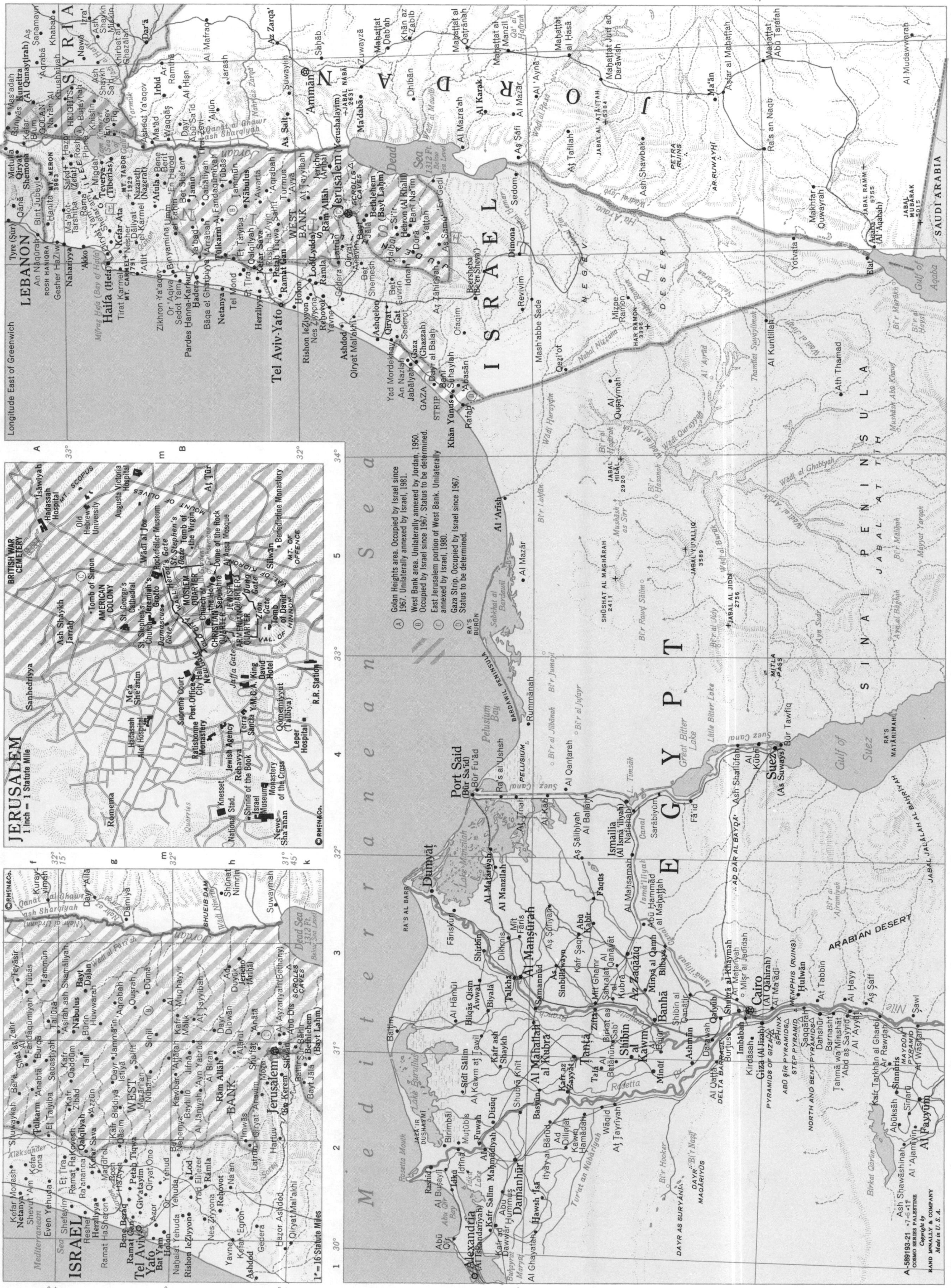

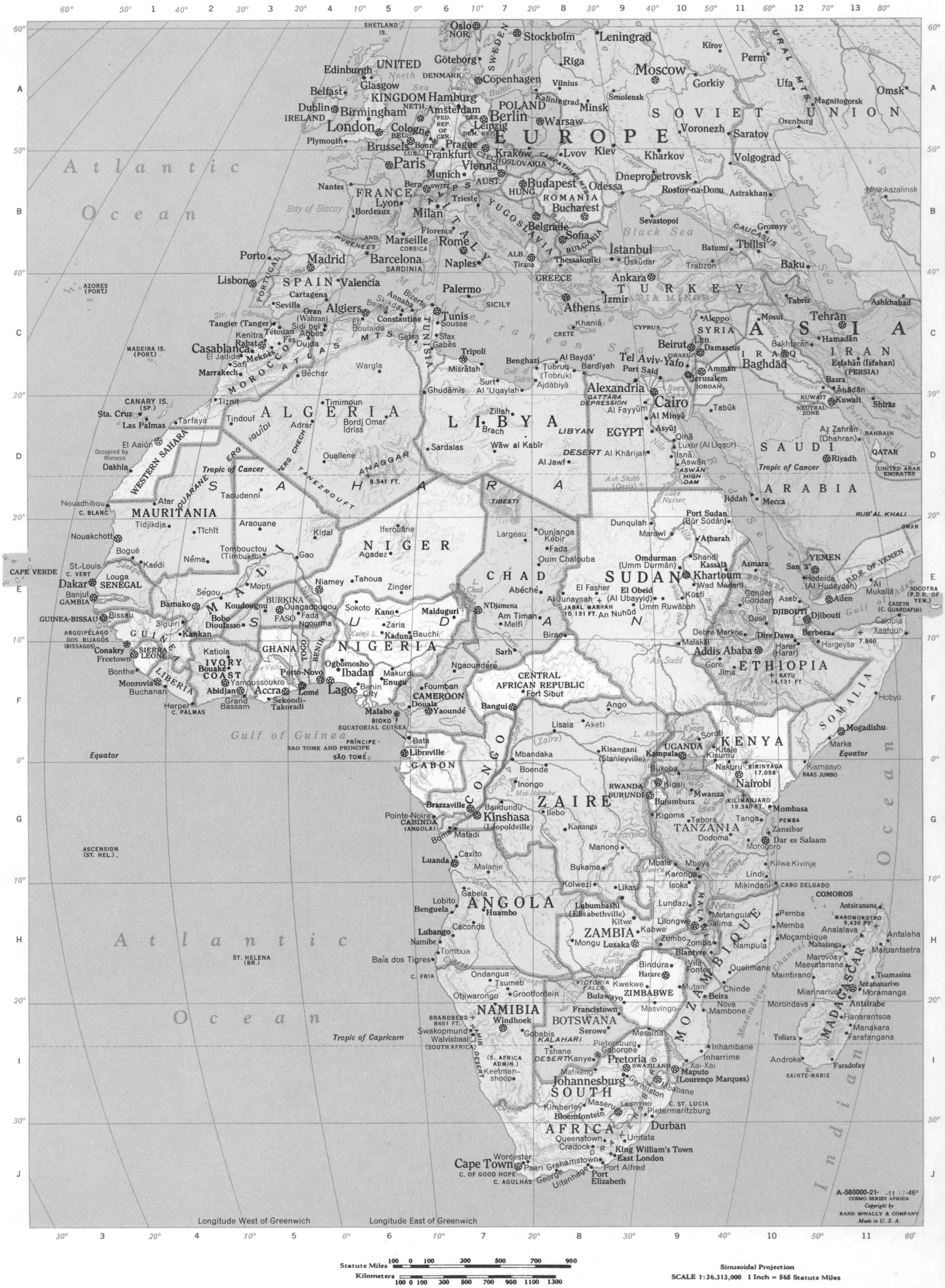

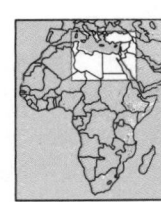

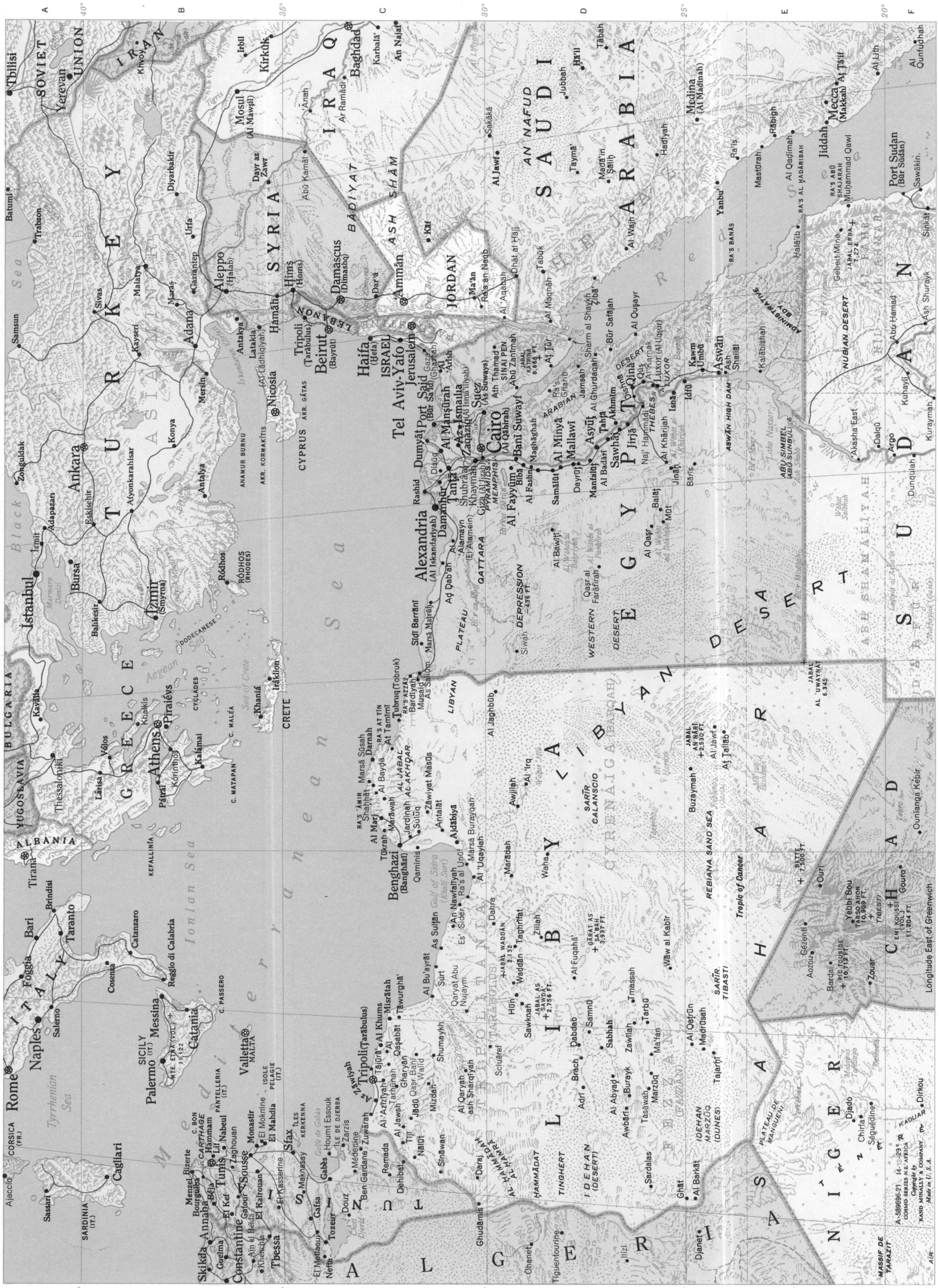

Sinusoidal Projection
SCALE 1:11,400,000   1 Inch = 180 Statute Miles

Statute Miles   50   0   50   100   150   200   250

50   0   50   100   150   200   250   300

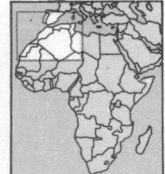

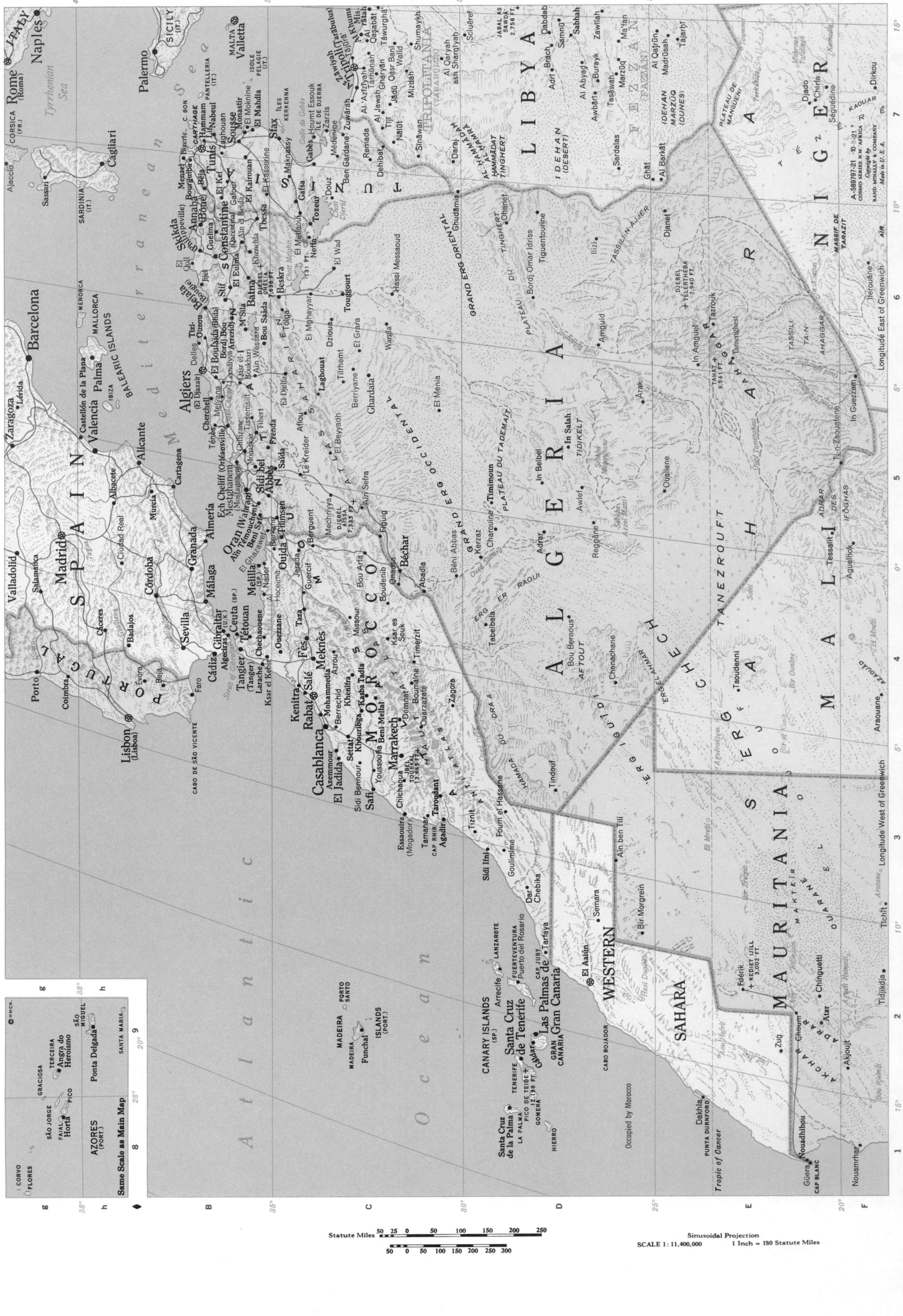

Statute Miles   50 25 0   50   100   150   200   250

50 0 50 100 150 200 250 300

Sinusoidal Projection
SCALE 1: 11,400,000   1 Inch = 180 Statute Miles

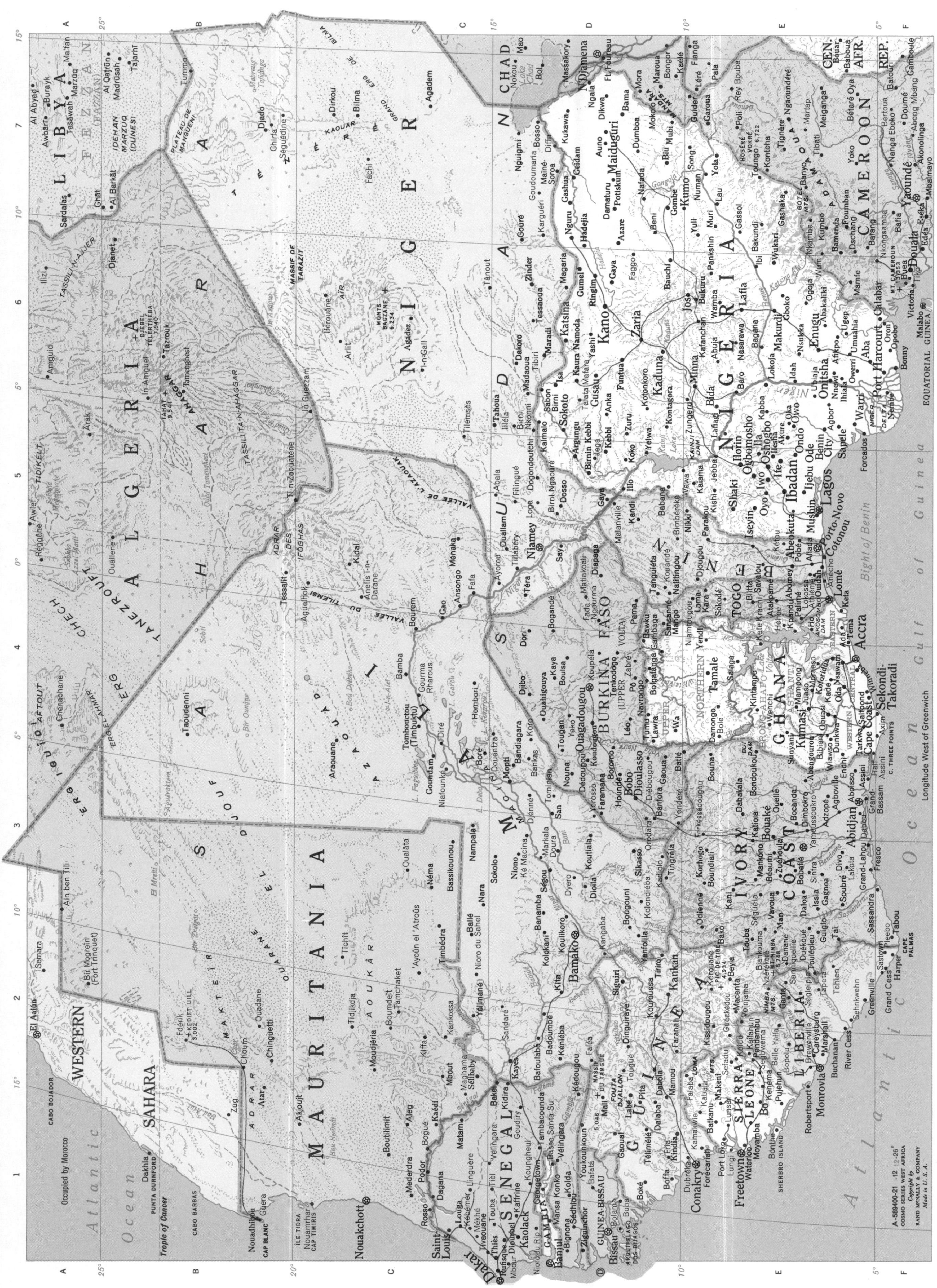

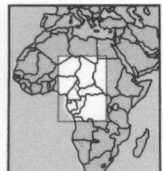

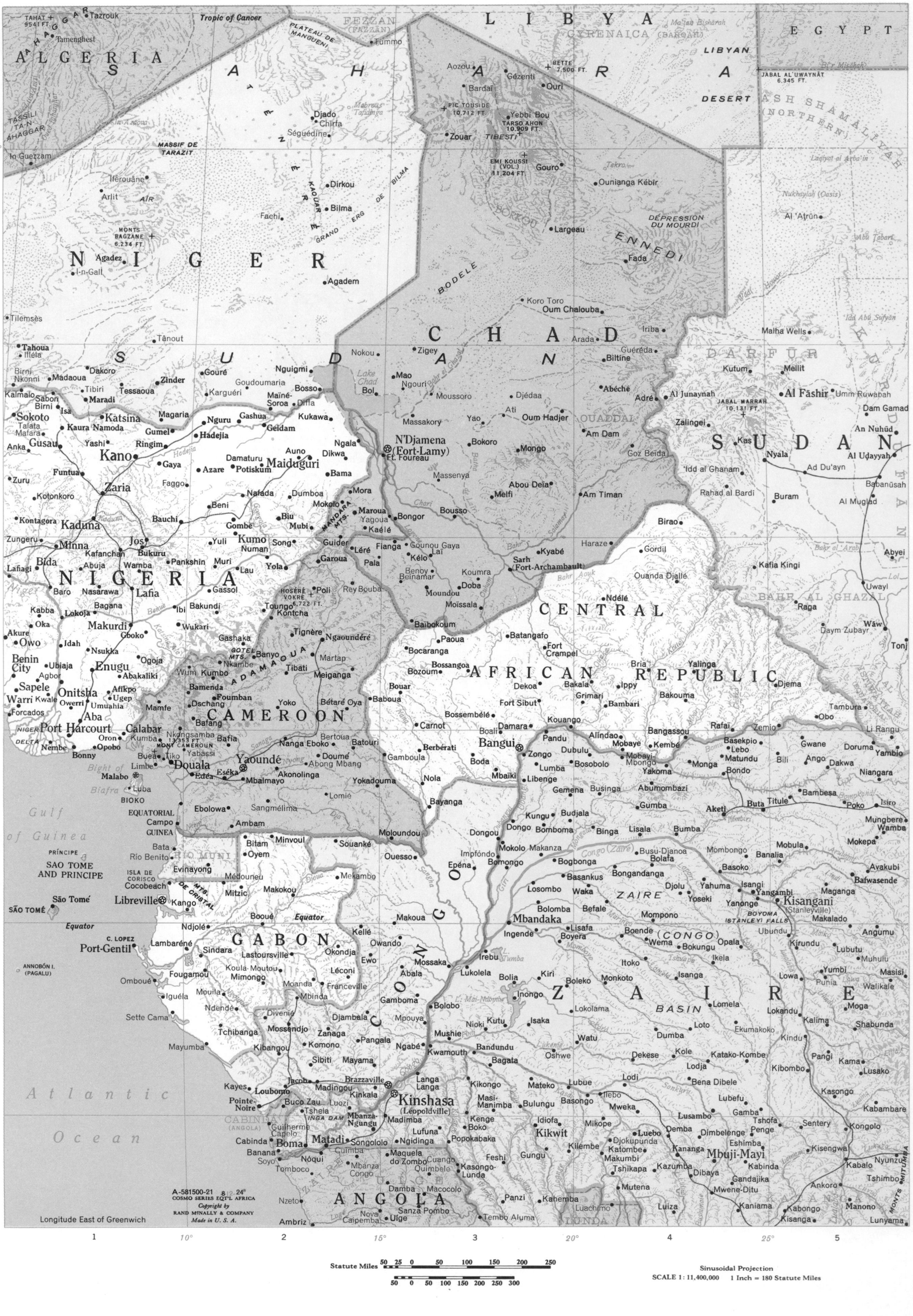

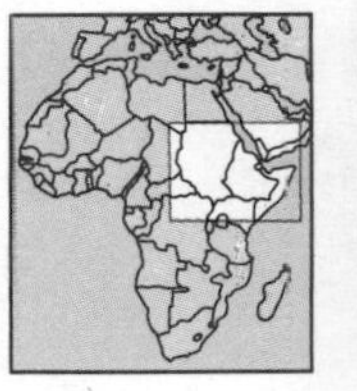

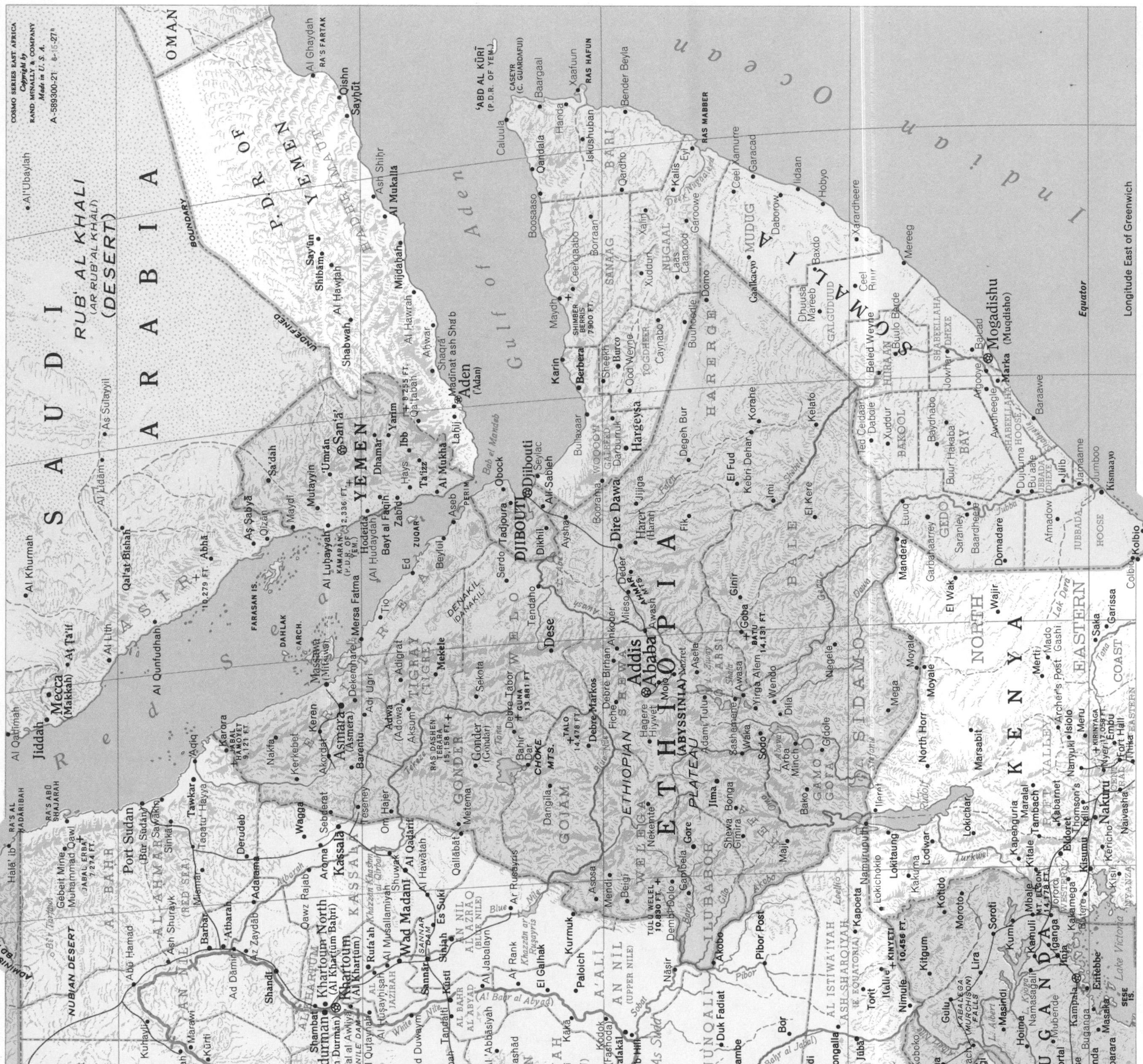

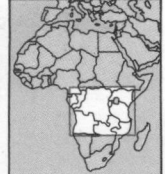

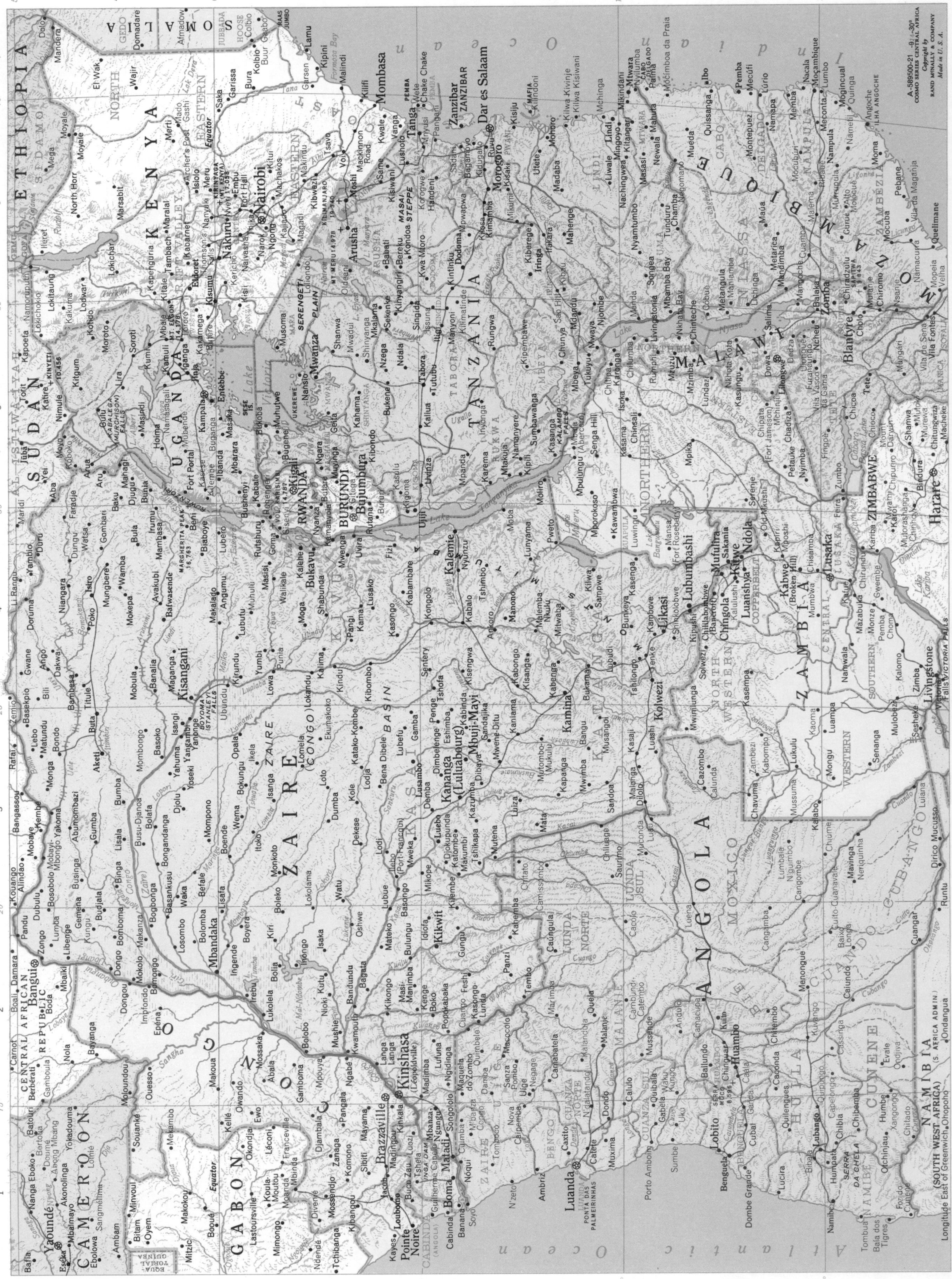

CENTRAL AFRICA

Statute Miles

Sinusoidal Projection

SCALE 1: 11,400,000   1 Inch = 180 Statute Miles

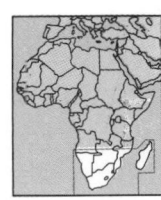
Same Scale as Main Map

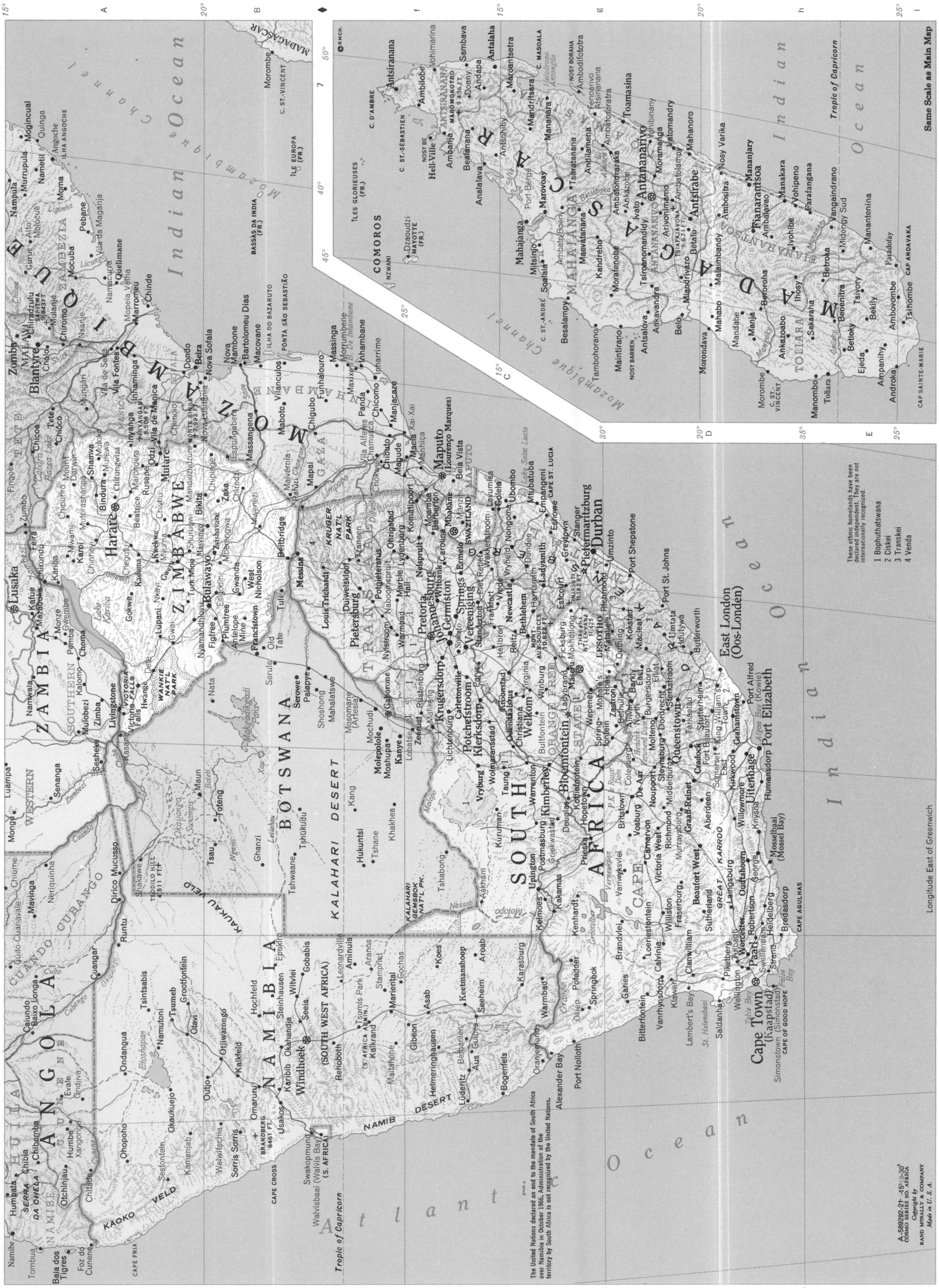

Sinusoidal Projection
SCALE 1:11,400,000   1 Inch = 180 Statute Miles

Statute Miles
Kilometers

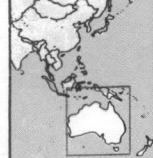

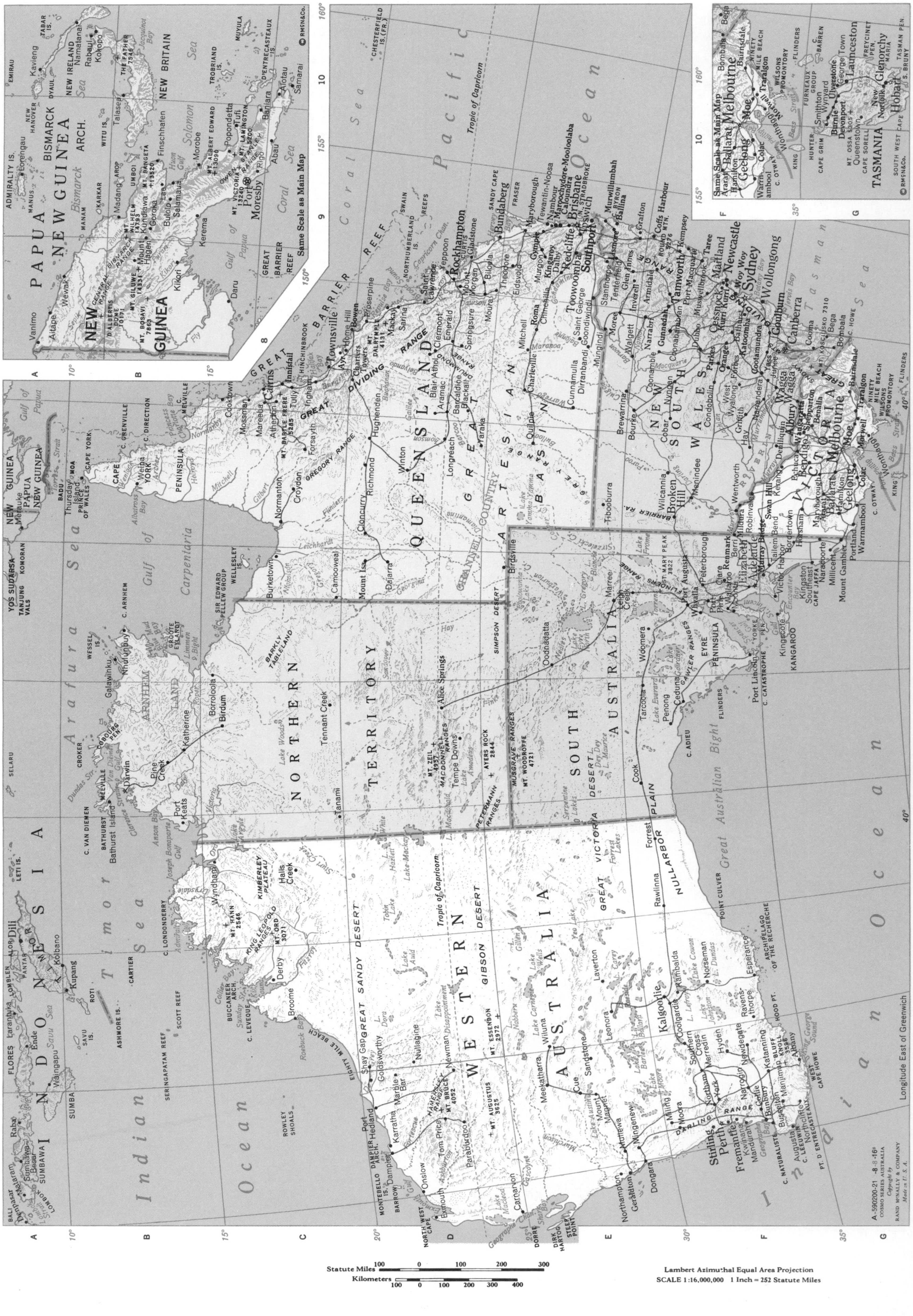

Statute Miles
100 0 100 200 300

Kilometers
100 0 100 200 300 400

Lambert Azimuthal Equal Area Projection
SCALE 1:16,000,000   1 Inch = 252 Statute Miles

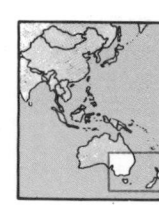

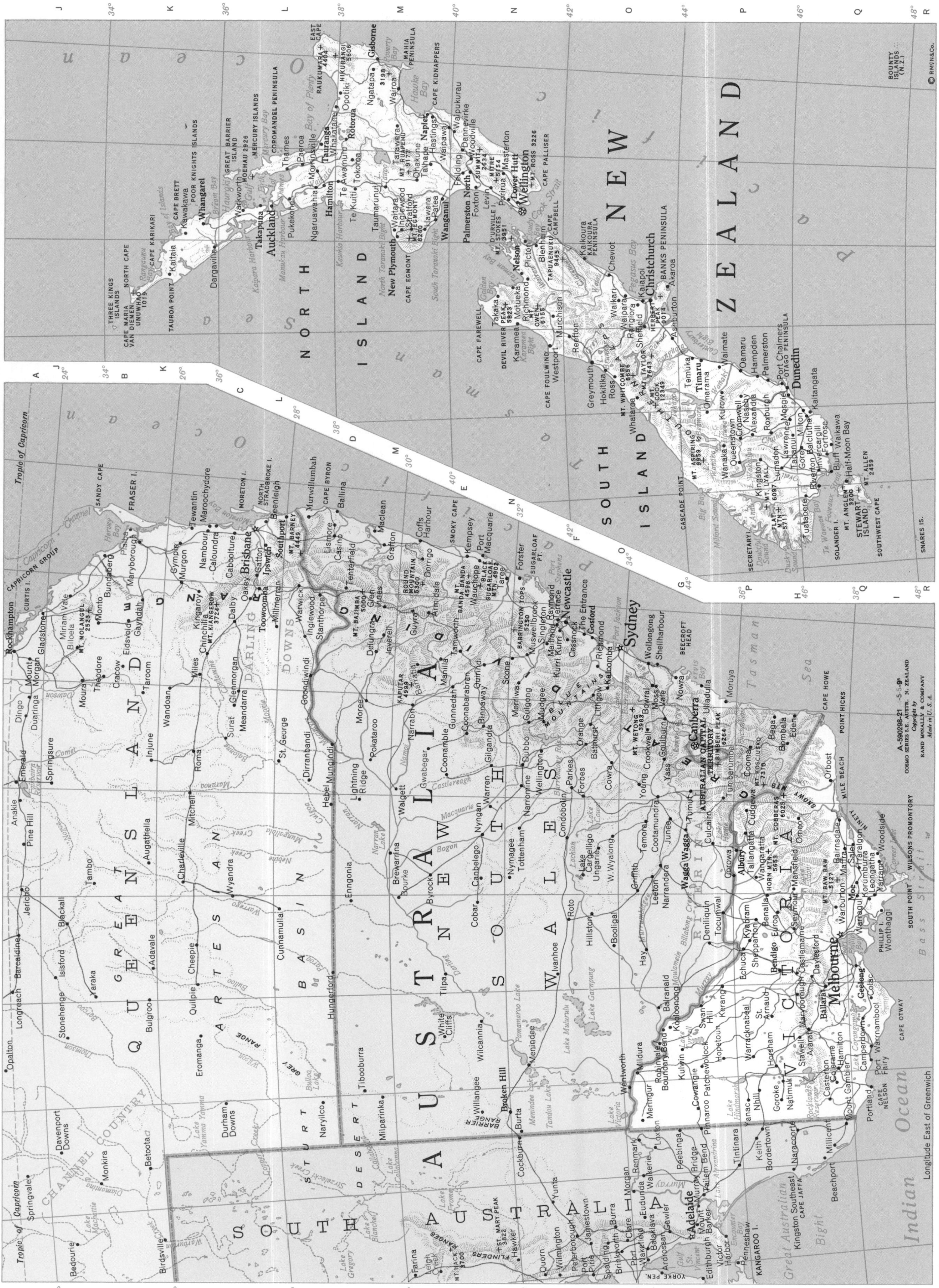

NORTH ISLAND
SOUTH ISLAND
NEW ZEALAND
SOUTH AUSTRALIA
NEW SOUTH WALES
QUEENSLAND
VICTORIA
AUSTRALIAN CAPITAL TERRITORY
Tasman Sea
Indian Ocean
Great Australian Bight
Bass Strait
Cook Strait
Tropic of Capricorn
Sydney
Melbourne
Adelaide
Brisbane
Canberra
Auckland
Wellington
Christchurch
Dunedin
Longitude East of Greenwich
A-590298-21 -5-5-9
COSMO SERIES S.E. AUSTR. - N. ZEALAND
Copyright by RAND McNALLY & COMPANY
Made in U. S. A.
Lambert Conformal Conic Projection
SCALE 1 : 8,000,000 1 Inch = 126 Statute Miles
Statute Miles 50 0 50 100 150
Kilometers 50 0 50 100 200

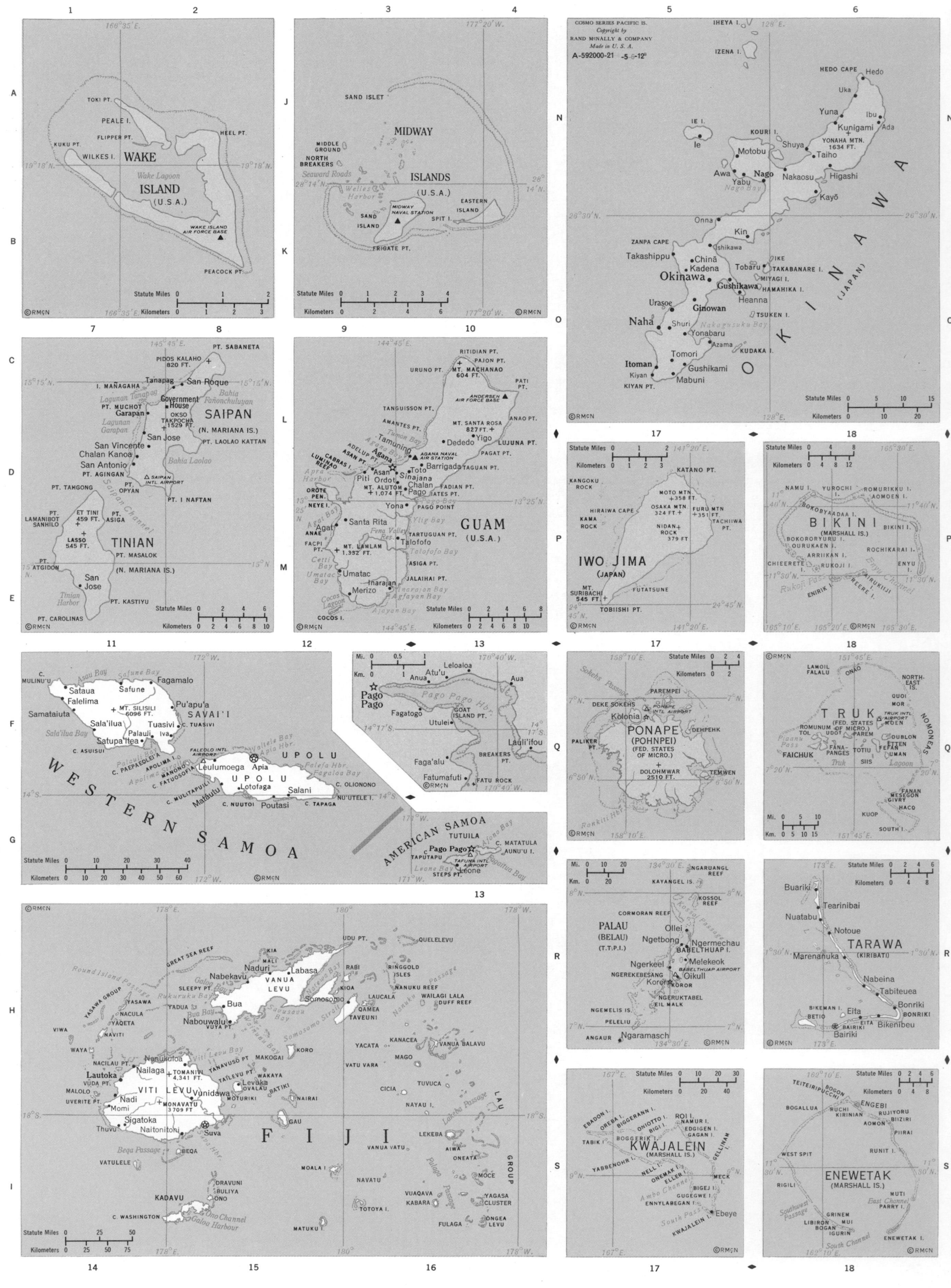

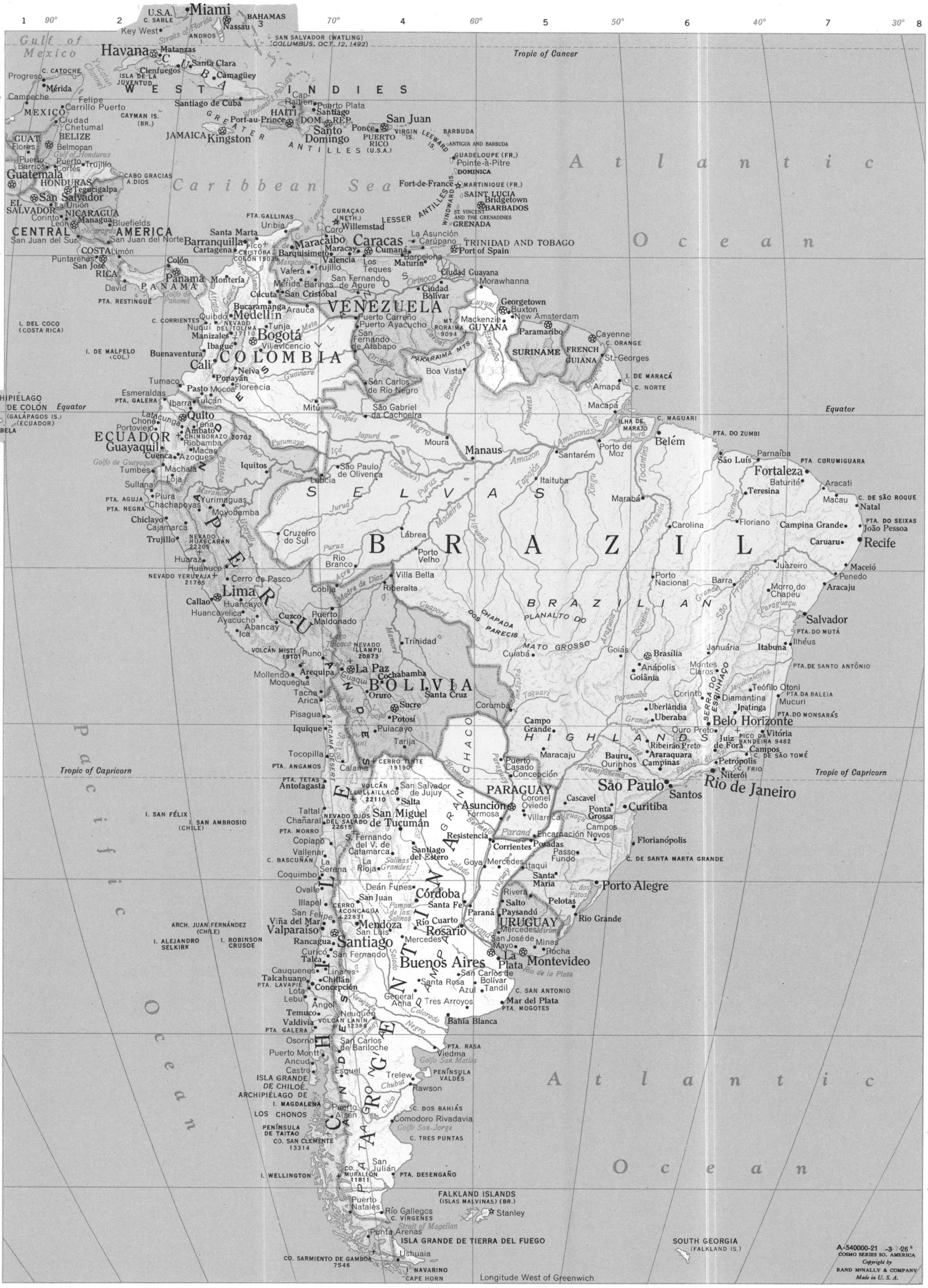

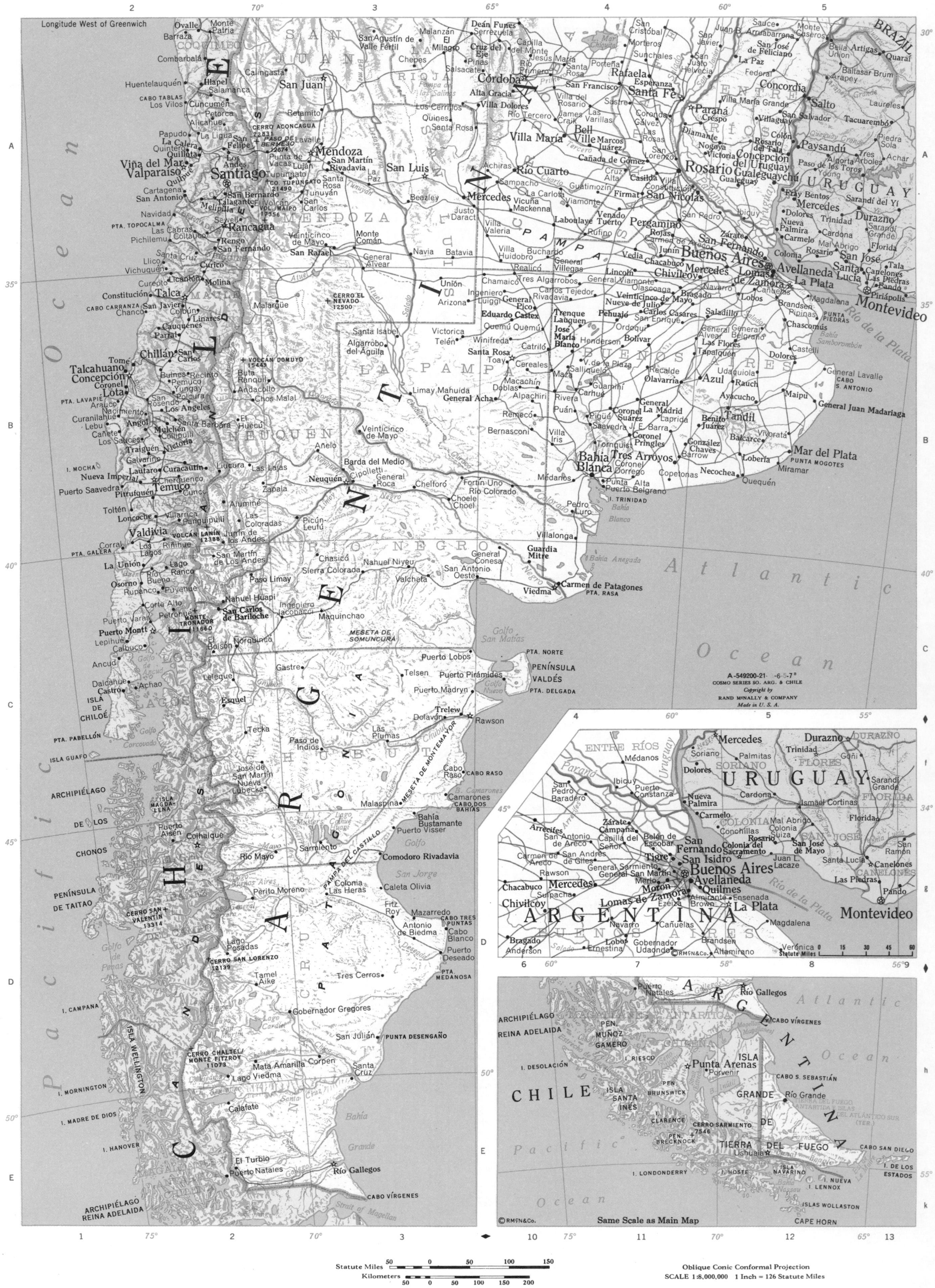

Oblique Conic Conformal Projection
SCALE 1:8,000,000   1 Inch = 126 Statute Miles

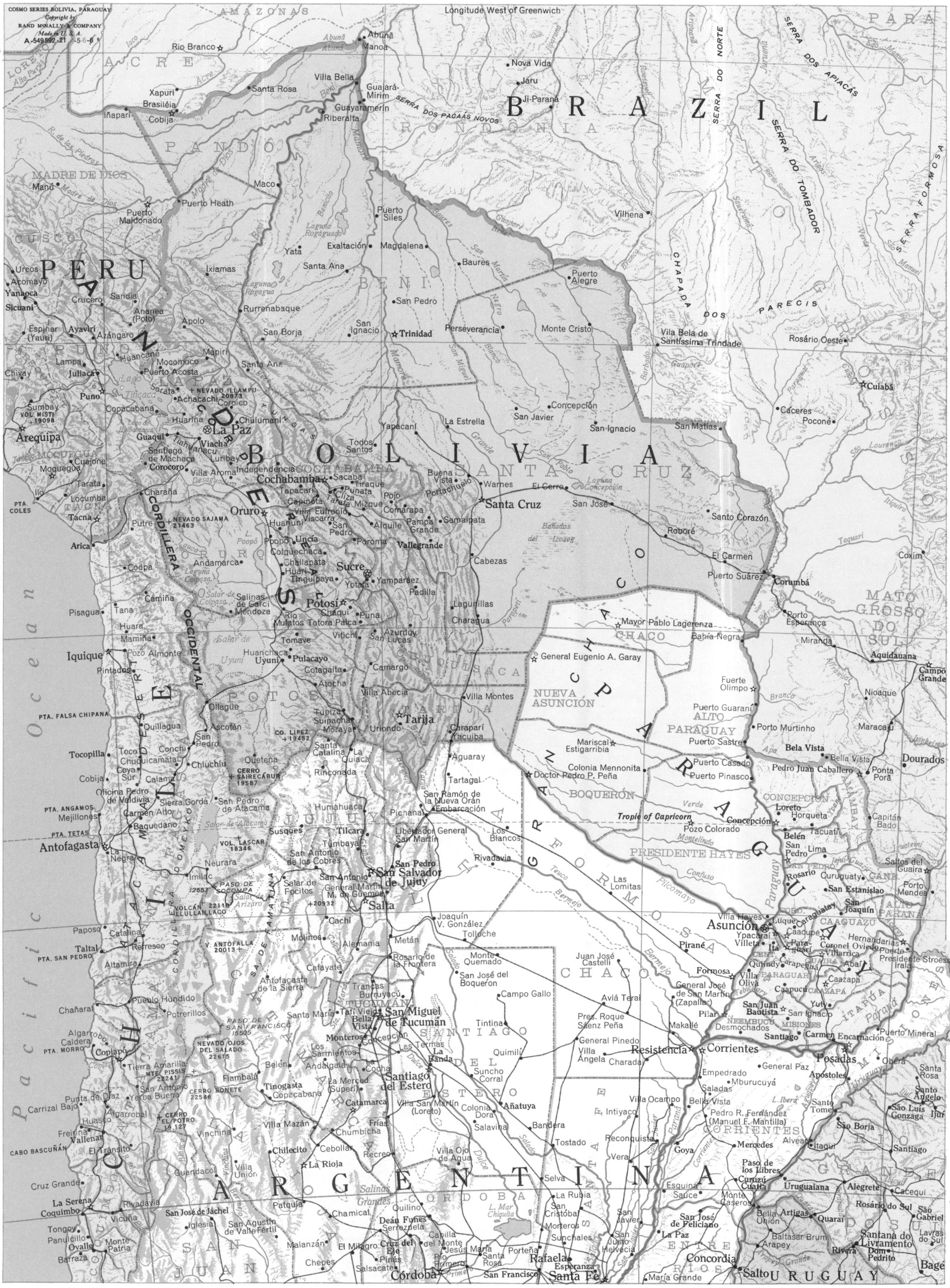

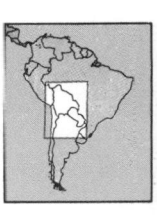

Oblique Conic Conformal Projection
SCALE 1:8,000,000 1 Inch = 126 Statute Miles

Statute Miles 50 0 50 100 150
Kilometers 50 0 50 100 150 200

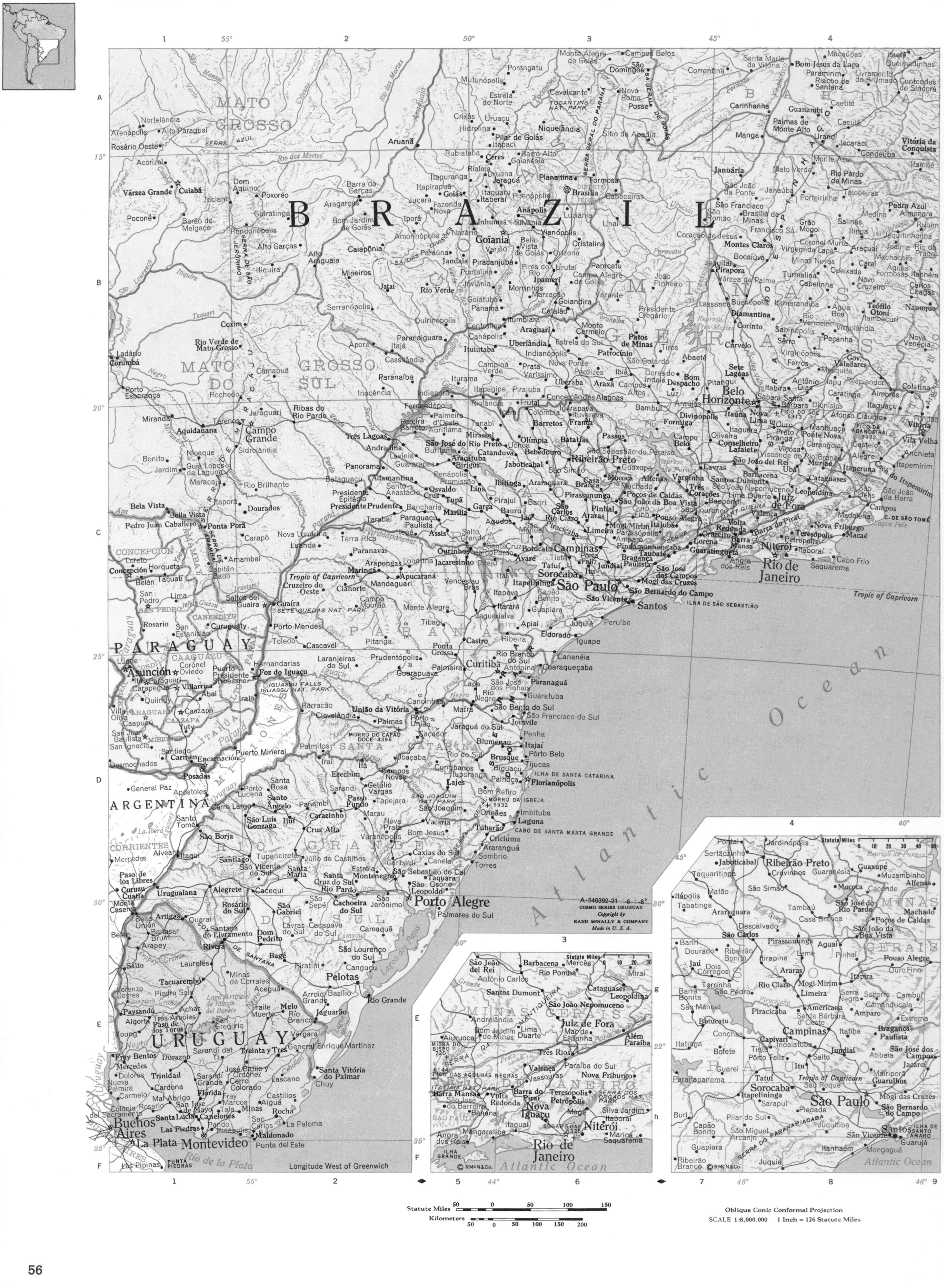

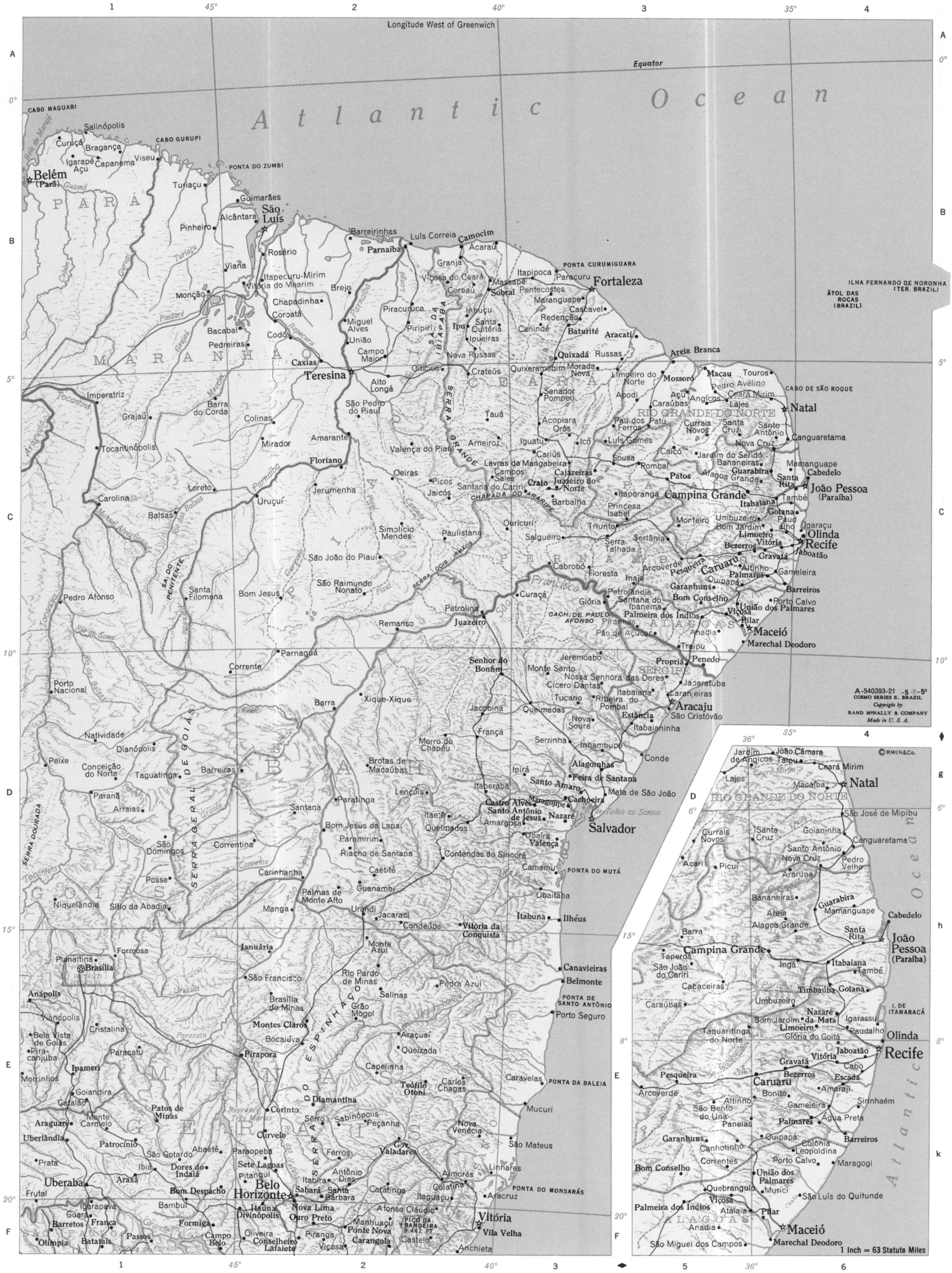

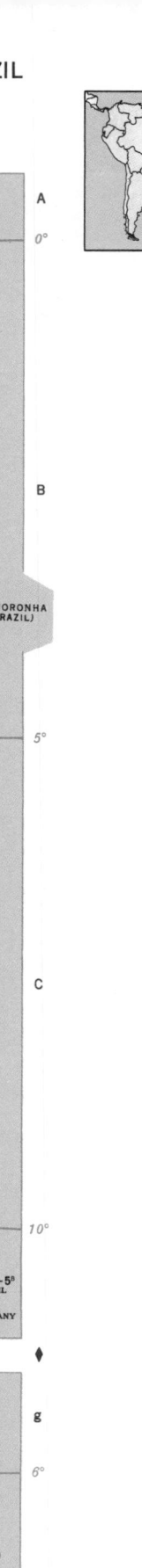

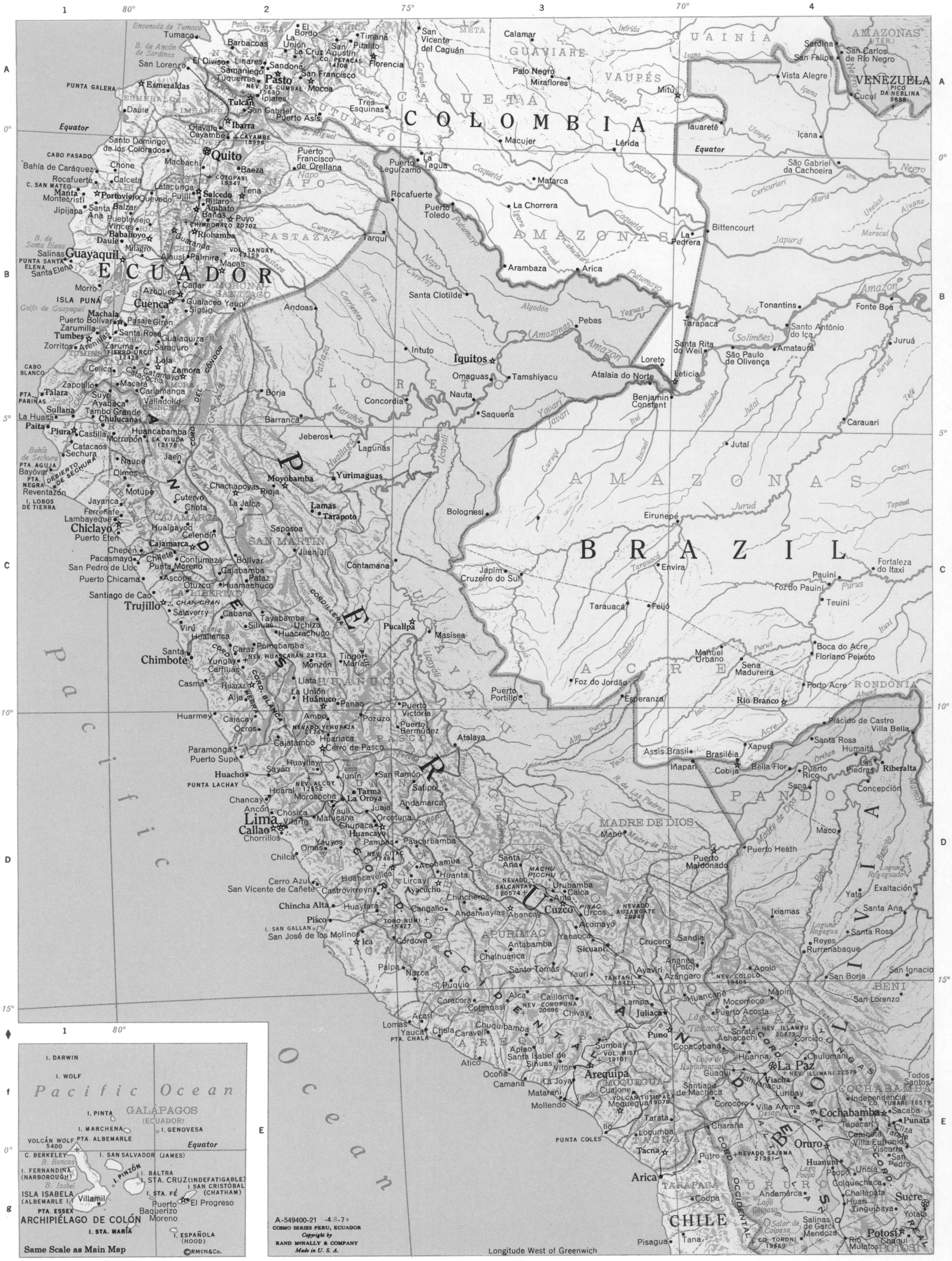

COLOMBIA

VENEZUELA
PICO DA NEBLINA
9888

ECUADOR

BRAZIL
AMAZONAS

ACRE

RONDONIA

PERU

BOLIVIA

CUZCO
MACHU PICCHU

MADRE DE DIOS

PANDO

BENI

COCHABAMBA

ORURO

CHILE

Pacific Ocean

Quito

Guayaquil

Cuenca

Lima
Callao

Trujillo

Chimbote

Iquitos

Arequipa

La Paz

Cochabamba

Oruro

Potosí

Sucre

Inset (lower left):

Pacific Ocean

GALÁPAGOS
(ECUADOR)

ARCHIPIÉLAGO DE COLÓN

Same Scale as Main Map

I. DARWIN
I. WOLF
I. PINTA
I. MARCHENA   I. GENOVESA
VOLCÁN WOLF   PTA. ALBEMARLE
5400
C. BERKELEY   I. SAN SALVADOR (JAMES)
B. Bancas
I. FERNANDINA   I. PINZÓN   BALTRA
(NARBOROUGH)   STA. CRUZ (INDEFATIGABLE)
B. Isabel   I. SAN CRISTÓBAL (CHATHAM)
ISLA ISABELA   I. STA. FÉ   El Progreso
(ALBEMARLE I.)
Villamil   Puerto
PTA. ESSEX   Baquerizo
                 Moreno
I. STA. MARÍA
I. ESPAÑOLA (HOOD)

A-549400-21   -4-8-7°
COSMO SERIES PERU, ECUADOR
Copyright by
RAND McNALLY & COMPANY
Made in U.S.A.

Longitude West of Greenwich

Statute Miles   50   0   50   100   150
Kilometers   50   0   50   100   150   200

Oblique Conic Conformal Projection
SCALE 1:8,000,000   1 Inch = 126 Statute Miles

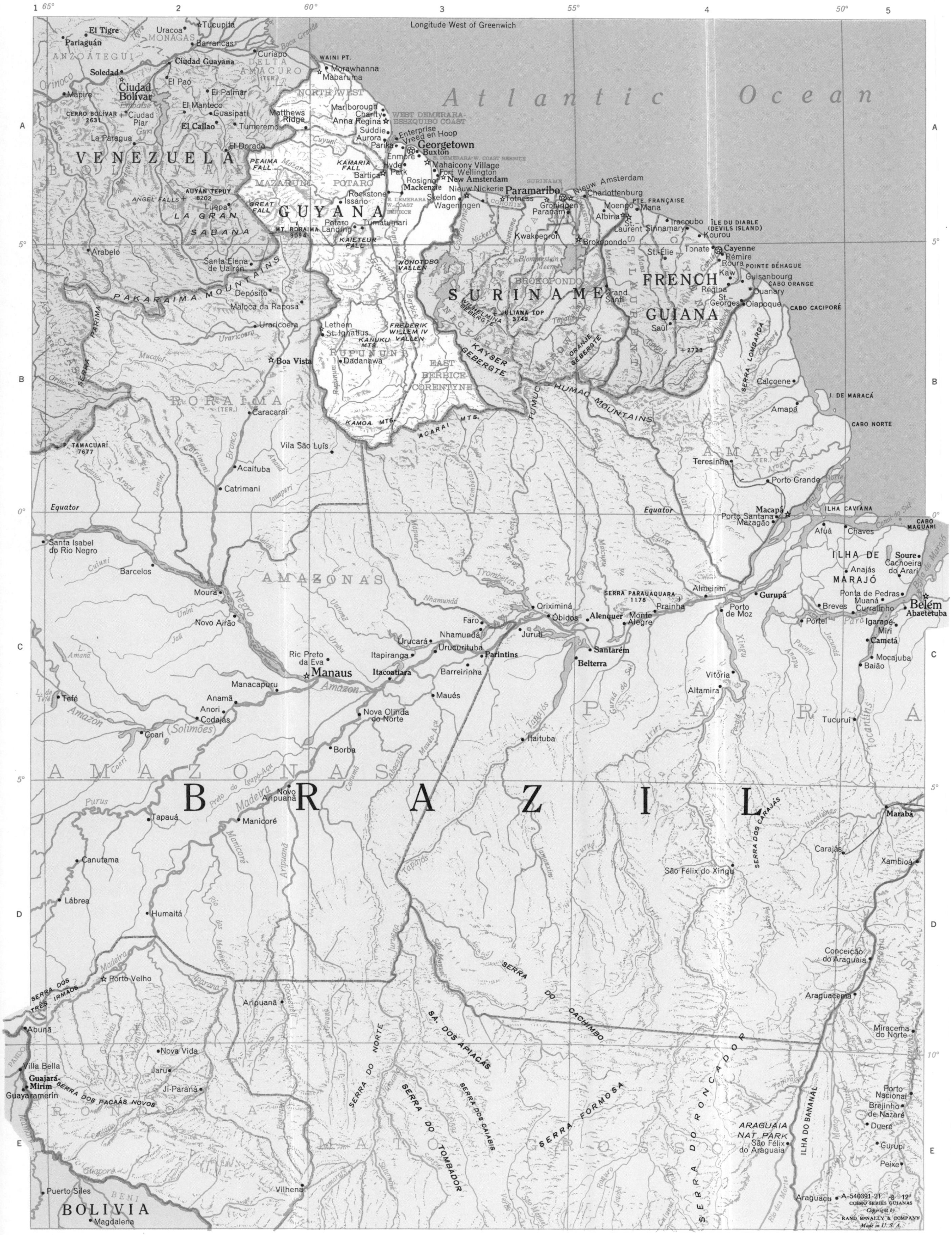

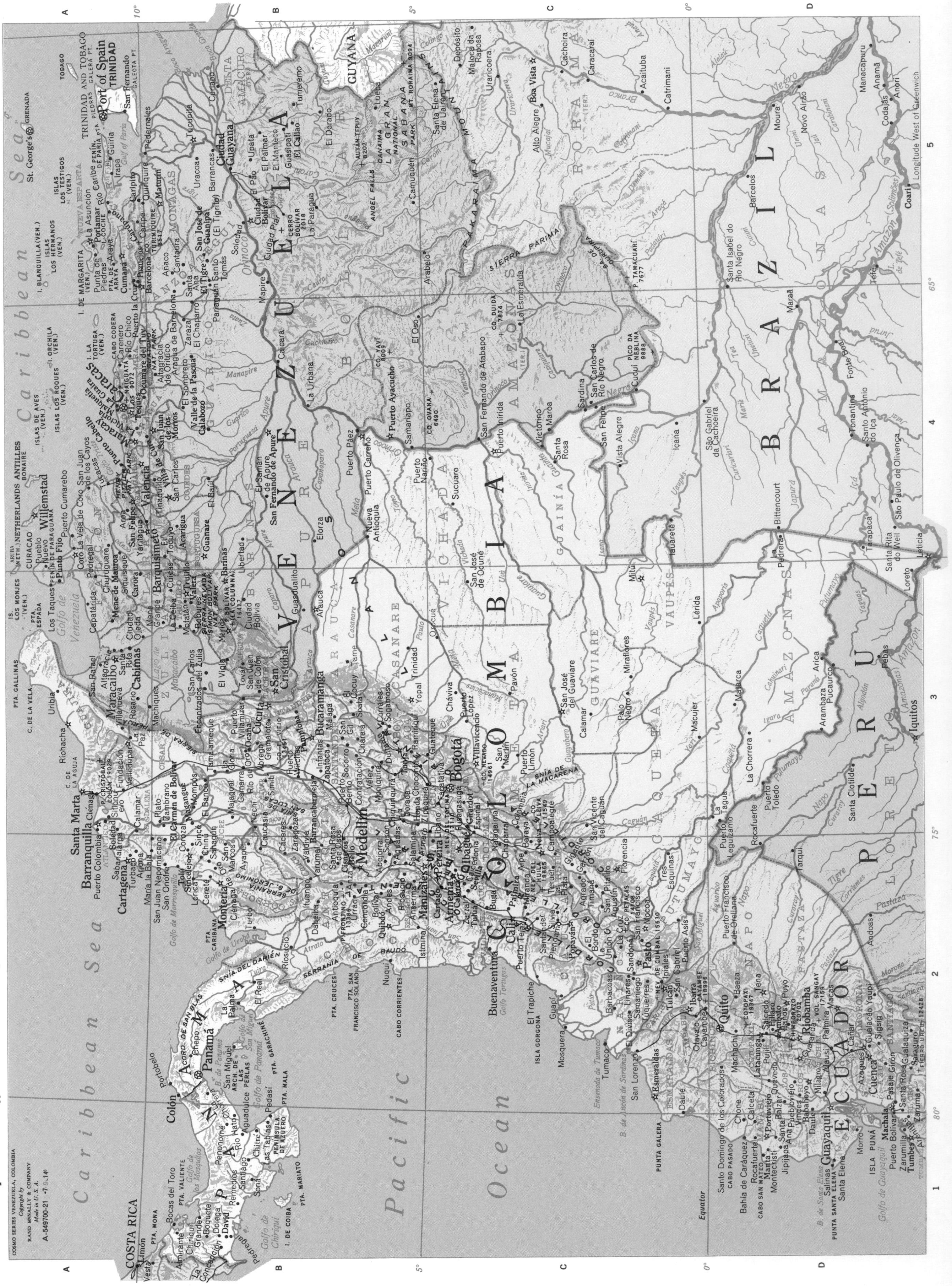

Statute Miles 50 0 50 100 150

Kilometers 50 0 50 100 150 200

Oblique Conic Conformal Projection
SCALE 1:8,000,000 1 Inch = 126 Statute Miles

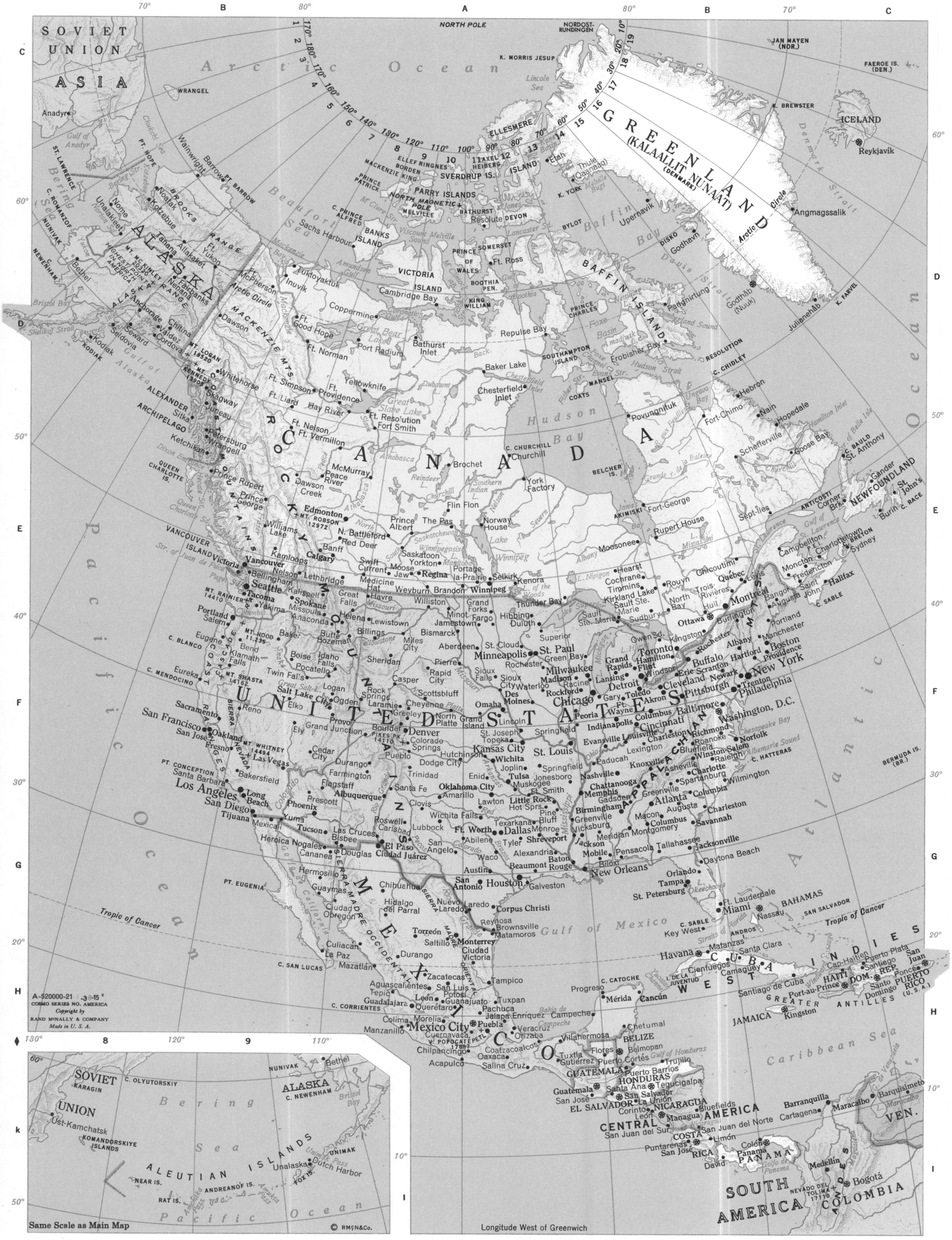

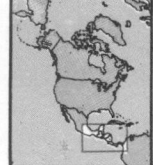

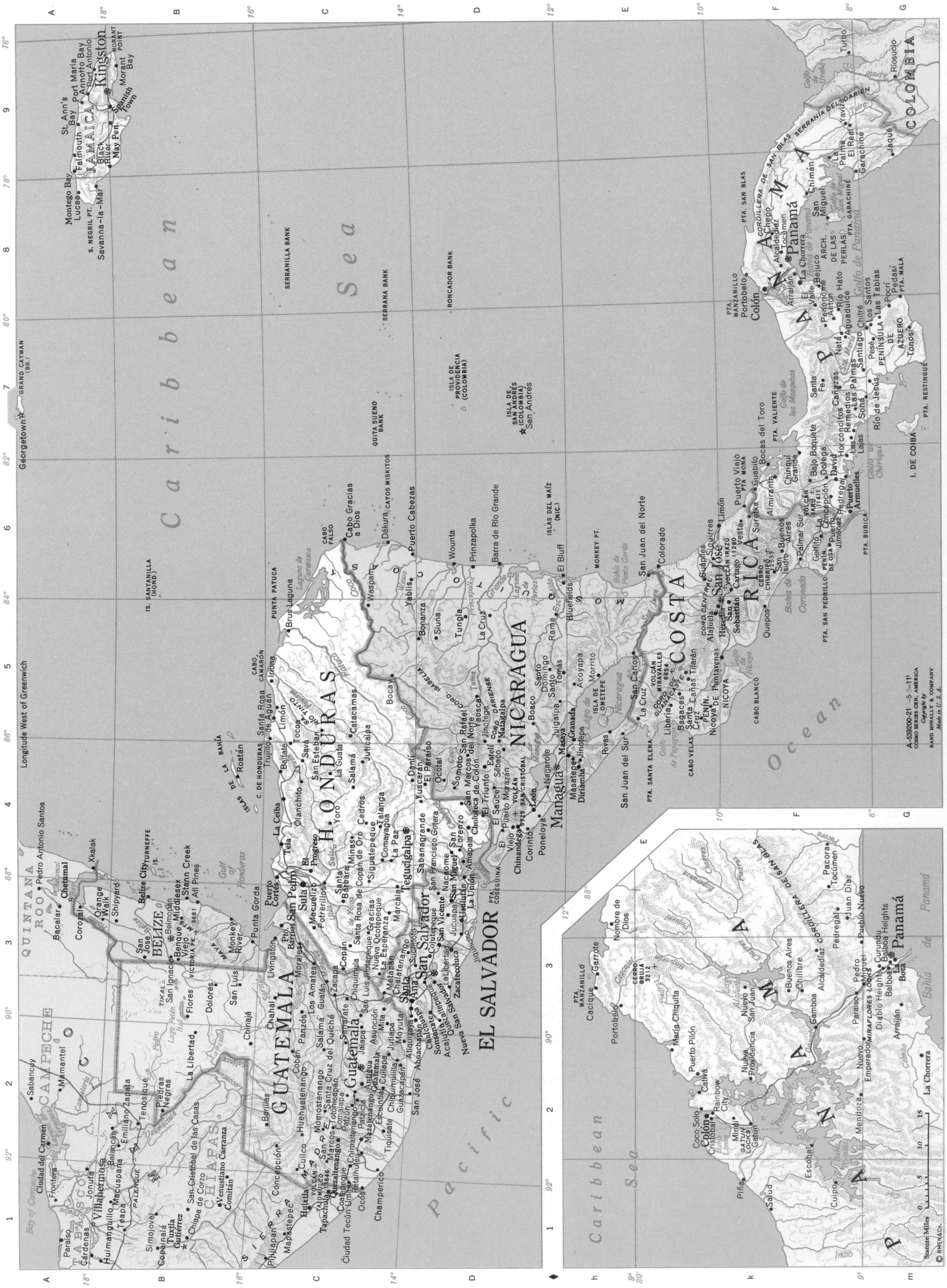

Statute Miles 25 0 25 75 125
Kilometers 25 0 25 75 125 175

Oblique Conic Conformal Projection
SCALE 1:6,000,000 1 Inch = 95 Statute Miles

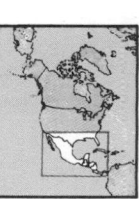

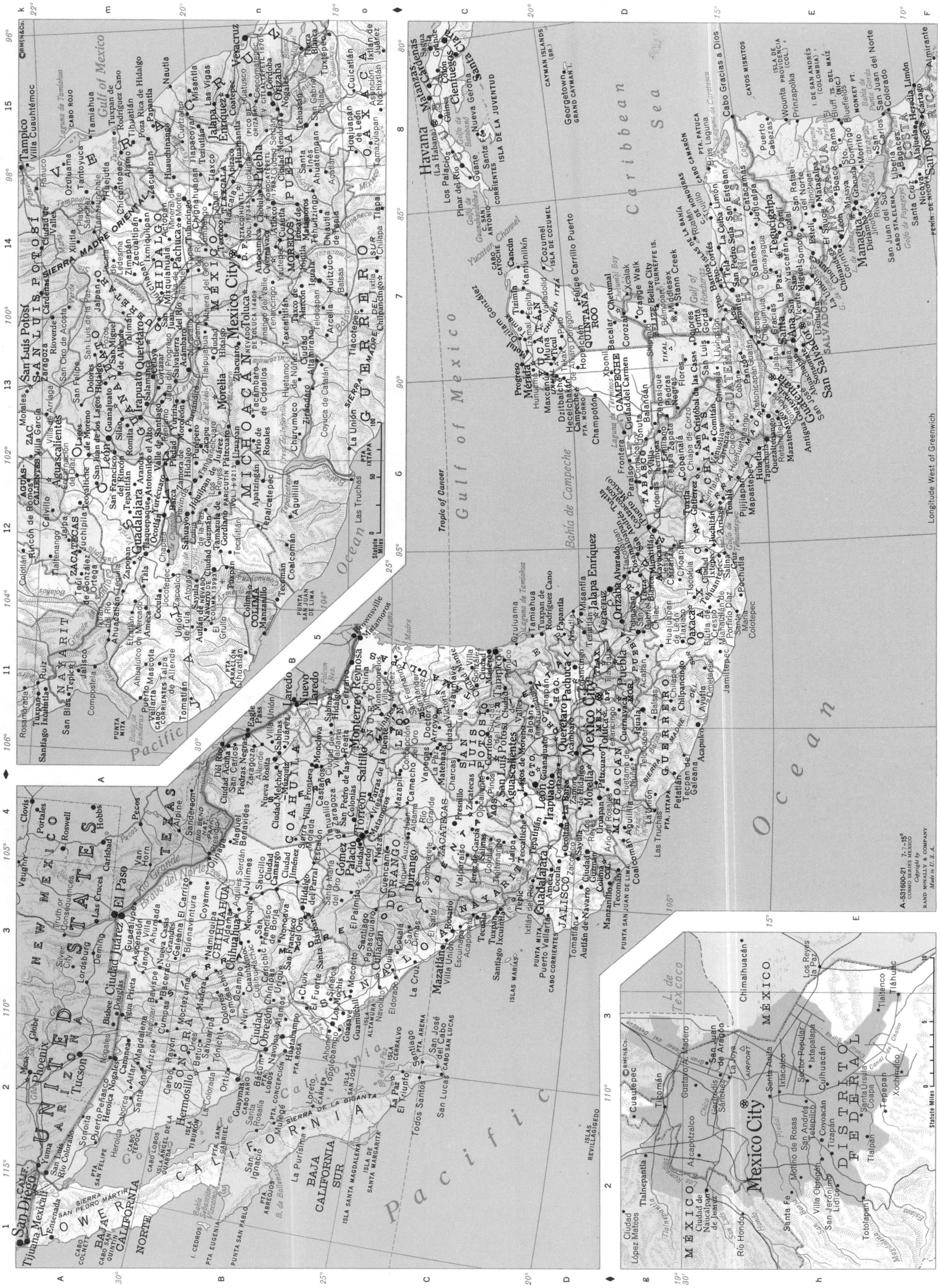

Oblique Conic Conformal Projection
SCALE 1:12,000 000 1 Inch = 189 Statute Miles

Statute Miles 50 25 0 50 100 150 200 250

Kilometers 50 0 100 200 300

Statute Miles 25 0 25 75 125

Kilometers 25 0 25 75 125 175

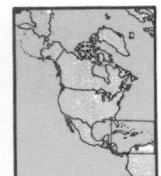

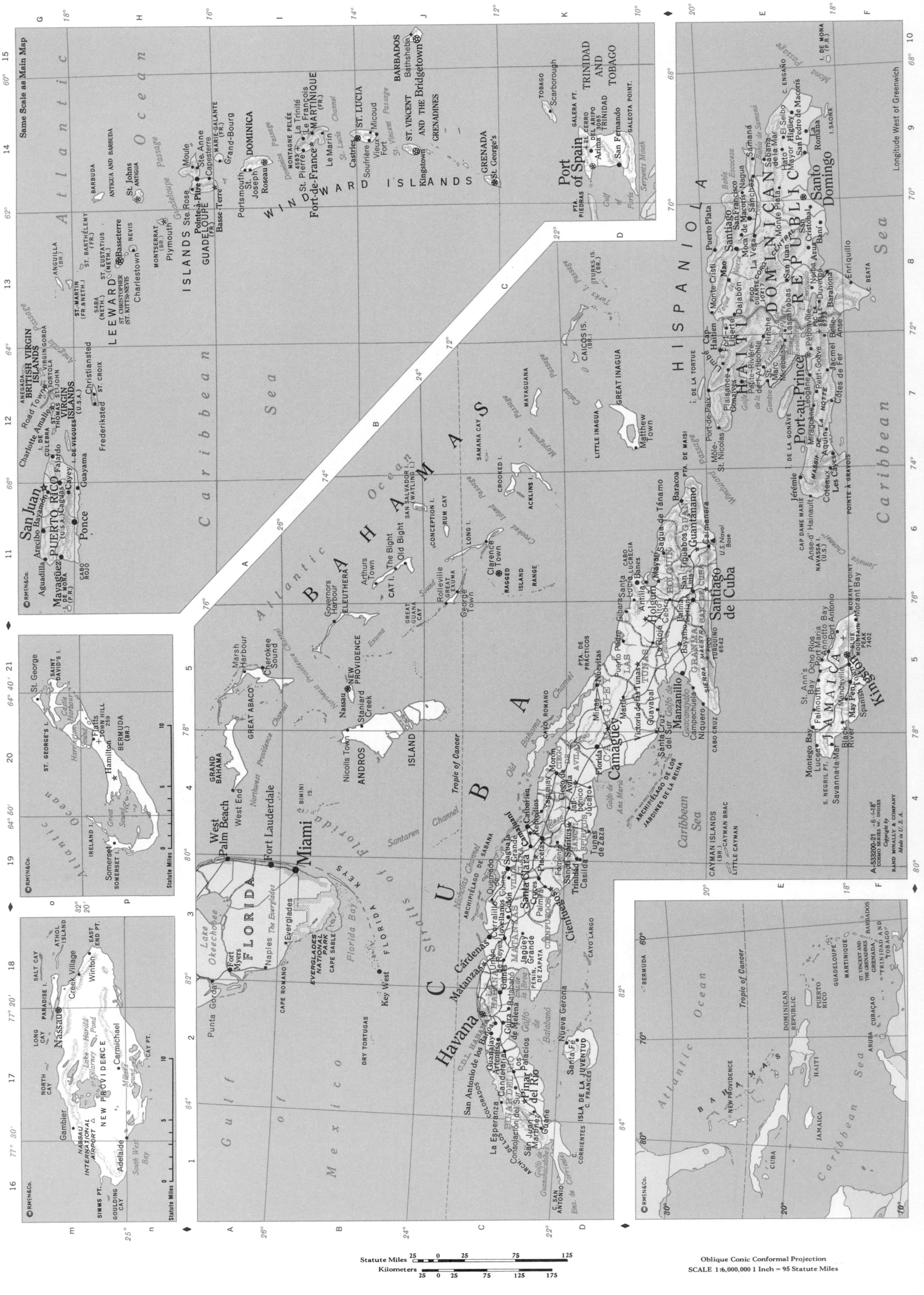

Oblique Conic Conformal Projection

SCALE 1:6,000,000 1 Inch = 95 Statute Miles

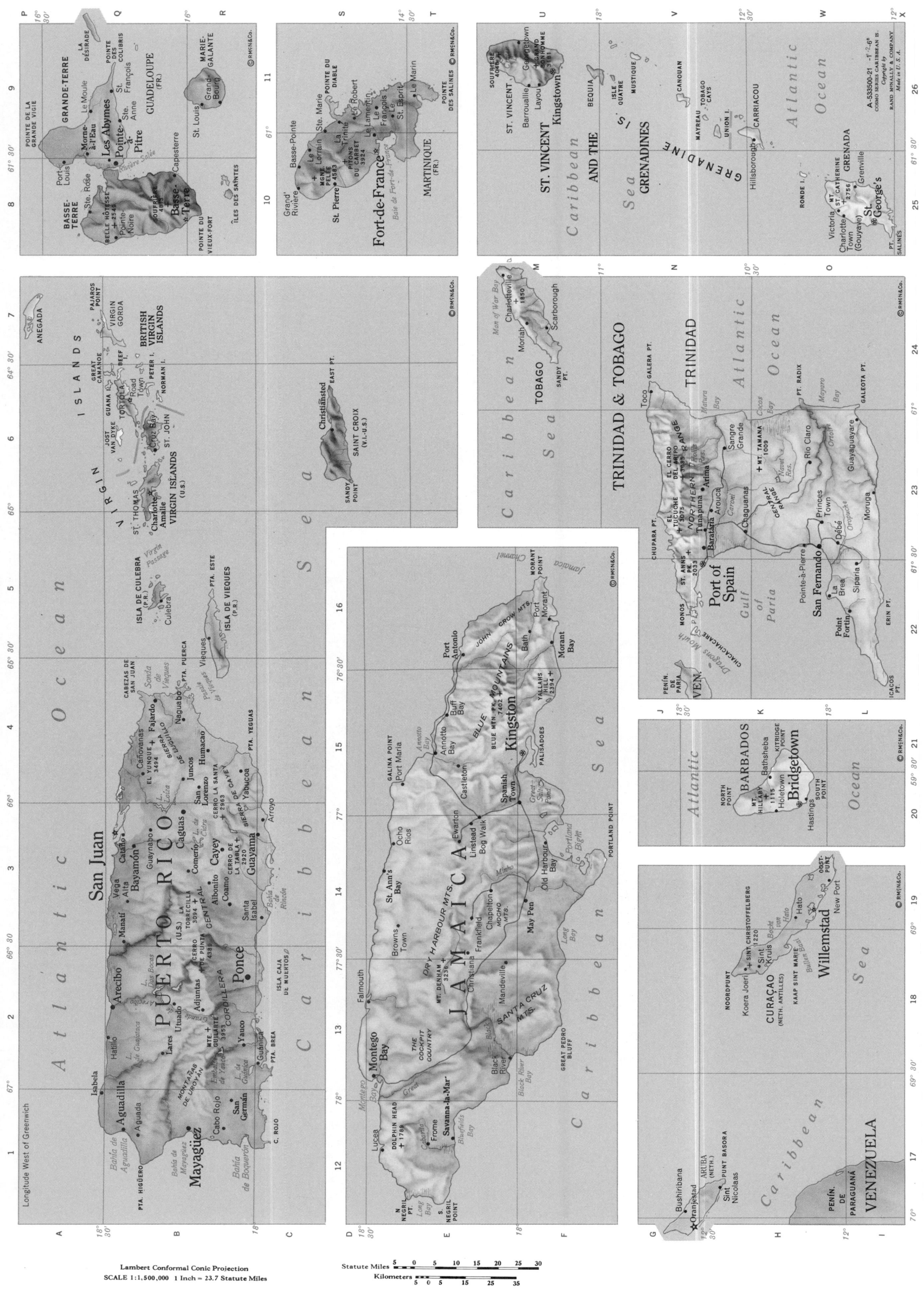

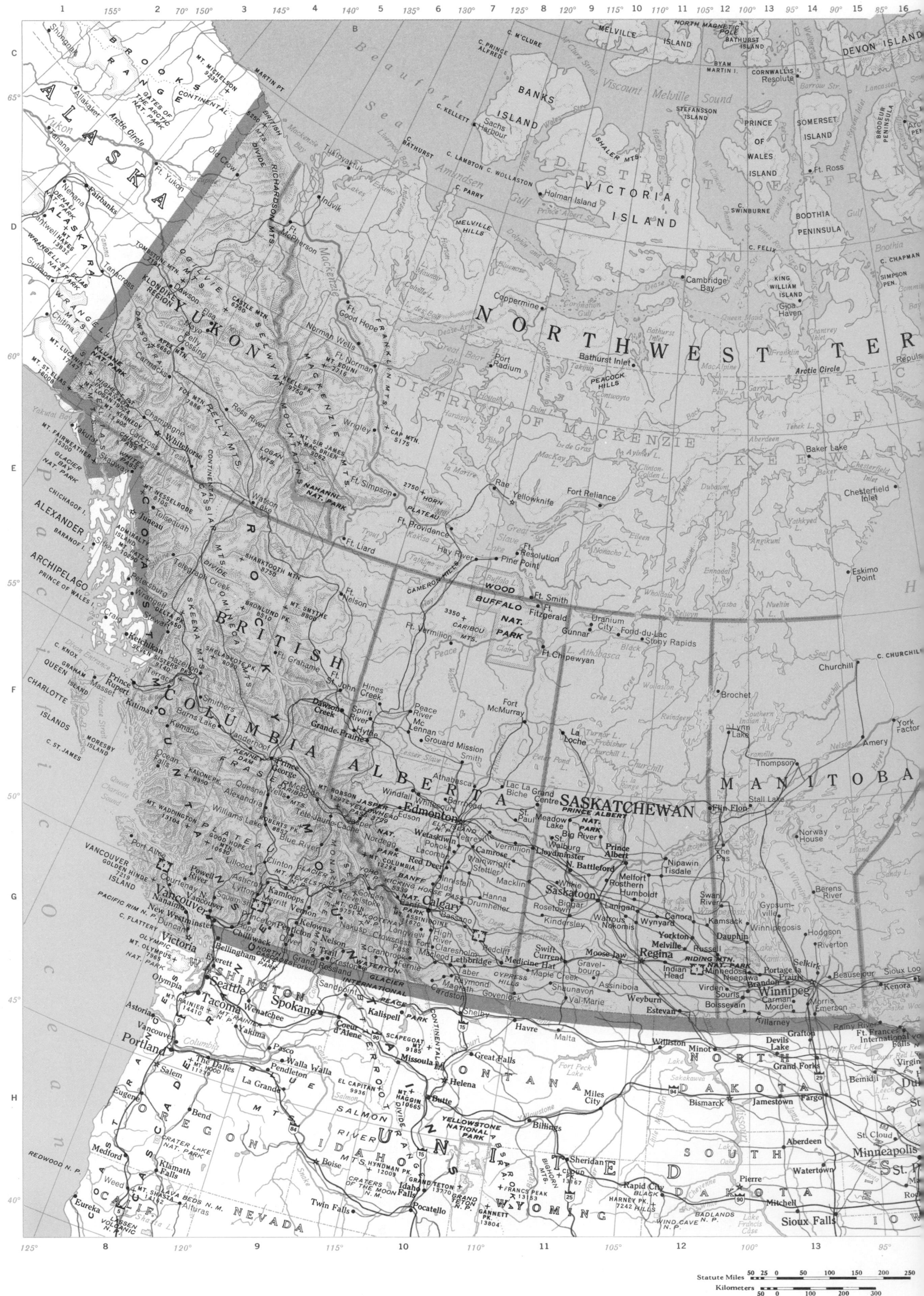

Lambert Conformal Conic Projection
SCALE 1:12,000,000   1 Inch = 189 Statute Miles

A-520200-72 -8-8-10⁸⁰
COSMO SERIES CANADA
Copyright by
RAND McNALLY & COMPANY
Made in U.S.A.

Longitude West of Greenwich

67

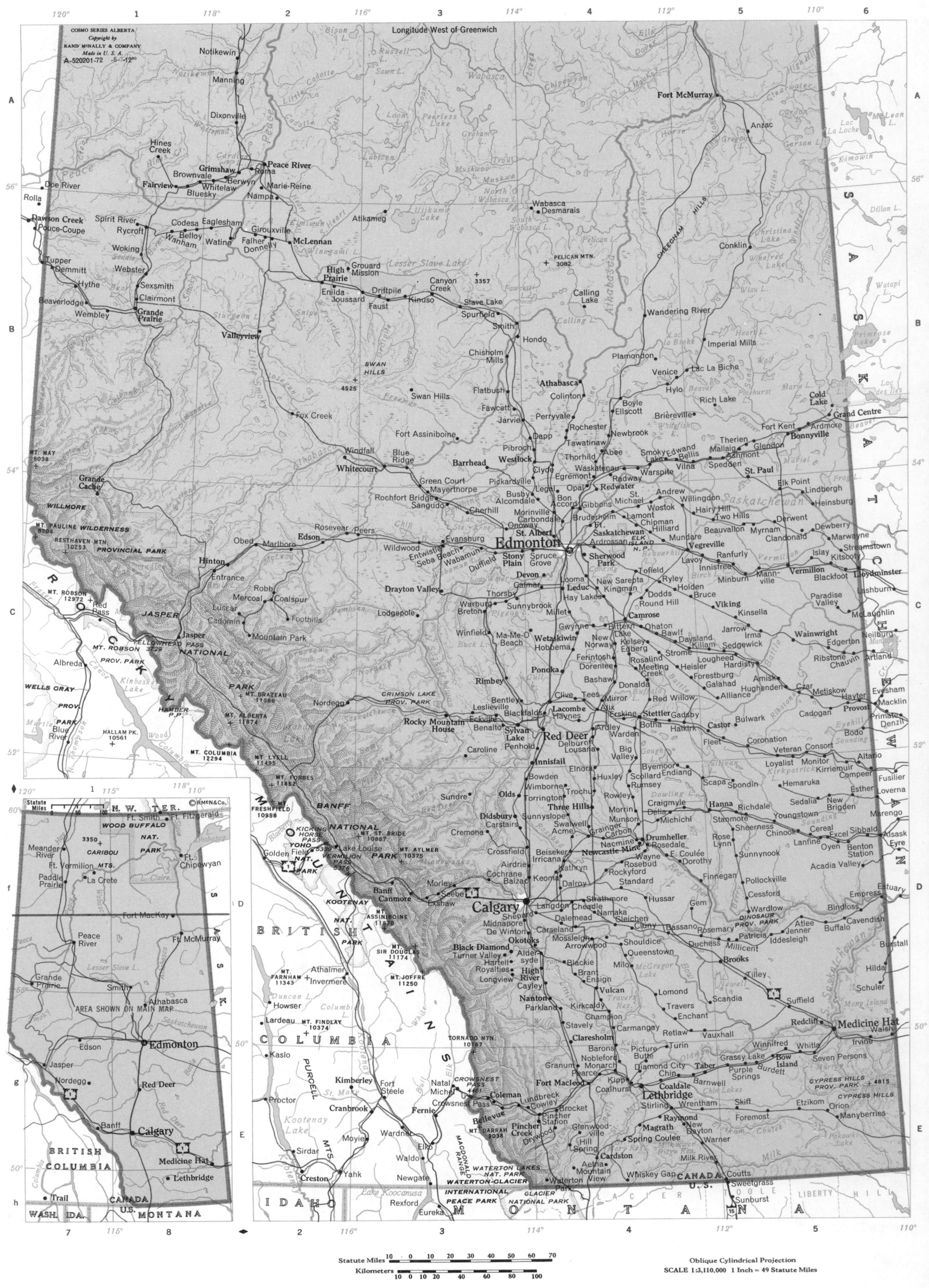

Oblique Cylindrical Projection
SCALE 1:3,110,000   1 Inch = 49 Statute Miles

Oblique Cylindrical Projection
SCALE 1:4,255,000 1 Inch = 67 Statute Miles

Statute Miles 10 0 10 20 30 40 50 60 70 80 90 100

Kilometers 10 0 10 20 40 60 80 100 120 140

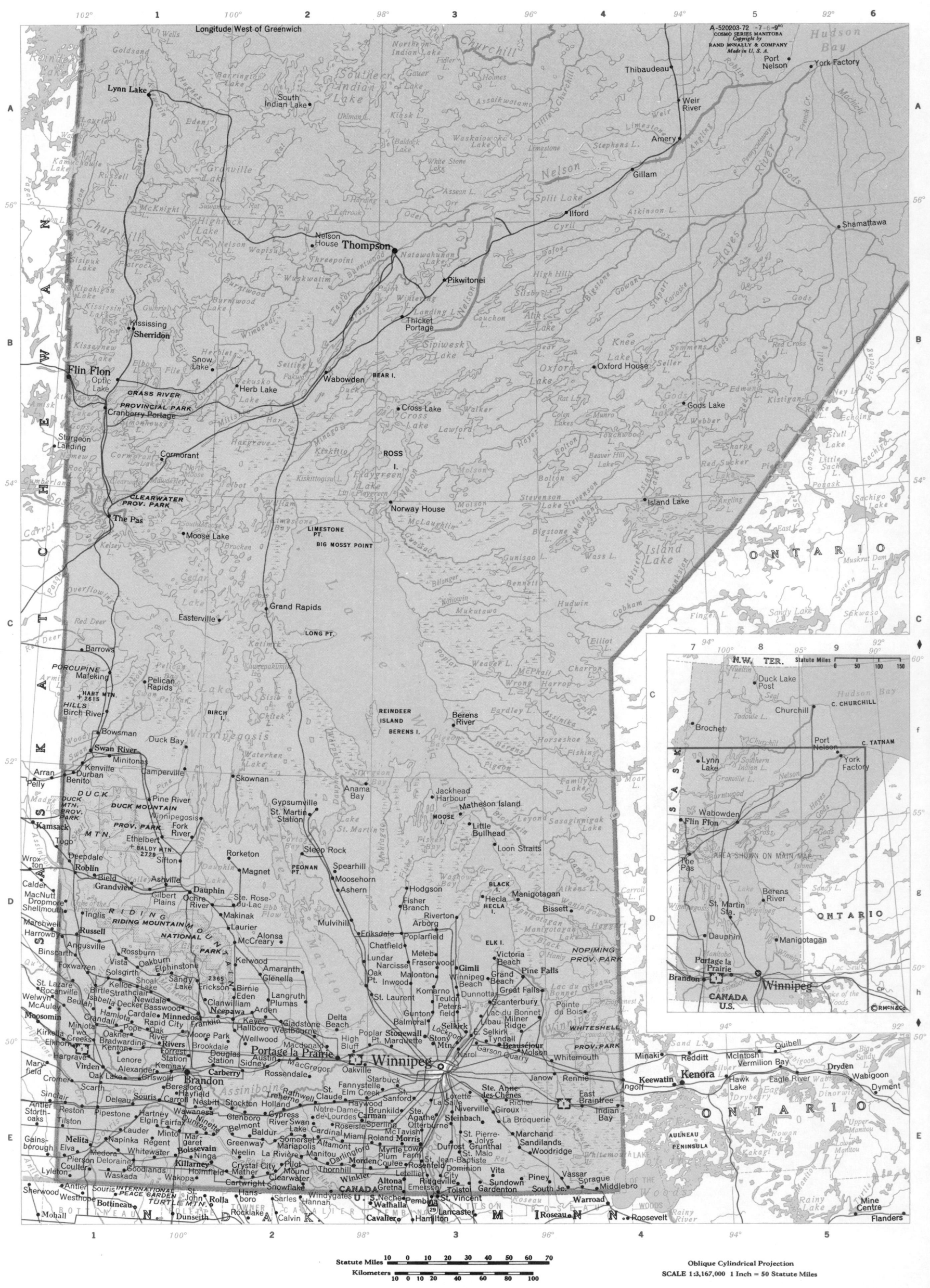

Manitoba

A-520203-72 -7-6-9⁹ᵗʰ
COSMO SERIES MANITOBA
Copyright by
RAND McNALLY & COMPANY
Made in U. S. A.

Oblique Cylindrical Projection
SCALE 1:3,167,000 1 Inch = 50 Statute Miles

Statute Miles
Kilometers

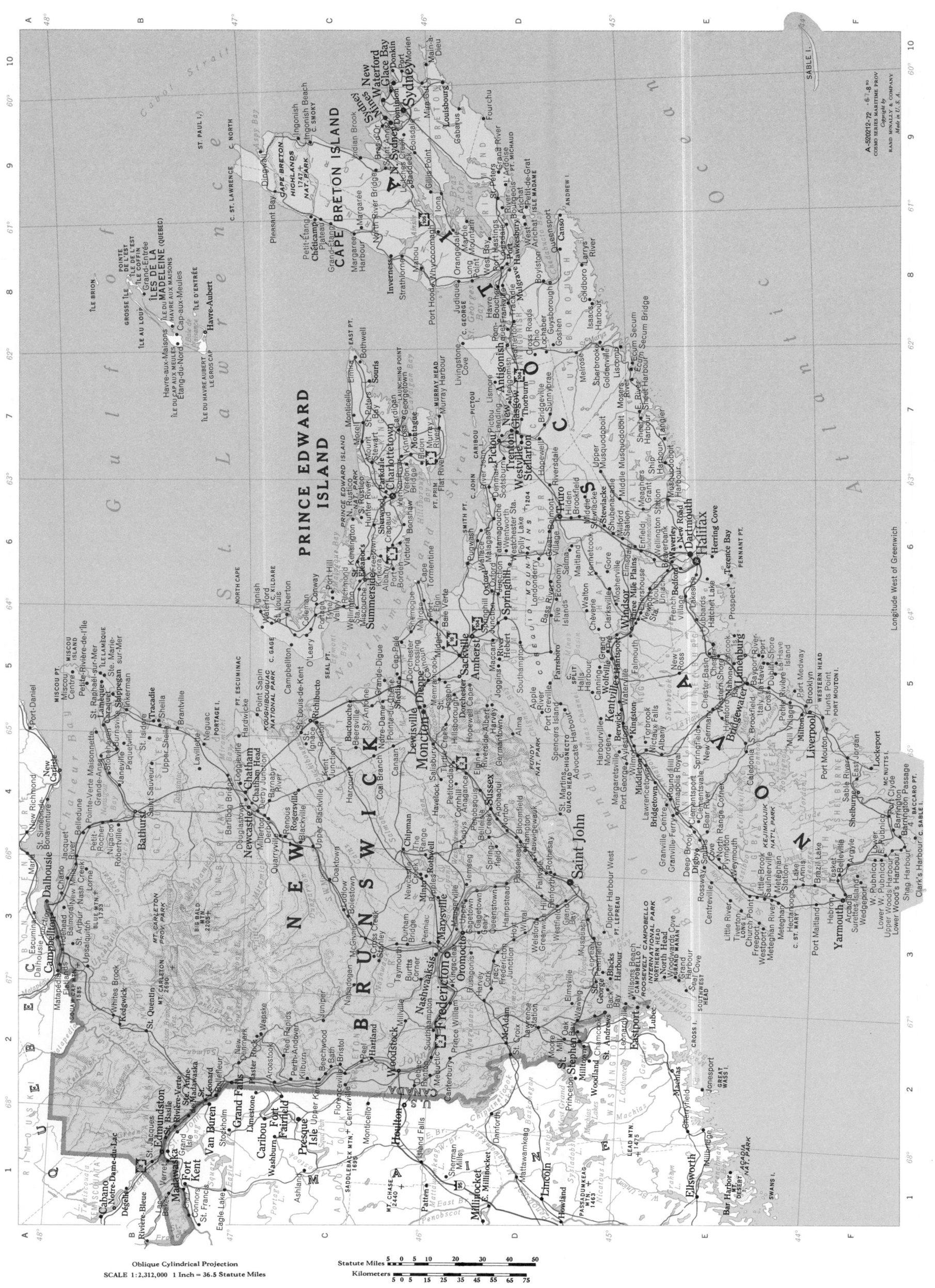

Oblique Cylindrical Projection
SCALE 1:2,312,000 1 Inch = 36.5 Statute Miles

Statute Miles
Kilometers

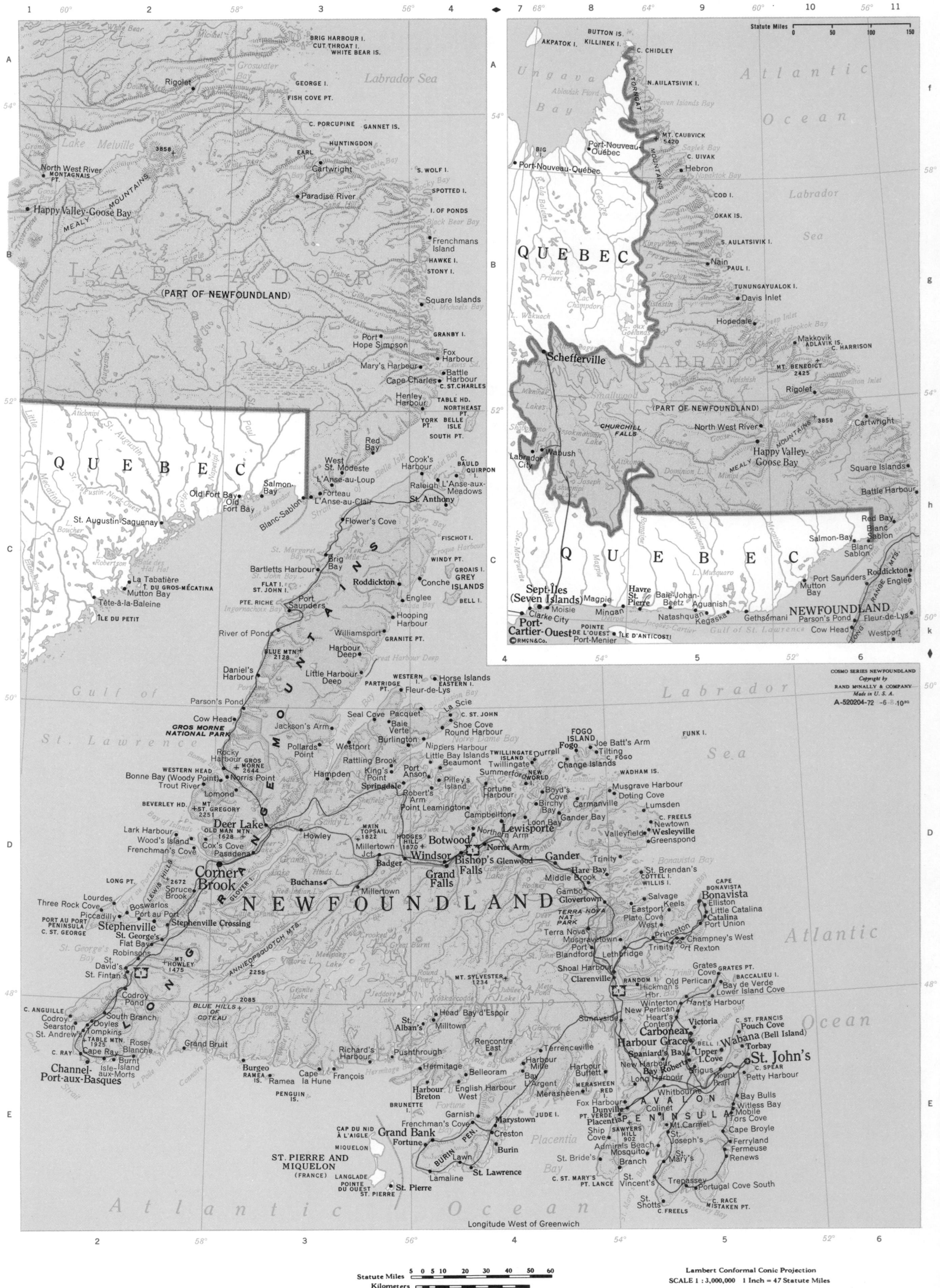

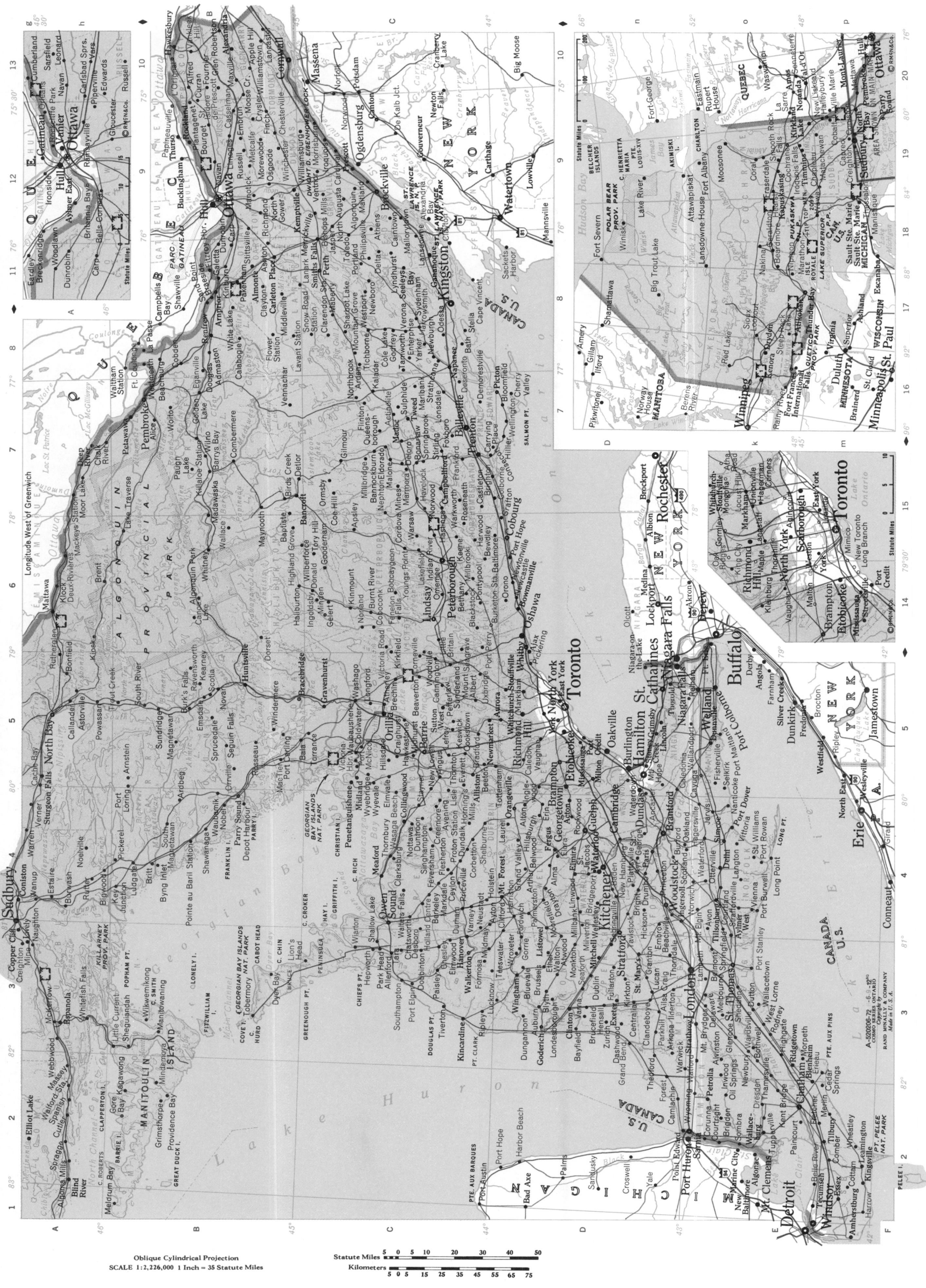

Oblique Cylindrical Projection
SCALE 1:2,226,000 1 Inch = 35 Statute Miles

Statute Miles
Kilometers

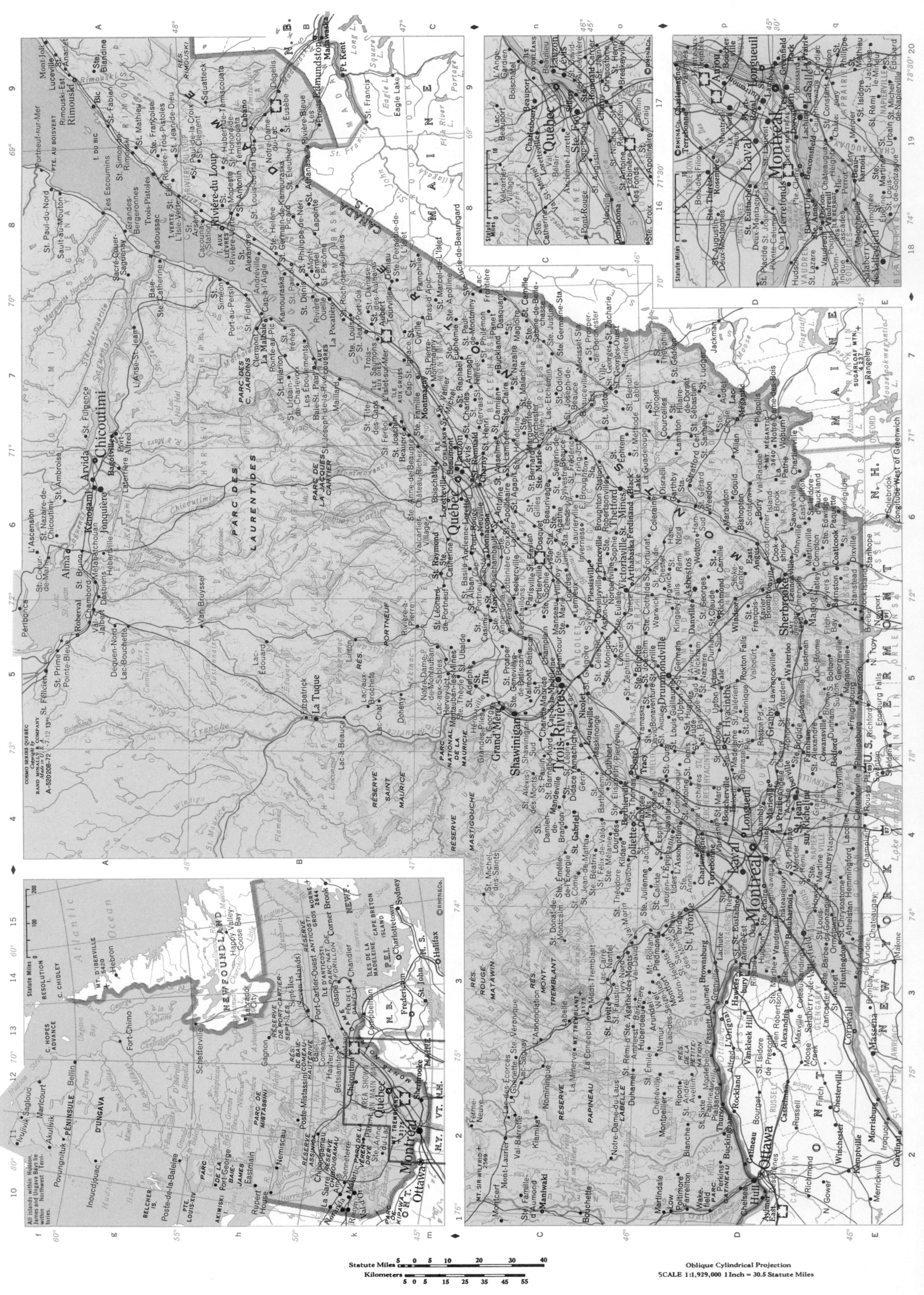

Statute Miles 5 0 5 10 20 30 40
Kilometers 5 0 5 15 25 35 45 55

Oblique Cylindrical Projection
SCALE 1:1,929,000 1 Inch = 30.5 Statute Miles

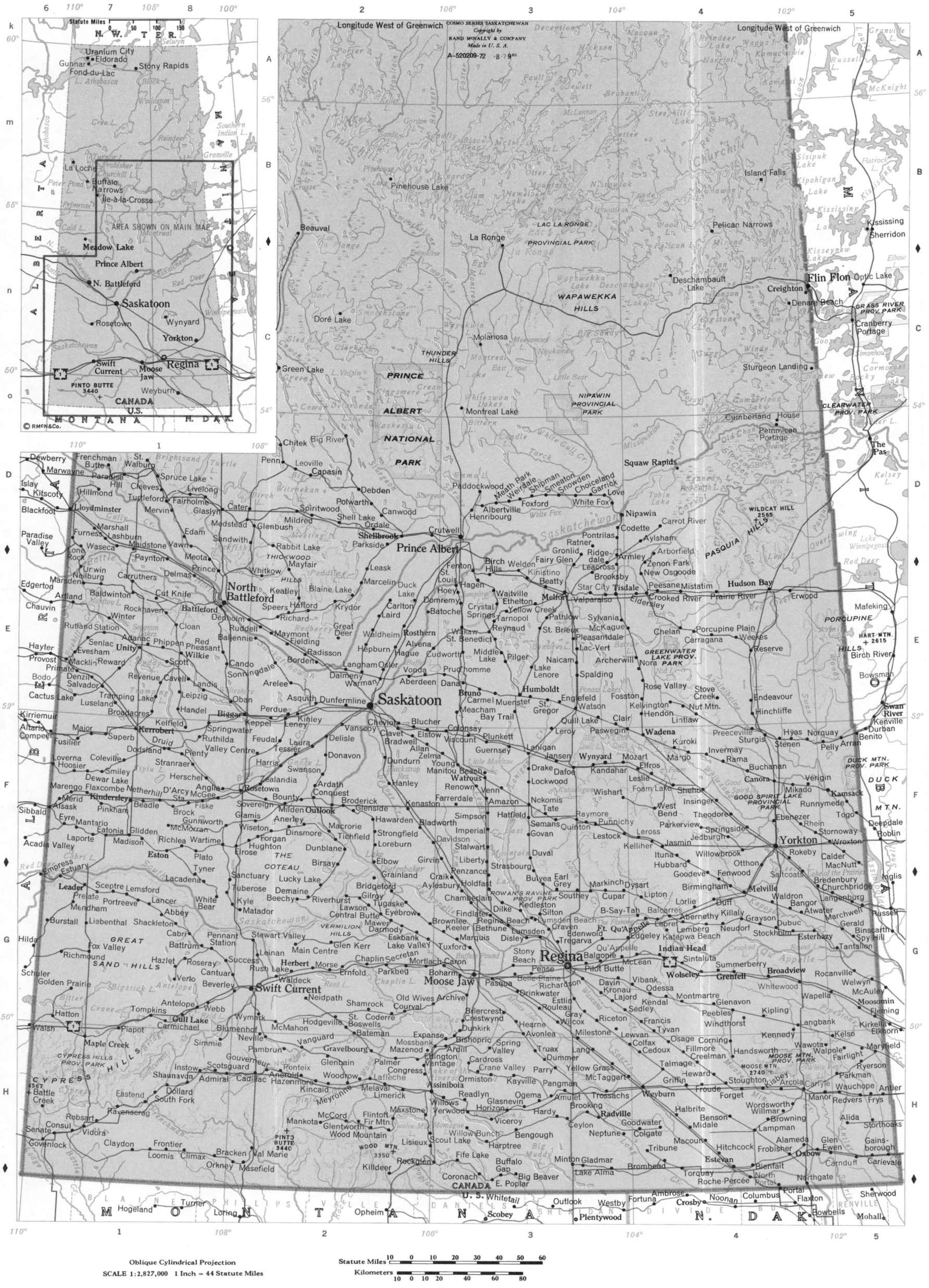

Oblique Cylindrical Projection
SCALE 1:2,827,000   1 Inch = 44 Statute Miles

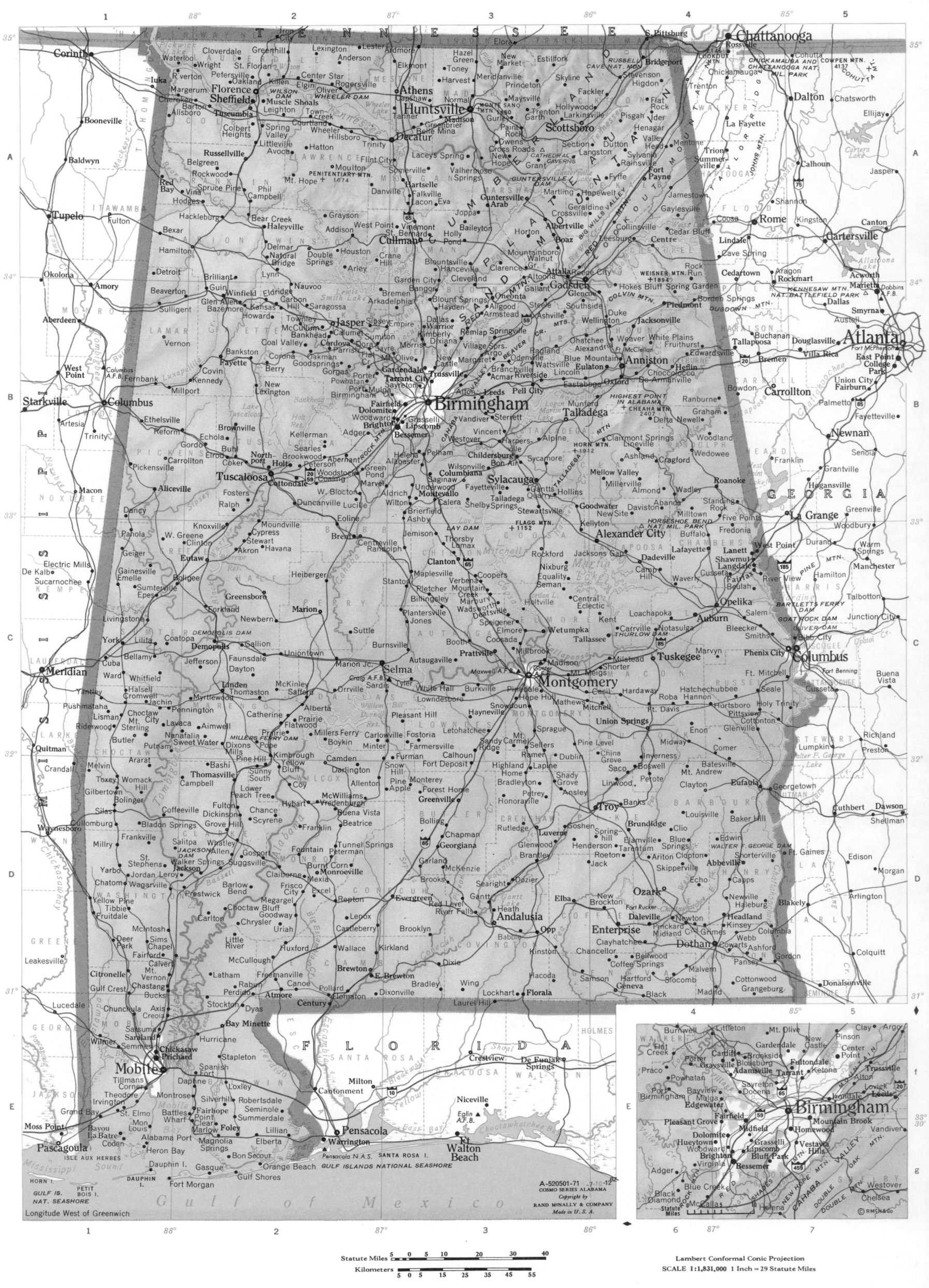

Statute Miles 5 0 5 10 20 30 40
Kilometers 5 0 5 15 25 35 45 55

Lambert Conformal Conic Projection
SCALE 1:1,831,000 1 Inch = 29 Statute Miles

A-520501-71 -7-10-12
COSMO SERIES ALABAMA
Copyright by
RAND M9NALLY & COMPANY
Made in U.S.A.

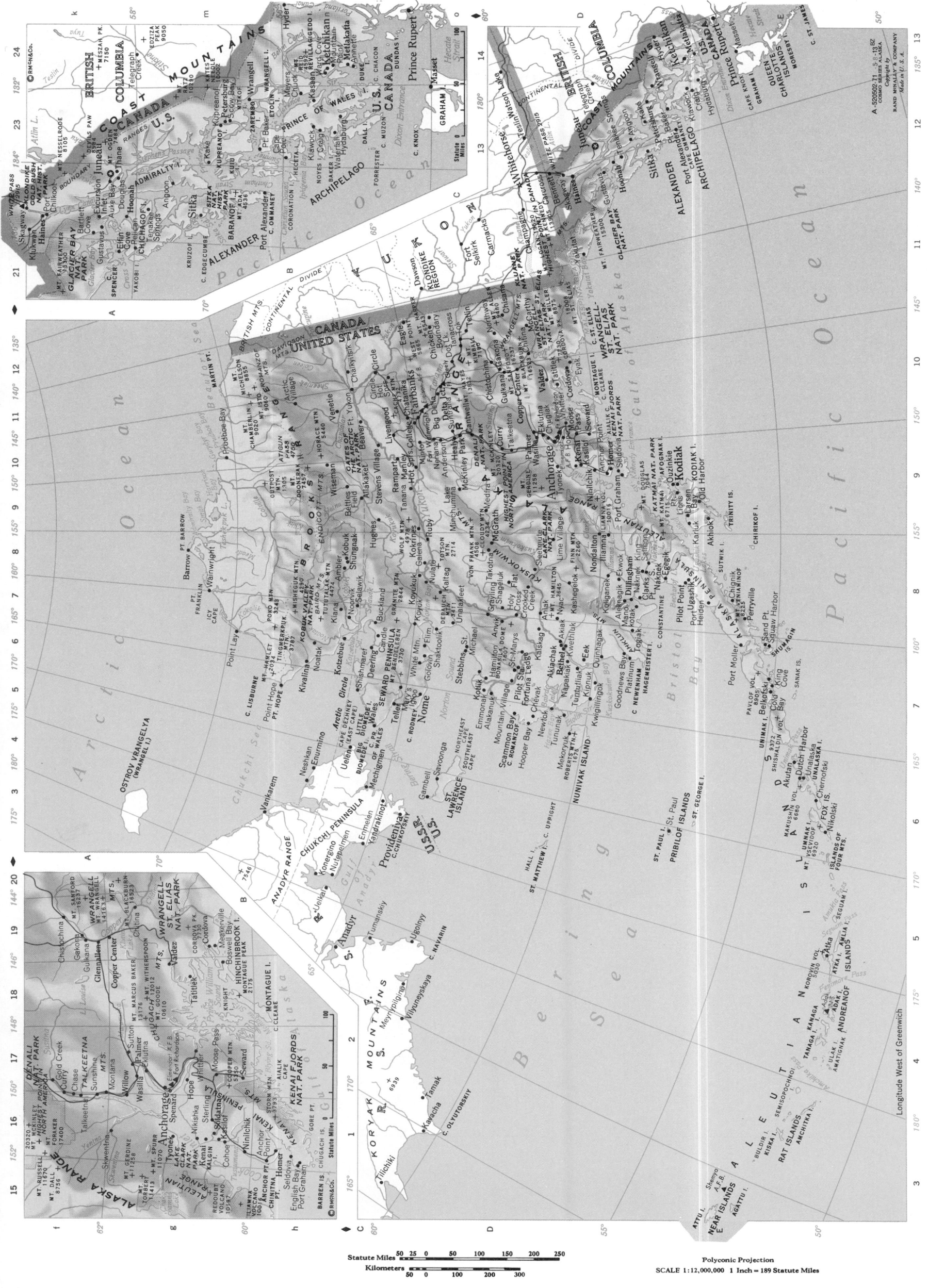

Statute Miles 50 25 0 50 100 150 200 250

Kilometers 50 0 100 200 300

Polyconic Projection
SCALE 1:12,000,000 1 Inch = 189 Statute Miles

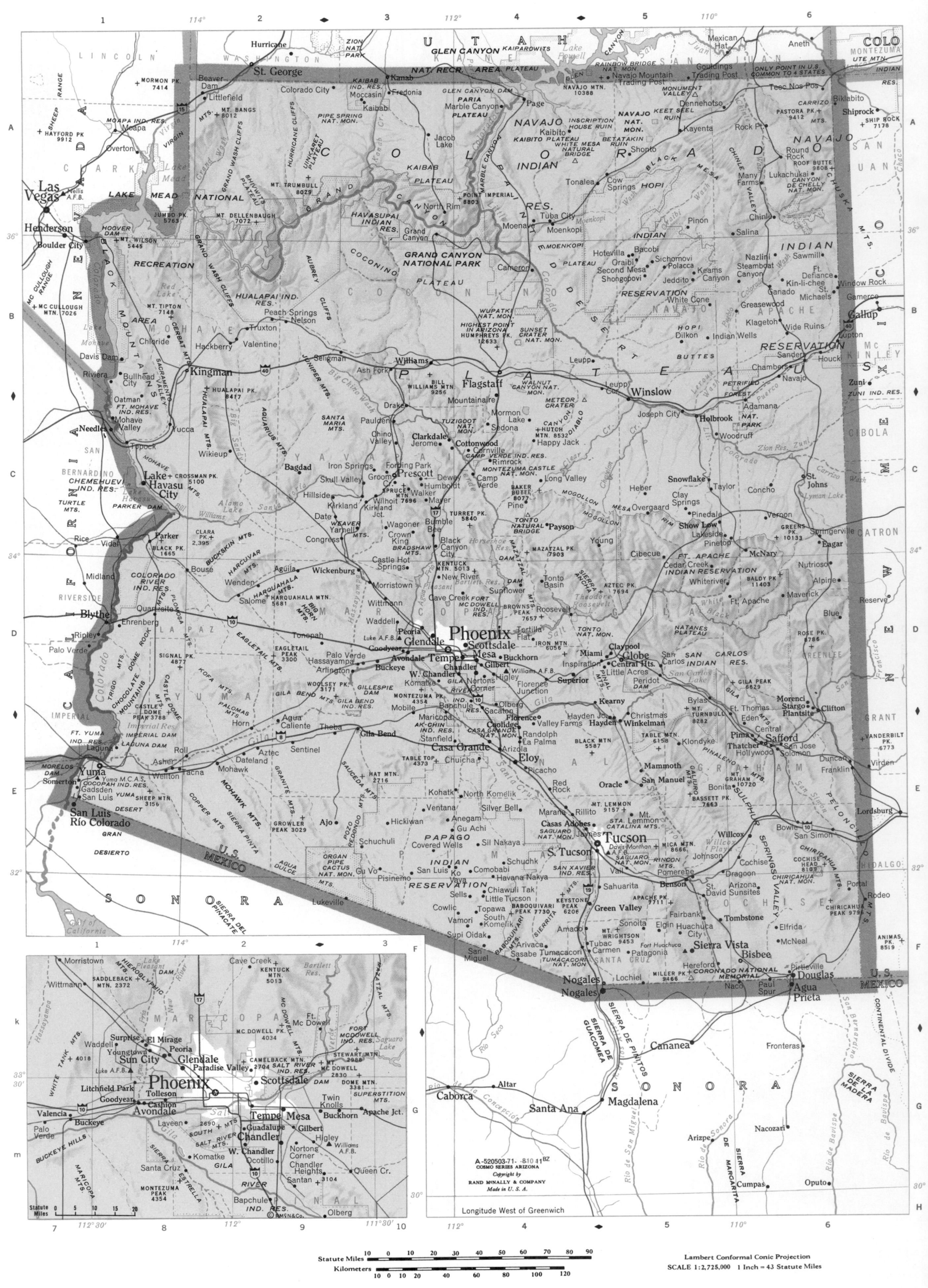

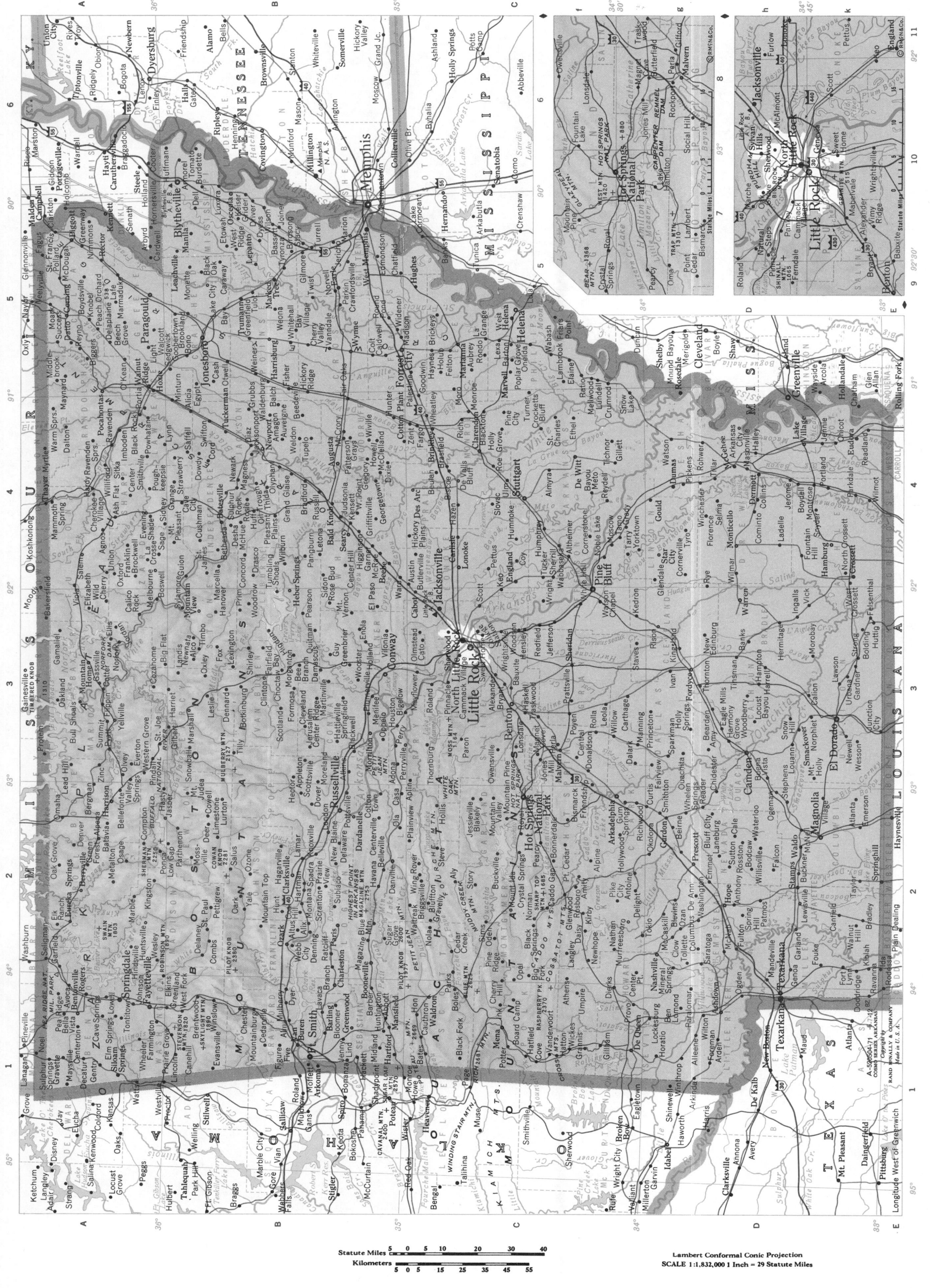

Lambert Conformal Conic Projection
SCALE 1:1,832,000 1 Inch = 29 Statute Miles

Statute Miles
Kilometers

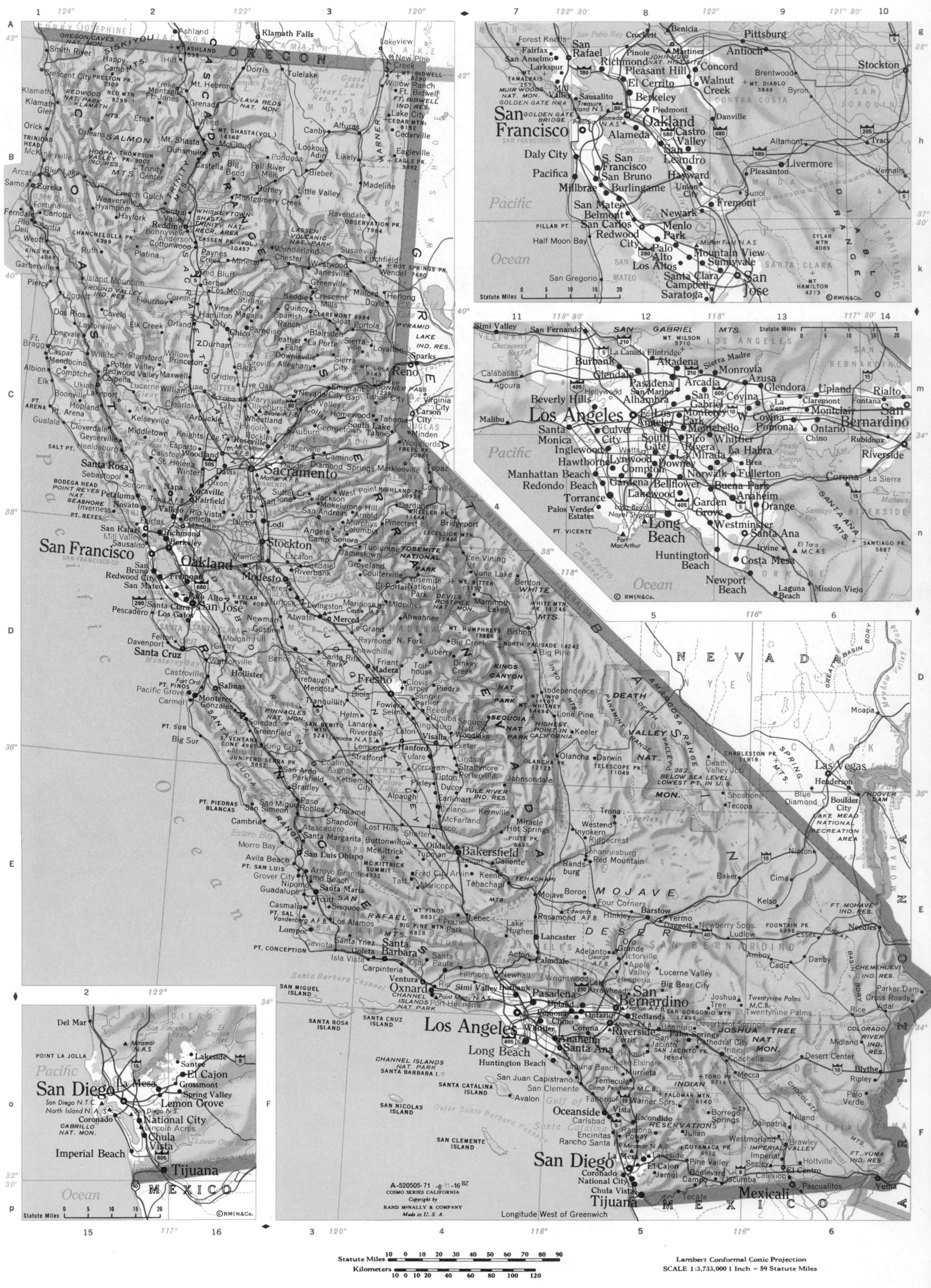

Lambert Conformal Conic Projection
SCALE 1:3,733,000 1 Inch = 59 Statute Miles

A-520505-71 -8-11-16 BZ
COSMO SERIES CALIFORNIA
Copyright by
RAND McNALLY & COMPANY
Made in U.S.A.

Longitude West of Greenwich

Statute Miles 5   0   5 10   20   30   40   50

Kilometers 5 0 5 15 25 35 45 55 65 75

Lambert Conformal Conic Projection
SCALE 1:2,186,000   1 Inch = 34.5 Statute Miles

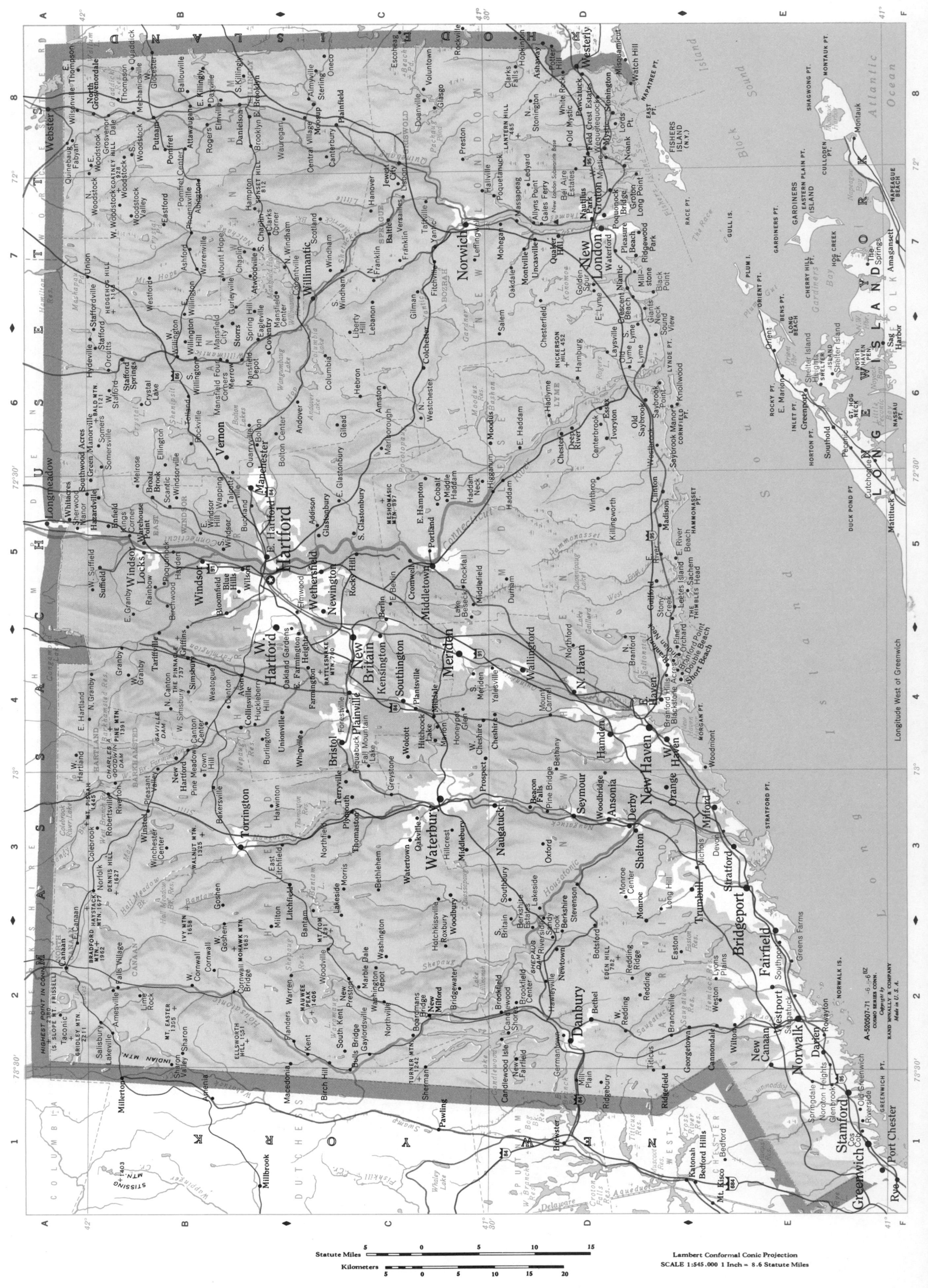

Statute Miles

Kilometers

Lambert Conformal Conic Projection
SCALE 1:545,000 1 Inch = 8.6 Statute Miles

A-500607.71
COSMO SERIES CONN.
Copyright ©
RAND M�NALLY & COMPANY
Made in U.S.A.

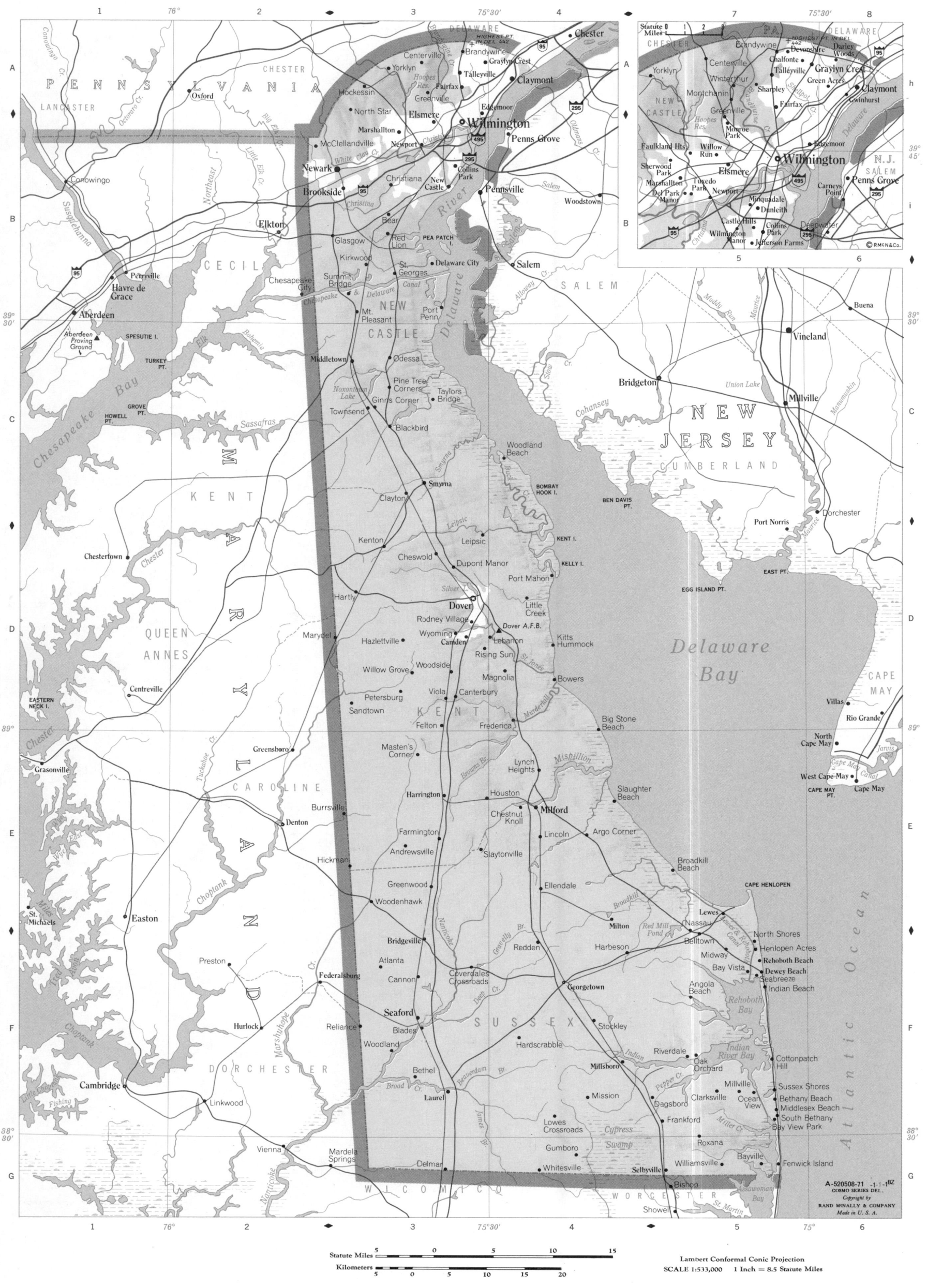

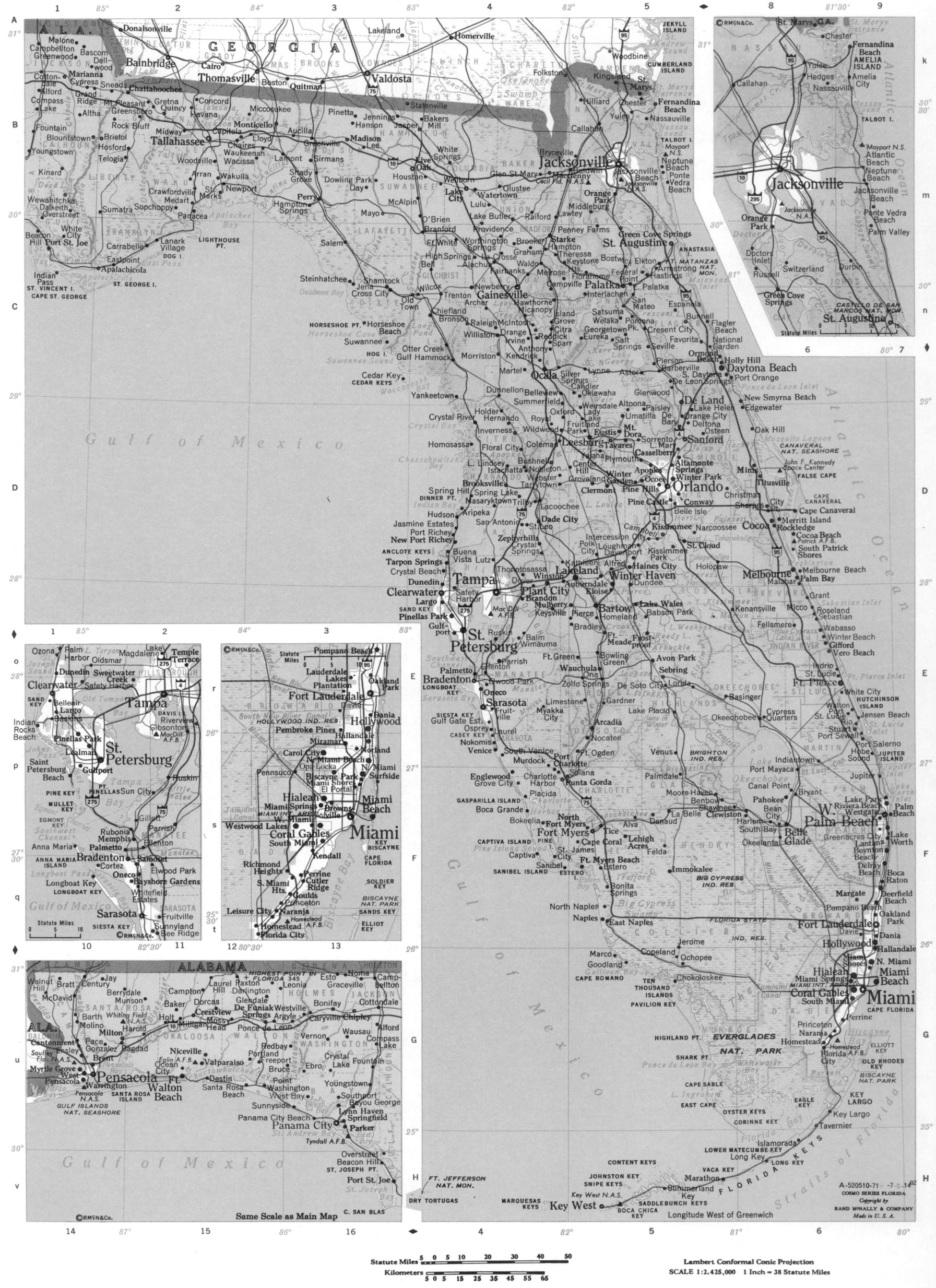

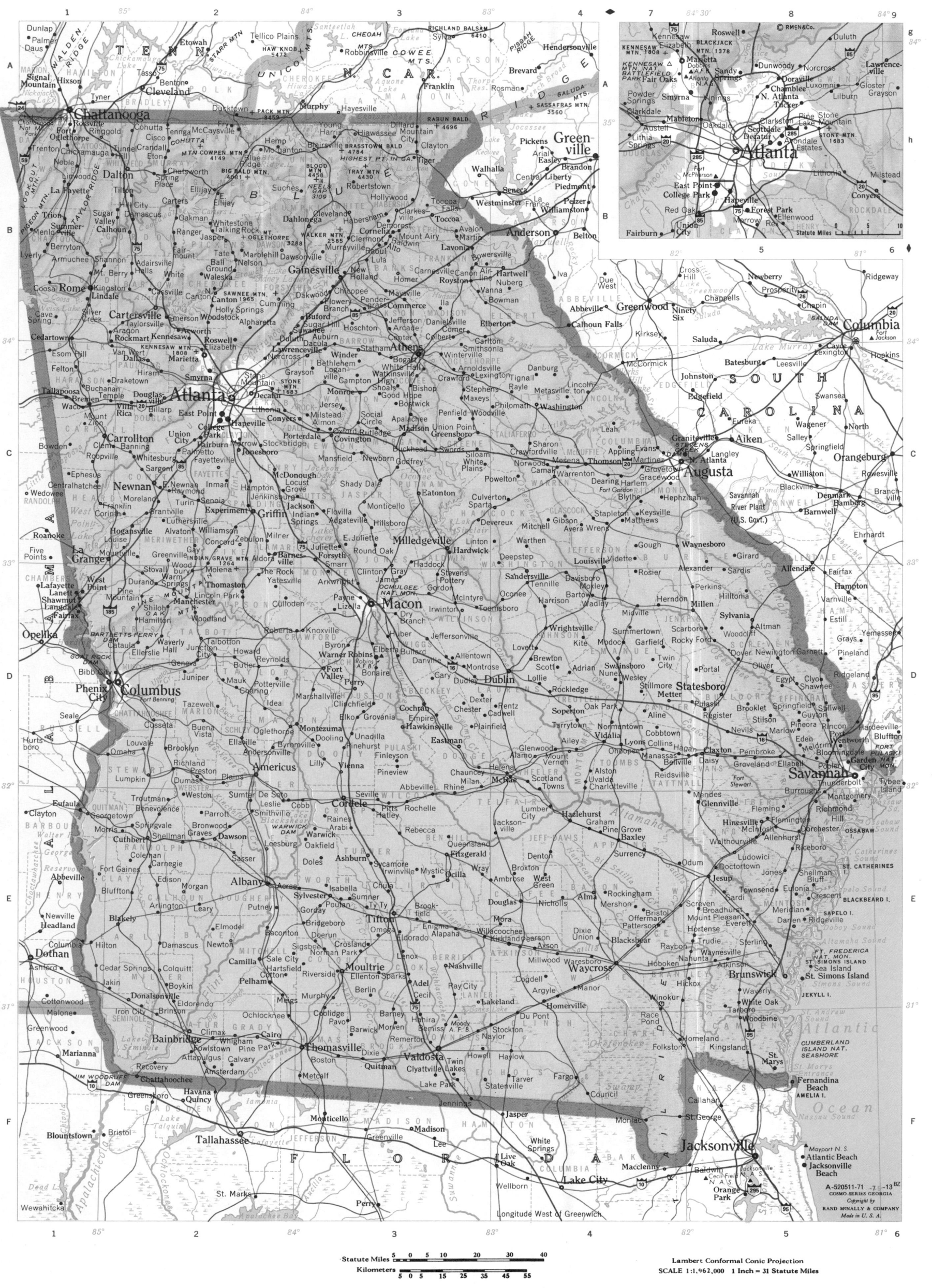

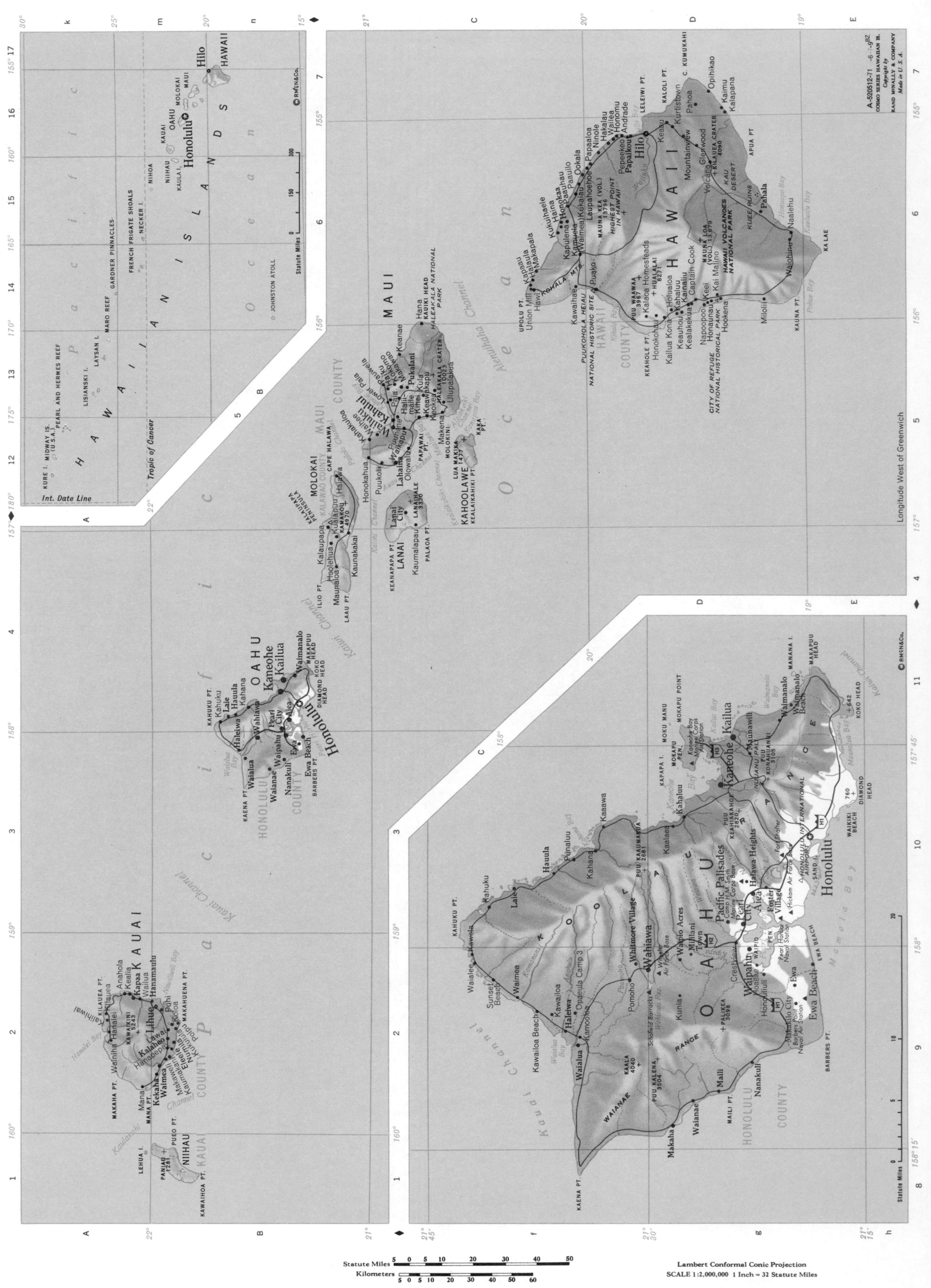

Statute Miles 5 0 5 10 20 30 40 50
Kilometers 5 0 5 10 20 30 40 50 60

Lambert Conformal Conic Projection
SCALE 1:2,000,000 1 Inch = 32 Statute Miles

A-500512-71 -6- .9⁸²
COSMO SERIES HAWAIIAN IS.
Copyright by
RAND M¢NALLY & COMPANY
Made in U.S.A.

© RM¢N&Co.

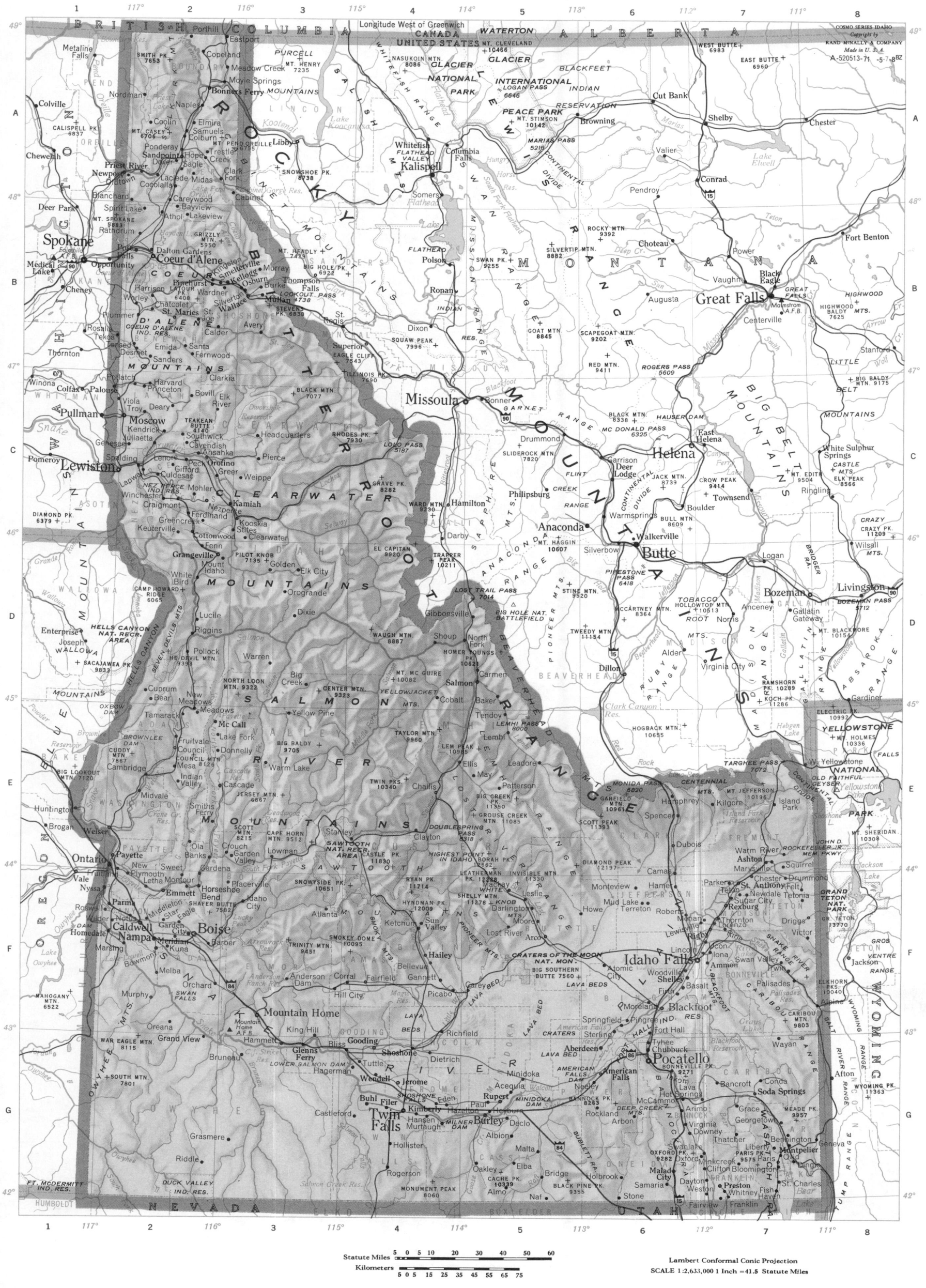

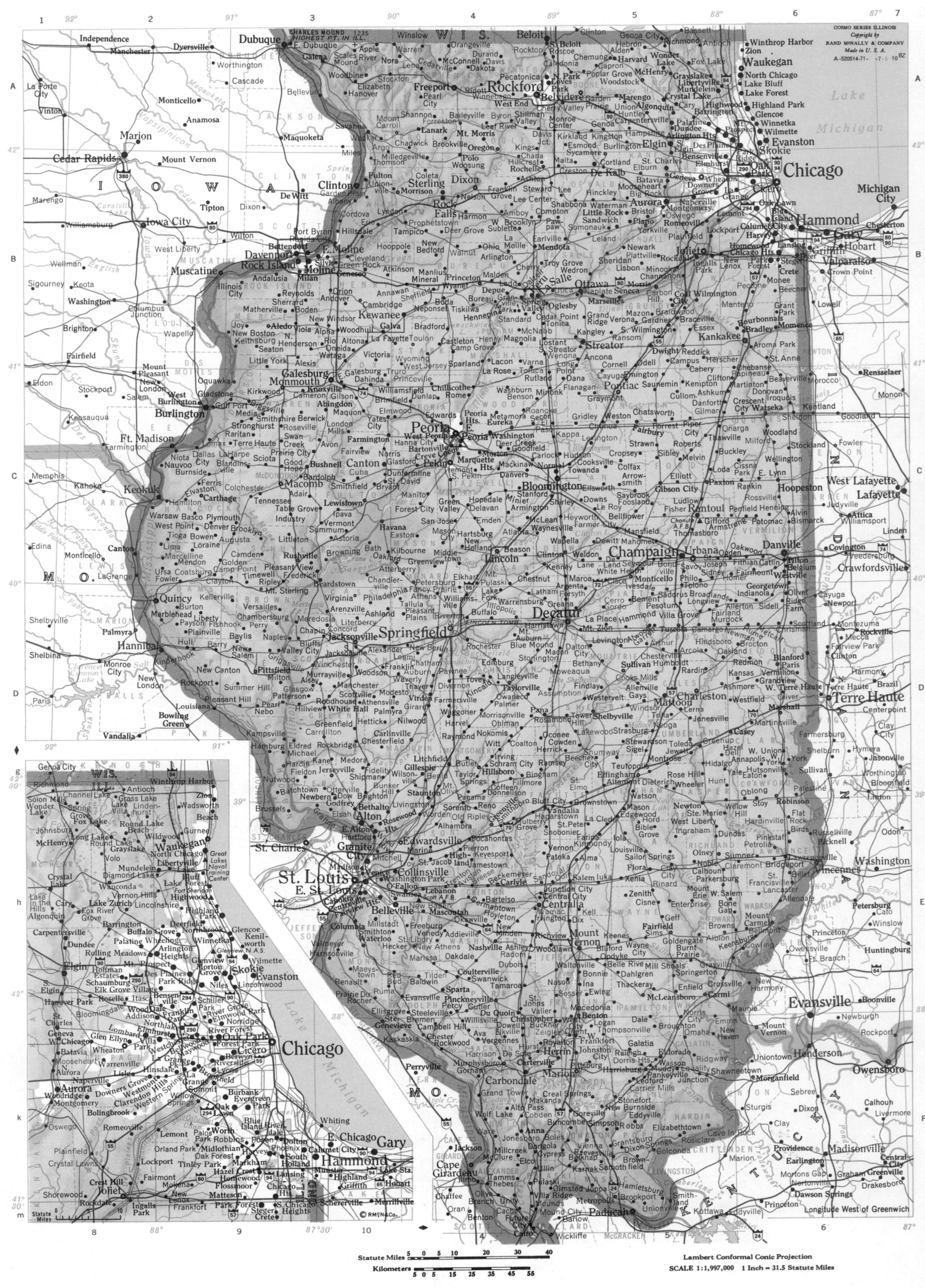

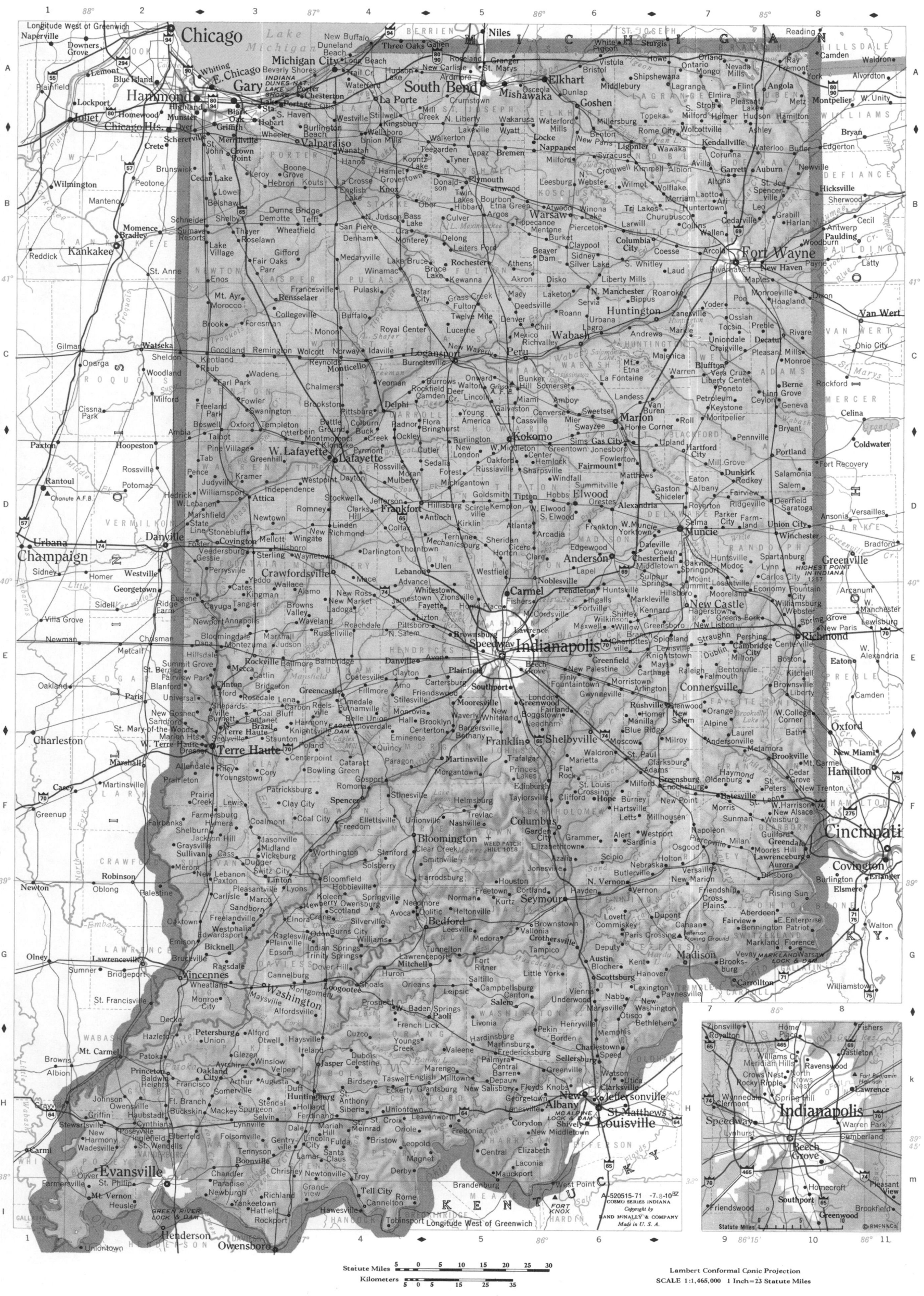

Copyright by
RAND M^{c}NALLY & COMPANY
Made in U.S.A.

Statute Miles 5 0 5 10 15 20 25 30

Kilometers 5 0 5 15 25 35

Lambert Conformal Conic Projection
SCALE 1:1,465,000 : 1 Inch=23 Statute Miles

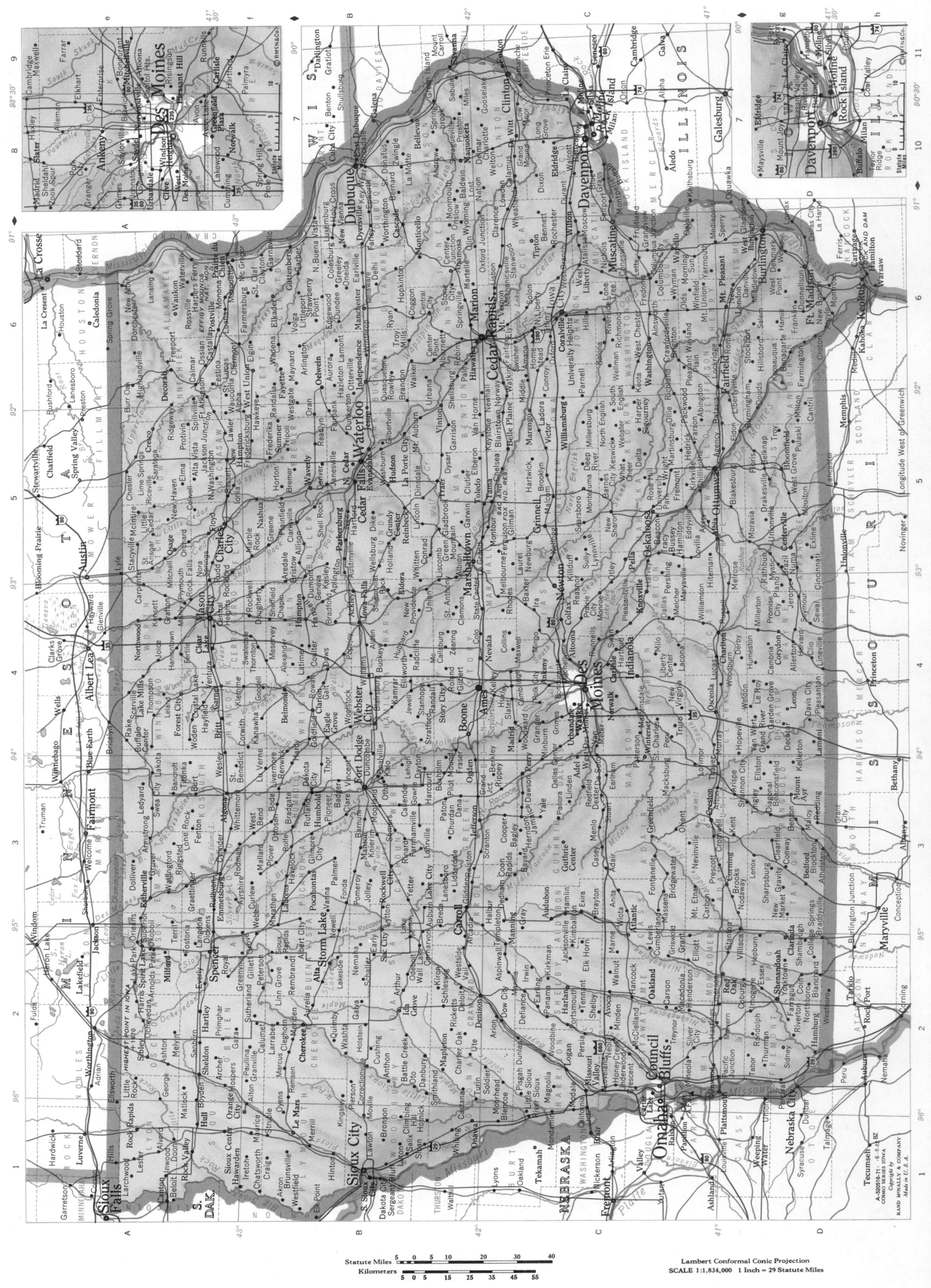

Statute Miles
Kilometers

Lambert Conformal Conic Projection
SCALE 1:1,834,000   1 Inch = 29 Statute Miles

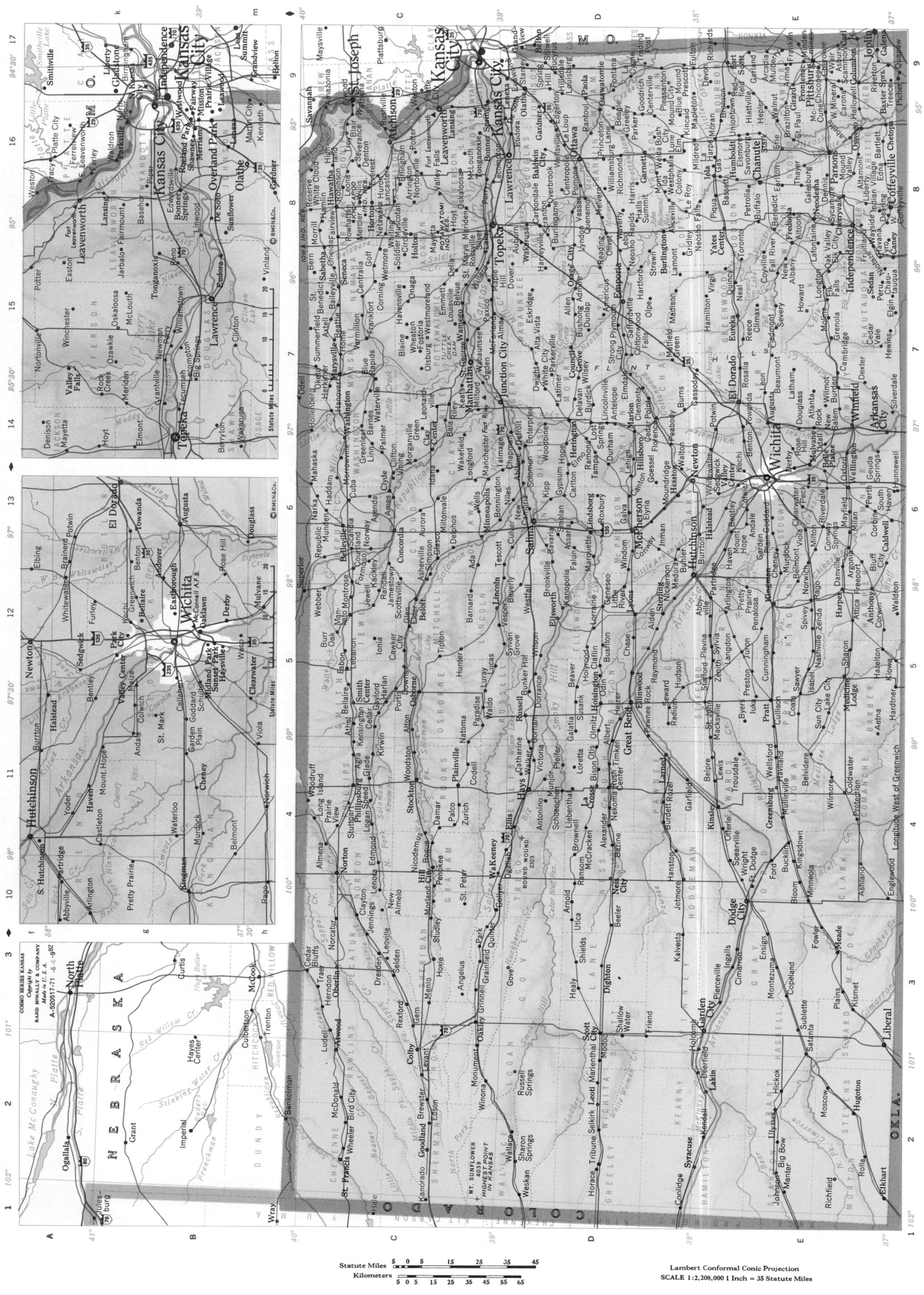

Statute Miles
Kilometers

Lambert Conformal Conic Projection
SCALE 1:2,208,000 1 Inch = 35 Statute Miles

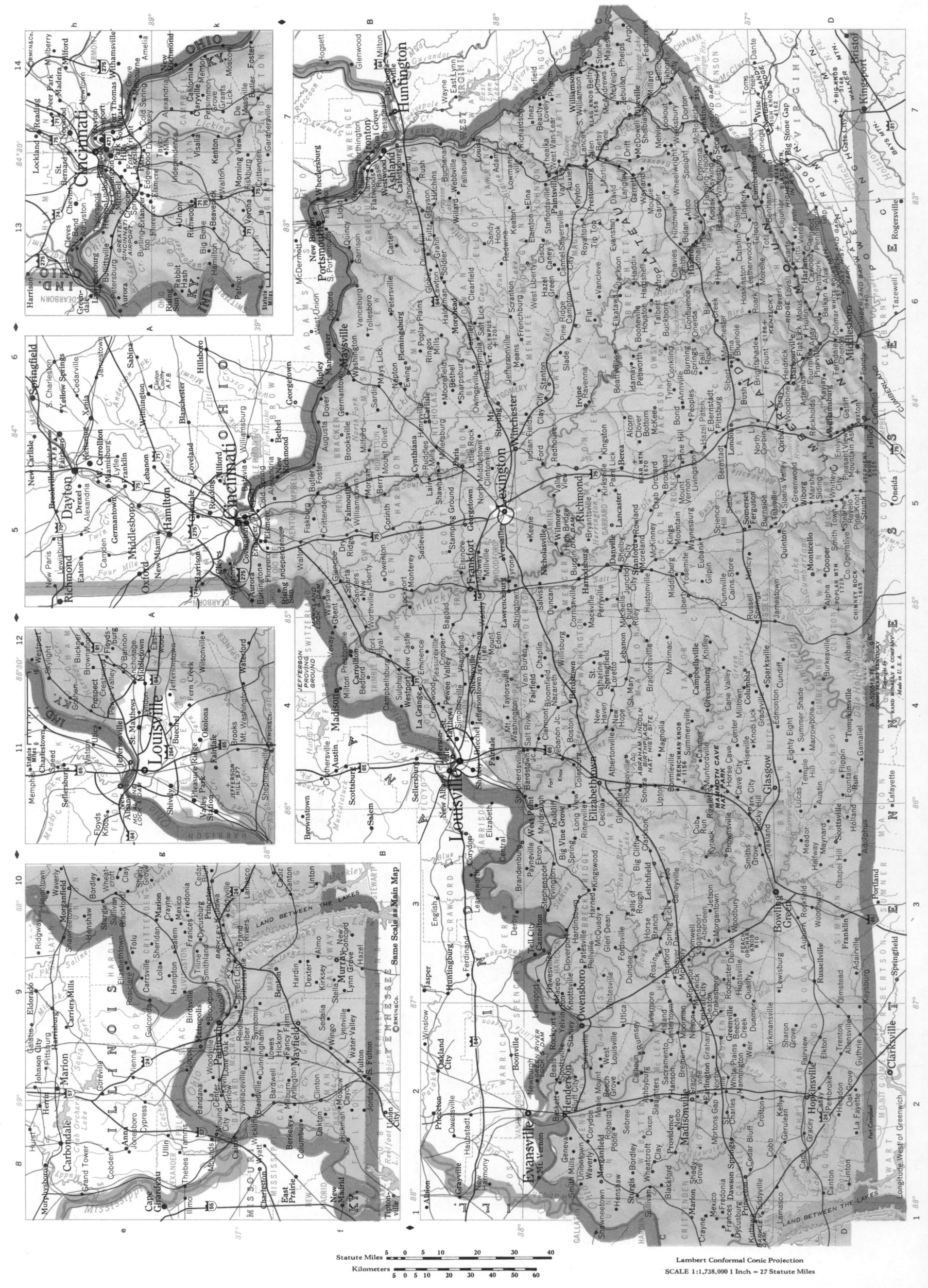

Statute Miles 5 0 5 10 20 30 40
Kilometers 5 0 5 10 20 30 40 50 60

Lambert Conformal Conic Projection
SCALE 1:1,738,000 1 Inch = 27 Statute Miles

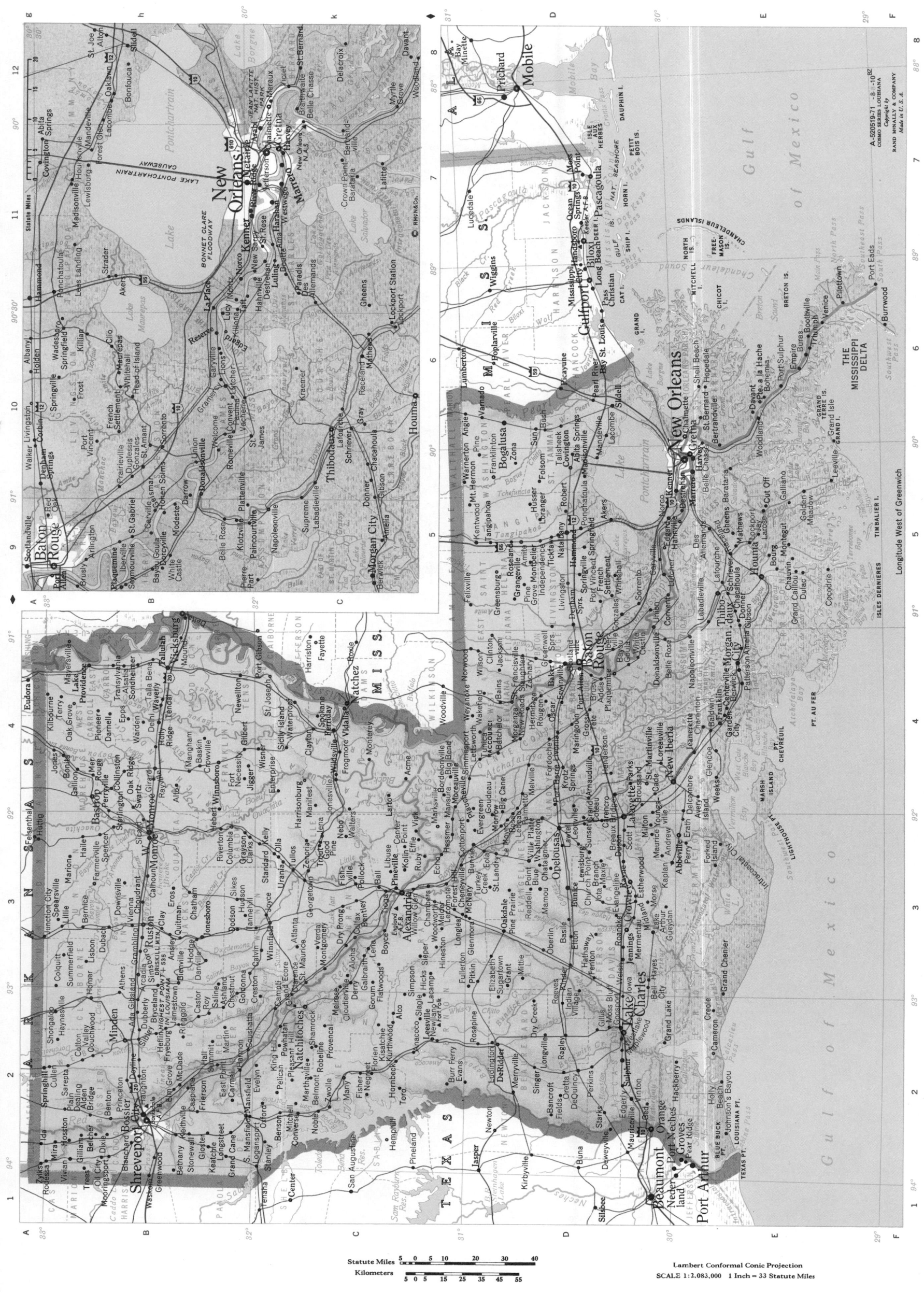

Statute Miles

Kilometers

Lambert Conformal Conic Projection
SCALE 1:2,083,000   1 Inch = 33 Statute Miles

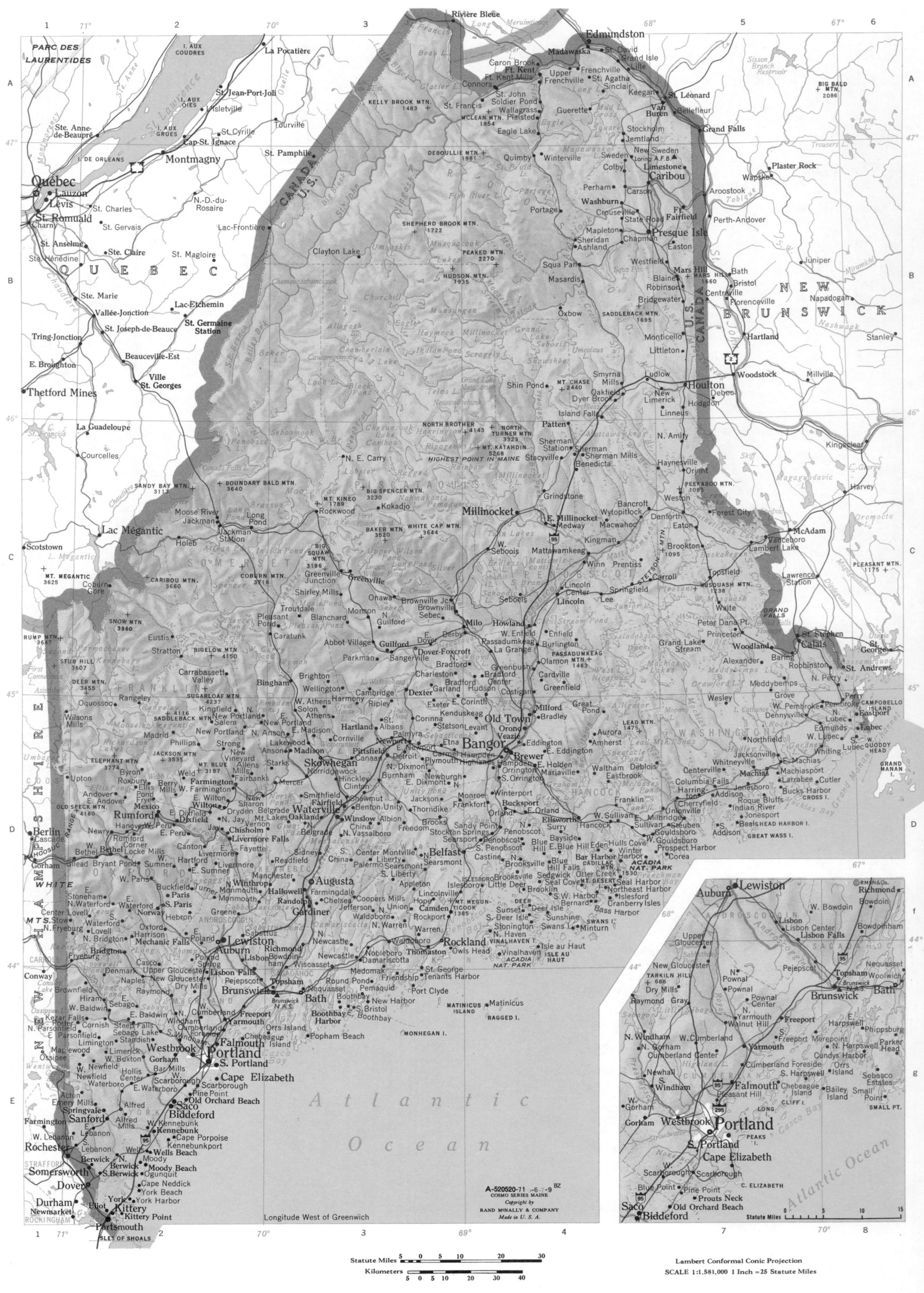

MAINE

Statute Miles 5 0 5 10 20 30
Kilometers 5 0 5 10 20 30 40

A-520520-71 -6- -9
COSMO SERIES MAINE
Copyright by
RAND MCNALLY & COMPANY
Made in U.S.A.

Lambert Conformal Conic Projection
SCALE 1:1,581,000 1 Inch = 25 Statute Miles

Longitude West of Greenwich

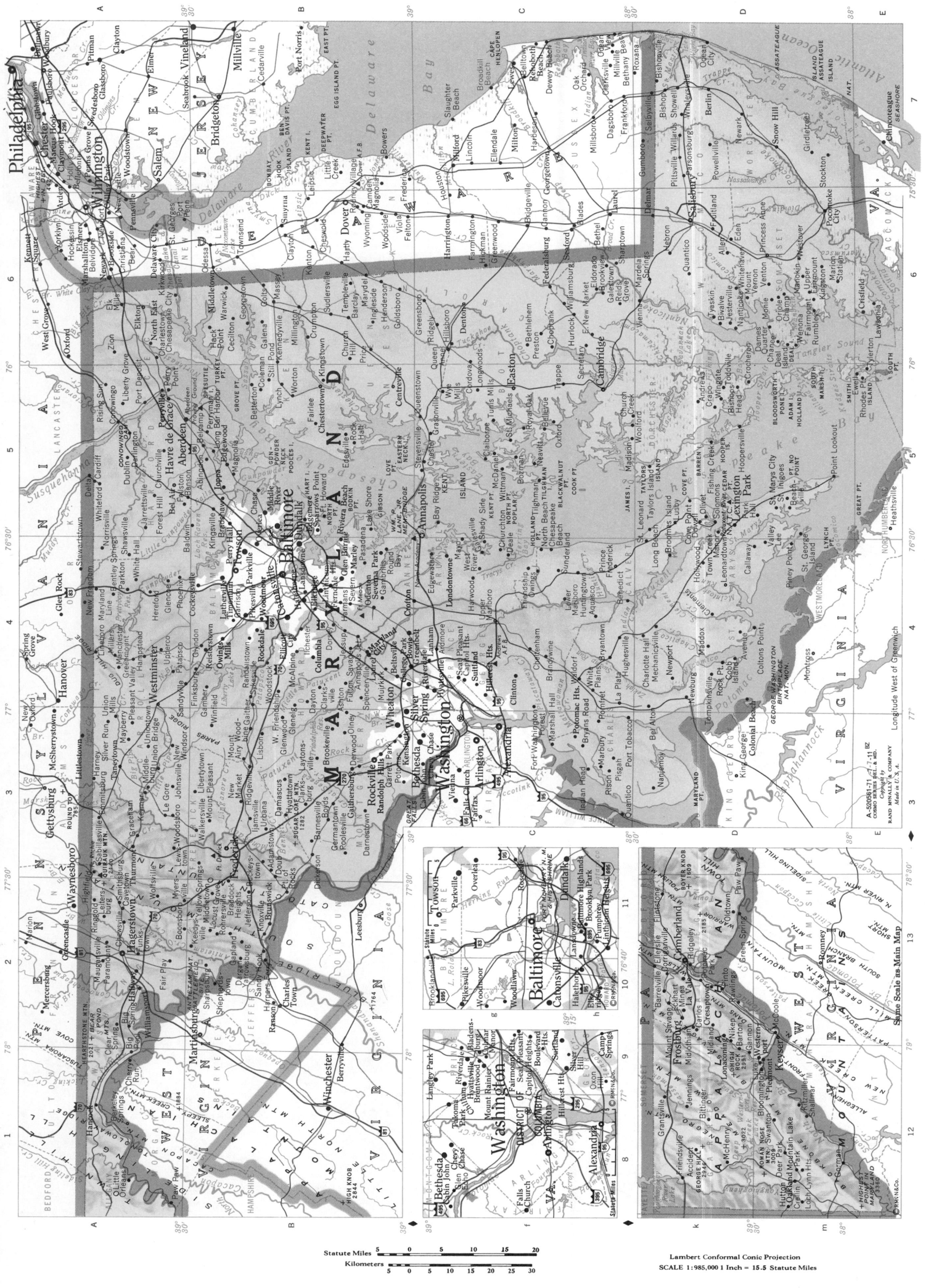

Lambert Conformal Conic Projection
SCALE 1:985,000 1 Inch = 15.5 Statute Miles

Statute Miles
Kilometers

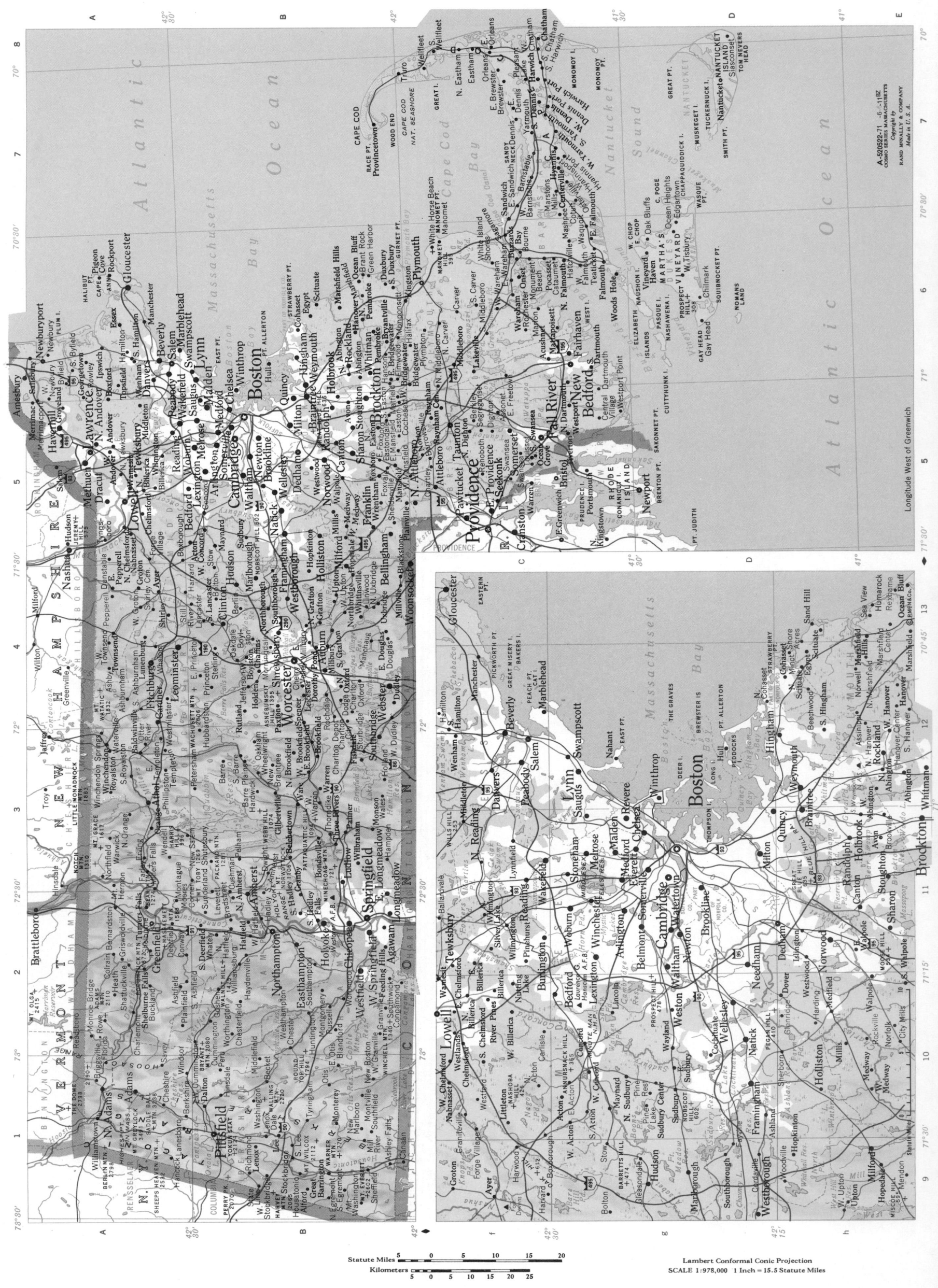

Statute Miles 5 0 5 10 15 20
Kilometers 5 0 5 10 15 20 25

Lambert Conformal Conic Projection
SCALE 1:978,000   1 Inch = 15.5 Statute Miles

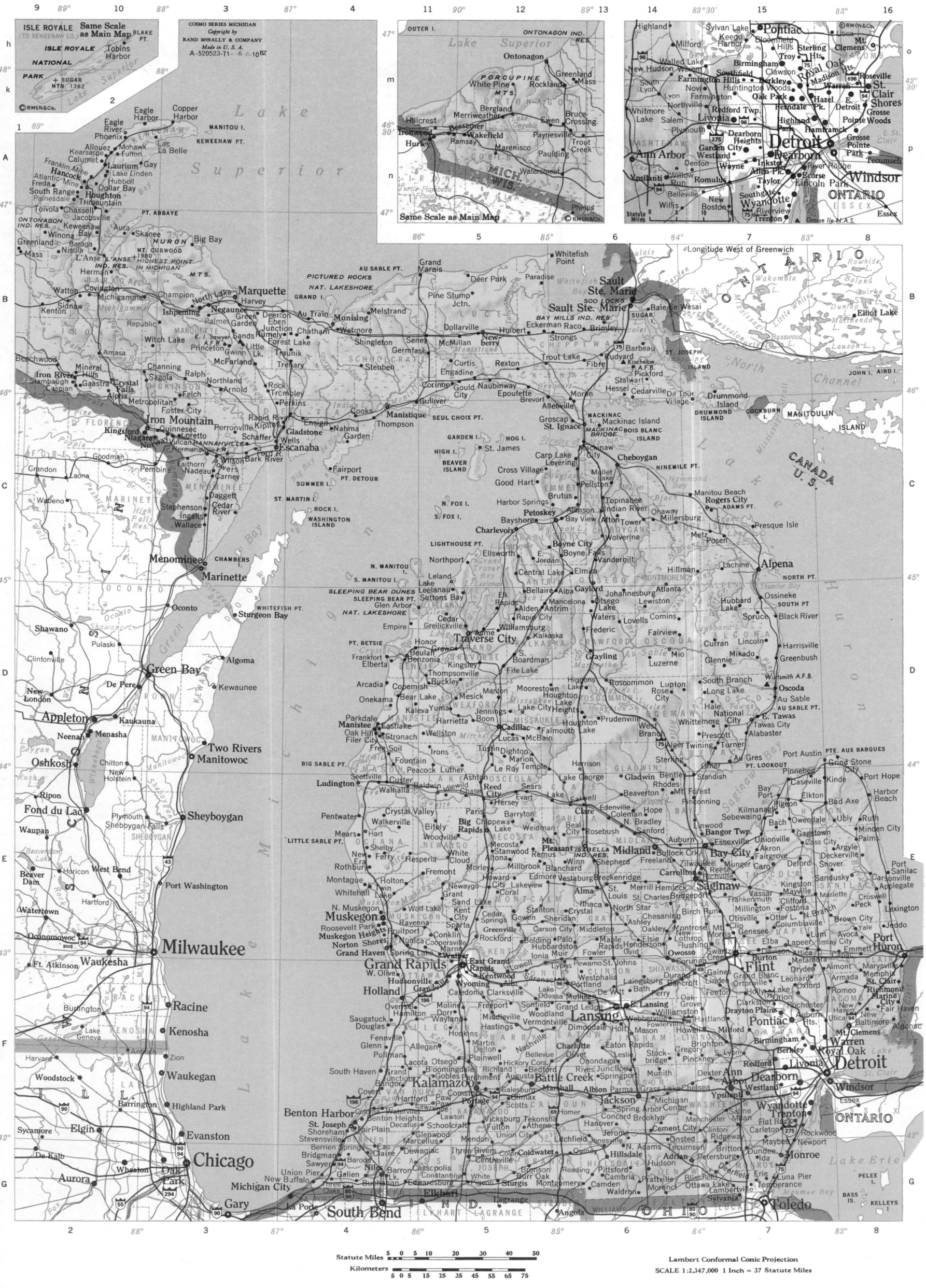

Statute Miles 5 0 5 10 20 30 40 50

Kilometers 5 0 5 15 25 35 45 55 65 75

Lambert Conformal Conic Projection
SCALE 1:2,347,000 1 Inch = 37 Statute Miles

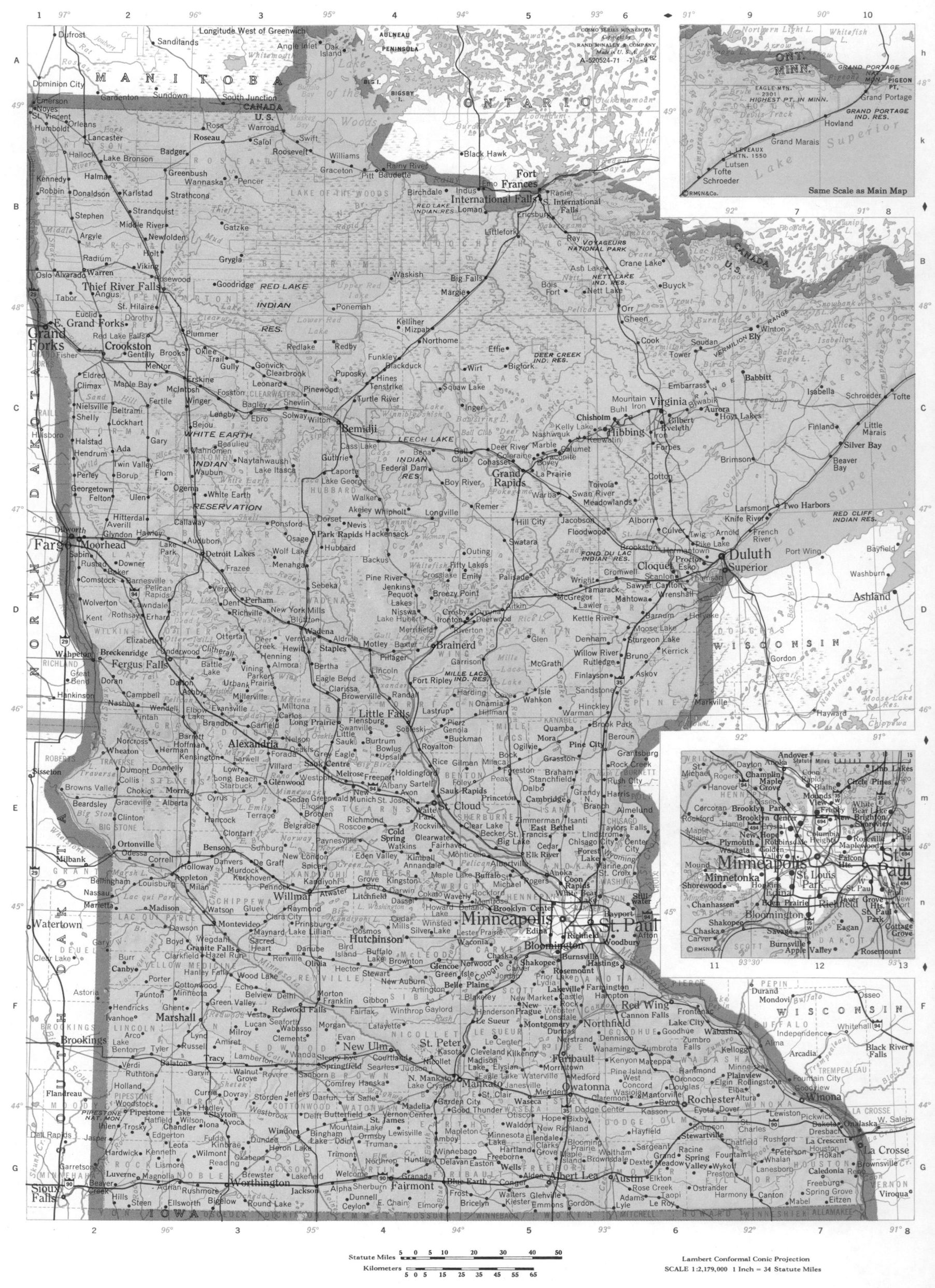

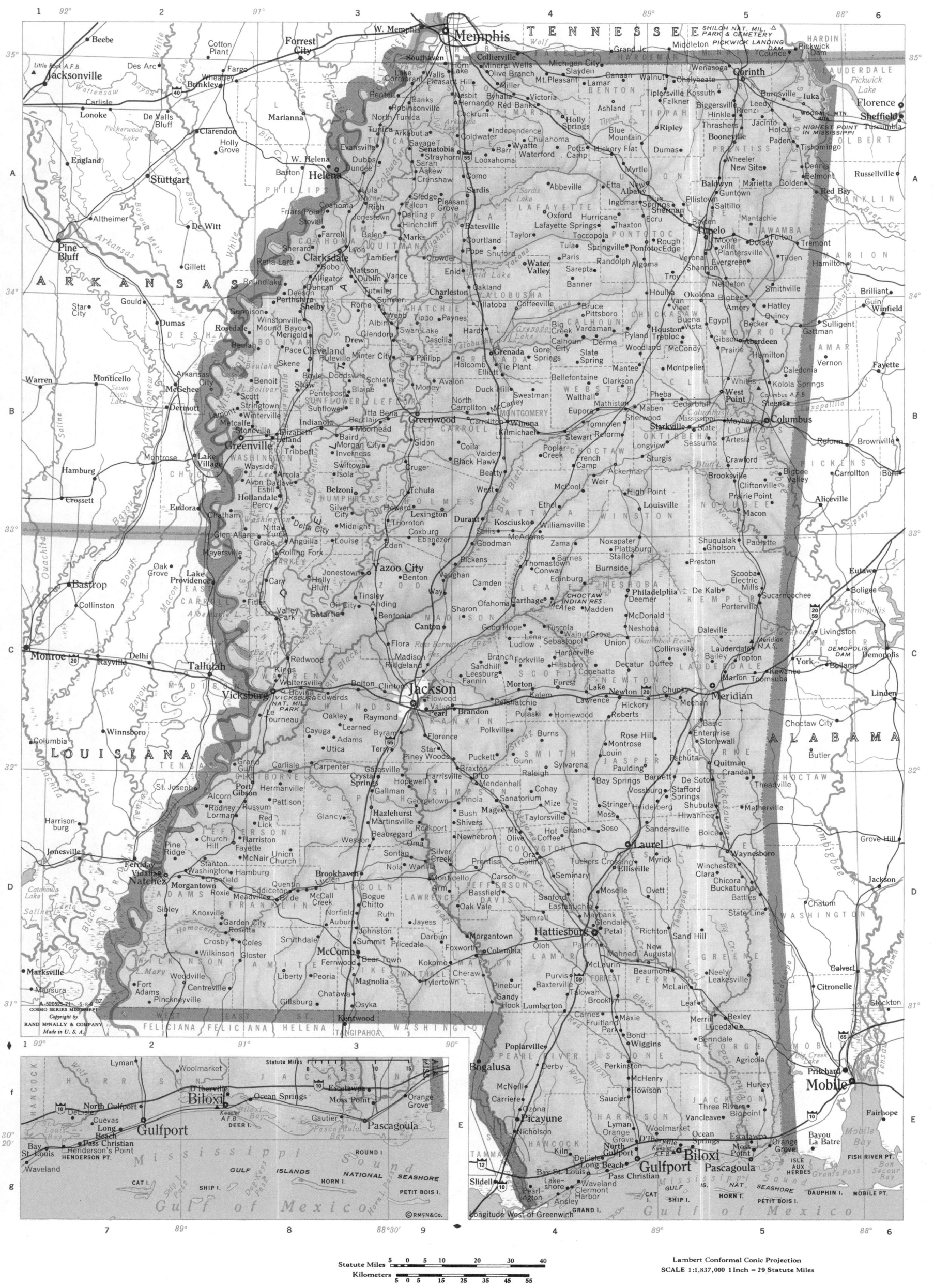

Lambert Conformal Conic Projection
SCALE 1:1,837,000 1 Inch = 29 Statute Miles

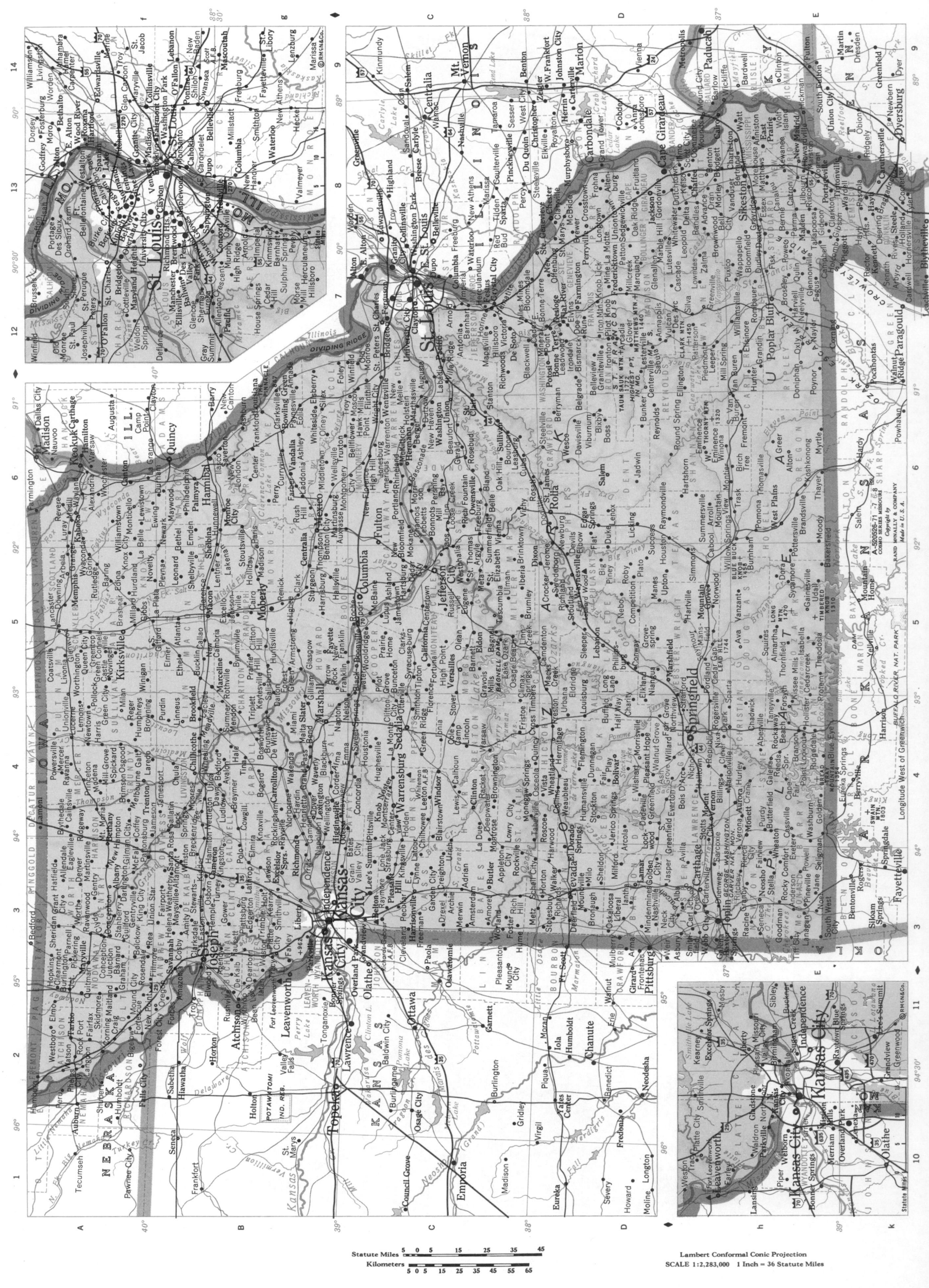

Statute Miles 5 0 5   15   25   35   45
Kilometers 5 0 5 15 25 35 45 55 65

Lambert Conformal Conic Projection
SCALE 1:2,283,000   1 Inch = 36 Statute Miles

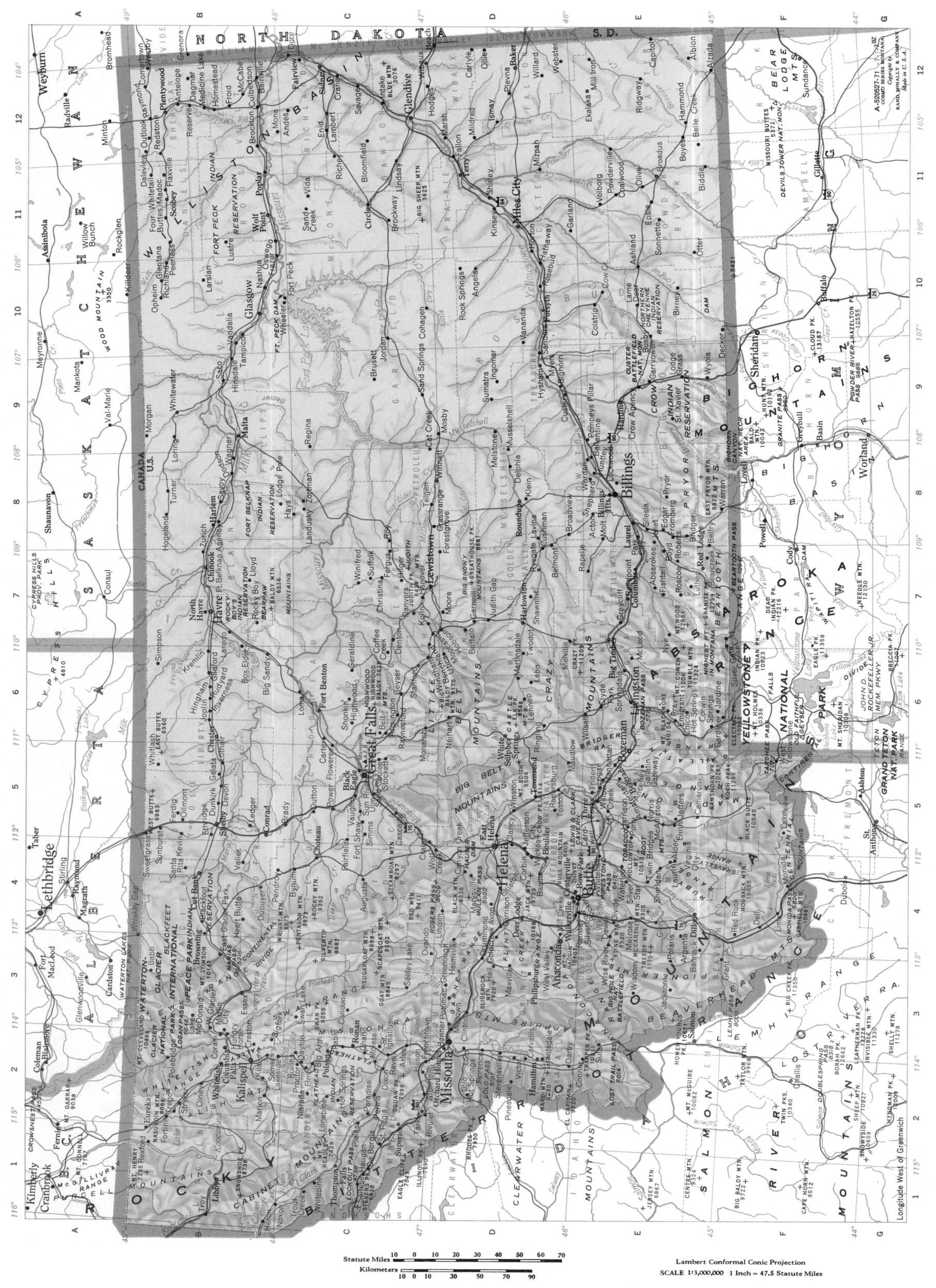

Statute Miles 10 0 10 20 30 40 50 60 70
Kilometers 10 0 10 30 50 70 90

Lambert Conformal Conic Projection
SCALE 1:3,000,000   1 Inch = 47.5 Statute Miles

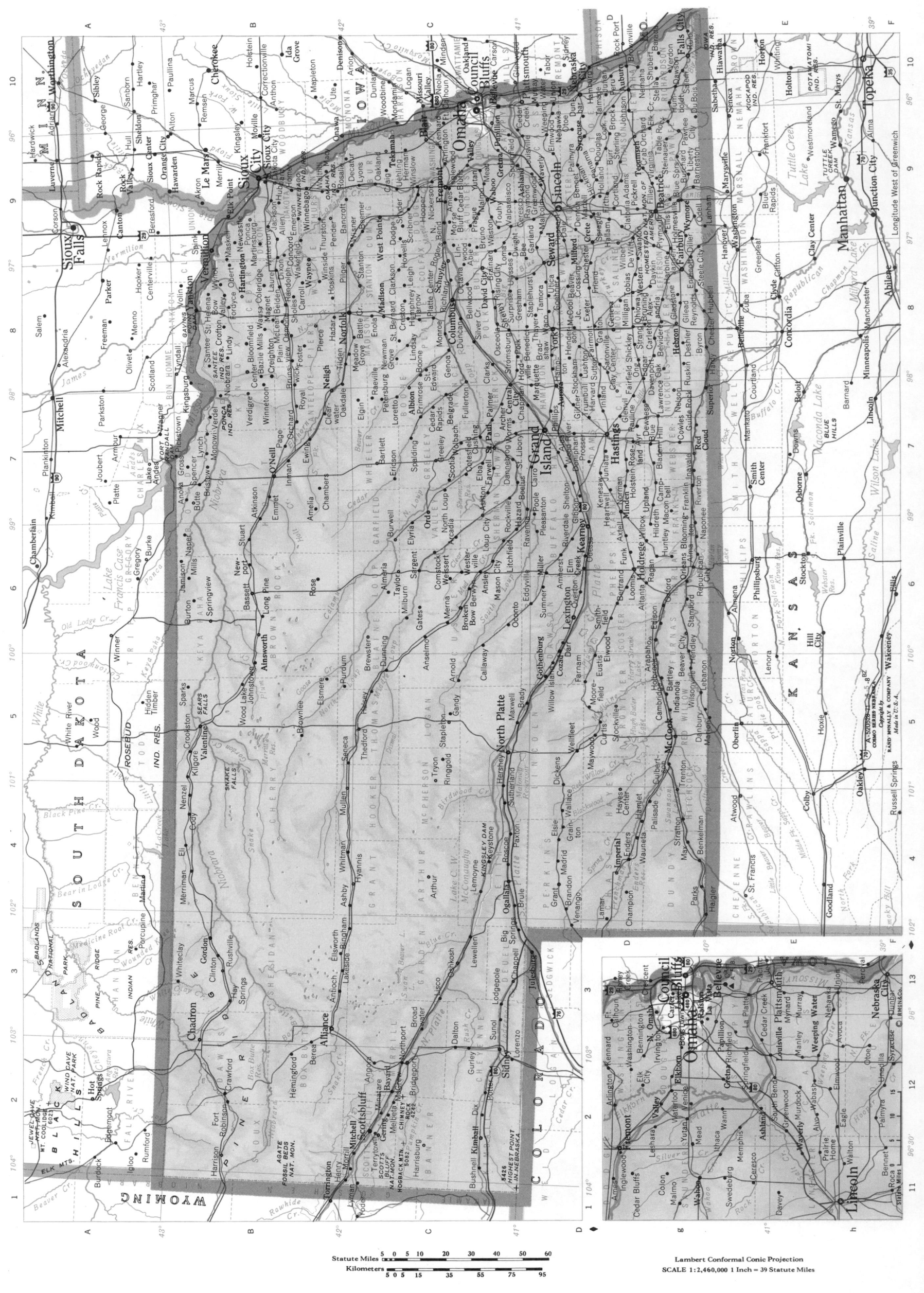

Statute Miles 5 0 5 10   20   30   40   50   60
Kilometers 5 0 5 15   35   55   75   95

Lambert Conformal Conic Projection
SCALE 1:2,460,000 1 Inch = 39 Statute Miles

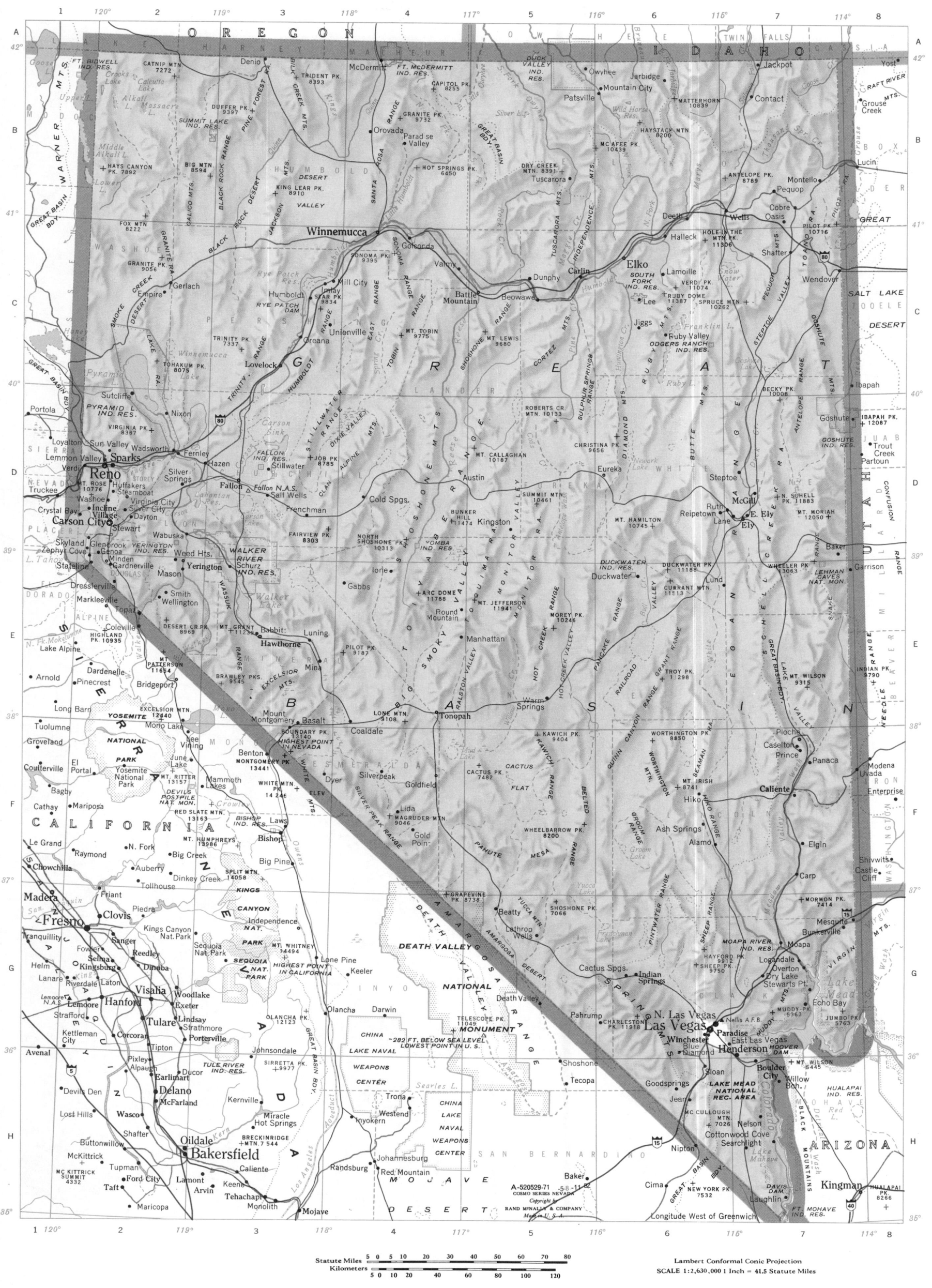

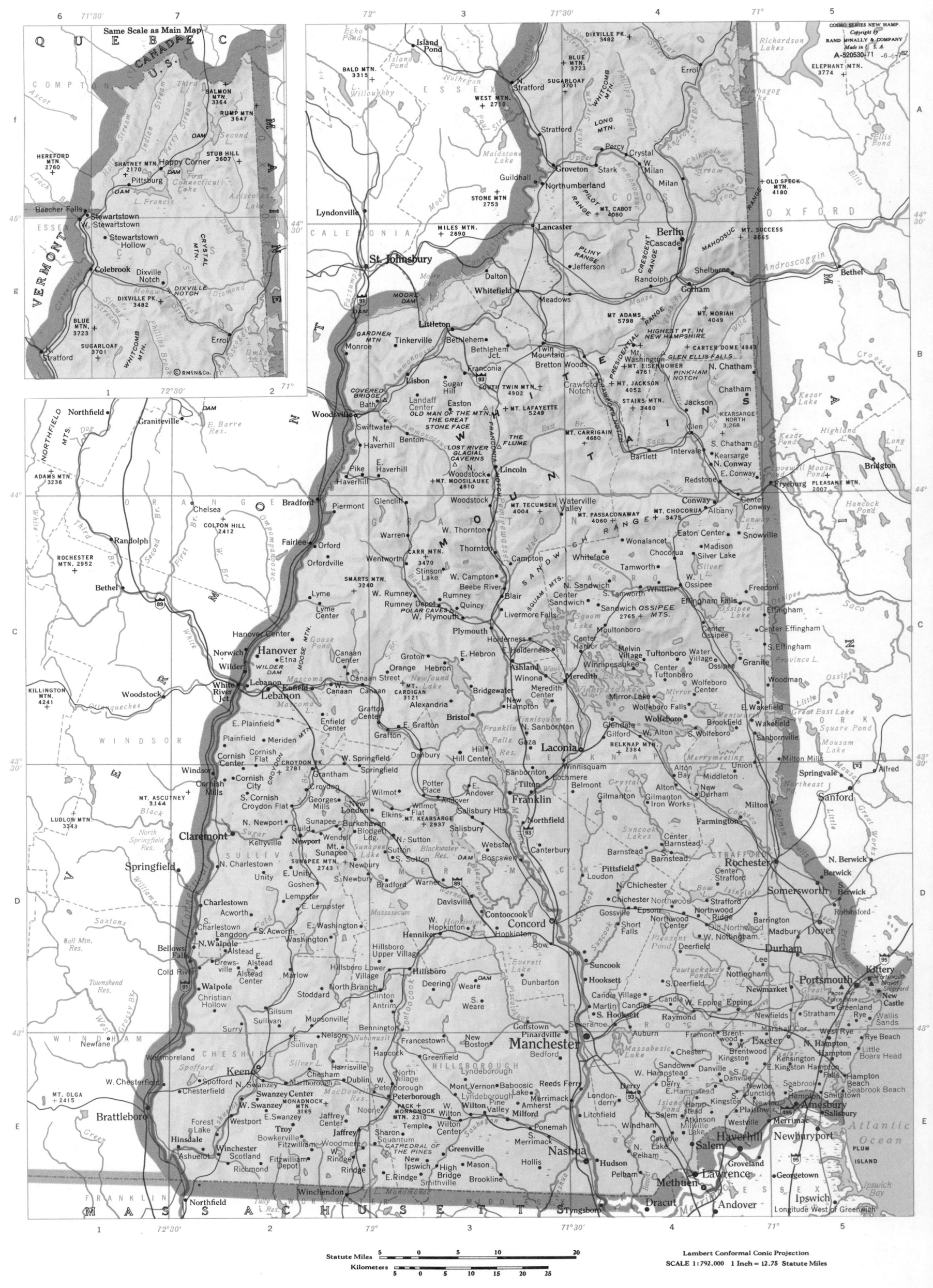

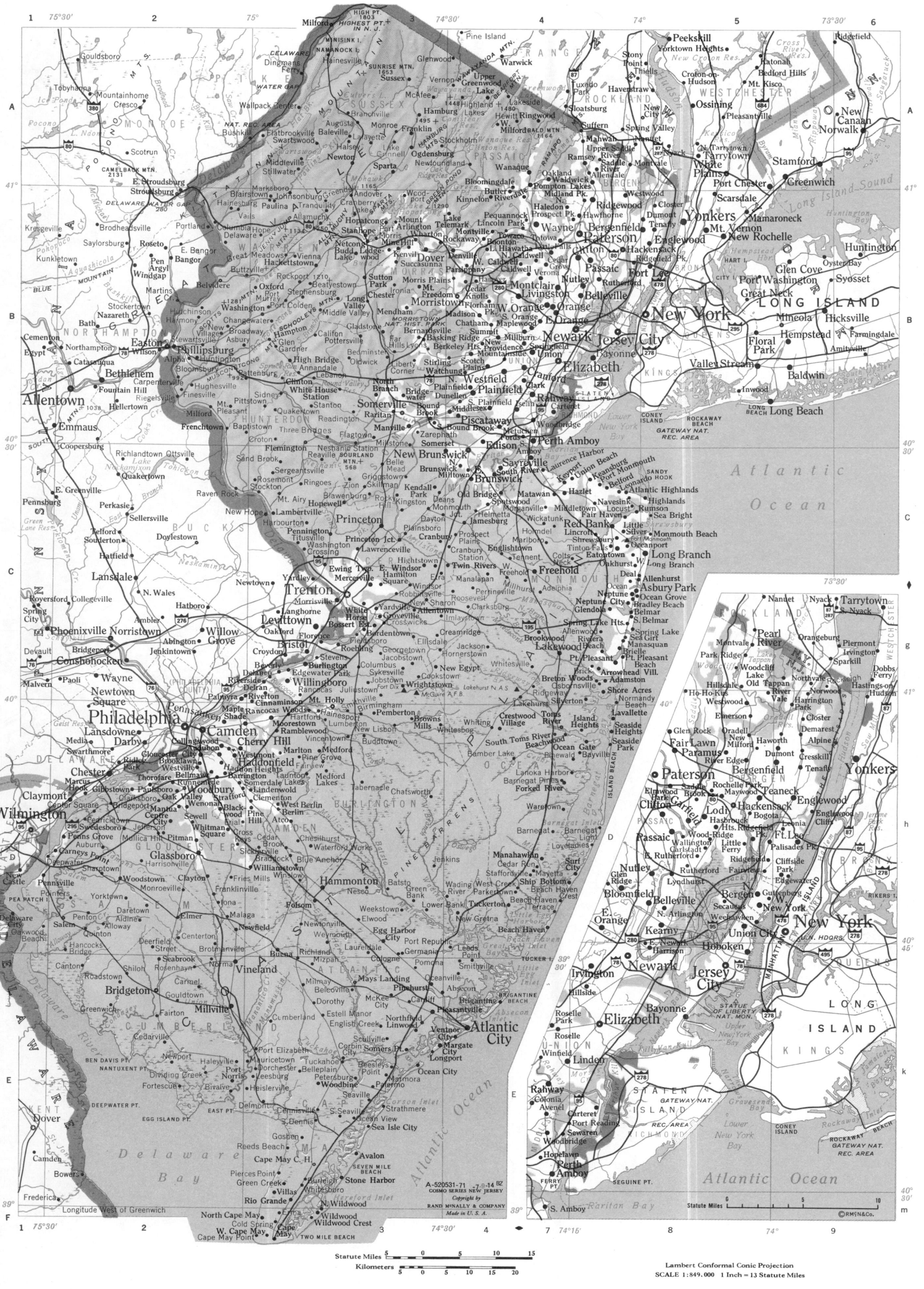

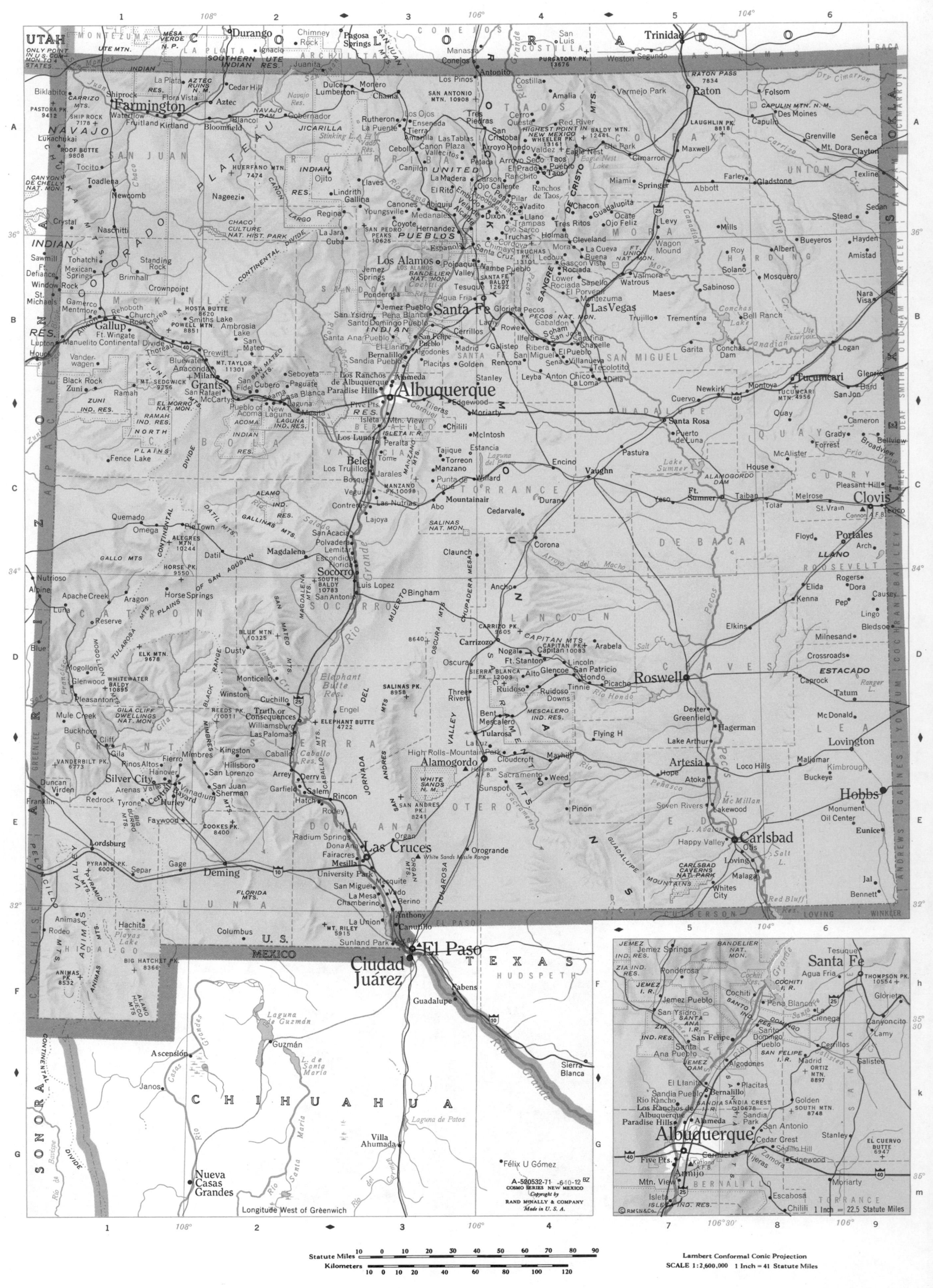

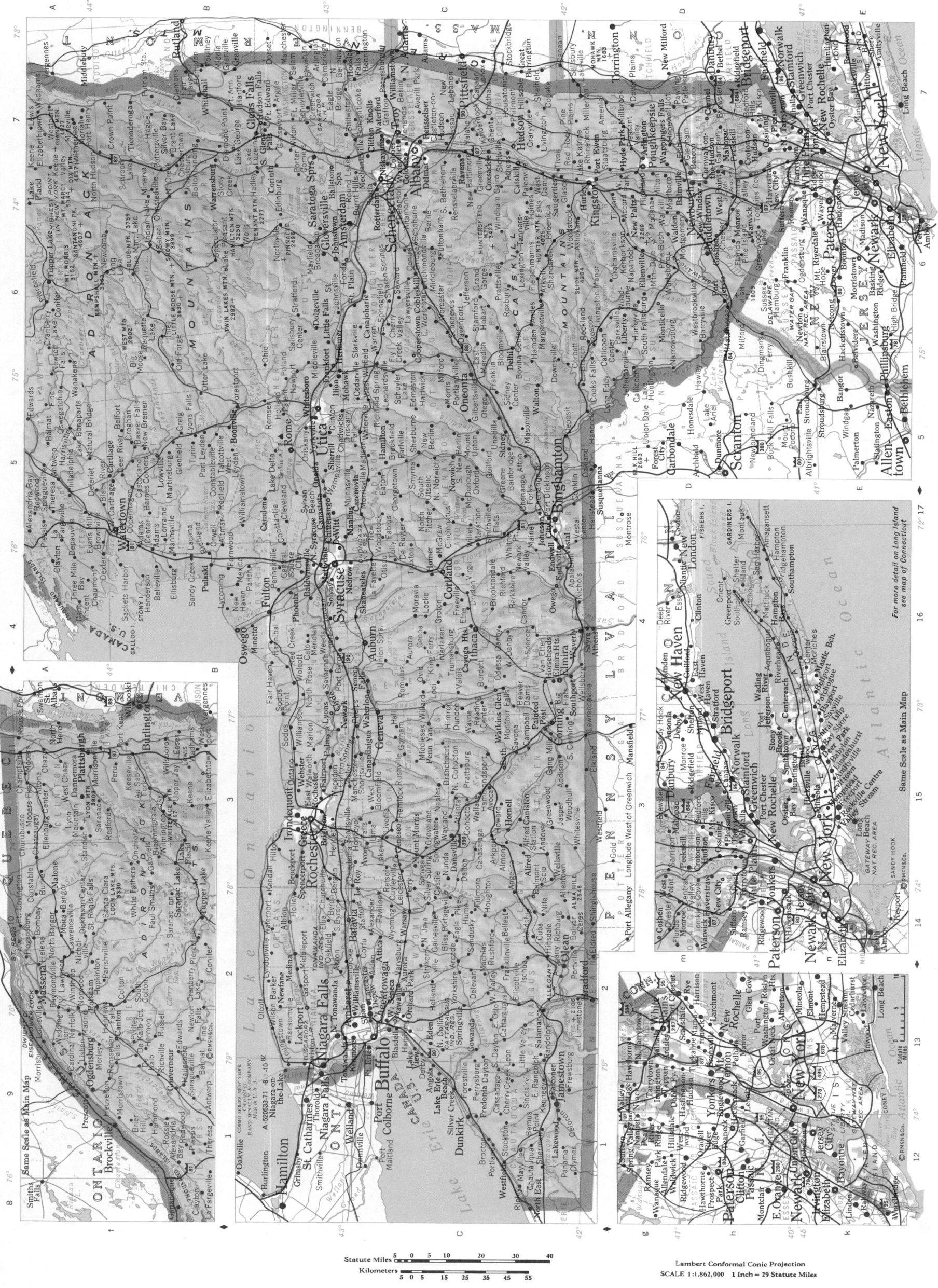

Statute Miles

Kilometers

Lambert Conformal Conic Projection
SCALE 1:1,862,000   1 Inch = 29 Statute Miles

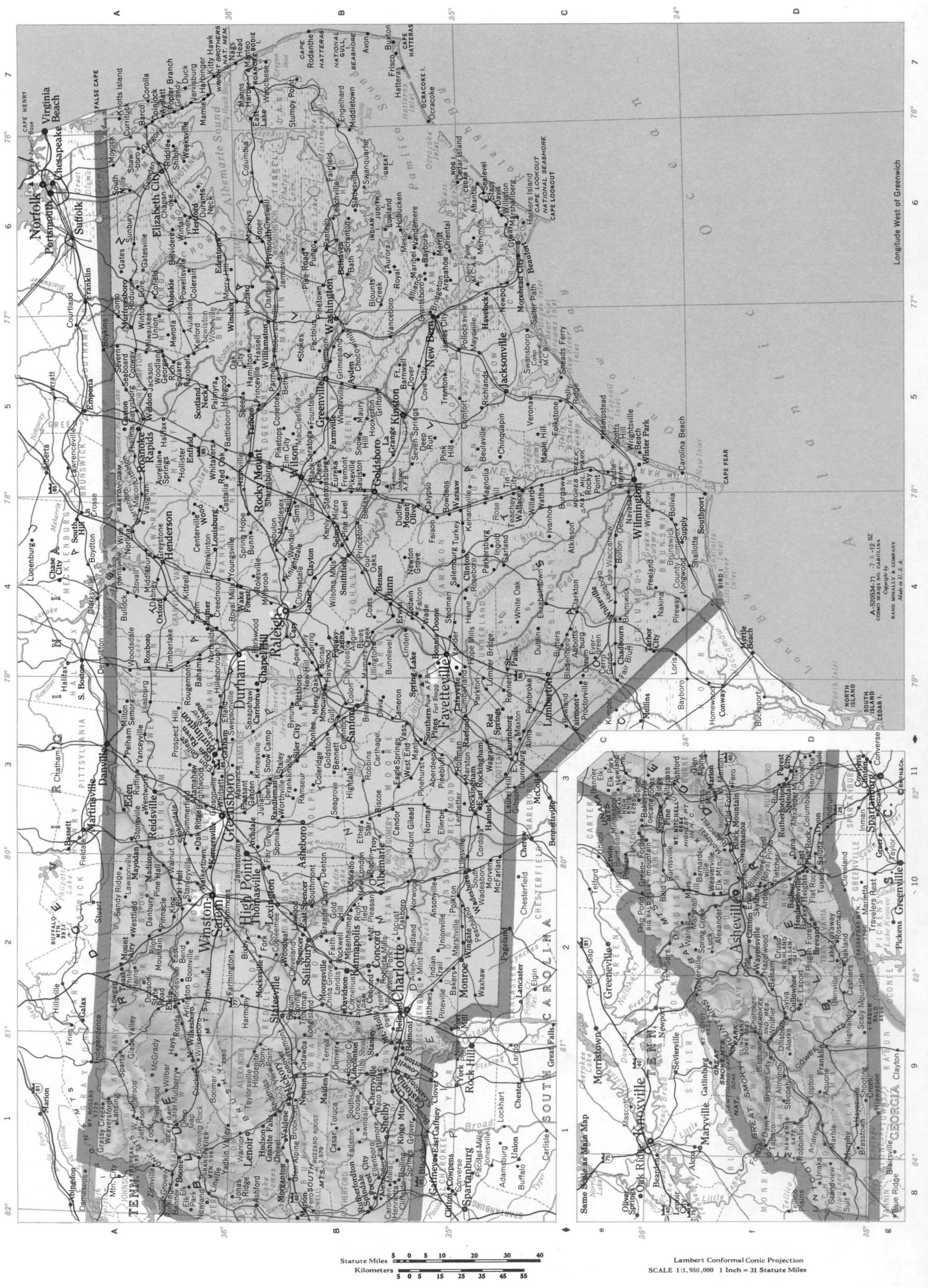

Statute Miles 5 0 5 10 20 30 40
Kilometers 5 0 5 15 25 35 45 55

Lambert Conformal Conic Projection
SCALE 1:1,950,000 1 Inch = 31 Statute Miles

Same Scale as Main Map

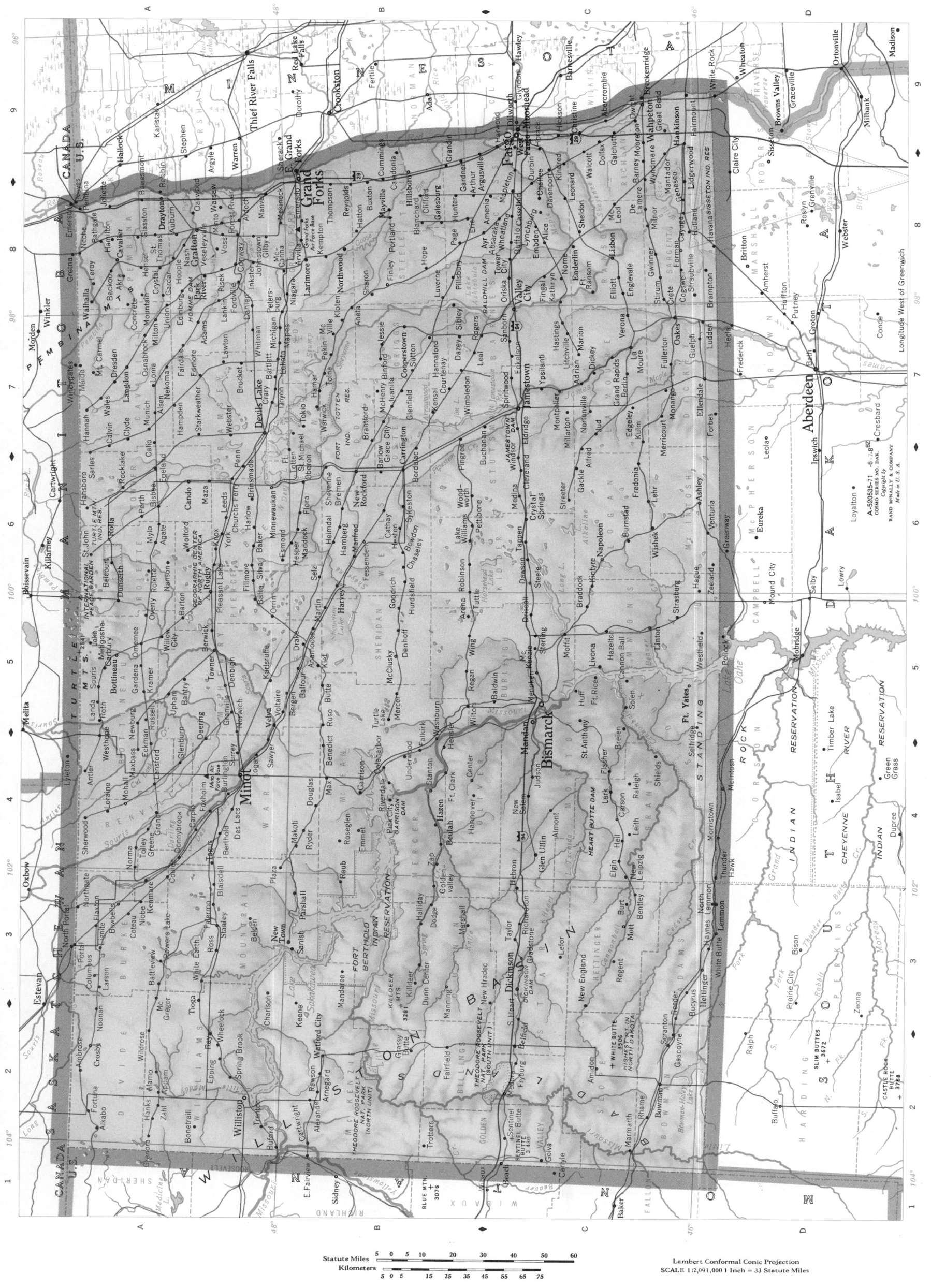

A-500535-71 -6 -8
COMO SERIES NO. DAK.
Copyright by
RAND McNALLY & COMPANY
Made in U.S.A.

Statute Miles
Kilometers

Lambert Conformal Conic Projection
SCALE 1:2,091,000 1 Inch = 33 Statute Miles

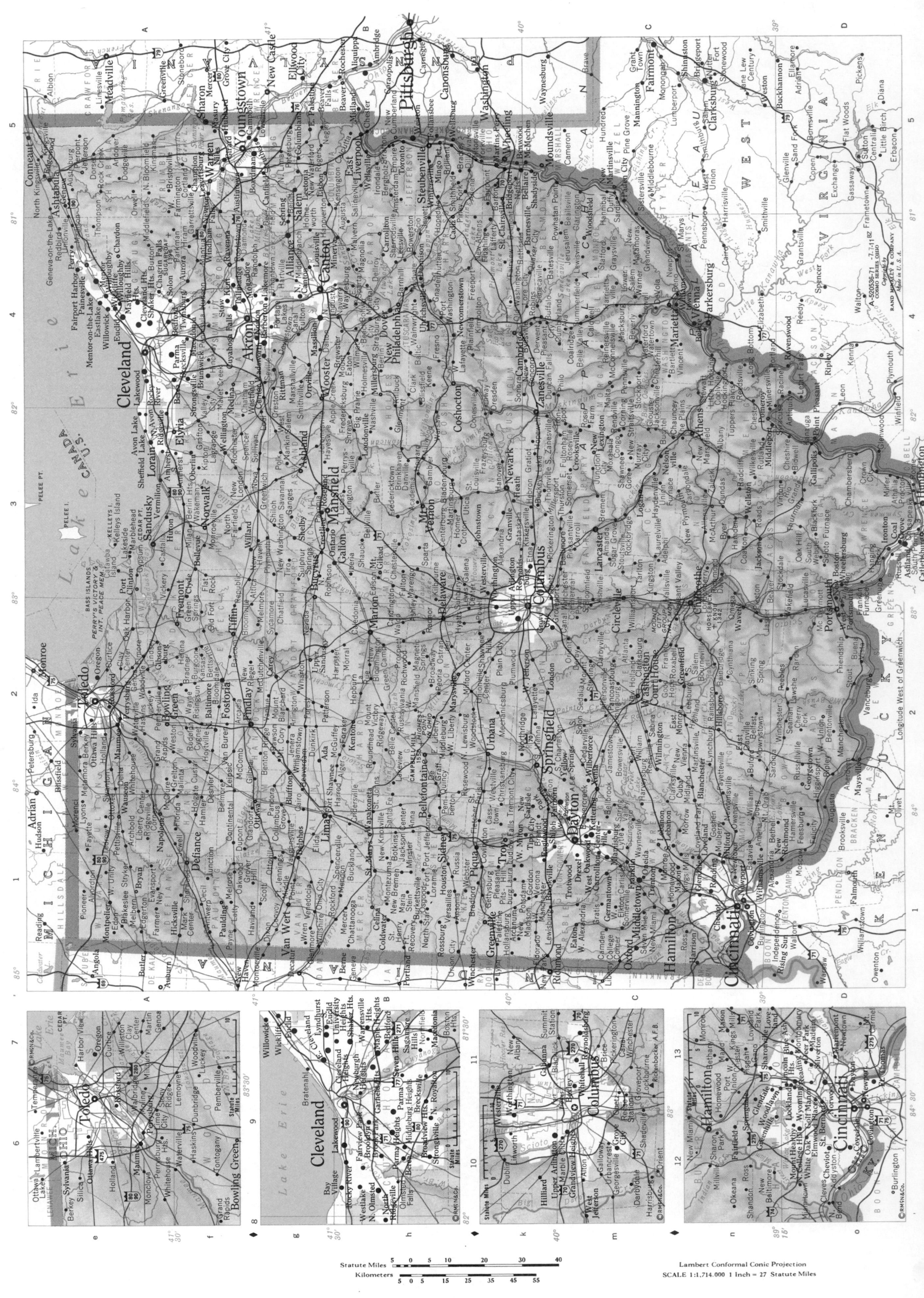

Statute Miles
Kilometers

Lambert Conformal Conic Projection
SCALE 1:1,714,000 1 Inch = 27 Statute Miles

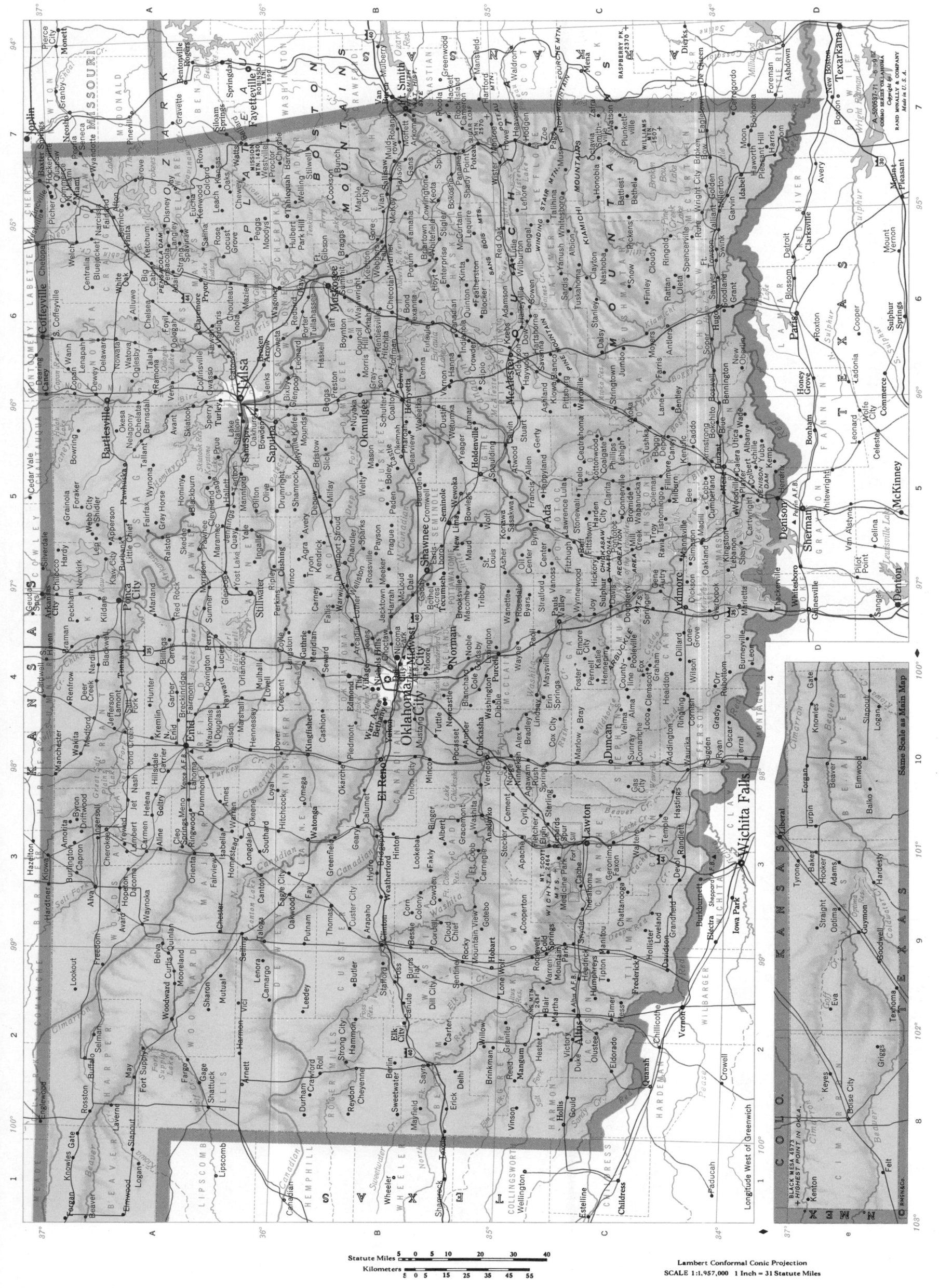

Statute Miles

Kilometers

Lambert Conformal Conic Projection
SCALE 1:1,957,000 1 Inch = 31 Statute Miles

Statute Miles 5 0 5 10 20 30 40 50
Kilometers 5 0 5 15 25 35 45 55 65 75

Lambert Conformal Conic Projection
SCALE 1:2,329,000 1 Inch = 37 Statute Miles

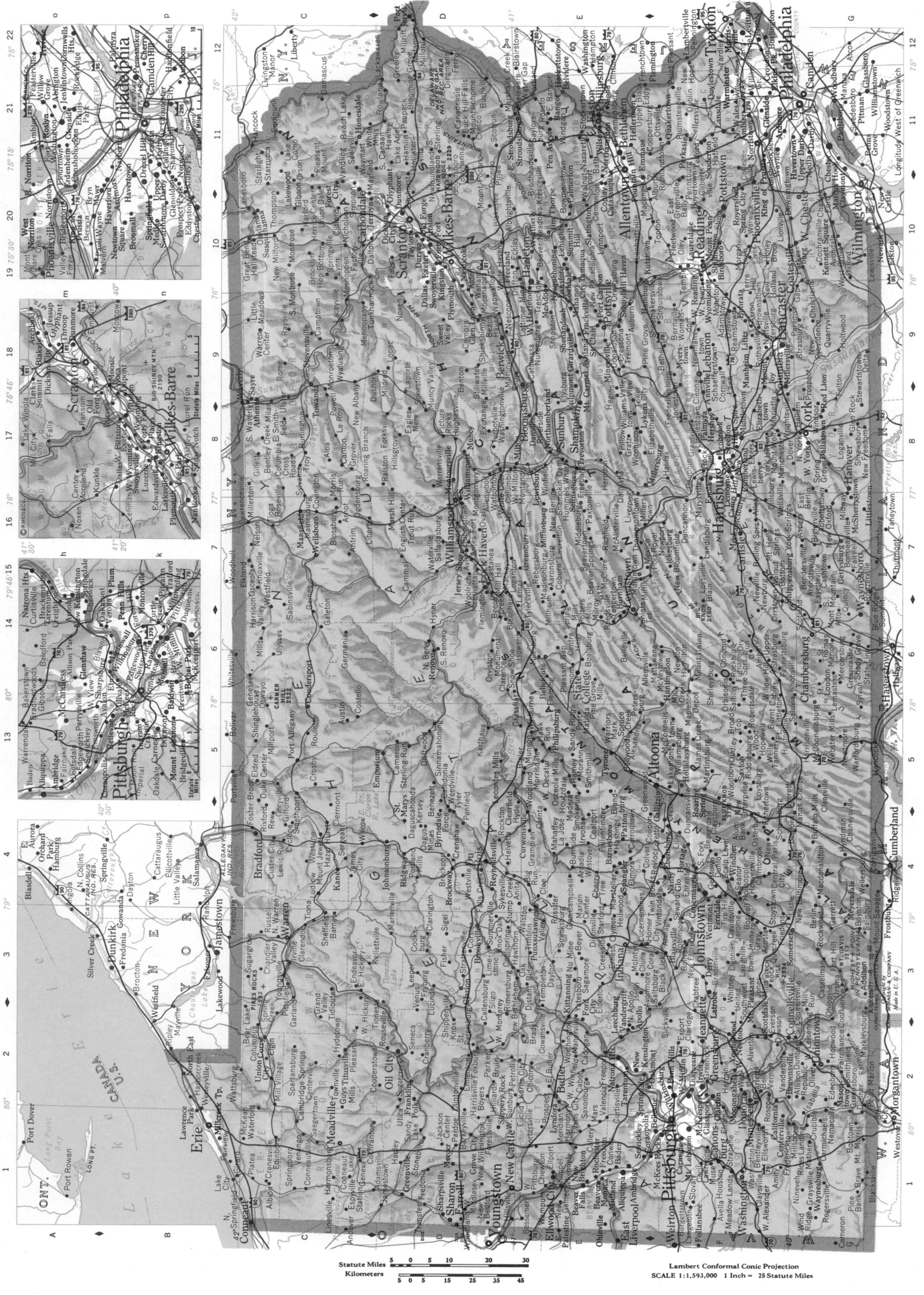

Statute Miles

Kilometers

Lambert Conformal Conic Projection
SCALE 1:1,593,000   1 Inch = 25 Statute Miles

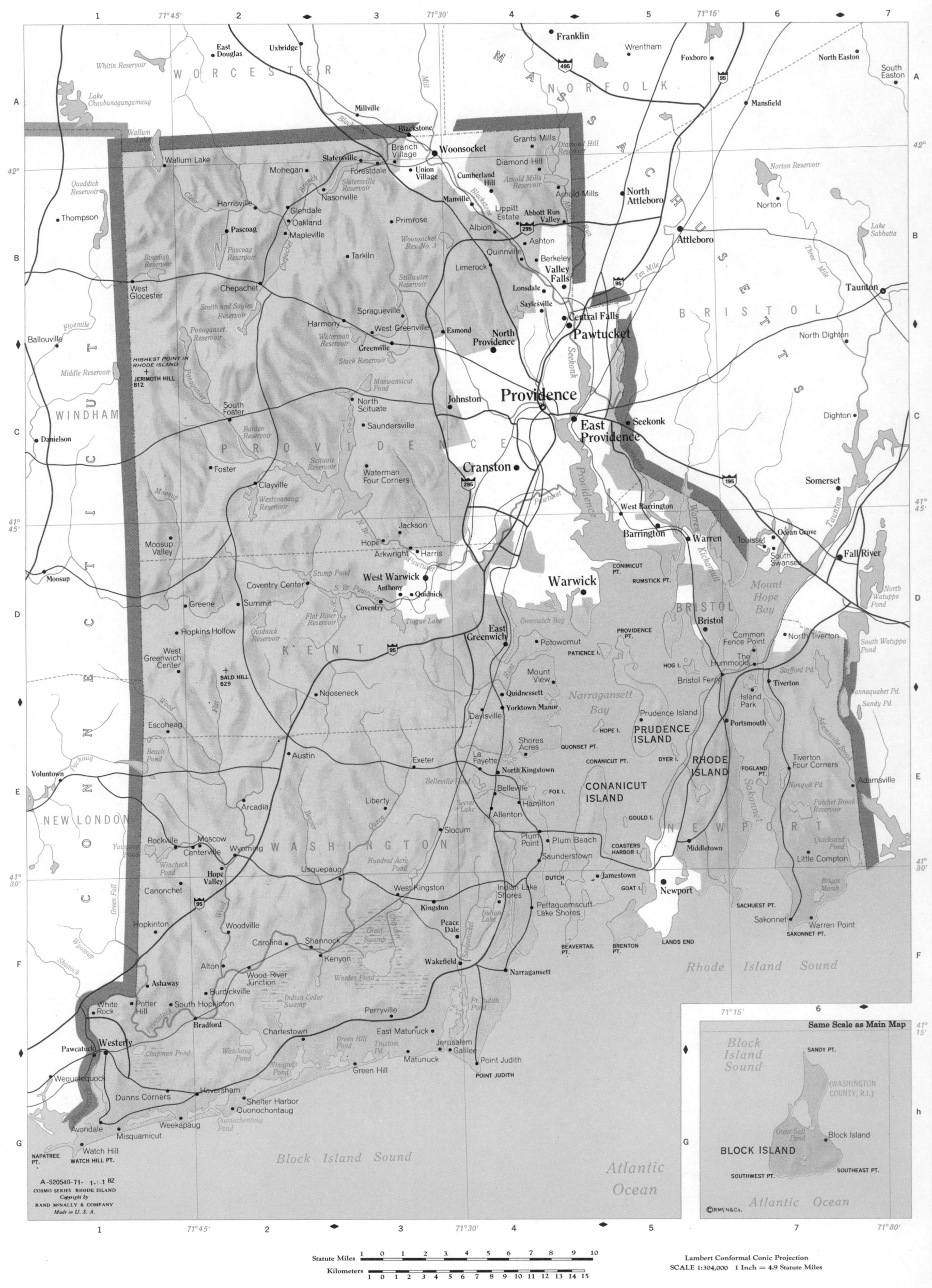

Statute Miles 1 0 1 2 3 4 5 6 7 8 9 10

Kilometers 1 0 1 2 3 4 5 6 7 8 9 10 11 12 13 14 15

Lambert Conformal Conic Projection
SCALE 1:304,000   1 Inch = 4.9 Statute Miles

A-520540-71- 1-1-1 BZ
COSMO SERIES RHODE ISLAND
Copyright by
RAND McNALLY & COMPANY
Made in U.S.A.

Same Scale as Main Map

Block
Island
Sound

(WASHINGTON
COUNTY, R.I.)

BLOCK ISLAND

©RM&N&Co.

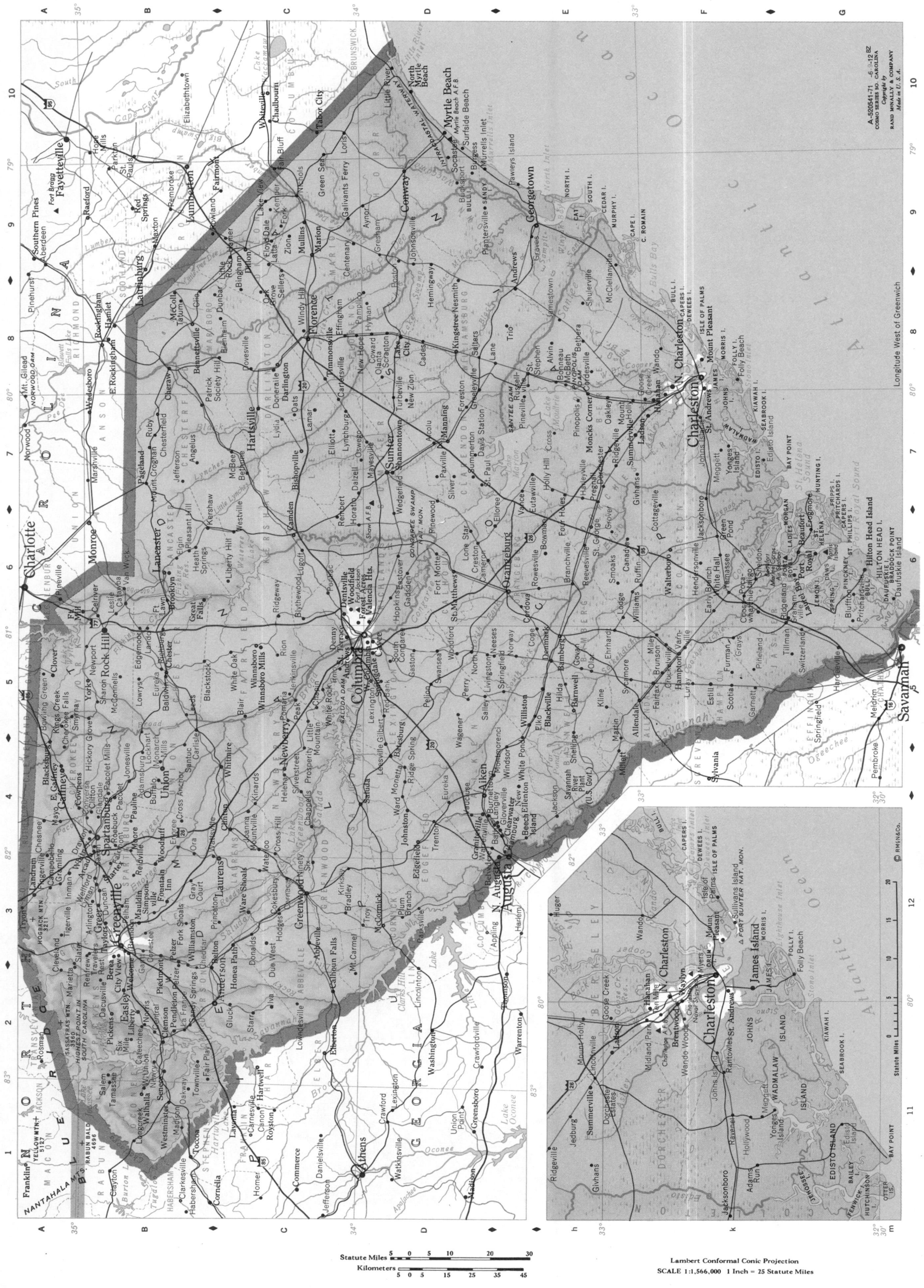

Statute Miles

Kilometers

Lambert Conformal Conic Projection
SCALE 1:1,566,000   1 Inch = 25 Statute Miles

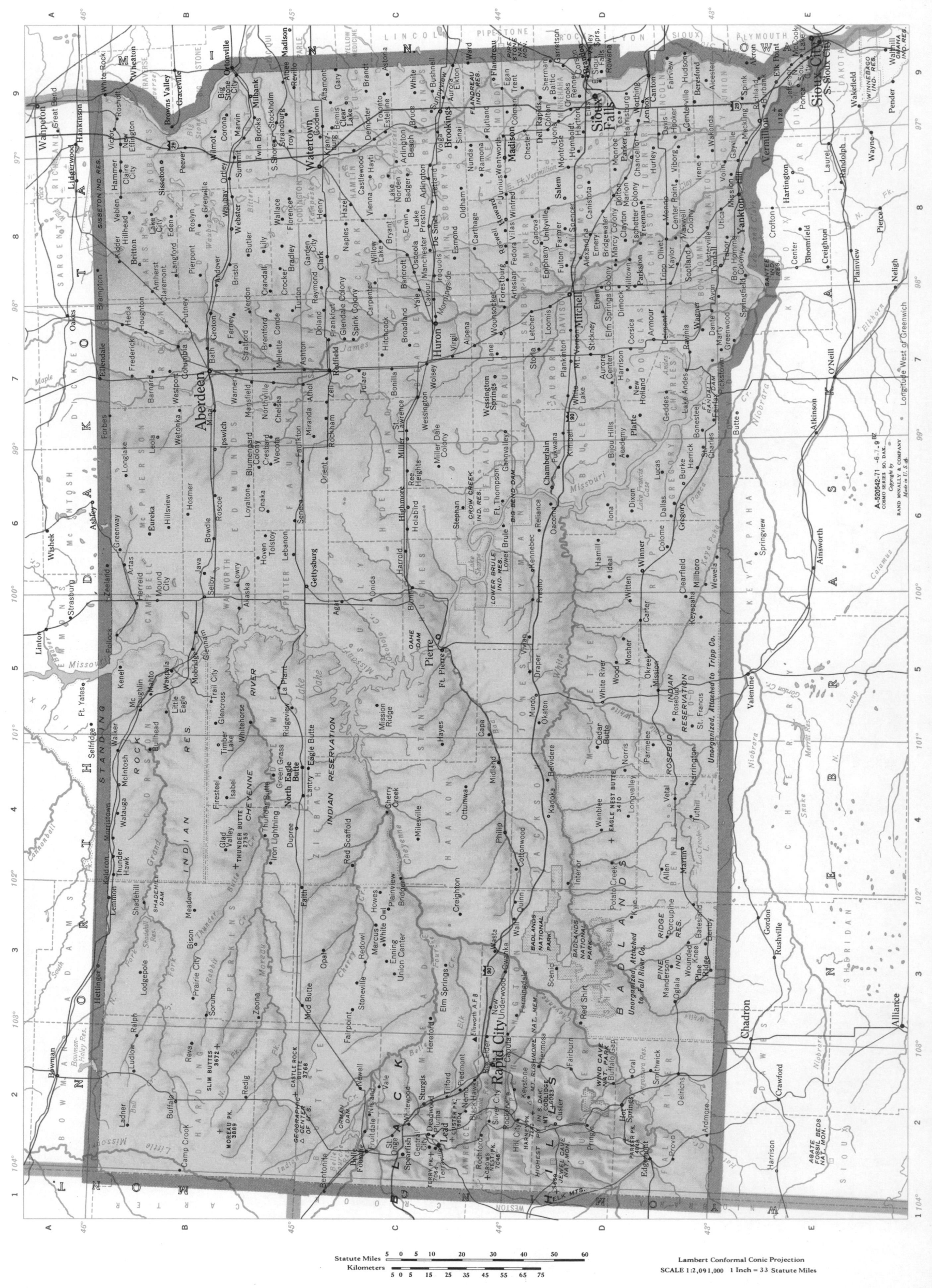

Statute Miles 5 0 5 10 20 30 40 50 60
Kilometers 5 0 5 15 25 35 45 55 65 75

Lambert Conformal Conic Projection
SCALE 1:2,091,000   1 Inch = 33 Statute Miles

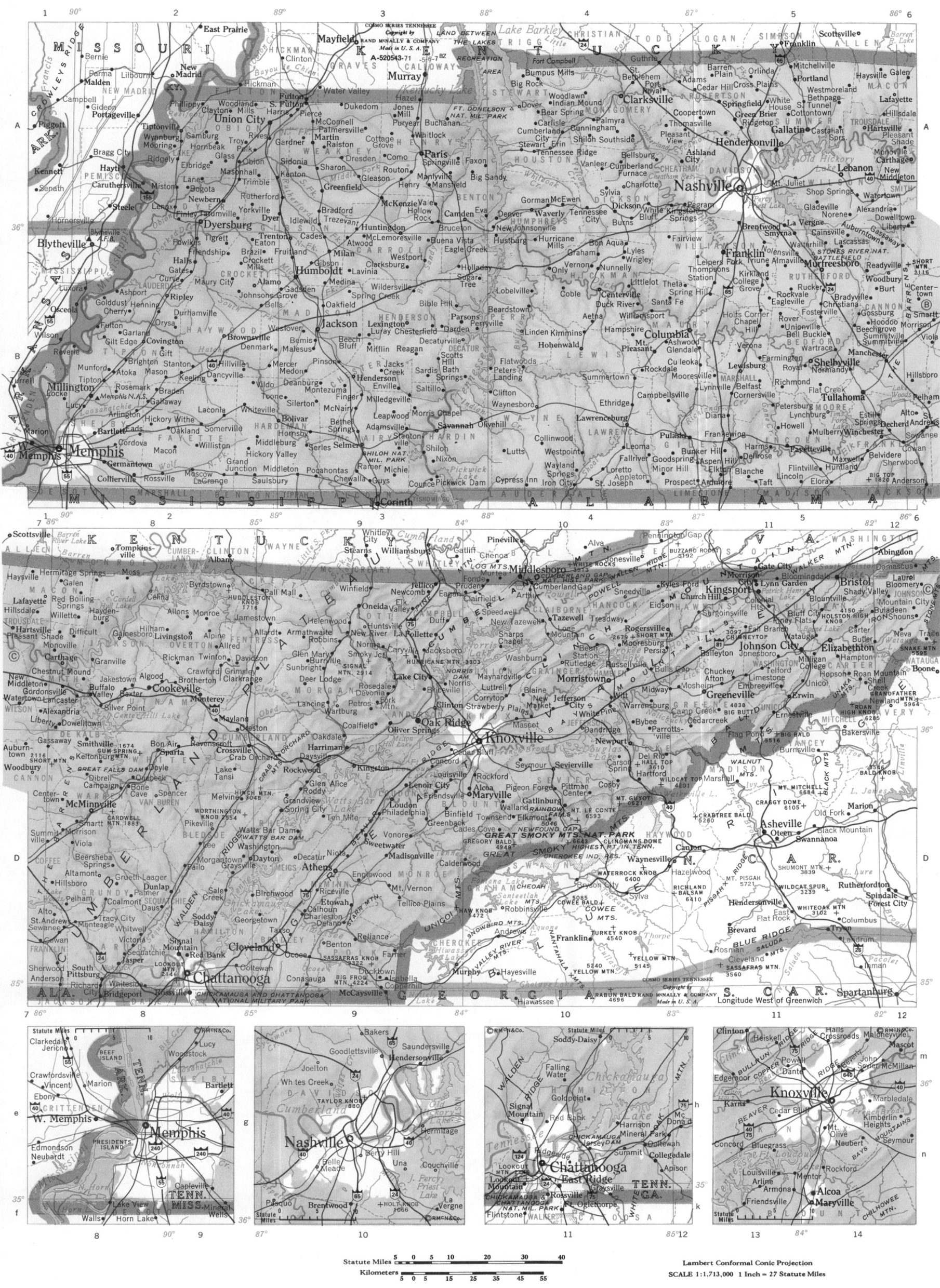

Lambert Conformal Conic Projection
SCALE 1:1,713,000 1 Inch = 27 Statute Miles

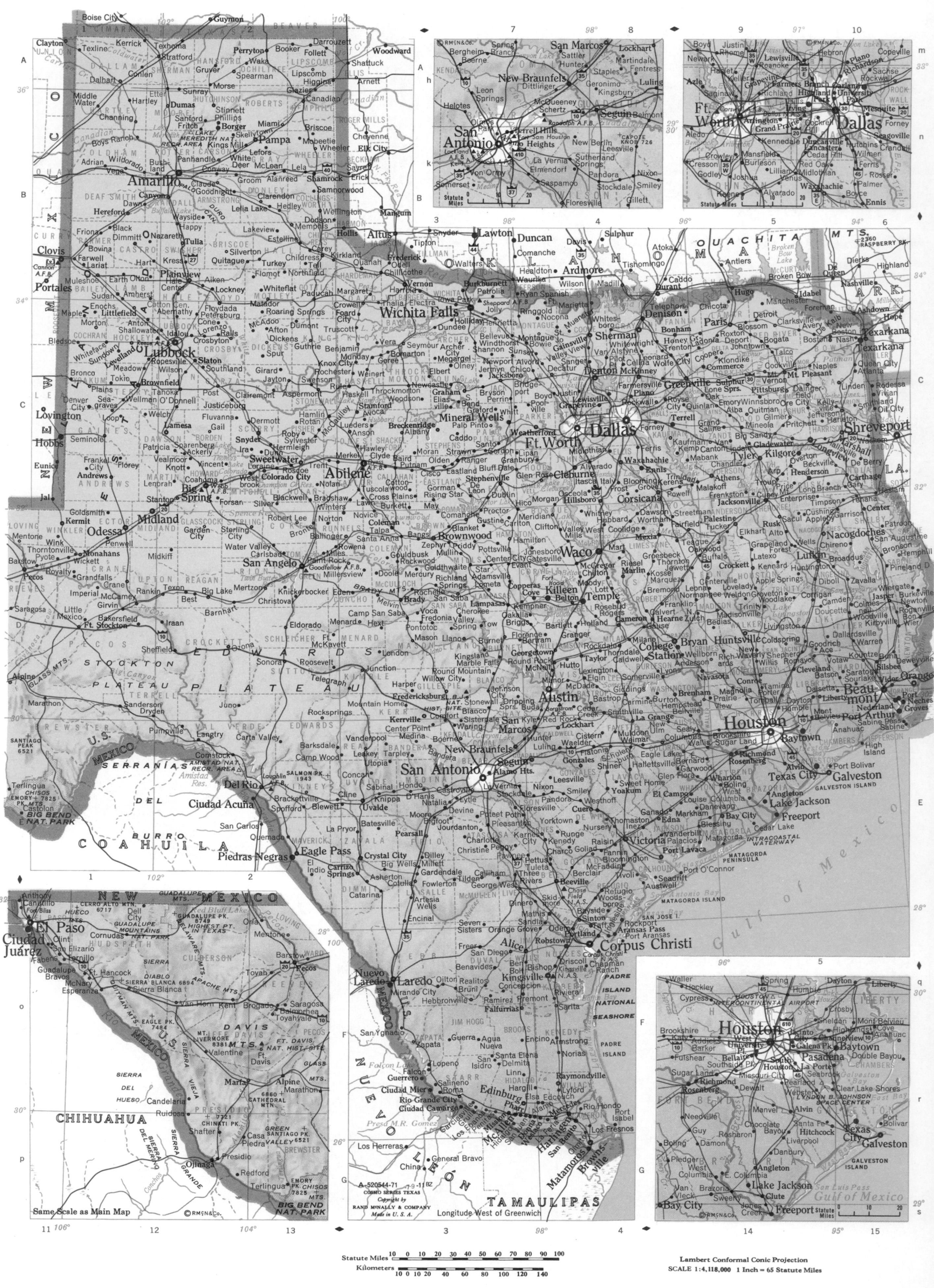

Statute Miles 10 0 10 20 30 40 50 60 70 80 90 100
Kilometers 10 0 10 20 40 60 80 100 120 140

Lambert Conformal Conic Projection
SCALE 1:4,118,000 1 Inch = 65 Statute Miles

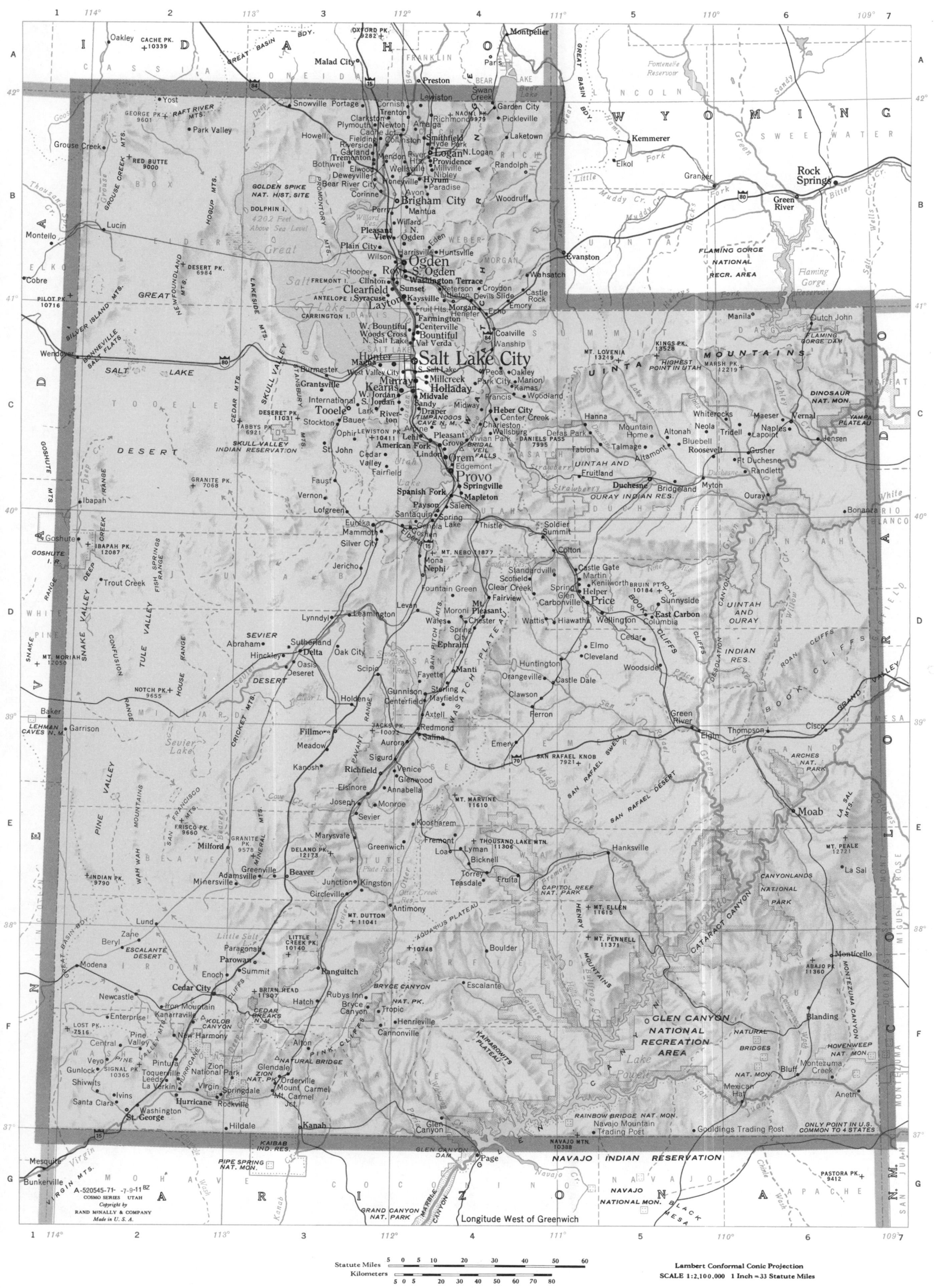

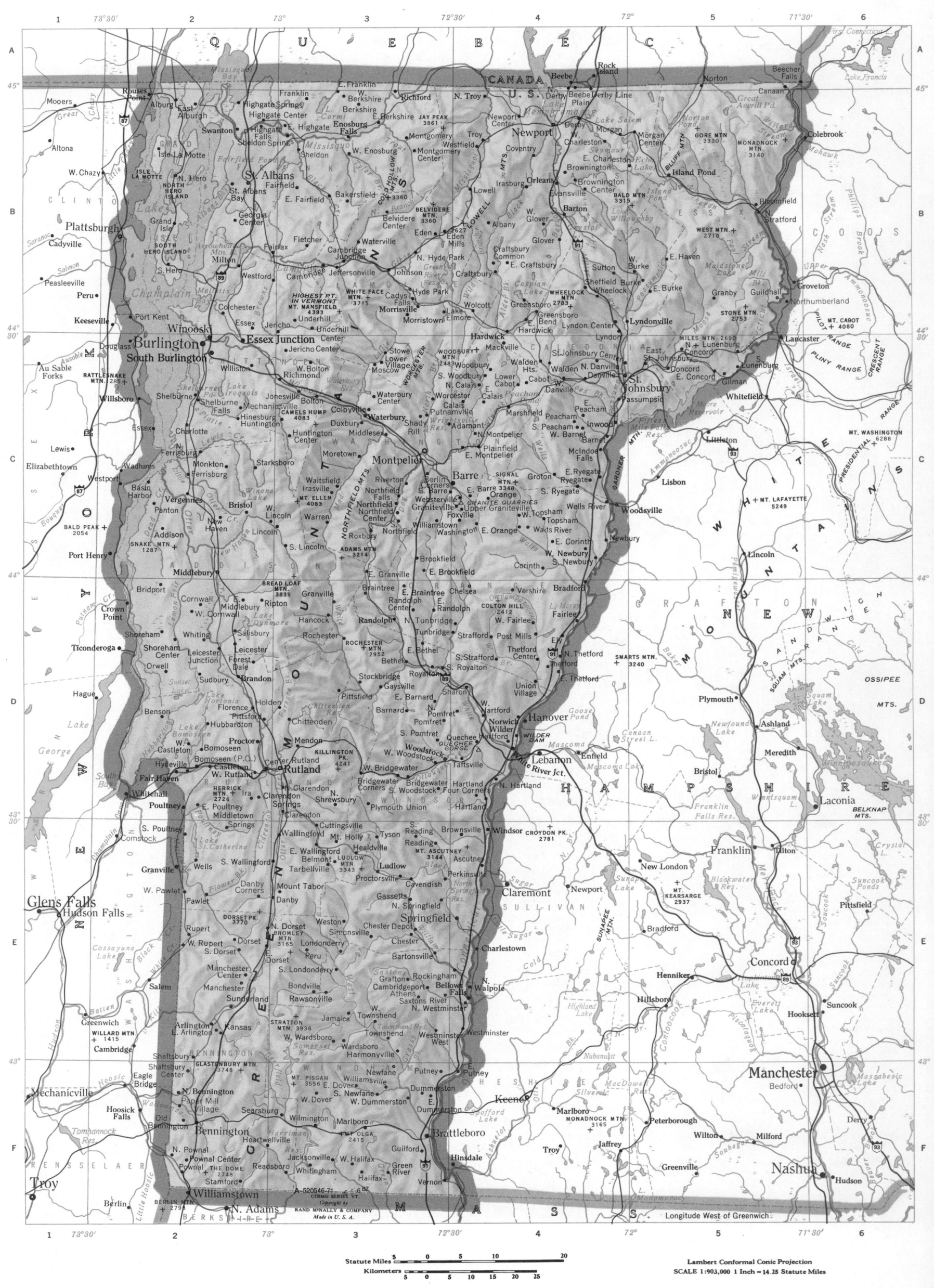

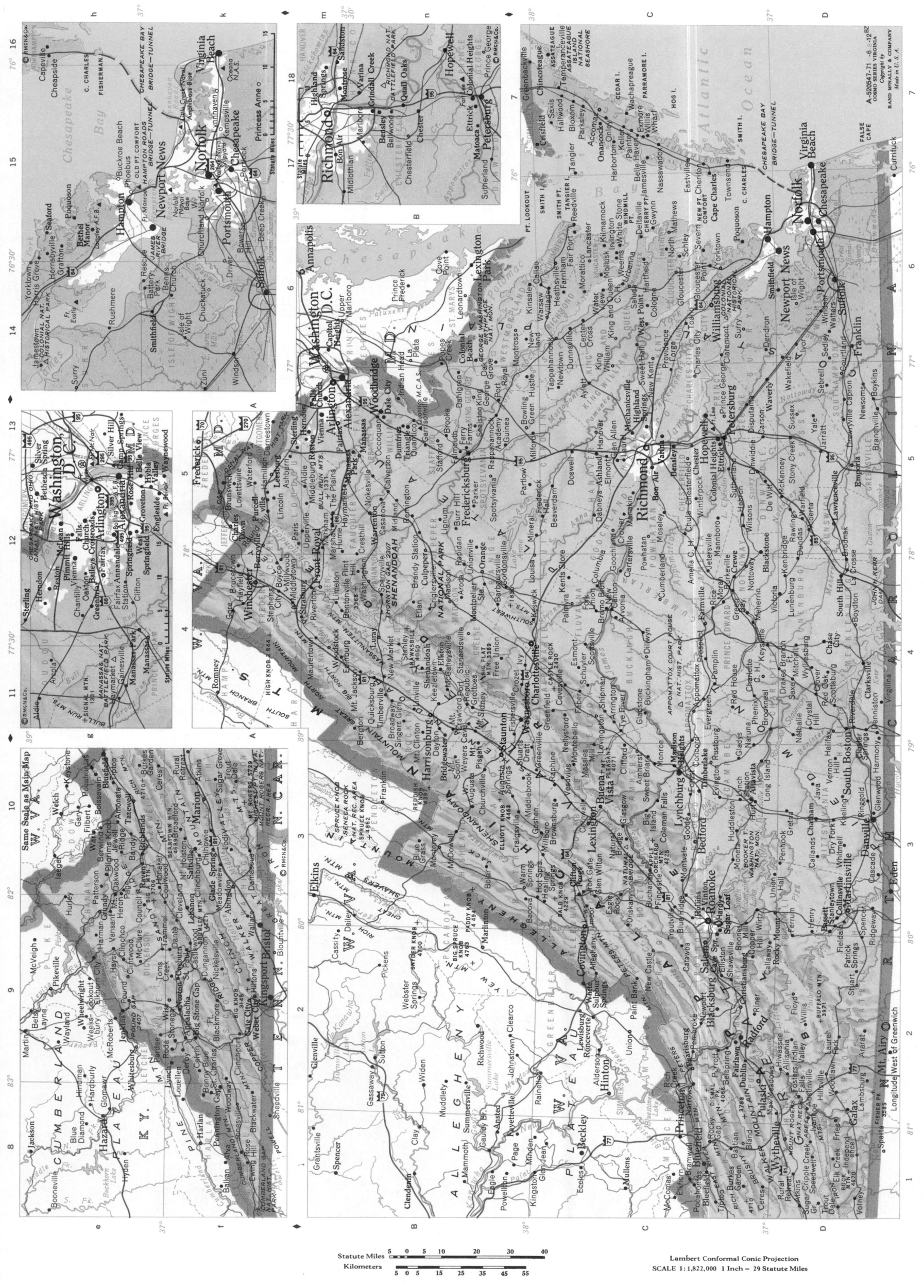

Statute Miles

Kilometers

Lambert Conformal Conic Projection
SCALE 1:1,822,000 1 Inch = 29 Statute Miles

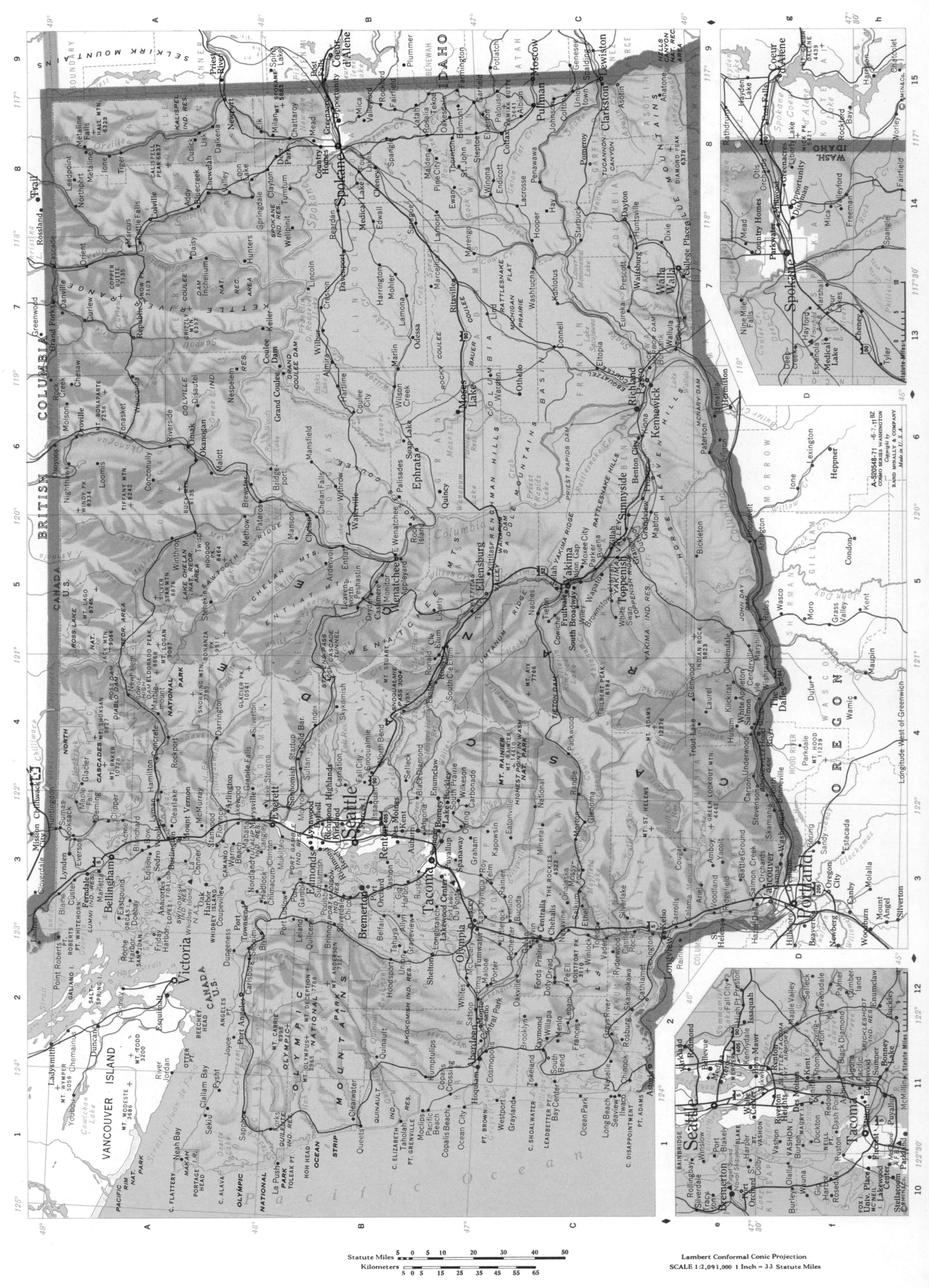

Lambert Conformal Conic Projection
SCALE 1:2,091,000 1 Inch = 33 Statute Miles

Statute Miles
Kilometers

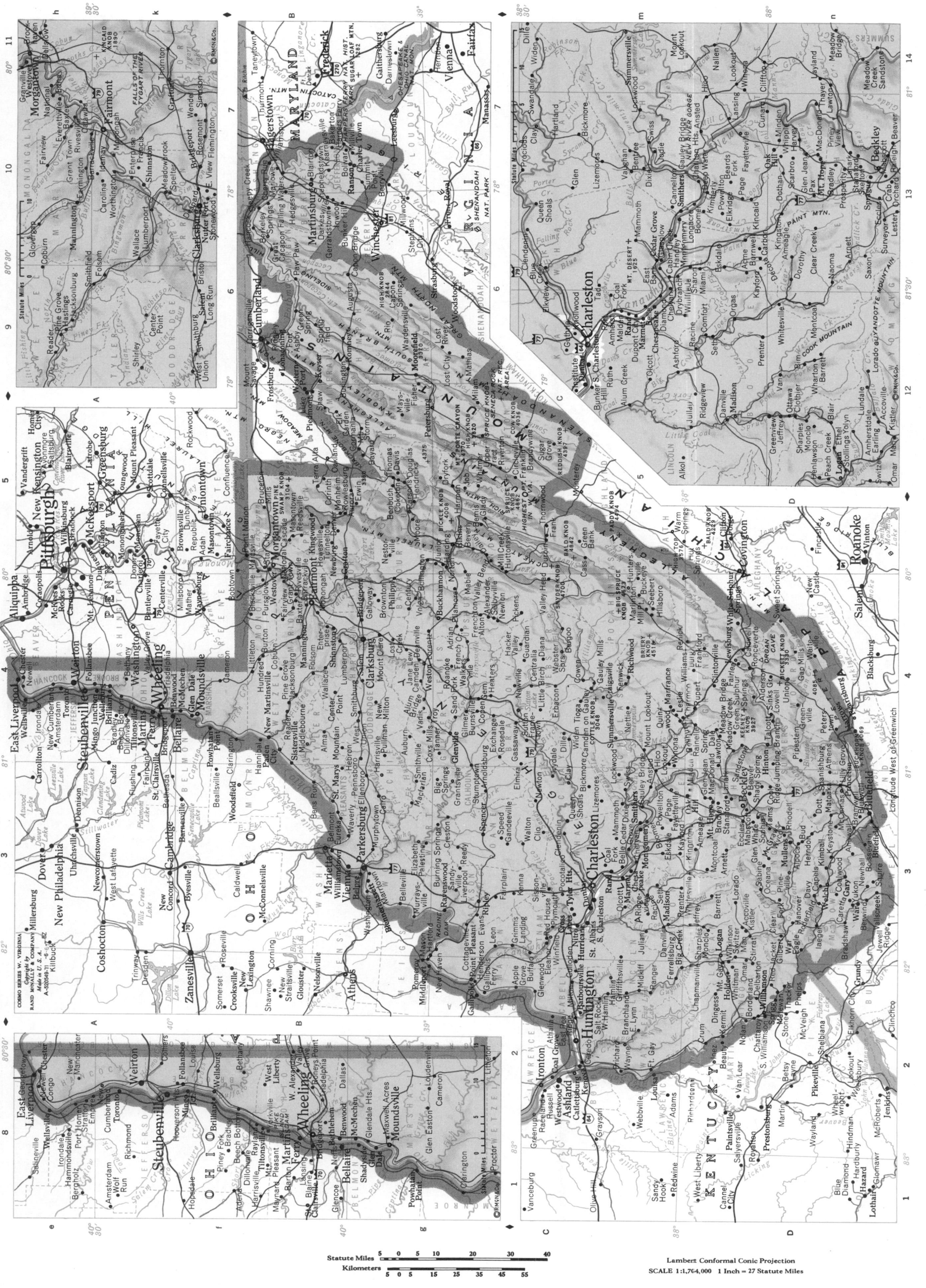

Statute Miles
Kilometers

Lambert Conformal Conic Projection
SCALE 1:1,764,000   1 Inch = 27 Statute Miles

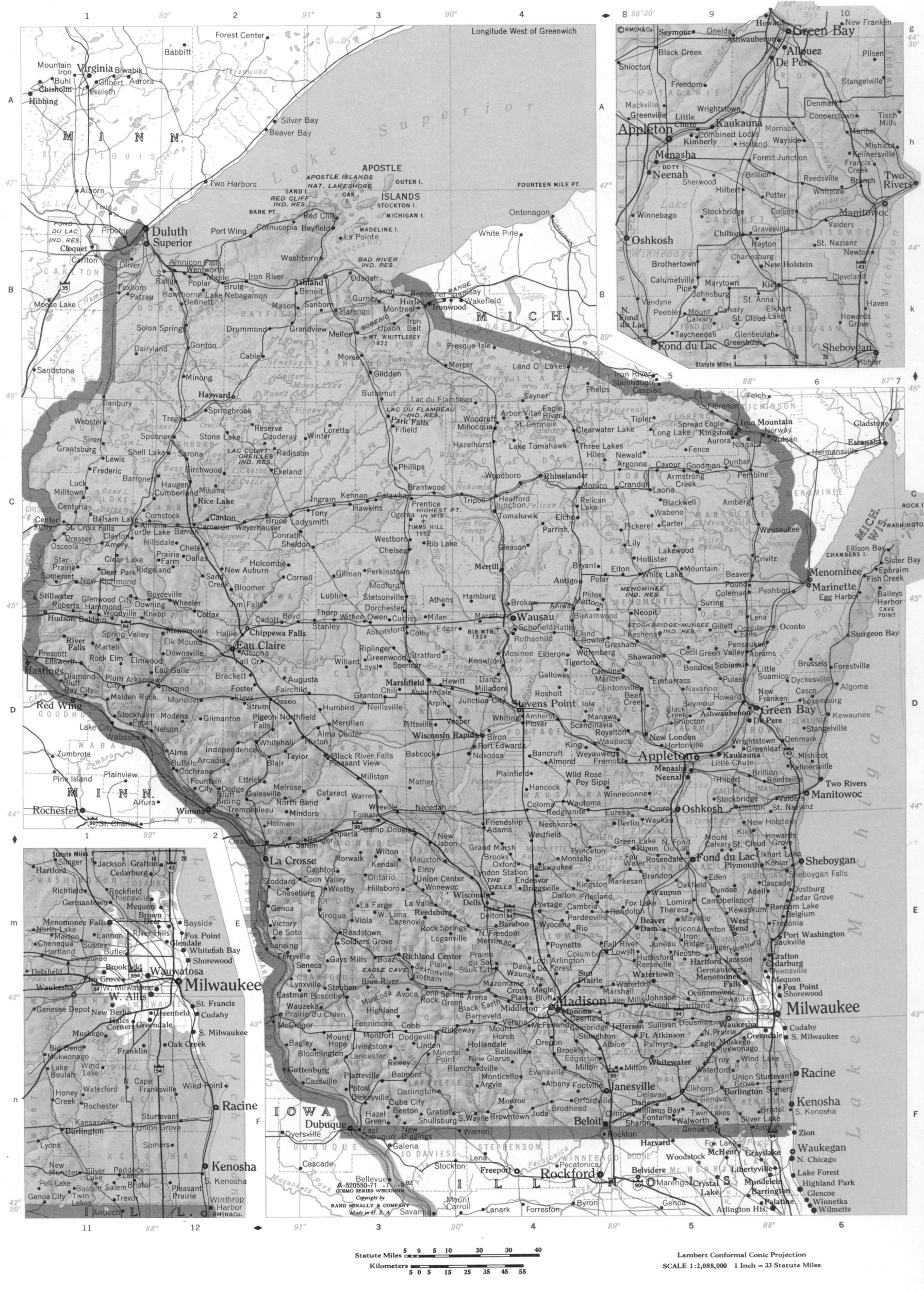

Lambert Conformal Conic Projection
SCALE 1:2,088,000   1 Inch = 33 Statute Miles

Statute Miles

Kilometers

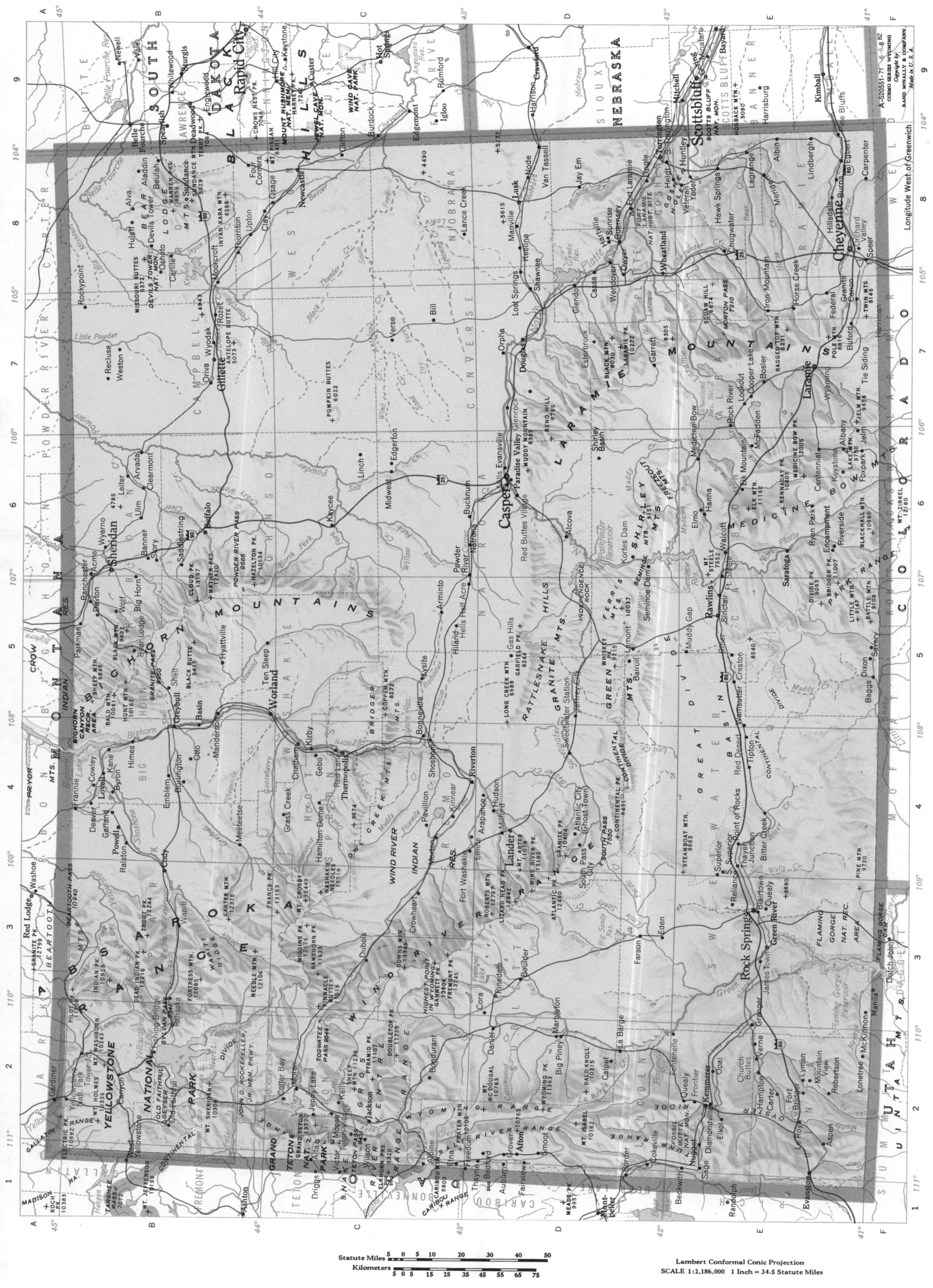

Statute Miles

Kilometers

Lambert Conformal Conic Projection
SCALE 1:2,186,000   1 Inch = 34.5 Statute Miles

Longitude West of Greenwich

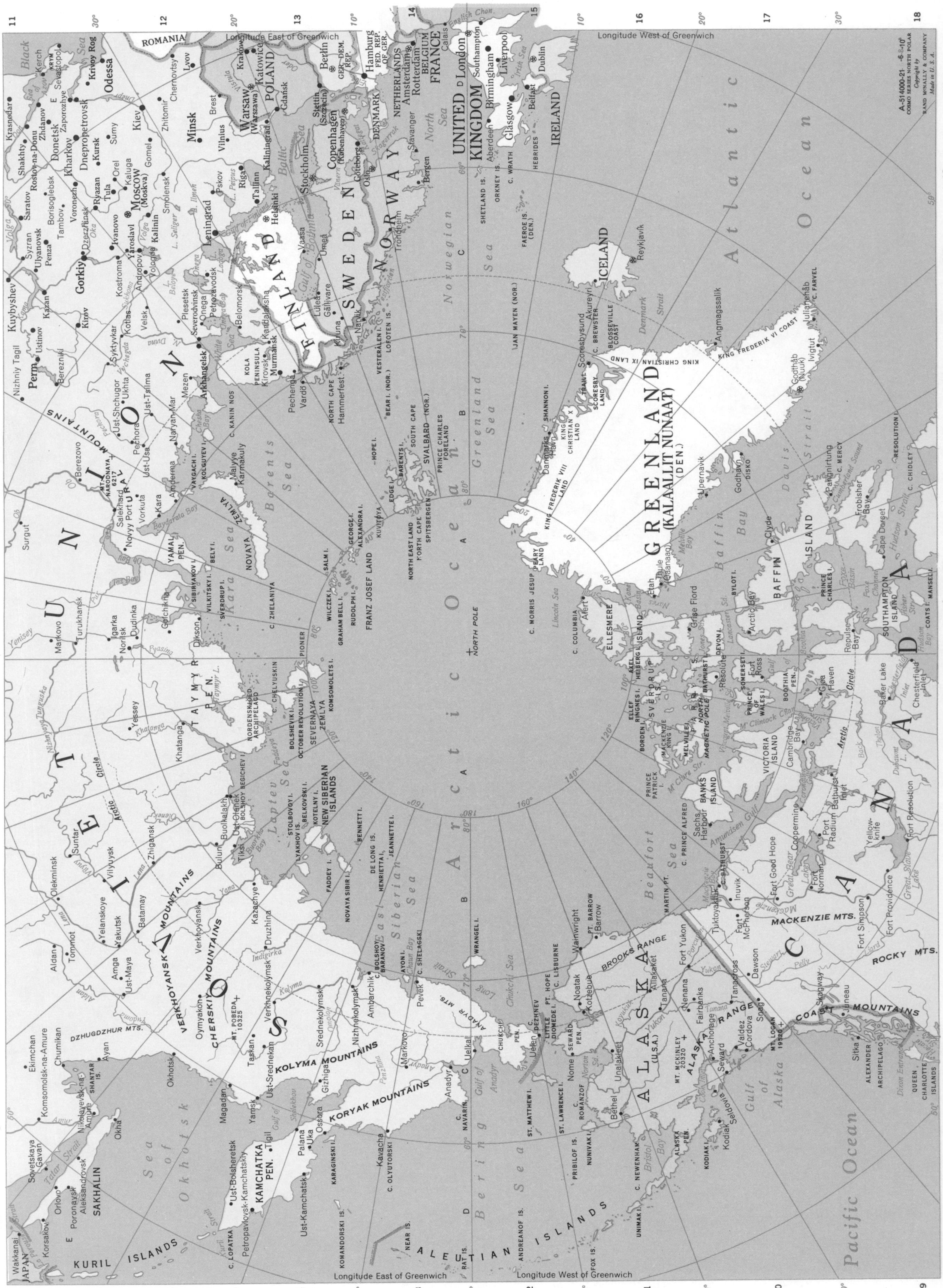

INDEX TO WORLD REFERENCE MAPS

INTRODUCTION TO THE INDEX

This universal index includes in a single alphabetical list approximately 78,000 names of features that appear on the reference maps. Each name is followed by the name of the country or continent in which it is located, a map-reference key and a page reference.

Names The names of cities appear in the index in regular type. The names of all other features appear in *italics*, followed by descriptive terms (hill, mtn., state) to indicate their nature.

Names that appear in shortened versions on the maps due to space limitations are spelled out in full in the index. The portions of these names omitted from the maps are enclosed in brackets — for example, Acapulco [de Juárez].

Abbreviations of names on the maps have been standardized as much as possible. Names that are abbreviated on the maps are generally spelled out in full in the index.

Country names and names of features that extend beyond the boundaries of one country are followed by the name of the continent in which each is located. Country designations follow the names of all other places in the index. The locations of places in the United States, Canada, and the United Kingdom are further defined by abbreviations that indicate the state, province, or political division in which each is located.

All abbreviations used in the index are defined in the List of Abbreviations below.

Alphabetization Names are alphabetized in the order of the letters of the English alphabet. Spanish *ll* and *ch*, for example, are not treated as distinct letters. Furthermore, diacritical marks are disregarded in alphabetization — German or Scandinavian *ä* or *ö* are treated as *a* or *o*.

The names of physical features may appear inverted, since they are always alphabetized under the proper, not the generic, part of the name, thus: 'Gibraltar, Strait of'. Otherwise every entry, whether consisting of one word or more, is alphabetized as a single continuous entity. 'Lakeland', for example, appears after 'La Crosse' and before 'La Salle'. Names beginning with articles (Le Havre, Den Helder, Al Manşūrah) are not inverted. Names beginning 'Mc' are alphabetized as though spelled 'Mac', and names beginning 'St.', 'Ste.' and 'Sainte' as though spelled 'Saint'.

In the case of identical names, towns are listed first, then political divisions, then physical features. Entries that are completely identical are listed alphabetically by country name.

Map-Reference Keys and Page References The map-reference keys and page references are found in the last two columns of each entry.

Each map-reference key consists of a letter and number. The letters appear along the sides of the maps. Lowercase letters indicate reference to inset maps. Numbers appear across the tops and bottoms of the maps.

Map reference keys for point features, such as cities and mountain peaks, indicate the locations of the symbols. For extensive areal features, such as countries or mountain ranges, locations are given for the approximate centers of the features. Those for linear features, such as canals and rivers, are given for the locations of the names.

Names of some important places or features that are omitted from the maps due to space limitations are included in the index. Each of these places is identified by an asterisk (*) preceding the map-reference key.

The page number generally refers to the main map for the country in which the feature is located. Page references to two-page maps always refer to the left-hand page.

LIST OF ABBREVIATIONS

Ab., Can.	Alberta, Can.	Den.	Denmark	Kir.	Kiribati	Nmb.	Namibia	St. Hel.	St. Helena
Afg.	Afghanistan	*dep.*	dependency, colony	Ks., U.S.	Kansas, U.S.	Nor.	Norway	St. Luc.	St. Lucia
Afr.	Africa	*depr.*	depression	Kuw.	Kuwait	Norf. I.	Norfolk Island	*stm.*	stream (river, creek)
Ak., U.S.	Alaska, U.S.	*dept.*	department, district	Ky., U.S.	Kentucky, U.S.	N.S., Can.	Nova Scotia, Can.	S. Tom./P.	Sao Tome and
Al., U.S.	Alabama, U.S.	*des.*	desert	*l.*	lake, pond	N.T., Can.	Northwest		Principe
Alb.	Albania	Dji.	Djibouti	La., U.S.	Louisiana, U.S.		Territories, Can.	St. P./M.	St. Pierre and
Alg.	Algeria	Dom.	Dominica	Leb.	Lebanon	Nv., U.S.	Nevada, U.S.		Miquelon
Am. Sam.	American Samoa	Dom. Rep.	Dominican Republic	Leso.	Lesotho	N.Y., U.S.	New York, U.S.	*strt.*	strait, channel,
anch.	anchorage	Ec.	Ecuador	Lib.	Liberia	N.Z.	New Zealand		sound
And.	Andorra	El Sal.	El Salvador	Liech.	Liechtenstein	Oc.	Oceania	St. Vin.	St. Vincent and the
Ang.	Angola	Eng., U.K.	England, U.K.	Lux.	Luxembourg	Oh., U.S.	Ohio, U.S.		Grenadines
Ant.	Antarctica	Eq. Gui.	Equatorial Guinea	Ma., U.S.	Massachusetts,	Ok., U.S.	Oklahoma, U.S.	Sur.	Suriname
Antig.	Antigua and	*est.*	estuary		U.S.	On., Can.	Ontario, Can.	*sw.*	swamp, marsh
	Barbuda	Eth.	Ethiopia	Madag.	Madagascar	Or., U.S.	Oregon, U.S.	Swaz.	Swaziland
Ar., U.S.	Arkansas, U.S.	Eur.	Europe	Malay.	Malaysia	Pa., U.S.	Pennsylvania, U.S.	Swe.	Sweden
Arg.	Argentina	Faer. Is.	Faeroe Islands	Mald.	Maldives	Pak.	Pakistan	Switz.	Switzerland
Aus.	Austria	Falk. Is.	Falkland Islands	Marsh. Is.	Marshall Islands	Pan.	Panama	Tai.	Taiwan
Austl.	Australia	Fin.	Finland	Mart.	Martinique	Pap. N. Gui.	Papua New Guinea	Tan.	Tanzania
Az., U.S.	Arizona, U.S.	Fl., U.S.	Florida, U.S.	Maur.	Mauritania	Para.	Paraguay	T./C. Is.	Turks and Caicos
b.	bay, gulf, inlet,	*for.*	forest, moor	May.	Mayotte	P.D.R.Yem.	People's Democratic		islands
	lagoon	Fr.	France	Mb., Can.	Manitoba, Can.		Republic of Yemen	*ter.*	territory
Bah.	Bahamas	F.R.Ger.	Federal Republic of	Md., U.S.	Maryland, U.S.	P.E., Can.	Prince Edward	Thai.	Thailand
Bahr.	Bahrain		Germany	Me., U.S.	Maine, U.S.		Island, Can.	Tn., U.S.	Tennessee, U.S.
Barb.	Barbados	Fr. Gu.	French Guiana	Mex.	Mexico	*pen.*	peninsula	Tok.	Tokelau
B.A.T.	British Antarctic	Fr. Poly.	French Polynesia	Mi., U.S.	Michigan, U.S.	Phil.	Philippines	Trin.	Trinidad and
	Territory	F.S.A.T.	French Southern	Micron.	Federated States of	Pit.	Pitcairn		Tobago
B.C., Can.	British Columbia,		and Antarctic		Micronesia	*pl.*	plain, flat	T.T.P.I.	Trust Territory of
	Can.		Territory	Mid. Is.	Midway Islands	*plat.*	plateau, highland		the Pacific Islands
Bdi.	Burundi	Ga., U.S.	Georgia, U.S.	*mil.*	military installation	Pol.	Poland	Tun.	Tunisia
Bel.	Belgium	Gam.	Gambia	Mn., U.S.	Minnesota, U.S.	Port.	Portugal	Tur.	Turkey
Ber.	Bermuda	Ger.D.R.	German Democratic	Mo., U.S.	Missouri, U.S.	P.Q., Can.	Quebec, Can.	Tx., U.S.	Texas, U.S.
Bhu.	Bhutan		Republic	Mon.	Monaco	P.R.	Puerto Rico	U.A.E.	United Arab
B.I.O.T.	British Indian Ocean	Gib.	Gibraltar	Mong.	Mongolia	*prov.*	province, region		Emirates
	Territory	Grc.	Greece	Monts.	Montserrat	*reg.*	physical region	Ug.	Uganda
Bngl.	Bangladesh	Gren.	Grenada	Mor.	Morocco	*res.*	reservoir	U.K.	United Kingdom
Bol.	Bolivia	Grnld.	Greenland	Moz.	Mozambique	Reu.	Reunion	Ur.	Uruguay
Boph.	Bophuthatswana	Guad.	Guadeloupe	Mrts.	Mauritius	*rf.*	reef, shoal	U.S.	United States
Bots.	Botswana	Guat.	Guatemala	Ms., U.S.	Mississippi, U.S.	R.I., U.S.	Rhode Island, U.S.	Ut., U.S.	Utah, U.S.
Braz.	Brazil	Gui.	Guinea	Mt., U.S.	Montana, U.S.	Rom.	Romania	Va., U.S.	Virginia, U.S.
Bru.	Brunei	Gui.-B.	Guinea-Bissau	*mth.*	river mouth or	Rw.	Rwanda	*val.*	valley, watercourse
Bul.	Bulgaria	Guy.	Guyana		channel	S.A.	South America	Vat.	Vatican City
c.	cape, point	Hi., U.S.	Hawaii, U.S.	*mtn.*	mountain	S. Afr.	South Africa	Ven.	Venezuela
Ca., U.S.	California, U.S.	*hist.*	historic site, ruins	*mts.*	mountains	Sau. Ar.	Saudi Arabia	V.I., Br.	Virgin Islands,
Cam.	Cameroon	*hist. reg.*	historic region	Mwi.	Malawi	S.C., U.S.	South Carolina, U.S.		British
Can.	Canada	H.K.	Hong Kong	N.A.	North America	*sci.*	scientific station	Viet.	Vietnam
Cay. Is.	Cayman Islands	Hond.	Honduras	N.B., Can.	New Brunswick,	Scot., U.K.	Scotland, U.K.	V.I.U.S.	Virgin Islands (U.S.)
Cen. Afr.	Central African	Hung.	Hungary		Can.	S.D., U.S.	South Dakota, U.S.	*vol.*	volcano
Rep.	Republic	*i.*	island	N.C., U.S.	North Carolina, U.S.	Sen.	Senegal	Vt., U.S.	Vermont, U.S.
Chile	Chile	Ia., U.S.	Iowa, U.S.	N. Cal.	New Caledonia	Sey.	Seychelles	Wa., U.S.	Washington, U.S.
Christ. I.	Christmas Island	I.C.	Ivory Coast	N.D., U.S.	North Dakota, U.S.	Sing.	Singapore	Wales, U.K.	Wales, U.K.
clf.	cliff, escarpment	Ice.	Iceland	Ne., U.S.	Nebraska, U.S.	Sk., Can.	Saskatchewan,	Wal./F.	Wallis and Futuna
co.	county, parish	*ice*	ice feature, glacier	Neth.	Netherlands		Can.	Wi., U.S.	Wisconsin, U.S.
Co., U.S.	Colorado, U.S.	Id., U.S.	Idaho, U.S.	Neth. Ant.	Netherlands Antilles	S. Kor.	South Korea	W. Sah.	Western Sahara
Col.	Colombia	Il., U.S.	Illinois, U.S.	Nf., Can.	Newfoundland, Can.	S.L.	Sierra Leone	W. Sam.	Western Samoa
Com.	Comoros	In., U.S.	Indiana, U.S.	N.H., U.S.	New Hampshire,	S. Mar.	San Marino	*wtfl.*	waterfall
C.R.	Costa Rica	Indon.	Indonesia		U.S.	Sol. Is.	Solomon Islands	W.V., U.S.	West Virginia, U.S.
crat.	crater	I. of Man	Isle of Man	Nic.	Nicaragua	Som.	Somalia	Wy., U.S.	Wyoming, U.S.
Ct., U.S.	Connecticut, U.S.	Ire.	Ireland	Nig.	Nigeria	Sov. Un.	Soviet Union	Yk., Can.	Yukon Territory,
ctry.	country	*is.*	islands	N. Ire., U.K.	Northern Ireland,	Sp. N. Afr.	Spanish North		Can.
C.V.	Cape Verde	Isr.	Israel		U.K.		Africa	Yugo.	Yugoslavia
Cyp.	Cyprus	Isr. Occ.	Israeli Occupied	N.J., U.S.	New Jersey, U.S.	Sri L.	Sri Lanka	Zam.	Zambia
Czech.	Czechoslovakia		Territories	N. Kor.	North Korea	*state*	state, republic,	Zimb.	Zimbabwe
D.C., U.S.	District of Columbia,	Jam.	Jamaica	N.M., U.S.	New Mexico, U.S.		canton		
	U.S.	Jord.	Jordan	N. Mar. Is.	Northern Mariana	St. C.-N.	St. Christopher-		
De., U.S.	Delaware, U.S.	Kam.	Kampuchea		Islands		Nevis		

INDEX

A

Name	Map Ref	Page
Aachen, F.R.Ger.	C3	18
Aalen, F.R.Ger.	D5	18
A'ali an Nil (Upper Nile), prov., Sud.	D3	47
Aalsmeer, Neth.	B4	17
Aalst (Alost), Bel.	B6	16
Aalten, Neth.	C6	17
Äänekcski, Fin.	F11	14
Aarau, Switz.	E4	18
Aare, stm., Switz.	E3	18
Aargau, state, Switz.	B4	20
Aaronsburg, Pa., U.S.	E7	115
Aarschot, Bel.	D4	17
Aba, China	E5	31
Aba, Nig.	E6	45
Aba, Zaire	A5	48
Abacaxis, stm., Braz.	C3	59
Ābādān, Iran	B4	38
Ābādeh, Iran	F6	39
Abadla, Alg.	C4	44
Abaetė, Braz.	B3	56
Abaetetuba, Braz.	C5	59
Abagnar Qi, China	C7	32
Abag Qi, China	C6	32
Abaí, Para.	E4	55
Abajo Peak, mtn., Ut., U.S.	F6	121
Abakaliki, Nig.	E6	45
Abakan, Sov. Un.	D12	29
Abala, Congo	B2	48
Abala, Niger	D5	45
Abancay, Peru	D3	58
Abanda, Al., U.S.	B4	78
Abanilla, Spain	C5	22
Abano Terme, Italy	B3	23
Abarqū, Iran	F6	39
' Abasān, Isr. Occ.	C6	41
Abashiri, Japan	C13	31
Abau, Pap. N. Gui.	m12	50
Abaya, Lake, l., Eth.	D4	47
Abbaye, Point, c., Mi., U.S.	B2	99
Abbeville, Fr.	B4	16
Abbeville, Al., U.S.	D4	78
Abbeville, Ga., U.S.	E3	87
Abbeville, La., U.S.	E3	95
Abbeville, Ms., U.S.	A4	101
Abbeville, S.C., U.S.	C3	117
Abbeville, co., S.C., U.S.	C2	117
Abbey, Sk., Can.	G1	75
Abbeydorney, Ire.	E2	11
Abbeyfeale, Ire.	E2	11
Abbey Head, c., Scot., U.K.	F5	13
Abbeyleix, Ire.	E4	11
Abbiategrasso, Italy	B2	23
Abbotsford, B.C., Can.	f13	69
Abbotsford, Wi., U.S.	D3	126
Abbott, Ar., U.S.	B1	81
Abbott Butte, mtn., Or., U.S.	E4	114
Abbott Run, stm., U.S.	B4	116
Abbott Run Valley, R.I., U.S.	B4	116
Abbottsburg, N.C., U.S.	C4	110
Abbottstown, Pa., U.S.	G7	115
Abbyville, Ks., U.S.	E5	93
' Abd al Kūrī, i., P.D.R.Yem.	D5	38
Abdulino, Sov. Un.	E19	8
Abe, Lake, l., Afr.	C5	47
Abéché, Chad	C4	46
Abee, Ab., Can.	B4	68
Abejorral, Col.	B2	60
Abengourou, I.C.	E4	45
Åbenrå, Den.	C3	15
Abeokuta, Nig.	E5	45
Aberayron, Wales, U.K.	B3	12
Aberchirder, Scot., U.K.	C6	13
Abercorn, P.Q., Can.	D5	74
Abercrombie, N.D., U.S.	C9	111
Aberdare, Wales, U.K.	E5	10
Aberdaron, Wales, U.K.	B3	12
Aberdeen, Sk., Can.	E2	75
Aberdeen, S. Afr.	D3	49
Aberdeen, Scot., U.K.	D5	10
Aberdeen, Id., U.S.	G6	89
Aberdeen, In., U.S.	G8	91
Aberdeen, Ky., U.S.	C3	94
Aberdeen, Md., U.S.	A5	97
Aberdeen, Ms., U.S.	B5	101
Aberdeen, N.C., U.S.	B3	110
Aberdeen, Oh., U.S.	D2	112
Aberdeen, S.D., U.S.	B7	118
Aberdeen, Wa., U.S.	C2	124
Aberdeen Lake, l., N.T., Can.	D13	66
Aberdeen Proving Ground, mil., Md., U.S.	A5	97
Aberdovey, Wales, U.K.	B3	12
Aberfeldy, Scot., U.K.	D5	13
Aberfoyle, Scot., U.K.	D4	13
Abergavenny, Wales, U.K.	E5	10
Abernant, Al., U.S.	B2	78
Abernathy, Tx., U.S.	C2	120
Abernethy, Sk., Can.	G4	75
Abert, Lake, l., Or., U.S.	E6	114
Abertillery, Wales, U.K.	C4	12
Abert Rim, clf, Or., U.S.	E6	114
Aberystwyth, Wales, U.K.	D4	10
Abesville, Mo., U.S.	E4	102
Abhā, Sau. Ar.	D4	38
Abhar, Iran	C4	39
Abidjan, I.C.	E4	45
Abie, Ne., U.S.	C9	104
Abilene, Ks., U.S.	D6	93
Abilene, Tx., U.S.	C3	120
Abingdon, Eng., U.K.	C3	90
Abingdon, Il., U.S.	C3	90
Abingdon, Ia., U.S.	C5	92
Abingdon, Va., U.S.	f10	123
Abington, Ct., U.S.	B7	84
Abington, Ma., U.S.	B6	98
Abington [Township], Pa., U.S.	o21	115
Abiquiu, N.M., U.S.	A3	108
Abisko, Swe.	C8	14
Abita Springs, La., U.S.	D5	95
Abitibi, stm., On., Can.	o19	73
Abitibi, Lake, l., Can.	G16	66
Ablon, Fr.	h10	16
Abloviak Fiord, P.Q., Can.	f8	72
Aboisso, I.C.	E4	45
Abomey, Benin	E5	45
Abong Mbang, Cam.	E2	46
Abongabong, mtn., Indon.	J2	35
Abony, Hung.	B5	24
Abou Deïa, Chad	C3	46
Aboyne, Scot., U.K.	C6	13
Abraham Lake, res., Ab., Can.	C2	68
Abraham Lincoln Birthplace National Historic Site, hist., Ky., U.S.	C4	94
Abrams, Wi., U.S.	D5	126
Abrantes, Port.	C1	22
Åbrego, Col.	B3	60
Abreojos, Punta, c., Mex.	B2	63
Abruzzi, hist reg., Italy	C4	23
Absaraka, N.D., U.S.	C8	111
Absaroka Range, mts., U.S.	F7	127
Absarokee, Mt., U.S.	E7	103
Absecon, N.J., U.S.	E4	107
Absecon Inlet, b., N.J., U.S.	E4	107
Abū 'Alī, i., Sau. Ar.	H4	39
Abu Dhabi (Abū Ẓaby), U.A.E.	C5	38
Abū Dīs, Isr. Occ.	h12	41
Abū Ḥadd, Bi'r, well, Eg.	E6	43
Abū Ḥadrīyah, Sau. Ar.	C4	38
Abū Ḥamad, Sud.	D3	47
Abū Ḥammād al Maḥaṭṭah, Eg.	D3	41
Abū Ḥummuṣ, Eg.	C2	41
Abuja, Nig.	E6	45
Abū Kabīr, Eg.	D3	41
Abū Kamāl, Syria	B4	38
Abū Kershola, Sud.	C3	47
Abū Khawf, Mushāsh, well, Eg.	E6	43
Abū Mūsá, i., U.A.E.	I7	39
Abūksāh, Eg.	E2	41
Abumombazi, Zaire	A3	48
Abuná, Braz.	A2	55
Abuná (Abunã), stm., S.A.	A2	55
Abū Qīr, Eg.	C2	41
Abū Qir Bay, b., Eg.	C2	41
Abū Qurqāṣ, Eg.	I8	40
Abu Shajarah, Ra's, c., Sud.	A4	47
Abu Simbel (Abū Sunbul), hist., Eg.	E6	43
Abū Sufyān, 'Idd, well, Sud.	B2	47
Abū Ṭabarī, well, Sud.	B2	47
Abū 'Urūq, well, Sud.	B3	47
Abū Zanīmah, Eg.	D6	43
Åbybro, Den.	A3	15
Åbyei, Sud.	D2	47
Abyssinia see Ethiopia, cty., Afr.	D4	47
Academia, Oh., U.S.	B3	112
Academy, S.D., U.S.	D6	118
Acadia, co., La., U.S.	D3	95
Acadia National Park, Me., U.S.	D4	96
Acadia Valley, Ab., Can.	D5	68
Acaituba, Braz.	B2	59
Acajutla, El Sal.	D3	62
Acámbaro, Mex.	C4	63
Acaponeta, Mex.	C3	63
Acapulco [de Juárez], Mex.	D4	63
Acarai Mountains, mts., S.A.	B3	59
Acaraú, Braz.	B2	57
Acaray, stm., Para.	E5	55
Acari, Braz.	h5	57
Acarí, Peru	E3	58
Acarigua, Ven.	B4	60
Acatlán [de Osorio], Mex.	D5	63
Acayucan, Mex.	D6	63
Accident, Md., U.S.	k12	97
Accomack, co., Va., U.S.	C7	123
Accomac, Va., U.S.	C7	123
Accord, N.Y., U.S.	D6	109
Accord Pond, l., Ma., U.S.	h12	98
Accoville, W.V., U.S.	D3	125
Accra, Ghana	E4	45
Accrington (Hyndburn), Eng., U.K.	A5	12
Ace, Tx., U.S.	D5	120
Aceguá, Ur.	E2	56
Acequia, Id., U.S.	G5	89
Achacachi, Bol.	C2	55
Achalpur (Ellichpur), India	G6	37
Achao, Chile	C2	54
Achar, Ur.	E1	56
Acharacle, Scot., U.K.	D3	13
Acheng, China	B10	31
Achenkirch, Aus.	B7	20
Achen Lake, l., Aus.	B7	20
Achern, F.R.Ger.	E3	19
Achicourt, Fr.	B2	17
Achille, Ok., U.S.	D5	113
Achill Head, c., Ire.	D1	11
Achill Island, i., Ire.	D2	10
Achill Sound, Ire.	D2	10
Achinsk, Sov. Un.	D12	29
Achiras, Arg.	A4	54
Achisay, Sov. Un.	E7	28
Achtubinsk, Sov. Un.	D3	28
Acıpayam, Tur.	D7	25
Acireale, Italy	F5	23
Ackerly, Tx., U.S.	C2	120
Ackerman, Ms., U.S.	B4	101
Acklins Island, i., Bah.	C6	64
Ackley, Ia., U.S.	B4	92
Acmar, Ab., Can.	D4	68
Acme, Ab., Can.	D4	68
Acme, La., U.S.	C4	95
Acme, Mi., U.S.	D5	99
Acme, Wa., U.S.	A3	124
Acme, W.V., U.S.	m13	125
Acme, Wy., U.S.	B6	127
Acoma Indian Reservation, N.M., U.S.	C2	108
Acomayo, Peru	D3	58
Aconcagua, Cerro, mtn., Arg.	A3	54
Acopiara, Braz.	C3	57
Acorizal, Braz.	B1	56
Acosta, Braz.	F3	115
Acoyapa, Nic.	E5	62
Acquaviva, Switz.	D6	21
Acqui [Terme], Italy	B2	23
Acre, state, Braz.	B2	55
Acre, stm., S.A.	C4	58
Actinolite, On., Can.	C7	73
Acton, On., Can.	D4	73
Acton, Ca., U.S.	E4	82
Acton, Me., U.S.	E2	96
Acton, Mt., U.S.	D5	103
Acton Vale, P.Q., Can.	D5	74
Actopan, Mex.	m14	63
Açu, Braz.	C3	57
Acushnet, Ma., U.S.	C6	98
Acworth, Ga., U.S.	B2	87
Acworth, N.H., U.S.	D2	106
Ada, Ghana	E5	45
Ada, Japan	N6	62
Ada, Ks., U.S.	C6	93
Ada, La., U.S.	C2	95
Ada, Mn., U.S.	C2	100
Ada, Oh., U.S.	B2	112
Ada, Ok., U.S.	C5	113
Ada, Yugo.	C5	24
Ada, co., Id., U.S.	F2	89
Ada, Cape, c., Sov. Un.	G19	8
Ada, Mount, mtn., Ak., U.S.	m22	79
Adair, Il., U.S.	C3	90
Adair, Ia., U.S.	C3	92
Adair, Ok., U.S.	A6	113
Adair, co., Ia., U.S.	C3	92
Adair, co., Ky., U.S.	C4	94
Adair, co., Mo., U.S.	A5	102
Adair, co., Ok., U.S.	B7	113
Adairsville, Ga., U.S.	B2	87
Adairville, Ky., U.S.	D3	94
Adak, Island, i., Ak., U.S.	E4	79
Adak Naval Station, mil., Ak., U.S.	E4	79
Adamant, Vt., U.S.	C3	122
Adamantina, Braz.	C2	56
Adamaoua, mts., Afr.	D2	46
Adam Island, i., Md., U.S.	D5	97
Adami Tulu, Eth.	D4	47
Adams, In., U.S.	F6	91
Adams, Ky., U.S.	B7	94
Adams, Ma., U.S.	A1	98
Adams, Mn., U.S.	G6	100
Adams, Ne., U.S.	D9	104
Adams, N.Y., U.S.	B4	109
Adams, N.D., U.S.	A7	111
Adams, Ok., U.S.	e9	113
Adams, Or., U.S.	B8	114
Adams, Tn., U.S.	A4	119
Adams, Wi., U.S.	E4	126
Adams, co., U.S.	B6	83
Adams, co., Co., U.S.	B6	83
Adams, co., Id., U.S.	E2	89
Adams, co., Il., U.S.	D2	90
Adams, co., In., U.S.	C8	91
Adams, co., Ia., U.S.	C3	92
Adams, co., Ms., U.S.	D2	101
Adams, co., Ne., U.S.	D7	104
Adams, co., N.D., U.S.	C3	111
Adams, co., Oh., U.S.	D2	112
Adams, co., Pa., U.S.	G7	115
Adams, co., Wa., U.S.	B7	124
Adams, co., Wi., U.S.	D4	126
Adams, Mount, mtn., N.H., U.S.	B4	106
Adams, Mount, mtn., Wa., U.S.	C4	124
Adams Bridge, rf., Asia	G6	36
Adams Center, N.Y., U.S.	B5	109
Adams City, Co., U.S.	*B6	83
Adams Lake, l., B.C., Can.	D8	69
Adams Mountain, mtn., Ma., U.S.	A2	98
Adams Mountain, mtn., Vt., U.S.	C3	122
Adams Point, c., Mi., U.S.	C7	99
Adams Run, S.C., U.S.	k11	117
Adamston, N.J., U.S.	C4	107
Adamstown, Md., U.S.	B3	97
Adamstown, Pa., U.S.	F9	115
Adamsville, P.Q., Can.	D5	74
Adamsville, Al., U.S.	f7	78
Adamsville, Oh., U.S.	B3	112
Adamsville, R.I., U.S.	E6	116
Adamsville, Tn., U.S.	B3	119
Adamsville, Tx., U.S.	D3	120
Adamsville, Ut., U.S.	E3	121
Adamsville Brook, stm., R.I., U.S.	E6	116
Adana, Tur.	D10	40
Adanac, Sk., Can.	E1	75
Adapazarı, Tur.	B8	40
Adarama, Sud.	B4	47
Adare, Ire.	E3	11
Adare, Cape, c., Ant.	B30	7
Adavale, Austl.	B5	51
Adda, stm., Italy	B2	23
Aḍ Ḍab'ah, Eg.	C5	43
Ad Dabbah, Sud.	B3	47
Ad Dahnā', des., Sau. Ar.	C4	38
Ad Dāmir, Sud.	B4	47
Ad Dār al Ḥamrā', Sau. Ar.	I11	40
Ad Dibdibah, pl., Sau. Ar.	G3	39
Addicks Barker, Tx., U.S.	r14	120
Addieville, Il., U.S.	E4	90
Ad Dilinjāt, Eg.	D2	41
Addington, Ok., U.S.	C4	113
Addis, La., U.S.	D4	95
Addis Ababa, Eth.	D4	47
Addison, Al., U.S.	A2	78
Addison, Ct., U.S.	C5	84
Addison, Il., U.S.	k8	90
Addison, Me., U.S.	D5	96
Addison, N.Y., U.S.	C3	109
Addison, Pa., U.S.	G3	115
Addison, Tx., U.S.	*n10	120
Addison, Vt., U.S.	C2	122
Addison, co., Vt., U.S.	C2	122
Ad Dīwānīyah, Iraq	E4	38
Ad Du'ayn, Sud.	C3	47
Ad Duwaym, Sud.	C4	47
Ad Duyūk, Isr. Occ.	h12	41
Addy, Wa., U.S.	A8	124
Addyston, Oh., U.S.	o12	112
Adel, Ga., U.S.	E3	87
Adel, Ia., U.S.	C3	92
Adel, Or., U.S.	E7	114
Adelaide, Austl.	F6	50
Adelaide, Bah.	m17	64
Adelaide Island, i., Ant.	C6	7
Adelanto, Ca., U.S.	E5	82
Adelboden, Switz.	D4	21
Adélie Coast, Ant.	C26	7
Adell, Wi., U.S.	E6	126
Adelphi, Oh., U.S.	C3	112
Adelphia, N.J., U.S.	C4	107
Adelup Point, c., Guam	L9	52
Aden ('Adan), P.D.R.Yem.	D4	38
Aden, Gulf of, b.	D4	38
Adena, Oh., U.S.	B5	112
Adenau, F.R.Ger.	C1	19
Adgateville, Ga., U.S.	C3	87
Adger, Al., U.S.	B2	78
Adi, i., Indon.	F9	35
Adi Ugri, Eth.	C4	47
Adıyaman, Tur.	C12	40
Adige, stm., Italy	B3	23
Adigrat, Eth.	C4	47
Ädilābād, India	H7	37
Adin, Ca., U.S.	B3	82
Adirondack Mountains, mts., N.Y., U.S.	A6	109
Adjud, Rom.	B8	24
Adjuntas, P.R.	B7	65
Adlavik Islands, is., Nf., Can.	g10	72
Adliswil, Switz.	C3	21
Admaston, On., Can.	B8	73
Admiral, Sk., Can.	H1	75
Admirals Beach, Nf., Can.	E5	72
Admiralty Bay, b., Ak., U.S.	A9	79
Admiralty Gulf, b., Austl.	B4	50
Admiralty Inlet, b., N.T., Can.	B15	66
Admiralty Island, i., Ak., U.S.	m22	79
Admiralty Islands, is., Pap. N. Gui.	h12	50
Admire, Ks., U.S.	D7	93
Adobe Acres, N.M., U.S.	B3	108
Adobe Creek, stm., Co., U.S.	C7	83
Adobe Creek Reservoir, res., Co., U.S.	C7	83
Adok, Sud.	D3	47
Adolphus, Ky., U.S.	D3	94
Adona, Ar., U.S.	B3	81
Ádoni, India	*E6	36
Adony, Hung.	B4	24
Adorf, Ger.D.R.	C7	19
Adour, stm., Fr.	F3	16
Adowa see Adwa, Eth.	C4	47
Adra, Spain	D4	22
Adrano, Italy	F5	23
Adrar, Alg.	D4	44
Adrar, reg., Maur.	B2	45
Adré, Chad	C4	46
Adrī, Libya	D2	43
Adria, Italy	B4	23
Adrian, Ga., U.S.	D4	87
Adrian, Mi., U.S.	G6	99
Adrian, Mn., U.S.	G3	100
Adrian, Mo., U.S.	C3	102
Adrian, N.D., U.S.	C7	111
Adrian, Or., U.S.	D9	114
Adrian, Tx., U.S.	B1	120
Adrian, W.V., U.S.	C4	125
Adriatic Sea, Eur.	G12	8
Adrigole, Ire.	F2	11
Advance, In., U.S.	D4	91
Advance, Mo., U.S.	D8	102
Advocate Harbour, N.S., Can.	D5	71
Adwa (Adowa), Eth.	C4	47
Adzopé, I.C.	E4	45
Æbelø, i., Den.	C4	15
Aegean Sea, Eur.	C5	40
Aegina see Aíyina, i., Grc.	D4	25
Ærø, i., Den.	D4	15
Ærøskøbing, Den.	D4	15
Aerzen, F.R.Ger.	F2	19
Aesch, Ab., Can.	E4	68
Aetna, Ab., Can.	E4	68
Aetna, Tn., U.S.	B4	119
Afars and Issas see Djibouti, ctry., Afr.	D5	47
Affoltern am Albis, Switz.	*B5	21
Affton, Mo., U.S.	*f13	102
Afghanistan, ctry., Asia	B3	36
Afgooye, Som.	E6	47
' Afif, Sau. Ar.	C4	38
Afikpo, Nig.	E6	45
Aflou, Alg.	C5	44
Afmadow, Som.	E5	47
Afognak Island, i., Ak., U.S.	D9	79
Afono Bay, b., Am. Sam.	G13	52
Afonso Cláudio, Braz.	F8	42
Africa		
Afton, De., U.S.	*A4	85
Afton, Ia., U.S.	C3	92
Afton, Mn., U.S.	C6	99
Afton, Mo., U.S.	C3	92
Afton, N.Y., U.S.	C5	109
Afton, Ok., U.S.	A7	113
Afton, Tn., U.S.	C11	119
Afton, Tx., U.S.	C2	120
Afton, Wy., U.S.	D2	127
Aftout, reg., Alg.	D4	44
Afuá, Braz.	C4	59
'Afula, Isr.	B7	41
Afyon, Tur.	C7	40
Agadem, Niger	C6	45
Agadez, Niger	C6	45
Agadir, Mor.	C3	44
Agana, Guam	L9	52
Agana Bay, b., Guam	L9	52
Agana Heights, Guam	*L9	52
Agana Naval Air Station, mil., Guam	L10	52
Agar, India	F5	37
Agar, S.D., U.S.	C5	118
Agartala, India	D9	36
Agassiz, B.C., Can.	E7	69
Agassiz, Cape, c., Ant.	B4	56
Agat, Guam	M9	52
Agat Bay, b., Guam	M9	52
Agate, Co., U.S.	B6	83
Agate, N.D., U.S.	A6	111
Agate Beach, Or., U.S.	C2	114
Agate Fossil Beds National Monument, Ne., U.S.	B2	104
Agattu Island, i., Ak., U.S.	E2	79
Agawam, Ma., U.S.	B2	98
Agawam, Ok., U.S.	C4	113
Agbor, Nig.	E6	45
Agboville, I.C.	E4	45
Agde, Fr.	F5	16
Agematsu, Japan	n16	33
Agen, Fr.	E4	16
Agency, Ia., U.S.	D5	92
Agency, Mo., U.S.	B3	102
Agenda, Ks., U.S.	C6	93
Ageo, Japan	*I9	33
Ageri, Lake, l., Switz.	B4	20
Agersø, i., Den.	C5	15
Agfayan Bay, b., Guam	M10	52
Aghā Jārī, Iran	F4	39
Aghleam, Ire.	C1	11
Agincourt (part of Scarborough), On., Can.	k15	73
Agingan, Puntan, c., N. Mar. Is.	D7	52
Aginskoye, Sov. Un.	A7	31
Agira, Italy	F5	23
Agno, Phil.	n12	34
Agno, stm., Phil.	o13	34
Agnone, Italy	D5	23
Agnos, Ar., U.S.	A4	81
Agogna, stm., Italy	B2	23
Agordo, Italy	m11	23
Agoura, Ca., U.S.	m11	82
Ägra, India	C6	36
Agra, Ks., U.S.	C4	93
Agra, Ok., U.S.	B5	113
Agrado, Col.	C2	60
Ağrı (Karaköse), Tur.	*C14	40
Agri, stm., Italy	D6	23
Agria Point, c., Phil.	o13	34
Agricola, Ms., U.S.	E5	101
Agrigento, Italy	F4	23
Agrinion, Grc.	C3	25
Agripoli, Italy	D5	23
Agryz, Sov. Un.	D19	8
Água Boa, Braz.	B4	56
Aguada, P.R.	B1	65
Aguadas, Col.	B2	60
Aguadilla, P.R.	G11	64
Aguadilla, Bahía de, b., P.R.	B1	65
Aguadulce, Pan.	F7	62
Agua Dulce Mountains, mts., Az., U.S.	E2	80
Agua Fria, N.M., U.S.	B3	108
Agua Fria, stm., Az., U.S.	D3	80
Aguaí, Braz.	m8	56
Aguán, stm., Hond.	C4	62
Aguanish, P.Q., Can.	h9	72
Agua Nueva, Tx., U.S.	F3	120
Aguapey, stm., Arg.	E4	55
Água Preta, Braz.	k6	57
' Akasha East, Sud.	A3	47
Agua Prieta, Mex.	A3	63
Aguaray, Arg.	D3	55
Aguarico, stm., S.A.	B2	58
Aguas Formosas, Braz.	B4	56
Aguascalientes, Mex.	C4	63
Aguascalientes, state, Mex.	C4	63
Agudos, Braz.	C3	56
Agueda, Port.	B1	22
Águeda, stm., Eur.	B2	22
Aguelhok, Mali	B3	45
Aguêraktem, well, Mali	B3	45
Aguilar, Co., U.S.	D6	83
Aguilar, Spain	D3	22
Águilas, Spain	D5	22
Aguililla, Mex.	D4	63
Aguja, Cabo de la, c., Col.	A3	60
Aguja, Punta, c., Peru	C1	58
Agulhas, Cape, c., S. Afr.	D3	49
Agulhas Negras, Pico das, mtn., Braz.	h5	56
Ahaggar, mts., Alg.	E6	44
Ahaggar, Tassili ta-n-, plat., Alg.	E6	44
Ahar, Iran	B3	39
Ahascragh, Ire.	D3	11
Ahaus, F.R.Ger.	A2	19
Ahirli, Tur.	C6	25
Ahlen, F.R.Ger.	C3	18
Ahlhorn, F.R.Ger.	F2	19
Ahmadābād (Ahmedabad), India	D5	36
Ahmadnagar, India	E5	36
Ahmadpur East, Pak.	C5	36
Ahmar, 'Erg el, des., Afr.	E4	44
Ahmar Mountains, mts., Eth.	D5	47
Ahmek Lake, l., On., Can.	B5	73
Ahome, Mex.	B3	63
Ahoskie, N.C., U.S.	A6	110
Ahousat, B.C., Can.	E4	69
Ahrensbök, F.R.Ger.	D4	15
Ahrweiler, F.R.Ger.	C3	18
Ahsahka, Id., U.S.	C2	89
Ahtanum Creek, stm., Wa., U.S.	C5	124
Ahuacatlán, Mex.	m11	63
Ahuachapán, El Sal.	E7	63
Ahualulco de Mercado, Mex.	m11	63
Åhus, Swe.	C8	15
Ahvāz (Nāsiri), Iran	C3	39
Ahvenanmaa (Åland), is., Fin.	G9	14
Ahwahnee, Ca., U.S.	D4	82
Aḥwar, P.D.R.Yem.	C6	47
Aialik, Cape, c., Ak., U.S.	D10	79
Aibonito, P.R.	B3	65
Aichach, F.R.Ger.	E6	19
Aiea, Hi., U.S.	B4	88
Aigen [in Mühlkreis], Aus.	D6	18
Aigle, Switz.	E3	18
Aiguá, Ur.	E2	56
Aigues-Mortes, Fr.	F6	16
Aiguilles, Fr.	C2	20
Aihui (Heihe), China	A10	31
Aija, Peru	C2	58
Aikawa, Japan	G9	33
Aiken, S.C., U.S.	D4	117
Aiken, Tx., U.S.	B2	120
Aiken, co., S.C., U.S.	D4	117
Aikens Lake, l., Mb., Can.	D4	70
Ailey, Ga., U.S.	D4	87
Ailsa Craig, On., Can.	D3	73
Aimorés, Braz.	B4	56
Ain, dept., Fr.	C1	20
Ain, stm., Fr.	C1	20
Aïn ben Tili, Maur.	A3	45
Aïn Témouchent, Alg.	B4	44
Aïn Wessara, Alg.	B5	44
Aïn Sefra, Alg.	C4	44
Aipe, Col.	C2	60
Aiquile, Bol.	C2	55
Aïr, mts., Niger	C6	45
Airabu, i., Indon.	K7	35
Airaines, Fr.	E1	17
Airdrie, Ab., Can.	D3	68
Airdrie, Scot., U.K.	E5	13
Aire, stm., Fr.	B5	16
Aire, stm., Eng., U.K.	A6	12
Aire-sur-l'Adour, Fr.	F3	16
Aire-[-sur-la-Lys], Fr.	B5	16
Air Force Island, i., N.T., Can.	C18	66
Airline, Ga., U.S.	B2	87
Air Park West, Ne., U.S.	D9	104
Airukiiji Island, i., Marsh Is.	P18	52
Aisch, stm., F.R.Ger.	D5	19
Aisén del General Carlos Ibáñez del Campo, prov., Chile	D2	54
Aishihik Lake, l., Yk., Can.	D5	66
Aisne, dept., Fr.	B5	16
Aisne, stm., Fr.	B5	16
Aïssa, Djebel, mtn., Alg.	C4	44
Aitape, Pap. N. Gui.	h11	50
Aitkin, Mn., U.S.	D5	100
Aitkin, co., Mn., U.S.	D5	100
Aitolikón, Grc.	C3	25
Aiud, Rom.	B6	24
Aiuruoca, Braz.	m11	56
Aiuruoca, stm., Braz.	m11	56
Aiwa, i., Fiji	l16	52
Aix, Mount, mtn., Wa., U.S.	C4	124
Aix-en-Provence, Fr.	F6	16
Aix-les-Bains, Fr.	C6	20
Aiyáleo, Grc.	h11	25
Aiyina (Aegina), i., Grc.	D4	25
Aíyion, Grc.	C4	25
Aizu-takada, Japan	H9	33
Aizu-wakamatsu, Japan	H9	33
Ajaccio, Fr.	D2	23
Ajaccio, Gulf of, b., Fr.	D2	23
Ajanta, India	D6	36
Ajax, On., Can.	D6	73
Ajax Bay, b., Guam	M9	52
Ajdābiyā, Libya	C4	43
'Ajlūn, Jord.	B7	41
Ajmer, India	C5	36
Ajo, Az., U.S.	E3	80
Akaishi-sammyaku, mts., Japan	n17	33
Akalkot, India	I6	37
Ajanta, India		
Akaroa, N.Z.	O14	51
Akaska, S.D., U.S.	B5	118
Akashi, Japan	I7	33
Akçaabat (Polathane), Tur.	B12	40
Akçadağ, Tur.	C11	40
Ak-Chin Indian Reservation, Az., U.S.	E3	80
Akdağmadeni, Tur.	C10	40
Akechi, Japan	n16	33
Akeley, Mn., U.S.	C4	100
Aken, Ger.D.R.	B7	19
Akers, La., U.S.	D5	95
Aketi, Zaire	A3	48
Akhaltsikhe, Sov. Un.	B14	40
Akharnaí, Grc.	g11	25
Akhḍar, Al Jabal al, mts., Libya	C4	43
Akhḍar, Al Jabal al, mts., Oman	C5	38
Akhelóös, stm., Grc.	C3	25
Akhiok, Ak., U.S.	D9	79
Akhisar, Tur.	C6	40
Akhmīm, Eg.	C3	38
Akhtopol, Bul.	D8	24
Akhtyrka, Sov. Un.	F10	27
Aki, Japan	J6	33
Akiachak, Ak., U.S.	C7	79
Akimiski Island, i., N.T., Can.	F16	66
Akjoujt, Maur.	C2	45
Akkeshi, Japan	E12	33
' Akko, Isr.	F10	40
Aklun Mountains, mts., Ak., U.S.	D7	79
Akō, Japan	J6	33
Akobo, stm., Afr.	D3	47
Akola, India	D6	36
Akonolinga, Cam.	E2	46
Akordat, Eth.	B4	47
Akosombo Dam, Ghana	E5	45
Akpatok Island, i., N.T., Can.	D19	66
Akra, N.D., U.S.	A8	111
Akranes, Ice.	n21	14
Akrítas, Ákra, c., Grc.	D3	40
Akron, Al., U.S.	C2	78
Akron, Co., U.S.	A7	83
Akron, In., U.S.	B5	91
Akron, Ia., U.S.	B1	92
Akron, Mi., U.S.	E7	99
Akron, N.Y., U.S.	B2	109
Akron, Oh., U.S.	A4	112
Akron, Pa., U.S.	F9	115
Aksaray, Tur.	C10	40
Akşehir, Tur.	C8	40
Akşehir Gölü, l., Tur.	C8	40
Akseki, Tur.	D8	40
Aksenovo-Zilovskoye, Sov. Un.	D14	29
Aksha, Sov. Un.	A7	31
Akshimrau, Sov. Un.	E4	28
Aksoran, Mount, mtn., Sov. Un.	F24	8
Aksu, China	E11	29
Aksum, Eth.	C4	47
Aktogay, Sov. Un.	D9	29
Aktumsyk, Sov. Un.	D5	28
Aktyubinsk, Sov. Un.	f11	74
Akure, Nig.	E6	45
Akureyri, Ice.	n23	14
Akuseki Island, i., Japan	L4	33
Akutan, Ak., U.S.	E6	79
Akyab see Sittwe, Burma	D9	36
Alabama, state, U.S.	C3	78
Alabama, stm., Al., U.S.	C2	78
Alabaster, Al., U.S.	B3	78
Alabaster, Mi., U.S.	E7	99
Alabat, i., Phil.	o14	34
Al 'Abbāsīyah, Sud.	C3	47
Al Abyaḍ, Libya	D2	43
Alachua, Fl., U.S.	C4	86
Alachua, co., Fl., U.S.	C4	86
Aladdin, Wy., U.S.	B8	127
Al Abyār, Libya	F3	40
Alagoa Grande, Braz.	C3	57
Alagôas, state, Braz.	C3	57
Alagoinhas, Braz.	B4	56
Alagón, Spain	B5	22
Alagón, stm., Spain	B2	22
Al 'Ajrūd, well, Eg.	D6	41
Alajuela, C.R.	E5	62
Alajuela, Lago, res., Pan.	k11	62
Alakol, Lake, l., Sov. Un.	D10	28
Alalakeiki Channel, strt., Hi., U.S.	C5	88
Al-Alamayn, Eg.	B2	43
Alalaú, stm., Braz.	C2	59
Alamance, co., N.C., U.S.	B3	110
' Alam ar Rūm, Ra's, c., Egypt	G6	40
Alameda, Sk., Can.	H4	75
Alameda, Ca., U.S.	h8	82
Alameda, N.M., U.S.	B3	108
Alameda, co., Ca., U.S.	D3	82
Alameda Naval Air Station, mil., Ca., U.S.	h8	82
Al 'Āmirīyah, Eg.	G7	40
Alamito Creek, stm., Tx., U.S.	p12	120
Alamo, Ga., U.S.	D4	87
Alamo, Mex.	m15	63
Alamo, Nv., U.S.	F6	105
Alamo, N.D., U.S.	A2	111
Alamo, Tn., U.S.	B2	119
Alamo, Tx., U.S.	F3	120
Alamo Heights, Tx., U.S.	k7	120
Alamo Hueco Mountains, mtn., N.M., U.S.	F1	108
Alamo Indian Reservation, N.M., U.S.	C2	108
Alamo Lake, res., Az., U.S.	C2	80

Name	Map Ref	Page
Alamos, Mex.	B3	63
Alamosa, Co., U.S.	D5	83
Alamosa, co., Co., U.S.	D5	83
Alamosa, stm., Co., U.S.	D4	83
Alamosa Creek, stm., N.M., U.S.	D2	108
Alamosa East, Co., U.S.	D5	83
Åland see Ahvenanmaa, is., Fin.	G9	14
Alanreed, Tx., U.S.	B2	120
Alanson, Mi., U.S.	C6	99
Alanya, Tur.	D9	40
Alaotra, Lac, l., Madag.	g9	49
Alapaha, Ga., U.S.	E3	87
Alapaha, stm., U.S.	E3	87
Alapayevsk, Sov. Un.	B6	28
Al ʿAqabah, Jord.	C3	38
Al ʿArīsh, Eg.	C6	43
Alasdair, Sgùrr, mtn., Scot., U.K.	C2	13
Alaşehir, Tur.	C7	40
Alaska, state, U.S.	C9	79
Alaska, Gulf of, b., Ak., U.S.	D10	79
Alaska Peninsula, pen., Ak., U.S.	D8	79
Alaska Range, mts., Ak., U.S.	C9	79
Alassio, Italy	C2	23
Alatna, stm., Ak., U.S.	B9	79
Al ʿAṭrūn, Sud.	B2	47
Alatyr, Sov. Un.	D16	27
Alausi, Ec.	B2	58
Alava, Cape, c., Wa., U.S.	A1	124
Alaverdi, Sov. Un.	B15	40
Al ʿAynā, Jord.	D7	41
Al ʿAyyāṭ, Eg.	E3	41
Al ʿAyzarīyah (Bethany), Isr. Occ.	h12	41
Al ʿAzīzīyah, Libya	C2	43
Alb, stm., F.R.Ger.	A5	21
Alba, Italy	B2	23
Alba, Mi., U.S.	D6	99
Alba, Mo., U.S.	D3	102
Alba, Pa., U.S.	C8	115
Alba, Tx., U.S.	E5	120
Albacete, Spain	C5	22
Al Badārī, Eg.	D6	43
Alba de Tormes, Spain	B3	22
Al Baḍārī, Iraq	B4	38
Ålbæk, Den.	A4	15
Ålbæk Bugt, b., Den.	A4	15
Al Bahnasā, Eg.	H8	40
Al Baḥr al Abyaḍ, prov., Sud.	C3	47
Al Baḥr al Aḥmar (Red Sea), prov., Sud.	A4	47
Alba Iulia, Rom.	B6	24
Al Bājūr, Eg.	D3	41
Albalate [del Arzobispo], Spain	B5	22
Al Ballaḥ, Eg.	D4	41
Albanel, Lac, l., P.Q., Can.	F18	66
Albani, Colli, hills, Italy	h9	23
Albania, ctry., Eur.	B2	40
Albano, Lake, l., Italy	h9	23
Albano Laziale, Italy	D4	23
Albany, Austl.	F2	50
Albany, N.S., Can.	C6	71
Albany, P.E., Can.	C6	71
Albany, Ca., U.S.	*h8	82
Albany, Ga., U.S.	E2	87
Albany, Il., U.S.	B3	90
Albany, In., U.S.	D7	91
Albany, Ky., U.S.	D4	94
Albany, La., U.S.	g10	95
Albany, Mo., U.S.	A3	102
Albany, N.H., U.S.	C4	106
Albany, N.Y., U.S.	C7	109
Albany, Oh., U.S.	C3	112
Albany, Or., U.S.	C3	114
Albany, Tx., U.S.	C3	120
Albany, Vt., U.S.	B4	122
Albany, Wy., U.S.	E6	127
Albany, co., N.Y., U.S.	C6	109
Albany, co., Wy., U.S.	E7	127
Albany, stm., On., Can.	o18	73
Al Barkāt, Libya	E2	43
Al Batānūn, Eg.	D2	41
Albatross Bay, b., Austl.	B7	50
Al Batrūn, Leb.	E10	40
Al Bawīṭī, Eg.	D5	43
Al Bayḍā, Libya	C4	43
Albee, U.S.	B9	118
Albemarle, N.C., U.S.	B2	110
Albemarle, co., Va., U.S.	C4	123
Albemarle, Punta, c., Ec.	f5	58
Albemarle Lake, l., Ms., U.S.	C2	101
Albemarle Sound, strt., N.C., U.S.	A6	110
Albenga, Italy	B2	23
Alberche, stm., Spain	B3	22
Alberga (part of Eskilstuna), Swe.	u34	14
Albergaria-a-Velha, Port.	B1	22
Albersdorf, F.R.Ger.	D3	15
Albert, Fr.	B5	16
Albert, Ks., U.S.	D4	93
Albert, N.M., U.S.	B6	108
Albert, co., N.B., Can.	D5	71
Albert, Lake, l., Afr.	A5	48
Alberta, Al., U.S.	C2	78
Alberta, Mn., U.S.	E2	100
Alberta, Va., U.S.	D5	123
Alberta, prov., Can.	C4	68
Alberta, Mount, mtn., Ab., Can.	C2	68
Albert Canyon, B.C., Can.	D9	69
Albert City, Ia., U.S.	B3	92
Albert Edward, Mount, mtn., Pap. N. Gui.	k12	50
Albert Lea, Mn., U.S.	G5	100
Albert Markham, Mount, mtn., Ant.	A28	7
Albert Nile, stm., Ug.	A5	48
Alberton, P.E., Can.	C5	71
Albert, Mt., U.S.	C2	103
Albertson, N.Y., U.S.	k13	109
Albertville, Fr.	D7	75
Albertville, Fr.	E7	16
Albertville, Al., U.S.	A3	78
Albertville, Mn., U.S.	E5	100
Albeuve, Switz.	C3	21
Albi, Fr.	F5	16
Albia, Ia., U.S.	C5	92
Albin, Wy., U.S.	E8	127
Albino, Italy	E8	21
Albion, Id., U.S.	G5	89
Albion, Il., U.S.	E5	90
Albion, In., U.S.	B7	91
Albion, Me., U.S.	D3	96

Name	Map Ref	Page
Albion, Mi., U.S.	F6	99
Albion, Ne., U.S.	C7	104
Albion, N.Y., U.S.	B2	109
Albion, Pa., U.S.	C6	113
Albion, R.I., U.S.	B4	116
Albion, Wi., U.S.	C8	124
Al Bīrah, Isr. Occ.	h11	41
Alborán, i., Spain	E4	22
Ålborg, Den.	I3	14
Ålborg Bugt, b., Den.	B4	15
Alborn, Mn., U.S.	D6	100
Albox, Spain	D4	22
Albreda, B.C., Can.	C8	69
Al Bu'ayrāt, Libya	C3	43
Albufeira, Port.	D1	22
Al Buhayrah, prov., Sud.	D2	47
Al Bunbah, Libya	F4	40
Albuñol, Spain	D4	22
Albuquerque, N.M., U.S.	B3	108
Al Buraymi, Oman	C5	38
Alburg, Vt., U.S.	B2	122
Alburnett, Ia., U.S.	B6	92
Alburquerque, Spain	C2	22
Alburtis, Pa., U.S.	F10	115
Albury, Austl.	G8	50
Al Buṣayrī, Eg.	C2	41
Alca, Peru	E3	58
Alcabideche, Port.	f9	22
Alcácer do Sal, Port.	C1	22
Alcácer do Sal, Port.	B6	22
Alcalá [de Guadaira], Spain	D3	22
Alcalá de Henares, Spain	B4	22
Alcalá de los Gazules, Spain	D3	22
Alcalá la Real, Spain	D4	22
Alcaldediaz, Pan.	F8	62
Alcamo, Italy	F4	23
Alcanadre, stm., Spain	B5	22
Alcanar, Spain	B6	22
Alcañiz, Spain	B5	22
Alcântara, Braz.	B2	57
Alcantarilla, Spain	D5	22
Alcaraz, Spain	C4	22
Alcaudete, Spain	D3	22
Alcázar de San Juan, Spain	C4	22
Alcester, S.D., U.S.	D9	118
Alcira, Spain	C5	22
Alco, Ar., U.S.	B3	81
Alco, La., U.S.	C2	95
Alcoa, Tn., U.S.	D10	119
Alcobendas, Spain	o17	22
Alcochete, Port.	f10	22
Alcolu, S.C., U.S.	D7	117
Alcomdale, Ab., Can.	C4	68
Alcona, co., Mi., U.S.	D7	99
Alcorcón, Spain	p17	22
Alcorisa, Spain	B5	22
Alcorn, Ms., U.S.	D2	101
Alcorn, co., Ms., U.S.	A5	101
Alcova, Wy., U.S.	D6	127
Alcovy, stm., Ga., U.S.	C3	87
Alcoy, Spain	C5	22
Alcoy, Nevado, mtn., Peru	D2	58
Alda, Ne., U.S.	D7	104
Aldama, Mex.	B3	63
Aldan, Sov. Un.	D15	29
Aldan, stm., Sov. Un.	C16	29
Aldan Plateau, plat., Sov. Un.	D15	29
Al Dār al Bayḍāʾ, hist., Eg.	D3	41
Aldeburgh, Eng., U.K.	B9	12
Alden, Ia., U.S.	B4	92
Alden, Il., U.S.	A5	90
Alden, Ks., U.S.	D5	93
Alden, Mi., U.S.	D5	99
Alden, Mn., U.S.	G5	100
Alden, N.Y., U.S.	C2	109
Alderney, i., Guernsey	F5	10
Alder Brook, stm., Vt., U.S.	B4	122
Aldershot, Eng., U.K.	E6	10
Alderson, W.V., U.S.	D4	125
Aldersyde, Ab., Can.	D4	68
Aldie, Va., U.S.	B5	123
Aldine, N.J., U.S.	D2	107
Aldora, Ga., U.S.	C2	87
Aldrich, Al., U.S.	B3	78
Aldrich, Mn., U.S.	D4	100
Aledo, Il., U.S.	B3	90
Aledo, Tx., U.S.	n9	120
Aleg, Maur.	C2	45
Alegre, Braz.	C4	56
Alegrete, Braz.	D1	56
Alegros Mountain, mtn., N.M., U.S.	C2	108
Alejandro Selkirk, Isla, i., Chile	G2	53
Aleknagik, Ak., U.S.	D8	79
Aleksandriya, Sov. Un.	G9	27
Aleksandrov, Sov. Un.	C12	27
Aleksandrovskoye, Sov. Un.	A9	28
Aleksandrovsk-[Sakhalinskiy], Sov. Un.	D17	29
Aleksandrów [Kujawski], Pol.	B5	26
Aleksandrów [Łódzki], Pol.	C5	26
Aleksin, Sov. Un.	D11	27
Aleksinac, Yugo.	D5	24
Alemania, Arg.	B3	56
Além Paraíba, Braz.	g6	56
Alençon, Fr.	C4	16
Alenquer, Braz.	C4	59
Alenquer, Port.	C1	22
Alentejo, hist reg., Port.	C2	22
Alenuihaha Channel, strt., Hi., U.S.	C5	88
Aleppo (Ḥalab), Syria	B2	38
Aléria, Fr.	C2	23
Alert, N.T., Can.	k39	66
Alert, N.T., Can.	F6	91
Alert Bay, B.C., Can.	D4	69
Alessandria, Italy	B2	23
Ålestrup, Den.	B3	15
Alhos Vedros, Port.	f9	22
Ålesund, Nor.	F2	14
Alet, Fr.	F5	16
Aleutian Islands, is., Ak., U.S.	E3	79
Aleutian Range, mts., Ak., U.S.	D8	79
Alex, Ok., U.S.	C4	113
Alexander, Ar., U.S.	C3	81
Alexander, Il., U.S.	D3	90
Alexander, Ks., U.S.	D4	93
Alexander, Me., U.S.	C5	96
Alexander, N.Y., U.S.	C2	109
Alexander, N.D., U.S.	B2	111

Name	Map Ref	Page
Alexander, W.V., U.S.	C4	125
Alexander, Ks., U.S.	F4	90
Alexander, co., N.C., U.S.	B1	110
Alicudi, i., Italy	f10	41
Alexander, Lake, l., Mn., U.S.	D4	100
Alexander Archipelago, is., Ak., U.S.	D12	79
Alexander Bay, S. Afr.	C2	49
Alexander City, Al., U.S.	C4	78
Alexander Island, i., Ant.	B5	7
Alexander Mills, N.C., U.S.	B1	110
Alexandra, N.Z.	P12	51
Alexandretta see İskenderun, Tur.	D11	40
Alexandretta, Gulf of, b., Tur.	D10	40
Alexandria, B.C., Can.	C6	69
Alexandria, On., Can.	B10	73
Alexandria (Al Iskandarīyah), Eg.	B2	38
Alexandria, Rom.	D7	24
Alexandria, Al., U.S.	B4	78
Alexandria, In., U.S.	D6	91
Alexandria, Ky., U.S.	B5	94
Alexandria, La., U.S.	C3	95
Alexandria, Mn., U.S.	E3	100
Alexandria, Mo., U.S.	A6	102
Alexandria, Ne., U.S.	D8	104
Alexandria, N.H., U.S.	C3	106
Alexandria, Oh., U.S.	B3	112
Alexandria, Pa., U.S.	E5	115
Alexandria, S.D., U.S.	D8	118
Alexandria, Tn., U.S.	A5	119
Alexandria, Va., U.S.	B5	123
Alexandria Bay, N.Y., U.S.	A5	109
Alexandrina, Lake, l., Austl.	G2	51
Alexandroúpolis, Grc.	B5	40
Alexis, Il., U.S.	B3	90
Alexis, stm., Nf., Can.	B3	72
Alexis Creek, B.C., Can.	C6	69
Aley, stm., Sov. Un.	E25	8
Aleysk, Sov. Un.	D11	29
Alfalfa, co., Ok., U.S.	A3	113
Al Fallūjah, Iraq	F14	40
Al Fandaqūmīyah, Isr. Occ.	B7	41
Alfaro, Spain	A5	22
Al Fashn, Eg.	D6	43
Alfatar, Bul.	D8	24
Al Fāw, Iraq	G4	39
Al Fayyūm, Eg.	C3	38
Alfeld, F.R.Ger.	B4	19
Alfenas, Braz.	C3	56
Alfiós (Alpheus), stm., Grc.	D3	25
Alfonsine, Italy	E8	20
Alford, Eng., U.K.	A8	12
Alford, Scot., U.K.	C6	13
Alford, Fl., U.S.	B1	86
Alford, In., U.S.	H3	91
Alfordsville, In., U.S.	G4	91
Alfortville, Fr.	g10	16
Alfred, On., Can.	B10	73
Alfred, Me., U.S.	E2	96
Alfred, N.Y., U.S.	C3	109
Alfred, N.D., U.S.	C6	111
Alfred Mills, Me., U.S.	E2	96
Alfred Station, N.Y., U.S.	C3	109
Al Fujayrah, U.A.E.	C5	38
Al Fuqahāʾ, Libya	D3	43
Algarrobal, Chile	E1	55
Algarrobo, Chile	E1	55
Algarrobo del Águila, Arg.	B3	54
Algarve, hist reg., Port.	D1	22
Algeciras, Spain	D3	22
Algemesí, Spain	C5	22
Alger, Mi., U.S.	D6	99
Alger, Oh., U.S.	B2	112
Alger, co., Mi., U.S.	B4	99
Algeria, ctry., Afr.	D5	44
Al Ghaydah, Eg.	D2	41
Al Ghaydah, P.D.R.Yem.	B7	47
Alghero, Italy	D2	23
Al Ghurdaqah, Eg.	D6	43
Algiers (El Djazair), Alg.	B5	44
Algoa Bay, b., S. Afr.	D4	49
Algodón, stm., Peru	B3	58
Algodones, N.M., U.S.	B3	108
Algoma, Ms., U.S.	A4	101
Algoma, Wi., U.S.	D6	126
Algoma Mills, On., Can.	p18	73
Algona, Ia., U.S.	A3	92
Algona, Wa., U.S.	B3	124
Algonac, Mi., U.S.	F8	99
Algonquin, Il., U.S.	A5	90
Algonquin Park, On., Can.	B6	73
Algonquin Provincial Park, On., Can.	B6	73

Name	Map Ref	Page
Aliceville, Al., U.S.	B1	78
Aliceville, Ks., U.S.	D8	93
Alicia, Ar., U.S.	B4	81
Alicudi, i., Italy	E5	23
Alīgarh, India	C6	36
Alīgūdarz, Iran	E4	39
Alindao, Cen. Afr. Rep.	E4	46
Aline, Ga., U.S.	D4	87
Aline, Ok., U.S.	A3	113
Alingsås, Swe.	I5	14
Alīpur Duār, India	D12	37
Al ʿIrq, Libya	D4	43
Al-Sabieh, Dji.	C5	47
Al Istiwaʿiyah al Gharbīyah (Western Equatoria), prov., Sud.	D2	47
Al Istiwaʿiyah ash Sharqiyah (Eastern Equatoria), prov., Eg.	E3	47
Alistráti, Grc.	B4	25
Aliwal North, S. Afr.	D4	49
Alix, Ab., Can.	C4	68
Alix, Ar., U.S.	B2	81
Al Jabalayn, Sud.	C3	47
Al Jāfūrah, des., Sau. Ar.	I5	39
Al Jaghbūb, Libya	D4	43
Al Jahrah, Kuw.	G3	39
Al Jānīyah, Isr. Occ.	h11	41
Al Jawf, Libya	E4	43
Al Jawf, Sau. Ar.	C3	38
Al Jawsh, Libya	C2	43
Al Jazīrah, prov., Sud.	C3	47
Aljezur, Port.	D1	22
Al Jithāmīyah, Sau. Ar.	I13	40
Al Jubayl, Sau. Ar.	H4	39
Al Junaynah, Sud.	C1	47
Al Kāb, Eg.	D4	41
Alkabo, N.D., U.S.	A2	111
Al Kahfah, Sau. Ar.	I14	40
Alkali Lake, l., Or., U.S.	E6	114
Alkaline Lake, l., N.D., U.S.	C6	111
Al Karak, Jord.	G10	40
Al Karnak, Eg.	D6	43
Al Kawm aṭ Ṭawīl, Eg.	C3	41
Al Kāzimīyah, Iraq	B4	38
Al Khābūr, stm., Syria	B4	38
Al Khāburah, Oman	C5	38
Al Khāliṣ, Iraq	E15	40
Al Khandaq, Sud.	B3	47
Al Khārijah, Eg.	C3	38
Al Khartūm, prov., Sud.	B3	47
Al Khaṣab, Oman	C5	38
Al Khums, Libya	C2	43
Al Khurmah, Sau. Ar.	C4	38
Al Khushnīyah, Syria	A7	41
Al Kubr, Eg.	B4	38
Al Kubrī, Eg.	D4	41
Al Kūfah, Iraq	D4	41
Al Kuntillah, Eg.	E6	41
Al Kūt, Iraq	D4	38
Al Maʿādī, Eg.	E3	41
Al-Maʿāniyah, well, Iraq	B4	38
Alma-Ata, Sov. Un.	E10	29
Alma Center, Wi., U.S.	D3	126
Almada, Port.	C1	22
Almadén, Spain	C3	22
Al Mafraq, Jord.	F11	40
Al Maḥallah al Kubrā, Eg.	C3	38
Al Maḥmūdīyah, Eg.	C2	41
Al Maḥmūdīyah, Iraq	F15	40
Al Maḥsamah, Eg.	E6	43
Al Maḥtab, Sau. Ar.	C3	38
Al Manṣūrah, Eg.	B3	38
Al Maqnah, Sau. Ar.	D4	41
Almanor, Lake, l., Ca., U.S.	B3	82
Almansa, Spain	C5	22
Almanzora, stm., Spain	D4	22
Al Marj, Libya	C4	43
Al Maṣīrah, i., Oman	C5	38
Al Maṭarīyah, Eg.	C3	41
Al Maṭarīyah, Eg.	D3	41
Al Mayadīn, Syria	B4	38
Almazán, Spain	B4	22
Al Mazār, Jord.	C7	41
Al Mazār, Jord.	C7	41
Almeirim, Braz.	C4	59
Almeirim, Port.	C1	22
Almelo, Neth.	A7	16
Almelund, Mn., U.S.	E6	100
Almena, Ks., U.S.	C4	93
Almena, Wi., U.S.	C1	126
Almendralejo, Spain	C2	22
Almería, Spain	D4	22
Almería, stm., Spain	D4	22
Almería, Gulf of, b., Spain	D4	22
Almetyevsk, Sov. Un.	*D8	29
Älmhult, Swe.	J6	14
Al Minyā, Eg.	C3	38
Al Miqdādīyah, Iraq	B7	38
Almira, Wa., U.S.	B7	124
Almirante, Pan.	F6	62
Almirante Brown, Arg.	g7	54
Almirós, Grc.	C4	25
Almo, Id., U.S.	G5	89
Almodôvar, Port.	D1	22
Almodóvar [del Campo], Spain	C3	22
Almogía, Spain	D3	22
Almonaster [la Real], Spain	D2	22
Almond, N.C., U.S.	f9	110
Almond, N.Y., U.S.	C3	109
Almond, Wi., U.S.	D4	126
Almont, Mi., U.S.	F7	99
Almont, N.D., U.S.	C4	111
Almonte, Spain	D2	22
Almora, India	C6	36
Almoradí, Spain	C5	22
Al Mubarraz, Sau. Ar.	H4	39
Al Mudawwarah, Jord.	C2	38
Al Mughayir, Isr. Occ.	g12	41
Al Mukallā, P.D.R.Yem.	D4	38
Al Mukhā, Yemen	E4	38
Almuñécar, Spain	D4	22

Name	Map Ref	Page
Allenton, Wi., U.S.	E5	126
Allentown, Ga., U.S.	D3	87
Allentown, N.J., U.S.	C3	107
Allentown, N.Y., U.S.	C2	109
Allenville, Il., U.S.	D5	90
Allenville, In., U.S.	E11	115
Allenwood, N.J., U.S.	C4	107
Allenwood, Pa., U.S.	D8	115
Alleppey, India	G6	36
Aller, stm., Eur.	B4	18
Allerton, Ia., U.S.	D4	92
Allerton, Point, c., Ma., U.S.	E11	115
Allgäuer Alps, mts., Eur.	B9	21
Al Lidām, Sau. Ar.	A5	47
Allier, stm., Fr.	D5	16
Al Līfīyah, well, Asia	B4	38
Alligator, stm., N.C., U.S.	B6	110
Alligator Lake, l., Me., U.S.	D4	96
Allihies, Ire.	F1	11
Allingåbro, Den.	C8	15
Allinge, Den.	C8	15
Allison, Co., U.S.	D3	83
Allison, Ia., U.S.	B5	92
Allison, N.M., U.S.	B1	108
Allison, Pa., U.S.	G2	115
Allison Harbour, B.C., Can.	D4	69
Allisonia, Va., U.S.	D2	123
Allison Park, Pa., U.S.	h14	115
Alliston, On., Can.	C5	73
Al Līth, Sau. Ar.	B5	10
Alloa, Scot., U.K.	B5	10
Allons, Tn., U.S.	C8	119
Allouez, Mi., U.S.	A2	99
Allouez, Wi., U.S.	h9	126
Alloway, N.J., U.S.	D2	107
Alloway Creek, stm., N.J., U.S.	D2	107
All Pines, Belize	B3	62
Allred, Tn., U.S.	C8	119
Allsboro, Al., U.S.	A1	78
Allschwil, Switz.	A4	21
Al Luḥayyah, Yemen	E4	38
Alluwe, Ok., U.S.	A6	113
Allyn, Wa., U.S.	B3	124
Alma, N.B., Can.	D4	73
Alma, On., Can.	D4	73
Alma, P.Q., Can.	A6	71
Alma, Ar., U.S.	B1	81
Alma, Co., U.S.	B4	83
Alma, Ga., U.S.	E4	87
Alma, Il., U.S.	E5	90
Alma, Ks., U.S.	C7	93
Alma, Mi., U.S.	E6	99
Alma, Mo., U.S.	B4	102
Alma, Ne., U.S.	D6	104
Alma, Ok., U.S.	C3	110
Alma, W.V., U.S.	B4	125
Alma, Wi., U.S.	D2	126
Al-Maʿāniyah, well, Iraq	B4	38
Almaciga, Ven.	A3	60
Almaguer, Col.	B2	58
Almagro, Spain	C4	22
Almagro, Isla, i., Mex.	C3	63
Almaty see Alma-Ata, Sov. Un.	E10	29
Altai Mountains, mts., Asia	B2	31
Al Qaḍārif, Sud.	C4	47
Al Qaḍīmah, Sau. Ar.	C3	38
Al Qāʾim, Iraq	E13	40
Al Qāmishlī, Syria	B4	38
Al Qanāyāt, Eg.	D3	41
Al Qaryah ash Sharqīyah, Libya	C2	43
Al Qaryatayn, Syria	E11	40
Al Qaṣabāt, Libya	C2	43
Al Qaṣr, Eg.	C2	38
Al Qaṭīf, Sau. Ar.	H4	39
Al Qaṭrūn, Libya	E2	43
Al Qayyāʾ, Eg.	D1	41
Al Quṭayyibah, well, Sau. Ar.	H14	40
Al Qunfudhah, Sau. Ar.	D4	38
Al Qurnah, Iraq	F3	39
Al Quṣaymah, Eg.	D6	41
Al Quṣayr, Eg.	C3	38
Al Quṭaynah, Sud.	C3	47
Alrø, Den.	C4	15
Als, Den.	B4	15
Als, i., Den.	D3	15
Alsace, hist reg., Fr.	C7	16
Alsask, Sk., Can.	F1	75
Alsasua, Spain	A4	22
Alsdorf, F.R.Ger.	C3	18
Alsea, Or., U.S.	C3	114
Alsek, stm., N.A.	D5	66
Alsen, N.D., U.S.	A7	111
Alsenbrück-Langmeil, F.R.Ger.	D3	19
Alsey, Il., U.S.	D3	90
Alsike (part of Uppsala), Swe.	t35	14
Alsip, Il., U.S.	*k9	90
Alstead, N.H., U.S.	D2	106
Alstead, stm., Sk., Can.	B2	75
Alstead Center, N.H., U.S.	D2	106
Alston, Eng., U.K.	F6	13
Alston, Ga., U.S.	D4	87
Alta, Ia., U.S.	B2	92
Alta, Ut., U.S.	*C4	121
Alta, Wy., U.S.	C2	127
Altadena, Ca., U.S.	m12	82
Altagracia, Ven.	A3	60
Altagracia de Orituco, Ven.	B2	60
Altai Mountains, mts., Asia	B2	31
Altamaha Sound, strt., Ga., U.S.	E5	87
Altamahaw, N.C., U.S.	A3	110
Altamira, Braz.	C4	59
Altamira, Chile	B2	55
Altamira, Arg.	g7	54
Altamont, Mb., Can.	E2	70
Altamont, Il., U.S.	D5	90
Altamont, Ks., U.S.	E8	93
Altamont, N.Y., U.S.	C6	109
Altamont, Or., U.S.	E5	114
Altamont, S.D., U.S.	C9	118
Altamont, Tn., U.S.	D8	119
Altamont, Ut., U.S.	C5	121
Altamonte Springs, Fl., U.S.	D5	86
Altamura, Italy	D6	23
Altamura, Isla, i., Mex.	C3	63
Altapass, N.C., U.S.	f10	110
Altar, Mex.	A2	63
Altario, Ab., Can.	D5	68
Alta Vista, Ks., U.S.	D7	93
Alta Vista, Va., U.S.	C3	123
Altay, China	B2	31
Altay, Mong.	—	—
Altdorf, Switz.	E4	18
Altdorf [bei Nürnberg], F.R.Ger.	D6	19
Altefähr, Ger.D.R.	A8	20
Altenberg, Ger.D.R.	C8	19
Altenbruch, F.R.Ger.	B4	18
Altenburg, Ger.D.R.	C6	18
Altenkirchen, Ger.D.R.	D8	102
Altenkirchen, Ger.D.R.	D7	15
Altenmarkt [an der Alz], F.R.Ger.	A8	20
Altenmarkt [an der Alz], F.R.Ger.	E7	20
Alten do Chão, Port.	C2	22
Altha, Fl., U.S.	B1	86
Altheim, Aus.	C4	81
Altheimer, Ar., U.S.	D3	57
Altkirch, Fr.	D5	87
Altman, N.Y., U.S.	B5	109
Altmühl, stm., F.R.Ger.	D5	19
Altnaharra, Scot., U.K.	B4	13

Name	Map Ref	Page
Alto, Ga., U.S.	B3	87
Alto, La., U.S.	B4	95
Alto, Mi., U.S.	F5	99
Alto, N.M., U.S.	D4	108
Alto, Tn., U.S.	D8	119
Alto, Tx., U.S.	D5	120
Alto Araguaia, Braz.	B2	56
Alto Cedro, Cuba	D5	64
Alto Garças, Braz.	B2	56
Alto Longá, Braz.	C2	57
Alto Molócuè, Moz.	A6	49
Altomünster, F.R.Ger.	A7	20
Alton, Or., Can.	D4	73
Alton, Eng., U.K.	C7	12
Alton, Al., U.S.	B3	78
Alton, Il., U.S.	E3	90
Alton, Ia., U.S.	B2	92
Alton, Ks., U.S.	C5	93
Alton, La., U.S.	h12	95
Alton, Mo., U.S.	E6	102
Alton, N.H., U.S.	D4	106
Alton, Oh., U.S.	m10	112
Alton, R.I., U.S.	F2	116
Alton, Ut., U.S.	F3	121
Alton, W.V., U.S.	C4	125
Altona, Mb., Can.	E3	70
Altona (part of Hamburg), F.R.Ger.	E3	15
Altona, Il., U.S.	B3	90
Altona, In., U.S.	B7	91
Altona, N.Y., U.S.	f11	109
Altona, Ut., U.S.	C5	121
Alton Bay, N.H., U.S.	D4	106
Altoona, Al., U.S.	A3	78
Altoona, Fl., U.S.	D5	86
Altoona, Ia., U.S.	C4	92
Altoona, Ks., U.S.	E8	93
Altoona, Pa., U.S.	E5	115
Altoona, Wi., U.S.	D2	126
Alto Paraguai, Braz.	A1	56
Alto Paraguay, dept., Para.	D4	55
Alto Paraná, dept., Para.	D5	55
Alto Pass, Il., U.S.	F4	90
Alto Purus, stm., Peru	D3	58
Altötting, F.R.Ger.	A8	20
Altrincham, Eng., U.K.	A5	12
Altro, Ky., U.S.	C6	94
Altstätten, Switz.	B5	20
Āltūn Kūprī, Iraq	E15	40
Altun Tagh (Altyn Tagh), mts., China	D2	31
Alt Zachun, Ger.D.R.	E5	15
Al 'Ubaylah, Sau. Ar.	C5	38
Al Uqayyah, Sud.	C2	47
Alum Bank, Pa., U.S.	F4	115
Alum Bridge, W.V., U.S.	B4	125
Alum Creek, W.V., U.S.	m12	125
Alum Creek, stm., Oh., U.S.	k11	112
Aluminé, Arg.	D2	54
Alum Rock, Ca., U.S.	*k9	82
Alupka, Sov. Un.	I10	27
Al 'Uqaylah, Libya	C3	43
Al 'Uqayr, Sau. Ar.	I5	39
Alutom, Mount, hill, Guam.	L9	52
Al 'Uzayr, Iraq	F3	39
Alva, Fl., U.S.	F5	86
Alva, Ky., U.S.	D6	94
Alva, Ok., U.S.	A3	113
Alva, Wy., U.S.	B8	127
Alvand, Kūh-e, mtn., Iran	D4	39
Alvarado, Mex.	D5	63
Alvarado, Tx., U.S.	B2	100
Alvaton, Ga., U.S.	C2	87
Älvdalen, Swe.	G6	14
Alvear, Arg.	E4	55
Alvena, Sk., Can.	E2	75
Alverca, Port.	f9	22
Alverton, Pa., U.S.	F2	115
Alvesta, Swe.	B8	15
Alvin, Il., U.S.	C6	90
Alvin, S.C., U.S.	E8	117
Alvin, Tx., U.S.	E5	120
Alvinston, On., Can.	E3	73
Alvo, Ne., U.S.	h12	104
Alvord, Ia., U.S.	A1	92
Alvord, Tx., U.S.	C4	120
Alvord Lake, l., Or., U.S.	E8	114
Alvordton, Oh., U.S.	A1	112
Älvsborg, co., Swe.	A6	15
Älvsered, Swe.	A6	15
Älvsjö (part of Stockholm), Swe.	t36	14
Al Wajh, Sau. Ar.	C3	38
Alwar, India	C6	36
Al Wāsiṭah, Eg.	E3	41
Alxa Zuoqi, China	D6	31
Alyat, Sov. Un.	F3	28
Alyth, Scot., U.K.	D5	13
Alytus, Sov. Un.	A8	26
Alz, stm., F.R.Ger.	E12	15
Alzada, Mt., U.S.	E12	103
Alzey, F.R.Ger.	D3	19
Ama, La., U.S.	k11	95
Amacuzac, stm., Mex.	n14	63
Amadeus, Lake, l., Austl.	D5	50
Amadi, Sud.	D3	47
Amadjuak Lake, l., N.T., Can.	C18	66
Amado, Az., U.S.	F4	80
Amador, co., Ca., U.S.	C3	82
Amagansett, N.Y., U.S.	n16	109
Amagasaki, Japan	o14	33
Amager, i., Den.	C6	15
Amagon, Ar., U.S.	B4	81
Amaha, Sud.	n18	33
Amahai, Indon.	F7	34
Amakusa Sea, Japan	J4	33
Åmål, Swe.	H5	14
Amalfi, Italy	D5	23
Amalga, Ut., U.S.	B4	121
Amalia, N.M., U.S.	A4	108
Amaliás, Grc.	D3	40
Amalner, India	G5	37
Amambaí, Braz.	C1	56
Amambaí, Serra de, mts., S.A.	D4	55
Amambay, dept., Para.	D4	55
Amami-Ō Island, i., Japan	F10	31
Amana, Ia., U.S.	C6	92
Amaná, Lago, l., Braz.	C2	59
Amancey, Fr.	B1	21
Amanda, Oh., U.S.	C3	112
Amangeldy, Sov. Un.	C7	28
Amantea, Italy	E6	23
Amantes Point, c., Guam	L10	52
Amapá, Braz.	B4	59
Amapá, ter., Braz.	B4	59
Amapala, Hond.	D4	62
Amaraji, Braz.	k6	57
Amarante, Braz.	C2	57
Amaranth, Mb., Can.	D2	70
Amargosa, Braz.	D3	57
Amargosa, stm., U.S.	D5	82
Amargosa Desert, des., U.S.	G5	105
Amargosa Range, mts., U.S.	G5	105
Amarillo, Tx., U.S.	B2	120
Amaro, Mount, mtn., Italy	C5	23
Amaroúsion, Grc.	g11	25
Amasa, Mi., U.S.	B2	99
Amasra, Tur.	B9	40
Amasya, Tur.	B10	40
Amataurá, Braz.	B4	58
Amatignak Island, i., Ak., U.S.	E4	79
Amatsu-kominato, Japan	n19	33
Amazon (Solimões) (Amazonas), stm., S.A.	D5	53
Amazonas, state, Braz.	C2	59
Amazonas, dept., Col.	D3	60
Amazonas, dept., Peru	C2	58
Amazonas, ter., Ven.	C4	60
Amazonia, Mo., U.S.	B3	102
Ambājōgāi (Moninabad), India	H6	37
Ambala, India	B6	36
Ambalavao, Madag.	h9	49
Ambam, Cam.	E2	46
Ambanja, Madag.	f9	49
Ambarchik, Sov. Un.	C19	29
Ambato, Ec.	B2	58
Ambato Boeny, Madag.	g9	49
Ambatolampy, Madag.	g9	49
Ambatondrazaka, Madag.	g9	49
Ambatosoratra, Madag.	g9	49
Amber, Ok., U.S.	B4	113
Amberg, F.R.Ger.	D5	18
Amberg, Wi., U.S.	C6	126
Ambérieu [-en-Bugey], Fr.	E6	16
Amberson, Pa., U.S.	F6	115
Ambert, Fr.	E5	16
Ambia, In., U.S.	D2	91
Ambikāpur, India	D7	36
Ambil Island, i., Phil.	p13	34
Ambilobe, Madag.	f9	49
Amble, Eng., U.K.	E7	13
Ambler, Ak., U.S.	B8	79
Ambler, Pa., U.S.	F11	115
Ambo, Peru	D2	58
Ambo Channel, strt., Marsh Is.	S17	52
Ambodifototra, Madag.	g9	49
Amboina see Ambon, Indon.	F7	34
Amboise, Fr.	D4	16
Ambon (Amboina), Indon.	F7	34
Ambon, i., Indon.	F7	34
Ambositra, Madag.	h9	49
Ambovombe, Madag.	h9	49
Amboy, Ca., U.S.	E6	82
Amboy, Il., U.S.	B4	90
Amboy, In., U.S.	C6	91
Amboy, Mn., U.S.	G4	100
Amboy, Wa., U.S.	D3	124
Ambridge, Pa., U.S.	E1	115
Ambriz, Ang.	C1	48
Ambrose, Ga., U.S.	E3	87
Ambrose, N.D., U.S.	A2	111
Ambrosia Lake, N.M., U.S.	B2	108
Ambur, Indon.	F8	34
Amchitka Island, i., Ak., U.S.	E3	79
Amchitka Pass, strt., Ak., U.S.	E4	79
Amden, Switz.	B7	21
Amderma, Sov. Un.	C9	29
Ameagle, W.V., U.S.	D3	125
Ameca, Mex.	C4	63
Ameca, stm., Mex.	m11	63
Amecameca [de Juárez], Mex.	n14	63
Ameland, i., Neth.	A6	16
Amelia, La., U.S.	E4	95
Amelia, Ne., U.S.	B7	104
Amelia, Oh., U.S.	C1	112
Amelia, co., Va., U.S.	C4	123
Amelia City, Fl., U.S.	k9	86
Amelia Court House, Va., U.S.	C5	123
Amelia Island, i., Fl., U.S.	k9	86
Amelinghausen, F.R.Ger.	E4	15
Amendolara, Italy	E6	23
Amenia, N.Y., U.S.	D7	109
Amenia, N.D., U.S.	B8	111
American, stm., Ca., U.S.	C3	82
American, South Fork, stm., Ca., U.S.	C3	82
Americana, Braz.	m8	56
American Falls, Id., U.S.	G6	89
American Falls Dam, Id., U.S.	G6	89
American Falls Reservoir, res., Id., U.S.	F5	89
American Fork, Ut., U.S.	C4	121
American Highland, plat., Ant.	B20	7
American Samoa, dep., Oc.	G11	2
Americus, Ga., U.S.	D2	87
Americus, Ks., U.S.	D7	93
Americus, Mo., U.S.	C6	102
Amersfoort, Neth.	A6	16
Amery, Mb., Can.	A4	70
Amery, Wi., U.S.	C1	126
Amery Ice Shelf, Ant.	C20	7
Ames, Ia., U.S.	B4	92
Ames, Ks., U.S.	C6	93
Ames, Ne., U.S.	C9	104
Ames, Ok., U.S.	A3	113
Amesbury, Ma., U.S.	A6	98
Amesville, Ct., U.S.	B2	84
Åmfissa, Grc.	C4	25
Amga, Sov. Un.	D8	33
Amguid, Alg.	D6	44
Amgun, stm., Sov. Un.	D16	29
Amherst, Sk., Can.	D5	71
Amherst, N.S., Can.	A8	83
Amherst, Me., U.S.	D4	96
Amherst, Ma., U.S.	B2	98
Amherst, Ne., U.S.	D6	104
Amherst, N.H., U.S.	E3	106
Amherst, Oh., U.S.	A3	112
Amherst, S.D., U.S.	B8	118
Amherst, Tx., U.S.	B1	120
Amherst, Va., U.S.	C3	123
Amherst, Wi., U.S.	D4	126
Amherst, co., Va., U.S.	C3	123
Amherstburg, On., Can.	E1	73
Amherstdale, W.V., U.S.	n12	125
Amiata, Monte, mtn., Italy	C3	23
Amidon, N.D., U.S.	C2	111
Amiens, Fr.	C5	16
Aminuis, Nmb.	B2	48
'Āmir, Ra's, c., Libya	C4	43
Amirante Islands, is., Sey.	G24	2
Amiret, Mn., U.S.	F3	100
Amir Kabir Dam, Iran	C5	39
Amisk, Ab., Can.	C5	68
Amisk Lake, l., Sk., Can.	C4	75
Amistad, N.M., U.S.	B6	108
Amistad National Recreation Area, Tx., U.S.	E2	120
Amistad Reservoir, res., N.A.	E2	120
Amite, La., U.S.	D5	95
Amite, co., Ms., U.S.	D3	101
Amite, stm., La., U.S.	D5	95
Amity, Ar., U.S.	C2	81
Amity, Mo., U.S.	B3	102
Amity, Or., U.S.	B3	114
Amity, Pa., U.S.	F1	115
Amityville, N.Y., U.S.	E7	109
Amlekhganj, Nepal	C7	36
Amlwch, Wales, U.K.	A3	12
'Ammān, Jord.	B3	38
Ammanford, Wales, U.K.	C3	12
Ammeloe, F.R.Ger.	A1	19
Ammendorf, Ger.D.R.	B6	19
Ammer Lake, l., F.R.Ger.	D5	18
Ammókhostos (Famagusta), Cyp.	E9	40
Ammon, Id., U.S.	F7	89
Ammonoosuc, stm., N.H., U.S.	B3	106
Amne Machin Shan see A'nyêmaqên Mountains, mts., China	E4	31
Amnicon Falls, Wi., U.S.	B2	126
Amo, In., U.S.	E5	91
Āmol, Iran	C6	39
Amonate, Va., U.S.	e10	123
Amoret, Mo., U.S.	C3	102
Amorgós, i., Grc.	D5	40
Amorinópolis, Braz.	B2	56
Amorita, Ok., U.S.	A3	113
Amory, Ms., U.S.	B5	101
Amos, P.Q., Can.	k11	74
Amoy see Xiamen, China	G8	31
Ampanihy, Madag.	h8	49
Amparo, Braz.	C3	56
Ampelókipoi, Grc.	*B4	25
Amper, stm., F.R.Ger.	E6	19
Ampezzo, Italy	B6	22
Amposta, Spain	E6	22
Amrāvati (Amraoti), India	D6	36
Amreli, India	G3	37
Amriswil, Switz.	A7	21
Amritsar, India	B5	36
Amroha, India	C7	37
Amrum, i., F.R.Ger.	A4	18
Amsteg, Switz.	C6	21
Amsterdam, Neth.	A6	16
Amsterdam, Ga., U.S.	F2	87
Amsterdam, Mo., U.S.	C3	102
Amsterdam, Mt., U.S.	E5	103
Amsterdam, N.Y., U.S.	C6	109
Amsterdam, Oh., U.S.	B5	112
Amsterdam, Île, i., F.S.A.T.	I2	2
Amstetten, Aus.	D7	18
Amston, Ct., U.S.	C6	84
Am Timan, Chad	C4	46
Amu Darya, stm., Asia	F9	29
Amukta Pass, strt., Ak., U.S.	E5	79
Amulet, Sk., Can.	H3	75
Amund Ringnes Island, i., N.T., Can.	m32	66
Amundsen Bay, b., Ant.	C17	7
Amundsen Gulf, b., N.T., Can.	B8	66
Amundsen-Scott, sci., Ant.	A17	7
Amundsen Sea, Ant.	B36	7
Amuntai, Indon.	F5	34
Amur (Heilong Jiang), stm., Asia	E16	29
Amvrakía, Gulf of, b., Grc.	C3	25
Amy, Ar., U.S.	D3	81
Amzi, Oued ti-n-, val., Afr.	D5	44
Anabar, stm., Sov. Un.	B14	29
'Anabtā, Isr. Occ.	f11	41
Anaco, Ven.	B5	60
Anacoco, La., U.S.	C2	95
Anacoco, Bayou, stm., La., U.S.	D2	95
Anaconda, Mt., U.S.	D4	103
Anaconda, N.M., U.S.	B2	108
Anaconda Range, mts., Mt., U.S.	E3	103
Anacortes, Wa., U.S.	A3	124
Anacostia, stm., U.S.	C4	97
Anacostia, Northwest Branch, stm., Md., U.S.	B3	97
Anacuao, Mount, mtn., Phil.	n13	34
Anadarko, Ok., U.S.	B3	113
Anadia, Braz.	C3	57
Anadyr, Sov. Un.	C20	29
Anadyr, Gulf of, b., Sov. Un.	C21	29
Anadyr Mountains, mts., Sov. Un.	C20	14
Anae, i., Guam	M9	52
Anáfi (Anaphe), i., Grc.	D5	40
Anagance, N.B., Can.	D4	71
'Ānah, Iraq	E13	40
Anaheim, Ca., U.S.	F5	82
Anahim Lake, B.C., Can.	C5	69
Anahola, Hi., U.S.	A2	88
Anahuac, Tx., U.S.	E5	120
Anahulu, stm., Hi., U.S.	f9	88
Anajás, Braz.	C5	59
Anak, N. Kor.	G2	33
Anakāpalle, India	E7	36
Anakie, Austl.	A6	51
Anaklia, Sov. Un.	A13	40
Analalava, Madag.	f9	49
Anamã, Braz.	D2	59
Anama Bay, Mb., Can.	D2	70
Ana María, Golfo de, b., Cuba	D4	64
Anambas Islands, is., Indon.	E3	34
Anamoose, N.D., U.S.	B5	111
Anamosa, Ia., U.S.	B6	92
Anamur, Tur.	D9	40
Anamur Burnu, c., Tur.	D9	40
Ananea (Poto), Peru	D3	58
Anantapur, India	F6	36
Anantnāg, India	B6	36
Ananyev, Sov. Un.	H8	27
Anao Point, c., Guam	L10	52
Anapa, Sov. Un.	I11	27
Anaphe see Anáfi, i., Grc.	D5	40
Anápolis, Braz.	B3	56
Anapu, stm., Braz.	*C4	59
Anār, Iran	F7	39
Anārak, Iran	E6	39
Anār Darreh, Afg.	E10	39
Anastasia Island, i., Fl., U.S.	C5	86
Anatone, Wa., U.S.	C8	124
Añatuya, Arg.	B3	55
Anauá, Braz.	B2	59
Anawalt, W.V., U.S.	D3	125
Ancash, dept., Peru	C2	58
Ancaster, On., Can.	D5	73
Ancenis, Fr.	D3	16
Ancha, Sierra, mts., Az., U.S.	D4	80
Anchieta, Braz.	C4	56
Anching see Anqing, China	E8	31
Anchorage, Ak., U.S.	C10	79
Anchorage, Ky., U.S.	g11	94
Anchor Point, Ak., U.S.	D9	79
Anchor Point, c., Ak., U.S.	h15	79
Ancienne-Lorette, P.Q., Can.	C6	74
Anclote Keys, is., Fl., U.S.	D4	86
Anco, Ky., U.S.	C6	94
Ancón, Peru	D2	58
Ancona, Italy	C4	23
Ancón de Sardinas, Bahía de, b., S.A.	C2	60
Ancud, Chile	C2	54
Ancud, Golfo de, b., Chile	C2	54
Anda, China	B10	31
Andacollo, Arg.	B2	54
Andahuaylas, Peru	D3	58
Andale, Ks., U.S.	E6	93
Andalgalá, Arg.	E2	55
Åndalsnes, Nor.	F2	14
Andalusia, Al., U.S.	D3	78
Andalusia, Il., U.S.	B3	90
Andalusia, hist reg., Spain	D3	22
Andaman and Nicobar Islands, ter., India	*F9	36
Andaman Islands, is., India	F9	36
Andaman Sea, Asia	F10	36
Andamarca, Bol.	C2	55
Andamarca, Peru	D3	58
Andavaka, Cap, c., Madag.	i9	49
Andebu, Nor.	p28	14
Andeer, Switz.	C7	21
Andenne, Bel.	D5	17
Andermatt, Switz.	C6	21
Andernach, F.R.Ger.	C3	18
Anderson Air Force Base, mil., Guam.	L10	52
Anderslöv, Swe.	C7	15
Anderson, Arg.	g6	54
Anderson, Al., U.S.	A2	78
Anderson, Ak., U.S.	C10	79
Anderson, Ca., U.S.	B2	82
Anderson, In., U.S.	D6	91
Anderson, Mo., U.S.	E3	102
Anderson, S.C., U.S.	B2	117
Anderson, Tn., U.S.	D8	119
Anderson, Tx., U.S.	D4	120
Anderson, co., Ks., U.S.	D8	93
Anderson, co., Ky., U.S.	C4	94
Anderson, co., S.C., U.S.	B2	117
Anderson, co., Tn., U.S.	C9	119
Anderson, co., Tx., U.S.	D5	120
Anderson, stm., In., U.S.	H4	91
Anderson, Mount, mtn., Wa., U.S.	B2	124
Anderson Ranch Reservoir, res., Id., U.S.	F3	89
Andersonville, Ga., U.S.	D2	87
Andersonville, In., U.S.	F7	91
Andes, Col.	B2	60
Andes, N.Y., U.S.	C6	109
Andes, mts., S.A.	E4	53
Andes, Lake, l., S.D., U.S.	D7	118
Andfjorden, strt., Nor.	C7	14
Andhra Pradesh, state, India	E6	36
Andikíthira, i., Grc.	E4	39
Andilamena, Madag.	g9	49
Andimeshk, Iran	E4	39
Andīmeshk, Rom.	A19	—
Andizhan, Sov. Un.	E10	29
Andkhvoy, Afg.	A4	36
Andoas, Peru	B2	58
Andong, S. Kor.	D10	31
Andorra, And.	A6	22
Andorra, ctry., Eur.	A6	22
Andover, Eng., U.K.	C6	12
Andover, Ct., U.S.	C6	84
Andover, Il., U.S.	B3	90
Andover, Ks., U.S.	g12	93
Andover, Me., U.S.	D2	96
Andover, Mn., U.S.	m12	100
Andover, N.H., U.S.	D3	106
Andover, N.Y., U.S.	C3	109
Andover, N.J., U.S.	B3	107
Andover, Oh., U.S.	A5	112
Andover, S.D., U.S.	B8	118
Andøya, i., Nor.	C6	14
Andradina, Braz.	C2	56
Andraitx, Spain	C7	22
Andreanof Islands, is., Ak., U.S.	E4	79
Andréville, P.Q., Can.	B8	74
Andrew, Ab., Can.	C4	68
Andrew, Ia., U.S.	B7	92
Andrew, co., Mo., U.S.	A3	102
Andrew Island, i., N.S., Can.	D9	71
Andrews, In., U.S.	C6	91
Andrews, Md., U.S.	D5	97
Andrews, N.C., U.S.	f9	110
Andrews, S.C., U.S.	E8	117
Andrews, Tx., U.S.	C1	120
Andrews, co., Tx., U.S.	C1	120
Andrews Air Force Base, mil., Md., U.S.	C4	97
Andreyevka, Sov. Un.	D8	33
Andreyevka, Sov. Un.	G11	27
Andria, Italy	D6	23
Androka, Madag.	h8	49
Andropov (Rybinsk), Sov. Un.	D5	26
Ándros, i., Grc.	D5	40
Androscoggin, co., Me., U.S.	D2	96
Androscoggin, stm., Me., U.S.	E4	100
Androscoggin Lake, l., Me., U.S.	D2	96
Andros Island, i., Bah.	B5	64
Andújar, Spain	D3	22
Angela, Mt., U.S.	D10	103
Ángel de la Guarda, Isla, i., Mex.	B2	63
Angeles, Phil.	o13	34
Angeles, Ky., U.S.	g11	94
Angeles Point, c., Wa., U.S.	A2	124
Ängelholm, Swe.	I5	14
Angelica, N.Y., U.S.	C2	109
Angelina, co., Tx., U.S.	D5	120
Angels Camp, Ca., U.S.	C3	82
Angelus, Ks., U.S.	C3	93
Angelus, S.C., U.S.	B7	117
Ångermanälven, stm., Swe.	F7	14
Angermünde, Ger.D.R.	B6	18
Angers, Fr.	D3	16
Angicos, Braz.	C3	57
Angie, La., U.S.	D6	95
Angle Inlet, Mn., U.S.	A3	100
Anglesey, i., Wales, U.K.	D4	10
Angleton, Tx., U.S.	E5	120
Anglia, Sk., Can.	F1	75
Angliers, P.Q., Can.	G17	66
Angling, stm., Mb., Can.	A5	70
Angling Lake, l., Mb., Can.	C5	70
Ango, Zaire	A4	48
Angoche, Moz.	A6	49
Angoche, Ilha, i., Moz.	A6	49
Angol, Chile	B2	54
Angola, In., U.S.	A8	91
Angola, N.Y., U.S.	C1	109
Angola, ctry., Afr.	D2	48
Angola Beach, De., U.S.	F5	85
Angola Swamp, sw., N.C., U.S.	C5	110
Angoon, Ak., U.S.	D13	79
Angostura Reservoir, res., S.D., U.S.	D2	118
Angoulême, Fr.	E4	16
Angren, Sov. Un.	E10	29
Angra do Heroísmo, Port.	g9	44
Angra dos Reis, Braz.	C4	56
Anguang, China	B10	32
Anguilla, Ms., U.S.	C3	101
Anguilla, ctry., N.A.	G13	64
Anguillara [Sabazia], Italy	g8	23
Anguille, Cape, c., Nf., Can.	E2	72
Angumu, Zaire	B4	48
Angus, On., Can.	C5	73
Angusville, Mb., Can.	D1	70
Anguy, China	J4	32
Anhui, prov., China	E8	31
Anhwei see Anhui, prov., China	E8	31
Aniak, Ak., U.S.	C8	79
Aniche, Fr.	B6	16
Aniene (Teverone), stm., Italy	F1	108
Animas, N.M., U.S.	F1	108
Animas, stm., Co., U.S.	D3	83
Animas, Lake, l., S.D., U.S.	D7	118
Animas Mountains, mts., N.M., U.S.	F1	108
Animas Peak, mtn., N.M., U.S.	F1	108
Animas Valley, val., N.M., U.S.	F1	108
Anina, Rom.	C2	24
Anita, Ia., U.S.	C3	92
Anita, Pa., U.S.	D4	115
Aniva, Sov. Un.	C11	33
Aniva, Cape, c., Sov. Un.	C11	33
Aniva Bay, b., Sov. Un.	C11	33
Aniwa, Wi., U.S.	C4	126
Anizy-le-Château, Fr.	E3	17
Anjār, India	o16	33
Anjō, Japan	o16	33
Anjou, P.Q., Can.	p19	74
Anjou, hist reg., Fr.	D3	16
Anju, N. Kor.	G2	33
Anjum, Neth.	A6	17
Anka, Nig.	F6	45
Ankang, China	E7	31
Ankara, Tur.	C9	40
Ankavandra, Madag.	g9	49
Ankazoabo, Madag.	h8	49
Ankazobe, Madag.	g9	49
Ankeny, Ia., U.S.	C4	92
Anklam, Ger.D.R.	B6	18
Ankober, Eth.	D4	47
Ankoro, Zaire	C4	48
An Loc, Viet.	G7	35
Anlong, China	F6	31
Anlu, China	I5	32
Ann, Cape, c., Ant.	C18	7
Ann, Cape, c., Ma., U.S.	A6	98
Anna, Sov. Un.	F13	27
Anna, Il., U.S.	F4	90
Anna, Oh., U.S.	B1	112
Anna, Tx., U.S.	C4	120
Anna, Lake, res., Va., U.S.	B5	123
Annaba (Bône), Alg.	B6	44
Annabella, Ut., U.S.	E3	121
Annaberg-Buchholz, Ger.D.R.	E11	40
An Nabk, Syria	B3	38
Annaburg, Ger.D.R.	B8	19
Annada, Mo., U.S.	B7	102
An Nafūd, des., Sau. Ar.	C4	38
An Najaf, Iraq	B4	38
An Nakhl, Eg.	B1	120
Annalee Heights, Va., U.S.	*B5	123
Anna Maria, Fl., U.S.	p10	86
Anna Maria Island, i., Fl., U.S.	q10	86
An Nāqūrah, Leb.	A7	41
An Nāsiriyah, Iraq	H2	75
Annawan, Il., U.S.	B4	90
An Nawfaliyah, Libya	F6	121
An Nazlah, Isr. Occ.	C6	41
An Nabk, Syria	n13	34
Anna Regina, Guy.	A3	59
Annecy, Fr.	E7	16
Annecy, Lake, l., Fr.	B9	31
Annecy-le-Vieux, Fr.	E1	21
Annemasse, Fr.	D7	16
Annette, Ak., U.S.	n24	79
An Nhon, Viet.	F8	35
Annieopsquotch Mountains, mts., Nf., Can.	D3	72
An Nīl, prov., Sud.		
An Nīl al Azraq (Blue Nile), prov., Sud.	C3	47
Anniston, Al., U.S.	B4	78
Anniston, Mo., U.S.	E8	102
Annobón see Pagalu (Pagalu), i., Eq. Gui.	F1	46
Annona, Tx., U.S.	C5	120
Annone, Lago di, l., Italy	E7	21
Annotto Bay, Jam.	E15	65
Annotto Bay, b., Jam.	E15	65
Annsjön, l., Swe.	u33	14
An Nuhūd, Sud.	C2	47
An Nu'māniyah, Iraq	E2	39
Annville, Ky., U.S.	C6	94
Annville, Pa., U.S.	F8	115
Anoka, Mn., U.S.	E5	100
Anoka, Ne., U.S.	B7	104
Anoka, co., Mn., U.S.	E5	100
Anori, Braz.	C2	59
Áno Viánnos, Grc.	E5	25
Anóyia, Grc.	E5	25
Anping, China	E6	32
Anqing, China	E8	31
Anqiu, China	D10	32
Ansbach, F.R.Ger.	D5	18
Anse d'Hainault, Haiti	E6	64
Anselmo, Ne., U.S.	C6	104
Anserma, Col.	B2	60
Anshan, China	C9	31
Anshun, China	F6	31
Ansley, Al., U.S.	D3	78
Ansley, Ne., U.S.	C6	104
Anson, Me., U.S.	D3	96
Anson, Tx., U.S.	C3	120
Anson, co., N.C., U.S.	B2	110
Anson Bay, b., Austl.	B5	50
Ansong, S. Kor.	H3	33
Ansonia, Ct., U.S.	D3	84
Ansonia, Oh., U.S.	B1	112
Ansonville, On., Can.	G16	66
Ansonville, N.C., U.S.	B2	110
Ansted, W.V., U.S.	C3	125
Ansudu, Indon.	F9	34
Anta, Peru	D3	58
Antabamba, Peru	D3	58
Antakya (Antioch), Tur.	D11	40
Antalaha, Madag.	f10	49
Antalät, well, Libya	G3	43
Antalya, Tur.	D8	40
Antalya, Gulf of, b., Tur.	D8	40
Antananarivo, Madag.	g9	49
Antananarivo, prov., Madag.	g9	49
Antarctica	A19	7
Antarctic Peninsula, pen., Ant.	C6	7
Antelope, Sk., Can.	G1	75
Antelope, Ks., U.S.	D7	93
Antelope, Mt., U.S.	B12	103
Antelope, Or., U.S.	C6	114
Antelope, S.D., U.S.	*D5	118
Antelope, co., Ne., U.S.	B7	104
Antelope Butte, mtn., Wy., U.S.	B7	127
Antelope Creek, stm., Wy., U.S.	C7	127
Antelope Lake, l., Sk., Can.	G1	75
Antelope Mine, Zimb.	B4	49
Antelope Peak, mtn., Nv., U.S.	B7	105
Antelope Range, mts., Nv., U.S.	D7	105
Antelope Reservoir, res., Or., U.S.	E9	114
Antelope Wash, val., Nv., U.S.	D5	105
Antequera, Spain	D3	22
Antero, Mount, mtn., Co., U.S.	C4	83
Antero Reservoir, res., Co., U.S.	C5	83
Antes Fort, Pa., U.S.	D7	115
Anthon, Ia., U.S.	B2	92
Anthony, Fl., U.S.	C4	86
Anthony, Ks., U.S.	E5	93
Anthony, N.M., U.S.	F3	108
Anthony, R.I., U.S.	D4	116
Anthony Creek, stm., W.V.,	D4	125
Anti-Atlas, mts., Mor.	C3	44
Antibes, Fr.	F7	16
Anticosti, Île d', i., P.Q., Can.	k14	74
Anticosti, Réserve, P.Q., Can.	k14	74
Antietam Creek, stm., Md.,	B2	97
Antietam National Battlefield Site, hist., Md., U.S.	B2	97
Antigo, Wi., U.S.	C4	126
Antigonish, N.S., Can.	D8	71
Antigonish, co., N.S., Can.	D8	71
Antigua, i., Antig.	H14	64
Antigua and Barbuda, ctry., N.A.	H14	64
Antigua Guatemala, Guat.	E6	63
Antilla, Cuba	D6	64
Antimony, Ut., U.S.	E3	121
Antioch see Antakya, Tur.	D11	40
Antioch, Ca., U.S.	h9	82
Antioch, Il., U.S.	A5	90
Antioch, Ne., U.S.	B3	104
Antioquia, Col.	B2	60
Antioquia, dept., Col.	B2	60
Antler, Sk., Can.	H5	75
Antler, N.D., U.S.	A4	111
Antler, stm., N.A.	E1	70
Antofagasta, Chile	D1	55
Antofagasta, prov., Chile	D1	55
Antofagasta de la Sierra, Arg.	E2	55
Antofalla, Volcán, vol., Arg.	E2	55
Antoine, Ar., U.S.	C2	81
Antón, Pan.	F7	63
Anton, Co., U.S.	B7	83
Anton, Tx., U.S.	C1	120
Anton Chico, N.M., U.S.	B4	108
Antongila, Helodrano, b., Madag.	g9	49
Antonia, Braz.	C7	102
Antonina, Braz.	A7	56
Antonino, Ks., U.S.	D4	93
António Carlos, Braz.	m20	56
António de Biedma, Arg.	B4	56
António Dias, Braz.	B4	56
Antonito, Co., U.S.	D5	83
Antony, Fr.	g10	16
Antora Peak, mtn., Co., U.S.	C4	83
Antratsit, Sov. Un.	q22	14

Name	Map Ref	Page
Antrim, N. Ire., U.K.	C5	11
Antrim, Mi., U.S.	D5	99
Antrim, N.H., U.S.	D3	106
Antrim, Pa., U.S.	C7	115
Antrim, co., Mi., U.S.	C5	99
Antsalova, Madag.	g8	49
Antsirabe, Madag.	g9	49
Antsiranana, Madag.	f9	49
Antsiranana, prov., Madag.	f9	49
Antsohihy, Madag.	f9	49
An Tuc, Viet.	C3	34
Antwerp (Antwerpen), Bel.	B5	16
Antwerp, N.Y., U.S.	A5	109
Antwerp, Oh., U.S.	A1	112
Antwerp, prov., Bel.	C4	17
Antwerpen see Antwerp, Bel.	B5	16
Anua, Am. Sam.	F13	52
An Uaimh (Navan), Ire.	D3	10
Anuradhapura, Sri L.	G7	36
Anvers Island, i., Ant.	C6	7
Anvik, Ak., U.S.	C7	79
Anxi, China	F8	31
Anxi, China	C4	31
Anyang, China	D7	31
A'nyêmaqên Mountains, mts., China	D4	31
Anyi, China	G4	32
Anykščiai, Sov. Un.	A8	26
Anza, Col.	B2	60
Anza, Mt., Italy	E5	21
Anzac, Ab., Can.	A5	68
Anzhero-Sudzhensk, Sov. Un.	D11	29
Anzin, Fr.	D3	17
Anzio, Italy	D4	23
Anzoátegui, state, Ven.	B5	60
Aoji-ri, N. Kor.	E5	33
Aomoen Island, i., Marsh Is.	P18	52
Aomon, i., Marsh Is.	S18	52
Aomori, Japan	C13	33
Aoral, mtn., Kam.	C2	34
Aosta, Italy	B1	23
Aou Hofrit, well, W. Sah.	E2	44
Aouk, Bahr, Afr.	D3	46
Aoukâr, reg., Maur.	C2	45
Aoyama, Japan	o15	33
Aozou, Chad	A3	46
Apa, stm., S.A.	D4	55
Apache, Ok., U.S.	C3	113
Apache, co., Az., U.S.	B6	80
Apache Creek, N.M., U.S.	D1	108
Apache Junction, Az., U.S.	m9	80
Apache Peak, mtn., Az., U.S.	F5	80
Apalachee, Ga., U.S.	C3	87
Apalachee Bay, b., Fl., U.S.	B2	86
Apalachicola, stm., Fl., U.S.	B1	86
Apalachicola, Fl., U.S.	C2	86
Apalachicola Bay, b., Fl., U.S.	C2	86
Apalachin, N.Y., U.S.	C4	109
Apan, Mex.	n14	63
Apaporis, stm., S.A.	D3	60
Aparri, Phil.	B6	34
Apatin, Yugo.	C4	24
Apatity, Sov. Un.	D15	14
Apatzingán [de la Constitución], Mex.	n12	63
Apeldoorn, Neth.	A6	16
Apennines, mts., Italy	C4	14
Apennine Tunnel, Italy	B3	23
Apérathos, Grc.	D5	25
Apex, N.C., U.S.	B4	110
Apex Mountain, mtn., Yk., Can.	D5	66
Api, mtn., Nepal	C8	37
Apia, W. Sam.	F12	52
Apiacás, Serra dos, plat., Braz.	E3	59
Apia Harbour, b., W. Sam.	F12	52
Apiaí, Braz.	C3	56
Apishapa, stm., Co., U.S.	D6	83
Apison, Tn., U.S.	h11	119
Apizaco, Mex.	n14	63
Aplao, Peru	E3	58
Aplin, Ar., U.S.	C3	81
Aplington, Ia., U.S.	B5	92
Apo, Mount, mtn., Phil.	D7	34
Apodi, Braz.	C3	57
Apohaqui, N.B., Can.	D4	71
Apolda, Ger.D.R.	C5	18
Apolima Island, i., W. Sam.	F11	52
Apolima Strait, strt., W. Sam.	F11	52
Apollo, Pa., U.S.	E2	115
Apolo, Bol.	D5	55
Apopka, Fl., U.S.	D5	86
Apopka, Lake, l., Fl., U.S.	D5	86
Aporé, stm., Braz.	B2	56
Aporé, Braz.	B2	56
Apostle Islands, is., Wi., U.S.	A3	126
Apostle Islands National Lakeshore, Wi., U.S.	A3	126
Apóstoles, Arg.	E4	55
Apostólou Andréa, Akrotírion, c., Cyp.	E10	40
Appalachia, Va., U.S.	f9	123
Appalachian Mountains, mts., N.A.	C11	76
Appam, N.D., U.S.	A2	111
Appanoose, co., Ia., U.S.	D5	92
Appenzell, Switz.	E4	18
Appenzell-Ausser Rhoden, state, Switz.	B5	20
Appenzell-Inner Rhoden, state, Switz.	B5	20
Apperson, Ok., U.S.	A5	113
Appingedam, Neth.	A6	17
Apple, stm., Wi., U.S.	C1	126
Apple, Eng., U.K.	F6	13
Appleby, Tx., U.S.	D5	120
Apple Creek, Oh., U.S.	B4	112
Applecross, Scot., U.K.	C3	13
Applegate, Mi., U.S.	E8	99
Applegate, Or., U.S.	E3	114
Applegate, stm., Or., U.S.	E3	114
Apple Grove, W.V., U.S.	C2	125
Apple Hill, On., Can.	B10	73
Apple Orchard Mountain, mtn., Va., U.S.	C3	123
Apple River, N.S., Can.	D5	71
Apple River, Il., U.S.	A3	90
Apple Springs, Tx., U.S.	D5	120
Appleton, Me., U.S.	D3	96
Appleton, Mn., U.S.	E2	100
Appleton, Tn., U.S.	B4	119
Appleton, Wa., U.S.	D4	124
Appleton, Wi., U.S.	D5	126
Appleton City, Mo., U.S.	C3	102
Apple Valley, Ca., U.S.	E5	82
Apple Valley, Mn., U.S.	n12	100
Apple Valley, N.D., U.S.	*C5	111
Applewood, Co., U.S.	B5	83
Appleyard, Wa., U.S.	B5	124
Appling, Ga., U.S.	C4	87
Appling, co., Ga., U.S.	E4	87
Appomattox, Va., U.S.	C4	123
Appomattox, co., Va., U.S.	C4	123
Appomattox, stm., Va., U.S.	C4	123
Appomattox Court House National Historical Park, Va., U.S.	C4	123
Apra Harbor, b., Guam	L9	52
Aprelsk, Sov. Un.	D14	29
Aprilia, Italy	D4	23
Apsheron Peninsula, pen., Sov. Un.	G19	8
Apsley, On., Can.	C6	73
Apt, Fr.	F6	16
Apua Point, c., Hi., U.S.	D6	88
Apucarana, Braz.	C2	56
Apulia, hist reg., Italy	D6	23
Apure, state, Ven.	B4	60
Apure, stm., Ven.	B4	60
Apurímac, dept., Peru	D3	58
Apurímac, stm., Peru	D3	58
Aqaba, Gulf of, b.	C3	38
' Aqīq, Sud.	B4	47
' Aqrabā, Syria	A8	41
' Aqrabah, Isr. Occ.	B7	41
Aquarius Mountains, mts., Az., U.S.	C2	80
Aquarius Plateau, plat., Ut., U.S.	E4	121
Aquasco, Md., U.S.	C4	97
Aquebogue, N.Y., U.S.	n16	109
Aquidauana, Braz.	C1	56
Aquila see L'Aquila, Italy	C4	23
Aquileia, Italy	D9	20
Aquiles Serdán, Mex.	B3	63
Aquin, Haiti	E7	64
Aquone, N.C., U.S.	f9	110
Arab, Al., U.S.	A3	78
' Arab, Bahr al, stm., Sud.	D2	47
' Arab, Khalīj al, b., Egypt	G7	40
' Arab, Shatt al, stm., Iraq	B4	38
Arabelo, Ven.	C5	60
Arabi, Ga., U.S.	E3	87
Arabi, La., U.S.	k11	95
Arabian Desert, des., Eg.	C3	38
Arabian Sea	H9	30
Araçá, stm., Braz.	B2	59
Aracaju, Braz.	D3	57
Aracati, Braz.	B3	57
Araçatuba, Braz.	C2	56
Aracena, Spain	D2	22
Aracruz, Braz.	B4	56
Araçuaí, Braz.	B4	56
Arad, Rom.	B5	24
Arada, Chad	B4	46
Arafura Sea	G7	6
Aragarças, Braz.	B2	56
Arago, Or., U.S.	D2	114
Arago, Cape, c., Or., U.S.	D2	114
Aragon, Ga., U.S.	B1	87
Aragon, N.M., U.S.	D1	108
Aragón, hist reg., Spain	B5	22
Aragón, stm., Spain	A5	22
Aragua, state, Ven.	A4	60
Araguacema, Braz.	D5	59
Araguaçu, Braz.	E5	59
Aragua de Barcelona, Ven.	B5	60
Araguaia, stm., Braz.	D6	53
Araguaia, Braço Menor, stm., Braz.	E5	59
Araguaia National Park, Braz.	E4	59
Araguao, Boca, mth., Ven.	B5	60
Araguari, Braz.	B3	56
Araguari, stm., Braz.	B4	56
Arai, Japan	H9	33
Arai, Japan	o16	33
' Arak, Alg.	D5	44
' Arāk, Iran	B5	38
Arakan Range, mts., Burma	E9	36
Arakhthos, stm., Grc.	C3	25
Araks, stm., Asia	B3	39
Aral Sea, Sov. Un.	E9	29
Aralsk, Sov. Un.	D6	28
Arambaza, Col.	D3	60
' Arān, Iran	D5	39
Aranda de Duero, Spain	B4	22
Arandas, Mex.	m12	63
Aran Island, i., Ire.	C2	10
Aran Islands, is., Ire.	D2	10
Aranjuez, Spain	B4	22
Aransas, co., Tx., U.S.	E4	120
Aransas Bay, b., Tx., U.S.	E4	120
Aransas Pass, Tx., U.S.	F4	120
Araouane, Mali	C4	45
Arapaho, Ok., U.S.	B3	113
Arapahoe, Co., U.S.	C8	83
Arapahoe, N.C., U.S.	B6	110
Arapahoe, Ne., U.S.	D6	104
Arapahoe, Wy., U.S.	D4	127
Arapahoe, co., Co., U.S.	B6	83
Arapey, Ur.	E1	56
Arapey Grande, stm., Ur.	E1	56
Arapiraca, Tur.	C12	40
Arapongas, Braz.	C2	56
Araranguá, Braz.	D3	56
Araraquara, Braz.	C3	56
Araras, Braz.	h6	57
Ararat, Austl.	G7	50
Ararat, Va., U.S.	D2	123
Ararat, Mount, mtn., Tur.	C15	40
Araripe, Chapada do, plat., Braz.	C3	57
Araruna, Braz.	h6	57
Arauca, Col.	B3	60
Arauca, dept., Col.	B3	60
Arauca, stm., S.A.	B3	60
Araujós, Braz.	D3	56
Aravá, Braz.	D3	56
Araya, Chile	B2	54
Araya, Point, c., Ca., U.S.	A5	60
Araya, Punta de, c., Ven.	A5	60
Arba Minch, Eth.	D4	47
Arboga, Swe.	t33	14
Arbois, Fr.	D6	16
Arboles, Mo., U.S.	D3	83
Arbon, Switz.	E4	18
Arbon, Id., U.S.	G6	89
Arborea (Mussolinia), Italy	E2	23
Arborfield, Sk., Can.	D4	75
Arbor Vitae, Wi., U.S.	C4	126
Arbroath, Scot., U.K.	B5	10
Arbuckle, Ca., U.S.	C2	82
Arbuckle, Lake, l., Fl., U.S.	E5	86
Arbuckle Mountains, mts., Ok., U.S.	C4	113
Arbuckles, Lake of the, res., Ok., U.S.	C4	113
Arbyrd, Mo., U.S.	E7	102
Arc, Bayou des, stm., Ar., U.S.	B4	81
Arcachon, Fr.	E3	16
Arcade, Ca., U.S.	c3	82
Arcade, Ga., U.S.	B3	87
Arcade, N.Y., U.S.	C2	109
Arcadia, Ca., U.S.	m12	82
Arcadia, Fl., U.S.	E5	86
Arcadia, In., U.S.	D5	91
Arcadia, Ks., U.S.	E9	93
Arcadia, La., U.S.	B3	95
Arcadia, Mi., U.S.	D4	99
Arcadia, Ne., U.S.	C6	104
Arcadia, Oh., U.S.	A2	112
Arcadia, Ok., U.S.	B4	113
Arcadia, Pa., U.S.	E4	115
Arcadia, R.I., U.S.	E2	116
Arcadia, S.C., U.S.	B4	117
Arcadia, Wi., U.S.	D2	126
Arcanum, Oh., U.S.	C1	112
Arcata, Ca., U.S.	B1	82
Arc Dome, mtn., Nv., U.S.	E4	105
Arcelia, Mex.	n13	63
Arcey, Fr.	A2	21
Archambault, Lac, l., P.Q., Can.	C3	74
Archbald, Pa., U.S.	m18	115
Archbold, Oh., U.S.	A1	112
Archdale, N.C., U.S.	B3	110
Archer, Fl., U.S.	C4	86
Archer, Ia., U.S.	A2	92
Archer, Ne., U.S.	C7	104
Archer, co., Tx., U.S.	C3	120
Archer, stm., Austl.	B7	50
Archer City, Tx., U.S.	C3	120
Archer's Post, Kenya	A6	48
Arches National Park, Ut., U.S.	E6	121
Archidona, Spain	D3	22
Archie, Mo., U.S.	C3	102
Archie, Sk., Can.	G3	75
Archuleta, co., Co., U.S.	D3	83
Arcis-sur-Aube, Fr.	C6	16
Arco, Id., U.S.	F5	89
Arco, Mn., U.S.	F2	100
Arcola, Sk., Can.	H4	75
Arcola, Il., U.S.	D5	90
Arcola, In., U.S.	B7	91
Arcola, Ms., U.S.	B3	101
Arcola, Mo., U.S.	D4	102
Arcola, Va., U.S.	g11	123
Arcos de la Frontera, Spain	D3	22
Arcot, India	F6	36
Arcoverde, Braz.	C3	57
Arctic Bay, N.T., Can.	B16	66
Arctic Ocean	A1	128
Arctic Village, Ak., U.S.	B10	79
Arcueil, Fr.	g10	16
Arda, stm., Eur.	E7	24
Ardabīl (Ardebil), Iran	B4	38
Ardagh, Ire.	E2	11
Ardahan, Tur.	B14	40
Ardakān, Iran	B5	38
Ardakān, Iran	E6	39
Ardath, Sk., Can.	F2	75
Ardatov, Sov. Un.	D16	27
Ardbeg, On., Can.	B4	73
Ardebil see Ardabīl, Iran	B4	38
Arden, Mb., Can.	D2	70
Arden, On., Can.	C8	73
Arden, Den.	B3	15
Arden, Ar., U.S.	D2	81
Arden, Ca., U.S.	*C3	82
Arden, N.C., U.S.	f10	110
Arden Hills, Mn., U.S.	*m12	100
Ardennes, dept., Fr.	E4	17
Ardennes, reg., Eur.	D6	16
Ardenno, Italy	C5	20
Ardenvoir, Wa., U.S.	B5	124
Ardestān, Iran	E6	39
Ardglass, N. Ire., U.K.	C6	11
Ardila, stm., Eur.	C2	22
Ardill, Sk., Can.	H3	75
Ardino, Bul.	E7	24
Ardley, Ab., Can.	C4	68
Ardmore, Ab., Can.	B5	68
Ardmore, Ire.	F4	11
Ardmore, Al., U.S.	A3	78
Ardmore, Md., U.S.	C4	97
Ardmore, Ok., U.S.	C4	113
Ardmore, Pa., U.S.	F11	115
Ardmore, S.D., U.S.	D2	118
Ardmore, Tn., U.S.	B5	119
Ardnamurchan, Point of, c., Scot., U.K.	D2	13
Ardnaree, Ire.	C2	11
Ardnave Point, c., Scot., U.K.	E2	13
Ardoch, N.D., U.S.	A8	111
Ardpatrick, Ire.	F4	11
Ardres, Fr.	D1	17
Ardrossan, Austl.	G1	51
Ardrossan, Ab., Can.	C4	68
Ardrossan, Scot., U.K.	C4	10
Ards, Al., U.S.	A2	78
Ardsley, N.Y., U.S.	g13	109
Ardsley, Eng., U.K.	h9	13
Ardud, Rom.	B3	24
Areado, Braz.	h6	57
Aredale, Ia., U.S.	B5	92
Areia, Braz.	h6	57
Areia Branca, Braz.	B3	57
Arelee, Sk., Can.	E2	75
Arena, N.D., U.S.	B5	111
Arena, Wi., U.S.	E4	126
Arena, Point, c., Ca., U.S.	C2	82
Arena, Punta, c., Mex.	C3	63
Arenac, co., Mi., U.S.	D7	99
Arenápolis, Braz.	A1	56
Arenas de San Pedro, Spain	B3	22
Arenas Valley, N.M., U.S.	E1	108
Arendal, Nor.	H3	14
Arendonk, Bel.	C5	17
Arendsee, Ger.D.R.	B5	18
Arendtsville, Pa., U.S.	G7	115
Arenillas, Ec.	B3	58
Arenzville, Il., U.S.	c3	90
Arequipa, Peru	E3	58
Arequipa, dept., Peru	E3	58
Arezzo, Italy	C3	23
Ares, Spain	A2	22
Argalastí, Grc.	C4	25
Arganda, Spain	p18	22
Argelès-Gazost, Fr.	F3	16
Argen, stm., F.R.Ger.	A8	21
Argenta, Italy	B3	23
Argenta, Il., U.S.	D5	90
Argentan, Fr.	C4	16
Argentat, Fr.	E4	16
Argenteuil, Fr.	C5	16
Argenteuil, co., P.Q., Can.	D3	74
Argentina, ctry., S.A.	G4	53
Argentino, Lago, l., Arg.	E2	54
Argenton-sur-Creuse, Fr.	D4	16
Argeș, stm., Rom.	C7	24
Arghandāb, stm., Afg.	E13	39
Arghandāb, Band-e, res., Afg.	E13	39
Argo, Sud.	B3	47
Argo, Al., U.S.	B3	78
Argo, Il., U.S.	A3	90
Argo Corner, De., U.S.	E4	85
Argolis, Gulf of, b., Grc.	D4	25
Argonia, Ks., U.S.	E6	93
Argonne, Wi., U.S.	C5	126
Argonne, reg., Fr.	C6	16
Argonne, Forêt d', for., Fr.	E4	17
Árgos, Grc.	D4	40
Árgos, In., U.S.	B5	91
Árgos Orestikón, Grc.	B3	25
Argostólion, Grc.	C3	40
Argun, stm., Asia	D14	29
Argungu, Nig.	D5	45
Argusville, N.D., U.S.	B9	111
Argyle, N.S., Can.	F4	71
Argyle, Fl., U.S.	u15	86
Argyle, Ga., U.S.	E4	87
Argyle, Ia., U.S.	D6	92
Argyle, Mi., U.S.	E8	99
Argyle, Mn., U.S.	B2	100
Argyle, Mo., U.S.	C5	102
Argyle, N.Y., U.S.	B7	109
Argyle, Wi., U.S.	F4	126
Argyle, Lake, res., Austl.	C4	50
Árhus, Den.	I4	14
Århus, co., Den.	B4	15
Århus Bugt, b., Den.	B4	15
Ari, In., U.S.	B7	91
Ariake Bay, b., Japan	K5	33
Ariano Irpino, Italy	D5	23
Ariano nel Polesine, Italy	E8	20
Ariari, stm., Col.	C3	60
Arica, Chile	C1	55
Arica, Col.	D3	60
Arichat, N.S., Can.	D9	71
Ariège, stm., Fr.	F4	16
Ariel, Wa., U.S.	D3	124
Aries, stm., Rom.	B6	24
Arikaree, stm., U.S.	B8	83
Arima, Trin.	K14	64
Arimo, Id., U.S.	G6	89
Arinos, stm., Braz.	B4	55
Ario de Rosales, Mex.	D4	63
Aripeka, Fl., U.S.	D4	86
Aripo, El Cerro del, mtn., Trin.	K14	64
Aripuanã, Braz.	D2	59
Aripuanã, stm., Braz.	D2	59
Arisaig, Scot., U.K.	D3	13
' Arīsh, Wādī al, val., Eg.	D4	41
Arispe, Ia., U.S.	D3	92
Ariton, Al., U.S.	D4	78
Arivaca, Az., U.S.	F4	80
Arivonimamo, Madag.	g9	49
Arizaro, Salar de, pl., Arg.	D2	55
Arizona, Arg.	B3	54
Arizona, state, U.S.	C4	80
Arizona Sunsites, Az., U.S.	F6	80
Arizpe, Mex.	A2	63
Arjay, Ky., U.S.	D6	94
Arjeplog, Swe.	D8	14
Arjona, Col.	A2	60
Arjona, Spain	D3	22
Arkabutla, Ms., U.S.	A3	101
Arkabutla Lake, res., Ms., U.S.	A4	101
Arkadelphia, Al., U.S.	B3	78
Arkadelphia, Ar., U.S.	C2	81
Arkaig, Loch, l., Scot., U.K.	D3	13
Arkalyk, Sov. Un.	D7	28
Arkansas, co., Ar., U.S.	C4	81
Arkansas, state, U.S.	C3	81
Arkansas, stm., U.S.	C9	76
Arkansas, Salt Fork, stm., U.S.	A3	113
Arkansas City, Ar., U.S.	D4	81
Arkansas City, Ks., U.S.	E6	93
Arkansaw, Wi., U.S.	D1	126
Arkelstorp, Swe.	B8	15
Arkhangelsk, Sov. Un.	C7	29
Arkhangelskoye, Sov. Un.	F13	27
Arkhara, Sov. Un.	B5	33
Árki, i., Grc.	D6	25
Arkinda, Ar., U.S.	D1	81
Arklow, Ire.	D3	10
Arkoma, Ok., U.S.	B7	113
Arkona, Kap (The Skaw), c., Ger.D.R.	D7	15
Arkonam, India	F6	36
Arkport, N.Y., U.S.	C3	109
Arkville, N.Y., U.S.	C6	109
Arkwright, Ga., U.S.	D3	87
Arkwright, R.I., U.S.	D3	116
Arlanza, stm., Spain	A4	22
Arlanzón, stm., Spain	A4	22
Arlberg Tunnel, Aus.	E5	18
Arlee, Mt., U.S.	C2	103
Arles, Fr.	F6	16
Arley, Al., U.S.	A2	78
Arlington, Az., U.S.	D3	80
Arlington, Ga., U.S.	E2	87
Arlington, Il., U.S.	B4	90
Arlington, Ia., U.S.	B6	92
Arlington, Ky., U.S.	f9	94
Arlington, Ma., U.S.	B5	98
Arlington, Mn., U.S.	F4	100
Arlington, Ne., U.S.	C9	104
Arlington, N.Y., U.S.	D7	109
Arlington, Oh., U.S.	B2	112
Arlington, Or., U.S.	B6	114
Arlington, S.C., U.S.	B3	117
Arlington, S.D., U.S.	C8	118
Arlington, Tn., U.S.	B2	119
Arlington, Tx., U.S.	n9	120
Arlington, Vt., U.S.	E2	122
Arlington, Va., U.S.	B5	123
Arlington, Wa., U.S.	A3	124
Arlington, co., Va., U.S.	g12	123
Arlington, Lake, res., Tx., U.S.	n9	120
Arlington Beach, Sk., Can.	G3	75
Arlington Heights, Il., U.S.	A5	90
Arlit, Niger	C6	45
Arlon, Bel.	C6	16
Arly, stm., Fr.	D2	20
Arm, Ms., U.S.	D3	101
Arm, stm., Sk., Can.	F3	75
Arma, Ks., U.S.	E9	93
Armada, Mi., U.S.	F8	99
Armagh, P.Q., Can.	C7	74
Armagh, N. Ire., U.K.	C3	10
Armagh, Pa., U.S.	F3	115
Armathwaite, Tn., U.S.	C9	119
Armavir, Sov. Un.	E7	29
Armenia, Col.	C2	60
Armenia, state, Sov. Un.	E7	29
Armenia, Cuba	C2	64
Armenía, stm., Mex.	n12	63
Armero, Col.	B3	60
Armidale, Austl.	F9	50
Armijo, N.M., U.S.	k7	108
Armington, Il., U.S.	C4	90
Arminto, Wy., U.S.	C5	127
Armit Lake, l., Can.	C1	70
Armley, Sk., Can.	D3	75
Armonk, N.Y., U.S.	*g13	109
Armorel, Ar., U.S.	B6	81
Armour, S.D., U.S.	D7	118
Armstead, Al., U.S.	B3	78
Armstrong, B.C., Can.	D8	69
Armstrong, Fl., U.S.	C5	86
Armstrong, Il., U.S.	C6	90
Armstrong, Ia., U.S.	A3	92
Armstrong, Mo., U.S.	B5	102
Armstrong, Ok., U.S.	C5	113
Armstrong, Tx., U.S.	F4	120
Armstrong, co., Pa., U.S.	E2	115
Armstrong, co., Tx., U.S.	B2	120
Armstrong Creek, Wi., U.S.	C5	126
Armstrong Creek, stm., W.V., U.S.	m13	125
Armstrong Station, On., Can.	F15	66
Armuchee, Ga., U.S.	B1	87
Armuchee, stm., Ga., U.S.	B1	87
Armyansk, Sov. Un.	H9	27
Arnaud, stm., P.Q., Can.	E18	66
Arnaudville, La., U.S.	D4	95
Arneburg, Ger.D.R.	F5	15
Arnedo, Spain	A4	22
Arnegard, N.D., U.S.	B2	111
Arneiroz, Braz.	A5	48
Arnett, Ok., U.S.	A2	113
Arnett, W.V., U.S.	n13	125
Arney, stm., N. Ire., U.K.	C4	11
Arnhem, Neth.	C5	16
Arnhem, Cape, c., Austl.	B6	50
Arnhem Land, reg., Austl.	B6	50
Árnissa, Grc.	B3	25
Arno, stm., Italy	C3	23
Arnold, Ca., U.S.	C3	82
Arnold, Ks., U.S.	D4	93
Arnold, Mi., U.S.	B3	99
Arnold, Mo., U.S.	C7	102
Arnold, Ne., U.S.	C6	104
Arnold, Pa., U.S.	h14	115
Arnold Mills Reservoir, res., R.I., U.S.	B4	116
Arnoldsburg, W.V., U.S.	C3	125
Arnolds Park, Ia., U.S.	A2	92
Arnoldsville, Ga., U.S.	C3	87
Arnot, Pa., U.S.	C7	115
Arnouville, Fr.	g10	16
Arnøya, i., Nor.	B9	14
Arnprior, On., Can.	B8	73
Arnsberg, F.R.Ger.	C8	18
Arnstadt, Ger.D.R.	C5	18
Arø, i., Den.	C3	15
Aroa, Ven.	A4	60
Aroab, Nmb.	C2	49
Arock, Or., U.S.	E9	114
Aroda, Va., U.S.	B4	123
Aroma Park, Il., U.S.	B6	90
Aron, stm., Fr.	D5	17
Aroostook, N.B., Can.	C2	71
Aroostook, co., Me., U.S.	B4	96
Aroostook, stm., N.A.	B4	96
Aroya, i., Pap. N. Gui.	k12	50a
Āros, Nor.	p28	14
Arosa, Switz.	F5	18
Arouca, Trin.	N23	65
Arp, Tx., U.S.	C5	120
Arpajon, Fr.	F2	17
Arpin, Wi., U.S.	D3	126
Arques, Fr.	D2	17
Arques-la-Bataille, Fr.	C4	16
' Arrābah, Isr. Occ.	B7	41
Arrah, India	C7	36
Ar Rahad, Sud.	C3	47
Arraiján, Pan.	F8	62
Arraias, Braz.	B5	57
Ar Ruţbah, Iraq	B4	38
Ar Ruwaytī, hist., Jord.	D7	41
Ārs, Den.	B3	15
Árma, Grc.	g10	25
Arsenyev, Sov. Un.	D6	33
Arsi, prov., Eth.	C4	47
Ārstad, Swe.	B6	15
Árta, Grc.	C3	40
Árta, dept., Grc.	*C3	25
Artas, S.D., U.S.	B6	118
Artashat, Sov. Un.	B2	39
Arțayyān, well, Sau. Ar.	H13	40
Artem, Sov. Un.	E16	29
Artemisa, Cuba	C2	64
Artemovsk, Sov. Un.	E27	8
Artemovskiy, Sov. Un.	B6	28
Artena, Italy	h9	23
Arter, Mount, mtn., Wy., U.S.	D4	127
Artern, Ger.D.R.	B6	19
Artesia, Ca., U.S.	*n12	82
Artesia, Ms., U.S.	B5	101
Artesia, N.M., U.S.	E5	108
Artesian, S.D., U.S.	C8	118
Artesia Wells, Tx., U.S.	E3	120
Arth, Switz.	B4	20
Arthabaska, P.Q., Can.	C6	74
Arthabaska, co., P.Q., Can.	C6	74
Arthur, On., Can.	D4	73
Arthur, Il., U.S.	D5	90
Arthur, Ia., U.S.	B2	92
Arthur, Ne., U.S.	C4	104
Arthur, N.D., U.S.	B8	111
Arthur, Tn., U.S.	C10	119
Arthur, co., Ne., U.S.	C4	104
Arthur, Lake, l., La., U.S.	D3	95
Arthur, Lake, res., Pa., U.S.	E1	115
Arthur Kill, stm., N.J., U.S.	k8	107
Arthurs Town, Bah.	B6	64
Artibonite, stm., Haiti	E7	64
Artigas, Ur.	E1	56
Artland, Sk., Can.	E1	75
Artois, hist reg., Fr.	B5	16
Artois, Collines de l', hills, Fr.	D2	17
Artvin, Tur.	B13	40
Aru, Zaire	A5	48
Arua, Ug.	A5	48
Aruanã, Braz.	A2	56
Aruba, ctry., N.A.	H17	65
Arucas, Spain	m14	22
Aru Islands, is., Indon.	G8	34
Arun, stm., Eng., U.K.	D7	13
Arunachal Pradesh, ter., India	C10	36
Arundel, P.Q., Can.	D3	74
Arundel, Eng., U.K.	D7	13
Arundel Village, Md., U.S.	*h11	97
Arusha, Tan.	B6	48
Arusha, prov., Tan.	B6	48
Aruwimi, stm., Zaire	A4	48
Arva, Ire.	D4	11
Arvada, Co., U.S.	B5	83
Arvada, Wy., U.S.	B6	127
Arvayheer, Mong.	B7	31
Arve, stm., Eur.	D2	20
Arvida, P.Q., Can.	A6	74
Arvidsjaur, Swe.	E8	14
Arvigo, Switz.	D7	21
Arvika, Swe.	H5	14
Arvilla, N.D., U.S.	B8	111
Arvin, Ca., U.S.	E4	82
Arvonia, Va., U.S.	C4	123
Arxan, China	B8	31
Arys, Sov. Un.	E9	29
Arzamas, Sov. Un.	D14	27
Arzgir, Sov. Un.	I15	27
Arzúa, Spain	A1	22
Aš, Czech.	C2	26
Aså, Den.	A4	15
Asab, Nmb.	C2	49
Asahi, Mount, mtn., Japan	E11	33
Asahikawa, Japan	C13	31
Asan, Guam	L9	52
Asan Bay, b., S. Kor.	H3	33
Asan Point, c., Guam	L9	52
Asansol, India	D8	36
Asau Bay, b., W. Sam.	F11	52
Asbach, F.R.Ger.	C2	19
Asbestos, P.Q., Can.	D6	74
Asbury, Mo., U.S.	D3	102
Asbury Park, N.J., U.S.	C4	107
Ascención, Mex.	A3	63
Ascension, co., La., U.S.	D5	95
Ascension, i., St. Hel.	G4	42
Aschaffenburg, F.R.Ger.	D4	18
Aschersleben, Ger.D.R.	C5	18
Ascoli Piceno, Italy	D6	21
Ascona, Switz.	D6	21
Ascope, Peru	C2	58
Ascotán, Chile	D2	55
Ascot-Corner, P.Q., Can.	D6	74
Ascutney, Vt., U.S.	E4	122
Ascutney, Mount, mtn., Vt., U.S.	E4	122
Aseb, Eth.	D4	47
Asela, Eth.	C4	47
Äsele, Swe.	E7	14
Asenovgrad, Bul.	E7	24
Asfar, Tall al, mtn., Jord.	D7	41
Asha, Sov. Un.	B5	28
Ashanti, prov., Ghana	E4	45
Ashaway, R.I., U.S.	F1	116
Ashbourne, Eng., U.K.	A6	12
Ashburn, Ga., U.S.	E3	87
Ashburn, Mo., U.S.	B6	102
Ashburn, Va., U.S.	A5	123
Ashburton, N.Z.	O13	51
Ashburton, stm., Austl.	D2	50
Ashby, Al., U.S.	B3	78
Ashby, Mn., U.S.	D2	100
Ashby, Ne., U.S.	B4	104
Ashbyburg, Ky., U.S.	C2	94
Ashcroft, B.C., Can.	D7	69
Ashdod, Isr.	B7	41
Ashdot Ya'aqov, Isr.	B7	41
Ashdown, Ar., U.S.	D1	81
Ashe, co., N.C., U.S.	A1	110
Asheboro, N.C., U.S.	B3	110
Ashepoo, stm., S.C., U.S.	F6	117
Asher, Ok., U.S.	C5	113
Ashern, Mb., Can.	D2	70
Asherton, Tx., U.S.	E3	120
Asherville, Ks., U.S.	C6	93
Asheville, N.C., U.S.	f10	110
Ashfield, Ma., U.S.	A2	98
Ash Flat, Ar., U.S.	A4	81
Ashford, Eng., U.K.	C8	12
Ashford, Al., U.S.	D4	78
Ashford, Ct., U.S.	B7	84
Ashford, W.V., U.S.	m12	125
Ash Fork, Az., U.S.	B3	80

Name	Map Ref	Page
Ash Grove, Mo., U.S.	D4	102
Ashikaga, Japan	H9	33
Ashington, Eng., U.K.	E7	13
Ashio, Japan	H9	33
Ashizuri, Cape, c., Japan	J6	33
Ashkhabad, Sov. Un.	F8	29
Ashkum, Il., U.S.	C6	90
Ash Lake, Mn., U.S.	B6	100
Ashland, Al., U.S.	B4	78
Ashland, Ca., U.S.	*h8	82
Ashland, Il., U.S.	D3	90
Ashland, Ks., U.S.	E4	93
Ashland, Ky., U.S.	B7	94
Ashland, La., U.S.	B2	95
Ashland, Me., U.S.	B4	96
Ashland, Ma., U.S.	g10	98
Ashland, Ms., U.S.	A4	101
Ashland, Mo., U.S.	C5	102
Ashland, Mt., U.S.	E10	103
Ashland, Ne., U.S.	C9	104
Ashland, N.H., U.S.	C3	106
Ashland, Oh., U.S.	B3	112
Ashland, Ok., U.S.	C5	113
Ashland, Or., U.S.	E4	114
Ashland, Pa., U.S.	E9	115
Ashland, Va., U.S.	C5	123
Ashland, Wi., U.S.	B3	126
Ashland, co., Oh., U.S.	B3	112
Ashland, co., Wi., U.S.	B3	126
Ashland, Mount, mtn., Or., U.S.	E4	114
Ashland City, Tn., U.S.	A4	119
Ashland Reservoir, res., Ma., U.S.	h10	98
Ashley, Il., U.S.	E4	90
Ashley, In., U.S.	A7	91
Ashley, Mi., U.S.	E6	99
Ashley, Mo., U.S.	B6	102
Ashley, N.D., U.S.	C6	111
Ashley, Oh., U.S.	B3	112
Ashley, Pa., U.S.	n17	115
Ashley, co., Ar., U.S.	D4	81
Ashley, stm., S.C., U.S.	F7	117
Ashley Creek, stm., Ut., U.S.	C6	121
Ashley Falls, Ma., U.S.	B1	98
Ashmont, Ab., Can.	B5	68
Ashmore, Il., U.S.	D5	90
Ashmore Islands, is., Austl.	B3	50
Ashmūn, Eg.	D2	41
Ashnola, stm., N.A.	A5	124
Ashokan, N.Y., U.S.	D6	109
Ashokan Reservoir, res., N.Y., U.S.	D6	109
Ashport, Tn., U.S.	B2	119
Ashqelon, Isr.	B3	38
Ash Shabakah, Iraq	B4	38
Ash Shabb, well, Eg.	E5	43
Ash Shallāl, Eg.	E6	43
Ash Shallūfah, Eg.	D4	41
Ash Shamāliyah (Northern), prov., Sud.	B2	47
Ash Shāriqah, U.A.E.	C5	38
Ash Sharqāt, Iraq	B4	38
Ash Shaṭrah, Iraq	F3	39
Ash Shaṭṭ, Egypt	G9	40
Ash Shawāshinah, Eg.	E2	41
Ash Shawbak, Jord.	D7	41
Ash Shaykh Jarrāḥ (part of Jerusalem), Isr. Occ.	m14	41
Ash Shaykh Miskīn, Syria	B8	41
Ash Shaykh Sa'd, Syria	B7	41
Ash Shiḥr, P.D.R.Yem.	D4	38
Ash Shumlul, Sau. Ar.	H3	39
Ash Shurayk, Sud.	B3	47
Ash Springs, Nv., U.S.	F6	105
Ashtabula, Oh., U.S.	A5	112
Ashtabula, co., Oh., U.S.	A5	112
Ashtabula, Lake, res., N.D., U.S.	B8	111
Ashton, On., Can.	B8	73
Ashton, Id., U.S.	E7	89
Ashton, Il., U.S.	B4	90
Ashton, Ia., U.S.	A2	92
Ashton, Md., U.S.	B3	97
Ashton, Mi., U.S.	E5	99
Ashton, Ne., U.S.	C7	104
Ashton, R.I., U.S.	B4	116
Ashton, S.D., U.S.	C7	118
Ashuanipi Lake, l., Nf., Can.	h8	72
Ashuelot, N.H., U.S.	E2	106
Ashuelot, stm., N.H., U.S.	E2	106
Ashville, Ab., Can.	D1	70
Ashville, Al., U.S.	B3	78
Ashville, Oh., U.S.	C3	112
Ashwaubenon, Wi., U.S.	D5	126
Ashwood, Or., U.S.	C6	114
Ashwood, Tn., U.S.	B4	119
Asia	E11	30
Asiago, Italy	D7	20
Asia Minor, reg., Tur.	C10	40
Asifābād, India	H7	37
Asiga, Puntan, c., N. Mar. Is.	D7	52
Asiga Point, c., Guam	M10	52
Asinara, Gulf of, b., Italy	D2	23
Asinara Island, i., Italy	D2	23
Asino, Sov. Un.	B11	28
'Asīr, reg., Sau. Ar.	D4	38
'Aṣīrah ash Shamāliyah, Isr. Occ.	g12	41
Asker, Nor.	p28	14
Askersund, Swe.	H6	14
Askew, Ms., U.S.	A3	101
Askham, S. Afr.	C3	49
Askim, Nor.	p29	14
Askim, Swe.	A5	15
Askival, mtn., Scot., U.K.	D2	13
Askö, i., Swe.	u35	14
Askov, Mn., U.S.	D6	100
Āsmār, Afg.	D15	39
Asmara (Asmera), Eth.	B4	47
Asnæs, Den.	C5	15
Asnebumskit Hill, hill, Ma., U.S.	B4	98
Åsnen, l., Swe.	B8	15
Asnières [-sur-Seine], Fr.	C5	16
Asopós, stm., Grc.	g11	25
Asosa, Eth.	G13	47
Asotin, Wa., U.S.	C8	124
Asotin, co., Wa., U.S.	C8	124
Asotin Creek, stm., Wa., U.S.	C8	124
Aspe, Spain	C5	22
Aspen, Co., U.S.	B4	83
Aspen Butte, mtn., Or., U.S.	E4	114
Aspen Hill, Md., U.S.	*B3	97
Aspen Hill, Tn., U.S.	B4	119
Asperg, F.R.Ger.	E4	19
Aspermont, Tx., U.S.	C2	120
Aspers, Pa., U.S.	G7	115
Aspinwall, Ia., U.S.	C2	92
Aspinwall, Pa., U.S.	k14	115
Aspiring, Mount, mtn., N.Z.	P12	51
Aspres [-sur-Buëch], Fr.	E1	20
Asprópirgos, Grc.	g11	25
Aspy Bay, b., N.S., Can.	C9	71
Asquith, Sk., Can.	E2	75

Assabet, stm., Ma., U.S.	g9	98
Aṣ Ṣabyā, Sau. Ar.	D4	38
Aṣ Ṣaff, Eg.	E3	41
Aṣ Ṣāfī, Jord.	C7	41
Assaikwatamo, stm., Mb., Can.	A3	70
Aṣ Ṣāliḥīyah, Eg.	D4	41
Aṣ Sallūm, Eg.	B2	38
Aṣ Salmān, Iraq	B4	38
Aṣ Salṭ, Jord.	F10	40
Assam, state, India	C9	36
Aṣ Samū', Isr. Occ.	C7	41
Aṣ Ṣanamayn, Syria	A8	41
Assaria, Ks., U.S.	D6	93
Assateague Island, i., U.S.	D7	97
Assateague Island National Seashore, U.S.	D7	97
Assawoman Bay, b., Md., U.S.	D7	97
Assawompset Pond, l., Ma., U.S.	C6	98
Assean Lake, l., Mb., Can.	A3	70
Assen, Neth.	A7	16
Assens, Den.	B4	15
Assens, Den.	C3	15
Aṣ Sinbillāwayn, Eg.	D3	41
Assini, I.C.	E4	45
Assiniboia, Sk., Can.	H3	75
Assiniboine, stm., Can.	E2	70
Assiniboine, Mount, mtn., Can.	D3	68
Assinica, Réserve, P.Q., Can.	h11	74
Assinika, stm., Mb., Can.	C4	70
Assinippi, Ma., U.S.	h12	98
Assis, Braz.	C2	56
Assis Brasil, Braz.	D4	58
Assisi, Italy	C4	23
Asso, Italy	E7	21
Assonet, Ma., U.S.	C5	98
Aṣ Suez, reg., Sud.	D3	47
Aṣ Sūfīyah, Eg.	B4	38
Aṣ Sulaymānīyah, Iraq	C4	38
Aṣ Sulaymānīyah, Sau. Ar.	C4	38
Aṣ Sulayyil, Sau. Ar.	A6	47
Aṣ Sulṭān, Libya	C3	43
Aṣ Summān, plat., Sau. Ar.	H3	39
Assumption, Il., U.S.	D4	90
Assumption, co., La., U.S.	E4	95
As Suwaydā', Syria	F11	40
Astakós, Grc.	C3	25
Āstārā, Iran	B4	39
Astipálaia, i., Grc.	D6	40
Asti, Italy	B2	23
Astipálaia, i., Grc.	D6	40
Aston, Pa., U.S.	*p20	115
Aston-Jonction, P.Q., Can.	C5	74
Astor, Fl., U.S.	C5	86
Astorga, Spain	A2	22
Astoria, Il., U.S.	C3	90
Astoria, Or., U.S.	A3	114
Astoria, S.D., U.S.	C9	118
Astorville, On., Can.	A5	73
Astrakhan, Sov. Un.	E7	29
Astura, stm., Italy	h9	23
Asturias, hist reg., Spain	A2	22
Asuisui, Cape, c., W. Sam.	F11	52
Asuke, Japan	n16	33
Asunción, Para.	E4	55
Asunción Mita, Guat.	C3	62
Asunción Nochixtlán, Mex.	o15	63
Asunden, l., Swe.	A7	15
Aswān, Eg.	C3	38
Aswān High Dam, Eg.	C3	38
Asyūṭ, Eg.	C3	38
Atacama, prov., Chile	E2	55
Atacama, Salar de, pl., Chile	D2	55
Atacama Desert, des., Chile	D2	55
Ata'īṭah, Jabal al, mtn., Jord.	G10	40
Atakpamé, Togo	E5	45
Atalaia, Braz.	k5	57
Atalaia do Norte, Braz.	B3	58
Atalándi, Grc.	C4	25
Atalaya, Peru	D3	58
Atalissa, Ia., U.S.	C6	92
Atami, Japan	n18	33
Ataq, Maur.	B2	45
'Aṭārūt, Isr. Occ.	h11	41
Atascadero, Ca., U.S.	E3	82
Atascosa, co., Tx., U.S.	E3	120
Atáviros, mtn., Grc.	D6	25
'Aṭbarah, Sud.	B3	47
'Aṭbarah, stm., Afr.	B4	47
Atbasar, Sov. Un.	D9	29
Atchafalaya, stm., La., U.S.	D4	95
Atchafalaya Bay, b., La., U.S.	E4	95
Atchison, Ks., U.S.	C8	93
Atchison, co., Ks., U.S.	C8	93
Atchison, co., Mo., U.S.	A2	102
Atco, N.J., U.S.	D3	107
Atgidon, Puntan, c., N. Mar. Is.	E7	52
Ath, Bel.	D3	17
Athabasca, Ab., Can.	B4	68
Athabasca, stm., Ab., Can.	f8	68
Athabasca, Lake, l., Can.	m7	75
Athalia, Oh., U.S.	D3	112
Athalmer, B.C., Can.	D10	69
Athapapuskow Lake, l., Mb., Can.	A1	70
Atha Road (part of Pickering), On., Can.	k15	73
Athboy, Ire.	D5	11
Athelstan, P.Q., Can.	D3	74
Athena, Or., U.S.	B8	114
Athenry, Ire.	D3	11
Athens, On., Can.	C9	73
Athens (Athínai), Grc.	D4	40
Athens, Al., U.S.	A3	78
Athens, Ga., U.S.	C2	81
Athens, Il., U.S.	C3	87
Athens, In., U.S.	D4	90
Athens, La., U.S.	B5	91
Athens, Me., U.S.	B2	95
Athens, Mi., U.S.	D3	96
Athens, N.Y., U.S.	F5	99
Athens, Oh., U.S.	C7	109
Athens, Pa., U.S.	C3	112
Athens, Tn., U.S.	C8	115
Athens, Tx., U.S.	D9	119
Athens, Vt., U.S.	C5	120
Athens, W.V., U.S.	E3	122
Athens, co., Oh., U.S.	D3	125
Atherley, On., Can.	C3	112
Atherton, Austl.	C5	73
Atherton, Ca., U.S.	C8	51
Athertonville, Ky., U.S.	*k8	82
Athi, stm., Kenya	C4	94
Athínai see Athens, Grc.	B6	48
Athlone, Ire.	D3	10
Athok, Burma	E10	36

Athol, Id., U.S.	B2	89
Athol, Ks., U.S.	C5	93
Athol, Ma., U.S.	A3	98
Athol, S.D., U.S.	C7	118
Athol Island, i., Bah.	m18	64
Ath Thamad, Eg.	D6	43
Athy, Ire.	D3	10
Ati, Chad	C3	46
Atibaia, Braz.	m8	56
Atico, Peru	E3	58
Aticonipi, Lac, l., P.Q., Can.	C2	72
Atikameg, Ab., Can.	B3	68
Atik Lake, l., Mb., Can.	B4	70
Atikonak Lake, l., Nf., Can.	h8	72
Atimonan, Phil.	p13	34
Atiquizaya, El Sal.	D3	62
Atka, Ak., U.S.	E5	79
Atka Island, i., Ak., U.S.	E5	79
Atkarsk, Sov. Un.	F15	27
Atkins, Ar., U.S.	B3	81
Atkins, Va., U.S.	D1	123
Atkinson, Ga., U.S.	E5	87
Atkinson, Il., U.S.	B3	90
Atkinson, Ne., U.S.	B7	104
Atkinson, N.H., U.S.	E4	106
Atkinson, N.C., U.S.	C4	110
Atkinson, co., Ga., U.S.	E5	87
Atkinson, Lake, l., Mb., Can.	A4	70
Atlanta, Ar., U.S.	D2	81
Atlanta, Ga., U.S.	C2	87
Atlanta, Id., U.S.	F3	89
Atlanta, Il., U.S.	C4	90
Atlanta, In., U.S.	D5	91
Atlanta, Ks., U.S.	E7	93
Atlanta, La., U.S.	C3	95
Atlanta, Mi., U.S.	C6	99
Atlanta, Mo., U.S.	B5	102
Atlanta, Ne., U.S.	D6	104
Atlanta, N.Y., U.S.	C3	109
Atlanta, Oh., U.S.	C2	112
Atlanta, Tx., U.S.	C5	120
Atlantic, Ia., U.S.	C2	92
Atlantic, N.C., U.S.	C6	110
Atlantic, co., N.J., U.S.	E3	107
Atlantic Beach, Fl., U.S.	m9	86
Atlantic City, N.J., U.S.	E4	107
Atlantic City, Wy., U.S.	D4	127
Atlantic Highlands, N.J., U.S.	C4	107
Atlantic Mine, Mi., U.S.	A2	99
Atlántico, dept., Col.	A2	60
Atlantic Ocean	G8	5
Atlantic Peak, mtn., Wy., U.S.	D3	127
Auglaize, co., Oh., U.S.	A1	112
Auglaize, stm., Oh., U.S.	A1	112
Atlas Mountains, mts., Afr.	C4	44
Atlas Saharien, mts., Alg.	C5	44
Atlee, Ab., Can.	D5	68
Atlin, B.C., Can.	m16	69
Atlin Lake, l., Can.	E6	66
'Atlit, Isr.	B6	41
Atlixco, Mex.	n14	63
Atmore, Al., U.S.	D2	78
Atna Peak, mtn., B.C., Can.	C3	69
Atocha, Bol.	D2	55
Atoka, N.M., U.S.	E5	108
Atoka, Ok., U.S.	C5	113
Atoka, Tn., U.S.	B2	119
Atoka, co., Ok., U.S.	C5	113
Atoka Reservoir, res., Ok., U.S.	C5	113
Atomic City, Id., U.S.	F6	89
Atotonilco el Alto, Mex.	m12	63
Atoyac, Mex.	m12	63
Atoyac, stm., Mex.	n14	63
Atrak (Atrek), stm., Asia	B5	38
Ätran, stm., Swe.	B6	15
Atrato, stm., Col.	B2	60
Atrek (Atrak), stm., Asia	C7	39
Atsugi, Japan	n18	33
Atsukeshi Bay, b., Japan	E12	33
Atsuma, Japan	E10	33
Atsumi, Japan	o16	33
Atsumi Bay, b., Japan	o16	33
At Tabbīn, Eg.	E3	41
Aṭ Ṭafīlah, Jord.	G10	40
Aṭ Ṭā'if, Sau. Ar.	C4	38
Attala, co., Ms., U.S.	B4	101
Attalla, Al., U.S.	A3	78
Aṭ Ṭallāb, Libya	E4	43
Aṭ Ṭallāb, Libya	C4	43
Attapu, Laos	C3	34
Attapulgus, Ga., U.S.	F2	87
'Aṭṭārah, Isr. Occ.	h11	41
Attawapiskat, On., Can.	n19	73
Attawapiskat, stm., On., Can.	n18	73
Attean Pond, l., Me., U.S.	C2	96
Atterberry, Il., U.S.	D3	90
Attica, In., U.S.	D3	91
Attica, Mi., U.S.	E7	99
Attica, N.Y., U.S.	C2	109
Attica, Oh., U.S.	A3	112
Attica, hist reg., Grc.	g11	25
Attigny, Fr.	E4	17
Attikamagen Lake, l., Nf., Can.	g8	72
Aṭ Ṭīnah, Eg.	C4	41
Attleboro, Ma., U.S.	C5	98
Attleborough, Eng., U.K.	B9	12
Attu Island, i., Ak., U.S.	E2	79
Aṭ Ṭūr, Eg.	D6	43
Aṭ Ṭūr, Isr. Occ.	m14	41
Aṭ Ṭurayf, Sau. Ar.	B3	38
Aṭ Ṭuwayyah, Sau. Ar.	I13	40
Attymon, Ire.	D3	11
Atui, Uad, val., Afr.	B2	45
Ātu'au, Am. Sam.	F13	52
Ātvidaberg, Swe.	H6	14
Atwater, Sk., Can.	G4	75
Atwater, Ca., U.S.	D3	82
Atwater, Mn., U.S.	E4	100
Atwater, Oh., U.S.	D7	73
Atwood, Co., U.S.	A7	84
Atwood, Il., U.S.	D5	90
Atwood, Ks., U.S.	C2	93
Atwood, Tn., U.S.	B3	119
Atwood Lake, res., Oh., U.S.	B4	112
Atwoodville, Ct., U.S.	B7	84
Aua, Am. Sam.	F13	52
Auau Channel, strt., Hi., U.S.	C5	88
Aubagne, Fr.	F4	17
Aube, dept., Fr.	F4	17
Aube, stm., Fr.	E5	16
Aubenas, Fr.	E6	16
Aubervilliers, Fr.	g10	16
Aubigny-sur-Nère, Fr.	D5	16
Aubin, Fr.	E5	16
Aubrey, P.Q., Can.	D4	74

Aubrey, Ar., U.S.	C5	81
Aubrey Cliffs, clf, Az., U.S.	B2	80
Auburn, On., Can.	D3	73
Auburn, Al., U.S.	C4	78
Auburn, Ca., U.S.	C3	82
Auburn, Ga., U.S.	B3	87
Auburn, Il., U.S.	D4	90
Auburn, In., U.S.	B7	91
Auburn, Ia., U.S.	B2	92
Auburn, Ks., U.S.	D8	93
Auburn, Ky., U.S.	D3	94
Auburn, Me., U.S.	D2	96
Auburn, Ma., U.S.	B4	98
Auburn, Mi., U.S.	E6	99
Auburn, Ms., U.S.	D3	101
Auburn, Ne., U.S.	D10	104
Auburn, N.H., U.S.	D4	106
Auburn, N.Y., U.S.	C4	109
Auburn, N.D., U.S.	A8	111
Auburn, Pa., U.S.	E9	115
Auburn, Wa., U.S.	B3	124
Auburn, W.V., U.S.	B4	125
Auburn, Wy., U.S.	D1	127
Auburndale, Fl., U.S.	D5	86
Auburndale, Wi., U.S.	D3	126
Auburn Heights, Mi., U.S.	F7	99
Auburntown, Tn., U.S.	B5	119
Aubusson, Fr.	E5	16
Auch, Fr.	F4	17
Auchel, Fr.	D2	17
Auchterarder, Scot., U.K.	D5	13
Aucilla, Fl., U.S.	B3	86
Aucilla, stm., Fl., U.S.	B3	86
Auckland, N.Z.	L15	51
Auckland Islands, is., N.Z.	J8	2
Aude, dept., Fr.	F5	16
Aude, stm., Fr.	F5	16
Audet, P.Q., Can.	D7	74
Audierne, Fr.	C1	16
Audincourt, Fr.	D7	16
Audrain, co., Mo., U.S.	B6	102
Audubon, Ia., U.S.	C3	92
Audubon, Mn., U.S.	D3	100
Audubon, N.J., U.S.	D2	107
Audubon, co., Ia., U.S.	C2	92
Audun-le-Roman, Fr.	E5	17
Aue, Ger.D.R.	C6	18
Auerbach, Ger.D.R.	C7	19
Augathella, Austl.	B6	51
Auggen, F.R.Ger.	A4	21
Aughnacloy, N. Ire., U.K.	C5	11
Aughrim, Ire.	E5	11
Aughty, Slieve, mts., Ire.	D3	11
Auglaize, co., Oh., U.S.	A1	112
Au Gres, Mi., U.S.	D7	99
Augsburg, F.R.Ger.	D5	18
Augusta, Austl.	F2	50
Augusta, Italy	F5	23
Augusta, Ar., U.S.	B4	81
Augusta, Ga., U.S.	C5	87
Augusta, Il., U.S.	C3	90
Augusta, Ks., U.S.	E7	93
Augusta, Ky., U.S.	B6	94
Augusta, Me., U.S.	D3	96
Augusta, Mi., U.S.	F5	99
Augusta, Mo., U.S.	C7	102
Augusta, Mt., U.S.	C4	103
Augusta, Oh., U.S.	B4	112
Augusta, W.V., U.S.	B6	125
Augusta, Wi., U.S.	D2	126
Augusta, co., Va., U.S.	B3	123
Augusta Springs, Va., U.S.	B3	123
Augusta Victoria Hospital, Isr. Occ.	m14	41
Augustenborg, Den.	D3	15
Augustów, Pol.	B7	26
Augustus, Mount, mtn., Austl.	D2	50
Aulander, N.C., U.S.	A5	110
Auld, Lake, l., Austl.	D3	50
Aulendorf, F.R.Ger.	B5	20
Aulnay-sous-Bois, Fr.	g11	16
Aulne, stm., Fr.	C2	16
Aulneau Peninsula, pen., On., Can.	E4	70
Aulnoye [-Aymeries], Fr.	D3	17
Ault, Co., U.S.	A6	83
Ault, Piz, mtn., Switz.	E7	21
Aumale, Fr.	E2	17
Aumsville, Or., U.S.	k12	114
Auneuil, Fr.	E2	17
Auning, Den.	B4	15
Auno, Nig.	D7	45
Aunu'u Island, i., Am. Sam.	K6	35
Aur, i., Malay.	K6	35
Auraiya, India	D7	37
Aurangābād, India	B3	37
Auray, Fr.	D2	16
Aurelia, Ia., U.S.	B2	92
Aurelian Springs, N.C., U.S.	A5	110
Aurich, F.R.Ger.	C2	18
Auriflama, Braz.	C3	56
Aurillac, Fr.	C5	16
Aurland, Nor.	C2	14
Aurora, On., Can.	C5	73
Aurora, Guy.	A3	59
Aurora, Co., U.S.	B6	83
Aurora, Il., U.S.	B5	90
Aurora, In., U.S.	F8	91
Aurora, Me., U.S.	D6	96
Aurora, Mn., U.S.	C6	100
Aurora, Mo., U.S.	E4	102
Aurora, Ne., U.S.	D7	104
Aurora, N.Y., U.S.	C4	109
Aurora, N.C., U.S.	B6	110
Aurora, Oh., U.S.	A4	112
Aurora, S.D., U.S.	C8	118
Aurora, Ut., U.S.	E4	121
Aurora, W.V., U.S.	B5	125
Aurora, co., S.D., U.S.	D7	118
Aurora Center, S.D., U.S.	D7	118
Aurora by the Sea, N.J., U.S.	C2	49
Aus, Nmb.	D6	99
Au Sable, stm., Mi., U.S.	f11	109
Ausable, stm., N.Y., U.S.	D6	99
Au Sable, North Branch, stm., Mi., U.S.	f11	109
Au Sable Forks, N.Y., U.S.	B4	99
Au Sable Point, c., Mi., U.S.	D7	99
Au Sable Point, c., Mi., U.S.		
Auschwitz see Oświęcim, Pol.	D9	20
Austell, Ga., U.S.	h7	87
Austin, Mb., Can.	E2	70
Austin, In., U.S.	G6	91
Austin, Ky., U.S.	D4	94
Austin, Mn., U.S.	G6	100
Austin, Nv., U.S.	D4	105
Austin, Oh., U.S.	C8	114

Austin, Pa., U.S.	C5	115
Austin, R.I., U.S.	E2	116
Austin, Tx., U.S.	D4	120
Austin, co., Tx., U.S.	E4	120
Austin, Lake, l., Austl.	E2	50
Austinburg, Oh., U.S.	A5	112
Austinville, Ia., U.S.	B5	92
Austinville, Va., U.S.	D2	123
Australia, ctry., Oc.	E6	50
Australian Capital Territory, ter., Austl.	G7	51
Austria, ctry., Eur.	E7	18
Axial Basin, Co., U.S.	A2	83
Austwell, Tx., U.S.	E4	120
Axim, Ghana	F4	45
Autauga, co., Al., U.S.	C3	78
Autaugaville, Al., U.S.	C3	78
Auth, Ne., U.S.	D10	104
Authie, stm., Fr.	D2	17
Autlán de Navarro, Mex.	D4	63
Autun, Fr.	D6	16
Auvergne, Ar., U.S.	B4	81
Auvergne, hist reg., Fr.	E5	16
Auvergne Mountains, mts., Fr.	E5	16
Auvers [-sur-Oise], Fr.	E2	17
Aux Barques, Pointe, c., Mi., U.S.	D8	99
Auxerre, Fr.	D5	16
Auxi-le-Château, Fr.	D2	17
Auxonne, Fr.	D6	16
Auxvasse, Mo., U.S.	B6	102
Auzangate, Nevado, mtn., Peru	D3	58
Ava, Il., U.S.	F4	90
Ava, Mo., U.S.	E5	102
Ava, Oh., U.S.	C4	112
Avakubi, Zaire	A4	48
Avalon, Fr.	D5	16
Avalon, Ca., U.S.	F4	82
Avalon, Ms., U.S.	B3	101
Avalon, Mo., U.S.	B4	102
Avalon, N.J., U.S.	E3	107
Avalon, Pa., U.S.	h13	115
Avalon, Lake, res., N.M., U.S.	E5	108
Avalon Peninsula, pen., Nf., Can.	E5	72
Avanos, Tur.	C10	40
Avant, Ok., U.S.	A5	113
Avard, Ok., U.S.	A3	113
Avaré, Braz.	C3	56
Avdira, Grc.	B1	112
Avella, Pa., U.S.	F1	115
Avellaneda, Arg.	A5	54
Avellino, Italy	D5	23
Avenal, Ca., U.S.	E3	82
Avenel, N.J., U.S.	k7	107
Avening, On., Can.	C4	73
Avenue, Md., U.S.	D4	97
Avera, Ga., U.S.	C4	87
Averill Park, N.Y., U.S.	C7	109
Aversa, Italy	D5	23
Avery, Id., U.S.	B3	89
Avery, Ok., U.S.	A5	113
Avery, Tx., U.S.	C5	120
Avery, co., N.C., U.S.	A1	110
Avery Island, La., U.S.	E4	95
Avesnes, Fr.	D3	17
Avesta, Swe.	G7	14
Avezzano, Italy	C4	23
Aviemore, Scot., U.K.	D5	13
Avigliano, Italy	D5	23
Avignon, Fr.	F6	16
Ávila, Spain	B3	22
Avila Beach, Ca., U.S.	E3	82
Avilés, Spain	A3	22
Avilla, In., U.S.	B7	91
Avilla, Mo., U.S.	D3	102
Avis, Pa., U.S.	D7	115
Aviston, Il., U.S.	E4	90
Avize, Fr.	F4	17
Avlón, Grc.	g11	25
Avoca, On., Can.	B7	73
Avoca, Ar., U.S.	A1	81
Avoca, Ia., U.S.	C2	92
Avoca, Mi., U.S.	E8	99
Avoca, N.Y., U.S.	C3	109
Avoca, Pa., U.S.	D10	115
Avoca, Tx., U.S.	C3	120
Avoca, Wi., U.S.	E3	126
Avocado Heights, Ca., U.S.	*m13	82
Avola, B.C., Can.	D5	69
Avola, Italy	F5	23
Avon, On., Can.	B5	54
Avon, Ct., U.S.	B4	84
Avon, Il., U.S.	C3	90
Avon, Ia., U.S.	e8	92
Avon, Ma., U.S.	B5	98
Avon, Mn., U.S.	E4	100
Avon, N.Y., U.S.	C3	109
Avon, N.C., U.S.	B7	110
Avon, Oh., U.S.	A3	112
Avon, S.D., U.S.	D7	118
Avon, co., Eng., U.K.	E5	12
Avon, stm., Austl.	F2	50
Avon, stm., Eng., U.K.	E6	12
Avon, stm., Eng., U.K.	E6	12
Avon, stm., Scot., U.K.	C5	13
Avon, Point, c., Oh., U.S.	A3	112
Avondale, Az., U.S.	*C3	80
Avondale, Co., U.S.	C6	83
Avondale, Mo., U.S.	h10	102
Avondale, Pa., U.S.	*C1	115
Avondale, R.I., U.S.	G10	115
Avondale Estates, Ga., U.S.	h8	87
Avon Lake, Oh., U.S.	A3	112
Avon Lake, Oh., U.S.	A3	112
Avonmore, Pa., U.S.	F2	115
Avon Park, Fl., U.S.	E5	86
Avoyelles, co., La., U.S.	C3	95
Avranches, Fr.	D5	16
Awa Island, i., Japan	G9	33
Awaji, Japan	o14	33
Awaji Island, i., Japan	I7	33

'Awartā, Isr. Occ.	B7	41
Awasa, Eth.	D4	47
Awash, Eth.	D5	47
Awash, stm., Eth.	C5	47
Awbārī, Libya	D2	43
Awdheegle, Som.	E5	47
Awe, Loch, l., Scot., U.K.	D3	13
Awjilah, Libya	D4	43
Awlef, Alg.	D5	44
Axel, Neth.	C3	17
Axel Heiberg Island, i., N.T., Can.	m33	66
Axim, Ghana	F4	45
Axiós (Vardar), stm., Eur.	B4	40
Axis, Al., U.S.	E1	78
Axminster, Eng., U.K.	D2	17
Axson, Ga., U.S.	E4	87
Axtell, Ks., U.S.	C7	93
Axtell, Ne., U.S.	D6	104
Axtell, Ut., U.S.	D4	121
Aÿ, Fr.	C5	16
Ay, stm., Sov. Un.	B5	28
Ayabaca, Peru	B2	58
Ayabe, Japan	n14	33
Ayacucho, Arg.	B5	54
Ayacucho, Peru	D3	58
Ayacucho, dept., Peru	D3	58
Ayaguz, Sov. Un.	E11	29
Ayamonte, Spain	D2	22
Ayan, Sov. Un.	D16	29
Ayapel, Col.	B2	60
Ayaviri, Peru	D3	58
Aycliffe, Eng., U.K.	F7	13
Aydar, stm., Sov. Un.	G12	27
Ayden, N.C., U.S.	B5	110
Aydin, Tur.	D6	40
Aydlett, N.C., U.S.	A7	110
Ayer, Ma., U.S.	A4	98
Ayers Cliff, P.Q., Can.	D5	74
Ayers Rock, mtn., Austl.	E5	50
Ayía, Grc.	C6	25
Ayía Paraskeví, Grc.	C6	25
Ayiásos, Grc.	C6	25
Áyioi Theódhoroi, Grc.	h10	25
Áyios Dhimítrios, Grc.	g11	25
Áyios Evstrátios, i., Grc.	C5	25
Áyios Nikólaos, Grc.	E5	25
Aylen Lake, l., On., Can.	B7	73
Aylesbury, Sk., Can.	G3	75
Aylesbury, Eng., U.K.	E6	10
Aylesford, N.S., Can.	D5	71
Aylett, Va., U.S.	C5	123
Aylmer, Mount, mtn., Ab., Can.	D3	68
Aylmer East, P.Q., Can.	D2	74
Aylmer Lake, l., N.T., Can.	D11	66
Aylmer West, On., Can.	E4	73
Aylsham, Sk., Can.	D4	75
'Ayn Yabrūd, Isr. Occ.	h11	41
Ayon Island, i., Sov. Un.	B9	29
Ayora, Spain	C5	22
Ayorou, Niger	D2	100
'Ayoûn el 'Atroûs, Maur.	C3	45
Ayr, Austl.	C8	50
Ayr, On., Can.	D4	73
Ayr, Scot., U.K.	C4	10
Ayr, Ne., U.S.	D7	104
Ayr, N.D., U.S.	B8	111
Ayre, Point of, c., I. of Man	F4	13
Ayrshire, Ia., U.S.	A3	92
Aysary, Sov. Un.	C8	29
Aysha, Eth.	C5	47
Ayton, On., Can.	C4	73
Ayton, Bul.	D8	24
Ayu Islands, is., Indon.	E8	34
Ayutla [de los Libres], Mex.	D5	63
Ayvacık, Tur.	C6	40
Ayvalık, Tur.	C6	40
Azalea Park, Fl., U.S.	*D5	86
Azalia, In., U.S.	F6	91
Azamagama, Japan	O5	52
Azangaro, Peru	D3	58
Azamgarh, India	D9	37
Azaouâd, reg., Mali	C4	45
Azaouak, Vallée de l', val., Afr.	D5	45
Azare, Nig.	D7	45
Āžar Shahr, Iran	A2	38
Azcapotzalco (part of Mexico City), Mex.	h9	63
Azemmour, Mor.	C3	44
Azerbaijan, hist reg., Iran	B4	38
Azerbaijan S.S.R., state, Sov. Un.	E7	29
Azizcohos Lake, l., Me., U.S.	C1	96
Azogues, Ec.	B2	58
Azores, is., Port.	g9	44
Azov, Sov. Un.	H12	27
Azov, Sea of, Sov. Un.	E6	29
Azrou, Mor.	C3	44
Aztec, N.M., U.S.	A2	108
Aztec, Az., U.S.	C3	80
Aztec Peak, mtn., Az., U.S.	D5	80
Aztec Ruins National Monument, N.M., U.S.	A1	108
Azua, Dom. Rep.	E8	64
Azuaga, Spain	C3	22
Azuay, prov., Ec.	B2	58
Azuero, Peninsula de, pen., Pan.	G7	62
Azul, Arg.	B5	54
Azul, Cordillera, mts., Peru	C2	58
Azul, Serra, plat., Braz.	A2	56
Azurduy, Bol.	c3	55
Azusa, Ca., U.S.	m13	82
Az Zabdānī, Syria	F11	40
Az Zāhirīyah, Isr. Occ.	C6	41
Az Zaqāzīq, Eg.	B3	38
Az Zāwiyah, Libya	B3	43
'Azzāz, Ra's, c., Libya	C4	43
Azzel Matti, Sebkha, pl., Alg.	D5	44
Az Zubayr, Iraq	F3	39
'Azzūn, Isr. Occ.	g11	41

B

Baal, F.R.Ger.	C6	17
Baar, Switz.	B6	21
Baardheere, Som.	E5	47
Baargaal, Som.	C7	47
Baarle-Hertog, Bel.	C4	17
Baarn, Neth.	N5	52
Baba Burnu, c., Tur.	C6	40
Babadag, Rom.	C9	24
Babaeski, Tur.	B6	40

Name	Map Ref	Page
Babahoyo, Ec.	B2	58
Babana, Nig.	D5	45
Babanüsah, Sud.	C2	47
Babar Islands, is., Indon.	G7	34
Babati, Tan.	B6	48
Babayevo, Sov. Un.	B11	27
Babb, Mt., U.S.	B3	103
Babb Creek, stm., Pa., U.S.	C7	115
Babbie, Al., U.S.	D3	78
Babbitt, Mn., U.S.	C7	100
Babbitt, Nv., U.S.	E3	105
Babcock, Wi., U.S.	D3	126
Babelthuap International Airport, Palau	R17	52
Babelthuap Island, i., Palau	R17	52
Babenhausen, F.R.Ger.	A6	19
Babi, i., Indon.	K2	35
Babine, stm., B.C., Can.	B4	69
Babine Lake, l., B.C., Can.	B5	69
Babine Range, mts., B.C., Can.	B4	69
Babo, Indon.	F8	34
Bābol, Iran	B5	38
Bābol Sar, Iran	C6	39
Baboosic Lake, N.H., U.S.	E3	106
Baboquivari Mountains, mts., Az., U.S.	F4	80
Baboquivari Peak, mtn., Az., U.S.	F4	80
Baboua, Cen. Afr. Rep.	D2	46
Babson Park, Fl., U.S.	E5	86
Babuskin, Sov. Un.	A6	31
Babuyan Islands, is., Phil.	B6	34
Babyak, Bul.	E6	24
Babylon, N.Y., U.S.	n15	109
Baca, co., Co., U.S.	D8	83
Bacabal, Braz.	B2	57
Bacajá, stm., Braz.	C4	59
Bacalar, Mex.	D7	63
Bacan, i., Indon.	F7	34
Bacău, Rom.	B8	24
Baccalieu Island, i., Nf., Can.	D5	72
Baccarat, Fr.	C7	16
Baccaro Point, c., N.S., Can.	F4	71
Bacerac, Mex.	A3	63
Bach, Mi., U.S.	E7	99
Bacharach, F.R.Ger.	C2	19
Bach Long Vi, i., Viet.	B7	35
Back, stm., N.T., Can.	C12	66
Back, stm., S.C., U.S.	h12	117
Bac Kan, Viet.	A6	35
Bačka Palanka, Yugo.	C4	24
Bačka Topola, Yugo.	C4	24
Back Bay, N.B., Can.	D3	71
Backbone Mountain, mtn., U.S.	m12	97
Backnang, F.R.Ger.	E4	19
Backoo, N.D., U.S.	A8	111
Backus, Mn., U.S.	D4	100
Bac Lieu, Viet.	D3	35
Bac Ninh, Viet.	A3	34
Bacnotan, Phil.	n13	34
Bacobi, Az., U.S.	B5	80
Bacolod, Phil.	C6	34
Bacon, co., Ga., U.S.	E4	87
Baconton, Ga., U.S.	E2	87
Bacoor, Phil.	o13	34
Bacova, Va., U.S.	B3	123
Bac Quang, Viet.	A6	35
Bacqueville-en-Caux, Fr.	E9	12
Bácsalmás, Hung.	B4	24
Bácum, Mex.	B2	63
Bad, stm., S.D., U.S.	C5	118
Bad, stm., Wi., U.S.	B3	126
Bad Aibling, F.R.Ger.	C2	20
Badajoz, Spain	C2	22
Badalona, Spain	B7	22
Badanah, Sau. Ar.	B4	38
Bad Axe, Mi., U.S.	E8	99
Bad Bergzabern, F.R.Ger.	D2	19
Bad Berneck, F.R.Ger.	C6	19
Bad Bramstedt, F.R.Ger.	E3	15
Baddeck, N.S., Can.	C9	71
Bad Doberan, Ger.D.R.	A5	18
Bad Düben, Ger.D.R.	B7	19
Baden, On., Can.	D4	73
Baden, Switz.	E1	115
Baden, Pa., U.S.	E1	115
Baden, hist reg., F.R.Ger.	D4	18
Baden [bei Wien], Aus.	D8	18
Baden-Baden, F.R.Ger.	D4	18
Baden-Württemberg, state, F.R.Ger.	D4	19
Bad Freienwalde, Ger.D.R.	B7	18
Bad Friedrichshall, F.R.Ger.	D4	19
Badgastein, Aus.	E6	18
Badger, Nf., Can.	D3	72
Badger, Mn., U.S.	B2	100
Badger, S.D., U.S.	C8	118
Badger, stm., Co., U.S.	B7	83
Bad Godesberg, F.R.Ger.	C2	19
Bad Hersfeld, F.R.Ger.	C4	19
Bad Homburg [vor der Höhe], F.R.Ger.	C4	18
Bad Honnef, F.R.Ger.	C2	19
Bad Hönningen, F.R.Ger.	C2	19
Badia Polesine, Italy	D7	20
Badīn, Pak.	B2	37
Badin, N.C., U.S.	B2	110
Badin Lake, res., N.C., U.S.	B2	110
Bad Ischl, Aus.	E6	18
Bad Kissingen, F.R.Ger.	C5	18
Bad Kreuznach, F.R.Ger.	D3	18
Badlands, hills, S.D., U.S.	D3	118
Badlands, reg., U.S.	C2	111
Badlands National Park, S.D., U.S.	D3	118
Bad Langensalza, Ger.D.R.	C5	18
Bad Lauterberg, F.R.Ger.	B5	19
Bad Leonfelden, Aus.	E9	19
Bad Liebenwerda, Ger.D.R.	B8	19
Bad Lippspringe, F.R.Ger.	D4	19
Bad Mergentheim, F.R.Ger.	D4	19
Bad Münstereifel, F.R.Ger.	C1	19
Bad Muskau, Ger.D.R.	B9	19
Bad Neustadt [an der Saale], F.R.Ger.	C5	19
Bad Oeynhausen, F.R.Ger.	A3	19
Bad Oldesloe, F.R.Ger.	E4	15
Ba Don, Viet.	D7	35
Badong, China	E7	31
Bad Orb, F.R.Ger.	C4	19
Badoumbé, Mali	D2	45
Bad Pyrmont, F.R.Ger.	B4	19
Bad Ragaz, Switz.	E2	21
Badrah, Iraq	E2	39
Bad Reichenhall, F.R.Ger.	E6	18
Bad River Indian Reservation, Wi., U.S.	B3	126
Bad Salzuflen, F.R.Ger.	A4	19
Bad Salzungen, Ger.D.R.	C5	18
Bad Schandau, Ger.D.R.	C9	19
Bad Segeberg, F.R.Ger.	E4	15
Bad Sülze, Ger.D.R.	D6	15
Bad Tennstedt, Ger.D.R.	B5	19
Bad Tölz, F.R.Ger.	E5	18
Badu, i., Austl.	A7	50
Badulla, Sri L.	G7	36
Badwater Creek, stm., Wy., U.S.	C5	127
Bad Wildungen, F.R.Ger.	B4	19
Bad Windsheim, F.R.Ger.	D5	19
Bad Wörishofen, F.R.Ger.	B6	20
Bad Wurzach, F.R.Ger.	B5	20
Baena, Spain	D3	22
Baependi, Braz.	C4	56
Baeza, Ec.	B2	58
Baeza, Spain	D4	22
Bafang, Cam.	D2	46
Bafatá, Gui.-B.	D2	45
Baffin Bay, b., N.A.	B14	61
Baffin Bay, b., Tx., U.S.	E4	120
Baffin Island, i., N.T., Can.	C18	66
Baffin Island National Park, N.T., Can.	C19	66
Bafia, Cam.	E2	46
Bafoulabé, Mali	D2	45
Bafoussam, Cam.	*D2	46
Bāfq, Iran	B5	38
Bafra, Tur.	B10	40
Bafra Burnu, c., Tur.	B11	40
Bāft, Iran	G8	39
Bafwasende, Zaire	A4	48
Bagabag, Phil.	n13	34
Bagaces, C.R.	E7	63
Bagamoyo, Tan.	C6	48
Bagana, Nig.	E6	45
Bagansiapi-api, Indon.	E2	34
Bagata, Zaire	B2	48
Bagdad, Az., U.S.	C2	80
Bagdad, Fl., U.S.	u14	86
Bagdad, Ky., U.S.	B4	94
Baghdād, Iraq	B4	38
Bāgherhāt, Bngl.	F12	31
Bagheria, Italy	E4	23
Baghlān, Afg.	A4	36
Bagley, Ia., U.S.	C3	92
Bagley, Mn., U.S.	C3	100
Bagley, Wi., U.S.	F2	126
Bagnacavallo, Italy	E7	20
Bagnara [Calabra], Italy	E5	23
Bagnell Dam, Mo., U.S.	C5	102
Bagnères-de-Bigorre, Fr.	F4	16
Bagnères-de-Luchon, Fr.	F4	16
Bagnolet, Fr.	g10	16
Bagnols, Fr.	E6	16
Bâgø, i., Den.	C3	15
Bagoé, stm., Afr.	D3	45
Bagolino, Italy	D6	20
Bagot, co., P.Q., Can.	D5	74
Bagrationovsk, Sov. Un.	A6	26
Baguio, Phil.	B6	34
Bagzane, Monts, mts., Niger	C6	45
Bahamas, ctry., N.A.	B5	64
Bahāwalnagar, Pak.	C4	37
Bahāwalpur, Pak.	C5	36
Bahia, state, Braz.	D2	57
Bahía Blanca, Arg.	B4	54
Bahía Bustamante, Arg.	D3	54
Bahía de Caráquez, Ec.	B1	58
Bahía Negra, Para.	D4	55
Bahir Dar, Eth.	C4	47
Bahraich, India	D8	37
Bahrain, ctry., Asia	C5	38
Bahr al Ghazāl, prov., Sud.	D2	47
Bahr aṣ Ṣāfī, des., Asia	D4	38
Bahrīyah, Al Wāḥāt al, well, Eg.	D5	43
Bāhū Kalāt, Iran	I10	39
Baía dos Tigres, Ang.	E1	48
Baia-Mare, Rom.	B6	24
Baião, Braz.	C5	59
Baíbokoum, Chad	D3	46
Baicheng, China	B9	31
Baie-Comeau, P.Q., Can.	k13	74
Baie-Comeau-Hauterive, Réserve de la, P.Q., Can.	h13	74
Baie de Wasai, Mi., U.S.	B6	99
Baie-d'Urfé, P.Q., Can.	q19	74
Baie-James, Parc de la, P.Q., Can.	h11	74
Baie-Johan-Beetz, P.Q., Can.	h9	72
Baiersbronn, F.R.Ger.	E3	19
Baie-Sainte-Catherine, P.Q., Can.	A8	74
Baie-Saint-Paul, P.Q., Can.	B7	74
Baie Verte, N.B., Can.	C5	71
Baie Verte, Nf., Can.	D3	72
Baihe, China	H4	32
Baikal, Lake, l., Sov. Un.	D13	29
Baikal Mountains, mts., Sov. Un.	D13	29
Baikunthapur, India	F9	37
Bailén, Spain	C4	22
Bǎileşti, Rom.	C6	24
Bailey, Co., U.S.	B5	83
Bailey, Ms., U.S.	C5	101
Bailey, N.C., U.S.	B4	110
Bailey, co., Tx., U.S.	B1	120
Bailey Brook, stm., Me., U.S.	B2	96
Bailey Island, i., Me., U.S.	g8	96
Bailey Island, i., S.C., U.S.	k11	117
Baileys Crossroads, Va., U.S.	g12	123
Baileys Harbor, Wi., U.S.	C6	126
Baileyton, Al., U.S.	A3	78
Baileyton, Tn., U.S.	C11	119
Baileyville, Ks., U.S.	C7	93
Bailieborough, Ire.	D5	11
Bailundo, Ang.	D2	48
Bainbridge, Ga., U.S.	F2	87
Bainbridge, In., U.S.	E4	91
Bainbridge, N.Y., U.S.	C5	109
Bainbridge, Oh., U.S.	C2	112
Bainbridge Island, i., Wa., U.S.	e10	124
Bains, La., U.S.	D4	95
Bainville, Mt., U.S.	B12	103
Baiquan, China	B10	31
Baird, Ms., U.S.	B3	101
Baird, Tx., U.S.	C3	120
Bairdford, Pa., U.S.	h14	115
Baird Inlet, b., Ak., U.S.	C7	79
Baird Mountains, mts., Ak., U.S.	B7	79
Bairiki, Kir.	R18	52
Bairiki, i., Kir.	R18	52
Bairin Youqi, China	C8	31
Bairin Zuoqi, China	B8	32
Bairnsdale, Austl.	G8	50
Bairoil, Wy., U.S.	D5	127
Baise, stm., Fr.	F4	16
Baixo Longa, Ang.	E2	48
Baja, Hung.	B4	24
Baja California Norte, state, Mex.	A1	63
Baja California Sur, state, Mex.	B2	63
Bajimba, Mount, mtn., Austl.	A9	51
Bajmok, Yugo.	C4	24
Bajo Boquete, Pan.	F6	62
Bajram-Ali, Sov. Un.	C11	39
Bakala, Cen. Afr. Rep.	D4	46
Bakar, Yugo.	C2	24
Bakel, Sen.	D2	45
Baker, Ca., U.S.	E5	82
Baker, Fl., U.S.	u15	86
Baker, La., U.S.	D4	95
Baker, Mn., U.S.	D6	100
Baker, Mt., U.S.	D12	103
Baker, Nv., U.S.	D7	105
Baker, N.D., U.S.	A6	111
Baker, Ok., U.S.	e9	113
Baker, Or., U.S.	C9	114
Baker, co., Fl., U.S.	B4	86
Baker, co., Ga., U.S.	E2	87
Baker, co., Or., U.S.	C9	114
Baker, stm., N.H., U.S.	C3	106
Baker, Mount, mtn., Wa., U.S.	A4	124
Baker Butte, mtn., Az., U.S.	C4	80
Baker Hill, Al., U.S.	D4	78
Baker Island, i., Oc.	F11	6
Baker Island, i., Ak., U.S.	n22	79
Baker Lake, N.T., Can.	D13	66
Baker Lake, l., N.T., Can.	D13	66
Baker Lake, l., Me., U.S.	B3	96
Baker Lake, res., Wa., U.S.	A4	124
Baker Mountain, mtn., Me., U.S.	C3	96
Bakers, N.C., U.S.	B2	110
Bakers Bayou, stm., Ar., U.S.	k11	81
Bakersfield, Ca., U.S.	E4	82
Bakersfield, Mo., U.S.	E5	102
Bakersfield, Vt., U.S.	B3	122
Bakers Island, i., Ma., U.S.	f12	98
Bakers Mill, Fl., U.S.	B4	86
Bakerstown, Pa., U.S.	h14	115
Bakersville, Ct., U.S.	B3	84
Bakersville, N.C., U.S.	e10	110
Bakewell, Eng., U.K.	A6	12
Bakhchisaray, Sov. Un.	I9	27
Bakhmut, Sov. Un.	q21	27
Bakhtārān (Kermānshāh), Iran		
Bakir, stm., Tur.	C6	25
Bako, Eth.	D4	47
Bako, I.C.	E3	45
Bakony Mountains, mts., Hung.	B3	24
Bakouma, Cen. Afr. Rep.	D4	46
Bakoye, stm., Afr.	D3	45
Baku, Sov. Un.	E7	29
Baku, Zaire	A5	48
Bakundi, Nig.	E7	45
Bakungan, Indon.	K2	35
Bala, On., Can.	B5	73
Bala, Isr. Occ.	f11	41
Bâlâ, Tur.	C9	40
Bala, Wales, U.K.	B4	12
Bala, Ks., U.S.	C7	93
Balabac Island, i., Phil.	D5	34
Balabac Strait, strt., Asia	D5	34
Balabalangan Islands, is., Indon.	F5	34
Balad, Iraq	D2	39
Balaghāt, India	G8	37
Balaguer, Spain	B6	22
Balaka, Mwi.	D6	48
Balakhna, Sov. Un.	D17	8
Balakhta, Sov. Un.	D27	8
Balaklava, Austl.	G2	51
Balakleya, Sov. Un.	G11	27
Balakovo, Sov. Un.	*D7	29
Bala Morghāb, Afg.	D11	39
Balancán [de Domínguez], Mex.	D6	63
Balanga, Phil.	o13	34
Balaoan, Phil.	n13	34
Balashov, Sov. Un.	F14	27
Balasore, India	D8	36
Bālāt, Eg.	D5	43
Balaton, Lake, l., Hung.	B3	24
Balayan, Phil.	o13	34
Balayan Bay, b., Phil.	p13	34
Balboa, Pan.	m11	62
Balboa Heights, Pan.	m11	62
Balbriggan, Ire.	D5	11
Balcarce, Arg.	B5	54
Balcarres, Sk., Can.	G4	75
Balch, Ar., U.S.	B4	81
Balch Springs, Tx., U.S.	*n10	120
Balclutha, N.Z.	Q12	51
Bald Creek, N.C., U.S.	f10	110
Bald Eagle Lake, l., Mn., U.S.	m12	100
Bald Eagle Lake, l., Mn., U.S.	C7	100
Baldegger Lake, l., Switz.	B5	21
Bald Hill, hill, R.I., U.S.	D2	116
Baldhill Dam, N.D., U.S.	B7	111
Bald Knob, Ar., U.S.	B4	81
Bald Knob, mtn., W.V., U.S.	c3	123
Bald Knob, mtn., W.V., U.S.	C5	125
Bald Knoll, mtn., Wy., U.S.	C2	127
Bald Mountain, mtn., Ct., U.S.	B6	84
Bald Mountain, mtn., N.J., U.S.	A4	107
Bald Mountain, mtn., Or., U.S.	C9	114
Bald Mountain, mtn., Vt., U.S.	B5	122
Bald Mountain, mtn., Wy., U.S.	B5	127
Bald Mountains, mts., N.C., U.S.	f10	110
Baldock Lake, l., Mb., Can.	A3	70
Baldour, Mb., Can.	E2	70
Balm, Fl., U.S.	E4	86
Balmat, N.Y., U.S.	A5	109
Baldwin, Fl., U.S.	B5	86
Baldwin, Ga., U.S.	B3	87
Baldwin, Il., U.S.	E4	90
Baldwin, La., U.S.	E4	95
Baldwin, Md., U.S.	B5	97
Baldwin, Mi., U.S.	E5	99
Baldwin, N.Y., U.S.	*E7	109
Baldwin, N.D., U.S.	B5	111
Baldwin, Pa., U.S.	k13	115
Baldwin, S.C., U.S.	B5	117
Baldwin, Wi., U.S.	D1	126
Baldwin, co., Al., U.S.	E2	78
Baldwin, co., Ga., U.S.	C3	87
Baldwin City, Ks., U.S.	D8	93
Baldwin Heights, In., U.S.	H2	91
Baldwin Lake, l., Wi., U.S.	C1	126
Baldwin Park, Ca., U.S.	*E4	82
Baldwinsville, N.Y., U.S.	B4	109
Baldwinton, Sk., Can.	E1	75
Baldwinville, Ma., U.S.	A3	98
Baldwyn, Ms., U.S.	A5	101
Baldy Mountain, mtn., B.C., Can.	D7	69
Baldy Mountain, mtn., Mb., Can.	D1	70
Baldy Mountain, mtn., Mt., U.S.	B7	103
Baldy Mountain, mtn., N.M., U.S.	A4	108
Baldy Peak, mtn., Az., U.S.	D6	80
Bale, prov., Eth.	D5	47
Balearic Islands, is., Spain	C7	22
Baleia, Ponta da, c., Braz.	E3	57
Baleine, Grande rivière de la, stm., P.Q., Can.	g11	74
Baleine, Rivière à la, stm., P.Q., Can.	g13	74
Baler, Phil.	o13	34
Baler Bay, b., Phil.	o13	34
Baleshare, i., Scot., U.K.	C1	13
Balesin, i., Phil.	o14	34
Baleville, N.J., U.S.	A3	107
Balfate, Hond.	C4	62
Balfour, N.C., U.S.	f10	110
Balfour, N.D., U.S.	B5	111
Balgonie, Sk., Can.	G3	75
Bali, India	E4	37
Bali, i., Indon.	G5	34
Balikesir, Tur.	C6	40
Balikpapan, Indon.	F5	34
Balingen, F.R.Ger.	A4	20
Balintang Channel, strt., Phil.	B6	34
Bali Sea, Indon.	G5	34
Baliuag, Phil.	o13	34
Balje, F.R.Ger.	B4	18
Baljennie, Sk., Can.	E2	75
Balkan Mountains, mts., Eur.	D7	24
Balkh, Afg.	A4	36
Balkhash, Sov. Un.	E10	29
Balkhash, Lake, l., Sov. Un.	E10	29
Balki, Sov. Un.	H10	27
Balko, Ok., U.S.	e10	113
Ball, La., U.S.	C3	95
Balla, Isr. Occ.	D2	11
Ballachulish, Scot., U.K.	D3	13
Ballagh, Ire.	E4	11
Ballaghaderreen, Ire.	D3	11
Ballantine, Mt., U.S.	E8	103
Ballantrae, Scot., U.K.	C4	10
Ballarat (Ballaarat), Austl.	G7	50
Ballard, Ok., U.S.	A7	113
Ballard, co., Ky., U.S.	e8	94
Ballard, Lake, l., Austl.	E3	50
Ballardvale, Ma., U.S.	f11	98
Ballater, Scot., U.K.	B5	10
Ballé, Mali	C3	45
Ballenas, Bahía de b., Mex.	B2	63
Ballenstedt, Ger.D.R.	B6	19
Balleny Islands, is., Ant.	C29	7
Ballerup, Den.	C6	15
Ball Ground, Ga., U.S.	B2	87
Ballia, India	E10	37
Ballina, Austl.	E9	50
Ballina, Ire.	C2	10
Ballina, Ire.	E3	11
Ballinalack, Ire.	D4	11
Ballinamore, Ire.	C4	11
Ballinascarthy, Ire.	F3	11
Ballinasloe, Ire.	D2	10
Ballindine, Ire.	F3	11
Ballineen, Ire.	F3	11
Ballingarry, Ire.	D4	11
Ballingeary, Ire.	F2	11
Ballinger, Tx., U.S.	D3	120
Ballinluig, Scot., U.K.	D5	13
Ballinrobe, Ire.	C2	10
Ballinskelligs Bay, b., Ire.	F1	11
Ballintra, Ire.	C3	11
Ballisodare, Ire.	C3	11
Ball Mountain Lake, res., Vt., U.S.	E3	122
Ballouville, Ct., U.S.	B8	84
Ballston, Or., U.S.	B3	114
Ballston Spa, N.Y., U.S.	B7	109
Ballwin, Mo., U.S.	f12	102
Bally, Pa., U.S.	F10	115
Ballybofey, Ire.	C4	11
Ballybunion, Ire.	E2	11
Ballycanew, Ire.	E5	11
Ballycastle, Ire.	C2	10
Ballycastle, N. Ire., U.K.	C3	10
Ballyconneely, Ire.	E3	11
Ballyconnell, Ire.	C4	11
Ballycroy, Ire.	C2	11
Ballyduff, Ire.	E3	11
Ballyferriter, Ire.	E1	11
Ballygar, Ire.	E3	11
Ballygorman, Ire.	B4	11
Ballyhaunis, Ire.	E3	11
Ballyheige Bay, b., Ire.	E2	11
Ballyjamesduff, Ire.	D4	11
Ballykelly, N. Ire., U.K.	C4	11
Ballylongford, Ire.	E2	11
Ballymahon, Ire.	E4	11
Ballymena, N. Ire., U.K.	C3	11
Ballymoney, N. Ire., U.K.	B5	11
Ballymore, Ire.	E4	11
Ballymurray, Ire.	C3	11
Ballynahinch, N. Ire., U.K.	C6	11
Ballyneety, Ire.	E3	11
Ballynoe, Ire.	F3	11
Ballytore, Ire.	D5	11
Ballyvaughan, Ire.	D2	11
Ballyvourney, Ire.	F2	11
Balm, Fl., U.S.	p11	86
Balmat, N.Y., U.S.	f9	109
Balmazújváros, Hung.	B4	24
Balmhorn, mtn., Switz.	D4	21
Balmoral, Mb., Can.	D3	70
Balmoral, N.B., Can.	B3	71
Balmoral Castle, Scot., U.K.	c3	13
Balmorhea, Tx., U.S.	o13	120
Balmville, N.Y., U.S.	D6	109
Balonne, stm., Austl.	E8	50
Bālotra, India	C5	36
Balrāmpur, India	D9	37
Balranald, Austl.	G4	51
Balş, Rom.	C7	24
Balsam, N.C., U.S.	f9	110
Balsam Lake, Wi., U.S.	C1	126
Balsam Lake, l., On., Can.	C6	73
Balsam Lake, l., Wi., U.S.	C1	126
Balsas, Braz.	C1	57
Balsas, Mex.	D5	63
Balsas, stm., Braz.	C1	57
Balsas, stm., Mex.	D4	63
Balsas, Rio das, stm., Braz.	D1	57
Balsthal, Switz.	B4	21
Balta, Sov. Un.	H7	27
Balta, N.D., U.S.	A5	111
Baltasar Brum, Ur.	E1	56
Baltic, Ct., U.S.	C7	84
Baltic, Oh., U.S.	B4	112
Baltic, S.D., U.S.	D9	118
Baltic Sea, Eur.	I8	14
Baltīm, Eg.	C3	41
Baltimore, On., Can.	C6	73
Baltimore, Ire.	F2	11
Baltimore, Md., U.S.	B4	97
Baltimore, Oh., U.S.	C3	112
Baltimore, co., Md., U.S.	B4	97
Baltimore Highlands, Md., U.S.	h11	97
Baltinglass, Ire.	E5	11
Baltiysk, Sov. Un.	A5	26
Baltra, Isla, i., Ec.	g5	58
Baltrum, F.R.Ger.	A7	17
Baluchistan, hist reg., Asia	C3	36
Balya, Tur.	C6	25
Balzac, Ab., Can.	D3	68
Balzar, Ec.	B2	58
Balzers, Liech.	B8	21
Bam, Iran	C5	38
Bama, Nig.	D7	45
Bamako, Mali	D3	45
Bamba, Mali	C4	45
Bambang, Phil.	n13	34
Bambari, Cen. Afr. Rep.	D4	46
Bamberg, F.R.Ger.	D5	18
Bamberg, S.C., U.S.	E5	117
Bamberg, co., S.C., U.S.	E5	117
Bamber Lake, N.J., U.S.	D4	107
Bambesa, Zaire	A4	48
Bambui, Braz.	C3	56
Bamburgh, Eng., U.K.	D2	13
Bamenda, Cam.	D2	46
Bam Lake, l., China	e10	113
Bampūr, Iran	H10	39
Bampūr, stm., Iran	H9	39
Bân, Càrn, mtn., Scot., U.K.	C4	13
Banagher, Ire.	E4	11
Banahao, Mount, mtn., Phil.	o13	34
Banalia, Zaire	A4	48
Banamba, Mali	D3	45
Banana, Zaire	C1	48
Bananal, Braz.	h5	56
Bananal, Ilha do, i., Braz.	D4	59
Bananeiras, Braz.	C2	57
Banana River, b., Fl., U.S.	D6	86
Banās, stm., India	E4	37
Banās, Ra's, c., Eg.	C3	38
Banbridge, N. Ire., U.K.	C5	11
Banbury, Eng., U.K.	D6	10
Banchory, Scot., U.K.	C6	13
Bancos, Bahía, b., Ec.	g5	58
Bancroft, On., Can.	B7	73
Bancroft, Id., U.S.	G7	89
Bancroft, Ia., U.S.	A3	92
Bancroft, Mi., U.S.	F6	99
Bancroft, S.D., U.S.	C8	118
Bancroft, Wi., U.S.	D4	126
Bānda, India	H8	37
Banda Aceh (Kutaraja), Indon.	k11	34
Banda Banda, Mount, mtn., Austl.	E9	51
Banda Islands, is., Indon.	F7	34
Bandama, stm., I.C.	E3	45
Bandana, Ky., U.S.	e9	94
Bandar see Machilipatnam, India	C5	36
Bandar 'Abbās, Iran	C5	38
Bandar Baharu, Malay.	J4	35
Bandar-e Anzalī (Bandar-e Pahlavī), Iran	F5	39
Bandar-e Deylam, Iran	F5	39
Bandar-e Khomeynī (Bandar-e Shāhpūr), Iran	F5	39
Bandar-e Lengeh, Iran	H7	39
Bandar-e Māhshahr, Iran	*F4	39
Bandar-e Pahlavī see Bandar-e Anzalī, Iran	B4	38
Bandar-e Rīg, Iran	G5	39
Bandar-e Shāh see Bandar-e Torkeman, Iran	B5	38
Bandar-e Shāhpūr see Bandar-e Khomeynī, Iran	F4	39
Bandar-e Torkeman (Bandar-e Shāh), Iran	B5	38
Bandar Maharani see Muar, Malay.	K5	35
Bandar Seri Begawan (Brunei), Bru.	E4	34
Banda Sea, Indon.	G7	34
Bande, Spain	A2	22
Banded Peak, mtn., Co., U.S.	D3	83
Bandeira, Pico da, mtn., Braz.	C4	56
Bandelier National Monument, N.M., U.S.	B3	108
Bandera, Arg.	D4	54
Bandera, Tx., U.S.	E3	120
Bandera, co., Tx., U.S.	E3	120
Banderas, Bahía de b., Mex.	m11	63
Bandholm, Den.	D6	15
Bāndīkūi, India	D6	37
Bandırma, Tur.	B3	40
Bandon, Ire.	F3	11
Bandon, stm., Ire.	F3	11
Bandon, Or., U.S.	D2	114
Bandung, Indon.	G3	34
Banes, Cuba	D6	64
Banff, Ab., Can.	D3	68
Banff, Scot., U.K.	B6	13
Banff National Park, Ab., Can.	D2	68
Banfora, Burkina	E4	45
Bangalore, India	F3	36
Bangassou, Cen. Afr. Rep.	E4	46
Bangangté, Cam.	D2	46
Bangeta, Mount, mtn., Pap. N. Gui.	k12	50
Banggai, Indon.	F6	34
Banggi, Island, i., Malay.	D5	34
Bangka, i., Indon.	F3	34
Bangkalan, Indon.	G4	34
Bangkok (Krung Thep), Thai.	C2	34
Bangladesh, ctry., Asia	D9	36
Bangong Lake, l., China	C6	36
Bangor, Sk., Can.	G4	75
Bangor, N. Ire., U.K.	C7	11
Bangor, Wales, U.K.	D4	10
Bangor, Al., U.S.	B3	78
Bangor, Me., U.S.	D4	96
Bangor, Mi., U.S.	F4	99
Bangor, N.Y., U.S.	f10	109
Bangor, Pa., U.S.	E11	115
Bangor, Wi., U.S.	E3	126
Bangor Erris, Ire.	C2	11
Bangor Township, Mi., U.S.	E7	99
Bangs, Tx., U.S.	D3	120
Bangs, Mount, mtn., Az., U.S.	A2	80
Bang Saphan, Thai.	C1	34
Bangu, Zaire	C3	48
Bangued, Phil.	B6	34
Bangui, Cen. Afr. Rep.	E3	46
Bangweulu, Lake, l., Zam.	D4	48
Banhã, Eg.	B3	38
Ban Hat Yai see Hat Yai, Thai.	D2	34
Baní, Dom. Rep.	E8	64
Bani, stm., Mali	D3	45
Bani, India	n12	34
Baniara, Pap. N. Gui.	k12	50
Banister, stm., Va., U.S.	D4	123
Banī Na'īm, Isr. Occ.	C7	41
Banī Suhaylah, Isr. Occ.	C6	41
Banī Suwayf, Eg.	C3	38
Bāniyās, Syria	B3	38
Banja Luka, Yugo.	C3	24
Banjarmasin, Indon.	F4	34
Banjul, Gam.	D1	45
Bankeryd, Swe.	A8	15
Bankfoot, Scot., U.K.	D5	13
Bankhead, Al., U.S.	A2	78
Bankhead Lake, res., Al., U.S.	B2	78
Banks, Al., U.S.	D4	78
Banks, Ar., U.S.	D3	81
Banks, Id., U.S.	E2	89
Banks, Ms., U.S.	A3	101
Banks, Or., U.S.	g11	114
Banks, co., Ga., U.S.	B3	87
Banksian, stm., Can.	C4	70
Banks Island, i., B.C., Can.	C2	69
Banks Island, i., N.T., Can.	B8	66
Banks Lake, l., Ga., U.S.	E3	87
Banks Lake, res., Wa., U.S.	B6	124
Banks Peninsula, pen., N.Z.	O14	51
Bankstown, Austl.	*F9	50
Bānkura, India	D8	36
Bann, stm., N. Ire., U.K.	E4	11
Bannack, Mt., U.S.	E4	103
Ban Na San, Thai.	D1	34
Banner, Ms., U.S.	A4	101
Banner, Wy., U.S.	B6	127
Banner, co., Ne., U.S.	C2	104
Banner Elk, N.C., U.S.	A1	110
Banning, Ca., U.S.	F5	82
Bannister, Mi., U.S.	E6	99
Bannockburn, On., Can.	C7	73
Bannock, co., Id., U.S.	G6	89
Bannock Peak, mtn., Id., U.S.	F6	89
Bannock Range, mts., Id., U.S.	G6	89
Bannu, Pak.	B5	36
Bañolas, Spain	*A7	22
Baños, Ec.	B2	58
Bansha, Ire.	E3	11
Banská Bystrica, Czech.	D5	26
Banská Štiavnica, Czech.	D5	26
Bansko, Bul.	E6	24
Bānswāra, India	F5	37
Bantam, Ct., U.S.	C3	84
Bantam, stm., Ct., U.S.	C3	84
Bantam Lake, l., Ct., U.S.	C3	84
Banteer, Ire.	E3	11
Bantry, Ire.	F2	11
Bantry, N.D., U.S.	A5	111
Bantry Bay, b., Ire.	F1	11
Banyak Islands, is., Indon.	m11	34
Banyo, Cam.	D2	46
Banyuwangi, Indon.	G4	34
Banzare Coast, Ant.	C25	7
Baochang, China	E6	31
Baode, China	E7	32
Baodi, China	E7	32
Baoding, China	E7	31
Baoji, China	E3	31
Bao Ha, Viet.	A6	35
Baojing, China	E7	31
Baokang, China	E7	31
Baoshan, China	F4	31
Baoting, China	C8	35
Baotou, China	C6	31
Bapaume, Fr.	D2	17
Bapchule, Az., U.S.	D4	80
Baptiste, On., Can.	B6	73
Baptistown, N.J., U.S.	B2	107
Bāqa el Gharbiyya, Isr.	B7	41
Ba'qūbah, Iraq	B4	38
Baquedano, Chile	D2	55
Bar, Fr.		
Bar, Sov. Un.	G6	27
Bar, Yugo.	D4	24
Baraawe, Som.	E5	47
Barabil, India	F10	37
Baraboo, Wi., U.S.	E4	126
Baraboo, stm., Wi., U.S.	E3	126
Baracaldo, Spain	A4	22
Baracoa, Cuba	D6	64
Baradero, Arg.	f7	54
Baraga, Mi., U.S.	B2	99
Baraga, co., Mi., U.S.	B2	99
Bārah, Sud.	C3	47
Barahona, Dom. Rep.	E8	64
Barajas de Madrid, Spain	p17	22
Bārākot, India	G10	37
Bāran, India	E6	37
Baranagar, India	*D8	36
Baranof Island, i., Ak., U.S.	m22	79
Baranov, Cape, c., Sov. Un.	C34	128
Baranovichi, Sov. Un.	E9	26
Barão de Melgaço, Braz.	B6	56
Barataria, Trin.	N23	65
Barataria, La., U.S.	E5	95
Barataria, Bayou, stm., La., U.S.	k11	95
Barataria Bay, b., La., U.S.	E6	95
Barat Daya Islands, is., Indon.	G7	34
Baraya, Col.	C2	60
Barbacena, Braz.	C3	56
Barbacoas, Col.	C1	60

Name	Map Ref	Page
Barbados, ctry., N.A.	J15	64
Barbalha, Braz.	C3	57
Barbar, Sud.	B3	47
Barbastro, Spain	A6	22
Barbate [de Franco], Spain	D3	22
Barbeau, Mi., U.S.	B6	99
Barbeau Peak, mtn., N.T., Can.	k37	67
Barber, Ar., U.S.	B1	81
Barber, co., Ks., U.S.	E5	93
Barbers Point, c., Hi., U.S.	B3	88
Barbers Point Naval Air Station, mil., Hi., U.S.	g9	88
Barberton, S. Afr.	C5	49
Barberton, Oh., U.S.	A4	112
Barberville, Fl., U.S.	C5	86
Barbezieux, Fr.	E3	16
Barbour, co., Al., U.S.	D4	78
Barbour, co., W.V., U.S.	B4	125
Barboursville, Va., U.S.	B4	123
Barboursville, W.V., U.S.	C2	125
Barbourville, Ky., U.S.	D6	94
Barbuda, i., Antig.	H14	64
Barby, Ger.D.R.	B6	19
Barca de Alva, Port.	B2	22
Barcaldine, Austl.	D8	50
Barcarena, Port.	f9	22
Barcarrota, Spain	G2	22
Barcellona [Pozzo di Gotto], Italy	E5	23
Barcelona, Spain	B7	22
Barcelona, Ven.	A5	60
Barcelonnette, Fr.	E7	16
Barcelos, Braz.	C2	59
Barcelos, Port.	B1	22
Barclay, Md., U.S.	B6	97
Barco, N.C., U.S.	A7	110
Barcoo, stm., Austl.	D7	50
Barcroft, Lake, res., Va., U.S.	g12	123
Bard, N.M., U.S.	B6	108
Barda del Medio, Arg.	B3	54
Bardaï, Chad	A3	46
Bardawīl, Sabkhat al, sw., Eg.	C5	41
Bardawīl Peninsula, spit, Eg.	C4	41
Bardejov, Czech.	D6	26
Barden Reservoir, res., R.I., U.S.	C2	116
Bardi, Italy	E5	20
Bardīyah, Libya	C5	43
Bardolph, Il., U.S.	C3	90
Bardonecchia, Italy	D2	20
Bardsey Island, i., Wales, U.K.	B3	12
Bardstown, Ky., U.S.	C4	94
Bardstown Junction, Ky., U.S.	C4	94
Bardswell Group, is., B.C., Can.	C3	69
Bardwell, Ky., U.S.	f9	94
Bardwell Lake, res., Tx., U.S.	C4	120
Bare Hill Pond, l., Ma., U.S.	g9	98
Bareilly, India	C6	36
Barenburg, F.R.Ger.	F2	15
Barentin, Fr.	C4	16
Barents, i., Nor.	B12	128
Barents Sea, Eur.	B6	29
Barentu, Eth.	B4	47
Barfleur, Pointe de, c., Fr.	C3	16
Bargarh, India	G9	37
Bargersville, In., U.S.	E5	91
Barguzin, Sov. Un.	D13	29
Bar Harbor, Me., U.S.	D4	96
Bari, Italy	D6	23
Bari, prov., Som.	D4	47
Barillas, Guat.	C2	62
Barinas, Ven.	B3	60
Barinas, state, Ven.	B4	60
Baring, Me., U.S.	C5	96
Baring, Mo., U.S.	A5	102
Baripāda, India	D8	36
Bariri, Braz.	C3	56
Bārīs, Eg.	E6	43
Barisāl, Bngl.	D9	36
Barisan Mountains, mts., Indon.	F2	34
Barito, stm., Indon.	F4	34
Barium Springs, N.C., U.S.	B2	110
Barkan, Ra's-e c., Iran	G4	39
Barker, N.Y., U.S.	B2	109
Barker Heights, N.C., U.S.	f10	110
Barkerville, B.C., Can.	C7	69
Barkeyville, Pa., U.S.	D2	115
Barkhamsted Reservoir, res., Ct., U.S.	B3	84
Barkley, Lake, res., U.S.	f10	94
Barkley Dam, Ky., U.S.	e9	94
Barkley Sound, strt., B.C., Can.	E5	69
Barkly East, S. Afr.	H5	49
Barkly Tableland, plat., Austl.	C6	50
Barkmere, P.Q., Can.	D3	74
Barkol, China	C3	31
Bark Point, c., Wi., U.S.	B2	126
Bark River, Mi., U.S.	C3	99
Barksdale, Tx., U.S.	E2	120
Barksdale Air Force Base, mil., La., U.S.	B2	95
Bar Lake, l., Sk., Can.	B2	75
Bar-le-Duc, Fr.	C6	16
Barlee, Lake, l., Austl.	E2	50
Barletta, Italy	D6	23
Barling, Ar., U.S.	B1	81
Barlow, Ky., U.S.	e8	94
Barlow, N.D., U.S.	B6	111
Barlow, Or., U.S.	h12	114
Barmer, India	C5	36
Bar Mills, Me., U.S.	E2	96
Barmouth, Wales, U.K.	D4	10
Barna, Ire.	D2	11
Barnaby River, N.B., Can.	C4	71
Barnard, Ks., U.S.	C5	93
Barnard, Mo., U.S.	A3	102
Barnard, S.D., U.S.	B7	118
Barnard, Vt., U.S.	D3	122
Barnard Castle, Eng., U.K.	C4	12
Barnardsville, N.C., U.S.	f10	110
Barnasht, Eg.	C3	41
Barnaul, Sov. Un.	D11	29
Barnegat, N.J., U.S.	D4	107
Barnegat Bay, b., N.J., U.S.	D4	107
Barnegat Inlet, b., N.J., U.S.	D4	107
Barnegat Light, N.J., U.S.	D4	107
Barnegat Pines, N.J., U.S.	D4	107
Barne Inlet, b., Ant.	g40	7
Barnes, Ks., U.S.	C7	93
Barnes, Pa., U.S.	C3	115
Barnes, co., N.D., U.S.	B7	111
Barnes City, Ia., U.S.	C5	92
Barnes Corners, N.Y., U.S.	b5	109
Barnes Creek, stm., La., U.S.	D2	95
Barnes Sound, strt., Fl., U.S.	G6	86
Barneston, Ne., U.S.	D9	104
Barnesville, Ga., U.S.	C2	87
Barnesville, Md., U.S.	B3	97
Barnesville, Mn., U.S.	D2	100
Barnesville, Oh., U.S.	C4	112
Barnet (part of London), Eng., U.K.	k12	10
Barnet, Vt., U.S.	C4	122
Barnett, Mo., U.S.	C5	102
Barneveld, Neth.	B5	17
Barneveld, Wi., U.S.	E4	126
Barney, Ga., U.S.	F3	87
Barney, N.D., U.S.	C8	111
Barney, Mount, mtn., Austl.	D9	51
Barnhart, Mo., U.S.	C7	102
Barnhart, Tx., U.S.	D2	120
Barnhill, Oh., U.S.	B4	112
Barnsdall, Ok., U.S.	A5	113
Barnsley, Eng., U.K.	A6	12
Barnstable, Ma., U.S.	C7	98
Barnstable, co., Ma., U.S.	C7	98
Barnstaple, Eng., U.K.	E4	10
Barnstaple Bay, b., Eng., U.K.	C3	12
Barnstead, N.H., U.S.	D4	106
Barnston, P.Q., Can.	D6	74
Barnum, Ia., U.S.	B3	92
Barnum, Mn., U.S.	D6	100
Barnwell, Ab., Can.	E4	68
Barnwell, S.C., U.S.	E5	117
Barnwell, co., S.C., U.S.	E5	117
Baro, Nig.	E6	45
Baro, stm., Afr.	D3	47
Baroda (Vadodara), India	D5	36
Baroda, Mi., U.S.	G4	99
Baron, Ok., U.S.	B7	113
Barons, Ab., Can.	E4	68
Barquisimeto, Ven.	A4	60
Barr, Fr.	C7	16
Barr, Co., U.S.	B6	83
Barr, Ra's al, c., Eg.	C3	41
Barra, Braz.	h5	57
Barra, Braz.	D2	57
Barra, i., Scot., U.K.	B3	10
Barra, Sound of, strt., Scot., U.K.	C1	13
Barra, Austl.	E8	51
Barra Bonita, Braz.	m7	56
Barração, Braz.	D2	56
Barrackville, W.V., U.S.	B4	125
Barrackpore, India	F12	37
Barra de Río Grande, Nic.	D6	62
Barra de Corda, Braz.	C1	57
Barra do Garças, Braz.	B2	56
Barra do Pirai, Braz.	C4	56
Barra Head, c., Scot., U.K.	B3	10
Barra Mansa, Braz.	C4	56
Barranca, Peru	B2	58
Barranca, N.M., U.S.	A3	108
Barrancabermeja, Col.	B2	58
Barrancas, Ven.	B3	60
Barrancas, Peru	*D2	58
Barrancos, Port.	C2	22
Barranqueras, Col.	A3	60
Barranquilla, Col.	A2	54
Barraza, Chile	A2	54
Barre, Ma., U.S.	B3	98
Barre, Vt., U.S.	C4	122
Barre des Écrins, mtn., Fr.	E7	16
Barre Falls Reservoir, res., Ma., U.S.	B4	98
Barreiras, Braz.	D2	57
Barreirinha, Braz.	C3	59
Barreirinhas, Braz.	B2	57
Barreiro, Port.	C1	22
Barreiros, Braz.	C4	57
Barrelville, Md., U.S.	k13	97
Barren, co., Ky., U.S.	D4	94
Barren, stm., Ky., U.S.	C3	94
Barren, Nosy, is., Madag.	g8	49
Barren Island, i., Md., U.S.	D5	97
Barren Islands, is., Ak., U.S.	h15	79
Barren Plain, Tn., U.S.	A5	119
Barren River Lake, res., Ky., U.S.	D3	94
Barren Plains, Ma., U.S.	B3	98
Barretos, Braz.	C3	56
Barrett, Mn., U.S.	E3	100
Barrett, W.V., U.S.	D3	125
Barretts Hill, hill, Ma., U.S.	g9	98
Barrhead, Ab., Can.	B3	68
Barrhead, Scot., U.K.	E4	13
Barrhill, Scot., U.K.	E4	13
Barrie, On., Can.	C5	73
Barrie Island, i., On., Can.	B2	73
Barrier Bay, b., Ant.	C21	7
Barrière, B.C., Can.	D7	69
Barrier Lake, l., Sk., Can.	E4	75
Barrier Range, mts., Austl.	F7	50
Barrigada, Guam	L10	52
Barrington, N.S., Can.	F4	71
Barrington, Il., U.S.	A5	90
Barrington, N.H., U.S.	D4	106
Barrington, N.J., U.S.	D2	107
Barrington, R.I., U.S.	D5	116
Barrington, co., R.I., U.S.	C5	116
Barrington Lake, l., Mb., Can.	A1	70
Barrington Passage, N.S., Can.	F4	71
Barrington Tops, mtn., Austl.	F8	51
Barrio Obrero Industrial, Peru	*D2	58
Barrio Alto, Braz.	B3	56
Barron, Wi., U.S.	C2	126
Barron, co., Wi., U.S.	C2	126
Barronett, Wi., U.S.	C2	126
Barrouallie, St. Vin.	U26	65
Barrow, Arg.	B4	54
Barrow, Ak., U.S.	A8	79
Barrow, co., Ga., U.S.	B3	87
Barrow, i., Austl.	D2	50
Barrow, stm., Ire.	D3	10
Barrow, Point, c., Ak., U.S.	A8	79
Barrow-in-Furness, Eng., U.K.	C5	10
Barrows, Mb., Can.	C1	70
Barrow Strait, strt., N.T., Can.	B14	66
Barrowsville, Ma., U.S.	C5	98
Barrueco de Santullán, Spain	A3	22
Barry (Vale of Glamorgan), Wales, U.K.	C4	12
Barry, Il., U.S.	D2	90
Barry, co., Mi., U.S.	F5	99
Barry, co., Mo., U.S.	E4	102
Barrys Bay, On., Can.	B7	73
Barryton, Mi., U.S.	E5	99
Barryville, N.Y., U.S.	D6	109
Bârsa, India	E6	36
Barsinghausen, F.R.Ger.	A4	19
Barse, i., Den.	C3	15
Barstow, Ca., U.S.	E5	82
Barstow, Tx., U.S.	D1	120
Bar-sur-Aube, Fr.	C6	16
Bartelso, Il., U.S.	E4	90
Barth, Ger.D.R.	B5	19
Bartholomew, co., In., U.S.	F6	91
Bartholomew, Bayou, stm., U.S.	D4	81
Bartibog Bridge, N.B., Can.	B4	71
Bartica, Guy.	A3	59
Bartin, Tur.	B9	40
Bartle Frere, Mount, mtn., Austl.	C8	50
Bartlesville, Ok., U.S.	A6	113
Bartlett, Il., U.S.	*k8	90
Bartlett, Ks., U.S.	E8	93
Bartlett, Ne., U.S.	C7	104
Bartlett, N.H., U.S.	B4	106
Bartlett, N.D., U.S.	A7	111
Bartlett, Oh., U.S.	C4	112
Bartlett, Tn., U.S.	B2	119
Bartlett, Tx., U.S.	D4	120
Bartlett Cove, Ak., U.S.	k22	79
Bartlett Reservoir, res., Az., U.S.	D4	80
Bartletts Ferry Dam, U.S.	C4	78
Bartletts Harbour, Nf., Can.	C3	72
Bartley, Ne., U.S.	D5	104
Bartolomeu Dias, Moz.	B6	49
Barton, Al., U.S.	A2	78
Barton, Ar., U.S.	C5	81
Barton, Md., U.S.	k12	97
Barton, N.D., U.S.	A5	111
Barton, Oh., U.S.	B5	112
Barton, Vt., U.S.	B4	122
Barton, co., Ks., U.S.	D5	93
Barton, co., Mo., U.S.	D3	102
Barton, stm., Vt., U.S.	B4	122
Barton-on-Humber, Eng., U.K.	A7	12
Bartonville, Vt., U.S.	C3	122
Bartonville, Il., U.S.	C4	90
Bartow, Fl., U.S.	E5	86
Bartow, Ga., U.S.	D4	87
Bartow, co., Ga., U.S.	B2	87
Bartoszyce, Pol.	A6	26
Barú, Volcán, vol., Pan.	F6	62
Barun Su, China	C4	32
Barus, Indon.	K3	35
Baruth, Ger.D.R.	A8	19
Baruun-Urt, Mong.	B7	31
Barvas, Scot., U.K.	A3	10
Barvenkovo, Sov. Un.	G11	27
Barview, Or., U.S.	*D2	114
Barwāni, India	F5	37
Barwick, Ga., U.S.	F3	87
Barwon, stm., Austl.	E8	50
Barybino, Sov. Un.	n17	27
Barycz, stm., Pol.	C4	26
Basalt, Co., U.S.	B3	83
Basalt, Id., U.S.	F6	89
Basalt, Nv., U.S.	E3	105
Basankusu, Zaire	A2	48
Basbulak, Sov. Un.	E6	28
Basco, Phil.	A6	34
Basco, Il., U.S.	C2	90
Bascom, Fl., U.S.	B1	86
Bascom, Oh., U.S.	A2	112
Basehor, Ks., U.S.	k16	93
Basekpio, Zaire	A3	48
Basel, Switz.	E3	18
Basel-Land, state, Switz.	B3	20
Basel-Stadt, state, Switz.	B3	20
Bashākerd, Kūhhā-ye, mts., Iran	H9	39
Bashan Lake, l., Ct., U.S.	D6	84
Bashaw, Ab., Can.	C4	68
Bashi, Al., U.S.	D2	78
Bashi Channel, strt., Asia	A6	34
Basiad Bay, b., Phil.	o14	34
Basilan, Phil.	D6	34
Basilan Island, i., Phil.	D6	34
Basildon, Eng., U.K.	C8	12
Basile, La., U.S.	D3	95
Basilicata, hist reg., Italy	D6	23
Basilio, Braz.	E2	56
Basin, Mt., U.S.	D4	103
Basin, Wy., U.S.	B4	127
Basinger, Fl., U.S.	E5	86
Basingstoke, Eng., U.K.	E6	10
Basin Harbor, Vt., U.S.	C2	122
Basin Lake, l., Sk., Can.	E3	75
Baška, Yugo.	C2	24
Baskahegan Lake, l., Me., U.S.	C5	96
Baskatong, Réservoir, res., P.Q., Can.	k11	74
Baskett, Ky., U.S.	C2	94
Baskin, Fl., U.S.	p10	86
Baskin, La., U.S.	B4	95
Basking Ridge, N.J., U.S.	B3	107
Basoko, Zaire	A3	48
Basongo, Zaire	B3	48
Basora, Punt, c., Neth. Ant.	H17	65
Basque Provinces, hist reg., Spain	A4	22
Basra (Al Başrah), Iraq	B4	38
Bas-Rhin, dept., Fr.	F7	17
Bassano, Ab., Can.	D4	68
Bassano del Grappa, Italy	B3	23
Bassas da India, rf., Reu.	B6	49
Bassein, Burma	E9	36
Bassein, mth., Burma	D1	35
Basse-Pointe, Mart.	S10	65
Basse Santa Su, Gam.	D2	45
Basse-Terre, Guad.	I14	64
Basseterre, St. C.-N.	H13	64
Basse-Terre, i., Guad.	Q8	65
Bassett, Ar., U.S.	B5	81
Bassett, Ia., U.S.	A5	92
Bassett, Ks., U.S.	E8	93
Bassett, Ne., U.S.	B6	104
Bassett, Va., U.S.	D3	123
Bassett, Wi., U.S.	n11	126
Bassett Creek, stm., Al., U.S.	D2	78
Bassett Peak, mtn., Az., U.S.	E5	80
Bass Harbor, Me., U.S.	D4	96
Bassikounou, Maur.	C3	45
Bass Islands, is., Oh., U.S.	A3	112
Bass Lake, In., U.S.	B4	91
Bass River, N.S., Can.	D6	71
Bass Strait, strt., Austl.	n15	50
Bassum, F.R.Ger.	F2	15
Basswood, Mb., Can.	D1	70
Basswood Lake, l., Mn., U.S.	B7	100
Bästad, Swe.	B6	15
Bastak, Iran	H7	39
Bastelica, Fr.	C4	20
Basti, India	D9	37
Bastian, Va., U.S.	C1	123
Bastogne, Bel.	B6	16
Bastrop, La., U.S.	B4	95
Bastrop, Tx., U.S.	D4	120
Bastrop, co., Tx., U.S.	D4	120
Bastuträsk, Swe.	E9	14
Basyūn, Eg.	D2	41
Bata, Eq. Gui.	E1	46
Bataan, Phil.	p13	34
Bataan Peninsula, pen., Phil.	o13	34
Batabanó, Cuba	C2	64
Batabanó, Golfo de, b., Cuba	C2	64
Bataguaçu, Braz.	C2	56
Batāla, India	B6	36
Batamay, Sov. Un.	C15	29
Batang, China	E4	31
Batangafo, Cen. Afr. Rep.	D3	46
Batangas, Phil.	C6	34
Batanghari, stm., Indon.	F2	34
Batan Islands, is., Phil.	A6	34
Bátaszék, Hung.	B4	24
Batatais, Braz.	C3	56
Batavia, Arg.	A3	54
Batavia, Ar., U.S.	A2	81
Batavia, Il., U.S.	B5	90
Batavia, Ia., U.S.	D5	92
Batavia, N.Y., U.S.	C2	109
Batavia, Oh., U.S.	C1	112
Bataysk, Sov. Un.	H12	27
Batchelor, La., U.S.	D4	95
Batchtown, Il., U.S.	D3	90
Batdambang, Kam.	C2	34
Bateman, Sk., Can.	G2	75
Bates, Ar., U.S.	C1	81
Bates, Or., U.S.	C8	114
Bates, co., Mo., U.S.	C3	102
Batesburg, S.C., U.S.	D4	117
Bates City, Mo., U.S.	C3	102
Batesland, S.D., U.S.	D3	118
Batesville, Ar., U.S.	B4	81
Batesville, In., U.S.	F7	91
Batesville, Ms., U.S.	A4	101
Batesville, Oh., U.S.	C4	112
Batesville, Tx., U.S.	E3	120
Bath, N.B., Can.	C2	71
Bath, On., Can.	C8	73
Bath, Jam.	F16	65
Bath, Eng., U.K.	E5	10
Bath, Il., U.S.	C3	90
Bath, In., U.S.	E8	91
Bath, Me., U.S.	E3	96
Bath, Mi., U.S.	F6	99
Bath, N.H., U.S.	B3	106
Bath, N.Y., U.S.	C3	109
Bath, N.C., U.S.	B6	110
Bath, Pa., U.S.	E11	115
Bath, S.C., U.S.	D4	117
Bath, S.D., U.S.	B7	118
Bath, co., Ky., U.S.	B6	94
Bath, co., Va., U.S.	B3	123
Bathgate, Scot., U.K.	E5	13
Bathgate, N.D., U.S.	A8	111
Bathsheba, Barb.	J15	64
Bath Springs, Tn., U.S.	B3	119
Bathurst, Austl.	F8	50
Bathurst, N.B., Can.	B4	71
Bathurst see Banjul, Gam.	D1	45
Bathurst, i., Austl.	B6	50
Bathurst, Cape, c., N.T., Can.	B7	66
Bathurst Inlet, N.T., Can.	C11	66
Bathurst Inlet, b., N.T., Can.	C11	66
Bathurst Island, Austl.	B6	50
Bathurst Island, i., N.T., Can.	m31	66
Batié, Burkina	E4	45
Batiki, i., Fiji	H15	52
Batiscan, P.Q., Can.	C5	74
Batiscan, stm., P.Q., Can.	B5	74
Batkanu, S.L.	E4	45
Batman, Tur.	*D13	40
Batna, Alg.	B6	44
Batoche, Sk., Can.	E2	75
Baton Rouge, La., U.S.	D4	95
Batouri, Cam.	E2	46
Batson, Tx., U.S.	D5	120
Batsto, N.J., U.S.	D3	107
Batsto, stm., N.J., U.S.	D3	107
Batten Kill, stm., Vt., U.S.	E2	122
Battery Park, Va., U.S.	k14	123
Batticaloa, Sri L.	G7	36
Battiest, Ok., U.S.	C7	113
Battle, stm., Can.	F11	66
Battleboro, N.C., U.S.	A5	110
Battle Creek, Sk., Can.	H1	75
Battle Creek, Ia., U.S.	B2	92
Battle Creek, Mi., U.S.	F5	99
Battle Creek, Ne., U.S.	C8	104
Battle Creek, stm., N.A.	B7	103
Battleford, Sk., Can.	E1	75
Battle Ground, In., U.S.	C4	91
Battle Ground, Wa., U.S.	D3	124
Battle Harbour, Nf., Can.	B4	72
Battle Lake, Mn., U.S.	D3	100
Battlement Mesa, mtn., Co., U.S.	B2	83
Battle Mountain, Nv., U.S.	C5	105
Battle Mountain, mtn., Wy., U.S.	E5	127
Battles, Al., U.S.	D5	101
Battles Wharf, Al., U.S.	E2	78
Battleview, N.D., U.S.	A3	111
Battonya, Hung.	B5	24
Battrum, Sk., Can.	G1	75
Batu, mtn., Eth.	D4	47
Batuc, Mex.	B2	63
Batu Islands, is., Indon.	F1	34
Batumi, Sov. Un.	E7	28
Batu Pahat, Malay.	L5	35
Baturaja, Indon.	F2	34
Baturino, Sov. Un.	B11	28
Baturité, Braz.	B3	57
Bat Yam, Isr.	g9	41
Bauan, Phil.	p13	34
Bauang, Phil.	B6	34
Baubau, Indon.	D6	45
Bauchi, Nig.	D6	45
Baudó, Serranía de, mts., Col.	B2	60
Bauer, Ut., U.S.	C3	121
Bauer Coulee, val., Wa., U.S.	B7	124
Baugé, Fr.	C4	16
Bauld, Cape, c., Nf., Can.	C4	72
Bauma, Switz.	C3	45
Baunei, Italy	B2	23
Baures, Bol.	B3	55
Baures, stm., Bol.	B3	55
Baurtregaum, mtn., Ire.	E2	11
Bauru, Braz.	C3	56
Bautzen, Ger.D.R.	C7	18
Bauxite, Ar., U.S.	C3	81
Bavaria, Ks., U.S.	D6	93
Bavaria, hist reg., F.R.Ger.	B7	20
Bavarian Alps, mts., Eur.	B7	20
Båven, l., Swe.	t34	14
Bavispe, Bel.	B6	16
Baw Baw, Mount, mtn., Austl.	H6	51
Bawcomville, La., U.S.	*B3	95
Bawean, i., Indon.	C1	86
Bawku, Ghana	D4	45
Bawlf, Ab., Can.	C4	68
Baxdo, Som.	D4	47
Baxian, China	E7	32
Baxley, Ga., U.S.	E4	87
Baxter, Ia., U.S.	C4	92
Baxter, Ky., U.S.	D6	94
Baxter, Mn., U.S.	D4	100
Baxter, Tn., U.S.	C8	119
Baxter, W.V., U.S.	A3	125
Baxter, co., Ar., U.S.	A3	81
Baxter Springs, Ks., U.S.	E9	93
Baxterville, Co., U.S.	D4	83
Baxterville, Ms., U.S.	D4	101
Bay, Ar., U.S.	B5	81
Bay, prov., Som.	E5	47
Bay, co., Fl., U.S.	u16	86
Bay, co., Mi., U.S.	E6	99
Bay al Kabīr, Wādī, val., Libya	C2	43
Bayambang, Phil.	o13	34
Bayamo, Cuba	D5	64
Bayamón, P.R.	G11	64
Bayan, China	C3	33
Bayanaul, Sov. Un.	C9	28
Bayanga, Cen. Afr. Rep.	E3	46
Bayanhongor, Mong.	B5	31
Bayan Obo, China	D3	32
Bayard, Ia., U.S.	C3	92
Bayard, Ne., U.S.	C2	104
Bayard, N.M., U.S.	E1	108
Bayard, W.V., U.S.	B5	125
Bayberry, N.Y., U.S.	B4	109
Bayble, Scot., U.K.	B2	13
Bayboro, N.C., U.S.	B6	110
Bay Bulls, Nf., Can.	E5	72
Bayburt, Tur.	B13	40
Bay Center, Wa., U.S.	C2	124
Bay City, Mi., U.S.	E7	99
Bay City, Or., U.S.	B3	114
Bay City, Tx., U.S.	E5	120
Bay City, Wi., U.S.	D1	126
Bay de Verde, Nf., Can.	D5	72
Baydhabo, Som.	E5	47
Baydrag, stm., Mong.	B4	31
Bayeux, Fr.	C3	16
Bayfield, On., Can.	D3	73
Bayfield, Co., U.S.	D3	83
Bayfield, Wi., U.S.	B3	126
Bayfield, co., Wi., U.S.	B2	126
Bay Head, N.J., U.S.	*C4	107
Bayindir, Tur.	C6	25
Baykonyr, Sov. Un.	D7	28
Bay L'Argent, Nf., Can.	E4	72
Baylis, Il., U.S.	D3	90
Baylor, co., Tx., U.S.	C3	120
Baymak, Sov. Un.	C5	28
Bay Minette, Al., U.S.	E2	78
Bayombong, Phil.	n13	34
Bayonne, Fr.	F3	16
Bayonne, N.J., U.S.	B4	107
Bayou Bodcau Reservoir, res., La., U.S.	B2	95
Bayou D'Arbonne Lake, res., La., U.S.	B3	95
Bayou George, Fl., U.S.	u16	86
Bayou Goula, La., U.S.	D4	95
Bayou La Batre, Al., U.S.	E1	78
Bayóvar, Peru	C1	58
Bay Point, c., S.C., U.S.	G7	117
Bayport, N.S., Can.	E5	71
Bay Port, Mi., U.S.	E7	99
Bayport, Mn., U.S.	E6	100
Bayport, N.Y., U.S.	n15	109
Bayramiç, Tur.	C6	25
Bayrampaşa, Tur.	*B7	40
Bayreuth, F.R.Ger.	D5	18
Bay Ridge, Md., U.S.	C5	97
Bayrischzell, F.R.Ger.	B7	20
Bay Roberts, Nf., Can.	E5	72
Bays, Lake of, l., On., Can.	B5	73
Bay Saint Louis, Ms., U.S.	E4	101
Bayshore, Mi., U.S.	C5	99
Bay Shore, N.Y., U.S.	E7	109
Bayshore Gardens, Fl., U.S.	q10	86
Bayside, Tx., U.S.	E4	120
Bayside, Wi., U.S.	m12	126
Bays Mountains, mtn., Tn., U.S.	C10	119
Bays Mountains, mtn., Tn., U.S.	n14	119
Bay Springs, Ms., U.S.	D4	101
Baysun, Sov. Un.	B13	39
Bayt al Faqīh, Yemen	g12	41
Bayt Dajan, Isr. Occ.	g12	41
Baytīlū, Isr. Occ.	h11	41
Bayt Jālā, Isr. Occ.	C7	41
Baytown, Tx., U.S.	E5	120
Bay Trail, Sk., Can.	E3	75
Bayview, Al., U.S.	f7	78
Bayview, Id., U.S.	B2	89
Bay View, Mi., U.S.	C5	99
Bay View, Ms., U.S.	A3	111
Bay View Park, De., U.S.	F5	85
Bay Village, Oh., U.S.	h9	112
Bayville, De., U.S.	F5	85
Bayville, N.J., U.S.	D4	107
Bayville, N.Y., U.S.	*E7	109
Bayzah, Bi'r, well, Eg.	D6	43
Baza, Spain	D5	22
Bazaruto, Ilha do i., Moz.	B6	49
Bazemore, Al., U.S.	B2	78
Bazhong, China	E8	31
Bazile Mills, Ne., U.S.	B8	104
Bazine, Ks., U.S.	D4	93
Bazmān, Kūh-e, mtn., Iran	G10	39
Baztán, Spain	A5	22
Be, Nosy, i., Madag.	f9	49
Beach, Il., U.S.	h9	90
Beach, N.D., U.S.	C1	111
Beachburg, On., Can.	B8	73
Beach City, Oh., U.S.	B4	112
Beachville, On., Can.	D4	73
Beachwood, N.J., U.S.	D4	107
Beachwood, Oh., U.S.	*h10	112
Beachy Head, c., Eng., U.K.	D8	12
Beacon, Ia., U.S.	C5	92
Beacon, N.Y., U.S.	D7	109
Beacon Falls, Ct., U.S.	D3	84
Beacon Hill, Fl., U.S.	C1	86
Beaconsfield, P.Q., Can.	q19	74
Beadle, Sk., Can.	F1	75
Beadle, co., S.D., U.S.	C7	118
Beagh, Slieve, hill, N. Ire., U.K.	C4	11
Beagle, Ks., U.S.	D9	93
Beagle, Canal, strt., S.A.	h12	54
Bealanana, Madag.	f9	49
Beal City, Mi., U.S.	E6	99
Beale Air Force Base, mil., Ca., U.S.	C3	82
Beallsville, Oh., U.S.	C4	112
Beals, Ky., U.S.	C2	94
Beals, Me., U.S.	D5	96
Bean Lake, Mo., U.S.	B3	102
Bean Station, Tn., U.S.	C10	119
Bear, De., U.S.	B3	85
Bear, i., Ire.	F2	11
Bear, i., Nor.	B13	128
Bear, stm., U.S.	B3	121
Bearcreek, Mt., U.S.	E7	103
Bear Creek, Wi., U.S.	D5	126
Bear Creek, stm., U.S.	E2	93
Bear Creek, stm., Al., U.S.	A1	78
Bear Creek, stm., Or., U.S.	E4	114
Bear Creek, stm., Wy., U.S.	E4	127
Bearden, Ar., U.S.	D3	81
Bearden, Ok., U.S.	B5	113
Beardmore, On., Can.	o18	73
Beardmore Glacier, Ant.	A30	7
Beards Fork, W.V., U.S.	m13	125
Beardsley, Mn., U.S.	E2	100
Beardstown, Il., U.S.	C3	90
Beardstown, Tn., U.S.	B4	119
Bearfort Mountain, mtn., N.J., U.S.	A4	107
Bear Inlet, b., N.C., U.S.	C5	110
Bear Island, i., Mb., Can.	B3	70
Bear Lake, Mi., U.S.	D4	99
Bear Lake, co., Id., U.S.	G7	89
Bear Lake, l., Ab., Can.	B1	68
Bear Lake, l., B.C., Can.	A4	69
Bear Lake, l., Mb., Can.	B4	70
Bear Lake, l., B.C., Can.	A4	121
Bear Lake, l., Wi., U.S.	C1	126
Bear Lodge Mountains, mts., Wy., U.S.	B8	127
Bear Mountain, mtn., Ar., U.S.	f7	81
Bear Mountain, mtn., Ca., U.S.	C5	94
Bear Mountain, mtn., Ma., U.S.	A3	98
Bear Mountain, mtn., Or., U.S.	D4	114
Béarn, hist reg., Fr.	F3	16
Bear Peninsula, pen., Ant.	B7	7
Bear Pond Mountains, mts., Md., U.S.	A2	97
Bear River, Ns., Can.	E4	71
Bear River City, Ut., U.S.	B3	121
Bear Spring, Tn., U.S.	A4	119
Bear Swamp, sw., Ma., U.S.	h11	98
Bear Tooth Pass, Wy., U.S.	B3	127
Beartooth Range, mts., U.S.	E7	103
Bear Town, Ms., U.S.	D3	101
Beartown Mountain, mtn., Va., U.S.	f10	123
Beas de Segura, Spain	C4	22
Beason, Il., U.S.	C4	90
Beata, Cabo, c., Dom. Rep.	F8	64
Beaton, B.C., Can.	D9	69
Beatrice, Al., U.S.	D2	78
Beatrice, Ne., U.S.	D9	104
Beatrice, Zimb.	A5	49
Beatton, stm., B.C., Can.	A7	69
Beatty, Sk., Can.	E3	75
Beatty, Nv., U.S.	G5	105
Beattyville, Ky., U.S.	C6	94
Beattystown, N.J., U.S.	B3	107
Beaucaire, Fr.	F6	16
Beauceville-Est, P.Q., Can.	C7	74
Beaucoup Creek, stm., La., U.S.	B3	—
Beaufort, Fr.	D7	16
Beaufort, Malay.	D5	34
Beaufort, Mo., U.S.	C6	102
Beaufort, N.C., U.S.	C6	110
Beaufort, S.C., U.S.	G6	117
Beaufort, co., N.C., U.S.	B5	110
Beaufort, co., S.C., U.S.	G6	117
Beaufort Island, i., Ant.	e38	7
Beaufort Marine Corps Air Station, mil., S.C., U.S.	F6	117
Beaufort Sea, N.A.	B10	79
Beaufort West, S. Afr.	D3	49
Beaugency, Fr.	C4	16
Beauharnois, P.Q., Can.	D4	74
Beauharnois, co., P.Q., Can.	D4	74
Beaulieu, P.Q., Can.	n17	74
Beaulieu, Scot., U.K.	A3	12
Beauly, Scot., U.K.	C4	13
Beauly, stm., Scot., U.K.	A3	12
Beaumaris, Wales, U.K.	A3	12
Beaumont, Bel.	D4	17
Beaumont, Nf., Can.	D4	72
Beaumont, Fr.	F4	16
Beaumont, Ca., U.S.	*F5	82
Beaumont, Ks., U.S.	E7	93
Beaumont, Ms., U.S.	D5	101
Beaumont, Tx., U.S.	D6	120
Beaumont [-sur-Oise], Fr.	E2	17
Beaune, Fr.	D6	16
Beaupré, P.Q., Can.	B7	74
Beauregard, Bel.	D4	17
Beauregard, co., La., U.S.	D2	95
Beaurivage, Mb., Can.	D3	70
Beausejour, Mb., Can.	D3	70
Beauty, Ky., U.S.	C7	94
Beauvais, Fr.	E2	16
Beauval, Sk., Can.	B2	75
Beauval, Fr.	D2	17
Beauvallon, Ab., Can.	C5	68
Beaver, Ak., U.S.	B10	79
Beaver, Ok., U.S.	*A2	113
Beaver, Oh., U.S.	C3	112
Beaver, Pa., U.S.	E1	115
Beaver, Ut., U.S.	E3	121
Beaver, W.V., U.S.	D3	125
Beaver, Wi., U.S.	C6	126
Beaver, co., Ok., U.S.	e10	113
Beaver, co., Pa., U.S.	E1	115
Beaver, co., Ut., U.S.	E2	121
Beaver, stm., Can.	B2	75
Beaver, stm., N.Y., U.S.	A6	109
Beaver, stm., R.I., U.S.	E2	116
Beaver, stm., U.S.	E6	71
Beaver Bank, N.S., Can.	E6	71
Beaver Bay, Mn., U.S.	C7	100
Beaver Brook, stm., U.S.	E4	106
Beaver City, Ne., U.S.	D6	104

Name	Map Ref	Page

Beaver Creek, B.C., Can. — E5 69
Beaver Creek, Mn., U.S. — G2 100
Beavercreek, Oh., U.S. — C1 112
Beaver Creek, stm., Sk., Can. — F2 75
Beaver Creek, stm., U.S. — E4 104
Beaver Creek, stm., U.S. — C8 127
Beaver Creek, stm., Ia., U.S. — e8 92
Beaver Creek, stm., Ky., U.S. — C7 94
Beaver Creek, stm., Mo., U.S. — A2 97
Beaver Creek, stm., Mt., U.S. — E5 102
Beaver Creek, stm., Mt., U.S. — B9 103
Beaver Creek, stm., Ne., U.S. — C7 104
Beaver Creek, stm., N.D., U.S. — C1 111
Beaver Creek, stm., N.D., U.S. — C5 111
Beaver Creek, stm., Ok., U.S. — C3 113
Beaver Creek, stm., Tn., U.S. — m13 119
Beaver Creek, stm., Wy., U.S. — D4 127
Beaver Creek Mountains, mts., Al., U.S. — B3 78
Beaver Crossing, Ne., U.S. — D8 104
Beaverdale, Pa., U.S. — F4 115
Beaver Dam, Az., U.S. — A2 80
Beaver Dam, In., U.S. — B5 91
Beaver Dam, Ky., U.S. — C3 94
Beaver Dam, Oh., U.S. — B2 112
Beaverdam, Ut., U.S. — *B3 121
Beaverdam, Va., U.S. — C5 123
Beaver Dam, Wi., U.S. — E5 126
Beaverdam Branch, stm., De., U.S. — F3 85
Beaverdam Lake, res., Wi., U.S. — E5 126
Beaver Dams, N.Y., U.S. — C4 109
Beaverdell, B.C., Can. — E8 69
Beaver Falls, N.Y., U.S. — B5 109
Beaver Falls, Pa., U.S. — E1 115
Beaverhead, co., Mt., U.S. — E3 103
Beaverhead, stm., Mt., U.S. — E4 103
Beaverhead Mountains, mts., U.S. — D5 89
Beaver Hill Lake, l., Mb., Can. — C4 68
Beaver Island, i., Mi., U.S. — C4 70
Beaver Lake, l., Ab., Can. — C5 99
Beaver Lake, res., Ar., U.S. — A2 81
Beaverlick, Ky., U.S. — k13 94
Beaverlodge, Ab., Can. — B1 68
Beaver Meadows, Pa., U.S. — E10 115
Beaver Point, Co., U.S. — A5 83
Beaver Ridge, mtn., Pa., U.S. — D9 119
Beaver Run Reservoir, res., Pa., U.S. — F2 115
Beaver Springs, Pa., U.S. — E7 115
Beavertail Point, c., R.I., U.S. — F4 116
Beaverton, On., Can. — C5 73
Beaverton, Al., U.S. — B1 78
Beaverton, Mi., U.S. — E6 99
Beaverton, Or., U.S. — B4 114
Beavertown, Pa., U.S. — E7 115
Beaverville, Il., U.S. — C6 90
Beazley, Arg. — A3 54
Bebedouro, Braz. — C3 56
Bebra, F.R.Ger. — C4 19
Bécancour, P.Q., Can. — C5 74
Bécancour, stm., P.Q., Can. — C6 74
Beccles, Eng., U.K. — B9 12
Bečej, Yugo. — C5 24
Becerreá, Spain — A2 22
Béchar, Alg. — C4 44
Becharof Lake, l., Ak., U.S. — D8 79
Bechyně, Czech. — D9 19
Beckemeyer, Il., U.S. — E4 90
Becker, Mn., U.S. — E5 100
Becker, Ms., U.S. — B5 101
Becker, co., Mn., U.S. — D3 100
Becket, Ma., U.S. — B1 98
Beckham, co., Ok., U.S. — B2 113
Beckley, W.V., U.S. — D3 125
Beckum, F.R.Ger. — B3 19
Beckville, Tx., U.S. — C5 120
Beckwith Creek, stm., La., U.S. — D2 95
Becky Peak, mtn., Nv., U.S. — D7 105
Bedale, Eng., U.K. — F7 13
Bédarieux, Fr. — F5 16
Bedburg, F.R.Ger. — C1 19
Bederkesa, F.R.Ger. — E2 15
Bedford, N.S., Can. — E6 71
Bedford, P.Q., Can. — D5 74
Bedford, Eng., U.K. — D6 10
Bedford, In., U.S. — G5 91
Bedford, Ia., U.S. — D3 92
Bedford, Ky., U.S. — B4 94
Bedford, Ma., U.S. — B5 98
Bedford, Mi., U.S. — F5 99
Bedford, Mo., U.S. — A4 102
Bedford, N.H., U.S. — E3 106
Bedford, Oh., U.S. — A4 112
Bedford, Pa., U.S. — F4 115
Bedford, Tx., U.S. — *n9 120
Bedford, Va., U.S. — C3 123
Bedford, Wy., U.S. — D2 127
Bedford, co., Pa., U.S. — G4 115
Bedford, co., Tn., U.S. — B5 119
Bedford, co., Va., U.S. — C3 123
Bedford Heights, Oh., U.S. — *h9 112
Bedford Hills, N.Y., U.S. — D7 109
Bedfordshire, co., Eng., U.K. — B7 12
Bedias, Tx., U.S. — D5 120
Bedlington, Eng., U.K. — C6 10
Bedminster, N.J., U.S. — B3 107
Bedourie, Austl. — B2 51
Bedrock, Co., U.S. — C2 83
Bedzin, Pol. — g10 26
Bee, Ne., U.S. — C8 104
Bee, co., Tx., U.S. — E4 120
Beebe, P.Q., Can. — D5 74
Beebe, Ar., U.S. — B4 81
Beebe Plain, Vt., U.S. — A4 122
Beebe Plain, N.H., U.S. — C3 106
Bee Branch, Ar., U.S. — B3 81
Beech Bluff, Tn., U.S. — B3 119
Beech Creek, Ky., U.S. — C2 94
Beech Creek, Pa., U.S. — D6 115
Beecher, Il., U.S. — B6 90
Beecher, Mi., U.S. — E7 99
Beecher City, Il., U.S. — D5 90
Beechey Head, c., B.C., Can. — h12 69
Beech Fork, stm., Ky., U.S. — C4 94
Beech Grove, In., U.S. — E5 91
Beech Grove, Ky., U.S. — C2 94
Beechgrove, Tn., U.S. — B5 119
Beech Island, S.C., U.S. — E4 117
Beechwood, N.B., Can. — C2 71
Beechwood, Ma., U.S. — h12 98
Beechwood, Mi., U.S. — B3 99
Beechy, Sk., Can. — G2 75
Beecroft Head, c., Austl. — B8 51
Beedeville, Ar., U.S. — B4 81
Beef Island, i., Tn., U.S. — e8 119

Beef Island, i., V.I., Br. — B6 65
Beek, Neth. — D5 17
Beeler, Ks., U.S. — D3 93
Beelitz, Ger.D.R. — A7 19
Beemer, Ne., U.S. — C9 104
Beenleigh, Austl. — C9 51
Bee Ridge, Fl., U.S. — q11 86
Beersheba (Be'er Sheva'), Isr. — B3 38
Beersheba Springs, Tn., U.S. — D8 119
Beersville, N.B., Can. — C4 71
Beesley Point, N.J., U.S. — E3 107
Beeton, On., Can. — C5 73
Beetzendorf, Ger.D.R. — F5 15
Beeville, Tx., U.S. — E4 120
Befale, Zaire — A3 48
Beg, Lough, l., N. Ire., U.K. — C5 11
Bega, Austl. — G8 50
Begicheva, i., Sov. Un. — B3 128
Béhague, Pointe, c., Fr. Gu. — B4 59
Behäla (South Suburban), India — *D8 36
Behbehān, Iran — F5 39
Behm Canal, strt., Ak., U.S. — n24 79
Behshahr, Iran — C6 39
Bei'an, China — B10 31
Beigi, Eth. — D3 47
Beihai, China — G6 31
Beijing see Peking, China — D8 31
Beili, China — C8 35
Beilngries, F.R.Ger. — D6 19
Beinamar, Chad — D3 46
Beira, Moz. — A5 49
Beira, hist reg., Port. — B2 22
Beirne, Ar., U.S. — D2 81
Beirut (Bayrūt), Leb. — B3 38
Beiseker, Ab., Can. — D4 68
Beitbridge, Zimb. — B5 49
Beius, Rom. — B6 24
Béja, Port. — C2 22
Béja, Tun. — B6 44
Bejaïa (Bougie), Alg. — B6 44
Béjar, Spain — B3 22
Bejestān, Iran — D9 39
Bejou, Mn., U.S. — C3 100
Bejuco, Pan. — F8 62
Bekabad, Sov. Un. — G22 8
Bekdash, Sov. Un. — E4 28
Békés, Hung. — B5 24
Békéscsaba, Hung. — B5 24
Bekily, Madag. — h9 49
Bela, India — E8 37
Bela, Pak. — C4 36
Bela Crkva, Yugo. — C5 24
Belaga, Malay. — E4 34
Bel Air, Md., U.S. — B5 97
Bel Air, Ks., U.S. — g12 93
Bel Aire Estates, Ct., U.S. — D7 84
Belalcázar, Spain — C3 22
Bel Alton, Md., U.S. — D4 97
Bélanger, stm., Mb., Can. — C3 70
Belanger, stm., Sk., Can. — B2 75
Belas, Port. — f9 22
Bela Vista, Braz. — C1 56
Bela Vista, Moz. — C5 49
Bela Vista de Goiás, Braz. — B3 56
Belawan, Indon. — E1 34
Belaya Glina, Sov. Un. — H13 27
Belaya Tserkov, Sov. Un. — G8 27
Belcamp, Md., U.S. — B5 97
Belcher, Ky., U.S. — C7 94
Belcher, La., U.S. — B2 95
Belcherāgh, Afg. — D12 39
Belcher Islands, is., N.T., Can. — E17 66
Belchertown, Ma., U.S. — B3 98
Belcourt, N.D., U.S. — A6 111
Belcoville, N.J., U.S. — E3 107
Belden, Ms., U.S. — A5 101
Belden, Ne., U.S. — B8 104
Belding, Mi., U.S. — E5 99
Belecke, F.R.Ger. — B3 19
Beled Weyne, Som. — E6 47
Belém (Pará), Braz. — B1 57
Belém, Port. — f9 22
Belén, Arg. — E2 55
Belén, Para. — D4 55
Belen, Ms., U.S. — A3 101
Belen, N.M., U.S. — C3 108
Belén, Ur. — E1 56
Belén de Escobar, Arg. — g7 54
Belenkoye, Sov. Un. — q20 27
Belev, Sov. Un. — E11 27
Belfair, Wa., U.S. — B3 124
Belfast, N. Ire., U.K. — C4 10
Belfast, Me., U.S. — D3 96
Belfast, N.Y., U.S. — C2 109
Belfast, N.C., U.S. — B5 110
Belfast, Oh., U.S. — C2 112
Belfast, Tn., U.S. — B5 119
Belfast Lough, b., N. Ire., U.K. — C6 11
Belfield, N.D., U.S. — C2 111
Belford, Eng., U.K. — E7 13
Belford, N.J., U.S. — C4 107
Belfort, ter., Fr. — D7 16
Belfort, N.Y., U.S. — B5 109
Belfry, Ky., U.S. — C7 94
Belfry, Mt., U.S. — E8 103
Belgaum, India — E5 36
Belgica Mountains, mts., Ant. — B16 7
Belgium, Il., U.S. — C6 90
Belgium, Wi., U.S. — E6 126
Belgium, ctry., Eur. — B6 16
Belgorod, Sov. Un. — F11 27
Belgorod-Dnestrovskiy, Sov. Un. — H8 27
Belgrade, Mn., U.S. — E3 100
Belgrade, Mt., U.S. — E5 103
Belgrade (Beograd), Yugo. — C5 24
Belgrade Lakes, Me., U.S. — D3 96
Belgreen, Al., U.S. — A2 78
Belhaven, N.C., U.S. — B6 110
Belice, stm., Italy — F4 23
Beli Lom, stm., Bul. — D8 24
Belington, W.V., U.S. — B5 125
Belitung, i., Indon. — F3 34
Belize, ctry., N.A. — D7 63
Belize, stm., Belize — B3 62
Belize City, Belize — D7 63
Belkino, Sov. Un. — B11 33
Belknap, Il., U.S. — F5 90
Belknap, co., N.H., U.S. — C3 106
Belknap Crater, crat., Or., U.S. — C5 114
Belknap Mountain, mtn., N.H., U.S. — C4 106
Belkovski, stm., Sov. Un. — B1 128

Bell, Ca., U.S. — *E4 82
Bell, Fl., U.S. — C4 86
Bell, co., Ky., U.S. — D6 94
Bell, co., Tx., U.S. — D4 120
Bella Bella, B.C., Can. — C3 69
Bellac, Fr. — D4 16
Bella Coola, B.C., Can. — C4 69
Bella Coola, stm., B.C., Can. — C4 69
Bellagio, Italy — D5 20
Bellahy, Ire. — D3 11
Bellair, Fl., U.S. — *m8 86
Bellaire, Ks., U.S. — C5 93
Bellaire, Mi., U.S. — D5 99
Bellaire, Oh., U.S. — B5 112
Bellaire, Tx., U.S. — r14 120
Bellano, Italy — D7 21
Bellary, India — E6 36
Bella Unión, Ur. — E1 56
Bella Vista, Arg. — E4 55
Bella Vista, Arg. — E2 55
Bella Vista, Para. — D4 55
Bella Vista, Ar., U.S. — A1 81
Bellbrook, Oh., U.S. — C1 112
Bell Buckle, Tn., U.S. — B5 119
Bell City, La., U.S. — D3 95
Bell City, Mo., U.S. — D8 102
Belle, Mo., U.S. — C6 102
Belle, W.V., U.S. — C3 125
Belle, stm., La., U.S. — k9 95
Belleair, Fl., U.S. — p10 86
Belle-Anse, Haiti — E7 64
Belle Bay, b., Nf., Can. — E4 72
Belle Center, Oh., U.S. — B2 112
Belle Chasse, La., U.S. — E5 95
Bellechasse, co., P.Q., Can. — C7 74
Belle Creek, Mt., U.S. — E11 103
Belledune, N.B., Can. — B4 71
Belleek, N. Ire., U.K. — C3 11
Bellefleur, N.B., Can. — B2 71
Bellefontaine, Ms., U.S. — B4 101
Bellefontaine, Oh., U.S. — B2 112
Bellefontaine Neighbors, Mo., U.S. — *f13 102
Bellefonte, Ar., U.S. — A2 81
Bellefonte, De., U.S. — *A3 85
Bellefonte, Pa., U.S. — E6 115
Belle Fourche, S.D., U.S. — C2 118
Belle Fourche, stm., U.S. — C3 118
Belle Fourche Reservoir, res., S.D., U.S. — C2 118
Bellegarde, Fr. — D6 16
Belle Glade, Fl., U.S. — F6 86
Belle Haven, Va., U.S. — C7 123
Belleherbe, Fr. — B2 21
Belle Hôtesse, mtn., Guad. — Q8 65
Belle Isle, Fl., U.S. — D5 86
Belle Isle, i., Nf., Can. — C4 72
Belle Isle, Strait of, strt., Nf., Can. — C3 72
Belleisle Creek, N.B., Can. — D4 71
Belle Mead, N.J., U.S. — C3 107
Belle Meade, Tn., U.S. — g10 119
Belle Mina, Al., U.S. — A3 78
Bellemoor, De., U.S. — *B3 85
Bellemore, Nf., Can. — E4 72
Belleplaine, N.J., U.S. — E3 107
Belle-Plaine, Sk., Can. — G3 75
Belle Plaine, Ia., U.S. — C5 92
Belle Plaine, Ks., U.S. — E6 93
Belle Plaine, Mn., U.S. — F5 100
Belle River, Il., U.S. — E5 90
Belle River, On., Can. — E2 73
Belle Rose, La., U.S. — D4 95
Belleu, Fr. — E3 17
Belle Union, Il., U.S. — E4 91
Belle Valley, Oh., U.S. — C4 112
Belle Vernon, Pa., U.S. — F2 115
Belleview, Fl., U.S. — C4 86
Belleview, Mo., U.S. — D7 102
Belle View, Va., U.S. — g12 123
Belleville, N.S., Can. — F4 71
Belleville, On., Can. — C7 73
Belleville, Fr. — D6 16
Belleville, Ar., U.S. — B2 81
Belleville, Il., U.S. — E4 90
Belleville, Ks., U.S. — C6 93
Belleville, Mi., U.S. — p15 99
Belleville, N.J., U.S. — B4 107
Belleville, N.Y., U.S. — B4 109
Belleville, Pa., U.S. — E6 115
Belleville, R.I., U.S. — E4 116
Belleville, W.V., U.S. — B3 125
Belleville Pond, l., R.I., U.S. — E4 116
Belleville [-sur-Meuse], Fr. — E5 17
Belle Yella, Lib. — E3 45
Bellflower, Ca., U.S. — n12 82
Bellflower, Il., U.S. — C5 90
Bellflower, Mo., U.S. — B6 102
Bell Gardens, Ca., U.S. — *n12 82
Bellin, P.Q., Can. — f12 74
Bellingham, Eng., U.K. — E6 13
Bellingham, Ma., U.S. — B5 98
Bellingham, Wa., U.S. — A3 124
Bellingshausen Sea, Ant. — B3 7
Bellinzona, Switz. — E4 18
Bell-Irving, stm., B.C., Can. — A3 69
Bell Island, i., Nf., Can. — E5 72
Bell Island, i., Nf., Can. — E5 72
Bellmawr, N.J., U.S. — D2 107
Bellmead, Tx., U.S. — *D4 120
Bellmore, N.Y., U.S. — *m15 109
Bellona, Col. — B2 60
Bellows Falls, Vt., U.S. — E4 122
Bellport, N.Y., U.S. — n16 109
Bell Ranch, N.M., U.S. — B5 108
Bells, Tn., U.S. — B2 119
Bells Corners, On., Can. — h12 73
Bells Creek, stm., W.V., U.S. — *m13 125
Bellshill, Scot., U.K. — *E4 13
Belltown, De., U.S. — F5 85
Bell Ville, Arg. — A4 54
Bellville, Ga., U.S. — D5 87

Bellville, Oh., U.S. — B3 112
Bellville, Tx., U.S. — E4 120
Bellvue, Co., U.S. — A5 83
Bellwood, Al., U.S. — D4 78
Bellwood, Il., U.S. — k9 90
Bellwood, Ne., U.S. — C8 104
Bellwood, Pa., U.S. — E5 115
Bellwood, Va., U.S. — n18 123
Belly, stm., N.A. — E4 68
Belmar, N.J., U.S. — C4 107
Belmond, Ia., U.S. — B4 92
Belmont, Mb., Can. — E2 70
Belmont, N.S., Can. — D6 71
Belmont, On., Can. — E3 73
Belmont, Ca., U.S. — h8 82
Belmont, La., U.S. — C2 95
Belmont, Ma., U.S. — g11 98
Belmont, N.H., U.S. — D4 106
Belmont, N.Y., U.S. — C2 109
Belmont, N.C., U.S. — B1 110
Belmont, Oh., U.S. — B4 112
Belmont, Tx., U.S. — k8 120
Belmont, Vt., U.S. — E3 122
Belmont, W.V., U.S. — B3 125
Belmont, Wi., U.S. — F3 126
Belmont, Zaire — A4 48
Belmont, co., Oh., U.S. — C4 112
Belmonte, Braz. — E3 57
Belmont Heights, Ut., U.S. — *C4 121
Belmopan, Belize — D7 63
Belmore, Oh., U.S. — A2 112
Belmullet, Ire. — C1 11
Bel-Nor, Mo., U.S. — f13 102
Belo, Madag. — g8 49
Belogorsk, Sov. Un. — D15 29
Belo Horizonte, Braz. — B4 56
Beloit, Ia., U.S. — A1 92
Beloit, Ks., U.S. — C5 93
Beloit, Oh., U.S. — B5 112
Beloit, Wi., U.S. — F4 126
Beloit North, Wi., U.S. — F4 126
Belokany, Sov. Un. — B16 40
Belomorsk, Sov. Un. — C6 29
Belopolye, Sov. Un. — F10 27
Beloretsk, Sov. Un. — D8 29
Belovo, Sov. Un. — E26 8
Beloye, Lake, l., Sov. Un. — A11 27
Belozersk, Sov. Un. — B11 27
Belp, Switz. — C4 21
Belpre, Ks., U.S. — A6 12
Belpre, Oh., U.S. — C4 112
Belshaw, In., U.S. — B3 91
Belspring, Va., U.S. — C2 123
Belt, Mt., U.S. — C6 103
Belted Range, mts., Nv., U.S. — F5 105
Belterra, Braz. — C4 59
Belton, Mo., U.S. — C3 102
Belton, S.C., U.S. — B3 117
Belton, Tx., U.S. — D4 120
Belton Lake, res., Tx., U.S. — D4 120
Beltra, Ire. — C3 11
Beltrami, co., Mn., U.S. — B3 100
Beltsville, Md., U.S. — B4 97
Beltsy, Sov. Un. — H6 27
Belukha, Mount, mtn., Sov. Un. — E11 29
Belumut, mtn., Malay. — L5 35
Belvedere, S.C., U.S. — D4 117
Belvedere Marittimo, Italy — E5 23
Belvedere Park, Ga., U.S. — *h8 87
Belvidere, De., U.S. — *B3 85
Belvidere, Il., U.S. — A5 90
Belvidere, Ne., U.S. — D8 104
Belvidere, N.J., U.S. — B2 107
Belvidere, N.C., U.S. — A6 110
Belvidere, S.D., U.S. — D4 118
Belvidere, Tn., U.S. — B5 119
Belvidere Center, Vt., U.S. — B3 122
Belview, Mn., U.S. — F3 100
Belvue, Ks., U.S. — C7 93
Belwood, On., Can. — D4 73
Belyando, stm., Austl. — D8 50
Belyy, Sov. Un. — D9 27
Belyy Bom, Sov. Un. — E26 8
Belyy Island, i., Sov. Un. — B9 29
Belyy Yar, Sov. Un. — B11 28
Belzig, Ger.D.R. — A7 19
Belzoni, Ms., U.S. — B3 101
Bembèzar, stm., Spain — C3 22
Bement, Il., U.S. — D5 90
Bemidji, Mn., U.S. — C4 100
Bemidji, Lake, l., Mn., U.S. — C4 100
Bemis, S.D., U.S. — C9 118
Bemis, Tn., U.S. — B3 119
Bemis, W.V., U.S. — C5 125
Bemus Point, N.Y., U.S. — C1 109
Benāb, Iran — C3 39
Benagerie, Austl. — G8 50
Benalla, Austl. — G9 50
Benalto, Ab., Can. — C3 68
Benavente, Spain — A3 22
Benavides, Tx., U.S. — F3 120
Benbane Head, c., N. Ire., U.K. — B5 11
Benbaun, mtn., Ire. — D2 11
Benbecula, i., Scot., U.K. — C1 13
Ben Bolt, Tx., U.S. — F3 120
Benbow, Fl., U.S. — F5 86
Benbrook, Tx., U.S. — *n9 120
Benbrook Lake, res., Tx., U.S. — *n9 120
Benchland, Mt., U.S. — C7 103
Ben Davis Point, c., N.J., U.S. — E2 107
Bendeleben, Mount, mtn., Ak., U.S. — B7 79
Bender Beyla, Som. — E8 47
Bendersville, Pa., U.S. — G7 115
Bendery, Sov. Un. — H7 27
Bendigo, Austl. — G7 50
Bendorf, F.R.Ger. — C2 19
Bene Beraq, Isr. — g10 41
Bene Berit, Isr. — B7 41
Benedict, Md., U.S. — C4 97
Benedict, Ne., U.S. — C8 104
Benedict, N.D., U.S. — B4 111

Benedict, Mount, mtn., Nf., Can. — g10 72
Benedicta, Me., U.S. — C4 96
Benenitra, Madag. — h9 49
Beneraird, hill, Scot., U.K. — E4 13
Benešov, Czech. — D3 26
Benestroff, Fr. — F6 17
Benevento, Italy — D5 23
Benevolence, Ga., U.S. — E2 87
Benewah, co., Id., U.S. — B2 89
Benezett, Pa., U.S. — D5 115
Benfeld, Fr. — A3 20
Bengal, Ok., U.S. — C6 113
Bengal, hist reg., Asia — D8 36
Bengal, Bay of, b., Asia — F8 36
Bengbu, China — E8 31
Benghazi (Banghāzī), Libya — C4 43
Bengkalis, Indon. — E2 34
Bengkalis, i., Indon. — L5 35
Bengkulu, Indon. — F2 34
Bengo, dept., Ang. — C1 48
Bengough, Sk., Can. — H3 75
Benguela, Ang. — D1 48
Benguela, dept., Ang. — D1 48
Benham, Ky., U.S. — D7 94
Ben Hill, co., Ga., U.S. — E3 87
Beni, Nig. — D7 45
Beni, Zaire — A4 48
Beni, dept., Bol. — B2 55
Béni, stm., Bol. — B2 55
Béni Abbas, Alg. — C4 44
Benicarló, Spain — B6 22
Benicia, Ca., U.S. — C2 82
Benito, stm., Bol. — B2 55
Beni Mellal, Mor. — C3 44
Benin, ctry., Afr. — E5 45
Benin, Bight of, Afr. — E5 45
Benin City, Nig. — E6 45
Benisa, Spain — C6 22
Beni Saf, Alg. — B4 44
Benito, Mb., Can. — D1 70
Benito Juárez, Arg. — D5 55
Benjamin, Tx., U.S. — C3 120
Benjamin Constant, Braz. — B3 58
Benkelman, Ne., U.S. — D4 104
Benkovac, Yugo. — C2 20
Benld, Il., U.S. — D4 90
Ben Lomond, Ar., U.S. — D1 81
Benmore, Lake, res., N.Z. — P12 51
Benmore Head, c., N. Ire., U.K. — B5 11
Bennett, Ne., U.S. — D9 104
Bennett, Co., U.S. — B6 83
Bennett, Ia., U.S. — C7 92
Bennett, N.C., U.S. — B3 110
Bennett, co., S.D., U.S. — D4 118
Bennett Creek, stm., Md., U.S. — B3 97
Bennett Island, i., Sov. Un. — B18 29
Bennett Lake, l., Mb., Can. — C3 70
Bennettsbridge, Ire. — E4 11
Bennettsville, S.C., U.S. — B8 117
Bennington, Id., U.S. — G7 89
Bennington, Ne., U.S. — C9 104
Bennington, N.H., U.S. — E3 106
Bennington, Ok., U.S. — C5 113
Bennington, Vt., U.S. — F2 122
Bennington, co., Vt., U.S. — E2 122
Bennion, Ut., U.S. — *C4 121
Benns Church, Va., U.S. — k14 123
Benoit, Ms., U.S. — B2 101
Benoit, Wi., U.S. — B2 126
Bénoué (Benue), stm., Afr. — E7 45
Benoy, Chad — D3 46
Benque Viejo, Belize — D7 63
Bensalem, Pa., U.S. — *F12 115
Bensberg, F.R.Ger. — C2 19
Bensenville, Il., U.S. — B6 90
Bensheim, F.R.Ger. — C3 19
Bensley, Va., U.S. — C5 123
Benson, Sk., Can. — H4 75
Benson, Az., U.S. — F5 80
Benson, Il., U.S. — C4 90
Benson, La., U.S. — C2 95
Benson, Md., U.S. — A5 97
Benson, Mn., U.S. — E3 100
Benson, N.C., U.S. — B4 110
Benson, Vt., U.S. — D2 122
Benson, co., N.D., U.S. — A6 111
Bent, N.M., U.S. — B5 108
Bent, co., Co., U.S. — D7 83
Bentham, Eng., U.K. — A2 19
Bentinck, i., Burma — G2 35
Bentiu, Sud. — D2 47
Bentley, Ab., Can. — C3 68
Bentley, Ks., U.S. — E6 93
Bentley, La., U.S. — C3 95
Bentley, N.D., U.S. — C3 111
Bentley, Ok., U.S. — C6 113
Bentley Creek, Pa., U.S. — C8 115
Bentley Springs, Md., U.S. — A4 97
Bentleyville, Pa., U.S. — F1 115
Benton, N.B., Can. — C2 71
Benton, Ar., U.S. — C3 81
Benton, Ca., U.S. — D4 82
Benton, Il., U.S. — E5 90
Benton, Ks., U.S. — E6 93
Benton, Ky., U.S. — f9 94
Benton, La., U.S. — B2 95
Benton, Me., U.S. — D3 96
Benton, Ms., U.S. — C3 101
Benton, Mo., U.S. — D8 102
Benton, Pa., U.S. — D9 115
Benton, Tn., U.S. — D9 119
Benton, Wi., U.S. — F3 126
Benton, co., Ar., U.S. — A1 81
Benton, co., In., U.S. — C3 91
Benton, co., Ia., U.S. — B5 92
Benton, co., Mn., U.S. — E4 100
Benton, co., Ms., U.S. — A4 101
Benton, co., Mo., U.S. — C4 102
Benton, co., Or., U.S. — C3 114
Benton, co., Tn., U.S. — A3 119
Benton, co., Wa., U.S. — C6 124
Benton City, Mo., U.S. — B6 102
Benton City, Wa., U.S. — C6 124
Benton Harbor, Mi., U.S. — F4 99
Benton Heights, Mi., U.S. — F4 99
Bentonia, Ms., U.S. — C3 101
Bentonville, Ar., U.S. — A1 81
Bentonville, Oh., U.S. — D2 112
Bentonville, Va., U.S. — B4 123
Bentree, W.V., U.S. — m13 125

Bent's Old Fort National Historic Site, hist., Co., U.S. — C7 83
Benue (Bénoué), stm., Afr. — E6 45
Benwee Head, c., Ire. — C2 11
Benwood, W.V., U.S. — f8 125
Benxi, China — C9 31
Benzie, co., Mi., U.S. — D4 99
Benzonia, Mi., U.S. — D4 99
Beo, Indon. — E7 34
Béoumi, I.C. — E3 45
Beowawe, Nv., U.S. — C5 105
Beppu, Japan — J5 33
Beqa, i., Fiji — I15 52
Beqa Passage, strt., Fiji — I14 52
Berach, stm., India — E5 37
Berat, Alb. — B2 25
Berau, F.R.Ger. — A5 21
Berau Bay, b., Indon. — F8 34
Berbera, Som. — C6 47
Berbérati, Cen. Afr. Rep. — E3 46
Berbice, stm., Guy. — B3 59
Bercher, Switz. — C2 21
Berchogur, Sov. Un. — D5 28
Berchtesgaden, F.R.Ger. — E6 18
Berck, Fr. — B4 16
Berclair, Tx., U.S. — E4 120
Berdichev, Sov. Un. — D5 29
Berdsk, Sov. Un. — C10 28
Berdyansk, Sov. Un. — H11 27
Berea, Ky., U.S. — C5 94
Berea, Ne., U.S. — B3 104
Berea, Oh., U.S. — A4 112
Berea, S.C., U.S. — B3 117
Berebere, Indon. — E7 34
Beregovo, Sov. Un. — G4 27
Bereku, Tan. — B6 48
Berens, stm., Can. — C3 70
Berens Island, i., Mb., Can. — C3 70
Berens River, Mb., Can. — C3 70
Beresford, Mb., Can. — E1 70
Beresford, S.D., U.S. — D9 118
Berettyóújfalu, Hung. — B5 24
Berezhany, Sov. Un. — G5 27
Berezina, stm., Sov. Un. — E7 27
Berezna, Sov. Un. — F8 27
Berezniki, Sov. Un. — D8 29
Berezovo, Sov. Un. — C9 29
Berg, Nor. — q27 14
Berga, Spain — A6 22
Berga, Swe. — B8 15
Bergama, Tur. — C6 25
Bergamasque Alps, mts., Italy — A2 21
Bergamo, Italy — A2 21
Bergedorf, F.R.Ger. — B5 18
Bergen see Mons, Bel. — F3 15
Bergen, F.R.Ger. — B5 18
Bergen, Nor. — G1 14
Bergen, N.Y., U.S. — B3 109
Bergen, N.D., U.S. — A5 111
Bergen, co., N.J., U.S. — A4 107
Bergen [auf Rügen], Ger.D.R. — A6 18
Bergenfield, N.J., U.S. — h8 107
Bergen op Zoom, Neth. — B6 16
Berger, Mo., U.S. — C6 102
Bergerac, Fr. — E4 16
Bergholz, Oh., U.S. — B5 112
Bergisch Gladbach, F.R.Ger. — C2 19
Bergkamen, F.R.Ger. — B2 19
Bergland, Mi., U.S. — m12 99
Bergman, Ar., U.S. — A2 81
Bergstrom Air Force Base, mil., Tx., U.S. — D4 120
Bergton, Va., U.S. — B4 123
Berguent, Mor. — C4 44
Bergün, Switz. — C8 21
Berhampore, India — D8 36
Berhampur, India — E7 36
Bering Sea — D32 128
Bering Strait, strt. — C5 79
Berino, N.M., U.S. — E3 108
Berislav, Sov. Un. — H9 27
Berja, Spain — D5 22
Berkane, Mor. — C4 44
Berkeley, Ca., U.S. — D2 82
Berkeley, Il., U.S. — *k9 90
Berkeley, I.C. — f8 94
Berkeley, Mo., U.S. — f13 102
Berkeley, R.I., U.S. — B4 116
Berkeley, co., S.C., U.S. — E8 117
Berkeley, co., W.V., U.S. — B6 125
Berkeley, Cabo, c., Ec. — I5 58
Berkeley Heights, N.J., U.S. — B4 107
Berkeley Springs, W.V., U.S. — B6 125
Berkey, Oh., U.S. — A2 112
Berkley, Ma., U.S. — C5 98
Berkley, Mi., U.S. — F7 99
Berkner Island, i., Ant. — B7 7
Berkovitsa, Bul. — F6 24
Berks, co., Pa., U.S. — F9 115
Berkshire, Ma., U.S. — A1 98
Berkshire, N.Y., U.S. — C4 109
Berkshire, Vt., U.S. — B3 122
Berkshire, co., Ma., U.S. — B1 98
Berkshire, co., Eng., U.K. — C6 12
Berkshire Estates, Ct., U.S. — D2 84
Berkshire Hills, hills, Ma., U.S. — A1 98
Berland, stm., Ab., Can. — C1 68
Berleburg, F.R.Ger. — B3 19
Berlenga Islands, is., Port. — C1 22
Berlin (East), Ger.D.R. — A7 19
Berlin (West), F.R.Ger. — B6 18
Berlin, Ct., U.S. — C4 84
Berlin, Md., U.S. — D7 97
Berlin, Ma., U.S. — B4 98
Berlin, N.H., U.S. — B4 106
Berlin, N.J., U.S. — D3 107
Berlin, N.Y., U.S. — C7 109
Berlin, N.D., U.S. — D7 111
Berlin, Oh., U.S. — B4 112
Berlin, Pa., U.S. — G3 115
Berlin, Wi., U.S. — E5 126
Berlin, Mount, mtn., Ant. — B35 7
Berlin Corners, Vt., U.S. — C3 122
Berlin Heights, Oh., U.S. — A3 112
Berlin Lake, res., Oh., U.S. — A4 112
Berlin Mountain, mtn., U.S. — A1 98
Berlin [West], state, F.R.Ger. — F7 15
Bermejo, Arg. — A3 54
Bermejo, stm., S.A. — E4 55
Bermeo, Spain — A4 22
Bermuda, dep., N.A. — F14 61
Bermuda, I.C. — p20 64
Bern, Switz. — E3 18
Bern, Ks., U.S. — C8 93
Bern, state, Switz. — C3 20
Bernalillo, N.M., U.S. — B3 108

Name	Map Ref	Page

Bernalillo, co., N.M., U.S. C3 108
Bernam, stm., Malay. K4 35
Bernard, Ia., U.S. B7 92
Bernard, Me., U.S. D4 96
Bernard Lake, l., On., Can. B5 73
Bernardston, Ma., U.S. A2 98
Bernardsville, N.J., U.S. B3 107
Bernasconi, Arg. B4 54
Bernau [am Chiemsee], F.R.Ger. B8 20
Bernau [bei Berlin], Ger.D.R. B6 18
Bernay, Fr. C4 16
Bernburg, Ger.D.R. C5 18
Berndorf, Aus. E8 18
Berne, In., U.S. C8 91
Berne, N.Y., U.S. C6 109
Berneray, i., Scot., U.K. C1 13
Bernese Alps, mts., Switz. E3 18
Bernice, La., U.S. B3 95
Bernice, Ok., U.S. A7 113
Bernie, Mo., U.S. E8 102
Bernina, Piz, mtn., Eur. C5 20
Bernina Pass, Switz. C6 20
Bernville, Pa., U.S. F9 115
Beroroha, Madag. h9 49
Beroun, Czech. D3 26
Beroun, Mn., U.S. E6 100
Berounka, stm., Czech. C3 26
Berrechid, Mor. C3 44
Berre [-l'Étang], Fr. F6 16
Berri, Austl. F7 50
Berrien, co., Ga., U.S. E3 87
Berrien, co., Mi., U.S. F4 99
Berrien Springs, Mi., U.S. G4 99
Berriyane, Alg. C5 44
Berry, Al., U.S. B2 78
Berry, Ky., U.S. B5 94
Berry, hist reg., Fr. D4 16
Berry Creek, stm., Ab., Can. D5 68
Berrydale, Fl., U.S. u14 86
Berryessa, Lake, res., Ca., U.S. C2 82
Berry Hill, Tn., U.S. g10 119
Berryman, Mo., U.S. D6 102
Berryton, Ga., U.S. B1 87
Berryton, Ks., U.S. m14 93
Berryville, Ar., U.S. A2 81
Berryville, Va., U.S. A5 123
Bersenbrück, F.R.Ger. B7 17
Bershad, Sov. Un. G7 27
Bertha, Mn., U.S. D3 100
Berthier, co., P.Q., Can. C4 74
Berthierville, P.Q., Can. C4 74
Berthold, N.D., U.S. A4 111
Berthoud, Co., U.S. A5 83
Berthoud Pass, Co., U.S. B5 83
Bertie, co., N.C., U.S. A5 110
Bertoua, Cam. E2 46
Bertraghboy Bay, b., Ire. D2 11
Bertram, Tx., U.S. D4 120
Bertrand, Mi., U.S. *G5 99
Bertrand, Mo., U.S. E8 102
Bertrand, Ne., U.S. D6 104
Bertrandville, La., U.S. E5 95
Bertrix, Bel. C6 16
Berwick, N.S., Can. D5 71
Berwick, Il., U.S. C3 90
Berwick, Ia., U.S. e8 92
Berwick, La., U.S. E4 95
Berwick, Me., U.S. E2 96
Berwick, N.D., U.S. A5 111
Berwick, Pa., U.S. D9 115
Berwick-upon-Tweed, Eng., U.K. C6 10
Berwind, W.V., U.S. D3 125
Berwyn, Ab., Can. A2 68
Berwyn, Il., U.S. k9 90
Berwyn, Ne., U.S. C6 104
Berwyn, Pa., U.S. o20 115
Beryl, Ut., U.S. F2 121
Besalampy, Madag. g8 49
Besançon, Fr. D7 16
Besar Hantu, mtn., Malay. K4 35
Beskid Mountains, mts., Eur. D5 26
Beskra, Alg. C6 44
Besnard Lake, l., Sk., Can. D5 72
Besni, Tur. D11 40
Bessèges, Fr. E6 16
Bessemer, Al., U.S. B3 78
Bessemer, Mi., U.S. n11 99
Bessemer, Pa., U.S. E1 115
Bessemer City, N.C., U.S. B1 110
Bessie, Ok., U.S. B3 113
Best, Tx., U.S. D2 120
Bestfield, De., U.S. *B3 85
Bestobe, Sov. Un. C8 28
Betafo, Madag. g9 49
Betanzos, Spain A1 22
Bétaré Oya, Cam. D2 46
Betatakin Ruin, hist., Az., U.S. A5 80
Bet Guvrin, Isr. C6 41
Bethalto, Il., U.S. E3 90
Bethanien, Nmb. C2 49
Bethany, On., Can. C6 73
Bethany see Al 'Ayzarīyah, Isr. Occ. h12 41
Bethany, Ct., U.S. D4 84
Bethany, Il., U.S. D5 90
Bethany, La., U.S. B1 95
Bethany, Mo., U.S. A3 102
Bethany, Ok., U.S. B4 113
Bethany, W.V., U.S. A4 125
Bethany Beach, De., U.S. F5 85
Bethel, Ak., U.S. C7 79
Bethel, Ct., U.S. D2 84
Bethel, De., U.S. F3 85
Bethel, Ky., U.S. B6 94
Bethel, Me., U.S. D2 96
Bethel, Mo., U.S. B5 102
Bethel, N.C., U.S. B5 110
Bethel, Oh., U.S. D1 112
Bethel, Ok., U.S. C7 113
Bethel, Pa., U.S. F9 115
Bethel, Vt., U.S. D3 122
Bethel Acres, Ok., U.S. *C2 113
Bethel Park, Pa., U.S. k14 115
Bethel Springs, Tn., U.S. B3 119
Bethera, S.C., U.S. E8 117
Bethesda, Wales, U.K. A3 12
Bethesda, Oh., U.S. B4 81
Bethesda, Md., U.S. C3 97
Bethlehem (Bayt Laḥm), Isr. Occ. G10 40
Bethlehem, S. Afr. C4 49
Bethlehem, Ct., U.S. C3 84
Bethlehem, Ga., U.S. C3 87
Bethlehem, In., U.S. G7 91
Bethlehem, Md., U.S. C6 97
Bethlehem, N.H., U.S. B3 106
Bethlehem, Pa., U.S. E11 115
Bethlehem, W.V., U.S. f8 125

Bethlehem Junction, N.H., U.S. B3 106
Bethpage, N.Y., U.S. *E7 109
Bethpage, Tn., U.S. A5 119
Bethune, Sk., Can. G3 75
Béthune, Fr. B5 16
Bethune, Co., U.S. B8 83
Bethune, S.C., U.S. C7 117
Betioky, Madag. h8 49
Betio, i., Kir. R18 52
Bet Neḥemya, Isr. h10 41
Betong, Thai. D2 34
Betoota, Austl. B3 51
Betpak-Dala, des., Sov. Un. D7 28
Betroka, Madag. h9 49
Bet Sh'ean, Isr. B7 41
Bet Shemesh, Isr. C6 41
Betsiamites, P.Q., Can. k13 74
Betsiboka, stm., Madag. g9 49
Betsie, Point, c., Mi., U.S. D4 99
Betsy Layne, Ky., U.S. C7 94
Bette, mtn., Libya E3 43
Bettendorf, Ia., U.S. C7 92
Betterton, Md., U.S. B5 97
Bettiah, India D10 37
Bettles Field, Ak., U.S. B9 79
Bettsville, Oh., U.S. A2 112
Bettyhill, Scot., U.K. A4 10
Betül, India D6 36
Betwa, stm., India D6 36
Betzdorf, F.R.Ger. C2 19
Beulah, Mb., Can. D1 70
Beulah, Al., U.S. C4 78
Beulah, Co., U.S. C6 83
Beulah, Mi., U.S. D4 99
Beulah, Ms., U.S. B3 101
Beulah, N.D., U.S. B4 111
Beulah, Wy., U.S. B8 127
Beulah, Lake, l., Ms., U.S. B3 101
Beulaville, N.C., U.S. C5 110
B. Everett Jordan Lake, res., N.C., U.S. B3 110
Beverley, Sk., Can. G2 75
Beverley, Eng., U.K. D6 10
Beverley Head, c., Nf., Can. D2 72
Beverly, Ks., U.S. C6 93
Beverly, Ky., U.S. D6 94
Beverly, Ma., U.S. A6 98
Beverly, N.J., U.S. C3 107
Beverly, Oh., U.S. C4 112
Beverly, Tn., U.S. m14 119
Beverly, W.V., U.S. C5 125
Beverly Hills, Ca., U.S. m12 82
Beverly Hills, Mi., U.S. *o15 99
Beverly Shores, In., U.S. A4 91
Beverstedt, F.R.Ger. E2 15
Beverwijk, Neth. A6 16
Bewdley, On., Can. C6 73
Bex, Switz. D3 21
Bexhill-on-Sea, Eng., U.K. D8 12
Bexley, Oh., U.S. m11 112
Beya, Sov. Un. E27 8
Béziers, Fr. F5 16
Bezmer, Bul. D8 24
Bezons, Fr. g9 16
Bhachau, India F3 37
Bhadra, India C6 36
Bhadrachalam, India I8 37
Bhadrakh, India G11 37
Bhag, Pak. C4 36
Bhagalpur, India C8 36
Bhakkar, Pak. B5 36
Bhaktapur, Nepal C8 36
Bhamo, Burma D10 36
Bhandara, India G7 37
Bharatpur, India C6 36
Bhatinda, India B5 37
Bhatpara, India D8 36
Bhaunagar, India D5 36
Bhawanipatna, India H9 37
Bheigeir, Beinn, hill, Scot., U.K. E2 13
Bhilai (Bhilainagar), India *D7 36
Bhilai, India G8 37
Bhima, stm., India E6 36
Bhind, India C6 36
Bhiwani, India C6 36
Bhola, Bngl. F13 37
Bhopal, India B6 36
Bhor, India E5 36
Bhubaneswar, India D8 36
Bhuj, India D4 36
Bhumiphol (Yanhee) Dam, Thai. D3 35
Bhusawal, India G5 37
Bhutan, ctry., Asia C9 36
Bia, mtn., Laos B2 34
Biaboye, Zaire A4 48
Biafra, Bight of, Afr. E1 46
Biak, i., Indon. F9 34
Biała, stm., Pol. h10 26
Biała Podlaska, Pol. B7 26
Biała Przemsza, stm., Pol. g11 26
Białogard, Pol. A4 26
Białystok, Pol. B7 26
Bian, Bidean nam, mtn., Scot., U.K. D4 13
Bianco, Italy E6 23
Biankouma, I.C. E3 44
Biarritz, Fr. F3 16
Biasca, Switz. C4 20
Bibā, Eg. D6 43
Bibai, Japan E10 33

Bickleton, Wa., U.S. D5 124
Bickmore, W.V., U.S. C3 125
Bicknell, In., U.S. G3 91
Bicknell, Ut., U.S. E4 121
Bicoli, Indon. E7 34
Bicske, Hung. B4 24
Bida, Nig. E6 45
Bīdar, India E6 36
Biddeford, Me., U.S. E2 96
Biddiyā, Isr. Occ. g11 41
Biddle, Mt., U.S. E11 103
Bideford, Eng., U.K. E4 10
Bidwell, Oh., U.S. D3 112
Bidwell, Mount, mtn., Ca., U.S. B3 82
Bié, dept., Ang. D2 48
Bieber, Ca., U.S. B3 82
Biebrza, stm., Pol. B7 26
Biedenkopf, F.R.Ger. C3 19
Biel, Switz. E3 18
Biel, Switz. D5 21
Biel (Bienne), Lake, l., Switz. D5 21
Bielawa, Pol. C4 26
Bield, Mb., Can. D1 70
Bielefeld, F.R.Ger. B4 18
Biella, Italy B2 23
Bielsko-Biała, Pol. D5 26
Bielsk Podlaski, Pol. B7 26
Bienfait, Sk., Can. H4 75
Bien Hoa, Viet. G7 35
Bienville, La., U.S. B3 95
Bienville, co., La., U.S. B2 95
Bienville, Lac, l., P.Q., Can. g12 74
Bierawka, stm., Pol. g9 26
Bière, Switz. C1 21
Bieruń Nowy, Pol. g10 26
Bieruń Stary, Pol. g10 26
Biese, stm., Ger.D.R. F5 15
Bietigheim, F.R.Ger. E4 19
Bièvre, stm., Fr. g9 16
Bièvres, Fr. h9 16
Biferno, stm., Italy D5 23
Big, stm., Sk., Can. D2 75
Big, stm., Mo., U.S. c7 102
Biga, Tur. B6 25
Big A Mountain, mtn., Va., U.S. e9 123
Big Arm, Mt., U.S. C2 103
Big Bald, mtn., U.S. f10 110
Big Bald, mtn., Ga., U.S. B2 87
Big Bald Mountain, mtn., N.B., Can. B2 71
Big Baldy Mountain, mtn., Mt., U.S. D6 103
Big Bay, Mi., U.S. B3 99
Big Bay, i., N.Z. P11 51
Big Bay De Noc, b., Mi., U.S. C4 99
Big Bear City, Ca., U.S. E5 82
Bigbee Valley, Ms., U.S. B5 101
Big Belt Mountains, mts., Mt., U.S. D5 103
Big Bend, Ca., U.S. B3 82
Big Bend, La., U.S. C4 95
Big Bend, Wi., U.S. n11 126
Beykoz, Tur. B7 25
Beyla, Gui. E3 45
Beylul, Eth. C5 47
Big Bend Dam, S.D., U.S. C6 118
Big Bend National Park, Tx., U.S. E1 120
Big Birch Lake, l., Mn., U.S. E4 100
Big Black, stm., Me., U.S. B3 96
Big Black, stm., Ms., U.S. C3 101
Big Blue, stm., In., U.S. E6 91
Big Bone, Ky., U.S. k13 94
Big Bow, Ks., U.S. E2 93
Big Burro Mountains, mts., N.M., U.S. E1 108
Big Butt, mtn., Tn., U.S. C11 119
Big Cabin, Ok., U.S. A6 113
Big Cabin Creek, stm., Ok., U.S. A6 113
Big Canyon, val., Tx., U.S. D1 120
Big Chino Wash, val., Az., U.S. B3 80
Big Clifty, Ky., U.S. C3 94
Big Coal, stm., W.V., U.S. C3 125
Big Corney Bayou, stm., U.S. B3 81
Big Costilla Peak, mtn., N.M., U.S. A4 108
Big Creek, B.C., Can. D6 69
Big Creek, Ca., U.S. D4 82
Big Creek, Id., U.S. D3 89
Big Creek, Ky., U.S. C6 94
Big Creek, W.V., U.S. C2 125
Big Creek, stm., B.C., Can. D6 69
Big Creek, stm., Ar., U.S. C5 81
Big Creek, stm., In., U.S. G7 91
Big Creek, stm., In., U.S. H2 91
Big Creek, stm., Ks., U.S. C4 93
Big Creek, stm., La., U.S. B4 95
Big Creek, stm., Mo., U.S. C3 102
Big Creek, stm., Tn., U.S. e8 119
Big Creek Lake, res., Al., U.S. E1 78
Big Creek Peak, mtn., Id., U.S. E5 89
Big Cypress Indian Reservation, Fl., U.S. F5 86
Big Cypress Swamp, sw., Fl., U.S. F5 86
Big Darby Creek, stm., Oh., U.S. C2 112
Big Delta, Ak., U.S. C10 79
Big Dry Creek, stm., Mt., U.S. C10 103
Big Duke Dam, N.C., U.S. B2 110
Big Eau Pleine, stm., Wi., U.S. D3 126
Big Eau Pleine Reservoir, res., Wi., U.S. D4 126
Bigej Island, i., Marsh Is. S17 52
Big Elk Creek, stm., Md., U.S. A6 97
Bigelow, Ar., U.S. B3 81
Bigelow, Mn., U.S. G3 100
Bigelow, Mo., U.S. A2 102
Bigelow, Mount, mtn., Me., U.S. C2 96
Big Escambia Creek, stm., U.S. D2 78
Big Falls, Mn., U.S. B5 100
Big Flat Mountain, mtn., Va., U.S. B4 123
Big Flats, N.Y., U.S. C4 109
Bigfoot, Tx., U.S. E3 120
Bigfork, Mn., U.S. C5 100
Bigfork, Mt., U.S. B2 103
Big Fork, stm., Mn., U.S. B5 100
Big Frog Mountain, mtn., Tn., U.S. D9 119
Biggar, Sk., Can. E1 75
Biggar, Scot., U.K. F5 13
Biggerann Island, i., Marsh Is S17 52
Biggers, Ar., U.S. A5 81
Biggersville, Ms., U.S. A5 101

Biggleswade, Eng., U.K. B7 12
Biggs, Ca., U.S. C3 82
Biggs, Or., U.S. B6 114
Biggsville, Il., U.S. C3 90
Big Gull Lake, l., On., Can. C8 73
Big Gully Creek, stm., Sk., Can. D1 75
Big Hatchet Peak, mtn., N.M., U.S. F1 108
Big Hole, stm., Mt., U.S. E4 103
Big Hole National Battlefield, hist., Mt., U.S. E3 103
Bighorn, Mt., U.S. D9 103
Big Horn, co., Mt., U.S. E9 103
Big Horn, co., Wy., U.S. B4 127
Bighorn, stm., U.S. B6 76
Bighorn Canyon National Recreation Area, U.S. F8 103
Bighorn Lake, res., U.S. B6 103
Bighorn Mountains, mts., U.S. B5 127
Big Horn Mountains, mts., Az., U.S. D2 80
Bigi Island, i., Marsh Is S17 52
Big Island, Va., U.S. C3 123
Big Island, i., N.T., Can. D18 66
Big Island, i., N.T., Can. f8 72
Big Kandiyohi Lake, l., Mn., U.S. F4 100
Big Knob, mtn., Pa., U.S. F6 115
Big Knob, mtn., Pa., U.S. f9 123
Big Lake, Mn., U.S. E5 100
Big Lake, Tx., U.S. D2 120
Big Lake, l., Me., U.S. C5 96
Bigler, Pa., U.S. E5 115
Biglerville, Pa., U.S. G7 115
Big Lookout Mountain, mtn., Or., U.S. C9 114
Big Lost, stm., Id., U.S. F5 89
Big Moose, N.Y., U.S. B6 109
Big Mossy Point, c., Mb., Can. C2 70
Big Mountain, mtn., Nv., U.S. B2 105
Big Muddy, stm., Il., U.S. F4 90
Big Muddy Creek, stm., Mt., U.S. B12 103
Big Muddy Lake, l., Sk., Can. H3 75
Big Nemaha, stm., Ne., U.S. D10 104
Bignona, Sen. D1 45
Big North Mountain, mts., Va., U.S. A4 123
Big Otter, stm., Va., U.S. C3 123
Big Pine, Ca., U.S. D4 82
Big Pine Creek, stm., In., U.S. D3 91
Big Pine Lake, l., Mn., U.S. D3 100
Big Pine Mountain, mtn., Ca., U.S. E4 82
Big Piney, Wy., U.S. D2 127
Big Piney, stm., Mo., U.S. D5 102
Big Piney Creek, stm., Ar., U.S. B2 81
Big Pipe Creek, stm., Md., U.S. A3 97
Bigpoint, Ms., U.S. E5 101
Big Pool, Md., U.S. A1 97
Big Prairie, Oh., U.S. B3 112
Big Quill Lake, l., Sk., Can. F3 75
Big Raccoon Creek, stm., In., U.S. E4 91
Big Rapids, Mi., U.S. E5 99
Big Rib, stm., Wi., U.S. C3 126
Big River, Sk., Can. D2 75
Big Rock, Il., U.S. B5 90
Big Rock, Tn., U.S. B7 119
Big Rock Mountain, mtn., Ar., U.S. .... B1 ...
Big Run, Pa., U.S. E4 115
Big Run, stm., W.V., U.S. C4 99
Big Sable Point, c., Mi., U.S. D4 99
Big Sandy, Mt., U.S. B6 103
Big Sandy, Tn., U.S. A3 119
Big Sandy, Tx., U.S. C5 120
Big Sandy, stm., U.S. C2 125
Big Sandy, stm., Az., U.S. C2 80
Big Sandy, stm., Wy., U.S. D3 127
Big Sandy Creek, stm., Co., U.S. C8 83
Big Sandy Creek, stm., Mt., U.S. B6 103
Big Sandy Creek, stm., W.V., U.S. C3 125
Big Sandy Lake, l., On., Can. E5 70
Big Sandy Lake, l., Sk., Can. C3 75
Big Sandy Reservoir, res., Wy., U.S. D3 127
Big Satilla Creek, stm., Ga., U.S. E4 87
Big Savage Mountain, mtn., U.S. k12 97
Big Sheep Mountain, mtn., Mt., U.S. C11 103
Big Shiney Mountain, mtn., U.S. e8 119
Big Sioux, stm., U.S. E9 118
Big Slough, stm., Ga., U.S. F2 87
Big Smoky Valley, val., Nv., U.S. E4 105
Big Snowy Mountains, mts., Mt., U.S. D7 103
Big Southern Butte, mtn., Id., U.S. F5 89
Big South Fork, stm., Ky., U.S. k13 94
Big Spencer Mountain, mtn., Me., U.S. C3 96
Big Spring, Ky., U.S. C3 94
Big Spring, Tx., U.S. C2 120
Big Springs, Ks., U.S. k15 93
Big Springs, Ne., U.S. C4 104
Big Spruce Knob, mtn., W.V., U.S. C4 125
Big Squaw Mountain, mtn., Me., U.S. C3 96
Bigstick Lake, l., Sk., Can. G1 75
Big Stone, co., Mn., U.S. E2 100
Bigstone, stm., Mb., Can. B4 70
Big Stone Beach, Ct., U.S. D4 85
Big Stone City, S.D., U.S. B9 118
Big Stone Gap, Va., U.S. f9 123
Big Stone Lake, l., Mn., U.S. E2 100
Bigstone Lake, l., Mb., Can. C4 70
Big Stone Lake, l., U.S. E2 100
Big Sur, Ca., U.S. D3 82
Big Sunflower, stm., Ms., U.S. B3 101
Big Thompson, stm., Co., U.S. A5 83
Big Timber, Mt., U.S. E7 103
Big Top, mtn., Tn., U.S. n17 119
Big Trout Lake, On., Can. n17 73
Big Trout Lake, l., On., Can. n17 73
Biguaçu, Braz. D3 56
Birdseye, In., U.S. H4 91

Big Walnut Creek, stm., Oh., U.S. m11 112
Big Wells, Tx., U.S. E3 120
Big Wills Creek, stm., Al., U.S. A3 78
Big Wills Valley, val., Al., U.S. A4 78
Bigwood, On., Can. A4 73
Big Wood, stm., Id., U.S. F4 89
Bihać, Yugo. C2 24
Bihar, India C8 36
Bihār, state, India D8 36
Bijagós, Arquipélago dos, is., Gui.-B. D1 45
Bijapur, India E6 36
Bijār, Iran D3 39
Bijeljina, Yugo. C4 24
Bijelo Polje, Yugo. D4 24
Bijie, China F6 31
Bijnor, India C7 37
Bijou Creek, stm., Co., U.S. B6 83
Bijou Hills, S.D., U.S. D6 118
Bikaner, India C5 36
Bikeman Island, i., Kir. R18 52
Bikenibeu, Kir. R18 52
Bikin, Sov. Un. B11 31
Bikin, stm., Sov. Un. C7 33
Bikini, atoll, Marsh Is. F10 6
Bikini Island, i., Marsh Is. P18 52
Bikita, Zimb. B5 49
Bilaspur, India D10 37
Bilauktaung Range, mts., Asia C1 34
Bilbao, Spain A2 22
Bilbays, Eg. D3 41
Bildudalur, Ice. n21 14
Bileća, Yugo. D4 24
Bilecik, Tur. B5 25
Biłgoraj, Pol. C7 26
Bili, Zaire A4 48
Bilin, Burma E10 36
Bilk Creek Mountains, mts., U.S. B3 105
Bill, Wy., U.S. C7 127
Billerica, Ma., U.S. A5 98
Billet, Il., U.S. E6 90
Billings, Mo., U.S. D4 102
Billings, Mt., U.S. E8 103
Billings, Ok., U.S. A4 113
Billings, co., N.D., U.S. B2 111
Billingsley, Al., U.S. C3 78
Billings Heights, Mt., U.S. E8 103
Bill Williams, stm., Az., U.S. C1 80
Bill Williams Mountain, mtn., Az., U.S. B3 80
Bilma, Niger C7 45
Biloela, Austl. D9 50
Biloxi, Ms., U.S. E5 101
Biloxi, stm., Ms., U.S. E4 101
Biloxi Bay, b., Ms., U.S. f8 101
Bilqās Qism Awwal, Eg. C3 41
Biltine, Chad C4 46
Biltmore Forest, N.C., U.S. f10 110
Bilugyun, i., Burma D2 35
Bilzen, Bel. D5 17
Bimberéké, Benin D5 45
Bimberi Peak, mtn., Austl. G7 51
Bimini Islands, is., Bah. E7 37
Bīna-Etāwa, India I7 37
Binalonan, Phil. n13 34
Biñan, Phil. o13 34
Bindloss, Ab., Can. D5 68
Bindura, Zimb. A5 49
Binfield, N.D., U.S. A3 111
Binford, N.D., U.S. B7 111
Binga, Zaire A4 48
Binga, Monte, mtn., Afr. A5 49
Bingamon Creek, stm., W.V., U.S. k10 125
Bingen, F.R.Ger. D3 18
Bingen, Ok., U.S. B3 113
Bingham, Me., U.S. C3 96
Bingham, co., Id., U.S. F6 89
Bingham Lake, Mn., U.S. G3 100
Binghamton, N.Y., U.S. C5 109
Bingley, Eng., U.K. G7 13
Binhai, China E8 31
Binjai, Indon. m11 34
Binnaway, Austl. E7 51
Binningen, Switz. A4 21
Bintan, i., Indon. L6 35
Bintang, mtn., Malay. J4 35
Bintuhan, Indon. F2 34
Bintulu, Malay. E4 34
Binxian, China D6 31
Binxian, China D5 31
Binyamina, Isr. B6 41
Binzhou, China D10 31
Biobío, prov., Chile D2 56
Biobío, stm., Chile D2 56
Bioko, i., Eq. Gui. E1 46
Biola, Ca., U.S. D4 82
Bippus, In., U.S. C6 91
Bīr, India H5 37
Bir al Uzam, Libya G4 40
Birao, Cen. Afr. Rep. C8 36
Biratnagar, Nepal C8 36
Birch, stm., W.V., U.S. C4 125
Birchdale, Mn., U.S. B4 100
Birch Hill, Ct., U.S. C2 84
Birch Hills, Sk., Can. D3 75
Birch Island, B.C., Can. D8 69
Birch Island, i., Mb., Can. C2 70
Birch Lake, l., Sk., Can. D1 75
Birch Lake, l., On., Can. C7 100
Birch River, Mb., Can. C1 70
Birch Run, Mi., U.S. E7 99
Birch Tree, Mo., U.S. E6 102
Birchwood, Ct., U.S. B5 84
Birchwood, Wi., U.S. C2 126
Birchwood City, Wi., U.S. D1 126
Birchwood Park, De., U.S. *B3 85
Bird City, Ks., U.S. C2 93
Bird Creek, stm., U.S. A6 113
Bird Island, Mn., U.S. F4 100
Bird Island, i., N.C., U.S. .... D5 ...
Birds, Il., U.S. E6 90
Birdsboro, Pa., U.S. F10 115
Birds Creek, On., Can. B7 73
Birdseye, In., U.S. H4 91
Birdsong, Ar., U.S. C5 81

Birdsville, Austl. E6 50
Birdsville, Ky., U.S. e9 94
Birdtail Creek, stm., Mb., Can. D1 70
Birdtown, N.C., U.S. f9 110
Birdum, Austl. C5 50
Birdwood, stm., Ne., U.S. C4 104
Birecik, Tur. D11 40
Breuen, Indon. J2 35
Bīrganj, Nepal D10 37
Birigui, Braz. C2 56
Birimbāl, Eg. C2 41
Bīrjand, Iran B5 38
Birk, Wādī, val., Sau. Ar. D3 41
Birkat as Sab', Eg. D2 19
Birkenfeld, F.R.Ger. F3 17
Birkenfeld, Or., U.S. B3 114
Birkenhead, Eng., U.K. D5 10
Bīrlad, Rom. B8 24
Birmingham, Sk., Can. G4 75
Birmingham, Eng., U.K. D6 10
Birmingham, India C5 36
Birmingham, Al., U.S. B3 78
Birmingham, Ia., U.S. D6 92
Birmingham, Mi., U.S. F7 99
Birmingham, Mo., U.S. h11 102
Birmingham, N.J., U.S. D3 107
Bir Mogrein (Fort Trinquet), Maur. A2 45
Birnamwood, Wi., U.S. C4 126
Birney, Mt., U.S. E10 103
Birni Ngaouré, Niger D5 45
Birni Kebbi, Nig. D5 45
Birni Nkonni, Niger D6 45
Birobidzhan, Sov. Un. E16 29
Biron, Wi., U.S. D4 126
Birr, Switz. B3 20
Birs, stm., Switz. B3 20
Birsk, Sov. Un. D20 8
Birtle, Mb., Can. D1 70
Biruuta, Mong. A6 32
Bisbee, Ar., U.S. C2 87
Bisbee, N.D., U.S. A6 111
Biscay, Bay of, Eur. G8 8
Biscayne, Key, i., Fl., U.S. s13 86
Biscayne Bay, b., Fl., U.S. G6 86
Biscayne Gardens, Fl., U.S. *s13 86
Biscayne National Monument, Fl., U.S. G6 86
Biscayne Park, Fl., U.S. s13 86
Bisceglie, Italy D6 23
Bischheim, Fr. F7 17
Bischofshofen, Aus. B9 20
Bischofswerda, Ger.D.R. B9 19
Bischwiller, Fr. F7 17
Biscoe, Ar., U.S. C4 81
Biscoe, N.C., U.S. B3 110
Biscoe Islands, is., Ant. C6 7
Biševo, i., Yugo. D3 24
Bishārah, Ma'tan, well, Libya E4 43
Bishnupur, India F11 37
Bishop, Ca., U.S. D4 82
Bishop, Ga., U.S. C3 87
Bishop, Md., U.S. D7 97
Bishop, Tx., U.S. F4 120
Bishop Auckland, Eng., U.K. F7 13
Bishopric, Sk., Can. H3 75
Bishop's Castle, Eng., U.K. B5 12
Bishop's Falls, Nf., Can. D4 72
Bishops Head, Md., U.S. D5 97
Bishop's Stortford, Eng., U.K. E7 10
Bishopton, P.Q., Can. D6 74
Bishopville, Md., U.S. D7 97
Bishopville, S.C., U.S. C7 117
Bismarck, Ar., U.S. C2 81
Bismarck, Il., U.S. C6 90
Bismarck, Mo., U.S. D7 102
Bismarck, N.D., U.S. C5 111
Bismarck, Cape, c., Grnld. A16 128
Bismarck Archipelago, is., Pap. N. Gui. h12 50
Bismarck Range, mts., Pap. N. Gui. k11 50
Bismarck Sea, Pap. N. Gui. h12 50
Bismark, Ger.D.R. F5 15
Bison, Ks., U.S. D4 93
Bison, Ok., U.S. A4 113
Bison, S.D., U.S. B3 118
Bison Peak, mtn., Co., U.S. B5 83
Bissau, Gui.-B. D1 45
Bissett, Mb., Can. D4 70
Bistcho Lake, l., Ab., Can. f7 68
Bistineau, Lake, res., La., U.S. B2 95
Bistrița, Rom. B7 24
Bistrița, stm., Rom. B7 24
Bitam, Gabon E2 46
Bitburg, F.R.Ger. E6 17
Bitche, Fr. E7 17
Bitely, Mi., U.S. E5 99
Bitlis, Tur. C14 40
Bitola, Yugo. E5 24
Bitonto, Italy D6 23
Bittencourt, Braz. B4 58
Bitter Creek, stm., Wy., U.S. E4 127
Bitterfeld, Ger.D.R. B7 19
Bitterfontein, S. Afr. D2 49
Bitter Lake, l., S.D., U.S. B8 118
Bitter Lake, l., Sk., Can. D3 75
Bitterroot, stm., Mt., U.S. D2 103
Bitterroot Range, mts., U.S. B3 89
Bittinger, Md., U.S. k12 97
Bituing, Indon. E7 34
Bityug, stm., Sov. Un. F13 27
Biu, Nig. D7 45
Bivalve, Md., U.S. D6 97
Bivalve, N.J., U.S. E2 107
Biwabik, Mn., U.S. C6 100
Biwa Lake, l., Japan n15 33
Bixby, Mn., U.S. G5 100
Bixby, N.C., U.S. B2 110
Bixby, Ok., U.S. B6 113
Biya, stm., Sov. Un. E26 8
Biyalā, Eg. C3 41
Biyang, China H5 32
Biysk, Sov. Un. D11 29
Bizak, Kūh-e, mtn., Iran D10 39
Bjargtangar, Ice. .... n20 ...
Bjelovar, Yugo. C2 24
Bjerringbro, Den. B3 15
Bjork Lake, l., U.S. E4 75
Black, Al., U.S. D4 78
Black, Tx., U.S. B1 120
Black, stm., N.A. B3 96
Black, stm., Az., U.S. D5 80
Black, stm., Ar., U.S. B4 81

Name	Map Ref	Page
Black, stm., La., U.S.	C4	95
Black, stm., Mi., U.S.	E8	99
Black, stm., N.Y., U.S.	B4	109
Black, stm., N.C., U.S.	C4	110
Black, stm., S.C., U.S.	D8	117
Black, stm., Vt., U.S.	E3	122
Black, stm., Wi., U.S.	D3	126
Black, Bayou, stm., La., U.S.	E5	95
Blackall, Austl.	D8	50
Black Bear Bay, b., Nf., Can.	B4	72
Black Bear Creek, stm., Ok., U.S.	A4	113
Black Bear Island Lake, l., Sk., Can.	B3	75
Blackbird, De., U.S.	C3	85
Blackburn, Eng., U.K.	D5	10
Blackburn, Mo., U.S.	B4	102
Blackburn, Ok., U.S.	A5	113
Blackburn, Mount, mtn., Ak., U.S.	C11	79
Black Butte, mtn., Or., U.S.	F5	103
Black Butte, mtn., Wy., U.S.	B5	127
Black Butte Lake, res., Ca., U.S.	C2	82
Black Butte Ranch, Or., U.S.	C5	114
Black Canyon, val., Co., U.S.	C3	83
Black Canyon City, Az., U.S.	C3	80
Black Canyon of the Gunnison National Monument, Co., U.S.	C3	83
Black Creek, B.C., Can.	E5	69
Black Creek, N.C., U.S.	B5	110
Black Creek, Wi., U.S.	D5	126
Black Creek, stm., U.S.	B1	108
Black Creek, stm., Ms., U.S.	D4	101
Black Creek, stm., S.C., U.S.	B7	117
Black Diamond, Ab., Can.	D3	68
Black Diamond, Al., U.S.	g6	78
Black Diamond, Wa., U.S.	B3	124
Black Down Hills, hills, Eng., U.K.	E5	10
Blackduck, Mn., U.S.	C4	100
Black Eagle, Mt., U.S.	C5	103
Black Earth, Wi., U.S.	E4	126
Blackey, Ky., U.S.	C7	94
Blackfalds, Ab., Can.	C4	68
Blackfeet Indian Reservation, Mt., U.S.	B4	103
Blackfoot, Ab., Can.	C5	68
Blackfoot, Id., U.S.	F6	89
Blackfoot, Mt., U.S.	B4	103
Blackfoot, stm., Mt., U.S.	C3	103
Blackfoot Mountains, mts., Id., U.S.	F7	89
Blackfoot Reservoir, res., Id., U.S.	G7	89
Blackford, Ky., U.S.	C2	94
Blackford, co., In., U.S.	D7	91
Black Forest, Co., U.S.	C6	83
Black Forest, mts., F.R.Ger.	E4	18
Blackfork, Oh., U.S.	D3	112
Blackhall Mountain, mtn., Wy., U.S.	E6	127
Black Hawk, Ms., U.S.	B3	101
Black Hawk, S.D., U.S.	C2	118
Black Hawk, co., Ia., U.S.	B5	92
Blackhead Bay, b., Nf., Can.	D5	72
Black Hills, mts., U.S.	C2	118
Blackie, Ab., Can.	D4	68
Black Island, i., Ant.	f38	7
Black Island, i., Mb., Can.	D3	70
Black Jack, Mo., U.S.	*f13	102
Blackjack Mountain, mtn., U.S.	h7	87
Black Lake, P.Q., Can.	C6	74
Black Lake, l., Sk., Can.	m7	75
Black Lake, l., Mi., U.S.	C6	99
Black Lake, l., N.Y., U.S.	f9	109
Black Lake Bayou, stm., La., U.S.	B2	95
Blacklick, Oh., U.S.	m11	112
Black Lick, Pa., U.S.	F3	115
Blacklick Estates, Oh., U.S.	m11	112
Black Mesa, mtn., Az., U.S.	A5	80
Black Mesa, mtn., Az., U.S.	e8	113
Black Mingo Creek, stm., S.C., U.S.	D9	117
Blackmore, Mount, mtn., Mt., U.S.	E6	103
Black Mountain, N.C., U.S.	f10	110
Black Mountain, mtn., Az., U.S.	D7	94
Black Mountain, mtn., Az., U.S.	E4	80
Black Mountain, mtn., Co., U.S.	A5	83
Black Mountain, mtn., Id., U.S.	C3	89
Black Mountain, mtn., Mt., U.S.	D4	103
Black Mountain, mtn., Or., U.S.	B7	114
Black Mountain, mtn., Wy., U.S.	B5	127
Black Mountain, mtn., Wy., U.S.	D7	127
Black Mountains, mts., Wales, U.K.	C4	12
Black Mountains, mts., Az., U.S.	B5	81
Black Oak, Ar., U.S.	B5	81
Black Oak, In., U.S.	A3	91
Black Peak, mtn., Az., U.S.	C1	80
Black Pine Peak, mtn., Id., U.S.	G5	89
Black Point, Ct., U.S.	D7	84
Black Point Beach Club, Ct., U.S.	*D7	84
Black Pond, l., Me., U.S.	B3	96
Blackpool, Eng., U.K.	D5	10
Black Range, mts., N.M., U.S.	D2	108
Black River, Jam.	E5	65
Black River, Mi., U.S.	D7	99
Black River, N.Y., U.S.	A5	109
Black River Bay, b., Jam.	F13	65
Black River Falls, Wi., U.S.	D3	126
Black Rock, Ar., U.S.	A4	81
Black Rock, N.M., U.S.	B1	108
Black Rock Desert, des., Nv., U.S.	B3	105
Black Rock Range, mts., Nv., U.S.	B3	105
Blacksburg, S.C., U.S.	A4	117
Blacksburg, Va., U.S.	C2	123
Black Sea	G15	8
Blacks Fork, stm., U.S.	E3	127
Blackshear, Ga., U.S.	E4	87
Blackshear, Lake, res., Ga., U.S.	E2	87
Blacksod Bay, b., Ire.	C1	10
Black Springs, Ar., U.S.	C2	81
Black Springs, Nv., U.S.	*D2	105
Black Squirrel Creek, stm., Co., U.S.	C6	83
Blackstairs Mountain, mtn., Ire.	E5	11
Blackstairs Mountains, mts., Ire.	E5	11
Blackstock, On., Can.	C6	73
Blackstock, S.C., U.S.	B5	117
Blackstone, Ma., U.S.	B4	98
Blackstone, Va., U.S.	C5	123
Blackstone, stm., Ab., Can.	C2	68
Blackstone, stm., R.I., U.S.	B4	116
Blackstrap Reservoir, res., Sk., Can.	F2	75
Black Sugarloaf Mountain, mtn., Austl.	E9	51
Blacksville, W.V., U.S.	B4	125
Black Thunder Creek, stm., Wy., U.S.	C8	127
Blacktown, Austl.	*F9	50
Blackville, N.B., Can.	C4	71
Blackville, S.C., U.S.	E5	117
Black Volta (Volta Noire), stm., Afr.	E4	45
Blackwalnut Point, c., Md., U.S.	C5	97
Black Warrior, stm., Al., U.S.	C2	78
Blackwater, Ire.	E5	11
Blackwater, Mo., U.S.	C5	102
Blackwater, Va., U.S.	f8	123
Blackwater, stm., Ire.	E5	11
Blackwater, stm., Fl., U.S.	u15	86
Blackwater, stm., Md., U.S.	D5	97
Blackwater, stm., N.H., U.S.	D3	106
Blackwater, stm., Va., U.S.	D6	123
Blackwater Reservoir, res., N.H., U.S.	D3	106
Blackwater Reservoir, res., Scot., U.K.	D4	13
Blackwell, Ar., U.S.	B3	81
Blackwell, Mo., U.S.	C7	102
Blackwell, Ok., U.S.	A4	113
Blackwell, Tx., U.S.	C2	120
Blackwell, W.V., U.S.	C5	125
Blackwood, N.J., U.S.	D2	107
Blackwood Creek, stm., Ne., U.S.	D4	104
Bladen, Ne., U.S.	D7	104
Bladen, co., N.C., U.S.	C4	110
Bladenboro, N.C., U.S.	C4	110
Bladensburg, Md., U.S.	f9	97
Bladensburg, Oh., U.S.	B3	112
Blades, De., U.S.	F3	85
Bladon Springs, Al., U.S.	D1	78
Bladworth, Sk., Can.	F2	75
Blaenbeery, stm., B.C., Can.	D2	68
Blagnac, Fr.	F4	16
Blagodarnoye, Sov. Un.	D2	24
Blagoevgrad (Gorna Dzhumaya), Bul.	D6	24
Blagoveshchensk, Sov. Un.	D20	8
Blagoveshchensk, Sov. Un.	D15	29
Blain, Fr.	D3	16
Blain, Pa., U.S.	F7	115
Blaine, Ks., U.S.	C7	93
Blaine, Me., U.S.	B5	96
Blaine, Mn., U.S.	m12	100
Blaine, Tn., U.S.	C10	119
Blaine, Wa., U.S.	A3	124
Blaine, co., Id., U.S.	F4	89
Blaine, co., Mt., U.S.	B7	103
Blaine, co., Ne., U.S.	C6	104
Blaine, co., Ok., U.S.	B3	113
Blaine Creek, stm., Ky., U.S.	B7	94
Blainville-sur-l'Eau, Fr.	F6	17
Blair, Ks., U.S.	C8	93
Blair, Ne., U.S.	C9	104
Blair, Ok., U.S.	C2	113
Blair, S.C., U.S.	C5	117
Blair, W.V., U.S.	n12	125
Blair, Wi., U.S.	D2	126
Blair, co., Pa., U.S.	E5	115
Blair Athol, Austl.	D8	50
Blair-Athol, Scot., U.K.	E5	13
Blairgowrie, Scot., U.K.	B5	10
Blairsburg, Ia., U.S.	B4	92
Blairsden, Ca., U.S.	C3	82
Blairstown, Ia., U.S.	C5	92
Blairstown, Mo., U.S.	C4	102
Blairstown, N.J., U.S.	B3	107
Blairsville, Ga., U.S.	B3	87
Blairsville, Pa., U.S.	F3	115
Blairton, W.V., U.S.	B7	125
Blaj, Rom.	B6	24
Blake Island, i., Wa., U.S.	e11	124
Blakely, Ga., U.S.	E2	87
Blakely, Pa., U.S.	m18	115
Blake Point, c., Mi., U.S.	h10	99
Blakesburg, Ia., U.S.	D5	92
Blakeslee, Oh., U.S.	A1	112
Blakeslee, Pa., U.S.	D10	115
Blâmont, Fr.	F6	17
Blanc, Cap, c., Afr.	B1	45
Blanc, Cap, c., Tun.	D7	16
Blanc, Mont, mtn., Eur.	E7	16
Blanca, Co., U.S.	D5	83
Blanca, Bahía, b., Arg.	B4	54
Blanca, Cordillera, mtn., Peru	E3	58
Blanca, Sierra, mtn., Tx., U.S.	o12	120
Blanca Peak, mtn., Co., U.S.	D5	83
Blanchard, Id., U.S.	A2	89
Blanchard, Ia., U.S.	D2	92
Blanchard, La., U.S.	B2	95
Blanchard, Me., U.S.	C3	96
Blanchard, Mi., U.S.	E5	99
Blanchard, N.D., U.S.	B8	111
Blanchard, Ok., U.S.	B4	113
Blanchard, Wa., U.S.	A3	124
Blanchard, stm., Oh., U.S.	A1	112
Blanchardville, Wi., U.S.	F4	126
Blanche, P.Q., Can.	D2	74
Blanche, Tn., U.S.	B5	119
Blanche, Lake, l., Austl.	E6	50
Blanchester, Oh., U.S.	C2	112
Blanco, N.M., U.S.	A2	108
Blanco, Tx., U.S.	D3	120
Blanco, co., Tx., U.S.	D3	120
Blanco, stm., Arg.	E2	55
Blanco, stm., Mex.	n15	63
Blanco, Cabo, c., C.R.	B1	58?
Blanco, Cabo, c., Peru	B1	58
Blanco, Cabo, c., U.S.	E2	114
Blanc-Sablon, P.Q., Can.	C3	72
Bland, Mo., U.S.	C6	102
Bland, Va., U.S.	C1	123
Bland, co., Va., U.S.	C1	123
Blandburg, Pa., U.S.	E5	115
Blandford, Ma., U.S.	B2	98
Blandford Forum, Eng., U.K.	D5	12
Blanding, Ut., U.S.	F6	121
Blandinsville, Il., U.S.	C3	90
Blandville, Ky., U.S.	f9	94
Blanford, In., U.S.	E2	91
Blangkejeren, Indon.	K2	35
Blangy-sur-Bresle, Fr.	E9	12
Blankenberge, Bel.	C3	17
Blankenburg, Ger.D.R.	C5	18
Blankenfelde, Ger.D.R.	A8	19
Blankenheim, F.R.Ger.	C1	19
Blanquefort, Fr.	D3	120
Blanquilla, Isla, i., Ven.	A5	60
Blantyre, Mwi.	E5	48
Blarney, Ire.	F3	11
Blasdell, N.Y., U.S.	C2	109
Blato, Yugo.	D3	24
Blaubeuren, F.R.Ger.	E4	19
Blauvelt, N.Y., U.S.	*g13	109
Blåvands Huk, c., Den.	C2	15
Blawnox, Pa., U.S.	k14	115
Blaye, Fr.	E3	16
Blażowa, Pol.	D7	26
Błaszki, Pol.	E4	15?
Bledów, Pol.	g10	26
Bleckley, co., Ga., U.S.	D3	87
Bled, Yugo.	B2	24
Bledsoe, Tx., U.S.	C1	120
Bledsoe, co., Tn., U.S.	D8	119
Bleecker, Al., U.S.	C4	78
Bleicherode, Ger.D.R.	B5	19
Blekinge, co., Swe.	B8	15
Blencoe, Ia., U.S.	C1	92
Blende, Co., U.S.	C6	83
Blendecques, Fr.	D2	17
Blenheim, On., Can.	E3	73
Blenheim, N.Z.	N14	51
Blenheim, S.C., U.S.	B8	117
Blennerhassett, W.V., U.S.	B3	125
Blessing, Tx., U.S.	E4	120
Blessington, Ire.	D5	11
Bletchley, Eng., U.K.	C7	12
Blevins, Ar., U.S.	D2	81
Blija, Neth.	A5	17
Blind, stm., La., U.S.	h10	95
Blind River, On., Can.	A2	73
Bliss, Id., U.S.	G4	89
Bliss, N.Y., U.S.	C2	109
Blissfield, Mi., U.S.	G7	99
Blissfield, Oh., U.S.	B4	112
Blitta, Togo	E5	45
Blocher, In., U.S.	G6	91
Block, Ok., U.S.	B6	113
Block Island, R.I., U.S.	h7	116
Block Island Sound, strt., U.S.	G2	116
Blockton, Ia., U.S.	D3	92
Blodgett, Mo., U.S.	D8	102
Blodgett Landing, N.H., U.S.	D2	106
Bloedel, B.C., Can.	D5	69
Bloemfontein, S. Afr.	C4	49
Blois, Fr.	D4	16
Blokhus, Den.	A3	15
Blomberg, F.R.Ger.	B4	19
Blommestein Meer, res., Sur.	B8	87?
Blönduós, Ice.	n22	14
Błonie, Pol.	m13	26
Blood Mountain, mtn., Ga., U.S.	B3	87
Bloodsworth Island, i., Md., U.S.	D5	97
Bloodvein, stm., Can.	D3	70
Bloody Foreland, c., Ire.	B3	11
Bloom, Ks., U.S.	E4	93
Bloom, Slieve, mts., Ire.	D4	11
Bloomdale, Oh., U.S.	A2	112
Bloomer, Ar., U.S.	B1	81
Bloomer, Wi., U.S.	C2	126
Bloomfield, N.B., Can.	D4	71
Bloomfield, On., Can.	D7	73
Bloomfield, Ct., U.S.	B5	84
Bloomfield, In., U.S.	F4	91
Bloomfield, Ia., U.S.	D5	92
Bloomfield, Ky., U.S.	C4	94
Bloomfield, Mo., U.S.	E8	102
Bloomfield, Mt., U.S.	C12	103
Bloomfield, Ne., U.S.	B8	104
Bloomfield, N.J., U.S.	h8	107
Bloomfield, N.M., U.S.	A2	108
Bloomfield, Vt., U.S.	B5	122
Bloomfield Hills, Mi., U.S.	o15	99
Bloomfield Township, Mi., U.S.	*F7	99
Bloomingburg, Oh., U.S.	C2	112
Bloomingdale, Ga., U.S.	D5	87
Bloomingdale, Il., U.S.	k8	90
Bloomingdale, In., U.S.	E3	91
Bloomingdale, Mi., U.S.	F5	99
Bloomingdale, N.J., U.S.	A4	107
Bloomingdale, N.Y., U.S.	f10	109
Bloomingdale, Tn., U.S.	C11	119
Blooming Grove, Pa., U.S.	D11	115
Blooming Grove, Tx., U.S.	C4	120
Blooming Prairie, Mn., U.S.	G5	100
Bloomington, Ca., U.S.	*m14	82
Bloomington, Id., U.S.	G7	89
Bloomington, Il., U.S.	C4	90
Bloomington, In., U.S.	F4	91
Bloomington, Md., U.S.	m12	97
Bloomington, Mn., U.S.	F5	100
Bloomington, Ne., U.S.	D6	104
Bloomington, Tx., U.S.	E4	120
Bloomington, Ut., U.S.	*F2	121
Bloomington, Wi., U.S.	F3	126
Bloomington, Lake, res., Il., U.S.	C5	90
Bloomsburg, Pa., U.S.	E9	115
Bloomsbury, N.J., U.S.	B2	107
Bloomsdale, Mo., U.S.	C7	102
Bloomville, Oh., U.S.	A2	112
Blossburg, Al., U.S.	f7	78
Blossburg, Pa., U.S.	C7	115
Blosseville Coast, Grnld.	C17	128
Blossom, Tx., U.S.	C5	120
Blount, co., Al., U.S.	B3	78
Blount, co., Tn., U.S.	D10	119
Blount Springs, Al., U.S.	A3	78
Blountstown, Fl., U.S.	B1	86
Blountsville, Al., U.S.	A3	78
Blountville, Tn., U.S.	C11	119
Blovice, Czech.	D8	19
Blowing Rock, N.C., U.S.	A1	110
Bloxom, Va., U.S.	C7	123
Bluebird, Sk., Can.	E2	75?
Bluewood, Sk., Can.	E2	75
Bludenz, Aus.	E4	18
Blue, Ok., U.S.	C5	113
Blue, stm., In., U.S.	H5	91
Blue, stm., Mo., U.S.	k10	102
Blue, stm., Ok., U.S.	C5	113
Blue, Mount, mtn., Me., U.S.	D2	96
Blue Anchor, N.J., U.S.	D3	107
Blue Ash, Oh., U.S.	o13	112
Bluebell, Ut., U.S.	C5	121
Blueberry, stm., B.C., Can.	A7	69
Blue Buck Knob, hill, Mo., U.S.	E5	102
Blue Buck Point, c., La., U.S.	E2	95
Blue Creek, Al., U.S.	g6	78
Blue Creek, Wa., U.S.	A8	124
Blue Creek, W.V., U.S.	m13	125
Blue Creek, stm., Ne., U.S.	C3	104
Blue Creek, stm., W.V., U.S.	m13	125
Blue Cypress Lake, l., Fl., U.S.	E6	86
Blue Diamond, Nv., U.S.	G6	105
Blue Earth, Mn., U.S.	G4	100
Blue Earth, co., Mn., U.S.	G4	100
Blue Earth, stm., Mn., U.S.	G4	100
Bluefield, Va., U.S.	C1	123
Bluefield, W.V., U.S.	D3	125
Blue Ciega Bay, b., Fl., U.S.	p10	86
Bluefields, Nic.	E8	63
Bluefields Bay, b., Jam.	E12	65
Blue Grass, Ia., U.S.	C7	92
Blue Grass, Va., U.S.	B3	123
Blue Hill, Me., U.S.	D4	96
Blue Hill, Ne., U.S.	D7	104
Blue Hill Falls, Me., U.S.	D4	96
Blue Hill Range, hills, Ma., U.S.	h11	98
Blue Hills, Ct., U.S.	B5	84
Blue Hills of Couteau, hills, Nf., Can.	E3	72
Bluehole, Ky., U.S.	C6	94
Blue Island, Il., U.S.	B6	90
Bluejacket, Ok., U.S.	A6	113
Bluejoint Lake, l., Or., U.S.	E7	114
Blue Knob, mtn., Pa., U.S.	F4	115
Blue Mesa Reservoir, res., Co., U.S.	C3	83
Blue Mound, Il., U.S.	D4	90
Blue Mound, Ks., U.S.	D8	93
Blue Mountain, Al., U.S.	B4	78
Blue Mountain, Ar., U.S.	B2	81
Blue Mountain, Co., U.S.	A2	83
Blue Mountain, Ms., U.S.	A4	101
Blue Mountain, mtn., N.B., Can.	B3	71
Blue Mountain, mtn., Nf., Can.	C3	72
Blue Mountain, mtn., Ar., U.S.	C1	81
Blue Mountain, mtn., Mt., U.S.	C12	103
Blue Mountain, mtn., N.H., U.S.	A4	106
Blue Mountain, mtn., N.M., U.S.	D2	108
Blue Mountain, mtn., N.Y., U.S.	B6	109
Blue Mountain, mtn., Pa., U.S.	F6	115
Blue Mountain Lake, N.Y., U.S.	B6	109
Blue Mountain Lake, res., Ar., U.S.	B2	81
Blue Mountain Peak, mtn., Jam.	E5	64
Blue Mountains, mts., Austl.	F8	51
Blue Mountains, mts., Jam.	E15	65
Blue Mountains, mts.,	A4	76
Blue Mud Bay, b., Austl.	B6	50
Blue Nile, stm., Afr.	C3	47
Blue Point, Me., U.S.	g7	96
Blue Rapids, Ks., U.S.	C7	93
Blue Ridge, Ga., U.S.	B2	87
Blue Ridge, In., U.S.	E6	91
Blue Ridge, Va., U.S.	C3	123
Blue Ridge, mtn.,	C11	76
Blue Ridge Lake, res., Ga., U.S.	B2	87
Blue Ridge Summit, Pa., U.S.	G7	115
Blue River, B.C., Can.	C8	69
Blue River, Or., U.S.	C4	114
Blue River, Wi., U.S.	E3	126
Bluesky, Ab., Can.	A1	68
Blue Springs, Al., U.S.	D4	78
Blue Springs, Mo., U.S.	h11	102
Blue Springs, Ne., U.S.	D9	104
Bluestone, stm., W.V., U.S.	D3	125
Bluestone Lake, res., U.S.	D3	125
Bluevale, On., Can.	D3	73
Bluewater, N.M., U.S.	B2	108
Bluewell, W.V., U.S.	D3	125
Bluff, N.Z.	Q12	51
Bluff, Ut., U.S.	F6	121
Bluff City, Ar., U.S.	D2	81
Bluff City, Il., U.S.	E4	90
Bluff City, Ks., U.S.	E6	93
Bluff City, Ky., U.S.	C2	94
Bluff City, Tn., U.S.	C11	119
Bluff Creek, stm., Ks., U.S.	E4	93
Bluff Creek, stm., Ok., U.S.	A4	113
Bluff Dale, Tx., U.S.	C3	120
Bluffdale, Ut., U.S.	*C4	121
Bluff Knoll, mtn., Austl.	F2	50
Bluff Lake, res., Ms., U.S.	B5	101
Bluff Mountain, mtn., Vt., U.S.	B5	122
Bluff Park, Al., U.S.	g7	78
Bluffs, Il., U.S.	D3	90
Bluffton, Ar., U.S.	C2	81
Bluffton, Ga., U.S.	E2	87
Bluffton, In., U.S.	C7	91
Bluffton, Mn., U.S.	D3	100
Bluffton, Oh., U.S.	B2	112
Bluffton, S.C., U.S.	G6	117
Blum, Tx., U.S.	C4	120
Blunt, S.D., U.S.	C6	118
Blunt, Or., U.S.	B2	59?
Blying Sound, strt., Ak., U.S.	h17	79
Blyth, On., Can.	D3	73
Blyth, Eng., U.K.	C6	10
Blythe, Ca., U.S.	F6	82
Blythedale, Mo., U.S.	A3	102
Blytheville, Ar., U.S.	B6	81
Blytheville Air Force Base, mil., Ar., U.S.	B6	81
Blythewood, S.C., U.S.	C6	117
Bo, S.L.	G4	45
Boac, Phil.	C7	34
Boaco, Nic.	E7	63
Bo'ai (Qinghua), China	G5	32
Boali, Cen. Afr. Rep.	B3	46
Boalsburg, Pa., U.S.	E6	115
Boardman, Oh., U.S.	A5	112
Boardman, Or., U.S.	B7	114
Boardman, stm., Mi., U.S.	D5	99
Boaz, Al., U.S.	A3	78
Boaz, Wi., U.S.	E3	126
Bobbili, India	E7	36
Bobbio, Italy	E5	20
Bobcaygeon, On., Can.	C6	73
Bobigny, Fr.	g10	16
Böblingen, F.R.Ger.	E4	19
Bobo, Ms., U.S.	A3	101
Bobo Dioulasso, Burkina	D4	45
Bóbr, stm., Pol.	C3	26
Bobrinets, Sov. Un.	D6	24?
Bobrka, Sov. Un.	G5	27
Bobruysk, Sov. Un.	E7	27
Bobtown, Pa., U.S.	G2	115
Boca Chica Key, i., Fl., U.S.	H5	86
Boca Ciega Bay, b., Fl., U.S.	p10	86
Bôca do Acre, Braz.	C4	58
Boca Grande, Fl., U.S.	F4	86
Bocaiúva, Braz.	B4	56
Bocanda, I.C.	E4	45
Bocaranga, Cen. Afr. Rep.	D3	46
Boca Raton, Fl., U.S.	F6	86
Bocas del Toro, Pan.	F6	62
Bocay, Nic.	C5	62
Boccea (Buxus), Italy	h8	23
Bochnia, Pol.	D6	26
Bocholt, F.R.Ger.	B1	19
Bochov, Czech.	C8	19
Bochum, F.R.Ger.	C3	18
Bochum, F.R.Ger.	B2	19
Bock, Mn., U.S.	E5	100
Bockhorn, F.R.Ger.	E2	15
Bockum-Hövel, F.R.Ger.	B2	19
Boda, Cen. Afr. Rep.	E3	46
Bodafors, Swe.	A8	15
Bodaybo, Sov. Un.	D14	29
Bodcau Creek, stm., Ar., U.S.	D2	81
Boddam, Scot., U.K.	C7	13
Bode, Ia., U.S.	B3	92
Bode, stm., Ger.D.R.	B6	19
Bodega Head, c., Ca., U.S.	C2	82
Bodele, reg., Chad	B3	46
Boden, Swe.	E9	14
Boden, Il., U.S.	B3	90
Boderg, Lough, l., Ire.	D2	10
Bodie Island, i., N.C., U.S.	B7	110
Bodine, Mount, mtn., B.C., Can.	B5	69
Bodkin Point, c., Md., U.S.	B5	97
Bodmin, Eng., U.K.	E4	10
Bodmin Moor, mor., Eng., U.K.	E4	10
Bodo, Ab., Can.	C5	68
Bodø, Nor.	D6	14
Bodrog, stm., Eur.	A5	24
Boen, Swe.	B6?	109?
Boende, Zaire	B3	48
Boerne, Tx., U.S.	E3	120
Bœuf, stm., La., U.S.	C4	95
Bœuf, Bayou, stm., La., U.S.	B5	95
Bœuf, Lake, l., La., U.S.	k10	95
Bofete, Braz.	m7	56
Boffa, Gui.	D2	45
Bogalusa, La., U.S.	D6	95
Bogan, stm., Austl.	E6	51
Bogandé, Burkina	D4	45
Bogard, Mo., U.S.	B4	102
Bogart, Ga., U.S.	C3	87
Bogata, Tx., U.S.	C5	120
Bogatynia, Pol.	C9	19
Bogbonga, Zaire	A2	48
Bogen, F.R.Ger.	E7	19
Bogenfels, Nmb.	C2	49
Bogense, Den.	C4	15
Boger City, N.C., U.S.	B1	110
Bogodukhov, Sov. Un.	F10	27
Bogon, i., Marsh Is.	S18	52
Bogor, Indon.	G3	34
Bogorodsk, Sov. Un.	E12	27
Bogorodsk, Sov. Un.	C14	27
Bogotá, Col.	C3	60
Bogotol, Sov. Un.	D26	8
Bogra, Bngl.	D8	36?
Boguchany, Sov. Un.	D28	8
Bogué, Maur.	C2	45
Bogue, Ks., U.S.	C4	93
Bogue Chitto, Ms., U.S.	D3	101
Bogue Chitto, stm., U.S.	D5	95
Bogue Inlet, b., N.C., U.S.	C5	110
Bogue Phalia, stm., Ms., U.S.	B3	101
Boguslav, Sov. Un.	G8	27
Bo Hai, b., China	B10	28?
Bohain-en-Vermandois, Fr.	C5	16
Bohemia, La., U.S.	E6	95
Bohemia, N.Y., U.S.	*n15	109
Bohemia, hist reg., Czech.	D6	18
Bohemian Forest, mts., Eur.	D6	18
Bohemian-Moravian Highlands, plat., Czech.	D3	26
Böhme, stm., F.R.Ger.	F3	15
Böhmte, F.R.Ger.	A3	19
Bohol, i., Phil.	D7	34
Boiestown, N.B., Can.	C3	71
Boiling Springs, N.C., U.S.	B1	110
Boiling Springs, Pa., U.S.	F7	115
Bois, Rio dos, stm., Braz.	B2	56
Bois Blanc Island, i., Mi., U.S.	C6	99
Bois Brule, stm., Wi., U.S.	B2	126
Boischatel, P.Q., Can.	C6	74
Bois-Colombes, Fr.	g10	16
Boisdale, Loch, b., Scot., U.K.	C1	13
Boise, Id., U.S.	F2	89
Boise, co., Id., U.S.	F3	89
Boise City, Ok., U.S.	e8	113
Boise Fort, Mn., U.S.	B5	100
Boissevain, Mb., Can.	E1	70
Boissevain, Va., U.S.	e10	123
Boistfort Peak, mtn., Wa., U.S.	C2	124
Boizenburg, Ger.D.R.	B5	18?
Bojeador, Cabo, c., Phil.	B7	34
Bojnürd, Iran	B5	38
Bokchito, Ok., U.S.	D5	113
Boké, Gui.	D2	45
Bokeelia, Fl., U.S.	F4	86
Bokhoma, Ok., U.S.	D7	113
Boko, Zaire	C2	48
Bokobyaadaa Island, i., Marsh Is.	P18	52
Bokoro, Chad	C3	46
Bokororyuru Island, i., Marsh Is.	P18	52
Bokoshe, Ok., U.S.	B7	113
Bokungu, Zaire	B3	48
Bol, Chad	C2	46
Bolafa, Zaire	A3	48
Bolama, Gui.-B.	D1	45
Bolaños, stm., Mex.	m12	63
Bolar, Va., U.S.	B3	123
Bolbec, Fr.	C4	16
Bolckow, Mo., U.S.	A3	102
Bole, Ghana	E4	45
Boleko, Zaire	B2	48
Boles, Ar., U.S.	C1	81
Boles, Il., U.S.	F5	90
Boles, N.M., U.S.	*E4	108
Bolesławiec, Pol.	C3	26
Boley, Ok., U.S.	B5	113
Bolgatanga, Ghana	D4	45
Bolgrad, Sov. Un.	I7	27
Boli, China	B11	31
Bolia, Zaire	B2	48
Boligee, Al., U.S.	C1	78
Bolinao, Phil.	n12	34
Bolinao, Cape, c., Phil.	n12	34
Boling, Tx., U.S.	E5	120
Bolingbrook, Il., U.S.	k8	90
Bolinger, Al., U.S.	D1	78
Bolivar, Arg.	B4	54
Bolívar, Col.	B2	60
Bolivar, Mo., U.S.	D4	102
Bolivar, N.Y., U.S.	C2	109
Bolivar, Oh., U.S.	B4	112
Bolivar, Pa., U.S.	F3	115
Bolivar, Tn., U.S.	B3	119
Bolívar, W.V., U.S.	B7	125
Bolívar, state, Ven.	B6	60
Bolivar, co., Ms., U.S.	B2	101
Bolívar, dept., Col.	B2	60
Bolívar, prov., Ec.	B2	58
Bolívar, Cerro, mtn., Ven.	B6	60
Bolivar, Lake, l., Ms., U.S.	B3	101
Bolívar, Pico, mtn., Ven.	B3	60
Bolivia, N.C., U.S.	C4	110
Bolivia, ctry., S.A.	C2	55
Bolkhov, Sov. Un.	E11	27
Bollebygd, Swe.	A6	15
Bollène, Fr.	E6	16
Bolligen, Switz.	C4	21
Bolling, Al., U.S.	D3	78
Bollinger, co., Mo., U.S.	D7	102
Bollnäs, Swe.	G7	14
Bollullos [del Condado], Spain	D2	22
Bolmen, l., Swe.	B7	15
Bolnisi, Sov. Un.	B15	40
Bolobo, Zaire	B2	48
Bologna, Italy	B3	23
Bologoye, Sov. Un.	C10	27
Bolomba, Zaire	A2	48
Bolon, Lake, l., Sov. Un.	B8	33
Bolotnoye, Sov. Un.	B10	28
Bolovens, Plateau des, plat., Laos	E7	35
Bolsena, Lake, l., Italy	C3	23
Bolshaya Kamenka, stm., Un.	q22	27
Bolshevik, i., Sov. Un.	B4	128
Bolshoy Irgiz, stm., Sov. Un.	G8	27
Bolshoy Uzen, stm., Sov. Un.	D3	28
Bolshoy Yugan, stm., Sov. Un.	D3	28
Bolsward, Neth.	A5	17
Bolton, Eng., U.K.	D5	10
Bolton, Ms., U.S.	C3	101
Bolton, N.C., U.S.	C4	110
Bolton, Vt., U.S.	C3	122
Bolton Center, Ct., U.S.	B6	84
Bolton Lakes, l., Ct., U.S.	B6	84
Bolton Landing, N.Y., U.S.	B7	109
Bolu, Tur.	B4	40
Bolus Head, c., Ire.	F1	11
Bolvadin, Tur.	C8	40
Bolzano, Italy	A3	23
Boma, Zaire	C1	48
Bomarton, Tx., U.S.	C3	120
Bombala, Austl.	G8	50
Bombay, India	E5	36
Bombay Hook Island, i., De., U.S.	C4	85
Bomboma, Zaire	A2	48
Bom Conselho, Braz.	B3	56
Bom Despacho, Braz.	B3	56
Bom Jardim, Braz.	B3	56
Bom Jardim de Goiás, Braz.	B2	56
Bom Jardim de Minas, Braz.	g5	56
Bom Jesus, Braz.	D2	56
Bom Jesus, Braz.	B3	56
Bom Jesus da Lapa, Braz.	A4	56
Bomokandi, stm., Zaire	A2	48
Bomongo, Zaire	A2	48
Bomoseen, Vt., U.S.	D2	122
Bomoseen, Lake, l., Vt., U.S.	D2	122
Bomu, stm., Afr.	A4	46
Bon, Cap, c., Tun.	B7	44
Bon Accord, Ab., Can.	C4	68
Bonaigarh, India	G10	37
Bon Air, Al., U.S.	B3	78
Bon Air, Tn., U.S.	D8	119
Bon Air, Va., U.S.	C5	123
Bonaire, i., Neth. Ant.	A4	60
Bonanza, Nic.	C5	62
Bonanza, Or., U.S.	B1	81?
Bonanza, Ut., U.S.	D6	121
Bonanza City, Co., U.S.	C4	83
Bonanza Peak, mtn., Wa., U.S.	A5	124
Bonaparte, Ia., U.S.	D6	92
Bonaparte, stm., B.C., Can.	D7	69
Bonaparte, Mount, mtn., Wa., U.S.	A6	124
Bonaparte Lake, l., B.C., Can.	D7	69
Bon Aqua, Tn., U.S.	B4	119
Bonar Bridge, Scot., U.K.	A3	22?
Bonarlaw, On., Can.	C7	73
Bonasila Dome, mtn., Ak., U.S.	C7	79
Bonavista, Nf., Can.	D5	72
Bonavista, Cape, c., Nf., Can.	D5	72

Name | Map Ref | Page

Bonavista Bay, b., Nf., Can. D5 72
Bond, Co., U.S. B4 83
Bond, Ky., U.S. C6 94
Bond, Ms., U.S. E4 101
Bond, Ok., U.S. B6 113
Bond, co., Il., U.S. E4 90
Bondeno, Italy E7 20
Bondo, Zaire A3 48
Bondoukou, I.C. E4 45
Bondsville, Ma., U.S. B3 98
Bonduel, Wi., U.S. D5 126
Bondurant, Ia., U.S. C4 92
Bondurant, Wy., U.S. C2 127
Bondville, Il., U.S. C5 90
Bondville, Vt., U.S. E3 122
Bondy, Fr. g10 16
Bone, Gulf of, b., Indon. F6 34
Bone Cave, Tn., U.S. D8 119
Bone Gap, Il., U.S. E6 90
Bone Lake, l., Wi., U.S. C1 126
Bone Rate Islands, is., Indon. G6 34
Bonesteel, S.D., U.S. D7 118
Bonete, Cerro, mtn., Arg. E2 55
Bonetraill, N.D., U.S. A2 111
Bonfield, On., Can. A5 73
Bonfouca, La., U.S. h12 95
Bonga, Eth. D4 47
Bongandanga, Zaire A3 48
Bongor, Chad C3 46
Bonham, Tx., U.S. C4 120
Bon Homme, co., S.D., U.S. D8 118
Bon Homme Colony, S.D., U.S. E8 118
Bonifacio, Fr. D2 23
Bonifacio, Strait of, strt., Eur. D2 23
Bonifay, Fl., U.S. u16 86
Bonilla, S.D., U.S. C7 118
Bonin Islands, is., Japan E8 6
Bonita, La., U.S. B4 95
Bonita Springs, Fl., U.S. F5 86
Bonito, Braz. C1 56
Bonito, Braz. k6 57
Bonlee, N.C., U.S. B3 110
Bonn, F.R.Ger. C3 18
Bonneau, S.C., U.S. E8 117
Bonneauville, Pa., U.S. G7 115
Bonne Bay (Woody Point), Nf., Can. D3 72
Bonne Bay, b., Nf., Can. D3 72
Bonne Idee, Bayou, stm., La., U.S. B4 95
Bonner, Mt., U.S. D3 103
Bonner, co., Id., U.S. A2 89
Bonnerdale, Ar., U.S. C2 81
Bonners Ferry, Id., U.S. A2 89
Bonner Springs, Ks., U.S. C9 93
Bønnerup Strand, Den. B4 15
Bonne-sur-Ménoge, Fr. D1 21
Bonnet, Lac du, l., Mb., Can. D4 70
Bonnétable, Fr. C4 16
Bonnet Clare Floodway, La., U.S. h11 95
Bonne Terre, Mo., U.S. D7 102
Bonneville, Fr. C2 20
Bonneville, Or., U.S. B5 114
Bonneville, co., Id., U.S. F7 89
Bonneville Dam, U.S. B4 114
Bonneville Peak, mtn., Id., U.S. F6 89
Bonneville Salt Flats, pl., Ut., U.S. C2 121
Bonnevoie-Sud, Lux. *E6 17
Bonney Lake, Wa., U.S. B3 124
Bonnie, Il., U.S. E5 90
Bonnie Doone, N.C., U.S. B4 110
Bonnieville, Ky., U.S. C4 94
Bonnots Mill, Mo., U.S. C6 102
Bonny, Nig. F6 45
Bonny Blue, Va., U.S. f8 123
Bonny Reservoir, res., Co., U.S. B8 83
Bonnyville, Ab., Can. B5 68
Bono, Ar., U.S. B5 81
Bono, Oh., U.S. *A2 112
Bonorva, Italy D2 23
Bonriki, Kir. R18 52
Bonriki, i., Kir. R18 52
Bons, Fr. D1 21
Bonsal, N.C., U.S. B4 110
Bon Secour, Al., U.S. E2 78
Bonshaw, P.E., Can. C6 71
Bontang, Indon. E5 34
Bonthe, S.L. E2 45
Bon Wier, Tx., U.S. D6 120
Book Cliffs, clf, U.S. D6 121
Booker, Tx., U.S. A2 120
Booker T. Washington National Monument, Va., U.S. C3 123
Booligal, Austl. F5 51
Boolyglass, Ire. E4 11
Boomer, N.C., U.S. A1 110
Boomer, W.V., U.S. C3 125
Boon, Mi., U.S. D5 99
Boone, Co., U.S. C6 83
Boone, Ia., U.S. B4 92
Boone, Ne., U.S. C8 104
Boone, N.C., U.S. A1 110
Boone, co., Ar., U.S. A2 81
Boone, co., Il., U.S. A5 90
Boone, co., In., U.S. D4 91
Boone, co., Ia., U.S. B3 92
Boone, co., Ky., U.S. B5 94
Boone, co., Mo., U.S. B5 102
Boone, co., Ne., U.S. C7 104
Boone, co., W.V., U.S. C3 125
Boone, stm., Ia., U.S. B4 92
Boone Grove, In., U.S. B3 91
Boone Lake, res., Tn., U.S. C11 119
Boones Mill, Va., U.S. C3 123
Booneville, Ar., U.S. B2 81
Booneville, Ky., U.S. C6 94
Booneville, Ms., U.S. A5 101
Boonsboro, Md., U.S. A2 97
Boons Pond, l., Ma., U.S. g10 98
Boonton, N.J., U.S. B4 107
Boonville, Ca., U.S. C2 82
Boonville, In., U.S. H3 91
Boonville, Mo., U.S. C5 102
Boonville, N.Y., U.S. B5 109
Boonville, N.C., U.S. A2 110
Boorama, Som. C5 47
Boosaaso, Som. C6 47
Booth, Al., U.S. C3 78
Boothbay, Me., U.S. E3 96
Boothbay Harbor, Me., U.S. E3 96
Boothby, Cape, c., Ant. C18 7
Boothia, Gulf of, b., N.T., Can. B14 66
Boothia Peninsula, pen., N.T., Can. B14 66
Booths Creek, stm., W.V., U.S. h11 125
Boothville, La., U.S. E6 95
Boothwyn, Pa., U.S. *G11 115
Bootle, Eng., U.K. A4 12
Boué, Gabon F2 46
Bophuthatswana, ctry., Afr. C4 49
Bopolu, Lib. E2 45
Boppard, F.R.Ger. C3 18
Boquerón, dept., Para. D3 55
Boquerón, stm., Pan. k11 62
Boquerón, Bahía de, b., P.R. B1 65
Bor, Sud. D3 47
Bor, Yugo. C6 24
Boraha, Nosy, i., Madag. g10 49
Borah Peak, mtn., Id., U.S. E5 89
Borås, Swe. I5 14
Borāzjān, Iran G5 39
Borba, Braz. C3 59
Borculo, Neth. B6 17
Bordeaux, Fr. E3 16
Bordelonville, La., U.S. C4 95
Borden, Sk., Can. E2 75
Borden, In., U.S. H6 91
Borden, co., Tx., U.S. C2 120
Borden Island, i., N.T., Can. m29 66
Borden Peninsula, pen., N.T., Can. B16 66
Borden Springs, Al., U.S. B4 78
Bordentown, N.J., U.S. C3 107
Borderland, W.V., U.S. D2 125
Borders, prov., Scot., U.K. E5 13
Bordertown, Austl. G7 50
Bordighera, Italy C1 23
Bordj Bou Arreridj, Alg. B5 44
Bordj Omar Idriss, Alg. D6 44
Bordley, Ky., U.S. C2 94
Bordulac, N.D., U.S. B7 111
Boré, Mali C4 45
Boren, l., Swe. u33 14
Borensberg, Swe. u33 14
Borgå, Fin. G11 14
Börger, F.R.Ger. B7 17
Borger, Neth. B6 17
Borger, Tx., U.S. B2 120
Borgholm, Swe. I7 14
Borghorst, F.R.Ger. A2 19
Borg Mountain, mtn., Ant. B12 7
Borgne, stm., Switz. D3 21
Borgne, Lake, b., La., U.S. D6 95
Borgomanero, Italy B2 23
Borgo Piave, Italy k9 23
Borgosesia, Italy E5 21
Borgo Val di Taro, Italy B2 23
Borgo Val Sugana, Italy C7 20
Boring, Or., U.S. B4 114
Borislav, Sov. Un. G4 27
Borisoglebsk, Sov. Un. D7 29
Borisov, Sov. Un. D7 27
Borispol, Sov. Un. F8 27
Borja, Peru B2 58
Borja, Spain B5 22
Borjas Blancas, Spain B6 22
Borken, F.R.Ger. B4 19
Borken, F.R.Ger. B1 19
Børkop, Den. C3 15
Borkou, hist reg., Chad B3 46
Borkum, F.R.Ger. A6 17
Borkum, i., F.R.Ger. B3 18
Borlänge, Swe. G6 14
Bormes, Fr. F7 16
Bormida, stm., Italy E4 20
Bormio, Italy C6 20
Borna, Ger.D.R. B7 19
Borne, Neth. B6 17
Borneo (Kalimantan), i., Asia E4 34
Bornheim, F.R.Ger. C1 19
Bornholm, co., Den. C8 15
Bornholm, i., Den. J6 14
Bornholmsgat, strt., Eur. C8 15
Bornos, Spain D3 22
Bornova, Tur. *C6 40
Borobudur, hist., Indon. G4 34
Boromlya, Sov. Un. F10 27
Boromo, Burkina D4 45
Boron, Ca., U.S. E5 82
Borovan, Bul. D6 24
Borovichi, Sov. Un. D6 29
Borovskoye, Sov. Un. q21 27
Borraan, Som. C6 47
Borrby, Swe. C8 15
Borre, Den. D6 15
Borrego Springs, Ca., U.S. F5 82
Borris, Ire. E5 11
Borrisokane, Ire. E3 11
Borrisoleigh, Ire. E4 11
Borroloola, Austl. C6 50
Borşa, Rom. B7 24
Bort-les-Orgues, Fr. E6 16
Borūjen, Iran F5 39
Borūjerd, Iran B4 38
Borup, Mn., U.S. C2 100
Borzhomi, Sov. Un. B14 40
Borzna, Sov. Un. F9 27
Borzonasca, Italy E5 20
Borzya, Sov. Un. A8 31
Bosa, Italy D2 23
Bosanska Dubica, Yugo. C3 24
Bosanska Gradiška, Yugo. C3 24
Bosanska Kostajnica, Yugo. C3 24
Bosanski Novi, Yugo. C3 24
Bosanski Petrovac, Yugo. C3 24
Bosanski Šamac, Yugo. C4 24
Bosavi, Mount, mtn., Pap. N. Gui. k11 50
Boscawen, N.H., U.S. D3 106
Boscobel, Wi., U.S. E3 126
Boshan, China D8 31
Boshrūyeh, Iran E8 39
Boskovice, Czech. D4 26
Bosler, Wy., U.S. E7 127
Bosna, stm., Yugo. C4 24
Bosnia, hist reg., Yugo. C3 24
Bosnik, Indon. F9 34
Bosobolo, Zaire A2 48
Bosporus, strt. B7 40
Bosque, N.M., U.S. C3 108
Bosque, co., Tx., U.S. D4 120
Boss, Mo., U.S. D6 102
Bossangoa, Cen. Afr. Rep. D3 46
Bossembélé, Cen. Afr. Rep. D3 46
Bossert Estates, N.J., U.S. C3 107
Bossier, co., La., U.S. B2 95
Bossier City, La., U.S. B2 95
Bosso, Niger C2 46
Bosso, Dallol, val., Niger D5 45
Bostāneh, Ra's-e, c., Iran H7 39
Bosten Lake, l., China C2 31
Boston, Eng., U.K. D6 10
Boston, Ga., U.S. F3 87
Boston, In., U.S. E8 91
Boston, Ky., U.S. C4 94
Boston, Ma., U.S. B5 98
Boston Bar, B.C., Can. E7 69
Boston Bay, b., Ma., U.S. B6 98
Boston Heights, Oh., U.S. h9 112
Boston Mountains, mts., Ar., U.S. B2 81
Bostonnais, stm., P.Q., Can. B5 74
Bostwick, Fl., U.S. C5 86
Bostwick, Ga., U.S. C3 87
Boswarlos, Nf., Can. D2 72
Boswell, B.C., Can. E9 69
Boswell, Al., U.S. D4 78
Boswell, Ar., U.S. A3 81
Boswell, In., U.S. C3 91
Boswell, Ok., U.S. C6 113
Boswell, Pa., U.S. F3 115
Bosworth, Mo., U.S. B4 102
Botany Bay, b., Austl. F9 50
Boteti, stm., Bots. B3 49
Botetourt, co., Va., U.S. C3 123
Botev, mtn., Bul. D7 24
Botevgrad, Bul. D6 24
Botha, Ab., Can. C4 68
Bothell, Wa., U.S. B3 124
Bothnia, Gulf of, b., Eur. F9 14
Bothwell, On., Can. E3 73
Bothwell, P.E., Can. C7 71
Botkins, Oh., U.S. B1 112
Botkyrka, Swe. t35 14
Botolan, Phil. o13 34
Botoşani, Rom. B8 24
Botsford, Ct., U.S. D2 84
Botswana, ctry., Afr. B3 49
Bottineau, N.D., U.S. A5 111
Bottineau, co., N.D., U.S. A4 111
Bottrop, F.R.Ger. B1 19
Botucatu, Braz. C3 56
Botwood, Nf., Can. D4 72
Bouaflé, I.C. E3 45
Bouaké, I.C. E3 45
Bouar, Cen. Afr. Rep. D3 46
Bou Arfa, Mor. C4 44
Bou Bernous, Alg. D4 44
Boucau, Fr. F3 16
Boucher, Lac l., P.Q., Can. C2 72
Boucherville, P.Q., Can. D4 74
Bouchette, P.Q., Can. C2 74
Boudenib, Mor. C4 44
Boû Djébéha, well, Mali C4 45
Boudreaux, Lake, l., La., U.S. E5 95
Boudry, Switz. C2 21
Bougainville, i., Pap. N. Gui. G9 6
Bougouni, Mali D3 45
Bouillon, Bel. E5 17
Boulder, Co., U.S. A5 83
Boulder, Mt., U.S. D4 103
Boulder, Ut., U.S. F4 121
Boulder, Wy., U.S. D3 127
Boulder, co., Co., U.S. A5 83
Boulder City, Nv., U.S. H7 105
Boulder Hill, Il., U.S. *B5 90
Boulevard, Ca., U.S. F5 82
Boulevard Heights, Md., U.S. f9 97
Bouligny, Fr. E5 17
Boulogne-Billancourt, Fr. C5 16
Boulogne-sur-Mer, Fr. B4 16
Boulsa, Burkina D4 45
Boumaine, Mor. C3 44
Boumdeït, Maur. C2 45
Bouna, I.C. E4 45
Boundary, Ak., U.S. C11 79
Boundary, co., Id., U.S. A2 89
Boundary Bald Mountain, mtn., Me., U.S. C2 96
Boundary Bay, b., Wa., U.S. A3 124
Boundary Bend, Austl. G4 51
Boundary Peak, mtn., Nv., U.S. F3 105
Boundary Ranges, mts., N.A. k22 79
Bound Brook, N.J., U.S. B3 107
Boundiali, I.C. E3 45
Bountiful, Ut., U.S. C4 121
Bounty, Sk., Can. F2 75
Bounty Islands, is., N.Z. Q17 51
Bourbeuse, stm., Mo., U.S. C6 102
Bourbon, In., U.S. B5 91
Bourbon, Mo., U.S. C6 102
Bourbon, co., Ks., U.S. E9 93
Bourbon, co., Ky., U.S. B5 94
Bourbonnais, Il., U.S. B6 90
Bourbonnais, hist reg., Fr. D5 16
Bourbonne-les-Bains, Fr. D6 16
Bourem, Mali C4 45
Bourg, La., U.S. E5 95
Bourg-de-Péage, Fr. E6 16
Bourg [-en-Bresse], Fr. D6 16
Bourges, Fr. D5 16
Bourget, On., Can. B9 73
Bourget, Lake, l., Fr. E6 16
Bourg-la-Reine, Fr. g10 16
Bourgoin [-Jallieu], Fr. E6 16
Bourg-Saint-Andéol, Fr. E6 16
Bourg-Saint-Maurice, Fr. D2 20
Bou Rjeïmat, well, Maur. C2 45
Bourke, Austl. F8 50
Bourne, Eng., U.K. B7 12
Bourne, Ma., U.S. C6 98
Bournemouth, Eng., U.K. E6 10
Bourneville, Oh., U.S. C2 112
Bou Saâda, Alg. B5 44
Bouse, Az., U.S. D2 80
Bousso, Chad D3 46
Boutilimit, Maur. C2 45
Boutte, La., U.S. k11 95
Bouvet, i., Ant. D13 7
Bovey, Mn., U.S. C5 100
Bovill, Id., U.S. C2 89
Bovina, Ms., U.S. C3 101
Bovina, Tx., U.S. B1 120
Bovina Center, N.Y., U.S. C6 109
Bow, N.H., U.S. D3 106
Bow, Wa., U.S. A3 124
Bow, stm., Ab., Can. D4 68
Bowbells, N.D., U.S. A3 111
Bowden, Ab., Can. D4 68
Bowden, Ok., U.S. A5 113
Bowdens, N.C., U.S. B4 110
Bowdish Reservoir, res., R.I., U.S. B1 116
Bowdle, S.D., U.S. B6 118
Bowdoin, Me., U.S. f8 96
Bowdoinham, Me., U.S. D3 96
Bowdon, Ga., U.S. C1 87
Bowdon, N.D., U.S. B6 111
Bowen, Austl. C8 50
Bowen, Il., U.S. C2 90
Bowers, De., U.S. D4 85
Bowerston, Oh., U.S. B4 112
Bowersville, Ga., U.S. B3 87
Bowersville, Oh., U.S. C2 112
Bowesmont, N.D., U.S. A8 111
Bowie, Az., U.S. E6 80
Bowie, Co., U.S. C3 83
Bowie, Md., U.S. B4 97
Bowie, Tx., U.S. C4 120
Bowie, co., Tx., U.S. C5 120
Bowie Creek, stm., Ms., U.S. D4 101
Bow Island, Ab., Can. E5 68
Bowkerville, N.H., U.S. E2 106
Bow Lake, l., N.H., U.S. D4 106
Bowlegs, Ok., U.S. B5 113
Bowler, Wi., U.S. D5 126
Bowling Green, Fl., U.S. E5 86
Bowling Green, In., U.S. F4 91
Bowling Green, Ky., U.S. D3 94
Bowling Green, Mo., U.S. B6 102
Bowling Green, Oh., U.S. A2 112
Bowling Green, S.C., U.S. A5 117
Bowling Green, Va., U.S. B5 123
Bowlus, Mn., U.S. E4 100
Bowman, Ga., U.S. B3 87
Bowman, N.D., U.S. C2 111
Bowman, S.C., U.S. E6 117
Bowman, co., N.D., U.S. C2 111
Bowman Creek, stm., Pa., U.S. m16 115
Bowman-Haley Lake, res., N.D., U.S. C2 111
Bowman Island, i., Ant. C23 7
Bowmanstown, Pa., U.S. E10 115
Bowmanville, On., Can. D6 73
Bow Mar, Co., U.S. *B5 83
Bowmont, Id., U.S. F2 89
Bowmore, Scot., U.K. E2 13
Bowokan Islands, is., Indon. F6 34
Bowral, Austl. G8 51
Bowring, Ok., U.S. A5 113
Bowron, stm., B.C., Can. C7 69
Bowron Lake Provincial Park, B.C., Can. C7 69
Bowser Lake, l., B.C., Can. A3 69
Bowsman, Mb., Can. C1 70
Bowstring Lake, l., Mn., U.S. C5 100
Bow Valley, Ne., U.S. B8 104
Boxborough, Ma., U.S. A5 98
Box Butte, co., Ne., U.S. B2 104
Box Butte Creek, stm., Ne., U.S. B3 104
Box Butte Reservoir, res., Ne., U.S. B2 104
Box Elder, Mt., U.S. B6 103
Box Elder, S.D., U.S. C2 118
Box Elder, co., Ut., U.S. B2 121
Box Elder Creek, stm., Co., U.S. A6 83
Box Elder Creek, stm., Mt., U.S. C8 103
Boxelder Creek, stm., Mt., U.S. E12 103
Boxford, Ma., U.S. A6 98
Boxholm, Ia., U.S. B3 92
Boxian, China E8 31
Boxmeer, Neth. C5 17
Boxtel, Neth. B6 16
Boyacá, dept., Col. B3 60
Boyang, China J7 32
Boyce, La., U.S. C3 95
Boyce, Tx., U.S. n10 120
Boyce, Va., U.S. A4 123
Boyceville, Wi., U.S. C1 126
Boyd, Mn., U.S. F3 100
Boyd, Mt., U.S. E7 103
Boyd, Tx., U.S. C4 120
Boyd, Wi., U.S. D2 126
Boyd, co., Ky., U.S. B7 94
Boyd, co., Ne., U.S. B7 104
Boydell, Ar., U.S. D4 81
Boyden, Ia., U.S. A2 92
Boyd Glacier, Ant. B34 7
Boyd Lake, l., Me., U.S. C4 96
Boyds, Md., U.S. B3 97
Boyd's Cove, Nf., Can. D4 72
Boydsville, Ar., U.S. A5 81
Boydton, Va., U.S. D4 123
Boyer, stm., Ia., U.S. C2 92
Boyera, Zaire B2 48
Boyer Knob, mtn., Md., U.S. k13 97
Boyero, Co., U.S. C7 83
Boyers, Pa., U.S. D2 115
Boyertown, Pa., U.S. F10 115
Boyes, Mt., U.S. E11 103
Boykin, Al., U.S. C2 78
Boykin, Ga., U.S. E2 87
Boykins, Va., U.S. D5 123
Boyle, Ab., Can. B4 68
Boyle, Ire. C2 10
Boyle, Ms., U.S. B3 101
Boyle, co., Ky., U.S. C5 94
Boylston, N.S., Can. D8 71
Boylston, Ma., U.S. B4 98
Boyne, stm., Ire. D5 11
Boyne City, Mi., U.S. C6 99
Boyne Falls, Mi., U.S. C6 99
Boynton, Ok., U.S. B6 113
Boynton, Pa., U.S. G3 115
Boynton Beach, Fl., U.S. F6 86
Boyoma Falls (Stanley Falls), wtfl, Zaire A4 48
Boy River, Mn., U.S. C4 100
Boysen Reservoir, res., Wy., U.S. C4 127
Boys Ranch, Tx., U.S. B1 120
Boys Town, Ne., U.S. g12 104
Boz, Cape, c., Tur. B7 25
Bozcaada, Tur. C6 25
Bozca Island (Tenedos), i., Tur. C6 25
Bozdoğan, Tur. D7 25
Bozeman, Mt., U.S. E5 103
Bozeman Pass, Mt., U.S. E6 103
Bozman, Md., U.S. C5 97
Bozoum, Cen. Afr. Rep. D3 46
Bozovici, Rom. C5 24
Bozqūsh, Kūh-e, mts., Iran C3 39
Bozüyük, Tur. C8 40
Bra, Italy B1 23
Brabant, prov., Bel. D4 17
Brabant, i., Ant. C6 7
Brabant Lake, l., Sk., Can. A4 75
Brač, i., Yugo. D3 24
Bracadale, Scot., U.K. D4 13
Bracadale, Loch, b., Scot., U.K. C2 13
Bracciano, Italy g8 23
Bracciano, Lake, l., Italy C4 23
Bracebridge, On., Can. B5 73
Braceville, Il., U.S. B5 90
Brach, Libya D2 43
Bracken, Sk., Can. H1 75
Bracken, co., Ky., U.S. B5 94
Bracken Lake, l., Mb., Can. C2 70
Brackenridge, Pa., U.S. h15 115
Brackett, Wi., U.S. D2 126
Brackettville, Tx., U.S. E2 120
Brackley, Eng., U.K. B6 12
Bracknell, Eng., U.K. C7 12
Brackwede, F.R.Ger. B3 19
Brad, Rom. B6 24
Bradano, stm., Italy D6 23
Braddock, N.J., U.S. D3 107
Braddock, N.D., U.S. C5 111
Braddock, Pa., U.S. k14 115
Braddock Heights, Md., U.S. B2 97
Braddock Point, c., S.C., U.S. G6 117
Braddyville, Ia., U.S. D2 92
Braden, Tn., U.S. B2 119
Bradenton, Fl., U.S. E4 86
Bradenville, Pa., U.S. F3 115
Bradford, On., Can. C5 73
Bradford, Eng., U.K. D6 10
Bradford, Ar., U.S. B4 81
Bradford, Il., U.S. B4 90
Bradford, Ia., U.S. B4 92
Bradford, Me., U.S. C4 96
Bradford, N.H., U.S. D3 106
Bradford, Oh., U.S. B1 112
Bradford, Pa., U.S. C4 115
Bradford, R.I., U.S. F2 116
Bradford, Tn., U.S. A3 119
Bradford, Vt., U.S. D4 122
Bradford, co., Fl., U.S. C4 86
Bradford, co., Pa., U.S. C8 115
Bradford Mountain, mtn., Ct., U.S. B2 84
Bradfordsville, Ky., U.S. C4 94
Bradfordwoods, Pa., U.S. h13 115
Bradgate, Ia., U.S. B3 92
Bradley, Al., U.S. D3 78
Bradley, Ar., U.S. D2 81
Bradley, Ca., U.S. E3 82
Bradley, Fl., U.S. E5 86
Bradley, Il., U.S. B6 90
Bradley, Me., U.S. D4 96
Bradley, Oh., U.S. B5 112
Bradley, Ok., U.S. C4 113
Bradley, S.C., U.S. C3 117
Bradley, S.D., U.S. B8 118
Bradley, W.V., U.S. D3 125
Bradley, co., Ar., U.S. D3 81
Bradley, co., Tn., U.S. D9 119
Bradley Beach, N.J., U.S. C4 107
Bradleyton, Al., U.S. D3 78
Bradner, Oh., U.S. A2 112
Brador, Baie de, b., P.Q., Can. C3 72
Bradshaw, Md., U.S. B5 97
Bradshaw, Ne., U.S. D8 104
Bradshaw, Tx., U.S. C3 120
Bradshaw, W.V., U.S. D3 125
Bradshaw Mountains, mts., Az., U.S. C3 80
Bradstreet, Ma., U.S. B2 98
Bradwardine, Mb., Can. D1 70
Bradwell, Sk., Can. F2 75
Brady, Mt., U.S. B5 103
Brady, Ne., U.S. C5 104
Brady, Tx., U.S. D3 120
Bradyville, Tn., U.S. B5 119
Brædstrup, Den. C3 15
Braemar, Scot., U.K. D5 13
Braeside, On., Can. B8 73
Braga, Port. B1 22
Bragado, Arg. B4 54
Bragança, Braz. B1 57
Bragança, Port. B2 22
Bragança Paulista, Braz. C3 56
Braggadocio, Mo., U.S. E8 102
Braggs, Ok., U.S. B6 113
Braham, Mn., U.S. E5 100
Brāhmani, stm., India D7 36
Brahmaputra (Yarlung Zangbo Jiang), stm., Asia C9 36
Braidwood, Il., U.S. B5 90
Brăila, Rom. C8 24
Brainard, Ne., U.S. C9 104
Braine-le-Comte, Bel. D4 17
Brainerd, Ks., U.S. g12 93
Brainerd, Mn., U.S. D4 100
Braintree, Eng., U.K. C8 12
Braintree, Ma., U.S. B5 98
Braintree, Vt., U.S. D3 122
Braithwaite, La., U.S. k12 95
Brake, F.R.Ger. B4 18
Brakel, F.R.Ger. B4 19
Brakpan, S. Afr. *C4 49
Bralorne, B.C., Can. D6 69
Braman, Ok., U.S. A4 113
Bramming, Den. C2 15
Brampton, On., Can. D5 73
Brampton, Eng., U.K. F6 13
Brampton, N.D., U.S. D8 111
Bramsche, F.R.Ger. B7 17
Bramwell, W.V., U.S. D3 125
Branch, Nf., Can. E5 72
Branch, Ar., U.S. B2 81
Branch, La., U.S. D3 95
Branch, Wi., U.S. h10 126
Branch, co., Mi., U.S. G5 99
Branch, stm., R.I., U.S. B3 116
Branch, stm., Wi., U.S. h10 126
Branch Lake, l., Me., U.S. D4 96
Branchland, W.V., U.S. C2 125
Branchport, N.Y., U.S. C3 109
Branch Village, R.I., U.S. B3 116
Branchville, Al., U.S. B3 78
Branchville, Ct., U.S. D2 84
Branchville, S.C., U.S. E6 117
Branchville, Va., U.S. D5 123
Branco, stm., Braz. B3 55
Branco, stm., Braz. D4 55
Branco, stm., Braz. C2 55
Brandberg, mtn., Nmb. B1 49
Brande, Den. C3 15
Brandenburg, Ger.D.R. B6 18
Brandenburg, Ky., U.S. C3 94
Brandenburg, hist reg., Ger.D.R. B6 18
Brandon, Mb., Can. E2 70
Brandon, Co., U.S. C8 83
Brandon, Fl., U.S. E4 86
Brandon, Ia., U.S. B6 92
Brandon, Mn., U.S. E3 100
Brandon, Ms., U.S. C4 101
Brandon, Ne., U.S. D4 104
Brandon, S.C., U.S. B3 117
Brandon, S.D., U.S. D9 118
Brandon, Vt., U.S. D2 122
Brandon, Wi., U.S. E5 126
Brandon Head, c., Ire. E1 11
Brandon Mountain, mtn., Ire. D1 10
Brandsen, Arg. B5 54
Brandsville, Mo., U.S. E6 102
Brandt, Oh., U.S. C1 112
Brandt, S.D., U.S. C9 118
Brandvlei, S. Afr. D3 49
Brandy Peak, mtn., Or., U.S. E3 114
Brandýs nad Labem, Czech. C9 19
Brandýs-Stará Boleslav, Czech. n18 26
Brandy Station, Va., U.S. B5 123
Brandywine, Md., U.S. C4 97
Brandywine, W.V., U.S. C5 125
Brandywine Creek, stm., U.S. A3 85
Branford, Ct., U.S. D4 84
Branford, Fl., U.S. C4 86
Branford Hills, Ct., U.S. D4 84
Branford Point, Ct., U.S. D4 84
Braniewo, Pol. A5 26
Bransfield Strait, strt., Ant. C7 7
Brańsk, Pol. B7 26
Branson, Co., U.S. D7 83
Branson, Mo., U.S. E4 102
Brant, Ab., Can. D4 68
Brant, co., On., Can. D4 73
Brantford, On., Can. D4 73
Brantford, N.D., U.S. B7 111
Brant Lake, N.Y., U.S. B7 109
Brantley, Al., U.S. D3 78
Brantley, co., Ga., U.S. E4 87
Brant Rock, Ma., U.S. B6 98
Brantville, N.B., Can. B5 71
Brantwood, Wi., U.S. C3 126
Bras-d'Apic, P.Q., Can. C7 74
Bras-d'Or, N.S., Can. C9 71
Bras d'Or Lake, l., N.S., Can. D9 71
Brasfield, Ar., U.S. C4 81
Brashear, Mo., U.S. A5 102
Brasiléia, Braz. B2 55
Brasília, Braz. B3 56
Brasília de Minas, Braz. B4 56
Braşov (Oraşul-Stalin), Rom. C7 24
Brasstown, N.C., U.S. f9 110
Brasstown Bald, mtn., Ga., U.S. B3 87
Brassua Lake, res., Me., U.S. C3 96
Bratenahl, Oh., U.S. g9 112
Bratislava, Czech. D4 26
Bratsk, Sov. Un. D13 29
Bratsk Reservoir, res., Sov. Un. D13 29
Bratslav, Sov. Un. G7 27
Bratt, Fl., U.S. u14 86
Brattleboro, Vt., U.S. F3 122
Braunau [am Inn], Aus. D6 18
Braunfels, F.R.Ger. C3 19
Braunschweig, F.R.Ger. B5 18
Brave, Pa., U.S. G1 115
Bråviken, b., Swe. u34 14
Brawley, Ca., U.S. F6 82
Brawley Peaks, mts., Nv., U.S. E3 105
Braxton, Ms., U.S. C4 101
Braxton, co., W.V., U.S. C4 125
Bray, Ire. D3 10
Bray, Ok., U.S. C4 113
Bray Head, c., Ire. F1 11
Braymer, Mo., U.S. B4 102
Brayton, Ia., U.S. C3 92
Brazeau, stm., Ab., Can. C2 68
Brazeau, Mount, mtn., Ab., Can. C2 68
Brazil, In., U.S. E3 91
Brazil, Ia., U.S. D5 92
Brazil, Tn., U.S. B2 119
Brazil, ctry., S.A. D5 53
Brazilian Highlands, plat., Braz. E5 53
Brazil Lake, N.S., Can. F4 71
Brazilton, Ks., U.S. E9 93
Brazoria, Tx., U.S. r14 120
Brazoria, co., Tx., U.S. E5 120
Brazos, co., Tx., U.S. D4 120
Brazos, stm., Tx., U.S. D4 120
Brazzaville, Congo B2 48
Brčko, Yugo. C4 24
Brda, stm., Pol. B4 26
Brea, Ca., U.S. n13 82
Brea, Punta, c., P.R. C2 65
Bread Loaf Mountain, mtn., Vt., U.S. D3 122
Breakenridge, Mount, mtn., B.C., Can. E7 69
Breakers Point, c., Am. Sam. F13 52
Breakeyville, P.Q., Can. o17 74
Bream Bay, b., N.Z. K15 51
Breared, Swe. B7 15
Breathitt, co., Ky., U.S. C6 94
Breaux Bridge, La., U.S. D4 95
Brechin, On., Can. C5 73
Brechin, Scot., U.K. B5 10
Breckenridge, P.Q., Can. h12 74
Breckenridge, Co., U.S. B4 83
Breckenridge, Mi., U.S. E6 99
Breckenridge, Mn., U.S. D2 100
Breckenridge, Mo., U.S. B4 102
Breckenridge, Ok., U.S. A4 113
Breckenridge, Tx., U.S. C3 120
Breckenridge Hills, Mo., U.S. *f13 102
Breckinridge, co., Ky., U.S. C3 94
Brecknock, Peninsula, pen., Chile h11 54
Brecksville, Oh., U.S. A4 112
Břeclav, Czech. D4 26
Brecon (Brecknock), Wales, U.K. E5 10
Brecon Beacons, mtn., Wales, U.K. E5 10
Breda, Neth. B6 16
Breda, Ia., U.S. B3 92
Bredasdorp, S. Afr. D3 49
Bredenbury, Sk., Can. G4 75
Bredstedt, F.R.Ger. D2 15
Bredy, Sov. Un. E21 8
Bree, Bel. C5 17
Breese, Il., U.S. E4 90
Breezy Point, Mn., U.S. D4 100
Bregalnica, stm., Yugo. E6 24
Bregenz, Aus. E4 18
Bregenzerach, stm., Aus. B8 21
Bregovo, Bul. C6 24
Breiðafjördur, b., Ice. n21 14
Breid Bay, b., Ant. B15 7
Breien, N.D., U.S. C5 111
Breil, Fr. F7 16
Breisach, F.R.Ger. A3 20
Brejinho de Nazaré, Braz. E5 59
Brejo, Braz. B2 57
Bremen, F.R.Ger. B4 18
Bremen, Al., U.S. B2 78
Bremen, Ga., U.S. C1 87
Bremen, Il., U.S. F4 90
Bremen, In., U.S. B5 91
Bremen, Ky., U.S. C2 94
Bremen, N.D., U.S. B6 111
Bremen, Oh., U.S. C3 112
Bremen, state, F.R.Ger. E2 15
Bremer, Ia., U.S. B5 92
Bremer, co., Ia., U.S. B5 92
Bremerhaven (Wesermünde), F.R.Ger. B4 18
Bremerton, Wa., U.S. B3 124
Bremervörde, F.R.Ger. E3 15
Bremo Bluff, Va., U.S. C4 123
Bremond, Tx., U.S. D4 120
Breña, Peru *D2 58
Brenham, Tx., U.S. D4 120
Brenish, Scot., U.K. B1 13
Brenner Pass, Eur. A3 23
Brent, On., Can. A6 73
Brent, Al., U.S. C2 78
Brent, Fl., U.S. u14 86
Brenta, stm., Italy D7 20
Brentford, S.D., U.S. B7 118
Brenton, W.V., U.S. *D3 125
Brenton Point, c., R.I., U.S. F5 116
Brentwood, Eng., U.K. k13 10
Brentwood, Ca., U.S. h9 82
Brentwood, Md., U.S. f9 97
Brentwood, Mo., U.S. f13 102
Brentwood, N.H., U.S. E4 106

Name	Map Ref	Page
Brentwood, N.Y., U.S.	E7	109
Brentwood, Oh., U.S.	*o12	112
Brentwood, Pa., U.S.	k14	115
Brentwood, S.C., U.S.	k11	117
Brentwood, Tn., U.S.	A5	119
Brescia, Italy	B3	23
Breskens, Neth.	C3	17
Breslau see Wrocław, Pol.	C4	26
Bresle, stm, Fr.	E9	12
Bressanone, Italy	A3	23
Bressuire, Fr.	D3	16
Brest, Fr.	C1	16
Brest (Brest-Litovsk), Sov. Un.	D5	29
Breteuil, Fr.	C3	68
Brétigny [-Notre-Dame], Fr.	F2	17
Breton, Ab., Can.	C3	68
Breton, Pertuis, strt., Fr.	D3	16
Breton Islands, is., La., U.S.	E5	95
Breton Sound, strt, La., U.S.	E6	95
Breton Woods, N.J., U.S.	C4	107
Brett, Cape, c., N.Z.	K15	51
Bretton Woods, N.H., U.S.	B4	106
Breuil, Italy	D3	20
Brevard, N.C., U.S.	f10	110
Brevard, co., Fl., U.S.	E6	86
Breves, Braz.	C4	59
Brevik (part of Porsgrunn), Nor.	p27	14
Břevnov (part of Prague), Czech.	n17	26
Brevoort Lake, l., Mi., U.S.	B6	99
Brevort, Mi., U.S.	B5	99
Brewarrina, Austl.	E8	50
Brewer, Me., U.S.	D4	96
Brewer, Mo., U.S.	D8	102
Brewerville, Lib.	E2	45
Brewster, Ks., U.S.	C2	93
Brewster, Ma., U.S.	C7	98
Brewster, Mn., U.S.	G3	100
Brewster, Ne., U.S.	C6	104
Brewster, N.Y., U.S.	D7	109
Brewster, Oh., U.S.	B4	112
Brewster, Wa., U.S.	A6	124
Brewster, co., Tx., U.S.	E1	120
Brewster, Kap, c., Grnld.	B18	61
Brewster Islands, is., Ma., U.S.	g12	98
Brewton, Al., U.S.	D2	78
Brewton, Ab., U.S.	D4	87
Brezhnev (Naberezhnye Chelny), Sov. Un.	D8	29
Brežice, Yugo.	C2	24
Březnice, Czech.	D8	19
Brezno, Czech.	D5	26
Bria, Cen. Afr. Rep.	D4	46
Brian Boru Peak, mtn., B.C., Can.	B4	69
Briançon, Fr.	E7	16
Brian Head, mtn., Ut., U.S.	F3	121
Briarcliff, Pa., U.S.	p20	115
Briarcliff Manor, N.Y., U.S.	*D7	109
Briare, Fr.	D5	16
Briartown, Ok., U.S.	B6	113
Brice, Oh., U.S.	m11	112
Bricelyn, Mn., U.S.	G5	100
Briceville, Tn., U.S.	C9	119
Brickeys, Ar., U.S.	C5	81
Brick [Township], N.J., U.S.	C4	107
Bridal Veil, Or., U.S.	B4	114
Bridal Veil Falls, wtfl, Ut., U.S.	C4	121
Bride, stm., Ire.	E3	11
Bridesville, B.C., Can.	E8	69
Bridge, stm., B.C., Can.	D6	69
Bridgeboro, Ga., U.S.	E3	87
Bridge City, La., U.S.	*E5	95
Bridge Creek, stm., Sk., Can.	H1	75
Bridgeford, Sk., Can.	G2	75
Bridgehampton, N.Y., U.S.	n16	109
Bridge Lake, B.C., Can.	D7	69
Bridgeland, Ut., U.S.	C5	121
Bridgend, Wales, U.K.	C4	12
Bridgeport, On., Can.	D4	73
Bridgeport, Al., U.S.	A4	78
Bridgeport, Ca., U.S.	E5	82
Bridgeport, Ct., U.S.	E3	84
Bridgeport, Il., U.S.	E6	90
Bridgeport, Mi., U.S.	E7	99
Bridgeport, Ne., U.S.	C2	104
Bridgeport, N.J., U.S.	D2	107
Bridgeport, Oh., U.S.	B5	112
Bridgeport, Ok., U.S.	B3	113
Bridgeport, Or., U.S.	C9	114
Bridgeport, Pa., U.S.	o20	115
Bridgeport, Tx., U.S.	C4	120
Bridgeport, Wa., U.S.	A6	124
Bridgeport, W.V., U.S.	B4	125
Bridger, Mt., U.S.	E8	103
Bridger, S.D., U.S.	C4	118
Bridger Mountains, mts., Wy., U.S.	C5	127
Bridger Peak, mtn., Wy., U.S.	E5	127
Bridger Range, mts., Mt., U.S.	E6	103
Bridgeton, In., U.S.	E3	91
Bridgeton, Mo., U.S.	C7	102
Bridgeton, N.J., U.S.	E2	107
Bridgeton, N.C., U.S.	B5	110
Bridgetown, Barb.	J15	64
Bridgetown, N.S., Can.	E4	71
Bridgetown, Oh., U.S.	*o12	112
Bridgeview, Il., U.S.	*k9	90
Bridgeville, N.S., Can.	D7	71
Bridgeville, De., U.S.	F3	85
Bridgeville, Pa., U.S.	k13	115
Bridgewater, N.S., Can.	E5	71
Bridgewater, Ct., U.S.	C2	84
Bridgewater, Ia., U.S.	C3	92
Bridgewater, Me., U.S.	B5	96
Bridgewater, Ma., U.S.	C6	98
Bridgewater, N.H., U.S.	C3	106
Bridgewater, S.D., U.S.	D8	118
Bridgewater, Vt., U.S.	D3	122
Bridgewater, Va., U.S.	B4	123
Bridgewater Corners, Vt., U.S.	D3	122
Bridgman, Mi., U.S.	G4	99
Bridgnorth, Eng., U.K.	B5	12
Bridgton, Me., U.S.	D2	96
Bridgwater, Eng., U.K.	E5	10
Bridgwater Bay, b., Eng., U.K.	E5	10
Bridlington, Eng., U.K.	C6	10
Bridport, Eng., U.K.	*o5	12
Brielle, N.J., U.S.	C4	107
Brienz, Switz.	E4	18
Brienz, Lake, l., Switz.	C5	21
Brier Creek, stm., Ga., U.S.	C5	87
Briercrest, Sk., Can.	G3	75
Brièreville, Al., U.S.	B5	68
Brierfield, Al., U.S.	B3	78
Brier Hill, N.Y., U.S.	f9	109
Briery Knob, mtn., W.V., U.S.	C4	125
Brig, Fr.	E5	17
Brigantine, N.J., U.S.	E4	107
Brigantine Beach, N.J., U.S.	E4	107
Brig Bay, Nf., Can.	C3	72
Brigden, On., Can.	E2	73
Brigg, Eng., U.K.	A7	12
Briggs, Ne., U.S.	*C10	104
Briggs, Tx., U.S.	D4	120
Briggsdale, Co., U.S.	A6	83
Briggs Marsh, sw., R.I., U.S.	F6	116
Briggsville, Ar., U.S.	C2	81
Briggsville, Ma., U.S.	A1	98
Briggsville, Wi., U.S.	E4	126
Brigham City, Ut., U.S.	B3	121
Brig Harbour Island, i., Nf., Can.	A3	72
Bright, On., Can.	D4	73
Brighton, On., Can.	C7	73
Brighton, Eng., U.K.	E6	10
Brighton, Al., U.S.	B3	78
Brighton, Co., U.S.	B6	83
Brighton, Il., U.S.	D3	90
Brighton, Ia., U.S.	C6	92
Brighton, Me., U.S.	C3	96
Brighton, Mi., U.S.	F7	99
Brighton, N.Y., U.S.	B3	109
Brighton, Or., U.S.	B3	114
Brighton, Tn., U.S.	B2	119
Brighton, Ut., U.S.	*C4	121
Brighton Indian Reservation, Fl., U.S.	E5	86
Brightsand Lake, l., Sk., Can.	D1	75
Brightshade, Ky., U.S.	C6	94
Brignoles, Fr.	F7	16
Brigus, Nf., Can.	E5	72
Brihuega, Spain	B4	22
Brilhante, stm., Braz.	C1	56
Brilliant, B.C., Can.	E9	69
Brilliant, Al., U.S.	A2	78
Brilliant, Oh., U.S.	B5	112
Brillion, Wi., U.S.	D5	126
Brilon, F.R.Ger.	B3	19
Brimfield, Il., U.S.	C4	90
Brimfield, Ma., U.S.	*B3	98
Brimhall, N.M., U.S.	B1	108
Brimley, Mi., U.S.	B6	99
Brimson, Mn., U.S.	C7	100
Brimson, Mo., U.S.	A4	102
Brindisi, Italy	D6	23
Bringhurst, In., U.S.	C5	91
Brinje, Yugo.	C2	24
Brinkhaven, Oh., U.S.	B3	112
Brinkley, Ar., U.S.	C4	81
Brinkman, Ok., U.S.	B2	113
Brinktown, Mo., U.S.	C5	102
Brinkworth, Austl.	F2	51
Brinnon, Wa., U.S.	B3	124
Brinsmade, N.D., U.S.	A6	111
Brinson, Ga., U.S.	F2	87
Brion, Île, i., P.Q., Can.	B8	71
Brione (Verzasca), Switz.	D6	21
Brioude, Fr.	E5	16
Brisbane, Austl.	E9	50
Briscoe, Tx., U.S.	B2	120
Briscoe, co., Tx., U.S.	B2	120
Brissago, Switz.	D6	21
Bristol, N.B., Can.	C2	71
Bristol, Eng., U.K.	E5	10
Bristol, Co., U.S.	C8	83
Bristol, Ct., U.S.	C4	84
Bristol, Fl., U.S.	B2	86
Bristol, Ga., U.S.	E4	87
Bristol, Il., U.S.	*B5	90
Bristol, In., U.S.	A6	91
Bristol, Me., U.S.	*E3	96
Bristol, N.H., U.S.	C3	106
Bristol, R.I., U.S.	D5	116
Bristol, S.D., U.S.	B8	118
Bristol, Tn., U.S.	C11	119
Bristol, Vt., U.S.	C2	122
Bristol, Va., U.S.	f9	123
Bristol, Wi., U.S.	F5	126
Bristol, co., Ma., U.S.	C5	98
Bristol, co., R.I., U.S.	D5	116
Bristol Bay, b., Ak., U.S.	D7	79
Bristol Channel, strt., U.K.	E4	10
Bristol Ferry, R.I., U.S.	D5	116
Bristol [Township], Pa., U.S.	F12	115
Bristolville, Oh., U.S.	A5	112
Bristow, In., U.S.	H4	91
Bristow, Ia., U.S.	B5	92
Bristow, Ne., U.S.	B7	104
Bristow, Ok., U.S.	B5	113
Britannia Bay (part of Ottawa), On., Can.	h12	73
Britannia Beach, B.C., Can.	E6	69
Britannia Range, mts., Ant.	B28	7
British Antarctic Territory, dep., S.A.	*C7	7
British Columbia, prov., Can.	C6	69
British Indian Ocean Territory, dep., Afr.	*G25	2
British Mountains, mts., N.A.	B12	79
British Virgin Islands, dep., N.A.	G12	64
Britstown, S. Afr.	D3	49
Britt, On., Can.	B4	73
Britt, Ia., U.S.	A4	92
Brittany, hist reg., Fr.	C2	16
Britton, Mi., U.S.	G7	99
Britton, S.D., U.S.	B8	118
Brive [-la-Gaillarde], Fr.	E4	16
Briviesca, Spain	A4	22
Brixham, Eng., U.K.	D4	12
Brno, Czech.	D4	19
Broa, Ensenada de la, b., Cuba	C3	64
Broach, India	D5	36
Broad, stm., Ga., U.S.	B4	87
Broad, stm., S.C., U.S.	C5	117
Broadacres, Sk., Can.	E1	75
Broadalbin, N.Y., U.S.	B6	109
Broadback, stm., P.Q., Can.	F17	66
Broad Bay, b., Scot., U.K.	B2	13
Broadbent, Or., U.S.	E2	114
Broad Brook, Ct., U.S.	B5	84
Broad Creek, stm., De., U.S.	F3	85
Broadus, Mt., U.S.	E11	103
Broadview, Sk., Can.	G4	75
Broadview, Il., U.S.	*k9	90
Broadview, Mt., U.S.	D9	103
Broadview, N.M., U.S.	C6	108
Broadview Heights, Oh., U.S.	h9	112
Broadview Park, Fl., U.S.	*r13	86
Broadwater, Ne., U.S.	C3	104
Broadwater, co., Mt., U.S.	D5	103
Broadway, N.J., U.S.	B2	107
Broadway, N.C., U.S.	B3	110
Broadway, Oh., U.S.	B2	112
Broadway, Va., U.S.	B4	123
Broager, Den.	D3	15
Brochet, Mb., Can.	f7	70
Brocken, mtn., Ger.D.R.	B5	19
Brocket, Ab., Can.	E4	68
Brocket, N.D., U.S.	A7	111
Brock Island, i., N.T., Can.	m29	66
Brockport, N.Y., U.S.	B3	109
Brockport, Pa., U.S.	D4	115
Brockton, Ma., U.S.	B5	98
Brockton, Mt., U.S.	B12	103
Brockton Reservoir, res., Ma., U.S.	h11	98
Brockville, On., Can.	C9	73
Brockway, Mt., U.S.	C11	103
Brockway, Pa., U.S.	D4	115
Brockwell, Ar., U.S.	A4	81
Brocton, Il., U.S.	D6	90
Brocton, N.Y., U.S.	C1	109
Broderick, Sk., Can.	F2	75
Broderick, Ca., U.S.	*C3	82
Brodeur Peninsula, pen., N.T., Can.	B15	66
Brodhead, Ky., U.S.	C5	94
Brodhead, Wi., U.S.	F4	126
Brodheadsville, Pa., U.S.	E11	115
Brodick, Scot., U.K.	E3	13
Brodnax, Va., U.S.	D4	123
Brodnica, Pol.	B5	26
Brody, Sov. Un.	F5	27
Brogan, Or., U.S.	C9	114
Brogue, Pa., U.S.	G8	115
Broken Arrow, Ok., U.S.	A6	113
Broken Bow, Ne., U.S.	C6	104
Broken Bow, Ok., U.S.	C7	113
Broken Bow Lake, res., Ok., U.S.	C7	113
Broken Hill, Austl.	F7	50
Brokopondo, Sur.	A3	59
Brokopondo, dept., Sur.	B3	59
Brome, P.Q., Can.	D5	74
Brome, F.R.Ger.	F4	15
Brome, co., P.Q., Can.	D5	74
Brome, Lac, l., P.Q., Can.	D5	74
Bromhead, Sk., Can.	H4	75
Bromide, Ok., U.S.	C5	113
Bromley (part of London), Eng., U.K.	m13	10
Bromptonville, P.Q., Can.	D6	74
Bromsgrove, Eng., U.K.	B5	12
Bromyard, Eng., U.K.	B5	12
Bronaugh, Mo., U.S.	D3	102
Bronco, Tx., U.S.	C1	120
Brønderslev, Den.	A3	15
Bronlund Peak, mtn., B.C., Can.	E7	66
Bronnitsy, Sov. Un.	n18	27
Brønnøysund, Nor.	D6	14
Bronson, Fl., U.S.	C4	86
Bronson, Ia., U.S.	B1	92
Bronson, Ks., U.S.	E8	93
Bronson, Mi., U.S.	G5	99
Bronson, Tx., U.S.	D6	120
Bronte, Tx., U.S.	D2	120
Bronwood, Ga., U.S.	E2	87
Bronx, co., N.Y., U.S.	E7	109
Bronxville, N.Y., U.S.	h13	109
Brook, In., U.S.	C3	91
Brookdale, Mb., Can.	D2	70
Brooke, Va., U.S.	B5	123
Brooke, co., W.V., U.S.	A4	125
Brooker, Fl., U.S.	C4	86
Brookeville, Md., U.S.	B3	97
Brookfield, N.S., Can.	D6	71
Brookfield, Ct., U.S.	D2	84
Brookfield, Ga., U.S.	E3	87
Brookfield, Il., U.S.	*k9	90
Brookfield, Ma., U.S.	B3	98
Brookfield, Mo., U.S.	B4	102
Brookfield, N.H., U.S.	C4	106
Brookfield, N.Y., U.S.	C5	109
Brookfield, Va., U.S.	B5	123
Brookfield, Vt., U.S.	*D5	123
Brookfield, Wi., U.S.	m11	126
Brookfield Center, Ct., U.S.	D2	84
Brookford, N.C., U.S.	B1	110
Brookhaven, Ms., U.S.	D3	101
Brookhaven, Pa., U.S.	*p20	115
Brookhaven, W.V., U.S.	h11	125
Brooking, Sk., Can.	H3	75
Brookings, Or., U.S.	E2	114
Brookings, S.D., U.S.	C9	118
Brookings, co., S.D., U.S.	C9	118
Brookland, Ar., U.S.	B5	81
Brooklandville, Md., U.S.	g10	97
Brooklawn, N.J., U.S.	D2	107
Brooklet, Ga., U.S.	D5	87
Brooklin, On., Can.	D6	73
Brookline, Ma., U.S.	B5	98
Brookline, N.H., U.S.	E3	106
Brookline Station, Mo., U.S.	D4	102
Brooklyn, N.S., Can.	E5	71
Brooklyn, Al., U.S.	D3	78
Brooklyn, Ct., U.S.	B8	84
Brooklyn, Ga., U.S.	D2	87
Brooklyn, Il., U.S.	E3	90
Brooklyn, In., U.S.	E5	91
Brooklyn, Ia., U.S.	C5	92
Brooklyn, Md., U.S.	B4	97
Brooklyn, Mi., U.S.	F6	99
Brooklyn, Ms., U.S.	D4	101
Brooklyn, Oh., U.S.	h9	112
Brooklyn, Pa., U.S.	C10	115
Brooklyn, Wi., U.S.	F4	126
Brooklyn Center, Mn., U.S.	m12	100
Brooklyn Park, Md., U.S.	h11	97
Brooklyn Park, Mn., U.S.	m12	100
Brookmere, B.C., Can.	E7	69
Brookneal, Va., U.S.	C4	123
Brookpark, Oh., U.S.	h9	112
Brook Park, Mn., U.S.	E5	100
Brookport, Il., U.S.	F5	90
Brookridge, Ca., U.S.	*B6	83
Brooks, Ab., Can.	D5	68
Brooks, Ga., U.S.	C2	87
Brooks, Ia., U.S.	D3	92
Brooks, Ky., U.S.	g11	94
Brooks, Me., U.S.	D3	96
Brooks, Mn., U.S.	C2	100
Brooks, Or., U.S.	m12	114
Brooks, Wi., U.S.	E4	126
Brooks, co., Ga., U.S.	F3	87
Brooks, co., Tx., U.S.	F3	120
Brooks Air Force Base, mil., Tx., U.S.	k7	120
Brooksburg, In., U.S.	G7	91
Brooksby, Sk., Can.	E3	75
Brooks Crossing, Mi., U.S.	m12	99
Brookside, Al., U.S.	f7	78
Brookside, Co., U.S.	C5	83
Brookside, De., U.S.	B3	85
Brooks Peninsula, pen., B.C., Can.	D4	69
Brooks Place, Ma., U.S.	*B5	98
Brooks, Ne., U.S.	D10	104
Brooks Range, mts., Ak., U.S.	B9	79
Brookston, In., U.S.	C4	91
Brookston, Mn., U.S.	D6	100
Brooksville, Fl., U.S.	D4	86
Brooksville, Ky., U.S.	B5	94
Brooksville, Me., U.S.	D4	96
Brooksville, Ms., U.S.	B5	101
Brooksville, Ok., U.S.	B5	113
Brooktondale, N.Y., U.S.	C4	109
Brookview, Md., U.S.	C6	97
Brookville, In., U.S.	F8	91
Brookville, Ks., U.S.	D6	93
Brookville, Oh., U.S.	C1	112
Brookville, Pa., U.S.	D3	115
Brookville Lake, res., In., U.S.	E7	91
Brookwood, Al., U.S.	B2	78
Brookwood, N.J., U.S.	C4	107
Broom, Loch, b., Scot., U.K.	B4	10
Broomall, Pa., U.S.	p20	115
Broome, Austl.	C3	50
Broome, co., N.Y., U.S.	C5	109
Broomes Island, Md., U.S.	D4	97
Broomfield, Co., U.S.	B5	83
Brooten, Mn., U.S.	E3	100
Brora, Scot., U.K.	B5	13
Brora, stm., Scot., U.K.	B4	13
Brösarp, Swe.	C8	15
Broseley, Mo., U.S.	E7	102
Brosna, stm., Ire.	C4	11
Brossard, P.Q., Can.	q20	74
Brotas de Macaúbas, Braz.	D2	57
Brothers, Or., U.S.	D6	114
Brothertown, Wi., U.S.	k9	126
Brotmanville, N.J., U.S.	D2	107
Brou, Fr.	C4	16
Brough, Eng., U.K.	F6	13
Brough Head, c., Scot., U.K.	A5	13
Broughton Station, P.Q., Can.	C6	74
Broussard, La., U.S.	D4	95
Brovst, Den.	A3	15
Broward, co., Fl., U.S.	F6	86
Browardale, Fl., U.S.	r13	86
Browerville, Mn., U.S.	D4	100
Brown, co., Il., U.S.	D3	90
Brown, co., In., U.S.	F5	91
Brown, co., Ks., U.S.	C8	93
Brown, co., Mn., U.S.	F4	100
Brown, co., Ne., U.S.	B6	104
Brown, co., Oh., U.S.	D2	112
Brown, co., S.D., U.S.	B7	118
Brown, co., Tx., U.S.	D3	120
Brown, co., Wi., U.S.	D6	126
Brown, Point, c., Wa., U.S.	C1	124
Brown City, Mi., U.S.	E8	99
Brown Deer, Wi., U.S.	m12	126
Brownell, Ks., U.S.	D4	93
Brownfield, Il., U.S.	F5	90
Brownfield, Me., U.S.	E2	96
Brownfield, Tx., U.S.	C1	120
Brownfields, La., U.S.	*D4	95
Browning, Sk., Can.	H4	75
Browning, Il., U.S.	C3	90
Browning, Mo., U.S.	A4	102
Browning, Mt., U.S.	B3	103
Browning Entrance, strt., B.C., Can.	C2	69
Brownington, Mo., U.S.	C4	102
Brownington Center, Vt., U.S.	B4	122
Brownlee, Sk., Can.	G3	75
Brownlee, Ne., U.S.	B5	104
Brownlee Dam, U.S.	E2	89
Brownlee Reservoir, res., U.S.	C10	114
Browns, Il., U.S.	E6	90
Browns, stm., Vt., U.S.	B2	122
Browns Branch, stm., De., U.S.	E3	85
Brownsboro, Al., U.S.	A3	78
Brownsboro, Tx., U.S.	C5	120
Brownsburg, In., U.S.	E5	91
Brownsburg, P.Q., Can.	D3	74
Brownsdale, Mn., U.S.	G6	100
Browns Inlet, b., N.C., U.S.	C5	110
Browns Mills, N.J., U.S.	D3	107
Browns Peak, mtn., Az., U.S.	D4	80
Browns Town, Jam.	E14	65
Brownstown, Il., U.S.	E5	90
Brownstown, In., U.S.	G5	91
Brownstown, Wa., U.S.	C5	124
Brownstown Head, c., Ire.	E4	11
Browns Valley, Ca., U.S.	C3	82
Browns Valley, Mn., U.S.	E1	100
Brownsville, Fl., U.S.	s13	86
Brownsville, Ky., U.S.	C3	94
Brownsville, La., U.S.	B3	95
Brownsville, Mn., U.S.	G7	100
Brownsville, Or., U.S.	C4	114
Brownsville, Pa., U.S.	F2	115
Brownsville, Tn., U.S.	B2	119
Brownsville, Tx., U.S.	G4	120
Brownsville, Vt., U.S.	E4	122
Brownsville, Wi., U.S.	E5	126
Brownton, Mn., U.S.	F4	100
Brownvale, Ab., Can.	A2	68
Brownville, Me., U.S.	C4	96
Brownville, N.Y., U.S.	A5	109
Brownville Junction, Me., U.S.	C3	96
Brown Willy, hill, Eng., U.K.	D8	102
Brownwood, Tx., U.S.	D3	120
Brownwood, Lake, res., Tx., U.S.	D3	120
Broxton, Ga., U.S.	E4	87
Broyhill Park, Va., U.S.	*B5	123
Brozas, Spain	B4	22
Bruay [-en-Artois], Fr.	B9	16
Bruce, Ab., Can.	C4	68
Bruce, Ms., U.S.	B4	101
Bruce, S.D., U.S.	C9	118
Bruce, Wi., U.S.	C2	126
Bruce, co., On., Can.	C3	73
Bruce, Mount, mtn., Austl.	D2	50
Bruce Crossing, Mi., U.S.	m12	99
Bruce Lake, l., In., U.S.	B5	91
Brucefield, On., Can.	D3	73
Bruceton, Tn., U.S.	A3	119
Bruceton Mills, W.V., U.S.	B5	125
Brucetown, Va., U.S.	A4	123
Bruceville, In., U.S.	G3	91
Bruchsal, F.R.Ger.	D4	18
Bruck, Aus.	B8	20
Brück, Ger.D.R.	A7	19
Bruck [an der Leitha], Aus.	D8	18
Bruck [an der Mur], Aus.	E7	18
Brückenau, F.R.Ger.	C4	19
Bruderheim, Ab., Can.	C4	68
Bruges see Brugge, Bel.	B5	16
Brugg, Switz.	B5	21
Brugge (Bruges), Bel.	B5	16
Brühl, F.R.Ger.	C1	19
Bruin Point, mtn., Ut., U.S.	D5	121
Bruja, Cerro, mtn., Pan.	k11	62
Brule, Ne., U.S.	C4	104
Brule, Wi., U.S.	B2	126
Brule, co., S.D., U.S.	D6	118
Brule, stm., U.S.	C5	126
Brûlé Lake, l., Ab., Can.	C2	68
Brule Lake, l., Mn., U.S.	k9	100
Brumath, Fr.	C7	16
Brumley, Mo., U.S.	C5	102
Brumley Mountain, mtn., Va., U.S.	f9	123
Brundidge, Al., U.S.	D4	78
Bruneau, Id., U.S.	G3	89
Bruneau, stm., U.S.	G3	89
Brunei, ctry., Asia	E4	34
Brunei Bay, b., Asia	D5	34
Brunete, Spain	p16	22
Brunette Island, i., Nf., Can.	E4	72
Bruni, Tx., U.S.	F3	120
Brunico, Italy	C7	20
Brunkild, Mb., Can.	E3	70
Brünig, Switz.	C5	21
Brunnen, Switz.	C6	21
Brunner, Lake, l., N.Z.	O13	51
Bruno, Sk., Can.	E3	75
Bruno, Mn., U.S.	D6	100
Brunsbüttel, F.R.Ger.	E3	15
Brunson, S.C., U.S.	F5	117
Brunswick, Ga., U.S.	E5	87
Brunswick, In., U.S.	B2	91
Brunswick, Me., U.S.	E3	96
Brunswick, Md., U.S.	B2	97
Brunswick, Mo., U.S.	B4	102
Brunswick, Ne., U.S.	B8	104
Brunswick, N.C., U.S.	C4	110
Brunswick, Oh., U.S.	A4	112
Brunswick, co., N.C., U.S.	C4	110
Brunswick, co., Va., U.S.	D5	123
Brunswick, Peninsula, pen., Chile	h11	54
Brunswick Naval Air Station, mil., Me., U.S.	E3	96
Brunswick see Braunschweig, F.R.Ger.	B5	18
Bruree, Ire.	E3	11
Brusett, Mt., U.S.	C9	103
Brush, Co., U.S.	A7	83
Brushy Mountain, mtn., Va., U.S.	C1	123
Brushy Mountains, mts., N.C., U.S.	B1	110
Brusly, La., U.S.	D4	95
Brusque, Braz.	D3	56
Brussels (Bruxelles), Bel.	B6	16
Brussels, On., Can.	D3	73
Brussels, Wi., U.S.	D6	126
Brusson, Italy	E4	21
Bruton, Eng., U.K.	C5	12
Brutus, Mi., U.S.	B6	99
Bruyères, Fr.	A2	20
Bryan, Oh., U.S.	A1	112
Bryan, Tx., U.S.	D4	120
Bryan, co., Ga., U.S.	D5	87
Bryan, co., Ok., U.S.	D5	113
Bryans Road, Md., U.S.	C3	97
Bryant, Ar., U.S.	C3	81
Bryant, Fl., U.S.	F6	86
Bryant, Il., U.S.	C3	90
Bryant, In., U.S.	D8	91
Bryant, S.D., U.S.	C8	118
Bryant, Wi., U.S.	C4	126
Bryant Creek, stm., Mo., U.S.	E5	102
Bryant Mountain, mtn., Ma., U.S.	B2	98
Bryantown, Md., U.S.	C4	97
Bryant Pond, Me., U.S.	D2	96
Bryantsville, Ky., U.S.	C5	94
Bryce Canyon, Ut., U.S.	F3	121
Bryce Canyon National Park, Ut., U.S.	F3	121
Bryceville, Fl., U.S.	B5	86
Brynica, stm., Pol.	g9	26
Bryn Mawr, Pa., U.S.	o20	115
Bryn Mawr, Wa., U.S.	e11	124
Bryson, Tx., U.S.	C3	120
Bryson City, N.C., U.S.	f9	110
Brzeg, Pol.	D6	26
Brzeziny, Pol.	D6	26
B-Say-Tah, Sk., Can.	G4	75
Bu'aale, Som.	H15	52
Bua Bay, b., Fiji	G1	52
Buariki, Kir.	R18	52
Bübiyān, i., Kuw.	C4	40
Buca, Tur.	*C6	40
Bucaramanga, Col.	B4	60
Buccaneer Archipelago, is., Austl.	C3	50
Buchach, Sov. Un.	G5	27
Buchanan, Lib.	E2	45
Buchanan, Ga., U.S.	C1	87
Buchanan, Mi., U.S.	G4	99
Buchanan, N.D., U.S.	B7	111
Buchanan, Tn., U.S.	A3	119
Buchanan, Va., U.S.	C3	123
Buchanan, co., Ia., U.S.	B6	92
Buchanan, co., Mo., U.S.	B3	102
Buchanan, co., Va., U.S.	e9	123
Buchanan, Lake, l., Austl.	D8	50
Buchan Ness, c., Scot., U.K.	C7	13
Buchans, Nf., Can.	D3	72
Buchardo, Arg.	A4	54
Bucharest (București), Rom.	C8	24
Buchboden, Aus.	B8	21
Buchen, F.R.Ger.	D4	19
Buchenberg, F.R.Ger.	A9	21
Buchholz, F.R.Ger.	E3	15
Buchloe, F.R.Ger.	E5	18
Buchs, Switz.	B5	20
Buchtel, Oh., U.S.	C3	112
Buckatunna, Ms., U.S.	D5	101
Buck Creek, In., U.S.	D4	91
Buck Creek, stm., Ga., U.S.	D2	87
Buck Creek, stm., In., U.S.	m11	91
Buck Creek, stm., Ky., U.S.	C5	94
Bückeburg, F.R.Ger.	A4	19
Buckeye, Az., U.S.	D3	80
Buckeye, Ia., U.S.	B4	92
Buckeye, W.V., U.S.	C4	125
Buckeye Hills, hills, Az., U.S.	m7	80
Buckeye Lake, Oh., U.S.	C3	112
Buckeystown, Md., U.S.	B3	97
Buckfield, Me., U.S.	D2	96
Buckhannon, W.V., U.S.	C4	125
Buckhaven, Scot., U.K.	B5	10
Buck Hall, Ga., U.S.	C3	87
Buck Hill Falls, Pa., U.S.	D11	115
Buckhorn, Az., U.S.	D4	80
Buckhorn, Ky., U.S.	C6	94
Buckhorn, N.M., U.S.	D1	108
Buckhorn Knob, mtn., W.V., U.S.	C6	125
Buckhorn Lake, res., Ky., U.S.	C6	94
Buckie, Scot., U.K.	B5	10
Buckingham, P.Q., Can.	D2	74
Buckingham, Eng., U.K.	C6	12
Buckingham, co., Va., U.S.	C4	123
Buckinghamshire, co., Eng., U.K.	C7	12
Buck Lake, l., Ab., Can.	C3	68
Buckland, P.Q., Can.	C7	74
Buckland, Ak., U.S.	B7	79
Buckland, Ma., U.S.	A2	98
Buckland, Oh., U.S.	B1	112
Buckley, Il., U.S.	C5	90
Buckley, Mi., U.S.	D5	99
Buckley, Wa., U.S.	B3	124
Bucklin, Ks., U.S.	E4	93
Bucklin, Mo., U.S.	B5	102
Buckman, Mn., U.S.	E4	100
Bucknell Manor, Va., U.S.	*B5	123
Buckner, Ar., U.S.	D2	81
Buckner, Il., U.S.	F4	90
Buckner, Ky., U.S.	g12	94
Buckner, Mo., U.S.	h11	102
Bucks, Al., U.S.	D1	78
Bucks, co., Pa., U.S.	F11	115
Bucks Harbor, Me., U.S.	D5	96
Buckskin, In., U.S.	H3	91
Buckskin Mountains, mts., Az., U.S.	C2	80
Bucksport, Me., U.S.	D4	96
Bucksport, S.C., U.S.	D9	117
Buckville, Ar., U.S.	C2	81
Bucoda, Wa., U.S.	C3	124
Buco Zau, Ang.	B1	48
Buctouche, N.B., Can.	C5	71
Bucyrus, Ks., U.S.	D9	93
Bucyrus, N.D., U.S.	C3	111
Bucyrus, Oh., U.S.	B3	112
Buda, Il., U.S.	B4	90
Buda, Tx., U.S.	D4	120
Budapest, Hung.	B4	24
Budd Coast, Ant.	C24	7
Budd Lake, l., N.J., U.S.	B3	107
Buddon Ness, c., Scot., U.K.	D6	13
Buddonovsk, Sov. Un.	G17	8
Buddtown, N.J., U.S.	D3	107
Bude, Eng., U.K.	E4	10
Bude, Ms., U.S.	D3	101
Bude Bay, b., Eng., U.K.	D3	12
Budjala, Zaire	A2	48
Budrio, Italy	B3	23
Budyně [nad Ohří], Czech.	n17	26
Buea, Cam.	E1	46
Buechel, Ky., U.S.	B4	94
Buena, N.J., U.S.	D3	107
Buena, Wa., U.S.	C5	124
Buenaventura, Col.	C2	60
Buenaventura, Mex.	B3	63
Buena Vista, Bol.	C3	55
Buena Vista, Co., U.S.	C5	83
Buena Vista, Fl., U.S.	D4	86
Buena Vista, Ga., U.S.	D2	87
Buena Vista, Ms., U.S.	B5	101
Buena Vista, Va., U.S.	C3	123
Buena Vista, co., Ia., U.S.	B2	92
Bueno, stm., Chile	C2	54
Buenópolis, Braz.	B4	56
Buenos Aires, Arg.	A5	54
Buenos Aires, C.R.	B6	64
Buenos Aires, Lago (Lago General Carrera), l., S.A.	D2	54
Bueyeros, N.M., U.S.	B6	108
Buffalo, Ab., Can.	D5	68
Buffalo, Il., U.S.	D4	90
Buffalo, Ia., U.S.	C7	92
Buffalo, Ks., U.S.	E8	93
Buffalo, Ky., U.S.	C4	94
Buffalo, Mn., U.S.	E5	100
Buffalo, Mo., U.S.	D4	102
Buffalo, N.Y., U.S.	C2	109
Buffalo, Oh., U.S.	C4	112
Buffalo, Ok., U.S.	A2	113
Buffalo, S.C., U.S.	B4	117
Buffalo, S.D., U.S.	B2	118
Buffalo, Tn., U.S.	A3	119
Buffalo, Tx., U.S.	D4	120
Buffalo, W.V., U.S.	C3	125
Buffalo, Wi., U.S.	D2	126
Buffalo, Wy., U.S.	B6	127
Buffalo, co., Ne., U.S.	D6	104
Buffalo, co., S.D., U.S.	C6	118
Buffalo, co., Wi., U.S.	D2	126
Buffalo, stm., Ar., U.S.	B3	81
Buffalo, stm., Mn., U.S.	D2	100

Name	Map Ref	Page
Buffalo, stm., Tn., U.S.	B4	119
Buffalo, stm., Wi., U.S.	D2	126
Buffalo Bill Reservoir, res., Wy., U.S.	B3	127
Buffalo Center, Ia., U.S.	A4	92
Buffalo Creek, Co., U.S.	B5	83
Buffalo Creek, stm., W.V., U.S.	f8	125
Buffalo Creek, stm., W.V., U.S.	h10	125
Buffalo Creek, stm., W.V., U.S.	n12	125
Buffalo Gap, Sk., Can.	H3	75
Buffalo Gap, Sk., Can.	D2	118
Buffalo Grove, Il., U.S.	h9	90
Buffalo Lake, Mn., U.S.	F4	100
Buffalo Lake, l., Ab., Can.	C4	68
Buffalo Lake, l., N.T., Can.	D9	66
Buffalo Lake, res., Tx., U.S.	B1	120
Buffalo Lake, res., Wi., U.S.	E4	126
Buffalo Mills, Pa., U.S.	G4	115
Buffalo Mountain, mtn., Va., U.S.	D2	123
Buffalo Narrows, Sk., Can.	m7	75
Buffalo Pound Lake, l., Sk., Can.	G3	75
Buffalo Valley, Tn., U.S.	C8	119
Buff Bay, Jam.	E15	65
Buffer Lake, l., Sk., Can.	E2	75
Buffumville Lake, res., Ma., U.S.	B4	98
Buford, Co., U.S.	B3	83
Buford, Ga., U.S.	B2	87
Buford, Oh., U.S.	C2	112
Buford, Wy., U.S.	E7	127
Bug, stm., Eur.	E4	27
Buga, Col.	C2	60
Buganga, Ug.	B5	48
Bugembe, Ug.	*A5	48
Bugene, Tan.	B5	48
Bugio, i., Port.	h12	22
Bugliaga, Indon.	D5	21
Bugojnc, Yugo.	C3	24
Bugsuk Island, i., Phil.	D5	34
Bugt, China	C9	32
Bugulma, Sov. Un.	C4	28
Buguruslan, Sov. Un.	C4	28
Buhl, Al., U.S.	D7	16
Bühl, F.R.Ger.	E3	19
Buhl, Al., U.S.	B2	78
Buhl, Id., U.S.	G4	89
Buhl, Mn., U.S.	C6	100
Bühlertal, F.R.Ger.	D6	93
Buhler, Ks., U.S.	E3	19
Bühlertal, F.R.Ger.	B8	24
Buhuşi, Rom.	E4	45
Bui Dam, Ghana	B4	110
Buies Creek, N.C., U.S.	B4	12
Builth Wells, Wales, U.K.	A6	17
Buitenpost, Neth.	D3	22
Bujalance, Spain	B4	48
Bujumbura, Bdi.	C4	48
Bukama, Zaire	B5	48
Bukavu, Zaire	B5	48
Bukene, Tan.	F9	29
Bukhara, Sov. Un.	F2	34
Bukittinggi, Indon.	B5	48
Bukoba, Tan.	B7	24
Bukovina, hist reg., Eur.	E6	45
Bukuru, Nig.	F8	34
Bula, Indon.	A4	48
Bula, Zaire	A6	21
Bülach, Switz.	e10	110
Buladean, N.C., U.S.	C11	119
Buladeen, Tn., U.S.	C6	94
Bulan, Ky., U.S.	E3	79
Bulawayo, Zimb.	D7	24
Buldir Island, i., Ak., U.S.	B5	31
Bulgan, Mong.	I15	52
Bulgaria, ctry., Eur.	B4	69
Bulgroo, Austl.	B4	69
Buliya, i., Fiji	B4	69
Bulkley, stm., B.C., Can.	E3	68
Bulkley Ranges, mts., B.C., Can.	D6	17
Bull, stm., B.C., Can.	C3	22
Bullange see Büllingen, Bel.	D3	87
Bullaque, stm., Spain	C5	22
Bullard, Ga., U.S.	C2	19
Bullas, Spain	E6	105
Bullaxaar, Som.	B2	118
Bullay, F.R.Ger.	C3	20
Bull Creek, stm., Nv., U.S.	H18	65
Bull Creek, stm., S.D., U.S.	F5	121
Bulle, Switz.	B4	118
Bullen Baai, b., Neth. Ant.	B1	80
Bullfrog Creek, stm., Ut., U.S.	D6	17
Bullhead, S.D., U.S.	G6	117
Büllingen (Bullange), Bel.	F8	117
Bull Island, i., S.C., U.S.	D9	117
Bullitt, co., Ky., U.S.	C4	94
Bullittsville, Ky., U.S.	h13	94
Bull Mountain, mtn., Mt., U.S.	D4	103
Bullock, co., Ga., U.S.	D5	87
Bullock, N.C., U.S.	A4	110
Bullock, co., Al., U.S.	C4	78
Bullock Creek, Mi., U.S.	E6	99
Bulloo, stm., Austl.	E7	50
Bulloo Lake, l., Austl.	D4	51
Bull Run, stm., Va., U.S.	g11	123
Bull Run Mountains, mts., Va., U.S.	B5	123
Bullrun High Mountain, Tn., U.S.	m13	119
Bullrun Rock, mtn., Or., U.S.	F8	117
Bulls Bay, b., S.C., U.S.	C1	84
Bulls Bridge, Ct., U.S.	C10	119
Bulls Gap, Tn., U.S.	A3	81
Bull Shoals, Ar., U.S.	A3	81
Bull Shoals Lake, res., Ga., U.S.	h8	87
Bull Sluice Lake, res., Ga., U.S.	C9	114
Bully Creek Reservoir, res., Or., U.S.	B2	54
Bulnes, Chile	k12	50
Bulolo, Pap. N. Gui.	G4	37
Bulsär, India	C4	49
Bultfontein, S. Afr.	B15	29
Bulun, Sov. Un.	D4	120
Bulungu, Zaire	B2	48
Bulwark, Ab., Can.	C5	68
Bulyea, Sk., Can.	G3	75
Bumba, Zaire	A3	48
Bumping, stm., Wa., U.S.	C4	124
Bumpus Mills, Tn., U.S.	A4	119
Buna, Tx., U.S.	D6	120
Bunbury, Austl.	F2	50
Bunch, Ok., U.S.	C5	102
Bunche Park, Fl., U.S.	B7	113
Buncombe, Il., U.S.	*s13	86
Buncombe, co., N.C., U.S.	F5	90
Buncrana, Ire.	f10	110
Bundaberg, Austl.	B4	11
Bünde, F.R.Ger.	D9	50

Bündi, India	E5	37
Bundick Creek, stm., La., U.S.	D2	95
Bundoran, Ire.	C3	11
Bunessan, Scot., U.K.	D2	13
Bungay, Eng., U.K.	B9	12
Bunger Hills, hills, Ant.	C23	7
Bungo Strait, strt., Japan	J6	33
Bunguran Selatan Islands, is., Indon.	E3	34
Bunguran Utara Islands, is., Indon.	E3	34
Bunia, Zaire	A5	48
Bunker, Mo., U.S.	D6	102
Bunker Hill, Il., U.S.	D4	90
Bunker Hill, In., U.S.	C5	91
Bunker Hill, Ks., U.S.	D5	93
Bunker Hill, Or., U.S.	*D2	114
Bunker Hill, Tn., U.S.	B5	119
Bunker Hill, W.V., U.S.	B5	125
Bunker Hill, mtn., Nv., U.S.	D4	105
Bunkerville, Nv., U.S.	G7	105
Bunkeya, Zaire	D4	48
Bunkie, La., U.S.	D3	95
Bunn, N.C., U.S.	B4	110
Bunnahowen, Ire.	C2	11
Bunnell, Fl., U.S.	C5	86
Bunnlevel, N.C., U.S.	B4	110
Bunnyconnellan, Ire.	B3	11
Buntharik, Thai.	E10	37
Buntingford, Eng., U.K.	m7	56
Buol, Indon.	*f11	124
Buon Me Thuot, Viet.	C3	34
Buor-Khaya Bay, b., Sov. Un.	B1	128
Bura, Kenya	B7	48
Buram, Sud.	C2	47
Buras, La., U.S.	E6	95
Buraydah, Sau. Ar.	C4	38
Burayk, Libya	D2	43
Burbank, Ca., U.S.	E4	82
Burbank, Il., U.S.	k9	90
Burbank, Ok., U.S.	A5	113
Burbank, S.D., U.S.	E9	118
Burbank, Wa., U.S.	C6	124
Burchard, Ne., U.S.	D9	104
Burco, Som.	D6	47
Burdekin, stm., Austl.	C8	50
Burden, Ks., U.S.	E7	93
Burdett, Ab., Can.	E5	68
Burdett, Ks., U.S.	D4	93
Burdett, N.Y., U.S.	C4	109
Burdette, Ar., U.S.	B6	81
Burdick, Ks., U.S.	D7	93
Burdickville, R.I., U.S.	F2	116
Burdur, Tur.	D8	40
Burdwän, India	D8	36
Bureau, Il., U.S.	B4	90
Bureau, co., Il., U.S.	B4	90
Burein Mountains, mts., Sov. Un.	B6	33
Büren, F.R.Ger.	B3	19
Büren, Switz.	B3	21
Bureya, Sov. Un.	B10	31
Bureya, stm., Sov. Un.	A5	33
Burford, On., Can.	D4	73
Burg, Ger.D.R.	A6	19
Burg, F.R.Ger.	D5	15
Burgas, Bul.	D8	24
Burgas, Gulf of, b., Bul.	C5	110
Burgaw, N.C., U.S.	C5	110
Burgdorf, F.R.Ger.	F3	15
Burgdorf, Switz.	E3	18
Burgeo, Nf., Can.	D4	49
Burgersdorp, S. Afr.	D9	117
Burgess, S.C., U.S.	D7	12
Burgess Hill, Eng., U.K.	F1	115
Burgettstown, Pa., U.S.	A8	20
Burghausen, F.R.Ger.	C5	13
Burghead, Scot., U.K.	C5	94
Burgin, Ky., U.S.	B4	51
Burglengenfeld, F.R.Ger.	A2	112
Burgos, Phil.	n12	34
Burgos, Spain	A4	22
Burgstädt, Ger.D.R.	A2	19
Burgsteinfurt, F.R.Ger.	I8	14
Burgsvik, Swe.	D6	16
Burgundy, hist reg., Fr.	D6	36
Burhänpur, India	E2	15
Burhave, F.R.Ger.	E10	37
Burhi Gandak, stm., India	m7	56
Buri, Braz.	*f6	62
Burica, Punta, c., N.A.	*f11	124
Burien, Wa., U.S.	C9	119
Burin, Isr. Occ.	g12	41
Burin Peninsula, pen., Nf., Can.	E4	72
Buriram, Thai.	C2	56
Buritama, Braz.	G7	40
Burj al 'Arab, Eg.	B3	120
Burkburnett, Tx., U.S.	B3	89
Burke, Id., U.S.	f10	109
Burke, N.Y., U.S.	D6	118
Burke, S.D., U.S.	B5	122
Burke, Vt., U.S.	*B5	123
Burke, Va., U.S.	C4	87
Burke, co., Ga., U.S.	B1	110
Burke, co., N.C., U.S.	A3	111
Burke Channel, strt., B.C., Can.	C4	69
Burke City, Mo., U.S.	f13	102
Burke Island, i., Ant.	B2	7
Burkes Garden, Va., U.S.	C1	123
Burkesville, Ky., U.S.	D4	94
Burket, In., U.S.	B6	91
Burketon Station (part of Newcastle), On., Can.	C6	73
Burketown, Austl.	C3	120
Burkett, Tx., U.S.	B3	120
Burkettsville, Oh., U.S.	D6	120
Burkeville, Tx., U.S.	C4	87
Burkeville, Va., U.S.	A4	45
Burkina Faso, ctry., Afr.	B2	54
Burk's Falls, On., Can.	C3	78
Burkville, Al., U.S.	C3	78
Burleigh, co., N.D., U.S.	C5	111
Burleson, Tx., U.S.	n9	120
Burleson, co., Tx., U.S.	D4	120
Burley, Id., U.S.	f10	124
Burley, Wa., U.S.	h8	93
Burlingame, Ca., U.S.	D7	73
Burlingame, Ks., U.S.	D5	73
Burlington, Nf., Can.	C1	126
Burlington, On., Can.	D5	73
Burlington, Ct., U.S.	B4	84
Burlington, Ia., U.S.	D6	92
Burlington, Il., U.S.	A5	90
Burlington, In., U.S.	D5	91
Burlington, Ks., U.S.	D8	93
Burlington, Ky., U.S.	A5	94
Burlington, Me., U.S.	C4	96
Burlington, Ma., U.S.	f11	98

Burlington, N.J., U.S.	C3	107
Burlington, N.C., U.S.	A3	110
Burlington, N.D., U.S.	A4	111
Burlington, Ok., U.S.	A3	113
Burlington, Pa., U.S.	C8	115
Burlington, Vt., U.S.	C2	122
Burlington, Wa., U.S.	A3	124
Burlington, W.V., U.S.	B6	125
Burlington, Wi., U.S.	F5	126
Burlington, Wy., U.S.	B4	127
Burlington, co., N.J., U.S.	D3	107
Burlington Beach, In., U.S.	B3	91
Burlington Junction, Mo., U.S.	A2	102
Burlyu-Tobe, Sov. Un.	D9	28
Burma, ctry., Asia	D10	36
Burnaby, B.C., Can.	C2	69
Burnaby Island, i., B.C., Can.	C2	69
Burnet, Tx., U.S.	D3	120
Burnet, co., Tx., U.S.	D3	120
Burnett, In., U.S.	E3	91
Burnett, co., Wi., U.S.	C1	126
Burnett, stm., Austl.	B8	51
Burnettsville, In., U.S.	C4	91
Burney, Ca., U.S.	B3	82
Burney, In., U.S.	F6	91
Burneyville, Ok., U.S.	D4	113
Burnham, Me., U.S.	D3	96
Burnham, Mo., U.S.	E6	102
Burnham, Pa., U.S.	E6	115
Burnham-on-Sea, Eng., U.K.	C5	12
Burnie, Austl.	o15	50
Burning Springs, Ky., U.S.	C6	94
Burning Springs, W.V., U.S.	C3	125
Burnley, Eng., U.K.	D5	10
Burns, Co., U.S.	B4	83
Burns, Ks., U.S.	D7	93
Burns, Or., U.S.	D7	114
Burns, Tn., U.S.	A4	119
Burns, Wy., U.S.	E8	127
Burns City, In., U.S.	G4	91
Burns Flat, Ok., U.S.	B2	113
Burnside, Il., U.S.	C2	90
Burnside, Ky., U.S.	D5	94
Burnside, Ky., U.S.	E4	115
Burns Lake, B.C., Can.	B5	69
Burns Paiute Indian Reservation, Or., U.S.	D7	114
Burnstad, N.D., U.S.	C6	111
Burnsville, N.B., Can.	B4	71
Burnsville, Al., U.S.	C3	78
Burnsville, Mn., U.S.	F5	100
Burnsville, Ms., U.S.	A5	101
Burnsville, N.C., U.S.	f10	110
Burnsville, W.V., U.S.	C4	125
Burnsville Lake, res., W.V., U.S.	C4	125
Burnt Cabins, Pa., U.S.	F6	115
Burnt Corn, Al., U.S.	D2	78
Burnt Hills, N.Y., U.S.	C7	109
Burnt Island, Nf., Can.	E2	72
Burntisland, Scot., U.K.	D5	13
Burnt Mills, Lake, l., Va., U.S.	k14	123
Burnt Prairie, Il., U.S.	E5	90
Burnt River, On., Can.	C6	73
Burntside Lake, l., Mn., U.S.	C6	100
Burntwood, stm., Mb., Can.	B2	70
Burntwood Lake, l., Mb., Can.	B1	70
Burnwell, Al., U.S.	f6	78
Burnwell, W.V., U.S.	m13	125
Burqä, Isr. Occ.	f11	41
Burr, Mn., U.S.	F2	100
Burr, Ne., U.S.	D9	104
Burra, Austl.	F2	51
Burragorang, Lake, l., Austl.	G8	51
Burray, i., Scot., U.K.	B6	13
Burrendong Reservoir, res., Austl.	F7	51
Burr Ferry, La., U.S.	C2	95
Burr Hill, Va., U.S.	B5	123
Burriana, Spain	C5	22
Burr Oak, Ia., U.S.	A6	92
Burr Oak, Ks., U.S.	C5	93
Burr Oak, Mi., U.S.	G5	99
Burr Oak Reservoir, res., Oh., U.S.	C3	112
Burroughs, Ga., U.S.	E5	87
Burrow Head, c., Scot., U.K.	F4	13
Burrows, In., U.S.	C5	91
Burrton, Ks., U.S.	D6	93
Burruyacú, Arg.	E3	55
Burrville, Tn., U.S.	C9	119
Burrwood, La., U.S.	F6	95
Burry Port, Wales, U.K.	C3	12
Bursa, Tur.	B7	40
Būr Safājah, Eg.	C3	38
Bursey, Mount, mtn., Ant.	B35	7
Burstall, Sk., Can.	G1	75
Burt, Ia., U.S.	A3	92
Burt, N.D., U.S.	C3	111
Burt, co., Ne., U.S.	C9	104
Burta, Austl.	F3	51
Bür Tawfīq, Eg.	E4	41
Burt Lake, l., Mi., U.S.	C6	99
Burton, B.C., Can.	D9	90
Burton, Il., U.S.	E7	99
Burton, Mi., U.S.	B6	104
Burton, Ne., U.S.	A4	112
Burton, Oh., U.S.	D4	120
Burton, Tx., U.S.	f11	124
Burton, Wa., U.S.	B4	125
Burton, co., Ga., U.S.	B3	87
Burton-on-Trent, Eng., U.K.	D6	10
Burtonport, Ire.	C6	11
Burträsk, Swe.	E9	14
Burtrum, Mn., U.S.	E4	100
Burtts Corner, N.B., Can.	C3	71
Burtus, Eg.	D3	41
Buru, i., Indon.	F7	34
Burük, Wädī al, val., Eg.	D5	41
Burullus, Lake, l., Eg.	A5	41
Burūn, Ra's, c., Eg.	C5	41
Bururi, Bdi.	B5	48
Burwash, On., Can.	A4	73
Burwell, Ne., U.S.	C6	104
Bury, P.Q., Can.	D6	74
Bury, Eng., U.K.	D5	11
Burynshik, Sov. Un.	D4	28
Bury Saint Edmunds, Eng., U.K.	D7	10
Busby, Ab., Can.	C4	68
Busby, Mt., U.S.	E10	103
Büschfeld, F.R.Ger.	D1	19
Bush, Ky., U.S.	C6	94
Bush, La., U.S.	D6	95
Bush City, Ks., U.S.	D8	93
Büsheler, Iran	G5	39
Bushenyi, Ug.	B5	48
Bushimaie, stm., Zaire	C4	48
Bushiribana, Aruba	G17	65
Bushkill, Pa., U.S.	D11	115
Bushland, Tx., U.S.	B1	120
Bushmills, N. Ire., U.K.	B6	11

Bushnell, Fl., U.S.	D4	86
Bushnell, Il., U.S.	C3	90
Bushnell, Ne., U.S.	C2	104
Bushnell, S.D., U.S.	C9	118
Bushong, Ks., U.S.	D7	93
Bush River, b., Md., U.S.	B5	97
Bushton, Ks., U.S.	D5	93
Businga, Zaire	A3	48
Busk, Sov. Un.	G5	27
Busko [Zdrój], Pol.	C6	26
Buşrá ash Shām, Syria	F11	40
Bussang, Fr.	A2	21
Busselton, Austl.	F2	50
Busseto, Italy	E6	20
Bussey, Ia., U.S.	C5	92
Bussum, Neth.	A6	16
Busto Arsizio, Italy	B2	23
Busu-Djanoa, Zaire	A3	48
Büsum, F.R.Ger.	D2	15
Buta, Zaire	A3	48
Buta Ranquil, Arg.	B3	54
Butare, Rw.	B5	48
Buṭayhah, Syria	B7	48
Bute, i., Scot., U.K.	E3	13
Butedale, B.C., Can.	C3	69
Bute Inlet, b., B.C., Can.	D5	69
Butere, Kenya	A5	48
Butha Qi, China	B9	31
Buthier, stm., Italy	B3	31
Butkhāk, Afg.	D3	20
Butler, Al., U.S.	D14	39
Butler, Ga., U.S.	C1	78
Butler, In., U.S.	D2	87
Butler, Ky., U.S.	D4	91
Butler, Mo., U.S.	B8	91
Butler, N.J., U.S.	B5	94
Butler, Oh., U.S.	C3	102
Butler, Pa., U.S.	A4	107
Butler, S.D., U.S.	B3	112
Butler, Tn., U.S.	E2	115
Butler, Wi., U.S.	B8	118
Butler, co., Al., U.S.	C11	119
Butler, co., Ia., U.S.	m11	126
Butler, co., Ks., U.S.	D3	78
Butler, co., Ky., U.S.	B5	92
Butler, co., Mo., U.S.	E7	93
Butler, co., Ne., U.S.	C4	94
Butler, co., Oh., U.S.	E7	102
Butler, co., Pa., U.S.	C8	104
Butler's Bridge, Ire.	C1	112
Butner, N.C., U.S.	E2	115
Butovo, Sov. Un.	A4	110
Buttahatchee, stm., U.S.	n17	27
Butte, Mt., U.S.	B5	101
Butte, Ne., U.S.	E4	103
Butte, N.D., U.S.	B7	104
Butte, co., Ca., U.S.	B5	111
Butte, co., Id., U.S.	C3	82
Butte, co., S.D., U.S.	F5	89
Butte des Morts, Lake, l., Wi., U.S.	C2	118
Butte Falls, Or., U.S.	D5	126
Butte Mountains, mts., Nv., U.S.	E4	114
Butterfield, Ar., U.S.	D6	105
Butterfield, Mn., U.S.	g8	81
Butternut, Wi., U.S.	G4	100
Butternut Lake, l., Wi., U.S.	E4	102
Butters, N.C., U.S.	C3	126
Butterworth, Malay.	C4	110
Butterworth, Transkei	D2	34
Buttevant, Ire.	D4	49
Button Islands, is., N.T., Can.	E3	11
Buttonwillow, Ca., U.S.	f8	72
Butts, co., Ga., U.S.	E4	82
Butuan, Phil.	C3	87
Butung, i., Indon.	D7	34
Buturlinovka, Sov. Un.	F6	34
Butzbach, F.R.Ger.	F13	27
Bützow, Ger.D.R.	C3	19
Buuhoodle, Som.	B5	18
Cabot Head, c., On., Can.	D6	47
Buur Gaabo, Som.	A3	73
Buur Hakaba, Som.	E6	47
Buxtehude, F.R.Ger.	F5	47
Buxton, Guy.	E5	47
Buxton, Eng., U.K.	B4	18
Buxton, N.C., U.S.	A3	59
Buxton, N.D., U.S.	A6	12
Buxton, Or., U.S.	B7	110
Buxton, Mount, mtn., B.C., Can.	B8	111
Buy, Sov. Un.	g11	114
Buyck, Mn., U.S.	C3	69
Buynaksk, Sov. Un.	*E2	96
Buyr Nuur, l., Asia	B6	100
Büyükliman see Vakfikebir, Tur.	B8	31
Büyükmenderes, stm., Tur.	B12	40
Buzachi Peninsula, pen., Sov. Un.	D7	40
Buzău, Rom.	E4	28
Buzău, stm., Rom.	C8	24
Buzaymah, Libya	C8	24
Buzet, Yugo.	E4	43
Buzuluk, Sov. Un.	C1	24
Buzzard Roost, mtn., N.C.	C4	28
Buzzards Bay, Ma., U.S.	B1	110
Buzzards Bay, b., Ma., U.S.	C6	98
Byala, Bul.	D7	24
Byala Slatina, Bul.	D6	24
Byam Martin Island, i., N.T., Can.	B10	79
Byars, Ok., U.S.	C4	113
Bybee, Tn., U.S.	C10	119
Bydgoszcz, Pol.	B5	26
Byelorussia (White Russia), state, Sov. Un.	D5	29
Byemoor, Ab., Can.	C4	68
Byers, Co., U.S.	B6	83
Byers, Tx., U.S.	E5	93
Byesville, Oh., U.S.	C4	112
Byfield, Ma., U.S.	A6	98
Byglandsfjord, Nor.	H2	14
Bykhov, Sov. Un.	n18	27
Bykovo, Sov. Un.	G15	27
Bylas, Az., U.S.	D5	80
Bylot Island, i., N.T., Can.	B17	66
Byng, Ok., U.S.	C5	113
Byng Inlet, On., U.S.	B4	73
Bynum, Mt., U.S.	C4	103
Bynumville, Mo., U.S.	B5	102
Byram, Ms., U.S.	C3	101
Byrdstown, Tn., U.S.	C8	119
Byron, Ca., U.S.	h9	82
Byron, Ga., U.S.	D3	87
Byron, Il., U.S.	A4	90
Byron, Me., U.S.	D2	96
Byron, Mn., U.S.	F6	100
Byron, Ne., U.S.	D8	104
Byron, N.Y., U.S.	B2	109
Byron, Ok., U.S.	A3	113
Byron, Wy., U.S.	B4	127
Byron, Cape, c., Austl.	E9	50
Byrum, Den.	A5	15
Byström, Neth.	n18	26
Bytom, Pol.	C5	26
Bytów, Pol.	A4	26
Byzantium see İstanbul, Tur.	B7	40

C

Byrdstown, Tn., U.S.	C8	119
Byrnedale, Pa., U.S.	D4	115
Byrock, Austl.	E6	51
Byromville, Ga., U.S.	D3	87
Cade, Il., U.S.	h9	82
Cadi, Ang.	D3	87
Cader Idris, mtn., Wales, U.K.	B4	12
Cades, S.C., U.S.	D8	117
Cades, Tn., U.S.	B3	119
Cades Cove, Tn., U.S.	D10	119
Cadet, Mo., U.S.	C7	102
Cadillac, Sk., Can.	H2	75
Cadillac, Fr.	E3	16
Cadillac, Mi., U.S.	D5	99
Cadillac Mountain, mtn., Me., U.S.	D4	96
Cádiz, Spain	D2	22
Cadiz, Ky., U.S.	D2	94
Cadiz, Oh., U.S.	B4	112
Cadiz, Gulf of, b., Eur.	D2	22
Cadogan, Ab., Can.	C5	68
Cadogan, Pa., U.S.	E2	115
Cadomin, Ab., Can.	C2	68
Cadott, Wi., U.S.	D2	126
Cadotte, stm., Ab., Can.	A2	68
Cadron Creek, stm., Ar., U.S.	B3	81
Cadwell, Ga., U.S.	D3	87
Cadys Falls, Vt., U.S.	B3	122
Caen, Fr.	C3	16
Caernarfon, Wales, U.K.	D4	10
Caernarfon Bay, b., Wales, U.K.	D4	10
Caerphilly (Rhymney Valley), Wales, U.K.	C4	12
Caesar Creek Lake, res., Oh., U.S.	C2	112
Caetité, Braz.	A4	56
Cafayate, Arg.	E2	55
Cagayan, stm., Phil.	B6	34
Cagayan de Oro, Phil.	D6	34
Cagayan Islands, is., Phil.	D6	34
Cagayan Sulu Island, i., Phil.	D5	34
Cagiallo, Switz.	D6	21
Cagles Mill Lake, res., In., U.S.	F4	91
Cagnarita, stm., Jam.	E12	65
Cagli, Italy	C4	23
Cagliari, Italy	E2	23
Cagliari, Gulf of, b., Italy	E2	23
Cagnes-sur-Mer, Fr.	F7	16
Caguán, stm., Col.	G11	64
Caguas, P.R.	C3	60
Cahaba, stm., Al., U.S.	C2	78
Cahaba Heights, Al., U.S.	*B3	78
Cahaba Valley, val., Al., U.S.	B3	78
Caha Mountains, mts., Ire.	F2	11
Caherdaniel, Ire.	F1	11
Cahir, Ire.	E4	11
Cahirciveen, Ire.	F1	11
Cahokia, Il., U.S.	E3	90
Cahone, Co., U.S.	D2	83
Cahore Point, c., Ire.	E5	11
Cahors, Fr.	E4	16
Cahuinari, stm., Col.	?	?
Caiabis, Serra dos, plat., Braz.	E3	59
Caiapônia, Braz.	B2	56
Caibarién, Cuba	C4	64
Caibo, Braz.	B7	35
Caicara, Ven.	B4	60
Caicedonia, Col.	C2	60
Caicó, Braz.	C3	57
Caicos Islands, is., T./C. Is.	D8	64
Caicos Passage, strt., N.A.	C7	64
Cailloma, Peru	E3	58
Caillou Bay, b., La., U.S.	E5	95
Caillou Lake, l., La., U.S.	E5	95
Caimanera, Cuba	E6	64
Caiman Point, c., Phil.	o12	34
Caimito, stm., Pan.	m11	62
Caimito, Cuba	C4	71
Cains Store, Ky., U.S.	C5	94
Cainsville, Mo., U.S.	A4	102
Cainsville, Tn., U.S.	B5	119
Caintown, On., Can.	C9	73
Cairnbrook, Pa., U.S.	F4	115
Cairngorm Mountains, mts., Scot., U.K.	C5	13
Cairns, Austl.	C8	50
Cairnsmore of Carsphairn, Scot., U.K.	E4	13
Cairn Table, mtn., Scot., U.K.	E5	13
Cairo (Al Qāhirah), Eg.	C3	38
Cairo, Ga., U.S.	F2	87
Cairo, Il., U.S.	F4	90
Cairo, Ne., U.S.	B5	102
Cairo, N.Y., U.S.	C7	104
Cairo, Oh., U.S.	B1	112
Cairo, W.V., U.S.	B3	125
Caja de Muertos, Isla, i., P.R.	E2	48
Cajamarca, Peru	C2	58
Cajamarca, dept., Peru	C2	58
Cajazeiras, Braz.	C3	57
Čajniče, Yugo.	D4	24
Čakovec, Yugo.	B3	24
Čakovice, Czech.	n18	26
Calabar, Nig.	F6	45
Calabasas, Ca., U.S.	m11	82
Calabogie, On., Can.	B8	73
Calabozo, Ven.	B4	60
Calafat, Rom.	E6	24
Calafate, Arg.	D2	54
Calais, Fr.	C4	16
Calais, Me., U.S.	C6	96
Calais, Vt., U.S.	C4	122
Calama, Chile	D2	55
Calamar, Col.	A3	60
Calamar, Col.	C3	60
Calamba, Phil.	o13	34
Calamian Group, is., Phil.	C6	34
Calamocha, Spain	B5	22
Calamus, stm., Ne., U.S.	B6	104
Cañas, Spain	A5	22
Calanda, Spain	B5	22
Calanscio, Sarīr, dés., Libya	D4	43
Calapan, Phil.	o14	34
Calárași, Rom.	C8	24
Calarcá, Col.	C2	60
Calasparra, Spain	C5	22
Calatayud, Spain	B5	22
Calau, Ger.D.R.	B8	19
Calauag, Phil.	p14	34
Calauag Bay, stm., Phil.	o14	34
Calaveras, co., Ca., U.S.	C3	82
Calavo Gardens, Ca., U.S.	*o16	82
Calbe, Ger.D.R.	B6	19

Name — Map Ref — Page

Calbuco, Chile C2 54
Calca, Peru D3 58
Calcasieu, co., La., U.S. D2 95
Calcasieu, stm., La., U.S. D2 95
Calcasieu Lake, l., La., U.S. E2 95
Calcasieu Pass, strt., La., U.S. E2 95
Calceta, Ec. B1 58
Calchaquí, stm., Arg. E2 55
Calçoene, Braz. B4 59
Calcutta, India D8 36
Calcutta, Oh., U.S. B5 112
Calcutta Lake, l., Nv., U.S. B2 105
Caldaro, Italy C7 20
Caldas, dept., Col. B2 60
Caldas da Rainha, Port. C1 22
Calder, Sk., Can. F5 75
Calder, Id., U.S. B2 89
Calder, stm., Eng., U.K. A6 12
Calder, Loch, l., Scot., U.K. B5 13
Caldera, Chile E1 55
Calderwood, Tn., U.S. D10 119
Caldron Falls Reservoir, res., Wi., U.S. C5 126
Caldwell, Ar., U.S. B5 81
Caldwell, Id., U.S. F2 89
Caldwell, Ks., U.S. E6 93
Caldwell, N.J., U.S. B4 107
Caldwell, Oh., U.S. C4 112
Caldwell, Tx., U.S. D4 120
Caldwell, W.V., U.S. D4 125
Caldwell, co., Ky., U.S. C2 94
Caldwell, co., La., U.S. B3 95
Caldwell, co., Mo., U.S. B3 102
Caldwell, co., N.C., U.S. B1 110
Caldwell, co., Tx., U.S. E4 120
Cale, Ar., U.S. D2 81
Caledon, On., Can. D5 73
Caledon, N. Ire., U.K. C5 11
Caledonia, N.S., Can. E4 71
Caledonia, On., Can. D5 73
Caledonia, Il., U.S. A5 90
Caledonia, Mi., U.S. F5 99
Caledonia, Mn., U.S. G7 100
Caledonia, Ms., U.S. B5 101
Caledonia, N.Y., U.S. C3 109
Caledonia, N.D., U.S. B9 111
Caledonia, Oh., U.S. B3 112
Caledonia, Pa., U.S. D5 115
Caledonia, co., Vt., U.S. C4 122
Caledonian Canal, Scot., U.K. B4 10
Calella, Spain B7 22
Calenzana, Fr. C2 23
Calera, Al., U.S. B3 78
Calera, Ok., U.S. D5 113
Caleta Olivia, Arg. D3 54
Calexico, Ca., U.S. F6 82
Calf of Man, i., I. of Man C4 10
Calgary, Ab., Can. D3 68
Calhan, Co., U.S. B6 83
Calheta, Port. h11 22
Calhoun, N.B., Can. C5 71
Calhoun, Al., U.S. C3 78
Calhoun, Ga., U.S. B2 87
Calhoun, Il., U.S. E5 90
Calhoun, Ky., U.S. C2 94
Calhoun, La., U.S. B3 95
Calhoun, Mo., U.S. C4 102
Calhoun, Tn., U.S. D9 119
Calhoun, co., Al., U.S. B4 78
Calhoun, co., Ar., U.S. D3 81
Calhoun, co., Fl., U.S. B1 86
Calhoun, co., Ga., U.S. E2 87
Calhoun, co., Il., U.S. D3 90
Calhoun, co., Ia., U.S. B3 92
Calhoun, co., Mi., U.S. F5 99
Calhoun, co., Ms., U.S. B4 101
Calhoun, co., S.C., U.S. D6 117
Calhoun, co., Tx., U.S. E4 120
Calhoun, co., W.V., U.S. C3 125
Calhoun City, Ms., U.S. B4 101
Calhoun Falls, S.C., U.S. C2 117
Cali, Col. C2 60
Calico Mountains, mts., Nv., U.S. B2 105
Calico Rock, Ar., U.S. A3 81
Calicut (Kozhikode), India F6 36
Caliente, Ca., U.S. E4 82
Caliente, Nv., U.S. F7 105
Califon, N.J., U.S. B3 107
California, Ky., U.S. k14 94
California, Mo., U.S. C5 102
California, Pa., U.S. F2 115
California, state, U.S. D4 82
California, Golfo de, b., Mex. B2 63
California Aqueduct, Ca., U.S. E4 82
California Junction, Ia., U.S. C1 92
California Oil Camp, Co., U.S. A2 83
Calingasta, Arg. A3 54
Calio, N.D., U.S. A7 111
Calion, Ar., U.S. D3 81
Calipatria, Ca., U.S. F6 82
Calispell Peak, mtn., Wa., U.S. A8 124
Calistoga, Ca., U.S. C2 82
Callabonna, stm., Austl. D3 51
Callabonna, Lake, l., Austl. D3 51
Callaghan, Mount, mtn., Nv., U.S. D5 105
Callahan, Fl., U.S. B5 86
Callahan, Ks., U.S. g12 93
Callahan, co., Tx., U.S. C3 120
Callan, Ire. E4 11
Callan, Slieve, hill, Ire. E3 11
Callander, On., Can. A5 73
Callander, Scot., U.K. B4 10
Callands, Va., U.S. D3 123
Callao, Peru D2 58
Callao, Mo., U.S. B5 102
Callao, Va., U.S. C6 123
Callao, dept., Peru *D2 58
Callaway, Fl., U.S. *u16 86
Callaway, Md., U.S. D4 97
Callaway, Mn., U.S. D3 100
Callaway, Ne., U.S. C6 104
Callaway, Va., U.S. C2 123
Callaway, co., Mo., U.S. C6 102
Callender, Ia., U.S. B3 92
Callensburg, Pa., U.S. D2 115
Callery, Pa., U.S. E1 115
Callicoon, N.Y., U.S. D5 109
Callicoon Center, N.Y., U.S. D6 109
Calliham, Tx., U.S. E3 120
Calling Lake, Ab., Can. B4 68
Calling Lake, l., Ab., Can. B4 68
Calloway, co., Ky., U.S. f9 94
Calmar, Ab., Can. C4 68
Calmar, Ia., U.S. A6 92
Calne, Eng., U.K. C5 12
Caloocan, Phil. o13 34
Caloosahatchee, stm., Fl., U.S. F5 86
Caloundra, Austl. E9 50
Calpella, Ca., U.S. C2 82
Calpet, Wy., U.S. D2 127
Caltagirone, Italy F5 23
Caltanissetta, Italy F5 23
Caltra, Ire. D3 11
Caluire [-et-Cuire], Fr. E6 16
Calulo, Ang. D1 48
Calumet, P.Q., Can. D3 74
Calumet, Al., U.S. B2 78
Calumet, Ia., U.S. B2 92
Calumet, Mi., U.S. A2 99
Calumet, Mn., U.S. C5 100
Calumet, Ok., U.S. B3 113
Calumet, co., Wi., U.S. D5 126
Calumet, Lake, l., Il., U.S. k9 90
Calumet City, Il., U.S. B6 90
Calumet Park, Il., U.S. *k9 90
Calumet Sag Channel, Il., U.S. k9 90
Calumetville, Wi., U.S. k9 126
Calunda, Ang. D3 48
Caluula, Som. C7 47
Calvary, Ga., U.S. F2 87
Calvary, Wi., U.S. k9 126
Calvert, Al., U.S. D1 78
Calvert, Tx., U.S. D4 120
Calvert, co., Md., U.S. C4 97
Calvert City, Ky., U.S. e9 94
Calvert Island, i., B.C., Can. D3 69
Calverton, Md., U.S. B4 97
Calverton, Va., U.S. B5 123
Calverton Park, Mo., U.S. f13 102
Calvi, Fr. C2 23
Calvillo, Mex. m12 63
Calvin, La., U.S. C3 95
Calvin, N.D., U.S. A7 111
Calvin, Ok., U.S. C5 113
Calvinia, S. Afr. D2 49
Calvörde, Ger.D.R. A6 19
Calw, F.R.Ger. E3 19
Calwa, Ca., U.S. *D4 82
Calypso, N.C., U.S. B4 110
Calzada de Calatrava, Spain C4 22
Cam, stm., Eng., U.K. D7 10
Camabatela, Ang. C2 48
Camacho, Mex. C4 63
Camacupa, Ang. D2 48
Camagüey, Cuba D5 64
Camagüey, prov., Cuba D5 64
Camajuaní, Cuba C4 64
Camak, Ga., U.S. C4 87
Camamu, Braz. D3 57
Camaná, Peru E3 58
Camanche, Ia., U.S. C7 92
Camanducaia, Braz. m8 56
Camano Island, i., Wa., U.S. A3 124
Camapuã, Braz. B2 56
Camaquã, Braz. E2 56
Camaquã, stm., Braz. E2 56
Camararé, stm., Braz. E3 59
Camargo, Bol. D2 55
Camargo, Il., U.S. D5 90
Camargo, Ok., U.S. A2 113
Camarillo, Ca., U.S. *E4 82
Camarón, Cabo, c., Hond. D7 63
Camarones, Arg. C3 54
Camarones, Bahía, b., Arg. C3 54
Camas, Wa., U.S. D3 124
Camas, co., Id., U.S. F4 89
Camas Valley, Or., U.S. D3 114
Ca Mau, Cape, c., Viet. D2 34
Cambay, India F4 37
Camberwell, Austl. *G8 50
Cambodia see Kampuchea, ctry., Asia C3 34
Camborne [-Redruth], Eng., U.K. E4 10
Cambra, Pa., U.S. D9 115
Cambrai, Fr. B5 16
Cambria, Ca., U.S. E3 82
Cambria, Ia., U.S. D4 92
Cambria, Mi., U.S. G6 99
Cambria, Wi., U.S. E4 126
Cambria, co., Pa., U.S. E4 115
Cambrian Mountains, mts., Wales, U.K. D5 10
Cambrian Park, Ca., U.S. *D3 82
Cambridge, On., Can. D4 73
Cambridge, Eng., U.K. D7 10
Cambridge, Id., U.S. E2 89
Cambridge, Il., U.S. B3 90
Cambridge, Ia., U.S. C4 92
Cambridge, Ks., U.S. E7 93
Cambridge, Me., U.S. C3 96
Cambridge, Md., U.S. C5 97
Cambridge, Ma., U.S. B5 98
Cambridge, Mn., U.S. E5 100
Cambridge, Ne., U.S. D5 104
Cambridge, N.Y., U.S. B7 109
Cambridge, Oh., U.S. B4 112
Cambridge, Vt., U.S. B3 122
Cambridge, Wi., U.S. E4 126
Cambridge Bay, N.T., Can. C12 66
Cambridge City, In., U.S. E7 91
Cambridge Junction, Vt., U.S. B3 122
Cambridgeport, Vt., U.S. E3 122
Cambridge Reservoir, res., Ma., U.S. g10 98
Cambridgeshire, co., Eng., U.K. B7 12
Cambridge Springs, Pa., U.S. C1 115
Cambuí, Braz. m8 56
Cambundi-Catembo (Nova Gaia), Ang. D2 48
Camden, Al., U.S. D2 78
Camden, Ar., U.S. D3 81
Camden, De., U.S. D3 85
Camden, Il., U.S. C3 90
Camden, In., U.S. C4 91
Camden, Me., U.S. D3 96
Camden, Mi., U.S. G6 99
Camden, Ms., U.S. C4 101
Camden, Mo., U.S. B3 102
Camden, N.J., U.S. D2 107
Camden, N.Y., U.S. B5 109
Camden, N.C., U.S. A6 110
Camden, Oh., U.S. C1 112
Camden, S.C., U.S. C6 117
Camden, Tn., U.S. A3 119
Camden, Tx., U.S. D5 120
Camden, W.V., U.S. B4 125
Camden, co., Ga., U.S. F5 87
Camden, co., Mo., U.S. C5 102
Camden, co., N.J., U.S. D3 107
Camden, co., N.C., U.S. A6 110
Camden on Gauley, W.V., U.S. C4 125
Camdenton, Mo., U.S. D5 102
Camelback Mountain, mtn., Az., U.S. k9 80
Camels Hump, mtn., Vt., U.S. C3 122
Camerino, Italy C4 23
Cameron, Az., U.S. B4 80
Cameron, Il., U.S. C3 90
Cameron, La., U.S. E2 95
Cameron, Mo., U.S. B3 102
Cameron, Mt., U.S. E5 103
Cameron, N.C., U.S. B3 110
Cameron, Ok., U.S. B7 113
Cameron, Pa., U.S. D5 115
Cameron, S.C., U.S. D6 117
Cameron, Tx., U.S. D4 120
Cameron, W.V., U.S. B4 125
Cameron, Wi., U.S. C2 126
Cameron, co., La., U.S. E2 95
Cameron, co., Pa., U.S. D5 115
Cameron, co., Tx., U.S. F4 120
Cameron Hills, hills, Can. E9 66
Cameron Island, i., N.T., Can. m31 66
Cameroon, ctry., Afr. D2 46
Cameroun, Mont, mtn., Cam. E1 46
Cametá, Braz. C5 59
Camiling, Phil. o13 34
Camilla, Ga., U.S. E2 87
Camiña, Chile C2 55
Caminha, Port. B1 22
Camino, Ca., U.S. C3 82
Camissombo (Verissimo Sarmento), Ang. C3 48
Camlachie, On., Can. D2 73
Cammack Village, Ar., U.S. C3 81
Cammal, Pa., U.S. D7 115
Camocim, Braz. B2 57
Camooweal, Austl. C6 50
Camopi, stm., Fr. Gu. B4 59
Camp, co., Tx., U.S. C5 120
Campagna di Roma, reg., Italy h9 23
Campaign, Tn., U.S. D8 119
Campana, Arg. g7 54
Campana, Isla, i., Chile D1 54
Campanario, Spain C3 22
Campania, hist reg., Italy D5 23
Campania Island, i., B.C., Can. C3 69
Campasak, Laos C3 34
Campbell, Al., U.S. D2 78
Campbell, Ca., U.S. k8 82
Campbell, Fl., U.S. D5 86
Campbell, Mn., U.S. D2 100
Campbell, Mo., U.S. E7 102
Campbell, Ne., U.S. D7 104
Campbell, N.Y., U.S. C3 109
Campbell, Oh., U.S. A5 112
Campbell, co., Ky., U.S. B5 94
Campbell, co., S.D., U.S. B5 118
Campbell, co., Tn., U.S. C9 119
Campbell, co., Va., U.S. C3 123
Campbell, co., Wy., U.S. B7 127
Campbell, Cape, c., N.Z. N15 51
Campbellford, On., Can. C7 73
Campbell Hill, Il., U.S. F4 90
Campbell Hill, hill, Oh., U.S. B2 112
Campbell Island, B.C., Can. C3 69
Campbell Island, i., B.C., Can. C3 69
Campbell Island, i., N.Z. J8 2
Campbell Lake, l., Or., U.S. E7 114
Campbellpore, Pak. B5 36
Campbell River, B.C., Can. D5 69
Campbells Bay, P.Q., Can. B8 73
Campbellsburg, In., U.S. G5 91
Campbellsburg, Ky., U.S. B4 94
Campbells Creek, stm., W.V., U.S. m13 125
Campbellsport, Wi., U.S. E5 126
Campbellsville, Ky., U.S. C4 94
Campbellsville, Tn., U.S. B4 119
Campbellton, N.B., Can. A3 71
Campbellton, Nf., Can. D4 72
Campbellton, P.E., Can. C5 71
Campbellton, Fl., U.S. B1 86
Campbelltown, Austl. *F9 50
Campbeltown, Scot., U.K. C4 10
Camp Creek, Tn., U.S. C11 119
Camp Crook, S.D., U.S. B2 118
Camp Douglas, Wi., U.S. E3 126
Campeche, Mex. D6 63
Campeche, state, Mex. D6 63
Campeche, Bahía de, b., Mex. C6 63
Campechuela, Cuba D5 64
Camperdown, Austl. I4 51
Campertogno, Italy E5 21
Camperville, Mb., Can. D1 70
Camp Grove, Il., U.S. B4 90
Cam Pha, Viet. A3 34
Camp Hill, Al., U.S. C4 78
Camp Hill, Pa., U.S. F8 115
Camp H. M. Smith Marine Corps Base, mil., Hi., U.S. g10 88
Camp Howard Ridge, mtn., Id., U.S. D2 89
Campiglia Marittima, Italy C3 23
Campina Grande, Braz. C3 57
Campinas, Braz. C3 56
Campina Verde, Braz. B3 56
Campion, Co., U.S. A5 83
Campione d'Italia, Italy D4 20
Camp Lejeune Marine Corps Base, mil., N.C., U.S. C5 110
Campo, Cam. E1 46
Campo, Ca., U.S. F5 82
Campo, Co., U.S. D8 83
Campoalegre, Col. C2 60
Campo Alegre de Goiás, Braz. B3 56
Campobasso, Italy D5 23
Campobello, S.C., U.S. A3 117
Campobello Island, i., N.B., Can. E3 71
Campo Belo, Braz. C3 56
Campo de Criptana, Spain C4 22
Campodolcino, Italy D7 21
Campo Gallo, Arg. E3 55
Campo Grande, Braz. C2 56
Campo Maior, Braz. B2 57
Campo Maior, Port. C2 22
Campo Mourão, Braz. C2 56
Campo Real, Spain p18 22
Campos, Braz. C4 56
Campos Altos, Braz. B3 56
Camposampiero, Italy D7 20
Campos Belos, Braz. A3 56
Campos Novos, Braz. D2 56
Campos Sales, Braz. C2 57
Campo Tencia, mtn., Switz. D6 21
Campo Tures, Italy C7 20
Camp Pendleton Marine Corps Base, mil., Ca., U.S. F5 82
Camp Point, Il., U.S. C2 90
Camp San Saba, Tx., U.S. D3 120
Camp Sherman, Or., U.S. C5 114
Camp Springs, Md., U.S. f9 97
Campti, La., U.S. C2 95
Campton, Fl., U.S. v15 86
Campton, Ga., U.S. C3 87
Campton, Ky., U.S. C6 94
Campton, N.H., U.S. C3 106
Camptown, Pa., U.S. C9 115
Campus, Il., U.S. B5 90
Camp Verde, Az., U.S. C4 80
Camp Verde Indian Reservation, Az., U.S. C4 80
Campville, Fl., U.S. C4 86
Camp Wood, Tx., U.S. E2 120
Cam Ranh, Viet. G8 35
Cam Ranh Bay, b., Viet. G8 35
Camrose, Ab., Can. C4 68
Camuquén, Ven. B5 60
Canaan, N.B., Can. C4 71
Canaan, Ct., U.S. A2 84
Canaan, In., U.S. G7 91
Canaan, Me., U.S. D3 96
Canaan, Ms., U.S. A4 101
Canaan, N.H., U.S. C2 106
Canaan, N.Y., U.S. C7 109
Canaan, Vt., U.S. A5 122
Canaan, stm., N.B., Can. C4 71
Canaan Center, N.H., U.S. C2 106
Canaan Street, N.H., U.S. C2 106
Canada, Ky., U.S. *C7 94
Canada, ctry., N.A. E13 66
Canada Bay, b., Nf., Can. C3 72
Cañada de Gómez, Arg. A4 54
Canada Falls Lake, res., Me., U.S. C2 96
Canadensis, Pa., U.S. D11 115
Canadian, Ok., U.S. B6 113
Canadian, Tx., U.S. B2 120
Canadian, co., Ok., U.S. B3 113
Canadian, stm., U.S. C7 76
Canadys, S.C., U.S. E6 117
Canaima National Park, Ven. B5 60
Canajoharie, N.Y., U.S. C6 109
Çanakkale, Tur. B6 40
Canale, Italy E3 20
Canal Flats, B.C., Can. D10 69
Canal Fulton, Oh., U.S. B4 112
Canalou, Mo., U.S. E8 102
Canal Point, Fl., U.S. F6 86
Canal Winchester, Oh., U.S. C3 112
Canandaigua, N.Y., U.S. C3 109
Canandaigua Lake, l., N.Y., U.S. C3 109
Cananea, Mex. A2 63
Cananéia, Braz. D3 56
Canápolis, Braz. B3 56
Cañar, Ec. B2 58
Cañar, prov., Ec. B2 58
Canary Islands, is., Spain m14 22
Cañas, C.R. E5 62
Canaseraga, N.Y., U.S. C3 109
Canastota, N.Y., U.S. B5 109
Canaveral, Cape, c., Fl., U.S. D6 86
Canaveral National Seashore, Fl., U.S. D6 86
Canavieiras, Braz. E3 57
Cañazas, Pan. F7 62
Canazei, Italy C7 20
Canbelego, Austl. E6 51
Canberra, Austl. G8 50
Canby, Ca., U.S. B3 82
Canby, Mn., U.S. F2 100
Canby, Or., U.S. B4 114
Cancale, Fr. C3 16
Canche, stm., Fr. D1 17
Cancún, Mex. C7 63
Candeias, stm., Braz. D2 59
Candelaria, Cuba C2 64
Candelaria, Phil. o12 34
Candelaria, Tx., U.S. o12 120
Candelaria, stm., Mex. A2 62
Candeleda, Spain B3 22
Candia see Iráklion, Grc. E5 40
Candia, N.H., U.S. D4 106
Candiac, P.Q., Can. q19 74
Candia Village, N.H., U.S. D4 106
Candle, Ak., U.S. B7 79
Candle Lake, l., Sk., Can. D3 75
Candler, Fl., U.S. C5 86
Candler, co., Ga., U.S. D4 87
Candlewood, Lake, l., Ct., U.S. D1 84
Candlewood Isle, Ct., U.S. D2 84
Candlewood Knolls, Ct., U.S. *D2 84
Candlewood Shores, Ct., U.S. D2 84
Candlewood Trails, Ct., U.S. *C2 84
Cando, Sk., Can. E1 75
Cando, N.D., U.S. A6 111
Candor, N.Y., U.S. C4 109
Candor, N.C., U.S. B3 110
Cane, stm., La., U.S. C2 95
Canea see Khaniá, Grc. E5 40
Canehill, Ar., U.S. B1 81
Canela, Braz. D2 56
Canelones, Ur. E1 56
Canelones, dept., Ur. g8 54
Canendiyu, dept., Para. D4 55
Cañete, Chile B2 54
Cane Valley, Ky., U.S. C4 94
Caney, Ks., U.S. E8 93
Caney, Ky., U.S. C6 94
Caney, Ok., U.S. C5 113
Caney, stm., Ok., U.S. A5 113
Caney Creek, stm., Tx., U.S. r14 120
Caney Fork, stm., Tn., U.S. C8 119
Caneyville, Ky., U.S. C3 94
Canfield, Ar., U.S. D2 81
Canfield, Oh., U.S. A5 112
Cangallo, Peru D3 58
Cangamba, Ang. D2 48
Cangas, Spain A1 22
Cangas de Narcea, Spain A2 22
Cangas de Onís, Spain A3 22
Cangombe, Ang. D3 48
Canguaretama, Braz. C3 57
Canguçu, Braz. E2 56
Cangzhou, China D8 31
Canhotinho, Braz. k5 57
Caniapiscau, stm., P.Q., Can. g13 74
Caniapiscau, Lac, l., P.Q., Can. h12 74
Canicanian, Phil. o14 34
Canicattì, Italy F4 23
Caniles, Spain D4 22
Canim Lake, B.C., Can. D7 69
Canim Lake, l., B.C., Can. D7 69
Canindé, Braz. B3 57
Canindé, stm., Braz. C2 57
Canistear Reservoir, res., N.J., U.S. A4 107
Canisteo, N.Y., U.S. C3 109
Canisteo, stm., N.Y., U.S. C3 109
Canistota, S.D., U.S. D8 118
Canjilon, N.M., U.S. A3 108
Çankırı, Tur. B9 40
Canlaon Volcano, vol., Phil. C6 34
Canmore, Ab., Can. D3 68
Canna, i., Scot., U.K. B3 10
Canna, Sound of, strt., Scot., U.K. C2 13
Cannelburg, In., U.S. G5 91
Cannel City, Ky., U.S. C6 94
Cannelton, In., U.S. I4 91
Cannelton, W.V., U.S. m13 125
Cannes, Fr. F7 16
Cannes, Bayou des, stm., La., U.S. D3 95
Canneto sull'Oglio, Italy D6 20
Canning, Scot., U.K. C4 13
Canning, Austl. *F2 50
Canning, N.S., Can. D5 71
Cannington, On., Can. C5 73
Cannock (Cannock Chase), Eng., U.K. B5 12
Cannon, De., U.S. F3 85
Cannon, co., Tn., U.S. B5 119
Cannon, stm., Mn., U.S. F5 100
Cannon Air Force Base, mil., N.M., U.S. C6 108
Cannonball, N.D., U.S. C5 111
Cannonball, stm., N.D., U.S. C5 111
Cannon Beach, Or., U.S. B3 114
Cannondale, Ct., U.S. E2 84
Cannon Falls, Mn., U.S. F6 100
Cannonsburg, Ky., U.S. B7 94
Cannonsville Reservoir, res., N.Y., U.S. C5 109
Cannonville, Ut., U.S. F3 121
Canoas, stm., Braz. D2 56
Canoe, B.C., Can. D8 69
Canoe, Al., U.S. D2 78
Canoe, stm., B.C., Can. C8 69
Canoe Lake, On., Can. B6 73
Canoinhas, Braz. D2 56
Canon, Ga., U.S. B3 87
Canonchet, R.I., U.S. F1 116
Canon City, Co., U.S. C5 83
Canones, N.M., U.S. A3 108
Canon Plaza, N.M., U.S. A3 108
Canonsburg, Pa., U.S. F1 115
Canoochee, stm., Ga., U.S. D5 87
Canora, Sk., Can. F4 75
Canosa [di Puglia], Italy D6 23
Canouan, i., St. Vin. V26 65
Canova, S.D., U.S. D8 118
Cañovanas, P.R. B4 65
Canso, N.S., Can. D8 71
Cantabrian Mountains, mts., Spain A3 22
Cantanhede, Port. B1 22
Cantário, stm., Braz. E2 59
Cantaura, Ven. B5 60
Canterbury, Austl. *F9 50
Canterbury, N.B., Can. D2 71
Canterbury, Eng., U.K. E7 10
Canterbury, Ct., U.S. C8 84
Canterbury, De., U.S. D3 85
Canterbury, N.H., U.S. D3 106
Canterbury Bight, N.Z. P13 51
Can Tho, Viet. G6 35
Canton (Guangzhou), China G7 31
Canton, Ct., U.S. B4 84
Canton, Ga., U.S. B2 87
Canton, Il., U.S. C3 90
Canton, In., U.S. G5 91
Canton, Ks., U.S. D6 93
Canton, Ky., U.S. D2 94
Canton, Me., U.S. D2 96
Canton, Ma., U.S. B5 98
Canton, Mi., U.S. *p15 99
Canton, Mn., U.S. G7 100
Canton, Ms., U.S. C3 101
Canton, Mo., U.S. A6 102
Canton, N.J., U.S. E2 107
Canton, N.Y., U.S. f9 109
Canton, N.C., U.S. f10 110
Canton, Oh., U.S. B4 112
Canton, Ok., U.S. A3 113
Canton, Pa., U.S. C8 115
Canton, S.D., U.S. D9 118
Canton, Tx., U.S. C5 120
Canton, Wi., U.S. C2 126
Canton Center, Ct., U.S. B4 84
Canton Lake, res., Ok., U.S. A3 113
Cantonment, Fl., U.S. u14 86
Cantril, Ia., U.S. D5 92
Cantù, Italy B2 23
Cantuar, Sk., Can. G1 75
Cantwell, Ak., U.S. C10 79
Cañuelas, Arg. B5 54
Canumã, stm., Braz. C3 59
Canutama, Braz. D2 59
Canute, Ok., U.S. B2 113
Canutillo, Tx., U.S. o11 120
Canwood, Sk., Can. D2 75
Cany-Barville, Fr. E8 12
Canyon, Tx., U.S. B2 120
Canyon, co., Id., U.S. F2 89
Canyoncito, N.M., U.S. h9 108
Canyon City, Or., U.S. C8 114
Canyon Creek, Ab., Can. B3 68
Canyon Creek, Mt., U.S. D4 103
Canyon de Chelly National Monument, Az., U.S. A6 80
Canyon Ferry Lake, res., Mt., U.S. D5 103
Canyon Lake, Tx., U.S. E3 120
Canyon Lake, res., Tx., U.S. E3 120
Canyonlands National Park, Ut., U.S. E6 121
Canyonville, Or., U.S. E3 114
Cao Bang, Viet. A7 35
Caonao, stm., Cuba D4 64
Caorle, Italy D8 20
Capac, Mi., U.S. F8 99
Çapakçur see Bingöl, Tur. C13 40
Cap-à-l'Aigle, P.Q., Can. B7 74
Capanaparo, stm., S.A. B4 60
Capanema, Braz. B1 57
Capão Bonito, Braz. C3 56
Capão Doce, Morro do, mtn., Braz. D2 56
Caparica, Port. f9 22
Caparo, stm., Ven. B3 60
Capasin, Sk., Can. D2 75
Capatárida, Ven. A3 60
Cap-aux-Meules, P.Q., Can. B8 71
Cap aux Meules, Île du, i., P.Q., Can. B8 71
Capbreton, Fr. F3 16
Cap-Chat, P.Q., Can. G19 66
Cap-de-la-Madeleine, P.Q., Can. C5 74
Capdenac-Gare, Fr. E5 16
Cape, prov., S. Afr. D3 49
Cape Barren, i., Austl. o15 50
Cape Breton, co., N.S., Can. D9 71
Cape Breton Highlands National Park, N.S., Can. C9 71
Cape Breton Island, i., N.S., Can. C9 71
Cape Broyle, Nf., Can. E5 72
Cape Canaveral, Fl., U.S. D6 86
Cape Charles, Nf., Can. B4 72
Cape Charles, Va., U.S. C6 123
Cape Coast, Ghana E4 45
Cape Cod Bay, b., Ma., U.S. C7 98
Cape Cod Canal, Ma., U.S. C6 98
Cape Cod National Seashore, Ma., U.S. C7 98
Cape Coral, Fl., U.S. F5 86
Cape Dorset, N.T., Can. D17 66
Cape Elizabeth, Me., U.S. E2 96
Cape Fair, Mo., U.S. E4 102
Cape Fear, stm., N.C., U.S. C4 110
Cape Girardeau, Mo., U.S. D8 102
Cape Girardeau, co., Mo., U.S. D8 102
Cape Hatteras National Seashore, N.C., U.S. B7 110
Cape Horn Mountain, mtn., Id., U.S. E3 89
Cape Island, i., S.C., U.S. E9 117
Cape la Hune, Nf., Can. E3 72
Capelinha, Braz. B4 56
Capelongo, Ang. E2 48
Cape Lookout National Seashore, N.C., U.S. C6 110
Capels, W.V., U.S. D3 125
Cape May, N.J., U.S. F3 107
Cape May, co., N.J., U.S. E3 107
Cape May Court House, N.J., U.S. E3 107
Cape May Point, N.J., U.S. F3 107
Cape Neddick, Me., U.S. E2 96
Cape Pole, Ak., U.S. n23 79
Cape Porpoise, Me., U.S. E2 96
Cape Ray, Nf., Can. E2 72
Capers Inlet, b., S.C., U.S. k12 117
Capers Island, i., S.C., U.S. G6 117
Capers Island, i., S.C., U.S. F8 117
Cape Sable Island, i., N.S., Can. F4 71
Capesterre, Guad. H14 64
Cape Tormentine, N.B., Can. C6 71
Cape Town (Kaapstad), S. Afr. D2 49
Cape Verde, ctry., Afr. E3 42
Capeville, Va., U.S. h16 123
Cape Vincent, N.Y., U.S. A4 109
Cape York Peninsula, pen., Austl. B7 50
Cap-Haïtien, Haiti E7 64
Capibaribe, stm., Braz. k5 57
Capilla del Monte, Arg. A4 54
Capilla del Señor, Arg. g7 54
Capim, stm., Braz. B1 57
Capinota, Bol. C2 55
Capitan, N.M., U.S. D4 108
Capitán Bado, Para. D4 55
Capitan Mountains, mts., N.M., U.S. D4 108
Capitan Peak, mtn., N.M., U.S. D4 108
Capitol, Mt., U.S. E12 103
Capitola, Ca., U.S. *D3 82
Capitola, Fl., U.S. B2 86
Capitol Heights, Ia., U.S. e8 92
Capitol Heights, Md., U.S. C4 97
Capitol Peak, mtn., Nv., U.S. B4 105
Capitol Reef National Park, Ut., U.S. E4 121
Capivari, Braz. m8 56
Capleville, Tn., U.S. e9 119
Cap Mountain, mtn., N.T., Can. D8 66
Capon Bridge, W.V., U.S. B6 125
Capon Springs, W.V., U.S. B6 125
Capote Knob, mtn., Tx., U.S. k8 120
Cap-Pelé, N.B., Can. C5 71
Cappoquin, Ire. E4 11
Capraia, i., Italy C2 23
Caprara, Point, c., Italy D2 23
Capreol, On., Can. p19 73
Caprera, i., Italy D2 23
Capri, i., Italy D5 23
Capricorn Channel, strt., Austl. D9 50
Capricorn Group, is., Austl. A8 51
Caprock, N.M., U.S. D6 108
Capron, Il., U.S. A5 90
Capron, Ok., U.S. A3 113
Capron, Va., U.S. D5 123
Cap-Rouge, P.Q., Can. n17 74
Cap-Saint-Ignace, P.Q., Can. B7 74
Cap-Santé, P.Q., Can. C6 74
Capshaw, Al., U.S. A3 78
Captain Cook, Hi., U.S. D6 88
Captiva, Fl., U.S. F4 86
Captiva Island, i., Fl., U.S. F4 86
Capua, Italy D5 23
Capulin, N.M., U.S. A6 108
Capulin Mountain National Monument, N.M., U.S. A6 108
Caputa, S.D., U.S. D3 118
Caquetá, dept., Col. C3 60
Caquetá (Japurá), stm., S.A. D3 60
Car, Slieve, mtn., Ire. C2 11
Carabaña, Spain p18 22
Carabanchel Bajo, Spain p17 22
Carabinani, stm., Braz. D5 60
Carabobo, state, Ven. A4 60
Caracal, Rom. C7 24
Caracaraí, Braz. B2 59
Caracas, Ven. A4 60
Caraguatay, Para. E4 55
Caraí, Braz. B4 56
Carajás, Braz. D5 59
Carajás, Serra dos, mts., Braz. C4 59
Carangola, Braz. C4 56
Caransebeş, Rom. C6 24
Carapari, Bol. D3 55
Carapeguá, Para. E4 55
Carapó, Braz. C1 56
Caraquet, N.B., Can. B5 71
Caratasca, Laguna de, b., Hond. D8 63
Caratinga, Braz. B4 56
Caratunk, Me., U.S. C3 96
Carauari, Braz. B4 58
Caraúbas, Braz. h5 57
Caraúbas, Braz. C3 57
Caravaca, Spain C5 22
Caravelas, Braz. E3 57
Caraveli, Peru E3 58
Caraway, Ar., U.S. B5 81
Caraz, Peru C2 58
Carazinho, Braz. D2 56
Carballino, Spain A1 22
Carballo, Spain A1 22
Carberry, Mb., Can. E2 70
Carbet, Pitons du, mts., Mart. S10 65
Carbó, Mex. B2 63
Carbon, Ab., Can. D4 68
Carbon, In., U.S. E3 91
Carbon, Ia., U.S. C3 92
Carbon, W.V., U.S. m13 125
Carbon, co., Mt., U.S. E7 103
Carbon, co., Pa., U.S. E10 115
Carbon, co., Ut., U.S. D5 121
Carbon, co., Wy., U.S. E5 127
Carbonado, Wa., U.S. B3 124
Carbonara, Cape, c., Italy E2 23
Carbondale, Ab., Can. C4 68
Carbondale, Co., U.S. B3 83
Carbondale, Il., U.S. F4 90
Carbondale, Ks., U.S. D8 93
Carbondale, Oh., U.S. C3 112
Carbondale, Pa., U.S. C10 115
Carbonear, Nf., Can. E5 72
Carbon Hill, Al., U.S. B2 78
Carbon Hill, Il., U.S. B5 90

Name	Map Ref	Page
Carbonia, Italy	E2	23
Carbonne, Fr.	F4	16
Carbonville, Ut., U.S.	D5	121
Carbury, N.D., U.S.	A5	111
Carcagente, Spain	C5	22
Carcans, Étang de b., Fr.	E3	16
Carcassonne, Fr.	F5	16
Carchi, prov., Ec.	A2	58
Carcross, Yk., Can.	D6	66
Çardak, Tur.	D7	25
Cardale, Mb., Can.	D1	70
Cárdenas, Cuba	C3	64
Cárdenas, Mex.	m14	63
Cárdenas, Mex.	D6	63
Çardi, Tur.	C7	25
Cardiel, Lago, l., Arg.	D2	54
Cardiff, Wales, U.K.	E5	10
Cardiff, Al., U.S.	i7	78
Cardiff, Md., U.S.	A5	97
Cardiff, N.J., U.S.	E3	107
Cardiff-By-The-Sea, Ca., U.S.	*F5	82
Cardigan, P.E., Can.	C7	71
Cardigan, Wales, U.K.	D4	10
Cardigan, Mount, mtn., N.H., U.S.	C3	106
Cardigan Bay, b., P.E., Can.	C7	71
Cardigan Bay, b., Wales, U.K.	D4	10
Cardinal, Mb., Can.	E2	70
Cardinal, On., Can.	C9	73
Cardinal Lake, l., Ab., Can.	A2	68
Cardington, Oh., U.S.	B3	112
Cardona, Ur.	E1	56
Cardross, Sk., Can.	H3	75
Cardston, Ab., Can.	E4	68
Cardville, Me., U.S.	C4	96
Cardwell, Mo., U.S.	E7	102
Cardwell, Mt., U.S.	E5	103
Cardwell Mountain, mtn., Tn., U.S.	D8	119
Carega, mtn., Italy	D7	20
Carei, Rom.	B6	24
Carencro, La., U.S.	D3	95
Careno, Ven.	A4	60
Carentan, Fr.	C3	16
Caretta, W.V., U.S.	D3	125
Carey, Id., U.S.	F5	89
Carey, Oh., U.S.	B2	112
Carey, Tx., U.S.	B2	120
Carey, Lake, l., Austl.	E3	50
Careysburg, Lib.	E2	45
Careywood, Id., U.S.	A2	89
Carhaix, Fr.	C2	16
Carhuás, Peru	C2	58
Carhué, Arg.	B4	54
Cariamanga, Ec.	B2	58
Cariati, Italy	E6	23
Caribana, Punta, c., Col.	B2	60
Caribbean Sea	B3	53
Cariboo Mountains, mts., B.C., Can.	C7	69
Caribou, Me., U.S.	B5	96
Caribou, co., Id., U.S.	G7	89
Caribou Island, i., N.S., Can.	D7	71
Caribou Lake, l., Me., U.S.	C3	96
Caribou Mountain, mtn., Id., U.S.	F7	89
Caribou Mountain, mtn., Me., U.S.	C2	96
Caribou Mountains, mts., Ab., Can.	f7	68
Caribou Range, mts., Id., U.S.	F7	89
Carichic, Mex.	B3	63
Carievale, Sk., Can.	H5	75
Carignan, Fr.	E5	17
Carinhanha, Braz.	A4	56
Carini, Italy	E4	23
Carinish, Scot., U.K.	C1	13
Carinthia, hist reg., Aus.	E6	18
Caripe, Ven.	A5	60
Caripito, Ven.	A5	60
Carius, Braz.	C3	57
Carl Blackwell, Lake, res., Ok., U.S.	A4	113
Carle Place, N.Y., U.S.	*n15	109
Carleton, Mi., U.S.	F7	99
Carleton, Ne., U.S.	D8	104
Carleton, co., N.B., Can.	C2	71
Carleton, Mount, mtn., N.B., Can.	B3	71
Carleton Place, On., Can.	B8	73
Carletonville, S. Afr.	C4	49
Carlile, Wy., U.S.	B8	127
Carlin, Nv., U.S.	C5	105
Carlingford, Ire.	C5	11
Carlingford Lough, b., Eur.	C5	11
Carlinville, Il., U.S.	D4	90
Carlisle, Eng., U.K.	C5	10
Carlisle, Ar., U.S.	C4	81
Carlisle, Ia., U.S.	G3	91
Carlisle, Ia., U.S.	C4	92
Carlisle, Ky., U.S.	B5	94
Carlisle, Ma., U.S.	f10	98
Carlisle, Ms., U.S.	C3	101
Carlisle, Oh., U.S.	C1	112
Carlisle, Pa., U.S.	F7	115
Carlisle, S.C., U.S.	B5	117
Carlisle, co., Ky., U.S.	f8	94
Carlit, Pic, mtn., Fr.	F4	16
Carl Junction, Mo., U.S.	D3	102
Carlock, Il., U.S.	C4	90
Carloforte, Italy	E2	23
Carlos, Md., U.S.	k13	97
Carlos, Mn., U.S.	E3	100
Carlos Casares, Arg.	B4	54
Carlos Chagas, Braz.	B4	56
Carlos City, In., U.S.	D7	91
Carlos Tejedor, Arg.	B4	54
Carlotta, Ca., U.S.	B1	82
Carlow, Ire.	D3	10
Carlow, co., Ire.	E5	11
Carloway, Scot., U.K.	B2	13
Carlsbad, Al., U.S.	C2	78
Carlsbad, Ca., U.S.	F5	82
Carlsbad, N.M., U.S.	E5	108
Carlsbad, Tx., U.S.	D2	120
Carlsbad Caverns National Park, N.M., U.S.	E5	108
Carlsbad Springs, On., Can.	h13	73
Carlsborg, Wa., U.S.	A2	124
Carlstadt, N.J., U.S.	h8	107
Carlton, Sk., Can.	E2	75
Carlton, Eng., U.K.	B6	12
Carlton, Al., U.S.	D2	78
Carlton, Ga., U.S.	B3	87
Carlton, Ks., U.S.	D6	93
Carlton, Mn., U.S.	D6	100
Carlton, Or., U.S.	B3	114
Carlton, Tx., U.S.	D3	120
Carlton, co., Mn., U.S.	D6	100
Carluke, Scot., U.K.	E5	13
Carlyle, Sk., Can.	H4	75
Carlyle, Il., U.S.	E4	90
Carlyle, Mt., U.S.	D12	103
Carlyle Lake, res., Il., U.S.	E4	90
Carmacks, Yk., Can.	D5	66
Carmagnola, Italy	B1	23
Carman, Mb., Can.	E2	70
Carmangay, Ab., Can.	D4	68
Carmanville, Nf., Can.	D4	72
Carmarthen, Wales, U.K.	E4	10
Carmarthen Bay, b., Wales, U.K.	E4	10
Carmaux, Fr.	E5	16
Carmel, Sk., Can.	E3	75
Carmel, Ca., U.S.	D3	82
Carmel, In., U.S.	E5	91
Carmel, Me., U.S.	D3	96
Carmel, N.J., U.S.	E2	107
Carmel, N.Y., U.S.	D7	109
Carmel, Mount, mtn., Isr.	B7	41
Carmel Head, c., Wales, U.K.	A3	12
Carmelo, Ur.	E1	56
Carmen, Az., U.S.	F4	80
Carmen, Id., U.S.	D5	89
Carmen, Ok., U.S.	A3	113
Carmen, Isla, i., Mex.	B2	63
Carmen, Río del, stm., Chile	E1	55
Carmen Alto, Chile	D2	55
Carmen de Areco, Arg.	A5	54
Carmen [del Paraná], Para.	E4	55
Carmen de Patagones, Arg.	C4	54
Carmer Hill, hill, Pa., U.S.	C6	115
Carmi, Il., U.S.	E5	90
Carmi, Lake, l., Vt., U.S.	B3	122
Carmichael, Bah.	m17	64
Carmichael, Sk., Can.	G1	75
Carmichael, Ca., U.S.	*C3	82
Carmichaels, Pa., U.S.	G2	115
Carmine, Tx., U.S.	D4	120
Carmona, Spain	D3	22
Carnarvon, Austl.	D1	50
Carnarvon, S. Afr.	D3	49
Carnarvon, Ia., U.S.	B2	92
Carnation, Wa., U.S.	B4	124
Carnaxide, Port.	f9	22
Carndonagh, Ire.	B4	11
Carnegie, Ga., U.S.	E2	87
Carnegie, Ok., U.S.	B3	113
Carnegie, Pa., U.S.	F1	115
Carnegie, Lake, l., Austl.	E3	50
Carnes, Al., U.S.	E4	101
Carnesville, Ga., U.S.	B3	87
Carnew, Ire.	E5	11
Carney, Mi., U.S.	C3	99
Carneys Point, N.J., U.S.	D2	107
Carnforth, Eng., U.K.	B5	12
Carnlough, N. Ire., U.K.	C6	11
Carnot, Cen. Afr. Rep.	D3	46
Carnot, Cape, c., Austl.	*F1	115
Carnoustie, Scot., U.K.	D6	13
Carnsore Point, c., Ire.	D3	10
Carnuel, N.M., U.S.	B3	108
Caro, Mi., U.S.	E7	99
Carol City, Fl., U.S.	s13	86
Caroleen, N.C., U.S.	B1	110
Carolina, Braz.	C1	57
Carolina, P.R.	*B4	65
Carolina, S. Afr.	C5	49
Carolina, R.I., U.S.	F2	116
Carolina, W.V., U.S.	k10	125
Carolina Beach, N.C., U.S.	C5	110
Carolinas, Puntan, c., N. Mar. Is.	E7	52
Caroline, Ab., Can.	C3	68
Caroline, Wi., U.S.	D5	126
Caroline, co., Md., U.S.	C6	97
Caroline, co., Va., U.S.	C5	123
Caroline, atoll, Kir.	G13	6
Caroline Islands, is., T.T.P.I.	F8	6
Caron, Sk., Can.	G3	75
Carona, Ks., U.S.	E9	93
Caroni, stm., Trin.	N23	65
Caroni, stm., Ven.	B5	60
Carora, Ven.	A3	60
Carouge, Switz.	E3	18
Carp, On., Can.	B8	73
Carpathian Mountains, mts., Eur.	F13	8
Carpentaria, Gulf of b., Austl.	A4	50
Carpenter, Ia., U.S.	A4	92
Carpenter, S.D., U.S.	C8	118
Carpenter, Wy., U.S.	E8	127
Carpenter Dam, Ar., U.S.	g7	81
Carpentersville, Il., U.S.	A5	90
Carpentersville, N.J., U.S.	B2	107
Carpentras, Fr.	E6	16
Carpi, Italy	B3	23
Carpinteria, Ca., U.S.	E4	82
Carpio, N.D., U.S.	A4	111
Carp Lake, l., B.C., Can.	A6	83
Carr, Co., U.S.	A6	83
Carrabassett Valley, Me., U.S.	D2	96
Carrabelle, Fl., U.S.	C2	86
Carradale, Scot., U.K.	E3	13
Carragana, Sk., Can.	E4	75
Carranntuohill, mtn., Ire.	D2	10
Carranza, Cabo, c., Chile	B2	54
Carrara, Italy	B3	23
Carrboro, N.C., U.S.	B3	110
Carriacou, i., Gren.	W26	65
Carrickfergus, N. Ire., U.K.	C4	10
Carrickmacross, Ire.	D5	11
Carrick-on-Shannon, Ire.	D3	11
Carrick[-on-Suir], Ire.	D3	10
Carrie, Mount, mtn., Wa., U.S.	B2	124
Carrier, P.Q., Can.	o17	74
Carrier, Ok., U.S.	A3	113
Carriere, Ms., U.S.	E4	101
Carrier Mills, Il., U.S.	F5	90
Carrigaholt, Ire.	D2	11
Carrigaline, Ire.	F3	11
Carrigan, Mount, mtn., N.H., U.S.	B4	106
Carrigan Head, c., Ire.	C3	11
Carrington, N.D., U.S.	B6	111
Carrington Island, i., Ut., U.S.	C3	121
Carrión, stm., Spain	A3	22
Carrión de los Condes, Spain	A3	22
Carrizal Bajo, Chile	E1	55
Carrizo Creek, stm., U.S.	A1	120
Carrizo Mountain, mtn., N.M., U.S.	A6	80
Carrizo Mountains, mts., U.S.	A6	80
Carrizo Springs, Tx., U.S.	E3	120
Carrizo Wash, val., U.S.	C6	80
Carrizozo, N.M., U.S.	D4	108
Carr Mountain, mtn., N.H., U.S.	C3	106
Carroll, Mb., Can.	E1	70
Carroll, Ia., U.S.	B3	92
Carroll, Me., U.S.	C4	96
Carroll, Ne., U.S.	B8	104
Carroll, Oh., U.S.	C3	112
Carroll, co., Ar., U.S.	A2	81
Carroll, co., Ga., U.S.	C1	87
Carroll, co., Il., U.S.	A4	90
Carroll, co., In., U.S.	C4	91
Carroll, co., Ia., U.S.	B3	92
Carroll, co., Ky., U.S.	B4	94
Carroll, co., Md., U.S.	A3	97
Carroll, co., Ms., U.S.	B4	101
Carroll, co., Mo., U.S.	B4	102
Carroll, co., N.H., U.S.	C4	106
Carroll, co., Oh., U.S.	B4	112
Carroll, co., Tn., U.S.	B3	119
Carroll, co., Va., U.S.	D2	123
Carroll Lake, l., Can.	D4	70
Carrolls, Wa., U.S.	C3	124
Carrollton, Al., U.S.	B1	78
Carrollton, Ga., U.S.	C1	87
Carrollton, Il., U.S.	D3	90
Carrollton, Ky., U.S.	B4	94
Carrollton, Mi., U.S.	E7	99
Carrollton, Ms., U.S.	B4	101
Carrollton, Mo., U.S.	B4	102
Carrollton, Oh., U.S.	B4	112
Carrollton, Tx., U.S.	*n10	120
Carrolltown, Pa., U.S.	E4	115
Carron, stm., Scot., U.K.	C5	13
Carron, Loch, b., Scot., U.K.	B4	10
Carrot, stm., Can.	D4	75
Carrot River, Sk., Can.	D4	75
Carrowmore, Lough, l., Ire.	C2	11
Carrsville, Ky., U.S.	e9	94
Carruthers, Sk., Can.	E1	75
Carrville, Al., U.S.	C4	78
Carry Falls Reservoir, res., N.Y., U.S.	f10	109
Carrying Place, On., Can.	C7	73
Carşamba, Tur.	B11	40
Carseland, Ab., Can.	D4	68
Carson, Ca., U.S.	*E4	82
Carson, Ia., U.S.	C2	92
Carson, Me., U.S.	B4	96
Carson, Ms., U.S.	D4	101
Carson, N.M., U.S.	A4	108
Carson, N.D., U.S.	C4	111
Carson, Va., U.S.	C5	123
Carson, Wa., U.S.	D4	124
Carson, co., Tx., U.S.	B2	120
Carson, stm., Nv., U.S.	D2	105
Carson City, Mi., U.S.	E6	99
Carson City, Nv., U.S.	D2	105
Carson Lake, l., Nv., U.S.	D3	105
Carson Sink, l., Nv., U.S.	D3	105
Carson Spring, Tn., U.S.	D10	119
Carsonville, Mi., U.S.	E8	99
Carstairs, Ab., Can.	D3	68
Carswell Air Force Base, mil., Tx., U.S.	n9	120
Cartagena, Chile	A2	54
Cartagena, Col.	A2	60
Cartagena, Spain	D5	22
Cartago, Col.	C2	60
Cartago, C.R.	F8	63
Carta Valley, Tx., U.S.	E2	120
Cartaxo, Port.	C1	22
Cartaya, Spain	D2	22
Carter, Ky., U.S.	B6	94
Carter, Mt., U.S.	C6	103
Carter, Ok., U.S.	B2	113
Carter, S.D., U.S.	D5	118
Carter, Tn., U.S.	C11	119
Carter, Wi., U.S.	C5	126
Carter, Wy., U.S.	E3	127
Carter, co., Ky., U.S.	B6	94
Carter, co., Mo., U.S.	E7	102
Carter, co., Mt., U.S.	E12	103
Carter, co., Ok., U.S.	C4	113
Carter, co., Tn., U.S.	C11	119
Carter Dome, mtn., N.H., U.S.	B4	106
Carteret, N.J., U.S.	B4	107
Carteret, co., N.C., U.S.	C6	110
Carter Lake, Ia., U.S.	C2	92
Carter Mountain, mtn., Wy., U.S.	B3	127
Carters, Ga., U.S.	B2	87
Cartersburg, In., U.S.	E5	91
Carters Lake, res., Ga., U.S.	B2	87
Cartersville, Ga., U.S.	B2	87
Cartersville, S.C., U.S.	C7	117
Cartersville, Va., U.S.	C4	123
Carterville, Il., U.S.	F4	90
Carterville, Mo., U.S.	D3	102
Carthage, Ar., U.S.	C3	81
Carthage, Il., U.S.	C2	90
Carthage, In., U.S.	E6	91
Carthage, Ms., U.S.	C4	101
Carthage, Mo., U.S.	D3	102
Carthage, N.Y., U.S.	B5	109
Carthage, N.C., U.S.	B3	110
Carthage, S.D., U.S.	C8	118
Carthage, Tn., U.S.	C5	119
Carthage, Tx., U.S.	C5	120
Carthage, hist., Tun.	B7	44
Cartier, i., Austl.	B3	50
Cartwright, Mb., Can.	E2	70
Cartwright, Nf., Can.	B3	72
Cartwright, N.D., U.S.	B2	111
Cartwright, Ok., U.S.	D5	113
Caruaru, Braz.	C3	57
Carúpano, Ven.	A5	60
Caruthers, Ca., U.S.	D4	82
Caruthersville, Mo., U.S.	E8	102
Carver, Ma., U.S.	C6	98
Carver, Mn., U.S.	F5	100
Carver, co., Mn., U.S.	F5	100
Carver Ranch Estates, Fl., U.S.	*r13	86
Carville, La., U.S.	h9	95
Carvin, Fr.	D2	17
Cary, Ga., U.S.	B3	87
Cary, Il., U.S.	A5	90
Cary, Ms., U.S.	C3	101
Cary, N.C., U.S.	B4	110
Caryville, Fl., U.S.	u16	86
Caryville, Tn., U.S.	C9	119
Casa, Ar., U.S.	B2	81
Casablanca, Mor.	C3	44
Casa Branca, Braz.	C3	56
Casa Grande, Az., U.S.	E4	80
Casa Grande National Monument, Az., U.S.	E4	80
Casale Monferrato, Italy	B2	23
Casalmaggiore, Italy	B3	23
Casanare, dept., Col.	B3	60
Casanare, stm., Col.	B3	60
Casanova, Va., U.S.	B5	123
Casa Piedra, Tx., U.S.	p12	120
Casar, N.C., U.S.	B1	110
Casarano, Italy	D7	23
Casas Adobes, Az., U.S.	*E5	80
Casca, Braz.	B3	56
Cascade, B.C., Can.	E8	69
Cascade, Co., U.S.	C6	83
Cascade, Id., U.S.	E2	89
Cascade, Ia., U.S.	B6	92
Cascade, Mo., U.S.	D7	102
Cascade, Mt., U.S.	C5	103
Cascade, N.H., U.S.	B4	106
Cascade, Va., U.S.	D3	123
Cascade, W.V., U.S.	B5	125
Cascade, Wi., U.S.	E5	126
Cascade, co., Mt., U.S.	C5	103
Cascade Locks, Or., U.S.	B5	114
Cascade Point, c., N.Z.	O12	51
Cascade Range, mts., N.A.	B3	76
Cascade Reservoir, res., Id., U.S.	E3	89
Cascade Summit, Or., U.S.	D4	114
Cascade Tunnel, Wa., U.S.	B4	124
Cascadia, Or., U.S.	C4	114
Cascais, Port.	C1	22
Cascais Bay, b., Port.	f9	22
Cascajal, stm., Pan.	h11	62
Cascavel, Braz.	C2	56
Cascavel, Braz.	B3	57
Cascilla, Ms., U.S.	B3	101
Casco, Me., U.S.	D2	96
Casco, Wi., U.S.	D6	126
Casco Bay, b., Me., U.S.	E3	96
Caselton, Nv., U.S.	F7	105
Caserta, Italy	D5	23
Caseville, Mi., U.S.	E7	99
Casey, Il., U.S.	D6	90
Casey, Ia., U.S.	C3	92
Casey, co., Ky., U.S.	C5	94
Casey, sci., Ant.	C24	7
Casey, Mount, mtn., Id., U.S.	A2	89
Casey Bay, b., Ant.	C17	7
Casey Key, i., Fl., U.S.	E4	86
Caseyr (Cape Guardafui), c., Som.	C7	47
Cash, Ar., U.S.	B5	81
Cashel, Ire.	C3	10
Cashel, Ire.	D2	11
Cashiers, N.C., U.S.	f9	110
Cashion, Az., U.S.	m8	80
Cashion, Ok., U.S.	B4	113
Cashmere, Wa., U.S.	B5	124
Cashton, Wi., U.S.	E3	126
Cashtown, Pa., U.S.	G7	115
Casiguran, Phil.	n14	34
Casiguran Sound, strt., Phil.	n13	34
Casilda, Arg.	A4	54
Casilda, Cuba	D4	64
Casino, Austl.	D9	51
Casiquiare, stm., Ven.	C4	60
Casma, Peru	C2	58
Casmalia, Ca., U.S.	E3	82
Caspar, Ca., U.S.	C2	82
Caspe, Spain	B5	22
Casper, Wy., U.S.	D6	127
Caspian, Mi., U.S.	B2	99
Caspiana, La., U.S.	B2	95
Caspian Depression, pl., Sov. Un.	E8	29
Caspian Lake, l., Vt., U.S.	B4	122
Caspian Sea	E8	29
Cass, In., U.S.	F3	91
Cass, W.V., U.S.	C5	125
Cass, co., Il., U.S.	D3	90
Cass, co., In., U.S.	C5	91
Cass, co., Ia., U.S.	C3	92
Cass, co., Mi., U.S.	G4	99
Cass, co., Mn., U.S.	D4	100
Cass, co., Mo., U.S.	C3	102
Cass, co., Ne., U.S.	D9	104
Cass, co., N.D., U.S.	C8	111
Cass, co., Tx., U.S.	C5	120
Cass, stm., Mi., U.S.	E7	99
Cassà [de la Selva], Spain	B7	22
Cassai (Kasai), stm., Afr.	D3	48
Cass City, Mi., U.S.	E7	99
Cassel, Fr.	D2	17
Cassel see Kassel, F.R.Ger.	C4	18
Casselberry, Fl., U.S.	D5	86
Casselman, On., Can.	B9	73
Casselman, stm., Pa., U.S.	G3	115
Casselton, N.D., U.S.	C8	111
Cassia, co., Id., U.S.	G5	89
Cassiar, B.C., Can.	m17	69
Cassiar Mountains, mts., Can.	E6	66
Cassidy, B.C., Can.	f12	69
Cassilândia, Braz.	B2	56
Cassinga, Ang.	D2	48
Cassino, Italy	D4	23
Cass Lake, Mn., U.S.	C4	100
Cass Lake, l., Mn., U.S.	C4	100
Cassoday, Ks., U.S.	D7	93
Cassopolis, Mi., U.S.	G4	99
Casstown, Oh., U.S.	B1	112
Cassville, Ga., U.S.	B2	87
Cassville, Mo., U.S.	E4	102
Cassville, Wi., U.S.	F3	126
Castalia, Ia., U.S.	A6	92
Castalia, N.C., U.S.	A4	110
Castalia, Oh., U.S.	A3	112
Castalian Springs, Tn., U.S.	A5	119
Castana, Ia., U.S.	B1	92
Castanea, Pa., U.S.	D7	115
Castanheira de Pêra, Port.	C1	22
Castaños, Mex.	B4	63
Castel di Guido, Italy	h8	23
Castelfranco Emilia, Italy	E7	20
Castelfranco Veneto, Italy	D7	20
Castel Gandolfo, Italy	h9	23
Castel Giuliano, Italy	g8	23
Casteljaloux, Fr.	E4	16
Castella, Ca., U.S.	B2	82
Castellamonte, Italy	B2	23
Castelli, Arg.	B5	54
Castellón de la Plana, Spain	C5	22
Castel Madama, Italy	h9	23
Castelnaudary, Fr.	F4	16
Castelo, Braz.	C4	56
Castelo Branco, Port.	C2	22
Castelo de Vide, Port.	C2	22
Castel San Pietro dell'Emilia, Italy	E7	20
Castelvetrano, Italy	F4	23
Casterton, Austl.	H3	51
Castile, N.Y., U.S.	C2	109
Castillo, Pampa del, Arg.	D3	54
Castillo de San Marcos National Monument, Fl., U.S.	n9	86
Castillos, Ur.	C6	56
Castine, Me., U.S.	D4	96
Castione [della Presolana], Italy	E9	21
Castle Air Force Base, mil., Ca., U.S.	D3	82
Castlebar, Ire.	D2	10
Castlebay, Scot., U.K.	D1	13
Castlebellingham, Ire.	D5	11
Castleberry, Al., U.S.	D2	78
Castleblayney, Ire.	C5	11
Castlecomer, Ire.	E4	11
Castle Dale, Ut., U.S.	D4	121
Castlederg, N. Ire., U.K.	C4	11
Castle Dome Mountains, mts., Az., U.S.	D1	80
Castle Dome Peak, mtn., Az., U.S.	D1	80
Castle Douglas, Scot., U.K.	C5	10
Castleford, Id., U.S.	G4	89
Castleford, Eng., U.K.	H12	12
Castlegar, B.C., Can.	E9	69
Castlegregory, Ire.	E1	11
Castle Harbour, b., Ber.	o20	64
Castle Hayne, N.C., U.S.	C5	110
Castle Hills, De., U.S.	i7	85
Castle Hot Springs, Az., U.S.	D3	80
Castleisland, Ire.	E2	11
Castlemaine, Austl.	H5	51
Castlemaine, Ire.	E2	11
Castle Mountain, mtn., Yk., Can.	D5	66
Castle Mountains, mts., Mt., U.S.	D6	103
Castle Park, Ca., U.S.	*o15	82
Castle Peak, mtn., Co., U.S.	B4	83
Castle Peak, mtn., Id., U.S.	E4	89
Castle Peak, mtn., Mo., U.S.	f13	102
Castlepollard, Ire.	D4	11
Castlerea, Ire.	D3	10
Castlereagh, N. Ire., U.K.	*C6	11
Castlereagh, stm., Austl.	E7	51
Castle Rock, Co., U.S.	B6	83
Castle Rock, Mn., U.S.	F5	100
Castle Rock, Wa., U.S.	C3	124
Castle Rock, mtn., Or., U.S.	C8	114
Castle Rock, mtn., Va., U.S.	C4	123
Castle Rock Butte, mtn., S.D., U.S.	B2	118
Castle Rock Lake, res., Wi., U.S.	E4	126
Castle Shannon, Pa., U.S.	*k13	115
Castleton, On., Can.	C7	73
Castleton, Il., U.S.	B4	90
Castleton, Ks., U.S.	g11	93
Castleton, Vt., U.S.	D2	122
Castleton on Hudson, N.Y., U.S.	C7	109
Castletown, I. of Man	F4	13
Castletownroche, Ire.	E3	11
Castlewellan, N. Ire., U.K.	C6	11
Castlewood, S.D., U.S.	C8	118
Castlewood, Va., U.S.	f9	123
Castor, Ab., Can.	C5	68
Castor, La., U.S.	B2	95
Castor, stm., Mo., U.S.	D7	102
Castor Creek, stm., La., U.S.	B3	95
Castorland, N.Y., U.S.	B5	109
Castres, Fr.	F5	16
Castries, St. Luc.	J14	64
Castro, Braz.	C3	56
Castro, Chile	C2	54
Castro, co., Tx., U.S.	B1	120
Castro Alves, Braz.	D3	57
Castro Marim, Port.	D2	22
Castro [del Río], Spain	D3	22
Castro-Urdiales, Spain	A4	22
Castro Valley, Ca., U.S.	h8	82
Castro Verde, Port.	D1	22
Castrovillari, Italy	E6	23
Castroville, Ca., U.S.	D3	82
Castroville, Tx., U.S.	E3	120
Castrovirreyna, Peru	D2	58
Castuera, Spain	C3	22
Caswell, co., N.C., U.S.	A3	110
Catacamas, Hond.	E7	63
Catacaos, Peru	C1	58
Cataguases, Braz.	C4	56
Catahoula, co., La., U.S.	C3	95
Catahoula Lake, l., La., U.S.	C3	95
Catalão, Braz.	B5	56
Catalca, Tur.	B7	40
Catalina, Nf., Can.	D5	72
Catalina, Chile	A3	54
Catalina Foothills, Az., U.S.	*E5	80
Catalonia, hist reg., Spain	B6	22
Catamarca, Arg.	B3	54
Catamarca, prov., Arg.	E2	55
Catamayo, Ec.	A2	58
Catanduanes, i., Phil.	C6	34
Catanduva, Braz.	C3	56
Catania, Italy	F5	23
Catania, Gulf of, b., Italy	F5	23
Cataño, P.R.	B3	65
Catanzaro, Italy	E6	23
Cataouatche, Lake, l., La., U.S.	k11	95
Cataract, In., U.S.	F4	91
Cataract, Wi., U.S.	D3	126
Cataract Canyon, val., Ut., U.S.	E5	121
Catarina, Tx., U.S.	E3	120
Catarroja, Spain	E3	91
Catasauqua, Pa., U.S.	E11	115
Catastrophe, Cape, c., Austl.	F6	50
Catawba, Wi., U.S.	C3	126
Catawba, co., N.C., U.S.	B1	110
Catawba, stm., S.C., U.S.	B6	117
Catawba, South Fork, stm., N.C., U.S.	B1	110
Catawba Island, Oh., U.S.	A3	112
Catawissa, Pa., U.S.	E9	115
Catbalogan, Phil.	C6	34
Cat Ba, i., Viet.	D4	34
Cateechee, S.C., U.S.	B2	117
Catete, Ang.	C2	48
Cathance Lake, l., Me., U.S.	D5	96
Catharine, Ks., U.S.	C5	93
Cathay, N.D., U.S.	B6	111
Cathedral Bluffs, clf, Co., U.S.	B5	113
Cathedral Caverns, Al., U.S.	A3	78
Cathedral City, Ca., U.S.	F5	82
Cathedral Mountain, mtn., Tx., U.S.	o13	120
Cathedral of the Pines, N.H., U.S.	E3	106
Catherine, Al., U.S.	C2	78
Catherine, Lake, res., Ar., U.S.	C3	81
Cathlamet, Wa., U.S.	C2	124
Cat Island, i., Bah.	B6	64
Cat Island, i., Ma., U.S.	f12	98
Cat Island, i., Ms., U.S.	E4	101
Cat Island, i., S.C., U.S.	E9	117
Cativá, Pan.	k11	62
Catlettsburg, Ky., U.S.	B7	94
Catlin, Il., U.S.	C6	90
Catlin, In., U.S.	E3	91
Catnip Mountain, mtn., Nv., U.S.	B2	105
Cato, N.Y., U.S.	B4	109
Catoche, Cabo, c., Mex.	C7	63
Catoctin Mountain, mtn., U.S.	B2	97
Catonsville, Md., U.S.	B4	97
Catoosa, Ok., U.S.	A6	113
Catoosa, co., Ga., U.S.	B1	87
Catriló, Arg.	B4	54
Catrimani, Braz.	B2	59
Catrimani, stm., Braz.	B2	59
Catron, co., N.M., U.S.	D1	108
Catskill, N.Y., U.S.	C7	109
Catskill Mountains, mts., N.Y., U.S.	C6	109
Catt, Mount, mtn., B.C., Can.	B3	69
Cattaraugus, N.Y., U.S.	C2	109
Cattaraugus, co., N.Y., U.S.	C2	109
Cattaraugus Creek, stm., N.Y., U.S.	C2	109
Cattaraugus Indian Reservation, N.Y., U.S.	C2	109
Cattolica, Italy	C4	23
Catumbela, stm., Ang.	D1	48
Catwick, Îles, is., Viet.	f9	72
Caubvick, Mount, mtn., Can.	C2	60
Cauca, dept., Col.	B2	60
Cauca, stm., Col.	B2	60
Caucasia, Col.	B2	60
Caucasus Mountains, mts., Sov. Un.	E7	29
Cauchon Lake, l., Mb., Can.	B3	70
Caucomgomoc Lake, l., Me., U.S.	B3	96
Caudebec, Fr.	C4	16
Caudry, Fr.	B5	16
Caughnawaga, P.Q., Can.	D4	74
Caulfield, Austl.	*G8	50
Caúngula, Ang.	C2	48
Cauquenes, Chile	B2	54
Caura, stm., Ven.	B5	60
Causey, N.M., U.S.	D6	108
Caussade, Fr.	E4	16
Cauthron, Ar., U.S.	C1	81
Caution, Cape, c., B.C., Can.	D4	69
Cauto, stm., Cuba	D5	64
Cauvery, stm., India	F6	36
Cavaillon, Fr.	F6	16
Cavalcante, Braz.	A3	56
Cavalier, N.D., U.S.	A8	111
Cavalier, co., N.D., U.S.	A7	111
Cavalla, stm., Afr.	E3	45
Cavallo, stm., Italy	C8	20
Cavan, Ire.	C3	10
Cavan, co., Ire.	D4	11
Cavarzere, Italy	B4	23
Cave City, Ar., U.S.	B4	81
Cave City, Ky., U.S.	C4	94
Cave Creek, Az., U.S.	D4	80
Cave In Rock, Il., U.S.	F5	90
Cave Junction, Or., U.S.	E3	114
Cavell, Sk., Can.	E1	75
Cavendish, Ab., Can.	D5	68
Cavendish, Id., U.S.	C2	89
Cavendish, Vt., U.S.	E3	122
Cave Point, c., Wi., U.S.	D6	126
Cave Run Lake, res., Ky., U.S.	B6	94
Cave Spring, Ga., U.S.	B1	87
Cave Spring, Va., U.S.	C2	123
Cave Springs, Ar., U.S.	A1	81
Cavetown, Md., U.S.	A2	97
Caviana, Ilha, i., Braz.	B4	59
Cavite, Phil.	o13	34
Cavour, Wi., U.S.	C5	126
Cawdor, Scot., U.K.	D5	13
Cawker City, Ks., U.S.	C5	93
Cawood, Ky., U.S.	D6	94
Cawston, B.C., Can.	E8	69
Caxias, Braz.	B2	57
Caxias do Sul, Braz.	B6	56
Cayambe, Ec.	A2	58
Cayambe, vol., Ec.	A2	58
Cayce, Ky., U.S.	f8	94
Cayce, S.C., U.S.	D5	117
Cayenne, Fr. Gu.	B8	59
Cayenne, ter., Fr. Gu.	B4	59
Cayeux-sur-Mer, Fr.	D9	12
Cayey, P.R.	G11	64
Cayey, Sierra de, mts., P.R.	B3	65
Cayley, Ab., Can.	D4	68
Cayman Brac, i., Cay. Is.	E4	64
Cayman Islands, dep., N.A.	D8	63
Caynabo, Som.	D6	47
Cay Point, c., Bah.	n17	64
Cayuga, On., Can.	E5	73
Cayuga, In., U.S.	E2	91
Cayuga, Ms., U.S.	C3	101
Cayuga, co., N.Y., U.S.	C4	109
Cayuga Heights, N.Y., U.S.	C4	109
Cayuga Lake, l., N.Y., U.S.	C4	109
Cazalla de la Sierra, Spain	C2	123
Cazenovia, N.Y., U.S.	C5	109
Cazombo, Ang.	D4	48
Cazorla, Spain	D4	22
Cea, stm., Spain	A3	22
Ceanannus Mór (Kells), Ire.	C5	11
Ceará, state, Braz.	C3	57
Ceará see Fortaleza, Braz.	B4	57
Ceará-Mirim, stm., Braz.	g6	57
Cebaco, i., Pan.	C2	62
Cebollatí, stm., Ur.	E2	56
Cebolla Creek, stm., Co., U.S.	C3	83
Cebollatí, Ur.	E2	56
Cebreros, Spain	B3	22
Cebu, Phil.	C6	34
Cebu, i., Phil.	C6	34
Cecil, Al., U.S.	C3	78
Cecil, Ga., U.S.	E3	87
Cecil, Oh., U.S.	A1	112
Cecil, Pa., U.S.	F1	115

Name	Map Ref	Page
Cecil, Wi., U.S.	D5	126
Cecil, co., U.S.	A6	97
Cecil Field Naval Air Station, mil., Fl., U.S.	B5	86
Cecilia, Ky., U.S.	C4	94
Ceciliton, Md., U.S.	B6	97
Cecina, Italy	C3	23
Cedar, Ks., U.S.	C5	93
Cedar, Mi., U.S.	D5	99
Cedar, Mn., U.S.	E5	100
Cedar, co., Ia., U.S.	C6	92
Cedar, co., Mo., U.S.	D4	102
Cedar, co., Ne., U.S.	B8	104
Cedar, stm., Ne., U.S.	C6	92
Cedar, stm., Ne., U.S.	B7	104
Cedar, stm., Ne., U.S.	B4	124
Cedar Bluff, Al., U.S.	A4	78
Cedar Bluff, Ky., U.S.	C2	94
Cedar Bluff, Tn., U.S.	D9	119
Cedar Bluff Reservoir, res., Ks., U.S.	D4	93
Cedar Bluffs, Ks., U.S.	C3	93
Cedar Bluffs, Ne., U.S.	C9	104
Cedar Breaks National Monument, Ut., U.S.	F3	121
Cedar Brook, N.J., U.S.	D3	107
Cedarburg, Wi., U.S.	E6	126
Cedarbutte, S.D., U.S.	D4	118
Cedar City, Mo., U.S.	C5	102
Cedar City, Ut., U.S.	F2	121
Cedar Creek, Az., U.S.	D5	80
Cedarcreek, Mo., U.S.	E5	102
Cedarcreek, Ne., U.S.	C9	104
Cedar Creek, Tn., U.S.	C11	119
Cedar Creek, Tx., U.S.	D4	120
Cedar Creek, stm., Co., U.S.	A7	83
Cedar Creek, stm., In., U.S.	B7	91
Cedar Creek, stm., Ia., U.S.	D6	92
Cedar Creek, stm., Mo., U.S.	C5	102
Cedar Creek, stm., N.J., U.S.	D4	107
Cedar Creek, stm., N.D., U.S.	C3	111
Cedar Creek, stm., Oh., U.S.	e7	112
Cedar Creek Lake, res., Tx., U.S.	C4	120
Cedar Crest, N.M., U.S.	k8	108
Cedaredge, Co., U.S.	C3	83
Cedar Falls, Ia., U.S.	B5	92
Cedar Gap, Mo., U.S.	D5	102
Cedar Grove, In., U.S.	F8	91
Cedar Grove, N.J., U.S.	B4	107
Cedar Grove, W.V., U.S.	C3	125
Cedar Grove, Wi., U.S.	E6	126
Cedar Hill, Mo., U.S.	g12	102
Cedar Hill, N.M., U.S.	A2	108
Cedar Hill, Tn., U.S.	A5	119
Cedar Hill, Tx., U.S.	n10	120
Cedarhurst, N.Y., U.S.	k13	109
Cedar Hills, Or., U.S.	*h12	114
Cedar Island, i., N.C., U.S.	C6	110
Cedar Island, i., S.C., U.S.	E9	117
Cedar Island, i., Va., U.S.	C7	123
Cedar Key, Fl., U.S.	C3	86
Cedar Keys, is., Fl., U.S.	C3	86
Cedar Knolls, N.J., U.S.	B4	107
Cedar Lake, In., U.S.	B3	91
Cedar Lake, l., On., Can.	A6	73
Cedar Lake, res., Mb., Can.	C1	70
Cedar Lake, res., Il., U.S.	F4	90
Cedar Mills, Mn., U.S.	F4	100
Cedar Mountain, mtn., Ca., U.S.	B3	82
Cedar Mountains, mts., Ut., U.S.	C2	121
Cedar Point, Il., U.S.	B4	90
Cedar Point, c., Md., U.S.	D5	97
Cedar Point, c., Md., U.S.	e7	112
Cedar Point, c., Oh., U.S.	A3	112
Cedar Rapids, Ia., U.S.	C6	92
Cedar Rapids, Ne., U.S.	C7	104
Cedar River, Mi., U.S.	C3	99
Cedar Run, Pa., U.S.	D4	107
Cedar Springs, On., Can.	E2	73
Cedar Springs, Ga., U.S.	E1	87
Cedar Springs, Mi., U.S.	E5	99
Cedar Swamp, sw., Ma., U.S.	f11	98
Cedartown, Ga., U.S.	B1	87
Cedarvale, B.C., Can.	B3	69
Cedar Vale, Ks., U.S.	E7	93
Cedarvale, N.M., U.S.	C4	108
Cedar Valley, Ut., U.S.	C3	121
Cedarville, Ar., U.S.	B1	81
Cedarville, Ca., U.S.	B3	82
Cedarville, Il., U.S.	A4	90
Cedarville, Ma., U.S.	*C6	98
Cedarville, N.J., U.S.	E2	107
Cedarville, N.Y., U.S.	C5	109
Cedarville, Oh., U.S.	C2	112
Cedoux, Sk., Can.	H4	75
Cedros, Hond.	C4	62
Cedros, Isla, i., Mex.	F5	50
Ceduna, Austl.	F5	50
Ceel Buur, Som.	E6	47
Ceel Xamurre, Som.	D6	47
Ceepeecee, B.C., Can.	C4	69
Ceerigaabo, Som.	C6	47
Cefalù, Italy	E5	23
Cega, stm., Spain	B3	22
Cegléd, Hung.	B4	24
Ceglie Messapico, Italy	D6	23
Cehegín, Spain	C5	22
Čelákovice, Czech.	n18	26
Celaya, Mex.	m13	63
Celebes (Sulawesi), i., Indon.	F6	34
Celebes Sea, Indon.	E6	34
Celendín, Peru	H4	91
Celestine, Ind.	H4	91
Celica, Ec.	B2	58
Celina, Oh., U.S.	B1	112
Celina, Tn., U.S.	C8	119
Celina, Tx., U.S.	C4	120
Celje, Yugo.	B2	24
Celle, F.R.Ger.	B5	18
Cellina, stm., Italy	C8	23
Celoron, N.Y., U.S.	C1	109
Cemaes Head, c., Wales, U.K.	B3	12
Cement, Ok., U.S.	C3	113
Cement City, Mi., U.S.	F6	99
Cementon, Pa., U.S.	E10	115
Cemişgezek, Tur.	C12	40
Cenderawasih Bay, b., Indon.	F9	34
Cenon, Fr.	E3	16
Centenary, S.C., U.S.	C9	117
Centennial, Wy., U.S.	E6	127
Centennial Lake, res., On., Can.	B7	73
Centennial Mountains, mts., Id., U.S.	E7	89
Center, Co., U.S.	D4	83
Center, Ga., U.S.	B3	87
Center, In., U.S.	D5	91
Center, Ky., U.S.	C4	94
Center, Mo., U.S.	B6	102
Center, Ne., U.S.	B8	104
Centuria, Wi., U.S.	C1	126
Center, N.D., U.S.	B4	111
Center, Ok., U.S.	C5	113
Center, Tx., U.S.	D5	120
Center Barnstead, N.H., U.S.	D4	106
Centerbrook, Ct., U.S.	D6	84
Centerburg, Oh., U.S.	B3	112
Center City, Mn., U.S.	E6	100
Center City, Tx., U.S.	D3	120
Center Conway, N.H., U.S.	C4	106
Center Creek, Ut., U.S.	C4	121
Center Cross, Va., U.S.	C6	123
Centereach, N.Y., U.S.	n15	109
Center Effingham, N.H., U.S.	C4	106
Centerfield, Ut., U.S.	D4	121
Center Harbor, N.H., U.S.	C4	106
Center Hill, Ar., U.S.	B4	81
Center Hill, Fl., U.S.	D5	86
Center Hill Lake, res., Tn., U.S.	C8	119
Center Junction, Ia., U.S.	B6	92
Center Line, Mi., U.S.	*p15	99
Center Moriches, N.Y., U.S.	n16	109
Center Mountain, mtn., Id., U.S.	D3	89
Center Ossipee, N.H., U.S.	C4	106
Center Point, Al., U.S.	f7	78
Center Point, Ar., U.S.	C2	81
Centerpoint, In., U.S.	F3	91
Center Point, Ia., U.S.	B6	92
Center Point, La., U.S.	C3	95
Center Point, S.D., U.S.	D8	118
Center Point, Tx., U.S.	E3	120
Center Point, W.V., U.S.	B4	125
Center Ridge, Ar., U.S.	B3	81
Center Rutland, Vt., U.S.	D2	122
Center Sandwich, N.H., U.S.	C4	106
Center Square, N.J., U.S.	D2	107
Center Star, Al., U.S.	A2	78
Center Strafford, N.H., U.S.	D4	106
Centerton, Ar., U.S.	A1	81
Centerton, In., U.S.	E5	91
Centerton, N.J., U.S.	D2	107
Centertown, Ky., U.S.	C3	94
Centertown, Mo., U.S.	C5	102
Centerview, Mo., U.S.	C4	102
Centerville, Ar., U.S.	B2	81
Centerville, De., U.S.	A3	85
Centerville, Ia., U.S.	D5	92
Centerville, Ks., U.S.	D8	93
Centerville, La., U.S.	E4	95
Centerville, Me., U.S.	D5	96
Centerville, Mo., U.S.	D7	102
Centerville, Nv., U.S.	*E2	105
Centerville, N.C., U.S.	A4	110
Centerville, Oh., U.S.	C1	112
Centerville, Pa., U.S.	C2	115
Centerville, Pa., U.S.	F2	115
Centerville, R.I., U.S.	E2	116
Centerville, S.D., U.S.	D9	118
Centerville, Tn., U.S.	B4	119
Centerville, Tx., U.S.	D5	120
Centerville, Ut., U.S.	C4	121
Centerville, Wa., U.S.	C4	124
Cento, Italy	E7	20
Centrahoma, Ok., U.S.	C5	113
Central, Al., U.S.	C3	78
Central, Az., U.S.	E6	80
Central, In., U.S.	H5	91
Central, N.M., U.S.	E1	108
Central, S.C., U.S.	B2	117
Central, Ut., U.S.	F2	121
Central, prov., Ghana	E4	45
Central, prov., Kenya	B6	48
Central, prov., Mwi.	D4	48
Central, prov., Scot., U.K.	D4	13
Central, prov., Zam.	D4	48
Central, dept., Para.	E4	55
Central, Cordillera, mts., Col.	E5	60
Central, Cordillera, mts., C.R.	E5	62
Central, Cordillera, mts., Dom. Rep.	E8	64
Central, Cordillera, mts., P.R.	B2	65
Central, Massif, mts., Fr.	E5	16
Central African Republic, ctry., Afr.	D4	46
Central Barren, In., U.S.	H5	91
Central Bridge, N.Y., U.S.	C6	109
Central Butte, Sk., Can.	G2	75
Central City, Il., U.S.	E4	90
Central City, Ia., U.S.	B6	92
Central City, Ky., U.S.	C2	94
Central City, Ne., U.S.	C7	104
Central City, Pa., U.S.	F4	115
Central City, S.D., U.S.	C2	118
Central Falls, R.I., U.S.	B4	116
Centralhatchee, Ga., U.S.	C1	87
Central Heights, Az., U.S.	D5	80
Central Heights, In., U.S.	A4	92
Centralia, On., Can.	D3	73
Centralia, Il., U.S.	E4	90
Centralia, Ks., U.S.	C7	93
Centralia, Mo., U.S.	B5	102
Centralia, Ok., U.S.	A6	113
Centralia, Wa., U.S.	C3	124
Centralia, W.V., U.S.	C4	125
Centralina, Braz.	D5	57
Central Islip, N.Y., U.S.	n15	109
Central Lake, Mi., U.S.	C5	99
Central Makrān Range, mts., Pak.	D3	36
Central Park, Wa., U.S.	C2	124
Central Point, Or., U.S.	E4	114
Central Range, mts., Pap. N. Gui.	h11	50
Central Range, hills, Trin.	O23	65
Central Siberian Uplands, plat., Sov. Un.	C13	29
Central Square, N.Y., U.S.	B4	109
Central Valley, Ca., U.S.	B2	82
Central Valley, N.Y., U.S.	D6	109
Central Village, Ct., U.S.	C8	84
Central Village, Ma., U.S.	C5	98
Centre, Al., U.S.	A4	78
Centre, co., Pa., U.S.	D6	115
Centre City, N.J., U.S.	D2	107
Centre Hall, Pa., U.S.	E7	115
Centre Peak, mtn., B.C., Can.	B4	69
Centreville, N.B., Can.	C2	71
Centreville, N.S., Can.	E3	71
Centreville, Al., U.S.	C2	78
Centreville, Md., U.S.	B5	97
Centreville, Mi., U.S.	G5	99
Centreville, Ms., U.S.	D2	101
Centreville, Va., U.S.	*B5	123
Centropolis, Ks., U.S.	D8	93
Century, Fl., U.S.	u14	86
Century, W.V., U.S.	B4	125
Cephalonia see Kefallinía, i., Grc.	C3	40
Cephisus see Kifisós, stm., Grc.	g9	25
Ceram, i., Indon.	F7	34
Ceram Sea, Indon.	F7	34
Cerbat Mountains, mts., Az., U.S.	B1	80
Čerčany, Czech.	o18	26
Cereal, Ab., Can.	D5	68
Cereales, Arg.	B4	54
Ceredo, W.V., U.S.	C2	125
Ceres, Braz.	B3	56
Ceres, Italy	D3	20
Ceres, Ca., U.S.	D3	82
Ceres, N.Y., U.S.	C2	109
Ceres, Ok., U.S.	A4	113
Ceresco, Ne., U.S.	C9	104
Cereté, Col.	B2	60
Cerignola, Italy	D5	23
Cerknica, Yugo.	C2	24
Cernavodă, Rom.	C9	24
Cernay, Fr.	D7	16
Cerralvo, Mex.	B5	63
Cerralvo, Isla, i., Mex.	C3	63
Cërrku, Alb.	B2	25
Cerrillos, N.M., U.S.	B3	108
Cerritos, Mex.	F5	16
Cerritos, Ca., U.S.	*E4	82
Cerro, N.M., U.S.	A4	108
Cerro Alto Mountain, mtn., Tx., U.S.	o12	120
Cerro Azul, Peru	D2	58
Cerro Colorado, Ur.	E1	56
Cerro de Pasco, Peru	D2	58
Cerro Gordo, Il., U.S.	D5	90
Cerro Gordo, N.C., U.S.	C4	110
Cerro Gordo, co., Ia., U.S.	A4	92
Cêrro Largo, Braz.	D2	56
Cervantes, Phil.	B6	34
Cervera del Río Alhama, Spain	A5	22
Cerveteri, Italy	g8	23
Cervignano del Friuli, Italy	D9	20
Cervione, Italy	C2	23
Cesar, dept., Col.	B3	60
Cesena, Italy	B4	23
Cesenatico, Italy	B4	23
Česká Kamenice, Czech.	C9	19
Česká Lípa, Czech.	C3	26
Česká Třebová, Czech.	D4	19
České Budějovice, Czech.	D4	19
Český Brod, Czech.	n18	26
Český Krumlov, Czech.	D3	26
Česma, stm., Yugo.	C3	24
Çeşme, Tur.	C6	25
Cessford, Ab., Can.	D5	68
Cessnock, Austl.	F9	50
Cestos, stm., Lib.	E3	45
Cetina, stm., Yugo.	D3	24
Cetinje, Yugo.	D4	24
Cetraro, Italy	E5	23
Cetti Bay, b., Guam	M9	52
Ceuta, Sp. N. Afr.	B4	44
Cévennes, reg., Fr.	E5	16
Cevio, Switz.	C4	20
Ceyhan, Tur.	*D10	40
Ceyhan, stm., Tur.	D11	40
Ceylon, On., Can.	C4	73
Ceylon, Sk., Can.	H3	75
Ceylon, In., U.S.	C8	91
Ceylon, Mn., U.S.	G4	100
Ceylon see Sri Lanka, ctry., Asia	G7	36
Chabařovice, Czech.	C8	19
Chacabuco, Arg.	A4	54
Chacachacare, i., Trin.	N22	65
Chacahoula, La., U.S.	E5	95
Chachapoyas, Peru	C2	58
Chāchārān, Pak.	C3	37
Chachoengsao, Thai.	F4	35
Chāchro, Pak.	E3	37
Chaco, prov., Arg.	E3	55
Chaco, dept., Para.	D3	55
Chaco, stm., N.M., U.S.	A1	108
Chaco Culture National Historic Park, N.M., U.S.	A2	108
Chacon, N.M., U.S.	A4	108
Chacon, Cape, c., Ak., U.S.	n24	79
Chacuaco Creek, stm., Co., U.S.	D7	83
Chad, ctry., Afr.	B3	46
Chad, Lake, l., Afr.	C2	46
Chadbourn, N.C., U.S.	C4	110
Chadds Ford, Pa., U.S.	G10	115
Chadileuvú, stm., Arg.	B3	54
Chadiza, Zam.	D5	48
Chadron, Ne., U.S.	B3	104
Chadwick, Il., U.S.	A4	90
Chadwick, Mo., U.S.	E4	102
Chadwicks, N.Y., U.S.	B5	109
Chaeryŏng, N. Kor.	G2	33
Chaffee, Mo., U.S.	D8	102
Chaffee, N.D., U.S.	C8	111
Chaffee, co., Co., U.S.	C4	83
Chaffin, Ma., U.S.	B4	98
Chaffois, Fr.	C1	21
Chāgai Hills, mts., Asia	G11	39
Chagny, Fr.	D6	16
Chagodoshcha, stm., Sov. Un.	B10	27
Chagos Archipelago, is., B.I.O.T.	G25	2
Chagres, stm., Pan.	k11	62
Chagrin Falls, Oh., U.S.	A4	112
Chaguanas, Trin.	N23	65
Chagyl, Sov. Un.	E5	28
Chahal, Guat.	C3	62
Chāhār Borjak, Afg.	B3	36
Chāh Bahār, Iran	I10	39
Chaibāsā, India	D8	36
Chainat, Thai.	C10	31
Chaîne Annamitique, mts., Asia	B3	34
Chaiyaphum, Thai.	B2	34
Chakachamna Lake, l., Ak., U.S.	g15	79
Chakradharpur, India	D8	36
Chakwāl, Pak.	B5	36
Chala, Peru	E3	58
Chala, Punta, c., Peru	E3	58
Chalan Kanoa, N. Mar. Is.	L10	52
Chalan Pago, Guam	L10	52
Chalatenango, El Sal.	C3	62
Chalcis see Khalkís, Grc.		
Chalco, Canal de, Mex.	h9	63
Chalfonte, De., U.S.	h7	85
Chalhuanca, Peru	D3	58
Chaling, China	K5	32
Chalke see Khálki, i., Grc.	D6	25
Chalk River, On., Can.	A7	73
Chalkyitsik, Ak., U.S.	B11	79
Challans, Fr.	D3	16
Challapata, Bol.	C2	55
Challis, Id., U.S.	E4	89
Chalmers, In., U.S.	C4	91
Chalmette, La., U.S.	E6	95
Châlons-sur-Marne, Fr.	C6	16
Chalon-sur-Saône, Fr.	D6	16
Chaltel, Cerro see Fitzroy, Monte, mtn., S.A.	D2	54
Chālūs, Iran	C5	39
Chamberino, N.M., U.S.	E3	108
Chamberlain, Sk., Can.	G3	75
Chamberlain, S.D., U.S.	D6	118
Chamberlain Lake, l., Me., U.S.	B3	96
Chamberlin, Mount, mtn., Ak., U.S.	B10	79
Chambers, Az., U.S.	B6	80
Chambers, co., Al., U.S.	C4	78
Chambers, co., Tx., U.S.	E5	120
Chambersburg, Il., U.S.	D3	90
Chambersburg, Oh., U.S.	D3	112
Chambersburg, Pa., U.S.	G6	115
Chambers Island, i., Wi., U.S.	C6	126
Chambéry, Fr.	E6	16
Chambeshi, stm., Zam.	D5	48
Chamblee, Ga., U.S.	h8	87
Chambly, P.Q., Can.	D4	74
Chambly, Fr.	E2	17
Chambly, co., P.Q., Can.	D4	74
Chambord, P.Q., Can.	A5	74
Chamcook, N.B., Can.	D2	71
Chamical, Arg.	F2	55
Chamisal, N.M., U.S.	A4	108
Chamois, Mo., U.S.	C6	102
Chamonix [-Mont-Blanc], Fr.	E7	16
Champ, Md., U.S.	D6	97
Champagne, hist reg., Fr.	C5	16
Champagney, Fr.	A2	21
Champagnole, Fr.	D6	16
Champaign, Il., U.S.	C5	90
Champaign, co., Il., U.S.	C5	90
Champaign, co., Oh., U.S.	B2	112
Champdoré, Lac, l., P.Q., Can.	g8	72
Champerico, Guat.	C2	62
Champéry, Switz.	D2	21
Champex, Switz.	D3	21
Champigneulles, Fr.	F6	17
Champigny-sur-Marne, Fr.	g11	16
Champion, Ab., Can.	D4	68
Champion, Mi., U.S.	B3	99
Champion, Ne., U.S.	D4	104
Champion, Oh., U.S.	A5	112
Champion Creek Reservoir, res., Tx., U.S.	C2	120
Champlain, N.Y., U.S.	f11	109
Champlain, co., P.Q., Can.	B4	74
Champlain, Lake, l., N.A.	B2	122
Champlin, Mn., U.S.	m12	100
Champlitte [-et-le-Prélot], Fr.	D6	16
Champney's West, Nf., Can.	D5	72
Champoton, Mex.	D6	63
Chamraj, India	F10	37
Chana, Il., U.S.	B4	90
Chañaral, Chile	E1	55
Chanārān, Iran	C9	39
Chancay, Peru	D2	58
Chance, Md., U.S.	D6	97
Chancellor, Al., U.S.	D4	78
Chancellor, S.D., U.S.	D8	118
Chanchelulla Peak, mtn., Ca., U.S.	B2	82
Chanco, Chile	B2	54
Chanda see Chandrapur, India	C6	36
Chandalar, stm., Ak., U.S.	B10	79
Chandausi, India	C7	37
Chandeleur Islands, is., La., U.S.	E7	95
Chandeleur Sound, strt., La., U.S.	E6	95
Chandigarh, India	*B6	36
Chandigarh, ter., India	*B6	36
Chandler, P.Q., Can.	k14	74
Chandler, Az., U.S.	D4	80
Chandler, In., U.S.	H3	91
Chandler, Mn., U.S.	G3	100
Chandler, Ok., U.S.	B5	113
Chandler, Tx., U.S.	C5	120
Chandler Heights, Az., U.S.	m9	80
Chandlers Valley, Pa., U.S.	C3	115
Chandlerville, Il., U.S.	C3	90
Chandos Lake, l., On., Can.	C7	73
Chāndpur, Bngl.	D9	36
Chandrakona, India	E6	36
Chandrapur, India	C6	36
Chaneysville, Pa., U.S.	G5	115
Chang, i., Thai.	F5	35
Changane, stm., Moz.	B5	49
Changbai Mountains, mts., Asia	E3	33
Changchou see Zhangzhou, China	G8	31
Changchun, China	C10	31
Changde, China	F7	31
Change Islands, Nf., Can.	D4	72
Changewater, N.J., U.S.	B3	107
Changhua, China	I8	31
Chang Jiang see Yangtze, stm., China	E8	31
Changjin, N. Kor.	F3	33
Changli, China	L8	32
Changling, China	B10	31
Changning, China	D7	32
Changsha, China	F7	31
Changshu, China	F2	33
Changsŏng [-up], N. Kor.	F2	33
Changshou, China	F8	31
Changting, China		
Changwu, China	D6	31
Changxing, China	I8	32
Changyŏn [-ŭp], N. Kor.	G2	33
Changzhi, China	D7	31
Changzhou, China	E8	31
Channahon, Il., U.S.	B5	90
Chanhassen, Mn., U.S.	n11	100
Channel Country, reg., Austl.	D6	50
Channel Islands, is., Eur.	F5	10
Channel Islands National Park, Ca., U.S.	F4	82
Channel Lake, Il., U.S.	H8	90
Channel-Port-aux-Basques, Nf., Can.	E2	72
Channelview, Tx., U.S.	r14	120
Channing, Mi., U.S.	B2	99
Channing, Tx., U.S.	B1	120
Chantada, Spain	A2	22
Chanthaburi, Thai.	C2	34
Chantilly, Fr.	C5	16
Chantilly, Va., U.S.	g12	123
Chantrey Inlet, b., N.T., Can.	C13	66
Chanute, Ks., U.S.	E8	93
Chanute Air Force Base, mil., Il., U.S.	C5	90
Chany, Lake, l., Sov. Un.	D10	29
Chao'an, China	G8	31
Chao Lake, l., China	I7	32
Chao Phraya, stm., Thai.	C2	34
Chaor He, stm., China	B9	31
Chaoyang, China	C9	31
Chapadinha, Braz.	B2	57
Chapala, Mex.	m12	63
Chapala, Lago de, l., Mex.	m12	63
Chaparral, Col.	C2	60
Chapayevsk, Sov. Un.	C3	28
Chapel Hill, De., U.S.	*B3	85
Chapel Hill, Ky., U.S.	D3	94
Chapel Hill, N.C., U.S.	B3	110
Chapel Hill, Tn., U.S.	B5	119
Chapelle, N.M., U.S.	B4	108
Chapel Square, Va., U.S.	*B5	123
Chapelton, Jam.	E14	65
Chapin, Il., U.S.	D3	90
Chapin, S.C., U.S.	C5	117
Chapleau, On., Can.	p19	73
Chaplin, Sk., Can.	G2	75
Chaplin, Ct., U.S.	B7	84
Chaplin, Ky., U.S.	C4	94
Chaplin, stm., Ky., U.S.	C4	94
Chaplin Lake, l., Sk., Can.	G2	75
Chaplygin, Sov. Un.	E12	27
Chapman, Al., U.S.	D3	78
Chapman, Ks., U.S.	D6	93
Chapman, Ne., U.S.	C7	104
Chapman, Cape, c., N.T., Can.	C15	66
Chapman Pond, l., R.I., U.S.	F1	116
Chapman Ranch, Tx., U.S.	F4	120
Chapmanville, W.V., U.S.	C2	125
Chappaqua, N.Y., U.S.	*D7	109
Chappaquiddick Island, i., Ma., U.S.	D7	98
Chappell, Ne., U.S.	C3	104
Chappells, S.C., U.S.	C4	117
Chāprota, India	C7	36
Chaqui, Bol.	C2	55
Char, well, Maur.	B2	45
Charadai, Arg.	E4	55
Charagua, Bol.	C3	55
Charalá, Col.	C6	60
Charaña, Bol.	C2	55
Charcas, Mex.	C4	63
Charco, Tx., U.S.	E4	120
Charcot Island, i., Ant.	C5	7
Chard, Eng., U.K.	D5	12
Chardon, Oh., U.S.	A4	112
Chardzhou, Sov. Un.	F9	29
Charente, stm., Fr.	E3	16
Charenton, La., U.S.	E4	95
Charenton-le-Pont, Fr.	g10	16
Charette, P.Q., Can.	C5	74
Chari, stm., Afr.	C3	46
Charikar, Afg.	A4	36
Charing, Ga., U.S.	D2	87
Chariton, Ia., U.S.	C4	92
Chariton, co., Mo., U.S.	B4	102
Chariton, stm., U.S.	A5	102
Charity, Mo., U.S.	D4	102
Charlemagne, P.Q., Can.	D4	74
Charlemont, Ma., U.S.	A2	98
Charleroi, Bel.	B6	16
Charleroi, Pa., U.S.	F2	115
Charles, co., Md., U.S.	C3	97
Charles, Cape, c., Va., U.S.	C6	123
Charles, stm., Ma., U.S.	B5	98
Charles A. Goodwin Dam, Ct., U.S.	B3	84
Charlesbourg, P.Q., Can.	n17	74
Charlesburg, Wi., U.S.	k9	126
Charles City, Ia., U.S.	A5	92
Charles City, Va., U.S.	C5	123
Charles City, co., Va., U.S.	C5	123
Charles Mill Lake, res., Oh., U.S.	B3	112
Charles Mix, co., S.D., U.S.	D7	118
Charles Mound, hill, Il., U.S.	A3	90
Charleston, Ar., U.S.	B1	81
Charleston, Il., U.S.	D5	90
Charleston, Me., U.S.	C4	96
Charleston, Ms., U.S.	A3	101
Charleston, Mo., U.S.	E8	102
Charleston, Or., U.S.	D2	114
Charleston, S.C., U.S.	F8	117
Charleston, Tn., U.S.	D9	119
Charleston, W.V., U.S.	C3	125
Charleston, co., S.C., U.S.	F7	117
Charleston Air Force Base, mil., S.C., U.S.	k11	117
Charleston Naval Shipyard, mil., S.C., U.S.	k12	117
Charleston Park, Nv., U.S.	*G6	105
Charleston Peak, mtn., Nv., U.S.	G6	105
Charlestown, St. C.-N.	H13	64
Charlestown, In., U.S.	H6	91
Charlestown, Md., U.S.	A6	97
Charlestown, N.H., U.S.	D2	106
Charlestown, R.I., U.S.	F2	116
Charles Town, W.V., U.S.	B7	125
Charlestown, Austl.	E8	50
Charleville, Austl.	E8	50
Charleville-Mézières, Fr.	C6	16
Charlevoix, Mi., U.S.	C5	99
Charlevoix, Lake, l., Mi., U.S.	C5	99
Charlevoix-Est, co., P.Q., Can.	A7	74
Charlevoix-Ouest, co., P.Q., Can.	B7	74
Charlie Lake, B.C., Can.	A7	69
Charlieu, Fr.	D6	16
Charlo, N.B., Can.	B3	71
Charlo, Mt., U.S.	C2	103
Charlotte, Ia., U.S.	C7	92
Charlotte, Mi., U.S.	F6	99
Charlotte, N.C., U.S.	B2	110
Charlotte, Tn., U.S.	A4	119
Charlotte, Tx., U.S.	E3	120
Charlotte, Vt., U.S.	C2	122
Charlotte, co., N.B., Can.	D3	71
Charlotte, co., Fl., U.S.	F5	86
Charlotte, co., Va., U.S.	C4	123
Charlotte Amalie, V.I.U.S.	G12	64
Charlotte Court House, Va., U.S.	C4	123
Charlotte Hall, Md., U.S.	D4	97
Charlotte Harbor, Fl., U.S.	F4	86
Charlotte Harbor, b., Fl., U.S.	F4	86
Charlotte Lake, l., B.C., Can.	C4	69
Charlottenburg, Sur.	A4	59
Charlottesville, In., U.S.	E6	91
Charlottesville, Va., U.S.	B4	123
Charlottetown, P.E., Can.	C6	71
Charlotte Town (Gouyave), Gren.	W25	65
Charlotteville, Trin.	M24	65
Charlotteville, Ga., U.S.	D4	87
Charlson, N.D., U.S.	A3	111
Charlton, Ma., U.S.	B4	98
Charlton, co., Ga., U.S.	F4	87
Charlton City, Ma., U.S.	B4	98
Charlton Depot, Ma., U.S.	B4	98
Charlton Heights, W.V., U.S.	m13	125
Charlton Island, i., N.T., Can.	n20	73
Charly [-sur-Marne], Fr.	F3	17
Charmco, W.V., U.S.	C4	125
Charmes, Fr.	C7	16
Charmey, Switz.	C3	21
Charny, P.Q., Can.	C6	74
Charouine, Alg.	D4	44
Charquemont, Fr.	B2	21
Charron Lake, l., Mb., Can.	C4	70
Charsadda, Pak.	B4	36
Charsk, Sov. Un.	D10	28
Charter Oak, Ia., U.S.	B2	92
Charters Towers, Austl.	D8	50
Chartierville, P.Q., Can.	D6	74
Chartley, Ma., U.S.	C5	98
Chartres, Fr.	C4	16
Charysh, stm., Sov. Un.	C10	28
Chascomús, Arg.	B5	54
Chase, B.C., Can.	D8	69
Chase, Ks., U.S.	D5	93
Chase, Md., U.S.	B5	97
Chase, Mi., U.S.	E5	99
Chase, co., Ks., U.S.	D7	93
Chase, co., Ne., U.S.	D4	104
Chase, Mount, mtn., Me., U.S.	B4	96
Chase City, Va., U.S.	D4	123
Chaseburg, Wi., U.S.	E2	126
Chase Field Naval Air Station, mil., Tx., U.S.	E4	120
Chaseley, N.D., U.S.	B6	111
Chase River, B.C., Can.	f12	69
Chasicó, Arg.	C3	54
Chaska, Mn., U.S.	F5	100
Chasov Yar, Sov. Un.	q20	27
Chassahowitzka Bay, b., Fl., U.S.	D4	86
Chassell, Mi., U.S.	A2	99
Chasseral, mtn., Switz.	B3	20
Chasseron, Mont, mtn., Switz.	C2	21
Chataignier, La., U.S.	D3	95
Chatanika, Ak., U.S.	B10	79
Chatawa, Ms., U.S.	D3	101
Châteaubriant, Fr.	D3	16
Château d'Oex, Switz.	D3	21
Château-du-Loir, Fr.	D4	16
Châteaudun, Fr.	C4	16
Chateaugay, N.Y., U.S.	f10	109
Château-Gontier, Fr.	D3	16
Châteauguay, P.Q., Can.	D4	74
Châteauguay, co., P.Q., Can.	D4	74
Châteauguay Heights, P.Q., Can.	q19	74
Châteauneuf, Fr.	D5	16
Château-Renault, Fr.	D4	16
Château-Richer, P.Q., Can.	C6	74
Châteauroux, Fr.	D4	16
Château-Salins, Fr.	F6	17
Château-Thierry, Fr.	C5	16
Châtel, Fr.	D2	21
Châtellerault, Fr.	D4	16
Châtel-Saint-Denis, Switz.	C2	21
Chatfield, Mb., Can.	D3	70
Chatfield, Ar., U.S.	B5	81
Chatfield, Mn., U.S.	G6	100
Chatfield, Oh., U.S.	B3	112
Chatham, N.B., Can.	B4	71
Chatham, On., Can.	E2	73
Chatham, Eng., U.K.	E7	10
Chatham, Il., U.S.	D4	90
Chatham, La., U.S.	B3	95
Chatham, Ma., U.S.	C8	98
Chatham, Mi., U.S.	B3	99
Chatham, N.J., U.S.	B4	107
Chatham, N.Y., U.S.	C7	109
Chatham, Va., U.S.	D4	123
Chatham, co., Ga., U.S.	E5	87
Chatham, co., N.C., U.S.	B3	110
Chatham Islands, is., N.Z.	I11	6
Chatham Sound, strt., B.C., Can.	B1	69
Chatham Strait, strt., Ak., U.S.	m22	79
Châtillon, Italy	D3	20
Châtillon-sur-Seine, Fr.	E8	28
Chatkal Range, mts., Sov. Un.	E8	28
Chatom, Al., U.S.	D1	78
Chatrapur, India	H10	37
Chatsworth, On., Can.	C4	73
Chatsworth, Ga., U.S.	B2	87
Chatsworth, Il., U.S.	C5	90
Chatsworth, N.J., U.S.	D3	107
Chatsworth Reservoir, res., Ca., U.S.	m11	82
Chattahoochee, Fl., U.S.	B2	87
Chattahoochee, co., Ga., U.S.	D1	87
Chattahoochee, stm., U.S.	E1	87
Chattanooga, Ok., U.S.	C3	113
Chattanooga, Tn., U.S.	D8	119
Chattaroy, Wa., U.S.	B8	124
Chattaroy, W.V., U.S.	D2	125
Chatteris, Eng., U.K.	B8	12
Chattooga, co., Ga., U.S.	B1	87
Chattooga, stm., U.S.	B1	117
Chatuge Lake, res., U.S.	g9	110
Chaudière, stm., P.Q., Can.	C7	74

Name — Map Ref — Page

Chauk, Burma D9 36
Chaumont, Fr. C6 16
Chaumont, N.Y., U.S. A4 109
Chaun Bay, b., Sov. Un. B34 128
Chauncey, Ga., U.S. D3 87
Chauncey, Oh., U.S. C3 112
Chauncy Lake, l., Ma., U.S. g9 98
Chauny, Fr. C5 16
Chau Phu, Viet. C3 34
Chautauqua, Ks., U.S. E7 93
Chautauqua, N.Y., U.S. C1 109
Chautauqua, S.D., U.S. *D8 118
Chautauqua, co., Ks., U.S. E7 93
Chautauqua, co., N.Y., U.S. C1 109
Chautauqua Lake, l., N.Y., U.S. C1 109
Chauvigny, Fr. D4 16
Chauvin, Ab., Can. C5 68
Chauvin, La., U.S. E5 95
Chavanga, Sov. Un. D17 14
Chaves, Braz. C5 59
Chaves, Port. B2 22
Chaves, co., N.M., U.S. D5 108
Chavies, Ky., U.S. C6 94
Chavinda, Mex. m12 63
Cháviva, Col. C3 60
Chavuma, Zam. D3 48
Chazelles, Fr. E6 16
Chazy, N.Y., U.S. f11 109
Cheadle, Ab., Can. D4 68
Cheaha Mountain, mtn., Al., U.S. B4 78
Cheam (part of London), Eng., U.K. m12 10
Cheapside, Va., U.S. h16 123
Cheat, Shavers Fork, stm., W.V., U.S. B5 125
Cheatham, co., Tn., U.S. A4 119
Cheatham Reservoir, res., Tn., U.S. A4 119
Cheat Mountain, mtn., W.V., U.S. C5 125
Cheb, Czech. C2 26
Chebacco Lake, l., Ma., U.S. f12 98
Chebanse, Il., U.S. C6 90
Chebeague Island, Me., U.S. E2 96
Cheboksary, Sov. Un. D7 29
Cheboygan, Mi., U.S. C6 99
Cheboygan, co., Mi., U.S. C6 99
Chech, 'Erg, des., Afr. E4 44
Chechaouene, Mor. B3 44
Chechŏn, S. Kor. H4 33
Checotah, Ok., U.S. B6 113
Chedabucto Bay, b., N.S., Can. D8 71
Cheddar, Eng., U.K. C5 12
Cheddar, S.C., U.S. B3 117
Cheduba Island, i., Burma E9 36
Cheecham Hills, hills, Ab., Can. B5 68
Cheektowaga, N.Y., U.S. C2 109
Cheepie, Austl. C5 51
Cheeseman Lake, res., Co., U.S. B5 83
Chegutu, Zimb. A5 49
Chehalem Mountains, mts., Or., U.S. h12 114
Chehalis, Wa., U.S. C3 124
Chehalis, stm., Wa., U.S. C2 124
Cheju, S. Kor. J3 33
Cheju Island, i., S. Kor. D10 31
Cheju Strait, strt., S. Kor. J3 33
Chekhov, Sov. Un. C10 33
Chekiang see Zhejiang, prov., China F9 31
Chekunda, Sov. Un. A6 33
Chela, Serra da, mtn., Ang. E1 48
Chelan, Sk., Can. E4 75
Chelan, Wa., U.S. B5 124
Chelan, co., Wa., U.S. B4 124
Chelan, Lake, l., Wa., U.S. A5 124
Chelan Falls, Wa., U.S. B5 124
Chelan Mountains, mts., Wa., U.S. A5 124
Cheleiros, Port. f9 22
Cheleken, Sov. Un. B6 39
Cheleken, pen., Sov. Un. B6 39
Chelforó, Arg. B3 54
Chélia, Djebel, mtn., Alg. B6 44
Chéliff, Oued, stm., Alg. B5 44
Chelkar, Sov. Un. E8 29
Chelles, Fr. F2 17
Chełm, Pol. C7 26
Chełmno, Pol. B5 26
Chelmsford, Eng., U.K. E7 10
Chelmsford, Ma., U.S. A5 98
Chełmża, Pol. B5 26
Chelsea, P.Q., Can. D2 74
Chelsea (part of London), Eng., U.K. m12 10
Chelsea, Al., U.S. g7 78
Chelsea, Ia., U.S. C5 92
Chelsea, Me., U.S. D3 96
Chelsea, Ma., U.S. B5 98
Chelsea, Mi., U.S. F6 99
Chelsea, Ok., U.S. A6 113
Chelsea, S.D., U.S. B7 118
Chelsea, Vt., U.S. D4 122
Chelsea, Wi., U.S. C3 126
Chelsea Estates, De., U.S. *B3 85
Cheltenham, Eng., U.K. E5 10
Cheltenham, Md., U.S. C4 97
Cheltenham Township, Pa., U.S. *o21 115
Chelva, Spain C5 22
Chelyabinsk, Sov. Un. D9 29
Chelyan, W.V., U.S. C3 125
Chelyuskin, Cape, c., Sov. Un. B13 29
Chelyuskintsy Ice Tongue, Ant. C21 7
Chemainus, B.C., Can. E6 69
Chemal, Sov. Un. E26 8
Chemehuevi Indian Reservation, Ca., U.S. E6 82
Chemillé, Fr. D3 16
Chemin Craig, P.Q., Can. o17 74
Chemnitz see Karl-Marx-Stadt, Ger.D.R. C6 18
Chemquasabamticook Lake (Ross Lake), l., Me., U.S. B3 96
Chemult, Or., U.S. D5 114
Chemung, Il., U.S. A5 90
Chemung, co., N.Y., U.S. C4 109
Chemung, stm., Pa., U.S. C8 115
Chemung Lake, l., On., Can. C6 73
Chenāb, stm., Asia B5 36
Chenachane, Alg. D4 44
Chenango, co., N.Y., U.S. C5 109
Chenango, stm., N.Y., U.S. C5 109
Chenango Bridge, N.Y., U.S. C5 109
Chenango Forks, N.Y., U.S. C5 109
Chene, Bayou, stm., La., U.S. k9 95
Chenequa, Wi., U.S. m11 126
Chenes, River Aux, b., La., U.S. k12 95
Chénéville, P.Q., Can. D2 74
Cheney, Ks., U.S. E6 93
Cheney, Wa., U.S. B8 124
Cheney Reservoir, res., Ks., U.S. E6 93
Cheneyville, La., U.S. C3 95
Chengchou see Zhengzhou, China E7 31
Chengde, China C8 31
Chengdu (Chengtu), China E5 31
Chenggu, China E6 31
Chenghai, China G8 31
Chengkou, China I3 32
Chengmai, China C8 35
Chengshan Point, c., China D9 31
Chengtu see Chengdu, China E5 31
Chenoa, Il., U.S. C5 90
Chenoa, Ky., U.S. D6 94
Chenôve, Fr. D6 16
Chenoweth, Or., U.S. B5 114
Chenxi, China F7 31
Chenxian, China F7 31
Chepachet, R.I., U.S. B2 116
Chepachet, stm., R.I., U.S. B2 116
Chepén, Peru C2 58
Chepes, Arg. A3 54
Chepo, Pan. F8 62
Chepstow, Wales, U.K. E5 10
Cheptsa, stm., Sov. Un. D19 8
Chequamegon Bay, b., Wi., U.S. B3 126
Cher, stm., Fr. D4 16
Cheraw, Co., U.S. C7 83
Cheraw, S.C., U.S. B8 117
Cherbourg, Fr. C3 16
Cherchell, Alg. B5 44
Cherdyn, Sov. Un. A5 28
Cheremkhovo, Sov. Un. D13 29
Cherepanovo, Sov. Un. C10 28
Cherepovets, Sov. Un. D6 29
Cherhill, Ab., Can. C3 68
Cheriton, Va., U.S. C7 123
Cherkassy, Sov. Un. G9 27
Cherkessk, Sov. Un. G17 8
Cherlakskiy, Sov. Un. C8 28
Chernigov, Sov. Un. D6 29
Chernigovka, Sov. Un. H11 27
Chernigovka, Sov. Un. D6 33
Chernobay, Sov. Un. G9 27
Chernobyl, Sov. Un. F8 27
Chernogorsk, Sov. Un. E27 8
Chernomorskoye, Sov. Un. I9 27
Chernovtsy, Sov. Un. E5 29
Chernoye, Sov. Un. r32 14
Chernyakhovsk (Insterburg), Sov. Un. D3 27
Cherokee, Al., U.S. A2 78
Cherokee, Ia., U.S. B2 92
Cherokee, Ks., U.S. E9 93
Cherokee, N.C., U.S. f9 110
Cherokee, Ok., U.S. A3 113
Cherokee, Tx., U.S. D3 120
Cherokee, co., Al., U.S. A4 78
Cherokee, co., Ga., U.S. B2 87
Cherokee, co., Ia., U.S. B2 92
Cherokee, co., Ks., U.S. E9 93
Cherokee, co., N.C., U.S. f8 110
Cherokee, co., Ok., U.S. B6 113
Cherokee, co., S.C., U.S. A4 117
Cherokee, co., Tx., U.S. D5 120
Cherokee Falls, S.C., U.S. A4 117
Cherokee Indian Reservation, N.C., U.S. f9 110
Cherokee Lake, res., Tn., U.S. C10 119
Cherokees, Lake O' The, res., Ok., U.S. A7 113
Cherokee Sound, Bah. A5 64
Cherokee Village, Ar., U.S. *A4 81
Cherquenco, Chile B2 54
Cherrapunji, India C9 36
Cherry, Il., U.S. B4 90
Cherry, Tn., U.S. B2 119
Cherry, co., Ne., U.S. B4 104
Cherry Creek, N.Y., U.S. C1 109
Cherry Creek, S.D., U.S. C4 118
Cherry Creek, stm., Co., U.S. B6 83
Cherry Creek, stm., S.D., U.S. C3 118
Cherryfield, Me., U.S. D5 96
Cherry Fork, Oh., U.S. D2 112
Cherry Grove, Or., U.S. g11 114
Cherry Hill, N.J., U.S. D2 107
Cherry Hills Village, Co., U.S. *B6 83
Cherry Point, c., Va., U.S. C6 123
Cherry Point Marine Corps Air Station, mil., N.C., U.S. C6 110
Cherry Run, W.V., U.S. B6 125
Cherry Tree, Pa., U.S. E4 115
Cherryvale, Ks., U.S. E8 93
Cherry Valley, On., Can. D7 73
Cherry Valley, Ar., U.S. B5 81
Cherry Valley, Il., U.S. A5 90
Cherry Valley, Ma., U.S. B4 98
Cherry Valley, N.Y., U.S. C6 109
Cherryville, N.C., U.S. B1 110
Cherskiy Mountains, mts., Sov. Un. C17 29
Chesaning, Mi., U.S. E6 99
Chesapeake, Oh., U.S. D3 112
Chesapeake, Va., U.S. D6 123
Chesapeake, W.V., U.S. C3 125
Chesapeake and Delaware Canal, U.S. B3 85
Chesapeake Bay, b., U.S. C12 76
Chesapeake Bay Bridge-Tunnel, Va., U.S. D7 123
Chesapeake Beach, Md., U.S. C4 97
Chesapeake City, Md., U.S. A6 97
Chesaw, Wa., U.S. A6 124
Chesdin, Lake, res., Va., U.S. C5 123
Chesha Bay, b., Sov. Un. B18 8
Chesham, Eng., U.K. k11 10
Chesham, N.H., U.S. E2 106
Cheshire, Ct., U.S. D4 84
Cheshire, Ma., U.S. A1 98
Cheshire, Oh., U.S. D3 112
Cheshire, co., Eng., U.K. A5 12
Cheshire, co., N.H., U.S. E2 106
Cheshire Reservoir, res., Ma., U.S. A1 98
Cheshunt, Eng., U.K. k12 10
Chesilhurst, N.J., U.S. D3 107
Chesley, On., Can. C3 73
Chesnee, S.C., U.S. A4 117
Chester, N.S., Can. E5 71
Chester, Eng., U.K. D5 10
Chester, Ar., U.S. B1 81
Chester, Ca., U.S. B3 82
Chester, Ct., U.S. D6 84
Chester, Fl., U.S. B5 86
Chester, Ga., U.S. D3 87
Chester, Id., U.S. F7 89
Chester, Il., U.S. F4 90
Chester, Ia., U.S. A5 92
Chester, Md., U.S. C5 97
Chester, Ma., U.S. B2 98
Chester, Mt., U.S. B6 103
Chester, Ne., U.S. D8 104
Chester, N.H., U.S. E4 106
Chester, N.J., U.S. B3 107
Chester, N.Y., U.S. D6 109
Chester, Oh., U.S. C4 112
Chester, Ok., U.S. A3 113
Chester, Pa., U.S. G11 115
Chester, S.C., U.S. B5 117
Chester, S.D., U.S. D9 118
Chester, Ut., U.S. D4 121
Chester, Vt., U.S. E3 122
Chester, Va., U.S. C5 123
Chester, W.V., U.S. A4 125
Chester, co., Pa., U.S. G10 115
Chester, co., S.C., U.S. B5 117
Chester, co., Tn., U.S. B3 119
Chester, stm., Md., U.S. B5 97
Chester Basin, N.S., Can. E5 71
Chester Depot, Vt., U.S. E3 122
Chesterfield, Eng., U.K. D6 10
Chesterfield, Il., U.S. D3 90
Chesterfield, In., U.S. D6 91
Chesterfield, Ma., U.S. B2 98
Chesterfield, N.H., U.S. E2 106
Chesterfield, S.C., U.S. B7 117
Chesterfield, Tn., U.S. B3 119
Chesterfield, Va., U.S. C5 123
Chesterfield, co., S.C., U.S. B7 117
Chesterfield, co., Va., U.S. C5 123
Chesterfield, Îles, is., N. Cal. H9 6
Chesterfield Inlet, N.T., Can. D14 66
Chesterfield Inlet, b., N.T., Can. D14 66
Chesterhill, Oh., U.S. C4 112
Chesterton, In., U.S. A3 91
Chestertown, Md., U.S. B5 97
Chestertown, N.Y., U.S. B7 109
Chester Township, Pa., U.S. *p20 115
Chesterville, On., Can. B9 73
Chesterville, Il., U.S. D5 90
Chesterville, Oh., U.S. B3 112
Chestnut, Il., U.S. C4 90
Chestnut, La., U.S. B2 95
Chestnut Hill Estates, De., U.S. *B3 85
Chestnut Knoll, De., U.S. E4 85
Chestnut Mound, Tn., U.S. C8 119
Chesuncook Lake, l., Me., U.S. C3 96
Cheswick, Pa., U.S. h14 115
Cheswold, De., U.S. D3 85
Chetac, Lake, l., Wi., U.S. C2 126
Chetco, stm., Or., U.S. E2 114
Chetek, Wi., U.S. C2 126
Chetek, Lake, l., Wi., U.S. C2 126
Chéticamp, N.S., Can. C8 71
Chetopa, Ks., U.S. E8 93
Chetumal, Mex. D7 63
Chetumal Bay, b., N.A. D7 63
Chetwynd, B.C., Can. B7 69
Chevak, Ak., U.S. C6 79
Chevelon Creek, stm., Az., U.S. C5 80
Cheverie, N.S., Can. D5 71
Cheverly, Md., U.S. *C4 97
Cheviot, Sk., Can. E2 75
Cheviot, N.Z. O14 51
Cheviot, Oh., U.S. C1 112
Cheviot Hills, hills, U.K. C5 10
Chevreuil, Bayou, stm., La., U.S. k10 95
Chevreuil, Point, c., La., U.S. E4 95
Chevy Chase, Md., U.S. C3 97
Chewack, stm., Wa., U.S. A5 124
Chewalla, Tn., U.S. B3 119
Chewelah, Wa., U.S. A8 124
Chewsville, Md., U.S. A2 97
Chewton, Pa., U.S. E1 115
Cheyenne, Ok., U.S. B2 113
Cheyenne, Wy., U.S. E8 127
Cheyenne, co., Co., U.S. C8 83
Cheyenne, co., Ks., U.S. C2 93
Cheyenne, co., Ne., U.S. C2 104
Cheyenne, stm., U.S. C4 118
Cheyenne, Dry Fork, stm., Wy., U.S. C7 127
Cheyenne Canon, Co., U.S. *C6 83
Cheyenne River Indian Reservation, S.D., U.S. B4 118
Cheyenne Wells, Co., U.S. C8 83
Chhatarpur, India E7 37
Chhindwāra, India F7 37
Chhukha Dzong, Bhu. D12 37
Chi, stm., Thai. E6 35
Chiang Kham, Thai. C4 35
Chiang Khong, Thai. A2 34
Chiang Mai, Thai. B1 34
Chiang Rai, Thai. B1 34
Chiapa de Corzo, Mex. D6 63
Chiapas, state, Mex. D6 63
Chiari, Italy B2 23
Chiasso, Switz. E7 21
Chiatura, Sov. Un. A14 40
Chiautla de Tapia, Mex. n14 63
Chiavari, Italy B2 23
Chiavenna, Italy C5 20
Chiawuli Tak, Az., U.S. F4 80
Chiba, Japan D13 31
Chibemba, Ang. E1 48
Chibia, Ang. E1 48
Chiblow Lake, l., On., Can. A1 73
Chibougamau, P.Q., Can. k12 74
Chibougamau, Réserve, P.Q., Can. k12 74
Chibuto, Moz. B5 49
Chibuzhang Lake, l., China B9 36
Chicago, Il., U.S. B6 90
Chicago Heights, Il., U.S. B6 90
Chicago Ridge, Il., U.S. *k9 90
Chicago Sanitary and Ship Canal, Il., U.S. k8 90
Chicamacomico, stm., Md., U.S. D6 97
Chicapa, stm., Afr. C3 48
Chichagof Island, i., Ak., U.S. m22 79
Chichaoua, Mor. C3 44
Chicheng, China D6 32
Chichén Itzá, hist., Mex. C7 63
Chichester, Eng., U.K. E6 10
Chichester, N.H., U.S. D4 106
Chichibu, Japan n18 33
Chickahominy, stm., Va., U.S. C5 123
Chickamauga, Ga., U.S. B1 87
Chickamauga and Chattanooga National Military Park, U.S. k11 119
Chickamauga Dam, Tn., U.S. h11 119
Chickamauga Lake, res., Tn., U.S. D8 119
Chickasaw, Al., U.S. E1 78
Chickasaw, co., Ia., U.S. A5 92
Chickasaw, co., Ms., U.S. B5 101
Chickasawhay, stm., Ms., U.S. D5 101
Chickasaw National Recreation Area, Ok., U.S. C5 113
Chickasha, Ok., U.S. B4 113
Chickasha, Lake, res., Ok., U.S. B3 113
Chicken, Ak., U.S. C11 79
Chickwolnepy Stream, stm., N.H., U.S. A4 106
Chiclana [de da Frontera], Spain D2 22
Chiclayo, Peru C2 58
Chico, Ca., U.S. C3 82
Chico, Tx., U.S. C4 120
Chico, Wa., U.S. B3 124
Chico, stm., Arg. C3 54
Chico, stm., Arg. D3 54
Chico, stm., Mex. h9 63
Chicoa, Moz. A5 49
Chico Creek, stm., Co., U.S. C6 83
Chico Hot Springs, Mt., U.S. E6 103
Chicomo, Moz. B5 49
Chicontepec, Mex. m14 63
Chicopee, Ga., U.S. B3 87
Chicopee, Ks., U.S. E9 93
Chicopee, Ma., U.S. B2 98
Chicora, Ms., U.S. D5 101
Chicora, Pa., U.S. E2 115
Chicot, co., Ar., U.S. D4 81
Chicot, Lake, l., Ar., U.S. D4 81
Chicota, Tx., U.S. C5 120
Chicot Island, i., La., U.S. E6 95
Chicoutimi, P.Q., Can. A6 74
Chicoutimi, co., P.Q., Can. A7 74
Chicoutimi, stm., P.Q., Can. A6 74
Chidester, Ar., U.S. D2 81
Chidley, Cape, c., Can. f8 72
Chieerete Island, i., Marsh Is. P18 52
Chiefland, Fl., U.S. C4 86
Chiefs Point, c., On., Can. C3 73
Chiem Lake, l., F.R.Ger. E6 18
Chien, Bayou de, stm., Ky., U.S. f8 94
Chieri, Italy B1 23
Chiers, stm., Eur. E5 17
Chiese, stm., Italy D6 20
Chieti, Italy C5 23
Chifeng, China C8 31
Chigasaki, Japan *I9 33
Chigirin, Sov. Un. G9 27
Chignahuapan, Mex. n14 63
Chignecto, Cape, c., N.S., Can. D5 71
Chignecto Bay, b., Can. D5 71
Chignik, Ak., U.S. D8 79
Chigubo, Moz. B5 49
Chigwell, Eng., U.K. k13 10
Chihli, Gulf of (Bo Hai), b., China D8 31
Chihuahua, Mex. B3 63
Chihuahua, state, Mex. B3 63
Chii, Mount, mtn., S. Kor. I3 33
Chikaskia, stm., U.S. A4 113
Chikura, Japan o18 33
Chilapa [de Alvarez], Mex. D5 63
Chilca, Peru D2 58
Chilcotin, stm., B.C., Can. C6 69
Childersburg, Al., U.S. B3 78
Childress, Tx., U.S. B2 120
Childress, co., Tx., U.S. B2 120
Chile, ctry., S.A. G3 53
Chilecito, Arg. E2 55
Chilete, Peru C2 58
Chilhowee, Mo., U.S. C4 102
Chilhowee Mountain, mtn., Tn., U.S. n14 119
Chilhowie, Va., U.S. f10 123
Chili, In., U.S. C5 91
Chili, N.M., U.S. *A3 108
Chili, Wi., U.S. D3 126
Chilibre, Pan. k11 62
Chili Center, N.Y., U.S. *B3 109
Chililabombwe (Bancroft), Zam. D4 48
Chilili, N.M., U.S. C3 108
Chilka Lake, l., India H10 37
Chilkat Pass, B.C., Can. E5 66
Chilko, stm., B.C., Can. D6 69
Chilko Lake, l., B.C., Can. D5 69
Chillán, Chile B2 54
Chilli, Sov. Un. E7 28
Chillicothe, Il., U.S. C4 90
Chillicothe, Ia., U.S. C5 92
Chillicothe, Mo., U.S. B4 102
Chillicothe, Oh., U.S. C3 112
Chillicothe, Tx., U.S. B3 120
Chilliwack, B.C., Can. E7 69
Chilliwack, stm., N.A. A4 124
Chillum, Md., U.S. f9 97
Chilmark, Ma., U.S. D6 98
Chilocco, Ok., U.S. A4 113
Chiloé, Isla de, i., Chile C2 54
Chiloquin, Or., U.S. E5 114
Chilpancingo [de los Bravos], Mex. D5 63
Chilton, Tx., U.S. D4 120
Chilton, Wi., U.S. D5 126
Chilton, co., Al., U.S. C3 78
Chiluage, Ang. C3 48
Chilumba, Mwi. D5 48
Chilung (Keelung), Tai. F9 31
Chilwa, Lake, l., Afr. E6 48
Chimacum, Wa., U.S. A3 124
Chimalhuacán, Mex. h10 63
Chimaltenango, Guat. C2 62
Chimán, Pan. F8 62
Chimay, Bel. D4 17
Chimayo, N.M., U.S. A4 108
Chimbay, Sov. Un. E8 29
Chimborazo, prov., Ec. B2 58
Chimborazo, vol., Ec. B2 58
Chimbote, Peru C2 58
Chimkent, Sov. Un. E9 29
Chimney Rock, Co., U.S. D3 83
Chimney Rock, mtn., Ky., U.S. D5 94
Chimney Rock, mtn., Ne., U.S. C2 104
Chimneytop, mtn., Tn., U.S. C11 119
Chimoio, Moz. A5 49
Chin, Ab., Can. E4 68
Chin, Cape, c., On., Can. B3 73
Chinā, Japan O5 52
China, Mex. B5 63
China, Me., U.S. D3 96
China, ctry., Asia E6 31
China Grove, N.C., U.S. B2 110
Chinajá, Guat. D6 63
China Lake, l., Me., U.S. D3 96
Chinan see Jinan, China D8 31
Chinandega, Nic. E7 63
Chinati Peak, mtn., Tx., U.S. p12 120
Chincha Alta, Peru D2 58
Chincheros, Peru D3 58
Chinchilla, Austl. E9 50
Chinchilla [de Monte Aragón], Spain C5 22
Chincoteague, Va., U.S. C7 123
Chincoteague Bay, b., U.S. D7 97
Chinde, Moz. A6 49
Chindo, S. Kor. I3 33
Chindwin, stm., Burma C10 36
Chingola, Zam. D4 48
Chinguar, Ang. D2 48
Chinguetti, Maur. B2 45
Chinhae, S. Kor. I4 33
Chinhoyi, Zimb. A5 49
Chiniot, Pak. B5 36
Chínipas, Mex. B3 63
Chinit, stm., Kam. F6 35
Chinitna Point, c., Ak., U.S. h15 79
Chinju, S. Kor. D10 31
Chinko, stm., Cen. Afr. Rep. D4 46
Chin Lakes, l., Ab., Can. E4 68
Chinle, Az., U.S. A6 80
Chinle Valley, val., Az., U.S. A6 80
Chinle Wash, val., U.S. A6 80
Chinnampo see Nampo, N. Kor. D10 31
Chino, Ca., U.S. F5 82
Chinon, Fr. D4 16
Chinook, Ab., Can. D5 68
Chinook, Mt., U.S. B7 103
Chinook, Wa., U.S. C2 124
Chinook, Lake, res., Or., U.S. C5 114
Chinook Cove, B.C., Can. D7 69
Chino Valley, Az., U.S. C3 80
Chinquapin, N.C., U.S. C5 110
Chinsali, Zam. D5 48
Chinteche, Mwi. D5 48
Chinú, Col. B2 60
Chioco, Moz. A5 49
Chioggia, Italy B4 23
Chios see Khíos, i., Grc. C5 40
Chipata (Fort Jameson), Zam. D5 48
Chipewyan, stm., Ab., Can. A4 68
Chipinge, Zimb. B5 49
Chipita Park, Co., U.S. C6 83
Chip Lake, l., Ab., Can. C3 68
Chipley, Fl., U.S. u16 86
Chipman, Ab., Can. C4 68
Chipman, N.B., Can. C4 71
Chipola, stm., Fl., U.S. B1 86
Chippenham, Eng., U.K. C5 12
Chippewa, co., Mi., U.S. B6 99
Chippewa, co., Mn., U.S. E3 100
Chippewa, co., Wi., U.S. C2 126
Chippewa, stm., Mn., U.S. E3 100
Chippewa, stm., Wi., U.S. D2 126
Chippewa, East Branch, stm., Mn., U.S. E3 100
Chippewa, East Fork, stm., Wi., U.S. C3 126
Chippewa, Lake, l., Wi., U.S. C2 126
Chippewa Falls, Wi., U.S. D2 126
Chippewa Lake, Mi., U.S. E5 99
Chipping Norton, Eng., U.K. C6 12
Chipuriro, Zimb. A5 49
Chiputneticook Lakes, l., N.A. C5 96
Chipuxet, stm., R.I., U.S. F3 116
Chiquimula, Guat. E7 63
Chiquimulilla, Guat. C2 62
Chiquinquirá, Col. B3 60
Chira, stm., S.A. B1 58
Chiradzulu, Mwi. E6 48
Chirchik, Sov. Un. E7 28
Chiredzi, Zimb. B5 49
Chireno, Tx., U.S. D5 120
Chirfa, Niger B7 45
Chiricahua Mountains, mts., Az., U.S. E6 80
Chiricahua National Monument, Az., U.S. F6 80
Chiricahua Peak, mtn., Az., U.S. F6 80
Chirikof Island, i., Ak., U.S. D8 79
Chiriquí, Golfo de, b., Pan. G6 62
Chiriquí Grande, Pan. F6 62
Chiromo, Mwi. E6 48
Chirpan, Bul. D7 24
Chirripó, Cerro, mtn., C.R. F6 62
Chirundu, Zimb. A4 49
Chisago, co., Mn., U.S. E6 100
Chisago City, Mn., U.S. E6 100
Chisamba, Zam. D4 48
Chisana, Ak., U.S. C11 79
Chisholm, Me., U.S. D2 96
Chisholm, Mn., U.S. C6 100
Chisholm Mills, Ab., Can. B3 68
Chișineu-Criș, Rom. B5 24
Chisos Mountains, mts., Tx., U.S. E1 120
Chistochina, Ak., U.S. C11 79
Chistopol, Sov. Un. B4 28
Chita, Sov. Un. D14 29
Chitado, Ang. E1 48
Chitato, Ang. C3 48
Chitek, Sk., Can. D2 75
Chitek Lake, l., Mb., Can. C2 70
Chitembo, Ang. D2 48
Chitina, Ak., U.S. C11 79
Chitina, stm., Ak., U.S. g19 79
Chitipa, Mwi. C5 48
Chitradurga, India F6 36
Chitrāl, Pak. A5 36
Chitré, Pan. G7 62
Chittagong, Bngl. D9 36
Chittenango, N.Y., U.S. B5 109
Chittenden, Vt., U.S. D3 122
Chittenden, co., Vt., U.S. C2 122
Chittenden Reservoir, res., Vt., U.S. D3 122
Chittoor, India F6 36
Chitungwiza, Zimb. A5 49
Chíuchíu, Chile D2 55
Chiumbe, stm., Afr. C3 48
Chiúme, Ang. E3 48
Chiusi, Italy C3 23
Chivasso, Italy B1 23
Chivay, Peru E3 58
Chivhu, Zimb. A5 49
Chivilcoy, Arg. A4 54
Chivington, Co., U.S. C8 83
Chixoy, stm., Guat. C2 62
Chizhapka, stm., Sov. Un. B9 28
Chloride, Az., U.S. B1 80
Chmielnik, Pol. C6 26
Choapa, stm., Chile A2 54
Choapan, Mex. D5 63
Chobe, stm., Afr. A3 49
Choccolocco, Al., U.S. B4 78
Choccolocco Creek, stm., Al., U.S. B3 78
Chochiwŏn, S. Kor. H3 33
Chocó, dept., Col. B2 60
Chocolate Mountains, mts., U.S. F6 82
Chocontá, Col. B3 60
Chocorua, N.H., U.S. C4 106
Chocorua, Mount, mtn., N.H., U.S. C4 106
Chocowinity, N.C., U.S. B5 110
Choctaw, Ar., U.S. B3 81
Choctaw, Ok., U.S. B4 113
Choctaw, co., Al., U.S. C1 78
Choctaw, co., Ms., U.S. B4 101
Choctaw, co., Ok., U.S. C6 113
Choctawhatchee, East Fork, stm., Al., U.S. D4 78
Choctawhatchee, West Fork, stm., Al., U.S. D4 78
Choctawhatchee Bay, b., Fl., U.S. u15 86
Choctaw Indian Reservation, Ms., U.S. C4 101
Chodzież, Pol. B4 26
Choele Choel, Arg. B3 54
Choiceland, Sk., Can. D3 75
Choiseul, i., Sol.Is. G9 6
Choisy-le-Roi, Fr. g10 16
Choix, Mex. B3 63
Chojna, Pol. B3 26
Chojnice, Pol. B4 26
Chojnów, Pol. C3 26
Chōkai, Mount, mtn., Japan G10 33
Choke Mountains, mts., Eth. C4 47
Chokio, Mn., U.S. E2 100
Chokoloskee, Fl., U.S. G5 86
Chokwé, Moz. B5 49
Cholame, Ca., U.S. E3 82
Cholet, Fr. D3 16
Cholo, Mwi. E6 48
Cholula [de Rivadabia], Mex. n14 63
Choluteca, Hond. E7 63
Choluteca, stm., Hond. D4 62
Choma, Zam. E4 48
Chomo Lhāri, mtn., Asia D12 37
Chomutov, Czech. C2 26
Chŏnan, S. Kor. H3 33
Chon Buri, Thai. C2 34
Chone, Ec. B1 58
Chong'an, China K8 32
Chŏngjin, N. Kor. C10 31
Chŏngju, N. Kor. G2 33
Chŏngju, S. Kor. D10 31
Chongqing (Chungking), China F6 31
Chongren, China K6 32
Chongsŏng [-nodongjaru], N. Kor. E4 33
Chŏnju, S. Kor. D10 31
Chonos, Archipiélago de los, is., Chile C2 54
Chonzie, Ben, mtn., Scot., U.K. D5 13
Chopim, stm., Braz. D2 56
Choptank, Md., U.S. C6 97
Choptank, stm., Md., U.S. C6 97
Chorrillos, Peru D2 58
Chortkov, Sov. Un. G5 27
Chorwŏn, N. Kor. D10 31
Chŏrwŏn, S. Kor. G3 33
Chorzów, Pol. C5 26
Chosan, N. Kor. F2 33
Chōshi, Japan I10 33
Chosica, Peru D2 58
Chos Malal, Arg. B2 54
Choszczno, Pol. B3 26
Chota, Peru C2 58
Choteau, Mt., U.S. C4 103
Chotětov, Czech. n18 26
Choudrant, La., U.S. B3 95
Choudrant, Bayou, stm., La., U.S. B3 95
Choum, Maur. B2 45
Choushan Islands see Zhoushan Islands, is., China E9 31
Chouteau, Ok., U.S. A6 113
Chouteau, co., Mt., U.S. C6 103
Chowan, co., N.C., U.S. A6 110
Chowan, stm., N.C., U.S. A6 110
Chowchilla, Ca., U.S. D3 82
Choybalsan, Mong. B7 31
Choyr, Mong. B6 31
Chrisman, Il., U.S. D6 90
Chrisney, In., U.S. H3 91
Christchurch, N.Z. O14 51
Christchurch, Eng., U.K. D6 12
Christian, co., Il., U.S. D4 90
Christian, co., Ky., U.S. D2 94
Christian, co., Mo., U.S. E4 102
Christiana, Jam. E14 65
Christiana, S. Afr. C4 49
Christiana, De., U.S. B3 85
Christiana, Pa., U.S. G9 115
Christiana, Tn., U.S. B5 119
Christian Hollow, N.H., U.S. D2 106
Christian Island, i., On., Can. C4 73
Christiansburg, Oh., U.S. B1 112
Christiansburg, Va., U.S. C2 123
Christiansfeld, Den. C3 15
Christian Sound, strt., Ak., U.S. n22 79
Christiansted, V.I.U.S. H12 64
Christina, Mt., U.S. C7 103
Christina, stm., Ab., Can. A5 68
Christina, stm., De., U.S. B3 85
Christina, Lake, l., Mn., U.S. D3 100
Christina Lake, l., Ab., Can. B5 68
Christina Peak, mtn., Nv., U.S. D6 105
Christine, N.D., U.S. C9 111
Christine, Tx., U.S. E3 120
Christmas, Fl., U.S. D5 86
Christmas Island, dep., Oc. G6 6
Christmas Island see Kiritimati Island, i., Kir. F12 6
Christmas Lake, l., Or., U.S. D6 114
Christmas Valley, Or., U.S. D6 114
Christopher, Il., U.S. F4 90
Christoval, Tx., U.S. D2 120
Chromo, Co., U.S. D4 83
Chrudim, Czech. D3 26
Chrysler, Al., U.S. D2 78
Chrzanów, Pol. g10 26
Chu, Sov. Un. E8 28
Chu, stm., Sov. Un. G23 8
Chubbuck, Id., U.S. G6 89
Chubut, prov., Arg. C3 54
Chubut, stm., Arg. C3 54
Chu Chua, B.C., Can. D7 69
Chuckey, Tn., U.S. C11 119
Chudovo, Sov. Un. B8 27
Chugach Islands, is., Ak., U.S. h16 79
Chugach Mountains, mts., Ak., U.S. g18 79
Chuguyev, Sov. Un. G11 27
Chugwater, Wy., U.S. E8 127
Chugwater Creek, stm., Wy., U.S. E8 127
Chuichu, Az., U.S. E4 80
Chuius Mountain, mtn., B.C., Can. B5 69
Chukai, Malay. J5 35
Chukchi Sea C32 128
Chukotsk Peninsula, pen., Sov. Un. C32 128
Chula, Ga., U.S. E3 87
Chula, Mo., U.S. B4 102
Chula, Va., U.S. C5 123

Name	Map Ref	Page
Chula Vista, Ca., U.S.	F5	82
Chulucanas, Peru	B1	58
Chulumani, Bol.	C2	55
Chulym, Sov. Un.	B10	28
Chulym, stm., Sov. Un.	D11	29
Chumbicha, Arg.	E2	55
Chumikan, Sov. Un.	D16	29
Chumphon, Thai.	G3	35
Chumysh, stm., Sov. Un.	C10	28
Chun'an, China	J8	32
Chunchŏn, S. Kor.	H3	33
Chunchula, Al., U.S.	E1	78
Chungju, S. Kor.	H3	33
Chungking see Chongqing, China	F6	31
Chungmu, S. Kor.	H4	33
Chunky, Ms., U.S.	C5	101
Chunya, Tan.	C5	48
Chuoi, i., Viet.	H6	35
Chupaca, Peru	D2	58
Chupadera Mesa, mtn., N.M., U.S.	D3	108
Chupadero, N.M., U.S.	*B4	108
Chupara Point, c., Trin.	N23	65
Chuquibamba, Peru	E3	58
Chuquicamata, Chile	D2	55
Chuquisaca, dept., Bol.	C2	55
Chur, Switz.	E4	18
Churchbridge, Sk., Can.	G5	75
Church Creek, Md., U.S.	C5	97
Church Hill, Md., U.S.	B6	97
Church Hill, Ms., U.S.	D2	101
Church Hill, Tn., U.S.	C11	119
Churchill, Mb., Can.	f9	70
Churchill, Oh., U.S.	*A5	112
Churchill, co., Nv., U.S.	D3	105
Churchill, stm., Can.	E13	66
Churchill, stm., Nf., Can.	h9	72
Churchill, Cape, c., Mb., Can.	f9	70
Churchill, Mount, mtn., B.C., Can.	E6	69
Churchill Falls, wtfl, Nf., Can.	h8	72
Churchill Lake, l., Sk., Can.	m7	75
Churchill Lake, l., Me., U.S.	B3	96
Church Mountain, mtn., B.C., Can.	f14	69
Church Point, N.S., Can.	E3	71
Church Point, La., U.S.	D3	95
Church Rock, N.M., U.S.	B1	108
Churchs Ferry, N.D., U.S.	A6	111
Church Stretton, Eng., U.K.	B5	12
Churchton, Md., U.S.	C4	97
Churchville, Md., U.S.	A5	97
Churchville, N.Y., U.S.	B3	109
Churchville, Va., U.S.	B3	123
Churdan, Ia., U.S.	B3	92
Churu, India	C5	37
Churubusco, In., U.S.	B7	91
Churubusco, N.Y., U.S.	f11	109
Churuguara, Ven.	A4	60
Churumuco, Mex.	n13	63
Chushul, India	B6	36
Chuska Mountains, mts., Az., U.S.	A6	80
Chusovaya, stm., Sov. Un.	D20	8
Chusovoy, Sov. Un.	B5	28
Chust, Sov. Un.	G23	8
Chuxian, China	H8	32
Chuxiong, China	F5	31
Chuy, Ur.	E2	56
Ciano d'Enza, Italy	E6	20
Cianorte, Braz.	C2	56
Cibecue, Az., U.S.	C5	80
Cibola, co., N.M., U.S.	C1	108
Cibolo Creek, stm., Tx., U.S.	h7	120
Çiçekdağı, Tur.	C10	40
Cicero, Il., U.S.	B6	90
Cicero, In., U.S.	D5	91
Cícero Dantas, Braz.	D3	57
Ciche, Sgùrr na, mtn., Scot., U.K.	D3	13
Cicia, i., Fiji	H16	52
Cide, Tur.	B9	40
Cidra, Lago de, res., P.R.	B3	65
Ciechanów, Pol.	B6	26
Ciego de Avila, Cuba	D4	64
Ciego de Avila, prov., Cuba	C4	64
Ciempozuelos, Spain	B4	22
Ciénaga, Col.	A3	60
Ciénaga de Oro, Col.	B2	60
Cienfuegos, Cuba	C3	64
Cienfuegos, prov., Cuba	C3	64
Cieszyn, Pol.	D5	26
Cieza, Spain	C5	22
Ciężkowice, Pol.	g10	26
Cigüela, stm., Spain	C4	22
Cihanbeyli, Tur.	C9	40
Cihuatlán, Mex.	n11	63
Cilacap, Indon.	G3	34
Cili, China	J4	32
Cima, Ca., U.S.	E6	82
Cimarron, Co., U.S.	C3	83
Cimarron, Ks., U.S.	E3	93
Cimarron, N.M., U.S.	A5	108
Cimarron, co., Ok., U.S.	e8	113
Cimarron, stm., U.S.	C8	76
Cimarron, North Fork, stm., U.S.	E2	93
Cîmpina, Rom.	C7	24
Cîmpulung, Rom.	C7	24
Cîmpulung Moldovenesc, Rom.	B7	24
Cincinnati, Ia., U.S.	D5	92
Cincinnati, Oh., U.S.	C1	112
Cincinnatus, N.Y., U.S.	C5	109
Cinconsine, Lac, l., P.Q., Can.	B4	74
Çine, Tur.	D7	25
Cinnaminson, N.J., U.S.	D3	107
Cintalapa [de Figueroa], Mex.	D6	63
Cinto, Monte, mtn., Fr.	C2	23
Cipolletti, Arg.	B3	54
Circle, Ak., U.S.	B11	79
Circle, Mt., U.S.	C11	103
Circle Hot Springs, Ak., U.S.	B11	79
Circle Pines, Mn., U.S.	m12	100
Circleville, Ks., U.S.	C8	93
Circleville, Oh., U.S.	C3	112
Circleville, Ut., U.S.	E3	121
Circleville, W.V., U.S.	C5	125
Cirebon, Indon.	G3	34
Cirencester, Eng., U.K.	E6	10
Cirí, stm., Pan.	m10	62
Cisco, Ga., U.S.	B2	87
Cisco, Il., U.S.	C5	90
Cisco, Tx., U.S.	C3	120
Cisco, Ut., U.S.	E6	121
Ciskei, ctry., Afr.	D4	49
Cisne, Il., U.S.	E5	90
Cisneros, Col.	B2	60
Cisnes, stm., Chile	C2	54
Cispus, stm., Wa., U.S.	C4	124
Cissna Park, Il., U.S.	C6	90
Cistern, Tx., U.S.	E4	120
Cisterna di Latina, Italy	h9	23
Cistierna, Spain	A3	22
Citac, Nevado, mtn., Peru	D2	58
Citlaltépetl, Volcán (Pico de Orizaba), vol., Mex.	n15	63
Citra, Fl., U.S.	C4	86
Citronelle, Al., U.S.	D1	78
Citrus, co., Fl., U.S.	D4	86
Citrus Heights, Ca., U.S.	*C3	82
Cittadella, Italy	B3	23
Città di Castello, Italy	C4	23
City Mills, Ma., U.S.	h10	98
City of Commerce, Ca., U.S.	n12	82
City of Refuge National Historical Park, Hi., U.S.	D5	88
City Point, Fl., U.S.	D6	86
City View, S.C., U.S.	B3	117
Ciudad Acuña, Mex.	B4	63
Ciudad Altamirano, Mex.	n13	63
Ciudad Bolívar, Ven.	B5	60
Ciudad Bolivia, Ven.	B3	60
Ciudad Camargo, Mex.	B3	63
Ciudad de la Habana, prov., Cuba	C2	64
Ciudad del Carmen, Mex.	D6	63
Ciudad del Maíz, Mex.	C5	63
Ciudad de Naucalpan de Juárez, Mex.	h9	63
Ciudad de Valles, Mex.	C5	63
Ciudad de Villaldama, Mex.	B4	63
Ciudad Guayana, Ven.	B5	60
Ciudad Guzmán, Mex.	D4	63
Ciudad Ixtepec, Mex.	D5	63
Ciudad Jiménez, Mex.	B4	63
Ciudad Juárez, Mex.	A3	63
Ciudad Lerdo, Mex.	C4	63
Ciudad López Mateos, Mex.	g9	63
Ciudad Madero, Mex.	C5	63
Ciudad Mante, Mex.	C5	63
Ciudad Melchor Múzquiz, Mex.	B4	63
Ciudad Mendoza, Mex.	n15	63
Ciudad Obregón, Mex.	B3	63
Ciudad Ojeda, Ven.	A3	60
Ciudad Piar, Ven.	B5	60
Ciudad Real, Spain	C4	22
Ciudad Rodrigo, Spain	B2	22
Ciudad Serdán, Mex.	n15	63
Ciudad Victoria, Mex.	C5	63
Cividale del Friuli, Italy	A4	23
Civitanova Marche, Italy	C4	23
Civitavecchia, Italy	C3	23
Civray, Fr.	D4	16
Çivril, Tur.	C7	40
Cizre, Tur.	D14	40
C.J. Strike Reservoir, res., Id., U.S.	G3	89
Clackamas, Or., U.S.	h12	114
Clackamas, co., Or., U.S.	B4	114
Claflin, Ks., U.S.	D5	93
Clacton-on-Sea, Eng., U.K.	C9	12
Claiborne, Al., U.S.	D2	78
Claiborne, Md., U.S.	C5	97
Claiborne, co., La., U.S.	B2	95
Claiborne, co., Ms., U.S.	D3	101
Claiborne, co., Tn., U.S.	C10	119
Claiborne, Lake, res., La., U.S.	B3	95
Clair, N.B., Can.	B1	71
Clair, Sk., Can.	E3	75
Claire, Lac, l., Ab., Can.	f8	68
Claire City, S.D., U.S.	B8	118
Clair Engle Lake, l., Ca., U.S.	B2	82
Clair-Mel City, Fl., U.S.	*E4	86
Clairton, Pa., U.S.	F2	115
Clallam, co., Wa., U.S.	A1	124
Clallam Bay, Wa., U.S.	A1	124
Clamart, Fr.	g10	16
Clamecy, Fr.	D5	16
Clam Lake, l., Sk., Can.	B3	75
Clam Lake, l., Wi., U.S.	C1	126
Clan Alpine Mountains, mts., Nv., U.S.	D4	105
Clancy, Mt., U.S.	D5	103
Clandeboye, On., Can.	D3	73
Clandonald, Ab., Can.	C5	68
Clanton, Al., U.S.	C3	78
Clanwilliam, Mb., Can.	D2	70
Clanwilliam, S. Afr.	D2	49
Clapperton Island, i., On., Can.	A2	73
Clara, Ire.	D4	11
Clara, Ms., U.S.	D5	101
Clara City, Mn., U.S.	F3	100
Clara Peak, mtn., Az., U.S.	C2	80
Clare, Austl.	F6	50
Clare, Mi., U.S.	D6	99
Clare, Ut., U.S.	D4	121
Clare, co., Ire.	E3	11
Clare, co., Mi., U.S.	E6	99
Clare, stm., Ire.	D3	11
Clarecastle (Clare), Ire.	E3	11
Claregalway, Ire.	D3	11
Clare Island, i., Ire.	C1	11
Claremont, Ca., U.S.	m13	82
Claremont, Il., U.S.	E6	90
Claremont, Mn., U.S.	F6	100
Claremont, N.H., U.S.	D2	106
Claremont, N.C., U.S.	B1	110
Claremont, S.D., U.S.	B7	118
Claremont, Va., U.S.	C6	123
Claremont, mtn., Ca., U.S.	C3	82
Claremore, Ok., U.S.	A6	113
Claremorris, Ire.	D2	10
Clarence, Al., U.S.	A3	78
Clarence, Ia., U.S.	C6	92
Clarence, La., U.S.	C2	95
Clarence, Mo., U.S.	B5	102
Clarence, Pa., U.S.	D6	115
Clarence, stm., N.Z.	O14	51
Clarence, Isla, i., Chile	h11	54
Clarence Cannon Lake, res., Mo., U.S.	B6	102
Clarence Island, i., B.A.T.	C7	7
Clarence Strait, strt., Austl.	B5	50
Clarence Strait, strt., Ak., U.S.	n23	79
Clarence Town, Bah.	C6	64
Clarenceville, P.Q., Can.	D4	74
Clarendon, Ar., U.S.	C4	81
Clarendon, Pa., U.S.	C3	115
Clarendon, Tx., U.S.	B2	120
Clarendon, Vt., U.S.	D2	122
Clarendon, co., S.C., U.S.	D7	117
Clarendon, stm., Vt., U.S.	E2	122
Clarendon Hills, Il., U.S.	k9	90
Clarendon Station, On., Can.	C8	73
Clarenville, Nf., Can.	D4	72
Claresholm, Ab., Can.	D4	68
Claridge, Pa., U.S.	F2	115
Clarie Coast, Ant.	C26	7
Clarinda, Ia., U.S.	D2	92
Clarington, Oh., U.S.	C5	112
Clarington, Pa., U.S.	D3	115
Clarion, Ia., U.S.	B4	92
Clarion, Pa., U.S.	D3	115
Clarion, co., Pa., U.S.	D3	115
Clarissa, Mn., U.S.	D4	100
Clarita, Ok., U.S.	C5	113
Clark, Co., U.S.	A4	83
Clark, Mo., U.S.	B5	102
Clark, N.J., U.S.	B4	107
Clark, Oh., U.S.	B4	112
Clark, S.D., U.S.	C8	118
Clark, co., Ar., U.S.	C2	81
Clark, co., Id., U.S.	E6	89
Clark, co., Il., U.S.	D6	90
Clark, co., In., U.S.	H6	91
Clark, co., Ks., U.S.	E4	93
Clark, co., Ky., U.S.	C5	94
Clark, co., Mo., U.S.	A6	102
Clark, co., Nv., U.S.	G6	105
Clark, co., Oh., U.S.	C2	112
Clark, co., S.D., U.S.	C8	118
Clark, co., Wa., U.S.	D3	124
Clark, co., Wi., U.S.	D3	126
Clark, Lake, l., Ak., U.S.	C9	79
Clark, Point, c., On., Can.	C3	73
Clark Colony, S.D., U.S.	*C8	118
Clarkdale, Az., U.S.	C3	80
Clarkdale, Ga., U.S.	h7	87
Clarke, co., Al., U.S.	D2	78
Clarke, co., Ga., U.S.	C3	87
Clarke, co., Ia., U.S.	D4	92
Clarke, co., Ms., U.S.	C5	101
Clarke, co., Va., U.S.	A4	123
Clarke City, P.Q., Can.	h8	72
Clarke Lake, l., Sk., Can.	C2	75
Clarkesville, Ga., U.S.	B3	87
Clarkfield, Mn., U.S.	F3	100
Clark Fork, Id., U.S.	A2	89
Clark Fork, stm., U.S.	C1	103
Clarkia, Id., U.S.	B2	89
Clark Mountain, mtn., Mo., U.S.	D7	102
Clarkrange, Tn., U.S.	C8	119
Clarks, La., U.S.	B3	95
Clarks, Ne., U.S.	C8	104
Clarks, stm., Ky., U.S.	f9	94
Clarks, West Fork, stm., Ky., U.S.	f9	94
Clarksboro, N.J., U.S.	D2	107
Clarksburg, On., Can.	C4	73
Clarksburg, In., U.S.	F7	91
Clarksburg, Md., U.S.	B3	97
Clarksburg, Mo., U.S.	C5	102
Clarksburg, N.J., U.S.	C4	107
Clarksburg, Oh., U.S.	C2	112
Clarksburg, Tn., U.S.	B3	119
Clarksburg, W.V., U.S.	B4	125
Clarksdale, Ms., U.S.	A3	101
Clarksdale, Mo., U.S.	B3	102
Clarks Falls, Ct., U.S.	D8	84
Clarks Grove, Mn., U.S.	G5	100
Clark's Harbour, N.S., Can.	F4	71
Clarks Hill, In., U.S.	D4	91
Clarkson, Ky., U.S.	C3	94
Clarkson, Ne., U.S.	C8	104
Clarks Point, Ak., U.S.	D8	79
Clarks Summit, Pa., U.S.	m18	115
Clarkston, Ga., U.S.	h8	87
Clarkston, Mi., U.S.	F7	99
Clarkston, Ut., U.S.	B3	121
Clarkston, Wa., U.S.	C8	124
Clarksville, N.S., Can.	D6	71
Clarksville, Ar., U.S.	B2	81
Clarksville, De., U.S.	F5	85
Clarksville, Ia., U.S.	B5	92
Clarksville, In., U.S.	H6	91
Clarksville, Md., U.S.	B4	97
Clarksville, Mi., U.S.	F5	99
Clarksville, Mo., U.S.	B7	102
Clarksville, Oh., U.S.	C2	112
Clarksville, Tn., U.S.	A4	119
Clarksville, Tx., U.S.	C5	120
Clarksville, Va., U.S.	D4	123
Clarkton, Mo., U.S.	E8	102
Clarkton, N.C., U.S.	C4	110
Claryville, Ky., U.S.	k14	94
Clashmore, Ire.	E4	11
Clatonia, Ne., U.S.	D9	104
Clatskanie, Or., U.S.	A3	114
Clatsop, co., Or., U.S.	A3	114
Claude, Tx., U.S.	B2	120
Claudy, N. Ire., U.K.	C4	11
Claunch, N.M., U.S.	C3	108
Clausthal-Zellerfeld, F.R.Ger.	C5	18
Clavet, Sk., Can.	F2	75
Clawson, Mi., U.S.	o15	99
Clawson, Ut., U.S.	D4	121
Claxton, Ga., U.S.	D5	87
Clay, Al., U.S.	f7	78
Clay, Ca., U.S.	C3	82
Clay, La., U.S.	B3	95
Clay, N.Y., U.S.	B4	109
Clay, Wy., U.S.	B8	127
Clay, co., Al., U.S.	B4	78
Clay, co., Ar., U.S.	A5	81
Clay, co., Fl., U.S.	B5	86
Clay, co., Ga., U.S.	E2	87
Clay, co., Il., U.S.	E5	90
Clay, co., In., U.S.	F3	91
Clay, co., Ia., U.S.	A2	92
Clay, co., Ks., U.S.	C6	93
Clay, co., Ky., U.S.	C6	94
Clay, co., Mn., U.S.	D2	100
Clay, co., Ms., U.S.	B5	101
Clay, co., Mo., U.S.	B3	102
Clay, co., Ne., U.S.	D7	104
Clay, co., N.C., U.S.	f9	110
Clay, co., S.D., U.S.	E8	118
Clay, co., Tn., U.S.	C8	119
Clay, co., Tx., U.S.	C3	120
Clay, co., W.V., U.S.	C3	125
Clay Center, Ks., U.S.	C6	93
Clay Center, Ne., U.S.	D7	104
Clay Center, Oh., U.S.	A2	112
Clay City, Il., U.S.	E5	90
Clay City, In., U.S.	F3	91
Clay City, Ky., U.S.	C6	94
Clay Creek, stm., Co., U.S.	D8	83
Clay Creek, stm., S.D., U.S.	D3	118
Claydon, Sk., Can.	H1	75
Clayhatchee, Al., U.S.	D4	78
Clay Head, c., I. of Man	F4	13
Claypool, Az., U.S.	D5	80
Claypool, In., U.S.	B6	91
Claysburg, Pa., U.S.	F5	115
Clay Springs, Az., U.S.	C5	80
Claysville, Pa., U.S.	F1	115
Clayton, On., Can.	B8	73
Clayton, Al., U.S.	D4	78
Clayton, De., U.S.	C3	85
Clayton, Ga., U.S.	B3	87
Clayton, Id., U.S.	E4	89
Clayton, Il., U.S.	C3	90
Clayton, In., U.S.	E4	91
Clayton, Ks., U.S.	C3	93
Clayton, La., U.S.	C4	95
Clayton, Mo., U.S.	C7	102
Clayton, N.J., U.S.	D2	107
Clayton, N.M., U.S.	A6	108
Clayton, N.Y., U.S.	A4	109
Clayton, N.C., U.S.	B4	110
Clayton, Ok., U.S.	C6	113
Clayton, S.D., U.S.	D8	118
Clayton, Tn., U.S.	A2	119
Clayton, Wa., U.S.	B8	124
Clayton, Wi., U.S.	C1	126
Clayton, co., Ga., U.S.	C2	87
Clayton, co., Ia., U.S.	B6	92
Clayton Lake, Me., U.S.	B3	96
Claytor Lake, res., Va., U.S.	C2	123
Clayville, R.I., U.S.	C2	116
Clear, i., Ire.	F2	11
Clear, stm., Ab., Can.	A1	68
Clear, stm., R.I., U.S.	B2	116
Clear, Cape, c., Ire.	E2	10
Clear, Lake, l., On., Can.	B7	73
Clear Boggy Creek, stm., Ok., U.S.	C5	113
Clear Brook, B.C., Can.	f13	69
Clearbrook, Mn., U.S.	C3	100
Clear Creek, In., U.S.	F4	91
Clear Creek, W.V., U.S.	n13	125
Clear Creek, co., Co., U.S.	B5	83
Clear Creek, stm., Az., U.S.	C4	80
Clear Creek, stm., Tn., U.S.	C9	119
Clear Creek, stm., Wy., U.S.	B6	127
Cleare, Cape, c., Ak., U.S.	D10	79
Clearfield, Ia., U.S.	D3	92
Clearfield, Ky., U.S.	B6	94
Clearfield, Pa., U.S.	D5	115
Clearfield, S.D., U.S.	D5	118
Clearfield, Ut., U.S.	B3	121
Clearfield, co., Pa., U.S.	D5	115
Clear Fork, W.V., U.S.	D3	125
Clear Fork, stm., W.V., U.S.	n13	125
Clear Lake, Ca., U.S.	C2	82
Clear Lake, Ia., U.S.	A4	92
Clear Lake, Mn., U.S.	E5	100
Clear Lake, S.D., U.S.	C9	118
Clearlake, Wa., U.S.	A3	124
Clear Lake, Wi., U.S.	C1	126
Clear Lake, l., Mb., Can.	D1	70
Clear Lake, l., Ca., U.S.	A4	92
Clear Lake, l., Ut., U.S.	D3	121
Clear Lake, res., Ca., U.S.	C2	82
Clear Lake City, Tx., U.S.	r14	120
Clear Lake Reservoir, res., Ca., U.S.	B3	82
Clear Lake Shores, Tx., U.S.	r15	120
Clearmont, Mo., U.S.	A2	102
Clearmont, Wy., U.S.	B6	127
Clear Spring, Md., U.S.	A2	97
Clear Stream, stm., N.H., U.S.	A4	106
Clearview, Ok., U.S.	B5	113
Clearview City, Ks., U.S.	g12	93
Clearville, Pa., U.S.	G5	115
Clearwater, B.C., Can.	D7	69
Clearwater, Fl., U.S.	E4	86
Clearwater, Id., U.S.	C3	89
Clearwater, Ks., U.S.	E6	93
Clearwater, Mn., U.S.	E4	100
Clearwater, Ne., U.S.	B7	104
Clearwater, S.C., U.S.	E4	117
Clearwater, Wa., U.S.	B1	124
Clearwater, co., Id., U.S.	C3	89
Clearwater, co., Mn., U.S.	C3	100
Clearwater, stm., Ab., Can.	D3	68
Clearwater, stm., Can.	A5	68
Clearwater, stm., B.C., Can.	C7	69
Clearwater, stm., Mn., U.S.	C3	100
Clearwater Lake, Wi., U.S.	C4	126
Clearwater Lake, l., B.C., Can.	C7	69
Clearwater Lake, l., Mb., Can.	B1	70
Clearwater Lake, res., Mo., U.S.	D7	102
Clearwater Mountains, mts., Id., U.S.	C2	89
Clearwater Provincial Park, Mb., Can.	C1	70
Cleaton, Ky., U.S.	C2	94
Cleator Moor, Eng., U.K.	F5	13
Cleburne, Tx., U.S.	C4	120
Cleburne, co., Al., U.S.	B4	78
Cleburne, co., Ar., U.S.	B3	81
Cle Elum, Wa., U.S.	B4	124
Cle Elum, stm., Wa., U.S.	B4	124
Cle Elum Lake, res., Wa., U.S.	B4	124
Cleethorpes, Eng., U.K.	A7	12
Cleggan, Ire.	D1	11
Cleghorn, Ia., U.S.	B2	92
Cleland Heights, De., U.S.	*B3	85
Clem, Ga., U.S.	C1	87
Clementon, N.J., U.S.	D3	107
Clements, Ks., U.S.	D7	93
Clements, Md., U.S.	D4	97
Clements, Mn., U.S.	F3	100
Clementsvale, N.S., Can.	E4	71
Clemmons, N.C., U.S.	A2	110
Clemons, Ia., U.S.	B4	92
Clemons, N.Y., U.S.	B7	109
Clemscott, Ok., U.S.	C4	113
Clemson, S.C., U.S.	B2	117
Clendenin, W.V., U.S.	C3	125
Clendening Reservoir, res., Oh., U.S.	B4	112
Cleo Springs, Ok., U.S.	A3	113
Clermont, Austl.	D8	50
Clermont, P.Q., Can.	B7	74
Clermont, Fr.	E2	74
Clermont, Fl., U.S.	D5	86
Clermont, Ga., U.S.	B3	87
Clermont, Ia., U.S.	A6	92
Clermont, Ky., U.S.	C4	94
Clermont, co., Oh., U.S.	C1	112
Clermont-Ferrand, Fr.	E5	16
Clermont Harbor, Ms., U.S.	E4	101
Clermont-l'Hérault, Fr.	F5	16
Clerval, Fr.	D6	17
Clervaux, Lux.	B7	17
Clevedon, Eng., U.K.	C5	12
Cleveland, Al., U.S.	A3	78
Cleveland, Ar., U.S.	B3	81
Cleveland, Ga., U.S.	B3	87
Cleveland, Il., U.S.	B3	90
Cleveland, Mn., U.S.	F5	100
Cleveland, Ms., U.S.	B3	101
Cleveland, Mo., U.S.	C3	102
Cleveland, N.M., U.S.	A4	108
Cleveland, N.Y., U.S.	B5	109
Cleveland, N.C., U.S.	B2	110
Cleveland, N.D., U.S.	C6	111
Cleveland, Oh., U.S.	A4	112
Cleveland, Ok., U.S.	A5	113
Cleveland, S.C., U.S.	A2	117
Cleveland, Tn., U.S.	D9	119
Cleveland, Tx., U.S.	D5	120
Cleveland, Ut., U.S.	D5	121
Cleveland, Va., U.S.	f9	123
Cleveland, Wi., U.S.	k10	126
Cleveland, co., Eng., U.K.	F7	13
Cleveland, co., Ar., U.S.	D3	81
Cleveland, co., N.C., U.S.	B1	110
Cleveland, co., Ok., U.S.	B4	113
Cleveland, Mount, mtn., Mt., U.S.	B3	103
Cleveland Heights, Oh., U.S.	A4	112
Cleveland Hills, hills, Eng., U.K.	F7	13
Clevelândia, Braz.	D2	56
Clever, Mo., U.S.	D4	102
Cleves see Kleve, F.R.Ger.	C3	18
Cleves, Oh., U.S.	o12	112
Clewiston, Fl., U.S.	F6	86
Clichy, Fr.	g10	16
Cliff, N.M., U.S.	E1	108
Cliff Island, i., Me., U.S.	g7	96
Clifford, On., Can.	D4	73
Clifford, In., U.S.	F6	91
Clifford, Mi., U.S.	E7	99
Clifford, N.D., U.S.	B8	111
Clifford, Pa., U.S.	C10	115
Clifford, Va., U.S.	C3	123
Cliffside, N.C., U.S.	B1	110
Cliffside Park, N.J., U.S.	h9	107
Cliffwood Beach, N.J., U.S.	*C4	107
Clifton, Az., U.S.	D6	80
Clifton, Co., U.S.	B2	83
Clifton, Id., U.S.	G7	89
Clifton, Il., U.S.	C6	90
Clifton, N.J., U.S.	B4	107
Clifton, S.C., U.S.	B4	117
Clifton, Tn., U.S.	B4	119
Clifton, Tx., U.S.	D4	120
Clifton, Va., U.S.	g12	123
Clifton, W.V., U.S.	C1	126
Clifton City, Mo., U.S.	C4	102
Clifton Forge, Va., U.S.	C3	123
Clifton Heights, Pa., U.S.	*p20	115
Clifton Hill, Mo., U.S.	B5	102
Clifton Knolls, N.Y., U.S.	C7	109
Clifton Springs, N.Y., U.S.	C3	109
Cliftonville, Ms., U.S.	B5	101
Climax, Sk., Can.	H1	75
Climax, Co., U.S.	B4	83
Climax, Ga., U.S.	F2	87
Climax, Ks., U.S.	E7	93
Climax, Mi., U.S.	F5	99
Climax, Mn., U.S.	C2	100
Climax Springs, Mo., U.S.	C4	102
Climbing Hill, Ia., U.S.	B1	92
Clinch, co., Ga., U.S.	F4	87
Clinch, stm., U.S.	D9	119
Clinchco, Va., U.S.	e9	123
Clinchfield, Ga., U.S.	D3	87
Clinch Mountain, mtn., U.S.	C10	119
Clinchport, Va., U.S.	f9	123
Clingmans Dome, mtn., U.S.	D10	119
Clint, Tx., U.S.	o11	120
Clinton, B.C., Can.	D7	69
Clinton, On., Can.	D3	73
Clinton, Ar., U.S.	B3	81
Clinton, Ct., U.S.	D5	84
Clinton, Il., U.S.	C5	90
Clinton, In., U.S.	E3	91
Clinton, Ia., U.S.	C7	92
Clinton, Ks., U.S.	D8	93
Clinton, Ky., U.S.	f9	94
Clinton, La., U.S.	D4	95
Clinton, Me., U.S.	D3	96
Clinton, Md., U.S.	C4	97
Clinton, Ma., U.S.	B4	98
Clinton, Mi., U.S.	F7	99
Clinton, Mn., U.S.	E2	100
Clinton, Ms., U.S.	C3	101
Clinton, Mo., U.S.	C4	102
Clinton, Mt., U.S.	D2	103
Clinton, N.J., U.S.	B3	107
Clinton, N.Y., U.S.	B5	109
Clinton, N.C., U.S.	C4	110
Clinton, Oh., U.S.	A4	112
Clinton, Ok., U.S.	B3	113
Clinton, S.C., U.S.	C4	117
Clinton, Tn., U.S.	C9	119
Clinton, Ut., U.S.	B3	121
Clinton, Wi., U.S.	F5	126
Clinton, co., Il., U.S.	E4	90
Clinton, co., In., U.S.	D4	91
Clinton, co., Ia., U.S.	C7	92
Clinton, co., Ky., U.S.	D4	94
Clinton, co., Mi., U.S.	F6	99
Clinton, co., Mo., U.S.	B3	102
Clinton, co., N.Y., U.S.	f11	109
Clinton, co., Oh., U.S.	C2	112
Clinton, co., Pa., U.S.	D6	115
Clinton-Colden Lake, l., N.T., Can.	D11	66
Clinton Lake, res., Ks., U.S.	m15	93
Clinton Reservoir, res., N.J., U.S.	A4	107
Clinton Township, Mi., U.S.	*F8	99
Clintonville, Ky., U.S.	B5	94
Clintonville, Pa., U.S.	D2	115
Clintonville, W.V., U.S.	D4	125
Clintonville, Wi., U.S.	D5	126
Clintwood, Va., U.S.	e9	123
Clio, Al., U.S.	D4	78
Clio, Ia., U.S.	D4	92
Clio, Mi., U.S.	E7	99
Clio, S.C., U.S.	B8	117
Clio, W.V., U.S.	C3	125
Cliza, Bol.	C2	55
Cloan, Sk., Can.	E1	75
Cloe, Pa., U.S.	E3	115
Cloghan, Ire.	C4	11
Cloghan, Ire.	D4	11
Cloghane, Ire.	E1	11
Clogheen, Ire.	E1	11
Clogher Head, c., Ire.	D5	11
Clonakilty, Ire.	E2	10
Clonakilty Bay, b., Ire.	E2	10
Cloncurry, Austl.	D7	50
Clones, Ire.	C4	11
Clonmany, Ire.	B4	11
Clonmel, Ire.	D3	10
Clonmellon, Ire.	D4	11
Clontarf, Mn., U.S.	E3	100
Cloone, Ire.	D4	11
Cloppenburg, F.R.Ger.	F2	15
Clopton, Al., U.S.	D4	78
Cloquet, Mn., U.S.	D6	100
Cloquet, stm., Mn., U.S.	D6	100
Closter, N.J., U.S.	B5	107
Clothier, W.V., U.S.	n12	125
Cloud, co., Ks., U.S.	C6	93
Cloud Chief, Ok., U.S.	B3	113
Cloudcroft, N.M., U.S.	E4	108
Cloud Peak, mtn., Wy., U.S.	B5	127
Cloudy, Ok., U.S.	C6	113
Cloudy Bay, b., N.Z.	N15	51
Cloudy Mountain, mtn., Ak., U.S.	C8	79
Cloutierville, La., U.S.	C3	95
Clover, S.C., U.S.	A5	117
Clover, Va., U.S.	D4	123
Clover Bottom, Ky., U.S.	C5	94
Cloverdale, B.C., Can.	f13	69
Cloverdale, Al., U.S.	A2	78
Cloverdale, Ca., U.S.	C2	82
Cloverdale, In., U.S.	E4	91
Cloverdale, Or., U.S.	B3	114
Cloverdale, Va., U.S.	*C3	123
Cloverleaf, Tx., U.S.	*r14	120
Cloverport, Ky., U.S.	C3	94
Clovis, Ca., U.S.	D4	82
Clovis, N.M., U.S.	C6	108
Clow, Ar., U.S.	D2	81
Cloyne, Ire.	F3	11
Cluanie, Loch, l., Scot., U.K.	D3	13
Cluj-Napoca, Rom.	B6	24
Clune, Pa., U.S.	E3	115
Cluny, Ab., Can.	D4	68
Cluny, Fr.	D6	16
Cluses, Fr.	D2	21
Clusone, Italy	D5	21
Cluster Springs, Va., U.S.	D4	123
Clute, Tx., U.S.	r14	120
Clutha, stm., N.Z.	P12	51
Clutier, Ia., U.S.	B5	92
Clwyd, co., Wales, U.K.	A4	12
Clyattville, Ga., U.S.	F3	87
Clyde, Ab., Can.	B4	68
Clyde, N.T., Can.	B19	66
Clyde, Ks., U.S.	C6	93
Clyde, Mo., U.S.	A3	102
Clyde, N.Y., U.S.	B4	109
Clyde, N.C., U.S.	f10	110
Clyde, N.D., U.S.	A7	111
Clyde, Oh., U.S.	A3	112
Clyde, Tx., U.S.	C3	120
Clyde, stm., N.S., Can.	E4	71
Clyde, stm., Scot., U.K.	E4	13
Clyde, Firth of, est., Scot., U.K.	C4	10
Clydebank, Scot., U.K.	C4	10
Clyde Park, Mt., U.S.	E6	103
Clymer, N.Y., U.S.	C1	109
Clymer, Pa., U.S.	E3	115
Cnoc Moy, hill, Scot., U.K.	E3	13
Cnossus, hist., Grc.	E5	25
Côa, stm., Port.	B2	22
Coachella, Ca., U.S.	F5	82
Coachella Canal, Ca., U.S.	F3	11
Coachford, Ire.	F3	11
Coahoma, Ms., U.S.	A3	101
Coahoma, Tx., U.S.	C2	120
Coahoma, co., Ms., U.S.	A3	101
Coahuayana, stm., Mex.	n12	63
Coahuila, state, Mex.	B4	63
Coal, co., Ok., U.S.	C5	113
Coal, stm., W.V., U.S.	C3	125
Coal Bluff, In., U.S.	E3	91
Coal Branch, N.B., Can.	C4	71
Coal City, Il., U.S.	B5	90
Coal City, In., U.S.	F3	91
Coalcomán [de Matamoros], Mex.	D4	63
Coal Creek, stm., In., U.S.	E3	91
Coal Creek, stm., Ok., U.S.	B6	113
Coaldale, Ab., Can.	E4	68
Coaldale, Co., U.S.	C5	83
Coaldale, Nv., U.S.	E4	105
Coaldale, Pa., U.S.	E10	115
Coalfield, Tn., U.S.	C9	119
Coal Fork, stm., W.V., U.S.	m13	125
Coalgate, Ok., U.S.	C5	113
Coalgood, Ky., U.S.	D6	94
Coal Grove, Oh., U.S.	D3	112
Coal Harbour, B.C., Can.	D4	69
Coalhurst, Ab., Can.	E4	68
Coaling, Al., U.S.	B2	78
Coalinga, Ca., U.S.	D3	82
Coalmont, B.C., Can.	A4	83
Coalmont, Tn., U.S.	D8	119
Coalport, Pa., U.S.	E5	115
Coalridge, Oh., U.S.	C4	112
Coalton, Il., U.S.	D5	90
Coalton, Oh., U.S.	C3	112
Coalville, Eng., U.K.	B6	12
Coalville, Ut., U.S.	C4	121
Coalwood, W.V., U.S.	D3	125
Coamo, P.R.	B3	65
Coari, Braz.	C2	59
Coari, stm., Braz.	C2	59
Coast, prov., Kenya	B6	48
Coasters Harbor Island, i., R.I., U.S.	E5	116
Coast Mountains, mts., N.A.	E6	66
Coast Ranges, mts., U.S.	B3	76
Coatbridge, Scot., U.K.	C4	10
Coatepec, Mex.	n15	63
Coatepeque, Guat.	C2	62
Coatesville, Pa., U.S.	G10	115
Coaticook, P.Q., Can.	D6	74
Coatney Hill, mtn., Ct., U.S.	B7	84
Coatopa, Al., U.S.	C1	78
Coats, Ks., U.S.	E5	93

Name	Map Ref	Page
Coats, N.C., U.S.	B4	110
Coatsburg, Il., U.S.	C2	90
Coats Island, i., N.T., Can.	D16	66
Coats Land, reg., Ant.	B9	7
Coatsville, Mo., U.S.	A5	102
Coatzacoalcos (Puerto México), Mex.	D6	63
Cobalt, On., Can.	p19	73
Cobalt, Ct., U.S.	C5	84
Cobalt, Id., U.S.	D4	89
Cobán, Guat.	D6	63
Cobar, Austl.	F8	50
Cobb, Ga., U.S.	E3	87
Cobb, Ky., U.S.	D2	94
Cobb, Ok., U.S.	C5	113
Cobb, Wi., U.S.	F3	126
Cobb, co., Ga., U.S.	C2	87
Cobb, stm., Mn., U.S.	G5	100
Cobberas, Mount, mtn., Austl.	H7	51
Cobb Island, Md., U.S.	D4	97
Cobble Hill, B.C., Can.	g12	69
Cobble Mountain Reservoir, res., Ma., U.S.	B2	98
Cobbosseecontee Lake, l., Me., U.S.	D3	96
Cobbtown, Ga., U.S.	D4	87
Cobden, On., Can.	B8	73
Cobden, Il., U.S.	F4	90
Cobequid Mountains, mts., N.S., Can.	D5	71
Cobh, Ire.	E2	10
Cobham, Eng., U.K.	m12	10
Cobham, stm., Can.	C4	70
Cobija, Bol.	B2	55
Cobija, Chile	D2	55
Coble, Tn., U.S.	B4	119
Coblence see Koblenz, F.R.Ger.	C3	18
Cobleskill, N.Y., U.S.	C6	109
Coboconk, On., Can.	C6	73
Cobourg, On., Can.	D6	73
Cobourg Peninsula, pen., Austl.	B5	50
Cobre, Nv., U.S.	B7	105
Côbuè, Moz.	D6	48
Cobun Creek, stm., W.V., U.S.	h11	125
Coburg, Austl.	*G7	50
Coburg, F.R.Ger.	C5	18
Coburg, Ia., U.S.	D2	92
Coburg, Or., U.S.	C3	114
Coburg island, i., N.T., Can.	m36	66
Coburn, Pa., U.S.	E7	115
Coburn Gore, Me., U.S.	C2	96
Coburn Mountain, mtn., Me., U.S.	C2	96
Cocentaina, Spain	C5	22
Cochabamba, Bol.	C2	55
Cochabamba, dept., Bol.	C2	55
Coche, isla, i., Ven.	A5	60
Cocheco, stm., N.H., U.S.	D5	106
Cochem, F.R.Ger.	C2	19
Cochesett, Ma., U.S.	B5	98
Cochetcpa Creek, stm., Co., U.S.	C4	83
Cochetcpa Hills, mts., Co., U.S.	C4	83
Cochin, India	G6	36
Cochin China, hist. reg., Viet.	H6	35
Cochincs Point, c., Phil.	o13	34
Cochise, Az., U.S.	E6	80
Cochise, co., Az., U.S.	F5	80
Cochise Head, mtn., Az., U.S.	E6	80
Cochiti, N.M., U.S.	h8	108
Cochiti Indian Reservation, N.M., U.S.	h8	108
Cochiti Reservoir, res., N.M., U.S.	B3	108
Cochituate, Ma., U.S.	g10	98
Cochituate, Lake, l., Ma., U.S.	g10	98
Cochran, Ga., U.S.	D3	87
Cochran, co., Tx., U.S.	C1	120
Cochrane, Ab., Can.	D3	68
Cochrane, On., Can.	o19	73
Cochrane, Wi., U.S.	D2	126
Cochrane, co., On., Can.	o19	73
Cochranton, Pa., U.S.	C1	115
Cochranville, Pa., U.S.	G10	115
Cockburn, Austl.	F3	51
Cocke, co., Tn., U.S.	D10	119
Cockermouth, Eng., U.K.	F5	13
Cockeysville, Md., U.S.	B4	97
Cockpit Country, reg., Jam.	E13	65
Cockrell Hill, Tx., U.S.	n10	120
Cockrum, Ms., U.S.	A4	101
Coco, stm., N.A.	E8	63
Coco, Isla del, i., C.R.	C2	53
Cocoa, Fl., U.S.	D6	86
Cocoa Beach, Fl., U.S.	D6	86
Cocoa West, Fl., U.S.	*D6	86
Cocobeach, Gabon	E1	46
Cocolalla, Id., U.S.	A2	89
Coconino, co., Az., U.S.	B3	80
Coconino Plateau, plat., Az., U.S.	B3	80
Coconut Creek, Fl., U.S.	*F6	86
Cocopah Indian Reservation, Az., U.S.	E1	80
Cocos Bay, b., Trin.	O23	65
Cocos Island i., Guam	M9	52
Cocos Islands (Keeling Islands), is., Ec.	G3	2
Cocos Lagoon, b., Guam	M9	52
Coco Solo, Pan.	k11	62
Cocula, Mex.	C4	63
Cod, Cape, c., Ma., U.S.	C7	98
Codajás, Braz.	C4	59
Codell, Ks., U.S.	C4	93
Coden, Al., U.S.	E1	78
Codera, Cabo, c., Ven.	A4	60
Coderre, Sk., Can.	G2	75
Codesa, Ab., Can.	B1	68
Codette, Sk., Can.	D3	75
Codigoro, Italy	E8	23
Codington, co., S.D., U.S.	C8	118
Cod Island, i., Nf., Can.	g9	72
Codó, Braz.	B2	57
Codogno, Italy	B2	23
Codpa, Chile	C2	55
Codroipo, Italy	D8	20
Codroy, Nf., Can.	E2	72
Codroy Pond, Nf., Can.	D2	72
Cody, Ne., U.S.	B4	104
Cody, Wy., U.S.	B3	127
Codys, N.B., Can.	D4	71
Coeburn, Va., U.S.	f9	123
Coe Hill, On., Can.	C7	73
Coesse, In., U.S.	B7	91
Coesfeld, F.R.Ger.	C3	18
Coeur d'Alene, Id., U.S.	B2	89
Coeur d'Alene, stm., Id., U.S.	B2	89
Coeur d'Alene Indian Reservation, Id., U.S.	B2	89
Coeur d'Alene Lake, res., Id., U.S.	B2	89
Coeur d'Alene Mountains, mts., Id., U.S.	B2	89
Coevorden, Neth.	B6	17
Coffee, co., Al., U.S.	D3	78
Coffee, co., Ga., U.S.	E4	87
Coffee, co., Tn., U.S.	B5	119
Coffee Creek, Mt., U.S.	C6	103
Coffeen, Il., U.S.	D4	90
Coffee Springs, Al., U.S.	D4	78
Coffeeville, Al., U.S.	D1	78
Coffeeville, Ms., U.S.	B4	101
Coffey, Mo., U.S.	A3	102
Coffey, co., Ks., U.S.	D8	93
Coffeyville, Ks., U.S.	E8	93
Coffin, Île, i., P.Q., Can.	B8	71
Coffin Bay, Austl.	F9	50
Coffs Harbour, Austl.	F9	50
Cofield, N.C., U.S.	A6	110
Cogdell, Ga., U.S.	E4	87
Coggon, Ia., U.S.	B6	92
Coghinas, stm., Italy	D2	23
Cognac, Fr.	E3	16
Cogswell, N.D., U.S.	C8	111
Cohagen, Mt., U.S.	C10	103
Cohansey, stm., N.J., U.S.	E2	107
Cohasset, Ma., U.S.	B6	98
Cohasset, Mn., U.S.	C5	100
Cohocton, N.Y., U.S.	C3	109
Cohocton, stm., N.Y., U.S.	C3	109
Cohoe, Ak., U.S.	g16	79
Cohoes, N.Y., U.S.	C7	109
Cohoon, Lake, res., Va., U.S.	k14	123
Cohutta, Ga., U.S.	B2	87
Cohutta Mountain, mtn., Ga., U.S.	B2	87
Coiba, Isla de, i., Pan.	G7	62
Coig, stm., Arg.	E2	54
Coihaique, Chile	D2	54
Coila, Ms., U.S.	B4	101
Coimbatore, India	F6	36
Coimbra, Port.	B1	22
Coín, Spain	D3	22
Coin, Ia., U.S.	D2	92
Coinjock, N.C., U.S.	A7	110
Coipasa, Laguna, l., Bol.	C2	55
Coipasa, Salar de, pl., S.A.	C2	55
Coire, Loch, l., Scot., U.K.	B4	13
Cojedes, state, Ven.	B4	60
Cojutepeque, El Sal.	D3	62
Cokato, Mn., U.S.	E4	100
Coke, co., Tx., U.S.	D2	120
Coker, Al., U.S.	B2	78
Cokesbury, S.C., U.S.	C3	117
Coketon, W.V., U.S.	B5	125
Cokeville, Wy., U.S.	E2	127
Colàba Point, c., India	H4	37
Colac, Austl.	G7	51
Colares, Port.	f9	22
Colatina, Braz.	E8	57
Colbeck, Cape, c., Ant.	B33	7
Colbert, Ga., U.S.	B3	87
Colbert, Ok., U.S.	D5	113
Colbert, co., Al., U.S.	A2	78
Colbert Heights, Al., U.S.	A2	78
Colbio, Som.	F5	47
Colborne, On., Can.	C7	73
Colbún, Chile	B2	54
Colburn, Id., U.S.	A2	89
Colburn, In., U.S.	C4	91
Colby, Ks., U.S.	C2	93
Colby, Me., U.S.	B4	96
Colby, Wi., U.S.	D3	126
Colbyville, Vt., U.S.	C3	122
Colchester, Eng., U.K.	E7	10
Colchester, Ct., U.S.	C6	84
Colchester, Il., U.S.	C3	90
Colchester, Vt., U.S.	B2	122
Colchester, co., N.S., Can.	D6	71
Cold, stm., N.H., U.S.	C4	106
Cold, stm., N.H., U.S.	D2	106
Cold Bay, Ak., U.S.	E7	79
Cold Fell, mtn., Eng., U.K.	F6	13
Cold Hollow Mountains, mts., Vt., U.S.	B3	122
Colditz, Ger.D.R.	B7	19
Cold Lake, Ab., Can.	B5	68
Cold Lake, l., Can.	B5	68
Cold River, N.H., U.S.	D2	106
Cold Spring, Ky., U.S.	h13	94
Cold Spring, Mn., U.S.	E4	100
Cold Spring, N.J., U.S.	F3	107
Cold Spring, N.Y., U.S.	D7	109
Cold Spring Harbor, N.Y., U.S.	*n15	109
Cold Springs, Nv., U.S.	D2	105
Coldspring, Tx., U.S.	D5	120
Coldstream, Scot., U.K.	E6	13
Cold Stream Pond, l., Me., U.S.	C4	96
Coldwater, On., Can.	C5	73
Coldwater, Ks., U.S.	E4	93
Coldwater, Mi., U.S.	G5	99
Coldwater, Ms., U.S.	A4	101
Coldwater, Oh., U.S.	B1	112
Coldwater, stm., Ms., U.S.	A3	101
Coldwater Creek, stm., U.S.	e9	113
Cole, Ok., U.S.	B4	113
Cole, co., Mo., U.S.	C5	102
Colebrook, Ct., U.S.	B3	84
Coleharbor, N.D., U.S.	B4	111
Cole Lake, On., Can.	C8	73
Colebrook River Lake, res., Ct., U.S.	A3	84
Cole Camp, Mo., U.S.	C4	102
Coleen, stm., Ak., U.S.	B11	79
Colegrove, Pa., U.S.	C4	115
Coleman, Ab., Can.	E3	68
Coleman, Fl., U.S.	D4	86
Coleman, Mi., U.S.	E6	99
Coleman, P.E., Can.	C5	71
Coleman, Tx., U.S.	D3	120
Coleman, Wi., U.S.	D5	126
Coleman, co., Tx., U.S.	D3	120
Coleman Falls, Va., U.S.	C3	123
Colemerik, Tur.	D14	40
Coleraine, Austl.	H3	51
Coleraine, P.Q., Can.	D6	74
Coleraine, N. Ire., U.K.	G6	10
Coleridge, Ne., U.S.	B8	104
Coleridge, N.C., U.S.	B3	110
Coles, Ms., U.S.	D2	101
Coles, co., Il., U.S.	D5	90
Coles, Punta, c., Peru	E3	58
Colesberg, S. Afr.	B7	91
Colesburg, Ia., U.S.	B6	92
Colesburg, Ky., U.S.	C4	94
Coleta, Il., U.S.	B4	90
Coleville, Sk., Can.	F1	75
Coleville, Ca., U.S.	C4	82
Colfax, Sk., Can.	H4	75
Colfax, Ca., U.S.	C3	82
Colfax, Il., U.S.	C5	90
Colfax, In., U.S.	D4	91
Colfax, Ia., U.S.	C4	92
Colfax, La., U.S.	C3	95
Colfax, N.D., U.S.	C9	111
Colfax, Wa., U.S.	C8	124
Colfax, Wi., U.S.	D2	126
Colfax, co., Ne., U.S.	C8	104
Colfax, co., N.M., U.S.	A5	108
Colgate, Sk., Can.	H4	75
Colhué Huapi, Lago, l., Arg.	D3	54
Colibris, Pointe des, c., Guad.	Q9	65
Colico, Italy	C5	20
Colima, Mex.	D4	63
Colima, state, Mex.	D4	63
Colima, Nevado de, mtn., Mex.	n12	63
Colinas, Braz.	C2	57
Colinet, Nf., Can.	E5	72
Colinton, Ab., Can.	B4	68
Coll, i., Scot., U.K.	B3	10
Collbran, Co., U.S.	B3	83
College, Ak., U.S.	B10	79
College City, Ar., U.S.	*A5	81
College Corner, Oh., U.S.	C1	112
Collegedale, Tn., U.S.	h11	119
College Grove, Tn., U.S.	B5	119
College Park, Ga., U.S.	C2	87
College Park, Md., U.S.	C4	97
College Place, Wa., U.S.	C7	124
College Springs, Ia., U.S.	D2	92
College Station, Ar., U.S.	*C3	81
College Station, Tx., U.S.	D4	120
Collegeville, Ar., U.S.	*C3	81
Collegeville, In., U.S.	C3	91
Collegeville, Pa., U.S.	F11	115
College Ward, Ut., U.S.	*B4	121
Colleyville, Tx., U.S.	*n9	120
Collie, Austl.	F2	50
Collier Bay, b., Austl.	C3	50
Colliers, W.V., U.S.	f8	125
Collierville, Tn., U.S.	B2	119
Collin, co., Tx., U.S.	C4	120
Collingdale, Pa., U.S.	p20	115
Collingsworth, co., Tx., U.S.	B2	120
Collingwood, On., Can.	C4	73
Collins, Ar., U.S.	D4	81
Collins, Ga., U.S.	D4	87
Collins, Ia., U.S.	C4	92
Collins, Ms., U.S.	D4	101
Collins, Mo., U.S.	D4	102
Collins, Wi., U.S.	h10	126
Collins Park, De., U.S.	B3	85
Collinston, La., U.S.	B4	95
Collinston, Ut., U.S.	B3	121
Collinsville, Ct., U.S.	B4	84
Collinsville, Il., U.S.	E4	90
Collinsville, Ok., U.S.	A6	113
Collinsville, Va., U.S.	D3	123
Collinwood, Tn., U.S.	B4	119
Collipulli, Chile	B2	54
Collis, Mn., U.S.	E2	100
Collooney, Ire.	C3	11
Collyer, Ks., U.S.	C3	93
Colman, S.D., U.S.	D9	118
Colmar, Fr.	C7	16
Colmar, Ky., U.S.	D6	94
Colmar Manor, Md., U.S.	f9	97
Colmenar de Oreja, Spain	B4	22
Colmenar Viejo, Spain	B4	22
Colmesneil, Tx., U.S.	D5	120
Colnett, Cabo, c., Mex.	A1	63
Cologne (Köln), F.R.Ger.	C3	18
Cologne, Mn., U.S.	F5	100
Cologne, N.J., U.S.	D3	107
Cologne, Va., U.S.	C6	123
Coloma, Mi., U.S.	F4	99
Colombes, Fr.	g10	16
Colômbia, Braz.	C3	56
Colombia, Col.	C3	60
Colombia, ctry., S.A.	C3	60
Colombo, Sri L.	G6	36
Colome, S.D., U.S.	D6	118
Colón, Arg.	A5	54
Colón, Cuba	C3	64
Colón, Pan.	F8	62
Colon, Ne., U.S.	g11	104
Colon, N.C., U.S.	B3	110
Colón, Archipiélago de (Galapagos Islands), is., Ec.	g5	58
Colona, Co., U.S.	C3	83
Colona, N.J., U.S.	k7	107
Colonia, dept., Ur.	g8	54
Colonia del Sacramento, Ur.	E1	56
Colonia Dora, Arg.	E3	55
Colonia Las Heras, Arg.	D3	54
Colonial Beach, Va., U.S.	B6	123
Colonia Leopoldina, Braz.	k6	57
Colonial Heights, Tn., U.S.	C11	119
Colonial Heights, Va., U.S.	C5	123
Colonial National Historical Park, Va., U.S.	C6	123
Colonial Park, Pa., U.S.	*F8	115
Colonia Mennonita, Para.	D5	55
Colonia Suiza, Ur.	g8	54
Colonna, Italy	h9	23
Colonna, Capo, c., Italy	E6	23
Colonsay, Sk., Can.	F3	75
Colonsay, i., Scot., U.K.	B3	10
Colony, Ok., U.S.	B3	113
Colorado, C.R.	C6	53
Colorado, co., Tx., U.S.	E4	120
Colorado, state, U.S.	B5	83
Colorado, stm., Arg.	D3	54
Colorado, stm., N.A.	D5	76
Colorado, stm., Tx., U.S.	D3	120
Colorado City, Az., U.S.	A3	80
Colorado City, Co., U.S.	D6	83
Colorado City, Tx., U.S.	C2	120
Colorado City, Lake, res., Tx.	C2	120
Colorado National Monument,	B2	83
Colorado Plateau, plat., U.S.	F5	23
Colorado River Aqueduct, Ca., U.S.		
Colorado River Indian Reservation, Az., U.S.	D1	80
Colorados, Archipiélago de los, is., Cuba	C1	64
Colorado Springs, Co., U.S.	C6	83
Colotlán, Mex.	C4	63
Colquechaca, Bol.	C2	55
Colquitt, Ga., U.S.	E2	87
Colquitt, co., Ga., U.S.	E3	87
Colrain, Ma., U.S.	A2	98
Colstrip, Mt., U.S.	E10	103
Colt, Ar., U.S.	B5	81
Coltauco, Chile	A2	54
Colter Bay, Wy., U.S.	C2	127
Colton, Ca., U.S.	*E5	82
Colton, N.Y., U.S.	f10	109
Colton, Or., U.S.	B4	114
Colton, S.D., U.S.	D9	118
Colton, Wa., U.S.	C8	124
Colton, Lake, mtn., Vt., U.S.	D4	122
Coltons Point, Md., U.S.	D4	97
Colts Neck, N.J., U.S.	C4	107
Columbia, Al., U.S.	D4	78
Columbia, Ca., U.S.	C3	82
Columbia, Ct., U.S.	C6	84
Columbia, Il., U.S.	E3	90
Columbia, Ky., U.S.	C4	94
Columbia, La., U.S.	B3	95
Columbia, Md., U.S.	B4	97
Columbia, Ms., U.S.	D4	101
Columbia, Mo., U.S.	C5	102
Columbia, N.C., U.S.	B6	110
Columbia, Pa., U.S.	F9	115
Columbia, S.C., U.S.	C5	117
Columbia, S.D., U.S.	B7	118
Columbia, Tn., U.S.	B5	119
Columbia, co., Ar., U.S.	D2	81
Columbia, co., Fl., U.S.	B4	86
Columbia, co., Ga., U.S.	C4	87
Columbia, co., N.Y., U.S.	C7	109
Columbia, co., Or., U.S.	B3	114
Columbia, co., Pa., U.S.	D9	115
Columbia, co., Wa., U.S.	C7	124
Columbia, co., Wi., U.S.	E4	126
Columbia, stm., N.A.	A3	76
Columbia, Mount, mtn., N.T., Can.	k37	66
Columbia, Mount, mtn., Co., U.S.	C2	68
Columbia Basin, Wa., U.S.	C6	124
Columbia City, In., U.S.	B7	91
Columbia City, Or., U.S.	B4	114
Columbia Cross Roads, Pa., U.S.	C8	115
Columbia Falls, Me., U.S.	D5	96
Columbia Falls, Mt., U.S.	B2	103
Columbia Heights, Mn., U.S.	m12	100
Columbia Lake, l., B.C., Can.	D10	69
Columbia Lake, res., Ct., U.S.	C6	84
Columbia Mountains, mts., B.C., Can.	C7	69
Columbiana, Oh., U.S.	B5	112
Columbiana, co., Oh., U.S.	B5	112
Columbiaville, Mi., U.S.	E7	99
Columbus, Ar., U.S.	D2	81
Columbus, Ga., U.S.	D2	87
Columbus, In., U.S.	F6	91
Columbus, Ks., U.S.	E9	93
Columbus, Ky., U.S.	f8	94
Columbus, Ms., U.S.	B5	101
Columbus, Mt., U.S.	E7	103
Columbus, Ne., U.S.	C8	104
Columbus, N.M., U.S.	F2	108
Columbus, N.C., U.S.	f10	110
Columbus, N.D., U.S.	A3	111
Columbus, Oh., U.S.	C2	112
Columbus, Pa., U.S.	C2	115
Columbus, Tx., U.S.	E4	120
Columbus, Wi., U.S.	E4	126
Columbus, co., N.C., U.S.	C4	110
Columbus Air Force Base, mil., Ms., U.S.	B5	101
Columbus City, Ia., U.S.	C6	92
Columbus Grove, Oh., U.S.	B1	112
Columbus Junction, Ia., U.S.	C6	92
Columbus Lake, Ms.,	B5	101
Colusa, Ca., U.S.	C2	82
Colusa, co., Ca., U.S.	C2	82
Colver, Pa., U.S.	E4	115
Colville, Wa., U.S.	A8	124
Colville, Ak., U.S.	B9	79
Colville, stm., Wa., U.S.	A8	124
Colville Indian Reservation, Wa., U.S.	A6	124
Colville, Lake, l., N.T., Can.	C7	66
Colvin Mountain, mtn., Al., U.S.	A3	78
Colvos Passage, strt., Wa., U.S.	f10	124
Colwell, Ks., U.S.	E6	93
Colwood, B.C., Can.	h12	69
Colwyn Bay, Wales, U.K.	A4	12
Colyell Creek, stm., La., U.S.	h10	95
Comacchio, Italy	B4	23
Comacchio, Valli di, b., Italy	B4	23
Comal, co., Tx., U.S.	E3	120
Comalapa, Guat.	E6	63
Comalcalco, Mex.	D6	63
Coman, Mount, mtn., Ant.	B6	7
Comanche, Ok., U.S.	C4	113
Comanche, Tx., U.S.	D3	120
Comanche, co., Ks., U.S.	E4	93
Comanche, co., Ok., U.S.	C3	113
Comanche, co., Tx., U.S.	D3	120
Comarapa, Bol.	C3	55
Comayagua, Hond.	E7	63
Combahee, stm., S.C., U.S.	F6	117
Combarbalá, Chile	A2	54
Combeaufontaine, Fr.	B1	20
Comber, N. Ire., U.K.	H7	10
Comber, On., Can.	E2	73
Combermere, On., Can.	B7	73
Combined Locks, Wi., U.S.	h9	126
Combs, Ar., U.S.	B2	81
Combs, Ky., U.S.	C6	94
Comer, Al., U.S.	C4	78
Comer, Ga., U.S.	B3	87
Comerío, P.R.	B3	65
Comet, stm., Austl.	B7	51
Comfort, N.C., U.S.	B5	110
Comfort, Tx., U.S.	E3	120
Comfort, W.V., U.S.	m12	125
Comfrey, Mn., U.S.	F4	100
Comilla, Bngl.	D9	36
Comines, Bel.	C1	17
Comino, Cape, c., Italy	D2	23
Comins, Mi., U.S.	D6	99
Cominto, Ar., U.S.	D4	81
Comitán [de Domínguez], Mex.	F6	82
Comite, stm., La., U.S.	*D4	95
Commack, N.Y., U.S.	*n15	109
Commentry, Fr.	D5	16
Commerce, Ga., U.S.	B3	87
Commerce, Mo., U.S.	D8	102
Commerce, Ok., U.S.	A7	113
Commerce, Tx., U.S.	C5	120
Commerce City, Co., U.S.	B6	83
Commercial Point, Oh., U.S.	C2	112
Commercy, Fr.	C6	16
Commewijne, dept., Sur.	A4	59
Commiskey, In., U.S.	G6	91
Commissaires, Lac des, l., P.Q., Can.	B2	98
Committee Bay, b., N.T., Can.	C15	66
Common Fence Point, R.I., U.S.	D6	116
Commonwealth Bay, b., Ant.	C27	7
Commonwealth Range, mts., Ant.	A30	7
Communism Peak, mtn., Sov. Un.	F10	29
Como, Italy	B2	23
Como, Co., U.S.	B5	83
Como, Ms., U.S.	A4	101
Como, N.C., U.S.	A5	110
Como, Tn., U.S.	A3	119
Como, Lake, l., Italy	B2	23
Comobabi, Az., U.S.	E4	80
Comodoro Rivadavia, Arg.	D3	54
Comorin, Cape, c., India	G6	36
Comoros, ctry., Afr.	H10	42
Comox, B.C., Can.	E5	69
Compass Lake, Fl., U.S.	B1	86
Compeer, Ab., Can.	D5	68
Competition, Mo., U.S.	D5	102
Compiègne, Fr.	C5	16
Compostela, Mex.	m11	63
Comptche, Ca., U.S.	C2	82
Compton, P.Q., Can.	D6	74
Compton, Ar., U.S.	A2	81
Compton, Ca., U.S.	n12	82
Compton, Il., U.S.	B4	90
Compton, co., P.Q., Can.	D6	74
Comstock, Mn., U.S.	D2	100
Comstock, Ne., U.S.	C6	104
Comstock, Wi., U.S.	C1	126
Comté, stm., Fr. Gu.	B4	59
Conakry, Gui.	E2	45
Conanicut Island, i., R.I., U.S.	E5	116
Conanicut Point, c., R.I., U.S.	E5	116
Conasauga, Tn., U.S.	D9	119
Concan, Tx., U.S.	E3	120
Concarneau, Fr.	D2	16
Conceição das Alagoas, Braz.	B3	56
Conceição do Araguaia, Braz.	D10	57
Conceição do Norte, Braz.	D1	57
Concepción, Bol.	C3	55
Concepción, Chile	D2	54
Concepción, Guat.	D6	63
Concepción, Para.	D5	55
Concepción, Phil.	o13	34
Concepción, dept., Para.	D4	55
Concepción, Laguna, l., Bol.	C3	55
Concepción, Punta, c., Mex.	B2	63
Concepción del Oro, Mex.	C5	63
Concepción del Uruguay, Arg.	A5	54
Conception, Point, c., Ca., U.S.	E3	82
Conception Bay, b., Nf., Can.	E5	72
Conception Island, i., Bah.	C6	64
Conception Junction, Mo., U.S.	A3	102
Conchas, Braz.	m7	56
Conchas Dam, N.M., U.S.	B5	108
Conchas Lake, res., N.M., U.S.	B5	108
Conche, Nf., Can.	C4	72
Conchi, Chile	A3	55
Conchillas, Ur.	g7	54
Concho, Az., U.S.	C6	80
Concho, co., Tx., U.S.	D3	120
Concho, stm., Tx., U.S.	D3	120
Conchos, stm., Mex.	B4	63
Con Co, i., Viet.	D9	34
Conconully, Wa., U.S.	A6	124
Concord, Ar., U.S.	B3	81
Concord, Ca., U.S.	h8	82
Concord, Fl., U.S.	B2	86
Concord, Ga., U.S.	C2	87
Concord, Il., U.S.	D3	90
Concord, Ky., U.S.	B6	94
Concord, Ma., U.S.	B5	98
Concord, Mi., U.S.	F6	99
Concord, Mo., U.S.	g13	102
Concord, N.H., U.S.	D3	106
Concord, N.C., U.S.	B2	110
Concord, Pa., U.S.	D9	115
Concord, Vt., U.S.	C5	122
Concord, stm., Ma., U.S.	A5	98
Concordia, Arg.	A5	54
Concordia, Col.	B3	58
Concordia, Peru	B3	58
Concordia, Mo., U.S.	C4	102
Concordia, co., La., U.S.	C4	95
Concordia, Ks., U.S.	C6	93
Concrete, N.D., U.S.	A8	111
Concrete, Wa., U.S.	A4	124
Conda, Id., U.S.	G7	89
Condamine, stm., Austl.	E9	50
Conde, Braz.	D9	57
Conde, S.D., U.S.	B7	118
Condé-[sur-l'Escaut], Fr.	B5	16
Condé-sur-Marne, Fr.	C5	16
Condé-sur-Noireau, Fr.	C3	16
Condino, Italy	D5	20
Condom, Fr.	E4	16
Condon, Mt., U.S.	C3	103
Condon, Or., U.S.	B6	114
Cóndor, Cordillera del, mts., S.A.	B2	58
Cone, Tx., U.S.	C2	120
Conecuh, co., Al., U.S.	D2	78
Conecuh, stm., Al., U.S.	D3	78
Conejos, Co., U.S.	D4	83
Conejos, co., Co., U.S.	D4	83
Conejos, stm., Co., U.S.	D4	83
Conemaugh, Pa., U.S.	F4	115
Conemaugh River Lake, res., Pa., U.S.	F3	115
Conestee, S.C., U.S.	B3	117
Conesus, N.Y., U.S.	C3	109
Conesville, Oh., U.S.	B3	112
Conetoe, N.C., U.S.	B5	110
Confluence, Pa., U.S.	G3	115
Confolens, Fr.	D4	16
Confusion Bay, b., Nf., Can.	C4	72
Confusion Range, mts., Ut.	D2	121
Confuso, stm., Para.	D4	55
Cong, Ire.	D2	11
Congamond, Ma., U.S.	B2	98
Congamond Lakes, l., U.S.	A4	84
Congaree, stm., S.C., U.S.	D6	117
Congaree Swamp National Monument, S.C., U.S.	D6	117
Conger, Mn., U.S.	G5	100
Congers, N.Y., U.S.	*D7	109
Congleton, Eng., U.K.	A5	12
Congo, Oh., U.S.	C3	112
Congo, W.V., U.S.	e8	125
Congo, ctry., Afr.	B2	48
Congo (Zaire), stm., Afr.	B2	48
Congress, Sk., Can.	H2	75
Congress, Az., U.S.	C3	80
Conifer, N.Y., U.S.	A6	109
Conil [de la Frontera], Spain	D2	22
Coniston, On., Can.	A4	73
Coniston Water, l., Eng., U.K.	F5	13
Conklin, Ab., Can.	B5	68
Conklin, Mi., U.S.	E5	99
Conklin, N.Y., U.S.	C5	109
Conlen, Tx., U.S.	A1	120
Conn, Lough, l., Ire.	C2	10
Connaught, hist. reg., Ire.	D2	11
Conneaut, Oh., U.S.	A5	112
Conneaut Creek, stm., Oh., U.S.	A5	112
Conneaut Lake, Pa., U.S.	C1	115
Conneaut Lake, l., Pa., U.S.	C1	115
Conneautville, Pa., U.S.	C1	115
Connecticut, state, U.S.	C5	84
Connecticut, stm., U.S.	C5	84
Connell, Wa., U.S.	C7	124
Connellsville, Pa., U.S.	F2	115
Connelly Springs, N.C., U.S.	B1	110
Connellys Mo., U.S.	A5	102
Conner, Mt., U.S.	E2	103
Connersville, In., U.S.	E7	91
Connerville, Ok., U.S.	C5	113
Connoire Bay, b., Nf., Can.	E3	72
Connors, N.B., Can.	B1	71
Conococheague Creek, stm., Md., U.S.	A2	97
Conover, N.C., U.S.	B1	110
Conover, Wi., U.S.	C5	126
Conowingo, Md., U.S.	A5	97
Conowingo Dam, Md., U.S.	A5	97
Conquest, Sk., Can.	F2	75
Conrad, Ia., U.S.	B5	92
Conrad, Mt., U.S.	B5	103
Conrath, Wi., U.S.	C2	126
Conroe, Tx., U.S.	D5	120
Conroy, Ia., U.S.	C6	92
Consecon, On., Can.	C7	73
Conselheiro Lafaiete, Braz.	C6	57
Consett, Eng., U.K.	F7	13
Conshohocken, Pa., U.S.	F11	115
Consolación del Sur, Cuba	C2	64
Con Son, is., Viet.	D3	34
Consort, Ab., Can.	C5	68
Constable, N.Y., U.S.	f10	109
Constableville, N.Y., U.S.	B5	109
Constance see Konstanz, F.R.Ger.	E4	18
Constance, Ky., U.S.	*A7	94
Constance, Lake, l., Eur.	E4	18
Constanța, Rom.	C9	24
Constantia, N.Y., U.S.	B5	109
Constantina, Spain	D3	22
Constantine (Qacentina), Alg.	B6	44
Constantine, Mi., U.S.	G5	99
Constantine, Cape, c., Ak., U.S.	D8	79
Constantinople see İstanbul, Tur.	B7	40
Constitución, Chile	B2	54
Consuegra, Spain	C4	22
Consul, Sk., Can.	H1	75
Contact, Nv., U.S.	B7	105
Contai, India	G11	37
Contamana, Peru	D3	58
Contas, Rio de, stm., Braz.	C8	57
Contendas do Sincorá, Braz.	A4	56
Content Keys, is., Fl., U.S.	H5	86
Continental, Oh., U.S.	A1	112
Continental Divide, N.M., U.S.	B1	108
Continental Peak, mtn., Wy., U.S.	D4	127
Continental Reservoir, res., Co., U.S.	D3	83
Contoocook, N.H., U.S.	D3	106
Contoocook, stm., N.H., U.S.	D3	106
Contra Costa, co., Ca., U.S.	D3	82
Contratación, Col.	D6	60
Contrecoeur, P.Q., Can.	D4	74
Contreras, N.M., U.S.	C3	108
Contrexéville, Fr.	A1	20
Contumazá, Peru	B2	58
Contwoyto Lake, l., N.T., Can.	C10	66
Convent, La., U.S.	D5	95
Converse, In., U.S.	C6	91
Converse, La., U.S.	C2	95
Converse, S.C., U.S.	A4	117
Converse, co., Wy., U.S.	C7	127
Convoy, Oh., U.S.	B1	112
Conway, P.E., Can.	C6	71
Conway, Wales, U.K.	A3	12
Conway, Ar., U.S.	B3	81
Conway, Fl., U.S.	D5	86
Conway, Ia., U.S.	D3	92
Conway, Ma., U.S.	A2	98
Conway, Mo., U.S.	D5	102
Conway, N.H., U.S.	B4	106
Conway, N.C., U.S.	A5	110
Conway, N.D., U.S.	A8	111
Conway, Pa., U.S.	E1	115
Conway, S.C., U.S.	D9	117
Conway, Tx., U.S.	B2	120
Conway, Wa., U.S.	A3	124
Conway, co., Ar., U.S.	B3	81
Conway, Lake, res., Ar., U.S.	B3	81
Conway, Lake, l., N.H., U.S.	C4	106
Conway Springs, Ks., U.S.	E6	93
Conyers, Ga., U.S.	C3	87
Cooch Behâr, India	C8	36
Cook, Austl.	F5	50
Cook, Mn., U.S.	C6	100
Cook, Ne., U.S.	D9	104
Cook, co., Ga., U.S.	E3	87
Cook, co., Il., U.S.	B6	90
Cook, co., Mn., U.S.	k9	100
Cook, Cape, c., B.C., Can.	D3	69
Cook, Mount, mtn., N.Z.	O13	51
Cooke, co., Tx., U.S.	C4	120
Cooke City, Mt., U.S.	E7	103
Cookes Peak, mtn., N.M., U.S.	E2	108
Cookeville, Tn., U.S.	C8	119
Cook Ice Shelf, Ant.	C28	7
Cooking Lake, l., Ab., Can.	C4	68

Name	Map Ref	Page
Cook Inlet, b., Ak., U.S.	D9	79
Cook Islands, ctry., Oc.	G12	6
Cook Mountain, mtn., W.V., U.S.	n12	125
Cook Point, c., Md., U.S.	C5	97
Cooks, Mi., U.S.	C4	99
Cooksburg, Pa., U.S.	D3	115
Cooks Falls, N.Y., U.S.	D6	109
Cook's Harbour, Nf., Can.	C4	72
Cookshire, P.Q., Can.	D6	74
Cooks Mills, Il., U.S.	D5	90
Cookson, Ok., U.S.	B7	113
Cookstown, On., Can.	C5	73
Cookstown, N. Ire., U.K.	C5	11
Cookstown, N.J., U.S.	C3	107
Cook Strait, strt., N.Z.	N15	51
Cooksville, Il., U.S.	C5	90
Cooktown, Austl.	C8	50
Cookville, Tx., U.S.	C5	120
Coolaney, Ire.	C3	11
Cooleemee, N.C., U.S.	B2	110
Coolgardie, Austl.	F3	50
Coolidge, Az., U.S.	E4	80
Coolidge, Ga., U.S.	E3	87
Coolidge, Ks., U.S.	D2	93
Coolidge, Tx., U.S.	D4	120
Coolidge, Mount, mtn., S.D., U.S.	D2	118
Coolin, Id., U.S.	A2	89
Cool Ridge, W.V., U.S.	D3	125
Coolspring, Pa., U.S.	D3	115
Coolville, Oh., U.S.	C4	112
Cooma, Austl.	G8	50
Coonabarabran, Austl.	F8	50
Coonamble, Austl.	F8	50
Coon Rapids, Ia., U.S.	C3	92
Coon Rapids, Mn., U.S.	E5	100
Coon Valley, Wi., U.S.	E2	126
Cooper, Ia., U.S.	C3	92
Cooper, Tx., U.S.	C5	120
Cooper, co., Mo., U.S.	C5	102
Cooper, stm., S.C., U.S.	F8	117
Cooper, East Branch, stm., S.C., U.S.	E8	117
Cooper, West Branch, stm., S.C., U.S.	E8	117
Co Operative, Ky., U.S.	D5	94
Cooper City, Fl., U.S.	*F6	86
Cooper Creek, stm., Austl.	E7	50
Cooper Mountain, mtn., Ak., U.S.	g17	79
Cooper Road, La., U.S.	*B2	95
Coopers, Al., U.S.	C3	78
Coopersburg, Pa., U.S.	F11	115
Coopers Mills, Me., U.S.	D3	96
Cooperstown, N.Y., U.S.	C6	109
Cooperstown, N.D., U.S.	B7	111
Cooperstown, Pa., U.S.	D2	115
Cooperstown, Wi., U.S.	h10	126
Coopersville, Mi., U.S.	E5	99
Cooperton, Ok., U.S.	C3	113
Coopertown, Tn., U.S.	A5	119
Coos, co., N.H., U.S.	A4	106
Coos, co., Or., U.S.	D2	114
Coos, stm., Or., U.S.	D2	114
Coosa, co., Al., U.S.	B3	78
Coosa, co., Ga., U.S.	B1	87
Coosa, stm., U.S.	C3	78
Coosada, Al., U.S.	C3	78
Coosawattee, stm., Ga., U.S.	B2	87
Coosawhatchie, S.C., U.S.	F6	117
Coosawhatchie, stm., S.C., U.S.	F5	117
Coos Bay, Or., U.S.	D2	114
Cootamundra, Austl.	F8	50
Cootehill, Ire.	C4	11
Cooter, Mo., U.S.	E8	102
Copacabana, Arg.	E2	55
Copacabana, Bol.	C2	55
Copainalá, Mex.	D6	63
Copake, N.Y., U.S.	C7	109
Copalis Beach, Wa., U.S.	B1	124
Copalis Crossing, Wa., U.S.	B1	124
Copán, Hond.	C3	62
Copan, Ok., U.S.	A6	113
Copan Reservoir, res., Ok., U.S.	A6	113
Cope, Co., U.S.	B8	83
Cope, S.C., U.S.	E5	117
Copeland, Fl., U.S.	G5	86
Copeland, Ks., U.S.	E3	93
Copemish, Mi., U.S.	D5	99
Copen, W.V., U.S.	C4	125
Copenhagen (København), Den.	J5	14
Copenhagen, N.Y., U.S.	B5	109
Copetonas, Arg.	B4	54
Copeville, Tx., U.S.	m10	120
Copiah, co., Ms., U.S.	D3	101
Copiapó, Chile	E1	55
Copiapó, stm., Chile	E1	55
Copinsay, i., Scot., U.K.	B6	13
Coplay, Pa., U.S.	E10	115
Copparo, Italy	B3	23
Coppename, stm., Sur.	A3	59
Copper, stm., Ak., U.S.	C11	79
Copperas Cove, Tx., U.S.	D4	120
Copper Butte, mtn., Wa., U.S.	A7	124
Copper Center, Ak., U.S.	C10	79
Copper Cliff, On., Can.	A3	73
Copper Harbor, Mi., U.S.	A3	99
Copperhill, Tn., U.S.	D9	119
Copper Hill, Va., U.S.	C2	123
Coppermine, N.T., Can.	C9	66
Coppermine, stm., N.T., Can.	C10	66
Copper Mountain, B.C., Can.	E7	69
Copper Mountain, mtn., Wy., U.S.	C5	127
Copper Mountains, mts., Az., U.S.	E2	80
Copper Ridge, mtn., Tn., U.S.	m13	119
Copper Ridge, mtn., Va., U.S.	f9	123
Copperton, Ut., U.S.	*C3	121
Coppet, Switz.	D1	21
Copton Creek, stm., Ab., Can.	B1	68
Coqên, China	B10	37
Coquet, stm., Eng., U.K.	E7	13
Coquille, Or., U.S.	D2	114
Coquimbo, Chile	E1	55
Coquimbo, prov., Chile	F1	55
Cora, Wy., U.S.	D3	127
Corabia, Rom.	D7	24
Coração de Jesus, Braz.	B4	56
Coracora, Peru	E3	58
Coral, On., Can.	o19	73
Coral, Mi., U.S.	E5	99
Coral, Pa., U.S.	F3	115
Coral Gables, Fl., U.S.	G6	86
Coral Sea, Oc.	G9	6
Coralville, Ia., U.S.	C6	92
Coralville Lake, res., Ia., U.S.	C5	92
Coram, Mt., U.S.	B2	103
Coram, N.Y., U.S.	*n15	109
Corangamite, Lake, l., Austl.	I4	51
Coraopolis, Pa., U.S.	E1	115
Corato, Italy	D6	23
Corbeil [-Essonnes], Fr.	C5	16
Corbeny, Fr.	E3	17
Corbett, N.Y., U.S.	C5	109
Corbetton, On., Can.	C4	73
Corbie, Fr.	C5	16
Corbin, Ky., U.S.	D5	94
Corbin, Mt., U.S.	D4	103
Corby, Eng., U.K.	B7	12
Corcoran, Ca., U.S.	D4	82
Corcoran, Mn., U.S.	m11	100
Corcovado, Golfo, b., Chile	C2	54
Cord, Ar., U.S.	B4	81
Cordaville, Ma., U.S.	g9	98
Cordele, Ga., U.S.	E3	87
Cordell, Ok., U.S.	B3	113
Cordell Hull Lake, res., Tn., U.S.	C8	119
Corder, Mo., U.S.	B4	102
Cordesville, S.C., U.S.	E8	117
Cordillera, dept., Para.	D4	55
Cordón, Phil.	n13	34
Córdoba, Arg.	A4	54
Córdoba, prov., Arg.	A4	54
Córdoba, dept., Col.	B2	60
Córdoba, Spain	D3	22
Córdoba, Peru	D2	58
Cordova, Al., U.S.	B2	78
Cordova, Ak., U.S.	C10	79
Cordova, Il., U.S.	B3	90
Cordova, Md., U.S.	C6	97
Cordova, Ne., U.S.	*D8	104
Cordova, N.M., U.S.	A4	108
Cordova, N.C., U.S.	C3	110
Cordova, S.C., U.S.	E6	117
Cordova, Tn., U.S.	B2	119
Cordova Mines, On., Can.	C7	73
Cordova Peak, mtn., Ak., U.S.	C10	79
Corea, Me., U.S.	D5	96
Coreaú, Braz.	B2	57
Corella, Spain	A5	22
Corfu see Kérkira, i., Grc.	C2	40
Cori, Italy	h9	23
Corigliano, Italy	E6	23
Corinna, Me., U.S.	D3	96
Corinne, Mi., U.S.	B5	99
Corinne, Ut., U.S.	B3	121
Corinne, W.V., U.S.	*D3	125
Corinth see Kórinthos, Grc.	D4	40
Corinth, Ga., U.S.	C2	87
Corinth, Ky., U.S.	B5	94
Corinth, Ms., U.S.	A5	101
Corinth, N.Y., U.S.	B7	109
Corinth, Vt., U.S.	C4	122
Corinth, W.V., U.S.	B5	125
Corinth, Bay of, b., Grc.	h9	25
Corinth, Gulf of, b., Grc.	C4	25
Corinth Canal, Grc.	h10	25
Corinto, Braz.	B4	56
Corinto, Nic.	E7	63
Corisco, Isla de, i., Eq. Gui.	E1	46
Cork, Ire.	E2	10
Cork, N.B., Can.	D3	71
Cork, co., Ire.	F3	11
Corleone, Italy	B6	40
Cormeilles-en-Parisis, Fr.	g9	16
Cormorant, Mb., Can.	B1	70
Cormorant Lake, l., Mb., Can.	B1	70
Corn, Ok., U.S.	B3	113
Cornaca, S.C., U.S.	C3	117
Cornelia, Ga., U.S.	B3	87
Cornelius, N.C., U.S.	B2	110
Cornelius, Or., U.S.	g11	114
Cornell, Il., U.S.	C5	90
Cornell, Wi., U.S.	C2	126
Corner Brook, Nf., Can.	D3	72
Corner Inlet, b., Austl.	I6	51
Cornersville, Tn., U.S.	B5	119
Cornerville, Ar., U.S.	D4	81
Cornfield Point, c., Ct., U.S.	D6	84
Cornhill, N.B., Can.	D4	71
Cornimont, Fr.	B2	40
Corning, Sk., Can.	H4	75
Corning, Ar., U.S.	A5	81
Corning, Ca., U.S.	C2	82
Corning, Ia., U.S.	D3	92
Corning, Ks., U.S.	C7	93
Corning, Mo., U.S.	A2	102
Corning, N.Y., U.S.	C3	109
Cornish, Me., U.S.	E2	96
Cornish, N.H., U.S.	D2	106
Cornish, Ut., U.S.	B4	121
Cornish Center, N.H., U.S.	D2	106
Cornish Flat, N.H., U.S.	D2	106
Cornish Mills, N.H., U.S.	D2	106
Cornville, Ky., U.S.	C5	94
Cornwall, On., Can.	B10	73
Cornville, Me., U.S.	D3	96
Cornwall, Ct., U.S.	B2	84
Cornwall, Pa., U.S.	F9	115
Cornwall, Vt., U.S.	D2	122
Cornwall, co., Eng., U.K.	D3	12
Cornwall Bridge, Ct., U.S.	B2	84
Cornwall Island, i., N.T., Can.	m33	66
Cornwallis Island, i., N.T., Can.	m32	66
Cornwall-on-Hudson, N.Y., U.S.	D6	109
Cornwells Heights, Pa., U.S.	o22	115
Coro, Ven.	A4	60
Coroaci, Braz.	B2	57
Coroatá, Braz.	D6	57
Corocoro, Bol.	C2	55
Coroico, Bol.	C2	55
Corolla, N.C., U.S.	A7	110
Coromandel, Braz.	E2	57
Coromandel Coast, India	F7	36
Coromandel Peninsula, pen., N.Z.	L15	51
Corona, Al., U.S.	B2	78
Corona, Ca., U.S.	F5	82
Corona, N.M., U.S.	C4	108
Corona, S.D., U.S.	B9	118
Coronach, Sk., Can.	H3	75
Coronado, Ca., U.S.	F5	82
Coronado, Bahía de, b., C.R.	F6	62
Coronado National Memorial, Az., U.S.	F5	80
Coronation, Ab., Can.	C5	68
Coronation Gulf, b., N.T., Can.	C10	66
Coronation Island, i., B.A.T.	C8	7
Coronation Island, i., Ak., U.S.	n22	79
Coronda, Arg.	A4	54
Coronel, Chile	B2	54
Coronel Dorrego, Arg.	B4	54
Coronel Murta, Braz.	B4	56
Coronel Oviedo, Para.	E4	55
Coronel Pringles, Arg.	B4	54
Coronel Suárez, Arg.	B4	54
Coronie, dept., Sur.	A3	59
Coropuna, Nevado, mtn., Peru	E3	58
Corowa, Austl.	G6	51
Corozal, Belize	D7	63
Corozal, Col.	B2	60
Corpen, Arg.	D3	54
Corps, Fr.	E1	20
Corpus Christi, Tx., U.S.	F4	120
Corpus Christi Naval Air Station, mil., Tx., U.S.	F4	120
Corral, Chile	B2	54
Corral, Id., U.S.	F4	89
Corral de Almaguer, Spain	C4	22
Corrales, Col.	B3	60
Corralillo, Cuba	C3	64
Corraun, Ire.	D2	11
Corravillers, Fr.	B2	20
Correctionville, Ia., U.S.	B2	92
Correll, Mn., U.S.	E2	100
Corrente, Braz.	D1	57
Correntes, Braz.	A4	56
Correntina, Braz.	k5	57
Corrib, Lough, l., Ire.	D2	10
Corrientes, Arg.	E4	55
Corrientes, prov., Arg.	E4	55
Corrientes, stm., Arg.	E4	55
Corrientes, stm., S.A.	B2	58
Corrientes, Cabo, c., Col.	B2	60
Corrientes, Cabo, c., Cuba	D1	64
Corrientes, Cabo, c., Mex.	C3	63
Corrientes, Ensenada de, b., Cuba	D1	64
Corrigan, Tx., U.S.	D5	120
Corriganville, Md., U.S.	k13	97
Corry, Pa., U.S.	C2	115
Corryton, Tn., U.S.	C10	119
Corse, Cap, c., Fr.	C2	23
Corsica, Pa., U.S.	D3	115
Corsica, S.D., U.S.	D7	118
Corsica, i., Fr.	C2	23
Corsicana, Tx., U.S.	C4	120
Corson, S.D., U.S.	D9	118
Corson, co., S.D., U.S.	B4	118
Corson Inlet, b., N.J., U.S.	E3	107
Cortazar, Mex.	C4	63
Corte, Fr.	C2	23
Corte Alto, Chile	C2	54
Cortegana, Spain	D2	22
Corte Madera, Ca., U.S.	*h7	82
Cortemilia, Italy	E4	20
Cortes [de la Frontera], Spain	D3	22
Cortez, Co., U.S.	D2	83
Cortez, Fl., U.S.	q10	86
Cortez Mountains, mts., Nv., U.S.	C5	105
Cortina d'Ampezzo, Italy	A4	23
Cortland, Il., U.S.	B5	90
Cortland, Ne., U.S.	D9	104
Cortland, N.Y., U.S.	C4	109
Cortland, Oh., U.S.	A5	112
Cortland, co., N.Y., U.S.	C4	109
Cortona, Italy	C3	23
Çoruh, stm., Asia	B13	40
Çorum, Tur.	B10	40
Corumbá, Braz.	B3	56
Corumbá, stm., Braz.	B3	56
Corunna, On., Can.	E2	73
Corunna, Mi., U.S.	F6	99
Corvallis, Mt., U.S.	D2	103
Corvallis, Or., U.S.	C3	114
Corvo, i., Port.	g8	44
Corwin Springs, Mt., U.S.	E6	103
Corwith, Ia., U.S.	B4	92
Cory, In., U.S.	F3	91
Corydon, Ia., U.S.	D4	92
Corydon, In., U.S.	H5	91
Corydon, Ky., U.S.	C2	94
Coryell, co., Tx., U.S.	D4	120
Cos see Kos, i., Grc.	D6	40
Cosalá, Mex.	C3	63
Cosamaloapan [de Carpio], Mex.	D5	63
Cosby, Mo., U.S.	A3	102
Cosby, Tn., U.S.	D10	119
Coscomatepec [de Bravo], Mex.	n15	63
Cosegüina, Punta, c., Nic.	D4	62
Cosenza, Italy	E6	23
Coshocton, Oh., U.S.	B4	112
Coshocton, co., Oh., U.S.	B4	112
Cosmopolis, Wa., U.S.	C2	124
Cosmos, Mn., U.S.	F4	100
Cosne, Fr.	D5	16
Cossatot, stm., Ar., U.S.	C1	81
Cossatot Mountains, mtn., Ar., U.S.	C2	81
Cossonay, Switz.	C2	20
Costa Mesa, Ca., U.S.	n13	82
Costa Rica, ctry., N.A.	F6	62
Costello, Pa., U.S.	C5	115
Costelloe, Ire.	D2	11
Costigan, Me., U.S.	C4	96
Costilla, N.M., U.S.	A4	108
Costilla, co., Co., U.S.	D5	83
Coswig, Ger.D.R.	B8	19
Coswig, Ger.D.R.	B7	19
Cotabato, Phil.	D6	34
Cotagaita, Bol.	D2	55
Cotahuasi, Peru	E3	58
Coteau, N.D., U.S.	A3	111
Coteau-Landing, P.Q., Can.	D3	74
Coteaux, Haiti	E6	64
Côtes de Fer, Haiti	E7	64
Cotesfield, Ne., U.S.	C7	104
Cotija de la Paz, Mex.	n12	63
Cotonou, Benin	E5	45
Cotopaxi, prov., Ec.	B2	58
Cotopaxi, vol., Ec.	B2	58
Cotswold Hills, hills, Eng., U.K.	E5	10
Cottage Grove, Mn., U.S.	n13	100
Cottage Grove, Or., U.S.	D3	114
Cottage Grove, Tn., U.S.	A3	119
Cottage Grove Reservoir, res., Or., U.S.	D3	114
Cottageville, S.C., U.S.	F7	117
Cottageville, W.V., U.S.	C3	125
Cottam, On., Can.	E2	73
Cottbus, Ger.D.R.	C7	18
Cottel Island, i., Nf., Can.	D5	72
Cotter, Ar., U.S.	A3	81
Cottian Alps, mts., Eur.	E7	16
Cottingham (Haltemprice), Eng., U.K.	G8	13
Cottle, co., Tx., U.S.	B2	120
Cottle Knob, mtn., W.V., U.S.	C4	125
Cottleville, Mo., U.S.	f12	102
Cotton, Ga., U.S.	E2	87
Cotton, Mn., U.S.	C6	100
Cotton, co., Ok., U.S.	C3	113
Cotton Center, Tx., U.S.	B1	120
Cotton Plant, Ar., U.S.	B4	81
Cottonport, La., U.S.	C3	95
Cottontown, Tn., U.S.	A5	119
Cotton Valley, La., U.S.	B2	95
Cottonwood, Al., U.S.	D4	78
Cottonwood, Az., U.S.	C3	80
Cottonwood, Ca., U.S.	B2	82
Cottonwood, Id., U.S.	C2	89
Cottonwood, Mn., U.S.	F3	100
Cottonwood, Ok., U.S.	C5	113
Cottonwood, S.D., U.S.	D4	118
Cottonwood, Tx., U.S.	C3	120
Cottonwood, co., Mn., U.S.	F3	100
Cottonwood, stm., Ks., U.S.	D7	93
Cottonwood, stm., Mn., U.S.	F3	100
Cottonwood Cove, Nv., U.S.	H7	105
Cottonwood Creek, stm., Wy., U.S.	C4	127
Cottonwood Creek, stm., Wy., U.S.	D2	127
Cottonwood Falls, Ks., U.S.	D7	93
Cottonwood Heights, Ut., U.S.	*C4	121
Cottonwood Wash, val., Ut., U.S.	F6	121
Cotuit, Ma., U.S.	C7	98
Cotulla, Tx., U.S.	E3	120
Couchiching, Lake, l., On., Can.	C5	73
Couchwood, La., U.S.	B2	95
Coudekerque-Branche, Fr.	B5	16
Couderay, Wi., U.S.	C2	126
Coudersport, Pa., U.S.	C5	115
Coudres, Île aux, i., P.Q., Can.	B7	74
Couëron, Fr.	D3	16
Cougar, Wa., U.S.	C3	124
Cougar Reservoir, res., Or., U.S.	C4	114
Coulee, N.D., U.S.	A3	111
Coulee City, Wa., U.S.	B6	124
Coulee Creek, stm., Wa., U.S.	g13	124
Coulee Dam, Wa., U.S.	B7	124
Coulee Dam National Recreation Area, Wa., U.S.	A7	124
Coulman Island, i., Ant.	B29	7
Coulommiers, Fr.	C5	16
Coulter, Mb., Can.	E1	70
Coulter, Ar., U.S.	B4	92
Coulterville, Il., U.S.	E4	90
Coulterville, Ca., U.S.	D2	82
Coulwood, Va., U.S.	f9	123
Counce, Tn., U.S.	B3	119
Council, Id., U.S.	E2	89
Council, Va., U.S.	e9	123
Council Bluffs, Ia., U.S.	C2	92
Council Grove, Ks., U.S.	D7	93
Council Grove Lake, res., Ks., U.S.	D7	93
Council Hill, Ok., U.S.	B6	113
Council Mountain, mtn., Id., U.S.	E2	89
Country Club Hills, Il., U.S.	*k9	90
Country Homes, Wa., U.S.	B8	124
Countryside, Il., U.S.	*k9	90
Countyline, Ok., U.S.	C4	113
Coupar Angus, Scot., U.K.	B5	10
Coupeville, Wa., U.S.	A3	124
Coupon, Pa., U.S.	E4	115
Courantyne, stm., S.A.	A3	59
Courbevoie, Fr.	g10	16
Courcelles, P.Q., Can.	D7	74
Courland Lagoon, b., Sov. Un.	D2	20
Courmayeur, Italy	D2	20
Coursan, Fr.	F5	16
Courtenay, B.C., Can.	E5	69
Courtenay, N.D., U.S.	B7	111
Courtland, On., Can.	E4	73
Courtland, Al., U.S.	A2	78
Courtland, Ca., U.S.	C3	82
Courtland, Ks., U.S.	C6	93
Courtland, Mn., U.S.	F4	100
Courtland, Ms., U.S.	A4	101
Courtland, Va., U.S.	D5	123
Courtmacsherry, Ire.	F3	11
Courtrai see Kortrijk, Bel.	B5	16
Courtright, On., Can.	E2	73
Courval, Sk., Can.	G2	75
Coushatta, La., U.S.	B2	95
Coutances, Fr.	C3	16
Coutras, Fr.	E3	16
Coutts, Ab., Can.	E5	68
Couvin, Bel.	D4	17
Cove, Scot., U.K.	C3	13
Cove, Ar., U.S.	C1	81
Cove, Or., U.S.	B9	114
Cove City, N.C., U.S.	B5	110
Cove Creek, stm., Ut., U.S.	E3	121
Covedale, Oh., U.S.	o12	112
Cove Island, i., On., Can.	B3	73
Covelo, Ca., U.S.	C2	82
Coventry, Eng., U.K.	D6	10
Coventry, Ct., U.S.	B6	84
Coventry, De., U.S.	*B3	85
Coventry, R.I., U.S.	D3	116
Coventry, Vt., U.S.	B4	122
Cove Point, Md., U.S.	D5	97
Cove Point, c., Md., U.S.	D5	97
Coverdales Crossroads, De., U.S.	F3	85
Covered Wells, Az., U.S.	E3	80
Covert, Mi., U.S.	F4	99
Covesville, Va., U.S.	C4	123
Covina, Ca., U.S.	m13	82
Covington, Ga., U.S.	C3	87
Covington, In., U.S.	D3	91
Covington, Ky., U.S.	A5	94
Covington, La., U.S.	D5	95
Covington, Mi., U.S.	B2	99
Covington, Oh., U.S.	B1	112
Covington, Tn., U.S.	B2	119
Covington, Va., U.S.	C3	123
Covington, Wa., U.S.	f11	124
Covington, co., Al., U.S.	D3	78
Covington, co., Ms., U.S.	D4	101
Cowal, Lake, l., Austl.	F6	51
Cowan, In., U.S.	D7	91
Cowan, Tn., U.S.	B5	119
Cowan, stm., Sk., Can.	C2	75
Cowan, Lake, l., Austl.	F3	50
Cowan Knob, mtn., Ar., U.S.	B2	81
Cowangie, Austl.	G3	51
Cowan Lake, l., Sk., Can.	C2	75
Cowansville, P.Q., Can.	D5	74
Coward, S.C., U.S.	D8	117
Cowarts, Al., U.S.	D4	78
Cow Creek, stm., Ks., U.S.	D5	93
Cow Creek, stm., Wa., U.S.	C7	124
Cowden, Il., U.S.	D5	90
Cowden, Ok., U.S.	B3	113
Cowdenbeath, Scot., U.K.	D5	13
Cowdrey, Co., U.S.	A4	83
Cowee Mountains, mts., N.C., U.S.	f9	110
Cowen, W.V., U.S.	C4	125
Cowen, Mount, mtn., Mt., U.S.	E6	103
Cowes, Eng., U.K.	E6	10
Coweta, Ok., U.S.	B6	113
Coweta, co., Ga., U.S.	C2	87
Cowgill, Mo., U.S.	B4	102
Cow Head, Nf., Can.	D3	72
Cowiche, Wa., U.S.	C5	124
Cowichan Bay, B.C., Can.	g12	69
Cowichan Lake, l., B.C., Can.	E5	69
Cowikee Creek, stm., Al., U.S.	C4	78
Cow Knob, mtn., W.V., U.S.	C5	125
Cow Lakes, l., Or., U.S.	D9	114
Cowles, Ne., U.S.	D7	104
Cowley, Ab., Can.	E3	68
Cowley, Wy., U.S.	B4	127
Cowley, co., Ks., U.S.	E7	93
Cowlic, Az., U.S.	F4	80
Cowling, Il., U.S.	E6	90
Cowlington, Ok., U.S.	B7	113
Cowlitz, co., Wa., U.S.	C3	124
Cowlitz, stm., Wa., U.S.	C3	124
Cowpasture, stm., Va., U.S.	B3	123
Cowpen Mountain, mtn., Ga., U.S.	B2	87
Cowpens, S.C., U.S.	A4	117
Cowra, Austl.	F7	51
Cowskin Creek, stm., Ks., U.S.	g11	93
Cox Springs, Az., U.S.	A5	80
Coxburg, Ms., U.S.	B3	101
Coxim, Braz.	B2	56
Coxsackie, N.Y., U.S.	C7	109
Cox's Cove, Nf., Can.	D2	72
Coxs Mills, W.V., U.S.	B4	125
Coy, Al., U.S.	D2	78
Coy, Ar., U.S.	C4	81
Coyame, Mex.	C4	63
Coyanosa Draw, val., Tx., U.S.	D1	120
Coya Sur, Chile	D2	55
Coyle, Ok., U.S.	B4	113
Coyoacán (part of Mexico City), Mex.	h9	63
Coyote, N.M., U.S.	A3	108
Coyote Basin, Co., U.S.	A2	83
Coyuca de Catalán, Mex.	n13	63
Coyville, Ks., U.S.	E8	93
Cozad, Ne., U.S.	D6	104
Cozahome, Ar., U.S.	A3	81
Cozumel, Mex.	C7	63
Cozumel, Isla de, i., Mex.	D7	63
Crab Creek, stm., Wa., U.S.	B7	124
Crab Orchard, Ky., U.S.	C5	94
Crab Orchard, Ne., U.S.	D9	104
Crab Orchard, Tn., U.S.	D9	119
Crab Orchard Lake, res., Il., U.S.	F4	90
Crab Orchard Mountains, mts., Tn., U.S.	D8	119
Crabtree, Or., U.S.	C4	114
Crabtree, Pa., U.S.	F3	115
Crabtree Mills, P.Q., Can.	D4	74
Cracking, stm., Sk., Can.	A3	75
Cracow, Austl.	B8	51
Cradock, S. Afr.	D4	49
Crafton, Pa., U.S.	k13	115
Craftsbury, Vt., U.S.	B4	122
Craftsbury Common, Vt., U.S.	B4	122
Cragford, Al., U.S.	B4	78
Craig, Ak., U.S.	D13	79
Craig, Co., U.S.	A3	83
Craig, Ia., U.S.	B1	92
Craig, Mo., U.S.	A2	102
Craig, Mt., U.S.	C5	103
Craig, Ne., U.S.	C9	104
Craig, Ok., U.S.	A6	113
Craig, co., Ok., U.S.	A6	113
Craig, co., Va., U.S.	C2	123
Craig Air Force Base, mil., Al., U.S.	C3	78
Craig Creek, stm., Va., U.S.	C2	123
Craigellachie, B.C., Can.	D8	69
Craighead, co., Ar., U.S.	B5	81
Craighouse, Scot., U.K.	C3	13
Craighurst, On., Can.	C5	73
Craigmont, Id., U.S.	C2	89
Craigmyle, Ab., Can.	D4	68
Craigsville, Va., U.S.	C3	123
Craigsville, W.V., U.S.	C4	125
Craigville, In., U.S.	C7	91
Craik, Sk., Can.	F3	75
Crail, Scot., U.K.	B6	10
Crailsheim, F.R.Ger.	D5	18
Craiova, Rom.	D6	24
Cramerton, N.C., U.S.	B1	110
Cranberry Isles, Me., U.S.	D4	96
Cranberry Lake, N.Y., U.S.	A6	109
Cranberry Lake, l., N.Y., U.S.	A6	109
Cranberry Portage, Mb., Can.	B1	70
Cranbrook, B.C., Can.	E10	69
Cranbury, N.J., U.S.	C4	107
Crandall, Ga., U.S.	B2	87
Crandall, Tx., U.S.	n10	120
Crandall, S.D., U.S.	B8	118
Crandon, Wi., U.S.	C5	126
Crane, Az., U.S.	E1	80
Crane, In., U.S.	G4	91
Crane, Mo., U.S.	E4	102
Crane, Tx., U.S.	D1	120
Crane, co., Tx., U.S.	D1	120
Crane Creek, stm., Oh., U.S.	e7	112
Crane Creek Reservoir, res., Id., U.S.	E2	89
Crane Hill, Al., U.S.	A2	78
Crane Lake, Mn., U.S.	B6	100
Crane Lake, l., Sk., Can.	G1	75
Crane Lake, l., Il., U.S.	C3	90
Crane Lake, l., Mn., U.S.	B6	100
Crane Mountain, mtn., Or., U.S.	E6	114
Crane Prairie Reservoir, res., Or., U.S.	D5	114
Cranesville, Pa., U.S.	C1	115
Cranfield, Ms., U.S.	D2	101
Cranford, N.J., U.S.	B4	107
Cransac, Fr.	E5	16
Cranston, R.I., U.S.	C4	116
Cranstown, Cape, c., Grnld.	B20	128
Crapaud, P.E., Can.	C6	71
Crapo, Md., U.S.	D5	97
Crary, N.D., U.S.	A7	111
Crary Mountains, mts., Ant.	B1	7
Craryville, N.Y., U.S.	C7	109
Crasna, stm., Eur.	B6	24
Crater Lake, Or., U.S.	E4	114
Crater Lake, l., Or., U.S.	E4	114
Crater Lake, l., St. Vin.	U26	65
Crater Lake National Park, Or., U.S.	E4	114
Craters of the Moon National Monument, Id., U.S.	F5	89
Crateús, Braz.	C2	57
Crato, Braz.	C3	57
Craughwell, Ire.	D3	11
Craven, Sk., Can.	G3	75
Craven, co., N.C., U.S.	B5	110
Cravinhos, Braz.	k8	56
Crawford, Co., U.S.	C3	83
Crawford, Ga., U.S.	C3	87
Crawford, Ms., U.S.	B5	101
Crawford, Ne., U.S.	B2	104
Crawford, Ok., U.S.	B2	113
Crawford, Tn., U.S.	C8	119
Crawford, co., Ar., U.S.	B1	81
Crawford, co., Ga., U.S.	D3	87
Crawford, co., Il., U.S.	D6	90
Crawford, co., In., U.S.	H4	91
Crawford, co., Ia., U.S.	B2	92
Crawford, co., Ks., U.S.	E9	93
Crawford, co., Mi., U.S.	D6	99
Crawford, co., Mo., U.S.	D6	102
Crawford, co., Oh., U.S.	B3	112
Crawford, co., Pa., U.S.	C1	115
Crawford, co., Wi., U.S.	E3	126
Crawford Bay, B.C., Can.	E9	69
Crawford Lake, l., Me., U.S.	C5	96
Crawford Notch, N.H., U.S.	B4	106
Crawford Notch State Park, N.H., U.S.	B4	106
Crawfordsville, Ar., U.S.	B5	81
Crawfordsville, In., U.S.	D4	91
Crawfordsville, Ia., U.S.	C6	92
Crawfordsville, Or., U.S.	C4	114
Crawfordville, Fl., U.S.	B2	86
Crawfordville, Ga., U.S.	C4	87
Crawley, Eng., U.K.	C7	12
Crayne, Ky., U.S.	e9	94
Crazy Mountains, mts., Mt., U.S.	D6	103
Crazy Peak, mtn., Mt., U.S.	D6	103
Crazy Woman Creek, stm., Wy., U.S.	B6	127
Creal Springs, Il., U.S.	F5	90
Creamridge, N.J., U.S.	C3	107
Crean Lake, l., Sk., Can.	C2	75
Crediton, Eng., U.K.	D4	12
Cree, stm., Sk., Can.	E11	66
Creede, Co., U.S.	D4	83
Creedmoor, N.C., U.S.	A4	110
Creek, co., Ok., U.S.	B5	113
Creekside, Pa., U.S.	E3	115
Creel Village, Bah.	m18	64
Cree Lake, l., Sk., Can.	m7	75
Creelman, Sk., Can.	H4	75
Creemore, On., Can.	C4	73
Cregganbaun, Ire.	D2	11
Creighton, Sk., Can.	n13	125
Creighton, Mo., U.S.	C3	102
Creighton, Ne., U.S.	B8	104
Creighton, Pa., U.S.	h14	115
Creighton, S.D., U.S.	C3	118
Creighton Mine, On., Can.	A3	73
Creil, Fr.	C5	16
Crellin, Md., U.S.	m12	97
Crema, Italy	B2	23
Cremona, Ab., Can.	D3	68
Cremona, Italy	B3	23
Crenshaw, Ms., U.S.	A3	101
Crenshaw, co., Al., U.S.	D3	78
Creola, Al., U.S.	E1	78
Creole, La., U.S.	E2	95
Crépy-en-Valois, Fr.	E2	16
Cres, i., Yugo.	C2	24
Cresaptown, Md., U.S.	k13	97
Cresbard, S.D., U.S.	B7	118
Crescent, Ga., U.S.	E5	87
Crescent, Ia., U.S.	C2	92
Crescent, Ok., U.S.	B4	113
Crescent, Or., U.S.	D5	114
Crescent, Lake, l., Wa., U.S.	A2	124
Crescent City, Ca., U.S.	B1	82
Crescent City, Fl., U.S.	C5	86
Crescent City, Il., U.S.	C6	90
Crescent Lake, Or., U.S.	D5	114
Crescent Lake, l., Fl., U.S.	C5	86
Crescent Lake, l., Or., U.S.	D5	114
Crescent Mills, Ca., U.S.	B3	82
Crescent Range, mtn., N.H., U.S.	B4	106
Crescent Springs, Ky., U.S.	h13	94
Crescent Spur, B.C., Can.	C7	69
Cresco, Ia., U.S.	A5	92
Cresco, Pa., U.S.	D11	115
Cressona, Pa., U.S.	E9	115
Crest, Fr.	E6	16
Cresta, Switz.	D6	21
Crested Butte, Co., U.S.	C4	83
Cresthaven, Fl., U.S.	*F6	86
Crest Hill, Il., U.S.	k8	90
Crestline, Oh., U.S.	B3	112
Creston, B.C., Can.	E9	69
Creston, Nf., Can.	E4	72
Creston, Il., U.S.	B5	90
Creston, Ia., U.S.	C3	92
Creston, Oh., U.S.	B4	112
Creston, Wa., U.S.	B7	124
Creston, W.V., U.S.	C3	125
Creston, Wy., U.S.	E5	127

Name	Map Ref	Page
Crestone, Co., U.S.	D5	83
Crestone Peak, mtn., Co., U.S.	D5	83
Crestview, Fl., U.S.	u15	86
Crestview, Ky., U.S.	g10	88
Crestwood, Il., U.S.	*k9	90
Crestwood, Ky., U.S.	B4	94
Crestwood, Mo., U.S.	*f13	102
Crestwood Village, N.J., U.S.	D4	107
Crestwynd, Sk., Can.	G3	75
Creswell, N.C., U.S.	B6	110
Creswell, Or., U.S.	D3	114
Crete, Il., U.S.	B6	90
Crete, Ne., U.S.	D9	104
Crete, N.D., U.S.	C8	111
Crete, i., Grc.	E5	40
Crete, Sea of, Grc.	D5	40
Créteil, Fr.	g10	16
Cretone, Italy	g9	23
Creus, Cape, c., Spain	A7	22
Creuse, stm., Fr.	D4	16
Creutzwald, Fr.	C7	16
Crevasse Valley Glacier, Ant.	B34	7
Creve Coeur, Il., U.S.	C4	90
Creve Coeur, Mo., U.S.	*f13	102
Crèvecœur-le-Grand, Fr.	E2	17
Crevillente, Spain	C5	22
Crewe, Eng., U.K.	D5	10
Crewe, Va., U.S.	C4	123
Crewkerne, Eng., U.K.	D5	12
Criciúma, Braz.	D3	56
Cricket, N.C., U.S.	A1	110
Cricket Mountains, mts., Ut., U.S.	E3	121
Cridersville, Oh., U.S.	B1	112
Crieff, Scot., U.K.	B5	10
Criffell, mtn., Scot., U.K.	F5	13
Criglersville, Va., U.S.	B4	123
Crikvenica, Yugo.	C2	24
Crimea, pen., Sov. Un.	E6	29
Crimmitschau, Ger.D.R.	C7	18
Crimson Lake Provincial Park, Ab., Can.	C3	68
Crinan, Scot., U.K.	D3	13
Cripple Creek, Co., U.S.	C5	83
Cripple Creek, Va., U.S.	D1	123
Crişana-Maramureş, hist reg., Rom.	B6	24
Crisfield, Md., U.S.	E6	97
Crisp, co., Ga., U.S.	E3	87
Criss Creek, B.C., Can.	D7	69
Crissolo, Italy	E3	20
Cristal, Monts de, mts., Gabon	E2	46
Cristalina, Braz.	B3	56
Cristóbal, Pan.	k11	62
Cristóbal Colón, Pico, mtn., Col.	A3	60
Crişu Alb, stm., Eur.	B5	24
Crittenden, Ky., U.S.	B5	94
Crittenden, co., Ar., U.S.	B5	81
Crittenden, co., Ky., U.S.	e9	94
Crivitz, Ger.D.R.	E5	15
Crivitz, Wi., U.S.	C6	126
Crixás, Braz.	A3	56
Crna, stm., Yugo.	E5	24
Črnomelj, Yugo.	C2	24
Croatia, hist reg., Yugo.	C2	24
Croche, stm., P.Q., Can.	A5	74
Crocheron, Md., U.S.	D5	97
Crocker, Mo., U.S.	D5	102
Crocker, co., U.S.	B8	118
Crockett, Ca., U.S.	g8	82
Crockett, Tx., U.S.	D5	120
Crockett, co., Tn., U.S.	B2	119
Crockett, co., Tx., U.S.	D2	120
Crockett Mills, Tn., U.S.	B2	119
Crocketts Bluff, Ar., U.S.	C4	81
Crocketville, S.C., U.S.	F5	117
Crofton, Ky., U.S.	C2	94
Crofton, Md., U.S.	B4	97
Crofton, Ne., U.S.	B8	104
Croghan, N.Y., U.S.	B5	109
Croghan Mountain, mtn., Ire.	E5	11
Crohy Head, c., Ire.	C3	11
Croix, Fr.	D3	17
Croix, Lac la, l., Mn., U.S.	B6	100
Croker, i., Austl.	B5	50
Croker, Cape, c., On., Can.	C4	73
Cromarty, Scot., U.K.	B4	10
Cromer, Mb., Can.	E1	70
Cromer, Eng., U.K.	B9	12
Cromona, Ky., U.S.	C7	94
Cromwell, N.Z.	P12	51
Cromwell, Al., U.S.	C1	78
Cromwell, Ct., U.S.	C5	84
Cromwell, In., U.S.	B6	91
Cromwell, Ia., U.S.	C3	92
Cromwell, Ky., U.S.	C3	94
Cromwell, Mn., U.S.	D6	100
Cromwell, Ok., U.S.	B5	113
Crook, Eng., U.K.	F7	13
Crook, Co., U.S.	A8	83
Crook, co., Or., U.S.	C6	114
Crook, co., Wy., U.S.	B8	127
Crooked, stm., B.C., Can.	B6	69
Crooked, stm., Or., U.S.	C6	114
Crooked Creek, Ak., U.S.	C8	79
Crooked Creek, stm., U.S.	E3	93
Crooked Creek, stm., Ar., U.S.	A3	81
Crooked Creek, stm., Pa., U.S.	k10	91
Crooked Creek, stm., Pa., U.S.	C7	115
Crooked Creek Lake, res., Pa., U.S.	E3	115
Crooked Island, i., Bah.	C6	64
Crooked Island Passage, strt., Bah.	C6	64
Crooked Lake, l., Nf., Can.	D3	72
Crooked Lake, l., Sk., Can.	G4	75
Crooked Lake, l., Fl., U.S.	E5	86
Crooked Lake, l., Mn., U.S.	B7	100
Crooked River, Sk., Can.	E4	75
Crooks, S.D., U.S.	D9	118
Crooks Lake, l., Nv., U.S.	B2	105
Crookston, Mn., U.S.	C2	100
Crookston, Ne., U.S.	B5	104
Crookstown, Ire.	F3	11
Crooksville, Oh., U.S.	C3	112
Crookwell, Austl.	G7	51
Croom, Ire.	E3	11
Cropper, Ky., U.S.	B4	94
Cropsey, Il., U.S.	C5	90
Croque Harbour, b., Nf., Can.	C4	72
Crosby, Mb., Can.	D5	100
Crosby, Ms., U.S.	D2	101
Crosby, N.D., U.S.	A2	111
Crosby, Pa., U.S.	C5	115
Crosby, Tx., U.S.	r14	120
Crosby, co., Tx., U.S.	*C2	120
Crosby, Mount, mtn., Wy., U.S.	C3	127
Crosbyton, Tx., U.S.	C2	120
Crosland, Ga., U.S.	E3	87
Cross, S.C., U.S.	E7	117
Cross, co., Ar., U.S.	B5	81

Cross, stm., Afr.	E6	45
Cross, Cape, c., Nmb.	B1	49
Cross Anchor, S.C., U.S.	B4	117
Cross Bay, b., Mb., Can.	C2	70
Crossbost, Scot., U.K.	B2	13
Cross City, Fl., U.S.	C3	86
Cross Creek, N.B., Can.	C3	71
Cross Creek, stm., W.V., U.S.	f8	125
Crossett, Ar., U.S.	D4	81
Cross Fell, mtn., Eng., U.K.	F6	13
Crossfield, Ab., Can.	D3	68
Crosshaven, Ire.	F3	11
Cross Hill, S.C., U.S.	C4	117
Cross Island, i., Me., U.S.	D5	96
Cross Keys, N.J., U.S.	D2	107
Cross Lake, Mb., Can.	B3	70
Crosslake, Mn., U.S.	D4	100
Cross Lake, l., Mb., Can.	B3	70
Cross Lake, l., Me., U.S.	A4	96
Cross Lanes, W.V., U.S.	C3	125
Crossman Peak, mtn., Az., U.S.	C1	80
Cross Mill, N.C., U.S.	f10	110
Crossmolina, Ire.	C2	11
Cross Mountains, mtn., Ar., U.S.	C1	81
Cross Plains, In., U.S.	G7	91
Cross Plains, Tn., U.S.	A5	119
Cross Plains, Tx., U.S.	C3	120
Cross Plains, Wi., U.S.	E4	126
Crossroads, N.M., U.S.	D6	108
Cross Roads Ohio, Tn., U.S.	D7	71
Cross Sound, strt., Ak., U.S.	k21	79
Cross Timbers, Mo., U.S.	C4	102
Crosstown, Ms., U.S.	D8	102
Cross Village, Mi., U.S.	C5	99
Crossville, Al., U.S.	A4	78
Crossville, Il., U.S.	E5	90
Crossville, Tn., U.S.	D8	119
Crosswicks, N.J., U.S.	C3	107
Croswell, Mi., U.S.	E8	99
Crothersville, In., U.S.	G6	91
Croton, Ia., U.S.	D6	92
Croton, N.J., U.S.	B3	107
Croton, Oh., U.S.	B3	112
Croton (Croton), Italy	E6	23
Croton-on-Hudson, N.Y., U.S.	D7	109
Crottendorf, Ger.D.R.	C7	19
Crouch, Id., U.S.	E3	89
Crouse, N.C., U.S.	B1	110
Crouseville, Me., U.S.	B4	96
Crow, stm., Mn., U.S.	F4	100
Crow, North Fork, stm., Mn., U.S.	E4	100
Crow Agency, Mt., U.S.	E9	103
Crow Creek, stm., U.S.	A6	83
Crow Creek Indian Reservation, S.D., U.S.	C6	118
Crowder, Ms., U.S.	A3	101
Crowder, Ok., U.S.	B6	113
Crowduck Lake, l., Mb., Can.	D4	70
Crowell, Tx., U.S.	C3	120
Crowheart, Wy., U.S.	C3	127
Crow Indian Reservation, Mt., U.S.	E9	103
Crowley, Co., U.S.	C7	83
Crowley, La., U.S.	D3	95
Crowley, Tx., U.S.	n9	120
Crowley, co., Co., U.S.	C7	83
Crowley, Lake, res., Ca., U.S.	D4	82
Crowleys Ridge, mtn., U.S.	B5	81
Crown City, Oh., U.S.	D3	112
Crown King, Az., U.S.	C3	80
Crown Point, In., U.S.	B3	91
Crown Point, La., U.S.	k11	95
Crown Point, N.Y., U.S.	*C10	104
Crownpoint, N.M., U.S.	B1	108
Crown Point, N.Y., U.S.	B7	109
Crow Peak, mtn., Mt., U.S.	D5	103
Crowsnest, B.C., Can.	E10	69
Crowsnest Pass, Ab., Can.	E3	68
Crowsnest Pass, Can.	E3	68
Crows Nest Peak, mtn., S.D., U.S.	C2	118
Crowville, La., U.S.	B4	95
Crow Wing, co., Mn., U.S.	D4	100
Crow Wing, stm., Mn., U.S.	D4	100
Croydon, Austl.	C7	50
Croydon (part of London), Eng., U.K.	E6	10
Croydon, N.H., U.S.	D2	106
Croydon, Pa., U.S.	F12	115
Croydon, Ut., U.S.	B4	121
Croydon Flat, N.H., U.S.	D2	106
Croydon Peak, mtn., N.H., U.S.	D2	106
Crozet, Va., U.S.	B4	123
Crozet, Îles, is., F.S.A.T.	J24	2
Crozier, Va., U.S.	C5	123
Crozon, Fr.	C1	16
Cruachan, Ben, mtn., Scot., U.K.	D3	13
Cruagh, i., Ire.	D1	11
Crucero, Peru	D3	58
Cruces, Cuba	C3	64
Cruces, Punta, c., Col.	B2	60
Crucible, Pa., U.S.	G1	115
Cruden Bay, Scot., U.K.	B6	10
Cruger, Ms., U.S.	B3	101
Crulai, Fr.	D2	125
Crumlin, N. Ire., U.K.	C5	11
Crummock Water, l., Eng., U.K.	F5	13
Crump Lake, l., Or., U.S.	E7	114
Crumpton, Md., U.S.	B6	97
Crumrod, Ar., U.S.	C5	81
Crumstown, In., U.S.	A5	91
Cruseilles, Fr.	C2	20
Crusheen, Ire.	E3	11
Cruso, N.C., U.S.	f10	110
Crutwell, Sk., Can.	D2	75
Cruz, Cabo, c., Cuba	E5	64
Cruz Alta, Arg.	A4	54
Cruz Alta, Braz.	D2	56
Cruz Bay, V.I.U.S.	B6	65
Cruz del Eje, Arg.	A4	54
Cruzeiro, Braz.	C4	56
Cruzeiro do Oeste, Braz.	C2	56
Cruzeiro do Sul, Braz.	C3	58
Cruz Grande, Chile	E1	55
Crysler, On., Can.	B9	73
Crystal, Mi., U.S.	E6	99
Crystal, Mn., U.S.	m12	100
Crystal, N.D., U.S.	A8	111
Crystal, stm., Co., U.S.	B3	83
Crystal Bay, Nv., U.S.	D1	105
Crystal Bay, b., Fl., U.S.	D4	86
Crystal Beach, Fl., U.S.	o10	86
Crystal City, Mb., Can.	E2	70
Crystal City, Mo., U.S.	C7	102
Crystal City, Tx., U.S.	E3	120
Crystal Falls, Mi., U.S.	B2	99
Crystal Hill, Va., U.S.	D4	123
Crystal Lake, Ct., U.S.	B6	84

Crystal Lake, Fl., U.S.	u16	86
Crystal Lake, Il., U.S.	A5	90
Crystal Lake, Ia., U.S.	A4	92
Crystal Lake, l., Ct., U.S.	B6	84
Crystal Lake, l., Mi., U.S.	D4	99
Crystal Lake, l., N.H., U.S.	D4	106
Crystal Lake, l., Vt., U.S.	B4	122
Crystal Lawns, Il., U.S.	k8	90
Crystal Manor, Il., U.S.	k8	90
Crystal Mountain, mtn., N.H., U.S.	g7	106
Crystal Pond, res., Ct., U.S.	B7	84
Crystal River, Fl., U.S.	D4	86
Crystal Springs, Sk., Can.	E3	75
Crystal Springs, Ar., U.S.	C2	81
Crystal Springs, Fl., U.S.	D4	86
Crystal Springs, Ms., U.S.	D3	101
Crystal Springs, N.D., U.S.	C6	111
Crystal Valley, Mi., U.S.	E4	99
Csongrád, Hung.	B5	24
Csorna, Hung.	B3	24
Cuajone, Peru	E3	58
Cuamba, Moz.	D6	48
Cuando, stm., Afr.	H8	42
Cuando Cubango, dept., Ang.	E2	48
Cuangar, Ang.	E2	48
Cuango, Ang.	C2	48
Cuango, stm., Afr.	C2	48
Cuango (Kwango), stm., Afr.	C2	48
Cuanza, stm., Ang.	C2	48
Cuanza-Norte, dept., Ang.	C1	48
Cuanza-Sul, dept., Ang.	D1	48
Cuarto, stm., Arg.	A4	54
Cuauhtémoc, Mex.	B3	63
Cuautepec (part of Mexico City), Mex.	g9	63
Cuautla [Morelos], Mex.	n14	63
Cuba, Port.	C2	22
Cuba, Al., U.S.	C1	78
Cuba, Il., U.S.	C3	90
Cuba, Ks., U.S.	C6	93
Cuba, Mo., U.S.	C6	102
Cuba, N.M., U.S.	A3	108
Cuba, N.Y., U.S.	C2	109
Cuba, Oh., U.S.	C2	112
Cuba, ctry., N.A.	C4	64
Cuba City, Wi., U.S.	F3	126
Cubal, Ang.	D1	48
Cubero, N.M., U.S.	B2	108
Cub Run, Ky., U.S.	C4	94
Cucamonga, Ca., U.S.	*m13	82
Cuchara, Co., U.S.	D5	83
Cucharas, stm., Co., U.S.	D6	83
Cuchillo, N.M., U.S.	D2	108
Cuchivero, stm., Ven.	B4	60
Cucuí, Braz.	C4	60
Cúcuta, Col.	B3	60
Cudahy, Ca., U.S.	*E4	82
Cudahy, Wi., U.S.	F6	126
Cuddalore, India	F6	36
Cuddapah, India	F6	36
Cuddy Mountain, mtn., Id., U.S.	E2	89
Cudgewa, Austl.	H6	51
Cudworth, Sk., Can.	E3	75
Cue, Austl.	E2	50
Cuéllar, Spain	B3	22
Cuenca, Ec.	B2	58
Cuenca, Spain	B4	22
Cuenca, Sierra de, mts., Spain	B4	22
Cuencamé [de Ceniceros], Mex.	C4	63
Cuernavaca, Mex.	D5	63
Cuero, Tx., U.S.	E4	120
Cuervo, N.M., U.S.	B5	108
Cuetzalan, Mex.	m15	63
Cuevas, Ms., U.S.	f7	101
Cuevas [del Almanzora], Spain	D2	23
Cuglieri, Italy	B1	56
Cuiabá, Braz.	B1	56
Cuiabá, stm., Braz.	B1	56
Cuicas, Ven.	B3	60
Cuicatlán, Mex.	o15	63
Cuilapa, Guat.	C2	62
Cuilcagh, mtn., Eur.	C4	11
Cuilco, Guat.	C2	62
Cuillin Hills, hills, Scot., U.K.	C2	13
Cuimba, Ang.	C1	48
Cuipo, Pan.	k10	62
Cuito, stm., Ang.	E2	48
Cuíto-Cuanavale, Ang.	E2	48
Cuitzeo, Lago de, l., Mex.	n13	63
Cuiuni, stm., Braz.	C2	59
Cuivre, West Fork, stm., Mo., U.S.	B6	102
Culberson, co., Tx., U.S.	o12	120
Culbertson, Mt., U.S.	B12	103
Culbertson, Ne., U.S.	D5	104
Culcairn, Austl.	G6	51
Culdaff, Bay, b., Ire.	B4	11
Culdesac, Id., U.S.	C2	89
Culebra, P.R.	B5	65
Culebra, Isla de i., P.R.	G12	64
Culebra Peak, mtn., Co., U.S.	D5	83
Culgoa, stm., Austl.	E8	50
Culhuacán (part of Mexico City), Mex.	h9	63
Culiacán, Mex.	C3	63
Cúllar de Baza, Spain	D4	22
Cullen, Scot., U.K.	C6	13
Cullen, La., U.S.	B2	95
Culleoka, Tn., U.S.	B5	119
Cullera, Spain	C5	22
Cullion, N. Ire., U.K.	C5	11
Cullison, Ks., U.S.	E5	93
Cullman, Al., U.S.	A3	78
Cullman, co., Al., U.S.	A3	78
Culloden, Ga., U.S.	D2	81
Culloden, W.V., U.S.	C2	125
Cullom, Il., U.S.	C5	90
Cullomburg, Al., U.S.	D1	78
Cullowhee, N.C., U.S.	f9	110
Culoz, Fr.	D1	20
Culp Creek, Or., U.S.	D4	114
Culpeper, Va., U.S.	B5	123
Culpeper, co., Va., U.S.	B5	123
Cultus Lake, B.C., Can.	f14	69
Culuene, stm., Braz.	A5	56
Culver, In., U.S.	B5	91
Culver, Or., U.S.	C5	114
Culver, Point, c., Austl.	F3	50
Culver City, Ca., U.S.	m12	82
Culvers Lake, l., N.J., U.S.	A3	107
Culverton, Ga., U.S.	C4	87
Culzean Bay, b., Scot., U.K.	E4	13
Cumaná, Ven.	A5	60
Cumbal, Nevado de, mtn., Col.	A2	60
Cumberland, B.C., Can.	E5	69
Cumberland, On., Can.	g13	73
Cumberland, Ky., U.S.	D7	94
Cumberland, Md., U.S.	k13	97
Cumberland, N.C., U.S.	B4	110

Cumberland, Oh., U.S.	C4	112
Cumberland, R.I., U.S.	C5	113
Cumberland, Va., U.S.	C4	123
Cumberland, Wi., U.S.	C1	126
Cumberland, co., N.S., Can.	f12	124
Cumberland, co., N.S., Can.	D5	71
Cumberland, co., Il., U.S.	D5	90
Cumberland, co., Ky., U.S.	D4	94
Cumberland, co., Me., U.S.	E2	96
Cumberland, co., N.J., U.S.	E2	107
Cumberland, co., N.C., U.S.	B4	110
Cumberland, co., Pa., U.S.	F7	115
Cumberland, co., Tn., U.S.	D8	119
Cumberland, co., Va., U.S.	C4	123
Cumberland, stm., U.S.	C11	76
Cumberland, Lake, res., Ky., U.S.	D5	94
Cumberland, South Fork, stm., U.S.	E2	96
Cumberland Center, Me., U.S.	g7	96
Cumberland City, Tn., U.S.	A4	119
Cumberland Foreside, Me., U.S.	E2	96
Cumberland Furnace, Tn., U.S.	A4	119
Cumberland Gap, Tn., U.S.	C10	119
Cumberland Gap, Tn., U.S.	D6	94
Cumberland Gap National Historical Park, U.S.	D6	94
Cumberland Hill, R.I., U.S.	B4	116
Cumberland House, Sk., Can.	D4	75
Cumberland Island National Seashore, Ga., U.S.	B3	63
Cumberland Lake, l., Sk., Can.	C4	75
Cumberland Mountain, mtn., Tn., U.S.	C9	119
Cumberland Peninsula, pen., N.T., Can.	C20	66
Cumberland Plateau, plat., U.S.	D8	119
Cumberland Sound, strt., N.T., Can.	C19	66
Cumbernauld, Scot., U.K.	*E5	13
Cumbres Pass, Co., U.S.	D4	83
Cumbria, co., Eng., U.K.	F6	13
Cuming, co., Ne., U.S.	C9	104
Cumming, Ga., U.S.	B2	87
Cumming, Ia., U.S.	f8	92
Cummings, N.D., U.S.	B8	111
Cummington, Ma., U.S.	B2	98
Cumnock, N.C., U.S.	B3	110
Cumnock [and Holmhead], Scot., U.K.	E4	13
Cumpas, Mex.	A3	63
Çumra, Tur.	D9	40
Cunard, W.V., U.S.	m13	125
Cunco, Chile	B2	54
Cuncumén, Chile	A2	54
Cundiff, Ky., U.S.	D4	94
Cundinamarca, dept., Col.	C3	60
Cundiyo, N.M., U.S.	*B4	108
Cundys Harbor, Me., U.S.	g8	96
Cunene, dept., Ang.	E2	48
Cunene, stm., Afr.	E1	48
Cuneo, Italy	B1	23
Cuney, Tx., U.S.	C5	120
Cunnamulla, Austl.	E8	50
Cunningham, Ky., U.S.	f9	94
Cunningham, Tn., U.S.	A4	119
Cupar, Sk., Can.	G3	75
Cupar, Scot., U.K.	D5	13
Cupertino, Ca., U.S.	*k8	82
Cupica, Braz.	C3	57
Curaçá, i., Neth. Ant.	H18	65
Curaçá, Braz.	B3	54
Curaçó, stm., Arg.	B3	54
Curanilahue, Chile	B2	54
Curaray, stm., S.A.	B3	58
Curcubăta, mtn., Rom.	B6	24
Curdsville, Ky., U.S.	C2	94
Curecanti National Recreation Area, Co., U.S.	C3	83
Curepto, Chile	B2	54
Curiapo, Ven.	B5	60
Curicó, Chile	A2	54
Curicuriari, stm., Braz.	C4	60
Curimataú, stm., Braz.	h6	57
Curitiba, Braz.	D3	56
Curitibanos, Braz.	D2	56
Curlew, Ia., U.S.	B3	92
Curlew, Wa., U.S.	A7	124
Curlew, stm., Wa., U.S.	A7	124
Curlew Lake, l., Wa., U.S.	A7	124
Curon Venosta, Italy	C5	20
Currais Novos, Braz.	C3	57
Curralinho, Braz.	C5	59
Curran, On., Can.	B10	73
Curran, Mi., U.S.	D7	99
Currans, Ire.	E2	11
Currant, Nv., U.S.	E6	105
Currant Creek, stm., Co., U.S.	C5	83
Currant Mountain, mtn., Nv., U.S.	E6	105
Curreeney, Ire.	E4	11
Current, stm., U.S.	A5	81
Currie, Nv., U.S.	C7	105
Currie, Mn., U.S.	F3	100
Currituck, N.C., U.S.	A6	110
Currituck, co., N.C., U.S.	A6	110
Curry, co., N.M., U.S.	C6	108
Curry, co., Or., U.S.	E2	114
Curryville, Mo., U.S.	B6	102
Curtea-de-Argeş, Rom.	C7	24
Curtice, Oh., U.S.	A2	112
Curtici, Rom.	B5	24
Curtin, Or., U.S.	D3	114
Curtis, Ar., U.S.	D2	81
Curtis, Mi., U.S.	B5	99
Curtis, i., Austl.	D9	50
Curtiss, Wi., U.S.	D3	126
Curtisville, Pa., U.S.	E2	115
Curuá, stm., Braz.	C4	59
Curuá, stm., Braz.	C4	59
Curuá do Sul, stm., Braz.	C4	59
Curuçá, Braz.	B1	57
Çuruk, Yugo.	C5	24
Çuruğ, Yugo.	C5	24
Curuguaty, Para.	C2	56
Curumiguara, Ponta, c., Braz.	B3	57
Curundu, Pan.	m11	62
Curupira, Sierra de, mts., S.A.	C5	60
Curuzú Cuatiá, Arg.	A4	55
Curve, Tn., U.S.	B2	119
Curvelo, Braz.	B2	56
Curvèr, stm., Switz.	C8	21
Curwensville, Pa., U.S.	E4	115
Curwensville Lake, res., Pa., U.S.	E4	115
Curwood, Mount, mtn., Mi., U.S.	B2	99
Cushendall, N. Ire., U.K.	B5	11
Cushing, Ia., U.S.	B2	92
Cushing, Ne., U.S.	C7	104
Cushing, Ok., U.S.	B5	113

Cushing, Tx., U.S.	D5	120
Cushman, Ar., U.S.	B4	81
Cushman, Ma., U.S.	B2	98
Cushman, Lake, res., Wa., U.S.	B2	124
Cusick, Wa., U.S.	A8	124
Cusihuiriáchic, Mex.	B3	63
Cusset, Fr.	D5	16
Cusseta, Al., U.S.	C4	78
Cusseta, Ga., U.S.	D2	87
Custar, Oh., U.S.	A2	112
Custer, Mi., U.S.	E4	99
Custer, S.D., U.S.	D2	118
Custer, Wa., U.S.	A3	124
Custer, co., Co., U.S.	C5	83
Custer, co., Id., U.S.	E4	89
Custer, co., Mt., U.S.	D11	103
Custer, co., Ne., U.S.	C6	104
Custer, co., Ok., U.S.	B2	113
Custer, co., S.D., U.S.	D2	118
Custer Battlefield National Monument, Mt., U.S.	E9	103
Custer City, Ok., U.S.	B3	113
Custer City, Pa., U.S.	C4	115
Custer Peak, mtn., S.D., U.S.	C2	118
Cut Bank, Mt., U.S.	B4	103
Cutbank, stm., Ab., Can.	B1	68
Cut Bank Creek, stm., N.D., U.S.	A4	111
Cut Beaver Lake, l., Sk., Can.	D4	75
Cutchogue, N.Y., U.S.	m16	109
Cutervo, Peru	C2	58
Cuthbert, Ga., U.S.	E2	87
Cut Knife, Sk., Can.	E1	75
Cutler, On., Can.	A2	73
Cutler, Ca., U.S.	E4	90
Cutler, In., U.S.	C5	91
Cutler, Me., U.S.	D5	96
Cutler Ridge, Fl., U.S.	s13	86
Cutlerville, Mi., U.S.	*F5	99
Cut Off, La., U.S.	E5	95
Cutro, Italy	E6	23
Cutshin, Ky., U.S.	C6	94
Cuttack, India	D8	36
Cut Throat Island, i., Nf., Can.	A3	72
Cuttingsville, Vt., U.S.	D3	122
Cuttyhunk Island, i., Ma., U.S.	D6	98
Cutzamalá, stm., Mex.	n13	63
Cuvo, stm., Ang.	D1	48
Cuxhaven, F.R.Ger.	B4	18
Cuyahoga, co., Oh., U.S.	A4	112
Cuyahoga, stm., Oh., U.S.	A4	112
Cuyahoga Falls, Oh., U.S.	A4	112
Cuyama, stm., Ca., U.S.	E4	82
Cuyamaca Peak, mtn., Ca., U.S.	F5	82
Cuyamungue, N.M., U.S.	*B4	108
Cuyaba, Nic.	C6	62
Cuylerville, N.Y., U.S.	C3	109
Cuyo Islands, is., Phil.	C6	34
Cuyuna, Mn., U.S.	D5	100
Cuyuni, stm., S.A.	A3	59
Cuzco, Peru	D3	58
Cuzco, In., U.S.	H4	91
Cuzco, dept., Peru	D3	58
Cwmbran, Wales, U.K.	C5	12
C.W. McConaughy, Lake, res., Ne., U.S.	D5	104
Cybinka, Pol.	A9	19
Cyclone, Oh., U.S.	A2	112
Cygnet, Oh., U.S.	A2	112
Cylinder, Ia., U.S.	A3	92
Cynthiana, In., U.S.	H2	91
Cynthiana, Ky., U.S.	B5	94
Cynthiana, Oh., U.S.	C2	112
Cypress, Al., U.S.	C2	78
Cypress, Ca., U.S.	*n12	82
Cypress, Fl., U.S.	B1	86
Cypress, Il., U.S.	F4	90
Cypress, Tx., U.S.	r14	120
Cypress Bayou, stm., Ar., U.S.	B3	81
Cypress Creek, stm., Tx., U.S.	r14	120
Cypress Hills, hills, Can.	G10	66
Cypress Hills Provincial Park, Ab., Can.	E5	68
Cypress Hills Provincial Park, Sk., Can.	H1	75
Cypress Inn, Tn., U.S.	B4	119
Cypress Lake, l., Sk., Can.	H1	75
Cypress Lake, l., Fl., U.S.	D5	86
Cypress Quarters, Fl., U.S.	E6	86
Cypress River, Mb., Can.	E2	70
Cypress Swamp, sw., U.S.	F4	85
Cyprus, ctry., Asia	E9	40
Cyrenaica (Barqah), hist reg., Libya	A4	43
Cyril, Ok., U.S.	C3	113
Cyril, stm., Mb., Can.	B4	70
Cyrus, Mn., U.S.	E3	100
Czar, Ab., Can.	C5	68
Czarna, stm., Pol.	k14	26
Czarna Przemsza, stm., Pol.	g10	26
Czarnków, Pol.	B3	26
Czechoslovakia, ctry., Eur.	C6	24
Czechowice-Dziedzice, Pol.	h10	26
Czersk, Pol.	B4	26
Częstochowa, Pol.	C5	26
Człuchów, Pol.	B4	26

D

Da'an, China	B11	32
Daaquam, P.Q., Can.	C7	74
Dabakala, I.C.	E4	45
Daba Mountains, mts., China	I4	32
Dabdab, Libya	D2	43
Dabeiba, Col.	B2	60
Dabie (part of Szczecin), Pol.	B3	26
Dabie Mountains, mts., China	I5	32
Dáblice, Czech.	n18	26
Dabneys, Va., U.S.	C5	123
Dabola, Gui.	F3	45
Daborow, Pol.	D6	47
Dabou, I.C.	E4	45
Dąbrowa, I.C.	E4	45
Dąbrowa Białostocka, Pol.	B7	26
Dąbrowa Górnicza, Pol.	C5	26
Dąbrowa [Tarnowska], Pol.	C6	26
Dacca (Dhaka), Bngl.	D9	36
Dacono, F.R.Ger.	m11	62
Dacono, Co., U.S.	A6	83
Dadanawa, Guy.	B1	60
Daday, Tur.	B9	40
Dade, co., Fl., U.S.	G6	86
Dade, co., Ga., U.S.	B1	87
Dade, co., Mo., U.S.	D4	102
Dade City, Fl., U.S.	D4	86
Dadeville, Al., U.S.	C4	78
Dadeville, Mo., U.S.	D4	102
Dadra and Nagar Haveli, ter., India	*D5	36
Dādu, Pak.	C4	36

Daet, Phil.	o14	34
Dafoe, Sk., Can.	F3	75
Dafoe, stm., Mb., Can.	B4	70
Dagana, Sen.	C1	45
Dagenham (part of London), Eng., U.K.	k13	10
Daggett, Ca., U.S.	E5	82
Daggett, Mi., U.S.	C3	99
Daggett, co., Ut., U.S.	C6	121
Dagö see Tondi, depr., Afg.	E10	39
Dagmar, Mt., U.S.	B12	103
Dagsboro, De., U.S.	F5	85
Dagu, China	E7	32
Daguscahonda, Pa., U.S.	D4	115
Dagus Mines, Pa., U.S.	D4	115
Dāhānu, India	G4	37
Dahinda, Il., U.S.	C3	90
Dahlak Archipelago, is., Eth.	A8	111
Dahlen, N.D., U.S.	A8	111
Dahlgren, Il., U.S.	E5	90
Dahlgren, Va., U.S.	B5	123
Dahlonega, Ga., U.S.	B3	87
Dahme, Ger.D.R.	B8	19
Dahomey see Benin, ctry., Afr.	E5	45
Dahra, Libya	D3	43
Dahshūr, Eg.	E3	41
Dahūk, Iraq	D14	40
Daicheng, China	E7	32
Dailey, W.V., U.S.	C5	125
Daimiel, Spain	C4	22
Daingean, Ire.	D4	11
Daiō, Japan	o15	33
Daiō, Cape, c., Japan	I8	33
Dairen see Lüda, China	D9	31
Dairy, Or., U.S.	E5	114
Dairyland, Wi., U.S.	B1	126
Daisetta, Tx., U.S.	D5	120
Daisy, Ar., U.S.	C2	81
Daisy, Ga., U.S.	D5	87
Daisy, Ok., U.S.	C6	113
Daixian, China	D7	31
Dajabón, Dom. Rep.	E8	64
Dajarra, Austl.	D6	50
Dakar, Sen.	D1	45
Dakhilah, Al Wāḩāt ad, well, Eg.	D5	43
Dakhla, W. Sah.	E1	44
Dakoro, Niger	D6	45
Dakota, Il., U.S.	A4	90
Dakota, Mn., U.S.	G7	100
Dakota, co., Mn., U.S.	F5	100
Dakota, co., Ne., U.S.	B9	104
Dakota City, Ia., U.S.	B3	92
Dakota City, Ne., U.S.	B9	104
Dakwa, Zaire	A4	48
Dalaas, Aus.	B9	21
Dalaba, Gui.	D2	45
Dalälven, stm., Swe.	G6	14
Dalaman, stm., Tur.	D7	25
Dalandzadgad, Mong.	C5	31
Dalark, Ar., U.S.	C3	81
Dalarö, Swe.	C12	14
Da Lat, Viet.	C3	34
Dälbandin, Pak.	C3	36
Dalbeattie, Scot., U.K.	F5	13
D'Albertis Dome, mtn., Pap. N. Gui.	k11	52
Dalby, Mn., U.S.	E5	100
Dalby, Austl.	E9	50
Dalby, Swe.	C7	15
Dalcahue, Chile	C2	54
Dale, In., U.S.	H4	91
Dale, Ok., U.S.	B4	113
Dale, Or., U.S.	D4	78
Dale, co., Al., U.S.	D4	78
Dale City, Va., U.S.	B5	123
Dale Hollow Lake, res., U.S.	C8	119
Dalemead, Ab., Can.	D4	78
Daleville, Al., U.S.	D4	78
Daleville, In., U.S.	D6	91
Dalhart, Tx., U.S.	A1	120
Dalhousie, N.B., Can.	A3	71
Dalhousie, India	A5	37
Dalhousie Junction, N.B., Can.	A3	71
Dali, China	E6	31
Dalian see Lüda, China	D9	31
Dalías, Spain	D4	22
Daliburgh, Scot., U.K.	C1	13
Da Linh, Viet.	C3	34
Dāliyat el Karmel, Isr.	B7	41
Dalkeith, Scot., U.K.	E5	13
Dalkena, Wa., U.S.	B1	86
Dalkey, Ire.	D5	11
Dall, Mount, mtn., Ak., U.S.	f15	79
Dallardsville, Tx., U.S.	D5	120
Dallas, Al., U.S.	B3	78
Dallas, Ga., U.S.	C2	87
Dallas, N.C., U.S.	B1	110
Dallas, Or., U.S.	C3	114
Dallas, S.D., U.S.	D6	118
Dallas, Tx., U.S.	C4	120
Dallas, W.V., U.S.	f8	125
Dallas, Wi., U.S.	C2	126
Dallas, co., Al., U.S.	D3	81
Dallas, co., Ar., U.S.	D3	81
Dallas, co., Ia., U.S.	C3	92
Dallas, co., Mo., U.S.	D4	102
Dallas, co., Tx., U.S.	C4	120
Dallas Center, Ia., U.S.	C4	92
Dallas Naval Air Station, mil., Tx., U.S.	n9	120
Dallastown, Pa., U.S.	G8	115
Dall Island, i., Ak., U.S.	n23	79
Dalmally, Scot., U.K.	D4	13
Dalmatia, hist reg., Yugo.	D3	24
Dalmellington, Scot., U.K.	E4	13
Dalmeny, Sk., Can.	E2	75
Dalnerechensk, Sov. Un.	D11	30
Dalnyaya, Sov. Un.	D11	30
Dalou Mountains, mts., China	K2	32
Dalqū, Sud.	A3	47
Dalroy, Ab., Can.	D4	68
Dalrymple, Mount, mtn., Austl.	D8	50
Dalton, Ga., U.S.	A4	81
Dalton, Ma., U.S.	A1	98
Dalton, Mn., U.S.	D3	100
Dalton, Ne., U.S.	B5	104
Dalton, N.H., U.S.	B3	106
Dalton, N.Y., U.S.	C3	109
Dalton, Oh., U.S.	B4	112

Name	Map Ref	Page

Dalton, Pa., U.S. — C10 115
Dalton, Wi., U.S. — E4 126
Dalton City, Il., U.S. — D5 90
Daltonganj, India — D7 36
Dalton Gardens, Id., U.S. — B2 89
Dalton Iceberg Tongue, Ant. — C25 7
Dalwhinnie, Scot., U.K. — D4 13
Daly, stm., Austl. — B5 50
Daly City, Ca., U.S. — h8 82
Dalzell, Il., U.S. — B4 90
Dalzell, S.C., U.S. — C7 117
Damān, India — D5 36
Damanhūr, Eg. — C6 43
Damaqun Mountains, mts., China — D7 32
Damar, Ks., U.S. — C4 93
Damar, i., Indon. — G7 34
Damara, Cen. Afr. Rep. — D3 46
Damariscotta, Me., U.S. — D3 96
Damariscotta Lake, l., Me., U.S. — D3 96
Damascus (Dimashq), Syria — B3 38
Damascus, Ar., U.S. — B3 81
Damascus, Ga., U.S. — B2 87
Damascus, Ga., U.S. — E2 87
Damascus, Md., U.S. — B3 97
Damascus, Pa., U.S. — C11 115
Damascus, Va., U.S. — f10 123
Damascus Gate, hist., Isr. Occ. — m14 41
Damaturu, Nig. — D7 45
Damba, Ang. — C2 48
Dame Marie, Cap, c., Haiti — E6 64
Dames Quarter, Md., U.S. — D6 97
Dam Gamad, Sud. — C2 47
Dāmghān, Iran — B5 38
Damietta see Dumyāṭ, Eg. — B3 38
Damietta Branch, stm., Eg. — D3 41
Daming, China — F6 32
Dāmiyā, Jord. — g13 41
Damme, F.R.Ger. — B8 17
Dāmodar, stm., India — F10 37
Damoh, India — F7 37
Damon, Tx., U.S. — r14 120
Damongo, Ghana — E4 45
Dampier, Austl. — D2 50
Dampier Archipelago, is., Austl. — D2 50
Dampier Strait, strt., Indon. — F8 34
Damvant, Switz. — B2 21
Dan, stm., U.S. — D3 123
Dana, Sk., Can. — E3 75
Dana, In., U.S. — E3 91
Dana, Ia., U.S. — B3 92
Dana, N.C., U.S. — f10 110
Danané, I.C. — E3 45
Da Nang, Viet. — B3 34
Dānāpur, India — E10 37
Danburg, Ga., U.S. — C4 87
Danbury, Ct., U.S. — D2 84
Danbury, Ia., U.S. — B2 92
Danbury, Ne., U.S. — D5 104
Danbury, N.H., U.S. — C3 106
Danbury, N.C., U.S. — A2 110
Danbury, Tx., U.S. — r14 120
Danbury, Wi., U.S. — B1 126
Danby, Ca., U.S. — E6 82
Danby, N.Y., U.S. — C4 109
Danby, Vt., U.S. — E3 122
Danby Corners, Vt., U.S. — E2 122
Dancy, Al., U.S. — B1 78
Dancy, Wi., U.S. — D4 126
Dancyville, Tn., U.S. — B2 119
Dande, stm., Ang. — C1 48
Dandenong, Austl. — *G8 50
Dandong, China — C9 31
Dandridge, Tn., U.S. — C10 119
Dane, Wi., U.S. — E4 126
Dane, co., Wi., U.S. — E4 126
Danevang, Tx., U.S. — E4 120
Danfeng, China — H4 32
Danforth, Il., U.S. — C6 90
Danforth, Me., U.S. — C5 96
Danforth Hills, mts., Co., U.S. — A2 83
Dangila, Eth. — C4 47
Dangshan, China — G7 32
Dangtu, China — I8 32
Dangyang, China — I4 32
Dania, Fl., U.S. — F6 86
Daniel, Wy., U.S. — *C4 121
Daniel, Wy., U.S. — D2 127
Daniels, co., Mt., U.S. — B11 103
Daniel's Harbour, Nf., Can. — C3 72
Danielson, Ct., U.S. — B8 84
Daniels Pass, Ut., U.S. — C4 121
Danielsville, Ga., U.S. — B3 87
Danilov, Sov. Un. — B13 27
Danilovgrad, Yugo. — D4 24
Danjo Island, i., Japan — J4 33
Danli, Hond. — E7 63
Dannebrog, Ne., U.S. — C7 104
Dannemare, Fr. — A3 21
Dannemora, N.Y., U.S. — f11 109
Dannenberg, F.R.Ger. — E5 15
Dannevirke, N.Z. — N16 51
Dannike, Swe. — A7 15
Dans Mountain, mtn., Md., U.S. — k13 97
Dansville, N.Y., U.S. — C3 109
Dante, S.D., U.S. — D7 118
Dante, Va., U.S. — f9 123
Dantewāra, India — H8 37
Danube, stm., Eur. — G14 9
Danube Delta, Eur. — I7 27
Danubyu, Burma — D1 35
Danvers, Il., U.S. — C4 90
Danvers, Ma., U.S. — A6 98
Danvers, Mn., U.S. — E3 100
Danvers, Mt., U.S. — C7 103
Danville, P.Q., Can. — D5 74
Danville, Ar., U.S. — B2 81
Danville, Ca., U.S. — h9 82
Danville, Ga., U.S. — D3 87
Danville, Il., U.S. — C6 90
Danville, In., U.S. — E4 91
Danville, Ia., U.S. — D6 92
Danville, Ks., U.S. — E6 93
Danville, Ky., U.S. — C5 94
Danville, La., U.S. — *B3 95
Danville, N.H., U.S. — E4 106
Danville, Oh., U.S. — B3 112
Danville, Pa., U.S. — E8 115
Danville, Vt., U.S. — C4 122
Danville, Va., U.S. — D3 123
Danville, W.V., U.S. — C3 125
Danxian, China — E9 31
Danzhai, China — K2 31
Danzig see Gdańsk, Pol. — A5 26
Danzig, Gulf of, b., Eur. — A5 26
Daosa, India — D6 37
Daoxian, China — F7 31

Daphne, Al., U.S. — E2 78
Dapp, Ab., Can. — B4 68
Da Qaidam, China — D4 31
Darʼā, Syria — F11 40
Dārāb, Iran — G7 39
Darabani, Rom. — A8 24
Daraj, Libya — C2 43
Darasun, Sov. Un. — D14 29
Darawah, Eg. — D3 41
Darbandi Khan Dam, Iraq — D2 39
Darbhanga, India — C8 36
D'Arbonne, Bayou, stm., La., U.S. — B3 95
Darburruk, Som. — D5 47
Darby, Mt., U.S. — D2 103
Darby, Pa., U.S. — G11 115
Darbydale, Oh., U.S. — m10 112
Darbyville, Oh., U.S. — C2 112
Dardanelle, Ar., U.S. — B2 81
Dardanelle, Ca., U.S. — C4 82
Dardanelle Lake, res., Ar., U.S. — B2 81
Dardanelles, strt. — B5 40
Darden, N.C., U.S. — B6 110
Darden, Tn., U.S. — B3 119
Dardenne Creek, stm., Mo., U.S. — f12 102
Dare, co., N.C., U.S. — B7 110
Darende, Tur. — C11 40
Dar es Salaam, Tan. — C6 48
Daretown, N.J., U.S. — D2 107
Darfo, Italy — D6 20
Dārfūr al Janūbīyah (Southern Darfur), prov., Sud. — C1 47
Dārfūr ash Shamālīyah (Northern Darfur), prov., Sud. — B2 47
Darganata, Sov. Un. — A11 39
Dargaville, N.Z. — K14 51
Darhan, Mong. — B6 31
Darhan Mumingan Lianheqi, China — D4 32
Darien, Ct., U.S. — E2 84
Darien, Ga., U.S. — E5 87
Darien, Il., U.S. — *B6 90
Darien, Wi., U.S. — F5 126
Darien, Serranía del, mts. — F9 62
Darjeeling, India — C8 36
Darke, co., Oh., U.S. — B1 112
Darkesville, W.V., U.S. — B6 125
Darley Woods, De., U.S. — h8 85
Darling, Ms., U.S. — A3 101
Darling, stm., Austl. — F7 50
Darling Downs, reg., Austl. — C8 51
Darlingford, Mb., Can. — E2 70
Darling Range, mts., Austl. — F2 50
Darlington, Eng., U.K. — C6 10
Darlington, Al., U.S. — D2 78
Darlington, Fl., U.S. — v15 86
Darlington, Id., U.S. — F5 89
Darlington, In., U.S. — D4 91
Darlington, Md., U.S. — A5 97
Darlington, Mo., U.S. — A3 102
Darlington, S.C., U.S. — C8 117
Darlington, Wi., U.S. — F3 126
Darlington, co., S.C., U.S. — C8 117
Darmody, Sk., Can. — G2 75
Darmstadt, F.R.Ger. — D4 18
Darnah, Libya — C4 43
Darnell, La., U.S. — B4 95
Darnestown, Md., U.S. — B3 97
Darney, Fr. — A2 20
Darnley, Cape, c., Ant. — C19 7
Daro, Malay. — E4 34
Daroca, Spain — B2 22
Darr, Ne., U.S. — D6 104
Darrah, Mount, mtn., Can. — E3 68
Darreh Gaz, Iran — C9 39
Darrington, Wa., U.S. — A4 124
Darrouzett, Tx., U.S. — A2 120
Darrow, La., U.S. — h10 95
Darsser Ort, c., Ger.D.R. — D6 15
Dart, Cape, c., Ant. — B36 7
Dartmoor, for., Eng., U.K. — E5 10
Dartmouth, N.S., Can. — E6 71
Dartmouth, Eng., U.K. — E5 10
Dartmouth, Ma., U.S. — C5 98
Dartmouth Woods, De., U.S. — *A3 85
Daru, Pap. N. Gui. — k11 50
Daruvar, Yugo. — C3 24
Darvel Bay, b., Malay. — E5 34
Darwin, Austl. — B5 50
Darwin, Ca., U.S. — D5 82
Darwin, Mn., U.S. — E4 100
Darwin, Isla, i., Ec. — I5 58
Darwin Glacier, Ant. — A21 7
Dasht, stm., Pak. — C3 36
Dashwood, On., Can. — D3 73
Dasol Bay, b., Phil. — o12 34
Dassel, Mn., U.S. — E4 100
Datça, Tur. — D6 25
Dateland, Az., U.S. — E1 80
Datia, India — E7 37
Datian, China — L7 32
Datil, N.M., U.S. — C2 108
Datil Mountains, mts., N.M., U.S. — C2 108
Datong, China — D7 31
Datto, Ar., U.S. — A5 81
Datu, Cape, c., Asia — E3 34
Datze, stm., Ger.D.R. — E7 15
Daufuskie Island, S.C., U.S. — G6 117
Daufuskie Island, i., S.C., U.S. — G6 117
Daugava (Western Dvina), stm. — C5 27
Daugavpils (Dvinsk), Sov. Un. — D6 27
Daule, Ec. — A2 58
Daule, stm., Ec. — A2 58
Daun, F.R.Ger. — C5 19
Daund, India — H5 37
Daung, i., Burma — F3 35
Dauphin, Mb., Can. — D1 70
Dauphin, Pa., U.S. — F8 115
Dauphin, co., Pa., U.S. — F8 115
Dauphiné, hist. reg., Fr. — E6 16
Dauphin Island, Al., U.S. — E1 78
Dauphin Island, i., Al., U.S. — E1 78
Dauphin Lake, l., Mb., Can. — D2 70
Davant, La., U.S. — E6 95
Davao, Phil. — D7 34
Davao Gulf, b., Phil. — D7 34

Daveluyville, P.Q., Can. — C5 74
Davenport, Ca., U.S. — D2 82
Davenport, Fl., U.S. — D5 86
Davenport, Ia., U.S. — C7 92
Davenport, Ne., U.S. — D8 104
Davenport, N.Y., U.S. — C6 109
Davenport, N.D., U.S. — C8 111
Davenport, Ok., U.S. — B5 113
Davenport, Wa., U.S. — B7 124
Davenport Downs, Austl. — B3 51
Daventry, Eng., U.K. — B6 12
Davey, Ne., U.S. — h11 104
David, Pan. — F6 62
David, Ky., U.S. — C7 94
David City, Ne., U.S. — C8 104
David-Gorodok, Sov. Un. — E6 27
Davidson, Sk., Can. — F3 75
Davidson, N.C., U.S. — B2 110
Davidson, Ok., U.S. — C2 113
Davidson, co., N.C., U.S. — B2 110
Davidson, co., Tn., U.S. — A5 119
Davidson Mountains, mts., Ak., U.S. — B11 79
Davidsville, Pa., U.S. — F4 115
Davie, Fl., U.S. — F6 86
Davie, co., N.C., U.S. — B2 110
Davies Bay, b., Ant. — C26 7
Daviess, co., In., U.S. — G3 91
Daviess, co., Ky., U.S. — C2 94
Daviess, co., Mo., U.S. — B3 102
Davin, Sk., Can. — G3 75
Davis, Ca., U.S. — C3 82
Davis, Il., U.S. — A4 90
Davis, N.C., U.S. — C6 110
Davis, Ok., U.S. — C4 113
Davis, S.D., U.S. — D9 118
Davis, W.V., U.S. — B5 125
Davis, co., Ia., U.S. — D5 92
Davis, co., Ut., U.S. — C3 121
Davis, Mount, mtn., Pa., U.S. — G3 115
Davis Dam, Az., U.S. — B1 80
Davis Dam, U.S. — H7 105
Davis Inlet, Nf., Can. — g9 72
Davis Islands, is., Fl., U.S. — p11 86
Davis Junction, Il., U.S. — A4 90
Davis Lake, l., Or., U.S. — E5 114
Davis-Monthan Air Force Base, mil., Az., U.S. — E5 80
Davis Mountains, mts., Tx., U.S. — o12 120
Davison, Mi., U.S. — E7 99
Davison, co., S.D., U.S. — D7 118
Davis Sea, Ant. — C22 7
Davis Station, S.C., U.S. — D7 117
Davis Strait, strt., N.A. — C15 61
Daviston, Al., U.S. — B4 78
Davisville, N.H., U.S. — D3 106
Davisville, R.I., U.S. — E4 116
Davlekanovo, Sov. Un. — o17 26
Davos, Switz. — E4 18
Davy, W.V., U.S. — D3 125
Dawa, stm., Afr. — E5 47
Dawasir, Wādī ad, val., Sau. Ar. — C4 38
Dawes, co., Ne., U.S. — B2 104
Dawley, Eng., U.K. — B5 12
Dawn, Mo., U.S. — B4 102
Dawn, Tx., U.S. — B1 120
Dawna Range, mts., Burma — D3 35
Dawros Head, c., Ire. — C3 11
Daws Island, i., S.C., U.S. — G6 117
Dawson, Yk., Can. — D5 66
Dawson, Ga., U.S. — E2 87
Dawson, Il., U.S. — D5 90
Dawson, Ia., U.S. — C3 92
Dawson, Mn., U.S. — F2 100
Dawson, Ne., U.S. — D10 104
Dawson, N.D., U.S. — C6 111
Dawson, Pa., U.S. — F2 115
Dawson, Tx., U.S. — D4 120
Dawson, co., Ga., U.S. — B2 87
Dawson, co., Mt., U.S. — C11 103
Dawson, co., Ne., U.S. — D6 104
Dawson, co., Tx., U.S. — C1 120
Dawson, stm., Austl. — D8 50
Dawson, Mount, mtn., B.C., Can. — D9 69
Dawson Creek, B.C., Can. — B7 69
Dawson-Lambton Glacier, Ant. — B10 7
Dawson Range, mts., Yk., Can. — D5 66
Dawsonville, Ga., U.S. — B2 87
Dax, Fr. — F3 16
Daxian, China — E8 31
Day, Fl., U.S. — B3 86
Day, co., S.D., U.S. — B8 118
Daykin, Ne., U.S. — D8 104
Daylesford, Austl. — H5 51
Daym Zubayr, Sud. — D2 47
Dayong, China — J4 32
Dayr Abū Saʿīd, Jord. — B7 41
Dayr al Balaḥ, Isr. Occ. — C6 41
Dayr ʿAllā, Jord. — g13 41
Dayr az Zawr, Syria — B4 38
Dayr Dibwān, Isr. Occ. — h12 41
Dayr Istiyā, Isr. Occ. — g11 41
Dayrūṭ, Eg. — D6 43
Daysland, Ab., Can. — C4 68
Dayton, Al., U.S. — C2 78
Dayton, Id., U.S. — G7 89
Dayton, In., U.S. — D4 91
Dayton, Ia., U.S. — B3 92
Dayton, Ky., U.S. — h14 94
Dayton, Md., U.S. — B4 97
Dayton, Mn., U.S. — m12 100
Dayton, Nv., U.S. — D2 105
Dayton, N.J., U.S. — C3 107
Dayton, N.Y., U.S. — C1 109
Dayton, Oh., U.S. — C1 112
Dayton, Or., U.S. — B3 114
Dayton, Pa., U.S. — E3 115
Dayton, Tn., U.S. — D8 119
Dayton, Tx., U.S. — D5 120
Dayton, Va., U.S. — B4 123
Dayton, Wa., U.S. — C8 124
Dayton, Wy., U.S. — B5 127
Daytona Beach, Fl., U.S. — C5 86
Dayu, China — J1 32
Dayville, Ct., U.S. — B8 84
Dazey, N.D., U.S. — B7 111
De Aar, S. Afr. — H4 48
Dead, North Branch, stm., Me., U.S. — C2 96
Dead, South Branch, stm., Me., U.S. — C2 96
Dead Creek, stm., Vt., U.S. — C2 122
Dead Diamond, stm., N.H., U.S. — g7 106

Dead Indian Peak, mtn., Wy., U.S. — B3 127
Dead Lake, l., Mn., U.S. — D3 100
Dead Lake, res., Fl., U.S. — B1 86
Deadman Bay, b., Fl., U.S. — C3 86
Deadman Creek, stm., Wa., U.S. — g14 124
Dead Sea, l., Asia — B3 38
Deadwood, S.D., U.S. — C2 118
Deadwood Reservoir, res., Id., U.S. — E3 89
Deaf Smith, co., Tx., U.S. — B1 120
Deakin Bay, b., Ant. — C28 7
Deal, Eng., U.K. — C9 12
Deal, N.J., U.S. — C4 107
Deale, Md., U.S. — C4 97
Deal Island, Md., U.S. — D6 97
Deal Island, i., Md., U.S. — D6 97
Dean, stm., B.C., Can. — C4 69
Deanburg, Tn., U.S. — B3 119
Dean Channel, strt., B.C., Can. — C4 69
Deán Funes, Arg. — A4 54
Deans, N.J., U.S. — C3 107
Deanville, W.V., U.S. — B4 125
Dearborn, Mi., U.S. — F7 99
Dearborn, Mo., U.S. — B3 102
Dearborn, co., In., U.S. — F7 91
Dearborn Heights, Mi., U.S. — p15 99
Dearg, Beinn, mtn., Scot., U.K. — B4 10
Dearing, Ga., U.S. — C4 87
Dearing, Ks., U.S. — E8 93
De Armanville, Al., U.S. — B4 78
Deary, Id., U.S. — C2 89
Dease Arm, b., N.T., Can. — C8 66
Dease Lake, B.C., Can. — m17 69
Dease Strait, strt., N.T., Can. — C11 66
Death Valley, val., Ca., U.S. — D5 82
Death Valley Junction, Ca., U.S. — D5 82
Death Valley National Monument, U.S. — D5 82
Deatsville, Al., U.S. — C3 78
Deauville, Fr. — C3 16
Deaver, Wy., U.S. — B4 127
De Baca, co., N.M., U.S. — C5 108
Debaltsevo, Sov. Un. — q21 27
Debao, China — G6 31
Debar, Yugo. — E5 24
De Bary, Fl., U.S. — D5 86
Debauch Mountain, mtn., Ak., U.S. — C8 79
Debden, Sk., Can. — D2 75
Débé, Trin. — O23 65
Debec, N.B., Can. — C2 71
De Beque, Co., U.S. — B2 83
De Berry, Tx., U.S. — C5 120
Debica, Pol. — C6 26
Deblin, Pol. — C6 26
Deblois, Me., U.S. — D4 96
Debno, Pol. — B3 26
Debo, Lac, l., Mali — C4 45
De Borgia, Mt., U.S. — C1 103
Debovo, Bul. — D7 24
Debre Birhan, Eth. — D4 47
Debrecen, Hung. — B5 24
Debre Markos, Eth. — C4 47
Debre Tabor, Eth. — C4 47
De Cade, Lake, l., La., U.S. — E5 95
Decatur, Al., U.S. — A3 78
Decatur, Ar., U.S. — A1 81
Decatur, Ga., U.S. — C2 87
Decatur, Il., U.S. — D5 90
Decatur, In., U.S. — C8 91
Decatur, Ia., U.S. — D4 92
Decatur, Mi., U.S. — F5 99
Decatur, Ms., U.S. — C4 101
Decatur, Ne., U.S. — B9 104
Decatur, Tn., U.S. — D9 119
Decatur, Tx., U.S. — C4 120
Decatur, co., Ga., U.S. — F2 87
Decatur, co., In., U.S. — F6 91
Decatur, co., Ia., U.S. — D4 92
Decatur, co., Ks., U.S. — C3 93
Decatur, co., Tn., U.S. — B3 119
Decaturville, Tn., U.S. — B3 119
Deccan, plat., India — E6 36
Deception, Mount, mtn., Wa., U.S. — B2 124
Deception Lake, l., Sk., Can. — A3 75
Decherd, Tn., U.S. — B5 119
Dečín, Czech. — C3 26
Decize, Fr. — D5 16
Decker, Mb., Can. — D1 70
Decker, Mt., U.S. — E10 103
Decker Lake, B.C., Can. — B5 69
Deckers, Co., U.S. — B5 83
Deckerville, Mi., U.S. — E8 99
Declo, Id., U.S. — G5 89
De Cocksdorp, Neth. — A4 17
Decorah, Ia., U.S. — A6 92
Decota, W.V., U.S. — m13 125
DeCoursey, Ky., U.S. — h14 94
Dededo, Guam — L10 52
Dedemsvaart, Neth. — B6 17
Deder, Eth. — D5 47
Dedham, Ia., U.S. — C3 92
Dedham, Ma., U.S. — B5 98
Dédougou, Burkina — D4 45
Dedza, Mwi. — D5 48
Dee, stm., Scot., U.K. — B5 10
Dee, stm., U.K. — B5 10
Deel, stm., Ire. — C4 11
Deemer, Ms., U.S. — C4 101
Deep, stm., N.C., U.S. — B3 110
Deep Brook, N.S., Can. — E4 71
Deep Creek, stm., De., U.S. — F3 85
Deep Creek, stm., Md., U.S. — B3 97
Deep Creek, stm., Wa., U.S. — g13 124
Deep Creek Lake, res., Md., U.S. — k12 97
Deep Creek Mountains, mts., Id., U.S. — G6 89
Deep Creek Range, mts., Ut., U.S. — D2 121
Deep Fork, stm., Ok., U.S. — B5 113
Deep Gap, N.C., U.S. — A1 110
Deep Inlet, b., Nf., Can. — g10 72
Deep Red Creek, stm., Ok., U.S. — C3 113

Deep River, On., Can. — A7 73
Deep River, Ct., U.S. — D6 84
Deep River, Ia., U.S. — C5 92
Deep Run, N.C., U.S. — B5 110
Deepstep, Ga., U.S. — C4 87
Deepwater, Mo., U.S. — C4 102
Deepwater, N.J., U.S. — D2 107
Deep Water, W.V., U.S. — m13 125
Deer Creek, Il., U.S. — C4 90
Deer Creek, Mn., U.S. — D3 100
Deer Creek, stm., In., U.S. — C5 91
Deer Creek, stm., Md., U.S. — A5 97
Deer Creek, stm., Ms., U.S. — B3 101
Deer Creek, stm., Oh., U.S. — C2 112
Deer Creek Indian Reservation, Mn., U.S. — C5 100
Deerfield, Il., U.S. — h9 90
Deerfield, In., U.S. — D8 91
Deerfield, Ks., U.S. — E2 93
Deerfield, Ma., U.S. — A2 98
Deerfield, Mi., U.S. — G7 99
Deerfield, Mo., U.S. — D3 102
Deerfield, N.H., U.S. — D4 106
Deerfield, Oh., U.S. — A4 112
Deerfield, Wi., U.S. — E4 126
Deerfield, stm., U.S. — A2 98
Deerfield Beach, Fl., U.S. — F6 86
Deerfield Street, N.J., U.S. — D2 107
Deer Grove, Il., U.S. — B4 90
Deering, Ak., U.S. — B7 79
Deering, Mo., U.S. — E8 102
Deering, N.H., U.S. — D3 106
Deering, N.D., U.S. — A4 111
Deer Island, Or., U.S. — B4 114
Deer Island, pen., Ma., U.S. — g12 98
Deer Island, i., Ms., U.S. — f8 101
Deer Isle, Me., U.S. — D4 96
Deer Isle, i., Me., U.S. — D4 96
Deer Lake, Nf., Can. — D3 72
Deer Lake, l., Nf., Can. — D3 72
Deer Lake, l., Mn., U.S. — C5 100
Deer Lodge, Mt., U.S. — D4 103
Deer Lodge, Tn., U.S. — C9 119
Deer Lodge, co., Mt., U.S. — E3 103
Deer Mountain, mtn., Me., U.S. — C2 96
Deer Park, Al., U.S. — D1 78
Deer Park, Md., U.S. — m12 97
Deer Park, N.Y., U.S. — n15 109
Deer Park, Oh., U.S. — o13 112
Deer Park, Tx., U.S. — *r14 120
Deer Park, Wa., U.S. — B8 124
Deer Peak, mtn., Co., U.S. — C5 83
Deer Pond, l., Nf., Can. — D3 72
Deer River, Mn., U.S. — C5 100
Deer River, N.Y., U.S. — B5 109
Deerton, Mi., U.S. — B3 99
Deer Trail, Co., U.S. — B6 83
Deerwood, Mn., U.S. — D5 100
Deeson, Ms., U.S. — A3 101
Deeth, Nv., U.S. — B6 105
Deex Nugaaleed, stm., Som. — C5 47
Deferiet, N.Y., U.S. — A5 109
Defiance, Ia., U.S. — C2 92
Defiance, Mo., U.S. — f12 102
Defiance, Oh., U.S. — A1 112
Defiance, co., Oh., U.S. — A1 112
Defiance, Mount, mtn., Or., U.S. — B5 114
Deford, Mi., U.S. — E7 99
De Forest, Wi., U.S. — E4 126
De Funiak Springs, Fl., U.S. — u15 86
Dêgê, China — E4 31
Degeberga, Swe. — C8 15
Degeh Bur, Eth. — C5 47
Dégelis, P.Q., Can. — B9 74
Degerön, Swe. — u33 14
Degersheim, Switz. — B10 21
Deggendorf, F.R.Ger. — D6 18
De Graff, Oh., U.S. — B2 112
De Gray, Lake, res., Ar., U.S. — C2 81
De Grey, stm., Austl. — D2 50
Deh Bīd, Iran — C7 44
Dehibat, Tun. — C7 44
Dehiwala-Mount Lavinia, Sri L. — *G6 36
Deh Kord, Iran — C5 39
Dehlorān, Iran — C4 39
Dehpehk, i., Micron. — Q17 52
Dehra Dūn, India — E8 37
Deh Shū, Afg. — F11 39
Deinze, Bel. — D3 17
Dej, Rom. — B6 24
Dejvice (part of Prague), Czech. — n17 26
De Kalb, Ms., U.S. — C5 101
De Kalb, Mo., U.S. — B3 102
De Kalb, N.Y., U.S. — f9 109
De Kalb, Tx., U.S. — C5 120
De Kalb, co., Al., U.S. — A4 78
De Kalb, co., Ga., U.S. — C2 87
De Kalb, co., Il., U.S. — B5 90
De Kalb, co., In., U.S. — B7 91
De Kalb, co., Mo., U.S. — B3 102
De Kalb, co., Tn., U.S. — D7 119
De Kalb Junction, N.Y., U.S. — f9 109
Dekemhare, Eth. — C4 47
Dekese, Zaire — B3 48
Deke Sokehs, i., Micron. — Q17 52
Dekoa, Cen. Afr. Rep. — D3 46
Delacroix, La., U.S. — k12 95
Delafield, Wi., U.S. — m11 126
De Lamere, N.D., U.S. — C8 111
Delanco, N.J., U.S. — C3 107
De Land, Fl., U.S. — C5 86
Delano, Ca., U.S. — E4 82
Delano, Mn., U.S. — E5 100
Delano, Pa., U.S. — E9 115
Delano Peak, mtn., Ut., U.S. — E3 121
Delaplaine, Ar., U.S. — A5 81
Delārām, Afg. — E11 39
Delaronde Lake, l., Sk., Can. — C2 75
Delavan, Il., U.S. — C4 90
Delavan, Wi., U.S. — F5 126
Delavan Lake, l., Wi., U.S. — F5 126
Delaware, Oh., U.S. — B2 112
Delaware, co., In., U.S. — D7 91
Delaware, co., Ia., U.S. — B6 92

Delaware, co., N.Y., U.S. — C5 109
Delaware, co., Oh., U.S. — B2 112
Delaware, co., Ok., U.S. — A7 113
Delaware, co., Pa., U.S. — G11 115
Delaware, state, U.S. — D3 85
Delaware, stm., U.S. — E2 107
Delaware, stm., Ks., U.S. — C8 93
Delaware, East Branch, stm., N.Y., U.S. — C5 109
Delaware, West Branch, stm., N.Y., U.S. — C5 109
Delaware Bay, b., U.S. — C12 76
Delaware City, De., U.S. — B3 85
Delaware Lake, res., Oh., U.S. — B3 112
Delaware Mountains, mts., Tx., U.S. — o12 120
Delaware Water Gap, Pa., U.S. — E11 115
Delaware Water Gap, N.J., U.S. — B2 107
Delaware Water Gap National Recreation Area, U.S. — B2 107
Delbarton, W.V., U.S. — D2 125
Delburne, Ab., Can. — C4 68
Delcambre, La., U.S. — E4 95
Del City, Ok., U.S. — B4 113
Delco, N.C., U.S. — C4 110
Deleau, Mb., Can. — E1 70
Délémont, Switz. — E3 18
De Leon, Tx., U.S. — C3 120
De Leon Springs, Fl., U.S. — C5 86
Delevan, N.Y., U.S. — C2 109
Delft, Neth. — A6 16
Delft, Mn., U.S. — G3 100
Delfzijl, Neth. — A7 16
Delgada, Punta, c., Arg. — C4 54
Delgado, Cabo, c., Moz. — D7 48
Delgertsogt, Mong. — A2 32
Delhi, On., Can. — E4 73
Delhi, India — C6 36
Delhi, Ca., U.S. — D4 82
Delhi, La., U.S. — B4 95
Delhi, N.Y., U.S. — C6 109
Delhi, ter., India — *C6 36
Delhi Hills, Oh., U.S. — *o12 112
Delia, Ks., U.S. — C8 93
Delia, Ab., Can. — C4 68
Delicias, Mex. — *B3 63
Delight, Ar., U.S. — C2 81
Delilī Burun, c., Tur. — B8 40
Delingha, China — D4 31
Delisle, Sk., Can. — F2 75
De Lisle, Ms., U.S. — E4 101
Delitzsch, Ger.D.R. — C6 18
Dell, Ar., U.S. — B5 81
Dell, Mt., U.S. — F4 103
Dell City, Tx., U.S. — o12 120
Delle, Fr. — B3 20
Dellenbaugh, Mount, mtn., Az., U.S. — A2 80
Delles, Alg. — B5 44
Dell Rapids, S.D., U.S. — D9 118
Dellrose, Tn., U.S. — B5 119
Dellroy, Oh., U.S. — B4 112
Dellslow, W.V., U.S. — h11 125
Dellwood, Fl., U.S. — B1 86
Dellwood, Mo., U.S. — *t13 102
Delmar, Al., U.S. — A2 78
Del Mar, Ca., U.S. — o15 82
Delmar, Ia., U.S. — B7 92
Delmar, Md., U.S. — D6 97
Delmar, N.Y., U.S. — C7 109
Delmas, Sk., Can. — E1 75
Delmenhorst, F.R.Ger. — B4 18
Delmita, Tx., U.S. — F3 120
Delmont, N.J., U.S. — E3 107
Delmont, S.D., U.S. — D7 118
Del Norte, Co., U.S. — D4 83
Del Norte, co., Ca., U.S. — B2 82
Deloit, Ia., U.S. — B2 92
Delong, In., U.S. — B5 91
De Long Islands, is., Sov. Un. — B35 128
Deloraine, Mb., Can. — E1 70
Delorme, Lac, l., P.Q., Can. — F18 66
Delos see Dhílos, i., Grc. — D5 25
Del Park Manor, De., U.S. — i7 85
Delphi, In., U.S. — C4 91
Delphi Falls, N.Y., U.S. — C4 109
Delphos, Ks., U.S. — C6 93
Delphos, Oh., U.S. — B1 112
Delran, N.J., U.S. — C3 107
Delray Beach, Fl., U.S. — F6 86
Del Rio, Tn., U.S. — D10 119
Del Rio, Tx., U.S. — E2 120
Delson, P.Q., Can. — q19 74
Delta, On., Can. — C8 73
Delta, Al., U.S. — B4 78
Delta, Co., U.S. — C2 83
Delta, Ia., U.S. — C5 92
Delta, La., U.S. — B4 95
Delta, Mo., U.S. — D8 102
Delta, Oh., U.S. — A1 112
Delta, Pa., U.S. — G9 115
Delta, Ut., U.S. — D3 121
Delta, co., Co., U.S. — C2 83
Delta, co., Mi., U.S. — C3 99
Delta, co., Tx., U.S. — C5 120
Delta Amacuro, ter., Ven. — B6 60
Delta Barrage, Eg. — B3 41
Delta Beach, Mb., Can. — D2 70
Delta Junction, Ak., U.S. — C10 79
Delta Reservoir, res., N.Y., U.S. — B5 109
Deltaville, Va., U.S. — C6 123
Deltona, Fl., U.S. — D5 86
Delungra, Austl. — D4 51
Delvin, Ire. — C4 11
Delvina, Alb. — I4 24
Delyatin, Sov. Un. — G5 27
Demanda, Sierra de la, mtn., Spain — A4 22
Demarest, N.J., U.S. — h9 107
Demavend, Mount see Damāvand, Iran — B5 38
Demba, Zaire — C4 48
Dembī Dolo, Eth. — D4 47
Demer, stm., Bel. — D5 17
Demidov, Sov. Un. — A3 59
Demini, stm., Braz. — B2 59
Deming, N.M., U.S. — E2 108
Deming, Wa., U.S. — A3 124
Demirci, Tur. — E6 24
Demir Kapija, Yugo. — H6 24
Demmin, Ger.D.R. — B1 18
Demmitt, Ab., Can. — B1 68
Demnat, Mor. — C3 44
Demopolis, Al., U.S. — C2 78

Name	Map Ref	Page
Demopolis Dam, Al., U.S.	C2	78
Demorest, Ga., U.S.	B3	87
Demorestville, On., Can.	C7	73
De Mossville, Ky., U.S.	k14	94
Demotte, In., U.S.	B3	91
Dempo, mtn., Indon.	F2	34
Dempster, S.D., U.S.	C9	118
Dêmqog, China	A7	37
Demyanka, stm., Sov. Un.	B8	28
Denain, Fr.	B5	16
Denakil (Danakil), pl., Eth.	C5	47
Denali National Park, Ak., U.S.	C9	79
Denare Beach, Sk., Can.	C4	75
Denau, Sov. Un.	H22	8
Denbigh, Wales, U.K.	D5	10
Denbigh, N.D., U.S.	A5	111
Den Burg, Neth.	A4	17
Denby, S.D., U.S.	D3	118
Dendermonde, Bel.	C4	17
Dendron, Va., U.S.	C6	123
Denezhkin Kamen, Mount, mtn., Sov. Un.	A5	28
Dengkou, China	D2	32
Denham, In., U.S.	B4	91
Denham, Mn., U.S.	E13	65
Denham, Mount, mtn., Jam.	D5	95
Denham Springs, La., U.S.	A6	16
Den Helder, Neth.	B5	111
Denhoff, N.D., U.S.	E1	75
Denholm, Sk., Can.	A4	17
Den Hoorn, Neth.	C6	22
Denia, Spain	B8	74
Deniau, P.Q., Can.	G7	50
Deniliquin, Austl.	B3	105
Denio, Nv., U.S.	B2	92
Denison, Ia., U.S.	k14	93
Denison, Ks., U.S.	C4	120
Denison, Tx., U.S.	D5	113
Denison Dam, U.S.	D7	40
Denizli, Tur.	C22	7
Denman Glacier, Ant.	D6	71
Denmark, N.S., Can.	D6	92
Denmark, Ia., U.S.	E2	96
Denmark, Me., U.S.	E5	117
Denmark, S.C., U.S.	D2	119
Denmark, Tn., U.S.	B6	126
Denmark, Wi., U.S.	I3	14
Denmark, ctry., Eur.	C17	128
Denmark Strait, strt.	B3	81
Dennard, Ar., U.S.	B2	81
Denning, Ar., U.S.	E8	93
Dennis, Ks., U.S.	C7	98
Dennis, Ma., U.S.	A5	101
Dennis, Ms., U.S.	B3	84
Dennis Hill, mtn., Ct., U.S.	F5	100
Dennison, Mn., U.S.	B4	112
Dennison, Oh., U.S.	C7	98
Dennis Port, Ma., U.S.	E3	107
Dennisville, N.J., U.S.	*D5	13
Denny, Scot., U.K.	D5	96
Dennysville, Me., U.S.	C5	117
Denny Terrace, S.C., U.S.	B5	17
Den Oever, Neth.	G5	34
Denpasar, Indon.	D3	100
Dent, co., Mo., U.S.	D6	102
Denton, Ga., U.S.	E4	87
Denton, Ks., U.S.	C8	93
Denton, Mi., U.S.	p14	99
Denton, Mt., U.S.	C7	103
Denton, Ne., U.S.	D9	104
Denton, N.C., U.S.	B2	110
Denton, Tx., U.S.	C4	120
Denton, co., Tx., U.S.	C4	120
D'Entrecasteaux, Point, c., Austl.	F2	50
D'Entrecasteaux Islands, is., Pap. N. Gui.	k13	50
Dents Du Midi, mts., Switz.	D2	21
Dentsville, S.C., U.S.	C6	117
Denver, Ar., U.S.	A2	81
Denver, Co., U.S.	B6	83
Denver, Il., U.S.	C2	90
Denver, In., U.S.	C5	91
Denver, Ia., U.S.	B5	92
Denver, Mo., U.S.	A3	102
Denver, N.C., U.S.	B1	110
Denver, Pa., U.S.	F9	115
Denver, Tn., U.S.	A4	119
Denver, W.V., U.S.	B5	125
Denver, co., Co., U.S.	B6	83
Denver City, Tx., U.S.	C1	120
Denville, N.J., U.S.	B4	107
Denzil, Sk., Can.	E11	37
Deoghar, India	E11	37
De Panne, Bel.	A4	49
Departure Bay, B.C., Can.	f12	69
Depauville, N.Y., U.S.	A4	109
Depauw, In., U.S.	H5	91
De Pere, Wi., U.S.	D5	126
Depew, N.Y., U.S.	C2	109
Depew, Ok., U.S.	B5	113
Depoe Bay, Or., U.S.	C2	114
Deport, Tx., U.S.	C5	120
Deposit, N.Y., U.S.	C5	109
Depósito, Braz.	B2	59
Depot Harbour, On., Can.	B4	73
Depue, Il., U.S.	B4	90
Deputy, In., U.S.	G6	91
Dêqên, China	F4	31
De Queen, Ar., U.S.	C1	81
De Queen Lake, res., Ar., U.S.	C1	81
Dequen-Nord, P.Q., Can.	A5	74
De Quincy, La., U.S.	D2	95
Dera, Lak. stm., Afr.	E5	47
Dera Ghāzi Khān, Pak.	B5	36
Dera Ismāīl Khān, Pak.	B5	36
Derbent, Sov. Un.	E8	28
Derbetovka, Sov. Un.	I14	27
Derby, Austl.	C4	50
Derby, N.B., Can.	C4	71
Derby, Eng., U.K.	D6	10
Derby, Ct., U.S.	D3	84
Derby, In., U.S.	H4	91
Derby, Ia., U.S.	D4	92
Derby, Ks., U.S.	E6	93
Derby, Me., U.S.	C4	96
Derby, N.Y., U.S.	C2	109
Derby, Oh., U.S.	C2	112
Derby, Vt., U.S.	f9	109
Derby Junction, N.B., Can.	C4	71
Derby Line, Vt., U.S.	A4	122
Derbyshire, co., Eng., U.K.	A6	12
Derecske, Hung.	B5	24
Derg, Lough, l., Ire.	D2	10
Der Grabow, b., Ger.D.R.	D6	15
De Ridder, La., U.S.	D2	95
Derik, Tur.	D13	40
Derma, Ms., U.S.	B4	101
Dermott, Ar., U.S.	D4	81
Dernieres, Isles, is., La., U.S.	E5	95
Derravaragh, Lough, l., Ire.	D3	10
Derrieusseaux Creek, stm., Ar., U.S.	C3	81
Derry see Londonderry, N. Ire., U.K.	C3	10
Derry, La., U.S.	C3	95
Derry, N.H., U.S.	E4	106
Derry, N.M., U.S.	E2	108
Derry, Pa., U.S.	F3	115
Derrybrien, Ire	D3	11
Derryveagh Mountains, mts., Ire.	B3	11
Derudeb, Sud.	B4	47
De Ruyter, N.Y., U.S.	C5	109
Derventa, Yugo.	C3	24
Derwent, Ab., Can.	C5	68
Derwent, Oh., U.S.	C4	112
Derwent, stm., Eng., U.K.	F8	13
Derwent, stm., Eng., U.K.	F6	13
Derwent, stm., Eng., U.K.	F5	13
Derwood, Md., U.S.	B3	97
Derzhavinsk, Sov. Un.	C7	28
Desaguadero, stm., Arg.	A3	54
Desaguadero, stm., Bol.	C2	55
Des Allemands, La., U.S.	E5	95
Des Arc, Ar., U.S.	C4	81
Des Arc, Mo., U.S.	D7	102
Desbiens, P.Q., Can.	A6	74
Desboro, On., Can.	C3	73
Descalvado, Braz.	D4	16
Descartes, Fr.	D4	16
Deschaillons, P.Q., Can.	C5	74
Deschambault, P.Q., Can.	C6	74
Deschambault Lake, Sk., Can.	C4	75
Deschambault Lake, l., Sk., Can.	C4	75
Deschênes, P.Q., Can.	D2	74
Deschutes, co., Or., U.S.	D5	114
Deschutes, stm., Or., U.S.	B6	114
Dese, Eth.	C4	47
Deseado, stm., Arg.	D3	54
Desengaño, Punta, c., Arg.	D3	54
Desenzano del Garda, Italy	D6	20
Deseret, Ut., U.S.	D3	121
Deseret Peak, mtn., Ut., U.S.	C3	121
Deseronto, On., Can.	C7	73
Desert, Mount, mtn., W.V., U.S.	m13	125
Deserta Grande, i., Port.	h12	22
Desert Center, Ca., U.S.	F6	82
Desert Creek Peak, mtn., Nv., U.S.	E2	105
Desert Hot Springs, Ca., U.S.	F5	82
Desert Peak, mtn., Ut., U.S.	B2	121
Desert Valley, val., Nv., U.S.	B3	105
Desha, Ar., U.S.	B4	81
Desha, co., Ar., U.S.	D4	81
Deshler, Ne., U.S.	D8	104
Deshler, Oh., U.S.	A2	112
Desio, Italy	D5	20
Des Lacs, N.D., U.S.	A4	111
Des Lacs, stm., N.D., U.S.	A4	111
Desloge, Mo., U.S.	D7	102
Desmarais, Ab., Can.	B4	68
Des Moines, Ia., U.S.	C4	92
Des Moines, N.M., U.S.	A6	108
Des Moines, Wa., U.S.	B3	124
Des Moines, co., Ia., U.S.	D6	92
Des Moines, stm., U.S.	D5	92
Des Moines, East Fork, stm., U.S.	A3	92
Desolación, Isla, i., Chile	h11	54
Desolation Canyon, val., Ut., U.S.	D5	121
De Soto, Ga., U.S.	E2	87
De Soto, Il., U.S.	F4	90
De Soto, Ia., U.S.	C3	92
De Soto, Ks., U.S.	D9	93
De Soto, Mo., U.S.	D5	101
De Soto, Mo., U.S.	C7	102
De Soto, Tx., U.S.	*n10	120
De Soto, Wi., U.S.	E2	126
De Soto, co., Fl., U.S.	E5	86
De Soto, co., La., U.S.	B2	95
De Soto, co., Ms., U.S.	A3	101
De Soto City, Fl., U.S.	E5	86
Despard, W.V., U.S.	k10	125
Des Peres, Mo., U.S.	f13	102
Des Plaines, Il., U.S.	A6	90
Des Plaines, stm., U.S.	k8	90
Dessau, Ger.D.R.	C6	18
Destin, Fl., U.S.	u15	86
Destrehan, La., U.S.	E5	95
Desvres, Fr.	D1	17
Dete, Zimb.	A4	49
Detlor, On., Can.	B7	73
Detmold, F.R.Ger.	C4	18
Detour, Point, c., Mi., U.S.	C4	99
De Tour Village, Mi., U.S.	C7	99
Detroit, Al., U.S.	A1	78
Detroit, Ks., U.S.	D6	93
Detroit, Me., U.S.	D3	96
Detroit, Mi., U.S.	F7	99
Detroit, Or., U.S.	C4	114
Detroit, Tx., U.S.	C5	120
Detroit, stm., N.A.	F7	99
Detroit Lake, res., Or., U.S.	C4	114
Detroit Lakes, Mn., U.S.	D3	100
Detva, Czech.	D5	26
Deuel, co., Ne., U.S.	C3	104
Deuel, co., S.D., U.S.	C9	118
Deurne (part of Antwerp), Bel.	B6	16
Deux Frères, is., Viet.	H7	35
Deux-Montagnes, P.Q., Can.	p19	74
Deux-Montagnes, co., P.Q., Can.	D3	74
Deux Montagnes, Lac des, l., P.Q., Can.	q19	74
Deux-Rivières, On., Can.	A6	73
Deva, Rom.	C4	24
De Valls Bluff, Ar., U.S.	C4	81
Dévaványa, Hung.	B5	24
Deventer, Neth.	A7	16
Devereux, Ga., U.S.	C3	87
Deveron, stm., Scot., U.K.	C6	13
DeView, Bayou, stm., Ar., U.S.	B4	81
Devil River Peak, mtn., N.Z.	N14	51
Devils Elbow, Mo., U.S.	D5	102
Devils Island see Diable, Île du, i., Fr. Gu.	A4	59
Devils Lake, N.D., U.S.	A7	111
Devils Lake, l., N.D., U.S.	A6	111
Devils Paw, mtn., Ak., U.S.	k23	79
Devils Postpile National Monument, Ca., U.S.	D4	82
Devils Slide, Ut., U.S.	B4	121
Devils Tower, Wy., U.S.	B8	127
Devils Tower National Monument, Wy., U.S.	B8	127
Devil Track Lake, l., Mn., U.S.	k9	100
Devin, Bul.	E7	24
Devine, Tx., U.S.	E3	120
Devizes, Eng., U.K.	C6	12
Devol, Ok., U.S.	C3	113
Devola, Oh., U.S.	C4	112
Devolli, stm., Alb.	B3	25
Devon, Ab., Can.	C4	68
Devon, Ks., U.S.	E9	93
Devon, Mt., U.S.	B5	103
Devon, co., Eng., U.K.	*o20	99
Devon, co., Eng., U.K.	D4	12
Devonia, Tn., U.S.	C9	119
Devon Island, i., N.T., Can.	m34	66
Devonport, Austl.	o15	50
Devonshire, De., U.S.	h7	85
Dewalt, Tx., U.S.	r14	120
Dewar, Ok., U.S.	B6	113
Dewar Lake, Sk., Can.	F1	75
Dewberry, Ab., Can.	C5	68
Dewdney, B.C., Can.	E6	69
Deweese, Ne., U.S.	D7	104
Dewees Inlet, b., S.C., U.S.	k12	117
Dewees Island, i., S.C., U.S.	F8	117
Dewey, Az., U.S.	C3	80
Dewey, Il., U.S.	E4	103
Dewey, Ok., U.S.	A6	113
Dewey, co., Ok., U.S.	B2	113
Dewey, co., S.D., U.S.	B4	118
Dewey Beach, De., U.S.	F5	85
Dewey Lake, res., Ky., U.S.	C7	94
Deweyville, Tx., U.S.	D6	120
Deweyville, Ut., U.S.	B3	121
De Winton, Ab., Can.	D3	68
Dewitt, Il., U.S.	C5	90
De Witt, Ar., U.S.	C4	81
De Witt, Ia., U.S.	C7	92
De Witt, Mi., U.S.	F6	99
De Witt, Mo., U.S.	B4	102
De Witt, Ne., U.S.	D9	104
De Witt, N.Y., U.S.	B4	109
DeWitt, Va., U.S.	C5	123
De Witt, co., Il., U.S.	C4	90
De Witt, co., Tx., U.S.	E4	120
Dewsbury, Eng., U.K.	A6	12
Dexing, China	D3	87
Dexter, Ga., U.S.	C3	92
Dexter, Ia., U.S.	E7	93
Dexter, Ks., U.S.	f9	94
Dexter, Ky., U.S.	C3	96
Dexter, Me., U.S.	F7	99
Dexter, Mi., U.S.	G6	100
Dexter, Mn., U.S.	D5	108
Dexter, N.M., U.S.	A4	109
Dexter, N.Y., U.S.	D4	114
Dexter, Or., U.S.	C5	86
Dexter, Lake, l., Fl., U.S.	E5	50
Dey-Dey, Lake, l., Austl.	E8	39
Deyhūk, Iran	H6	39
Deyyer, Iran	E4	39
Dez, stm., Iran	E4	38
Dezfūl, Iran	C21	29
Dezhnev, Cape, c., Sov. Un.	D8	31
Dezhou, China	H10	40
Dhahab, Eg.	B5	92
Dhahran see Az Zahrān, Sau. Ar.	C4	38
Dhaka see Dacca, Bngl.	D9	36
Dhamār, Yemen	D4	38
Dhamtari, India	G8	37
Dhānbād, India	F11	37
Dhangarhi, Nepal	C8	37
D'Hanis, Tx., U.S.	E3	120
Dhankuta, Nepal	D11	37
Dhār, India	F5	37
Dharamjaygarh, India	D7	36
Dharmapuri, India	F6	36
Dharmsāla, India	B6	36
Dhārwār (part of Hubli-Dhārwār), India	E6	36
Dhāt al Hājj, Sau. Ar.	H11	40
Dhaulāgiri, mtn., Nepal	C7	36
Dhekélia, Grc.	g11	25
Dhenoúsa, i., Grc.	D5	25
Dhiban, Jord.	G10	40
Dhidhimótikhon, Grc.	B6	25
Dhilos (Delos), i., Grc.	D5	25
Dhimitsána, Grc.	D4	25
Dholpur, India	D6	37
Dhomhnuill, Sgùrr, mtn., Scot., U.K.	D3	13
Dhorāji, India	G3	37
Dhrépanon, Cape, c., Grc	C4	25
Dhubri, India	D12	37
Dhule, India	D5	36
Dhuusa Mareeb, Som.	D6	47
Día, i., Grc.	E5	25
Diable, Île du (Devils Island), i., Fr. Gu.	A4	59
Diable, Pointe du, c., Mart.	S11	65
Diablerets, mtn., Switz.	C4	18
Diablo, Canyon, val., Az., U.S.	C4	99
Diablo, Mount, mtn., Ca., U.S.	h9	82
Diablo Dam, Wa., U.S.	A4	124
Diablo Heights, Pan.	m11	62
Diablo Lake, res., Wa., U.S.	A4	124
Diablo Range, mts., Ca., U.S.	D3	82
Diagonal, Ia., U.S.	A4	54
Diamante, Arg.	E4	45
Diamantina, Braz.	D7	50
Diamantina, stm., Austl.	A4	112
Diamond, Oh., U.S.	a12	125
Diamond, W.V., U.S.	*n13	82
Diamond Bar, Ca., U.S.	E4	68
Diamond City, Ab., Can.	F12	37
Diamond Harbour, India	B4	88
Diamond Head, crat., Hi., U.S.	C7	34
Diamond Hill Reservoir, res., R.I., U.S.	A4	116
Diamond Lake, Il., U.S.	h9	90
Diamond Lake, l., Or., U.S.	D4	114
Diamond Mountains, mts., Nv., U.S.	D6	105
Diamond Peak, mtn., Id., U.S.	A3	83
Diamond Peak, mtn., Id., U.S.	E5	89
Diamond Peak, mtn., Or., U.S.	D4	114
Diamond Peak, mtn., Wa., U.S.	C8	124
Diamond Point, N.Y., U.S.	B7	109
Diamond Springs, Ca., U.S.	C3	82
Diamondville, Wy., U.S.	E2	127
Diana, Tn., U.S.	C5	125
Dianalund, Den.	C4	15
Dianbai, China	G7	89
Dianjiang, China	E8	32
Dianópolis, Braz.	D1	57
Diapaga, Burkina	C9	71
Diapitan Bay, b., Phil.	*o20	34
Diaz, Ar., U.S.	B4	81
Dibaya, Zaire	C3	48
Dibble, Ok., U.S.	B4	113
Dibble Iceberg Tongue, Ant.	C26	7
D'Iberville, Ms., U.S.	E7	24
D'Iberville, Lac, l., P.Q., Can.	g12	74
Diboll, Tx., U.S.	D5	120
Dibrell, Tn., U.S.	D8	119
Dibrugarh, India	C9	36
Dickens, Ia., U.S.	A2	92
Dickens, Ne., U.S.	D5	104
Dickens, Tx., U.S.	C2	120
Dickens, co., Tx., U.S.	C2	120
Dickenson, co., Va., U.S.	e9	123
Dickerson, Md., U.S.	B3	97
Dickey, N.D., U.S.	C7	111
Dickey, co., N.D., U.S.	C7	111
Dickeyville, Wi., U.S.	F3	126
Dickinson, Al., U.S.	D2	78
Dickinson, N.D., U.S.	C3	111
Dickinson, Tx., U.S.	r14	120
Dickinson, co., Ia., U.S.	A2	92
Dickinson, co., Ks., U.S.	D6	93
Dickinson, co., Mi., U.S.	B3	99
Dickinson Center, N.Y., U.S.	f10	109
Dickinson Dam, N.D., U.S.	C3	111
Dickson, Ok., U.S.	C5	113
Dickson, Tn., U.S.	A4	119
Dickson, co., Tn., U.S.	A4	119
Dickson City, Pa., U.S.	D10	115
Dicle (Tigris), stm., Asia	D13	40
Didcot, Ab., Can.	D3	68
Didwāna, India	D5	37
Die, Fr.	E6	16
Diébougou, Burkina	D4	45
Dieburg, F.R.Ger.	D3	19
Diefenbaker, Lake, res., Sk., Can.	F2	75
Diégo-Suarez see Antsiranana, Madag.	f9	49
Diekirch, Lux.	E6	17
Diemel, stm., F.R.Ger.	B3	19
Dien Bien Phu, Viet.	B5	35
Diepholz, F.R.Ger.	B4	18
Dieppe, N.B., Can.	C5	71
Dieppe, Fr.	C4	16
Dierks, Ar., U.S.	C1	81
Di'er Songhua, stm., China	D2	33
Diessen, F.R.Ger.	B7	20
Diest, Bel.	D5	17
Dieterich, Il., U.S.	D5	90
Dietikon, Switz.	D3	21
Dieuze, Fr.	F6	17
Diever, Neth.	B6	17
Diez, F.R.Ger.	E3	18
Diffa, Niger	D7	45
Differdange, Lux.	E5	17
Difficult, Tn., U.S.	C8	119
Digboi, India	C10	36
Digby, N.S., Can.	E4	71
Digby, co., N.S., Can.	E3	71
Dighton, Ks., U.S.	D3	93
Dighton, Ma., U.S.	C5	98
Dighton, Mi., U.S.	D5	99
Digne, Fr.	E7	16
Digoin, Fr.	D5	16
Digul, stm., Indon.	G10	34
Dijon, Fr.	D6	16
Dike, Ia., U.S.	B5	92
Dikhil, Dji.	C4	38
Dikili, Tur.	C6	25
Dikirnis, Eg.	C3	41
Diksmuide, Bel.	C2	17
Dikson, Sov. Un.	B11	29
Dikwa, Nig.	D7	45
Dila, Eth.	D4	47
Dili, Indon.	G7	34
Dilia, N.M., U.S.	B4	108
Di Linh, Viet.	G8	35
Dilke, Sk., Can.	G3	75
Dilkon, Az., U.S.	B5	80
Dillard, Ga., U.S.	D3	114
Dillard, Or., U.S.	B2	113
Dill City, Ok., U.S.	C4	125
Dille, W.V., U.S.	D9	104
Diller, Ne., U.S.	D3	120
Dilley, Tx., U.S.	G2	115
Dilliner, Pa., U.S.	C2	47
Dilling, Sud.	D1	19
Dillingen, F.R.Ger.	D5	18
Dillingen [an der Donau], F.R.Ger.	D8	79
Dillingham, Ak., U.S.	B4	83
Dillon, Co., U.S.	E4	103
Dillon, Mt., U.S.	C9	117
Dillon, S.C., U.S.	C9	117
Dillon, co., S.C., U.S.	B5	68
Dillon, stm., Can.	B3	112
Dillon Lake, l., Sk., Can.	B4	83
Dillon Lake, res., Oh., U.S.	B5	112
Dillon Reservoir, res., Co., U.S.	B4	83
Dillsboro, In., U.S.	F7	91
Dillsboro, N.C., U.S.	f9	110
Dillsburg, Pa., U.S.	F7	115
Dillwyn, Va., U.S.	C4	123
Dilman see Salmās, Iran	B2	39
Dilolo, Zaire	D4	48
Dilworth, Mn., U.S.	D2	100
Dimbelenge, Zaire	C4	48
Dimbokro, I.C.	E4	45
Dimashq see Damascus, Syria	D7	24
Dimitrovgrad, Bul.	D7	24
Dimitrovgrad, Yugo.	E3	120
Dimmit, co., Tx., U.S.	B1	120
Dimmitt, Tx., U.S.	D8	118
Dimock, S.D., U.S.	E7	41
Dimona, Isr.	F6	99
Dimondale, Mi., U.S.	C7	34
Dinagat, i., Phil.	E12	37
Dinājpur, Bngl.	C2	16
Dinan, Fr.	B6	16
Dinant, Bel.	C8	25
Dinar, Tur.	D5	99
Dinard, Fr.	C3	24
Dinaric Alps, mts., Yugo.	F6	36
Dindigul, India	E4	120
Dinero, Tx., U.S.	o13	34
Dingalan Bay, b., Phil.	D6	31
Dingbian, China	B2	125
Dingelstädt, Ger.D.R.	D6	31
Dingess, W.V., U.S.	E9	31
Dinghai, China	D1	10
Dingle, Ire.	G7	89
Dingle, Ire.	D1	10
Dingle Bay, b., Ire.	C4	125
Dingmans Ferry, Pa., U.S.	D12	115
Dingo, Austl.	A7	51
Dinguiraye, Gui.	C3	45
Dingwall, Scot., U.K.	D8	13
Dingxian, China	D4	31
Dingxin, China	C4	31
Dingxing, China	E6	32
Dinh Lap, Viet.	B7	35
Dinkelsbühl, F.R.Ger.	D5	19
Dinkey Creek, Ca., U.S.	D4	82
Dinklage, F.R.Ger.	F2	15
Dinner Point, c., Fl., U.S.	D4	86
Dinorwic Lake, l., On., Can.	E5	70
Dinosaur, Co., U.S.	A1	83
Dinosaur National Monument, U.S.	C6	121
Dinosaur Provincial Park, Ab., Can.	D5	68
Dinsdale, Ia., U.S.	B5	92
Dinslaken, F.R.Ger.	B1	19
Dinsmore, Sk., Can.	F2	75
Dinuba, Ca., U.S.	D4	82
Dinwiddie, Va., U.S.	C5	123
Dinwiddie, co., Va., U.S.	C5	123
Dioila, Mali	D3	45
Dionisio, Braz.	B4	56
Diourbel, Sen.	D1	45
Diphu Pass, Asia	C10	36
Diplo, Pak.	E2	37
Dipper Harbour West, N.B., Can.	D3	71
Dippoldiswalde, Ger.D.R.	C8	19
Diré, Mali	C4	45
Direction, Cape, c., Austl.	B7	50
Dire Dawa, Eth.	D5	47
Diriamba, Nic.	E7	63
Dirico, Ang.	E3	48
Dirk Hartog, i., Austl.	E1	50
Dirkou, Niger	C7	45
Dirmil, Tur.	D7	25
Dirranbandi, Austl.	E8	50
Dirty Devil, stm., Ut., U.S.	E5	121
Disappointment, Cape, c., Falk. Is.	D9	7
Disappointment, Cape, c., Wa., U.S.	C1	124
Disappointment, Lake, l., Austl.	D3	50
Disappointment Creek, stm., U.S.	D2	83
Discovery, Mount, mtn., Ant.	f39	7
Disentis (Mustér), Switz.	C4	20
Dishman, Wa., U.S.	g14	124
Dishnā, Eg.	D6	43
Disko, i., Grnld.	B6	91
Disko, i., Grnld.	C15	61
Disley, Sk., Can.	G3	75
Dismal, stm., Ne., U.S.	C5	104
Dismal Peak, mtn., Va., U.S.	C2	123
Disputanta, Va., U.S.	C5	123
Disraëli, P.Q., Can.	D6	74
Diss, Eng., U.K.	B9	12
Distant, Pa., U.S.	E3	115
District Heights-Forestville, Md., U.S.	f8	97
District of Columbia, dept.		
Distrito Especial (Bogotá), dept., Col.	C3	60
Distrito Federal (Federal District), state, Mex.	D5	63
Distrito Federal, dept., Arg.	g7	54
Distrito Federal, dept., Braz.	B3	56
Distrito Federal, dept., Ven.	A4	60
Disūq, Eg.	C6	43
Ditzum, F.R.Ger.	A7	17
Diu, India	D5	36
Divernon, Il., U.S.	D4	90
Dives-sur-Mer, Fr.	C3	16
Divide, co., N.D., U.S.	A2	111
Divide Peak, mtn., Wy., U.S.	E5	127
Dividing Creek, N.J., U.S.	E2	107
Dividing Creek, stm., Md., U.S.	D6	97
Divinópolis, Braz.	C4	56
Divion, Fr.	B9	17
Divisões, Serra das, hills, Braz.	B2	56
Divišov, Czech.	o18	26
Divnoye, Sov. Un.	I14	27
Divo, I.C.	E3	45
Divriği, Tur.	C12	40
Dix, Il., U.S.	C2	104
Dix, Ne., U.S.	C5	94
Dix Dam, Ky., U.S.	C5	94
Dix, stm., Ky., U.S.	C5	94
Dix, stm., Ky., U.S.	D1	19
Dixfield, Me., U.S.	D8	79
Dix Hills, N.Y., U.S.	*n15	109
Dixiana, Al., U.S.	B3	78
Dixie, Ga., U.S.	F3	87
Dixie, La., U.S.	B4	81
Dixie, Wa., U.S.	C8	119
Dixie, W.V., U.S.	C3	125
Dixie, co., Fl., U.S.	C3	86
Dixie Inn, La., U.S.	F7	91
Dixie Union, Ga., U.S.	E4	87
Dixie Valley, val., Nv., U.S.	D4	105
Dix Mountain, mtn., N.Y., U.S.	A7	109
Dixmont, Me., U.S.	D3	96
Dixon, Ca., U.S.	C3	82
Dixon, Il., U.S.	B4	90
Dixon, Ia., U.S.	C7	92
Dixon, Ky., U.S.	C2	94
Dixon, Mo., U.S.	D5	102
Dixon, Mt., U.S.	C2	103
Dixon, Ne., U.S.	B9	104
Dixon, N.M., U.S.	A4	108
Dixon, co., Ne., U.S.	B8	104
Dixon Entrance, strt., N.A.	B1	69
Dixon Springs, Il., U.S.	F5	90
Dixonville, Ab., Can.	A2	68
Dixonville, Pa., U.S.	E3	115
Dixville Notch, N.H., U.S.	g7	106
Dixville Notch, N.H., U.S.	g7	106
Dixville Peak, mtn., N.H., U.S.	g7	106
Dizy-le-Gros, Fr.	C5	16
Dizy-Magenta, Fr.	E12	65
Dja, stm., Afr.	E2	46
Djado, Niger	B7	45
Djakarta see Jakarta, Indon.	G3	34
Djakovica, Yugo.	B5	10
Djakovo, Yugo.	C3	24
Djambala, Congo	B1	48
Djanet, Alg.	E6	44
Djaravica, mtn., Yugo.	D5	24
Djelfa, Alg.	C5	28
Djema, Cen. Afr. Rep.	D5	46
Djenné, Mali	D4	45
Djerba, Île de, i., Tun.	C7	44
Djerid, Chott, sw., Tun.	C6	44
Djibo, Burkina	D4	45
Djibouti, Dji.	C5	47
Djibouti, ctry., Afr.	C5	47
Djokupunda, Zaire	C3	48
Djolu, Zaire	A3	48
Djoua, stm., Afr.	E2	46
Djougou, Benin	E5	45
Djugu, Zaire	A5	48
Djurdjevac, Yugo.	B3	24
Djursholm, Swe.	t36	14
D'Lo, Ms., U.S.	D4	101
Długa, Pol.	k14	27
Dmitriyev-Lgovskiy, Sov. Un.	C11	27
Dmitrov, Sov. Un.	E10	27
Dmitrovsk-Orlovskiy, Sov. Un.	E10	27
Dnepr, stm., Sov. Un.	D5	29
Dneprodzerzhinsk, Sov. Un.	G10	27
Dnepropetrovsk, Sov. Un.	E6	29
Dnestr, stm., Sov. Un.	H7	27
Dnieper see Dnepr, stm., Sov. Un.		
Dno, Sov. Un.	D5	29
Doaktown, N.B., Can.	C7	71
Doany, Madag.	f9	49
Doba, Chad	D3	46
Dobbins Air Force Base, mil., Ga., U.S.	h7	87
Dobbinton, On., Can.	C3	73
Dobbs Ferry, N.Y., U.S.	g13	109
Döbeln, Ger.D.R.	C6	18
Doberai Peninsula, pen., Indon.	F8	34
Doberlug-Kirchhain, Ger.D.R.	B8	19
Doblas, Arg.	B4	54
Dobo, Indon.	G8	34
Doboj, Yugo.	C4	24
Doboy Sound, b., Ga., U.S.	E5	87
Dobřejovice, Czech.	o18	26
Dobříš, Czech.	D9	19
Dobrovice, Czech.	n18	26
Dobrovolsk, Sov. Un.	A7	26
Dobruja, reg., Eur.	C9	24
Dobrush, Czech.	D6	26
Dobšiná, Czech.	E7	26
Dobson, N.C., U.S.	A2	110
Dobson, stm., Braz.	E2	57
Docena, Al., U.S.	f7	78
Dock Junction, Ga., U.S.	E5	87
Dockton, Wa., U.S.	f11	124
Doctor Arroyo, Mex.	C4	63
Doctor Pedro P. Peña, Para.	D3	55
Doctors Inlet, Fl., U.S.	m8	86
Doctors Lake, l., Fl., U.S.	m8	86
Doctortown, Ga., U.S.	E5	87
Doddridge, Ar., U.S.	D2	81
Doddridge, co., W.V., U.S.	B4	125
Dodds, Ab., Can.	C4	68
Doddsville, Ms., U.S.	B3	101
Dodecanese, is., Grc.	D6	40
Dodge, Ne., U.S.	C9	104
Dodge, N.D., U.S.	B3	111
Dodge, Wi., U.S.	D2	126
Dodge, co., Ga., U.S.	G6	100
Dodge, co., Mn., U.S.	C9	104
Dodge, co., Ne., U.S.	E5	126
Dodge, co., Wi., U.S.	F6	100
Dodge Center, Mn., U.S.	E3	93
Dodge City, Ks., U.S.	A5	112
Dodgeville, Oh., U.S.	F3	126
Dodgeville, Wi., U.S.	C6	48
Dodoma, Tan.	C6	48
Dodoma, prov., Tan.	F1	75
Dodsland, Sk., Can.	B3	95
Dodson, La., U.S.	B8	103
Dodson, Mt., U.S.	B2	120
Dodson, Tx., U.S.	B6	7
Dodson Peninsula, pen., Ant.	A7	69
Doe River, B.C., Can.	E3	87
Doerun, Ga., U.S.	D7	102
Doe Run, Mo., U.S.	C6	17
Doetinchem, Neth.	C3	122
Dog, stm., Vt., U.S.	B8	36
Dogai Coring, l., China	D6	69
Dog Creek, B.C., Can.	C2	92
Dog Island, i., Fl., U.S.	g8	101
Dog Keys Pass, strt., Ms., U.S.	D2	70
Dog Lake, l., Mb., Can.	H6	33
Dogondoutchi, Niger	D5	45
Dōgo Yama, mtn., Japan	C15	40
Doha (Ad Dawhah), Qatar	C5	38
Dohad, India	F5	37
Doheny, P.Q., Can.	B5	74
Doiran, Lake, l., Eur.	B4	24
Dois Córregos, Braz.	m7	56
Dokkum, Neth.	A6	17
Doksy, Czech.	C9	19
Dol, Fr.	C3	16
Doland, S.D., U.S.	C7	118
Dolavón, Arg.	C3	54
Dolbeau, P.Q., Can.	G18	66
Dôle, Fr.	D6	16
Dolega, Pan.	F6	62
Doleib Hill, Sud.	D3	47
Dolgellau, Wales, U.K.	B4	12
Dolgeville, N.Y., U.S.	B6	109
Dolina, Sov. Un.	B13	31
Dolinskoye, Sov. Un.	B9	24
Dollar Bay, Mi., U.S.	A2	99
Dollard, Sk., Can.	H1	75
Dollart, b., Eur.	A7	17
Dolliver, Ia., U.S.	A3	92
Dolní Kubín, Czech.	D5	26
Dolohmwar, mtn., Micron.	Q17	52
Dolomite, Al., U.S.	B3	78
Dolomites, mts., Italy	A3	23
Dolores, Guat.	B5	54
Dolores, Mex.	B3	63
Dolores, Mex.	D2	63
Dolores, Ur.	E1	56
Dolores, co., Co., U.S.	D2	83
Dolores Hidalgo, Mex.	m13	63
Dolphin and Union Strait, strt., N.T., Can.	C9	66
Dolphin Island, i., Ut., U.S.	B3	121
Dolton, Il., U.S.	k9	90
Dolton, S.D., U.S.	D8	118
Dom, mtn., Switz.	D4	21
Dom Aquino, Braz.	B2	56
Domat-Ems, Switz.	C7	21
Domažlice, Czech.	D2	26
Dombarovskiy, Sov. Un.	C5	28
Dombasle[-sur-Meurthe], Fr.	F6	17
Dombe Grande, Ang.	D1	48
Dombóvár, Hung.	B4	24
Domburg, Neth.	C3	17
Dôme, Puy de, mtn., Fr.	E5	16

Name	Map Ref	Page
Dome Mountain, mtn., Az., U.S.	k9	80
Dome of the Rock, Isr. Occ.	m14	41
Dome Peak, mtn., Co., U.S.	B3	83
Dome Rock Mountains, mts., Az., U.S.	D1	80
Domeyko, Cordillera, mts., Chile	D2	55
Domfront, Fr.	C3	16
Dominica, ctry., N.A.	i14	64
Dominican Republic, ctry., N.A.	E8	64
Dominica Passage, strt., N.A.	I14	64
Dominion, N.S., Can.	C9	71
Dominion, Cape, c., N.T., Can.	C18	66
Dominion City, Mb., Can.	E3	70
Dominion Lake, l., Nf., Can.	h9	72
Dömitz, Ger.D.R.	B5	18
Dommel, stm., Eur.	C5	17
Domo, Eth.	D6	47
Domodedovo, Sov. Un.	n17	27
Domodossola, Italy	A2	23
Dom Pedrito, Braz.	C6	56
Dompierre [-sur-Authie], Fr.	D1	17
Domremy, Fr.	E3	75
Domuyo, Volcán, vol., Arg.	B2	54
Don, stm., Sov. Un.	H13	27
Don, stm., Scot., U.K.	C6	13
Dona Ana, N.M., U.S.	E3	108
Dona Ana, co., N.M., U.S.	E2	108
Donaghadee, N. Ire., U.K.	C4	10
Donald, On., Can.	C6	73
Donald, Or., U.S.	h12	114
Donalda, Ab., Can.	C4	68
Donalds, S.C., U.S.	C3	117
Donaldson, Ar., U.S.	C3	81
Donaldson, In., U.S.	B5	91
Donaldson, Mn., U.S.	B2	100
Donaldson, Pa., U.S.	E9	115
Donaldsonville, La., U.S.	D4	95
Donalsonville, Ga., U.S.	E2	87
Donard, Ire.	D5	11
Donard, Slieve, mtn., N. Ire., U.K.	C4	10
Donaueschingen, F.R.Ger.	B4	20
Donauwörth, F.R.Ger.	E5	19
Donavon, Sk., Can.	F2	75
Don Benito, Spain	C3	22
Doncaster, Eng., U.K.	D6	10
Doncaster and Templestowe, Austl.	*G8	50
Dondo, Ang.	C1	48
Dondo, Moz.	A5	49
Donegal, Ire.	C4	11
Donegal, co., Ire.	C4	11
Donegal Bay, b., Ire.	C2	11
Donegal Point, c., Ire.	E2	11
Doneraile, S.C., U.S.	C8	117
Donets Basin, Sov. Un.	q21	27
Donetsk, Sov. Un.	E6	29
Dongara, Austl.	E1	50
Dongchuan, China	F5	31
Dongco, China	B7	36
Dongfang, China	C8	35
Donggala, Indon.	F5	34
Dongguang, China	F7	32
Dong Hoi, Viet.	B3	34
Dongning, China	D5	33
Dongo, Zaire	A2	48
Dongola, Il., U.S.	F4	90
Dongou, Congo	A2	48
Dongping, China	D8	31
Dongsheng, China	D6	31
Dongtai, China	H9	32
Dongting Lake, l., China	F1	31
Dong Ujimqin Qi, China	B7	32
Dongxiang, China	J7	32
Dongxing, China	G6	31
Dongzhi, China	I7	32
Donington, Eng., U.K.	B7	12
Doniphan, Mo., U.S.	E7	102
Doniphan, Ne., U.S.	D7	104
Doniphan, co., Ks., U.S.	C8	93
Donji Vakuf, Yugo.	C3	24
Donkey Creek, stm., Wy., U.S.	B7	127
Donkin, N.S., Can.	C10	71
Donley, co., Tx., U.S.	B2	120
Donna, Tx., U.S.	F3	120
Donnacona, P.Q., Can.	C6	74
Donnellson, Il., U.S.	D4	90
Donnellson, Ia., U.S.	D6	92
Donnelly, Ab., Can.	B2	68
Donnelly, Id., U.S.	E2	89
Donnelly, Mn., U.S.	E2	100
Donner, La., U.S.	E5	95
Donner Pass, Ca., U.S.	C3	82
Donnybrook, N.D., U.S.	A4	111
Donora, Pa., U.S.	F2	115
Donovan, Il., U.S.	C6	90
Don Peninsula, pen., B.C., Can.	C3	69
Donzère, Fr.	E6	16
Dooagh, Ire.	D1	11
Doole, Tx., U.S.	D3	120
Dooling, Ga., U.S.	D3	87
Doolittle, Mo., U.S.	D6	102
Dooly, co., Ga., U.S.	D3	87
Doon, Ia., U.S.	A1	92
Doon, Loch, l., Scot., U.K.	E4	13
Doonbeg, Ire.	E2	11
Doonerak, Mount, mtn., Ak., U.S.	B9	79
Door, co., Wi., U.S.	D6	126
Doornik see Tournai, Bel.	D3	17
Dora, Al., U.S.	B2	78
Dora, Mo., U.S.	E5	102
Dora, N.M., U.S.	D6	108
Dora, Lake, l., Austl.	D3	50
Dora Baltea, stm., Italy	D2	100
Doran, Ms., U.S.	D2	100
Doraville, Ga., U.S.	h8	87
Dorbod, China	A11	32
Dorcas, Fl., U.S.	u15	86
Dorcheat, Bayou, stm., U.S.	B2	95
Dorchester, N.B., Can.	D5	71
Dorchester, Eng., U.K.	E5	10
Dorchester, Ia., U.S.	A6	92
Dorchester, Ne., U.S.	D8	104
Dorchester, N.J., U.S.	E3	107
Dorchester, Wi., U.S.	C3	126
Dorchester, co., Md., U.S.	D5	97
Dorchester, co., S.C., U.S.	E7	117
Dorchester, Cape, c., N.T., Can.	C17	66
Dorchester Crossing, N.B., Can.		
Dorchester Estates, Al., U.S.	k11	117
Dorcyville, La., U.S.	h9	95
Dordogne, stm., Fr.	E4	16
Dordrecht, Neth.	B6	16
Dordrecht, S. Afr.	D4	49
Doré, stm., Sk., Can.	C2	75
Doré, Lake, l., On., Can.	B7	73
Doré Lake, Sk., Can.	C2	75
Doré Lake, l., Sk., Can.	C2	75
Dorena, Or., U.S.	D4	114
Dorena Lake, res., Or., U.S.	D3	114
Dorenlee, Ab., Can.	C4	68
Dores, Scot., U.K.	C4	13
Dores do Indaiá, Braz.	B3	56
Dorfen, F.R.Ger.	A8	20
Dorgali, Italy	D2	23
Dörgön Lake, l., Mong.	B3	31
Dori, Burkina		
Dorion-Vaudreuil, P.Q., Can.	q18	74
Dormagen, F.R.Ger.	*C3	18
Dormans, Fr.	E3	17
Dormont, Pa., U.S.	k13	115
Dornbirn, Aus.	E4	18
Dornie, Scot., U.K.	C3	13
Dornoch, Scot., U.K.	B4	10
Dornoch Firth, est., Scot., U.K.	B5	10
Dorogobuzh, Sov. Un.	D9	27
Dorohoi, Rom.	B8	24
Dorothy, Ab., Can.	D4	68
Dorothy, Mn., U.S.	C2	100
Dorothy, N.J., U.S.	E3	107
Dorothy, W.V., U.S.	n13	125
Dorothy Pond, Ma., U.S.	B4	98
Dorr, Mi., U.S.	F5	99
Dorrance, Ks., U.S.	D5	93
Dorrigo, Austl.	E9	51
Dorris, Ca., U.S.	B3	82
Dorset, On., Can.	B6	73
Dorset, Oh., U.S.	A5	112
Dorset, Vt., U.S.	E2	122
Dorset, co., Eng., U.K.	D5	12
Dorset Peak, mtn., Vt., U.S.	E2	122
Dorsey, Md., U.S.	B4	97
Dorsey, Ms., U.S.	A5	101
Dorsten, F.R.Ger.	B1	19
Dortmund, F.R.Ger.	C3	18
Dortmund Ems Canal, F.R.Ger.	B7	17
Dörtyol, Tur.	D11	40
Dorum, F.R.Ger.	E2	15
Doruma, Zaire	A4	48
Dorval, P.Q., Can.	q19	74
Dos Bahías, Cabo, c., Arg.	C3	54
Dos Bocas, Lago, res., P.R.	B2	65
Dos Hermanas, Spain	D3	22
Dos Quebradas, Col.	*C2	60
Dosquet, P.Q., Can.	C6	74
Dos Rios, Ca., U.S.	C2	82
Dosse, stm., Ger.D.R.	E6	15
Dossor, Sov. Un.	D4	28
Doswell, Va., U.S.	C5	123
Dothan, Al., U.S.	D4	78
Dothan, W.V., U.S.	n13	125
Doting Cove, Nf., Can.	D5	72
Dot Lake, Ak., U.S.	C11	79
Dott, W.V., U.S.	D3	125
Doty, Wa., U.S.	C2	124
Douai, Fr.	B5	16
Douala, Cam.	E1	46
Douarnenez, Fr.	C1	16
Double Bayou, Tx., U.S.	r15	120
Double Beach, Ct., U.S.	D4	84
Double Mer, b., Nf., Can.	A2	72
Double Mountain, mtn., Al., U.S.		
Double Oak Mountain, mtn., Al., U.S.	g7	78
Doublespring Pass, Id., U.S.	E5	89
Doubletop Peak, mtn., Wy., U.S.		
Doubs, Md., U.S.	B3	97
Doubs, dept., Fr.	B20	
Doubs, stm., Eur.	D7	16
Doubtful Sound, strt., N.Z.	P11	51
Doucette, Tx., U.S.	D5	120
Doud, Ia., U.S.	D5	92
Doué, Fr.	D3	16
Douentza, Mali	D4	45
Dougherty, Ia., U.S.	B4	92
Dougherty, Ok., U.S.	C4	113
Dougherty, co., Ga., U.S.	E2	87
Douglas, On., Can.	B8	73
Douglas, I. of Man	C3	10
Douglas, S. Afr.	C3	49
Douglas, Scot., U.K.	E5	13
Douglas, Az., U.S.	F6	80
Douglas, Ga., U.S.	E4	87
Douglas, Ma., U.S.	B4	98
Douglas, Mi., U.S.	F4	99
Douglas, Mn., U.S.	F6	100
Douglas, N.D., U.S.	B4	111
Douglas, Ok., U.S.	A4	113
Douglas, W.V., U.S.	B5	125
Douglas, Wy., U.S.	D7	127
Douglas, co., Co., U.S.	B6	83
Douglas, co., Ga., U.S.	C2	87
Douglas, co., Il., U.S.	D5	90
Douglas, co., Ks., U.S.	D8	93
Douglas, co., Mn., U.S.	E3	100
Douglas, co., Mo., U.S.	E5	102
Douglas, co., Ne., U.S.	C9	104
Douglas, co., Nv., U.S.	E2	105
Douglas, co., Or., U.S.	D3	114
Douglas, co., S.D., U.S.	D7	118
Douglas, co., Wa., U.S.	B6	124
Douglas, co., Wi., U.S.	B2	126
Douglas, Mount, mtn., Ak., U.S.	D9	79
Douglas Channel, strt., B.C., Can.	C3	69
Douglas Creek, stm., Co., Can.	B2	83
Douglas Lake, B.C., Can.	D7	69
Douglas Lake, l., Mi., U.S.	C6	99
Douglas Lake, res., Tn., U.S.	D10	119
Douglas Point, c., On., Can.	C3	73
Douglas Station, Mb., Can.	E2	70
Douglass, Ks., U.S.	E7	93
Douglasville, Ga., U.S.	C2	87
Doullens, Fr.	B5	16
Doulus Head, c., Ire.	F1	11
Doumé, Cam.	E2	46
Dounreay, Scot., U.K.	B5	13
Dour, Bel.	D3	17
Doura, Mali	D3	45
Dourados, Braz.	F2	57
Dourados, Braz.	B1	56
Dourdan, Fr.	D5	16
Douro (Duero), stm., Eur.	B1	22
Douz, Tun.	C6	44
Dove Creek, Co., U.S.	D2	83
Dover, Eng., U.K.	E7	10
Dover, Ar., U.S.	B2	81
Dover, De., U.S.	D3	85
Dover, Fl., U.S.	D4	86
Dover, Ga., U.S.	D5	87
Dover, Id., U.S.	A2	89
Dover, Ks., U.S.	D8	93
Dover, Ky., U.S.	B6	94
Dover, Ma., U.S.	h10	98
Dover, Mn., U.S.	G6	100
Dover, Mo., U.S.	B4	102
Dover, N.H., U.S.	D5	106
Dover, N.J., U.S.	B3	107
Dover, N.C., U.S.	B5	110
Dover, Oh., U.S.	B4	112
Dover, Ok., U.S.	B4	113
Dover, Tn., U.S.	A4	119
Dover, stm., Ab., Can.	A4	68
Dover Air Force Base, mil., De., U.S.	D4	85
Dover-Foxcroft, Me., U.S.	C3	96
Dover Hill, In., U.S.	G4	91
Dover Plains, N.Y., U.S.	D7	109
Dovesville, S.C., U.S.	C8	117
Dovray, Mn., U.S.	F3	100
Dovrefjell, mts., Nor.	F3	14
Dow, Il., U.S.	D3	90
Dowagiac, Mi., U.S.	G4	99
Dow City, Ia., U.S.	C2	92
Dowell, Il., U.S.	F4	90
Dowell, Md., U.S.	D5	97
Dowelltown, Tn., U.S.	C8	119
Dowlatābād, Afg.	C13	39
Dowling Lake, l., Ab., Can.	D4	68
Dowling Park, Fl., U.S.	B3	86
Downer, Mn., U.S.	D2	100
Downers Grove, Il., U.S.	n12	82
Downey, Ca., U.S.	n12	82
Downey, Id., U.S.	G6	89
Downham Market, Eng., U.K.	B8	12
Downie, Ca., U.S.	C3	82
Downing, Mo., U.S.	A5	102
Downing, Wi., U.S.	C1	126
Downingtown, Pa., U.S.	F10	115
Downpatrick, N. Ire., U.K.	C4	10
Downpatrick Head, c., Ire.	C2	11
Downs, Il., U.S.	C5	90
Downs, Ks., U.S.	C5	93
Downs Mountain, mtn., Wy., U.S.	C3	127
Downsville, La., U.S.	B3	95
Downsville, N.Y., U.S.	C6	109
Downsville, Wi., U.S.	D2	126
Downton, Mount, mtn., B.C., Can.	C5	69
Dow Rūd, Iran	E4	39
Dows, Ia., U.S.	B4	92
Dowshī, Afg.	D14	39
Doyle, Ca., U.S.	B3	82
Doyle, Tn., U.S.	D8	119
Doyles, Nf., Can.	E2	72
Doylestown, Oh., U.S.	B4	112
Doylestown, Pa., U.S.	F11	115
Doyline, La., U.S.	B2	95
Doyon, N.D., U.S.	A7	111
Dozier, Al., U.S.	D3	78
Dra'a, Hamada du, des., Alg.	D3	44
Drâa, Oued, val., Afr.	D3	44
Drabenderhöhe, F.R.Ger.	C2	19
Drachten, Neth.	A6	17
Drăgănești-Vlașca, Rom.	C7	24
Draganovo, Bul.	D7	24
Drăgășani, Rom.	C7	24
Dragons Mouth, strt.	N22	65
Dragoon, Az., U.S.	E5	80
Drager, Den.	C6	15
Draguignan, Fr.	F7	16
Dragovgrad, Yugo.	B24	
Drain, Or., U.S.	D3	114
Drake, Sk., Can.	F3	75
Drake, Az., U.S.	C3	80
Drake, Co., U.S.	A5	83
Drake, N.D., U.S.	B5	111
Drakensberg, mts., Afr.	D4	49
Drake Passage, strt.	J16	2
Drake Peak, mtn., Or., U.S.	E6	114
Drakesboro, Ky., U.S.	C2	94
Drakes Branch, Va., U.S.	D4	123
Drakes Creek, stm., U.S.	D3	94
Drakes Creek, West Fork, stm., Ky., U.S.	D3	94
Drakesville, Ia., U.S.	D5	92
Draketown, Ga., U.S.	C1	87
Dráma, Grc.	B5	40
Drama, stm., Pol.	g9	26
Drammen, Nor.	G4	14
Drancy, Fr.	g10	16
Dranse, stm., Fr.	C2	20
Draper, S.D., U.S.	D5	118
Draperstown, N. Ire., U.K.	C5	11
Drasco, Ar., U.S.	B4	81
Drava (Drau), stm., Eur.	C4	24
Draveil, Fr.	F2	17
Dravuni, i., Fiji	I15	52
Drawsko [Pomorskie], Pol.	B3	26
Drayton, On., Can.	D4	73
Drayton, N.D., U.S.	A8	111
Drayton, S.C., U.S.	B4	117
Drayton Plains, Mi., U.S.	F7	99
Drayton Valley, Ab., Can.	C3	68
Dreamland Villa, Az., U.S.	*D4	80
Drebkau, Ger.D.R.	C7	18
Dreibergen, F.R.Ger.	D3	15
Drenthe, prov., Neth.	B6	17
Dresbach, Mn., U.S.	G7	100
Dresden, Ger.D.R.	C6	18
Dresden, Ks., U.S.	C3	93
Dresden, On., Can.	E2	73
Dresden, Oh., U.S.	B3	112
Dresden, Tn., U.S.	A3	119
Dresser, In., U.S.	F3	91
Dresser, Wi., U.S.	C1	126
Dresslerville, Nv., U.S.	E2	105
Dreux, Fr.	C4	16
Drew, Ms., U.S.	B3	101
Drew, co., Ar., U.S.	D4	81
Drewryville, Va., U.S.	D5	123
Drewsey, Or., U.S.	D8	114
Drews Reservoir, res., Or., U.S.	E6	114
Drewsville, N.H., U.S.	D2	106
Drexel, Mo., U.S.	C3	102
Drexel, N.C., U.S.	B1	110
Drexel, Oh., U.S.	C1	112
Drexel Hill, Pa., U.S.	p20	115
Driffield, Eng., U.K.	F8	115
Drift, Ky., U.S.	C7	94
Drifton, Pa., U.S.	D10	115
Driftpile, Ab., Can.	B3	68
Driftpile, stm., Ab., Can.	B3	68
Driftwood, Ok., U.S.	A3	113
Driftwood, Pa., U.S.	D5	115
Driftwood Creek, stm., Ne., U.S.	D4	104
Driggs, Id., U.S.	F7	89
Drimoleague, Ire.	F2	11
Drina, stm., Yugo.	C4	24
Drin Gulf, b., Alb.	B2	25
Drini, stm., Alb.	A3	25
Drinkwater, Sk., Can.	G3	75
Dripping Springs, Tx., U.S.	D3	120
Driscoll, N.D., U.S.	C5	111
Driscoll, Tx., U.S.	F4	120
Driskill Mountain, hill, La., U.S.	B3	95
Dröbak, Nor.	H4	14
Drobeta-Turnu-Severin, Rom.	C6	24
Drogheda, Ire.	D3	10
Drogobych, Sov. Un.	G4	27
Droitwich, Eng., U.K.	B5	12
Dromahair, Ire.	C3	11
Drôme, stm., Fr.	E6	16
Dromcliffe, Ire.	D4	11
Dromod, Ire.	C4	11
Dromore, N. Ire., U.K.	C4	11
Dromore West, Ire.	C3	11
Dronero, Italy	E3	20
Dronfield, Eng., U.K.	A6	12
Dronninglund, Den.	A4	15
Dropmore, Mb., Can.	D1	70
Druid, Sk., Can.	F1	75
Drulingen, Fr.	E2	19
Drumbeg, Scot., U.K.	B3	13
Drumbo, On., Can.	D4	73
Drumcliffe, Ire.	C3	11
Drumheller, Ab., Can.	D4	68
Drum Island, i., S.C., U.S.	k12	117
Drumlish, Ire.	D4	11
Drummond, Id., U.S.	F7	89
Drummond, Mt., U.S.	D3	103
Drummond, Ok., U.S.	A3	113
Drummond, Wi., U.S.	B2	126
Drummond, co., Can.	D5	74
Drummond, Lake, l., Va., U.S.	D6	123
Drummond Island, i., Mi., U.S.	B7	99
Drummond Island, i., Mi., U.S.	C7	99
Drummond Range, mts., Austl.	D8	51
Drummondville, P.Q., Can.	D5	74
Drummore, Scot., U.K.	F4	13
Drumquin, N. Ire., U.K.	C4	11
Drumright, Ok., U.S.	B5	113
Drumshanbo, Ire.	C3	11
Druzhina, Sov. Un.	C36	128
Druzhkovka, Sov. Un.	q20	27
Drwęca, stm., Pol.	B5	26
Dryad, Wa., U.S.	C2	124
Dryberry Lake, l., On., Can.	E5	70
Dry Branch, Ga., U.S.	D3	87
Drybranch, W.V., U.S.	m13	125
Dry Cimarron, stm., U.S.	A6	108
Dry Creek, La., U.S.	D2	95
Dry Creek, stm., Ks., U.S.	g12	93
Dry Creek Mountain, mtn., Nv., U.S.	B5	105
Dryden, On., Can.	o16	73
Dryden, Ar., U.S.	*B5	81
Dryden, Me., U.S.	D2	96
Dryden, Mi., U.S.	F7	99
Dryden, N.Y., U.S.	C4	109
Dryden, Tx., U.S.	D1	120
Dryden, Wa., U.S.	B5	124
Dry Fork, Va., U.S.	D3	123
Dryfork, W.V., U.S.	C5	125
Dry Fork, stm., Mo., U.S.	D6	102
Dry Fork, stm., W.V., U.S.	D3	125
Dry Fork, stm., W.V., U.S.	B5	125
Drygalski Island, i., Ant.	C22	7
Dry Harbour Mountains, mts., Jam.	E14	65
Drymen, Scot., U.K.	D4	13
Dry Mills, Me., U.S.	E2	96
Dry Prong, La., U.S.	C3	95
Dry Ridge, Ky., U.S.	B5	94
Dry Run, Pa., U.S.	F6	115
Dry Tortugas, is., Fl., U.S.	H5	86
Drywood, Ab., Can.	E4	68
Dschang, Cam.	D2	46
Duaihe, Hasi, well, W. Sah.	D2	44
Duaringa, Austl.	A7	51
Duarte, Ca., U.S.	*E5	82
Duarte, Pico, mtn., Dom. Rep.	D3	13
Duart Point, c., Scot., U.K.	D3	13
Dubā, Sau. Ar.	I10	40
Dubach, La., U.S.	B3	95
Dubai (Dubayy), U.A.E.	C5	38
Dubawnt, l., N.T., Can.	D12	66
Dubawnt, stm., N.T., Can.	D12	66
Dubba, Zaire	E4	13
Dubberly, La., U.S.	B2	95
Dubbo, Austl.	F8	50
Dübendorf, Switz.	B6	21
Dublin, On., Can.	D3	73
Dublin (Baile Átha Cliath), Ire.	D3	10
Dublin, Al., U.S.	*D3	82
Dublin, Ga., U.S.	D4	87
Dublin, In., U.S.	E7	91
Dublin, Md., U.S.	A5	97
Dublin, N.H., U.S.	A3	101
Dublin, N.C., U.S.	C4	110
Dublin, Pa., U.S.	F11	115
Dublin, Tx., U.S.	C3	120
Dublin, Va., U.S.	C2	123
Dublin, co., Ire.	D5	11
Dublin Bay, b., Ire.	D5	11
Dublin Shore, N.S., Can.	E5	71
Dublon, i., Micron.	Q18	52
Dubnica [nad Váhom], Czech.	E6	89
Dubois, Id., U.S.	H4	91
Dubois, In., U.S.	D4	104
Du Bois, Ne., U.S.	D4	104
Du Bois, Pa., U.S.	D4	115
Dubois, co., In., U.S.	H4	91
Duboistown, Pa., U.S.	D7	115
Dubossary, Sov. Un.	H7	27
Dubossary Reservoir, res., Sov. Un.	B9	24
Dubovka, Sov. Un.	G15	28
Dubrēka, Gui.	E2	45
Dubrovka, Sov. Un.	s31	14
Dubrovnik, Yugo.	D4	24
Dubuc, Sk., Can.	G4	75
Dubulu, Zaire	A3	48
Dubuque, Ia., U.S.	B7	92
Dubuque, co., Ia., U.S.	B7	92
Duchcov, Czech.	C5	18
Duchesne, co., Ut., U.S.	C5	121
Duchesne, stm., Ut., U.S.	C5	121
Duchess, Ab., Can.	D5	68
Ducie, atoll, Pit.	H14	6
Duck, N.C., U.S.	A7	110
Duck, stm., Tn., U.S.	B4	119
Duck Bay, Mb., Can.	C1	70
Duck Creek, stm., De., U.S.	C4	85
Duck Creek, stm., Nv., U.S.	D7	105
Duck Creek, stm., Oh., U.S.	C4	112
Duck Creek, stm., Wi., U.S.	h9	126
Duck Hill, Ms., U.S.	B4	101
Duck Lake, Sk., Can.	E2	75
Duck Lake, l., Mb., Can.	B2	70
Duck Lake, l., Me., U.S.	C4	96
Duck Lake Post, Mb., Can.	f8	70
Duck Mountain, hills, Mb., Can.	D1	70
Duck Mountain Provincial Park, Mb., Can.	D1	70
Duck Mountain Provincial Park, Sk., Can.	F5	75
Duck River, Tn., U.S.	B4	119
Ducktown, Tn., U.S.	D9	119
Duck Valley Indian Reservation, U.S.	B5	105
Duckwater, Nv., U.S.	E6	105
Duckwater Indian Reservation, Nv., U.S.	E6	105
Duckwater Peak, mtn., Nv., U.S.	E6	105
Ducor, Ca., U.S.	E4	82
Dudelange, Lux.	E6	17
Duderstadt, F.R.Ger.	B5	19
Dūdhi, India	E9	37
Dudinka, Sov. Un.	C11	29
Dudley, Eng., U.K.	D5	10
Dudley, Ma., U.S.	B4	98
Dudley, Mo., U.S.	E7	102
Dudley, N.C., U.S.	B4	110
Dudley, Pa., U.S.	F5	115
Dudweiler, F.R.Ger.	D2	19
Dueéckué, I.C.	E3	45
Duenweg, Mo., U.S.	D3	102
Duero (Douro), stm., Eur.	B3	22
Due West, S.C., U.S.	C3	117
Duff, Sk., Can.	G4	75
Duff, In., U.S.	H3	91
Duff, stm., U.S.	C9	119
Duffee, Ms., U.S.	C5	101
Duffern, co., On., Can.	C4	73
Dufferin, co., On., Can.	D3	73
Duffield, Ab., Can.	C3	68
Duff Reef, rf., Fiji	H16	52
Dufftown, Scot., U.K.	C5	13
Duffy, Oh., U.S.	C5	112
Dufrost, Mb., Can.	E3	70
Dufur, Or., U.S.	B5	114
Dugdemona, stm., La., U.S.	B3	95
Dugger, In., U.S.	F3	91
Dugi, i., Yugo.	C2	24
Dugort, Ire.	C1	11
Duhamel, P.Q., Can.	C2	74
Duich, Loch, b., Scot., U.K.	C3	13
Duida, Cerro, mtn., Ven.	C4	60
Duisburg, F.R.Ger.	C3	18
Duitama, Col.	C2	60
Duiwelskloof, S. Afr.	B5	49
Dujuuma, Som.	E8	47
Dūkan Dam, Iraq	C2	39
Duke, Al., U.S.	B4	78
Duke, Ok., U.S.	C2	113
Duke Center, Pa., U.S.	C5	115
Dukedom, Tn., U.S.	A3	119
Duke Island, i., Ak., U.S.	n24	79
Dukes, co., Ma., U.S.	D6	98
Duk Fadiat, Sud.	D3	47
Duki, Pak.	E14	55
Dukla Pass, Eur.	D6	26
Dulac, La., U.S.	E5	95
Dulce, N.M., U.S.	A2	108
Dulce, stm., Arg.	B3	55
Dülken, F.R.Ger.	C6	17
Dülmen, F.R.Ger.	B2	19
Duluth, Ga., U.S.	B2	87
Duluth, Mn., U.S.	D6	100
Dūmā, Isr. Occ.	g11	41
Dūmā, Syria	*F11	40
Dumaguete, Phil.	D6	34
Dumanwur, Indon.	B11	40
Dumaran Island, i., Phil.	C5	34
Dumas, Ar., U.S.	D4	81
Dumas, Ms., U.S.	A5	101
Dumas, Tx., U.S.	B2	120
Dumba, Zaire	E4	13
Dumbarton, Scot., U.K.	D7	93
Dumbarton, N.H., U.S.	D3	106
Dumbéaton, Scot., U.K.	E4	13
Dumbéa, N. Cal.		
Dumbleyung, Austl.	F2	50
Dumfries, Scot., U.K.	E5	13
Dumfries, Va., U.S.	B5	123
Dumfries and Galloway, prov., Scot., U.K.	E4	13
Dumka, India	E11	37
Dummer, I., F.R.Ger.	H3	75
Dümmer, l., F.R.Ger.	F2	15
Dummerston, Vt., U.S.	F3	122
Dumon, i.,	A5	91
Dumont, Mn., U.S.	E2	100
Dumont, Tx., U.S.	C2	120
Dumon-d'Urville, sci., Ant.	C27	7
Dumyāt (Damietta), Eg.	B3	38
Dunaff Head, c., Ire.	B4	11
Dunaföldvár, Hung.	B4	24
Dunaire, Sk., Can.	*h8	87
Dunajec, stm., Eur.	D6	34
Dunajská Streda, Czech.	B1	47
Dunany Point, c., Ire.	D5	11
Dunaújváros, Hung.	B4	24
Dunay, Sov. Un.	G6	33
Dunayevtsy, Sov. Un.	G6	27
Dunbar, Ky., U.S.	C5	94
Dunbar, Ne., U.S.	D9	104
Dunbar, Pa., U.S.	G2	115
Dunbar, S.C., U.S.	B8	117
Dunbar, W.V., U.S.	C3	125
Dunbarton, N.H., U.S.	D3	106
Dunbeath, Scot., U.K.	B5	13
Dunblane, Sk., Can.	F2	75
Dunbolyne, Ire.	D5	11
Duncan, B.C., Can.	f6	112
Duncan, Ms., U.S.	A3	101
Duncan, Ne., U.S.	C8	104
Duncan, Ok., U.S.	C4	113
Duncan, S.C., U.S.	B3	117
Duncan, stm., B.C., Can.	D9	69
Duncan Falls, Oh., U.S.	C4	112
Duncan Lake, l., B.C., Can.	D9	69
Duncannon, Pa., U.S.	F7	115
Duncansby Head, c., Scot., U.K.	A5	10
Duncansville, Pa., U.S.	F5	115
Duncanville, Al., U.S.	B2	78
Duncanville, Tx., U.S.	n10	120
Duncombe, Ia., U.S.	B4	92
Duncormick, Ire.	E5	11
Dundalk, On., Can.	C4	73
Dundalk, Ire.	C3	10
Dundalk, Md., U.S.	B4	97
Dundalk Bay, b., Ire.	D3	10
Dundas, On., Can.	D5	73
Dundas, Il., U.S.	E5	90
Dundas, Mn., U.S.	F5	100
Dundas, co., On., Can.	B9	73
Dundas, Va., U.S.	D4	123
Dundas Lake, l., Austl.	F3	50
Dundas Island, i., B.C., Can.	B2	69
Dundas Strait, strt., Austl.	C5	49
Dundee, S. Afr.	C5	49
Dundee, Scot., U.K.	D5	10
Dundee, Fl., U.S.	D5	86
Dundee, Il., U.S.	A5	90
Dundee, Ia., U.S.	B6	92
Dundee, Ky., U.S.	C3	94
Dundee, Mi., U.S.	G7	99
Dundee, Ms., U.S.	A3	101
Dundee, N.Y., U.S.	C4	109
Dundee, Or., U.S.	h11	114
Dundee, Tx., U.S.	C3	120
Dundee, Wi., U.S.	E5	126
Dundrum, Ire.	E3	11
Dundrum, Ire.	D5	11
Dundrum Bay, b., N. Ire., U.K.	C4	10
Dundurn, Sk., Can.	F2	75
Dundy, co., Ne., U.S.	D4	104
Dunedin, N.Z.	P13	51
Dunedin, Fl., U.S.	D4	86
Duneland Beach, In., U.S.	A4	91
Dunellen, N.J., U.S.	B4	107
Dunfanaghy, Ire.	B4	11
Dunfermline, Sk., Can.	E2	75
Dunfermline, Scot., U.K.	B5	10
Dungannon, On., Can.	D3	73
Dungannon, Va., U.S.	f9	123
Dungannon, N. Ire., U.K.	C4	11
Dungarvan, Ire.	E3	11
Dungarvan Harbour, b., Ire.	E4	11
Dungeness, c., Eng., U.K.	D8	12
Dungeness, stm., Wa., U.S.	A2	124
Dung Gate, hist., Isr. Occ.	m14	41
Dungiven, N. Ire., U.K.	C5	11
Dungloe, Ire.	C3	11
Dungu, Zaire	A4	48
Dunham, P.Q., Can.	D5	74
Dunhua, China	C10	31
Dunhuang, China	C3	31
Dunkard Creek, stm., U.S.	B4	125
Dunkeld, Scot., U.K.	D5	13
Dunkerque, Fr.	A4	16
Dunkerton, Ia., U.S.	B5	92
Dunkery Hill, hill, Eng., U.K.	C4	12
Dunkineely, Ire.	C3	11
Dunkirk, In., U.S.	D7	91
Dunkirk, N.Y., U.S.	C1	109
Dunkwa, Ghana	E4	45
Dún Laoghaire, Ire.	D3	10
Dunlap, Il., U.S.	C4	90
Dunlap, Ia., U.S.	C2	92
Dunlap, Ks., U.S.	D7	93
Dunlap, Tn., U.S.	D8	119
Dunlavin, Ire.	D5	11
Dunleer, Ire.	D5	11
Dunleith, De., U.S.	i7	85
Dunlo, Pa., U.S.	F4	115
Dunloup Creek, stm., W.V., U.S.	n13	125
Dunmanway, Ire.	F2	11
Dunmore, Scot., U.K.	C3	94
Dunmore, Pa., U.S.	D10	115
Dunmore, Lake, l., Vt., U.S.	D2	122
Dunmore East, Ire.	E5	11
Dunn, N.C., U.S.	B4	110
Dunn, Tx., U.S.	C2	120
Dunn, co., N.D., U.S.	B3	111
Dunn, co., Wi., U.S.	D2	126
Dunn Center, N.D., U.S.	B3	111
Dunnegan, Mo., U.S.	D4	102
Dunnellon, Fl., U.S.	C4	86
Dunning, Ne., U.S.	C5	104
Dun Loring Woods, Va., U.S.	*B5	123
Dunnottar, Mb., Can.	D3	70
Dunns Bridge, In., U.S.	B4	91
Dunns Corners, R.I., U.S.	G1	116
Dunnsville, Va., U.S.	C6	123
Dunnville, Ky., U.S.	C5	94
Dunnville, On., Can.	E5	73
Dunphy, Nv., U.S.	C5	105
Dunqula, Sud.	B3	47
Dunrea, Mb., Can.	E2	70
Dunrobin, On., Can.	B9	73
Duns, Scot., U.K.	E6	13
Dunseith, N.D., U.S.	A5	111
Dunsmuir, Ca., U.S.	B2	82
Dunstable, Ma., U.S.	A5	98
Dun-sur-Auron, Fr.	E5	17
Dun [-sur-Meuse], Fr.	E5	17
Dunvegan, On., Can.	C4	73
Dunvegan, Loch, b., Scot., U.K.	C2	13
Dunvegan Head, c., Scot., U.K.	C2	13
Dunville, Nf., Can.	E5	72
Dunwoody, Ga., U.S.	h8	87
Duolun, China	i6	31
Duong Dong, Viet.	G5	35
Du Page, co., Il., U.S.	B5	90
Du Page, stm., Il., U.S.	k8	90
Dupax, Phil.	n13	34
Duplessis, La., U.S.	h10	95
Duplin, co., N.C., U.S.	C5	110

Name	Map Ref	Page
Dupont, Co., U.S.	B6	83
Du Pont, Ga., U.S.	F4	87
Dupont, In., U.S.	G6	91
Dupont, La., U.S.	*D4	95
Dupont, Oh., U.S.	A1	112
Dupont, Pa., U.S.	n18	115
Du Pont, Wa., U.S.	B3	124
Dupont, Bayou, stm., La., U.S.	k11	95
Dupont City, W.V., U.S.	m12	125
Dupont Manor, De., U.S.	D3	85
Dupree, S.D., U.S.	B4	118
Dupuyer, Mt., U.S.	B4	103
Duquesne, Pa., U.S.	F2	115
Du Quoin, Il., U.S.	E4	90
Dūrā, Isr. Occ.	C7	41
Duran, N.M., U.S.	C4	108
Durance, stm., Fr.	F6	16
Durand, Ga., U.S.	D2	87
Durand, Il., U.S.	A4	90
Durand, Mi., U.S.	F6	99
Durand, Wi., U.S.	D2	126
Durango (Victoria de Durango), Mex.	C4	63
Durango, Co., U.S.	D3	83
Durango, state, Mex.	C4	63
Durant, Ia., U.S.	C7	92
Durant, Ms., U.S.	B4	101
Durant, Ok., U.S.	D5	113
Durants Neck, N.C., U.S.	A6	110
Duraton, stm., Spain	B4	22
Durazno, Ur.	E1	56
Durazno, dept., Ur.	f8	54
Durban, Mb., Can.	D1	70
Durban, S. Afr.	C5	49
Durbin, N.D., U.S.	C8	111
Durbin, W.V., U.S.	C5	125
Durbin Creek, stm., Fl., U.S.	m8	86
Düren, F.R.Ger.	C3	18
Durg, India	G8	37
Durgāpur, India	F11	37
Durham, On., Can.	C4	73
Durham, Eng., U.K.	C6	10
Durham, Ca., U.S.	C3	82
Durham, Ct., U.S.	D5	84
Durham, Ks., U.S.	D6	93
Durham, Mo., U.S.	B6	102
Durham, N.H., U.S.	D5	106
Durham, N.C., U.S.	B4	110
Durham, Ok., U.S.	B2	113
Durham, co., On., Can.	C6	73
Durham, co., Eng., U.K.	F7	13
Durham, co., N.C., U.S.	A4	110
Durham Bridge, N.B., Can.	C3	71
Durham Downs, Austl.	C3	51
Durham-Sud, P.Q., Can.	D5	74
Durhamville, Tn., U.S.	B2	119
Durkee, Or., U.S.	C9	114
Durmersheim, F.R.Ger.	E3	19
Durmitor, mtn., Yugo.	D4	24
Durness, Scot., U.K.	A4	10
Durness, Kyle of, b., Scot., U.K.	B4	13
Durnford, Punta, c., W. Sah.	E1	44
Dürrboden, Switz.	C8	21
Durrell, Nf., Can.	D4	72
Durrësi, Alb.	B2	25
Durrow, Ire.	E4	11
Durrus, Ire.	F2	11
Dursey, i., Ire.	F1	11
Dursunbey, Tur.	C7	25
Duru, Zaire	A4	48
Durūz, Jabal ad, mts., Syria	F11	40
D'Urville Island, i., N.Z.	N14	51
Duryea, Pa., U.S.	D10	115
Dushan, China	F6	31
Dushanbe, Sov. Un.	F9	29
Dushaymī, Jazā'ir, is., Eg.	C2	41
Dushore, Pa., U.S.	C9	115
Dusky Sound, strt., N.Z.	P11	51
Duson, La., U.S.	D3	95
Düsseldorf, F.R.Ger.	C3	18
Dustin, Ok., U.S.	B5	113
Dusty, N.M., U.S.	D2	108
Dutch Creek, stm., Ar., U.S.	C2	81
Dutchess, co., N.Y., U.S.	D7	109
Dutch Harbor, Ak., U.S.	E6	79
Dutch Island, i., R.I., U.S.	F4	116
Dutch John, Ut., U.S.	C6	121
Dutchtown, Mo., U.S.	D8	102
Dutton, On., Can.	E3	73
Dutton, Al., U.S.	A4	78
Dutton, Mt., U.S.	C5	103
Dutton, Mount, mtn., Ut., U.S.	E3	121
Dutzow, Mo., U.S.	C7	102
Duval, Sk., Can.	F3	75
Duval, co., Fl., U.S.	B5	86
Duval, co., Tx., U.S.	F3	120
Duvergé, Dom. Rep.	E8	64
Duvno, Yugo.	D3	24
Duxbury, Ma., U.S.	B6	98
Duxbury, Vt., U.S.	C3	122
Duyun, China	F6	31
Düzce, Tur.	B8	40
Dvina Bay, b., Sov. Un.	C16	8
Dvůr Králové [nad Labem], Czech.	C3	26
Dwārka, India	F2	37
Dwight, Il., U.S.	B5	90
Dwight, Ks., U.S.	D7	93
Dwight, Ma., U.S.	B3	98
Dwight, Ne., U.S.	C8	104
Dwight, N.D., U.S.	C9	111
Dwight D. Eisenhower Lock, N.Y., U.S.	f9	109
Dworshak Reservoir, res., Id., U.S.	C3	89
Dwyer, Wy., U.S.	D8	127
Dyakovo, Sov. Un.	r22	27
Dyatkovo, Sov. Un.	E10	27
Dyaul, i., Pap. N. Gui.	h13	50
Dyce, Scot., U.K.	C6	13
Dyckesville, Wi., U.S.	D6	126
Dycusburg, Ky., U.S.	e9	94
Dyer, Ar., U.S.	B1	81
Dyer, In., U.S.	A2	91
Dyer, Nv., U.S.	F3	105
Dyer, Tn., U.S.	A3	119
Dyer, co., Tn., U.S.	A2	119
Dyer Bay, On., Can.	B3	73
Dyer Bay, b., On., Can.	B3	73
Dyer Brook, Me., U.S.	B4	96
Dyer Island, i., R.I., U.S.	E5	116
Dyero, Mali	D3	45
Dyersburg, Tn., U.S.	A2	119
Dyersville, Ia., U.S.	B6	92
Dyess, Ar., U.S.	B5	81
Dyess Air Force Base, mil., Tx., U.S.	C3	120
Dyfed, co., Wales, U.K.	C3	12
Dyje, stm., Eur.	D3	26
Dykh-Tau, Mount, mtn., Sov. Un.	*E7	29
Dyment, On., Can.	E5	70
Dysart, Sk., Can.	G3	75
Dysart, Ia., U.S.	B5	92

Name	Map Ref	Page
Dzalaata, Mong.	B2	32
Dzamïn Üüd, Mong.	B4	32
Dzaoudzi, May.	f9	49
Dzaudzhikau see Ordzhonikidze, Sov. Un.	E7	29
Dzavhan, stm., Mong.	B3	31
Dzerzhinsk, Sov. Un.	E6	27
Dzerzhinsk, Sov. Un.	C14	27
Dzerzhinsk, Sov. Un.	q20	27
Dzhalal-Abad, Sov. Un.	E8	28
Dzhambul, Sov. Un.	E10	29
Dzhankoy, Sov. Un.	I10	27
Dzhebel, Sov. Un.	B7	39
Dzhetygara, Sov. Un.	C6	28
Dzhezkazgan, Sov. Un.	D7	28
Dzhizak, Sov. Un.	G22	8
Dzhugdzhur Mountains, mts., Sov. Un.	D16	29
Dzhungarian Alatau Mountains, mts., Asia	D9	28
Dzhusaly, Sov. Un.	D6	28
Działdowo, Pol.	B6	26
Działoszyce, Pol.	C6	26
Dzierżoniów, Pol.	C4	26
Dzilam González, Mex.	C7	63
Dzioua, Alg.	C6	44
Dzitbalché, Mex.	C6	63
Dzulfa, Sov. Un.	C15	40
Dzungaria, reg., China	B2	31
Dzuunmod, Mong.	B6	31

E

Name	Map Ref	Page
Eads, Co., U.S.	C8	83
Eads, Tn., U.S.	B2	119
Eagan, Mn., U.S.	n12	100
Eagan, Tn., U.S.	C10	119
Eagar, Az., U.S.	C6	80
Eagle, Ak., U.S.	C11	79
Eagle, Co., U.S.	B4	83
Eagle, Id., U.S.	F2	89
Eagle, Ne., U.S.	h12	104
Eagle, N.Y., U.S.	C2	109
Eagle, Wi., U.S.	F5	126
Eagle, co., Co., U.S.	B4	83
Eagle, stm., Nf., Can.	B2	72
Eagle Bend, Mn., U.S.	D3	100
Eagle Bridge, N.Y., U.S.	C7	109
Eagle Butte, S.D., U.S.	C4	118
Eagle Cave, Wi., U.S.	E3	126
Eagle City, Ok., U.S.	B3	113
Eagle Cliff, Wi., U.S.	B3	89
Eagle Creek, Tn., U.S.	B4	119
Eagle Creek, stm., Sk., Can.	F2	75
Eagle Creek, stm., In., U.S.	D5	91
Eagle Creek, stm., Ky., U.S.	B5	94
Eagle Creek Reservoir, res., In., U.S.	E5	91
Eagle Dam, In., U.S.	E4	91
Eagle Grove, Ia., U.S.	B4	92
Eagle Harbor, Mi., U.S.	A2	99
Eagle Key, i., Fl., U.S.	G6	86
Eagle Lake, Me., U.S.	A4	96
Eagle Lake, Mn., U.S.	F5	100
Eagle Lake, Tx., U.S.	E4	120
Eagle Lake, Wi., U.S.	*F5	126
Eagle Lake, l., On., Can.	E5	70
Eagle Lake, l., Ca., U.S.	B3	82
Eagle Lake, l., Me., U.S.	B3	96
Eagle Lake, l., Me., U.S.	A4	96
Eagle Lake, l., Ms., U.S.	C3	101
Eagle Lake, l., Wi., U.S.	C4	126
Eagle Mills, Ar., U.S.	D3	81
Eagle Mountain, mtn., Mn., U.S.	k9	100
Eagle Mountain Lake, res., Tx., U.S.	m9	120
Eagle Nest, N.M., U.S.	A4	108
Eagle Nest Butte, mtn., S.D., U.S.	D4	118
Eaglenest Lake, l., Can.	D4	70
Eagle Nest Lake, l., N.M., U.S.	A4	108
Eagle Pass, Tx., U.S.	E2	120
Eagle Peak, mtn., Ca., U.S.	B3	82
Eagle Peak, mtn., Tx., U.S.	o12	120
Eagle Point, Or., U.S.	E4	114
Eagle River, On., Can.	E5	70
Eagle River, Mi., U.S.	A2	99
Eagle River, Wi., U.S.	C4	126
Eagle Rock, Va., U.S.	C3	123
Eaglesham, Ab., Can.	B2	68
Eagles Mere, Pa., U.S.	D8	115
Eagle Springs, N.C., U.S.	B3	110
Eagletail Mountains, mts., Az., U.S.	D2	80
Eagletail Peak, mtn., Az., U.S.	D2	80
Eagleton Village, Tn., U.S.	*D10	119
Eagletown, Ok., U.S.	C7	113
Eagleville, Ca., U.S.	B3	82
Eagleville, Ct., U.S.	B6	84
Eagleville, Mo., U.S.	A4	102
Eagleville, Tn., U.S.	B5	119
Eakly, Ok., U.S.	B3	113
Ealing (part of London), Eng., U.K.	k12	10
Eardley, P.Q., Can.	g11	73
Eardley Lake, l., Mb., Can.	C3	70
Earle, Ar., U.S.	B5	81
Earl Grey, Sk., Can.	G3	75
Earl Park, In., U.S.	C3	91
Earlsboro, Ok., U.S.	B5	113
Earlton, Ks., U.S.	E8	93
Earlville, Il., U.S.	B5	90
Earlville, Ia., U.S.	B6	92
Earlville, N.Y., U.S.	C5	109
Early, Ia., U.S.	B2	92
Early, co., Ga., U.S.	E2	87
Early Branch, S.C., U.S.	F6	117
Earn, stm., Scot., U.K.	D5	13
Earn, Loch l., Scot., U.K.	E4	13
Earth, Tx., U.S.	B1	120
Easingwold, Eng., U.K.	F7	13
Easky, Ire.	C3	11
Easley, S.C., U.S.	B2	117
East, stm., On., Can.	B5	73
East, stm., Ct., U.S.	D5	84
East, stm., N.Y., U.S.	k13	109
East, stm., Wi., U.S.	h9	126
Eastaboga, Al., U.S.	B3	78
East Acton, Ma., U.S.	g10	98
East Alburgh, Vt., U.S.	B2	122
East Alstead, N.H., U.S.	D2	106
East Alton, Il., U.S.	E3	90
East Andover, Me., U.S.	D2	96
East Andover, N.H., U.S.	D3	106
East Angus, P.Q., Can.	D6	74

Name	Map Ref	Page
East Arlington, Vt., U.S.	E2	122
East Aurora, N.Y., U.S.	C2	109
East Baldwin, Me., U.S.	E2	96
East Bangor, Pa., U.S.	E11	115
East Bank, W.V., U.S.	m13	125
East Barnard, Vt., U.S.	D3	122
East Barre, Vt., U.S.	C4	122
East Baton Rouge, co., La., U.S.	D4	95
East Bay, b., Fl., U.S.	u16	86
East Bay, b., Tx., U.S.	R15	120
East Beckwith Mountain, mtn., Co., U.S.	C3	83
East Bend, N.C., U.S.	A2	110
East Berbice-Corentyne, dept., Guy.	B3	59
East Berlin, Ct., U.S.	C5	84
East Berlin, Pa., U.S.	G8	115
East Bernard, Tx., U.S.	E4	120
East Bernstadt, Ky., U.S.	C5	94
East Bethel, Mn., U.S.	E5	100
East Bethel, Vt., U.S.	D3	122
East Billerica, Ma., U.S.	f11	98
East Blue Hill, Me., U.S.	D4	96
East Bonne Terre, Mo., U.S.	D7	102
East Boothbay, Me., U.S.	E3	96
Eastborough, Ks., U.S.	g12	93
Eastbourne, Eng., U.K.	E7	10
East Brady, Pa., U.S.	E2	115
East Braintree, Mb., Can.	E4	70
East Braintree, Vt., U.S.	D3	122
East Branch, N.Y., U.S.	D5	109
East Branch Clarion River Lake, res., Pa., U.S.	C4	115
East Brewster, Ma., U.S.	C7	98
East Brewton, Al., U.S.	D2	78
East Bridgewater, Ma., U.S.	B6	98
East Brimfield Lake, res., Ma., U.S.	B3	98
East Brookfield, Me., U.S.	D4	96
East Brookfield, Ma., U.S.	B3	98
East Brookfield, Vt., U.S.	C3	122
East Brooklyn, Ct., U.S.	B8	84
East Broughton Station, P.Q., Can.	C6	74
East Brunswick, N.J., U.S.	C4	107
East Burke, Vt., U.S.	B5	122
East Butler, Pa., U.S.	E2	115
East Butte, mtn., Mt., U.S.	B5	103
East Cache Creek, stm., Ok., U.S.	C3	113
East Calais, Vt., U.S.	C4	122
East Canaan, Ct., U.S.	A2	84
East Candia, N.H., U.S.	D4	106
East Cape, c., Fl., U.S.	G5	86
East Cape, c., N.Z.	L17	51
East Carbon, Ut., U.S.	D5	121
East Carroll, co., La., U.S.	B4	95
East Chain, Mn., U.S.	G3	100
East Channel, strt., Marsh Is.	S18	52
East Charleston, Vt., U.S.	B5	122
East Chelmsford, Ma., U.S.	f10	98
Eastchester, N.Y., U.S.	*n15	109
East Chicago, In., U.S.	A3	91
East Chicago Heights, Il., U.S.	*k9	90
East China Sea, Asia	F10	31
East Chop, c., Ma., U.S.	D6	98
East Cleveland, Oh., U.S.	g9	112
East-Clifton, P.Q., Can.	D6	74
East Columbia, Tx., U.S.	r14	120
East Concord, Vt., U.S.	C5	122
East Conway, N.H., U.S.	B4	106
East Corinth, Me., U.S.	D3	96
East Corinth, Vt., U.S.	C4	122
East Cote Blanche Bay, b., La., U.S.	E4	95
East Coulee, Ab., Can.	D4	68
East Danville, Oh., U.S.	C2	112
East Demerara-West Coast Berbice, dept., Guy.	A3	59
East Dennis, Ma., U.S.	C7	98
East Dereham, Eng., U.K.	B8	12
East Derry, N.H., U.S.	E4	106
East Detroit, Mi., U.S.	p16	99
East Dixfield, Me., U.S.	D3	96
East Dixmont, Me., U.S.	D3	96
East Douglas, Ma., U.S.	B4	98
East Dover, Me., U.S.	C3	96
East Dover, Vt., U.S.	F3	122
East Dubuque, Il., U.S.	A3	90
East Dummerston, Vt., U.S.	F3	122
East Eddington, Me., U.S.	D4	96
East Ellijay, Ga., U.S.	B2	87
Eastend, Sk., Can.	H1	75
East End Point, c., Bah.	m18	64
East Enterprise, In., U.S.	G8	91
Easter, Mount, mtn., Ct., U.S.	B2	84
Easter Island see Pascua, Isla de, i., Chile	H15	6
East Olympia, Wa., U.S.	C3	124
Eastern, prov., Ghana	E5	45
Eastern, prov., Kenya	B6	48
Eastern, prov., Zam.	C5	49
Eastern Bay, b., Md., U.S.	C5	97
Eastern Channel, strt., Japan	J4	33
Eastern Ghāts, mts., India	E7	36
Eastern Island, i., Nf., Can.	A4	72
Eastern Island, i., Mid. Is.	K4	52
Eastern Neck Island, i., Md., U.S.	B5	97
Eastern Point, c., Ma., U.S.	f13	98
Easterville, Mb., Can.	C2	70
East Fairfield, Vt., U.S.	B3	122
East Fairview, N.D., U.S.	B1	111
East Falmouth, Ma., U.S.	C6	98
East Farmington Heights, Ct., U.S.	C2	94
East Feliciana, co., La., U.S.	D4	95
East Flanders, prov., Bel.	C3	17
East Flat Rock, N.C., U.S.	f10	110
East Flevoland, reg., Neth.	C5	17
Eastford, Ct., U.S.	B7	84
East Fork, stm., Wy., U.S.	D3	127
East Fork Lake, l., Oh., U.S.	C1	112
East Foxboro, Ma., U.S.	B5	98
East Franklin, Vt., U.S.	B3	122
East Freetown, Ma., U.S.	C6	98
East Frisian Islands, is., F.R.Ger.	B3	18
East Fultonham, Oh., U.S.	C3	112
East Gaffney, S.C., U.S.	A4	117
East Galesburg, Il., U.S.	C3	90
East, stm., Ct., U.S.	D5	84
East Germany see German Democratic Republic, ctry., Eur.	B6	18
East Glacier Park, Mt., U.S.	B3	103
East Glastonbury, Ct., U.S.	C5	84
East Glenville, N.Y., U.S.	*C7	109
East Grafton, N.H., U.S.	C3	106
East Granby, Ct., U.S.	B5	84
East Grand Forks, Mn., U.S.	C2	100
East Grand Rapids, Mi., U.S.	F5	99
East Granville, Vt., U.S.	C3	122

Name	Map Ref	Page
East Greenville, Pa., U.S.	F10	115
East Greenwich, R.I., U.S.	D4	116
East Grinstead, Eng., U.K.	C8	12
East Haddam, Ct., U.S.	D6	84
East Half Hollow Hills, N.Y., U.S.	*n15	109
East Hampden, Me., U.S.	*D4	96
East Hampstead, N.H., U.S.	E4	106
East Hampton, Ct., U.S.	C5	84
Easthampton, Ma., U.S.	B2	98
East Hampton, N.Y., U.S.	n16	109
East Hanover, N.J., U.S.	*B4	107
East Hardwick, Vt., U.S.	B4	122
East Harpswell, Me., U.S.	g8	96
East Hartford, Ct., U.S.	B5	84
East Haven, Ct., U.S.	D4	84
East Haven, Vt., U.S.	B5	122
East Haverhill, N.H., U.S.	B3	106
East Hebron, N.H., U.S.	C3	106
East Helena, Mt., U.S.	D5	103
East Hickory, Pa., U.S.	C3	115
East Highgate, Vt., U.S.	B3	122
East Hills, N.Y., U.S.	*E7	109
East Holden, Me., U.S.	D4	96
East Holderness, N.H., U.S.	C3	106
East Islip, N.Y., U.S.	*n15	109
East Jordan, Mi., U.S.	C5	99
East Jordan, N.S., Can.	*F4	71
East Juliette, Ga., U.S.	C3	87
East Kelowna, B.C., Can.	E8	69
East Kilbride, Scot., U.K.	B8	84
East Killingly, Ct., U.S.	B8	84
East Kingston, N.H., U.S.	E4	106
Eastlake, Mi., U.S.	D4	99
East Lake, N.C., U.S.	B7	110
Eastlake, Oh., U.S.	A4	112
East Lake, l., On., Can.	C5	70
East Lake Tohopekaliga, l., Fl., U.S.	D5	86
Eastbrook, Me., U.S.	D4	96
East Landing, Mi., U.S.	F6	99
East Laport, Il., U.S.	f9	110
East Las Vegas, Nv., U.S.	G6	105
East Laurinburg, N.C., U.S.	C3	110
East Lebanon, Me., U.S.	E2	96
East Lempster, N.H., U.S.	D2	106
East Litchfield, Ct., U.S.	B3	84
East Livermore, Me., U.S.	D2	96
East Liverpool, Oh., U.S.	B5	112
East Loch Roag, b., Scot., U.K.	B2	13
East Loch Tarbert, b., Scot., U.K.	C2	13
East London (Oos-Londen), S. Afr.	D4	49
East Longmeadow, Ma., U.S.	B2	98
East Los Angeles, Ca., U.S.	m12	82
East Lyme, Ct., U.S.	D7	84
East Lynn, Il., U.S.	C6	90
East Lynn, W.V., U.S.	C2	125
East Lynne, Mo., U.S.	C3	102
East Machias, Me., U.S.	D5	96
East Madison, Me., U.S.	D3	96
Eastmain, P.Q., Can.	h11	74
Eastmain, stm., P.Q., Can.	F18	66
Eastmain-Opinaca, Réservoir, res., P.Q., Can.	h11	74
Eastman, P.Q., Can.	D5	74
Eastman, Ga., U.S.	D3	87
Eastman, Wi., U.S.	E2	126
East Mansfield, Ma., U.S.	B5	98
East Marion, Ma., U.S.	*C6	98
East Marion, N.Y., U.S.	*m16	109
East Matunuck, R.I., U.S.	F3	116
East Meadow, N.Y., U.S.	*n15	109
East Meredith, N.Y., U.S.	C6	109
East Middlebury, Vt., U.S.	D2	122
East Millbury, Ma., U.S.	B4	98
East Millinocket, Me., U.S.	C4	96
East Moline, Il., U.S.	B3	90
East Monroe, Oh., U.S.	C2	112
East Montpelier, Vt., U.S.	C4	122
East Naples, Fl., U.S.	F5	86
East Newark, N.J., U.S.	k8	107
East New Market, Md., U.S.	C6	97
East Newnan, Ga., U.S.	C2	87
East Newport, Me., U.S.	D3	96
East New Portland, Me., U.S.	D2	96
East Nishnabotna, stm., Ia., U.S.	C2	92
East Norriton, Pa., U.S.	o20	115
East Northport, N.Y., U.S.	*n15	109
East Olympia, Wa., U.S.	C3	124
Easton, Ct., U.S.	D2	84
Easton, Ks., U.S.	*k15	93
Easton, Me., U.S.	B5	96
Easton, Md., U.S.	C5	97
Easton, Mo., U.S.	B3	102
Easton, N.H., U.S.	B3	106
Easton, Pa., U.S.	E11	115
Easton, Wa., U.S.	B4	124
Eastondale, Ma., U.S.	B5	98
Easton Reservoir, res., Ct., U.S.	D2	84
East Orange, N.J., U.S.	B4	107
East Orange, Vt., U.S.	C4	122
East Orland, Me., U.S.	D4	96
East Orleans, Ma., U.S.	C8	98
East Otis, Ma., U.S.	B1	98
East Otto, N.Y., U.S.	C2	109
Eastover, S.C., U.S.	D6	117
East Palatka, Fl., U.S.	C5	86
East Palestine, Oh., U.S.	B5	112
East Palo Alto, Ca., U.S.	*D2	82
East Parsonfield, Me., U.S.	E2	96
East Pass, strt., Fl., U.S.	u16	86
East Patchogue, N.Y., U.S.	*n16	109
East Peacham, Vt., U.S.	C4	122
East Pea Ridge, W.V., U.S.	C2	125
East Peoria, Il., U.S.	C4	90
East Pepperell, Ma., U.S.	A4	98
East Peru, Me., U.S.	D2	96
East Petersburg, Pa., U.S.	F9	115
East Pine, B.C., Can.	B7	69
East Pittsburgh, Pa., U.S.	k14	115
Eastpoint, Fl., U.S.	C2	86
East Point, Ga., U.S.	C2	87
East Point, la., U.S.	m13	94
East Point, c., P.E., Can.	C8	71
East Point, c., Ma., U.S.	E2	98
East Point, c., N.J., U.S.	E2	107
East Point, c., V.I.U.S.	G7	64
East Poland, Me., U.S.	D2	96
East Poplar, Sk., Can.	H3	75

Name	Map Ref	Page
Eastport, Nf., Can.	D5	72
Eastport, Id., U.S.	A2	89
Eastport, Me., U.S.	D6	96
Eastport, N.Y., U.S.	n16	109
East Portal, Co., U.S.	B5	83
East Poultney, Vt., U.S.	D2	122
East Prairie, Mo., U.S.	E8	102
East Princeton, Ma., U.S.	B4	98
East Prospect, Pa., U.S.	G8	115
East Providence, R.I., U.S.	C4	116
East Pryor Mountain, mtn., Mt., U.S.	E8	103
East Randolph, N.Y., U.S.	C2	109
East Randolph, Vt., U.S.	D3	122
East Range, mts., Nv., U.S.	C4	105
East Retford, Eng., U.K.	A7	12
East Ridge, Tn., U.S.	h11	119
East Rindge, N.H., U.S.	E3	106
East River, Ct., U.S.	D5	84
East River Mountain, mts., U.S.	C1	123
East River Sheet Harbour, N.S., Can.	E7	71
East Rochester, N.Y., U.S.	B3	109
East Rockaway, N.Y., U.S.	*k13	109
East Rockingham, N.C., U.S.	C3	110
East Rutherford, N.J., U.S.	h8	107
East Ryegate, Vt., U.S.	C4	122
East Saint Johnsbury, Vt., U.S.	C5	122
East Saint Louis, Il., U.S.	E3	90
East Salt Creek, stm., Co., U.S.	B2	83
East Sandwich, Ma., U.S.	C7	98
East Sebago, Me., U.S.	E2	96
East Selkirk, Mb., Can.	D3	70
East Siberian Sea, Sov. Un.	B18	29
Eastside, Or., U.S.	D2	114
East Sioux Falls, S.D., U.S.	D9	118
East Smithfield, Pa., U.S.	C8	115
Eastsound, Wa., U.S.	A3	124
East Sparta, Oh., U.S.	B4	112
East Spencer, N.C., U.S.	B2	110
East Springfield, N.Y., U.S.	C6	109
East Stoneham, Me., U.S.	D2	96
East Stroudsburg, Pa., U.S.	D11	115
East Sudbury, Ma., U.S.	g10	98
East Sullivan, Me., U.S.	D4	96
East Sullivan, N.H., U.S.	E2	106
East Sumner, Me., U.S.	D2	96
East Sussex, co., Eng., U.K.	D7	12
East Swanzey, N.H., U.S.	E2	106
East Tawas, Mi., U.S.	D7	99
East Templeton, Ma., U.S.	A4	98
East Thermopolis, Wy., U.S.	*C4	127
East Thetford, Vt., U.S.	D4	122
East Thompson, Ct., U.S.	A8	84
East Trout Lake, l., Sk., Can.	C3	75
East Troy, Wi., U.S.	F5	126
East Tustin, Ca., U.S.	n13	82
East Unity, N.H., U.S.	D2	106
East Vestal, N.Y., U.S.	C5	109
East View, W.V., U.S.	k10	125
East Wakefield, N.H., U.S.	C4	106
East Walker, stm., U.S.	E2	105
East Wallingford, Vt., U.S.	E3	122
East Walpole, Ma., U.S.	h11	98
East Wareham, Ma., U.S.	C6	98
East Washington, Pa., U.S.	F1	115
East Waterboro, Me., U.S.	E2	96
East Waterford, Me., U.S.	D2	96
East Wenatchee, Wa., U.S.	B5	124
East Wilton, Me., U.S.	D2	96
East Windsor, N.J., U.S.	C3	107
East Windsor Hill, Ct., U.S.	B5	84
Eastwood, Ky., U.S.	g12	94
Eastwood, Eng., U.K.	*F5	99
Eastwood Hills, Ut., U.S.	C4	121
East Woodstock, Ct., U.S.	B8	84
East Worcester, N.Y., U.S.	C6	109
East York, On., Can.	D5	73
Eaton, Co., U.S.	A6	83
Eaton, Il., U.S.	D6	90
Eaton, In., U.S.	D7	91
Eaton, N.Y., U.S.	C5	109
Eaton, Oh., U.S.	C1	112
Eaton, Tn., U.S.	B2	119
Eaton, co., Mi., U.S.	F6	99
Eaton Center, N.H., U.S.	C4	106
Eatonia, Sk., Can.	F1	75
Eaton Rapids, Mi., U.S.	F6	99
Eatonton, Ga., U.S.	C3	87
Eatontown, N.J., U.S.	C4	107
Eatonville, Wa., U.S.	C3	124
Eau Claire, Wi., U.S.	D2	126
Eau Claire, co., Wi., U.S.	D2	126
Eau Claire, Lac à l', l., P.Q., Can.	g11	74
Eau Galle, Wi., U.S.	D1	126
Eauze, Fr.	F6	16
Ebadon Island, i., Marsh Is.	S17	52
Ebb and Flow Lake, l., Mb., Can.	D2	70
Ebbw Vale (Blaenau Gwent), Wales, U.K.	C4	12
Ebeleben, Ger.D.R.	B5	19
Ebeltoft, Den.	B4	15
Ebenezer, Ms., U.S.	C3	101
Eben Junction, Mi., U.S.	B4	99
Ebensburg, Pa., U.S.	F4	115
Eberbach, F.R.Ger.	F9	19
Ebermannstadt, F.R.Ger.	B9	19
Ebersbach, Ger.D.R.	B8	19
Ebersbach, F.R.Ger.	E5	19
Eberswald[-Finow], Ger.D.R.	B6	18
Ebetsu, Japan	E10	33
Ebeye, Marsh Is.	S17	52
Ebingen, F.R.Ger.	E5	19
Eboli, Italy	D2	24
Ebolowa, Cam.	u16	45
Ebro, Mn., U.S.	C3	100
Ebro, stm., Spain	B4	22
Eccles, W.V., U.S.	n13	125
Eceabat, Tur.	I12	25
Echague, Phil.	n13	34
Echallens, Switz.	C2	21
Ech Cheliff (Orléansville), Alg.	B5	44
Echeconnee Creek, stm., Ga., U.S.	D3	87
Echigawa, Japan	n15	33
Echo, Al., U.S.	D4	78
Echo, La., U.S.	C3	95
Echo, Mn., U.S.	F3	100
Echo, Or., U.S.	B7	114
Echo, Ut., U.S.	C4	121
Echo Bay, Nv., U.S.	G7	105
Echoing, stm., Can.	B6	70
Echoing Lake, l., On., Can.	B5	70

Name	Map Ref	Page
Echola, Al., U.S.	B2	78
Echo Lake, l., Me., U.S.	D3	96
Echo Lake, l., Vt., U.S.	B5	122
Echols, co., Ga., U.S.	F4	87
Echt, Neth.	C5	17
Echt, Scot., U.K.	C6	13
Echuca, Austl.	G7	50
Écija, Spain	D3	22
Eckelson, N.D., U.S.	C7	111
Eckerman, Mi., U.S.	B5	99
Eckernförde, F.R.Ger.	A4	18
Eckernförder Bucht, b., F.R.Ger.	D4	15
Eckerty, In., U.S.	H4	91
Eckhart Mines, Md., U.S.	k13	97
Eckley, Pa., U.S.	A8	83
Eckley, Co., U.S.	E10	115
Eckman, N.D., U.S.	A4	111
Eckman, W.V., U.S.	*D3	125
Eckville, Ab., Can.	C3	78
Eclectic, Al., U.S.	C1	123
Eclipse Sound, strt., N.T., Can.	B17	66
Econfina, stm., Fl., U.S.	B3	86
Economy, N.S., Can.	D6	71
Economy, In., U.S.	E7	91
Ecorces, Rivière aux, stm., P.Q., Can.	A6	74
Ecorse, Mi., U.S.	p15	99
Ecru, Ms., U.S.	A4	101
Ector, co., Tx., U.S.	D1	120
Ecuador, ctry., S.A.	B2	58
Ecum Secum, N.S., Can.	E7	71
Ecum Secum Bridge, N.S., Can.	E7	71
Ed, Eth.	C5	47
Ed, Swe.	H5	14
Edam, Sk., Can.	D1	75
Edam, Neth.	B5	17
Eday, i., Scot., U.K.	A6	13
Edberg, Ab., Can.	C4	68
Edcouch, Tx., U.S.	F4	120
Eddiceton, Ms., U.S.	D3	101
Eddington, Me., U.S.	D4	96
Eddrachillis Bay, b., Scot., U.K.	B3	13
Eddy, co., N.M., U.S.	E5	108
Eddy, co., N.D., U.S.	B7	111
Eddystone, Pa., U.S.	p20	115
Eddyville, Il., U.S.	F5	90
Eddyville, Ia., U.S.	C5	92
Eddyville, Ky., U.S.	e9	94
Eddyville, Ne., U.S.	C6	104
Ede, Neth.	B5	17
Ede, Nig.	G6	45
Edéa, Cam.	E2	46
Eden, Austl.	H7	51
Eden, Mb., Can.	D2	70
Eden, Az., U.S.	E6	80
Eden, Ga., U.S.	D5	87
Eden, Id., U.S.	G4	89
Eden, Me., U.S.	D4	96
Eden, Md., U.S.	D6	97
Eden, N.Y., U.S.	C2	109
Eden, N.C., U.S.	A3	110
Eden, S.D., U.S.	B8	118
Eden, Tx., U.S.	D3	120
Eden, Ut., U.S.	B4	121
Eden, Vt., U.S.	B3	122
Eden, Wi., U.S.	E5	126
Eden, Wy., U.S.	D3	127
Eden, stm., Eng., U.K.	C5	10
Edenborn, Pa., U.S.	G2	115
Edenderry, Ire.	D3	10
Eden Hill, hill, De., U.S.	D2	84
Eden Lake, l., Mb., Can.	A1	70
Eden Mills, Vt., U.S.	B3	122
Eden Prairie, Mn., U.S.	n12	100
Eden Valley, Mn., U.S.	E4	100
Edenville, Mi., U.S.	E6	99
Edenwold, Sk., Can.	G3	75
Eder, stm., F.R.Ger.	C4	18
Edgar, Mt., U.S.	B5	97
Edgar, Ne., U.S.	D8	104
Edgar, Wi., U.S.	D4	126
Edgar, co., Il., U.S.	D6	90
Edgard, La., U.S.	D5	95
Edgar Springs, Mo., U.S.	D6	102
Edge, i., Nor.	B12	128
Edgecombe, co., N.C., U.S.	B5	110
Edgecumbe, Cape, c., Ak., U.S.	m21	79
Edgefield, S.C., U.S.	D4	117
Edgefield, co., S.C., U.S.	D4	117
Edgeley, Sk., Can.	G4	75
Edgeley, N.D., U.S.	C7	111
Edgemere, Md., U.S.	B5	97
Edgemont, Ar., U.S.	*B3	81
Edgemont, S.D., U.S.	D2	118
Edgemont, De., U.S.	A3	85
Edgemoor, S.C., U.S.	B5	117
Edgemoor, Tn., U.S.	m13	119
Edgerly, La., U.S.	D2	95
Edgerton, Ab., Can.	C5	68
Edgerton, Ks., U.S.	D8	93
Edgerton, Mn., U.S.	G2	100
Edgerton, Mo., U.S.	B3	102
Edgerton, Oh., U.S.	A1	112
Edgerton, Wi., U.S.	F4	126
Edgerton, Wy., U.S.	C6	127
Edgewater, Al., U.S.	f7	78
Edgewater, Co., U.S.	*B5	83
Edgewater, Fl., U.S.	C6	86
Edgewater, Md., U.S.	C4	97
Edgewater, N.J., U.S.	h9	107
Edgewater Park, N.J., U.S.	C3	107
Edgewood, B.C., Can.	E8	69
Edgewood, Il., U.S.	E5	90
Edgewood, Ia., U.S.	B6	92
Edgewood, Ky., U.S.	h13	94
Edgewood, Md., U.S.	B5	97
Edgewood, N.M., U.S.	B3	108
Edgewood, Oh., U.S.	A5	112
Edgewood, Pa., U.S.	k14	115
Edgeworth, Pa., U.S.	h13	115
Edgigen Island, i., Marsh Is.	S17	52
Edina, Mo., U.S.	A5	102
Edina, Mn., U.S.	n12	100
Edinboro, Pa., U.S.	C1	115
Edinburg, Il., U.S.	D4	90
Edinburg, In., U.S.	F6	91
Edinburg, Ms., U.S.	C4	101
Edinburg, N.D., U.S.	A8	111
Edinburg, N.Y., U.S.	B6	109
Edinburg, Tx., U.S.	F3	120
Edinburg, Va., U.S.	B4	123
Edinburgh, Scot., U.K.	C5	10

Name	Map Ref	Page
Edinburgh, In., U.S.	F6	91
Edirne, Tur.	B6	40
Edison, Ga., U.S.	E2	87
Edison, Ne., U.S.	D6	104
Edison, N.J., U.S.	B4	107
Edison, Oh., U.S.	B3	112
Edison, Wa., U.S.	A3	124
Edisto, stm., S.C., U.S.	E6	117
Edisto, North Fork, stm., S.C., U.S.	D5	117
Edisto, South Fork, stm., S.C., U.S.	E5	117
Edisto Island, S.C., U.S.	F7	117
Edisto Island, i., S.C., U.S.	F7	117
Edith, Mount, mtn., Mt., U.S.	D5	103
Edithburgh, Austl.	G1	51
Edmeston, N.Y., U.S.	C5	109
Edmond, Ks., U.S.	C4	93
Edmond, Ok., U.S.	B4	113
Edmonds, Wa., U.S.	B3	124
Edmondson, Ar., U.S.	B5	81
Edmondson Heights, Md., U.S.	g10	97
Edmonson, co., Ky., U.S.	C3	94
Edmonton, Ab., Can.	C4	68
Edmonton, Ky., U.S.	D4	94
Edmore, Mi., U.S.	E5	99
Edmore, N.D., U.S.	A7	111
Edmund Lake, l., Mb., Can.	B5	70
Edmunds, co., S.D., U.S.	B6	118
Edmundston, N.B., Can.	B1	71
Edna, Ks., U.S.	E8	93
Edna, Tx., U.S.	E4	120
Edna, W.V., U.S.	h10	125
Edolo, Italy	D9	21
Edon, Oh., U.S.	A1	112
Édouard, Lac, l., P.Q., Can.	C5	74
Edremit, Tur.	C6	25
Edremit, Gulf of, b., Tur.	C6	25
Edson, Ab., Can.	C2	68
Edson, Ks., U.S.	C2	93
Edson Butte, mtn., Or., U.S.	E2	114
Eduardo Castex, Arg.	D4	56
Eduni, Mount, mtn., N.T., Can.	D7	66
Edwall, Wa., U.S.	B8	124
Edward, Ab., Can.	B4	68
Edward, Lake, l., Afr.	B4	48
Edwards, On., U.S.	h13	73
Edwards, Co., U.S.	B4	83
Edwards, Il., U.S.	C4	90
Edwards, Ms., U.S.	C3	101
Edwards, N.Y., U.S.	A5	109
Edwards, co., Il., U.S.	E5	90
Edwards, co., Ks., U.S.	E4	93
Edwards, co., Tx., U.S.	E2	120
Edwards Air Force Base, mil., Ca., U.S.	E5	82
Edwardsburg, Mi., U.S.	G4	99
Edwards Butte, mtn., Or., U.S.	B3	114
Edwards Plateau, plat., Tx., U.S.	D2	120
Edwardsport, In., U.S.	G3	91
Edwardsville, Al., U.S.	B4	78
Edwardsville, Il., U.S.	E4	90
Edwardsville, Ks., U.S.	k16	93
Edwardsville, Pa., U.S.	n17	115
Edward VIII Bay, b., Ant.	C18	7
Edward VII Peninsula, pen., Ant.	B33	7
Edwin, Al., U.S.	D4	78
Edzell, Scot., U.K.	D6	13
Eek, Ak., U.S.	C7	79
Eeklo, Bel.	C3	17
Eel, stm., Ca., U.S.	B2	82
Eel, stm., In., U.S.	C6	91
Eel, stm., In., U.S.	F3	91
Eferding, Aus.	D7	18
Effie, Ca., U.S.	C3	95
Effie, Mn., U.S.	C5	100
Effigy Mounds National Monument, Ia., U.S.	A6	92
Effingham, Il., U.S.	D5	90
Effingham, Ks., U.S.	C8	93
Effingham, N.H., U.S.	C5	106
Effingham, S.C., U.S.	C8	117
Effingham, co., Ga., U.S.	D5	87
Effingham, co., Il., U.S.	D5	90
Effingham Falls, N.H., U.S.	C4	106
Efland, N.C., U.S.	A3	110
Eforie Nord, Rom.	C9	24
Eforie Sud (Vasile Roaită), Rom.	C9	24
Ega, stm., Spain	A4	22
Egadi Islands, is., Italy	E4	23
Egan, S.D., U.S.	D9	118
Egan Range, mts., Nv., U.S.	E7	105
Eganville, On., Can.	B7	73
Egbert, Wy., U.S.	E8	127
Egegik, Ak., U.S.	D8	79
Egeland, N.D., U.S.	A6	111
Egeln, Ger.D.R.	B6	19
Eger, Hung.	B5	24
Egersund, Nor.	H2	14
Egerton, Mount, mtn., Ant.	A28	7
Eggebek, F.R.Ger.	D3	15
Eggenfelden, F.R.Ger.	E7	19
Egg Harbor, Wi., U.S.	C6	126
Egg Harbor City, N.J., U.S.	D3	107
Egg Island Point, c., N.J., U.S.	E2	107
Egg Lake, l., Sk., Can.	C3	75
Egilsstadir, Ice.	n25	14
Égletons, Fr.	E8	16
Eglin Air Force Base, mil., Fl., U.S.	u15	86
Eglinton Island, i., N.T., Can.	m28	66
Eglisau, Switz.	A6	21
Egmond aan Zee, Neth.	B4	17
Egmont, Cape, c., N.Z.	M14	51
Egmont, Mount, mtn., N.Z.	M15	51
Egmont Bay, b., P.E., Can.	C5	71
Egmont Channel, strt., Fl., U.S.	p10	86
Egmont Key, i., Fl., U.S.	p10	86
Egnar, Co., U.S.	D2	83
Egremont, Ab., Can.	B4	68
Egremont, Eng., U.K.	F5	13
Eğridir, Tur.	D8	40
Eğridir Gölü, l., Tur.	C8	40
Egrigoz, mtn., Tur.	C7	25
Egtved, Den.	C3	15
Egypt, Ar., U.S.	B5	81
Egypt, Ga., U.S.	D5	87
Egypt, Ma., U.S.	B6	98
Egypt, Ms., U.S.	B5	101
Egypt, ctry., Afr.	C2	38
Egypt, Lake of, res., Il., U.S.	F5	90
Ehrenberg, Az., U.S.	D1	80
Ehrenfeld, Pa., U.S.	F4	115
Ehrhardt, S.C., U.S.	E5	117
Eibar, Spain	B4	22
Eibau, Ger.D.R.	C9	19
Eibenstock, Ger.D.R.	C7	19
Eichstätt, F.R.Ger.	D5	18
Eider, stm., F.R.Ger.	A4	18
Eidsberg, Nor.	H4	14
Eidson, Tn., U.S.	C10	119
Eidsvold, Austl.	E9	50
Eidsvoll, Nor.	G4	14
Eielson Air Force Base, mil., Ak., U.S.	C10	79
Eifel, mts., F.R.Ger.	C3	18
Eige, Càrn, mtn., Scot., U.K.	C3	13
Eigg, i., Scot., U.K.	B3	10
Eigg, Sound of, strt., Scot., U.K.	D2	13
Eightmile Creek, stm., Ks., U.S.	h12	93
Eights Coast, Ant.	B3	7
Eighty Eight, Ky., U.S.	D4	94
Eikeren, l., Nor.	p28	14
Eildon, Lake, res., Austl.	H6	51
Eileen Lake, l., N.T., Can.	D11	66
Eilenburg, Ger.D.R.	C6	18
Eiler Rasmussen, Cape, c., Grnld.	A16	128
Eil Malk, i., Palau	R17	52
Einbeck, F.R.Ger.	C4	18
Eindhoven, Neth.	B6	16
Einsiedeln, Switz.	B4	20
Eirunepé, Braz.	C4	58
Eisenach, Ger.D.R.	C5	18
Eisenberg, Ger.D.R.	C6	19
Eisenhower, Mount, mtn., N.H., U.S.	B4	106
Eisenhüttenstadt, Ger.D.R.	B7	18
Eisenstadt, Aus.	E8	18
Eiserfeld, F.R.Ger.	C2	19
Eisfeld, Ger.D.R.	C5	18
Eisleben, Ger.D.R.	C6	18
Eita, Kir.	R18	52
Eita, i., Kir.	R18	52
Eitorf, F.R.Ger.	C2	19
Eitzen, Mn., U.S.	G7	100
Ejby, Den.	C3	15
Ejea de los Caballeros, Spain	A5	22
Ejeda, Madag.	h8	49
Ejstrup, Den.	C3	15
Ejutla de Crespo, Mex.	D5	63
Ekalaka, Mt., U.S.	E12	103
Ekenäs, Fin.	G10	14
Ekeren, Bel.	C4	17
Ekhínos, Grc.	B5	25
Ekimchan, Sov. Un.	D16	29
Ekôln, i., Swe.	t35	14
Ekron, Ky., U.S.	C3	94
Eksjö, Swe.	I6	14
Ekumakoko, Zaire	B3	48
Ekwan, stm., On., Can.	F15	66
Ekwok, Ak., U.S.	D8	79
El Aaiún, W. Sah.	D2	44
Elaine, Ar., U.S.	C5	81
Elamanchili, India	I9	37
Elamton, Ky., U.S.	C6	94
Elamville, Al., U.S.	D4	78
Eland, Wi., U.S.	D4	126
El Arahal, Spain	D3	22
Elassón, Grc.	C4	25
Elat, Isr.	E6	41
Elâziğ, Tur.	C12	40
Elba, Al., U.S.	D3	78
Elba, Al., U.S.	G5	89
Elba, Mn., U.S.	F6	100
Elba, Ne., U.S.	C7	104
Elba, N.Y., U.S.	B2	109
Elba, i., Italy	C3	23
El Banco, Col.	B3	60
El Barco [de Avila], Spain	A2	22
Elbasani, Alb.	B3	40
El Baúl, Ven.	B4	60
Elbe (Labe), stm., Eur.	B4	18
Elberfeld, In., U.S.	H3	91
Elberon, Ia., U.S.	B5	92
Elbert, Co., U.S.	B6	83
Elbert, Tx., U.S.	C3	120
Elbert, co., Ga., U.S.	B4	87
Elbert, Mount, mtn., Co., U.S.	B4	83
Elberta, Al., U.S.	E2	78
Elberta, Ga., U.S.	D3	87
Elberta, Mi., U.S.	D4	99
Elberta, Ut., U.S.	D4	121
Elberton, Ga., U.S.	B4	87
Elbeuf, Fr.	C8	16
El Beyyadh, Alg.	C5	44
Elbing, Pol.	A5	26
Elbistan, Tur.	C11	40
Elblag, Pol.	A5	26
El Bluff, Nic.	E8	63
El Bolsón, Arg.	E2	54
El Bonillo, Spain	C4	22
El Bordo, Col.	C2	60
El Boulaïda (Blida), Alg.	B5	44
Elbow, Sk., Can.	F2	75
Elbow, stm., Ab., Can.	D3	68
Elbow Lake, Mn., U.S.	E3	100
Elbow Lake, l., Mb., Can.	B3	101
Elbridge, Tn., U.S.	A2	119
Elbrus, Mount, mtn., Sov. Un.	E7	29
Elburg, Neth.	B5	17
El Burgo de Osma, Spain	B4	22
Elburn, Il., U.S.	B5	90
Elburz Mountains, mts., Iran	B5	38
El Cajon, Ca., U.S.	F5	82
El Callao, Ven.	B5	60
El Campo, Tx., U.S.	E4	120
El Capitan, mtn., Mt., U.S.	D2	103
El Capitan Reservoir, res., Ca., U.S.	o16	82
El Carmen, Bol.	C4	55
El Carmen de Bolívar, Col.	C4	60
El Carrizo, Mex.	B3	63
El Cerrito, Ca., U.S.	h8	82
El Centro, Ca., U.S.	F6	82
El Cerro, Bol.	C5	55
El Chaparro, Ven.	B4	60
Elche, Spain	C5	22
Elcho, Wi., U.S.	C4	126
Elco, Il., U.S.	F4	90
El Cocuy, Col.	B3	60
El Cuervo Butte, mtn., N.M., U.S.	k9	108
Elda, Spain	C5	22
Elde, stm., Ger.D.R.	B5	18
Elderon, Wi., U.S.	D4	126
Eldersley, Sk., Can.	E4	75
Elderton, Pa., U.S.	E3	115
El Diviso, Col.	C2	60
El Djelfa, Alg.	B5	44
El Djouf, des., Afr.	B3	45
Eldon, P.E., Can.	C7	71
Eldon, Ia., U.S.	D5	92
Eldon, Mo., U.S.	C5	102
Eldora, Ia., U.S.	B4	92
Eldorado, Braz.	C7	56
Eldorado, On., Can.	C7	73
Eldorado, Sk., Can.	m7	75
Eldorado, Mex.	C3	63
El Dorado, Ar., U.S.	D3	81
Eldorado, Ga., U.S.	E3	87
Eldorado, Il., U.S.	F5	90
El Dorado, Ks., U.S.	E7	93
Eldorado, Md., U.S.	C6	97
Eldorado, N.C., U.S.	B2	110
Eldorado, Oh., U.S.	C1	112
Eldorado, Ok., U.S.	C2	113
Eldorado, Tx., U.S.	D2	120
El Dorado, Ven.	B5	60
El Dorado, co., Ca., U.S.	C3	82
Eldorado Peak, mtn., Wa., U.S.	A4	124
Eldorado Springs, Co., U.S.	B5	83
Eldorado Springs, Mc., U.S.	D3	102
Eldorendo, Ga., U.S.	E2	87
Eldred, Il., U.S.	D3	90
Eldred, Mn., U.S.	C2	100
Eldred, Pa., U.S.	C5	115
Eldridge, Al., U.S.	B2	78
Eldridge, Ia., U.S.	C7	92
Eldridge, Mo., U.S.	D5	102
Eldridge, N.D., U.S.	C7	111
Eleanor, W.V., U.S.	C3	125
Electra, Tx., U.S.	B3	120
Electric Mills, Ms., U.S.	C5	101
Electric Peak, mtn., Co., U.S.	C5	83
Electric Peak, mtn., Mt., U.S.	E6	103
Elektrogorsk, Sov. Un.	n18	27
Elektrostal, Sov. Un.	n18	27
El Encanto, Col.	C5	58
El Encanto Heights, Ca., U.S.	*E4	82
Elephant Butte, mtn., N.M., U.S.	D2	108
Elephant Butte Reservoir, res., N.M., U.S.	D2	108
Elephant Island, i., B.A.T.	C7	7
Elephant Mountain, mtn., Me., U.S.	D2	96
Eleuthera, i., Bah.	B5	64
Eleva, Wi., U.S.	D2	126
Eleven Mile Canyon Reservoir, res., Co., U.S.	C5	83
Eleven Point, stm., U.S.	A4	81
Elevsís (Eleusis), Grc.	g11	25
Elevsís, Gulf of, b., Grc.	g11	25
El Escorial, Spain	o16	22
El Eulma, Alg.	B6	44
Eleusis see Elevsís, Grc.	g11	25
Elfin Cove, Ak., U.S.	k21	79
Elfrida, Az., U.S.	F6	80
Elfros, Sk., Can.	F4	75
El Fud, Eth.	D5	47
El Fuerte, Mex.	B3	63
El Galhak, Sud.	C3	47
El Ghazawet, Alg.	B4	44
Elgin, Mb., Can.	E1	70
Elgin, N.B., Can.	D4	71
Elgin, Scot., U.K.	B5	10
Elgin, Al., U.S.	A2	78
Elgin, Az., U.S.	F5	80
Elgin, Il., U.S.	A5	90
Elgin, Ia., U.S.	B6	92
Elgin, Ks., U.S.	E7	93
Elgin, Mn., U.S.	F6	100
Elgin, Ne., U.S.	C7	104
Elgin, N.D., U.S.	C4	111
Elgin, Ok., U.S.	C3	113
Elgin, Or., U.S.	B9	114
Elgin, Pa., U.S.	C2	115
Elgin, S.C., U.S.	B6	117
Elgin, Tx., U.S.	D4	120
Elgin, co., On., Can.	E3	73
Elgon, Mount, mtn., Afr.	A5	48
El Grara, Alg.	C5	44
El Grullo, Mex.	n11	63
El Huecú, Arg.	B2	54
Eli, Ne., U.S.	B4	104
Eliasville, Tx., U.S.	C3	120
Elida, N.M., U.S.	D6	108
Elida, Oh., U.S.	B1	112
Elikón Óros (Helicon), mtn., Grc.	g9	25
Elila, stm., Zaire	B4	48
Elim, Ak., U.S.	C7	79
El Indio, Tx., U.S.	E2	120
Eliot, Me., U.S.	E2	96
Elisabethville see Lubumbashi, Zaire	D4	48
Elista, Sov. Un.	H15	27
Elizabeth, Austl.	F6	50
Elizabeth, Ar., U.S.	A3	81
Elizabeth, Co., U.S.	B6	83
Elizabeth, Il., U.S.	A3	90
Elizabeth, In., U.S.	H6	91
Elizabeth, La., U.S.	D3	95
Elizabeth, Mn., U.S.	D2	100
Elizabeth, N.J., U.S.	B4	107
Elizabeth, W.V., U.S.	B3	125
Elizabeth, Cape, c., Wa., U.S.	B1	124
Elizabeth City, N.C., U.S.	A6	110
Elizabeth Islands, is., Ma., U.S.	D6	98
Elizabethton, Tn., U.S.	C11	119
Elizabethtown, Il., U.S.	F5	90
Elizabethtown, In., U.S.	F6	91
Elizabethtown, Ky., U.S.	C4	94
Elizabethtown, N.Y., U.S.	A7	109
Elizabethtown, N.C., U.S.	C4	110
Elizabethtown, Pa., U.S.	F8	115
Elizabethville, Pa., U.S.	E8	115
El Jadida, Mor.	C3	44
Elk, Wa., U.S.	A8	124
Elk, Pol.	B7	26
Elk, co., Ks., U.S.	E7	93
Elk, co., Pa., U.S.	D4	115
Elk, stm., B.C., Can.	D10	69
Elk, stm., U.S.	A2	78
Elk, stm., Co., U.S.	A4	83
Elk, stm., Ks., U.S.	E7	93
Elk, stm., W.V., U.S.	C3	125
Elk, stm., Wi., U.S.	C3	126
Elk City, Id., U.S.	D3	89
Elk City, Ks., U.S.	E7	93
Elk City, Ne., U.S.	g12	104
Elk City, Ok., U.S.	B2	113
Elk City Lake, res., Ks., U.S.	E7	93
Elk Creek, Ne., U.S.	D9	104
Elk Creek, stm., Ok., U.S.	B2	113
Elk Creek, stm., S.D., U.S.	C3	118
El Kef, Tun.	B6	44
El Kere, Eth.	D5	47
Elk Falls, Ks., U.S.	E7	93
Elk Garden, W.V., U.S.	B5	125
Elk Grove, Ca., U.S.	C3	82
Elk Grove Village, Il., U.S.	h9	90
Elkhart, Il., U.S.	C4	90
Elkhart, In., U.S.	A6	91
Elkhart, Ia., U.S.	e8	92
Elkhart, Ks., U.S.	E2	93
Elkhart, Tx., U.S.	D5	120
Elkhart, co., In., U.S.	A6	91
Elkhart, Lake, Wi., U.S.	E5	126
Elkhead Mountains, mts., Co., U.S.	A8	83
Elkhorn, Mb., Can.	E1	70
Elkhorn, Ne., U.S.	g12	104
Elkhorn, Wi., U.S.	F5	126
Elkhorn, co., Ne., U.S.	B7	104
Elkhorn, North Fork, stm., Ne., U.S.	B8	104
Elkhorn, South Fork, stm., Ne., U.S.	B7	104
Elkhorn City, Ky., U.S.	C7	94
Elkhorn Peaks, mts., Id., U.S.	F7	89
Elkhovo, Bul.	D8	24
Elkin, N.C., U.S.	A2	110
Elkins, Ar., U.S.	A1	81
Elkins, N.H., U.S.	D3	106
Elkins, W.V., U.S.	C5	125
Elkins Park, Pa., U.S.	F11	115
Elk Island, i., Mb., Can.	D3	70
Elk Island National Park, Ab., Can.	C4	68
Elkland, Mo., U.S.	D4	102
Elkland, Pa., U.S.	C7	115
Elk Mills, Md., U.S.	A6	97
Elkmont, Al., U.S.	A3	78
Elkmont, Tn., U.S.	D10	119
Elk Mound, Wi., U.S.	D2	126
Elk Mountain, Wy., U.S.	E6	127
Elk Mountain, mtn., N.M., U.S.	D1	108
Elk Mountain, mtn., Wy., U.S.	E6	127
Elk Mountains, mts., Co., U.S.	B3	83
Elko, B.C., Can.	E10	69
Elko, Ga., U.S.	D3	87
Elko, Nv., U.S.	C6	105
Elko, S.C., U.S.	E5	117
Elko, co., Nv., U.S.	B6	105
Elk Park, N.C., U.S.	A1	110
Elk Peak, mtn., Mt., U.S.	D6	103
Elk Point, Ab., Can.	C5	68
Elk Point, S.D., U.S.	E9	118
Elk Ranch, Ar., U.S.	A2	81
Elk Rapids, Mi., U.S.	D5	99
Elkridge, Md., U.S.	B4	97
Elkridge, W.V., U.S.	m13	125
Elk River, Id., U.S.	C2	89
Elk River, Mn., U.S.	E5	100
Elk Springs, Co., U.S.	A2	83
Elkton, Fl., U.S.	C5	86
Elkton, Ky., U.S.	D2	94
Elkton, Md., U.S.	A6	97
Elkton, Mi., U.S.	E7	99
Elkton, Or., U.S.	D3	114
Elkton, S.D., U.S.	C9	118
Elkton, Tn., U.S.	B5	119
Elkton, Va., U.S.	B4	123
Elk Valley, Tn., U.S.	C9	119
Elkview, W.V., U.S.	m13	125
Elkville, Il., U.S.	F4	90
Ellaville, Ga., U.S.	D2	87
Ellamore, W.V., U.S.	C4	125
Ellef Ringnes Island, i., N.T., Can.	m31	66
Ellen, Mount, mtn., Ut., U.S.	E5	121
Ellen, Mount, mtn., Vt., U.S.	C3	122
Ellenboro, N.C., U.S.	B1	110
Ellenboro, W.V., U.S.	B3	125
Ellenburg Center, N.Y., U.S.	f11	109
Ellendale, De., U.S.	E4	85
Ellendale, Mn., U.S.	G5	100
Ellendale, N.D., U.S.	C7	111
Ellensburg, Wa., U.S.	C5	124
Ellenton, Fl., U.S.	E4	86
Ellenton, Ga., U.S.	E3	87
Ellenville, N.Y., U.S.	D6	109
Ellerbe, N.C., U.S.	B3	110
Ellershouse, N.S., Can.	E6	71
Ellerslie, Ga., U.S.	D2	87
Ellerslie, Md., U.S.	k13	97
Ellesmere Island, i., N.T., Can.	m35	66
Ellesmere Port, Eng., U.K.	A5	12
Ellettsville, In., U.S.	F4	91
Ellice Islands see Tuvalu, ctry., Oc.	G10	6
Ellicott City, Md., U.S.	B4	97
Ellicottville, N.Y., U.S.	C2	109
Ellijay, Ga., U.S.	B2	87
Ellington, Mo., U.S.	D7	102
Ellington, Ct., U.S.	B6	84
Ellinwood, Ks., U.S.	D5	93
Elliot, S. Afr.	H5	49
Elliot Lake, On., Can.	A2	73
Elliot Lake, l., On., Can.	A2	73
Elliott, Il., U.S.	C5	90
Elliott, Ms., U.S.	B4	101
Elliott, N.D., U.S.	C7	111
Elliott, S.C., U.S.	C7	117
Elliott, co., Ky., U.S.	B6	94
Elliott Bay, b., Wa., U.S.	e11	124
Elliott Key, i., Fl., U.S.	G6	86
Elliotts Knob, mtn., Va., U.S.	B3	123
Elliston, Nf., Can.	D5	72
Elliston, Mt., U.S.	D4	103
Elliston, Va., U.S.	C2	123
Ellisville, Il., U.S.	C3	90
Ellisville, Ms., U.S.	D4	101
Ellisville, Mo., U.S.	f12	102
Ellon, Scot., U.K.	B5	10
Ellore see Elūru, India	E7	36
Elloree, S.C., U.S.	D6	117
Ellport, Pa., U.S.	E1	115
Ellrich, Ger.D.R.	B5	19
Ells, stm., Ab., Can.	A4	68
Ellscott, Ab., Can.	B4	68
Ellsinore, Mo., U.S.	E7	102
Ellston, Ia., U.S.	D3	92
Ellsworth, Il., U.S.	C5	90
Ellsworth, Ia., U.S.	B4	92
Ellsworth, Ks., U.S.	D5	93
Ellsworth, Me., U.S.	D4	96
Ellsworth, Mi., U.S.	C5	99
Ellsworth, Pa., U.S.	F1	115
Ellsworth, Wi., U.S.	D1	126
Ellsworth, co., Ks., U.S.	D5	93
Ellsworth Air Force Base, mil., S.D., U.S.	C2	118
Ellsworth Hill, mtn., Ct., U.S.	*D3	84
Ellsworth Land, reg., Ant.	B4	7
Ellsworth Mountains, mts., Ant.	B4	7
Ellwangen, F.R.Ger.	D5	18
Ellwood City, Pa., U.S.	E1	115
Elma, Ia., U.S.	A5	92
Elma, Wa., U.S.	B2	124
Elma Center, N.Y., U.S.	C2	109
Elmali, Tur.	D7	25
El Manteco, Ven.	B5	60
Elm Creek, Mb., Can.	E2	70
Elm Creek, Ne., U.S.	D6	104
Elm Creek, stm., Mn., U.S.	G4	100
Elmdale, Ks., U.S.	D7	93
Elmendorf, Tx., U.S.	k7	120
Eimendorf Air Force Base, mil., Ak., U.S.	C10	79
El Menia, Alg.	C5	44
Elmer, Mo., U.S.	B5	102
Elmer, N.J., U.S.	D2	107
Elmer, Ok., U.S.	C2	113
El Metlaoui, Tun.	C6	44
El Mghayyar, Alg.	C6	44
Elm Grove, La., U.S.	B2	95
Elm Grove, Wi., U.S.	m11	126
Elmhurst, Il., U.S.	B6	90
Elmhurst, Pa., U.S.	D10	115
El Milagro, Arg.	A3	54
Elmira, On., Can.	D4	73
Elmira, P.E., Can.	C7	71
Elmira, In., U.S.	A7	91
Elmira, Mi., U.S.	C6	99
Elmira, N.Y., U.S.	C4	109
Elmira, W.V., U.S.	C4	125
Elmira Heights, N.Y., U.S.	C4	109
Elmo, Mo., U.S.	A2	102
Elmo, Ut., U.S.	D5	121
Elmodel, Ga., U.S.	E2	87
El Moknine, Tun.	B7	44
Elmont, Ks., U.S.	k14	93
Elmont, N.Y., U.S.	k13	109
Elmont, Va., U.S.	C5	123
El Monte, Ca., U.S.	*E4	82
Elmora, Pa., U.S.	E4	115
Elmore, Al., U.S.	C3	78
Elmore, Mn., U.S.	G4	100
Elmore, Oh., U.S.	A2	112
Elmore, co., Al., U.S.	C3	78
Elmore, co., Id., U.S.	F3	89
Elmore City, Ok., U.S.	C4	113
El Morro National Monument, N.M., U.S.	B1	108
El Mreiti, well, Maur.	B3	45
Elmsdale, N.S., Can.	E6	71
Elmshorn, F.R.Ger.	B4	18
Elm Springs, Ar., U.S.	A1	81
Elm Springs, S.D., U.S.	C3	118
Elm Springs Colony, S.D., U.S.	D8	118
Elmsvale, N.B., Can.	D3	71
Elmvale, On., Can.	C5	73
Elmwood, Ct., U.S.	B4	84
Elmwood, Il., U.S.	C4	90
Elmwood, Ne., U.S.	D9	104
Elmwood, Ok., U.S.	A1	113
Elmwood, Wi., U.S.	D1	126
Elmwood Park, Il., U.S.	k9	90
Elmwood Park, N.J., U.S.	h8	107
Elmwood Place, Oh., U.S.	o13	112
Elna, Ky., U.S.	C7	94
Elne, Fr.	F5	16
Elnora, Ab., Can.	D4	68
Elnora, In., U.S.	G3	91
El Nevado, Cerro, mtn., Arg.	B2	54
El Obeid (Al Ubayyiḍ), Sud.	C3	47
Elon College, N.C., U.S.	A3	110
Elora, On., Can.	D4	73
Elora, Tn., U.S.	B5	119
El Oro, Arg.	B2	54
Elorza, Ven.	B4	60
El Oso, Ven.	D8	60
Eloy, Az., U.S.	E4	80
El Palmar, Mex.	B3	63
El Palmito, Mex.	D6	63
El Pao, Ven.	B5	60
El Paraíso, Hond.	D4	62
El Pardo, Spain	o17	22
El Paso, Ar., U.S.	B3	81
El Paso, Il., U.S.	C4	90
El Paso, Tx., U.S.	o11	120
El Paso, co., Co., U.S.	C6	83
El Paso, co., Tx., U.S.	o11	120
Elphinstone, Mb., Can.	D1	70
El Pital, Cerro, mtn., N.A.	*C3	62
El Portal, Ca., U.S.	D4	82
El Portal, Fl., U.S.	s13	86
El Porvenir, N.M., U.S.	B4	108
El Prado, N.M., U.S.	A4	108
El Progreso, Ec.	g6	58
El Progreso, Hond.	C4	62
El Puerto de Santa María, Spain	D2	22
El Qoll, Alg.	B6	44
Elqui, stm., Chile	F1	55
Elrama, Pa., U.S.	F2	115
El Real, Pan.	F9	62
El Reno, Ok., U.S.	B4	113
El Rio, Ca., U.S.	E4	82
El Rito, N.M., U.S.	A3	108
Elrod, Al., U.S.	B2	78
Elrosa, Mn., U.S.	E4	100
Elrose, Sk., Can.	F1	75
Elroy, Wi., U.S.	E3	126
Elsa, Yk., Can.	D5	66
Elsa, Tx., U.S.	F4	120
Elsah, Il., U.S.	E3	90
El Salto, Mex.	C3	63
El Salvador, ctry., N.A.	E7	63
El Samán de Apure, Ven.	B4	60
El Sauce, Nic.	E7	63
Elsberry, Mo., U.S.	B7	102
El Segundo, Ca., U.S.	*n12	82
El Seibo, Dom. Rep.	E9	64
Elsie, Mi., U.S.	E6	99
Elsie, Ne., U.S.	D4	104
Elsinore see Helsingør, Den.	I5	14
Elsinore, Ky., U.S.	B5	94
Elsinore, Ut., U.S.	E3	121
Elsmere, De., U.S.	B3	85
Elsmere, Ky., U.S.	B5	94
Elsmere, Ne., U.S.	B5	104
Elsmore, Ks., U.S.	E8	93
El Sobrante, Ca., U.S.	*h8	82
El Sombrero, Ven.	B4	60
Elsterwerda, Ger.D.R.	C6	18
Elstow, Sk., Can.	F2	75
El Tarf, Alg.	F2	23
El Tigre, Ven.	B5	60
El Tocuyo, Ven.	B4	60
Elton, La., U.S.	D3	95
Elton, Wi., U.S.	C5	126
Eltopia, Wa., U.S.	C6	124
El Toro, Ca., U.S.	*n13	82
El Toro Marine Corps Air Station, mil., Ca., U.S.	n13	82
El Tránsito, Chile	E1	55
El Trapiche, Col.	C2	60
El Triunfo, Hond.	D4	62
El Triunfo, Mex.	C2	63
El Tucuche, mtn., Trin.	N23	65
El Turbio, Arg.	E2	54
Eltville, F.R.Ger.	C3	19
Elūru (Ellore), India	E7	36
Elva, Mb., Can.	E1	70
El Vado Reservoir, res., N.M., U.S.	A3	108
El Valle, Pan.	F7	62
El Valle, N.M., U.S.	*A4	108
Elvas, Port.	C2	22
Elvaston, Il., U.S.	C2	90
Elverson, Pa., U.S.	F10	115
Elverum, Nor.	G4	14
El Viejo, Nic.	D4	62
El Viejo, Cerro, mtn., Col.	B3	60
El Vigía, Ven.	B3	60
Elvins, Mo., U.S.	D7	102
El Volcán, Chile	A2	54
El Wad, Alg.	C6	44
El Wak, Kenya	A7	48
Elwell, Lake, res., Mt., U.S.	B5	103
Elwha, stm., Wa., U.S.	A2	124
Elwood, In., U.S.	D6	91
Elwood, Ks., U.S.	C9	93
Elwood, Ne., U.S.	D6	104
Elwood, N.J., U.S.	D3	107
Elwood, N.Y., U.S.	*n15	109
Elwood, Ut., U.S.	*B3	121
Elwood Park, Fl., U.S.	E4	86
Ely, Eng., U.K.	D7	10
Ely, Ia., U.S.	C6	92
Ely, Mn., U.S.	C7	100
Ely, Nv., U.S.	D7	105
Ely, Vt., U.S.	D4	122
Elyria, Ks., U.S.	D6	93
Elyria, Oh., U.S.	A3	112
Elysburg, Pa., U.S.	E8	115
Elysian, Mn., U.S.	F5	100
El Yunque, mtn., P.R.	B4	65
Elzach, F.R.Ger.	A2	20
Emämshahr (Shährūd), Iran	B5	38
Emanuel, co., Ga., U.S.	D4	87
Emba, Sov. Un.	D5	28
Emba, stm., Sov. Un.	D5	28
Embarcación, Arg.	D3	55
Embarrass, Mn., U.S.	C6	100
Embarrass, Wi., U.S.	D5	126
Embarrass, stm., Il., U.S.	D6	90
Embarrass, stm., Wi., U.S.	D5	126
Embden Pond, l., Me., U.S.	D3	96
Embetsu, Japan	D10	33
Embira, stm., Braz.	C3	58
Emblem, Wy., U.S.	B4	127
Embreeville, Tn., U.S.	C11	119
Embrun, On., Can.	B9	73
Embrun, Fr.	E7	16
Embu, Kenya	B6	48
Embudo, N.M., U.S.	A4	108
Emden, F.R.Ger.	B3	18
Emden, Il., U.S.	C4	90
Emden, Mo., U.S.	B6	102
Emerald, Austl.	D9	50
Emerald, N.D., U.S.	B8	111
Emerald, *D9	104	
Emerson, Mb., Can.	E3	70
Emerson, Ga., U.S.	B2	87
Emerson, Ia., U.S.	D2	92
Emerson, Ne., U.S.	B9	104
Emerson, N.J., U.S.	h8	107
Emery, S.D., U.S.	D8	118
Emery, Ut., U.S.	E4	121
Emery, co., Ut., U.S.	E5	121
Emery Mills, Me., U.S.	E2	96
Emet, Tur.	C7	25
Emida, Id., U.S.	B2	89
Emigrant, Mt., U.S.	E6	103
Emigrant Gap, Ca., U.S.	C3	82
Emiliano Zapata, Mex.	D6	63
Emilia-Romagna, prov., Italy	E6	20
Emilia-Romagna, hist reg., Italy	B3	23
Emily, Mn., U.S.	D5	100
Emily, Lake, l., Mn., U.S.	E3	100
Emine, Cape, c., Bul.	F4	91
Eminence, Ky., U.S.	B4	94
Eminence, Mo., U.S.	D6	102
Emirau, i., Pap. N. Gui.	h13	50
Emirdağ, Tur.	C8	40
Emison, Il., U.S.	G3	91
Emlenton, Pa., U.S.	D2	115
Emlichheim, F.R.Ger.	C3	18
Emlyn, Ky., U.S.	D5	94
Emma, Mo., U.S.	C4	102
Emma Lake, l., Sk., Can.	D2	75
Emmaus, Pa., U.S.	E11	115
Emmeline Lake, l., Sk., Can.	C2	75
Emmen, Neth.	A7	16
Emmen, Switz.	B5	21
Emmendingen, F.R.Ger.	A2	20
Emmerich, F.R.Ger.	C3	18

Name	Map Ref	Page
Emmet, Ar., U.S.	D2	81
Emmet, Ne., U.S.	B7	104
Emmet, N.D., U.S.	B4	111
Emmet, co., Ia., U.S.	A3	92
Emmet, co., Mi., U.S.	C6	99
Emmetsburg, Ia., U.S.	A3	92
Emmett, Id., U.S.	F2	89
Emmett, Ks., U.S.	C7	93
Emmett, Mi., U.S.	E8	99
Emmitsburg, Md., U.S.	A3	97
Emmonak, Ak., U.S.	C7	79
Emmons, Mn., U.S.	G5	100
Emmons, co., N.D., U.S.	C5	111
Emms, stm., Aus.	D7	18
Emory, Tx., U.S.	E5	120
Emory Peak, mtn., Tx., U.S.	E1	120
Empangeni, S. Afr.	C5	49
Empedrado, Arg.	E4	55
Empire, Al., U.S.	B2	78
Empire, Co., U.S.	B5	83
Empire, Ga., U.S.	D3	87
Empire, La., U.S.	E6	95
Empire, Mi., U.S.	D4	99
Empire, Nv., U.S.	C2	105
Empire, Oh., U.S.	B5	112
Empoli, Italy	C3	23
Emporia, Ks., U.S.	D7	93
Emporia, Va., U.S.	D5	123
Emporium, Pa., U.S.	D5	115
Empress, Ab., Can.	D5	68
Emptinne, Bel.	D5	17
Ems, stm., Eur.	B3	18
Emsdale, On., Can.	B5	73
Emsdetten, F.R.Ger.	B3	18
Ems Jade Canal, F.R.Ger.	A7	17
Emsworth, Pa., U.S.	h13	115
Emyvale, Ire.	C5	11
Ena, Japan	n16	33
Ena, Mount, mtn., Japan.	n16	33
Enard Bay, b., Scot., U.K.	B3	13
Encampment, Wy., U.S.	E6	127
Encanto, Cape, c., Phil.	o13	34
Encarnación, Para.	E4	55
Encarnación de Díaz, Mex.	m12	63
Enchant, Ab., Can.	D4	68
Enchi, Ghana	E4	45
Encinal, N.M., U.S.	*B2	108
Encinal, Tx., U.S.	E3	120
Encinitas, Ca., U.S.	F5	82
Encino, N.M., U.S.	C4	108
Encino, Tx., U.S.	F3	120
Encontrados, Ven.	B3	60
Encounter Bay, b., Austl.	G6	50
Endako, B.C., Can.	B5	69
Endako, stm., B.C., Can.	B5	69
Ende, Indon.	G6	34
Endeavor, Pa., U.S.	C3	115
Endeavor, Wi., U.S.	E4	126
Endeavour, Sk., Can.	E4	75
Endelave, Den.	C4	15
Endelave, i., Den.	C4	15
Enderby, B.C., Can.	D8	69
Enderby Land, reg., Ant.	C18	7
Enderlin, N.D., U.S.	C8	111
Enders, Ne., U.S.	D4	104
Enders Reservoir, res., Ne., U.S.	D4	104
Endiang, Ab., Can.	D4	68
Endicott, Ne., U.S.	D8	104
Endicott, N.Y., U.S.	C4	109
Endicott, Wa., U.S.	C8	124
Endicott Mountains, mts., Ak., U.S.	B9	79
Endless Lake, l., Me., U.S.	C4	96
Endwell, N.Y., U.S.	C4	109
Ene, stm., Peru	D3	58
Enebakk, Nor.	p29	14
Energetik, Sov. Un	C5	28
Enewetak, atoll, Marsh Is.	F9	6
Enewetak Island, i., Marsh Is.	S18	52
Enez, Tur.	B6	40
Enfield, Austl.	*F6	50
Enfield, N.S., Can.	E6	71
Enfield (part of London), Eng., U.K.	k12	10
Enfield, Ct., U.S.	B5	84
Enfield, Il., U.S.	E5	90
Enfield, Me., U.S.	C4	96
Enfield, N.H., U.S.	C2	106
Enfield, N.C., U.S.	A5	110
Enfield Center, N.H., U.S.	C2	106
Engadine, Mi., U.S.	B5	99
Engaño, Cabo, c., Dom. Rep.	E9	64
Engaru, Japan	D11	33
Engebi, i., Marsh Is.	S18	52
'En Gedi, Isr.	C7	41
Engelberg, Switz.	C4	20
Engelhard, N.C., U.S.	B7	110
Engels, Sov. Un.	F16	27
Engen, F.R.Ger.	A6	21
Engenina, F.R.Ger.	B7	41
' En Gev, Isr.	D4	17
Enghien, Bel.	g10	16
Enghien, Fr.	C4	81
England, Ar., U.S.	D6	10
England Air Force Base, mil., La., U.S.	C3	95
Englee, Nf., Can.	C3	72
Englefeld, Sk., Can.	E3	75
Engleside, Va., U.S.	g12	123
Englevale, N.D., U.S.	C8	111
Englewood, B.C., Can.	D4	69
Englewood, Co., U.S.	B6	83
Englewood, Fl., U.S.	F4	86
Englewood, Ks., U.S.	E4	93
Englewood, N.J., U.S.	B5	107
Englewood, Oh., U.S.	C1	112
Englewood, Tn., U.S.	D9	119
Englewood Cliffs, N.J., U.S.	h9	107
English, In., U.S.	H5	91
English Bay, Ak., U.S.	h16	79
English Bāzār, India	E12	37
English Center, Pa., U.S.	D7	115
English Coast, Ant.	B5	7
English Channel, strt., Eur.	F5	10
English Creek, N.J., U.S.	E3	107
English Harbour West, Nf., Can.	E4	72
English Lake, In., U.S.	B4	91
Englishtown, N.J., U.S.	C4	107
Enguera, Spain	C5	22
'En Harod, Isr.	B7	41
Enid, Ms., U.S.	A4	101
Enid, Mt., U.S.	C12	103
Enid, Ok., U.S.	A4	113
Enid Lake, res., Ms., U.S.	A4	101
Enigma, Ga., U.S.	E3	87
Enida, Ab., Can.	B2	68
Enirik Island, i., Marsh Is.	P18	52
Enix, N.C., U.S.	f10	110
'En Kerem, Isr.	h11	41
Enkhuizen, Neth.	B5	17
Enköping, Swe.	H7	14
Enmore, Guy.	A3	59
Enna, Italy	F5	23
Ennadai Lake, l., N.T., Can.	D12	66
Ennedi, plat., Chad	B4	46
Enell, Lough, l., Ire.	D4	11
Enngonia, Austl.	D5	51
Ennigerloh, F.R.Ger.	B3	19
Enning, S.D., U.S.	C3	118
Ennis, Ire.	D2	10
Ennis, Mt., U.S.	E5	103
Ennis, Tx., U.S.	C4	120
Enniscorthy, Ire.	D3	10
Enniskillen, N. Ire., U.K.	C3	10
Ennistymon, Ire.	D2	10
Enns, Aus.	D7	18
Enns, stm., Aus.	D7	18
Enoch, Ut., U.S.	F3	121
Enochs, Tx., U.S.	C1	120
Enola, Ar., U.S.	B3	81
Enola, Ne., U.S.	C8	104
Enola, Pa., U.S.	F8	115
Enon, Al., U.S.	C4	78
Enon, Oh., U.S.	C2	112
Enon, Tn., U.S.	A4	119
Enoree, S.C., U.S.	B4	117
Enoree, stm., S.C., U.S.	B3	117
Enos, In., U.S.	B3	91
Enosburg Falls, Vt., U.S.	B3	122
Enriquillo, Dom. Rep.	F8	64
Enriquillo, Lago, l., Dom. Rep.	E8	64
Enschede, Neth.	A7	16
Ensenada, Arg.	g8	54
Ensenada, Mex.	A1	63
Ensenada, N.M., U.S.	A3	108
Enshi, China	E6	31
Enshu Bay, b., Japan	I8	33
Ensign, Ab., Can.	D4	68
Ensign, Ks., U.S.	E3	93
Ensign, Mi., U.S.	C4	99
Ensisheim, Fr.	B3	20
Ensley, N.C., U.S.	u14	86
Entebbe, Ug.	A5	48
Enterprise, On., Can.	C8	73
Enterprise, Guy.	A3	59
Enterprise, Al., U.S.	D4	78
Enterprise, Il., U.S.	E5	90
Enterprise, Ia., U.S.	e8	92
Enterprise, Ks., U.S.	D6	93
Enterprise, La., U.S.	C4	95
Enterprise, Ms., U.S.	C5	101
Enterprise, Ok., U.S.	B6	113
Enterprise, Or., U.S.	B9	114
Enterprise, Ut., U.S.	F2	121
Enterprise, W.V., U.S.	B4	125
Entiat, Wa., U.S.	B5	124
Entiat, stm., Wa., U.S.	B5	124
Entiat, Lake, l., Wa., U.S.	B5	124
Entiat Mountains, mts., Wa., U.S.	B5	124
Entrance, Ab., Can.	C2	68
Entraygues, Fr.	E5	16
Entrée, Île d', i., P.Q., Can.	B8	71
Entre Minho e Douro, hist reg., Port.	B1	22
Entre Ríos, prov., Arg.	A5	54
Entwistle, Ab., Can.	C3	68
Enugu, Nig.	G7	45
Enumclaw, Wa., U.S.	B4	124
Envermeu, Fr.	E9	12
Envigado, Col.	*B2	60
Enville, Tn., U.S.	B3	119
Envira, Braz.	C3	58
Enyu Channel, strt., Marsh Is.	P18	52
Enyu Island, i., Marsh Is.	P18	52
Enz, stm., F.R.Ger.	D8	19
Enza, stm., Italy	E6	20
Enzan, Japan	n17	33
Eola, Ut., U.S.	D3	95
Eola Hills, hills, Or., U.S.	h11	114
Eolia, Mo., U.S.	B6	102
Eolie Islands, is., Italy	E5	23
Eoline, Al., U.S.	C2	78
Epe, Neth.	C5	17
Epéna, Congo	A2	48
Épernay, Fr.	C5	16
Epes, Al., U.S.	C1	78
Ephesus, Ga., U.S.	C1	87
Ephesus, hist., Tur.	D6	25
Ephraim, Ut., U.S.	D4	121
Ephraim, Wi., U.S.	C6	126
Ephrata, Pa., U.S.	F9	115
Ephrata, Wa., U.S.	B6	124
Épila, Spain	D5	22
Épinal, Fr.	C7	16
Épinay [-sur-Seine], Fr.	g10	16
Epiphany, S.D., U.S.	D8	118
Epirus, hist reg., Grc.	C3	25
Epoufette, Mi., U.S.	B5	99
Epping, Eng., U.K.	k13	10
Epping, N.H., U.S.	D4	106
Epping, N.D., U.S.	A2	111
Eppingen, F.R.Ger.	D3	19
Epps, La., U.S.	B3	95
Epsom, In., U.S.	G3	91
Epsom, N.H., U.S.	D4	106
Epsom [and Ewell], Eng., U.K.	m12	10
Epukiro, Nmb.	B2	49
Epworth, Ia., U.S.	B7	92
Eqlid, Iran	F6	39
Equality, Al., U.S.	C3	78
Equality, Il., U.S.	F5	90
Equatorial Guinea, ctry., Afr.	E1	46
Équeurdreville, Fr.	C3	16
Equinunk, Pa., U.S.	C11	115
Erath, La., U.S.	E3	95
Erath, co., Tx., U.S.	C3	120
Erba, Italy	D3	20
Erba, Jabal, mtn., Sud.	A4	47
Erbach, F.R.Ger.	D5	19
Erbacon, W.V., U.S.	C4	125
Erbendorf, F.R.Ger.	D7	19
Erciş, Tur.	C14	40
Erciyes Dağı, mtn., Tur.	C10	40
Érd, Hung.	B4	24
Erdek, Tur.	B6	25
Erdene, Mong.	C7	31
Erdene-Dzuu, Mong.	B5	31
Erdenetsagaan, Mong.	B6	32
Erdenheim, Pa., U.S.	o21	115
Erding, F.R.Ger.	D5	18
Erebus, Mount, mtn., Ant.	B29	7
Erechim, Braz.	D10	56
Ereğli, Tur.	B8	40
Ereğli, Tur.	C4	40
Erenhot, China	C4	32
Eresós, Grc.	C5	25
Erétria (Néa Psará), Grc.	g11	25
Erft, stm., F.R.Ger.	C4	18
Erfurt, Ger.D.R.	C5	18
Ergene, stm., Tur.	B6	40
Erhard, Mn., U.S.	D2	100
Eria, stm., Spain	A4	22
Erial, N.J., U.S.	D2	107
Eriboll, Loch, b., Scot., U.K.	B4	13
Erice, Italy	E4	23
Ericht, Loch, l., Scot., U.K.	D4	13
Erick, Ok., U.S.	B2	113
Erickson, B.C., Can.	E9	69
Erickson, Mb., Can.	D2	70
Ericsburg, Mn., U.S.	B5	100
Ericson, Ne., U.S.	C7	104
Erie, Co., U.S.	A5	83
Erie, Il., U.S.	B3	90
Erie, Ks., U.S.	E8	93
Erie, Mi., U.S.	G7	99
Erie, N.D., U.S.	B8	111
Erie, Pa., U.S.	B1	115
Erie, co., N.Y., U.S.	C2	109
Erie, co., Oh., U.S.	A3	112
Erie, co., Pa., U.S.	C1	115
Erie, Lake, l., N.A.	B11	76
Erieau, On., Can.	E3	73
Erie Canal, N.Y., U.S.	B5	109
Eriksdale, Mb., Can.	D2	70
Erimanthos, mtn., Grc.	D3	25
Erimo, Cape, c., Japan	C13	31
Erin, On., Can.	D4	73
Erin, Tn., U.S.	A4	119
Erin Point, c., Trin.	O22	65
Erin Springs, Ok., U.S.	C4	113
Eriskay, i., Scot., U.K.	C1	13
Erisort, Loch, b., Scot., U.K.	B2	13
Erithraí, Grc.	C4	25
Eritrea, prov., Eth.	B4	47
Erkelenz, F.R.Ger.	C6	17
Erken, l., Swe.	t36	14
Erlangen, F.R.Ger.	D5	18
Erlanger, Ky., U.S.	A5	94
Erling, Lake, res., Ar., U.S.	D2	81
Erma, N.J., U.S.	F3	107
Ermelo, Neth.	B5	17
Ermelo, S. Afr.	C5	49
Ermenak, Tur.	D9	40
Ermont, Fr.	g10	16
Ermoúpolis (Syros), Grc.	D5	25
Erne, Loch, l., N. Ire., U.K.	C3	10
Erne, Upper Lough, l., Eur.	C3	10
Emée, Fr.	C3	16
Ernest, Pa., U.S.	E3	115
Ernestina, Arg.	g7	54
Ernestville, Tn., U.S.	C11	119
Emfold, Sk., Can.	G2	75
Erode, India	*F6	36
Eromanga, Austl.	C4	51
Eros, La., U.S.	B3	95
Errigal, mtn., Ire.	C2	10
Erris Head, c., Ire.	C1	10
Errol, N.H., U.S.	A4	106
Errol Heights, Or., U.S.	*h12	114
Erskine, Ab., Can.	C4	68
Erskine, Mn., U.S.	C3	100
Erstein, Fr.	C7	16
Erstfeld, Switz.	C4	20
Erving, Ma., U.S.	A3	98
Erwin, N.C., U.S.	B4	110
Erwin, S.D., U.S.	C8	118
Erwin, Tn., U.S.	C11	119
Erwin, W.V., U.S.	B5	125
Erwinville, La., U.S.	D4	95
Erwood, Sk., Can.	E4	75
Erzincan, Tur.	C12	40
Erzurum, Tur.	C13	40
Esan, Cape, c., Japan	F10	33
Esashi, Japan	C13	31
Esashi, Japan	D11	33
Esbjerg, Den.	J3	14
Esbon, Ks., U.S.	C5	93
Escabosa, N.M., U.S.	m8	108
Escada, Braz.	k6	57
Escalante, Ut., U.S.	F4	121
Escalante, stm., Ut., U.S.	F4	121
Escalante Creek, stm., Co., U.S.	C2	83
Escalante Desert, des., Ut., U.S.	F2	121
Escalón, Mex.	B4	63
Escalon, Ca., U.S.	D3	82
Escambia, co., Al., U.S.	D2	78
Escambia, co., Fl., U.S.	u14	86
Escambia, stm., Fl., U.S.	u14	86
Escanaba, Mi., U.S.	C3	99
Escanaba, stm., Mi., U.S.	B3	99
Escarpada Point, c., Phil.	B7	34
Escatawpa, Ms., U.S.	E5	101
Escatawpa, stm., U.S.	D5	101
Eschede, F.R.Ger.	F4	15
Eschenbach, F.R.Ger.	D6	19
Escholzmatt, Switz.	C4	21
Esch-sur-Alzette, Lux.	C7	16
Eschwege, F.R.Ger.	C5	18
Eschweiler, F.R.Ger.	C6	17
Escobal, Pan.	k11	62
Escocesa, Bahía, b., Dom. Rep.	E9	64
Escoheag, R.I., U.S.	E1	116
Escondida, N.M., U.S.	C3	108
Escondido, stm., Nic.	D6	62
Escondido, Ca., U.S.	F5	82
Escondido, stm., Nic.	D6	62
Escoumins, Rivière des, stm., P.Q., Can.	A8	74
Escuinapa [de Hidalgo], Mex.	C3	63
Escuintla, Guat.	A3	71
Escuminac, P.Q., Can.	A3	71
Escuminac, Point, c., N.B., Can.	B5	71
Eséka, Cam.	E2	46
Esenler, Tur.	*B7	40
Esens, F.R.Ger.	A7	17
Eşfahān (Isfahan), Iran	B5	38
Esgueva, stm., Spain	B3	22
Esher, Eng., U.K.	m12	10
Eshima, Zaire	C5	48
Eshkāshem, Afg.	C15	39
Eshowe, S. Afr.	C5	49
Esigodini, Zimb.	D7	19
Esk, stm., Eng., U.K.	E6	13
Esk, stm., Eng., U.K.	B7	11
Eskbank, Sk., Can.	G2	75
Eskdale, W.V., U.S.	C3	125
Eskilstuna, Swe.	H7	14
Eskimo Lakes, l., N.T., Can.	D6	66
Eskimo Point, N.T., Can.	D14	66
Eskişehir, Tur.	C7	40
Esko, Mn., U.S.	D6	100
Eskridge, Ks., U.S.	D7	93
Esla, stm., Spain	B3	22
Eslāmābād, Iran	*D3	39
Eslarn, F.R.Ger.	D7	19
Eslava, stm., Mex.	h9	63
Eslöv, Swe.	I5	15
Eşme, Tur.	C4	40
Esmeralda, co., Nv., U.S.	F4	105
Esmeraldas, Ec.	A2	58
Esmeraldas, prov., Ec.	A2	58
Esmond, Il., U.S.	B5	90
Esmond, N.D., U.S.	A6	111
Esmond, R.I., U.S.	B4	116
Esmont, Va., U.S.	C4	123
Esom Hill, Ga., U.S.	B2	87
Espada, Punta, c., Col.	A6	60
Espanola, On., Can.	A3	73
Espanola, Fl., U.S.	C5	86
Espanola, N.M., U.S.	B3	108
Espanola, Wa., U.S.	g13	124
Española, Isla (Hood), i., Ec.	g6	58
Esparto, Ca., U.S.	C2	82
Esperance, Austl.	F3	50
Esperanza, Arg.	A4	54
Esperanza, Peru	C3	58
Esperanza, Tx., U.S.	o12	120
Esperanza, stm., Pan.	k12	62
Esperanza, sci., Ant.	C7	7
Espichel, Cape, c., Port.	C1	22
Espinal, Col.	C3	60
Espinhaço, Serra do, mts., Braz.	E6	53
Espírito Santo, state, Braz.	H10	6
Espíritu Santo, i., Vanuatu	*G11	14
Espita, Mex.	B1	22
Espoo, Fin.	B5	49
Esposende, Port.	D9	115
Espungabera, Moz.	C1	115
Espy, Pa., U.S.		
Espyville Station, Pa., U.S.		
Esquatzel Coulee, val., Wa., U.S.	C6	124
Esquel, Arg.	C2	54
Esquimalt, B.C., Can.	E6	69
Esquina, Arg.	F4	55
Essaouira (Mogador), Mor.	C3	44
Essen, Bel.	C4	17
Essen, F.R.Ger.	C3	18
Essendon, Austl.	*G7	50
Essendon, Mount, mtn., Austl.	D3	50
Essequibo, stm., Guy.	B3	59
Essex, On., Can.	E2	73
Essex, Ct., U.S.	D6	84
Essex, Il., U.S.	B5	90
Essex, Ia., U.S.	D2	92
Essex, Md., U.S.	B5	97
Essex, Ma., U.S.	A6	98
Essex, Mt., U.S.	B3	103
Essex, N.Y., U.S.	f11	109
Essex, co., On., Can.	E2	73
Essex, co., Eng., U.K.	C8	12
Essex, co., Ma., U.S.	A5	98
Essex, co., N.J., U.S.	B4	107
Essex, co., N.Y., U.S.	B7	109
Essex, co., Vt., U.S.	B5	122
Essex, co., Va., U.S.	C6	123
Essex Fells, N.J., U.S.	*B4	107
Essex Junction, Vt., U.S.	C2	122
Essexville, Mi., U.S.	E7	99
Esslingen, F.R.Ger.	D4	18
Essonne, dept., Fr.	F2	17
Es Suki, Sud.	C3	47
Est, Île de l', i., P.Q., Can.	B8	71
Est, Pointe de l', c., P.Q., Can.	B8	71
Estacada, Or., U.S.	B4	114
Estacado, Llano, pl., U.S.	C1	120
Estados, Isla de los, i., Arg.	h13	54
Eştahbānāt, Iran	G7	39
Estaire, On., Can.	A4	73
Estância, Braz.	D3	57
Estancia, N.M., U.S.	C3	108
Estand, Kūh-e, mtn., Iran	F9	39
Estarreja, Port.	B1	22
Estcourt, S. Afr.	C4	49
Este, Italy	D3	21
Este, Punta, c., P.R.	B5	65
Esteli, Nic.	E7	63
Estella, Spain	A4	22
Estelle, Tx., U.S.	C1	120
Estelline, S.D., U.S.	C9	118
Estelline, Tx., U.S.	B2	120
Estell Manor, N.J., U.S.	E3	107
Estepa, Spain	D3	22
Estepona, Spain	D2	22
Esterbrook, Wy., U.S.	D7	127
Esterhazy, Sk., Can.	G4	75
Esternay, Fr.	F3	17
Esternberg, Aus.	E8	19
Estero, Fl., U.S.	F5	86
Estero Bay, b., Ca., U.S.	E3	82
Estero Bay, b., Fl., U.S.	F5	86
Estero Island, i., Fl., U.S.	F5	86
Estes Park, Co., U.S.	A5	83
Estevan, Sk., Can.	H4	75
Estevan Group, is., B.C., Can.	C3	69
Estevan Point, B.C., Can.	E4	69
Esther, Ab., Can.	D5	68
Estherville, Ia., U.S.	A3	92
Estherwood, La., U.S.	D3	95
Estill, Ms., U.S.	B3	101
Estill, S.C., U.S.	F5	117
Estill, co., Ky., U.S.	C6	94
Estillfork, Al., U.S.	A3	78
Estill Springs, Tn., U.S.	B5	119
Estlin, Sk., Can.	G3	75
Estonia, state, Sov. Un.	D5	29
Estrées-Saint-Denis, Fr.	E2	17
Estrela, mtn., Port.	*B2	22
Estrela, Serra da, mts., Port.	B2	22
Estrela do Norte, Braz.	A3	56
Estrela do Sul, Braz.	B3	56
Estremadura, hist reg., Port.	C1	22
Estremadura, hist reg., Spain	C3	22
Estremoz, Port.	C2	22
Esztergom, Hung.	B4	24
Étain, Fr.	C6	16
Étalans, Fr.	B1	21
Étampes, Fr.	C5	16
Étang-du-Nord, P.Q., Can.	B8	71
Étaples, Fr.	B8	16
Eternity Range, mts., Ant.	C6	7
Ethel, On., Can.	D3	73
Ethel, Ar., U.S.	C4	81
Ethel, Ms., U.S.	B4	101
Ethel, Wa., U.S.	C3	124
Ethel, W.V., U.S.	n12	125
Ethelbert, Mb., Can.	D1	70
Ethelsville, Al., U.S.	B1	78
Ethelton, Sk., Can.	E3	75
Ether, N.C., U.S.	B3	110
Ethete, Wy., U.S.	C4	127
Ethiopia, ctry., Afr.	D4	47
Ethiopian Plateau, plat., Eth.	A4	47
Ethridge, Mt., U.S.	B5	103
Ethridge, Tn., U.S.	B4	119
Etive, Loch, l., Scot., U.K.	E7	13
Etla, Mex.		
Etna, Me., U.S.	D3	96
Etna, N.H., U.S.	C2	106
Etna, N.Y., U.S.	C4	109
Etna, Oh., U.S.	m13	112
Etna, Pa., U.S.	k14	115
Etna, Wy., U.S.	C1	127
Etna, Mount, mtn., Italy	F5	23
Etna Green, In., U.S.	B5	91
Etobicoke, On., Can.	D5	73
Etolin Island, i., Ak., U.S.	m23	79
Etolin Strait, strt., Ak., U.S.	C6	79
Eton, Ga., U.S.	B2	87
Etoshapan, pl., Nmb.	A2	49
Etowah, Tn., U.S.	D9	119
Etowah, co., Al., U.S.	A3	78
Etowah, stm., Ga., U.S.	B2	87
Etters, Pa., U.S.	F8	115
Ettington, Sk., Can.	H2	75
Et Tini, hill, N. Mar. Is.	D7	52
Eṭ Ṭira, Isr.	B6	41
Ettlingen, F.R.Ger.	E3	19
Ettrick, Sk., Can.	C5	123
Ettrick, Wi., U.S.	D3	126
Etzatlán, Mex.	m11	63
Etzikom Coulee, stm., Ab., Can.	E5	68
Eu, Fr.	B4	16
Euboea see Évvoia, i., Grc.	C4	40
Eucha, Ok., U.S.	A7	113
Euclid, Mn., U.S.	C2	100
Euclid, Oh., U.S.	A4	112
Eudora, Ar., U.S.	D4	81
Eudora, Ks., U.S.	D8	93
Eudora, Mo., U.S.	E4	102
Eudunda, Austl.	G2	51
Eufaula, Al., U.S.	D4	78
Eufaula, Ok., U.S.	B6	113
Eufaula Lake, res., Ok., U.S.	B6	113
Eugene, In., U.S.	E3	91
Eugene, Mo., U.S.	C5	102
Eugene, Or., U.S.	C3	114
Eugenia, Punta, c., Mex.	B1	63
Eulato, Al., U.S.	B3	78
Eulonia, Ga., U.S.	E5	87
Eunice, La., U.S.	D3	95
Eunice, N.M., U.S.	E6	108
Eupen, Bel.	B7	16
Euphrates (Firat), stm., Asia	B3	38
Eure, dept., Fr.	C4	16
Eure, stm., Fr.	C4	16
Eureka, N.T., Can.	m34	66
Eureka, Ca., U.S.	B1	82
Eureka, Il., U.S.	C4	90
Eureka, Ks., U.S.	E7	93
Eureka, Mo., U.S.	f12	102
Eureka, Mt., U.S.	B1	103
Eureka, Nv., U.S.	D6	105
Eureka, N.C., U.S.	B5	110
Eureka, S.D., U.S.	B6	118
Eureka, Ut., U.S.	D3	121
Eureka, Wa., U.S.	C7	124
Eureka, W.V., U.S.	B3	125
Eureka, Wi., U.S.	D5	126
Eureka, co., Nv., U.S.	C5	105
Eureka Sound, strt., N.T., Can.	m34	66
Eureka Springs, Ar., U.S.	A2	81
Europa, Île, i., Reu.	B7	49
Europa Point, c., Gib.		
Europe	E13	8
Euskirchen, F.R.Ger.	C3	18
Eustis, Fl., U.S.	D5	86
Eustis, Me., U.S.	C2	96
Eustis, Ne., U.S.	D5	104
Eutaw, Al., U.S.	C2	78
Eutawville, S.C., U.S.	E7	117
Eutin, F.R.Ger.	A5	18
Eutsuk Lake, l., B.C., Can.	C4	69
Eva, Al., U.S.	A3	78
Eva, Tn., U.S.	A3	119
Evan, Mn., U.S.	F4	100
Evançon, stm., Italy	E4	21
Evandale, N.B., Can.	D3	71
Evangeline, co., La., U.S.	D3	95
Evans, Co., U.S.	A6	83
Evans, Ga., U.S.	C4	87
Evans, La., U.S.	C2	95
Evans, W.V., U.S.	C3	125
Evans, co., Ga., U.S.	D5	87
Evans, Lac, l., P.Q., Can.	o20	73
Evans, Mount, mtn., Co., U.S.	B5	83
Evansburg, Ab., Can.	C3	68
Evans City, Pa., U.S.	E1	115
Evansdale, Ia., U.S.	B5	92
Evans Mills, N.Y., U.S.	A5	109
Evansport, Oh., U.S.	A1	112
Evanston, Il., U.S.	A6	90
Evanston, Wy., U.S.	E2	127
Evansville, In., U.S.	I2	91
Evansville, Mn., U.S.	D3	100
Evansville, Wi., U.S.	F4	126
Evansville, Wy., U.S.	D6	127
Evant, Tx., U.S.	D3	120
Evanton, Scot., U.K.	D4	13
Evarts, Ky., U.S.	D6	94
Eveleth, Mn., U.S.	C6	100
Evelyn, La., U.S.	C2	95
Evening Shade, Ar., U.S.	A4	81
Even Yehuda, Isr.	f10	41
Everard, Lake, l., Austl.	F5	50
Everard, Ks., U.S.	C8	93
Everest, Mount, mtn., Asia	C5	36
Everett, Ont., Can.	C5	73
Everett, Ma., U.S.	g11	98
Everett, Pa., U.S.	F5	115
Everett, Wa., U.S.	B3	124
Everett, Mount, mtn., Ma., U.S.	B1	98
Everett Lake, res., N.H., U.S.	D3	106
Everettville, W.V., U.S.	h10	125
Evergem, Bel.	C3	17
Everglades National Park, Fl., U.S.	G5	86
Evergreen, Al., U.S.	D3	78
Evergreen, Co., U.S.	B5	83
Evergreen, La., U.S.	D3	95
Evergreen, Ms., U.S.	A5	101
Evergreen, N.C., U.S.	C4	110
Evergreen Park, Il., U.S.	k9	90
Everly, Ia., U.S.	A2	92
Everson, Pa., U.S.	F2	115
Everson, Wa., U.S.	A3	124
Everton, Ar., U.S.	A3	81
Everton, Mo., U.S.	D4	102
Evesham, Sk., Can.	E1	75
Evesham, Eng., U.K.	B6	12
Évian-les-Bains, Fr.	C2	20
Évinayong, Eq. Gui.	E2	46
Evington, Va., U.S.	C3	123
Evolène, Switz.	D3	21
Évora, Port.	C2	22
Évreux, Fr.	C4	16
Évron, Fr.	C3	16
Évros (Maritsa) (Meriç), stm., Eur.	B6	25
Evrótas, stm., Grc.	D4	25
E.V. Spence Reservoir, res., Tx., U.S.	D2	120
Evstratios, i., Grc.	C4	40
Évvoia (Euboea), i., Grc.	C4	40
Évvoia, North Gulf of, b., Grc.	B3	88
Ewa, Hi., U.S.	B3	88
Ewa Beach, Hi., U.S.	g9	88
Ewan, Wa., U.S.	B8	124
Ewarton, Jam.	E14	65
Ewe, Loch, b., Scot., U.K.	C3	13
Ewell, Md., U.S.	E5	97
Ewen, Mi., U.S.	m12	99
Ewing, Il., U.S.	E5	90
Ewing, Ky., U.S.	B6	94
Ewing, Mo., U.S.	A6	102
Ewing, Ne., U.S.	B7	104
Ewing, Va., U.S.	f8	123
Ewing Township, N.J., U.S.	C3	107
Ewo, Congo	B1	48
Exaltación, Bol.	B2	55
Excel, Ab., Can.	D5	68
Excel, Al., U.S.	D2	78
Excello, Mo., U.S.	B5	102
Excelsior Mountain, mtn., Ca., U.S.	C4	82
Excelsior Mountains, mts., Nv., U.S.	E3	105
Excelsior Springs, Mo., U.S.	B3	102
Exchange, Pa., U.S.	D8	115
Exchange, W.V., U.S.	C4	125
Exe, stm., Eng., U.K.	D4	12
Executive Committee Range, mts., Ant.	B36	7
Exeland, Wi., U.S.	C2	126
Exeter, On., Can.	D3	73
Exeter, Eng., U.K.	E5	10
Exeter, Ca., U.S.	D4	82
Exeter, Me., U.S.	D3	96
Exeter, Mo., U.S.	E4	102
Exeter, Ne., U.S.	D8	104
Exeter, N.H., U.S.	E5	106
Exeter, N.C., U.S.	D10	115
Exeter, R.I., U.S.	E3	116
Exeter, co., N.H., U.S.	E5	106
Exira, Ia., U.S.	C3	92
Exline, Ia., U.S.	D5	92
Exmoor, for., Eng., U.K.	E5	10
Exmore, Va., U.S.	C7	123
Exmouth, Austl.	D1	50
Exmouth, Eng., U.K.	E5	10
Exmouth Gulf, b., Austl.	D1	50
Expanse, Sk., Can.	G3	75
Experiment, Ga., U.S.	C2	87
Exploits, stm., Nf., Can.	D3	72
Exploits, Bay of, b., Nf., Can.	D4	72
Export, Pa., U.S.	F2	115
Exshaw, Ab., Can.	D3	68
Extension, B.C., Can.	f12	69
Extrema, Braz.	m8	56
Exuma Sound, strt., Bah.	B5	64
Eyak, Ak., U.S.	C10	79
Eyebrow, Sk., Can.	G2	75
Eyehill Creek, stm., Can.	C5	68
Eyemouth, Scot., U.K.	C5	10
Eye Peninsula, pen., Scot., U.K.	B2	13
Eyl, Som.	D6	47
Eylar Mountain, mtn., Ca., U.S.	D3	82
Eynort, Loch, b., Scot., U.K.	C1	13
Eyota, Mn., U.S.	G6	100
Eyre, Sk., Can.	F1	75
Eyre, Lake, l., Austl.	D3	11
Eyre North, Lake, l., Austl.	F6	50
Eyre Peninsula, pen., Austl.	F6	50
Ezeiza, Arg.	g7	54
Ezine, Tur.	C6	40

F

Fabens, Tx., U.S.	o11	120
Faber, Va., U.S.	C4	123
Faber Lake, l., N.T., Can.	D9	66
Fabius, N.Y., U.S.	C5	109
Fabius, stm., Mo., U.S.	A6	102
Fåborg, Den.	C4	15
Fabriano, Italy	B1	81
Fabyan, Ct., U.S.	A8	84
Facatativá, Col.	C3	60
Fachi, Niger	C7	45
Facpi Point, c., Guam	M9	52
Factoryville, Pa., U.S.	C10	115
Fada, Chad	B4	46
Fada Ngourma, Burkina	D5	45
Faddeya Gulf, b., Sov. Un.	B17	29
Faddeeva Island, i., Sov. Un.	B3	128
Fadian Point, c., Guam	L10	52
Faenza, Italy	C1	81
Fafe, Port.	B1	22
Faga'alu, Am. Sam.	F13	52
Fagaitua Bay, b., Am. Sam.	G13	52
Fagamalo, W. Sam.	F11	52
Făgăraş, Rom.	C7	24
Fagatogo, Am. Sam.	F13	52
Fagelbro, Swe.	t36	14
Fagernes, Nor.		
Fagersta, Swe.	G6	14
Faggo, Nig.		
Faguibine, Lac, l., Mali	C4	45

Name	Map Ref	Page
Fagus, Mo., U.S.	E7	102
Fahan, Ire.	B4	11
Faial, i., Port.	g8	44
Faichuk, is., Micron.	Q18	52
Fä'id, Eg.	D4	41
Faido, Switz.	D6	21
Fairacres, N.M., U.S.	E3	108
Fairbairn Reservoir, res., Austl.	A7	51
Fairbank, Az., U.S.	F5	80
Fairbank, Ia., U.S.	B5	92
Fairbanks, Ak., U.S.	C10	79
Fairbanks, Fl., U.S.	C4	86
Fairbanks, In., U.S.	F2	91
Fairbanks, Me., U.S.	D2	96
Fair Bluff, N.C., U.S.	C3	110
Fairburn, Ga., U.S.	C2	87
Fairburn, S.D., U.S.	D2	118
Fairbury, Il., U.S.	C5	90
Fairbury, Ne., U.S.	D8	104
Fairchance, Pa., U.S.	G2	115
Fairchild, Wi., U.S.	D3	126
Fairchild Air Force Base, mil., Wa., U.S.	g13	124
Fairdale, Ky., U.S.	B4	94
Fairdale, N.D., U.S.	A7	111
Fairfax, Mb., Can.	E1	70
Fairfax, Al., U.S.	C4	78
Fairfax, Ca., U.S.	C2	82
Fairfax, De., U.S.	A3	85
Fairfax, Ia., U.S.	C6	92
Fairfax, Mn., U.S.	F4	100
Fairfax, Mo., U.S.	A2	102
Fairfax, Ok., U.S.	A5	113
Fairfax, S.C., U.S.	F5	117
Fairfax, S.D., U.S.	D7	118
Fairfax, Vt., U.S.	B2	122
Fairfax, Va., U.S.	B5	123
Fairfax, co., Va., U.S.	B5	123
Fairfax Station, Va., U.S.	g12	123
Fairfield, Austl.	*F9	51
Fairfield, Al., U.S.	B3	78
Fairfield, Ca., U.S.	C2	82
Fairfield, Ct., U.S.	E2	84
Fairfield, Id., U.S.	F4	89
Fairfield, Il., U.S.	E5	90
Fairfield, Ia., U.S.	C6	92
Fairfield, Ky., U.S.	C4	94
Fairfield, Me., U.S.	D3	96
Fairfield, Mt., U.S.	C5	103
Fairfield, Ne., U.S.	D7	104
Fairfield, N.J., U.S.	*B4	107
Fairfield, N.C., U.S.	B6	110
Fairfield, N.D., U.S.	B2	111
Fairfield, Oh., U.S.	n12	112
Fairfield, Pa., U.S.	G7	115
Fairfield, Tx., U.S.	D4	120
Fairfield, Ut., U.S.	C3	121
Fairfield, Vt., U.S.	B3	122
Fairfield, Wa., U.S.	B8	124
Fairfield, co., Ct., U.S.	D2	84
Fairfield, co., Oh., U.S.	C3	112
Fairfield, co., S.C., U.S.	C5	117
Fairfield Bay, Ar., U.S.	B3	81
Fairfield Pond, l., Vt., U.S.	B3	122
Fairgrove, Mo., U.S.	E7	99
Fair Grove, Mo., U.S.	D4	102
Fair Grove, N.C., U.S.	B2	110
Fairhaven, Ma., U.S.	C6	98
Fairhaven, Mi., U.S.	F8	99
Fairhaven, Mn., U.S.	E4	100
Fair Haven, N.J., U.S.	C4	107
Fair Haven, N.Y., U.S.	B4	109
Fair Haven, Vt., U.S.	D2	122
Fairholme, Sk., Can.	D1	75
Fairhope, Al., U.S.	E2	78
Fairland, Il., U.S.	D5	90
Fairland, In., U.S.	E6	91
Fairland, Ok., U.S.	A7	113
Fair Lawn, N.J., U.S.	h8	107
Fairlawn, Oh., U.S.	*A4	112
Fairlawn, Va., U.S.	C2	123
Fairlea, W.V., U.S.	D4	125
Fairlee, Md., U.S.	B5	97
Fairlee, Vt., U.S.	D4	122
Fairless Hills, Pa., U.S.	*F12	115
Fairmont, Il., U.S.	C6	90
Fairmont, Mn., U.S.	G4	100
Fairmont, Ne., U.S.	D8	104
Fairmont, N.C., U.S.	C3	110
Fairmont, S.C., U.S.	B3	117
Fairmont, W.V., U.S.	B4	125
Fairmount, Ga., U.S.	B2	87
Fairmount, Il., U.S.	C6	90
Fairmount, In., U.S.	D6	91
Fairmount, Ks., U.S.	k16	93
Fairmount, Md., U.S.	D6	97
Fairmount, N.Y., U.S.	*B4	109
Fairmount, N.D., U.S.	C9	111
Fairmount Heights, Md., U.S.	f9	97
Fair Oaks, Ca., U.S.	*C3	82
Fair Oaks, Ga., U.S.	h7	87
Fair Oaks, In., U.S.	B3	91
Fairoaks, Pa., U.S.	h13	115
Fair Plain, Mi., U.S.	F4	99
Fair Plain, W.V., U.S.	C3	125
Fairplay, Co., U.S.	B5	83
Fair Play, Md., U.S.	A2	97
Fair Play, Mo., U.S.	D4	102
Fair Play, S.C., U.S.	B2	117
Fairpoint, Oh., U.S.	B5	112
Fairpoint, S.D., U.S.	C3	118
Fairport, Ia., U.S.	C7	92
Fairport, Mo., U.S.	B3	102
Fairport, N.Y., U.S.	B3	109
Fair Port, Va., U.S.	C6	123
Fairport Harbor, Oh., U.S.	A4	112
Fairton, N.J., U.S.	E2	107
Fairvale, N.B., Can.	D4	71
Fairview, Austl.	A1	68
Fairview, Ar., U.S.	*D4	81
Fairview, Il., U.S.	C3	90
Fairview, Ks., U.S.	C8	93
Fairview, Mi., U.S.	D6	99
Fairview, Mt., U.S.	C12	103
Fairview, N.J., U.S.	D3	117
Fairview, N.J., U.S.	h8	107
Fairview, N.Y., U.S.	*D7	109
Fairview, Oh., U.S.	B4	112
Fairview, Ok., U.S.	A3	113
Fairview, Or., U.S.	*B4	114
Fairview, S.D., U.S.	D9	118
Fairview, Tn., U.S.	B4	119
Fairview, Ut., U.S.	D4	121
Fairview, W.V., U.S.	B4	125
Fairview, Wy., U.S.	D2	127
Fairview Heights, Il., U.S.	E3	90
Fairview Park, In., U.S.	E3	91
Fairview Park, Oh., U.S.	g9	112
Fairview Peak, mtn., Nv., U.S.	D3	105
Fairview Peak, mtn., Or., U.S.	D4	114
Fairview Shores, Fl., U.S.	*D5	86
Fair Water, Wi., U.S.	E5	126
Fairway, Ks., U.S.	k16	93
Fairweather, Mount, mtn., N.A.	D12	79
Fairy Glen, Sk., Can.	D3	75
Faisalabad (Lyallpur), Pak.	B5	36
Faison, N.C., U.S.	B4	110
Faith, N.C., U.S.	B2	110
Faith, S.D., U.S.	B3	118
Faithorn, Mi., U.S.	C3	99
Faizābād (Fyzabad), India	C7	36
Fajardo, P.R.	G12	64
Fajr, Bi'r, well, Sau. Ar.	H11	40
Fakenham, Eng., U.K.	B8	12
Fakfak, Indon.	F8	34
Fakse, Den.	C6	15
Fakse Bugt, b., Den.	C6	15
Fakse Ladeplads, Den.	C6	15
Faku, China	C10	32
Fal, stm., Eng., U.K.	D3	12
Falaba, S.L.	E2	45
Falaise, Fr.	C3	16
Falalu, i., Micron.	Q18	52
Fălciu, Rom.	B9	24
Falcon, Co., U.S.	D2	81
Falcon, Co., U.S.	C6	83
Falcon, Ms., U.S.	A3	101
Falcon, N.C., U.S.	B4	110
Falcón, state, Ven.	A4	60
Falconer, N.Y., U.S.	C1	109
Falcon Heights, Mn., U.S.	n12	100
Falcon Heights, Or., U.S.	E5	114
Falcon Lake, res., N.A.	F3	120
Faléa, Mali	D2	45
Falefa Harbour, b., W. Sam.	F12	52
Falelima, W. Sam.	F11	52
Falémé, stm., Afr.	D2	45
Faleolo International Airport, W. Sam.	F12	52
Faleshty, Sov. Un.	B8	24
Falfurrias, Tx., U.S.	F3	120
Falher, Ab., Can.	B2	68
Falkenberg, Ger.D.R.	B8	19
Falkenberg, Swe.	B6	15
Falkenstein, Ger.D.R.	C7	19
Falkirk, Scot., U.K.	C5	10
Falkland, B.C., Can.	D8	69
Falkland Islands (Islas Malvinas), dep., S.A.	I5	53
Falkner, Ms., U.S.	A5	101
Falköping, Swe.	H5	14
Falkville, Al., U.S.	A3	78
Fall, F.R.Ger.	B7	20
Fall, stm., Ks., U.S.	E7	93
Fall Branch, Tn., U.S.	C11	119
Fallbrook, Ca., U.S.	F5	82
Fall City, Wa., U.S.	B4	124
Fall Creek, Wi., U.S.	D2	126
Fall Creek, stm., In., U.S.	k10	91
Fallentimber, Pa., U.S.	E4	115
Falling Creek, stm., Va., U.S.	n17	123
Falling Rock Creek, stm., W.V., U.S.	m13	125
Falling Water, Tn., U.S.	h11	119
Falling Waters, W.V., U.S.	B7	125
Fallis, Ok., U.S.	B4	113
Fall Mountain Lake, Ct., U.S.	C4	84
Fällnäs, Swe.	u35	14
Fallon, Mt., U.S.	D11	103
Fallon, Nv., U.S.	D3	105
Fallon, co., Mt., U.S.	D12	103
Fallon Indian Reservation, Nv., U.S.	D3	105
Fallon Naval Air Station, mil., Nv., U.S.	D3	105
Fall River, Ks., U.S.	E7	93
Fall River, Ma., U.S.	C5	98
Fall River, Tn., U.S.	B4	119
Fall River, Wi., U.S.	E4	126
Fall River, co., S.D., U.S.	D2	118
Fall River Lake, res., Ks., U.S.	E7	93
Fall River Mills, Ca., U.S.	B3	82
Fall Rock, Ky., U.S.	C6	94
Falls, co., Tx., U.S.	D4	120
Fallsburg, Ky., U.S.	B7	94
Falls Church, Va., U.S.	g12	123
Falls City, Ne., U.S.	D10	104
Falls City, Or., U.S.	C3	114
Falls Creek, Pa., U.S.	D4	115
Falls of Rough, Ky., U.S.	C3	94
Fallston, N.C., U.S.	B1	110
Falls Village, Ct., U.S.	B2	84
Falmouth, N.S., Can.	E5	71
Falmouth, Jam.	E5	64
Falmouth, Eng., U.K.	E4	10
Falmouth, In., U.S.	E7	91
Falmouth, Ky., U.S.	B5	94
Falmouth, Me., U.S.	E2	96
Falmouth, Mi., U.S.	D5	99
Falmouth, Ma., U.S.	C6	98
Falmouth, Va., U.S.	B5	123
Falmouth Bay, b., Eng., U.K.	D2	12
False Bay, S. Afr.	H3	49
False Cape, c., Fl., U.S.	D6	86
False Cape, c., Va., U.S.	D7	123
False Chipana, Punta, c., Chile	A2	59
Falso, Cabo, c., Hond.	C5	64
Falster, i., Den.	C6	15
Fălticeni, Rom.	B8	24
Falun, Ks., U.S.	D6	93
Falun, Swe.	G6	14
Famagusta see Ammókhostos, Cyp.	E9	40
Famatina, Sierra de, mts., Arg.	E2	55
Family Lake, l., Mb., Can.	D4	70
Fanan, i., Micron.	Q18	52
Fancy Farm, Ky., U.S.	f9	94
Fancy Prairie, Il., U.S.	D4	90
Fang, Thai.	D4	34
Fangcheng, China	H5	32
Fangxian, China	E7	31
Fannettsburg, Pa., U.S.	F6	115
Fannin, Tx., U.S.	E4	120
Fannin, co., Ga., U.S.	B2	87
Fannin, co., Tx., U.S.	C4	120
Fanning Island see Tabuaeran Island, atoll, Kir.	F12	6
Fannūj, Iran	H9	39
Fanny Bay, B.C., Can.	E5	69
Fannystelle, Mb., Can.	E3	70
Fano, Italy	C4	23
Fanø, i., Den.	C2	15
Fanø Bugt, b., Den.	C2	15
Fañonchuluyan, Bahia, b., N. Mar. Is.	D8	52
Fan-si-pan, mtn., Viet.	A5	35
Fanwood, N.J., U.S.	*B4	107
Fāqūs, Eg.	D3	41
Faradje, Zaire	A4	48
Faradofay, Madag.	h9	49
Farafangana, Madag.	h9	49
Farāfirah, Al Wāḥat al, well, Eg.	C2	38
Farāh, Afg.	B3	36
Farah, stm., Afg.	B3	36
Farallon, Punta, c., Mex.	n11	63
Faramana, Burkina	D4	45
Faranah, Gui.	D2	45
Farasan Islands, is., Sau. Ar.	D4	38
Farber, Mo., U.S.	B6	102
Fareham, Eng., U.K.	D6	12
Farewell, Cape, c., N.Z.	N14	51
Fargo, Ga., U.S.	F4	87
Fargo, N.D., U.S.	C9	111
Fargo, Ok., U.S.	A2	113
Faribault, Mn., U.S.	F5	100
Faribault, co., Mn., U.S.	G4	100
Farīdpur, Bngl.	F12	37
Fārigh, Wādī al, val., Libya	G3	40
Farilhões Islands, is., Port.	C1	22
Farīmān, Iran	D9	39
Farina, Austl.	E2	51
Farina, Il., U.S.	E5	90
Farisita, Co., U.S.	D5	83
Fāriskūr, Eg.	C3	41
Farley, Ia., U.S.	B6	92
Farley, Ma., U.S.	A3	98
Farley, Mo., U.S.	B3	102
Farley, N.M., U.S.	A5	108
Farmer, Oh., U.S.	A1	112
Farmer, S.D., U.S.	D8	118
Farmer City, Il., U.S.	C5	90
Farmers, Ky., U.S.	B6	94
Farmers Branch, Tx., U.S.	n10	120
Farmersburg, In., U.S.	F3	91
Farmersburg, Ia., U.S.	B6	92
Farmersville, Al., U.S.	C3	78
Farmersville, Ca., U.S.	*D4	82
Farmersville, Il., U.S.	D4	90
Farmersville, Tx., U.S.	C4	120
Farmerville, La., U.S.	B3	95
Farmingdale, Me., U.S.	D3	96
Farmingdale, N.J., U.S.	*C4	107
Farmingdale, N.Y., U.S.	*n15	109
Farmington, Ar., U.S.	A1	81
Farmington, Ct., U.S.	C4	84
Farmington, De., U.S.	E3	85
Farmington, Il., U.S.	C3	90
Farmington, Ia., U.S.	D6	92
Farmington, Me., U.S.	D2	96
Farmington, Mi., U.S.	p15	99
Farmington, Mo., U.S.	D7	102
Farmington, N.H., U.S.	D4	106
Farmington, N.M., U.S.	A1	108
Farmington, N.C., U.S.	A2	110
Farmington, Pa., U.S.	G2	115
Farmington, Tn., U.S.	B5	119
Farmington, Ut., U.S.	C4	121
Farmington, Wa., U.S.	B8	124
Farmington, W.V., U.S.	h10	125
Farmington, stm., Ct., U.S.	B4	84
Farmington, West Branch, stm., U.S.	B4	84
Farmington Hills, Mi., U.S.	o15	99
Farmingville, N.Y., U.S.	*n15	109
Farmland, In., U.S.	D7	91
Farm Pond, l., Ma., U.S.	h10	98
Farmville, N.C., U.S.	B5	110
Farmville, Va., U.S.	C4	123
Farnam, Ne., U.S.	D5	104
Farnborough, Eng., U.K.	C6	12
Farne Islands, is., Eng., U.K.	C6	10
Farner, Tn., U.S.	D9	119
Farnham, P.Q., Can.	D5	74
Farnham, Va., U.S.	C6	123
Farnham, Mount, mtn., B.C., Can.	D9	69
Farnhamville, Ia., U.S.	B3	92
Färningen, Switz.	C6	21
Faro, Braz.	C3	59
Faro, Port.	D2	22
Farragut, Ia., U.S.	D2	92
Farrar, Ia., U.S.	e9	92
Farrar, stm., Scot., U.K.	C4	13
Farrāshband, Iran	G6	39
Farrell, Ms., U.S.	A3	101
Farrell, Pa., U.S.	D1	115
Farrellton, P.Q., Can.	D2	74
Farrerdale, Sk., Can.	F3	75
Farris, Ok., U.S.	C6	113
Farris, i., Nor.	p27	14
Farrukhābād, India	C6	36
Fars, hist. reg., Iran	C5	38
Fársala (Pharsalos), Grc.	C4	25
Fārsī, Afg.	E11	39
Farsø, Den.	B3	15
Farson, Ia., U.S.	C5	92
Farson, Wy., U.S.	D3	127
Fartak, Ra's, c., P.D.R.Yem.	H5	38
Fārup, Den.	B3	15
Farvel, Kap, c., Grnld.	D16	61
Farwell, Mi., U.S.	E6	99
Farwell, Mn., U.S.	E3	100
Farwell, Ne., U.S.	C7	104
Farwell, Tx., U.S.	B1	120
Fasā, Iran	D5	38
Fasano, Italy	D6	23
Fashoda see Kodok, Sudan	D3	74
Fāstēh, Ra's-e, c., Iran	I10	39
Fastov, Sov. Un.	F7	27
Fatehpur, India	C7	36
Fatsa, Tur.	B11	40
Fatumafuti, Am. Sam.	F11	52
Fatuosofia, Cape, c., W. Sam.	F11	52
Fatu Rock, rock, Am. Sam.	F13	52
Faucett, Mo., U.S.	B3	102
Faulenfürst, F.R.Ger.	A5	21
Faulk, co., S.D., U.S.	B6	118
Faulkner, co., Ar., U.S.	B3	81
Faulkton, S.D., U.S.	B6	118
Fauquier, B.C., Can.	E8	69
Fauquier, co., Va., U.S.	B5	123
Faust, Ab., Can.	B3	68
Favara, Italy	F4	23
Faverges, Fr.	D2	20
Faverney, Fr.	A1	21
Faversham, Eng., U.K.	C8	12
Favorita, Fl., U.S.	C6	86
Fawcett, Ab., Can.	B3	68
Fawcett Lake, l., Ab., Can.	B4	68
Fawnie Nose, mtn., B.C., Can.	C5	69
Fawnie Range, mts., B.C., Can.	C5	69
Faxaflói, b., Ice.	n21	14
Faxälven, stm., Swe.	F6	14
Faxon, Ok., U.S.	C3	113
Faxon, Tn., U.S.	A3	119
Fayd, Sau. Ar.	I14	40
Fayette, Al., U.S.	B2	78
Fayette, Ia., U.S.	B6	92
Fayette, Me., U.S.	D2	96
Fayette, Ms., U.S.	D2	101
Fayette, Mo., U.S.	B5	102
Fayette, Oh., U.S.	A1	112
Fayette, Ut., U.S.	D4	121
Fayette, co., Al., U.S.	B3	78
Fayette, co., Ga., U.S.	C2	87
Fayette, co., Il., U.S.	D4	90
Fayette, co., In., U.S.	E7	91
Fayette, co., Ia., U.S.	B6	92
Fayette, co., Ky., U.S.	B5	94
Fayette, co., Oh., U.S.	C2	112
Fayette, co., Pa., U.S.	G2	115
Fayette, co., Tn., U.S.	B2	119
Fayette, co., Tx., U.S.	E4	120
Fayette, co., W.V., U.S.	C3	125
Fayetteville, Al., U.S.	B3	78
Fayetteville, Ar., U.S.	A1	81
Fayetteville, Ga., U.S.	C2	87
Fayetteville, N.C., U.S.	B4	110
Fayetteville, Oh., U.S.	C2	112
Fayetteville, Pa., U.S.	G6	115
Fayetteville, Tn., U.S.	B5	119
Fayetteville, W.V., U.S.	C3	125
Faylakah, i., Kuw.	G4	39
Fays-Billot, Fr.	B1	20
Fayville, Ma., U.S.	g9	98
Fayville, Ma., U.S.	E1	108
Fazenda Nova, Braz.	B2	56
Fdérik, Maur.	B2	45
Fear, Cape, c., N.C., U.S.	D5	110
Feasterville, Pa., U.S.	o21	115
Feather, stm., Ca., U.S.	C3	82
Feather, Middle Fork, stm., Ca., U.S.	C3	82
Feather, Mount, mtn., Ant.	e40	7
Feather Falls, Ca., U.S.	C3	82
Featherston, Ok., U.S.	B6	113
Fécamp, Fr.	C4	16
Federal, Arg.	A5	54
Federal Dam, Mn., U.S.	C4	100
Federal Heights, Co., U.S.	*B6	83
Federalsburg, Md., U.S.	C6	97
Federal Way, Wa., U.S.	*f11	124
Fedora, S.D., U.S.	C8	118
Fedscreek, Ky., U.S.	C7	94
Feeding Hills, Ma., U.S.	B2	98
Feesburg, Oh., U.S.	D1	112
Fefan, i., Micron.	Q18	52
Fegen, Swe.	A7	15
Fehmarn, i., F.R.Ger.	A5	18
Fehmarn Strait, strt., Eur.	D5	15
Feia, Lagoa, b., Braz.	C4	56
Feijó, Braz.	C3	58
Feilding, N.Z.	N15	51
Feira (Luangwa), Zam.	E5	48
Feira de Santana, Braz.	D3	57
Fejø, i., Den.	D5	15
Felanitx, Spain	C7	22
Felch, Mi., U.S.	B3	99
Feldbach, Aus.	E7	15
Feldberg, Ger.D.R.	B3	19
Feldberg, mtn., F.R.Ger.	B4	20
Feldkirch, Aus.	D6	19
Felicity, Oh., U.S.	D1	112
Felipe Carrillo Puerto, Mex.	D7	63
Felix, Cape, c., N.T., Can.	C13	66
Felixstowe, Eng., U.K.	C9	12
Felixville, La., U.S.	D5	95
Fellbach, F.R.Ger.	E4	19
Fellingsbro, Swe.	t33	14
Fellowship, N.J., U.S.	*D3	107
Fellsmere, Fl., U.S.	E6	86
Ffestiniog, Wales, U.K.	D5	10
Felt, Id., U.S.	F7	89
Felton, Ca., U.S.	D2	82
Felton, De., U.S.	D3	85
Felton, Mn., U.S.	C1	100
Felton, Pa., U.S.	G8	115
Femø, i., Den.	D5	15
Femunden, l., Nor.	F4	14
Fena Valley Reservoir, res., Guam	M9	52
Fence, Wi., U.S.	C5	126
Fence, stm., Mi., U.S.	B2	99
Fence Lake, N.M., U.S.	C1	108
Fence Lake, l., Wi., U.S.	C4	126
Fenelon Falls, On., Can.	C6	73
Fengcheng, China	F8	31
Fengcheng, China	D11	32
Fengdu, China	E8	31
Fengjie, China	E8	31
Fengning, China	G4	31
Fengqing, China	H2	32
Fengxian, China	G2	32
Fengxiang, China	E8	31
Fenimore Pass, strt., Ak., U.S.	E4	79
Fenn, Id., U.S.	D2	89
Fennimore, Wi., U.S.	F3	126
Fennville, Mi., U.S.	F4	99
Fenoarivo Atsinanana, Madag.	g9	49
Fenton, Sk., Can.	D3	75
Fenton, Il., U.S.	A3	92
Fenton, La., U.S.	D3	95
Fenton, Mi., U.S.	F7	99
Fenton, Mo., U.S.	f13	102
Fentress, Tx., U.S.	E4	120
Fentress, co., Tn., U.S.	C9	119
Fenwick, W.V., U.S.	C4	125
Fenwick Island, De., U.S.	G5	85
Fenwick Island, i., S.C., U.S.	k11	117
Fenwood, Sk., Can.	G4	75
Feodosiya, Sov. Un.	I10	27
Fer, Point au, c., La., U.S.	E4	95
Ferbane, Ire.	D4	11
Ferdig, Mt., U.S.	B5	103
Ferdinand, Id., U.S.	C2	89
Ferdinand, In., U.S.	H4	91
Ferdinandshof, Ger.D.R.	B7	19
Ferdows, Iran	E7	39
Fère-Champenoise, Fr.	F3	17
Ferentino, Italy	H8	23
Fergana, Sov. Un.	E8	28
Fergana Mountains, mts., Sov. Un.	E8	28
Fergus, On., Can.	D4	73
Fergus, Mt., U.S.	C7	103
Fergus, co., Mt., U.S.	C7	103
Fergus Falls, Mn., U.S.	D2	100
Ferguson, b., B.C., Can.	D9	69
Ferguson, Ia., U.S.	C5	92
Ferguson, Ky., U.S.	C5	94
Ferguson, Mo., U.S.	C7	102
Ferintosh, Ab., Can.	C4	68
Ferkéssédougou, I.C.	E3	45
Ferme-Neuve, P.Q., Can.	C2	74
Fermeuse, Nf., Can.	E5	72
Fermo, Italy	C4	23
Fermoselle, Spain	B2	22
Fermoy, Ire.	D2	10
Fernandina, Isla (Narborough), i., Ec.	g5	58
Fernandina Beach, Fl., U.S.	B5	86
Fernando de Noronha, Ilha, i., Braz.	B4	57
Fernandópolis, Braz.	C2	56
Fernando Póo see Bioko, i., Eq. Gui.	E1	46
Fernán-Núñez, Spain	D3	22
Fernbank, Al., U.S.	B1	78
Ferndale, Ar., U.S.	h9	81
Ferndale, Ca., U.S.	B1	82
Ferndale, Ky., U.S.	D6	94
Ferndale, Md., U.S.	*B4	97
Ferndale, Mi., U.S.	P15	99
Ferndale, Pa., U.S.	F4	115
Ferndale, Wa., U.S.	A3	124
Ferney, S.D., U.S.	B7	118
Fernie, B.C., Can.	E10	69
Ferney, Nv., U.S.	D2	105
Fern Ridge Lake, res., Or., U.S.	C3	114
Ferns, Ire.	E5	11
Fernwood, Id., U.S.	B2	89
Fernwood, Ms., U.S.	D3	101
Fernwood, N.Y., U.S.	B4	109
Ferrara, Italy	B3	23
Ferreira do Alentejo, Port.	C1	22
Ferreira do Zézere, Port.	C1	22
Ferrellsburg, W.V., U.S.	C2	125
Ferreñafe, Peru	C2	58
Ferret, Fr.	A3	21
Ferriday, La., U.S.	C4	95
Ferriere, Italy	E5	20
Ferris, Il., U.S.	C2	90
Ferris, Tx., U.S.	C4	120
Ferris Mountains, mts., Wy., U.S.	D5	127
Ferron, Ut., U.S.	D4	121
Ferros, Braz.	B4	56
Fertown, Va., U.S.	D2	123
Ferry, Mi., U.S.	E4	99
Ferry, co., Wa., U.S.	A7	124
Ferry Farms, Va., U.S.	B5	123
Ferry Point, c., N.J., U.S.	k7	107
Ferryville, Wi., U.S.	E2	126
Fertile, Ia., U.S.	A4	92
Fertile, Mn., U.S.	C2	100
Fertília, Italy	D2	23
Fès, Mor.	C4	44
Feshi, Zaire	C2	48
Fessenden, N.D., U.S.	B6	111
Festina, Ia., U.S.	A6	92
Festus, Mo., U.S.	C7	102
Feteşti, Rom.	C8	24
Fethard, Ire.	E4	11
Fethiye, Tur.	D7	40
Fetisovo, Sov. Un.	E4	28
Fettercairn, Scot., U.K.	D6	13
Firth, Id., U.S.	F6	89
Feuchtwangen, F.R.Ger.	D5	19
Feudal, Sk., Can.	F2	75
Feuilles, Rivière aux, stm., P.Q., Can.	g12	74
Feurs, Fr.	E6	16
Feversham, On., Can.	C4	73
Feyzābād, Afg.	A5	36
Fezzan (Fazzān), hist. reg., Libya	D2	43
Fhada, Beinn, mtn., Scot., U.K.	B4	10
Fiambalá, Arg.	E2	55
Fianarantsoa, Madag.	h9	49
Fianarantsoa, prov., Madag.	h9	49
Fianga, Chad	D3	46
Fibre, Mi., U.S.	B6	99
Ficarolo, Italy	E7	20
Fiche, Eth.	D4	47
Fichtelgebirge, mts., F.R.Ger.	C6	19
Ficksburg, S. Afr.	C4	49
Fidalgo Island, i., Wa., U.S.	A3	124
Fidelity, Il., U.S.	D3	90
Fidenza, Italy	B3	23
Fidler Lake, l., Mb., Can.	A3	70
Fieldale, Va., U.S.	D3	123
Field Crest Estates, Ct., U.S.	D8	84
Fielding, Sk., Can.	E2	75
Fielding, Ut., U.S.	B3	121
Fieldon, Il., U.S.	D3	90
Fields, La., U.S.	D2	95
Fields, Or., U.S.	E8	114
Fields, Lake, l., La., U.S.	k10	95
Fields Lake, stm., Fl., U.S.	E4	10
Fieri, Alb.	I3	25
Fiery Urco, mtn., Ec.	C2	58
Fiesch, Switz.	D5	21
Fife, prov., Scot., U.K.	B5	10
Fife Lake, Mi., U.S.	D5	99
Fife Lake, Sk., Can.	H3	75
Fife Lake, l., Mi., U.S.	D5	99
Fife Ness, c., Scot., U.K.	B6	10
Fifteen Mile Falls Reservoir, res., N.H., U.S.	B4	127
Fifteenmile Creek, stm., Wy., U.S.	B4	127
Fifty Lakes, Mn., U.S.	D4	100
Fig Garden, Ca., U.S.	D4	82
Figeac, Fr.	E5	16
Figtree, Zimb.	B4	49
Figueira da Foz, Port.	B1	22
Figueras, Spain	A7	22
Figuig, Mor.	C4	44
Fiji, ctry., Oc.	H10	6
Fik, Eth.	D5	47
Fiksdal, Nor.	E2	14
Filadelfia, Para.	C4	59
Filer, Id., U.S.	G4	89
Filer City, Mi., U.S.	D4	99
Filey, Eng., U.K.	F8	12
Fili, Grc.	g11	25
Filiatrá, Grc.	D3	25
Filicudi, i., Italy	E5	23
Filingué, Niger	D5	45
Filisur, Switz.	C8	21
Filley, Ne., U.S.	D9	104
Fillmore, Sk., Can.	H4	75
Fillmore, Ca., U.S.	E4	82
Fillmore, Il., U.S.	D4	90
Fillmore, In., U.S.	E4	91
Fillmore, Mo., U.S.	A3	102
Fillmore, N.Y., U.S.	C2	109
Fillmore, N.D., U.S.	A6	111
Fillmore, Ut., U.S.	E3	121
Fillmore, co., Mn., U.S.	G6	100
Fillmore, co., Ne., U.S.	D8	104
Fimi, stm., Zaire	B2	48
Finale Emilia, Italy	E7	20
Fincastle, Va., U.S.	C3	123
Finch, On., Can.	B9	73
Findhorn, stm., Scot., U.K.	C5	13
Findlater, Sk., Can.	G3	75
Findlay, Il., U.S.	D5	90
Findlay, Oh., U.S.	A2	112
Findlay, Mount, mtn., B.C., Can.	D9	69
Fine, N.Y., U.S.	A5	109
Finesville, N.J., U.S.	B2	107
Fingal, N.D., U.S.	C8	111
Finger, Tn., U.S.	B3	119
Finger Lake, l., On., Can.	C5	70
Fingerville, S.C., U.S.	A3	117
Fingoè, Moz.	A5	49
Finike, Tur.	D8	40
Finisterre, Cape, c., Spain	A1	22
Finjasjön, l., Swe.	B7	15
Fink, stm., Austl.	E5	50
Finksburg, Md., U.S.	B4	97
Finland, Mn., U.S.	C7	100
Finland, ctry., Eur.	E12	14
Finland, Gulf of, b., Eur.	H12	14
Finlay, stm., B.C., Can.	m17	69
Finlayson, Mn., U.S.	D6	100
Finley, N.D., U.S.	B8	111
Finley, Ok., U.S.	C6	113
Finley, Tn., U.S.	A2	119
Finleyson, Ga., U.S.	D3	87
Finmoore, B.C., Can.	C6	69
Finn, stm., Ire.	C4	11
Finnegan, Ab., Can.	D4	68
Finney, co., Ks., U.S.	D3	93
Finn Mountain, mtn., Ak., U.S.	C8	79
Finnsburg, Vt., U.S.	C2	122
Finschhafen, Pap. N. Gui.	k12	50
Finspång, Swe.	u33	14
Finsteraarhorn, mtn., Switz.	C7	20
Finsterwalde, Ger.D.R.	C6	18
Fintona, N. Ire., U.K.	C4	11
Fintown, Ire.	C3	11
Fionn Loch, l., Scot., U.K.	C3	13
Fiq, Syria	F10	40
Firat (Euphrates), stm., Asia	B4	38
Fircrest, Wa., U.S.	f10	124
Fir, stm., Sk., Can.	D4	75
Firebaugh, Ca., U.S.	D3	82
Firenzuola, Italy	B3	23
Firesteel, S.D., U.S.	B4	118
Firestone, Co., U.S.	A6	83
Firmat, Arg.	A4	54
Firminy, Fr.	E6	16
Fir Mountain, Sk., Can.	H2	75
Firozabad, India	D7	37
Firozpur, India	B5	36
Firsby, Eng., U.K.	A8	12
Firsovo, Sov. Un.	C11	33
First Connecticut Lake, l., N.H., U.S.	f7	106
First Roach Pond, l., Me., U.S.	C3	96
Firth, Id., U.S.	F6	89
Firth, Ne., U.S.	D9	104
Firūzābād, Iran	G6	39
Firūz Kūh, Iran	B5	38
Fischot Island, i., Nf., Can.	C4	72
Firūz Kūh, Iran	C2	49
Fish, stm., Nmb.	A4	96
Fish, stm., Me., U.S.	A4	96
Fish Cove Point, c., Nf., Can.	A3	72
Fish Creek, Wi., U.S.	C6	126
Fisheating Creek, stm., Fl., U.S.	F5	86
Fisher, Ar., U.S.	B5	81
Fisher, Il., U.S.	C5	90
Fisher, La., U.S.	C2	95
Fisher, Mn., U.S.	C2	100
Fisher, Pa., U.S.	D3	115
Fisher, W.V., U.S.	B5	125
Fisher, co., Tx., U.S.	C2	120
Fisher, stm., On., Can.	D3	70
Fisher Bay, b., Mb., Can.	D3	70
Fisher Branch, Mb., Can.	D3	70
Fisher Glacier, Ant.	B19	7
Fishermans Island, i., Va., U.S.	h15	123
Fishers, In., U.S.	E5	91
Fishers Island, i., N.Y., U.S.	m16	109
Fishers Peak, mtn., Co., U.S.	D6	83
Fisher Strait, strt., N.T., Can.	D16	66
Fishersville, Va., U.S.	B4	123
Fishertown, Pa., U.S.	F4	115
Fishguard [and Goodwick], Wales, U.K.	E4	10
Fish Haven, Id., U.S.	G7	89
Fishhook, b., Mb., Can.	D3	70
Fishing Bay, b., Md., U.S.	D5	97
Fishing Creek, Md., U.S.	D5	97
Fishing Creek, stm., N.C., U.S.	A5	110
Fishing Creek, stm., Pa., U.S.	B5	117
Fishing Creek, stm., W.V., U.S.	B4	125
Fishing Creek, North Fork, stm., W.V., U.S.	h9	125
Fishing Creek, South Fork, stm., W.V., U.S.	h9	125
Fishing Creek Reservoir, res., S.C., U.S.	B6	117
Fishing Lake, l., Mb., Can.	C4	70
Fishing Lake, l., Sk., Can.	F4	75
Fishkill, N.Y., U.S.	D7	109
Fish River Lake, l., Me., U.S.	B4	96
Fish Springs Range, mts., Ut., U.S.	D2	121
Fishtail, Mt., U.S.	E7	103
Fishtail Point, c., Ant.	f39	7
Fishtrap Lake, res., Ky., U.S.	C7	94
Fisk, Mo., U.S.	E7	102
Fiskdale, Ma., U.S.	B3	98
Fiske, Sk., Can.	F1	75
Fismes, Fr.	C5	16
Fitch-Bay, P.Q., Can.	D5	74
Fitchburg, Ma., U.S.	A4	98
Fitchville, Ct., U.S.	C7	84

Name   Map Ref   Page

Fithian, Il., U.S. — C6 90
Fitler, Ms., U.S. — C2 101
Fittstown, Ok., U.S. — C5 113
Fitzgerald, Ga., U.S. — E3 87
Fitzhugh, Ok., U.S. — C5 113
Fitz Hugh Sound, strt., B.C., Can. — D4 69
Fitzpatrick, P.Q., Can. — B5 74
Fitz Roy, Arg. — D3 54
Fitzroy, stm., Austl. — D9 50
Fitzroy, stm., Austl. — C3 50
Fitzroy, Monte (Cerro Chaltel), mtn., S.A. — D2 54
Fitzroy Harbour, On., Can. — B8 73
Fitzwilliam, N.H., U.S. — E2 106
Fitzwilliam Depot, N.H., U.S. — D3 103
Fitzwilliam Island, i., On., Can. — B3 73
Fiume see Rijeka, Yugo. — C2 24
Fiumicino, Italy — h8 23
Five Island Lake, l., Ia., U.S. — A3 92
Five Islands, N.S., Can. — D5 71
Fivemile Creek, stm., Wy., U.S. — C4 127
Fivemiletown, N. Ire., U.K. — C4 11
Five Points, Al., U.S. — B4 78
Five Points, N.M., U.S. — B3 108
Fizi, Zaire — B4 48
Fjärås Kyrkby, Swe. — A6 15
Fjärdhundra, Swe. — t34 14
Fjerritslev, Den. — A3 15
Flagg Mountain, hill, Al., U.S. — C3 78
Flag Knob, mtn., Ky., U.S. — C7 94
Flagler, Co., U.S. — B7 83
Flagler, co., Fl., U.S. — C5 86
Flagler Beach, Fl., U.S. — C5 86
Flag Pond, Tn., U.S. — C11 119
Flagstaff, Az., U.S. — B4 80
Flagstaff Lake, l., Or., U.S. — E7 114
Flagtown, N.J., U.S. — B3 107
Flamand, Lac, l., P.Q., Can. — B4 74
Flambeau, stm., Wi., U.S. — C3 126
Flambeau, South Fork, stm., Wi., U.S. — C3 126
Flamborough Head, c., Eng., U.K. — C7 10
Flaming Gorge Dam, Ut., U.S. — C6 121
Flaming Gorge National Recreation Area, U.S. — E3 127
Flaming Gorge Reservoir, res., U.S. — E3 127
Flanagan, Il., U.S. — C5 90
Flanders, On., Can. — E5 70
Flanders, Ct., U.S. — C2 84
Flanders, N.J., U.S. — *B3 107
Flanders, hist reg., Eur. — B5 16
Flandreau, S.D., U.S. — C9 118
Flandreau Indian Reservation, S.D., U.S. — C9 118
Flannan Islands, is., Scot., U.K. — A3 10
Flåren, l., Swe. — A8 15
Flasher, N.D., U.S. — C4 111
Flat, Ak., U.S. — C8 79
Flat, Ky., U.S. — C6 94
Flat, Mo., U.S. — D6 102
Flat, stm., Mi., U.S. — E5 99
Flat, stm., N.C., U.S. — A4 110
Flat, stm., R.I., U.S. — E2 116
Flat Bay, Nf., Can. — D2 72
Flat Brook, stm., N.J., U.S. — A3 107
Flatbrookville, N.J., U.S. — A3 107
Flatbush, Ab., Can. — B3 68
Flat Creek, Al., U.S. — B2 78
Flat Creek, Tn., U.S. — B5 119
Flathead, co., Mt., U.S. — B2 103
Flathead, stm., N.A. — E10 69
Flathead, North Fork, stm., N.A. — B2 103
Flathead, South Fork, stm., Mt., U.S. — C3 103
Flathead Indian Reservation, Mt., U.S. — C2 103
Flathead Lake, l., Mt., U.S. — C2 103
Flathead Valley, val., Mt., U.S. — C2 103
Flat Island, i., Nf., Can. — C3 72
Flat Lake, l., Ab., Can. — B4 68
Flat Lake, l., La., U.S. — k9 95
Flatlands, N.B., Can. — B3 71
Flat Lick, Ky., U.S. — D6 94
Flat Mountain, mtn., N.Z. — P11 51
Flatonia, Tx., U.S. — E4 120
Flat River, P.E., Can. — C7 71
Flat River, Mo., U.S. — D7 102
Flat River Reservoir, res., R.I., U.S. — D3 116
Flat Rock, Al., U.S. — A4 78
Flat Rock, Il., U.S. — E6 90
Flat Rock, In., U.S. — F6 91
Flat Rock, Mi., U.S. — F7 99
Flat Rock, N.C., U.S. — f10 110
Flat Rock, Oh., U.S. — A3 112
Flatrock, stm., In., U.S. — F6 91
Flatrock Lake, l., Ms., U.S. — B1 70
Flattery, Cape, c., Wa., U.S. — A1 124
Flatts, Ber. — p20 64
Flatwoods, Ky., U.S. — B7 94
Flatwoods, La., U.S. — C3 95
Flatwoods, Tn., U.S. — B4 119
Flatwoods, W.V., U.S. — *C4 125
Flawil, Switz. — B5 20
Flaxcombe, Sk., Can. — F1 75
Flaxton, N.D., U.S. — A3 111
Flaxville, Mt., U.S. — B11 103
Fleet, Ab., Can. — C5 68
Fleet, Eng., U.K. — C7 12
Fleetwood, Eng., U.K. — G5 13
Fleetwood, N.C., U.S. — A1 110
Fleetwood, Pa., U.S. — F10 115
Fleischmanns, N.Y., U.S. — C6 109
Flekkefjord, Nor. — H2 14
Fleming, Sk., Can. — G5 75
Fleming, Co., U.S. — A8 83
Fleming, Ga., U.S. — E5 87
Fleming, Pa., U.S. — E6 115
Fleming, co., Ky., U.S. — B6 94
Fleming-Neon, Ky., U.S. — C7 94
Flemingsburg, Ky., U.S. — B6 94
Flemington, Ga., U.S. — E5 87
Flemington, Mo., U.S. — D4 102
Flemington, N.J., U.S. — B3 107
Flemington, Pa., U.S. — D7 115
Flemington, W.V., U.S. — k10 125
Flen, Swe. — t34 14
Flensburg, F.R.Ger. — A4 18
Flensburg, Mn., U.S. — E4 100
Flensburg Fjord, b., Eur. — D3 15
Flers, Fr. — C3 16
Flesherton, On., Can. — C4 73
Fletcher, On., Can. — E2 73
Fletcher, N.C., U.S. — f10 110
Fletcher, Oh., U.S. — B1 112
Fletcher, Vt., U.S. — B3 122
Fletcher Islands, is., Ant. — B3 7

Fleur-de-Lys, Nf., Can. — C3 72
Fleurier, Switz. — C2 20
Flieden, F.R.Ger. — C4 19
Flims, Switz. — C7 21
Flinders, stm., Austl. — C7 50
Flinders Island, i., Austl. — F5 50
Flinders Range, mts., Austl. — F6 50
Flin Flon, Mb., Can. — B1 70
Flint, Wales, U.K. — A4 12
Flint, In., U.S. — A7 91
Flint, Mi., U.S. — E7 99
Flint, stm., Ga., U.S. — E2 87
Flint City, Al., U.S. — A3 78
Flint Creek, stm., Al., U.S. — A3 78
Flint Creek Range, mts., Mt., U.S. — D3 103
Flinthill, Mo., U.S. — C7 102
Flint Hill, Va., U.S. — B4 123
Flint Hills, hills, Ks., U.S. — D7 93
Flint Island, i., Kir. — G12 6
Flintoft, Sk., Can. — H2 75
Flinton, On., Can. — C7 73
Flint Run, stm., W.V., U.S. — k9 125
Flintstone, Md., U.S. — k13 97
Flintville, Tn., U.S. — B5 119
Flipper Point, c., Wake I. — A2 52
Flippin, Ar., U.S. — A3 81
Flippin, Ky., U.S. — D4 94
Flixecourt, Fr. — D2 17
Flöha, Ger.D.R. — C8 19
Flom, Mn., U.S. — C2 100
Flomaton, Al., U.S. — D2 78
Flomot, Tx., U.S. — B2 120
Flood Range, mts., Ant. — B35 7
Floodwood, Mn., U.S. — D6 100
Flora, Il., U.S. — E5 90
Flora, In., U.S. — C4 91
Flora, Ms., U.S. — C3 101
Flora, N.D., U.S. — B6 111
Florahome, Fl., U.S. — C5 86
Floral, Al., U.S. — D3 78
Floral City, Fl., U.S. — D4 86
Floral Park, N.Y., U.S. — *k13 109
Flora Vista, N.M., U.S. — A1 108
Florala, Al., U.S. — D3 78
Florence (Firenze), Italy — C3 23
Florence, Al., U.S. — A2 78
Florence, Az., U.S. — D4 80
Florence, Ca., U.S. — *n12 82
Florence, Co., U.S. — C5 83
Florence, In., U.S. — G8 91
Florence, Ks., U.S. — D7 93
Florence, Ky., U.S. — A5 94
Florence, Ms., U.S. — C3 101
Florence, Mo., U.S. — C5 102
Florence, Mt., U.S. — D2 103
Florence, N.J., U.S. — C3 107
Florence, Or., U.S. — D2 114
Florence, S.C., U.S. — C8 117
Florence, S.D., U.S. — B8 118
Florence, Tx., U.S. — D4 120
Florence, Vt., U.S. — D2 122
Florence, Wa., U.S. — A3 124
Florence, Wi., U.S. — C5 126
Florence, co., S.C., U.S. — C8 117
Florence, co., Wi., U.S. — C5 126
Florence Junction, Az., U.S. — D4 80
Florenceville, N.B., Can. — C2 71
Florencia, Col. — C2 60
Florenville, Bel. — E5 17
Flores, Guat. — D7 63
Flores, dept., Ur. — f8 54
Flores, i., Indon. — G6 34
Flores, i., Port. — g8 44
Flores Island, i., B.C., Can. — E4 69
Flores Sea, Indon. — G6 34
Floresta, Braz. — C3 57
Floresville, Tx., U.S. — E3 120
Florham Park, N.J., U.S. — B4 107
Floriano, Braz. — C2 57
Floriano Peixoto, Braz. — C4 58
Florianópolis, Braz. — C3 57
Florida, Cuba — D4 64
Florida, Ma., U.S. — A1 98
Florida, N.M., U.S. — C3 108
Florida, N.Y., U.S. — D6 109
Florida, Oh., U.S. — A1 112
Florida, Ur. — E1 56
Florida, dept., Ur. — f8 54
Florida, state, U.S. — E5 86
Florida, Cape, c., Fl., U.S. — G6 86
Florida, Straits of, strt., N.A. — F11 76
Florida Bay, b., Fl., U.S. — H6 86
Floridablanca, Col. — *B3 60
Florida City, Fl., U.S. — G6 86
Florida Keys, is., Fl., U.S. — H6 86
Florida Mountains, mts., N.M., U.S. — E2 108
Florida State Indian Reservation, Fl., U.S. — F5 86
Florien, La., U.S. — C2 95
Florin, Ca., U.S. — *C3 82
Flórina (Phlorina), Grc. — B3 25
Floris, Ia., U.S. — D5 92
Florissant, Co., U.S. — C5 83
Florissant, Mo., U.S. — f13 102
Florissant Fossil Beds National Monument, Co., U.S. — C5 83
Flossmoor, Il., U.S. — k9 90
Flournoy, Ca., U.S. — C2 82
Flourtown, Pa., U.S. — o21 115
Flovilla, Ga., U.S. — C3 87
Flower Brook, stm., Vt., U.S. — E2 122
Floweree, Mt., U.S. — C5 103
Flower Hill, N.Y., U.S. — *E7 109
Flower's Cove, Nf., Can. — C3 72
Flower Station, On., Can. — B8 73
Flowery Branch, Ga., U.S. — B3 87
Flowood, Ms., U.S. — C3 101
Floyd, Ia., U.S. — A5 92
Floyd, N.M., U.S. — C6 108
Floyd, Va., U.S. — C2 123
Floyd, co., Ga., U.S. — B1 87
Floyd, co., In., U.S. — H6 91
Floyd, co., Ia., U.S. — A5 92
Floyd, co., Ky., U.S. — C7 94
Floyd, co., Tx., U.S. — B2 120
Floyd, co., Va., U.S. — D2 123
Floyd, stm., Ia., U.S. — B1 92
Floydada, Tx., U.S. — B2 120
Floyd Dale, S.C., U.S. — C9 117
Floydsburg, Ky., U.S. — g12 94
Floyds Fork, stm., Ky., U.S. — B4 94
Floyds Knobs, In., U.S. — H6 91
Fluchthorn, mtn., Eur. — C9 21
Fluessen, l., Neth. — B5 17
Flumendosa, stm., Italy — E2 23
Flums, Switz. — B6 21
Flushing, Mi., U.S. — E7 99
Flushing, Oh., U.S. — B4 112
Fluvanna, Tx., U.S. — C2 120
Fluvanna, co., Va., U.S. — C4 123
Fly, stm. — k11 50
Fly Creek, N.Y., U.S. — C6 109
Flyinge, Swe. — C7 15
Flying H, N.M., U.S. — D4 108

Foam Lake, Sk., Can. — F4 75
Foam Lake, l., Sk., Can. — F4 75
Foard, co., Tx., U.S. — B3 120
Foça, Tur. — C6 25
Foča, Yugo. — D4 24
Fochabers, Scot., U.K. — C5 13
Focșani, Rom. — C8 24
Foggia, Italy — D5 23
Fogland Point, c., R.I., U.S. — E6 116
Fogliano, Italy — k9 23
Fogo, Nf., Can. — D4 72
Fogo, Cape, c., Nf., Can. — D5 72
Fogo Island, i., Nf., Can. — D4 72
Föhr, i., F.R.Ger. — A4 18
Foix, Fr. — F4 16
Folcroft, Pa., U.S. — *p20 115
Foley, Al., U.S. — E2 78
Foley, Mn., U.S. — E5 100
Foley, Mo., U.S. — B7 102
Foley Island, i., N.T., Can. — C17 66
Foligno, Italy — C4 23
Folkestone, Eng., U.K. — E7 10
Folkston, Ga., U.S. — F4 87
Folkstone, N.C., U.S. — C5 110
Follansbee, W.V., U.S. — A4 125
Follett, Tx., U.S. — A2 120
Follonica, Italy — C3 23
Folly Beach, S.C., U.S. — F8 117
Folly Island, i., S.C., U.S. — F8 117
Folly Lake, N.S., Can. — D6 71
Folsom, Ca., U.S. — C3 82
Folsom, La., U.S. — D5 95
Folsom, N.J., U.S. — D3 107
Folsom, N.M., U.S. — A6 108
Folsom, Pa., U.S. — *p20 115
Folsom, W.V., U.S. — B4 125
Folsomville, In., U.S. — H3 91
Fomento, Cuba — C4 64
Fonda, Ia., U.S. — B3 92
Fonda, N.Y., U.S. — C6 109
Fond-du-Lac, Sk., Can. — m7 75
Fond du Lac, Wi., U.S. — E5 126
Fond du Lac, co., Wi., U.S. — E5 126
Fond du Lac Indian Reservation, Mn., U.S. — D6 100
Fonde, Ky., U.S. — D6 94
Fondi, Italy — D4 23
Fonsagrada, Spain — B3 22
Fonseca, Golfo de, b., N.A. — E7 63
Fontainebleau, Fr. — C5 16
Fontana, Ca., U.S. — m14 82
Fontana, Ks., U.S. — D9 93
Fontana, Wi., U.S. — F5 126
Fontana Dam, N.C., U.S. — f9 110
Fontana Lake, res., N.C., U.S. — f9 110
Fontanelle, Ia., U.S. — C3 92
Fontanet, In., U.S. — E3 91
Fonte Boa, Braz. — D4 60
Fontenay-le-Comte, Fr. — D3 16
Fontenay [-sous-Bois], Fr. — g10 16
Fontenelle, Wy., U.S. — E2 127
Fontenelle Reservoir, res., Wy., U.S. — D2 127
Foosland, Il., U.S. — C5 90
Foothill Farms, Ca., U.S. — *C3 82
Foothills, Ab., Can. — C2 68
Footville, Wi., U.S. — F4 126
Foping, China — H2 32
Forada, Mn., U.S. — E3 100
Foraker, Oh., U.S. — B2 112
Foraker, Ok., U.S. — A5 113
Foraker, Mount, mtn., Ak., U.S. — f16 79
Forbach, Fr. — C7 16
Forbes, Austl. — F8 50
Forbes, Mn., U.S. — C6 100
Forbes, Mo., U.S. — B2 102
Forbes, N.D., U.S. — D7 111
Forbes, Lac, l., P.Q., Can. — C3 74
Forbes, Mount, mtn., Ab., Can. — D2 68
Forcados, Nig. — E6 45
Forcalquier, Fr. — F6 16
Force, Pa., U.S. — D4 115
Forchheim, F.R.Ger. — D5 19
Ford, Scot., U.K. — D3 13
Ford, Ks., U.S. — E4 93
Ford, Ky., U.S. — C5 94
Ford, co., Il., U.S. — C5 90
Ford, co., Ks., U.S. — E4 93
Ford, stm., Mi., U.S. — C3 99
Ford City, Ca., U.S. — E4 82
Ford City, Pa., U.S. — E2 115
Fordland, Mo., U.S. — D5 102
Fordoche, La., U.S. — D4 95
Ford Ranges, mts., Ant. — B34 7
Ford River, Mi., U.S. — C3 99
Fords, N.J., U.S. — C4 107
Fords Prairie, Wa., U.S. — C3 124
Fordsville, Ky., U.S. — C3 94
Fordville, N.D., U.S. — A8 111
Fordwich, On., Can. — D3 73
Fordyce, Ar., U.S. — D3 81
Fordyce, Ne., U.S. — B8 104
Forécariah, Gui. — E2 45
Foreman, Ar., U.S. — D1 81
Foremost, Ab., Can. — E5 68
Foresman, In., U.S. — C3 91
Forest, Bel. — B6 16
Forest, On., Can. — D2 73
Forest, In., U.S. — D5 91
Forest, Ms., U.S. — C4 101
Forest, Oh., U.S. — B2 112
Forest, Tx., U.S. — D5 120
Forest, Va., U.S. — C3 123
Forest, co., Pa., U.S. — C3 115
Forest, co., Wi., U.S. — C5 126
Forest, stm., N.D., U.S. — A8 111
Forest Acres, S.C., U.S. — C6 117
Forestburg, Ab., Can. — C4 68
Forestburg, S.D., U.S. — C7 118
Forest City, Il., U.S. — C4 90
Forest City, Ia., U.S. — A4 92
Forest City, Mo., U.S. — B2 102
Forest City, N.C., U.S. — B1 110
Forest City, Pa., U.S. — C11 115
Forestdale, R.I., U.S. — B3 116
Forest Dale, Vt., U.S. — D2 122
Forest Glen, La., U.S. — h12 95
Forest Green, Mo., U.S. — B5 102
Forestgrove, Mt., U.S. — D7 103
Forest Grove, Or., U.S. — B3 114
Forest Hill, La., U.S. — C3 95
Forest Hill, Md., U.S. — A5 97
Forest Hill, Tx., U.S. — *n9 120
Forest Hills, Pa., U.S. — k14 115
Forest Home, Al., U.S. — D3 78
Forest Junction, Wi., U.S. — h9 126
Forest Knolls, Ca., U.S. — g7 82
Forest Lake, Mi., U.S. — B4 99
Forest Lake, Mn., U.S. — E6 100
Forest Lake, N.H., U.S. — E2 106
Foreston, Mn., U.S. — E5 100

Foreston, S.C., U.S. — D7 117
Forest Park, Ga., U.S. — h8 87
Forest Park, Il., U.S. — k9 90
Forest Park, La., U.S. — B3 95
Forest Park, Oh., U.S. — n12 112
Forestport, N.Y., U.S. — B5 109
Forest River, N.D., U.S. — A8 111
Forestville, Md., U.S. — *C4 97
Forestville, N.Y., U.S. — C1 109
Forestville, Pa., U.S. — D1 115
Forestville, Wi., U.S. — D6 126
Forfar, Scot., U.K. — B5 10
Forgan, Sk., Can. — F2 75
Forgan, Ok., U.S. — A1 113
Forges-les-Eaux, Fr. — C4 16
Forget, Sk., Can. — H4 75
Fork, N.C., U.S. — B2 110
Fork, S.C., U.S. — C9 117
Fork Creek, stm., W.V., U.S. — m12 125
Forked Deer, stm., Tn., U.S. — B2 119
Forked Deer, Middle Fork, stm., Tn., U.S. — D3 119
Forked Deer, North Fork, stm., Tn., U.S. — B3 119
Forked Deer, South Fork, stm., Tn., U.S. — B2 119
Forked Island, La., U.S. — E3 95
Forked River, N.J., U.S. — D4 107
Forkland, Al., U.S. — C2 78
Fork Mountain, Tn., U.S. — C9 119
Fork River, Mb., Can. — D1 70
Forks, Wa., U.S. — B1 124
Forks of Salmon, Ca., U.S. — B2 82
Fork Shoals, S.C., U.S. — B3 117
Forksville, Pa., U.S. — D8 115
Fork Union, Va., U.S. — C4 123
Forkville, Ms., U.S. — C4 101
Forlì, Italy — B4 23
Formby, Eng., U.K. — A4 12
Formello, Italy — g8 23
Formentera, i., Spain — C6 22
Formiga, Braz. — C3 56
Formigine, Italy — C4 20
Formosa, Arg. — B4 55
Formosa, Braz. — B3 56
Formosa, On., Can. — C3 73
Formosa, prov., Arg. — B4 55
Formosa, Serra, plat., Braz. — E4 59
Formosa Bay, b., Kenya — B7 48
Formosa see Taiwan, ctry., Asia — G9 31
Formoso, Ks., U.S. — C6 93
Formoso, stm., Braz. — E5 59
Fornovo di Taro, Italy — E6 20
Forres, Scot., U.K. — B5 10
Forrest, Austl. — F4 50
Forrest, Il., U.S. — C5 90
Forrest, N.M., U.S. — C6 108
Forrest, co., Ms., U.S. — D4 101
Forrest City, Ar., U.S. — B5 81
Forrester Island, i., Ak., U.S. — n23 79
Forrest Lakes, l., Austl. — E4 50
Forreston, Il., U.S. — A4 90
Forrest Station, Mb., Can. — E2 70
Forsan, Tx., U.S. — C2 120
Forsayth, Austl. — C7 50
Forst [Lausitz], Ger.D.R. — C7 18
Forsyth, Ga., U.S. — C3 87
Forsyth, Il., U.S. — D5 90
Forsyth, Mo., U.S. — E4 102
Forsyth, Mt., U.S. — D10 103
Forsyth, co., Ga., U.S. — B2 87
Forsyth, co., N.C., U.S. — A2 110
Fort Adams, Ms., U.S. — D2 101
Fort Albany, On., Can. — n19 73
Fortaleza, Braz. — B3 57
Fortaleza de Ituxi, Braz. — C4 58
Fort Ann, N.Y., U.S. — B7 109
Fort Apache, Az., U.S. — D6 80
Fort Apache Indian Reservation, Az., U.S. — D5 80
Fort-Archambault see Sarh, Chad — D3 46
Fort Ashby, W.V., U.S. — B6 125
Fort Assiniboine, Ab., Can. — B3 68
Fort Atkinson, Ia., U.S. — A6 92
Fort Atkinson, Wi., U.S. — F5 126
Fort Augustus, Scot., U.K. — C4 13
Fort Barnwell, N.C., U.S. — B5 110
Fort Belknap Agency, Mt., U.S. — B8 103
Fort Belknap Indian Reservation, Mt., U.S. — B8 103
Fort Belvoir, Va., U.S. — g12 123
Fort Benjamin Harrison, mil., In., U.S. — k10 91
Fort Benning, mil., Ga., U.S. — D2 87
Fort Benton, Mt., U.S. — C6 103
Fort Berthold Indian Reservation, N.D., U.S. — B3 111
Fort Bidwell, Ca., U.S. — B3 82
Fort Bidwell Indian Reservation, Ca., U.S. — B3 82
Fort Blackmore, Va., U.S. — f9 123
Fort Bliss, mil., Tx., U.S. — o11 120
Fort Bragg, Ca., U.S. — C2 82
Fort Bragg, mil., N.C., U.S. — B3 110
Fort Branch, In., U.S. — H2 91
Fort Bridger, Wy., U.S. — E2 127
Fort Calhoun, Ne., U.S. — C9 104
Fort Campbell, mil., U.S. — A4 119
Fort Carson, mil., Co., U.S. — C6 83
Fort-Chimo, P.Q., Can. — g13 74
Fort Chipewyan, Ab., Can. — f8 68
Fort Clark, N.D., U.S. — B4 111
Fort Clatsop National Memorial, hist., Or., U.S. — A3 114
Fort Cobb, Ok., U.S. — B3 113
Fort Cobb Reservoir, res., Ok., U.S. — B3 113
Fort Collins, Co., U.S. — A5 83
Fort Coulonge, P.Q., Can. — C6 74
Fort Covington, N.Y., U.S. — f10 109
Fort Crampel, Cen. Afr. Rep. — C4 46
Fort Davis, Al., U.S. — C4 78
Fort Davis, Tx., U.S. — *n9 120
Fort Davis National Historic Site, hist., Tx., U.S. — o13 120
Fort Defiance, Az., U.S. — B6 80
Fort-de-France, Mart. — I14 64
Fort-de-France, Baie de, b., Mart. — S10 65
Fort Deposit, Al., U.S. — D3 78
Fort Detrick, mil., Md., U.S. — B3 97

Fort Devens, mil., Ma., U.S. — f9 98
Fort Dix, mil., N.J., U.S. — C3 107
Fort Dodge, Ia., U.S. — B3 92
Fort Dodge, Ks., U.S. — D4 93
Fort Donelson National Military Park, Tn., U.S. — A4 119
Fort Duchesne, Ut., U.S. — C6 121
Forteau, Nf., Can. — C3 72
Fort Edward, N.Y., U.S. — B7 109
Fort Erie, On., Can. — E6 73
Fortescue, Mo., U.S. — A2 102
Fortescue, N.J., U.S. — E2 107
Fortescue, stm., Austl. — D2 50
Fortine, Mt., U.S. — B2 103
Fortín Uno, Arg. — B3 54
Fort Jackson, mil., S.C., U.S. — C6 117
Fort Jefferson National Monument, Fl., U.S. — H4 86
Fort Jennings, Oh., U.S. — B1 112
Fort Jones, Ca., U.S. — B2 82
Fort Kent, Ab., Can. — B5 68
Fort Kent, Me., U.S. — A4 96
Fort Kent Mills, Me., U.S. — A4 96
Fort Klamath, Or., U.S. — E5 114
Fort Knox, mil., Ky., U.S. — B4 94
Fort-Lamy see N'Djamena, Chad — C3 46
Fort Langley, B.C., Can. — f13 69
Fort Laramie, Wy., U.S. — D8 127
Fort Laramie National Historic Site, hist., Wy., U.S. — D8 127
Fort Lauderdale, Fl., U.S. — F6 86
Fort Lawn, S.C., U.S. — B6 117
Fort Leavenworth, mil., Ks., U.S. — C9 93
Fort Lee, N.J., U.S. — B5 107
Fort Lee, mil., Va., U.S. — C5 123
Fort Leonard Wood, mil., Mo., U.S. — D5 102
Fort Lewis, mil., Wa., U.S. — B3 124
Fort Liard, N.T., Can. — D8 66
Fort-Liberté, Haiti — E8 64
Fort Littleton, Pa., U.S. — F5 115
Fort Loramie, Oh., U.S. — B1 112
Fort Loudon, Pa., U.S. — G6 115
Fort Loudoun Lake, res., Tn., U.S. — D9 119
Fort Lupton, Co., U.S. — A6 83
Fort MacArthur, mil., Ca., U.S. — n12 82
Fort MacKay, Ab., Can. — f8 68
Fort Macleod, Ab., Can. — E4 68
Fort Madison, Ia., U.S. — D6 92
Fort Matanzas National Monument, Fl., U.S. — C5 86
Fort McClellan, mil., Al., U.S. — B4 78
Fort McDermitt Indian Reservation, Az., U.S. — B4 105
Fort McDowell Indian Reservation, Az., U.S. — D4 80
Fort McHenry National Monument And Historic Shrine, Md., U.S. — g11 97
Fort McKavett, Tx., U.S. — *D2 120
Fort McKinley, Oh., U.S. — *C1 112
Fort McMurray, Ab., Can. — A5 68
Fort McPherson, N.T., Can. — C6 66
Fort Meade, Fl., U.S. — E5 86
Fort Meade, mil., Md., U.S. — B4 97
Fort Meadow Reservoir, res., Ma., U.S. — g9 98
Fort Mill, S.C., U.S. — A6 117
Fort Miller, N.Y., U.S. — B7 109
Fort Mitchell, Al., U.S. — C4 78
Fort Mitchell, Ky., U.S. — h13 94
Fort Mohave Indian Reservation, U.S. — C1 80
Fort Monmouth, mil., N.J., U.S. — C4 107
Fort Monroe, mil., Va., U.S. — h15 123
Fort Morgan, Al., U.S. — E1 78
Fort Morgan, Co., U.S. — A7 83
Fort Motte, S.C., U.S. — D6 117
Fort Myer, mil., Va., U.S. — g12 123
Fort Myers, Fl., U.S. — F5 86
Fort Myers Beach, Fl., U.S. — F5 86
Fort Necessity, La., U.S. — B4 95
Fort Nelson, B.C., Can. — m18 69
Fort Norman, N.T., Can. — D7 66
Fort Ogden, Fl., U.S. — E5 86
Fort Oglethorpe, Ga., U.S. — B1 87
Fort Ord, mil., Ca., U.S. — D3 82
Fort Payne, Al., U.S. — A4 78
Fort Peck, Mt., U.S. — B10 103
Fort Peck Dam, Mt., U.S. — B10 103
Fort Peck Indian Reservation, Mt., U.S. — B11 103
Fort Peck Lake, res., Mt., U.S. — C9 103
Fort Pierce, Fl., U.S. — E6 86
Fort Pierce Inlet, b., Fl., U.S. — E6 86
Fort Pierre, S.D., U.S. — C5 118
Fort Plain, N.Y., U.S. — C6 109
Fort Polk, mil., La., U.S. — C2 95
Fort Portal, Ug. — A5 48
Fort Providence, N.T., Can. — D9 66
Fort Qu'Appelle, Sk., Can. — G4 75
Fort Randall Dam, S.D., U.S. — D7 118
Fort Ransom, N.D., U.S. — C8 111
Fort Recovery, Oh., U.S. — B1 112
Fort Reliance, N.T., Can. — D11 66
Fort Resolution, N.T., Can. — D10 66

Fortress Mountain, mtn., Wy., U.S. — B3 127
Fort Rice, N.D., U.S. — C5 111
Fort Richardson, mil., Ak., U.S. — C10 79
Fort Riley, mil., Ks., U.S. — C7 93
Fort Ripley, Mn., U.S. — D4 100
Fort Ritchie, mil., Md., U.S. — A3 97
Fort Ritner, In., U.S. — G5 91
Fort Robinson, Ne., U.S. — B2 104
Fort Rock, Or., U.S. — D5 114
Fortrose, N.Z. — Q12 51
Fortrose, Scot., U.K. — C4 13
Fort Ross, N.T., Can. — B14 66
Fort Saint James, B.C., Can. — B5 69
Fort Saint John, B.C., Can. — A7 69
Fort Sam Houston, mil., Tx., U.S. — k7 120
Fort Sandeman, Pak. — B4 36
Fort Saskatchewan, Ab., Can. — C4 68
Fort Scott, Ks., U.S. — E9 93
Fort Severn, On., Can. — n18 73
Fort Shafter, mil., Hi., U.S. — g10 88
Fort Shaw, Mt., U.S. — C5 103
Fort Shawnee, Oh., U.S. — B1 112
Fort Sheridan, mil., Il., U.S. — h9 90
Fort-Shevchenko, Sov. Un. — E4 28
Fort Sibut, Cen. Afr. Rep. — D3 46
Fort Sill, mil., Ok., U.S. — C3 113
Fort Simpson, N.T., Can. — D8 66
Fort Smith, Ab., Can. — f8 68
Fort Smith, N.T., Can. — D10 66
Fort Smith, Ar., U.S. — B1 81
Fort Stanton, N.M., U.S. — D4 108
Fort Steele, B.C., Can. — E10 69
Fort Steele, Wy., U.S. — E6 127
Fort Stewart, mil., Ga., U.S. — D5 87
Fort Stockton, Tx., U.S. — D1 120
Fort Sumner, N.M., U.S. — C5 108
Fort Sumter National Monument, S.C., U.S. — k12 117
Fort Supply, Ok., U.S. — A2 113
Fort Supply Lake, res., Ok., U.S. — A2 113
Fort Thomas, Az., U.S. — D6 80
Fort Thomas, Ky., U.S. — h14 94
Fort Thompson, S.D., U.S. — C6 118
Fort Totten, N.D., U.S. — B7 111
Fort Totten Indian Reservation, N.D., U.S. — B7 111
Fort Towson, Ok., U.S. — C6 113
Fortuna, Ca., U.S. — B1 82
Fortuna, Mo., U.S. — C5 102
Fortuna, N.D., U.S. — A2 111
Fortuna Ledge (Marshall), Ak., U.S. — C7 79
Fortune, Nf., Can. — E4 72
Fortune Bay, b., Nf., Can. — E4 72
Fortune Harbour, Nf., Can. — D4 72
Fort Union National Monument, N.M., U.S. — B5 108
Fort Valley, Ga., U.S. — D3 87
Fort Vermilion, Ab., Can. — f7 68
Fortville, In., U.S. — E6 91
Fort Wainwright, mil., Ak., U.S. — C10 79
Fort Walton Beach, Fl., U.S. — u15 86
Fort Washakie, Wy., U.S. — C4 127
Fort Washington, Pa., U.S. — o21 115
Fort Washington Forest, Md., U.S. — C4 97
Fort Wayne, In., U.S. — B7 91
Fort Wellington, Guy. — A3 59
Fort White, Fl., U.S. — C4 86
Fort William, Scot., U.K. — B4 10
Fort Wingate, N.M., U.S. — B1 108
Fort Worth, Tx., U.S. — C4 120
Fort Wright, Ky., U.S. — h13 94
Fort Yates, N.D., U.S. — C5 111
Forty Fort, Pa., U.S. — D10 115
Fort Yukon, Ak., U.S. — B10 79
Fort Yuma Indian Reservation, Ca., U.S. — F6 82
Foruk, Iran — H7 39
Foss, Ok., U.S. — B2 113
Fossano, Italy — B1 23
Fosser, Nor. — p29 14
Fossil, Or., U.S. — C6 114
Fossil Butte National Monument, Wy., U.S. — E2 127
Fossil Lake, l., Or., U.S. — D6 114
Fossombrone, Italy — C4 23
Foss Reservoir, res., Ok., U.S. — B2 113
Fosston, Sk., Can. — E4 75
Fosston, Mn., U.S. — C3 100
Foster, In., U.S. — D3 91
Foster, Ky., U.S. — B5 94
Foster, Mo., U.S. — C3 102
Foster, Ne., U.S. — B8 104
Foster, Or., U.S. — C4 114
Foster, Wi., U.S. — D2 126
Foster, co., N.D., U.S. — B6 111
Foster Brook, Pa., U.S. — C4 115
Foster City, Ca., U.S. — *h8 82
Foster City, Mi., U.S. — C3 99
Fosters, Al., U.S. — B2 78
Fosters Falls, Va., U.S. — D2 123
Fosters Pond, l., Ma., U.S. — f11 98
Foster Village, Hi., U.S. — g10 88
Fosterville, Tn., U.S. — B5 119
Fostoria, Al., U.S. — C3 78
Fostoria, Ia., U.S. — A2 92
Fostoria, Ks., U.S. — C7 93
Fostoria, Mi., U.S. — E7 99
Fostoria, Oh., U.S. — A2 112
Fougamou, Gabon — F2 46
Fougères, Fr. — C3 16
Foula, i., Scot., U.K. — C8 12
Foulness Island, i., Eng., U.K. — N13 51
Foulwind, Cape, c., N.Z. — N13 51
Foumban, Cam. — D2 46
Foum el Hassane, Mor. — D3 44
Foun, Mor. — D6 94
Fountain, Co., U.S. — C6 83
Fountain, Fl., U.S. — B1 86
Fountain, Mn., U.S. — G6 100
Fountain, N.C., U.S. — B5 110
Fountain, co., In., U.S. — D3 91
Fountain City, In., U.S. — E8 91
Fountain City, Wi., U.S. — D2 126
Fountain Creek, stm., Co., U.S. — C6 83
Fountain Green, Ut., U.S. — D4 121
Fountain Hill, Ar., U.S. — D4 81
Fountain Hill, Pa., U.S. — E11 115
Fountain Inn, S.C., U.S. — B3 117
Fountain Lake, Ar., U.S. — f8 81
Fountain Peak, mtn., Ca., U.S. — E6 82

Name	Map Ref	Page
Fountain Place, La., U.S.	D4	95
Fountain Run, Ky., U.S.	D4	94
Fountaintown, In., U.S.	E6	91
Fountain Valley, Ca., U.S.	*n13	103
Four Buttes, Mt., U.S.	B11	103
Fourchambault, Fr.	D5	16
Fourche, Ar., U.S.	*C3	81
Fourche, stm., Ar., U.S.	k10	81
Fourche LaFave, stm., Ar., U.S.	C2	81
Fourche Maline, stm., Ok., U.S.	C6	113
Fourche Mountain, mtn., Ar., U.S.	C2	81
Fourchu, N.S., Can.	D9	71
Four Corners, Mt., U.S.	E5	82
Four Corners, Or., U.S.	*C4	114
Four Corners, Wy., U.S.	B8	127
Four Lakes, Wa., U.S.	B8	124
Fourmies, Fr.	B6	16
Fourmile, Ky., U.S.	D6	94
Fourmile Creek, stm., Ia., U.S.	e8	92
Four Mountains, Islands of, is., Ak., U.S.	E6	79
Fournier, On., Can.	B10	73
Four Oaks, N.C., U.S.	B4	110
Fouta Djallon, reg., Gui.	D2	45
Foveaux Strait, strt., N.Z.	Q11	51
Fowey, Eng., U.K.	D3	12
Fowler, Ca., U.S.	D4	82
Fowler, Co., U.S.	C6	83
Fowler, Il., U.S.	C2	90
Fowler, In., U.S.	C3	91
Fowler, Ks., U.S.	E3	93
Fowler, Mi., U.S.	E6	99
Fowlerton, In., U.S.	D6	91
Fowlerton, Tx., U.S.	E3	120
Fowlerville, Mi., U.S.	F6	99
Fowlkes, Tn., U.S.	B2	119
Fowlstown, Ga., U.S.	F2	87
Fox, Ar., U.S.	B3	81
Fox, Ok., U.S.	C4	113
Fox, Or., U.S.	C7	114
Fox, stm., Mb., Can.	B4	70
Fox, stm., U.S.	B5	90
Fox, stm., U.S.	A6	102
Fox, stm., Mi., U.S.	B4	99
Fox, stm., Wi., U.S.	D5	126
Foxboro, On., Can.	C7	73
Foxboro, Ma., U.S.	B5	98
Foxboro, Wi., U.S.	B1	126
Fox Chapel, Pa., U.S.	*h14	115
Fox Creek, Ab., Can.	B2	68
Foxdale, I. of Man	F4	13
Foxe Basin, b., N.T., Can.	C17	66
Foxe Channel, strt., N.T., Can.	D16	66
Foxe Peninsula, pen., N.T., Can.	C17	66
Foxford, Sk., Can.	D3	75
Foxford, Ire.	D2	11
Fox Harbour, Nf., Can.	E5	72
Fox Harbour, Nf., Can.	B4	72
Foxholm, N.D., U.S.	A4	111
Fox Island, i., R.I., U.S.	E4	116
Fox Island, i., Wa., U.S.	f10	124
Fox Islands, is., Ak., U.S.	E6	79
Fox Lake, Il., U.S.	A5	90
Fox Lake, Wi., U.S.	E5	126
Fox Lake, l., U.S.	h8	90
Fox Mountain, mtn., Yk., Can.	D6	66
Fox Mountain, mtn., Nv., U.S.	B2	105
Foxpark, Wy., U.S.	E6	127
Fox Point, Wi., U.S.	E6	126
Fox River Grove, Il., U.S.	h8	90
Foxton, N.Z.	N15	51
Foxvale, Ma., U.S.	B5	98
Fox Valley, Sk., Can.	G1	75
Foxville, Vt., U.S.	C4	122
Foxwarren, Mb., Can.	D1	70
Foxworth, Ms., U.S.	D4	101
Foyil, Ok., U.S.	A6	113
Foyle, stm., Eur.	C4	11
Foyle, Lough, l., Eur.	C3	10
Foynes, Ire.	D2	10
Foz do Cunene, Ang.	E1	48
Foz do Iguaçu, Braz.	D2	56
Foz do Jordão, Braz.	C3	58
Foz do Paunini, Braz.	C4	58
Frackville, Pa., U.S.	E9	115
Fraga, Spain	B6	22
Fraile Muerto, Ur.	E2	56
Frametown, W.V., U.S.	C4	125
Framingham, Ma., U.S.	B5	98
Framnes Mountains, mts., Ant.	C19	7
Franca, Braz.	C3	56
França, Braz.	D2	57
Française, Pointe, c., Fr. Gu.	C5	58
Francavilla Fontana, Italy	D6	23
France, ctry., Eur.	D5	16
Frances, Ky., U.S.	e9	94
Francés, Cabo, c., Cuba	D2	64
Franceville, In., U.S.	C4	91
Franceville, Gabon	F2	46
Franche-Comté, hist reg., Fr.	D6	16
Francis, Sk., Can.	G4	75
Francis, Ok., U.S.	C5	113
Francis, Ut., U.S.	C4	121
Francis, W.V., U.S.	k10	125
Francis, Lake, l., N.H., U.S.	f7	106
Francis Case, Lake, res., S.D., U.S.	D6	118
Francisco, In., U.S.	H3	91
Francisco de Orellana, Ec.	B2	58
Francisco Sá, Braz.	B4	56
Francis Creek, Wi., U.S.	h10	126
Francistown, Bots.	B4	49
François, Nf., Can.	E3	72
François Lake, l., B.C., Can.	C5	69
Franconia, N.H., U.S.	B3	106
Franconia Notch, N.H., U.S.	B3	106
Franconville, Fr.	g9	16
Francs Peak, mtn., Wy., U.S.	C3	127
Franeker, Neth.	A5	17
Frank, W.V., U.S.	C5	125
Frankel City, Tx., U.S.	C1	120
Frankenberg, Ger.D.R.	D8	19
Frankenberg [-Eder], F.R.Ger.	C4	18
Frankenmuth, Mi., U.S.	E7	99
Frankenthal, F.R.Ger.	D4	18
Frankewing, Tn., U.S.	B5	119
Frankfield, Jam.	E14	65
Frankford see Kilcormac, Ire.	D4	11
Frankford, De., U.S.	C7	73
Frankford, Mo., U.S.	B6	102
Frankford, W.V., U.S.	D4	125
Frankford, On., Can.	C7	73
Frankfort, Il., U.S.	m9	90
Frankfort, In., U.S.	D4	91
Frankfort, Ks., U.S.	C7	93
Frankfort, Ky., U.S.	B5	94
Frankfort, Me., U.S.	D4	96
Frankfort, Mi., U.S.	D4	99
Frankfort, N.Y., U.S.	B5	109
Frankfort, Oh., U.S.	C2	112
Frankfort, S.D., U.S.	C7	118
Frankfurt [am Main], F.R.Ger.	C4	18
Frankfurt [an der Oder], Ger.D.R.	B7	18
Fränkische Saale, stm., F.R.Ger.	C5	19
Frank Lake, l., Ab., Can.	D4	68
Franklin, Al., U.S.	D2	78
Franklin, Az., U.S.	E6	80
Franklin, Ar., U.S.	A4	81
Franklin, Ct., U.S.	C7	84
Franklin, Ga., U.S.	C1	87
Franklin, Id., U.S.	G7	89
Franklin, Il., U.S.	F5	91
Franklin, In., U.S.	F5	91
Franklin, Ia., U.S.	E9	93
Franklin, Ks., U.S.	E9	93
Franklin, Ky., U.S.	D3	94
Franklin, La., U.S.	E4	95
Franklin, Me., U.S.	D4	96
Franklin, Ma., U.S.	B5	98
Franklin, Mn., U.S.	F4	100
Franklin, Mo., U.S.	B5	102
Franklin, Ne., U.S.	D7	104
Franklin, N.H., U.S.	D3	106
Franklin, N.J., U.S.	A3	107
Franklin, N.Y., U.S.	C5	109
Franklin, N.C., U.S.	f9	110
Franklin, Oh., U.S.	C1	112
Franklin, Pa., U.S.	D2	115
Franklin, Tn., U.S.	B5	119
Franklin, Tx., U.S.	D4	120
Franklin, Va., U.S.	D6	123
Franklin, W.V., U.S.	C5	125
Franklin, Wi., U.S.	n11	126
Franklin, dept., N.T., Can.	B15	66
Franklin, co., Al., U.S.	A2	78
Franklin, co., Ar., U.S.	B2	81
Franklin, co., Fl., U.S.	C2	86
Franklin, co., Ga., U.S.	B3	87
Franklin, co., Id., U.S.	G7	89
Franklin, co., Il., U.S.	E4	90
Franklin, co., In., U.S.	F7	91
Franklin, co., Ia., U.S.	B4	92
Franklin, co., Ks., U.S.	D8	93
Franklin, co., Ky., U.S.	B5	94
Franklin, co., La., U.S.	B4	95
Franklin, co., Me., U.S.	C2	96
Franklin, co., Ma., U.S.	A2	98
Franklin, co., Ms., U.S.	D3	101
Franklin, co., Mo., U.S.	C6	102
Franklin, co., Ne., U.S.	D7	104
Franklin, co., N.Y., U.S.	f10	109
Franklin, co., N.C., U.S.	A4	110
Franklin, co., Oh., U.S.	B2	112
Franklin, co., Pa., U.S.	G6	115
Franklin, co., Tn., U.S.	B5	119
Franklin, co., Tx., U.S.	C5	120
Franklin, co., Vt., U.S.	B2	122
Franklin, co., Va., U.S.	D3	123
Franklin, co., Wa., U.S.	C6	124
Franklin, Point, c., Ak., U.S.	A8	79
Franklin D. Roosevelt Lake, res., Wa., U.S.	B7	124
Franklin Falls Reservoir, res., N.H., U.S.	C3	106
Franklin Grove, Il., U.S.	B4	90
Franklinton, In., Can.	B4	73
Franklin Lake, l., N.T., Can.	C13	66
Franklin Lake, l., Nv., U.S.	C6	105
Franklin Lakes, N.J., U.S.	*B4	107
Franklin Mine, Wi., U.S.	A2	99
Franklin Mountains, mts., N.T., Can.	C8	66
Franklin Park, Il., U.S.	k9	90
Franklin Park, Pa., U.S.	h13	115
Franklin Square, N.Y., U.S.	*E7	109
Franklin Strait, strt., N.T., Can.	B13	66
Franklinton, La., U.S.	D5	95
Franklinton, N.C., U.S.	A4	110
Franklinville, N.J., U.S.	D2	107
Franklinville, N.Y., U.S.	C2	109
Franklinville, N.C., U.S.	B3	110
Frankston, Austl.	*G8	50
Frankston, Tx., U.S.	C5	120
Franksville, Wi., U.S.	n12	126
Frankton, In., U.S.	D6	91
Franktown, Co., U.S.	B6	83
Frankville, N.S., Can.	D8	71
Frankville, Al., U.S.	D1	78
Frannie, Wy., U.S.	B4	127
Franz Josef Land, is., Sov. Un.	B8	29
Frascati, Italy	D4	23
Fraser, Co., U.S.	B5	83
Fraser, Ia., U.S.	C3	92
Fraser, Mi., U.S.	*o16	99
Fraser, stm., B.C., Can.	E7	69
Fraser, stm., Nf., Can.	g9	72
Fraser, Mount, mtn., Can.	C8	69
Fraserburg, S. Afr.	D3	49
Fraserburgh, Scot., U.K.	B6	10
Fraserdale, On., Can.	o19	73
Fraser Lake, B.C., Can.	B5	69
Fraser Lake, l., B.C., Can.	B5	69
Fraser Plateau, plat., B.C., Can.	D6	69
Fraserwood, Mb., Can.	D3	70
Frasne, Fr.	E7	16
Frauenfeld, Switz.	E4	18
Fray Bentos, Ur.	E1	56
Fray Marcos, Ur.	E1	56
Frazee, Mn., U.S.	D3	100
Frazeysburg, Oh., U.S.	B3	112
Frazier Park, Ca., U.S.	E4	82
Freda, Mi., U.S.	A2	99
Frederic, Mi., U.S.	D6	99
Frederica, De., U.S.	D4	85
Frederica, Den.	J3	14
Frederick, Co., U.S.	A6	83
Frederick, Il., U.S.	C3	90
Frederick, Md., U.S.	B3	97
Frederick, Ok., U.S.	C2	113
Frederick, S.D., U.S.	B7	118
Frederick, co., Md., U.S.	A4	97
Frederick, co., Va., U.S.	A4	123
Frederick Hall, Va., U.S.	C5	123
Fredericksburg, In., U.S.	H5	91
Fredericksburg, Ia., U.S.	B5	92
Fredericksburg, Oh., U.S.	B4	112
Fredericksburg, Pa., U.S.	F9	115
Fredericksburg, Tx., U.S.	D3	120
Fredericksburg, Va., U.S.	B5	123
Frederick Sound, strt., Ak., U.S.	m23	79
Fredericktown, Mo., U.S.	D7	102
Fredericktown, Oh., U.S.	B3	112
Fredericktown, Pa., U.S.	F1	115
Fredericton, N.B., Can.	D3	71
Fredericton Junction, N.B., Can.	D3	71
Frederika, Ia., U.S.	B5	92
Frederiksberg, Den.	*J5	14
Frederiksberg, Den.	*J5	14
Frederikshavn, Den.	I4	14
Frederikssund, Den.	C6	15
Frederiksted, V.I.U.S.	H12	64
Frederiksværk, Den.	C6	15
Frederik Willem IV Vallen, wtfl, Sur.	B3	59
Fredonia, Al., U.S.	C4	78
Fredonia, Az., U.S.	A3	80
Fredonia, In., U.S.	H5	91
Fredonia, Ks., U.S.	E8	93
Fredonia, Ky., U.S.	C1	94
Fredonia, N.Y., U.S.	C1	109
Fredonia, N.D., U.S.	C6	111
Fredonia, Tx., U.S.	D3	120
Fredonia, Wi., U.S.	E6	126
Fredrikstad, Nor.	H4	14
Freeborn, Mn., U.S.	G5	100
Freeborn, co., Mn., U.S.	G5	100
Freeburg, Il., U.S.	E4	90
Freeburg, Mo., U.S.	C6	102
Freeburg, Pa., U.S.	E8	115
Freedom, Ca., U.S.	*D3	82
Freedom, In., U.S.	F4	91
Freedom, Me., U.S.	D3	96
Freedom, N.H., U.S.	C4	106
Freedom, Ok., U.S.	A2	113
Freedom, Pa., U.S.	E1	115
Freedom, Wi., U.S.	h9	126
Freedom, Wy., U.S.	D2	127
Freehold, N.J., U.S.	C4	107
Freeland, Mi., U.S.	E6	99
Freeland, N.C., U.S.	C4	110
Freeland, Pa., U.S.	D10	115
Freeland Park, In., U.S.	C3	91
Freelandville, In., U.S.	G3	91
Freel Peak, mtn., Ca., U.S.	C4	82
Freels, Cape, c., Nf., Can.	E5	72
Freels, Cape, c., Nf., Can.	D5	72
Freeman, Mo., U.S.	C3	102
Freeman, S.D., U.S.	D8	118
Freeman, Wa., U.S.	g14	124
Freeman, stm., Ab., Can.	B3	68
Freeman Lake, l., In., U.S.	C4	91
Freemansburg, Pa., U.S.	E11	115
Freemason Islands, is., La., U.S.	E7	95
Freemount, Ire.	E3	11
Freeport, Bah.	*A4	64
Freeport, N.S., Can.	E3	71
Freeport, Fl., U.S.	u15	86
Freeport, Il., U.S.	A4	90
Freeport, Ia., U.S.	A6	92
Freeport, Ks., U.S.	E6	93
Freeport, Me., U.S.	E2	96
Freeport, Mi., U.S.	F5	99
Freeport, Mn., U.S.	E4	100
Freeport, N.Y., U.S.	n15	109
Freeport, Oh., U.S.	B4	112
Freeport, Pa., U.S.	E2	115
Freeport, Tx., U.S.	F5	120
Freer, Tx., U.S.	F3	120
Free Soil, Mi., U.S.	D4	99
Freestone, co., Tx., U.S.	D4	120
Freetown, P.E., Can.	C6	71
Freetown, In., U.S.	G5	91
Freetown, S.L.	E2	45
Freetown, Ma., U.S.	C5	98
Free Union, Va., U.S.	B4	123
Freeville, N.Y., U.S.	C4	109
Freezeout Mountains, mts., Wy., U.S.	D6	127
Fregenal de la Sierra, Spain	C2	22
Fregene, Italy	h8	23
Freiberg, Ger.D.R.	C6	18
Freiberger Mulde, stm., Eur.	B8	19
Freiburg, F.R.Ger.	E3	15
Freiburg [im Breisgau], F.R.Ger.	D3	18
Freienbach, Switz.	B6	21
Freirina, Chile	E1	55
Freising, F.R.Ger.	D5	18
Freistadt, Aus.	D7	18
Freistadt, Ger.D.R.	B8	19
Freital, Ger.D.R.	C6	18
Fréjus, Fr.	F7	16
Fréjus Tunnel, Eur.	D2	20
Frelighsburg, P.Q., Can.	D5	74
Fremantle, Austl.	F2	50
Fremont, Ca., U.S.	D2	82
Fremont, Ia., U.S.	C5	92
Fremont, In., U.S.	A8	91
Fremont, Mi., U.S.	E5	99
Fremont, Mo., U.S.	E6	102
Fremont, Ne., U.S.	C9	104
Fremont, N.H., U.S.	E4	106
Fremont, N.C., U.S.	B5	110
Fremont, Oh., U.S.	A2	112
Fremont, Ut., U.S.	E4	121
Fremont, Wi., U.S.	D5	126
Fremont, co., Co., U.S.	C5	83
Fremont, co., Id., U.S.	E7	89
Fremont, co., Ia., U.S.	D2	92
Fremont, co., Wy., U.S.	C4	127
Fremont, stm., Ut., U.S.	E4	121
Fremont Island, i., Ut., U.S.	B3	121
Fremont Lake, l., Wy., U.S.	D3	127
Fremont Peak, mtn., Wy., U.S.	C3	127
French, On., Can.	A2	73
French Broad, stm., U.S.	D10	119
Frenchburg, Ky., U.S.	C6	94
French Camp, Ms., U.S.	B4	101
French Creek, W.V., U.S.	C4	125
French Creek, stm., Mb., Can.	A5	70
French Creek, stm., Pa., U.S.	C2	115
French Frigate Shoals, rf., Hi., U.S.	m14	88
French Guiana, dep., S.A.	B8	59
French Gulch, Ca., U.S.	B2	82
French Island, Wi., U.S.	*E2	126
French Lick, In., U.S.	G4	91
Frenchman, Nv., U.S.	E5	105
Frenchman, stm., N.A.	A8	103
Frenchman Butte, Sk., Can.	D1	75
Frenchman Creek, stm., U.S.	D4	104
Frenchman Hills, hills, Wa., U.S.	C6	124
Frenchman Knob, mtn., Ky., U.S.	C4	94
Frenchman Lake, l., Nv., U.S.	G6	105
Frenchman's Cove, Nf., Can.	E4	72
Frenchman's Cove, Nf., Can.	D2	72
Frenchmans Island, Nf., Can.	D3	72
Frenchpark, Ire.	C3	11
French Polynesia, dep., Oc.	H13	6
French River, Mn., U.S.	D7	100
French Settlement, La., U.S.	D5	95
French Southern and Antarctic Territories, dep., Afr.	*J1	2
Frenchton, W.V., U.S.	C4	125
Frenchtown, Mt., U.S.	C2	103
Frenchtown, N.J., U.S.	B2	107
Frenchville, Me., U.S.	A4	96
Frenda, Alg.	B5	44
Fresco, I.C.	E3	45
Fresco, stm., Braz.	D4	59
Fresnillo [de González Echeverría], Mex.	C4	63
Fresno, Ca., U.S.	D4	82
Fresno, Oh., U.S.	B4	112
Fresno, co., Ca., U.S.	D4	82
Fresno Reservoir, res., Mt., U.S.	B6	103
Freudenstadt, F.R.Ger.	D4	18
Frévent, Fr.	B5	16
Freyburg, Ger.D.R.	B6	19
Freycinet Peninsula, pen., Austl.	o15	50
Freyenstein, Ger.D.R.	E6	15
Freyming-Merlebach, Fr.	E6	17
Freyung, F.R.Ger.	E8	19
Fria, Gui.	D2	45
Fria, Cape, c., Nmb.	A1	49
Friant, Ca., U.S.	D4	82
Friars Point, Ms., U.S.	A3	101
Frías, Arg.	E2	55
Fribourg, Switz.	E3	18
Fribourg, state, Switz.	C3	20
Friday Harbor, Wa., U.S.	A2	124
Fridley, Mn., U.S.	m12	100
Fridtjof Nansen, Mount, mtn., Ant.	A32	7
Friedberg, F.R.Ger.	C4	18
Friedberg, Pa., U.S.	F3	115
Friedrichroda, Ger.D.R.	C5	19
Friedrichshafen, F.R.Ger.	E4	18
Friedrichskoog, F.R.Ger.	D2	15
Friedrichstadt, F.R.Ger.	D3	15
Friedrichsthal, F.R.Ger.	D2	19
Friend, Ks., U.S.	D3	93
Friend, Ne., U.S.	D8	104
Friendship, Ar., U.S.	C3	81
Friendship, In., U.S.	G7	91
Friendship, Me., U.S.	E3	96
Friendship, N.Y., U.S.	C2	109
Friendship, Oh., U.S.	D2	112
Friendship, Tn., U.S.	B2	119
Friendship, Wi., U.S.	E4	126
Friendsville, Md., U.S.	k12	97
Friendsville, Tn., U.S.	D9	119
Friendswood, Tx., U.S.	*r14	120
Fries, Va., U.S.	D2	123
Friesach, Aus.	E7	18
Friesack, Ger.D.R.	F6	15
Friesland, prov., Neth.	A5	17
Friesland, Wi., U.S.	E4	126
Fries Mills, N.J., U.S.	D2	107
Friesoythe, F.R.Ger.	A7	17
Frigate Point, c., Mid. Is.	K3	52
Frio, co., Tx., U.S.	E3	120
Frio, stm., Tx., U.S.	E3	120
Frio Draw, val., U.S.	C6	108
Fripps Island, i., S.C., U.S.	G7	117
Frisco, Co., U.S.	B4	83
Frisco, N.C., U.S.	B7	110
Frisco City, Al., U.S.	D2	78
Frisco Peak, mtn., Ut., U.S.	E2	121
Frissell, Mount, mtn., U.S.	A2	84
Fristoe, Mo., U.S.	C4	102
Fritch, Tx., U.S.	B2	120
Fritsla, Swe.	A6	15
Fritzlar, F.R.Ger.	C4	18
Friuli-Venezia Giulia, prov., Italy	C8	20
Frobisher, Sk., Can.	H4	75
Frobisher Bay, N.T., Can.	D19	66
Frobisher Bay, b., N.T., Can.	D19	66
Frobisher Lake, l., Sk., Can.	m7	75
Frog Lake, l., Ab., Can.	C5	68
Frogmore, La., U.S.	C4	95
Frogmore, S.C., U.S.	G6	117
Frohna, Mo., U.S.	D8	102
Froid, Mt., U.S.	B12	103
Frolovo, Sov. Un.	G14	27
Fromberg, Mt., U.S.	E8	103
Frome, Jam.	E12	65
Frome, Eng., U.K.	C5	12
Frome, stm., Eng., U.K.	D5	12
Frome, Lake, l., Austl.	F6	50
Frontenac, Mn., U.S.	F6	100
Frontenac, co., On., Can.	C8	73
Frontenac, co., P.Q., Can.	D7	74
Frontera, Mex.	D6	63
Frontier, Sk., Can.	H1	75
Frontier, Wy., U.S.	E2	127
Frontier, co., Ne., U.S.	D5	104
Frontignan, Fr.	F5	16
Frontino, Páramo, mtn., Col.	B2	60
Front Range, mts., Co., U.S.	A5	83
Front Royal, Va., U.S.	B4	123
Frosinone, Italy	D4	23
Frost, Tx., U.S.	C4	120
Frostburg, Md., U.S.	k13	97
Frostproof, Fl., U.S.	E5	86
Frøya, i., Nor.	E7	14
Fruges, Fr.	B4	16
Fruita, Co., U.S.	B2	83
Fruitdale, Al., U.S.	D1	78
Fruitdale, S.D., U.S.	C2	118
Fruit Heights, Ut., U.S.	B4	121
Fruithurst, Al., U.S.	B4	78
Fruitland, Id., U.S.	F2	89
Fruitland, Ia., U.S.	C6	92
Fruitland, Md., U.S.	D6	97
Fruitland, Mo., U.S.	D8	102
Fruitland, N.M., U.S.	A1	108
Fruitland, Tn., U.S.	B3	119
Fruitland Park, Fl., U.S.	D5	86
Fruitland Park, Ms., U.S.	E4	101
Fruitvale, B.C., Can.	E9	69
Fruitvale, Tn., U.S.	B3	119
Fruitvale, Wa., U.S.	C5	124
Fruitville, Fl., U.S.	E4	86
Frunze, Sov. Un.	H10	27
Frunze, Sov. Un.	E10	29
Frutal, Braz.	C3	56
Frutigen, Switz.	C4	21
Fry, Ga., U.S.	B2	87
Fryazevo, Sov. Un.	n18	27
Frýdek-Místek, Czech.	D5	26
Fryeburg, Me., U.S.	D2	96
Fryburg, Pa., U.S.	D2	115
Fryeburg, La., U.S.	B2	95
Frys, Sk., Can.	H5	75
Fuchou see Fuzhou, China	F8	31
Fuchū, Japan	*I9	33
Fuding, China	J7	32
Fuencarral, Spain	p17	22
Fuente-Álamo [de Murcia], Spain	D5	22
Fuente de Cantos, Spain	C2	22
Fuente el Saz, Spain	o17	22
Fuente Obejuna, Spain	C3	22
Fuentes [de Andalucía], Spain	D3	22
Fuentesaúco, Spain	B3	22
Fuentes [de Andalucía], Spain	D2	22
Fuerte, stm., Mex.	B3	63
Fuerte Olimpo, Para.	D4	55
Fuerteventura, i., Spain	m14	22
Fugou, China	G6	32
Fuhai, China	B2	31
Fuji, Japan	n17	33
Fuji, Mount, vol., Japan	I9	33
Fujian, prov., China	F8	31
Fujieda, Japan	o17	33
Fujimi, Japan	n17	33
Fujinomiya, Japan	n17	33
Fujisawa, Japan	*I9	33
Fuji-yoshida, Japan	n17	33
Fukagawa, Japan	E10	33
Fukuchiyama, Japan	I7	33
Fukue Island, i., Japan	J4	33
Fukui, Japan	D12	31
Fukuoka, Japan	E11	31
Fukushima, Japan	H10	33
Fukushima, Japan	I8	33
Fukuyama, Japan	I6	33
Fulaga, i., Fiji	I16	52
Fulaga Passage, strt., Fiji	I16	52
Fulda, F.R.Ger.	C4	18
Fulda, In., U.S.	H4	91
Fulda, Mn., U.S.	G3	100
Fulda, stm., F.R.Ger.	B4	19
Fuling, China	J2	32
Fullarton, On., Can.	D3	73
Fullerton, Ca., U.S.	n13	82
Fullerton, Ky., U.S.	B7	94
Fullerton, Ne., U.S.	C8	104
Fullerton, N.D., U.S.	C7	111
Fulshear, Tx., U.S.	r14	120
Fulton, Al., U.S.	D2	78
Fulton, Ar., U.S.	D2	81
Fulton, Il., U.S.	B3	90
Fulton, In., U.S.	C5	91
Fulton, Ks., U.S.	D9	93
Fulton, Ky., U.S.	f9	94
Fulton, Md., U.S.	B4	97
Fulton, Mi., U.S.	F5	99
Fulton, Mo., U.S.	C6	102
Fulton, Ms., U.S.	A5	101
Fulton, N.Y., U.S.	B4	109
Fulton, Oh., U.S.	B3	112
Fulton, S.D., U.S.	D8	118
Fulton, Tn., U.S.	B2	119
Fulton, Tx., U.S.	E4	120
Fulton, co., Ar., U.S.	A4	81
Fulton, co., Ga., U.S.	C2	87
Fulton, co., Il., U.S.	C3	90
Fulton, co., In., U.S.	B5	91
Fulton, co., Ky., U.S.	f8	94
Fulton, co., N.Y., U.S.	B6	109
Fulton, co., Oh., U.S.	A1	112
Fulton, co., Pa., U.S.	G5	115
Fultondale, Al., U.S.	f7	78
Fultonham, N.Y., U.S.	C6	109
Fultz, Ky., U.S.	B6	94
Fumay, Fr.	C6	16
Funabashi, Japan	n19	33
Funafuti, Tuvalu	G10	6
Funchal, Port.	h12	22
Fundación, Col.	A3	60
Fundão, Braz.	B4	56
Fundão, Port.	B2	22
Fundy, Bay of, b., Can.	D5	71
Fundy National Park, N.B., Can.	D4	71
Funhalouro, Moz.	B5	49
Funing, China	G6	31
Funing, China	H8	32
Funing Bay, b., China	K9	32
Funk, Ne., U.S.	D6	104
Funk Island, i., Nf., Can.	D5	72
Funkley, Mn., U.S.	C4	100
Funkstown, Md., U.S.	A2	97
Funtua, Nig.	D6	45
Fuping, China	E2	32
Fuqing, China	F8	31
Fuquay-Varina, N.C., U.S.	B4	110
Fur, i., Den.	B3	15
Furancungo, Moz.	D6	48
Furano, Japan	E11	33
Fürg, Iran	C5	38
Furka Pass, Switz.	C5	21
Furman, Al., U.S.	C3	78
Furman, S.C., U.S.	F5	117
Furmanov, Sov. Un.	C13	29
Furnas, co., Ne., U.S.	D6	104
Furnas, Represa de, res., Braz.	C5	56
Furneaux Group, is., Austl.	o15	50
Furqlus, Syria	B7	40
Fürstenfeld, Aus.	E8	18
Fürstenfeldbruck, F.R.Ger.	A7	20
Fürstenwalde [Spree], Ger.D.R.	B7	18
Fürth, F.R.Ger.	D5	18
Furth im Wald, F.R.Ger.	D7	19
Furukawa, Japan	H8	33
Fury Mountain, hill, Japan	P17	54
Fusagasugá, Col.	C3	60
Fushun [am See], Aus.	B9	20
Fushun, China	C9	31
Fusilier, Sk., Can.	F1	75
Fusong, China	E3	33
Füssen, F.R.Ger.	E5	18
Fusui, China	A7	35
Futatsune, rock, Japan	P17	52
Future City, Il., U.S.	F4	90
Fuwah, Eg.	C2	41
Fuxian, China	F3	32
Fuxian, China	E9	32
Fuxian Lake, l., China	G5	31
Fuxin, China	C9	31
Fuyang, China	E8	31
Fuyang, China	E8	31
Fuyu, China	B9	31
Fuyu, China	C2	33
Fuyuan, China	B7	33
Fuyun, China	B7	33
Fuzhou (Fuchou), China	F8	31
Fuzhou, China	J7	32
Fyffe, Al., U.S.	A4	78
Fyn, co., Den.	C4	15
Fyn, i., Den.	J4	14
Fyne, Loch, b., Scot., U.K.	B4	10

G

Name	Map Ref	Page
Gaalkacyo, Som.	D6	47
Gaastra, Mi., U.S.	B2	99
Gabaldon, N.M., U.S.	B4	108
Gabarus, N.S., Can.	D9	71
Gabbs, Nv., U.S.	E4	105
Gabela, Ang.	D1	48
Gabès, Tun.	C7	44
Gabès, Golfe de, b., Tun.	C7	44
Gąbin, Pol.	B5	26
Gabon, ctry., Afr.	F2	46
Gaborone, Bots.	B4	49
Gabriel, Mount, hill, Ire.	F2	11
Gabriels, N.Y., U.S.	f10	109
Gabriola, B.C., Can.	f12	69
Gabrovo, Bul.	D7	24
Gachsārān, Iran	F5	39
Gackle, N.D., U.S.	C6	111
Gacko, Yugo.	D4	24
Gadag, India	E6	36
Gadmen, Switz.	C5	21
Gadsby, Ab., Can.	C4	68
Gadsden, Al., U.S.	A3	78
Gadsden, Az., U.S.	E1	80
Gadsden, S.C., U.S.	D6	117
Gadsden, Tn., U.S.	B3	119
Gadsden, co., Fl., U.S.	B2	86
Gadyach, Sov. Un.	F10	27
Găești, Rom.	C7	24
Gaeta, Italy	D4	23
Gaeta, Gulf of, b., Italy	D4	23
Gaffney, S.C., U.S.	A4	117
Gafour, Tun.	B6	44
Gafsa, Tun.	C6	44
Gagan Island, i., Marsh Is.	S17	52
Gagarin, Sov. Un.	D10	27
Gage, Ok., U.S.	A2	113
Gage, co., Ne., U.S.	D9	104
Gage, Cape, c., P.E., Can.	C5	71
Gagetown, N.B., Can.	D3	71
Gagetown, Mi., U.S.	E7	99
Gaggenau, F.R.Ger.	E3	19
Gagliano del Capo, Italy	E7	23
Gagnoa, I.C.	E3	45
Gagnon, P.Q., Can.	h13	74
Gagny, Fr.	g11	16
Gahanna, Oh., U.S.	k11	112
Gaibānda, Bngl.	E12	37
Gail, Tx., U.S.	C2	120
Gail, stm., Aus.	C9	20
Gaildorf, F.R.Ger.	E3	19
Gaillac, Fr.	F4	16
Gaillard, Lake, l., Ct., U.S.	D5	84
Gaines, Mi., U.S.	F7	99
Gaines, Pa., U.S.	C7	115
Gaines, co., Tx., U.S.	C1	120
Gainesboro, Tn., U.S.	C8	119
Gaines Creek, stm., Ok., U.S.	C6	113
Gainesville, Al., U.S.	C1	78
Gainesville, Fl., U.S.	C4	86
Gainesville, Ga., U.S.	B3	87
Gainesville, Mo., U.S.	E5	102
Gainesville, N.Y., U.S.	C2	109
Gainesville, Tx., U.S.	C4	120
Gainesville, Va., U.S.	g11	123
Gainsborough, Sk., Can.	H5	75
Gainsborough, Eng., U.K.	D6	10
Gairdner, Lake, l., Austl.	F6	50
Gairloch, Scot., U.K.	C3	13
Gairloch, Loch, b., Scot., U.K.	C3	13
Gaither, Md., U.S.	B4	97
Gaithersburg, Md., U.S.	B3	97
Gaixian, China	C9	31
Gakona, Ak., U.S.	C10	79
Galahad, Ab., Can.	C5	68
Galápagar, Spain	o16	22
Galápagos, ter., Ec.	g5	58
Galapagos Islands see Colón, Archipiélago de, is., Ec.	g5	58
Galashiels, Scot., U.K.	C5	10
Galata, Mt., U.S.	B5	103
Galați (Galacz), Rom.	C9	24
Galatia, Il., U.S.	F5	90
Galatia, Ks., U.S.	D5	93
Galatina, Italy	D7	23
Galátsion, Grc.	*C4	25
Galax, Va., U.S.	D2	123
Galaxídhion, Grc.	C4	25
Gáldar, Spain	m14	22
Galeana, Mex.	A3	63
Galena, Ak., U.S.	C8	79
Galena, Il., U.S.	A3	90
Galena, Ks., U.S.	E9	93
Galena, Md., U.S.	B6	97
Galena, Mo., U.S.	E4	102
Galena, Oh., U.S.	B3	112
Galena Park, Tx., U.S.	r14	120
Galeota Point, c., Trin.	K14	64
Galera, Punta, c., Chile	B2	54
Galera, Punta, c., Trin.	A1	58
Galera Point, c., Trin.	K14	64
Galesburg, Il., U.S.	C3	90
Galesburg, Mi., U.S.	F5	99
Galesburg, N.D., U.S.	B8	111
Gales Creek, Or., U.S.	B3	114
Gales Ferry, Ct., U.S.	D7	84
Galesville, Md., U.S.	C4	97
Galesville, Wi., U.S.	D2	126
Galeton, Co., U.S.	A6	83
Galeton, Pa., U.S.	C6	115
Galeville, N.Y., U.S.	*B4	109
Galgaduud, prov., Som.	D6	47
Galiano Island, i., B.C., Can.	E6	69
Galich, Sov. Un.	B2	28

Name	Map Ref	Page

Galicia, hist reg., Eur. — D6 26
Galicia, hist reg., Spain — A2 22
Galien, Mi., U.S. — G4 99
Galilee, R.I., U.S. — F3 116
Galilee, hist reg., Isr. — B7 41
Galilee, Lake, l., U.S. — D8 50
Galilee, Sea of see Kinneret, Yam, l., Isr. — B7 41
Galina Point, c., Jam. — E15 65
Galion, Oh., U.S. — B3 112
Galisteo Creek, stm., N.M., U.S. — k8 108
Galite Channel, strt., Tun. — F2 23
Galiuro Mountains, mts., Az., U.S. — E5 80
Galivants Ferry, S.C., U.S. — C9 117
Gallan Head, c., Scot., U.K. — B1 13
Gallant, Al., U.S. — B3 78
Gallarate, Italy — B2 23
Gällaryd, Swe. — A8 15
Gallatin, Mo., U.S. — B4 102
Gallatin, Tn., U.S. — A5 119
Gallatin, co., Il., U.S. — F5 90
Gallatin, co., Ky., U.S. — B5 94
Gallatin, co., Mt., U.S. — E5 103
Gallatin, stm., Mt., U.S. — E5 103
Gallatin Gateway, Mt., U.S. — E5 103
Gallatin Range, mts., Mt., U.S. — E5 103
Gallaway, Tn., U.S. — B2 119
Galle, Sri L. — G7 36
Gállego, stm., Spain — A5 22
Gallegos, stm., Arg. — E2 54
Galley Head, c., Ire. — F3 11
Gallia, co., Oh., U.S. — D3 112
Galliano, La., U.S. — E5 95
Galliate, Italy — D4 20
Gallicano nel Lazio, Italy — h9 23
Gallina, N.M., U.S. — A3 108
Gallinas, Punta, c., Col. — A3 60
Gallinas Mountains, mts., N.M., U.S. — C2 108
Gallion, Al., U.S. — C2 78
Gallipoli, Italy — D6 23
Gallipoli Peninsula, pen., Tur. — B6 40
Gallipolis, Oh., U.S. — D3 112
Gallipolis Ferry, W.V., U.S. — C2 125
Gallitzin, Pa., U.S. — F4 115
Gällivare, Swe. — D9 14
Gallneukirchen, Aus. — E9 19
Gallo, stm., Spain — B5 22
Gallo Mountains, mts., N.M., U.S. — C1 108
Galloc Island, i., N.Y., U.S. — B4 109
Galloway, Oh., U.S. — m10 112
Galloway, W.V., U.S. — B4 125
Galloway, Wi., U.S. — D4 126
Galloway, Mull of, c., Scot., U.K. — F4 13
Gällstad, Swe. — A7 15
Gallup, N.M., U.S. — B1 108
Galoa Bay, b., Fiji — H15 52
Galoa Harbour, b., Fiji — I15 52
Galt, Ca., U.S. — C3 82
Galt, Ia., U.S. — B4 92
Galt, Mo., U.S. — A4 102
Galten, b., Swe. — t34 14
Galtür, Aus. — C6 20
Galtymore, mtn., Ire. — E3 11
Galty Mountains, mts., Ire. — D2 10
Galva, Il., U.S. — B3 90
Galva, Ia., U.S. — B2 92
Galva, Ks., U.S. — D6 93
Galvarino, Chile — B2 54
Galveston, In., U.S. — C5 91
Galveston, Tx., U.S. — E5 120
Galveston, co., Tx., U.S. — E5 120
Galveston Bay, b., Tx., U.S. — E5 120
Galveston Island, i., Tx., U.S. — E5 120
Gálvez, Arg. — A4 54
Galvin, Wa., U.S. — C2 124
Galway, Ire. — D2 10
Galway, co., Ire. — D2 11
Galway Bay, b., Ire. — D2 10
Gamaches, Fr. — E9 12
Gamagōri, Japan — o16 33
Gamaliel, Ar., U.S. — A3 81
Gamaliel, Ky., U.S. — D4 94
Gamarra, Col. — B3 60
Gamba, China — C12 37
Gamba, Zaire — B3 48
Gambaga, Ghana — D4 45
Gambela, Eth. — D3 47
Gambell, Ak., U.S. — C5 79
Gamber, Md., U.S. — B4 97
Gambia, ctry., Afr. — D1 45
Gambia, stm., Afr. — D2 45
Gambier, Bah. — m17 64
Gambier, Oh., U.S. — B3 112
Gambo, Nf., Can. — D4 72
Gamboa, Pan. — k11 62
Gamboma, Congo — B2 48
Gamboula, Cen. Afr. Rep. — E3 46
Gambrills, Md., U.S. — B4 97
Gameleira, Braz. — C3 57
Gamerco, N.M., U.S. — B1 108
Gammertingen, F.R.Ger. — A5 20
Gammon, stm., Can. — D4 70
Gamo Gofa, prov., Eth. — D4 47
Gamph, Slieve, mts., Ire. — C3 11
Ganado, Az., U.S. — B6 80
Ganado, Tx., U.S. — E4 120
Gananoque, On., Can. — C8 73
Gancheng, China — C8 35
Ganda, Ang. — D1 48
Gandajika, Zaire — C3 48
Gandak, stm., Asia — D10 37
Gandeeville, W.V., U.S. — C3 125
Gander, Nf., Can. — D4 72
Gander, stm., Nf., Can. — D4 72
Gander Bay, Nf., Can. — D4 72
Gander Lake, l., Nf., Can. — D4 72
Gandhinagar, India — D5 36
Gāndhi Sāgar, res., India — E5 37
Gandía, Spain — C5 22
Gandomak, Afg. — D14 39
Gandy, Ne., U.S. — C5 104
Gangāpur, India — D6 37
Gangaw, Burma — D9 36
Gangdise Mountains, mts., China — B9 37
Ganges, B.C., Can. — g12 69
Ganges, Fr. — F5 16
Ganges, Oh., U.S. — B3 112
Ganges, stm., Asia — D8 36
Ganges, Mouths of the, mth., Asia — D8 36
Gang Mills, N.Y., U.S. — C3 109
Gangtok, India — C8 36
Gangu, China — E6 31
Gani, Indon. — F7 34
Gan Jiang, stm., China — K6 32
Gannan, China — C1 33
Gannat, Fr. — D5 16
Gannet Islands, is., Nf., Can. — B3 72
Gannett Peak, mtn., Wy., U.S. — C3 127

Gannon, Md., U.S. — k12 97
Gannvalley, S.D., U.S. — C7 118
Gano, Oh., U.S. — n13 112
Gans, Ok., U.S. — B7 113
Gansevoort, N.Y., U.S. — B7 109
Gansu, prov., China — D5 31
Ganta, Lib. — E3 45
Gantt, Al., U.S. — D3 78
Gantt, S.C., U.S. — B3 117
Gantt Lake, res., Al., U.S. — D3 78
Gantts Quarry, Al., U.S. — B3 78
Ganyu, China — E8 31
Ganzhou, China — F7 31
Gao, Mali — C5 45
Gao'an, China — J6 32
Gaoil, Sliabh, mtn., Scot., U.K. — E3 13
Gaoua, Burkina — D4 45
Gaoual, Gui. — D2 45
Gaoyou, China — H8 32
Gaoyou Lake, l., China — H8 32
Gap, Fr. — E7 16
Gap, Pa., U.S. — G9 115
Gapan, Phil. — o13 34
Gapland, Md., U.S. — B2 97
Gap Mills, W.V., U.S. — D4 125
Gar, China — B7 36
Gara, Lough, l., Ire. — C3 11
Garacad, Som. — F8 62
Garachiné, Pan. — F8 62
Garachiné, Punta, c., Pan. — C3 57
Garanhuns, Braz. — D7 52
Garapan, N. Mar. Is. — D7 52
Garapan, Lagunan, b., N. Mar. Is. — D7 52
Garau, Canal de, Mex. — h9 63
Garautha, India — E7 47
Garbaharrey, Som. — E5 47
Garber, Ia., U.S. — B6 92
Garber, Ok., U.S. — A4 113
Garberville, Ca., U.S. — B2 82
Garbsen, F.R.Ger. — *B4 18
Garça, Braz. — C3 56
Garching [an der Alz], F.R.Ger. — A8 20
Garcia, Co., U.S. — D5 83
Garciasville, Tx., U.S. — F3 120
Gard, stm., Fr. — E6 16
Garda, Lake, l., Italy — B3 23
Gardanne, Fr. — F6 16
Gardar, N.D., U.S. — A8 111
Gardelegen, Ger.D.R. — B5 18
Garden, Mi., U.S. — C4 99
Garden, co., Ne., U.S. — C3 104
Gardena, Ca., U.S. — n12 82
Gardena, N.D., U.S. — A5 111
Garden City, Al., U.S. — A3 78
Garden City, Co., U.S. — *A6 83
Garden City, Ga., U.S. — D5 87
Garden City, Id., U.S. — F2 89
Garden City, In., U.S. — F6 91
Garden City, Ks., U.S. — E3 93
Garden City, La., U.S. — E4 95
Garden City, Mi., U.S. — p15 99
Garden City, Mn., U.S. — F4 100
Garden City, Mo., U.S. — C3 102
Garden City, N.Y., U.S. — *E7 109
Garden City, S.D., U.S. — C8 118
Garden City, Tx., U.S. — D2 120
Garden City, Ut., U.S. — B4 121
Garden City Park, N.Y., U.S. — *n15 109
Gardendale, Al., U.S. — B3 78
Gardendale, Tx., U.S. — E3 120
Garden Grove, Ca., U.S. — n13 82
Garden Grove, Ia., U.S. — D4 92
Garden Home, Or., U.S. — *B4 114
Garden Island, i., Mi., U.S. — C5 99
Garden of Gethsemane, Isr. Occ. — m14 41
Garden Plain, Il., U.S. — B3 90
Garden Plain, Ks., U.S. — E6 93
Garden Prairie, Il., U.S. — A5 90
Garden Reach, India — *D8 36
Gardenton, Mb., Can. — E3 70
Garden Valley, Id., U.S. — E3 89
Gardardentz — ...
Gardi, Ga., U.S. — E5 87
Gardiner, Me., U.S. — D3 96
Gardiner, Mt., U.S. — E6 103
Gardiner, Or., U.S. — D2 114
Gardiners Island, i., N.Y., U.S. — m16 109
Gardner, Ar., U.S. — B3 81
Gardner, Co., U.S. — D5 83
Gardner, Fl., U.S. — E5 86
Gardner, Il., U.S. — B5 90
Gardner, Ks., U.S. — D9 93
Gardner, Ma., U.S. — A4 98
Gardner, N.D., U.S. — B9 111
Gardner Canal, b., B.C., Can. — C3 69
Gardner Lake, l., Ct., U.S. — C6 84
Gardner Lake, l., Me., U.S. — D5 96
Gardner Mountain, mtn., N.H., U.S. — B3 106
Gardner Pinnacles, Hi., U.S. — k14 88
Gardnersville, Ky., U.S. — k14 94
Gardnerville, Nv., U.S. — E2 105
Gardone Riviera, Italy — D6 20
Gardone Val Trompia, Italy — D6 20
Garešnica, Yugo. — C3 24
Garfield, Ar., U.S. — A2 81
Garfield, Ga., U.S. — C4 87
Garfield, Ks., U.S. — D4 93
Garfield, Mn., U.S. — E3 100
Garfield, N.J., U.S. — h8 107
Garfield, N.M., U.S. — E2 108
Garfield, Wa., U.S. — B8 124
Garfield, co., Co., U.S. — B2 83
Garfield, co., Mt., U.S. — C9 103
Garfield, co., Ne., U.S. — C7 104
Garfield, co., Ok., U.S. — A4 113
Garfield, co., Ut., U.S. — F4 121
Garfield, co., Wa., U.S. — C8 124
Garfield Heights, Oh., U.S. — h9 112
Garfield Mountain, mtn., Mt., U.S. — F4 103
Garfield Park, De., U.S. — *B3 85
Garfield Peak, mtn., Wy., U.S. — C3 127
Gargaliáni, Grc. — D3 25
Gargano Peninsula, pen., Italy — D6 20
Gargnano, Italy — C3 23
Garibaldi, Braz. — D2 56
Garibaldi, Or., U.S. — B3 114
Garibaldi, Mount, mtn., B.C., Can. — E6 69
Garibaldi Provincial Park, B.C., Can. — D6 69
Garies, S. Afr. — D2 49
Garissa, Kenya — B6 48
Garita, N.M., U.S. — B5 108
Garland, Al., U.S. — D3 78
Garland, Ks., U.S. — E9 93
Garland, Me., U.S. — C3 96

Garland, Ne., U.S. — D9 104
Garland, N.C., U.S. — C4 110
Garland, Pa., U.S. — C3 115
Garland, Tn., U.S. — B2 119
Garland, Tx., U.S. — n10 120
Garland, Ut., U.S. — B3 121
Garland, Wy., U.S. — B4 127
Garland, co., Ar., U.S. — C2 81
Garmisch-Partenkirchen, F.R.Ger. — E5 18
Garmouth, Scot., U.K. — C5 13
Garnavillo, Ia., U.S. — B6 92
Garneill, Mt., U.S. — D7 103
Garner, Ar., U.S. — B4 81
Garner, Ia., U.S. — A4 92
Garner, Ky., U.S. — C7 94
Garner, N.C., U.S. — B4 110
Garnet Range, mts., Mt., U.S. — D3 103
Garnett, Ks., U.S. — D8 93
Garnett, S.C., U.S. — F5 117
Garnish, Nf., Can. — E4 72
Garnpung, Lake, l., Austl. — F4 51
Garo Hills, hills, India — E13 37
Garonne, stm., Eur. — E3 16
Garoowe, Som. — D4 47
Garou, Lac, l., Mali — C4 45
Garoua, Cam. — D2 46
Garrard, co., Ky., U.S. — C5 94
Garretson, S.D., U.S. — D9 118
Garrett, Il., U.S. — D5 90
Garrett, In., U.S. — B7 91
Garrett, Ky., U.S. — C7 94
Garrett, Pa., U.S. — G3 115
Garrett, Wy., U.S. — D7 127
Garrett, co., Md., U.S. — k12 97
Garrett Park, Md., U.S. — B3 97
Garrettsville, Oh., U.S. — A4 112
Garrick, Sk., Can. — D3 75
Garrison, Ia., U.S. — B5 92
Garrison, Ky., U.S. — B6 94
Garrison, Md., U.S. — B4 97
Garrison, Mn., U.S. — D5 100
Garrison, Mt., U.S. — D4 103
Garrison, N.Y., U.S. — D7 109
Garrison, N.D., U.S. — B4 111
Garrison, Tx., U.S. — D5 120
Garrison, Ut., U.S. — E1 121
Garrison Dam, N.D., U.S. — B4 111
Garrisonville, Va., U.S. — B5 123
Garristown, Ire. — C5 11
Garron Point, c., N. Ire., U.K. — B6 11
Garrote, Pan. — h11 62
Garrovillas, Spain — C2 22
Garruk, Pak. — C4 36
Garry, stm., Scot., U.K. — D5 13
Garry Lake, l., N.T., Can. — C13 66
Garryowen, Mt., U.S. — E9 103
Garsen, Kenya — B7 48
Garson Lake, l., Can. — A5 68
Garson Quarry, Mb., Can. — D3 70
Garstang, Eng., U.K. — G6 13
Garth, Al., U.S. — A3 78
Garthby Station (Beaulac), P.Q., Can. — D6 74
Gartz, Ger.D.R. — E8 15
Garut, Indon. — G3 34
Garvagh, N. Ire., U.K. — C5 11
Garve, Scot., U.K. — C4 13
Garvin, Mn., U.S. — F3 100
Garvin, Ok., U.S. — D7 113
Garvin, co., Ok., U.S. — C4 113
Garwin, Ia., U.S. — B5 92
Garwolin, Pol. — C6 26
Garwood, N.J., U.S. — *B4 107
Garwood, Tx., U.S. — E4 120
Gary, In., U.S. — A3 91
Gary, Mn., U.S. — C2 100
Gary, S.D., U.S. — C9 118
Gary, W.V., U.S. — D3 125
Garyarsa, China — B8 37
Garysburg, N.C., U.S. — A5 110
Garyville, La., U.S. — D5 95
Garza, co., Tx., U.S. — C2 120
Garza García, Mex. — *B4 63
Garza-Little Elm Reservoir, res., Tx., U.S. — C4 120
Garzón, Col. — C2 60
Gas, Ks., U.S. — E8 93
Gas City, In., U.S. — D6 91
Gasconade, Mo., U.S. — C6 102
Gasconade, co., Mo., U.S. — C6 102
Gasconade, stm., Mo., U.S. — C6 102
Gasconade, Osage Fork, stm., Mo., U.S. — D5 102
Gascony, hist reg., Fr. — E3 16
Gascoyne, N.D., U.S. — C2 111
Gascoyne, stm., Austl. — E2 50
Gashaka, Nig. — E7 45
Gasherbrum, mtn., Asia — *A6 36
Gas Hills, Wy., U.S. — D5 127
Gashua, Nig. — C5 46
Gasparilla Island, i., Fl., U.S. — F4 86
Gaspé, P.Q., Can. — k14 74
Gaspé, Cap, c., P.Q., Can. — G20 66
Gaspésie, Péninsule de la, pen., P.Q., Can. — k13 74
Gasport, N.Y., U.S. — B2 109
Gasque, Al., U.S. — E2 78
Gassaway, Tn., U.S. — B5 119
Gassaway, W.V., U.S. — C4 125
Gassets, Vt., U.S. — E3 122
Gassol, Nig. — E7 45
Gassville, Ar., U.S. — A3 81
Gaston, In., U.S. — D7 91
Gaston, N.C., U.S. — A5 110
Gaston, Or., U.S. — h11 114
Gaston, S.C., U.S. — D5 117
Gaston, co., N.C., U.S. — B1 110
Gaston, Lake, res., U.S. — A5 110
Gaston Dam, N.C., U.S. — A5 110
Gastonia, N.C., U.S. — B1 110
Gastre, Arg. — C3 54
Gata, Cabo de, c., Spain — B2 22
Gata, Sierra de, mts., Spain — B2 22
Gátas, Akrotírion, c., Cyp. — E9 40
Gatchina, Sov. Un. — B8 27
Gate, Ok., U.S. — A1 113
Gate City, Va., U.S. — f9 123
Gatehouse-of-Fleet, Scot., U.K. — F4 13
Gates, Ne., U.S. — C6 104
Gates, N.Y., U.S. — B3 109
Gates, N.C., U.S. — A6 110
Gates, Or., U.S. — C4 114
Gates, Tn., U.S. — B2 119
Gates, co., N.C., U.S. — A6 110
Gateshead, Eng., U.K. — C6 10
Gates of the Arctic National Park, Ak., U.S. — B9 79
Gatesville, N.C., U.S. — A6 110
Gatesville, Tx., U.S. — D4 120
Gateway, Ar., U.S. — *A2 81

Gateway, Co., U.S. — C2 83
Gateway, Or., U.S. — C5 114
Gatineau, P.Q., Can. — D2 74
Gatineau, co., P.Q., Can. — C2 74
Gatineau, stm., P.Q., Can. — D2 74
Gatineau, Parc, P.Q., Can. — D2 74
Gatliff, Ky., U.S. — D5 94
Gatlinburg, Tn., U.S. — D10 119
Gato, Co., U.S. — D3 83
Gattman, Ms., U.S. — B5 101
Gatton, Austl. — C9 51
Gatún, Pan. — k11 62
Gatún, Lago, res., Pan. — k11 62
Gatun Locks, Pan. — k11 62
Gatzke, Mn., U.S. — B3 100
Gau, i., Fiji — I15 52
Gauer Lake, l., Mb., Can. — A3 70
Gauhāti, India — C9 36
Gauja, stm., Sov. Un. — C5 27
Gaula, stm., Nor. — F4 14
Gauley, stm., W.V., U.S. — C3 125
Gauley Bridge, W.V., U.S. — C3 125
Gauley Mills, W.V., U.S. — C4 125
Gause, Tx., U.S. — D4 120
Gautier, Ms., U.S. — f8 101
Gavá, Spain — B7 22
Gávdhos, i., Grc. — E5 40
Gavins Point Dam, U.S. — B8 104
Gāvkhūnī, Bāţlāq-e, sw., Iran — E6 39
Gävle, Swe. — G7 14
Gävleborg, co., Swe. — G7 14
Gävlebukten, b., Swe. — G7 14
Gavrilov Posad, Sov. Un. — C13 27
Gawler, Austl. — G2 51
Gawler Ranges, mts., Austl. — F6 50
Gay, Ga., U.S. — C2 87
Gay, Mi., U.S. — A2 99
Gaya, India — D7 36
Gaya, Niger — D6 45
Gaya, Nig. — D6 45
Gay Head, Ma., U.S. — D6 98
Gay Head, c., Ma., U.S. — D6 98
Gaylesville, Al., U.S. — A4 78
Gaylord, Ks., U.S. — C5 93
Gaylord, Mi., U.S. — C6 99
Gaylord, Mn., U.S. — F4 100
Gaylord, Or., U.S. — E2 114
Gaylordsville, Ct., U.S. — C2 84
Gayndah, Austl. — B8 51
Gays, Il., U.S. — D5 90
Gays Mills, Wi., U.S. — E3 126
Gaysville, Vt., U.S. — D3 122
Gayville, S.D., U.S. — E8 118
Gaza (Ghazzah), Isr. Occ. — B3 38
Gaza, Ia., U.S. — A2 92
Gaza, dept., Moz. — B5 49
Gaza Strip, ter., Isr. Occ. — C6 41
Gaziantep, Tur. — D11 40
Gboko, Nig. — E6 45
Gdańsk (Danzig), Pol. — A5 26
Gdov, Sov. Un. — B6 27
Gdynia, Pol. — A5 26
Gearhart, Or., U.S. — A3 114
Gearhart Mountain, mtn., Or., U.S. — E6 114
Geary, N.B., Can. — D3 71
Geary, Ok., U.S. — B3 113
Geary, co., Ks., U.S. — D7 93
Geauga, co., Oh., U.S. — A4 112
Gebeit Mine, Sud. — B7 47
Gebze, Tur. — B7 25
Ged, La., U.S. — D2 95
Geddes, S.D., U.S. — D7 118
Gedera, Isr. — C6 41
Gedern, F.R.Ger. — C4 19
Gedinne, Bel. — E7 17
Gediz, Tur. — C7 40
Gediz, stm., Tur. — C6 40
Gedo, prov., Som. — E5 47
Gedser, Den. — D5 15
Geel, Bel. — C4 17
Geelong, Austl. — G7 50
Geetbets, Bel. — D5 17
Geff, Il., U.S. — E5 90
Gê'gyai, China — A8 37
Geidam, Nig. — D7 45
Geiger, Al., U.S. — C1 78
Geisenfeld, F.R.Ger. — E6 19
Geislingen, F.R.Ger. — D5 19
Geismar, La., U.S. — h9 95
Geistown, Pa., U.S. — F4 115
Geist Reservoir, res., In., U.S. — B5 91
Geita, Tan. — B5 48
Gejiu, China — F5 31
Gela, Italy — F5 23
Gelderland, prov., Neth. — C5 17
Geldermalsen, Neth. — C5 17
Geldern, F.R.Ger. — B2 19
Geldrop, Neth. — C5 17
Gelert, On., Can. — C6 73
Gelibolu (Gallipoli), Tur. — B6 40
Gelligaer, Wales, U.K. — C4 13
Gellinam Island, i., Marsh Is. — S17 52
Gelnhausen, F.R.Ger. — C4 19
Gelsenkirchen, F.R.Ger. — C3 18
Gelting, F.R.Ger. — A5 18
Gem, Ab., Can. — D5 68
Gem, In., U.S. — D6 91
Gem, Ks., U.S. — C3 93
Gem, W.V., U.S. — D3 125
Gem, co., Id., U.S. — E2 89
Gemas, Malay. — K5 35
Gembloux, Bel. — D4 17
Gemena, Zaire — A2 48
Gemert, Neth. — C5 17
Gemla, Swe. — H6 14
Gemlik, Tur. — B7 40
Gemona del Friuli, Italy — C9 20
Gemünden, F.R.Ger. — C4 19
Gem Village, Co., U.S. — D3 83
Genale (Jubba), stm., Afr. — D5 47
Genarp, Swe. — C7 15
Gene Autry, Ok., U.S. — C4 113
General Alvear, Arg. — B4 54
General Alvear, Arg. — A3 54
General Belgrano, Arg. — B5 54
General Carrera, Lago (Lago Buenos Aires), l., S.A. — D2 54
General Conesa, Arg. — B5 54
General Enrique Martínez, Ur. — E2 56
General Eugenio A. Garay, Para. — D3 55
General José de San Martín, Arg. — E4 55
General Juan Madariaga, Arg. — B5 54
General La Madrid, Arg. — B4 54
General Lavalle, Arg. — B5 54
General Martín Miguel de Güemes, Arg. — E4 55
General Paz, Arg. — E4 55
General Pico, Arg. — B4 54

General Pinedo, Arg. — E3 55
General Roca, Arg. — B3 54
General San Martín, Arg. — g7 54
General Sarmiento, Arg. — g7 54
General Tinio, Phil. — o13 34
General Toshevo, Bul. — D9 24
General Viamonte, Arg. — B4 54
General Villegas, Arg. — B4 54
Genesee, Id., U.S. — C2 89
Genesee, Mi., U.S. — E7 99
Genesee, Pa., U.S. — C6 115
Genesee, co., Mi., U.S. — E7 99
Genesee, co., N.Y., U.S. — B2 109
Genesee, stm., N.Y., U.S. — C2 109
Genesee Depot, Wi., U.S. — n11 126
Geneseo, Il., U.S. — B3 90
Geneseo, Ks., U.S. — D5 93
Geneseo, N.Y., U.S. — C3 109
Geneseo, N.D., U.S. — C8 111
Geneva (Genève), Switz. — E3 18
Geneva, Al., U.S. — D4 78
Geneva, Ga., U.S. — D2 87
Geneva, Id., U.S. — G7 89
Geneva, Il., U.S. — B5 90
Geneva, In., U.S. — C8 91
Geneva, Ia., U.S. — B4 92
Geneva, Ky., U.S. — C2 94
Geneva, Ne., U.S. — D8 104
Geneva, N.Y., U.S. — C4 109
Geneva, Oh., U.S. — A5 112
Geneva, Pa., U.S. — C1 115
Geneva, co., Al., U.S. — D4 78
Geneva, Lake, l., Wi., U.S. — F5 126
Geneva, Lake, l., Eur. — E3 18
Geneva-on-the-Lake, Oh., U.S. — A5 112
Genève, state, Switz. — E3 18
Genichesk, Sov. Un. — H10 27
Genil, stm., Spain — D3 22
Génissiat, Fr. — C1 20
Genk, Belg. — D5 17
Gennep, Neth. — C5 17
Gennevilliers, Fr. — g10 16
Genoa (Genova), Italy — D2 81
Genoa, Ar., U.S. — D2 81
Genoa, Co., U.S. — B7 83
Genoa, Il., U.S. — A5 90
Genoa, Ne., U.S. — C8 104
Genoa, Nv., U.S. — D2 105
Genoa, N.Y., U.S. — C4 109
Genoa, Oh., U.S. — A2 112
Genoa, Wi., U.S. — E2 126
Genoa, Gulf of, b., Italy — B2 23
Genoa City, Wi., U.S. — F5 126
Genola, Mn., U.S. — E4 100
Genola, Ut., U.S. — D4 121
Genolier, Switz. — D1 21
Genova, dept., Ec. — A2 58
Genovesa, Isla, i., Ec. — f6 58
Gent (Ghent), Bel. — B5 16
Gentbrugge (part of Gent), Bel. — C3 17
Genthin, Ger.D.R. — B6 18
Gentilly, Fr. — g10 16
Gentilly, Mn., U.S. — C2 100
Gentry, Ar., U.S. — A1 81
Gentry, Mo., U.S. — A3 102
Gentry, co., Mo., U.S. — A3 102
Gentryville, In., U.S. — H3 91
Genzano di Roma, Italy — h9 23
Geographe Bay, b., Austl. — F2 50
Geographe Channel, strt., Austl. — D1 50
Geographical Society Island, i., Grnld. — B16 128
Geokchay, Sov. Un. — G18 8
Geology...
George, S. Afr. — D3 49
George, i., Can. — B10 128
George, co., Ms., U.S. — E5 101
George, stm., P.Q., Can. — g13 74
George, Cape, c., N.S., Can. — D8 71
George, Lake, l., Austl. — G7 51
George, Lake, l., N.S., Can. — E3 71
George, Lake, l., Fl., U.S. — C5 86
George, Lake, l., N.Y., U.S. — B7 109
George Air Force Base, mil., Ca., U.S. — E5 82
George B. Stevenson Reservoir, res., Pa., U.S. — D6 115
George Hill, mtn., Md., U.S. — k12 97
George Island, i., Nf., Can. — A3 72
George Peak, mtn., Ut., U.S. — B2 121
Georges Mills, N.H., U.S. — D2 106
Georgesville, Oh., U.S. — m10 112
George Town, Austl. — o15 50
George Town, Bah. — C6 64
Georgetown, On., Can. — D5 73
Georgetown, P.E., Can. — C7 71
Georgetown, Cay. Is. — E5 65
Georgetown, Gam. — D2 45
Georgetown, Guy. — B7 59
George Town (Pinang), Malay. — U26 65
Georgetown, St. Vin. — U26 65
Georgetown, Ca., U.S. — C3 82
Georgetown, Co., U.S. — B5 83
Georgetown, Ct., U.S. — D2 84
Georgetown, De., U.S. — F4 85
Georgetown, Fl., U.S. — C5 86
Georgetown, Ga., U.S. — E1 87
Georgetown, Id., U.S. — G7 89
Georgetown, Il., U.S. — D6 90
Georgetown, In., U.S. — H6 91
Georgetown, Ky., U.S. — B5 94
Georgetown, La., U.S. — C3 95
Georgetown, Md., U.S. — B6 97
Georgetown, Ma., U.S. — A6 98
Georgetown, Ms., U.S. — D3 101
Georgetown, Oh., U.S. — D2 112
Georgetown, S.C., U.S. — E9 117
Georgetown, Tx., U.S. — D4 120
Georgetown, co., S.C., U.S. — E9 117
Georgeville, P.Q., Can. — D5 74
George V Coast, Ant. — C28 7
George VI Sound, strt., Ant. — B6 7
George Washington Birthplace National Monument, Va., U.S. — B6 123
George Washington Carver National Monument, Mo., U.S. — D3 102
George West, Tx., U.S. — E3 120
Georgia, state, Sov. Un. — E7 29
Georgia, state, U.S. — D3 87
Georgia, Strait of, strt., N.A. — E5 69
Georgia Center, Vt., U.S. — B2 122
Georgian Bay, b., On., Can. — B3 73
Georgian Bay Islands National Park, On., Can. — B3 73
Georgina, stm., Austl. — D6 50

Georgiu-Dez, Sov. Un. — F12 27
Georgiyevsk, Sov. Un. — G17 8
Gera, Ger.D.R. — C6 18
Geraardsbergen, Bel. — D3 17
Geral, Serra, clf, Braz. — D2 56
Gerald, Sk., Can. — G5 75
Gerald, Mo., U.S. — C6 102
Geral de Goiás, Serra, clf, Braz. — D1 57
Geraldine, Al., U.S. — A4 78
Geraldine, Mt., U.S. — C6 103
Geral do Paraná, Serra, mts., Braz. — A3 56
Geraldton, Austl. — E1 50
Geraldton, On., Can. — o18 73
Gérardmer, Fr. — A2 20
Gerber, Ca., U.S. — B2 82
Gerber Reservoir, res., Or., U.S. — E5 114
Gerbstedt, Ger.D.R. — B6 19
Gercüş, Tur. — D13 40
Gerdau, stm., F.R.Ger. — F4 15
Gerdine, Mount, mtn., Ak., U.S. — C9 79
Gerede, Tur. — B9 40
Gereh, Küh-e, mtn., Iran — F5 39
Gereshk, Afg. — B3 36
Gérgal, Spain — D4 22
Gering, Ne., U.S. — C2 104
Gérin, P.Q., Can. — C4 74
Gerlach, Nv., U.S. — C2 105
Gerlachovka, mtn., Czech. — D6 26
German Democratic Republic (East Germany), ctry., Eur. — B6 18
Germania, N.J., U.S. — D3 107
Germania, Wi., U.S. — C6 115
Germansen Lake, l., B.C., Can. — B5 69
Germantown, N.B., Can. — D5 71
Germantown, Il., U.S. — E4 90
Germantown, Ky., U.S. — B6 94
Germantown, Md., U.S. — B3 97
Germantown, Oh., U.S. — C1 112
Germantown, Tn., U.S. — B2 119
Germantown, Wi., U.S. — E5 126
Germany, Federal Republic of (West Germany), ctry., Eur. — C4 18
Germersheim, F.R.Ger. — D3 19
Germfask, Mi., U.S. — B5 99
Germiston, S. Afr. — C4 49
Gernrode, Ger.D.R. — B6 19
Gernsheim, F.R.Ger. — D3 19
Gero, Japan — n16 33
Gerolzhofen, F.R.Ger. — D5 19
Gerona, Spain — B7 22
Geronimo, Ok., U.S. — C3 113
Geronimo, Tx., U.S. — h8 120
Gerrardstown, W.V., U.S. — B6 125
Gersfeld, F.R.Ger. — C4 19
Gersthofen, F.R.Ger. — E5 19
Gertrudis Sánchez (part of Mexico City), Mex. — h9 63
Gerty, Ok., U.S. — C5 113
Gervais, Or., U.S. — B4 114
Gerze, Tur. — B10 40
Geseke, F.R.Ger. — B3 19
Gessie, In., U.S. — D3 91
Gesher HaZiw, Isr. — A7 41
Getafe, Spain — B4 22
Gethsémani, P.Q., Can. — h9 72
Gettysburg, Oh., U.S. — B1 112
Gettysburg, Pa., U.S. — G7 115
Gettysburg, S.D., U.S. — C6 118
Getúlio Vargas, Braz. — D2 56
Getz Ice Shelf, Ant. — B36 7
Geuda Springs, Ks., U.S. — E6 93
Gevelsberg, F.R.Ger. — B2 19
Gex, Fr. — C2 20
Geyser, Mt., U.S. — C6 103
Geyserville, Ca., U.S. — C2 82
Geyve, Tur. — B8 40
Ghabīyah, Wādī al, val., Eg. — E5 41
Ghaggar, stm., India — E5 37
Ghaghar Reservoir, res., India — E9 37
Ghāghra, stm., India — C7 36
Ghana, ctry., Afr. — E4 45
Ghanzi, Bots. — B3 49
Ghardaïa, Alg. — C5 44
Gharyān, Libya — C2 43
Ghāt, Libya — D2 43
Ghawr as Sharqīyah, Qanāt al, Jord. — B7 41
Ghazāl, Baḥr al, stm., Sud. — C3 47
Ghazal, Bahr el, stm., Chad — C3 46
Ghāzīābād, India — *C6 36
Ghazīpur, India — C6 37
Ghaznī, Afg. — B4 36
Gheen, Mn., U.S. — C6 100
Gheens, La., U.S. — E5 95
Ghent, Ky., U.S. — B4 94
Ghent, Mn., U.S. — F3 100
Ghent see Gent, Bel. — B5 16
Ghent, N.Y., U.S. — C7 109
Gheorghe Gheorghiu-Dej, Rom. — B8 24
Gheorgheni, Rom. — B7 24
Gherla, Rom. — B6 24
Ghilizane, Alg. — B5 44
Ghiló, Beinn a', mtn., Scot., U.K. — D5 13
Ghudāmis, Libya — C1 43
Ghūrīān, Afg. — D10 39
Gia Dinh, Viet. — C3 34
Giannutri, i., Italy — C3 23
Giant Mountain, mtn., N.Y., U.S. — A7 109
Giants Neck, Ct., U.S. — D7 84
Giaveno, Italy — D2 20
Gibara, Cuba — D5 64
Gibbon, Mn., U.S. — F4 100
Gibbon, Ne., U.S. — D7 104
Gibbons, Ab., Can. — C4 68
Gibbonsville, Id., U.S. — D5 89
Gibbs, Mo., U.S. — A5 102
Gibbstown, N.J., U.S. — D2 107
Gibeon, Nmb. — C2 49
Gibraléon, Spain — D2 22
Gibraltar, dep., Eur. — D3 22
Gibraltar, Strait of, strt. — E3 22
Gibsland, La., U.S. — B2 95
Gibson, Ga., U.S. — C4 87
Gibson, La., U.S. — E5 95
Gibson, N.C., U.S. — C3 110
Gibson, co., In., U.S. — H2 91
Gibson, co., Tn., U.S. — A3 119
Gibsonburg, Oh., U.S. — A2 112
Gibson City, Il., U.S. — C5 90
Gibson Desert, des., Austl. — D3 50
Gibsonia, Pa., U.S. — h14 115

Name — Map Ref — Page

Gibson Island, i., Md., U.S. B5 97
Gibsons, B.C., Can. E6 69
Gibsonton, Fl., U.S. p11 86
Gibsonville, N.C., U.S. A3 110
Giddings, Tx., U.S. D4 120
Gideon, Mo., U.S. E8 102
Gidole, Eth. D4 47
Gien, Fr. D5 16
Giessen, F.R.Ger. C4 18
Gifford, Ar., U.S. g8 81
Gifford, Fl., U.S. E6 86
Gifford, Id., U.S. C2 89
Gifford, Il., U.S. C5 90
Gifford, In., U.S. B3 91
Gifford, Pa., U.S. C4 115
Giffre, stm., Fr. D2 21
Gifhorn, F.R.Ger. F4 15
Gift, Tn., U.S. B2 119
Gifu, Japan D12 31
Giganta, Sierra de la, mts., Mex. B2 63
Gigante, Col. C2 60
Gigha, is., Scot., U.K. E3 13
Gig Harbor, Wa., U.S. B3 124
Giglio, i., Italy C3 23
Gihon, stm., Vt., U.S. B3 122
Gijón, Spain A3 22
Gila, N.M., U.S. E1 108
Gila, co., Az., U.S. D5 80
Gila, stm., U.S. D5 76
Gila Bend, Az., U.S. E3 80
Gila Bend Indian Reservation, Az., U.S. D3 80
Gila Bend Mountains, mts., Az., U.S. D2 80
Gila Cliff Dwellings National Monument, N.M., U.S. D1 108
Gila Mountains, mts., Az., U.S. D6 80
Gila Peak, mtn., Az., U.S. B6 80
Gila River Indian Reservation, Az., U.S. D4 80
Gilbert, Az., U.S. D4 80
Gilbert, Ar., U.S. B3 81
Gilbert, Ia., U.S. B4 92
Gilbert, La., U.S. B4 95
Gilbert, Mn., U.S. C6 100
Gilbert, Or., U.S. *B4 114
Gilbert, S.C., U.S. D5 117
Gilbert, W.V., U.S. D3 125
Gilbert, stm., Austl. C7 50
Gilbert, stm., Nf., Can. B3 72
Gilbert Islands see Kiribati, ctry., Oc. G11 6
Gilbert Islands, is., Kir. G10 6
Gilbertown, Al., U.S. D1 78
Gilbert Peak, mtn., Wa., U.S. C4 124
Gilbert Plains, Mb., Can. D1 70
Gilbertsville, Ky., U.S. f9 94
Gilbertsville, N.Y., U.S. C5 109
Gilbertsville, Pa., U.S. F10 115
Gilbertville, Ia., U.S. B5 92
Gilbertville, Ma., U.S. B3 98
Gilboa, Oh., U.S. A2 112
Gilby, N.D., U.S. A8 111
Gilchrist, Or., U.S. D5 114
Gilchrist, co., Fl., U.S. C4 86
Gilcrest, Co., U.S. A6 83
Gildford, Mt., U.S. B6 103
Gilead, Ct., U.S. C6 84
Gilead, Me., U.S. D2 96
Gilead, Ne., U.S. D8 104
Giles. co., Tn., U.S. B4 119
Giles, co., Va., U.S. C2 123
Gilford, N. Ire., U.K. C5 11
Gilford, N.H., U.S. C4 106
Gilford Island, i., B.C., Can. D4 69
Gilgandra, Austl. E7 51
Gilgit, Pak. A5 36
Gil Island, i., B.C., Can. C3 69
Gill, Co., U.S. A6 83
Gill, Lough, l., Ire. C3 11
Gillam, Mb., Can. A4 70
Gilleleje, Den. B6 15
Gillen, Lake, l., Austl. E3 50
Gillespie, Il., U.S. D4 90
Gillespie, co., Tx., U.S. D3 120
Gillespie Dam, Az., U.S. D3 80
Gillett, Ar., U.S. C4 81
Gillett, Fl., U.S. p10 86
Gillett, Pa., U.S. C8 115
Gillett, Tx., U.S. k8 120
Gillett, Wi., U.S. D5 126
Gillette, Wy., U.S. B7 127
Gillett Grove, Ia., U.S. A2 92
Gillham, Ar., U.S. C1 81
Gilliam, La., U.S. B2 95
Gillifilliam, Mo., U.S. B4 102
Gilliam, co., Or., U.S. B6 114
Gillingham, Eng., U.K. C8 12
Gillis, La., U.S. D2 95
Gillis Point, N.S., Can. C9 71
Gillsburg, Ms., U.S. D3 101
Gilly (part of Charleroi), Bel. B6 16
Gilman, Co., U.S. B4 83
Gilman, Ct., U.S. C7 84
Gilman, Il., U.S. C5 90
Gilman, Ia., U.S. C5 92
Gilman, Mn., U.S. E5 100
Gilman, Vt., U.S. C5 122
Gilman, Wi., U.S. C3 126
Gilman City, Mo., U.S. A4 102
Gilmanton, N.H., U.S. D4 106
Gilmanton, Wi., U.S. D2 126
Gilmanton Iron Works, N.H., U.S. D4 106
Gilmer, Tx., U.S. C5 120
Gilmer, W.V., U.S. C4 125
Gilmer, co., Ga., U.S. B2 87
Gilmer, co., W.V., U.S. C4 125
Gilmore, Ar., U.S. B5 81
Gilmore City, Ia., U.S. B3 92
Gilmour, On., Can. C7 73
Gilo, stm., Eth. D3 47
Gilpin, Ky., U.S. C5 94
Gilpin, co., Co., U.S. B5 83
Gilroy, Sk., Can. G2 75
Gilroy, Ca., U.S. D3 82
Gilson, Il., U.S. C3 90
Gilsum, N.H., U.S. D2 106
Gilt Edge, Tn., U.S. B2 119
Giltner, Ne., U.S. D7 104
Giluwe, Mount, mtn., Pap. N. Gui. k11 50
Gimli, Mb., Can. D3 70
Ginir, Eth. D5 47
Ginns Corner, De., U.S. C3 85
Ginosa, Italy D6 23
Ginowan, Japan O5 52
Ginzo [de Limia], Spain A2 22
Gioia del Colle, Italy D6 23
Gioiosa Ionica, Italy E6 23
Girard, Ga., U.S. C5 87
Girard, Il., U.S. D4 90
Girard, Ks., U.S. E9 93
Girard, La., U.S. B4 95
Girard, Oh., U.S. A5 112
Girard, Pa., U.S. B1 115
Girard, Tx., U.S. C2 120
Girardot, Col. C3 60
Girardville, Pa., U.S. E9 115
Girdletree, Md., U.S. D7 97
Gīreh, Kūh-e, mtn., Iran H8 39
Giresun, Tur. B12 40
Giri, stm., Zaire A2 48
Giridih, India D8 36
Girna, stm., India G5 37
Giromagny, Fr. D7 16
Girón, Ec. B2 58
Gironde, est., Fr. E3 16
Giroux, Mb., Can. E3 70
Girouxville, Ab., Can. B2 68
Girvan, Scot., U.K. C4 10
Girvin, Sk., Can. F3 75
Girvin, Tx., U.S. D1 120
Gisborne, N.Z. M17 51
Gisborne Lake, l., Nf., Can. E4 72
Giscome, B.C., Can. B6 69
Gisenyi, Rw. B4 48
Gislaved, Swe. A7 15
Gisors, Fr. C4 16
Gitega, Bdi. B4 48
Giulianova, Italy C4 23
Giurgiu, Rom. D7 24
Giv'atayim, Isr. g10 41
Give, Den. C3 15
Givet, Fr. B6 16
Givhans, S.C., U.S. E7 117
Givors, Fr. E6 16
Givry, i., Micron. Q18 52
Giza (Al Jīzah), Eg. B3 38
Giza, Pyramids of, hist., Egypt E3 41
Gīzāb, Afg. E13 39
Gizhiga, Sov. Un. C19 29
Giżycko, Pol. A6 26
Gjirokastra, Alb. B3 40
Gjoa Haven, N.T., Can. C13 66
Gjövik, Nor. G4 14
Glace Bay, N.S., Can. C10 71
Glacier, B.C., Can. D9 69
Glacier, Wa., U.S. A4 124
Glacier, co., Mt., U.S. B3 103
Glacier Bay, b., Ak., U.S. k21 79
Glacier Bay National Park, Ak., U.S. D12 79
Glacier National Park, B.C., Can. D9 69
Glacier National Park, Mt., U.S. B2 103
Glacier Peak, mtn., Wa., U.S. A4 124
Gladbeck, F.R.Ger. B1 19
Gladbrook, Ia., U.S. B5 92
Glade, Ks., U.S. C4 93
Glade Creek, stm., Wa., U.S. C6 124
Glade Creek, stm., W.V., U.S. n14 125
Glade Creek, stm., W.V., U.S. n13 125
Glade Park, Co., U.S. B2 83
Glades, co., Fl., U.S. F5 86
Glade Spring, Va., U.S. f10 123
Glade Valley, N.C., U.S. A1 110
Gladeville, Tn., U.S. A5 119
Gladewater, Tx., U.S. C5 120
Gladmar, Sk., Can. H3 75
Gladstone, Austl. D9 50
Gladstone, Mb., Can. D2 70
Gladstone, Il., U.S. C3 90
Gladstone, Mi., U.S. C4 99
Gladstone, Mo., U.S. h10 102
Gladstone, Ne., U.S. D8 104
Gladstone, N.J., U.S. B3 107
Gladstone, N.M., U.S. A6 108
Gladstone, N.D., U.S. C3 111
Gladstone, Or., U.S. B4 114
Gladstone, Va., U.S. C4 123
Glad Valley, S.D., U.S. B4 118
Gladwin, Mi., U.S. E6 99
Gladwin, co., Mi., U.S. D6 99
Glady, W.V., U.S. C5 125
Gladys, Va., U.S. C3 123
Glåma, stm., Nor. G5 14
Glamis, Sk., Can. F2 75
Glamoč, Yugo. C3 24
Glan, l., Swe. u33 14
Glan, stm., F.R.Ger. D2 19
Gland, Switz. D1 21
Glandorf, Oh., U.S. A1 112
Glanshammar (part of Örebro), Swe. t33 14
Glärnisch, mts., Switz. C4 20
Glarus, Switz. E4 18
Glarus, state, Switz. B5 20
Glarus Alps, mts., Switz. C6 21
Glasco, Ks., U.S. C6 93
Glasco, N.Y., U.S. C7 109
Glascock, co., Ga., U.S. C4 87
Glasford, Il., U.S. C4 90
Glasgo, Ct., U.S. C8 84
Glasgow, Scot., U.K. C4 10
Glasgow, Il., U.S. D3 90
Glasgow, Ky., U.S. C4 94
Glasgow, Mo., U.S. B5 102
Glasgow, Mt., U.S. B10 103
Glasgow, Va., U.S. C3 123
Glasgow, W.V., U.S. m13 125
Glasgow Village, Mo., U.S. *f13 102
Glaslyn, Sk., Can. D1 75
Glasnevin, Sk., Can. H3 75
Glass, Tn., U.S. A2 119
Glassboro, N.J., U.S. D2 107
Glasscock, co., Tx., U.S. D2 120
Glass Mountains, mts., Tx., U.S. D1 120
Glasson, Ire. D4 11
Glassport, Pa., U.S. F2 115
Glasston, N.D., U.S. A8 111
Glastenbury Mountain, mtn., Vt., U.S. F2 122
Glastonbury, Eng., U.K. C5 12
Glastonbury, Ct., U.S. C5 84
Glauchau, Ger.D.R. C6 18
Glazier, Tx., U.S. A2 120
Glazier Lake, l., Me., U.S. A3 96
Glazov, Sov. Un. B4 28
Glazypeau Mountain, mtn., Ar., U.S. f7 81
Gleason, Tn., U.S. A3 119
Gleason, Wi., U.S. C4 126
Gleasondale, Ma., U.S. g9 98
Gleichen, Ab., Can. D4 68
Glen, Mn., U.S. D5 100
Glen, Mt., U.S. E4 103
Glen, N.H., U.S. B4 106
Glen, W.V., U.S. m13 125
Glenade, Ire. C3 11
Glen Alice, Tn., U.S. D9 119
Glen Allan, Ms., U.S. B2 101
Glen Allen, Al., U.S. B2 78
Glenallen, Mo., U.S. D7 102
Glen Allen, Va., U.S. C5 123
Glen Alpine, N.C., U.S. B1 110
Glenamaddy, Ire. D3 11
Glenamoy, Ire. C2 11
Glénan, Îles de, is., Fr. D1 16
Glen Arbor, Mi., U.S. D4 99
Glenarm, N. Ire., U.K. C6 11
Glenavon, Sk., Can. G4 75
Glen Avon, Ca., U.S. m14 82
Glenbain, Sk., Can. H2 75
Glenbarr, Scot., U.K. E3 13
Glenbeigh, Ire. E2 11
Glenbeulah, Wi., U.S. k9 126
Glenboro, Mb., Can. E2 70
Glenbrook, Nv., U.S. D2 105
Glenburn, N.D., U.S. A4 111
Glen Burnie, Md., U.S. B4 97
Glenbush, Sk., Can. D2 75
Glen Campbell, Pa., U.S. E4 115
Glen Canyon, Ut., U.S. F4 121
Glen Canyon, val., U.S. G4 121
Glen Canyon Dam, Az., U.S. A4 80
Glen Canyon National Recreation Area, U.S. F5 121
Glencar, Ire. E2 11
Glen Carbon, Il., U.S. *E4 90
Glencliff, N.H., U.S. C3 106
Glencoe, On., Can. E3 73
Glencoe, Al., U.S. B4 78
Glencoe, Il., U.S. A6 90
Glencoe, Ky., U.S. B5 94
Glencoe, La., U.S. E4 95
Glencoe, Md., U.S. A4 97
Glencoe, Mn., U.S. F4 100
Glencoe, Mo., U.S. f12 102
Glencoe, N.M., U.S. D4 108
Glencoe, Ok., U.S. A5 113
Glencolumbkille, Ire. C3 11
Glen Cove, N.Y., U.S. h13 109
Glencross, S.D., U.S. B5 118
Glendale, Az., U.S. D3 80
Glendale, Ar., U.S. D4 81
Glendale, Ca., U.S. m12 82
Glendale, Co., U.S. *B6 83
Glendale, Fl., U.S. v15 86
Glendale, Ky., U.S. C4 94
Glendale, Ma., U.S. *B1 98
Glendale, Ms., U.S. D4 101
Glendale, Mo., U.S. *f13 102
Glendale, N.H., U.S. C4 106
Glendale, Oh., U.S. C1 112
Glendale, Or., U.S. E3 114
Glendale, R.I., U.S. B2 116
Glendale, S.C., U.S. B4 117
Glendale, Tn., U.S. B5 119
Glendale, Ut., U.S. F3 121
Glen Dale, W.V., U.S. B4 125
Glendale, Wi., U.S. m12 126
Glendale Colony, S.D., U.S. C7 118
Glendale Heights, Il., U.S. *k8 90
Glendale Heights, W.V., U.S. g8 125
Glen Dean, Ky., U.S. C3 94
Glendevey, Co., U.S. A5 83
Glendive, Mt., U.S. C12 103
Glendo, Wy., U.S. D7 127
Glendola, N.J., U.S. C4 107
Glendon, Ab., Can. B5 68
Glendora, Ca., U.S. m13 82
Glendora, Ms., U.S. B3 101
Glendora, N.J., U.S. *D2 107
Glendo Reservoir, res., Wy., U.S. D8 127
Glendowan, Ire. C4 11
Glen Easton, W.V., U.S. g8 125
Glen Echo, Md., U.S. f8 97
Glen Elder, Ks., U.S. C5 93
Glenelg, Scot., U.K. C3 13
Glenelg, Md., U.S. B4 97
Glenella, Mb., Can. D2 70
Glen Ellis Falls, wtfl, N.H., U.S. B4 106
Glen Ellyn, Il., U.S. k8 90
Glen Ewen, Sk., Can. H4 75
Glenfarne, Ire. C4 11
Glen Ferris, W.V., U.S. *C3 125
Glenfield, N.Y., U.S. B5 109
Glenfield, N.D., U.S. B7 111
Glenfinnan, Scot., U.K. D3 13
Glen Flora, Tx., U.S. E4 120
Glengad Head, c., Ire. B4 11
Glen Gardner, N.J., U.S. B3 107
Glengarriff, Ire. F2 11
Glengarry, co., On., Can. B10 73
Glenham, N.Y., U.S. D7 109
Glenham, S.D., U.S. B5 118
Glen Haven, Co., U.S. A5 83
Glen Head, N.Y., U.S. *h13 109
Glen Innes, Austl. E9 50
Glen Jean, W.V., U.S. D3 125
Glen Kerr, Sk., Can. G2 75
Glen Lake, l., Mi., U.S. D5 99
Glenluce, Scot., U.K. F4 13
Glen Lyon, Pa., U.S. D9 115
Glenmont, Oh., U.S. B3 112
Glenmora, La., U.S. D3 95
Glenmore, Oh., U.S. B1 112
Glenmorgan, Austl. C7 51
Glenn, Mi., U.S. F4 99
Glenn, co., Ca., U.S. C2 82
Glennallen, Ak., U.S. f19 79
Glennie, Mi., U.S. D7 99
Glennonville, Mo., U.S. E7 102
Glenns Ferry, Id., U.S. G3 89
Glennville, Ga., U.S. E5 87
Glenolden, Pa., U.S. p20 115
Glenoma, Wa., U.S. C3 124
Glenorchy, Austl. o15 50
Glenpool, Ok., U.S. B5 113
Glen Raven, N.C., U.S. A3 110
Glenridge, Ma., U.S. h10 98
Glen Ridge, N.J., U.S. h8 107
Glenrio, N.M., U.S. B6 108
Glen Robertson, On., Can. B10 73
Glen Rock, N.J., U.S. h8 107
Glen Rock, Pa., U.S. G8 115
Glenrock, Wy., U.S. D7 127
Glen Rose, Tx., U.S. C4 120
Glenrothes, Scot., U.K. D5 13
Glen Saint Mary, Fl., U.S. B4 86
Glens Falls, N.Y., U.S. B7 109
Glenshaw, Pa., U.S. h14 115
Glenside, Sk., Can. F2 75
Glenside, Pa., U.S. F11 115
Glentana, Mt., U.S. B10 103
Glenties, Ire. C3 11
Glentworth, Sk., Can. H2 75
Glen Ullin, N.D., U.S. C4 111
Glenview, Il., U.S. h9 90
Glenview Naval Air Station, mil., Il., U.S. h9 90
Glenvil, Ne., U.S. D7 104
Glenville, Ire. E3 11
Glenville, Mn., U.S. G5 100
Glenville, N.C., U.S. f9 110
Glenville, W.V., U.S. C4 125
Glen White, W.V., U.S. D3 125
Glen Wilton, Va., U.S. C3 123
Glenwood, Nf., Can. D4 72
Glenwood, Al., U.S. D3 78
Glenwood, Ar., U.S. C2 81
Glenwood, Fl., U.S. C5 86
Glenwood, Ga., U.S. D4 87
Glenwood, Il., U.S. *k9 90
Glenwood, In., U.S. E7 91
Glenwood, Ia., U.S. C2 92
Glenwood, Md., U.S. B3 97
Glenwood, Mn., U.S. E3 100
Glenwood, Mo., U.S. A5 102
Glenwood, N.M., U.S. D1 108
Glenwood, Or., U.S. B3 114
Glenwood, Ut., U.S. E4 121
Glenwood, Va., U.S. D3 123
Glenwood, Wa., U.S. C4 124
Glenwood, W.V., U.S. C2 125
Glenwood City, Wi., U.S. C1 126
Glenwood Farms, Va., U.S. *C5 123
Glenwood Springs, Co., U.S. B3 83
Glenwoodville, Ab., Can. E4 68
Gletsch, Switz. C5 21
Glezen, In., U.S. H3 91
Glidden, Sk., Can. F1 75
Glidden, Ia., U.S. B3 92
Glidden, Wi., U.S. B3 126
Glide, Or., U.S. D3 114
Glifádha, Grc. h11 25
Glin, Ire. E2 11
Glittertinden, mtn., Nor. G3 14
Gliwice, Pol. C5 26
Globe, Az., U.S. D5 80
Globe, Ky., U.S. B6 94
Globino, Sov. Un. G9 27
Głogów, Pol. C4 26
Glorenza, Italy A3 23
Glória, Braz. C3 57
Glória de Goitá, Braz. k6 57
Glorieta, N.M., U.S. B4 108
Glorieuses, Îles, is., Reu. f9 49
Glossop, Eng., U.K. A6 12
Glossopteris, Mount, mtn., Ant. A1 7
Gloster, Ga., U.S. h8 87
Gloster, La., U.S. B2 95
Gloster, Ms., U.S. D2 101
Glostrup, Den. C6 15
Gloucester, On., Can. h12 73
Gloucester, Eng., U.K. E5 10
Gloucester, Ma., U.S. A6 98
Gloucester, Va., U.S. C6 123
Gloucester, co., N.B., Can. B4 71
Gloucester, co., N.J., U.S. D2 107
Gloucester, co., Va., U.S. C6 123
Gloucester City, N.J., U.S. D2 107
Gloucester Point, Va., U.S. C6 123
Gloucestershire, co., Eng., U.K. C7 12
Glouster, Oh., U.S. C3 112
Glover, Mo., U.S. D7 102
Glover, Vt., U.S. B4 122
Glover Gap, W.V., U.S. h10 125
Glover Island, i., Nf., Can. D3 72
Gloversville, N.Y., U.S. B6 109
Glovertown, Nf., Can. D4 72
Gloverville, S.C., U.S. E4 117
Głubczyce, Pol. C4 26
Glubokoye, Sov. Un. D6 27
Głuchołazy, Pol. C4 26
Gluck, S.C., U.S. C2 117
Glücksburg, F.R.Ger. D3 15
Glückstadt, F.R.Ger. E3 15
Gluek, Mn., U.S. E3 100
Glukhov, Sov. Un. F9 27
Glussk, Sov. Un. E7 27
Glyndon, Md., U.S. B4 97
Glyndon, Mn., U.S. D2 100
Glyngøre, Den. B2 15
Glynn, co., Ga., U.S. E5 87
Gmunden, Aus. E6 18
Gnadenhutten, Oh., U.S. B4 112
Gnesta, Swe. t35 14
Gniezno, Pol. B4 26
Gnjilane, Yugo. D5 24
Gnoien, Ger.D.R. E6 15
Goa [,Damān and Diu], ter., India F5 36
Goālpāra, India D13 37
Goat Fell, mtn., Scot., U.K. E3 13
Goat Island, i., R.I., U.S. F5 116
Goat Island Point, c., Am. Sam. F13 52
Goat Mountain, mtn., Mt., U.S. C3 103
Goat Rock Dam, U.S. C4 78
Goba, Eth. D5 47
Gobabis, Nmb. B2 49
Gobernador, N.M., U.S. A2 108
Gobernador Gregores, Arg. D2 54
Gobernador Udaondo, Arg. g7 54
Gobi Desert, des., Asia C5 31
Gobles, Mi., U.S. F5 99
Gobō, Japan J7 33
Goch, F.R.Ger. C3 18
Gochas, Nmb. B2 49
Godāvari, stm., India E6 36
Godāvari, Mouths of the, mth., India E7 36
Godda, India E11 37
Goddard, Ks., U.S. E6 93
Goderich, On., Can. D3 73
Godfrey, On., Can. C8 73
Godfrey, Ga., U.S. C3 87
Godfrey, Il., U.S. E3 90
Godhavn, Grnld. C15 61
Godhra, India F4 37
Godley, Tx., U.S. n9 120
Gods, stm., Mb., Can. A5 70
Gods Lake, Mb., Can. B4 70
Gods Lake, l., Mb., Can. B4 70
Godthåb (Nuuk), Grnld. C15 61
Godwin, N.C., U.S. B4 110
Goehner, Ne., U.S. D8 104
Goélands, Lac aux, l., P.Q., Can. g8 72
Goes, Neth. C3 17
Goessel, Ks., U.S. D6 93
Goff, Ks., U.S. C8 93
Goff Creek, stm., Ok., U.S. e9 113
Goffstown, N.H., U.S. D3 106
Gogebic, co., Mi., U.S. n12 99
Gogebic, Lake, l., Mi., U.S. m12 99
Gogebic Range, hills, U.S. B3 126
Goglio, Italy D5 21
Gohfeld, F.R.Ger. A3 19
Göhren, Ger.D.R. D7 15
Goiana, Braz. C4 57
Goiandira, Braz. B3 56
Goianésia, Braz. B3 56
Goiânia, Braz. B3 56
Goianinha, Braz. h6 57
Goiás, Braz. B2 56
Goiás, state, Braz. B3 56
Goiatuba, Braz. B3 56
Goil, Loch, b., Scot., U.K. D4 13
Goito, Italy D6 20
Gojam, prov., Eth. C4 47
Gojō, Japan o14 33
Gökçeada, i., Tur. B5 25
Göksun, Tur. C11 40
Gokwe, Zimb. A4 49
Gol, Nor. G3 14
Gola, i., Ire. B3 11
Golam Head, c., Ire. D2 11
Golan Heights, ter., Syria A7 41
Golbaf, Iran C5 38
Golchikha, Sov. Un. B11 29
Golconda, Il., U.S. F5 90
Golconda, Nv., U.S. C4 105
Goldach, Switz. B7 21
Gołdap, Pol. A7 26
Goldbach, F.R.Ger. C4 19
Gold Bar, Wa., U.S. B4 124
Gold Beach, Or., U.S. E2 114
Goldberg, Ger.D.R. E6 15
Goldboro, N.S., Can. D8 71
Gold Bridge, B.C., Can. D6 69
Gold Coast see Southport, Austl. E9 50
Gold Creek, Ak., U.S. f17 79
Goldcreek, Mt., U.S. D4 103
Golddust, Tn., U.S. B2 119
Golden, B.C., Can. D9 69
Golden, Ire. E4 11
Golden, Co., U.S. B5 83
Golden, Il., U.S. C2 90
Golden, Ms., U.S. A5 101
Golden, Mo., U.S. E4 102
Golden, N.M., U.S. B3 108
Golden, Ok., U.S. C7 113
Golden Bay, b., N.Z. N14 51
Golden Beach, Fl., U.S. *G6 86
Golden City, Mo., U.S. D3 102
Goldendale, Wa., U.S. D5 124
Golden Ears Provincial Park, B.C., Can. E6 69
Goldengate, Il., U.S. E5 90
Golden Gate Bridge, Ca., U.S. h7 82
Golden Gate National Recreation Area, Ca., U.S. h7 82
Golden Hinde, mtn., B.C., Can. E5 69
Golden Lake, On., Can. B7 73
Golden Lake, l., On., Can. B7 73
Golden Meadow, La., U.S. E5 95
Golden Prairie, Sk., Can. G1 75
Golden Spike National Historic Site, hist., Ut., U.S. B3 121
Golden Spur, Ct., U.S. D7 84
Golden Valley, Mn., U.S. n12 100
Goldenvalley, N.D., U.S. B3 111
Golden Valley, co., Mt., U.S. D7 103
Golden Valley, co., N.D., U.S. B2 111
Goldenville, N.S., Can. D7 71
Goldfield, Ia., U.S. B4 92
Goldfield, Nv., U.S. F4 105
Gold Hill, N.C., U.S. B2 110
Gold Hill, Or., U.S. E3 114
Goldonna, La., U.S. B3 95
Goldsand Lake, l., Mb., Can. A1 70
Goldsboro, Md., U.S. B6 97
Goldsboro, N.C., U.S. B5 110
Goldsby, Ok., U.S. B4 113
Goldschmidt, Cape, c., Ant. g40 7
Goldsmith, In., U.S. D5 91
Goldsmith, Tx., U.S. D1 120
Goldston, N.C., U.S. B3 110
Goldsworthy, Austl. D2 50
Goldthwaite, Tx., U.S. D3 120
Goleen, Ire. F2 11
Golela, S. Afr. C5 49
Goleniów, Pol. B3 26
Goleta, Ca., U.S. E4 82
Golets-Skalistyy, Mount, mtn., Sov. Un. D14 29
Golfito, C.R. F6 62
Golf Manor, Oh., U.S. o13 112
Goliad, Tx., U.S. E4 120
Goliad, co., Tx., U.S. E4 120
Golling [an der Salzach], Aus. B9 20
Golmud, China D3 31
Golo, stm., Fr. C2 23
Golo Island, i., Phil. p13 34
Golovin, Ak., U.S. C7 79
Golpāyegān, Iran B5 38
Golspie, Scot., U.K. A5 10
Goltry, Ok., U.S. A3 113
Golts, Md., U.S. B6 97
Golva, N.D., U.S. C2 111
Golyamo Konare, Bul. D7 24
Goma, Zaire B4 48
Gomati, stm., India D9 37
Gombari, Zaire A4 48
Gombe, Nig. D7 45
Gomel, Sov. Un. D6 29
Gomera, i., Spain m13 22
Gómez Palacio, Mex. B4 63
Gommern, Ger.D.R. A6 19
Gonābād, Iran D9 39
Gonaïves, Haiti E7 64
Gonâve, Golfe de la, b., Haiti E7 64
Gonâve, Île de la, i., Haiti E7 64
Gonbad-e Qābūs, Iran C7 39
Gonda, India C7 36
Gonder (Gondar), Eth. C4 47
Gonder, prov., Eth. C4 47
Gondia, India G8 37
Gondrecourt-le-Château, Fr. F5 17
Gönen, Tur. B6 40
Gonesse, Fr. g10 16
Gongga Mountain (Minya Konka), mtn., China F5 31
Gongola, stm., Nig. D7 45
Goñi, Ur. f8 54
Gonvick, Mn., U.S. C3 100
Gonzales, Ca., U.S. D3 82
Gonzales, La., U.S. D5 95
Gonzales, Tx., U.S. E4 120
Gonzales, co., Tx., U.S. E4 120
Gonzalez, Fl., U.S. u14 86
González Chaves, Arg. B4 54
Goochland, Va., U.S. C5 123
Goochland, co., Va., U.S. C5 123
Goode, Va., U.S. C3 123
Goode, Mount, mtn., Ak., U.S. g18 79
Goodell, Ia., U.S. B4 92
Gooderham, On., Can. C6 73
Goodeve, Sk., Can. F4 75
Goodfellow Air Force Base, mil., Tx., U.S. D2 120
Goodfield, Il., U.S. C4 90
Good Hart, Mi., U.S. C5 99
Good Hope, Ga., U.S. C3 87
Good Hope, Il., U.S. C3 90
Good Hope, Ms., U.S. C4 101
Good Hope, Oh., U.S. C2 112
Good Hope, Cape of, c., S. Afr. D2 49
Good Hope Mountain, mtn., B.C., Can. D5 69
Goodhue, Mn., U.S. F6 100
Goodhue, co., Mn., U.S. F6 100
Gooding, Id., U.S. G4 89
Gooding, co., Id., U.S. F4 89
Goodland, Fl., U.S. G5 86
Goodland, In., U.S. C3 91
Goodland, Ks., U.S. C2 93
Goodland, Ok., U.S. D6 113
Goodlands, Mb., Can. E1 70
Goodlettsville, Tn., U.S. g10 119
Goodman, Ms., U.S. C4 101
Goodman, Mo., U.S. E3 102
Goodman, Wi., U.S. C5 126
Goodnews Bay, Ak., U.S. D7 79
Goodnight, Tx., U.S. B2 120
Good Pine, La., U.S. C3 95
Goodrich, Co., U.S. A6 83
Goodrich, Ks., U.S. D9 93
Goodrich, N.D., U.S. B5 111
Goodrich, Tx., U.S. D5 120
Goodridge, Mn., U.S. B3 100
Good Spirit Lake, l., Sk., Can. F4 75
Good Spirit Lake Provincial Park, Sk., Can. F4 75
Goodspring, Tn., U.S. B4 119
Goodsprings, Al., U.S. B2 78
Goodsprings, Nv., U.S. H6 105
Good Thunder, Mn., U.S. F4 100
Goodview, Mn., U.S. F7 100
Goodwater, Sk., Can. H4 75
Goodwater, Al., U.S. B3 78
Goodway, Al., U.S. D2 78
Goodwell, Ok., U.S. e9 113
Goodwin, Ar., U.S. C4 81
Goodwin, S.D., U.S. C9 118
Goodyear, Az., U.S. D3 80
Goole, Eng., U.K. A7 12
Goondiwindi, Austl. E9 50
Goor, Neth. B6 17
Goose, stm., Nf., Can. h9 72
Goose, stm., N.D., U.S. B8 111
Goose Bay, b., Nf., Can. B1 72
Gooseberry Creek, stm., Wy., U.S. B4 127
Goose Creek, S.C., U.S. F7 117
Goose Creek, stm., U.S. G5 89
Goose Creek, stm., Ne., U.S. B5 104
Goose Creek, stm., Va., U.S. C3 123
Goose Creek Reservoir, res., S.C., U.S. k11 117
Goose Island, i., B.C., Can. D3 69
Goose Lake, Ia., U.S. C7 92
Goose Lake, l., Mb., Can. B1 70
Goose Lake, l., Sk., Can. D4 75
Goose Lake, l., Sk., Can. F2 75
Goose Lake, l., U.S. B3 82
Goose Pond, l., N.H., U.S. C2 106
Gopālganj, India D10 37
Gopło Lake, l., Pol. B5 26
Göppingen, F.R.Ger. D4 18
Góra, Pol. C4 26
Góra Kalwaria, Pol. C6 26
Gorakhpur, India C7 36
Gorday, Ga., U.S. E3 87
Gördes, Tur. C7 25
Gordil, Cen. Afr. Rep. D4 46
Gordo, Al., U.S. B2 78
Gordon, Al., U.S. D4 78
Gordon, Ga., U.S. D3 87
Gordon, Mn., U.S. G5 100
Gordon, Ne., U.S. B3 104
Gordon, Oh., U.S. C1 112
Gordon, Tx., U.S. C3 120
Gordon, Wi., U.S. B2 126
Gordon, co., Ga., U.S. B2 87
Gordon Creek, stm., Ne., U.S. B5 104
Gordon Horne Peak, mtn., B.C., Can. D8 69
Gordon Lake, l., Ab., Can. A5 68
Gordon Lake, l., Sk., Can. B2 75
Gordonsville, Tn., U.S. C8 119
Gordonsville, Va., U.S. B4 123
Gordonville, Mo., U.S. D8 102
Gore, N.S., Can. D6 71
Gore, Eth. D4 47
Gore, N.Z. Q12 51
Gore, Oh., U.S. C3 112
Gore, Ok., U.S. B6 113
Gore, Va., U.S. A4 123
Gore Bay, On., Can. B2 73
Goree, Tx., U.S. C3 120
Gore Mountain, mtn., Vt., U.S. B5 122
Gore Point, c., Ak., U.S. h16 79
Gore Range, mts., Co., U.S. B4 83
Gore Springs, Ms., U.S. B4 101
Goreville, Il., U.S. F5 90
Gorey, Ire. D3 10
Gorgān (Asterābād), Iran B5 38
Gorgān, stm., Iran C7 39
Gorgān, Khalīj, b., Iran C6 39
Gorgas, Al., U.S. B2 78
Gorge High Dam, Wa., U.S. A4 124
Gorgona, Isla, i., Col. C2 60
Gorham, Il., U.S. F4 90
Gorham, Ks., U.S. D4 93
Gorham, Me., U.S. E2 96
Gorham, N.H., U.S. B4 106
Gorham, N.Y., U.S. C3 109
Gori, Sov. Un. E2 28
Gorin, Mo., U.S. A5 102
Gorinchem, Neth. C5 17
Goris, Sov. Un. B3 39
Gorizia, Italy B4 23
Gorki, Sov. Un. D8 27
Gorkiy, Sov. Un. D7 29
Gorkiy Reservoir, res., Sov. Un. D7 29
Gørlev, Den. C5 15
Gorlice, Pol. D6 26
Görlitz, Ger.D.R. C7 18
Gorlovka, Sov. Un. G12 27
Gorm, Loch, l., Scot., U.K. E2 13
Gorman, Md., U.S. m12 97
Gorman, Tn., U.S. A4 119
Gorman, Tx., U.S. C3 120
Gormania, W.V., U.S. B5 125
Gormley (part of Whitchurch-Stouffville), On., Can. k15 73
Gorna Oryakhovitsa, Bul. D7 24
Gornji Milanovac, Yugo. C5 24
Gorno-Altaysk, Sov. Un. D11 29
Gornozavodsk, Sov. Un. C10 33
Gorodenka, Sov. Un. G5 27
Gorodets, Sov. Un. D17 8
Gorodnya, Sov. Un. F8 27
Gorodok, Mong. A5 31
Gorodok, Sov. Un. D8 27
Gorodok, Sov. Un. G4 27
Goroka, Pap. N. Gui. k12 50
Goroke, Austl. H3 51
Gorontalo, Indon. E6 34
Gorrie, On., Can. D3 73
Gorskoye, Sov. Un. q21 27
Gort, Ire. D3 11
Gortahork, Ire. B3 11
Gorum, La., U.S. C3 95
Gorumna, i., Ire. D2 11
Goryn, stm., Sov. Un. F6 27

Name   **Map Ref**   **Page**

Gorzów [Wielkopolski], Pol. . B3 26
Gosford, Austl. F8 51
Goshen, N.S., Can. D8 71
Goshen, Al., U.S. D3 78
Goshen, Ct., U.S. B3 84
Goshen, In., U.S. A6 91
Goshen, Ky., U.S. g11 94
Goshen, Ma., U.S. B2 98
Goshen, N.H., U.S. D2 106
Goshen, N.J., U.S. E3 107
Goshen, N.Y., U.S. D6 109
Goshen, Oh., U.S. C1 112
Goshen, Or., U.S. D3 114
Goshen, Ut., U.S. D4 121
Goshen, Va., U.S. C3 123
Goshen, co., Wy., U.S. D8 127
Goshen Hole, Wy., U.S. D8 127
Goshogawara, Japan F10 33
Goshute Indian Reservation,
U.S. D7 105
Goshute Lake, l., Nv., U.S. . . C7 105
Goshute Mountains, mts., Nv.,
U.S. C7 105
Goslar, F.R.Ger. C5 18
Gosnell, Ar., U.S. *B6 81
Gosnells, Austl. *F2 50
Gosper, co., Ne., U.S. D6 104
Gospić, Yugo. C2 24
Gosport, Eng., U.K. D6 12
Gosport, Al., U.S. D2 78
Gosport, In., U.S. F4 91
Gossau, Switz. B7 21
Gossburg, Tn., U.S. B5 119
Gossville, N.H., U.S. D4 106
Gostivar, Yugo. E5 24
Gostyń, Pol. C4 26
Gostynin, Pol. B5 26
Gostynka, stm., Pol. g9 26
Gotebo, Ok., U.S. B3 113
Göteborg (Gothenburg), Swe. I4 14
Göteborg och Bohus, co.,
Swe. A5 15
Gotel Mountains, mts., Afr. . . D2 46
Gotemba, Japan n18 33
Gotha, Ger.D.R. C5 18
Gotham, Wi., U.S. E3 126
Gothenburg, Ne., U.S. D5 104
Gotland, i., Swe. I8 14
Gotō Islands, is., Japan . . . J4 33
Gotse Delchev, Bul. E6 24
Göttingen, F.R.Ger. C4 18
Gottwaldov (Zlín), Czech. . . . D4 26
Götzis, Aus. B8 21
Goubangzi, China D9 32
Gouda, Neth. A6 16
Goudeau, La., U.S. D3 95
Goudiry, Sen. D2 45
Goudoumaria, Niger D7 45
Goudswaard, Neth. C4 17
Gough, Ga., U.S. C4 87
Gough Island, i., St. Hel. . . . I9 5
Gough Lake, l., Ab., Can. . . . C4 68
Gouin, Réservoir, res., P.Q.,
Can. k12 74
Goulburn, Austl. F8 50
Gould, Ar., U.S. D4 81
Gould, Co., U.S. A4 83
Gould, Ok., U.S. C2 113
Gouldbusk, Tx., U.S. D3 120
Gould City, Mi., U.S. B5 99
Goulding Cay, i., Bah. m16 64
Gouldings Trading Post, Ut.,
U.S. F5 121
Gould Island, i., R.I., U.S. . . . E5 116
Goulds, Fl., U.S. s13 86
Gouldsboro, Me., U.S. D4 96
Gouldsboro, Pa., U.S. D11 115
Gouldtown, N.J., U.S. E2 107
Goulimme, Mor. D2 44
Gounamitz, stm., N.B., Can. . B2 71
Goundam, Mali C4 45
Gounou Gaya, Chad D3 46
Gourdon, Fr. E4 16
Gouré, Niger D7 45
Gourma Rharous, Mali C4 45
Gournay-en-Bray, Fr. C4 16
Gouro, Chad B3 46
Gouverneur, Sk., Can. H2 75
Gouverneur, N.Y., U.S. f9 109
Govan, Sk., Can. F3 75
Govan, S.C., U.S. E5 117
Gove, Ks., U.S. D3 93
Gove, co., Ks., U.S. D3 93
Goveniock, Sk., Can. H1 75
Governador Valadares, Braz. . B4 56
Government Camp, Or., U.S. . B5 114
Governors Harbour, Bah. . . . B5 64
Govind Balabh Pant Sāgar,
res., India F9 37
Gowan, stm., Mb., Can. B4 70
Gowanda, N.Y., U.S. C2 109
Gowen, Mi., U.S. E5 99
Gowen, Ok., U.S. C6 113
Gower, Mo., U.S. B3 102
Gowna, Lough, l., Ire. D3 10
Gowrie, Ia., U.S. B3 92
Goya, Arg. E4 55
Goz Beïda, Chad C4 46
Graaff-Reinet, S. Afr. D3 49
Grabill, In., U.S. B8 91
Grabow, Ger.D.R. E5 15
Gračac, Yugo. C2 24
Gračanica, Yugo. C4 24
Grace, Id., U.S. G7 89
Grace, Ms., U.S. C3 101
Grace, Mount, mtn., Ma., U.S. A3 98
Grace City, N.D., U.S. B7 111
Graceham, Md., U.S. A3 97
Gracemont, Ok., U.S. B3 113
Graceton, Mn., U.S. B3 100
Graceville, Fl., U.S. u16 86
Graceville, Mn., U.S. E2 100
Gracewood, Ga., U.S. C4 87
Gracey, Ky., U.S. D2 94
Gracias, Hond. E7 63
Graciosa, i., Port. g9 44
Gradačac, Yugo. C4 24
Gradizhsk, Sov. Un. D9 20
Grado, Italy D9 20
Grado, Spain A2 22
Grady, Ar., U.S. C3 81
Grady, N.M., U.S. C6 108
Grady, Ok., U.S. C4 113
Grady, co., Ga., U.S. F2 87
Grady, co., Ok., U.S. C4 113
Gradyville, Ky., U.S. C4 94
Graettinger, Ia., U.S. A3 92
Grafenau, F.R.Ger. E8 19
Graford, Tx., U.S. C3 120
Grafton, Austl. E9 50
Grafton, On., Can. D6 73
Grafton, Il., U.S. E3 90
Grafton, Ia., U.S. A4 92
Grafton, Ma., U.S. B4 98

Grafton, Ne., U.S. D8 104
Grafton, N.H., U.S. C3 106
Grafton, N.Y., U.S. C7 109
Grafton, N.D., U.S. A8 111
Grafton, Oh., U.S. A3 112
Grafton, Vt., U.S. E3 122
Grafton, Va., U.S. h15 123
Grafton, W.V., U.S. B4 125
Grafton, Wi., U.S. E6 126
Grafton, co., N.H., U.S. C3 106
Grafton Center, N.H., U.S. . . C3 106
Graham, Al., U.S. B4 78
Graham, Ca., U.S. *n12 82
Graham, Fl., U.S. C4 86
Graham, Ga., U.S. E4 87
Graham, Ky., U.S. C2 94
Graham, Mo., U.S. A2 102
Graham, N.C., U.S. A3 110
Graham, Ok., U.S. C4 113
Graham, Tn., U.S. B4 119
Graham, Tx., U.S. C3 120
Graham, Wa., U.S. B3 124
Graham, co., Az., U.S. E5 80
Graham, co., Ks., U.S. C4 93
Graham, co., N.C., U.S. f9 110
Graham, stm., B.C., Can. . . . A6 69
Graham Lake, l., Me., U.S. . . D4 96
Graham Lake, l., Me., U.S. . . E5 96
Graham, Mount, mtn., Az.,
U.S. E6 80
Graham Bell, i., Sov. Un. . . . A7 128
Graham Creek, stm., In., U.S. G6 91
Graham Island, i., B.C., Can. . C1 69
Graham Island, i., N.T., Can. . m33 66
Graham Lake, l., Ab., Can. . . A3 68
Graham Lake, l., Me., U.S. . . D4 96
Graham Land, reg., Ant. C6 7
Grahamstown, S. Afr. D4 49
Grahamsville, N.Y., U.S. D6 109
Grahamville, S.C., U.S. G6 117
Grahn, Ky., U.S. B6 94
Grainfield, Ks., U.S. C3 93
Grainger, co., Tn., U.S. C10 119
Grainland, Sk., Can. F2 75
Grainola, Ok., U.S. A5 113
Grain Valley, Mo., U.S. B3 102
Grajaú, Braz. C1 57
Grajaú, stm., Braz. B1 57
Grajewo, Pol. B7 26
Gram, Den. C3 15
Gramada, Bul. D6 24
Gramalote, Col. B3 60
Gramastetten, Aus. E9 19
Grambling, La., U.S. B3 95
Gramercy, La., U.S. h10 95
Gramling, S.C., U.S. A3 117
Grammer, In., U.S. F6 91
Grammichele, Italy F5 23
Grampian, Pa., U.S. E4 115
Grampian, prov., Scot., U.K. . C6 13
Grampian Mountains, mts.,
Scot., U.K. B4 10
Gramshi, Alb. B3 25
Gramzow, Ger.D.R. E8 15
Grand, Mount, mtn., Ant. . . . B29 7
Granada, Nic. E7 63
Granada, Spain D4 22
Granada, Co., U.S. C8 83
Granada, Mn., U.S. G4 100
Granard, Ire. D4 11
Granbury, Tx., U.S. C4 120
Granby, P.Q., Can. D5 74
Granby, Co., U.S. A5 83
Granby, Ct., U.S. B4 84
Granby, Ma., U.S. B2 98
Granby, Mo., U.S. E3 102
Granby, Vt., U.S. B5 122
Granby, Lake, res., Co., U.S. . A5 83
Granby Island, i., Nf., Can. . . E2 72
Gran Canal del Desagüe, Mex. g9 63
Gran Canaria, i., Spain n14 22
Gran Chaco, pl., S.A. D3 55
Grand, co., Co., U.S. A4 83
Grand, co., Ut., U.S. E6 121
Grand, stm., On., Can. D4 73
Grand, stm., Mi., U.S. E5 99
Grand, stm., Mo., U.S. A3 102
Grand, stm., Oh., U.S. A4 112
Grand, North Fork, stm., S.D.,
U.S. B2 118
Grand, South Fork, stm., S.D.,
U.S. B3 118
Grand Bahama, i., Bah. A4 64
Grand Bank, Nf., Can. E4 72
Grand-Bassam, I.C. E4 45
Grand Bay, N.B., Can. D3 71
Grand Bay, Al., U.S. E1 78
Grand Bayou, stm., La., U.S. . h9 95
Grand Bayou, stm., La., U.S. . k10 95
Grand Beach, Mb., Can. D3 70
Grand Bend, On., Can. D3 73
Grand Blanc, Mi., U.S. F7 99
Grand Bonhomme, mtn., St.
Vin. U26 65
Grand-Bourg, Guad. I14 64
Grand Bruit, Nf., Can. E2 72
Grand Caillou, La., U.S. E5 95
Grand Canal, China E8 31
Grand Canal, Ire. D4 11
Grand Cane, La., U.S. B2 95
Grand Canyon, Az., U.S. . . . A3 80
Grand Canyon, val., Az., U.S. . A3 80
Grand Canyon National Park,
Az., U.S. B3 80
Grand Cayman, i., Cay. Is. . . E8 63
Grand Centre, Ab., Can. B5 68
Grand Cess, Lib. F3 45
Grand Chenier, La., U.S. . . . E3 95
Grand Combin, mtn., Switz. . . D3 21
Grand Coteau, La., U.S. D3 95
Grand Coulee, Wa., U.S. . . . B6 124
Grand Coulee Dam, Wa., U.S. B6 124
Grande, stm., Arg. B3 54
Grande, stm., Arg. D2 55
Grande, stm., Bol. B2 56
Grande, stm., Braz. B2 56
Grande, Bahía, b., Arg. E3 54
Grande, Boca, mth., Ven. . . . B5 60
Grande, Ilha, i., Braz. h5 56
Grande, Rio, stm., N.A. E7 76
Grande, Serra, mts., Braz. . . C2 57
Grande-Anse, N.B., Can. . . . B4 71
Grande Cache, Ab., Can. . . . C1 68
Grande Ecore, La., U.S. C2 95
Grande de Arecibo, stm., P.R. B2 65
Grande [de Matagalpa], stm.,
Nic. E8 63
Grande de Santiago, stm.,
Mex. C3 63
Grande de Tarija, stm., S.A. . D3 55
Grande-Digue, N.B., Can. . . . C5 71
Grande-Ligne, P.Q., Can. . . . D4 74

Grand-Entrée, P.Q., Can. . . . B8 71
Grande Prairie, Ab., Can. . . . B1 68
Grand Erg de Bilma, des.,
Niger C7 45
Grand Erg Occidental, des.,
Alg. C5 44
Grand Erg Oriental, des., Alg. . C6 44
Grande Ronde, stm., U.S. . . . C8 124
Grandes, Salinas, pl., Arg. . . F2 55
Grandes-Bergeronnes, P.Q.,
Can. A8 74
Grandes-Piles, P.Q., Can. . . . C5 74
Grande-Étang, N.S., Can. . . . C8 71
Grande-Terre, i., Guad. Q9 65
Grande Vigie, Pointe de la, c.,
Guad. P9 65
Grand Falls, N.B., Can. B2 71
Grand Falls, Nf., Can. D4 72
Grandfalls, Tx., U.S. D1 120
Grand Falls, wtfl, Me., U.S. . . C5 96
Grand Falls, wtfl, Me., U.S. . . C5 96
Grand Falls Lake, l., N.A. . . . C5 96
Grandfather Mountain, mtn.,
N.C., U.S. A1 110
Grandfield, Ok., U.S. C3 113
Grand Forks, B.C., Can. E8 69
Grand Forks, N.D., U.S. B8 111
Grand Forks, co., N.D., U.S. . B8 111
Grand Forks Air Force Base,
mil., N.D., U.S. B8 111
Grand Glaise, Ar., U.S. B4 81
Grand Gorge, N.Y., U.S. C6 109
Grand Gulf, Ms., U.S. C2 101
Grand Harbour, N.B., Can. . . E3 71
Grand Haven, Mi., U.S. E4 99
Grand Hogback, mtn., Co.,
U.S. B3 83
Grandin, Mo., U.S. E7 102
Grandin, N.D., U.S. B9 111
Grand Island, Ne., U.S. D7 104
Grand Island, i., La., U.S. . . . D6 95
Grand Island, i., Mi., U.S. . . . B4 99
Granite Quarry, N.C., U.S. . . . B2 110
Grand Isle, La., U.S. E6 95
Grand Isle, Me., U.S. A4 96
Grand Isle, Vt., U.S. B2 122
Grand Isle, co., Vt., U.S. B2 122
Grand Isle, i., La., U.S. E6 95
Grand Junction, Co., U.S. . . . B2 83
Grand Junction, Ia., U.S. . . . B3 92
Grand Junction, Mi., U.S. . . . F4 99
Grand Junction, Tn., U.S. . . . B2 119
Grand lac Bostonnais, l., P.Q.,
Can. B5 74
Grand-Lahou, I.C. E3 45
Grand Lake, Co., U.S. A5 83
Grand Lake, La., U.S. D2 95
Grand Lake, l., N.B., Can. . . . D3 71
Grand Lake, l., Nf., Can. D3 72
Grand Lake, l., Nf., Can. D2 72
Grand Lake, l., La., U.S. E3 95
Grand Lake, l., La., U.S. E6 95
Grand Lake, l., Me., U.S. . . . C5 96
Grand Lake, l., Mi., U.S. C7 99
Grand Lake, l., Oh., U.S. . . . B1 112
Grand Lake Matagamon, l.,
Me., U.S. B4 96
Grand Lake Seboeis, l., Me.,
U.S. B4 96
Grand Lake Stream, Me., U.S. C5 96
Grand Ledge, Mi., U.S. F6 99
Grand Lieu, Lac de, l., Fr. . . . D3 16
Grand Manan Channel, strt.,
N.A. D6 96
Grand Manan Island, i., N.B.,
Can. E3 71
Grand Marais, Mi., U.S. B4 99
Grand Marais, Mn., U.S. k9 100
Grand Marsh, Wi., U.S. E4 126
Grand Meadow, Mn., U.S. . . . G6 100
Grand'Mère, P.Q., Can. C5 74
Grand Mesa, mtn., Co., U.S. . C2 83
Grand Mound, Ia., U.S. C7 92
Grand Pass, Mo., U.S. B4 102
Grand Portage, Mn., U.S. . . . k10 100
Grand Portage Indian
Reservation, Mn., U.S. . . . k10 100
Grand Portage National
Monument, Mn., U.S. h10 100
Grand Prairie, Tx., U.S. n10 120
Grand Pré, N.S., Can. D5 71
Grand Rapids, Mb., Can. . . . C2 70
Grand Rapids, Mi., U.S. F5 99
Grand Rapids, Mn., U.S. . . . C5 100
Grand Rapids, N.D., U.S. . . . C7 111
Grand Rapids, Oh., U.S. f6 112
Grand Ridge, Fl., U.S. B1 86
Grand Ridge, Il., U.S. B5 90
Grand River, N.S., Can. D9 71
Grand River, Ia., U.S. D4 92
Grand Rivers, Ky., U.S. f9 94
Grand' Rivière, Mart. S10 65
Grand Ronde, Or., U.S. B3 114
Grand Saline, Tx., U.S. C5 120
Grand Santi, Fr. Gu. B4 59
Grands-Jardins, Parc des,
P.Q., Can. B7 74
Grandson, Switz. C2 21
Grand Terrace, Ca., U.S. . . . *E5 82
Grand Terre Islands, is., La.,
U.S. E6 95
Grand Teton, mtn., Wy., U.S. . C2 127
Grand Teton National Park,
Wy., U.S. C2 127
Grand Tower, Il., U.S. F4 90
Grand Traverse, co., Mi., U.S. D5 99
Grand Traverse Bay, b., Mi.,
U.S. C5 99
Grand Traverse Bay, East
Arm, b., Mi., U.S. C5 99
Grand Traverse Bay, West
Arm, b., Mi., U.S. C5 99
Grand Valley, On., Can. D4 73
Grand Valley, Co., U.S. B2 83
Grand Valley, val., Co., U.S. . B2 83
Grandview, Mb., Can. D1 70
Grand View, Id., U.S. G2 89
Grandview, Il., U.S. D4 90
Grandview, In., U.S. I4 91
Grandview, Mo., U.S. C3 102
Grandview, Tn., U.S. D9 119
Grandview, Tx., U.S. C4 120
Grand View, Wi., U.S. B2 126
Grandview Heights, Oh., U.S. . m10 112
Grandville, Mi., U.S. F5 99
Grandvilliers, Fr. C4 16
Grand Wash, val., Az., U.S. . A2 80
Grand Wash Cliffs, clf, Az.,
U.S. B2 80
Grandy, Mn., U.S. E5 100
Grandy, N.C., U.S. A7 110
Grange, Eng., U.K. F6 13

Grangeburg, Al., U.S. D4 78
Grangemouth, Scot., U.K. . . . D5 13
Granger, In., U.S. A5 91
Granger, Ia., U.S. C4 92
Granger, Mo., U.S. A6 102
Granger, Tx., U.S. D4 120
Granger, Wa., U.S. C5 124
Granger, Wy., U.S. E3 127
Grangeville, La., U.S. D2 89
Grangeville, La., U.S. D5 95
Granite, Co., U.S. B4 83
Granite, Ok., U.S. C2 113
Granite, Or., U.S. C8 114
Granite, Ut., U.S. *C4 121
Granite, co., Mt., U.S. D3 103
Granite Canon, Wy., U.S. . . . E7 127
Granite City, Il., U.S. E3 90
Granite Falls, Mn., U.S. F3 100
Granite Falls, N.C., U.S. B1 110
Granite Falls, Wa., U.S. A4 124
Granite Harbor, b., Ant. e39 7
Granite Lake, res., Nf., Can. . D3 72
Granite Mountain, mtn., Ak.,
U.S. B7 79
Granite Mountain, mtn., Ar.,
U.S. k10 81
Granite Mountains, mts., Az.,
U.S. E2 80
Granite Mountains, mts., Wy.,
U.S. D5 127
Granite Park, Ut., U.S. C4 121
Granite Pass, Wy., U.S. B5 127
Granite Peak, mtn., Mt., U.S. . E7 103
Granite Peak, mtn., Nv., U.S. . C2 105
Granite Peak, mtn., Ut., U.S. . B4 105
Granite Peak, mtn., Ut., U.S. . C2 121
Granite Peak, mtn., Ut., U.S. . E3 121
Granite Point, c., Nf., Can. . . C3 72
Granite Range, mts., Nv., U.S. C2 105
Graniteville, Mo., U.S. D7 102
Graniteville, S.C., U.S. D4 117
Graniteville, Vt., U.S. C4 122
Granja, Braz. B2 57
Granja de Torrehermosa,
Spain C3 22
Granma, prov., Cuba D5 64
Grannis, Ar., U.S. C1 81
Grano, N.D., U.S. A4 111
Granollers, Spain B7 22
Gran Paradiso, mtn., Italy . . . D3 20
Gransee, Ger.D.R. E7 15
Grant, Al., U.S. A3 78
Grant, Co., U.S. B5 83
Grant, Fl., U.S. E6 86
Grant, Ia., U.S. C2 92
Grant, La., U.S. D3 95
Grant, Mi., U.S. E5 99
Grant, Mt., U.S. E3 103
Grant, Ne., U.S. D4 104
Grant, Ok., U.S. D6 113
Grant, co., Ar., U.S. C3 81
Grant, co., In., U.S. D6 91
Grant, co., Ks., U.S. E2 93
Grant, co., Ky., U.S. B5 94
Grant, co., Mn., U.S. E2 100
Grant, co., Ne., U.S. C4 104
Grant, co., N.M., U.S. E1 108
Grant, co., N.D., U.S. C4 111
Grant, co., Ok., U.S. A4 113
Grant, co., Or., U.S. C7 114
Grant, co., S.D., U.S. B8 118
Grant, co., Wa., U.S. B6 124
Grant, co., W.V., U.S. B5 125
Grant, co., Wi., U.S. F3 126
Grant City, Mo., U.S. A3 102
Grant Mound, Ia., U.S. A3 102
Grant, Mount, mtn., Nv., U.S. . E3 105
Grantham, Eng., U.K. D6 10
Grantham, N.H., U.S. D2 106
Granton, On., Can. D3 73
Granton, Wi., U.S. D3 126
Grantown-on-Spey, Scot., U.K. C5 13
Grant Park, Il., U.S. B6 90
Grant Range, mts., Nv., U.S. . E6 105
Grants, N.M., U.S. B2 108
Grantsboro, N.C., U.S. B6 110
Grantsburg, Il., U.S. F5 90
Grantsburg, Wi., U.S. C1 126
Grantsdale, Mt., U.S. D2 103
Grants Lick, Ky., U.S. k14 94
Grants Pass, Or., U.S. E3 114
Grantsville, Ut., U.S. C3 121
Grantsville, W.V., U.S. C3 125
Grantville, Ga., U.S. C2 87
Grantville, Ks., U.S. k14 93
Grantville, Pa., U.S. F8 115
Granum, Ab., Can. E4 68
Granville, Fr. C3 16
Granville, Il., U.S. B5 90
Granville, Ia., U.S. B2 92
Granville, Ma., U.S. B2 98
Granville, N.Y., U.S. B7 109
Granville, N.D., U.S. A5 111
Granville, Oh., U.S. B3 112
Granville, Tn., U.S. C8 119
Granville, Vt., U.S. D3 122
Granville, W.V., U.S. h11 125
Granville, co., N.C., U.S. A4 110
Granville Centre, N.S., Can. . E4 71
Granville Ferry, N.S., Can. . . E4 71
Granville Lake, l., Mb., Can. . A1 70
Grão Mogol, Braz. D7 56
Grapeland, Tx., U.S. D5 120
Grapeview, Wa., U.S. B3 124
Grapevine, Ky., U.S. C2 94
Grapevine, Tx., U.S. C4 120
Grapevine Lake, res., Tx., U.S. n9 120
Grapevine Peak, mtn., Nv.,
U.S. G5 105
Gras, Lac de l., N.T., Can. . . D10 66
Grasonville, Md., U.S. C5 97
Grass, stm., Mb., Can. B2 70
Grass, stm., N.Y., U.S. f9 109
Grass Creek, In., U.S. C5 91
Grass Creek, Wy., U.S. C4 127
Grasse, Fr. E7 16
Grasselli, Al., U.S. B3 78
Grassflat, Pa., U.S. D5 115
Grassington, Eng., U.K. F6 11
Grass Lake, Il., U.S. h8 90
Grass Lake, Mi., U.S. F6 99
Grass Lake, l., Il., U.S. h8 90
Grassrange, Mt., U.S. C8 103
Grass River Provincial Park,
Mb., Can. B1 70
Grasston, Mn., U.S. E5 100
Grass Valley, Ca., U.S. C3 82

Grass Valley, Or., U.S. B6 114
Grassy Brook, stm., Vt., U.S. . E3 122
Grassy Butte, N.D., U.S. B2 111
Grassy Creek, N.C., U.S. . . . A1 110
Grassy Lake, l., La., U.S. . . . k9 95
Gråsten, Den. D3 15
Grates Cove, Nf., Can. D5 72
Grates Point, c., Nf., Can. . . . D5 72
Gratiot, Oh., U.S. C3 112
Gratiot, Wi., U.S. F3 126
Gratiot, co., Mi., U.S. E6 99
Gratis, Oh., U.S. C1 112
Gratz, Pa., U.S. E8 115
Graubünden, state, Switz. . . . C5 20
Graulhet, Fr. F4 16
Gravatá, Braz. C3 57
Gravedona, Italy D7 21
Gravelbourg, Sk., Can. H2 75
Gravelines, Fr. D2 17
Gravelly, Ar., U.S. C2 81
Gravelly Branch, stm., De.,
U.S. F4 85
Gravelly Range, mts., Mt.,
U.S. E4 103
Gravenhurst, On., Can. C5 73
Grave Peak, mtn., Id., U.S. . . C4 89
Graves, Ga., U.S. E9 117
Graves, co., Ky., U.S. f9 94
Gravesend, Eng., U.K. E7 10
Gravette, Ar., U.S. A1 81
Gravina [in Puglia], Italy D6 23
Gravity, Ia., U.S. D3 92
Gravois, Pointe à, c., Haiti . . . E7 64
Gravois Mills, Mo., U.S. C5 102
Grawn, Mi., U.S. D5 99
Gray, Sk., Can. G3 75
Gray, Fr. D6 16
Gray, Ga., U.S. C3 87
Gray, Ia., U.S. C2 92
Gray, Ky., U.S. D5 94
Gray, Me., U.S. g7 96
Gray, co., Ks., U.S. E3 93
Gray, co., Tx., U.S. B2 120
Graybeck Mountain, mtn., Or.,
U.S. E3 114
Gray Court, S.C., U.S. B3 117
Gray Gables, Ma., U.S. *C6 98
Gray Horse, Ok., U.S. A5 113
Grayland, Wa., U.S. C1 124
Grayling, Ak., U.S. C7 79
Grayling, Mi., U.S. D6 99
Graylyn Crest, De., U.S. A3 85
Graymont, Il., U.S. C5 90
Grays, Eng., U.K. m13 11
Grays, Ar., U.S. B4 81
Grays Harbor, co., Wa., U.S. . B2 124
Grays Harbor, b., Wa., U.S. . . C1 124
Grayslake, Il., U.S. A5 90
Grays Lake, sw., Id., U.S. . . . F7 89
Grason, Sk., Can. G4 75
Grayson, Ky., U.S. B7 94
Grayson, Ga., U.S. C3 87
Grayson, Ky., U.S. B7 94
Grayson, La., U.S. B3 95
Grayson, Ok., U.S. B6 113
Grayson, co., Ky., U.S. C3 94
Grayson, co., Tx., U.S. C4 120
Grayson, co., Va., U.S. D1 123
Grayson Lake, res., Ky., U.S. . B7 94
Grayson Peak, mtn., Co., U.S. B5 83
Grays Peak, mtn., Co., U.S. . . B5 83
Grays River, Wa., U.S. C2 124
Gray Summit, Mo., U.S. g12 102
Graysville, Al., U.S. f7 78
Graysville, Oh., U.S. C4 112
Graysville, Pa., U.S. D8 115
Graysville, Tn., U.S. D8 119
Grayville, Il., U.S. E5 90
Graz, Aus. E7 18
Greasewood, Az., U.S. B6 80
Great, stm., Jam. E13 65
Great Abaco, i., Bah. A5 64
Great Alföld, pl., Hung. B5 24
Great Artesian Basin, Austl. . . E4 50
Great Australian Bight, Austl. . F4 50
Great Averill Pond, l., Vt., U.S. B5 122
Great Bahama, i., Bah. A4 64
Great Barrier Island, i., N.Z. . L15 51
Great Barrier Reef, rf., Austl. . C8 50
Great Barrington, Ma., U.S. . . B1 98
Great Basin, reg., U.S. D2 105
Great Bay, b., N.H., U.S. . . . D5 106
Great Bay, b., N.J., U.S. D4 107
Great Bear Lake, l., N.T., Can. C8 66
Great Bend, Ks., U.S. D5 93
Great Bend, N.D., U.S. C9 111
Great Bend, Pa., U.S. C10 115
Great Bay, b., U.S. D3 99
Great Bitter Lake, l., Eg. C4 41
Great Blasket, i., Ire. E1 11
Great Blue Hill, hill, Ma., U.S. B5 98
Great Burnt Lake, l., Nf., Can. D3 72
Great Cacapon, W.V., U.S. . . B6 125
Great Camanoe, i., V.I., Br. . . D5 65
Great Captain Island, i., Ct.,
U.S. E1 84
Great Channel, strt., Asia . . . G9 36
Great Deer, Ak., U.S. D12 79
Great Dismal Swamp, sw.,
U.S. D6 123
Great Divide Basin, Wy., U.S. E4 127
Great Dividing Range, mts.,
Austl. F9 50
Great Duck Island, i., On.,
Can. B2 73
Great East Lake, l., U.S. C5 106
Great Egg Harbor, stm., N.J.,
U.S. D3 107
Greater Antilles, is., N.A. . . . H13 61
Greater Cincinnati Airport, Ky.,
U.S. h13 94
Greater Khingan Range (Da
Hinggan Ling), mts., China . B9 31
Greater London, co., Eng.,
U.K. C7 12
Greater Manchester, co., Eng.,
U.K. *A5 12
Great Exuma, i., Bah. C6 64
Great Falls, stm., Guy. A2 59
Great Falls, Mb., Can. D3 70
Great Falls, Mt., U.S. C5 103
Great Falls, S.C., U.S. B6 117
Great Falls, wtfl, Md., U.S. . . B3 97
Great Falls Dam, Tn., U.S. . . D8 119
Great Guana Cay, i., Bah. . . . B5 64
Great Harbour Deep, b., Nf.,
Can. C3 72
Great Inagua, i., Bah. D7 64

Great Indian Desert (Thar
Desert), des., Asia C5 36
Great Island, spit, Ma., U.S. . C7 98
Great Island, i., N.C., U.S. . . B6 110
Great Karroo, plat., S. Afr. . . D3 49
Great Lakes Naval Training
Center, mil., Il., U.S. h9 90
Great Miami, stm., U.S. C1 112
Great Misery Island, i., Ma.,
U.S. f12 98
Great Moose Lake, l., Me.,
U.S. D3 96
Great Neck, N.Y., U.S. h13 109
Great Neck Estates, N.Y.,
U.S. *E7 109
Great Nicobar, i., India G9 36
Great North Mountain, mtn.,
U.S. C6 125
Great Pedro Bluff, c., Jam. . . F13 65
Great Pee Dee, stm., U.S. . . D9 117
Great Point, c., Ma., U.S. . . . D7 98
Great Pond, Me., U.S. D4 96
Great Pond, l., Ma., U.S. . . . D3 96
Great Pond, l., Ma., U.S. . . . h11 98
Great Pond, l., Ma., U.S. . . . h12 98
Great Quittacas Pond, l., Ma.,
U.S. C6 98
Great Ruaha, stm., Tan. C6 48
Great Sacandaga Lake, l.,
N.Y., U.S. C6 109
Great Saint Bernard Pass,
Eur. B1 23
Great Salt Lake, l., Ut., U.S. . B3 121
Great Salt Lake Desert, des.,
Ut., U.S. C2 121
Great Salt Plains Lake, res.,
Ok., U.S. A3 113
Great Salt Pond, b., R.I., U.S. h7 116
Great Salt Pond, l., Jam. F15 65
Great Sand Dunes National
Monument, Co., U.S. D5 83
Great Sand Hills, hills, Sk.,
Can. G1 75
Great Sandy Desert, des.,
Austl. D3 50
Great Sea Reef, rf., Fiji H15 52
Great Seneca Creek, stm.,
Md., U.S. B3 97
Great Skellig, rock, Ire. F1 11
Great Slave Lake, l., N.T.,
Can. D10 66
Great Smoky Mountains, mts.,
U.S. B8 119
Great Smoky Mountains
National Park, U.S. B8 119
Great Sound, strt., Ber. p19 64
Great Swamp, sw., R.I., U.S. . F3 116
Great Tenasserim, stm.,
Burma F3 35
Great Valley, val., U.S. C2 123
Great Victoria Desert, des.,
Austl. E4 50
Great Village, N.S., Can. . . . D6 71
Great Wall, hist., China C8 31
Great Wass Island, i., Me.,
U.S. D5 96
Great Yarmouth, Eng., U.K. . . D7 10
Great Zab, stm., Asia D14 40
Greece, ctry., Eur. C4 40
Gredos, Sierra de, mts., Spain B3 22
Greece, N.Y., U.S. B3 109
Greece, ctry., Eur. C4 40
Greeley, Co., U.S. A6 83
Greeley, Ia., U.S. B6 92
Greeley, Ks., U.S. D8 93
Greeley, Ne., U.S. C7 104
Greeley, co., Ks., U.S. D2 93
Greeley, co., Ne., U.S. C7 104
Greeleyville, S.C., U.S. D8 117
Greely Fiord, N.T., Can. k35 66
Green, Ks., U.S. C6 93
Green, Or., U.S. D3 114
Green, co., Ky., U.S. C4 94
Green, co., Wi., U.S. F4 126
Green, stm., N.B., Can. B1 71
Green, stm., Jam. A1 83
Green, stm., Il., U.S. B4 90
Green, stm., Ky., U.S. C2 94
Green, stm., Wa., U.S. B3 124
Green Acres, De., U.S. h8 85
Green Acres, Or., U.S. D2 114
Greenacres, Wa., U.S. B8 124
Greenacres City, Fl., U.S. . . . F6 86
Green Bank, N.J., U.S. D3 107
Green Bank, W.V., U.S. C5 125
Green Bay, Va., U.S. C4 123
Green Bay, Wi., U.S. D6 126
Green Bay, b., U.S. D3 99
Greenbelt, Md., U.S. C4 97
Greenbrier, Al., U.S. A3 78
Green Brier, Tn., U.S. A5 119
Greenbrier, co., W.V., U.S. . . D4 125
Greenbrier, stm., W.V., U.S. . D4 125
Green Brook, N.J., U.S. *B4 107
Greenburr, Pa., U.S. D7 115
Greenbush, Me., U.S. C4 96
Greenbush, Mn., U.S. B2 100
Greenbush, Mn., U.S. D7 99
Green Camp, Oh., U.S. B2 112
Greencastle, In., U.S. E4 91
Greencastle, Mo., U.S. A5 102
Greencastle, Pa., U.S. G6 115
Green City, Mo., U.S. A5 102
Green Court, Ab., Can. B3 68
Green Cove Springs, Fl., U.S. C5 86
Greencreek, Id., U.S. C2 89
Greendale, In., U.S. F8 91
Greendale, Ut., U.S. F6 121
Greendale, Wi., U.S. F6 126
Greendell, N.J., U.S. B3 107
Greene, Me., U.S. D2 96
Greene, N.Y., U.S. C5 109
Greene, co., Al., U.S. A4 78
Greene, co., Ar., U.S. A5 81
Greene, co., Ga., U.S. C3 87
Greene, co., Il., U.S. D3 90
Greene, co., In., U.S. F4 91
Greene, co., Ia., U.S. B3 92
Greene, co., Ms., U.S. D5 101
Greene, co., Mo., U.S. D4 102
Greene, co., N.Y., U.S. C6 109
Greene, co., N.C., U.S. B5 110
Greene, co., Oh., U.S. C2 112
Greene, co., Pa., U.S. G1 115

Name | Map Ref | Page

Greene, co., Tn., U.S. C11 119
Greene, co., Va., U.S. B4 123
Greeneville, Tn., U.S. C11 119
Green Fall, stm., U.S. F1 116
Greenfield, Ar., U.S. B5 81
Greenfield, Ca., U.S. D3 82
Greenfield, Il., U.S. D3 90
Greenfield, In., U.S. E6 91
Greenfield, Ia., U.S. C3 92
Greenfield, Me., U.S. C4 96
Greenfield, Ma., U.S. A2 98
Greenfield, Mo., U.S. D4 102
Greenfield, N.H., U.S. E3 106
Greenfield, N.M., U.S. D5 108
Greenfield, Oh., U.S. C2 112
Greenfield, Ok., U.S. B3 113
Greenfield, Tn., U.S. A3 119
Greenfield, Va., U.S. C4 123
Greenfield, Wi., U.S. n11 126
Greenfield Park, P.Q., Can. q20 74
Greenfield Plaza, Ia., U.S. e8 92
Green Forest, Ar., U.S. A2 81
Green Grass, S.D., U.S. B4 118
Green Harbor, Ma., U.S. B6 98
Greenhill, Al., U.S. A2 78
Greenhill, In., U.S. D3 91
Green Hill, R.I., U.S. G3 116
Green Hill Pond, l., R.I., U.S. G3 116
Greenhills, Oh., U.S. n12 112
Greenhorn, Or., U.S. C8 114
Greenhorn Creek, stm., Co., U.S. D6 83
Green Island, Ia., U.S. B7 92
Green Island, N.Y., U.S. *C7 109
Green Isle, Mn., U.S. F4 100
Green Lake, Sk., Can. C2 75
Green Lake, Ut., U.S. *C6 121
Green Lake, Wi., U.S. E5 126
Green Lake, co., Wi., U.S. E4 126
Green Lake, l., B.C., Can. D7 69
Green Lake, l., Sk., Can. C2 75
Green Lake, l., Me., U.S. D4 96
Green Lake, l., Wi., U.S. E5 126
Greenland, Ar., U.S. B1 81
Greenland, Mi., U.S. B1 99
Greenland, N.H., U.S. D5 106
Greenland (Kalaallit Nunaat), ctry., N.A. B16 61
Greenland Sea B15 128
Greenlaw, Scot., U.K. E6 13
Greenlawn, N.Y., U.S. *h13 109
Greenleaf, Ks., U.S. C7 93
Greenleaf, Wi., U.S. D5 126
Greenlee, co., Az., U.S. D6 80
Green Lookout Mountain, mtn., Wa., U.S. D3 124
Green Lowther, mtn., Scot., U.K. E5 13
Green Manorville, Ct., U.S. B5 84
Greenmount, Md., U.S. A4 97
Green Mountain, Ia., U.S. B5 92
Greenmountain, N.C., U.S. f10 110
Green Mountain Falls, Co., U.S. *C6 83
Green Mountain Reservoir, res., Co., U.S. B4 83
Green Mountains, mts., Vt., U.S. F2 122
Green Mountains, mts., Wy., U.S. D5 127
Greenock, Scot., U.K. C4 10
Greenock, Pa., U.S. F2 115
Greenore Point, c., Ire. E5 11
Greenough, Mt., U.S. D3 103
Greenough Point, c., On., Can. C3 73
Green Peter Lake, res., Or., U.S. C4 114
Green Pond, Al., U.S. B2 78
Green Pond, S.C., U.S. F6 117
Green Pond, l., N.J., U.S. A4 107
Green Pond Mountain, mtn., N.J., U.S. B3 107
Greenport, N.Y., U.S. m16 109
Green Ridge, Mo., U.S. C4 102
Green River, Ut., U.S. E5 121
Green River, Wy., U.S. E3 127
Green River Lake, res., Ky., U.S. C4 94
Green River Lock and Dam, U.S. I2 91
Green River Reservoir, res., Vt., U.S. B3 122
Green Rock, Il., U.S. B3 90
Greensboro, Al., U.S. C2 78
Greensboro, Fl., U.S. B2 86
Greensboro, Ga., U.S. C3 87
Greensboro, In., U.S. E7 91
Greensboro, Md., U.S. C6 97
Greensboro, N.C., U.S. A3 110
Greensboro, Pa., U.S. G2 115
Greensboro, Vt., U.S. B4 122
Greensboro Bend, Vt., U.S. B4 122
Greensburg, In., U.S. F7 91
Greensburg, Ks., U.S. E4 93
Greensburg, Ky., U.S. C4 94
Greensburg, La., U.S. D5 95
Greensburg, Pa., U.S. F2 115
Green Sea, S.C., U.S. C10 117
Greens Fork, In., U.S. E7 91
Greens Peak, mtn., Az., U.S. C6 80
Greenspond, Nf., Can. D5 72
Green Spring, W.V., U.S. B6 125
Green Springs, Oh., U.S. A2 112
Greenstone Point, c., Scot., U.K. C3 13
Green Sulphur Springs, W.V., U.S. D4 125
Greensville, co., Va., U.S. D5 123
Green Swamp, sw., N.C., U.S. C4 110
Greentop, Mo., U.S. A5 102
Greentown, In., U.S. D6 91
Green Tree, Pa., U.S. *k13 115
Greenup, Il., U.S. D5 90
Greenup, Ky., U.S. B7 94
Greenup, co., Ky., U.S. B6 94
Green Valley, Az., U.S. F5 80
Green Valley, Il., U.S. C4 90
Green Valley, Mn., U.S. F3 100
Green Valley, Wi., U.S. D5 126
Green Valley, val., Tx., U.S. p13 120
Greenview, Il., U.S. C4 90
Greenview, W.V., U.S. n12 125
Greenville, Lib. E3 45
Greenville, Al., U.S. D3 78
Greenville, Ca., U.S. B3 82
Greenville, De., U.S. A3 85
Greenville, Fl., U.S. B3 86
Greenville, Ga., U.S. C2 87
Greenville, Il., U.S. E4 90
Greenville, In., U.S. H6 91
Greenville, Ia., U.S. A2 92
Greenville, Ky., U.S. C2 94
Greenville, Me., U.S. C3 96
Greenville, Mi., U.S. E5 99
Greenville, Ms., U.S. B2 101
Greenville, Mo., U.S. D7 102
Greenville, N.H., U.S. E3 106
Greenville, N.Y., U.S. *n15 109
Greenville, N.C., U.S. B5 110
Greenville, Oh., U.S. B1 112
Greenville, Pa., U.S. D1 115
Greenville, R.I., U.S. C3 116
Greenville, S.C., U.S. B3 117
Greenville, Tx., U.S. C4 120
Greenville, Ut., U.S. E3 121
Greenville, Va., U.S. B3 123
Greenville, W.V., U.S. D4 125
Greenville, Wi., U.S. h8 126
Greenville, co., S.C., U.S. B3 117
Greenville Creek, stm., Oh., U.S. B1 112
Greenville Junction, Me., U.S. C3 96
Greenwald, Mn., U.S. E4 100
Greenwater Lake Provincial Park, Sk., Can. E4 75
Greenway, Mb., Can. E2 70
Greenway, Ar., U.S. A5 81
Greenwell Springs, La., U.S. D5 95
Greenwich (part of London), Eng., U.K. m13 10
Greenwich, Ct., U.S. E1 84
Greenwich, Ks., U.S. g12 93
Greenwich, N.J., U.S. E2 107
Greenwich, N.Y., U.S. B7 109
Greenwich, Oh., U.S. A3 112
Greenwich, Ut., U.S. E4 121
Greenwich, Va., U.S. *B5 123
Greenwich Bay, b., R.I., U.S. D4 116
Greenwich Hill, N.B., Can. D3 71
Greenwich Point, c., Ct., U.S. E1 84
Greenwood, B.C., Can. E8 69
Greenwood, Ar., U.S. B1 81
Greenwood, De., U.S. E3 85
Greenwood, Fl., U.S. B1 86
Greenwood, In., U.S. E5 91
Greenwood, Ky., U.S. D5 94
Greenwood, La., U.S. B2 95
Greenwood, Ms., U.S. B3 101
Greenwood, Mo., U.S. k11 102
Greenwood, Ne., U.S. D9 104
Greenwood, N.Y., U.S. C3 109
Greenwood, Pa., U.S. E5 115
Greenwood, S.C., U.S. C3 117
Greenwood, S.D., U.S. E7 118
Greenwood, Wi., U.S. D3 126
Greenwood, co., Ks., U.S. E7 93
Greenwood, co., S.C., U.S. C3 117
Greenwood, Lake, res., In., U.S. G4 91
Greenwood, Lake, res., S.C., U.S. C4 117
Greenwood Lake, N.Y., U.S. D6 109
Greenwood Lake, l., U.S. A4 107
Greenwood Lake, l., Mn., U.S. C7 100
Greenwood Village, Co., U.S. *B6 83
Greer, Id., U.S. C2 89
Greer, Mo., U.S. E6 102
Greer, S.C., U.S. B3 117
Greer, co., Ok., U.S. C2 113
Greers Ferry Lake, res., Ar., U.S. B3 81
Greeson, Lake, res., Ar., U.S. C2 81
Greetsiel, F.R.Ger. A7 17
Gregg, co., Tx., U.S. C5 120
Gregoire Lake, l., Ab., Can. A5 68
Gregory, Ar., U.S. B4 81
Gregory, Mi., U.S. F6 99
Gregory, N.C., U.S. A6 110
Gregory, S.D., U.S. D6 118
Gregory, co., S.D., U.S. D6 118
Gregory, stm., Austl. C6 50
Gregory, Lake, l., Austl. E6 50
Gregory Bald, mtn., Tn., U.S. D10 119
Gregory Range, mts., Austl. C7 50
Greifswald, Ger.D.R. A6 18
Greifswalder Bodden, b., Ger.D.R. D7 15
Greig, N.Y., U.S. B5 109
Greilickville, Mi., U.S. D5 99
Grein, Aus. D7 18
Greiz, Ger.D.R. C6 18
Grelton, Oh., U.S. A1 112
Gremyachinsk, Sov. Un. D20 8
Grenå, Den. B4 15
Grenada, Ca., U.S. B2 82
Grenada, Ms., U.S. B4 101
Grenada, co., Ms., U.S. B4 101
Grenada, ctry., N.A. J14 64
Grenada Lake, res., Ms., U.S. B4 101
Grenade, Fr. F4 16
Grenadine Islands, is., N.A. V26 65
Grenagh, Ire. E3 11
Grenay, Fr. D2 17
Grenchen, Switz. B3 20
Grenen (The Skaw), spit, Den. A4 15
Grenfell, Sk., Can. G4 75
Grenoble, Fr. E6 16
Grenola, Ks., U.S. E7 93
Grenora, N.D., U.S. A2 111
Grenville, P.Q., Can. D3 74
Grenville, Gren. W25 65
Grenville, N.M., U.S. A6 108
Grenville, S.D., U.S. B8 118
Grenville, co., On., Can. C9 73
Grenville, Cape, c., Austl. B7 50
Grenville, Point, c., Wa., U.S. B1 124
Grenville Channel, strt., B.C., Can. C3 69
Gresham, Ne., U.S. C8 104
Gresham, Or., U.S. B4 114
Gresham, S.C., U.S. D9 117
Gresham, Wi., U.S. D5 126
Gresham Park, Ga., U.S. *h8 87
Gretna, Mb., Can. E3 70
Gretna, Scot., U.K. F5 13
Gretna, Fl., U.S. B2 86
Gretna, La., U.S. E5 95
Gretna, Ne., U.S. C9 104
Gretna, Va., U.S. D3 123
Greven, F.R.Ger. A2 19
Grevená, Grc. B3 25
Grevenbroich, F.R.Ger. B1 19
Grevesmühlen, Ger.D.R. E5 15
Grey, co., On., Can. C4 73
Grey, stm., Nf., Can. E3 72
Grey, stm., N.Z. O13 51
Greybull, Wy., U.S. B4 127
Greybull, stm., Wy., U.S. B4 127
Greycliff, Mt., U.S. E7 103
Grey Eagle, Mn., U.S. E4 100
Grey Islands, is., Nf., Can. C4 72
Greylock, Mount, mtn., Ma., U.S. A1 98
Greymouth, N.Z. O13 51
Grey Range, mts., Austl. E7 50
Greys, stm., Wy., U.S. C2 127
Greystone, Ct., U.S. C3 84
Greytown, S. Afr. A4 110
Greytown, S. Afr. C5 49
Gribbell Island, i., B.C., Can. C3 69
Gridley, Ca., U.S. C3 82
Gridley, Il., U.S. C5 90
Gridley, Ks., U.S. D8 93
Gridley Mountain, mtn., Ct., U.S. A2 84
Griekwastad, S. Afr. C3 49
Griesheim, F.R.Ger. D3 19
Grieskirchen, Aus. D6 18
Griffin, Sk., Can. H4 75
Griffin, Ga., U.S. C2 87
Griffin, In., U.S. H2 91
Griffiss Air Force Base, mil., N.Y., U.S. B5 109
Griffith, Austl. F8 50
Griffith, In., U.S. A3 91
Griffith Island, i., On., Can. C4 73
Griffithsville, W.V., U.S. C3 125
Griffithville, Ar., U.S. B4 81
Grifton, N.C., U.S. B5 110
Griggs, Ok., U.S. e8 113
Griggs, co., N.D., U.S. B7 111
Griggstown, N.J., U.S. C3 107
Griggsville, Il., U.S. D3 90
Grigoriopol, Sov. Un. B9 24
Grijalva, stm., Mex. D6 63
Grim, Cape, c., Austl. o14 50
Grimari, Cen. Afr. Rep. D4 46
Grimes, Al., U.S. D4 78
Grimes, Ia., U.S. C4 92
Grimes, co., Tx., U.S. D4 120
Grimesland, N.C., U.S. B5 110
Grimma, Ger.D.R. C6 18
Grimmen, Ger.D.R. D7 15
Grimmialp, Switz. C4 21
Grimms Landing, W.V., U.S. C3 125
Grimsby, On., Can. D5 73
Grimsby, Eng., U.K. D6 10
Grímsey, i., Ice. m23 14
Grimshaw, Ab., Can. A2 68
Grimsley, Tn., U.S. C9 119
Grimstad, Nor. H3 14
Grimsthorpe, On., Can. B2 73
Grindall Creek, Va., U.S. n18 123
Grindelwald, Switz. C5 21
Grindsted, Den. C2 15
Grindstone, Me., U.S. C4 96
Grind Stone City, Mi., U.S. D8 99
Grinem, i., Marsh Is. S18 52
Grinnell, Ia., U.S. C5 92
Grinnell, Ks., U.S. C3 93
Grinnell Peninsula, pen., N.T., Can. m32 66
Grise Fiord, N.T., Can. m35 66
Gris-Nez, Cap, c., Fr. D9 12
Grissom Air Force Base, mil., In., U.S. C5 91
Griswold, Mb., Can. E1 70
Griswold, Ia., U.S. C2 92
Griswoldville, Ma., U.S. A2 98
Grizzly Mountain, mtn., Id., U.S. B2 89
Grizzly Mountain, mtn., Or., U.S. C6 114
Grizzly Mountain, mtn., Wa., U.S. A7 124
Groais Island, i., Nf., Can. C4 72
Grodków, Pol. C4 26
Grodno, Sov. Un. E4 27
Grodzisk Mazowiecki, Pol. m13 26
Grodzisk [Wielkopolski], Pol. B4 26
Groenlo, Neth. B6 17
Groesbeck, Oh., U.S. *o12 112
Groesbeck, Tx., U.S. D4 120
Groix, Île de, i., Fr. D2 16
Grójec, Pol. C6 26
Grombalia, Tun. F3 23
Gronau, F.R.Ger. B3 18
Gronau, F.R.Ger. A4 19
Groningen, Neth. A7 16
Groningen, Sur. A3 59
Groningen, prov., Neth. A6 17
Gronlid, Sk., Can. D3 75
Groom, Tx., U.S. B2 120
Groom Lake, l., Nv., U.S. F6 105
Groom Range, mts., Nv., U.S. F6 105
Groote Eylandt, i., Austl. B6 50
Grootfontein, Nmb. A2 49
Grootvloer, pl., S. Afr. C3 49
Groscap, Mi., U.S. C6 99
Grosio, Italy D9 21
Groslay, Fr. g10 16
Gros-Mécatina, Île du, i., P.Q., Can. C2 72
Gros Morne, mtn., Nf., Can. D3 72
Gros Morne National Park, Nf., Can. D3 72
Gross, Ne., U.S. B7 104
Grossbreitenbach, Ger.D.R. C6 19
Grosse Ile, Mi., U.S. *F7 99
Grosse Île, i., P.Q., Can. B8 71
Grosse Isle Naval Air Station, mil., Mi., U.S. p15 99
Grosse Laaber, stm., F.R.Ger. E7 19
Grossenhain, Ger.D.R. C6 18
Grosse Pointe, Mi., U.S. p16 99
Grosse Pointe Park, Mi., U.S. p16 99
Grosse Pointe Woods, Mi., U.S. p16 99
Grosser Arber, mtn., F.R.Ger. D8 19
Grosser Röder, stm., Ger.D.R. B8 19
Grosser Plön, l., F.R.Ger. D4 15
Grosser Priel, mtn., Aus. E7 18
Grosse Tete, La., U.S. D4 95
Grosseto, Italy C3 23
Grossevichi, Sov. Un. B9 33
Gross-Gerau, F.R.Ger. D4 19
Grossglockner, mtn., Aus. E6 18
Grossmont, Ca., U.S. o16 82
Grossostheim, F.R.Ger. D4 19
Grossräschen, Ger.D.R. B9 19
Grossröhrsdorf, Ger.D.R. B9 19
Grosvenor Dale, Ct., U.S. B8 84
Gros Ventre, stm., Wy., U.S. C2 127
Gros Ventre Range, mts., Wy., U.S. C2 127
Groswater Bay, b., Nf., Can. A3 72
Groton, Ct., U.S. D7 84
Groton, Ma., U.S. A4 98
Groton, N.H., U.S. C3 106
Groton, N.Y., U.S. C4 109
Groton, S.D., U.S. B7 118
Groton, Vt., U.S. C4 122
Groton Long Point, Ct., U.S. D7 84
Grottaferrata, Italy h9 23
Grottaglie, Italy D6 23
Grottoes, Va., U.S. B4 123
Grouard Mission, Ab., Can. B2 68
Grouse Creek, Ut., U.S. B2 121
Grouse Creek, stm., Ks., U.S. E7 93
Grouse Creek, stm., Ut., U.S. B2 121
Grouse Creek Mountain, mtn., Id., U.S. E5 89
Grouse Creek Mountains, mts., Ut., U.S. B2 121
Grovania, Ga., U.S. D3 87
Grove, Me., U.S. C5 96
Grove, Ok., U.S. A7 113
Grove City, Fl., U.S. F4 86
Grove City, Mn., U.S. E4 100
Grove City, Oh., U.S. C2 112
Grove City, Pa., U.S. D1 115
Grove Hill, Al., U.S. D2 78
Groveland, Ca., U.S. D3 82
Groveland, Fl., U.S. D5 86
Groveland, Ga., U.S. D5 87
Groveland, Ma., U.S. A5 98
Groveland, N.Y., U.S. C3 109
Grove Mountains, mts., Ant. B21 7
Grove Point, c., Md., U.S. B5 97
Groveport, Oh., U.S. C3 112
Grover, Co., U.S. A6 83
Grover, N.C., U.S. B1 110
Grover, Pa., U.S. C8 115
Grover, S.C., U.S. E6 117
Grover, Wy., U.S. D2 127
Grover City, Ca., U.S. E3 82
Grover Hill, Oh., U.S. A1 112
Grovertown, In., U.S. B4 91
Groves, Tx., U.S. E6 120
Grovespring, Mo., U.S. D5 102
Groveton, N.H., U.S. A3 106
Groveton, Tx., U.S. D5 120
Groveton, Va., U.S. g12 123
Groveton Gardens, Va., U.S. B5 123
Grovetown, Ga., U.S. C4 87
Groveville, N.J., U.S. C3 107
Growler Peak, mtn., Az., U.S. E2 80
Groznyy, Sov. Un. E7 29
Grubbs, Ar., U.S. B4 81
Grudovo, Bul. D8 24
Grudziądz, Pol. B5 26
Grues, Île aux, i., P.Q., Can. B7 74
Gruetli-Laager, Tn., U.S. D8 119
Gruinard Bay, b., Scot., U.K. C3 13
Grulla, Tx., U.S. F3 120
Grünberg, F.R.Ger. C4 19
Grundy, Va., U.S. e9 123
Grundy, co., Il., U.S. B5 90
Grundy, co., Ia., U.S. B5 92
Grundy, co., Mo., U.S. A4 102
Grundy, co., Tn., U.S. D8 119
Grundy Center, Ia., U.S. B5 92
Grünstadt, F.R.Ger. D3 19
Grunthal, Mb., Can. E3 70
Grüsch, Switz. C8 21
Gruver, Ia., U.S. A3 92
Gruver, Tx., U.S. A2 120
Gruyères, Switz. C3 21
Gruž (part of Dubrovnik), Yugo. D4 24
Gryazi, Sov. Un. E13 27
Gryazovets, Sov. Un. B13 27
Gryfice, Pol. B3 26
Gryfino, Pol. B3 26
Grygla, Mn., U.S. B3 100
Gstaad, Switz. C3 20
Guabito, Pan. F6 62
Guacanayabo, Golfo de, b., Cuba D5 64
Gu Achi, Az., U.S. E3 80
Guadalajara, Mex. C4 63
Guadalajara, Spain B4 22
Guadalcanal, Spain C3 22
Guadalcanal, i., Sol.Is. G9 6
Guadalentín, stm., Spain D5 22
Guadalhorce, stm., Spain D3 22
Guadalmena, stm., Spain C4 22
Guadalope, stm., Spain B5 22
Guadalquivir, stm., Spain D2 22
Guadalupe, Mex. *B4 63
Guadalupe, Az., U.S. m9 80
Guadalupe, Ca., U.S. E3 82
Guadalupe, Co., U.S. D4 83
Guadalupe, co., N.M., U.S. C5 108
Guadalupe, co., Tx., U.S. E4 120
Guadalupe, Isla de, i., Mex. E15 6
Guadalupe, Sierra de, mts., Spain C3 22
Guadalupe [Bravos], Mex. A3 63
Guadalupe Mountains, mts., U.S. E5 108
Guadalupe Mountains National Park, Tx., U.S. o12 120
Guadalupe Peak, mtn., Tx., U.S. o12 120
Guadalupita, N.M., U.S. A4 108
Guadarrama, stm., Spain p17 22
Guadarrama, Sierra de, mts., Spain B4 22
Guadeloupe, dep., N.A. H14 64
Guadeloupe Passage, strt., N.A. H14 64
Guadiana, stm., Eur. C3 22
Guadiana Menor, stm., Spain D4 22
Guadiela, stm., Spain B4 22
Guadilla, Bahía de, b., P.R. B1 65
Guadix, Spain D4 22
Guafo, Isla, i., Chile C2 54
Guagua, Phil. o13 34
Guainía, dept., Col. C4 60
Guainía, stm., S.A. C4 60
Guaira, Braz. C2 56
Guairá, dept., Para. E4 55
Guajará Mirim, Braz. E1 59
Guajataca, Lago de, res., P.R. B2 65
Guajira, dept., Col. A3 60
Gualaceo, Ec. B2 58
Gualala, Ca., U.S. C2 82
Gualán, Guat. D7 62
Gualaquiza, Ec. B2 58
Gualeguay, Arg. A5 54
Gualeguaychú, Arg. A5 54
Guam, dep., Oc. F8 6
Guamá, stm., Braz. B1 57
Guamini, Arg. B4 54
Guamúchil, Mex. B3 63
Guanacaste, Cordillera de, mts., C.R. E5 62
Guanahacabibes, Golfo de, b., Cuba C1 64
Guana Island, i., V.I., Br. B6 65
Guanajay, Cuba C2 64
Guanajuato, Mex. C4 63
Guanajuato, state, Mex. C4 63
Guanambi, Braz. A4 56
Guanare, Ven. B4 60
Guandacol, Arg. E2 55
Guandi, China E4 33
Guane, Cuba C1 64
Guang'an, China I2 32
Guangchang, China K7 32
Guangde, China I8 32
Guangdong, prov., China G7 31
Guanghua, China E7 31
Guangnan, China G6 31
Guangxi Zhuangzu, prov., China G6 31
Guangyuan, China E6 31
Guangzhou see Canton, China G7 31
Guánica, P.R. C2 65
Guánica, Laguna de, l., P.R. B2 65
Guano Lake, l., Or., U.S. E7 114
Guantánamo, Cuba D6 64
Guantánamo, prov., Cuba D6 64
Guanxian, China F6 32
Guanyun, China G8 32
Guapí, Col. C2 60
Guapiara, Braz. C3 56
Guápiles, C.R. E6 62
Guaporé (Iténez), stm., S.A. B3 55
Guaqui, Bol. C2 55
Guará, Braz. F1 57
Guara, Sierra de, mts., Spain A5 22
Guarabira, Braz. C3 57
Guaranda, Ec. B2 58
Guaranésia, Braz. k8 56
Guarapuava, Braz. D2 56
Guaraqueçaba, Braz. D3 56
Guararapes, Braz. C2 56
Guaratinguetá, Braz. C3 56
Guaratuba, Braz. D3 56
Guarda, Port. B2 22
Guardafui, Cape see Caseyr, c., Som. C7 47
Guardia Mitre, Arg. C4 54
Guardian, W.V., U.S. C4 125
Guareí, Braz. m7 56
Guareña, Spain C2 22
Guárico, state, Ven. B4 60
Guárico, stm., Ven. B4 60
Guarujá, Braz. n8 56
Guarulhos, Braz. m8 56
Guasave, Mex. B3 63
Guasdualito, Ven. B3 60
Guasipati, Ven. B5 60
Guastalla, Italy B3 23
Guatemala, Guat. E6 63
Guatemala, ctry., N.A. D6 63
Guateque, Col. C3 60
Guatimozín, Arg. A4 54
Guatopo National Park, Ven. A4 60
Guaviare, dept., Col. C3 60
Guaviare, stm., Col. C3 60
Guaxupé, Braz. C3 56
Guayabal, Cuba D5 64
Guayaguayare, Trin. O23 65
Guayama, P.R. H11 64
Guayaquil, Ec. B2 58
Guayaquil, Golfo de, b., S.A. B1 58
Guayaramerín, Bol. B2 55
Guayas, prov., Ec. B1 58
Guaymas, Mex. B2 63
Guaynabo, P.R. B3 65
Guazacapán, Guat. C2 62
Gubakha, Sov. Un. B5 28
Gubbio, Italy C4 23
Gubin, Pol. B9 19
Gucheng, China H4 32
Gúdar, Sierra de, mts., Spain B5 22
Gudauta, Sov. Un. A13 40
Gudenå, stm., Den. B3 15
Gudermes, Sov. Un. E3 28
Gudhjem, Den. C8 15
Güdür, India F6 36
Guebwiller, Fr. D7 16
Guéckédou, Gui. E2 45
Guelma, Alg. B6 44
Guelph, On., Can. D4 73
Guelph, N.D., U.S. C7 111
Guénette, P.Q., Can. C2 74
Güera, W. Sah. E1 44
Guercif, Mor. C4 44
Guéréda, Chad C4 46
Guéret, Fr. D4 16
Guerette, Me., U.S. A4 96
Guernica y Luno, Spain A4 22
Guernsey, Sk., Can. F3 75
Guernsey, Wy., U.S. D8 127
Guernsey, co., Oh., U.S. B4 112
Guernsey, dep., Eur. F5 10
Guernsey, i., Guernsey F3 10
Guerra, Tx., U.S. F3 120
Guerrero, state, Mex. D5 63
Guest Peninsula, pen., Ant. B34 7
Gueugnon, Fr. D6 16
Gueydan, La., U.S. D3 95
Guffey, Co., U.S. C5 83
Gugegwe Island, i., Marsh Is. S17 52
Gügerd, Kūh-e, mts., Iran D6 39
Gūh Kūh, mtn., Iran H9 39
Guia Lopes da Laguna, Braz. C1 56
Guibes, Nmb. C2 49
Guichi, China I7 32
Guide, China D5 31
Guider, Cam. D2 46
Guide Rock, Ne., U.S. D7 104
Guidong, China K5 32
Guidonia [Montecelio], Italy D4 23
Guiglo, I.C. E3 45
Guilarte, Monte, mtn., P.R. B2 65
Guild, N.H., U.S. D2 106
Guildford, Eng., U.K. E6 10
Guildhall, Vt., U.S. B5 122
Guilford, Ct., U.S. D5 84
Guilford, In., U.S. F8 91
Guilford, Me., U.S. C3 96
Guilford, Mo., U.S. A3 102
Guilford, N.Y., U.S. C5 109
Guilford, Vt., U.S. F3 122
Guilford, co., N.C., U.S. A3 110
Guilhermé Capelo, Ang. C1 48
Guilin, China F7 31
Guillaume-Delisle, Lac, l., P.Q., Can. E17 66
Guillestre, Fr. E2 20
Guimarães, Braz. B2 57
Guimarães, Port. B1 22
Guimba, Phil. o13 34
Guin, Al., U.S. B2 78
Guinea, Va., U.S. B5 123
Guinea, ctry., Afr. D2 45
Guinea, Gulf of, b., Afr. F6 42
Guinea-Bissau, ctry., Afr. D1 45
Güines, Cuba C2 64
Guînes, Fr. D1 17
Guingamp, Fr. C2 16
Guion, Ar., U.S. B4 81
Güira de Melena, Cuba C2 64
Guiratinga, Braz. B2 56
Güiria, Ven. A5 60
Guisanbourg, Fr. Gu. B4 59
Guisborough, Eng., U.K. F7 13
Guise, Fr. C5 16
Guist Creek, stm., Ky., U.S. B4 94
Guitiriz, Spain A2 22
Guixi, China J7 32
Guixian, China G6 31
Guiyang, China F6 31
Guizhou, prov., China F6 31
Gujan, Fr. E3 16
Gujarat, state, India D5 36
Gujrānwāla, Pak. B5 36
Gujrāt, Pak. *B5 36
Gulbarga, India E6 36
Guldborg, Den. D5 15
Gulf, N.C., U.S. B3 110
Gulf, co., Fl., U.S. C1 86
Gulf Breeze, Fl., U.S. *u14 86
Gulf Gate Estates, Fl., U.S. E4 86
Gulf Hammock, Fl., U.S. C4 86
Gulf Islands National Seashore, U.S. E5 101
Gulfport, Fl., U.S. E4 86
Gulf Port, Il., U.S. C2 90
Gulfport, Ms., U.S. E4 101
Gulf Shores, Al., U.S. E2 78
Gulgong, Austl. F7 51
Gulkana, Ak., U.S. C10 79
Gullion, Slieve, mtn., N. Ire., U.K. C5 11
Gull Island, i., N.C., U.S. B7 110
Gullivan Bay, b., Fl., U.S. G5 86
Gulliver, Mi., U.S. B5 99
Gull Lake, Sk., Can. G1 75
Gull Lake, l., Ab., Can. C4 68
Gull Lake, l., Mn., U.S. D4 100
Güllük, Tur. D6 40
Gully, Mn., U.S. C3 100
Gulu, Ug. A5 48
Gulyantsi, Bul. D7 24
Gulyaypole, Sov. Un. H11 27
Gumaca, Phil. p14 34
Gumba, Zaire A3 48
Gumboro, De., U.S. G4 85
Gumefens, Switz. C3 21
Gumel, Nig. D6 45
Gummersbach, F.R.Ger. B2 19
Gum Spring Mountain, mtn., Tn., U.S. D8 119
Gum Springs, Ar., U.S. C2 81
Gum Swamp Creek, stm., Ga., U.S. D3 87
Gümüşhane, Tur. B12 40
Guna, India E6 37
Guna, mtn., Eth. C4 47
Gundelfingen, F.R.Ger. E5 19
Güngören, Tur. *B7 40
Gungu, Zaire C2 48
Gunisao, stm., Mb., Can. C3 70
Gunisao Lake, l., Mb., Can. C3 70
Gunlock, Ut., U.S. F2 121
Gunn, Ms., U.S. C4 101
Gunnar, Sk., Can. m7 75
Gunnbjørn Fjeld, mtn., Grnld. *C17 128
Gunnedah, Austl. F9 50
Gunnison, Co., U.S. C4 83
Gunnison, Ms., U.S. B3 101
Gunnison, Ut., U.S. D4 121
Gunnison, co., Co., U.S. C3 83
Gunnison, stm., Co., U.S. C2 83
Gunnison, Mount, mtn., Co., U.S. C3 83
Gunnworth, Sk., Can. F1 75
Gunpowder Creek, stm., Ky., U.S. k13 94
Gunpowder Neck, c., Md., U.S. B5 97
Gunpowder River, b., Md., U.S. B5 97
Gunter Air Force Base, mil., Al., U.S. C3 78
Guntersville, Al., U.S. A3 78
Guntersville Dam, Al., U.S. A3 78
Guntersville Lake, res., Al., U.S. A3 78
Gunton, Mb., Can. D3 70
Guntown, Ms., U.S. A5 101
Guntūr, India E7 36
Gunungsitoli, Indon. L2 35
Günz, stm., F.R.Ger. A6 20
Günzburg, F.R.Ger. E5 19
Gunzenhausen, F.R.Ger. D5 19
Guoyang, China H7 32
Gura Humorului, Rom. B7 24
Gurdāspur, India A5 37
Gurdon, Ar., U.S. D2 81
Gurguéia, stm., Braz. C2 57
Guri, Embalse, res., Ven. B5 60
Gurjevsk, Sov. Un. E26 8
Gurk, stm., Aus. E7 18
Gurkha, Nepal C10 37
Gurley, Al., U.S. A3 78
Gurley, Ne., U.S. C3 104
Gurleyville, Ct., U.S. B7 84
Gurnee, Il., U.S. h9 90
Gurnet Point, c., Ma., U.S. B6 98
Gurney, Wi., U.S. B3 126
Gurué, Moz. A6 49
Gurupá, Braz. C4 59
Gurupi, Braz. E5 59
Gurupi, stm., Braz. B1 57
Gurupi, Cabo, c., Braz. B1 57
Guryev, Sov. Un. E8 29
Gusau, Nig. D6 45
Gusev, Sov. Un. A7 26
Gusher, Ut., U.S. C6 121
Gushi, China E8 31
Gushikami, Japan O5 52
Gushikawa, Japan O5 52
Gusinje, Yugo. D4 24
Gus-Khrustalnyy, Sov. Un. D13 27
Gustavo A. Madero (part of Mexico City), Mex. h9 63
Gustavus, Ak., U.S. D12 79
Güsten, Ger.D.R. B6 19
Gustine, Ca., U.S. D3 82
Gustine, Tx., U.S. D3 120
Güstrow, Ger.D.R. B6 18
Gutau, Aus. E9 19
Gütersloh, F.R.Ger. C4 18
Guthrie, Ky., U.S. D2 94
Guthrie, Mn., U.S. C4 100
Guthrie, Ok., U.S. B4 113
Guthrie, Tx., U.S. C2 120
Guthrie, W.V., U.S. m12 125
Guthrie, co., Ia., U.S. C3 92
Guthrie Center, Ia., U.S. C3 92
Guthrie Lake, l., Mb., Can. B1 70
Guttenberg, Ia., U.S. B6 92
Guttenberg, N.J., U.S. h8 107
Gu Vo, Az., U.S. E3 80
Guy, Ar., U.S. B3 81
Guy, Tx., U.S. r14 120
Guyana, ctry., S.A. A3 59
Guyandotte, stm., W.V., U.S. C2 125
Guyandotte Mountain, mtn., W.V., U.S. n12 125
Guyang, China D4 32
Guyenne, hist reg., Fr. E4 16
Guymon, Ok., U.S. e9 113
Guyot, Mount, mtn., U.S. D10 119
Guyra, Austl. E8 51
Guys, Tn., U.S. B3 119
Guysborough, N.S., Can. D8 71
Guysborough, co., N.S., Can. D3 71
Guys Mills, Pa., U.S. C2 115
Guyton, Ga., U.S. D5 87
Guyuan, China D6 32
Guyuan, China G2 32
Guzar, Sov. Un. B13 39

Name	Map Ref	Page

Gozhen, China — H7 32
Gvardeysk, Sov. Un. — A6 26
Gwabegar, Austl. — E7 51
Gwādar, Pak. — C3 36
Gwai, Zimb. — A4 49
Gwalior, India — C6 36
Gwanda, Zimb. — B4 49
Gwane, Zaire — A4 48
Gwda, stm., Pol. — B4 26
Gweebarra Bay, b., Ire. — C3 11
Gweesalia, Ire. — C2 11
Gwembe, Zam. — E4 48
Gwent, co., Wales, U.K. — C5 12
Gweru, Zimb. — A4 49
Gwinhurst, De., U.S. — h8 85
Gwinn, Mi., U.S. — B3 99
Gwinner, N.D., U.S. — C8 111
Gwinnett, co., Ga., U.S. — C2 87
Gwydyr b., Ak., U.S. — A10 79
Gwynedd, co., Wales, U.K. — A3 12
Gwynn, Va., U.S. — C6 123
Gwynne, Ab., Can. — C4 68
Gwynneville, In., U.S. — E6 91
Gwynns Falls, stm., Md., U.S. — g10 97
Gyangzê, China — C8 36
Gyaring Lake, l., China — E4 31
Gyaring Lake, l., China — B8 36
Gyirong, China — C10 37
Gympie, Austl. — E9 50
Gyöngyös, Hung. — B4 24
Győr (Raab), Hung. — B3 24
Gypsera, Switz. — C3 21
Gypsum, Co., U.S. — B4 83
Gypsum, Ks., U.S. — D6 93
Gypsum, Oh., U.S. — A3 112
Gypsumville, Mb., Can. — D2 70
Gyula, Hung. — B5 24

H

Haag [in Oberbayern], F.R.Ger. — A8 20
Haakon, co., S.D., U.S. — C4 118
Haaksbergen, Neth. — B6 17
Haamstede, Neth. — C3 17
Haapamäki, Fin. — F11 14
Haapsalu, Sov. Un. — B4 27
Ha Arava (Wādī al Jayb), val., Asia — D7 41
Haarlem, Neth. — A6 16
Haarlemmermeer, Neth. — A6 16
Hab, stm., Pak. — I13 39
Habermehl Peak, mtn., Ant. — B13 7
Habersham, Ga., U.S. — B3 87
Habersham, co., Ga., U.S. — B3 87
Haboru, China — D10 33
Hachiman, Japan — n15 33
Hachinohe, Japan — F10 33
Hachiōji, Japan — I9 33
Hachita, N.M., U.S. — F1 108
Hacienda Heights, Ca., U.S. — *n13 82
Hack, Mount, mtn., Austl. — E2 51
Hackberry, Az., U.S. — B2 80
Hackberry, La., U.S. — E2 95
Hackberry Creek, stm., Ks., U.S. — D3 93
Hackensack, Mn., U.S. — D4 100
Hackensack, N.J., U.S. — B4 107
Hackensack, stm., N.J., U.S. — h8 107
Hacker Valley, W.V., U.S. — C4 125
Hacketstown, Ire. — E5 11
Hackett, Ar., U.S. — B1 81
Hackettstown, N.J., U.S. — B3 107
Hackleburg, Al., U.S. — A2 78
Hackney (part of London), Eng., U.K. — k12 10
Hack Point, Md., U.S. — B6 97
Hacoda, l., U.S. — D3 78
Hacq, i., Micron. — Q18 52
Hadar, Ne., U.S. — B8 104
Ḥadārībah, Ra's al, c., Sud. — A4 47
Hadassah Alef Hospital, Isr. — m14 41
Hadd, Ra's al, c., Oman — C5 38
Haddam, Ct., U.S. — D5 84
Haddam, Ks., U.S. — C6 93
Haddington, Scot., U.K. — E6 13
Haddix, Ky., U.S. — C6 94
Haddock, Ga., U.S. — C3 87
Haddonfield, N.J., U.S. — D2 107
Haddon Heights, N.J., U.S. — D2 107
Hadejia, Nig. — D7 45
Hadejia, stm., Nig. — D6 45
Hadera, Isr. — F10 40
Haderslev, Den. — C3 15
Hadim, Tur. — D9 40
Ḥadīyah, Bi'r al, well, Eg. — D6 41
Ḥadīyah, Sau. Ar. — D7 43
Hadleigh, Eng., U.K. — B8 12
Hadley, Ma., U.S. — B2 98
Hadley, Mn., U.S. — F3 100
Hadley, N.Y., U.S. — B7 109
Hadley, Pa., U.S. — D1 115
Hadley Bay, b., N.T., Can. — B11 66
Hadley Lake, l., Me., U.S. — D5 96
Hadlock, Wa., U.S. — A3 124
Hadlyme, Ct., U.S. — D6 84
Ha Dong, Viet. — A3 34
Ḥaḍramawt, reg., P.D.R.Yem. — D4 38
Hadsten, Den. — B4 15
Hadsund, Den. — B4 15
Haeju, N. Kor. — C10 31
Haenam, S. Kor. — I3 33
Haerhpin see Harbin, China — B10 31
Hafford, Sk., Can. — E2 75
Ḥafira, Qā' al, pl., Jord. — C8 41
Hafnarfjördur, Ice. — n22 14
Haft Gel, Iran — F4 39
Hafun, Ras, c., Som. — C7 47
Hagan, Ga., U.S. — D5 87
Hagari, stm., India — F6 36
Hagarstown, Il., U.S. — E4 90
Hagemeister Island, i., Ak., U.S. — D7 79
Hagen, Sk., Can. — E3 75
Hagen, F.R.Ger. — C3 18
Hagenow, Ger.D.R. — E5 15
Hagensborg, B.C., Can. — C4 69
Hagere Hiywet, Eth. — D4 47
Hagerman, Id., U.S. — G4 89
Hagerman, N.M., U.S. — D5 108
Hagerman Corners, On., Can. — k15 73
Hagerstown, In., U.S. — E7 91
Hagerstown, Md., U.S. — A2 97
Hagersville, On., Can. — E4 73
Haggart Lake, l., On., Can. — D4 70
Haggin, Mount, mtn., Mt., U.S. — D3 103
Ha Giang, Viet. — A6 34
Hags Head, c., Ire. — E2 11
Hague, Sk., Can. — E2 75
Hague, N.Y., U.S. — B7 109
Hague, N.D., U.S. — C6 111
Hague, Cap de la, c., Fr. — C3 16
Haguenau, Fr. — C7 16

Hagues Peak, mtn., Co., U.S. — A5 83
Haï Hai, Baie des, b., P.Q., Can. — C2 72
Haï Hai, Lac, l., P.Q., Can. — A7 74
Hahira, Ga., U.S. — F3 87
Hahnville, La., U.S. — E5 95
Haicheng, China — G8 31
Haicheng, China — D10 32
Haichow Bay see Haizhou Bay, b., China — G8 32
Hai Duong, Viet. — B7 35
Haifa (Hefa), Isr. — B3 38
Haifa, Bay of see Hefa, Mifraẓ, b., Isr. — B6 41
Haigerloch, F.R.Ger. — A4 20
Haigler, Ne., U.S. — D4 104
Haikang, China — G6 31
Haikou, China — B4 34
Haiku, Hi., U.S. — C5 88
Hā'il, Sau. Ar. — C4 38
Hailar, China — B8 31
Haile, La., U.S. — B3 95
Hailesboro, N.Y., U.S. — f9 109
Hailey, Id., U.S. — F4 89
Haileybury, On., Can. — p20 73
Haileyville, Ok., U.S. — C6 113
Hailong, China — C10 31
Hailun, China — B10 31
Haimen, China — F9 31
Haimen, China — I9 32
Hainan Island, i., China — B3 34
Hainaut, prov., Bel. — D3 17
Haines, Ak., U.S. — D12 79
Haines, Or., U.S. — C9 114
Hainesburg, N.J., U.S. — B2 107
Haines City, Fl., U.S. — D5 86
Haines Falls, N.Y., U.S. — C6 109
Hainesport, N.J., U.S. — D3 107
Hainesville, N.J., U.S. — A3 107
Hainichen, Ger.D.R. — C8 19
Haining, China — I9 32
Haiphong, Viet. — A3 34
Hairy Hill, Ab., Can. — C5 68
Haiti, ctry., N.A. — E7 64
Haiyang, China — F9 32
Haiyuan, China — F1 32
Haizhou, China — E8 31
Haizhou Bay, b., China — G8 32
Hajdúböszörmény, Hung. — B5 24
Hajdúhadház, Hung. — B5 24
Hajdúnánás, Hung. — B5 24
Hajdúszoboszló, Hung. — B5 24
Hajiki, Cape, c., Japan — G9 33
Hajnówka, Pol. — B7 26
Hakken, Mount, mtn., Japan — I7 33
Hakodate, Japan — C13 31
Haku, Mount, mtn., Japan — m15 33
Halabjah, Iraq — D2 39
Ḥalā'ib, Eg. — E7 43
Halawa, Hi., U.S. — C6 88
Halawa, Cape, c., Hi., U.S. — B5 88
Halawa Heights, Hi., U.S. — g10 88
Halberstadt, Ger.D.R. — C5 18
Halbrite, Sk., Can. — H4 75
Halcon, Mount, mtn., Phil. — C6 34
Haldeman, Ky., U.S. — B6 94
Halden, Nor. — H4 14
Haldensleben, Ger.D.R. — B5 18
Haldimand, co., On., Can. — E5 73
Hale, Co., U.S. — B8 83
Hale, Mi., U.S. — D7 99
Hale, Mo., U.S. — B4 102
Hale, co., Al., U.S. — C2 78
Hale, co., Tx., U.S. — B2 120
Haleakala Crater, crat., Hi., U.S. — C5 88
Haleakala National Park, Hi., U.S. — C6 88
Haleburg, Al., U.S. — D4 78
Hale Center, Tx., U.S. — B2 120
Haledon, N.J., U.S. — *B4 107
Haleiwa, Hi., U.S. — B3 88
Hales Corners, Wi., U.S. — n11 126
Halesworth, Eng., U.K. — B9 12
Halethorpe, Md., U.S. — B4 97
Haleyville, Al., U.S. — A2 78
Haleyville, N.J., U.S. — E2 107
Half Assini, Ghana — E4 45
Half Hollow Hills, N.Y., U.S. — *h13 109
Half-Moon Bay, N.Z. — Q12 51
Half Moon Bay, Ca., U.S. — k8 82
Halfway, Ky., U.S. — D3 94
Halfway, Md., U.S. — A2 97
Half Way, Mo., U.S. — D4 102
Halfway, Or., U.S. — C9 114
Halfway, stm., B.C., Can. — A6 69
Halfway Nunatak, mtn., Ant. — f40 7
Haliburton, On., Can. — B6 73
Haliburton, co., On., Can. — B6 73
Halibut Point, c., Ma., U.S. — A6 98
Halifax, N.S., Can. — E6 71
Halifax, Eng., U.K. — D6 10
Halifax, Ma., U.S. — C6 98
Halifax, N.C., U.S. — A5 110
Halifax, Pa., U.S. — F8 115
Halifax, Va., U.S. — D4 123
Halifax, co., N.C., U.S. — A5 110
Halifax, co., Va., U.S. — D4 123
Halifax Bay, b., Austl. — C8 50
Haliimaile, Hi., U.S. — C5 88
Halkirk, Ab., Can. — C4 68
Hall, In., U.S. — E4 91
Hall, Mt., U.S. — D3 103
Hall, N.Y., U.S. — C3 109
Hall, co., Ga., U.S. — B3 87
Hall, co., Ne., U.S. — D7 104
Hall, co., Tx., U.S. — B2 120
Halla, Mount, mtn., S. Kor. — J3 33
Halladale, stm., Scot., U.K. — B5 13
Hallam, Ne., U.S. — D9 104
Hallam Peak, mtn., B.C., Can. — C8 69
Halland, co., Swe. — H5 15
Hallandale, Fl., U.S. — G6 86
Hallands Väderö, i., Swe. — H5 15
Hall Basin, b., N.A. — k39 66
Hallboro, Mb., Can. — D2 70
Halle, Ger.D.R. — C5 18
Halle, F.R.Ger. — A3 19
Halleck, Nv., U.S. — C6 105
Halle-Neustadt, Ger.D.R. — *C6 18
Hallett, Ok., U.S. — A5 113
Hallett, Cape, c., Ant. — B30 7
Hallettsville, Tx., U.S. — E4 120
Halley, Ar., U.S. — D4 81

Halley Bay, sci., Ant. — B10 7
Halliday, N.D., U.S. — B3 111
Hallie, Wi., U.S. — D2 126
Hallim, S. Kor. — J3 33
Hall Island, i., Ak., U.S. — C5 79
Hall Meadow Brook, stm., Ct., U.S. — B3 84
Hall Meadow Brook Reservoir, res., Ct., U.S. — B3 84
Hall Mountain, mtn., Wa., U.S. — A8 124
Hallock, Mn., U.S. — B2 100
Hallowell, Ks., U.S. — E9 93
Hallowell, Me., U.S. — D3 96
Hall Peninsula, pen., N.T., Can. — D19 66
Halls, Ga., U.S. — B2 87
Halls, Tn., U.S. — B2 119
Hallsberg, Swe. — t33 14
Hallsboro, N.C., U.S. — C4 110
Halls Creek, Austl. — C4 50
Halls Creek, stm., Ut., U.S. — F5 121
Halls Crossroads, Tn., U.S. — m14 119
Halls Harbour, N.S., Can. — D5 71
Halls Stream, stm., N.H., U.S. — f7 106
Halls Summit, Ks., U.S. — D8 93
Hallstead, Pa., U.S. — C10 115
Hall Summit, La., U.S. — B2 95
Hallsville, Mo., U.S. — B5 102
Hallsville, Oh., U.S. — C3 112
Hallsville, Tx., U.S. — C5 120
Hall Top, mtn., Tn., U.S. — D10 119
Halltown, Mo., U.S. — D4 102
Hallville, Ct., U.S. — C7 84
Hallwil Lake, l., Switz. — B4 20
Hallwood, Va., U.S. — C7 123
Halma, Mn., U.S. — B2 100
Halmahera, i., Indon. — E7 34
Halmahera Sea, Indon. — F7 34
Halmstad, Swe. — I5 14
Hals, Den. — A4 15
Halsell, Al., U.S. — C1 78
Halsey, Ne., U.S. — C5 104
Halsey, N.J., U.S. — A3 107
Halsey, Or., U.S. — C3 114
Halstad, Mn., U.S. — C2 100
Halstead, Eng., U.K. — C8 12
Halstead, Ks., U.S. — E6 93
Haltern, F.R.Ger. — B2 19
Haltia, mtn., Eur. — C9 14
Haltom City, Tx., U.S. — *n9 120
Halton, co., On., Can. — D5 73
Haltwhistle, Eng., U.K. — F6 13
Ham, Fr. — E3 17
Hamada, Japan — I6 33
Hamadān, Iran — B4 38
Hamāh, Syria — B3 38
Hamahika Island, i., Japan — O5 52
Hamamatsu, Japan — H9 33
Hamar, Nor. — G4 14
Hamber Provincial Park, B.C., Can. — C8 69
Hamblen, co., Tn., U.S. — C10 119
Hamburg, F.R.Ger. — B5 18
Hamburg, Ar., U.S. — D4 81
Hamburg, Ct., U.S. — D6 84
Hamburg, Il., U.S. — D3 90
Hamburg, Ia., U.S. — D2 92
Hamburg, Ms., U.S. — D2 101
Hamburg, N.J., U.S. — A3 107
Hamburg, N.Y., U.S. — C2 109
Hamburg, Pa., U.S. — E10 115
Hamburg, state, F.R.Ger. — E4 15
Hamburg Mountains, mts., N.J., U.S. — A3 107
Ḥamḍ, Wādī al, val., Sau. Ar. — C3 38
Hamden, Ct., U.S. — D4 84
Hamden, N.Y., U.S. — C6 109
Hamden, Oh., U.S. — C3 112
Hämeenlinna, Fin. — G11 14
Hamel, Mn., U.S. — m11 100
Hameln, F.R.Ger. — B4 18
Hamer, Id., U.S. — F6 89
Hamer, S.C., U.S. — A7 117
Hamersley Range, mts., Austl. — D2 50
Hamersville, Oh., U.S. — D2 112
Hamhŭng, N. Kor. — G3 33
Hami, China — C3 31
Hamill, Ia., U.S. — D6 92
Hamill, S.D., U.S. — D6 118
Hamilton, Austl. — G7 50
Hamilton, Ber. — p20 64
Hamilton, On., Can. — D5 73
Hamilton, N.Z. — L15 51
Hamilton, Scot., U.K. — C4 10
Hamilton, Al., U.S. — A2 78
Hamilton, Ga., U.S. — D2 87
Hamilton, Il., U.S. — C2 90
Hamilton, In., U.S. — A8 91
Hamilton, Ks., U.S. — E7 93
Hamilton, Ma., U.S. — A6 98
Hamilton, Mi., U.S. — F4 99
Hamilton, Mo., U.S. — B3 102
Hamilton, Mt., U.S. — D2 103
Hamilton, N.Y., U.S. — C5 109
Hamilton, N.C., U.S. — B5 110
Hamilton, N.D., U.S. — A8 111
Hamilton, Oh., U.S. — C1 112
Hamilton, Tx., U.S. — D3 120
Hamilton, Va., U.S. — A5 123
Hamilton, co., Fl., U.S. — B3 86
Hamilton, co., Il., U.S. — E5 90
Hamilton, co., In., U.S. — D5 91
Hamilton, co., Ia., U.S. — B4 92
Hamilton, co., Ks., U.S. — E2 93
Hamilton, co., Ne., U.S. — D7 104
Hamilton, co., N.Y., U.S. — B6 109
Hamilton, co., Oh., U.S. — C1 112
Hamilton, co., Tn., U.S. — D8 119
Hamilton, co., Tx., U.S. — D3 120
Hamilton, Lake, res., Ar., U.S. — C2 81
Hamilton, Mount, mtn., Ak., U.S. — C8 79
Hamilton, Mount, mtn., Ca., U.S. — k9 82
Hamilton, Mount, mtn., Nv., U.S. — D6 105
Hamilton City, Ca., U.S. — C2 82
Hamilton Dome, Wy., U.S. — C4 127
Hamilton Inlet, b., Nf., Can. — A2 72
Hamilton Mountain, mtn., N.Y., U.S. — B6 109

Hamilton Reservoir, res., Ma., U.S. — B3 98
Hamilton Sound, strt., Nf., Can. — D4 72
Hamilton Square, N.J., U.S. — C3 107
Hamiota, Mb., Can. — D1 70
Hamīrpur, India — C7 36
Hamīrpur, India — B6 37
Hamjŏng-ni, N. Kor. — G2 33
Ham Lake, Mn., U.S. — *m12 100
Hamler, Oh., U.S. — A1 112
Hamlet, In., U.S. — B4 91
Hamlet, Ne., U.S. — D4 104
Hamlet, N.C., U.S. — C3 110
Hamlet, Mount, mtn., Ak., U.S. — B6 79
Hamletsburg, Il., U.S. — F5 90
Hamlin, Ks., U.S. — C8 93
Hamlin, Pa., U.S. — D11 115
Hamlin, Tx., U.S. — C2 120
Hamlin, W.V., U.S. — C2 125
Hamlin, co., S.D., U.S. — C8 118
Hamlin Lake, l., Mi., U.S. — D4 99
Hamm [in Westfalen], F.R.Ger. — B7 18
Hammār, Hawr al, l., Iraq — F3 39
Hammarby, Swe. — t35 14
Hammarsjön, l., Swe. — C8 15
Hamme, Bel. — C4 17
Hammel, Den. — B3 15
Hammelburg, F.R.Ger. — C4 19
Hammer, S.D., U.S. — B8 118
Hammerfest, Nor. — B10 14
Hammett, Id., U.S. — G3 89
Hammon, Ok., U.S. — B2 113
Hammonasset, stm., Ct., U.S. — D5 84
Hammonasset Point, c., Ct., U.S. — D5 84
Hammond, Il., U.S. — D5 90
Hammond, In., U.S. — A2 91
Hammond, La., U.S. — D5 95
Hammond, Mn., U.S. — F6 100
Hammond, Mt., U.S. — E12 103
Hammond, N.Y., U.S. — f9 109
Hammond, Or., U.S. — A3 114
Hammond, Wi., U.S. — D1 126
Hammond Bay, b., Mi., U.S. — C6 99
Hammondsport, N.Y., U.S. — C3 109
Hammonton, N.J., U.S. — D3 107
Hamneda, Swe. — B7 15
Ham-Nord, P.Q., Can. — D6 74
Hamoyet, Jabal, mtn., Afr. — B4 47
Hampden, Nf., Can. — D3 72
Hampden, N.Z. — P13 51
Hampden, Me., U.S. — D4 96
Hampden, Ma., U.S. — B3 98
Hampden, Oh., U.S. — B3 112
Hampden, co., Ma., U.S. — B2 98
Hampden Highlands, Me., U.S. — D4 96
Hampshire, Il., U.S. — A5 90
Hampshire, Tn., U.S. — B4 119
Hampshire, co., Eng., U.K. — C6 12
Hampshire, co., Ma., U.S. — B2 98
Hampshire, co., W.V., U.S. — B6 125
Hampstead, N.B., Can. — D3 71
Hampstead (part of London), Eng., U.K. — k12 10
Hampstead, Md., U.S. — A4 97
Hampstead, N.H., U.S. — E4 106
Hampstead, N.C., U.S. — C5 110
Hampton, N.B., Can. — D4 71
Hampton, Ar., U.S. — D3 81
Hampton, Ct., U.S. — B7 84
Hampton, Fl., U.S. — C4 86
Hampton, Ga., U.S. — C2 87
Hampton, Ia., U.S. — B4 92
Hampton, Ky., U.S. — e9 94
Hampton, Ne., U.S. — D8 104
Hampton, N.H., U.S. — E5 106
Hampton, N.J., U.S. — B3 107
Hampton, S.C., U.S. — F5 117
Hampton, Tn., U.S. — C11 119
Hampton, Va., U.S. — C6 123
Hampton, co., S.C., U.S. — F5 117
Hampton Bays, N.Y., U.S. — n16 109
Hampton Beach, N.H., U.S. — E5 106
Hampton Butte, mtn., Or., U.S. — D6 114
Hampton Falls, N.H., U.S. — E5 106
Hampton Roads, Va., U.S. — k15 123
Hampton Roads Bridge-Tunnel, Va., U.S. — k15 123
Ḥamrā', Al Ḥammādah al, pl., Afr. — D2 43
Hams Fork, stm., Wy., U.S. — E2 127
Ham-Sud, P.Q., Can. — D6 74
Ham Tan, Viet. — G7 35
Hamtramck, Mi., U.S. — p15 99
Hamyang, S. Kor. — I3 33
Han, stm., Asia — H4 33
Hana, Hi., U.S. — C6 88
Hanahan, S.C., U.S. — F7 117
Hanalei, Hi., U.S. — A2 88
Hanalei Bay, b., Hi., U.S. — A2 88
Hanamaki, Japan — G10 33
Hanamaulu, Hi., U.S. — B2 88
Hanapepe, Hi., U.S. — B2 88
Hanau, F.R.Ger. — C4 19
Hanceville, B.C., Can. — D6 69
Hanceville, Al., U.S. — A3 78
Hancheng, China — G4 32
Hanchuan, China — E2 32
Hancock, Md., U.S. — A1 97
Hancock, Me., U.S. — D4 96
Hancock, Mi., U.S. — A2 99
Hancock, Mn., U.S. — E3 100
Hancock, N.H., U.S. — E3 106
Hancock, N.Y., U.S. — D5 109
Hancock, Vt., U.S. — D3 122
Hancock, Wi., U.S. — D4 126
Hancock, co., Ga., U.S. — C3 87
Hancock, co., Il., U.S. — C2 90
Hancock, co., In., U.S. — E6 91
Hancock, co., Ia., U.S. — A4 92
Hancock, co., Ky., U.S. — C3 94
Hancock, co., Me., U.S. — D4 96
Hancock, co., Ms., U.S. — E4 101
Hancock, co., Oh., U.S. — A2 112
Hancock, co., Tn., U.S. — C10 119
Hancock, co., W.V., U.S. — A4 125
Hancock, Mount, mtn., Ak., U.S. — C8 79
Hancock Pond, l., Me., U.S. — E2 96
Hancocks Bridge, N.J., U.S. — D2 107
Hand, co., S.D., U.S. — C6 118
Handa, Japan — o15 33
Handa, Som. — C7 47
Handa, i., Scot., U.K. — B4 13
Handan, China — D7 32
Handeni, Tan. — C6 48

Handley, W.V., U.S. — m13 125
Handsworth, Sk., Can. — H4 75
Haney, B.C., Can. — E6 69
Hanford, Ca., U.S. — D4 82
Hangchou see Hangzhou, China — E9 31
Hangchow Bay see Hangzhou Bay, b., China — I9 32
Hangelsberg, Ger.D.R. — F7 15
Hanging Rock, Oh., U.S. — D3 112
Hangingstone, stm., Ab., Can. — A5 68
Hangman Creek, stm., Wa., U.S. — B8 124
Hangö, Fin. — H10 14
Hangzhou (Hangchou), China — E9 31
Hangzhou Bay, b., China — I9 32
HaNiqra, Rosh, c., Asia — A7 41
Hanita, Isr. — A7 41
Hankinson, N.D., U.S. — C9 111
Hanks, N.D., U.S. — A2 111
Hanksville, Ut., U.S. — E5 121
Hanley, Sk., Can. — F2 75
Hanley Falls, Mn., U.S. — F3 100
Hanlontown, Ia., U.S. — A4 92
Hann, Mount, mtn., Austl. — C4 50
Hanna, Ab., Can. — D5 68
Hanna, In., U.S. — B4 91
Hanna, Ut., U.S. — C5 121
Hanna, Wy., U.S. — E6 127
Hanna City, Il., U.S. — C4 90
Hannaford, N.D., U.S. — B7 111
Hannah, N.D., U.S. — A7 111
Hannahville Indian Reservation, Mi., U.S. — C3 99
Hannawa Falls, N.Y., U.S. — f10 109
Hannibal, Mo., U.S. — B6 102
Hannibal, N.Y., U.S. — B4 109
Hannibal, Oh., U.S. — C5 112
Hannover, F.R.Ger. — B4 18
Hannover, N.D., U.S. — B4 111
Hanöbukten, b., Swe. — J6 14
Hanoi, Viet. — A3 34
Hanover, On., Can. — C3 73
Hanover, Ar., U.S. — B3 81
Hanover, Ct., U.S. — C7 84
Hanover, Il., U.S. — A3 90
Hanover, In., U.S. — G7 91
Hanover, Ks., U.S. — C7 93
Hanover, Me., U.S. — D2 96
Hanover, Mi., U.S. — F6 99
Hanover, Mn., U.S. — m11 100
Hanover, N.H., U.S. — C2 106
Hanover, N.M., U.S. — E1 108
Hanover, Oh., U.S. — B3 112
Hanover, Pa., U.S. — G8 115
Hanover, Va., U.S. — C5 123
Hanover, W.V., U.S. — D3 125
Hanover, co., Va., U.S. — C5 123
Hanover, hist. reg., F.R.Ger. — B4 18
Hanover, Isla, i., Chile — E2 54
Hanover Center, Ma., U.S. — h12 98
Hanover Center, N.H., U.S. — C2 106
Hanover Park, Il., U.S. — k8 90
Hanoverton, Oh., U.S. — B5 112
Hanover Township, N.J., U.S. — B4 107
Hansard, B.C., Can. — B7 69
Hansboro, N.D., U.S. — A6 111
Hansell, Ia., U.S. — B4 92
Hansen, Id., U.S. — G4 89
Hansford, co., Tx., U.S. — A2 120
Han Shui, stm., China — E7 31
Hanska, Mn., U.S. — F4 100
Hanson, Ky., U.S. — C2 94
Hanson, Ma., U.S. — B6 98
Hanson, Ok., U.S. — B7 113
Hanson, co., S.D., U.S. — D8 118
Hanson, Lake, l., Sk., Can. — C4 75
Hanstholm (Hansted), Den. — A2 15
Hanston, Ks., U.S. — D4 93
Hants, co., N.S., Can. — D6 71
Hant's Harbour, Nf., Can. — E5 72
Hantsport, N.S., Can. — D5 71
Hanyin, China — H3 32
Hanzhong, China — E8 31
Hao Binh, Viet. — B6 35
Haparanda, Swe. — E10 14
Hapeville, Ga., U.S. — C2 87
Happy, Tx., U.S. — B2 120
Happy Camp, Ca., U.S. — B2 82
Happy Corner, N.H., U.S. — f7 106
Happy Jack, Az., U.S. — C4 80
Happy Jack, La., U.S. — E6 95
Happyland, Ok., U.S. — C5 113
Happy Valley, Or., U.S. — *B4 114
Happy Valley-Goose Bay, Nf., Can. — B1 72

Hapsu, N. Kor. — F4 33
Haql, Sau. Ar. — C2 38
Ḥaraḍ, Sau. Ar. — C4 38
Häradsbäck, Swe. — B8 15
Harahan, La., U.S. — k11 95
Haralson, Ga., U.S. — C1 87
Haralson, co., Ga., U.S. — C1 87
Harare (Salisbury), Zimb. — A5 49
Haraze, Chad — D4 46
Harbeson, De., U.S. — F4 85
Harbin (Haerhpin), China — B10 31
Harbinger, N.C., U.S. — A7 110
Harboør, Den. — B2 15
Harbor Beach, Mi., U.S. — E8 99
Harborcreek, Pa., U.S. — B2 115
Harbor Springs, Mi., U.S. — C6 99
Harborton, Va., U.S. — C7 123
Harbor View, Oh., U.S. — e7 112
Harbour Breton, Nf., Can. — E4 72
Harbour Buffett, Nf., Can. — E4 72
Harbour Deep, Nf., Can. — C3 72
Harbour Grace, Nf., Can. — E5 72
Harbour Mille, Nf., Can. — E4 72
Harbourville, N.S., Can. — D5 71
Harburg (part of Hamburg), F.R.Ger. — E3 15
Hårby, Den. — C4 15
Harcourt, N.B., Can. — C4 71
Harcuvar Mountains, mts., Az., U.S. — D2 80
Harda, India — F6 37
Hardangerfjorden, Nor. — H1 14
Hardangerjøkulen, Nor. — G2 14
Hardangervidda, plat., Nor. — G2 14
Hardaway, Al., U.S. — C4 78
Hardee, co., Fl., U.S. — E5 86
Hardeeville, S.C., U.S. — G5 117
Hardeman, co., Tn., U.S. — B3 119
Hardeman, co., Tx., U.S. — B3 120
Harderwijk, Neth. — B6 17
Hardesty, Ok., U.S. — e9 113
Hardin, Il., U.S. — D3 90
Hardin, Ky., U.S. — f9 94
Hardin, Mo., U.S. — B4 102
Hardin, Mt., U.S. — E9 103
Hardin, co., Ia., U.S. — B4 92
Hardin, co., Il., U.S. — F5 90
Hardin, co., Ky., U.S. — C4 94
Hardin, co., Oh., U.S. — B2 112
Hardin, co., Tn., U.S. — B3 119
Hardin, co., Tx., U.S. — D5 120
Harding, Ma., U.S. — h10 98
Harding, Mn., U.S. — D4 100
Harding, W.V., U.S. — C5 125
Harding, co., N.M., U.S. — B5 108
Harding, co., S.D., U.S. — B2 118
Harding, Lake, res., U.S. — C4 78
Harding Lake, l., Mb., Can. — A2 70
Hardinsburg, In., U.S. — H5 91
Hardinsburg, Ky., U.S. — C3 94
Hardinville, Il., U.S. — E6 90
Hardisty, Ab., Can. — C5 68
Hardisty Lake, l., N.T., Can. — D9 66
Hardman, Or., U.S. — B7 114
Hardoi, India — D8 37
Hardshell, Ky., U.S. — C6 94
Hardtner, Ks., U.S. — E5 93
Hardwār, India — C6 36
Hardwick, Ga., U.S. — C3 87
Hardwick, Ma., U.S. — B3 98
Hardwick, Mn., U.S. — G2 100
Hardwick, Vt., U.S. — C4 122
Hardwicke, N.B., Can. — B5 71
Hardwood Ridge, mtn., Pa., U.S. — D11 115
Hardy, Sk., Can. — H3 75
Hardy, Ar., U.S. — A4 81
Hardy, Ia., U.S. — B3 92
Hardy, Ne., U.S. — D8 104
Hardy, Ok., U.S. — A5 113
Hardy, Va., U.S. — C3 123
Hardy, co., W.V., U.S. — B6 125
Hardy Lake, res., In., U.S. — G6 91
Hare Bay, Nf., Can. — D4 72
Hare Bay, b., Nf., Can. — C4 72
Haren, Neth. — A6 17
Harer (Harar), Eth. — D5 47
Harerge, prov., Eth. — D6 47
Harfleur, Fr. — C4 16
Harford, Pa., U.S. — C10 115
Harford, co., Md., U.S. — A5 97
Hargeysa, Som. — D5 47
Harghita, mtn., Rom. — B7 24
Hargrave, Mb., Can. — D1 70
Hargrave Lake, l., Mb., Can. — B2 70
Harihar, India — E3 36
Ḥarīr, Wādī al, val., Syria — B8 41
Ḥarīrūd, stm., Asia — B3 36
Harker Heights, Tx., U.S. — *D4 120
Harkers Island, N.C., U.S. — C6 110
Harlan, Ia., U.S. — C2 92
Harlan, In., U.S. — B8 91
Harlan, Ks., U.S. — C5 93
Harlan, Ky., U.S. — D6 94
Harlan, co., Ky., U.S. — D6 94
Harlan, co., Ne., U.S. — D6 104
Harlan County Lake, res., Ne., U.S. — E6 104
Harlech, Wales, U.K. — B3 12
Harlem, Fl., U.S. — F6 86
Harlem, Ga., U.S. — C4 87
Harleton, Tx., U.S. — C5 120
Harleyville, S.C., U.S. — E7 117
Harlingen, Neth. — A6 16
Harlingen, Tx., U.S. — F4 120
Harlow, Eng., U.K. — k13 10
Harlowton, Mt., U.S. — D7 103
Harman, Va., U.S. — e9 123
Harman, W.V., U.S. — C5 125
Harmans, Md., U.S. — B4 97
Harmon, Il., U.S. — B4 90
Harmon, Ok., U.S. — A2 113
Harmon, co., Ok., U.S. — C2 113
Harmon Creek, stm., W.V., U.S. — f8 125
Harmonsburg, Pa., U.S. — C1 115
Harmony, In., U.S. — E3 91
Harmony, Mn., U.S. — G6 100
Harmony, N.C., U.S. — B2 110
Harmony, R.I., U.S. — B3 116
Harmony Grove, Ar., U.S. — D3 81
Harmony Hills, De., U.S. — *B3 85
Harmonyville, Vt., U.S. — E3 122
Harned, Ky., U.S. — C3 94
Harnett, co., N.C., U.S. — B4 110
Harney, Or., U.S. — D7 114
Harney, co., Or., U.S. — D7 114
Harney, Lake, l., Fl., U.S. — D5 86
Harney, Lake, l., Or., U.S. — D7 114
Harney Peak, mtn., S.D., U.S. — D2 118
Härnösand, Swe. — F8 14
Haro, Spain — A4 22
Haro, Cabo, c., Mex. — D4 62
Harold, Fl., U.S. — u15 86
Harold Pond, l., Bah. — m17 64
Haro Strait, strt., Wa., U.S. — A2 124
Harper, Lib. — H4 45
Harper, Ks., U.S. — E5 93
Harper, Or., U.S. — D9 114
Harper, Tx., U.S. — D3 120
Harper, co., Ks., U.S. — E5 93
Harper, co., Ok., U.S. — A2 113
Harper, Mount, mtn., Ak., U.S. — C11 79
Harper Woods, Mi., U.S. — *p16 99
Harpers Ferry, Ia., U.S. — A6 92
Harpers Ferry, W.V., U.S. — B7 125
Harpers Ferry National Historical Park, W.V., U.S. — B7 125
Harpersville, Al., U.S. — B3 78
Harpster, Oh., U.S. — B2 112
Harpswell Center, Me., U.S. — *E3 96
Harptree, Sk., Can. — H3 75
Harquahala Mountain, mtn., Az., U.S. — D2 80
Harquahala Mountains, mts., Az., U.S. — D2 80
Harrah, Ok., U.S. — B4 113
Harran, Neth. — B6 17
Ḥarrah, Sau. Ar. — C5 38
Harray, Loch of, l., Scot., U.K. — A5 13
Harrell, Ar., U.S. — D3 81
Harricana, stm., Can. — F17 66
Harriet, Ar., U.S. — A3 81
Harrietta, Mi., U.S. — D5 99

Name	Map Ref	Page

Harriettsville, Oh., U.S. — C4 112
Harriman, Tn., U.S. — D9 119
Harriman, Wy., U.S. — E7 127
Harriman Reservoir, res., Vt., U.S. — F3 122
Harrington, De., U.S. — E8 85
Harrington, Me., U.S. — D5 96
Harrington, Wa., U.S. — B7 124
Harrington Park, N.J., U.S. — h9 107
Harrington Pond, l., Me., U.S. — C3 96
Harrington Sound, strt., Ber. — o20 64
Harriott Lake, l., Sk., Can. — A4 75
Harris, Sk., Can. — F2 75
Harris, Scot., U.K. — B3 10
Harris, Ia., U.S. — A2 92
Harris, Mn., U.S. — E6 100
Harris, Mo., U.S. — A4 102
Harris, Ok., U.S. — D7 113
Harris, R.I., U.S. — D3 116
Harris, Tn., U.S. — A3 119
Harris, co., Ga., U.S. — D2 87
Harris, co., Tx., U.S. — E5 120
Harris, Lake, l., Fl., U.S. — D5 86
Harris, Sound of, strt., Scot., U.K. — C1 13
Harrisburg, Ar., U.S. — B5 81
Harrisburg, Il., U.S. — F5 90
Harrisburg, Mo., U.S. — B5 102
Harrisburg, Ne., U.S. — C2 104
Harrisburg, Oh., U.S. — m10 112
Harrisburg, Or., U.S. — C3 114
Harrisburg, Pa., U.S. — F8 115
Harrisburg, S.D., U.S. — D9 118
Harris Grove, Va., U.S. — h15 123
Harris Hill, hill, Ma., U.S. — A3 98
Harrismith, S. Afr. — C4 49
Harrison, Ar., U.S. — A2 81
Harrison, Ga., U.S. — D4 87
Harrison, Id., U.S. — B2 89
Harrison, Il., U.S. — F4 90
Harrison, Me., U.S. — D2 96
Harrison, Mi., U.S. — D6 99
Harrison, Mt., U.S. — E5 103
Harrison, Ne., U.S. — B2 104
Harrison, N.J., U.S. — k8 107
Harrison, N.Y., U.S. — h13 109
Harrison, Oh., U.S. — C1 112
Harrison, S.D., U.S. — D7 118
Harrison, Tn., U.S. — h11 119
Harrison, co., In., U.S. — H5 91
Harrison, co., Ia., U.S. — C2 92
Harrison, co., Ky., U.S. — B5 94
Harrison, co., Ms., U.S. — E4 101
Harrison, co., Mo., U.S. — A3 102
Harrison, co., Oh., U.S. — B4 112
Harrison, co., Tx., U.S. — C5 120
Harrison, co., W.V., U.S. — B4 125
Harrison, Cape, c., Nf., Can. — g10 72
Harrison Bay, b., Ak., U.S. — A9 79
Harrisonburg, La., U.S. — C4 95
Harrisonburg, Va., U.S. — B4 123
Harrison Hot Springs, B.C., Can. — f14 69
Harrison Lake, l., B.C., Can. — E7 69
Harrison Valley, Pa., U.S. — C6 115
Harrisonville, Il., U.S. — E3 90
Harrisonville, Mo., U.S. — C3 102
Harrisonville, N.J., U.S. — D2 107
Harrisonville, Pa., U.S. — G5 115
Harriston, On., Can. — D4 73
Harriston, Ms., U.S. — D2 101
Harristown, Il., U.S. — D4 90
Harrisville, Ms., U.S. — D3 101
Harrisville, Mi., U.S. — D7 99
Harrisville, N.H., U.S. — E2 106
Harrisville, N.Y., U.S. — A5 109
Harrisville, Pa., U.S. — D1 115
Harrisville, R.I., U.S. — B2 116
Harrisville, Ut., U.S. — B4 121
Harrisville, W.V., U.S. — B3 125
Harrod, Oh., U.S. — B2 112
Harrodsburg, In., U.S. — F4 91
Harrodsburg, Ky., U.S. — C5 94
Harrods Creek, stm., Ky., U.S. — g11 94
Harrogate, Eng., U.K. — C6 10
Harrold, S.D., U.S. — C6 118
Harrold, Tx., U.S. — B3 120
Harrop Lake, l., Mb., Can. — C4 70
Harrow, On., Can. — E2 73
Harrowby, Mb., Can. — D1 70
Harrowsmith, On., Can. — C8 73
Harrys, stm., Nf., Can. — D2 72
Harry S. Truman Reservoir, res., Mo., U.S. — C4 102
Harry Strunk Lake, res., Ne., U.S. — D5 104
Harsin, Iran — D3 39
Harstad, Nor. — C7 14
Hart, Mi., U.S. — E4 99
Hart, Tx., U.S. — B1 120
Hart, co., Ga., U.S. — B4 87
Hart, co., Ky., U.S. — C4 94
Hart, Lake, l., Fl., U.S. — D5 86
Hartell, Ab., Can. — D3 68
Hartfield, Va., U.S. — C6 123
Hartford, Al., U.S. — D4 78
Hartford, Ar., U.S. — B1 81
Hartford, Ct., U.S. — B5 84
Hartford, Il., U.S. — E3 90
Hartford, Ia., U.S. — *G8 92
Hartford, Ks., U.S. — D8 93
Hartford, Ky., U.S. — C3 94
Hartford, Me., U.S. — D2 96
Hartford, Mi., U.S. — F4 99
Hartford, N.J., U.S. — D3 107
Hartford, N.Y., U.S. — B7 109
Hartford, S.D., U.S. — D9 118
Hartford, Tn., U.S. — D10 119
Hartford, Vt., U.S. — D4 122
Hartford, Wi., U.S. — E5 126
Hartford, W.V., U.S. — C2 125
Hartford, co., Ct., U.S. — B4 84
Hartford City, In., U.S. — D7 91
Hartha, Ger.D.R. — B7 19
Hartington, Ne., U.S. — B8 104
Hart Island, i., Md., U.S. — B5 97
Hart Lake, l., Or., U.S. — E7 114
Hartland, N.B., Can. — C2 71
Hartland, Me., U.S. — D3 96
Hartland, Mi., U.S. — F7 99
Hartland, Mn., U.S. — G5 100
Hartland, Vt., U.S. — D4 122
Hartland, W.V., U.S. — m13 125
Hartland Four Corners, Vt., U.S. — D4 122
Hartland Point, c., Eng., U.K. — E4 10
Hartley, Ia., U.S. — A2 92
Hartley, Tx., U.S. — B1 120
Hartley, co., Tx., U.S. — B1 120
Hartline, Wa., U.S. — B6 124
Hartly, De., U.S. — D3 85
Hartman, Ar., U.S. — B2 81

Hartman, Co., U.S. — C8 83
Hart Mountain, mtn., Mb., Can. — C1 70
Hartney, Mb., Can. — E1 70
Hartsburg, Il., U.S. — C4 90
Hartsburg, Mo., U.S. — C5 102
Hartsdale, N.Y., U.S. — *n15 109
Hartsel, Co., U.S. — B5 83
Hartselle, Al., U.S. — A3 78
Hartsfield, Ga., U.S. — E3 87
Hartshorn, Mo., U.S. — D6 102
Hartshorne, Ok., U.S. — C6 113
Hartsville, In., U.S. — F6 91
Hartsville, S.C., U.S. — C7 117
Hartsville, Tn., U.S. — A5 119
Hartville, Mo., U.S. — D5 102
Hartville, Oh., U.S. — B4 112
Hartville, Wy., U.S. — D8 127
Hartwell, Ga., U.S. — B4 87
Hartwell Lake, res., U.S. — B1 117
Hartwick, Ia., U.S. — C5 92
Hartwick, N.Y., U.S. — C5 109
Har Us Lake, l., Mong. — B3 31
Harüt, stm., Afg. — E10 39
Harvard, Id., U.S. — C2 89
Harvard, Il., U.S. — A5 90
Harvard, Ia., U.S. — D4 92
Harvard, Ma., U.S. — B4 98
Harvard, Ne., U.S. — D7 104
Harvard, Mount, mtn., Co., U.S. — C4 83
Harvel, Il., U.S. — D4 90
Harvest, Al., U.S. — A3 78
Harvey, N.B., Can. — D5 71
Harvey, N.B., Can. — D3 71
Harvey, Il., U.S. — B6 90
Harvey, Ia., U.S. — C5 92
Harvey, La., U.S. — E5 95
Harvey, Mi., U.S. — B3 99
Harvey, N.D., U.S. — B6 111
Harvey, W.V., U.S. — n13 125
Harvey, co., Ks., U.S. — D6 93
Harvey Lake, res., Pa., U.S. — m16 115
Harvey Mountain, mtn., U.S. — B1 98
Harveysburg, Oh., U.S. — C1 112
Harveys Creek, stm., Pa., U.S. — n16 115
Harveyville, Ks., U.S. — D8 93
Harwich, Ma., U.S. — C7 98
Harwich, Eng., U.K. — E7 10
Harwich Port, Ma., U.S. — C7 98
Harwinton, Ct., U.S. — B3 84
Harwood, On., Can. — C6 73
Harwood, Md., U.S. — C4 97
Harwood, Mo., U.S. — D3 102
Harwood, N.D., U.S. — C9 111
Harwood Heights, Il., U.S. — *k9 90
Haryāna, state, India — C6 36
Harzgerode, Ger.D.R. — B6 19
Harz Mountains, mts., Eur. — C5 18
Hasa, Wādī al, val., Jord. — D7 41
Hasanah, Bi'r, well, Eg. — D5 41
Hasan Dağı, mtn., Tur. — C10 40
Hasan Kīādeh, Iran — C4 39
Hasbrouck Heights, N.J., U.S. — h8 107
Hasdo, stm., India — F9 37
Hase, stm., F.R.Ger. — B3 18
Haselünne, F.R.Ger. — B3 18
Hashimoto, Japan — o14 33
Hashtpar, Iran — C4 39
Haskell, Ar., U.S. — C3 81
Haskell, Ok., U.S. — B6 113
Haskell, Tx., U.S. — C3 120
Haskell, co., Ks., U.S. — E3 93
Haskell, co., Ok., U.S. — B6 113
Haskell, co., Tx., U.S. — C3 120
Haskins, Oh., U.S. — A2 112
Haslach, Aus. — E9 19
Hasle, Den. — C8 15
Haslemere, Eng., U.K. — C7 12
Haslett, Mi., U.S. — *F6 99
Haslev, Den. — C6 15
Hassan, India — F6 36
Hassayampa, stm., Az., U.S. — D3 80
Hasselt, N.C., U.S. — B5 110
Hasselt, Bel. — B6 16
Hasselt, Neth. — B6 17
Hassfurt, F.R.Ger. — C5 19
Hassi Messaoud, Alg. — C6 44
Hassleben, Ger.D.R. — E7 15
Hässleholm, Swe. — I5 14
Hassloch, F.R.Ger. — B8 19
Hastings, Barb. — K20 65
Hastings, On., Can. — C7 73
Hastings, N.Z. — M16 51
Hastings, Eng., U.K. — E7 10
Hastings, Fl., U.S. — C5 86
Hastings, Ia., U.S. — C2 92
Hastings, Mi., U.S. — F5 99
Hastings, Mn., U.S. — F6 100
Hastings, Ne., U.S. — D7 104
Hastings, Ok., U.S. — C3 113
Hastings, Pa., U.S. — E4 115
Hastings, W.V., U.S. — h9 125
Hastings, co., On., Can. — C7 73
Hastings-on-Hudson, N.Y., U.S. — h13 109
Hästveda, Swe. — B7 15
Hasty, Ar., U.S. — A2 81
Hasty, Co., U.S. — C7 83
Haswell, Co., U.S. — C7 83
Hatboro, Pa., U.S. — *F11 115
Hatch, N.M., U.S. — E2 108
Hatch, Ut., U.S. — F3 121
Hatchechubbee, Al., U.S. — C4 78
Hatchet Lake, l., Sk., Can. — m8 75
Hatchie, stm., Tn., U.S. — B2 119
Hatchville, Ma., U.S. — C6 98
Hatch Wash, val., Ut., U.S. — E6 121
Hat Creek, stm., S.D., U.S. — E2 118
Hateg, Rom. — C6 24
Hatfield, Sk., Can. — F3 75
Hatfield, Ar., U.S. — C1 81
Hatfield, In., U.S. — I3 91
Hatfield, Ma., U.S. — B2 98
Hatfield, Mn., U.S. — G2 100
Hatfield, Pa., U.S. — F11 115
Hāthras, India — D7 37
Ha Tien, Viet. — G6 35
Ha Tinh, Viet. — C8 35
Hatillo, P.R. — B2 65
Hatley, Ga., U.S. — B5 101
Hatley, Wi., U.S. — D4 126
Hat Mountain, mtn., Az., U.S. — E3 80
Hato, Neth. Ant. — H19 65

Hato, Bocht van, b., Neth. Ant. — H19 65
Hato Mayor [del Rey], Dom. Rep. — E9 64
Hatta, India — E7 37
Hattem, Neth. — B6 17
Hatteras, N.C., U.S. — B7 110
Hatteras, Cape, c., N.C., U.S. — B7 110
Hatteras Inlet, b., N.C., U.S. — B7 110
Hattfjelldal, Nor. — E6 14
Hattiesburg, Ms., U.S. — D4 101
Hattieville, Ar., U.S. — B3 81
Hattingen, F.R.Ger. — *C3 18
Hatton, Sk., Can. — G1 75
Hatton, Al., U.S. — A2 78
Hatton, Ar., U.S. — C1 81
Hatton, N.D., U.S. — B8 111
Hatvan, Hung. — B4 24
Hat Yai (Ban Hat Yai), Thai. — D2 34
Hatzic, B.C., Can. — f13 69
Hau Bon, Viet. — F8 35
Haubourdin, Fr. — D3 17
Haubstadt, In., U.S. — H2 91
Haugan, Mt., U.S. — C1 103
Haugen, Wi., U.S. — C2 126
Haugesund, Nor. — H1 14
Haughton, La., U.S. — B2 95
Haultain, stm., Sk., Can. — A2 75
Hauppauge, N.Y., U.S. — *n15 109
Hauraki Gulf, b., N.Z. — L15 51
Hausach, F.R.Ger. — A4 20
Hauser, Or., U.S. — D2 114
Hauser Dam, Mt., U.S. — D5 103
Haus Stock, mtn., Switz. — C7 21
Haut, Isle au, i., Me., U.S. — D4 96
Haut Atlas, mts., Mor. — C3 44
Haute-Marne, dept., Fr. — A1 20
Hauterive, P.Q., Can. — k13 74
Hautes-Alpes, dept., Fr. — E2 20
Haute-Saône, dept., Fr. — B2 20
Haute-Savoie, dept., Fr. — C2 20
Hautes Fagnes, mts., Eur. — D6 17
Hautmont, Fr. — B5 16
Haut-Rhin, dept., Fr. — B3 20
Hauula, Hi., U.S. — B4 88
Hauzenberg, F.R.Ger. — E8 19
Havana (La Habana), Cuba — C2 64
Havana, Al., U.S. — C2 78
Havana, Ar., U.S. — B2 81
Havana, Fl., U.S. — B2 86
Havana, Il., U.S. — C3 90
Havana, Ks., U.S. — E8 93
Havana, N.D., U.S. — D8 111
Havana Nakya, Az., U.S. — E4 80
Havasu, Lake, res., U.S. — C1 80
Havasupai Indian Reservation, Az., U.S. — A3 80
Havel, stm., Eur. — F6 15
Havelberg, Ger.D.R. — F6 15
Havelock, N.B., Can. — D4 71
Havelock, On., Can. — C7 73
Havelock, Ia., U.S. — B3 92
Havelock, N.C., U.S. — C6 110
Haven, Ks., U.S. — E6 93
Haven, Wi., U.S. — k10 126
Haverford [Township], Pa., U.S. — o20 115
Haverfordwest, Wales, U.K. — C3 12
Haverhill, Eng., U.K. — B8 12
Haverhill, Ma., U.S. — A5 98
Haverhill, N.H., U.S. — B2 106
Haversham, R.I., U.S. — C2 116
Haverstraw, N.Y., U.S. — D7 109
Havertown, Pa., U.S. — G11 115
Haviland, Ks., U.S. — E4 93
Haviland, Oh., U.S. — A1 112
Havířov, Czech. — *D5 26
Havlíčkuv Brod, Czech. — D3 26
Havre-Aubert, P.Q., Can. — B8 71
Havre Aubert, Île du, i., P.Q., Can. — B8 71
Havre-aux-Maisons, P.Q., Can. — B8 71
Havre aux Maisons, Île du, i., P.Q., Can. — B8 71
Havre Boucher, N.S., Can. — D8 71
Havre de Grace, Md., U.S. — A5 97
Havre North, Mt., U.S. — B7 103
Havre Saint Pierre, P.Q., Can. — h9 72
Havza, Tur. — B10 40
Hawaii, co., Hi., U.S. — D6 88
Hawaii, state, U.S. — C5 88
Hawaii, i., Hi., U.S. — D6 88
Hawaiian Gardens, Ca., U.S. — *n12 82
Hawaiian Islands, is., Hi., U.S. — m14 88
Hawaii Volcanoes National Park, Hi., U.S. — D6 88
Hawarden, Sk., Can. — F2 75
Hawarden, Ia., U.S. — A1 92
Hawea, Lake, l., N.Z. — P12 51
Hawera, N.Z. — M15 51
Hawes, Eng., U.K. — F6 13
Hawesville, Ky., U.S. — C3 94
Hawi, Hi., U.S. — C6 88
Hawick, Scot., U.K. — C5 10
Hawke Bay, b., N.Z. — M16 51
Hawke Island, i., Nf., Can. — B4 72
Hawker, Austl. — E2 51
Hawkes, Mount, mtn., Ant. — A7 7
Hawkesbury, On., Can. — B10 73
Hawkesbury Island, i., B.C., Can. — C3 69
Hawkestone, On., Can. — C5 73
Hawkeye, Ia., U.S. — B6 92
Hawkins, Wi., U.S. — C2 126
Hawkins, co., Tn., U.S. — C11 119
Hawkinsville, Ga., U.S. — D3 87
Hawk Lake, On., Can. — E5 70
Haw Knob, mtn., U.S. — D9 119
Hawk Point, Mo., U.S. — C6 102
Hawksbill, mtn., Va., U.S. — B4 123
Hawk Springs, Wy., U.S. — D8 127
Hawley, Mn., U.S. — D2 100
Hawley, Tx., U.S. — C3 120
Hawleyville, Ct., U.S. — D2 84
Haworth, N.J., U.S. — h9 107
Haworth, Ok., U.S. — D7 113
Haw River, N.C., U.S. — A3 110
Hawsh 'Īsā, Eg. — B3 41
Hawthorn, Fl., U.S. — C4 86
Hawthorne, Fl., U.S. — C4 86
Hawthorne, Nv., U.S. — E3 105
Hawthorne, N.J., U.S. — B4 107
Hawthorne, N.Y., U.S. — g13 109
Hawthorne, Wi., U.S. — B2 126
Haxtun, Co., U.S. — A8 83
Hay, Austl. — F7 50
Hay, Wa., U.S. — *C8 124
Hay, stm., Austl. — D6 50

Hay, stm., Can. — E9 66
Hayange, Fr. — C7 16
Haybes, Fr. — D4 17
Hayden, Al., U.S. — B3 78
Hayden, Az., U.S. — E5 80
Hayden, Co., U.S. — A3 83
Hayden, Id., U.S. — *B2 89
Hayden, In., U.S. — G6 91
Haydenburg, Tn., U.S. — C8 119
Hayden Lake, l., Id., U.S. — B2 89
Haydenville, Ma., U.S. — B2 98
Haydenville, Oh., U.S. — C3 112
Hayes, La., U.S. — D3 95
Hayes, S.D., U.S. — C4 118
Hayes, co., Ne., U.S. — D4 104
Hayes, stm., Mb., Can. — A5 70
Hayes, Mount, mtn., Ak., U.S. — C10 79
Hayes Center, Ne., U.S. — D4 104
Hayesville, N.C., U.S. — f9 110
Hayesville, Oh., U.S. — B3 112
Hayesville, Or., U.S. — *C4 114
Hayfield, Mb., Can. — E1 70
Hayfield, Ia., U.S. — A4 92
Hayfield, Mn., U.S. — G6 100
Hayford, Wa., U.S. — g13 124
Hayfork, Ca., U.S. — B2 82
Hayford Peak, mtn., Nv., U.S. — G6 105
Hay Island, i., On., Can. — C4 73
Hay Lakes, Ab., Can. — C4 68
Haylow, Ga., U.S. — F4 87
Haymana, Tur. — C9 40
Haymarket, Va., U.S. — B5 123
Haymock Lake, l., Me., U.S. — B3 96
Haymond, In., U.S. — F7 91
Haynes, Ab., Can. — C4 68
Haynes, Ar., U.S. — C5 81
Haynes, N.D., U.S. — D3 111
Haynesville, La., U.S. — B2 95
Haynesville, Me., U.S. — C5 96
Hayneville, Al., U.S. — C3 78
Hay-on-Wye, Wales, U.K. — B4 12
Hay River, N.T., Can. — D9 66
Hays, Ks., U.S. — C4 93
Hays, Mt., U.S. — C8 103
Hays, N.C., U.S. — A1 110
Hays, co., Tx., U.S. — D3 120
Hays Canyon Peak, mtn., Nv., U.S. — B2 105
Haysi, Va., U.S. — e9 123
Haysī, Bi'r al, well, Eg. — E6 41
Hay Springs, Ne., U.S. — B3 104
Haystack Mountain, mtn., Ct., U.S. — B3 84
Haystack Mountain, mtn., U.S. — B6 105
Haysville, In., U.S. — H4 91
Haysville, Ks., U.S. — g12 93
Haysville, Tn., U.S. — A5 119
Hayter, Ab., Can. — C5 68
Hayti, Mo., U.S. — E8 102
Hayti, S.D., U.S. — C8 118
Hayti Heights, Mo., U.S. — E8 102
Hayton, Wi., U.S. — h9 126
Hayward, Ca., U.S. — h8 82
Hayward, Ok., U.S. — A4 113
Hayward, Wi., U.S. — C2 126
Hayward Addition, S.D., U.S. — *D8 118
Haywards Heath, Eng., U.K. — C7 12
Haywood, Mb., Can. — E2 70
Haywood, N.C., U.S. — B3 110
Haywood, Ok., U.S. — C6 113
Haywood, co., N.C., U.S. — f9 110
Haywood, co., Tn., U.S. — B2 119
Hazard, Ky., U.S. — C6 94
Hazard, Ne., U.S. — C6 104
Hazardville, Ct., U.S. — B5 84
Hazārībāgh, India — E10 37
Hazawzā', Sabkhat, l., Sau. Ar. — G12 40
Hazebrouck, Fr. — B5 16
Hazel, Ky., U.S. — f9 94
Hazel, S.D., U.S. — C8 118
Hazel Crest, Il., U.S. — k9 90
Hazel Dell, Il., U.S. — D5 90
Hazel Dell, Wa., U.S. — D3 124
Hazel Green, Al., U.S. — A3 78
Hazel Green, Ky., U.S. — C6 94
Hazel Green, Wi., U.S. — F3 126
Hazel Hurst, Pa., U.S. — C4 115
Hazelhurst, Ms., U.S. — D3 101
Hazelhurst, N.C., U.S. — f9 110
Hazel Park, Mi., U.S. — p15 99
Hazel Run, Mn., U.S. — F2 100
Hazelton, B.C., Can. — B4 69
Hazelton, Id., U.S. — G4 89
Hazelton, Ks., U.S. — E5 93
Hazelton, N.D., U.S. — C5 111
Hazelton Peak, mtn., Wy., U.S. — B5 127
Hazelwood, Mo., U.S. — *f13 102
Hazelwood, N.C., U.S. — f9 110
Hazen, Ar., U.S. — C4 81
Hazen, Nv., U.S. — D2 105
Hazen, N.D., U.S. — B4 111
Hazen, stm., Nf., Can. — B3 72
Hazen Bay, b., Ak., U.S. — C6 79
Hazenmore, Sk., Can. — H2 75
Hazen Strait, strt., N.T., Can. — m29 66
Hazlehurst, Al., U.S. — E4 87
Hazlehurst, Ms., U.S. — D3 101
Hazlet, Sk., Can. — G1 75
Hazlet, N.J., U.S. — C4 107
Hazleton, In., U.S. — H2 91
Hazleton, Ia., U.S. — B6 92
Hazleton, Pa., U.S. — E10 115
Hazlett, Lake, l., Austl. — D4 50
Hazlettville, De., U.S. — D3 85
Hazor, Isr. — B7 41
Hazor Ashdod, Isr. — D3 41
Head Bay d'Espoir, Nf., Can. — E4 72
Head Harbor Island, i., Me., U.S. — D5 96
Headland, Al., U.S. — D4 78
Headley, Mount, mtn., Mt., U.S. — C1 103
Head of Island, La., U.S. — h10 95
Headrick, Ok., U.S. — C2 113
Heafford Junction, Wi., U.S. — C4 126
Healdsburg, Ca., U.S. — C2 82
Healdton, Ok., U.S. — C4 113
Healdville, Vt., U.S. — E3 122
Healing Springs, Va., U.S. — C3 123
Healy, Ak., U.S. — C10 79
Healy, Ks., U.S. — D3 93
Heanor, Eng., U.K. — (---)
Heard, co., Ga., U.S. — C1 87
Heard Island, i., Austl. — j1 2
Hearne, Sk., Can. — G3 75
Hearne, Tx., U.S. — D4 120
Hearst, On., Can. — o19 73

Hearst Island, i., Ant. — C6 7
Heart, stm., Ab., Can. — B2 68
Heart, stm., N.D., U.S. — C3 111
Heart Butte, Mt., U.S. — B4 103
Heart Butte Dam, N.D., U.S. — C4 111
Hearthstone Mountain, mtn., Md., U.S. — A2 97
Heart Lake, l., Ab., Can. — B5 68
Heart Lake, l., Wy., U.S. — B2 127
Heart's Content, Nf., Can. — E5 72
Heartwell, Ne., U.S. — D7 104
Heaters, W.V., U.S. — C4 125
Heath, Al., U.S. — D3 78
Heath, Ma., U.S. — A2 98
Heath, Oh., U.S. — B3 112
Heath Springs, S.C., U.S. — B6 117
Heathsville, Va., U.S. — C6 123
Heaton, N.D., U.S. — B6 111
Heavener, Ok., U.S. — C7 113
Hebbronville, Tx., U.S. — F3 120
Hebel, Austl. — G8 51
Heber, Az., U.S. — C5 80
Heber City, Ut., U.S. — C4 121
Heber Springs, Ar., U.S. — B3 81
Hebert, La., U.S. — B4 95
Hébertville, P.Q., Can. — A6 74
Hebgen Lake, res., Mt., U.S. — F5 103
Hebo, Or., U.S. — B3 114
Hebrides, Sea of the, Scot., U.K. — B3 10
Hebron, Nf., Can. — f9 72
Hebron, N.S., Can. — F3 71
Hebron (Al Khalīl), Isr. Occ. — G10 40
Hebron, Ct., U.S. — C6 84
Hebron, Il., U.S. — A5 90
Hebron, In., U.S. — B3 91
Hebron, Ky., U.S. — h13 94
Hebron, Me., U.S. — D2 96
Hebron, Md., U.S. — D6 97
Hebron, Ne., U.S. — D8 104
Hebron, N.H., U.S. — C3 106
Hebron, N.D., U.S. — C3 111
Hebron, Oh., U.S. — C3 112
Hebron, Tx., U.S. — m10 120
Hebron, W.V., U.S. — B3 125
Heby, Swe. — t34 14
Hecate Strait, strt., B.C., Can. — C2 69
Hecelchakán, Mex. — C6 63
Heceta Island, i., Ak., U.S. — n23 79
Hechingen, F.R.Ger. — D4 18
Hechtel, Bel. — C5 17
Hechuan, China — E8 31
Hecker, Il., U.S. — E4 90
Hecklingen, Ger.D.R. — B6 19
Hecla, Mb., Can. — D3 70
Hecla, S.D., U.S. — B7 118
Hecla Island, i., Mb., Can. — D3 70
Hectanooga, N.S., Can. — E3 71
Hector, Ar., U.S. — B3 81
Hector, Mn., U.S. — F4 100
Hede, Swe. — F5 14
Hedemora, Swe. — G6 14
Hedensted, Den. — C3 15
He Devil, mtn., Id., U.S. — D2 89
Hedgehog Hill, hill, Ct., U.S. — B7 84
Hedges, Fl., U.S. — k8 86
Hedgesville, W.V., U.S. — B7 125
Hedley, B.C., Can. — E7 69
Hedley, Tx., U.S. — B2 120
Hedo, Japan — N6 52
Hedon, Eng., U.K. — A7 12
Hedo Cape, c., Japan — N6 52
Hedrick, Ia., U.S. — C5 92
Heek, F.R.Ger. — A2 19
Heel Point, c., Wake I. — A2 52
Heeney, Co., U.S. — B4 83
Heerde, Neth. — B6 17
Heerenveen, Neth. — A6 16
Heerlen, Neth. — D6 17
Heessen, F.R.Ger. — B2 19
Hefa, Mifraz (Bay of Haifa), b., Isr. — B6 41
Hefei, China — E8 31
Heflin, Al., U.S. — B4 78
Heflin, La., U.S. — B2 95
Hegang, China — B11 31
Hegins, Pa., U.S. — E9 115
Heide, F.R.Ger. — A4 18
Heidelberg, Austl. — *G8 50
Heidelberg, P.Q., Can. — D3 74
Heidelberg, S. Afr. — D3 49
Heidelberg, Ms., U.S. — D5 101
Heiden, Switz. — B8 21
Heidenau, Ger.D.R. — B7 19
Heidenheim, F.R.Ger. — D5 18
Heidrick, Ky., U.S. — D6 94
Heil, N.D., U.S. — C4 111
Heilbron, S. Afr. — D4 49
Heilbronn, F.R.Ger. — D4 18
Heiligenblut, Aus. — H13 (---)
Heiligenhafen, F.R.Ger. — A5 18
Heiligenstadt, Ger.D.R. — C5 18
Heilongjiang, prov., China — B10 31
Heilong Jiang (Amur), stm., Asia — B10 31
Heilungkiang see Heilongjiang, prov., China — B10 31
Heilwood, Pa., U.S. — E4 115
Heimbach, F.R.Ger. — D6 17
Heimdal, N.D., U.S. — B6 111
Heimenkirch, F.R.Ger. — A8 21
Heinola, Fin. — G12 14
Heinsberg, F.R.Ger. — C6 17
Heinsburg, Ab., Can. — C5 68
Heiskell, Tn., U.S. — m13 119
Heisler, Ab., Can. — C4 68
Heislerville, N.J., U.S. — E3 107
Heizer, Ks., U.S. — D5 93
Hejaz, reg., Sau. Ar. — E7 32
Hejan, China — E7 32
Hekla, Mount, vol., Ice. — n23 14
Hel, Pol. — A4 26
Helagsfjället, mtn., Swe. — F5 14
Helan Mountains, mts., China — D6 31
Helbra, Ger.D.R. — B6 19
Helena, Al., U.S. — B3 78
Helena, Ar., U.S. — C5 81
Helena, Ca., U.S. — B2 82
Helena, Ga., U.S. — D4 87
Helena, Mo., U.S. — B3 102
Helena, Mt., U.S. — D5 103
Helena, N.Y., U.S. — f10 109
Helena, Oh., U.S. — A2 112
Helena, Ok., U.S. — A3 113

Heli, China — C5 33
Helicon see Elikón Óros, mtn., Grc. — g9 25
Helix, Or., U.S. — B8 114
Hellam, Pa., U.S. — G8 115
Hellenthal, F.R.Ger. — D6 17
Hellertown, Pa., U.S. — E11 115
Hellín, Spain — C5 22
Hells Canyon, val., U.S. — B10 114
Hells Canyon National Recreation Area, U.S. — B10 114
Hell-Ville, Madag. — f9 49
Helm, Ca., U.S. — D3 82
Helmand, stm., Asia — B3 36
Helmbrechts, F.R.Ger. — C6 19
Helmer, Id., U.S. — *C2 89
Helmer, In., U.S. — A7 91
Helmeringhausen, Nmb. — C2 49
Helmetta, N.J., U.S. — C4 107
Helmond, Neth. — B6 17
Helmsdale, Scot., U.K. — A5 10
Helmsley, Eng., U.K. — F7 13
Helmstedt, F.R.Ger. — B5 18
Helmville, Mt., U.S. — D4 103
Helotes, Tx., U.S. — h7 120
Helper, Ut., U.S. — D5 121
Helsingborg, Swe. — I5 14
Helsinger, Den. — I5 14
Helsinki, Fin. — G11 14
Helston, Eng., U.K. — D2 12
Heltonville, In., U.S. — G5 91
Helvecia, Arg. — A4 54
Helvellyn, mtn., Eng., U.K. — F6 13
Helvetia, Pa., U.S. — D4 115
Helvick Head, c., Ire. — E4 11
Hemaruka, Ab., Can. — D5 68
Hematite, Mo., U.S. — C7 102
Hemau, F.R.Ger. — D6 19
Hemel Hempstead, Eng., U.K. — k12 10
Hemet, Ca., U.S. — F5 82
Hemford, N.S., Can. — E5 71
Hemingford, Ne., U.S. — B2 104
Hemingway, S.C., U.S. — D9 117
Hemlock, In., U.S. — D5 91
Hemlock, Mi., U.S. — E6 99
Hemlock, N.Y., U.S. — C3 109
Hemlock Reservoir, res., Ct., U.S. — E2 84
Hemmesta, Swe. — t36 14
Hemmingford, P.Q., Can. — D4 74
Hemnesberget, Nor. — D5 14
Hemphill, Tx., U.S. — D6 120
Hemphill, co., Tx., U.S. — B2 120
Hemple, Mo., U.S. — B3 102
Hempstead, N.Y., U.S. — n15 109
Hempstead, Tx., U.S. — D4 120
Hempstead, co., Ar., U.S. — D2 81
Henagar, Al., U.S. — A4 78
Henan, prov., China — E7 31

Henderson, Arg. — B4 54
Henderson, Al., U.S. — D3 78
Henderson, Co., U.S. — B6 83
Henderson, Ia., U.S. — C2 92
Henderson, Ky., U.S. — C2 94
Henderson, La., U.S. — D4 95
Henderson, Md., U.S. — B6 97
Henderson, Mn., U.S. — F5 100
Henderson, Ne., U.S. — D8 104
Henderson, Nv., U.S. — G7 105
Henderson, N.Y., U.S. — A4 109
Henderson, N.C., U.S. — A4 110
Henderson, Tn., U.S. — B3 119
Henderson, Tx., U.S. — C5 120
Henderson, W.V., U.S. — C3 125
Henderson, co., Il., U.S. — C3 90
Henderson, co., Ky., U.S. — C2 94
Henderson, co., N.C., U.S. — f10 110
Henderson, co., Tn., U.S. — B3 119
Henderson, co., Tx., U.S. — C5 120
Henderson's Point, Ms., U.S. — g7 101
Hendersonville, N.C., U.S. — f10 110
Hendersonville, Tn., U.S. — A5 119
Hendījān, Iran — F4 39
Hendley, Ne., U.S. — D6 104
Hendon, Sk., Can. — E4 75
Hendorābī, i., Iran — H6 39
Hendricks, Mn., U.S. — F2 100
Hendricks, W.V., U.S. — B5 125
Hendricks, co., In., U.S. — E4 91
Hendrix, Ok., U.S. — D5 113
Hendrum, Mn., U.S. — C2 100
Hendry, co., Fl., U.S. — F5 86
Hengelo, Neth. — A7 16
Hengshan, China — K5 32
Hengshan, China — F3 32
Hengyang, China — F7 31
Hénin-Beaumont, Fr. — D2 17

Henlawson, W.V., U.S. — n12 125
Henley Harbour, Nf., Can. — B4 72
Henley-on-Thames, Eng., U.K. — C7 12
Henlopen, Cape, c., De., U.S. — E5 85
Henlopen Acres, De., U.S. — F5 85
Hennebont, Fr. — D2 16
Hennef, F.R.Ger. — C2 19
Hennepin, Il., U.S. — B4 90
Hennepin, Ok., U.S. — C4 113
Hennepin, co., Mn., U.S. — E5 100
Hennessey, Ok., U.S. — A4 113
Henniker, N.H., U.S. — D3 106
Henning, Il., U.S. — C6 90
Henning, Mn., U.S. — D3 100
Henning, Tn., U.S. — B2 119
Henricoburg, Va., U.S. — C5 123
Henrico, co., Va., U.S. — C5 123
Henrietta, N.Y., U.S. — B3 109
Henrietta, N.C., U.S. — B1 110
Henrietta, Tx., U.S. — C3 120
Henrietta, i., Sov. Un. — B35 128
Henrietta Maria, Cape, c., On., Can. — n19 73
Henrieville, Ut., U.S. — F4 121
Henry, Il., U.S. — B4 90
Henry, Ne., U.S. — C1 104
Henry, S.D., U.S. — C8 118
Henry, co., Al., U.S. — D4 78
Henry, co., Ga., U.S. — C2 87
Henry, co., Il., U.S. — B3 90

Name	Map Ref	Page
Henry, co., In., U.S.	E7	91
Henry, co., Ia., U.S.	C6	92
Henry, co., Ky., U.S.	B4	94
Henry, co., Mo., U.S.	C4	102
Henry, co., Oh., U.S.	A1	112
Henry, co., Tn., U.S.	A3	119
Henry, co., Va., U.S.	D3	123
Henry, Mount, mtn., Mt., U.S.	B1	103
Henryetta, Ok., U.S.	B6	113
Henry Kater, Cape, c., N.T., Can.	C19	66
Henry Mountains, mts., Ut., U.S.	E5	121
Henry Pittier National Park, Ven.	A4	60
Henrys Fork, stm., U.S.	E2	127
Henryville, P.Q., Can.	D4	74
Henryville, In., U.S.	G6	91
Henryville, Ky., U.S.	B5	94
Hensall, On., Can.	D3	73
Hensel, N.D., U.S.	A8	111
Henshaw, Ky., U.S.	e9	94
Hensler, N.D., U.S.	B4	111
Hensley, Ar., U.S.	C3	81
Henson Creek, stm., Md., U.S.	f9	97
Hentiyn Mountains, mts., Mong.	B6	31
Henzada, Burma	E10	36
Hepburn, On., Can.	E2	75
Hepburn, Ia., U.S.	D2	92
Hepburn, Oh., U.S.	B2	112
Hephzibah, Ga., U.S.	C4	87
Hepler, Ks., U.S.	E9	93
Heppenheim, F.R.Ger.	D3	19
Heppner, Or., U.S.	B7	114
Hepu, China	G6	31
Hepworth, On., Can.	C3	73
Heqing, China	F5	31
Herät, Afg.	B3	36
Herbert, Sk., Can.	G2	75
Herbertingen, F.R.Ger.		
Herbert Peak, mtn., N.Z.	O14	51
Herbes, Isle aux, i., Al., U.S.	E1	78
Herb Lake, l., Mb., Can.	B2	70
Herblay, Fr.	g9	16
Herblet Lake, l., Mb., Can.	B2	70
Herborn, F.R.Ger.	C3	19
Herceg-Novi, Yugo.	D4	24
Hercegovina, hist reg., Yugo.	D4	24
Herculaneum, Mo., U.S.	C7	102
Hercules, Ca., U.S.	*g8	82
Herdecke, F.R.Ger.	B2	19
Heredia, C.R.	E8	63
Hereford, Eng., U.K.	D5	10
Hereford, Az., U.S.	F5	80
Hereford, Co., U.S.	A6	83
Hereford, Md., U.S.	A4	97
Hereford, Or., U.S.	C8	114
Hereford, S.D., U.S.	C3	118
Hereford, Tx., U.S.	B1	120
Hereford and Worcester, co., Eng., U.K.	B5	12
Hereford Inlet, b., N.J., U.S.	E3	107
Hérémence, Switz.	C4	22
Herencia, Spain	C4	17
Herentals, Bel.	C6	15
Herford, F.R.Ger.	B4	18
Héricourt, Fr.	B2	20
Hérimoncourt, Fr.	B2	21
Herington, Ks., U.S.	D7	93
Herisau, Switz.	E4	18
Heritage Range, mts., Ant.	B4	7
Heritage Village, Ct., U.S.	D3	84
Herkimer, Ks., U.S.	C7	93
Herkimer, N.Y., U.S.	B6	109
Herkimer, co., N.Y., U.S.	B5	109
Herman, Mn., U.S.	B2	99
Herman, Ne., U.S.	E2	100
Herman, Pa., U.S.	C9	104
Hermann, Mo., U.S.	C6	102
Hermano Peak, mtn., Co., U.S.	D2	83
Hermansville, Mi., U.S.	C3	99
Hermantown, Mn., U.S.	D6	100
Hermanville, Ms., U.S.	D3	101
Hermeskeil, F.R.Ger.	D1	19
Herminie, Pa., U.S.	F2	115
Hermiston, Or., U.S.	B7	114
Hermitage, Nf., Can.	E4	72
Hermitage, Ar., U.S.	D3	81
Hermitage, La., U.S.	D4	95
Hermitage, Mo., U.S.	D4	102
Hermitage, Pa., U.S.	*D1	115
Hermitage Bay, b., Nf., Can.	E3	72
Hermitage Springs, Tn., U.S.	C8	119
Hermleigh, Tx., U.S.	C2	120
Hermon, Me., U.S.	*D4	96
Hermon, N.Y., U.S.	f9	109
Hermon, Mount, mtn., Asia	F11	40
Hermosa, S.D., U.S.	D2	118
Hermosa Beach, Ca., U.S.	*n12	82
Hermosillo, Mex.	B2	63
Hernád, stm., Eur.	A5	24
Hernandarias, Para.	E5	55
Hernández, N.M., U.S.	A3	108
Hernando, Fl., U.S.	D4	86
Hernando, Ms., U.S.	A4	101
Hernando, co., Fl., U.S.	D4	86
Herndon, Ga., U.S.	C3	87
Herndon, Ia., U.S.	C3	92
Herndon, Ks., U.S.	C3	93
Herndon, Pa., U.S.	D2	94
Herndon, Va., U.S.	E8	115
Herndon, W.V., U.S.	B5	123
Herne, F.R.Ger.	D3	125
Herning, Den.	B2	19
Heroa's Gate, hist., Isr Occ.	I3	14
Heroica Caborca, Mex.	m14	41
Heroica Nogales, Mex.	A2	63
Heron, Mt., U.S.	A2	63
Heron Bay, Al., U.S.	B1	103
Heron Lake, Mn., U.S.	E1	78
Hérouville, P.Q., Can.	G3	100
Herreid, S.D., U.S.	C5	74
Herrenberg, F.R.Ger.	B5	118
Herrick, Il., U.S.	D5	90
Herrick, S.D., U.S.	D6	118
Herrick Center, Pa., U.S.	C11	115
Herrick Creek, stm., B.C., Can.	B7	69
Herrick Mountain, mtn., Vt., U.S.	D2	122
Herriman, Ut., U.S.	*C3	121
Herrin, Il., U.S.	F4	90
Herring Bay, b., Md., U.S.	C4	97
Herring Cove, N.S., Can.	E6	71
Herring Run, stm., Md., U.S.	g11	97
Herrington Lake, res., Ky., U.S.	C5	94
Hersbruck, F.R.Ger.	D6	19
Herschel, Sk., Can.	F1	75
Herscher, Il., U.S.	B5	90
Hersey, Mi., U.S.	E5	99
Hershey, Ne., U.S.	C5	104
Hershey, Pa., U.S.	F8	115
Herstal, Bel.	B6	16
Herten, F.R.Ger.	*C3	18
Hertford, Eng., U.K.	E6	10
Hertford, N.C., U.S.	A6	110
Hertford, co., N.C., U.S.	A5	110
Hertfordshire, co., Eng., U.K.	C7	12
Hervás, Spain	B3	22
Hervey Bay, b., Austl.	D9	50
Hervey-Jonction, P.Q., Can.	C5	74
Herxheim, F.R.Ger.	D3	19
Herzberg, Ger.D.R.	F7	15
Herzberg, Ger.D.R.	B8	19
Herzberg [am Harz], F.R.Ger.	B5	19
Herzliyya, Isr.	F10	40
Herzogenaurach, F.R.Ger.	D5	19
Herzogenbuchsee, Switz.	B4	21
Hesdin, Fr.	D2	17
Hesel, F.R.Ger.	A7	17
Hess, Ok., U.S.	B6	113
Hessel, Mi., U.S.	B6	99
Hesselager, Den.	C4	15
Hessele, l., Fr.	B5	15
Hessen, state, F.R.Ger.	C3	19
Hessmer, La., U.S.	C3	95
Hesston, Ks., U.S.	D6	93
Hetland, S.D., U.S.	C8	118
Hettick, Il., U.S.	D3	90
Hettinger, N.D., U.S.	D3	111
Hettinger, co., N.D., U.S.	C3	111
Hettstedt, Ger.D.R.	B6	19
Heusler, N.D., U.S.	I2	91
Heuvelton, N.Y., U.S.	f9	109
Heves, Hung.	B5	24
Heward, Sk., Can.	H4	75
Hewins, Ks., U.S.	E7	93
Hewitt, Mn., U.S.	D3	100
Hewitt, N.J., U.S.	A4	107
Hewitt, Tx., U.S.	*D4	120
Hewitt, Wi., U.S.	D3	126
Hewlett, N.Y., U.S.	*n14	109
Hexian, China	G7	31
Hexigten Qi, China	C7	32
Hext, Tx., U.S.	D3	120
Heyang, China	G4	32
Heyburn, Id., U.S.	G5	89
Heyworth, Il., U.S.	C5	90
Heze, China	G2	32
Hialeah, Fl., U.S.	G6	86
Hiawassee, Ga., U.S.	B3	87
Hiawatha, Ks., U.S.	C8	93
Hiawatha, Ut., U.S.	D4	121
Hiawatha Camp, Co., U.S.	A2	83
Hibbard, In., U.S.	B5	91
Hibbing, Mn., U.S.	C6	100
Hickam Air Force Base, mil., Hi., U.S.	g10	88
Hickiwan, Az., U.S.	E3	80
Hickman, De., U.S.	E3	85
Hickman, Ky., U.S.	f8	94
Hickman, Ne., U.S.	D9	104
Hickman, co., Ky., U.S.	f8	94
Hickman, co., Tn., U.S.	B4	119
Hickman's Harbour, Nf., Can.	D5	72
Hickok, Ks., U.S.	E2	93
Hickory, Ky., U.S.	f9	94
Hickory, Ms., U.S.	C4	101
Hickory, N.C., U.S.	B1	110
Hickory, Ok., U.S.	C5	113
Hickory, co., Mo., U.S.	D4	102
Hickory Corners, Mi., U.S.	F5	99
Hickory Flat, Ms., U.S.	A4	101
Hickory Grove, S.C., U.S.	B5	117
Hickory Hills, Il., U.S.	*k9	90
Hickory Plains, Ar., U.S.	C4	81
Hickory Ridge, Ar., U.S.	B5	81
Hickory Valley, Tn., U.S.	B2	119
Hickory Withe, Tn., U.S.	B2	119
Hickox, Ga., U.S.	E5	87
Hicks, La., U.S.	C2	95
Hicks, Point, c., Austl.	H7	51
Hickson, On., Can.	D4	73
Hickson Lake, l., Sk., Can.	A3	75
Hicksville, N.Y., U.S.	E7	109
Hicksville, Oh., U.S.	A1	112
Hico, Tx., U.S.	D3	120
Hico, W.V., U.S.	C3	125
Hida, stm., Japan	n16	33
Hidalgo, Il., U.S.	D5	90
Hidalgo, Tx., U.S.	F3	120
Hidalgo, state, Mex.	C5	63
Hidalgo, co., N.M., U.S.	F1	108
Hidalgo, co., Tx., U.S.	F3	120
Hidalgo del Parral, Mex.	B3	63
Hiddenite, N.C., U.S.	B1	110
Hiddensee, i., Ger.D.R.	D7	15
Hideaway Park, Co., U.S.	B5	83
Hidrolina, Braz.	A3	56
Hieroglyphic Mountains, mts., Az., U.S.	k8	80
Hierro, i., Spain	n13	22
Higashi, Japan	N6	52
Higashiizu, Japan	o18	33
Higashiōsaka, Japan	I7	33
Higbee, Mo., U.S.	B5	102
Higden, Ar., U.S.	B3	81
Higdon, Al., U.S.	A4	78
Higganum, Ct., U.S.	D5	84
Higgins, Tx., U.S.	A2	120
Higgins Lake, Mi., U.S.	D6	99
Higgins Lake, l., Mi., U.S.	D6	99
Higgins Millpond, res., Md., U.S.	C6	97
Higginson, Ar., U.S.	B4	81
Higginsport, Oh., U.S.	D2	112
Higginsville, Mo., U.S.	B4	102
High Bluff, Mb., Can.	D2	70
High Bridge, N.J., U.S.	C5	99
High Bridge, N.H., U.S.	E3	106
High Bridge, N.J., U.S.	B3	107
Highfalls, N.C., U.S.	B3	110
High Falls Reservoir, res., Wi., U.S.	C5	126
Highfield, Md., U.S.	A3	97
Highgate Falls, Vt., U.S.	B2	122
High Hill, On., Can.	E3	73
High Hill, Mo., U.S.	C6	102
High Hill, stm., Can.	A5	68
High Hill Lake, l., Mb., Can.	B4	70
High Island, Tx., U.S.	E5	120
High Island, i., Mi., U.S.	C5	99
High Knob, mtn., W.V., U.S.	C5	125
Highland, Ca., U.S.	*E5	82
Highland, Il., U.S.	E4	90
Highland, In., U.S.	A3	91
Highland, Ks., U.S.	C8	93
Highland, Mi., U.S.	o14	99
Highland, N.Y., U.S.	D7	109
Highland, Oh., U.S.	C2	112
Highland, Wi., U.S.	E3	126
Highland, prov., Scot., U.K.	B4	13
Highland, co., Oh., U.S.	C2	112
Highland, co., Va., U.S.	B3	123
Highland Falls, N.Y., U.S.	*D6	109
Highland Grove, On., Can.	B6	73
Highland Heights, Oh., U.S.	*g10	112
Highland Home, Al., U.S.	D3	78
Highland Lake, l., Me., U.S.	g7	96
Highland Lakes, N.J., U.S.	A4	107
Highland Park, Il., U.S.	A6	90
Highland Park, Mi., U.S.	p15	99
Highland Park, N.J., U.S.	*C4	107
Highland Park, Tx., U.S.	n10	120
Highland Peak, mtn., Ca., U.S.	C4	82
Highland Point, c., Fl., U.S.	G5	86
Highlands, N.J., U.S.	C5	107
Highlands, N.C., U.S.	f9	110
Highlands, Tx., U.S.	r14	120
Highlands, co., Fl., U.S.	E5	86
Highland Springs, Va., U.S.	C5	123
Highlands, Austl.	F5	51
Highlandville, Ia., U.S.	A6	92
Highmore, S.D., U.S.	C6	118
High Point, Ms., U.S.	B4	101
High Point, Mo., U.S.	C5	102
High Point, N.C., U.S.	B2	110
High Prairie, Ab., Can.	B2	68
High Ridge, Mo., U.S.	g12	102
High River, Ab., Can.	D4	68
Highrock Lake, l., Mb., Can.	B1	70
High Rock Lake, res., N.C., U.S.	B2	110
High Rolls Mountain Park, N.M., U.S.	E4	108
High Shoals, Ga., U.S.	C3	87
High Shoals, N.C., U.S.	B1	110
High Spire, Pa., U.S.	F8	115
High Springs, Fl., U.S.	C4	86
High Tatra Mountains, mts., Eur.	D5	26
High Top, mtn., W.V., U.S.	C5	125
Hightstown, N.J., U.S.	C3	107
High Willhays, mtn., Eng., U.K.	D3	12
Highwood, Il., U.S.	A6	90
Highwood, Mt., U.S.	C6	103
Highwood Baldy, mtn., Mt., U.S.	C6	103
Highwood Mountains, mts., Mt., U.S.	C6	103
High Wycombe, Eng., U.K.	E6	10
Higley, Az., U.S.	D4	80
Higüero, Punta, c., P.R.	B1	65
Higüey, Dom. Rep.	E9	64
Hiiraan, prov., Som.	E6	47
Hiiumaa, i., Sov. Un.	B4	27
Hiko, Nv., U.S.	F6	105
Hikone, Japan	n15	33
Hiko Range, mts., Nv., U.S.	F6	105
Hikurangi, mtn., N.Z.	L17	51
Hilāl, Jabal, mts., Eg.	D5	41
Hiland, Wy., U.S.	C5	127
Hilbert, Wi., U.S.	D5	126
Hilda, Ab., Can.	D5	68
Hilda, S.C., U.S.	E5	117
Hildale, Ut., U.S.	F3	121
Hildburghausen, Ger.D.R.	C5	18
Hilden, N.S., Can.	D6	71
Hilden, F.R.Ger.	B1	19
Hildesheim, F.R.Ger.	B4	18
Hildreth, Ne., U.S.	D6	104
Hiles, Wi., U.S.	C5	126
Hilger, Mt., U.S.	C7	103
Hilham, Tn., U.S.	C8	119
Hill, N.H., U.S.	C3	106
Hill, co., Mt., U.S.	B6	103
Hill, co., Tx., U.S.	D4	120
Hill see Al Hillah, Iraq	B4	38
Hillaby, Mount, mtn., Barb.	K20	65
Hillared, Swe.	A7	15
Hill City, Id., U.S.	F3	89
Hill City, Ks., U.S.	C4	93
Hill City, Mn., U.S.	D5	100
Hill City, S.D., U.S.	D2	118
Hillcrest, Il., U.S.	B4	90
Hillcrest, Mi., U.S.	m11	99
Hillcrest, N.Y., U.S.	*n15	109
Hillcrest Center, Ca., U.S.	*E4	82
Hillcrest Heights, Md., U.S.	f9	97
Hillegom, Neth.	B4	17
Hillerage, Ne., U.S.	*C2	104
Hillerød, Den.	C6	15
Hillesheim, F.R.Ger.	C1	19
Hillhead, S.D., U.S.	B8	118
Hilliard, Ab., Can.	C4	68
Hilliard, Fl., U.S.	B5	86
Hilliard, Oh., U.S.	k10	112
Hilliards, Pa., U.S.	D2	115
Hillier, On., Can.	D7	73
Hillisburg, In., U.S.	D5	91
Hill Lake, l., Ar., U.S.	h10	81
Hillman, Mi., U.S.	C7	99
Hillman, Mn., U.S.	D5	100
Hillmond, Sk., Can.	D1	75
Hilirose, Co., U.S.	A7	83
Hills, Ia., U.S.	C6	92
Hills, Mn., U.S.	G2	100
Hillsboro, Al., U.S.	A2	78
Hillsboro, Ga., U.S.	C3	87
Hillsboro, Il., U.S.	D4	90
Hillsboro, In., U.S.	D3	91
Hillsboro, Ia., U.S.	D6	92
Hillsboro, Ks., U.S.	D6	93
Hillsboro, Md., U.S.	C6	97
Hillsboro, Ms., U.S.	C4	101
Hillsboro, Mo., U.S.	C7	102
Hillsboro, N.H., U.S.	D3	106
Hillsboro, N.M., U.S.	E2	108
Hillsboro, N.D., U.S.	B8	111
Hillsboro, Oh., U.S.	C2	112
Hillsboro, Or., U.S.	B4	114
Hillsboro, Tn., U.S.	B5	119
Hillsboro, Tx., U.S.	D4	120
Hillsboro, W.V., U.S.	C4	125
Hillsboro, Wi., U.S.	E3	126
Hillsboro Canal, Fl., U.S.	F6	86
Hillsborough, N.B., Can.	C5	71
Hillsborough, Gren.	W25	65
Hillsborough, St. Vin.	W26	65
Hillsborough, Ca., U.S.	*h8	82
Hillsborough, N.C., U.S.	A3	110
Hillsborough, co., Fl., U.S.	E4	86
Hillsborough, co., N.H., U.S.	E3	106
Hillsborough Bay, b., P.E.I., Can.	C6	71
Hillsborough Lower Village, N.H., U.S.	D3	106
Hillsborough Upper Village, N.H., U.S.	D3	106
Hixon, B.C., Can.	C6	69
Hixton, Wi., U.S.	D2	126
Hills Creek Lake, res., Or., U.S.	D4	114
Hillsdale, On., Can.	C5	73
Hillsdale, Il., U.S.	B3	90
Hillsdale, In., U.S.	E3	91
Hillsdale, Ks., U.S.	D9	93
Hillsdale, Mi., U.S.	G6	99
Hillsdale, N.J., U.S.	g8	107
Hillsdale, N.Y., U.S.	C7	109
Hillsdale, Ok., U.S.	A4	113
Hillsdale, Tn., U.S.	A5	119
Hillsdale, Wi., U.S.	C2	126
Hillsdale, co., Mi., U.S.	G6	99
Hillside, Az., U.S.	C3	80
Hillside, Co., U.S.	C5	83
Hillside, Il., U.S.	*k9	90
Hillside, N.J., U.S.	k8	107
Hillside Heights, De., U.S.	*B3	85
Hill Spring, Ab., Can.	E4	68
Hillsview, S.D., U.S.	B6	118
Hillsville, Pa., U.S.	D1	115
Hillsville, Va., U.S.	D2	123
Hilltonia, Ga., U.S.	D5	87
Hilltown, N. Ire., U.K.	C5	11
Hillview, Il., U.S.	D3	90
Hillview, Ky., U.S.	g11	94
Hillview, Tn., U.S.	g12	102
Hilo, Hi., U.S.	D6	88
Hilo Bay, b., Hi., U.S.	k12	97
Hilpotstein, F.R.Ger.	D6	19
Hilton, Ab., Can.	E1	87
Hilton, N.Y., U.S.	B3	109
Hilton Head Island, S.C., U.S.	G6	117
Hilton Head Island, i., S.C., U.S.	f9	123
Hiltons, Va., U.S.	A6	16
Hilversum, Neth.	C6 ·	94
Hima, Ky., U.S.	C8	36
Himachal Pradesh, state, India	I3	33
Himalayas, mts., Asia	C3	107
Himeji, Japan	H8	33
Himi, Japan	C4	109
Himrod, N.Y., U.S.	E7	64
Hinche, Haiti	C8	50
Hinchinbrook, i., Austl.	g18	79
Hinchinbrook Island, i., Ak., U.S.	E4	75
Hinckley, Eng., U.K.	E6	10
Hinckley, Il., U.S.	B5	90
Hinckley, Me., U.S.	D3	96
Hinckley, Mn., U.S.	D6	100
Hinckley, Oh., U.S.	A4	112
Hinckley, Ut., U.S.	D3	121
Hinckley Reservoir, res., N.Y., U.S.	B5	109
Hindiyah Barrage, Iraq	F15	40
Hindman, Ky., U.S.	C7	94
Hindmarsh, Lake, l., Austl.	G3	51
Hinds, co., Ms., U.S.	C3	101
Hindsboro, Il., U.S.	D5	90
Hinds Lake, l., Nf., Can.	D3	72
Hindsville, Ar., U.S.	A2	81
Hindubägh, Pak.	B4	36
Hindu Kush, mts., Asia	A4	100
Hines, Or., U.S.	D7	114
Hinesburg, Vt., U.S.	C2	122
Hines Creek, Ab., Can.	A1	68
Hines Creek, stm., Ab., Can.	A1	68
Hineston, La., U.S.	C3	95
Hinesville, Ga., U.S.	E5	87
Hingham, Ma., U.S.	B6	98
Hingham, Mt., U.S.	B6	103
Hingham Bay, b., Ma., U.S.	g12	98
Hingoli, India	H6	37
Hinis, Tur.	C13	40
Hinkle, Ms., U.S.	A5	101
Hinkley, Ca., U.S.	E5	82
Hinnom, Valley of, val., Isr. Occ.	m14	41
Hinnøya, i., Nor.	C6	14
Hinojosa [del Duque], Spain	C6	17
Hinsdale, Il., U.S.	k9	90
Hinsdale, Ma., U.S.	B1	98
Hinsdale, Mt., U.S.	B9	103
Hinsdale, N.H., U.S.	E2	106
Hinsdale, N.Y., U.S.	C2	109
Hinsdale, co., Co., U.S.	D3	83
Hinterrhein, Switz.	C7	21
Hinterrhein, stm., Switz.	C7	21
Hinton, Ab., Can.	C2	68
Hinton, Ok., U.S.	B3	113
Hinton, W.V., U.S.	D4	125
Hirado Island, i., Japan	J4	33
Hiraiwa Cape, c., Japan	P17	52
Hirakata, Japan	*I7	33
Hirākud, res., India	G9	37
Hiram, Ga., U.S.	C2	87
Hiram, Me., U.S.	E2	96
Hiram, Oh., U.S.	A4	112
Hiratsuka, Japan	n17	33
Hīrlău, Rom.	B8	24
Hiroo, Japan	E11	33
Hirosaki, Japan	C13	31
Hiroshima, Japan	E11	31
Hirschberg see Jelenia Góra, Pol.		
Hirson, Fr.	C6	16
Hîrşova, Rom.	C8	24
Hirtshals, Den.	A3	15
Hisār, India	A5	36
Hisārönü, Tur.	B9	40
Hiseville, Ky., U.S.	C5	94
Hispaniola, i., N.A.	E8	64
Hīt, Iraq	F14	40
Hitachi, Japan	D13	31
Hitchcock, S.D., U.S.	H4	75
Hitchcock, Tx., U.S.	C4	84
Hitchcock, co., Ne., U.S.	D4	104
Hitchcock Lake, Ct., U.S.	B7	94
Hitchin, Eng., U.K.	B7	94
Hitchins, Ky., U.S.	B6	113
Hitchita, Ok., U.S.	C5	92
Hiteman, Ia., U.S.	F3	14
Hitoyoshi, Japan	F3	14
Hitra, i., Nor.	B8	24
Hitterdal, Mn., U.S.	D2	100
Hittisau, Aus.	B8	21
Hitzacker, F.R.Ger.	D5	86
Hiwannee, Ms., U.S.	D5	101
Hiwasse, Ar., U.S.	A1	81
Hiwassee, Va., U.S.	D2	123
Hiwassee, stm., Tn., U.S.	D9	119
Hiwassee Lake, res., N.C., U.S.	f8	110
Hjallerup, Den.	A4	15
Hjälmaren, l., Swe.	H7	14
Hjälmseryd, Swe.	H6	14
Hjo, Swe.	G6	14
Hjørring, Den.	A3	15
Hkakabo Razi, mtn., Burma	C10	36
Hlohovec, Czech.	D4	26
Ho, Ghana	E5	45
Hoaeae, Hi., U.S.	g9	88
Hoagland, In., U.S.	C8	91
Hoai Nhon, Viet.	C3	34
Hoback, stm., Wy., U.S.	C3	127
Hobart, Austl.	o15	50
Hobart, In., U.S.	A3	91
Hobart, N.Y., U.S.	C6	109
Hobart, Ok., U.S.	B2	113
Hobart, Wi., U.S.	h9	98
Hobbema, Ab., Can.	C4	68
Hobbies, Mt., U.S.	*B3	108
Hobbs, N.M., U.S.	E6	108
Hobbs, In., U.S.	D6	91
Hobbsville, In., U.S.	k8	107
Hobe Sound, Fl., U.S.	E6	86
Hoboken (part of Antwerp), Bel.	B6	16
Hoboken, Ga., U.S.	E4	87
Hoboken, N.J., U.S.	k8	107
Hobro, Den.	B3	15
Hobson, Mt., U.S.	D7	103
Hobson Lake, l., B.C., Can.	C7	69
Hobucken, N.C., U.S.	B6	110
Hobyo, Som.	D6	47
Hochdorf, Switz.	E4	18
Hochfeld, Nmb.	B2	49
Hochfelden, Fr.	F7	17
Ho Chi Minh City (Saigon), Viet.	C3	34
Höchst (part of Frankfurt am Main), F.R.Ger.	C3	19
Höchstadt [an der Aisch], F.R.Ger.	D5	19
Hockenheim, F.R.Ger.	D3	19
Hockerville, Ok., U.S.	A7	113
Hockessin, De., U.S.	A3	85
Hocking, co., Oh., U.S.	C3	112
Hocking, stm., Oh., U.S.	C3	112
Hockinson, Wa., U.S.	D3	82
Hockley, Tx., U.S.	q14	120
Hockley, co., Tx., U.S.	C1	120
Hoddesdon, Eng., U.K.	B5	96
Hodeida (Al Hudaydah), Yemen	D4	38
Hodgdon, Me., U.S.	B5	96
Hodge, La., U.S.	B3	95
Hodgeman, co., Ks., U.S.	D4	93
Hodgenville, Ky., U.S.	C4	94
Hodges, Al., U.S.	A2	78
Hodges, S.C., U.S.	C3	117
Hodges Hill, hill, Nf., Can.	D4	72
Hodges Village Reservoir, res., Ma., U.S.	B4	98
Hodgeville, Sk., Can.	G2	75
Hodgson, Mb., Can.	D3	70
Hódmezővásárhely, Hung.	B5	24
Hodonín, Czech.	D4	26
Hoehne, Co., U.S.	D6	83
Hoek van Holland, Neth.	D4	17
Hoensbroek, Neth.	D5	17
Hoeryŏng, N. Kor.	E3	33
Hof, F.R.Ger.	C5	18
Hof, Nor.	p28	14
Hoffman, N.C., U.S.	B3	110
Hoffman, Mn., U.S.	E3	100
Hoffman Estates, Il., U.S.	h8	90
Hofgeismar, F.R.Ger.	A4	101
Höfn, Ice.	n25	14
Hofsjökull, Ice.	n23	14
Hōfu, Japan	I5	33
Höganäs, Swe.	C2	87
Hogansville, Ga., U.S.	C2	87
Hogback Mountain, mtn., Mt., U.S.	F4	103
Hogback Mountain, mtn., Ne., U.S.	C2	104
Hogback Mountain, mtn., S.C., U.S.	A3	117
Hog Island, i., Fl., U.S.	r3	86
Hog Island, i., Mi., U.S.	C5	99
Hog Island, i., N.C., U.S.	B6	110
Hog Island, i., R.I., U.S.	D5	116
Hog Island, i., Va., U.S.	C7	123
Hogup Mountains, mts., Ut., U.S.	B2	121
Hoh, stm., Wa., U.S.	B2	127
Hohenwald, Tn., U.S.	B4	119
Hohe Tauern, mts., Aus.	E6	19
Hoh Head, c., Wa., U.S.	B1	124
Hohhot, China	C7	31
Hohoe, Ghana	E5	45
Ho-Ho-Kus, N.J., U.S.	h8	107
Hohwachter Bucht, b., F.R.Ger.	B8	24
Hoi An, Viet.	B3	34
Hoima, Ug.	A5	48
Hoisington, Ks., U.S.	D5	93
Hoi Xuan, Viet.	B6	35
Højer, Den.	D2	15
Hokah, Mn., U.S.	G7	100
Hokes Bluff, Al., U.S.	B4	78
Hokitika, N.Z.	O13	51
Hokkaidō, i., Japan	C13	31
Hokksund, Nor.	A5	35
Holabird, S.D., U.S.	C6	118
Holbæk, Den.	C5	15
Holbeach, Eng., U.K.	B8	12
Holbrook, Az., U.S.	C5	80
Holbrook, Id., U.S.	G6	89
Holbrook, Ma., U.S.	B5	98
Holbrook, Ne., U.S.	D5	104
Holbrook, N.Y., U.S.	*n15	109
Holcomb, Il., U.S.	B5	90
Holcomb, Ks., U.S.	E3	93
Holcomb, Mo., U.S.	E8	102
Holcomb, Wi., U.S.	C2	126
Holden, Ab., Can.	C4	68
Holden, Ma., U.S.	g10	95
Holden, Mo., U.S.	C4	102
Holden, Ut., U.S.	D3	121
Holden, W.V., U.S.	D2	125
Holden Heights, Fl., U.S.	D5	86
Holdenville, Ok., U.S.	B5	113
Holder, Fl., U.S.	D4	86
Holderness, N.H., U.S.	C3	106
Holdfast, Sk., Can.	G3	75
Holdingford, Mn., U.S.	E4	100
Holdrege, Ne., U.S.	D6	104
Hole in the Mountain Peak, mtn., Nv., U.S.	C6	105
Hölen, Nor.	p28	14
Holetown, Barb.	K20	65
Holgate, Oh., U.S.	A1	112
Holguín, Cuba	D5	64
Holguín, prov., Cuba	D5	64
Holiday, Fl., U.S.	*D4	86
Holiday, Ut., U.S.	*C4	121
Holladay, Tn., U.S.	B3	119
Holladay, Ut., U.S.	C4	121
Holland, Mb., Can.	E2	70
Holland, Ar., U.S.	B3	81
Holland, In., U.S.	H3	91
Holland, Ia., U.S.	B5	92
Holland, Ky., U.S.	E3	94
Holland, Ma., U.S.	B3	98
Holland, Mi., U.S.	F4	99
Holland, Mn., U.S.	F2	100
Holland, Ne., U.S.	D9	104
Holland, N.Y., U.S.	C2	109
Holland, Oh., U.S.	A2	112
Holland, Tx., U.S.	D4	120
Holland, Wi., U.S.	h9	126
Holland see Netherlands, ctry., Eur.	A6	16
Hollandale, Ms., U.S.	B3	101
Hollandale, Wi., U.S.	F4	126
Holland Centre, On., Can.	C4	73
Holland Island, i., Md., U.S.	D5	97
Holland Patent, N.Y., U.S.	B5	109
Holland Point, c., Md., U.S.	C4	97
Holland Straits, strt., Md., U.S.	D5	97
Hollansburg, Oh., U.S.	C1	112
Hollenberg, Ks., U.S.	C7	93
Holley, N.Y., U.S.	B2	109
Hollick-Kenyon Plateau, plat., Ant.	B2	7
Holliday, Mo., U.S.	B5	102
Holliday, Tx., U.S.	C3	120
Hollidaysburg, Pa., U.S.	F5	115
Hollins, Al., U.S.	B3	78
Hollins, Va., U.S.	C3	123
Hollis, N.H., U.S.	E3	106
Hollis, Ok., U.S.	C2	113
Hollis Center, Me., U.S.	E2	96
Hollister, Ca., U.S.	D3	82
Hollister, Id., U.S.	G4	89
Hollister, Mo., U.S.	E4	102
Hollister, N.C., U.S.	A5	110
Hollister, Ok., U.S.	C3	113
Hollister, Wi., U.S.	C5	126
Holloman Air Force Base, mil., N.M., U.S.	E3	108
Holloway, Mn., U.S.	E3	100
Holloway Terrace, De., U.S.	*B3	85
Hollow Rock, Tn., U.S.	A3	119
Hollowtop Mountain, mtn., Mt., U.S.	E4	103
Hollsopple, Pa., U.S.	F4	115
Hollum, Neth.	A5	17
Holly, Co., U.S.	C8	83
Holly, Mi., U.S.	F7	99
Holly Beach, La., U.S.	E2	95
Holly Bluff, Ms., U.S.	C3	101
Holly Grove, Ar., U.S.	C4	81
Holly Hill, Fl., U.S.	C5	86
Holly Hill, S.C., U.S.	E7	117
Holly Pond, Al., U.S.	A3	78
Holly Ridge, La., U.S.	B4	95
Holly Ridge, N.C., U.S.	C5	110
Holly Shelter Swamp, sw., N.C., U.S.	C5	110
Holly Springs, Ga., U.S.	D3	81
Holly Springs, Ms., U.S.	A4	101
Holly Springs, N.C., U.S.	B4	110
Hollywood, Al., U.S.	A4	78
Hollywood, Az., U.S.	E6	80
Hollywood, Ca., U.S.	C2	81
Hollywood (part of Los Angeles), Ca., U.S.	m12	82
Hollywood, Fl., U.S.	F6	86
Hollywood, Md., U.S.	D4	97
Hollywood Indian Reservation, Fl., U.S.	r13	86
Holman, N.M., U.S.	A4	108
Holman Island, N.T., Can.	B9	66
Holmdel, N.J., U.S.	C4	107
Holmes, co., Fl., U.S.	u16	86
Holmes, co., Ms., U.S.	B3	101
Holmes, co., Oh., U.S.	B4	112
Holmes, Mount, mtn., Wy., U.S.	B2	127
Holmestrand, Nor.	p28	14
Holmes Lake, l., Mb., Can.	A3	70
Holmestvand, Nor.	B1	124
Holmfield, Mb., Can.	E2	70
Holmsbu, Nor.	p28	14
Holmsund, Swe.	F9	14
Holon, Isr.	B6	41
Holopaw, Fl., U.S.	D5	86
Holroyd, Austl.	*F9	51
Holroyd, stm., Austl.	B7	50
Holstebro, Den.	I3	14
Holsted, Den.	C2	15
Holstein, On., Can.	C4	73
Holstein, Ia., U.S.	B2	92
Holstein, Mo., U.S.	C6	102
Holstein, Ne., U.S.	D7	104
Holston, stm., Tn., U.S.	C11	119
Holston, Middle Fork, stm., Va., U.S.	f10	123
Holston High Knob, mtn., Tn., U.S.	C11	119
Holsworthy, Eng., U.K.	D3	12
Holt, Al., U.S.	B2	78
Holt, Fl., U.S.	u15	86
Holt, Mi., U.S.	F6	99
Holt, Mo., U.S.	B3	102
Holt, co., Mo., U.S.	A2	102
Holt, co., Ne., U.S.	B7	104
Holt Knob, mtn., Tn., U.S.	g10	119
Holton, In., U.S.	F7	91
Holton, Ks., U.S.	C8	93
Holton, Mi., U.S.	E4	99
Holt Reservoir, res., Al., U.S.	B2	78
Holts Summit, Mo., U.S.	C5	102
Holtville, Ca., U.S.	F6	82
Holtwood, Pa., U.S.	G9	115
Holualoa, Hi., U.S.	D6	88

Name	Map Ref	Page
Holycross, Ire.	E4	11
Holy Cross, Ak., U.S.	C8	79
Holy Cross, Ia., U.S.	B7	92
Holy Cross, Mountain of the, mtn., Co., U.S.	B4	83
Holyhead, Wales, U.K.	D4	10
Holy Island, i., Eng., U.K.	C6	10
Holy Island, i., Wales, U.K.	D4	10
Holyoke, Co., U.S.	A8	83
Holyoke, Ma., U.S.	B2	98
Holyoke, Mn., U.S.	D6	100
Holyoke Range, hills, Ma., U.S.	B2	98
Holyrood, Ks., U.S.	D5	93
Holy Sepulchre, The Church of the, Isr. Occ.	m14	41
Holy Trinity, Al., U.S.	C4	78
Holzgau, Aus.	B9	21
Holzkirchen, F.R.Ger.	B7	20
Holzminden, F.R.Ger.	C4	18
Homalin, Burma	D9	36
Homberg, F.R.Ger.	B4	19
Homberg, F.R.Ger.	B1	19
Hombetsu, Japan	E11	33
Hombori, Mali	C4	45
Hombourg-Haut, Fr.	E6	17
Homburg, F.R.Ger.	D2	19
Home, Ks., U.S.	C7	93
Home Bay, b., N.T., Can.	C19	66
Home Corner, In., U.S.	C6	91
Homécourt, Fr.	C6	16
Homecroft, In., U.S.	m10	91
Home Gardens, Ca., U.S.	*n13	82
Home Hill, Austl.	C8	50
Homelake, Co., U.S.	D4	83
Homeland, Fl., U.S.	E5	86
Homeland, Ga., U.S.	F4	87
Home Place, In., U.S.	E5	91
Homer, Ak., U.S.	D9	79
Homer, Ga., U.S.	B3	87
Homer, Il., U.S.	C6	90
Homer, In., U.S.	E6	91
Homer, La., U.S.	B2	95
Homer, Mi., U.S.	F6	99
Homer, Ne., U.S.	B9	104
Homer, N.Y., U.S.	C4	109
Homer City, Pa., U.S.	E3	115
Homerville, Ga., U.S.	E4	87
Homer Youngs Peak, mtn., Mt., U.S.	E3	103
Homestead, Fl., U.S.	G6	86
Homestead, Ia., U.S.	C6	92
Homestead, Mt., U.S.	B12	103
Homestead, Ok., U.S.	A3	113
Homestead Air Force Base, mil., Fl., U.S.	k14	115
Homestead National Monument of America, Ne., U.S.	D9	104
Hometown, Il., U.S.	*k9	90
Homewood, Al., U.S.	g7	78
Homewood, Ca., U.S.	C3	82
Homewood, Il., U.S.	B6	90
Homewood, Ms., U.S.	C4	101
Homewood, Oh., U.S.	C1	112
Homeworth, Oh., U.S.	B4	112
Hominy, Ok., U.S.	A5	113
Hominy Creek, stm., Ok., U.S.	A5	113
Homme Dam, N.D., U.S.	A8	111
Hommura, Japan	o18	33
Homochitto, stm., Ms., U.S.	D2	101
Homosassa, Fl., U.S.	D4	86
Homs (Ḥimṣ), Syria	B3	38
Hon, Ar., U.S.	C1	81
Honaker, Va., U.S.	e10	123
Honan see Henan, prov., China	E7	31
Honaunau, Hi., U.S.	D6	88
Honaz, mtn., Tur.	D7	40
Honda, Col.	B3	60
Hondo, Ab., Can.	B4	68
Hondo, N.M., U.S.	D4	108
Hondo, Tx., U.S.	E3	120
Hondo, stm., Mex.	h9	63
Hondo, stm., N.A.	A3	62
Hondo, Rio, stm., N.M., U.S.	D4	108
Honduras, ctry., N.A.	D7	63
Honduras, Cabo de, c., Hond.	D7	63
Honduras, Gulf of, b., N.A.	D7	63
Honea Path, S.C., U.S.	C3	117
Hönefoss, Nor.	G4	14
Honeoye, Ks., U.S.	C3	109
Honesdale, Pa., U.S.	C11	115
Honey Brook, Pa., U.S.	F10	115
Honey Creek, Ia., U.S.	C2	92
Honey Creek, Wi., U.S.	n11	126
Honey Grove, Tx., U.S.	C5	120
Honey Lake, l., Ca., U.S.	B3	82
Honeymoon Bay, B.C., Can.	g11	69
Honeypot Glen, Ct., U.S.	C4	84
Honeyville, Ut., U.S.	B3	121
Honfleur, Fr.	C4	16
Heng, Den.	C5	15
Hong'an, China	I6	32
Honga River, b., Md., U.S.	D5	97
Hon Gay, Viet.	B7	35
Honghu, China	F7	31
Hong Kong, dep., Asia	G7	31
Hongshui He, stm., China	F3	33
Hongwŏn, N. Kor.	F3	33
Hongze Lake, l., China	D5	31
Honiara, Sol.Is.	G9	6
Honichin Hural, Mong.	C3	32
Honiton, Eng., U.K.	D4	12
Hönö, i., Swe.	A5	15
Honobia, U.S.	C7	113
Honokaa, Hi., U.S.	D6	88
Honokahua, Hi., U.S.	B5	88
Honokohau, Hi., U.S.	C7	88
Honolulu, co., Hi., U.S.	B4	88
Honolulu, co., Hi., U.S.	g9	88
Honolulu International Airport, Hi., U.S.	g10	88
Honomu, Hi., U.S.	D6	88
Honor, Mi., U.S.	D4	99
Honoraville, Al., U.S.	D3	78
Honoululi, Hi., U.S.	g9	88
Honshū, i., Japan	D12	31
Honuapo Bay, b., Hi., U.S.	D6	88
Hood, co., Tx., U.S.	C4	120
Hood, Mount, mtn., Or., U.S.	B5	114
Hood Canal, b., Wa., U.S.	B2	124
Hoodoo, In., U.S.	A4	68
Hoodoo Peak, mtn., Wa., U.S.	A5	124
Hood Point, Austl.		
Hood River, Or., U.S.	B5	114
Hood River, co., Or., U.S.	B5	114
Hoodsport, Wa., U.S.	B2	124
Hoogeveen, Neth.	B6	17
Hoogezand, Neth.	A6	17
Hooghly, stm., India	D8	36
Hookena, Hi., U.S.	D6	88

Name	Map Ref	Page
Hooker, Ok., U.S.	e9	113
Hooker, S.D., U.S.	D8	118
Hooker, co., Ne., U.S.	C4	104
Hooker, Bi'r, well, Eg.	D2	41
Hooker, Mount, mtn., Can.	C8	69
Hookerton, N.C., U.S.	B5	110
Hook Head, c., Ire.	E5	11
Hooksett, N.H., U.S.	D4	106
Hoolehua, Hi., U.S.	B4	88
Hoonah, Ak., U.S.	D12	79
Hoopa Valley Indian Reservation, Ca., U.S.	B2	82
Hooper, Co., U.S.	D5	83
Hooper, Ne., U.S.	C9	104
Hooper, Ut., U.S.	B3	121
Hooper, Wa., U.S.	C7	124
Hooper Bay, Ak., U.S.	C6	79
Hooper Creek, stm., Ne., U.S.	h12	104
Hooper Islands, is., Md., U.S.	D5	97
Hooper Strait, strt., Md., U.S.	D5	97
Hoopersville, Md., U.S.	D5	97
Hoopeston, Il., U.S.	C6	90
Hooping Harbour, Nf., Can.	C3	72
Hoople, N.D., U.S.	A8	111
Hooppole, Il., U.S.	B4	90
Hoosac Range, mts., U.S.	A1	98
Hoosic, stm., U.S.	C7	109
Hoosick Falls, N.Y., U.S.	C7	109
Hoosier, Sk., Can.	F1	75
Hoosic Range, mts., U.S.	C4	109
Hoover, Al., U.S.		
Hoover Dam, U.S.	G7	105
Hoover Reservoir, res., Oh., U.S.	B3	112
Hooverson Heights, W.V., U.S.	f8	125
Hooversville, Pa., U.S.	F4	115
Hopa, Tur.	B13	40
Hopatcong, N.J., U.S.	B3	107
Hopatcong, Lake, l., N.J., U.S.	A3	107
Hop Bottom, Pa., U.S.	C10	115
Hope, B.C., Can.	E7	69
Hope, Ak., U.S.	C10	79
Hope, Ar., U.S.	D2	81
Hope, Id., U.S.	A2	89
Hope, In., U.S.	F6	91
Hope, Ks., U.S.	D6	93
Hope, Me., U.S.	D3	96
Hope, Mi., U.S.	E6	99
Hope, Mn., U.S.	G5	100
Hope, N.M., U.S.	E5	108
Hope, N.D., U.S.	B8	111
Hope, i., Nor.	B12	128
Hope, Ben, mtn., Scot., U.K.	A4	10
Hope, Loch, l., Scot., U.K.	B4	13
Hope, Point, c., Ak., U.S.	B6	79
Hopedale, Nf., Can.	g9	72
Hopedale, Il., U.S.	C4	90
Hopedale, La., U.S.	E6	95
Hopedale, Ma., U.S.	B4	98
Hopedale, Oh., U.S.	B5	112
Hopeh see Hebei, prov., China	D8	31
Hope Hull, Al., U.S.	C3	78
Hope Island, i., B.C., Can.	D4	69
Hope Island, i., R.I., U.S.	E5	116
Hopelawn, N.J., U.S.	k7	107
Hopelchén, Mex.	D7	63
Hope Mills, N.C., U.S.	C4	110
Hopeton, Ok., U.S.	A3	113
Hopetoun, Austl.	G4	51
Hopetown, S. Afr.	C3	49
Hope Valley, R.I., U.S.	E2	116
Hopeville, Ia., U.S.	D4	92
Hopewell, N.S., Can.	D7	71
Hopewell, N.J., U.S.	D3	101
Hopewell, N.J., U.S.	C3	107
Hopewell, Oh., U.S.	C3	112
Hopewell, Pa., U.S.	F5	115
Hopewell, Va., U.S.	C5	123
Hopewell Cape, N.B., Can.	D5	71
Hopewell Junction, N.Y., U.S.	D7	109
Hopi Buttes, mtn., Az., U.S.	B5	80
Hopi Indian Reservation, Az., U.S.	A5	80
Hopkins, Mi., U.S.	F5	99
Hopkins, Mn., U.S.	n12	100
Hopkins, Mo., U.S.	A3	102
Hopkins, co., Ky., U.S.	C2	94
Hopkins, co., Tx., U.S.	C5	120
Hopkinsville, Ky., U.S.	D2	94
Hopkinton, Ia., U.S.	B6	92
Hopkinton, Ma., U.S.	B4	98
Hopkinton, N.H., U.S.	D3	106
Hopkinton, N.Y., U.S.	f10	109
Hopkinton, R.I., U.S.	F1	116
Hopkinton Lake, res., N.H., U.S.	D3	106
Hopland, Ca., U.S.	C2	82
Hopwood, Pa., U.S.	G2	115
Hoquiam, Wa., U.S.	C2	124
Horace, Ks., U.S.	D2	93
Horace, N.D., U.S.	C9	111
Horace Mountain, mtn., Ak., U.S.	B10	79
Horatio, Ar., U.S.	D1	81
Horatio, S.C., U.S.	C6	117
Horaždovice, Czech.	D8	19
Horb, F.R.Ger.	E3	19
Hørby, Den.	A4	15
Hörby, Swe.	C7	15
Horconcitos, Pan.	F6	62
Hord, Il., U.S.	E5	90
Hordville, Ne., U.S.	C8	104
Horgen, Switz.	E4	18
Horicon, Wi., U.S.	E5	126
Horine, Mo., U.S.	C7	102
Horizon, Sk., Can.	H3	75
Hörle, Swe.	A7	15
Horlick Mountains, mts., Ant.	A36	7
Hormoz, i., Iran	H8	39
Hormoz, Kūh-e, mtn., Iran	H7	39
Hormuz, Strait of, strt., Asia	C5	38
Horn, Aus.	D7	18
Horn, i., Ice.	m21	14
Horn, Cape, c., Chile	k12	54
Hornavan, l., Swe.	D7	14
Hornbeak, Tn., U.S.	A2	119
Hornbeck, La., U.S.	C2	95
Hornburg, F.R.Ger.	A5	19
Horncastle, Eng., U.K.	A7	12
Hornell, N.Y., U.S.	C3	109
Hornerstown, N.J., U.S.	C3	107
Hornersville, Mo., U.S.	E7	102
Horn Head, c., Ire.	B4	11
Hornick, Ia., U.S.	B1	92
Horning's Mills, On., Can.	C4	73
Horní Počernice, Czech.	n18	26
Horn Island, i., Ms., U.S.	E5	101

Name	Map Ref	Page
Horn Island Pass, strt., Ms., U.S.	g8	101
Horn Lake, Ms., U.S.	A3	101
Horn Mountain, mtn., Al., U.S.	B3	78
Horn Pond, l., Ma., U.S.	g11	98
Hornsby, Tn., U.S.	B3	119
Hornsbyville, Va., U.S.	h15	123
Hornsea, Eng., U.K.	D6	10
Hornslet, Den.	B4	15
Hörnum, F.R.Ger.	A4	18
Hořovice, Czech.	D8	19
Horqin Youyi Qianqi, China	A10	32
Horqin Youyi Zhongqi, China	B9	32
Horqueta, Para.	D4	55
Horred, Swe.	A6	15
Horry, co., S.C., U.S.	D10	117
Horse, stm., Ab., Can.	A5	68
Horse, stm., Ab., Can.	C6	84
Horse Branch, Ky., U.S.	C3	94
Horse Cave, Ky., U.S.	C4	94
Horse Creek, Wy., U.S.	E7	127
Horse Creek, stm., U.S.	E8	127
Horse Creek, stm., Co., U.S.	C7	83
Horse Creek, stm., Wy., U.S.	D4	102
Horse Creek Reservoir, res., Co., U.S.	C7	83
Horsefly, B.C., Can.	C7	69
Horsefly Lake, l., B.C., Can.	C7	69
Horsehead Lake, l., N.D., U.S.	B6	111
Horseheads, N.Y., U.S.	C4	109
Horse Heaven Hills, hills, Wa., U.S.	C6	124
Horse Islands, Nf., Can.	C4	72
Horse Mountain, mtn., N.M., U.S.	D1	108
Horsens, Den.	J3	14
Horseshoe Beach, Fl., U.S.	C3	86
Horseshoe Bend, Id., U.S.	F2	89
Horseshoe Bend National Military Park, Al., U.S.	C4	78
Horseshoe Cove, b., Fl., U.S.	C3	86
Horseshoe Lake, l., Mb., Can.	C3	70
Horseshoe Point, c., Fl., U.S.	C3	86
Horseshoe Reservoir, res., Az., U.S.	C4	80
Horse Springs, N.M., U.S.	D1	108
Horsham, Austl.	G7	50
Horsham, Eng., U.K.	C7	12
Horsham, Pa., U.S.	*F11	115
Horšovský Týn, Czech.	D7	19
Horta, Port.	g8	44
Hortense, Ga., U.S.	E5	87
Horton, Al., U.S.	A3	78
Horton, In., U.S.	D5	91
Horton, Ks., U.S.	C8	93
Horton, Mo., U.S.	D3	102
Horton, stm., N.T., Can.	C8	66
Hortonia, Lake, l., Vt., U.S.	D2	122
Hortonville, Wi., U.S.	D5	126
Horwich, Eng., U.K.	C5	15
Horwin, Switz.	B5	21
Hoschton, Ga., U.S.	B3	87
Hoséré Vokré, mtn., Cam.	D2	46
Hosford, Fl., U.S.	B2	86
Hoshāb, Pak.	H11	39
Hoshiārpur, India	B6	36
Hoskins, Ne., U.S.	B8	104
Hoskins, Or., U.S.	C3	114
Hoskinston, Ky., U.S.	C6	94
Hosmer, B.C., Can.	E10	69
Hosmer, S.D., U.S.	B6	118
Hospers, Ia., U.S.	A2	92
Hospital, Ire.	E3	11
Hospitalet, Spain	B7	22
Hosston, La., U.S.	B2	95
Hosta Butte, mtn., N.M., U.S.	B1	108
Hoste, Isla, i., Chile	k12	54
Hot, Thai.	C3	35
Hotaka, Mount, mtn., Japan	H8	33
Hotan, China	A6	36
Hotan He, stm., China	A7	36
Hotchkiss, Co., U.S.	C3	83
Hotchkissville, Ct., U.S.	C3	84
Hot Coffee, Ms., U.S.	D4	101
Hot Creek Range, mts., Nv., U.S.	E5	105
Hot Creek Valley, val., Nv., U.S.	E5	105
Hötensleben, Ger.D.R.	A6	19
Hotevilla, Az., U.S.	B5	80
Hoting, Swe.	E7	14
Hot Springs, co., Ar., U.S.	C2	81
Hot Springs, Mt., U.S.	C2	103
Hot Springs, N.C., U.S.	f10	110
Hot Springs, S.D., U.S.	D2	118
Hot Springs, Va., U.S.	C3	123
Hot Springs, co., Wy., U.S.	C4	127
Hot Springs National Park, Ar., U.S.	C2	81
Hot Springs National Park, Ar., U.S.	C2	81
Hot Springs Peak, mtn., Ca., U.S.	B3	82
Hot Springs Peak, mtn., Nv., U.S.	B4	105
Hot Sulphur Springs, Co., U.S.	A4	83
Hottah Lake, l., N.T., Can.	C9	66
Hotte, Massif de la, mts., Haiti	E7	64
Houck, Az., U.S.	B6	80
Houffalize, Bel.	D5	17
Houghton, Mi., U.S.	A2	99
Houghton, N.Y., U.S.	C2	109
Houghton, co., Mi., U.S.	A2	99
Houghton Lake, Mi., U.S.	D6	99
Houghton Lake, l., Mi., U.S.	D6	99
Houghton Lake Heights, Mi., U.S.	D6	99
Houghtonville, Ma., U.S.	*A1	98
Houilles, Fr.	g9	16
Houlka, Ms., U.S.	A4	101
Houltonville, La., U.S.	h11	95
Houmé, Burkina	F5	45
Houmt Essouk, Tun.	C7	44
Houndé, Burkina	F5	45
Hourn, Loch, b., Scot., U.K.	C3	13
Housatonic, Ma., U.S.	B1	98
Housatonic, stm., U.S.	D3	84
House, N.M., U.S.	C6	108
House, stm., Ab., Can.	B4	68
House Range, mts., Ut., U.S.	D2	121
House Springs, Mo., U.S.	g12	102
Houston, De., U.S.	E3	85

Name	Map Ref	Page
Houston, In., U.S.	F5	91
Houston, Mn., U.S.	G7	100
Houston, Ms., U.S.	B4	101
Houston, Mo., U.S.	D6	102
Houston, Pa., U.S.	F1	115
Houston, Tx., U.S.	E5	120
Houston, co., Al., U.S.	D4	78
Houston, co., Ga., U.S.	D3	87
Houston, co., Mn., U.S.	G7	100
Houston, co., Tn., U.S.	A4	119
Houston, co., Tx., U.S.	D5	120
Houston, co., La., U.S.	D2	95
Houston, Lake, res., Tx., U.S.	r14	120
Houstonia, Mo., U.S.	C4	102
Houston Intercontinental Airport, Tx., U.S.	r14	120
Houtzdale, Pa., U.S.	E5	115
Hovd, Mong.	B3	31
Hovd, stm., Mong.	B3	31
Hövelhof, F.R.Ger.	C4	18
Hoven, S.D., U.S.	B6	118
Hovenweep National Monument, Ut., U.S.	F6	121
Hovland, Mn., U.S.	k10	100
Hövsgöl Lake, l., Mong.	A5	31
Howar, Wādī, val., Afr.	B2	47
Howard, Al., U.S.	B2	78
Howard, Co., U.S.	C5	83
Howard, Ga., U.S.	D2	87
Howard, Ks., U.S.	E7	93
Howard, Ms., U.S.	B3	101
Howard, N.Y., U.S.	C3	109
Howard, Oh., U.S.	B3	112
Howard, Pa., U.S.	D6	115
Howard, S.D., U.S.	C8	118
Howard, Wi., U.S.	D5	126
Howard, co., Ar., U.S.	C2	81
Howard, co., In., U.S.	C5	91
Howard, co., Ia., U.S.	A5	92
Howard, co., Md., U.S.	B4	97
Howard, co., Mo., U.S.	B5	102
Howard, co., Ne., U.S.	C7	104
Howard, co., Tx., U.S.	C2	120
Howard City, Mi., U.S.	E5	99
Howard Hanson Reservoir, res., Wa., U.S.	B4	124
Howard Lake, Mn., U.S.	E4	100
Howard Prairie Lake, res., Or., U.S.	E4	114
Howards Grove-Millersville, Wi., U.S.	E6	126
Howardville, Mo., U.S.	E8	102
Howe, Id., U.S.	F6	89
Howe, In., U.S.	A7	91
Howe, Ok., U.S.	C7	113
Howe, Cape, c., Austl.	G9	50
Howell, Mi., U.S.	F7	99
Howell, Tn., U.S.	B5	119
Howell, Ut., U.S.	B3	121
Howell, co., Mo., U.S.	D6	102
Howells, Ne., U.S.	C8	104
Howes, S.D., U.S.	C3	118
Howe Sound, strt., B.C., Can.	E6	69
Howesville, W.V., U.S.	B5	125
Howick, P.Q., Can.	D4	74
Howison, Ms., U.S.	E4	101
Howland, Me., U.S.	C4	96
Howland Island, i., Oc.	F11	6
Howley, Nf., Can.	D3	72
Howley, Mount, mtn., Nf., Can.	D2	72
Howrah, India	D8	36
Howser, B.C., Can.	D9	69
Howson Peak, mtn., B.C., Can.	B4	69
Howth (part of Dublin), Ire.	D5	11
Hoxie, Ar., U.S.	A5	81
Hoxie, Ks., U.S.	C3	93
Höxter, F.R.Ger.	C4	18
Hoy, i., Scot., U.K.	A5	10
Hoya, F.R.Ger.	B4	18
Hoyerswerda, Ger.D.R.	C7	18
Hoylake, Eng., U.K.	A4	12
Hoyleton, Il., U.S.	E4	90
Hoyo, Sierra del, mts., Spain	o17	22
Hoyt, N.B., Can.	D3	71
Hoyt, Co., U.S.	A6	83
Hoyt, Ks., U.S.	C8	93
Hoyt, Ok., U.S.	B6	113
Hoyt Lakes, Mn., U.S.	C6	100
Hoytville, Oh., U.S.	A2	112
Hradec Králové, Czech.	C3	26
Hranice, Czech.	D4	26
Hrubieszów, Pol.	C7	26
Hsinchu, Tai.	G9	31
Hsipaw, Burma	A2	35
Huacho, Peru	D2	58
Huachuca City, Az., U.S.	F5	80
Huacrachuco, Peru	C2	58
Huade, China	D5	32
Huadian, China	C10	31
Hua Hin, Thai.	C1	34
Huai'an (Huaicheng), China	H8	32
Huaide, China	C9	31
Huailai, China	D6	32
Huainan, China	E8	31
Huaiyang, China	H6	32
Huaiyuan, China	H7	32
Huajuapan de León, Mex.	D5	63
Hualahuises, Mex.	D6	88
Hualalai, vol., Hi., U.S.		
Hualapai Indian Reservation, Az., U.S.	B2	80
Hualapai Mountains, mts., Az., U.S.	C2	80
Hualapai Peak, mtn., Az., U.S.	C2	80
Hualgayoc, Peru	C2	58
Hualien, Tai.	G9	31
Huallaga, stm., Peru	C2	58
Huallanca, Peru	C2	58
Huamachuco, Peru	C2	58
Huamantla, Mex.	n15	63
Huambo, Ang.	D2	48
Huambo, dept., Ang.	D2	48
Huancabamba, Peru	C2	58
Huancavelica, Peru	D2	58
Huancavelica, dept., Peru	D2	58
Huancayo, Peru	D2	58
Huanchaca, Bol.	C3	57
Huangchuan, China	H6	32
Huang He (Yellow), stm., China	D8	31
Huangling, China	E8	31
Huangmei, China	I6	32
Huangping, China	K2	32
Huangxian, China	F9	32
Huangyan, China	J9	32
Huangyuan, China	D5	31

Name	Map Ref	Page
Huanjiang, China	G6	31
Huanta, Peru	D3	58
Huánuco, Peru	C2	58
Huánuco, dept., Peru	C2	58
Huara, Chile	F5	57
Huaral, Peru	D2	58
Huaraz, Peru	C2	58
Huari, Bol.	C2	55
Huariaca, Peru	D2	58
Huarina, Bol.	C2	55
Huarmey, Peru	D2	58
Huascarán, Nevado, mtn., Peru	C2	58
Huasco, Chile	E1	55
Huasco, stm., Chile	E1	55
Huatabampo, Mex.	E4	62
Huatusco [de Chicuellar], Mex.	n15	63
Huauchinango, Mex.	m14	63
Huaxian, China	G6	32
Huayllay, Peru	D2	58
Huaytará, Peru	D2	58
Huayuan, China	J3	32
Hubbard, Sk., Can.	F4	75
Hubbard, Ia., U.S.	B4	92
Hubbard, Mn., U.S.	D4	100
Hubbard, Ne., U.S.	B9	104
Hubbard, Oh., U.S.	A5	112
Hubbard, Or., U.S.	B4	114
Hubbard, co., Mn., U.S.	C4	100
Hubbard Creek Lake, res., Tx., U.S.	C3	120
Hubbard Lake, Mi., U.S.	D7	99
Hubbard Lake, l., Mi., U.S.	D7	99
Hubbards, N.S., Can.	E5	71
Hubbardston, Ma., U.S.	B3	98
Hubbardston, Mi., U.S.	E6	99
Hubbardton, stm., Vt., U.S.	D2	122
Hubbell, Mi., U.S.	A2	99
Hubbell, Ne., U.S.	D8	104
Hubei, prov., China	E8	31
Huben, Aus.	C8	20
Huber, Ga., U.S.	D3	87
Huberdeau, P.Q., Can.	D3	74
Huber Heights, Oh., U.S.	*C1	112
Huber South, Oh., U.S.	*C1	112
Hubli [-Dhārwār], India	E6	36
Huckleberry Hill, Ct., U.S.	B4	84
Huckleberry Mountain, mtn., Or., U.S.	D4	114
Huddersfield, Eng., U.K.	D6	10
Huddinge, Swe.	*H7	14
Huddleston, Va., U.S.	C3	123
Huddleston Knob, mtn., Tn., U.S.	C8	119
Huddy, Ky., U.S.	C7	94
Hude, F.R.Ger.	B4	18
Hudgin Creek, stm., Ar., U.S.	D3	81
Hudiksvall, Swe.	G7	14
Hudson, P.Q., Can.	D3	74
Hudson, Co., U.S.	A6	83
Hudson, Fl., U.S.	D4	86
Hudson, Il., U.S.	C5	90
Hudson, In., U.S.	A7	91
Hudson, Ia., U.S.	B5	92
Hudson, Ma., U.S.	B4	98
Hudson, Mi., U.S.	G6	99
Hudson, N.H., U.S.	E4	106
Hudson, N.Y., U.S.	C7	109
Hudson, N.C., U.S.	B1	110
Hudson, Oh., U.S.	A4	112
Hudson, S.D., U.S.	D9	118
Hudson, Wi., U.S.	D1	126
Hudson, Wy., U.S.	C4	127
Hudson, co., N.J., U.S.	B4	107
Hudson, stm., U.S.	E7	109
Hudson, stm., Ga., U.S.	B3	87
Hudson Bay, Sk., Can.	E4	75
Hudson Bay, b., Can.	D15	66
Hudson Falls, N.Y., U.S.	B7	109
Hudson Hope, B.C., Can.	A6	69
Hudson Lake, In., U.S.	A4	91
Hudson Mountain, mtn., Me., U.S.	B3	96
Hudson Mountains, mts., Ant.	B2	7
Hudson Strait, strt., Can.	D18	66
Hudsonville, Mi., U.S.	F5	99
Hudspeth, co., Tx., U.S.	o12	120
Hudwin Lake, l., Mb., Can.	C3	70
Hue, Viet.	B3	34
Huebin, S.D., U.S.	B6	118
Huehuetenango, Guat.	D6	63
Hünfeld, F.R.Ger.	C4	19
Huejutla [de Reyes], Mex.	m14	63
Huelma, Spain	D2	22
Huelva, Spain	D2	22
Huentelauquén, Chile	E1	55
Huércal-Overa, Spain	D5	22
Huerfano, co., Co., U.S.	D6	83
Huerfano, stm., Co., U.S.	D6	83
Huerfano Mountain, mtn., N.M., U.S.	A2	108
Huerva, stm., Spain	B5	22
Huesca, Spain	B5	22
Huéscar, Spain	D4	22
Huetamo de Núñez, Mex.	D4	63
Huete, Spain	B4	22
Hueytown, Al., U.S.	g6	78
Huff, N.D., U.S.	C5	111
Huffakers, Nv., U.S.	D2	105
Huger, S.C., U.S.	h12	117
Huggins, Butler Lake, res., Ne., U.S.		
Hughenden, Austl.	D7	50
Hughenden, Ab., Can.	C5	68
Hughes, Ak., U.S.	B9	79
Hughes, co., Ok., U.S.	B5	113
Hughes, co., S.D., U.S.	C5	118
Hughes, stm., Md., U.S.	A1	70
Hughes, North Fork, stm., W.V., U.S.	B3	125
Hughes, South Fork, stm., W.V., U.S.	B3	125
Hughesville, Md., U.S.	C4	97
Hughesville, Mo., U.S.	C4	102
Hughesville, N.J., U.S.	B3	107
Hughson, Ca., U.S.	D3	82
Hugo, Co., U.S.	B7	83
Hugo, Mn., U.S.	m13	100
Hugo, Ok., U.S.	C6	113
Hugo Lake, res., Ok., U.S.	C6	113
Hugoton, Ks., U.S.	E2	93
Huguley, Al., U.S.	*C4	78
Huichang, China	F8	31
Huichapan, Mex.	m14	63
Huíchŏn, N. Kor.	F3	33

Name	Map Ref	Page
Huila, dept., Ang.	D2	48
Huila, dept., Col.	C2	60
Huila, Nevado del, mtn., Col.	C2	60
Huili, China	F5	31
Huimanguillo, Mex.	B1	62
Huimin, China	D8	31
Huiñaimarca, Lago de l., S.A.	E4	58
Huinan, China	E3	33
Huitzuco [de los Figueroa], Mex.	n14	63
Huixtla, Mex.	D6	63
Huizen, Neth.	B5	17
Huizhou, China	G7	31
Hukou, China	F8	31
Hukuntsi, Bots.	B3	49
Hulah Lake, res., Ok., U.S.	A5	113
Hulan, China	B10	31
Hulbert, Mi., U.S.	B5	99
Hulbert, Ok., U.S.	B6	113
Hulen, Ky., U.S.	D6	94
Hulett, Wy., U.S.	B8	127
Hulin, China	C6	33
Hull, P.Q., Can.	D2	74
Hull (Kingston-upon-Hull), Eng., U.K.	D6	10
Hull, Il., U.S.	D2	90
Hull, Ia., U.S.	A1	92
Hull, Ma., U.S.	B6	98
Hull, co., P.Q., Can.	D2	74
Hull Glacier, Ant.	B35	7
Hulls Cove, Me., U.S.	D4	96
Hulst, Neth.	C4	17
Huludao, China	C9	31
Hulun Lake, l., China	B8	31
Hulwān, Eg.	E3	41
Huma, China	A10	31
Humacao, P.R.	B4	65
Humahuaca, Arg.	D2	55
Humaitá, Braz.	D5	59
Humansdorp, S. Afr.	D3	49
Humansville, Mo., U.S.	D4	102
Humarock, Ma., U.S.	h13	98
Humbe, Ang.	E1	48
Humber, stm., Eng., U.K.	D6	10
Humberside, co., Eng., U.K.	G8	13
Humbird, Wi., U.S.	D3	126
Humble, Tx., U.S.	E5	120
Humboldt, Sk., Can.	E3	75
Humboldt, Il., U.S.	D5	90
Humboldt, Ia., U.S.	B3	92
Humboldt, Ks., U.S.	E8	93
Humboldt, Ne., U.S.	D10	104
Humboldt, Nv., U.S.	C5	105
Humboldt, S.D., U.S.	D8	118
Humboldt, Tn., U.S.	B3	119
Humboldt, co., Ca., U.S.	B2	82
Humboldt, co., Ia., U.S.	B3	92
Humboldt, co., Nv., U.S.	B3	105
Humboldt, stm., Nv., U.S.	C3	105
Humboldt, North Fork, stm., Nv., U.S.	B6	105
Humboldt Mountains, mts., Ant.	B14	7
Humboldt Range, mts., Nv., U.S.	C3	105
Hume, Il., U.S.	D6	90
Hume, Mo., U.S.	C3	102
Hume, N.Y., U.S.	C2	109
Hume, Va., U.S.	B5	123
Hume, Lake, res., Austl.	G6	51
Humenné, Czech.	D6	26
Humeston, Ia., U.S.	D4	92
Hummels Wharf, Pa., U.S.	E8	115
Humnoke, Ar., U.S.	C4	81
Humpata, Ang.	E1	48
Humphrey, Ar., U.S.	C4	81
Humphrey, Ne., U.S.	C8	104
Humphreys, Mo., U.S.	A4	102
Humphreys, co., Ms., U.S.	B3	101
Humphreys, co., Tn., U.S.	A4	119
Humphreys, Mount, mtn., Ca., U.S.	D4	82
Humphreys Peak, mtn., Az., U.S.	B4	80
Humpolec, Czech.	D8	26
Humptulips, Wa., U.S.	B2	124
Hūn, Libya	D3	43
Húnaflói, b., Ice.	n22	14
Hunan, prov., China	F7	31
Hunchun, China	C11	31
Hundested, Den.	C5	15
Hundred, W.V., U.S.	B4	125
Hundred Acre Pond, l., R.I., U.S.	E3	116
Hunedoara, Rom.	C6	24
Hünfeld, F.R.Ger.	C4	19
Hungary, ctry., Eur.	B4	24
Hungerford, Austl.	D5	51
Hüngnam, N. Kor.	D10	31
Hungry Hill, mtn., Ire.	F2	11
Hungry Horse, Mt., U.S.	B2	103
Hungry Horse Reservoir, res., Mt., U.S.	B3	103
Huningue, Fr.		
Hunish, Rubha, c., Scot., U.K.	C2	13
Hunjiang, China	C10	31
Hunn, i., Swe.	u33	14
Hunnewell, Ks., U.S.	E6	93
Hunnewell, Mo., U.S.	B6	102
Hunsrück, mts., F.R.Ger.	D8	12
Hunstanton, Eng., U.K.	I13	12
Hunt, China	E2	81
Hunt, Il., U.S.	C5	90
Hunt, co., Tx., U.S.	C4	120
Hunt, stm., R.I., U.S.	C4	116
Hunte, stm., F.R.Ger.	F2	15
Hunter, Ar., U.S.	C5	81
Hunter, Ks., U.S.	C5	93
Hunter, N.D., U.S.	B8	111
Hunter, Ok., U.S.	A4	113
Hunter, i., Austl.	o14	50
Hunterdon, co., N.J., U.S.	B3	107
Hunter Island, i., B.C., Can.	D3	69
Hunter Mountain, mtn., N.Y., U.S.	C6	109
Hunters, Wa., U.S.	A7	124
Huntersfield Mountain, mtn., N.Y., U.S.	C6	109
Huntersville, W.V., U.S.	C4	125
Huntertown, In., U.S.	B7	91
Huntingburg, In., U.S.	H4	91
Huntingdon, P.Q., Can.	D3	74
Huntingdon, B.C., Can.	f13	69
Huntingdon, Eng., U.K.	I12	12
Huntingdon, Pa., U.S.	F6	115
Huntingdon, Tn., U.S.	A3	119
Huntingdon, co., P.Q., Can.	D3	74
Huntingdon, co., Pa., U.S.	F5	115
Huntingdon Island, i., Nf., Can.	B3	72

Huntingdon Valley, Pa., U.S. *o21 115
Hunting Island, i., S.C., U.S. G7 117
Huntington, Ar., U.S. B1 81
Huntington, In., U.S. C7 91
Huntington, Ma., U.S. B2 98
Huntington, N.J., U.S. B2 107
Huntington, N.Y., U.S. E7 109
Huntington, Or., U.S. C9 114
Huntington, Tx., U.S. D5 120
Huntington, Ut., U.S. D5 121
Huntington, Vt., U.S. C3 122
Huntington, W.V., U.S. C2 125
Huntington, co., In., U.S. C6 91
Huntington Bay, N.Y., U.S. *E7 109
Huntington Beach, Ca., U.S. F4 82
Huntington Center, Vt., U.S. C3 122
Huntington Creek, stm., Nv., U.S. C6 105
Huntington Lake, res., In., U.S. C7 91
Huntington Park, Ca., U.S. *E4 82
Huntington Station, N.Y., U.S. *E7 109
Huntington Woods, Mi., U.S. p15 99
Huntingtown, Md., U.S. C4 97
Huntland, Tn., U.S. B5 119
Huntley, Il., U.S. A5 90
Huntley, Mn., U.S. G4 100
Huntley, Mt., U.S. E8 103
Huntley, Ne., U.S. D6 104
Huntley, Wy., U.S. E8 127
Huntly, Scot., U.K. B5 10
Hunt Mountain, mtn., Wy., U.S. B5 127
Hunts Point, N.S., Can. F5 71
Huntsville, On., Can. B5 73
Huntsville, Al., U.S. A3 78
Huntsville, Ar., U.S. A2 81
Huntsville, In., U.S. E6 91
Huntsville, Ky., U.S. C3 94
Huntsville, Mo., U.S. B5 102
Huntsville, Tn., U.S. C9 119
Huntsville, Tx., U.S. D5 120
Huntsville, Ut., U.S. B4 121
Hunucmá, Mex. C7 63
Hunyuan, China D7 31
Huon Gulf, b., Pap. N. Gui. k12 50
Huoshan, China I7 32
Huoxian, China F4 32
Hupeh see Hubei, prov., China E7 31
Ḥuraydīn, Wādī, val., Eg. D6 41
Hurd, Cape, c., On., Can. B3 73
Hurdland, Mo., U.S. A5 102
Hurdsfield, N.D., U.S. B6 111
Hure Qi, China C9 32
Hurley, Ms., U.S. E5 101
Hurley, Mo., U.S. E4 102
Hurley, N.M., U.S. E1 108
Hurley, N.Y., U.S. D6 109
Hurley, S.D., U.S. D8 118
Hurley, Va., U.S. e9 123
Hurley, Wi., U.S. B3 126
Hurleyville, N.Y., U.S. D6 109
Hurliness, Scot., U.K. B5 13
Hurlock, Md., U.S. C6 97
Hurmägai, Pak. G12 39
Huron, In., U.S. G4 91
Huron, Ks., U.S. C8 93
Huron, Oh., U.S. A3 112
Huron, S.D., U.S. C7 118
Huron, co., On., Can. D3 73
Huron, co., Mi., U.S. E7 99
Huron, co., Oh., U.S. A3 112
Huron, stm., Mi., U.S. p14 99
Huron, Lake, l., N.A. B11 76
Huron Mountains, hills, Mi., U.S. B3 99
Hurricane, In., U.S. E2 78
Hurricane, Ms., U.S. A4 101
Hurricane, Ut., U.S. F2 121
Hurricane, W.V., U.S. C2 125
Hurricane Cliffs, clf, U.S. A2 80
Hurricane Creek, stm., Ar., U.S. C3 81
Hurricane Creek, stm., Ga., U.S. E4 87
Hurricane Mills, Tn., U.S. B4 119
Hurricane Mountain, mtn., Tn., U.S. C9 119
Hurst, Il., U.S. F4 90
Hurst, Tx., U.S. *n9 120
Hurstville, Austl. *F9 50
Hurt, Va., U.S. C3 123
Hürth, F.R.Ger. C1 19
Hurtsboro, Al., U.S. C4 78
Hurup, Den. B2 15
Huşi, Rom. B9 24
Huskvarna (part of Jönköping), Swe. I6 14
Huson, Mt., U.S. C2 103
Hussar, Ab., Can. D4 68
Husser, La., U.S. D5 95
Hustburg, Tn., U.S. B4 119
Hustisford, Wi., U.S. E5 126
Hustle, Va., U.S. B5 123
Hustontown, Pa., U.S. F5 115
Hustonville, Ky., U.S. C5 94
Husum, F.R.Ger. A4 18
Husum, Wa., U.S. D4 124
Hutchins, Tx., U.S. n10 120
Hutchinson, Ks., U.S. D6 93
Hutchinson, Mn., U.S. F4 100
Hutchinson, N.J., U.S. B2 107
Hutchinson, co., S.D., U.S. D8 118
Hutchinson, co., Tx., U.S. B2 120
Hutchinson Island, i., Fl., U.S. E6 86
Hutchinson Island, i., S.C., U.S. k11 117
Hutch Mountain, mtn., Az., U.S. C4 80
Hutsonville, Il., U.S. D6 90
Hüttental, F.R.Ger. C3 19
Huttig, Ar., U.S. D3 81
Hutto, Tx., U.S. D4 120
Hutton, Md., U.S. m12 97
Huttonsville, W.V., U.S. C5 125
Huttwil, Switz. B4 21
Hutuo He, stm., China D8 31
Huu, Indon. G5 34
Huwwärah, Isr. Occ. g12 41
Huxford, Al., U.S. D2 78
Huxley, Ab., Can. C4 68
Huxley, Ia., U.S. C4 92
Huy, Bel. B6 16
Huzgan, Iran F4 39
Hvalpsund, Den. B2 15
Hvannadalshnúkur, mtn., Ice. n24 14
Hvar, i., Yugo. D3 24
Hvidbjerg, Den. B2 15
Hvide Sande, Den. C2 15
Hvitstein, Nor. p28 14
Hvittingfoss (part of Kongsberg), Nor. p28 14
Hwange, Zimb. A4 49
Hwang Ho see Huang He, stm., China D8 31

I

Hyak, Wa., U.S. B4 124
Hyampom, Ca., U.S. B2 82
Hyannis, Ma., U.S. C7 98
Hyannis, Ne., U.S. C4 104
Hyannis Port, Ma., U.S. C7 98
Hyargas Lake, l., Mong. B3 31
Hyas, Sk., Can. F4 75
Hyatts, Oh., U.S. B2 112
Hyattstown, Md., U.S. B3 97
Hyattsville, Md., U.S. C4 97
Hyattville, Wy., U.S. B5 127
Hybart, Al., U.S. D2 78
Hybla Valley, Va., U.S. g12 123
Hydaburg, Ak., U.S. D13 79
Hyde, Pa., U.S. D5 115
Hyde, co., N.C., U.S. B6 110
Hyde, co., S.D., U.S. C6 118
Hyde Park, Austl. F2 50
Hyde Park, Guy. A3 59
Hyde Park, N.Y., U.S. D7 109
Hyde Park, Ut., U.S. B4 121
Hyde Park, Vt., U.S. B3 122
Hyder, Ak., U.S. D13 79
Hyderābād, India E6 36
Hyderābād, Pak. C4 36
Hydetown, Pa., U.S. C2 115
Hydeville, Ct., U.S. B6 84
Hydeville, Vt., U.S. D2 122
Hydra see Ídhra, i., Grc. D4 25
Hydraulic, B.C., Can. C7 69
Hydro, Ok., U.S. B3 113
Hyères, Fr. F7 16
Hyères, Îles d', is., Fr. F7 16
Hyesan, N. Kor. C10 31
Hygiene, Co., U.S. A5 83
Hylo, Ab., Can. B4 68
Hyman, S.C., U.S. D8 117
Hymera, In., U.S. F3 91
Hyndman, Pa., U.S. G4 115
Hyndman Peak, mtn., Id., U.S. F4 89
Hyner, Pa., U.S. D6 115
Hyōpchōn, S. Kor. I4 33
Hyrum, Ut., U.S. B4 121
Hyrynsalmi, Fin. E13 14
Hysham, Mt., U.S. D9 103
Hythe, Ab., Can. B1 68
Hythe, Eng., U.K. C9 12
Hyvinkää, Fin. *G11 14

I

Iaco (Yaco), stm., S.A. D4 58
Iaeger, W.V., U.S. D3 125
Ialomiţa, stm., Rom. C8 24
Iamonia, Lake, l., Fl., U.S. B2 86
Iantha, Mo., U.S. D3 102
Iapu, Braz. B4 56
Iatan, Mo., U.S. B2 102
Iates Point, c., Guam L10 52a
Iatt, Lake, res., La., U.S. C3 95
Iauaretê, Braz. C4 60
Iba, Phil. o12 34
Ibadan, Nig. E5 45
Ibagué, Col. C2 60
Ibanda, Ug. B5 48
Ibapah, Ut., U.S. C2 121
Ibapah Peak, mtn., Ut., U.S. D2 121
Ibarra, Ec. A2 58
Ibb, Yemen C5 47
Ibbenbüren, F.R.Ger. A2 19
Iberá, Laguna, l., Arg. E4 55
Iberia, Mo., U.S. C5 102
Iberia, co., La., U.S. E4 95
Iberville, P.Q., Can. D4 74
Iberville, co., P.Q., Can. D4 74
Iberville, co., La., U.S. D4 95
Iberville, Mont d', mtn., Can. g14 74
Ibi, Nig. E6 45
Ibi, stm., Japan n15 33
Ibiá, Braz. B3 56
Ibiapaba, Serra da, mts., Braz. B2 57
Ibicuí, Braz. D1 56
Ibicuy, Arg. A5 54
Ibirapuitã, stm., Braz. E1 56
Ibitinga, Braz. C3 56
Ibiza, Spain C6 22
Ibiza, i., Spain C6 22
Ibo, Moz. D7 48
Ibri, Oman C5 38
Ibu, Japan N6 52
Ica, Peru D2 58
Ica, dept., Peru D2 58
Içá (Putumayo), stm., S.A. D4 60
Icacos Point, c., Trin. O22 65
Içana, Braz. A4 58
Içana (Isana), stm., S.A. C4 60
Ice Harbor Dam, Wa., U.S. C7 124
Iceland, ctry., Eur. n23 14
Icém, Braz. C3 56
Icó, Braz. B7 69
Ichikawa, Japan n18 33
Ichinomiya, Japan n15 33
Ichinoseki, Japan G10 33
Ichnya, Sov. Un. F9 27
Icicle Creek, stm., Wa., U.S. B5 124
Ickesburg, Pa., U.S. F7 115
Icó, Braz. C3 57
Icy Cape, c., Ak., U.S. A7 79
Icy Strait, strt., Ak., U.S. k22 79
Ida, La., U.S. A2 95
Ida, Mi., U.S. G7 99
Ida, co., Ia., U.S. B2 92
Ida, Lake, l., Mn., U.S. D3 100
Ida, Mount, mtn., Grc. E5 25
Idabel, Ok., U.S. D7 113
Idah, Nig. E6 45
Idaho, co., Id., U.S. D3 89
Idaho, state, U.S. E3 89
Idaho City, Id., U.S. F3 89
Idaho Falls, Id., U.S. F6 89
Idaho Springs, Co., U.S. B5 83
Idalia, Tx., U.S. B8 83
Idalou, Tx., U.S. C2 120
Idamay, W.V., U.S. k10 125
Idana, Ks., U.S. C6 93
Idanha, Or., U.S. C4 114
Idanha-a-Nova, Port. C2 22
Idar-Oberstein, F.R.Ger. D2 19
Idaville, In., U.S. C4 91
Idaville, Or., U.S. B3 114
Idd al Ghanam, Sud. C1 47
Ideal, Ga., U.S. D2 87
Ideal, S.D., U.S. D6 118
Idehan, des., Libya D2 43

Ider, Al., U.S. A4 78
Ider, stm., Mong. B4 31
Idfinā, Eg. C2 41
Idfū, Eg. C3 38
Ídhra (Hydra), i., Grc. D4 25
Idi, Indon. D1 34
Idiofa, Zaire C2 48
Idkū, Eg. C2 41
Idkū Lake, l., Eg. C2 41
Idlewild, Mi., U.S. E5 99
Idlewild, Tn., U.S. A3 119
Idleyld Park, Or., U.S. D3 114
Idlib, Syria E11 40
Idnah, Isr. Occ. C6 41
Idria, Yugo. B2 24
Idrigill Point, c., Scot., U.K. C2 13
Idritsa, Sov. Un. C7 27
Idro, Lake, l., Italy D6 20
Idutywa, Transkei D4 49
Ie, Japan N5 52
Ie Island, i., Japan N5 52
Iepê, Braz. C2 56
Ieper (Ypres), Bel. B5 16
Ierápetra, Grc. E5 40
Ierisós, Grc. B4 25
Iesi (Jesi), Italy C4 23
Ifakara, Tan. C6 48
Ife, Nig. E5 45
Iferouâne, Niger D8 28
Ifôghas, Adrar des, mts., Afr. B5 45
Iganga, Ug. C4 57
Igaraçu, Braz. D3 60
Igara Paraná, stm., Col. C3 56
Igarapava, Braz. B1 57
Igarapé Açu, Braz. C5 59
Igarapé-Miri, Braz. C11 29
Igarka, Sov. Un. C15 40
Iğdir, Tur. E6 44
Igharghar, Oued, val., Afr. D6 44
Igharghar, Oued, val., Alg. F2 55
Iglesia, Arg. E2 23
Iglesias, Italy D3 83
Iglino, Sov. Un. B6 40
Igny, Fr. h9 16
Igoumenítsa, Grc. C3 25
Igra, Sov. Un. B4 28
Igreja, Morro da, mtn., Braz. D2 56
Iguaçu, stm., S.A. D2 56
Iguala, Mex. D5 63
Igualada, Spain B6 22
Iguape, Braz. D2 56
Iguassu Falls, wtfl, S.A. C2 56
Iguatemi, stm., Braz. C3 57
Iguatu, Braz. F1 46
Iguidi, 'Erg, dunes, Afr. D3 44
Igurin, i., Marsh Is. S18 52a
Ih Bogd Mountain, mtn., Mong. C5 31
Iheya Island, i., Japan N5 52
Ihiala, Nig. G2 100
Iida, Japan n16 33
Iijima, Japan n16 33
Iisalmi, Fin. F12 14
Iizuka, Japan J5 33
Ijamsville, Md., U.S. B3 97
Ijebu Ode, Nig. E5 45
Ijill, Kediet, mtn., Maur. B2 45
Ijmuiden, Neth. B4 17
IJssel, stm., Neth. B6 17
IJsselmeer (Zuider Zee), l., Neth. A6 16
Ijui, Braz. D2 56
Ijuí, stm., Braz. D2 56
Ikaría, i., Grc. G10 14
Ikast, Den. B3 15
Ike, i., Japan O6 52
Ikeda, Japan o14 33
Ikela, Zaire B3 48
Ikhtiman, Bul. D6 24
Iki Island, i., Japan J4 33
Ila, Nig. E5 45
Ila, Ga., U.S. B3 87
Ilagan, Phil. B6 34
Ilām, Iran E3 39
Ilanz, Switz. E4 18
Ilasco, Mo., U.S. B6 102
Iława, Pol. D3 91
Ilchester, Md., U.S. B4 97
Ilderton, On., Can. D3 73
Île-à-la-Crosse, Sk., Can. m7 75
Île-à-la-Crosse, Lac, l., Sk., Can. B2 75
Ilebo (Port-Francqui), Zaire B3 48
Île-de-France, hist reg., Fr. C5 16
Ilek, stm., Sov. Un. E20 8
Île Perrot, P.Q., Can. q19 74
Ileret, Kenya A6 48
Île (Isana), stm., S.A. C4 60
Iles, Lac des, l., Sk., Can. B6 68
Ilesha, Nig. E5 45
Ilfeld, N.M., U.S. B4 108
Ilford, Mb., Can. B7 69
Ilfracombe, Eng., U.K. E4 10
Ilgin, Tur. C8 40
Ilhavo, Port. B1 22
Ilhéus, Braz. D3 57
Ili, stm., Asia E10 29
Independencia, Bol. C2 55
Inderborskiy, Sov. Un. A6 28
Index, Wa., U.S. B4 124
India, ctry., Asia D6 36
Indiahoma, Ok., U.S. C3 113
Indian, stm., De., U.S. F4 85
Indian, stm., Mi., U.S. B4 99
Indian, stm., N.Y., U.S. A5 109
Indiana, Pa., U.S. E3 115
Indiana, co., Pa., U.S. E3 115
Indiana, state, U.S. C5 91
Indiana Dunes National Lakeshore, In., U.S. A3 91
Indian Agency, Co., U.S. D3 83
Indianapolis, In., U.S. E5 91
Indian Bay, Mb., Can. E4 70
Indian Bay, b., Phil. D6 86
Indian Beach, De., U.S. F5 85
Indian Brook, stm., F.R.Ger. D5 18
Indian Cedar Swamp, sw., R.I., U.S. F2 116
Indian Cove, Ct., U.S. *D4 84
Indian Creek, stm., Ak., U.S. H5 91
Indian Creek, stm., Md., U.S. C4 97
Indian Creek, stm., Oh., U.S. C1 112
Indian Creek, stm., S.D., U.S. B8 118
Indian Creek, stm., Tn., U.S. B3 119
Indian Creek, stm., W.V., U.S. k9 125
Indian Grave Mountain, hill, Ga., U.S. C2 87

Illnau, Switz. B6 21
Illo, Nig. D5 45
Illora, Spain D4 22
Ilmen, Lake, l., Sov. Un. B8 27
Ilmenau, Ger.D.R. C5 18
Ilmenau, F.R.Ger. B5 18
Ilo, Peru E3 58
Iloilo, Phil. C6 34
Ilorin, Nig. E5 45
Ilovaysk, Sov. Un. r21 27
Iloviya, Sov. Un. D2 28
Ilsenburg, Ger.D.R. B5 19
Ilubabor, prov., Eth. D3 47
Ilwaco, Wa., U.S. C1 124
Ilwaki, Indon. G7 34
Iłża, Pol. C6 26
Imabari, Japan I6 33
Imabetsu, Japan C11 39
Imambaba, Sov. Un. C11 39
Iman, stm., Sov. Un. B11 31
Imandra, Lake, l., Sov. Un. B15 14
Imatra, Fin. *G13 14
Imazu, Japan n14 33
Imbābah (part of Giza), Eg. D3 41
Imbabura, prov., Ec. A2 58
Imbituba, Braz. D3 56
Imbituva, Braz. B6 56
Imbler, Or., U.S. B9 114
Imboden, Ar., U.S. A4 81
Ime, Beinn, mtn., Scot., U.K. D4 13
Imgyt Marsh, sw., Sov. Un. D8 28
Imi, Eth. D5 47
Imilac, Chile C3 105
Imlay, Nv., U.S. C3 105
Imlay City, Mi., U.S. E7 99
Imlaystown, N.J., U.S. B8 15
Immeln, l., Swe. B8 15
Immenstadt, F.R.Ger. E5 18
Immokalee, Fl., U.S. F5 86
Imnaha, Or., U.S. B10 114
Imnaha, stm., Or., U.S. B10 114
Imogene, Ia., U.S. D2 92
Imola, Italy B3 23
Imotski, Yugo. D3 24
Imperatriz, Braz. C1 57
Imperia, Italy C2 23
Imperia, prov., Italy C2 23
Imperial, Sk., Can. F3 75
Imperial, Ca., U.S. F6 82
Imperial, Mo., U.S. C7 102
Imperial, Ne., U.S. D4 104
Imperial, Pa., U.S. k13 115
Imperial, co., Ca., U.S. F6 82
Imperial Beach, Ca., U.S. o15 82
Imperial Dam, U.S. E1 80
Imperial Mills, Ab., Can. B5 68
Imperial Reservoir, res., U.S. E1 80
Imperial Valley, val., Ca., U.S. F6 82
Impfondo, Congo A2 48
Imphal, India D6 36
Imst, Aus. E5 18
Imus, Phil. o13 34
' Imwās, Isr. Occ. h11 41
Ina, Japan n16 33
Ina, Il., U.S. E5 90
Ina, stm., Pol. B3 26
Inagh, Phil. o12 34
Inajá, Braz. C3 57
I-n-Alei, well, Mali C4 45
In Amguel, Alg. E6 44
Inanwatan, Indon. F8 34
Iñapari, Peru D4 58
Inarajan, Guam M9 52a
Inarajan Bay, b., Guam M10 52a
Inari, Fin. C12 14
Inari, l., Fin. C12 14
Inavale, Ne., U.S. D7 104
Inawashiro, Sov. Un. H10 33
In Azaoua, well, Niger B6 45
In Belbel, Alg. D5 44
Inca, Spain C7 22
Incastro, stm., Italy h9 23
Ince Burun, c., Tur. A10 40
Incesu, Tur. C10 40
Inch, Ire. E2 11
Inchard, Loch, b., Scot., U.K. B3 13
Inchelium, Wa., U.S. A7 124
Inchŏn, S. Kor. D10 31
Incline Village, Nv., U.S. D2 105
Indaiatuba, Braz. m8 56
Indalsälven, stm., Swe. F7 14
Indaw, Burma D10 36
Independence, Ca., U.S. D4 82
Independence, Ia., U.S. B6 92
Independence, Ks., U.S. E8 93
Independence, Ky., U.S. B5 94
Independence, Mo., U.S. B3 102
Independence, Ms., U.S. A4 101
Independence, Oh., U.S. *h9 112
Independence, Or., U.S. C3 114
Independence, Va., U.S. D1 123
Independence, Wi., U.S. D2 126
Independence, co., Ar., U.S. B4 81
Independence, stm., N.Y., U.S. B5 109
Independence Mountains, mts., Nv., U.S. C5 105
Independence National Historical Park, Pa., U.S. p21 115
Independence Rock, mtn., Wy., U.S. D5 127

Indian Harbour Beach, Fl., U.S. *D6 86
Indian Head, Sk., Can. G4 75
Indian Head, Md., U.S. C3 97
Indian Heights, In., U.S. *D5 91
Indian Hills, Co., U.S. *B5 83
Indian Island, i., N.C., U.S. B6 110
Indian Lake, N.Y., U.S. B6 109
Indian Lake, l., Mi., U.S. C4 99
Indian Lake, l., N.Y., U.S. B6 109
Indian Lake, l., Oh., U.S. B2 112
Indian Lake Shores, R.I., U.S. F4 116
Indian Mound, Tn., U.S. A4 119
Indian Mound Beach, Ma., U.S. C6 98
Indian Mountain, mtn., Ct., U.S. B2 84
Indian Neck, Ct., U.S. D4 84
Indian Ocean G2 2
Indianola, Il., U.S. D6 90
Indianola, Ia., U.S. C4 92
Indianola, Ms., U.S. B3 101
Indianola, Ne., U.S. D5 104
Indianola, Ok., U.S. B6 113
Indianópolis, Braz. B3 56
Indian Peak, mtn., Ut., U.S. E2 121
Indian Peak, mtn., Wy., U.S. B3 127
Indian Pond, l., Me., U.S. D3 96
Indian Pond, l., Me., U.S. C3 96
Indian Pond, l., Me., U.S. C3 96
Indian Prairie Canal, Fl., U.S. E5 86
Indian Ridge Estates, Az., U.S. E5 80
Indian River, On., Can. C6 73
Indian River, Me., U.S. D5 96
Indian River, Mi., U.S. C6 99
Indian River, co., Fl., U.S. E6 86
Indian River, b., Fl., U.S. D6 86
Indian River Bay, b., De., U.S. F5 85
Indian Rocks Beach, Fl., U.S. p10 86
Indian Springs, Ga., U.S. C3 87
Indian Springs, Nv., U.S. G6 105
Indian Stream, stm., N.H., U.S. f7 106
Indiantown, Fl., U.S. E6 86
Indian Trail, N.C., U.S. B2 110
Indian Valley, Id., U.S. E2 89
Indian Valley, Va., U.S. D2 123
Indian Village, N.Y., U.S. C4 109
Indian Village, La., U.S. D3 95
Indian Wells, Az., U.S. B5 80
Indiaporã, Braz. B2 56
Indigirka, stm., Sov. Un. C17 29
Indio, Ca., U.S. F5 82
Indio, stm., Pan. k10 62
Indochina, reg., Asia B3 34
Indonesia, ctry., Asia F5 34
Indore, India o13 34
Indragiri, stm., Indon. G3 34
Indramayu, Indon. E7 36
Indrāvati, stm., India E6 86
Indrio, Fl., U.S. E6 86
Indus, Mn., U.S. B5 100
Indus, stm., Asia D8 13
Industry, Il., U.S. C3 90
Inebolu, Tur. B9 40
Inecik, Tur. n14 33
Inegöl, Tur. C7 94
Inez, Ky., U.S. C7 94
Inez, Tx., U.S. E4 120
Infanta, Phil. o12 34
Infanta, Phil. o13 34
Infantas, Col. B3 60
Infiernillo, Presa del, res., Mex. D4 63
Infiesto, Spain A3 22
Ingá, Braz. h6 57
Inga Dam, Zaire C1 48
Ingalls, Ar., U.S. D3 81
Ingalls, In., U.S. E6 91
Ingalls, Ks., U.S. E3 93
Ingalls, Mi., U.S. C3 99
Ingalls Park, Il., U.S. B5 90
Ingelheim, F.R.Ger. D3 19
Ingende, Zaire B3 48
Ingeniero Jacobacci, Arg. C3 54
Ingeniero Luiggi, Arg. B4 54
Ingenika, stm., B.C., Can. C5 69
Inger, Mn., U.S. C4 100
Ingersheim, Fr. A3 20
Ingersoll, On., Can. D4 73
Ingham, Austl. A3 113
Ingham, co., Mi., U.S. F6 99
Ingleside, Md., U.S. B5 97
Ingleside, Tx., U.S. F4 120
Inglewood, Austl. D5 73
Inglewood, On., Can. D5 73
Inglewood, N.Z. M15 51
Inglewood, Ca., U.S. n12 82
Inglewood, Ne., U.S. C9 104
Inglis, Mb., Can. D1 70
Ingoda, stm., Sov. Un. B7 31
Ingold, N.C., U.S. C4 110
Ingoldsby, On., Can. C6 73
Ingolstadt, F.R.Ger. D5 18
Ingomar, Ms., U.S. A4 101
Ingomar, Mt., U.S. D9 103
Ingonish Beach, N.S., Can. C9 71
Ingonish Bay, b., Nf., Can. C9 71
Ingraham, Lake, l., Fl., U.S. G5 86
Ingram, Pa., U.S. k13 115
Ingram, Tx., U.S. E3 120
Ingrid Christensen Coast, Ant. C20 7
In Guezzam, Alg. F6 44
Ingul, stm., Sov. Un. H9 27
Ingulets, Sov. Un. H9 27
Inguri, stm., Sov. Un. I6 27
Inhambane, Moz. F6 49
Inhambane, prov., Moz. F6 49
Inhambane, Baía de, b., Moz. F7 49
Inhambupe, Braz. F11 57
Inhaminga, Moz. A6 49
Inharrime, Moz. F6 49
Inhuçu, Braz. B3 57
Inhumas, Braz. B4 56
Iniesta, Spain C5 22
Inírida, stm., Col. D1 58

Inistioge, Ire. E4 11
Injasuti, mtn., Afr. C4 49
Injune, Austl. B7 51
Inkerman, N.B., Can. B5 71
Inkom, Id., U.S. G6 89
Inkster, Mi., U.S. p15 99
Inkster, N.D., U.S. A8 111
Inle Lake, l., Burma B3 35
Inman, Ga., U.S. C2 87
Inman, Ks., U.S. D6 93
Inman, Ne., U.S. B7 104
Inman, S.C., U.S. A3 117
Inn, stm., Eur. D6 18
Innerkip, On., Can. D2 13
Inner Hebrides, is., Scot., U.K. D2 13
Innerleithen, Scot., U.K. E5 13
Inner Mongolia (Nei Mongol), prov., China C7 31
Inner Sound, strt., Scot., U.K. B4 10
Inniscrone, Ire. C2 11
Innisfail, Ab., Can. C4 68
Innisfail, Austl. C8 50
Innisfree, Ab., Can. C5 68
Inniswold, La., U.S. *D4 95
Innokentyevskiy, Sov. Un. B10 33
Innsbruck, Aus. E5 18
Ino, Japan J6 33
Inocência, Braz. B2 56
Inola, Ok., U.S. A6 113
Inongo, Zaire B3 48
Inoucdjouac, P.Q., Can. g11 74
Inowrocław, Pol. B5 26
Ins, Switz. B3 21
In Salah, Alg. D5 44
Insch, Scot., U.K. C6 13
Inscription House Ruin, hist., Az., U.S. A5 80
Insein, Burma E10 36
Insinger, Sk., Can. F4 75
Inspiration, Az., U.S. D5 80
Institute, W.V., U.S. m12 125
Instow, Sk., Can. H1 75
Inta, Sov. Un. B21 8
Intercession City, Fl., U.S. D5 86
Interior, S.D., U.S. D4 118
Interlachen, Fl., U.S. C5 86
Interlaken, Switz. E3 18
Interlaken, Ma., U.S. *B1 98
Interlaken, N.Y., U.S. C4 109
International Falls, Mn., U.S. B5 100
International Peace Garden, N.A. A5 111
Intersection Mountain, mtn., Can. C8 69
Interval, N.H., U.S. B4 106
Inthanon, mtn., Thai. B1 34
Intiyaco, Arg. E3 55
Intracoastal City, La., U.S. E3 95
Intracoastal Waterway, U.S. E4 95
Introbio, Italy E7 21
Intuto, Peru B3 58
Inútil, Bahía, b., Chile h12 54
Inuvik, N.W. Ter., Can. C6 66
Inveraray, Scot., U.K. B4 10
Inver Bay, b., Ire. C3 11
Invercargill, N.Z. Q12 51
Inverell, Austl. E9 50
Invergarry, Scot., U.K. C4 13
Invergordon, Scot., U.K. C4 13
Inver Grove Heights, Mn., U.S. n12 100
Inverkeithing, Scot., U.K. E4 13
Invermay, Sk., Can. F4 75
Invermere, B.C., Can. D9 69
Inverness, P.Q., Can. C6 74
Inverness, N.S., Can. C6 71
Inverness, Scot., U.K. C4 78
Inverness, Ca., U.S. C2 82
Inverness, Fl., U.S. D4 86
Inverness, Il., U.S. B3 101
Inverness, Ms., U.S. B3 101
Inverness, Mt., U.S. B6 103
Inverness, co., N.S., Can. C6 71
Inverurie, Scot., U.K. C6 13
Invisible Mountain, mtn., Id., U.S. F5 89
Inwood, Mb., Can. D3 70
Inwood, On., Can. E2 73
Inwood, Fl., U.S. *D5 86
Inwood, Ia., U.S. A1 92
Inwood, N.Y., U.S. k13 109
Inwood, Vt., U.S. C4 122
Inwood, W.V., U.S. B6 125
Inyanga, Zimb. A5 49
Inyangani, mtn., Zimb. A5 49
Inyan Kara Creek, stm., Wy., U.S. B8 127
Inyan Kara Mountain, mtn., Wy., U.S. B8 127
Inyo, co., Ca., U.S. D5 82
Inyo, Mount, mtn., Ca., U.S. D5 82
Inyokern, Ca., U.S. E5 82
Inyo Mountains, mts., Ca., U.S. D4 82
Inyonga, Tan. C5 48
Inza, Sov. Un. E16 27
Inzana Lake, l., B.C., Can. B5 69
Inza, Grc. C3 40
Ioánnina, Grc. C3 40
Iokanga, Sov. Un. D18 14
Iola, Ks., U.S. E8 93
Iola, Tx., U.S. D4 120
Iola, Wi., U.S. D4 126
Iona, Id., U.S. F7 89
Iona, Mn., U.S. G3 100
Iona, S.D., U.S. D7 118
Iona, i., Scot., U.K. E3 13
Ione, Ca., U.S. C3 82
Ione, Or., U.S. A6 83
Ione, Nv., U.S. E4 105
Ione, Wa., U.S. B7 114
Ionia, Ia., U.S. A5 92
Ionia, Mi., U.S. F5 99
Ionia, Mo., U.S. C4 102
Ionia, co., Mi., U.S. F5 99
Ionian Islands, is., Grc. C3 40
Ionian Sea, Eur. H12 5
Iós, i., Grc. D5 40
Iosco, co., Mi., U.S. D7 99
Iota, La., U.S. D3 95
Iowa, La., U.S. D2 95
Iowa, co., Ia., U.S. C5 92
Iowa, co., Wi., U.S. E3 126
Iowa, state, U.S. B4 92
Iowa, stm., Ia., U.S. C5 92
Iowa, West Branch, stm., Ia., U.S. B4 92
Iowa City, Ia., U.S. C6 92

Name	Map Ref	Page

Iowa Falls, Ia., U.S. — B4 92
Iowa Indian Reservation, U.S. — C8 93
Iowa Lake, l., U.S. — A3 92
Iowa Park, Tx., U.S. — C3 120
Ipameri, Braz. — B3 56
Ipava, Il., U.S. — C3 90
Ipel' (Ipoly), stm., Eur. — D5 26
Iphigenia Bay, b., Ak., U.S. — n22 79
Ipiales, Col. — C2 60
Ipirá, Braz. — D3 57
Ipoh, Malay. — E2 34
Ipoly (Ipel'), stm., Eur. — E5 26
Iporá, Braz. — B2 56
Ippy, Cen. Afr. Rep. — D4 46
Ipsala, Tur. — B6 25
Ipswich, Austl. — E9 50
Ipswich, Eng., U.K. — D7 10
Ipswich, Ma., U.S. — A6 98
Ipswich, S.D., U.S. — B6 118
Ipswich, stm., Ma., U.S. — A5 98
Ipu, Braz. — B2 57
Ipueiras, Braz. — B2 57
Iquique, Chile — D1 55
Iquitos, Peru — B3 58
Ira, Ia., U.S. — C4 92
Ira, Tx., U.S. — C2 120
Ira, Vt., U.S. — D2 122
Iraan, Tx., U.S. — D2 120
Iracoubo, Fr. Gu. — A4 59
Iraí, Braz. — D2 56
Iráklion (Candia), Grc. — E5 40
Irala, Para. — E5 55
Iran, ctry., Asia — C4 38
Iran, Plateau of, plat., Asia — B5 38
Iran Mountains, mts., Asia — E4 34
Trānshahr, Iran — H10 39
Irapa, Ven. — A5 60
Irapuato, Mex. — C4 63
Iraq, ctry., Asia — B4 38
Irasburg, Vt., U.S. — B4 122
Irasville, Vt., U.S. — C3 122
Irazú, Volcán, vol., C.R. — F6 62
Irbid, Jord. — B3 38
Irbîl, Iraq — B4 38
Irbit, Sov. Un. — D21 8
Irebu, Zaire — B2 48
Iredell, co., N.C., U.S. — B2 110
Ireland, In., U.S. — H3 91
Ireland, ctry., Eur. — D3 10
Ireland Island, i., Ber. — p19 64
Irene, S.D., U.S. — D8 118
Ireton, Ia., U.S. — B1 92
Irgiz, Sov. Un. — H9 28
Irgiz, stm., Sov. Un. — D6 28
Iri, S. Kor. — I3 33
Irian Jaya, prov., Indon. — F9 34
Iriba, Chad — B4 46
Iriklinskoye Reservoir, res., Sov. Un. — C5 28
Iringa, Tan. — C6 48
Iringa, prov., Tan. — C6 48
Iriomote Island, i., Japan — G9 31
Irion, co., Tx., U.S. — D2 120
Iriona, Hond. — C5 62
Iriri, stm., Braz. — C4 59
Irish, Mount, mtn., Nv., U.S. — F6 105
Irish Sea, Eur. — D4 10
Irkutsk, Sov. Un. — D13 29
Irma, Ab., Can. — C5 68
Irmo, S.C., U.S. — C5 117
Irō, Cape, c., Japan — I9 33
Iron, Mn., U.S. — C6 100
Iron, co., Mi., U.S. — C6 100
Iron, co., Mo., U.S. — D7 102
Iron, co., Ut., U.S. — F2 121
Iron, co., Wi., U.S. — B3 126
Iron Belt, Wi., U.S. — B3 126
Iron City, Ga., U.S. — E2 87
Iron City, Tn., U.S. — B4 119
Irondale, Al., U.S. — f7 78
Irondale, Mo., U.S. — D7 102
Irondale, Oh., U.S. — B5 112
Irondequoit, N.Y., U.S. — B3 109
Iron Gate, Va., U.S. — C3 123
Iron Gate, val., Eur. — C6 24
Iron Gate Reservoir, res., Ca., U.S. — C5 82? ... B2 82
Ironia, N.J., U.S. — B3 107
Iron Lightning, S.D., U.S. — B4 118
Iron Mountain, Mi., U.S. — C2 99
Iron Mountain, Mo., U.S. — D7 102
Iron Mountain, Wy., U.S. — E7 127
Iron Mountain, mtn., Az., U.S. — D1 123
Iron Mountains, mts., U.S. — D1 123
Iron Ridge, Wi., U.S. — E5 126
Iron River, Mi., U.S. — B2 99
Iron River, Wi., U.S. — B2 126
Irons, Mi., U.S. — D5 99
Ironside, P.Q., Can. — h12 73
Ironside, Or., U.S. — C9 114
Ironspot, Oh., U.S. — C3 112
Iron Springs, Az., U.S. — C3 80
Ironton, Mn., U.S. — D5 100
Ironton, Mo., U.S. — D7 102
Ironton, Oh., U.S. — D3 112
Ironwood, Mi., U.S. — n11 99
Iroquois, Il., U.S. — C6 90
Iroquois, S.D., U.S. — C8 118
Iroquois, co., Il., U.S. — C6 90
Iroquois, stm., U.S. — C6 90
Iroquois, Lake, l., Vt., U.S. — B2 122
Iroquois Falls, On., Can. — o19 73
Irrawaddy, stm., Burma — D10 36
Irrawaddy, Mouths of the, mth., Burma — E10 36
Irricana, Ab., Can. — D4 68
Irrigon, Or., U.S. — B7 114
Irt, stm., Eng., U.K. — F5 13
Irthing, stm., Eng., U.K. — F6 13
Irtysh, Sov. Un. — C8 28
Irtysh, stm., Sov. Un. — D9 29
Irumu, Zaire — A4 48
Irún, Spain — A5 22
Irvine, Ab., Can. — E5 68
Irvine, Ca., U.S. — n13 82
Irvine, Fl., U.S. — C4 86
Irvine, Ky., U.S. — C6 94
Irvine, Pa., U.S. — C3 115
Irvine, stm., Scot., U.K. — E4 13
Irvines Landing, B.C., Can. — E5 69
Irving, Il., U.S. — D4 90
Irving, Tx., U.S. — n10 120
Irvington, Al., U.S. — E1 78
Irvington, Il., U.S. — E4 90
Irvington, Ky., U.S. — C3 94
Irvington, Ne., U.S. — g12 104
Irvington, N.J., U.S. — k8 107
Irvington, N.Y., U.S. — g13 109
Irvington, Va., U.S. — C6 123
Irvona, Pa., U.S. — E5 115
Irwin, Id., U.S. — F7 89
Irwin, Ia., U.S. — C2 92

Irwin, Pa., U.S. — F2 115
Irwin, co., Ga., U.S. — E3 87
Irwinton, Ga., U.S. — D3 87
Irwinville, Ga., U.S. — E3 87
Isa, Nig. — D6 45
Isaac Lake, l., B.C., Can. — C7 69
Isaacs Harbour, N.S., Can. — D8 71
Isabel, Ks., U.S. — E5 93
Isabel, S.D., U.S. — B4 118
Isabel, Bahia, b., Ec. — g5 58
Isabel, Mount, mtn., Wy., U.S. — D2 127
Isabela, P.R. — A1 65
Isabela (Albemarle Island), i., Ec. — g5 58
Isabelia, Cordillera, mts., Nic. — D5 62
Isabella, Ga., U.S. — E3 87
Isabella, Mb., Can. — D1 70
Isabella, Mn., U.S. — C7 100
Isabella, Mo., U.S. — E5 102
Isabella, Ok., U.S. — A3 113
Isabella, Pa., U.S. — G2 115
Isabella, Tn., U.S. — D9 119
Isabella, co., Mi., U.S. — E6 99
Isabella Indian Reservation, Mi., U.S. — E6 99
Isabella Lake, l., Mn., U.S. — C7 100
Isaccea, Rom. — C9 24
Isachsen, N.T., Can. — m31 66
Isafjardardjúp, Ice. — m21 14
Isafjördur, Ice. — m21 14
Isahaya, Japan — J5 33
Isaka, Zaire — B2 48
Isana (Içana), stm., S.A. — C4 60
Isanga, Zaire — A3 48
Isangi, Zaire — A3 48
Isanti, Mn., U.S. — E5 100
Isanti, co., Mn., U.S. — E5 100
Isar, stm., Eur. — D6 18
Isarco, stm., Italy — A3 23
'Īsāwīyah, Isr. Occ. — m14 41
Isbergues, Fr. — D2 17
Isbister, stm., Mb., Can. — C4 70
Ischgl, Aus. — B9 21
Ischia, i., Italy — D4 23
Ischua, N.Y., U.S. — C2 109
Ise (Uji-yamada), Japan — I8 33
Ise, stm., F.R.Ger. — F4 15
Ise Bay, b., Japan — o15 33
Isefjord, b., Den. — C5 15
Isel, stm., Aus. — E6 18
Iselin, N.J., U.S. — B4 107
Iselin, Pa., U.S. — E3 115
Isen, stm., F.R.Ger. — A8 20
Isenthal, Switz. — C6 21
Iseo, Lake, l., Italy — B3 23
Isère, dept., Fr. — D1 20
Isère, stm., Fr. — E6 16
Iserlohn, F.R.Ger. — B2 19
Isernia, Italy — D4 23
Isesaki, Japan — H9 33
Iseyin, Nig. — D6 45
Isfahan see Eşfahān, Iran — B5 38
Ishikari Bay, b., Japan — E10 33
Ishikawa, Japan — O5 52
Ishim, Sov. Un. — D9 29
Ishim, stm., Sov. Un. — D9 29
Ishimbay, Sov. Un. — C5 28
Ishinomaki, Japan — D13 33
Ishioka, Japan — m19 33
Ishpeming, Mi., U.S. — B3 99
Isigny-sur-Mer, Fr. — C3 16
Isil-Kul, Sov. Un. — C8 28
Isinglass, stm., N.H., U.S. — D4 106
Isiolo, Kenya — A6 48
Isiro, Zaire — A4 48
Isisford, Austl. — B5 51
İskenderun (Alexandretta), Tur. — D10 40
İskilip, Tur. — B10 40
Iskitim, Sov. Un. — E25 8
Iskŭr, stm., Bul. — D6 24
Iskushuban, Som. — C7 47
Iskwatikan Lake, l., Sk., Can. — B3 75
Isla Cristina, Spain — D2 22
Islāmābād, Pak. — B5 36
Islamorada, Fl., U.S. — H6 86
Island, Ky., U.S. — C2 94
Island, co., Wa., U.S. — A3 124
Island Beach, N.J., U.S. — D4 107
Island-Brook, P.Q., Can. — D6 74
Island City, Or., U.S. — B8 114
Island Creek, Ma., U.S. — *B6 98
Island Falls, Sk., Can. — B4 75
Island Falls, Me., U.S. — B4 96
Island Grove, Fl., U.S. — C4 86
Island Heights, N.J., U.S. — D4 107
Island Lake, Mb., Can. — C4 70
Island Lake, l., Mb., Can. — C4 70
Island Lake, stm., Mb., Can. — C4 70
Island Park, Id., U.S. — E7 89
Island Park, N.Y., U.S. — *E7 109
Island Park, R.I., U.S. — E6 116
Island Park Reservoir, res., Id., U.S. — E7 89
Island Pond, Vt., U.S. — B5 122
Island Pond, l., N.H., U.S. — E4 106
Islands, Bay of, b., Can. — D2 72
Islands, Bay of, b., N.Z. — K15 51
Isla Vista, Ca., U.S. — E4 82
Islay, Ab., Can. — C5 68
Islay, i., Scot., U.K. — E3 10
Islay, Sound of, strt., Scot., U.K. — E3 13
Isle, Mn., U.S. — D5 100
Isle, stm., Fr. — E6 16
Isle-aux-Haut, Me., U.S. — D4 96
Isle-aux-Morts, Nf., Can. — E2 72
Isle La Motte, Vt., U.S. — B2 122
Isle of Man, ctry., Eur. — C4 10
Isle of Palms, S.C., U.S. — k12 117
Isle of Wight, U.S. — D6 123
Isle of Wight, co., Eng., U.K. — D6 123
Isle of Wight, co., Va., U.S. — D6 123
Isle of Wight Bay, b., Md., U.S. — D7 97
Isle Pierre, B.C., Can. — C6 69
Isle Royale National Park, Mi., U.S. — h9 99
Islesboro, Me., U.S. — D4 96
Islesboro Island, i., Me., U.S. — D4 96
Islesford, Me., U.S. — D4 96
Isleta, N.M., U.S. — C3 108
Isleta Indian Reservation, N.M., U.S. — C3 108
Isleton, Ca., U.S. — C3 82
Islington, Ma., U.S. — h11 98
Islip, N.Y., U.S. — *n15 109
Islip Terrace, N.Y., U.S. — *n15 109
Ismael Cortinas, Ur. — f5 54
Ismailia, Eg. — B3 38
Ismā' ilīyah Canal, Eg. — B3 41
Ismay, Mt., U.S. — D12 103
Isnā, Eg. — C3 38
Isny, F.R.Ger. — A9 21
Isoka, Zam. — D5 48
Isola, Ms., U.S. — B3 101

Isola della Scala, Italy — D7 20
Isola di Capo Rizzuto, Italy — E6 23
Isonzo, stm., Eur. — A4 23
Isparta, Tur. — D8 40
İspir, Tur. — B13 40
Israel, ctry., Asia — B3 38
Israel, stm., N.H., U.S. — B3 106
Israeli Occupied Areas, dep., Asia — B7 41
Issano, Guy. — A3 59
Issaquah, Wa., U.S. — B3 124
Issaquena, co., Ms., U.S. — C2 101
Issia, I.C. — E3 45
Issoire, Fr. — E5 16
Issoudun, Fr. — D4 16
Issuna, Tan. — C5 48
Issy, Fr. — g10 16
İstanbul (Constantinople) (Byzantium), Tur. — B7 40
Istiaía, Grc. — C4 25
Istmina, Col. — C2 60
Isto, Mount, mtn., Ak., U.S. — B11 79
Istokpoga, Lake, l., Fl., U.S. — E5 86
Istranca Mountains, mts., Tur. — B6 25
Istres, Fr. — F6 16
Istrian Peninsula, pen., Yugo. — C1 24
Itá, Braz. — D2 56
Itá, Para. — E4 55
Itabaiana, Braz. — C3 57
Itabaiana, Braz. — D3 57
Itabaianinha, Braz. — D3 57
Itabapoana, stm., Braz. — C4 56
Itaberaba, Braz. — D2 57
Itaberaí, Braz. — B3 56
Itabira, Braz. — B4 56
Itaboraí, Braz. — C4 56
Itaborai, Braz. — D3 57
Itacaiunas, stm., Braz. — D4 59
Itacoatiara, Braz. — C3 59
Itacuaí, stm., Braz. — C3 58
Itaeté, Braz. — A4 57
Itaguaçu, Braz. — B4 56
Itaguari, Braz. — h6 56
Itaguara, Braz. — C4 56
Itaguaí, Braz. — C3 56
Itaguí, Col. — *B2 60
Itaituba, Braz. — C3 59
Itaituba, Braz. — B2 56
Itajaí, Braz. — D3 56
Itajubá, Braz. — C3 56
Italy, Tx., U.S. — C4 120
Italy, ctry., Eur. — C4 23
Italy Cross, N.S., Can. — E5 71
Itamaracá, Ilha de, i., Braz. — h6 57
Itamarandiba, Braz. — B4 56
Itambacuri, Braz. — B4 56
Itambé, Braz. — B4 56
Itanhaém, Braz. — n8 56
Itapaci, Braz. — A3 56
Itapagipe, Braz. — B3 56
Itapecuru, stm., Braz. — B2 57
Itapecuru-Mirim, Braz. — B2 57
Itapemirim, Braz. — C4 56
Itaperuna, Braz. — C4 56
Itapetinga, Braz. — C3 56
Itapetininga, stm., Braz. — m7 56
Itapeva, Braz. — C3 56
Itapicuru, stm., Braz. — D3 57
Itapipoca, Braz. — B3 57
Itapiranga, Braz. — m8 56
Itapiranga, Braz. — C3 59
Itapirapuã, Braz. — B2 56
Itápolis, Braz. — k7 56
Itaporã, Braz. — C2 56
Itaporanga, Braz. — C3 57
Itapuã, Braz. — E4 55
Itapuranga, Braz. — B3 56
Itaquari, Braz. — n9 56
Itarana, Braz. — B4 56
Itararé, Braz. — C3 56
Itararé, stm., Braz. — C3 56
Itārsi, India — F6 37
Itasca, Il., U.S. — k8 90
Itasca, Tx., U.S. — C4 120
Itasca, co., Mn., U.S. — C5 100
Itasca, Lake, l., Mn., U.S. — C3 100
Itatiaia National Park, Braz. — h5 56
Itatiba, Braz. — m8 56
Itatinga, Braz. — m7 56
Itaúna, Braz. — B3 56
Itawamba, co., Ms., U.S. — A5 101
Itéa, Grc. — B3 25
Iténez (Guaporé), stm., S.A. — B3 55
Itenhém, Braz. — B4 56
Ithaca, Mi., U.S. — E6 99
Ithaca, Ne., U.S. — g11 104
Ithaca, N.Y., U.S. — C4 109
Ithaca see Itháki, i., Grc. — B3 25
Itháki, Grc. — C3 25
Itháki (Ithaca), i., Grc. — C3 25
Itigi, Tan. — C5 48
Itimbiri, stm., Zaire — A3 48
Itinga, Braz. — B4 56
Itiquira, Braz. — B2 56
Itiquira, stm., Braz. — *B1 56
Itiquira, Braz. — B2 56
Itirapina, Braz. — m8 56
Itu, Braz. — B2 56
Ituango, Col. — B2 60
Ituí, stm., Braz. — B3 58
Ituiutaba, Braz. — B3 56
Itumbiara, Braz. — B4 56
Ituna, Sk., Can. — F4 75
Ituporanga, Braz. — D3 56
Iturama, Braz. — B3 56
Ituverava, Braz. — C4 56
Ituxi, stm., Braz. — C4 59
Ityāy al Bārūd, Eg. — D2 41
Itzehoe, F.R.Ger. — B4 18
Iuka, Il., U.S. — E5 90
Iuka, Ms., U.S. — A5 101
Iva, S.C., U.S. — C2 117
Iva, W. Sam. — F11 52
Ivaí, stm., Braz. — B7 37
Ivalo, Fin. — C12 14
Ivan, Ar., U.S. — G5 91
Ivanec, Yugo. — B7 92
Ivangrad, Yugo. — F2 100
Ivanhoe, Austl. — F5 51
Ivanhoe, Ca., U.S. — F2 100
Ivanhoe, Mn., U.S. — F2 100
Ivanhoe, Va., U.S. — D2 123
Ivano-Frankovsk, Sov. Un. — G5 27
Ivanovichi, Sov. Un. — D7 33

Ivanovka, Sov. Un. — q21 27
Ivanovka, Sov. Un. — A4 33
Ivanovo, Sov. Un. — D7 29
Ivanteyevka, Sov. Un. — n17 27
Ivato, Madag. — g9 49
Ivaylovgrad, Bul. — E8 24
Ivdel, Sov. Un. — A6 28
Ivesdale, Il., U.S. — D5 90
Ivigtut, Grnld. — C19 128
Ivinheima, stm., Braz. — C2 56
Ivins, Ut., U.S. — F2 121
Ivohibe, Madag. — h9 49
Ivor, Va., U.S. — D6 123
Ivory Coast, ctry., Afr. — E3 45
Ivoryton, Ct., U.S. — D6 84
Ivrea, Italy — B1 23
Ivujivik, P.Q., Can. — f11 74
Ivy Mountain, mtn., Ct., U.S. — B3 84
Ivydale, W.V., U.S. — C3 125
Ivyton, Ky., U.S. — C7 94
Ivywild, Co., U.S. — C6 83
Iwaki (Taira), Japan — H10 33
Iwaki, Mount, mtn., Japan — F10 33
Iwakuni, Japan — I6 33
Iwamizawa, Japan — E10 33
Iwanai, Japan — E10 33
Iwo, Nig. — E5 45
Iwo Jima, i., Japan — E8 6
Iwŏn, N. Kor. — F4 33
Ixelles (Elsene), Bel. — *D4 17
Ixiamas, Bol. — B2 55
Ixmiquilpan, Mex. — m14 63
Ixtacalco (part of Mexico City), Mex. — h9 63
Ixtacihuatl, vol., Mex. — n14 63
Ixtapa, Punta, c., Mex. — D4 63
Ixtapalapa (part of Mexico City), Mex. — h9 63
Ixtlán de Juárez, Mex. — o15 63
Ixtlán del Río, Mex. — C4 63
Izabal, Lago de, l., Guat. — D7 63
Izad Khvāst, Iran — F6 39
Izamal, Mex. — C7 63
Izard, co., Ar., U.S. — A4 81
Izberbash, Sov. Un. — E3 28
Izegem, Bel. — D3 17
Izena Island, i., Japan — N5 52
Izhevsk see Ustinov, Sov. Un. — D8 29
Izhma, stm., Sov. Un. — C19 8
Izmail, Sov. Un. — I7 27
İzmir (Smyrna), Tur. — C6 40
İzmit (Kocaeli) (Nicomedia), Tur. — B7 40
İznik (Nicaea), Tur. — B7 40
İznik Lake, l., Tur. — B7 40
Izozog, Bañados de, sw., Bol. — C3 55
Izra', Syria — o14 41
Izúcar de Matamoros, Mex. — n14 63
Izuhara, Japan — I4 33
Izu Islands, is., Japan — D8 6
Izumo, Japan — I6 33
Izyum, Sov. Un. — G11 27

J

Jabal al Awliyā', Sud. — B3 47
Jabalón, stm., Spain — C4 22
Jabalpur, India — D6 36
Jabālyah, Isr. Occ. — C6 41
Jablonec [nad Nisou], Czech. — C3 26
Jablonná, Czech. — o17 26
Jablunkov Pass, Czech. — D5 26
Jaboatão, Braz. — C4 57
Jaboticabal, Braz. — C3 56
Jabrīn, i., Iran — C5 38
Jaca, Spain — A5 22
Jacala de Ledesma, Mex. — m14 63
Jacaraci, Braz. — D2 57
Jacaré, stm., Braz. — D2 57
Jacareí, Braz. — m9 56
Jacarezinho, Braz. — C2 56
Jagādhri, India — B7 37
Jachin, Al., U.S. — C1 78
Jáchymov, Czech. — C2 26
Jaciara, Braz. — B1 56
Jacinto, Ms., U.S. — A5 101
Jacinto City, Tx., U.S. — r14 120
Jack, Al., U.S. — D4 78
Jack, co., Tx., U.S. — C3 120
Jackfish Lake, l., Sk., Can. — D1 75
Jackhead Harbour, Mb., Can. — D3 70
Jackman, Me., U.S. — C2 96
Jackman Station, Me., U.S. — C2 96
Jack Mountain, mtn., Mt., U.S. — D4 103
Jack Mountain, mtn., Va., U.S. — B3 123
Jack Mountain, mtn., Wa., U.S. — A5 124
Jackpot, Nv., U.S. — B7 105
Jacksboro, Tn., U.S. — C9 119
Jacksboro, Tx., U.S. — C3 120
Jacks Creek, Tn., U.S. — B3 119
Jacks Mountain, mtn., Pa., U.S. — E6 115
Jackson, Al., U.S. — D2 78
Jackson, Ca., U.S. — C3 82
Jackson, Ga., U.S. — C3 87
Jackson, Ky., U.S. — C6 94
Jackson, La., U.S. — D4 95
Jackson, Me., U.S. — D3 96
Jackson, Mi., U.S. — F6 99
Jackson, Mn., U.S. — G3 100
Jackson, Mo., U.S. — D8 102
Jackson, Ne., U.S. — B9 104
Jackson, N.H., U.S. — B4 106
Jackson, N.C., U.S. — A5 110
Jackson, Oh., U.S. — C3 112
Jackson, S.C., U.S. — E4 117
Jackson, Tn., U.S. — B3 119
Jackson, Wi., U.S. — E5 126
Jackson, Wy., U.S. — C2 127
Jackson, co., Al., U.S. — A3 78
Jackson, co., Ar., U.S. — B4 81
Jackson, co., Co., U.S. — A4 83
Jackson, co., Fl., U.S. — B1 86
Jackson, co., Ga., U.S. — B3 87
Jackson, co., Il., U.S. — F4 90
Jackson, co., In., U.S. — G5 91
Jackson, co., Ia., U.S. — B7 92
Jackson, co., Ks., U.S. — C8 93
Jackson, co., Ky., U.S. — C6 94
Jackson, co., Mi., U.S. — F6 99
Jackson, co., Mn., U.S. — G3 100
Jackson, co., Mo., U.S. — B3 102

Jackson, co., N.C., U.S. — f9 110
Jackson, co., Oh., U.S. — C3 112
Jackson, co., Ok., U.S. — C2 113
Jackson, co., Or., U.S. — E4 114
Jackson, co., S.D., U.S. — D4 118
Jackson, co., Tn., U.S. — C8 119
Jackson, co., Tx., U.S. — E4 120
Jackson, co., W.V., U.S. — C3 125
Jackson, co., Wi., U.S. — D3 126
Jackson, stm., Va., U.S. — C3 123
Jackson, Lake, l., Fl., U.S. — E5 86
Jackson, Lake, l., Fl., U.S. — B2 86
Jackson, Mount, mtn., N.H., U.S. — B6 7
Jackson, Port, b., Austl. — F8 51
Jacksonboro, S.C., U.S. — F7 117
Jacksonburg, W.V., U.S. — B4 125
Jackson Center, Oh., U.S. — B1 112
Jackson Center, Pa., U.S. — D1 115
Jackson Dam, Al., U.S. — D2 78
Jackson Hill, In., U.S. — F3 91
Jackson Junction, Ia., U.S. — A5 92
Jackson Lake, res., Ga., U.S. — C3 87
Jackson Lake, res., Wy., U.S. — C2 127
Jackson Mountain, mtn., Me., U.S. — D2 96
Jackson Mountains, mts., Nv., U.S. — B3 105
Jacksonport, Ar., U.S. — B4 81
Jackson's Arm, Nf., Can. — D3 72
Jacksons Gap, Al., U.S. — C4 78
Jacksonville, Al., U.S. — B4 78
Jacksonville, Ar., U.S. — C3 81
Jacksonville, Fl., U.S. — B5 86
Jacksonville, Ga., U.S. — E4 87
Jacksonville, Il., U.S. — D3 90
Jacksonville, Me., U.S. — D5 96
Jacksonville, Mo., U.S. — B5 102
Jacksonville, N.C., U.S. — C5 110
Jacksonville, Oh., U.S. — C3 112
Jacksonville, Or., U.S. — E4 114
Jacksonville, Tx., U.S. — D5 120
Jacksonville, Vt., U.S. — F3 122
Jacksonville Beach, Fl., U.S. — B5 86
Jacksonville Naval Air Station, mil., Fl., U.S. — B5 86
Jacks Peak, mtn., Ut., U.S. — E3 121
Jacktown, Ok., U.S. — B4 113
Jacmel, Haiti — E7 64
Jacob, Congo — B1 48
Jacobābād, Pak. — C4 36
Jacobina, Braz. — D2 57
Jacob Lake, Az., U.S. — A3 80
Jacobson, Mn., U.S. — D5 100
Jacobstown, N.J., U.S. — C3 107
Jacobsville, Mi., U.S. — B2 99
Jacques-Cartier, stm., P.Q., Can. — B6 74
Jacques-Cartier, Détroit de, strt., P.Q., Can. — h8 72
Jacques-Cartier, Mont, mtn., P.Q., Can. — G19 66
Jacques-Cartier, Parc de la, P.Q., Can. — B6 74
Jacquet, stm., N.B., Can. — B3 71
Jacquet River, N.B., Can. — B4 71
Jacquinot Bay, b., Pap. N. Gui. — k13 50
Jacuí, stm., Braz. — D2 56
Jacuípe, stm., Braz. — D3 57
Jacumba, Ca., U.S. — F5 82
Jacundá, stm., Braz. — C4 59
Jadabpur, India — *D8 36
Jade Bay, b., F.R.Ger. — B4 18
Jadū, Libya — C2 43
Jādwin, Mo., U.S. — D6 102
Jægerspris, Den. — C5 15
Jaén, Peru — C2 58
Jaén, Spain — D4 22
Jaffa, Cape, c., Austl. — G6 50
Jaffa Gate, hist., Isr. Occ. — m14 41
Jaffna, Sri L. — G7 36
Jaffrey, N.H., U.S. — E2 106
Jaffrey Center, N.H., U.S. — E2 106
Jagdalpur, India — E7 36
Jagin, stm., Iran — H9 39
Jagst, stm., F.R.Ger. — D4 19
Jaguarão, Braz. — C6 54
Jaguariaíva, Braz. — C3 56
Jagüey Grande, Cuba — C3 64
Jahrom, Iran — C5 38
Jailolo, Indon. — E7 34
Jaipur, India — D8 36
Jaisalmer, India — C5 36
Jajce, Yugo. — C3 24
Jājpur, India — D8 36
Jakarta (Djakarta), Indon. — G3 34
Jakestown, Tn., U.S. — C8 119
Jakobstad, Fin. — F10 14
Jalaihai Point, c., Guam — M10 52
Jalālābād, Afg. — B5 36
Jalālah al Baḥrīyah, Jabal, plat., Eg. — E4 41
Jalapa, Guat. — E6 63
Jalapa Enríquez, Mex. — D5 63
Jalaun, India — C6 36
Jaldak, Afg. — D1 37
Jalesar, India — D6 36
Jālgaon, India — m11 63
Jalisco, state, Mex. — C3 63
Jālna, India — J7 36
Jalón, stm., Spain — B5 22
Jālor, India — D5 36
Jalpa, Mex. — C4 63
Jalpaiguri, India — D12 37
Jalpan, Mex. — C5 63
Jālū, Wāḥat, well, Libya — D5 43
Jālūlā', Iraq — B4 38
Jamaame, Som. — B8 47
Jamaica, Ia., U.S. — C3 92
Jamaica, ctry., N.A. — E6 64
Jamaica Channel, strt., N.A. — E12 64
Jamalpur, Bngl. — E12 37
Jamanxim, stm., Braz. — D3 59
Jamari, stm., Braz. — B3 57
Jambi, Indon. — F3 34
Jambuair, Cape, c., Indon. — D1 34
James, Ia., U.S. — B1 92
James, stm., U.S. — A8 76
James, stm., U.S. — D7 111
James, stm., Mo., U.S. — E4 102
James, stm., S.D., U.S. — D8 118
James, stm., Va., U.S. — C4 123
James Bay, b., Can. — F16 66
James Branch, stm., De., U.S. — F3 85

Jamesburg, N.J., U.S. — C4 107
James City, N.C., U.S. — B5 110
James City, Pa., U.S. — C4 115
James City, co., Va., U.S. — C6 123
James Craik, Arg. — A4 54
James Creek, Pa., U.S. — F5 115
James Island, B.C., Can. — g12 69
James Island, S.C., U.S. — k12 117
James Island, S.C., U.S. — C5 97
James Island, i., S.C., U.S. — F8 117
Jameson, Mo., U.S. — A4 102
Jamesport, Mo., U.S. — B4 102
James River Bridge, Va., U.S. — k15 123
James Ross Island, i., Ant. — C7 7
James Ross Strait, strt., N.T., Can. — C13 66
Jamestown, Austl. — F2 51
Jamestown, Ire. — D3 11
Jamestown, Al., U.S. — A4 78
Jamestown, Ar., U.S. — *B4 81
Jamestown, Ca., U.S. — D3 82
Jamestown, Co., U.S. — A5 83
Jamestown, Il., U.S. — E4 90
Jamestown, In., U.S. — E4 91
Jamestown, Ks., U.S. — C6 93
Jamestown, Ky., U.S. — D4 94
Jamestown, La., U.S. — B2 95
Jamestown, Mo., U.S. — C5 102
Jamestown, N.Y., U.S. — C1 109
Jamestown, N.C., U.S. — B3 110
Jamestown, N.D., U.S. — C7 111
Jamestown, Oh., U.S. — C2 112
Jamestown, Pa., U.S. — D1 115
Jamestown, R.I., U.S. — F5 116
Jamestown, S.C., U.S. — E8 117
Jamestown, Tn., U.S. — C9 119
James Town, Wy., U.S. — B2 127
Jamestown Dam, N.D., U.S. — C7 111
Jamestown Reservoir, res., N.D., U.S. — C7 111
Jamesville, N.C., U.S. — B6 110
Jamesville, Va., U.S. — C7 123
Jamieson, Or., U.S. — C9 114
Jamiltepec, Mex. — D5 63
Jamison, Ne., U.S. — B6 104
Jammā' īn, Isr. Occ. — g11 41
Jammerbugten, b., Den. — A3 15
Jammu, India — B5 36
Jammu and Kashmir, dep., Asia — A6 36
Jāmnagar (Navanagar), India — D5 36
Jāmpur, Pak. — C3 37
Jamsah, Eg. — D6 43
Jamshedpur, India — D8 36
Jämshög, Swe. — B8 15
Jamul, Ca., U.S. — F5 82
Jamuna, stm., Bngl. — E12 37
Janaúba, Braz. — B4 56
Jandaia, Braz. — B2 56
Jandaq, Iran — D7 39
Jandiatuba, stm., Braz. — C3 58
Jándula, stm., Spain — C4 22
Jane, Mo., U.S. — E3 102
Jane Lew, W.V., U.S. — B4 125
Janesville, Ca., U.S. — B3 82
Janesville, Il., U.S. — D5 90
Janesville, Ia., U.S. — B5 92
Janesville, Wi., U.S. — F5 126
Janeville, N.B., Can. — B4 71
Jangipur, India — E12 37
Janīn, Isr. Occ. — B7 41
Jan Lake, l., Sk., Can. — C4 75
Jan Mayen, i., Nor. — B15 128
Janos, Mex. — A3 63
Jánoshalma, Hung. — B4 24
Janów Lubelski, Pol. — C7 26
Jansen, Sk., Can. — F3 75
Jansen, Co., U.S. — D6 83
Jansen, Ne., U.S. — D8 104
Januária, Braz. — B4 56
Japan, ctry., Asia — D12 31
Japan, Sea of, Asia — C12 31
Japaratuba, Braz. — D3 57
Japurá (Caquetá), stm., S.A. — D4 60
Jaqué, Pan. — G8 62
Jarábulus, Syria — D12 40
Jaraguá, Braz. — B3 56
Jaraguá do Sul, Braz. — D3 56
Jaral del Progreso, Mex. — m13 63
Jarales, N.M., U.S. — C3 108
Jarama, stm., Spain — B4 22
Jaramānah, Syria — *F11 40
Jarash, Jord. — B7 41
Jarbidge, Nv., U.S. — B6 105
Jarbidge, East Fork, stm., U.S. — B6 105
Jardim, Braz. — C1 56
Jardim de Angicos, Braz. — g6 57
Jardim do Seridó, Braz. — C4 57
Jardinah, Libya — C4 43
Jardinópolis, Braz. — k8 56
Jardines de la Reina, Archipiélago de los, is., Cuba — D4 64
Järfälla, Swe. — *H7 14
Jargalang, China — C10 32
Jargalant, Mong. — B7 31
Jarnac, Fr. — E5 16
Jarny, Fr. — C6 17
Jarocin, Pol. — C3 26
Jaroměř, Czech. — C3 26
Jaroso, Co., U.S. — D5 83
Jarratt, Va., U.S. — D5 123
Jarrell, Tx., U.S. — D4 120
Jarrettsville, Md., U.S. — A5 97
Jarrow, Eng., U.K. — B3 55? — B5 55
Jaru, Braz. — B3 55
Jarud Qi, China — C9 31
Jarvie, Ab., Can. — B4 68
Jarvis, On., Can. — E4 73
Jarvis, i., Oc. — G12 61
Jarvisburg, N.C., U.S. — A7 110
Jäsk, Iran — I8 39
Jasło, Pol. — F5 26
Jasmine Estates, Fl., U.S. — D4 86
Jason Peninsula, pen., Ant. — C7 7
Jasonville, In., U.S. — F3 91
Jasper, Ab., Can. — C1 68
Jasper, On., Can. — C9 73
Jasper, Al., U.S. — B2 78
Jasper, Ar., U.S. — B2 81
Jasper, Fl., U.S. — B4 86
Jasper, Ga., U.S. — B2 87

Index

Name	Map Ref	Page

Jasper, In., U.S. — H4 91
Jasper, Mn., U.S. — G2 100
Jasper, Mo., U.S. — D3 102
Jasper, N.Y., U.S. — C3 109
Jasper, Oh., U.S. — C2 112
Jasper, Or., U.S. — D4 114
Jasper, Tn., U.S. — D8 119
Jasper, Tx., U.S. — D6 120
Jasper, co., Ga., U.S. — C3 87
Jasper, co., Il., U.S. — D5 90
Jasper, co., In., U.S. — B3 91
Jasper, co., Ia., U.S. — C4 92
Jasper, co., Ms., U.S. — C4 101
Jasper, co., Mo., U.S. — D3 102
Jasper, co., S.C., U.S. — G5 117
Jasper, co., Tx., U.S. — D5 120
Jasper Lake, l., Ab., Can. — C1 68
Jasper National Park, Ab., Can. — C1 68
Jastarnia. Pol. — A5 26
Jastrzebia Góra, Pol. — A5 26
Jastrzębie-Zdrój, Pol. — h9 26
Jászapáti, Hung. — B5 24
Jászberény, Hung. — B4 24
Jataí, Braz. — B2 56
Jāti, Pak. — E2 37
Jatibonico, Cuba — D4 64
Játiva, Spain — C5 22
Jatni, India — G10 37
Jatobá, stm., Braz. — E4 59
Jaú, Braz. — C3 56
Jaú, stm., Braz. — C2 59
Jauaperi, stm., Braz. — B2 59
Jaumave, Mex. — C5 63
Jaunpur, India — C7 36
Java, S.D., U.S. — B6 118
Java, Va., U.S. — D3 123
Java (Jawa), i., Indon. — G3 34
Javari see Yavari, stm., S.A. — B3 58
Java Sea, Indon. — G4 34
Jávea, Spain — C6 22
Jawhār, India — H4 37
Jawor, Pol. — C4 26
Jaworzno, Pol. — g10 26
Jay, Fl., U.S. — u14 86
Jay, Me., U.S. — D2 96
Jay, Ok., U.S. — A7 113
Jay, co., In., U.S. — D7 91
Jayanca, Peru — C2 58
Jaya Peak, mtn., Indon. — F9 34
Jayapura (Sukarnapura), Indon. — F10 34
Jay Em, Wy., U.S. — D8 127
Jayess, Ms., U.S. — D3 101
Jay Peak, mtn., Vt., U.S. — B3 122
Jayton, Tx., U.S. — C2 120
Jaz Mūriān, Hāmūn-e, l., Iran — H9 39
J. B. Thomas, Lake, res., Tx., U.S. — C2 120
Jean, Nv., U.S. — H6 105
Jeanerette, La., U.S. — E4 95
Jean Lafitte National Historical Park, La., U.S. — k12 95
Jeannette, Pa., U.S. — F2 115
Jeannette Island, i., Sov. Un. — B35 128
Jebba, Nig. — E5 45
Jeberos, Peru — C2 58
Jedburg, S.C., U.S. — h11 117
Jedburgh, Sk., Can. — F4 75
Jedburgh, Scot., U.K. — C5 10
Jeddito, Az., U.S. — B5 80
Jeddo, Mi., U.S. — E8 99
Jeddore Lake, res., Nf., Can. — D3 72
Jedrzejów, Pol. — C6 26
Jeetze, stm., Eur. — B5 18
Jeff, Ky., U.S. — C6 94
Jeff Davis, co., Ga., U.S. — E4 87
Jeff Davis, co., Tx., U.S. — o12 120
Jeffers, Mn., U.S. — F3 100
Jeffers, Mt., U.S. — E5 103
Jefferson, Al., U.S. — C2 78
Jefferson, Ar., U.S. — C3 81
Jefferson, Co., U.S. — B5 83
Jefferson, Ga., U.S. — B3 87
Jefferson, Ia., U.S. — B3 92
Jefferson, Me., U.S. — D3 96
Jefferson, N.H., U.S. — B4 106
Jefferson, N.C., U.S. — A1 110
Jefferson, Oh., U.S. — A4 112
Jefferson, Or., U.S. — C3 114
Jefferson, Pa., U.S. — *F2 115
Jefferson, S.C., U.S. — B7 117
Jefferson, S.D., U.S. — E9 118
Jefferson, Tx., U.S. — C5 120
Jefferson, Wi., U.S. — E5 126
Jefferson, co., Al., U.S. — B3 78
Jefferson, co., Ar., U.S. — C3 81
Jefferson, co., Co., U.S. — B5 83
Jefferson, co., Fl., U.S. — B3 86
Jefferson, co., Ga., U.S. — C4 87
Jefferson, co., Id., U.S. — F6 89
Jefferson, co., Il., U.S. — E5 90
Jefferson, co., In., U.S. — G6 91
Jefferson, co., Ks., U.S. — C8 93
Jefferson, co., Ky., U.S. — B4 94
Jefferson, co., La., U.S. — E5 95
Jefferson, co., Ms., U.S. — D2 101
Jefferson, co., Mo., U.S. — C7 102
Jefferson, co., Mt., U.S. — D4 103
Jefferson, co., Ne., U.S. — D8 104
Jefferson, co., N.Y., U.S. — A5 109
Jefferson, co., Oh., U.S. — B5 112
Jefferson, co., Ok., U.S. — C4 113
Jefferson, co., Or., U.S. — C5 114
Jefferson, co., Pa., U.S. — D3 115
Jefferson, co., Tn., U.S. — C10 119
Jefferson, co., Tx., U.S. — E5 120
Jefferson, co., Wa., U.S. — B2 124
Jefferson, co., W.V., U.S. — B7 125
Jefferson, co., Wi., U.S. — E5 126
Jefferson, stm., Mt., U.S. — E5 103
Jefferson, Mount, mtn., Id., U.S. — E7 89
Jefferson, Mount, mtn., Nv., U.S. — E5 105
Jefferson, Mount, mtn., Or., U.S. — C5 114
Jefferson City, Mo., U.S. — C5 102
Jefferson City, Mt., U.S. — D5 103
Jefferson City, Tn., U.S. — C10 119
Jefferson Davis, co., La., U.S. — D3 95
Jefferson Davis, co., Ms., U.S. — D4 101
Jefferson Farms, De., U.S. — i7 85
Jefferson Hill, hill, Ky., U.S. — g11 94
Jefferson Manor, Va., U.S. — *B5 123

Jefferson Proving Ground, mil., In., U.S. — G7 91
Jeffersontown, Ky., U.S. — B4 94
Jefferson Village, Va., U.S. — *B5 123
Jeffersonville, Ga., U.S. — D3 87
Jeffersonville, In., U.S. — H6 91
Jeffersonville, Ky., U.S. — C6 94
Jeffersonville, N.Y., U.S. — D6 109
Jeffersonville, Oh., U.S. — C2 112
Jeffersonville, Vt., U.S. — B3 122
Jeffrey, W.V., U.S. — D3 125
Jeffrey City, Wy., U.S. — D5 127
Jeffries Creek, stm., S.C., U.S. — C8 117
Jega, Nig. — D5 45
Jehossee Island, i., S.C., U.S. — k11 117
Jejui-Guazú, stm., Para. — D4 55
Jēkabpils, Sov. Un. — C5 27
Jekyll Island, i., Ga., U.S. — E5 87
Jelenia Góra (Hirschberg), Pol. — C3 26
Jelgava (Yelgava), Sov. Un. — C4 27
Jellico, Tn., U.S. — C9 119
Jelling, Den. — C3 15
Jelm, Wy., U.S. — E6 127
Jelm Mountain, mtn., Wy., U.S. — E7 127
Jelöya, i., Nor. — p28 14
Jemaja, i., Indon. — K6 35
Jember, Indon. — G4 34
Jemez, stm., N.M., U.S. — k7 108
Jemez Dam, N.M., U.S. — k7 108
Jemez Indian Reservation, N.M., U.S. — h7 108
Jemez Pueblo, N.M., U.S. — B3 108
Jemez Springs, N.M., U.S. — B3 108
Jemison, Al., U.S. — C3 78
Jemseg, N.B., Can. — D3 71
Jemtland, Me., U.S. — A4 96
Jena, Ger.D.R. — C5 18
Jena, Fl., U.S. — C3 86
Jena, La., U.S. — C3 95
Jenaz, Switz. — C8 21
Jenbach, Aus. — B7 20
Jendouba, Tun. — F2 23
Jenera, Oh., U.S. — B2 112
Jenison, Mi., U.S. — *F5 99
Jenkins, Ky., U.S. — C7 94
Jenkins, Mn., U.S. — D4 100
Jenkins, N.J., U.S. — D3 107
Jenkinsburg, Ga., U.S. — C2 87
Jenkinsville, S.C., U.S. — C5 117
Jenkintown, Pa., U.S. — o21 115
Jenks, Ok., U.S. — A6 113
Jenner, Ab., Can. — D5 68
Jenners, Pa., U.S. — F3 115
Jennie, Ar., U.S. — D4 81
Jennings, Fl., U.S. — B3 86
Jennings, Ks., U.S. — C3 93
Jennings, La., U.S. — D3 95
Jennings, Md., U.S. — k12 97
Jennings, Mi., U.S. — D5 99
Jennings, Mo., U.S. — f13 102
Jennings, Ok., U.S. — A5 113
Jennings, co., In., U.S. — G6 91
Jennings Lodge, Or., U.S. — *B4 114
Jenny Jump Mountain, mtn., N.J., U.S. — B3 107
Jenny Lind, Ar., U.S. — B1 81
Jensen, Ut., U.S. — C6 121
Jensen Beach, Fl., U.S. — E6 86
Jeptha Knob, hill, Ky., U.S. — B4 94
Jequié, Braz. — C8 57
Jequitaí, Braz. — D6 57
Jequitinhonha, Braz. — B4 56
Jequitinhonha, stm., Braz. — E2 57
Jerada, Mor. — C4 44
Jérémie, Haiti — E6 64
Jeremoabo, Braz. — D7 57
Jerez de García Salinas, Mex. — C4 63
Jerez de la Frontera, Spain — I2 22
Jerez de los Caballeros, Spain — C2 22
Jericho, Austl. — A6 51
Jericho (Arīḥā), Isr. Occ. — C7 41
Jericho, Ar., U.S. — B5 81
Jericho, N.Y., U.S. — *E7 109
Jericho, Vt., U.S. — B3 122
Jericho Center, Vt., U.S. — C3 122
Jerico Springs, Mo., U.S. — D4 102
Jerimoth Hill, hill, R.I., U.S. — C1 116
Jermyn, Pa., U.S. — C10 115
Jermyn, Tx., U.S. — C3 120
Jerome, Az., U.S. — C3 80
Jerome, Id., U.S. — G4 89
Jerome, Ia., U.S. — D4 92
Jerome, Mi., U.S. — F6 99
Jerome, Mo., U.S. — D6 102
Jerome, Pa., U.S. — F4 115
Jerome, co., Id., U.S. — G4 89
Jeromesville, Oh., U.S. — B3 112
Jersey, co., Il., U.S. — D3 90
Jersey, dep., Eur. — F5 10
Jersey City, N.J., U.S. — B4 107
Jersey Mountain, mtn., Id., U.S. — E3 89
Jersey Shore, Pa., U.S. — D7 115
Jerseyville, Il., U.S. — D3 90
Jerumenha, Braz. — E5 57
Jerusalem (Yerushalayim), Isr. — B3 38
Jerusalem, Ar., U.S. — B3 81
Jerusalem, Oh., U.S. — C4 112
Jervis Bay, b., Austl. — G9 50
Jervis Inlet, b., B.C., Can. — D6 69
Jesenice Reservoir, res., Czech. — C7 19
Jesenice, Czech. — C4 26
Jessamine, co., Ky., U.S. — C5 94
Jessen, Ger.D.R. — B7 19
Jessie, N.D., U.S. — B7 111
Jessie, Ar., U.S. — C2 81
Jessnitz, Ger.D.R. — B7 19
Jessore, Bngl. — F12 37
Jessup, Md., U.S. — B4 97
Jessup, Pa., U.S. — m18 115
Jesterville, Md., U.S. — D6 97
Jesup, Ga., U.S. — E5 87
Jesup, Ia., U.S. — B5 92
Jesus, Lake, l., Fl., U.S. — D5 86
Jésus, Île, i., P.Q., Can. — p19 74
Jesús Carranza, Mex. — D5 63
Jesús María, Arg. — A4 54
Jesús María, Peru — *D2 54
Jet, Ok., U.S. — A3 113
Jetersville, Va., U.S. — C4 123
Jetmore, Ks., U.S. — D4 93
Jette, Bel. — D4 17
Jeumont, Fr. — D4 17
Jever, F.R.Ger. — B3 18
Jewel Cave National Monument, S.D., U.S. — D2 118
Jewell, Ia., U.S. — B4 92

Jewell, Ks., U.S. — C5 93
Jewell, co., Ks., U.S. — C5 93
Jewell Ridge, Va., U.S. — e10 123
Jewett, Il., U.S. — D5 90
Jewett, Oh., U.S. — B4 112
Jewett, Tx., U.S. — D4 120
Jewett City, Ct., U.S. — C8 84
Jewett Lake, l., Sk., Can. — A3 75
Jeypore, India — E7 36
Jeziorka, stm., Pol. — m14 26
Jhal, Pak. — C1 37
Jhālawār, India — E6 37
Jhal Jhao, Pak. — D6 36
Jhang Maghiāna, Pak. — B4 37
Jhang Sadar, Pak. — *B5 36
Jhānsi, India — C6 36
Jhawāni, Nepal — D10 37
Jhelum, Pak. — B5 36
Jhelum, stm., Asia — B5 36
Jhūnjhunu, India — C5 37
Jialing Jiang, stm., China — E6 31
Jiamusi, China — B11 31
Ji'an, China — F7 31
Ji'an, China — D12 32
Jianchang, China — D11 32
Jiande, China — J8 32
Jiangling, China — E7 31
Jiangmen, China — G7 31
Jiangsu, prov., China — E9 31
Jiangxi, prov., China — F8 31
Jiangyin (Chengjiang), China — I9 32
Jiangyou, China — E5 31
Jianli, China — J5 32
Jianning, China — K7 32
Jian'ou, China — F8 31
Jianping, China — C8 31
Jianshi, China — I3 32
Jianshui, China — G5 31
Jianyang, China — K8 32
Jiaohe, China — E3 33
Jiaozhou Bay, b., China — F9 32
Jiaozuo, China — D7 31
Jiashan, China — H8 32
Jiaxian, China — H3 32
Jiaxing, China — E9 31
Jiayi, China — I5 32
Jicarilla Indian Reservation, N.M., U.S. — A2 108
Jičín, Czech. — C3 26
Jiddah, Sau. Ar. — D3 38
Jiddī, Jabal al, mtn., Eg. — D5 41
Jīdū, Bi'r al, well, Eg. — D5 41
Jiek'kevarri, mtn., Nor. — C8 14
Jiexiu, China — F4 32
Jieyang, China — G8 31
Jifnā, Isr. Occ. — h11 41
Jigger, La., U.S. — B4 95
Jiggs, Nv., U.S. — C6 105
Jihlava, Czech. — D3 26
Jihočeský, prov., Czech. — D9 19
Jijel, Alg. — B6 44
Jijiga, Eth. — G2 47
Jijona, Spain — C5 22
Jilbānah, Bi'r al, well, Eg. — D4 41
Jilib, Som. — C8 47
Jilin, China — C10 31
Jilin, prov., China — C10 31
Jiloca, stm., Spain — B5 22
Jílové u Prahy, Czech. — o18 26
Jima, Eth. — D4 47
Jimbolia, Rom. — C5 24
Jimena [de la Frontera], Spain — D3 22
Jim Falls, Wi., U.S. — C2 126
Jim Hogg, co., Tx., U.S. — F3 120
Jim Lake, res., N.D., U.S. — B7 111
Jimo, China — F9 32
Jim Thorpe, Pa., U.S. — E10 115
Jim Wells, co., Tx., U.S. — F3 120
Jināḥ, Eg. — D6 43
Jinan (Tsinan), China — D8 31
Jincheng, China — G5 32
Jindřichův Hradec, Czech. — D3 26
Jingbian, China — F3 32
Jingchuan, China — G2 32
Jingde, China — I8 32
Jingdezhen, China — F8 31
Jing He, stm., China — G3 32
Jinghong, China — G3 32
Jingmen, China — I5 32
Jingning, China — G1 32
Jingshan, China — I5 32
Jingxi, China — D9 32
Jingxian, China — I8 32
Jingxing, China — K3 32
Jingziguan, China — H4 32
Jinhua, China — F8 31
Jining, China — C3 31
Jining, China — D8 31
Jinja, Ug. — A5 48
Jinniu, China — I6 32
Jinotega, Nic. — E7 63
Jinotepe, Nic. — E7 63
Jinsha Jiang, stm., China — F4 31
Jinshi, China — J4 32
Jinta, China — C4 31
Jinxian, China — D9 32
Jinyun, China — J9 32
Jinzhou, China — C9 31
Ji-Paraná, Braz. — E5 59
Jiparaná, stm., Braz. — D2 59
Jipijapa, Ec. — B1 58
Jiquilisco, El Sal. — D3 62
Jiquilpan de Juárez, Mex. — n12 63
Jirjā, Eg. — C3 38
Jirkov, Czech. — B7 19
Jisr ash Shughūr, Syria — E11 40
Jiu, stm., Rom. — C6 24
Jiujiang, China — F8 31
Jiuquan, China — D4 31
Jiurongcheng, China — F10 32
Jiwani, Rās, c., Pak. — I10 39
Jixi, China — B11 31
Jixian, China — G6 32
Jizera, stm., Czech. — C9 19
Joaçaba, Braz. — B4 56
Joaíma, Braz. — B4 56
Joanna, S.C., U.S. — C4 117
João Belo see Xai-Xai, Moz. — C5 49
João Câmara, Braz. — g6 57
João Pessoa (Paraíba), Braz. — C6 57
João Pinheiro, Braz. — C4 56
Joaquín V. González, Arg. — E3 55
Job, W.V., U.S. — D3 123
Job Peak, mtn., Nv., U.S. — D3 105
Jobstown, N.J., U.S. — C3 107
Jocassee, Lake, res., U.S. — B1 117
Jocotepec, Mex. — m12 63
Jódar, Spain — D4 22
Jo Daviess, co., Il., U.S. — A3 90

Jodhpur, India — C5 36
Jodie, W.V., U.S. — m13 125
Jodoigne, Bel. — D4 17
Joe Batt's Arm, Nf., Can. — D4 72
Joensuu, Fin. — F13 14
Joes, Co., U.S. — B8 83
Joes Brook, stm., Vt., U.S. — C4 122
Joes Creek, stm., W.V., U.S. — m12 125
Joetsu, Japan — H9 33
Jœuf, Fr. — C6 16
Joffre, Mount, mtn., Can. — D3 68
Joggins, N.S., Can. — D5 71
Jogjakarta see Yogyakarta, Indon. — G4 34
Johannesburg, S. Afr. — C4 49
Johannesburg, Ca., U.S. — E5 82
Johannesburg, Mi., U.S. — D6 99
John, Cape, c., N.S., Can. — D6 71
John Crow Mountains, mts., Jam. — E16 65
John Day, Or., U.S. — C8 114
John Day, stm., Or., U.S. — B6 114
John Day, North Fork, stm., Or., U.S. — C7 114
John Day, South Fork, stm., Or., U.S. — D5 114
John Day Dam, U.S. — C6 114
John Day Fossil Beds National Monument, Or., U.S. — C6 114
John F. Kennedy Space Center, sci., Fl., U.S. — D6 86
John H. Kerr Dam, Va., U.S. — D4 123
John H. Kerr Reservoir, res., U.S. — D4 123
John Martin Reservoir, res., Co., U.S. — C7 83
John Muir National Historical Site, hist., Ca., U.S. — h8 82
John o'Groats, Scot., U.K. — B5 13
John Redmond Reservoir, res., Ks., U.S. — D8 93
Johns Island, S.C., U.S. — F7 117
Johns Island, i., S.C., U.S. — F7 117
Johnson, Ar., U.S. — A1 81
Johnson, In., U.S. — H2 91
Johnson, Ks., U.S. — E2 93
Johnson, Ne., U.S. — D10 104
Johnson, Vt., U.S. — B3 122
Johnson, Wa., U.S. — C8 124
Johnson, co., Ar., U.S. — B2 81
Johnson, co., Ga., U.S. — D4 87
Johnson, co., Il., U.S. — F5 90
Johnson, co., In., U.S. — F5 91
Johnson, co., Ia., U.S. — C6 92
Johnson, co., Ks., U.S. — D9 93
Johnson, co., Ky., U.S. — C7 94
Johnson, co., Mo., U.S. — C4 102
Johnson, co., Ne., U.S. — D9 104
Johnson, co., Tn., U.S. — C12 119
Johnson, co., Tx., U.S. — C4 120
Johnson, co., Wy., U.S. — B6 127
Johnsonburg, Pa., U.S. — D4 115
Johnson City, N.Y., U.S. — C5 109
Johnson City, Tn., U.S. — C11 119
Johnson City, Tx., U.S. — D3 120
Johnson Creek, Wi., U.S. — E5 126
Johnsondale, Ca., U.S. — E4 82
Johnson's Bayou, La., U.S. — E2 95
Johnsons Grove, Tn., U.S. — B2 119
Johnsonville, S.C., U.S. — D9 117
Johns Pass, strt., Fl., U.S. — p10 86
Johnston, R.I., U.S. — C4 116
Johnston, S.C., U.S. — D4 117
Johnston, co., N.C., U.S. — B4 110
Johnston, co., Ok., U.S. — C5 113
Johnston, i., Oc. — E11 6
Johnston City, Il., U.S. — F5 90
Johnstone, Scot., U.K. — *E4 13
Johnstone Strait, strt., B.C., Can. — D4 69
Johnston Key, i., Fl., U.S. — H5 86
Johnston's Point, c., Scot., U.K. — E3 13
Johnstown, Co., U.S. — A6 83
Johnstown, Ne., U.S. — B5 104
Johnstown, N.Y., U.S. — B6 109
Johnstown, N.D., U.S. — A8 111
Johnstown, Oh., U.S. — B3 112
Johnstown, Pa., U.S. — F4 115
Johnsville, Md., U.S. — A3 97
Johntown, Tx., U.S. — C5 120
Johnville, P.Q., Can. — D6 74
John W. Flannagan Reservoir, res., Va., U.S. — e9 123
Johor, state, Malay. — K5 35
Johor Baharu, Malay. — E2 34
Joice, Ia., U.S. — A4 92
Joigny, Fr. — D5 16
Joiner, Ar., U.S. — B5 81
Joinville, Braz. — D3 56
Joinville, Fr. — C6 16
Joinville Island, i., Ant. — C7 7
Jojutla, Mex. — n14 63
Jokkmokk, Swe. — D8 14
Jolfā, Iran — B2 39
Joliet, Il., U.S. — B5 90
Joliet, Mt., U.S. — E8 103
Joliette, P.Q., Can. — C4 74
Joliette, N.D., U.S. — A8 111
Joliette, co., P.Q., Can. — C3 74
Jolley, Ia., U.S. — B3 92
Jolo, Phil. — D6 34
Jomalig Island, i., Phil. — o14 34
Jomda, China — E4 31
Jonas Ridge, N.C., U.S. — A1 110
Jonava, Sov. Un. — A8 26
Jones, Al., U.S. — C3 78
Jones, La., U.S. — B4 95
Jones, Ok., U.S. — B4 113
Jones, co., Ga., U.S. — C3 87
Jones, co., Ia., U.S. — B6 92
Jones, co., Ms., U.S. — D4 101
Jones, co., N.C., U.S. — B5 110
Jones, co., S.D., U.S. — D5 118
Jones, co., Tx., U.S. — C3 120
Jonesboro, Ar., U.S. — A5 81
Jonesboro, Ga., U.S. — C2 87
Jonesboro, Il., U.S. — F4 90
Jonesboro, In., U.S. — D6 91
Jonesboro, La., U.S. — B3 95
Jonesboro, Tn., U.S. — C11 119
Jonesboro, Tx., U.S. — D5 120
Jonesborough, Tn., U.S. — C11 119
Jonesburg, Mo., U.S. — C6 102
Jones Creek, Tx., U.S. — s14 120
Jones Mill, Ar., U.S. — C3 81
Jones Mills, Pa., U.S. — F2 115
Jones Mountains, mts., Ant. — B3 7

Jonesport, Me., U.S. — D5 96
Jones Sound, strt., N.T., Can. — m34 66
Jonestown, Ms., U.S. — A3 101
Jonestown, Pa., U.S. — F9 115
Jonesville, Ga., U.S. — C3 87
Jonesville, La., U.S. — C4 95
Jonesville, Mi., U.S. — G6 99
Jonesville, N.C., U.S. — A2 110
Jonesville, S.C., U.S. — B4 117
Jonesville, Vt., U.S. — C3 122
Jonesville, Va., U.S. — f8 123
Jönköping, Swe. — I6 14
Jönköping, co., Swe. — A8 15
Jonquière, P.Q., Can. — A6 74
Jonuta, Mex. — D6 63
Jonzac, Fr. — E3 16
Joplin, Mo., U.S. — D3 102
Joplin, Mt., U.S. — B6 103
Joppa, Al., U.S. — A3 78
Joppa, Il., U.S. — F5 90
Joppa, Md., U.S. — B5 97
Jordan, Al., U.S. — D1 78
Jordan, Ar., U.S. — A3 81
Jordan, Ky., U.S. — f8 94
Jordan, Mn., U.S. — F5 100
Jordan, Mt., U.S. — C10 103
Jordan, N.Y., U.S. — B4 109
Jordan, ctry., Asia — B7 41
Jordan, stm., Ut., U.S. — C4 121
Jordan Creek, stm., U.S. — E9 114
Jordan Lake, res., Al., U.S. — C3 78
Jordan Valley, Or., U.S. — D9 114
Jorhāt, India — C9 36
Jörn, Swe. — E9 14
Jornado del Muerto, des., N.M., U.S. — D3 108
Jos, Nig. — E6 45
José Battle y Ordóñez, Ur. — E1 56
José de San Martín, Arg. — C2 54
José María Blanco, Arg. — B4 54
Joseph, Or., U.S. — B9 114
Joseph, Ut., U.S. — E3 121
Joseph, Lac, l., Nf., Can. — h8 72
Joseph, Lake, l., On., Can. — B5 73
Joseph Bonaparte Gulf, b., Austl. — B4 50
Joseph City, Az., U.S. — C5 80
Josephine, co., Or., U.S. — E3 114
Josephville, Mo., U.S. — f12 102
Joshua, Tx., U.S. — n9 120
Joshua Tree, Ca., U.S. — E5 82
Joshua Tree National Monument, Ca., U.S. — F6 82
Josselin, Fr. — C2 16
Jost Van Dyke, i., V.I., Br. — G2 14
Jostedalsbreen, Nor. — F6 14
Jotunheimen, mts., Nor. — G3 14
Jourdanton, Tx., U.S. — E3 120
Joussard, Ab., Can. — B3 68
Joux, Lake, l., Switz. — C2 20
Jouy-en-Josas, Fr. — g9 16
Jovellanos, Cuba — C6 64
Joviânia, Braz. — B3 56
Jowhar, Som. — C5 47
Joy, Il., U.S. — B3 90
Joy, Ok., U.S. — C4 113
Joyce, La., U.S. — C3 95
Joyce, Wa., U.S. — A2 124
J. Percy Priest Lake, res., Tn., U.S. — A5 119
Juab, co., Ut., U.S. — D2 121
Juaja, Peru — D2 58
Juan Aldama, Mex. — C4 63
Juan B. Arruabarrena, Arg. — A5 54
Juan de Fuca, Strait of, strt., N.A. — A1 124
Juan Díaz (part of Panamá), Pan. — k12 62
Juan E. Barra, Arg. — B4 54
Juan Fernández, Archipiélago, is., Chile — G2 53
Juanita, N.D., U.S. — B7 111
Juan José Castelli, Arg. — B4 55
Juanjuí, Peru — C2 58
Juan L. Lacaze, Ur. — g8 54
Juárez, Mex. — B4 63
Juaso, Ghana — E4 45
Juazeiro, Braz. — C2 57
Juazeiro do Norte, Braz. — E8 57
Jūbā, Sud. — E3 47
Jubba (Genale), stm., Afr. — E5 47
Jubbada Dhexe, prov., Som. — E5 47
Jubbada Hoose, prov., Som. — E5 47
Jubilee Lake, l., Nf., Can. — D4 72
Juby, Cap, c., Mor. — D2 44
Júcar, stm., Spain — C5 22
Juçara, Braz. — B4 56
Júcaro, Cuba — D4 64
Juchipila, stm., Mex. — m12 63
Juchitán [de Zaragoza], Mex. — D5 63
Jucuapa, El Sal. — D3 62
Jucuruçu, Braz. — C6 18

Julian Alps, mts., Eur. — C2 24
Juliana Top, mtn., Sur. — C3 59
Julianehåb, Grnld. — C16 61
Jülich, F.R.Ger. — D6 17
Juliette, Ga., U.S. — C3 87
Julimes, Mex. — B3 63
Julita, Swe. — t34 14
Júlio de Castilhos, Braz. — D2 56
Juliustown, N.J., U.S. — C3 107
Jullundur, India — B6 36
Julu, China — F6 32
Jumayl, Bi'r, well, Eg. — D5 41
Jumboo, Som. — F5 47
Jumbo Peak, mtn., Nv., U.S. — G7 105
Jumet (part of Charleroi), Bel. — B6 16
Jumilla, Spain — C5 22
Jump, stm., Wi., U.S. — C3 126
Jump, North Fork, stm., Wi., U.S. — C3 126
Jump, South Fork, stm., Wi., U.S. — C3 126
Jumping Branch, W.V., U.S. — D4 125
Jumping Lake, l., Sk., Can. — E3 75
Junāgadh, India — D5 36
Juncos, P.R. — B4 65
Junction, Il., U.S. — F5 90
Junction, Oh., U.S. — A1 112
Junction, Tx., U.S. — D3 120
Junction, Ut., U.S. — E3 121
Junction City, Ar., U.S. — D3 81
Junction City, Ga., U.S. — D2 87
Junction City, Il., U.S. — E4 90
Junction City, Ks., U.S. — C7 93
Junction City, Ky., U.S. — C5 94
Junction City, La., U.S. — A3 95
Junction City, Oh., U.S. — C3 112
Junction City, Or., U.S. — C3 114
Junction City, Wi., U.S. — D4 126
Jundiaí, Braz. — G5 56
Juneau, Ak., U.S. — D13 79
Juneau, Wi., U.S. — E5 126
Juneau, co., Wi., U.S. — E3 126
June in Winter, Lake, l., Fl., U.S. — E5 86
June Lake, Ca., U.S. — D4 82
Jungfrau, mtn., Switz. — E3 18
Junglinster, Lux. — E6 17
Juniata, Ne., U.S. — D7 104
Juniata, Pa., U.S. — F7 115
Juniata, co., Pa., U.S. — F7 115
Juniata, Raystown Branch, stm., Pa., U.S. — F5 115
Juniata Terrace, Pa., U.S. — E6 115
Junín, Arg. — A4 54
Junín, Peru — D2 58
Junín, dept., Peru — D2 58
Junín, Lago, l., Peru — D2 58
Junín de los Andes, Arg. — B2 54
Junior, W.V., U.S. — C5 125
Juniper, N.B., Can. — C2 71
Juniper Mountains, mts., Az., U.S. — B2 80
Junipero Serra Peak, mtn., Ca., U.S. — D3 82
Juntura, Or., U.S. — D8 114
Jupiter, Fl., U.S. — F6 86
Jupiter Inlet, b., Fl., U.S. — F6 86
Jupiter Island, i., Fl., U.S. — E6 86
Juquiá, Braz. — C3 56
Juquitiba, Braz. — m8 56
Jura, state, Switz. — B3 20
Jura, dept., Fr. — C1 20
Jura, i., Scot., U.K. — C4 10
Jura, Sound of, strt., Scot., U.K. — C4 10
Jura Mountains, mts., Eur. — E3 18
Jurbarkas, Sov. Un. — A7 26
Jurf ad Darāwīsh, Jord. — G10 40
Juruá, Braz. — B4 58
Juruá, stm., S.A. — B4 58
Juruena, stm., Braz. — B3 59
Juruena, stm., Braz. — D3 59
Juruti, Braz. — D6 59
Juskatla, B.C., Can. — C1 69
Jussey, Fr. — C2 20
Justice, Il., U.S. — *k9 90
Justiceburg, Tx., U.S. — C2 120
Justin, Tx., U.S. — C4 120
Juta Daract, Arg. — A3 54
Jutaí, Braz. — C4 58
Jutaí, stm., Braz. — B4 58
Jüterbog, Ger.D.R. — C6 18
Jutiapa, Guat. — E7 63
Jutiapa, Hond. — E7 63
Juticalpa, Hond. — I13 14
Jutland, pen., Den. — I3 14
Juventud, Isla de la (Isle of Pines), i., Cuba — D2 64
Juxian, China — G8 32
Juyongguan Pass, China — D7 32
Jyderup, Den. — D5 24
Južna Morava, stm., Yugo. — F11 14
Jyväskylä, Fin. — F11 14

K

K2 (Godwin Austen), mtn., Asia — A6 36
Kaaawa, Hi., U.S. — f10 88
Kaala, mtn., Hi., U.S. — f9 88
Kaaluku Bay, b., Hi., U.S. — E6 88
Kaaumakua, Puu, mtn., Hi., U.S. — f10 88
Kabala, S.L. — F2 45
Kabale, Ug. — B4 48
Kabalega Falls (Murchison Falls), wtfl, Ug. — A5 48
Kabalo, Zaire — C4 48
Kabambare, Zaire — C4 48
Kabara, i., Fiji — I16 52
Kabarnet, Kenya — E6 48
Kabba, Nig. — E6 45
Kabetogama Lake, l., Mn., U.S. — B5 100
Kabinda, Zaire — C4 48
Kabompo, Zam. — D4 48
Kabompo, stm., Zam. — D4 48
Kabong, Malay. — E4 34
Kabongo, Zaire — C4 48
Kabul, Afg. — C3 36
Kabul, stm., Asia — D14 39
Kabwe (Broken Hill), Zam. — D5 48
Kaches Lake, res., Wa., U.S. — B4 124
Kachug, Sov. Un. — D13 29
Kadan, Czech. — C5 26
Kadan, Burma — C2 35
Kadavu, i., Fiji — I15 52
Kade, Ghana — E4 45

Name	Map Ref	Page
Kadena, Japan	O5	52
Kadet Channel, strt., Eur.	A6	18
Kadhimaïn (part of Baghdād), Iraq	F15	40
Kading, stm., Laos	C6	35
Kadinhani, Tur.	C9	40
Kadiolo, Mali	D3	45
Kadiri, India	F6	36
Kadoka, S.D., U.S.	D4	118
Kadoma, Zimb.	A4	49
Kaduna, Nig.	D6	45
Kaduna, stm., Nig.	D6	45
Kāduqlī, Sud.	C2	47
Kaédi, Maur.	C2	45
Kaélé, Cam.	C2	46
Kaena Point, c., Hi., U.S.	B3	88
Kaeryŏng, S. Kor.	H4	33
Käf, Sau. Ar.	B3	38
Kafanchan, Nig.	E6	45
Käfar Jar Ghar, mtn., Afg.	E13	39
Kaffrine, Sen.	D1	45
Kafia Kingi, Sud.	D1	47
Kafr ad Dawwār, Eg.	C2	41
Kafr ash Shaykh, Eg.	C2	41
Kafr az Zayyāt, Eg.	D2	41
Kafr Mālik, Isr. Occ.	h12	41
Kafr Qaddūm, Isr. Occ.	g11	41
Kafr Qāsim, Isr.	g10	41
Kafr Şaqr, Eg.	D3	41
Kafr Salīm, Eg.	C2	41
Kafr Ṭarkhān al Gharbī, Eg.	E3	41
Kafr Zībād, Isr. Occ.	g11	41
Kafue, Zam.	E4	48
Kafue, stm., Zam.	E4	48
Kagan, Sov. Un.	B12	39
Kagawong, On., Can.	B2	73
Kagera, stm., Afr.	B5	48
Kağızman, Tur.	B14	40
Kagoshima, Japan	E11	31
Kagoshima Bay, b., Japan	K5	33
Kagul, Sov. Un.	I7	27
Kahakuloa, Hi., U.S.	B5	88
Kahaluu, Hi., U.S.	D6	88
Kahaluu, Hi., U.S.	g10	88
Kahama, Tan.	B5	48
Kahana, Hi., U.S.	B4	88
Kahana Bay, b., Hi., U.S.	f10	88
Kahayan, stm., Indon.	F4	34
Kahemba, Zaire	C2	48
Kahla, Ger.D.R.	C6	19
Kahlotus, Wa., U.S.	C7	124
Kahnūj, Iran	C5	38
Kahoka, Mo., U.S.	A6	102
Kahoolawe, i., Hi., U.S.	C5	88
Kahuku, Hi., U.S.	B4	88
Kahuku Point, c., Hi., U.S.	B4	88
Kahului, Hi., U.S.	C5	88
Kahului Bay, b., Hi., U.S.	C5	88
Kaiama, Nig.	E5	45
Kaiapoi, N.Z.	O14	51
Kaibab, Az., U.S.	A3	80
Kaibab Indian Reservation, Az., U.S.	A3	80
Kaibab Plateau, plat., Az., U.S.	A3	80
Kaibito, Az., U.S.	A4	80
Kaibito Plateau, plat., Az., U.S.	A4	80
Kaieteur Fall, wtfl, Guy.	A3	59
Kaifeng, China	E7	31
Kaihua, China	J8	32
Kai Islands, is., Indon.	G8	34
Kaikoura, N.Z.	O14	51
Kaikoura Peninsula, pen., N.Z.	O14	51
Kailahun, S.L.	E2	45
Kailas Range see Gangdise Mountains, mts., China	B9	37
Kailu, China	C9	32
Kailua, Hi., U.S.	B4	88
Kailua Bay, b., Hi., U.S.	g11	88
Kailua Kona, Hi., U.S.	D6	88
Kaimana, Indon.	F8	34
Kaimu, Hi., U.S.	D7	88
Kainaliu, Hi., U.S.	D6	88
Kainan, Japan	I7	33
Kainji Dam, Nig.	E5	45
Kainji Lake, res., Nig.	D5	45
Kaintragarh, India	G10	37
Kaipara Harbour, b., N.Z.	L15	51
Kaiparowits Plateau, plat., Ut., U.S.	F4	121
Kaipokok Bay, b., Nf., Can.	g10	72
Kaiserslautern, F.R.Ger.	D3	18
Kaiserstuhl, Switz.	A5	21
Kaišiadorys, Sov. Un.	A8	26
Kaitaia, N.Z.	K14	51
Kaitangata, N.Z.	Q12	51
Kaithal, India	C6	37
Kaiwi Channel, strt., Hi., U.S.	B4	88
Kaixian, China	E6	31
Kaiyuan, China	C11	32
Kaizuka, Japan	o14	33
Kajaani, Fin.	E12	14
Kajakī, Band-e, res., Afg.	E12	39
Kajiado, Kenya	B6	48
Kajikazawa, Japan	n17	33
Kākā, Sud.	C3	47
Kakamas, S. Afr.	C3	49
Kakamega, Kenya	A5	48
Kake, Ak., U.S.	D13	79
Kakegawa, Japan	o17	33
Kakhovka, Sov. Un.	H9	27
Kakhovka Reservoir, res., Sov. Un.	E6	29
Kākināda (Cocanada), India	E7	36
Kakisa Lake, l., N.T., Can.	D9	66
Kakogawa, Japan	*I7	33
Kakuma, Kenya	A5	48
Kakwa, stm., Can.	B1	68
Kälabäka, Grc.	C3	25
Kalabakan, Malay.	E5	34
Kalábishah, Eg.	E6	43
Kalach, Sov. Un.	F13	27
Kalach-na-Donu, Sov. Un.	G14	27
Kaladar, On., Can.	C7	73
Ka Lae, c., Hi., U.S.	E6	88
Kalahari Desert, des., Afr.	B3	49
Kalahari Gemsbok National Park, S. Afr.	C3	49
Kalaheo, Hi., U.S.	B2	88
Kalaho, Pidos, hill, N. Mar. Is.	C8	52
Kalai-Mor, Sov. Un.	D11	39
Kälak, Iran	I9	39
Kalama, Wa., U.S.	C3	124
Kalamaki, Grc.	D4	40
Kalamariá, Grc.	*B4	25
Kalamazoo, Mi., U.S.	F5	99
Kalamazoo, co., Mi., U.S.	F5	99
Kalamazoo, stm., Mi., U.S.	F5	99
Kalambo Falls, wtfl, Afr.	C5	48
Kalandula, Ang.	C2	48
Kalaoa Homesteads, Hi., U.S.	D6	88
Kalaotoa, i., Indon.	G6	34
Kalapana, Hi., U.S.	D7	88
Kalasin, Thai.	D5	35
Kalät, Pak.	C4	36
Kalaupapa, Hi., U.S.	B5	88
Kalaupapa Peninsula, pen., Hi., U.S.	B5	88
Kalavárda, Grc.	C4	25
Kalawao, co., Hi., U.S.	B5	88
Kalb, Ra's al, c., P.D.R.Yem.	C5	38
Kalbā', U.A.E.	C5	38
Kalecik, Tur.	B9	40
Kaleden, B.C., Can.	E8	69
Kalegauk, i., Burma	E2	35
Kalehe, Zaire	B4	48
Kaleköy, Tur.	B5	25
Kalemie (Albertville), Zaire	C4	48
Kalena, Puu, mtn., Hi., U.S.	g9	88
Kaleva, Mi., U.S.	D4	99
Kalevala, Sov. Un.	E14	14
Kalewa, Burma	D9	36
Kalgalaksha, Sov. Un.	E16	14
Kalgin Island, i., Ak., U.S.	g16	79
Kalgoorlie, Austl.	F3	50
Kalibo, Phil.	C6	34
Kalihiwai, Hi., U.S.	A2	88
Kalima, Zaire	B4	48
Kálimnos, Grc.	D6	25
Kálimnos, i., Grc.	D6	40
Kalinin, Sov. Un.	D6	29
Kaliningrad, Sov. Un.	n17	27
Kaliningrad (Königsberg), Sov. Un.	D5	29
Kalininsk, Sov. Un.	F15	27
Kalinkovichi, Sov. Un.	E7	27
Kalis, Som.	D6	47
Kalispel Indian Reservation, Wa., U.S.	A8	124
Kalispell, Mt., U.S.	B2	103
Kalisz, Pol.	C5	26
Kaliua, Tan.	C5	48
Kalixälven, stm., Swe.	D10	14
Kalkaska, Mi., U.S.	D5	99
Kalkaska, co., Mi., U.S.	D5	99
Kalkfeld, Nmb.	A2	49
Kalkrand, Nmb.	B2	49
Kallithéa, Grc.	h11	25
Kallsjön, l., Swe.	F5	14
Kalmalo, Nig.	D6	45
Kalmar, Swe.	I7	14
Kalmar, Swe.	t35	14
Kalmarsund, strt., Swe.	I7	14
Kalmykovo, Sov. Un.	D4	28
Kalo, La., U.S.	B3	92
Kalocsa, Hung.	B3	24
Kalohi Channel, strt., Hi., U.S.	C4	88
Kaloli Point, c., Hi., U.S.	D7	88
Kalomo, Zam.	E4	48
Kalona, Ia., U.S.	C6	92
Kalone Peak, mtn., B.C., Can.	C4	69
Kälpi, India	C7	37
Kalskag, Ak., U.S.	C7	79
Kaltag, Ak., U.S.	C8	79
Kaluga, Sov. Un.	D6	29
Kalulushi, Zam.	D4	48
Kalundborg, Den.	C5	15
Kalush, Sov. Un.	G5	27
Kałuszyn, Pol.	B6	26
Kalvarija, Sov. Un.	A7	26
Kalvehave, Den.	D6	15
Kalvesta, Ks., U.S.	D3	93
Kalvsjön, l., Swe.	A7	15
Kalyān, India	H4	37
Kama, Zaire	B4	48
Kama, stm., Sov. Un.	D8	29
Kamaing, Burma	C10	36
Kamaishi, Japan	D13	31
Kamakou, mtn., Hi., U.S.	B5	88
Kamakura, Japan	n18	33
Kamalia, Pak.	E2	45
Kamananui Stream, stm., Hi., U.S.	f9	88
Kamaniskeg Lake, l., On., Can.	B7	73
Kamanjab, Nmb.	A1	49
Kamanyola, Zaire	B4	48
Kamarán, i., P.D.R.Yem.	D4	38
Kama Reservoir, res., Sov. Un.	D8	29
Kämärhäti, India	*D8	36
Kamaria Fall, wtfl, Guy.	A3	59
Kama Rock, i., Japan	P17	52
Kamarod, Pak.	C3	36
Kamas, Ut., U.S.	C4	121
Kamatsi Lake, l., Sk., Can.	A4	75
Kambalda, Austl.	F3	50
Kambing, i., Indon.	G7	34
Kambove, Zaire	D4	48
Kamchatka Peninsula, pen., Sov. Un.	D18	29
Kamenets-Podolskiy, Sov. Un.	G6	27
Kamenjak, Cape, c., Yugo.	C1	22
Kamenka, Sov. Un.	G7	27
Kamenka, Sov. Un.	C2	28
Kamen-na-Obi, Sov. Un.	D11	29
Kamensk-Shakhtinskiy, Sov. Un.	G13	27
Kamenz, Ger.D.R.	D9	29
Kamenz, Ger.D.R.	C7	18
Kameoka, Japan	o14	33
Kämet, mtn., Asia	B7	37
Kamiah, Id., U.S.	C2	89
Kamiak Butte, mtn., Wa., U.S.	C8	124
Kamień Pomorski, Pol.	B3	26
Kamina, Zaire	C4	48
Kamioka, Japan	m16	33
Kamloops, B.C., Can.	D7	69
Kamloops, l., Japan	I6	33
Kamo, Sov. Un.	B15	40
Kamoa Mountains, mts., Guy.	B3	59
Kamoolawe, i., Hi., U.S.	C5	88
Kamouraska, P.Q., Can.	B8	74
Kamouraska, co., P.Q., Can.	B8	74
Kampala, Ug.	A5	48
Kampar, Malay.	L6	34
Kampar, stm., Indon.	E2	34
Kampen, Neth.	C5	17
Kampeska, Lake, l., S.D., U.S.	C8	118
Kamphaeng Phet, Thai.	D3	35
Kampong Cham, Kam.	C4	35
Kampong Chhnang, Kam.	C4	35
Kampong Khleang, Kam.	F6	35
Kampong Saom (Sihanoukville), Kam.	C2	34
Kampong Saom Bay, b., Kam.	C2	34
Kampong Spoe, Kam.	G6	35
Kampong Thum, Kam.	C4	35
Kampot, Kam.	C2	34
Kampsville, Il., U.S.	D3	90
Kampuchea, ctry., Asia	C3	34
Kamrar, Ia., U.S.	B4	92
Kamsack, Sk., Can.	F5	75
Kamuchawie Lake, l., Can.	A4	75
Kamuela (Waimea), Hi., U.S.	C6	88
Kamuli, Ug.	A5	48
Kamyshevakha, Sov. Un.	q21	27
Kamyshin, Sov. Un.	F15	27
Kamyshlov, Sov. Un.	B6	28
Kanab, Ut., U.S.	F3	121
Kanab Creek, stm., U.S.	A3	80
Kanabec, co., Mn., U.S.	E5	100
Kanacea, i., Fiji	H16	52
Kanaga Island, i., Ak., U.S.	E4	79
Kanairiktok, stm., Nf., Can.	g9	72
Kananaskis, stm., Ab., Can.	D3	68
Kanash, Sov. Un.	D16	27
Kanauga, Oh., U.S.	D3	112
Kanawha, Ia., U.S.	B4	92
Kanawha, co., W.V., U.S.	C3	125
Kanawha, stm., W.V., U.S.	C3	125
Kanayama, Japan	n16	33
Kanazawa, Japan	D12	31
Kanchanaburi, Thai.	E3	35
Kānchenjunga, mtn., Asia	C8	36
Kānchipuram (Conjeeveram), India	F7	36
Kānchrāpāra, India	*D8	36
Kandahar (Qandahār), Afg.	B4	36
Kandahar, Sk., Can.	F3	75
Kandalaksha, Sov. Un.	C9	29
Kandalaksha Bay, b., Sov. Un.	B15	8
Kandangan, Indon.	F5	34
Kandel, F.R.Ger.	D3	19
Kandern, F.R.Ger.	A4	21
Kandersteg, Switz.	C3	20
Kandi, Benin	D5	45
Kandira, Tur.	B8	40
Kandla, India	E4	100
Kandräch, Pak.	C3	36
Kandreho, Madag.	g9	49
Kandy, Sri L.	G7	36
Kane, Pa., U.S.	C4	115
Kane, co., Il., U.S.	B5	90
Kane, co., Ut., U.S.	F3	121
Kane Basin, strt., N.A.	m38	66
Kaneohe, Hi., U.S.	B4	88
Kaneohe Bay, b., Hi., U.S.	g10	88
Kaneohe Bay Marine Corps Air Station, mil., Hi., U.S.	g10	88
Kanevskaya, Sov. Un.	H12	27
Kang, Bots.	B3	49
Kanga, Malay.	I4	35
Kangaba, Mali	D3	45
Kangal, Tur.	C11	40
Kangaroo, i., Austl.	G6	50
Kangbao, China	C7	31
Kangding, China	E5	31
Kangdong, N. Kor.	G3	33
Kangean Islands, is., Indcn.	G5	34
Kanggye, N. Kor.	C10	31
Kanggye, II., U.S.	B5	90
Kangnūng, S. Kor.	D10	31
Kango, Gabon	A2	48
Kangrinboqê Mountain, mtn., China	B8	37
Kani, Burma	A1	35
Kani, I.C.	E3	45
Kaniama, Zaire	C3	48
Kanin Nos, Cape, c., Sov. Un.	C7	29
Kanjiža, Yugo.	B5	24
Kankakee, Il., U.S.	B6	90
Kankakee, co., Il., U.S.	B6	90
Kankakee, stm., U.S.	B5	90
Kanken, Gui.	D3	45
Kanker, India	D7	36
Kankossa, Maur.	C2	45
Kannapolis, N.C., U.S.	B2	110
Kannauj, India	D7	37
Kano, Nig.	D6	45
Kanopolis, Ks., U.S.	D5	93
Kanopolis Lake, res., Ks., U.S.	D5	93
Kanorado, Co., U.S.	C1	93
Kanosh, Ut., U.S.	E3	121
Kanoya, Japan	K5	33
Känpur, India	C7	36
Kansas, Al., U.S.	B2	78
Kansas, Oh., U.S.	B2	90
Kansas, Ok., U.S.	A2	112
Kansas, Ok., U.S.	A7	113
Kansas, state, U.S.	D5	93
Kansas, stm., Ks., U.S.	C7	93
Kansas City, Ks., U.S.	C9	93
Kansas City, Mo., U.S.	B3	102
Kansasville, Wi., U.S.	n11	126
Kansk, Sov. Un.	D12	29
Kansu see Gansu, prov., China	D5	31
Kantang, Thai.	D1	35
Kanton Island, i., Kir.	G11	6
Kantunilkin, Mex.	C7	63
Kanturk, Ire.	I3	11
Kanuku Mountains, mts., Guy.	B3	59
Kanuma, Japan	H9	33
Kanye, Bots.	B4	49
Kaohsiung, Tai.	G9	31
Kaoko Veld, plat., Nmb.	A1	49
Kaolack, Sen.	D1	45
Kaoma, Zam.	D3	48
Kaouar, reg., Niger	C7	45
Kapaa, Hi., U.S.	A2	88
Kapaau, Hi., U.S.	C6	88
Kapal, Sov. Un.	F24	8
Kapandrition, Grc.	g11	25
Kapanga, Zaire	C4	48
Kapapa Island, i., Hi., U.S.	g10	88
Kapéllion, Grc.	g10	25
Kapenguria, Kenya	A5	48
Kapfenberg, Aus.	E7	18
Kapiri Mposhi, Zam.	D4	48
Kapit, Malay.	E4	34
Kaplan, La., U.S.	D3	95
Kaplice, Czech.	E9	19
Kapoeta, Sud.	E3	47
Kaposvár, Hung.	B3	24
Kaposvar Creek, stm., Sk., Can.	g4	75
Kapowsin, Wa., U.S.	C3	124
Kappa, Il., U.S.	C4	90
Kapsan, N. Kor.	F3	33
Kapuas, stm., Indon.	E4	34
Kapulena, Hi., U.S.	C6	88
Kapuskasing, On., Can.	o19	73
Kapustin Yar, Sov. Un.	D3	28
Kaputar, mtn., Austl.	E8	51
Kapuvár, Hung.	B3	24
Kara, Sov. Un.	C9	29
Kara, mtn., Tur.	D9	40
Karabash, Sov. Un.	D21	8
Kara-Bogaz-Gol, Sov. Un.	E4	28
Kara-Bogaz-Gol Gulf, b., Sov. Un.	E4	28
Karabük, Tur.	*B9	40
Karachev, Sov. Un.	E10	27
Karāchi Cantonment, Pak.	D4	36
Karāchi, Pak.	D4	36
Karad, India	C2	36
Karaganda, Sov. Un.	E10	29
Karagayly, Sov. Un.	D19	29
Karaj, Iran	D5	39
Karakas, Sov. Un.	D10	28
Karakelong, i., Indon.	E7	34
Karakoram Pass, Asia	A6	36
Karakoram Range, mts., Asia	A6	36
Karaköse see Ağrı, Tur.	C14	40
Kara-Kum, des., Sov. Un.	E8	29
Kara-Kum Canal, Sov. Un.	H21	8
Karaman, Tur.	D9	40
Karamay, China	B1	31
Karamea, N.Z.	N14	51
Karamea Bight, N.Z.	N13	51
Karamürsel, Tur.	B7	40
Karapinar, Tur.	D9	40
Karasburg, Nmb.	C2	49
Kara Sea, Sov. Un.	B9	29
Karasu, Tur.	C6	28
Karasu, Tur.	B8	40
Karasuk, Sov. Un.	C9	28
Karatal, stm., Sov. Un.	D9	29
Karatau Range, mts., Sov. Un.	E7	28
Karatobe, Sov. Un.	D4	28
Karatsu, Japan	J4	33
Karaul, Sov. Un.	D5	29
Karaulkeldy, Sov. Un.	D5	29
Karawanken, mts., Eur.	F1	18
Karbalā', Iraq	F15	40
Karcag, Hung.	B4	24
Karczew, Pol.	m14	26
Kardhítsa, Grc.	C3	40
Karema, Tan.	C5	48
Karesuando (part of Kiruna), Swe.	C10	14
Kargasok, Sov. Un.	D11	29
Kargat, Sov. Un.	D25	8
Kargil, India	B6	36
Kargopol, Sov. Un.	A12	27
Karguéri, Niger	D7	45
Kariaí, Grc.	B5	25
Kariba, Zimb.	A4	49
Kariba, Lake, res., Afr.	A4	49
Karibib, Nmb.	B2	49
Karīkāl, India	F6	36
Karikari, Cape, c., N.Z.	K14	51
Karimata Archipelago, is., Indon.	F3	34
Karimata Strait, strt., Indon.	F3	34
Karimunjawa Islands, is., Indon.	G4	34
Karin, Som.	C6	47
Karisimbi, Volcán, vol., Afr.	B4	48
Káristos, Grc.	C5	40
Kariya, Japan	o15	33
Karkal, Iran	D10	39
Karkar, i., Pap. N. Gui.	h12	50
Karkaralinsk, Sov. Un.	E10	29
Karkheh, stm., Iran	E3	39
Karkinit Gulf, b., Sov. Un.	I9	27
Karl-Marx-Stadt (Chemnitz), Ger.D.R.	C6	18
Karlobag, Yugo.	C2	24
Karloske, stm., Mb., Can.	B4	70
Karlovac, Yugo.	C2	24
Karlovo, Bul.	D7	24
Karlovy Vary, Czech.	I6	14
Karlsborg, Swe.	H6	14
Karlshamn, Swe.	I6	14
Karlskoga, Swe.	H6	14
Karlskrona, Swe.	I6	14
Karlsruhe, F.R.Ger.	A5	111
Karlsruhe, N.D., U.S.	A5	111
Karlstad, Mn., U.S.	B2	100
Karlstadt, F.R.Ger.	D4	19
Karlstad, Swe.	H5	14
Karluk, Ak., U.S.	D9	79
Karnāl, India	*C6	36
Karnālī, stm., Nepal	C8	37
Karnataka, state, India	F6	36
Karnes, co., Tx., U.S.	E4	120
Karnes City, Tx., U.S.	E4	120
Karnobat, Bul.	D8	24
Karns, Tn., U.S.	n13	119
Kärnten, state, Aus.	C9	20
Karonga, Mwi.	A4	49
Karonga, Mwi.	C5	48
Karora, Sud.	B4	47
Karow, Ger.D.R.	E6	15
Kárpathos, i., Grc.	E6	40
Karpenision, Grc.	C3	25
Kars, Tur.	B14	40
Karsakpay, Sov. Un.	E9	29
Karsha, Sov. Un.	C4	28
Karshi, Sov. Un.	D8	29
Karstädt, Ger.D.R.	E5	15
Karthaus, Pa., U.S.	D5	115
Kartuzy, Pol.	A5	26
Kārūn, stm., Iran	F4	39
Karval, Co., U.S.	C7	83
Karvia, Fin.	F10	14
Karviná, Czech.	D5	26
Kārwār, India	F5	36
Kas, Sud.	C1	47
Kas, Tur.	D7	40
Kasaan, Ak., U.S.	n23	79
Kasai, hist reg., Zaire	B3	48
Kasai (Cassai), stm., Afr.	B2	48
Kasaji, Zaire	D4	48
Kasama, Bots.	A4	49
Kasama, Zaire	D5	48
Kasanga, Tan.	C5	48
Kasaragod, India	F3	36
Kasba Lake, l., N.T., Can.	D12	66
Kasba Tadla, Mor.	C3	44
Kasese, Ug.	A5	48
Kāshān, Iran	B5	38
Kashi, China	F10	29
Kashihara, Japan	o14	33
Kashima, Japan	n19	33
Kāshīpur, India	C7	37
Kashira, Sov. Un.	D12	27
Kashirka, stm., Sov. Un.	n18	27
Kashiwazaki, Japan	H9	33
Kāshmar (Turshīz), Iran	B5	38
Kashmor, Pak.	C2	37
Kasimov, Sov. Un.	D13	27
Kaskaskia, Il., U.S.	F4	90
Kaskaskia, stm., Il., U.S.	D5	90
Kaskö, Fin.	F9	14
Kaslo, B.C., Can.	E9	69
Kasongo, Zaire	B4	48
Kasongo-Lunda, Zaire	C2	48
Kásos, i., Grc.	E6	40
Kasota, Mn., U.S.	F5	100
Kassalā, Sud.	B4	47
Kassalā, prov., Sud.	B4	47
Kassandra, Gulf of, b., Grc.	B4	25
Kassel (Cassel), F.R.Ger.	C4	18
Kasson, Mn., U.S.	F6	100
Kastamonu, Tur.	B9	40
Kastoria, Grc.	B3	40
Kástron, Grc.	g10	25
Kasukabe, Japan	n18	33
Kasulu, Tan.	B5	48
Kasumi, Japan	I7	33
Kasumiga-Ura, l., Japan	H10	33
Kasungu, Mwi.	D5	48
Kasūr, Pak.	B5	36
Katahdin, Mount, mtn., Me., U.S.	C4	96
Katako-Kombe, Zaire	B3	48
Katanga, hist reg., Zaire	C4	48
Katanning, Austl.	F2	50
Katano Point, c., Japan	P17	52
Katata, Japan	n14	33
Katepwa Beach, Sk., Can.	G4	75
Katerini, Grc.	B4	40
Kates Needle, mtn., Ak., U.S.	m24	79
Katha, Burma	D10	36
Katherine, Austl.	B5	50
Kāthiāwār, pen., India	D4	36
Kathleen, Fl., U.S.	D4	86
Kathmandu, Nepal	C8	36
Kathryn, Ab., Can.	D4	68
Kathryn, N.D., U.S.	C8	111
Kathua, India	A5	37
Katie, India	C4	113
Katihār, India	E11	37
Katiimik Lake, l., Mb., Can.	C2	70
Katiola, I.C.	E3	45
Katire, Sud.	E3	47
Katlehong, S. Afr.	*C4	49
Katmai, Mount, mtn., Ak., U.S.	D9	79
Katmai National Park, Ak., U.S.	D9	79
Kato Alepokhórion, Grc.	g10	25
Katokhí, Grc.	C3	25
Katombe, Zaire	C3	48
Katoomba, Austl.	F9	50
Katoúna, Grc.	C3	25
Katowice (Stalinogród), Pol.	C5	26
Kātrīnā, Jabal, mtn., Eg.	D6	43
Katrine, Loch, l., Scot., U.K.	D4	13
Katrineholm, Swe.	H7	14
Katsina, Nig.	D6	45
Katsina Ala, stm., Afr.	E6	45
Katsuta, Japan	m15	33
Katsuyama, Japan	m15	33
Kattakurgan, Sov. Un.	H22	8
Kattegat, strt., Eur.	I4	14
Katun, stm., Sov. Un.	E26	8
Katwijk aan Zee, Neth.	B4	17
Katy, Tx., U.S.	r14	120
Kau, Indon.	E7	34
Kauai, co., Hi., U.S.	B1	88
Kauai, i., Hi., U.S.	A2	88
Kauai Channel, strt., Hi., U.S.	B3	88
Kau Desert, des., Hi., U.S.	D6	88
Kaufbeuren, F.R.Ger.	E5	18
Kaufman, Tx., U.S.	C4	120
Kaufman, co., Tx., U.S.	C4	120
Kauhajoki, Fin.	F10	14
Kauhava, Fin.	F10	14
Kaukauna, Wi., U.S.	D5	126
Kaukauna, Wi., U.S.	D5	126
Kaukauveld, plat., Afr.	D5	72
Kaula Island, i., Hi., U.S.	m15	88
Kaulakahi Channel, strt., Hi., U.S.	A2	88
Kauliranta, Fin.	D10	14
Kaunakakai, Hi., U.S.	B5	88
Kauna Point, c., Hi., U.S.	D6	88
Kaunas, Sov. Un.	A6	26
Kaura Namoda, Nig.	D6	45
Kautokeino, Nor.	C10	14
Kavacha, Sov. Un.	C19	29
Kavaja, Alb.	A4	49
Kavála, Grc.	B5	40
Kavála, Gulf of, b., Grc.	B5	40
Kavarna, Bul.	D9	24
Kavieng, Pap. N. Gui.	h13	50
Kavīr, Dasht-e, des., Iran	B5	38
Kävlinge, Swe.	I5	14
Kaw, Fr. Gu.	B4	59
Kawagama Lake, l., On., Can.	B6	73
Kawagoe, Japan	n18	33
Kawaguchi, Japan	n18	33
Kawaihae, Hi., U.S.	C6	88
Kawaihae Bay, b., Hi., U.S.	C5	88
Kawaihoa Point, c., Hi., U.S.	B1	88
Kawailoa, Hi., U.S.	f9	88
Kawailoa Beach, Hi., U.S.	f9	88
Kawakawa, N.Z.	K15	51
Kawambwa, Zam.	C4	48
Kawardha, India	F8	37
Kawasaki, Japan	D12	31
Kawhia, N.Z.	M15	51
Kawich Peak, mtn., Nv., U.S.	F5	105
Kawich Range, mts., Nv., U.S.	F5	105
Kawkarein, Burma	D3	35
Kaw Lake, res., Ok., U.S.	A5	113
Kawm Hamādah, Eg.	D2	41
Kawm Umbū, Eg.	E6	43
Kawthaung, Burma	F10	35
Kay, co., Ok., U.S.	A4	113
Kaya, Burkina	D5	45
Kayangel Islands, is., Palau	R17	52
Kaycee, Wy., U.S.	C6	127
Kayenta, Az., U.S.	A5	80
Kayes, Congo	B1	48
Kayes, Mali	D2	45
Kayford, W.V., U.S.	C3	125
Kayjay, Ky., U.S.	D6	94
Kayl, Lux.	F9	17
Kaysō, S.D., U.S.	D8	118
Kayō, Japan	N6	52
Kayseri, Tur.	C10	40
Kaysville, Ut., U.S.	B4	121
Kayuagung, Indon.	F2	34
Kayville, Sk., Can.	H3	75
Kazachye, Sov. Un.	B16	29
Kazakevichevo, Sov. Un.	B7	33
Kazakh Hills, hills, Sov. Un.	D7	28
Kazakh S.S.R., state, Sov. Un.	E9	29
Kazalinsk, Sov. Un.	D6	28
Kazan, Sov. Un.	D7	29
Kazan, stm., N.T., Can.	D12	66
Kazanlŭk, Bul.	D7	24
Kāzerūn, Iran	G5	39
Kazi-Magomed, Sov. Un.	E3	28
Kazimierz [Dolny], Pol.	C6	26
Kazincbarcika, Hung.	A5	24
Kazym, stm., Sov. Un.	C22	8
Kadyně, Czech.	D8	19
Kéa, Grc.	D5	40
Kéa, i., Grc.	D5	40
Keaau, Hi., U.S.	D6	88
Keady, N. Ire., U.K.	C5	11
Keahiakahoe, Puu, mtn., Hi., U.S.	g10	88
Keahole Point, c., Hi., U.S.	D5	88
Kealaikahiki Channel, strt., Hi., U.S.	C5	88
Kealaikahiki Point, c., Hi., U.S.	C5	88
Kealakekua, Hi., U.S.	D6	88
Kealia, Hi., U.S.	A2	88
Keams Canyon, Az., U.S.	B5	80
Keanapapa Point, c., Hi., U.S.	C4	88
Keansburg, N.J., U.S.	C4	107
Kearney, On., Can.	B5	73
Kearney, Mo., U.S.	B3	102
Kearney, Ne., U.S.	D6	104
Kearney, co., Ne., U.S.	D7	104
Kearneysville, W.V., U.S.	B7	125
Kearny, Az., U.S.	D5	80
Kearny, N.J., U.S.	h8	107
Kearny, co., Ks., U.S.	D2	93
Kearsarge, Mi., U.S.	A2	99
Kearsarge, N.H., U.S.	B4	106
Kearsarge, Mount, mtn., N.H., U.S.	D3	106
Kearsarge North, mtn., N.H., U.S.	B4	106
Keatchie, La., U.S.	B2	95
Keatley, Sk., Can.	E2	75
Keaton, Ky., U.S.	C7	94
Keats, Ks., U.S.	C7	93
Kebbi, Nig.	D5	45
Kébémer, Sen.	C1	45
Kebnekaise, mtn., Swe.	D8	14
Kebock Head, c., Scot., U.K.	B2	13
Kebri Dehar, Eth.	D5	47
Kecskemét, Hung.	B4	24
Kedah, state, Malay.	J4	35
Kedainiai, Sov. Un.	A8	26
Keddie, Ca., U.S.	B3	82
Kedgwick, N.B., Can.	B2	71
Kedgwick, stm., N.B., Can.	B2	71
Kedleston, Sk., Can.	G3	75
Kediri, Indon.	G5	34
Kedong, China	B3	33
Kédougou, Sen.	D2	45
Keefers, B.C., Can.	D7	69
Keego Harbor, Mi., U.S.	o15	99
Keei, Hi., U.S.	D6	88
Keele Peak, mtn., Yk., Can.	C7	66
Keeler, Ca., U.S.	D5	82
Keeline, Wy., U.S.	D8	127
Keeling, Va., U.S.	D3	123
Keelung see Chilung, Tai.	F9	31
Keene, Ca., U.S.	E4	82
Keene, Ky., U.S.	C5	94
Keene, N.H., U.S.	E2	106
Keene, N.Y., U.S.	A7	109
Keene, N.D., U.S.	B3	111
Keenesburg, Co., U.S.	A6	83
Keene Valley, N.Y., U.S.	f11	109
Keeney Knob, mtn., W.V., U.S.	D4	125
Keensburg, Il., U.S.	E6	90
Keeper Hill, mtn., Ire.	I4	11
Keeseville, N.Y., U.S.	f11	109
Keesler Air Force Base, mil., Ms., U.S.	E5	101
Keetmanshoop, Nmb.	C2	49
Keet Seel Ruin, hist., Az., U.S.	A5	80
Keewatin, On., Can.	E4	70
Keewatin, Mn., U.S.	C5	100
Keewatin, dept., N.T., Can.	D13	66
Keewatin, stm., Mb., Can.	A1	70
Kefa, prov., Eth.	D4	47
Kefallinía (Cephalonia), i., Grc.	C3	40
Kefar Ata, Isr.	C4	41
Kefar Blum, Isr.	A7	41
Kefar 'Eqron, Isr.	h10	41
Kefar Monash, Isr.	f10	41
Kefar Sava, Isr.	B6	41
Kefar Yona, Isr.	f10	41
Kef City, Ok., U.S.	o21	14
Ke Ga, Cape, c., Viet.	F8	35
Kegonsa, Lake, l., Wi., U.S.	F4	126
Keho Lake, l., Ab., Can.	E4	68
Kehsi Mansam, Burma	D6	10
Keilor, Austl.	*G7	51
Keimoes, S. Afr.	C3	49
Keitele, l., Fin.	F11	14
Keith, Austl.	H3	51
Keith, Scot., U.K.	B5	10
Keith, co., Ne., U.S.	C4	104
Keithley Creek, B.C., Can.	C7	69
Keithville, La., U.S.	B2	95
Kejimkujik Lake, l., N.S., Can.	E4	71
Kejimkujik National Park, N.S., Can.	E4	71
Kekaha, Hi., U.S.	B2	88
Kékes, mtn., Hung.	*B5	24

Name	Map Ref	Page
Kelafo, Eth.	D5	47
Kelan, China	E4	32
Kelang, Malay.	E2	34
Kelantan, state, Malay.	J4	35
Kelantan, stm., Malay.	J5	35
Keldron, S.D., U.S.	B4	118
Kelfield, Sk., Can.	F1	75
Kelford, N.C., U.S.	A5	110
Kelheim, F.R.Ger.	E6	19
Kelibia, Tun.	F3	23
Kelkit, stm., Tur.	B11	40
Kell, Il., U.S.	E5	90
Kellé, Congo	B1	48
Kellenhusen, F.R.Ger.	D5	15
Keller, Tx., U.S.	n9	120
Keller, Va., U.S.	C7	123
Keller, Wa., U.S.	A7	124
Keller Lake, l., Sk., Can.	A2	75
Kellerman, Al., U.S.	B2	78
Kellerton, Ia., U.S.	D3	92
Kellerville, Il., U.S.	D3	90
Kellett, Cape, c., N.T., Can.	B7	66
Kellettville, Pa., U.S.	D3	115
Kelley, Ia., U.S.	C4	92
Kelleys Island, Oh., U.S.	A3	112
Kelleys Island, i., Oh., U.S.	A3	112
Kelliher, Sk., Can.	F4	75
Kelliher, Mn., U.S.	C4	100
Kellmünz, F.R.Ger.	A6	20
Kellnersville, Wi., U.S.	D6	126
Kelloe, Mb., Can.	D1	70
Kellogg, Id., U.S.	B2	89
Kellogg, Ia., U.S.	C5	92
Kellogg, Mn., U.S.	F6	100
Kells see Ceanannus Mór, Ire.	D5	11
Kelly, Ky., U.S.	D2	94
Kelly, La., U.S.	C3	95
Kelly, Wy., U.S.	C2	127
Kelly Air Force Base, mil., Tx., U.S.	k7	120
Kelly Brook Mountain, mtn., Me., U.S.	A3	96
Kelly Island, i., De., U.S.	D4	85
Kelly Lake, B.C., Can.	B7	69
Kelly Lake, Mn., U.S.	C5	100
Kellyton, Al., U.S.	C3	78
Kellyville, N.H., U.S.	D2	106
Kellyville, Ok., U.S.	B5	113
Kellyville, Tx., U.S.	C5	120
Kelme, Sov. Un.	A7	26
Kélo, Chad	D3	46
Kelowna, B.C., Can.	E8	69
Kelsey, Ab., Can.	C4	68
Kelsey Bay, B.C., Can.	D4	69
Kelsey Lake, l., Mb., Can.	C1	70
Kelseyville, Ca., U.S.	C2	82
Kelso, Sk., Can.	H5	75
Kelso, Scot., U.K.	C5	10
Kelso, Ca., U.S.	E6	82
Kelso, Mo., U.S.	D8	102
Kelso, Wa., U.S.	C3	124
Keltie, Mount, mtn., Ant.	f40	7
Keltonburg, Tn., U.S.	D8	119
Keluang, Malay.	E2	34
Kelvington, Sk., Can.	E4	75
Kelwood, Mb., Can.	D2	70
Kem, Sov. Un.	E16	14
Kem, stm., Sov. Un.	C15	8
Ké Macina, Mali	D3	45
Kemano, B.C., Can.	C4	69
Kembé, Cen. Afr. Rep.	E4	46
Kemerovo, Sov. Un.	D11	29
Kemi, Fin.	E11	14
Kemijärvi, Fin.	D12	14
Kemijärvi, l., Fin.	D12	14
Kemijoki, stm., Fin.	D11	14
Kemme, well, Libya	E3	43
Kemmerer, Wy., U.S.	E2	127
Kemnath, F.R.Ger.	D6	19
Kemnay, Mb., Can.	E1	70
Kemp, Ok., U.S.	D5	113
Kemp, Tx., U.S.	C4	120
Kemp, Lake, res., Tx., U.S.	C3	120
Kemp Coast, Ant.	C18	7
Kempen, F.R.Ger.	C6	17
Kemper, S.C., U.S.	C9	117
Kemper, co., Ms., U.S.	C5	101
Kempner, Tx., U.S.	D4	120
Kemp Peninsula, pen., Ant.	B6	7
Kempsey, Austl.	F9	50
Kempshall Mountain, mtn., N.Y., U.S.	A6	109
Kempten [in Allgäu], F.R.Ger.	E5	18
Kempton, Il., U.S.	C5	90
Kempton, In., U.S.	D5	91
Kempton, N.D., U.S.	B8	111
Kemptville, On., Can.	B9	73
Kenai, Ak., U.S.	C9	79
Kenai Fjords National Park, Ak., U.S.	D10	79
Kenai Mountains, mts., Ak., U.S.	h16	79
Kenai Peninsula, pen., Ak., U.S.	h16	79
Kenamu, stm., Nf., Can.	B1	72
Kenansville, Fl., U.S.	E6	86
Kenansville, N.C., U.S.	C5	110
Kenaston, Sk., Can.	F2	75
Kenbridge, Va., U.S.	D4	123
Kendal, Sk., Can.	G4	75
Kendal, Eng., U.K.	C5	10
Kendall, Fl., U.S.	s13	86
Kendall, N.Y., U.S.	B2	109
Kendall, Wi., U.S.	E3	126
Kendall, co., Il., U.S.	B5	90
Kendall, co., Tx., U.S.	E3	120
Kendall Park, N.J., U.S.	C3	107
Kendallville, In., U.S.	B7	91
Kendari, Indon.	F6	34
Kendrāpāra, India	D8	36
Kendrick, Id., U.S.	C2	89
Kendrick, Ok., U.S.	B5	113
Kenduskeag, Me., U.S.	D4	96
Kenedy, Tx., U.S.	E4	120
Kenedy, co., Tx., U.S.	F4	120
Kenefic, Ok., U.S.	C5	113
Kenel, S.D., U.S.	B5	118
Kenema, S.L.	D2	45
Kenesaw, Ne., U.S.	D7	104
Kenge, Zaire	B2	48
Kēng Tung, Burma	D10	36
Kenhardt, S. Afr.	C3	49
Kéniéba, Mali	C2	45
Kenilworth, Il., U.S.	h9	90
Kenilworth, N.J., U.S.	*B4	107
Kenilworth, Ut., U.S.	D5	121
Kenimekh, Sov. Un.	A12	39
Kenly, N.C., U.S.	B4	110
Kenmare, Ire.	E2	11
Kenmare, N.D., U.S.	A3	111
Kenmare, stm., Ire.	E1	11
Kenmore, N.Y., U.S.	*C2	109
Kenmore, Wa., U.S.	*B3	124
Kenna, N.M., U.S.	D6	108
Kenna, W.V., U.S.	C3	125
Kennaday Peak, mtn., Wy., U.S.	E6	127
Kennan, Wi., U.S.	C3	126
Kennard, In., U.S.	E6	91
Kennard, Ne., U.S.	C9	104
Kennard, Tx., U.S.	D5	120
Kennebago Lake, l., Me., U.S.	C2	96
Kennebec, S.D., U.S.	D5	118
Kennebec, co., Me., U.S.	D3	96
Kennebec, stm., Me., U.S.	D3	96
Kennebunk, Me., U.S.	E2	96
Kennebunkport, Me., U.S.	E2	96
Kennedale, Tx., U.S.	n9	120
Kennedy, Sk., Can.	G4	75
Kennedy, Al., U.S.	B2	78
Kennedy, Mn., U.S.	B2	100
Kennedy, N.Y., U.S.	C1	109
Kennedy, Mount, mtn., Yk., Can.	D5	66
Kennedy Channel, strt., N.A.	k38	66
Kennedy Entrance, strt., Ak., U.S.	D9	79
Kennedy Heights, La., U.S.	*E5	95
Kennedy Lake, l., Sk., Can.	D4	75
Kennedyville, Md., U.S.	B6	97
Kennesaw, Ga., U.S.	B2	87
Kennesaw Mountain, mtn., Ga., U.S.	C2	87
Kennesaw Mountain National Battlefield Park, Ga., U.S.	h7	87
Kennet, stm., Eng., U.K.	C6	12
Kennetcook, N.S., Can.	D6	71
Kenneth, Ks., U.S.	m16	93
Kenneth, Mn., U.S.	G2	100
Kennett, Mo., U.S.	E7	102
Kennett Square, Pa., U.S.	G10	115
Kennewick, Wa., U.S.	C6	124
Kenney, Il., U.S.	C4	90
Kenney Dam, B.C., Can.	C5	69
Kennisis Lake, l., On., Can.	B6	73
Kennydale, Wa., U.S.	e11	124
Keno, Or., U.S.	E5	114
Kénogami, P.Q., Can.	A6	74
Kénogami, Lac, l., P.Q., Can.	A6	74
Kenora, On., Can.	o16	73
Kenora, On., Can.	o17	73
Kenosha, Wi., U.S.	F6	126
Kenosha, co., Wi., U.S.	F5	126
Kenova, W.V., U.S.	C2	125
Ken Rock, Il., U.S.	A4	90
Kensal, N.D., U.S.	B7	111
Kensett, Ar., U.S.	B4	81
Kensett, Ia., U.S.	A4	92
Kensico Reservoir, res., N.Y., U.S.	g13	109
Kensington, P.E., Can.	C6	71
Kensington (part of London), Eng., U.K.	k12	10
Kensington, Ca., U.S.	*h8	82
Kensington, Ct., U.S.	C4	84
Kensington, Ks., U.S.	C4	93
Kensington, Md., U.S.	B3	97
Kensington, Mn., U.S.	E3	100
Kensington, N.H., U.S.	E5	106
Kensington, Oh., U.S.	B5	112
Kent, Al., U.S.	C4	78
Kent, Ct., U.S.	C2	84
Kent, In., U.S.	G6	91
Kent, Mn., U.S.	D2	100
Kent, Oh., U.S.	A4	112
Kent, Or., U.S.	B6	114
Kent, Tx., U.S.	o12	120
Kent, Wa., U.S.	B3	124
Kent, co., N.B., Can.	C4	71
Kent, co., On., Can.	E2	73
Kent, co., Eng., U.K.	C8	12
Kent, co., De., U.S.	D3	85
Kent, co., Md., U.S.	B5	97
Kent, co., Mi., U.S.	E5	99
Kent, co., R.I., U.S.	D2	116
Kent, co., Tx., U.S.	C2	120
Kent Bridge, On., Can.	E2	73
Kent City, Mi., U.S.	E5	99
Kent Island, i., De., U.S.	D4	85
Kent Island, i., Md., U.S.	C5	97
Kent Junction, N.B., Can.	C4	71
Kentland, In., U.S.	C3	91
Kenton, Mb., Can.	E1	70
Kenton, De., U.S.	D3	85
Kenton, Ky., U.S.	k14	94
Kenton, Oh., U.S.	B2	112
Kenton, Tn., U.S.	A2	119
Kenton, co., Ky., U.S.	B5	94
Kent Point, c., Md., U.S.	C5	97
Kents Store, Va., U.S.	C4	123
Kentucky, state, U.S.	C4	94
Kentucky, stm., Ky., U.S.	B5	94
Kentucky, Middle Fork, stm., Ky., U.S.	C6	94
Kentucky, North Fork, stm., Ky., U.S.	C6	94
Kentucky, South Fork, stm., Ky., U.S.	C6	94
Kentucky Dam, Ky., U.S.	e9	94
Kentucky Lake, res., U.S.	C10	76
Kentucky Ridge, mtn., Ky., U.S.	D6	94
Kentville, N.S., Can.	D5	71
Kentwood, La., U.S.	D5	95
Kentwood, Mi., U.S.	F5	99
Kenvil, N.J., U.S.	B3	107
Kenvir, Ky., U.S.	D7	94
Kenwood, Oh., U.S.	*A7	113
Kenwood, Ok., U.S.	A6	113
Kenya, ctry., Afr.	A6	48
Kenya, Mount see Kirinyaga, mtn., Kenya	B6	48
Kenyon, Mn., U.S.	F6	100
Kenyon, R.I., U.S.	F2	116
Keo, Ar., U.S.	C3	81
Keokea, Hi., U.S.	C5	88
Keokuk, Ia., U.S.	D6	92
Keokuk, co., Ia., U.S.	C5	92
Keokuk Lock and Dam, U.S.	D6	92
Keoma, Ab., Can.	D4	68
Keonjhargarh, India	G10	37
Keosauqua, Ia., U.S.	D6	92
Keota, Co., U.S.	A6	83
Keota, Ia., U.S.	C5	92
Keowee, Lake, l., S.C., U.S.	B2	117
Kepno, Pol.	C5	21
Keppel, Sk., Can.	E2	75
Kerala, state, India	F4	36
Kerang, Austl.	G7	50
Keratsínion, Grc.	*D4	25
Kerby, Or., U.S.	E3	114
Kerch, Sov. Un.	E6	29
Kerchemya, Sov. Un.	C19	8
Kerch Strait, strt., Sov. Un.	I11	27
Kerema, Pap. N. Gui.	k12	50
Keremeos, B.C., Can.	E8	69
Kerempe Burnu, c., Tur.	A9	40
Keren, Eth.	B4	47
Kerend, Iran	D3	39
Kerens, Tx., U.S.	C4	120
Kerguélen, Îles, is., F.S.A.T.	J1	2
Kerhonkson, N.Y., U.S.	D6	109
Kericho, Kenya	B6	48
Kerinci, mtn., Indon.	F2	34
Kerkebet, Eth.	B4	47
Kerkenna, Îles, is., Tun.	C7	44
Kerkhoven, Mn., U.S.	E3	100
Kerki, Sov. Un.	H22	8
Kérkira, Grc.	C2	40
Kérkira (Corfu), i., Grc.	C2	40
Kerkrade, Neth.	B7	16
Kermadec Islands, is., N.Z.	I11	6
Kermān, Iran	B5	38
Kermānshāh see Bakhtarān, Iran	B4	38
Kerme, Gulf of, b., Tur.	D6	25
Kermit, Tx., U.S.	D1	120
Kermit, W.V., U.S.	D2	125
Kermode, Mount, mtn., B.C., Can.	C2	69
Kern, co., Ca., U.S.	E4	82
Kern, stm., Ca., U.S.	E4	82
Kernersville, N.C., U.S.	A2	110
Kernville, Ca., U.S.	E4	82
Kernville, Or., U.S.	C3	114
Kérouané, Gui.	E3	45
Kerpen, F.R.Ger.	C1	19
Kerr, co., Tx., U.S.	D3	120
Kerr, Lake, l., Fl., U.S.	C5	86
Kerrick, Mn., U.S.	D6	100
Kerrick, Tx., U.S.	A1	120
Kerrobert, Sk., Can.	F1	75
Kerrville, Tx., U.S.	D3	120
Kerry, co., Ire.	E2	11
Kerry Head, c., Ire.	E2	11
Kersey, Co., U.S.	A6	83
Kersey, Pa., U.S.	D4	115
Kershaw, S.C., U.S.	B6	117
Kershaw, co., S.C., U.S.	C6	117
Kersley, B.C., Can.	C6	69
Kerteminde, Den.	I8	15
Kerulen, stm., Asia	B7	31
Kerzaz, Alg.	D4	44
Kerzers, Switz.	C3	21
Keşan, Tur.	B6	40
Kesch, Piz, mtn., Switz.	C5	20
Kesennuma, Japan	G10	33
Kesh, N. Ire., U.K.	C4	11
Keshan, China	B10	31
Keshena, Wi., U.S.	D5	126
Keşiş Tepesi, mtn., Tur.	C12	40
Kesley, Ia., U.S.	B5	92
Kestenga, Sov. Un.	E14	14
Keswick, On., Can.	C5	73
Keswick, Eng., U.K.	F5	13
Keswick, Ia., U.S.	C5	92
Keswick, Va., U.S.	B4	123
Keszthely, Hung.	B3	24
Ket, stm., Sov. Un.	B10	28
Ketapang, Indon.	F4	34
Ketchikan, Ak., U.S.	D13	79
Ketchum, Id., U.S.	F4	89
Ketchum, Ok., U.S.	A6	113
Kete Krachi, Ghana	E4	45
Ketona, Al., U.S.	f7	78
Kétou, Benin	A6	45
Kętrzyn, Pol.	A6	21
Kettering, Eng., U.K.	C1	12
Kettering, Oh., U.S.	C1	112
Kettle, stm., N.A.	E8	69
Kettle, stm., Mn., U.S.	D6	100
Kettle Creek, stm., Pa., U.S.	D6	115
Kettle Creek Lake, l., Pa., U.S.	D6	115
Kettle Falls, Wa., U.S.	A7	124
Kettleman City, Ca., U.S.	E4	82
Kettle River, Mn., U.S.	D6	100
Kettle River Range, mts., Wa., U.S.	A7	124
Kettwig, F.R.Ger.	B1	19
Kety, Pol.	D5	26
Ketzin, Ger.D.R.	A7	19
Keuka Lake, l., N.Y., U.S.	C3	109
Keuterville, Id., U.S.	C2	89
Kevil, Ky., U.S.	e9	94
Kevin, Mt., U.S.	B5	103
Kewanee, Il., U.S.	B4	90
Kewanee, Ms., U.S.	C5	101
Kewanee, Mo., U.S.	E8	102
Kewanna, In., U.S.	B5	91
Kewaskum, Wi., U.S.	E5	126
Kewaunee, Wi., U.S.	D6	126
Kewaunee, co., Wi., U.S.	D6	126
Keweenaw, co., Mi., U.S.	A2	99
Keweenaw Bay, Mi., U.S.	B2	99
Keweenaw Bay, b., Mi., U.S.	B2	99
Keweenaw Point, c., Mi., U.S.	A3	99
Key, Lough, l., Ire.	C3	11
Keyapaha, S.D., U.S.	D5	118
Keya Paha, co., Ne., U.S.	A5	104
Keya Paha, stm., U.S.	A5	104
Keyes, Mb., Can.	D2	70
Keyes, Ok., U.S.	e8	113
Keyesport, Il., U.S.	E4	90
Keyhole Reservoir, res., Wy., U.S.	B8	127
Key Junction, On., Can.	B4	73
Key Largo, Fl., U.S.	G6	86
Keymar, Md., U.S.	A3	97
Keynsham, Eng., U.K.	C5	12
Keyport, N.J., U.S.	C4	107
Keysburg, Ky., U.S.	D2	94
Keyser, W.V., U.S.	B6	125
Keystone, In., U.S.	C7	91
Keystone, Ia., U.S.	C5	92
Keystone, Ne., U.S.	C4	104
Keystone, S.D., U.S.	D2	118
Keystone, W.V., U.S.	D3	125
Keystone Heights, Fl., U.S.	C4	86
Keystone Lake, res., Ok., U.S.	A5	113
Keystone Peak, mtn., Az., U.S.	F4	80
Keysville, Ga., U.S.	C4	87
Keysville, Va., U.S.	C4	123
Keytesville, Mo., U.S.	B5	102
Key West, Fl., U.S.	H5	86
Key West, La., U.S.	B7	95
Key West Naval Air Station, mil., Fl., U.S.	H5	86
Kezar Falls, Me., U.S.	E2	96
Kezar Lake, l., Me., U.S.	D2	96
Kezar Pond, l., Me., U.S.	D2	96
Kezhma, Sov. Un.	D13	29
Kežmarok, Czech.	D6	26
Khabab, Syria	A8	41
Khabarovsk, Sov. Un.	E16	29
Khabīs see Shāhdād, Iran	F8	39
Khachmas, Sov. Un.	E3	28
Khaidhárion, Grc.	*C4	25
Khairpur, Pak.	B4	36
Khakhea, Bots.	B3	49
Khalándrion, Grc.	*C4	25
Khalia, Grc.	g11	25
Khálki (Chalke), i., Grc.	D6	25
Khalkidhikí Penninsula, pen., Grc.	B4	25
Khalkís, Grc.	C4	40
Khalūf, Oman	C5	38
Khambhāliya, India	D5	36
Khambhāt, Gulf of, b., India	D5	36
Khāmgaon, India	G6	37
Khammam, India	I8	37
Khānābād, Afg.	A4	36
Khānaqīn, Iraq	B4	38
Khān az Zabīb, Jord.	C8	41
Khānderi, i., India	H4	37
Khandwa, India	D6	36
Khanh Hung, Viet.	D3	34
Khaniá (Canea), Grc.	E5	40
Khaniá, Gulf of, b., Grc.	E4	25
Khanka, Lake, l., Asia	B11	31
Khānpur, Pak.	C5	36
Khanty-Mansiysk, Sov. Un.	A7	28
Khān Yūnus, Isr. Occ.	C6	41
Kharagpur, India	D8	36
Khārān, Pak.	G12	39
Kharānaq, Iran	E7	39
Kharg Island see Khārk, Jazīreh-Ye, i., Iran	C4	38
Khargon, India	G5	37
Khariār, India	G5	37
Khārijah, Al Wāḥāt al, well, Eg.	C3	38
Khārk, Jazīreh-Ye (Kharg Island), i., Iran	C4	38
Kharkov, Sov. Un.	D6	29
Kharmān, Kūh-e, mtn., Iran	G6	39
Kharmanli, Bul.	E7	24
Kharovsk, Sov. Un.	B13	29
Khartoum (Al Kharṭūm), Sud.	B3	47
Khartoum North (Al Kharṭūm Baḥrī), Sud.	B3	47
Khartsyzsk, Sov. Un.	q21	27
Khasavyurt, Sov. Un.	G18	8
Khāsh, Afg.	D6	36
Khāsh, Iran	G10	39
Khāsh, stm., Afg.	B3	36
Khashm al Qirbah, Khazzān, res., Sud.	C4	47
Khashuri, Sov. Un.	B14	40
Khasi Hills, mts., India	C9	36
Khaskovo, Bul.	E7	24
Khatanga, Sov. Un.	B13	29
Khatanga, stm., Sov. Un.	B13	29
Khavast, Sov. Un.	I11	27
Khaybar, Sau. Ar.	C3	38
Khemmarat, Thai.	D6	35
Khenchla, Alg.	B6	44
Khenifra, Mor.	C3	44
Kherson, Sov. Un.	H9	27
Kheta, stm., Sov. Un.	B12	29
Khieo, mtn., Thai.	E4	35
Khilchipur, India	I6	37
Khilok, Sov. Un.	D14	29
Khimki, Sov. Un.	C6	40
Khíos (Chios), i., Grc.	C5	40
Khíos (Chios), i., Grc.	C5	40
Khirbat al Ghazālah, Syria	B8	41
Khisfīn, Syria	B7	41
Khiva, Sov. Un.	E6	28
Khlebarovo, Bul.	D8	24
Khmelnik, Sov. Un.	G7	27
Khmelnitskiy, Sov. Un.	G6	27
Khoai, i., Viet.	H6	35
Khodzheyli, Sov. Un.	E5	28
Kholm, Afg.	B4	36
Kholm, Sov. Un.	C8	27
Kholmsk, Sov. Un.	E17	29
Khomeyn, Iran	E5	39
Khomeynishahr, Iran	E5	39
Khon Kaen, Thai.	B2	34
Khoper, stm., Sov. Un.	F14	27
Khor, stm., Sov. Un.	B12	31
Khóra Sfakíon, Grc.	E5	40
Khorinsk, Sov. Un.	A6	31
Khorog, Sov. Un.	F10	29
Khorol, Sov. Un.	G9	27
Khorramābād, Iran	E4	39
Khorramshahr, Iran	E4	39
Khotin, Sov. Un.	G6	27
Khouribga, Mor.	C3	44
Khowst, Afg.	B4	36
Khram Yai, i., Thai.	F4	35
Khrisoúpolis, Grc.	B5	25
Khromtau, Sov. Un.	E9	28
Khu Khan, Thai.	E6	35
Khulna, Bngl.	D8	36
Khunzakh, Sov. Un.	A16	40
Khūrān, strt., Iran	H7	39
Khurda, India	G10	37
Khurja, India	G14	40
Khūryān Mūryān (Kuria Muria Is.), is., Oman	D5	38
Khushāb, Pak.	A4	36
Khust, Sov. Un.	G4	27
Khuzdār, Pak.	B6	38
Khvāf, Iran	E7	39
Khvor, Iran	E7	39
Khvormūj, Iran	G5	39
Khvoy, Iran	E5	39
Khwae Noi, stm., Thai.	B1	34
Khyber Pass, Asia	B5	36
Kia, i., Sol. Is.	H15	52
Kiamichi, stm., Ok., U.S.	C6	113
Kiamika, P.Q., Can.	C2	74
Kiamika, stm., P.Q., Can.	C2	74
Kiana, Ak., U.S.	B7	79
Kiangarow, Mount, mtn., Austl.	C8	51
Kiangsi see Jiangxi, prov., China	F8	31
Kiangsu see Jiangsu, prov., China	F8	31
Kiantajärvi, l., Fin.	E13	14
Kiask Lake, l., Mb., Can.	A3	70
Kiáton, Grc.	D3	25
Kiawah Island, i., S.C., U.S.	F7	117
Kibangou, Congo	B1	48
Kibau, Tan.	C6	48
Kiberege, Tan.	C6	48
Kibombo, Zaire	B5	48
Kibondo, Tan.	B6	48
Kibwezi, Kenya	B6	48
Kičevo, Yugo.	E5	24
Kickamuit, stm., R.I., U.S.	D5	116
Kickapoo, stm., Wi., U.S.	E3	126
Kickapoo, Lake, res., Tx., U.S.	C3	120
Kickapoo Creek, stm., Il., U.S.	C4	90
Kickapoo Indian Reservation, Ks., U.S.	C8	93
Kicking Horse Pass, Can.	D2	68
Kidal, Mali	C5	45
Kidder, Mo., U.S.	B3	102
Kidder, S.D., U.S.	B8	118
Kidder, co., N.D., U.S.	C6	111
Kidderminster, Eng., U.K.	D5	10
Kidira, Sen.	C3	45
Kidnappers, Cape, c., N.Z.	M16	51
Kidron, Valley of, val., Isr. Occ.	m14	41
Kidsgrove, Eng., U.K.	A5	12
Kidugallo, Tan.	C6	48
Kidwelly, Wales, U.K.	C3	12
Kiefer, Ok., U.S.	B5	113
Kiel, F.R.Ger.	A5	18
Kiel, Wi., U.S.	E5	126
Kiel Bay, b., F.R.Ger.	A5	18
Kiel Canal, F.R.Ger.	A4	18
Kielce, Pol.	C6	26
Kienthal, Switz.	C4	21
Kiester, Mn., U.S.	G5	100
Kiev, Sov. Un.	D6	29
Kiev Reservoir, res., Sov. Un.	F8	27
Kiffa, Maur.	C2	45
Kifisiá, Grc.	g11	25
Kifisós (Cephisus), stm., Grc.	g9	25
Kifisós, stm., Grc.	g11	25
Kifrī, Iraq	E15	40
Kigali, Rw.	B5	48
Kigi, Tur.	C13	40
Kigoma, Tan.	B4	48
Kigoma, prov., Tan.	B5	48
Kiholo Bay, b., Hi., U.S.	D5	88
Kii Strait, strt., Japan	J7	33
Kikinda, Yugo.	C5	24
Kikori, Pap. N. Gui.	k11	50
Kikori, stm., Pap. N. Gui.	k11	50
Kikwit, Zaire	C2	48
Kila, Mt., U.S.	B2	103
Kilauea, Hi., U.S.	A2	88
Kilauea Crater, crat., Hi., U.S.	D6	88
Kilauea Point, c., Hi., U.S.	A2	88
Kilbeggan, Ire.	D4	11
Kilbourne, Il., U.S.	C4	90
Kilbourne, La., U.S.	B4	95
Kilbrannan Sound, strt., Scot., U.K.	E3	13
Kilburn, N.B., Can.	C2	71
Kilcar, Ire.	C3	11
Kilchoan, Scot., U.K.	D2	13
Kilchu, N. Kor.	F4	33
Kilcock, Ire.	D5	11
Kilcolgan, Ire.	D3	11
Kilconnell, Ire.	D3	11
Kilcoole, Ire.	D5	11
Kilcormac (Frankford), Ire.	D4	11
Kilcullen, Ire.	D5	11
Kildare, Ire.	D5	11
Kildare, Ok., U.S.	A4	113
Kildare, co., Ire.	D5	11
Kildare, Cape, c., P.E., Can.	C6	71
Kildorrery, Ire.	E3	11
Kildysart, Ire.	E2	11
Kilembe, Ug.	A5	48
Kilembe, Zaire	C2	48
Kilfenora, Ire.	D2	11
Kilfinane, Ire.	E3	11
Kilgarvan, Ire.	F2	11
Kilgore, Ne., U.S.	B5	104
Kilgore, Tx., U.S.	C5	120
Kilifi, Kenya	B6	48
Kilimanjaro, prov., Tan.	B6	48
Kilimanjaro, mtn., Tan.	B6	48
Kilimatinde, Tan.	C5	48
Kilindoni, Tan.	C6	48
Kilis, Tur.	D11	40
Kiliya, Sov. Un.	I7	27
Kilkee, Ire.	D2	11
Kilkeel, N. Ire., U.K.	C6	11
Kilkenny, Mn., U.S.	F5	100
Kilkenny, co., Ire.	E4	11
Kilkerrin, Ire.	D3	11
Kilkieran Bay, b., Ire.	D2	11
Kilkís, Grc.	B4	25
Kill, Ire.	D5	11
Killadoon, Ire.	C1	11
Killala, Ire.	C2	11
Killala Bay, b., Ire.	C2	11
Killaloe, Ire.	E3	11
Killaloe Station, On., Can.	B7	73
Killally, Sk., Can.	G4	75
Killam, Ab., Can.	C5	68
Killam, Tx., U.S.	E2	120
Killarney, Mb., Can.	E2	70
Killarney, Ire.	E2	11
Killarney, Lake, l., Bah.	m17	64
Killarney Provincial Park, On., Can.	A3	73
Killbuck, Oh., U.S.	B4	112
Killdeer, N.D., U.S.	B3	111
Killdeer Mountains, mts., N.D., U.S.	B3	111
Killduff, Ia., U.S.	C5	92
Killeen, Tx., U.S.	D4	120
Killen, Al., U.S.	A2	78
Killenaule, Ire.	E4	11
Killeshandra, Ire.	C4	11
Killeter, N. Ire., U.K.	C4	11
Killian, La., U.S.	D5	95
Killik, stm., Ak., U.S.	B9	79
Killimor, Ire.	D3	11
Killin, Scot., U.K.	D4	13
Killíni, Grc.	E3	25
Killington Peak, mtn., Vt., U.S.	D3	122
Killingworth, Ct., U.S.	D5	84
Killíni, Grc.	D3	25
Killorglin, Ire.	E2	11
Killybegs, Ire.	C3	11
Killyleagh, N. Ire., U.K.	C6	11
Kilmacthomas, Ire.	E4	11
Kilmaine, Ire.	D2	11
Kilmallock, Ire.	E3	11
Kilmanagh, Mi., U.S.	E7	99
Kilmarnock, Scot., U.K.	C4	10
Kilmarnock, Va., U.S.	C6	123
Kilmelford, Scot., U.K.	D3	13
Kilmez, Sov. Un.	B4	28
Kilmichael, Ms., U.S.	B4	101
Kiln, Ms., U.S.	E4	101
Kilrea, N. Ire., U.K.	C5	11
Kilrush, Ire.	D2	11
Kilsyth, Scot., U.K.	E4	13
Kiltamagh, Ire.	D3	11
Kiltoom, Ire.	D3	11
Kilwa, Zaire	C4	48
Kilwa Kisiwani, Tan.	C6	48
Kilwa Kivinje, Tan.	C6	48
Kim, Co., U.S.	D7	83
Kimamba, Tan.	C6	48
Kimball, Mn., U.S.	E4	100
Kimball, Ne., U.S.	C2	104
Kimball, S.D., U.S.	D7	118
Kimball, W.V., U.S.	D3	125
Kimball, co., Ne., U.S.	C2	104
Kimball, Mount, mtn., Ak., U.S.	C11	79
Kimballton, Ia., U.S.	C2	92
Kimberley, B.C., Can.	E9	69
Kimberley, S. Afr.	C4	49
Kimberley Plateau, plat., Austl.	C4	50
Kimberlin Heights, Tn., U.S.	n14	119
Kimberly, Al., U.S.	B3	78
Kimberly, Id., U.S.	G4	89
Kimberly, Or., U.S.	C7	114
Kimberly, W.V., U.S.	m13	125
Kimberly, Wi., U.S.	h9	126
Kimble, co., Tx., U.S.	D3	120
Kimbolton, Oh., U.S.	B4	112
Kimbrough, Al., U.S.	C2	78
Kimbrough, N.M., U.S.	E6	108
Kimch'aek (Sŏngjin), N. Kor.	C10	31
Kimchŏn, S. Kor.	H4	33
Kimesville, N.C., U.S.	B3	110
Kími, Grc.	C5	25
Kimiwan Lake, l., Ab., Can.	B2	68
Kimmel, In., U.S.	B6	91
Kimmins, Tn., U.S.	B4	119
Kimmswick, Mo., U.S.	g13	102
Kimowin, stm., Ab., Can.	A6	68
Kimry, Sov. Un.	C11	27
Kin, Japan	O5	52
Kinabalu, Mount, mtn., Malay.	D5	34
Kinard, Fl., U.S.	B1	86
Kinards, S.C., U.S.	C4	117
Kinbasket Lake, l., B.C., Can.	D8	69
Kinbrace, Scot., U.K.	B5	13
Kinbrae, Mn., U.S.	G3	100
Kinburn, On., Can.	B8	73
Kincaid, Il., U.S.	D4	90
Kincaid, Ks., U.S.	D8	93
Kincaid, W.V., U.S.	m13	125
Kincaid, Lake, res., Il., U.S.	C3	90
Kincardine, On., Can.	C3	73
Kincheloe Air Force Base, mil., Mi., U.S.	B6	99
Kinchafoonee Creek, stm., Ga., U.S.	E2	87
Kinde, Mi., U.S.	E8	99
Kinder, La., U.S.	D3	95
Kinderhook, Il., U.S.	D2	90
Kinderhook, N.Y., U.S.	C7	109
Kinder Scout, mtn., Eng., U.K.	A6	12
Kindersley, Sk., Can.	F1	75
Kindia, Gui.	D2	45
Kindred, N.D., U.S.	C9	111
Kindu, Zaire	B4	48
Kineo, Mount, mtn., Me., U.S.	C3	96
Kineshma, Sov. Un.	C14	29
King, N.C., U.S.	A2	110
King, Wi., U.S.	D4	126
King, co., Tx., U.S.	C2	120
King, co., Wa., U.S.	B4	124
King, i., Austl.	G7	50
King and Queen, co., Va., U.S.	C6	123
King and Queen Court House, Va., U.S.	C6	123
King Christian IX Land, reg., Grnld.	C18	128
King Christian X Land, reg., Grnld.	B17	128
King City, On., Can.	k14	73
King City, Ca., U.S.	D3	82
King City, Mo., U.S.	A3	102
King Cove, Ak., U.S.	E7	79
King David Hotel, Isr.	m14	41
King Ferry, N.Y., U.S.	C4	109
Kingfield, Me., U.S.	D2	96
Kingfisher, Ok., U.S.	B4	113
Kingfisher, co., Ok., U.S.	B3	113
King Frederik VI Coast, Grnld.	C19	128
King Frederik VIII Land, reg., Grnld.	B17	128
King George, Va., U.S.	B5	123
King George, co., Va., U.S.	B5	123
King George, Mount, mtn., B.C., Can.	D10	69
King George Island, i., B.A.T.	C7	7
King George Sound, strt., Austl.	G2	50
King Hill, Id., U.S.	F3	89
King Island, i., B.C., Can.	C4	69
King Lear Peak, mtn., Nv., U.S.	B3	105
King Leopold Ranges, mts., Austl.	C4	50
Kingman, Ab., Can.	C4	68
Kingman, Az., U.S.	B1	80
Kingman, Ks., U.S.	E5	93
Kingman, Me., U.S.	C4	96
Kingman, co., Ks., U.S.	E5	93
King Mountain, mtn., Ok., U.S.	C2	113
King Mountain, mtn., Or., U.S.	D8	114
King of Prussia, Pa., U.S.	F11	115
King Peak, mtn., Ca., U.S.	B1	82
Kings, Il., U.S.	A4	90
Kings, Ms., U.S.	C3	101
Kings, co., N.B., Can.	D4	71
Kings, co., N.S., Can.	D5	71
Kings, co., P.E., Can.	C7	71
Kings, co., Ca., U.S.	D4	82
Kings, co., N.Y., U.S.	E7	109
Kings, stm., Ar., U.S.	A2	81
Kings, stm., Ca., U.S.	D4	82
Kings, stm., Nv., U.S.	B3	105
Kingsburg, Ca., U.S.	D4	82
Kingsbury, Tx., U.S.	h8	120
Kingsbury, co., S.D., U.S.	C8	118

Name — Map Ref — Page

Kings Canyon National Park, Ca., U.S. — D4 82
Kingsclear, N.B., Can. — D3 71
Kings Corner, Ct., U.S. — B5 84
Kingscote, Austl. — G6 50
Kings Creek, S.C., U.S. — A5 117
Kingsdown, Ks., U.S. — E4 93
Kingsey-Falls, P.Q., Can. — D5 74
Kingsford, Mi., U.S. — C2 99
Kingsgate, B.C., Can. — E9 69
Kingsland, Ar., U.S. — D3 81
Kingsland, Ga., U.S. — F5 87
Kingsland, Tx., U.S. — D3 120
Kingsley, Ia., U.S. — B2 92
Kingsley, Mi., U.S. — D5 99
Kingsley Dam, Ne., U.S. — C4 104
Kingsmere Lake, I., Sk., Can. — C2 75
Kings Mill, Tx., U.S. — B2 120
Kings Mills, Oh., U.S. — C1 112
Kings Mountain, Ky., U.S. — C5 94
Kings Mountain, N.C., U.S. — B1 110
King Sound, strt., Austl. — C3 50
Kings Park, Va., U.S. — *B5 123
Kings Park West, Va., U.S. — B5 123
Kings Peak, mtn., Ut., U.S. — C5 121
King's Point, Nf., Can. — D3 72
Kings Point, N.Y., U.S. — *E7 109
Kingsport, Tn., U.S. — C11 119
Kingston, N.S., Can. — E5 71
Kingston, On., Can. — C8 73
Kingston, Jam. — F5 64
Kingston, N.Z. — P12 51
Kingston, Ar., U.S. — A2 81
Kingston, Ga., U.S. — B2 87
Kingston, Id., U.S. — B2 89
Kingston, Il., U.S. — A5 90
Kingston, Ky., U.S. — C5 94
Kingston, Md., U.S. — D6 97
Kingston, Ma., U.S. — C6 98
Kingston, Mi., U.S. — E7 99
Kingston, Mn., U.S. — E4 100
Kingston, Mo., U.S. — B3 102
Kingston, Nv., U.S. — D5 105
Kingston, N.H., U.S. — E4 106
Kingston, N.J., U.S. — C3 107
Kingston, N.Y., U.S. — D6 109
Kingston, Oh., U.S. — C3 112
Kingston, Ok., U.S. — D5 113
Kingston, Pa., U.S. — D10 115
Kingston, R.I., U.S. — F3 116
Kingston, Tn., U.S. — D9 119
Kingston, Ut., U.S. — E3 121
Kingston, W.V., U.S. — D3 125
Kingston, Wi., U.S. — E5 126
Kingston Southeast, Austl. — G6 50
Kingston Springs, Tn., U.S. — A4 119
Kingston-upon-Thames (part of London), Eng., U.K. — m12 10
Kingstown, St. Vin. — J14 64
Kingstown, Md., U.S. — B5 97
Kingstree, S.C., U.S. — D8 117
Kings Valley, Or., U.S. — C3 114
Kingsville, On., Can. — E2 73
Kingsville, Md., U.S. — B5 97
Kingsville, Mo., U.S. — C3 102
Kingsville, Oh., U.S. — A5 112
Kingsville, Tx., U.S. — F4 120
Kingsville Naval Air Station, mil., Tx., U.S. — F4 120
Kingswood, Ky., U.S. — C3 94
Kington, Eng., U.K. — B4 12
Kingurutik Lake, I., Nf., Can. — g9 72
Kingussie, Scot., U.K. — B4 10
King William, Va., U.S. — C5 123
King William, co., Va., U.S. — C5 123
King William Island, i., N.T., Can. — C13 66
King William's Town, S. Afr. — D4 49
Kingwood, W.V., U.S. — B5 125
Kinistino, Sk., Can. — E3 75
Kinkaid Lake, res., Il., U.S. — F4 90
Kinkala, Congo — B1 48
Kinkora, P.E., Can. — C6 71
Kinley, Sk., Can. — E2 75
Kin-Li-Chee, Az., U.S. — B6 80
Kinloch, Mo., U.S. — f13 102
Kinlochewe, Scot., U.K. — C3 13
Kinloch Hourn, Scot., U.K. — C3 13
Kinmount, On., Can. — C6 73
Kinmundy, Il., U.S. — E5 90
Kinnaird, B.C., Can. — E9 69
Kinnairds Head, c., Scot., U.K. — B6 10
Kinnear, Wy., U.S. — C4 127
Kinnelon, N.J., U.S. — B4 107
Kinneret, Yam (Sea of Galilee), l., Isr. — B7 41
Kinney, co., Tx., U.S. — E2 120
Kinomoto, Japan — n15 33
Kinosaki, Japan — I7 33
Kinrooi, Bel. — C5 17
Kinross, P.E., Can. — C7 71
Kinross, Scot., U.K. — D5 13
Kinsale, Ire. — E2 10
Kinsale, Va., U.S. — B6 123
Kinsale, Old Head of, c., Ire. — E2 10
Kinsella, Ab., Can. — C5 68
Kinsey, Al., U.S. — D4 78
Kinsey, Mt., U.S. — D11 103
Kinshasa (Léopoldville), Zaire — B2 48
Kinsley, Ks., U.S. — E4 93
Kinsman, Oh., U.S. — A5 112
Kinston, Al., U.S. — D3 78
Kinston, N.C., U.S. — B5 110
Kinta, Ok., U.S. — B6 113
Kintampo, Ghana — E4 45
Kintinku, Tan. — C6 48
Kintore, Scot., U.K. — C6 13
Kintyre, N.D., U.S. — C6 111
Kintyre, Mull of, c., Scot., U.K. — E3 13
Kinuso, Ab., Can. — B3 68
Kinvara, Ire. — D3 11
Kinyangiri, Tan. — C6 48
Kinyeti, mtn., Sud. — E3 47
Kinzia, Or., U.S. — C6 114
Kioa, i., Fiji — H15 52
Kiona, Wa., U.S. — C6 124
Kiosk, On., Can. — A6 73
Kiowa, Co., U.S. — B6 83
Kiowa, Ks., U.S. — E5 93
Kiowa, co., Co., U.S. — C8 83
Kiowa, co., Ks., U.S. — E4 93
Kiowa, co., Ok., U.S. — C2 113
Kiowa Creek, stm., Co., U.S. — B6 83
Kiowa Creek, stm., Ok., U.S. — A1 113
Kipahigan Lake, I., Can. — B5 75
Kipahulu, Hi., U.S. — *C5 88
Kipapa Stream, stm., Hi., U.S. — g9 88
Kiparissía, Grc. — D3 25
Kiparissía, Gulf of, b., Grc. — D3 25
Kipawa, Parc de, P.Q., Can. — k11 74

Kipembawe, Tan. — C5 48
Kipili, Tan. — C5 48
Kipini, Kenya — B7 48
Kipling, Sk., Can. — G4 75
Kipling, Mi., U.S. — C3 99
Kipnuk, Ak., U.S. — C7 79
Kipp, Ab., Can. — E4 68
Kipp, Ks., U.S. — D6 93
Kipton, Oh., U.S. — A3 112
Kipushi, Zaire — D4 48
Kirby, Ar., U.S. — C2 81
Kirby, Tx., U.S. — *E3 120
Kirby, Wy., U.S. — C4 127
Kirbyville, Tx., U.S. — D6 120
Kirchberg, Switz. — B4 21
Kirchdorf, Ger.D.R. — E5 15
Kirchhain, F.R.Ger. — C3 19
Kirchheimbolanden, F.R.Ger. — D2 19
Kirchheim [unter Teck], F.R.Ger. — E4 19
Kirchhundem, F.R.Ger. — B3 19
Kirdāsah, Eg. — D3 41
Kirensk, Sov. Un. — D13 29
Kirghiz S.S.R., state, Sov. Un. — E10 29
Kirgiz Range, mts., Sov. Un. — E8 28
Kiri, Zaire — B2 48
Kiribati, ctry., Oc. — G11 6
Kirikkale, Tur. — C9 40
Kirin see Jilin, prov., China — C10 31
Kirinía, Cyp. — E9 40
Kirinian, i., Marsh Is. — S18 52
Kirinyaga (Mount Kenya), mtn., Kenya — B6 48
Kirk, Co., U.S. — B8 83
Kırkağaç, Tur. — B10 40
Kirkby Lonsdale, Eng., U.K. — F6 13
Kirkby Stephen, Eng., U.K. — F6 13
Kirkcaldy, Ab., Can. — D4 68
Kirkcaldy, Scot., U.K. — B5 10
Kirkcolm, Scot., U.K. — F3 13
Kirkcudbright, Scot., U.K. — C5 10
Kirkcudbright Bay, b., Scot., U.K. — F4 13
Kirkella, Mb., Can. — D1 70
Kirkenes, Nor. — C13 14
Kirkersville, Oh., U.S. — C3 112
Kirkfield, On., Can. — C6 73
Kirkintilloch, Scot., U.K. — E4 13
Kirkoswald, Eng., U.K. — F6 13
Kirkland, Al., U.S. — D2 78
Kirkland, Az., U.S. — C3 80
Kirkland, Ga., U.S. — E4 87
Kirkland, Il., U.S. — A5 90
Kirkland, Tn., U.S. — B5 119
Kirkland, Tx., U.S. — B2 120
Kirkland, Wa., U.S. — B3 124
Kirkland Lake, On., Can. — o19 73
Kirklareli, Tur. — B6 40
Kirklin, In., U.S. — D5 91
Kirkman, Ia., U.S. — C2 92
Kirkmansville, Ky., U.S. — D2 94
Kirkpatrick, Mount, mtn., Ant. — A29 7
Kirkpatrick Lake, I., Ab., Can. — D5 68
Kirksey, Ky., U.S. — f9 94
Kirksey, S.C., U.S. — C3 117
Kirksville, Mo., U.S. — A5 102
Kirkton, On., Can. — D3 73
Kirkton of Glenisla, Scot., U.K. — D5 13
Kirkūk, Iraq — B4 38
Kirkville, Ia., U.S. — C5 92
Kirkwall, Scot., U.K. — A5 10
Kirkwood, S. Afr. — D4 49
Kirkwood, De., U.S. — B3 85
Kirkwood, Il., U.S. — C3 90
Kirkwood, Mo., U.S. — f13 102
Kirn, F.R.Ger. — D3 18
Kiron, Ia., U.S. — B2 92
Kirov, Sov. Un. — D7 29
Kirova, Zaliv, b., Sov. Un. — B4 39
Kirovabad, Sov. Un. — E7 29
Kirovakan, Sov. Un. — B15 40
Kirovograd, Sov. Un. — B6 28
Kirovohrad, Sov. Un. — G9 27
Kirovsk, Sov. Un. — C6 29
Kirriemuir, Ab., Can. — D5 68
Kirriemuir, Scot., U.K. — D5 13
Kirsanov, Sov. Un. — E14 27
Kırşehir, Tur. — C10 40
Kirthar Range, mts., Pak. — C4 36
Kirtland, N.M., U.S. — A1 108
Kirtland, Oh., U.S. — *C1 112
Kirtland Air Force Base, mil., N.M., U.S. — k7 108
Kiruna, Swe. — D9 14
Kirundu, Zaire — B4 48
Kirwin, Ks., U.S. — C4 93
Kirwin Reservoir, res., Ks., U.S. — C4 93
Kiryū, Japan — H9 33
Kisaki, Tan. — C6 48
Kisanga, Zaire — C4 48
Kisangani (Stanleyville), Zaire — A4 48
Kisarazu, Japan — n18 33
Kisatchie, La., U.S. — C2 95
K.I. Sawyer Air Force Base, mil., Mi., U.S. — B3 99
Kisbey, Sk., Can. — H4 75
Kiselevsk, Sov. Un. — C11 28
Kisengwa, Zaire — C4 48
Kishanganj, India — D11 37
Kishangarh, India — C5 36
Kishi, Nig. — E5 45
Kishinev, Sov. Un. — E6 29
Kishiwada, Japan — o14 33
Kishorganj, Bngl. — D9 36
Kisii, Kenya — B5 48
Kisiju, Tan. — C6 48
Kisiwa Creek, stm., Ks., U.S. — g11 93
Kiskani, Tan. — D6 48
Kiska Island, i., Ak., U.S. — E3 79
Kiskatinaw, stm., B.C., Can. — B7 69
Kiskittogisu Lake, I., Mb., Can. — B2 70
Kiskitto Lake, I., Mb., Can. — B2 70
Kiskőrös, Hung. — B4 24
Kiskundorozsma (part of Szeged), Hung. — B5 24
Kiskunfélegyháza, Hung. — B4 24
Kiskunhalas, Hung. — E4 24
Kiskunmajsa, Hung. — E4 24
Kislovodsk, Sov. Un. — E2 28
Kismayo, Som. — F5 47
Kismet, Ks., U.S. — E3 93
Kiso-sammyaku, mts., Japan — m16 33
Kissamos, Grc. — E4 25
Kissee Mills, Mo., U.S. — E4 102
Kisseynew Lake, I., Can. — B1 70
Kissidougou, Gui. — G3 45
Kissimmee, Fl., U.S. — D5 86
Kissimmee, stm., Fl., U.S. — E5 86
Kissimmee, Lake, I., Fl., U.S. — E5 86
Kissimmee Park, Fl., U.S. — D5 86

Kississing, Mb., Can. — B1 70
Kississing, stm., Mb., Can. — B1 70
Kississing Lake, I., Mb., Can. — B1 70
Kisslegg, F.R.Ger. — A8 21
Kistefjellet, mtn., Nor. — C8 14
Kistigan Lake, I., Mb., Can. — B5 70
Kistler, W.V., U.S. — D3 125
Kistrand, Nor. — B11 14
Kisújszállás, Hung. — B5 24
Kisumu, Kenya — A5 48
Kita, Mali — D3 45
Kita, Mount, mtn., Japan — I9 33
Kita-ibaraki, Japan — H10 33
Kita-iwo, i., Japan — E8 6
Kitakyūshū, Japan — E11 31
Kitale, Kenya — A5 48
Kitami, Japan — E11 33
Kitangani, Tan. — D6 48
Kit Carson, Co., U.S. — C8 83
Kit Carson, co., Co., U.S. — B8 83
Kitchell, In., U.S. — E8 91
Kitchener, On., Can. — D4 73
Kite, Ga., U.S. — D4 87
Kitgum, Ug. — A5 48
Kíthira, Grc. — D4 25
Kíthira (Cythera), i., Grc. — D4 40
Kíthnos, i., Grc. — D5 40
Kitimat, B.C., Can. — B3 69
Kitridge Point, c., Barb. — K21 65
Kitsap, co., Wa., U.S. — B3 124
Kitscoty, Ab., Can. — C5 68
Kittanning, Pa., U.S. — E2 115
Kittatinny Mountain, mtn., U.S. — B2 107
Kittery, Me., U.S. — E2 96
Kittery Point, Me., U.S. — E2 96
Kittilä, Fin. — D11 14
Kittitas, Wa., U.S. — C5 124
Kittitas, co., Wa., U.S. — B5 124
Kittitas Valley, val., Wa., U.S. — B5 124
Kittrell, N.C., U.S. — A4 110
Kitts, Ky., U.S. — D6 94
Kitts Hummock, De., U.S. — D4 85
Kittson, co., Mn., U.S. — B2 100
Kitty Hawk, N.C., U.S. — A7 110
Kitty Hawk Bay, b., N.C., U.S. — A7 110
Kitui, Kenya — B6 48
Kitwanga, B.C., Can. — B3 69
Kitwe, Zam. — D4 48
Kitzbühel, Aus. — E6 18
Kitzingen, F.R.Ger. — D5 18
Kitzmiller, Md., U.S. — m12 97
Kivalina, Ak., U.S. — B7 79
Kivu, hist reg., Zaire — B4 48
Kivu, Lac, l., Afr. — B4 48
Kiya, stm., Sov. Un. — D26 8
Kiyan, Japan — O5 33
Kiyan Point, c., Japan — O5 52
Kıyıköy, Tur. — B7 40
Kiyiu Lake, l., Sk., Can. — F1 75
Kizel, Sov. Un. — B8 28
Kizil, stm., Tur. — B10 40
Kizlyar, Sov. Un. — E8 28
Kizyl-Arvat, Sov. Un. — F8 29
Kjaekan, Nor. — C10 14
Kjellerup, Den. — B3 15
Kjelvik, Nor. — B12 14
Kladno, Czech. — C3 26
Klagenfurt, Aus. — E7 18
Klagetoh, Az., U.S. — B6 80
Klaipėda (Memel), Sov. Un. — D3 27
Klamath, co., Or., U.S. — E5 114
Klamath, stm., U.S. — B2 82
Klamath Falls, Or., U.S. — E5 114
Klamath Glen, Ca., U.S. — B2 82
Klamath Mountains, mts., U.S. — E2 114
Klanxbüll, F.R.Ger. — D1 15
Klarälven, stm., Eur. — G5 14
Klatovy, Czech. — D2 26
Klawer, S. Afr. — D2 49
Klawock, Ak., U.S. — D13 79
Kleberg, co., Tx., U.S. — F4 120
Kleena Kleene, B.C., Can. — D5 69
Klein, Tx., U.S. — *D5 120
Kleinburg, On., Can. — k14 73
Klemme, Ia., U.S. — A4 92
Klerksdorp, S. Afr. — C4 49
Kletnya, Sov. Un. — E9 27
Kletsk, Sov. Un. — E6 27
Kleve (Cleves), F.R.Ger. — C3 18
Klibreck, Ben, mtn., Scot., U.K. — C4 13
Klíčany, Czech. — n17 26
Klickitat, Wa., U.S. — D4 124
Klickitat, co., Wa., U.S. — D4 124
Klickitat, stm., Wa., U.S. — C4 124
Klimovsk, Sov. Un. — n17 27
Klin, Sov. Un. — C11 27
Klinaklini, stm., B.C., Can. — D5 69
Kline, S.C., U.S. — E5 117
Klingenthal, Ger.D.R. — C7 19
Klínovec, mtn., Czech. — C7 19
Klintsy, Sov. Un. — E9 27
Klippan, Swe. — B7 15
Klitmøller, Den. — A2 15
Ključ, Yugo. — C3 24
Kłobuck, Pol. — C5 26
Kloch Lake, I., B.C., Can. — A6 73
Klock, On., Can. — A6 73
Kłodnica, stm., Pol. — g9 26
Kłodzko, Pol. — C4 26
Klondike, Tx., U.S. — C5 120
Klondike, hist. reg., Yk., Can. — D5 66
Klondike Gold Rush National Historical Park, U.S. — k22 79
Klondike Region, hist reg., Yk., Can. — D5 66
Klondyke, Az., U.S. — E5 80
Klos, Alb. — B3 25
Klostermansfeld, Ger.D.R. — B6 19
Klosterneuburg, Aus. — D8 18
Klosters, Switz. — B6 21
Kloten, Switz. — B4 21
Kloten, N.D., U.S. — B7 111
Klötze, Ger.D.R. — F5 15
Klotzsche, Ger.D.R. — B7 19
Klotzville, La., U.S. — h9 95
Kluane Lake, l., Yk., Can. — D5 66
Kluane National Park, Yk., Can. — D5 66
Kluczbork, Pol. — C5 26
Klukwan, Ak., U.S. — k22 79
Klutina Lake, l., Ak., U.S. — g19 79
Klütz, Ger.D.R. — E6 15
Klyazma, stm., Sov. Un. — C13 27
Klyuchevskaya Sopka, vol., Sov. Un. — D18 29
Knapp, Wi., U.S. — D1 126
Knapp Creek, stm., W.V., U.S. — C5 125
Knaresborough, Eng., U.K. — F7 13
Knee Lake, I., Mb., Can. — B4 70
Knee Lake, I., Sk., Can. — B1 75
Knesebeck, F.R.Ger. — F4 15
Knesset, Isr. — m14 41

Knezha, Bul. — D7 24
Knickerbocker, Tx., U.S. — D2 120
Knierim, Ia., U.S. — B3 92
Knife, stm., N.D., U.S. — B3 111
Knife River, Mn., U.S. — D7 100
Knin, Yugo. — C3 24
Knippa, Tx., U.S. — E3 120
Knislinge, Swe. — B8 15
Knittelfeld, Aus. — E7 18
Knob Creek, stm., Ky., U.S. — g11 94
Knobel, Ar., U.S. — A5 81
Knob Lick, Ky., U.S. — C4 94
Knob Lick, Mo., U.S. — D7 102
Knobly Mountain, mtn., W.V., U.S. — B5 125
Knob Noster, Mo., U.S. — C4 102
Knobsville, Pa., U.S. — F6 115
Knockadoon Head, c., Ire. — F4 11
Knockalongy, mtn., Ire. — C3 11
Knockanefune, hill, Ire. — E2 11
Knocklong, Ire. — E3 11
Knockmealdown Mountains, mts., Ire. — D2 10
Knokke [-Heist], Bel. — C3 17
Knollwood, Ct., U.S. — D6 84
Knollwood, W.V., U.S. — m12 125
Knops Pond, l., Ma., U.S. — f9 98
Knott, co., Ky., U.S. — C6 94
Knotts Island, N.C., U.S. — A7 110
Knottsville, Ky., U.S. — C3 94
Knowles, Ok., U.S. — A1 113
Knowlton, Wi., U.S. — D4 126
Knox, Austl. — *G8 50
Knox, In., U.S. — B4 91
Knox, N.D., U.S. — A6 111
Knox, Pa., U.S. — D2 115
Knox, co., In., U.S. — G3 91
Knox, co., Ky., U.S. — D6 94
Knox, co., Me., U.S. — D4 96
Knox, co., Mo., U.S. — A5 102
Knox, co., Ne., U.S. — B8 104
Knox, co., Oh., U.S. — B3 112
Knox, co., Tn., U.S. — C10 119
Knox, co., Tx., U.S. — C3 120
Knox, Cape, c., B.C., Can. — B1 69
Knox City, Mo., U.S. — A5 102
Knox City, Tx., U.S. — C3 120
Knox Coast, Ant. — C23 7
Knox Dale, Pa., U.S. — D3 115
Knoxville, Al., U.S. — C2 78
Knoxville, Ar., U.S. — B2 81
Knoxville, Ga., U.S. — D3 87
Knoxville, Il., U.S. — C3 90
Knoxville, Ia., U.S. — C4 92
Knoxville, Md., U.S. — B2 97
Knoxville, Pa., U.S. — C7 115
Knoxville, Tn., U.S. — D10 119
Knurów, Pol. — g9 26
Knutsford, S. Afr. — D3 49
Knyazhevo, Sov. Un. — B7 27
Knysna, S. Afr. — D3 49
Ko, Mount, mtn., Sov. Un. — C8 33
Kobayashi, Japan — K5 33
Kōbe, Japan — E11 31
Kobelyaki, Sov. Un. — G10 27
Kobenhavn, co., Den. — C6 15
Koboko, Ug. — A5 48
Kobona, Sov. Un. — r32 14
Kobrin, Sov. Un. — E5 27
Kobroor, i., Indon. — G8 34
Kobuk, Ak., U.S. — B8 79
Kobuk, stm., Ak., U.S. — B7 79
Kobuk Valley National Park, Ak., U.S. — B8 79
Kobuleti, Sov. Un. — B13 40
Kōca, stm., Tur. — B7 40
Kocaba, stm., Czech. — o17 26
Kocaeli see Izmit, Tur. — B7 40
Kočani, Yugo. — D5 24
Kocasinan, Tur. — *B7 40
Koceljeva, Yugo. — C2 24
Kočevje, Yugo. — B1 24
Kōchi, Japan — E11 31
Kocher, stm., F.R.Ger. — B5 18
Koch Peak, mtn., Mt., U.S. — E5 103
Kock, Pol. — C7 26
Kodak, Ky., U.S. — C6 94
Kodari, Nepal — D10 37
Kodiak, Ak., U.S. — D9 79
Kodiak Island, i., Ak., U.S. — D9 79
Kodok (Fashoda), Sud. — D3 47
Koes, Nmb. — C2 49
Koettlitz Glacier, Ant. — f39 7
Kofa Mountains, mts., Az., U.S. — D2 80
Kofiefontein, S. Afr. — C3 49
Koforidua, Ghana — E4 45
Kōfu, Japan — I9 33
Kogaluk, stm., Nf., Can. — g9 72
Køge, Den. — C6 15
Køge Bugt, b., Den. — C6 15
Kohala Mountains, mts., Hi., U.S. — C6 88
Kohatk, Az., U.S. — E4 80
Kohima, India — D7 37
Kohler, Wi., U.S. — E6 126
Kohtla-Järve, Sov. Un. — B6 27
Koidu, S.L. — E2 45
Köinge, Swe. — A6 15
Ko Island, i., Japan — F9 33
Koili Range, mts., Hi., U.S. — f10 88
Kōje Island, i., S. Kor. — I4 33
Kojetín, Czech. — D5 26
Kokand, Sov. Un. — E9 29
Kokanee Glacier Provincial Park, B.C., Can. — E9 69
Kokas, Indon. — F8 34
Kokemäki, Fin. — C13 14
Kokkola, Fin. — F10 14
Koko, Nig. — D5 45
Koko Head, c., Hi., U.S. — B4 88
Kokolik, stm., Ak., U.S. — B7 79
Kokomo, Hi., U.S. — C5 88
Kokomo, In., U.S. — D5 91
Kokomo, Ms., U.S. — D3 101

Koko Nor see Qinghai Lake, l., China — D4 31
Kokopo, Pap. N. Gui. — h13 50
Kokosing, stm., Oh., U.S. — B3 112
Kokrines, Ak., U.S. — C9 79
Kōksan, N. Kor. — G3 33
Koksilah, B.C., Can. — g12 69
Koksoak, stm., P.Q., Can. — E19 66
Kokstad, S. Afr. — D4 49
Ko Lanta, i., Thai. — I3 35
Kola, Sov. Un. — C15 14
Kolaka, Indon. — F7 34
Kola Peninsula, pen., Sov. Un. — C6 29
Kolār Gold Fields, India — F6 36
Kolari, Fin. — D10 14
Kolárovo, Czech. — E4 26
Kolåsen, Swe. — E7 14
Kolāyat, India — D4 37
Kolbäck, Swe. — t34 14
Kolbio, Kenya — B7 48
Kolbuszowa, Pol. — C6 26
Kolchugino, Sov. Un. — C12 27
Kolczewo, Pol. — E8 15
Kolda, Sen. — D2 45
Koldewey, i., Grnld. — B16 128
Kolding, Den. — C3 15
Kole, Zaire — B3 48
Koleč, Czech. — n17 26
Kolezhma, Sov. Un. — E16 14
Kolguyev Island, i., Sov. Un. — C7 29
Kolhāpur, India — E5 36
Koliganek, Ak., U.S. — D8 79
Kolimbine, stm., Afr. — C2 45
Kolín, Czech. — C3 26
Kolin, La., U.S. — C3 95
Kölleda, Ger.D.R. — B6 19
Kolno, Pol. — B6 26
Kolo, Pol. — B5 26
Koloa, Hi., U.S. — B2 88
Kolob Canyon, val., Ut., U.S. — F2 121
Kołobrzeg, Pol. — A3 26
Kolokani, Mali — D3 45
Kolola Springs, Ms., U.S. — B5 101
Kolomna, Sov. Un. — C12 27
Kolomyya, Sov. Un. — G5 27
Kolondiéba, Mali — D3 45
Kolonia, Micron. — Q17 52
Kolonodale, Indon. — F6 34
Kolp, stm., Sov. Un. — B10 27
Kolpashevo, Sov. Un. — B10 28
Kolpino, Sov. Un. — s31 14
Kolwa, Pak. — C3 36
Kolwezi, Zaire — D4 48
Kolyberovo, Sov. Un. — n18 27
Kolyma, stm., Sov. Un. — C18 29
Kolyma Mountains, mts., Sov. Un. — C18 29
Komádi, Hung. — B5 24
Komandorski Islands, is., Sov. Un. — D19 29
Komarno, Mb., Can. — D3 70
Komárno, Czech. — E5 26
Komárom, Hung. — D7 26
Komárom, Hung. — B4 24
Komló, Hung. — B4 24
Kommunarsk, Sov. Un. — G12 27
Komodo, i., Indon. — G5 34
Komoé, stm., Afr. — E4 45
Komono, Congo — B1 48
Komoran, i., Indon. — G9 34
Komotiní, Grc. — B5 40
Komsomolets, i., Sov. Un. — A4 128
Komsomolsk [-na-Amure], Sov. Un. — D16 29
Konahuanui, Puu, mtn., Hi., U.S. — g10 88
Konar, stm., Asia — A5 36
Konar-e Khāş, Afg. — D15 39
Konawa, Ok., U.S. — C5 113
Kondinskoye, Sov. Un. — B7 28
Kondoa, Tan. — B6 48
Kondopoga, Sov. Un. — F16 14
Kondratyeva, Sov. Un. — C9 28
Kong, i., Kam. — I5 35
Kong, stm., Asia — C3 34
Kongju, S. Kor. — H3 33
Kongolo, Zaire — C4 48
Kongor, Sud. — D3 47
Kongsberg, Nor. — H3 14
Kongsvinger, Nor. — G5 14
Königsberg see Kaliningrad, Sov. Un. — D5 29
Königsbrück, Ger.D.R. — B8 19
Königslutter, F.R.Ger. — A5 19
Königs Wusterhausen, Ger.D.R. — A8 19
Konin, Pol. — B5 26
Konispol, Alb. — B3 25
Kōnitsa, Grc. — B3 25
Köniz, Switz. — C3 21
Konjic, Yugo. — D4 24
Konkouré, stm., Gui. — G2 45
Konnarock, Va., U.S. — D2 123
Könnern, Ger.D.R. — B6 19
Konomoc, Lake, res., Ct., U.S. — D7 84
Konosha, Sov. Un. — A13 27
Konotop, Sov. Un. — F9 27
Konotop, Pol. — B3 26
Końskie, Pol. — C6 26
Konstancin-Jeziorna, Pol. — m14 26
Konstantinovka, Sov. Un. — q20 27
Konstanz (Constance), F.R.Ger. — E4 18
Kontagora, Nig. — D6 45
Kontich, Bel. — C4 17
Kontiomäki, Fin. — E13 14
Kontum, Viet. — C3 34
Konyang, S. Kor. — I3 33
Konzhakovskiy Kamen, mtn., Sov. Un. — B5 28
Koocanusa, Lake, res., N.A. — B1 103
Koochiching, co., Mn., U.S. — B4 100
Koolau Range, mts., Hi., U.S. — f10 88
Kooloonong, Austl. — G4 51
Koosharem, Ut., U.S. — E4 121
Kooskia, Id., U.S. — C3 89
Kootenai, Id., U.S. — *A2 89
Kootenai, co., Id., U.S. — B2 89
Kootenay, stm., N.A. — E10 69
Kootenay National Park, B.C., Can. — E9 69

Kopet Mountains, mts., Asia — B8 39
Kopeysk, Sov. Un. — B6 28
Köping, Swe. — H6 14
Köppany, stm., Hung. — B4 24
Koppel, Pa., U.S. — E1 115
Koprivnica, Yugo. — B3 24
Kopychintsy, Sov. Un. — G6 27
Korab, mtn., Eur. — E5 24
Korahe, Eth. — D5 47
Korarou, Lac, l., Mali — C4 45
Korba, Tun. — F3 23
Korbach, F.R.Ger. — B3 19
Korbu, mtn., Malay. — J4 35
Korça, Alb. — B3 40
Korčula, i., Yugo. — D3 24
Kord Kūy, Iran — C7 39
Korea, North, ctry., Asia — D10 31
Korea, South, ctry., Asia — D10 31
Korea Bay, b., Asia — D9 31
Korea Strait, strt., Asia — E10 31
Korets, Sov. Un. — F6 27
Korhogo, I.C. — E3 45
Kori Creek, stm., India — F2 37
Koridhallós, Grc. — *D4 25
Kórinthos (Corinth), Grc. — D4 40
Kōriyama, Japan — H10 33
Korkino, Sov. Un. — E21 8
Korkuteli, Tur. — D8 40
Korla, China — C2 31
Kormakíti, Akrotírion, c., Cyp. — B3 24
Körmend, Hung. — B3 24
Kornat, i., Yugo. — D2 24
Korneuburg, Aus. — D8 18
Kornwestheim, F.R.Ger. — E4 19
Koro, Mali — D4 45
Koro, i., Fiji — H15 52
Korogwe, Tan. — C6 48
Koronis, Lake, l., Mn., U.S. — E4 100
Koropion, Grc. — h11 25
Koror, Palau — R17 52
Koror, i., Palau — R17 52
Korosten, Sov. Un. — F7 27
Korotoyak, Sov. Un. — F12 27
Korovin Volcano, vol., Ak., U.S. — E5 79
Korsakov, Sov. Un. — E17 29
Korsør, Den. — C5 15
Kortrijk (Courtrai), Bel. — B5 16
Korumburra, Austl. — I5 51
Koryak Mountains, mts., Sov. Un. — C19 29
Kos, Grc. — D6 40
Kos (Cos), i., Grc. — D6 40
Koschagyl, Sov. Un. — D4 28
Kościan, Pol. — B4 26
Kościerzyna, Pol. — A4 26
Kosciusko, Ms., U.S. — B4 101
Kosciusko, co., In., U.S. — B6 91
Kosciusko, Mount, mtn., Austl. — G8 50
Koshiki Islands, is., Japan — K4 33
Koshkonong, Lake, l., Wi., U.S. — F5 126
Košice, Czech. — D6 26
Košíře (part of Prague), Czech. — n17 26
Koskaecodde Lake, l., Nf., Can. — D4 72
Kosŏng, N. Kor. — G4 33
Kosovska Mitrovica, Yugo. — D5 24
Kosrae, i., Micron. — F9 6
Kösslarn, F.R.Ger. — A9 20
Kossol Passage, strt., Palau — R17 52
Kossol Reef, rf., Palau — R17 52
Kossuth, Ms., U.S. — A5 101
Kossuth, co., Ia., U.S. — A3 92
Kostelec, Czech. — o18 26
Kostelec, Czech. — n18 26
Kostroma, Sov. Un. — B7 29
Kostrzyn, Pol. — A4 26
Koszalin, Pol. — A3 26
Kőszeg, Hung. — B3 24
Kota, India — C6 36
Kota Baharu, Malay. — D2 34
Kotabaru, Indon. — F5 34
Kota Kinabalu, Malay. — D5 34
Kotatengah, Indon. — L4 35
Kotel, Bul. — D8 24
Kotelnich, Sov. Un. — B8 29
Kotelnikovo, Sov. Un. — H14 27
Kotelnyy, i., Sov. Un. — B16 29
Köthen, Ger.D.R. — C5 18
Kotido, Ug. — A5 48
Kotka, Fin. — G12 14
Kotlas, Sov. Un. — C7 29
Kotlik, Ak., U.S. — C7 79
Kotonkoro, Nig. — D6 45
Kotor, Yugo. — D4 24
Kotor Bay, b., Yugo. — D4 24
Kotor Varoš, Yugo. — C3 24
Kotovsk, Sov. Un. — E13 27
Kotovsk, Sov. Un. — H7 27
Kotri, Pak. — C4 36
Kottagūdem, India — E6 36
Kotte, Sri L. — *G6 36
Kotto, stm., Cen. Afr. Rep. — D5 45
Kotzebue, Ak., U.S. — B7 79
Kotzebue Sound, strt., Ak., U.S. — B7 79
Kötzting, F.R.Ger. — D7 18
Kouandé, Benin — D5 45
Kouchibouguacis, stm., N.B., Can. — C4 71
Kouchibouguac National Park, N.B., Can. — C5 71
Koudougou, Burkina — D4 45
Koula-Moutou, Gabon — F2 46
Koulikoro, Mali — D3 45
Koumra, Chad — D3 45
Koundheul, Sen. — D2 45
Kounradskiy, Sov. Un. — D6 29
Kountze, Tx., U.S. — D5 120
Koupéla, Burkina — D4 45
Kouri Island, i., Japan — N6 52
Kouroussa, Gui. — G3 45
Kourou, Fr. Gu. — A4 59
Koussi, Emi, mtn., Chad — D3 46
Koutiala, Mali — D3 45
Kouvola, Fin. — G12 14
Ko Vaya, Az., U.S. — E4 80
Kovel, Sov. Un. — F5 27
Kovrov, Sov. Un. — C13 27
Kowloon, H.K. — G7 31
Köyceğiz, Tur. — C7 40
Koyuk, Ak., U.S. — C7 79
Koyukuk, stm., Ak., U.S. — B8 79
Kozan, Tur. — D10 40

Name	Map Ref	Page
Kozáni, Grc.	B3	25
Kozelsk, Sov. Un.	D10	27
Kozienice, Pol.	C6	26
Koźle, Pol.	C5	26
Kozloduy, Bul.	D6	24
Kozuchów, Pol.	C3	26
Kôzu Island, i., Japan	I9	33
Kpandu, Ghana	E5	45
Kra, Isthmus of, Asia	C1	34
Kracheh, Kam.	C3	34
Kraemer, La., U.S.	k10	95
Kragerö, Nor.	H3	14
Kragujevac, Yugo.	D5	24
Kraków, Pol.	C5	26
Krakower, I., Ger.D.R.	E6	15
Kraljevo. Yugo.	D5	24
Královské Vinohrady (part of Prague), Czech.	n17	26
Kralupy [nad Vltavou], Czech.	n17	26
Králův Dvůr, Czech.	o17	26
Kramatorsk, Sov. Un.	G11	27
Kramer, In., U.S.	D3	91
Kramer, N.D., U.S.	A5	111
Kranidhion, Grc.	D4	25
Kranj, Yugo.	B2	24
Kranzburg, S.D., U.S.	C9	118
Kraslice, Czech.	C2	26
Krasnaya Polyana, Sov. Un.	q22	27
Kraśnik, Pol.	C7	26
Krasnoarmeysk, Sov. Un.	G15	27
Krasnoarmeysk, Sov. Un.	F15	27
Krasnoarmeysk, Sov. Un.	C7	28
Krasnodar, Sov. Un.	E6	29
Krasnogorsk, Sov. Un.	B11	33
Krasnogorsk, Sov. Un.	G10	27
Krasnogvardeyskoye, Sov. Un.	I13	27
Krasnokamsk, Sov. Un.	B5	28
Krasnoselkup, Sov. Un.	B25	8
Krasnoselye, Sov. Un.	G9	27
Krasnoslobodsk, Sov. Un.	D14	27
Krasnoslobodsk, Sov. Un.	G9	27
Krasnoturinsk, Sov. Un.	B6	28
Krasnoural'sk, Sov. Un.	B5	28
Krasnoufimsk, Sov. Un.	D21	8
Krasnovishersk, Sov. Un.	A5	28
Krasnovodsk, Sov. Un.	E8	29
Krasnoyarsk, Sov. Un.	D12	29
Krasnoye Selo, Sov. Un.	s31	14
Krasnoznamenskiy, Sov. Un.	C7	28
Krasnystaw, Pol.	C7	26
Krasnyy Kholm, Sov. Un.	B11	27
Krasny Kut, Sov. Un.	q21	27
Krasnyy Kut, Sov. Un.	C3	28
Krasnyy Liman, Sov. Un.	q20	27
Krasnyy Luch, Sov. Un.	q21	27
Krasnyy Sulin, Sov. Un.	H13	27
Krasnyy Yar, Sov. Un.	F15	27
Kratovo, Yugo.	D6	24
Kraul Mountains, mts., Ant.	B11	7
Krebs, Ok., U.S.	C6	113
Krefeld, F.R.Ger.	C3	18
Kremenchug Reservoir, res., Sov. Un.	E5	29
Kremenets, Sov. Un.	F5	27
Kremennaya, Sov. Un.	p21	27
Kremikovsti, Bul.	D6	24
Kremlin, Mt., U.S.	B6	103
Kremlin, Ok., U.S.	A4	113
Kremmling, Co., U.S.	A4	83
Krems [am der Donau], Aus.	D7	18
Kresgeville, Pa., U.S.	E10	115
Kress, Tx., U.S.	B2	120
Kreuzlingen, Switz.	B5	20
Krichev, Sov. Un.	E8	27
Kriens, Switz.	B4	21
Krilon, Cape, c., Sov. Un.	D11	33
Krilon Peninsula, pen., Sov. Un.	C10	33
Krishna, stm., India	E6	36
Krishnagiri, India	F6	36
Krishnanagar, India	F12	37
Kristiansand, Nor.	H2	14
Kristianstad, Swe.	I6	14
Kristianstad, co., Swe.	B7	15
Kristiansund, Nor.	F2	14
Kristinestad, Fin.	F9	14
Kriva Palanka, Yugo.	D6	24
Krivoy Rog, Sov. Un.	E6	29
Križevci, Yugo.	B3	24
Krk, i., Yugo.	C2	24
Krka, stm., Yugo.	D3	24
Krnov, Czech.	C4	26
Krokeaí, Grc.	D4	25
Krokstadelva, Nor.	p28	14
Krolevets, Sov. Un.	F9	27
Kroměříž, Czech.	D4	26
Kromy, Sov. Un.	E10	27
Kronach, F.R.Ger.	C6	19
Kronau, Sk., Can.	G3	75
Kronoberg, co., Swe.	B8	15
Kronshtadt, Sov. Un.	B7	27
Kroonstad, S. Afr.	C4	49
Kröpelin, Ger.D.R.	D5	15
Kropotkin, Sov. Un.	I13	29
Krosno, Pol.	D6	26
Krosno Odrzańskie, Pol.	B3	26
Krotoszyn, Pol.	C4	26
Krotz Springs, La., U.S.	D4	95
Krško, Yugo.	C2	24
Kruger National Park, S. Afr.	B5	49
Krugersdorp, S. Afr.	C4	49
Kruja, Alb.	B2	25
Krumbach, F.R.Ger.	A6	20
Krumovgrad, Bul.	E7	24
Kruševac, Yugo.	E7	24
Kruševo, Yugo.	E5	24
Kruszwica, Pol.	C4	26
Kruzof Island, i., Ak., U.S.	m21	79
Krydor, Sk., Can.	E2	75
Krymsk, Sov. Un.	I11	27
Krynica, Pol.	D6	26
Krynki, Pol.	b7	26
Ksar el Kebir, Mor.	B3	44
Ksar es Souk, Mor.	C4	44
Kuala Dungun, Malay.	J5	35
Kuala Kangsar, Malay.	J4	35
Kuala Kerau, Malay.	K5	35
Kualakurun, Indon.	F4	34
Kuala Lipis, Malay.	E2	34
Kuala Lumpur, Malay.	E2	34
Kualapuu, Hi., U.S.	B4	88
Kuala Terengganu, Malay.	D2	34
Kuandang, Indon.	E6	34
Kuandian, China	D11	31
Kuantan, Malay.	E2	34
Kuba, Sov. Un.	E3	29
Kuban, stm., Sov. Un.	I13	27
Kubitzer Bodden, b., Ger.D.R.	D7	15
Kubokawa, Japan	J6	33
Kuching, Malay.	E4	34
Kuchinoerabu Island, i., Japan	K5	33
Kuchino Island, i., Japan	L4	33
Kuçovë see Stalin, Alb.	B2	25
Küçükçekmece, Tur.	*B7	40
Küçükköy, Tur.	*B7	40
Küçükmenderes, stm., Tur.	C6	25
Kudaka Island, i., Japan	O5	52
Kudat, Malay.	D5	34
Kudirkos Naumiestis, Sov. Un.	A4	26
Kudus, Indon.	G4	34
Kudymkar, Sov. Un.	B4	28
Kuee Ruins, hist., Hi., U.S.	D6	88
Kufstein, Aus.	E6	18
Kûh, Ra's al, c., Iran	I8	39
Kuhayfī, Sud.	B3	47
Kuhēsi, Alb.	A3	25
Kuhestān, Afg.	D10	39
Kūhpāyeh, Iran	E6	39
Kūhrān, Kūh-e, mtn., Iran	H9	39
Kuito, Ang.	D2	48
Kuiu Island, i., Ak., U.S.	m23	79
Kuji, Japan	F10	33
Kujū, Mount, mtn., Japan	J5	33
Kukawa, Nig.	D7	45
Kuki, Japan	m18	33
Kukuihaele, Hi., U.S.	B2	88
Kukuiula, Hi., U.S.	B2	88
Kuku Point, c., Wake I.	A1	52
Kula, Bul.	D6	24
Kula, Tur.	C7	25
Kula, Hi., U.S.	C5	88
Kula, Yugo.	C4	24
Kula Kangri, mtn., Bhu.	C9	36
Kulebaki, Sov. Un.	D14	27
Kulim, Malay.	J4	35
Kulltorp, Swe.	A7	15
Kulm, N.D., U.S.	C7	111
Kulmbach, F.R.Ger.	C5	18
Kulpmont, Pa., U.S.	E9	115
Kulunda, Sov. Un.	C9	28
Kulunda, Lake, l., Sov. Un.	C9	28
Kulwin, Austl.	G4	51
Kulyab, Sov. Un.	H22	8
Küm, stm., S. Kor.	H3	33
Kuma, stm., Sov. Un.	F18	8
Kumagaya, Japan	m18	33
Kumai, Indon.	F4	34
Kumamoto, Japan	E11	31
Kumano Bay, b., Japan	J8	33
Kumanovo, Yugo.	D5	24
Kumasi, Ghana	E4	45
Kumba, Cam.	E1	46
Kumbakonam, India	F6	36
Kumbo, Cam.	D2	46
Kumhwa, S. Kor.	G3	33
Kumi, Ug.	A5	48
Kumihama, Japan	n14	33
Kumkale, Tur.	C6	40
Kumla, Swe.	H6	14
Kummerower Lake, l., Ger.D.R.	E6	15
Kumo, Nig.	E7	45
Kumukahi, Cape, c., Hi., U.S.	D7	88
Kuna, Id., U.S.	F2	89
Kundar, stm., Asia	B2	37
Kundiawa, Pap. N. Gui.	k11	50
Kuneitra (Al Qunayţirah), Syria	F10	40
Kunggyü Lake, l., China	B9	37
Kunghit Island, i., B.C., Can.	C2	69
Kungrad, Sov. Un.	E5	28
Kungsbacka, Swe.	A6	15
Kungsör, Swe.	t34	14
Kungu, Zaire	A2	48
Kungur, Sov. Un.	B5	28
Kunia, Hi., U.S.	g9	88
Kunigami, Japan	N6	52
Kunimi, Mount, mtn., Japan	J5	33
Kunkle, Oh., U.S.	m17	115
Kunlun Mountains, mts., China	F11	30
Kunming, China	F5	31
Kunsan, S. Kor.	D10	31
Kunszentmárton, Hung.	B5	24
Künzelsau, F.R.Ger.	D4	19
Kuolayarvi, Sov. Un.	D13	14
Kuop, atoll, Micron.	Q18	52
Kuopio, Fin.	F12	14
Kupa, stm., Yugo.	C2	24
Kupang, Indon.	G6	34
Kupino, Sov. Un.	C9	28
Kupreanof, Ak., U.S.	m23	79
Kupreanof Island, i., Ak., U.S.	m23	79
Kupyansk, Sov. Un.	G11	27
Kur, stm., Asia	B7	33
Kura, stm., Asia	E3	28
Kurashiki, Japan	I6	33
Kurashevo, Sov. Un.	q20	27
Kuray, Sov. Un.	D9	28
Kuraymah, Sud.	B3	47
Kuraymah, Jord.	f13	41
Kurdistan, hist reg., Asia	B4	38
Kurdufān al Janūbīyah (Southern Kurdufan), prov., Sud.	C2	47
Kurdufān ash Shamālīyah (Northern Kurdufan), prov., Sud.	C2	47
Kürdzhali, Bul.	E7	24
Kure, Japan	E11	31
Kure Island, i., Hi., U.S.	k12	88
Kuressaare, Sov. Un.	B4	27
Kureyka, stm., Sov. Un.	C12	29
Kurgaldzhinskiy, Sov. Un.	C8	28
Kurgan, Sov. Un.	D9	29
Kurganinsk, Sov. Un.	G17	8
Kurgan-Tyube, Sov. Un.	H22	8
Kuria Muria Islands see Khūryān Mūryān, is., Oman	A6	20
Kuriğrām, Bngl.	E12	37
Kuril Islands, is., Sov. Un.	E17	29
Kuril Strait, strt., Sov. Un.	D18	29
Kurilskaya, Cape, c., Sov. Un.	H18	8
Kurmuk, Sud.	C3	47
Kurnool, India	E6	36
Kuro Island, i., Japan	K4	33
Kurovskoye, Sov. Un.	n18	27
Kurów, N.Z.	P13	51
Kurri Kurri, Austl.	F9	50
Kuršumlija, Yugo.	D5	24
Kurtalan, Tur.	D13	40
Kürtí, Sud.	B3	47
Kurtistown, Hi., U.S.	D6	88
Kurtz, In., U.S.	G6	91
Kuruman, S. Afr.	C3	49
Kurunegala, Sri L.	G7	36
Kusadası, Tur.	D6	25
Kusakaki Island, i., Japan	K4	33
Kusatsu, Japan	n14	33
Kushchevskaya, Sov. Un.	H12	27
Kushima, Japan	J7	33
Kushimoto, Japan	J7	33
Kushiro, Japan	C13	31
Kushka, Sov. Un.	F9	29
Kushmurun, Sov. Un.	C6	28
Kushmurun, Lake, l., Sov. Un.	C6	28
Kuskokwim, stm., Ak., U.S.	C8	79
Kuskokwim Bay, b., Ak., U.S.	D7	79
Kuskokwim Mountains, mts., Ak., U.S.	C8	79
Kuş Island, i., Tur.	B6	25
Küsnacht, Switz.	B6	21
Küssnacht [am Rigi], Switz.	B7	21
Kustanay, Sov. Un.	D9	29
Kustī, Sud.	C3	47
Kut, i., Thai.	G5	35
Kuta, Alb.	B2	25
Kutacane, Indon.	K2	35
Kütahya, Tur.	C7	40
Kutaisi, Sov. Un.	G17	8
Kutawagan Lake, l., Sk., Can.	F3	75
Kūt Barrage, Iraq	D2	59
Kutch, Gulf of, b., India	D4	36
Kutch, Rann of, pl., Asia	D4	36
Kutina, Yugo.	C3	24
Kutná Hora, Czech.	D3	26
Kutno, Pol.	B5	26
Kuttawa, Ky., U.S.	e9	94
Kutu, Zaire	B2	48
Kutum, Sud.	C1	47
Kuturaja see Banda Aceh, Indon.	k11	34
Kuty, Sov. Un.	A7	24
Kutztown, Pa., U.S.	E10	115
Kuŭm-ni, N. Kor.	G2	33
Kuusamo, Fin.	E13	14
Kuvandyk, Sov. Un.	E20	8
Kuvango (Capelongo), Ang.	D2	48
Kuwait, Kuw.	C4	38
Kuwait, ctry., Asia	C4	38
Kuwait Bay, b., Kuw.	G4	39
Kuwana, Japan	I8	33
Kuybyshev, Sov. Un.	B9	28
Kuybyshev, Sov. Un.	D8	29
Kuybyshev, Sov. Un.	H12	27
Kuybyshev Reservoir, res., Sov. Un.	D7	29
Küysanjaq, Iraq	D15	40
Kuyto, l., Sov. Un.	E14	14
Kuznetsk, Sov. Un.	E16	27
Kuznetsk Basin, Sov. Un.	D25	8
Kuznetsovo, Sov. Un.	C10	33
Kuzomen, Sov. Un.	D17	14
Kvarner, b., Yugo.	C2	24
Kvismare Kanal, Swe.	t33	14
Kvitøya, i., Nor.	A11	128
Kwai see Khwae Noi, stm., Thai.	E3	35
Kwajalein, atoll, Marsh Is.	F10	6
Kwajalein Island, i., Marsh Is.	S17	52
Kwakoegron, Sur.	A3	59
Kwale, Kenya	B6	48
Kwa Mashu, S. Afr.	*C5	49
Kwamouth, Zaire	B2	48
Kwa Mtoro, Tan.	C6	48
Kwangju, S. Kor.	D10	31
Kwango (Cuango), stm., Afr.	C2	48
Kwangsi Chuang see Guangxi Zhuangzu, prov., China	G6	31
Kwangtung see Guangdong, prov., China	G7	31
Kwatisore, Indon.	F8	34
Kweichow see Guizhou, prov., China	F6	31
Kwekwe, Zimb.	A4	49
Kwenge, stm., Afr.	C2	48
Kwethluk, Ak., U.S.	C7	79
Kwidzyn, Pol.	B5	26
Kwigillingok, Ak., U.S.	D7	79
Kwilu, stm., Afr.	B2	48
Kwinana, Austl.	F2	50
Kyabé, Chad	D3	46
Kyabram, Austl.	H5	51
Kyaiklat, Burma	E10	36
Kyaikto, Burma	D2	35
Kyakhta, Sov. Un.	D13	29
Kyaukpadaung, Burma	B1	35
Kyaukpyu, Burma	E9	36
Kyaukse, Burma	D10	36
Kybartai, Sov. Un.	A7	26
Kyje, stm., Sov. Un.	n18	26
Kyle, Sk., Can.	G1	75
Kyle, S.D., U.S.	D3	118
Kyle, Tx., U.S.	E4	120
Kyle [of Lochalsh], Scot., U.K.	C5	13
Kyles Ford, Tn., U.S.	C10	119
Kylestrome, Scot., U.K.	B3	13
Kyll, stm., F.R.Ger.	E6	17
Kyllburg, F.R.Ger.	E6	17
Kyōga, Cape, c., Japan	I7	33
Kyoga, Lake, l., Ug.	A5	48
Kyōmipo see Songnim, N. Kor.	G2	33
Kyonggi Bay, b., Asia	H2	33
Kyŏngju, S. Kor.	D10	31
Kyŏngsŏng, N. Kor.	F4	33
Kyōto, Japan	D12	31
Kyritz, Ger.D.R.	E5	15
Kyrkjebö, Nor.	G1	14
Kyrock, Ky., U.S.	C3	94
Kyshtovka, Sov. Un.	D24	8
Kyshtym, Sov. Un.	C4	28
Kyuquot, B.C., Can.	D4	69
Kyuquot Sound, strt., B.C., Can.	E4	69
Kyūroku Island, i., Japan	F9	33
Kyūshū, i., Japan	E11	31
Kyustendil, Bul.	D6	24
Kyzyl, Sov. Un.	D12	29
Kyzyl-Kiya, Sov. Un.	I18	8
Kyzyl-Kum, des., Sov. Un.	E9	29
Kyzyltas Mountains, mts., Sov. Un.	D9	28
Kzyl-Orda, Sov. Un.	E9	29

L

Name	Map Ref	Page
Laa [an der Thaya], Aus.	D8	18
Laage, Ger.D.R.	E6	15
La Almunia de Doña Godina, Spain	C2	22
La Araucanía, prov., Chile	B2	54
Laas Caanood, Som.	F7	47
La Asunción, Ven.	A5	60
Laau Point, c., Hi., U.S.	B4	88
Labadie, Mo., U.S.	C7	102
Labadieville, La., U.S.	E5	95
La Banda, Arg.	E3	55
La Barca, Mex.	G8	62
La Barge, Wy., U.S.	D2	127
La Barge Creek, stm., Wy., U.S.	D2	127
Labasa, Fiji	H15	52
La Baule-Escoublac, Fr.	D3	16
Labe (Elbe), stm., Eur.	C7	18
Labelle, P.Q., Can.	D6	74
La Belle, Fl., U.S.	F5	86
La Belle, Mo., U.S.	A6	102
Labelle, co., P.Q., Can.	C2	74
La Belle-Île, i., Fr.	D2	16
Laberge, Lake, l., Yk., Can.	D5	66
Labette, Ks., U.S.	E8	93
Labette, co., Ks., U.S.	E8	93
Labette Creek, stm., Ks., U.S.	E8	93
Labin, Yugo.	C2	24
La Bisbal, Spain	B7	22
Labo, Phil.	o14	34
Labo, Mount, mtn., Phil.	p14	34
La Boca, Pan.	m11	64
La Bolt, S.D., U.S.	*B9	118
Labouheyre, Fr.	E3	16
Laboulaye, Arg.	A4	54
Labrador, reg., Nf., Can.	g9	72
Labrador City, Nf., Can.	h8	72
La Brea, Trin.	O22	65
La Broquerie, Mb., Can.	E3	70
Labuan Island, i., Malay.	D5	34
Labuha, Indon.	F7	34
Labuhanbilik, Indon.	K4	35
Labuk Bay, b., Malay.	D5	34
Lac-à-Beauce, P.Q., Can.	B5	74
La Calera, Chile	A2	54
Lacamp, La., U.S.	C3	95
La Canada Flintridge, Ca., U.S.	m12	82
La Capelle [-en-Thiérache], Fr.	E3	17
La Carlota, Arg.	A4	54
La Carolina, Spain	C4	22
Lac-aux-Brochets, P.Q., Can.	B5	74
Lac-aux-Sables, P.Q., Can.	C5	74
Lac-Baker, N.B., Can.	B1	71
Lac-Beauport, P.Q., Can.	n17	74
Lac-Bouchette, P.Q., Can.	A5	74
Lac-Brome, P.Q., Can.	D5	74
Laccadive, Minicoy and Amindivi Islands see Lakshadweep, ter., India	*F5	36
Laccadive Islands see Lakshadweep, is., India	F5	36
Lac-Carré, P.Q., Can.	C3	74
Lac-Chat, P.Q., Can.	B5	74
Lac Courte Oreilles Indian Reservation, Wi., U.S.	C2	126
Lac-des-Écorces, P.Q., Can.	C2	74
Lac-des-Seize-Îles, P.Q., Can.	D3	74
Lac du Bonnet, Mb., Can.	D3	70
Lac du Flambeau, Wi., U.S.	C4	126
Lac du Flambeau Indian Reservation, Wi., U.S.	C3	126
Lac-Édouard, P.Q., Can.	B5	74
La Ceiba, Hond.	D7	63
La Ceiba, Ven.	B3	60
La Center, Ky., U.S.	e9	94
Lac-Etchemin, P.Q., Can.	C7	74
Lacey, Wa., U.S.	B3	124
Laceys Spring, Al., U.S.	A3	78
Laceyville, Pa., U.S.	C9	115
Lac-Frontière, P.Q., Can.	C7	74
La Chambre, Fr.	D2	20
Lachapelle [-sous-Rougemont], Fr.	A3	21
La Charité, Fr.	D5	16
La Chartre, Fr.	D5	16
La Chaux-de-Fonds, Switz.	E3	18
Lachay, Punta, c., Peru	D2	58
Lachen, Switz.	B6	21
Lachine, P.Q., Can.	D4	74
Lachlan, stm., Austl.	F8	50
La Chorrera, Col.	D3	60
La Chorrera, Pan.	F8	62
Lachute, P.Q., Can.	D3	74
Laçi, Alb.	B2	25
La Cienega, N.M., U.S.	h8	108
La Ciotat, Fr.	F6	16
La Cisa Pass, Italy	B2	23
Lackawanna, N.Y., U.S.	C2	109
Lackawanna, co., Pa., U.S.	D10	115
Lackawaxen, Pa., U.S.	D12	115
Lackland Air Force Base, mil., Tx., U.S.	k7	120
Lac La Belle, Mi., U.S.	A2	99
Lac La Biche, Ab., Can.	B5	68
Lac la Ronge Provincial Park, Sk., Can.	B3	75
Laclede, Id., U.S.	A2	89
Laclede, Il., U.S.	E5	90
Laclede, Mo., U.S.	D5	102
Laclede, co., Mo., U.S.	D5	102
Lac-Mégantic, P.Q., Can.	D6	74
La Cocha, Arg.	E3	55
Lacolle, P.Q., Can.	D4	74
La Colorada, Mex.	C4	62
Lacomb, Or., U.S.	C4	114
Lacombe, Ab., Can.	C4	68
Lacombe, La., U.S.	D6	95
Lacon, Il., U.S.	B4	90
Lacona, Ia., U.S.	C4	92
La Concepción, Pan.	F6	62
La Conception, P.Q., Can.	C2	74
Laconia, In., U.S.	H5	91
Laconia, N.H., U.S.	C4	106
Laconia, Tn., U.S.	B2	119
Laconia, Gulf of, b., Grc.	E5	25
La Conner, Wa., U.S.	A3	124
La Coruña, Spain	A1	22
Lacota, Mi., U.S.	F4	99
La Courneuve, Fr.	g10	17
Lacq, Fr.	F3	16
Lac qui Parle, co., Mn., U.S.	F2	100
Lac qui Parle, West Branch, stm., Mn., U.S.	F2	100
La Creek Lake, l., S.D., U.S.	D4	118
La Crescent, Mn., U.S.	G7	100
La Crescenta, Ca., U.S.	*m12	82
La Crete, Ab., Can.	f7	68
La Crosse, Ar., U.S.	A4	81
La Crosse, In., U.S.	B4	91
La Crosse, Ks., U.S.	D4	93
La Crosse, Va., U.S.	D4	123
La Crosse, Wi., U.S.	E2	126
La Crosse, co., Wi., U.S.	E2	126
La Crosse, stm., Wi., U.S.	E3	126
La Cruz, Col.	G3	60
La Cruz, C.R.	E5	63
La Cruz, Mex.	E6	62
La Cruz [de Río Grande], Nic.	D5	63
Lac-Saguay, P.Q., Can.	C2	74
Lac-Saint-Jean-Est, co., P.Q., Can.	A6	74
Lac-Saint-Jean-Ouest, co., P.Q., Can.	A5	74
Lac-Vert, Sk., Can.	E3	75
La Cygne, Ks., U.S.	D9	93
Ladário, Braz.	B1	56
Ladder Creek, stm., Ks., U.S.	D2	93
Laddonia, Mo., U.S.	B6	102
Ladelle, Ar., U.S.	D4	81
Ladera Heights, Ca., U.S.	*m12	82
La Désirade, i., Guad.	Q9	65
Ladies Island, i., S.C., U.S.	G6	117
Ladispoli, Italy	h8	23
Ladner, B.C., Can.	E6	69
Ladner, S.D., U.S.	B2	118
Ladnun, India	D5	37
La Dorada, Col.	B3	60
Ladoga, Ia., U.S.	C5	92
Ladoga, Lake, l., Sov. Un.	C6	29
Ladoga, Tx., U.S.	C5	120
Ladora, Ia., U.S.	C5	92
Ladson, S.C., U.S.	F7	117
Ladue, Mo., U.S.	C4	102
Ladybank, Scot., U.K.	D5	13
Ladybrand, S. Afr.	C4	49
Ladysmith, B.C., Can.	E6	69
Ladysmith, S. Afr.	C4	49
Ladysmith, Wi., U.S.	C2	126
Lae, Pap. N. Gui.	k12	50
La Esmeralda, Ven.	C4	60
Læsø, i., Den.	A4	15
La Esperanza, Cuba	C2	64
La Esperanza, Hond.	C3	62
La Estrada, Spain	A1	22
La Estrella, Bol.	C3	55
La Farge, Wi., U.S.	E3	126
LaFargeville, N.Y., U.S.	A5	109
Lafayette, Al., U.S.	C4	78
Lafayette, Ca., U.S.	*h8	82
Lafayette, Co., U.S.	B5	83
Lafayette, Il., U.S.	B4	90
Lafayette, In., U.S.	D4	91
Lafayette, Ky., U.S.	D2	94
Lafayette, La., U.S.	D3	95
Lafayette, Mn., U.S.	F4	100
Lafayette, N.J., U.S.	A3	107
Lafayette, N.Y., U.S.	C4	109
Lafayette, N.C., U.S.	B4	110
Lafayette, Oh., U.S.	C2	112
Lafayette, Or., U.S.	B3	114
Lafayette, R.I., U.S.	E4	116
Lafayette, Tn., U.S.	A5	119
Lafayette, co., Ar., U.S.	D2	81
Lafayette, co., Fl., U.S.	C3	86
Lafayette, co., Mo., U.S.	B4	102
Lafayette, co., Ms., U.S.	A4	101
Lafayette, co., Wi., U.S.	F3	126
Lafayette, Mount, mtn., N.H., U.S.	B3	106
Lafayette Hill, Pa., U.S.	*o20	115
Lafayette Southwest, La., U.S.	*D3	95
Lafe, Ar., U.S.	A5	81
La Fère, Fr.	E3	17
La Feria, Tx., U.S.	F4	120
La Ferté-Bernard, Fr.	C4	16
La Ferté-Macé, Fr.	C3	16
La Ferté-sous-Jouarre, Fr.	A5	17
Lafferty, Oh., U.S.	B4	112
Lafia, Nig.	E6	45
Lafiagi, Nig.	E6	45
Lafitte, La., U.S.	k11	95
Laflèche, Sk., Can.	H2	75
La Flèche, Fr.	C4	16
La Follette, Tn., U.S.	C9	119
La Fontaine, In., U.S.	C6	91
Lafourche, La., U.S.	E5	95
Lafourche, co., La., U.S.	E5	95
Lafourche, Bayou, stm., La., U.S.	E5	95
La France, S.C., U.S.	B2	117
La Galite, i., Tun.	F2	23
Lagan, stm., Swe.	I5	14
Lage, F.R.Ger.	B3	19
Lågen, stm., Nor.	G3	14
Lagg, Scot., U.K.	E3	13
Laggan, Bay, b., Scot., U.K.	E2	13
Laggan, Loch, res., Scot., U.K.	D4	13
Laghouat, Alg.	C5	44
Lago, Mount, mtn., Wa., U.S.	A5	124
Lagoa, Port.	D1	22
Lagoa Vermelha, Braz.	B6	57
Lago Posadas, Arg.	D2	54
Lago Ranco, Chile	B2	54
Lagos, Nig.	E5	45
Lagos, Port.	D1	22
Lagos de Moreno, Mex.	G9	62
La Grand'Combe, Fr.	D6	16
La Grande, Or., U.S.	B8	114
La Grande, stm., P.Q., Can.	h11	72
La Grande Deux, Réservoir, res., P.Q., Can.	h11	72
La Grande Quatre, Réservoir, res., P.Q., Can.	F18	66
Lagrange, Fl., U.S.	D6	86
La Grange, Ga., U.S.	C1	87
La Grange, Ky., U.S.	B4	94
La Grange, Me., U.S.	C4	96
La Grange, Mo., U.S.	A6	102
La Grange, N.C., U.S.	B5	110
La Grange, Oh., U.S.	A3	112
La Grange, Tx., U.S.	E4	120
Lagrange, Wy., U.S.	E8	127
Lagrange, co., In., U.S.	A7	91
La Grange Highlands, Il., U.S.	*k9	90
La Grange Park, Il., U.S.	k9	90
La Gran Sabana, pl., Ven.	C6	61
Lagro, In., U.S.	C6	91
La Grulla, Tx., U.S.	F3	120
La Grue, Bayou, stm., Ar., U.S.	C4	81
La Guadeloupe (Saint-Évariste), P.Q., Can.	D7	74
La Guaira, Ven.	A4	60
Laguardia, Spain	A3	22
La Guata, Hond.	C4	62
Laguna, N.M., U.S.	C3	108
Laguna Beach, Ca., U.S.	F5	82
Laguna Dam, U.S.	E1	80
Laguna Hills, Ca., U.S.	*n13	82
Laguna Indian Reservation, N.M., U.S.	C2	108
Lagunas, Peru	C2	58
Lagunillas, Bol.	C3	55
La Habana, prov., Cuba	C2	64
La Habra, Ca., U.S.	n13	82
Lahad Datu, Malay.	E5	34
Lahaina, Hi., U.S.	C5	88
La Harpe, Il., U.S.	C3	90
La Harpe, Ks., U.S.	E8	93
Lahat, Indon.	F2	34
Lahave, N.S., Can.	E5	71
La Have Island, i., N.S., Can.	E5	71
La Have, stm., N.S., Can.	E5	71
Laheria Sarai, India	D10	37
Lahij, P.D.R.Yem.	C5	39
Lāhījān, Iran	C5	39
Lahinch, Ire.	E2	11
Lahn, stm., F.R.Ger.	C4	18
Laholm, Swe.	B7	15
Lahoma, Ok., U.S.	A3	113
Lahontan Reservoir, res., Nv., U.S.	D2	105
Lahore, Pak.	C5	36
Lahore Cantonment, Pak.	*B5	36
Lahr, F.R.Ger.	D3	18
Lahri, Pak.	C4	36
Lahti, Fin.	G11	14
La Huaca, Peru	B1	58
Laï, Chad	D3	46
Lai Chau, Viet.	A5	35
Laichow Bay see Laizhou Bay, b., China	D8	31
Laide, Scot., U.K.	C3	13
Laidon, Loch, l., Scot., U.K.	D4	13
Laie, Hi., U.S.	B4	88
Laifeng, China	J3	32
L'Aigle, Fr.	C4	16
L'Aigle Creek, stm., Ar., U.S.	D3	81
Laingsburg, S. Afr.	D3	49
Laingsburg, Mi., U.S.	F6	99
Lair, Ky., U.S.	B5	94
Laird, Sk., Can.	E2	75
Laird, Co., U.S.	A8	83
Lairg, Scot., U.K.	A4	10
Laïri, Batha de, stm., Chad	F7	34
Laiwui, Indon.	F7	34
Laiyang, China	D9	31
Laizhou Bay, b., China	C2	58
La Jalca, Peru	C2	58
La Jara, Co., U.S.	D5	83
La Jara, N.M., U.S.	A3	108
La Joie, Point, c., Port.	f9	22
Lajes, Braz.	D2	56
Lajes, Braz.	C3	57
La Jolla, Point, c., Ca., U.S.	o15	82
Lajord, Sk., Can.	G3	75
La Jose, Pa., U.S.	E4	115
Lajosmizse, Hung.	B4	24
La Joya (part of Mexico City), Mex.	h9	63
La Joya, Peru	E3	58
Lajoya, N.M., U.S.	C3	108
La Junta, Co., U.S.	D7	83
Lake, Ms., U.S.	C4	101
Lake, co., Ca., U.S.	C2	82
Lake, co., Co., U.S.	B4	83
Lake, co., Fl., U.S.	D5	86
Lake, co., Il., U.S.	A5	90
Lake, co., In., U.S.	B3	91
Lake, co., Mi., U.S.	E5	99
Lake, co., Mn., U.S.	C7	100
Lake, co., Mt., U.S.	C2	103
Lake, co., Oh., U.S.	A4	112
Lake, co., Or., U.S.	E6	114
Lake, co., S.D., U.S.	C8	118
Lake, co., Tn., U.S.	A2	119
Lake Alfred, Fl., U.S.	D5	86
Lake Alma, Sk., Can.	H3	75
Lake Andes, S.D., U.S.	D7	118
Lake Ann, Mi., U.S.	D4	99
Lake Annis, N.S., Can.	E4	71
Lake Ariel, Pa., U.S.	D11	115
Lake Arrowhead, Ca., U.S.	E5	82
Lake Arthur, La., U.S.	D3	95
Lake Arthur, N.M., U.S.	D5	108
Lake Barcroft, Va., U.S.	B5	123
Lake Benton, Mn., U.S.	G2	100
Lake Beschta, Ct., U.S.	C5	84
Lake Beulah, Wi., U.S.	n11	126
Lake Bluff, Il., U.S.	A6	90
Lake Bonaparte, N.Y., U.S.	A5	109
Lake Bronson, Mn., U.S.	B2	100
Lake Butler, Fl., U.S.	B4	86
Lake Cargelligo, Austl.	F6	51
Lake Charles, La., U.S.	D2	95
Lake Chelan National Recreation Area, Wa., U.S.	A5	124
Lake City, Ar., U.S.	B5	81
Lake City, Co., U.S.	D3	83
Lake City, Fl., U.S.	B4	86
Lake City, Ia., U.S.	B3	92
Lake City, Mi., U.S.	D5	99
Lake City, Mn., U.S.	F6	100
Lake City, Pa., U.S.	B1	115
Lake City, S.C., U.S.	D8	117
Lake City, Tn., U.S.	C9	119
Lake Clark National Park, Ak., U.S.	C9	79
Lake Como, Pa., U.S.	C11	115
Lake Cormorant, Ms., U.S.	A3	101
Lake Cowichan, B.C., Can.	g11	69
Lakecreek, Or., U.S.	E4	114
Lake Creek, stm., Wa., U.S.	F4	100
Lake Crystal, Mn., U.S.	F4	100
Lake Delta, N.Y., U.S.	B5	109
Lake Delton, Wi., U.S.	E4	126
Lake District, reg., Eng., U.K.		
Lake Elmo, Mn., U.S.	*n13	100
Lake Elmore, Vt., U.S.	B3	122
Lake Elsinore, Ca., U.S.	F5	82
Lake Erie Beach, N.Y., U.S.	C1	109
Lakefield, P.Q., Can.	G3	100
Lake Forest, Fl., U.S.	*s13	86
Lake Forest, Il., U.S.	A6	90
Lake Fork, Il., U.S.	E2	89
Lake Fork, Oh., U.S.	D3	83
Lake Fork, stm., Ut., U.S.	C5	121
Lake Geneva, Wi., U.S.	F5	126
Lake George, Mi., U.S.	E6	99
Lake George, Mn., U.S.	C4	100
Lake George, N.Y., U.S.	B7	109
Lake Grinnell, N.J., U.S.	A3	107

Name	Map Ref	Page

Lake Grove, N.Y., U.S. — *E7 109
Lake Hamilton, Ar., U.S. — g7 81
Lake Harbour, N.T., Can. — D19 66
Lake Havasu City, Az., U.S. — C1 80
Lake Helen, Fl., U.S. — D5 86
Lake Hiawatha, N.J., U.S. — B4 107
Lake Hubert, Mn., U.S. — D4 100
Lake Hughes, Ca., U.S. — E4 82
Lake Huntington, N.Y., U.S. — D5 109
Lakehurst, N.J., U.S. — C4 107
Lakehurst Naval Air Station, mil., N.J., U.S. — C4 107
Lake Itasca, Mn., U.S. — C3 100
Lake Jackson, Tx., U.S. — E5 120
Lake Katrine, N.Y., U.S. — D7 109
Lakeland, Fl., U.S. — D5 86
Lakeland, Ga., U.S. — E3 87
Lake Leelanau, Mi., U.S. — D5 99
Lake Lenore, Sk., Can. — E3 75
Lake Lillian, Mi., U.S. — F4 100
Lake Lindsey, Fl., U.S. — D4 86
Lake Linden, Mi., U.S. — A2 99
Lake Louise, Ab., Can. — D2 68
Lake Luzerne, N.Y., U.S. — B7 109
Lake Magdalene, Fl., U.S. — o11 86
Lake Mary, Fl., U.S. — D5 86
Lake Mcdonald, Mt., U.S. — B3 103
Lake Mead National Recreation Area, U.S. — H7 105
Lake Meredith National Recreation Area, Tx., U.S. — B2 120
Lake Metigoshe, N.D., U.S. — A5 111
Lake Mills, Ia., U.S. — A4 92
Lake Mills, Wi., U.S. — E5 126
Lake Minchumina, Ak., U.S. — C9 79
Lakemont, Pa., U.S. — F5 115
Lakemore, Oh., U.S. — A4 112
Lake Mountain, mtn., Wy., U.S. — E6 127
Lakenan, Mo., U.S. — B5 102
Lake Nebagamon, Wi., U.S. — B2 126
Lake Norden, S.D., U.S. — C8 118
Lake Odessa, Mi., U.S. — F5 99
Lake Of The Woods, co., Mn., U.S. — B4 100
Lake Orion, Mi., U.S. — F7 99
Lake Oswego, Or., U.S. — B4 114
Lake Ozark, Mo., U.S. — C5 102
Lake Park, Fl., U.S. — F6 86
Lake Park, Ga., U.S. — F3 87
Lake Park, Ia., U.S. — A2 92
Lake Park, Mn., U.S. — D2 100
Lake Placid, Fl., U.S. — E5 86
Lake Placid, N.Y., U.S. — A7 109
Lake Pleasant, N.Y., U.S. — B6 109
Lake Pontchartrain Causeway, La., U.S. — h11 95
Lakeport, Ca., U.S. — C2 82
Lake Preston, S.D., U.S. — C8 118
Lake Providence, La., U.S. — B4 95
Lake Range, mts., Nv., U.S. — C2 105
Lakeridge, Va., U.S. — *E2 105
Lake Ridge, Va., U.S. — B5 123
Lake River, On., Can. — n19 73
Lake Ronkonkoma, N.Y., U.S. — *n15 109
Lake Shore, Md., U.S. — B5 97
Lakeshore, Ms., U.S. — E4 101
Lake Shore, Ut., U.S. — *C4 121
Lakeside, N.S., Can. — E6 71
Lakeside, Az., U.S. — C6 80
Lakeside, Ca., U.S. — F5 82
Lakeside, Ct., U.S. — *B5 83
Lakeside, Ct., U.S. — D3 84
Lakeside, Ct., U.S. — C3 84
Lakeside, Ia., U.S. — B2 92
Lakeside, Mt., U.S. — B2 103
Lakeside, Ne., U.S. — B3 104
Lakeside, N.J., U.S. — A4 107
Lakeside, Oh., U.S. — A3 112
Lakeside, Or., U.S. — D2 114
Lakeside, Va., U.S. — *C5 123
Lakeside Mountains, mts., Ut., U.S. — B3 121
Lakeside Park, Ky., U.S. — h13 94
Lake Station, In., U.S. — A3 91
Lake Station, Ok., U.S. — A5 113
Lake Stevens, Wa., U.S. — A3 124
Lake Superior Provincial Park, On., Can. — p18 73
Lake Swamp, stm., S.C., U.S. — D8 117
Lake Tansi, Tn., U.S. — D8 119
Lake Telemark, N.J., U.S. — B4 107
Lake Tomahawk, Wi., U.S. — C4 126
Laketon, In., U.S. — C6 91
Laketown, Ut., U.S. — B4 121
Lake Toxaway, N.C., U.S. — f10 110
Lake Traverse, On., Can. — B6 73
Lake Valley, Sk., Can. — G2 75
Lake Valley, val., Nv., U.S. — E7 105
Lakeview, Ga., U.S. — *B1 87
Lakeview, Id., U.S. — B2 89
Lakeview, Mi., U.S. — E5 99
Lakeview, Mt., U.S. — F5 103
Lake View, N.Y., U.S. — C2 109
Lakeview, Oh., U.S. — B2 112
Lakeview, Or., U.S. — E6 114
Lake View, S.C., U.S. — C9 117
Lake View, Tx., U.S. — B2 120
Lake Villa, Il., U.S. — h8 90
Lake Village, Ar., U.S. — D4 81
Lake Village, In., U.S. — B3 91
Lakeville, Ct., U.S. — B2 84
Lakeville, In., U.S. — A5 91
Lakeville, Ma., U.S. — C6 98
Lakeville, Mn., U.S. — F5 100
Lakeville, N.Y., U.S. — C3 109
Lake Waccamaw, N.C., U.S. — C4 110
Lake Wales, Fl., U.S. — E5 86
Lake Williams, N.D., U.S. — B6 111
Lake Winola, Pa., U.S. — m17 115
Lake Wissota, Wi., U.S. — *D2 126
Lakewood, Ca., U.S. — n12 82
Lakewood, Co., U.S. — B5 83
Lakewood, Il., U.S. — D5 90
Lakewood, Me., U.S. — D3 96
Lakewood, N.J., U.S. — C4 107
Lakewood, N.M., U.S. — E5 108
Lakewood, N.Y., U.S. — C1 109
Lakewood, Oh., U.S. — A4 112
Lakewood, Pa., U.S. — C10 115
Lakewood, Wa., U.S. — A3 124
Lakewood Center, Wa., U.S. — B3 124
Lake Worth, Fl., U.S. — F6 86
Lake Worth Inlet, b., Fl., U.S. — F7 86
Lake Zurich, Il., U.S. — h8 90
Lakhī, Afg. — B3 36
Lakhīmpur, India — C7 36
Lakhpat, India — F2 37
Lakhta (part of Leningrad), Sov. Un. — r31 14

Lakin, Ks., U.S. — E2 93
Lakota, I.C. — E3 45
Lakota, Ia., U.S. — A3 92
Lakota, N.D., U.S. — A7 111
Laksefjorden, Nor. — B12 14
Lakshadweep (Laccadive, Minicoy and Amīndivi Islands), ter., India — *F5 36
Lakshadweep (Laccadive Islands), is., India — F5 36
La Laguna, Spain — m13 22
Lālī, Iran — E4 39
La Libertad, El Sal. — D3 62
La Libertad, Guat. — B2 62
La Libertad, dept., Peru — C2 58
La Ligua, Chile — A2 54
Lalín, Spain — A1 22
La Línea, Spain — D3 22
Lalitpur, India — D6 36
Lalitpur, Nepal — C8 36
La Loche, Sk., Can. — m7 75
La Loche, Lac, l., Sk., Can. — A6 68
La Loma, N.M., U.S. — B4 108
La Louvière, Bel. — D4 17
La Luz, N.M., U.S. — D4 108
La Macarena, Serranía de, mts., Col. — C3 60
La Machine, Fr. — D5 16
La Maddalena, Italy — D2 23
La Madera, N.M., U.S. — A3 108
Lama-Kara, Togo — E5 45
La Malbaie, P.Q., Can. — B7 74
Lamaline, Nf., Can. — E4 72
La Mancha, reg., Spain — C4 22
Lamanibot Sanhilo, Puntan, c., N. Mar. Is. — D7 52
Lamar, Ar., U.S. — B2 81
Lamar, Co., U.S. — C8 83
Lamar, In., U.S. — H4 91
Lamar, Ms., U.S. — A4 101
Lamar, Mo., U.S. — D3 102
Lamar, Ne., U.S. — D4 104
Lamar, Ok., U.S. — B5 113
Lamar, Pa., U.S. — D7 115
Lamar, S.C., U.S. — C7 117
Lamar, co., Al., U.S. — B1 78
Lamar, co., Ga., U.S. — C2 87
Lamar, co., Ms., U.S. — D4 101
Lamar, co., Tx., U.S. — C5 120
Lamar, stm., Wy., U.S. — B2 127
Lamarche, Fr. — A1 20
La Marmora, Punta, mtn., Italy — D2 23
La Marque, Tx., U.S. — *r15 120
Lamas, Peru — C2 58
Lamasco, Ky., U.S. — f10 94
La Mauricie, Parc National de, P.Q., Can. — C5 74
Lamb, co., Tx., U.S. — B1 120
Lamballe, Fr. — C2 16
Lambaréné, Gabon — F2 46
Lambay i., Ire. — D5 11
Lambayeque, Peru — C2 58
Lambayeque, dept., Peru — C2 58
Lambert, Ms., U.S. — A3 101
Lambert, Mt., U.S. — C12 103
Lambert, Ok., U.S. — A3 113
Lambert Glacier, Ant. — B19 7
Lambert Lake, Me., U.S. — C5 96
Lamberton, Mn., U.S. — F3 100
Lambert's Bay, S. Afr. — D2 49
Lambertville, Mi., U.S. — G7 99
Lambertville, N.J., U.S. — C3 107
Lambeth, On., Can. — E3 73
Lambeth (part of London), Eng., U.K. — m12 10
Lambourn, Eng., U.K. — C6 12
Lambrecht (Pfalz), F.R.Ger. — D3 19
Lambro, stm., Italy — D5 20
Lambrook, Ar., U.S. — C5 81
Lambsburg, Va., U.S. — D2 123
Lamb's Head, c., Ire. — F1 11
Lambton, P.Q., Can. — D6 74
Lambton, co., On., Can. — E2 73
Lambton, Cape, c., N.T., Can. — B8 66
Lamdessar-Timur, Indon. — G8 34
Lame Deer, Mt., U.S. — E10 103
Lamego, Port. — B2 22
Lameque, N.B., Can. — B5 71
Lameque, Île, i., N.B., Can. — B5 71
La Merced (Superí), Arg. — B5 54
La Mesa, Ca., U.S. — F5 82
La Mesa, N.M., U.S. — E3 108
Lamesa, Tx., U.S. — C2 120
Lamia, Grc. — C4 40
La Minerve, P.Q., Can. — C3 74
Lamington, Mount, mtn., Pap. N. Gui. — k12 50
La Mirada, Ca., U.S. — *E4 82
Lamlam, Mount, mtn., Guam — M9 52
La'nga Lake, l., China — B7 36
Langa Langa, Zaire — B2 48
Langanes, c., Ice. — m25 14
Langarūd, Iran — C5 39
Lāngås, Swe. — B6 15
Langbank, Sk., Can. — G4 75
Lang Bay, B.C., Can. — E5 69
Langdale, Al., U.S. — C4 78
Langdon, Ab., Can. — D4 68
Langdon, Ia., U.S. — A2 92
Langdon, Ks., U.S. — E5 93
Langdon, Mo., U.S. — A2 102
Langdon, N.H., U.S. — D2 106
Langdon, N.D., U.S. — A7 111
L'Ange-Gardien, P.Q., Can. — n17 74
Langeland, i., Den. — B7 15
Langelandsbaelt, strt., Den. — B7 15
Langeloth, Pa., U.S. — F1 115
Langen, F.R.Ger. — E5 19
Langenau, F.R.Ger. — D6 18
Langenburg, Sk., Can. — G5 75
Langenselbold, F.R.Ger. — C4 19
Langenthal, Switz. — E3 20
Langenzenn, F.R.Ger. — D5 19
Langeoog, F.R.Ger. — A7 19
Langeoog, i., F.R.Ger. — B3 18
Langerak, strt., Den. — H3 14
Langesund, Nor. — H3 14
Langeten, stm., Switz. — B4 21
Langford, B.C., Can. — h12 69
Langford, S.D., U.S. — B8 118
Länghalsen, l., Swe. — u34 14
Länghammet, Swe. — u34 14
Langholm, Scot., U.K. — A7 12
Langhorne, Pa., U.S. — F12 115
Langjökull, Ice. — n22 14
Langkawi, i., Malay. — I3 35
Langkha Tuk, mtn., Thai. — I4 35
Langlade, i., St. P./M. — E3 72
Langlade, co., Wi., U.S. — C4 126
Langley, B.C., Can. — f13 69
Langley, Ar., U.S. — C2 81
Langley, Ky., U.S. — C7 94
Langley, Ok., U.S. — A6 113
Langley, S.C., U.S. — E4 117

Lanao, Lake, l., Phil. — D6 34
Lanare, Ca., U.S. — D4 82
Langley Air Force Base, mil., Va., U.S. — h15 123
Lanark, On., Can. — C8 73
Lanark, Scot., U.K. — C5 10
Lanark, Il., U.S. — A4 90
Lanark, W.V., U.S. — D3 125
Lanark, co., On., Can. — B8 73
Lanark Village, Fl., U.S. — C2 86
Lancang, China — G4 31
Lancashire, De., U.S. — *A4 85
Lancashire, Eng., U.K. — G6 13
Lancaster, On., Can. — B10 73
Lancaster, Eng., U.K. — C5 10
Lancaster, Ca., U.S. — E4 82
Lancaster, Il., U.S. — E6 90
Lancaster, Ks., U.S. — C8 93
Lancaster, Ky., U.S. — C5 94
Lancaster, Ma., U.S. — B4 98
Lancaster, Mo., U.S. — A5 102
Lancaster, N.H., U.S. — B3 106
Lancaster, N.Y., U.S. — C2 109
Lancaster, Oh., U.S. — C3 112
Lancaster, Pa., U.S. — F9 115
Lancaster, S.C., U.S. — B6 117
Lancaster, Tn., U.S. — C8 119
Lancaster, Tx., U.S. — n10 120
Lancaster, Va., U.S. — C6 123
Lancaster, Wi., U.S. — F3 126
Lancaster, co., Ne., U.S. — D9 104
Lancaster, co., Pa., U.S. — G9 115
Lancaster, co., S.C., U.S. — B6 117
Lancaster, co., Va., U.S. — C6 123
Lancaster Sound, strt., N.T., Can. — B15 66
Lance Creek, De., U.S. — *A3 85
Lance, Point, c., Nf., Can. — E4 72
Lance Creek, Wy., U.S. — C8 127
Lance Creek, stm., Wy., U.S. — C8 127
Lancer, Sk., Can. — G1 75
Lancer, Ky., U.S. — C7 94
Lanchou see Lanzhou, China — D5 31
Lanciano, Italy — C5 23
Lancing, Tn., U.S. — C8 119
Landa, N.D., U.S. — A5 111
Landaff Center, N.H., U.S. — B3 106
Landau [an der Isar], F.R.Ger. — D6 18
Landau [in der Pfalz], F.R.Ger. — D4 18
Land Between the Lakes, U.S. — f9 94
Landeck, Aus. — E5 18
Landen, Bel. — D5 17
Lander, Wy., U.S. — D4 127
Lander, co., Nv., U.S. — C4 105
Landerneau, Fr. — C1 16
Landes, In., U.S. — C6 91
Landing Lake, l., Mb., Can. — B3 70
Landis, Sk., Can. — E1 75
Landis, N.C., U.S. — B2 110
Landisburg, Pa., U.S. — F7 115
Landividiau, Fr. — C1 16
Lando, S.C., U.S. — B5 117
Land O' Lakes, Wi., U.S. — B4 126
Landquart, Switz. — C8 21
Landquart, stm., Switz. — C8 21
Landsberg, F.R.Ger. — D5 18
Land's End, c., Eng., U.K. — F4 10
Lands End, c., R.I., U.S. — F5 116
Landshut, F.R.Ger. — D6 18
Landskrona, Swe. — J5 14
Landsman Creek, stm., Co., U.S. — B8 83
Landsort, Swe. — u35 14
Landusky, Mt., U.S. — C8 103
Lane, Il., U.S. — C5 90
Lane, Ks., U.S. — D8 93
Lane, Nv., U.S. — D7 105
Lane, Ok., U.S. — C6 113
Lane, S.C., U.S. — D8 117
Lane, S.D., U.S. — C7 118
Lane, Tn., U.S. — A2 119
Lane, co., Ks., U.S. — D3 93
Lane, co., Or., U.S. — C4 114
Laneburg, Ar., U.S. — D2 81
La Negra, Chile — B5 54
Lanesboro, Ma., U.S. — A1 98
Lanesboro, Mn., U.S. — G7 100
Lanesboro, Pa., U.S. — C10 115
Lanesville, In., U.S. — H6 91
Lanett, Al., U.S. — C4 78
Lanfine, Ab., Can. — D5 68
Lang, Sk., Can. — H3 75
Langå, Den. — B3 15

Langley, Wa., U.S. — A3 124
Langley Park, Md., U.S. — f9 97
Langlois, Or., U.S. — E2 114
Langleyville, Il., U.S. — D4 90
Langnau [im Emmental], Switz. — E5 16
Langogne, Fr. — E5 16
Langon, Fr. — E3 16
Langøya, i., Nor. — C6 14
Langres, Fr. — D6 16
Langres, Plateau de, plat., Fr. — D6 16
Langruth, Mb., Can. — D2 70
Langsa, Indon. — E1 34
Lang Son, Viet. — B7 35
Langstaff, On., Can. — k15 73
Langston, Al., U.S. — A3 78
Langston, Ok., U.S. — B4 113
Langton, On., Can. — E4 73
Langtry, Tx., U.S. — E2 120
Languedoc, hist reg., Fr. — F5 16
L'Anguille, stm., Ar., U.S. — B5 81
Langzhong, China — E6 31
Lanham, Md., U.S. — C4 97
Lanier, co., Ga., U.S. — E3 87
Lanigan, Sk., Can. — F3 75
Lanigan Creek, stm., Sk., Can. — F3 75
Lanin, Volcán, vol., S.A. — B2 54
Lankaran, Sov. Un. — A8 111
Lanklaar, Bel. — C5 17
Lannion, Fr. — C2 16
Lannon, Wi., U.S. — m11 126
L'Annonciation, P.Q., Can. — C3 74
Lanoka Harbor, N.J., U.S. — D4 107
Lansdale, Pa., U.S. — F11 115
Lansdowne, On., Can. — C8 73
Lansdowne, Md., U.S. — B4 97
Lansdowne, Pa., U.S. — *p20 115
Lansdowne House, On., Can. — n18 73
L'Anse, Mi., U.S. — B2 99
L'Anse-au-Clair, Nf., Can. — C3 72
L'Anse-au-Loup, Nf., Can. — C3 72
L'Anse-aux-Meadows, Nf., Can. — C4 72
L'Anse Indian Reservation, Mi., U.S. — B2 99
L'Anse-Saint-Jean, P.Q., Can. — A7 74
Lansford, N.D., U.S. — A4 111
Lansford, Pa., U.S. — E10 115
Lansing, Il., U.S. — B6 90
Lansing, Ia., U.S. — A6 92
Lansing, Ks., U.S. — C9 93
Lansing, Mi., U.S. — F6 99
Lansing, N.C., U.S. — A1 110
Lansing, W.V., U.S. — m13 125
Lanslebourg, Fr. — D2 20
Lantana, Fl., U.S. — F6 86
Lantana, Cuba — D5 64
Lantern Hill, hill, Ct., U.S. — D8 84
Lantry, S.D., U.S. — B4 118
Lanuvio, Italy — h9 23
Lanxi, China — F8 31
Lanxi, China — A12 32
Lao, Ut., U.S. — C3 121
Lao Cai, Viet. — A6 35
Laoag, Phil. — B6 34
Laoighis, co., Ire. — I5 11
Laolao, Bahia, b., N. Mar. Is. — D8 52
Laolao Kattan, Puntan, c., N. Mar. Is. — D8 52
Laon, Fr. — C5 16
Laona, Wi., U.S. — C5 126
La Oroya, Peru — D2 58
Laos, ctry., Asia — B2 34
Laotto, In., U.S. — B7 91
Lapa, Braz. — D3 56
La Palma, Pan. — F8 62
La Palma, Az., U.S. — E4 80
La Palma, Ca., U.S. — *n12 82
La Palma, i., Spain — m13 22
La Palma [del Condado], Spain — D2 22
La Paloma, Ur. — E2 56
La Pampa, prov., Arg. — B3 54
La Paragua, Ven. — B5 60
La Pasión, stm., Guat. — B2 62
La Passe, On., Can. — B8 73
La Patrie, P.Q., Can. — D6 74
La Paz, Arg. — A5 54
La Paz, Arg. — A3 54
La Paz, Bol. — G5 58
La Paz, Col. — A3 60
La Paz, Hond. — E7 63
La Paz, Mex. — C2 63
La Paz, Mex. — E7 63
La Paz, Phil. — B5 34
Lapaz, In., U.S. — C5 91
La Paz, dept., Bol. — G5 58
La Paz, Bahía de, b., Mex. — D2 63
La Pedrera, Col. — D4 60
La Perouse Strait, strt., Asia — D10 33
La Piedad [Cavadas], Mex. — m12 63
Lapine, Al., U.S. — D3 78
La Pine, Or., U.S. — D5 114
La Place, Il., U.S. — D5 90
La Place, La., U.S. — h11 95
Lapland, reg., Eur. — C11 14
La Plant, S.D., U.S. — B5 118
La Plata, Arg. — C5 54
La Plata, Col. — F5 60
La Plata, Md., U.S. — C4 97
La Plata, Mo., U.S. — A5 102
La Plata, N.M., U.S. — A1 108
La Plata, co., Co., U.S. — D3 83
La Plata Mountains, mts., Co., U.S. — D3 83
La Pobla de Lillet, Spain — A6 22
La Pocatière, P.Q., Can. — B7 74
La Poile Bay, b., Nf., Can. — E2 72
Lapoint, Ut., U.S. — C6 121
La Pointe, Wi., U.S. — B3 126
Lapointe [-Station], P.Q., Can. — A8 74
La Pola [de Gordón], Spain — A3 22
Laporte, Ca., U.S. — C3 82
Laporte, Co., U.S. — A5 83
La Porte, In., U.S. — A4 91
Laporte, Mn., U.S. — C4 100
La Porte, Pa., U.S. — D9 115
La Porte, Tx., U.S. — r14 120
La Porte, co., In., U.S. — A4 91
La Porte City, Ia., U.S. — B5 92
Läppe, Swe. — t33 14
Lappeenranta, Fin. — G13 14
La Prairie, P.Q., Can. — D4 74

La Prairie, Mn., U.S. — C5 100
Laprairie, co., P.Q., Can. — D4 74
Laprida, Arg. — B4 54
La Pryor, Tx., U.S. — E3 120
Lāpseki, Tur. — B6 40
La Puebla, Spain — C7 22
La Puebla de Montalbán, Spain — C3 22
La Puente, Ca., U.S. — *m13 82
La Puente, N.M., U.S. — A3 108
La Purísima, Mex. — B2 63
La Push, Wa., U.S. — B1 124
Laqīyat al Arba'in, Sud. — B2 47
La Quiaca, Arg. — D2 55
Lār, Iran — C5 38
Lara, state, Ven. — A3 60
Laramie, Wy., U.S. — E7 127
Laramie, co., Wy., U.S. — E8 127
Laramie, stm., U.S. — E7 127
Laramie Mountains, mts., Wy., U.S. — D7 127
Laramie Peak, mtn., Wy., U.S. — D7 127
Laranjeiras, Braz. — D3 57
Laranjeiras do Sul, Braz. — D2 56
Larantuka, Indon. — G6 34
Larap, Phil. — o14 34
Larche Pass, Eur. — E2 20
Larchmont, N.Y., U.S. — h13 109
Larchmont North, N.Y., U.S. — *h13 109
Larchwood, Ia., U.S. — A1 92
Lardeau, B.C., Can. — D9 69
L'Ardoise, N.S., Can. — D9 71
Laredo, Spain — A4 22
Laredo, Mo., U.S. — A4 102
Laredo, Tx., U.S. — F3 120
Laredo Sound, strt., B.C., Can. — C3 69
La Réole, Fr. — E4 16
Lares, P.R. — B2 65
Largeau, Chad — B3 46
Largentière, Fr. — E6 16
Largo, Fl., U.S. — E4 86
Largo, Cañon, val., N.M., U.S. — A2 108
Largo, Cayo, i., Cuba — D3 64
Largo, Key, i., Fl., U.S. — G6 86
Largs, Scot., U.K. — E4 13
Lariat, Tx., U.S. — B1 120
La Ricamarie, Fr. — E6 16
Larimer, co., Co., U.S. — A5 83
Larimore, N.D., U.S. — B8 111
Larino, Italy — D5 23
La Rioja, Arg. — E2 55
La Rioja, Cuba — D5 64
La Rioja, prov., Arg. — E2 55
Lárisa, Grc. — C4 40
Laristan, hist reg., Iran — C5 38
La Rivière, Mb., Can. — E2 70
Lark, N.D., U.S. — C4 111
Larkana, Pak. — C3 36
Larkinsville, Al., U.S. — A3 78
Larkspur, Co., U.S. — B6 83
Larnaca see Lárnax, Cyp. — B3 38
Larnaca (Larnaca), Cyp. — B3 38
Larne, N. Ire., U.K. — C4 10
Larned, Ks., U.S. — D4 93
Larose, La., U.S. — E5 95
Larrabee, Ia., U.S. — B2 92
Larrys River, N.S., Can. — D8 71
Larsen Bay, Ak., U.S. — D9 79
Larsen Ice Shelf, Ant. — C6 7
Larslan, Mt., U.S. — B10 103
Larsmont, Mn., U.S. — D7 100
Larson, N.D., U.S. — A3 111
Larto, La., U.S. — C4 95
La Rubia, Arg. — F3 55
La Rue, Oh., U.S. — B2 112
Larue, co., Ky., U.S. — C4 94
Laruns, Fr. — F3 16
Larvik, Nor. — H3 14
Larwill, In., U.S. — B6 91
Laryak, Sov. Un. — C25 8
La Sagra, mtn., Spain — D4 22
La Sal, Ut., U.S. — E6 121
La Salle, Mb., Can. — E3 70
La Salle, P.Q., Can. — q19 74
LaSalle, Il., U.S. — B4 90
La Salle, Co., U.S. — A6 83
La Salle, Mn., U.S. — F4 100
La Salle, co., Il., U.S. — B5 90
La Salle, co., La., U.S. — C3 95
La Salle, co., Tx., U.S. — E3 120
Las Animas, Co., U.S. — C7 83
Las Animas, co., Co., U.S. — D6 83
La Sarre, P.Q., Can. — k11 74
Lasbela, Pak. — A5 108
Las Cabras, Chile — A2 54
Lascahobas, Haiti — E8 64
Lascano, Ur. — C7 56
Lascassas, Tn., U.S. — B5 119
Lascar, Volcán, vol., Chile — D2 55
L'Ascension, P.Q., Can. — A6 74
La Scie, Nf., Can. — D4 72
Las Colorados, Arg. — B2 54
Las Cruces, N.M., U.S. — E3 108
La Serena, Chile — E1 55
La Seyne [-sur-Mer], Fr. — F6 16
Las Flores, Arg. — B5 54
Lashburn, Sk., Can. — D1 75
Lashio, Burma — D10 35
La Sila, reg., Italy — E6 23
Las Lajas, Arg. — B2 54
Las Lajas, Pan. — F7 62
Las Lomitas, Arg. — D3 55
Las Marismas, sw., Spain — D2 22
La Solana, Spain — C4 22
La Spezia, Italy — E5 20
Las Piedras, Ven. — r14 120
Las Piedras, Río de, stm., Peru — D3 58
Las Plumas, Arg. — C3 54
Las Rosas, Arg. — A4 54
Las Rozas de Madrid, Spain — p17 22

Lassance, Braz. — B4 56
Lassen, co., Ca., U.S. — B3 82
Lassen Peak, vol., Ca., U.S. — B3 82
Lassen Volcanic National Park, Ca., U.S. — B3 82
Lasso, hill, N. Mar. Is. — D7 52
L'Assomption, P.Q., Can. — D4 74
L'Assomption, co., P.Q., Can. — D4 74
Las Tablas, Pan. — G7 62
Las Tablas, N.M., U.S. — A3 108
Last Chance, Co., U.S. — B7 83
Las Termas, Arg. — E3 55
Last Mountain Lake, l., Sk., Can. — F3 75
Lastoursville, Gabon — F2 46
Lastovo, i., Yugo. — D3 24
Lastrup, F.R.Ger. — B7 17
Lastrup, Mn., U.S. — D4 100
Las Tunas, prov., Cuba — D5 64
Las Varillas, Arg. — A4 54
Las Vegas, Nv., U.S. — G6 105
Las Vegas, N.M., U.S. — B4 108
Las Vigas, Mex. — n15 63
La Tabatière, P.Q., Can. — C2 72
Latacunga, Ec. — B2 58
Latady Island, i., Ant. — B5 7
La Tagua, Col. — D3 60
Latah, Wa., U.S. — B8 124
Latah, co., Id., U.S. — C2 89
Latakia (Al-Lādhiqīyah), Syria — B3 38
Laterrière, P.Q., Can. — A6 74
La Teste-de-Buch, Fr. — E3 16
Latexo, Tx., U.S. — D5 120
Latham, Il., U.S. — D4 90
Latham, Ks., U.S. — E7 93
Latham, N.Y., U.S. — *n15 109
Lathrop, Mo., U.S. — B3 102
Lathrop Wells, Nv., U.S. — G5 105
Latimer, Ks., U.S. — D7 93
Latimer, co., Ok., U.S. — C6 113
Latina, Italy — D4 23
Latium, hist reg., Italy — C4 23
Laton, Ca., U.S. — D4 82
Latoritsa (Latorica), stm., Sov. Un. — D7 26
La Torrecilla, mtn., P.R. — B3 65
La Tortuga, Isla, i., Ven. — A4 60
Latour, Mo., U.S. — C3 102
La Tour-du-Pin, Fr. — E6 16
Latour Peak, mtn., Id., U.S. — B2 89
La Tremblade, Fr. — E3 16
La Trinité, Mart. — I14 64
Latrobe, Pa., U.S. — F3 115
Latrun, Isr. Occ. — C6 41
Latta, S.C., U.S. — C9 117
Lattimer Mines, Pa., U.S. — E10 115
Lattimore, N.C., U.S. — B1 110
Latty, Oh., U.S. — A1 112
La Tuque, P.Q., Can. — B5 74
Latvia, state, Sov. Un. — D5 29
Lau, Nig. — E7 45
Lauca, stm., Bol. — C2 55
Laucala, i., Fiji — H16 52
Lauchhammer, Ger.D.R. — B8 19
Laud, In., U.S. — B7 91
Lauda, F.R.Ger. — D4 19
Lauder, Scot., U.K. — E6 13
Lauderdale, co., Al., U.S. — A2 78
Lauderdale, co., Ms., U.S. — C5 101
Lauderdale, co., Tn., U.S. — B2 119
Lauderdale Lakes, Fl., U.S. — r13 86
Lauderhill, Fl., U.S. — *r13 86
Lauf [an der Pegnitz], F.R.Ger. — D6 19
Laufen, F.R.Ger. — B8 20
Laufen, Switz. — E2 20
Lauffen, F.R.Ger. — D4 19
Laughery Creek, stm., In., U.S. — F7 91
Laughlin Air Force Base, mil., Tx., U.S. — E2 120
Laughlin Peak, mtn., N.M., U.S. — A5 108
Laughlintown, Pa., U.S. — F3 115
Lau Group, is., Fiji — I16 52
Laupen, F.R.Ger. — E5 19
Lauli'ifou, Am. Sam. — F13 52
Launceston, Austl. — o15 50
Launceston, Eng., U.K. — E4 10
Launching Point, c., P.E., Can. — C7 71
La Unión, Col. — C2 60
La Unión, El Sal. — E7 63
La Unión, Mex. — D4 63
La Unión, Peru — C2 58
La Unión, Spain — D5 22
Laupahoehoe, Hi., U.S. — D6 88
Laupheim, F.R.Ger. — D4 18
Laura, Sk., Can. — F2 75
Laura, Oh., U.S. — C1 112
La Urbana, Ven. — B4 60
Laurberg, Den. — B3 15
Laurel, On., Can. — D4 73
Laurel, De., U.S. — F4 85
Laurel, Fl., U.S. — E4 86
Laurel, In., U.S. — F7 91
Laurel, Md., U.S. — B4 97
Laurel, Mt., U.S. — E8 103
Laurel, Ne., U.S. — B8 104
Laurel, co., Ky., U.S. — C5 94
Laurel Bay, S.C., U.S. — G6 117
Laurel Bloomery, Tn., U.S. — C12 119
Laurel Creek, stm., W.V., U.S. — n14 125
Laurel Creek, stm., W.V., U.S. — m12 125
Laureldale, N.J., U.S. — D3 107
Laureldale, Pa., U.S. — F10 115
Laureles, Ur. — E1 56
Laurel Fork, stm., W.V., U.S. — C5 125
Laurel Hill, N.C., U.S. — C3 110
Laurel Mountain, mtn., W.V., U.S. — B5 125
Laurel River Lake, res., Ky., U.S. — D5 94
Laurel Run, Pa., U.S. — n17 115
Laurelton, N.Y., U.S. — E7 115
Laurelwood Academy, Or., U.S. — h11 114
Laurence G. Hanscom Air Force Base, mil., Ma., U.S. — g10 98
Laurence Harbor, N.J., U.S. — C4 107

Name	Map Ref	Page
Laurencekirk, Scot., U.K.	D6	13
Laurens, Ia., U.S.	B3	92
Laurens, S.C., U.S.	C3	117
Laurens, co., Ga., U.S.	D4	87
Laurens, co., S.C., U.S.	C4	117
Laurentides, P.Q., Can.	D4	74
Laurentides, Parc des, P.Q., Can.	B6	74
Laurentum, hist., Italy	h8	23
Lauria Inferiore, Italy	D5	23
Laurie, stm., Mb., Can.	A1	70
Laurie Island, i., B.A.T.	C8	7
Laurie Lake, l., Can.	A1	70
Laurier, Mb., Can.	D2	70
Laurier, P.Q., Can.	C6	74
Laurierville, P.Q., Can.	C6	74
Laurin, Mt., U.S.	E4	103
Laurinburg, N.C., U.S.	C3	110
Lauritzen Bay, b., Ant.	C28	7
Laurium see Lávrion, Grc.	D5	25
Laurium, Mi., U.S.	A2	99
Lausanne, Switz.	E3	18
Lauscha, Ger.D.R.	C6	19
Laut, i., Indon.	F5	34
Laut, i., Indon.	J8	35
Lautaro, Chile	B2	54
Lauterbach, F.R.Ger.	C4	19
Lauterbrunnen, Switz.	C4	21
Lauterecken, F.R.Ger.	D2	19
Laut Kecil Islands, is., Indon.	F5	34
Lautoka, Fiji	H14	52
Lauzon, P.Q., Can.	C6	74
Lava Beds National Monument, Ca., U.S.	B3	82
Lavaca, Ar., U.S.	C1	78
Lavaca, Ar., U.S.	B1	81
Lavaca, co., Tx., U.S.	E4	120
Lava Hot Springs, Id., U.S.	G6	89
Laval, P.Q., Can.	D4	74
Laval, Fr.	C3	16
La Vale, Md., U.S.	k13	97
La Valle, Wi., U.S.	E3	126
La Valley, Co., U.S.	D5	83
Lavaltrie, P.Q., Can.	D4	74
Lävän, i., Iran	H6	39
Lavant, stm., Aus.	E7	18
Lavant Station, On., Can.	B8	73
Lavapié, Punta, c., Chile	B2	54
Lävar Meydän, pl., Iran	F7	39
Lavaur, Fr.	F4	16
Lavaveix-les-Mines, Fr.	D5	16
Laveen, Az., U.S.	m8	80
La Vega, Dom. Rep.	E8	64
La Veia de Coro, Ven.	A4	60
Lavelanet, Fr.	F4	16
Lavello, Italy	D5	23
L'Avenir, P.Q., Can.	D5	74
La Vérendrye, Parc de, P.Q., Can.	k11	74
La Vergne, Tn., U.S.	A5	119
La Verkin, Ut., U.S.	F2	121
La Verne, Ca., U.S.	m13	82
Laverne, Ok., U.S.	A2	113
La Vernia, Tx., U.S.	E3	120
Laverton, Austl.	E3	50
La Veta, Co., U.S.	D5	83
Laviana, Spain	A3	22
La Victoria, Peru	*D2	58
La Victoria, Ven.	A4	60
Lavieille, Lake, l., On., Can.	B6	73
Lavillette, N.B., Can.	B4	71
Lavina, Mt., U.S.	D8	103
Lavinia, Braz.	C2	56
Lavinia, Tn., U.S.	B3	119
La Vista, Ga., U.S.	h8	87
La Vista, Ne., U.S.	g12	104
La Viuda, mtn., Peru	C2	58
Lavonia, Ga., U.S.	B3	87
Lavon Lake, res., Tx., U.S.	m10	120
Lavoy, Ab., Can.	C5	68
Lavras, Braz.	C4	56
Lavras da Mangabeira, Braz.	C3	57
Lavras do Sul, Braz.	E2	56
Lávrion (Laurium), Grc.	D5	25
Lavumisa, Swaz.	C5	49
Lawai, Hi., U.S.	B2	88
Lawen, Or., U.S.	D8	114
Lawers, Ben, mtn., Scot., U.K.	D4	13
Lawford Lake, l., Mb., Can.	B3	70
Lawit, mtn., Malay.	J5	35
Lawler, Ia., U.S.	A5	92
Lawler, Mn., U.S.	D5	100
Lawn, Nf., Can.	E4	72
Lawn, Pa., U.S.	F8	115
Lawn, Tx., U.S.	C3	120
Lawndale, Ca., U.S.	*E4	82
Lawndale, N.C., U.S.	B1	110
Lawnside, N.J., U.S.	*D2	107
Lawra, Ghana	D4	45
Lawrence, N.Z.	P12	51
Lawrence, In., U.S.	E5	91
Lawrence, Ks., U.S.	D8	93
Lawrence, Ma., U.S.	A5	98
Lawrence, Mi., U.S.	F4	99
Lawrence, Ms., U.S.	C4	101
Lawrence, Ne., U.S.	D7	104
Lawrence, N.Y., U.S.	k13	109
Lawrence, co., Al., U.S.	F1	115
Lawrence, co., Al., U.S.	A2	78
Lawrence, co., Ar., U.S.	A4	81
Lawrence, co., Il., U.S.	E6	90
Lawrence, co., In., U.S.	G4	91
Lawrence, co., Ky., U.S.	B7	94
Lawrence, co., Ms., U.S.	D3	101
Lawrence, co., Mo., U.S.	D4	102
Lawrence, co., Oh., U.S.	D3	112
Lawrence, co., Pa., U.S.	E1	115
Lawrence, co., S.D., U.S.	C2	118
Lawrence, co., Tn., U.S.	B4	119
Lawrenceburg, In., U.S.	F8	91
Lawrenceburg, Ky., U.S.	B5	94
Lawrenceburg, Tn., U.S.	B4	119
Lawrence Park, Pa., U.S.	B1	115
Lawrence Station, On., Can.	D2	73
Lawrencetown, N.S., Can.	E4	71
Lawrenceville, On., Can.	E3	73
Lawrenceville, Ga., U.S.	C3	87
Lawrenceville, Il., U.S.	E6	90
Lawrenceville, N.J., U.S.	C3	107
Lawrenceville, N.Y., U.S.	f10	109
Lawrenceville, Pa., U.S.	C7	115
Lawrenceville, Va., U.S.	D5	123
Lawshe, Oh., U.S.	D2	112
Lawson, Mo., U.S.	B3	102
Lawson, Ar., U.S.	D3	81
Lawsonia, Md., U.S.	E6	97
Lawsonville, N.C., U.S.	A2	110
Lawtell, La., U.S.	D3	95
Lawtey, Fl., U.S.	B4	86
Lawton, Ky., U.S.	B1	92
Lawton, Ky., U.S.	B6	94
Lawton, Mi., U.S.	F5	99
Lawton, N.D., U.S.	A7	111
Lawton, Ok., U.S.	C3	113
Lawton, W.V., U.S.	D4	125
Lawyersville, N.Y., U.S.	C6	109
Lawz, Jabal al, mtn., Sau. Ar.	H10	40
Laxou, Fr.	C7	16
Lay, Cap, c., Viet.	D7	35
Lay Dam, Al., U.S.	C3	78
Lay Lake, res., Al., U.S.	B3	78
Layland, W.V., U.S.	n14	125
Layou, St. Vin.	U26	65
Laysan Island, i., Hi., U.S.	k13	88
Laysville, Ct., U.S.	D6	84
Layton, Ut., U.S.	B4	121
Laytonsville, Md., U.S.	B3	97
Laytonville, Ca., U.S.	C2	82
Lazdijai, Sov. Un.	A7	26
Lazear, Co., U.S.	C3	83
Łaziska Górne, Pol.	g9	26
Lea, co., N.M., U.S.	D6	108
Lea, stm., Eng., U.K.	k12	10
Leach, Ok., U.S.	A7	113
Leachville, Ar., U.S.	B5	81
Leacross, Sk., Can.	D3	75
Lead, S.D., U.S.	C2	118
Leadbetter Point, c., Wa., U.S.	C1	124
Leader, Sk., Can.	G1	75
Lead Hill, Ar., U.S.	A3	81
Lead Hill, hill, Mo., U.S.	D5	102
Lead Mountain, mtn., Me., U.S.	D4	96
Lead Mountain Ponds, l., Me., U.S.	D4	96
Leadore, Id., U.S.	E5	89
Leadville, Co., U.S.	B4	83
Leadwood, Mo., U.S.	D7	102
Leaf, stm., Ms., U.S.	D5	101
Leaf River, Il., U.S.	A4	90
League City, Tx., U.S.	*r14	120
Leah, Ga., U.S.	C4f	87
Leake, co., Ms., U.S.	C4	101
Leakesville, Ms., U.S.	D5	101
Leakey, Tx., U.S.	E3	120
Leal, N.D., U.S.	B7	111
Lealman, Fl., U.S.	p10	86
Leamington, On., Can.	E2	73
Leamington (Royal Leamington Spa), Eng., U.K.	D6	10
Leamington, Ut., U.S.	D3	121
Leane, Lough, l., Ire.	E2	11
Leapwood, Tn., U.S.	B3	119
Learned, Ms., U.S.	C3	101
Leary, Ga., U.S.	E2	87
Leasburg, Mo., U.S.	C6	102
Leasburg, N.C., U.S.	A3	110
Leaside (part of East York), On., Can.	m15	73
Leask, Sk., Can.	D2	75
Leatherhead, Eng., U.K.	m12	10
Leatherman Peak, mtn., Id., U.S.	E5	89
Leatherwood, Ky., U.S.	C6	94
L'Eau Frais Creek, stm., Ar., U.S.	C3	81
Leavenworth, In., U.S.	H5	91
Leavenworth, Ks., U.S.	C9	93
Leavenworth, Wa., U.S.	B5	124
Leavenworth, co., Ks., U.S.	C8	93
Leavittsburg, Oh., U.S.	A5	112
Leawood, Ks., U.S.	k16	93
Łeba, Pol.	A4	26
Lebam, Wa., U.S.	C2	124
Lebanon, De., U.S.	D4	85
Lebanon, Il., U.S.	E4	90
Lebanon, In., U.S.	D5	91
Lebanon, Ks., U.S.	C5	93
Lebanon, Ky., U.S.	C4	94
Lebanon, Mo., U.S.	D5	102
Lebanon, Ne., U.S.	D5	104
Lebanon, N.H., U.S.	C2	106
Lebanon, Oh., U.S.	C1	112
Lebanon, Or., U.S.	C4	114
Lebanon, Pa., U.S.	F9	115
Lebanon, S.D., U.S.	B6	118
Lebanon, Tn., U.S.	A5	119
Lebanon, Va., U.S.	f9	123
Lebanon, co., Pa., U.S.	F8	115
Lebanon, ctry., Asia	B3	38
Lebanon Junction, Ky., U.S.	C4	94
Lebeau, La., U.S.	D4	95
Lebec, Ca., U.S.	E4	82
Lebedin, Sov. Un.	F10	27
Lebedyan, Sov. Un.	E12	27
Le Biot, Fr.	D2	21
Le Blanc, Fr.	D4	16
Le Blanc-Mesnil, Fr.	g10	16
Lebo, Ks., U.S.	D8	93
Lebo, Zaire	A3	48
Łębork, Pol.	A4	26
Le Bourg-d'Oisans, Fr.	D2	20
Le Bourget, Fr.	g10	16
Le Bouscat, Fr.	E3	16
Le Brassus, Switz.	C1	21
Lebret, Sk., Can.	G4	75
Lebrija, Spain	D2	22
Lebu, Chile	B2	54
Lebyazhye, Sov. Un.	B7	28
Le Cateau, Fr.	B5	16
Lecce, Italy	D7	23
Lecco, Italy	B2	23
Lecco, Lake, l., Italy	E7	21
Le Center, Mn., U.S.	F5	100
Lech, stm., Eur.	D5	18
Le Chambon-Feugerolles, Fr.	E6	16
Le-Château, Fr.	E3	16
Lechbruck, F.R.Ger.	B6	20
Le Chesnay, Fr.	g9	16
Le Chesne, Fr.	E4	17
Leck, F.R.Ger.	A5	19
Le Claire, Ia., U.S.	C7	92
Leclercville, P.Q., Can.	C6	74
Lecompte, La., U.S.	C3	95
Lecompton, Ks., U.S.	C8	93
Léconi, Gabon	F2	46
Leconte, Mount, mtn., Tn., U.S.	D10	119
Lecontes Mills, Pa., U.S.	D5	115
Le Coteau, Fr.	D6	16
Le Creusot, Fr.	D6	16
Le Croisic, Fr.	D2	16
Le Crotoy, Fr.	B4	16
Lectoure, Fr.	F4	16
Łęczyca, Pol.	C4	26
Ledbetter, N.C., U.S.	C3	110
Ledbury, Eng., U.K.	B5	12
Lečdice, Czech.	n17	20
Ledeberg (part of Gent), Bel.	D3	17
Ledesma, Spain	B2	22
Ledford, Il., U.S.	F5	90
Ledger, Mt., U.S.	B5	103
Ledgewood, N.J., U.S.	B3	107
Ledo, India	C10	36
Ledoux, N.M., U.S.	B4	108
Leduc, Ab., Can.	C4	68
Ledyard, Ct., U.S.	D7	84
Ledyard, Ia., U.S.	A3	92
Lee, Fl., U.S.	B3	86
Lee, Il., U.S.	B5	90
Lee, Me., U.S.	C4	96
Lee, Ma., U.S.	B1	98
Lee, Nv., U.S.	C6	105
Lee, N.H., U.S.	D4	106
Lee, Tn., U.S.	D8	119
Lee, co., Al., U.S.	C4	78
Lee, co., Ar., U.S.	C5	81
Lee, co., Fl., U.S.	F5	86
Lee, co., Ga., U.S.	E2	87
Lee, co., Il., U.S.	B4	90
Lee, co., Ia., U.S.	D6	92
Lee, co., Ky., U.S.	C6	94
Lee, co., Ms., U.S.	A5	101
Lee, co., N.C., U.S.	B3	110
Lee, co., S.C., U.S.	C7	117
Lee, co., Tx., U.S.	D4	120
Lee, co., Va., U.S.	f8	123
Lee, stm., Ire.	E2	10
Lee, Lake, l., Ms., U.S.	B3	101
Lee Center, Il., U.S.	B4	90
Leechburg, Pa., U.S.	E2	115
Leech Lake, l., Sk., Can.	F4	75
Leech Lake, l., Mn., U.S.	C4	100
Leech Lake Indian Reservation, Mn., U.S.	C4	100
Leechville, N.C., U.S.	B6	110
Lee Creek, stm., U.S.	B1	81
Leedey, Ok., U.S.	B2	113
Leedom Estates, De., U.S.	*B3	85
Leeds, Eng., U.K.	D6	10
Leeds, Al., U.S.	B3	78
Leeds, N.D., U.S.	A6	111
Leeds, S.C., U.S.	B5	117
Leeds, Ut., U.S.	F2	121
Leeds, co., On., Can.	C8	73
Leeds Point, N.J., U.S.	E4	107
Leeds-Village, P.Q., Can.	C6	74
Leek, Eng., U.K.	A5	12
Leelanau, co., Mi., U.S.	D5	99
Leelanau, Lake, l., Mi., U.S.	C5	99
Leenane, Ire.	D2	11
Lee Park, Pa., U.S.	n17	115
Leer, F.R.Ger.	B3	18
Leesburg, Al., U.S.	A4	78
Leesburg, Fl., U.S.	D5	86
Leesburg, Ga., U.S.	E2	87
Leesburg, In., U.S.	B6	91
Leesburg, N.J., U.S.	E3	107
Leesburg, Oh., U.S.	C2	112
Leesburg, Va., U.S.	A5	123
Lees Landing, La., U.S.	h11	95
Lees Summit, Mo., U.S.	C3	102
Leesville, Ct., U.S.	*C6	84
Leesville, In., U.S.	G5	91
Leesville, La., U.S.	C2	95
Leesville, Oh., U.S.	B4	112
Leesville, S.C., U.S.	D4	117
Leesville, Tx., U.S.	E4	120
Leesville Lake, res., Va., U.S.	C3	123
Leetes Island, Ct., U.S.	D5	84
Leeton, Austl.	G6	51
Leeton, Mo., U.S.	C4	102
Leetonia, Oh., U.S.	B5	112
Leetsdale, Pa., U.S.	h13	115
Leeuwarden, Neth.	A6	16
Leeuwin, Cape, c., Austl.	F2	50
Leeville, La., U.S.	E5	95
Lee Vining, Ca., U.S.	D4	82
Leeward Islands, is., N.A.	H13	64
Le Ferriere, Italy	h9	23
Leffingwell, Ct., U.S.	C7	84
Leflore, Ok., U.S.	C7	113
Le Flore, co., Ok., U.S.	C7	113
Lefors, Tx., U.S.	B2	120
Le François, Mart.	I14	64
Lefroy, On., Can.	C5	73
Lefroy, Lake, l., Austl.	F3	50
Legal, Ab., Can.	C4	68
Leganés, Spain	p17	22
Legau, F.R.Ger.	E5	18
Legazpi, Phil.	C6	34
Leggett, Ca., U.S.	C2	82
Leghorn see Livorno, Italy	C3	23
Legionowo, Pol.	k13	26
Legnago, Italy	D7	20
Legnano, Italy	B2	23
Legnica (Liegnitz), Pol.	C4	26
Le Gore, Ind.	A3	97
Le Grand, Ca., U.S.	D3	82
Le Grand, Ia., U.S.	B5	92
Le Grand-Quevilly, Fr.	g10	16
Leh, India	B6	36
Le Havre, Fr.	C4	16
Lehi, Ut., U.S.	C4	121
Lehigh, Ia., U.S.	B3	92
Lehigh, Ks., U.S.	D6	93
Lehigh, Ok., U.S.	C5	113
Lehigh, co., Pa., U.S.	E10	115
Lehigh, stm., Pa., U.S.	E10	115
Lehigh Acres, Fl., U.S.	F5	86
Lehighton, Pa., U.S.	E10	115
Lehman, Pa., U.S.	n16	115
Lehman Caves National Monument, Nv., U.S.	C7	105
Lehr, N.D., U.S.	C6	111
Lehrte, F.R.Ger.	B4	18
Lehua Island, i., Hi., U.S.	A1	88
Leiah, Pak.	E3	37
Leibnitz, Aus.	E7	18
Leicester, Eng., U.K.	D6	10
Leicester, Ma., U.S.	B4	98
Leicester, N.Y., U.S.	C3	109
Leicester, Vt., U.S.	D2	122
Leicester Junction, Vt., U.S.	D2	122
Leicestershire, co., Eng., U.K.	B6	12
Leichhardt, Austl.	*F9	50
Leichhardt, stm., Austl.	C7	50
Leiden, Neth.	A6	16
Leigh, Ne., U.S.	C8	104
Leigh Creek, Austl.	F6	50
Leighton, Al., U.S.	A2	78
Leinan, Sk., Can.	G2	75
Leine, stm., Eur.	B4	18
Leinster, hist reg., Ire.	D4	11
Leinster, Mount, mtn., Ire.	I5	11
Leipalingis, Sov. Un.	A7	26
Leipers Fork, Tn., U.S.	B5	119
Leipsic, De., U.S.	D3	85
Leipsic, In., U.S.	G5	91
Leipsic, Oh., U.S.	A2	112
Leipsic, stm., De., U.S.	C3	85
Leipzig, Sk., Can.	E1	75
Leipzig, Ger.D.R.	C6	18
Leiria, Port.	C1	22
Leisnig, Ger.D.R.	C6	19
Leisure City, Fl., U.S.	s13	86
Leitchfield, Ky., U.S.	C9	71
Leiter, Wy., U.S.	B6	127
Leitersburg, Md., U.S.	A3	97
Leiters Ford, In., U.S.	B5	91
Leith (part of Edinburgh), Scot., U.K.	E5	13
Leith, N.D., U.S.	C4	111
Leitha, stm., Eur.	B3	24
Leitrim, co., Ire.	C3	11
Leiva, Cerro, mtn., Col.	C3	60
Leizhou Bay, b., China	B9	35
Lejunior, Ky., U.S.	D6	94
Lek, stm., Neth.	C4	17
Leka, i., Nor.	E14	14
Lekeba, i., Fiji	I16	52
Leksand, Swe.	G6	14
Leksula, Indon.	F7	34
Lela, Tx., U.S.	B2	120
Le Lamentin, Mart.	S10	65
Leland, Il., U.S.	B5	90
Leland, Ia., U.S.	A4	92
Leland, Ms., U.S.	B3	101
Leland, Mi., U.S.	C5	99
Leland, Ok., U.S.	B6	113
Leland, Tx., U.S.	C4	120
Leleiwi Point, c., Hi., U.S.	D7	88
Leleque, Arg.	C2	54
Lelia Lake, Tx., U.S.	B2	120
Leloaloa, Am. Sam.	F13	52
Le Locle, Switz.	E3	18
Le Lorrain, Mart.	S10	65
Leloup, Ks., U.S.	D8	93
Lelystad, Neth.	F2	121
Le Maire, Estrecho de, strt., Arg.	h12	54
Le Mans, Fr.	C4	16
Le Marin, Mart.	I14	64
Le Mars, Fr.	B1	92
Lemasters, Pa., U.S.	G6	115
Lemay, Mo., U.S.	*g13	102
Lembach, Fr.	F7	17
Lemberg, Sk., Can.	G4	75
Lemdiyya, Alg.	B5	44
Leme, Braz.	m8	56
Lemelerveld, Neth.	B6	17
Lemery, Phil.	p13	34
Lemesós (Limassol), Cyp.	E9	40
Lemgo, F.R.Ger.	B4	18
Lemhi, Id., U.S.	E5	89
Lemhi, co., Id., U.S.	E5	89
Lemhi, stm., Id., U.S.	E5	89
Lemhi Pass, Id., U.S.	E5	89
Lemhi Range, mts., Id., U.S.	E5	89
Lemieux, P.Q., Can.	C5	74
Lemitar, N.M., U.S.	C3	108
Lemmer, Neth.	B5	17
Lemmon, S.D., U.S.	B3	118
Lemmon, Mount, mtn., Az., U.S.	E5	80
Lemmon Valley, Nv., U.S.	D2	105
Lemnos see Límnos, i., Grc.	C5	40
Lemon, Lake, l., In., U.S.	F5	91
Lemon Fair, stm., Vt., U.S.	C2	122
Lemon Grove, Ca., U.S.	o15	82
Lemon Island, i., S.C., U.S.	G6	117
Lemons, Mo., U.S.	A4	102
Lemont, Il., U.S.	B5	90
Lemont, Pa., U.S.	E6	115
Lemonweir, stm., Wi., U.S.	D3	126
Lemoore, Ca., U.S.	D4	82
Lemoore Naval Air Station, mil., Ca., U.S.	D4	82
Le Moyen, La., U.S.	D3	95
Lemoyne, Ne., U.S.	C4	104
Lemoyne, Oh., U.S.	f7	112
Lempa, stm., N.A.	D3	62
Lem Peak, mtn., Id., U.S.	E5	89
Lempster, N.H., U.S.	D2	106
Lemsford, Sk., Can.	G1	75
Lemvig, Den.	B2	15
Léré, Chad	D2	46
Lena, Il., U.S.	A4	90
Lena, La., U.S.	C3	95
Lena, Ms., U.S.	C4	101
Lena, Wi., U.S.	D5	126
Lena, stm., Sov. Un.	C15	29
Lena, Il., U.S.	B3	90
Lenapah, Ok., U.S.	A6	113
Lenawee, co., Mi., U.S.	G6	99
Lençóis, Braz.	D7	57
Lendinara, Italy	D7	20
Lenexa, Ks., U.S.	D9	93
Leney, Sk., Can.	E2	75
Lengby, Mn., U.S.	C3	100
Lengede, F.R.Ger.	A5	19
Lengerich, F.R.Ger.	A2	19
Lenghu, China	D3	31
Lenhartsville, Pa., U.S.	E10	115
Leninabad, Sov. Un.	E9	29
Leninakan, Sov. Un.	E2	28
Leningrad, Sov. Un.	C6	29
Leningradskaya, sci., Ant.	C28	7
Lenino, Sov. Un.	n17	27
Leninogorsk, Sov. Un.	D11	29
Lenin Peak, mtn., Sov. Un.	*F10	29
Leninsk, Sov. Un.	G15	27
Leninsk-Kuznetskiy, Sov. Un.	D11	29
Leninskoye, Sov. Un.	C7	29
Lenkoran, Sov. Un.	C3	39
Lenk, Switz.	F7	29
Lenne, stm., F.R.Ger.	B6	113
Lennox, S.D., U.S.	B2	19
Lennox, Isla, i., Chile	D9	118
Lennox and Addington, co., On., Can.	k12	54
Lennoxville, P.Q., Can.	C7	73
Lenoir, N.C., U.S.	D6	74
Lenoir, co., N.C., U.S.	B1	110
Lenoir City, Tn., U.S.	B5	110
Lenora, Ks., U.S.	D9	119
Lenorah, Tx., U.S.	C3	93
Lenore, Mb., Can.	C2	120
Lenore, Id., U.S.	E1	70
Lenore Lake, l., Sk., Can.	C2	89
Lenore Lake, l., Wa., U.S.	E3	75
Lenox, Ga., U.S.	B6	124
Lenox, Ia., U.S.	E3	87
Lenox, Ma., U.S.	D3	92
Lenox, Mo., U.S.	B1	98
Lenox, Tn., U.S.	D6	102
Lenox Dale, Ma., U.S.	A2	119
Lens, Fr.	B1	98
Lentner, Mo., U.S.	B5	16
Lenzburg, Il., U.S.	B5	102
Lenzen, Ger.D.R.	E4	90
Lenzerheide, Switz.	E5	15
Léo, Burkina	C8	21
Léogâne, Haiti	D4	45
Leola, S.D., U.S.	E7	64
Leola, Tn., U.S.	B7	118
Leoma, Tn., U.S.	B4	119
Leominster, Eng., U.K.	B5	12
Leominster, Ma., U.S.	A4	98
León, Nic.	E7	63
León, Spain	A3	22
Leon, Ia., U.S.	D4	92
Leon, Ks., U.S.	E7	93
Leon, N.Y., U.S.	C1	109
Leon, Ok., U.S.	D4	113
Leon, W.V., U.S.	C3	125
Leon, co., Fl., U.S.	B2	86
Leon, co., Tx., U.S.	D4	120
León, hist reg., Spain	B3	22
León [de los Aldamas], Mex.	C4	63
Leona, Ks., U.S.	C8	93
Leona, Tx., U.S.	D5	120
Leonard, On., Can.	h13	73
Leonard, Mi., U.S.	F7	99
Leonard, Mn., U.S.	C3	100
Leonard, Mo., U.S.	B5	102
Leonard, N.D., U.S.	C8	111
Leonard, Ok., U.S.	B6	113
Leonard, Tx., U.S.	C4	120
Leonardo, N.J., U.S.	C4	107
Leonardsville, N.Y., U.S.	C5	109
Leonardsville, N.B., Can.	E3	71
Leonardtown, Md., U.S.	D4	97
Leonardville, Nmb.	B2	49
Leonberg, F.R.Ger.	E3	19
León [de los Aldamas], Mex.	C4	63
Leone, Am. Sam.	G13	52
Leone Bay, b., Am. Sam.	G13	52
Leonforte, Italy	F5	23
Leonia, Fl., U.S.	u15	86
Leonia, N.J., U.S.	h9	107
Leonidas, Mi., U.S.	F5	99
Leonidhion, Grc.	D4	25
Leonora, Austl.	E3	50
Leonville, La., U.S.	D4	95
Leoti, Ks., U.S.	D2	93
Leoville, Sk., Can.	D2	75
Lepanto, Ar., U.S.	B5	81
Lepe, Spain	D2	22
Lepel, Sov. Un.	D7	27
Le Petit-Quevilly, Fr.	C4	16
Lépihué, Chile	C2	54
Leping, China	J7	32
L'Épiphanie, P.Q., Can.	D4	74
Le-Plain-de-Coravillers, Fr.	A2	21
Le Plessis-Belleville, Fr.	E2	17
Le Plessis-Robinson, Fr.	G10	16
Le Pont, Switz.	C1	21
Lepontine Alps, mts., Eur.	A2	23
Le Portel, Fr.	D9	12
Lepreau, N.B., Can.	D3	71
Lepreau, Point, c., N.B., Can.	D3	71
Lepsinsk, Sov. Un.	F25	8
Le Puy [-en-Velay], Fr.	E5	16
Le Quesnoy, Fr.	D3	17
Lequire, Ok., U.S.	B6	113
Le Raincy, Fr.	g11	16
Le Raysville, Pa., U.S.	C9	115
Lercara Friddi, Italy	F4	23
Léré, Chad	D2	46
Lérida, Col.	C3	60
Lérida, Spain	B6	22
Lérida, Spain	A4	22
Lerma, stm., Mex.	m13	63
Lerna, Il., U.S.	D5	90
Lerna, Il., U.S.	D5	90
Léros, i., Grc.	D6	40
Leross, Sk., Can.	F4	75
Leroux Wash, val., Az., U.S.	B5	80
Leroy, Sk., Can.	F3	75
Leroy, Al., U.S.	D1	78
Le Roy, Il., U.S.	C5	90
Leroy, Ks., U.S.	D8	93
Le Roy, La., U.S.	B3	91
Le Roy, Mi., U.S.	E5	99
Le Roy, Mn., U.S.	G6	100
Le Roy, N.Y., U.S.	C3	109
Leroy, N.D., U.S.	A8	111
Le Roy, Pa., U.S.	C8	115
Lerum, Swe.	A6	15
Le Russey, Fr.	D2	21
Lerwick, Scot., U.K.	g10	13
Lery, Lake, l., La., U.S.	k12	95
Les Abymes, Guad.	Q8	65
Le Saint-Esprit, Mart.	S11	65
Lesbos see Lésvos, i., Grc.	C5	40
Les Cayes, Haiti	E7	64
Les Diablerets, Switz.	B2	21
Les Éboulements, P.Q., Can.	B7	74
Les Echelles, Fr.	D1	20
Les Escoumins, P.Q., Can.	A8	74
Les Étroits, P.Q., Can.	o16	74
Les Fonds, P.Q., Can.		
Leshan, China	F7	31
Les Haudères, Switz.	C3	21
Les Lilas, Fr.	g10	16
Lesneven, Fr.	C1	16
Lesnoy, Sov. Un.	B4	28
Lesogorsk, Sov. Un.	B11	33
Lesotho, ctry., Afr.	C4	49
Lesozavodsk, Sov. Un.	E16	29
Lesparre, Fr.	E3	16
Les Pont-de-Cé, Fr.	D3	16
Les Rousses, Fr.	D1	21
Les Sables-d'Olonne, Fr.	D3	16
Lesser Antilles, is.	B4	53
Lesser Khingan Range (Xiao Hinggan Ling), mts., China	B10	31
Lesser Slave Lake, l., Ab., Can.	B3	68
Lesser Sunda Islands (Nusa Tenggara), is., Indon.	G5	34
Lessines, Bel.	D3	17
Lester, Al., U.S.	A2	78
Lester, Ia., U.S.	A1	92
Lester, W.V., U.S.	n13	125
Lester Prairie, Mn., U.S.	F4	100
Lesterville, Mo., U.S.	D7	102
Lesterville, S.D., U.S.	D8	118
Lestock, Sk., Can.	F3	75
Le Sueur, Mn., U.S.	F5	100
Le Sueur, co., Mn., U.S.	F5	100
Les Verrières, Switz.	C1	21
Lésvos (Lesbos), i., Grc.	C5	40
Leszno, Pol.	C4	26
Letart Falls, Oh., U.S.	D4	112
Letcher, S.D., U.S.	D7	118
Letcher, co., Ky., U.S.	C7	94
Le Teil, Fr.	E6	16
Letellier, Mb., Can.	E3	70
Letha, Id., U.S.	F2	89
Lethbridge, Ab., Can.	E4	68
Lethbridge, Nf., Can.	D5	72
Lethem, Guy.	B2	60
Le Thillot, Fr.	B2	20
Letiahau, stm., Bots.	B3	49
Leticia, Col.	D4	60
Leti Islands, is., Indon.	G7	34
Leto, Fl., U.S.	*E4	86
Letohatchee, Al., U.S.	C3	78
Letona, Ar., U.S.	B4	81
Letpadan, Burma	E10	36
Le Tréport, Fr.	B4	16
Le Touquet-Paris-Plage, Fr.	D9	17
Le Tourneau, U.S.	C3	101
Letterfrack, Ire.	D2	11
Letterkenny, Ire.	C3	10
Lettermullen, Ire.	D2	11
Letts, Ia., U.S.	C6	92
Letts, In., U.S.	F6	91
Lettsworth, La., U.S.	D4	95
Leucadia, Ca., U.S.	*F5	82
Leucas see Levkás, i., Grc.	C3	40
Leuctra see Lévktra, Grc.	g10	25
Leukerbad, Switz.	D4	21
Leuk, Switz.	D4	21
Leukerbad, Switz.	D4	21
Leupp, Az., U.S.	B5	80
Leupp Corner, Az., U.S.	B5	80
Leuser, mtn., Indon.	m11	34
Leushinskiy Tuman, Lake, l., Sov. Un.	B6	28
Leutkirch, F.R.Ger.	E6	20
Leuven (Louvain), Bel.	B6	16
Leuze, Bel.	D3	17
Levádhia, Grc.	C4	40
Levallois-Perret, Fr.	g10	16
Levan, Ut., U.S.	D4	121
Levanger, Nor.	F4	14
Levanna, mtn., Eur.	E7	16
Levant, Ks., U.S.	C2	93
Levant, Me., U.S.	D4	96
Leveaux Mountain, mtn., Mn., U.S.	k9	100
Levelland, Tx., U.S.	C1	120
Leven, Scot., U.K.	B5	13
Leveque, Cape, c., Austl.	C3	50
Leverett, Ma., U.S.	B2	98
Leverett Glacier, Ant.	A32	7
Levering, Mi., U.S.	C6	99
Leverkusen, F.R.Ger.	B1	19
Levice, Czech.	D5	26
Levick, Mount, mtn., Ant.	B29	7
Levie, Fr.	C1	21
Levier, Fr.	E5	16
Le Vigan, Fr.	E5	16
Levin, N.Z.	N15	51
Lévis, P.Q., Can.	C6	74
Lévis, co., P.Q., Can.	C6	74
Levisa Fork, stm., U.S.	C7	94
Levittown, N.Y., U.S.	E7	109
Levittown, Pa., U.S.	F12	115
Lévka, Grc.	C3	40
Lévkas, Grc.	C3	40
Lévktra (Leuctra), Grc.	g10	25
Levoča, Czech.	D6	26
Levuka, Fiji	H15	52
Levy, co., Fl., U.S.	C4	86
Levy Lake, l., Fl., U.S.	C4	86
Lewellen, Ne., U.S.	C4	104
Lewes, Eng., U.K.	E7	10
Lewes, De., U.S.	E5	85
Lewes and Rehoboth Canal, De., U.S.	F5	85
Lewis, In., U.S.	F3	91
Lewis, Ia., U.S.	C2	92
Lewis, Ks., U.S.	E4	93
Lewis, co., Id., U.S.	C2	89
Lewis, co., Ky., U.S.	B6	94
Lewis, co., Mo., U.S.	A6	102
Lewis, co., N.Y., U.S.	B5	109
Lewis, co., Tn., U.S.	B4	119
Lewis, co., Wa., U.S.	C4	124
Lewis, co., W.V., U.S.	C4	125
Lewis, i., Scot., U.K.	A3	10
Lewis, Butt of, c., Scot., U.K.	A3	10
Lewis and Clark, co., Mt., U.S.	C4	103
Lewis and Clark Cavern, Mt., U.S.	D5	103
Lewis and Clark Lake, res., U.S.	E8	118
Lewisberry, Pa., U.S.	F8	115
Lewisburg, Ky., U.S.	D3	94
Lewisburg, Oh., U.S.	C1	112
Lewisburg, Pa., U.S.	E8	115
Lewisburg, Tn., U.S.	B5	119
Lewisburg, W.V., U.S.	D4	125
Lewis Center, Oh., U.S.	B2	112
Lewis Creek, stm., Sk., Can.	D2	75
Lewis Creek, stm., Vt., U.S.	C2	122
Lewis Hills, hills, Nf., Can.	D2	72
Lewis Lake, l., Wy., U.S.	B2	127
Lewisport, Ky., U.S.	C3	94

Name	Map Ref	Page
Lewisporte, Nf., Can.	D4	72
Lewis Range, mts., N.A.	A5	76
Lewis Run, Pa., U.S.	C4	115
Lewis Smith Lake, res., Al., U.S.	B2	78
Lewiston, Id., U.S.	C1	89
Lewiston, Me., U.S.	D2	96
Lewiston, Mi., U.S.	D6	99
Lewiston, Mn., U.S.	G7	100
Lewiston, N.Y., U.S.	B1	109
Lewiston, Ut., U.S.	B4	121
Lewiston Peak, mtn., Ut., U.S.	C3	121
Lewiston Woodville, N.C., U.S.	A5	110
Lewistown, Il., U.S.	C3	90
Lewistown, Md., U.S.	A3	97
Lewistown, Mo., U.S.	A6	102
Lewistown, Mt., U.S.	C7	103
Lewistown, Pa., U.S.	E6	115
Lewisville, N.B., Can.	C5	71
Lewisville, Ar., U.S.	D2	81
Lewisville, Id., U.S.	F6	89
Lewisville, In., U.S.	E7	91
Lewisville, Mn., U.S.	G4	100
Lewisville, Oh., U.S.	C4	112
Lewisville Lake, res., Tx., U.S.	C4	120
Lewvan, Sk., Can.	G3	75
Lexa, Ar., U.S.	C5	81
Lexington, Al., U.S.	A2	78
Lexington, Ga., U.S.	C3	87
Lexington, Il., U.S.	C5	90
Lexington, In., U.S.	G6	91
Lexington, Ky., U.S.	B5	94
Lexington, Ma., U.S.	B5	98
Lexington, Mi., U.S.	E8	99
Lexington, Ms., U.S.	B3	101
Lexington, Mo., U.S.	B4	102
Lexington, Ne., U.S.	D6	104
Lexington, N.Y., U.S.	C6	109
Lexington, N.C., U.S.	B2	110
Lexington, Oh., U.S.	B3	112
Lexington, Ok., U.S.	B4	113
Lexington, Or., U.S.	B7	114
Lexington, S.C., U.S.	D5	117
Lexington, Tn., U.S.	B3	119
Lexington, Tx., U.S.	D4	120
Lexington, Va., U.S.	C3	123
Lexington, Wa., U.S.	C3	124
Lexington, co., S.C., U.S.	D5	117
Lexington Park, Md., U.S.	D5	97
Leyba, N.M., U.S.	B4	108
Leyburn, Eng., U.K.	F7	13
Leyond, stm., Mb., Can.	D3	70
Leysin, Switz.	D2	21
Leyte, i., Phil.	C6	34
Leżajsk, Pol.	C7	26
Lezha, Alb.	B2	40
Lézignan, Fr.	F5	16
Lgov, Sov. Un.	F10	27
Lhasa, China	F3	31
L'Haÿ-les-Roses, Fr.	g10	14
Lhazê, China	C11	37
Lhokseumawe, Indon.	k11	34
Lhoksukon, Indon.	J2	35
Liangcheng, China	D5	32
Liangping, China	I2	32
Lianhua, China	K5	32
Lianjiang, China	B9	35
Lianyungang, China	E8	31
Lianyuan, China	G8	32
Liaocheng, China	E9	32
Liaodong Bay, b., China	C9	31
Liao He, stm., China	C9	31
Liaoning, prov., China	C9	31
Liaotung Bay see Liaodong Bay, b., China	E9	32
Liaotung Peninsula, pen., China	D9	31
Liaoyang, China	C9	31
Liaoyuan, China	C10	31
Liard, stm., Can.	E4	17
Liart, Fr.	E4	17
Liathach, mtn., Scot., U.K.	C3	13
Líbano, Col.	C2	60
Libau, Mb., Can.	D3	70
Libby, Mt., U.S.	B1	103
Libčice [nad Vltavou], Czech.	n17	26
Libčhov, Czech.	n17	26
Libenge, Zaire	A2	48
Liberal, Ks., U.S.	E3	93
Liberal, Mo., U.S.	D3	102
Liberec, Czech.	C3	26
Liberia, C.R.	E7	63
Liberia, ctry., Afr.	E3	45
Libertad, Ven.	B4	60
Libertador General Bernardo O'Higgins, prov., Chile	A2	54
Libertador General San Martín, Arg.	D3	55
Liberty, Sk., Can.	F3	75
Liberty, Id., U.S.	G7	89
Liberty, Il., U.S.	D2	90
Liberty, In., U.S.	E8	91
Liberty, Ky., U.S.	C5	94
Liberty, Me., U.S.	D3	96
Liberty, Ms., U.S.	D3	101
Liberty, Mo., U.S.	B3	102
Liberty, Ne., U.S.	D9	104
Liberty, N.Y., U.S.	D6	109
Liberty, N.C., U.S.	B3	110
Liberty, Pa., U.S.	C7	115
Liberty, S.C., U.S.	B2	117
Liberty, Tn., U.S.	C8	119
Liberty, Tx., U.S.	D5	120
Liberty, co., Fl., U.S.	B5	124
Liberty, co., Ga., U.S.	E5	87
Liberty, co., Mt., U.S.	B5	103
Liberty, co., Tx., U.S.	D5	120
Liberty Acres, Ca., U.S.	*n12	82
Liberty Center, Ia., U.S.	C7	91
Liberty Center, Oh., U.S.	A1	112
Liberty Corner, N.J., U.S.	B3	107
Liberty Grove, Md., U.S.	A5	97
Liberty Hill, Ct., U.S.	C6	84
Liberty Hill, S.C., U.S.	C6	117
Liberty Lake, Wa., U.S.	g14	124
Liberty Lake, res., Md., U.S.	A4	97
Liberty Mills, In., U.S.	B6	91
Libertytown, Md., U.S.	B3	97
Libertyville, Il., U.S.	A6	90
Libertyville, Ia., U.S.	D5	92
Libiron, i., Marsh Is.	S18	52
Liblar, F.R.Ger.	C1	19
Libourne, Fr.	E4	16
Libramont, Bel.	E5	17
Libreville, Gabon	E1	46
Libušín, Czech.	n17	26
Libya, ctry., Afr.	C5	45
Libyan Desert, des., Afr.	C4	43
Libyan Plateau, plat., Afr.	B4	43
Licantén, Chile	B2	54
Licata, Italy	F4	23
Lice, Tur.	C13	40
Licenza, Italy	g9	23
Lichfield, Eng., U.K.	B6	12
Lichinga, Moz.	D6	48
Lichtenburg, S. Afr.	C4	49
Lichtenfels, F.R.Ger.	C6	19
Lichtenstein, Ger.D.R.	C7	19
Lick Creek, stm., Tn., U.S.	C11	119
Licking, Mo., U.S.	D6	102
Licking, co., Oh., U.S.	B3	112
Licking, stm., Ky., U.S.	B6	94
Licking, North Fork, stm., Ky., U.S.	B5	94
Licking, South Fork, stm., Ky., U.S.	B5	94
Licosa, Point, c., Italy	D5	23
Licungó, stm., Moz.	A6	49
Lida, Sov. Un.	E5	27
Lida, Lake, l., Mn., U.S.	D3	100
Liddel, stm., U.K.	E6	13
Lidderdale, Ia., U.S.	B3	92
Lidgerwood, N.D., U.S.	C8	111
Lidhult, Swe.	B7	15
Lidice, Czech.	C3	26
Lidingö, Swe.	H8	14
Lidköping, Swe.	H5	14
Lido di Roma, Italy	h8	23
Lidzbark Warmiński, Pol.	A6	26
Liebenthal, Sk., Can.	G1	75
Liebenthal, Ks., U.S.	D4	93
Lieberose, Ger.D.R.	B9	19
Liechtenstein, ctry., Eur.	E14	4
Liège (Luik), Bel.	B6	16
Liège, prov., Bel.	D5	17
Liege, stm., Ab., Can.	A4	68
Liegnitz see Legnica, Pol.	C4	26
Lieksa, Fin.	F14	14
Lienen, F.R.Ger.	A2	19
Lienz, Aus.	E6	19
Liepāja, Sov. Un.	C3	27
Lier (Lierre), Bel.	B6	16
Lierneux, Bel.	D5	17
Lierre see Lier, Bel.	B6	16
Liestal, Switz.	E3	18
Liévin, Fr.	D2	17
Lièvre, Rivière du, stm., P.Q., Can.	D2	74
Lièvres, Île aux, i., P.Q., Can.	B8	74
Liffey, stm., Ire.	D3	10
Lifford, Ire.	*C3	10
Liftwood, De., U.S.	*A3	85
Light, Ar., U.S.	A5	81
Lighthouse Inlet, b., S.C., U.S.	k12	117
Lighthouse Point, Fl., U.S.	*F6	86
Lighthouse Point, c., Fl., U.S.	C2	86
Lighthouse Point, c., Mi., U.S.	E3	99
Lighthouse Point, c., Mi., U.S.	C5	99
Lightning Creek, stm., Wy., U.S.	C8	127
Lightning Ridge, Austl.	D6	51
Lignite, N.D., U.S.	A3	111
Lignum, Va., U.S.	B5	123
Ligny-en-Barrois, Fr.	F5	17
Ligonha, stm., Moz.	E6	48
Ligonier, In., U.S.	B6	91
Ligonier, Pa., U.S.	F3	115
Ligovo (part of Leningrad), Sov. Un.	s31	14
Liguria, prov., Italy	E4	20
Liguria, hist reg., Italy	B2	23
Ligurian Apennines, mts., Italy	E4	20
Ligurian Sea, Eur.	C2	23
Lihue, Hi., U.S.	B2	88
Lijiang, China	F5	31
Lijin, China	F8	32
Likasi, Zaire	D4	48
Likely, B.C., Can.	C7	69
Likely, Ca., U.S.	B3	82
Likhoslavl, Sov. Un.	n18	27
Likino-Dulevo, Sov. Un.	E8	102
Lilbourn, Mo., U.S.	h8	87
Liliburn, Ga., U.S.	h8	87
L'Île-Rousse, Fr.	C2	23
Lilesville, N.C., U.S.	C3	110
Liling, China	K5	32
Lille, Fr.	B5	16
Lille, Me., U.S.	A4	96
Lille Bælt, strt., Den.	C3	15
Lillehammer, Nor.	G4	14
Lillers, Fr.	D2	17
Lillesand, Nor.	H3	14
Lillestrøm, Nor.	H4	14
Lillian, Al., U.S.	E2	78
Lillian, Tx., U.S.	n9	120
Lillie, La., U.S.	B3	95
Lillington, N.C., U.S.	B4	110
Lillionah, Lake, l., Ct., U.S.	C2	84
Lilly, Pa., U.S.	F4	115
Lilly Fork, stm., W.V., U.S.	m13	125
Lilly Grove, W.V., U.S.	D3	125
Lilongwe, Mwi.	D5	48
Lily, Ky., U.S.	C5	94
Lily, S.D., U.S.	B8	118
Lily, Wi., U.S.	C5	126
Lim, stm., Yugo.	D4	24
Lima, Para.	D4	55
Lima, Peru	D2	58
Lima, Mt., U.S.	F5	103
Lima, N.Y., U.S.	C3	109
Lima, Oh., U.S.	B1	112
Lima, dept., Peru	D2	58
Lima, stm., Eur.	D2	22
Lima Duarte, Braz.	C4	57
Limanowa, Pol.	D6	26
Lima Reservoir, res., Mt., U.S.	F4	103
Limassol see Lemesós, Cyp.	B5	11
Limavady, N. Ire., U.K.	B5	11
Limay, stm., Arg.	B3	54
Limay Mahuida, Arg.	B3	54
Limbach [-Oberfrohna], Ger.D.R.	C7	19
Limbe, Cam.	E1	46
Limbé, Haiti	E7	64
Limburg, F.R.Ger.	C4	18
Limburg, prov., Bel.	D5	17
Limburg, prov., Neth.	D5	17
Lime City, Oh., U.S.	e6	112
Limedale, In., U.S.	E4	91
Limeil-Brévannes, Fr.	h10	16
Limeira, Braz.	C3	56
Limerick, Sk., Can.	H2	75
Limerick, Ire.	D2	10
Limerick, Me., U.S.	E2	96
Limerick, R.I., U.S.	B3	116
Lime Rock, Ct., U.S.	B2	84
Lime Springs, Ia., U.S.	A5	92
Limestone, Ar., U.S.	B2	81
Limestone, Fl., U.S.	E5	86
Limestone, Me., U.S.	B5	96
Limestone, N.Y., U.S.	C2	109
Limestone, Pa., U.S.	D3	115
Limestone, co., Al., U.S.	A2	78
Limestone, co., Tx., U.S.	D4	120
Limestone Bay, b., Mb., Can.	C2	70
Limestone Lake, l., Mb., Can.	A4	70
Limestone Point, pen., Mb., Can.	C2	70
Limeton, Va., U.S.	B4	123
Lime Village, Ak., U.S.	C8	79
Limfjorden, strt., Den.	B3	15
Limmen Bight, Austl.	B6	50
Límnos (Lemnos), i., Grc.	C5	40
Limoeiro, Braz.	C3	57
Limoeiro do Norte, Braz.	C3	57
Limoges, On., Can.	B9	73
Limoges, Fr.	E4	16
Limón, C.R.	E8	63
Limón, Hond.	D7	63
Limon, Co., U.S.	B6	83
Limón, Bahia, b., Pan.	k11	62
Limousin, hist reg., Fr.	E4	16
Limousin Plateau, plat., Fr.	E4	16
Limoux, Fr.	F5	16
Limpopo, stm., Afr.	B5	49
Linah, Sau. Ar.	H14	40
Linares, Chile	B2	54
Linares, Col.	C2	60
Linares, Mex.	C5	63
Linares, Spain	C4	22
Linares, Braz.	E2	57
Linaro, Cape, c., Italy	D2	23
Lince, Peru	*D2	58
Linchuan, China	F8	31
Lincoln, Arg.	A4	54
Lincoln, On., Can.	D5	73
Lincoln, Eng., U.K.	D6	10
Lincoln, Al., U.S.	B3	78
Lincoln, Ar., U.S.	B1	81
Lincoln, Ca., U.S.	C3	82
Lincoln, De., U.S.	E4	85
Lincoln, Id., U.S.	F7	89
Lincoln, Il., U.S.	C4	90
Lincoln, Ks., U.S.	C5	93
Lincoln, Me., U.S.	C4	96
Lincoln, Ma., U.S.	g10	98
Lincoln, Mi., U.S.	D7	99
Lincoln, Mo., U.S.	C4	102
Lincoln, Mt., U.S.	D4	103
Lincoln, Ne., U.S.	D9	104
Lincoln, N.M., U.S.	D4	108
Lincoln, Tn., U.S.	B5	119
Lincoln, Vt., U.S.	C3	122
Lincoln, Va., U.S.	A5	123
Lincoln, Wa., U.S.	B7	124
Lincoln, co., Ar., U.S.	D4	81
Lincoln, co., Co., U.S.	C7	83
Lincoln, co., Ga., U.S.	C4	87
Lincoln, co., Id., U.S.	G4	89
Lincoln, co., Ks., U.S.	C5	93
Lincoln, co., Ky., U.S.	C5	94
Lincoln, co., La., U.S.	B3	95
Lincoln, co., Me., U.S.	D3	96
Lincoln, co., Mn., U.S.	F2	100
Lincoln, co., Ms., U.S.	D3	101
Lincoln, co., Mo., U.S.	B7	102
Lincoln, co., Mt., U.S.	B1	103
Lincoln, co., Ne., U.S.	D5	104
Lincoln, co., Nv., U.S.	F6	105
Lincoln, co., N.M., U.S.	D4	108
Lincoln, co., N.C., U.S.	B1	110
Lincoln, co., Ok., U.S.	B5	113
Lincoln, co., Or., U.S.	C3	114
Lincoln, co., S.D., U.S.	D9	118
Lincoln, co., Tn., U.S.	B5	119
Lincoln, co., Wa., U.S.	B7	124
Lincoln, co., W.V., U.S.	C2	125
Lincoln, co., Wi., U.S.	C4	126
Lincoln, co., Wy., U.S.	D2	127
Lincoln, Mount, mtn., Co., U.S.	B4	83
Lincoln Acres, Ca., U.S.	o15	82
Lincoln Center, Me., U.S.	C4	96
Lincoln Center, Ks., U.S.	C5	93
Lincoln City, In., U.S.	H4	91
Lincoln City, Or., U.S.	C2	114
Lincoln Heights, Oh., U.S.	o13	112
Lincoln Park, Co., U.S.	C5	83
Lincoln Park, Ga., U.S.	D2	87
Lincoln Park, Mi., U.S.	p15	99
Lincoln Park, N.J., U.S.	B4	107
Lincoln Park, Nv., U.S.	*D2	105
Lincoln Sea, N.A.	A15	61
Lincolnshire, Il., U.S.	h9	90
Lincolnshire, co., Eng., U.K.	A7	12
Lincoln Tomb State Memorial, hist., Il., U.S.	D4	90
Lincolnton, Ga., U.S.	C4	87
Lincolnton, N.C., U.S.	B1	110
Lincoln Village, Ca., U.S.	*g10	82
Lincoln Village, Oh., U.S.	*m10	112
Lincolnville, Me., U.S.	D3	96
Lincolnville, S.C., U.S.	h11	117
Lincoln Wolds, hills, Eng., U.K.	h9	90
L'Incudine, mtn., Fr.	D2	23
Lind, Wa., U.S.	*C3	82
Linda, Ca., U.S.	C3	82
Lindale, Ga., U.S.	B1	87
Lindale, Tx., U.S.	C5	120
Lindau, F.R.Ger.	E4	18
Lindbergh, Ab., Can.	C5	68
Linden, Al., U.S.	C2	78
Linden, Ca., U.S.	D3	82
Linden, In., U.S.	D4	91
Linden, Mi., U.S.	F7	99
Linden, N.J., U.S.	k8	107
Linden, N.C., U.S.	B4	110
Linden, Pa., U.S.	D7	115
Linden, Tn., U.S.	B4	119
Linden, Wi., U.S.	F3	126
Lindenhurst, Il., U.S.	h8	90
Lindenhurst, N.Y., U.S.	n15	109
Lindenwold, N.J., U.S.	D3	107
Linderöd, Swe.	C3	15
Lindesberg, Swe.	H6	14
Lindi, Tan.	C7	48
Lindi, stm., Zaire	A5	48
Lindian, China	A11	32
Lindlar, F.R.Ger.	B2	19
Lindome, Swe.	A6	15
Lindon, Co., U.S.	B7	83
Lindon, Ut., U.S.	C4	121
Lindow, Ger.D.R.	F6	15
Lindrith, N.M., U.S.	A2	108
Lindsay, On., Can.	C6	73
Lindsay, Ca., U.S.	D4	82
Lindsay, Ne., U.S.	C8	104
Lindsay, Ok., U.S.	C4	113
Lindsborg, Ks., U.S.	D6	93
Lindsay, Oh., U.S.	A2	112
Lindstrom, Mn., U.S.	E6	100
Lindy, Md., U.S.	B8	104
Linefork, Ky., U.S.	C7	94
Linesville, Pa., U.S.	C1	115
Lineville, Al., U.S.	B4	78
Lineville, Ia., U.S.	D4	92
Linfen, China	D7	31
Linganore Creek, stm., Md., U.S.	B3	97
Lingao, China	B8	35
Lingayen, Phil.	B6	34
Lingayen Gulf, b., Phil.	n13	34
Lingen, F.R.Ger.	B3	18
Lingga Archipelago, is., Indon.	F2	34
Lingle, Wy., U.S.	D8	127
Linglestown, Pa., U.S.	F8	115
Lingling, China	F7	31
Lingo, N.M., U.S.	D6	108
Lingshan, China	G6	31
Linguère, Sen.	C1	45
Lingwu, China	E2	32
Lingyuan, China	C8	31
Linh, mtn., Viet.	B3	34
Linhai, China	F9	31
Linhares, Braz.	E2	57
Linhe, China	D2	32
Linjiang, China	F3	33
Linkou, China	B11	31
Linköping, Swe.	H6	14
Linlithgow, Scot., U.K.	E5	13
Linn, Ks., U.S.	C6	93
Linn, Mo., U.S.	C6	102
Linn, Tx., U.S.	F3	120
Linn, co., Ia., U.S.	B6	92
Linn, co., Ks., U.S.	D9	93
Linn, co., Mo., U.S.	B4	102
Linn, co., Or., U.S.	C4	114
Linn Creek, Mo., U.S.	C5	102
Linneus, Me., U.S.	B5	96
Linneus, Mo., U.S.	B4	102
Linn Grove, In., U.S.	C7	91
Linn Grove, Ia., U.S.	B2	92
Linnhe, Loch, b., Scot., U.K.	D4	13
Lino Lakes, Mn., U.S.	m12	100
Linqing, China	D8	31
Linru, China	G5	32
Lins, Braz.	C5	56
Linstead, Jam.	E14	65
Lintan, China	E5	31
Lintao, China	D5	31
Linth, stm., Switz.	B5	20
Linthal, Switz.	C7	21
Linthicum Heights, Md., U.S.	B4	97
Lintlaw, Sk., Can.	E4	75
Linton, P.Q., Can.	B5	74
Linton, Ga., U.S.	C3	87
Linton, In., U.S.	F3	91
Linton, Ky., U.S.	D2	94
Linton, N.D., U.S.	C5	111
Linville, N.C., U.S.	A1	110
Linville, Va., U.S.	B4	123
Linwood, On., Can.	D4	73
Linwood, Ks., U.S.	m15	93
Linwood, Mi., U.S.	E7	99
Linwood, Ne., U.S.	C9	104
Linwood, N.J., U.S.	E3	107
Linwood, N.C., U.S.	B2	110
Linworth, Oh., U.S.	k10	112
Linxi, China	C9	32
Linxia, China	D5	31
Linyi, China	D8	31
Linz, Aus.	D7	18
Lions, La., U.S.	h10	95
Lions, Gulf of, b., Fr.	F6	16
Lion's Head, On., Can.	C3	73
Lionville, Pa., U.S.	F10	115
Lipa, Phil.	C6	34
Lipari, Italy	E5	23
Lipari, Italy	E5	23
Lipetsk, Sov. Un.	D6	29
Lipez, Cerro, mtn., Bol.	D2	55
Lipik, Yugo.	C3	24
Liping, China	F6	31
Lipno Reservoir, res., Czech.	E9	19
Lipova, Rom.	B5	24
Lippe, stm., F.R.Ger.	C4	18
Lippstadt, F.R.Ger.	B3	18
Lipscomb, Al., U.S.	B3	78
Lipscomb, Tx., U.S.	A2	120
Lipscomb, co., Tx., U.S.	A2	120
Lipsós, i., Grc.	D6	25
Lipton, Sk., Can.	G4	75
Lipu, China	A5	48
Li Rangu, Sud.	E2	47
Liri, stm., Italy	D4	23
Liria, Spain	C5	22
Liro, stm., Italy	D7	21
Lisala, Zaire	A3	48
Lisbon (Lisboa), Port.	C1	22
Lisbon, Ct., U.S.	C7	84
Lisbon, Ia., U.S.	C6	92
Lisbon, Me., U.S.	D2	96
Lisbon, Md., U.S.	B3	97
Lisbon, N.H., U.S.	B3	106
Lisbon, N.Y., U.S.	f9	109
Lisbon, N.D., U.S.	C8	111
Lisbon, Oh., U.S.	B5	112
Lisbon Center, Me., U.S.	D2	96
Lisbon Falls, Me., U.S.	D2	96
Lisbon Ferry, N.J., U.S.	h8	107
Lisburn, N. Ire., U.K.	C6	11
Lisburne, Cape, c., Ak., U.S.	B6	79
Liscannor Bay, b., Ire.	E2	11
Liscarney, Ire.	D2	11
Lisco, Ne., U.S.	C3	104
Liscomb, N.S., Can.	D7	71
Liscomb, Ia., U.S.	B5	92
Lisdoonvarna, Ire.	D2	11
Lishi, China	E2	32
Lishu, China	C11	31
Lishui, China	F8	31
Lisianski Island, i., Hi., U.S.	k13	88
Lisichansk, Sov. Un.	q21	27
Lisieux, Sk., Can.	H2	75
Lisieux, Fr.	C4	16
Liskeard, Eng., U.K.	D3	12
L'Isle, On., Can.	C5	73
L'Isle, Switz.	C1	21
L'Isle [-sur-le-Doubs], Fr.	B2	20
L'Islet, P.Q., Can.	B8	74
L'Islet-sur-Mer, P.Q., Can.	B7	74
L'Isle-Verte, P.Q., Can.	A8	74
Lisman, Al., U.S.	C1	78
Lismore, Austl.	E9	50
Lismore, N.S., Can.	D7	71
Lismore, Ire.	E4	11
Lismore, i., Scot., U.K.	D3	13
Lismore, i., Scot., U.K.	C4	11
Listafjorden, b., Nor.	H2	14
Lister, B.C., Can.	E9	69
Listie, Pa., U.S.	F3	115
Listowel, On., Can.	D4	73
Listowel, Ire.	D2	10
Litang, China	F5	31
Litava, stm., Czech.	o16	26
Litchfield, On., Can.	B3	82
Litchfield, Ct., U.S.	C3	84
Litchfield, Il., U.S.	D4	90
Litchfield, Mi., U.S.	F6	99
Litchfield, Mn., U.S.	E4	100
Litchfield, Ne., U.S.	C6	104
Litchfield, N.H., U.S.	E4	106
Litchfield, co., Ct., U.S.	B2	84
Litchfield Park, Az., U.S.	m8	80
Litchfield, N.D., U.S.	C7	111
Liteň, Czech.	o17	26
Literberry, Il., U.S.	D3	90
Lithgow, Austl.	F8	51
Lithia Springs, Ga., U.S.	h7	87
Lithinon, Cape, c., Grc.	E5	25
Lithonia, Ga., U.S.	C2	87
Lithuania, state, Sov. Un.	D5	29
Lititz, Pa., U.S.	F9	115
Litókhoron, Grc.	C4	25
Litoměřice, Czech.	D4	26
Litomyšl, Czech.	t35	14
Litslena, Swe.	B5	21
Littau, Switz.	B5	21
Little, stm., U.S.	D7	113
Little, stm., U.S.	C7	84
Little, stm., Ga., U.S.	E3	87
Little, stm., Ky., U.S.	D2	94
Little, stm., La., U.S.	C3	95
Little, stm., N.C., U.S.	B3	110
Little, stm., Ok., U.S.	B5	113
Little, stm., S.C., U.S.	C2	117
Little, stm., Tn., U.S.	n14	119
Little, stm., Vt., U.S.	C3	122
Little, stm., Va., U.S.	D2	123
Little Acres, Az., U.S.	D5	80
Little Alföld, pl., Hung.	B3	24
Little America, Wy., U.S.	*E3	127
Little Andaman, i., India	F9	36
Little Arkansas, stm., Ks., U.S.	D6	93
Little Bay Islands, Nf., Can.	D3	72
Little Bear Lake, l., Sk., Can.	C3	75
Little Beaver Creek, stm., Ks., U.S.	C2	93
Little Belt Mountains, mts., Mt., U.S.	D6	103
Little Bighorn, stm., U.S.	E9	103
Little Birch, W.V., U.S.	C4	125
Little Bitter Lake, l., Eg.	D4	41
Little Black, stm., Me., U.S.	A3	96
Little Blue, stm., In., U.S.	H5	91
Little Blue, stm., Ne., U.S.	E3	107
Little Boars Head, N.H., U.S.	E5	106
Little Bow, stm., Ab., Can.	D4	68
Little Britain, On., Can.	C6	73
Little Brook, N.S., Can.	E3	71
Little Bullhead, Mb., Can.	D3	70
Little Cacapon, stm., W.V., U.S.	B6	125
Little Cadotte, stm., Ab., Can.	A2	68
Little Canada, Mn., U.S.	*m12	100
Little Carpathians, mts., Czech.	D4	26
Little Catalina, Nf., Can.	D5	72
Little Cayman, i., Cay. Is.	E3	64
Little Cedar, Ia., U.S.	A5	92
Little Cedar, stm., Ia., U.S.	A5	92
Little Chief, Sk., Can.	C5	97
Little Choptank River, b., Md., U.S.	C5	97
Little Churchill, stm., Mb., Can.	A4	70
Little Chute, Wi., U.S.	D5	126
Little Coal, stm., W.V., U.S.	C3	125
Little Colorado, stm., Az., U.S.	B4	80
Little Compton, R.I., U.S.	D6	116
Little Creek, De., U.S.	D4	85
Little Creek Naval Amphibious Base, mil., Va., U.S.	k15	123
Little Creek Peak, mtn., Ut., U.S.	F3	121
Little Current, On., Can.	C4	96
Little Deer Isle, Me., U.S.	D4	96
Little Diomede Island, i., Ak., U.S.	B6	79
Little Dry Creek, stm., Mt., U.S.	C10	103
Little Eagle, S.D., U.S.	B5	118
Little Egg Harbor, b., N.J., U.S.	D4	107
Little Egg Inlet, b., N.J., U.S.	E4	107
Little Falls, Mn., U.S.	E4	100
Little Falls, N.J., U.S.	B4	107
Little Falls, N.Y., U.S.	B6	109
Little Ferry, N.J., U.S.	h8	107
Little Fishing Creek, stm., W.V., U.S.	h9	125
Littlefork, Mn., U.S.	B5	100
Little Fork, stm., Mn., U.S.	B5	100
Little Frog Mountain, mtn., Tn., U.S.	D9	119
Little Goose Creek, stm., Wy., U.S.	B6	127
Little Grand Lake, l., Nf., Can.	D3	72
Little Gunpowder Falls, stm., Md., U.S.	A4	97
Littlehampton, Eng., U.K.	D7	12
Little Harbour Deep, Nf., Can.	D3	72
Little Hocking, Oh., U.S.	C4	112
Little Humboldt, stm., Nv., U.S.	B4	105
Little Humboldt, North Fork, stm., Nv., U.S.	B4	105
Little Humboldt, South Fork, stm., Nv., U.S.	B5	105
Little Inagua, i., Bah.	D7	64
Little Kanawha, stm., W.V., U.S.	C4	125
Little Kanawha, West Fork, stm., W.V., U.S.	B3	125
Little Lake, Mi., U.S.	B3	99
Little Lake, l., La., U.S.	E5	95
Littlelot, Tn., U.S.	B4	119
Little Lynches, stm., S.C., U.S.	C7	117
Little Manatee, stm., Fl., U.S.	p11	86
Little Manitou Lake, l., Sk., Can.	F3	75
Little Marais, Mn., U.S.	C7	100
Little Mazarn Creek, stm., Ar., U.S.	g7	81
Little Meadows, Pa., U.S.	C9	115
Little Mecatina, stm., Can.	h9	72
Little Mexico, Tx., U.S.	D1	120
Little Miami, stm., Oh., U.S.	C1	112
Little Miami, East Fork, stm., Oh., U.S.	C1	112
Little Miami, Todd Fork, stm., Oh., U.S.	C1	112
Little Minch, strt., Scot., U.K.	B3	10
Little Missouri, stm., U.S.	A7	76
Little Missouri, stm., Ar., U.S.	D2	81
Little Moose Mountain, mtn., N.Y., U.S.	B6	109
Little Mountain, S.C., U.S.	C5	117
Little Mountain, mtn., Wy., U.S.	E3	127
Little Muddy, stm., Il., U.S.	E4	90
Little Muddy, stm., N.D., U.S.	A2	111
Little Orleans, Md., U.S.	A1	97
Little Osage, stm., U.S.	E9	93
Little Otter Creek, stm., Vt., U.S.	C2	122
Little Pee Dee, stm., S.C., U.S.	C9	117
Little Pigeon Creek, stm., In., U.S.	I3	91
Little Pipe Creek, stm., Md., U.S.	A3	97
Little Playgreen Lake, l., Mb., Can.	B3	70
Littleport, Ia., U.S.	B6	92
Little Quill Lake, l., Sk., Can.	F3	75
Little Rann of Kutch, pl., India	F3	37
Little Red, stm., Ar., U.S.	B4	81
Little Red, Middle Fork, stm., Ar., U.S.	B3	81
Little River, Sk., Can.	E3	71
Little River, Al., U.S.	D2	78
Little River, Ks., U.S.	D5	93
Little River, S.C., U.S.	D10	117
Little River, co., Ar., U.S.	D1	81
Little River Inlet, b., S.C., U.S.	C3	81
Little Rock, Ar., U.S.	C3	81
Little Rock, Ia., U.S.	A2	92
Little Rock, S.C., U.S.	C9	117
Littlerock, Wa., U.S.	C2	124
Little Rock, stm., U.S.	A1	92
Little Rock Air Force Base, mil., Ar., U.S.	C3	81
Little Sable Point, c., Mi., U.S.	E4	99
Little Sachigo Lake, l., Can.	B5	70
Little Saint Bernard Pass, Eur.	E7	16
Little Salt Lake, l., Ut., U.S.	F3	121
Little Sand Creek, stm., Mn., U.S.	D6	100
Little Sandy, stm., Ky., U.S.	B6	94
Little Sandy Creek, stm., Wy., U.S.	D3	127
Little Sauk, Mn., U.S.	E4	100
Little Sebago Lake, l., Me., U.S.	g7	96
Little Silver, N.J., U.S.	C4	107
Little Sioux, Ia., U.S.	C1	92
Little Sioux, stm., Ia., U.S.	B2	92
Little Sioux, West Fork, stm., Ia., U.S.	B2	92
Little Smoky, stm., Ab., Can.	B2	68
Little Snake, stm., U.S.	A2	83
Little Southwest Miramichi, stm., N.B., Can.	C3	71
Little Spokane, stm., Wa., U.S.	B8	124
Littlestown, Pa., U.S.	G7	115
Little Suamico, Wi., U.S.	D6	126
Little Tallapoosa, stm., U.S.	B4	78
Little Tennile Creek, stm., W.V., U.S.	k10	123
Little Tennessee, stm., U.S.	D9	119
Littleton, Al., U.S.	f7	78
Littleton, Co., U.S.	B6	83
Littleton, Il., U.S.	C3	90
Littleton, Me., U.S.	B5	96
Littleton, Ma., U.S.	f10	98
Littleton, N.H., U.S.	B3	106
Littleton, N.C., U.S.	A5	110
Littleton, W.V., U.S.	B4	125
Little Tucson, Az., U.S.	F4	80
Little Valley, Ca., U.S.	B3	82
Little Valley, N.Y., U.S.	C2	109
Littleville, Al., U.S.	A2	78
Little Wabash, stm., Il., U.S.	E5	90
Little Walnut, stm., Ks., U.S.	g13	93
Little West Fork, stm., Tn., U.S.	A4	119
Little White, stm., S.D., U.S.	D5	118
Little Wolf, stm., Wi., U.S.	D4	126
Little Wood, stm., Id., U.S.	F4	89
Little York, Il., U.S.	B3	90
Little York, N.J., U.S.	G6	91
Little Zab, stm., Asia	E15	40
Littoria see Latina, Italy	D4	23
Litvínov, Czech.	C2	26
Liuba, China	E2	32
Liucheng, China	G6	31
Liucura, Chile	C11	32
Liuhe, China	C11	31
Liupan Mountains, mts., China	F1	31
Liuyang, China	J5	32
Liuzhou, China	G6	31
Livelong, Sk., Can.	D1	75
Liveoak, On., Can.	A3	73
Livengood, Ak., U.S.	B10	79
Livenza, stm., Italy	D8	20
Live Oak, Ca., U.S.	C3	82
Live Oak, Fl., U.S.	B4	86
Live Oak, Tx., U.S.	*E3	120
Live Oak, co., Tx., U.S.	E3	120
Live Oak Manor, Fl., U.S.	*E5	95
Livermore, Ca., U.S.	D3	82
Livermore, Ia., U.S.	B3	92
Livermore, Ky., U.S.	C2	94
Livermore, Me., U.S.	D2	96

Name — Map Ref — Page

Livermore, Mount, mtn., Tx., U.S. — o12 120
Livermore Falls, Me., U.S. — D2 96
Livermore Falls, N.H., U.S. — D3 106
Liverpool, Austl. — *F9 50
Liverpool, N.S., Can. — E5 71
Liverpool, Eng., U.K. — D5 10
Liverpool, Pa., U.S. — E7 115
Liverpool, Tx., U.S. — r14 120
Liverpool, W.V., U.S. — C3 125
Liverpool Bay, b., N.T., Can. — B7 66
Livigno, Italy — C9 21
Livingston, Guat. — D7 63
Livingston, Al., U.S. — C1 78
Livingston, Ca., U.S. — D3 82
Livingston, Il., U.S. — E4 90
Livingston, Ky., U.S. — C5 94
Livingston, La., U.S. — D5 95
Livingston, Mt., U.S. — E6 103
Livingston, N.J., U.S. — B4 107
Livingston, N.Y., U.S. — C7 109
Livingston, S.C., U.S. — D5 117
Livingston, Tn., U.S. — C8 119
Livingston, Tx., U.S. — D5 120
Livingston, Wi., U.S. — F3 126
Livingston, co., Il., U.S. — C5 90
Livingston, co., Ky., U.S. — e9 94
Livingston, co., La., U.S. — D5 95
Livingston, co., Mi., U.S. — F7 99
Livingston, co., Mo., U.S. — B4 102
Livingston, co., N.Y., U.S. — C3 109
Livingston, Lake, res., Tx., U.S. — D5 120
Livingstone, Zam. — E4 48
Livingstone Cove, N.S., Can. — D8 71
Livingstone Falls, wtfl, Afr. — *C1 48
Livingstonia, Mwi. — D5 48
Livingston Island, i., B.A.T. — C6 7
Livingston Manor, N.Y., U.S. — D6 109
Livno, Yugo. — D3 24
Livny, Sov. Un. — E11 27
Livona, N.D., U.S. — C5 111
Livonia, In., U.S. — G5 91
Livonia, La., U.S. — D4 95
Livonia, Mi., U.S. — F7 99
Livonia, Mo., U.S. — A5 102
Livonia, N.Y., U.S. — C3 109
Livorno (Leghorn), Italy — C3 23
Livramento do Brumado, Braz. — A4 56
Livry-Gargan, Fr. — g11 16
Liwale, Tan. — C6 48
Lixian, China — J4 32
Liyang, China — I8 32
Lizard Creek, stm., Ia., U.S. — B3 92
Lizard Head Pass, Co., U.S. — D3 83
Lizard Head Peak, mtn., Wy., U.S. — D3 127
Lizard Point, c., Eng., U.K. — F4 10
Lizella, Ga., U.S. — D3 87
Lizemores, W.V., U.S. — C3 125
Lizton, In., U.S. — E4 91
Ljubljana, Yugo. — B2 24
Ljubuški, Yugo. — D3 24
Ljungby, Swe. — I5 14
Ljusdal, Swe. — G7 14
Ljusterö, Swe. — t36 14
Llandeilo, Wales, U.K. — C4 12
Llandovery, Wales, U.K. — C4 12
Llandrindod Wells, Wales, U.K. — D5 10
Llandudno, Wales, U.K. — D5 10
Llanelli, Wales, U.K. — E4 10
Llanes, Spain — A3 22
Llanfyllin, Wales, U.K. — B4 12
Llangefni, Wales, U.K. — A3 12
Llangollen, Wales, U.K. — B4 12
Llangollen Estates, De., U.S. — *B3 85
Llangynog, Wales, U.K. — B4 12
Llanidloes, Wales, U.K. — B4 12
Llano, N.M., U.S. — A4 108
Llano, Tx., U.S. — D3 120
Llano, co., Tx., U.S. — D3 120
Llano, stm., Tx., U.S. — D3 120
Llanos, pl., S.A. — B3 60
Llanquihue, Lago, l., Chile — C2 54
Llanrwst, Wales, U.K. — A4 12
Llata, Peru — C2 58
Llaves, N.M., U.S. — A3 108
Llerena, Spain — C2 22
Lleyn Peninsula, pen., Wales, U.K. — D4 10
Llico, Chile — A2 55
Llobregat, stm., Spain — B6 22
Lloyd, Fl., U.S. — B2 86
Lloyd, Ky., U.S. — B7 94
Lloyd, Mt., U.S. — B7 103
Lloyd Harbor, N.Y., U.S. — *E7 109
Lloydminster, Ab., Can. — C5 68
Lloydminster, Sk., Can. — D1 75
Lloyds, stm., Nf., Can. — D3 72
Lluchmayor, Spain — C7 22
Llullaillaco, Volcán, vol., S.A. — D2 55
Lo, stm., Viet. — B6 35
Loa, Ut., U.S. — E4 121
Loa, stm., Chile — D2 55
Loachapoka, Al., U.S. — C4 78
Loami, Il., U.S. — D4 90
Loange, stm., Afr. — C2 48
Lobatse, Bots. — C4 49
Löbau, Ger.D.R. — C7 18
Lobaye, stm., Cen. Afr. Rep. — E3 46
Lobelville, Tn., U.S. — B4 119
Lobenstein, Ger.D.R. — C6 19
Loberia, Arg. — D5 54
Lobito, Ang. — D1 48
Lobnya, Sov. Un. — m17 27
Lobo, Phil. — p13 34
Lobos, Arg. — B5 54
Lobos, Cabo, c., Mex. — B2 63
Lobos, Punta, c., Mex. — B2 63
Lobos de Tierra, Isla, i., Peru — C1 58
Lobster Lake, l., Me., U.S. — C3 96
Loburg, Ger.D.R. — A7 19
Locarno, Switz. — E4 18
Lochaber, N.S., Can. — D7 71
Lochaline, Scot., U.K. — D3 13
Locharron, Scot., U.K. — D3 13
Lochdonhead, Scot., U.K. — D3 13
Lochem, Neth. — D6 17
Loches, Fr. — D4 16
Lochgilphead, Scot., U.K. — D3 13
Lochinver, Scot., U.K. — B3 13
Loch Lomond, Va., U.S. — B5 123
Loch Lynn Heights, Md., U.S. — m12 97
Lochmaben, Scot., U.K. — E5 13
Lochmere, N.H., U.S. — D3 106
Lochnagar, mtn., Scot., U.K. — D5 13
Lochranza, Scot., U.K. — E3 13
Loch Raven Reservoir, res., Md., U.S. — B4 97
Lochsa, stm., Id., U.S. — C3 89
Lochy, Loch, l., Scot., U.K. — D4 13
Lockbourne, Oh., U.S. — m11 112
Locke, In., U.S. — B5 91
Locke, N.Y., U.S. — C4 109

Locke, Tn., U.S. — B1 119
Locke Mills, Me., U.S. — D2 96
Lockeport, N.S., Can. — F4 71
Lockerbie, Scot., U.K. — E5 13
Lockesburg, Ar., U.S. — D1 81
Lockhart, Al., U.S. — D3 78
Lockhart, Fl., U.S. — *D5 86
Lockhart, Mn., U.S. — C2 100
Lockhart, S.C., U.S. — B5 117
Lockhart, Tx., U.S. — E4 120
Lockland, Oh., U.S. — o13 112
Lockney, Tx., U.S. — B2 120
Lockport, Mb., Can. — D3 70
Lockport, Il., U.S. — B5 90
Lockport, Ky., U.S. — B5 94
Lockport, La., U.S. — E5 95
Lockport, N.Y., U.S. — B2 109
Lockridge, Ia., U.S. — C6 92
Lock Springs, Mo., U.S. — B4 102
Lockwood, Sk., Can. — F3 75
Lockwood, Mo., U.S. — D4 102
Lockwood, Mt., U.S. — E8 103
Lockwood, W.V., U.S. — C3 125
Loco, Ok., U.S. — C4 113
Loco Hills, N.M., U.S. — E6 108
Locumba, Peru — E3 58
Locust, N.J., U.S. — C4 107
Locust, N.C., U.S. — B2 110
Locust Bayou, Ar., U.S. — D3 81
Locust Creek, stm., Mo., U.S. — B4 102
Locust Fork, stm., Al., U.S. — B3 78
Locust Grove, Ga., U.S. — C2 87
Locust Grove, Md., U.S. — D6 97
Locust Grove, N.Y., U.S. — *C7 109
Locust Hill (part of Markham), On., Can. — k15 73
Lod, Isr. — G10 40
Loda, Il., U.S. — C5 90
Loděnice, stm., Czech. — n17 26
Löderup, Swe. — C8 15
Lodève, Fr. — F5 16
Lodeynoye Pole, Sov. Un. — A9 27
Lodge, S.C., U.S. — E6 117
Lodge Creek, stm., N.A. — B7 103
Lodge Grass, Mt., U.S. — E9 103
Lodgepole, Ab., Can. — C3 68
Lodgepole, Ne., U.S. — C3 104
Lodgepole, S.D., U.S. — B3 118
Lodgepole Creek, stm., U.S. — C3 104
Lodhran, Pak. — C5 36
Lodi, Italy — B2 23
Lodi, Ca., U.S. — C3 82
Lodi, N.J., U.S. — h8 107
Lodi, N.Y., U.S. — C4 109
Lodi, Oh., U.S. — A3 112
Lodi, Wi., U.S. — E4 126
Lodi, Zaire — B3 48
Lodja, Zaire — B3 48
Lodore, Canyon of, val., Co., U.S. — A2 83
Lods, Fr. — B2 20
Lodwar, Kenya — A6 48
Łódź, Pol. — C5 26
Loeches, Spain — p18 22
Loei, Thai. — D4 35
Loeli, i., Sud. — D3 47
Loeriesfontein, S. Afr. — D2 49
Lofer, Aus. — B8 20
Lofoten, is., Nor. — C5 14
Loftus, Eng., U.K. — F8 13
Loga, Niger — D5 45
Logan, Il., U.S. — F5 90
Logan, Ia., U.S. — C2 92
Logan, Ks., U.S. — C4 93
Logan, Mt., U.S. — E5 103
Logan, N.M., U.S. — B6 108
Logan, N.D., U.S. — A4 111
Logan, Oh., U.S. — C3 112
Logan, Ok., U.S. — A1 113
Logan, Ut., U.S. — B4 121
Logan, W.V., U.S. — D3 125
Logan, co., Ar., U.S. — B2 81
Logan, co., Co., U.S. — A7 83
Logan, co., Il., U.S. — C4 90
Logan, co., Ks., U.S. — D2 93
Logan, co., Ky., U.S. — D3 94
Logan, co., Ne., U.S. — C5 104
Logan, co., N.D., U.S. — C6 111
Logan, co., Oh., U.S. — B2 112
Logan, co., Ok., U.S. — B4 113
Logan, co., W.V., U.S. — D3 125
Logan, Mount, mtn., Yk., Can. — D4 66
Logan, Mount, mtn., Wa., U.S. — A5 124
Logan Creek, stm., Ne., U.S. — B9 104
Logandale, Nv., U.S. — G7 105
Logan Martin Lake, res., Al., U.S. — B3 78
Logan Mountains, mts., Yk., Can. — D7 66
Logan Pass, Mt., U.S. — B2 103
Logansport, In., U.S. — C5 91
Logansport, Ky., U.S. — C3 94
Logansport, La., U.S. — C2 95
Loganton, Pa., U.S. — D7 115
Loganville, Ga., U.S. — C3 87
Loganville, Wi., U.S. — E3 126
Loge, stm., Ang. — C1 48
Loggieville, N.B., Can. — B4 71
Log Lane Village, Co., U.S. — A7 83
Logone, stm., Afr. — C3 46
Logroño, Spain — A4 22
Logrosán, Spain — C3 22
Løgstør, Den. — B3 15
Løgumkloster, Den. — C3 15
Lohals, Den. — C4 15
Lohardaga, India — D7 36
Lohr, F.R.Ger. — B5 19
Lohrville, Ia., U.S. — B3 92
Loi, mtn., Laos — B5 35
Loikaw, Burma — C2 34
Loir, stm., Fr. — D4 16
Loíza, Lago, res., P.R. — B3 65
Loja, Ec. — B2 58
Loja, Spain — D3 22
Loja, prov., Ec. — B2 58
Lokandu, Zaire — B4 48
Lokan tekojärvi, res., Fin. — C13 14
Lokeren, Bel. — C3 17
Lokhvitsa, Sov. Un. — F9 27
Lokichokio, Kenya — A6 48
Lokichar, Kenya — A6 48
Lokitaung, Kenya — A6 48
Løkken, Den. — A3 15
Lokoja, Nig. — E6 45
Lokolama, Zaire — B2 48
Lokoro, stm., Zaire — B3 48
Lokossa, Benin — E5 45
Lol, stm., Sud. — D2 47
Lola, Ky., U.S. — e9 94

Lola, Mount, mtn., Ca., U.S. — C3 82
Loliondo, Tan. — B6 48
Lolland, i., Den. — J4 14
Lollar, F.R.Ger. — C3 19
Lollie, Ga., U.S. — D4 87
Lolo, Mt., U.S. — D2 103
Lolo Hot Springs, Mt., U.S. — D2 103
Lolo Pass, U.S. — C4 89
Lom, Bul. — D6 24
Loma, Co., U.S. — B2 83
Loma, Mt., U.S. — C6 103
Loma, Ne., U.S. — C9 104
Loma, N.D., U.S. — A7 111
Loma Linda, Ca., U.S. — *E5 82
Lomami, stm., Zaire — B3 48
Loma Mountains, mts., S.L. — G3 45
Loman, Mn., U.S. — B5 100
Lomas, Peru — C6 92
Lomas de Zamora, Arg. — A5 54
Lomax, Al., U.S. — C3 78
Lomax, Il., U.S. — C2 90
Lombard, Il., U.S. — k8 90
Lombarda, Serra, plat., Braz. — B4 59
Lombardia, prov., Italy — B2 23
Lombardy, hist reg., Italy — B2 23
Lomblen, i., Indon. — G6 34
Lombok, i., Indon. — G5 34
Lombok Strait, strt., Indon. — E5 45
Lomé, Togo — E5 45
Lomela, Zaire — B3 48
Lomela, stm., Zaire — B3 48
Lometa, Tx., U.S. — D3 120
Lomié, Cam. — E2 46
Lomira, Wi., U.S. — E5 126
Lomita, Ca., U.S. — *E4 82
Lommel, Bel. — C5 17
Lomond, Ab., Can. — D4 68
Lomond, Nf., Can. — D3 72
Lomond, Loch, l., Scot., U.K. — D4 13
Lomonosov, Sov. Un. — s30 14
Lomonosova, Sov. Un. — C7 28
Lompoc, Ca., U.S. — E3 82
Lom Sak, Thai. — D4 35
Łomża, Pol. — B7 26
Lonaconing, Md., U.S. — k13 97
Loncoche, Chile — B2 54
Londesborough, On., Can. — D3 73
London, Eng., U.K. — E6 10
London, Ar., U.S. — B2 81
London, In., U.S. — E6 91
London, Ky., U.S. — C5 94
London, Oh., U.S. — C2 112
London, Tx., U.S. — D3 120
London (Heathrow) Airport, Eng., U.K. — m12 10
Londonderry, N.S., Can. — D6 71
Londonderry (Derry), N. Ire., U.K. — C3 10
Londonderry, N.H., U.S. — E4 106
Londonderry, Vt., U.S. — E3 122
Londonderry, Cape, c., Austl. — k11 54
Londonderry, Isla, i., Chile — A2 83
London Mills, Il., U.S. — C3 90
Londontowne, Md., U.S. — C4 97
Londrina, Braz. — C2 56
Lone Elm, Ks., U.S. — D8 93
Lone Grove, Ok., U.S. — C4 113
Lone Jack, Mo., U.S. — C3 102
Lonely Island, i., On., Can. — B3 73
Lone Mountain, Tn., U.S. — C10 119
Lone Mountain, mtn., Nv., U.S. — E4 105
Lone Oak, Ky., U.S. — e9 94
Lone Oak, Tx., U.S. — C5 120
Lone Pine, Ca., U.S. — D4 82
Lonepine, Mt., U.S. — C2 103
Lone Rock, Sk., Can. — D1 75
Lone Rock, Wi., U.S. — E3 126
Lone Star, S.C., U.S. — D6 117
Lone Tree, Ia., U.S. — C6 92
Lonetree, Wy., U.S. — E2 127
Lone Tree Creek, stm., Co., U.S. — A6 83
Lone Wolf, Ok., U.S. — C2 113
Long, co., Ga., U.S. — E5 87
Longá, stm., Ang. — D1 48
Longá, stm., Braz. — D6 57
Longacre, W.V., U.S. — m13 125
Longarone, Italy — C8 20
Long Bar Harbor, Md., U.S. — B5 97
Long Bay, b., Jam. — E12 65
Long Bay, b., Jam. — F14 65
Long Beach, In., U.S. — A4 91
Long Beach, Md., U.S. — D5 97
Long Beach, Ms., U.S. — E3 100
Long Beach, N.Y., U.S. — g7 101
Long Beach, Wa., U.S. — E7 109
Long Beach Naval Shipyard, mil., Ca., U.S. — n12 82
Longboat Key, Fl., U.S. — q10 86
Longboat Key, i., Fl., U.S. — E4 86
Longboat Pass, strt., Fl., U.S. — q10 86
Long Bottom, Oh., U.S. — C4 112
Long Branch (part of Etobicoke), On., Can. — m14 73
Long Branch, N.J., U.S. — C5 107
Long Branch, Tx., U.S. — C5 120
Longbranch, Wa., U.S. — B3 124
Long Cay, i., Bah. — m17 64
Long Creek, Or., U.S. — C7 114
Longcreek, S.C., U.S. — B1 117
Long Creek, stm., N.A. — H3 75
Long Creek Mountain, mtn., Wy., U.S. — D5 127
Longdale, Ok., U.S. — A3 113
Long Eaton, Eng., U.K. — B6 12
Long Eddy, N.Y., U.S. — D5 109
Longford, On., Can. — C5 73
Longford, Ire. — C6 11
Longford, Ks., U.S. — C6 93
Longford, co., Ire. — C6 11
Long Grove, Ia., U.S. — C7 92
Long Harbour, Nf., Can. — E5 72
Long Hill, Ct., U.S. — D7 84
Longiram, Indon. — F5 34
Long Island, Indon. — p14 34
Longisland, N.C., U.S. — C4 93
Long Island, i., N.S., Can. — E3 71
Long Island, i., Bah. — C10 64
Long Island, i., N.B., Can. — E3 71
Long Island, i., Me., U.S. — g7 96
Long Island, i., Ma., U.S. — g12 98
Long Island, i., N.Y., U.S. — E7 109
Long Island Sound, strt., U.S. — E7 109
Long Key, Fl., U.S. — H6 86
Long Key, i., Fl., U.S. — H6 86
Longlac, On., Can. — G15 66
Longli, China — F9 32
Long Lake, Il., U.S. — h8 90

Long Lake, Mi., U.S. — D7 99
Long Lake, N.Y., U.S. — B6 109
Longlake, S.D., U.S. — B6 118
Long Lake, Wi., U.S. — C5 126
Long Lake, l., Me., U.S. — A4 96
Long Lake, l., Me., U.S. — D2 96
Long Lake, l., Mi., U.S. — D5 99
Long Lake, l., Mi., U.S. — C7 99
Long Lake, l., Mn., U.S. — D4 100
Long Lake, l., N.Y., U.S. — B6 109
Long Lake, l., N.D., U.S. — C6 111
Long Lake, l., Wa., U.S. — f10 124
Long Lake Colony, S.D., U.S. — *B7 118
Long Lane, Mo., U.S. — D5 102
Longleaf, La., U.S. — C3 95
Longlin, China — G6 31
Longmeadow, Ma., U.S. — B2 98
Longmont, Co., U.S. — A5 83
Long Mountain, mtn., Mo., U.S. — E5 102
Long Mountain, mtn., N.H., U.S. — A4 106
Long Pine, Ne., U.S. — B6 104
Long Point, N.S., Can. — D8 71
Long Point, On., Can. — E4 73
Long Point, Il., U.S. — B5 90
Long Point, c., Mb., Can. — C2 70
Long Point, c., Nf., Can. — D2 72
Long Point, pen., On., Can. — E4 73
Long Pond, l., Me., U.S. — C3 96
Long Pond, l., Me., U.S. — C2 96
Long Pond, l., Ma., U.S. — C6 98
Long Pond, l., Ma., U.S. — C6 98
Long Pond, res., Fl., U.S. — C4 86
Longport, N.J., U.S. — E3 107
Long Prairie, Mn., U.S. — E4 100
Longquan, China — F8 31
Long Range Mountains, mts., Nf., Can. — D2 72
Longreach, Austl. — D7 50
Longridge, Eng., U.K. — G6 13
Long Run, W.V., U.S. — k9 125
Longs Peak, mtn., Co., U.S. — A5 83
Long Strait, strt., Sov. Un. — B20 29
Longstreet, La., U.S. — B2 95
Longton, Ks., U.S. — E7 93
Longtown, Eng., U.K. — E6 13
Longtown, Mo., U.S. — D8 102
Longueau, Fr. — E2 17
Longueuil, P.Q., Can. — D4 74
Longuyon, Fr. — C6 16
Longvale, Ca., U.S. — C2 82
Long Valley, Az., U.S. — C4 80
Long Valley, N.J., U.S. — B3 107
Longvalley, S.D., U.S. — D4 118
Longview, Ab., Can. — D3 68
Longview, Il., U.S. — D5 90
Long View, Ky., U.S. — C4 94
Longview, Ms., U.S. — B5 101
Long View, N.C., U.S. — B1 110
Longview, Tx., U.S. — C5 120
Longview, Wa., U.S. — C3 124
Longville, La., U.S. — D2 95
Longville, Mn., U.S. — C4 100
Longwood, Fl., U.S. — *D5 86
Longwood, N.C., U.S. — C4 110
Longwoods, Md., U.S. — C5 97
Longwy, Fr. — C6 16
Longxian, China — G2 32
Long Xuyen, Viet. — I8 35
Longyan, China — F8 31
Longyao, China — F6 32
Longzhen, China — B3 33
Longzhou, China — C10 36
Lonkin, Burma — C4 81
Lonoke, Ar., U.S. — C4 81
Lonoke, co., Ar., U.S. — C4 81
Lönsdal, Nor. — D6 14
Lonsdale, On., Can. — C7 73
Lonsdale, Mn., U.S. — F5 100
Lonsdale, R.I., U.S. — B4 116
Lons-le-Saunier, Fr. — D6 16
Lontzen, Bel. — D5 17
Looe, Eng., U.K. — D3 12
Loogootee, In., U.S. — G4 91
Lookeba, Ok., U.S. — B3 113
Lookout, Ca., U.S. — B3 82
Lookout, Ky., U.S. — C7 94
Lookout, W.V., U.S. — C4 125
Lookout, Cape, c., N.C., U.S. — C6 114
Lookout, Point, c., Mi., U.S. — d7 99
Lookout Mountain, Tn., U.S. — h11 119
Lookout Mountain, mtn., Or., U.S. — C6 114
Lookout Pass, U.S. — B3 89
Lookout Point Lake, res., Or., U.S. — D4 114

Loranger, La., U.S. — D5 95
Lorca, Spain — D5 22
Lord Howe Island, i., Austl. — I9 6
Lordsburg, N.M., U.S. — E1 108
Loreauville, La., U.S. — D4 95
Lore City, Oh., U.S. — C4 112
Lorena, Braz. — C3 56
Lorengau, Pap. N. Gui. — h12 50
Lorentz, W.V., U.S. — B4 125
Lorenzo, Id., U.S. — F7 89
Lorenzo, Ne., U.S. — C2 104
Lorenzo, Tx., U.S. — C2 120
Lorenzo Geyres, Ur. — E1 56
Loreto, Braz. — C1 57
Loreto, Col. — D6 60
Loreto, Italy — C4 23
Loreto, Mex. — B2 63
Loreto, Para. — D5 58
Loreto, dept., Peru — B3 58
Loretta, Ks., U.S. — D4 93
Loretta, Wi., U.S. — C3 126
Loretto, Mb., Can. — E3 70
Loretto, Ky., U.S. — C4 94
Loretto, Mi., U.S. — C3 99
Loretto, Ne., U.S. — C7 104
Loretto, Pa., U.S. — F4 115
Loretto, Tn., U.S. — B4 119
Lorica, Col. — B2 60
Lorida, Fl., U.S. — E5 86
Lorient, Fr. — D2 16
L'Orignal, On., Can. — B10 73
Loring, Mt., U.S. — B9 103
Loring Air Force Base, mil., Me., U.S. — B5 96
Loris, S.C., U.S. — C10 117
Lorlie, Sk., Can. — G4 75
Lorman, Ms., U.S. — D2 101
Lorn, Firth of, est., Scot., U.K. — B4 10
Lorne, N.B., Can. — B3 71
Lorneville, On., Can. — C5 73
Lorquin, Fr. — F6 17
Lorraine, Ks., U.S. — D5 93
Lorraine, N.Y., U.S. — B5 109
Lorraine, Al., U.S. — D4 78
Lorraine, hist reg., Fr. — C6 16
Lorraine, Co., U.S. — B5 83
Lorraine Plateau, plat., Fr. — C7 16
Lorsch, F.R.Ger. — D3 19
Lorup, F.R.Ger. — B7 17
Los Alamitos, Ca., U.S. — *F5 82
Los Alamos, Ca., U.S. — B3 82
Los Alamos, N.M., U.S. — B3 108
Los Alamos, co., N.M., U.S. — B3 108
Los Altos, Ca., U.S. — k8 82
Los Altos, Oh., U.S. — k8 82
Los Altos Hills, Ca., U.S. — *k8 82
Los Andes, Chile — A2 54
Los Ángeles, Chile — B2 54
Los Angeles, Ca., U.S. — E4 82
Los Angeles, co., Ca., U.S. — E4 82
Los Angeles Aqueduct, Ca., U.S. — E4 82
Los Banos, Ca., U.S. — D3 82
Los Blancos, Arg. — D3 55
Los Cerrillos, Arg. — A3 54
Los Ebanos, Tx., U.S. — F3 120
Los Fresnos, Tx., U.S. — F4 120
Los Gatos, Ca., U.S. — D2 82
Los Hermanos, Islas, is., Ven. — A5 60
Lošinj, i., Yugo. — C2 24
Los Lagos, Chile — B2 54
Los Lagos, prov., Chile — C2 54
Los Lunas, N.M., U.S. — C3 108
Los Mochis, Mex. — B3 63
Los Molinos, Ca., U.S. — B2 82
Los Monjes, Islas, is., Ven. — A3 60
Los Nietos, Ca., U.S. — *n12 82
Los Ojos, N.M., U.S. — A3 108
Los Padillas, N.M., U.S. — *B3 108
Los Palacios, Cuba — C2 64
Los Palacios [y Villafranca], Spain — D3 22
Los Peares, Spain — A2 22
Los Pinos, N.M., U.S. — A3 108
Los Pinos, stm., Co., U.S. — D3 83
Los Ranchos de Albuquerque, N.M., U.S. — B3 108
Los Remedios, stm., Mex. — g9 63
Los Reyes [de Salgado], Mex. — D4 63
Los Reyes la Paz, Mex. — h10 63
Los Ríos, prov., Ec. — B2 58
Los Roques, Islas, is., Ven. — A4 60
Los Santos, Pan. — G7 62
Los Santos [de Maimona], Spain — C2 22
Los Sarmientos, Arg. — E2 55
Los Sauces, Chile — B2 54
Lossiemouth, Scot., U.K. — C5 13
Lössnitz, Ger.D.R. — C7 19
Lost, stm., Wa., U.S. — A5 124
Lost, stm., W.V., U.S. — B6 125
Lostant, Il., U.S. — B4 90
Los Taques, Ven. — A3 60
Lostine, Or., U.S. — B9 114
Lost Nation, Ia., U.S. — C7 92
Lost City, W.V., U.S. — B6 125
Lost Creek, stm., Ar., U.S. — C3 81
Lost Creek, stm., Wy., U.S. — D5 127
Lost Hills, Ca., U.S. — E4 82
Lost Peak, mtn., Ut., U.S. — F2 121
Lost Ranger Peak, mtn., Co., U.S. — A4 83
Lost River, Id., U.S. — F5 89
Lost River Glacial Caverns, N.H., U.S. — B3 106
Lost River Range, mts., Id., U.S. — e8 89

Lott, Tx., U.S. — D4 120
Lotung, Tai. — G9 31
Louang Namtha, Laos — B4 35
Louangphrabang, Laos — B2 34
Louann, Ar., U.S. — D3 81
Loubomo, Congo — B1 48
Loudenville, W.V., U.S. — g8 125
Loudon, N.H., U.S. — D4 106
Loudon, Tn., U.S. — D9 119
Loudon, co., Tn., U.S. — D9 119
Loudonville, N.Y., U.S. — *C7 109
Loudonville, Oh., U.S. — B3 112
Loudoun, co., Va., U.S. — A5 123
Loudun, Fr. — D4 16
Louga, Sen. — C1 45
Loughborough, Eng., U.K. — D6 10
Lougheed, Ab., Can. — C5 68
Lougheed Island, i., N.T., Can. — m31 66
Loughman, Fl., U.S. — D5 86
Loughrea, Ire. — D2 11
Loughros More Bay, b., Ire. — D1 11
Louin, Ms., U.S. — C4 101
Louisa, Ky., U.S. — B7 94
Louisa, Va., U.S. — B4 123
Louisa, co., Ia., U.S. — C6 92
Louisa, co., Va., U.S. — C5 123
Louisa, Lake, l., Fl., U.S. — D5 86
Louisburg, N.S., Can. — D10 71
Louisburg, Ks., U.S. — D9 93
Louisburg, Mn., U.S. — E2 100
Louisburg, N.C., U.S. — A4 110
Louisburgh, Ire. — D2 11
Louisdale, N.S., Can. — D8 71
Louise, Ga., U.S. — C2 87
Louise, Ms., U.S. — C3 101
Louise, Tx., U.S. — E4 120
Louise, W.V., U.S. — f8 125
Louise, Lake, l., Ak., U.S. — f18 79
Louise Island, i., B.C., Can. — C2 69
Louiseville, P.Q., Can. — C5 74
Louisiade Archipelago, is., Pap. N. Gui. — G9 6
Louisiana, Mo., U.S. — B6 102
Louisiana, state, U.S. — C3 95
Louisiana Point, c., La., U.S. — E2 95
Louis Trichardt, S. Afr. — B4 49
Louisville, Al., U.S. — D4 78
Louisville, Co., U.S. — B5 83
Louisville, Ga., U.S. — C4 87
Louisville, Il., U.S. — E5 90
Louisville, Ks., U.S. — C7 93
Louisville, Ky., U.S. — B4 94
Louisville, Ms., U.S. — B4 101
Louisville, Ne., U.S. — D9 104
Louisville, N.Y., U.S. — f9 109
Louisville, Oh., U.S. — B4 112
Louisville, Tn., U.S. — D9 119
Louis-XIV, Pointe, c., P.Q., Can. — h11 74
Loukhi, Sov. Un. — D15 14
Loulé, Port. — D1 22
Louny, Czech. — C2 26
Loup, co., Ne., U.S. — C6 104
Loup, stm., Ne., U.S. — C8 104
Loup, Île au, i., P.Q., Can. — B8 71
Loup, Rivière du, stm., P.Q., Can. — B8 74
Loup, Rivière du, stm., P.Q., Can. — C4 74
Lourdes, Nf., Can. — D2 72
Lourdes, Fr. — F3 16
Lourdes, P.Q., Can. — C6 74
Lourdes, P.Q., Can. — C4 74
Lourenço Marques see Maputo, Moz. — C5 49
Loures, Port. — f9 22
Lousã, Port. — B1 22
Lousana, Ab., Can. — C4 68
Louth, Ire. — B5 11
Louth, Eng., U.K. — B6 12
Louth, co., Ire. — D5 11
Loutrá Aidhipsoú, Grc. — C4 25
Loutrákion, Grc. — D4 25
Loutre, Bayou de, stm., La., U.S. — B3 95
Louvain see Leuven, Bel. — B6 16
Louviers, Fr. — C4 16
Louviers, Co., U.S. — B6 83
Lovat, stm., Sov. Un. — C8 27
Love, co., Ok., U.S. — C4 113
Love, stm., Ok., U.S. — D4 113
Lovech, Bul. — D7 24
Lovelaceville, Ky., U.S. — f9 94
Loveladies, N.J., U.S. — D4 107
Lovelady, Tx., U.S. — D5 120
Loveland, Co., U.S. — A5 83
Loveland, Ia., U.S. — C2 92
Loveland, Oh., U.S. — n13 112
Lovell, Me., U.S. — D2 96
Lovell, Ok., U.S. — A4 113
Lovell, Wy., U.S. — B5 127
Lovells, Mi., U.S. — D6 99
Lovelock, Nv., U.S. — C3 105
Lovely, W.V., U.S. — C7 94
Lovenia, Mount, mtn., Ut., U.S. — C5 121
Love Point, c., Md., U.S. — B5 97
Lovern, Sk., Can. — F1 75
Loves Park, Il., U.S. — A4 90
Lovett, Ga., U.S. — D4 87
Lovettsville, Va., U.S. — A5 123
Lovewell Pond, l., Me., U.S. — D2 96
Lovick, Al., U.S. — f7 78
Lovilia, Ia., U.S. — C5 92
Loving, N.M., U.S. — E5 108
Loving, co., Tx., U.S. — D1 120
Lovingston, Va., U.S. — C4 123
Lovington, Il., U.S. — D5 90
Lovington, N.M., U.S. — e8 108
Lovosice, Czech. — C9 19
Low, Cape, c., N.T., Can. — D15 66
Lowa, stm., Zaire — B5 48
Lowden, Ia., U.S. — C6 92
Lowell, Ar., U.S. — A1 81
Lowell, In., U.S. — B3 91
Lowell, Ma., U.S. — A5 98
Lowell, Mi., U.S. — F5 99
Lowell, N.C., U.S. — B1 110
Lowell, Oh., U.S. — C4 112
Lowell, Or., U.S. — D4 114
Lowell, Vt., U.S. — B4 122
Lowell, Wi., U.S. — E5 126
Lowell, Lake, res., Id., U.S. — F2 89

Name	Map Ref	Page

Lowell Mountains, mts., Vt., U.S. — B4 122
Lowellville, Oh., U.S. — A5 112
Lower Arrow Lake, l., B.C., Can. — E8 69
Lower Bank, N.J., U.S. — D3 107
Lower Brule, S.D., U.S. — C6 118
Lower Brule Indian Reservation, S.D., U.S. — C6 118
Lower Burrell, Pa., U.S. — *h15 115
Lower Cabot, Vt., U.S. — C4 122
Lower California, pen., Mex. — B2 63
Lower East Pubnico, N.S., Can. — F4 71
Lower Hutt, N.Z. — N15 51
Lower Island Cove, Nf., Can. — D5 72
Lower Klamath Lake, l., Ca., U.S. — B3 82
Lower Manitou Lake, l., On., Can. — E5 70
Lower Marlboro, Md., U.S. — C4 97
Lower Matecumbe Key, i., Fl., U.S. — H6 86
Lower Merion Township, Pa., U.S. — *F11 115
Lower Monumental Lake, res., Wa., U.S. — C7 124
Lower New York Bay, b., N.J., U.S. — B4 107
Lower Otay Reservoir, res., Ca., U.S. — o16 82
Lower Paia, Hi., U.S. — C5 88
Lower Peach Tree, Al., U.S. — D2 78
Lower Red Lake, l., Mn., U.S. — C3 100
Lower Rice Lake, l., Mn., U.S. — C3 100
Lower Salem, Oh., U.S. — C4 112
Lower Salmon Dam, Id., U.S. — G4 89
Lower Village, Vt., U.S. — C3 122
Lower West Pubnico, N.S., Can. — F4 71
Lower Wilson Pond, l., Me., U.S. — C3 96
Lower Wood's Harbour, N.S., Can. — F4 71
Lowes, Ky., U.S. — f9 94
Lowestoft, Eng., U.K. — D7 10
Lowgap, N.C., U.S. — A2 110
Łowicz, Pol. — B5 26
Lowland, N.C., U.S. — B6 110
Lowman, Id., U.S. — E3 89
Lowmansville, Ky., U.S. — C7 94
Low Moor, Ia., U.S. — C7 92
Lowndes, Mo., U.S. — D7 102
Lowndes, co., Al., U.S. — C3 78
Lowndes, co., Ga., U.S. — F3 87
Lowndes, co., Ms., U.S. — B5 101
Lowndesboro, Al., U.S. — C3 78
Lowndesville, S.C., U.S. — C2 117
Lowry, Mn., U.S. — E3 100
Lowry, S.D., U.S. — B6 118
Lowry Air Force Base, mil., Co., U.S. — B6 83
Lowry City, Mo., U.S. — C4 102
Lowrys, S.C., U.S. — B5 117
Low Tatra Mountains, mts., Czech. — D5 26
Lowville, N.Y., U.S. — B5 109
Low Water Lake, l., Ab., Can. — C3 68
Loxley, Al., U.S. — E2 78
Loxton, Austl. — G3 51
Loyal, Ok., U.S. — B3 113
Loyal, Wi., U.S. — D3 126
Loyalist, Ab., Can. — D5 68
Loyall, Ky., U.S. — D6 94
Loyalsock Creek, stm., Pa., U.S. — D8 115
Loyalton, Ca., U.S. — C3 82
Loyalton, S.D., U.S. — B6 118
Loyalty Islands, is., N. Cal. — H10 6
Loysburg, Pa., U.S. — F5 115
Loysville, Pa., U.S. — F7 115
Loznica, Yugo. — C4 24
Lozovaya, Sov. Un. — G9 27
Lozovaya, Sov. Un. — G11 27
Lozoya, Canal of, Spain — o17 22
Lualaba, stm., Zaire — B4 48
Luama, stm., Zaire — B4 48
Lua Makika, crat., Hi., U.S. — C5 88
Luampa, stm., Zam. — E3 48
Lu'an, China — I7 32
Luana, Ia., U.S. — A6 92
Lüeyang, China — H2 32
Luanda, Braz. — C2 56
Luanda, dept., Ang. — C1 48
Luanda, Braz. — C2 56
Luang, mtn., Thai. — D1 34
Luang Chiang Dao, mtn., Thai. — C3 35
Luanginga, stm., Afr. — D5 48
Luan He, stm., China — C8 31
Luanian, China — D4 32
Luapula, prov., Zam. — D5 48
Luarca, Spain — A2 22
Luashi, Zaire — D3 48
Luau, Ang. — D3 48
Lubaczów, Pol. — C7 26
Lubang, Phil. — p14 34
Lubang, i., Phil. — p13 34
Lubang Islands, is., Phil. — C6 34
Lubango, Ang. — D1 48
Lubao, Phil. — o13 34
Lubartów, Pol. — C7 26
Lubawa, Pol. — B5 26
Lübbecke, F.R.Ger. — A3 19
Lübben, Ger.D.R. — C6 18
Lübbenau, Ger.D.R. — B8 19
Lubbock, Tx., U.S. — C2 120
Lubbock, co., Tx., U.S. — C2 120
Lubec, Me., U.S. — D6 96
Lübeck Bay, b., Eur. — A5 18
Lubefu, Zaire — B4 48
Lubero, Zaire — B4 48
Lubicon Lake, l., Ab., Can. — A3 68
Lubilash, stm., Zaire — C3 48
Lubin, Pol. — C7 26
Lublin, Wi., U.S. — C3 126
Lublin, Pol. — C7 26
Lubliniec, Pol. — C5 26
Lubny, Sov. Un. — F9 27
Luboń, Pol. — B4 26
Lubsko, Pol. — C5 26
Lübtheen, Ger.D.R. — E5 15
Lubudi, Zaire — D4 48
Lubudi, stm., Zaire — C3 48
Lubue, Braz. — B2 48
Lubumbashi (Élisabethville), Zaire — D4 48
Lubutu, Zaire — B4 48
Lucama, N.C., U.S. — B4 110
Lucan, On., Can. — D3 73
Lucan, Ire. — D5 11

Lucan, Mn., U.S. — F3 100
Lucania, Mount, mtn., Yk., Can. — D4 66
Lucas, Ia., U.S. — C4 92
Lucas, Ks., U.S. — C5 93
Lucas, Ky., U.S. — D3 94
Lucas, Mi., U.S. — D5 99
Lucas, Oh., U.S. — B3 112
Lucas, S.D., U.S. — D6 118
Lucas, co., Ia., U.S. — C4 92
Lucas, co., Oh., U.S. — A2 112
Lucasville, Oh., U.S. — D3 112
Lucca, Italy — C3 23
Lucé, Fr. — C4 16
Luce, co., Mi., U.S. — B5 99
Luce Bay, b., Scot., U.K. — C4 10
Lucedale, Ms., U.S. — E5 101
Lucena, Phil. — C6 34
Lucena, Spain — D3 22
Lucena del Cid, Spain — B5 22
Lučenec, Czech. — D5 26
Lucera, Italy — D5 23
Lucerne, Ca., U.S. — C2 82
Lucerne, Co., U.S. — A6 83
Lucerne, In., U.S. — C5 91
Lucerne, Mo., U.S. — A4 102
Lucernemines, Pa., U.S. — E3 115
Lucerne, Lake of, l., Switz. — E4 18
Lucerne Valley, Ca., U.S. — E5 82
Luceville, P.Q., Can. — A9 74
Luchou see Luzhou, China — F6 31
Lüchow, F.R.Ger. — F5 15
Luchuan, China — A9 35
Lucien, Ms., U.S. — D3 101
Lucien, Ok., U.S. — A4 113
Lucile, Id., U.S. — D2 89
Lucille, Al., U.S. — B2 78
Lucinda, Pa., U.S. — D2 115
Lucipara Islands, is., Indon. — G7 34
Lucira, Ang. — D1 48
Luck, Wi., U.S. — C1 126
Luckau, Ger.D.R. — C6 18
Luckenwalde, Ger.D.R. — B6 18
Luckey, Oh., U.S. — A2 112
Luck Lake, l., Sk., Can. — F2 75
Lucknow, On., Can. — D3 73
Lucknow, India — C7 36
Lucky Lake, Sk., Can. — G3 75
Lucky MacCamp, Wy., U.S. — *D5 127
Lucky Peak Lake, res., Id., U.S. — F3 89
Luçon, Fr. — D3 16
Lucrecia, Cabo, c., Cuba — D6 64
Lucy, La., U.S. — h10 95
Lucy, Tn., U.S. — B2 119
Lüda (Dairen), China — D9 31
Luda Kamchiya, stm., Bul. — D8 24
Ludden, N.D., U.S. — C7 111
Ludell, Ks., U.S. — C3 93
Lüdenscheid, F.R.Ger. — B2 19
Lüderitz, Nmb. — C2 49
Ludgate, On., Can. — B4 73
Ludhiāna, India — B6 36
Luding, China — F5 31
Lüdinghausen, F.R.Ger. — B2 19
Ludington, Mi., U.S. — E4 99
Ludlow, N.B., Can. — C3 71
Ludlow, Eng., U.K. — D5 10
Ludlow, Il., U.S. — C5 90
Ludlow, Ky., U.S. — h13 94
Ludlow, Me., U.S. — B4 96
Ludlow, Ma., U.S. — B3 98
Ludlow, Mo., U.S. — B4 102
Ludlow, Pa., U.S. — C4 115
Ludlow, S.D., U.S. — B2 118
Ludlow, Vt., U.S. — E3 122
Ludlow Falls, Oh., U.S. — B1 112
Ludlow Mountain, mtn., Vt., U.S. — E3 122
Ludowici, Ga., U.S. — E5 87
Ludvika, Swe. — G6 14
Ludwigsburg, F.R.Ger. — D4 18
Ludwigshafen [am Rhein], F.R.Ger. — D4 18
Ludwigslust, Ger.D.R. — B5 18
Luebo, Zaire — C3 48
Lueders, Tx., U.S. — C3 120
Luena, Ang. — E3 48
Luepa, Ven. — B5 60
Lufkin, Tx., U.S. — D5 120
Lufuna, Zaire — C2 48
Luga, Sov. Un. — B7 27
Luga, stm., Sov. Un. — B7 27
Lugan, stm., Sov. Un. — q22 27
Luganchik, stm., Sov. Un. — q22 27
Lugano, Switz. — E4 18
Lugano, Lake, l., Eur. — E7 21
Lugar, Ger.D.R. — C7 19
Lugenda, stm., Moz. — D6 48
Lugnaquillia Mountian, mtn., Ire. — D3 10
Lugo, Italy — B3 23
Lugo, Spain — A2 22
Lugoff, S.C., U.S. — C6 117
Lugoj, Rom. — C5 24
Lugovoy, Sov. Un. — E8 28
Luhuo, China — E5 31
Luiana, Ang. — E3 48
Luidhorn, Neth. — A6 17
Luik see Liège, Bel. — B6 16
Luing, i., Scot., U.K. — D3 13
Luís Correia, Braz. — D7 57
Luís Gomes, Braz. — C3 57
Luis Lopez, N.M., U.S. — D3 108
Luiza, Zaire — C3 48
Lujuna Point, c., Guam — L10 52
Lukachukai, Az., U.S. — A6 80
Luke, Md., U.S. — m12 97
Luke Air Force Base, mil., Az., U.S. — D3 80
Lukenie, stm., Zaire — B4 48
Lukeville, Az., U.S. — F3 80
Lukolela, Zaire — B3 48
Lukovit, Bul. — D7 24
Łuków, Pol. — C7 26
Lukoyanov, Sov. Un. — D15 27
Lukuga, stm., Zaire — C4 48
Lukulu, Zam. — D4 48
Lula, Ga., U.S. — B3 87
Lula, Ms., U.S. — A3 101
Lula, Ok., U.S. — C5 113
Luleå, Swe. — E10 14
Luleälven, stm., Swe. — D9 14
Lüleburgaz, Tur. — B6 40
Luling, La., U.S. — k11 95
Luling, Tx., U.S. — E4 120
Lulong, China — D8 31
Lulu, Fl., U.S. — B4 86
Lulua, stm., Zaire — C3 48

Luluabourg see Kananga, Zaire — C3 48
Lum, Mi., U.S. — E7 99
Lumba, Zaire — A2 48
Lumbala N'guimbo, Ang. — D3 48
Lumber, stm., U.S. — C9 117
Lumber Bridge, N.C., U.S. — C3 110
Lumber City, Ga., U.S. — E4 87
Lumberport, W.V., U.S. — B4 125
Lumberton, Ms., U.S. — D4 101
Lumberton, N.J., U.S. — D3 107
Lumberton, N.M., U.S. — A3 108
Lumberton, N.C., U.S. — C3 110
Lumbo, Moz. — E7 48
Lumby, B.C., Can. — D8 69
Luminao Reef, rf., Guam — L9 52
Lumpkin, Ga., U.S. — D2 87
Lumpkin, co., Ga., U.S. — B2 87
Lumsden, Nf., Can. — D5 72
Lumsden, Sk., Can. — G3 75
Lumsden, Scot., U.K. — C6 13
Lumsden, N.Z. — P12 51
Lumsden Beach, Sk., Can. — G3 75
Lumut, Point, c., Indon. — F3 34
Luna, Mn., U.S. — F5 100
Luna, co., N.M., U.S. — E2 108
Luna Pier, Mi., U.S. — G7 99
Lund, B.C., Can. — D5 69
Lund, Swe. — J5 14
Lund, Nv., U.S. — E6 105
Lunda Norte, dept., Ang. — C2 48
Lunda Sul, dept., Ang. — D3 48
Lundazi, Zam. — D5 48
Lundbreck, Ab., Can. — E3 68
Lundby, Den. — C5 15
Lunderskov, Den. — C3 15
Lundu, Malay. — E3 34
Lundy, i., Eng., U.K. — E4 10
Lune, stm., Eng., U.K. — F6 13
Lünen, F.R.Ger. — B2 19
Lunenburg, N.S., Can. — E5 71
Lunenburg, Ma., U.S. — A4 98
Lunenburg, Vt., U.S. — C5 122
Lunenburg, Va., U.S. — D4 123
Lunenburg, co., N.S., Can. — E5 71
Lunenburg, co., Va., U.S. — D4 123
Lunéville, Fr. — C7 16
Lunga, stm., Zam. — D4 48
Lungué-Bungo, stm., Afr. — D3 48
Lūni, stm., India — C5 36
Luning, Nv., U.S. — E3 105
Lunino, Sov. Un. — E15 27
Lunsar, S.L. — E2 45
Lunyama, Zaire — C4 48
Luocheng, China — D8 31
Luoding, China — A9 35
Luohe, China — E7 31
Luoning, China — G4 32
Luoshan, China — H6 32
Luoyang, China — E7 31
Luozi, Zaire — B1 48
Lupani, Zimb. — A4 49
Lupeni, Rom. — C6 24
Lupton, Az., U.S. — B6 80
Lupton, Mi., U.S. — D6 99
Lupus, Mo., U.S. — C5 102
Luque, Para. — E4 55
Luquillo, Sierra de, mts. P.R. — B4 65
Lūrah, stm., Afg. — B4 36
Luray, Ks., U.S. — C5 93
Luray, Mo., U.S. — A6 102
Luray, S.C., U.S. — F5 117
Luray, Tn., U.S. — B3 119
Luray, Va., U.S. — B4 123
Lure, Fr. — D7 16
Lure, Lake, res., N.C., U.S. — f10 110
Lurgan, N. Ire., U.K. — C3 10
Luribay, Bol. — C2 55
Lúrio, Moz. — D7 48
Lúrio, stm., Moz. — D6 48
Lurton, Ar., U.S. — B2 81
Lusaka, Zam. — E4 48
Lusaka, prov., Zam. — E4 48
Lusambo, Zaire — B3 48
Lusby, Md., U.S. — D5 97
Luscar, Ab., Can. — C1 68
Luseland, Sk., Can. — E1 75
Lushan, China — H5 32
Lushan, China — F8 34
Lushnja, Alb. — B2 25
Lushoto, Tan. — B6 48
Lüshun, China — D9 31
Lusignan, Fr. — F5 16
Lusk, Wy., U.S. — D8 127
Lustre, Mt., U.S. — B11 103
Lüt, Dasht-e, des., Iran — B5 38
Lutcher, La., U.S. — D5 95
Lutesville, Mo., U.S. — D8 102
Luther, Mi., U.S. — D5 99
Luther, Ok., U.S. — B4 113
Luthersburg, Pa., U.S. — D4 115
Luthersville, Ga., U.S. — C2 87
Lutherville-Timonium, Md., U.S. — B4 97
Lutie, Ok., U.S. — C6 113
Lütjenburg, F.R.Ger. — D4 15
Luton, Eng., U.K. — E6 10
Lutong, Malay. — E4 34
Lutsen, Mn., U.S. — k9 100
Luttrell, Tn., U.S. — C10 119
Lutts, Tn., U.S. — B4 119
Lutugino, Sov. Un. — q22 27
Lutz, Fl., U.S. — D4 86
Lützow-Holm Bay, b., Ant. — C16 7
Luuq, Som. — E5 47

Luvua, stm., Zaire — C4 48
Luverne, Al., U.S. — D3 78
Luverne, Ia., U.S. — A3 92
Luverne, Mn., U.S. — G2 100
Luverne, N.D., U.S. — B8 111
Luwingu, Zam. — D5 48
Luwuk, Indon. — F6 34
Luxapallila Creek, stm., U.S. — B5 101
Luxembourg, prov., Bel. — E5 17
Luxembourg, ctry., Eur. — C7 16
Luxembourg, Lux. — C7 16
Luxembourg, Ia., U.S. — B6 92
Luxemburg, Wi., U.S. — D6 126
Luxi, China — F7 31
Luxomni, Ga., U.S. — h8 87
Luxor (Al Uqsur), Eg. — C3 43
Luxor, hist., Egypt — D6 43
Luxora, Ar., U.S. — B6 81
Luz, Braz. — B3 56
Luza, Sov. Un. — A3 28
Luza, stm., Sov. Un. — A3 28
Luzern, Switz. — E4 18
Luzern, state, Switz. — B4 20
Luzerne, Mi., U.S. — D6 99
Luzerne, Pa., U.S. — n17 115
Luzerne, co., Pa., U.S. — D9 115
Luzhou (Luchow), China — F6 31
Luziânia, Braz. — B3 56
Lužnice, stm., Eur. — D6 26
Luzon, i., Phil. — B6 34
Luzon Strait, strt., Asia — A6 34
Lvov, Sov. Un. — E5 29
Lyakhov Islands, is., Sov. Un. — B1 128
Lyall, Mount, mtn., N.Z. — P11 51
Lyallpur see Faisalabad, Pak. — B5 36
Lyaskovets, Bul. — D7 24
Lybster, Scot., U.K. — B5 13
Lychen, Ger.D.R. — E7 15
Lycksele, Swe. — E8 14
Lycoming, N.Y., U.S. — B4 109
Lycoming, co., Pa., U.S. — D7 115
Lycoming Creek, stm., Pa., U.S. — D7 115
Lydenburg, S. Afr. — C5 49
Lydia, Mn., U.S. — F5 100
Lydia, S.C., U.S. — C7 117
Lydick, In., U.S. — A4 91
Lyell, Mount, mtn., Ca., U.S. — D4 82
Lyell Island, i., B.C., Can. — C2 69
Lyerly, Ga., U.S. — B1 87
Lyford, Tx., U.S. — F4 120
Lygnern, l., Swe. — A6 15
Lykens, Pa., U.S. — E8 115
Lyle, Mn., U.S. — G6 100
Lyle, Wa., U.S. — D4 124
Lyles, Tn., U.S. — B4 119
Lyleton, Mb., Can. — E1 70
Lyman, Ms., U.S. — E4 101
Lyman, Ne., U.S. — C1 104
Lyman, S.C., U.S. — B3 117
Lyman, Ut., U.S. — E4 121
Lyman, Wa., U.S. — A3 124
Lyman, Wy., U.S. — E2 127
Lyman, co., S.D., U.S. — D6 118
Lyman Lake, res., Az., U.S. — C6 80
Lyme, Ct., U.S. — D6 84
Lyme, N.H., U.S. — C2 106
Lyme Bay, b., Eng., U.K. — D5 12
Lyme Center, N.H., U.S. — C2 106
Lymington, Eng., U.K. — D6 12
Łyna, stm., Eur. — B6 26
Lynch, Ky., U.S. — D7 94
Lynch, Md., U.S. — B5 97
Lynch, Ne., U.S. — B7 104
Lynchburg, N.D., U.S. — C8 111
Lynchburg, Oh., U.S. — C2 112
Lynchburg, S.C., U.S. — C7 117
Lynchburg, Tn., U.S. — B5 119
Lynchburg, Va., U.S. — C3 123
Lynches, stm., S.C., U.S. — D8 117
Lynch Heights, De., U.S. — E4 85
Lynch Station, Va., U.S. — C3 123
Lynd, Mn., U.S. — F3 100
Lyndeborough, N.H., U.S. — E3 106
Lynden, Wa., U.S. — A3 124
Lyndhurst, On., Can. — C8 73
Lyndhurst, N.J., U.S. — h8 107
Lyndon, Ks., U.S. — D8 93
Lyndon, Ky., U.S. — g11 94
Lyndon, Il., U.S. — B4 90
Lyndon, Vt., U.S. — B4 122
Lyndon B. Johnson National Historical Site, hist., Tx., U.S. — D3 120
Lyndon B. Johnson Space Center, sci., Tx., U.S. — r14 120
Lyndon Center, Vt., U.S. — B4 122
Lyndon Station, Wi., U.S. — E4 126
Lyndonville, N.Y., U.S. — B2 109
Lyndonville, Vt., U.S. — B4 122
Lyndora, Pa., U.S. — E2 115
Lyngby [Tårbæk], Den. — C6 15
Lynn, Al., U.S. — A2 78
Lynn, Ar., U.S. — A4 81
Lynn, In., U.S. — D8 91
Lynn, Ma., U.S. — B6 98
Lynn, Pa., U.S. — C10 115
Lynn, co., Tx., U.S. — C2 120
Lynn Canal, b., Ak., U.S. — k22 79
Lynndyl, Ut., U.S. — D3 121
Lynne Acres, Md., U.S. — B4 97
Lynnfield, Ma., U.S. — f11 98
Lynn Garden, Tn., U.S. — C11 119
Lynn Grove, Ky., U.S. — f9 94
Lynn Haven, Fl., U.S. — u16 86
Lynnhaven Roads, b., Va., U.S. — k15 123
Lynnport, Pa., U.S. — E10 115
Lynnville, Ia., U.S. — C5 92
Lynnville, In., U.S. — H3 91
Lynnville, Tn., U.S. — B4 119
Lynnwood, Wa., U.S. — B3 124
Lynton, Eng., U.K. — C4 12
Lynwood, Ca., U.S. — n12 82
Lynxville, Wi., U.S. — E2 126
Lyoffans, Fr. — A2 21
Lyon, Fr. — E6 16
Lyon, Ms., U.S. — A3 101
Lyon, co., Ia., U.S. — A1 92
Lyon, co., Ks., U.S. — D7 93
Lyon, co., Ky., U.S. — C1 94
Lyon, co., Mn., U.S. — F3 100
Lyon, co., Nv., U.S. — D2 105
Lyon Creek, stm., Ks., U.S. — D7 93
Lyon Mountain, N.Y., U.S. — f11 109
Lyon Mountain, mtn., N.Y., U.S. — f11 109
Lyonnais, hist. reg., Fr. — E6 16
Lyons, Co., U.S. — A5 83
Lyons, Ga., U.S. — D4 87
Lyons, Il., U.S. — k9 90
Lyons, In., U.S. — G3 91
Lyons, Ks., U.S. — D5 93
Lyons, Mi., U.S. — F6 99
Lyons, Ne., U.S. — C9 104
Lyons, N.Y., U.S. — B3 109
Lyons, Oh., U.S. — A1 112
Lyons, Or., U.S. — C4 114
Lyons, S.D., U.S. — D9 118
Lyons, Tx., U.S. — D4 120
Lyons, Wi., U.S. — n11 126
Lyons Falls, N.Y., U.S. — B5 109
Lyons Plains, Ct., U.S. — E2 84
Lyracrompane, Ire. — E2 11
Lys, stm., Eur. — D3 17

Lysá [nad Labem], Czech. — n18 26
Lysaya Gora, Sov. Un. — G8 27
Lysekil, Swe. — H4 14
Lysite, Wy., U.S. — C5 127
Lyss, Switz. — B3 21
Lysva, Sov. Un. — D8 29
Lytham Saint Anne's, Eng., U.K. — A5 12
Lytle, Oh., U.S. — C1 112
Lytle, Tx., U.S. — E3 120
Lytton, B.C., Can. — D7 69
Lytton, Ia., U.S. — B3 92
Lyubar, Sov. Un. — G6 27
Lyubertsy, Sov. Un. — n17 27
Lyudinovo, Sov. Un. — E10 27

M

Ma, stm., Asia — A2 34
Ma'ād, Jord. — B7 41
Maalaea, Hi., U.S. — *C5 88
Maalaea Bay, b., Hi., U.S. — C5 88
Ma'alot-Tarshiha, Isr. — B7 41
Maam Cross, Ire. — D2 11
Maamoura, Cap, c., Tun. — F3 23
Ma'ān, Jord. — G10 40
Maas, Ire. — C3 11
Maas (Meuse), stm., Eur. — B6 16
Maaseik, Bel. — C5 17
Maastricht, Neth. — B6 16
Mabana, Wa., U.S. — A3 124
Mabaruma, Guy. — A3 59
Mabber, Ras, c., Som. — D7 47
Mabel, Mn., U.S. — G7 100
Mabel Lake, l., B.C., Can. — D8 69
Mabelvale, Ar., U.S. — k10 81
Maben, Ms., U.S. — B4 101
Maberly, On., Can. — C8 73
Mabie, W.V., U.S. — C5 125
Mableton, Ga., U.S. — h7 87
Mablethorpe, Eng., U.K. — A8 12
Mabote, Moz. — B5 49
Mabou, N.S., Can. — C8 71
Mabrous Tafidinga, well, Niger — B7 45
Mabscott, W.V., U.S. — D3 125
Mabton, Wa., U.S. — C6 124
Mabuni, Japan — O5 52
Macachin, Arg. — B4 54
Macadam, N.B., Can. — D2 71
Macaé, Braz. — C4 56
Macaíba, Braz. — g6 57
Macalelon, Phil. — p14 34
Macapá, Braz. — B4 59
Macará, Ec. — B2 58
MacArthur, Oh., U.S. — C3 112
Macas, Ec. — B2 58
Macau, Braz. — C3 57
Macau, dep., Asia — G7 31
Macau, Braz. — C3 57
Macaúbas, Braz. — A4 56
McAuley, Mb., Can. — D1 70
McBain, Mi., U.S. — D5 99
McBaine, Mo., U.S. — C5 102
McBee, S.C., U.S. — C7 117
McBride, B.C., Can. — C7 69
McBride, Mo., U.S. — D8 102
McCabe, Mt., U.S. — B12 103
Maccagno [Superiore], Italy — D6 21
McCall, Id., U.S. — E2 89
McCall Creek, Ms., U.S. — D3 101
McCallsburg, Ia., U.S. — B4 92
McCamey, Tx., U.S. — D1 120
McCammon, Id., U.S. — G6 89
McCandless, Pa., U.S. — h13 115
McCanna, N.D., U.S. — A8 111
Maccarese, Italy — h8 23
McCarley, Ms., U.S. — B3 101
McCarr, Ky., U.S. — C7 94
McCarthy, Ak., U.S. — C11 79
McCartney Mountain, mtn., Mt., U.S. — E4 103
McCartys, N.M., U.S. — B2 108
McCaskill, Ar., U.S. — D2 81
McCauley Island, i., B.C., Can. — C2 69
McCaulley, Tx., U.S. — C2 120
McCaysville, Ga., U.S. — B2 87
McChord Air Force Base, mil., Wa., U.S. — f11 124
McClain, co., Ok., U.S. — C4 113
McClave, Co., U.S. — C8 83
McCleary, Wa., U.S. — B2 124
McClellan Air Force Base, mil., Ca., U.S. — C3 82
McClelland, Ar., U.S. — B4 81
McClelland, Ia., U.S. — C2 92
McClellanville, S.C., U.S. — E9 117
McClintock, Mount, mtn., Ant. — A28 7
McCloud, Ca., U.S. — B2 82
McClure, Il., U.S. — F4 90
McClure, Oh., U.S. — A2 112
McClure, Pa., U.S. — E7 115
McClure, Va., U.S. — e9 123
McClusky, N.D., U.S. — B5 111
McColl, S.C., U.S. — B8 117
McComas, W.V., U.S. — D3 125
McComb, Ms., U.S. — D3 101
McComb, Oh., U.S. — A2 112
McCone, co., Mt., U.S. — C11 103
McConnell, Tn., U.S. — A3 119
McConnell Air Force Base, mil., Ks., U.S. — g12 93
McConnells, S.C., U.S. — B5 117
McConnellsburg, Pa., U.S. — G6 115
McConnelsville, Oh., U.S. — C4 112
McCook, Ne., U.S. — D5 104

McCook, co., S.D., U.S. — D8 118
McCook Lake, S.D., U.S. — E9 118
McCool, Ms., U.S. — B4 101
McCoole, Md., U.S. — m13 97
McCool Junction, Ne., U.S. — D8 104
McCord, Sk., Can. — H2 75
McCordsville, In., U.S. — E6 91
McCormick, S.C., U.S. — D3 117
McCormick, co., S.C., U.S. — D3 117
McCoy, Co., U.S. — B4 83
McCracken, Ks., U.S. — D4 93
McCracken, co., Ky., U.S. — e9 94
McCreary, Mb., Can. — D2 70
McCreary, co., Ky., U.S. — D5 94
McCrory, Ar., U.S. — B4 81
McCulloch, co., Tx., U.S. — D3 120
Macculloch, Cape, c., N.T., Can. — B18 66
McCullough, Al., U.S. — D2 78
McCullough Mountain, mtn., Nv., U.S. — H6 105
McCullum, Al., U.S. — B2 78
McCune, Ks., U.S. — E8 93
McCurtain, Ok., U.S. — B7 113
McCurtain, co., Ok., U.S. — C7 113
McCutchenville, Oh., U.S. — B2 112
McDade, Tx., U.S. — D4 120
McDaniel, Md., U.S. — C5 97
McDavid, Fl., U.S. — u14 86
McDermitt, Nv., U.S. — B4 105
McDermott, Oh., U.S. — D2 112
Macdhui, Ben, mtn., Scot., U.K. — B4 10
MacDill Air Force Base, mil., Fl., U.S. — E4 86
Macdonald, Mb., Can. — D2 70
McDonald, Ks., U.S. — C2 93
McDonald, Ms., U.S. — C4 101
McDonald, N.M., U.S. — D6 108
McDonald, Tn., U.S. — h12 119
MacDonald, W.V., U.S. — D3 125
McDonald, co., Mo., U.S. — E3 102
Macdonald, Lake, l., Austl. — D4 50
McDonald Creek, stm., Mt., U.S. — B4 103
McDonald Islands, is., Austl. — J1 2
Macdonald Range, mts., B.C., Can. — E10 69
MacDonaldton, Pa., U.S. — G4 115
Macdonnell Ranges, mts., Austl. — D5 50
McDonough, Ga., U.S. — C2 87
McDonough, N.Y., U.S. — C5 109
McDonough, co., Il., U.S. — C3 90
McDougall, Mount, mtn., Wy., U.S. — C2 127
McDowell, Ky., U.S. — C7 94
McDowell, co., N.C., U.S. — f10 110
McDowell, co., W.V., U.S. — D3 125
McDowell Mountains, mts., Az., U.S. — k9 80
McDowell Peak, mtn., Az., U.S. — k9 80
MacDowell Reservoir, res., N.H., U.S. — E2 106
Macduff, Scot., U.K. — C6 13
McDuffie, co., Ga., U.S. — C4 87
Mace, In., U.S. — D4 91
Macedon, N.Y., U.S. — B3 109
Macedonia, Ct., U.S. — B2 84
Macedonia, Il., U.S. — E5 90
Macedonia, Oh., U.S. — A4 112
Macedonia, hist. reg., Eur. — B4 25
Maceió, Braz. — C3 57
McElhattan, Pa., U.S. — D7 115
McElroy Creek, stm., W.V. — k9 125
Macenta, Gui. — E3 45
Maceo, Ky., U.S. — C3 94
Macerata, Italy — C4 23
Maces Bay, b., N.B., Can. — D3 71
McEwen, Tn., U.S. — A4 119
McFadden, Wy., U.S. — E6 127
McFaddin, Tx., U.S. — E4 120
McFall, Mo., U.S. — A3 102
McFarlan, N.C., U.S. — C3 110
MacFarlane, W.V., U.S. — B3 125
McFarland, Ca., U.S. — E4 82
McFarland, Wi., U.S. — E4 126
McFarland, Mi., U.S. — B3 99
McGaheysville, Va., U.S. — B4 123
McGee, Ms., U.S. — F1 75
McGehee, Ar., U.S. — D4 81
McGill, Nv., U.S. — D7 105
McGillivray, B.C., Can. — D6 69
McGillicuddy's Reeks, mts., Ire. — E2 10
McGivney, N.B., Can. — C3 71
McGrady, N.C., U.S. — A1 110
McGrath, Ak., U.S. — C8 79
McGrath, Mn., U.S. — D5 100
McGraw, N.Y., U.S. — C4 109
McGraws, W.V., U.S. — D3 125
MacGregor, Mb., Can. — E2 70
McGregor, Ia., U.S. — A6 92
McGregor, Mn., U.S. — D5 100
McGregor, N.D., U.S. — A3 111
McGregor, Tx., U.S. — D4 120
McGregor, stm., B.C., Can. — B7 69
McGregor Lake, l., Ab., Can. — D4 68
McGrew, Ne., U.S. — C2 104
McGuffey, Oh., U.S. — B2 112
McGuire, Mount, mtn., Id., U.S. — D4 89
McGuire Air Force Base, mil., N.J., U.S. — C3 107
Mach, Pak. — C4 36
Machačkala, Sov. Un.? — B6 28
Machachi, Ec. — B2 58
Machado, Braz. — C3 56
Machakos, Kenya — B6 48
Machala, Ec. — B2 58
Machanao, Mount, hill, Guam — L10 52
Machattie, Lake, l., Austl. — B2 51
Macheng, China — E7 31
McHenry, Il., U.S. — A5 90
McHenry, Md., U.S. — k12 97
McHenry, Ms., U.S. — E4 101
McHenry, N.D., U.S. — B7 111
McHenry, co., Il., U.S. — A5 90
McHenry, co., N.D., U.S. — A5 111
Machias, Me., U.S. — D5 96
Machias, N.Y., U.S. — C2 109
Machias, stm., Me., U.S. — D5 96
Machias Bay, b., Me., U.S. — D5 96
Machias Lakes, l., Me., U.S. — D5 96
Machiasport, Me., U.S. — D5 96
Machichi, stm., Mb., Can. — A6 70

Name	Map Ref	Page
Machico, Port.	h12	22
Machilipatnam (Bandar), India	E7	36
Mchinga, Tan.	C6	48
Mchinji, Mwi.	D5	48
Machiques, Ven.	A3	60
Macho, Arroyo del, val., N.M., U.S.	C4	108
Machrihanish, Scot., U.K.	E3	13
McHue, Ar., U.S.	B4	81
Machu Picchu, hist., Peru	D3	58
Machynlleth, Wales, U.K.	B4	12
Macia, Moz.	C5	49
Măcin, Rom.	C9	24
Macina, reg., Mali	D4	45
McIndoe Falls, Vt., U.S.	C4	122
McIntire, Ia., U.S.	A5	92
McIntosh, Al., U.S.	D1	78
McIntosh, Fl., U.S.	C4	86
McIntosh, Ga., U.S.	E5	87
McIntosh, Mn., U.S.	C3	100
McIntosh, N.M., U.S.	C3	108
McIntosh, S.D., U.S.	C5	111
McIntosh, co., Ga., U.S.	E5	87
McIntosh, co., N.D., U.S.	C6	111
McIntosh, co., Ok., U.S.	B6	113
McIntosh Lake, l., Sk., Can.	B3	75
McIntosh Run, stm., Md., U.S.	D4	97
McIntyre, Ga., U.S.	D3	87
McIntyre, Pa., U.S.	E3	115
Macintyre, stm., Austl.	D7	51
Mack, Co., U.S.	B2	83
McKague, Sk., Can.	E4	75
Mackay, Austl.	D8	50
Mackay, Id., U.S.	F5	89
MacKay, stm., Ab., Can.	A4	68
Mackay, Lake, l., Austl.	D4	50
MacKay Lake, l., N.T., Can.	D10	66
McKean, Pa., U.S.	C1	115
McKean, co., Pa., U.S.	C4	115
McKee, Ky., U.S.	C6	94
McKee City, N.J., U.S.	E3	107
McKeesport, Pa., U.S.	F2	115
McKees Rocks, Pa., U.S.	F1	115
McKenney, Va., U.S.	D5	123
McKenzie, Guy.	A3	59
McKenzie, Al., U.S.	D3	78
McKenzie, N.D., U.S.	C5	111
McKenzie, Tn., U.S.	A3	119
Mackenzie, dept., N.T., Can.	D11	66
McKenzie, co., N.D., U.S.	B2	111
Mackenzie, stm., N.T., Can.	C6	66
McKenzie, stm., Or., U.S.	C4	114
MacKenzie Bay, b., Ant.	C20	7
Mackenzie Bay, b., Can.	C5	66
McKenzie Bridge, Or., U.S.	C4	114
Mackenzie King Island, i., N.T., Can.	m29	66
Mackenzie Mountains, mts., Can.	D7	66
McKerrow, On., Can.	A3	73
Mackey, In., U.S.	H3	91
Mackeys, N.C., U.S.	B6	110
Mackeys Station, On., Can.	A7	73
Mackeyville, Pa., U.S.	D7	115
Mackinac, co., Mi., U.S.	B5	99
Mackinac, Straits of, strt., Mi., U.S.	C6	99
Mackinac Bridge, Mi., U.S.	C6	99
Mackinac Island, Mi., U.S.	C6	99
Mackinac Island, i., Mi., U.S.	C6	99
Mackinaw, Il., U.S.	C4	90
Mackinaw, stm., Il., U.S.	C4	90
Mackinaw City, Mi., U.S.	C6	99
McKinley, Al., U.S.	C2	78
McKinley, co., N.M., U.S.	B1	108
McKinley, Mount, mtn., Ak., U.S.	C9	79
McKinley Park, Ak., U.S.	C10	79
McKinleyville, Ca., U.S.	B1	82
McKinney, Ky., U.S.	C5	94
McKinney, Tx., U.S.	C4	120
McKinney, Lake, l., Ks., U.S.	E2	93
McKinnon, Wy., U.S.	E3	127
Mackinnon Road, Kenya	B6	48
Mackittrick, Ca., U.S.	E4	82
McKittrick, Ca., U.S.	E4	82
McKittrick Summit, mtn., Ca., U.S.	E4	82
Macklin, Sk., Can.	E1	75
McKnight Lake, l., Mb., Can.	A1	70
Macksburg, Oh., U.S.	C4	112
Macks Creek, Mo., U.S.	D5	102
Macksville, Ks., U.S.	E5	93
Mackville, Ky., U.S.	C4	94
Mackville, Wi., U.S.	h9	126
McLain, Ms., U.S.	D5	101
McLaughlin, Ab., Can.	C5	68
McLaughlin, S.D., U.S.	B5	118
McLaughlin, stm., Mb., Can.	C3	70
McLaurin, Ms., U.S.	D4	101
Maclean, Austl.	D9	51
McLean, Sk., Can.	G3	75
McLean, Il., U.S.	C4	90
McLean, Ne., U.S.	B8	104
McLean, Tx., U.S.	B2	120
McLean, Va., U.S.	g12	123
McLean, co., Il., U.S.	C4	90
McLean, co., Ky., U.S.	C2	94
McLean, co., N.D., U.S.	B4	111
McLean Lake, l., Sk., Can.	A6	68
McLean Mountain, mtn., Me., U.S.	A4	96
McLeansboro, Il., U.S.	E5	90
Maclean Strait, strt., N.T., Can.	m31	66
Maclear, S. Afr.	D4	49
McLemoresville, Tn., U.S.	B3	119
McLennan, Ab., Can.	B2	68
McLennan, co., Tx., U.S.	D4	120
McLennan Lake, l., Sk., Can.	B3	75
McLeod, N.D., U.S.	C8	111
McLeod, co., Mn., U.S.	F4	100
McLeod, stm., Ab., Can.	C2	68
Macleod, Lake, l., Austl.	D1	50
McLeod Lake, B.C., Can.	B6	69
McLeod Lake, l., B.C., Can.	B6	69
McLoud, Ok., U.S.	B4	113
McLoughlin, Mount, mtn., Or., U.S.	D4	114
McLouth, Ks., U.S.	C8	93
McMahon, Sk., Can.	G2	75
McMechen, W.V., U.S.	B4	125
McMillan, Mi., U.S.	B5	99
McMillan, Lake, res., N.M., U.S.	E5	108
McMillin, Wa., U.S.	f11	124
McMinn, co., Tn., U.S.	D9	119
McMinnville, Or., U.S.	B3	114
McMinnville, Tn., U.S.	D8	119
McMorran, Sk., Can.	F1	75
McMullen, co., Tx., U.S.	E3	120
McMurdo, sci., Ant.	B29	7
McMurdo Sound, strt., Ant.	B29	7
McNab, Ar., U.S.	D2	81
McNabb, Il., U.S.	B4	90
McNair, Ms., U.S.	D2	101
McNairy, Tn., U.S.	B3	119
McNairy, co., Tn., U.S.	B3	119
McNary, Az., U.S.	C6	80
McNary, Tx., U.S.	D3	95
McNary Dam, U.S.	B7	114
McNaughton Lake, res., B.C., Can.	C8	69
McNeal, Az., U.S.	F6	80
McNeil, Ar., U.S.	D2	81
McNeil, Tx., U.S.	D4	120
McNeil, Mount, mtn., B.C., Can.	B2	69
McNeil Island, i., Wa., U.S.	f10	124
McNulty, Or., U.S.	*B4	114
McNutt, Sk., Can.	F5	75
McNutts Island, i., N.S., Can.	F4	71
Maco, Bol.	B2	55
Macocolo, Ang.	C2	48
Macomb, Il., U.S.	C3	90
Macomb, Ok., U.S.	B4	113
Macomb, co., Mi., U.S.	F8	99
Mâcon, Fr.	D6	16
Macon, Ga., U.S.	D3	87
Macon, Il., U.S.	D5	90
Macon, Ms., U.S.	B5	101
Macon, Mo., U.S.	B5	102
Macon, N.C., U.S.	A4	110
Macon, Tn., U.S.	B2	119
Macon, co., Al., U.S.	C4	78
Macon, co., Ga., U.S.	D2	87
Macon, co., Il., U.S.	D4	90
Macon, co., Mo., U.S.	B5	102
Macon, co., N.C., U.S.	f9	110
Macon, co., Tn., U.S.	A5	119
Macon, Bayou, stm., U.S.	B4	95
Macoun, Sk., Can.	H4	75
Macoun Lake, l., Sk., Can.	A4	75
Macoupin, co., Il., U.S.	D4	90
Macoupin Creek, stm., Il., U.S.	D3	90
Macovane, Moz.	B6	49
McPhail, stm., Mb., Can.	C3	70
McPherson, Ks., U.S.	D6	93
McPherson, co., Ks., U.S.	D6	93
McPherson, co., Ne., U.S.	C4	104
McPherson, co., S.D., U.S.	B6	118
McQuady, Ky., U.S.	C3	94
Macquarie, stm., Austl.	F8	50
Macquarie Island, i., Austl.	J7	2
McQueeney, Tx., U.S.	h7	120
McRae, Ar., U.S.	B4	81
McRae, Ga., U.S.	D4	87
McRoberts, Ky., U.S.	C7	94
Macroom, Ire.	E2	10
Macrorie, Sk., Can.	F2	75
McSherrystown, Pa., U.S.	G7	115
McTaggart, Sk., Can.	H3	75
McTavish, Mb., Can.	E3	70
MacTier, On., Can.	B5	73
Macujer, Col.	G3	60
Macuelizo, Hond.	C3	62
Macungie, Pa., U.S.	E10	115
McVeigh, Ky., U.S.	C7	94
McVeytown, Pa., U.S.	F6	115
McVille, N.D., U.S.	B7	111
Macwahoc, Me., U.S.	C4	96
McWilliams, Al., U.S.	D2	78
Macy, In., U.S.	C5	91
Macy, Ne., U.S.	B9	104
Mad, stm., Ca., U.S.	B2	82
Mad, stm., Ct., U.S.	B3	84
Mad, stm., N.H., U.S.	C3	106
Mad, stm., Oh., U.S.	C2	112
Mad, stm., Vt., U.S.	C3	122
Ma'dabā, Jord.	C7	41
Madaba, Tan.	C6	48
Madagascar, ctry., Afr.	g9	49
Mada'in Şālih, Sau. Ar.	D7	43
Madalena, Braz.	C4	56
Madame, Isle, i., N.S., Can.	D9	71
Madang, Pap. N. Gui.	k12	50
Madaoua, Niger	D6	45
Madāripur, Bngl.	F13	37
Madawaska, On., Can.	B7	73
Madawaska, Me., U.S.	A4	96
Madawaska, co., N.B., Can.	B1	71
Madawaska, stm., On., Can.	B9	74
Madawaska, stm., On., Can.	B7	73
Madawaska Lake, l., Me., U.S.	A4	96
Madaya, Burma	A2	35
Madbury, N.H., U.S.	D5	106
Madden, Ms., U.S.	C4	101
Maddock, N.D., U.S.	B6	111
Maddox, Md., U.S.	D4	97
Madeira, Oh., U.S.	o13	112
Madeira, i., Port.	h11	22
Madeira, stm., S.A.	D2	59
Madeira Islands, is., Port.	C1	44
Madeleine, Îles de la, is., P.Q., Can.	B8	71
Madelia, Mn., U.S.	F4	100
Madeline Island, i., Wi., U.S.	B3	126
Madera, Mex.	B3	63
Madera, Ca., U.S.	D3	82
Madera, Pa., U.S.	E5	115
Madera, co., Ca., U.S.	D4	82
Madgaon, India	E5	36
Madge Lake, l., Sk., Can.	D1	70
Madhupur, India	E11	37
Madhya Pradesh, state, India	D6	36
Madimba, Zaire	C2	48
Madīnat ash Sha'b, P.D.R.Yem.	D4	38
Madingou, Congo	B1	48
Madison, Al., U.S.	A3	78
Madison, Ar., U.S.	B5	81
Madison, Ca., U.S.	C3	82
Madison, Ct., U.S.	D5	84
Madison, Fl., U.S.	B3	86
Madison, Ga., U.S.	C3	87
Madison, In., U.S.	G7	91
Madison, Ks., U.S.	D7	93
Madison, Me., U.S.	D3	96
Madison, Md., U.S.	C5	97
Madison, Mn., U.S.	E2	100
Madison, Mo., U.S.	C5	102
Madison, Ne., U.S.	C8	104
Madison, N.H., U.S.	C4	106
Madison, N.J., U.S.	B4	107
Madison, N.Y., U.S.	C5	109
Madison, N.C., U.S.	A3	110
Madison, Oh., U.S.	A4	112
Madison, S.C., U.S.	B1	117
Madison, S.D., U.S.	C8	118
Madison, W.V., U.S.	C3	125
Madison, Wi., U.S.	E4	126
Madison, co., Al., U.S.	A3	78
Madison, co., Ar., U.S.	B2	81
Madison, co., Fl., U.S.	B3	86
Madison, co., Ga., U.S.	B3	87
Madison, co., Id., U.S.	F7	89
Madison, co., Il., U.S.	E4	90
Madison, co., In., U.S.	D6	91
Madison, co., Ia., U.S.	C3	92
Madison, co., Ky., U.S.	C5	94
Madison, co., La., U.S.	B4	95
Madison, co., Ms., U.S.	C4	101
Madison, co., Mo., U.S.	D7	102
Madison, co., Mt., U.S.	E5	103
Madison, co., Ne., U.S.	C8	104
Madison, co., N.Y., U.S.	C5	109
Madison, co., N.C., U.S.	f10	110
Madison, co., Oh., U.S.	C2	112
Madison, co., Tn., U.S.	B3	119
Madison, co., Tx., U.S.	D5	120
Madison, co., Va., U.S.	B4	123
Madison, stm., Mt., U.S.	E5	103
Madisonburg, Pa., U.S.	E7	115
Madison Heights, Mi., U.S.	o15	99
Madison Heights, Va., U.S.	C3	123
Madison Lake, Mn., U.S.	F5	100
Madison Range, mts., Mt., U.S.	E5	103
Madisonville, Ky., U.S.	C2	94
Madisonville, La., U.S.	D5	95
Madisonville, Tn., U.S.	D9	119
Madisonville, Tx., U.S.	D5	120
Madiun, Indon.	G4	34
Madoc, On., Can.	C7	73
Madoc, Mt., U.S.	B11	103
Mado Gashi, Kenya	A6	48
Madon, stm., Fr.	A2	20
Madona, Sov. Un.	C6	27
Madonna di Campiglio, Italy	C6	20
Madrakah, Ra's al, c., Oman	D5	38
Madras, India	F7	36
Madras, Or., U.S.	C5	114
Madras see Tamil Nadu, state, India	G6	36
Madre, Laguna, b., Mex.	C5	63
Madre, Laguna, b., Tx., U.S.	F4	120
Madre, Sierra, mts., N.A.	D6	63
Madre, Sierra, mts., Phil.	B6	34
Madre de Dios, dept., Peru	D3	58
Madre de Dios, Isla, i., Chile	E1	54
Madre del Sur, Sierra, mts., Mex.	D4	63
Madre Occidental, Sierra, mts., Mex.	B3	63
Madre Oriental, Sierra, mts., Mex.	C5	63
Madrid, Spain	B4	22
Madrid, Al., U.S.	D4	78
Madrid, Ia., U.S.	C4	92
Madrid, Me., U.S.	D2	96
Madrid, N.Y., U.S.	f9	109
Madridejos, Spain	C4	22
Madrūsah, Libya	I9	43
Madura, i., Indon.	G4	34
Madurai, India	G6	36
Maebashi, Japan	D12	31
Mae Hong Son, Thai.	C3	35
Maella, Spain	B6	22
Maengsan, N. Kor.	G3	33
Maeser, Ut., U.S.	C6	121
Maesteg, Wales, U.K.	C4	12
Maestra, Sierra, mts., Cuba	D5	64
Maevatanana, Madag.	g9	49
Maeystown, Il., U.S.	E3	90
Ma'fan, Libya	D2	43
Mafeking, Mb., Can.	C1	70
Mafeking see Mafikeng, S. Afr.	C4	49
Maffra, Austl.	H6	51
Mafia, i., Tan.	C6	48
Mafikeng, S. Afr.	C4	49
Mafra, Braz.	D3	56
Mafra, Port.	C1	22
Magadan, Sov. Un.	D18	29
Magadi, Kenya	B6	48
Magadi, Lake, l., Kenya	B6	48
Magaguadavic Lake, l., N.B., Can.	D2	71
Magaiza, Moz.	C3	82
Magallanes y Antártica Chilena, prov., Chile	h11	54
Maganga, Zaire	A4	48
Magangué, Col.	B3	60
Magaria, Niger	D6	45
Magat, stm., Phil.	n13	34
Magazine, Ar., U.S.	B2	81
Magazine Mountain, mtn., Ar., U.S.	B2	81
Magdalena, Arg.	B5	54
Magdalena, Bol.	B3	55
Magdalena, N.M., U.S.	C2	108
Magdalena, dept., Col.	A3	60
Magdalena, stm., Col.	B3	60
Magdalena, stm., Mex.	h9	63
Magdalena, Isla, i., Chile	C2	54
Magdalena [de Kino], Mex.	A2	63
Magdalena del Mar, Peru	*D2	58
Magdalena Mountains, mts., N.M., U.S.	D2	108
Magdeburg, Ger.D.R.	B5	18
Magdi'el, Isr.	g10	41
Magé, Braz.	h6	56
Magee, Ms., U.S.	D4	101
Magelang, Indon.	G4	34
Magellan, Strait of (Estrecho de Magallanes), strt., S.A.	h11	54
Mageney, Ire.	E5	11
Magenta, Italy	B2	23
Maggia, stm., Switz.	C3	15
Maggie Creek, stm., Nv., U.S.	C5	105
Maggiore, Lake, l., Eur.	A2	23
Maghāghah, Eg.	D6	43
Maghama, Maur.	C2	45
Maghera, N. Ire., U.K.	C5	11
Magherafelt, N. Ire., U.K.	C5	11
Magic Reservoir, res., Id., U.S.	F4	89
Magilligan Point, c., N. Ire., U.K.	B5	11
Maglaj, Yugo.	C4	24
Maglić, Yugo.	D5	24
Maglie, Italy	D7	23
Magna, Ut., U.S.	C3	121
Magness, Ar., U.S.	B4	81
Magnet, Mb., Can.	D2	70
Magnet, Ne., U.S.	B8	104
Magnetawan, On., Can.	B4	73
Magnetawan, stm., On., Can.	B4	73
Magnet Cove, Ar., U.S.	C3	81
Magnetic Springs, Oh., U.S.	B2	112
Magnitogorsk, Sov. Un.	D9	27
Magnolia, Ar., U.S.	D2	81
Magnolia, De., U.S.	D4	85
Magnolia, Il., U.S.	B4	90
Magnolia, Ia., U.S.	C2	92
Magnolia, Ky., U.S.	C4	94
Magnolia, Md., U.S.	B5	97
Magnolia, Ms., U.S.	D3	101
Magnolia, N.J., U.S.	*D2	107
Magnolia, N.C., U.S.	C4	110
Magnolia, Oh., U.S.	B4	112
Magnolia, Tx., U.S.	D5	120
Magnolia Springs, Al., U.S.	E2	78
Mago, i., Fiji	H16	52
Magoffin, co., Ky., U.S.	C6	94
Magog, P.Q., Can.	D5	74
Magothy River, b., Md., U.S.	B4	97
Magoúla, Grc.	g11	25
Magpie, P.Q., Can.	h8	72
Magpie, stm., P.Q., Can.	h8	72
Magrath, Ab., Can.	E4	68
Magruder Mountain, mtn., Nv., U.S.	F4	105
Maguari, Cabo, c., Braz.	B1	57
Magude, Moz.	C5	49
Magwe, Burma	B3	35
Mahābād, Iran	B4	38
Mahabo, Madag.	h8	49
Mahaffey, Pa., U.S.	E4	115
Mahagi, Zaire	A5	48
Mahaicony Village, Guy.	A3	59
Mahajanga, Madag.	g9	49
Mahajanga, prov., Madag.	g9	49
Mahakam, stm., Indon.	F5	34
Mahalapye, Bots.	B4	49
Mahallāt, Iran	E5	39
Mahanadi, stm., India	D7	36
Mahanoro, Madag.	g9	49
Mahanoy City, Pa., U.S.	E9	115
Maharashtra, state, India	D6	36
Maha Sarakham, Thai.	B2	34
Mahaska, Ks., U.S.	C6	93
Mahaska, co., Ia., U.S.	C5	92
Mahattat Abū Ţarafah, Jord.	E7	41
Mahattat al Ḩasā, Jord.	D7	41
Mahattat al Manzil, Jord.	C8	41
Mahattat al Qaţrānah, Jord.	G11	40
Mahattat Dab'ah, Jord.	C8	41
Mahbubnagar, India	E6	36
Mahe, India	F6	36
Mahenge, Tan.	C6	48
Mahi, stm., India	D5	36
Mahia Peninsula, pen., N.Z.	M16	51
Mahned, Ms., U.S.	C3	101
Mahnomen, Mn., U.S.	C3	100
Mahnomen, co., Mn., U.S.	C3	100
Mahogany Mountain, mtn., Or., U.S.	D9	114
Mahomet, Il., U.S.	C5	90
Mahón, Spain	C8	22
Mahone Bay, N.S., Can.	E5	71
Mahoning, co., Oh., U.S.	B5	112
Mahoning, stm., U.S.	A5	112
Mahoosuc Range, mts., N.H., U.S.	B4	106
Mahopac, N.Y., U.S.	D7	109
Mahto, S.D., U.S.	B5	118
Mahtowa, Mn., U.S.	D6	100
Mahuta, Tan.	D6	48
Mahuva, India	G3	37
Mahwah, N.J., U.S.	A4	107
Maîche, Fr.	B2	20
Maicurú, stm., Braz.	C4	59
Maida, N.D., U.S.	A7	111
Maiden, N.C., U.S.	B1	110
Maidenhead, Eng., U.K.	C7	12
Maiden Rock, Wi., U.S.	D1	126
Maidens, rock, N. Ire., U.K.	C6	11
Maidstone, Sk., Can.	D1	75
Maidstone, Eng., U.K.	E7	10
Maidstone, Lake, l., Vt., U.S.	B5	122
Maidsville, W.V., U.S.	B5	125
Maiduguri, Nig.	D7	45
Maihar, India	E8	37
Maikala Range, mts., India	F8	37
Maiko, stm., Zaire	B5	48
Maikoor, i., Indon.	G8	34
Maili, Hi., U.S.	g9	88
Maili Point, c., Hi., U.S.	g9	88
Maillard, P.Q., Can.	B7	74
Mailly-et-Chazelot, Fr.	A1	21
Main, stm., F.R.Ger.	D4	18
Main, stm., N. Ire., U.K.	C5	11
Main-à-Dieu, N.S., Can.	D10	71
Mainburg, F.R.Ger.	D5	18
Main Centre, Sk., Can.	G2	75
Main Channel, strt., On., Can.	B3	73
Mai-Ndombe, Lac, l., Zaire	B2	48
Maine, N.Y., U.S.	C4	109
Maine, hist reg., Fr.	C4	16
Maine, state, U.S.	C3	96
Mainesburg, Pa., U.S.	C7	115
Maïné-Soroa, Niger	D7	45
Mainland, i., Scot., U.K.	g10	10
Mainland, i., Scot., U.K.	A5	10
Mainland, i., Mb., Can.	C4	70
Main Pass, strt., La., U.S.	E6	95
Maintirano, Madag.	g8	49
Main Topsail, mtn., Nf., Can.	C2	54
Mainz (Mayence), F.R.Ger.	D4	18
Maipo, Volcán, vol., S.A.	B5	54
Maipú, Arg.	B5	54
Maiquetía, Ven.	A4	60
Maira, stm., Italy	E3	20
Mairiporã, Braz.	m8	56
Mairum, Pak.	G11	37
Maisí, Cabo, c., Cuba	D6	64
Maisonnette, N.B., Can.	B4	71
Maisons-Laffitte, Fr.	g9	16
Maitland, Austl.	F9	50
Maitland, N.S., Can.	D6	71
Maitland, Fl., U.S.	*D5	86
Maitland, Mo., U.S.	A2	102
Maitland, stm., On., Can.	D3	73
Maíz, Islas del, is., Nic.	E8	63
Maize, Ks., U.S.	g12	93
Maizuru, Japan	I7	33
Majagual, Col.	B3	60
Majene, Indon.	F5	34
Majenica, In., U.S.	C6	91
Maji, Eth.	D4	47
Major, Sk., Can.	F1	75
Major, co., Ok., U.S.	A3	113
Majuro, atoll, Marsh Is.	F10	6
Makaha, Hi., U.S.	g9	88
Makaha Point, c., Hi., U.S.	A2	88
Makah Indian Reservation, Wa., U.S.	A1	124
Makahuena Point, c., Hi., U.S.	B2	88
Makakilo City, Hi., U.S.	g9	88
Makalado, Zaire	C2	48
Makallé, Arg.	E4	55
Makalū, mtn., Asia	*C8	38
Makanda, Il., U.S.	F4	90
Makanza, Zaire	A2	48
Makapala, Hi., U.S.	C6	88
Makapuu Head, c., Hi., U.S.	B4	88
Makarov, Sov. Un.	B13	31
Makarska, Yugo.	D3	24
Makasar see Ujung Pandang, Indon.	G5	34
Makassar Strait, strt., Indon.	F5	34
Makat, Sov. Un.	E8	29
Makawao, Hi., U.S.	C5	88
Makaweli, Hi., U.S.	B2	88
Makeni, S.L.	E2	45
Makeyevka, Sov. Un.	E6	29
Makgadikgadi Pans, pl., Bots.	B4	49
Makharadze, Sov. Un.	B14	40
Makhfar Quwayrah, Jord.	E7	41
Makindu, Kenya	B6	48
Makinak, Mb., Can.	D2	70
Makinsk, Sov. Un.	C8	28
Makkinga, Neth.	B6	17
Makkovik, Nf., Can.	g10	72
Makkum, Neth.	A5	17
Makó, Hung.	C6	24
Makokou, Gabon	E2	46
Makoti, N.D., U.S.	B4	111
Makoua, Congo	A2	48
Maków [Mazowiecki], Pol.	B6	26
Makteïr, reg., Maur.	B2	45
Mākū, Iran	B4	38
Makumbi, Zaire	C3	48
Makurazaki, Japan	K5	33
Makurdi, Nig.	E6	45
Makushin Volcano, vol., Ak., U.S.	E6	79
Mal Abrigo, Ur.	E1	56
Mala, Punta, c., Pan.	G8	62
Malabang, Phil.	o13	34
Malabar, Fl., U.S.	D6	86
Malabar Coast, India	B2	36
Malabo, Eq. Gui.	E1	46
Malacca see Melaka, Malay.	E2	34
Malacca, Strait of, strt., Asia	E2	34
Malad City, Id., U.S.	G6	89
Malafede, stm., Italy	h8	23
Málaga, Col.	B3	60
Málaga, Spain	D3	22
Malaga, N.J., U.S.	D2	107
Malaga, N.M., U.S.	E5	108
Málaga Bay, b., Spain	D3	22
Malagash, N.S., Can.	D6	71
Malagón, Spain	C4	22
Malaimbandy, Madag.	h9	49
Malaita, i., Sol.Is.	G9	6
Malakāl, Sud.	D3	47
Malakoff, Fr.	g10	16
Malakoff, Tx., U.S.	C4	120
Malalbergo, Italy	E7	20
Malan, Indon.	G4	34
Malang, Indon.	G4	34
Malange, Ang.	C2	48
Malanje, dept., Ang.	C2	48
Malanville, Benin	D5	45
Malanzán, Arg.	A3	54
Mala Panew, stm., Pol.	f9	26
Mälaren, l., Swe.	t34	14
Malargüe, Arg.	B3	54
Malartic, P.Q., Can.	k11	74
Malaspina, Arg.	C3	54
Malaspina Glacier, Ak., U.S.	D11	79
Malatya, Tur.	C12	40
Malawi, ctry., Afr.	A5	49
Malaya Vishera, Sov. Un.	B9	27
Malaybalay, Phil.	D7	34
Malāyer, Iran	D4	39
Malay Peninsula, pen., Asia	D2	34
Malaysia, ctry., Asia	E4	34
Malazgirt, Tur.	C14	40
Malbaie, stm., P.Q., Can.	B7	74
Mal Bay, b., Ire.	E3	10
Malbork, Pol.	A5	26
Malchin, Ger.D.R.	B6	18
Malchow, Ger.D.R.	B6	18
Malcolm, Ne., U.S.	D9	104
Malcom, Ia., U.S.	C5	92
Malden, Il., U.S.	B4	90
Malden, Ma., U.S.	B5	98
Malden, Mo., U.S.	E8	102
Malden, Wa., U.S.	B8	124
Malden, W.V., U.S.	m12	125
Malden Island, i., Kir.	G12	6
Maldives, ctry., Asia	G5	36
Maldon, Eng., U.K.	E7	10
Maldonado, Ur.	C6	56
Malè, Italy	C6	20
Maléa, Ákra, c., Grc.	g10	25
Malegaon, India	C2	36
Malema, Moz.	A6	49
Malemba-Nkulu, Zaire	C4	48
Malesherbes, Fr.	C5	16
Malesus, Tn., U.S.	B3	119
Malha Wells, Sud.	B2	47
Malheur, co., Or., U.S.	D9	114
Malheur, stm., Or., U.S.	D9	114
Malheur Lake, l., Or., U.S.	D8	114
Mali, Gui.	C4	45
Mali, ctry., Afr.	C4	45
Mali, i., Burma	F3	35
Mali, i., Fiji	H15	52
Malibu, Ca., U.S.	m11	82
Mālīhah, Bi'r, well, Eg.	E5	41
Malik, Wādī al, val., Sud.	B3	47
Malin, Ire.	B4	11
Malin, Sov. Un.	F7	27
Malin, Or., U.S.	E5	114
Malinau, Indon.	E5	34
Malindi, Kenya	B7	48
Malines see Mechelen, Bel.	B6	16
Malin Head, c., Ire.	B4	11
Malinmore Head, c., Ire.	C3	10
Malino, Sov. Un.	n18	27
Malinyi, Tan.	C6	48
Maliwun, Burma	F10	36
Malja, Eth.	D4	47
Majiang, N.M., U.S.	A6	108
Maljamar, N.M., U.S.	E6	108
Malkangiri, India	H8	37
Malkara, Tur.	E8	24
Malko Tŭrnovo, Bul.	E8	24
Mallaig, Ab., Can.	B5	68
Mallaig, Scot., U.K.	B3	10
Mallaig, Eg.	D3	38
Mallersdorf, F.R.Ger.	D6	18
Malles Venosta, Italy	C6	20
Mallet Creek, Oh., U.S.	A4	112
Malletts Bay, b., Vt., U.S.	B2	122
Mallorca, i., Spain	C7	22
Mallorytown, On., Can.	C9	73
Malmédy, Bel.	B7	16
Malmö, Swe.	t34	14
Malmköping, Swe.	J5	14
Malmo, Ne., U.S.	C9	104
Malmöhus, co., Swe.	C7	15
Malmstrom Air Force Base, mil., Mt., U.S.	C5	103
Malmyzh, Sov. Un.	B12	31
Maloarkhangelsk, Sov. Un.	E11	27
Maloggia (Maloja), Switz.	D8	21
Maloja Pass, Switz.	C5	20
Malolo, i., Fiji	H14	52
Malolos, Phil.	o13	34
Malone, On., Can.	C7	73
Malone, Fl., U.S.	B1	86
Malone, N.Y., U.S.	f10	109
Malone, Wa., U.S.	C2	124
Maloney Reservoir, res., Ne., U.S.	C5	104
Malonga, Zaire	D3	48
Malonno, Italy	D9	21
Malonton, Mb., Can.	D3	70
Maloy, Ia., U.S.	D3	92
Maloyaroslavets, Sov. Un.	D11	27
Malpelo, Isla de, i., Col.	C2	53
Malpeque Bay, b., P.E., Can.	C6	71
Mālpura, India	D5	37
Malsch, F.R.Ger.	E3	19
Malta, Id., U.S.	G5	89
Malta, Il., U.S.	B5	90
Malta, Mt., U.S.	B9	103
Malta, Oh., U.S.	C4	112
Malta, ctry., Eur.	H11	8
Malta Bend, Mo., U.S.	B4	102
Maltahöhe, Nmb.	B2	49
Maltepe, Tur.	*B6	40
Malton (part of Mississauga), On., Can.	m14	73
Malton, Eng., U.K.	C6	10
Malvern, Eng., U.K.	B5	12
Malvern, Ar., U.S.	C3	81
Malvern, Ia., U.S.	D2	92
Malvern, Oh., U.S.	B4	112
Malvern, Pa., U.S.	o19	115
Malverne, N.Y., U.S.	k13	109
Malvérnia, Moz.	B5	49
Malyye Karmakuly, Sov. Un.	B9	128
Malyy Uzen, stm., Sov. Un.	D3	28
Mamala Bay, b., Hi., U.S.	g10	88
Mamamguape, Braz.	C3	57
Mamba, Japan	m17	33
Mambasa, Zaire	A5	48
Mamberamo, stm., Indon.	F9	34
Mamelodi, S. Afr.	*C4	49
Ma-Me-O Beach, Ab., Can.	C4	68
Mamers, Fr.	C4	16
Mamers, N.C., U.S.	B4	110
Mamfe, Came.	D1	46
Mamiña, Chile	D2	55
Mammoth, Az., U.S.	E5	80
Mammoth, W.V., U.S.	C3	125
Mammoth, Ut., U.S.	D3	121
Mammoth Cave National Park, Ky., U.S.	C4	94
Mammoth Lakes, Ca., U.S.	D4	82
Mammoth Spring, Ar., U.S.	A4	81
Mamonovo, Sov. Un.	A5	26
Mamoré, stm., S.A.	B2	55
Mamou, Gui.	D2	45
Mamou, La., U.S.	D3	95
Mampong, Ghana	E4	45
Mamry, Lake, l., Pol.	A6	26
Mamuju, Indon.	F5	34
Man, I.C.	E3	45
Man, W.V., U.S.	D3	125
Man, Isle of, i., I. of Man	D4	7
Mana, Fr. Gu.	B8	59
Mana, Hi., U.S.	A2	88
Manabí, prov., Ec.	C2	60
Manacacías, stm., Col.	C3	60
Manacapuru, Braz.	C2	59
Manacor, Spain	C7	22
Manado, Indon.	E6	34
Mañagaha, Isleta, i., N. Mar.	D7	52
Managua, Nic.	E7	63
Managua, Lago de, l., Nic.	D4	62
Manahawkin, N.J., U.S.	D4	107
Manakara, Madag.	h9	49
Manam, i., Pap. N. Gui.	h12	50
Manama, Bahr.	C5	38
Manana Island, i., Hi., U.S.	g11	88
Manandona, Madag.	g9	49
Manantenina, Madag.	h9	49
Manantico Creek, stm., N.J., U.S.	E3	107
Manapire, stm., Ven.	B4	60
Manas He, stm., China	B2	31
Manas Lake, l., China	B2	31
Manasquan, N.J., U.S.	C4	107
Manasquan, stm., N.J., U.S.	C4	107
Manassa, Co., U.S.	D5	83
Manassas, Va., U.S.	B5	123
Manassas, Ga., U.S.	D5	87
Manassas National Battlefield Park, U.S.	g11	123
Manassas Park, Va., U.S.	B5	123
Manatee, co., Fl., U.S.	E4	86
Manatee, stm., Fl., U.S.	E4	86
Manatí, P.R.		
Manaus, Braz.	D8	40
Manavgat, Tur.		
Manawan Lake, l., Sk., Can.	B4	75
Mancelona, Mi., U.S.	D5	99
Mancha Real, Spain	D4	22
Manchaug, Ma., U.S.	B4	98
Manchester, Eng., U.K.	D5	12
Manchester, Ga., U.S.	D2	87
Manchester, Ia., U.S.	B6	92
Manchester, Ky., U.S.	C6	94
Manchester, Ma., U.S.	A6	98
Manchester, Md., U.S.	A4	97
Manchester, Mi., U.S.	F6	99
Manchester, Mo., U.S.	f12	102

Name	Map Ref	Page
Manchester, N.H., U.S.	E4	106
Manchester, N.Y., U.S.	C3	109
Manchester, Oh., U.S.	D2	112
Manchester, Ok., U.S.	A3	113
Manchester, Pa., U.S.	F8	115
Manchester, S.D., U.S.	C8	118
Manchester, Tn., U.S.	B5	119
Manchester, Tx., U.S.	C5	120
Manchester, Vt., U.S.	E2	122
Manchester Center, Vt., U.S.	E2	122
Manchuria, hist. reg., China	B10	31
Mancos, Co., U.S.	D2	83
Mancos, stm., U.S.	D2	83
Manda, Tan.	D5	48
Mandabe, Madag.	h8	49
Mandaguari, Braz.	C2	56
Mandal, Nor.	H2	14
Mandalay, Burma	D10	36
Mandalgovi, Mong.	B6	31
Mandalī, Iraq	E2	39
Mandalya, Gulf of, b., Tur.	D6	25
Mandan, N.D., U.S.	C5	111
Mandar, Gulf of, b., Indon.	F5	34
Mandara Mountains, mts., Afr.	C2	46
Mandasor, India	D6	36
Mandeb, Bab el, strt.	D4	38
Mandel, Afg.	E10	39
Mandera, Kenya	A7	48
Manderfeld, Bel.	D6	17
Manderson, S.D., U.S.	D3	118
Manderson, Wy., U.S.	B5	127
Mandeure, Fr.	B2	21
Mandeville, P.Q., Can.	C4	74
Mandeville, Jam.	E5	64
Mandeville, Ar., U.S.	D2	81
Mandeville, La., U.S.	D5	95
Mandidzudzure, Zimb.	A5	49
Mandimba, Moz.	D6	48
Mandla, India	F8	37
Mandø, i., Den.	C2	15
Mándra, Grc.	C4	25
Mandritsara, Madag.	g9	49
Mandurah, Austl.	F2	50
Manduria, Italy	D6	23
Māndvi (Cutch Māndvi), India	D4	36
Manes, Mo., U.S.	D5	102
Manfalūt, Eg.	C3	38
Manfred, N.D., U.S.	B6	111
Manfredonia, Italy	D5	23
Manfredonia, Gulf of, b., Italy	D6	23
Manga, Braz.	A4	56
Mangalia, Rom.	D9	24
Mangalore, India	F5	36
Mangaratiba, Braz.	h5	56
Mangatarem, Phil.	o13	34
Mangerton Mountain, mtn., Ire.	F2	11
Mangham, La., U.S.	B4	95
Mangkalihat, Cape, c., Indon.	E5	34
Mangoche, Mwi.	D6	48
Mangoky, stm., Madag.	h8	49
Mangole, i., Indon.	F7	34
Mangualde, Port.	B2	22
Mangueni, Plateau de, plat., Niger	B7	45
Mangum, Ok., U.S.	C2	113
Manhasset, N.Y., U.S.	*h13	109
Manhattan, Ks., U.S.	C7	93
Manhattan, Mt., U.S.	E5	103
Manhattan, Nv., U.S.	E4	105
Manhattan Beach, Ca., U.S.	n12	82
Manhattan Island, i., N.Y., U.S.	h13	109
Manheim, Pa., U.S.	F9	115
Manheim, W.V., U.S.	B5	125
Manhiça, Moz.	C5	49
Manhuaçu, Braz.	C4	56
Maniago, Italy	C8	20
Maniamba, Moz.	D6	48
Manica, dept., Moz.	A5	49
Manicoré, Braz.	D2	59
Manicoré, stm., Braz.	D2	59
Manicouagan, stm., P.Q., Can.	G19	66
Manicouagan, Réservoir, res., P.Q., Can.	F19	66
Manifest, La., U.S.	C4	95
Manigotagan, Mb., Can.	D3	70
Manigotagan, stm., Can.	D3	70
Manigotagan Lake, l., Mb., Can.	D4	70
Manila, Phil.	C6	34
Manila, Ar., U.S.	B5	81
Manila, Ut., U.S.	C6	121
Manila Bay, b., Phil.	o13	34
Manilla, Austl.	E8	51
Manilla, In., U.S.	E6	91
Manilla, Ia., U.S.	C2	92
Manipur, state, India	D9	36
Manisa, Tur.	C6	40
Manistee, Mi., U.S.	D4	99
Manistee, co., Mi., U.S.	D4	99
Manistee, stm., Mi., U.S.	D5	99
Manistique, Mi., U.S.	C4	99
Manistique, stm., Mi., U.S.	B4	99
Manistique Lake, l., Mi., U.S.	B5	99
Manito, Il., U.S.	C4	90
Manitoba, prov., Can.	C3	70
Manitoba, Lake, l., Mb., Can.	D2	70
Manitou, Mb., Can.	E2	70
Manitou, Ok., U.S.	C3	113
Manitou, stm., On., Can.	E5	70
Manitou Lake, l., On., Can.	C3	70
Manitou Beach, Sk., Can.	F3	75
Manitou Beach, Mi., U.S.	G7	99
Manitou Island, i., Mi., U.S.	A3	99
Manitou Lake, l., On., Can.	A6	73
Manitou Lake, l., On., Can.	E1	75
Manitoulin, co., On., Can.	B2	73
Manitoulin Island, i., On., Can.	B2	73
Manitou Springs, Co., U.S.	C6	83
Manitowaning, On., Can.	B3	73
Manitowoc, Wi., U.S.	D6	126
Manitowoc, co., Wi., U.S.	h10	126
Manitowoc, stm., Wi., U.S.	h10	126
Manitowoc, North Branch, stm., Wi., U.S.	h9	126
Manitowoc, South Branch, stm., Wi., U.S.	k9	126
Maniwaki, P.Q., Can.	C2	74
Manizales, Col.	B2	60
Manja, Madag.	h8	49
Manjacaze, Moz.	B5	49
Manjimup, Austl.	F2	50
Mānjra, stm., India	E6	36
Mankato, Ks., U.S.	C5	93
Mankato, Mn., U.S.	F5	100
Mankono, I.C.	E3	45
Mankota, Sk., Can.	H2	75
Manley, Ne., U.S.	h12	104
Manlius, Il., U.S.	B4	90
Manlius, N.Y., U.S.	C5	109
Manlléu, Spain	A7	22
Manly, Ia., U.S.	A4	92
Manlyville, Tn., U.S.	A3	119
Manmād, India	G5	37
Mannar, Sri L.	G6	36
Mannar, Gulf of, b., Asia	G6	36
Mannboro, Va., U.S.	C5	123
Mannheim, F.R.Ger.	D4	18
Manning, Ab., Can.	A2	68
Manning, Ar., U.S.	C3	81
Manning, Ia., U.S.	C2	92
Manning, N.D., U.S.	B3	111
Manning, Or., U.S.	g11	114
Manning, S.C., U.S.	D7	117
Manning Provincial Park, B.C., Can.	E7	69
Mannington, Ky., U.S.	C2	94
Mannington, W.V., U.S.	B4	125
Manns Choice, Pa., U.S.	G4	115
Manns Creek, stm., W.V., ...	n14	125
Mannsville, N.Y., U.S.	B4	109
Mannsville, Ok., U.S.	C5	113
Mannville, Ab., Can.	C5	68
Manns Harbor, N.C., U.S.	B7	110
Manns, stm., Italy	E2	23
Mannu, stm., Italy	E2	23
Manoa, Bol.	A2	55
Man of War Bay, b., Trin.	M24	65
Manokin, Md., U.S.	D6	97
Manokin, stm., Md., U.S.	D6	97
Manokotak, Ak., U.S.	D8	79
Manokwari, Indon.	F8	34
Manombo, Madag.	h8	49
Manomet, Ma., U.S.	C6	98
Manomet Hill, hill, Ma., U.S.	C6	98
Manomet Point, c., Ma., U.S.	C6	98
Manono, Zaire	C3	48
Manono, i., W. Sam.	F11	52
Manor, Sk., Can.	H4	75
Manor, Ga., U.S.	E4	87
Manor, Tx., U.S.	D4	120
Manorhamilton, Ire.	C3	11
Manorhaven, N.Y., U.S.	*h13	109
Manorville, Pa., U.S.	E2	115
Manosque, Fr.	F6	16
Manotick, On., Can.	B9	73
Manouane, Lac, l., P.Q., Can.	h12	74
Manp'o, N. Kor.	F3	33
Manresa, Spain	B6	22
Mansa (Fort Roseberry), Zam.	D4	48
Mansa Konko, Gam.	D1	45
Mânsarp, Swe.	A8	15
Mansel Island, i., N.T., Can.	D17	66
Mansfield, Austl.	H6	51
Mansfield, Eng., U.K.	D6	10
Mansfield, Ar., U.S.	B1	81
Mansfield, Ga., U.S.	C3	87
Mansfield, Il., U.S.	C5	90
Mansfield, La., U.S.	B2	95
Mansfield, Ma., U.S.	B5	98
Mansfield, Mo., U.S.	D5	102
Mansfield, Oh., U.S.	B3	112
Mansfield, Pa., U.S.	C7	115
Mansfield, S.D., U.S.	B7	118
Mansfield, Tn., U.S.	A3	119
Mansfield, Tx., U.S.	n9	120
Mansfield, Wa., U.S.	B6	124
Mansfield, Mount, mtn., Vt., U.S.	B3	122
Mansfield Center, Ct., U.S.	B7	84
Mansfield Depot, Ct., U.S.	B6	84
Mansfield Four Corners, Ct., U.S.	B6	84
Mansfield Hollow Lake, res., Ct., U.S.	B7	84
Manso, stm., Braz.	B2	56
Manson, Ia., U.S.	B3	92
Manson, Wa., U.S.	B5	124
Manson, stm., B.C., Can.	B5	69
Manson Creek, B.C., Can.	B5	69
Mansonville, P.Q., Can.	D5	74
Mansura, La., U.S.	C3	95
Mantachie, Ms., U.S.	A5	101
Mantador, N.D., U.S.	C9	111
Mantagao, stm., Mb., Can.	D3	70
Mantario, Sk., Can.	F1	75
Mantaro, stm., Peru	D3	58
Manteca, Ca., U.S.	D3	82
Mantee, Ms., U.S.	B4	101
Manteo, N.C., U.S.	B7	110
Manter, Ks., U.S.	E2	93
Mantes [-la-Jolie], Fr.	C4	16
Manthani, India	H7	37
Manti, Ut., U.S.	D4	121
Mantiqueira, Serra da, mts., Braz.	C4	56
Manton, Mi., U.S.	D5	99
Mantorville, Mn., U.S.	F6	100
Mantua (Mantova), Italy	B3	23
Mantua, N.J., U.S.	D2	107
Mantua, Oh., U.S.	A4	112
Mantua, Ut., U.S.	B4	121
Mantua Hills, Va., U.S.	*B5	123
Manú, Peru	D3	58
Manuel Benavides, Mex.	B4	63
Manuel Urbano, Braz.	C4	58
Manui, i., Indon.	F6	34
Manukau Harbour, b., N.Z.	L15	51
Manulla, stm., Ire.	D2	11
Manumuskin, stm., N.J., U.S.	D2	107
Manus, i., Pap. N. Gui.	h12	50
Manvel, N.D., U.S.	A8	111
Manvel, Tx., U.S.	r14	120
Manville, N.J., U.S.	B3	107
Manville, R.I., U.S.	B4	116
Manville, Wy., U.S.	D8	127
Many, La., U.S.	C2	95
Manyara, Lake, l., Tan.	B6	48
Manyberries, Ab., Can.	E5	68
Manych, stm., Sov. Un.	H13	27
Manych Lake, l., Sov. Un.	H14	27
Many Farms, Az., U.S.	A6	80
Many Island Lake, l., Can.	D5	68
Manyoni, Tan.	C5	48
Manzanares, Spain	C4	22
Manzanares, stm., Braz.	o17	22
Manzanares Canal, Spain	p17	22
Manzanillo, Cuba	D5	64
Manzanillo, Mex.	D4	63
Manzanillo, Punta, c., Pan.	F8	62
Manzanita, Indon.	B3	114
Manzanola, Co., U.S.	C7	83
Manzano, N.M., U.S.	C3	108
Manzano Mountains, mts., N.M., U.S.	C3	108
Manzano Peak, mtn., N.M., U.S.	C3	108
Manzhouli, China	B10	31
Manziana, Italy	g8	23
Manzilah, Lake, l., Eg.	C3	41
Manzini, Swaz.	C5	49
Mao, Chad	C3	46
Mao, Dom. Rep.	E8	64
Maoke Mountains, mts., Indon.	F9	34
Maoming, China	G7	31
Mapastepec, Mex.	D6	63
Mapaville, Mo., U.S.	C7	102
Maple (part of Vaughan), On., Can.	k14	73
Maple, stm., U.S.	A7	118
Maple, stm., Ia., U.S.	B2	92
Maple, stm., N.D., U.S.	C8	111
Maple, Wi., U.S.	B2	126
Maple Bay, Mn., U.S.	C2	100
Maple Bluff, Wi., U.S.	E4	126
Maple Creek, Sk., Can.	H1	75
Maple Creek, stm., Ne., U.S.	C9	104
Maple Falls, Wa., U.S.	A3	124
Maple Grove, Mn., U.S.	m12	100
Maple Heights, Oh., U.S.	h9	112
Maple Hill, Ks., U.S.	C7	93
Maple Hill, N.C., U.S.	C5	110
Maple Island, Mn., U.S.	G5	100
Maple Lake, Mn., U.S.	E5	100
Maple Mount, Ky., U.S.	C2	94
Maple Plain, Mn., U.S.	m11	100
Maple Rapids, Mi., U.S.	E6	99
Maple Shade, N.J., U.S.	D2	107
Maplesville, Al., U.S.	C3	78
Mapleton, Ia., U.S.	B2	92
Mapleton, Ks., U.S.	D9	93
Mapleton, Me., U.S.	B4	96
Mapleton, Mn., U.S.	G5	100
Mapleton, N.D., U.S.	C8	111
Mapleton, Or., U.S.	C3	114
Mapleton, Ut., U.S.	C4	121
Mapleton Depot, Pa., U.S.	F6	115
Maple Valley, Wa., U.S.	f11	124
Mapleville, R.I., U.S.	B2	116
Maplewood, Me., U.S.	E2	96
Maplewood, Mn., U.S.	n12	100
Maplewood, Mo., U.S.	f13	102
Maplewood, N.J., U.S.	B4	107
Mapuera, stm., Braz.	C3	59
Maputo (Lourenço Marques), Moz.	C5	49
Maputo, dept., Moz.	C5	49
Maqārīyūs, Dayr, hist., Eg.	D2	41
Maquela do Zombo, Ang.	C2	48
Maquinchao, Arg.	C3	54
Maquoketa, Ia., U.S.	B7	92
Maquoketa, stm., Ia., U.S.	B6	92
Maquoketa, North Fork, stm., Ia., U.S.	B7	92
Maquon, Il., U.S.	C3	90
Mar, Serra do, clf, Braz.	D3	56
Mara, prov., Tan.	B5	48
Maraā, Braz.	D4	60
Marabá, Braz.	D5	59
Maracá, Ilha de, i., Braz.	B4	59
Maracaibo, Ven.	A3	60
Maracaibo, Lago de, l., Ven.	B3	60
Maracaju, Braz.	C1	56
Maracaju, Serra de, hills, S.A.	C1	56
Maracay, Ven.	A4	60
Maradi, Niger	D6	45
Marāgheh, Iran	B4	38
Maragogi, Braz.	k6	57
Maragojipe, Braz.	D3	57
Marais des Cygnes, stm., U.S.	D8	93
Marajó, Baía de, b., Braz.	C5	59
Marajó, Ilha de, i., Braz.	C5	59
Maramec, Ok., U.S.	A5	113
Marana, Az., U.S.	E4	80
Marand, Iran	B4	38
Maranguape, Braz.	B3	57
Maranhão, state, Braz.	B1	57
Marano, Laguna di, b., Italy	D9	20
Maranoa, stm., Austl.	E8	50
Marañón, stm., Peru	B2	58
Maraş, Tur.	D11	40
Mărăşeşti, Rom.	C8	24
Marathón, Grc.	g11	25
Marathon, Fl., U.S.	H5	86
Marathon, Ia., U.S.	B3	92
Marathon, N.Y., U.S.	C4	109
Marathon, Tx., U.S.	D1	120
Marathon, Wi., U.S.	D4	126
Marathon, co., Wi., U.S.	D4	126
Maratua, i., Indon.	E5	34
Marau, Braz.	D2	56
Maravilla de Ocampo, Mex.	n13	63
Marāwah, Libya	C4	43
Marāwī, Sud.	B3	47
Marbach [am Neckar], F.R.Ger.	E4	19
Marbella, Spain	D3	22
Marble, Ar., U.S.	A2	81
Marble, Co., U.S.	B3	83
Marble, Mn., U.S.	C5	100
Marble, N.C., U.S.	f9	110
Marble Bar, Austl.	D2	50
Marble Canyon, Az., U.S.	A4	80
Marble Canyon, val., Az., U.S.	A4	80
Marble City, Ok., U.S.	B7	113
Marble Cliff, Oh., U.S.	m10	112
Marble Dale, Ct., U.S.	C2	84
Marble Falls, Tx., U.S.	D3	120
Marble Hall, S. Afr.	B4	49
Marblehead, Il., U.S.	D2	90
Marblehead, Ma., U.S.	B6	98
Marblehead, Oh., U.S.	A3	112
Marblehill, Ga., U.S.	B2	87
Marble Hill, Mo., U.S.	D8	102
Marblemount, Wa., U.S.	A4	124
Marble Mountain, N.S., Can.	D8	71
Marble Rock, Ia., U.S.	B5	92
Marbleton, P.Q., Can.	D6	74
Marbleton, Wy., U.S.	D2	127
Marburg, F.R.Ger.	C4	18
Marbury, Al., U.S.	C3	78
Marbury, Md., U.S.	C3	97
Marcala, Hond.	G7	62
Marcaria, Italy	D6	20
Marceline, Mo., U.S.	B5	102
Marcella, Ar., U.S.	B4	81
Marcelline, Il., U.S.	C2	90
Marcellus, Mi., U.S.	F5	99
Marcellus, N.Y., U.S.	C4	109
March, Eng., U.K.	B8	12
March Air Force Base, mil., Ca., U.S.	F5	82
Marche, hist. reg., Fr.	D4	16
Marche-en-Famenne, Bel.	D5	17
Marchena, Spain	D3	22
Marchena, Isla, i., Ec.	I5	58
Marches, hist. reg., Italy	C4	23
Mar Chiquita, Laguna, l., Arg.	A4	54
Marco, Fl., U.S.	G5	86
Marco, In., U.S.	G3	91
Marcola, Or., U.S.	C4	114
Marcos Juárez, Arg.	A4	54
Marcus, Ia., U.S.	B2	92
Marcus, Wa., U.S.	A7	124
Marcus Baker, Mount, mtn., Ak., U.S.	g18	79
Marcus Hook, Pa., U.S.	G11	115
Marcy, Mount, mtn., N.Y., U.S.	A7	109
Marcy Colony, S.D., U.S.	D8	118
Mardān, Pak.	B5	36
Mar de Espanha, Braz.	g6	56
Mardela Springs, Md., U.S.	D6	97
Mar del Plata, Arg.	B5	54
Mardin, Tur.	D13	40
Marechal Deodoro, Braz.	C3	57
Maree, Loch, l., Scot., U.K.	C3	13
Mareeba, Austl.	C8	50
Marenanuka, Kir.	R18	52
Marengo, Sk., Can.	F1	75
Marengo, Il., U.S.	A5	90
Marengo, In., U.S.	H5	91
Marengo, Ia., U.S.	C5	92
Marengo, Oh., U.S.	B3	112
Marengo, Wa., U.S.	B7	124
Marengo, Wi., U.S.	B3	126
Marengo, co., Al., U.S.	C2	78
Marenisco, Mi., U.S.	n12	99
Marennes, Fr.	E3	16
Maretz, Fr.	D3	17
Mareuil-sur-Ourcq, Fr.	E3	17
Marfa, Tx., U.S.	o12	120
Margai Lake, l., China	A8	36
Marganets, Sov. Un.	H10	27
Margaree, N.S., Can.	C8	71
Margaree Harbour, N.S., Can.	C8	71
Margaret, Mb., Can.	E2	70
Margaret, Al., U.S.	B3	78
Margaret, Tx., U.S.	B3	120
Margaretville, N.S., Can.	D4	71
Margaretville, N.Y., U.S.	C6	109
Margarita, Isla de, i., Ven.	A5	60
Margate, Eng., U.K.	E7	10
Margate, Fl., U.S.	F6	86
Margate City, N.J., U.S.	E3	107
Margerum, Al., U.S.	A1	78
Margherita Peak, mtn., Afr.	A4	48
Marghī, Afg.	D13	39
Marghūb, Küh-e, mtn., Iran	E8	39
Margie, Mn., U.S.	B5	100
Margilan, Sov. Un.	E10	29
Margny-lès-Compiègne, Fr.	E2	17
Margo, Dasht-i, des., Afg.	F11	39
Margrethe, Lake, l., Mi., U.S.	D6	99
Marguerite Bay, b., Ant.	C6	7
Maria, i., Austl.	o15	50
María Chiquita, Pan.	k11	62
Mariager, Den.	B3	15
Mariager Fjord, Den.	B4	15
Mariah Hill, in., U.S.	H4	91
Marian, Lake, l., Fl., U.S.	E5	86
Mariana Islands, is., Oc.	E8	6
Marianna, Ar., U.S.	C5	81
Marianna, Fl., U.S.	B1	86
Marianna, Pa., U.S.	F1	115
Mariánské Lázně, Czech.	D2	26
Mariapolis, Mb., Can.	E2	70
Marias, stm., Mt., U.S.	B4	103
Marias, Islas, is., Mex.	C3	63
Marias Pass, Mt., U.S.	B3	103
Maria Stein, Oh., U.S.	B1	112
Maria van Diemen, Cape, c., N.Z.	K14	51
Mariaville, Me., U.S.	D4	96
Maribel, N.C., U.S.	B6	110
Maribel, Wi., U.S.	h10	126
Maribo, Den.	D5	15
Maribor, Yugo.	B2	24
Maricá, Braz.	h6	56
Maricaban Island, i., Phil.	p13	34
Maricopa, Az., U.S.	E3	80
Maricopa, Ca., U.S.	E4	82
Maricopa, co., Az., U.S.	D3	80
Maricopa Mountains, mts., Az., U.S.	m7	80
Maricourt (Wakeham Bay), P.Q., Can.	f12	74
Marié, stm., Braz.	D4	60
Mariedamm, Swe.	u33	14
Marie Byrd Land, reg., Ant.	B1	7
Mariefred, Swe.	t35	14
Marie-Galante, i., Guad.	I14	64
Marieham, Fin.	G8	14
Marie Lake, l., Ab., Can.	B5	68
Mariembourg, Bel.	D4	17
Mariemont, Oh., U.S.	o13	112
Marienberg, Ger.D.R.	C8	19
Marienthal, Nmb.	B2	49
Marienthal, Ks., U.S.	D3	93
Marienville, Pa., U.S.	D3	115
Marie-Reine, Ab., Can.	A2	68
Maries, co., Mo., U.S.	C6	102
Mariestad, Swe.	H5	14
Marietta, Ga., U.S.	C2	87
Marietta, In., U.S.	F6	91
Marietta, Mn., U.S.	E2	100
Marietta, Ms., U.S.	A5	101
Marietta, Oh., U.S.	C4	112
Marietta, Ok., U.S.	D4	113
Marietta, S.C., U.S.	A2	117
Marietta, Wa., U.S.	A3	124
Marieville, P.Q., Can.	D4	74
Marīvān, Iran	D3	39
Mariveles, Phil.	o13	34
Marj 'Uyūn, Leb.	F10	40
Mark, Il., U.S.	B4	90
Marka, Som.	A5	47
Marka Kul, l., Sov. Un.	B2	31
Markala, Mali	F4	45
Markam, China	F4	31
Markaryd, Swe.	I5	14
Mark Center, Oh., U.S.	A1	112
Markdale, On., Can.	C4	73
Marked Tree, Ar., U.S.	B5	81
Markerwaard, reg., Neth.	C5	17
Markesan, Wi., U.S.	E5	126
Market Drayton, Eng., U.K.	B5	12
Market Harborough, Eng., U.K.	I12	12
Markethill, N. Ire., U.K.	C5	11
Market Rasen, Eng., U.K.	A7	12
Market Weighton, Eng., U.K.	G8	13
Markham, On., Can.	B5	73
Markham, Il., U.S.	k9	90
Markham, Tx., U.S.	E5	120
Markham, Va., U.S.	B5	123
Markham, Mount, mtn., Ant.	A29	7
Marki, Pol.	k14	26
Markinch, Sk., Can.	F4	75
Markkleeberg, Ger.D.R.	B7	19
Markland, In., U.S.	G8	91
Markland Lock and Dam, U.S.	B8	94
Markle, In., U.S.	B6	110
Markleeville, Ca., U.S.	C4	82
Markleville, In., U.S.	D6	91
Markleysburg, Pa., U.S.	G3	115
Markneukirchen, Ger.D.R.	h6	56
Markópoulon, Grc.	h11	25
Markovka, Sov. Un.	G12	27
Markovo, Sov. Un.	C20	29
Markovo, Sov. Un.	C11	29
Markranstädt, Ger.D.R.	B7	19
Marks, Ms., U.S.	A3	101
Marksboro, N.J., U.S.	B3	107
Marksville, La., U.S.	C3	95
Marktheidenfeld, F.R.Ger.	C4	19
Marktredwitz, F.R.Ger.	D6	19
Markville, Mn., U.S.	D6	100
Marl, F.R.Ger.	*C3	18
Marlbank, On., Can.	C7	73
Marlboro, Ab., Can.	C2	68
Marlboro, N.J., U.S.	C4	107
Marlboro, N.Y., U.S.	D6	109
Marlboro, Vt., U.S.	E2	122
Marlboro, Va., U.S.	n17	123
Marlboro, co., S.C., U.S.	B8	117
Marlborough, Guy.	A3	59
Marlborough, Eng., U.K.	C6	12
Marlborough, Ct., U.S.	C6	84
Marlborough, Ma., U.S.	B4	98
Marlborough, N.H., U.S.	E2	106
Marle, Fr.	E2	17
Marlene Village, Or., U.S.	*B4	114
Marlette, Mi., U.S.	E7	99
Marlin, Tx., U.S.	D4	120
Marlin, Wa., U.S.	B7	124
Marlinton, W.V., U.S.	C4	125
Marlow, Ger.D.R.	D6	15
Marlow, Eng., U.K.	C6	12
Marlow, N.H., U.S.	E2	106
Marlow, Ok., U.S.	C4	113
Marlowe, W.V., U.S.	A6	125
Marlton, N.J., U.S.	D3	107
Marmande, Fr.	A5	81?
Marmara, Sea of, Tur.	B7	40
Marmara Island, i., Tur.	E8	20
Marmaris, Tur.	D7	40
Marmarth, N.D., U.S.	C2	111
Marmelos, Rio dos, stm., Braz.	E6	100
Marmet, W.V., U.S.	C3	125
Marmolada, mtn., Italy	C6	20
Marmora, On., Can.	C7	73
Marmora, N.J., U.S.	E3	107
Marmore, stm., Italy	E4	21
Marnay, Fr.	B1	20
Marnaz, Fr.	D2	21
Marne, F.R.Ger.	E3	15
Marne, Ia., U.S.	C2	92
Marne, Mi., U.S.	E5	99
Marne, dept., Fr.	F4	17
Marne, stm., Fr.	C5	16
Marne au Rhin, Canal de la, Fr.	F4	17
Maroa, Il., U.S.	C5	90
Maroa, Ven.	C4	60
Maroantsetra, Madag.	g9	49
Maromokotro, mtn., Madag.	f9	49
Marondera, Zimb.	A5	49
Marone, Italy	E9	21
Maroni, stm., S.A.	B4	59
Maroochydore-Mooloolaba, Austl.	E9	50
Maro Reef, rf., Hi., U.S.	k13	88
Maroua, Cam.	C2	46
Marovoay, Madag.	g9	49
Marowijne, dept., Sur.	B4	59
Marquam, Or., U.S.	B4	114
Marquand, Mo., U.S.	D7	102
Marquesas Islands, is., Fr. Poly.	G13	6
Marquesas Keys, is., Fl., U.S.	H4	86
Marquette, Ia., U.S.	A6	92
Marquette, Mi., U.S.	B3	99
Marquette, Ne., U.S.	C8	104
Marquette, co., Mi., U.S.	B3	99
Marquette, co., Wi., U.S.	E4	126
Marquette Heights, Il., U.S.	C4	90
Marquez, Tx., U.S.	D4	120
Marquis, Sk., Can.	G3	75
Marquise, Fr.	D9	12
Marrah, Jabal, mts., Sud.	C1	47
Marrakech, Mor.	B4	43
Marree, Austl.	E6	50
Marrero, La., U.S.	E5	95
Marrickville, Austl.	*F9	50
Marriott, La., U.S.	*B3	121
Marromeu, Moz.	A6	49
Marrowbone, Ky., U.S.	D4	94
Marrtown, W.V., U.S.	B3	125
Mars, Rivière à, stm., P.Q., Can.	A7	74
Marsabit, Kenya	A6	48
Marsá Burayqah, Libya	C3	43
Marsala, Italy	F4	23
Marsá Maţrūḩ, Eg.	B2	38
Marsá Süsah, Libya	C4	43
Marsden, Sk., Can.	E1	75
Marseillan, Fr.	F5	16
Marseille, Fr.	F6	16
Marseilles, Il., U.S.	B5	90
Marshall, Lib.	E2	45
Marshall, Ar., U.S.	B3	81
Marshall, Il., U.S.	D6	90
Marshall, In., U.S.	E3	91
Marshall, Mi., U.S.	F6	99
Marshall, Mn., U.S.	F3	100
Marshall, Mo., U.S.	B4	102
Marshall, N.C., U.S.	f10	110
Marshall, N.D., U.S.	B3	111
Marshall, Ok., U.S.	A4	113
Marshall, Tx., U.S.	C5	120
Marshall, Va., U.S.	B5	123
Marshall, Wa., U.S.	g13	124
Marshall, co., Al., U.S.	A3	78
Marshall, co., Il., U.S.	B4	90
Marshall, co., In., U.S.	B5	91
Marshall, co., Ia., U.S.	C4	92
Marshall, co., Ks., U.S.	C7	93
Marshall, co., Ky., U.S.	f9	94
Marshall, co., Mn., U.S.	B2	100
Marshall, co., Ms., U.S.	A4	101
Marshall, co., Ok., U.S.	C5	113
Marshall, co., S.D., U.S.	B8	118
Marshall, co., Tn., U.S.	B5	119
Marshall, co., W.V., U.S.	B4	125
Marshallberg, N.C., U.S.	C6	110
Marshall Corner, N.J., U.S.	C3	107
Marshall Islands, ter., T.T.P.I.	F10	6
Marshalls Creek, Pa., U.S.	D11	115
Marshallton, De., U.S.	B3	85
Marshallton, Pa., U.S.	B5	92
Marshallville, Ga., U.S.	D3	87
Marshallville, Oh., U.S.	B4	112
Marshes Siding, Ky., U.S.	D5	94
Marshfield, Ma., U.S.	B6	98
Marshfield, Mo., U.S.	D5	102
Marshfield, Vt., U.S.	C4	122
Marshfield, Wi., U.S.	D3	126
Marshfield Hills, Ma., U.S.	B6	98
Marsh Harbour, Bah.	A5	64
Mars Hill, In., U.S.	m14	91
Mars Hill, Me., U.S.	B5	96
Mars Hill, N.C., U.S.	f10	110
Marsh Island, i., La., U.S.	E3	95
Marsh Lake, res., Mn., U.S.	E2	100
Marsh Peak, mtn., Ut., U.S.	C6	121
Marshville, N.C., U.S.	C2	110
Marshyhope Creek, stm., Md., U.S.	C6	97
Marsing, Id., U.S.	F2	89
Marstal, Den.	D4	15
Marsteller, Pa., U.S.	E4	115
Marston, Mo., U.S.	E8	102
Marston, N.C., U.S.	C3	110
Marstons Mills, Ma., U.S.	C7	98
Mart, Tx., U.S.	D4	120
Martaban, Burma	E10	36
Martaban, Gulf of, b., Burma	E10	36
Martap, Cam.	D2	46
Martapura, Indon.	C4	86?
Martel, Fl., U.S.	C4	86
Martelange, Bel.	E5	17
Martell, Ia., U.S.	D9	104
Martelle, Ia., U.S.	B6	92
Martha, Ok., U.S.	C2	113
Marthasville, Mo., U.S.	C6	102
Martha's Vineyard, i., Ma., U.S.	D6	98
Marthaville, La., U.S.	C2	95
Martí, Cuba	D5	64
Martignano, Lake, l., Italy	g8	23
Martigny[-Ville], Switz.	F6	16
Martigues, Fr.	F6	16
Martin, Czech.	D5	87?
Martin, Ky., U.S.	C7	94
Martin, La., U.S.	B2	95
Martin, Mi., U.S.	F5	99

Name	Map Ref	Page
Martin, N.D., U.S.	B5	111
Martin, Oh., U.S.	e7	112
Martin, S.C., U.S.	E5	117
Martin, S.D., U.S.	D4	118
Martin, Tn., U.S.	A3	119
Martin, Ut., U.S.	D5	121
Martin, co., Fl., U.S.	E6	86
Martin, co., In., U.S.	G4	91
Martin, co., Ky., U.S.	C7	94
Martin, co., Mn., U.S.	G4	100
Martin, co., N.C., U.S.	B5	110
Martin, co., Tx., U.S.	C2	120
Martina [Franca], Italy	D6	23
Martin City, Mt., U.S.	B3	103
Martindale, P.Q., Can.	D2	74
Martindale, Tx., U.S.	h8	120
Martinez, Ca., U.S.	C2	82
Martinez, Ga., U.S.	C4	87
Martinique, dep., N.A.	I14	64
Martin Lake, res., Al., U.S.	C4	78
Martin Peninsula, pen., Ant.	B1	7
Martin Point, c., Ak., U.S.	A11	79
Martinsburg, In., U.S.	H5	91
Martinsburg, Ia., U.S.	C5	92
Martinsburg, Ne., U.S.	B6	102
Martinsburg, N.Y., U.S.	B9	104
Martinsburg, Oh., U.S.	B5	109
Martinsburg, Pa., U.S.	B3	112
Martinsburg, Pa., U.S.	F5	115
Martinsburg, W.V., U.S.	B7	125
Martinsdale, Mt., U.S.	D6	103
Martins Ferry, Oh., U.S.	B5	112
Martins Pond, l., Ma., U.S.	f11	98
Martinsville, Il., U.S.	D6	90
Martinsville, In., U.S.	F5	91
Martinsville, Ms., U.S.	D3	101
Martinsville, Mo., U.S.	A3	102
Martinsville, Oh., U.S.	C2	112
Martinsville, Va., U.S.	D3	123
Martinton, Il., U.S.	C5	90
Martinville, P.Q., Can.	D6	74
Martofte, Den.	C4	15
Martos, Spain	D4	22
Martre, Lac la, l., N.T., Can.	D9	66
Martwick, Ky., U.S.	C2	94
Marty, S.D., U.S.	E7	118
Marudi, Malay.	E4	34
Ma'rūf, Afg.	B4	36
Marugame, Japan	I6	33
Marum, Neth.	A6	17
Marumsco Creek, stm., Md., U.S.	D6	97
Mārūn, stm., Iran	F4	39
Marvast, Iran	F7	39
Marv Dasht, Iran	G6	39
Marvejols, Fr.	E5	16
Marvel, Al., U.S.	B2	78
Marvel, Co., U.S.	D2	83
Marvell, Ar., U.S.	C5	81
Marvin, S.D., U.S.	B9	118
Marvine, Mount, mtn., Ut., U.S.	E4	121
Marvyn, Al., U.S.	C4	78
Marwayne, Ab., Can.	C5	68
Mary, Sov. Un.	F9	29
Mary, Lake, l., Mn., U.S.	E3	100
Mary, Lake, l., Ms., U.S.	D2	101
Maryborough, Austl.	E9	50
Maryborough, Austl.	G7	50
Marydel, De., U.S.	D3	85
Marydel, Md., U.S.	B6	97
Maryfield, Sk., Can.	H5	75
Maryland, state, U.S.	B4	97
Maryland City, Md., U.S.	B4	97
Maryland Heights, Mo., U.S.	f13	102
Maryland Line, Md., U.S.	A4	97
Maryland Point, c., Md., U.S.	D3	97
Maryport, Eng., U.K.	C5	10
Marys, stm., Nv., U.S.	B6	105
Mary's Harbour, Nf., Can.	B4	72
Mary's Igloo, Ak., U.S.	B6	79
Marys Peak, mtn., Or., U.S.	C3	114
Marystown, Nf., Can.	E4	72
Marysvale, Ut., U.S.	E3	121
Marysville, B.C., Can.	E10	69
Marysville, N.B., Can.	D3	71
Marysville, Ca., U.S.	C3	82
Marysville, Id., U.S.	E7	89
Marysville, In., U.S.	G6	91
Marysville, Ks., U.S.	C7	93
Marysville, Mi., U.S.	F8	99
Marysville, Mt., U.S.	D4	103
Marysville, Oh., U.S.	B2	112
Marysville, Pa., U.S.	F8	115
Marysville, Wa., U.S.	A3	124
Marytown, Wi., U.S.	k9	126
Maryūt, Buḥayrat, l., Eg.	C1	41
Maryville, Ky., U.S.	*g11	94
Maryville, Mo., U.S.	A3	102
Maryville, Tn., U.S.	D10	119
Marzagão, Braz.	B3	56
Marzūq, Libya	D2	43
Marzūq, Idehan, dunes, Libya	E2	43
Mas'adah, Afg.	A7	41
Masai Steppe, pl., Tan.	B6	48
Masaka, Ug.	B5	48
Masalembo-Besar, i., Indon.	G4	34
Masalok, Puntan, c., N. Mar. Is.	D7	52
Masan, S. Kor.	D10	31
Masardis, Me., U.S.	B4	96
Masaryktown, Fl., U.S.	D4	86
Masasi, Tan.	D6	48
Masatepe, Nic.	E4	62
Masaya, Nic.	E7	63
Masbate, Phil.	C6	34
Masbate, i., Phil.	C6	34
Mascarene Islands, is., Afr.	H24	2
Mascoma, stm., N.H., U.S.	C2	106
Mascoma Lake, l., N.H., U.S.	C2	106
Mascot, Tn., U.S.	C10	119
Mascota, Mex.	m11	63
Mascouche, P.Q., Can.	D4	74
Mascoutah, Il., U.S.	E4	90
Mascuspana, Mex.	B1	62
Masefield, Sk., Can.	H2	75
Maseru, Leso.	C4	49
Mash'abbe Sade, Isr.	D6	41
Masham, Eng., U.K.	F7	13
Mashapaug Pond, l., Ct., U.S.	A7	84
Mashhad, Iran	B5	38
Mashīz, Iran	G8	39
Mashkel, Hāmūn-i-, l., Pak.	G11	39
Māshkīd, stm., Asia	H11	39
Mashpee, Ma., U.S.	C7	98
Mashra' ar Raqq, Sud.	D2	47
Masi-Manimba, Zaire	B2	48
Masindi, Ug.	A5	48
Masisea, Peru	C3	58
Masisi, Zaire	B4	48
Masjed Soleymān, Iran	B4	38
Mask, Lough, l., Ire.	H3	11
Maskanah, Syria	D12	40
Maskell, Ne., U.S.	B9	104
Maskinongé, P.Q., Can.	C4	74
Maskinongé, co., P.Q., Can.	C4	74
Masnières, Fr.	D3	17
Masoala, Cap, c., Madag.	g10	49
Mason, Il., U.S.	E5	90
Mason, Mi., U.S.	F6	99
Mason, Nv., U.S.	E2	105
Mason, N.H., U.S.	E3	106
Mason, Oh., U.S.	C1	112
Mason, Ok., U.S.	B5	113
Mason, Tn., U.S.	B2	119
Mason, Tx., U.S.	D3	120
Mason, W.V., U.S.	B2	125
Mason, co., Il., U.S.	C4	90
Mason, co., Ky., U.S.	B6	94
Mason, co., Mi., U.S.	D4	99
Mason, co., Tx., U.S.	D3	120
Mason, co., Wa., U.S.	B2	124
Mason, co., W.V., U.S.	C2	125
Mason City, Il., U.S.	C4	90
Mason City, Ia., U.S.	A4	92
Mason City, Ne., U.S.	C6	104
Masonhall, Tn., U.S.	A2	119
Masontown, Pa., U.S.	G2	115
Masontown, W.V., U.S.	B5	125
Masonville, Ar., U.S.	D4	81
Masonville, Co., U.S.	A5	83
Masonville, N.Y., U.S.	C5	109
Massa, Italy	B3	23
Massabesic Lake, l., N.H., U.S.	E4	106
Massac, co., Il., U.S.	F5	90
Massachusetts, state, U.S.	B4	98
Massachusetts Bay, b., Ma., U.S.	B6	98
Massacre Lake, l., Nv., U.S.	B2	105
Massaemett Mountain, mtn., U.S.	A2	98
Massafra, Italy	D6	23
Massakory, Chad	C3	46
Massa Marittima, Italy	C3	23
Massangena, Moz.	B5	49
Massapê, Braz.	B2	57
Massapequa, N.Y., U.S.	*E7	109
Massapequa Park, N.Y., U.S.	*E7	109
Massapoag Lake, l., Ma., U.S.	h11	98
Massasecum, Lake, l., N.H., U.S.	D3	106
Massawa (Mitsiwa), Eth.	B4	47
Massena, Ia., U.S.	C3	92
Massena, N.Y., U.S.	f10	109
Massenya, Chad	C3	46
Masset, B.C., Can.	C1	69
Masset Inlet, b., B.C., Can.	C1	69
Massey, On., Can.	A2	73
Masseys Mill, Va., U.S.	C3	123
Massillon, Oh., U.S.	B4	112
Massinga, Moz.	B6	49
Massive, Mount, mtn., Co., U.S.	B4	83
Masson Island, i., Ant.	C22	7
Masten's Corner, De., U.S.	E3	85
Mastergeehy, Ire.	F1	11
Masterton, N.Z.	N15	51
Mastic, N.Y., U.S.	*n16	109
Mastic Beach, N.Y., U.S.	n16	109
Mastigouche, Réserve, P.Q., Can.	C4	74
Mastūrah, Sau. Ar.	C3	38
Masuria, reg., Pol.	B6	26
Masvingo (Nyanda), Zimb.	B5	49
Mata Amarilla, Arg.	D2	54
Mata de São João, Braz.	D3	57
Matadi, Zaire	C1	48
Matador, Sk., Can.	G2	75
Matador, Tx., U.S.	B2	120
Matagalpa, Nic.	E7	63
Matagorda, Tx., U.S.	E5	120
Matagorda Bay, b., Tx., U.S.	E4	120
Matagorda Island, i., Tx., U.S.	E4	120
Matagorda Peninsula, pen., Tx., U.S.	E5	120
Matak, i., Indon.	K7	35
Matam, Sen.	C2	45
Matamoros, Pa., U.S.	D12	115
Matamoros, Mex.	B5	63
Matamoros [de la Laguna], Mex.	B4	63
Matane, P.Q., Can.	k13	74
Matanuska, stm., Ak., U.S.	g18	79
Matanzas, Cuba	C3	64
Matanzas, prov., Cuba	C3	64
Matanzas Inlet, b., Fl., U.S.	C5	86
Matão, Braz.	k7	56
Matapédia, P.Q., Can.	B3	71
Matara, Sri L.	G7	36
Mataram, Indon.	G5	34
Matarani, Peru	E3	58
Matarca, Col.	D3	60
Matārīmah, Ra's, c., Eg.	E4	41
Mataró, Spain	B7	22
Matatiele, S. Afr.	D4	49
Matatula, Cape, c., Am. Sam.	G13	52
Mataútu, W. Sam.	F12	52
Matawan, N.J., U.S.	C4	107
Matawin, stm., P.Q., Can.	C4	74
Matehuala, Mex.	C4	63
Mateke, Zaire	B2	48
Matera, Italy	D6	23
Mátészalka, Hung.	B6	24
Mateur, Tun.	F2	23
Matewan, W.V., U.S.	D2	125
Matfield Green, Ks., U.S.	D7	93
Mather, Mb., Can.	E2	70
Mather, Pa., U.S.	G1	115
Mather Air Force Base, mil., Ca., U.S.	C3	82
Mather Peaks, mts., Wy., U.S.	B5	127
Matherville, Il., U.S.	B3	90
Matherville, Ms., U.S.	D5	101
Matheson, Co., U.S.	B7	83
Matheson Island, Mb., Can.	D3	70
Mathews, Al., U.S.	D3	78
Mathews, Va., U.S.	C6	123
Mathews, co., Va., U.S.	C6	123
Mathews, Lake, l., Ca., U.S.	n14	82
Mathias, W.V., U.S.	B5	125
Mathis, Tx., U.S.	E4	120
Mathiston, Ms., U.S.	B4	101
Mathura (Muttra), India	C6	36
Mati, stm., Alb.	B2	25
Matiakoali, Burkina	D5	45
Matinenda Lake, l., On., Can.	A2	73
Matinicus, Me., U.S.	E4	96
Matinicus Island, i., Me., U.S.	E3	96
Matlock, Eng., U.K.	A6	12
Matlock, Ia., U.S.	A2	92
Matoaca, Va., U.S.	n18	123
Matoaka, W.V., U.S.	D3	125
Mato Grosso, state, Braz.	B4	55
Mato Grosso, Planalto do, plat., Braz.	E5	53
Mato Grosso do Sul, state, Braz.	B2	56
Matosinhos, Port.	B1	22
Mato Verde, Braz.	B4	56
Maṭraḥ, Oman	C5	38
Matrosovo, Sov. Un.	B11	33
Matsqui, B.C., Can.	f13	69
Matsudo, Japan	*l9	33
Matsue, Japan	D11	31
Matsuida, Japan	m17	33
Matsumae, Japan	F10	33
Matsumoto, Japan	H9	33
Matsuyama, Japan	E11	31
Matsuzaka, Japan	I8	33
Matsuzaki, Japan	o17	33
Mattamiscontis Lake, l., Me., U.S.	C4	96
Mattapoisett, Ma., U.S.	C6	98
Mattaponi, stm., Va., U.S.	C5	123
Mattawa, On., Can.	A6	73
Mattawamkeag, Me., U.S.	C4	96
Mattawamkeag, stm., Me., U.S.	C4	96
Mattawamkeag, East Branch, stm., Me., U.S.	C4	96
Mattawamkeag, West Branch, stm., Me., U.S.	C4	96
Mattawamkeag Lake, l., Me., U.S.	C4	96
Mattawana, Pa., U.S.	F6	115
Mattawoman Creek, stm., Md., U.S.	C3	97
Matterhorn, mtn., Eur.	B1	23
Matterhorn, mtn., Nv., U.S.	B6	105
Matterson Inlet, b., Ant.	g40	7
Matter Vispa, stm., Switz.	D4	21
Matteson, Il., U.S.	k9	90
Matthews, Ga., U.S.	C4	87
Matthews, In., U.S.	D7	91
Matthews, Mo., U.S.	E8	102
Matthews, N.C., U.S.	B2	110
Matthews Mountain, mtn., Mo., U.S.	D6	102
Matthews Ridge, Guy.	A2	59
Matthew Town, Bah.	D7	64
Mattituck, N.Y., U.S.	n16	109
Mattoon, Il., U.S.	D5	90
Mattoon, Wi., U.S.	C4	126
Mattoon, Lake, res., Il., U.S.	D5	90
Mattson, Ms., U.S.	A3	101
Mattydale, N.Y., U.S.	B4	109
Matucana, Peru	D2	58
Matuku Island, i., Fiji.	I15	52
Matundu, Zaire	A3	48
Matunuck, R.I., U.S.	G3	116
Matura Bay, b., Trin.	N23	65
Maturín, Ven.	B5	60
Maúa, Moz.	D6	48
Mauban, Phil.	o13	34
Maubeuge, Fr.	B5	16
Ma-Ubin, Burma	D1	35
Mauchline, Scot., U.K.	E4	13
Mauckport, In., U.S.	H5	91
Maud, Scot., U.K.	B5	10
Maud, Oh., U.S.	n13	112
Maud, Ok., U.S.	B5	113
Maudlow, Mt., U.S.	D5	103
Maués, Braz.	C3	59
Maués-Açu, stm., Braz.	C3	59
Mauganj, India	E8	37
Maugansville, Md., U.S.	A2	97
Maugerville, N.B., Can.	D3	71
Maughold Head, c., I. of Man	F4	13
Maui, co., Hi., U.S.	B5	88
Maui, i., Hi., U.S.	C6	88
Mauk, Ga., U.S.	D2	87
Mauldin, S.C., U.S.	B3	117
Maule, prov., Chile	B2	54
Mauléon [-Licharre], Fr.	F3	16
Maumakeogh, hill, Ire.	C2	11
Maumee, Oh., U.S.	A2	112
Maumee, stm., U.S.	A2	112
Maumee Bay, b., U.S.	A2	112
Maumelle, Lake, res., Ar., U.S.	C3	81
Maun, Bots.	A3	49
Mauna Kea, vol., Hi., U.S.	D6	88
Maunaloa, Hi., U.S.	B4	88
Mauna Loa, vol., Hi., U.S.	D6	88
Maunalua Bay, b., Hi., U.S.	g10	88
Maunath Bhanjan, India	E9	37
Maunawili, Hi., U.S.	g10	88
Maungdaw, Burma	D9	36
Maunie, Il., U.S.	E5	90
Maunoir, Lac, l., N.T., Can.	C8	66
Maupin, Or., U.S.	B5	114
Maurepas, La., U.S.	h10	95
Maurepas, Lake, l., La., U.S.	D5	95
Maurertown, Va., U.S.	B4	123
Maurice, La., U.S.	D3	95
Maurice, stm., N.J., U.S.	E2	107
Maurice, Lake, l., Austl.	E5	50
Mauricetown, N.J., U.S.	E2	107
Mauritania, ctry., Afr.	C2	45
Mauritius, ctry., Afr.	H24	2
Maury, N.C., U.S.	B5	110
Maury, co., Tn., U.S.	B4	119
Maury City, Tn., U.S.	B2	119
Mauston, Wi., U.S.	E3	126
Mauterndorf, Aus.	H13	19
Mauwee Peak, mtn., Ct., U.S.	C2	84
Maverick, co., Tx., U.S.	E2	120
Mavinga, Ang.	E3	48
Mawdesley Lake, l., Mb., Can.	B1	70
Mawer, Sk., Can.	G2	75
Mawlaik, Burma	D9	36
Mawson, sci., Ant.	C19	7
Mawson Coast, Ant.	C19	7
Mawson Escarpment, clf, Ant.	D19	7
Mawson Glacier, Ant.	e40	7
Mawson Peninsula, pen., Ant.	C28	7
Max, Ne., U.S.	D4	104
Max, N.D., U.S.	B4	111
Maxbass, N.D., U.S.	A4	111
Maxcanú, Mex.	C6	63
Maxeys, Ga., U.S.	C3	87
Maxinkuckee, Lake, l., In., U.S.	B5	91
Maxixe, Moz.	B6	49
Max Meadows, Va., U.S.	D2	123
Maxstone, Sk., Can.	H2	75
Maxton, N.C., U.S.	C3	110
Maxville, On., Can.	B10	73
Maxville, Mt., U.S.	D3	103
Maxwell, Ca., U.S.	C2	82
Maxwell, In., U.S.	E6	91
Maxwell, Ia., U.S.	C4	92
Maxwell, Ne., U.S.	C5	104
Maxwell, N.M., U.S.	A5	108
Maxwell, Tn., U.S.	B5	119
Maxwell Acres, W.V., U.S.	g8	125
Maxwell Air Force Base, mil., Al., U.S.	C3	78
Maxwell Colony, S.D., U.S.	D8	118
May, Id., U.S.	E5	89
May, Ok., U.S.	A2	113
May, Tx., U.S.	C3	120
May, Isle of, i., Scot., U.K.	D5	10
Maya, Mesa de, mtn., Co., U.S.	D7	83
Mayaguana, i., Bah.	C7	64
Mayaguana Passage, strt., Bah.	C7	64
Mayagüez, P.R.	G11	64
Mayagüez, Bahía de, b., P.R.	B1	65
Mayama, Congo	B1	48
Maya Mountains, mts., N.A.	B3	62
Mayarí, Cuba	D6	64
Mayaro Bay, b., Trin.	O24	65
Maybank, Ms., U.S.	D4	101
Maybee, Mi., U.S.	F7	99
Maybell, Co., U.S.	A2	83
Mayberry, Ms., U.S.	A3	97
Maybeury, W.V., U.S.	*D3	125
Maybole, Scot., U.K.	C4	10
Maydh, Som.	C6	47
Maydī, Yemen	B3	38
Maydūm, Pyramid, hist., Egypt	E3	41
Mayen, F.R.Ger.	C3	18
Mayence see Mainz, F.R.Ger.	D4	18
Mayenne, Fr.	D3	16
Mayenne, co., Fr.	D3	16
Mayenne, stm., Fr.	C3	16
Mayer, Az., U.S.	C3	80
Mayersville, Ms., U.S.	C2	101
Mayerthorpe, Ab., Can.	C3	68
Mayes, co., Ok., U.S.	A6	113
Mayesville, S.C., U.S.	D7	117
Mayetta, Ks., U.S.	C8	93
Mayetta, N.J., U.S.	D4	107
Mayfair, Sk., Can.	E2	75
Mayfield, Ks., U.S.	E6	93
Mayfield, Ky., U.S.	f9	94
Mayfield, N.Y., U.S.	B4	109
Mayfield, Ok., U.S.	C10	113
Mayfield, Pa., U.S.	C10	115
Mayfield, Ut., U.S.	D4	121
Mayfield Heights, Oh., U.S.	A4	112
Mayfield, Lake, res., Wa., U.S.	C3	124
Mayflower, Ar., U.S.	C3	81
Mayger, Or., U.S.	A3	114
Mayhew, Ms., U.S.	B5	101
Mayhill, N.M., U.S.	E4	108
Maykain, Sov. Un.	C9	28
Mayking, Ky., U.S.	C7	94
Maykop, Sov. Un.	G17	8
Mayland, Tn., U.S.	C8	119
Maymont, Sk., Can.	E2	75
Maymyo, Burma	D10	36
Maynard, Ia., U.S.	B6	92
Maynard, Ky., U.S.	D3	94
Maynard, Ma., U.S.	B5	98
Maynard, Mn., U.S.	F3	100
Maynardville, Tn., U.S.	C10	119
Mayne, B.C., Can.	g12	69
Mayne River, Ab., Can.	f7	68
Maynooth, On., Can.	B7	73
Maynooth, Ire.	D5	11
Mayo, Yk., Can.	D5	66
Mayo, Fl., U.S.	C3	86
Mayo, Md., U.S.	C4	97
Mayo, S.C., U.S.	A4	117
Mayo, co., Ire.	C2	11
Mayo, stm., Arg.	D2	54
Mayodan, N.C., U.S.	A3	110
Mayo Lake, l., Yk., Can.	D6	66
Mayon Volcano, vol., Phil.	C6	34
Mayor Pablo Lagerenza, Para.	A3	55
Mayotte, dep., Afr.	f9	49
May Park, Or., U.S.	B8	114
May Pen, Jam.	F5	64
Mayport Naval Station, mil., Fl., U.S.	B5	86
Mayreau, i., St. Vin.	V26	65
Mayrhofen, Aus.	B7	20
Mays, In., U.S.	E7	91
Mays Landing, N.J., U.S.	E3	107
Mays Lick, Ky., U.S.	B6	94
Maysel, W.V., U.S.	C3	125
Maysville, Al., U.S.	A3	78
Maysville, Ar., U.S.	A1	81
Maysville, Ga., U.S.	B3	87
Maysville, Ky., U.S.	B6	94
Maysville, Mo., U.S.	B3	102
Maysville, N.C., U.S.	C5	110
Maysville, Ok., U.S.	C4	113
Mayville, Mi., U.S.	E7	99
Mayville, N.Y., U.S.	C1	109
Mayville, N.D., U.S.	B8	111
Mayville, Or., U.S.	C6	114
Mayville, Wi., U.S.	E5	126
Maywood, Il., U.S.	k9	90
Maywood, Ne., U.S.	D5	104
Maywood, N.J., U.S.	h8	107
Maywood Park, Or., U.S.	B4	114
Maza, N.D., U.S.	A6	111
Mazabuka, Zam.	E4	48
Mazagão, Braz.	C4	59
Mazapil, Mex.	F5	63
Mazara del Vallo, Italy	F4	23
Mazār-e Sharīf, Afg.	A4	36
Mazār'ā Nūbānī, Isr. Occ.	g11	41
Mazar Creek, stm., Sk., Can.	g7	91
Mazarrón, Spain	D5	22
Mazaruni, stm., Guy.	A3	59
Mazaruni-Potaro, dept., Guy.	A3	59
Mazatenango, Guat.	C3	63
Mazatlán, Mex.	C3	63
Mazatzal Mountains, mts., Az., U.S.	C4	80
Mazatzal Peak, mtn., Az., U.S.	C4	80
Mažeikiai, Sov. Un.	A4	27
Mazenod, Sk., Can.	H2	75
Mazeppa, Mn., U.S.	F6	100
Mazgirt, Tur.	C12	40
Mazie, Ok., U.S.	A6	113
Mazomanie, Wi., U.S.	E4	126
Mazon, Il., U.S.	B5	90
Mazzarino, Italy	F5	23
Mbabane, Swaz.	C5	49
Mbaïki, Cen. Afr. Rep.	E3	46
Mbala (Abercorn), Zam.	C5	48
Mbale, Ug.	A5	48
Mbalmayo, Cam.	E2	46
Mbamba Bay, Tan.	D5	48
Mbandaka, Zaire	A2	48
M'banza Congo, Ang.	C1	48
Mbanza-Ngungu, Zaire	C1	48
Mbarara, Ug.	B5	48
Mbari, stm., Cen. Afr. Rep.	D4	46
Mberengwa, Zimb.	B4	49
Mbeya, Tan.	C5	48
Mbeya, prov., Tan.	C5	48
Mbinda, Congo	B1	48
Mbour, Sen.	D1	45
Mbout, Maur.	C2	45
Mbuji-Mayi, Zaire	C3	48
Mburucuyá, Arg.	E4	55
Mdandu, Tan.	C5	48
Mdantsane, Ciskei	*D4	49
Me, i., Viet.	C6	35
Meacham, Sk., Can.	E3	75
Meacham, Or., U.S.	B8	114
Mead, Co., U.S.	A6	83
Mead, Ne., U.S.	C9	104
Mead, Ok., U.S.	D5	113
Mead, Wa., U.S.	B8	124
Mead, Lake, res., U.S.	A1	80
Meade, Ks., U.S.	E3	93
Meade, co., Ks., U.S.	E3	93
Meade, co., Ky., U.S.	C3	94
Meade, co., S.D., U.S.	C3	118
Meade, stm., Ak., U.S.	B8	79
Meade Peak, mtn., Id., U.S.	G7	89
Meaden Peak, mtn., Co., U.S.	A3	83
Meadow, Tx., U.S.	C1	120
Meadow, Ut., U.S.	E3	121
Meadow, stm., W.V., U.S.	C4	125
Meadow Bridge, W.V., U.S.	D4	125
Meadowbrook, W.V., U.S.	k10	125
Meadow Creek, W.V., U.S.	D4	125
Meadow Creek, stm., W.V., U.S.	n14	125
Meadow Grove, Ne., U.S.	B8	104
Meadow Lake, Sk., Can.	n7	75
Meadow Lands, Pa., U.S.	F1	115
Meadow Mountain, mtn., U.S.	k12	97
Meadowview, Va., U.S.	f10	123
Meadville, Ms., U.S.	D3	101
Meadville, Mo., U.S.	B4	102
Meadville, Pa., U.S.	C1	115
Meaford, On., Can.	C4	73
Meagher, co., Mt., U.S.	D6	103
Meaghers Grant, N.S., Can.	E6	71
Mealy Mountains, mts., Nf., Can.	h9	72
Meander River, Ab., Can.	f7	68
Means, Ky., U.S.	C6	94
Mearim, stm., Braz.	C1	57
Mears, Mi., U.S.	E4	99
Me'a She'arim (part of Jerusalem), Isr.	m14	41
Meaux, Fr.	C5	16
Mebane, N.C., U.S.	A3	110
Mecca (Makkah), Sau. Ar.	C3	38
Mecca, Ca., U.S.	F5	82
Mecca, In., U.S.	E3	91
Mechanic Falls, Me., U.S.	D2	96
Mechanicsburg, In., U.S.	D5	91
Mechanicsburg, Oh., U.S.	B2	112
Mechanicsburg, Pa., U.S.	F7	115
Mechanicsville, Ct., U.S.	B8	84
Mechanicsville, Ia., U.S.	C6	92
Mechanicsville, Md., U.S.	D4	97
Mechanicsville, Vt., U.S.	C2	122
Mechanicville, N.Y., U.S.	C7	109
Mechant, Lake, l., La., U.S.	E4	95
Mechelen (Malines), Bel.	B6	16
Mechernich, F.R.Ger.	C6	18
Meck Island, i., Marsh. Is.	S17	52
Mecklenburg, co., N.C., U.S.	B2	110
Mecklenburg, co., Va., U.S.	D4	123
Mecklenburg, hist reg., Ger.D.R.	B5	18
Mecklenburg Bay, b., Eur.	D5	15
Meconta, Moz.	D6	48
Mecosta, Mi., U.S.	E5	99
Mecosta, co., Mi., U.S.	E5	99
Mecúfi, Moz.	D7	48
Medak, India	H7	37
Medan, Indon.	E1	34
Medanales, N.M., U.S.	A3	108
Médanos, Arg.	I7	54
Medanosa, Punta, c., Arg.	D3	54
Medart, Fl., U.S.	B2	86
Meddybemps, Me., U.S.	C5	96
Meddybemps Lake, l., Me., U.S.	C5	96
Medeglia, Switz.	F4	21
Medellín, Col.	B2	60
Medemblik, Neth.	B5	17
Médenine, Tun.	C7	44
Mederdra, Maur.	B1	45
Medfield, Ma., U.S.	h10	98
Medford, Mn., U.S.	F5	100
Medford, Ma., U.S.	g11	98
Medford, N.J., U.S.	D3	107
Medford, Ok., U.S.	A4	113
Medford, Or., U.S.	E4	114
Medford, Wi., U.S.	C3	126
Medford Lakes, N.J., U.S.	D3	107
Medgidia, Rom.	C9	24
Media, Il., U.S.	B3	90
Media, Pa., U.S.	G11	115
Mediapolis, Ia., U.S.	C6	92
Mediaş, Rom.	B7	24
Medical Lake, Wa., U.S.	B8	124
Medicina, Italy	E7	20
Medicine Bow, Wy., U.S.	E6	127
Medicine Bow, stm., Wy., U.S.	E6	127
Medicine Bow Mountains, mts., U.S.	E6	127
Medicine Bow Peak, mtn., Wy., U.S.	E6	127
Medicine Creek, stm., Mo., U.S.	B4	102
Medicine Creek, stm., Ne., U.S.	D5	104
Medicine Lake, Mt., U.S.	B12	103
Medicine Lodge, Ks., U.S.	E5	93
Medicine Lodge, stm., U.S.	E4	93
Medicine Park, Ok., U.S.	C3	113
Medill, Mo., U.S.	A6	102
Medina (Al Madīnah), Sau. Ar.	C3	38
Medina, N.Y., U.S.	B2	109
Medina, N.D., U.S.	C6	111
Medina, Oh., U.S.	A4	112
Medina, Tn., U.S.	B3	119
Medina, Tx., U.S.	E3	120
Medina, Wa., U.S.	e11	124
Medina, co., Oh., U.S.	A4	112
Medina, co., Tx., U.S.	E3	120
Medina, stm., Tx., U.S.	k7	120
Medina del Campo, Spain	B3	22
Medina de Ríoseco, Spain	B3	22
Medina-Sidonia, Spain	D3	22
Mediterranean Sea	H12	8
Medjerda, stm., Tun.	F2	23
Medjerda, Monts de la, mts., Afr.	F2	23
Medje, el Bab, Tun.	F2	23
Mednogorsk, Sov. Un.	C5	28
Medomak, Me., U.S.	D3	96
Medon, Tn., U.S.	B3	119
Medora, Il., U.S.	D3	90
Medora, In., U.S.	G5	91
Medora, Ks., U.S.	D6	93
Medora, N.D., U.S.	C2	111
Médouneu, Gabon	E2	46
Medstead, Sk., Can.	D1	75
Meductic, N.B., Can.	D2	71
Meduxnekeag, North Branch, stm., N.A.	B5	96
Medveditsa, stm., Sov. Un.	F15	27
Medvedovskaya, Sov. Un.	I12	27
Medvezhi Islands, is., Sov. Un.	B19	29
Medvezhyegorsk, Sov. Un.	C6	29
Medway, Ma., U.S.	B5	98
Medway, Me., U.S.	C4	96
Medway, stm., N.S., Can.	E5	71
Medzhibozh, Sov. Un.	G6	27
Meekatharra, Austl.	E2	50
Meeker, Ok., U.S.	B5	113
Meeker, Co., U.S.	A3	83
Meeker, co., Mn., U.S.	E4	100
Meelpaeg Lake, res., Nf., Can.	D3	72
Meerane, Ger.D.R.	C6	18
Meerbusch, F.R.Ger.	*C3	18
Meerle, Bel.	C4	17
Meersburg, F.R.Ger.	A7	21
Meerut, India	C6	36
Meeteetse, Wy., U.S.	B4	127
Meeting Creek, Ab., Can.	C4	68
Meeting Lake, l., Sk., Can.	D2	75
Meeyomoot Lake, l., Sk., Can.	C3	75
Mega, Eth.	E4	47
Megali Canal, Grc.	g10	25
Megalópolis, Grc.	D4	25
Mégantic, co., P.Q., Can.	C6	74
Mégantic, Lac, l., P.Q., Can.	D7	74
Mégantic, Mont, mtn., P.Q., Can.	D7	74
Megargel, Al., U.S.	D2	78
Megargel, Tx., U.S.	C3	120
Mégève, Fr.	E2	21
Meggett, S.C., U.S.	F7	117
Meghalaya, state, India	C9	36
Megunticook, Mount, mtn., Me., U.S.	D3	96
Mehadia, Rom.	D5	24
Mehar, Pak.	C3	38
Mehekar, India	G6	37
Meherpur, Bngl.	F12	37
Meherrin, Va., U.S.	C4	123
Meherrin, stm., U.S.	A4	110
Mehlville, Mo., U.S.	f13	102
Mehoopany, Pa., U.S.	C9	115
Mehrān, Iran	E3	39
Mehrān, stm., Iran	F4	39
Mehsāna, India	D5	36
Mehun-sur-Yèvre, Fr.	D5	16
Meiganga, Cam.	D2	46
Meighen Island, i., N.T., Can.	K32	66
Meigs, Ga., U.S.	E2	87
Meigs, co., Oh., U.S.	C3	112
Meigs, co., Tn., U.S.	D9	119
Meiktila, Burma	D10	36
Meiners Oaks, Ca., U.S.	*E4	82
Meinerzhagen, F.R.Ger.	C4	18
Meiningen, Ger.D.R.	C6	18
Meissen, Ger.D.R.	C7	18
Meitan, China	K2	32
Meixian (Meizhou), China	G8	31
Mejillones, Chile	D1	55
Mekambo, Gabon	A2	48
Mekele, Eth.	F2	47
Mékhé, Sen.	C1	45
Mekhtar, Pak.	E1	38
Mekinac, Lac, l., P.Q., Can.	B5	74
Mekinock, N.D., U.S.	A8	111
Meknès, Mor.	B4	44
Mekong, stm., Asia	H13	39
Mekong, Mouths of the, mth., Viet.	D3	34
Melaka (Malacca), Malay.	M6	34
Melaka, state, Malay.	K5	35
Mélambes, Grc.	n8	25
Melba, Id., U.S.	F2	89
Melbern, Oh., U.S.	A1	112
Melbeta, Ne., U.S.	C2	104
Melbourne, Austl.	G8	50
Melbourne, On., Can.	E3	73
Melbourne, Ar., U.S.	A4	81
Melbourne, Fl., U.S.	D6	86
Melbourne, Ia., U.S.	C4	92
Melbourne, Ky., U.S.	h14	94
Melbourne Beach, Fl., U.S.	D6	86
Melcher, Ia., U.S.	C4	92
Melchor, Mex.	D3	63
Meldorf, F.R.Ger.	C9	15
Meldrum Bay, On., Can.	B1	73
Meleb, Mb., Can.	D3	70

Name	Map Ref	Page
Melekeok, Palau	R17	52
Melekess, Sov. Un.	E18	8
Melenki, Sov. Un.	D13	27
Mélèzes, Rivière aux, stm., P.Q., Can.	g12	74
Melfi, Chad	C3	46
Melfi, Italy	D5	23
Melfort, Sk., Can.	E3	75
Melghir, Chott, l., Alg.	C6	44
Melilla, Sp. N. Afr.	B4	44
Melipilla, Chile	A2	54
Mélisey, Fr.	A2	21
Melita, Mb., Can.	E1	70
Melito di Porto Salvo, Italy	F5	23
Melitopol, Sov. Un.	H10	27
Mella, stm., Italy	D6	20
Melle, Fr.	D3	16
Melle, F.R.Ger.	A3	19
Mellen, Wi., U.S.	B3	126
Mellette, S.D., U.S.	B7	118
Mellette, co., S.D., U.S.	D5	118
Mellit, Sud.	C2	47
Mellor Glacier, Ant.	B19	7
Mellott, In., U.S.	D3	91
Mellow Valley, Al., U.S.	B4	78
Mellrichstadt, F.R.Ger.	C5	19
Mellum, i., F.R.Ger.	E2	15
Mellwood, Ar., U.S.	C5	81
Melmore, Oh., U.S.	A2	112
Mělník, Czech.	n18	26
Melo, Ur.	E2	56
Melocheville, P.Q., Can.	q19	74
Melrose, N.B., Can.	C6	71
Melrose, N.S., Can.	D7	71
Melrose, Ct., U.S.	B5	84
Melrose, Fl., U.S.	C4	86
Melrose, Ia., U.S.	D4	92
Melrose, La., U.S.	C3	95
Melrose, Ma., U.S.	B5	98
Melrose, Mn., U.S.	E4	100
Melrose, N.M., U.S.	C6	108
Melrose, Oh., U.S.	A1	112
Melrose, Wi., U.S.	D3	126
Melrose Park, Fl., U.S.	r13	86
Melrose Park, Il., U.S.	*k9	90
Mels, Switz.	B7	21
Melstone, Mt., U.S.	D9	103
Melstrand, Mi., U.S.	B4	99
Melsungen, F.R.Ger.	B4	19
Melton Hill Lake, res., Tn., U.S.	D9	119
Melton Mowbray, Eng., U.K.	B7	12
Melun, Fr.	C5	16
Melvaig, Scot., U.K.	C3	13
Melvern, Ks., U.S.	D8	93
Melvern Lake, res., Ks., U.S.	D8	93
Melville, Austl.	*F2	50
Melville, Sk., Can.	G4	75
Melville, La., U.S.	D4	95
Melville, Mt., U.S.	D7	103
Melville, N.Y., U.S.	*n15	109
Melville, i., Austl.	B5	50
Melville, Cape, c., Austl.	B7	50
Melville, Lake, l., Nf., Can.	B2	72
Melville Bugt, b., Grnld.	B14	61
Melville Hills, hills, N.T., Can.	C8	66
Melville Island, i., N.T., Can.	m30	66
Melville Peninsula, pen., N.T., Can.	C16	66
Melvin, Al., U.S.	D1	78
Melvin, Il., U.S.	C5	90
Melvin, Ia., U.S.	A2	92
Melvin, Ky., U.S.	C7	94
Melvin, Tx., U.S.	D3	120
Melvin, Lough, l., Eur.	C3	11
Melvindale, Mi., U.S.	*p7	99
Melvine, Tn., U.S.	D8	119
Melvin Village, N.H., U.S.	C4	106
Melyana, Alg.	B5	44
Mélykút, Hung.	B4	24
Memba, Moz.	D7	48
Memmingen, F.R.Ger.	E5	18
Mempawah, Indon.	E3	34
Memphis, Fl., U.S.	p10	86
Memphis, In., U.S.	H6	91
Memphis, Mi., U.S.	F8	99
Memphis, Mo., U.S.	A5	102
Memphis, Ne., U.S.	g12	104
Memphis, Tn., U.S.	B1	119
Memphis, Tx., U.S.	B2	120
Memphis, hist., Eg.	C3	38
Memphis Naval Air Station, mil., Tn., U.S.	B2	119
Memphremagog, Lake, l., N.A.	B5	74
Memramcook, N.B., Can.	C5	71
Mena, Ar., U.S.	C1	81
Menahga, Mn., U.S.	D3	100
Menai Strait, strt., Wales, U.K.	A3	12
Ménaka, Mali	C5	45
Menan, Id., U.S.	F7	89
Menands, N.Y., U.S.	C7	109
Menard, Tx., U.S.	D3	120
Menard, co., Il., U.S.	C4	90
Menard, co., Tx., U.S.	D3	120
Menasha, Wi., U.S.	D5	126
Mendawai, stm., Indon.	F4	34
Mende, Fr.	E5	16
Menden, F.R.Ger.	B2	19
Mendenhall, Ms., U.S.	D4	101
Mendes, Sk., Can.	G1	75
Mendham, N.J., U.S.	B3	107
Mendi, Eth.	D4	47
Mendip Hills, hills, Eng., U.K.	C5	12
Mendocino, Ca., U.S.	C2	82
Mendocino, co., Ca., U.S.	C2	82
Mendon, Il., U.S.	D2	90
Mendon, Ma., U.S.	h9	98
Mendon, Mi., U.S.	F5	99
Mendon, Mo., U.S.	B4	102
Mendon, Oh., U.S.	B1	112
Mendon, Ut., U.S.	B4	121
Mendon, Vt., U.S.	D3	122
Mendota, Ca., U.S.	D3	82
Mendota, Il., U.S.	B4	90
Mendota, Lake, l., Wi., U.S.	E4	126
Mendota Heights, Mn., U.S.	*m13	100
Mendoza, Arg.	A3	54
Mendoza, Pan.	k11	62
Mendoza, prov., Arg.	A3	54
Mendrisio, Switz.	E6	21
Mene de Mauroa, Ven.	A3	60
Mene Grande, Ven.	C3	60
Menemen, Tur.	C6	25
Menen, Bel.	D3	17
Menfi, Italy	F4	23
Mengcheng, China	E8	31
Menggala, Indon.	F3	34
Menghai, China	B4	35
Menglian, China	B4	35
Mengzi, China	G5	31
Menifee, Ar., U.S.	B3	81
Menifee, co., Ky., U.S.	C6	94
Menihek Lakes, l., Nf., Can.	g8	72
Menindee, Austl.	F7	50
Menindee Lake, l., Austl.	F4	51
Menlo, Ga., U.S.	B1	87
Menlo, Ia., U.S.	C3	92
Menlo, Ks., U.S.	C3	93
Menlo, Wa., U.S.	C2	124
Menlo Park, Ca., U.S.	k8	82
Menno, S.D., U.S.	D8	118
Meno, Ok., U.S.	A3	113
Menominee, Mi., U.S.	C3	99
Menominee, co., Mi., U.S.	C3	99
Menominee, co., Wi., U.S.	C5	126
Menominee, stm., U.S.	C6	126
Menominee Indian Reservation, Wi., U.S.	C5	126
Menomonee, stm., Wi., U.S.	m11	126
Menomonee Falls, Wi., U.S.	E5	126
Menomonie, Wi., U.S.	D2	126
Menongue, Ang.	D2	48
Menor, Mar, b., Spain	D5	22
Menorca, i., Spain	C8	22
Mentana, Italy	g9	23
Mentawai Islands, is., Indon.	F1	34
Mentmore, N.M., U.S.	B1	108
Menton, Fr.	F7	16
Mentone, Al., U.S.	A4	78
Mentone, In., U.S.	B5	91
Mentone, Tx., U.S.	D1	120
Mentor, Ky., U.S.	k14	94
Mentor, Mn., U.S.	C2	100
Mentor, Oh., U.S.	A4	112
Mentor, Tn., U.S.	n13	119
Mentor-on-the-Lake, Oh., U.S.	A4	112
Menzel Bourguiba, Tun.	B6	44
Menzies, Mount, mtn., Ant.	B19	7
Menziken, Switz.	B5	21
Meoqui, Mex.	B3	63
Meota, Sk., Can.	D1	75
Meppel, Neth.	A7	16
Meppen, F.R.Ger.	B3	18
Meqerghane, Sebkha, pl., Alg.	D5	44
Mequinenza, Embalse de, res., Sp.	B11	22
Mequon, Wi., U.S.	E6	126
Merabolo, Gulf of, b., Grc.	E5	25
Meramec, stm., Mo., U.S.	C7	102
Merano, Italy	A3	23
Merate, Italy	E7	21
Merauke, Indon.	G10	34
Meraux, La., U.S.	k12	95
Mercāra, India	F6	36
Merced, Ca., U.S.	D3	82
Merced, co., Ca., U.S.	D3	82
Merced, stm., Ca., U.S.	D3	82
Mercedes, Arg.	A3	54
Mercedes, Arg.	A5	54
Mercedes, Tx., U.S.	F4	120
Mercedes, Ur.	E1	56
Mercer, Me., U.S.	D3	96
Mercer, Mo., U.S.	A4	102
Mercer, N.D., U.S.	B5	111
Mercer, Oh., U.S.	B1	112
Mercer, Pa., U.S.	D1	115
Mercer, Wi., U.S.	B3	126
Mercer, co., Il., U.S.	B3	90
Mercer, co., Ky., U.S.	C5	94
Mercer, co., Mo., U.S.	A4	102
Mercer, co., N.J., U.S.	C3	107
Mercer, co., N.D., U.S.	B4	111
Mercer, co., Oh., U.S.	B1	112
Mercer, co., Pa., U.S.	D1	115
Mercer, co., W.V., U.S.	D3	125
Mercer Island, i., Wa., U.S.	e11	124
Mercersburg, Pa., U.S.	G6	115
Mercerville, N.J., U.S.	C3	107
Merchantville, N.J., U.S.	*D2	107
Merchtem (Saint-Philomène), P.Q., Can.	D4	74
Mercier, Ks., U.S.	C8	93
Mercoal, Ab., Can.	C2	68
Mercury Bay, b., N.Z.	L15	51
Mercury Islands, is., N.Z.	L15	51
Mercy, Cape, c., N.T., Can.	D20	66
Meredith, Co., U.S.	B4	83
Meredith, N.H., U.S.	C3	106
Meredith, Lake, l., Co., U.S.	C7	83
Meredith, Lake, res., Tx., U.S.	B2	120
Meredith Center, N.H., U.S.	C3	106
Meredosia, Il., U.S.	D3	90
Meredosia Lake, l., Il., U.S.	D3	90
Mereeg, Som.	H4	47
Merefa, Sov. Un.	G11	27
Merepoint, Me., U.S.	g7	96
Mergui, Burma	F10	36
Mergui Archipelago, is., Burma	F10	36
Mergui (Maritsa) (Évros), stm., Eur.	B6	25
Meriç, Tur.	F1	75
Mérida, Mex.	C7	63
Mérida, Spain	C2	22
Mérida, Ven.	B3	60
Mérida, state, Ven.	B3	60
Meriden, Ct., U.S.	C4	84
Meriden, Ia., U.S.	B2	92
Meriden, Ks., U.S.	C8	93
Meriden, Mn., U.S.	F5	100
Meriden, N.H., U.S.	C2	106
Meriden, Wy., U.S.	E8	127
Meridian, Ga., U.S.	E5	87
Meridian, Id., U.S.	F2	89
Meridian, Ms., U.S.	C5	101
Meridian, N.Y., U.S.	B4	109
Meridian, Ok., U.S.	B4	113
Meridian, Tx., U.S.	D4	120
Meridian Hills, In., U.S.	k10	91
Meridian Naval Air Station, mil., Ms., U.S.	C5	101
Meridianville, Al., U.S.	A3	78
Mérignac, Fr.	E3	16
Mérigold, Ms., U.S.	B3	101
Merigomish, N.S., Can.	D7	71
Merikarvia, Fin.	G9	14
Meringur, Austl.	G3	51
Merino, Co., U.S.	A7	83
Merion Station, Pa., U.S.	*p20	115
Meriwether, co., Ga., U.S.	C2	87
Merizo, Guam	M9	52
Merkel, Tx., U.S.	C2	120
Merkine, Sov. Un.	A8	26
Merksem (part of Antwerp), Bel.	B6	16
Merksplas, Bel.	C4	17
Merlin, On., Can.	E2	73
Merlin, Or., U.S.	E3	114
Merlo, Arg.	g7	54
Mermentau, La., U.S.	D3	95
Mermentau, stm., La., U.S.	E3	95
Mern, Den.	C6	15
Merna, Ne., U.S.	C6	104
Merom, In., U.S.	F2	91
Meron, Mount, mtn., Isr.	A7	41
Merredin, Austl.	F2	50
Merriam, In., U.S.	B7	91
Merriam, Ks., U.S.	k16	93
Merrick, N.Y., U.S.	*n15	109
Merrick, co., Ne., U.S.	C7	104
Merrick, mtn., Scot., U.K.	E4	13
Merrick Brook, stm., Ct., U.S.	C7	84
Merrickville, On., Can.	C9	73
Merricourt, N.D., U.S.	C7	111
Merrifield, Mn., U.S.	D4	100
Merrifield, Va., U.S.	*B5	123
Merrill, Ia., U.S.	B1	92
Merrill, Mi., U.S.	E6	99
Merrill, Ms., U.S.	E5	101
Merrill, Or., U.S.	E5	114
Merrill, Wi., U.S.	C4	126
Merrillan, Wi., U.S.	D3	126
Merrillville, In., U.S.	B3	91
Merrimac, Ky., U.S.	C4	94
Merrimac, Ma., U.S.	A5	98
Merrimac, Wi., U.S.	E4	126
Merrimack, N.H., U.S.	E4	106
Merrimack, co., N.H., U.S.	D3	106
Merrimack, stm., U.S.	A5	98
Merrimacport, Ma., U.S.	A5	98
Merriman, Ne., U.S.	B4	104
Merrimon, N.C., U.S.	C6	110
Merritt, B.C., Can.	D7	69
Merritt, N.C., U.S.	B6	110
Merritt Island, Fl., U.S.	D6	86
Merritt Reservoir, res., Ne., U.S.	B5	104
Merriwa, Austl.	F8	51
Merriweather, Mi., U.S.	m12	99
Merrouge, La., U.S.	B4	95
Merrow, Ct., U.S.	B6	84
Merry Hill, N.C., U.S.	A6	110
Merrymeeting Lake, l., N.H., U.S.	D4	106
Merry Oaks, N.C., U.S.	B3	110
Merryville, La., U.S.	D2	95
Mersa Fatma, Eth.	B5	47
Merseburg, Ger.D.R.	C5	18
Mersey, stm., Eng., U.K.	D5	10
Merseyside, co., Eng., U.K.	A4	12
Mershon, Ga., U.S.	E4	87
Mersin, Tur.	D10	40
Mersing, Malay.	E2	34
Merthyr Tydfil, Wales, U.K.	E5	10
Merti, Kenya	A6	48
Mértola, Port.	D3	22
Merton, Wi., U.S.	m11	126
Mertz Glacier, Ant.	C27	7
Mertzon, Tx., U.S.	D2	120
Méru, Fr.	C5	16
Méru, Kenya	A6	48
Meru, Mount, mtn., Tan.	B6	48
Mervelier, Switz.	B4	21
Merville, Fr.	D2	17
Mervin, Sk., Can.	D1	75
Merwin Lake, res., Wa., U.S.	C3	124
Méry [-sur-Seine], Fr.	F3	17
Merzifon, Tur.	B10	40
Merzig, F.R.Ger.	E6	17
Meyersdale, Pa., U.S.	G3	115
Mesa, Az., U.S.	D4	80
Mesa, Co., U.S.	B2	83
Mesa, Id., U.S.	E2	89
Mesa, co., Co., U.S.	C2	83
Mesabi Range, hills, Mn., U.S.	C6	100
Mesagne, Italy	D6	23
Mesa Mountain, mtn., Co., U.S.	D4	83
Mesa Verde National Park, Co., U.S.	D2	83
Mescalero, N.M., U.S.	D4	108
Mescalero Indian Reservation, N.M., U.S.	D4	108
Mesegon, i., Micron.	Q18	52
Mesena, Ga., U.S.	C4	87
Meservey, Ia., U.S.	B4	92
Meshcherskoye, Sov. Un.	n17	27
Meshchovsk, Sov. Un.	D10	27
Meshkovskaya, Sov. Un.	G13	27
Meshomasic Mountain, mtn., Ct., U.S.	C5	84
Meshoppen, Pa., U.S.	C9	115
Mesic, N.C., U.S.	B6	110
Mesick, Mi., U.S.	D5	99
Mesilinka, stm., B.C., Can.	A5	69
Mesilla, N.M., U.S.	E3	108
Mesita, N.M., U.S.	B2	108
Mesita, Co., U.S.	D5	83
Mesocco, Switz.	C5	20
Mesolóngion, Grc.	C3	40
Mesopotamia, Braz.	B4	56
Mesquite, Nv., U.S.	G7	105
Mesquite, N.M., U.S.	E3	108
Mesquite, Tx., U.S.	n10	120
Messasonkee Lake, l., Me., U.S.	D3	96
Messápion Óros, mtn., Grc.	g10	25
Messen, Switz.	B3	21
Messina, Italy	E5	23
Messina, S. Afr.	B5	49
Messina, Strait of, strt., Italy	E5	23
Messíni, Grc.	D3	25
Messíni, Gulf of, b., Grc.	D4	25
Messkirch, F.R.Ger.	B5	20
Mesta (Néstos), stm., Eur.	C4	21
Mestghanem (Mostaganem), Alg.	B5	44
Mestre, Italy	B4	23
Mesudiye, Tur.	B11	40
Meta, Col.	C5	102
Meta, dept., Col.	C3	60
Meta, stm., S.A.	B4	60
Métabetchouan, P.Q., Can.	A6	74
Meta Pond, l., Nf., Can.	D4	72
Metairie, La., U.S.	k11	95
Metaline, Wa., U.S.	A8	124
Metaline Falls, Wa., U.S.	A8	124
Metamora, Il., U.S.	C4	90
Metamora, Mi., U.S.	F7	99
Metamora, Oh., U.S.	A2	112
Metán, Arg.	E3	55
Metangula, Moz.	D5	48
Metapán, El Sal.	C3	62
Metaponto, Italy	D6	23
Metarica, Moz.	D6	48
Métascouac, Lac, l., P.Q., Can.	B6	74
Metasville, Ga., U.S.	C4	87
Metcalf, Ga., U.S.	F3	87
Metcalf, Il., U.S.	D6	90
Metcalfe, On., Can.	B9	73
Metcalfe, Ms., U.S.	B2	101
Metcalfe, co., Ky., U.S.	C4	94
Metchosin, B.C., Can.	h12	69
Metedeconk, North Branch, stm., N.J., U.S.	C4	107
Metedeconk, South Branch, stm., N.J., U.S.	C3	107
Meteghan, N.S., Can.	E3	71
Meteghan River, N.S., Can.	E3	71
Meteghan Station, N.S., Can.	E3	71
Metema, Eth.	B2	122
Meteor Crater, crat., Az., U.S.	C4	80
Methóni, Grc.	D3	25
Methow, Wa., U.S.	A5	124
Methow, stm., Wa., U.S.	A5	124
Methuen, Ma., U.S.	A5	98
Metiskow, Ab., Can.	C5	68
Metković, Yugo.	D3	24
Metlakatla, Ak., U.S.	D13	79
Meto, Bayou, stm., Ar., U.S.	C4	81
Metolius, Or., U.S.	C5	114
Metonga, Lake, l., Wi., U.S.	C5	126
Metropolis, Il., U.S.	F5	90
Metropolitana, prov., Chile	A2	54
Metsovon, Grc.	C3	25
Mettawee, stm., U.S.	E2	122
Metten, F.R.Ger.	E7	19
Metter, Ga., U.S.	D4	87
Mettet, Bel.	D4	17
Mettingen, F.R.Ger.	A2	19
Mettmann, F.R.Ger.	B1	19
Mettuchen, N.J., U.S.	B4	107
Metulla, Isr.	A7	41
Metz, Fr.	C7	16
Metz, In., U.S.	A8	91
Metz, Mi., U.S.	C7	99
Metz, Mo., U.S.	D3	102
Metzeral, Fr.	B3	20
Metzger, Or., U.S.	h12	114
Meudon, Fr.	g9	16
Meulaboh, Indon.	m11	34
Meung, Fr.	D4	16
Meureudu, Indon.	J2	35
Meurthe, stm., Fr.	D7	16
Meurthe-et-Moselle, dept., Fr.	F6	17
Meuse, dept., Fr.	E5	17
Meuse (Maas), stm., Eur.	C6	16
Meuse, Côtes de, mtn., Fr.	C6	16
Meuselwitz, Ger.D.R.	B7	19
Mexia, Al., U.S.	D2	78
Mexia, Lake, res., Tx., U.S.	D4	120
Mexicali, Mex.	A1	63
Mexican Hat, Ut., U.S.	F6	121
Mexican Springs, N.M., U.S.	B1	108
Mexico, In., U.S.	C5	91
Mexico, Ky., U.S.	e9	94
Mexico, Me., U.S.	D2	96
Mexico, Mo., U.S.	B6	102
Mexico, N.Y., U.S.	B4	109
Mexico, Pa., U.S.	E7	115
México, state, Mex.	D5	63
Mexico, ctry., Mex.	D5	63
Mexico, Gulf of, b., N.A.	G11	61
Mexico City, Mex.	D5	63
Meydān-e Gel, pl., Iran	G7	39
Meydānī, Ra's-e, c., Iran	C5	38
Meyers Chuck, Ak., U.S.	n23	79
Meyisti, i., Grc.	D7	25
Meymaneh, Afg.	A4	36
Meyrin, Switz.	D1	21
Meyronne, Sk., Can.	H2	75
Mèze, Fr.	F5	16
Mezen, Sov. Un.	C7	29
Mezen, stm., Sov. Un.	C7	29
Mezen Bay, b., Sov. Un.	B17	8
Mézenc, Mont, mtn., Fr.	E6	16
Mezhdurechenskiy, Sov. Un.	B7	28
Meziadin Lake, l., B.C., Can.	A3	69
Mézières, Switz.	C2	21
Mezőkövesd, Hung.	B4	24
Mezőtúr, Hung.	B5	24
Mezzana, Italy	C3	20
Mezzolombardo, Italy	C7	20
Mga, Sov. Un.	s32	14
Mglin, Sov. Un.	E9	27
Mhór, Beinn, mtn., Scot., U.K.	C1	13
Mhór, Loch, l., Scot., U.K.	C4	13
Mhow, India	F5	37
Miahuatlán de Porfirio Díaz, Mex.	D5	63
Miajadas, Spain	C3	22
Miājlar, India	D3	37
Miami, Mb., Can.	E2	70
Miami, Az., U.S.	D5	80
Miami, Fl., U.S.	G6	86
Miami, In., U.S.	C5	91
Miami, Mo., U.S.	B4	102
Miami, N.M., U.S.	A5	108
Miami, Ok., U.S.	A7	113
Miami, Tx., U.S.	B2	120
Miami, W.V., U.S.	m13	125
Miami, co., In., U.S.	C5	91
Miami, co., Ks., U.S.	D9	93
Miami, co., Oh., U.S.	B1	112
Miami Beach, Fl., U.S.	G6	86
Miami Canal, Fl., U.S.	F6	86
Miami International Airport, Fl., U.S.	G6	86
Miamisburg, Oh., U.S.	C1	112
Miami Shores, Fl., U.S.	s13	86
Miami Springs, Fl., U.S.	s13	86
Miamitown, Oh., U.S.	o12	112
Miāndowāb, Iran	B4	38
Miandrivazo, Madag.	q9	49
Miāneh, Iran	B5	38
Miangas Island, i., Indon.	D7	34
Miān Kāleh, Shebh-e Jazīreh-ye, pen., Iran	C6	39
Mianning, China	F5	31
Miānwāli, Pak.	D4	36
Mianyang, China	E5	31
Mianyang, China	I5	30
Miarinarivo, Madag.	q9	49
Miass, Sov. Un.	B6	28
Miass, stm., Sov. Un.	B6	28
Miastko, Pol.	A4	26
Mica, Wa., U.S.	B8	124
Mica Mountain, mtn., Az., U.S.	E5	80
Micanopy, Fl., U.S.	C4	86
Micco, Fl., U.S.	E6	86
Miccosukee, Fl., U.S.	B2	86
Miccosukee, Lake, res., Fl., U.S.	B2	86
Michael, Il., U.S.	D3	90
Michael, Lake, l., Nf., Can.	A2	72
Michalovce, Czech.	D6	26
Michaud Point, c., N.S., Can.	D9	71
Michel, B.C., Can.	E10	69
Michelson, Mount, mtn., Ak., U.S.	B11	79
Michendorf, Ger.D.R.	A8	19
Michichi, Ab., Can.	D4	68
Michie, Tn., U.S.	B3	119
Michigamme, Mi., U.S.	B2	99
Michigamme, Lake, l., Mi., U.S.	B2	99
Michigamme Reservoir, Mi., U.S.	B2	99
Michigan, N.D., U.S.	A7	111
Michigan, state, U.S.	E6	99
Michigan, stm., Co., U.S.	A4	83
Michigan, Lake, l., U.S.	B10	76
Michigan Center, Mi., U.S.	F6	99
Michigan City, In., U.S.	A4	91
Michigan Island, i., Wi., U.S.	B3	126
Michigan Prairie, reg., Wa., U.S.	C7	124
Michigantown, In., U.S.	D5	91
Michoacán, state, Mex.	D4	63
Michurin, Bul.	D8	24
Michurinsk, Sov. Un.	E13	27
Micoud, St. Luc.	J14	64
Micro, N.C., U.S.	B4	110
Micronesia, Federated States of, ter., T.T.P.I.	F9	6
Midai, i., Indon.	K7	35
Midale, Sk., Can.	H4	75
Midas, Id., U.S.	A2	89
Middelburg, Neth.	B5	16
Middelburg, S. Afr.	D4	49
Middelfart, Den.	C3	15
Middelharnis, Neth.	C4	17
Middelkerke, Bel.	C2	17
Middle, stm., B.C., Can.	B5	69
Middle, stm., Ia., U.S.	C3	92
Middle, stm., Mn., U.S.	B2	100
Middle Andaman, i., India	F9	36
Middleboro, Ma., U.S.	C6	98
Middlebourne, W.V., U.S.	B4	125
Middlebranch, Oh., U.S.	B4	112
Middlebro, Mb., Can.	E4	70
Middle Brook, Nf., Can.	D4	72
Middlebrook, Va., U.S.	B3	123
Middleburg, Fl., U.S.	B5	86
Middleburg, Ky., U.S.	C5	94
Middleburg, N.Y., U.S.	C6	109
Middleburg, N.C., U.S.	A4	110
Middleburg, Oh., U.S.	E7	115
Middleburg, Pa., U.S.	E7	115
Middleburg, Tn., U.S.	B3	119
Middleburgh, N.Y., U.S.	C6	109
Middleburg Heights, Oh., U.S.	h9	112
Middlebury, Ct., U.S.	C3	84
Middlebury, In., U.S.	A6	91
Middlebury, Vt., U.S.	C2	122
Middlefield, Ct., U.S.	C5	84
Middlefield, Ma., U.S.	B1	98
Middlefield, Oh., U.S.	A4	112
Middle Granville, N.Y., U.S.	B7	109
Middle Ground, rf., Mid. Is.	J3	52
Middle Haddam, Ct., U.S.	C5	84
Middle Island Creek, stm., W.V., U.S.	B3	125
Middle Lake, Sk., Can.	E3	75
Middle Loup, stm., Ne., U.S.	C5	104
Middle Musquodoboit, N.S., Can.	D6	71
Middle Nodaway, stm., Ia., U.S.	C2	92
Middle Park, val., Co., U.S.	A4	83
Middle Patuxent, stm., Md., U.S.	B4	97
Middleport, Oh., U.S.	C3	112
Middleport, N.Y., U.S.	B2	109
Middleport, Oh., U.S.	C3	112
Middle Raccoon, stm., Ia., U.S.	C3	92
Middle River, Md., U.S.	B5	97
Middle River, Mn., U.S.	B2	100
Middlesboro, Ky., U.S.	D6	94
Middlesbrough (Teesside), Eng., U.K.	C6	10
Middlesex, Belize	D7	63
Middlesex, N.J., U.S.	B4	107
Middlesex, N.Y., U.S.	C3	109
Middlesex, N.C., U.S.	B4	110
Middlesex, Vt., U.S.	C3	122
Middlesex, co., Ct., U.S.	D5	84
Middlesex, co., Ma., U.S.	B4	98
Middlesex, co., N.J., U.S.	C4	107
Middlesex, co., Va., U.S.	C6	123
Middlesex Fells Reservation, Ma., U.S.	g11	98
Middle Stewiacke, N.S., Can.	D6	71
Middleton, N.S., Can.	E4	71
Middleton, Id., U.S.	F2	89
Middleton, Ma., U.S.	A5	98
Middleton, Tn., U.S.	B3	119
Middleton, Wi., U.S.	E4	126
Middletown, Ct., U.S.	C5	84
Middletown, De., U.S.	C3	85
Middletown, Il., U.S.	C4	90
Middletown, In., U.S.	D6	91
Middletown, Ky., U.S.	g11	94
Middletown, Md., U.S.	B2	97
Middletown, Mo., U.S.	B6	102
Middletown, N.J., U.S.	C4	107
Middletown, N.Y., U.S.	D6	109
Middletown, Oh., U.S.	C1	112
Middletown, Pa., U.S.	F8	115
Middletown, R.I., U.S.	E4	116
Middletown, Va., U.S.	A4	123
Middletown Springs, Vt., U.S.	E2	122
Middleville, Mi., U.S.	F5	99
Middleville, N.J., U.S.	B3	107
Middleville, N.Y., U.S.	B6	109
Midfield, Al., U.S.	g7	78
Midgic, N.B., Can.	D5	71
Mid Glamorgan, co., Wales, U.K.	C4	12
Midi d'Ossau, Pic du, mtn., Fr.	F3	16
Midkiff, Tx., U.S.	D2	120
Midkiff, W.V., U.S.	C2	125
Midland, Ab., Can.	*C3	68
Midland, On., Can.	C5	73
Midland, Ar., U.S.	B1	81
Midland, In., U.S.	F3	91
Midland, La., U.S.	D3	95
Midland, Mi., U.S.	E6	99
Midland, N.C., U.S.	B2	110
Midland, Oh., U.S.	C2	112
Midland, Pa., U.S.	E1	115
Midland, S.D., U.S.	C4	118
Midland, Tx., U.S.	D1	120
Midland, Va., U.S.	B5	123
Midland, co., Mi., U.S.	E6	99
Midland, co., Tx., U.S.	D1	120
Midland Basin, Co., U.S.	A2	83
Midland City, Al., U.S.	D4	78
Midland Park, Ks., U.S.	g12	93
Midland Park, N.J., U.S.	B4	107
Midland Park, S.C., U.S.	k11	117
Midleton, Ire.	E2	10
Midlothian, Il., U.S.	k9	90
Midlothian, Md., U.S.	k13	97
Midlothian, Tx., U.S.	C4	120
Midlothian, Va., U.S.	m17	123
Midnapore, Ab., Can.	D3	68
Midnapore, India	D8	36
Midnight, Ms., U.S.	B3	101
Midongy Sud, Madag.	h9	49
Midpines, Ca., U.S.	D4	82
Midvale, Id., U.S.	E2	89
Midvale, Oh., U.S.	B4	112
Midvale, Ut., U.S.	C4	121
Midville, Ga., U.S.	D4	87
Midway, B.C., Can.	E8	69
Midway, Al., U.S.	C4	78
Midway, De., U.S.	F5	85
Midway, Ky., U.S.	B5	94
Midway, Or., U.S.	*B4	114
Midway, Pa., U.S.	G7	115
Midway, Ut., U.S.	C11	119
Midway, Ut., U.S.	C4	121
Midway Islands, dep., Oc.	E11	6
Midway Naval Station, mil., Mid. Is.	K3	52
Midway Range, mts., B.C., Can.	E8	69
Midwest, Wy., U.S.	C6	127
Midwest City, Ok., U.S.	B4	113
Midyat, Tur.	D13	40
Miechów, Pol.	C6	26
Miedzychód, Pol.	B3	26
Międzyrzec [Podlaski], Pol.	C7	26
Międzyrzecz, Pol.	B3	26
Międzyrzecze, Pol.	g10	26
Międzyzdroje, Pol.	B3	26
Mielec, Pol.	C6	26
Mien, i., Swe.	B8	15
Mienia, stm., Pol.	m14	26
Mier, In., U.S.	C6	91
Miercurea Ciuc, Rom.	B7	24
Mieres, Spain	A3	22
Miesbach, F.R.Ger.	B7	20
Mieso, Eth.	D5	47
Mifflin, Pa., U.S.	E7	115
Mifflin, Tn., U.S.	B3	119
Mifflin, co., Pa., U.S.	E6	115
Mifflinburg, Pa., U.S.	E7	115
Mifflintown, Pa., U.S.	E7	115
Mifflinville, Pa., U.S.	D9	115
Migdal, Isr.	B7	41
Migennes, Fr.	D5	16
Migliarino, Italy	E7	20
Miguel Alemán, Presa, res., Mex.	n15	63
Miguel Alves, Braz.	B2	57
Miguel Auza, Mex.	C4	63
Mihai Viteazu, Rom.	C9	24
Mihama, Japan	o15	39
Mijares, stm., Spain	B5	22
Mijdahah, P.D.R.Yem.	C6	47
Mijdaḩah, P.D.R.Yem.	C6	47
Mikado, Sk., Can.	F4	75
Mikado, Mi., U.S.	D7	99
Mikana, Wi., U.S.	C2	126
Mikha Tskhakaya, Sov. Un.	A14	40
Mikhaylov, Sov. Un.	D12	27
Mikhaylov, Cape, c., Ant.	C24	7
Mikhaylovgrad, Bul.	D6	24
Mikhaylovka, Sov. Un.	H10	27
Mikhaylovskiy, Sov. Un.	C9	28
Mikindani, Tan.	D7	48
Mikkalo, Or., U.S.	B6	114
Mikkeli, Fin.	G12	14
Mikołów, Pol.	g9	26
Mikonos, Grc.	D5	25
Míkonos, i., Grc.	C3	48
Mikope, Zaire	C3	48
Mikulov, Czech.	C6	26
Mikumi, Tan.	C6	48
Mikura Island, i., Japan	J9	33
Milaca, Mn., U.S.	E5	100
Milagro, Ec.	D2	60
Milam, co., Tx., U.S.	D4	120
Milam, co., Tx., U.S.	D4	120
Milan, P.Q., Can.	D6	74
Milan (Milano), Italy	D4	23
Milan, Ga., U.S.	D3	87
Milan, Il., U.S.	B3	90
Milan, In., U.S.	F7	91
Milan, Ks., U.S.	E6	93
Milan, Mi., U.S.	F7	99
Milan, Mo., U.S.	A4	102
Milan, N.H., U.S.	A4	106
Milan, N.M., U.S.	B2	108
Milan, Oh., U.S.	A3	112
Milan, Tn., U.S.	B3	119
Milan, Wi., U.S.	D3	126
Milano, Tx., U.S.	D4	120
Milâs, Tur.	D6	25
Milazzo, Italy	E5	23
Milbank, S.D., U.S.	B9	118
Milbanke Sound, strt., B.C., Can.	C3	69
Milbridge, Me., U.S.	D5	96
Milburn, Ne., U.S.	C6	104
Milburn, Ok., U.S.	C5	113
Milden, Sk., Can.	F2	75
Mildenhall, Eng., U.K.	B8	12
Mildmay, On., Can.	C3	73
Mildred, Ks., U.S.	D9	93
Mildred, Mt., U.S.	D12	103
Mildred, Pa., U.S.	D9	115
Mildura, Austl.	F7	50
Miléai, Grc.	C8	51
Miles, Austl.	E9	50
Miles, Ia., U.S.	B7	92
Miles, Tx., U.S.	D2	120
Milesburg, Pa., U.S.	E6	115
Miles City, Mt., U.S.	D11	103
Miles Mountain, mtn., Vt., U.S.	C5	122
Milestone, Sk., Can.	G3	75
Milesville, S.D., U.S.	C4	118
Miletus, hist., Tur.	D6	25
Milevsko, Czech.	F5	117
Miley, S.C., U.S.	F5	117
Milfay, Ok., U.S.	B5	113
Milford, Ca., U.S.	B3	82
Milford, Ct., U.S.	E3	84

183

Name — Map Ref — Page

Milford, De., U.S. E4 85
Milford, Il., U.S. C6 90
Milford, In., U.S. B6 91
Milford, Ia., U.S. A2 92
Milford, Ks., U.S. C7 93
Milford, Ky., U.S. B5 94
Milford, Me., U.S. D4 96
Milford, Ma., U.S. B4 98
Milford, Mi., U.S. F7 99
Milford, Mo., U.S. D3 102
Milford, Ne., U.S. D8 104
Milford, N.H., U.S. E3 106
Milford, N.J., U.S. B2 107
Milford, N.Y., U.S. C6 109
Milford, Oh., U.S. C1 112
Milford, Pa., U.S. D12 115
Milford, Ut., U.S. E2 121
Milford, Va., U.S. B5 123
Milford Center, Oh., U.S. B2 112
Milford Haven, Wales, U.K. E4 10
Milford Lake, res., Ks., U.S. C6 93
Milford Sound, strt., N.Z. P11 51
Milford Station, N.S., Can. D6 71
Milh, Ra's al, c., Libya F5 40
Milicz, Pol. C4 26
Mililani Town, Hi., U.S. g9 88
Miling, Austl. F2 50
Milk, stm., N.A. B8 103
Milk Creek, stm., Co., U.S. A3 83
Milk River, Ab., Can. E4 68
Milk River Ridge Reservoir, res., Ab., Can. E4 68
Mill, stm., Ma., U.S. h9 98
Milladore, Wi., U.S. D4 126
Millard, Ky., U.S. C7 94
Millard, Mo., U.S. A5 102
Millard, co., Ut., U.S. D2 121
Millars Sound, strt., Bah. n17 64
Millarton, N.D., U.S. C7 111
Millau, Fr. E5 16
Millbank, On., Can. D4 73
Millboro, S.D., U.S. D6 118
Millboro, Va., U.S. C3 123
Millbrae, Ca., U.S. h8 82
Millbridge, On., Can. C7 73
Millbrook, On., Can. C6 73
Millbrook, Al., U.S. C3 78
Millbrook, Mi., U.S. E5 99
Millbrook, N.Y., U.S. D7 109
Mill Brook, stm., Vt., U.S. B5 122
Millburn, N.J., U.S. B4 107
Millbury, Ma., U.S. B4 98
Millbury, Oh., U.S. e7 112
Mill City, Nv., U.S. C3 105
Mill City, Or., U.S. C4 114
Mill City, Pa., U.S. m17 115
Millcreek, Il., U.S. F4 90
Mill Creek, In., U.S. A4 91
Millcreek, Mo., U.S. D7 102
Mill Creek, Ok., U.S. C5 113
Mill Creek, Pa., U.S. F6 115
Millcreek, Ut., U.S. C4 121
Mill Creek, W.V., U.S. C5 125
Mill Creek, stm., In., U.S. F4 91
Mill Creek, stm., Ks., U.S. C6 93
Mill Creek, stm., Ks., U.S. C7 93
Mill Creek, stm., N.J., U.S. D4 107
Mill Creek, stm., Oh., U.S. B2 112
Mill Creek, stm., Tn., U.S. G10 119
Mill Creek, stm., W.V., U.S. C3 125
Mill Creek, stm., W.V., U.S. m13 125
Millcreek Township, Pa., U.S. B1 115
Milldale, Ct., U.S. C4 84
Milledgeville, Ga., U.S. C3 87
Milledgeville, Il., U.S. B4 90
Milledgeville, Tn., U.S. B3 119
Mille Îles, Rivière des, stm., P.Q., Can. p19 74
Mille Lacs, co., Mn., U.S. E5 100
Mille Lacs Indian Reservation, Mn., U.S. D5 100
Mille Lacs Lake, l., Mn., U.S. D5 100
Millen, Ga., U.S. D5 87
Miller, Ms., U.S. A4 101
Miller, Ne., U.S. D6 104
Miller, Oh., U.S. D3 112
Miller, S.D., U.S. C7 118
Miller, co., Ar., U.S. D2 81
Miller, co., Ga., U.S. E2 87
Miller, co., Mo., U.S. C5 102
Miller, Mount, mtn., Ak., U.S. C11 79
Miller Creek, stm., De., U.S. F5 85
Miller Dale Colony, S.D., U.S. C6 118
Millerovo, Sov. Un. G13 27
Miller Peak, mtn., Az., U.S. F5 80
Miller Run, stm., Vt., U.S. B4 122
Millers, Md., U.S. A4 97
Millers, stm., Ma., U.S. A3 98
Millersburg, In., U.S. A6 91
Millersburg, Ia., U.S. C5 92
Millersburg, Ky., U.S. B5 94
Millersburg, Mi., U.S. C6 99
Millersburg, Oh., U.S. B4 112
Millersburg, Pa., U.S. E8 115
Millers Falls, Ma., U.S. A3 98
Millers Ferry, Al., U.S. C2 78
Millers Ferry Dam, Al., U.S. C2 78
Millersport, Oh., U.S. C3 112
Millerstown, Pa., U.S. E7 115
Millersview, Tx., U.S. D3 120
Millersville, Oh., U.S. *n12 112
Millersville, Pa., U.S. F9 115
Millerton, N.B., Can. C4 71
Millerton, Ia., U.S. D4 92
Millerton, N.Y., U.S. D7 109
Millerton, Ok., U.S. D6 113
Millerton, Pa., U.S. C8 115
Millertown, Nf., Can. D3 72
Millertown Junction, Nf., Can. D3 72
Millerville, Al., U.S. B4 78
Millerville, Mn., U.S. D3 100
Millet, Ab., Can. C4 68
Millett, S.C., U.S. E4 117
Millett, Tx., U.S. E3 120
Mill Grove, In., U.S. D7 91
Mill Grove, Mo., U.S. A4 102
Mill Hall, Pa., U.S. D7 115
Millheim, Pa., U.S. E7 115
Millhousen, In., U.S. F7 91
Millhurst, N.J., U.S. C4 107
Millicent, Austl. G7 50
Millicent, Ab., Can. D5 68
Milligan, Fl., U.S. u15 86
Milligan, Ne., U.S. D8 104
Milligan College, Tn., U.S. C11 119
Milliken, Co., U.S. A6 83
Millington, Md., U.S. B6 97
Millington, Mi., U.S. E7 99
Millington, Or., U.S. D2 114
Millington, Tn., U.S. B2 119
Millinocket, Me., U.S. C4 96
Millinocket Lake, l., Me., U.S. C4 96
Millinocket Lake, l., Me., U.S. B4 96
Mill Iron, Mt., U.S. E12 103
Millis, Ma., U.S. B5 98
Mill Island, i., Ant. C23 7
Millmerran, Austl. C8 51
Millom, Eng., U.K. F5 13
Mill Point, W.V., U.S. C4 125
Millport, Scot., U.K. E4 13
Millport, Al., U.S. B1 78
Millport, Pa., U.S. C5 115
Millrift, Pa., U.S. D12 115
Mill River, Ma., U.S. B1 98
Mill Run, Pa., U.S. G3 115
Millry, Al., U.S. D1 78
Mills, Ne., U.S. B6 104
Mills, N.M., U.S. A5 108
Mills, Pa., U.S. C6 115
Mills, Wy., U.S. D6 127
Mills, co., Ia., U.S. C2 92
Mills, co., Tx., U.S. D3 120
Millsboro, De., U.S. F4 85
Millsboro, Pa., U.S. G1 115
Mill Shoals, Il., U.S. E5 90
Mills Lake, l., N.T., Can. D9 66
Mill Spring, Mo., U.S. D7 102
Millstadt, Il., U.S. E3 90
Millston, Wi., U.S. D3 126
Millstone, N.J., U.S. B3 107
Millstone, stm., N.J., U.S. C4 107
Millstreet, Ire. E2 11
Milltown, Nf., Can. E4 72
Milltown, Al., U.S. B4 78
Milltown, In., U.S. H5 91
Milltown, Ky., U.S. C4 94
Milltown, Mt., U.S. D3 103
Milltown, N.J., U.S. C4 107
Milltown, S.D., U.S. D8 118
Milltown, Wi., U.S. C1 126
Millvale, Pa., U.S. k14 115
Mill Valley, Ca., U.S. D2 82
Mill Village, N.S., Can. E5 71
Mill Village, Pa., U.S. C2 115
Millville, N.B., Can. C2 71
Millville, De., U.S. F5 85
Millville, Ky., U.S. B5 94
Millville, Ma., U.S. B4 98
Millville, N.J., U.S. E2 107
Millville, Oh., U.S. n12 112
Millville, Pa., U.S. D9 115
Millville, Ut., U.S. B4 121
Millville, W.V., U.S. B7 125
Millville Lake, N.H., U.S. E4 106
Millwood, Ga., U.S. E4 87
Millwood, Oh., U.S. B3 112
Millwood, Va., U.S. A4 123
Millwood, Wa., U.S. g14 124
Millwood Lake, res., Ar., U.S. D1 81
Milmay, N.J., U.S. E3 107
Milner, B.C., Can. f13 69
Milner, Co., U.S. A3 83
Milner, Ga., U.S. C2 87
Milner Dam, Id., U.S. G5 89
Milner Ridge, Mb., Can. D3 70
Milnesand, N.M., U.S. D6 108
Milnor, N.D., U.S. C8 111
Milo, Ab., Can. D4 68
Milo, Ia., U.S. C4 92
Milo, Me., U.S. C4 96
Milo, Mo., U.S. D3 102
Milo, Or., U.S. E3 114
Milolii, Hi., U.S. D6 88
Milos, i., Grc. D5 40
Milparinka, Austl. D3 51
Milpitas, Ca., U.S. *k9 82
Milroy, In., U.S. F7 91
Milroy, Mn., U.S. F3 100
Milroy, Pa., U.S. E6 115
Milstead, Al., U.S. C4 78
Milstead, Ga., U.S. C3 87
Miltenberg, F.R.Ger. D4 19
Milton, N.S., Can. E5 71
Milton, On., Can. D5 73
Milton, N.Z. Q12 51
Milton, Ct., U.S. B2 84
Milton, De., U.S. E4 85
Milton, Fl., U.S. u14 86
Milton, Il., U.S. D3 90
Milton, In., U.S. E7 91
Milton, Ia., U.S. D5 92
Milton, Ks., U.S. E6 93
Milton, Ky., U.S. B4 94
Milton, La., U.S. D3 95
Milton, Ma., U.S. B5 98
Milton, N.H., U.S. D5 106
Milton, N.Y., U.S. D7 109
Milton, N.C., U.S. A3 110
Milton, N.D., U.S. A7 111
Milton, Pa., U.S. D8 115
Milton, Vt., U.S. B2 122
Milton, Wa., U.S. f11 124
Milton, W.V., U.S. C2 125
Milton, Wi., U.S. F5 126
Milton, Lake, l., Oh., U.S. A4 112
Miltona, Mn., U.S. D3 100
Miltona, Lake, l., Mn., U.S. D3 100
Milton-Freewater, Or., U.S. B8 114
Milton Mills, N.H., U.S. C5 106
Milton Reservoir, res., Co., U.S. A6 83
Miltonvale, Ks., U.S. C6 93
Miltown Malbay, Ire. E2 11
Milverton, On., Can. D4 73
Milwaukee, N.C., U.S. A5 110
Milwaukee, Wi., U.S. E6 126
Milwaukee, co., Wi., U.S. E6 126
Milwaukee, stm., Wi., U.S. m12 126
Milwaukie, Or., U.S. B4 114
Mimbres, N.M., U.S. E2 108
Mimbres Mountains, mts., N.M., U.S. E2 108
Mimico (part of Etobicoke), On., Can. m15 73
Mimizan, Fr. E3 16
Mimoň, Czech. C9 19
Mimongo, Gabon F2 46
Mimosa Park, La., U.S. *E5 95
Mims, Fl., U.S. D6 86
Mina, Nv., U.S. E3 105
Mina, S.D., U.S. B7 118
Mina' al Aḥmadi, Kuw. C4 38
Mīnāb, Iran H8 39
Minago, stm., Mb., Can. B2 70
Minaki, On., Can. E4 70
Minamata, Japan J5 33
Minami-iwo, i., Japan E8 6
Minami-Tori Island, i., Japan E9 6
Minas, Cuba D5 64
Minas, Ur. E1 56
Minas Basin, b., N.S., Can. D5 71
Minas Channel, strt., N.S., Can. D5 71
Minas de Corrales, Ur. E1 56
Minas de Oro, Hond. C4 62
Minas de Riotinto, Spain D2 22
Minas Gerais, state, Braz. B4 56
Minas Novas, Braz. B4 56
Minatare, Ne., U.S. C2 104
Minatitlán, Mex. D6 63
Minbu, Burma D9 36
Minburn, Ab., Can. C5 68
Minburn, Ia., U.S. C3 92
Mincio, stm., Italy D6 20
Minco, Ok., U.S. B4 113
Mindanao, i., Phil. D6 34
Mindanao Sea, Phil. D6 34
Mindel, stm., F.R.Ger. A6 20
Mindelheim, F.R.Ger. A6 20
Mindemoya, On., Can. B2 73
Minden, On., Can. C6 73
Minden, F.R.Ger. B4 18
Minden, Ia., U.S. C2 92
Minden, La., U.S. B2 95
Minden, Ne., U.S. D7 104
Minden, Nv., U.S. E2 105
Minden, W.V., U.S. D3 125
Minden City, Mi., U.S. E8 99
Mindenmines, Mo., U.S. D3 102
Mindi, Pan. k11 62
Mindoro, Wi., U.S. D2 126
Mindoro, i., Phil. C6 34
Mindoro Strait, strt., Phil. C6 34
Mine Centre, On., Can. E5 70
Minechoag Mountain, hill, Ma., U.S. B3 98
Minehead, Eng., U.K. E5 10
Mine Head, c., Ire. F4 11
Mine Hill, N.J., U.S. B3 107
Mineiros, Braz. B2 56
Mine La Motte, Mo., U.S. D7 102
Mineola, Ia., U.S. C2 92
Mineola, N.Y., U.S. E7 109
Mineola, Tx., U.S. C5 120
Miner, Mo., U.S. E8 102
Miner, co., S.D., U.S. D8 118
Mineral, Ca., U.S. B3 82
Mineral, Il., U.S. B4 90
Mineral, Va., U.S. B5 123
Mineral, Wa., U.S. C3 124
Mineral, co., Co., U.S. D4 83
Mineral, co., Mt., U.S. C1 103
Mineral, co., Nv., U.S. E3 105
Mineral, co., W.V., U.S. B6 125
Mineral City, Oh., U.S. B4 112
Mineral del Monte, Mex. m14 63
Mineral del Oro, Mex. n13 63
Mineral Hills, Mi., U.S. B2 99
Mineral Mountains, mts., Ut., U.S. E3 121
Mineral Park, Tn., U.S. h11 119
Mineral Point, Mo., U.S. D7 102
Mineral Point, Wi., U.S. F3 126
Mineral Springs, Ar., U.S. D2 81
Mineral Wells, Ms., U.S. A4 101
Mineral Wells, Tx., U.S. C3 120
Minersville, Oh., U.S. C4 112
Minersville, Pa., U.S. E9 115
Minersville, Ut., U.S. E3 121
Minerva, N.Y., U.S. B7 109
Minerva, Oh., U.S. B4 112
Minervino Murge, Italy D6 23
Minetto, N.Y., U.S. B4 109
Mineville, N.Y., U.S. A7 109
Mingan, P.Q., Can. h8 72
Mingechaur, Sov. Un. G18 8
Mingechaur Reservoir, res., Sov. Un. E3 28
Mingenew, Austl. E2 50
Mingo, Ia., U.S. C4 92
Mingo, co., W.V., U.S. D2 125
Mingo Junction, Oh., U.S. B5 112
Mingoyo, Tan. D6 48
Mingshui, China C4 31
Mingshui, China C2 33
Minho (Miño), stm., Eur. B1 22
Minho, stm., Jam. E14 65
Minicoy Island, i., India G5 36
Minidoka, Id., U.S. G5 89
Minidoka, co., Id., U.S. G5 89
Minidoka Dam, Id., U.S. G5 89
Minier, Il., U.S. C4 90
Miniota, Mb., Can. D1 70
Minipi Lake, l., Nf., Can. h9 72
Minisink Island, i., N.J., U.S. A3 107
Minitonas, Mb., Can. C1 70
Minna, Nig. E6 45
Minna Bluff, pen., Ant. B29 7
Minneapolis, Ks., U.S. C6 93
Minneapolis, Mn., U.S. F5 100
Minneapolis, N.C., U.S. e11 110
Minnedosa, Mb., Can. D2 70
Minnedosa, stm., Mb., Can. D1 70
Minnehaha, co., S.D., U.S. D9 118
Minneiska, Mn., U.S. F7 100
Minneola, Ks., U.S. E3 93
Minneota, Mn., U.S. F3 100
Minnesota, state, U.S. E4 100
Minnesota, stm., Mn., U.S. F2 100
Minnesota Lake, Mn., U.S. G5 100
Minnetonka, Mn., U.S. n12 100
Minnetonka, Lake, l., Mn., U.S. n11 100
Minnewanka, Lake, l., Ab., Can. D3 68
Minnewaska, Lake, l., Mn., U.S. E3 100
Minnewaukan, N.D., U.S. A6 111
Mino, Japan n15 33
Miño (Minho), stm., Eur. A1 22
Minocqua, Wi., U.S. C4 126
Minokamo, Japan n15 33
Minong, Wi., U.S. B2 126
Minonk, Il., U.S. C4 90
Minooka, Il., U.S. B5 90
Minor Hill, Tn., U.S. B4 119
Minot, Ma., U.S. h12 98
Minot, N.D., U.S. A4 111
Minot Air Force Base, mil., N.D., U.S. A4 111
Minqin, China D5 31
Minquadale, De., U.S. i7 85
Minsen, F.R.Ger. A7 17
Minsk, Sov. Un. D5 29
Mińsk Mazowiecki, Pol. B6 26
Minster, Oh., U.S. B1 112
Minter, Al., U.S. C2 78
Minter City, Ms., U.S. B3 101
Mint Hill, N.C., U.S. B2 110
Minto, Mb., Can. E1 70
Minto, N.B., Can. C3 71
Minto, Ak., U.S. C10 79
Minto, N.D., U.S. A8 111
Minto, Lac, l., P.Q., Can. g11 74
Minton, Sk., Can. H3 75
Minturn, Ar., U.S. B4 81
Minturn, Co., U.S. B4 83
Minturn, Me., U.S. D4 96
Minturno, Italy D4 23
Minūf, Eg. D3 41
Minusinsk, Sov. Un. D12 29
Minute Man National Historical Park, Ma., U.S. g10 98
Minvoul, Gabon E2 46
Minyā al Qamḥ, Eg. D3 41
Minya Konka see Gongga Mountain, mtn., China F5 31
Mio, Mi., U.S. D6 99
Miquelon, i., St. P./M. E3 72
Mira, Port. B1 22
Mira, La., U.S. B2 95
Mira, stm., Port. D1 22
Mira, stm., S.A. A2 58
Miracema do Norte, Braz. D5 59
Miracle Hot Springs, Ca., U.S. E4 82
Mirador, Braz. C2 57
Miraflores, Col. C3 60
Miraflores, Peru *D2 58
Miraflores Locks, Pan. m11 62
Miragoâne, Haiti E7 64
Mira Gut, N.S., Can. C10 71
Miraí, Braz. g6 56
Miraj, India E5 36
Mira Loma, Ca., U.S. *m13 82
Miramar, Arg. B5 54
Miramar, Fl., U.S. s13 86
Miramar Naval Air Station, mil., Ca., U.S. F5 82
Miramichi Bay, b., N.B., Can. B4 71
Miranda, Braz. C1 56
Miranda, Col. C2 60
Miranda, S.D., U.S. C7 118
Miranda, state, Ven. A4 60
Miranda, stm., Braz. C1 56
Miranda de Ebro, Spain A4 22
Miranda do Douro, Port. B2 22
Mirande, Fr. F4 16
Mirandela, Port. B2 22
Mirando City, Tx., U.S. F3 120
Mirandola, Italy E7 20
Mirassol, Braz. C3 56
Miravalles, Volcán, vol., C.R. E5 62
Mirbāţ, Oman D5 38
Mirebalais, Haiti E7 64
Mirecourt, Fr. C7 16
Mirepoix, Fr. F4 16
Mirgorod, Sov. Un. G9 27
Miri, Malay. E4 34
Miriam Vale, Austl. B8 51
Mirim, Lagoa, b., S.A. E2 56
Mírina, Grc. C5 40
Mirnyy, sci., Ant. C22 7
Mirond Lake, l., Sk., Can. B4 75
Mirow, Ger.D.R. E6 15
Mīrpur, Pak. C2 37
Mīrpur Khās, Pak. E2 37
Mirror, Ab., Can. C4 68
Mirror Lake, N.H., U.S. C4 106
Mirror Lake, l., N.H., U.S. C4 106
Mirzāpur, India C7 36
Misāḩah, Bi'r, well, Eg. E5 43
Misakubo, Japan n16 33
Misantla, Mex. D5 63
Misburg, F.R.Ger. A4 19
Miscoe Hill, hill, Ma., U.S. h9 98
Miscou Centre, N.B., Can. B5 71
Miscouche, P.E., Can. C6 71
Miscou Island, i., N.B., Can. B5 71
Miscou Point, c., N.B., Can. A5 71
Misenheimer, N.C., U.S. B2 110
Mishan, China D6 33
Mishawaka, In., U.S. A5 91
Misheguk Mountain, mtn., Ak., U.S. B7 79
Mishicot, Wi., U.S. D6 126
Mishima, Japan I9 33
Misiones, prov., Arg. E5 55
Misiones, dept., Para. E4 55
Miskitos, Cayos, is., Nic. E8 63
Miskolc, Hung. A5 24
Mismār, Sud. B4 47
Misool, i., Indon. F7 34
Mispillion, stm., De., U.S. E4 85
Misquamicut, R.I., U.S. G1 116
Mişr al Jadīdah (Heliopolis) (part of Cairo), Eg. D3 41
Misrātah, Libya C3 43
Missaukee, co., Mi., U.S. D5 99
Missaukee, Lake, l., Mi., U.S. D5 99
Missinaibi, stm., On., Can. G16 66
Mission, Ks., U.S. m16 93
Mission, S.D., U.S. D5 118
Mission, Tx., U.S. F3 120
Mission City, B.C., Can. E6 69
Mission Hill, S.D., U.S. E8 118
Mission Hills, Ks., U.S. *k16 93
Mission Mountain, mtn., Ok., U.S. A7 115
Mission Range, mts., Mt., U.S. C3 103
Mission Ridge, S.D., U.S. C5 118
Mission Viejo, Ca., U.S. n13 82
Missipuskiow, stm., Sk., Can. D4 75
Missisquoi, co., P.Q., Can. D5 74
Missisquoi, stm., Vt., U.S. B3 122
Missisquoi Bay, b., Vt., U.S. A2 122
Mississauga, On., Can. D5 73
Mississinewa, stm., U.S. D7 91
Mississinewa Lake, res., In., U.S. C6 91
Mississippi, co., Ar., U.S. B5 81
Mississippi, co., Mo., U.S. E8 102
Mississippi, state, U.S. C4 101
Mississippi, stm., U.S. D9 76
Mississippi Delta, La., U.S. E6 95
Mississippi Lake, l., On., Can. B8 73
Mississippi Sound, strt., U.S. E5 101
Mississippi State, Ms., U.S. B5 101
Missoula, Mt., U.S. D2 103
Missoula, co., Mt., U.S. D2 103
Missour, Mor. C4 44
Missouri, state, U.S. C5 102
Missouri, stm., U.S. B8 76
Missouri Buttes, mtn., Wy., U.S. B8 127
Missouri City, Mo., U.S. h11 102
Missouri City, Tx., U.S. r14 120
Missouri Valley, Ia., U.S. C2 92
Mistaken Point, c., Nf., Can. E5 72
Mistassini, Lac, l., P.Q., Can. h12 74
Mistassini, Parc de, P.Q., Can. h12 74
Mistastin Lake, l., Nf., Can. g9 72
Mistatim, Sk., Can. E4 75
Mistelbach [an der Zaya], Aus. D8 18
Misti, Volcán, vol., Peru E3 58
Miston, Tn., U.S. A2 119
Mistretta, Italy F5 23
Mita, Punta, c., Mex. C3 63
Mitaka, Japan *I9 33
Mitake, Japan I8 33
Mitcham, Austl. *F6 50
Mitchell, Austl. E8 50
Mitchell, On., Can. D3 73
Mitchell, Ga., U.S. C4 87
Mitchell, Il., U.S. E3 90
Mitchell, In., U.S. G5 91
Mitchell, Ia., U.S. A5 92
Mitchell, La., U.S. C2 95
Mitchell, Ne., U.S. C2 104
Mitchell, Or., U.S. C6 114
Mitchell, S.D., U.S. D7 118
Mitchell, co., Ga., U.S. E2 87
Mitchell, co., Ia., U.S. A5 92
Mitchell, co., Ks., U.S. C5 93
Mitchell, co., N.C., U.S. e10 110
Mitchell, co., Tx., U.S. C2 120
Mitchell, stm., Austl. C7 50
Mitchell, Lake, l., Mi., U.S. D5 99
Mitchell, Lake, res., Al., U.S. C3 78
Mitchell, Mount, mtn., N.C., U.S. f10 110
Mitchell Island, i., La., U.S. E6 95
Mitchellsburg, Ky., U.S. C5 94
Mitchellville, Ia., U.S. C4 92
Mitchellville, Tn., U.S. A5 119
Mitchelstown, Ire. D2 10
Mīt Fāris, Eg. C3 41
Mīt Ghamr, Eg. D3 41
Mitilíni, Grc. C6 40
Mitishto, stm., Mb., Can. B2 70
Mitkof Island, i., Ak., U.S. m23 79
Mitla Pass, Eg. E4 41
Mito, Japan H10 33
Mitra do Bispo, mtn., Braz. h5 56
Mitre, mtn., N.Z. N15 51
Mitry-Mory, Fr. E2 17
Mitsinjo, Madag. g9 49
Mittelland Canal, Eur. B5 18
Mittenwald, F.R.Ger. B7 20
Mittersill, Aus. B8 20
Mitterteich, F.R.Ger. D6 18
Mittie, La., U.S. D3 95
Mittlerer Isar Kanal, F.R.Ger. A7 20
Mittweida, Ger.D.R. C6 18
Mitú, Col. C3 60
Mitumba, Monts, mts., Zaire C4 48
Mitwaba, Zaire C4 48
Mitzic, Gabon E2 46
Miura, Japan n18 33
Mixquiahuala, Mex. m14 63
Mixteco, stm., Mex. o14 63
Miyagi Island, i., Japan O5 52
Miyake Island, i., Japan I9 33
Miyako, Japan G10 33
Miyakonojō, Japan K5 33
Miyazaki, Japan K5 33
Miyazu, Japan n14 33
Mizdah, Libya C2 43
Mize, Ms., U.S. D4 101
Mizen Head, c., Ire. F2 11
Mizil, Rom. C8 24
Mizoram, ter., India D9 36
Mizpah, Mn., U.S. C4 100
Mizpah, N.J., U.S. E3 107
Mizpah Creek, stm., Mt., U.S. E11 103
Mizpe Ramon, Isr. G10 40
Mizque, Bol. C2 55
Mjölby, Swe. H6 14
Mjøsa, l., Nor. G4 14
Mkalama, Tan. B5 48
Mladá Boleslav, Czech. C3 26
Mława, Pol. B6 26
Mljet, i., Yugo. D3 24
Mnichovo Hradiště, Czech. C9 19
Mnyusi, Tan. C6 48
Mo, Nor. D6 14
Moa, i., Austl. B7 50
Moab, Ut., U.S. E6 121
Moala Island, i., Fiji I15 52
Moamba, Moz. C5 49
Moanda, Gabon F2 46
Moapa, Nv., U.S. G7 105
Moapa River Indian Reservation, Nv., U.S. G7 105
Moark, Ar., U.S. A5 81
Moar Lake, l., Can. D4 70
Moate, Ire. D4 11
Moba, Zaire C4 48
Mobara, Japan n19 33
Mobaye, Cen. Afr. Rep. E4 46
Mobayi-Mbongo, Zaire A3 48
Mobeetie, Tx., U.S. B2 120
Moberly, Mo., U.S. B5 102
Moberly Lake, B.C., Can. B7 69
Moberly Lake, l., B.C., Can. B7 69
Mobile, Nf., Can. E5 72
Mobile, Al., U.S. E1 78
Mobile, Az., U.S. D3 80
Mobile, co., Al., U.S. E1 78
Mobile, stm., Al., U.S. E1 78
Mobile Bay, b., Al., U.S. E1 83
Mobridge, S.D., U.S. B5 118
Mobula, Zaire A4 48
Moca, Dom. Rep. E8 64
Mocajuba, Braz. C5 59
Moçambique, Moz. D7 48
Moçâmedes see Namibe, Ang. E1 48
Mocanaqua, Pa., U.S. D9 115
Moccasin, Az., U.S. A3 80
Moccasin, Mt., U.S. C7 103
Moce, i., Fiji I16 52
Mocha, Isla, i., Chile B2 54
Moc Hoa, Viet. G6 35
Mocho Mountains, mts., Jam. E14 65
Mochudi, Bots. B4 49
Mocímboa da Praia, Moz. D7 48
Möckeln, l., Swe. B8 15
Mocksville, N.C., U.S. B2 110
Moclips, Wa., U.S. B1 124
Môco, Serra, mtn., Ang. D2 48
Mocoa, Col. C2 60
Mococa, Braz. C3 56
Mocomoco, Bol. C2 55
Mocorito, Mex. B3 63
Moctezuma, Mex. B3 63
Moctezuma, stm., Mex. m14 63
Mocuba, Moz. A6 49
Mocubúri, Moz. D6 48
Modale, Ia., U.S. C2 92
Modane, Fr. D2 20
Model, Co., U.S. D6 83
Model Reservoir, res., Co., U.S. D6 83
Modena, Italy B3 23
Modena, Mo., U.S. A4 102
Modena, N.Y., U.S. D6 109
Modena, Ut., U.S. F2 121
Modena, Wi., U.S. D2 126
Modeste, La., U.S. h9 95
Modesto, Ca., U.S. D3 82
Modesto, Il., U.S. D4 90
Modica, Italy F5 23
Modlin, Pol. k13 26
Mödling, Aus. D8 18
Modoc, Ga., U.S. D4 87
Modoc, In., U.S. D7 91
Modoc, Ks., U.S. D2 93
Modoc, co., Ca., U.S. B3 82
Modoc Point, Or., U.S. E5 114
Modřany, Czech. o17 26
Moe, Austl. G8 50
Moehau, mtn., N.Z. L15 51
Moen, i., Micron. Q18 52
Moenave, Az., U.S. A4 80
Moengo, Sur. A4 59
Moenkopi, Az., U.S. A4 80
Moenkopi Plateau, plat., Az., U.S. B4 80
Moenkopi Wash, val., Az., U.S. A5 80
Moerbeke, Bel. C3 17
Moers, F.R.Ger. B1 19
Moesa, stm., Switz. D7 21
Moeskroen see Mouscron, Bel. B5 16
Moffat, Scot., U.K. E5 13
Moffat, Co., U.S. C5 83
Moffat, co., Co., U.S. A2 83
Moffat Tunnel, Co., U.S. B5 83
Moffett, Ok., U.S. B7 113
Moffett Field Naval Air Station, mil., Ca., U.S. k8 82
Moffit, N.D., U.S. C5 111
Moga, Zaire B4 48
Mogadishu (Muqdisho), Som. E6 47
Mogadore, Oh., U.S. A4 112
Mogaung, Burma C10 36
Mogi das Cruzes, Braz. C3 56
Mogielnica, Pol. C6 26
Mogilev, Sov. Un. D6 29
Mogilev-Podolskiy, Sov. Un. G6 27
Mogilno, Pol. B4 26
Mogi-Mirim, Braz. C3 56
Mogincual, Moz. A7 49
Mogocha, Sov. Un. D14 29
Mogochin, Sov. Un. B10 28
Mogok, Burma D10 36
Mogollon, N.M., U.S. D1 108
Mogollon Mesa, mtn., Az., U.S. C4 80
Mogollon Mountains, mts., N.M., U.S. D1 108
Mogollon Rim, clf, Az., U.S. C5 80
Mogote, Co., U.S. D4 83
Mogotes, Punta, c., Arg. B5 54
Mogpog, Phil. p13 34
Moguer, Spain D2 22
Mohács, Hung. C4 24
Mohale's Hoek, Leso. D4 49
Mohall, N.D., U.S. A4 111
Mohammedia, Mor. C3 44
Mohave, co., Az., U.S. B1 80
Mohave, Lake, res., U.S. H7 105
Mohave Mountains, mts., Az., U.S. C1 80
Mohave Valley, Az., U.S. C1 80
Mohawk, Mi., U.S. A2 99
Mohawk, N.Y., U.S. C5 109
Mohawk, stm., N.H., U.S. g7 106
Mohawk, stm., N.Y., U.S. C6 109
Mohawk Lake, l., N.J., U.S. A3 107
Mohawk Mountain, mtn., Ct., U.S. B2 84
Mohawk Mountains, mts., Az., U.S. E2 80
Mohe, China A9 31
Mohegan, Ct., U.S. D7 84
Mohegan, R.I., U.S. B2 116
Mohican, stm., Oh., U.S. B3 112
Mohican, Black Fork, stm., Oh., U.S. B3 112
Mohican, Clear Fork, stm., Oh., U.S. B3 112
Mohill, Ire. D4 11
Mohler, Wa., U.S. B7 124
Mohnton, Pa., U.S. F10 115
Mohoro, Tan. C6 48
Moiese, Mt., U.S. C2 103
Moinești, Rom. B8 24
Moinkum Desert, des., Sov. Un. E8 28
Mointy, Sov. Un. D8 28
Moira, N.Y., U.S. f10 109
Moisie, P.Q., Can. h8 72
Moisie, stm., P.Q., Can. h8 72
Moissac, Fr. E4 16
Moïssala, Chad D3 46
Moita, Port. f10 22
Mojave, Ca., U.S. E4 82
Mojave, stm., Ca., U.S. E5 82
Mojave Desert, des., Ca., U.S. E5 82
Moji-Guaçu, stm., Braz. k8 56
Mojo, Eth. D4 47
Mokameh, India E10 37
Mokane, Mo., U.S. C6 102
Mokapu Peninsula, pen., Hi., U.S. g10 88
Mokapu Point, c., Hi., U.S. g11 88
Mokelumne, stm., Ca., U.S. C3 82
Mokelumne Hill, Ca., U.S. C3 82
Mokena, Il., U.S. k9 90
Mokepa, Zaire A4 48
Mokhotlong, Leso. C4 49
Mokochu, mtn., Thai. E3 35
Mokolo, Cam. C2 46
Mokolo, Zaire A2 48
Mokpo, S. Kor. E10 31
Moksha, stm., Sov. Un. D14 27
Moku Manu, i., Hi., U.S. g11 88
Mol, Bel. C5 17
Mol, Yugo. C5 24
Mola [di Bari], Italy D6 23
Molalla, Or., U.S. B4 114
Molangul, Mount, mtn., Austl. B8 51
Molanosa, Sk., Can. C3 75
Moláoi, Grc. D4 25
Molasses Pond, l., Me., U.S. D4 96
Molat, i., Yugo. C2 24
Mold, Wales, U.K. A4 12
Moldau see Vltava, stm., Czech. D3 26
Moldavia, state, Sov. Un. E5 29
Moldavia, hist reg., Rom. B8 24
Molde, Nor. F2 14
Moldova, stm., Rom. B8 24
Moldoveanu, mtn., Rom. C7 24
Molega Lake, l., N.S., Can. E5 71
Molena, Ga., U.S. C2 87
Molenbeek-Saint Jean, Bel. *D4 17
Molepolole, Bots. B4 49
Môle-Saint-Nicolas, Haiti E7 64
Molfetta, Italy D6 23
Molina, Chile B2 54
Molina, Co., U.S. B2 83
Molina de Aragón, Spain B5 22
Molina de Segura, Spain C5 22
Moline, Il., U.S. B3 90
Moline, Ks., U.S. E7 93
Moline, Mi., U.S. F5 99
Moline, Oh., U.S. e6 112
Molinella, Italy E7 20
Molino, Fl., U.S. u14 86
Molino de Rosas (part of Mexico City), Mex. h9 63
Molinos, Arg. E2 55
Moliro, Zaire C5 48
Molise, hist reg., Italy C5 23
Moliterno, Italy D5 23
Möll, stm., Aus. C9 20
Mölle, Swe. B6 15
Mollendo, Peru E3 58

Name	Map Ref	Page
Mollusk, Va., U.S.	C6	123
Mölndal, Swe.	I4	14
Molochansk, Sov. Un.	H10	27
Molodechno, Sov. Un.	D6	27
Molokai, i., Hi., U.S.	B5	88
Molokini, i., Hi., U.S.	C5	88
Molopo, stm., Afr.	C3	49
Moloundou, Cam.	E3	46
Molsheim, Fr.	F7	17
Molson, Mb., Can.	D3	70
Molson, Wa., U.S.	A6	124
Molson, stm., Mb., Can.	C4	91
Molson Lake, l., Mb., Can.	B3	70
Molt, Mt., U.S.	E8	103
Molteno, S. Afr.	D4	49
Moluccas (Maluku), is., Indon.	F7	34
Molucca Sea, Indon.	E7	34
Molus, Ky., U.S.	D6	94
Moma, Moz.	A6	49
Mombasa, Kenya	B6	48
Mombetsu, Japan	D11	33
Mombongo, Zaire	A3	48
Momboyo, stm., Zaire	B2	48
Momchilgrad, Bul.	E7	24
Momence, Il., U.S.	B6	90
Momi, Fiji	H14	52
Momostenango, Guat.	C2	62
Mompog Pass, strt., Phil.	p14	34
Mompono, Zaire	A3	48
Mompós, Col.	B3	60
Møn, i., Den.	C6	15
Mona, Ut., U.S.	D4	121
Mona, Isla de, i., P.R.	G11	64
Mona, Punta, c., C.R.	F6	62
Monaca, Pa., U.S.	E1	115
Monaco, ctry., Eur.	F7	16
Monadhliath Mountains, mts., Scot., U.K.	C4	13
Monadnock, Mount, mtn., N.H., U.S.	E2	106
Monadnock Mountain, mtn., Vt., U.S.	B5	122
Monagas, state, Ven.	B5	60
Monaghan, Ire.	C5	11
Monaghan, co., Ire.	C4	11
Monahans, Tx., U.S.	D1	120
Monamolin, Ire.	E5	11
Monango, N.D., U.S.	C7	111
Mona Passage, strt., N.A.	E10	64
Monarch, Ab., Can.	E4	68
Monarch, Mt., U.S.	C6	103
Monarch Mills, S.C., U.S.	B4	117
Monarch Mountain, mtn., B.C., Can.	D5	69
Monarch Pass, Co., U.S.	C4	83
Monashee Mountains, mts., B.C., Can.	D8	69
Monastir, Tun.	B7	44
Monastyrshchina, Sov. Un.	D8	27
Monavatu, mtn., Fiji	H14	52
Moncalieri, Italy	B1	23
Monção, Braz.	B1	57
Moncey, Fr.	B1	21
Monchegorsk, Sov. Un.	D15	14
Mönchengladbach, F.R.Ger.	C3	18
Monchique, Port.	D1	22
Monchique, Serra de, mts., Port.	D1	22
Moncks Corner, S.C., U.S.	E7	117
Monclo, D., U.S.	D3	125
Monclova, Mex.	B4	63
Monclova, Oh., U.S.	e6	112
Moncton, N.B., Can.	C5	71
Moncure, N.C., U.S.	B3	110
Mondamin, Ia., U.S.	C1	92
Mondego, stm., Port.	B1	22
Mondego, Cabo, c., Port.	B1	22
Mond Lake, l., Aus.	B9	20
Mondoñedo, Spain	A2	22
Mondorf-les-Bains, Lux.	E6	17
Mondovì, Italy	B1	23
Mondovi, Wi., U.S.	D2	126
Monee, Il., U.S.	B6	90
Monegaw Springs, Mo., U.S.	C4	102
Monemvasía, Grc.	D4	25
Moneron Island, i., Sov. Un.	C10	33
Monessen, Pa., U.S.	F2	115
Moneta, Va., U.S.	C3	123
Monett, Mo., U.S.	E4	102
Monetta, S.C., U.S.	D4	117
Monette, Ar., U.S.	B5	81
Money, Ms., U.S.	B3	101
Moneymore, N. Ire., U.K.	C5	11
Monfalcone, Italy	A4	23
Monforte de Lemos, Spain	A2	22
Monfort Heights, Oh., U.S.	o12	112
Monga, Zaire	A3	48
Mongaguá, Braz.	n8	56
Mongala, stm., Zaire	A3	48
Mongalla, Sud.	D3	47
Möng Hsat, Burma	B3	35
Monghyr, India	C8	36
Möng Mit, Burma	D10	36
Mongo, Chad	C3	46
Mongo, In., U.S.	A7	91
Mongolia (part of Markham), On., U.S.	k15	73
Mongolia, ctry., Asia	B5	31
Mongolia, Plateau of, plat., Mong.	B6	31
Möng Pan, Burma	B3	35
Mongu, Zam.	E3	48
Möng Yu, Burma	D10	36
Monhegan Island, i., Me., U.S.	E3	96
Mönh Hayrhan Mountain, mtn., Mong.	B3	31
Moniac, Ga., U.S.	F4	87
Moniaive, Scot., U.K.	E5	13
Monico, Wi., U.S.	C4	126
Monida Pass, U.S.	E6	89
Monie, Md., U.S.	D6	97
Moninabad see Ambājogāi, India	H6	37
Moniquirá, Col.	B3	60
Moniteau, co., Mo., U.S.	C5	102
Monitor, Ab., Can.	D5	68
Monitor, Or., U.S.	h12	114
Monitor, Wa., U.S.	B5	124
Monitor Range, mts., Nv., U.S.	E5	105
Monitor Valley, val., Nv., U.S.	D5	105
Monivea, Ire.	D3	11
Monkey Point, c., Nic.	E8	63
Monkey River, Belize	B3	62
Monkira, Austl.	D3	51
Monkoto, Zaire	B3	48
Monkton, On., Can.	D3	73
Monkton, Vt., U.S.	C2	122
Mon Louis, Al., U.S.	E1	78
Monmouth, Wales, U.K.	C5	12
Monmouth, Il., U.S.	C3	90
Monmouth, Me., U.S.	D2	96
Monmouth, co., N.J., U.S.	C4	107
Monmouth Beach, N.J., U.S.	C5	107
Monmouth Junction, N.J., U.S.	C3	107
Monmouth Mountain, mtn., B.C., Can.	D6	69
Monnickendam, Neth.	B5	17
Monnow, stm., U.K.	C5	12
Mono, co., Ca., U.S.	D4	82
Mono Lake, l., Ca., U.S.	D4	82
Monomonac, Lake, l., U.S.	E3	106
Monomoy Island, i., Ma., U.S.	C7	98
Monomoy Point, c., Ma., U.S.	C7	98
Monon, In., U.S.	C4	91
Monona, Ia., U.S.	A6	92
Monona, Wi., U.S.	E4	126
Monona, co., Ia., U.S.	B1	92
Monongah, W.V., U.S.	B4	125
Monongahela, Pa., U.S.	F2	115
Monongahela, stm., U.S.	G2	115
Monongahela, co., W.V., U.S.	B4	125
Monopoli, Italy	D6	23
Monor, Hung.	B4	24
Monóvar, Spain	C5	22
Monowi, Ne., U.S.	B7	104
Monowice, Pol.	g10	26
Monponsett, Ma., U.S.	B6	98
Monreale, Italy	E4	23
Monroe, Ar., U.S.	C4	81
Monroe, Ct., U.S.	D3	84
Monroe, Ga., U.S.	C3	87
Monroe, Ia., U.S.	C4	92
Monroe, La., U.S.	B3	95
Monroe, Me., U.S.	D3	96
Monroe, Mi., U.S.	G7	99
Monroe, Ne., U.S.	C8	104
Monroe, N.H., U.S.	B2	106
Monroe, N.J., U.S.	A3	107
Monroe, N.Y., U.S.	D6	109
Monroe, N.C., U.S.	C2	110
Monroe, Oh., U.S.	C1	112
Monroe, Ok., U.S.	C7	113
Monroe, Or., U.S.	C3	114
Monroe, S.D., U.S.	D8	118
Monroe, Tn., U.S.	C8	119
Monroe, Ut., U.S.	E3	121
Monroe, Va., U.S.	C3	123
Monroe, Wa., U.S.	B4	124
Monroe, Wi., U.S.	F4	126
Monroe, co., Al., U.S.	D2	78
Monroe, co., Ar., U.S.	C4	81
Monroe, co., Fl., U.S.	G5	86
Monroe, co., Ga., U.S.	D3	87
Monroe, co., Il., U.S.	E3	90
Monroe, co., In., U.S.	F4	91
Monroe, co., Ia., U.S.	D5	92
Monroe, co., Ky., U.S.	D4	94
Monroe, co., Mi., U.S.	G7	99
Monroe, co., Ms., U.S.	B5	101
Monroe, co., Mo., U.S.	B5	102
Monroe, co., N.Y., U.S.	B3	109
Monroe, co., Oh., U.S.	C4	112
Monroe, co., Pa., U.S.	D11	115
Monroe, co., Tn., U.S.	D9	119
Monroe, co., W.V., U.S.	D4	125
Monroe, co., Wi., U.S.	E3	126
Monroe Bridge, Ma., U.S.	A2	98
Monroe Center, Ct., U.S.	D3	84
Monroe Center, Il., U.S.	A5	90
Monroe City, In., U.S.	G3	91
Monroe City, Mo., U.S.	B6	102
Monroe Lake, res., In., U.S.	F5	91
Monroe Park, De., U.S.	h7	85
Monroeton, Pa., U.S.	C9	115
Monroeville, Al., U.S.	D2	78
Monroeville, In., U.S.	C8	91
Monroeville, N.J., U.S.	D2	107
Monroeville, Oh., U.S.	A3	112
Monroeville, Pa., U.S.	k14	115
Monrovia, Lib.	E2	45
Monrovia, Ca., U.S.	m13	82
Monrovia, In., U.S.	E5	91
Mons (Bergen), Bel.	B5	16
Monsará, Ponta do, c., Braz.	E3	57
Monschau, F.R.Ger.	D6	17
Monselice, Italy	D7	20
Monsey, N.Y., U.S.	*m14	109
Møns Klint, clf, Den.	D6	15
Monson, Me., U.S.	C3	96
Monson, Ma., U.S.	B3	98
Montabaur, F.R.Ger.	C2	19
Montagnais Point, c., Nf., Can.	B1	72
Montagnana, Italy	D7	20
Montague, P.E., Can.	C7	71
Montague, Ca., U.S.	B2	82
Montague, Ma., U.S.	A2	98
Montague, Mi., U.S.	E4	99
Montague, Tx., U.S.	C4	120
Montague, co., Tx., U.S.	C4	120
Montague Island, i., Ak., U.S.	D10	79
Montague Lake, l., Sk., Can.	H3	75
Montague Peak, mtn., Ak., U.S.	g18	79
Montague Strait, strt., Ak., U.S.	h18	79
Montalbán, Spain	B5	22
Montalegre, Port.	B2	22
Mont Alto, Pa., U.S.	G6	115
Montalto, mtn., Italy	E5	23
Montana, Ak., U.S.	g17	79
Montana, state, U.S.	D7	103
Montana-Vermala, Switz.	D3	21
Montánchez, Spain	C2	22
Montandon, Pa., U.S.	E8	115
Montargis, Fr.	D5	16
Montataire, Fr.	E2	17
Montauban, Fr.	C5	16
Montauban-les-Mines, P.Q., Can.	C5	74
Montauk, N.Y., U.S.	m17	109
Montbard, Fr.	D6	16
Montbéliard, Fr.	D7	16
Mont Belvieu, Tx., U.S.	E5	120
Montblanch, Spain	B6	22
Mont Blanc Tunnel, Eur.	E7	16
Montbrison, Fr.	E6	16
Montcalm, co., P.Q., Can.	C3	74
Montcalm, co., Mi., U.S.	E5	99
Montcalm, Pic de, mtn., Fr.	F4	16
Mont-Carmel, P.Q., Can.	B8	74
Montceau-les-Mines, Fr.	E6	16
Mont Cenis Pass, Fr.	E7	16
Montcerf, P.Q., Can.	C1	74
Montchanin, Fr.	D6	16
Montchanin, De., U.S.	h7	85
Montclair, Ca., U.S.	m13	82
Montclair, N.J., U.S.	B4	107
Mont Clare, Pa., U.S.	o19	115
Montcornet, Fr.	C5	16
Mont-de-Marsan, Fr.	F3	16
Montdidier, Fr.	C5	16
Monteagle, Tn., U.S.	D8	119
Monte Alegre, Braz.	C2	56
Monte Alegre, Braz.	C4	59
Monte Alegre de Goiás, Braz.	A3	56
Monte Azul, Braz.	B4	56
Montebello, P.Q., Can.	D2	74
Montebello, Ca., U.S.	m12	82
Montebello, Va., U.S.	C3	123
Montebello Islands, is., Austl.	D2	50
Montebelluna, Italy	D8	20
Monte Carmelo, Braz.	B3	56
Monte Caseros, Arg.	A5	54
Montecatini Terme, Italy	C3	23
Montecito, Ca., U.S.	*E4	82
Monte Comán, Arg.	A3	54
Monte Creek, B.C., Can.	D8	69
Monte Cristi, Dom. Rep.	E8	64
Montecristi, Ec.	B1	58
Montecristo, Bol.	B3	55
Montecristo, i., Italy	C3	23
Montefrío, Spain	D3	22
Montego Bay, Jam.	E5	64
Montego Bay, b., Jam.	E13	65
Montegut, La., U.S.	E5	95
Monteiro, Braz.	C3	57
Monteith, Mount, mtn., B.C., Can.	B6	69
Montelavar, Port.	f9	22
Montélimar, Fr.	E6	16
Montelindo, stm., Para.	D4	55
Montellano, Spain	D3	22
Montello, Nv., U.S.	C8	105
Montello, Wi., U.S.	E4	126
Montemayor, Meseta de, plat., Arg.	C3	54
Montemorelos, Mex.	B5	63
Montemor-o-Novo, Port.	C1	22
Montenegro, Braz.	D2	56
Montenegro, hist reg., Yugo.	D4	24
Monte Patria, Chile	A2	54
Monte Plata, Dom. Rep.	E9	64
Monte Porzio Catone, Italy	h9	23
Montepuez, Moz.	D6	48
Montepulciano, Italy	C3	23
Monte Quemado, Arg.	E3	55
Montereau [-faut-Yonne], Fr.	C5	16
Monterey, Al., U.S.	D3	78
Monterey, Ca., U.S.	D3	82
Monterey, In., U.S.	B4	91
Monterey, Ky., U.S.	B5	94
Monterey, La., U.S.	C4	95
Monterey, Ma., U.S.	B1	98
Monterey, Tn., U.S.	C8	119
Monterey, Va., U.S.	B3	123
Monterey, co., Ca., U.S.	D3	82
Monterey Bay, b., Ca., U.S.	D2	82
Monterey Park, Ca., U.S.	m12	82
Montería, Col.	B2	60
Monteros, Arg.	E2	55
Monterotondo, Italy	g9	23
Monterrey, Mex.	B4	63
Montesano, Wa., U.S.	C2	124
Monte Sano Mountain, mtn., Al., U.S.	A3	78
Monte Sant'Angelo, Italy	D5	23
Monte Santo, Braz.	D3	57
Monte Santu, Capo di, c., Italy	D2	23
Montes Claros, Braz.	B4	56
Montevallo, Al., U.S.	B3	78
Montevarchi, Italy	C3	23
Montevideo, Mn., U.S.	F3	100
Montevideo, Ur.	E1	56
Monteview, Id., U.S.	F6	89
Monte Vista, Co., U.S.	D4	83
Montezuma, Ga., U.S.	D2	87
Montezuma, In., U.S.	E3	91
Montezuma, Ia., U.S.	C5	92
Montezuma, Ks., U.S.	E3	93
Montezuma, N.M., U.S.	B4	108
Montezuma, Oh., U.S.	B1	112
Montezuma, co., Co., U.S.	D2	83
Montezuma Canyon, val., Ut., U.S.	F6	121
Montezuma Castle National Monument, Az., U.S.	C4	80
Montezuma Creek, Ut., U.S.	F6	121
Montezuma Peak, mtn., Az., U.S.	D3	80
Montfaucon, Switz.	B3	21
Montfort, P.Q., Can.	D3	74
Montfort, Wi., U.S.	F3	126
Montfort-sur-Meu, Fr.	C3	16
Montgomery see Sähiwäl, Pak.	B5	36
Montgomery, Wales, U.K.	B4	12
Montgomery, Al., U.S.	C3	78
Montgomery, Ga., U.S.	E5	87
Montgomery, Il., U.S.	B5	90
Montgomery, In., U.S.	G3	91
Montgomery, La., U.S.	C3	95
Montgomery, Ma., U.S.	B2	98
Montgomery, Mi., U.S.	G6	99
Montgomery, Mn., U.S.	F5	100
Montgomery, N.Y., U.S.	D6	109
Montgomery, Oh., U.S.	o13	112
Montgomery, Pa., U.S.	D8	115
Montgomery, Vt., U.S.	B3	122
Montgomery, W.V., U.S.	C3	125
Montgomery, co., Al., U.S.	C3	78
Montgomery, co., Ar., U.S.	C2	81
Montgomery, co., Ga., U.S.	D4	87
Montgomery, co., Il., U.S.	D4	90
Montgomery, co., In., U.S.	D4	91
Montgomery, co., Ia., U.S.	C2	92
Montgomery, co., Ks., U.S.	E8	93
Montgomery, co., Ky., U.S.	B6	94
Montgomery, co., Md., U.S.	B3	97
Montgomery, co., Ms., U.S.	B4	101
Montgomery, co., Mo., U.S.	C6	102
Montgomery, co., N.Y., U.S.	C6	109
Montgomery, co., N.C., U.S.	B3	110
Montgomery, co., Oh., U.S.	C1	112
Montgomery, co., Pa., U.S.	F11	115
Montgomery, co., Tn., U.S.	A4	119
Montgomery, co., Tx., U.S.	D5	120
Montgomery, co., Va., U.S.	C2	123
Montgomery Center, Vt., U.S.	B3	122
Montgomery City, Mo., U.S.	C6	102
Montgomery Creek, Ca., U.S.	B3	82
Montgomery Village, Md., U.S.	*B3	97
Monthermé, Fr.	E4	17
Monthey, Switz.	C2	20
Monticello, P.E., Can.	C7	71
Monticello, Ar., U.S.	D4	81
Monticello, Fl., U.S.	B3	86
Monticello, Ga., U.S.	C3	87
Monticello, Il., U.S.	C5	90
Monticello, In., U.S.	C4	91
Monticello, Ia., U.S.	B6	92
Monticello, Ky., U.S.	D5	94
Monticello, Me., U.S.	B5	96
Monticello, Mn., U.S.	E5	100
Monticello, Ms., U.S.	D3	101
Monticello, Mo., U.S.	A6	102
Monticello, N.M., U.S.	D2	108
Monticello, N.Y., U.S.	D6	109
Monticello, Ut., U.S.	F6	121
Monticello, Wi., U.S.	F4	126
Mont Ida, Ks., U.S.	D8	93
Montier, Mo., U.S.	D6	102
Montier-en-Der, Fr.	F4	17
Montiers-sur-Saulx, Fr.	F5	17
Montignac, Fr.	E4	16
Montigny [-lés-Metz], Fr.	C7	16
Montijo, Port.	C1	22
Montijo, Spain	C2	22
Montilla, Spain	D3	22
Monti Verdi, Ut., U.S.	*B4	121
Montivilliers, Fr.	C4	16
Mont-Joli, P.Q., Can.	A9	74
Mont-Laurier, P.Q., Can.	C2	74
Montluçon, Fr.	D5	16
Montmagny, P.Q., Can.	C7	74
Montmagny, co., P.Q., Can.	C7	74
Montmartre, Sk., Can.	G4	75
Montmédy, Fr.	E5	17
Montmélian, Fr.	D2	20
Montmirail, Fr.	F3	17
Montmorenci, In., U.S.	D3	91
Montmorenci, S.C., U.S.	D4	117
Montmorency, Fr.	g10	16
Montmorency, co., Mi., U.S.	C6	99
Montmorency, stm., P.Q., Can.	B6	74
Montmorency Number One, co., P.Q., Can.	B6	74
Montmorency Number Two, co., P.Q., Can.	C7	74
Montmorillon, Fr.	D4	16
Montney, B.C., Can.	A7	69
Monto, Austl.	B8	51
Montone, stm., Italy	B3	23
Montoro, Spain	C3	22
Montour, co., Pa., U.S.	D8	115
Montour Falls, N.Y., U.S.	C4	109
Montoursville, Pa., U.S.	D8	115
Montoya, N.M., U.S.	B5	108
Montpelier, Id., U.S.	G7	89
Montpelier, In., U.S.	C7	91
Montpelier, Ia., U.S.	C7	92
Montpelier, La., U.S.	D5	95
Montpelier, Ms., U.S.	B5	101
Montpelier, N.D., U.S.	C7	111
Montpelier, Oh., U.S.	A1	112
Montpelier, Vt., U.S.	C3	122
Montpelier Station, Va., U.S.	B4	123
Montpellier, P.Q., Can.	D2	74
Montpellier, Fr.	F5	16
Montréal, P.Q., Can.	D4	74
Montreal, Wi., U.S.	B3	126
Montréal, Île de, i., P.Q., Can.	q19	74
Montreal Lake, Sk., Can.	C3	75
Montreal Lake, l., Sk., Can.	C3	75
Montréal-Nord, P.Q., Can.	p19	74
Montreat, N.C., U.S.	f10	110
Montreuil, Fr.	C5	16
Montreuil [-sous-Bois], Fr.	C5	16
Montreuil-sur-Mer, Fr.	B4	16
Montreux, Switz.	E3	18
Montricher, Switz.	C1	21
Mont-Rolland, P.Q., Can.	D3	74
Mont-Royal, P.Q., Can.	p19	74
Mont-Saint-Martin, Fr.	C6	16
Mont-Saint-Michel, Fr.	C3	16
Montserrat, Mo., U.S.	C4	102
Montserrat, dep., N.A.	H13	64
Montserrat, mtn., Spain	B6	22
Mont-Tremblant see Sähiwäl, Pak.	B5	36
Mont-Tremblant, Réserve, P.Q., Can.	C3	74
Montvale, N.J., U.S.	A4	107
Montvale, Va., U.S.	C3	123
Mont Vernon, N.H., U.S.	E3	106
Montville, Ct., U.S.	D7	84
Montville, Ma., U.S.	B1	98
Montville, N.J., U.S.	A4	107
Montz, La., U.S.	h11	95
Montzen, Bel.	D5	17
Monument, Co., U.S.	B6	83
Monument, Ks., U.S.	C2	93
Monument, N.M., U.S.	E6	108
Monument, Or., U.S.	C7	114
Monument, Pa., U.S.	D6	115
Monument Beach, Ma., U.S.	C6	98
Monument Heights, Va., U.S.	*C5	123
Monument Peak, mtn., Co., U.S.	B3	83
Monument Peak, mtn., Id., U.S.	G4	89
Monument Valley, val., Az., U.S.	*F5	121
Monywa, Burma	D10	36
Monza, Italy	B2	23
Monze, Zam.	E4	48
Monze, Cape, c., Pak.	I13	39
Monzón, Peru	C2	58
Monzón, Spain	B6	22
Moodus, Ct., U.S.	D6	84
Moodus Reservoir, res., U.S.	C6	84
Moody, Me., U.S.	E2	96
Moody, Mo., U.S.	E6	102
Moody, Tx., U.S.	D4	120
Moody, co., S.D., U.S.	C9	118
Moody Air Force Base, mil., Ga., U.S.	F3	87
Moody Beach, Me., U.S.	E2	96
Moodys, Ok., U.S.	A7	113
Mooers, N.Y., U.S.	f11	109
Mooers Forks, N.Y., U.S.	f11	109
Moon, Va., U.S.	C6	123
Moonachie, N.J., U.S.	*B4	107
Moonie, stm., Austl.	C7	51
Moon Lake, l., Ms., U.S.	A3	101
Moon Run, Pa., U.S.	k13	115
Moonta, Austl.	F6	50
Moora, Austl.	F2	50
Moorabbin, Austl.	*G8	50
Moorcroft, Wy., U.S.	B8	127
Moore, Id., U.S.	F5	89
Moore, Mt., U.S.	D7	103
Moore, Ok., U.S.	B4	113
Moore, S.C., U.S.	B4	117
Moore, Tx., U.S.	E3	120
Moore, W.V., U.S.	B5	125
Moore, co., N.C., U.S.	B3	110
Moore, co., Tn., U.S.	B5	119
Moore, co., Tx., U.S.	B2	120
Moore Dam, U.S.	B3	106
Moorefield, On., Can.	D4	73
Moorefield, Ky., U.S.	B6	94
Moorefield, Ne., U.S.	D5	104
Moorefield, W.V., U.S.	B6	125
Moore Haven, Fl., U.S.	F5	86
Mooreland, In., U.S.	E7	91
Mooreland, Ok., U.S.	A2	113
Moore Mill, N.B., Can.	D2	71
Moore Park, Mb., Can.	D2	70
Moore Reservoir, res., U.S.	B3	106
Mooresburg, Tn., U.S.	C10	119
Moores Corner, Ma., U.S.	A3	98
Moores Creek National Military Park, N.C., U.S.	C4	110
Moores Hill, In., U.S.	F7	91
Moorestown, Mi., U.S.	D5	99
Moorestown, N.J., U.S.	D3	107
Mooresville, In., U.S.	E5	91
Mooresville, Mo., U.S.	B4	102
Mooresville, N.C., U.S.	B2	110
Mooresville, Pa., U.S.	B5	119
Mooreton, N.D., U.S.	C9	111
Mooreville, Ms., U.S.	A5	101
Moorhead, Ia., U.S.	C2	92
Moorhead, Mn., U.S.	D2	100
Moorhead, Ms., U.S.	B3	101
Mooring, Tn., U.S.	A2	119
Mooringsport, La., U.S.	B2	95
Moor Lake, On., Can.	A7	73
Moorland, Ia., U.S.	B3	92
Moorman, Ky., U.S.	C2	94
Moosburg, F.R.Ger.	E6	19
Moose, Wy., U.S.	C2	127
Moose, stm., N.H., U.S.	B4	106
Moose, stm., N.Y., U.S.	B5	109
Moose, stm., Vt., U.S.	B5	122
Moose Creek, On., Can.	B10	73
Moose Factory, On., Can.	F16	66
Moosehead Lake, l., Me., U.S.	C3	96
Mooseheart, Il., U.S.	B5	90
Moose Heights, B.C., Can.	C6	69
Moose Hill, hill, Ma., U.S.	h11	98
Moosehorn, Mb., Can.	D2	70
Moose Island, i., Mb., Can.	D3	70
Moose Jaw, Sk., Can.	G3	75
Moose Jaw, stm., Sk., Can.	G3	75
Moose Lake, Mb., Can.	C3	70
Moose Lake, Mn., U.S.	D6	100
Moose Lake, l., Mb., Can.	C1	68
Moose Lake, l., Wi., U.S.	B2	126
Mooseleuk Stream, stm., Me., U.S.	B4	96
Mooselookmeguntic Lake, l., Me., U.S.	D2	96
Moose Mountain, mtn., Sk., Can.	H4	75
Moose Mountain, mtn., N.H., U.S.	C2	106
Moose Mountain Creek, stm., Sk., Can.	H4	75
Moose Mountain Provincial Park, Sk., Can.	H4	75
Moose Pass, Ak., U.S.	C10	79
Moose River, Me., U.S.	C2	96
Moosic, Pa., U.S.	m18	115
Moosilauke, Mount, mtn., N.H., U.S.	B3	106
Moosomin, Sk., Can.	G5	75
Moosonee, On., Can.	o19	73
Moosup, Ct., U.S.	C8	84
Moosup, stm., U.S.	C10	115
Moosup Valley, R.I., U.S.	D1	116
Mopang Lake, l., Me., U.S.	D5	96
Mopeia Velha, Moz.	A6	49
Mopti, Mali	E4	45
Moquegua, Peru	E3	58
Moquegua, dept., Peru	E3	58
Mór, Hung.	B4	24
Mor, i., Micron.	Q18	52
Mor, Glen, val., Scot., U.K.	D8	13
Mór, Sgùrr, mtn., Scot., U.K.	C3	13
Mora, Swe.	F6	14
Mora, Mn., U.S.	E5	100
Mora, N.M., U.S.	A5	108
Mora, co., N.M., U.S.	A5	108
Mora, stm., N.M., U.S.	A5	108
Morača, stm., Yugo.	D4	24
Morādābād, India	F8	37
Morada Nova, Braz.	D7	57
Mora de Ebro, Spain	B6	22
Mora de Rubielos, Spain	B5	22
Morafenobe, Madag.	E8	49
Moraga, Ca., U.S.	*D2	82
Moraine, Oh., U.S.	*C1	112
Morales, Guat.	C3	62
Morales, Mex.	k13	63
Moramanga, Madag.	E9	49
Moran, In., U.S.	E8	93
Moran, Ks., U.S.	E8	93
Moran, Tx., U.S.	C3	120
Morann, Pa., U.S.	E5	115
Morant Bay, Jam.	A5	80
Morant Point, c., Jam.	F5	64
Morar, Loch, l., Scot., U.K.	C3	13
Morat, Lake, l., Switz.	C2	20
Morata de Tajuña, Spain	p18	22
Moratalla, Spain	C5	22
Morattico, Va., U.S.	C6	123
Moratuwa, Sri L.	*G6	36
Morava, stm., Eur.	D5	20
Moravia, Ia., U.S.	D5	92
Moravia, N.Y., U.S.	C4	109
Moravia, hist reg., Czech.	D4	26
Morawhanna, Guy.	A3	59
Moraya, Bol.	D2	55
Moray Firth, b., Scot., U.K.	D9	13
Morbach, F.R.Ger.	C2	19
Morbegno, Italy	D4	20
Mordāb, i., Iran	B7	38
Morden, Mb., Can.	E2	70
Morden, N.S., Can.	D5	71
More, Ben, mtn., Scot., U.K.	E7	13
More, Ben, mtn., Scot., U.K.	C3	13
More, Ben, mtn., Scot., U.K.	D4	13
More Assynt, Ben, mtn., Scot., U.K.	A4	10
Moreau, South Fork, stm., S.D., U.S.	B2	118
Moreau Peak, mtn., S.D., U.S.	B2	118
Moreauville, La., U.S.	C4	95
Morecambe, Eng., U.K.	F6	13
Morecambe Bay, b., Eng., U.K.	D5	10
Moree, Austl.	E8	50
Morehead, Ky., U.S.	B6	94
Morehead City, N.C., U.S.	C6	110
Morehouse, Mo., U.S.	E8	102
Morehouse, co., La., U.S.	B4	95
Mörel, Switz.	D5	21
Moreland, Ar., U.S.	B2	81
Moreland, Ga., U.S.	C2	87
Moreland, Id., U.S.	F6	89
Moreland, Ky., U.S.	C5	94
Morelia, Mex.	D4	63
Morell, P.E., Can.	C7	71
Morella, Spain	B5	22
Morelos, state, Mex.	D5	63
Morena, Sierra, mts., Spain	C3	22
Morenci, Az., U.S.	D6	80
Morenci, Mi., U.S.	G6	99
Moresby Island, i., B.C., Can.	C2	69
Moreton Bay, b., Austl.	C9	51
Moreton-in-Marsh, Eng., U.K.	J11	12
Moreton Island, i., Austl.	C9	51
Moretown, Vt., U.S.	C3	122
Moreuil, Fr.	E2	17
Morey, Lake, l., Vt., U.S.	D4	122
Morey Peak, mtn., Nv., U.S.	E5	105
Morez, Fr.	D7	16
Mórfou, Cyp.	E9	40
Morgan, Austl.	G2	51
Morgan, Ga., U.S.	E2	87
Morgan, Ky., U.S.	B5	94
Morgan, Mn., U.S.	F4	100
Morgan, Tx., U.S.	C4	120
Morgan, Ut., U.S.	B4	121
Morgan, co., Al., U.S.	A3	78
Morgan, co., Co., U.S.	A7	83
Morgan, co., Ga., U.S.	C3	87
Morgan, co., Il., U.S.	D3	90
Morgan, co., In., U.S.	F5	91
Morgan, co., Ky., U.S.	C6	94
Morgan, co., Mo., U.S.	C5	102
Morgan, co., Oh., U.S.	C4	112
Morgan, co., Tn., U.S.	C9	119
Morgan, co., Ut., U.S.	B4	121
Morgan, co., W.V., U.S.	B6	125
Morgan Center, Vt., U.S.	B5	122
Morgan City, La., U.S.	E4	95
Morgan City, Ms., U.S.	B3	101
Morganfield, Ky., U.S.	C2	94
Morgan Hill, Ca., U.S.	D3	82
Morgan Island, i., S.C., U.S.	G6	117
Morgan Point, c., Ct., U.S.	E4	84
Morganton, Ga., U.S.	B2	87
Morganton, N.C., U.S.	B1	110
Morgantown, In., U.S.	F5	91
Morgantown, Ky., U.S.	C3	94
Morgantown, Ms., U.S.	D4	101
Morgantown, Pa., U.S.	F10	115
Morgantown, Tn., U.S.	C6	119
Morgantown, W.V., U.S.	B5	125
Morganville, Ks., U.S.	C6	93
Morganville, N.J., U.S.	C4	107
Morganza, La., U.S.	D4	95
Morges, Switz.	C2	20
Morghāb, stm., Asia	A3	36
Morhange, Fr.	F6	17
Mori, Japan	E10	33
Moriah, Trin.	M24	65
Moriah, N.Y., U.S.	A7	109
Moriah, Mount, mtn., Nv., U.S.	D7	105
Moriah, Mount, mtn., N.H., U.S.	B4	106
Moriarty, N.M., U.S.	C3	108
Morice, stm., B.C., Can.	B4	69
Morice Lake, l., B.C., Can.	B4	69
Moriguchi, Japan	*I7	33
Morin-Heights, P.Q., Can.	D3	74
Morinville, Ab., Can.	C4	68
Morioka, Japan	D13	31
Morisset-Station, P.Q., Can.	C7	74
Morjärv, Swe.	D10	14
Morkill, stm., B.C., Can.	C7	69
Morlaix, Fr.	C2	16
Morland, Ks., U.S.	C3	93
Morley, Ab., Can.	D3	68
Morley, Mi., U.S.	E5	99
Morley, Mo., U.S.	D8	102
Morley, N.Y., U.S.	f9	109
Mormon Lake, Az., U.S.	C4	80
Mormon Peak, mtn., Nv., U.S.	G7	105
Morne-à-l'Eau, Guad.	Q9	65
Morningside, S.D., U.S.	C7	118
Morning Sun, Ia., U.S.	C6	92
Mornington, Isla, i., Chile	D1	54
Mornington View, Ky., U.S.	k14	94
Moro, Ar., U.S.	C5	81
Moro, Or., U.S.	B6	114
Morobay, Ar., U.S.	D3	81
Morobe, Pap. N. Gui.	k12	50
Morocco, In., U.S.	C3	91
Morocco, ctry., Afr.	B4	45
Morococha, Peru	C2	58
Moro Creek, stm., Ar., U.S.	D3	81
Morogoro, Tan.	C6	48
Morogoro, prov., Tan.	C6	48
Moro Gulf, b., Phil.	D6	34
Moroleón, Mex.	m13	63
Morombe, Madag.	F8	49
Morón, Cuba	C8	64
Mörön, Mong.	B6	31
Morona, stm., Peru	B2	58
Morona-Santiago, prov., Ec.	B3	58
Morondava, Madag.	F8	49
Morón de la Frontera, Spain	D3	22
Morong, Phil.	o13	34
Moroni, Com.	C8	49
Morotai, i., Indon.	E7	34
Moroto, Ug.	A6	48
Morozovsk, Sov. Un.	G13	27
Morpeth, Eng., U.K.	E7	13
Morral, Oh., U.S.	B2	112
Morrill, Ks., U.S.	C8	93
Morrill, Ne., U.S.	C2	104
Morrill, co., Ne., U.S.	C2	104
Morrilton, Ar., U.S.	B3	81
Morrin, Ab., Can.	D4	68
Morrinhos, Braz.	C4	56
Morrinsville, N.Z.	B5	51
Morris, Al., U.S.	B3	78
Morris, Ct., U.S.	C3	84

Name	Map Ref	Page

Morris, Ga., U.S. — E2 87
Morris, Il., U.S. — B5 90
Morris, In., U.S. — F7 91
Morris, Mn., U.S. — E3 100
Morris, N.Y., U.S. — C5 109
Morris, Ok., U.S. — B6 113
Morris, co., Ks., U.S. — D7 93
Morris, co., N.J., U.S. — B3 107
Morris, co., Tx., U.S. — C5 120
Morris, Mount, mtn., N.Y., U.S. — A6 109
Morrisburg, On., Can. — C9 73
Morris Chapel, Tn., U.S. — B3 119
Morrisdale, Pa., U.S. — E5 115
Morris Island, i., S.C., U.S. — F8 117
Morris Jesup, Kap, c., Grnld. — A17 61
Morrison, Co., U.S. — B5 83
Morrison, Il., U.S. — B4 90
Morrison, Mo., U.S. — C6 102
Morrison, Ok., U.S. — A4 113
Morrison, Tn., U.S. — D8 119
Morrison, Wi., U.S. — h10 126
Morrison, co., Mn., U.S. — D4 100
Morrison City, Tn., U.S. — C11 119
Morrisonville, Il., U.S. — D4 90
Morrisonville, N.Y., U.S. — f11 109
Morris Plains, N.J., U.S. — B4 107
Morris Run, Pa., U.S. — C7 115
Morriston, Fl., U.S. — C4 86
Morristown, Az., U.S. — D3 80
Morristown, In., U.S. — E6 91
Morristown, Mn., U.S. — F5 100
Morristown, N.J., U.S. — B4 107
Morristown, N.Y., U.S. — f9 109
Morristown, S.D., U.S. — B4 118
Morristown, Tn., U.S. — C10 119
Morristown, Vt., U.S. — B3 122
Morristown National Historical Park, N.J., U.S. — B3 107
Morrisville, Mo., U.S. — D4 102
Morrisville, N.Y., U.S. — C5 109
Morrisville, Pa., U.S. — F12 115
Morrisville, Vt., U.S. — B3 122
Morro, Ec. — B1 58
Morro, Punta, c., Chile — E1 55
Morro, Punta, c., Mex. — D6 63
Morro Bay, Ca., U.S. — E3 82
Morro do Chapéu, Braz. — D2 57
Morropón, Peru — C2 58
Morrosquillo, Golfo de b., Col. — B2 60
Morrow, Ga., U.S. — C2 87
Morrow, La., U.S. — D3 95
Morrow, Oh., U.S. — C1 112
Morrow, co., Oh., U.S. — B3 112
Morrow, co., Or., U.S. — B7 114
Morrowville, Ks., U.S. — C6 93
Morrumbene, Moz. — B6 49
Mors, i., Den. — B2 15
Morse, Sk., Can. — G2 75
Morse, La., U.S. — D3 95
Morse, Tx., U.S. — A2 120
Morse, Wi., U.S. — B3 126
Morse Bluff, Ne., U.S. — C9 104
Morse Mill, Mo., U.S. — g12 102
Morse Reservoir, res., In., U.S. — D5 91
Morses Creek, stm., N.J., U.S. — k8 107
Morshansk, Sov. Un. — E13 27
Mortagne, Fr. — C4 16
Mortara, Italy — B2 23
Morteau, Fr. — D7 16
Morteros, Arg. — A4 54
Mortes, Rio das, stm., Braz. — E4 59
Mortlach, Sk., Can. — G2 75
Morton, Il., U.S. — C4 90
Morton, Mn., U.S. — F4 100
Morton, Ms., U.S. — C4 101
Morton, Tx., U.S. — C1 120
Morton, Wa., U.S. — C3 124
Morton, co., Ks., U.S. — E2 93
Morton, co., N.D., U.S. — C4 111
Morton Grove, Il., U.S. — h9 90
Morton Pass, Wy., U.S. — E7 127
Mortons Gap, Ky., U.S. — C2 94
Moruga, Trin. — O23 65
Morundah, Austl. — G8 51
Morvan Mountains, mts., Fr. — D6 16
Morven, Ga., U.S. — F3 87
Morven, N.C., U.S. — C2 110
Morven, Mont, mtn., Fr. — E7 16
Morvi, India — F3 37
Morwell, Austl. — G8 50
Moryakovskiy Zaton, Sov. Un. — B10 28
Morye, Sov. Un. — r32 14
Mosalsk, Sov. Un. — D10 27
Mosbach, F.R.Ger. — D4 19
Mosby, Mo., U.S. — h11 102
Mosby, Mt., U.S. — D9 103
Mosca, Co., U.S. — D5 83
Moscarello, Italy — k9 23
Moscos Islands, is., Burma — F10 36
Moscow (Moskva), Sov. Un. — D6 29
Moscow, Ar., U.S. — C4 81
Moscow, Id., U.S. — C2 89
Moscow, In., U.S. — F6 91
Moscow, Ia., U.S. — C6 92
Moscow, Ks., U.S. — E2 93
Moscow, Ky., U.S. — f8 94
Moscow, Oh., U.S. — D1 112
Moscow, Pa., U.S. — m18 115
Moscow, R.I., U.S. — E2 116
Moscow, Tn., U.S. — B2 119
Moscow, Vt., U.S. — C3 122
Moscow Mills, Mo., U.S. — C7 102
Mosel (Moselle), stm., Eur. — D3 18
Moseley, Va., U.S. — C5 123
Moselle, Ms., U.S. — D4 101
Moselle, dept., Fr. — E6 17
Moselle (Mosel), stm., Eur. — C7 16
Mosers River, N.S., Can. — E7 71
Moses Coulee, val., Wa., U.S. — B6 124
Moses Lake, l., Wa., U.S. — B6 124
Mosgiel, N.Z. — P13 51
Moshi, Tn., U.S. — C11 119
Mosher, S.D., U.S. — D5 118
Mosherville, N.S., Can. — E6 71
Moshi, Tan. — B6 48
Moshupa, Bots. — B4 49
Mosier, Or., U.S. — B5 114
Mosinee, Wi., U.S. — D4 126
Mosjöen, Nor. — E5 14
Moskva, stm., Sov. Un. — n18 27
Mosley Creek, stm., B.C., Can. — D5 69
Mosomane (Artesia), Bots. — B4 49
Mosonmagyaróvár, Hung. — B3 24
Mosquera, Col. — C2 60
Mosquero, N.M., U.S. — B6 108
Mosquito, Nf., Can. — E5 72
Mosquito Coast, N.A. — D6 62
Mosquito Creek, stm., Ia., U.S. — C2 92

Mosquito Creek Lake, res., Oh., U.S. — A5 112
Mosquito Lagoon, b., Fl., U.S. — D6 86
Mosquitos, Golfo de los, b., Pan. — F7 62
Moss, Nor. — H4 14
Moss, Ms., U.S. — D4 101
Moss, Tn., U.S. — C8 119
Mossbank, Sk., Can. — H3 75
Moss Bluff, La., U.S. — D2 95
Mosselbaai (Mossel Bay), S. Afr. — D3 49
Mossendjo, Congo — B1 48
Mossleigh, Ab., Can. — D4 68
Mossman, Austl. — C8 50
Mossoró, Braz. — C3 57
Moss Point, Ms., U.S. — E5 101
Moss Vale, Austl. — G8 51
Mossville, Ar., U.S. — B2 81
Mossy, stm., Mb., Can. — D2 70
Mossy, stm., Sk., Can. — C4 75
Mossy Head, Fl., U.S. — u15 86
Mossyrock, Wa., U.S. — C3 124
Most, Czech. — C2 26
Mostar, Yugo. — D3 24
Mostefa, Cap, c., Tun. — F3 23
Móstoles, Spain — p17 22
Mosul (Al Mawşil), Iraq — B4 38
Moswansicut Pond, l., R.I., U.S. — C3 116
Motagua, stm., N.A. — E6 63
Motala, Swe. — H6 14
Motatán, Ven. — B3 60
Motherwell, Scot., U.K. — C5 10
Motīhāri, India — D10 37
Motilla del Palancar, Spain — C5 22
Motley, Mn., U.S. — D4 100
Motley, co., Tx., U.S. — B2 120
Motobu, Japan — N5 52
Motomachi, Japan — o18 33
Moto Mountain, hill, Japan — P17 52
Motril, Spain — D4 22
Motru, stm., Rom. — C6 24
Motul [de Felipe Carrillo Puerto], Mex. — C7 63
Motupe, Peru — C2 58
Moturiki, i., Fiji — H15 52
Mou, Den. — B4 15
Mouaskar, Alg. — B5 44
Moúdhros (Mudros), Grc. — C5 25
Moudjéria, Maur. — C2 45
Moudon, Switz. — C2 20
Moudouk, Switz. — F2 46
Mouila, Gabon — F2 46
Moulamein Billabong Creek, stm., Austl. — G5 51
Mould Bay, N.T., Can. — m28 66
Moule, Guad. — H14 64
Moulins, Fr. — D5 16
Moulmein, Burma — E10 36
Moulouya, Oued, stm., Mor. — C4 44
Moulton, Al., U.S. — A2 78
Moulton, Ia., U.S. — D5 92
Moultonboro, N.H., U.S. — C4 106
Moultrie, Ga., U.S. — E3 87
Moultrie, co., Il., U.S. — D5 90
Moultrie, Lake, res., S.C., U.S. — E7 117
Mound, La., U.S. — B4 95
Mound, Mn., U.S. — n11 100
Mound Bayou, Ms., U.S. — B3 101
Mound City, Il., U.S. — F4 90
Mound City, Ks., U.S. — D9 93
Mound City, Mo., U.S. — A2 102
Mound City, S.D., U.S. — B5 118
Mound City Group National Monument, Oh., U.S. — C2 112
Moundou, Chad — D3 46
Moundridge, Ks., U.S. — D6 93
Mounds, Il., U.S. — F4 90
Mounds, Ok., U.S. — B5 113
Mounds View, Mn., U.S. — m12 100
Moundsville, W.V., U.S. — B4 125
Mound Valley, Ks., U.S. — E8 93
Moundville, Al., U.S. — C2 78
Moundville, Mo., U.S. — D3 102
Mountain, N.D., U.S. — A8 111
Mountain, W.V., U.S. — B4 125
Mountain, Wi., U.S. — C5 126
Mountainair, N.M., U.S. — C3 108
Mountain Ash, Ky., U.S. — D5 94
Mountainboro, Al., U.S. — A3 78
Mountain Brook, Al., U.S. — g7 78
Mountainburg, Ar., U.S. — B1 81
Mountain City, Ga., U.S. — B3 87
Mountain City, Nv., U.S. — B6 105
Mountain City, Tn., U.S. — C12 119
Mountain Dale, N.Y., U.S. — D6 109
Mountain Fork, stm., U.S. — C7 113
Mountain Grove, On., Can. — C8 73
Mountain Grove, Mo., U.S. — D5 102
Mountain Home, Ar., U.S. — A3 81
Mountain Home, Id., U.S. — F3 89
Mountainhome, Pa., U.S. — D11 115
Mountain Home, Tx., U.S. — D3 120
Mountain Home Air Force Base, mil., Id., U.S. — F3 89
Mountain Iron, Mn., U.S. — C6 100
Mountain Lake, Mn., U.S. — G4 100
Mountain Lake, l., Sk., Can. — B3 75
Mountain Lake Park, Md., U.S. — m12 97
Mountain Lakes, N.J., U.S. — *B4 107
Mountain Nile (Al Baḩr al Jabal), stm., Sud. — D3 47
Mountain Park, Ab., Can. — C2 68
Mountain Park, Ok., U.S. — C3 113
Mountain Pine, Ar., U.S. — C2 81
Mountain Point, Ak., U.S. — n24 79
Mountain Springs, Nv., U.S. — *G6 105
Mountain Valley, U.S. — C2 81
Mountain View, Ab., Can. — E4 68
Mountain View, Ar., U.S. — B3 81
Mountain View, Ca., U.S. — k8 82
Mountain View, Co., U.S. — *B5 83
Mountain View, Hi., U.S. — D6 88
Mountain View, Mo., U.S. — D6 102
Mountain View, N.M., U.S. — C3 108
Mountain View, Wy., U.S. — E2 127
Mountain Village, Ak., U.S. — C7 79
Mount Airy, Ga., U.S. — B3 87
Mount Airy, Md., U.S. — B3 97
Mount Airy, N.J., U.S. — C3 107

Mount Airy, N.C., U.S. — A2 110
Mount Albert, On., Can. — C5 73
Mount Angel, Or., U.S. — B4 114
Mount Arlington, N.J., U.S. — B3 107
Mount Assiniboine Provincial Park, B.C., Can. — D10 69
Mount Athos, ter., Grc. — B5 25
Mount Auburn, Il., U.S. — D4 90
Mount Auburn, Ia., U.S. — B5 92
Mount Ayr, In., U.S. — C3 91
Mount Ayr, Ia., U.S. — D3 92
Mount Barker, Austl. — G2 51
Mount Bellew, Ire. — D3 11
Mount Berry, Ga., U.S. — B1 87
Mount Blanchard, Oh., U.S. — B2 112
Mount Brydges, On., U.S. — E3 73
Mount Calvary, Wi., U.S. — E5 126
Mount Carleton Provincial Park, N.B., Can. — B3 71
Mount Carmel, Nf., Can. — E5 72
Mount Carmel, Al., U.S. — C3 78
Mount Carmel, Il., U.S. — E6 90
Mount Carmel, In., U.S. — F8 91
Mount Carmel, N.D., U.S. — A7 111
Mount Carmel, Oh., U.S. — o13 112
Mount Carmel, Pa., U.S. — E9 115
Mount Carmel, S.C., U.S. — C2 117
Mount Carmel, Ut., U.S. — F3 121
Mount Carmel Junction, Ut., U.S. — F3 121
Mount Carroll, Il., U.S. — A4 90
Mount Clare, W.V., U.S. — B4 125
Mount Clemens, Mi., U.S. — F8 99
Mount Clinton, Va., U.S. — B4 123
Mount Cory, Oh., U.S. — B2 112
Mount Crawford, Va., U.S. — B4 123
Mount Croghan, S.C., U.S. — B7 117
Mount Darwin, Zimb. — A5 49
Mount Desert, Me., U.S. — *D4 96
Mount Desert Island, i., Me., U.S. — D4 96
Mount Dora, Fl., U.S. — D5 86
Mount Dora, N.M., U.S. — A6 108
Mount Eaton, Oh., U.S. — B4 112
Mount Eden, Ky., U.S. — B4 94
Mount Elgin, On., Can. — E4 73
Mount Enterprise, Tx., U.S. — D5 120
Mount Ephraim, N.J., U.S. — *D2 107
Mount Erie, Il., U.S. — E5 90
Mount Etna, In., U.S. — C6 91
Mount Etna, Ia., U.S. — C3 92
Mount Forest, On., Can. — D4 73
Mount Forest, Mi., U.S. — E6 99
Mount Freedom, N.J., U.S. — B3 107
Mount Gambier, Austl. — G7 50
Mount Gay, W.V., U.S. — D2 125
Mount Gilead, N.C., U.S. — B3 110
Mount Gilead, Oh., U.S. — B3 112
Mount Hagen, Pap. N. Gui. — k11 50
Mount Healthy, Oh., U.S. — o12 112
Mount Hebron, Ca., U.S. — B2 82
Mount Hermon, La., U.S. — D5 95
Mount Hermon, Ma., U.S. — A3 98
Mount Heron, Va., U.S. — e9 123
Mount Holly, Ar., U.S. — D3 81
Mount Holly, N.J., U.S. — D3 107
Mount Holly, N.C., U.S. — B1 110
Mount Holly, S.C., U.S. — E7 117
Mount Holly, Vt., U.S. — E3 122
Mount Holly Springs, Pa., U.S. — F7 115
Mount Hood, Or., U.S. — B5 114
Mount Hope, On., Can. — D5 73
Mount Hope, Al., U.S. — A2 78
Mount Hope, Ks., U.S. — E6 93
Mount Hope, W.V., U.S. — D3 125
Mount Hope, stm., Ct., U.S. — B7 84
Mount Hope Bay, b., U.S. — D6 116
Mount Horeb, Wi., U.S. — E4 126
Mount Ida, Ar., U.S. — C2 81
Mount Idaho, Id., U.S. — D2 89
Mount Isa, Austl. — D6 50
Mount Jackson, Va., U.S. — B4 123
Mount Jewett, Pa., U.S. — C4 115
Mount Joy, Ia., U.S. — h10 92
Mount Joy, Pa., U.S. — F9 115
Mount Judea, Ar., U.S. — B2 81
Mount Juliet, Tn., U.S. — A5 119
Mount Kisco, N.Y., U.S. — D7 109
Mountlake Terrace, Wa., U.S. — *B3 124
Mount Lebanon, Pa., U.S. — F1 115
Mount Lemmon, Az., U.S. — E5 80
Mount Lookout, W.V., U.S. — C4 125
Mount Magnet, Austl. — E2 50
Mount Meigs, Al., U.S. — C3 78
Mountmellick, Ire. — D4 11
Mount Montgomery, Nv., U.S. — F3 105
Mount Morgan, Austl. — D9 50
Mount Moriah, Mo., U.S. — A4 102
Mount Morris, Il., U.S. — A4 90
Mount Morris, Mi., U.S. — E7 99
Mount Morris, N.Y., U.S. — C3 109
Mount Morris, Pa., U.S. — G1 115
Mount of Olives, hill, Isr. Occ. — m14 41
Mount Olive, Al., U.S. — B3 78
Mount Olive, Il., U.S. — D4 90
Mount Olive, Ms., U.S. — D4 101
Mount Olive, N.C., U.S. — B4 110
Mount Olive, Tn., U.S. — n14 119
Mount Olivet, Ky., U.S. — B5 94
Mount Orab, Oh., U.S. — C2 112
Mount Pearl, Nf., Can. — E5 72
Mount Penn, Pa., U.S. — F10 115
Mount Pleasant, Fl., U.S. — B2 86
Mount Pleasant, Ga., U.S. — D5 87
Mount Pleasant, Ia., U.S. — D6 92
Mount Pleasant, Mi., U.S. — E6 99
Mount Pleasant, Ms., U.S. — A4 101
Mount Pleasant, N.J., U.S. — B2 107
Mount Pleasant, N.C., U.S. — B2 110
Mount Pleasant, Oh., U.S. — B5 112
Mount Pleasant, Pa., U.S. — F2 115
Mount Pleasant, S.C., U.S. — F8 117
Mount Pleasant, Tn., U.S. — B4 119
Mount Pleasant, Tx., U.S. — C5 120
Mount Pleasant, Ut., U.S. — D4 121
Mount Pocono, Pa., U.S. — D11 115
Mount Prospect, Il., U.S. — A6 90
Mount Pulaski, Il., U.S. — C4 90
Mountrail, co., N.D., U.S. — A3 111
Mount Rainier, Md., U.S. — f9 97
Mount Rainier National Park, Wa., U.S. — C4 124
Mount Revelstoke National Park, B.C., Can. — D8 69
Mount Robson Provincial Park, B.C., Can. — C8 69
Mount Rogers National Recreation Area, Va., U.S. — D1 123
Mount Rushmore National Memorial, hist., S.D., U.S. — G2 118
Mount Savage, Md., U.S. — k13 97
Mount's Bay, b., Eng., U.K. — D2 12

Mount Shasta, Ca., U.S. — B2 82
Mount Sidney, Va., U.S. — B4 123
Mount Solon, Va., U.S. — B3 123
Mount Sterling, Al., U.S. — C1 78
Mount Sterling, Il., U.S. — D3 90
Mount Sterling, Ky., U.S. — B6 94
Mount Stewart, P.E., Can. — C7 71
Mount Storm, W.V., U.S. — B5 125
Mount Summit, In., U.S. — D7 91
Mount Sunapee, N.H., U.S. — D2 106
Mount Tabor, N.J., U.S. — B4 107
Mount Uniacke, N.S., Can. — E6 71
Mount Union, Ia., U.S. — C6 92
Mount Union, Pa., U.S. — F6 115
Mount Upton, N.Y., U.S. — C5 109
Mount Vernon, Al., U.S. — D1 78
Mount Vernon, Ar., U.S. — B3 81
Mount Vernon, Ga., U.S. — D4 87
Mount Vernon, Il., U.S. — E5 90
Mount Vernon, In., U.S. — I2 91
Mount Vernon, Ia., U.S. — C6 92
Mount Vernon, Ky., U.S. — C5 94
Mount Vernon, Me., U.S. — D3 96
Mount Vernon, Md., U.S. — D6 97
Mount Vernon, Mo., U.S. — D4 102
Mount Vernon, N.Y., U.S. — h13 109
Mount Vernon, Oh., U.S. — B3 112
Mount Vernon, Or., U.S. — C7 114
Mount Vernon, S.D., U.S. — D7 118
Mount Vernon, Tn., U.S. — D9 119
Mount Vernon, Tx., U.S. — C5 120
Mount Vernon, Wa., U.S. — A3 124
Mount Victory, Oh., U.S. — B2 112
Mount View, R.I., U.S. — D4 116
Mountville, S.C., U.S. — C4 117
Mount Washington, Ky., U.S. — B4 94
Mount Washington, Ma., U.S. — B1 98
Mount Wolf, Pa., U.S. — F8 115
Mount Zion, Ga., U.S. — C1 87
Mount Zion, Il., U.S. — D5 90
Moura, Austl. — D8 50
Moura, Braz. — C2 59
Mourdi, Dépression du, depr., Chad — B4 46
Mourmelon-le-Grand, Fr. — E4 17
Mourne Mountains, mts., N. Ire., U.K. — C3 10
Mouscron (Moeskroen), Bel. — C2 22
Mousie, Ky., U.S. — C7 94
Moussoro, Chad — C3 46
Mouthe, Fr. — C1 21
Moûtiers[-Tarentaise], Fr. — E7 16
Mouy, Fr. — E2 21
Moville, Ire. — B4 11
Moville, Ia., U.S. — B1 92
Moweaqua, Il., U.S. — D4 90
Mower, co., Mn., U.S. — G6 100
Mowrystown, Oh., U.S. — C2 112
Moxahala, Oh., U.S. — C3 112
Moxee City, Wa., U.S. — C5 124
Moxico, geog. reg., Ang. — D3 48
Moxie Pond, l., Me., U.S. — C3 96
Moxley, Ga., U.S. — D4 87
Moy, Scot., U.K. — C4 13
Moy, stm., Ire. — C2 11
Moyale, Eth. — E4 47
Moyale, Kenya — A6 48
Moyamba, S.L. — E2 45
Moyers, Ok., U.S. — C6 113
Moyeuvre-[Grande], Fr. — C7 16
Moyie, B.C., Can. — E10 69
Moyie Springs, Id., U.S. — A2 89
Moynalty, Ire. — D5 11
Moyo, Ug. — h11 41
Moyobamba, Peru — C2 58
Moyock, N.C., U.S. — A6 110
Moyuta, Guat. — C2 62
Moza, Isr. — h11 41
Mozambique, ctry., Afr. — H9 42
Mozambique Channel, strt., Afr. — H10 42
Mozart, Sk., Can. — F3 75
Mozdok, Sov. Un. — E2 28
Mozelle, Ky., U.S. — C6 94
Mozhaysk, Sov. Un. — D11 27
Mozhga, Sov. Un. — D19 8
Mozyr, Sov. Un. — E7 27
Mpanda, Tan. — C5 48
Mpika, Zam. — D5 48
Mporokoso, Zam. — C5 48
Mpouya, Congo — B2 48
Mpraeso, Ghana — D4 11
Mpulungu, Zam. — C5 48
Mpwapwa, Tan. — C6 48
Mragowo, Pol. — B6 26
Mšec, Czech. — n16 26
Mšenélázně, Czech. — n17 26
M'Sila, Alg. — B5 44
Msta, stm., Sov. Un. — B9 27
Mstislavl, Sov. Un. — D6 33
Mtakuja, Tan. — C5 48
Mtsensk, Sov. Un. — E11 27
Mtubatuba, S. Afr. — C5 49
Mtwara, Tan. — D6 48
Mtwara, prov., Tan. — D6 48
Muar (Bandar Maharani), Malay. — K5 35
Muaratewe, Indon. — F5 34
Mubārak, Jabal, mtn., Asia — F4 41
Mubende, Ug. — A5 48
Mubi, Nig. — F8 45
Mucajaí, stm., Braz. — B2 59
Mücheln, Ger.D.R. — D6 18
Muchkapskiy, Sov. Un. — F14 27
Muchot, Puntan, c., N. Mar. Is. — F7 52
Much Wenlock (Wenlock), Eng., U.K. — B3 10
Muck, i., Scot., U.K. — B3 10
Muckalee Creek, stm., Ga., U.S. — D2 87
Muckleshoot Indian Reservation, Wa., U.S. — f11 124
Muconda, Ang. — D3 48
Mucuri, Braz. — E3 57
Mucuri, stm., Braz. — E3 57
Mucusso, Ang. — E3 48
Mud, stm., Ky., U.S. — C3 94

Mud, stm., Mn., U.S. — B3 100
Mud, stm., W.V., U.S. — C2 125
Muda, stm., Malay. — I4 35
Mudanjiang, China — C10 31
Mudan Jiang, stm., China — D4 33
Mudanya, Tur. — B7 25
Mud Butte, S.D., U.S. — C3 118
Mud Creek, stm., Al., U.S. — g6 78
Mud Creek, stm., Co., U.S. — D8 83
Mud Creek, stm., Ne., U.S. — C6 104
Mud Creek, stm., Ok., U.S. — C4 113
Muddy, Il., U.S. — F5 90
Muddy Boggy Creek, stm., Ok., U.S. — C6 113
Muddy Creek, stm., Ks., U.S. — k14 93
Muddy Creek, stm., Ut., U.S. — E4 121
Muddy Creek, stm., Wy., U.S. — D6 127
Muddy Creek, stm., Wy., U.S. — E2 127
Muddy Creek, stm., Wy., U.S. — E5 127
Muddy Creek, stm., Wy., U.S. — C4 127
Muddy Creek Mountain, mtn., Ar., U.S. — C2 81
Muddy Lake, l., Sk., Can. — E1 75
Muddy Mountain, mtn., Wy., U.S. — D6 127
Muddy Mountains, mts., Nv., U.S. — G7 105
Muddy Peak, mtn., Nv., U.S. — G7 105
Müden, F.R.Ger. — F4 15
Mudgee, Austl. — F7 51
Mudjatik, stm., Sk., Can. — A2 75
Mud Lake, l., Id., U.S. — F6 89
Mud Lake, l., Me., U.S. — A4 96
Mud Lake, l., Nv., U.S. — F4 105
Mud Lick Creek, stm., Ky., U.S. — k13 94
Mudon, Burma — E10 36
Mudros see Moúdhros, Grc. — C5 25
Mudug, prov., Som. — D6 47
Mueda, Moz. — D6 48
Muenster, Sk., Can. — E3 75
Muenster, Tx., U.S. — C4 120
Muff, Ire. — B4 11
Mufulira, Zam. — D4 48
Mugardos, Spain — A1 22
Mugia, Spain — A1 22
Muğla, Tur. — D7 40
Mugodzhary Mountains, hills, Sov. Un. — D5 28
Muhammad Qawl, Sud. — A4 47
Mühlacker, F.R.Ger. — D6 18
Mühldorf, F.R.Ger. — D6 18
Muhlenberg, co., Ky., U.S. — C2 94
Mühlhausen [in Thüringen], Ger.D.R. — C5 18
Mühlig-Hofmann Mountains, mts., Ant. — B13 7
Muhulu, Zaire — B4 48
Muhutwe, Tan. — B5 48
Mui, i., Marsh Is. — S18 52
Muine Bheag, Ire. — E5 11
Muir, Mi., U.S. — E6 99
Muirkirk, Scot., U.K. — C4 13
Muirkirk, Md., U.S. — B4 97
Muir Woods National Monument, Ca., U.S. — h7 82
Mukachevo, Sov. Un. — G4 27
Mukah, Malay. — E4 34
Mukden see Shenyang, China — C9 31
Mukilteo, Wa., U.S. — B3 124
Mukutawa, stm., Mb., Can. — C3 70
Mukwonago, Wi., U.S. — F5 126
Mula, Spain — C5 22
Mulanje, Mwi. — E6 48
Mulberry, Fl., U.S. — E4 86
Mulberry, In., U.S. — D4 91
Mulberry, Ks., U.S. — E9 93
Mulberry, N.C., U.S. — A1 110
Mulberry, Oh., U.S. — C1 112
Mulberry, Tn., U.S. — B5 119
Mulberry, stm., Ar., U.S. — B1 81
Mulberry Fork, stm., Al., U.S. — B3 78
Mulberry Grove, Il., U.S. — E4 90
Mulberry Mountain, mtn., Ar., U.S. — B3 81
Mulchén, Chile — B2 54
Mulde, stm., Ger.D.R. — C6 18
Muldoon, Tx., U.S. — E4 120
Muldraugh, Ky., U.S. — C4 94
Muldrow, Ok., U.S. — B7 113
Mule Creek, N.M., U.S. — D1 108
Mulegé, Mex. — B2 63
Muleshoe, Tx., U.S. — B1 120
Mulga, Al., U.S. — B3 78
Mulgrave, N.S., Can. — D8 71
Mulhacén, mtn., Spain — D8 22
Mulhall, Ok., U.S. — A4 113
Mülheim [an der Ruhr], F.R.Ger. — C3 18
Mulhouse, Fr. — D7 16
Muling, China — C11 31
Muling He, stm., China — D6 33
Mulino, Or., U.S. — B4 114
Mulinu'u, Cape, c., W. Sam. — F11 52
Mulitapu'ili, Cape, c., W. Sam. — F12 52
Mull, i., Scot., U.K. — B4 10
Mull, Sound of, strt., Scot., U.K. — B3 10
Mullaghcleevaun, mtn., Ire. — D5 11
Mullan, Id., U.S. — B3 89
Mullan Pass, Mt., U.S. — D4 103
Mullen, Ne., U.S. — B4 104
Mullens, W.V., U.S. — D3 125
Muller Mountains, mts., Indon. — E5 34
Mullet Key, i., Fl., U.S. — p10 86
Mullet Lake, l., Mi., U.S. — C6 99
Mullet Peninsula, pen., Ire. — C1 11
Mullett Lake, l., Mi., U.S. — C6 99
Mullewa, Austl. — E2 50
Mull Head, c., Scot., U.K. — A6 13
Mullica, stm., N.J., U.S. — D3 107
Mullica Hill, N.J., U.S. — D2 107
Mullin, Tx., U.S. — D3 120
Mullinavat, Ire. — E4 11
Mullingar, Ire. — D4 11
Mullins, S.C., U.S. — C9 117
Mullinville, Ks., U.S. — E4 93
Müllrose, Ger.D.R. — A9 19
Mulobezi, Zam. — E4 48
Mulranny (Mallranny), Ire. — C2 11
Multán, Pak. — E4 36
Multnomah, co., Or., U.S. — B4 114
Mulurulu, Lake, l., Austl. — F4 51
Mulvane, Ks., U.S. — E6 93
Mulvihill, Mb., Can. — D2 70
Mumbwa, Zam. — D4 48

Muna, Mex. — C7 63
Münchberg, F.R.Ger. — C6 19
Münchenstein, Switz. — A4 21
Munchŏn, N. Kor. — G3 33
Muncie, In., U.S. — D7 91
Muncy, Pa., U.S. — D8 115
Mundare, Ab., Can. — C4 68
Munday, Tx., U.S. — C3 120
Mundelein, Il., U.S. — A5 90
Münden, F.R.Ger. — C4 18
Munden, Ks., U.S. — C6 93
Munford, Al., U.S. — B4 78
Munford, Tn., U.S. — B2 119
Munfordville, Ky., U.S. — C4 94
Mungallala Creek, stm., Austl. — D6 51
Mungári, Moz. — A5 49
Mungbere, Zaire — A4 48
Mungindi, Austl. — E8 51
Munger, Ms., U.S. — E7 99
Munhango, Ang. — k14 115
Munich (München), F.R.Ger. — D5 19
Munich, N.D., U.S. — A7 111
Munising, Mi., U.S. — B4 99
Munith, Mi., U.S. — F6 99
Munjor, Ks., U.S. — D4 93
Munnsville, N.Y., U.S. — C5 109
Muñoz, Phil. — o13 34
Muñoz Gamero, Península, pen., Chile — h11 54
Munro Lake, l., Mb., Can. — B4 70
Munsan-ni, S. Kor. — H3 33
Munsan, F.R.Ger. — E4 19
Münsingen, Switz. — C4 21
Munson, Ab., Can. — D4 68
Munson, Fl., U.S. — u15 86
Munster, In., U.S. — A2 91
Munster, hist reg., Ire. — E3 11
Münster [in Westfalen], F.R.Ger. — C3 18
Munsungan Lake, l., Me., U.S. — B3 96
Muntenia, hist reg., Rom. — C7 24
Muntok, Indon. — F3 34
Munuscong Lake, l., Mi., U.S. — B6 99
Muonio, Fin. — D10 14
Muonio, stm., Eur. — D10 14
Muotathal, Switz. — C6 21
Mur (Mura), stm., Eur. — B2 24
Mura (Mur), stm., Eur. — B3 24
Murakami, Japan — G9 33
Murākh, Bi'r, well, Eg. — E6 41
Murano, Italy — D8 20
Murashi, Sov. Un. — B3 28
Murat, mtn., Tur. — C13 40
Murau, Aus. — E7 18
Muravera, Italy — E2 23
Muravyevo, Sov. Un. — C11 33
Mürcheh Khvort, Iran — E5 11
Murchison, N.Z. — N14 51
Murchison Falls see Kabalega Falls, wtfl, Ug. — A5 48
Murcia, Spain — C5 22
Murcia, hist reg., Spain — C5 22
Murcki, Pol. — C2 81
Murderkill, stm., De., U.S. — D5 85
Murdo, S.D., U.S. — D5 118
Murdock, Fl., U.S. — E4 86
Murdock, Il., U.S. — D5 90
Murdock, Ks., U.S. — E6 93
Murdock, Mn., U.S. — E3 100
Mureş, stm., Eur. — C5 24
Muret, Fr. — F4 16
Murewa, Zimb. — A5 49
Murfreesboro, Ar., U.S. — C2 81
Murfreesboro, N.C., U.S. — A5 110
Murfreesboro, Tn., U.S. — B5 119
Murgha Kibzai, Pak. — E4 36
Mürgo, Hämün-i, l., Pak. — H12 39
Murgon, Austl. — E9 51
Muri, Switz. — C4 21
Muriaé, Braz. — C4 56
Murici, Braz. — k6 57
Muriel Lake, l., Ab., Can. — B5 68
Müritz Lake, l., Ger.D.R. — B6 18
Murmansk, Sov. Un. — C9 29
Murnau, F.R.Ger. — B7 20
Muroran, Japan — C13 31
Muros, Spain — A1 22
Muroto, Japan — J7 33
Muroto, Cape, c., Japan — J7 33
Murphy, Id., U.S. — F2 89
Murphy, Mo., U.S. — g13 102
Murphy, N.C., U.S. — f8 110
Murphy, Or., U.S. — E3 114
Murphy Island, i., S.C., U.S. — E9 117
Murphys, Ca., U.S. — C3 82
Murphysboro, Il., U.S. — F4 90
Murphytown, W.V., U.S. — B3 125
Murr, Bi'r, well, Eg. — E6 43
Murray, Id., U.S. — B3 89
Murray, Ky., U.S. — f9 94
Murray, Ut., U.S. — C4 121
Murray, co., Ga., U.S. — B2 87
Murray, co., Mn., U.S. — F3 100
Murray, co., Ok., U.S. — C4 113
Murray, stm., B.C., Can. — B7 69
Murray, Lake, res., Ok., U.S. — C4 113
Murray, Lake, res., S.C., U.S. — C4 117
Murray Bridge, Austl. — G6 50
Murray City, Oh., U.S. — C3 112
Murray Harbour, P.E., Can. — D7 71
Murray Head, c., P.E., Can. — D7 71
Murray Lake, l., Ab., Can. — E5 68
Murray River, P.E., Can. — D7 71
Murraysburg, S. Afr. — D3 49
Murrayville, B.C., Can. — f13 69
Murrayville, Il., U.S. — D3 90
Murrells Inlet, S.C., U.S. — D9 117
Murrhardt, F.R.Ger. — C4 21
Murrieta, Ca., U.S. — F5 82
Murrumbidgee, stm., Austl. — F8 51
Murrupula, Moz. — D6 48
Murrysville, Pa., U.S. — *k15 115
Mursala, i., Indon. — K3 35
Murska Sobota, Yugo. — B2 24
Murtaugh, Id., U.S. — G4 89

Name	Map Ref	Page
Murten, Switz.	C3	21
Murtle Lake, l., B.C., Can.	C8	69
Murud, India	E5	36
Murwāra, India	D7	36
Murwillumbah, Austl.	E9	50
Mürz, stm., Aus.	E7	18
Mürzzuschlag, Aus.	E7	18
Muş, Tur.	C13	40
Musaid, Libya	C4	43
Musala, mtn., Bul.	D6	24
Musan, N. Kor.	C10	31
Musangoli, Zaire	C3	48
Mūsā Qal'eh, Afg.	E12	39
Muscat, Oman	C5	38
Muscatatuck, stm., In., U.S.	G5	91
Muscatatuck, Vernon Fork, stm., In., U.S.	G6	91
Muscatine, Ia., U.S.	C6	92
Muscatine, co., Ia., U.S.	C6	92
Muscle Shoals, Al., U.S.	A2	78
Musclow, Mount, mtn., B.C., Can.	C4	69
Muscoda, Wi., U.S.	E3	126
Muscogee, co., Ga., U.S.	D2	87
Musconetcong, stm., N.J., U.S.	B4	107
Musconetcong Mountain, mtn., N.J., U.S.	B2	107
Muscooten Bay, l., Il., U.S.	C3	90
Muscotah, Ks., U.S.	C8	93
Muscoy, Ca., U.S.	*E5	82
Muse, Ok., U.S.	C7	113
Muse, Pa., U.S.	F1	115
Musgrave Harbour, Nf., Can.	D5	72
Musgrave Ranges, mts., Austl.	E5	50
Musgravetown, Nf., Can.	D5	72
Mushie, Zaire	B2	48
Mushin, Nig.	E5	45
Mushketovo, Sov. Un.	r20	27
Musi, stm., Indon.	F2	34
Muskeg Bay, b., Mn., U.S.	B3	100
Muskeget Channel, strt., Ma., U.S.	D7	98
Musket Island, i., Ma., U.S.	D7	98
Muskego, Wi., U.S.	F5	126
Muskego Lake, l., Wi., U.S.	n11	126
Muskegon, Mi., U.S.	E4	99
Muskegon, co., Mi., U.S.	E4	99
Muskegon, stm., Mi., U.S.	E4	99
Muskegon Heights, Mi., U.S.	E4	99
Muskegon Lake, l., Mi., U.S.	E4	99
Muskingum, co., Oh., U.S.	B4	112
Muskingum, stm., Oh., U.S.	C4	112
Muskö, Swe.	u36	14
Muskogee, Ok., U.S.	B6	113
Muskogee, co., Ok., U.S.	B6	113
Muskoka, co., On., Can.	B5	73
Muskoka, Lake, l., On., Can.	C5	73
Muskrat Dam Lake, res., On., Can.	C6	70
Muskwa, stm., Ab., Can.	A3	68
Muskwa Lake, l., Ab., Can.	A3	68
Musoma, Tan.	B5	48
Musquacook Lakes, l., Me., U.S.	B3	96
Musquaro, Lac, l., P.Q., Can.	h14	74
Musquash, N.B., Can.	D3	71
Musquash Mountain, mtn., Me., U.S.	C5	96
Musquodoboit Harbour, N.S., Can.	E6	71
Musselburgh, Scot., U.K.	C5	10
Musselshell, Mt., U.S.	D9	103
Musselshell, co., Mt., U.S.	D8	103
Musselshell, stm., Mt., U.S.	D9	103
Mussende, Ang.	C3	48
Mussidan, Fr.	E4	16
Mussolinia see Arborea, Italy	E2	23
Mussoorie, India	B6	36
Mussuma, Ang.	D3	48
Mustafakemalpaşa, Tur.	B7	40
Mustang, Ok., U.S.	B4	113
Musters, Lago, l., Arg.	D3	54
Mustinka, stm., Mn., U.S.	E2	100
Mustique, i., St. Vin.	V26	65
Mustvee, Sov. Un.	B6	27
Muswellbrook, Austl.	F9	50
Mût, Eg.	D5	43
Mut, Tur.	D9	40
Mutá, Ponta do, c., Braz.	D3	57
Mutare, Zimb.	A5	49
Mutayyin, Yemen	B5	47
Mutena, Zaire	C3	48
Muti, i., Marsh Is.	S18	52
Mutoko, Zimb.	A5	49
Mutombo-Mukulu, Zaire	C3	48
Mutorashanga, Zimb.	A5	49
Mutsu, Japan	F10	33
Mutsu Bay, b., Japan	F10	33
Mutton Bay, P.Q., Can.	C2	72
Mutton Mountains, mts., Or., U.S.	C5	114
Mutual, Ok., U.S.	A2	113
Muṭūbis, Eg.	C2	41
Mutunópolis, Braz.	A3	56
Mutzig, Fr.	F7	17
Muxima, Ang.	C1	48
Muyinga, Bdi.	B5	48
Muynak, Sov. Un.	E5	28
Muyula, i., Pap. N. Gui.	k13	50a
Muzaffargarh, Pak.	B3	37
Muzaffarnagar, India	*C6	36
Muzaffarpur, India	C8	37
Muzambinho, Braz.	k8	57
Muzayyinah, Nuwaybi'al, well, Egypt	H10	43
Muzhi, Sov. Un.	B21	8
Muzon, Cape, c., Ak., U.S.	n23	79
Muztag, mtn., China	A8	36
Muztag, mtn., China	A7	36
Muztagata, mtn., China	F10	29
Mvuma, Zimb.	A5	49
Mwadui, Tan.	B5	48
Mwami, Zimb.	A5	49
Mwanza, Tan.	B5	48
Mwanza, prov., Tan.	C5	48
Mwaya, Tan.	C5	48
Mweelrea, mtn., Ire.	D2	11
Mweka, Zaire	C4	48
Mwene-Ditu, Zaire	C4	48
Mwenezi, Zimb.	B5	49
Mwenga, Zaire	B5	48
Mweru, Lake, l., Afr.	C4	48
Mwimba, Zaire	C4	48
Mwinilunga, Zam.	D3	48
Myakka, stm., Fl., U.S.	E4	86
Myakka City, Fl., U.S.	E4	86
Myanaung, Burma	D1	35
Myaungmya, Burma	D1	35
Mycenae, hist. see Mikínai, Grc.		
Myerstown, Pa., U.S.	F9	115
Myersville, Md., U.S.	B2	97
Myingyan, Burma	D10	36
Myitkyinā, Burma	C10	36
Myitnge, stm., Burma	B2	35
Myjava, Czech.	D4	26
Mylo, N.D., U.S.	A6	111
Mymensingh, Bngl.	D9	36
Mynaral, Sov. Un.	D8	28
Mynard, Ne., U.S.	h13	104
Myrick, Ms., U.S.	D5	101
Myrnam, Ab., Can.	C5	68
Myrtle, Mb., Can.	E3	70
Myrtle, Ms., U.S.	A4	101
Myrtle, Mo., U.S.	E6	102
Myrtle Beach, S.C., U.S.	D10	117
Myrtle Beach Air Force Base, mil., S.C., U.S.	D10	117
Myrtle Creek, Or., U.S.	D3	114
Myrtle Grove, Fl., U.S.	u14	86
Myrtle Grove, La., U.S.	k12	95
Myrtle Point, Or., U.S.	D2	114
Myrtlewood, Al., U.S.	C2	78
Mysen, Nor.	p29	14
Myślenice, Pol.	D5	26
Myślibórz, Pol.	B3	26
Mysłowice, Pol.	g10	26
Mysore, India	F6	36
Mysore see Karnataka, state, India	F6	36
Mystic, Ct., U.S.	D8	84
Mystic, Ga., U.S.	E3	87
Mystic, Ia., U.S.	D5	92
Mystic Lakes, l., Ma., U.S.	g11	98
Myszków, Pol.	f10	26
My Tho, Viet.	C3	34
Mytilene see Mitilíni, Grc.	C6	40
Mytishchi, Sov. Un.	n17	27
Myton, Ut., U.S.	C5	121
Mže, stm., Czech.	D8	19
Mzimba, Mwi.	D5	48
Mzuzu, Mwi.	D5	48

N

Name	Map Ref	Page
Naab, stm., F.R.Ger.	D7	19
Naalehu, Hi., U.S.	D6	88
Naamans Garden, De., U.S.	*A3	85
Na'an, Isr.	h10	41
Naantali, Fin.	G10	14
Naas, Ire.	D3	10
Nabā, Jabal (Mount Nebo), mtn., Jord.	C7	41
Nabadwīp, India	*D8	36
Nabb, In., U.S.	G6	91
Nabberu, Lake, l., Austl.	E3	50
Nabburg, F.R.Ger.	D7	19
Nabeina, Kir.	R18	52
Nabekavu, Fiji	H15	52
Naberezhnye Chelny see Brezhnev, Sov. Un.	D8	29
Nabeul, Tur.	B7	44
Nabi Shuayb, Mount, mtn., Yemen	*D4	38
Nabnasset, Ma., U.S.	A5	98
Naboomspruit, S. Afr.	B4	49
Nabouwalu, Fiji	H15	52
Nabq, Eg.	H10	40
Nacala, Moz.	D7	48
Nacaome, Hond.	D4	62
Naches, Wa., U.S.	C5	124
Naches, stm., Wa., U.S.	C5	124
Nachingwea, Tan.	D6	48
Náchod, Czech.	C4	26
Nacimiento, Chile	B2	54
Nacimiento Reservoir, res., Ca., U.S.	E3	82
Nacka, Swe.	*H8	14
Nacmine, Ab., Can.	D4	68
Naco, Az., U.S.	F6	80
Nacogdoches, Tx., U.S.	D5	120
Nacogdoches, co., Tx., U.S.	D5	120
Nacozari [de García], Mex.	A3	63
Nadbai, Fiji	H14	52
Nadarzyn, Pol.	m13	26
Nadeau, Mi., U.S.	C3	99
Naden Harbour, b., B.C., Can.	B1	69
Nadi, Fiji	H14	52
Nadiād, India	F4	37
Nădlac, Rom.	B5	24
Nador, Mor.	B4	44
Nadori, Fiji	H15	52
Nadvornaya, Sov. Un.	G5	27
Næstved, Den.	J4	14
Nafada, Nig.	D7	45
Nafishah, Eg.	D4	38
Nafishah, Eg.	D4	41
Nafūsah, Jabal, hills, Libya		
Naga, Phil.	C6	34
Naga Hills, mts., Asia	C10	36
Nāgāland, state, India	*C9	36
Nagano, Japan	D12	31
Nagaoka, Japan	D12	31
Nagappattinam, India	F6	36
Nagar, India	B6	36
Nagar, Nic.	D4	62
Nagar Pārkar, Pak.	D5	36
Nagasaki, Japan	E10	31
Nāgaur, India	D4	37
Nageezi, N.M., U.S.	A2	108
Nāgercoil, India	G6	36
Nagles Mountains, mts., Ire.	E3	11
Nago, Japan	N5	52
Nagog Pond, l., Ma., U.S.	f10	98
Nagold, F.R.Ger.	E3	19
Nagoya, Japan	D12	31
Nagpur, India	D6	36
Nagqu, China	E3	31
Nags Head, N.C., U.S.	B7	110
Nagua, Dom. Rep.	E9	64
Naguabo, P.R.	B4	65
Naguilian, Phil.	n13	34
Nagykanizsa, Hung.	B3	24
Nagykőrös, Hung.	B4	24
Naha, Japan	N5	52
Nahalat Yehuda, Isr.	h10	41
Nahanni National Park, N.T., Can.	D7	66
Nahariyya, Isr.	B7	41
Nahāvand, Iran	D4	39
Nahe, stm., F.R.Ger.	D3	18
Nahma, Mi., U.S.	C4	99
Nahmakanta Lake, l., Me., U.S.	C3	96
Nahuel Huapí, Arg.	C2	54
Nahuel Huapí, Lago, l., Arg.	C2	54
Nahunta, Ga., U.S.	E5	87
Naic, Phil.	o13	34
Naiguatá, Pico, mtn., Ven.	A4	60
Naihāti, India	*D8	36
Nailaga, Fiji	H14	52
Nain, Nf., Can.	g9	72
Nā'īn, Iran	E6	39
Naini Tāl, India	C7	37
Nairai, i., Fiji	H15	52
Nairn, Scot., U.K.	B5	10
Nairn, stm., Scot., U.K.	C4	13
Nairobi, Kenya	B6	48
Naitonitoni, Fiji	l15	52
Naivasha, Kenya	B6	48
Najafābād, Iran	E5	39
Naj' Hammādi, Eg.	D6	43
Najībābād, India	C7	37
Najin, N. Kor.	C11	31
Najran, well, Sau. Ar.	D4	38
Nakadōri Island, i., Japan	J4	33
Nakagusuku Bay, b., Japan	O5	52
Nakaminato, Japan	m19	33
Nakamura, Japan	J6	33
Nakaosu, Japan	N6	52
Nakatsu, Japan	J5	33
Nakfa, Eth.	B4	47
Nakhichevan, Sov. Un.	F3	28
Nakhodka, Sov. Un.	E6	33
Nakhon Chai Si, stm., Thai.	E4	35
Nakhon Pathom, Thai.	F3	35
Nakhon Phanom, Thai.	B2	34
Nakhon Ratchasima, Thai.	C2	34
Nakhon Sawan, Thai.	B1	34
Nakhon Si Thammarat, Thai.	D2	34
Nakina, On., Can.	o18	73
Nakina, N.C., U.S.	C4	110
Nakina, Ak., U.S.	f9	72
Naknek, Ak., U.S.	D8	79
Naknek Lake, l., Ak., U.S.	D8	79
Nakono Island, i., Japan	L4	33
Nakskov, Den.	J4	14
Naktong [nad Notecią], Pol.	B4	26
Naku, S. Kor.	I3	33
Nakuru, Kenya	B6	48
Nakusp, B.C., Can.	D9	69
Nāl, stm., Pak.	C4	36
Nalchik, Sov. Un.	F4	28
Nallen, W.V., U.S.	m14	125
Nalón, stm., Spain	A2	22
Nālūt, Libya	C2	43
Nam, stm., Asia	B3	35
Nam, stm., S. Kor.	I4	33
Namacurra, Moz.	D6	48
Namak, Daryācheh-ye, l., Iran	D5	39
Namak, Kavīr-e, des., Iran	D8	39
Namaka, Ab., Can.	D4	68
Namakan Lake, l., N.A.	B6	100
Namakzār, Daryācheh-ye, l., Asia	D10	39
Namangan, Sov. Un.	E10	29
Namanock Island, i., N.J., U.S.	A3	107
Namanyere, Tan.	C6	48
Namasagali, Ug.	A5	48
Namatanai, Pap. N. Gui.	h13	50a
Nambe Pueblo, N.M., U.S.	B4	108
Nambour, Austl.	E9	50
Namcha Barwa, mtn., China	F4	31
Nam Dinh, Viet.	A3	34
Nämdö, i., Swe.	t36	14
Nam Du Islands, is., Viet.	H6	35
Namekagon, stm., Wi., U.S.	B2	126
Namekagon Lake, l., Wi., U.S.	B2	126
Namen see Namur, Bel.	B6	16
Nameti, Moz.	A6	49
Namib Desert, des., Nmrb.	B1	49
Namibe (Moçâmedes), Ang.	E1	48
Namibe, dept., Ang.	E1	48
Namibia (South West Africa), Afr.	B2	49
Namiquipa, Mex.	B3	63
Nam Lake, l., China	E3	31
Namlea, Indon.	F7	34
Namoi, stm., Austl.	F8	50
Nampa, Ab., Can.	A2	68
Nampa, Id., U.S.	F2	89
Nampala, Mali	C3	45
Nampo (Chinnampo), N. Kor.	D10	31
Nampula, Moz.	A6	49
Nampula, dept., Moz.	D6	48
Namsen, stm., Nor.	E4	14
Namsos, Nor.	E4	14
Nam Tok, Thai.	E3	35
Namu, B.C., Can.	C4	69
Namu Island, i., Marsh Is.	P18	52
Namur (Namen), Bel.	B6	16
Namur, P.Q., Can.	D3	74
Namur, prov., Bel.	A7	17
Namur Island, i., Marsh Is.	S17	52
Namutoni, Nmb.	A2	49
Namwala, Zam.	E4	48
Namwŏn, S. Kor.	I3	33
Namysłów, Pol.	C4	26
Nan, Thai.	C4	35
Nan, stm., Thai.	B2	34
Nana, stm., Cen. Afr. Rep.	D3	46
Nanafalia, Al., U.S.	C2	78
Nanaimo, B.C., Can.	E5	69
Nanakuli, Hi., U.S.	B3	88
Nanam, N. Kor.	H8	33
Nanango, Austl.	E9	50
Nanatsu Island, i., Japan	H8	33
Nance, co., Ne., U.S.	C7	104
Nanchang, China	F8	31
Nancheng, China	F8	31
Nanchong, China	E8	31
Nanchuan, China	J2	32
Nancy, Fr.	C7	16
Nancy, Ky., U.S.	C5	94
Nancy Creek, stm., Ga., U.S.	h8	87
Nānded, India	H6	37
Nandurbār, India	G5	37
Nanfeng, China	K7	32
Nanga Eboko, Cam.	E2	46
Nanga Parbat, mtn., Pak.	A5	36
Nangis, Fr.	F2	17
Nangong, China	F6	32
Nang Rong, Thai.	C2	34
Nanhua, China	F5	31
Nanjemoy, Md., U.S.	C3	97
Nanjing (Nanking), China	E8	31
Nankin, Oh., U.S.	B3	112
Nanking see Nanjing, China	E8	31
Nanning, China	B10	30
Nanoose Bay, B.C., Can.	f11	69
Nanowin, stm., Mb., Can.	C3	70
Nansemond, stm., Va., U.S.	k14	123
Nansen Sound, strt., N.T., Can.	k33	66
Nanshan see Qilian Mountains, mts., China	D4	31
Nansio, Tan.	B5	48
Nantais, Lac, l., P.Q., Can.	A6	111
Nanterre, Fr.	g9	16
Nantes, Fr.	D3	16
Nanteuil-le-Haudouin, Fr.	E2	17
Nantian, China	J9	32
Nanticoke, On., Can.	E4	73
Nanticoke, Md., U.S.	D6	97
Nanticoke, Pa., U.S.	D10	115
Nanticoke, stm., U.S.	D6	97
Nanton, Ab., Can.	D4	68
Nantong, China	E9	31
Nantua, Fr.	D6	16
Nantucket, Ma., U.S.	D7	98
Nantucket, co., Ma., U.S.	D7	98
Nantucket Island, i., Ma., U.S.	D7	98
Nantucket Sound, strt., Ma., U.S.	C7	98
Nantuxent Point, c., N.J., U.S.	E2	107
Nantwich, Eng., U.K.	A5	12
Nanty Glo, Pa., U.S.	F4	115
Nanuet, N.Y., U.S.	g12	109
Nanukuloa, Fiji	H15	52
Nanuku Passage, strt., Fiji	H16	52
Nanuku Reef, rf., Fiji	H16	52
Nanuque, Braz.	B4	56
Nanyang, China	E7	31
Nanyuki, Kenya	A6	48
Nanzhang, China	I4	32
Nao, Cape, c., Spain	C6	22
Naoli He, stm., China	C6	33
Naoma, W.V., U.S.	n13	125
Naomi Peak, mtn., Ut., U.S.	B4	121
Náousa, Grc.	B4	25
Napa, Ca., U.S.	C2	82
Napa, co., Ca., U.S.	C2	82
Napa, stm., Ca., U.S.	C2	82
Napadogan, N.B., Can.	C3	71
Napakiak, Ak., U.S.	C7	79
Napanee, On., Can.	C8	73
Napanoch, N.Y., U.S.	D6	109
Napatree Point, c., R.I., U.S.	G1	116
Napavine, Wa., U.S.	C3	124
Nape, Laos	C6	35
Naper, Ne., U.S.	B6	104
Naperville, Il., U.S.	B5	90
Napetipi, stm., Can.	C2	72
Napf, mtn., Switz.	C4	21
Napier, N.Z.	M16	51
Napier Mountains, mts., Ant.	C18	7
Napierville, P.Q., Can.	D4	74
Napierville, co., P.Q., Can.	D4	74
Napinka, Mb., Can.	E1	70
Naplate, Il., U.S.	B5	90
Naples (Napoli), Italy	D5	23
Naples, Fl., U.S.	F5	86
Naples, Id., U.S.	A2	89
Naples, Me., U.S.	E2	96
Naples, N.Y., U.S.	C3	109
Naples, S.D., U.S.	C8	118
Naples, Tx., U.S.	C5	120
Naples, Ut., U.S.	C6	121
Naples, Gulf of, b., Italy	D5	23
Napo, prov., Ec.	B2	58
Napo, stm., S.A.	B3	58
Napoleon, In., U.S.	F7	91
Napoleon, Mo., U.S.	B3	102
Napoleon, N.D., U.S.	C6	111
Napoleon, Oh., U.S.	A1	112
Napoleonville, La., U.S.	E4	95
Naponee, Ne., U.S.	D6	104
Nappanee, In., U.S.	B5	91
Nara, Mali	C3	45
Nāra Canal, Pak.	D2	37
Naracoorte, Austl.	G8	50
Narail, Bngl.	D7	36
Naramata, B.C., Can.	E8	69
Naranja, Fl., U.S.	G6	86
Naranjo, stm., Mex.	D4	63
Narathiwat, Thai.	D2	34
Nara Visa, N.M., U.S.	B6	108
Narberth, Wales, U.K.	C3	12
Narberth, Pa., U.S.	p20	115
Narbonne, Fr.	F5	16
Narcissa, Ok., U.S.	A7	113
Narcisse, Mb., Can.	D3	70
Narcoossee, Fl., U.S.	D5	86
Nardin, Pa., U.S.	A4	113
Nardò, Italy	D6	23
Narew, stm., Eur.	B6	26
Nārī, Jabal an, hills, Libya	E4	43
Nariño, dept., Col.	C2	60
Narita, Japan	n19	33
Narka, Ks., U.S.	C6	93
Narmada, stm., India	D6	36
Narodnaya, Mount, mtn., Sov. Un.	C9	29
Naro-Fominsk, Sov. Un.	D11	27
Narok, Kenya	B6	48
Narol, Pol.	D3	70
Narrabri, Austl.	F8	50
Narragansett, R.I., U.S.	F4	116
Narragansett Bay, b., R.I., U.S.	D5	116
Narraguagus, stm., Me., U.S.	D5	96
Narran, stm., Austl.	D6	51
Narrandera, Austl.	F8	50
Narran Lake, l., Austl.	D6	51
Narraway, stm., Can.	B7	69
Narrogin, Austl.	F2	50
Narromine, Austl.	F7	50
Narrows, Va., U.S.	C2	123
Narrowsburg, N.Y., U.S.	D5	109
Narsimhapur, India	I8	37
Naruna, Va., U.S.	C3	123
Narva, Sov. Un.	B7	27
Narvik, Nor.	C7	14
Naryan-Mar, Sov. Un.	D7	29
Naryilco, Austl.	D3	51
Narym, Sov. Un.	D25	8
Naryn, Sov. Un.	E9	29
Naryn, stm., Asia	E9	29
Narynkol, Sov. Un.	E10	29
Na Sam, Viet.	A3	34
Nasarawa, Nig.	E6	45
Nase, Japan	F10	31
Naseby, N.Z.	P13	51
Naselle, Wa., U.S.	C2	124
Nash, N.D., U.S.	A8	111
Nash, Tx., U.S.	C5	120
Nash, co., N.C., U.S.	A4	110
Nash Creek, N.B., Can.	B3	71
Nash Stream, stm., N.H., U.S.	B4	106
Nashawena Island, i., Ma., U.S.	D6	98
Nashoba Hill, hill, Ma., U.S.	f10	98
Nashua, Ia., U.S.	B5	92
Nashua, Mn., U.S.	E2	100
Nashua, Mt., U.S.	B10	103
Nashua, N.H., U.S.	E4	106
Nashua, stm., U.S.	E3	106
Nashville, Ar., U.S.	D2	81
Nashville, Ga., U.S.	E3	87
Nashville, Il., U.S.	E4	90
Nashville, In., U.S.	F5	91
Nashville, Ks., U.S.	E5	93
Nashville, Mi., U.S.	F5	99
Nashville, Mo., U.S.	D3	102
Nashville, N.C., U.S.	B5	110
Nashville, Oh., U.S.	B3	112
Nashville, Tn., U.S.	A5	119
Nashwaak, stm., N.B., Can.	C3	71
Nashwaaksis, N.B., Can.	D3	71
Nashwauk, Mn., U.S.	C5	100
Našice, Yugo.	C4	24
Nasielsk, Pol.	B6	26
Nasīf, Bi'r, well, Eg.	D2	41
Näsijärvi, l., Fin.	G10	14
Nāsik, India	E5	36
Nāsir, Sud.	D3	47
Nāsiri see Ahvāz, Iran	B4	38
Naskaupi, stm., Nf., Can.	g9	72
Nason, Il., U.S.	E5	90
Nasonville, R.I., U.S.	B3	116
Nass, stm., B.C., Can.	E7	66
Nassau, Bah.	B5	64
Nassau, De., U.S.	E5	85
Nassau, Mn., U.S.	E2	100
Nassau, N.Y., U.S.	C7	109
Nassau, co., Fl., U.S.	B5	86
Nassau, co., N.Y., U.S.	E7	109
Nassau, stm., Fl., U.S.	k8	86
Nassau, Bahía, b., Chile	k12	54
Nassau International Airport, Bah.	m17	64
Nassau Shores, N.Y., U.S.	*n15	109
Nassau Sound, b., Fl., U.S.	B5	86
Nassauville, Fl., U.S.	B5	86
Nassawadox, Va., U.S.	C7	123
Nassawango Creek, stm., Md., U.S.	D6	97
Nasser, Lake, res., Afr.	E6	43
Nässjö, Swe.	I6	14
Nasugbu, Phil.	o13	34
Nasukoin Mountain, mtn., Mt., U.S.	B2	103
Nata, Bots.	B4	49
Natá, Pan.	F7	62
Natagaima, Col.	C2	60
Natal, Braz.	C3	57
Natal, B.C., Can.	E10	69
Natal, prov., S. Afr.	C5	49
Natalbany, La., U.S.	D5	95
Natalia, Tx., U.S.	E3	120
Natanes Plateau, plat., Az., U.S.	D5	80
Natashquan, P.Q., Can.	h9	72
Natashquan, stm., Can.	h9	72
Natawahunan Lake, l., Mb., Can.	B3	70
Natchez, Ms., U.S.	D2	101
Natchitoches, La., U.S.	C2	95
Natchitoches, co., La., U.S.	C2	95
Natewa Bay, b., Fiji	H15	52
Nathalie, Va., U.S.	D4	123
Nathrop, Co., U.S.	C4	83
Natick, Ma., U.S.	B5	98
Natimuk, Austl.	H3	51
Nation, stm., B.C., Can.	B5	69
National, W.V., U.S.	B4	125
National City, Mi., U.S.	D7	99
National Gardens, Fl., U.S.	C5	86
National Park, N.J., U.S.	*D2	107
Natitingou, Benin	E8	45
Natividade, Braz.	D1	57
Natoma, Ks., U.S.	C4	93
Natron, Lake, l., Afr.	B6	48
Natrona, Wy., U.S.	D5	127
Natrona, co., Wy., U.S.	D5	127
Natrona Heights, Pa., U.S.	E2	115
Nättarö, i., Swe.	u36	14
Nattaung, mtn., Burma	C5	35
Natural Bridge, Al., U.S.	A2	78
Natural Bridge, N.Y., U.S.	A5	109
Natural Bridge, Va., U.S.	C3	123
Natural Bridge, Ut., U.S.	F3	121
Natural Bridges National Monument, Ut., U.S.	F5	121
Naturaliste, Cape, c., Austl.	F1	50
Natural Steps, Ar., U.S.	h10	81
Naturita, Co., U.S.	C2	83
Naubinway, Mi., U.S.	C5	99
Nauders, Aus.	B5	19
Nauen, Ger.D.R.	C5	18
Naugatuck, Ct., U.S.	D3	84
Naugatuck, stm., Ct., U.S.	C3	84
Naughton, On., Can.	A3	73
Naumburg [an der Saale], Ger.D.R.	C5	18
Naunhof, Ger.D.R.	B7	19
Naupactus see Návpaktos, Grc.	C3	25
Nauru, ctry., Oc.	G10	6
Naushon Island, i., Ma., U.S.	D6	98
Nauta, Peru	B3	58
Nautilus Park, Ct., U.S.	D7	84
Nautla, Mex.	C5	63
Nauvoo, Al., U.S.	B2	78
Nauvoo, Il., U.S.	C2	90
Nauwigewauk, N.B., Can.	D4	71
Nava, Lake, l., Spain	A3	22
Nava del Rey, Spain	D6	20
Navahermosa, Spain	C3	22
Navajo, co., Az., U.S.	B5	80
Navajo Dam, N.M., U.S.	A2	108
Navajo Indian Reservation, U.S.	A4	80
Navajo Mountain, mtn., Ut., U.S.	F5	121
Navajo National Monument, Az., U.S.	A2	80
Navajo Reservoir, res., U.S.	A2	108
Navalcarnero, Spain	B3	22
Navalmoral de la Mata, Spain	C3	22
Navan see An Uaimh, Ire.	D3	10
Navarino, Wi., U.S.	D5	126
Navarino, Isla, i., Chile	k12	54
Navarre, Fl., U.S.	u15	86
Navarre, hist. reg., Spain	A5	22
Navarro, co., Tx., U.S.	C4	120
Navas de Tolosa, Spain	G5	115
Navasota, Tx., U.S.	D4	120
Navasota, stm., Tx., U.S.	D4	120
Navassa, N.C., U.S.	C4	110
Navassa Island, i., N.A.	E7	64
Navatu, rf., Fiji	I16	52
Navävekvarn, Swe.	u34	14
Naver, stm., Scot., U.K.	B4	13
Naver, Loch, l., Scot., U.K.	B4	13
Navesink, N.J., U.S.	C4	107
Navet Reservoir, res., Trin.	O23	65
Navia, Arg.	A3	54
Navia, stm., Spain	A2	22
Navidad, Chile	A2	54
Naviti, i., Fiji	H14	52
Navojoa, Mex.	B3	63
Navolato, Mex.	C3	63
Návpaktos (Naupactus), Grc.	C3	25
Návplion, Grc.	D4	25
Navrongo, Ghana	F5	45
Navsāri, India	G4	37
Nawá, Syria	B8	41
Nawābshāh, Pak.	D2	37
Nawāda, India	E10	37
Nawāh, Afg.	E13	39
Nawiliwili Bay, b., Hi., U.S.	B2	88
Náxos, Grc.	D5	40
Náxos, i., Grc.	D5	40
Nay, Fr.	F3	16
Nayarit, state, Mex.	C3	63
Nayau Island, i., Fiji	H16	52
Nāy Band, Iran	C5	38
Nāy Band, Iran	E8	39
Nāy Band, Kūh-e, mtn., Iran	E8	39
Nāy Band, Ra's-e, c., Iran	H6	39
Naylor, Ga., U.S.	F3	87
Naylor, Mo., U.S.	E7	102
Nayoro, Japan	D11	33
Naytahwaush, Mn., U.S.	C3	100
Nazaré, Braz.	D3	57
Nazaré, Port.	C1	22
Nazaré da Mata, Braz.	h6	57
Nazareth (Nazerat), Isr.	B3	38
Nazareth, Ky., U.S.	C4	94
Nazareth, Pa., U.S.	E11	115
Nazareth, Tx., U.S.	B1	120
Nazário, Braz.	B3	56
Nazas, Mex.	B4	63
Nazas, stm., Mex.	B4	63
Nazca, Peru	D3	58
Nazilli, Tur.	D7	40
Nazimovo, Sov. Un.	D27	8
Naziya, Sov. Un.	s32	14
Nazko, stm., B.C., Can.	C6	69
Nazlini, Az., U.S.	B6	80
Nazret, Eth.	D4	47
Nazyvayevsk, Sov. Un.	D8	28
Ncheu, Mwi.	D5	48
Ndala, Tan.	B5	48
N'dalatando, Ang.	C1	48
Ndélé, Cen. Afr. Rep.	D4	46
Ndendé, Gabon	F2	46
N'Djamena (Fort-Lamy), Chad	C3	46
Ndjolé, Gabon	F2	46
Ndola, Zam.	D4	48
Neagh, Lough, l., N. Ire., U.K.	C3	10
Neah Bay, Wa., U.S.	A1	124
Néa Ionía, Grc.	*C4	25
Neales, stm., Austl.	E6	50
Néa Liósia, Grc.	*C4	25
Néa Páfos, Cyp.	E9	40
Néa Palátia, Grc.	g11	25
Neápolis, Grc.	D4	25
Neápolis, Grc.	C4	25
Néa Psará see Erétria, Grc.	g11	25
Near Islands, is., Ak., U.S.	E2	79
Néa Smírni, Grc.	*D4	25
Neath, Wales, U.K.	E5	10
Neavitt, Md., U.S.	C5	97
Neba, Japan	n16	33
Nebel, stm., Ger.D.R.	E6	15
Nebine Creek, stm., Austl.	D6	51
Nebit-Dag, Sov. Un.	B7	39
Neblina, Pico da, mtn., S.A.	C4	60
Nebo, Il., U.S.	D3	90
Nebo, Ky., U.S.	C2	94
Nebo, N.C., U.S.	B1	110
Nebo, Mo., U.S.	D5	102
Nebo, Mount see Nabā, Jabal, mtn., Jord.	C7	41
Nebo, Mount, mtn., Ut., U.S.	D4	121
Nebraska, state, U.S.	C6	104
Nebraska City, Ne., U.S.	D10	104
Nebuželý, Czech.	n18	19
Necedah, Wi., U.S.	D3	126
Nechako, stm., B.C., Can.	C5	69
Nechako Range, mts., B.C., Can.	C5	69
Neches, stm., Tx., U.S.	D5	120
Nechí, Col.	B3	60
Nechí, stm., Col.	B3	60
Nechranice Reservoir, res., Czech.	C8	19
Neckar, stm., F.R.Ger.	D4	18
Neckarsulm, F.R.Ger.	D4	19
Neck City, Mo., U.S.	D3	102
Necker Island, i., Hi., U.S.	m15	88
Necochea, Arg.	B5	54
Nederland, Co., U.S.	B5	83
Nederland, Tx., U.S.	E6	120
Neder Rijn, mth., Neth.	C5	17
Nedrow, N.Y., U.S.	C4	109
Needham, Ma., U.S.	B5	98
Needham, stm.	g11	98
Needle Mountain, mtn., Wy., U.S.	B3	127
Needles, Ca., U.S.	E6	82
Needmore, In., U.S.	G4	91
Needmore, Pa., U.S.	G6	115
Needville, Tx., U.S.	r14	120
Neelin, Mb., Can.	E2	70
Neels Gap, Ga., U.S.	B2	87
Neely, Ms., U.S.	D5	101
Neelyville, Mo., U.S.	E7	102
Neembucú, dept., Para.	E4	55
Neenah, Wi., U.S.	D5	126
Neepawa, Mb., Can.	D2	70
Neerpelt, Bel.	B7	17
Neeses, S.C., U.S.	D5	117
Neffs, Oh., U.S.	B5	112
Neffsville, Pa., U.S.	F9	115
Nefta, Tun.	C6	44
Neftegorsk, Sov. Un.	G16	9
Nefyn, Wales, U.K.	A3	12
Negage, Ang.	C2	48
Negaunee, Mi., U.S.	B3	99
Negele, Eth.	D4	47
Negeri Sembilan, state, Malay.	K5	35
Negev Desert, des., Isr.	D6	41
Negley, Oh., U.S.	B5	112
Negomano, Moz.	D6	48
Negombo, Sri L.	*G6	36
Negotin, Yugo.	C6	24
Negra, Cordillera, mts., Peru	C1	58
Negra, Punta, c., Peru	C1	58
Negreet, La., U.S.	C2	95
Negreira, Spain	A1	22
Negro, stm., Arg.	B4	54
Negro, stm., Bol.	B3	55
Negro, stm., Braz.	B1	56

Name | Map Ref | Page

Negro, stm., Braz. — D2 56
Negro, stm., S.A. — D4 53
Negro, stm., S.A. — E1 56
Negro Mountain, mtn. Md., U.S. — k12 97
Negros, i., Phil. — D6 34
Negru-Vodă, Rom. — D9 24
Neguac, N.B., Can. — B4 71
Nehalem, Or., U.S. — B3 114
Nehalem, stm., Or., U.S. — A3 114
Nehawka, Ne., U.S. — D10 104
Nehbandān, Iran — F10 39
Nehe, China — B2 33
Neheim-Hüsten, F.R.Ger. —
Neiba, Dom. Rep. — E8 64
Neiden, Nor. — C13 14
Neidpath, Sk., Can. — G2 75
Neihart, Mt., U.S. — D6 103
Neihuang, China — G6 32
Neijiang, China — F6 31
Neilburg, Sk., Can. — E1 75
Neill Point, c., Wa., U.S. — f11 124
Neillsville, Wi., U.S. — D3 126
Nei Monggol see Inner Mongolia, prov., China — C7 31
Neisse, stm., Eur. — C7 18
Neiva, Col. — C2 60
Neixiang, China — E7 31
Nejd, reg., Sau. Ar. — C4 38
Nejdek, Czech. — C7 19
Nekemte, Eth. — D4 47
Nekoma, Ks., U.S. — D4 93
Nekoma, N.D., U.S. — A7 111
Nekoosa, Wi., U.S. — D4 126
Nekso, Den. — C8 15
Nelagony, Ok., U.S. — A5 113
Nelidovo, Sov. Un. — C9 27
Neligh, Ne., U.S. — B7 104
Nellis Air Force Base, mil., Nv., U.S. — G6 105
Nell Island, i., Marsh Is. — S17 52
Nellore, India — F7 36
Nellysford, Va., U.S. — C4 123
Nelma, Sov. Un. — C9 33
Nelson, B.C., Can. — E9 69
Nelson, N.Z. — N14 51
Nelson, Az., U.S. — B2 80
Nelson, Ga., U.S. — B2 87
Nelson, Il., U.S. — B4 90
Nelson, Ky., U.S. — C2 94
Nelson, Mo., U.S. — B4 102
Nelson, Ne., U.S. — D7 104
Nelson, Nv., U.S. — H7 105
Nelson, N.H., U.S. — E2 106
Nelson, Pa., U.S. — C7 115
Nelson, Wi., U.S. — D1 126
Nelson, co., Ky., U.S. — C4 94
Nelson, co., N.D., U.S. — B7 111
Nelson, co., Va., U.S. — C4 123
Nelson, stm., Mb., Can. — A4 70
Nelson, Cape, i., Austl. — I3 51
Nelson Forks, B.C., Can. — m18 69
Nelson House, Mb., Can. — B2 70
Nelson Lake, i., Mb., Can. — B2 70
Nelsonville, Oh., U.S. — C3 112
Nelspruit, S. Afr. — C5 49
Néma, Maur. — C3 45
Nemacolin, Pa., U.S. — G2 115
Nemadji, stm., U.S. — B1 126
Nemaha, Ia., U.S. — B2 92
Nemaha, Ne., U.S. — D10 104
Nemaha, co., Ks., U.S. — C7 93
Nemaha, co., Ne., U.S. — D10 104
Nemakščiai, Sov. Un. — A7 26
Neman, Sov. Un. — A7 26
Neman (Nemunas), stm., Sov. Un. — E5 27
Nembe, Nig. — F6 45
Nemeiben Lake, i., Sk., Can. — B3 75
Nemi, Lake, i., Italy — h9 23
Nemiscau, P.Q., Can. — h11 74
Nemo, S.D., U.S. — C2 118
Nemours, Fr. — C5 16
Nemunas (Neman), stm., Sov. Un. — D4 27
Nemuro, Japan — C14 31
Nemuro Strait, strt., Asia — D12 33
Nenagh, Ire. — D2 10
Nenana, Ak., U.S. — C10 79
Nendeln, Liech. — B8 21
Nene, stm., Eng., U.K. — B8 12
Nenjiang, China — B10 31
Nenzel, Ne., U.S. — B4 104
Nenzing, Aus. — B8 21
Neodesha, Ks., U.S. — E8 93
Neoga, Il., U.S. — D5 90
Neola, Ia., U.S. — C2 92
Neola, Ut., U.S. — C5 121
Néon Karlovásion, Grc. — D6 25
Neopit, Wi., U.S. — D5 126
Neosho, Mo., U.S. — E3 102
Neosho, Wi., U.S. — E5 126
Neosho, co., Ks., U.S. — E8 93
Neosho, stm., Ok., U.S. — A6 113
Neosho Falls, Ks., U.S. — D8 93
Neosho Rapids, Ks., U.S. — D8 93
Neotsu, Or., U.S. — B3 114
Nepal, ctry., Asia — C7 36
Nepālganj, Nepal — C8 37
Nepaug, Ct., U.S. — *B4 84
Nepaug Reservoir, res., Ct., U.S. — B3 84
Nepewassi Lake, i., On., Can. — A4 73
Nephi, Ut., U.S. — D4 121
Nephton, On., Can. — C7 73
Nepisiguit, stm., N.B., Can. — B3 71
Nepisiguit Bay, b., N.B., Can. — B4 71
Nepomuk, Czech. — D8 19
Neponset, Il., U.S. — B4 90
Neponset, stm., Ma., U.S. — h11 98
Nepton, Ky., U.S. — B6 94
Neptune, Sk., Can. — H3 75
Neptune, N.J., U.S. — C4 107
Neptune Beach, Fl., U.S. — B5 86
Neptune City, N.J., U.S. — C4 107
Nera, stm., Italy — C4 23
Nérac, Fr. — D3 17
Nerchinsk, Sov. Un. — D14 29
Nerchinskiy Zavod, Sov. Un. — A8 31
Nerekhta, Sov. Un. — C13 27
Neretva, stm., Yugo. — D3 23
Neriquinha, Ang. — E3 48
Neris, stm., Sov. Un. — D6 27
Nerja, Spain — D4 22
Nerpichye, Sov. Un. — B12 34
Nerstrand, Mn., U.S. — F5 100
Nerva, Spain — D2 22
Nes, Neth. — A5 17
Nesbit, Ms., U.S. — A3 101
Nesbitt, Mb., Can. — E2 70
Nesco, N.J., U.S. — D3 107
Nesconset, N.Y., U.S. — *n15 109
Nescopeck, Pa., U.S. — D9 115

Nesebŭr, Bul. — D8 24
Neshanic, stm., N.J., U.S. — C3 107
Neshanic Station, N.J., U.S. — B3 107
Nesher, Isr. — B7 41
Neshkoro, Wi., U.S. — E4 126
Neshoba, Ms., U.S. — C4 101
Neskia Beach, Or., U.S. — E2 114
Neskaupstadur, Ice. — n26 14
Neskowin, Or., U.S. — B3 114
Nesle, Fr. — E2 17
Nesmith, S.C., U.S. — D8 117
Nesodden, Nor. — p28 14
Nesowadnehunk, i., Me., U.S. — B3 96
Nespelem, Wa., U.S. — A7 124
Nesquehoning, Pa., U.S. — E10 115
Ness, co., Ks., U.S. — D4 93
Ness, Loch, l., Scot., U.K. — C4 13
Ness City, Ks., U.S. — D4 93
Nesselrode, Mount, mtn., N.A. — E6 66
Nesselwang, F.R.Ger. — B6 20
Nesslau, Switz. — B5 20
Nessmersiel, F.R.Ger. — A7 17
Nesterov, Sov. Un. — C7 26
Nesterov, Sov. Un. — A7 26
Nestório, Grc. — B3 25
Nestorville, W.V., U.S. — B5 125
Néstos (Mesta), stm., Eur. — B5 25
Nesvizh, Sov. Un. — E6 27
Nes Ziyyona, Isr. — C6 41
Netanya, Isr. — B6 41
Netarts, Or., U.S. — B3 114
Netawaka, Ks., U.S. — C8 93
Netcong, N.J., U.S. — B3 107
Netherhill, Sk., Can. — F1 75
Netherlands, ctry., Eur. — A6 16
Netherlands Antilles, ctry., N.A. — A4 60
Nethy Bridge, Scot., U.K. — C5 13
Netolice, Czech. — D9 19
Netrakona, Bngl. — E13 37
Nettilling Lake, l., N.T., Can. — C18 66
Nett Lake, Mn., U.S. — B5 100
Nett Lake, l., Mn., U.S. — B5 100
Nett Lake Indian Reservation, Mn., U.S. — B6 100
Nettleton, Ms., U.S. — A5 101
Nettleton, Mo., U.S. — B4 102
Nettuno, Italy — k9 23
Netvořice, Czech. — o18 26
Netzahualcóyotl, Mex. — *D5 63
Neubeckum, F.R.Ger. — B3 19
Neubrandenburg, Ger.D.R. — B6 18
Neuchâtel, Switz. — E3 18
Neuchâtel, state, Switz. — C2 20
Neuchâtel, Lake, l., Switz. — E3 18
Neudorf, Sk., Can. — G4 75
Neuenegg, Switz. — C3 21
Neuenkirchen, F.R.Ger. — E3 15
Neuenrade, F.R.Ger. — B2 19
Neuenburg, F.R.Ger. — E6 17
Neufchâteau, Bel. — E5 17
Neufchâteau, Fr. — C6 16
Neufchâtel-en-Bray, Fr. — C4 16
Neufchâtel-sur-Aisne, Fr. — E4 17
Neufelden, Aus. — D6 18
Neugersdorf, Ger.D.R. — C9 19
Neuharlingersiel, F.R.Ger. — A7 17
Neuhaus, Ger.D.R. — E4 15
Neuhaus, Ger.D.R. — C4 19
Neuilly [-sur-Seine], Fr. — g11 16
Neu-Isenburg, F.R.Ger. — C3 19
Neukirchen am Grossvenediger, Aus. — B8 20
Neumarkt, F.R.Ger. — D5 18
Neumarkt-Sankt Veit, F.R.Ger. — A8 20
Neumünster, F.R.Ger. — A4 18
Neunburg vorm Wald, F.R.Ger. — D7 19
Neunkirch, Switz. — A6 21
Neunkirchen, Aus. — E8 18
Neunkirchen, F.R.Ger. — D2 19
Neuquén, Arg. — B3 54
Neuquén, prov., Arg. — B3 54
Neuquén, stm., Arg. — B3 54
Neurara, Chile — D2 55
Neuruppin, Ger.D.R. — B6 18
Neusiedler Lake, l., Eur. — E8 18
Neuss, F.R.Ger. — B1 19
Neustadt, On., Can. — C4 73
Neustadt, Ger.D.R. — B9 19
Neustadt, Ger.D.R. — C6 19
Neustadt, F.R.Ger. — E4 18
Neustadt, F.R.Ger. — C4 19
Neustadt am Rübenberge, F.R.Ger. — F3 15
Neustadt [an der Aisch], F.R.Ger. — D5 18
Neustadt [an der Dosse], Ger.D.R. — B6 18
Neustadt an der Waldnaab, F.R.Ger. — D7 19
Neustadt an der Weinstrasse, F.R.Ger. — D4 18
Neustadt [bei Coburg], F.R.Ger. — C5 18
Neustadt-Glewe, Ger.D.R. — E5 15
Neustadt [in Holstein], F.R.Ger. — A5 18
Neustrelitz, Ger.D.R. — B6 18
Neu-Ulm, F.R.Ger. — D5 18
Neuville, P.Q., Can. — C6 74
Neuville-lès-Dieppe, Fr. — E9 12
Neuville, i., F.R.Ger. — E2 15
Neuwied, F.R.Ger. — C3 18
Neva, Tn., U.S. — C12 119
Neva, stm., Sov. Un. — s31 14
Nevada, Ia., U.S. — B4 92
Nevada, Mo., U.S. — D3 102
Nevada, Oh., U.S. — B2 112
Nevada, co., Ar., U.S. — D2 81
Nevada, state, U.S. — D5 105
Nevada, Sierra, mts., Spain — D4 22
Nevada, Sierra, mts., Ca., U.S. — D4 82
Nevada City, Ca., U.S. — C3 82
Nevada Mills, In., U.S. — A7 91
Nevado, Cerro, mtn., Col. — C3 60
Nevado Illampu, mtn., Bol. — C2 55
Nevel, Sov. Un. — C7 27
Nevelsk, Sov. Un. — B13 31
Nevelski, Mount, mtn., Sov. Un. — A11 33
Nevers, Fr. — D5 16
Neversink, stm., N.Y., U.S. — D6 109
Neversink Reservoir, res., N.Y., U.S. — D6 109
Nevesinje, Yugo. — D4 24
Neville, Sk., Can. — H2 75
Neville, Fr. — E8 12

Nevis, Ga., U.S. — D5 87
Nevinnomyssk, Sov. Un. — G17 8
Nevinville, Ia., U.S. — C3 92
Nevis, i., St. C.-N. — H13 64
Nevis, Ben, mtn., Scot., U.K. — C3 13
Nevis, Loch, b., Scot., U.K. — C3 13
Nevşehir, Tur. — C10 40
New, stm., U.S. — C3 125
New, stm., Az., U.S. — k8 80
New, stm., N.C., U.S. — C5 110
Newala, Tan. — D6 48
New Albany, In., U.S. — H6 91
New Albany, Ks., U.S. — E8 93
New Albany, Ms., U.S. — A4 101
New Albany, Oh., U.S. — k11 112
New Albin, Ia., U.S. — A6 92
Newald, Wi., U.S. — C5 126
New Almelo, Ks., U.S. — C3 93
New Alsace, In., U.S. — F8 91
New Amsterdam, Guy. — A3 59
Newark, Eng., U.K. — D6 10
Newark, Ar., U.S. — B4 81
Newark, Ca., U.S. — h8 82
Newark, De., U.S. — B3 85
Newark, Il., U.S. — B5 90
Newark, Md., U.S. — D7 97
Newark, Mo., U.S. — A6 102
Newark, N.J., U.S. — B4 107
Newark, N.Y., U.S. — B3 109
Newark, Oh., U.S. — B3 112
Newark, Tx., U.S. — m9 120
Newark Bay, b., N.J., U.S. — k8 107
Newark Lake, l., Nv., U.S. — D6 105
Newark Valley, N.Y., U.S. — C4 109
New Athens, Il., U.S. — E4 90
New Athens, Oh., U.S. — B4 112
New Auburn, Mn., U.S. — F4 100
New Auburn, Wi., U.S. — C2 126
New Augusta, Ms., U.S. — D4 101
Newaygo, Mi., U.S. — E5 99
Newaygo, co., Mi., U.S. — E5 99
New Baden, Il., U.S. — E4 90
New Baltimore, Mi., U.S. — F8 99
New Baltimore, N.Y., U.S. — C7 109
New Baltimore, Oh., U.S. — n12 112
New Baltimore, Pa., U.S. — G4 115
New Bedford, Il., U.S. — B4 90
New Bedford, Ma., U.S. — C6 98
New Bedford, Pa., U.S. — D1 115
Newberg, Or., U.S. — B4 114
New Berlin, Il., U.S. — D4 90
New Berlin, N.Y., U.S. — C5 109
New Berlin, Pa., U.S. — E7 115
New Berlin, Tx., U.S. — k7 120
New Berlin, Wi., U.S. — n11 126
Newbern, Al., U.S. — C2 78
Newbern, Il., U.S. — D3 90
New Bern, N.C., U.S. — B5 110
Newbern, Tn., U.S. — A2 119
Newberry, Fl., U.S. — C4 86
Newberry, Mi., U.S. — B5 99
Newberry, S.C., U.S. — C4 117
Newberry, co., S.C., U.S. — C4 117
Newberry Springs, Ca., U.S. — E5 82
New Bethlehem, Pa., U.S. — D3 115
New Blaine, Ar., U.S. — B2 81
New Bloomfield, Mo., U.S. — C5 102
New Bloomfield, Pa., U.S. — F7 115
New Bloomington, Oh., U.S. — B2 112
New Boston, Ga., U.S. — C3 87
New Boston, Ia., U.S. — D6 92
New Boston, Ma., U.S. — B1 98
New Boston, Mi., U.S. — p15 99
New Boston, N.H., U.S. — E3 106
New Boston, Oh., U.S. — D3 112
New Boston, Tx., U.S. — C5 120
New Braintree, Ma., U.S. — B3 98
New Braunfels, Tx., U.S. — E3 120
New Bremen, N.Y., U.S. — B5 109
New Bremen, Oh., U.S. — B1 112
New Bridge, Or., U.S. — C9 114
Nevis Brigden, Ab., Can. — D5 68
New Brighton, Mn., U.S. — m12 100
New Brighton, Pa., U.S. — E1 115
New Britain, Ct., U.S. — C4 84
New Britain, i., Pap. N. Gui. — k13 50
New Brockton, Al., U.S. — D4 78
Newbrook, Ab., Can. — B4 68
New Brunswick, N.J., U.S. — C4 107
New Brunswick, prov., Can. — C3 71
New Buffalo, Mi., U.S. — G4 99
Newburg, Ia., U.S. — C5 92
Newburg, Md., U.S. — D4 97
Newburg, Mo., U.S. — D6 102
Newburg, N.D., U.S. — A5 111
Newburg, Pa., U.S. — F6 115
Newburg, W.V., U.S. — B5 125
Newburg, Wi., U.S. — E5 126
Newburgh, On., Can. — C8 73
Newburgh, Scot., U.K. — C7 13
Newburgh, In., U.S. — I3 91
Newburgh, Me., U.S. — D4 96
Newburgh, N.Y., U.S. — D6 109
Newburgh Heights, Oh., U.S. — h9 112
New Burnside, Il., U.S. — F5 90
Newbury, On., Can. — E3 73
Newbury, Eng., U.K. — E6 10
Newbury, Ma., U.S. — A6 98
Newbury, N.H., U.S. — D2 106
Newbury, Vt., U.S. — C4 122
Newburyport, Ma., U.S. — A6 98
New Caledonia, dep., Oc. — H10 6
New Cambria, Ks., U.S. — D6 93
New Cambria, Mo., U.S. — B5 102
New Canaan, Ct., U.S. — E2 84
New Canton, Il., U.S. — D2 90
New Canton, Va., U.S. — C4 123
New Carlisle, P.Q., Can. — A4 71
New Carlisle, In., U.S. — A4 91
New Carlisle, Oh., U.S. — C1 112
New Carrollton, Md., U.S. — *C4 97
New Cassel, N.Y., U.S. — *n15 109
New Castle, hist reg., Spain — C4 22
Newcastle, Austl. — F8 51
Newcastle, N.B., Can. — B4 71
Newcastle, On., Can. — D6 73
Newcastle, Ire. — E4 10
Newcastle, S. Afr. — C5 49
Newcastle, N. Ire., U.K. — C6 11
Newcastle, Ca., U.S. — C3 82
Newcastle, Co., U.S. — B3 83
Newcastle, De., U.S. — B3 85
Newcastle, Ok., U.S. — B4 113
Newcastle, Tx., U.S. — C3 120

Newcastle, Ut., U.S. — F2 121
New Castle, Va., U.S. — C2 123
New Castle, Wy., U.S. — C8 127
New Castle, co., De., U.S. — B3 85
Newcastle Creek, N.B., Can. — C3 71
Newcastle Emlyn, Wales, U.K. — B3 12
Newcastle Mine, Ab., Can. — D4 68
Newcastle-on-Tyne, Eng., U.K. — C6 10
Newcastle-under-Lyme, Eng., U.K. — A5 12
Newcastle West, Ire. — E2 11
Newcestown, Ire. — F3 11
New City, N.Y., U.S. — D6 109
New Columbia, Pa., U.S. — D8 115
Newcomb, N.M., U.S. — A1 108
Newcomb, N.Y., U.S. — B6 109
Newcomb, Tn., U.S. — A7 119
Newcomerstown, Oh., U.S. — B4 112
New Concord, Ky., U.S. — f9 94
New Concord, Oh., U.S. — C4 112
New Cumberland, Pa., U.S. — F8 115
New Cumberland, W.V., U.S. — A4 125
New Cumnock, Scot., U.K. — C4 10
Newdale, Mb., Can. — D1 70
Newdale, Id., U.S. — F7 89
New Dayton, Ab., Can. — E4 68
New Delhi, India — C6 36
New Denmark, N.B., Can. — C2 71
New Denver, B.C., Can. — D9 69
New Diggings, Wi., U.S. — F3 126
New Durham, N.H., U.S. — D4 106
New Edinburg, Ar., U.S. — D3 81
New Effington, S.D., U.S. — B9 118
New Egypt, N.J., U.S. — C3 107
Newell, Al., U.S. — B4 78
Newell, Ar., U.S. — D3 81
Newell, Ia., U.S. — B2 92
Newell, S.D., U.S. — C2 118
Newell, W.V., U.S. — A4 125
Newell, Lake, l., Ab., Can. — D5 68
New Ellenton, S.C., U.S. — E4 117
Newellton, La., U.S. — B4 95
New England, N.D., U.S. — C3 111
New Enterprise, Pa., U.S. — F5 115
New Era, Mi., U.S. — E4 99
Newe Sha'anan, Isr. — m14 41
New Fairfield, Ct., U.S. — D2 84
Newfane, N.Y., U.S. — B2 109
Newfane, Vt., U.S. — F3 122
Newfield, Me., U.S. — E2 96
Newfield, N.J., U.S. — D2 107
Newfields, N.H., U.S. — D5 106
New Florence, Mo., U.S. — C6 102
New Florence, Pa., U.S. — F3 115
Newfolden, Mn., U.S. — B2 100
New Forest, for., Eng., U.K. — D6 12
Newfound Gap, U.S. — f9 110
Newfound Lake, l., N.H., U.S. — C3 106
Newfoundland, N.J., U.S. — A4 107
Newfoundland, i., Can. — D11 72
Newfoundland, prov., Can. — D4 72
Newfoundland Mountains, mts., Ut., U.S. — B2 121
New Franken, Wi., U.S. — D6 126
New Franklin, Mo., U.S. — B5 102
New Freedom, Pa., U.S. — G8 115
New Galilee, Pa., U.S. — E1 115
New Galloway, Scot., U.K. — C4 10
Newgate, B.C., Can. — E10 69
New Gate, hist., Isr. — m14 41
New Germany, N.S., Can. — E5 71
New Glarus, Wi., U.S. — F4 126
New Glasgow, N.S., Can. — D7 71
New Gloucester, Me., U.S. — E2 96
New Goshen, In., U.S. — E3 91
New Gretna, N.J., U.S. — D4 107
New Guinea, i. — G8 6
Newhalem, Wa., U.S. — A4 124
Newhall, Ca., U.S. — E4 82
Newhall, Ia., U.S. — C6 92
Newhall, W.V., U.S. — D3 125
New Hamburg, On., Can. — D4 73
New Hampshire, state, U.S. — C3 106
New Hampton, Ia., U.S. — A5 92
New Hampton, Mo., U.S. — A3 102
New Hampton, N.H., U.S. — C3 106
New Hanover, co., N.C., U.S. — C5 110
New Hanover, i., Pap. N. Gui. — h12 50
New Harbor, Me., U.S. — E3 96
New Harbour, Nf., Can. — E5 72
New Harmony, In., U.S. — H2 91
New Harmony, Ut., U.S. — F2 121
New Hartford, Ct., U.S. — B4 84
New Hartford, Ia., U.S. — B5 92
New Haven, Ct., U.S. — D4 84
New Haven, Il., U.S. — F5 90
New Haven, In., U.S. — B7 91
New Haven, Ky., U.S. — C4 94
New Haven, Mi., U.S. — F8 99
New Haven, Mo., U.S. — C6 102
New Haven, N.Y., U.S. — B4 109
New Haven, W.V., U.S. — C3 125
New Haven, co., Ct., U.S. — D3 84
New Haven, stm., Vt., U.S. — C2 122
New Haven Harbor, b., Ct., U.S. — E4 84
New Hazelton, B.C., Can. — B4 69
Newhebron, Ms., U.S. — D4 101
New Hebrides see Vanuatu, ctry., Oc. — H10 6
New Hill, N.C., U.S. — B4 110
New Holland, Ga., U.S. — B3 87
New Holland, Il., U.S. — C4 90
New Holland, Oh., U.S. — C2 112
New Holland, Pa., U.S. — F9 115
New Holland, S.D., U.S. — D7 118
New Holstein, Wi., U.S. — E5 126
New Hope, Al., U.S. — A3 78
Newhope, Ar., U.S. — C2 81
New Hope, Ky., U.S. — C4 94
New Hope, Pa., U.S. — F12 115
New Hope Mountain, mtn., Al., U.S. — g7 78
New Hradec, N.D., U.S. — B3 111
New Hudson, Mi., U.S. — o14 99
New Hyde Park, N.Y., U.S. — *E7 109
New Iberia, La., U.S. — D4 95
Newington, Ct., U.S. — C5 84
Newington, Ga., U.S. — D5 87
New Inlet, b., N.C., U.S. — D5 110
New Inn, Ire. — E4 11
New Ipswich, N.H., U.S. — E3 106
New Ireland, i., Pap. N. Gui. — h13 50
New Johnsonville, Tn., U.S. — A4 119

New Kensington, Pa., U.S. — E2 115
New Kent, Va., U.S. — C5 123
New Kent, co., Va., U.S. — C5 123
Newkirk, Ok., U.S. — A4 113
Newkirk, N.M., U.S. — B5 108
New Knoxville, Oh., U.S. — B1 112
New Laguna, N.M., U.S. — B2 108
New Lake, l., N.C., U.S. — B6 110
Newland, N.C., U.S. — A1 110
New Lebanon, In., U.S. — F3 91
New Lebanon, N.Y., U.S. — C7 109
New Leipzig, N.D., U.S. — C4 111
New Lenox, Il., U.S. — B6 90
New Lexington, Oh., U.S. — C3 112
New Liberty, Ky., U.S. — B5 94
New Lima, Ok., U.S. — B5 113
New Lisbon, In., U.S. — E7 91
New Lisbon, N.J., U.S. — D3 107
New Lisbon, Wi., U.S. — E3 126
New Liskeard, On., Can. — p20 73
Newllano, La., U.S. — C2 95
New London, Ct., U.S. — D7 84
New London, Ia., U.S. — D6 92
New London, Mn., U.S. — E4 100
New London, Mo., U.S. — B6 102
New London, N.H., U.S. — D3 106
New London, N.C., U.S. — B2 110
New London, Oh., U.S. — A3 112
New London, Wi., U.S. — D5 126
New London, co., Ct., U.S. — C7 84
New London Submarine Base, mil., Ct., U.S. — D7 84
New Lothrop, Mi., U.S. — E6 99
New Lowell, On., Can. — C5 73
New Madison, Oh., U.S. — C1 112
New Madrid, Mo., U.S. — E8 102
New Madrid, co., Mo., U.S. — E8 102
Newman, Austl. — D2 50
Newman, Ca., U.S. — D3 82
Newman, Il., U.S. — D6 90
Newman, Ks., U.S. — k15 93
New Manchester, W.V., U.S. — e8 125
Newman Grove, Ne., U.S. — C8 104
Newman Lake, l., Wa., U.S. — B8 124
Newmanstown, Pa., U.S. — F9 115
New Marion, In., U.S. — F7 91
Newmarket, On., Can. — C5 73
Newmarket, Ire. — E2 11
Newmarket, Eng., U.K. — B8 12
Newmarket, Al., U.S. — A3 78
Newmarket, Ga., U.S. — E2 87
New Market, Al., U.S. — E4 91
New Market, Ia., U.S. — D3 92
New Market, Md., U.S. — B3 97
New Market, Mn., U.S. — F5 100
New Market, N.H., U.S. — D5 106
New Market, Tn., U.S. — C10 119
New Market, Va., U.S. — B4 123
Newmarket-on-Fergus, Ire. — E3 11
New Marlboro, Ma., U.S. — B1 98
New Marshfield, Oh., U.S. — C3 112
New Martinsville, W.V., U.S. — B4 125
New Matamoras, Oh., U.S. — C4 112
New Meadows, Id., U.S. — D2 89
New Melle, Mo., U.S. — C7 102
New Mexico, state, U.S. — C3 108
New Miami, Oh., U.S. — C1 112
New Middletown, In., U.S. — H5 91
New Milford, Ct., U.S. — C2 84
New Milford, N.J., U.S. — h8 107
New Milford, Pa., U.S. — C10 115
New Mills, N.B., Can. — B3 71
New Milton, W.V., U.S. — B4 125
New Minden, Il., U.S. — E4 90
New Munich, Mn., U.S. — E4 100
New Munster, Wi., U.S. — n11 126
Newnans Lake, l., Fl., U.S. — C4 86
Newnata, Ar., U.S. — B4 81
New Norfolk, Austl. — o15 50
New Norway, Ab., Can. — C4 68
New Offenburg, Mo., U.S. — D7 102
New Orleans, La., U.S. — E5 95
New Orleans Naval Air Station, mil., La., U.S. — k11 95
New Osgoode, Sk., Can. — D4 75
New Oxford, Pa., U.S. — G7 115
New Palestine, In., U.S. — E6 91
New Paltz, N.Y., U.S. — D6 109
New Paris, In., U.S. — B6 91
New Paris, Oh., U.S. — C1 112
New Paris, Pa., U.S. — F4 115
New Perlican, Nf., Can. — E5 72
New Philadelphia, Oh., U.S. — B4 112
New Philadelphia, Pa., U.S. — E9 115
New Pine Creek, Ca., U.S. — B3 82
New Pine Creek, Or., U.S. — E6 114
New Plymouth, N.Z. — M15 51
New Plymouth, Id., U.S. — F2 89
New Plymouth, Oh., U.S. — C3 112
New Point, In., U.S. — F7 91
New Point, Mo., U.S. — A2 102
New Point Comfort, c., Va., U.S. — C6 123
Newport, Ire. — D2 11
Newport, Ire. — E3 11
Newport, Eng., U.K. — E6 10
Newport, Wales, U.K. — E5 10
Newport, Ar., U.S. — B4 81
Newport, De., U.S. — B3 85
Newport, Fl., U.S. — B2 86
Newport, In., U.S. — E3 91
Newport, Ky., U.S. — A5 94
Newport, Me., U.S. — D3 96
Newport, Mi., U.S. — G7 99
Newport, Mn., U.S. — n13 100
Newport, Ne., U.S. — B6 104
Newport, N.H., U.S. — D2 106
Newport, N.C., U.S. — C6 110
Newport, Oh., U.S. — C4 112
Newport, Or., U.S. — C2 114
Newport, Pa., U.S. — F7 115
Newport, R.I., U.S. — F5 116
Newport, Tn., U.S. — D10 119
Newport, Tx., U.S. — C3 120
Newport, Vt., U.S. — B4 122
Newport, Wa., U.S. — A8 124
Newport, co., R.I., U.S. — E5 116
Newport Beach, Ca., U.S. — n13 82
Newport Hills, Wa., U.S. — *e11 124
Newport News, Va., U.S. — D6 123

New Providence, Ia., U.S. — B4 92
New Providence, N.J., U.S. — B4 107
New Providence, i., Bah. — B5 64
Newquay, Eng., U.K. — E4 10
New Quay, Wales, U.K. — B3 12
New Raymer, Co., U.S. — A7 83
New Richland, Mn., U.S. — G5 100
New Richmond, P.Q., Can. — A4 71
New Richmond, In., U.S. — D4 91
New Richmond, Oh., U.S. — D1 112
New Richmond, Wi., U.S. — C1 126
New Riegel, Oh., U.S. — A2 112
New River, Az., U.S. — D3 80
New River, Tn., U.S. — C9 119
New River Gorge, val., W.V., U.S. — m13 125
New River Inlet, b., N.C., U.S. — C5 110
New Road, N.S., Can. — E6 71
New Roads, La., U.S. — D4 95
New Rochelle, N.Y., U.S. — E7 109
New Rockford, N.D., U.S. — B6 111
New Ross, N.S., Can. — E5 71
New Ross, Ire. — D3 10
New Ross, In., U.S. — E4 91
New Ross, Ire. — C3 10
Newry, Me., U.S. — D2 96
Newry, S.C., U.S. — B2 117
New Salem, In., U.S. — D3 90
New Salem, Ks., U.S. — E7 93
New Salem, Ma., U.S. — A3 98
New Salem, N.D., U.S. — C4 111
New Salisbury, In., U.S. — H5 91
New Sarepta, Ab., Can. — C4 68
New Sarpy, La., U.S. — k11 95
New Sharon, Ia., U.S. — C5 92
New Sharon, Me., U.S. — D2 96
New Sharon, N.J., U.S. — C3 107
New Siberian Islands, is., Sov. Un. — B18 29
New Site, Al., U.S. — B4 78
New Site, Ms., U.S. — A5 101
New Smyrna Beach, Fl., U.S. — C6 86
Newsoms, Va., U.S. — D5 123
New South Wales, state, Austl. — F8 50
New Straitsville, Oh., U.S. — C3 112
New Sweden, Me., U.S. — B4 96
New Tazwell, Tn., U.S. — C10 119
Newtok, Ak., U.S. — C7 79
Newton, Al., U.S. — D4 78
Newton, Ga., U.S. — E2 87
Newton, Il., U.S. — E5 90
Newton, Ia., U.S. — C4 92
Newton, Ks., U.S. — D6 93
Newton, Ma., U.S. — B5 98
Newton, Ms., U.S. — C4 101
Newton, N.J., U.S. — A3 107
Newton, N.C., U.S. — B1 110
Newton, Tx., U.S. — D6 120
Newton, Ut., U.S. — B4 121
Newton, W.V., U.S. — C3 125
Newton, Wi., U.S. — k10 126
Newton, co., Ar., U.S. — B2 81
Newton, co., Ga., U.S. — C3 87
Newton, co., In., U.S. — B3 91
Newton, co., Ms., U.S. — C4 101
Newton, co., Mo., U.S. — E3 102
Newton, co., Tx., U.S. — D6 120
Newton Abbot, Eng., U.K. — D4 12
Newton Falls, N.Y., U.S. — A6 109
Newton Falls, Oh., U.S. — A5 112
Newton Grove, N.C., U.S. — B4 110
Newton Hamilton, Pa., U.S. — F6 115
Newton Junction, N.H., U.S. — E4 106
Newton Lake, res., Il., U.S. — E5 90
Newton Stewart, Scot., U.K. — F4 13
Newtonsville, Oh., U.S. — C1 112
Newtonville, On., Can. — D6 73
Newtonville, In., U.S. — H4 91
Newtonville, Ma., U.S. — g10 98
Newtown, Wales, U.K. — D5 10
Newtown, In., U.S. — D3 91
Newtown, Mo., U.S. — A4 102
New Town, N.D., U.S. — B3 111
Newtown, Oh., U.S. — C1 112
Newtown, Va., U.S. — C5 123
Newtownabbey, N. Ire., U.K. — C6 11
Newtownards, N. Ire., U.K. — C4 10
Newtown Crommelin, N. Ire., U.K. — C5 11
Newtown Hamilton, N. Ire. — C5 11
Newtownmountkennedy, Ire. — C5 11
New Town Square, Pa., U.S. — p20 115
Newtownstewart, N. Ire., U.K. — C5 11
New Trenton, In., U.S. — F8 91
New Ulm, Mn., U.S. — F4 100
New Ulm, Tx., U.S. — E4 120
New Underwood, S.D., U.S. — C3 118
New Vienna, Ia., U.S. — B6 92
New Vienna, Oh., U.S. — C2 112
New Village, N.J., U.S. — B2 107
Newville, Al., U.S. — D4 78
Newville, In., U.S. — B8 91
Newville, Pa., U.S. — F7 115
New Vineyard, Me., U.S. — D2 96
New Virginia, Ia., U.S. — C4 92
New Washington, In., U.S. — G6 91
New Washington, Oh., U.S. — B3 112
New Washoe City, Nv., U.S. — *D2 105
New Waterford, N.S., Can. — C9 71
New Waterford, Oh., U.S. — B5 112
New Waverly, Tx., U.S. — D5 120
New Westminster, B.C., Can. — E6 69
New Whiteland, In., U.S. — E5 91
New Wilmington, Pa., U.S. — D1 115
New Windsor, Il., U.S. — B3 90
New Windsor, Md., U.S. — A3 97
New Windsor, N.Y., U.S. — D6 109
New Woodstock, N.Y., U.S. — C5 109
New World Island, i., Nf., Can. — D4 72
New York, N.Y., U.S. — k13 109
New York, co., N.Y., U.S. — k13 109
New York, state, U.S. — C6 109
New York Mills, Mn., U.S. — D3 100
New Zealand, ctry., Oc. — N14 51
New Zion, S.C., U.S. — D7 117
Neya, Sov. Un. — B2 30
Neye Island, i., Guam — M9 52
Ney Lake, l., Can. —
Neyriz, Iran — C5 38
Neyshābūr, Iran — B5 38
Nezperce, Id., U.S. — *C2 89
Nez Perce, co., Id., U.S. — C2 89

Name	Map Ref	Page
Nez Perce Indian Reservation, Id., U.S.	C2	89
Nezpique, Bayou, stm., La., U.S.	D3	95
Ngabang, Indon.	E3	34
Ngabé, Congo	B2	48
Ngala, Nig.	D7	45
Ngami, Lake, l., Bots.	B3	49
Ngangla Ringco Lake, l., China	B7	36
Ngangzê Lake, l., China	B11	37
Ngara, Tan.	B5	48
Ngaramasch, Palau	R17	52
Ngaruangl Reef, rf., Palau	R17	52
Ngaruawahia, N.Z.	L15	51
Ngatapa, N.Z.	M16	51
Ngemelis Islands, is., Palau	R17	52
Ngerekebesang, i., Palau	R17	52
Ngerkeel, Palau	R17	52
Ngermechau, Palau	R17	52
Ngeruktabel, i., Palau	R17	52
Ngetbong, Palau	R17	52
Ngidinga, Zaire	C2	48
Ngong, Kenya	B6	48
Ngoring Lake, l., China	D4	31
Ngounié, stm., Gabon	F2	46
Ngouri, Chad	C3	46
Nguigmi, Niger	D7	45
Nguru, Nig.	D7	45
Nhamundá, Braz.	C3	59
Nhamundá, stm., Braz.	C3	59
Nha Trang, Viet.	C3	34
Nhill, Austl.	H3	51
Nhulunbuy, Austl.	B6	50
Niafounké, Mali	C4	45
Niagara, N.D., U.S.	B8	111
Niagara, Wi., U.S.	C6	126
Niagara, co., On., Can.	D5	73
Niagara, co., N.Y., U.S.	B2	109
Niagara, stm., N.A.	B1	109
Niagara Falls, On., Can.	D5	73
Niagara Falls, N.Y., U.S.	B1	109
Niagara-on-the-Lake, On., Can.	D5	73
Niamey, Niger	D5	45
Niamtougou, Togo	E5	45
Niangara, Zaire	A4	48
Niangua, Mo., U.S.	D5	102
Niangua, stm., Mo., U.S.	D5	102
Niantic, Ct., U.S.	D7	84
Niarada, Mt., U.S.	C2	103
Nias, i., Indon.	E1	34
Niassa, dept., Moz.	D6	48
Nibe, Den.	B3	15
Nibley, Ut., U.S.	B4	121
Nicaragua, ctry., N.A.	E7	63
Nicaragua, Lago de, l., Nic.	E7	63
Nicastro (Lamezia Terme), Italy	F11	23
Nicatous Lake, l., Me., U.S.	C4	96
Nice, Fr.	F7	16
Niceville, Fl., U.S.	u15	86
Nichicun, Lac, l., P.Q., Can.	h12	74
Nichinan, Japan	K5	33
Nicholas, co., Ky., U.S.	B5	94
Nicholas, co., W.V., U.S.	C4	125
Nicholas Channel, strt., N.A.	C7	64
Nicholasville, Ky., U.S.	C5	94
Nicholls, Ga., U.S.	E4	87
Nichols, Ia., U.S.	C6	92
Nichols, Mo., U.S.	D4	102
Nichols, N.Y., U.S.	C4	109
Nichols Hills, Ok., U.S.	B4	113
Nicholson, Ms., U.S.	E4	101
Nicholson, Pa., U.S.	C10	115
Nicholson, stm., Austl.	C6	50
Nicholville, N.Y., U.S.	f10	109
Nickajack Lake, res., Tn., U.S.	l9	123
Nickerie, dept., Sur.	B3	59
Nickerie, stm., Sur.	A3	59
Nickerson, Ks., U.S.	D5	93
Nickerson, Ne., U.S.	C9	104
Nickerson Hill, hill, Ct., U.S.	B4	84
Nicobar Islands, is., India	G9	36
Nicodemus, Ks., U.S.	C4	93
Nicola, B.C., Can.	D7	69
Nicola, stm., B.C., Can.	D7	69
Nicolet, P.Q., Can.	C5	74
Nicolet, co., P.Q., Can.	C5	74
Nicolet, stm., P.Q., Can.	C5	74
Nicolet, Lake, l., Mi., U.S.	B6	99
Nicollet, Mn., U.S.	F4	100
Nicollet, co., Mn., U.S.	F4	100
Nicolls Town, Bah.	B4	64
Nicoma Park, Ok., U.S.	B4	113
Nicosia (Levkosía), Cyp.	E9	40
Nicosia [Sicilia], Italy	F5	23
Nicotera, Italy	E5	23
Nicoya, C.R.	I6	62
Nicoya, Golfo de, b., C.R.	F5	62
Nicoya, Península de, pen., C.R.	F7	63
Nictaux Falls, N.S., Can.	E4	71
Nida, stm., Pol.	C6	26
Nid à l'Aigle, Cap du, c., St. P./M.	E3	72
Nidan Rock, i., Japan	P17	52
Nidd, stm., Eng., U.K.	F11	13
Nidda, F.R.Ger.	C3	19
Nidda, stm., F.R.Ger.	C4	19
Nidwalden, state, Switz.	C4	20
Nidzica, Pol.	B6	26
Niebüll, F.R.Ger.	D2	15
Niederbronn-les-Bains, Fr.	F7	17
Niedermarsberg, F.R.Ger.	C3	19
Niedersachsen, state, F.R.Ger.	F3	15
Nielsville, Mn., U.S.	C2	100
Nienburg, F.R.Ger.	B4	18
Niers, stm., F.R.Ger.	C6	17
Nierstein, F.R.Ger.	D3	19
Niesky, Ger.D.R.	B9	19
Nieszawa, Pol.	B5	26
Nietleben, Ger.D.R.	B6	19
Nieuw Amsterdam, Sur.	B6	59
Nieuweroord, Neth.	B6	17
Nieuw Nickerie, Sur.	B3	59
Nieuwpoort, Bel.	C2	17
Nigadoo, N.B., Can.	B4	71
Nigde, Tur.	D10	40
Nigel Island, i., B.C., Can.	C6	69
Niger, ctry., Afr.	C6	45
Niger, stm., Afr.	F6	45
Niger Delta, Nig.	F6	45
Nigeria, ctry., Afr.	F6	45
Nigg, Scot., U.K.	C5	13
Nighthawk, Wa., U.S.	A6	124
Nigríta, Grc.	H11	39
Nihoa, i., Hi., U.S.	m15	88
Nihon see Japan, Asia		
Niigata, Japan	D12	31
Niihama, Japan	J6	33
Niihau, i., Hi., U.S.	B1	88
Nii Island, i., Japan	I9	33
Niimi, Japan	I6	33
Nijar, Spain	D4	22
Nijkerk, Neth.	B5	17
Nijmegen, Neth.	B6	16
Nikaia, Grc.	*D4	25
Nikep, Md., U.S.	k13	97
Nikishka, Ak., U.S.	g16	79
Nikitinka, Sov. Un.	D9	29
Nikitovka, Sov. Un.	q21	27
Nikki, Benin	E5	45
Nikkō, Japan	D12	31
Nikolayev, Sov. Un.	E6	29
Nikolayevsk, Sov. Un.	F15	27
Nikolayevsk [-na-Amure], Sov. Un.	D17	29
Nikolsk, Sov. Un.	B3	28
Nikolski, Ak., U.S.	E6	79
Nikonovskoye, Sov. Un.	n18	27
Nikopol, Bul.	D7	24
Nikopol, Sov. Un.	H10	27
Niksar, Tur.	B11	40
Nikšić, Yugo.	D4	24
Niland, Ca., U.S.	F6	82
Nile, N.Y., U.S.	C2	109
Nile, stm., Afr.	D9	42
Nileh, Küh-e, mtn., Iran	E5	39
Niles, Il., U.S.	h9	90
Niles, Ks., U.S.	D6	93
Niles, Mi., U.S.	G4	99
Niles, Oh., U.S.	A5	112
Nilvange, Fr.	E6	17
Nilwood, Il., U.S.	D4	90
Nimach, India	E5	37
Nimba, Mont, mtn., Afr.	E3	45
Nimba Mountains, mts., Afr.	E3	45
Nîmes, Fr.	F6	16
Nimmons, Ar., U.S.	A5	81
Nimpkish, stm., B.C., Can.	D4	69
Nimrin, Wādī, val., Jord.	h13	41
Nimrod Glacier, Ant.	A29	7
Nimrod Lake, res., Ar., U.S.	C2	81
Nimule, Sud.	E3	47
Ninemile Creek, stm., Ks., U.S.	k15	93
Nine Mile Creek, stm., Ut., U.S.	D5	121
Nine Mile Falls, Wa., U.S.	g13	124
Ninemile Point, c., Mi., U.S.	C6	99
Ninette, Mb., Can.	E2	70
Ninety Six, S.C., U.S.	C3	117
Ninety Mile Beach, Austl.	G8	50
Nineveh, Pa., U.S.	G1	115
Nineveh, hist., Iraq	B4	38
Ninga, Mb., Can.	E2	70
Ning'an, China	C10	31
Ningbo, China	F9	31
Ningde, China	F8	31
Ningdu, China	K6	32
Ninghai, China	J9	32
Ninghua, China	K7	32
Ningjin, China	F6	32
Ningming, China	A7	35
Ningqiang, China	H2	32
Ningsia Hui see Ningxia Huizu, prov., China	D6	31
Ningwu, China	D7	31
Ningxia Huizu, prov., China	D6	31
Ningxian, China	D6	31
Ninh Binh, Viet.	A3	34
Niniget Pond, l., R.I., U.S.	G2	116
Ninilchik, Ak., U.S.	C9	79
Ninnekah, Ok., U.S.	C4	113
Ninnescah, North Fork, stm., Ks., U.S.	E5	93
Ninnescah, South Fork, stm., Ks., U.S.	E5	93
Ninnis Glacier, Ant.	C27	7
Ninole, Hi., U.S.	D6	88
Ninove, Bel.	D4	17
Nioaque, Braz.	C1	56
Niobe, N.D., U.S.	A3	111
Niobrara, Ne., U.S.	B7	104
Niobrara, co., Wy., U.S.	C8	127
Niobrara, stm., U.S.	B7	104
Nioki, Zaire	B2	48
Niono, Mali	D4	45
Nioro du Rip, Sen.	D1	45
Nioro du Sahel, Mali	C3	45
Niort, Fr.	D3	16
Niota, Il., U.S.	C2	90
Niota, Tn., U.S.	D9	119
Niotaze, Ks., U.S.	E7	93
Nipawin, Sk., Can.	D4	75
Nipawin Provincial Park, Sk., Can.	C3	75
Nipekamew Lake, l., Sk., Can.	C3	75
Nipew Lake, l., Sk., Can.	B3	75
Nipigon, On., Can.	o17	73
Nipigon, Lake, l., On., Can.	o17	73
Nipishish Lake, l., Nf., Can.	g9	72
Nipissing, co., On., Can.	A6	73
Nipissing, Lake, l., On., Can.	A5	73
Nipomo, Ca., U.S.	E3	82
Nippers Harbour, Nf., Can.	D4	72
Nipple Mountain, mtn., Co., U.S.	D2	83
Nipton, Ca., U.S.	E6	82
Niquelândia, Braz.	A3	56
Niquero, Cuba	D5	64
Nirasaki, Japan	n17	33
Nirmal, India	H7	37
Nirmali, India	D11	37
Niš, Yugo.	D5	24
Nisa, Port.	C2	22
Nišava, stm., Eur.	D6	24
Nishinomiya, Japan	*I7	33
Nishio, Japan	o16	33
Nísiros, i., Grc.	D6	25
Niskayuna, N.Y., U.S.	C7	109
Nisland, S.D., U.S.	C2	118
Nisqually, stm., Wa., U.S.	C3	124
Nissan, stm., Swe.	B7	15
Nissan Bredning, b., Den.	B7	15
Nissum Fjord, Den.	B2	15
Nisswa, Mn., U.S.	D4	100
Nistowiak Lake, l., Sk., Can.	B3	75
Nisula, Mi., U.S.	B2	99
Niterói, Braz.	C7	56
Nith, stm., Scot., U.K.	E5	13
Nitra, Czech.	D5	26
Nitra, stm., Czech.	D5	26
Nitro, W.V., U.S.	C3	125
Nitta Yuma, Ms., U.S.	B3	101
Nittenau, F.R.Ger.	*D4	19
Niue, ctry., Oc.	H11	6
Niverville, P.Q., Can.	k11	74
Nivernais, hist reg., Fr.	D5	16
Nivernais, Côtes du, hills, Fr.	D5	16
Niverville, Mb., Can.	E3	70
Nivskiy, Sov. Un.	D15	14
Niwot, Co., U.S.	A5	83
Nixa, Mo., U.S.	D4	102
Nixburg, Al., U.S.	C3	78
Nixon, Nv., U.S.	D2	105
Nixon, Tn., U.S.	B3	119
Nixon, Tx., U.S.	E4	120
Nizāmābād, India	H7	37
Nizām Sāgar, res., India	H7	37
Nizōgan, stm., Afg.	E11	39
Nizhnemozero, Sov. Un.	E18	14
Nizhnekamsk, Sov. Un.	*D8	29
Nizhnekolymsk, Sov. Un.	C19	29
Nizhne-Leninskoye, Sov. Un.	C6	33
Nizhneudinsk, Sov. Un.	D12	31
Nizhneye, Sov. Un.	q21	27
Nizhniy Chir, Sov. Un.	G14	27
Nizhniy Lomov, Sov. Un.	E14	27
Nizhniy Pyandzh, Sov. Un.	H22	8
Nizhniy Tagil, Sov. Un.	D9	29
Nizhnyaya Tunguska, stm., Sov. Un.	C12	29
Nizhnyaya Tura, Sov. Un.	D21	8
Nizmennyy, Cape, c., Sov. Un.	E7	33
Nizza Monferrato, Italy	E4	20
Nizzana, Nahal, val., Isr.	D6	41
Njombe, Tan.	C5	48
Njurunda, Swe.	F7	14
Nkambe, Cam.	D2	46
Nkayi, Zimb.	A4	49
Nkhata Bay, Mwi.	D5	48
Nkhota Kota, Mwi.	D5	48
Nkongsamba, Cam.	E1	46
Nnewi, Nig.	F6	45
Noākhāli, Bngl.	F13	37
Noank, Ct., U.S.	D8	84
Noasca, Italy	D3	20
Noatak, Ak., U.S.	B7	79
Noatak, stm., Ak., U.S.	B7	79
Nobel, On., Can.	E4	73
Nobeoka, Japan	J5	33
Noble, Il., U.S.	E5	90
Noble, La., U.S.	C2	95
Noble, Ok., U.S.	B4	113
Noble, co., In., U.S.	B7	91
Noble, co., Oh., U.S.	C4	112
Noble, co., Ok., U.S.	A4	113
Nobleboro, Me., U.S.	D3	96
Nobleford, Ab., Can.	E4	68
Nobles, co., Mn., U.S.	G3	100
Noblesville, In., U.S.	D6	91
Nobleton, Fl., U.S.	D4	86
Noboribetsu, Japan	E10	33
Nobscot Hill, hill, Ma., U.S.	B5	98
Nocatee, Fl., U.S.	E5	86
Nocona, Tx., U.S.	C4	120
Nodaway, co., Mo., U.S.	A3	102
Nodaway, stm., U.S.	A2	102
Node, Wy., U.S.	D8	127
Noel, Mo., U.S.	E3	102
Noel Paul's Brook, stm., Nf., Can.	D3	72
Noelville, On., Can.	A4	73
Nogal, N.M., U.S.	D4	108
Nogales, Mex.	n15	63
Nogales, Az., U.S.	F5	80
Nogara, Italy	D7	20
Nōgata, Japan	J5	33
Nogent-en-Bassigny, Fr.	C6	16
Nogent-le-Rotrou, Fr.	C4	16
Nogent [-sur-Marne], Fr.	g10	16
Nogent-sur-Seine, Fr.	C5	16
Noginsk, Sov. Un.	D12	27
Nogoyá, Arg.	A5	54
Nohar, India	F6	36
Noheji, Japan	F10	33
Noirmoutier, Île de, i., Fr.	D2	16
Noisy-le-Sec, Fr.	g10	16
Nojima, Cape, c., Japan	I9	33
Nokesville, Va., U.S.	B5	123
Nok Kundi, Pak.	G11	39
Nokomis, Sk., Can.	F3	75
Nokomis, Fl., U.S.	E4	86
Nokomis, Il., U.S.	D4	90
Nokomis, Lake, res., Wi., U.S.	C4	126
Nokou, Chad	C2	46
Nokrek, mtn., India	E13	37
Nola, Cen. Afr. Rep.	D3	46
Nola, Italy	D5	23
Nolan, Ms., U.S.	D3	101
Nolan, Tx., U.S.	C2	120
Nolan, W.V., U.S.	D2	125
Nolan, co., Tx., U.S.	C2	120
Nolensville, Tn., U.S.	B5	119
Nolichucky, stm., Tn., U.S.	C10	119
Nolin, stm., Ky., U.S.	C3	94
Nolin Lake, res., Ky., U.S.	C3	94
Nolinsk, Sov. Un.	B3	28
Noma, Fl., U.S.	u16	86
Noma, Cape, c., Japan	K5	33
Nomans Land, i., Ma., U.S.	D6	98
Nombre de Dios, Pan.	h12	62
Nomény, Fr.	F6	17
Nomgon, Mong.	C1	32
Nominingue, P.Q., Can.	C2	74
Nomonea, is., Micron.	Q18	52
Nonacho Lake, l., N.T., Can.	D11	66
Nondalton, Ak., U.S.	C8	79
Nonesuch, stm., Me., U.S.	g7	96
Nong'an, China	C10	31
Nong Khai, Thai.	B2	34
Nongoma, S. Afr.	C5	49
Nonoava, Mex.	B3	63
Nonquit Pond, l., R.I., U.S.	E6	116
Nonsuch, Wa., U.S.	A3	124
Nooksack, North Fork, stm., Wa., U.S.	A4	124
Nooksack, South Fork, stm., Wa., U.S.	A3	124
Noonan, N.D., U.S.	A2	111
Noone, N.H., U.S.	E3	106
Noordpunt, c., Neth. Ant.	H18	65
Noordwijk-Binnen, Neth.	B4	17
Noorvik, Ak., U.S.	B7	79
Nootka Island, i., Can.	E4	69
Nootka Sound, strt., B.C., Can.	E4	69
Nopiming Provincial Park, Mb., Can.	D3	70
Noquebay, Lake, l., Wi., U.S.	C6	126
Nóqui, Ang.	C2	48
Nora, Swe.	H6	14
Nora, Il., U.S.	A4	90
Noranda, P.Q., Can.	k11	74
Nora Springs, Ia., U.S.	A5	92
Norbertville, P.Q., Can.	C6	74
Norborne, Mo., U.S.	B4	102
Norcatur, Ks., U.S.	C3	93
Norco, Ca., U.S.	*n13	82
Norco, La., U.S.	D5	95
Norcross, Ga., U.S.	C2	87
Norcross, Mn., U.S.	E2	100
Nord, dept., Fr.	D2	17
Nord, Canal du, Fr.	D3	17
Nordborg, Den.	C3	15
Nordegg, Ab., Can.	C2	68
Nordegg, stm., Ab., Can.	C3	68
Norden, F.R.Ger.	B3	18
Nordenham, F.R.Ger.	B4	18
Norderney, F.R.Ger.	A7	17
Norderney, i., F.R.Ger.	B3	18
Norderstedt, F.R.Ger.	*B5	18
Nordhausen, Ger.D.R.	C5	18
Nordhorn, F.R.Ger.	B3	18
Nordjylland, co., Den.	B3	15
Nordland, Wa., U.S.	A3	124
Nordmaling, Swe.	F8	14
Nördlingen, F.R.Ger.	D5	18
Nordostrundingen, c., Grnld.	A19	61
Nordreisa, Nor.	C9	14
Nordrhein-Westfalen, state, F.R.Ger.	B2	19
Nordstrand, i., F.R.Ger.	A4	18
Nore, stm., Ire.	D3	10
Norene, Tn., U.S.	A5	119
Norfolk, Ct., U.S.	B3	84
Norfolk, Ma., U.S.	h10	98
Norfolk, Ne., U.S.	B8	104
Norfolk, N.Y., U.S.	f9	109
Norfolk, Va., U.S.	D6	123
Norfolk, co., On., Can.	E4	73
Norfolk, co., Eng., U.K.	B8	12
Norfolk, co., Ma., U.S.	B5	98
Norfolk Island, dep., Oc.	H10	6
Norfolk Naval Base, mil., Va., U.S.	k15	123
Norfolk Naval Shipyard, mil., Va., U.S.	k15	123
Norfork, Ar., U.S.	A3	81
Norfork Dam, Ar., U.S.	A3	81
Norfork Lake, res., U.S.	A3	81
Norge, Ok., U.S.	C4	113
Norias, Tx., U.S.	F4	120
Norilsk, Sov. Un.	C11	29
Norland, Fl., U.S.	s13	86
Norlina, N.C., U.S.	A4	110
Norma, N.J., U.S.	E2	107
Norma, N.D., U.S.	A4	111
Norman, Tn., U.S.	C9	119
Norman, Al., U.S.	A3	78
Norman, In., U.S.	G5	91
Norman, Ne., U.S.	D7	104
Norman, N.C., U.S.	B3	110
Norman, Ok., U.S.	B4	113
Norman, co., Mn., U.S.	C2	100
Norman, stm., Austl.	B7	50
Normanby, stm., Austl.	B7	50
Normandy, Mo., U.S.	f13	102
Normandy, Tn., U.S.	B5	119
Normandy, Hills of, hills, Fr.	C3	16
Normandy Beach, N.J., U.S.	C4	107
Normangee, Tx., U.S.	D4	120
Norman Island, i., V.I., Br.	B6	65
Norman Park, Ga., U.S.	E3	87
Normanton, Austl.	C7	50
Normantown, W.V., U.S.	C4	125
Norman Wells, N.T., Can.	C7	66
Norphlet, Ar., U.S.	D3	81
Norquincó, Arg.	C2	54
Norquay, Sk., Can.	F4	75
Norrahammar, Swe.	A8	15
Nørre Aby, Den.	C3	15
Norridge, Il., U.S.	k9	90
Norridgewock, Me., U.S.	D3	96
Norris, Mt., U.S.	E5	103
Norris, S.C., U.S.	B2	117
Norris, S.D., U.S.	D4	118
Norris, Tn., U.S.	C9	119
Norris Arm, Nf., Can.	D4	72
Norris City, Il., U.S.	F5	90
Norris Dam, Tn., U.S.	C9	119
Norris Lake, res., Tn., U.S.	C10	119
Norris Point, Nf., Can.	D3	72
Norristown, Pa., U.S.	F11	115
Norrköping, Swe.	H7	14
Norrland, Swe.	H8	14
Norseman, Austl.	F3	50
Norte, Cabo, c., Braz.	B5	59
Norte, Canal do, strt., Braz.	B4	59
Norte, Punta, c., Arg.	C4	54
Norte, Serra do, plat., Braz.	E3	59
Norte de Santander, dept., Col.	B3	60
Nortelândia, Braz.	A1	56
North, S.C., U.S.	D5	117
North, Va., U.S.	C6	123
North, stm., Nf., Can.	D3	72
North, stm., Al., U.S.	B2	78
North, stm., Ia., U.S.	C3	92
North, stm., Ma., U.S.	h12	98
North, stm., Ma., U.S.	B5	98
North, stm., W.V., U.S.	B6	125
North Abington, Ma., U.S.	B6	98
North Acton, Ma., U.S.	f10	98
North Adams, Ma., U.S.	A1	98
North Albany, Or., U.S.	k11	114
Northallerton, Eng., U.K.	F7	13
Northam, Austl.	F2	50
North America	E11	61
North Amherst, Ma., U.S.	B2	98
North Amityville, N.Y., U.S.	*n15	109
North Andaman, i., India	F9	36
North and Bent Pyramids, hist., Egypt	E3	41
North Andrews Gardens, Fl., U.S.	*r13	86
North Anson, Me., U.S.	D3	96
North Apollo, Pa., U.S.	E2	115
North Arapaho Peak, mtn., Co., U.S.	A5	83
North Arlington, N.J., U.S.	h8	107
North Atlanta, Ga., U.S.	h8	87
North Attleboro, Ma., U.S.	C5	98
North Augusta, On., Can.	C9	73
North Augusta, S.C., U.S.	D4	117
North Aulatsivik Island, i., Nf., Can.	f9	72
North Aurora, Il., U.S.	k8	90
North Avondale, Co., U.S.	C6	83
North Babylon, N.Y., U.S.	*n15	109
North Baltimore, Oh., U.S.	A2	112
North Bangor, N.Y., U.S.	f10	109
North Battleford, Sk., Can.	E1	75
North Bay, On., Can.	A5	73
North Beach, Md., U.S.	C4	97
North Belgrade, Me., U.S.	D3	96
North Bellmore, N.Y., U.S.	*n15	109
North Belmont, N.C., U.S.	B1	110
North Bend, B.C., Can.	E7	69
North Bend, Ne., U.S.	C9	104
North Bend, Oh., U.S.	o12	112
North Bend, Or., U.S.	D2	114
North Bend, Pa., U.S.	D6	115
North Bend, Wi., U.S.	D2	126
North Bennington, Vt., U.S.	F2	122
North Bergen, N.J., U.S.	h8	107
North Berwick, Scot., U.K.	D6	13
North Berwick, Me., U.S.	E2	96
North Billerica, Ma., U.S.	A5	98
North Bloomfield, Oh., U.S.	A5	112
North Bonneville, Wa., U.S.	D4	124
North Borneo see Sabah, state, Malay.	A3	124
North Braddock, Pa., U.S.	*k14	115
North Bradford, Me., U.S.	C4	96
North Bradley, Mi., U.S.	E6	99
North Branch, Mi., U.S.	E7	99
North Branch, Mn., U.S.	E6	100
North Branch, N.H., U.S.	D3	106
North Branch, N.J., U.S.	B3	107
North Branford, Ct., U.S.	D4	84
North Breakers, rf., Mid. Is.	J3	52
North Bridgeton, Me., U.S.	D2	96
North Brookfield, Ma., U.S.	B3	98
North Brother, mtn., Me., U.S.	C4	96
North Brunswick, N.J., U.S.	C4	107
North Buena Vista, Ia., U.S.	B7	92
North Caldwell, N.J., U.S.	B4	107
North Canadian, stm., Ok., U.S.	A5	113
North Canton, Ct., U.S.	B4	84
North Canton, Ga., U.S.	B2	87
North Canton, Oh., U.S.	B4	112
North Cape, Wi., U.S.	n11	126
North Cape, c., P.E., Can.	B6	71
North Cape, c., N.Z.	K14	51
North Cape, c., Nor.	B11	14
North Cape, c., N.C., U.S.	A13	128
North Cape May, N.J., U.S.	F3	107
North Carolina, state, U.S.	B3	110
North Carrollton, Ms., U.S.	B4	101
North Carver, Ma., U.S.	C6	98
North Cascades National Park, Wa., U.S.	A4	124
North Cay, i., Bah.	m17	64
North Channel, strt., On., Can.	A2	73
North Channel, strt., U.K.	C3	10
North Charleston, S.C., U.S.	F8	117
North Charlestown, N.H., U.S.	D2	106
North Chatham, N.H., U.S.	B4	106
North Chicago, Il., U.S.	A6	90
North Chichester, N.H., U.S.	D4	106
North City, Wa., U.S.	*B3	124
North Clarendon, Vt., U.S.	D3	122
Northcliffe, Austl.	F2	50
North Cohasset, Ma., U.S.	g12	98
North Cohocton, N.Y., U.S.	C3	109
North College Hill, Oh., U.S.	o12	112
North Collins, N.Y., U.S.	C2	109
North Concord, Vt., U.S.	B5	122
North Conway, N.H., U.S.	B4	106
North Corbin, Ky., U.S.	D5	94
Northcote, Austl.	*G8	50
North Creek, N.Y., U.S.	B7	109
North Crossett, Ar., U.S.	D4	81
North Crows Nest, In., U.S.	k10	91
North Dakota, state, U.S.	B5	111
North Danville, Vt., U.S.	C4	122
North Dartmouth, Ma., U.S.	C6	98
North Decatur, Ga., U.S.	*h8	87
North Dighton, Ma., U.S.	C5	98
North Dixmont, Me., U.S.	D3	96
North Downs, hills, Eng., U.K.	C4	12
North Druid Hills, Ga., U.S.	h8	87
North Eagle Butte, S.D., U.S.	B4	118
North East, Md., U.S.	A6	97
North East, Pa., U.S.	B2	115
Northeast, stm., Md., U.S.	A6	97
Northeast Cape, c., Ak., U.S.	C6	79
Northeast Cape Fear, stm., N.C., U.S.	C5	110
North East Carry, Me., U.S.	C3	96
Northeastern, prov., Kenya	A6	48
North Eastham, Ma., U.S.	C8	98
Northeast Henrietta, N.Y., U.S.	B3	109
Northeast Islands, is., Micron.		
North East Land, i.,	A13	128
Northeast Point, c., Nf., Can.	B4	72
Northeast Polder, reg., Neth.	B5	17
North East Point, l., N.H., U.S.	D5	106
Northeast Providence Channel, strt., Bah.	B5	64
North Edisto, stm., S.C., U.S.	k11	117
North Egremont, Ma., U.S.	B1	98
Northeim, F.R.Ger.	C4	18
North English, Ia., U.S.	C5	92
North Enid, Ok., U.S.	A4	113
Northern, prov., Ghana	D5	48
Northern, prov., Mwi.	D5	48
Northern, prov., Zam.	D5	48
Northern Arm, Nf., Can.	D4	72
Northern Cheyenne Indian Reservation, Mt., U.S.	E10	103
Northern Donets, stm., Sov. Un.	G13	27
Northern Dvina, stm., Sov. Un.	E7	29
Northern Head, c., N.B., Can.	E3	71
Northern Indian Lake, l., Mb., Can.	A3	70
Northern Ireland, ter., U.K.	C3	10
Northern Mariana Islands, ter., T.T.P.I.	E8	6
Northern Range, mts., Trin.	N23	65
Northern Sporades, is., Grc.	C5	25
Northern Territory, ter., Austl.	C5	50
North Esk, stm., Scot., U.K.	E6	13
North Fairfield, Oh., U.S.	A3	112
North Fair Oaks, Ca., U.S.	k8	82
North Falmouth, Ma., U.S.	C6	98
North Ferrisburg, Vt., U.S.	C2	122
Northfield, B.C., Can.	f12	69
Northfield, Ct., U.S.	C3	84
Northfield, Il., U.S.	*h9	90
Northfield, Me., U.S.	D5	96
Northfield, Ma., U.S.	A3	98
Northfield, Mn., U.S.	F5	100
Northfield, N.H., U.S.	D3	106
Northfield, N.J., U.S.	E3	107
Northfield, Tx., U.S.	B2	120
Northfield, Vt., U.S.	C3	122
Northfield, Wi., U.S.	D2	126
Northfield Center, Vt., U.S.	C3	122
Northfield Falls, Vt., U.S.	C3	122
Northfield Mountains, mts., Vt., U.S.	C3	122
North Fond du Lac, Wi., U.S.	E5	126
Northford, Ct., U.S.	D4	84
North Foreland, c., Eng., U.K.	E7	10
North Fork, Ca., U.S.	D4	82
North Fork, Id., U.S.	D5	89
North Fork Reservoir, res., Or., U.S.	B4	114
North Fort Myers, Fl., U.S.	F5	86
North Fox Island, i., Mi., U.S.	C5	99
North Franklin, Ct., U.S.	C7	84
North Freedom, Wi., U.S.	E4	126
North Frisian Islands, is., Eur.	A4	18
North Fryeburg, Me., U.S.	D2	96
North Galiano, B.C., Can.	f12	69
Northgate, Sk., Can.	H4	75
Northgate, N.D., U.S.	A3	111
Northglenn, Co., U.S.	B6	83
North Gorham, Me., U.S.	g7	96
North Gower, On., Can.	B9	73
North Grafton, Ma., U.S.	B4	98
North Granby, Ct., U.S.	B4	84
North Great River, N.Y., U.S.	*n18	109
North Grosvenordale, Ct., U.S.	B8	84
North Gulfport, Ms., U.S.	E4	101
North Halawa Stream, stm., Hi., U.S.	g10	88
North Haledon, N.J., U.S.	B4	107
North Hampton, N.H., U.S.	E5	106
North Hanover, Ma., U.S.	h12	98
North Harpswell, Me., U.S.	g8	96
North Hartland, Vt., U.S.	D4	122
North Hartland Reservoir, res., Vt., U.S.	D4	122
North Hatfield, Ma., U.S.	B2	98
North Hatley, P.Q., Can.	D6	74
North Haven, Ct., U.S.	D4	84
North Haven, Me., U.S.	D3	96
North Haverhill, N.H., U.S.	B2	106
North Head, N.B., Can.	E3	71
North Henderson, Il., U.S.	B3	90
North Hero, Vt., U.S.	B2	122
North Hero Island, i., Vt., U.S.	B2	122
North Highlands, Ca., U.S.	*C3	82
North Holland, prov., Neth.	B4	17
North Holston, Va., U.S.	f10	123
North Horn Lake, l., Tn., U.S.	e8	119
North Horr, Kenya	A6	48
North Hudson, N.Y., U.S.	B7	109
North Hudson, Wi., U.S.	*C1	126
North Hyde Park, Vt., U.S.	B3	122
North Industry, Oh., U.S.	B4	112
North Inlet, b., S.C., U.S.	E9	117
North Island, i., N.Z.	M15	51
North Island, i., S.C., U.S.	E9	117
North Island Naval Air Station, mil., Ca., U.S.	o15	82
North Islands, is., La., U.S.	E7	95
North Java, N.Y., U.S.	C2	109
North Jay, Me., U.S.	D2	96
North Judson, In., U.S.	B4	91
North Kansas City, Mo., U.S.	h10	102
North Kingstown, R.I., U.S.	E4	116
North Kingsville, Oh., U.S.	A5	112
North Komelik, Az., U.S.	E4	80
North La Junta, Co., U.S.	C7	83
Northlake, Il., U.S.	k9	90
North Lake, Wi., U.S.	*m11	126
Northland, Wi., U.S.	C4	126
North Laramie, stm., Wy., U.S.	D7	127
North Las Vegas, Nv., U.S.	G6	105
North Lauderdale, Fl., U.S.	*r13	86
North La Veta Pass, Co., U.S.	D5	83
North Lawrence, N.Y., U.S.	f10	109
North Lemmon, N.D., U.S.	D3	111
North Liberty, In., U.S.	A5	91
North Liberty, Ia., U.S.	C6	92
North Lima, Oh., U.S.	B5	112
North Lindenhurst, N.Y., U.S.	*n15	109
North Little Rock, Ar., U.S.	C3	81
North Logan, Ut., U.S.	B4	121
North Loon Mountain, mtn., Id., U.S.	D3	89
North Loup, Ne., U.S.	C7	104
North Loup, stm., Ne., U.S.	B5	104
North Lubec, Me., U.S.	D5	96
North Magnetic Pole, N.T., Can.	m31	66
North Mamm Peak, mtn., Co., U.S.	B3	83
North Manchester, In., U.S.	C6	91
North Manitou Island, i., Mi., U.S.	C4	99
North Mankato, Mn., U.S.	F4	100
North Marshfield, Ma., U.S.	h12	98
North Massapequa, N.Y., U.S.	*E7	109
North Miami, Fl., U.S.	G6	86
North Miami, Ok., U.S.	A7	113
North Miami Beach, Fl., U.S.	s13	86
North Middleboro, Ma., U.S.	C6	98
North Middletown, Ky., U.S.	B5	94
North Monmouth, Me., U.S.	D3	96
North Montpelier, Vt., U.S.	C4	122
Northmoor, Mo., U.S.	h10	102
North Moose Lake, l., Mb., Can.	B1	70
North Mountain, mtn., Pa., U.S.	D9	115
North Muskegon, Mi., U.S.	E4	99
North Myrtle Beach, S.C., U.S.	D10	117
North Naples, Fl., U.S.	F5	86
North Negril Point, c., Jam.	E12	65
North Newcastle, Me., U.S.	D3	96
North New Hyde Park, N.Y., U.S.	*E7	109
North Newport, N.H., U.S.	D2	106

Name — Map Ref — Page

North New Portland, Me., U.S. D2 96
North New River Canal, Fl., U.S. F6 86
North Norwich, N.Y., U.S. C5 109
North Oaks, Ca., U.S. *E4 82
North Ogden, Ut., U.S. B4 121
North Olmsted, Oh., U.S. h9 112
North Omaha, Ne., U.S. g13 104
Northome, Mn., U.S. C4 100
North Orange, Ma., U.S. A3 98
North Oxford, Ma., U.S. B4 98
North Palisade, mtn., Ca., U.S. D4 82
North Palm Beach, Fl., U.S. *F6 86
North Park, Il., U.S. A4 90
North Park, val., Co., U.S. A4 83
North Parsonfield, Me., U.S. E2 96
North Pass, strt., La., U.S. E7 95
North Patchogue, N.Y., U.S. *n15 109
North Pembroke, Ma., U.S. B6 98
North Pitcher, N.Y., U.S. C5 109
North Plainfield, N.J., U.S. B4 107
North Plains, Or., U.S. B4 114
North Plains, pl., N.M., U.S. C1 108
North Platte, Ne., U.S. C5 104
North Platte, stm., U.S. B7 76
North Point, c., Barb. K20 65
North Point, c., Md., U.S. B5 97
North Point, c., Md., U.S. C5 97
North Point, c., Mi., U.S. C7 99
North Pole A1 128
North Pomfret, Vt., U.S. D4 122
North Pond, l., Me., U.S. D3 96
North Pond, l., Ma., U.S. h9 98
Northport, Al., U.S. B2 78
North Port, Fl., U.S. *D4 86
Northport, Mi., U.S. C5 99
Northport, Ne., U.S. C2 104
Northport, N.Y., U.S. *n15 109
Northport, Wa., U.S. A8 124
North Portal, Sk., Can. H4 75
North Powder, Or., U.S. B9 114
North Pownal, Me., U.S. g7 96
North Pownal, Vt., U.S. F2 122
North Prairie, Wi., U.S. F5 126
North Providence, R.I., U.S. C4 116
North Raccoon, stm., Ia., U.S. C3 92
North Range Corner, N.S., Can. E4 71
North Reading, Ma., U.S. f11 98
North Richland Hills, Tx., U.S. n9 120
Northridge, Oh., U.S. C2 112
North Ridgeville, Oh., U.S. A3 112
North Rim, Az., U.S. A3 80
North River Bridge, N.S., Can. C9 71
North Riverside, Il., U.S. *k9 90
North Robinson, Oh., U.S. B3 112
North Ronaldsay, i., Scot., U.K. A5 10
Northrop, Mn., U.S. G4 100
North Rose, N.Y., U.S. B4 109
North Royalton, Oh., U.S. h9 112
North Rustico, P.E., Can. C6 71
North Salem, In., U.S. E4 91
North Salem, N.H., U.S. E4 106
North Salt Lake, Ut., U.S. C4 121
North Sanbornton, N.H., U.S. C3 106
North Sandwich, N.H., U.S. C4 106
North Santee, stm., S.C., U.S. E9 117
North Saskatchewan, stm., Can. F10 66
North Schell Peak, mtn., Nv., U.S. D7 105
North Scituate, Ma., U.S. h12 98
North Scituate, R.I., U.S. C3 116
North Sea, Eur. D9 8
Norths Highland, plat., Ant. C25 7
North Shores, De., U.S. F5 85
North Shoshone Peak, mtn., Nv., U.S. D4 105
North Shrewsbury, Vt., U.S. D3 122
Northside, N.C., U.S. A4 110
North Sioux City, S.D., U.S. E9 118
North Skunk, stm., Ia., U.S. C5 92
North Sound, strt., Ire. D2 11
North Sound, strt., Scot., U.K. A6 13
North Spicer Island, i., N.T., Can. C17 66
North Springfield, Pa., U.S. B1 115
North Springfield, Vt., U.S. E3 122
North Springfield, Va., U.S. *B5 123
North Springfield Reservoir, res., Vt., U.S. E4 122
North Star, De., U.S. A3 85
North Star, Mi., U.S. E6 99
North Star, Oh., U.S. B1 112
North Stonington, Ct., U.S. D8 84
North St. Paul, Mn., U.S. m13 100
North Stradbroke, i., Austl. E9 50
North Stratford, N.H., U.S. A3 106
North Sudbury, Ma., U.S. g10 98
North Sutton, N.H., U.S. D3 106
North Swansea, Ma., U.S. C5 98
North Swanzey, N.H., U.S. E2 106
North Sydney, Austl. *F9 50
North Sydney, N.S., Can. C9 71
North Syracuse, N.Y., U.S. B4 109
North Taranaki Bight, N.Z. M15 51
North Tarrytown, N.Y., U.S. D7 109
North Tea Lake, l., On., Can. B5 73
North Terre Haute, In., U.S. E3 91
North Tewksbury, Ma., U.S. A5 98
North Thetford, Vt., U.S. D4 122
North Thompson, stm., B.C., Can. D8 69
North Tolsta, Scot., U.K. B2 13
North Tonawanda, N.Y., U.S. B2 109
North Troy, Vt., U.S. B4 122
North Truro, Ma., U.S. *B7 98
North Tunbridge, Vt., U.S. D4 122
North Tunica, Ms., U.S. A3 101
North Turner Mountain, mtn., Me., U.S. C4 96
North Twin Lake, l., Nf., Can. D4 72
North Twin Lake, l., Wi., U.S. B4 126
North Tyne, stm., Eng., U.K. E6 13
North Uist, i., Scot., U.K. B3 10
Northumberland, N.H., U.S. A3 106
Northumberland, Pa., U.S. E8 115
Northumberland, co., N.B., Can. B3 71
Northumberland, co., On., Can. C7 73
Northumberland, co., Eng., U.K. E6 13
Northumberland, co., Pa., U.S. D8 115
Northumberland, co., Va., U.S. C6 123
Northumberland Isles, is., Austl. D9 50
Northumberland Strait, strt., Can. C6 71
North Umpqua, stm., Or., U.S. D3 114
North Uxbridge, Ma., U.S. B4 98
Northvale, N.J., U.S. g9 109
North Valley Stream, N.Y., U.S. *n15 109

North Vancouver, B.C., Can. E6 69
North Vassalboro, Me., U.S. D3 96
North Vernon, In., U.S. F6 91
North Versailles, Pa., U.S. *k14 115
North Village, N.H., U.S. E3 106
Northville, Ct., U.S. C2 84
Northville, Mi., U.S. p15 99
Northville, N.Y., U.S. B6 109
Northville, S.D., U.S. B7 118
North Wabasca Lake, l., Ab., Can. A4 68
North Waldoboro, Me., U.S. D3 96
North Wales, Pa., U.S. F11 115
North Walpole, N.H., U.S. D2 106
North Walsham, Eng., U.K. D7 10
North Wantagh, N.Y., U.S. *n15 109
North Warren, Pa., U.S. C3 115
North Waterford, Me., U.S. D2 96
North Webster, In., U.S. B6 91
Northway, Ak., U.S. C11 79
North West, dept., Guy. A3 59
North West Cape, c., Austl. D1 50
North Westchester, Ct., U.S. C6 84
North-Western, prov., Zam. D4 48
Northwest Highlands, plat., Scot., U.K. B4 10
North Westminster, Vt., U.S. E4 122
Northwest Miramichi, stm., N.B., Can. B3 71
Northwest Polder, reg., Neth. B5 17
Northwest Providence Channel, strt., Bah. A4 64
North West River, Nf., Can. B1 72
Northwest Territories, prov., Can. C13 66
Northwest Upsalquitch, stm., N.B., Can. B3 71
Northwich, Eng., U.K. A5 12
North Wildwood, N.J., U.S. E3 107
North Wilkesboro, N.C., U.S. A1 110
North Wilmington, Ma., U.S. f11 98
North Windham, Ct., U.S. C7 84
North Windham, Me., U.S. E2 96
Northwood, Ia., U.S. A4 92
Northwood, N.H., U.S. D4 106
Northwood, N.D., U.S. B8 111
Northwood, Oh., U.S. *c7 112
Northwood Center, N.H., U.S. D4 106
Northwood Ridge, N.H., U.S. D4 106
Northwoods, Mo., U.S. *f13 102
North Woodstock, Ct., U.S. B8 84
North Woodstock, N.H., U.S. B3 106
North Yarmouth, Me., U.S. g7 96
North York, On., Can. D5 73
North York, Pa., U.S. G8 115
North York Moors, hills, Eng., U.K. C6 10
North Yorkshire, co., Eng., U.K. F7 13
North Zulch, Tx., U.S. D4 120
Norton, N.B., Can. D4 71
Norton, Eng., U.K. F8 13
Norton, Ks., U.S. C4 93
Norton, Ma., U.S. C5 98
Norton, Oh., U.S. A4 112
Norton, Tx., U.S. D2 120
Norton, Va., U.S. f9 123
Norton, W.V., U.S. C5 125
Norton, co., Ks., U.S. C4 93
Norton Air Force Base, mil., Ca., U.S. E5 82
Norton Bay, b., Ak., U.S. C7 79
Norton Creek, stm., Al., U.S. B1 78
Norton Pond, l., Vt., U.S. B5 122
Norton Reservoir, res., Ks., U.S. C3 93
Nortons Corner, Az., U.S. D4 80
Norton Shores, Mi., U.S. E4 99
Norton Sound, strt., Ak., U.S. C6 79
Nortonville, Ks., U.S. C8 93
Nortonville, Ky., U.S. C2 94
Nortonville, N.D., U.S. C7 111
Nortorf, F.R.Ger. D3 15
Norvegia, Cape, c., Ant. B11 7
Norwalk, Ct., U.S. n12 82
Norwalk, Ca., U.S. E2 84
Norwalk, Ia., U.S. C4 92
Norwalk, Oh., U.S. A3 112
Norwalk, Wi., U.S. E3 126
Norwalk Islands, is., Ct., U.S. E2 84
Norway, In., U.S. C4 91
Norway, Ia., U.S. C6 92
Norway, Ks., U.S. C6 93
Norway, Me., U.S. D2 96
Norway, Mi., U.S. C3 99
Norway, Or., U.S. D2 114
Norway, S.C., U.S. E5 117
Norway, ctry., Eur. F4 14
Norway House, Mb., Can. C3 70
Norway Lake, l., Mn., U.S. E3 100
Norwegian Bay, b., N.T., Can. m33 66
Norwegian Sea, Eur. C14 128
Norwell, Ma., U.S. h12 98
Norwich, On., Can. E4 73
Norwich, Eng., U.K. D7 10
Norwich, Ct., U.S. C7 84
Norwich, Ks., U.S. E6 93
Norwich, N.Y., U.S. C5 109
Norwich, N.D., U.S. A5 111
Norwich, Vt., U.S. D4 122
Norwood, On., Can. C7 73
Norwood, Ca., U.S. C2 83
Norwood, Co., U.S. C4 87
Norwood, Ga., U.S. C4 87
Norwood, La., U.S. D4 95
Norwood, Ma., U.S. B5 98
Norwood, Mn., U.S. F5 100
Norwood, N.J., U.S. h9 107
Norwood, N.Y., U.S. f10 109
Norwood, N.C., U.S. B2 110
Norwood, Oh., U.S. o13 112
Norwood, Pa., U.S. p20 115
Norwottock, Mount, mtn., Ma., U.S. B3 98
Nosbonsing, Lake, l., On., Can. A5 73
Noshiro, Japan F9 33
Nösjön, l., Swe. A6 15
Nossa Senhora das Dores, Braz. D3 57
Nossen, Ger.D.R. B8 19
Noss Head, c., Scot., U.K. C5 13
Nossob, stm., Afr. C3 49
Nosy Varika, Madag. h9 49
Notch Hill, B.C., Can. D8 69
Notch Mountain, mtn., Ma., U.S. A3 98
Notch Peak, mtn., Ut., U.S. D2 121
Noteć, stm., Pol. B3 26
Notikewin, Ab., Can. A2 68
Notikewin, stm., Ab., Can. A1 68

Noto, Italy F5 23
Noto, Gulf of, b., Italy F5 23
Notodden, Nor. H3 14
Noto Island, i., Japan H8 33
Notoue, Kir. R18 52
Noto Peninsula, pen., Japan D12 31
Notre-Dame, N.B., Can. C5 71
Notre Dame, Monts, mts., P.Q., Can. k13 74
Notre Dame Bay, b., Nf., Can. D4 72
Notre-Dame-de-Lourdes, Mb., Can. E2 70
Notre-Dame-de-Montauban, P.Q., Can. C5 74
Notre-Dame-des-Bois, P.Q., Can. D6 74
Notre-Dame-du-Lac, P.Q., Can. B9 74
Notre-Dame-du-Laus, P.Q., Can. C2 74
Nottawa, On., Can. C4 73
Nottawasaga Bay, b., On., C4 73
Nottaway, stm., P.Q., Can. h11 74
Nottely Lake, res., Ga., U.S. B2 87
Nottingham, Eng., U.K. D6 10
Nottingham, N.H., U.S. D4 106
Nottingham Island, i., N.T., Can. D17 66
Nottinghamshire, co., Eng., U.K. A7 12
Nottoway, Va., U.S. C4 123
Nottoway, co., Va., U.S. C4 123
Nottoway, stm., Va., U.S. D5 123
Notukeu Creek, stm., Sk., Can. H2 75
Notus, Id., U.S. F2 89
Nouadhibou, Maur. B1 45
Nouakchott, Maur. C1 45
Nouamrhar, Maur. C1 45
Nouméa, N. Cal. H10 6
Nouna, Burkina D4 45
Noupoort, S. Afr. D3 49
Noutonice, Czech. n17 26
Nouvelle-France, Cap de c., P.Q., Can. D18 66
Nouzonville, Fr. C6 16
Nova, Oh., U.S. A3 112
Nova Caipemba, Ang. C1 48
Nova Cruz, Braz. C3 57
Nova Friburgo, Braz. C4 56
Nova Iguaçu, Braz. h6 56
Nova Lima, Braz. C4 56
Nova Londrina, Braz. C2 56
Nova Lusitânia, Moz. A5 49
Nova Mambone, Moz. B6 49
Nova Olinda do Norte, Braz. C3 57
Nova Ponte, Braz. B3 56
Nova Prata, Braz. D2 56
Novar, On., Can. B5 73
Novara, Italy B2 23
Nova Roma, Braz. A3 56
Nova Russas, Braz. C2 57
Nova Scotia, prov., Can. D6 71
Nova Sofala, Moz. B5 49
Nova Soure, Braz. D3 57
Novate Mezzola, Italy D7 21
Novato, Ca., U.S. C2 82
Nova Varoš, Yugo. D4 24
Nova Venécia, Braz. B4 56
Nova Vida, Braz. B3 55
Novaya Astrakhan, Sov. Un. p21 27
Novaya Kazanka, Sov. Un. F18 8
Novaya Ladoga, Sov. Un. A9 27
Novaya Lyalya, Sov. Un. D9 29
Novaya Odessa, Sov. Un. H8 27
Novaya Sibir Island, i., Sov. Un. B17 29
Novaya Zemlya, is., Sov. Un. B8 29
Nova Zagora, Bul. D8 24
Novelda, Spain C5 22
Novelty, Mo., U.S. A5 102
Nové Město [nad Váhom], Czech. D4 26
Nové Strašecí, Czech. C8 19
Nové Zámky, Czech. E5 26
Novgorod, Sov. Un. D5 28
Novgorod-Severskiy, Sov. Un. E9 27
Novi, Mex. p15 99
Novice, Tx., U.S. D3 120
Novigrad, Yugo. C2 24
Novi Ligure, Italy B2 23
Novinger, Mo., U.S. A5 102
Novi Pazar, Bul. D8 24
Novi Pazar, Yugo. D5 24
Novi Sad, Yugo. C4 24
Novo, stm., Braz. g6 56
Novo Airão, Braz. C2 59
Novoaltaysk, Sov. Un. E25 8
Novoanninskiy, Sov. Un. C2 28
Novo Aripuaná, Braz. C3 59
Novoaydar, Sov. Un. G12 27
Novocherkassk, Sov. Un. H13 27
Nôvo Cruzeiro, Braz. B4 56
Novoekonomicheskoye, Sov. Un. q20 27
Novograd-Volynskiy, Sov. Un. F6 27
Novogrudok, Sov. Un. E5 27
Novokazalinsk, Sov. Un. E6 28
Novokubyshevsk, Sov. Un. *D7 29
Novokuybyshevsk, Sov. Un. B7 33
Novokuznetsk, Sov. Un. D11 29
Novo Mesto, Yugo. C2 24
Novomirgorod, Sov. Un. G8 27
Novomoskovsk, Sov. Un. G10 27
Novomoskovsk, Sov. Un. D6 29
Novopokrovskaya, Sov. Un. I13 27
Novorossiysk, Sov. Un. I6 29
Novo-Selo, Bul. C6 24
Novoshakhtinsk, Sov. Un. H12 27
Novosibirsk, Sov. Un. D11 29
Novosibirsk Reservoir, res., Sov. Un. C10 28
Novosil, Sov. Un. E11 27
Novotroitsk, Sov. Un. D6 29
Novoukrainka, Sov. Un. G8 27
Novoyeniseyskaya, Sov. Un. B11 33
Novozybkov, Sov. Un. E8 27

Nowra-Bomaderry, Austl. G8 50
Nowshāk, mtn., Asia k17 39
Nowy Dwór, Pol. B6 26
Nowy Targ, Pol. D6 26
Nowy Sącz, Pol. D6 26
Nowy Tomyśl, Pol. B4 26
Noxapater, Ms., U.S. C4 101
Noxen, Pa., U.S. D9 115
Noxon, Mt., U.S. C1 103
Noxon Reservoir, res., Mt., U.S. C1 103
Noxontown Lake, res., De., U.S. C3 85
Noxubee, co., Ms., U.S. B5 101
Noxubee, stm., U.S. B5 101
Noya, Spain A1 22
Noyes, Mn., U.S. B1 100
Noyes Island, i., Ak., U.S. n22 79
Noyon, Fr. C5 16
Nozeroy, Fr. C1 21
Nsanje, Mwi. E6 48
Nsawam, Ghana E4 45
Nsukka, Nig. E6 45
Ntem, stm., Afr. E2 46
Nuatabu, Kir. R18 52
Nubanusit Lake, l., N.H., U.S. D2 106
Nubārīyah, Tur'at an, Eg. B3 41
Nuberg, Ga., U.S. B4 87
Nubian Desert, des., Sud. A3 47
Nuckolls, co., Ne., U.S. D7 104
Nucla, Co., U.S. C2 83
Nueces, co., Tx., U.S. F4 120
Nueces, stm., Tx., U.S. E3 120
Nueltin Lake, l., Can. D13 66
Nueva Antioquia, Col. B4 60
Nueva Asunción, dept., Para. D3 55
Nueva Casas Grandes, Mex. A3 63
Nueva Esparta, state, Ven. A5 60
Nueva Gerona, Cuba D2 64
Nueva Imperial, Chile B2 54
Nueva Lubecka, Arg. C2 54
Nueva Ocotepeque, Hond. C3 62
Nueva Palmira, Ur. E1 56
Nueva Providencia, Pan. k11 62
Nueva Rosita, Mex. B4 63
Nueva San Salvador, El Sal. D3 62
Nueve de Julio, Arg. B4 54
Nuevitas, Cuba D5 64
Nuevo, Golfo de, b., Arg. C4 54
Nuevo Emperador, Pan. m11 62
Nuevo Laredo, Mex. B5 63
Nuevo León, state, Mex. B5 63
Nuevo San Juan, Pan. k11 62
Nūḥ, Rās, c., Pak. I11 39
Nukhayb, Iraq G14 40
Nukhaylah, well, Sud. B2 47
Nuits, Fr. D6 16
Nukhayb, Iraq G14 40
Nuku'alofa, Tonga H11 6
Nukus, Sov. Un. E5 28
Nulato, Ak., U.S. C8 79
Nules, Spain C5 22
Nulhegan, stm., Vt., U.S. B5 122
Nullagine, Austl. D3 50
Nullarbor Plain, pl., Austl. F4 50
Numa, Ia., U.S. D5 92
Numan, Nig. E7 45
Numazu, Japan I9 33
Numfoor, i., Indon. F8 34
Numila, Hi., U.S. B2 88
Nu Mine, Pa., U.S. E3 115
Nunawading, Austl. *G8 50
Nuneaton, Eng., U.K. B6 12
Nunez, Ga., U.S. D4 87
Nunica, Mi., U.S. E4 99
Nunivak Island, i., Ak., U.S. D6 79
Nunn, Co., U.S. A6 83
Nunnelly, Tn., U.S. B4 119
Nuoro, Italy D2 23
Nuqui, Col. B2 60
Nura, stm., Sov. Un. E23 8
Nuremberg see Nürnberg, F.R.Ger. D5 18
Nuremberg, Pa., U.S. E9 115
Nuri, Mex. B3 63
Nürtingen, F.R.Ger. D5 18
Nus, Italy E3 21
Nusaybin, Tur. D13 40
Nushki, Pak. C4 36
Nusle (part of Prague), Czech. n17 26
Nut Lake, l., Sk., Can. E4 75
Nutley, N.J., U.S. B4 107
Nut Mountain, Sk., Can. E4 75
Nutrioso, Az., U.S. D6 80
Nutter Fort, W.V., U.S. k10 125
Nutting Lake, Ma., U.S. f10 98
Nutwood, Il., U.S. D3 90
Nuuanu Pali, Hi., U.S. g10 88
Nu'utele Island, i., W. Sam. G12 6
Nuutoi, Cape, i., W. Sam. G12 6
Nuwara-Eliya, Sri L. B5 113
Nuyaka, Ok., U.S. B5 113
Nüzvīd, India I8 37
Nyac, Ak., U.S. C8 79
Nyack, N.Y., U.S. D7 109
Nyala, Sud. C1 47
Nyamandhlovu, Zimb. A4 49
Nyamtumbo, Tan. D6 48
Nyandoma, Sov. Un. C7 29
Nyanza, Rw. B4 48
Nyanza, prov., Kenya B5 48
Nyasa, Lake, l., Afr. D5 48
Nyborg, Swe. I6 14
Nyda, Sov. Un. B23 8
Nye, Mt., U.S. E7 103
Nye, co., Nv., U.S. E5 105
Nyeri, Kenya B5 48
Nyima, Tan. D5 48
Nyimba, Zam. D5 48
Nyíregyháza, Hung. B5 24
Nykøbing, Den. I3 14
Nykøbing Falster, Den. C5 15
Nykøbing Sjælland, Den. H7 14
Nyköping, Swe. H8 14
Nylstroom, S. Afr. B4 49
Nymagee, Austl. F6 51
Nymburk, Czech. E5 26
Nynäshamn, Swe. H8 14
Nyngan, Austl. F6 51
Nyon, Switz. E3 18
Nyong, stm., Cam. E2 46
Nýřany, Czech. D1 26
Nýrsko, Czech. D8 19

Nysa, Pol. C4 26
Nyssa, Or., U.S. D9 114
Nysted, Den. D5 15
Nyunzu, Zaire C4 48
Nzega, Tan. B5 48
Nzérékoré, Gui. E3 45
N'zeto, Ang. C1 48
Nzwani, i., Com. f8 49

O

Oacoma, S.D., U.S. D6 118
Oahe, Lake, res., U.S. A7 76
Oahe Dam, S.D., U.S. C5 118
Oahu, i., Hi., U.S. B4 88
Oakalla, Tx., U.S. D4 120
Oak Bay, B.C., Can. h12 69
Oak Bay, N.B., Can. D2 71
Oak Bluffs, Ma., U.S. D6 98
Oakboro, N.C., U.S. B2 110
Oak Brook, Il., U.S. *k9 90
Oakburn, Mb., Can. D1 70
Oak City, Ut., U.S. D3 121
Oak Creek, Co., U.S. A4 83
Oak Creek, Wi., U.S. n12 126
Oakdale, Ca., U.S. D3 82
Oakdale, Ct., U.S. D7 84
Oakdale, Ga., U.S. h8 87
Oakdale, Il., U.S. E4 90
Oakdale, La., U.S. D3 95
Oakdale, Ma., U.S. B4 98
Oakdale, Mn., U.S. *n13 100
Oakdale, Ne., U.S. B8 104
Oakdale, N.Y., U.S. *n15 109
Oakdale, Pa., U.S. k13 115
Oakdale, Tn., U.S. D9 119
Oakengates, Eng., U.K. B5 12
Oakes, N.D., U.S. C7 111
Oakesdale, Wa., U.S. B8 124
Oakey, Austl. C8 51
Oakfield, Ga., U.S. E3 87
Oakfield, Me., U.S. B4 96
Oakfield, N.Y., U.S. B2 109
Oakfield, Tn., U.S. B3 119
Oakfield, Wi., U.S. E5 126
Oakford, Il., U.S. C4 90
Oak Forest, Il., U.S. *k9 90
Oak Grove, Ar., U.S. A2 81
Oak Grove, Ky., U.S. D2 94
Oak Grove, La., U.S. B4 95
Oak Grove, Mi., U.S. F7 99
Oak Grove, Or., U.S. B4 114
Oak Grove, S.C., U.S. C8 117
Oak Grove, Va., U.S. B6 123
Oakham, Eng., U.K. B7 12
Oakham, Ma., U.S. B3 98
Oak Harbor, Oh., U.S. A2 112
Oak Harbor, Wa., U.S. A3 124
Oak Hill, De., U.S. *B3 85
Oak Hill, Fl., U.S. D6 86
Oak Hill, Ks., U.S. *C6 93
Oak Hill, Oh., U.S. D3 112
Oak Hill, W.V., U.S. D3 125
Oak Hill, mtn., Ma., U.S. f9 98
Oakhurst, N.J., U.S. C4 107
Oakhurst, Ok., U.S. A5 113
Oak Island, i., Wi., U.S. B3 126
Oak Lake, Mb., Can. E1 70
Oak Lake, l., Mb., Can. E1 70
Oakland, On., Can. D4 73
Oakland, Al., U.S. A2 78
Oakland, Ar., U.S. A3 81
Oakland, Fl., U.S. *F6 86
Oakland, Il., U.S. D5 90
Oakland, Ia., U.S. C2 92
Oakland, Ky., U.S. C3 94
Oakland, Me., U.S. D3 96
Oakland, Md., U.S. m12 97
Oakland, Ne., U.S. C9 104
Oakland, N.J., U.S. A4 107
Oakland, Ok., U.S. C5 113
Oakland, Or., U.S. D3 114
Oakland, Pa., U.S. C10 115
Oakland, R.I., U.S. B2 116
Oakland, Tn., U.S. B2 119
Oakland, co., Mi., U.S. F7 99
Oakland City, In., U.S. H3 91
Oakland Gardens, Ct., U.S. D5 84
Oakland Park, Fl., U.S. r13 86
Oak Lane Manor, De., U.S. *A3 85
Oak Lawn, Il., U.S. B6 90
Oak Lawn, Il., U.S. g12 93
Oakleigh, Austl. *G8 50
Oakley, Id., U.S. G5 89
Oakley, Ks., U.S. C3 93
Oakley, Mi., U.S. E6 99
Oakley, S.C., U.S. E6 117
Oakley, Ut., U.S. C4 121
Oaklyn, N.J., U.S. *D2 107
Oakman, Al., U.S. B2 78
Oakman, Ga., U.S. B2 87
Oakmont, Pa., U.S. E2 115
Oak Mountain, mtn., Tn., U.S. h11 119
Oakner, Mb., Can. D1 70
Oak Orchard, De., U.S. F5 85
Oak Park, Il., U.S. B6 90
Oak Park, Il., U.S. *k9 90
Oak Park, Mi., U.S. p15 99
Oak Point, Mb., Can. D2 70
Oak Ridge, La., U.S. B4 95
Oak Ridge, Mo., U.S. D8 102
Oak Ridge, N.C., U.S. A3 110
Oak Ridge, Or., U.S. D4 114
Oak Ridge, Tn., U.S. C9 119
Oak Ridge Reservoir, res., N.J., U.S. A3 107
Oak Ridges (part of Richmond Hill), On., Can. k15 73
Oak River, Mb., Can. D1 70
Oaks, Ok., U.S. A7 113
Oakton, Ky., U.S. f8 94
Oaktown, In., U.S. G3 91
Oak Vale, Ms., U.S. D4 101
Oak View, W.V., U.S. *D4 125
Oak Valley, N.J., U.S. *D2 107
Oakville, Mb., Can. E2 70
Oakville, Ct., U.S. C3 84
Oakville, Ia., U.S. C6 92
Oakville, Mo., U.S. g13 102

Oakville, Wa., U.S. C2 124
Oakway, S.C., U.S. B1 117
Oakwood, Ga., U.S. B3 87
Oakwood, Il., U.S. C6 90
Oakwood, N.D., U.S. A8 111
Oakwood, Oh., U.S. A1 112
Oakwood, Oh., U.S. C1 112
Oakwood, Ok., U.S. B3 113
Oakwood, Tx., U.S. D5 120
Oakwood, Va., U.S. e9 123
Oakwood Beach, N.J., U.S. D1 107
Oamaru, N.Z. P13 51
Ōamishirasato, Japan n19 33
Oark, Ar., U.S. B2 81
Oasis, Ut., U.S. D3 121
Oatman, Az., U.S. C1 80
Oats, S.C., U.S. C7 117
Oaxaca, state, Mex. D5 63
Oaxaca [de Juárez], Mex. D5 63
Ob, stm., Sov. Un. C9 29
Oba, On., Can. G16 66
Obama, Japan n14 33
Oban, Scot., U.K. E1 75
Oban, Sk., Can. B4 10
O'Bannon, Ky., U.S. g11 94
Ob Bay, b., Sov. Un. C10 29
Obed, Ab., Can. C2 68
Obed, stm., Tn., U.S. C9 119
Ober, In., U.S. B4 91
Oberá, Arg. E4 55
Oberammergau, F.R.Ger. B7 20
Oberdrauburg, Aus. C8 20
Oberhausen, F.R.Ger. C3 18
Oberkirch, F.R.Ger. E3 19
Oberlin, La., U.S. D3 95
Oberlin, Oh., U.S. A3 112
Obernai, Fr. C7 16
Obernburg [am Main], F.R.Ger. D4 19
Oberösterreich, state, Aus. B6 111
Oberstaufen, F.R.Ger. B6 20
Oberstdorf, F.R.Ger. E5 18
Obetz, Oh., U.S. C3 112
Óbidos, Braz. C3 59
Obihiro, Japan C13 31
Obi Islands, is., Indon. F7 34
Obion, Tn., U.S. A2 119
Obion, co., Tn., U.S. A2 119
Obion, Tn., U.S. A2 119
Obion, Middle Fork, stm., Tn., U.S. A3 119
Obion, Rutherford Fork, stm., Tn., U.S. A3 119
Obion, South Fork, stm., Tn., U.S. A3 119
Obion Creek, stm., Ky., U.S. f9 94
Oblachnaya, Mount, mtn., Sov. Un. E7 33
Oblong, Il., U.S. D6 90
Obluchye, Sov. Un. E16 29
Obo, Cen. Afr. Rep. D5 46
Obock, Dji. C5 47
Oborniki, Pol. B4 26
Oboyan, Sov. Un. F11 27
O'Brien, Fl., U.S. B4 86
O'Brien, co., Ia., U.S. A2 92
Observation Peak, mtn., Ca., U.S. B3 82
Obuasi, Ghana E4 45
Obwalden, state, Switz. C4 20
Ocala, Fl., U.S. C4 86
Ocampo, Mex. B3 63
Ocaña, Col. B3 60
Ocaña, Spain A5 108
Occidental, Cordillera, mts., Col. C2 60
Occidental, Cordillera, mts., Peru D3 53
Occidental, Cordillera, mts., S.A. C2 55
Occoquan, Va., U.S. B5 123
Ocean, co., N.J., U.S. C4 107
Ocean, co., N.J., U.S. D4 107
Ocean, co., W.V., U.S. D3 125
Oceana, co., Mi., U.S. E4 99
Oceana Naval Air Station, mil., Va., U.S. k15 123
Ocean Bluff, Ma., U.S. B6 98
Ocean City, Fl., U.S. u15 86
Ocean City, Md., U.S. D7 97
Ocean City, N.J., U.S. E3 107
Ocean Falls, B.C., Can. C4 69
Ocean Gate, N.J., U.S. D4 107
Ocean Grove, Ma., U.S. *C5 98
Ocean Grove, N.J., U.S. C4 107
Ocean Heights, Ma., U.S. D6 98
Ocean Park, Wa., U.S. C1 124
Ocean Port, N.J., U.S. C4 107
Oceanside, Ca., U.S. F5 82
Oceanside, N.Y., U.S. *E7 109
Ocean Springs, Ms., U.S. E5 101
Ocean View, De., U.S. F5 85
Oceanville, N.J., U.S. E4 107
Ochamchira, Sov. Un. A13 41
Ochelata, Ok., U.S. A6 113
Ocheyedan, Ia., U.S. A2 92
Ocheyedan, stm., Ia., U.S. A2 92
Ochil Hills, hills, Scot., U.K. D5 13
Ochlocknee, Ga., U.S. F2 87
Ochlockonee, stm., Fl., U.S. B2 86
Ochoco Lake, res., Or., U.S. C6 114
Ochopee, Fl., U.S. G5 86
Ocho Rios, Jam. E9 64
Ochre River, Mb., Can. D2 70
Ochtrup, F.R.Ger. A2 19
Ockelbo, Swe. G7 14
Ockley, In., U.S. C4 91
Ocmulgee, stm., Ga., U.S. D3 87
Ocmulgee National Monument, Ga., U.S. D3 87
Ocna-Sibiului, Rom. C7 24
Ocnele Mari, Rom. D7 24
Oconee, Ga., U.S. D3 87
Oconee, Il., U.S. D4 90
Oconee, co., Ga., U.S. C3 87

Name	Map Ref	Page

Oconee, co., S.C., U.S. — B1 117
Oconee, stm., Ga., U.S. — C3 87
Oconee, Lake, res., Ga., U.S. — C3 87
Oconomowoc, Wi., U.S. — E5 126
Oconto, Ne., U.S. — C6 104
Oconto, Wi., U.S. — D6 126
Oconto, co., Wi., U.S. — D5 126
Oconto, stm., Wi., U.S. — D5 126
Oconto Falls, Wi., U.S. — D5 126
Ocós, Guat. — C1 62
Ocotal, Nic. — E7 63
Ocotillo, Az., U.S. — m9 80
Ocracoke, N.C., U.S. — B7 110
Ocracoke Inlet, b., N.C., U.S. — B6 110
Ocracoke Island, i., N.C., U.S. — B7 110
Ocros, Peru — D2 58
Octavia, Ne., U.S. — C8 104
Octavia, Ok., U.S. — C7 113
Octeville, Fr. — C3 16
October Revolution Island, i., Sov. Un. — B4 128
Octoraro Creek, stm., U.S. — A5 97
Ocumare del Tuy, Ven. — A4 60
Oda, Ghana — E4 45
Odanah, Wi., U.S. — B3 126
Ōdate, Japan — F10 33
Odawara, Japan — n18 33
Odd, W.V., U.S. — *D3 125
Odda, Nor. — G2 14
Odebolt, Ia., U.S. — B2 92
Odei, stm., Mb., Can. — A3 70
Odell, Il., U.S. — B5 90
Odell, Ne., U.S. — D9 104
Odell, Or., U.S. — B5 114
Odell, Tx., U.S. — B3 120
Odell Lake, l., Or., U.S. — E5 114
Odem, Tx., U.S. — F4 120
Odemira, Port. — D1 22
Ödemiş, Tur. — C7 40
Oden, Ar., U.S. — C2 81
Odendaalsrus, S. Afr. — C4 49
Odensala, Swe. — t35 14
Odensbacken (part of Örebro), Swe. — t33 14
Odense, Den. — J4 14
Odense, stm., Den. — C4 15
Odenton, Md., U.S. — B4 97
Odenville, Al., U.S. — B3 78
Odenwald, mts., F.R.Ger. — D3 19
Oder (Odra), stm., Eur. — B5 18
Oder Spree Canal, Ger.D.R. — A9 19
Odessa, On., Can. — C8 73
Odessa, Sov. Un. — E6 29
Odessa, ..., ... — C3 85
Odessa, Fl., U.S. — *D4 86
Odessa, Mn., U.S. — E2 100
Odessa, Mo., U.S. — C4 102
Odessa, Ne., U.S. — D6 104
Odessa, N.Y., U.S. — C4 109
Odessa, Tx., U.S. — D1 120
Odessa, Wa., U.S. — B7 124
Odgers Ranch Indian Reservation, Nv., U.S. — C6 105
Odiel, stm., Spain — D2 22
Odienné, I.C. — E3 45
Odin, Il., U.S. — E4 90
Odin, Ks., U.S. — D5 93
Odin, Mn., U.S. — G4 100
Odin, Mount, mtn., B.C., Can. — D8 69
Odivelas, Port. — f9 22
Odobești, Rom. — C8 24
Odon, In., U.S. — G4 91
O'Donnell, Tx., U.S. — C2 120
Odorheiu Secuiesc, Rom. — B7 24
Odra (Oder), stm., Eur. — B3 26
Odum, Ga., U.S. — E4 87
Odzi, Zimb. — A5 49
Oebisfelde, Ger.D.R. — A5 19
Oeiras, Braz. — C2 57
Oeiras, Port. — f9 22
Oelde, F.R.Ger. — B3 19
Oelrichs, S.D., U.S. — D2 118
Oelsnitz [im Erzgebirge], Ger.D.R. — C6 18
Oelsnitz [im Vogtland], Ger.D.R. — C6 18
Oelwein, Ia., U.S. — B6 92
Oensingen, Switz. — B4 21
Oesede, F.R.Ger. — A3 19
Oettingen [in Bayern], F.R.Ger. — E5 19
Oeyon Island, i., S. Kor. — H2 33
Ofahoma, Ms., U.S. — C4 101
O'Fallon, Il., U.S. — E4 90
O'Fallon, Mo., U.S. — f12 102
O'Fallon Creek, stm., Mt., U.S. — D12 113
Ofanto, stm., Italy — D5 23
Ofaqim, Isr. — C6 41
Offaly, co., Ire. — C4 11
Offenbach [am Main], F.R.Ger. — D4 18
Offenburg, F.R.Ger. — D3 18
Offence, Mount of, hist., Isr. Occ. — m14 41
Offerle, Ks., U.S. — E4 93
Offerman, Ga., U.S. — E4 87
Offutt Air Force Base, mil., Ne., U.S. — g3 104
Oficina Pedro de Valdivia, Chile — D2 55
Oftringen, Switz. — B4 21
Ōfunato, Japan — G10 33
Oga, Japan — G9 33
Ōgaki, Japan — l8 33
Ogallah, Ks., U.S. — D4 93
Ogallala, Ne., U.S. — C4 104
Oga Peninsula, pen., Japan — G10 33
Ogbomosho, Nig. — E6 45
Ogden, Ar., U.S. — D1 81
Ogden, Ia., U.S. — B3 92
Ogden, Ks., U.S. — C6 93
Ogden, Ut., U.S. — B4 121
Ogden, Mount, mtn., Ak., U.S. — k23 79
Ogdensburg, N.J., U.S. — A3 107
Ogdensburg, N.Y., U.S. — f9 109
Ogdensburg, Wi., U.S. — D5 126
Ogeechee, stm., Ga., U.S. — D5 87
Ogema, Sk., Can. — H3 75
Ogema, Wi., U.S. — C3 126
Ogemaw, co., Mi., U.S. — D6 99
Ogilvie Mountains, mts., Yk., Can. — D5 66
Oglala, S.D., U.S. — D3 118
Ogle, co., Il., U.S. — A4 90
Oglesby, Il., U.S. — B4 90
Oglesby, Tx., U.S. — D4 120
Oglethorpe, Ga., U.S. — D2 87
Oglethorpe, co., Ga., U.S. — C3 87
Oglethorpe, Mount, mtn., U.S. — B2 87

Oglio, stm., Italy — B3 23
Ognon, stm., Fr. — B1 20
Ogoamas, mtn., Indon. — E6 34
Ogoja, Nig. — E6 45
Ogoki, stm., On., Can. — o18 73
Ogooué, stm., Afr. — F2 46
Ogosta, stm., Bul. — D6 24
Ogrodzieniec, Pol. — g11 26
Ogulin, Yugo. — C2 24
Ogunquit, Me., U.S. — E2 96
Ogurchinskiy, i., Sov. Un. — B6 39
Ohakune, N.Z. — M15 51
Ohanet, Alg. — D6 44
O'Hanly, stm., Mb., Can. — D4 70
Ōhara, Japan — n19 33
Ohatchee, Al., U.S. — B3 78
Ohaton, Ab., Can. — C4 68
O'Higgins, Lago (Lago San Martín), l., S.A. — D2 54
Ohio, Co., U.S. — C4 83
Ohio, Il., U.S. — B4 90
Ohio, N.Y., U.S. — B6 109
Ohio, co., In., U.S. — G7 91
Ohio, co., Ky., U.S. — C3 94
Ohio, co., W.V., U.S. — A4 125
Ohio, state, U.S. — B3 112
Ohio, stm., U.S. — C11 76
Ohio Brush Creek, stm., Oh., U.S. — D2 112
Ohio City, Oh., U.S. — B1 112
Ohio Peak, mtn., Co., U.S. — C3 83
Ohiopyle, Pa., U.S. — G3 115
Ohioville, Pa., U.S. — E1 115
Ohiowa, Ne., U.S. — D8 104
Ohlman, Il., U.S. — D4 90
Ohoopee, Ga., U.S. — D4 87
Ohoopee, stm., Ga., U.S. — D4 87
Ohopoho, Nmb. — A1 49
Ohře, stm., Eur. — C2 26
Ohrid, Yugo. — E5 24
Ohrid, Lake, l., Eur. — E5 24
Ohrigstad, S. Afr. — B5 49
Öhringen, F.R.Ger. — D4 19
Oiapoque (Oyapock), stm., S.A. — B4 59
Oich, stm., Scot., U.K. — C4 13
Oies, Île aux, i., P.Q., Can. — B7 74
Oikull, Palau — R17 52
Oil Center, N.M., U.S. — E6 108
Oil City, Ca., U.S. — B2 95
Oil City, La., U.S. — B2 95
Oil City, Ms., U.S. — C3 101
Oil City, Pa., U.S. — D2 115
Oil Creek, stm., Pa., U.S. — C2 115
Oildale, Ca., U.S. — E4 82
Oilmont, Mt., U.S. — B5 103
Oil Springs, On., Can. — E2 73
Oilton, Ok., U.S. — A5 113
Oilton, Tx., U.S. — F3 120
Oil Trough, Ar., U.S. — B4 81
Oir, Beinn an, mtn., Scot., U.K. — E3 13
Oise, dept., Fr. — E2 17
Oise, stm., Eur. — C5 16
Oiseau, stm., Can. — D4 70
Oisemont, Fr. — E9 12
Ō Island, i., Japan — I9 33
Ō Island, i., Japan — F9 33
Oita, Japan — J5 33
Oiticica, Braz. — C2 57
Ojai, Ca., U.S. — E4 82
Ojinaga, Mex. — B4 63
Ojocaliente, Mex. — C4 63
Ojo Caliente, N.M., U.S. — A3 108
Ojo Feliz, N.M., U.S. — A4 108
Ojo Sarco, N.M., U.S. — A4 108
Ojos del Salado, Nevado, mtn., S.A. — E2 55
Oka, P.Q., Can. — D3 74
Oka, Nig. — E6 45
Oka, stm., Sov. Un. — C14 27
Okaba, Indon. — G9 34
Okabena, Mn., U.S. — G3 100
Okahandja, Nmb. — B2 49
Okak Islands, is., Nf., Can. — g9 72
Okaloosa, co., Fl., U.S. — u15 86
Okamanpeedan Lake, l., U.S. — A3 92
Okanagan Centre, B.C., Can. — D8 69
Okanagan Falls, B.C., Can. — E8 69
Okanagan Lake, l., B.C., Can. — D8 69
Okanagan Landing, B.C., Can. — D8 69
Okanagan Range, mts., N.A. — E7 69
Okanogan, Wa., U.S. — A6 124
Okanogan, co., Wa., U.S. — A6 124
Okanogan, stm., N.A. — A6 124
Okapilco Creek, stm., Ga., U.S. — E3 87
Okāra, Pak. — B4 37
Okarche, Ok., U.S. — B4 113
Okatibbee Reservoir, res., Ms., U.S. — C5 101
Okatoma Creek, stm., Ms., U.S. — D4 101
Okaton, S.D., U.S. — D5 118
Okauchee, Wi., U.S. — *E5 126
Okauchee Lake, Wi., U.S. — *E5 126
Okaukuejo, Nmb. — A2 49
Okavango, stm., Afr. — H7 42
Okavango Swamps, sw., Bots. — A3 49
Okawville, Il., U.S. — E4 90
Okay, Ok., U.S. — B6 113
Okaya, Japan — H8 33
Okayama, Japan — E11 31
Okazaki, Japan — o16 33
O'Kean, Ar., U.S. — A5 81
Okeana, Oh., U.S. — n12 112
Okęcie (Airport of Warsaw), Pol. — m13 26
Okeechobee, Fl., U.S. — E6 86
Okeechobee, co., Fl., U.S. — E6 86
Okeechobee, Lake, l., Fl., U.S. — F6 86
Okeene, Ok., U.S. — A3 113
Okefenokee Swamp, sw., U.S. — F4 87
Okehampton, Eng., U.K. — K9 13
Okemah, Ok., U.S. — B5 113
Okemos, Mi., U.S. — *F6 99
Oker, stm., F.R.Ger. — A5 19
Okesa, Ok., U.S. — A5 113
Oketo, Ks., U.S. — C7 93
Okfuskee, co., Ok., U.S. — B5 113
Okha, India — D4 36
Okha, Sov. Un. — D17 29
Okhotsk, Sov. Un. — D17 29
Okhotsk, Sea of, Asia — D17 29
Okiep, S. Afr. — C2 49
Oki Islands, is., Japan — D11 31
Okinawa Island, i., Japan — F10 31
Oklahoma, co., Ok., U.S. — B4 113
Oklahoma, state, U.S. — B4 113
Oklahoma City, Ok., U.S. — B4 113
Oklawaha, Fl., U.S. — C5 86
Oklawaha, stm., Fl., U.S. — C5 86
Oklawaha, Lake, res., Fl., U.S. — C5 86
Oklee, Mn., U.S. — C3 100

Okmulgee, Ok., U.S. — B6 113
Okmulgee, co., Ok., U.S. — B5 113
Okoboji, Ia., U.S. — A2 92
Okobojo Creek, stm., S.D., U.S. — C5 118
Okolona, Ar., U.S. — D2 81
Okolona, Ky., U.S. — g11 94
Okolona, Ms., U.S. — B5 101
Okondja, Gabon — F2 46
Okotoks, Ab., Can. — D4 68
Okreek, S.D., U.S. — D5 118
Oktaha, Ok., U.S. — B6 113
Oktibbeha, co., Ms., U.S. — B5 101
Oktyabrsk, Sov. Un. — D5 28
Oktyabrskiy, Sov. Un. — C4 28
Okulovka, Sov. Un. — B9 27
Okuma Bay, b., Ant. — B32 7
Okuniew, Pol. — k14 26
Okushiri, Japan — E9 33
Okushiri Island, i., Japan — E9 33
Ola, Ar., U.S. — B2 81
Ola, Id., U.S. — E2 89
Olancha, Ca., U.S. — D5 82
Olancha Peak, mtn., Ca., U.S. — D4 82
Olanchito, Hond. — C4 62
Öland, i., Swe. — I7 14
Olanta, Pa., U.S. — E4 115
Olanta, S.C., U.S. — D8 117
Olar, S.C., U.S. — E5 117
Olascoaga, Arg. — B4 54
Olathe, Co., U.S. — C3 83
Olathe, Ks., U.S. — D9 93
Olavarría, Arg. — B4 54
Oława, Pol. — C4 26
Olazagutía, Spain — A4 22
Olberg, Az., U.S. — D4 80
Olbernhau, Ger.D.R. — C8 19
Olbia, Italy — D2 23
Olcott, N.Y., U.S. — B2 109
Olcott, W.V., U.S. — C3 125
Old Bahama Channel, strt., N.A. — C4 64
Old Bennington, Vt., U.S. — F2 122
Old Bethpage, N.Y., U.S. — *n15 109
Old Bight, Bah. — B6 64
Old Bridge, N.J., U.S. — C4 107
Old Castile, hist reg., Spain — B2 22
Old Crow, Yk., Can. — C5 66
Oldeani, Tan. — B6 48
Oldenburg, F.R.Ger. — B3 18
Oldenburg, In., U.S. — F7 91
Oldenburg [in Holstein], F.R.Ger. — A5 18
Oldenzaal, Neth. — B6 17
Old Faithful Geyser, Wy., U.S. — B2 127
Old Forge, N.Y., U.S. — B6 109
Old Forge, Pa., U.S. — D10 115
Old Fort, N.C., U.S. — f10 110
Old Fort, Oh., U.S. — A2 112
Old Fort Bay, P.Q., Can. — C3 72
Oldham, Eng., U.K. — D5 10
Oldham, S.D., U.S. — C8 118
Oldham, co., Ky., U.S. — B4 94
Oldham, co., Tx., U.S. — B1 120
Oldham Village, Ma., U.S. — *B6 98
Old Harbor, Ak., U.S. — D9 79
Old Harbour Bay, Jam. — F14 65
Old Hickory Lake, res., Tn., U.S. — A5 119
Old Lyme, Ct., U.S. — D6 84
Oldman, stm., Ab., Can. — E4 68
Old Man Mountain, mtn., Nf., U.S. — D3 72
Old Man of the Mountain, — B3 106
Oldmans Creek, stm., N.J., U.S. — D2 107
Old Meldrum, Scot., U.K. — D6 13
Old Mkushi, Zam. — D4 48
Old Monroe, Mo., U.S. — C7 102
Old Mystic, Ct., U.S. — D8 84
Old Northwood, N.H., U.S. — D4 106
Old Orchard Beach, Me., U.S. — E2 96
Old Perlican, Nf., Can. — D5 72
Old Point Comfort, c., Va., U.S. — h15 123
Old Rhodes Key, i., Fl., U.S. — G6 86
Old Ripley, Il., U.S. — E4 90
Old River Lake, l., Ar., U.S. — k10 81
Olds, Ab., Can. — D3 68
Olds, Ia., U.S. — C6 92
Old Saybrook, Ct., U.S. — D6 84
Oldsmar, Fl., U.S. — o10 86
Old Speck Mountain, mtn., Me., U.S. — D2 96
Old Tampa Bay, b., Fl., U.S. — p10 86
Old Tappan, N.J., U.S. — g9 107
Old Tate, Bots. — B4 49
Old Topsail Inlet, b., N.C., U.S. — C5 110
Old Town, Fl., U.S. — C4 86
Old Town, Id., U.S. — A1 89
Old Town, Me., U.S. — C4 96
Oldtown, Md., U.S. — k13 97
Old Washington, Oh., U.S. — B4 112
Old Wives, Sk., Can. — G3 75
Old Wives Lake, l., Sk., Can. — G2 75
Olean, Mo., U.S. — C5 102
Olean, N.Y., U.S. — C2 109
O'Leary, P.E., Can. — C5 71
Olecko, Pol. — A7 26
Oleiros, Spain — A2 22
Olekma, stm., Sov. Un. — D15 29
Olëkminsk, Sov. Un. — C15 29
Olenëk, stm., Sov. Un. — C14 29
Olentangy, stm., Oh., U.S. — B3 112
Oléron, Île d', i., Fr. — E3 16
Oleśnica, Pol. — C4 26
Olesno, Pol. — C5 26
Oleta, Ok., U.S. — C12 113
Olga, Sov. Un. — n19 33
Olga, Mount, mtn., Vt., U.S. — F3 122
Ólgiy, Mong. — B2 31
Ólgod, Den. — C2 15
Olhão, Port. — D2 22
Olifants, stm., Afr. — B5 49
Olímpia, Braz. — C3 56
Olin, Ia., U.S. — B6 92
Olinda, Braz. — C4 57
Olionono, Cape, c., W. Sam. — A5 22
Olite, Spain — A5 22
Oliva, Spain — C5 22
Oliva de la Frontera, Spain — C2 22
Olivais, Port. — f9 22
Olive, Mt., U.S. — E11 103
Olive, Ok., U.S. — A5 113

Olive, Ok., U.S. — A5 113
Olive Branch, Il., U.S. — F4 90
Olive Branch, Ms., U.S. — A4 101
Olive Hill, Ky., U.S. — B6 94
Olivehurst, Ca., U.S. — C3 82
Oliveira, Braz. — C4 56
Olivenza, Spain — C2 22
Oliver, B.C., Can. — E8 69
Oliver, Al., U.S. — A2 78
Oliver, Ga., U.S. — D5 87
Oliver, Il., U.S. — D6 90
Oliver, Pa., U.S. — G2 115
Oliver, Wi., U.S. — B1 126
Oliver, co., N.D., U.S. — B4 111
Oliver Dam, U.S. — C5 78
Oliver Springs, Tn., U.S. — C9 119
Olivet, On., Can. — D6 90
Olivet, Ks., U.S. — D8 93
Olivet, Md., U.S. — D5 97
Olivet, Mi., U.S. — F6 99
Olivet, S.D., U.S. — D8 118
Olivette, Mo., U.S. — *f13 102
Olivia, Mn., U.S. — F4 100
Olivia, N.C., U.S. — B3 110
Olivone, Switz. — C4 20
Öljaren, l., Swe. — t34 14
Olkusz, Pol. — g11 26
Ollagüe, Chile — D2 55
Ollei, Palau — R17 52
Ollie, Ia., U.S. — C5 92
Olmitz, Ks., U.S. — D5 93
Olmos, Peru — C2 58
Olmos Park, Tx., U.S. — k7 120
Olmstead, Ky., U.S. — D3 94
Olmstead, Ut., U.S. — *C4 121
Olmsted, co., Mn., U.S. — G6 100
Olmsted Falls, Oh., U.S. — h9 112
Olmstedville, N.Y., U.S. — B7 109
Olney, Il., U.S. — E5 90
Olney, Md., U.S. — B3 97
Olney, Mo., U.S. — C5 102
Olney, Mt., U.S. — B2 103
Olney, Tx., U.S. — C3 120
Olney Springs, Co., U.S. — C7 83
Oloh, Ms., U.S. — D4 101
Olomouc, Czech. — C6 26
Olongapo, Phil. — o13 34
Oloron, Gave d', stm., Fr. — F3 16
Oloron-Sainte-Marie, Fr. — F3 16
Olot, Spain — A7 22
Olowalu, Hi., U.S. — C5 88
Olpe, F.R.Ger. — B2 19
Olpe, Ks., U.S. — D7 93
Olsburg, Ks., U.S. — C7 93
Olše, stm., Eur. — h9 26
Olshany, Sov. Un. — F10 27
Olst, Neth. — B6 17
Olsztyn (Allenstein), Pol. — B6 26
Olt, stm., Rom. — C7 24
Olten, Switz. — E3 18
Oltenia, hist reg., Rom. — C6 24
Oltenița, Rom. — C8 24
Oltet, stm., Rom. — C6 24
Oltu, Tur. — B13 40
Olustee, Fl., U.S. — B4 86
Olustee, Ok., U.S. — C2 113
Olvenstedt, Ger.D.R. — A6 19
Olvera, Spain — D3 22
Olympia, Ky., U.S. — B6 94
Olympia, Wa., U.S. — B3 124
Olympia, hist., Grc. — D3 25
Olympia Heights, Fl., U.S. — *s13 86
Olympic Mountains, mts., Wa., U.S. — B2 124
Olympic National Park, Wa., U.S. — B2 124
Olympus, Mount, mtn., Grc. — B4 40
Olympus, Mount, mtn., Ky., U.S. — B6 94
Olympus, Mount, mtn., U.S. — B2 124
Olyphant, Ar., U.S. — B4 81
Olyphant, Pa., U.S. — D10 115
Olyutorsky, Cape, c., Sov. Un. — D20 29
Oma, Ar., U.S. — g7 81
Oma, Ms., U.S. — D3 101
Omae, Cape, c., Japan — o17 33
Omaguas, Peru — B3 58
Omaha, Ga., U.S. — D1 87
Omaha, Il., U.S. — F5 90
Omaha, Ne., U.S. — C10 104
Omaha Indian Reservation, Ne., U.S. — B9 104
Omak, Wa., U.S. — A6 124
Omak Lake, l., Wa., U.S. — A6 124
Oman, cry., Asia — C5 38
Oman, Gulf of, b., Asia — C6 38
Omar, W.V., U.S. — D3 125
Omaruru, Nmb. — P12 51
Omarama, N.Z. — — —
Omatako, stm., Nmb. — A4 —
Omdurman (Umm Durmān), Sud. — B3 47
Omega, Ga., U.S. — E3 87
Omega, N.M., U.S. — C1 108
Omega, Oh., U.S. — C3 112
Omegna, Italy — E5 21
Omemee, On., Can. — C6 73
Omemee, N.D., U.S. — A5 111
Omeo, Austl. — H6 51
Omer, Mi., U.S. — D7 99
Ometepe, Isla de, i., Nic. — E5 62
Ometepec, Mex. — D5 63
Om Hajer, Eth. — C4 47
Omineca, stm., B.C., Can. — B5 69
Omineca Mountains, mts., B.C., Can. — A4 69
Omingo Lake, l., On., Can. — I9 33
Ōmiya, Japan — o15 33
Ommaney, Cape, c., Ak., U.S. — D12 79
Ommen, Neth. — B6 17
Ómolos, mtn., Cyp. — E9 40
Omolon, stm., Sov. Un. — C18 29
Omonono, Cape, c., W. Sam. — A5 22
Ompompanoosuc, West Branch, stm., Vt., U.S. — D4 122
Omro, Wi., U.S. — D5 126
Omsk, Sov. Un. — D10 29
Opole, Pol. — C4 26

Ōmuta, Japan — J5 33
Omutninsk, Sov. Un. — D19 8
Ona, Fl., U.S. — E5 86
Onaga, Ks., U.S. — C7 93
Onaka, S.D., U.S. — B6 118
Onalaska, Wa., U.S. — C3 124
Onalaska, Wi., U.S. — E2 126
Onamia, Mn., U.S. — D5 100
Onancock, Va., U.S. — C7 123
Onao, i., Micron. — Q18 52
Onarga, Il., U.S. — C6 90
Onawa, Ia., U.S. — B1 92
Onawa, Me., U.S. — C3 96
Onawa, Lake, l., Me., U.S. — C3 96
Onaway, Mi., U.S. — C6 99
Onchiota, N.Y., U.S. — f10 109
Onda, Spain — C5 22
Ondangua, Nmb. — A2 49
Ondava, stm., Czech. — D6 26
Ondjiva (Ngiva), Ang. — E2 48
Ondo, Nig. — E5 45
Öndörhaan, Mong. — B7 31
Oneata, i., Fiji — I16 52
Oneco, Ct., U.S. — C8 84
Oneco, Fl., U.S. — E4 86
Onega, stm., Sov. Un. — C16 8
Onega, Lake, l., Sov. Un. — C6 29
One Hundred Fifty Mile House, B.C., Can. — C7 69
One Hundred Mile House, B.C., Can. — D7 69
Oneida, Ar., U.S. — C5 81
Oneida, Il., U.S. — B3 90
Oneida, Ks., U.S. — C8 93
Oneida, Ky., U.S. — C6 94
Oneida, N.Y., U.S. — B5 109
Oneida, Oh., U.S. — C1 112
Oneida, Tn., U.S. — C9 119
Oneida, Wi., U.S. — g9 126
Oneida, co., Id., U.S. — G6 89
Oneida, co., N.Y., U.S. — B5 109
Oneida, co., Wi., U.S. — C4 126
Oneida Lake, l., N.Y., U.S. — B5 109
O'Neill, Ne., U.S. — B7 104
Onekama, Mi., U.S. — D4 99
Oneonta, Al., U.S. — B3 78
Oneonta, N.Y., U.S. — C5 109
Ong, Ne., U.S. — D8 104
Ongea Levu, i., Fiji — I16 52
Ongiin Hiid, Mong. — B5 31
Ongjin, N. Kor. — H2 33
Ongjin, stm., Mong. — B5 31
Onitsha, Nig. — E6 45
Oniotto Island, i., Marsh Is. — S17 52
Onley, Va., U.S. — C7 123
Only, Ia., U.S. — B4 119
Onna, Japan — O5 52
Ono, Japan — n15 33
Ono, i., Fiji — I15 52
Ono Channel, strt., Fiji — I15 52
Onomichi, Japan — I6 33
Onondaga, Mi., U.S. — F6 99
Onondaga, co., N.Y., U.S. — C4 109
Onondaga Indian Reservation, N.Y., U.S. — C4 109
Onota Lake, l., Ma., U.S. — B1 98
Onoway, Ab., Can. — C3 68
Onset, Ma., U.S. — C6 98
Onslow, Austl. — D2 50
Onslow, Ia., U.S. — B6 92
Onslow, co., N.C., U.S. — C5 110
Onslow Bay, b., N.C., U.S. — C5 110
Onsŏng [-ŭp], N. Kor. — E4 33
Onsted, Mi., U.S. — F6 99
Ontake, Mount, mtn., Japan — n16 33
Ontario, Ca., U.S. — E5 82
Ontario, N.Y., U.S. — B3 109
Ontario, Oh., U.S. — B3 112
Ontario, Or., U.S. — C10 114
Ontario, co., On., Can. — C5 73
Ontario, co., N.Y., U.S. — C3 109
Ontario, prov., Can. — C6 73
Ontario, Lake, l., N.A. — B12 76
Ontonum, Sov. Un. — g7 81
Ontonagon, Mi., U.S. — m12 99
Ontonagon, co., Mi., U.S. — m12 99
Ontonagon Indian Reservation, Mi., U.S. — C5 91
Onward, In., U.S. — C5 91
Oodnadatta, Austl. — E6 50
Ood Weyne, Som. — D6 47
Ooldea, Austl. — F5 50
Oolitic, In., U.S. — G4 91
Oologah, Ok., U.S. — A6 113
Oologah Lake, res., Ok., U.S. — A6 113
Ooltewah, Tn., U.S. — D8 119
Ooltgensplaat, Neth. — C4 17
Oostburg, Neth. — C3 17
Oostburg, Wi., U.S. — E6 126
Oostende (Ostende), Bel. — B5 16
Oosterend, Neth. — A4 17
Oosterend, Neth. — A5 17
Oosterhout, Neth. — C4 17
Oosterschelde, b., Bel. — B5 16
Oostmahorn, Neth. — A6 17
Oost-Vlieland, Neth. — A5 17
Oostvoorne, Neth. — C4 17
Ootacamund, India — F6 36
Ootsa Lake, B.C., Can. — C4 69
Ootsa Lake, l., B.C., Can. — C4 69
Opal, Ab., Can. — C4 68
Opal, S.D., U.S. — C3 118
Opal, Wy., U.S. — E2 127
Opala, Zaire — B5 48
Opal Cliffs, Ca., U.S. — *D3 82
Opa-Locka, Fl., U.S. — s13 86
Opalton, Austl. — A4 51
Opava, Czech. — D4 26
Opdyke, Il., U.S. — E5 90
Opelika, Al., U.S. — C4 78
Opelousas, La., U.S. — D3 95
Opeongo, stm., On., Can. — B6 73
Opeongo Lake, l., On., Can. — I9 33
Opequon Creek, stm., W.V., U.S. — B6 125
Ophir, Or., U.S. — E2 114
Opihikao, Hi., U.S. — D7 88
Opiscotéo, Lac, l., P.Q., Can. — F19 66
Opobo, Nig. — F6 45
Opochka, Sov. Un. — C7 27
Opoczno, Pol. — C5 26
Opole, Pol. — C4 26

Opole Lubelskie, Pol. — C7 26
Opotiki, N.Z. — M16 51
Opp, Al., U.S. — D3 78
Oppdal, Nor. — F3 14
Oppelo, Ar., U.S. — B3 81
Opportunity, Wa., U.S. — B8 124
Optic Lake, Mb., Can. — B1 70
Optima, Ok., U.S. — e9 113
Optima Reservoir, res., Ok., U.S. — e9 113
Opyan, Puntan, c., N. Mar. Is. — C3 52
Oquawka, Il., U.S. — C3 90
Oquossoc, Me., U.S. — D2 96
Ora, Italy — C7 20
Ora, In., U.S. — B4 91
Ora, Ms., U.S. — D4 101
Oracle, Az., U.S. — E5 80
Oradea, Rom. — B5 24
Oradell, N.J., U.S. — h8 107
Oradell Reservoir, res., N.J., U.S. — h9 107
Orai, India — E7 37
Oraibi, Az., U.S. — B5 80
Oraibi Wash, val., Az., U.S. — A5 80
Oral, S.D., U.S. — D2 118
Oran (Wahran), Alg. — B4 44
Oran, Ia., U.S. — B5 92
Oran, Mo., U.S. — D8 102
Orange, Austl. — F8 50
Orange, Fr. — E6 16
Orange, Ca., U.S. — n13 82
Orange, Ct., U.S. — D3 84
Orange, In., U.S. — E7 91
Orange, Ma., U.S. — A3 98
Orange, N.H., U.S. — C3 106
Orange, N.J., U.S. — B4 107
Orange, Tx., U.S. — D6 120
Orange, Vt., U.S. — C4 122
Orange, co., Ca., U.S. — F5 82
Orange, co., Fl., U.S. — D5 86
Orange, co., In., U.S. — G4 91
Orange, co., N.Y., U.S. — D6 109
Orange, co., N.C., U.S. — A3 110
Orange, co., Tx., U.S. — D6 120
Orange, co., Vt., U.S. — D3 122
Orange, co., Va., U.S. — C4 49
Orange, Cabo, c., Braz. — B4 59
Orange Beach, Al., U.S. — E2 78
Orangeburg, S.C., U.S. — E6 117
Orangeburg, co., S.C., U.S. — E6 117
Orange City, Fl., U.S. — D5 86
Orange City, Ia., U.S. — B1 92
Orangedale, N.S., Can. — D8 71
Orange Free State, prov., S. Afr. — C4 49
Orange Grove, Ms., U.S. — E5 101
Orange Grove, Tx., U.S. — F4 120
Orange Lake, Fl., U.S. — C4 86
Orange Lake, l., Fl., U.S. — C4 86
Orangevale, Ca., U.S. — *C3 82
Orangeville, On., Can. — D4 73
Orangeville, Il., U.S. — A4 90
Orangeville, Ut., U.S. — D4 121
Orange Walk, Belize — D7 63
Orani, Phil. — o13 34
Oranienbaum, Ger.D.R. — B7 19
Oranienburg, Ger.D.R. — B6 18
Oranje Gebergte, mts., Sur. — B4 59
Oranjemund, Nmb. — C2 49
Oranjestad, Aruba — G17 65
Oranmore, Ire. — D3 11
Or 'Aqiva, Isr. — B6 41
Orăștie, Rom. — C6 24
Oravița, Rom. — C5 24
Orba, stm., Italy — E4 20
Orbe, Switz. — C2 21
Orbetello, Italy — C3 23
Orbey, Fr. — A3 20
Orbigo, stm., Spain — A3 22
Orbisonia, Pa., U.S. — F6 115
Orbost, Austl. — H7 51
Örby, Swe. — A6 15
Orcas Island, i., Wa., U.S. — A3 124
Orchard, Co., U.S. — A6 83
Orchard, Id., U.S. — F2 89
Orchard, Ne., U.S. — B7 104
Orchard City, Co., U.S. — C3 83
Orchard Farm, Mo., U.S. — f13 102
Orchard Homes, Mt., U.S. — D2 103
Orchard Mesa, Co., U.S. — *B2 83
Orchard Park, N.Y., U.S. — C2 109
Orchards, Wa., U.S. — D3 124
Orchard Valley, Wy., U.S. — E8 127
Orchies, Fr. — D7 17
Orchila, Isla, i., Ven. — A4 60
Orcotuna, Peru — D2 58
Orcutt, Ca., U.S. — E3 82
Orcutts, Ct., U.S. — B6 84
Ord, Ne., U.S. — C7 104
Ord, Mount, mtn., Austl. — C4 50
Ordale, Sk., Can. — D2 75
Ordenes, Spain — A2 22
Orderville, Ut., U.S. — F3 121
Ording, F.R.Ger. — D2 15
Ordoqui, Arg. — B4 54
Ordos Desert, des., China — D6 31
Ordot, Guam — L10 52
Ordu, Tur. — B11 40
Orduña, Spain — A4 22
Ordway, Co., U.S. — C7 83
Ordzhonikidze (Dzaudzhikau), Sov. Un. — E7 29
Oreana, Il., U.S. — D5 90
Oreana, Nv., U.S. — C3 105
Oreba Island, i., Marsh Is. — S17 52
Örebro, Swe. — H6 14
Ore City, Tx., U.S. — C5 120
Oregon, Il., U.S. — A4 90
Oregon, Mo., U.S. — B2 102
Oregon, Oh., U.S. — A2 112
Oregon, Wi., U.S. — F4 126
Oregon, co., Mo., U.S. — C6 102
Oregon, state, U.S. — C6 114
Oregon Caves National Monument, Or., U.S. — E2 114
Oregon City, Or., U.S. — B4 114
Oregon Inlet, b., N.C., U.S. — B7 110
Öregrund, Swe. — A5 —
Orehoved, Den. — D5 15
Orekhov, Sov. Un. — H10 27
Orekhovo, Bul. — D6 24
Orekhovo-Zuyevo, Sov. Un. — D12 27
Orel, Sov. Un. — D6 29
Oreland, Pa., U.S. — *o21 115
Ore Mountains, mts., Eur. — D8 18
Orenburg, Sov. Un. — D9 28
Orense, Spain — A2 22
Orestes, In., U.S. — D6 91
Orestiás, Grc. — B6 40

Name	Map Ref	Page
Øresund (The Sound), strt., Eur.	J5	14
Øreti, stm., N.Z.	P12	51
Oretta, La., U.S.	D2	95
Orford, N.H., U.S.	C2	106
Orford, Mont., mtn., P.Q., Can.	D5	74
Orford Ness, c., Eng., U.K.	B9	12
Orfordville, N.H., U.S.	C2	106
Orfordville, Wi., U.S.	F4	126
Organ, N.M., U.S.	E3	108
Organ Cave, W.V., U.S.	D4	125
Organ Mountains, mts., N.M., U.S.	E3	108
Organ Pipe Cactus National Monument, Az., U.S.	E3	80
Orgas, W.V., U.S.	m12	125
Orgaz, Spain	C4	22
Orgelet, Fr.	C1	20
Orgeyev, Sov. Un.	H7	27
Orgūn, Afg.	B4	36
Orhon, stm., Mong.	B5	31
Orick, Ca., U.S.	B1	82
Orient, Il., U.S.	F5	90
Orient, Ia., U.S.	C3	92
Orient, Me., U.S.	C5	96
Orient, N.Y., U.S.	m16	109
Orient, Oh., U.S.	C2	112
Orient, S.D., U.S.	C6	118
Orient, Wa., U.S.	A7	124
Orienta, Ok., U.S.	A3	113
Oriental, N.C., U.S.	B6	110
Oriental, Cordillera, mts., Col.	C3	60
Orihuela, Spain	C5	22
Orillia, On., Can.	C5	73
Orinda, Ca., U.S.	*h8	82
Orinoco, stm., S.A.	B5	60
Oriole, Md., U.S.	D6	97
Orion, Ab., Can.	E5	68
Orion, Phil.	o13	34
Orion, Il., U.S.	B3	90
Oriska, N.D., U.S.	C8	111
Oriskany, N.Y., U.S.	B5	109
Oriskany, Va., U.S.	C3	123
Oriskany Falls, N.Y., U.S.	C5	109
Orissa, state, India	E7	36
Oristano, Italy	E2	23
Oristano, Gulf of, b., Italy	E2	23
Orivesi, l., Fin.	F13	14
Oriximiná, Braz.	C3	59
Orizaba, Mex.	D5	63
Orizona, Braz.	B3	56
Orkanger, Nor.	F3	14
Örkelljunga, Swe.	B7	15
Orkla, stm., Nor.	F4	14
Orkney, Sk., Can.	H2	75
Orkney, prov., Scot., U.K.	A5	13
Orkney Islands, is., Scot., U.K.	A5	10
Orla, Tx., U.S.	o13	120
Orland, Ca., U.S.	C2	82
Orland, In., U.S.	A7	91
Orland, Me., U.S.	D4	96
Orlando, Fl., U.S.	D5	86
Orlando, Ok., U.S.	A4	113
Orland Park, Il., U.S.	k9	90
Orleães, Braz.	D3	56
Orléanais, hist reg., Fr.	D4	16
Orleans, On., Can.	h12	73
Orléans, Fr.	D4	16
Orleans, Ca., U.S.	B2	82
Orleans, In., U.S.	G5	91
Orleans, Ia., U.S.	A2	92
Orleans, Ma., U.S.	C7	98
Orleans, Mn., U.S.	B2	100
Orleans, Ne., U.S.	D6	104
Orleans, Vt., U.S.	B4	122
Orleans, co., La., U.S.	E6	95
Orleans, co., N.Y., U.S.	B2	109
Orleans, co., Vt., U.S.	B4	122
Orléans, Île d', i., P.Q., Can.	C6	74
Orlik Reservoir, res., Czech.	D9	19
Orlinda, Tn., U.S.	A5	119
Orlová, Czech.	*D5	26
Orlovo, Sov. Un.	E17	29
Orly, Fr.	h10	16
Orlyak, Bul.	D8	24
Orman Dam, S.D., U.S.	C2	118
Ormāra, Pak.	C3	36
Ormāra, Rās, c., Pak.	I12	39
Ormiston, Sk., Can.	H3	75
Ormond Beach, Fl., U.S.	C5	86
Ormond By The Sea, Fl., U.S.	*C5	86
Ormsby, On., Can.	C7	73
Ormsby, Mn., U.S.	G4	100
Ormskirk, Eng., U.K.	A5	12
Ormstown, P.Q., Can.	D3	74
Ornans, Fr.	B2	20
Orne, stm., Fr.	C3	16
Orneta, Pol.	A6	26
Örnö, Swe.	t36	14
Örnö, i., Swe.	t36	14
Örnsköldsvik, Swe.	F8	14
Orø, i., Den.	C5	15
Orocué, Col.	C3	60
Orodara, Burkina	D4	45
Orofino, Id., U.S.	C2	89
Oro Grande, Ca., U.S.	E5	82
Orograude, N.M., U.S.	E3	108
Orohena, mtn., Fr. Poly.	*H13	6
Oromocto, N.B., Can.	D3	71
Oromocto Lake, l., N.B., Can.	D2	71
Oron, Nig.	F6	45
Oron-la-Ville, Switz.	C2	21
Orono, On., Can.	D6	73
Orono, Me., U.S.	D4	96
Orono, Mn., U.S.	*n11	100
Oronoco, Mn., U.S.	F6	100
Oronogo, Mo., U.S.	D3	102
Oronsay, i., Scot., U.K.	D2	13
Oropuche, stm., Trin.	O23	65
Oroquieta, Phil.	D6	34
Orós, Braz.	C3	57
Orosei, Gulf of, b., Italy	D2	23
Orosháza, Hung.	B5	24
Orote Peninsula, pen., Guam	L9	52
Orovada, Nv., U.S.	B4	105
Oroville, Ca., U.S.	C3	82
Oroville, Wa., U.S.	A6	124
Oroville, Lake, res., Ca., U.S.	C3	82
Orpington (part of London), Eng., U.K.	m13	10
Orr, Mn., U.S.	B6	100
Orrick, Mo., U.S.	B3	102
Orrin, N.D., U.S.	A5	111
Orrington, Me., U.S.	D4	96
Orr Lake, l., Mb., Can.	A3	70
Orrs Island, Me., U.S.	E3	96
Orrstown, Pa., U.S.	F6	115
Orrum, N.C., U.S.	C4	110
Orrville, On., Can.	B5	73
Orrville, Al., U.S.	C2	78
Orrville, Oh., U.S.	B4	112
Orsa, Swe.	G6	14
Orsay, Fr.	F2	17
Orsha, Sov. Un.	D8	27
Orsières, Switz.	C3	20
Orsk, Sov. Un.	D8	29
Orson, Pa., U.S.	C11	115
Orşova, Rom.	C6	24
Ørsted, Den.	B4	15
Örsundsbro, Swe.	t35	14
Orta, Lake, l., Italy	D4	20
Ortaca, Tur.	D7	25
Orta [San Giulio], Italy	E5	21
Ortegal, Cape, c., Spain	A2	22
Orthez, Fr.	F3	16
Ortigueira, Spain	A2	22
Orting, Wa., U.S.	B3	124
Ortisei, Italy	C7	20
Ortiz, Mex.	B2	63
Ortiz, Co., U.S.	D4	83
Ortiz Mountain, mtn., N.M., U.S.	k8	108
Ortley, S.D., U.S.	B8	118
Ortoire, stm., Trin.	O23	65
Ortona, Italy	C5	23
Ortonville, Mi., U.S.	F7	99
Ortonville, Mn., U.S.	E2	100
Orūmīyeh (Urmia), Iran	B4	38
Oruro, Bol.	C2	55
Oruro, dept., Bol.	C2	55
Orvieto, Italy	C4	23
Orviston, Pa., U.S.	D6	115
Orwell, N.Y., U.S.	B4	109
Orwell, Oh., U.S.	A5	112
Orwell, Vt., U.S.	D2	122
Orwigsburg, Pa., U.S.	E9	115
Or Yehuda, Isr.	g10	41
Orysa, Tn., U.S.	B2	119
Orzesze, Pol.	g9	26
Osa, Peninsula de, pen., C.R.	F6	62
Osage, Sk., Can.	H4	75
Osage, Ia., U.S.	A5	92
Osage, Mn., U.S.	D3	100
Osage, Ok., U.S.	A5	113
Osage, Wy., U.S.	C8	127
Osage, co., Ks., U.S.	D8	93
Osage, co., Mo., U.S.	C6	102
Osage, co., Ok., U.S.	A5	113
Osage, stm., Mo., U.S.	C3	102
Osage Beach, Mo., U.S.	C5	102
Osage City, Ks., U.S.	D8	93
Osage Creek, stm., Ar., U.S.	A2	81
Ōsaka, Japan	E12	31
Ōsaka Bay, b., Japan	o14	33
Osaka Mountain, hill, Japan	P17	52
Osakis, Mn., U.S.	E3	100
Osakis, Lake, l., Mn., U.S.	E3	100
Osawatomie, Ks., U.S.	D9	93
Osborne, Ks., U.S.	C5	93
Osborne, co., Ks., U.S.	C5	93
Osbornsville, N.J., U.S.	C4	107
Osburn, Id., U.S.	B3	89
Osby, Swe.	B8	15
Oscar, La., U.S.	D4	95
Oscar, Ok., U.S.	D4	113
Osceola, Ar., U.S.	A5	91
Osceola, In., U.S.	C4	92
Osceola, Ia., U.S.	C4	102
Osceola, Mo., U.S.	C8	104
Osceola, Ne., U.S.	C7	115
Osceola, Pa., U.S.	C8	118
Osceola, S.D., U.S.	C4	120
Osceola, Tx., U.S.	C1	126
Osceola, Wi., U.S.	E5	86
Osceola, co., Fl., U.S.	A2	92
Osceola, co., Ia., U.S.	E5	99
Osceola, co., Mi., U.S.	E5	115
Osceola Mills, Pa., U.S.	C6	18
Oschatz, Ger.D.R.	B5	18
Oschersleben, Ger.D.R.	D7	99
Oscoda, Mi., U.S.	D6	99
Oscoda, co., Mi., U.S.	D3	108
Oscura Mountains, mts., N.M., U.S.	C8	19
Osek, Czech.	r31	14
Oselki, Sov. Un.	F7	91
Osgood, In., U.S.	A4	102
Osgood, Oh., U.S.	B1	112
Osgoode, On., Can.	B9	73
Osh, Sov. Un.	E10	29
Oshamambe, Japan	E10	33
Oshawa, On., Can.	D6	73
O-shima, i., Japan	J7	33
Oshkosh, Ne., U.S.	C3	104
Oshkosh, Wi., U.S.	D5	126
Oshnovīyeh, Iran	C2	39
Oshogbo, Nig.	E5	45
Oshoto, Wy., U.S.	B8	127
Oshtorān Kūh, mtn., Iran	E4	39
Oshwe, Zaire	B2	48
Osijek, Yugo.	C4	24
Osilinka, stm., B.C., Can.	A5	69
Osinniki, Sov. Un.	E26	8
Osipovichi, Sov. Un.	E7	27
Oskaloosa, Ia., U.S.	C5	92
Oskaloosa, Ks., U.S.	C8	93
Oskarshamn, Swe.	I7	14
Oskol, stm., Sov. Un.	G11	27
Oskū, Iran	C2	39
Osler, Sk., Can.	E2	75
Oslo, Nor.	H4	14
Oslo, Mn., U.S.	B1	100
Oslofjorden, Nor.	H4	14
Osmānābād, India	H6	37
Osmancik, Tur.	B10	40
Osmaneli, Tur.	B7	25
Osmaniye, Tur.	D11	40
Osmond, Ne., U.S.	B8	104
Osnabrock, N.D., U.S.	A7	111
Osnabrück, F.R.Ger.	B4	18
Osório, Braz.	D2	56
Osorno, Chile	C2	54
Osoyoos, B.C., Can.	E8	69
Osoyoos, Lake, l., Wa., U.S.	A6	124
Ospika, stm., B.C., Can.	A6	69
Osprey, Fl., U.S.	E4	86
Ossa, Mount, mtn., Austl.	o15	50
Ossabaw Island, i., Ga., U.S.	E5	87
Ossabaw Sound, strt., Ga., U.S.	E6	87
Osseo, Mn., U.S.	m12	100
Osseo, Wi., U.S.	D2	126
Ossian, In., U.S.	C7	91
Ossian, Ia., U.S.	A6	92
Ossineke, Mi., U.S.	D7	99
Ossining, N.Y., U.S.	D7	109
Ossipee, N.H., U.S.	C4	106
Ossipee, co., N.H., U.S.	C5	106
Ossipee Lake, l., N.H., U.S.	C4	106
Ossipee Mountains, mts., N.H., U.S.	C4	106
Ossokmanuan Lake, l., Nf., Can.	h8	72
Ossora, Sov. Un.	D34	128
Östaná, Swe.	t36	14
Ostashkov, Sov. Un.	C9	27
Osteen, Fl., U.S.	D5	86
Ostende see Oostende, Bel.	B5	16
Osterburg, Ger.D.R.	B5	18
Osterburg, Pa., U.S.	F4	115
Osterode, F.R.Ger.	B5	19
Östersund, Swe.	F6	14
Osterville, Ma., U.S.	C7	98
Osterwieck, Ger.D.R.	B5	19
Ostia Antica, Italy	h8	23
Ostiglia, Italy	D7	20
Ostrach, F.R.Ger.	B5	20
Ostrander, Mn., U.S.	G6	100
Ostrander, Oh., U.S.	B2	112
Ostrava, Czech.	D5	26
Ostróda, Pol.	B5	26
Ostrog, Sov. Un.	F6	27
Ostrogozhsk, Sov. Un.	F12	27
Ostrołęka, Pol.	B6	26
Ostrov, Czech.	C2	26
Ostrov, Rom.	C8	24
Ostrov, Sov. Un.	C7	27
Ostrowiec [Świętokrzyski], Pol.	C6	26
Ostrów Lubelski, Pol.	C7	26
Ostrów Mazowiecka, Pol.	B6	26
Ostrów Wielkopolski, Pol.	C4	26
Ostrzeszów, Pol.	C4	26
Ostseebad Graal-Müritz, Ger.D.R.	D6	15
Ostseebad Rerik, Ger.D.R.	D5	15
Ostuni, Italy	D6	23
Ōsuka, Japan	o16	33
Osüm, stm., Bul.	D7	24
Osumi, stm., Alb.	B3	25
Ōsumi Islands, is., Japan	E11	31
Ōsumi Strait, strt., Japan	K5	33
Osuna, Spain	D3	22
Osvaldo Cruz, Braz.	C2	56
Oswayo, Pa., U.S.	C5	115
Oswegatchie, Ct., U.S.	*D7	84
Oswegatchie, N.Y., U.S.	A5	109
Oswegatchie, stm., N.Y., U.S.	B5	109
Oswego, Il., U.S.	B5	90
Oswego, Ks., U.S.	E8	93
Oswego, Mt., U.S.	B11	103
Oswego, N.Y., U.S.	B4	109
Oswego, S.C., U.S.	C7	117
Oswego, co., N.Y., U.S.	B4	109
Oswego, stm., N.J., U.S.	D4	107
Oswego, stm., N.Y., U.S.	B4	109
Oswestry, Eng., U.K.	D5	10
Oświęcim (Auschwitz), Pol.	C5	26
Osyka, Ms., U.S.	D3	101
Otago Peninsula, pen., N.Z.	P13	51
Ōtaki, Japan	n19	33
Otar, Sov. Un.	E9	28
Otaru, Japan	C13	31
Otava, stm., Czech.	D8	19
Otavalo, Ec.	A2	58
Otavi, Nmb.	*o15	82
Otchinjau, Ang.	E1	48
Oteen, N.C., U.S.	f10	110
Otego, N.Y., U.S.	C5	109
Otero, co., Co., U.S.	D7	83
Otero, co., N.M., U.S.	E3	108
Othello, Wa., U.S.	C6	124
Otho, Ia., U.S.	B3	92
Othonoí, i., Grc.	C2	25
Óthris Mountains, mts., Grc.	E5	45
oti, stm., Afr.	E5	45
Otis, Co., U.S.	A8	83
Otis, In., U.S.	A4	91
Otis, Ks., U.S.	D4	93
Otis, Ma., U.S.	B1	98
Otisco, In., U.S.	G6	91
Otisco, Mn., U.S.	G5	100
Otisco, N.Y., U.S.	C4	109
Otis Orchards, Wa., U.S.	g14	124
Otis Reservoir, res., Ma., U.S.	B1	98
Otisville, Mi., U.S.	E7	99
Otjiwarongo, Nmb.	B2	49
Otley, Ia., U.S.	C4	92
Otočac, Yugo.	C2	24
Otoe, Ne., U.S.	D9	104
Otoe, co., Ne., U.S.	D9	104
Otra, stm., Nor.	H2	14
Otradnoye, Sov. Un.	s31	14
Otranto, Italy	D7	23
Otranto, Strait of, strt., Eur.	B2	40
Otsego, Mi., U.S.	F5	99
Otsego, co., Mi., U.S.	C6	99
Otsego, co., N.Y., U.S.	C5	109
Otsego Lake, Mi., U.S.	D6	99
Otsego Lake, l., N.Y., U.S.	C6	109
Ōtsu, Japan	o14	33
Ōtsuki, Japan	n17	33
Ottauquechee, stm., Vt., U.S.	D4	122
Ottawa, On., Can.	B9	73
Ottawa, Il., U.S.	B5	90
Ottawa, Ks., U.S.	D8	93
Ottawa, Oh., U.S.	A1	112
Ottawa, W.V., U.S.	n12	125
Ottawa, co., Ks., U.S.	C6	93
Ottawa, co., Mi., U.S.	F4	99
Ottawa, co., Oh., U.S.	A2	112
Ottawa, co., Ok., U.S.	A7	113
Ottawa, stm., Can.	G17	66
Ottawa, stm., Oh., U.S.	A1	112
Ottawa, stm., Oh., U.S.	e6	112
Ottawa-Carleton, co., On., Can.	B9	73
Ottawa Hills, Oh., U.S.	e6	112
Ottawa Islands, is., N.T., Can.	E16	66
Ottawa Lake, Mi., U.S.	G7	99
Otter, Mt., U.S.	E10	103
Otter, stm., Ab., Can.	A2	68
Otter, stm., Eng., U.K.	D3	91
Otterbein, In., U.S.	D3	91
Otterburg, F.R.Ger.	E2	106
Otter Brook, stm., N.H., U.S.	E2	106
Otter Brook Lake, l., N.H., U.S.	E2	106
Otterburne, Mb., Can.	E3	70
Otter Creek, Fl., U.S.	C4	86
Otter Creek, stm., Ut., U.S.	E4	121
Otter Creek, stm., Vt., U.S.	C2	122
Otter Creek Reservoir, res., Ut., U.S.	E4	121
Otter Islands, is., S.C., U.S.	m11	117
Otter Lake, Mi., U.S.	E7	99
Otter Lake, N.Y., U.S.	A5	109
Otter Lake, l., Sk., Can.	B3	75
Otter River, Ma., U.S.	A3	98
Otterndorf, F.R.Ger.	F5	100
Ottersberg, F.R.Ger.	C4	106
Otter Tail, co., Mn., U.S.	D2	100
Otter Tail, stm., Mn., U.S.	D2	100
Otter Tail Lake, l., Mn., U.S.	D3	100
Otterup, Den.	C4	15
Otterville, On., Can.	E4	73
Otterville, Il., U.S.	D3	90
Otterville, Ia., U.S.	B6	92
Otterville, Mo., U.S.	C4	102
Otthon, Sk., Can.	F4	75
Ottignies, Bel.	D4	17
Otto, Wy., U.S.	B4	127
Ottokee, Oh., U.S.	A1	112
Ottone, Italy	E5	20
Ottoson, Ia., U.S.	B3	92
Ottoville, Oh., U.S.	B1	112
Ottsville, Pa., U.S.	F11	115
Ottumwa, Ia., U.S.	C5	92
Ottumwa, S.D., U.S.	C2	118
Otuzco, Peru	C2	58
Otway, Cape, c., Austl.	G7	50
Otway, Seno, b., Chile	h11	54
Otwell, Ar., U.S.	B5	81
Otwell, In., U.S.	H3	91
Otwock, Pol.	m14	26
Ötztal Alps, mts., Eur.	C6	20
Ötztal Ach, stm., Aus.	B6	20
Ou, stm., Laos	B5	35
Ouachita, co., Ar., U.S.	D3	81
Ouachita, co., La., U.S.	B3	95
Ouachita, stm., U.S.	D9	76
Ouachita, Lake, res., Ar., U.S.	C2	81
Ouachita Mountains, mts., U.S.	D9	76
Ouadane, Maur.	B2	45
Ouaddaï, hist reg., Chad	o16	33
Ouagadougou, Burkina	D7	24
Ouahigouya, Burkina	B3	25
Ouaka, stm., Cen. Afr. Rep.	E11	31
Oualâta, Maur.	K5	33
Ouallam, Niger	D3	22
Ouallene, Alg.	E5	44
Ouanary, Fr. Gu.	B4	59
Ouanda Djallé, Cen. Afr. Rep.	*D7	84
Ouarane, reg., Maur.	B3	45
Ouarzazate, Mor.	C3	44
Oubangui (Ubangi), stm., Afr.	A2	48
Ouddorp, Neth.	C3	17
Oudenaarde, Bel.	D3	17
Oude-Pekela, Neth.	A6	17
Oudtshoorn, S. Afr.	D3	49
Ouellé, I.C.	E4	45
Ouelle, stm., P.Q., Can.	B8	74
Ouémé, stm., Benin	E5	45
Ouesso, Congo	A2	48
Ouest, Pointe de l', c., P.Q., Can.	k8	72
Ouest, Pointe du, c., St. P./M.	E3	72
Ouezzane, Mor.	C3	44
Oughter, Lough, l., Ire.	D3	10
Ougherard, Ire.	D2	11
Ouham, stm., Afr.	D3	45
Ouidah, Benin	E5	45
Oujda, Mor.	C4	44
Oullins, Fr.	E6	16
Oulu, Fin.	E11	14
Oulujärvi, l., Fin.	E12	14
Oum Chalouba, Chad	B4	46
Oum Hadjer, Chad	C3	46
Ounâne, Bîr, well, Mali	C3	46
Ounasjoki, stm., Fin.	D11	14
Ounianga Kébir, Chad	B4	46
Ouray, Co., U.S.	C3	83
Ouray, Ut., U.S.	C6	121
Ouray, co., Co., U.S.	C3	83
Ouray, Mount, mtn., Co., U.S.	D2	96
Ouri, Chad	A3	46
Ouricuri, Braz.	C2	57
Ourinhos, Braz.	C3	56
Ourique, Port.	D1	22
Ouro Fino, Braz.	C3	56
Ouro Prêto, Braz.	C4	56
Ourthe, stm., Bel.	D5	17
Ourukaen Island, i., Marsh Is.	P18	52
Ouse, stm., Eng., U.K.	D7	10
Ouse, stm., Eng., U.K.	F7	11
Outagamie, co., Wi., U.S.	D5	126
Outer Hebrides, is., Scot., U.K.	B3	10
Outer Island, i., Wi., U.S.	A3	126
Outer Santa Barbara Passage, strt., Ca., U.S.	F4	82
Outes, Spain	A1	22
Outing, Mn., U.S.	D5	100
Outjo, Nmb.	B2	49
Outlook, Sk., Can.	F2	75
Outlook, Mt., U.S.	B12	103
Outlook, Wa., U.S.	C5	124
Outpost Mountain, mtn., Ak., U.S.	B9	79
Outreau, Fr.	B4	16
Outremont, P.Q., Can.	p19	74
Ouville-la-Rivière, Fr.	E8	17
Ouzinkie, Ak., U.S.	D9	79
Ovada, Italy	B2	23
Oval, Pa., U.S.	D7	115
Ovalau, i., Fiji	H15	52
Ovalle, Chile	A2	54
Ovana, Cerro, mtn., Ven.	C4	60
Ovando, Mt., U.S.	C3	103
Ovar, Port.	B1	22
Overath, F.R.Ger.	D8	92
Overbrook, Ks., U.S.	D8	93
Overbrook, Ok., U.S.	C4	113
Overflowing, stm., Can.	C5	80
Overgaard, Az., U.S.	C5	80
Overijse, Bel.	D4	17
Overijssel, prov., Neth.	C6	17
Overisel, Mi., U.S.	F4	99
Overland, Mo., U.S.	f13	102
Overland Park, Ks., U.S.	m16	93
Overlea, Md., U.S.	B5	97
Overly, N.D., U.S.	A5	111
Overstreet, Fl., U.S.	C1	86
Overton, Nv., U.S.	G7	105
Overton, Tx., U.S.	C5	120
Overton, co., Tn., U.S.	C8	119
Övertorneå, Swe.	D10	14
Ovett, Ms., U.S.	D4	101
Ovid, Co., U.S.	A8	83
Ovid, Mi., U.S.	E6	99
Ovid, N.Y., U.S.	C4	109
Oviedo, Spain	A3	22
Oviedo, Fl., U.S.	D5	86
Ovruch, Sov. Un.	F8	27
Owando, Congo	B2	48
Owaneco, Il., U.S.	D4	90
Owanka, S.D., U.S.	D3	118
Owasco, N.Y., U.S.	C4	109
Owasco Lake, l., N.Y., U.S.	C4	109
Owasso, Ok., U.S.	A6	113
Owatonna, Mn., U.S.	F5	100
Owbeh, Afg.	D11	39
Owego, N.Y., U.S.	C4	109
Owen, Wi., U.S.	D3	126
Owen, co., In., U.S.	F4	91
Owen, co., Ky., U.S.	B5	94
Owen, Lake, l., Wi., U.S.	B2	126
Owen, Mount, mtn., N.Z.	N14	51
Owen, Mount, mtn., Co., U.S.	C3	83
Owendale, Mi., U.S.	E7	99
Owens, stm., Ca., U.S.	D4	82
Owensboro, Ky., U.S.	C2	94
Owensburg, In., U.S.	G4	91
Owens Creek, stm., Md., U.S.	A3	97
Owens Cross Roads, Al., U.S.	A3	78
Owens Lake, l., Ca., U.S.	D5	82
Owensville, In., U.S.	H2	91
Owensville, Mo., U.S.	C6	102
Owensville, Oh., U.S.	C1	112
Owenton, Ky., U.S.	B5	94
Owerri, Nig.	E6	45
Owey, i., Ire.	B3	11
Owikeno Lake, l., B.C., Can.	D4	69
Owings, Md., U.S.	C4	97
Owings Mills, Md., U.S.	B4	97
Owingsville, Ky., U.S.	B6	94
Owl Creek, stm., Wy., U.S.	C4	127
Owl Creek Mountains, mts., Wy., U.S.	C4	127
Owls Head, Me., U.S.	D3	96
Owo, Nig.	E6	45
Owosso, Mi., U.S.	E6	99
Owsley, co., Ky., U.S.	C6	94
Owyhee, Nv., U.S.	B5	105
Owyhee, co., Id., U.S.	G2	89
Owyhee, stm., U.S.	E9	114
Owyhee, Lake, res., Or., U.S.	D9	114
Owyhee, North Fork, stm., U.S.	E9	114
Owyhee, South Fork, stm., U.S.	G2	89
Owyhee Dam, Or., U.S.	D9	114
Owyhee Mountains, mts., U.S.	G2	89
Öxabäck, Swe.	A6	15
Oxbow, Sk., Can.	B4	96
Oxbow, Me., U.S.	B10	114
Oxbow Dam, U.S.	E2	89
Oxford, N.S., Can.	D6	71
Oxford, Eng., U.K.	E6	10
Oxford, Al., U.S.	B4	78
Oxford, Ct., U.S.	D3	84
Oxford, Fl., U.S.	D4	86
Oxford, Ga., U.S.	C3	87
Oxford, Id., U.S.	G6	89
Oxford, In., U.S.	C3	91
Oxford, Ia., U.S.	C6	92
Oxford, Ks., U.S.	E6	93
Oxford, Me., U.S.	D2	96
Oxford, Md., U.S.	C5	97
Oxford, Ma., U.S.	B4	98
Oxford, Mi., U.S.	F7	99
Oxford, Ms., U.S.	A4	101
Oxford, Ne., U.S.	D6	104
Oxford, N.J., U.S.	B3	107
Oxford, N.Y., U.S.	C5	109
Oxford, N.C., U.S.	A4	110
Oxford, Oh., U.S.	C1	112
Oxford, Pa., U.S.	G10	115
Oxford, Wi., U.S.	E4	126
Oxford, co., On., Can.	D4	73
Oxford, co., Me., U.S.	D2	96
Oxford House, Mb., Can.	B4	70
Oxford Junction, Ia., U.S.	C7	92
Oxford Junction, N.S., Can.	D6	71
Oxford Lake, l., Mb., Can.	B4	70
Oxford Peak, mtn., Id., U.S.	G6	89
Oxfordshire, co., Eng., U.K.	C6	12
Oxly, Mo., U.S.	E7	102
Oxnard, Ca., U.S.	E4	82
Oxon Hill, Md., U.S.	f9	97
Oyace, Italy	E3	21
Oyama, B.C., Can.	D8	69
Oyama, Japan	m18	33
Oyapock (Oiapoque), stm., S.A.	B4	59
Oyat, stm., Sov. Un.	A10	27
Oyem, Gabon	A2	48
Oyen, Ab., Can.	D5	68
Øyeren, l., Nor.	p29	14
Oykel Bridge, Scot., U.K.	C4	13
Oykel, stm., Scot., U.K.	C4	13
Oymyakon, Sov. Un.	C17	29
Oyo, Nig.	E5	45
Oyonnax, Fr.	D6	16
Oyster Bay, N.Y., U.S.	E7	109
Oyster Keys, is., Fl., U.S.	G6	86
Oyster Ridge, mtn., Wy., U.S.	E2	127
Ozamiz, Phil.	D6	34
Ozan, Ar., U.S.	C2	81
Ozark, Al., U.S.	D4	78
Ozark, Ar., U.S.	B2	81
Ozark, Mo., U.S.	D4	102
Ozark, co., Mo., U.S.	E5	102
Ozark Escarpment, clf, U.S.	B4	81
Ozark Plateau, plat., U.S.	C9	76
Ozark Reservoir, res., U.S.	B1	81
Ozarks, Lake of the, res., Mo., U.S.	C5	102
Ożarowice, Pol.	g10	26
Ozaukee, co., Wi., U.S.	E6	126
Ózd, Hung.	A5	24
Ozernyy, Sov. Un.	C6	28
Ozette Lake, l., Wa., U.S.	A1	124
Ozieri, Italy	D2	23
Ozona, Fl., U.S.	o10	86
Ozona, Tx., U.S.	D2	120
Ozorków, Pol.	C5	26
Ozuluama, Mex.	C5	63

P

Name	Map Ref	Page
Paar, stm., F.R.Ger.	E6	19
Paarl, S. Afr.	D2	49
Paauhau, Hi., U.S.	C6	88
Paauilo, Hi., U.S.	C6	88
Pabbay, i., Scot., U.K.	C1	13
Pabianice, Pol.	C5	26
Pablo, Mt., U.S.	C2	103
Pablo, Bngl.	D8	36
Pacaás Novos, Serra dos, mts., Braz.	C4	59
Pacajá, stm., Braz.	C4	59
Pacasmayo, Peru	C2	58
Pace, Fl., U.S.	u14	86
Pace, Ms., U.S.	B3	101
Pachaug Pond, l., Ct., U.S.	C8	84
Pachmarhi, India	F7	37
Pachuca [de Soto], Mex.	C5	63
Pachuta, Ms., U.S.	C5	101
Pacific, B.C., Can.	B3	69
Pacific, Mo., U.S.	C7	102
Pacific, Wa., U.S.	f11	124
Pacific, co., Wa., U.S.	C2	124
Pacific Beach, Wa., U.S.	B1	124
Pacifica, Ca., U.S.	h8	82
Pacific City, Or., U.S.	B3	114
Pacific Creek, stm., Wy., U.S.	D3	127
Pacific Grove, Ca., U.S.	D3	82
Pacific Islands, Trust Territory of the, dep., Oc.	F9	6
Pacific Junction, Ia., U.S.	C2	92
Pacific Ocean	E11	6
Pacific Palisades, Hi., U.S.	g10	88
Pacific Ranges, mts., B.C., Can.	D4	69
Pacific Rim National Park, B.C., Can.	E5	69
Packard Mountain, hill, Ma., U.S.	B3	98
Pack Monadnock Mountain, mtn., N.H., U.S.	E3	106
Packwaukee, Wi., U.S.	E4	126
Packwood, Ia., U.S.	C5	92
Packwood, Wa., U.S.	C4	124
Pacolet, S.C., U.S.	B4	117
Pacolet, stm., S.C., U.S.	A4	117
Pacolet Mills, S.C., U.S.	B4	117
Pacora, Pan.	k12	62
Pacora, stm., Pan.	k12	62
Pacov, Czech.	D9	19
Pacquet, Nf., Can.	D4	72
Pactola Reservoir, res., S.D., U.S.	C2	118
Pactolus, N.C., U.S.	B5	110
Paczków, Pol.	C4	26
Padang, Indon.	F2	34
Padang, i., Indon.	L5	35
Padang Endau, Malay.	K5	35
Padangpanjang, Indon.	E1	34
Padangsidempuan, Indon.	E1	34
Padauiri, stm., Braz.	B2	59
Paddle Prairie, Ab., Can.	f7	68
Paddling Lake, l., Sk., Can.	E2	75
Paddock Lake, Wi., U.S.	n11	126
Paddockwood, Sk., Can.	D3	75
Paddy Knob, mtn., U.S.	C5	125
Paden, Ms., U.S.	A5	101
Paden, Ok., U.S.	B5	113
Paden City, W.V., U.S.	B4	125
Paderborn, F.R.Ger.	C4	18
Pad Idan, Pak.	C4	36
Padilla, Bol.	C3	55
Padova (Padua), Italy	B3	23
Padre Island, i., Tx., U.S.	F4	120
Padre Island National Seashore, Tx., U.S.	F4	120
Padroni, Co., U.S.	A7	83
Padstow, Eng., U.K.	D3	12
Paducah, Ky., U.S.	e9	94
Paducah, Tx., U.S.	B2	120
Paektu, Mount, mtn., Asia	F4	33
Paepaeloe'i'a, Cape, c., W. Sam.	F11	52
Paeroa, N.Z.	L15	51
Paestum, hist., Italy	D5	23
Pafúri, Moz.	B5	49
Pag, i., Yugo.	C2	24
Pagai Selatan, i., Indon.	F2	34
Pagai Utara, i., Indon.	F2	34
Pagasitikós Kólpos (Gulf of Vólos), b., Grc.	C4	40
Pagatan, Indon.	F4	34
Pagat Point, c., Guam	L10	52
Page, Az., U.S.	A4	80
Page, Ne., U.S.	B7	104
Page, N.D., U.S.	B8	111
Page, Ok., U.S.	C7	113
Page, W.V., U.S.	C3	125
Page, co., Ia., U.S.	D2	92
Page, co., Va., U.S.	B4	123
Pageland, S.C., U.S.	B7	117
Page Manor, Oh., U.S.	*C1	112
Pagny [-sur-Moselle], Fr.	F5	17
Pagoda Bay, b., Guam	M10	52
Pagoda Peak, mtn., Co., U.S.	A3	83
Pagoda Point, c., Burma	G9	36
Pago Pago, Am. Sam.	G13	52
Pago Pago Harbor, b., Am. Sam.	F13	52
Pagosa Point, c., Guam	M10	52
Pagosa Springs, Co., U.S.	D3	83
Paguate, N.M., U.S.	B2	108
Pahala, Hi., U.S.	D6	88
Pahang, state, Malay.	K5	35
Pahang, stm., Malay.	E2	34
Pahārpur, Pak.	A3	37
Pahaska, Wy., U.S.	B3	127
Pahoa, Hi., U.S.	D7	88
Pahokee, Fl., U.S.	F6	86
Pahrump, Nv., U.S.	G6	105
Pahute Mesa, mtn., Nv., U.S.	F5	105
Paia, Hi., U.S.	C5	88
Paignton, Eng., U.K.	D4	12
Päijänne, l., Fin.	G11	14
Pailolo Channel, strt., Hi., U.S.	B5	88
Paincourt, On., Can.	E2	73
Paincourtville, La., U.S.	k9	95
Painesdale, Mi., U.S.	A2	99
Painesville, Oh., U.S.	A4	112
Paint, stm., Mi., U.S.	B2	99
Paint Bank, Va., U.S.	C2	123
Paint Creek, stm., Oh., U.S.	C2	112
Paint Creek, stm., Oh., U.S.	m13	125
Paint Creek, North Fork, stm., Oh., U.S.	C2	112
Paint Creek Lake, res., Oh., U.S.	C2	112
Painted Desert, des., Az., U.S.	B4	80
Painted Post, N.Y., U.S.	C3	109
Painted Rock Reservoir, res., Az., U.S.	D3	80
Painter, Va., U.S.	C7	123
Paint Lick, Ky., U.S.	C5	94
Paint Mountain, W.V., U.S.	n13	125
Paint Rock, Al., U.S.	A3	78
Paint Rock, Tx., U.S.	D2	120
Paintsville, Ky., U.S.	C7	94
Paisley, On., Can.	C3	73
Paisley, Scot., U.K.	E4	13
Paisley, Fl., U.S.	D5	86
Paisley, Or., U.S.	E6	114
Paita, Peru	C1	58
Pajala, Swe.	D10	14

Index

Name	Map Ref	Page
Pajarito, N.M., U.S.	*B3	108
Pajaros Point, c., V.I., Br.	A7	65
Pajon Point, c., Guam	L10	52
Pakanbaru, Indon.	E2	34
Pakhra, stm., Sov. Un.	n17	27
Pakistan, ctry., Asia	C4	36
Pakokku, Burma	D9	36
Pakra, stm., Yugo.	C3	24
Pakowki Lake, l., Ab., Can.	E5	68
Pakwa Lake, l., Mb., Can.	D2	70
Pakxe, Laos	B3	34
Pala, Chad	D2	46
Palacios, Tx., U.S.	E4	120
Palafrugell, Spain	B7	22
Palagruža, is., Yugo.	D3	24
Palaiokhóra, Grc.	E4	25
Palaión Fáliron, Grc.	h11	25
Palamás, Grc.	C4	25
Palamós, Spain	B7	22
Palana, Sov. Un.	D18	29
Palanga, Sov. Un.	D3	27
Palangkaraya, Indon.	F4	34
Pālanpur, India	D5	36
Palaoa Point, c., Hi., U.S.	C4	88
Palapag, Phil.	C7	34
Palapye, Bots.	B4	49
Palas del Rey, Spain	A2	22
Palatine, Il., U.S.	A5	90
Palatka, Fl., U.S.	C5	86
Palau (Belau), ter., T.T.P.I.	F8	6
Palauig, Phil.	o12	34
Palauig Point, c., Phil.	o12	34
Palauli (Vailoa), W. Sam.	F11	52
Palauli Bay, b., W. Sam.	F11	52
Palawan, i., Phil.	C5	34
Palazzolo Acreide, Italy	F5	23
Palco, Ks., U.S.	C4	93
Palembang, Indon.	F2	34
Palena, stm., S.A.	C2	54
Palencia, Spain	A3	22
Palenque, hist., Mex.	B2	62
Palenville, N.Y., U.S.	C6	109
Palermo, Italy	E4	23
Palermo, Me., U.S.	D3	96
Palermo, N.J., U.S.	E3	107
Palermo, N.D., U.S.	A3	111
Palestine, Ar., U.S.	C5	81
Palestine, Ct., U.S.	*D2	84
Palestine, Il., U.S.	D6	90
Palestine, Oh., U.S.	B1	112
Palestine, Tx., U.S.	D5	120
Palestine, W.V., U.S.	B3	125
Palestine, hist reg, Asia	G10	40
Palestine, Lake, res., Tx., U.S.	C5	120
Palestrina, Italy	h9	23
Paletwa, Burma	D9	36
Pälezgïr Chauki, Pak.	B2	36
Pālghāt, India	F6	36
Palhoça, Braz.	D3	57
Pāli, India	E4	37
Palidoro (Baebiana), Italy	h8	23
Palikea, mtn., Hi., U.S.	g9	88
Paliker Point, c., Micron.	Q17	52
Palimé, Togo	E5	45
Palisade, Co., U.S.	B2	83
Palisade, Mn., U.S.	D5	100
Palisade, Nv., U.S.	D4	104
Palisades, Id., U.S.	F7	89
Palisades, Wa., U.S.	B6	124
Palisades Park, N.J., U.S.	h8	107
Palisades Reservoir, res., U.S.	F7	89
Palisadoes, spit, Jam.	F15	65
Paliseul, Bel.	E5	19
Pālitāna, India	G3	37
Palk Strait, strt., Asia	G6	36
Pallaskenry, Ire.	E3	11
Pallasovka, Sov. Un.	D3	28
Palling, B.C., Can.	B5	69
Palliser, Cape, c., N.Z.	N15	51
Pall Mall, Tn., U.S.	C9	119
Palma, Moz.	D7	48
Palma, stm., Braz.	D1	57
Palma del Río, Spain	D5	22
Palma [de Mallorca], Spain	C7	22
Palmares, Braz.	D2	56
Palmar Sur, C.R.	F6	62
Palmas, Braz.	D2	56
Palmas, Cape, c., Lib	F3	45
Palmas de Monte Alto, Braz.	A4	56
Palm Bay, Fl., U.S.	D6	86
Palm Beach, Fl., U.S.	F6	86
Palm Beach, co., Fl., U.S.	F6	86
Palm Beach Gardens, Fl., U.S.	F6	86
Palmdale, Ca., U.S.	E4	82
Palmdale, Fl., U.S.	F5	86
Palm Desert, Ca., U.S.	*F5	82
Palmeira, Braz.	D2	57
Palmeira d'Oeste, Braz.	D2	57
Palmeira dos Indios, Braz.	C3	57
Palmeirinhas, Ponta das, c., Ang.	C1	48
Palmer, Sk., Can.	H2	75
Palmer, Ak., U.S.	C10	79
Palmer, Il., U.S.	D4	90
Palmer, Ia., U.S.	B3	92
Palmer, Ks., U.S.	C6	93
Palmer, Ma., U.S.	B3	98
Palmer, Mi., U.S.	B3	99
Palmer, Ms., U.S.	D4	101
Palmer, Ne., U.S.	C8	104
Palmer, Tn., U.S.	D8	119
Palmer, Tx., U.S.	n10	120
Palmer, Wa., U.S.	f12	124
Palmeras do Sul, Braz.	B6	57
Palmer Lake, Co., U.S.	B6	83
Palmer Land, reg., Ant.	B7	7
Palmer Park, Md., U.S.	*C4	97
Palmerston, On., Can.	D4	73
Palmerston, N.Z.	P13	51
Palmerston North, N.Z.	N15	51
Palmerton, Pa., U.S.	E10	115
Palmersville, Tn., U.S.	A3	119
Palmetto, Fl., U.S.	E4	86
Palmetto, Ga., U.S.	C2	87
Palmetto, La., U.S.	D4	95
Palmi, Italy	E5	23
Palmira, Col.	C3	60
Palmira, Cuba	C3	64
Palmira, Ec.	C3	60
Palmitos, Braz.	D2	57
Palms, Mi., U.S.	E8	99
Palms, Isle of, i., S.C., U.S.	F8	117
Palm Springs, Ca., U.S.	F5	82
Palm Valley, Fl., U.S.	m9	86
Palmyra, Il., U.S.	D3	90
Palmyra, In., U.S.	H5	91
Palmyra, Me., U.S.	D3	96
Palmyra, Mo., U.S.	B6	102
Palmyra, Ne., U.S.	D9	104
Palmyra, N.J., U.S.	C2	107
Palmyra, N.Y., U.S.	B3	109
Palmyra, N.C., U.S.	A5	110
Palmyra, Pa., U.S.	F8	115
Palmyra, Tn., U.S.	A4	119
Palmyra, Va., U.S.	C4	123
Palmyra, Wi., U.S.	F5	126
Palmyra, atoll, Oc.	F12	6
Palmyras Point, c., India	G11	37
Palo (Alsium), Italy	h8	23
Palo, Ia., U.S.	B6	92
Palo Alto, Ca., U.S.	D2	82
Palo Alto, co., Ia., U.S.	A3	92
Palo Duro Canyon, val., Tx., U.S.	B2	120
Paloich, Sud.	C3	47
Palomar Mountain, mtn., Ca., U.S.	F5	82
Palomas Mountains, mts., Az., U.S.	D2	80
Palombara Sabina, Italy	g9	23
Palo Negro, Col.	C3	60
Palo Pinto, Tx., U.S.	C3	120
Palo Pinto, co., Tx., U.S.	C3	120
Palopo, Indon.	F6	34
Palos, Cape, c., Spain	D5	22
Palos Heights, Il., U.S.	*k9	90
Palos Hills, Il., U.S.	*k9	90
Palos Park, Il., U.S.	k9	90
Palos Verdes Estates, Ca., U.S.	n12	82
Palourde, Lake, l., La., U.S.	k9	95
Palouse, Wa., U.S.	C8	124
Palouse, stm., Wa., U.S.	C7	124
Palo Verde, Az., U.S.	D3	80
Palo Verde, Ca., U.S.	F6	82
Palpa, Peru	D3	58
Pålsboda, Swe.	t33	14
Pama, Burkina	D5	45
Pamamaroo Lake, l., Austl.	F4	51
Pambrun, Sk., Can.	H2	75
Pamekasan, Indon.	G4	34
Pamiers, Fr.	F4	16
Pamir, mts., Asia	F10	29
Pamlico, co., N.C., U.S.	B6	110
Pamlico, stm., N.C., U.S.	B6	110
Pamlico Sound, strt., N.C., U.S.	B6	110
Pampa, Tx., U.S.	B2	120
Pampa, reg., Arg.	G4	53
Pampa Grande, Bol.	C3	55
Pampanga, stm., Phil.	o13	34
Pampas, Peru	D3	58
Pampilhosa do Botão, Port.	B1	22
Pamplico, S.C., U.S.	D8	117
Pamplin, Va., U.S.	C4	123
Pamplona, Col.	B3	60
Pamplona, Spain	A5	22
Pamunkey, stm., Va., U.S.	C5	123
Pana, Il., U.S.	D4	90
Panaca, Fl., U.S.	B2	86
Panache, Lake, l., On., Can.	A3	73
Panagyurishte, Bul.	D7	24
Panaitan, i., Indon.	G3	34
Panaji (Panjim) (Nova Goa), India	E5	36
Panama, Braz.	B3	56
Panamá, Pan.	F8	62
Panama, Il., U.S.	D4	90
Panama, Ne., U.S.	C9	104
Panama, N.Y., U.S.	C1	109
Panama, Ok., U.S.	B7	113
Panama, ctry., N.A.	F8	62
Panamá, Bahía de, b., Pan.	F8	62
Panamá, Golfo de, b., Pan.	F8	62
Panama Canal, Pan.	k11	62
Panama City, Fl., U.S.	u16	86
Panama City Beach, Fl., U.S.	u16	86
Panambi, Braz.	D2	56
Panamint Range, mts., Ca., U.S.	D5	82
Panao, Peru	C2	58
Panarea, i., Italy	E5	23
Panaro, stm., Italy	B3	23
Panay, i., Phil.	C6	34
Pancake Range, mts., Nv., U.S.	E6	105
Pančevo, Yugo.	C5	24
Pancoastburg, Oh., U.S.	C2	112
Panda, Moz.	B5	49
Pandharpur, India	D5	36
Pāndhurna, India	G7	37
Pando, Ur.	E1	56
Pando, dept., Bol.	B2	55
Pandora, Oh., U.S.	B2	112
Pandora, Tx., U.S.	E4	120
Pandu, Zaire	B2	48
Panelas, Braz.	k5	57
Panet, P.Q., Can.	C7	74
Panevežys, Sov. Un.	D5	27
Panfilov, Sov. Un.	E10	29
Pangala, Congo	B1	48
Pangani, Tan.	C6	48
Pangburn, Ar., U.S.	B4	81
Pangi, Zaire	B4	48
Pañginay, Phil.	o13	34
Pangkalanbuun, Indon.	F4	34
Pangkalpinang, Indon.	F3	34
Pangman, Sk., Can.	H3	75
Pangnirtung, N.T., Can.	C19	66
Pangsau Pass, Asia	C10	36
Panguipulli, Chile	B2	54
Panguitch, Ut., U.S.	F3	121
Panhandle, Tx., U.S.	B2	120
Paniau, mtn., Hi., U.S.	B1	88
Panié, Mont, mtn., N. Cal.	*H10	6
Pānihāti, India	*D8	37
Paniqui, Phil.	C6	34
Panj, stm., Asia	k17	39
Panjāb, Afg.	D13	39
Panjgūr, Pak.	C3	36
Panjim see Panaji, India	E5	36
Panjnad, Pak.	G13	39
Pankey, Ar., U.S.	h10	81
Pankeyville, Il., U.S.	F5	90
Pankshin, Nig.	B1	48
Panmunjom, N. Kor.	H3	33
Panna, India	D7	37
Panola, Al., U.S.	C1	78
Panola, co., Ms., U.S.	A3	101
Panola, co., Tx., U.S.	C5	120
Panora, Ia., U.S.	C3	92
Panorama, Braz.	D2	56
Pansey, Al., U.S.	D4	78
Panshan, China	D9	32
Panshi, China	C11	32
Pantar, i., Indon.	G6	34
Pantego, N.C., U.S.	B6	110
Pantelleria, Italy	F3	23
Pantelleria, i., Italy	F4	23
Panthersville, Ga., U.S.	*h8	87
Pantin, Fr.	g10	16
Panton, Vt., U.S.	C2	122
Pánuco, Mex.	C5	63
Pánuco, stm., Mex.	k14	63
Panulcillo, Chile	F1	55
Panzi, Zaire	C2	48
Panzos, Guat.	D7	63
Pão de Açúcar, Braz.	C3	57
Paola, Italy	E6	23
Paola, Ks., U.S.	D9	93
Paoli, In., U.S.	G5	91
Paoli, Ok., U.S.	C4	113
Paoli, Pa., U.S.	o20	115
Paonia, Co., U.S.	C3	83
Paoua, Cen. Afr. Rep.	D4	46
Paoy Pet, Kam.	F5	35
Pápa, Hung.	B3	24
Papaaloa, Hi., U.S.	D6	88
Papagayo, Golfo de, b., C.R.	E7	63
Papago Indian Reservation, Az., U.S.	E3	80
Papaikou, Hi., U.S.	D6	88
Papantla [de Olarte], Mex.	C5	63
Papawai Point, c., Hi., U.S.	C5	88
Papeete, Fr. Poly.	H13	6
Papenburg, F.R.Ger.	B8	18
Papillion, Ne., U.S.	C9	104
Papineau, co., P.Q., Can.	D2	74
Papineau Labelle, Réserve, P.Q., Can.	C2	74
Papineauville, P.Q., Can.	D2	74
Paposo, Chile	E1	55
Papua, Gulf of, b., Pap. N. Gui.	k11	50
Papua New Guinea, ctry., Oc.	G8	6
Papudo, Chile	A2	54
Papun, Burma	E10	36
Paquetville, N.B., Can.	B4	71
Pará see Belém, Braz.	B1	57
Pará, state, Braz.	C4	59
Pará, dept., Sur.	A3	59
Pará, stm., Braz.	C5	59
Paraburdoo, Austl.	D2	50
Paracale, Phil.	o14	34
Paracatu, Braz.	D3	56
Paracatu, stm., Braz.	B3	56
Parke, co., In., U.S.	E3	91
Paracel Islands, is., Asia	B4	34
Parachute, Co., U.S.	B2	83
Paracín, Yugo.	D5	24
Paracuru, Braz.	B2	57
Paradis, La., U.S.	k11	95
Paradise, Ca., U.S.	C3	82
Paradise, Ks., U.S.	C5	93
Paradise, Mi., U.S.	B5	99
Paradise, Mt., U.S.	C2	103
Paradise, Nv., U.S.	G6	105
Paradise, Ut., U.S.	B4	121
Paradise, stm., Nf., Can.	D3	72
Paradise Hill, Sk., Can.	D1	75
Paradise Hills, N.M., U.S.	B3	108
Paradise Island, i., Bah.	m18	64
Paradise River, Nf., Can.	B4	72
Paradise Valley, Ab., Can.	C5	68
Paradise Valley, Az., U.S.	k9	80
Paradise Valley, Nv., U.S.	B4	105
Paradise Valley, Wy., U.S.	D6	127
Paradox, Co., U.S.	C2	83
Paragon, In., U.S.	F4	91
Paragonah, Ut., U.S.	F3	121
Paragould, Ar., U.S.	A5	81
Paragua, stm., Ven.	B5	60
Paraguaçu, stm., Braz.	D3	57
Paraguaçu Paulista, Braz.	C2	56
Paraguaná, Península de, pen., Ven.	A4	60
Paraguari, Para.	E4	55
Paraguari, dept., Para.	E4	55
Paraguay, ctry., S.A.	D4	55
Paraguay (Paraguai), stm., S.A.	D4	55
Paraíba, state, Braz.	C3	57
Paraíba, stm., Braz.	h6	57
Paraíba do Sul, stm., Braz.	g6	56
Paraíso, Pan.	k11	62
Paraisópolis, Braz.	C3	56
Parakou, Benin	E5	45
Paraiso, Braz.	D6	57
Paramaribo, Sur.	A3	59
Paramonga, Peru	D3	58
Paramount, Ca., U.S.	*n12	82
Paramount, Md., U.S.	A2	97
Paramus, N.J., U.S.	h8	107
Paran, Nahal, val.	D6	41
Paraná, Arg.	A4	54
Paraná, Braz.	D1	57
Paraná, state, Braz.	C2	56
Paraná, stm., Braz.	D1	57
Paraná, stm., S.A.	G5	53
Paranaguá, Braz.	D3	56
Paranaíba, Braz.	B2	56
Paranaíba, stm., Braz.	B2	56
Paranaiguara, Braz.	B2	56
Paranam, Sur.	A3	59
Paranavaí, Braz.	C2	56
Paraopeba, Braz.	E2	57
Parapetí, stm., Bol.	C3	55
Parauaquara, Serra, hill, Braz.	C4	59
Paray-le-Monial, Fr.	D6	16
Parbati, stm., India	H6	37
Parbhani, India	H6	37
Parchim, Ger.D.R.	B5	18
Parchment, Mi., U.S.	F5	99
Parczew, Pol.	C7	26
Pardee, Va., U.S.	e9	123
Pardeeville, Wi., U.S.	E4	126
Pardes Hanna-Karkur, Isr.	B6	41
Pardo, stm., Braz.	C3	56
Pardo, stm., Braz.	D1	57
Pardo, stm., Braz.	D2	56
Pardoe, Pa., U.S.	D1	115
Pardubice, Czech.	E15	18
Parecis, Chapada dos, mts., Braz.	B4	59
Parem, i., Micron.	Q18	52
Parempei, i., Micron.	Q17	52
Parent, P.Q., Can.	k12	74
Parepare, Indon.	F5	34
Párga, Grc.	C3	40
Pargo, Ponta do, c., Port.	h11	22
Pargolovo, Sov. Un.	r31	14
Paria, stm., U.S.	A4	80
Paria, Gulf of, b.	A5	60
Paria, Península de, pen., Ven.	A5	60
Pariaguán, Ven.	B5	60
Paria Plateau, plat., Az., U.S.	A4	80
Paricutín, vol., Mex.	n12	63
Parigi, Indon.	F6	34
Parika, Guy.	A3	59
Parima, Serra (Sierra Parima), mts., S.A.	B2	59
Parima, Sierra (Serra Parima), mts., S.A.	C5	60
Pariñas, Punta, c., Peru	B1	58
Parintins, Braz.	C3	59
Paris, On., Can.	D4	73
Paris, Fr.	C5	16
Paris, Ar., U.S.	B2	81
Paris, Id., U.S.	G7	89
Paris, Il., U.S.	D6	90
Paris, Ky., U.S.	B5	94
Paris, Me., U.S.	D2	96
Paris, Mi., U.S.	E5	99
Paris, Ms., U.S.	A4	101
Paris, Mo., U.S.	B5	102
Paris, Tn., U.S.	A3	119
Paris, Tx., U.S.	C5	120
Paris, Va., U.S.	A5	123
Paris Crossing, In., U.S.	G6	91
Parish, N.Y., U.S.	B4	109
Parishville, N.Y., U.S.	f10	109
Parisville, P.Q., Can.	C5	74
Park, Ks., U.S.	C3	93
Park, co., Co., U.S.	B5	83
Park, co., Mt., U.S.	E6	103
Park, co., Wy., U.S.	B3	127
Park, stm., N.D., U.S.	A8	111
Park City, Ks., U.S.	g12	93
Park City, Ky., U.S.	C4	94
Park City, Mt., U.S.	E8	103
Park City, Ut., U.S.	C4	121
Parkdale, Ar., U.S.	D4	81
Parkdale, P.E., Can.	C6	71
Parkdale, Mi., U.S.	D4	99
Parkdale, Or., U.S.	B5	114
Parker, Az., U.S.	C1	80
Parker, Co., U.S.	B6	83
Parker, Fl., U.S.	u16	86
Parker, Id., U.S.	F7	89
Parker, Ks., U.S.	D9	93
Parker, Pa., U.S.	D2	115
Parker, S.D., U.S.	D8	118
Parker, Wa., U.S.	C5	124
Parker, co., Tx., U.S.	C4	120
Parker City, In., U.S.	D7	91
Parker Dam, Ca., U.S.	E6	82
Parker Dam, U.S.	C1	80
Parker Peak, mtn., S.D., U.S.	D2	118
Parkers Prairie, Mn., U.S.	D3	100
Parkersburg, Ia., U.S.	B5	92
Parkersburg, Il., U.S.	E5	90
Parkersburg, W.V., U.S.	B3	125
Parkertown, N.J., U.S.	D4	107
Parkerview, Sk., Can.	F4	75
Parkerville, Ks., U.S.	D7	93
Parkes, Austl.	F8	50
Parkesburg, Pa., U.S.	G10	115
Park Falls, Wi., U.S.	C3	126
Park Forest, Il., U.S.	B6	90
Park Forest South, Il., U.S.	B6	90
Park Hall, Md., U.S.	D5	97
Park Head, On., Can.	C3	73
Park Hill, Ok., U.S.	B7	113
Parkhill, On., Can.	D3	73
Park Hills, Ky., U.S.	h13	94
Parkin, Ar., U.S.	B5	81
Parkland, Ab., Can.	D4	68
Parkland, Wa., U.S.	f11	124
Park Layne, Oh., U.S.	C1	112
Parkman, Sk., Can.	H5	75
Parkman, Me., U.S.	C3	96
Parkman, Oh., U.S.	A4	112
Parkman, Wy., U.S.	B5	127
Park Place, Or., U.S.	h12	114
Park Plateau, plat., Co., U.S.	D6	83
Park Range, mts., Co., U.S.	A4	83
Park Rapids, Mn., U.S.	D3	100
Park Ridge, Il., U.S.	B6	90
Park Ridge, N.J., U.S.	g8	107
Park River, N.D., U.S.	A8	111
Parkrose, Or., U.S.	B4	114
Parks, Ar., U.S.	C2	81
Parks, La., U.S.	D4	95
Parkside, Sk., Can.	D2	75
Parksley, Va., U.S.	C7	123
Parkston, S.D., U.S.	D8	118
Parksville, B.C., Can.	E5	69
Parksville, N.Y., U.S.	D6	109
Parksville, S.C., U.S.	D3	117
Parkton, Md., U.S.	A4	97
Parkton, N.C., U.S.	C3	110
Park Valley, Ut., U.S.	B2	121
Parkville, Md., U.S.	B4	97
Parkville, Mo., U.S.	B3	102
Parkwater, Wa., U.S.	g14	124
Parkway, Ca., U.S.	*C3	82
Parkwood, N.C., U.S.	A4	110
Parla, Spain	p17	22
Parlākimidi, India	H10	37
Parle, Lac qui, l., Mn., U.S.	E2	100
Parlier, Ca., U.S.	D4	82
Parma, Italy	B3	23
Parma, Id., U.S.	F2	89
Parma, Mi., U.S.	F6	99
Parma, Mo., U.S.	E8	102
Parma, Oh., U.S.	A4	112
Parma, stm., Italy	E6	20
Parma Heights, Oh., U.S.	h9	112
Parmachene Lake, l., Me., U.S.	C2	96
Parmele, N.C., U.S.	B5	110
Parmelee, S.D., U.S.	D5	118
Parmer, co., Tx., U.S.	B1	120
Parnaguá, Braz.	F6	59
Parnaíba, Braz.	B2	57
Parnaíba, stm., Braz.	C3	57
Parnamirim, Braz.	E3	57
Parnassós, mtn., Grc.	C4	25
Parnell, Ia., U.S.	C5	92
Parnell, Mo., U.S.	A3	102
Pärnu, Sov. Un.	B5	27
Paro, Bhu.	C8	36
Paroo, stm., Austl.	F7	50
Páros, Grc.	D5	25
Páros, i., Grc.	D5	40
Parowan, Ut., U.S.	F3	121
Par Pond, res., S.C., U.S.	D5	117
Parr, In., U.S.	B3	91
Parral, Chile	B2	54
Parramatta, Austl.	*F9	50
Parramore Island, i., Va., U.S.	C7	123
Parras de la Fuente, Mex.	B4	63
Parrett, stm., Eng., U.K.	C5	12
Parris Island, i., S.C., U.S.	G6	117
Parrish, Al., U.S.	B2	78
Parrish, Fl., U.S.	E4	86
Parrish, Wi., U.S.	C4	126
Parrott, Ga., U.S.	E2	87
Parrott, Va., U.S.	C2	123
Parrottsville, Tn., U.S.	C10	119
Parrsboro, N.S., Can.	D5	71
Parrs Ridge, mtn., Md., U.S.	B3	97
Parry, Sk., Can.	H3	75
Parry, Cape, c., N.T., Can.	B8	66
Parry, Mount, mtn., B.C., Can.	C3	69
Parry Island, i., On., Can.	B4	73
Parry Islands, is., N.T., Can.	m29	66
Parry Sound, On., Can.	B4	73
Parry Sound, co., On., Can.	B5	73
Parsberg, F.R.Ger.	D5	18
Parseta, stm., Pol.	A3	26
Parshall, Co., U.S.	A4	83
Parshall, N.D., U.S.	B3	111
Parsippany, N.J., U.S.	B4	107
Parsnip, stm., B.C., Can.	B6	69
Parsons, Ks., U.S.	E8	93
Parsons, Tn., U.S.	B3	119
Parsons, W.V., U.S.	B5	125
Parsonsburg, Md., U.S.	D7	97
Parson's Peak, mtn., Id., U.S.	G7	89
Parson's Pond, Nf., Can.	C3	72
Partābgarh, India	E5	37
Partenen, Aus.	C6	20
Parthenay, Fr.	D3	16
Parthenon, Ar., U.S.	B2	81
Partinico, Italy	E4	23
Partlow, Va., U.S.	B5	123
Partree, Ire.	D2	11
Partridge, Ks., U.S.	g12	93
Partridge Point, c., Nf., Can.	C3	72
Paru, stm., Braz.	C4	59
Paru de Oeste, stm., Braz.	C3	59
Parys, S. Afr.	G5	48
Pasadena, Nf., Can.	D3	72
Pasadena, Ca., U.S.	E4	82
Pasadena, Md., U.S.	B4	97
Pasadena, Tx., U.S.	r14	120
Pasado, Cabo, c., Ec.	B1	58
Pa Sak, stm., Thai.	D4	35
Pasay, Phil.	o14	34
Pascagoula, Ms., U.S.	E5	101
Pascagoula, stm., Ms., U.S.	D5	101
Pascagoula Bay, b., Ms., U.S.	f8	101
Paşcani, Rom.	B9	24
Pasco, Wa., U.S.	C6	124
Pasco, co., Fl., U.S.	D4	86
Pasco, dept., Peru	C2	58
Pascoag, R.I., U.S.	B2	116
Pascoag Reservoir, res., R.I., U.S.	B2	116
Pascola, Mo., U.S.	E8	102
Pascua, Isla de (Easter Island), i., Chile	H15	6
Pas-de-Calais, dept., Fr.	D2	17
Pasewalk, Ger.D.R.	B7	18
Pashkovo, Sov. Un.	B11	31
Pasig, Phil.	o13	34
Pasłęk, Pol.	A5	26
Pasni, Pak.	C3	36
Paso de Indios, Arg.	C3	53
Paso de los Libres, Arg.	E4	55
Paso de los Toros, Ur.	E1	56
Paso Limay, Arg.	E2	54
Paso Robles, Ca., U.S.	E3	82
Pasquia Hills, hills, Sk., Can.	D1	75
Pasquia, stm., Can.	D5	75
Pasquotank, co., N.C., U.S.	A6	110
Pasrūr, Pak.	B5	36
Passaconaway, Mount, mtn., N.H., U.S.	C4	106
Passadumkeag, Me., U.S.	C4	96
Passadumkeag Mountain, mtn., Me., U.S.	C4	96
Passage East, Ire.	E5	11
Passage West, Ire.	F3	11
Passaic, N.J., U.S.	B4	107
Passaic, co., N.J., U.S.	A4	107
Passaic, stm., N.J., U.S.	h8	107
Passamaquoddy Bay, b., Me., U.S.	C6	96
Passau, F.R.Ger.	D6	18
Pass Christian, Ms., U.S.	E4	101
Passekeag, N.B., Can.	D4	71
Passero, Cape, c., Italy	F5	23
Passo Fundo, Braz.	B6	56
Passos, Braz.	C3	57
Passumpsic, Vt., U.S.	C4	122
Passumpsic, stm., Vt., U.S.	C4	122
Passy, Fr.	E2	21
Pastaza, prov., Ec.	B2	58
Pastaza, stm., S.A.	B2	58
Pasto, Col.	C3	60
Pastora Peak, mtn., Az., U.S.	A6	80
Pastura, N.M., U.S.	C5	108
Pasuruan, Indon.	G4	34
Paswegin, Sk., Can.	F4	75
Patagonia, Az., U.S.	F5	80
Patagonia, reg., Arg.	E3	53
Pātan, India	I4	37
Patan see Lalitpur, Nepal		
Patapsco, stm., Md., U.S.	B4	97
Patapsco, North Branch, stm., Md., U.S.	A4	97
Pataskala, Oh., U.S.	C3	112
Patea, N.Z.	M15	51
Pateley Bridge, Eng., U.K.	F7	13
Patensie, S. Afr.	H4	48
Paternò, Italy	F5	23
Pateros, Wa., U.S.	A6	124
Paterson, N.J., U.S.	B4	107
Paterson, Wa., U.S.	D6	124
Patesville, Ky., U.S.	C3	94
Pathānkot, India	B6	36
Pathfinder Reservoir, res., Wy., U.S.	D6	127
Pathfork, Ky., U.S.	D6	94
Pathlow, Sk., Can.	E3	75
Patía, stm., Col.	C3	60
Patiāla, India	D6	36
Patiāli, India	G8	37
Patience Island, i., R.I., U.S.	D4	116
Pati Point, c., Guam	l11	52
Patman, Lake, res., Tx., U.S.	C5	120
Patmos, Ar., U.S.	D2	81
Pátmos, i., Grc.	D6	40
Patna, India	G11	37
Patnanongan Island, i., Phil.	o14	34
Patoka, Il., U.S.	E4	90
Patoka, In., U.S.	H2	91
Patoka, stm., In., U.S.	H3	91
Patoka Lake, res., In., U.S.	H4	91
Paton, Ia., U.S.	B3	92
Patos, Braz.	E3	57
Patos, Lagoa dos, b., Braz.	E2	56
Patos de Minas, Braz.	B3	56
Patos, Alb.	B2	25
Patquía, Arg.	F2	55
Pátrai (Patras), Grc.	C3	40
Pátrai, Gulf of see Patraikós Kólpos, b., Grc.	C3	40
Patraikós Kólpos (Gulf of Pátrai), b., Grc.	C3	40
Patras see Pátrai, Grc.	C3	40
Patricia, Ab., Can.	D5	68
Patricia, Tx., U.S.	C1	120
Patrick, S.C., U.S.	B7	117
Patrick, co., Va., U.S.	D2	123
Patrick Air Force Base, mil., Fl., U.S.	D6	86
Patricksburg, In., U.S.	F4	91
Patrick Springs, Va., U.S.	D2	123
Patriot, In., U.S.	G8	91
Patrocinio, Braz.	B3	56
Patroon, Tx., U.S.	D6	120
Patsaliga Creek, stm., Al., U.S.	D3	78
Patsville, Nv., U.S.	B6	105
Pattani, Thai.	I4	34
Pattani, stm., Thai.	I4	35
Pattaquattic Hill, hill, Ma., U.S.	B3	98
Patten, Me., U.S.	C4	96
Pattenburg, N.J., U.S.	B2	107
Patterson, Ar., U.S.	B4	81
Patterson, Ga., U.S.	E4	87
Patterson, Id., U.S.	E5	89
Patterson, Il., U.S.	D3	90
Patterson, La., U.S.	E4	95
Patterson, Mo., U.S.	D7	102
Patterson, N.Y., U.S.	D7	109
Patterson, Va., U.S.	e10	123
Patterson Creek, stm., W.V., U.S.	B5	125
Pattison, Ms., U.S.	D3	101
Patton, Mo., U.S.	D7	102
Patton, Pa., U.S.	E4	115
Pattonsburg, Mo., U.S.	A3	102
Pattullo, Mount, mtn., B.C., Can.	A3	69
Patu, Braz.	C3	57
Patuākhāli, Bngl.	F13	37
Patuca, stm., Hond.	D8	63
Patuca, Punta, c., Hond.	D8	63
Patuxent, stm., Md., U.S.	D4	97
Patuxent River Naval Air Test Center, mil., Md., U.S.	D5	97
Patzau, Wi., U.S.	B1	126
Pátzcuaro, Mex.	n13	63
Pátzcuaro, Lago de, l., Mex.	n13	63
Patzicía, Guat.	C2	62
Patzún, Guat.	C2	62
Pau, Fr.	F3	16
Pau, Gave de, stm., Fr.	F3	16
Paucarbamba, Peru	D3	58
Paudalho, Braz.	C3	57
Pau dos Ferros, Braz.	E3	57
Paugh Lake, On., Can.	B7	73
Pauillac, Fr.	E3	16
Pauini, Braz.	C4	58
Pauk, Burma	D9	36
Paul, Id., U.S.	G5	89
Paul Island, i., Nf., Can.	g9	72
Paulatuk, N.T., Can.	C5	62
Paulden, Az., U.S.	C3	80
Paulding, Ms., U.S.	C4	101
Paulding, Oh., U.S.	A1	112
Paulding, co., Ga., U.S.	C2	87
Paulding, co., Oh., U.S.	A1	112
Paulding Bay, b., Ant.	C25	7
Paulette, Ms., U.S.	B5	101
Paulina, La., U.S.	h10	95
Paulina, Or., U.S.	C7	114
Paulina Mountains, mts., Or., U.S.	D5	114
Paulina Peak, mtn., Or., U.S.	E5	114
Pauline, Ne., U.S.	D7	104
Pauline, Mount, mtn., Can.	C1	68
Paulins Kill, stm., N.J., U.S.	A3	107
Paulista, Braz.	C3	57
Paulistana, Braz.	B2	57
Paull, stm., Sk., Can.	B3	75
Paull Lake, l., Sk., Can.	A3	75
Paulo Afonso, Cachoeira de, wtfl, Braz.	C3	57
Paulsboro, N.J., U.S.	D2	107
Paul Smiths, N.Y., U.S.	f10	109
Paulstown, Ire.	E4	11
Paul Stream, stm., Vt., U.S.	B5	122
Pauls Valley, Ok., U.S.	C4	113
Paungde, Burma	E10	36
Paupack, Pa., U.S.	D11	115
Pauto, stm., Col.	B2	71
Pauwela, Hi., U.S.	C5	88
Pavant Range, mts., Ut., U.S.	E3	121
Pāveh, Iran	B2	38
Pavia, Italy	B3	23
Pavilion, B.C., Can.	D7	69
Pavilion, N.Y., U.S.	C2	109
Pavillion, Wy., U.S.	C4	127
Pavlodar, Sov. Un.	D10	29
Pavlof Volcano, vol., Ak., U.S.	D7	79
Pavlograd, Sov. Un.	G10	27
Pavlovo, Sov. Un.	D14	27
Pavlovsk, Sov. Un.	s31	14
Pavlovsk, Sov. Un.	F13	27
Pavlovskaya, Sov. Un.	H13	27
Pavlovski Posad, Sov. Un.	n18	27
Pavo, Ga., U.S.	F3	87
Pawcatuck, Ct., U.S.	D8	84
Pawcatuck, stm., R.I., U.S.	G1	116
Paw Creek, N.C., U.S.	B2	110
Pawhuska, Ok., U.S.	A5	113
Pawlet, Vt., U.S.	E2	122
Pawley's Island, S.C., U.S.	E9	117
Pawling, N.Y., U.S.	D7	109
Pawłowice, Pol.	h9	26

Name — Map Ref — Page

Pawn, stm., Burma C2 35
Pawnee, Il., U.S. D4 90
Pawnee, Ok., U.S. A5 113
Pawnee, Tx., U.S. E4 120
Pawnee, co., Ks., U.S. D4 93
Pawnee, co., Ne., U.S. D9 104
Pawnee, co., Ok., U.S. A5 113
Pawnee, stm., Ks., U.S. D3 93
Pawnee City, Ne., U.S. D9 104
Pawnee Creek, stm., Co., U.S. A7 83
Pawnee Rock, Ks., U.S. D5 93
Pawpaw, Il., U.S. B5 90
Paw Paw, Mi., U.S. F5 99
Paw Paw, W.V., U.S. B6 125
Paw Paw, stm., Mi., U.S. F4 99
Pawpaw Creek, stm., W.V., U.S. h10 125
Pawtuckaway Pond, l., N.H., U.S. D4 106
Pawtucket, R.I., U.S. C4 116
Pawtuxet, stm., R.I., U.S. C4 116
Pawtuxet, North Branch, stm., R.I., U.S. D3 116
Pawtuxet, South Branch, stm., R.I., U.S. D3 116
Pax, W.V., U.S. n13 125
Paxico, Ks., U.S. C7 93
Paxoí, i., Grc. C3 25
Paxton, Fl., U.S. u15 86
Paxton, Il., U.S. C5 90
Paxton, In., U.S. F3 91
Paxton, Ma., U.S. B4 98
Paxton, Ne., U.S. C4 104
Paxtonville, Pa., U.S. E7 115
Paxville, S.C., U.S. D7 117
Payerne, Switz. C2 21
Payette, Id., U.S. E2 89
Payette, co., Id., U.S. E2 89
Payette, North Fork, stm., Id., U.S. E2 89
Payette, South Fork, stm., Id., U.S. E3 89
Payette Lake, res., Id., U.S. E3 89
Payne, Ga., U.S. D3 87
Payne, Oh., U.S. A1 112
Payne, co., Ok., U.S. A4 113
Payne, Lac, l., P.Q., Can. g12 74
Paynes, Ms., U.S. B3 101
Paynes Creek, Ca., U.S. B3 82
Paynesville, Mn., U.S. E4 100
Paynesville, Mo., U.S. B7 102
Payneville, Ky., U.S. C3 94
Paynton, Sk., Can. D1 75
Paysandú, Ur. E1 56
Payson, Az., U.S. C4 80
Payson, Il., U.S. D2 90
Payson, Ok., U.S. B5 113
Payson, Ut., U.S. C4 121
Pazardzhik, Bul. D7 24
Pazin, Yugo. C1 24
Pea, stm., Al., U.S. D3 78
Peabody, Ks., U.S. D6 93
Peabody, Ma., U.S. A6 98
Peabody, stm., N.H., U.S. B4 106
Peace, stm., Can. E9 66
Peace, stm., Fl., U.S. E5 86
Peace Dale, R.I., U.S. F3 116
Peace River, Ab., Can. A2 68
Peach, co., Ga., U.S. D3 87
Peacham, Vt., U.S. C4 122
Peacham Pond, res., Vt., U.S. C4 122
Peach Creek, W.V., U.S. D5 125
Peachland, B.C., Can. E8 69
Peachland, N.C., U.S. C2 110
Peach Orchard, Ar., U.S. A5 81
Peach Orchard, Ga., U.S. *C4 87
Peach Orchard Knob, mtn., Ky., U.S. C3 94
Peach Point, c., Ma., U.S. f12 98
Peach Springs, Az., U.S. B2 80
Peachtree City, Ga., U.S. *C2 87
Peacock, Mi., U.S. D5 99
Peacock Hills, hills, N.T., Can. C10 66
Peacock Point, c., Wake I. B2 52
Peacock Sound, strt., Ant. B2 7
Peaima Fall, wtfl, Guy. A2 59
Peak, S.C., U.S. C5 117
Peaked Mountain, mtn., Me., U.S. B4 96
Peaks Island, i., Me., U.S. g7 96
Peale, Mount, mtn., Ut., U.S. E6 121
Peale Island, i., Wake I. A2 52
Pea Patch Island, i., De., U.S. B3 85
Pearce, Ab., Can. E4 68
Pearcy, Ar., U.S. C2 81
Pea Ridge, Ar., U.S. A1 81
Pea Ridge National Military Park, Ar., U.S. A1 81
Pearisburg, Va., U.S. C2 123
Pearl, Il., U.S. D3 90
Pearl, Ms., U.S. C3 101
Pearl, stm., U.S. D3 101
Pearland, Tx., U.S. r14 120
Pearl and Hermes Reef, rf., Hi., U.S. k12 88
Pearl City, Hi., U.S. B4 88
Pearl City, Il., U.S. A4 90
Pearl Harbor, b., Hi., U.S. B3 88
Pearl Harbor Naval Station, mil., Hi., U.S. g10 88
Pearlington, Ms., U.S. E4 101
Pearl River, La., U.S. D6 95
Pearl River, N.Y., U.S. g12 109
Pearl River, co., Ms., U.S. E4 101
Pearsall, Tx., U.S. E3 120
Pearsoll Peak, mtn., Or., U.S. E3 114
Pearson, Ar., U.S. B3 81
Pearson, Ga., U.S. E4 87
Peary Channel, strt., N.T., Can. m30 66
Peary Land, reg., Grnld. A18 128
Pease, Mn., U.S. E5 100
Pease, stm., Tx., U.S. B3 120
Pease Air Force Base, mil., N.H., U.S. D5 106
Pebane, Moz. A6 49
Pebas, Peru B3 58
Pebworth, Ky., U.S. C6 94
Peć, Yugo. D5 24
Peçanha, Braz. B4 56
Pecatonica, Il., U.S. A4 90
Pecatonica, stm., U.S. A4 90
Pecatonica, East Branch, stm., Wi., U.S. F4 126
Pechenga, Sov. Un. C6 29
Pechora, Sov. Un. B20 8
Pechora, stm., Sov. Un. C8 29
Pechora Bay, b., Sov. Un. B19 8
Peck, Id., U.S. C2 89
Peck, Ks., U.S. E6 93
Peck, Mi., U.S. E8 99
Peckerwood Lake, res., Ar., U.S. C4 81
Peckham, Ok., U.S. A4 113
Pecos, N.M., U.S. B4 108
Pecos, Tx., U.S. D1 120
Pecos, co., Tx., U.S. D1 120
Pecos, stm., U.S. D7 76
Pecos National Monument, N.M., U.S. B4 108
Pécs, Hung. B4 24
Peculiar, Mo., U.S. C3 102
Pedasí, Pan. G7 62
Peddocks Island, i., Ma., U.S. g12 98
Pedernales, Ven. B5 60
Pedra Azul, Braz. B4 56
Pedregal (part of Panamá), Pan. k12 62
Pedregal, Pan. F6 62
Pedregal, Ven. A3 60
Pedreiras, Braz. B2 57
Pedricktown, N.J., U.S. D2 107
Pedro Afonso, Braz. C1 57
Pedro Antonio Santos, Mex. A3 62
Pedro Avelino, Braz. C3 57
Pedro Juan Caballero, Para. D4 55
Pedro Luro, Arg. B4 54
Pedro Miguel, Pan. k11 62
Pedro R. Fernández (Manuel F. Mantilla), Arg. E4 55
Pedro Velho, Braz. h6 57
Peebinga, Austl. G3 51
Peebles, Sk., Can. G4 75
Peebles, Scot., U.K. C5 10
Peebles, Oh., U.S. D2 112
Peebles, Wi., U.S. k9 126
Peekaboo Mountain, hill, Me., U.S. C5 96
Peekskill, N.Y., U.S. D7 109
Peel, N.B., Can. C2 71
Peel, I. of Man F4 13
Peel, co., On., Can. D5 73
Peel, stm., Can. C5 66
Peel Fell, mtn., Eng., U.K. E6 13
Pe Ell, Wa., U.S. C2 124
Peel Sound, strt., N.T., Can. B13 66
Peene, stm., Ger.D.R. B6 18
Peer, Bel. C5 17
Peerless, Mt., U.S. B11 103
Peerless Lake, l., Ab., Can. A3 68
Peers, Ab., Can. C3 68
Peesane, Sk., Can. E4 75
Peetz, Co., U.S. A7 83
Peever, S.D., U.S. B9 118
Pefferlaw, On., Can. C5 73
Pegan Hill, hill, Ma., U.S. g10 98
Pegasus Bay, b., N.Z. O14 51
Pegau, Ger.D.R. B7 19
Pegs, Ok., U.S. A6 113
Peggy, Tx., U.S. E3 120
Pegnitz, F.R.Ger. D6 19
Pegnitz, stm., F.R.Ger. D5 18
Pego, Spain C5 22
Pegram, Tn., U.S. A4 119
Pegu, Burma E10 36
Pegu Yoma, mts., Burma C1 35
Pehčevo, Yugo. E6 24
Pehuajó, Arg. B4 54
Peine, F.R.Ger. B5 18
Peiping see Peking, China D8 31
Peipus, Lake, l., Sov. Un. D6 29
Peixe, Braz. D1 57
Peixian, China G7 32
Peixian, China G7 32
Pejepscot, Me., U.S. E2 96
Pekalongan, Indon. G3 34
Pekan, Malay. E2 34
Pekin, Il., U.S. C4 90
Pekin, In., U.S. G5 91
Pekin, N.D., U.S. B7 111
Peking (Beijing), China D8 31
Pelabuhan Kelang, Malay. K4 35
Pélagos, i., Grc. C5 25
Pelahatchie, Ms., U.S. C4 101
Pelaihari, Indon. F4 34
Pelat, Mont, mtn., Fr. E7 16
Pelée, Montagne, mtn., Mart. I14 64
Pelee Island, i., On., Can. F2 73
Peleliu, i., Palau R17 52
Pelham, On., Can. D5 73
Pelham, Al., U.S. B3 78
Pelham, Ga., U.S. E2 87
Pelham, Ma., U.S. B3 98
Pelham, N.H., U.S. E4 106
Pelham, N.Y., U.S. *h13 109
Pelham, N.C., U.S. A3 110
Pelham, S.C., U.S. B3 117
Pelham, Tn., U.S. D8 119
Pelham Manor, N.Y., U.S. h13 109
Pelhřimov, Czech. D3 26
Pelican, Ak., U.S. m21 79
Pelican, La., U.S. C2 95
Pelican Bay, b., Mb., Can. C1 70
Pelican Lake, Wi., U.S. C4 126
Pelican Lake, l., Ab., Can. B4 68
Pelican Lake, l., Mb., Can. C1 70
Pelican Lake, l., Sk., Can. B4 75
Pelican Lake, l., Mn., U.S. D4 100
Pelican Lake, l., Mn., U.S. D3 100
Pelican Lake, l., Mn., U.S. B6 100
Pelican Lake, l., Mn., U.S. E5 100
Pelican Lake, l., Wi., U.S. C4 126
Pelican Mountain, mtn., Ab., Can. B4 68
Pelican Narrows, Sk., Can. B4 75
Pelican Rapids, Mb., Can. C1 70
Pelican Rapids, Mn., U.S. D2 100
Péligre, Lac de, res., Haiti E8 64
Pelion, S.C., U.S. D5 117
Pella, Ia., U.S. C5 92
Pell City, Al., U.S. B3 78
Pellice, stm., Italy E3 20
Pell Lake, Wi., U.S. n11 126
Pellston, Mi., U.S. C6 99
Pellville, Ky., U.S. C3 94
Pellworm, i., F.R.Ger. A4 18
Pelly, Sk., Can. F5 75
Pelly, stm., Yk., Can. D5 66
Pelly Crossing, Yk., Can. D5 66
Pelly Lake, l., N.T., Can. C12 66
Pelly Mountains, mts., Yk., Can. D6 66
Peloncillo Mountains, mts., U.S. E1 108
Peloponnesos, hist reg., Grc. D4 25
Pelotas, Braz. E2 56
Pelotas, stm., Braz. D2 56
Pel'ovo, Bul. D7 24
Pelton, Lake, l., La., U.S. E5 95
Pelusium, hist., Eg. C4 41
Pelusium Bay, b., Eg. C4 41
Pelzer, S.C., U.S. B3 117
Pemadumcook Lake, l., Me., U.S. C3 96
Pemanggil, i., Malay. K6 35
Pemaquid, Me., U.S. E3 96
Pematangsiantar, Indon. m11 34
Pemba, Moz. D7 48
Pemba, Zam. E4 48
Pemba, prov., Tan. C6 48
Pemba, i., Tan. C6 48
Pemberton, B.C., Can. D6 69
Pemberton, N.J., U.S. D3 107
Pemberton, Oh., U.S. B1 112
Pemberville, Oh., U.S. A2 112
Pembina, N.D., U.S. A8 111
Pembina, co., N.D., U.S. A8 111
Pembina, stm., Ab., Can. C3 68
Pembina, stm., N.A. E2 70
Pembina Mountains, mts., N.A. A7 111
Pembine, Wi., U.S. C6 126
Pembroke, On., Can. B7 73
Pembroke, Wales, U.K. E4 10
Pembroke, Ga., U.S. D5 87
Pembroke, Ky., U.S. D2 94
Pembroke, Me., U.S. D5 96
Pembroke, Ma., U.S. B6 98
Pembroke, N.Y., U.S. B2 109
Pembroke, N.C., U.S. C3 110
Pembroke, Va., U.S. C2 123
Pembroke Pines, Fl., U.S. r13 86
Pembuang, stm., Indon. F4 34
Pemigewasset, stm., N.H., U.S. C3 106
Pemigewasset, East Branch, stm., N.H., U.S. B3 106
Pemiscot, co., Mo., U.S. E8 102
Pemmican Portage, Sk., Can. D4 75
Pemuco, Chile B2 54
Pena Blanca, N.M., U.S. B3 108
Penafiel, Port. B1 22
Peñafiel, Spain B3 22
Peñalara, mtn., Spain B4 22
Penalosa, Ks., U.S. E5 93
Penamacor, Port. B2 22
Penápolis, Braz. C2 56
Peñaranda de Bracamonte, Spain B3 22
Pen Argyl, Pa., U.S. E11 115
Peñarroya-Pueblonuevo, Spain C3 22
Peñas, Cape, c., Spain A3 22
Penas, Golfo de, b., Chile D2 54
Penasco, N.M., U.S. A4 108
Peñasco, Rio, stm., N.M., U.S. E4 108
Penbrook, Pa., U.S. F8 115
Pence, In., U.S. D2 91
Pencer, Mn., U.S. B3 100
Penck Trough, val., Ant. B12 7
Pendéli (Pentelicus), mtn., Grc. g11 25
Pendembu, S.L. E2 45
Pender, Ne., U.S. B9 104
Pender, co., N.C., U.S. C4 110
Pendergrass, Ga., U.S. B3 87
Pender Island, B.C., Can. g12 69
Pendleton, In., U.S. E6 91
Pendleton, Or., U.S. B8 114
Pendleton, S.C., U.S. B2 117
Pendleton, co., Ky., U.S. B5 94
Pendleton, co., W.V., U.S. C5 125
Pendley Hills, Ga., U.S. h8 87
Pend Oreille, co., Wa., U.S. A8 124
Pend Oreille, stm., N.A. A8 124
Pend Oreille, Lake, l., Id., U.S. A2 89
Pend Oreille, Mount, mtn., Id., U.S. A2 89
Pendroy, Mt., U.S. B4 103
Penedo, Braz. D3 57
Penetanguishene, On., Can. C5 73
Peneus see Piniós, stm., Grc. C4 40
Pengalengan, Indon. G3 34
Penfield, Ga., U.S. C3 87
Penfield, Il., U.S. C6 90
Penfield, N.Y., U.S. *B3 109
Penfield, Pa., U.S. D4 115
Peng'an, China I2 32
Penganga, stm., India H6 37
Penge, Zaire C3 48
Pengibu, i., Indon. L7 35
Penglai, China F9 32
Pengshui, China J3 32
Penguin Islands, is., Nf., Can. E3 72
Penha, Braz. D3 56
Penhold, Ab., Can. C4 68
Penhook, Va., U.S. D3 123
Peniche, Port. C1 22
Penicuik, Scot., U.K. E5 13
Peninsula, Oh., U.S. A4 112
Peninsular Malaysia, hist reg., Malay. E2 34
Penitas, Tx., U.S. F3 120
Penitente, Serra do, hills, Braz. C1 57
Penitentiary Mountain, hill, Al., U.S. A2 78
Pénjamo, Mex. m13 63
Penn, Sk., Can. D2 75
Penn, N.D., U.S. A6 111
Penn Acres, De., U.S. *B3 85
Pennant Point, c., N.S., Can. E6 71
Pennant Station, Sk., Can. G1 75
Pennask Mountain, mtn., B.C., Can. E7 69
Penne, Italy C4 23
Pennell, Mount, mtn., Ut., U.S. F5 121
Pennellville, N.Y., U.S. B4 109
Penner, stm., India F6 36
Penneshaw, Austl. G1 51
Penney Farms, Fl., U.S. C5 86
Pennfield, N.B., Can. D3 71
Penn Hills, Pa., U.S. k14 115
Penniac, N.B., Can. C3 71
Pennine Alps, mts., Eur. C3 21
Pennines, mts., Eng., U.K. C5 10
Pennington, Al., U.S. C1 78
Pennington, N.J., U.S. C3 107
Pennington, co., Mn., U.S. B2 100
Pennington, co., S.D., U.S. D2 118
Pennington Gap, Va., U.S. f8 123
Pennock, Mn., U.S. E3 100
Pennsauken, N.J., U.S. D2 107
Pennsboro, W.V., U.S. B4 125
Pennsburg, Pa., U.S. F11 115
Penns Grove, N.J., U.S. D2 107
Pennsuco, Fl., U.S. s13 86
Pennsville, N.J., U.S. D1 107
Pennsville, Oh., U.S. C4 112
Pennsylvania, state, U.S. E7 115
Penn Valley, Pa., U.S. o20 115
Pennville, In., U.S. D7 91
Penny, B.C., Can. C7 69
Penn Yan, N.Y., U.S. C3 109
Pennycutaway, stm., Mb., Can. A5 70
Penobscot, Me., U.S. D4 96
Penobscot, co., Me., U.S. C4 96
Penobscot, stm., Me., U.S. C4 96
Penobscot, East Branch, stm., Me., U.S. C4 96
Penobscot, North Branch, stm., Me., U.S. B2 96
Penobscot, West Branch, stm., Me., U.S. C3 96
Penobscot Bay, b., Me., U.S. D3 96
Penobscot Lake, l., Me., U.S. C2 96
Penobsquis, N.B., Can. D4 71
Penokee, Ks., U.S. C4 93
Penong, Austl. F5 50
Penonomé, Pan. F7 62
Penrhyn, Cape, c., N.T., Can. C16 66
Penrith, Austl. *F9 50
Penrith, Eng., U.K. F6 13
Pensacola, Fl., U.S. u14 86
Pensacola, Ok., U.S. A6 113
Pensacola Bay, b., Fl., U.S. u14 86
Pensacola Dam, Ok., U.S. A6 113
Pensacola Mountains, mts., Ant. A6 7
Pensacola Naval Air Station, mil., Fl., U.S. u14 86
Pensaukee, Wi., U.S. D6 126
Pense, Sk., Can. G3 75
Pentagon Mountain, mtn., Mt., U.S. C3 103
Pentecostes, Braz. B3 57
Pentelicus see Pendéli, mtn., Grc. g11 25
Penticton, B.C., Can. E8 69
Pentland Firth, strt., Scot., U.K. A5 10
Pentland Hills, hills, Scot., U.K. E5 13
Penton, N.J., U.S. D2 107
Pentwater, Mi., U.S. E4 99
Penwell, Tx., U.S. D1 120
Penza, Sov. Un. D7 29
Penzance, Sk., Can. F3 75
Penzance, Eng., U.K. E4 10
Penzberg, F.R.Ger. E5 18
Penzhina, stm., Sov. Un. C19 29
Penzlin, Ger.D.R. E7 15
Peoa, Ut., U.S. C4 121
Peonan Point, c., Mb., Can. D2 70
Peoples, Ky., U.S. C5 94
Peoria, Az., U.S. D3 80
Peoria, Il., U.S. C4 90
Peoria, Oh., U.S. B2 112
Peoria, Ok., U.S. A7 113
Peoria, co., Il., U.S. C4 90
Peoria Heights, Il., U.S. C4 90
Peotone, Il., U.S. B6 90
Pep, N.M., U.S. D6 108
Pepacton Reservoir, res., N.Y., U.S. C6 109
Pepeekeo, Hi., U.S. D6 88
Pepin, Wi., U.S. D1 126
Pepin, co., Wi., U.S. D2 126
Pepin, Lake, l., U.S. D1 126
Pepper Creek, stm., De., U.S. F5 85
Pepperell, Ma., U.S. A4 98
Pepper Pike, Oh., U.S. *h10 112
Peqini, Alb. B2 25
Pequabuck, Ct., U.S. C4 84
Pequannock, N.J., U.S. B4 107
Pequení, stm., Pan. k12 62
Pequest, stm., N.J., U.S. B2 107
Pequop Mountains, mts., Nv., U.S. C7 105
Pequot Lakes, Mn., U.S. D4 100
Perabumulih, Indon. F2 34
Perak, state, Malay. J4 35
Perak, stm., Malay. J4 35
Perakhóra, Grc. g9 25
Perales, stm., Spain p16 22
Perales de Tajuña, Spain p18 22
Peralta, N.M., U.S. C3 108
Pérama, Grc. h11 25
Percival, Ia., U.S. D2 92
Percy, Il., U.S. E4 90
Percy, N.H., U.S. A4 106
Perdido, Al., U.S. D2 78
Perdido, mtn., Spain A6 22
Perdido, stm., U.S. E2 78
Perdido Bay, b., Al., U.S. E2 78
Perdizes, Braz. B3 56
Perdue, Sk., Can. E2 75
Perea, N.M., U.S. B1 108
Pereira, Col. C2 60
Pereira Barreto, Braz. C2 56
Perekop, Sov. Un. H9 27
Pere Marquette, stm., Mi., U.S. E4 99
Peremennyy, Cape, c., Ant. C23 7
Perené, stm., Peru D3 58
Pereslavl-Zalesskiy, Sov. Un. C12 27
Pereyaslav-Khmelnitskiy, Sov. Un. F8 27
Perez, Phil. o14 34
Pergamino, Arg. A4 54
Pergine Valsugana, Italy A3 23
Perham, Me., U.S. B4 96
Perham, Mn., U.S. D3 100
Péribonca, P.Q., Can. A5 74
Peridot, Az., U.S. D5 80
Périgueux, Fr. E4 16
Perijá, Sierra de, mts., S.A. B3 60
Perim, i., P.D.R.Yem. D4 38
Peristérion, Grc. g11 25
Perito Moreno, Arg. D2 54
Perkam, Cape, c., Indon. F9 34
Perkasie, Pa., U.S. F11 115
Perkins, P.Q., Can. D2 74
Perkins, Ga., U.S. D5 87
Perkins, Mi., U.S. C3 99
Perkins, Ok., U.S. B4 113
Perkins, co., Ne., U.S. D4 104
Perkins, co., S.D., U.S. B3 118
Perkinston, Ms., U.S. E4 101
Perkinstown, Wi., U.S. C3 126
Perkinsville, Vt., U.S. E3 122
Perla, Ar., U.S. C3 81
Perlas, Archipiélago de las, is., Pan. F8 62
Perlas, Laguna de, b., Nic. E8 63
Perleberg, Ger.D.R. B5 18
Perley, Mn., U.S. C2 100
Perlis, state, Malay. I4 35
Perl-Mack, Co., U.S. *B6 83
Perm, Sov. Un. D8 29
Perma, Mt., U.S. C2 103
Përmeti, Alb. B3 25
Pernambuco, state, Braz. C3 57
Pernell, Ok., U.S. C4 113
Pernik, Bul. D6 24
Péronne, Fr. C5 16
Perot, Bayou, stm., La., U.S. k11 95
Perote, Al., U.S. D4 78
Perpignan, Fr. F5 16
Perquimans, co., N.C., U.S. A6 110
Perrin, Tx., U.S. C3 120
Perrine, Fl., U.S. G6 86
Perrineville, N.J., U.S. C4 107
Perris, Ca., U.S. F5 82
Perro, Laguna del, l., N.M., U.S. C4 108
Perronville, Mi., U.S. C3 99
Perros-Guirec, Fr. C2 16
Perrot, Île, i., P.Q., Can. q19 74
Perry, Ar., U.S. B3 81
Perry, Fl., U.S. B3 86
Perry, Ga., U.S. D3 87
Perry, Il., U.S. D3 90
Perry, Ia., U.S. C3 92
Perry, Ks., U.S. C8 93
Perry, La., U.S. E3 95
Perry, Me., U.S. D5 96
Perry, Mi., U.S. F6 99
Perry, Mo., U.S. B6 102
Perry, N.Y., U.S. C2 109
Perry, Oh., U.S. A4 112
Perry, Ok., U.S. A4 113
Perry, S.C., U.S. D5 117
Perry, Ut., U.S. B3 121
Perry, co., Al., U.S. C2 78
Perry, co., Ar., U.S. C3 81
Perry, co., Il., U.S. E4 90
Perry, co., In., U.S. H4 91
Perry, co., Ky., U.S. C6 94
Perry, co., Ms., U.S. D4 101
Perry, co., Mo., U.S. D8 102
Perry, co., Oh., U.S. C3 112
Perry, co., Pa., U.S. F7 115
Perry, co., Tn., U.S. B4 119
Perrydale, Or., U.S. B3 114
Perry Hall, Md., U.S. B5 97
Perry Heights, Oh., U.S. *B4 112
Perry Lake, res., Ks., U.S. C8 93
Perryman, Md., U.S. B5 97
Perry Peak, mtn., Ma., U.S. B1 98
Perry Point, Md., U.S. A5 97
Perrysburg, N.Y., U.S. C1 109
Perrysburg, Oh., U.S. A2 112
Perrysburg Heights, Oh., U.S. e6 112
Perry Stream, stm., N.H., U.S. f7 106
Perry's Victory and International Peace Memorial, hist., Oh., U.S. A2 112
Perrysville, In., U.S. D3 91
Perrysville, Oh., U.S. B3 112
Perrysville, Pa., U.S. h13 115
Perryton, Tx., U.S. A2 120
Perryvale, Ab., Can. B4 68
Perryville, Ak., U.S. D8 79
Perryville, Ar., U.S. B3 81
Perryville, Ky., U.S. C5 94
Perryville, La., U.S. B4 95
Perryville, Md., U.S. A5 97
Perryville, Mo., U.S. D8 102
Perryville, R.I., U.S. F3 116
Perryville, Tn., U.S. B3 119
Persan, Fr. E2 17
Persepolis, hist., Iran G6 39
Perseverancia, Bol. B3 55
Pershing, In., U.S. E7 91
Pershing, Ia., U.S. C4 92
Pershing, Mo., U.S. C6 102
Pershing, co., Nv., U.S. C3 105
Persia, Ia., U.S. C2 92
Persia, Tn., U.S. C10 119
Persian Gulf, b., Asia C5 38
Persimmon Grove, Ky., U.S. k14 94
Person, co., N.C., U.S. A3 110
Perstorp, Swe. B7 15
Pertek, Tur. C12 40
Perth, Austl. F2 50
Perth, On., Can. C8 73
Perth, Scot., U.K. B5 10
Perth, Ks., U.S. E6 93
Perth, N.D., U.S. A6 111
Perth, co., On., Can. D3 73
Perth Amboy, N.J., U.S. B4 107
Perth-Andover, N.B., Can. C2 71
Perthshire, Ms., U.S. B3 101
Pertuis, Fr. F6 16
Peru, Il., U.S. B4 90
Peru, In., U.S. C5 91
Peru, Ia., U.S. C4 92
Peru, Ks., U.S. E7 93
Peru, Me., U.S. *D2 96
Peru, Ma., U.S. B1 98
Peru, Ne., U.S. D10 104
Peru, N.Y., U.S. f11 109
Peru, Vt., U.S. E3 122
Peru, ctry., S.A. C2 58
Perugia, Italy C4 23
Peruíbe, Braz. C3 56
Peruque, Mo., U.S. f12 102
Péruwelz, Bel. D3 17
Pervomaysk, Sov. Un. q21 27
Pervomaysk, Sov. Un. G8 27
Pervouralsk, Sov. Un. D8 29
Pesaro, Italy C4 23
Pescadero, Ca., U.S. D2 82
Pescara, Italy C5 23
Pescara, stm., Italy C4 23
Peschanyy, Cape, c., Sov. Un. G19 8
Peschanyy, Cape, c., Sov. Un. B10 33
Pesé, Pan. G7 62
Peshastin, Wa., U.S. B5 124
Peshāwar, Pak. B5 36
Peshkopija, Alb. B3 25
Peshtera, Bul. D7 24
Peshtigo, Wi., U.S. C6 126
Peshtigo, stm., Wi., U.S. C5 126
Peski, Sov. Un. n18 27
Peski, Sov. Un. F14 27
Peski, Sov. Un. C7 28
Peso da Régua, Port. B2 22
Pesotum, Il., U.S. D5 90
Pesqueira, Braz. C3 57
Pessac, Fr. E3 16
Petaca, N.M., U.S. A3 108
Petacas, Cerro, mtn., Col. C2 60
Petah Tiqwa, Isr. B6 41
Petal, Ms., U.S. D4 101
Petaluma, Ca., U.S. C2 82
Pétange, Lux. E5 17
Petatlán, Mex. D4 63
Petauke, Zam. D5 48
Petawawa, On., Can. B7 73
Petawawa, stm., On., Can. A6 73
Peterí Itzá, Lago, l., Guat. B3 62
Petenwell Lake, res., Wi., U.S. D4 126
Peterborough, Austl. F6 50
Peterborough, On., Can. C6 73
Peterborough, Eng., U.K. D6 10
Peterborough, N.H., U.S. E3 106
Peterborough, co., On., Can. C6 73
Peter Dare Point, Me., U.S. C5 96
Peterhead, Scot., U.K. B6 10
Peter I Island, i., Ant. C3 7
Peter Island, i., V.I., Br. B6 65
Peterlee, Eng., U.K. F7 13
Peterman, Al., U.S. D2 78
Petermann Ranges, mts., Austl. E4 50
Peter Pond Lake, l., Sk., Can. m7 75
Petersburg, Ak., U.S. D13 79
Petersburg, De., U.S. D3 85
Petersburg, Il., U.S. C4 90
Petersburg, In., U.S. H3 91
Petersburg, Ky., U.S. h13 94
Petersburg, Mi., U.S. G7 99
Petersburg, Ne., U.S. C7 104
Petersburg, N.J., U.S. E3 107
Petersburg, N.Y., U.S. C7 109
Petersburg, N.D., U.S. A8 111
Petersburg, Oh., U.S. B5 112
Petersburg, Pa., U.S. E5 115
Petersburg, Tn., U.S. B5 119
Petersburg, Tx., U.S. C2 120
Petersburg, Va., U.S. C5 123
Petersburg, W.V., U.S. C5 125
Peters Creek, stm., W.V., U.S. m14 125
Petersdorf, F.R.Ger. D5 15
Petersfield, Mb., Can. D3 70
Petersfield, Eng., U.K. C7 12
Petersham, Ma., U.S. B3 98
Peters Landing, Tn., U.S. B4 119
Peters Mountain, mtn., U.S. D4 125
Peterson, Al., U.S. B2 78
Peterson, Ia., U.S. B2 92
Peterson, Mn., U.S. G7 100
Peterson, Ut., U.S. B4 121
Peterson Field, mil., Co., U.S. C6 83
Peterstown, W.V., U.S. D4 125
Petersville, Al., U.S. A2 78
Petersville, Ky., U.S. B6 94
Peter the Great Bay, b., Sov. Un. C11 31
Petilia Policastro, Italy E6 23
Pétionville, Haiti E7 64
Petit, Île du, i., P.Q., Can. C2 72
Petit Bois Island, i., Ms., U.S. E5 101
Petitcodiac, N.B., Can. D4 71
Petitcodiac, stm., N.B., Can. C5 71
Petit-de-Grat, N.S., Can. D9 71
Petite Amite, stm., La., U.S. h10 95
Petite-Nation, Réserve de la, P.Q., Can. D3 74
Petite Rivière, N.S., Can. E5 71
Petite-Rivière-de-l'Artibonite, Haiti E7 64
Petite-Rivière-de-l'Île, N.B., Can. B5 71
Petit-Étang, N.S., Can. C9 71
Petit-Goâve, Haiti E7 64
Petit Jean, stm., Ar., U.S. B2 81
Petit Jean Mountain, mtn., Ar., U.S. C2 81
Petit Lac Des Allemands, l., La., U.S. k11 95
Petit Lake, l., La., U.S. k12 95
Petit-Rocher, N.B., Can. B4 71
Petitsikapau Lake, l., Nf., Can. g8 72
Peto, Mex. C7 63
Petorca, Chile A2 54
Petoskey, Mi., U.S. C6 99
Petra, hist., Jord. D7 41
Petras, Mount, mtn., Ant. B36 7
Petrey, Al., U.S. D3 78
Petrich, Bul. E6 24
Petrified Forest National Park, Az., U.S. B6 80
Petrikov, Sov. Un. E7 27
Petrila, Rom. C6 24
Petrinja, Yugo. C3 24
Petrodvorets, Sov. Un. s30 14
Petrohué, Chile C2 54
Petrokrepost, Sov. Un. B8 27
Petrolândia, Braz. C3 57
Petroleum, In., U.S. C7 91
Petroleum, co., Mt., U.S. C8 103
Petrolia, On., Can. E2 73
Petrolia, Il., U.S. E6 90
Petrolia, Ks., U.S. E8 93
Petrolia, Pa., U.S. D2 115
Petrolia, Tx., U.S. B3 120
Petrolina, Braz. C2 57
Petropavlovsk, Sov. Un. D9 29
Petropavlovsk [-Kamchatskiy], Sov. Un. D18 29
Petrópolis, Braz. C4 56
Petros, Tn., U.S. C9 119
Petroșani, Rom. C6 24
Petrovgrad see Zrenjanin, Yugo. C5 24
Petrovsk, Sov. Un. E15 27
Petrovsk-Zabaykalskiy, Sov. Un. D13 29
Petrozavodsk, Sov. Un. C6 29
Pettaquamscutt Lake Shores, R.I., U.S. F4 116
Pettibone, N.D., U.S. B6 111
Pettigo, Ire. C4 11
Pettigrew, Ar., U.S. B2 81
Pettingell Peak, mtn., Co., U.S. B5 83
Pettis, co., Mo., U.S. C4 102
Pettisville, Oh., U.S. A1 112
Petneu, Aus. B9 21
Pettus, Tx., U.S. E4 120
Petty Harbour, Nf., Can. E5 72
Petukhovo, Sov. Un. D9 28
Pevek, Sov. Un. C33 128
Pevely, Mo., U.S. g13 102
Pewamo, Mi., U.S. E6 99
Pewaukee, Wi., U.S. E5 126
Pewaukee Lake, l., Wi., U.S. m11 126
Pewee Valley, Ky., U.S. B4 94
Peyton, Co., U.S. B6 83
Pézenas, Fr. F5 16
Pfaffenhofen [an der Ilm], F.R.Ger. E6 19
Pfäffikon, Switz. B6 21
Pfarrkirchen, F.R.Ger. D6 18
Pfeifer, Ks., U.S. D4 93
Pforzheim, F.R.Ger. D4 18
Pfunds, Aus. C6 20
Pfungstadt, F.R.Ger. D3 19
Phalodi, India C5 36
Phaltan, India I5 37
Phangan, i., Thai. H4 35
Phanom Dongrak, Thiu Khao, mts., Asia E5 35
Phan Rang, Viet. C3 34
Phan Thiet, Viet. C3 34
Pharoah, Ok., U.S. B5 113
Pharr, Tx., U.S. F3 120
Pharsalus see Fársala, Grc. C4 25
Phatthalung, Thai. D2 34
Pheba, Ms., U.S. B5 101
Phelps, Ky., U.S. C7 94
Phelps, N.Y., U.S. C3 109
Phelps, Wi., U.S. B4 126
Phelps, co., Mo., U.S. D6 102
Phelps, co., Ne., U.S. D6 104
Phelps City, Mo., U.S. A2 102
Phelps Lake, l., N.C., U.S. B6 110
Phenix, Va., U.S. C4 123
Phenix City, Al., U.S. C4 78
Phet Buri, Thai. C1 34
Phetchabun, Thai. B2 34
Phetchabun, Thiu Khao, mts., Thai. E4 35
Phichit, Thai. D4 35
Philadelphia, Il., U.S. D3 90
Philadelphia, Ms., U.S. C4 101
Philadelphia, Mo., U.S. B6 102
Philadelphia, N.Y., U.S. A5 109
Philadelphia, Pa., U.S. G11 115
Philadelphia, Tn., U.S. D9 119

Name	Map Ref	Page
Philadelphia, co., Pa., U.S.	G12	115
Philadelphia Naval Shipyard; mil., Pa., U.S.	P21	115
Phil Campbell, Al., U.S.	A2	78
Philip, S.D., U.S.	C4	118
Philippeville see Skikda, Alg.	B6	44
Philippeville, Bel.	A6	17
Philippi, W.V., U.S.	B4	125
Philippi Glacier, Ant.	C21	7
Philippines, ctry., Asia	C6	34
Philippine Sea	E7	6
Philipsburg, P.Q., Can.	D4	74
Philipsburg, Mt., U.S.	D3	103
Philipsburg, Pa., U.S.	E5	115
Philipsville, On., Can.	C8	73
Philleo Lake, l., Wa., U.S.	h14	124
Phillip Island, i., Austl.	I5	51
Phillippy, Tn., U.S.	A2	119
Phillips, Me., U.S.	D2	96
Phillips, Ne., U.S.	D7	104
Phillips, Ok., U.S.	C5	113
Phillips, Tx., U.S.	B2	120
Phillips, Wi., U.S.	C3	126
Phillips, co., Ar., U.S.	C5	81
Phillips, co., Co., U.S.	A8	83
Phillips, co., Ks., U.S.	C4	93
Phillips, co., Mt., U.S.	B8	103
Phillips Brook, stm., N.H., U.S.	A4	106
Phillipsburg, Ks., U.S.	C4	93
Phillipsburg, Mo., U.S.	D5	102
Phillipsburg, N.J., U.S.	B2	107
Phillipston, Ma., U.S.	A3	98
Philmont, N.Y., U.S.	C7	109
Philo, Il., U.S.	C5	90
Philo, Oh., U.S.	C4	112
Philomath, Ga., U.S.	C4	87
Philomath, Or., U.S.	C3	114
Philpott Reservoir, res., Va., U.S.	D2	123
Phippen, Sk., Can.	E1	75
Phippsburg, Co., U.S.	A4	83
Phippsburg, Me., U.S.	g8	96
Phitsanulok, Thai.	B2	34
Phlorina see Flórina, Grc.	B3	25
Phlox, Wi., U.S.	C4	126
Phnom Penh, Kam.	C2	34
Phoenicia, N.Y., U.S.	C6	109
Phoenix, Az., U.S.	D3	80
Phoenix, Il., U.S.	k9	90
Phoenix, Md., U.S.	A4	97
Phoenix, N.Y., U.S.	A2	99
Phoenix, N.Y., U.S.	B4	109
Phoenix, Or., U.S.	E4	114
Phoenix Islands, is., Kir.	G11	6
Phoenixville, Pa., U.S.	F10	115
Phong, stm., Thai.	D5	35
Phongsali, Laos	B5	35
Phrae, Thai.	B2	34
Phra Nakhon Si Ayutthaya, Thai.	E4	35
Phu Cuong, Viet.	G7	35
Phuket, Thai.	D1	34
Phuket, i., Thai.	I3	35
Phumi Samraong, Kam.	E5	35
Phu Quoc, i., Viet.	G6	35
Phu Tho, Viet.	B6	35
Phutthaisong, Thai.	E5	35
Phu Vinh, Viet.	H7	35
Piaanu Pass, strt., Micron.	Q18	52
Piacenza, Italy	B2	23
Pialba, Austl.	B9	51
Pianguan, China	E4	32
Pianosa, i., Italy	C3	23
Pianosa Island, i., Italy	C5	23
Piapot, Sk., Can.	H1	75
Piaseczno, Pol.	m14	26
Piastów, Pol.	m13	26
Piatra-Neamţ, Rom.	B8	24
Piatt, co., Il., U.S.	D5	90
Piauí, state, Braz.	C2	57
Piauí, stm., Braz.	C2	57
Piave, stm., Italy	A4	23
Piazza Armerina, Italy	F5	23
Pibor, stm., Afr.	D3	47
Pibor Post, Sud.	D3	47
Pibroch, Ab., Can.	B4	68
Picabo, Id., U.S.	F4	89
Picacho, Az., U.S.	E4	80
Picacho, N.M., U.S.	D4	108
Picard, P.Q., Can.	B8	74
Picardy, hist. reg., Fr.	C5	16
Picayune, Ms., U.S.	E4	101
Piccadilly, Nf., Can.	D2	72
Piceance Creek, stm., Co., U.S.	B2	83
Pichanal, Arg.	D3	55
Picher, Ok., U.S.	A7	113
Pichilemu, Chile	A2	54
Pichincha, prov., Ec.	B4	58
Pickardville, Ab., Can.	B4	68
Pickaway, co., Oh., U.S.	C2	112
Pick City, N.D., U.S.	B4	111
Pickelville, Ut., U.S.	B4	121
Pickens, Ar., U.S.	D4	81
Pickens, Ms., U.S.	C3	101
Pickens, Ok., U.S.	C6	113
Pickens, S.C., U.S.	B2	117
Pickens, W.V., U.S.	C4	125
Pickens, co., Al., U.S.	B1	78
Pickens, co., Ga., U.S.	B2	87
Pickens, co., S.C., U.S.	B2	117
Pickensville, Al., U.S.	B1	78
Pickerel, On., Can.	B4	73
Pickerel, Wi., U.S.	C5	126
Pickerel, stm., On., Can.	A4	73
Pickerel Lake, l., Wi., U.S.	C5	126
Pickering, On., Can.	D5	73
Pickering, Eng., U.K.	F8	13
Pickering, Mo., U.S.	A3	102
Pickerington, Oh., U.S.	C3	112
Pickett, co., Tn., U.S.	C8	119
Pickford, Mi., U.S.	B6	99
Pickrell, Ne., U.S.	D9	104
Pickstown, S.D., U.S.	D7	118
Pickwick, Mn., U.S.	G7	100
Pickwick Dam, Tn., U.S.	B3	119
Pickwick Lake, res., U.S.	A6	101
Pickworth Point, c., Ma., U.S.	f12	98
Pico, i., Port.	g8	44
Pico, Ponta do, mtn., Port.	*g8	44
Pico Rivera, Ca., U.S.	n12	82
Picos, Braz.	C2	57
Picton, N.Z.	N14	51
Picton, N.S., Can.	D7	71
Pictou, N.S., Can.	D7	71
Pictou Island, i., N.S., Can.	D7	71
Pictou Landing, N.S., Can.	D7	71
Picture Butte, Ab., Can.	E4	68
Pictured Rocks National Lakeshore, Mi., U.S.	B4	99
Picture Rocks, Pa., U.S.	D8	115
Picuí, Braz.	h5	57
Picún Leufú, Arg.	B3	54

Name	Map Ref	Page
Pidálion, Akrotírion, c., Cyp.	E10	40
Pidurutalagala, mtn., Sri L.	G7	36
Piedade, Braz.	m8	56
Piedal, stm., Mex.	h9	63
Piedmont, P.Q., Can.	D3	74
Piedmont, Al., U.S.	B4	78
Piedmont, Ca., U.S.	h8	82
Piedmont, Ks., U.S.	E7	93
Piedmont, Mo., U.S.	D7	102
Piedmont, Ok., U.S.	B4	113
Piedmont, S.C., U.S.	B3	117
Piedmont, S.D., U.S.	C2	118
Piedmont, W.V., U.S.	B5	125
Piedmont, hist. reg., Italy	B1	23
Piedmont Lake, res., Oh., U.S.	B4	112
Piedra, Ca., U.S.	D4	82
Piedra, stm., Co., U.S.	D3	83
Piedrabuena, Spain	C3	22
Piedras, stm., Pan.	k11	62
Piedras, stm., Pan.	k12	62
Piedras, Punta, c., Arg.	B5	54
Piedras, Punta, c., Ven.	A5	60
Piedras Blancas, Point, c., Ca., U.S.	E3	82
Piedras Negras, Guat.	D6	63
Piedras Negras, Mex.	B4	63
Piedra Sola, Ur.	E1	56
Piekary Śląskie, Pol.	g9	26
Pieksämäki, Fin.	F12	14
Pielinen, l., Fin.	F13	14
Piemonte, prov., Italy	D3	20
Piendamó, Col.	C2	60
Pierce, Co., U.S.	A6	83
Pierce, Fl., U.S.	E5	86
Pierce, Ne., U.S.	B8	104
Pierce, Tn., U.S.	A3	119
Pierce, co., Ga., U.S.	E4	87
Pierce, co., Ne., U.S.	B8	104
Pierce, co., N.D., U.S.	A5	111
Pierce, co., Wa., U.S.	C3	124
Pierce, co., Wi., U.S.	D1	126
Pierce, Lake, l., Fl., U.S.	E5	86
Pierce City, Mo., U.S.	E3	102
Piercefield, N.Y., U.S.	A6	109
Pierce Lake, l., Can.	B5	70
Pierce Pond, l., Me., U.S.	C2	96
Pierces Point, N.J., U.S.	E3	107
Pierceton, In., U.S.	B6	91
Pierceville, In., U.S.	F7	91
Pierceville, Ks., U.S.	E3	93
Piercy, Ca., U.S.	C2	82
Piermont, N.H., U.S.	C3	106
Pierowall, Scot., U.K.	A6	13
Pierpont, Oh., U.S.	A5	112
Pierpont, S.D., U.S.	B8	118
Pierre, S.D., U.S.	C5	118
Pierre, Bayou, stm., Ms., U.S.	D3	101
Pierrefitte-sur-Aire, Fr.	F5	17
Pierrefonds, P.Q., Can.	q19	74
Pierre Part, La., U.S.	k9	95
Pierreville, P.Q., Can.	C5	74
Pierron, Il., U.S.	E4	90
Pierson, Mb., Can.	E1	70
Pierson, Fl., U.S.	C5	86
Pierson, Ia., U.S.	B2	92
Pierz, Mn., U.S.	E4	100
Piešťany, Czech.	D4	26
Pietermaritzburg, S. Afr.	C5	49
Pietersburg, S. Afr.	B4	49
Pie Town, N.M., U.S.	C1	108
Pietrasanta, Italy	C3	23
Piet Retief, S. Afr.	C5	49
Pietrosu, mtn., Rom.	B7	24
Pietrosul, mtn., Rom.	B7	24
Pieve di Cadore, Italy	A4	23
Pigeon, Mi., U.S.	E7	99
Pigeon, stm., Mb., Can.	C3	70
Pigeon, stm., In., U.S.	f9	110
Pigeon, stm., In., U.S.	A6	91
Pigeon, stm., Mn., U.S.	h10	100
Pigeon, stm., Wi., U.S.	k10	126
Pigeon Bay, b., Mb., Can.	C3	70
Pigeon Cove, Ma., U.S.	A6	98
Pigeon Creek, stm., Al., U.S.	D3	78
Pigeon Creek, stm., In., U.S.	H3	91
Pigeon Falls, Wi., U.S.	D2	126
Pigeon Forge, Tn., U.S.	D10	119
Pigeon Lake, l., Ab., Can.	C4	68
Pigeon Mountain, mtn., U.S.	B1	87
Pigeon Point, c., Mn., U.S.	h10	100
Pigg, stm., Va., U.S.	D3	123
Piggott, Ar., U.S.	A5	81
Piguë, Arg.	B4	54
Piirai, i., Marsh Is.	S18	52
Pijijiapan, Mex.	D6	63
Pike, N.H., U.S.	B2	106
Pike, N.Y., U.S.	C2	109
Pike, co., Al., U.S.	D4	78
Pike, co., Ar., U.S.	C2	81
Pike, co., Ga., U.S.	C2	87
Pike, co., Il., U.S.	D3	90
Pike, co., In., U.S.	H3	91
Pike, co., Ky., U.S.	C7	94
Pike, co., Ms., U.S.	D3	101
Pike, co., Mo., U.S.	B6	102
Pike, co., Oh., U.S.	C2	112
Pike, co., Pa., U.S.	D11	115
Pike, stm., Wi., U.S.	C6	126
Pike City, Mn., U.S.	C2	81
Pike Island Dam, U.S.	f8	125
Pike Lake, Mn., U.S.	D6	100
Pike Road, Al., U.S.	C3	78
Pike Rock, N.C., U.S.	B6	110
Pikes Peak, mtn., Co., U.S.	C5	83
Pikes Rocks, mtn., Pa., U.S.	C3	115
Pikesville, Md., U.S.	B4	97
Piketon, S. Afr.	D2	49
Piketon, Oh., U.S.	C2	112
Pikeville, Ky., U.S.	C7	94
Pikeville, N.C., U.S.	B5	110
Pikeville, Tn., U.S.	D8	119
Pikou, China	E10	32
Pikwitonei, Mb., Can.	B3	70
Piła, Pol.	B3	26
Pilar, Braz.	C3	57
Pilar, Para.	E4	55
Pilar, N.M., U.S.	A4	108
Pilar de Goiás, Braz.	A3	56
Pilar do Sul, Braz.	m8	56
Pilatus, mtn., Switz.	C4	20
Pilcomayo, stm., S.A.	E4	55
Pilger, Sk., Can.	E3	75
Pilger, Ne., U.S.	B8	104
Pilgrim, Ky., U.S.	C7	94
Pilgrim Gardens, Pa., U.S.	*p20	115
Pilibhīt, India	C7	37
Pilica, stm., Pol.	C5	26
Pillager, Mn., U.S.	D4	100
Pillaro, Ec.	B2	58
Pillar Point, c., Ca., U.S.	k7	82
Pilley's Island, Nf., Can.	D4	72
Pillow, Pa., U.S.	E8	115
Pillsbury, N.D., U.S.	B8	111

Name	Map Ref	Page
Pílos, Grc.	D3	25
Pilot Butte, Sk., Can.	G3	75
Pilot Grove, Mo., U.S.	C5	102
Pilot Knob, Mo., U.S.	D7	102
Pilot Knob, Ar., U.S.	C1	81
Pilot Knob, mtn., Ar., U.S.	B2	81
Pilot Knob, mtn., Id., U.S.	D3	89
Pilot Mound, Mb., Can.	E2	70
Pilot Mound, Ia., U.S.	B3	92
Pilot Mountain, N.C., U.S.	A2	110
Pilot Peak, mtn., Nv., U.S.	E4	105
Pilot Peak, mtn., Nv., U.S.	B7	105
Pilot Peak, mtn., Wy., U.S.	B3	127
Pilot Point, Ak., U.S.	D8	79
Pilot Point, Tx., U.S.	C4	120
Pilot Range, mts., Nv., U.S.	B7	105
Pilot Range, mts., N.H., U.S.	A4	106
Pilot Rock, Or., U.S.	B8	114
Pilot Station, Ak., U.S.	C7	79
Pilottown, La., U.S.	E6	95
Pilsen, Wi., U.S.	h10	126
Pima, Az., U.S.	E6	80
Pima, co., Az., U.S.	E3	80
Pimmit Hills, Va., U.S.	g12	123
Pimpri-Chinchwad, India	*E5	36
Pina, Pan.	k10	62
Pinal, co., Az., U.S.	E4	80
Pinaleno Mountains, mts., Az., U.S.	E5	80
Pinal Mountains, mts., Az., U.S.	D5	80
Pinang see George Town, Malay.	D2	34
Pinang, state, Malay.	J4	35
Pinang, i., Malay.	D2	34
Pınarbaşı, Tur.	C11	41
Pinar del Río, Cuba	C2	64
Pinar del Río, prov., Cuba	C2	64
Pinardville, N.H., U.S.	E3	106
Pinás, Arg.	A3	54
Pinatubo, Mount, mtn., Phil.	o13	34
Pincher Creek, Ab., Can.	E4	68
Pincher Station, Ab., Can.	E4	68
Pinckard, Al., U.S.	D4	78
Pinckney, Mi., U.S.	F7	99
Pinckney Island, i., S.C., U.S.	G6	117
Pinckneyville, Il., U.S.	E4	90
Pinconning, Mi., U.S.	E7	99
Pindall, Ar., U.S.	A3	81
Pindamonhangaba, Braz.	C3	56
Pindaré, stm., Braz.	B1	57
Pindus Mountains, mts., Grc.	C3	40
Pine, Az., U.S.	C4	80
Pine, Co., U.S.	B5	83
Pine, La., U.S.	D5	95
Pine, stm., B.C., Can.	B6	69
Pine, stm., Mi., U.S.	D1	70
Pine, stm., Mi., U.S.	D7	99
Pine, stm., Mi., U.S.	D5	99
Pine, stm., N.H., U.S.	C4	106
Pine, stm., Wi., U.S.	C5	126
Pine Apple, Al., U.S.	D3	78
Pine Bank, Pa., U.S.	G1	115
Pine Barrens, reg., N.J., U.S.	D3	107
Pine Bluff, Ar., U.S.	C3	81
Pinebluff, N.C., U.S.	B3	110
Pine Bluffs, Wy., U.S.	E8	127
Pine Bridge, Ct., U.S.	D3	84
Pinebur, Ms., U.S.	D4	101
Pine Bush, N.Y., U.S.	D6	109
Pine Castle, Fl., U.S.	D5	86
Pine City, Ar., U.S.	C4	81
Pine City, Mn., U.S.	E6	100
Pine City, Wa., U.S.	B8	124
Pine Creek, Austl.	B6	50
Pine Creek, stm., Ab., Can.	B4	68
Pine Creek, stm., Nv., U.S.	C5	105
Pine Creek, stm., Pa., U.S.	C6	115
Pine Creek, stm., Wa., U.S.	B8	124
Pine Creek Lake, res., Ok., U.S.	C6	113
Pinecrest, Ca., U.S.	C4	82
Pinedale, Al., U.S.	D3	78
Pinedale, Az., U.S.	C5	80
Pinedale, Wy., U.S.	D3	127
Pine Falls, Mb., Can.	D3	70
Pine Forest Range, mts., Nv., U.S.	B3	105
Pine Grove, Ga., U.S.	C4	87
Pine Grove, La., U.S.	D5	95
Pine Grove, N.J., U.S.	D3	107
Pine Grove, W.V., U.S.	B4	125
Pine Grove Mills, Pa., U.S.	E6	115
Pine Hall, N.C., U.S.	A2	110
Pine Hill, Austl.	A6	51
Pine Hill, N.J., U.S.	D2	78
Pine Hill, Ky., U.S.	C5	94
Pine Hill, N.J., U.S.	D3	107
Pine Hills, Fl., U.S.	D5	86
Pine, Pointe aux, c., On., Can.	p15	73
Pinehouse Lake, Sk., Can.	B2	75
Pinehouse Lake, l., Sk., Can.	B2	75
Pinehurst, Ga., U.S.	D3	87
Pinehurst, Id., U.S.	B3	89
Pinehurst, Ma., U.S.	f11	98
Pinehurst, N.C., U.S.	B3	110
Pinehurst Lake, l., Ab., Can.	B5	68
Pine Island, Mn., U.S.	F6	100
Pine Island, i., Fl., U.S.	F4	86
Pine Island, i., Fl., U.S.	D6	86
Pine Island Bay, b., Ant.	C1	7
Pine Island Sound, strt., Fl., U.S.	F4	86
Pine Key, i., Fl., U.S.	p10	86
Pine Knot, Ky., U.S.	D5	94
Pine Lake, Ga., U.S.	h8	87
Pine Lake, Ma., U.S.	g10	98
Pine Lake, l., In., U.S.	A4	91
Pine Lake, l., Wi., U.S.	C4	126
Pine Lawn, Mo., U.S.	f13	102
Pine Level, Al., U.S.	C3	78
Pine Level, N.C., U.S.	B4	110
Pinellas, co., Fl., U.S.	D4	86
Pinellas Park, Fl., U.S.	p10	86
Pine Meadow, Ct., U.S.	B4	84
Pine Mountain, Ga., U.S.	C2	87
Pine Mountain, mtn., U.S.	D6	94
Pine Mountain, mtn., Ct., U.S.	B4	84
Pine Mountain, mtn., Or., U.S.	D6	114
Pine Mountain, mtn., Tn., U.S.	C9	119
Pine Mountain, mtn., Wy., U.S.	E3	127
Pine Mountain, hills, Ok., U.S.	C6	113
Pineora, Ga., U.S.	D5	87
Pine Orchard, Ct., U.S.	D4	84
Pine Plains, N.Y., U.S.	D7	109
Pine Point, N.T., Can.	D10	66

Name	Map Ref	Page
Pine Point, Me., U.S.	E2	96
Pine Point, N.C., U.S.	D5	95
Piner Bay, b., Ant.	C27	7
Pine Rest, Ma., U.S.	g10	98
Pine Ridge, Ar., U.S.	C2	81
Pine Ridge, Ky., U.S.	C6	94
Pine Ridge, Ms., U.S.	D2	101
Pine Ridge, S.D., U.S.	D3	118
Pine Ridge Indian Reservation, S.D., U.S.	D3	118
Pine River, Mb., Can.	D1	70
Pine River, Mn., U.S.	D4	100
Pinerolo, Italy	B1	23
Pines, Isle of see Juventud, Isla de la, i., Cuba	D2	64
Pines, Lake o' the, res., Tx., U.S.	C5	120
Pinesdale, Mt., U.S.	D2	103
Pine Stump Junction, Mi., U.S.	B5	99
Pine Swamp Knob, mtn., W.V., U.S.	B5	125
Pinetop, Az., U.S.	C6	80
Pinetops, N.C., U.S.	B5	110
Pinetown, N.C., U.S.	B6	110
Pine Tree Corners, De., U.S.	C3	85
Pinetta, Fl., U.S.	B3	86
Pine Valley, Ca., U.S.	F5	82
Pine Valley, N.H., U.S.	E3	106
Pine Valley, Ut., U.S.	F2	121
Pine Valley Mountains, mts., Ut., U.S.	F2	121
Pineview, Ga., U.S.	D3	87
Pine Village, In., U.S.	D3	91
Pineville, Ky., U.S.	D6	94
Pineville, La., U.S.	C3	95
Pineville, Mo., U.S.	E3	102
Pineville, N.C., U.S.	B2	110
Pineville, S.C., U.S.	E7	117
Pineville, W.V., U.S.	D3	125
Pinewald, N.J., U.S.	D4	107
Pinewood, Fl., U.S.	s13	86
Pinewood, Mn., U.S.	C3	100
Pinewood, S.C., U.S.	D7	117
Piney, Mb., Can.	E3	70
Piney Creek, stm., W.V., U.S.	n13	125
Piney Flats, Tn., U.S.	C11	119
Piney Fork, Oh., U.S.	B5	112
Piney Fork, stm., W.V., U.S.	h9	125
Piney Point, Md., U.S.	D4	97
Piney View, W.V., U.S.	n13	125
Piney Woods, Ms., U.S.	C3	101
Pingding, China	B1	34
Pingdingshan, China	F5	32
Pingdu, China	H5	32
Pingjiang, China	D8	31
Pingle, China	J5	32
Pingli, China	G7	31
Pingliang, China	D7	31
Pingluo, China	D3	31
Pingnan, China	E2	32
Pingquan, China	G7	31
Pingree, Id., U.S.	D8	32
Pingree, N.D., U.S.	F6	89
Pingwu, China	B7	111
Pingxiang, China	E5	31
Pingxiang, China	G6	31
Pinhal, Braz.	F7	31
Pinhal Novo, Port.	C3	56
Pinheiro, Braz.	f10	22
Pinhel, Port.	B1	57
Piñi, i., Indon.	B2	22
Piniós (Peneus), stm., Grc.	E1	34
Pink Cliffs, clf, Ut., U.S.	C4	40
Pinkham Notch, N.H., U.S.	F3	121
Pink Hill, N.C., U.S.	B4	106
Pinkstaff, Il., U.S.	B5	110
Pinnacle, Ar., U.S.	E6	90
Pinnacle, N.C., U.S.	C3	81
Pinnacle, mtn., N.Y., U.S.	A2	110
Pinnacle Buttes, mtn., Wy., U.S.	B6	109
Pinnacles National Monument, U.S.	C3	127
Pinnaroo, Austl.	D3	82
Pinneberg, F.R.Ger.	G3	51
Pinnebog, Mi., U.S.	E3	15
Pinola, Ms., U.S.	E7	99
Pinole, Ca., U.S.	D4	101
Pinon, Az., U.S.	h8	82
Piñon, Fr.	B5	80
Pinon, N.M., U.S.	E3	17
Pinopolis, S.C., U.S.	A5	80
Pinos, Mex.	E7	117
Pinos, Mount, mtn., Ca., U.S.	C4	63
Pinos, Point, c., Ca., U.S.	E4	82
Pinos Altos, N.M., U.S.	D2	82
Pinos, Spain	E1	108
Pinos-Puente, Spain	C5	22
Pinotepa Nacional, Mex.	D4	22
Pinsk, Sov. Un.	D5	63
Pinsk Marshes, sw., Sov. Un.	E6	27
Pinta, Isla, i., Ec.	f7	58
Pinta, Sierra, mts., Az., U.S.	f5	58
Pintados, Chile	E2	80
Pinto, Spain	D2	55
Pinto Butte, mtn., Sk., Can.	p17	22
Pinto Creek, stm., Sk., Can.	k13	97
Pintura, Ut., U.S.	H2	75
Pintwater Range, mts., Nv., U.S.	F2	121
Pinware, stm., Nf., Can.	G6	105
Pinzolo, China	C3	72
Pinzón, Isla, i., Ec.	C6	20
Piombino, Italy	g5	58
Pioneer, La., U.S.	C3	23
Pioneer, Oh., U.S.	B4	95
Pioneer Mine, B.C., Can.	A1	112
Pioneer Mountains, mts., Id., U.S.	D6	69
Pionki, Pol.	F5	89
Piopolis, P.Q., Can.	C6	26
Piotrków [Trybunalski], Pol.	D7	74
Piove di Sacco, Italy	C5	26
Pipe, Wi., U.S.	D8	20
Piper City, Il., U.S.	k9	126
Piper Creek, stm., In., U.S.	C6	90
Piper, dept., Peru	k16	93
Piperi, i., Grc.	C5	25
Piperton, Tn., U.S.	B2	119
Pipe Spring National Monument, Az., U.S.	A3	80
Pipestem, W.V., U.S.	D4	125

Name	Map Ref	Page
Pipestem Creek, stm., N.D., U.S.	B6	111
Pipestone, Mb., Can.	E1	70
Pipestone, Mn., U.S.	G2	100
Pipestone, co., Mn., U.S.	F2	100
Pipestone Creek, stm., Can.	E1	70
Pipestone National Monument, Mn., U.S.	G2	100
Pipestone Pass, Mt., U.S.	E4	103
Pipinas, Arg.	B5	54
Pipmuacan, Réservoir, res., P.Q., Can.	k12	74
Piqua, Ks., U.S.	E8	93
Piqua, Oh., U.S.	B1	112
Piquiri, stm., Braz.	C2	56
Piracanjuba, Braz.	B3	56
Piracicaba, Braz.	C3	56
Piracicaba, stm., Braz.	m8	56
Piracuruca, Braz.	B2	57
Piraeus see Piraiévs, Grc.	D4	40
Piraiévs (Piraeus), Grc.	D4	40
Piraju, Braz.	C3	56
Pirajuba, Braz.	C3	56
Pirajuí, Braz.	C3	56
Piramida, Mount, mtn., Sov. Un.	D12	29
Piran, Yugo.	C1	24
Pirané, Arg.	E4	55
Piranga, Braz.	C3	56
Piranhas, Braz.	C3	57
Pirapora, Braz.	B4	56
Pirassununga, Braz.	C3	56
Piratini, Braz.	E2	56
Pirenópolis, Braz.	B3	56
Pires do Rio, Braz.	B3	56
Pírgos, Grc.	D3	40
Piriápolis, Ur.	E1	56
Pirin Mountains, mts., Bul.	E6	24
Piripiri, Braz.	B2	57
Pirmasens, F.R.Ger.	D3	18
Pirna, Ger.D.R.	C6	18
Pirot, Yugo.	D27	8
Pirovskoye, Sov. Un.	D27	8
Pirtleville, Az., U.S.	F6	80
Piru, Indon.	F7	34
Piryatin, Sov. Un.	F9	27
Pisa, Italy	C3	23
Pisa, hist., Peru	C23	58
Pisagua, Chile	C1	55
Pisar, Pol.	D6	26
Piscataqua, stm., N.H., U.S.	D5	106
Piscataquis, co., Me., U.S.	C3	96
Piscataway, N.J., U.S.	B4	107
Piscataway Creek, stm., Md., U.S.	C4	97
Pisciotta, Italy	D5	23
Pisco, Peru	D2	58
Piseco Lake, l., N.Y., U.S.	B6	109
Písek, Czech.	D3	26
Pisek, N.D., U.S.	A8	111
Pisgah, Al., U.S.	A4	78
Pisgah, Ia., U.S.	C2	92
Pisgah, Md., U.S.	C3	97
Pisgah, Oh., U.S.	n13	112
Pisgah, Mount, mtn., Ct., U.S.	B3	84
Pisgah, Mount, mtn., Vt., U.S.	F3	122
Pisgah, Mount, mtn., Wy., U.S.	C3	127
Pisgah Forest, N.C., U.S.	f10	110
Pishin, Pak.	B4	36
Pishtin, Pak.	B4	36
Pishukan, Rās, c., Pak.	I11	39
Pisinemo, Az., U.S.	E3	80
Pismo Beach, Ca., U.S.	E3	82
Pisogne, Italy	D6	20
Pissis, Monte, mtn., Arg.	C2	54
Pisticci, Italy	D6	23
Pistoia, Italy	C3	23
Pistol River, Or., U.S.	E2	114
Pisuerga, stm., Spain	A3	22
Pisz, Pol.	B6	26
Pita, Gui.	B3	82
Pitalito, Col.	C2	60
Pitangui, Braz.	B4	56
Pitcairn, dep., Oc.	H14	6
Piteälven, stm., Swe.	E9	14
Piteşti, Rom.	C7	24
Pithiviers, Fr.	C5	16
Piti, Guam	L9	52
Pitkin, co., Co., U.S.	B4	83
Pitman, N.J., U.S.	D2	107
Pitofsquén, Chile	B2	54
Piton des Neiges, Reu.	C1	112
Pitt, co., N.C., U.S.	B5	110
Pitt Island, i., B.C., Can.	C3	69
Pitts, Ga., U.S.	D3	87
Pittsboro, In., U.S.	E5	91
Pittsboro, Ms., U.S.	B4	101
Pittsboro, N.C., U.S.	B3	110
Pittsburg, Il., U.S.	g9	90
Pittsburg, Ks., U.S.	E9	93
Pittsburg, Tx., U.S.	C5	120
Pittsburg, co., Ok., U.S.	C6	113
Pittsburgh, Pa., U.S.	F1	115
Pittsfield, Il., U.S.	D3	90
Pittsfield, Ma., U.S.	B1	98
Pittsfield, N.H., U.S.	D4	106
Pittsfield, Vt., U.S.	D3	122
Pittston, Pa., U.S.	D10	115
Pittstown, N.J., U.S.	B3	107
Pittsview, Oh., U.S.	C4	112
Pittsville, Md., U.S.	D7	97
Pittsville, Wi., U.S.	D3	126
Pittsylvania, co., Va., U.S.	D3	123
Piura, Peru	B1	58
Piura, dept., Peru	A1	58
Piúte, co., Ut., U.S.	E3	121
Piute Peak, mtn., Ca., U.S.	E4	82
Piute Reservoir, res., Ut., U.S.	E3	121
Pithān, Nepal	C9	37
Piva, stm., Yugo.	D4	24
Pixley, Ca., U.S.	E4	82
Pizzo, Italy	E6	23

Name	Map Ref	Page
P. K. le Roux Dam, res., S. Afr.	D3	49
Placentia, Nf., Can.	E5	72
Placentia, Ca., U.S.	*n13	82
Placentia Bay, b., Nf., Can.	E4	72
Placer, co., Ca., U.S.	C3	82
Placerville, Ca., U.S.	C3	82
Placerville, Co., U.S.	C2	83
Placerville, Id., U.S.	F3	89
Placetas, Cuba	C4	64
Placid, Lake, l., Fl., U.S.	E5	86
Placid, Lake, l., N.Y., U.S.	f11	109
Placida, Fl., U.S.	F4	86
Plácido de Castro, Braz.	D4	58
Plaffeien, Switz.	C3	21
Plain, Wi., U.S.	E3	126
Plain City, Oh., U.S.	B2	112
Plain City, Ut., U.S.	B3	121
Plain Dealing, La., U.S.	B2	95
Plainfield, Ct., U.S.	C8	84
Plainfield, Il., U.S.	B5	90
Plainfield, In., U.S.	E5	91
Plainfield, Ia., U.S.	B5	92
Plainfield, Ma., U.S.	A2	98
Plainfield, N.H., U.S.	C2	106
Plainfield, N.J., U.S.	B4	107
Plainfield, Oh., U.S.	B4	112
Plainfield, Vt., U.S.	C4	122
Plainfield, Wi., U.S.	D4	126
Plainfield Heights, Mi., U.S.	E5	99
Plains, Ga., U.S.	D2	87
Plains, Ks., U.S.	E3	93
Plains, Mt., U.S.	C2	103
Plains, Pa., U.S.	n17	115
Plains, Tx., U.S.	C1	120
Plainsboro, N.J., U.S.	C3	107
Plainview, Mn., U.S.	F6	100
Plainview, Ne., U.S.	B8	104
Plainview, N.Y., U.S.	*E7	109
Plainview, S.D., U.S.	C3	118
Plainview, Tx., U.S.	B2	120
Plainville, Ct., U.S.	C4	84
Plainville, Ks., U.S.	C4	93
Plainville, Il., U.S.	D2	90
Plainville, In., U.S.	G3	91
Plainville, Ks., U.S.	C4	93
Plainville, Ma., U.S.	B5	98
Plainwell, Mi., U.S.	F5	99
Plaisance, P.Q., Can.	D2	74
Plaisance, Haiti	E7	64
Plaisance, Baie de, b., P.Q., Can.	B8	71
Plaisance-du-Gers, Fr.	F4	16
Plaisted, Me., U.S.	A4	96
Plaistow, N.H., U.S.	E4	106
Plamondon, Ab., Can.	B4	68
Planá, Czech.	D7	19
Planalto, Braz.	B3	56
Plane, stm., Ger.D.R.	A7	19
Plankinton, S.D., U.S.	D7	118
Plano, Il., U.S.	B5	90
Plano, Ia., U.S.	D4	92
Plano, Tx., U.S.	C4	120
Plantagenet, On., Can.	B9	73
Plant City, Fl., U.S.	r13	86
Plantation, Fl., U.S.	C3	78
Plantersville, Al., U.S.	A5	101
Plantersville, S.C., U.S.	D9	117
Plantsite, Az., U.S.	D6	80
Plantsville, Ct., U.S.	C4	84
Plaquemine, La., U.S.	E6	95
Plaquemines, co., La., U.S.	E6	95
Plasencia, Spain	B4	22
Plaster Rock, N.B., Can.	C2	71
Plastun, Sov. Un.	D8	33
Plasy, Czech.	D8	19
Plata, mtn., Switz.	D8	21
Plata, Río de la, est., S.A.	B5	54
Platea, Grc.	C1	115
Plateau, stm., B.C., Can.	B3	82
Plateau City, Co., U.S.	B3	83
Plateau Creek, stm., Co., U.S.	B3	83
Platina, Ca., U.S.	B2	82
Platinum, Ak., U.S.	D7	79
Platner, Co., U.S.	A7	83
Plato, Sk., Can.	F1	75
Plato, Col.	B5	60
Plato, Mo., U.S.	D5	102
Platón Sánchez, Mex.	m14	63
Platte, S.D., U.S.	D7	118
Platte, co., Mo., U.S.	C8	104
Platte, co., Ne., U.S.	B3	127
Platte, co., Wy., U.S.	D8	104
Platte, stm., U.S.	C6	104
Platte, stm., Mn., U.S.	D4	100
Platte, stm., Mo., U.S.	A3	102
Platte Center, Ne., U.S.	C8	104
Platte City, Mo., U.S.	B3	102
Plattenville, La., U.S.	k9	95
Platter, Ok., U.S.	D5	113
Platteville, Wi., U.S.	F3	126
Plattling, F.R.Ger.	E7	19
Plattsburg, Ms., U.S.	C4	101
Plattsburg, Mo., U.S.	B3	110
Plattsburgh, N.Y., U.S.	f11	109
Plattsburgh Air Force Base, mil., N.Y., U.S.	f11	109
Plattsmouth, Ne., U.S.	D10	104
Plattsville, On., Can.	D4	73
Plattville, Il., U.S.	B5	90
Plaucheville, La., U.S.	D4	95
Plauen, Ger.D.R.	C6	18
Plauer, l., Ger.D.R.	E6	15
Playas Lake, l., N.M., U.S.	F2	108
Playgreen Lake, l., Mb., Can.	B2	70
Plaza, N.D., U.S.	A4	111
Pleasant, stm., Me., U.S.	C3	96
Pleasant, stm., Me., U.S.	D3	96
Pleasant, Mount, mtn., Va., U.S.	C3	123
Pleasant Bay, N.S., Can.	C9	71
Pleasantdale, Sk., Can.	E3	75
Pleasant Dale, Ne., U.S.	D9	104
Pleasant Gap, Pa., U.S.	E6	115
Pleasant Garden, N.C., U.S.	B3	110
Pleasant Grove, Al., U.S.	g7	78
Pleasant Grove, Ms., U.S.	A3	101
Pleasant Grove, Ut., U.S.	C4	121
Pleasant Hill, Al., U.S.	h8	82
Pleasant Hill, Il., U.S.	D3	90
Pleasant Hill, La., U.S.	C2	95
Pleasant Hill, Mo., U.S.	e8	92
Pleasant Hill, Me., U.S.	g7	96
Pleasant Hill, Mo., U.S.	C3	102
Pleasant Hill, Oh., U.S.	D7	113

Name	Map Ref	Page
Pleasant Hill, S.C., U.S.	B6	117
Pleasant Hills, Pa., U.S.	*k14	115
Pleasant Hope, Mo., U.S.	D4	102
Pleasant Lake, Ar., U.S.	A5	81
Pleasant Lake, In., U.S.	A7	91
Pleasant Lake, Ma., U.S.	C7	98
Pleasant Lake, N.D., U.S.	A6	111
Pleasant Lake, l., Me., U.S.	C5	96
Pleasant Lake, l., N.H., U.S.	D4	106
Pleasant Mills, In., U.S.	C8	91
Pleasant Mount, Pa., U.S.	C11	115
Pleasanton, Ca., U.S.	h9	82
Pleasanton, Ia., U.S.	D4	92
Pleasanton, Ks., U.S.	D9	93
Pleasanton, Ne., U.S.	D6	104
Pleasanton, N.M., U.S.	D1	108
Pleasanton, Tx., U.S.	E3	120
Pleasant Plain, Ia., U.S.	C6	92
Pleasant Plains, Ar., U.S.	B4	81
Pleasant Plains, Il., U.S.	D4	90
Pleasant Pond, Me., U.S.	C3	96
Pleasant Pond, l., Me., U.S.	E6	97
Pleasant Prairie, Wi., U.S.	n12	126
Pleasants, co., W.V., U.S.	B3	125
Pleasant Shade, Tn., U.S.	C8	119
Pleasant Valley, Ct., U.S.	B4	84
Pleasant Valley, Ia., U.S.	D11	115
Pleasant Valley, Ia., U.S.	g11	92
Pleasant Valley, Md., U.S.	A3	97
Pleasant Valley, Mo., U.S.	h11	102
Pleasant Valley, Nv., U.S.	*D2	105
Pleasant Valley, N.Y., U.S.	D7	109
Pleasant Valley, Oh., U.S.	C2	112
Pleasant View, Co., U.S.	*B5	83
Pleasant View, In., U.S.	C3	90
Pleasant View, In., U.S.	m11	91
Pleasant View, Ky., U.S.	D5	94
Pleasant View, Tn., U.S.	A4	119
Pleasant View, Ut., U.S.	B3	121
Pleasant View, Wi., U.S.	D3	126
Pleasantville, In., U.S.	G3	91
Pleasantville, Ia., U.S.	C4	92
Pleasantville, N.J., U.S.	E3	107
Pleasantville, N.Y., U.S.	D7	109
Pleasantville, Oh., U.S.	C3	112
Pleasantville, Pa., U.S.	C2	115
Pleasure Beach, Ct., U.S.	D7	84
Pleasure Ridge Park, Ky., U.S.	g11	94
Pleasureville, Ky., U.S.	B4	94
Pledger, Tx., U.S.	r14	120
Pleebo, Lib.	F3	45
Pleiku, Viet.	F7	35
Plenița, Rom.	C6	24
Plenty, Sk., Can.	F1	75
Plenty, Bay of, b., N.Z.	L16	51
Plentywood, Mt., U.S.	B12	103
Plérin, Fr.	C2	16
Plesetsk, Sov. Un.	C7	29
Plessis, N.Y., U.S.	A5	109
Plessisville, P.Q., Can.	C6	74
Pleszew, Pol.	C4	26
Plétipi, Lac, l., P.Q., Can.	h12	74
Plettenberg, F.R.Ger.	B2	19
Pleven, Bul.	D7	24
Plevna, Ks., U.S.	E5	93
Plevna, Mo., U.S.	B5	102
Plevna, Mt., U.S.	D12	103
Pliny Range, mts., N.H., U.S.	B4	106
Pljevlja, Yugo.	D4	24
Plochingen, F.R.Ger.	E4	19
Płock, Pol.	B5	26
Ploërmel, Fr.	D2	16
Ploiești, Rom.	C8	24
Plomárion, Grc.	C6	25
Plomb du Cantal, mtn., Fr.	E5	16
Plombières-les-Bains, Fr.	B2	20
Plomosa Mountains, mts., Az., U.S.	D1	80
Plön, F.R.Ger.	D4	15
Plonge, Lac la, l., Sk., Can.	B2	75
Płońsk, Pol.	B6	26
Plougastel, Fr.	C1	16
Plovdiv, Bul.	D7	24
Plover, Ia., U.S.	*B3	92
Plover, Wi., U.S.	D4	126
Plover, stm., Wi., U.S.	D4	126
Pluck, Ire.	C4	11
Plum, Pa., U.S.	k14	115
Pluma, S.D., U.S.	C2	118
Plumas, Mb., Can.	D2	70
Plumas, co., Ca., U.S.	B3	82
Plum Bayou, stm., Ar., U.S.	k10	81
Plum Beach, R.I., U.S.	E4	116
Plum Branch, S.C., U.S.	D3	117
Plum Bridge, N. Ire., U.K.	C4	11
Plum City, Wi., U.S.	D1	126
Plum Coulee, Mb., Can.	E3	70
Plum Creek, stm., Ne., U.S.	D6	104
Plumerville, Ar., U.S.	B3	81
Plum Island, i., Ma., U.S.	A6	98
Plummer, Id., U.S.	B2	89
Plummer, Mn., U.S.	C2	100
Plum Point, R.I., U.S.	E4	116
Plumsteadville, Pa., U.S.	F11	115
Plumtree, Zimb.	B4	49
Plumwood, Oh., U.S.	B2	112
Plunkett, Sk., Can.	F3	75
Plunkettville, Ok., U.S.	C7	113
Plush, Or., U.S.	E7	114
Plymouth, Monts.	h13	64
Plymouth, Eng., U.K.	E4	10
Plymouth, Ct., U.S.	C3	84
Plymouth, Fl., U.S.	D5	86
Plymouth, Il., U.S.	C3	90
Plymouth, In., U.S.	B5	91
Plymouth, Ia., U.S.	A4	92
Plymouth, Ks., U.S.	D7	93
Plymouth, Me., U.S.	D3	96
Plymouth, Mi., U.S.	p15	99
Plymouth, Mn., U.S.	m12	100
Plymouth, Ne., U.S.	D9	104
Plymouth, N.H., U.S.	C3	106
Plymouth, N.C., U.S.	B6	110
Plymouth, Oh., U.S.	A3	112
Plymouth, Pa., U.S.	D10	115
Plymouth, Ut., U.S.	B3	121
Plymouth, W.V., U.S.	C3	125
Plymouth, Wi., U.S.	E6	126
Plymouth, co., Ia., U.S.	B1	92
Plymouth, co., Ma., U.S.	C6	98
Plymouth Bay, b., Ma., U.S.	*C6	98
Plymouth Meeting, Pa., U.S.	*o20	115
Plympton, R.I., Can.	*k14	115
Plympton, Ma., U.S.	C6	98
Plzeň, Czech.	D2	26
Pô, Burkina	D4	45
Po, Italy	B3	23
Po, stm., Italy	B5	123
Po, Mouths of the, mth., Italy	B4	100
Poamoho Stream, stm., Hi., U.S.	f9	88
Pobé, Benin	E5	45
Pobeda, Mount, mtn., Sov. Un.	C36	128
Pobedino, Sov. Un.	B11	33
Pobedy, Peak, mtn., Asia	E11	29
Poca, W.V., U.S.	*C3	125
Pocahontas, Ar., U.S.	A5	81
Pocahontas, Il., U.S.	E4	90
Pocahontas, Ia., U.S.	B3	92
Pocahontas, Tn., U.S.	B3	119
Pocahontas, Va., U.S.	e10	123
Pocahontas, co., Ia., U.S.	B3	92
Pocahontas, co., W.V., U.S.	C4	125
Pocasset, Ma., U.S.	C6	98
Pocatalico, W.V., U.S.	C3	125
Pocatalico, stm., W.V., U.S.	C3	125
Pocatello, Id., U.S.	G6	89
Pochep, Sov. Un.	E9	27
Pochutla, Mex.	D5	63
Pocola, Ok., U.S.	B7	113
Pocola, Ok., U.S.	B7	113
Pocomoke, stm., Md., U.S.	D7	97
Pocomoke City, Md., U.S.	D6	97
Pocomoke Sound, strt., Md., U.S.	E6	97
Poconé, Braz.	B1	56
Pocono Mountains, hills, Pa., U.S.	E11	115
Pocono Pines, Pa., U.S.	D11	115
Poços de Caldas, Braz.	C3	56
Pocotopaug Lake, res., Ct., U.S.	C6	84
Pocrí, Pan.	G7	62
Pocumtuck Mountain, mtn., Ma., U.S.	A2	98
Podbořany, Czech.	C8	19
Podgornoye, Sov. Un.	D25	8
Podhořany, Czech.	n17	26
Podkamennaya Tunguska, Sov. Un.	C27	8
Podkamennaya Tunguska, stm., Sov. Un.	C12	29
Podolsk, Sov. Un.	D11	27
Podor, Sen.	C2	45
Podporozhye, Sov. Un.	G16	14
Poe, In., U.S.	C7	91
Poel, i., Ger.D.R.	E5	15
Pofadder, S. Afr.	C2	49
Poggibonsi, Italy	C3	23
Pöggstall, Aus.	D7	18
Pogradeci, Alb.	B3	25
Pogranichnoye, Sov. Un.	A11	33
Pogranichnyy, Sov. Un.	D5	33
Pohang, S. Kor.	D10	31
Pohue Bay, b., Hi., U.S.	E6	88
Poinsett, co., Ar., U.S.	B5	81
Poinsett, Lake, l., Fl., U.S.	D6	86
Poinsett, Cape, c., Ant.	C24	7
Poinsett, Lake, l., S.D., U.S.	C8	118
Point Arena, Ca., U.S.	C2	82
Point Baker, Ak., U.S.	D13	79
Point Blue, La., U.S.	D3	95
Point Cedar, Ar., U.S.	C2	81
Point Clear, Al., U.S.	E2	78
Pointe a la Hache, La., U.S.	E6	95
Pointe-à-Pierre, Trin.	O23	65
Pointe-à-Pitre, Guad.	H14	64
Pointe au Baril Station, On., Can.	B4	73
Pointe-au-Pic, P.Q., Can.	B7	74
Pointe-aux-Trembles, P.Q., Can.	p20	74
Pointe-Bleue, P.Q., Can.	A5	74
Pointe-Calumet, P.Q., Can.	q19	74
Pointe-Claire, P.Q., Can.	D4	74
Pointe Coupee, co., La., U.S.	D4	95
Pointe-des-Cascades, P.Q., Can.	q19	74
Pointe du Bois, Mb., Can.	D4	70
Pointe-du-Chêne, N.B., Can.	C5	71
Pointe-du-Lac, P.Q., Can.	C5	74
Point Edward, On., Can.	D2	73
Pointe-Noire, Congo	B1	48
Pointe-Noire, Guad.	Q8	65
Pointers, N.J., U.S.	D2	107
Pointe-Verte, N.B., Can.	B4	71
Point Fortin, Trin.	O22	65
Point Hope, Ak., U.S.	B6	79
Point Imperial, mtn., Az., U.S.	A4	80
Point Independence, Ma., U.S.	*C6	98
Point Judith, R.I., U.S.	G4	116
Point Judith Pond, l., R.I., U.S.	F4	116
Point Lake, l., N.T., Can.	C10	66
Point Leamington, Nf., Can.	D4	72
Point Lookout, Md., U.S.	D5	97
Point Lookout, Md., U.S.	E4	102
Point Marion, Pa., U.S.	G2	115
Point Mugu Naval Air Station, mil., Ca., U.S.	E4	82
Point of Rocks, Md., U.S.	B2	97
Point of Rocks, Wy., U.S.	E4	127
Point Pelee National Park, On., Can.	F2	73
Point Pleasant, N.J., U.S.	C4	107
Point Pleasant, W.V., U.S.	C2	125
Point Pleasant Beach, N.J., U.S.	C4	107
Point Reyes National Seashore, Ca., U.S.	C2	82
Point Roberts, Wa., U.S.	A2	124
Point Sapin, N.B., Can.	C5	71
Point Washington, Fl., U.S.	u15	86
Poipu, Hi., U.S.	B2	88
Poirino, Italy	E3	20
Poison Creek, stm., Wy., U.S.	C5	127
Poisson Blanc, Lac du, res., P.Q., Can.	C2	74
Poissy, Fr.	C5	16
Poitiers, Fr.	D4	16
Poitou, hist reg., Fr.	D3	16
Poix, Fr.	E1	17
Pojo, Bol.	C3	55
Pojoaque Valley, N.M., U.S.	B3	108
Pokaran, India	C5	36
Pokataroo, Austl.	D7	51
Pokegama Lake, l., Mn., U.S.	C5	100
Pokegama Lake, l., Wi., U.S.	C2	126
Pokhara, Nepal	C9	37
Pokkye-ri, N. Kor.	G3	33
Poko, Zaire	A4	48
Poko Mountain, mtn., Ak., U.S.	B7	79
Pokrov, Sov. Un.	n19	27
Pokrovskoye, Sov. Un.	H12	27
Polacca, Az., U.S.	B5	80
Polān, Iran	F4	91
Poland, In., U.S.	F4	91
Poland, Me., U.S.	*D2	96
Poland, N.Y., U.S.	B5	109
Poland, ctry., Eur.	C5	26
Poland Spring, Me., U.S.	D2	96
Polar, Wi., U.S.	C5	126
Polar Bear Provincial Park, On., Can.	n18	73
Polaris, Mt., U.S.	E3	103
Polar Record Glacier, Ant.	C20	7
Polar Times Glacier, Ant.	C20	7
Polathane see Akçaabat, Tur.	B12	40
Polbain, Scot., U.K.	B3	13
Polch, F.R.Ger.	C2	19
Polcura, Chile	B2	54
Polebridge, Mt., U.S.	B2	103
Polecat Creek, stm., Ok., U.S.	B5	113
Pol-e Khomrī, Afg.	A4	36
Polesella, Italy	E7	20
Polessk, Sov. Un.	A6	26
Polevskoy, Sov. Un.	D21	8
Polgár, Hung.	B5	24
Poli, Cam.	D2	46
Police, Pol.	B3	26
Policastro, Gulf of, b., Italy	E5	23
Police, Pol.	B3	26
Poligny, Fr.	D6	16
Políkhnitos, Grc.	C6	25
Polillo, Phil.	o13	34
Polillo Islands, is., Phil.	B6	34
Polillo Strait, strt., Phil.	o13	34
Pólis, Cyp.	E9	40
Polígyros, Grc.	B4	25
Polk, Ne., U.S.	C8	104
Polk, Oh., U.S.	B3	112
Polk, Pa., U.S.	D2	115
Polk, Tn., U.S.	A2	119
Polk, co., Ar., U.S.	C1	81
Polk, co., Fl., U.S.	E5	86
Polk, co., Ga., U.S.	C1	87
Polk, co., Ia., U.S.	C4	92
Polk, co., Mn., U.S.	C2	100
Polk, co., Mo., U.S.	D4	102
Polk, co., N.C., U.S.	C8	104
Polk, co., N.C., U.S.	f10	110
Polk, co., Or., U.S.	C3	114
Polk, co., Tn., U.S.	D9	119
Polk, co., Tx., U.S.	D5	120
Polk, co., Wi., U.S.	C1	126
Polk City, Fl., U.S.	D5	86
Polk City, Ia., U.S.	C4	92
Polkton, N.C., U.S.	B2	110
Polkville, Ms., U.S.	C4	101
Pollard, Al., U.S.	D2	78
Pollard, Ar., U.S.	A5	81
Pollards Point, Nf., Can.	D3	72
Pollensa, Spain	C7	22
Pollock, Id., U.S.	D2	89
Pollock, La., U.S.	C3	95
Pollock, Mo., U.S.	A4	102
Pollock, S.D., U.S.	B5	118
Pollocksville, N.C., U.S.	B5	110
Pollockville, Ab., Can.	D5	68
Polo, Il., U.S.	B4	90
Polo, Mo., U.S.	B3	102
Polochic, stm., Guat.	C3	62
Pologi, Sov. Un.	H11	27
Polonnoye, Sov. Un.	F6	27
Polotsk, Sov. Un.	D7	27
Polson, Mt., U.S.	C2	103
Poltava, Sov. Un.	E6	29
Poltimore, P.Q., Can.	D2	74
Polunochnoye, Sov. Un.	A6	28
Polvadera, N.M., U.S.	C3	108
Polwarth, Sk., Can.	D2	75
Polyarnyy, Sov. Un.	C15	14
Pomabamba, Peru	C2	58
Pomarão, Port.	D2	22
Pomaria, S.C., U.S.	C5	117
Pomba, stm., Braz.	g6	56
Pombal, Braz.	C3	57
Pombal, Port.	C1	22
Pomerania, hist reg., Pol.	B5	26
Pomeranian Bay, b., Eur.	D8	15
Pomerene, Az., U.S.	E5	80
Pomeroy, N. Ire., U.K.	C5	11
Pomeroy, Ia., U.S.	B3	92
Pomeroy, Oh., U.S.	C3	112
Pomeroy, Wa., U.S.	B8	124
Pomezia, Italy	h9	23
Pomfret, Ct., U.S.	B8	84
Pomfret, Md., U.S.	C3	97
Pomfret, Vt., U.S.	D3	122
Pomfret Center, Ct., U.S.	B8	84
Pomme de Terre, stm., Mn., U.S.	E3	100
Pomme de Terre, stm., Mo., U.S.	D4	102
Pomme de Terre Lake, res., Mo., U.S.	D4	102
Pomoho, Hi., U.S.	f9	88
Pomona, Ca., U.S.	E5	82
Pomona, Ks., U.S.	D8	93
Pomona, Mo., U.S.	E6	102
Pomona, N.J., U.S.	E3	107
Pomona Lake, res., Ks., U.S.	D7	93
Pomona Park, Fl., U.S.	C5	86
Pomorie, Bul.	D8	24
Pompano Beach, Fl., U.S.	F6	86
Pompano Beach Highlands, Fl., U.S.	*F6	86
Pompeii, hist., Italy	D5	23
Pompeyevka, Sov. Un.	B3	33
Pompeys Pillar, Mt., U.S.	E9	103
Pompton Lakes, N.J., U.S.	A4	107
Pomquet, N.S., Can.	D8	71
Ponaganset, Stm., R.I., U.S.	C2	116
Ponaganset Reservoir, res., R.I., U.S.	C2	116
Ponape (Pohnpei), i., Micron.	F9	6
Ponape International Airport, Micron.	Q17	52
Ponask, stm., On., Can.	B5	70
Ponask Lake, l., On., Can.	B5	70
Ponass Lakes, l., Sk., Can.	E4	75
Ponca, Ar., U.S.	A2	81
Ponca, Ne., U.S.	B9	104
Ponca City, Ok., U.S.	A4	113
Ponca Creek, stm., U.S.	A6	104
Ponca Indian Reservation, Ne., U.S.	B7	104
Ponce, P.R.	H11	64
Ponce de Leon, Fl., U.S.	u16	86
Ponce de Leon Bay, b., Fl., U.S.	G5	86
Ponce de Leon Inlet, b., Fl., U.S.	*C6	86
Poncha Pass, Co., U.S.	C4	83
Poncha Springs, Co., U.S.	C4	83
Ponchatoula, La., U.S.	D5	95
Pond, stm., Ky., U.S.	C2	94
Pond, West Fork, stm., Ky., U.S.	C2	94
Pond Creek, Ok., U.S.	A3	113
Pond Creek, stm., Co., U.S.	C1	83
Pond Creek, stm., Ky., U.S.	g11	94
Pondera, co., Mt., U.S.	B4	103
Ponderay, Id., U.S.	A2	89
Ponderosa, N.M., U.S.	B3	108
Pond Fork, stm., W.V., U.S.	D3	125
Pond Fork, West Fork, stm., W.V., U.S.	n12	125
Pondicherry, ter., India	*F6	36
Pondicherry, ter., India	F6	36
Pond Inlet, N.T., Can.	B17	66
Ponds, Island of, i., Nf., Can.	B4	72
Pone Island, i., Md., U.S.	D5	97
Poneloya, Nic.	D4	62
Ponemah, Mn., U.S.	B4	100
Poneto, In., U.S.	C7	91
Ponferrada, Spain	A2	22
Pongoma, Sov. Un.	E16	14
Ponhook Lake, l., N.S., Can.	E5	71
Ponkapog Pond, l., Ma., U.S.	h11	98
Ponoka, Ab., Can.	C4	68
Ponoy, Sov. Un.	D19	14
Ponoy, stm., Sov. Un.	B16	8
Pons, Fr.	E3	16
Ponsford, Mn., U.S.	D3	100
Ponta Delgada, Port.	B3	26
Ponta de Pedras, Braz.	C5	59
Ponta Grossa, Braz.	D2	56
Pontal, Braz.	k7	56
Pontalina, Braz.	B3	56
Pont-à-Mousson, Fr.	C7	16
Ponta Porã, Braz.	C1	56
Pontarlier, Fr.	D7	16
Pontchartrain, Lake, l., La., U.S.	D5	95
Pont-de-Roide, Fr.	B2	20
Pontedera, Italy	C3	23
Ponte de Sor, Port.	C1	22
Ponte di Legno, Italy	C6	20
Pontefract, Eng., U.K.	A6	12
Ponteix, Sk., Can.	H2	75
Ponte Nova, Braz.	C4	56
Pontevedra, Spain	A1	22
Ponte Vedra Beach, Fl., U.S.	B5	86
Pontfaverger-Moronvilliers, Fr.	E4	17
Pontiac, Il., U.S.	C5	90
Pontiac, Mi., U.S.	F7	99
Pontiac, S.C., U.S.	C6	117
Pontianak, Indon.	F3	34
Pontic Mountains, mts., Tur.	B11	40
Pontivy, Fr.	C2	16
Pont-l'Abbé, Fr.	D1	16
Pontoise, Fr.	C5	16
Pontoosuc Lake, l., Ma., U.S.	B1	98
Pontotoc, Ms., U.S.	A4	101
Pontotoc, Tx., U.S.	D3	120
Pontotoc, co., Ms., U.S.	A4	101
Pontotoc, co., Ok., U.S.	C5	113
Pontremoli, Italy	B2	23
Pontresina, Switz.	C3	23
Pontrilas, Sk., Can.	D3	75
Pont-Rouge, P.Q., Can.	C6	74
Pont-Sainte-Maxence, Fr.	E2	17
Pontypool, P.Q., Can.	C6	73
Pontypool (Torfaen), Wales, U.K.	C4	12
Pontypridd (Taff-Ely), Wales, U.K.	C4	12
Pony, Mt., U.S.	E5	103
Ponza, i., Italy	D4	23
Ponziane Islands, is., Italy	D4	23
Poole, Eng., U.K.	E5	10
Poole, Ky., U.S.	C2	94
Poole, Ne., U.S.	D7	104
Pooler, Ga., U.S.	D5	87
Pooles Island, i., Md., U.S.	B5	97
Pooleville, Md., U.S.	B3	97
Pooleville, Oh., U.S.	C4	113
Poolewe, Scot., U.K.	C3	13
Pooley Island, i., B.C., Can.	C3	69
Poolowanna Lake, l., Austl.	E6	50
Poolville, Tx., U.S.	C4	120
Poona see Pune, India	E5	36
Poopó, Bol.	C3	55
Poopó, Lago, l., Bol.	K15	51
Poor Knights Islands, is., N.Z.	P13	51
Pootatuck Park, Ct., U.S.	*D2	84
Popasnaya, Sov. Un.	q21	27
Popayán, Col.	C2	60
Pope, Ms., U.S.	A4	101
Pope, co., Ar., U.S.	B2	81
Pope, co., Il., U.S.	F5	90
Pope, co., Mn., U.S.	E3	100
Pope Air Force Base, mil., N.C., U.S.	B3	110
Popejoy, Ia., U.S.	B4	92
Poperinge, Bel.	D2	17
Popham Beach, Me., U.S.	E3	96
Popham Point, c., On., Can.	B3	73
Poplar, Mt., U.S.	B11	103
Poplar, N.C., U.S.	e10	110
Poplar, Wi., U.S.	B2	126
Poplar, stm., N.A.	B11	103
Poplar, West Fork, stm., U.S.	B11	103
Poplar Bluff, Mo., U.S.	E7	102
Poplar Branch, N.C., U.S.	A7	110
Poplar Creek, Ms., U.S.	B4	101
Poplarfield, Mb., Can.	D3	70
Poplar Grove, Ar., U.S.	C5	81
Poplar Grove, Il., U.S.	A5	90
Poplar Island, i., Md., U.S.	C5	97
Poplar Mountain, mtn., Ky., U.S.	D6	94
Poplar Plains, Ky., U.S.	B6	94
Poplar Point, Mb., Can.	D3	70
Poplarville, Ms., U.S.	E4	101
Popo, co., Il., U.S.		
Popocatépetl, Volcán, vol., Mex.	n14	63
Popokabaka, Zaire	C2	48
Popondetta, Pap. N. Gui.	k12	50
Popovo, Bul.	D8	24
Poppel, Bel.	C5	17
Popple, stm., Wi., U.S.	C5	126
Poprad, Czech.	*D6	26
Poquetanuck, Ct., U.S.	D7	84
Poquonock, Ct., U.S.	B5	84
Poquonock Bridge, Ct., U.S.	D7	84
Poquoson, Va., U.S.	C6	123
Porali, stm., Pak.	H13	39
Porangatu, Braz.	A3	56
Porbandar, India	D2	36
Porcher Island, i., B.C., Can.	C2	69
Porcuna, Spain	D3	22
Porcupine, S.D., U.S.	D3	118
Porcupine, stm., N.A.	B11	79
Porcupine, Cape, c., Nf., Can.	B3	72
Porcupine Hills, hills, Can.	E5	75
Porcupine Mountains, mts., Mi., U.S.	m12	99
Porcupine Plain, Sk., Can.	E4	75
Pordenone, Italy	D7	20
Poreč, Yugo.	B1	24
Pori, Fin.	G9	14
Porirua, N.Z.	N15	51
Porjus, Swe.	C8	14
Porkhov, Sov. Un.	C7	27
Porkkala, Fin.	G11	14
Porlamar, Ven.	A5	60
Porlezza, Italy	D2	23
Pornic, Fr.	D2	16
Poroma, Bol.	C3	55
Poronaysk, Sov. Un.	E17	29
Poroshiri, Mount, mtn., Japan	E11	33
Porpoise Bay, b., Ant.	C25	7
Porrentruy, Switz.	E3	18
Porsangen, Nor.	B12	14
Porsgrunn, Nor.	p27	14
Portachuelo, Bol.	C3	55
Portadown, N. Ire., U.K.	C3	10
Portadown, N. Ire., U.K.	C6	11
Portaferry, N. Ire., U.K.	C6	11
Portage, P.E., Can.	C5	71
Portage, In., U.S.	A3	91
Portage, Me., U.S.	B4	96
Portage, Mi., U.S.	F5	99
Portage, Pa., U.S.	F4	115
Portage, Ut., U.S.	B3	121
Portage, Wi., U.S.	E4	126
Portage, co., Oh., U.S.	A4	112
Portage, co., Wi., U.S.	D4	126
Portage, stm., Oh., U.S.	B2	112
Portage, North Branch, stm., Oh., U.S.	f7	102
Portage Des Sioux, Mo., U.S.	f13	102
Portage Head, c., Wa., U.S.	A1	124
Portage Island, i., N.B., Can.	B4	71
Portage Lake, l., Me., U.S.	B4	96
Portage Lakes, Oh., U.S.	B4	112
Portage la Prairie, Mb., Can.	E2	70
Portageville, Mo., U.S.	E8	102
Portageville, N.Y., U.S.	C2	109
Portal, Az., U.S.	F6	80
Portal, Ga., U.S.	D5	87
Portal, N.D., U.S.	A3	111
Portales, N.M., U.S.	C6	108
Port Alexander, Ak., U.S.	D13	79
Port-Alfred, P.Q., Can.	A7	74
Port Alfred (Kowie), S. Afr.	D4	49
Port Alice, B.C., Can.	D4	69
Port Allegany, Pa., U.S.	C5	115
Port Allen, La., U.S.	D4	95
Port Amherst, W.V., U.S.	m12	125
Port Angeles, Wa., U.S.	A2	124
Port Antonio, Jam.	E5	64
Port Aransas, Tx., U.S.	F4	120
Port Arthur see Lüshun, China	D9	31
Port Arthur, Tx., U.S.	E6	120
Portaskaig, Scot., U.K.	E2	13
Port Augusta, Austl.	F6	50
Port-au-Persil, P.Q., Can.	B8	74
Port-au-Port, Nf., Can.	D2	72
Port au Port Bay, b., Nf., Can.	D2	72
Port au Port Peninsula, pen., Nf., Can.	D2	72
Port-au-Prince, Haiti	E7	64
Port Austin, Mi., U.S.	D7	99
Port Barre, La., U.S.	D4	95
Port-Bergé, Madag.	g9	49
Port Birmingham, Al., U.S.	B2	78
Port Blair, India	F9	36
Port Blakely, Wa., U.S.	e11	124
Port Blandford, Nf., Can.	D4	72
Port Bolivar, Tx., U.S.	E5	120
Port Borden, P.E., Can.	C6	71
Port Burwell, On., Can.	E4	73
Port Byron, Il., U.S.	B3	90
Port Byron, N.Y., U.S.	B4	109
Port Carbon, Pa., U.S.	E9	115
Port Carling, On., Can.	B5	73
Port-Cartier-Ouest, P.Q., Can.	h13	74
Port-Cartier-Sept-Îles, Réserve de, P.Q., Can.	h13	74
Port Chalmers, N.Z.	P13	51
Port Charlotte, Fl., U.S.	F4	86
Port Chester, N.Y., U.S.	E7	109
Port Clements, B.C., Can.	C1	69
Port Clinton, Oh., U.S.	D1	70
Port Clyde, N.S., Can.	F4	71
Port Clyde, Me., U.S.	E3	96
Port Colborne, On., Can.	E5	73
Port Colden, N.J., U.S.	B3	107
Port Coquitlam, B.C., Can.	E6	69
Port Credit, On., Can.	D5	73
Port-Daniel, P.Q., Can.	A5	71
Port-de-Bouc, Fr.	F6	16
Port-de-Paix, Haiti	E7	64
Port Deposit, Md., U.S.	A5	97
Port Dickinson, N.Y., U.S.	C5	109
Port Dickson, Malay.	E2	34
Port Dover, On., Can.	E4	73
Port Eads, La., U.S.	E6	95
Port Edward, B.C., Can.	B2	69
Port Edwards, Wi., U.S.	D4	126
Port Elgin, N.B., Can.	C5	71
Port Elgin, On., Can.	C3	73
Port Elizabeth, S. Afr.	D4	49
Port Ellen, Scot., U.K.	E2	13
Porteña, Arg.	A4	54
Porter, Al., U.S.	B2	78
Porter, In., U.S.	A3	91
Porter, Me., U.S.	E2	96
Porter, Mn., U.S.	F2	100
Porter, Ok., U.S.	B6	113
Porter, Tx., U.S.	D5	120
Porter, Wa., U.S.	C2	124
Porter, co., In., U.S.	A3	91
Porter Corners, N.Y., U.S.	B7	109
Porter Creek, stm., W.V., U.S.	m13	125
Porterdale, Ga., U.S.	C3	87
Porter Lake, l., Sk., Can.	A2	75
Porterville, Ca., U.S.	D4	82
Porterville, Ms., U.S.	C5	101
Port Essington, B.C., Can.	B2	69
Port Ewen, N.Y., U.S.	D7	109
Port Fairy, Austl.	I4	51
Port Gamble, Wa., U.S.	B3	124
Port Gamble Indian Reservation, Wa., U.S.	B3	124
Port-Gentil, Gabon	F1	46
Port George, N.S., Can.	D4	71
Port Gibson, Ms., U.S.	D3	101
Port Glasgow, Scot., U.K.	E4	13
Port Graham, Ak., U.S.	D9	79
Port Greville, N.S., Can.	D5	71
Port Hammond, B.C., Can.	f13	69
Port Harcourt, Nig.	F6	45
Port Hardy, B.C., Can.	D4	69
Port Hastings, N.S., Can.	D8	71
Port Hawkesbury, N.S., Can.	D8	71
Porthcawl, Wales, U.K.	C4	12
Port Hedland, Austl.	D3	50
Port Heiden, Ak., U.S.	D8	79
Port Henry, N.Y., U.S.	A7	109
Port Hill, P.E., Can.	C6	71
Porthill, Id., U.S.	A2	89
Port Hood, N.S., Can.	C8	71
Port Hope, On., Can.	D6	73
Port Hope, Mi., U.S.	E8	99
Port Hope Simpson, Nf., Can.	B3	72
Port Hueneme, Ca., U.S.	E4	82
Port Huron, Mi., U.S.	F8	99
Portia, Ar., U.S.	A4	81
Portimão, Port.	D1	22
Port Isabel, Tx., U.S.	F4	120
Port Jefferson, N.Y., U.S.	n15	109
Port Jefferson Station, N.Y., U.S.	*n15	109
Port Jervis, N.Y., U.S.	D6	109
Port Keats, Austl.	B4	50
Port Kent, N.Y., U.S.	f11	109
Portland, Austl.	G7	50
Portland, On., Can.	C8	73
Portland, Al., U.S.	D4	81
Portland, Co., U.S.	C5	83
Portland, Ct., U.S.	C5	84
Portland, In., U.S.	D8	91
Portland, Me., U.S.	E2	96
Portland, Mi., U.S.	F6	99
Portland, Mo., U.S.	C6	102
Portland, N.Y., U.S.	C1	109
Portland, N.D., U.S.	B8	111
Portland, Or., U.S.	B4	114
Portland, Pa., U.S.	E11	115
Portland, Tn., U.S.	A5	119
Portland, Tx., U.S.	F4	120
Portland, Bill of, c., Eng., U.K.	E5	10
Portland Canal, b., N.A.	B2	69
Portland Creek Pond, l., Nf., Can.	C3	72
Portland Inlet, b., B.C., Can.	B2	69
Portland Mills, Pa., U.S.	D4	115
Portland Point, c., Jam.	F14	65
Portlandville, N.Y., U.S.	C6	109
Portlaoise, Ire.	D3	10
Port Lavaca, Tx., U.S.	E4	120
Portlaw, Ire.	E4	11
Port Leyden, N.Y., U.S.	B5	109
Port Lincoln, Austl.	F6	50
Port Lions, Ak., U.S.	D9	79
Port Loko, S.L.	E2	45
Port Loring, On., Can.	B4	73
Port-Louis, Fr.	D2	16
Port-Louis, Guad.	Q8	65
Port Louis, Mrts.	H24	2
Port Ludlow, Wa., U.S.	B3	124
Port Macquarie, Austl.	F9	50
Port Madison Indian Reservation, Wa., U.S.	B3	124
Portmadoc, Wales, U.K.	B3	12
Portmagee, Ire.	F1	11
Portmahomack, Scot., U.K.	C5	13
Port Maitland, N.S., Can.	F3	71
Port Maitland, On., Can.	E5	73
Port Maria, Jam.	E5	64
Port Matilda, Pa., U.S.	E5	115
Port Mayaca, Fl., U.S.	F6	86
Port McNicoll, On., Can.	C5	73
Port Medway, N.S., Can.	E5	71
Port Mellon, B.C., Can.	E6	69
Port-Menier, P.Q., Can.	k8	72
Port Moller, Ak., U.S.	D7	79
Port Monmouth, N.J., U.S.	C4	107
Morant, Jam.	F16	65
Port Moresby, Pap. N. Gui.	k12	50
Port Morien, N.S., Can.	C10	71
Port Morris, N.J., U.S.	B3	107
Port Mouton Island, i., N.S., Can.	F5	71
Port Murray, N.J., U.S.	B3	107
Portnahaven, Scot., U.K.	E2	13
Port Neches, Tx., U.S.	E6	120
Port Nelson, Mb., Can.	A5	70
Portneuf, P.Q., Can.	C6	74
Portneuf, Réserve, P.Q., Can.	B5	74
Portneuf-sur-Mer, P.Q., Can.	A8	74
Port Nolloth, S. Afr.	C2	49
Port-Nouveau-Québec, P.Q., Can.	f8	72
Porto, Port.	B1	22
Porto Acre, Braz.	C4	58
Porto Alegre, Braz.	E2	56
Porto Alexandre see Tombua, Ang.	E1	48
Porto Amboim, Ang.	D1	48
Porto Belo, Braz.	D3	56
Portobelo, Pan.	F8	62
Porto Calvo, Braz.	C3	57
Porto O'Connor, Tx., U.S.	E4	120
Porto de Moz, Braz.	C4	59
Pôrto de Mós, Port.	C1	22
Porto Esperança, Braz.	B1	56
Porto Feliz, Braz.	A4	54
Portoferraio, Italy	C3	23
Portofino, Italy	B2	23
Port of Ness, Scot., U.K.	B2	13
Port of Spain, Trin.	K14	64
Porto Garibaldi, Italy	E7	20
Porto Grande, Braz.	B4	23
Portogruaro, Italy	D7	20
Portola, Ca., U.S.	C3	82
Porto Lucena, Braz.	D1	56
Portomaggiore, Italy	B3	23
Porto Mendes, Braz.	C2	56
Porto Murtinho, Braz.	D4	55
Porto Nacional, Braz.	C5	59
Porto-Novo, Benin	E5	45
Porto Orange, Fl., U.S.	C6	86
Port Orchard, Wa., U.S.	B3	124
Port Orford, Or., U.S.	E2	114
Porto Santana, Braz.	B4	59
Porto Santo, i., Port.	g12	22
Portoscuso, Italy	E3	23
Porto Seguro, Braz.	B3	57
Porto Torres, Italy	D2	23
Porto União, Braz.	D2	56
Porto-Vecchio, Fr.	n24	22a
Porto Velho, Braz.	C5	58
Portovíejo, Ec.	B1	58
Portpatrick, Scot., U.K.	F3	13
Port Penn, De., U.S.	B3	85
Port Perry, On., Can.	C6	73
Port Phillip Bay, b., Austl.	G7	50
Port Pirie, Austl.	F6	50
Port Radium, N.T., Can.	C9	66
Port Reading, N.J., U.S.	k8	107
Portree, Scot., U.K.	C2	13
Portreeve, Sk., Can.	G1	75
Port Renfrew, B.C., Can.	E5	69
Port Republic, N.J., U.S.	D4	107
Port Republic, Va., U.S.	B4	123
Port Rexton, Nf., Can.	D5	72
Port Richey, Fl., U.S.	D4	86

Name	Map Ref	Page

Port Rowan, On., Can. — E4 73
Port Royal, Ky., U.S. — B4 94
Port Royal, Pa., U.S. — E7 115
Port Royal, S.C., U.S. — G6 117
Port Royal, Tn., U.S. — A4 119
Port Royal, Va., U.S. — B5 123
Port Royal Island, i., S.C., U.S. — G6 117
Port Royal Sound, strt., S.C., U.S. — G6 117
Portrush, N. Ire., U.K. — B5 11
Port Said (Būr Saʿīd), Eg. — B3 38
Port Saint Lucie, Fl., U.S. — E6 86
Port Saint Joe, Fl., U.S. — C1 86
Port Saint Johns, Transkei — D4 49
Port-Saint-Louis [-du-Rhône], Fr. — F6 16
Port Salerno, Fl., U.S. — E6 86
Portsalon, Ire. — B4 11
Port Sanilac, Mi., U.S. — E8 99
Port Saunders, Nf., Can. — C3 72
Port Sewall, Fl., U.S. — E6 86
Port Shepstone, S. Afr. — D5 49
Port Simpson, B.C., Can. — B2 69
Portsmouth, Dom. — I14 64
Portsmouth, Eng., U.K. — E6 10
Portsmouth, Ia., U.S. — C2 92
Portsmouth, N.H., U.S. — D5 106
Portsmouth, Oh., U.S. — D3 112
Portsmouth, R.I., U.S. — E6 116
Portsmouth, Va., U.S. — D6 123
Portsmouth Naval Shipyard, mil., Me., U.S. — D5 106
Portsoy, Scot., U.K. — C6 13
Port Stanley, On., Can. — E3 73
Port Sudan (Būr Sūdān), Sud. — B4 47
Port Sulphur, La., U.S. — E6 95
Port-sur-Saône, Fr. — B2 20
Port Talbot (Afan), Wales, U.K. — C4 12
Porttipahdan Reservoir, res., Fin. — C12 14
Port Tobacco Village, Md., U.S. — C3 97
Port Townsend, Wa., U.S. — A3 124
Portugal, ctry., Eur. — C1 22
Portugal Cove South, Nf., Can. — E5 72
Portugalete, Spain — A4 22
Portuguesa, state, Ven. — B4 60
Portuguesa, stm., Ven. — B4 60
Portumna, Ire. — D3 11
Port Union, Nf., Can. — D5 72
Port Union, Oh., U.S. — n13 112
Port-Vendres, Fr. — F5 16
Port-Vila, Vanuatu — ʼH10 6
Portville, N.Y., U.S. — C2 109
Port Vincent, La., U.S. — D5 95
Port Vue, Pa., U.S. — *k14 115
Port Wakefield, Austl. — G2 51
Port Washington, N.Y., U.S. — h13 109
Port Washington, Oh., U.S. — B4 112
Port Washington, Wi., U.S. — E6 126
Port Wentworth, Ga., U.S. — D5 87
Port William, Scot., U.K. — F4 13
Port William, Oh., U.S. — C2 112
Port Wing, Wi., U.S. — B2 126
Porum, Ok., U.S. — B6 113
Porvenir, Chile — h11 54
Porz, F.R.Ger. — C2 19
Posadas, Arg. — E4 55
Posadas, Spain — D3 22
Poschiavo, Switz. — D9 21
Posen, Il., U.S. — k9 90
Posen, Mi., U.S. — C7 99
Posey, co., In., U.S. — H2 91
Poseyville, In., U.S. — H2 91
Poshekhonye-Volodarsk, Sov. Un. — B12 27
Poso, Indon. — F6 34
Poso, Lake, l., Indon. — F6 34
Posòng, S. Kor. — I3 33
Posse, Braz. — A3 56
Pössneck, Ger.D.R. — C6 19
Post, Or., U.S. — C6 114
Post, Tx., U.S. — C2 120
Poste-de-la-Baleine, P.Q., Can. — g14 74
Poste-Mistassini, P.Q., Can. — h12 74
Post Falls, Id., U.S. — B2 89
Postmasburg, S. Afr. — C3 49
Post Mills, Vt., U.S. — D4 122
Poston, S.C., U.S. — D9 117
Postville, Ia., U.S. — A6 92
Potaro Landing, Guy. — A3 59
Potato Creek, S.D., U.S. — D4 118
Potawatomi Indian Reservation, Ks., U.S. — C8 93
Potchefstroom, S. Afr. — C4 49
Poteau, Ok., U.S. — B7 113
Poteau, stm., U.S. — C1 81
Poteau Mountain, mtn., U.S. — C1 81
Poteet, Tx., U.S. — E3 120
Potenza, Italy — D5 23
Potenza, stm., Italy — C4 23
Potgietersrus, S. Afr. — B4 49
Poth, Tx., U.S. — E3 120
Potholes Reservoir, res., Wa., U.S. — B6 124
Poti, Sov. Un. — G17 8
Poti, stm., Braz. — B2 57
Potiskum, Nig. — D7 45
Potlatch, Id., U.S. — C2 89
Potlatch, stm., Id., U.S. — C6 90
Potomac, Il., U.S. — C6 90
Potomac, Md., U.S. — B3 97
Potomac, Mt., U.S. — D3 103
Potomac, stm., U.S. — D4 97
Potomac, North Branch, stm., U.S. — m12 97
Potomac, South Branch, stm., U.S. — B6 125
Potomac, South Branch, North Fork, stm., U.S. — C5 125
Potomac, South Branch, South Fork, stm., U.S. — B6 125
Potomac Heights, Md., U.S. — C3 97
Potomac Park, Md., U.S. — k13 97
Potosí, Bol. — C2 55
Potosi, Mo., U.S. — D7 102
Potosi, Wi., U.S. — F3 126
Potosí, dept., Bol. — D2 55
Potrerillos, Chile — E2 55
Potrerillos, Hond. — G4 63
Potro, Cerro el, mtn., S.A. — E2 55
Potsdam, Ger.D.R. — B6 18
Potsdam, N.Y., U.S. — f10 109
Pottawatomie, co., Ks., U.S. — C7 93
Pottawatomie, co., Ok., U.S. — B4 113
Pottawattamie, co., Ia., U.S. — C2 92
Potter, Ks., U.S. — C1 81
Potter, Ne., U.S. — C8 93
Potter, stm., Mn., U.S. — C2 104
Potter, Wi., U.S. — h9 126

Potter, co., Pa., U.S. — C6 115
Potter, co., S.D., U.S. — B6 118
Potter, co., Tx., U.S. — B2 120
Potter Hill, R.I., U.S. — F1 116
Potter Place, N.H., U.S. — D3 106
Pottersville, Mo., U.S. — E5 102
Pottersville, N.J., U.S. — B3 107
Pottersville, N.Y., U.S. — B7 109
Potter Valley, Ca., U.S. — C2 82
Potterville, Mi., U.S. — F6 99
Potts Camp, Ms., U.S. — A4 101
Potts Creek, stm., U.S. — C2 123
Pottstown, Pa., U.S. — F10 115
Pottsville, Ar., U.S. — B2 81
Pottsville, Pa., U.S. — E9 115
Pottsville, Tx., U.S. — D3 120
Potwin, Ks., U.S. — E6 93
Pouce-Coupe, B.C., Can. — B7 69
Pouch Cove, Nf., Can. — E5 72
Poughkeepsie, Ar., U.S. — A4 81
Poughkeepsie, N.Y., U.S. — D7 109
Poulan, Ga., U.S. — E3 87
Poulsbo, Wa., U.S. — B3 124
Poultney, Vt., U.S. — D2 122
Poultney, stm., Vt., U.S. — D2 122
Pound, Va., U.S. — e9 123
Pound, Wi., U.S. — C5 126
Pound Gap, U.S. — C7 94
Pouso Alegre, Braz. — G6 56
Poutasi, W. Sam. — G12 52
Pouthisat, Kam. — C2 34
Pouxeux, Fr. — A2 20
Povungnituk, P.Q., Can. — f11 74
Powassan, On., Can. — A5 73
Poway, Ca., U.S. — F5 82
Powder, stm., U.S. — A6 76
Powder, Middle Fork, stm., Wy., U.S. — C6 127
Powder, North Fork, stm., Wy., U.S. — C6 127
Powder, South Fork, stm., Wy., U.S. — C6 127
Powderhorn, Co., U.S. — C3 83
Powder River, Wy., U.S. — C6 127
Powder River Pass, Wy., U.S. — B5 127
Powderly, Mt., U.S. — E11 103
Powder Wash, Co., U.S. — A2 83
Powe, Mo., U.S. — E3 102
Powell, Mo., U.S. — E3 102
Powell, Oh., U.S. — B2 112
Powell, Pa., U.S. — C9 115
Powell, Tn., U.S. — m13 119
Powell, Tx., U.S. — C4 120
Powell, Wy., U.S. — B4 127
Powell, co., Ky., U.S. — C6 94
Powell, co., Mt., U.S. — D4 103
Powell, stm., U.S. — C10 119
Powell, Lake, res., U.S. — F5 121
Powell, Mount, mtn., Co., U.S. — B4 83
Powell Butte, Or., U.S. — C5 114
Powellhurst, Or., U.S. — *B4 114
Powell Mountain, mtn., N.M., U.S. — B1 108
Powell Park, reg., Co., U.S. — A2 83
Powellsville, N.C., U.S. — A6 110
Powellville, W.V., U.S. — C3 125
Powellville, Md., U.S. — D7 97
Powelton, Ga., U.S. — C4 87
Power, Mt., U.S. — C5 103
Power, co., Id., U.S. — G5 89
Power Head, c., Ire. — F3 11
Powers, Or., U.S. — E2 114
Powers, Or., U.S. — E2 114
Powers Lake, N.D., U.S. — A3 111
Powersville, Mo., U.S. — A4 102
Poweshiek, co., Ia., U.S. — C5 92
Powhatan, La., U.S. — B2 78
Powhatan, Ar., U.S. — A4 81
Powhatan, Va., U.S. — C5 123
Powhatan, co., Va., U.S. — C5 123
Powhatan Point, Oh., U.S. — C5 112
Powhattan, Ks., U.S. — C8 93
Pownal, Me., U.S. — g7 96
Pownal, Vt., U.S. — F2 122
Pownal Center, Me., U.S. — g7 96
Pownal Center, Vt., U.S. — F2 122
Powys, co., Wales, U.K. — B4 12
Poxoréo, Braz. — B2 56
Poyang Lake, l., China — F8 33
Poyarkovo, Sov. Un. — C3 81
Poyen, Ar., U.S. — C3 81
Poygan, Lake, l., Wi., U.S. — D5 126
Poynette, Wi., U.S. — E4 126
Poynor, Mo., U.S. — E7 102
Poyntzpass, N. Ire., U.K. — C5 11
Poy Sippi, Wi., U.S. — D5 126
Požarevac, Yugo. — C5 24
Poza Rica de Hidalgo, Mex. — m15 63
Poznań, Pol. — B4 26
Pozo Almonte, Chile — D2 55
Pozoblanco, Spain — D3 22
Pozo Colorado, Para. — D4 55
Pozo Redondo Mountains, mts., U.S. — E3 80
Pozos, Mex. — m13 63
Pozuelo de Alarcón, Spain — p17 22
Pozuelos, Ven. — A5 60
Pozuzo, Peru — D2 58
Pozzallo, Italy — F5 23
Pozzuoli, Italy — D5 23
Prachatice, Czech. — E9 19
Prachin Buri, Thai. — C3 34
Prachuap Khiri Khan, Thai. — G3 35
Praco, Al., U.S. — f6 78
Prades, Fr. — F5 16
Prado Flood Control Basin, Ca., U.S. — n13 82
Præstø, Den. — C6 15
Praga (part of Warsaw), Pol. — k14 26
Prague (Praha), Czech. — C3 26
Prague, Ne., U.S. — C9 104
Prague, Ok., U.S. — B5 113
Prainha, Braz. — C4 59
Prairie, Al., U.S. — C2 78
Prairie, co., Ar., U.S. — C4 81
Prairie, co., Mt., U.S. — D11 103
Prairie, stm., Mn., U.S. — C5 100
Prairie, stm., Wi., U.S. — C4 126
Prairie Bayou, stm., Ar., U.S. — g7 81

Prairie City, Il., U.S. — C3 90
Prairie City, Ia., U.S. — C4 92
Prairie City, Or., U.S. — C8 114
Prairie City, S.D., U.S. — B3 118
Prairie Creek, In., U.S. — F3 91
Prairie Creek Reservoir, res., In., U.S. — D7 91
Prairie Dog Creek, stm., U.S. — C3 93
Prairie du Chien, Wi., U.S. — E2 126
Prairie Du Rocher, Il., U.S. — E3 90
Prairie du Sac, Wi., U.S. — E4 126
Prairie Farm, Wi., U.S. — C2 126
Prairie Grove, Ar., U.S. — B1 81
Prairie Hill, Mo., U.S. — B5 102
Prairie Home, Mo., U.S. — C5 102
Prairie Home, Ne., U.S. — h11 104
Prairie Point, Ms., U.S. — B5 101
Prairie River, Sk., Can. — E4 75
Prairies, Lake of the, res., Can. — F5 75
Prairies, Rivière des, stm., P.Q., Can. — p19 74
Prairieton, In., U.S. — F3 91
Prairie View, Ar., U.S. — B2 81
Prairie View, Ks., U.S. — C4 93
Prairie View, Tx., U.S. — D5 120
Prairie Village, Ks., U.S. — m16 93
Prairieville, La., U.S. — h10 95
Pran Buri, Thai. — C2 34
Praszka, Pol. — C5 26
Prata, Braz. — B3 56
Prater Mountain, mtn., Wy., U.S. — C2 127
Prato, Italy — C3 23
Prats-de-Mollo, Fr. — F5 16
Pratt, Ks., U.S. — E5 93
Pratt, W.V., U.S. — *C3 125
Pratt, co., Ks., U.S. — E5 93
Pratten, Switz. — A4 21
Prattsburg, N.Y., U.S. — C3 109
Prattsville, Ar., U.S. — C3 81
Prattsville, N.Y., U.S. — C6 109
Prattville, Al., U.S. — C3 78
Prattville, Mi., U.S. — G6 99
Pravdinsk, Sov. Un. — A6 26
Pravia, Spain — A2 22
Pray, Mt., U.S. — E6 103
Preble, co., Oh., U.S. — C1 112
Predazzo, Italy — C7 20
Preeceville, Sk., Can. — F4 75
Preetz, F.R.Ger. — D4 15
Pregel, stm., Sov. Un. — D3 27
Pregolya, stm., Sov. Un. — A6 26
Prelate, Sk., Can. — G1 75
Premana, Italy — D7 21
Premont, Tx., U.S. — F3 120
Prémontré, Fr. — E3 17
Premosello, Italy — D5 21
Prenjasi, Alb. — B3 25
Prenter, W.V., U.S. — C3 125
Prentice, Wi., U.S. — C3 126
Prentiss, Me., U.S. — C4 96
Prentiss, Ms., U.S. — D4 101
Prentiss, co., Ms., U.S. — A5 101
Prenzlau, Ger.D.R. — B6 18
Přerov, Czech. — D4 26
Prescott, On., Can. — C9 73
Prescott, Az., U.S. — C3 80
Prescott, Ar., U.S. — D2 81
Prescott, Ia., U.S. — C3 92
Prescott, Ks., U.S. — D9 93
Prescott, Mi., U.S. — D7 99
Prescott, Wa., U.S. — C7 124
Prescott, co., On., Can. — B10 73
Preshute, N.C., U.S. — A6 110
Presidencia Roque Sáenz Peña, Arg. — E3 55
Presidente Epitácio, Braz. — C2 56
Presidente Hayes, dept.ʼ, Para. — D4 55
Presidente Olegário, Braz. — B3 56
Presidente Prudente, Braz. — C2 56
Presidential Range, mts., N.H., U.S. — B4 106
Presidents Island, i., Tn., U.S. — e8 119
Presidio, Tx., U.S. — p12 120
Presidio, co., Tx., U.S. — o12 120
Presidio of San Francisco, mil., Ca., U.S. — h8 82
Preslav, Bul. — D8 24
Prešov, Czech. — D6 26
Presque Isle, Me., U.S. — B5 96
Presque Isle, Wi., U.S. — C7 99
Presque Isle, Wi., U.S. — B4 126
Presque Isle, co., Mi., U.S. — C6 99
Pressath, F.R.Ger. — D6 19
Prestatyn, Wales, U.K. — A4 12
Presteigne, Wales, U.K. — A3 78
Přeštice, Czech. — D3 81
Prestice, Czech. — D3 81
Preston, Austl. — *G8 50
Preston, Eng., U.K. — D5 10
Preston, Ct., U.S. — C8 84
Preston, Ga., U.S. — D2 87
Preston, Id., U.S. — G7 89
Preston, Ia., U.S. — B7 92
Preston, Ks., U.S. — E5 93
Preston, Ky., U.S. — B6 94
Preston, Md., U.S. — C6 97
Preston, Mn., U.S. — G6 100
Preston, Mo., U.S. — C5 101
Preston, Ok., U.S. — B6 113
Preston, co., W.V., U.S. — e10 124
Preston Peak, mtn., Ca., U.S. — B2 82
Prestonsburg, Ky., U.S. — C7 94
Prestwick, Scot., U.K. — F4 13
Preti, mtn., Italy — C8 20
Preto, stm., Braz. — h6 56
Prêto, stm., Braz. — D2 57
Prêto do Igapó-Açu, stm., Braz. — D2 59
Pretoria, S. Afr. — C4 49
Prettyboy Reservoir, res., Md., U.S. — A4 97
Pretty Prairie, Ks., U.S. — E5 93
Préveza, Grc. — B2 25
Prewitt, N.M., U.S. — B1 108
Prewitt Reservoir, res., Co., U.S. — A7 83
Prey Veng, Kam. — G6 35
Příbor, Czech. — D4 26
Pribilof Islands, is., Ak., U.S. — D5 79
Příbram, Czech. — D3 26
Price, Md., U.S. — B6 97
Price, Tx., U.S. — C5 120

Price, Ut., U.S. — D5 121
Price, co., Wi., U.S. — C3 126
Prices, stm., Ut., U.S. — D5 121
Pricedale, Ms., U.S. — D3 101
Price Inlet, b., S.C., U.S. — k12 117
Price Island, i., B.C., Can. — C3 69
Priceville, On., Can. — C4 73
Prichard, Al., U.S. — E1 78
Prichard, W.V., U.S. — C2 125
Priddy, Tx., U.S. — D3 120
Priego [de Córdoba], Spain — D3 22
Prienai, Sov. Un. — A7 26
Prieska, S. Afr. — C3 49
Priest Lake, l., Id., U.S. — A2 89
Priestley, Mount, mtn., B.C., Can. — B3 69
Priest Rapids Dam, Wa., U.S. — C6 124
Priest Rapids Lake, res., Wa., Can. — C6 124
Priest River, Id., U.S. — A2 89
Prievidza, Czech. — *D5 26
Prijedor, Yugo. — C3 24
Prijepolje, Yugo. — D4 24
Prikumsk, Sov. Un. — E2 28
Prilep, Yugo. — E5 24
Prilly, Switz. — C2 21
Priluki, Sov. Un. — F9 27
Prim, Point, c., P.E., Can. — C6 71
Primate, Sk., Can. — E1 75
Primero, stm., Arg. — A4 54
Primghar, Ia., U.S. — A2 92
Primolano, Italy — D7 20
Primorsk, Sov. Un. — A6 26
Primorsk, Sov. Un. — A7 27
Primorsko-Akhtarsk, Sov. Un. — H12 27
Primrose, Ne., U.S. — C7 104
Primrose, R.I., U.S. — B3 116
Primrose Lake, l., Can. — B6 68
Primrose, Sk., Can. — E1 75
Prince, co., P.E., Can. — C6 71
Prince, Lake, res., Va., U.S. — k14 123
Prince Albert, Sk., Can. — D3 75
Prince Albert Mountains, mts., Ant. — B29 7
Prince Albert National Park, Sk., Can. — C2 75
Prince Albert Sound, strt., N.T., Can. — B9 66
Prince Alfred, Cape, c., N.T., Can. — B9 66
Prince Charles Foreland, i., Nor. — B14 128
Prince Charles Island, i., N.T., Can. — C17 66
Prince Charles Mountains, mts., Ant. — B19 7
Prince Edward, co., On., Can. — C7 73
Prince Edward, co., Va., U.S. — C4 123
Prince Edward Island, prov., Can. — C6 71
Prince Edward Island National Park, P.E., Can. — C6 71
Prince Edward Islands, is., S. Afr. — J23 7
Prince Frederick, Md., U.S. — C4 97
Prince George, B.C., Can. — C6 69
Prince George, Va., U.S. — C5 123
Prince George, co., Va., U.S. — C5 123
Prince Georges, co., Md., U.S. — C4 97
Prince of Wales, i., Austl. — B7 50
Prince of Wales, Cape, c., Ak., U.S. — B6 79
Prince of Wales Island, i., N.T., Can. — B13 66
Prince of Wales Island, i., Ak., U.S. — n23 79
Prince of Wales Strait, strt., N.T., Can. — B9 66
Prince Olav Coast, Ant. — C17 7
Prince Patrick Island, i., N.T., Can. — m27 66
Prince Regent Inlet, b., N.T., Can. — B14 66
Prince Rupert, B.C., Can. — B2 69
Princess Isabel, Braz. — C3 57
Princesa Isabel, Braz. — C3 57
Princes Lakes, In., U.S. — F5 91
Princes Risborough, Eng., U.K. — C7 12
Princess Anne, Md., U.S. — D6 97
Princess Astrid Coast, Ant. — B14 7
Princess Charlotte Bay, b., Austl. — p12 120
Princess Martha Coast, Ant. — B11 7
Princess Ragnhild Coast, Ant. — B15 7
Princess Royal Channel, strt., B.C., Can. — C3 69
Princess Royal Island, i., B.C., Can. — C3 69
Princes Town, Trin. — O23 65
Princeton, B.C., Can. — E7 69
Princeton, Ca., U.S. — C2 82
Princeton, Fl., U.S. — G6 86
Princeton, Il., U.S. — B4 90
Princeton, In., U.S. — H2 91
Princeton, Ia., U.S. — C7 92
Princeton, Ky., U.S. — C2 94
Princeton, Me., U.S. — C5 96
Princeton, Mn., U.S. — E5 100
Princeton, Mo., U.S. — A4 102
Princeton, N.C., U.S. — B4 110
Princeton, N.J., U.S. — C3 107
Princeton, W.V., U.S. — D3 125
Princeton, Wi., U.S. — E4 126
Princeton, Mount, mtn., Co., U.S. — C4 83
Princeton Junction, N.J., U.S. — C3 107
Princeville, P.Q., Can. — C6 71
Princeville, Il., U.S. — C4 90
Principe, i., S. Tom./P. — E1 46
Principe Channel, strt., B.C., Can. — C3 69
Pringle, S.D., U.S. — D2 118
Pringsheim, Mn., U.S. — F3 100
Prinzapolka, Nic. — E8 63
Prinzapolka, stm., Nic. — D6 62
Prior Lake, Mn., U.S. — F5 100

Priozersk, Sov. Un. — A8 27
Pripyat, Sov. Un. — F7 27
Pripyat (Pripet), stm., Sov. Un. — B4 39
Prishib, Sov. Un. — D5 24
Priština, Yugo. — D5 24
Pritchards Island, i., S.C., U.S. — G6 117
Pritchett, Co., U.S. — D8 83
Pritzerber, B.R. — F6 15
Pritzwalk, Ger.D.R. — B6 18
Privas, Fr. — E6 16
Privert, Lac, l., P.Q., Can. — g8 72
Privas, Fr. — A1 22
Privolnoye, Sov. Un. — H9 27
Prizren, Yugo. — D5 24
Prizzi, Italy — F4 23
Probolinggo, Indon. — G4 34
Procida, Italy — G9 23
Procious, W.V., U.S. — m13 125
Procter, B.C., Can. — E9 69
Proctor, Mn., U.S. — D6 100
Proctor, Mt., U.S. — C2 103
Proctor, Ok., U.S. — B7 113
Proctor, Tx., U.S. — D3 120
Proctor, Vt., U.S. — D2 122
Proctor, W.V., U.S. — g8 125
Proctor Lake, res., Tx., U.S. — C3 120
Proctorsville, Vt., U.S. — E3 122
Proctorville, N.C., U.S. — C3 110
Proctorville, Oh., U.S. — D3 112
Proença-a-Nova, Port. — C2 22
Progreso, Mex. — C7 63
Prokhladnyy, Sov. Un. — E2 28
Prokopyevsk, Sov. Un. — D11 29
Prokuplje, Yugo. — D5 24
Prole, U.S. — f8 92
Proletarsk, Sov. Un. — q21 27
Proletarsk, Sov. Un. — H13 27
Prome (Pye), Burma — E10 36
Promise City, Ia., U.S. — D4 92
Promissão, Braz. — C3 56
Promontory Mountains, mts., Ut., U.S. — B3 121
Pronsfeld, F.R.Ger. — D6 17
Prophetstown, Il., U.S. — B4 90
Propriá, Braz. — D3 57
Prorer Wiek, b., Ger.D.R. — D7 15
Proserpine, Austl. — D8 50
Prosna, stm., Pol. — C5 26
Prosotsáni, Grc. — B4 25
Prospect, N.S., Can. — E6 71
Prospect, Ct., U.S. — C4 84
Prospect, In., U.S. — G4 91
Prospect, Ky., U.S. — g11 94
Prospect, Oh., U.S. — B2 112
Prospect, Or., U.S. — E4 114
Prospect, Pa., U.S. — E1 115
Prospect, Tn., U.S. — B4 119
Prospect, Va., U.S. — C4 123
Prospect Harbor, Me., U.S. — D4 96
Prospect Heights, Co., U.S. — *C5 83
Prospect Heights, Il., U.S. — *h9 90
Prospect Hill, N.C., U.S. — A3 110
Prospect Hill, mtn., Or., U.S. — k11 114
Prospect Hill, hill, Ma., U.S. — D6 98
Prospect Hill, hill, Ma., U.S. — g10 98
Prospect Park, N.J., U.S. — B4 107
Prospect Park, Pa., U.S. — p20 115
Prospect Plains, N.J., U.S. — C4 107
Prosperity, S.C., U.S. — C4 117
Prosperity, W.V., U.S. — n13 125
Prosser, Ne., U.S. — D7 104
Prosser, Wa., U.S. — C6 124
Prostějov, Czech. — D4 26
Frostki, Pol. — B7 26
Protection, Ks., U.S. — E4 93
Protem, Mo., U.S. — E5 102
Protivin, Ia., U.S. — A5 92
Proton Station, On., Can. — C4 73
Prouts Neck, Me., U.S. — g7 96
Provadiyska, stm., Bul. — D8 24
Provencal, La., U.S. — C2 95
Provence, hist reg., Fr. — F7 16
Providence, Fl., U.S. — C5 86
Providence, Ky., U.S. — C2 94
Providence, Ut., U.S. — B4 121
Providence, co., R.I., U.S. — C5 116
Providence, stm., R.I., U.S. — C5 116
Providence Bay, On., Can. — B2 73
Providence Forge, Va., U.S. — C5 123
Providence Point, c., R.I., U.S. — E5 116
Providencia, Isla de, i., Col. — D7 62
Province Lake, l., N.H., U.S. — C5 106
Provincetown, Ma., U.S. — B7 98
Provins, Fr. — C1 81
Provo, S.D., U.S. — D2 118
Provo, Ut., U.S. — C4 121
Provo, stm., Ut., U.S. — C5 121
Provost, Ab., U.S. — C5 68
Prowers, co., Co., U.S. — D8 83
Prozor, Yugo. — D3 24
Pruden, U.S. — C10 119
Prudence Island, i., R.I., U.S. — D5 116
Prudence Island, i., R.I., U.S. — D5 116
Prudentópolis, Braz. — D2 56
Prudenville, Mi., U.S. — D6 99
Prudhoe Bay, Ak., U.S. — A10 79
Prudhoe Bay, b., Ak., U.S. — A10 79
Prud'homme, Sk., Can. — E3 75
Prue, Ok., U.S. — A5 113
Prüm, F.R.Ger. — D6 17
Pruszków, Pol. — B6 26
Prut, stm., Eur. — B9 24
Pruzhany, Sov. Un. — E5 27
Prydz Bay, b., Ant. — C20 7
Pryor, Mt., U.S. — D6 83
Pryor, Ok., U.S. — A6 113
Pryor Mountains, mts., Mt., U.S. — E8 103
Przedbórz, Pol. — C5 26
Przemyśl, Pol. — D7 26
Przeworsk, Pol. — g10 26
Przeworz, Pol. — B9 19
Przhevalsk, Sov. Un. — E9 28
Psakhná, Grc. — C4 25
Psará, i., Grc. — C5 40
Pskov, Lake, l., Sov. Un. — D5 27
Pskov, Sov. Un. — D5 29
Ptich, stm., Sov. Un. — E7 27
Ptolemaís, Grc. — B3 25
Ptuj, Yugo. — B2 26
Puán, Arg. — B4 54
Puán, Arg. — B4 54
Pu'apu'a, W. Sam. — F11 52
Pucallpa, Peru — C3 58

Pucheng, China — K8 32
Pucheng, China — G6 32
Puck, Pol. — A5 26
Puckaway Lake, l., Wi., U.S. — E4 126
Puckett, Ms., U.S. — C4 101
Pudasjärvi, Fin. — E12 14
Pudoz, Sov. Un. — A11 27
Puebla, state, Mex. — D5 63
Puebla de Don Fadrique, Spain — D4 22
Puebla del Caramiñal, Spain — A1 22
Puebla [de Zaragoza], Mex. — D5 63
Pueblo, Co., U.S. — C6 83
Pueblo, co., Co., U.S. — C6 83
Pueblo Colorado Wash, val., Az., U.S. — B6 80
Pueblo Hundido, Chile — E1 55
Pueblo Libre, Peru — *D2 58
Pueblo Mountain, mtn., Or., U.S. — E8 114
Pueblo Mountains, mts., Or., U.S. — E8 114
Pueblo Nuevo (part of Panamá), Pan. — k11 62
Pueblo Nuevo, Ven. — A4 60
Pueblo Reservoir, res., Co., U.S. — C6 83
Puebloviejo, Ec. — B2 58
Puenteareas, Spain — A1 22
Puente-Ceso, Spain — A1 22
Puentedeume, Spain — E2 28
Puente-Genil, Spain — D3 22
Pueo Point, c., Hi., U.S. — B1 88
Puʼer, China — G5 31
Puerca, Punta, c., P.R. — B4 65
Puerco, stm., U.S. — C6 80
Puerco, Rio, stm., N.M., U.S. — B2 108
Puerto Acosta, Bol. — C5 55
Puerto Aisén, Chile — D2 54
Puerto Alegre, Bol. — B3 55
Puerto Armuelles, Pan. — F6 62
Puerto Asís, Col. — C2 60
Puerto Ayacucho, Ven. — B4 60
Puerto Baquerizo Moreno, Ec. — g6 58
Puerto Barrios, Guat. — D7 63
Puerto Belgrano, Arg. — B4 54
Puerto Bermúdez, Peru — D3 58
Puerto Berrío, Col. — B3 60
Puerto Bolívar, Ec. — B1 58
Puerto Cabello, Ven. — A4 60
Puerto Cabezas, Nic. — E8 63
Puerto Carreño, Col. — B4 60
Puerto Casado, Para. — D4 55
Puerto Chicama, Peru — C2 58
Puerto Colombia, Col. — A3 60
Puerto Constanza, Arg. — f7 54
Puerto Cortés, Hond. — D7 63
Puerto Cumarebo, Ven. — A4 60
Puerto de la Cruz, Spain — m13 22
Puerto del Rosario, Spain — m15 22
Puerto del Son, Spain — A1 22
Puerto de Luna, N.M., U.S. — C5 108
Puerto Deseado, Arg. — D3 54
Puerto Eten, Peru — C2 58
Puerto Guaraní, Para. — D4 55
Puerto Heath, Bol. — B2 55
Puerto Inírida, Col. — C4 60
Puerto Jiménez, C.R. — F6 62
Puerto la Cruz, Ven. — A5 60
Puerto Leguízamo, Col. — D3 60
Puerto Limón, Col. — C3 60
Puertollano, Spain — C3 22
Puerto Lobos, Arg. — C3 54
Puerto López, Col. — B3 60
Puerto Madryn, Arg. — C3 54
Puerto Maldonado, Peru — D4 58
Puerto México see Coatzacoalcos, Mex. — D6 63
Puerto Mineral, Arg. — E4 55
Puerto Montt, Chile — C2 54
Puerto Morazán, Nic. — D4 62
Puerto Nariño, Col. — C4 60
Puerto Natales, Chile — E2 54
Puerto Padre, Cuba — D6 64
Puerto Páez, Ven. — B4 60
Puerto Peñasco, Mex. — A2 63
Puerto Pilón, Pan. — k11 62
Puerto Pinasco, Para. — D4 55
Puerto Pirámides, Arg. — C4 54
Puerto Plata, Dom. Rep. — E8 64
Puerto Portillo, Peru — C3 58
Puerto Presidente Stroessner, Para. — E5 55
Puerto Princesa, Phil. — D5 34
Puerto Real, Spain — D2 22
Puerto Rico, ctry., N.A. — G11 64
Puerto Saavedra, Chile — B2 54
Puerto Sastre, Para. — D4 55
Puerto Siles, Bol. — *B2 55
Puerto Suárez, Bol. — C4 55
Puerto Supe, Peru — D2 58
Puerto Tejada, Col. — C3 60
Puerto Toledo, Col. — D3 60
Puerto Vallarta, Mex. — C3 63
Puerto Varas, Chile — C2 54
Puerto Victoria, Peru — C3 58
Puerto Viejo, C.R. — F6 62
Puerto Villamizar, Col. — B3 60
Puerto Visser, Arg. — D3 54
Puerto Wilches, Col. — B3 60
Puertoyano, Spain — C3 28
Puget Sound, strt., Wa., U.S. — B3 124
Puget Sound Naval Shipyard, mil., Wa., U.S. — e10 124
Puget-Théniers, Fr. — F7 16
Pugwash, N.S., Can. — D6 71
Puhi, Hi., U.S. — B2 88
Puhsi, China — K8 32
Puigcerdá, Spain — A6 22
Pujilí, Ec. — B2 58
Pujili, Ec. — B2 58
Pukalani, Hi., U.S. — C5 88
Pukaskwa National Park, On., Can. — o18 73
Pukch'ŏng, N. Kor. — F4 33
Pukeashun Mountain, mtn., B.C., Can. — B2 88
Pukekohe, N.Z. — L15 51
Pukhan, stm., Asia — H3 33
Pukou, China — H8 32
Puksubaek, Mount, mtn., N. Kor. — F3 33
Pukwana, S.D., U.S. — D6 118
Pula, Italy — E2 23
Pula, Cro. — C1 24
Pulacayo, Bol. — D2 55
Pulaski, Il., U.S. — F4 90
Pulaski, Ia., U.S. — D5 92
Pulaski, N.Y., U.S. — B4 109
Pulaski, Tn., U.S. — B4 119
Pulaski, Va., U.S. — C2 123

Name	Map Ref	Page
Pulaski, Wi., U.S.	D5	126
Pulaski, co., Ar., U.S.	C3	81
Pulaski, co., Ga., U.S.	D3	87
Pulaski, co., Il., U.S.	F4	90
Pulaski, co., In., U.S.	B4	91
Pulaski, co., Ky., U.S.	C5	94
Pulaski, co., Mo., U.S.	D5	102
Pulaski, co., Va., U.S.	C2	123
Putawy, Pol.	C6	26
Pulheim, F.R.Ger.	*C3	18
Pullman, Mi., U.S.	F4	99
Pullman, Wa., U.S.	C8	124
Pullman, W.V., U.S.	B4	125
Pulog, Mount, mtn., Phil.	B6	34
Pulozero, Sov. Un.	C15	14
Pułtusk, Pol.	B6	26
Puma Lake, l., China	C13	31
Pumphrey, Md., U.S.	h11	97
Pumpkin Buttes, mtn., Wy., U.S.	C7	127
Pumpkin Creek, stm., Mt., U.S.	E11	103
Pumpkin Creek, stm., Ne., U.S.	C2	104
Pumpville, Tx., U.S.	E2	120
Puna, Bol.	C2	55
Puná, Isla, l., Ec.	B1	58
Punakha, Bhu.	C8	36
Punat, Yugo.	C2	24
Punata, Bol.	C2	55
Punchaw, B.C., Can.	C6	69
Pune (Poona), India	E5	36
Pungo Lake, l., N.C., U.S.	B6	110
Pungsan, N. Kor.	F4	33
Punia, Zaire	B4	48
Punjab, state, India	B5	36
Punjab, prov., Pak.	B5	36
Punnichy, Sk., Can.	F3	75
Puno, Peru	E3	58
Puno, dept., Peru	E3	58
Punta, Cerro de, mtn., P.R.	B2	65
Punta Alta, Arg.	B4	54
Punta Arenas, Chile	h11	54
Punta de Díaz, Chile	E1	55
Punta del Este, Ur.	E2	56
Punta de Piedras, Ven.	A5	60
Punta de Vacas, Arg.	A3	54
Punta Gorda, Belize	D7	63
Punta Gorda, Fl., U.S.	F4	86
Punta Gorda, Bahía de, b., Nic.	E8	63
Punta Moreno, Peru	C2	58
Puntarenas, C.R.	E5	62
Punto Fijo, Ven.	A3	60
Puntzi Lake, l., B.C., Can.	C5	69
Punxsutawney, Pa., U.S.	E4	115
Puposky, Mn., U.S.	C4	100
Puquio, Peru	E3	58
Pur, stm., Sov. Un.	C10	29
Pūranpur, India	C8	37
Purcell, Mo., U.S.	D3	102
Purcell, Ok., U.S.	B4	113
Purcell Mountains, mts., N.A.	D9	69
Purcellville, Va., U.S.	A5	123
Purdham Hill, mtn., Ar., U.S.	h10	81
Purdin, Mo., U.S.	B4	102
Purdum, Ne., U.S.	B5	104
Purdy, Mo., U.S.	E4	102
Purépero, Mex.	n12	63
Purgatoire, stm., Co., U.S.	D7	83
Purgatoire Peak, mtn., Co., U.S.	D5	83
Puri, India	E8	36
Purmerend, Neth.	B4	17
Pūrna, stm., India	H6	37
Purnea, India	C8	36
Purple Springs, Ab., Can.	E5	68
Pursglove, W.V., U.S.	B4	125
Puruândiro, Mex.	m13	63
Purūlia, India	D8	36
Purus, stm., S.A.	D4	53
Purvis, Ms., U.S.	D3	101
Puryear, Tn., U.S.	A3	119
Puryŏng-dong, N. Kor.	F4	33
Pusan, S. Kor.	D10	31
Pushaw Lake, l., Me., U.S.	D4	96
Pushkin, Sov. Un.	C6	29
Pushkino, Sov. Un.	C11	27
Pushmataha, Al., U.S.	C1	78
Pushmataha, co., Ok., U.S.	C6	113
Pushthrough, Nf., Can.	E3	72
Pusiano, Lago di, l., Italy	E7	21
Püspökladány, Hung.	B5	24
Pustelnik, Pol.	k14	26
Pustynnaya, Sov. Un.	B8	28
Putao, Burma	C10	36
Puteaux, Fr.	g9	16
Putian, China	F8	31
Putilovo, Sov. Un.	s32	14
Puting, Cape, c., Indon.	F4	34
Putivl, Sov. Un.	F9	27
Putlitz, Ger.D.R.	E6	15
Putnam, Al., U.S.	C1	78
Putnam, Ct., U.S.	B8	84
Putnam, Ok., U.S.	B3	113
Putnam, Tx., U.S.	C3	120
Putnam, co., Fl., U.S.	C5	86
Putnam, co., Ga., U.S.	C3	87
Putnam, co., Il., U.S.	B4	90
Putnam, co., In., U.S.	E4	91
Putnam, co., Mo., U.S.	A4	102
Putnam, co., N.Y., U.S.	D7	109
Putnam, co., Oh., U.S.	B1	112
Putnam, co., Tn., U.S.	C8	119
Putnam, co., W.V., U.S.	C3	125
Putnam Station, N.Y., U.S.	B7	109
Putnamville, In., U.S.	E4	91
Putnamville, Vt., U.S.	C3	122
Putney, Ga., U.S.	E2	87
Putney, S.D., U.S.	B7	118
Putney, Vt., U.S.	F3	122
Putre, Chile	C2	55
Puttalam, Sri L.	G6	36
Putte, Neth.	C4	17
Püttlingen, F.R.Ger.	D1	19
Putumayo, dept., Col.	C2	60
Putumayo (Içá), stm., S.A.	D3	60
Pütürge, Tur.	C12	40
Puukohola Heiau National Historic Site, hist., Hi., U.S.	D6	88
Puukolii, Hi., U.S.	C5	88
Puulavesi, l., Fin.	G12	14
Puunene, Hi., U.S.	C5	88
Puurs, Bel.	C4	17
Puxico, Mo., U.S.	E7	102
Puyallup, Wa., U.S.	B3	124
Puyallup, stm., Wa., U.S.	C3	124
Puyang, China	G6	32
Puyehue, Chile	C2	54
Puyo, Ec.	B2	58
Pūzak, Jehil-e, l., Iran	F10	39
Pûzim, Ra's-e, c., Iran	I10	39
Pwani, prov., Tan.	C6	48
Pweto, Zaire	C5	48
Pwllheli, Wales, U.K.	D4	10
Pyaozero, l., Sov. Un.	D14	14
Pyapon, Burma	E10	36
Pyasina, stm., Sov. Un.	B12	29
Pyatigorsk, Sov. Un.	E2	28
Pyatt, Ar., U.S.	A3	81
Pyhäjärvi, l., Fin.	G10	14
Pyinmana, Burma	E10	36
Pyland, Ms., U.S.	B4	101
Pyles Fork, stm., W.V., U.S.	h10	125
Pymatuning Reservoir, res., U.S.	C1	115
Pyŏngchang, S. Kor.	H4	33
Pyŏngtaek, S. Kor.	H3	33
Pyŏngyang, N. Kor.	D10	31
Pyote, Tx., U.S.	D1	120
Pyramid Lake, l., Nv., U.S.	C2	105
Pyramid Lake Indian Reservation, Nv., U.S.	D2	105
Pyramid Mountains, mts., N.M., U.S.	E1	108
Pyramid Peak, mtn., N.M., U.S.	E1	108
Pyramid Peak, mtn., Wy., U.S.	C2	127
Pyramids, hist., Eg.	C3	38
Pyrenees, mts., Eur.	A6	22
Pyrites, N.Y., U.S.	f9	109
Pyrmont, In., U.S.	D4	91
Pyrzyce, Pol.	B3	26
Pyskowice, Pol.	g9	26
Pytalovo, Sov. Un.	C6	27
Pyu, Burma	E10	36

Q

Name	Map Ref	Page
Qabātiyah, Isr. Occ.	B7	41
Qā'emshahr, Iran	C6	39
Qahar Youyi Zhongqi, China	D5	32
Qaidam Pendi (Tsaidam Basin), reg., China	D3	31
Qalamshāh, Eg.	H8	40
Qalāt, Afg.	B4	36
Qal'at al Mu'azzam, Sau. Ar.	C3	38
Qal'at Bīshah, Sau. Ar.	C4	38
Qal'at Ṣāliḥ, Iraq	F3	39
Qal'at Sukkar, Iraq	F3	39
Qal'eh-ye Best, Afg.	F12	39
Qal'eh-ye Now, Afg.	D11	39
Qallābāt, Sud.	C4	47
Qalqīlya, Isr. Occ.	B6	41
Qalyūb, Eg.	B3	41
Qamdo, China	E4	31
Qamea, i., Fiji	H16	52
Qamīnis, Libya	C4	43
Qānā, Leb.	A7	41
Qandahār see Kandahar, Afg.	B4	36
Qandala, Som.	C6	47
Qārah, Egypt	H6	40
Qardho, Som.	D6	47
Qareh Sū, stm., Iran	D5	39
Qārū, i., Kuw.	G4	39
Qārūn, Birkat, l., Eg.	D6	43
Qaryat Abu Nujaym, Libya	C3	43
Qasr al Farāfirah, Eg.	C2	38
Qasr Banī Walīd, Libya	C2	43
Qasr el Boukhari, Alg.	B5	44
Qasr-e Shīrīn, Iran	D2	39
Qaṭabah, P.D.R.Yem.	D4	38
Qatar, ctry., Asia	C5	38
Qattara Depression, depr., Eg.	C2	38
Qāyen, Iran	E9	39
Qeshm, Iran	B4	38
Qeshm, Iran	H8	39
Qeshm, i., Iran	C5	38
Qeys, i., Iran	H6	39
Qezel Owzan, stm., Iran	C4	39
Qezi'ot, Isr.	D6	41
Qian'an, China	D8	32
Qianjiang, China	J3	32
Qianshan, China	I7	32
Qiantang Jiang, stm., China	J8	32
Qianxian, China	G3	32
Qianyang, China	F7	31
Qiaojia, China	F5	31
Qichun, China	I6	32
Qiemo, China	A8	36
Qijiang, China	J2	32
Qila Lādgasht, Pak.	C3	36
Qila Saifullāh, Pak.	B2	37
Qilian Mountains (Nan Shan), mts., China	D4	31
Qimen, China	J7	32
Qinā, Eg.	C3	38
Qing'an, China	J7	32
Qingdao (Tsingtao), China	D9	31
Qinghai, prov., China	D4	31
Qinghai Lake (Koko Nor), l., China	D4	31
Qingjian, China	D7	31
Qingjiang, China	E8	31
Qingjiang, China	J6	32
Qingliu, China	F8	31
Qingpu, China	E9	31
Qingyang, China	D6	31
Qingyuan, China	C11	32
Qinhuangdao, China	D8	31
Qin Ling (Tsinling Shan), mts., China	E6	31
Qinxian, China	F5	32
Qinyang, China	G5	32
Qinzhou, China	B8	35
Qiongshan, China	B4	34
Qiqian, China	A9	31
Qiqihar (Tsitsihar), China	B9	31
Qiryat 'Anavim, Isr.	C7	41
Qiryat Gat, Isr.	D4	41
Qiryat Mal'akhi, Isr.	C6	41
Qiryat Ono, Isr.	g10	41
Qiryat Shemona, Isr.	A7	41
Qiryat Yam, Isr.	B7	41
Qishn, P.D.R.Yem.	B7	47
Qishon, stm., Isr.	B7	41
Qitai, China	C2	31
Qiyang, China	F7	31
Qizan, Sau. Ar.	D4	38
Qizil Jilga, China	B6	36
Qnadsa, Alg.	C4	44
Qom, Iran	B5	38
Qom, Iran	E5	39
Qomemiyyut (Talbiya) (part of Jerusalem), Isr.	m14	41
Qomsheh, Iran	E5	39
Qondūz, Afg.	C14	39
Quabbin Reservoir, res., Ma., U.S.	B3	98
Quaco Head, c., N.B., Can.	D4	71
Quaddick, Ct., U.S.	B8	84
Quaddick Reservoir, res., Ct., U.S.	B8	84
Quail Oaks, Va., U.S.	n18	123
Quakenbrück, F.R.Ger.	B3	18
Quaker City, Oh., U.S.	C4	112
Quaker Hill, Ct., U.S.	D7	84
Quakertown, N.J., U.S.	B3	107
Quakertown, Pa., U.S.	F11	115
Qualicum Beach, B.C., Can.	E5	69
Quality, Ky., U.S.	C3	94
Quamba, Mn., U.S.	E5	100
Quanah, Tx., U.S.	B3	120
Quang Ngai, Viet.	B3	34
Quang Tri, Viet.	B3	34
Quan Long, Viet.	D3	34
Quannapowitt, Lake, l., Ma., U.S.	f11	98
Quantico, Md., U.S.	D6	97
Quantico, Va., U.S.	B5	123
Quantico Marine Corps Air Station, mil., Va., U.S.	B5	123
Quanzhou, China	F7	31
Quanzhou, China	G8	31
Quapaw, Ok., U.S.	A7	113
Qu'Appelle, Sk., Can.	G4	75
Qu'Appelle, stm., Can.	G4	75
Quaraí, Braz.	E1	56
Quaraí, stm., S.A.	E1	56
Quarles Mountains, mts., Indon.	F5	34
Quarryville, N.B., Can.	C4	71
Quarryville, Ct., U.S.	B6	84
Quarryville, Pa., U.S.	G9	115
Quartu Sant' Elena, Italy	E2	23
Quartz Mountain, mtn., Or., U.S.	D4	114
Quartzsite, Az., U.S.	D1	80
Quasqueton, Ia., U.S.	B6	92
Quassapaug, Lake, l., Ct., U.S.	C3	84
Quatre, Isle, i., St. Vin.	V26	65
Quatsino Sound, strt., B.C., Can.	D3	69
Quay, N.M., U.S.	C6	108
Quay, Ok., U.S.	A5	113
Quay, co., N.M., U.S.	C6	108
Qūchān, Iran	B5	38
Quealy, Wy., U.S.	E3	127
Québec, P.Q., Can.	C6	74
Québec, co., P.Q., Can.	B6	74
Quebec, prov., Can.	C5	74
Quebeck, Tn., U.S.	D8	119
Quechee, Vt., U.S.	D4	122
Quecreek, Pa., U.S.	F3	115
Quedlinburg, Ger.D.R.	C5	18
Queen, stm., R.I., U.S.	E3	116
Queen, Cape, c., N.T., Can.	D17	66
Queen Alexandra Range, mts., Ant.	A29	7
Queen Anne, Md., U.S.	C6	97
Queen Annes, co., Md., U.S.	C6	97
Queen Bess, Mount, mtn., B.C., Can.	D5	69
Queenborough [-in-Sheppey], Eng., U.K.	E7	10
Queen Charlotte, B.C., Can.	C1	69
Queen Charlotte Islands, is., B.C., Can.	C1	69
Queen Charlotte Mountains, mts., B.C., Can.	C1	69
Queen Charlotte Sound, strt., B.C., Can.	n17	69
Queen Charlotte Strait, strt., B.C., Can.	D4	69
Queen City, Mo., U.S.	A5	102
Queen City, Tx., U.S.	C5	120
Queen Creek, Az., U.S.	m9	80
Queen Elizabeth Islands, is., N.T., Can.	k30	66
Queen Fabiola Mountains, mts., Ant.	B16	7
Queen Mary Coast, Ant.	C22	7
Queen Maud Gulf, b., N.T., Can.	C12	66
Queen Maud Land, reg., Ant.	B15	7
Queen Maud Mountains, mts., Ant.	A31	7
Queens, co., N.B., Can.	D4	71
Queens, co., N.S., Can.	E4	71
Queens, co., P.E., Can.	C6	71
Queens, co., N.Y., U.S.	E7	109
Queensborough, On., Can.	C7	73
Queensferry see South Queensferry, Scot., U.K.	E5	13
Queen Shoals, W.V., U.S.	C3	125
Queensland, state, Austl.	D7	50
Queensport, N.S., Can.	D8	71
Queens Sound, strt., B.C., Can.	D3	69
Queenstown, Austl.	o15	50
Queenstown, Ab., Can.	D4	68
Queenstown, N.B., Can.	D3	71
Queenstown, N.Z.	P12	51
Queenstown, S. Afr.	D4	49
Queenstown, Md., U.S.	C5	97
Queen Victoria Sea, Eur.	A5	29
Queets, Wa., U.S.	B1	124
Queguay Grande, stm., Ur.	E2	56
Queimadas, Braz.	A4	56
Queimadinhas, Braz.	A4	56
Queixada, Braz.	B4	56
Quela, Ang.	C2	48
Quelelevu, i., Fiji	H16	52
Quelimane, Moz.	A6	49
Quemado, N.M., U.S.	C1	108
Quemado, Tx., U.S.	E2	120
Quemado de Güines, Cuba	C3	64
Quemú Quemú, Arg.	B4	54
Quenemo, Ks., U.S.	D8	93
Quentin, Ms., U.S.	D3	101
Quepos, C.R.	F5	62
Quequen, Arg.	B5	54
Querétaro, Mex.	C4	63
Querétaro, state, Mex.	C5	63
Querfurt, Ger.D.R.	B6	19
Quers, Fr.	A21	19
Quesada, Spain	D4	22
Queshan, China	H6	32
Quesnel, B.C., Can.	C6	69
Quesnel, stm., B.C., Can.	C7	69
Quesnel Lake, l., B.C., Can.	C7	69
Questa, N.M., U.S.	A4	108
Quetena, Bol.	D2	55
Quetico Provincial Park, On., Can.	o17	73
Quetta, Pak.	B4	36
Quevedo, Ec.	B2	58
Quezaltenango, Guat.	D3	62
Quezaltepeque, El Sal.	D3	62
Quezon City, Phil.	C6	34
Quibala, Ang.	D1	48
Quibdó, Col.	D3	60
Quibell, On., Can.	E5	70
Quiberon, Fr.	D2	16
Quiberon Peninsula, pen., Fr.	D2	16
Quicksand Pond, l., R.I., U.S.	E6	116
Quicksburg, Va., U.S.	B4	123
Quidnessett, R.I., U.S.	E4	116
Quidnick, R.I., U.S.	D3	116
Quidnick Reservoir, res., R.I., U.S.	D2	116
Quilá, Mex.	C3	63
Quilcene, Wa., U.S.	B3	124
Quilengues, Ang.	D1	48
Quileute Indian Reservation, Wa., U.S.	B1	124
Quilino, Arg.	F3	55
Quillagua, Chile	D2	55
Quillan, Fr.	F5	16
Quill Lake, Sk., Can.	E3	75
Quillota, Chile	A2	54
Quilmes, Arg.	g7	54
Quilon, India	G6	36
Quilpie, Austl.	E7	50
Quilpué, Chile	A2	54
Quilty, Ire.	E2	11
Quimbele, Ang.	C2	48
Quimby, Ia., U.S.	B2	92
Quimby, Me., U.S.	A4	96
Quimili, Arg.	E3	55
Quimper, Fr.	C1	16
Quimperlé, Fr.	D2	16
Quinaby, Or., U.S.	B4	114
Quinault, Wa., U.S.	B2	124
Quinault, stm., Wa., U.S.	B2	124
Quinault, Lake, l., Wa., U.S.	B2	124
Quinault Indian Reservation, Wa., U.S.	B1	124
Quincy, Ca., U.S.	C3	82
Quincy, Fl., U.S.	B2	86
Quincy, Il., U.S.	D2	90
Quincy, In., U.S.	F4	91
Quincy, Ks., U.S.	E8	93
Quincy, Ky., U.S.	B6	94
Quincy, Ma., U.S.	B5	98
Quincy, Mi., U.S.	G6	99
Quincy, Ms., U.S.	B5	101
Quincy, Mo., U.S.	C4	102
Quincy, Oh., U.S.	B2	112
Quincy, Or., U.S.	A3	114
Quincy, Pa., U.S.	G6	115
Quincy, Wa., U.S.	B6	124
Quincy Bay, b., Ma., U.S.	g12	98
Quindío, dept., Col.	C2	60
Quinebaug, Ct., U.S.	A8	84
Quinebaug, stm., Ct., U.S.	C8	84
Quines, Arg.	F3	55
Quinga, Moz.	A7	49
Quinhagak, Ak., U.S.	D7	79
Qui Nhon, Viet.	B3	34
Quinlan, Ok., U.S.	A3	113
Quinlan, Tx., U.S.	C4	120
Quinn, S.D., U.S.	D3	118
Quinn, stm., Nv., U.S.	B3	105
Quinn Canyon Range, mts., Nv., U.S.	F6	105
Quinnesec, Mi., U.S.	C3	99
Quinnipiac, stm., Ct., U.S.	D4	84
Quinnville, R.I., U.S.	B4	116
Quintana de la Serena, Spain	C4	22
Quintanar [de la Orden], Spain	C4	22
Quintana Roo, state, Mex.	D7	63
Quinter, Ks., U.S.	C3	93
Quintero, Chile	A2	54
Quinton, Sk., Can.	F3	75
Quinton, Ok., U.S.	B6	113
Quinton, N.J., U.S.	D2	107
Quinton, Ky., U.S.	D5	94
Quinwood, W.V., U.S.	C4	125
Quipapá, Braz.	C7	56
Quipungo, Ang.	D1	48
Quirauk Mountain, mtn., Md., U.S.	A2	97
Quirindi, Austl.	E9	51
Quirinópolis, Braz.	B2	56
Quissama, Moz.	B6	49
Quitaque, Tx., U.S.	B2	120
Quitman, Ar., U.S.	B3	81
Quitman, Ga., U.S.	F3	87
Quitman, La., U.S.	B3	95
Quitman, Ms., U.S.	C5	101
Quitman, Tx., U.S.	C5	120
Quitman, co., Ga., U.S.	E1	87
Quitman, co., Ms., U.S.	A3	101
Quitman Mountains, mts., Tx., U.S.	o12	120
Quito, Ec.	B2	58
Quixadá, Braz.	B3	57
Quixeramobim, Braz.	B3	57
Qulin, Mo., U.S.	E7	102
Quoi, i., Micron.	Q18	52
Quonnipaug Lake, l., Ct., U.S.	D5	84
Quonochontaug, R.I., U.S.	G2	116
Quonochontaug Pond, l., R.I., U.S.	G2	116
Quonset Point, c., R.I., U.S.	E4	116
Quorn, Austl.	F2	51
Qurayyah, Wādī, val., Eg.	D6	41
Qūş, Eg.	C3	38
Quṣrah, Isr. Occ.	g12	41
Quthing, Leso.	D4	49
Quxian, China	E6	31
Quxian, China	F8	31

R

Name	Map Ref	Page
Raab (Rába), stm., Eur.	B2	24
Raabs [an der Thaya], Aus.	D7	18
Raahe, Fin.	E11	14
Raalte, Neth.	B6	17
Ra'ananna, Isr.	g10	41
Raasay, i., Scot., U.K.	C6	13
Rab, i., Yugo.	C9	23
Raba, Indon.	G5	34
Rába (Raab), stm., Eur.	B3	24
Rabat, Mor.	C3	44
Rabaul, Pap. N. Gui.	h13	50
Rabbit Creek, stm., S.D., U.S.	B3	118
Rabbit Ears Pass, Co., U.S.	A4	83
Rabbit Hash, Ky., U.S.	k13	94
Rabbit Lake, Sk., Can.	C2	75
Rabi, i., Fiji	H16	52
Rābigh, Sau. Ar.	D2	38
Rabun, co., Ga., U.S.	B3	87
Rabun Bald, mtn., Ga., U.S.	B3	87
Rača, Yugo.	B5	24
Raccoon Creek, stm., Oh., U.S.	D3	112
Raccourci Island, i., La., U.S.	D4	95
Race, Cape, c., Nf., Can.	E5	72
Raceland, Ky., U.S.	B7	94
Raceland, La., U.S.	E5	95
Race Point, c., Ma., U.S.	B7	98
Race Pond, Ga., U.S.	F4	87
Rach Gia, Viet.	C2	34
Racibórz, Pol.	C5	26
Racine, Mn., U.S.	G6	100
Racine, Mo., U.S.	E3	102
Racine, Oh., U.S.	D4	112
Racine, W.V., U.S.	C3	125
Racine, Wi., U.S.	F6	126
Racine, co., Wi., U.S.	F5	126
Racine Dam,	C3	125
Račiněves, Czech.	n17	26
Racket, stm., Ab., Can.	C4	102
Raco, Mi., U.S.	B6	99
Rădăuţi, Rom.	B7	24
Radbuza, stm., Czech.	D8	19
Radcliff, Ky., U.S.	C4	94
Radcliffe, Ia., U.S.	B4	92
Råde, Nor.	p28	14
Radeberg, Ger.D.R.	C6	18
Radebeul, Ger.D.R.	B8	19
Radersburg, Mt., U.S.	D5	103
Radford, Va., U.S.	C2	123
Radisson, Sk., Can.	E2	75
Radisson, Wi., U.S.	C2	126
Radium, Mn., U.S.	B2	100
Radium Hot Springs, B.C., Can.	D9	69
Radium Springs, N.M., U.S.	E3	108
Radix, Point, c., Trin.	O24	65
Radley, Ks., U.S.	*E9	93
Radnice, Czech.	D8	19
Radnor, In., U.S.	C4	91
Radnor, Oh., U.S.	B2	112
Radnor Township, Pa., U.S.	*F11	115
Radom, Pol.	C6	26
Radom, Il., U.S.	E4	90
Radomir, Bul.	D6	24
Radomsko, Pol.	C5	26
Radomyshl, Sov. Un.	F7	27
Radoviš, Yugo.	E6	24
Radstadt, Aus.	E6	18
Radville, Sk., Can.	H3	75
Radway, Ab., Can.	B4	68
Radzionków, Pol.	g9	26
Radzymin, Pol.	k14	26
Radzyń [Podlaski], Pol.	C7	26
Rae, N.T., Can.	D9	66
Rãe Bareli, India	C7	36
Raeford, N.C.,-U.S.	C3	110
Raesfeld, F.R.Ger.	B1	19
Raeside, Lake, l., Austl.	E3	50
Rae Strait, strt., N.T., Can.	C14	66
Raeville, Ne., U.S.	C7	104
Rafaela, Arg.	A4	54
Rafah, Isr. Occ.	G10	41
Rafaï, Cen. Afr. Rep.	D4	46
Rafḥā', Sau. Ar.	H14	40
Rafsanjān, Iran	F8	39
Raft, stm., Id., U.S.	G5	89
Raft River Mountains, mts., Ut., U.S.	B2	121
Raga, Sud.	D2	47
Ragan, Ne., U.S.	D6	104
Ragay, Phil.	p14	34
Ragay Gulf, b., Phil.	p14	34
Ragged Island, i., Me., U.S.	E4	96
Ragged Island Range, is., Bah.	C6	64
Ragged Lake, l., Me., U.S.	C3	96
Ragged Top Mountain, mtn., Wy., U.S.	E7	127
Ragland, Al., U.S.	B3	78
Raglesville, In., U.S.	G4	91
Rago, Ks., U.S.	E5	93
Ragsdale, In., U.S.	G3	91
Ragunda, Swe.	F7	14
Ragusa, Italy	F5	23
Rahad al Bardī, Sud.	C1	47
Rahden, F.R.Ger.	F2	15
Rahīmyār Khān, Pak.	C5	36
Rahway, N.J., U.S.	B4	107
Rahway, stm., N.J., U.S.	k7	107
Rāichūr, India	E6	36
Raiford, Fl., U.S.	B4	86
Raigarh, India	D7	36
Railroad Valley, val., Nv., U.S.	E6	105
Raimbault, stm., P.Q., Can.	A5	74
Rainbow Bridge National Monument, hist., Ut., U.S.	F5	121
Rainbow City, Pan.	k11	62
Rainbow City, Al., U.S.	*A3	78
Rainbow Falls, wtfl, Tn., U.S.	D10	119
Rainbow Flowage, res., Wi., U.S.	C4	126
Rainbow Lake, l., Austl.	E3	50
Rainelle, W.V., U.S.	D4	125
Raines, Ks., U.S.	E3	87
Rainier, Or., U.S.	A4	114
Rainier, Wa., U.S.	C3	124
Rainier, Mount, mtn., Wa., U.S.	C4	124
Rains, co., Tx., U.S.	C5	120
Rainsboro, Oh., U.S.	C2	112
Rainsville, Al., U.S.	A4	78
Rainy, stm., N.A.	B5	100
Rainy Lake, l., N.A.	B5	100
Rainy River, On., Can.	o16	73
Rainy River, co., On., Can.	o16	73
Raipur, India	D7	36
Ra'īs, Sau. Ar.	D2	38
Raismes, Fr.	D3	17
Raja, Cape, c., Indon.	K2	33
Rajahmundry, India	E7	36
Rajang, stm., Malay.	E5	34
Rajapalaiyam, India	*G6	36
Rājasthān, state, India	D5	36
Rājkot, India	E11	37
Rāj-Nāndgaon, India	D6	36
Rajouri, India	C6	36
Rājpīpla, India	B3	36
Rājshāhi, Bngl.	O13	51
Rakaia, stm., N.Z.	E4	126
Rakan, Ra's, c., Qatar	C11	39
Raka Zangbo, stm., China	A4	92
Rake, Ia., U.S.	A4	92
Rakhov, Sov. Un.	A7	24
Rakkestad, Nor.	p29	14
Rakovník, Czech.	D6	18
Rakvere, Sov. Un.	B6	27
Raleigh, Fl., U.S.	C4	86
Raleigh, Il., U.S.	F5	90
Raleigh, Ms., U.S.	C4	101
Raleigh, N.C., U.S.	B4	110
Raleigh, N.D., U.S.	C4	111
Raleigh, W.V., U.S.	n13	125
Raleigh, co., W.V., U.S.	D3	125
Raleigh Bay, b., N.C., U.S.	B6	110
Raleigh Hills, Or., U.S.	*B4	114
Ralls, Tx., U.S.	C2	120
Ralls, co., Mo., U.S.	B6	102
Ralph, Al., U.S.	B2	78
Ralph, Mi., U.S.	B3	99
Ralph, S.D., U.S.	B2	118
Ralston, Ia., U.S.	B3	92
Ralston, Ne., U.S.	g12	104
Ralston, Ok., U.S.	A5	113
Ralston, Pa., U.S.	D8	115
Ralston, Tn., U.S.	A3	119
Ralston, Wy., U.S.	B4	127
Ralston Valley, val., Nv., U.S.	E4	105
Ram, stm., Ab., Can.	C3	68
Ram, Isr.	B7	41
Rama, Isr.	B7	41
Rama, Sask., Can.	F4	75
Rama, Nic.	E8	63
Ramādī Barrage, Iraq	F14	40
Ramah, Co., U.S.	B6	83
Ramah, N.M., U.S.	B1	108
Ramah Indian Reservation, N.M., U.S.	C1	108
Ramallah, Isr. Occ.	C7	41
Ramat Gan, Isr.	B6	41
Ramat HaKovesh, Isr.	g10	41
Ramat HaSharon, Isr.	g10	41
Rāmban, India	B6	36
Rambervillers, Fr.	C7	16
Rambleton Acres, De., U.S.	*B3	85
Ramblewood, N.J., U.S.	D3	107
Rambouillet, Fr.	C4	16
Ramea Islands, is., Nf., Can.	E3	72
Ramelton, Ire.	B4	11
Ramenskoye, Sov. Un.	D12	27
Ramer, Al., U.S.	C3	78
Ramer, Tn., U.S.	B3	119
Ramey, Pa., U.S.	E5	115
Rāmganga, stm., India	D7	37
Rāmhormoz, Iran	F4	39
Ramirez, Tx., U.S.	F3	120
Ramiriquí, Col.	B3	60
Ramla, Isr.	C6	41
Rāmpur, India	C6	36
Ramsey, I. of Man	C4	10
Ramsay, Mi., U.S.	n12	99
Ramsayville, On., Can.	h12	73
Ramsey, Eng., U.K.	B7	12
Ramsey, Il., U.S.	D4	90
Ramsey, Mn., U.S.	E5	100
Ramsey, N.J., U.S.	A4	107
Ramsey, co., Mn., U.S.	E5	100
Ramsey, co., N.D., U.S.	A7	111
Ramsgate, Eng., U.K.	E7	10
Ramshīr, Iran	F4	39
Ramshorn Peak, mtn., Mt., U.S.	E5	103
Ramshorn Peak, mtn., Wy., U.S.	C3	127
Ramu, stm., Pap. N. Gui.	k11	50
Rānāghāt, India	F12	37
Ranau, Indon.	F2	34
Ranburne, Al., U.S.	B4	78
Rancagua, Chile	A2	54
Rancharia, Braz.	C2	56
Rancheria Rock, mtn., Or., U.S.	C6	114
Ranchester, Wy., U.S.	B5	127
Ranchi, India	D8	36
Ranchito, N.M., U.S.	A4	108
Rancho Cordova, Ca., U.S.	*C3	82
Rancho Mirage, Ca., U.S.	*F5	82
Rancho Palos Verdes, Ca., U.S.	n12	82
Rancho Rinconado, Ca., U.S.	k8	82
Rancho Santa Fe, Ca., U.S.	F5	82
Ranchos de Taos, N.M., U.S.	A4	108
Ranco, Lago, l., Chile	C2	54
Rancocas, N.J., U.S.	C3	107
Rancocas Creek, stm., N.J., U.S.	C3	107
Rancocas Creek, South Branch, stm., N.J., U.S.	D3	107
Rancocas Woods, N.J., U.S.	A4	83
Rand, Co., U.S.	A4	83
Rand, W.V., U.S.	C3	125
Randalia, Ia., U.S.	B6	92
Randall, Ia., U.S.	B4	92
Randall, Ks., U.S.	C5	93
Randall, Mn., U.S.	D4	100
Randall, co., Tx., U.S.	B2	120
Randallstown, Md., U.S.	B4	97
Randen, F.R.Ger.	I4	14
Randers, Den.	D3	15
Randle, Wa., U.S.	C4	124
Randleman, N.C., U.S.	B3	110
Randles, Mo., U.S.	D8	102
Randlett, Ok., U.S.	C3	113
Randlett, Ut., U.S.	C6	121
Randolph, Al., U.S.	C3	78
Randolph, Az., U.S.	E4	80
Randolph, Ia., U.S.	D2	92
Randolph, Ks., U.S.	C7	93
Randolph, Me., U.S.	D3	96
Randolph, Ma., U.S.	B5	98
Randolph, Mn., U.S.	F5	100
Randolph, Ne., U.S.	B8	104
Randolph, N.H., U.S.	B4	106
Randolph, N.Y., U.S.	C2	109
Randolph, Ut., U.S.	B4	121
Randolph, Vt., U.S.	D3	122
Randolph, Wi., U.S.	E4	126
Randolph, co., Al., U.S.	B4	78
Randolph, co., Ar., U.S.	A4	81
Randolph, co., Ga., U.S.	E2	87
Randolph, co., Il., U.S.	E4	90
Randolph, co., In., U.S.	D8	91
Randolph, co., Mo., U.S.	B5	102
Randolph, co., N.C., U.S.	B3	110
Randolph, co., W.V., U.S.	C5	125
Randolph Air Force Base, mil., Tx., U.S.	h7	120
Randolph Center, Vt., U.S.	D3	122
Randolph Hills, Md., U.S.	B3	97
Random Island, i., Nf., Can.	D5	72
Random Lake, Wi., U.S.	E6	126
Randow, stm., Ger.D.R.	B7	18
Randsburg, Ca., U.S.	E5	82
Randwick, Austl.	*F9	50
Ranfurly, N.Z.	E4	126
Rangaunu Bay, b., N.Z.	K14	51

Name	Map Ref	Page
Rangeley, Me., U.S.	D2	96
Rangeley Lake, l., Me., U.S.	D2	96
Rangely, Co., U.S.	A2	83
Ranger, Ga., U.S.	B2	87
Ranger, Tx., U.S.	C3	120
Ranger, W.V., U.S.	C2	125
Ranger Lake, l., N.M., U.S.	D6	108
Rangiora, N.Z.	O14	51
Rangitata, stm., N.Z.	O13	51
Rangoon, Burma	E10	36
Rangpur, Bngl.	C8	36
Ranier, Mn., U.S.	B5	100
Rāniganj, India	D8	36
Rankin, Il., U.S.	C6	90
Rankin, Pa., U.S.	k14	115
Rankin, Tx., U.S.	D2	120
Rankin, co., Ms., U.S.	C4	101
Rannoch, Loch, res., Scot., U.K.	D4	13
Ransom, Il., U.S.	B5	90
Ransom, Ks., U.S.	D4	93
Ransom, Pa., U.S.	m17	115
Ransom, co., N.D., U.S.	C8	111
Ransomville, N.Y., U.S.	B2	109
Ranson, W.V., U.S.	B7	125
Rantauprapat, Indon.	K3	34
Rantekombola, mtn., Indon.	F6	34
Rantoul, Il., U.S.	C5	90
Rantoul, Ks., U.S.	D8	93
Ranum, Den.	B3	15
Raohe, China	B11	31
Raon [-l'Étape], Fr.	A2	20
Raoui, Erg er, des., Alg.	D4	44
Raoul, Ar., U.S.	B3	87
Rapallo, Italy	B2	23
Rāpch, stm., Iran	I9	39
Rapelje, Mt., U.S.	E7	103
Raphine, Va., U.S.	C3	123
Raphoe, Ire.	C4	11
Rapid, stm., Mn., U.S.	B4	100
Rapid, North Branch, stm., Mn., U.S.	B4	100
Rapidan, Va., U.S.	B4	123
Rapid City, Mb., Can.	D1	70
Rapid City, Mi., U.S.	D5	99
Rapid City, S.D., U.S.	C2	118
Rapides, co., La., U.S.	C3	95
Rapid River, Mi., U.S.	C4	99
Rapids City, Il., U.S.	B3	90
Rappahannock, co., Va., U.S.	B4	123
Rappahannock, stm., Va., U.S.	B5	123
Rappahannock Academy, Va., U.S.	B5	123
Rapperswil, Switz.	B6	21
Rāpti, stm., Asia	D9	37
Raquette, stm., N.Y., U.S.	f10	109
Raquette Lake, N.Y., U.S.	B6	109
Raquette Lake, l., N.Y., U.S.	B6	109
Rarden, Oh., U.S.	D2	112
Rardin, Il., U.S.	D5	90
Raritan, Il., U.S.	C3	90
Raritan, N.J., U.S.	B3	107
Raritan, stm., N.J., U.S.	C4	107
Raritan, South Branch, stm., N.J., U.S.	B3	107
Raritan Bay, b., N.J., U.S.	C4	107
Rasa, Punta, c., Arg.	C4	54
Ra's al 'Ayn, Syria	D13	40
Ra's al Khaymah, U.A.E.	C5	38
Ra's al Unūf, Libya	C3	43
Ra's al 'Ushsh, Eg.	C4	41
Ra's an Naqb, Jord.	C3	38
Ra's at Tannūrah, Sau. Ar.	C5	38
Rasbokil, Swe.	t35	14
Ras Dashen Terara, mtn., Eth.	F2	47
Raseiniai, Sov. Un.	A7	26
Ra's Gharib, Eg.	D6	43
Rashād, Sud.	C3	47
Rāshayyā, Leb.	F10	40
Rashīd (Rosetta), Eg.	B3	43
Rāshidah, Ma'tan, well, Libya	H3	40
Rashkov, Sov. Un.	B9	24
Rasht, Iran	A4	38
Raška, Yugo.	D5	24
Raška, stm., Yugo.	D5	24
Raso, Cabo, c., Arg.	C3	54
Raspberry Peak, mtn., Ar., U.S.	C1	81
Rasskazovo, Sov. Un.	E13	27
Rastatt, F.R.Ger.	D4	18
Rastede, F.R.Ger.	A8	17
Rastibonne Monastery, Isr.	m14	41
Raszyn, Pol.	m13	26
Rat, stm., Mb., Can.	E3	70
Rat Buri, Thai.	C1	34
Ratcliff, Ar., U.S.	B1	81
Ratekau, F.R.Ger.	E4	15
Rathbun, Ia., U.S.	D5	92
Rathbun Lake, res., Ia., U.S.	D5	92
Rathdrum, Id., U.S.	B2	89
Rathenow, F.R.Ger.	B6	18
Rathfriland, N. Ire., U.K.	C5	11
Rathkeale, Ire.	I4	11
Rathlin Island, i., N. Ire., U.K.	C3	10
Rathlin Sound, strt., N. Ire., U.K.	B5	11
Ráth Luirc, Ire.	E3	11
Rathmore, Ire.	E2	11
Rathmullen, Ire.	B4	11
Rathnew, Ire.	D5	11
Rathowen, Ire.	C4	11
Rathwell, Mb., Can.	E2	70
Ratingen, F.R.Ger.	C3	18
Ratio, Ar., U.S.	C5	81
Rat Islands, is., Ak., U.S.	E3	79
Rat Lake, l., Mb., Can.	B4	70
Ratlām, India	F5	37
Ratnāgiri, India	E5	37
Ratner, Sk., Can.	D3	75
Raton, N.M., U.S.	A5	108
Raton Pass, N.M., U.S.	A5	108
Rattenburg, Aus.	E5	18
Rattlesnake Creek, stm., Ks., U.S.	E4	93
Rattlesnake Creek, stm., Oh., U.S.	C2	112
Rattlesnake Creek, stm., Wa., U.S.	C6	124
Rattlesnake Flat, pl., Wa., U.S.	C7	124
Rattlesnake Hills, hills, Wa., U.S.	C6	124
Rattlesnake Hills, hills, Wy., U.S.	D5	127
Rattlesnake Mountain, mtn., Ct., U.S.		
Rattling Brook, Nf., Can.	D3	72
Rattray Head, c., Scot., U.K.	D11	13
Rättvik, Swe.	G6	14
Ratzeburg, F.R.Ger.	E4	15
Ratzeburger, l., Eur.	E4	15
Raub, Malay.	K4	35
Raub, In., U.S.	C3	91
Raub, N.D., U.S.	B3	111
Rauch, Arg.	B5	54
Rauer, i., Nor.	p28	14
Raufarhöfn, Ice.	m25	14
Raukumara, mtn., N.Z.	L17	51
Rauland, Nor.	H2	14
Rauma, Fin.	G9	14
Raurkela, India	F10	37
Rausu, Mount, mtn., Japan	D12	33
Rautalampi, Fin.	F12	14
Ravalli, co., Mt., U.S.	C2	103
Ravalli, co., Mt., U.S.	D2	103
Ravanna, Ar., U.S.	D1	81
Ravanna, Mo., U.S.	A4	102
Rāvar, Iran	B5	38
Rava-Russkaya, Sov. Un.	F4	27
Raven, Va., U.S.	e10	123
Ravendale, Ca., U.S.	B3	82
Ravenden, Ar., U.S.	A4	81
Ravenden Springs, Ar., U.S.	A4	81
Ravenel, S.C., U.S.	k11	117
Ravenglass, Eng., U.K.	F5	13
Ravenna, Italy	B4	23
Ravenna, Ky., U.S.	C6	94
Ravenna, Mi., U.S.	E5	99
Ravenna, Ne., U.S.	C7	104
Ravenna, Oh., U.S.	A4	112
Raven Park, reg., Co., U.S.	A2	83
Raven Rock, N.J., U.S.	C2	107
Ravensburg, F.R.Ger.	E4	18
Ravenscrag, Sk., Can.	H1	75
Ravenscroft, Tn., U.S.	D8	119
Ravensdale, Wa., U.S.	f12	124
Ravensthorpe, Austl.	F3	50
Ravenswood, In., U.S.	k10	91
Ravenswood, W.V., U.S.	C3	125
Ravensworth, On., Can.	B5	73
Ravenwood, Mo., U.S.	A3	102
Rāvi, stm., Asia	B4	37
Ravia, Ok., U.S.	C5	113
Ravinia, S.D., U.S.	D7	118
Rāwalpindi, Pak.	B5	36
Rāwalpindi Cantonment, Pak.	*B5	36
Rawa Mazowiecka, Pol.	C6	26
Rawāndūz, Iraq	D15	40
Rawdon, P.Q., Can.	C4	74
Rawd Sālim, Bi'r, well, Eg.	D5	41
Rawhide Creek, stm., Wy., U.S.	D8	127
Rawicz, Pol.		26
Rawlings, Md., U.S.	k13	97
Rawlings, Va., U.S.	D5	123
Rawlinna, Austl.	F4	50
Rawlins, Wy., U.S.	E5	127
Rawlins, co., Ks., U.S.	C2	93
Rawson, Arg.	g6	54
Rawson, Arg.	C3	54
Rawson, N.D., U.S.	B2	111
Rawson, Oh., U.S.	B2	112
Rawsonville, Vt., U.S.	E3	122
Ray, In., U.S.	A8	91
Ray, Mn., U.S.	B5	100
Ray, N.D., U.S.	A2	111
Ray, co., Mo., U.S.	B3	102
Ray, Cape, c., Nf., Can.	E2	72
Raya, mtn., Indon.	F4	34
Raya, i., Indon.	J1	35
Rāyagada, India	H9	37
Raychikhinsk, Sov. Un.	B4	33
Ray City, Ga., U.S.	E3	87
Raygorodka, Sov. Un.	q22	27
Rayle, Ga., U.S.	C4	87
Raymond, Ab., Can.	E4	68
Raymond, Ca., U.S.	D4	82
Raymond, Ia., U.S.	B5	92
Raymond, Il., U.S.	D4	90
Raymond, Ks., U.S.	D5	93
Raymond, Me., U.S.	E2	96
Raymond, Mn., U.S.	E3	100
Raymond, Ms., U.S.	C3	101
Raymond, Ne., U.S.	D9	104
Raymond, N.H., U.S.	D4	106
Raymond, S.D., U.S.	C8	118
Raymond, Wa., U.S.	C2	124
Raymond Terrace, Austl.	F8	51
Raymondville, Mo., U.S.	D6	102
Raymondville, N.Y., U.S.	f10	109
Raymondville, Tx., U.S.	F4	120
Raymore, Sk., Can.	F3	75
Raymore, Mo., U.S.	C3	102
Rayne, La., U.S.	D3	95
Rayner Glacier, Ant.	C17	7
Raynesford, Mt., U.S.	C6	103
Raynham, Ma., U.S.	C5	98
Raynham Center, Ma., U.S.	C5	98
Rayón, Mex.	B2	63
Rayong, Thai.	F4	35
Raytown, Mo., U.S.	h11	102
Rayville, La., U.S.	B4	95
Rayville, Mo., U.S.	B3	102
Razan, Iran	D4	38
Razgrad, Bul.	D8	24
Razlog, Bul.	D6	24
Razmak, Pak.	B4	36
Razorback Mountain, mtn., B.C., Can.	D5	69
Ré, Île de, i., Fr.	D3	16
Rea, Mo., U.S.	A3	102
Rea, Lough, l., Ire.	D3	11
Reader, Ar., U.S.	D2	81
Reader, W.V., U.S.	B4	125
Reader Lake, l., Mb., Can.	C1	70
Readfield, Me., U.S.	D3	96
Reading, Eng., U.K.	E6	10
Reading, Ks., U.S.	D8	93
Reading, Ma., U.S.	A5	98
Reading, Mi., U.S.	G6	99
Reading, Oh., U.S.	C1	112
Reading, Pa., U.S.	F10	115
Reading, Vt., U.S.	E3	122
Reading Center, N.Y., U.S.	C4	109
Readland, Ar., U.S.	D4	81
Readlyn, Sk., Can.	H3	75
Readlyn, Ia., U.S.	B5	92
Readsboro, Vt., U.S.	F3	122
Readstown, Wi., U.S.	E3	126
Readyville, Tn., U.S.	B5	119
Reagan, Tn., U.S.	B3	119
Reagan, co., Tx., U.S.	D2	120
Real, co., Tx., U.S.	E3	120
Real, Cordillera, mts., S.A.	B4	54
Realicó, Arg.	B4	54
Realitos, Tx., U.S.	F3	120
Reamstown, Pa., U.S.	F9	115
Reardan, Wa., U.S.	B8	124
Reasnor, Ia., U.S.	C4	92
Reata, Mex.	B4	63
Reaville, N.J., U.S.	C3	107
Rebecca, Ga., U.S.	E3	87
Rebersburg, Pa., U.S.	E7	115
Rebiana, well, Libya	E4	43
Rebiana Sand Sea, des., Libya	E3	43
Reboly, Sov. Un.	F14	14
Rebun Island, i., Japan	D10	33
Recalde, Arg.	B4	54
Recanati, Italy	C4	23
Recherche, Archipelago of the, is., Austl.	F3	50
Rechitsa, Sov. Un.	E8	27
Recife, Braz.	C4	57
Recinto, Chile	B2	54
Recklinghausen, F.R.Ger.	C3	18
Recluse, Wy., U.S.	B7	127
Recogne, Bel.	E5	17
Recovery, Ga., U.S.	F2	87
Recreo, Arg.	E2	55
Rector, Ar., U.S.	A5	81
Red, stm., Asia	G5	31
Red, stm., N.A.	A8	76
Red, stm., U.S.	D9	76
Red, stm., Ky., U.S.	C6	94
Red, stm., Tn., U.S.	A4	119
Red, Elm Fork, stm., U.S.	B2	113
Red, North Fork, stm., U.S.	B1	113
Red, Salt Fork, stm., U.S.	C2	113
Red, South Fork, stm., U.S.	A5	119
Red, West Fork, stm., U.S.	A4	119
Redang, i., Malay.	J5	35
Red Bank, N.J., U.S.	C4	107
Red Bank, S.C., U.S.	D5	117
Red Bank, Tn., U.S.	D8	119
Red Banks, Ms., U.S.	A4	101
Red Bay, Nf., Can.	C3	72
Red Bay, Al., U.S.	A1	78
Red Bay, b., N. Ire., U.K.	B6	11
Redbird, Ok., U.S.	B6	113
Red Bird, stm., Ky., U.S.	C6	94
Red Bluff, Ca., U.S.	B2	82
Red Bluff Lake, res., U.S.	o12	120
Red Boiling Springs, Tn., U.S.	C8	119
Red Butte, mtn., Ut., U.S.	B2	121
Red Buttes Village, Wy., U.S.	D6	127
Redby, Mn., U.S.	C4	100
Redcar, Eng., U.K.	F7	13
Red Cedar, stm., Wi., U.S.	C2	126
Red Cedar Lake, l., Wi., U.S.	C2	126
Redcliff, Ab., Can.	D5	68
Redcliff, Co., U.S.	B4	83
Red Cliff, Wi., U.S.	B3	126
Redcliffe, Austl.	E9	50
Red Cliff Indian Reservation, Wi., U.S.	B2	126
Red Cloud, Ne., U.S.	D7	104
Redcloud Peak, mtn., Co., U.S.	D3	83
Red Creek, N.Y., U.S.	B4	109
Red Creek, stm., Ms., U.S.	E4	101
Red Cross Lake, l., Mb., Can.	B5	70
Red Deer, Ab., Can.	C4	68
Red Deer, stm., Can.	D4	68
Red Deer, stm., Can.	E4	75
Red Deer Lake, l., Mb., Can.	C1	70
Reddell, La., U.S.	D3	95
Red Desert, Wy., U.S.	E4	127
Reddick, Fl., U.S.	C4	86
Reddick, Il., U.S.	B5	90
Redding, Ca., U.S.	B2	82
Redding, Ct., U.S.	D2	84
Redding, Ia., U.S.	D3	92
Redding Ridge, Ct., U.S.	D2	84
Reddish Knob, mtn., U.S.	C5	125
Redditt, On., Can.	B1	73
Rede, stm., Eng., U.K.	E6	13
Red Earth Lake, l., Sk., Can.	D4	75
Redenção, Braz.	B3	57
Redeye, stm., Mn., U.S.	D3	100
Redfield, Ar., U.S.	C3	81
Redfield, Ia., U.S.	C3	92
Redfield, Ks., U.S.	E9	93
Redfield, N.Y., U.S.	B5	109
Redfield, S.D., U.S.	C7	118
Redford, N.Y., U.S.	f11	109
Redford, Tx., U.S.	p12	120
Redford Township, Mi., U.S.	F7	99
Redgranite, Wi., U.S.	D4	126
Redhill, Eng., U.K.	m12	10
Red Hook, N.Y., U.S.	C7	109
Redhouse, Ky., U.S.	C5	94
Red House, Va., U.S.	C4	123
Red House, W.V., U.S.	C3	125
Redig, S.D., U.S.	B2	118
Red Indian Lake, l., Nf., Can.	D3	72
Redkey, In., U.S.	D7	91
Red Lake, On., Can.	o16	73
Red Lake, co., Mn., U.S.	C2	100
Red Lake, l., Az., U.S.	B1	80
Red Lake, l., Mn., U.S.	C2	100
Red Lake Falls, Mn., U.S.	C2	100
Red Lake Indian Reservation, Mn., U.S.	B3	100
Redlands, Ca., U.S.	E5	82
Red Level, Al., U.S.	D3	78
Red Lick, Ms., U.S.	D2	101
Red Lion, Pa., U.S.	G8	115
Red Lodge, Mt., U.S.	E7	103
Red Mill Pond, l., De., U.S.	F5	85
Redmon, Il., U.S.	D6	90
Redmond, Or., U.S.	C5	114
Redmond, Ut., U.S.	E4	121
Redmond, Wa., U.S.	e11	124
Red Mountain, mtn., U.S.	E5	82
Red Mountain, mtn., Al., U.S.	B3	78
Red Mountain, mtn., Mt., U.S.	C4	103
Red Mountain Pass, Co., U.S.	D3	83
Rednitz, stm., F.R.Ger.	D5	18
Red Oak, Ga., U.S.	h7	87
Red Oak, Ia., U.S.	D2	92
Red Oak, N.C., U.S.	A5	110
Red Oak, Ok., U.S.	C6	113
Red Oak, Tx., U.S.	n10	120
Red Oak, Va., U.S.	D4	123
Red Oaks, La., U.S.	h9	95
Redon, Fr.	D2	16
Redonda Islands, is., B.C., Can.	D5	69
Redondela, Spain	A1	22
Redondo, Port.	C2	22
Redondo, Wa., U.S.	f11	124
Redondo Beach, Ca., U.S.	n12	82
Redoubt Volcano, vol., Ak., U.S.	g15	79
Redowl, S.D., U.S.	C3	118
Red Peak, mtn., Co., U.S.	B4	83
Red Pheasant, Sk., Can.	E1	75
Red Rapids, N.B., Can.	C2	71
Red River, N.M., U.S.	A4	108
Red River, co., La., U.S.	B2	95
Red River, co., Tx., U.S.	C5	120
Red Rock, B.C., Can.	C6	69
Red Rock, Az., U.S.	E4	80
Red Rock, N.M., U.S.	E1	108
Red Rock, Ok., U.S.	A4	113
Red Rock, Tx., U.S.	E4	120
Red Rock, stm., Mt., U.S.	F4	103
Red Rock, Lake, res., Ia., U.S.	C4	92
Red Scaffold, S.D., U.S.	C4	118
Red Sea	C3	38
Red Shirt, S.D., U.S.	D3	118
Red Springs, N.C., U.S.	C3	110
Redstone, B.C., Can.	C6	69
Redstone, Co., U.S.	B3	83
Redstone, Mt., U.S.	B12	103
Redstone, N.H., U.S.	B4	106
Red Sucker, stm., Mb., Can.	B5	70
Red Sucker Lake, l., Mb., Can.	B5	70
Red Table Mountain, mts., Co., U.S.	B4	83
Redvale, Co., U.S.	C2	83
Redwater, Ab., Can.	C4	68
Redwater, stm., Mt., U.S.	C11	103
Red Willow, Ab., Can.	C4	68
Red Willow, co., Ne., U.S.	D5	104
Red Willow Creek, stm., Ne., U.S.	D5	104
Redwine, Ky., U.S.	B6	94
Red Wing, Co., U.S.	D5	83
Red Wing, Mn., U.S.	F6	100
Redwood, Ms., U.S.	C3	101
Redwood, N.Y., U.S.	A5	109
Redwood, co., Mn., U.S.	F3	100
Redwood, stm., Mn., U.S.	F3	100
Redwood City, Ca., U.S.	D2	82
Redwood Falls, Mn., U.S.	F3	100
Redwood National Park, Ca., U.S.	B2	82
Redwood Valley, Ca., U.S.	C2	82
Ree, Lough, l., Ire.	D2	10
Reece, Ks., U.S.	E7	93
Reece City, Al., U.S.	A3	78
Reed, Ok., U.S.	C2	113
Reed City, Mi., U.S.	E5	99
Reeder, N.D., U.S.	C3	111
Reed Lake, l., Sk., Can.	G2	75
Reedley, Ca., U.S.	D4	82
Reedpoint, Mt., U.S.	E7	103
Reeds, Plain of, pl., Viet.	G6	35
Reeds Beach, N.J., U.S.	E3	107
Reedsburg, Wi., U.S.	E3	126
Reeds Peak, mtn., N.M., U.S.	D2	108
Reedsport, Or., U.S.	D2	114
Reeds Spring, Mo., U.S.	E4	102
Reedsville, Pa., U.S.	E6	115
Reedsville, W.V., U.S.	B5	125
Reedsville, Wi., U.S.	D6	126
Reedurban, Oh., U.S.	B4	112
Reedville, Va., U.S.	C6	123
Reedy, W.V., U.S.	C3	125
Reedy Lake, l., Fl., U.S.	E5	86
Reefton, N.Z.	O13	51
Reelfoot Lake, l., Tn., U.S.	A2	119
Reese, stm., Nv., U.S.	C4	105
Reese Air Force Base, mil., Tx., U.S.	C1	120
Reese Station, Oh., U.S.	m11	112
Reeseville, Wi., U.S.	E5	126
Reese, Mi., U.S.	E7	99
Reesville, Oh., U.S.	C2	112
Reeth, Eng., U.K.	F7	13
Reeves, La., U.S.	D2	95
Reeves, co., Tx., U.S.	o13	120
Reevesville, S.C., U.S.	E6	117
Refugio, Tx., U.S.	E4	120
Refugio, co., Tx., U.S.	E4	120
Refresco, Chile	E2	55
Reform, Al., U.S.	B1	78
Reform, Ms., U.S.	B4	101
Reftele, Swe.	H5	15
Refton, Pa., U.S.	G9	115
Rega, stm., Pol.	B5	26
Regan, N.D., U.S.	C5	111
Regen, F.R.Ger.	D6	18
Regen, stm., F.R.Ger.	D6	18
Regensburg, F.R.Ger.	D6	18
Regent, N.D., U.S.	C3	111
Reggâne, Alg.	C5	44
Reggio di Calabria, Italy	E5	23
Reggio nell'Emilia, Italy	B3	23
Reghin, Rom.	B7	24
Regina, Sk., Can.	G3	75
Régina, Fr. Gu.	C8	59
Regina, Mt., U.S.	C9	103
Regina Beach, Sk., Can.	G3	75
Register, Ga., U.S.	D5	87
Regna, Swe.	u33	14
Regnitz, stm., F.R.Ger.	D5	18
Reguengos de Monsaraz, Port.	C2	22
Rehau, F.R.Ger.	C7	19
Rehavya (part of Jerusalem), Isr.	m14	41
Rehna, Ger.D.R.	E5	15
Rehoboth, Nmb.	B2	49
Rehoboth, Ma., U.S.	C5	98
Rehoboth, N.M., U.S.	B1	108
Rehoboth Beach, De., U.S.	F5	85
Reichenbach, Ger.D.R.	C6	19
Reichenbach, F.R.Ger.	A4	20
Reid, Mount, mtn., Ak., U.S.	n24	79
Reidland, Ky., U.S.	e9	94
Reids Grove, Md., U.S.	D6	97
Reidsville, Ga., U.S.	D4	87
Reidsville, N.C., U.S.	A3	110
Reidville, S.C., U.S.	B3	117
Reigate, Eng., U.K.	E6	10
Reims, Fr.	C6	16
Reina Adelaida, Archipiélago, is., Chile	E2	54
Reinach, Switz.	B5	21
Reinbeck, Ia., U.S.	B5	92
Reindeer, stm., Sk., Can.	B4	75
Reindeer Island, i., Mb., Can.	C3	70
Reindeer Lake, l., Can.	m8	75
Reinersville, Oh., U.S.	C4	112
Reinfeld, F.R.Ger.	E4	15
Reinosa, Spain	A3	22
Reinosa see Reynosa, Mex.	B5	63
Reisterstown, Md., U.S.	B4	97
Reit im Winkl, F.R.Ger.	B8	20
Reitz, S. Afr.	C4	49
Rekarne, Swe.	t34	14
Reliance, De., U.S.	F3	85
Reliance, S.D., U.S.	D6	118
Reliance, Tn., U.S.	D9	119
Reliance, Wy., U.S.	E3	127
Remada, Tun.	C7	44
Remagen, F.R.Ger.	C2	19
Remanso, Braz.	C2	57
Rembert, S.C., U.S.	C6	117
Rembertów (part of Warsaw), Pol.	k14	26
Rembrandt, Ia., U.S.	B2	92
Remecó, Arg.	B4	54
Remedios, Cuba	C4	64
Remedios, Pan.	F7	62
Remer, Mn., U.S.	C5	100
Remerton, Ga., U.S.	F3	87
Remeshk, Iran	H9	39
Remington, In., U.S.	C3	91
Remington, Va., U.S.	B5	123
Rémire, Fr. Gu.	B4	59
Remiremont, Fr.	C7	16
Remlap, Al., U.S.	B3	78
Remmel Dam, Ar., U.S.	g8	81
Rems, stm., F.R.Ger.	E4	19
Remscheid, F.R.Ger.	C3	18
Remsen, Ia., U.S.	B2	92
Remsen, N.Y., U.S.	B5	109
Remus, Mi., U.S.	E5	99
Rena Lara, Ms., U.S.	A3	101
Renault, Il., U.S.	E3	90
Renco, Ks., U.S.	k15	93
Rencontre East, Nf., Can.	E4	72
Rend Lake, res., Il., U.S.	E5	90
Rendsburg, F.R.Ger.	A4	18
Renedo, Spain	A4	22
Renens, Switz.	C2	21
Renews, Nf., Can.	E5	72
Renforth, N.B., Can.	D3	71
Renfrew, On., Can.	B8	73
Renfrew, S.C., U.S.	B3	117
Renfrew, co., On., Can.	B7	73
Rengo, Chile	A2	54
Reni, Sov. Un.	C9	24
Renick, W.V., U.S.	D4	125
Renick, Mo., U.S.	B5	102
Renish Point, c., Scot., U.K.	C2	13
Renmark, Austl.	F7	50
Renner, S.D., U.S.	D9	118
Rennerod, F.R.Ger.	C3	19
Rennert, N.C., U.S.	C3	110
Rennes, Fr.	D3	16
Rennick Bay, b., Ant.	C29	7
Rennick Glacier, Ant.	B29	7
Rennie, Mb., Can.	E4	70
Reno, Nv., U.S.	D2	105
Reno, Oh., U.S.	C4	112
Reno, co., Ks., U.S.	E5	93
Reno, stm., Italy	B4	23
Reno Hill, mtn., Wy., U.S.	D6	127
Reno Lake, l., Mn., U.S.	E3	100
Renova, Pa., U.S.	C4	71
Renovo, Pa., U.S.	D6	115
Renown, Sk., Can.	F3	75
Renshou, China	C5	31
Renville, Mn., U.S.	F4	100
Renville, co., Mn., U.S.	F4	100
Renville, co., N.D., U.S.	A4	111
Renwick, Ia., U.S.	B4	92
Repton, Al., U.S.	D2	78
Republic, Ks., U.S.	C6	93
Republic, Mi., U.S.	B3	99
Republic, Mo., U.S.	D4	102
Republic, Oh., U.S.	A2	112
Republic, Pa., U.S.	G2	115
Republic, Wa., U.S.	A7	124
Republic, co., Ks., U.S.	C6	93
Republican, North Fork, stm., U.S.	A8	83
Republican, South Fork, stm., U.S.	E4	104
Republic City, Ne., U.S.	D6	104
Repulse Bay, N.T., Can.	C15	66
Repulse Bay, b., Austl.	D8	50
Requena, Spain	C5	22
Requena, Tur.	B11	
Resang, Cape, c., Malay.	E2	34
Rescue, Va., U.S.	k14	123
Reserve, La., U.S.	h10	95
Reserve, Ks., U.S.	C8	93
Reserve, Mt., U.S.	B12	103
Reserve, N.M., U.S.	D1	108
Reserve Pond, l., Ma., U.S.	h11	98
Reshef, Isr.	g10	41
Resistencia, Arg.	E4	55
Resko, Pol.	B3	26
Resolution Island, i., N.T., Can.	D20	66
Resplendor, Braz.	B4	56
Resthaven Mountain, mtn., Ab., Can.	C1	68
Restigouche, co., N.B., Can.	B2	71
Restigouche, stm., Can.	B2	71
Restinga, Punta, c., Pan.	G7	62
Reston, Mb., Can.	E1	70
Reston, Va., U.S.	B5	123
Resülhinzir, c., Tur.	D10	40
Reszel, Pol.	a16	26
Retalhuleu, Guat.	E6	63
Retamito, Arg.	A3	54
Rethel, Fr.	C6	16
Réthimnon, Grc.		
Reti, Pak.	C2	37
Retiw...		
Retlaw, Ab., Can.	D4	68
Retsof, N.Y., U.S.	C3	109
Reubens, Id., U.S.	*C2	89
Reuland, Bel.	D6	17
Reunion, dep., Afr.	H24	2
Reus, Spain	B6	22
Reuss, stm., Switz.	B5	21
Reuterstadt Stavenhagen, Ger.D.R.	E6	15
Reutlingen, F.R.Ger.	D4	18
Reutte, Aus.	E5	18
Reva, S.D., U.S.	B2	118
Revda, Sov. Un.	B5	28
Revel, Fr.	F5	16
Revelo, Ky., U.S.	D5	94
Revelstoke, B.C., Can.	D8	69
Reventazón, Peru	C1	58
Revenue, Sk., Can.	E1	75
Revere, Ma., U.S.	g11	98
Revere, Mn., U.S.	F3	100
Revere, Mo., U.S.	A6	102
Reverie, Tn., U.S.	B2	119
Revigny [-sur-Ornain], Fr.	F4	17
Revillagigedo, Islas, is., Mex.	D2	63
Revillagigedo Island, i., Ak., U.S.	n24	79
Revillo, S.D., U.S.	B9	118
Revin, Fr.	C6	16
Revivim, Isr.	C6	41
Revloc, Pa., U.S.	F4	115
Řevnice, Czech.	o17	26
Rew, Pa., U.S.	C4	115
Rewa, India	D7	36
Reward, Sk., Can.	E1	75
Rewāri, India	C6	36
Rewey, Wi., U.S.	F3	126
Rex, Ga., U.S.	h8	87
Rex, Mount, mtn., Ant.	B5	7
Rexburg, Id., U.S.	F7	89
Rexford, Ks., U.S.	C3	93
Rexford, Mt., U.S.	B1	103
Rexhame, Ma., U.S.	h13	98
Rexton, N.B., Can.	C5	71
Rexton, Mi., U.S.	B5	99
Rey, Iran	D5	39
Rey Bouba, Cam.	D2	46
Reydell, Ar., U.S.	C4	81
Reydon, Ok., U.S.	B2	113
Reyes, Point, c., Ca., U.S.	C2	82
Reykjavík, Ice.	n22	14
Reyno, Ar., U.S.	A5	81
Reynolds, Ga., U.S.	D2	87
Reynolds, Il., U.S.	B3	90
Reynolds, In., U.S.	C4	91
Reynolds, Ne., U.S.	D8	104
Reynolds, N.D., U.S.	B8	111
Reynolds, co., Mo., U.S.	D6	102
Reynoldsburg, Oh., U.S.	C3	112
Reynoldsville, Pa., U.S.	D4	115
Reynosa (Reinosa), Mex.	B5	63
Rezā'īyeh see Orūmīyeh, Iran	D3	16
Rezé, Fr.	D3	16
Rēzekne, Sov. Un.	C6	27
Rezeny, Sov. Un.	B9	24
Rhaetian Alps, mts., Eur.	A3	23
Rhame, N.D., U.S.	C2	111
Rhea, co., Tn., U.S.	D9	119
Rheda-Wiedenbrück, F.R.Ger.	B3	19
Rheden, Neth.	A7	16
Rhein, Sk., Can.	F4	75
Rheine, F.R.Ger.	B3	18
Rheinfelden, Switz.	A4	21
Rheinhausen, F.R.Ger.	C4	18
Rheinland, hist reg., F.R.Ger.	C3	18
Rheinland-Pfalz, state, F.R.Ger.	C2	19
Rheinsberg, Ger.D.R.	E6	15
Rheinwaldhorn, mtn., Switz.	C5	20
Rhenen, Neth.	C6	17
Rheydt, F.R.Ger.	A3	20
Rhinau, Fr.	C7	17
Rhin Canal, Ger.D.R.	F6	15
Rhine, Ga., U.S.	D3	87
Rhine, stm., Eur.	C3	18
Rhinebeck, N.Y., U.S.	D7	109
Rhineland, Wi., U.S.	C4	126
Rhineland, hist reg., Eur.	C2	18
Rhinns Point, c., Scot., U.K.	E2	13
Rhinow, Ger.D.R.	F6	15
Rhir, Cap, c., Mor.	C3	44
Rhode Island, state, U.S.	E5	116
Rhode Island Sound, strt., U.S.	F5	116
Rhodell, W.V., U.S.	D3	125
Rhodes, Ia., U.S.	C4	92
Rhodes, Mi., U.S.	E6	99
Rhodes see Ródhos, i., Grc.	D7	40
Rhodesia see Zimbabwe, ctry., Afr.	A5	49
Rhodes Peak, mtn., Id., U.S.	C4	89
Rhodes Point, Md., U.S.	E5	97
Rhodhiss, N.C., U.S.	B1	110
Rhodope Mountains, mts., Eur.	E7	24
Rhome, Tx., U.S.	m9	120
Rhondda, Wales, U.K.	E6	16
Rhône, stm., Fr.	E6	16
Rhône au Rhin, Canal du, Fr.	C7	17
Rhum, i., Scot., U.K.	B3	10
Rhum, Sound of, strt., Scot., U.K.	D2	13
Rhyl, Wales, U.K.	C4	12
Rhymney, Wales, U.K.	J9	13
Riacho de Santana, Braz.	A4	56
Rialma, Braz.	B3	56
Rialto, Ca., U.S.	m14	82
Rianjo, Spain	A1	22
Riau Archipelago, is., Indon.	E2	34
Riaza, Spain	B4	22
Riaza, stm., Spain	A3	22
Ribadavia, Spain	A1	22
Ribadeo, Spain	A2	22
Ribadesella, Spain	A3	22
Ribas do Rio Pardo, Braz.	C2	56
Ribble, stm., Eng., U.K.	G6	13
Ribe, Den.	C2	15
Ribe, co., Den.	C2	15
Ribeauville, Fr.	C7	17
Ribeira, Braz.	C3	56
Ribeira do Pombal, Braz.	D3	57
Ribeirão Branco, Braz.	n7	56
Ribeirão Preto, Braz.	F4	56
Ribera, Italy	F4	23
Ribera, N.M., U.S.	B4	108
Ribérac, Fr.	E4	16
Rib Lake, Wi., U.S.	C3	126
Rib Mountain, mtn., Wi., U.S.	D6	126
Ribnitz-Damgarten, Ger.D.R.	D6	15
Ribstone Creek, stm., Ab., Can.	C5	68
Říčany, Czech.	o18	26

Name	Map Ref	Page

Rockwell, N.C., U.S. B2 110
Rockwell City, Ia., U.S. B3 92
Rockwell Park, N.C., U.S. B2 110
Rockwood, On., Can. D4 73
Rockwood, Al., U.S. A2 78
Rockwood, Il., U.S. F4 90
Rockwood, Me., U.S. C3 96
Rockwood, Mi., U.S. F7 99
Rockwood, Or., U.S. *B4 114
Rockwood, Pa., U.S. G3 115
Rockwood, Tn., U.S. D9 119
Rockwood, Tx., U.S. D3 120
Rocky, Ok., U.S. B2 113
Rocky, stm., Ab., Can. C2 68
Rocky, stm., N.C., U.S. B4 110
Rocky, stm., S.C., U.S. C2 117
Rocky, East Branch, stm., Oh., U.S. h9 112
Rocky, West Branch, stm., Oh., U.S. h9 112
Rocky Bay, b., Nf., Can. B4 72
Rocky Boy, Mt., U.S. B7 103
Rocky Boys Indian Reservation, Mt., U.S. B7 103
Rocky Comfort, Mo., U.S. E3 102
Rocky Coulee, val., Wa., U.S. B6 124
Rocky Creek, Fl., U.S. *o10 86
Rockyford, Ab., Can. D4 68
Rocky Ford, Co., U.S. C7 83
Rocky Ford, Ga., U.S. D5 87
Rocky Fork Lake, l., Oh., U.S. C2 112
Rocky Gap, Va., U.S. C1 123
Rocky Harbour, Nf., Can. D3 72
Rocky Hill, Ct., U.S. C5 84
Rocky Hill, Ky., U.S. C3 94
Rocky Hill, N.J., U.S. C3 107
Rocky Lake, l., Mb., Can. B1 70
Rocky Lake, l., Me., U.S. D5 96
Rocky Mount, N.C., U.S. B5 110
Rocky Mount, Va., U.S. C3 123
Rocky Mountain, mtn., Mt., U.S. C4 103
Rocky Mountain House, Ab., Can. C3 68
Rocky Mountain National Park, Co., U.S. A5 83
Rocky Mountains, mts., N.A. E9 61
Rocky Point, N.C., U.S. C5 110
Rocky Ripple, In., U.S. k10 91
Rocky River, Oh., U.S. A4 112
Rocky Top, mtn., Or., U.S. C4 114
Rocroi, Fr. E4 17
Roda, Va., U.S. f9 123
Rodach, F.R.Ger. C5 19
Rodanthe, N.C., U.S. B7 110
Rodarte, N.M., U.S. *A4 108
Rødby, Den. D5 15
Rødbyhavn, Den. D5 15
Roddickton, Nf., Can. C3 72
Rødding, Den. C3 15
Roddy, Tn., U.S. D9 119
Rødekro, Den. C3 15
Rodeo, Ca., U.S. *g8 82
Rodeo, N.M., U.S. F1 108
Roderfield, W.V., U.S. D3 125
Roderick Island, i., B.C., Can. C3 69
Rodessa, La., U.S. B2 95
Rodewisch, Ger.D.R. C7 19
Rodewisch, N.M., U.S. E2 108
Rodez, Fr. E5 16
Ródhos (Rhodes), i., Grc. D7 40
Roding, F.R.Ger. D7 19
Rodman, Ia., U.S. A3 92
Rodney, On., Can. E3 73
Rodney, Ms., U.S. D2 101
Rodney, Cape, c., Ak., U.S. C6 79
Rodney Pond, l., Nf., Can. D4 72
Rodney Village, De., U.S. D3 85
Roduco, N.C., U.S. A6 110
Roe, Ar., U.S. C4 81
Roebling, N.J., U.S. C3 107
Roebourne, Austl. D2 50
Roebuck, S.C., U.S. B4 117
Roebuck Bay, b., Austl. C3 50
Roeland Park, Ks., U.S. k16 93
Roermond, Neth. B6 16
Roeselare (Roulers), Bel. B5 16
Roessleville, N.Y., U.S. *C7 109
Roes Welcome Sound, strt., N.T., Can. D15 66
Roetgen, F.R.Ger. D6 17
Roff, Ok., U.S. C5 113
Rogachev, Sov. Un. E8 27
Rogagua, Laguna, l., Bol. B2 55
Rogáguado, Laguna, l., Bol. B2 55
Roganville, Tx., U.S. D6 120
Rogatica, Yugo. D4 24
Roger Mills, co., Ok., U.S. B2 113
Rogers, Ar., U.S. A1 81
Rogers, Ct., U.S. B8 84
Rogers, Mn., U.S. C9 104
Rogers, Ne., U.S. C9 104
Rogers, N.M., U.S. D6 108
Rogers, N.D., U.S. B7 111
Rogers, Oh., U.S. B5 112
Rogers, Tx., U.S. D4 120
Rogers, co., Ok., U.S. A6 113
Rogers, Mount, mtn., Va., U.S. f10 123
Rogers City, Mi., U.S. C7 99
Rogers Lake, res., Ct., U.S. D6 84
Rogerson, Id., U.S. G4 89
Rogers Pass, Mt., U.S. C4 103
Rogersville, N.B., Can. C4 71
Rogersville, Al., U.S. A2 78
Rogersville, Mo., U.S. D4 102
Rogersville, Pa., U.S. G1 115
Rogersville, Tn., U.S. C10 119
Roggen, Co., U.S. A6 83
Rogozhina, Alb. B2 25
Rogoźno, Pol. B4 26
Rogue, stm., Or., U.S. E2 114
Rogue River, Or., U.S. E3 114
Rohnert Park, Ca., U.S. *C2 82
Rohrersville, Md., U.S. B2 97
Rohri Canal, Pak. D2 37
Rohtak, India *C6 36
Rohwer, Ar., U.S. D4 81
Roi Et, Thai. B2 34
Roissy-en-France, Fr. g11 16
Rojas, Arg. A4 54
Rojo, Cabo, c., Mex. m15 63
Rojo, Cabo, c., P.R. H11 64
Rokan, stm., Indon. L4 32
Rokeby, Sk., Can. F4 75
Rokel, stm., S.L. F3 47
Rokitno, Sov. Un. F6 27
Rokycany, Czech. D7 19
Roland, Mb., Can. E3 70
Roland, Ia., U.S. B4 92
Roland, Ok., U.S. B7 113
Roland, Lake, res., Md., U.S. g11 97

Rolesville, N.C., U.S. B4 110
Rolette, N.D., U.S. A6 111
Rolette, co., N.D., U.S. A6 111
Rolfe, Ia., U.S. B3 92
Roll, Az., U.S. E2 80
Roll, In., U.S. C7 91
Roll, Ok., U.S. B2 113
Rolla, B.C., Can. B7 69
Rolla, Ar., U.S. C3 81
Rolla, Ks., U.S. E2 93
Rolla, Mo., U.S. D6 102
Rolla, N.D., U.S. A6 111
Rolle, Switz. E3 18
Rolleville, Bah. C6 64
Rollingbay, Wa., U.S. e10 124
Rollingstone, Mn., U.S. F7 100
Rollins, Mt., U.S. C2 103
Rollinsford, N.H., U.S. D5 106
Rolvsøya, i., Nor. B10 14
Roma, Austl. E8 50
Roma, Ab., Can. A2 68
Roma, Tx., U.S. F3 120
Romain, Cape, c., S.C., U.S. F9 117
Romaine, stm., Can. h9 72
Roman, Rom. B8 24
Romania, ctry., Eur. C7 24
Roman Nose Mountain, mtn., Md., U.S. m12 97
Roman Nose Mountain, mtn., Or., U.S. D3 114
Romano, Cape, c., Fl., U.S. G5 86
Romano, Cayo, i., Cuba C5 64
Romanshorn, Switz. A7 21
Romans [-sur-Isère], Fr. E6 16
Romanzof, Cape, c., Ak., U.S. C6 79
Romanzof Mountains, mts., Ak., U.S. B11 79
Romayor, Tx., U.S. D5 120
Rombauer, Mo., U.S. E7 102
Rome (Roma), Italy D4 23
Rome, Ga., U.S. B1 87
Rome, Il., U.S. C4 90
Rome, In., U.S. I4 91
Rome, Ia., U.S. D6 92
Rome, Ms., U.S. B3 101
Rome, N.Y., U.S. B5 109
Rome, Oh., U.S. D3 112
Rome, Pa., U.S. C9 115
Rome City, In., U.S. B7 91
Romema (part of Jerusalem), Isr. m14 41
Romeo, Co., U.S. D4 83
Romeo, Mi., U.S. F7 99
Romeoville, Il., U.S. k8 90
Romeville, La., U.S. h10 95
Romford (part of London), Eng., U.K. k13 10
Romilly, Fr. C5 16
Romita, Mex. m13 63
Romney, In., U.S. D4 91
Romney, W.V., U.S. B6 125
Romny, Sov. Un. F9 27
Rømø, i., Den. C2 15
Romona, In., U.S. F4 91
Romont, Switz. C2 21
Romorantin, Fr. D4 16
Rompin, stm., Malay. K5 33
Romsey, Eng., U.K. D6 12
Romulus, Mi., U.S. p15 99
Romulus, N.Y., U.S. C4 109
Romuncion, i., Micron. Q18 52
Romuriku Island, i., Marsh Is. P18 52
Ron, Viet. D7 35
Rona, i., Scot., U.K. C2 13
Rona, i., Scot., U.K. A3 13
Ronald, Wa., U.S. B4 124
Roncador, Serra do, plat., Braz. E4 59
Roncador Bank, Col. D7 62
Roncesvalles, W.V., U.S. D4 125
Ronciglione, Italy C4 23
Ronda, Spain D3 22
Ronda, N.C., U.S. A2 110
Rønde, Den. B4 15
Ronde Island, i., Gren. W25 65
Rondo, Ar., U.S. C5 81
Rondônia, state, Braz. E2 59
Rondonópolis, Braz. B2 56
Roneys Point, W.V., U.S. f8 125
Ronge, Lac la, l., Sk., Can. B3 75
Rongjiang, China L3 32
Rongxian, China G7 31
Ronkiti Harbor, b., Micron. Q17 52
Ronkonkoma, N.Y., U.S. *n15 109
Ron Ma, Cape, c., Viet. C7 35
Rønne, Den. J6 14
Ronne, stm., Swe. B6 15
Ronneburg, Ger.D.R. C7 19
Ronne Entrance, b., Ant. B5 7
Ronne Ice Shelf, Ant. B6 7
Ronse, Bel. B5 16
Ronuro, stm., Braz. E4 59
Roodepoort-Maraisburg, S. Afr. *C4 49
Roodeschool, Neth. A6 17
Roodhouse, Il., U.S. D3 90
Roof Butte, mtn., Az., U.S. A6 80
Rooks, co., Ks., U.S. C4 93
Roopville, Ga., U.S. C1 87
Roosendaal, Neth. B6 16
Roosevelt, Az., U.S. D4 80
Roosevelt, Mn., U.S. B3 100
Roosevelt, N.J., U.S. C4 107
Roosevelt, N.Y., U.S. *n15 109
Roosevelt, Ok., U.S. C2 113
Roosevelt, Ut., U.S. C5 121
Roosevelt, co., Mt., U.S. B11 103
Roosevelt, co., N.M., U.S. C6 108
Roosevelt, stm., Braz. D2 59
Roosevelt Campobello International Park, N.B., Can. E3 71
Roosevelt Island, i., Ant. B32 7
Roosevelt Park, Mi., U.S. E4 99
Rootstown, Oh., U.S. A4 112
Ropczyce, Pol. C6 26
Roper, In., U.S. B6 110
Roper, stm., Austl. B5 50
Ropesville, Tx., U.S. C1 120
Roque Bluffs, Me., U.S. D5 96
Roquetas, Spain B6 22
Rora Head, c., Scot., U.K. B5 13
Roraima, ter., Braz. A2 59
Roraima, Mount, mtn., S.A. A2 59

Rorke Lake, l., Can. B5 70
Rorketon, Mb., Can. D2 70
Røros, Nor. F4 14
Rorschach, Switz. E4 18
Rosa, La., U.S. D3 95
Rosa, Monte, mtn., Eur. B1 23
Rosa, Punta, c., Mex. B3 63
Rosales, Phil. o13 34
Rosalia, Ks., U.S. E7 93
Rosalia, Wa., U.S. B8 124
Rosalind, Ab., Can. C4 68
Rosamond, Ca., U.S. E4 82
Rosamond, Il., U.S. D4 90
Rosamorada, Mex. k11 63
Rosario, Arg. A4 54
Rosário, Braz. B2 57
Rosario, Mex. C3 63
Rosario, Para. D4 55
Rosario, Phil. p13 34
Rosario, Ur. E1 56
Rosario, Ven. A3 60
Rosario de la Frontera, Arg. E3 55
Rosario del Tala, Arg. A5 54
Rosário do Sul, Braz. E2 56
Rosário Oeste, Braz. A1 56
Rosati, Mo., U.S. C6 102
Rosburg, Wa., U.S. C2 124
Roscoe, Il., U.S. A5 90
Roscoe, Mn., U.S. E4 100
Roscoe, Mo., U.S. D4 102
Roscoe, Mt., U.S. E7 103
Roscoe, Ne., U.S. C4 104
Roscoe, N.Y., U.S. D6 109
Roscoe, Pa., U.S. F2 115
Roscoe, S.D., U.S. B6 118
Roscoe, Tx., U.S. C2 120
Roscoe Glacier, Ant. C22 7
Roscommon, Ire. D2 10
Roscommon, Mi., U.S. D6 99
Roscommon, co., Ire. D3 11
Roscommon, co., Mi., U.S. D6 99
Roscrea, Ire. D3 10
Rose, Ne., U.S. B6 104
Rose, Ok., U.S. A6 113
Rose, Mount, mtn., Nv., U.S. D2 105
Roseau, Dom. I14 64
Roseau, Mn., U.S. B3 100
Roseau, co., Mn., U.S. B3 100
Roseau, stm., N.A. E3 70
Roseau, South Fork, stm., Mn., U.S. B3 100
Roseau, Maur. C1 45
Rosebery, B.C., Can. D9 69
Rose-Blanche, Nf., Can. E2 72
Roseboro, N.C., U.S. C4 110
Rosebud, Ab., Can. D4 68
Rose Bud, Ar., U.S. B3 81
Rosebud, Mo., U.S. C6 102
Rosebud, Mt., U.S. D10 103
Rosebud, S.D., U.S. D5 118
Rosebud, Tx., U.S. D4 120
Rosebud, co., Mt., U.S. D10 103
Rosebud, stm., Ab., Can. D4 68
Rosebud Creek, stm., Mt., U.S. E10 103
Rosebud Indian Reservation, S.D., U.S. D5 118
Roseburg, Or., U.S. D3 114
Rosebush, Mi., U.S. E6 99
Rose City, Mi., U.S. D6 99
Rose Creek, Mn., U.S. G6 100
Rosedale, Ab., Can. D4 68
Rosedale, B.C., Can. f14 69
Rosedale, Co., U.S. *A6 83
Rosedale, In., U.S. E3 91
Rosedale, Md., U.S. g11 97
Rosedale, Ms., U.S. B2 101
Rosedale, N.Y., U.S. C4 113
Rosedale, Tn., U.S. C9 119
Rosedale, W.V., U.S. C4 125
Rosedale Colony, S.D., U.S. *D8 118
Rose Farm, Oh., U.S. C3 112
Rosegan, N.D., U.S. B4 111
Rose Hill, Il., U.S. D5 90
Rose Hill, Ks., U.S. C5 92
Rose Hill, Ks., U.S. E6 93
Rose Hill, Ms., U.S. C4 101
Rose Hill, N.C., U.S. C4 110
Rose Hill, Va., U.S. f8 123
Roseisle, Mb., Can. E2 70
Roseland, Ca., U.S. *C2 82
Roseland, Fl., U.S. E6 86
Roseland, La., U.S. A5 91
Roseland, La., U.S. D5 95
Roseland, Ne., U.S. D7 104
Roseland, N.J., U.S. *B4 107
Roseland, Oh., U.S. B3 112
Roselawn, In., U.S. B3 91
Roselle, Il., U.S. k8 90
Roselle, N.J., U.S. k7 107
Roselle Park, N.J., U.S. k7 107
Rosemark, Tn., U.S. B2 119
Rosemary, Ab., Can. D5 68
Rosemead, Ca., U.S. *m15 82
Rosemère, P.Q., Can. p19 74
Rosemont, N.J., U.S. C3 107
Rosemont, W.V., U.S. k10 125
Rosemount, Mn., U.S. F5 100
Rosenberg, Tx., U.S. E5 120
Rosendale, Mo., U.S. A3 102
Rosendale, Wi., U.S. E5 126
Roseneath, On., Can. C6 73
Rosenhayn, N.J., U.S. E2 107
Rosenheim, F.R.Ger. E6 18
Rose Peak, mtn., Az., U.S. D6 80
Rosepine, La., U.S. D2 95
Rose Point, c., B.C., Can. B2 69
Rose Prairie, B.C., Can. A7 69
Roseray, Sk., Can. G1 75
Rosetown, Sk., Can. F2 75
Rosetta see Rashîd, Eg. B3 38
Rosetta, Ms., U.S. D2 101
Rosetta Branch, stm., Ms., U.S. D2 101
Rosetta Mouth, mth., Eg. C2 41
Rose Valley, Sk., Can. E4 75
Rosevear, Ab., Can. C2 68
Roseville, Ca., U.S. C3 82
Roseville, Il., U.S. C3 90
Roseville, Mi., U.S. o16 99
Roseville, Oh., U.S. C3 112
Roseville, Pa., U.S. C8 115
Rosewood, Mn., U.S. B2 100
Rosewood, Oh., U.S. B1 112
Rosewood Heights, Il., U.S. *E3 90
Rosharon, Tx., U.S. r14 120
Rosholt, S.D., U.S. B9 118
Rosholt, Wi., U.S. D4 126

Rosh Pinna, Isr. B7 41
Rosiclare, Il., U.S. F5 90
Rosie, Ar., U.S. B4 81
Rosier, Ga., U.S. D4 87
Rosières-en-Santerre, Fr. E2 17
Rosignano Marittimo, Italy C3 23
Rosignol, Guy. A3 59
Rosiori de Vede, Rom. C7 24
Roskilde, Den. C6 15
Roskilde, co., Den. C6 15
Roslavl, Sov. Un. E9 27
Roslyn, Pa., U.S. o21 115
Roslyn, S.D., U.S. B8 118
Roslyn, Wa., U.S. B5 124
Roslyn Heights, N.Y., U.S. h13 109
Rosman, N.C., U.S. f10 110
Ross, Mn., U.S. B3 100
Ross, N.D., U.S. A3 111
Ross, Oh., U.S. C1 112
Ross, co., Oh., U.S. C2 112
Ross, Mount, mtn., N.Z. N15 51
Rossa, Switz. D7 21
Rossano, Italy E6 23
Ross Barnett Reservoir, res., Ms., U.S. C3 101
Rossburg, Oh., U.S. B1 112
Rossburn, Mb., Can. D1 70
Rosscarbery, Ire. F2 11
Ross Dam, Wa., U.S. A4 124
Rosseau, On., Can. B5 73
Rossendale, Mb., Can. E2 70
Rosser, Tx., U.S. n10 120
Rosses, Bay, b., Ire. B3 11
Rosses Point, Ire. B3 11
Ross Ice Shelf, Ant. A31 7
Rossignol, Lake, l., N.S., Can. E4 71
Rossiter, Pa., U.S. E4 115
Rossland, B.C., Can. E9 69
Rosslare, Ire. E5 11
Rosslau, Ger.D.R. B7 19
Rosslyn, Ire. A4 124
Rossmoor, Ca., U.S. *n12 82
Ross, Maur. C1 45
Ross-on-Wye, Eng., U.K. C5 12
Rossosh, Sov. Un. F12 27
Ross River, Yk., Can. D6 66
Ross Sea, Ant. B31 7
Rosston, Ar., U.S. D2 81
Rosston, Ok., U.S. A2 113
Ross Township, Pa., U.S. *E1 115
Rossville, Ga., U.S. B1 87
Rossville, Il., U.S. C6 90
Rossville, In., U.S. D4 91
Rossville, Ks., U.S. C8 93
Rossville, Tn., U.S. B2 119
Rosswein, Ger.D.R. C8 19
Rostock, Ger.D.R. A6 18
Rostov, Sov. Un. C12 27
Rostov-na-Donu, Sov. Un. E6 29
Roşul Pass, Rom. C7 24
Roswell, Ga., U.S. B2 87
Roswell, Id., U.S. F2 89
Roswell, N.M., U.S. D5 108
Roswell, S.D., U.S. C8 118
Rota, Spain D2 22
Rotan, Tx., U.S. C2 120
Rotenburg [an der Fulda], F.R.Ger. C5 19
Roth, F.R.Ger. D6 19
Roth, N.D., U.S. A5 111
Rothaar Mountains, mts., F.R.Ger. C4 18
Rothbury, Eng., U.K. E7 13
Rothbury, Mi., U.S. E4 99
Röthenbach [bei Sankt Wolfgang], F.R.Ger. D6 19
Röthenbach im Emmental, Switz. C4 21
Rothenburg [ob der Tauber], F.R.Ger. D5 18
Rothenthurm, Switz. B6 21
Rother, stm., Eng., U.K. D8 12
Rothera, sci., Ant. C6 7
Rotherham, Eng., U.K. A6 12
Rothes, Scot., U.K. C5 13
Rothesay, N.B., Can. D4 71
Rothesay, Scot., U.K. C4 10
Rothschild, Wi., U.S. D4 126
Rothsville, Pa., U.S. F9 115
Rothville, Mo., U.S. B4 102
Rothwell, N.B., Can. C3 71
Roto, Austl. F5 51
Rotondo, Monte, mtn., Fr. C2 23
Rotorua, N.Z. M16 51
Rott, stm., F.R.Ger. E6 19
Rottenburg, F.R.Ger. E3 19
Rottenmann, Aus. E7 19
Rotterdam, Neth. B6 16
Rotterdam, N.Y., U.S. C6 109
Rottumeroog, i., Neth. A6 17
Rottweil, F.R.Ger. D4 18
Roubaix, Fr. B5 16
Roubideau Creek, stm., Co., U.S. C2 83
Roudnice [nad Labem], Czech. n17 21
Rouen, Fr. C4 16
Rouge-Matawin, Réserve, P.Q., Can. C3 74
Rougemont, Fr. B2 20
Rough, stm., Ky., U.S. C3 94
Rough River Lake, res., Ky., U.S. C3 94
Rougon, La., U.S. D4 95
Rouleau, Sk., Can. G3 75
Roulers see Roeselare, Bel. B5 16
Roulette, Pa., U.S. C5 115
Round Head, Oh., U.S. B2 112
Round Hill, N.S., Can. E4 71
Round Hill, Va., U.S. A5 123
Round Island, i., Ms., U.S. g8 101
Round Island Passage, strt., Fiji H14 52
Round Lake, Il., U.S. h8 90
Round Lake, Mn., U.S. G3 100

Round Lake, N.Y., U.S. C7 109
Round Lake, l., On., Can. B7 73
Round Lake, l., Sk., Can. G4 75
Round Lake Beach, Il., U.S. h8 90
Round Mound, hill, Ks., U.S. D4 93
Round Mountain, Nv., U.S. E4 105
Round Mountain, Tx., U.S. D3 120
Round Mountain, mtn., Austl. F9 50
Round Oak, Ga., U.S. C3 87
Round Pond, Ar., U.S. B5 81
Round Pond, Me., U.S. E3 96
Round Pond, l., Nf., Can. D4 72
Round Rock, Az., U.S. A6 80
Round Rock, Tx., U.S. D4 120
Round Spring, Mo., U.S. D6 102
Roundstone, Ire. D2 11
Round Top Hill, mtn., Ma., U.S. B2 98
Roundup, Mt., U.S. D8 103
Round Valley Indian Reservation, Ca., U.S. C2 82
Round Valley Reservoir, res., N.J., U.S. B3 107
Roura, Fr. Gu. C8 59
Rousay, i., Scot., U.K. A5 10
Rouses Point, N.Y., U.S. f11 109
Rouseville, Pa., U.S. D2 115
Routon, Tn., U.S. A3 119
Routt, co., Co., U.S. A3 83
Rouville, co., P.Q., Can. D4 74
Rouyn, P.Q., Can. k11 74
Rouzerville, Pa., U.S. G6 115
Rovaniemi, Fin. D11 14
Rovato, Italy B3 23
Roven'ki, Sov. Un. G12 27
Roven'ki, Sov. Un. G12 27
Rover, Ar., U.S. C2 81
Rover, Tn., U.S. B5 119
Roveredo, Switz. D7 21
Rovereto, Italy B3 23
Rovigo, Italy B3 23
Rovinj, Yugo. C1 24
Rovno, Sov. Un. D5 29
Rovnoye, Sov. Un. F16 27
Row, Ia., U.S. A7 113
Rowan, Ia., U.S. B4 92
Rowan, co., Ky., U.S. B6 94
Rowan, co., N.C., U.S. B2 110
Rowan's Ravine Provincial Park, Sk., Can. G3 75
Rowe, Ma., U.S. A2 98
Rowe, N.M., U.S. B4 108
Rowena, S.D., U.S. D9 118
Rowena, Tx., U.S. D2 120
Rowesville, S.C., U.S. E6 117
Rowland, Ky., U.S. C6 94
Rowland, N.C., U.S. C3 110
Rowland Heights, Ca., U.S. *n13 82
Rowlesburg, W.V., U.S. B5 125
Rowlett, Tx., U.S. *n9 120
Rowletts, Ky., U.S. C4 94
Rowley, Ab., Can. D4 68
Rowley, In., U.S. A6 92
Rowley, Ma., U.S. A6 98
Rowley Shoals, rf., Austl. C2 50
Roxabell, Oh., U.S. C2 112
Roxana, De., U.S. C12 27
Roxana, N.C., U.S. C6 34
Roxboro, N.C., U.S. A4 110
Roxburgh, N.Z. P12 51
Roxbury, Ct., U.S. C2 84
Roxbury, Ks., U.S. D6 93
Roxbury, Me., U.S. D2 96
Roxbury, N.Y., U.S. C6 109
Roxbury, Vt., U.S. C3 122
Roxie, Ms., U.S. D2 101
Roxobel, N.C., U.S. A5 110
Roxton, Tx., U.S. C5 120
Roxton Falls, P.Q., Can. D5 74
Roxton Pond (Sainte-Pudentienne), P.Q., Can. D5 74
Roy, Mt., U.S. C8 103
Roy, N.M., U.S. B5 108
Roy, Ut., U.S. B3 121
Roy, Wa., U.S. B3 124
Roya, Peña, mtn., Spain B5 22
Royal, Ar., U.S. C2 81
Royal, Ia., U.S. A2 92
Royal, Ne., U.S. B7 104
Royal, Tn., U.S. B5 119
Royal, stm., Me., U.S. g7 96
Royal Canal, Ire. C4 11
Royal Center, In., U.S. C4 91
Royale, Isle, i., Mi., U.S. h9 99
Royal Gorge, val., Co., U.S. C5 83
Royal Oak, B.C., Can. h12 69
Royal Oak, Mi., U.S. F7 99
Royal Pines, Ct., U.S. f10 110
Royalston, Ma., U.S. A3 98
Royalton, Il., U.S. F4 90
Royalton, Mn., U.S. E4 100
Royalton, Vt., U.S. D3 122
Royalty, Tx., U.S. D1 120
Royan, Fr. E3 16
Royersford, Pa., U.S. F10 115
Royerton, In., U.S. D7 91
Royse City, Tx., U.S. C4 120
Royston, B.C., Can. E5 69
Royston, Ga., U.S. B3 87

Rucker, Tn., U.S. B5 119
Ruda, stm., Pol. g9 26
Ruda Śląska, Pol. g9 26
Rūdbār, Afg. B3 36
Rudd, Ia., U.S. A5 92
Ruddell, Sk., Can. E2 75
Ruddels Mills, Ky., U.S. B5 94
Rüdesheim, F.R.Ger. C3 18
Rudkøbing, Den. D4 15
Rudná, Czech. n17 21
Rudnichnyy, Sov. Un. B4 28
Rudnyy, Sov. Un. *D9 29
Rudolf, Lake, l., Afr. A6 48
Rudolph, Oh., U.S. A2 112
Rudolph, i., Sov. Un. A8 128
Rudolstadt, Ger.D.R. C5 18
Rūd Sar, Iran B5 38
Rudy, Ar., U.S. *B1 81
Rudyard, Mi., U.S. B6 99
Rudyard, Mt., U.S. B6 103
Rue, Fr. D9 12
Rueil-Malmaison, Fr. g9 16
Ruelle, Fr. E4 16
Rueun, Switz. C7 21
Rufā' Ar, Sud. C6 48
Rufe, Ok., U.S. C6 113
Ruffec, Fr. E4 16
Ruffin, N.C., U.S. A3 110
Ruffin, S.C., U.S. E6 117
Rufiji, stm., Tan. C6 48
Rufino, Arg. A4 54
Rufisque, Sen. D1 45
Rufus, Or., U.S. B6 114
Rufus Woods Lake, res., Wa., U.S. A6 124
Rugao, China H9 32
Rugby, Eng., U.K. B6 12
Rugby, N.D., U.S. A6 111
Rugeley, Eng., U.K. B6 12
Rügen, i., Ger.D.R. A6 18
Rugged Mountain, mtn., B.C., Can. D4 69
Rugozero, Sov. Un. E15 14
Ruhengeri, Rw. B5 48
Ruhla, Ger.D.R. C5 19
Ruhland, Ger.D.R. C4 18
Ruhr, stm., F.R.Ger. C4 18
RÜT, Afg. D13 39
Rui'an, China F9 31
Ruidosa, Tx., U.S. p12 120
Ruidoso, N.M., U.S. D4 108
Ruidoso Downs, N.M., U.S. D4 108
Ruiz, Mex. m11 63
Rujiyoru, i., Marsh Is. S18 52
Rukoji Island, i., Marsh Is. P18 52
Rukoji Pass, strt., Marsh Is. D2 120
Rukwa, prov., Tan. C5 48
Rukwa, Lake, l., Tan. C5 48
Rule, Tx., U.S. C3 120
Rule Creek, stm., Co., U.S. D7 83
Ruleville, Ms., U.S. B3 101
Rulo, Ne., U.S. D10 104
Rum, Il., U.S. E3 90
Ruma, Il., U.S. E3 90
Ruma, Yugo. C4 24
Rumbek, Sud. D2 47
Rumbley, Md., U.S. D6 97
Rumburk, Czech. C9 19
Rum Cay, i., Bah. C6 64
Rum Creek, stm., W.V., U.S. n12 125
Rumely, Mi., U.S. B3 99
Rumford, Me., U.S. D2 96
Rumilly, Fr. D1 20
Rummah, Wādī ar, val., Sau. Ar. C4 38
Rummānah, Eg. C4 41
Rummānah, Bi'r ar, well, Egypt G9 40
Rumney, N.H., U.S. C3 106
Rumney Depot, N.H., U.S. C3 106
Rumoi, Japan E10 33
Rumph, Mwi. D5 48
Rump Mountain, mtn., Me., U.S. C1 96
Rumsey, Ab., Can. D4 68
Rumsey, Ca., U.S. C2 82
Rumson, N.J., U.S. C4 107
Rumstick Point, c., R.I., U.S. D5 116
Runan, China H6 32
Runcorn, Eng., U.K. A5 12
Rung, i., Kam. G5 35
Runge, Tx., U.S. E4 120
Rungwa, Tan. C5 48
Runit Island, i., Marsh Is. S18 52
Runnells, Ia., U.S. C4 92
Runnels, co., Tx., U.S. D3 120
Runnemede, N.J., U.S. D2 107
Runnymede, Sk., Can. F5 75
Runtu, Nmb. D2 31
Ruoqiang, China D2 31
Ruo Shui, stm., China C5 54
Rupanco, Chile C2 54
Rupat, i., Indon. L4 33
Rupert, Id., U.S. G5 89
Rupert, Que. D6 17
Rupert, W.V., U.S. D4 125
Rupert, Rivière de, stm., P.Q., Can. h11 74
Rupert House, P.Q., Can. h11 74
Rupununi, dept., Guy. B3 59
Rupununi, stm., Guy. B3 59
Rur, stm., Eur. D6 17
Rural Hall, N.C., U.S. A2 110
Rural Retreat, Va., U.S. D1 123
Rurrenabaque, Bol. B2 55
Rusagonis, N.B., Can. D3 71
Ruşayriş, Khazzan ar, res., Afr. C3 47
Ruse, Bul. D7 24
Rusera, India E11 37
Rush, Ire. D3 10
Rush, co., In., U.S. *C6 83
Rush, Ky., U.S. B7 94
Rush, co., Ks., U.S. D4 93
Rush, co., In., U.S. E6 91
Rush, stm., Wi., U.S. D1 126
Rush Center, Ks., U.S. D4 93
Rush City, Mn., U.S. E6 100
Rush Creek, stm., Co., U.S. C7 83
Rush Creek, stm., Ne., U.S. D3 104
Rush Creek, stm., Oh., U.S. C3 112
Rush Creek, stm., Tx., U.S. C4 113
Rushden, Eng., U.K. B7 12
Rushford, N.Y., U.S. C2 109
Rush Hill, Mo., U.S. B6 102
Rush Lake, Sk., Can. G2 75
Rush Lake, l., On., Can. E5 100
Rush Lake, l., Wi., U.S. E5 126
Rush Valley, Nv., U.S. C3 121
Rushmere, Va., U.S. h14 123
Rushmore, U.S. G3 100

Rush Springs, Ok., U.S. C4 113
Rushsylvania, Oh., U.S. B2 112
Rush Valley, Ut., U.S. C3 121
Rushville, Il., U.S. C3 90
Rushville, In., U.S. E7 91
Rushville, Mo., U.S. B2 102
Rushville, Ne., U.S. B3 104
Rushville, N.Y., U.S. C3 109
Rusk, Tx., U.S. D5 120
Rusk, co., Tx., U.S. C5 120
Rusk, co., Wi., U.S. C2 126
Ruskin, Fl., U.S. E4 86
Ruskin, Ne., U.S. D8 104
Ruso, N.D., U.S. B5 111
Russas, Braz. B3 57
Russell, Mb., Can. D1 70
Russell, On., Can. B9 73
Russell, Ar., U.S. B4 81
Russell, Fl., U.S. m8 86
Russell, Ia., U.S. D4 92
Russell, Ks., U.S. D5 93
Russell, Ky., U.S. B7 94
Russell, Ma., U.S. B2 98
Russell, Mn., U.S. F3 100
Russell, N.Y., U.S. f9 109
Russell, N.D., U.S. A5 111
Russell, co., On., Can. B9 73
Russell, co., Al., U.S. C4 78
Russell, co., Ks., U.S. D5 93
Russell, co., Ky., U.S. C4 94
Russell, co., Va., U.S. f9 123
Russell, Mount, mtn., Ak., U.S. f16 79
Russell Cave National Monument, Al., U.S. A4 78
Russell Fork, stm., U.S. C7 94
Russellkonda, India H10 37
Russell Lake, I., Ab., Can. .. A3 68
Russell Lake, I., Mb., Can. .. A1 70
Russell Springs, Ks., U.S. .. D2 93
Russell Springs, Ky., U.S. .. C4 94
Russellville, Al., U.S. A2 78
Russellville, Ar., U.S. B2 81
Russellville, Il., U.S. E6 90
Russellville, In., U.S. E4 91
Russellville, Ky., U.S. D3 94
Russellville, Mo., U.S. C5 102
Russellville, Oh., U.S. D2 112
Russellville, Or., U.S. *B4 114
Russellville, S.C., U.S. E8 117
Russellville, Tn., U.S. C10 119
Rüsselsheim, F.R.Ger. D3 19
Russia, Oh., U.S. B1 112
Russian, stm., Ca., U.S. C2 82
Russian Soviet Federative Socialist Republic, state, Sov. Un. C12 29
Russiaville, In., U.S. D5 91
Russum, Ms., U.S. D2 101
Rustad, Mn., U.S. D2 100
Rustavi, Sov. Un. B15 40
Rustburg, Va., U.S. C3 123
Rustenburg, S. Afr. C4 49
Ruston, La., U.S. B3 95
Ruston, Wa., U.S. B3 124
Ruswil, Switz. B5 21
Ruszów, Pol. B10 19
Rutana, Bdi. B4 48
Rute, Spain D3 22
Ruteng, Indon. G6 34
Ruth, Ms., U.S. D3 101
Ruth, Nv., U.S. D6 105
Ruth, N.C., U.S. f11 110
Ruth, W.V., U.S. m12 125
Rutherford, N.J., U.S. B4 107
Rutherford, Tn., U.S. A3 119
Rutherford, co., N.C., U.S. .. B1 110
Rutherford, co., Tn., U.S. ... B5 119
Rutherfordton, N.C., U.S. ... B1 110
Rutherglen, On., Can. A5 73
Rutherglen, Scot., U.K. E4 13
Rutheron, N.M., U.S. A3 108
Ruthilda, Sk., Can. F1 75
Ruthin, Wales, U.K. A4 12
Ruthton, Mn., U.S. F2 100
Ruthven, Ia., U.S. A3 92
Rüti, Switz. B4 21
Rutland, B.C., Can. E8 69
Rutland, Il., U.S. C4 90
Rutland, Ia., U.S. B3 92
Rutland, Ma., U.S. B4 98
Rutland, N.D., U.S. C8 111
Rutland, Oh., U.S. C3 112
Rutland, S.D., U.S. C9 118
Rutland, Vt., U.S. D3 122
Rutland, co., Vt., U.S. D2 122
Rutland Station, Sk., Can. .. E1 75
Rutledge, Al., U.S. D3 78
Rutledge, Ga., U.S. C3 87
Rutledge, Mn., U.S. D6 100
Rutledge, Mo., U.S. A5 102
Rutledge, Tn., U.S. C10 119
Rutshuru, Zaire B4 48
Rutter, On., Can. A4 73
Ruvo [di Puglia], Italy D6 23
Ruvu, Tan. C6 48
Ruvuma, prov., Tan. D6 48
Ruvuma, stm., Afr. D6 48
Ruwenzori, mts., Afr. A4 48
Ruza, Sov. Un. D11 27
Ruzayevka, Sov. Un. D15 27
Ružomberok, Czech. B5 26
Rwanda, ctry., Afr. B5 48
Ry, Den. B3 15
Ryå, stm., Den. A3 15
Ryan, Ia., U.S. B6 92
Ryan, Ok., U.S. C4 113
Ryan Creek, stm., Al., U.S. .. A3 78
Ryan Park, Wy., U.S. E6 127
Ryan Peak, mtn., Id., U.S. .. F4 89
Ryazan, Sov. Un. D6 29
Ryazhsk, Sov. Un. E13 27
Rybachye, Sov. Un. E9 28
Rybatskoye (part of Leningrad), Sov. Un. s31 14
Rybinsk see Andropov, Sov. Un. D6 29
Rybnik, Pol. C5 26
Rybnitsa, Sov. Un. B9 24
Rychnov [nad Kněžnou], Czech. C4 26
Rycroft, Ab., Can. B1 68
Ryde, Austl. *F9 50
Ryde, Eng., U.K. E6 10
Ryder, N.D., U.S. B4 111
Ryderwood, Wa., U.S. C2 124
Rye, Eng., U.K. D8 12
Rye, Co., U.S. D6 83
Rye, N.H., U.S. D5 106
Rye, N.Y., U.S. h13 109
Rye Beach, N.H., U.S. E5 106

Ryegate, Mt., U.S. D7 103
Ryegate, Vt., U.S. C4 122
Rye Patch Dam, Nv., U.S. .. C3 105
Rye Patch Reservoir, res., Nv., U.S. C3 105
Ryerson, Sk., Can. H5 75
Rygge, Nor. p28 14
Ryley, Ab., Can. C4 68
Rylsk, Sov. Un. F10 27
Rynda, Sov. Un. C17 14
Ryomgård, Den. B4 15
Rypin, Pol. B5 26
Rysy, mtn., Eur. *D6 26
Ryōtsu, Japan G9 33
Ryukyu Islands, is., Japan .. F10 31
Rzązda, stm., Pol. k14 26
Rzepin, Pol. B3 26
Rzeszów, Pol. C6 26
Rzhev, Sov. Un. C10 27

S

Saale, stm., Eur. C5 18
Saaler Bodden, b., Ger.D.R. . D6 15
Saalfeld, Ger.D.R. C5 18
Saalfelden, Aus. B8 20
Saanen, Switz. D3 21
Saar, hist reg., F.R.Ger. D3 18
Saar, stm., Eur. E6 17
Saarbrücken, F.R.Ger. D3 18
Saarburg, F.R.Ger. E6 17
Saaremaa, i., Sov. Un. B4 27
Saarland, state, F.R.Ger. ... E6 17
Saarlouis, F.R.Ger. D3 18
Saas Almagell, Switz. D4 21
Saas Fee, Switz. D4 21
Saavedra, Arg. B4 54
Saba, i., Neth. Ant. H13 64
Šabac, Yugo. C4 24
Sabadell, Spain B7 22
Sabae, Japan n15 33
Sabael, N.Y., U.S. B6 109
Sabah (North Borneo), state, Malay. D5 34
Sa'bah, mtn., Libya D3 43
Sabana, Archipiélago de, is., Cuba C4 64
Sabana de la Mar, Dom. Rep. E9 64
Sabanagrande, Hond. D4 62
Sabanalarga, Col. A3 60
Sabaneta, Puntan, c., N. Mar. Is. C8 52
Sabang, Indon. k11 34
Sabará, Braz. B4 56
Sãbarmati, stm., India D5 36
Sabastiiyah, Isr. Occ. f11 41
Sabattus, Me., U.S. D2 96
Sabattus Pond, I., Me., U.S. . D2 96
Sabaudia, Italy D4 23
Sabbathday Pond, I., Me., U.S. g7 96
Sabetha, Ks., U.S. C8 93
Sabha, Libya D2 43
Sabillasville, Md., U.S. A3 97
Sabin, Mn., U.S. D2 100
Sabina, Oh., U.S. C2 112
Sabinal, Tx., U.S. E3 120
Sabinas, Mex. B4 63
Sabinas Hidalgo, Mex. B4 63
Sabine, Tx., U.S. E6 120
Sabine, W.V., U.S. D3 125
Sabine, co., La., U.S. C2 95
Sabine, co., Tx., U.S. D6 120
Sabine, stm., U.S. D6 120
Sabine, Mount, mtn., Ant. .. B29 7
Sabine Lake, I., U.S. E2 95
Sabine Pass, Tx., U.S. E6 120
Sabine Pass, strt., U.S. E2 95
Sabinópolis, Braz. B4 56
Sabinsville, Pa., U.S. C7 115
Sablé, Fr. D3 16
Sable, Cape, c., N.S., Can. .. H19 66
Sable, Cape, c., Fl., U.S. ... G5 86
Sable Island, i., N.S., Can. .. F10 71
Sable River, N.S., Can. F4 71
Sabon Birni, Nig. D6 45
Sabor, stm., Port. B2 22
Sabrãtah, Libya *C2 43
Sabrina Coast, Ant. C25 7
Sabula, Ia., U.S. B7 92
Sabula, Mo., U.S. D7 102
Sabzevār, Iran B5 38
Sac, co., Ia., U.S. B2 92
Sac, stm., Mo., U.S. D4 102
Sacaba, Bol. C2 55
Sacajawea, Lake, res., Wa., U.S. C7 124
Sacajawea Peak, mtn., Or., U.S. B9 114
Sacandaga Lake, I., N.Y., U.S. B6 109
Sac and Fox Indian Reservation, Ia., U.S. C5 92
Sacaton, Az., U.S. D4 80
Sacavém, Port. f9 22
Sac City, Ia., U.S. B2 92
Săcele, Rom. C7 24
Sachem Head, Ct., U.S. ... E5 84
Sachigo Lake, I., On., Can. .. C5 70
Sachse, Tx., U.S. n10 120
Sachs Harbour, N.T., Can. .. B8 66
Sachuest Point, c., R.I., U.S. . F6 116
Sacile, Italy D8 20
Sackets Harbor, N.Y., U.S. .. B4 109
Sackville, N.B., Can. D5 71
Saco, Al., U.S. D4 78
Saco, Me., U.S. E2 96
Saco, Mt., U.S. B9 103
Saco, East Branch, stm., N.H., U.S. B4 106
Sacramento, Ca., U.S. C3 82
Sacramento, Ky., U.S. C2 94
Sacramento, N.M., U.S. ... E4 108
Sacramento, co., Ca., U.S. .. C3 82
Sacramento, stm., Ca., U.S. . C3 82
Sacramento, stm., N.M., U.S. E4 108
Sacramento Mountains, mts., N.M., U.S. D4 108
Sacramento Valley, val., Az., U.S. B1 80
Sacramento Valley, val., Ca., U.S. C2 82
Sacré-Coeur-Saguenay, P.Q., Can. A8 74
Sacred Heart, Mn., U.S. ... F3 100
Sacrofano, Italy g8 23
Sacul, Tx., U.S. D5 120
Sa'dah, Yemen C3 38
Šadani, Tan. C6 48
Saddle (Burnt), stm., Ab., Can. B1 68
Saddle, stm., N.J., U.S. h8 107

Saddleback Mountain, mtn., Az., U.S. k8 80
Saddleback Mountain, mtn., Me., U.S. B4 96
Saddleback Mountain, mtn., Me., U.S. D2 96
Saddle Ball Mountain, mtn., Ma., U.S. A1 98
Saddle Brook, N.J., U.S. ... h8 107
Saddle Mountain, mtn., Or., U.S. B3 114
Saddle Mountains, mts., Wa., U.S. C5 124
Saddle River, N.J., U.S. A4 107
Saddlestring, Wy., U.S. B6 127
Sadieville, Ky., U.S. B5 94
Sadiya, India C10 36
Sado, stm., Port. C1 22
Sado, i., Japan D12 31
Sadorus, Il., U.S. D5 90
Sadská, Czech. n18 26
Sæby, Den. A4 15
Saegertown, Pa., U.S. C1 115
Safãjah, Bür, well, Egypt ... H9 40
Safety Harbor, Fl., U.S. E4 86
Safford, Al., U.S. C2 78
Safford, Az., U.S. E6 80
Saffron Walden, Eng., U.K. . B8 12
Safi, Mor. C3 44
Safid, stm., Iran C4 39
Safidäbeh, Iran F10 39
Safid Küh, Selseleh-ye, mts., Afg. D12 39
Safi Kuh, mts., Asia D14 39
Safonovo, Sov. Un. D9 27
Safrakköyü, Tur. *B7 40
Safranbolu, Tur. B9 40
Safune, W. Sam. F11 52
Safune Bay, b., W. Sam. ... F11 52
Saga, China J5 33
Saga, Japan J5 33
Sagadahoc, co., Me., U.S. .. E3 96
Sagaing, Burma D10 36
Sagamihara, Japan *I9 33
Sagami Sea, b., Japan n18 33
Sagamore, Ma., U.S. C6 98
Sagamore, Pa., U.S. E3 115
Sagamore Beach, Ma., U.S. . *C6 98
Sagamore Hills, Oh., U.S. .. h9 112
Saganaga Lake, I., Mn., U.S. B7 100
Sagara, India D3 37
Sagara, Japan o17 33
Saggart, Ire. D5 11
Sag Harbor, N.Y., U.S. m16 109
Sagle, Id., U.S. A2 89
Sagleipie, Lib. E3 45
Saglek Bay, b., Nf., Can. ... f9 72
Saglouc, P.Q., Can. f11 74
Sagola, Mi., U.S. B2 99
Sago de Tánamo, Cuba ... D6 64
Sagua la Grande, Cuba C3 64
Saguache, Co., U.S. C4 83
Saguache, co., Co., U.S. ... C4 83
Saguache Creek, stm., Co., U.S. C4 83
Saguaro National Monument (Tucson Mountain Section), Az., U.S. E4 80
Saguaro National Monument, Az., U.S. E5 80
Saguenay, co., P.Q., Can. .. A8 74
Saguenay, stm., P.Q., Can. . A7 74
Sagunto, Spain C5 22
Sahāb, Jord. C8 41
Sahagún, Col. B2 60
Sahagún, Spain B2 22
Sahand, Küh-e, mtn., Iran .. C3 39
Sahara, des., Afr. D6 42
Sahāranpur, India C6 36
Sāhiwāl (Montgomery), Pak. B5 36
Şahrajat al Kubrā, Eg. D3 41
Şahuaripa, Mex. B3 63
Sahuarita, Az., U.S. F5 80
Sahuayo [de Díaz], Mex. .. m12 63
Said, Sov. Un. E6 28
Saïda, Alg. C5 44
Sa'īdābād, Iran G7 39
Sa'īdābād, Bngl. C8 36
Saigō, Japan H6 33
Saigon see Ho Chi Minh City, Viet. C3 34
Saiki, Japan J5 33
Sailor Springs, Il., U.S. E5 90
Saimaa, I., Fin. G13 14
Saint Abb's Head, c., Scot., U.K. E6 13
Saint-Adelphe, P.Q., Can. .. C5 74
Saint-Affrique, Fr. F5 16
Saint-Agapit, P.Q., Can. ... C6 74
Saint Agatha, Me., U.S. ... A4 96
Sainte-Agathe, P.Q., Can. .. C6 74
Sainte-Agathe-des-Monts, P.Q., Can. C3 74
Sainte-Agnès-de-Dundee, P.Q., Can. D3 74
Saint-Aimé [Massueville], P.Q., Can. C4 74
Saint-Alban, P.Q., Can. C5 74
Saint Albans, Eng., U.K. ... C7 12
Saint Albans, Vt., U.S. B2 122
Saint Albans, W.V., U.S. ... C3 125
Saint Albans Bay, Vt., U.S. . B2 122
Saint Alban's Head, c., Eng., U.K. E5 10
Saint-Alexandre, P.Q., Can. . D4 74
Saint-Alexandre, P.Q., Can. . B8 74
Saint-Alexis-des-Monts, P.Q., Can. C4 74
Saint-Alphonse [-de-Granby], P.Q., Can. D5 74
Saint-Amand-les-Eaux, Fr. .. B5 16
Saint-Amand-Mont-Rond, Fr. D5 16
Saint Amant, La., U.S. h10 95
Saint-Amarin, Fr. B3 20
Saint-Ambroise, P.Q., Can. . A6 74
Saint-Anaclet, P.Q., Can. ... A9 74

Saint-André, Cap, c., Madag. g8 49
Saint-André-Avellin, P.Q., Can. D2 74
Saint-André-Est, P.Q., Can. . D3 74
Saint Andrew Bay, b., Fl., U.S. u16 86
Saint Andrews, N.B., Can. .. D2 71
Saint Andrew's, Nf., Can. ... E2 72
Saint Andrews, Scot., U.K. .. B5 10
Saint Andrews, S.C., U.S. ... C5 117
Saint Andrews, S.C., U.S. ... F7 117
Saint Andrews, Tn., U.S. ... D8 119
Saint Andrews Bay, b., Scot., U.K. D6 13
Saint Andrew Sound, strt., Ga., U.S. F5 87
Sainte-Angèle [-de-Monnoir], P.Q., Can. D4 74
Saint-Anicet, P.Q., Can. D3 74
Saint Ann, Mo., U.S. *f13 102
Saint Anna, Wi., U.S. k9 126
Sainte-Anne, Guad. H14 64
Saint Anne, Il., U.S. B6 90
Sainte-Anne, Lac, I., Ab., Can. C3 68
Sainte-Anne-de-Beaupré, P.Q., Can. B7 74
Sainte-Anne-de-la-Pérade, P.Q., Can. C5 74
Sainte Anne-de-Madawaska, N.B., Can. B1 71
Sainte Anne-des-Chênes, Mb., Can. E3 70
Sainte-Anne [-des-Plaines], P.Q., Can. D4 74
Sainte-Anne-du-Lac, P.Q., Can. k11 74
Sainte-Anne du Nord, stm., P.Q., Can. B7 74
Saint Anns, N.S., Can. C9 71
Saint Ann's Bay, Jam. E5 64
Saint Anns Peak, mtn., Trin. . N23 65
Saint-Anselme, P.Q., Can. .. C7 74
Saint Ansgar, Ia., U.S. A5 92
Saint Anthony, Nf., Can. ... C4 72
Saint Anthony, Id., U.S. ... F7 89
Saint Anthony, In., U.S. ... H4 91
Saint Anthony, Ia., U.S. ... B4 92
Saint Anthony, N.D., U.S. .. C5 111
Saint Antoine, N.B., Can. ... C5 71
Saint-Antoine [-de-Tilly], P.Q., Can. C6 74
Saint-Antoine [-sur-Richelieu], P.Q., Can. D4 74
Saint-Antonin, P.Q., Can. ... B8 74
Saint-Apollinaire (Francoeur), P.Q., Can. C7 74
Sainte-Apolline, P.Q., Can. .. C7 74
Saint Arnaud, Austl. H4 51
Saint-Arsène, P.Q., Can. ... B8 74
Saint Arthur, N.B., Can. B3 71
Saint-Athanase, P.Q., Can. . B8 74
Saint-Aubert, P.Q., Can. B7 74
Saint-Augustin, P.Q., Can. .. o17 74
Saint Augustin, Sask., Can. . C2 72
Saint-Augustin-Deux-Montagnes, P.Q., Can. .. p19 74
Saint Augustine, Fl., U.S. .. C5 86
Saint Augustin-Nord-Ouest, stm., P.Q., Can. C2 72
Saint Augustin-Saguenay, P.Q., Can. C2 72
Saint Austell, Eng., U.K. ... D3 12
Saint-Avold, Fr. C7 16
Sainte-Barbe, P.Q., Can. ... D3 74
Saint-Barnabé-Nord, P.Q., Can. C5 74
Saint-Barnabé-Sud, P.Q., Can. D5 74
Saint-Barthélemy, P.Q., Can. C4 74
Saint-Barthélemy, i., Guad. . H13 64
Saint Basile, N.B., Can. B1 71
Saint-Basile, P.Q., Can. C6 74
Sainte-Béatrix, P.Q., Can. .. C4 74
Saint Bees Head, c., Eng., U.K. C5 10
Saint Benedict, Sk., Can. ... E3 75
Saint Benedict, Ia., U.S. ... A3 92
Saint Benedict, Ks., U.S. ... C7 93
Saint Benedict, Or., U.S. ... h12 114
Saint-Benoît-Labre, P.Q., Can. C7 74
Saint-Bernard, P.Q., Can. .. C6 74
Saint Bernard, Al., U.S. A3 78
Saint Bernard, La., U.S. E6 95
Saint Bernard, Ne., U.S. ... C8 104
Saint Bernard, Oh., U.S. ... o13 112
Saint Bernard, co., La., U.S. . E6 95
Saint Bernice, In., U.S. E2 91
Saint Bethlehem, Tn., U.S. . A4 119
Sainte-Blandine, P.Q., Can. . A9 74
Saint Boswells, Sk., Can. ... G2 75
Saint Brendan's, Nf., Can. .. D5 72
Saint Bride, Mount, mtn., Ab., Can. D3 68
Saint Bride's, Nf., Can. E4 72
Saint Brides Bay, b., Wales, U.K. E4 10
Saint-Brieuc, Fr. C2 16
Saint Brieux, Sk., Can. E3 75
Sainte-Brigide [-d'Iberville], P.Q., Can. D4 74
Sainte-Brigitte [-des-Saults], P.Q., Can. C5 74
Saint-Bruno, P.Q., Can. A6 74
Saint-Calais, Fr. D4 16
Saint-Calixte, P.Q., Can. ... D4 74
Saint-Camille, P.Q., Can. ... D6 74
Saint-Camille [-de-Bellechasse], P.Q., Can. .. C7 74
Saint-Casimir, P.Q., Can. ... C5 74
Saint Catharines, On., Can. . D5 73
Saint Catherine, Ky., U.S. .. B5 94
Saint Catherine, Lake, I., Vt., U.S. E2 122
Saint Catherine, Mount, mtn., Gren. W25 65
Saint Catherines Island, i., Ga., U.S. E5 87
Saint Catherine's Point, c., Eng., U.K. E6 12
Saint Catherines Sound, strt., Ga., U.S. E5 87
Saint-Célestin (Annaville), P.Q., Can. C5 74
Saint-Césaire, P.Q., Can. ... D4 74
Saint-Chamond, Fr. E6 16
Saint Charles, Ar., U.S. C4 81
Saint Charles, Id., U.S. G7 89
Saint Charles, Il., U.S. B5 90
Saint Charles, Ky., U.S. C2 94
Saint Charles, Mi., U.S. E6 99

Saint Charles, Mn., U.S. ... G6 100
Saint Charles, Mo., U.S. ... C7 102
Saint Charles, S.D., U.S. ... D6 118
Saint Charles, Va., U.S. f8 123
Saint Charles, co., La., U.S. . E5 95
Saint Charles, co., Mo., U.S. C7 102
Saint Charles, Cape, c., Nf., Can. B4 72
Saint-Chély-d'Apcher, Fr. .. E5 16
Saint Christopher (Saint Kitts)-Nevis, ctry., N.A. H13 64
Saint-Chrysostome, P.Q., Can. D4 74
Saint Clair, Mn., U.S. F5 100
Saint Clair, Mi., U.S. F8 99
Saint Clair, Mo., U.S. C6 102
Saint Clair, Pa., U.S. E9 115
Saint Clair, co., Al., U.S. ... B3 78
Saint Clair, co., Il., U.S. E3 90
Saint Clair, co., Mi., U.S. ... F8 99
Saint Clair, co., Mo., U.S. ... C4 102
Saint Clair, stm., N.A. E2 73
Saint Clair, Lake, I., N.A. ... E2 73
Saint Clair Shores, Mi., U.S. p16 99
Saint Clairsville, Oh., U.S. .. B5 112
Saint Claude, Mb., Can. ... E2 70
Saint-Claude, Fr. D6 16
Saint-Clément, P.Q., Can. .. B8 74
Saint Clements Creek, stm., Md., U.S. D4 97
Sainte-Clothilde, P.Q., Can. . D5 74
Saint Cloud, Fl., U.S. D5 86
Saint Cloud, Mn., U.S. E5 100
Saint Cloud, Wi., U.S. E5 126
Saint-Coeur-de-Marie, P.Q., Can. A6 74
Saint-Côme, P.Q., Can. C4 74
Saint-Constant, P.Q., Can. . q19 74
Saint Croix, N.B., Can. D2 71
Sainte-Croix, P.Q., Can. ... C6 74
Sainte-Croix, Switz. C2 20
Saint Croix, In., U.S. H4 91
Saint Croix, i., V.I.U.S. H12 64
Saint Croix, stm., N.A. C5 96
Saint Croix, co., Wi., U.S. .. C1 126
Saint Croix, Lake, I., U.S. .. D1 126
Saint Croix Falls, Wi., U.S. . C1 126
Saint Croix Stream, stm., Me., U.S. B4 96
Saint-Cuthbert, P.Q., Can. .. C4 74
Saint-Cyrille, P.Q., Can. D5 74
Saint-Cyrille [-de-L'Islet], P.Q., Can. B7 74
Saint-Cyr [-sur-Loire], Fr. .. D4 16
Saint-Damase, P.Q., Can. .. D4 74
Saint-Damase-des-Aulnaies, P.Q., Can. B7 74
Saint-Damien-de-Brandon, P.Q., Can. C4 74
Saint-Damien [-de-Buckland 96], P.Q., Can. C7 74
Saint David, Az., U.S. F5 80
Saint David, Il., U.S. C3 90
Saint David, Me., U.S. A4 96
Saint-David-de-l'Auberivière, P.Q., Can. n17 74
Saint David's, Nf., Can. D2 72
Saint David's, Wales, U.K. .. C2 12
Saint David's Head, c., Wales, U.K. E4 10
Saint David's Island, i., Ber. o21 64
Saint-David [-y-Yamaska], P.Q., Can. C5 74
Saint-Denis, Fr. C5 16
Saint-Denis, Reu. H24 2
Saint-Denis [-de-la-Bouteillerie], P.Q., Can. .. B8 74
Saint-Denis-Rivière-Richelieu, P.Q., Can. D4 74
Saint-Didace, P.Q., Can. ... C4 74
Saint-Dié, Fr. C7 16
Saint-Dizier, Fr. C6 16
Saint-Dominique, P.Q., Can. D5 74
Saint-Dominique, P.Q., Can. q18 74
Saint-Donat-de-Montcalm, P.Q., Can. C3 74
Saint Donatus, Ia., U.S. ... B7 92
Saint-Édouard [-de-Napierville], P.Q., Can. .. q19 74
Saint Edward, Ne., U.S. ... C8 104
Saint-Edwidge, P.Q., Can. .. D6 74
Sainte Eleanor's, P.E., Can. . C6 71
Sainte-Éleuthère, P.Q., Can. B8 74
Saint Elias, Cape, c., Ak., U.S. D11 79
Saint Elias, Mount, mtn., N.A. C11 79
Saint Elias Mountains, mts., N.A. C11 79
Saint-Élie, Fr. Gu. B4 59
Sainte-Élisabeth, P.Q., Can. . C4 74
Saint Elizabeth, Mo., U.S. .. C5 102
Saint Elmo, Il., U.S. E5 90
Saint Elmo, Il., U.S. D5 90
Sainte-Émélie-de-l'Énergie, P.Q., Can. C4 74
Saint-Émile, P.Q., Can. D3 74
Sainte-Émilie, P.Q., Can. ... C7 74
Saint-Esprit, P.Q., Can. C4 74
Saint-Étienne, Fr. E6 16
Saint-Étienne [-de-Beauharnois], P.Q., Can. .. q19 74
Sainte-Eulalie, P.Q., Can. .. C5 74
Saint-Euphémie, P.Q., Can. C7 74
Saint-Eusèbe, P.Q., Can. ... B9 74
Saint-Eustache, Mb., Can. .. E2 70
Saint-Eustache, P.Q., Can. . D4 74
Saint-Fabien, P.Q., Can. ... A9 74
Sainte-Famille, P.Q., Can. .. B7 74
Sainte-Famille-d'Aumond, P.Q., Can. C2 74
Saint-Faustin, P.Q., Can. ... C3 74
Saint-Félicien, P.Q., Can. ... A5 74
Saint-Ferdinand (Bernierville), P.Q., Can. C6 74
Saint-Ferréol [-les-Neiges], P.Q., Can. B7 74
Saint-Fidèle, P.Q., Can. B7 74
Saint Fintan's, Nf., Can. ... D2 72
Saint-Flavien, P.Q., Can. ... C6 74
Saint-Florent, Fr. C9 16
Saint Florian, Al., U.S. A2 78
Saint-Flour, Fr. E5 16
Saint-Foy, P.Q., Can. n17 74
Sainte-Foy-la-Grande, Fr. .. E4 16
Saint Francis, Ar., U.S. A5 81
Saint Francis, Ks., U.S. C2 93
Saint Francis, Me., U.S. ... A4 96
Saint Francis, Mn., U.S. ... E5 100

Saint Francis, S.D., U.S. ... D5 118
Saint Francis, Wi., U.S. n12 126
Saint Francis, co., Ar., U.S. . B5 81
Saint Francis, stm., N.A. ... B8 74
Saint Francis, stm., U.S. A5 81
Saint Francis, Cape, c., Nf., Can. E5 72
Saint Francisville, Il., U.S. .. E6 90
Saint Francisville, La., U.S. . D4 95
Saint-François, Guad. Q9 65
Saint Francois, co., Mo., U.S. D7 102
Saint-François, stm., P.Q., Can. D5 74
Saint-François, Lac, I., P.Q., Can. D6 74
Saint François Mountains, hills, Mo., U.S. D7 102
Saint-François-Xavier [-de-Brompton], P.Q., Can. . D5 74
Saint-Frédéric, P.Q., Can. .. C7 74
Saint Froid Lake, I., Me., U.S. B4 96
Saint-Fulgence, P.Q., Can. . A7 74
Saint-Gabriel, P.Q., Can. ... C4 74
Saint Gabriel, La., U.S. h9 95
Saint-Gaudens, Fr. F4 16
Saint-Gédéon, P.Q., Can. .. D7 74
Sainte Genevieve, Mo., U.S. D7 102
Sainte Genevieve, co., Mo., U.S. D7 102
Saint-Gènéviève-de-Batiscan, P.Q., Can. C5 74
Saint George, Austl. E8 50
Saint George, Ber. o20 64
Saint George, N.B., Can. ... D3 71
Saint George, On., Can. D4 73
Saint George, S.C., U.S. ... F4 87
Saint George, Ks., U.S. C7 93
Saint George, Me., U.S. D3 96
Saint George, S.C., U.S. ... E6 117
Saint George, Ut., U.S. F2 121
Saint George, Cape, c., Nf., Can. D2 72
Saint George, Cape, c., Fl., U.S. C1 86
Saint George Island, i., Ak., U.S. D6 79
Saint George Island, i., Fl., U.S. C2 86
Saint George's, Nf., Can. ... D2 72
Saint-Georges, Bel. D5 17
Saint George's, Nf., Can. ... C4 74
Saint-Georges, Fr. Gu. B4 59
Saint George's, Gren. J14 64
Saint-Georges, De., U.S. ... B3 85
Saint George's Bay, b., Nf., Can. D2 72
Saint Georges Bay, b., N.S., Can. D8 71
Saint George's Cathedral, Isr. m14 41
Saint George's Channel, strt., Eur. E3 10
Saint-Georges-Ouest, P.Q., Can. C7 74
Saint-Gérard, P.Q., Can. ... D6 74
Saint-Germain, P.Q., Can. .. D5 74
Saint-Germain, Wi., U.S. ... C4 126
Saint-Germain, Forêt de, Fr. g9 16
Saint-Germain-de-Kamouraska, P.Q., Can. B8 74
Saint-Germain-en-Laye, Fr. . g9 16
Sainte-Germaine-Station, P.Q., Can. C7 74
Saint-Gervais, P.Q., Can. ... C7 74
Saint-Gervais-les-Bains, Fr. . D7 16
Saint-Gilles (Sint-Gillis), Bel. *D4 17
Saint-Gilles-Croix-de-Vie, Fr. D3 16
Saint-Gilles-du-Gard, Fr. ... F6 16
Saint-Gingolph, Switz. D2 21
Saint-Girons, Fr. F4 16
Saint-Gobain, Fr. C5 16
Saint Gotthard Tunnel, Switz. E4 21
Saint Govan's Head, c., Wales, U.K. C3 12
Saint-Grégoire (Larochelle), P.Q., Can. C5 74
Saint Gregor, Sk., Can. E3 75
Saint Gregory, Mount, mtn., Nf., Can. D2 72
Saint-Guillaume-d'Upton, P.Q., Can. D5 74

Saint-Hélène [-de-Kamouraska], P.Q., Can. .. B8 74
Saint Helena, Ca., U.S. C2 82
Saint Helena, co., La., U.S. . D5 95
Saint Helena, dep., Afr. H5 42
Saint Helena Island, i., S.C., U.S. G6 117
Saint Helena Sound, strt., S.C., U.S. G7 117
Sainte-Hélène [-de-Kamouraska], P.Q., Can. B8 74
Saint Helens, Eng., U.K. ... A5 12
Saint Helens, Or., U.S. B4 114
Saint Helens, Mount, vol., Wa., U.S. C3 124
Saint Helier, Jersey F5 10
Saint-Hénédine [-de-Beauharnois], P.Q., Can. q19 74
Saint-Henri [-de-Lévis], P.Q., Can. C6 74
Saint Henry, Oh., U.S. B1 112
Saint-Herménégilde, P.Q., Can. D6 74
Saint-Hilaire, Fr. B2 21
Saint-Hilaire-de-Dorset, P.Q., Can. D7 74
Saint-Hippolyte, Fr. B2 21
Saint-Honoré, P.Q., Can. .. D7 74
Saint-Honoré-de-Témiscouata, P.Q., Can. B8 74
Saint-Hubert, Bel. D5 17
Saint-Hubert-de-Témiscouata, P.Q., Can. B8 74
Saint-Hugues, P.Q., Can. .. D5 74
Saint-Hyacinthe, P.Q., Can. D5 74
Saint-Hyacinthe, co., P.Q., Can. D5 74
Saint Ignace, Mi., U.S. C6 99
Saint Ignace Island, i., On., Can. o18 73
Saint Ignatius, Mt., U.S. ... C2 103
Saint Ignatius, Guy. B3 59
Saint-Ignace, N.B., Can. ... C5 71
Saint-Imier, Switz. B3 21
Saint-Irénée, P.Q., Can. ... B7 74
Saint Isidore, N.B., Can. ... B4 71
Saint-Isidore, P.Q., Can. ... q19 74
Saint-Isidore-d'Auckland, P.Q., Can. D6 74

Name	Map Ref	Page
Saint Isidore de Prescott, On., Can.	B10	73
Saint Ives, Eng., U.K.	B7	12
Saint Ives, Eng., U.K.	D2	12
Saint Jacob, Il., U.S.	E4	90
Saint Jacobs, On., Can.	D4	73
Saint Jacques, N.B., Can.	B1	71
Saint-Jacques, P.Q., Can.	D4	74
Saint-Jacques-le-Mineur, P.Q., Can.	q20	74
Saint James, Ar., U.S.	B4	81
Saint James, La., U.S.	k10	95
Saint James, Mi., U.S.	C5	99
Saint James, Mn., U.S.	G4	100
Saint James, Mo., U.S.	D6	102
Saint James, N.Y., U.S.	*n15	109
Saint James, co., La., U.S.	D5	95
Saint James, Cape, c., B.C., Can.	D2	69
Saint James City, Fl., U.S.	F4	86
Saint-Jean, co., P.Q., Can.	D4	74
Saint-Jean, stm., P.Q., Can.	A7	74
Saint-Jean, Lac, l., P.Q., Can.	A5	74
Saint Jean-Baptiste, Mb., Can.	E3	70
Saint-Jean-Chrysostome, P.Q., Can.	o17	74
Saint-Jean-d'Angély, Fr.	E3	16
Saint-Jean-de-Dieu, P.Q., Can.	A8	74
Saint-Jean-de-Luz, Fr.	F3	16
Saint-Jean-de-Matha, P.Q., Can.	C4	74
Saint-Jean-de-Maurienne, Fr.	D2	20
Saint-Jean-Port-Joli, P.Q., Can.	B7	74
Saint-Jean-sur-Richelieu, P.Q., Can.	D4	74
Saint-Jérôme, P.Q., Can.	D3	74
Saint Jo, Tx., U.S.	C4	120
Saint-Joachim, P.Q., Can.	B7	74
Saint-Joachim [-de-Courval], P.Q., Can.	D5	74
Saint Joe, Ar., U.S.	A3	81
Saint Joe, In., U.S.	B8	91
Saint Joe, La., U.S.	h12	95
Saint Joe, stm., Id., U.S.	B3	89
Saint John, N.B., Can.	D3	71
Saint John, In., U.S.	B3	91
Saint John, Ks., U.S.	E5	93
Saint John, Me., U.S.	A4	96
Saint John, N.D., U.S.	A6	111
Saint John, Wa., U.S.	B8	124
Saint John, co., N.B., Can.	D4	71
Saint John, i., V.I.U.S.	G12	64
Saint John, stm., N.A.	G19	66
Saint John, Cape, c., Nf., Can.	D4	72
Saint John, Lake, l., Nf., Can.	D4	72
Saint John, Southeast Branch, stm., N.A.	B2	96
Saint John Bay, b., Nf., Can.	C3	72
Saint John Island, i., Nf., Can.	C3	72
Saint John's, Antig.	H14	64
Saint John's, Nf., Can.	E5	72
Saint Johns, Az., U.S.	C6	80
Saint Johns, Il., U.S.	E4	90
Saint Johns, Mi., U.S.	F6	99
Saint Johns, Mo., U.S.	*f13	102
Saint Johns, Oh., U.S.	B1	112
Saint Johns, co., Fl., U.S.	C5	86
Saint Johns, stm., Fl., U.S.	B5	86
Saint Johnsbury, Vt., U.S.	C4	122
Saint Johnsbury Center, Vt., U.S.	C4	122
Saint John's Point, c., Ire.	C3	11
Saint John's Point, c., N. Ire., U.K.	C6	11
Saint Johnsville, N.Y., U.S.	B6	109
Saint John the Baptist, co., La., U.S.	D5	95
Saint Jones, stm., De., U.S.	D4	85
Saint Joseph, N.B., Can.	D5	71
Saint Joseph, Dom.	I14	64
Saint Joseph, Il., U.S.	C5	90
Saint Joseph, La., U.S.	C4	95
Saint Joseph, Mi., U.S.	F4	99
Saint Joseph, Mn., U.S.	E4	100
Saint Joseph, Mo., U.S.	B3	102
Saint Joseph, Tn., U.S.	B4	119
Saint Joseph, co., In., U.S.	A5	91
Saint Joseph, co., Mi., U.S.	G5	99
Saint-Joseph, P.Q., Can.	F5	99
Saint-Joseph, Lac, l., P.Q., Can.	n16	74
Saint Joseph, Lake, l., On., Can.	o17	73
Saint Joseph, Mart.	e18	64
Saint Joseph Bay, b., Fl., U.S.	C1	86
Saint-Joseph-de-Beauce, P.Q., Can.	C7	74
Saint-Joseph-de-la-Rive, P.Q., Can.	B7	74
Saint-Joseph-du-Lac, P.Q., Can.	p18	74
Saint Joseph Point, c., Fl., U.S.	v16	86
Saint Joseph's, Nf., Can.	E5	72
Saint Joseph Sound, strt., Fl., U.S.	o10	86
Saint-Jovite, P.Q., Can.	C3	74
Saint-Jude, P.Q., Can.	D5	74
Saint-Julien [-en-Genevois], Fr.	D1	21
Sainte-Julienne, P.Q., Can.	D4	74
Sainte-Julie-Station, P.Q., Can.	C6	74
Saint-Junien, Fr.	E4	16
Saint Just, Eng., U.K.	D2	12
Saint-Just-en-Chaussée, Fr.	E2	17
Sainte-Justine, P.Q., Can.	C7	74
Sainte-Justine [-de-Newton], P.Q., Can.	D3	74
Saint-Lambert, P.Q., Can.	q19	74
Saint-Lambert [-de-Lévis], P.Q., Can.	C6	74
Saint Landry, La., U.S.	D3	95
Saint Landry, co., La., U.S.	D3	95
Saint-Laurent, Mb., Can.	D3	70
Saint-Laurent, P.Q., Can.	p19	74
Saint-Laurent-Blangy, Fr.	D2	17
Saint-Laurent-de-la-Salanque, Fr.	F5	16
Saint-Laurent [-du-Maroni], Fr. Gu.	A4	59
Saint-Laurent [du Maroni], ter., Fr. Gu.	B4	59
Saint-Laurent-en-Grandvaux, Fr.	C1	20
Saint Lawrence, Austl.	D8	50
Saint Lawrence, Nf., Can.	E4	72
Saint Lawrence, S.D., U.S.	C7	118
Saint Lawrence, co., N.Y., U.S.	A5	109
Saint Lawrence, stm., N.A.	G19	66
Saint Lawrence, Cape, c., N.S., Can.	B9	71
Saint Lawrence, Gulf of, b., Can.	G20	66
Saint Lawrence Island, i., Ak., U.S.	C5	79
Saint Lawrence Islands National Park, On., Can.	C9	73
Saint Lazare, Mb., Can.	D1	70
Saint-Lazare, P.Q., Can.	q18	74
Saint Leo, Fl., U.S.	D4	86
Saint Leon, In., U.S.	F8	91
Saint-Léonard, N.B., Can.	B2	71
Saint-Léonard, P.Q., Can.	C5	74
Saint-Léonard, Fr.	E4	16
Saint-Léonard-de-Portneuf, P.Q., Can.	C6	74
Saint Lewis, stm., Nf., Can.	B3	72
Saint Lewis Sound, strt., Nf., Can.	B4	72
Saint Libory, Ne., U.S.	C7	104
Saint-Lô, Fr.	C3	16
Saint Louis, P.E., Can.	C5	71
Saint Louis, Sk., Can.	E3	75
Saint-Louis, Guad.	R9	65
Saint-Louis, Sen.	C1	45
Saint Louis, Mi., U.S.	E6	99
Saint Louis, Mo., U.S.	C7	102
Saint Louis, Ok., U.S.	B5	113
Saint Louis, co., Mn., U.S.	C6	100
Saint Louis, co., Mo., U.S.	C7	102
Saint Louis, stm., U.S.	D6	100
Saint-Louis, Lac, l., P.Q., Can.	q19	74
Saint Louis Bay, b., Ms., U.S.	f7	101
Saint Louis Crossing, In., U.S.	F6	91
Saint-Louis [-de-Bonsecours], P.Q., Can.	D5	74
Saint Louis-de-Gonzague, P.Q., Can.	D3	74
Saint Louis-de-Kent, N.B., Can.	C5	71
Saint-Louis-du-Ha! Ha!, P.Q., Can.	B8	74
Sainte-Louise, P.Q., Can.	B7	74
Saint Louis Park, Mn., U.S.	n12	100
Saint Louisville, Oh., U.S.	B3	112
Saint-Loup-sur-Semouse, Fr.	B2	20
Saint-Luc, Switz.	D4	21
Saint Lucas, Ia., U.S.	A6	92
Saint Lucia, ctry., N.A.	J14	64
Saint Lucia, Cape, c., S. Afr.	C5	49
Saint Lucia, Lake, l., S. Afr.	C5	49
Saint Lucia Channel, strt., N.A.	I14	64
Saint Lucie, co., Fl., U.S.	E6	86
Saint Lucie Canal, Fl., U.S.	F6	86
Sainte-Lucie-de-Beauregard, P.Q., Can.	C7	74
Saint Lucie Inlet, b., Fl., U.S.	E6	86
Sainte-Madeleine, P.Q., Can.	D4	74
Sainte-Magloire, P.Q., Can.	C7	74
Saint Magnus Bay, b., Scot., U.K.	g10	10
Saint-Maixent-l'École, Fr.	D3	16
Saint-Malachie [-Station], P.Q., Can.	C7	74
Saint Malo, Mb., Can.	E3	70
Saint Malo, Fr.	C2	16
Saint-Malo, Gulf of, b., Fr.	C2	16
Saint-Mandé, Fr.	g10	16
Saint-Marc, P.Q., Can.	C5	74
Saint-Marc, P.Q., Can.	D4	74
Saint-Marc, Haiti	E7	64
Saint-Marcel, P.Q., Can.	C7	74
Saint-Marcel-de-L'Islet, P.Q., Can.	C7	74
Saint-Marcellin, Fr.	E6	16
Saint Margaret Bay, b., Nf., Can.	C3	72
Saint Margaret's Hope, Scot., U.K.	B6	13
Saint-Marguerite, stm., P.Q., Can.	h8	72
Sainte-Marguerite, stm., P.Q., Can.	A7	74
Sainte-Marguerite-de-Dorchester, P.Q., Can.	C7	74
Sainte-Marguerite Nord-Est, stm., P.Q., Can.	A7	74
Sainte-Marie, P.Q., Can.	C6	74
Sainte-Marie, P.Q., Can.	C5	74
Sainte-Marie, Mart.	S11	65
Sainte-Marie, Il., U.S.	E5	90
Sainte-Marie, Cap, c., Madag.	i8	49
Sainte-Marie-aux-Mines, Fr.	A3	20
Sainte Marie-sur-Mer, N.B.	B5	71
Sainte-Martine, P.Q., Can.	D4	74
Saint Martin Island, i., Mi.	C4	99
Saint Martins, N.B., Can.	D4	71
Saint Martin Station, Mb.	D2	70
Saint-Martin-Boulogne, Fr.	D9	12
Saint Martin, co., La., U.S.	D4	95
Saint Martin, i., N.A.	G13	64
Saint Martin, Md., U.S.	D7	97
Saint Martin, Lake, l., Mb.	D2	70
Saint Martinville, La., U.S.	D4	95
Saint-Martory, Fr.	F4	16
Saint Mary, Ky., U.S.	C4	94
Saint Mary, Mo., U.S.	D8	102
Saint Mary, co., La., U.S.	E4	95
Saint Mary, stm., B.C., Can.	E2	68
Saint Mary, stm., N.A.	E4	68
Saint Mary, Cape, c., N.S.	E3	71
Saint Mary's, Nf., Can.	E5	72
Saint Mary's, On., Can.	D3	73
Saint Marys, Ak., U.S.	C7	79
Saint Marys, Ga., U.S.	F5	87
Saint Marys, In., U.S.	A5	91
Saint Marys, Ks., U.S.	C7	93
Saint Marys, Oh., U.S.	B1	112
Saint Marys, Pa., U.S.	D4	115
Saint Marys, W.V., U.S.	B3	125
Saint Marys, co., Md., U.S.	D4	97
Saint Marys, stm., N.S., Can.	D8	71
Saint Mary's, stm., U.S.	F5	87
Saint Marys, stm., U.S.	C8	91
Saint Marys, stm., Md., U.S.	D5	97
Saint Mary's, Cape, c., Nf., Can.	E4	72
Saint Mary's Bay, b., Nf., Can.	E5	72
Saint Marys Bay, b., N.S.	E3	71
Saint Marys City, Md., U.S.	D5	97
Saint Marys Entrance, strt., Ga., U.S.	F5	87
Saint-Mathieu, P.Q., Can.	A9	74
Saint-Mathieu, P.Q., Can.	q19	74
Saint Matthew Island, i., Ak., U.S.	C5	79
Saint Matthews, Ky., U.S.	B4	94
Saint Matthews, S.C., U.S.	D6	117
Saint-Maur-des-Fossés, Fr.	g10	16
Saint-Maurice, P.Q., Can.	C5	74
Saint-Maurice, Switz.	C3	20
Saint-Maurice, La., U.S.	C3	95
Saint-Maurice, co., P.Q., Can.	C4	74
Saint-Maurice, stm., P.Q., Can.	C5	74
Saint-Maurice, Réserve, P.Q., Can.	B4	74
Saint Meinrad, In., U.S.	H4	91
Sainte-Mélanie, P.Q., Can.	C4	74
Sainte-Memmie, Fr.	F4	17
Sainte-Menehould, Fr.	C6	16
Saint-Méthode [-de-Frontenac], P.Q., Can.	C6	74
Saint Michael, Ab., Can.	C4	68
Saint Michael, Ak., U.S.	C7	79
Saint Michael, Mn., U.S.	E5	100
Saint Michael, N.D., U.S.	B7	111
Saint Michaels, Az., U.S.	B6	80
Saint Michaels, Md., U.S.	C5	97
Saint Michaels Bay, b., Nf., Can.	B4	72
Saint-Michel, Fr.	E4	17
Saint-Michel, Fr.	D2	20
Saint-Michel [-de-Bellechasse], P.Q., Can.	C7	74
Saint-Michel-de-Napierville, P.Q., Can.	q19	74
Saint-Michel-des-Saints, P.Q., Can.	C4	74
Saint-Mihiel, Fr.	C6	16
Saint-Modeste, P.Q., Can.	B8	74
Sainte-Monique, P.Q., Can.	C5	74
Saint-Nazaire, P.Q., Can.	D5	74
Saint-Nazaire, Fr.	D2	16
Saint-Nazaire [-de-Buckland], P.Q., Can.	C7	74
Saint-Nazaire-de-Chicoutimi, P.Q., Can.	A6	74
Saint Nazianz, Wi., U.S.	D6	126
Saint Neots, Eng., U.K.	B7	12
Saint-Nérée, P.Q., Can.	C7	74
Saint-Nicolas see Sint-Niklaas, Bel.	B6	16
Saint-Nicolas, P.Q., Can.	o17	74
Saint-Nicolas-de-Port, Fr.	F6	17
Saint-Odilon, P.Q., Can.	C7	74
Saint Olaf, Ia., U.S.	B6	92
Saint-Omer, Fr.	B5	16
Saint Onge, S.D., U.S.	C2	118
Saintonge, hist reg., Fr.	E3	16
Saint-Ouen, Fr.	g10	16
Saint-Pacôme, P.Q., Can.	B8	74
Saint-Pamphile, P.Q., Can.	C8	74
Saint Paris, Oh., U.S.	B2	112
Saint-Pascal, P.Q., Can.	B8	74
Saint Patrice, Lac, l., P.Q., Can.	A7	73
Saint Paul, Ab., Can.	B5	68
Saint Paul, Ak., U.S.	D5	79
Saint Paul, Ar., U.S.	B2	81
Saint Paul, In., U.S.	F6	91
Saint Paul, Ks., U.S.	E8	93
Saint Paul, Mn., U.S.	F5	100
Saint Paul, Mo., U.S.	f12	102
Saint Paul, Ne., U.S.	C7	104
Saint Paul, Or., U.S.	h12	114
Saint Paul, S.C., U.S.	D7	117
Saint Paul, Va., U.S.	f9	123
Saint Paul, stm., Lib.	E2	45
Saint-Paul, Île, i., F.S.A.T.	I2	2
Saint-Paul-de-Chester, P.Q., Can.	D6	74
Saint-Paul-de-la-Croix, P.Q., Can.	B8	74
Saint-Paul-de-Montminy, P.Q., Can.	C7	74
Saint-Paulin, P.Q., Can.	C4	74
Saint Paul Island, i., N.S., Can.	B9	71
Saint Paul Park, Mn., U.S.	n12	100
Saint Pauls, N.C., U.S.	C4	110
Sainte-Perpétue-de-L'Islet, P.Q., Can.	B8	74
Saint Peter, Il., U.S.	E5	90
Saint Peter, Ks., U.S.	C3	93
Saint Peter, Mn., U.S.	F5	100
Saint Peter Port, Guernsey	F5	10
Saint Peters, N.S., Can.	D9	71
Saint Peters, Mo., U.S.	C7	102
Saint Peters Bay, P.E., Can.	C7	71
Saint Petersburg, Fl., U.S.	E4	86
Saint Petersburg, Pa., U.S.	D2	115
Saint Petersburg Beach, Fl., U.S.	p10	86
Saint-Philémon, P.Q., Can.	C7	74
Saint Philip, In., U.S.	I2	91
Saint-Philippe-de-Néri, P.Q., Can.	B8	74
Saint Phillips Island, i., S.C., U.S.	G6	117
Saint-Pie, P.Q., Can.	D5	74
Saint-Pierre, Mart.	I14	64
Saint-Pierre, St. P/M.	E3	72
Saint-Pierre, i., St. P/M.	E3	72
Saint-Pierre, Lac, l., P.Q., Can.	C5	74
Saint Pierre and Miquelon, dep., N.A.	E3	72
Saint-Pierre-d'Albigny, Fr.	E8	17
Saint-Pierre-en-Port, Fr.	E8	17
Saint-Pierre-Jolys, Mb.	F17	66
Saint-Pierre-Montmagny, P.Q., Can.	C7	74
Saint-Placide, P.Q., Can.	p18	74
Saint-Pol-de-Léon, Fr.	C2	17
Saint-Pol-sur-Mer, Fr.	C2	17
Saint-Pol [-sur-Ternoise], Fr.	B5	16
Saint-Pourçain, Fr.	F2	23
Saint-Prime, P.Q., Can.	A5	74
Saint-Prosper, P.Q., Can.	C7	74
Saint-Prosper-de-Dorchester, P.Q., Can.	C7	74
Saint Quentin, N.B., Can.	B2	71
Saint-Quentin, Fr.	C5	16
Saint-Raphaël, P.Q., Can.	C7	74
Saint-Raphaël, Fr.	F7	16
Saint-Raphaël-sur-Mer, N.B.	B5	71
Saint-Raymond, P.Q., Can.	C6	74
Saint-Rédempteur, P.Q., Can.	o17	74
Saint Regis, Mt., U.S.	C1	103
Saint Regis, stm., N.A.	f10	109
Saint Regis, West Branch, stm., N.Y., U.S.	f10	109
Saint Regis Falls, N.Y., U.S.	f10	109
Saint-Rémi, P.Q., Can.	D4	74
Saint-Rémi-d'Amherst, P.Q., Can.	C3	74
Saint-Rémi [-de-Tingwick], P.Q., Can.	D6	74
Saint-Roch [-de-Richelieu], P.Q., Can.	D4	74
Saint-Roch-des-Aulnaies, P.Q., Can.	B7	74
Sainte-Rose, Guad.	H14	64
Saint Rose, La., U.S.	k11	95
Sainte Rose-du-Lac, Mb., Can.	D2	70
Saint-Samuel [-Station], P.Q., Can.	D7	74
Saint Sanford, Mb., Can.	E3	70
Saint Sauveur, N.B., Can.	B4	71
Saint-Sauveur-des-Monts, P.Q., Can.	D3	74
Sainte-Savine, Fr.	C6	16
Saint-Sébastien, P.Q., Can.	D7	74
Saint-Sébastien, Cap, c., Madag.	f9	49
Saint-Sébastien [-sur-Loire], Fr.	D4	16
Saint-Sever, Fr.	F3	16
Saint-Séverin-de-Beauce, P.Q., Can.	C7	74
Saint Shotts, Nf., Can.	E5	72
Saint-Siméon, P.Q., Can.	B8	74
Saint-Siméon, Fr.	F3	17
Saint-Siméon-de-Bonaventure, P.Q., Can.	A4	71
Saint-Simon-de-Rimouski, P.Q., Can.	A8	74
Saint Simons Island, Ga., U.S.	E5	87
Saint Simons Island, i., Ga., U.S.	E5	87
Saint Simons Sound, strt., Ga., U.S.	E5	87
Saint-Sixte, P.Q., Can.	D2	74
Sainte-Sophie, P.Q., Can.	C6	74
Sainte-Sophie [-de-Lévrard], P.Q., Can.	C5	74
Saint Stephen, N.B., Can.	D2	71
Saint Stephen, S.C., U.S.	E8	117
Saint Stephens, In., U.S.	D1	78
Saint Stephen's Church, Isr. Occ.	m14	41
Saint Stephen's Gate, hist., Isr. Occ.	m14	41
Saint-Sylvère, P.Q., Can.	D6	74
Saint-Sylvestre, P.Q., Can.	D6	74
Saint Tammany, co., La., U.S.	D5	95
Sainte-Thècle, P.Q., Can.	C4	74
Saint-Théodore, P.Q., Can.	C4	74
Saint-Théophile, P.Q., Can.	D7	74
Sainte-Thérèse, P.Q., Can.	D4	74
Saint Thomas, On., Can.	E3	73
Saint Thomas, Mo., U.S.	C5	102
Saint Thomas, N.D., U.S.	A8	111
Saint Thomas, Pa., U.S.	G6	115
Saint Thomas, i., V.I.U.S.	G12	64
Saint-Thomas [-de-Joliette], P.Q., Can.	C4	74
Saint Timothée, P.Q., Can.	q18	74
Saint-Tite, P.Q., Can.	C5	74
Saint-Tite-des-Caps, P.Q., Can.	B7	74
Saint-Tropez, Fr.	F7	16
Saint-Ubalde, P.Q., Can.	C5	74
Saint-Urbain, P.Q., Can.	q19	74
Saint-Urbain-de-Charlevoix, P.Q., Can.	B7	74
Saint-Valère, P.Q., Can.	C5	74
Saint-Valérien, P.Q., Can.	D5	74
Saint-Valéry-sur-Somme, Fr.	B4	16
Saint-Vallier, P.Q., Can.	C7	74
Saint-Vallier, Fr.	E6	16
Sainte-Véronique, P.Q., Can.	C3	74
Saint-Victor, P.Q., Can.	C7	74
Saint Vincent, i., St. Vin.	U26	65
Saint-Vincent, Cape, c., Madag.	D8	49
Saint-Vincent, Cape, c., Port.	D1	22
Saint Vincent, Cape, c., Austl.	G6	50
Saint Vincent and the Grenadines, ctry., N.A.	J14	64
Saint Vincent Island, i., Fl., U.S.	C1	86
Saint Vincent Passage, strt., N.A.	J14	64
Saint Vincent's, Nf., Can.	E5	72
Saint-Vith, Bel.	D6	17
Saint Vrain, N.M., U.S.	C6	108
Saint Walburg, Sk., Can.	D1	75
Saint Wendelins, In., U.S.	H2	91
Saint Williams, On., Can.	E4	73
Saint Xavier, Mt., U.S.	E9	103
Saint-Yrieix-la-Perche, Fr.	E4	16
Saint-Zacharie, P.Q., Can.	C7	74
Saint-Zéphirin, P.Q., Can.	D5	74
Saipan, i., N. Mar. Is.	E8	6
Saipan Channel, strt., N. Mar. Is.	D7	52
Saipan International Airport, N. Mar. Is.	D7	52
Sairecabur, Cerro, mtn., S.A.	B2	55
Sajama, Nevado, mtn., Bol.	C2	55
Saka, Kenya	B6	48
Sa Kaeo, Thai.	F5	35
Sakai, Japan	H8	31
Sakākah, Sau. Ar.	C4	38
Sakakawea, Lake, res., N.D., U.S.	B3	111
Sakania, Zaire	D4	48
Sakaraha, Madag.	h8	49
Sakarya, stm., Tur.	B8	40
Sakata, Japan	D12	31
Sakchu, N. Kor.	F2	33
Sakhalin, i., Sov. Un.	D17	29
Sakiai, Sov. Un.	A7	26
Sakishima Islands, is., Japan	G9	31
Sakmara, stm., Sov. Un.	G9	28
Sakon Nakhon, Thai.	B2	34
Sakonnet, stm., R.I., U.S.	E6	116
Sakonnet Point, c., R.I., U.S.	F6	116
Sakskøbing, Den.	D5	15
Sakti, India	D7	36
Sal, stm., Sov. Un.	H14	27
Sal, Point, c., Ca., U.S.	E3	82
Sala, Swe.	H7	14
Salaberry-de-Valleyfield, P.Q., Can.	D3	74
Sala Consilina, Italy	D5	23
Saladas, Arg.	E4	55
Saladillo, Arg.	B5	54
Salado, stm., Arg.	B3	54
Salado, stm., Arg.	F3	55
Salado, stm., Mex.	B4	63
Salado, Arroyo, stm., Arg.	C3	54
Salado, Rio, stm., N.M., U.S.	D2	108
Salaga, Ghana	E4	45
Sala'ilua, W. Sam.	F11	52
Sala'ilua Bay, b., W. Sam.	F11	52
Şalālah, Oman	D5	38
Salamá, Guat.	C2	62
Salamá, Hond.	E7	63
Salamanca, Chile	A2	54
Salamanca, Mex.	m13	63
Salamanca, Spain	B3	22
Salamanca, N.Y., U.S.	C2	109
Salamat, Bahr, stm., Chad	C3	46
Salamaua, Pap. N. Gui.	k12	50
Salamina, Col.	B2	60
Salamís, Grc.	D4	25
Salamís, i., Grc.	h10	25
Salamonia, In., U.S.	D8	91
Salamonie, stm., In., U.S.	C6	91
Salamonie Lake, res., In., U.S.	C6	91
Salani, W. Sam.	G12	52
Salar de Pocitos, Arg.	D2	55
Salas, Spain	A2	22
Salavat, Sov. Un.	C5	28
Salaverry, Peru	C2	58
Salavina, Arg.	E3	55
Salawati, i., Indon.	F8	34
Sala y Gómez, Isla, i., Chile	H16	6
Salbris, Fr.	D5	16
Salcantay, Nevado, mtn., Peru	D3	58
Salcedo, Ec.	B2	58
Saldaña, S. Afr.	D2	49
Saldus, Sov. Un.	C4	27
Sale, Austl.	I6	51
Salé, Mor.	C3	44
Sale City, Ga., U.S.	E2	87
Salée, Rivière, strt., Guad.	Q8	65
Salekhard, Sov. Un.	C9	29
Salem, India	F6	36
Salem, Ar., U.S.	A4	81
Salem, Ct., U.S.	D6	84
Salem, Fl., U.S.	C3	86
Salem, Il., U.S.	E5	90
Salem, In., U.S.	G5	91
Salem, Ia., U.S.	D6	92
Salem, Ma., U.S.	A6	98
Salem, Mi., U.S.	p14	99
Salem, Mo., U.S.	D6	102
Salem, N.H., U.S.	E4	106
Salem, N.J., U.S.	D2	107
Salem, N.M., U.S.	E2	108
Salem, N.Y., U.S.	B7	109
Salem, Oh., U.S.	B5	112
Salem, Or., U.S.	C4	114
Salem, S.C., U.S.	B2	117
Salem, S.D., U.S.	D8	118
Salem, Ut., U.S.	C4	121
Salem, Va., U.S.	C2	123
Salem, W.V., U.S.	B4	125
Salem, co., N.J., U.S.	D2	107
Salem, stm., N.J., U.S.	D2	107
Salem, Lake, l., Vt., U.S.	B4	122
Salemburg, N.C., U.S.	B4	110
Salemi, Italy	F4	23
Salen, Scot., U.K.	D3	13
Salen, Scot., U.K.	D3	13
Salerno, Italy	D5	23
Salerno, Gulf of, b., Italy	D5	23
Salfit, Isr. Occ.	B7	41
Salford, Eng., U.K.	D5	10
Salgótarján, Hung.	A4	24
Salgueiro, Braz.	C3	57
Salida, Co., U.S.	C5	83
Salies-de-Béarn, Fr.	F3	16
Salihli, Tur.	D7	40
Salima, Mwi.	D5	49
Şalīmah, Wāḥat, well, Sud.	B1	51
Salin, Burma	B1	35
Salina, Az., U.S.	D6	80
Salina, Ks., U.S.	D6	93
Salina, Ut., U.S.	E4	121
Salina, Braz.	B1	56
Salina Cruz, Mex.	D5	63
Salinas, Ec.	B1	58
Salinas, stm., N.A.	B2	62
Salinas, Cape, c., Spain	C7	22
Salinas, Ca., U.S.	D3	82
Salinas, Braz.	m8	56
Salinas, Pampa de las, pl., Arg.	A3	54
Salinas de Garci Mendoza, Bol.	C2	55
Salinas National Monument, N.M., U.S.	C3	108
Salinas Peak, mtn., N.M., U.S.	D3	108
Saline, Mi., U.S.	F7	99
Saline, co., Ar., U.S.	C3	81
Saline, co., Il., U.S.	F5	90
Saline, co., Ks., U.S.	D6	93
Saline, co., Mo., U.S.	C4	102
Saline, co., Ne., U.S.	D8	104
Saline, stm., Ar., U.S.	C3	81
Saline, stm., Il., U.S.	F5	90
Saline, North Fork, stm., Il., U.S.	B3	111
Saline, South Fork, stm., Ar., U.S.	f8	81
Saline Bayou, stm., La., U.S.	B3	95
Saline Lake, res., La., U.S.	C3	95
Salineno, Tx., U.S.	F3	120
Salinópolis, Braz.	B1	57
Salins-les-Bains, Fr.	C6	16
Salisbury, Austl.	*F6	50
Salisbury, N.B., Can.	C5	71
Salisbury, Eng., U.K.	E6	10
Salisbury see Harare, Zimb.	A5	49
Salisbury Center, N.Y., U.S.	B6	109
Salisbury Heights, N.H., U.S.	D3	106
Salisbury Island, i., N.T., Can.	D17	66
Salisbury Plain, pl., Eng., U.K.	C6	12
Salish Mountains, mts., Mt., U.S.	B2	103
Salitpa, Al., U.S.	D1	78
Salix, La., U.S.	B1	92
Salkehatchie, stm., S.C., U.S.	E5	117
Salkum, Wa., U.S.	C3	124
Salladasburg, Pa., U.S.	D7	115
Sallanches, Fr.	D2	20
Salley, S.C., U.S.	D5	117
Sallis, Ms., U.S.	B4	101
Sallisaw, Ok., U.S.	B7	113
Sallūm, Khalīj as, b., Afr.	G5	40
Sallyana, Nepal	C9	37
Salm, i., Sov. Un.	B9	128
Salmās (Dīlmān), Iran	B2	39
Salmo, stm., B.C., Can.	E9	69
Salmon, Id., U.S.	D5	89
Salmon, stm., B.C., Can.	B6	69
Salmon, stm., N.B., Can.	C4	71
Salmon, stm., N.B., Can.	B2	71
Salmon, stm., N.A.	f10	109
Salmon, stm., Id., U.S.	D3	89
Salmon, Middle Fork, stm., Id., U.S.	E4	89
Salmon, South Fork, stm., Id., U.S.	E3	89
Salmon Arm, B.C., Can.	D8	69
Salmon-Bay, P.Q., Can.	C3	72
Salmon Creek, Wa., U.S.	D3	124
Salmon Creek Reservoir, res., Id., U.S.	G4	89
Salmon Falls, Ct., U.S.	D5	106
Salmon Falls Creek, stm., U.S.	G4	89
Salmon Mountain, mtn., N.H., U.S.	f7	106
Salmon Mountains, mts., Ca., U.S.	B2	82
Salmon Peak, mtn., Tx., U.S.	E2	120
Salmon Point, c., On., Can.	D7	73
Salmon River Mountains, mts., Id., U.S.	E3	89
Salmon River Reservoir, res., N.Y., U.S.	B5	109
Salmon Valley, B.C., Can.	B6	69
Salo, Fin.	G10	14
Salò, Italy	D6	20
Salol, Mn., U.S.	B3	100
Salome, Az., U.S.	D2	80
Salon-de-Provence, Fr.	F6	16
Salonika see Thessaloníki, Grc.	B4	40
Salonta, Rom.	B5	24
Salsacate, Arg.	A3	54
Salsette, i., India	H4	37
Salsk, Sov. Un.	H13	27
Salsomaggiore Terme, Italy	D4	80
Salt, stm., Az., U.S.	D4	80
Salt, stm., Ky., U.S.	C4	94
Salt, stm., Mo., U.S.	B6	102
Salt, Middle Fork, stm., Mo., U.S.	B5	102
Salt, North Fork, stm., Mo., U.S.	B5	102
Salt, South Fork, stm., Mo., U.S.	B5	102
Salta, Arg.	D2	55
Salta, prov., Arg.	D3	55
Saltash, Eng., U.K.	D3	12
Saltburn-by-the-Sea, Eng., U.K.	F8	13
Salt Cay, i., Bah.	m18	64
Saltcoats, Sk., Can.	F4	75
Saltcoats, Scot., U.K.	E4	13
Salt Creek, stm., Il., U.S.	C4	90
Salt Creek, stm., Ne., U.S.	f10	93
Salt Creek, stm., N.M., U.S.	h11	104
Salt Creek, stm., Oh., U.S.	D5	108
Salt Creek, stm., Wy., U.S.	C6	127
Saltee Islands, is., Ire.	E6	11
Salter Path, N.C., U.S.	C6	110
Salters, S.C., U.S.	D8	117
Saltese, Mt., U.S.	C1	103
Salt Fork, Ok., U.S.	A4	113
Saltholm, i., Den.	C6	15
Saltillo, Mex.	B4	63
Saltillo, In., U.S.	G5	91
Saltillo, Ms., U.S.	A5	101
Saltillo, Tn., U.S.	B3	119
Salt Lake, co., Ut., U.S.	C3	121
Salt Lake, l., Hi., U.S.	g10	88
Salt Lake City, Ut., U.S.	C4	121
Salt Lick, Ky., U.S.	B6	94
Salto, Braz.	m8	56
Salto, Ur.	F5	82
Salto Grande, Braz.	C3	56
Salton Sea, l., Ca., U.S.	F5	82
Saltonstall, Lake, l., Ct., U.S.	D4	84
Saltpond, Ghana	E4	45
Salt River Indian Reservation, Az., U.S.	k9	80
Salt River Range, mts., Wy., U.S.	D2	127
Salt Rock, W.V., U.S.	C2	125
Saltsjöbaden (part of Nacka), Swe.	t36	14
Saltspring Island, i., B.C., Can.	C6	69
Salt Springs, Fl., U.S.	C5	86
Saltville, Va., U.S.	f10	123
Salt Wells Creek, stm., Wy., U.S.	E4	127
Salud, Pan.	k10	62
Saluda, N.C., U.S.	f10	110
Saluda, S.C., U.S.	C4	117
Saluda, Va., U.S.	C6	123
Saluda, co., S.C., U.S.	C4	117
Saluda, stm., S.C., U.S.	C4	117
Salûr, India	C7	36
Salus, Ar., U.S.	B1	81
Saluvia, Pa., U.S.	F5	115
Saluzzo, Italy	D2	23
Salvador, Braz.	B9	57
Salvador, Sk., Can.	D1	75
Salvador, Lake, l., La., U.S.	E5	95
Salvage, Nf., Can.	D5	72
Salvatierra, Mex.	m13	63
Salwá, Baḥr as, b., Asia	I5	39
Salween (Nù Jiāng), stm., Asia	D10	36
Salyany, Sov. Un.	D2	28

Name	Map Ref	Page
Salyer, Ca., U.S.	B2	82
Salyersville, Ky., U.S.	C6	94
Salym Marsh, sw., Sov. Un.	B8	28
Salzach, stm., Eur.	E6	18
Salzburg, Aus.	E6	18
Salzburg, state, Aus.	B8	20
Salzgitter, F.R.Ger.	B5	18
Salzwedel, Ger.D.R.	B5	18
Sama [de Langreo], Spain	A3	22
Samaipata, Bol.	C3	55
Samalá, stm., Guat.	C2	62
Samálüt, Eg.	D6	43
Samaná, Dom. Rep.	E9	64
Samaná, Bahía de, b., Dom. Rep.	E9	64
Samana Cay, i., Bah.	C7	64
Samandaği, Tur.	D10	40
Samani, Japan	E11	33
Samaniego, Col.	C2	60
Samannūd, Eg.	D3	41
Samar, i., Phil.	C7	34
Samara, stm., Sov. Un.	C4	28
Samarai, Pap. N. Gui.	m13	50
Samarga, Sov. Un.	C9	33
Samaria, Id., U.S.	G6	89
Samarinda, Indon.	F5	34
Samariapo, Ven.	B4	60
Samarkand, Sov. Un.	F9	29
Sämarrä', Iraq	B4	38
Sämarrä Barrage, Iraq	E14	40
Samataiuta, W. Sam.	F11	52
Samaten, Fr.	F4	16
Samawäri, Pak.	C1	37
Sambalpur, India	D7	36
Sambar, Cape, c., Indon.	F4	34
Sambas, Indon.	E3.	34
Sambava, Madag.	f10	49
Sambhal, India	C7	37
Sämbhar, India	D5	37
Sambor, Sov. Un.	G4	27
Samborombón, Bahía, b., Arg.	B5	54
Sambre, stm., Eur.	D4	17
Samburg, Tn., U.S.	A2	119
Samch'ŏk, S. Kor.	H4	33
Samch'ŏnpo, S. Kor.	I4	33
Same, Tan.	B6	48
Samedan, Switz.	C5	20
Sammamish Lake, l., Wa., U.S.	e11	124
Samnorwood, Tx., U.S.	B2	120
Samnū, Libya	D2	43
Samoa, i., U.S.	B1	82
Samokov, Bul.	D6	24
Sámos, Grc.	D6	40
Sámos, i., Grc.	D6	40
Samoset, Fl., U.S.	q10	86
Samosir, i., Indon.	E1	34
Samoth, Il., U.S.	F5	90
Samothrace see Samothráki, i., Grc.		
Samothráki (Samothrace), i., Grc.	B5	40
Sampacho, Arg.	A4	54
Sampaloc Point, c., Phil.	o13	34
Sampit, Indon.	F4	34
Sampit, stm., S.C., U.S.	E9	117
Sampson, co., N.C., U.S.	B4	110
Sampwe, Zaire	C5	48
Sam Rayburn Reservoir, res., Tx., U.S.	D5	120
Samsang, China	B9	37
Samsø, i., Den.	C4	15
Samsø Bælt, strt., Den.	C4	15
Samson, Al., U.S.	D3	78
Samsun, Tur.	B11	40
Samtown, La., U.S.	*C3	95
Samtredia, Sov. Un.	A14	40
Samuels, Id., U.S.	A2	89
Samui, i., Thai.	H4	35
Samus, Sov. Un.	D25	8
Samut Sakhon, Thai.	C2	34
San, Mali	D4	45
San, stm., Asia	F7	35
San, stm., Eur.	C7	26
San'ā', Yemen	D4	38
Sanaag, prov., Som.	C6	47
San Acacia, N.M., U.S.	C3	108
San Acacio, Co., U.S.	D5	83
Sanaga, stm., Cam.	E2	46
San Agustín, Col.	C2	60
San Agustin, Cape, c., Phil.	D7	34
San Agustin, Plains of, pl., N.M., U.S.	C2	108
San Agustín de Valle Fértil, Arg.	A3	54
Sanak Islands, is., Ak., U.S.	E7	79
San Ambrosio, Isla, i., Chile	F3	53
Sanana, i., Indon.	F7	34
Sanandaj, Iran	B4	38
San Andreas, Ca., U.S.	C3	82
San Andrés, Col.	D7	62
San Andrés, Isla i., Col.	D7	62
San Andrés de Giles, Arg.	g7	54
San Andres Mountains, mts., N.M., U.S.	E3	108
San Andres Peak, mtn., N.M., U.S.	E3	108
San Andrés Tetepilco (part of Mexico City), Mex.	h9	63
San Andrés Tuxtla, Mex.	h12	54
San Andrés y Providencia, dept., Col.	*D7	62
San Angelo, Tx., U.S.	D2	120
San Anselmo, Ca., U.S.	h7	82
San Antonio, Arg.	D2	55
San Antonio, Chile	A2	54
San Antonio, Chile	E2	55
San Antonio, N. Mar. Is.	D7	52
San Antonio, Phil.	o13	34
San Antonio, Fl., U.S.	D4	86
San Antonio, N.M., U.S.	k8	108
San Antonio, Tx., U.S.	E3	120
San Antonio, co., Tx., U.S.	D5	124
San Antonio, Cabo, c., Arg.	D1	64
San Antonio, Cabo, c., Cuba	C6	22
San Antonio Abad, Spain	C6	22
San Antonio Bay, b., Tx., U.S.	E4	120
San Antonio de Areco, Arg.	g7	54
San Antonio de los Baños, Cuba	C2	64
San Antonio de los Cobres, Arg.	D2	55
San Antonio Mountain, mtn., N.M., U.S.	A3	108
San Antonio Oeste, Arg.	C4	54
Sanaranate, Guat.	C2	62
San Ardo, Ca., U.S.	D3	82
Sanatorium, Ms., U.S.	D4	101
San Augustine, Tx., U.S.	D5	120
San Augustine, co., Tx., U.S.	D5	120
San Bartolomeo [in Galdo], Italy	D5	23
San Benedetto del Tronto, Italy	C4	23
San Benito, Tx., U.S.	F4	120
San Benito, co., Ca., U.S.	D3	82
San Benito Mountain, mtn., Ca., U.S.	D3	82
San Bernardino, Switz.	D7	21
San Bernardino, Ca., U.S.	E5	82
San Bernardino, co., Ca., U.S.	E5	82
San Bernardo, Chile	A2	54
San Blas, Mex.	m11	63
San Blas, Cape, c., Fl., U.S.	v16	86
San Blas, Cordillera de, mts., Pan.	F8	62
San Blas, Punta, c., Pan.	F8	62
San Bonifacio, Italy	D7	20
San Borja, Bol.	B2	55
San Borja, stm., Mex.	h9	63
San Bruno, Ca., U.S.	D2	82
San Candido, Italy	C8	20
San Carlos, Arg.	A3	54
San Carlos, Chile	B2	54
San Carlos, Mex.	B4	63
San Carlos, Nic.	F5	64
San Carlos, Phil.	o13	34
San Carlos, Az., U.S.	D5	80
San Carlos, Ca., U.S.	k8	82
San Carlos, Ur.	E2	56
San Carlos, Ven.	B4	60
San Carlos de Bariloche, Arg.	C2	54
San Carlos del Zulia, Ven.	B3	60
San Carlos de Río Negro, Ven.	C4	60
San Carlos Indian Reservation, Az., U.S.	D5	80
San Carlos Lake, res., Az., U.S.	D5	80
San Cataldo, Italy	F4	23
Sancerre, Fr.	D5	16
Sánchez, Dom. Rep.	E9	64
San Ciro de Acosta, Mex.	m14	63
San Clemente, Spain	C4	22
San Clemente, Ca., U.S.	F5	82
San Clemente Island, i., Ca., U.S.	F4	82
San Cristóbal, Arg.	A4	54
San Cristóbal, Dom. Rep.	E8	64
San Cristóbal, N.M., U.S.	A4	108
San Cristóbal, Ven.	B3	60
San Cristóbal, Isla (Chatham), i., Ec.	g6	58
San Cristóbal, Volcán, vol., Nic.	D4	62
San Cristóbal de las Casas, Mex.	D6	63
Sancti-Spíritus, Cuba	D4	64
Sancti-Spíritus, prov., Cuba	D4	64
Sanctuary, Sk., Can.	G1	75
Sancy, Puy de, mtn., Fr.	E5	16
Sand, stm., Ab., Can.	o14	33
Sanda, Japan	E3	13
Sanda, i., Scot., U.K.	D5	34
San Daniele del Friuli, Italy	C9	20
Sandaré, Mali	D2	45
Sanday, i., Scot., U.K.	A5	10
Sanday Sound, b., Scot., U.K.	A6	13
Sandborn, In., U.S.	G3	91
Sand Brook, N.J., U.S.	C3	107
Sand Coulee, Mt., U.S.	C5	103
Sand Creek, Wi., U.S.	D2	126
Sand Creek, stm., In., U.S.	F6	91
Sand Creek, stm., Ks., U.S.	g12	93
Sand Creek, stm., Wy., U.S.	C7	127
Sand Draw, Wy., U.S.	*D4	127
Sande, Nor.	p28	14
Sandefjord, Nor.	p28	14
Sanders, Az., U.S.	B6	80
Sanders, Ky., U.S.	B5	94
Sanders, Mt., U.S.	D9	103
Sanders, co., Mt., U.S.	C1	103
Sanderson, Tx., U.S.	D1	120
Sandersville, Ga., U.S.	D4	87
Sandersville, Ms., U.S.	D4	101
Sandfly Lake, l., Sk., Can.	B2	75
Sandford, In., U.S.	E2	91
Sand Fork, W.V., U.S.	C4	125
Sandhammaren, c., Swe.	I6	15
Sand Hill, Mn., U.S.	h13	98
Sandhill, Ms., U.S.	C4	101
Sand Hill, stm., Mn., U.S.	C2	100
Sand Hill, stm., Nf., Can.	B3	72
Sandhill, Peru	D4	58
Sandia, Peru	F3	58
Sandia, Tx., U.S.	E4	120
Sandia Crest, mtn., N.M., U.S.	k8	108
Sandia Indian Reservation, N.M., U.S.	k7	108
Sandia Mountains, mts., N.M., U.S.	k8	108
Sandia Park, N.M., U.S.	k8	108
San Diego, Ca., U.S.	F5	82
San Diego, Tx., U.S.	F3	120
San Diego, co., Ca., U.S.	F5	82
San Diego, stm., Ca., U.S.	o15	82
San Diego, Cabo, c., Arg.	h12	54
San Diego Naval Station, mil., Ca., U.S.	o15	82
San Diego Naval Training Center, mil., Ca., U.S.	o15	82
Sandikli, Tur.	C8	40
Sandila, India	C7	36
Sandilands, Mb., Can.	E3	70
San Dimas, Mex.	E7	52
San Dimas, Ca., U.S.	*m13	82
Sand Island, i., Mid. Is.	K3	52
Sand Island, i., Hi., U.S.	g10	88
Sand Island, i., Wi., U.S.	B3	126
Sand Islet, i., Mid. Is.	J3	52
Sand Lake, Mi., U.S.	E5	99
Sand Key, i., Fl., U.S.	E4	86
Sandlick Creek, stm., W.V., U.S.	n13	125
Sand Mountain, mtn., U.S.	B3	78
Sandnes, Nor.	H1	14
Sandoa, Zaire	C3	48
Sandomierz, Pol.	C6	26
Sandon, B.C., Can.	D9	69
Sandoná, Col.	C2	60
Sandoval, Il., U.S.	E4	90
Sandoval, co., N.M., U.S.	B2	108
Sandover, stm., Austl.	D6	50
Sandown, Eng., U.K.	D6	12
Sandown, N.H., U.S.	E4	106
Sand Point, On., Can.	B8	73
Sand Point, Ak., U.S.	D7	79
Sandpoint, Id., U.S.	A2	89
Sands, Ms., U.S.	B3	101
Sands Key, i., Fl., U.S.	s3	86
Sandspit, B.C., Can.	C2	69
Sand Springs, Mt., U.S.	C9	103
Sand Springs, Ok., U.S.	A5	113
Sandston, Va., U.S.	m18	123
Sandstone, Austl.	E2	50
Sandstone, Mn., U.S.	D6	100
Sandstone, W.V., U.S.	D4	125
Sandtown, De., U.S.	D3	85
Sandusky, Mi., U.S.	E8	99
Sandusky, N.Y., U.S.	C2	109
Sandusky, Oh., U.S.	A3	112
Sandusky, co., Oh., U.S.	B2	112
Sandusky Bay, b., Oh., U.S.	A3	112
Sandvig, Den.	C8	15
Sandviken, Swe.	G7	14
Sandwich, Il., U.S.	B5	90
Sandwich, Ma., U.S.	C7	98
Sandwich Bay, b., Nf., Can.	B3	72
Sandwich Range, mts., N.H., U.S.	C3	106
Sandwick, B.C., Can.	E5	69
Sandwith, Sk., Can.	D1	75
Sandy, Or., U.S.	B4	114
Sandy, Ut., U.S.	C4	121
Sandy, stm., Me., U.S.	D2	96
Sandy Bay Mountain, mtn., Me., U.S.	C2	96
Sandy Brook, stm., Ct., U.S.	A3	84
Sandy Cape, c., Austl.	D9	50
Sandy Creek, N.Y., U.S.	B4	109
Sandy Creek, stm., Oh., U.S.	B4	112
Sandy Creek, stm., Ok., U.S.	C2	113
Sandy Hook, Ct., U.S.	D2	84
Sandy Hook, Ky., U.S.	B6	94
Sandy Hook, Ms., U.S.	D4	101
Sandy Hook, spit, N.J., U.S.	C5	107
Sandy Island, i., S.C., U.S.	D9	117
Sandy Lake, Mb., Can.	D1	70
Sandy Lake, Pa., U.S.	D1	115
Sandy Lake, l., Nf., Can.	D3	72
Sandy Lake, l., On., Can.	n16	73
Sandy Lake, l., Sk., Can.	B2	75
Sandy Neck, pen., Ma., U.S.	C7	98
Sandy Point, c., Trin.	M24	65
Sandy Point, c., R.I., U.S.	h7	116
Sandy Point, c., V.I.U.S.	C6	65
Sandy Pond, l., Ma., U.S.	g10	98
Sandy Ridge, Al., U.S.	C3	78
Sandy Ridge, N.C., U.S.	A2	110
Sandy Ridge, Pa., U.S.	E5	115
Sandy Ridge, mtn., Va., U.S.	e9	123
Sandy Springs, Ga., U.S.	h8	87
Sandy Springs, S.C., U.S.	B2	117
Sandyville, Md., U.S.	A4	97
Sandyville, W.V., U.S.	C3	125
San Elizario, Tx., U.S.	o11	120
San Enrique, Arg.	B4	54
San Estanislao, Para.	D5	55
San Esteban, Hond.	D7	63
San Fabian, Phil.	n13	34
San Felice sul Panaro, Italy	E7	20
San Felipe, Chile	A2	54
San Felipe, Col.	C4	60
San Felipe, Mex.	m13	63
San Felipe, Ven.	A4	60
San Felipe Indian Reservation, N.M., U.S.	k8	108
San Felipe Pueblo, N.M., U.S.	B3	108
San Feliú de Guixols, Spain	B7	22
San Félix, Isla, i., Chile	F2	53
San Fernando, Arg.	A5	54
San Fernando, Chile	A2	54
San Fernando, Mex.	C5	63
San Fernando, Phil.	o13	34
San Fernando, Phil.	B6	34
San Fernando, Spain	D2	22
San Fernando, Trin.	K14	64
San Fernando, Ca., U.S.	m12	82
San Fernando de Apure, Ven.	B4	60
San Fernando de Atabapo, Ven.	C4	60
San Fernando de Henares, Spain	p17	22
San Fidel, N.M., U.S.	B2	108
Sânfjället, mtn., Swe.	F5	14
Sânfjället National Park, Swe.	F5	14
Sanford, Co., U.S.	D5	83
Sanford, Fl., U.S.	D5	86
Sanford, Me., U.S.	E2	96
Sanford, Mi., U.S.	E6	99
Sanford, N.C., U.S.	B3	110
Sanford, Tx., U.S.	B2	120
Sanford, Mount, mtn., Ak., U.S.	C11	79
San Francisco, Arg.	A4	54
San Francisco, Col.	C2	60
San Francisco, Ca., U.S.	D2	82
San Francisco, co., Ca., U.S.	D2	82
San Francisco, stm., U.S.	D6	80
San Francisco, stm., Ca., U.S.	D2	82
San Francisco, Paso de, S.A.	E2	55
San Francisco Bay, b., Ca., U.S.	h8	82
San Francisco de Borja, Mex.	B3	63
San Francisco del Oro, Mex.	B3	63
San Francisco del Rincón, Mex.	m13	63
San Francisco de Macorís, Dom. Rep.	E8	64
San Francisco Gotera, El Sal.	D3	62
San Francisco Mountains, mts., Ut., U.S.	E2	121
San Francisco Solano, Punta, c., Col.	B2	60
San Gabriel, Ca., U.S.	m12	82
San Gabriel, Punta, c., Mex.	B2	63
San Gabriel Chilac, Mex.	D5	63
San Gabriel Mountains, mts., Ca., U.S.	m12	82
San Gallan, Isla, i., Peru	n13	125
Sangamner, India	H5	37
Sangamon, co., Il., U.S.	D4	90
Sangamon, stm., Il., U.S.	C3	90
Sangatte, Fr.	D9	12
Sang-e Mäsheh, Afg.	E13	39
Sangay, Volcán, vol., Ec.	B2	58
Sanger, Ca., U.S.	D4	82
Sanger, Tx., U.S.	C4	120
Sangerhausen, Ger.D.R.	C5	18
San Germán, P.R.	B1	65
Sangerville, Me., U.S.	C3	96
Sanggau, Indon.	E4	34
Sangha, stm., Afr.	A3	46
Sangihe, i., Indon.	E7	34
San Gil, Col.	C3	60
San Gimignano, Italy	C5	20
San Giovanni in Fiore, Italy	E6	23
San Giovanni in Persiceto, Italy	E7	20
Sangju, S. Kor.	H4	33
Sängli, India	*E5	36
Sangmélima, Cam.	E2	46
San Gorgonio Mountain, mtn., Ca., U.S.	E5	82
Sangre de Cristo Mountains, mts., U.S.	C6	76
San Gregorio, Ca., U.S.	k8	82
San Gregorio, Ur.	E1	56
Sangre Grande, Trin.	N23	65
Sangro, stm., Italy	D5	23
Sangrür, India	B5	37
Sangudo, Ab., Can.	C3	68
Sangue, Rio do, stm., Braz.	B4	55
Sangüesa, Spain	A5	22
Sanguinara, stm., Italy	h8	23
Sanhedriyya (part of Jerusalem), Isr.	m14	41
Sanibel, Fl., U.S.	F4	86
Sanibel Island, i., Fl., U.S.	F4	86
San Ignacio, Belize	B3	62
San Ignacio, Bol.	B2	55
San Ignacio, Bol.	C3	55
San Ignacio, Mex.	B2	63
San Ignacio, Para.	E4	55
Sanilac, co., Mi., U.S.	E8	99
San Ildefonso, Cape, c., Phil.	B6	34
San Ildefonso [o la Granja], Spain	B3	22
San Ildefonso Peninsula, pen., Phil.	n14	34
Sanish, N.D., U.S.	B3	111
San Isidro, Peru	g7	54
San Isidro, Tx., U.S.	F3	120
San Isidro [del General], C.R.	F6	62
Sanitz, Ger.D.R.	B12	18
Saniyah, Hawr as, l., Iraq	E3	39
San Jacinto, Ca., U.S.	F5	82
San Jacinto, co., Tx., U.S.	D5	120
San Jacinto, stm., Tx., U.S.	r14	120
San Jacinto Peak, mtn., Ca., U.S.	E5	82
San Javier, Arg.	A4	54
San Javier, Bol.	C3	55
San Javier, stm., Arg.	F3	55
San Javier [de Loncomilla], Chile	B2	54
San Jerónimo, Serranía de, mts., Col.	B2	60
San Jerónimo (part of Mexico City), Mex.	h9	63
Sanjiang, China	L3	32
Sanjō, Japan	H9	33
San Joaquín, Para.	A4	55
San Joaquin, Ca., U.S.	D3	82
San Joaquin, co., Ca., U.S.	D3	82
San Joaquin, stm., Ca., U.S.	D3	82
San Joaquin Valley, val., Ca., U.S.	D3	82
San Jon, N.M., U.S.	B6	108
San Jorge, Golfo, b., Arg.	F3	53
San José, Belize	B3	62
San José, C.R.	F5	62
San José, Guat.	E6	63
San Jose, N. Mar. Is.	D7	52
San Jose, N. Mar. Is.	E7	52
San Jose, Phil.	o13	34
San Jose, Phil.	o13	34
San Jose, Phil.	C6	34
San Jose, Az., U.S.	D3	80
San Jose, Ca., U.S.	D3	82
San Jose, Il., U.S.	C4	90
San Jose, N.M., U.S.	B4	108
San José, Isla, i., Mex.	B2	63
San José [de Chiquitos, Bol.]	B2	63
San José de Feliciano, Arg.	A5	54
San José de Guanipa (El Tigrito), Ven.	B5	60
San José de Jachal, Arg.	F2	55
San José del Boquerón, Arg.	E3	55
San José del Cabo, Mex.	C3	63
San José del Guaviare, Col.	C3	60
San José de los Molinos, Peru	D2	58
San José de Mayo, Ur.	E1	56
San José de Ocuné, Col.	C3	60
San Jose Island, i., Tx., U.S.	E4	120
San Juan, Arg.	g8	54
San Juan, Phil.	p13	34
San Juan, Phil.	n13	34
San Juan, P.R.	G11	64
San Juan, Co., U.S.	D6	83
San Juan, Tx., U.S.	F3	120
San Juan, prov., Arg.	A3	54
San Juan, co., Co., U.S.	D3	83
San Juan, co., N.M., U.S.	A1	108
San Juan, co., Ut., U.S.	F5	121
San Juan, co., Wa., U.S.	A3	124
San Juan, stm., Arg.	A3	54
San Juan, stm., B.C., Can.	g11	69
San Juan, stm., Co., U.S.	C2	60
San Juan, stm., N.A.	E8	63
San Juan, Cabezas de, c., P.R.	C6	76
San Juan Bautista, Para.	E4	55
San Juan Capistrano, Ca., U.S.	F5	82
San Juan de Aragón (part of Mexico City), Mex.	h9	63
San Juan de Colón, Ven.	B3	60
San Juan [de la Maguana], Dom. Rep.	E8	64
San Juan de Lima, Punta, c., Mex.	D4	63
San Juan del Norte, Nic.	F6	62
San Juan de los Cayos, Ven.	A4	60
San Juan de los Lagos, Mex.	m12	63
San Juan de los Morros, Ven.	B4	60
San Juan del Sur, Nic.	E7	62
San Juan Mountains, mts., Co., U.S.	D3	83
San Juan Nepomuceno, Col.	B2	60
San Juan Pueblo, N.M., U.S.	*A3	108
San Juan y Martínez, Cuba	C2	64
San Julián, Arg.	A4	54
San Justo, Arg.	A4	54
Sankarani, stm., Afr.	*D3	45
Sankt Anton [am Arlberg], Aus.	B6	20
Sankt Blasien, F.R.Ger.	A3	19
Sankt Gallen, Switz.	A4	18
Sankt Gallen, state, Switz.	B5	20
Sankt Gallenkirch, Aus.	B8	21
Sankt Georgen [im Attergau], Aus.	B9	20
Sankt Goarshausen, F.R.Ger.	C2	19
Sankt Johann [in Tirol], Aus.	B8	20
Sankt Margrethen, Switz.	B8	21
Sankt Michaelisdonn, F.R.Ger.	E3	15
Sankt Moritz, Switz.	E4	18
Sankt Olof, Swe.	C8	15
Sankt Pölten, Aus.	D7	18
Sankt Veit [an der Glan], Aus.	E7	18
Sankt Wendel, F.R.Ger.	D2	19
Sankuru, stm., Zaire	B3	48
San Leandro, Ca., U.S.	h8	82
San Lorenzo, Arg.	A4	54
San Lorenzo, Ec.	A2	58
San Lorenzo, Hond.	D4	62
San Lorenzo, P.R.	B4	65
San Lorenzo, Ca., U.S.	h8	82
San Lorenzo, N.M., U.S.	E2	108
San Lorenzo, Cerro, mtn., S.A.	D2	54
San Lorenzo de El Escorial, Spain	B3	22
San Lucas, Bol.	D2	55
San Lucas, Mex.	C2	63
San Lucas, Cabo, c., Mex.	C3	63
San Lucas, Serranía de, mts., Col.	B3	60
San Luis, Arg.	A3	54
San Luis, Cuba	D6	64
San Luis, Guat.	D7	63
San Luis, Az., U.S.	E3	80
San Luis, Co., U.S.	D5	83
San Luis, prov., Arg.	A3	54
San Luis, stm., Mex.	h9	63
San Luis, Point, c., Ca., U.S.	E3	82
San Luis Creek, stm., Co., U.S.	C5	83
San Luis de la Paz, Mex.	m13	63
San Luis Jilotepeque, Guat.	C3	62
San Luis Obispo, Ca., U.S.	E3	82
San Luis Obispo, co., Ca., U.S.	E3	82
San Luis Pass, strt., Tx., U.S.	r14	120
San Luis Peak, mtn., Co., U.S.	D4	83
San Luis Potosí, Mex.	C4	63
San Luis Potosí, state, Mex.	C4	63
San Luis Río Colorado, Mex.	A2	63
San Luis Valley, val., Co., U.S.	D4	83
San Manuel, Az., U.S.	E5	80
San Marco [in Lamis], Italy	D5	23
San Marcos, Col.	B2	60
San Marcos, Guat.	C2	62
San Marcos, Ca., U.S.	*F5	82
San Marcos, Tx., U.S.	E4	120
San Marcos, stm., Tx., U.S.	h8	120
San Marcos de Colón, Hond.	D4	62
San Marino, ctry., Eur.	C4	23
San Martín, Ca., U.S.	k8	82
San Martín, dept., Peru	C2	58
San Martín, stm., Bol.	B3	55
San Martín, Lago (Lago O'Higgins), l., S.A.	D2	54
San Martín de la Vega, Spain	p17	22
San Martín de los Andes, Arg.	C2	54
San Martino di Castrozza, Italy	C7	20
San Mateo, Spain	B6	22
San Mateo, Ca., U.S.	D2	82
San Mateo, Fl., U.S.	C5	86
San Mateo, N.M., U.S.	B2	108
San Mateo, co., Ca., U.S.	D2	82
San Mateo, Cabo, c., Ec.	B1	58
San Mateo Mountains, mts., N.M., U.S.	D2	108
San Mateo Mountains, mts., N.M., U.S.	B2	108
San Matías, Bol.	C4	55
San Matías, Golfo, b., Arg.	C4	54
Sanmen Bay, b., China	J9	32
Sanmenxia, China	E3	31
San Miguel, El Sal.	E7	63
San Miguel, Pan.	F8	62
San Miguel, Az., U.S.	F4	80
San Miguel, N.M., U.S.	E3	108
San Miguel, co., Co., U.S.	C3	62
San Miguel, co., N.M., U.S.	B5	108
San Miguel, stm., S.A.	D2	58
San Miguel de Allende, Mex.	m13	63
San Miguel de Tucumán, Arg.	E3	55
San Miguel Island, i., Ca., U.S.	E3	82
San Miguel Mountains, mts., Co., U.S.	D2	83
Sanming, China	K7	32
Sannär, Sud.	C3	47
San Narciso, Phil.	p14	34
San Narciso, Phil.	o13	34
Sannar Dam, Sud.	C3	47
San Nicholas, Phil.	n13	34
San Nicolas, Phil.	o13	34
San Nicolás [de los Arroyos], Arg.	A4	54
San Nicolás de los Garzas, Mex.	*B4	63
San Nicolas Island, i., Ca., U.S.	F4	82
Sanniquellie, Lib.	E3	45
Sannois, Fr.	g10	16
Sano, Japan	m18	33
Sanok, Pol.	D7	26
San Onofre, Col.	B2	60
San Pablo, Phil.	o13	34
San Pablo, Ca., U.S.	*h8	82
San Pablo, Co., U.S.	D5	83
San Pablo, stm., Bol.	C3	55
San Pablo Bay, b., Ca., U.S.	g8	82
San Patricio, N.M., U.S.	D4	108
San Patricio, Bayou, stm., La., U.S.	C2	95
San Pedrillo, Punta, c., C.R.	F6	62
San Pedro, Arg.	A5	54
San Pedro, Bol.	B3	55
San Pedro, Bol.	C3	55
San Pedro, Chile	A2	54
San Pedro, Para.	D4	55
San Pedro, N.M., U.S.	*B3	108
San Pedro, dept., Para.	D4	55
San Pedro, stm., Mex.	k11	63
San Pedro, stm., N.A.	E5	80
San Pedro, Punta, c., Chile	E1	55
San Pedro, Punta, c., Ec.	n12	63
San Pedro de Atacama, Chile	A3	54
San Pedro [de Buena Vista], Bol.	C2	55
San Pedro de las Colonias, Mex.	B4	63
San Pedro de Lloc, Peru	B2	58
San Pedro de Macorís, Dom. Rep.	E9	64
San Pedro Mártir, Sierra, mts., Mex.	A1	63
San Pedro Peaks, mts., N.M., U.S.	A3	108
San Pedro Sula, Hond.	D7	63
San Pedro Tlaquepaque see Tlaquepaque, Mex.	m12	63
Sanpete, co., Ut., U.S.	D4	121
San Pierre, In., U.S.	B4	91
San Pietro, i., Italy	E2	23
San Pitch Mountains, mts., Ut., U.S.	D4	121
Sanpoil, stm., Wa., U.S.	A7	124
Sanpoil, West Fork, stm., Wa., U.S.	A7	124
San Quintin, Phil.	o13	34
San Quintín, Cabo, c., Mex.	A1	63
San Rafael, Arg.	A3	54
San Rafael, Ca., U.S.	D2	82
San Rafael, N.M., U.S.	B2	108
San Rafael, Ven.	A3	60
San Rafael, Cerro, mtn., S.A.	D2	54
San Rafael del Norte, Nic.	E7	63
San Rafael Desert, des., Ut., U.S.	E5	121
San Rafael Knob, mtn., Ut., U.S.	E5	121
San Rafael Mountains, mts., Ca., U.S.	E4	82
San Rafael Swell, plat., Ut., U.S.	E5	121
San Ramón, Peru	D2	58
San Ramón, Ur.	g9	54
San Ramón de la Nueva Orán, Arg.	D3	55
San Remo, Italy	C1	23
San Remo, N.Y., U.S.	*n15	109
San Román, Spain	A2	22
San Roque, N. Mar. Is.	D8	52
San Roque, Spain	D3	22
San Rosendo, Chile	B2	54
San Saba, Tx., U.S.	D3	120
San Saba, co., Tx., U.S.	D3	120
San Salvador, Arg.	A5	54
San Salvador, El Sal.	E7	63
San Salvador (Watling Island), i., Bah.	B6	64
San Salvador, Isla (James), i., Ec.	g5	58
San Salvador de Jujuy, Arg.	D2	55
Sansanné-Mango, Togo	D5	45
Sans Bois Mountains, mts., Ok., U.S.	B6	113
San Sebastián (part of San José), C.R.	F5	62
San Sebastián, Spain	A5	22
San Sebastián, Cabo, c., Arg.	h12	54
San Sebastián de los Reyes, Spain	o17	22
Sansepolcro, Italy	C4	23
San Severo, Italy	D5	23
San Simeon, Ca., U.S.	E3	82
San Simon, Az., U.S.	E6	80
San Simon, stm., Az., U.S.	E6	80
Santa, Peru	C2	58
Santa, Id., U.S.	B2	89
Santa, stm., Peru	C2	58
Santa Ana, Bol.	B2	55
Santa Ana, Bol.	B1	58
Santa Ana, El Sal.	E7	63
Santa Ana, Mex.	A2	63
Santa Ana, Peru	D3	58
Santa Ana, Ca., U.S.	F5	82
Santa Ana, stm., Ca., U.S.	n13	82
Santa Ana [de Barcelona], Ven.	B5	60
Santa Ana Indian Reservation, N.M., U.S.	h7	108
Santa Ana Mountains, mts., Ca., U.S.	n13	82
Santa Ana Pueblo, N.M., U.S.	B3	108
Santa Anita (part of Mexico City), Mex.	h9	63
Santa Anna, Tx., U.S.	D3	120
Santa Bárbara, Braz.	B4	56
Santa Bárbara, Chile	D2	54
Santa Bárbara, Hond.	C3	62
Santa Barbara, Ca., U.S.	E4	82
Santa Barbara, co., Ca., U.S.	E3	82
Santa Barbara Channel, strt., Ca., U.S.	E3	82
Santa Bárbara d'Oeste, Braz.	m8	57
Santa Catalina, Arg.	D2	55
Santa Catalina, Gulf of, b., Ca., U.S.	F5	82
Santa Catalina Island, i., Ca., U.S.	F4	82
Santa Catalina Mountains, mts., Az., U.S.	E5	80
Santa Catarina, Mex.	*B4	63
Santa Catarina, state, Braz.	B7	56
Santa Catarina, Ilha de, i., Braz.	D3	56
Santa Clara, Cuba	C4	64
Santa Clara, Mex.	D2	82
Santa Clara, Ca., U.S.	D2	82
Santa Clara, N.Y., U.S.	f10	109
Santa Clara, Or., U.S.	*C3	114
Santa Clara, Ut., U.S.	F2	121
Santa Clara, co., Ca., U.S.	D3	82
Santa Clara, prov., Cuba	D3	54
Santa Clara, stm., Ca., U.S.	E4	82
Santa Clara Pueblo, N.M., U.S.	*B3	108
Santa Claus, In., U.S.	H4	91
Santa Clotilde, Peru	B3	58
Santa Coloma [de Cervelló], Spain	B7	22
Santa Coloma de Farnés, Spain	B7	22
Santa Croce, Cape, c., Italy	F5	23
Santa Cruz, Bol.	C3	55
Santa Cruz, Braz.	A3	54
Santa Cruz, Chile	A2	54
Santa Cruz, C.R.	F5	62
Santa Cruz, Phil.	o13	34
Santa Cruz, Phil.	p13	34
Santa Cruz, Phil.	o12	34
Santa Cruz, N.M., U.S.	B3	108
Santa Cruz, co., Az., U.S.	F5	80
Santa Cruz, dept., Bol.	C3	55
Santa Cruz, stm., Arg.	F2	53
Santa Cruz, stm., Az., U.S.	E4	80
Santa Cruz de la Palma, Spain	m13	42
Santa Cruz de la Zarza, Spain	C4	22
Santa Cruz del Quiché, Guat.	C2	62

Name	Map Ref	Page

Santa Cruz del Sur, Cuba — D5 64
Santa Cruz de Tenerife, Spain — m13 22
Santa Cruz do Rio Pardo, Braz. — C3 56
Santa Cruz [do Sul], Braz. — D2 56
Santa Cruz Island, i., Ca., U.S. — F4 82
Santa Cruz Islands, is., Sol.Is. — G10 6
Santa Cruz Mountains, mts., Jam. — F13 65
Santa Elena, Ec. — B1 58
Santa Elena, Tx., U.S. — F3 120
Santa Elena, Bahía de, b., Ec. — B1 58
Santa Elena, Cabo, c., C.R. — E7 63
Santa Elena, Punta, c., Ec. — B1 58
Santa Elena de Uairén, Ven. — C5 60
Santa Eugenia, Spain — A1 22
Santa Eulalia del Río, Spain — C6 22
Santa Fe, Arg. — A4 54
Santa Fé, Cuba — D2 64
Santa Fe (part of Mexico City), Mex. — h9 63
Santa Fe, Pan. — F7 62
Santa Fe, Spain — D4 22
Santa Fe, N.M., U.S. — B4 108
Santa Fe, Oh., U.S. — B1 112
Santa Fe, Tn., U.S. — B4 119
Santa Fe, Tx., U.S. — r14 120
Santa Fe, prov., Arg. — A4 54
Santa Fe, co., N.M., U.S. — B3 108
Santa Fe, stm., N.M., U.S. — h8 108
Santa Fe, Isla, i., Ec. — g5 58
Santa Fe Baldy, mtn., N.M., U.S. — B4 108
Santa Fe Springs, Ca., U.S. — *n12 82
Santa Filomena, Braz. — C1 57
Santai, China — E6 31
Santa Inés, Isla, i., Chile — h11 54
Santa Inés Ahuatempan, Mex. — n14 63
Santa Isabel, Arg. — B3 54
Santa Isabel see Malabo, Eq. Gui. — E1 46
Santa Isabel, P.R. — C3 65
Santa Isabel, Pico de, mtn., Eq. Gui. — *E1 46
Santa Isabel de Sihuas, Peru — E3 58
Santa Isabel do Rio Negro, Braz. — C5 59
Santa Lucía, Cuba — D6 64
Santa Lucía, Ur. — E1 56
Santa Lucía, stm., Ur. — g8 54
Santa Lucia Range, mts., Ca., U.S. — E3 82
Santa Magdalena, Isla, i., Mex. — C2 63
Santa Margarita, Isla de, i., Mex. — E3 82
Santa Margarita, Isla de, i., Mex. — C2 63
Santa María, Arg. — E2 55
Santa Maria, Braz. — D2 56
Santa Maria, Phil. — o13 34
Santa Maria, i., Port. — h9 44
Santa María, stm., Arg. — E2 55
Santa María, stm., Mex. — m14 63
Santa María, stm., Pan. — F7 62
Santa María, stm., Az., U.S. — C2 80
Santa María, Isla, i., Ec. — g5 58
Santa Maria [Capua Vetere], Italy — D5 23
Santa María Colotepec, Mex. — D5 63
Santa Maria da Vitória, Braz. — A4 56
Santa Maria del Oro, Mex. — B3 63
Santa Maria di Leuca, Cape, c., Italy — E7 23
Santa Maria Maggiore, Italy — D5 21
Santa Maria Mountains, mts., Az., U.S. — C3 80
Santa Marta, Col. — A3 60
Santa Marta, Col. — C2 22
Santa Marta Grande, Cabo de, c., Braz. — D3 56
Santa Monica, Ca., U.S. — m12 82
Santan, Az., U.S. — m9 80
Santana, Braz. — D2 57
Santana, Port. — h12 22
Santana, Coxilha de, hills, S.A. — E2 56
Santana do Cariri, Braz. — C3 57
Santana do Ipanema, Braz. — C3 57
Santana do Livramento, Braz. — E1 56
Santander, Col. — C2 60
Santander, Spain — A4 22
Santander, dept., Col. — B3 60
Santander Jiménez, Mex. — C5 63
Sant'Angelo Romano, Italy — g9 23
Santanilla, Islas, is., Hond. — B6 62
Santanoni Peak, mtn., N.Y., U.S. — A6 109
Sant'Antiocco, i., Italy — E2 23
Santañy, Spain — C7 22
Santa Paula, Ca., U.S. — E4 82
Santaquin, Ut., U.S. — D4 121
Santarém, Braz. — D7 59
Santarém, Port. — C1 22
Santaren Channel, strt., Bah. — B4 64
Santa Rita, Guam — M9 52
Santa Rita, Mt., U.S. — B4 103
Santa Rita, Ven. — A3 60
Santa Rita do Weil, Braz. — B4 58
Santa Rita Park, Ca., U.S. — D3 82
Santa Rosa, Arg. — D4 54
Santa Rosa, Arg. — A3 54
Santa Rosa, Bol. — B2 55
Santa Rosa, Col. — C4 60
Santa Rosa, Ca., U.S. — C2 82
Santa Rosa, Mo., U.S. — B3 102
Santa Rosa, N.M., U.S. — C5 108
Santa Rosa, co., Fl., U.S. — u14 86
Santa Rosa, Mount, hill, Guam — L10 52
Santa Rosa Beach, Fl., U.S. — u15 86
Santa Rosa de Aguán, Hond. — C5 62
Santa Rosa de Copán, Hond. — C3 62
Santa Rosa [de Río Primero], Arg. — A4 54
Santa Rosa Island, i., Ca., U.S. — F3 82
Santa Rosa Island, i., Fl., U.S. — u14 86
Santa Rosalía, Mex. — C3 63
Santa Rosa Range, mts., Nv., U.S. — B4 105
Santa Teresa Gallura, Italy — D2 23
Santa Úrsula Coapa (part of Mexico City), Mex. — h9 63
Santa Vitória do Palmar, Braz. — E1 56
Santa Ynez, Ca., U.S. — E3 82
Santee, U.S. — o16 82
Santee, Ne., U.S. — B8 104
Santee, S.C., U.S. — F7 117
Santee Dam, S.C., U.S. — E7 117
Santee Indian Reservation, Ne., U.S. — B8 104

Sant'Eufemia, Gulf of, b., Italy — E6 23
Santiago, Braz. — D2 56
Santiago, Chile — A2 54
Santiago, Mex. — C3 63
Santiago, Pan. — F7 62
Santiago, Para. — E4 55
Santiago, Phil. — n13 34
Santiago, stm., S.A. — B2 58
Santiago, Cape, c., Phil. — p13 34
Santiago de Cao, Peru — C2 58
Santiago [de Compostela], Spain — A1 22
Santiago de Cuba, Cuba — E6 64
Santiago de Cuba, prov., Cuba — D6 64
Santiago del Estero, Arg. — E3 55
Santiago del Estero, prov., Arg. — E3 55
Santiago [de los Caballeros], Dom. Rep. — E8 64
Santiago de Machaca, Bol. — C2 55
Santiago Island, i., Phil. — n12 34
Santiago Ixcuintla, Mex. — C3 63
Santiago Papasquiaro, Mex. — B3 63
Santiago Peak, mtn., Ca., U.S. — n13 82
Santiago Reservoir, res., Ca., U.S. — n13 82
Santiam Pass, Or., U.S. — C4 114
Santipur, India — F12 37
Santisteban del Puerto, Spain — C4 22
Santo, Tx., U.S. — B3 120
Santo Amaro, Braz. — D3 57
Santo Amaro, Ilha de, i., Braz. — m8 56
Santo Anastácio, Braz. — C2 56
Santo Ângelo, Braz. — D2 56
Santo Antônio, Braz. — C3 57
Santo Antônio, Ponta de, c., Braz. — E3 57
Santo Antônio do Içá, Braz. — D4 60
Santo Antônio de Jesus, Braz. — D3 57
Santo Corazón, Bol. — C4 55
Santo Domingo, Dom. Rep. — E9 64
Santo Domingo, stm., Mex. — n15 63
Santo Domingo de la Calzada, Spain — A4 22
Santo Domingo de los Colorados, Ec. — B2 58
Santo Domingo Indian Reservation, N.M., U.S. — h8 108
Santo Domingo Pueblo, N.M., U.S. — B3 108
Santoña, Spain — A4 22
Santos, Braz. — C3 56
Santos Dumont, Braz. — D4 57
Santo Tomás, Nic. — D5 62
Santo Tomás, Peru — D3 58
Santo Tomás, Ven. — B5 60
Santo Tomé, Arg. — E4 55
Santuit, Ma., U.S. — *C7 98
San Valentín, Cerro, mtn., Chile — D2 54
San Vicente, El Sal. — E7 63
San Vicente, N. Mar. Is. — D7 52
San Vicente de Alcántara, Spain — C2 22
San Vicente de Cañete, Peru — D2 58
San Vicente de la Barquera, Spain — A3 22
San Vicente del Caguán, Col. — C3 60
San Vicente Reservoir, res., Ca., U.S. — o16 82
San Vito al Tagliamento, Italy — B4 23
San Ygnacio, Tx., U.S. — F3 120
San Ysidro, N.M., U.S. — B3 108
Sanza Pombo, Ang. — C2 48
Sanzhan, China — B3 33
São Bento do Sul, Braz. — D3 56
São Bento do Una, Braz. — k5 57
São Bernardo do Campo, Braz. — G6 57
São Borja, Braz. — D1 56
São Carlos, Braz. — C3 56
São Cristóvão, Braz. — D3 57
São Domingos, Braz. — A3 56
São Félix do Araguaia, Braz. — E4 59
São Félix do Xingu, Braz. — D4 59
São Fidélis, Braz. — B4 56
São Francisco, Braz. — E2 56
São Francisco, stm., Braz. — C3 57
São Francisco do Sul, Braz. — D3 56
São Gabriel, Braz. — E2 56
São Gabriel da Cachoeira, Braz. — D4 60
São Gotardo, Braz. — B3 56
São Hill, Tan. — C6 48
São Jerônimo, Braz. — E2 56
São Jerônimo, Serra de, plat., Braz. — B2 56
São João da Barra, Braz. — C4 56
São João da Boa Vista, Braz. — C3 56
São João da Ponte, Braz. — B4 56
São João das Lampas, Port. — f9 22
São João del Rei, Braz. — C4 56
São João do Cariri, Braz. — h5 57
São João do Piauí, Braz. — h5 57
São João Nepomuceno, Braz. — C4 56
São Joaquim, Braz. — D3 56
São Joaquim National Park, Braz. — D2 56
São Jorge, i., Port. — g8 44
São José de Mipibu, Braz. — h6 57
São José do Barreiro, Braz. — h5 56
São José do Rio Pardo, Braz. — k8 56
São José do Rio Preto, Braz. — C3 56
São José dos Campos, Braz. — G6 57
São José dos Pinhais, Braz. — D3 56
São Leopoldo, Braz. — D2 56
São Lourenço, Braz. — C3 56
São Lourenço, stm., Braz. — B1 56
São Luís, Braz. — D3 59
São Luís, Braz. — E2 57
São Luís Gonzaga, Braz. — D2 56
São Manuel, Braz. — G4 57
São Manuel, stm., Braz. — D3 59
São Mateus, Braz. — E3 57
São Miguel, i., Port. — h9 44
São Miguel Arcanjo, Braz. — m7 56
São Miguel dos Campos, Braz. — k5 57
Saona, Isla, i., Dom. Rep. — E9 64
Saône, stm., Fr. — D6 16
São Paulo, Braz. — C3 56
São Paulo, state, Braz. — C3 56
São Paulo de Olivença, Braz. — D4 60
São Pedro, Braz. — m8 56
São Pedro do Piauí, Braz. — C2 57
São Raimundo Nonato, Braz. — C2 57
São Romão, Braz. — B3 56
São Roque, Braz. — m8 56
São Roque, Cabo de, c., Braz. — A6 57

Saorre, Mount, mtn., N.T., Can. — D16 66
São Sebastião, Ilha de, i., Braz. — C3 56
São Sebastião, Ponta, c., Moz. — B6 49
São Sebastião do Caí, Braz. — D2 56
São Sebastião do Paraíso, Braz. — C3 56
São Sepé, Braz. — E2 56
São Simão, Braz. — C3 56
São Tomé, S. Tom./P. — E1 46
São Tomé, i., S. Tom./P. — E1 46
São Tomé, Cabo de, c., Braz. — C4 56
São Tomé, Pico de, mtn., S. Tom./P. — *E1 46
Sao Tome and Principe, ctry., Afr. — E1 46
Saoura, Oued, val., Alg. — D4 44
São Vicente, Braz. — C3 56
São Vicente, Port. — h11 22
São Vicente do Braz. — D2 56
Sápai, Grc. — B5 25
Sapele, Nig. — E6 45
Sapello, N.M., U.S. — n13 108
Sapelo Island, i., Ga., U.S. — E5 87
Sapelo Sound, strt., Ga., U.S. — E5 87
Sapinero, Col. — C3 83
Sapitwa, mtn., Mwi. — E6 48
Saposoa, Peru — C2 58
Sapozhok, Sov. Un. — E13 27
Sappa Creek, stm., U.S. — E5 104
Sappa Creek, Middle Fork, stm., Ks., U.S. — C2 93
Sappa Creek, South Fork, stm., Ks., U.S. — C3 93
Sappemeer (part of Hoogezand), Neth. — A6 17
Sapphire Mountains, mts., Mt., U.S. — D3 103
Sappington, Mo., U.S. — f13 102
Sapporo, Japan — C13 31
Sapri, Italy — D5 23
Sapulpa, Ok., U.S. — B5 113
Saqqārah, Eg. — C3 41
Saqqez, Iran — C3 39
Saquarema, Braz. — C4 56
Saquena, Peru — B3 58
Saráb, Iran — C3 39
Sarābīyūm, Eg. — D4 41
Sara Buri, Thai. — E4 35
Saragossa, Tx., U.S. — D1 120
Saragossa, Al., U.S. — B2 78
Saraguro, Ec. — B2 58
Sarah, Ms., U.S. — A3 101
Sarajevo, Yugo. — D4 24
Sarakhs, Iran — C10 39
Saraktash, Sov. Un. — E20 8
Saraland, Al., U.S. — E1 78
Saramacca, dept., Sur. — B3 59
Saranac, Mi., U.S. — F5 99
Saranac, stm., N.Y., U.S. — f11 109
Saranac Inn, N.Y., U.S. — f10 109
Saranac Lake, N.Y., U.S. — f10 109
Saranac Lakes, l., N.Y., U.S. — f10 109
Saranda, Alb. — C3 40
Sarandí, stm., Ur. — D2 56
Sarandí del Yi, Ur. — E1 56
Sarandí Grande, Ur. — E1 56
Sarangani Bay, b., Phil. — D6 34
Sarangpur, India — F6 37
Saranley, Som. — E5 47
Sárapatak, Sov. Un. — D7 29
Sarapuí, Braz. — m8 56
Sarapul, Sov. Un. — B4 28
Sarasota, Fl., U.S. — E4 86
Sarasota, co., Fl., U.S. — E4 86
Sarasota Bay, b., Fl., U.S. — E4 86
Saratov, Sov. Un. — B9 28
Saratoga, Ar., U.S. — D2 81
Saratoga, Ca., U.S. — k8 82
Saratoga, In., U.S. — D8 91
Saratoga, N.C., U.S. — A5 92
Saratoga, N.C., U.S. — B5 110
Saratoga, Tx., U.S. — D5 120
Saratoga, Wy., U.S. — E6 127
Saratoga, co., N.Y., U.S. — B7 109
Saratoga Lake, l., N.Y., U.S. — C7 109
Saratoga National Historical Park, N.Y., U.S. — B7 109
Saratoga Springs, N.Y., U.S. — B7 109
Saratov, Sov. Un. — D7 29
Saravan, Iran — H11 39
Saravan, Laos — E7 35
Sarawak, state, Malay. — E4 34
Saray, Tur. — B6 25
Sarayköy, Tur. — D7 40
Sarbāz, Iran — C6 38
Sárbogárd, Hung. — B4 24
Sarca, stm., Italy — D6 20
Sarcelles, Fr. — g10 16
Sarcoxie, Mo., U.S. — D3 102
Sārda, stm., Asia — C8 37
Sardalas, Libya — C7 45
Sardegna, Col. — C4 60
Sardinia, i., Italy — F6 91
Sardis, B.C., Can. — f14 69
Sardis, Ms., U.S. — A4 101
Sardis, Tn., U.S. — B3 119
Sardis Lake, res., Ms., U.S. — A4 101
Sarektjåkkå, mtn., Swe. — D7 14
Sar-e Pol, Afg. — C12 39
Sarepta, La., U.S. — B2 95
Sarepta, Ms., U.S. — A4 101
Sargans, Switz. — B5 20
Sargent, Ga., U.S. — C2 87
Sargent, Ne., U.S. — C6 104
Sargent, co., N.D., U.S. — C8 111
Sargento Lores, Peru — C3 58
Sargodha, Pak. — A4 37
Sarh (Fort-Archambault), Chad — G8 34
Sarhad, Afg. — k17 39
Sārī, Iran — C6 39
Saría, i., Grc. — E6 25
Sarıkamış, Tur. — B14 40
Sarina, Austl. — D9 50
Sarine, stm., Switz. — C3 20
Sariñena, Spain — B5 22
Sarita, Tx., U.S. — F4 120
Sariwŏn, N. Kor. — G2 33
Sark, i., Guernsey — F5 54
Sarkad, Hung. — C11 40
Şarkışla, Tur. — B7 40
Şarköy, Tur. — B6 40
Sarlat, Fr. — E4 16
Sarles, N.D., U.S. — A6 111

Sarmiento, Arg. — D3 54
Sarmiento, Cerro, mtn., Chile — h11 54
Särna, Swe. — G5 14
Sarnen, Switz. — C4 20
Sarnen, Lake, l., Switz. — C4 20
Sarnia, On., Can. — E2 73
Sarny, Sov. Un. — F6 27
Särö, Swe. — A5 15
Saronic Gulf, b., Grc. — D4 25
Saronno, Italy — B2 23
Saronville, Ne., U.S. — D8 104
Saros, Gulf of, b., Tur. — B6 25
Sárospatak, Hung. — A5 24
Sarova, Sov. Un. — D14 27
Sarpsborg, Nor. — p29 14
Sarpy, co., Ne., U.S. — C9 104
Sarralbe, Fr. — F7 16
Sarrebourg, Fr. — F7 16
Sarreguemines, Fr. — C7 16
Sarre-Union, Fr. — F7 17
Sarria, Spain — A2 22
Sarstedt, F.R.Ger. — A4 19
Sartell, Mn., U.S. — E4 100
Sartène, Fr. — D2 23
Sarthe, stm., Fr. — D3 16
Sartrouville, Fr. — g9 16
Sarufutsu, Japan — D11 33
Sárvár, Hung. — B3 24
Sarvestān, Iran — G6 39
Sary-Ishikotrau Desert, des., Sov. Un. — D9 28
Sary-Ozek, Sov. Un. — E9 28
Sarysu, stm., Sov. Un. — D7 28
Sarzana, Italy — B2 23
Sasa, Az., U.S. — F4 80
Sasaginnigak Lake, l., Mb., Can. — D4 70
Sasakwa, Ok., U.S. — C5 113
Sāsarām, India — D7 36
Sasebo, Japan — E10 31
Sashemene, Eth. — D4 47
Saskatchewan, prov., Can. — E3 75
Saskatchewan, stm., Can. — F12 66
Saskatoon, Sk., Can. — E2 75
Sasovo, Sov. Un. — D13 27
Saspamco, Tx., U.S. — k7 120
Sassafras, stm., Md., U.S. — B5 97
Sassafras Mountain, mtn., U.S. — A2 117
Sassandra, I.C. — F3 45
Sassandra, stm., I.C. — E3 45
Sassari, Italy — D2 23
Sassenberg, F.R.Ger. — B3 19
Sasser, Ga., U.S. — E2 87
Sassnitz, Ger.D.R. — A6 18
Sasso Marconi, Italy — E7 20
Sassuolo, Italy — E6 20
Sastown, Lib. — F3 45
Sasu-ri, N. Kor. — F3 33
Sasykkol, Lake, l., Sov. Un. — D10 28
Satah Mountain, mtn., B.C., Can. — C5 69
Satanta, Ks., U.S. — E3 93
Sātāra, India — I4 37
Satartia, Ms., U.S. — C3 101
Sataua, W. Sam. — F11 52
Satellite Beach, Fl., U.S. — *D6 86
Säter, Swe. — G6 14
Satilla, stm., Ga., U.S. — E5 87
Satipo, Peru — D3 58
Satirlar, Tur. — D7 25
Satka, Sov. Un. — D8 29
Sätmāla Range, mts., India — H7 37
Satna, India — E8 37
Sátoraljaújhely, Hung. — A5 24
Sātpura Range, mts., India — D6 36
Satrup, F.R.Ger. — D3 15
Satsop, Wa., U.S. — B2 124
Satsuma, Al., U.S. — E1 78
Satsuma, Fl., U.S. — C5 86
Sattahip, Thai. — F4 35
Sattler, Tx., U.S. — h7 120
Satu Mare, Rom. — B6 24
Satun, Thai. — I4 35
Satura'itea, W. Sam. — F11 52
Saturna Island, i., B.C., Can. — E6 69
Satus Creek, stm., Wa., U.S. — C5 124
Sauce, Arg. — A5 54
Sauceda Mountains, mts., Az., U.S. — E3 80
Saucedas, Mex. — B3 63
Saucillo, Mex. — B3 63
Saudi Arabia, ctry., Asia — C4 38
Saufley Field Naval Air Station, mil., Fl., U.S. — u14 86
Saugatuck, Mi., U.S. — F4 99
Saugatuck, stm., Ct., U.S. — D2 84
Saugatucket, stm., R.I., U.S. — F4 116
Saugatuck Reservoir, res., Ct., U.S. — D2 84
Saugerties, N.Y., U.S. — C7 109
Saugus, Ca., U.S. — *E4 82
Saugus, Ma., U.S. — B5 98
Saugus, stm., Ma., U.S. — g11 98
Sauk, co., Wi., U.S. — E4 126
Sauk, stm., Mn., U.S. — E4 100
Sauk Centre, Mn., U.S. — E4 100
Sauk City, Wi., U.S. — E4 126
Sauk Rapids, Mn., U.S. — E4 100
Saukville, Wi., U.S. — E6 126
Saul, Fr. Gu. — C8 59
Saulgau, F.R.Ger. — D5 19
Saulgrub, F.R.Ger. — B7 20
Saulsbury, Tn., U.S. — B2 119
Saulspoort, S. Afr. — B5 110
Sault-au-Mouton, P.Q., Can. — A8 74
Sault Sainte Marie, On., Can. — p18 73
Sault Sainte Marie, Mi., U.S. — B6 99
Saulx [-de-Vesoul], Fr. — A1 21
Saumâtre, Étang, l., Haiti — E7 64
Saumur, Fr. — D3 16
Saundatti, India — D3 37
Saunders, co., Ne., U.S. — C9 104
Saunderstown, R.I., U.S. — E4 116
Saundersville, R.I., U.S. — C5 116
Saundersville, Tn., U.S. — g10 119
Saurimo, Ang. — C5 48
Sava, stm., Yugo. — B4 24
Savage, Mo., U.S. — D4 102
Savage, Ms., U.S. — A3 101
Savage, stm., Md., U.S. — k12 97

Savai'i, i., W. Sam. — G11 6
Savalou, Benin — E5 45
Savanna, Il., U.S. — A3 90
Savanna, Ok., U.S. — C6 113
Savannah, Ga., U.S. — D5 87
Savannah, Mo., U.S. — B3 102
Savannah, N.Y., U.S. — B4 109
Savannah, Oh., U.S. — B3 112
Savannah, Tn., U.S. — B3 119
Savannah, stm., U.S. — F5 117
Savannah River Plant, sci., S.C., U.S. — E4 117
Savanna-la-Mar, Jam. — E4 64
Savannakhet, Laos — D6 35
Savanna Lake, l., Md., U.S. — D6 97
Savannau, On., Can. — C4 21
Savarov, Sov. Un. — D14 27
Sāveh, Iran — D5 39
Säveni, Rom. — B8 24
Saverne, Fr. — C7 16
Saverton, Mo., U.S. — B6 102
Savery, Wy., U.S. — E5 127
Savigliano, Italy — B1 23
Savigny [-sur-Orge], Fr. — F2 17
Saville Dam, Ct., U.S. — B4 84
Savoie, dept., Fr. — D2 20
Savona, B.C., Can. — D7 69
Savona, Italy — B2 23
Savona, N.Y., U.S. — C3 109
Savonburg, Ks., U.S. — E8 93
Savonlinna, Fin. — G13 14
Savoonga, Ak., U.S. — C5 79
Savoy, Il., U.S. — C5 90
Savoy, Ma., U.S. — A1 98
Savran, Sov. Un. — G8 27
Sävsjö, Swe. — A8 15
Savur, Tur. — D13 40
Savusavu Bay, b., Fiji — H15 52
Savu Sea, Indon. — G6 34
Saw, Burma — D9 36
Sawahlunto, Indon. — F2 34
Sawākin, Sud. — D4 47
Sawankhalok, Thai. — B1 34
Sawatch Range, mts., Co., U.S. — B4 83
Sawda', Jabal as, hills, Libya — D3 43
Sawdirī, Sud. — C2 47
Sawel Mountain, mtn., N. Ire., U.K. — C4 11
Sawhāj, Eg. — D6 43
Sawknah, Libya — D3 43
Sawl, Eg. — E3 41
Sawmill, Az., U.S. — B6 80
Sawnee Mountain, mtn., Ga., U.S. — B2 87
Sawpit, Co., U.S. — D3 83
Sawyer, Lake, l., Ab., Can. — A3 68
Sawyer, Ks., U.S. — E5 93
Sawyer, Mi., U.S. — G4 99
Sawyer, Mn., U.S. — D6 100
Sawyer, N.D., U.S. — A4 111
Sawyer, Ok., U.S. — C6 113
Sawyer, co., Wi., U.S. — C2 126
Sawyers Hill, hill, Nf., Can. — E5 72
Sawyerville, P.Q., Can. — D6 74
Saxapahaw, N.C., U.S. — B3 110
Saxe, Va., U.S. — D4 123
Sexis, Va., U.S. — C7 123
Sexmundham, Eng., U.K. — B9 12
Sexon, W.V., U.S. — n13 125
Sexon, Wi., U.S. — B3 126
Saxonburg, Pa., U.S. — E2 115
Saxony, hist reg., Ger.D.R. — C6 18
Saxony-Anhalt, hist reg., Ger.D.R. — B6 19
Saxton, Ky., U.S. — D5 94
Saxton, Pa., U.S. — F5 115
Saxtons, stm., Vt., U.S. — E3 122
Saxtons River, Vt., U.S. — E3 122
Say, Niger — D5 45
Sayán, Peru — D2 58
Sayan Mountains, mts., Asia — D12 29
Saybrook, Il., U.S. — C5 90
Saybrook Manor, Ct., U.S. — D6 84
Saybrook Point, Ct., U.S. — D6 84
Saydā (Sidon), Leb. — B3 38
Şaydā, Iran — e8 22
Saye, Niger — D5 45
Sayhūt, P.D.R.Yem. — D5 38
Saylorsburg, Pa., U.S. — E11 115
Saylorville, Ia., U.S. — e8 92
Saylorville Lake, res., Ia., U.S. — C4 92
Sayner, Wi., U.S. — C4 126
Sayre, Al., U.S. — B3 78
Sayre, Ok., U.S. — B2 113
Sayre, Pa., U.S. — C8 115
Sayreton, Al., U.S. — f7 78
Sayreville, N.J., U.S. — C4 107
Sayr Usa, Mong. — C6 31
Sayula, Mex. — H8 63
Sayula, Laguna de, l., Mex. — m12 63
Say'ün, P.D.R.Yem. — D5 38
Sazani, i., Alb. — C2 40
Sázava, Czech. — o18 18
Sázava, stm., Czech. — D3 18
Sázliyka, stm., Bul. — D7 24

Scarville, Ia., U.S. — A4 92
Scauri, Italy — F4 23
Sceaux, Fr. — g10 16
Scenic, S.D., U.S. — D3 118
Sceptre, Sk., Can. — G1 75
Schaal, l., Eur. — C1 15
Schaefferstown, Pa., U.S. — F9 115
Schaerbeek (Schaarbeek), Bel. — *D4 17
Schaffer, Mi., U.S. — C3 99
Schaffhausen, Switz. — E4 18
Schaffhausen, state, Switz. — B4 20
Schagen, Neth. — B4 17
Schaghticoke, N.Y., U.S. — C7 109
Schaller, Ia., U.S. — B2 92
Schangnau, Switz. — C4 21
Schärding, Aus. — E8 19
Scharnhörn, i., F.R.Ger. — E2 15
Schaumburg, Il., U.S. — h8 90
Schefferville, P.Q., Can. — h13 74
Schell City, Mo., U.S. — C3 102
Schell Creek Range, mts., Nv., U.S. — D7 105
Schellsburg, Pa., U.S. — F4 115
Schenectady, N.Y., U.S. — C7 109
Schenectady, co., N.Y., U.S. — C6 109
Schenefeld, F.R.Ger. — D3 15
Schenevus, N.Y., U.S. — C5 109
Scherer, Lake, res., Ga., U.S. — C3 87
Schererville, In., U.S. — B3 91
Scherfede, F.R.Ger. — B4 19
Schertz, Tx., U.S. — h7 120
Scheveningen (part of The Hague), Neth. — B4 17
Schiedam, Neth. — B6 16
Schiermonnikoog, i., Neth. — A6 17
Schifferstadt, F.R.Ger. — D3 19
Schiller Park, Il., U.S. — k9 90
Schilpario, Italy — C6 20
Schiltigheim, Fr. — C7 16
Schio, Italy — B3 23
Schkeuditz, Ger.D.R. — B7 18
Schladming, Aus. — E6 18
Schlater, Ms., U.S. — B3 101
Schlei, b., F.R.Ger. — D3 15
Schleicher, co., Tx., U.S. — D2 120
Schleiz, Ger.D.R. — C6 19
Schleswig, Ia., U.S. — B2 92
Schleswig-Holstein, state, F.R.Ger. — D3 15
Schleswig-Holstein, hist reg., F.R.Ger. — A4 18
Schley, Va., U.S. — C6 123
Schley, co., Ga., U.S. — D2 87
Schlieren, Switz. — B4 21
Schlitz, F.R.Ger. — C4 19
Schloss Neuhaus, F.R.Ger. — B3 19
Schlüchtern, F.R.Ger. — C4 18
Schmalkalden, Ger.D.R. — C5 18
Schmölln, Ger.D.R. — C7 19
Schnackenburg, F.R.Ger. — E5 15
Schneeberg, Ger.D.R. — C7 19
Schneeberg, mtn., F.R.Ger. — C6 19
Schneider, In., U.S. — B3 91
Schoenchen, Ks., U.S. — D4 93
Schofield, Wi., U.S. — D4 126
Schofield Barracks, mil., Hi., U.S. — g9 88
Schoharie, N.Y., U.S. — C6 109
Schoharie, co., N.Y., U.S. — C6 109
Schoharie Creek, stm., N.Y., U.S. — C6 109
Scholls, Or., U.S. — h12 114
Schönbach, Aus. — D7 18
Schöneck, Ger.D.R. — C7 19
Schöngau, F.R.Ger. — E5 18
Schöningen, F.R.Ger. — B5 18
Schoodic Lake, l., Me., U.S. — C4 96
Schoolcraft, Mi., U.S. — F5 99
Schoolcraft, co., Mi., U.S. — B4 99
Schooleys Mountain, mtn., N.J., U.S. — B3 107
Schoonhoven, Neth. — C4 17
Schopfheim, F.R.Ger. — B3 20
Schorndorf, F.R.Ger. — C4 17
Schoten, Bel. — C4 17
Schötmar, F.R.Ger. — B3 19
Schouten Islands, is., Indon. — F9 34
Schramberg, F.R.Ger. — D4 19
Schram City, Il., U.S. — D4 90
Schriever, La., U.S. — E5 95
Schrobenhausen, F.R.Ger. — D5 18
Schroeder, Mn., U.S. — C8 100
Schroon Lake, N.Y., U.S. — B7 109
Schroon Lake, l., N.Y., U.S. — B7 109
Schuchk, Az., U.S. — E4 80
Schuchuli, Az., U.S. — E3 80
Schuler, Ab., Can. — D5 68
Schull, Ire. — F2 11
Schulte, Ks., U.S. — g12 93
Schülter, Ks., U.S. — B6 113
Schüpfheim, Switz. — B5 21
Schurz, Nv., U.S. — E3 105
Schussenried, F.R.Ger. — A8 21
Schüttorf, F.R.Ger. — A2 19
Schuyler, Ne., U.S. — C8 104
Schuyler, Va., U.S. — C4 123
Schuyler, co., Il., U.S. — C3 90
Schuyler, co., Mo., U.S. — A5 102
Schuyler, co., N.Y., U.S. — C4 109
Schuyler Lake, N.Y., U.S. — C5 109
Schuylerville, N.Y., U.S. — B7 109
Schuylkill, co., Pa., U.S. — E9 115
Schuylkill, stm., Pa., U.S. — F10 115
Schuylkill Haven, Pa., U.S. — E9 115
Schwabach, F.R.Ger. — D4 19
Schwäbische Alb, mts., F.R.Ger. — D4 19
Schwäbisch Gmünd, F.R.Ger. — D4 18
Schwäbisch Hall, F.R.Ger. — D4 18
Schwabmünchen, F.R.Ger. — A6 20
Schwandorf, F.R.Ger. — D6 18
Schwaner Mountains, mts., Indon. — F4 34
Schwarmstedt, F.R.Ger. — F3 15
Schwarza, stm., F.R.Ger. — A5 21
Schwarze Elster, stm., Ger.D.R. — B8 19
Schwarzenbach [an der Saale], F.R.Ger. — C6 19
Schwarzenberg, Ger.D.R. — C7 19
Schwarzenfeld, F.R.Ger. — D7 19
Schwarzheide, Ger.D.R. — B8 19
Schwedt, Ger.D.R. — B7 18
Schweich, F.R.Ger. — D2 19
Schweinfurt, F.R.Ger. — C5 18
Schwerin, Ger.D.R. — B5 18
Schwerin, Lake, l., Ger.D.R. — B5 18
Schwetzingen, F.R.Ger. — D3 19
Schwyz, Switz. — B5 20
Schwyz, state, Switz. — B4 20

Name	Map Ref	Page
Sciacca, Italy	F4	23
Science Hill, Ky., U.S.	C5	94
Scilly Isles, is., Eng., U.K.	F3	10
Scio, N.Y., U.S.	C3	109
Scio, Oh., U.S.	B4	112
Scio, Or., U.S.	C4	114
Sciota, Il., U.S.	C3	90
Scioto, co., Oh., U.S.	D3	112
Scioto, stm., Oh., U.S.	B2	112
Scioto Furnace, Oh., U.S.	D3	112
Scipio, In., U.S.	F6	91
Scipio, Ok., U.S.	B6	113
Scipio, Ut., U.S.	D3	121
Scircleville, In., U.S.	D5	91
Scituate, Ma., U.S.	B6	98
Scituate Reservoir, res., R.I., U.S.	C3	116
Sciuëref, Libya	D2	43
Scobey, Mt., U.S.	B11	103
Scofield, Ut., U.S.	D4	121
Scofield Reservoir, res., Ut., U.S.	D4	121
Scollard, Ab., Can.	D4	68
Scone, Austl.	F8	51
Scooba, Ms., U.S.	C5	101
Scopus, Mount, mtn., Isr.	m14	41
Scoresbysund, Grnld.	B17	128
Scotch Plains, N.J., U.S.	B4	107
Scotia, On., Can.	B5	73
Scotia, Ca., U.S.	B1	82
Scotia, Ne., U.S.	C7	104
Scotia, N.Y., U.S.	C7	109
Scotia, S.C., U.S.	F5	117
Scotland, On., Can.	D4	73
Scotland, Ar., U.S.	B3	81
Scotland, Ct., U.S.	C7	84
Scotland, Ga., U.S.	D4	87
Scotland, Il., U.S.	D6	90
Scotland, In., U.S.	G4	91
Scotland, N.H., U.S.	E2	106
Scotland, Pa., U.S.	G6	115
Scotland, S.D., U.S.	D8	118
Scotland, co., Mo., U.S.	A5	102
Scotland, co., N.C., U.S.	C3	110
Scotland, ter., U.K.	B4	10
Scotland Neck, N.C., U.S.	A5	110
Scotlandville, La., U.S.	D4	95
Scotrun, Pa., U.S.	D11	115
Scotsburn, N.S., Can.	D7	71
Scotsguard, Sk., Can.	H1	75
Scotstown, P.Q., Can.	D6	74
Scott, Sk., Can.	E1	75
Scott, Ar., U.S.	C3	81
Scott, Ga., U.S.	D4	87
Scott, La., U.S.	D3	95
Scott, Ms., U.S.	B2	101
Scott, Oh., U.S.	B1	112
Scott, co., Ar., U.S.	C1	81
Scott, co., Il., U.S.	D3	90
Scott, co., In., U.S.	G6	91
Scott, co., Ia., U.S.	C7	92
Scott, co., Ks., U.S.	D3	93
Scott, co., Ky., U.S.	B5	94
Scott, co., Mn., U.S.	F5	100
Scott, co., Ms., U.S.	C4	101
Scott, co., Mo., U.S.	D8	102
Scott, co., Tn., U.S.	C9	119
Scott, co., Va., U.S.	f9	123
Scott, i., Ant.	C31	7
Scott, sci., Ant.	B29	7
Scott, Cape, c., B.C., Can.	D3	69
Scott, Mount, mtn., Ok., U.S.	C3	113
Scott, Mount, mtn., Or., U.S.	E4	114
Scott Air Force Base, mil., Il., U.S.	E4	90
Scott City, Ks., U.S.	D3	93
Scott City, Mo., U.S.	D8	102
Scottdale, Ga., U.S.	h8	87
Scottdale, Pa., U.S.	F2	115
Scott Glacier, Ant.	C23	7
Scott Glacier, Ant.	A33	7
Scott Islands, is., B.C., Can.	D3	69
Scott Mountain, mtn., Id., U.S.	E3	89
Scott Peak, mtn., Id., U.S.	E6	89
Scott Reef, rf., Austl.	B3	50
Scott Reservoir, res., N.C., U.S.	A1	110
Scotts, Mi., U.S.	F5	99
Scottsbluff, Ne., U.S.	C2	104
Scotts Bluff, co., Ne., U.S.	C2	104
Scotts Bluff National Monument, Ne., U.S.	C2	104
Scottsboro, Al., U.S.	A3	78
Scottsburg, In., U.S.	G6	91
Scottsburg, Or., U.S.	D3	114
Scottsburg, Va., U.S.	D4	123
Scottsdale, Az., U.S.	D4	80
Scotts Hill, N.C., U.S.	C5	110
Scotts Hill, Tn., U.S.	B3	119
Scotts Mills, Or., U.S.	B4	114
Scotts Mountain, mtn., N.J., U.S.	B2	107
Scotts Valley, Ca., U.S.	*D2	82
Scottsville, Ar., U.S.	B2	81
Scottsville, Ks., U.S.	C6	93
Scottsville, Ky., U.S.	D3	94
Scottsville, N.Y., U.S.	B3	109
Scottsville, Va., U.S.	C4	123
Scott Township, Pa., U.S.	*k13	115
Scottville, Il., U.S.	D3	90
Scottville, Mi., U.S.	E4	99
Scourie, Scot., U.K.	B3	13
Scout Lake, Sk., Can.	H3	75
Scow Bay, Ak., U.S.	m23	79
Scraggly Lake, l., Me., U.S.	B4	96
Scranton, Ar., U.S.	B2	81
Scranton, Ia., U.S.	B3	92
Scranton, Ks., U.S.	D8	93
Scranton, Ky., U.S.	C6	94
Scranton, N.C., U.S.	B6	110
Scranton, N.D., U.S.	C2	111
Scranton, Pa., U.S.	D10	115
Scranton, S.C., U.S.	D8	117
Screven, Ga., U.S.	E4	87
Screven, co., Ga., U.S.	D5	87
Scribner, Ne., U.S.	C9	104
Scridain, Loch, b., Scot., U.K.	D2	13
Scrivia, stm., Italy	E4	20
Scugog, Lake, l., On., Can.	C6	73
Scullville, N.J., U.S.	E3	107
Scunthorpe, Eng., U.K.	D6	13
Scuol (Schuls), Switz.	E5	18
Scurry, co., Tx., U.S.	C2	120
Scutari see Shkodra, Alb.	A2	40
Scutari, Lake, l., Eur.	D4	24
Scyrene, Al., U.S.	D2	78
Scyros see Skíros, i., Grc.	C5	40
Seaboard, N.C., U.S.	A5	110
Seabreeze, De., U.S.	F5	85
Sea Bright, N.J., U.S.	C5	107
Seabrook, Md., U.S.	*C4	97
Seabrook, N.H., U.S.	E5	106
Seabrook, Tx., U.S.	r14	120
Seabrook Beach, N.H., U.S.	E5	106
Seabrook Island, i., S.C., U.S.	F7	117
Sea Cliff, N.Y., U.S.	*E7	109
Seadrift, Tx., U.S.	E4	120
Seaford, De., U.S.	F3	85
Seaford, N.Y., U.S.	*E7	109
Seaford, Va., U.S.	h15	123
Seaforth, On., Can.	D3	73
Seaforth, Mn., U.S.	F3	100
Seagoville, Tx., U.S.	n10	120
Sea Girt, N.J., U.S.	C4	107
Seagrave, On., Can.	C6	73
Seagraves, Tx., U.S.	C1	120
Seagrove, N.C., U.S.	B3	110
Seaham, Eng., U.K.	F7	13
Seahouses, Eng., U.K.	E7	13
Sea Isle City, N.J., U.S.	E3	107
Seal, stm., Mb., Can.	f8	70
Seal Bay, b., Ant.	B11	7
Seal Beach, Ca., U.S.	*n12	82
Seal Cove, N.B., Can.	E3	71
Seal Cove, Nf., Can.	D3	72
Seal Cove, Me., U.S.	D4	96
Seale, Al., U.S.	C4	78
Sealevel, N.C., U.S.	C6	110
Seal Harbor, Me., U.S.	D4	96
Seal Lake, l., Nf., Can.	g9	72
Seal Point, c., P.E., Can.	C5	71
Seal Rock, Or., U.S.	C2	114
Sealston, Va., U.S.	B5	123
Sealy, Tx., U.S.	E4	120
Seama, N.M., U.S.	B2	108
Seaman, Oh., U.S.	D2	112
Seaman Range, mts., Nv., U.S.	F6	105
Seanor, Pa., U.S.	F4	115
Searchlight, Nv., U.S.	H7	105
Searcy, Ar., U.S.	B4	81
Searcy, co., Ar., U.S.	B3	81
Searight, Al., U.S.	D3	78
Searles, Al., U.S.	B2	78
Searles, Mn., U.S.	F4	100
Searles Lake, l., Ca., U.S.	E5	82
Sears, Mi., U.S.	E5	99
Searsboro, Ia., U.S.	C5	92
Searsburg, Vt., U.S.	F3	122
Sears Falls, wtfl, Ne., U.S.	B5	104
Searsmont, Me., U.S.	D3	96
Searsport, Me., U.S.	D4	96
Searston, Nf., Can.	E2	72
Seaside, Ca., U.S.	*D3	82
Seaside, Or., U.S.	B3	114
Seaside Heights, N.J., U.S.	D4	107
Seaside Park, N.J., U.S.	D4	107
Seaton, Eng., U.K.	D4	12
Seaton, Il., U.S.	B3	90
Seat Pleasant, Md., U.S.	C4	97
Seattle, Wa., U.S.	B3	124
Seattle-Tacoma International Airport, Wa., U.S.	f11	124
Sea View, Ma., U.S.	*H13	98
Seaview, Wa., U.S.	C1	124
Seaward Roads, strt., Mid. Is.	J3	52
Seba Beach, Ab., Can.	C3	68
Sébaco, Nic.	D4	62
Sebago Lake, l., Me., U.S.	E2	96
Sebasco Estates, Me., U.S.	g8	96
Sebastian, Fl., U.S.	E6	86
Sebastian, co., Ar., U.S.	B1	81
Sebastian, Cape, c., Or., U.S.	E2	114
Sebastian Inlet, b., Fl., U.S.	E6	86
Sebastián Vizcaíno, Bahía, b., Mex.	B2	63
Sebasticook Lake, l., Me., U.S.	D3	96
Sebastopol, Ca., U.S.	C2	82
Sebastopol, Ms., U.S.	C4	101
Sebdérat, Eth.	B4	47
Sebec, Me., U.S.	C3	96
Sebec Lake, l., Me., U.S.	C3	96
Seben, Tur.	D10	31
Sebewaing, Mi., U.S.	E7	99
Şebinkarahisar, Tur.	B12	40
Sebnitz, Ger.D.R.	C7	18
Seboeis, Me., U.S.	C4	96
Seboeis, stm., Me., U.S.	B4	96
Seboeis Lake, l., Me., U.S.	*C4	96
Sebokeng, S. Afr.	g40	49
Seboomook Lake, l., Me., U.S.	C3	96
Seboyeta, N.M., U.S.	B2	108
Sebree, Ky., U.S.	C2	94
Sebrell, Va., U.S.	D5	123
Sebring, Fl., U.S.	E5	86
Sebring, Oh., U.S.	B4	112
Sebringville, On., Can.	D3	73
Secaucus, N.J., U.S.	h8	107
Secchia, stm., Italy	B3	23
Sechelt, B.C., Can.	E6	69
Sechura, Peru	C1	58
Sechura, Bahía de, b., Peru	C1	58
Sechura, Desierto de, des., Peru	C1	58
Seclin, Fr.	D3	17
Seco, Ky., U.S.	C7	94
Second Mesa, Az., U.S.	B5	80
Secor, Il., U.S.	C4	90
Secretan, Sk., Can.	G2	75
Secretary, Md., U.S.	C6	97
Secretary Island, i., N.Z.	P11	51
Section, Al., U.S.	A4	78
Sector Popular (part of Mexico City), Mex.	h9	63
Security, Co., U.S.	C6	83
Sedalia, Ab., Can.	D5	68
Sedalia, Co., U.S.	B6	83
Sedalia, In., U.S.	C4	91
Sedalia, Ky., U.S.	f9	94
Sedalia, Mo., U.S.	C4	102
Sedalia, Oh., U.S.	C2	112
Sedan, Fr.	C6	16
Sedan, Ks., U.S.	E7	93
Sedan, Mn., U.S.	E3	100
Sedan, N.M., U.S.	A6	108
Sedom, Isr.	C7	41
Sedona, Az., U.S.	C4	80
Sedot Yam, Isr.	B6	41
Sedro Woolley, Wa., U.S.	A3	124
Sedrun, Switz.	C6	21
Seebe, Ab., Can.	D3	68
Seeber, stm., Can.	C5	70
Seebert, W.V., U.S.	C4	125
Seehausen, Ger.D.R.	F5	15
Seeheim, Nmb.	C2	49
Seeis, Nmb.	B2	49
Seekonk, Ma., U.S.	C5	98
Seekonk, stm., R.I., U.S.	C4	116
Seeley, Ca., U.S.	F6	82
Seeley Lake, Mt., U.S.	C3	103
Seeleys Bay, On., Can.	C8	73
Seelow, Ger.D.R.	F8	15
Seelyville, In., U.S.	F3	91
Seelyville, Pa., U.S.	C11	115
Sées, Fr.	C4	16
Seesen, F.R.Ger.	B5	19
Seez, stm., Switz.	C7	21
Sefadu, S.L.	E2	45
Seferihisar, Tur.	C6	25
Segamat, Malay.	K5	35
Segbwema, S.L.	E2	45
Segesta, hist., Italy	F4	23
Segezha, Sov. Un.	F16	14
Segorbe, Spain	C5	22
Ségou, Mali	D3	45
Segovia, Spain	B3	22
Segozero, l., Sov. Un.	F15	14
Segré, Fr.	D3	16
Segre, stm., Eur.	B6	22
Segreganset, stm., Ma., U.S.	C5	98
Seguam Island, i., Ak., U.S.	E5	79
Seguam Pass, strt., Ak., U.S.	E5	79
Séguédine, Niger	B7	45
Séguéla, I.C.	E3	45
Seguin, Tx., U.S.	E4	120
Seguin Falls, On., Can.	B5	73
Segundo, Co., U.S.	D6	83
Segura, stm., Spain	C5	22
Seh Konj, Küh-e, mtn., Iran	F8	39
Sehnkwehn, Lib.	F6	45
Sehore, India	I6	37
Seibert, Co., U.S.	B8	83
Seiling, Ok., U.S.	A3	113
Seille, stm., Fr.	F6	17
Seinäjoki, Fin.	F10	14
Seine, stm., Fr.	C4	16
Seine, Bay of the, est., Fr.	C3	16
Seine-et-Marne, dept., Fr.	F3	17
Seixal, Port.	f9	22
Sejerby, Den.	C5	15
Sejero, i., Den.	C5	15
Sejero Bugt, b., Den.	C5	15
Sekenke, Tan.	B5	48
Seki, Japan	o15	33
Sekiu, Wa., U.S.	A1	124
Sekondi-Takoradi, Ghana	F4	45
Sekota, Eth.	C4	47
Selah, Wa., U.S.	C5	124
Selangor, state, Malay.	K4	35
Selanovtsi, Bul.	D7	24
Selaru, i., Indon.	G8	34
Selatan, Cape, c., Indon.	F4	34
Selatpanjang, Indon.	L5	35
Selawik, Ak., U.S.	B7	79
Selawik Lake, l., Ak., U.S.	B7	79
Selayar, i., Indon.	G6	34
Selb, F.R.Ger.	C6	18
Selbourne, Cape, c., Ant.	g40	7
Selby, Nor.	F4	14
Selby, Eng., U.K.	A6	12
Selby, S.D., U.S.	B5	118
Selbyville, De., U.S.	G5	85
Selbyville, W.V., U.S.	C4	125
Selde, Den.	B3	15
Selden, Ks., U.S.	C3	93
Selden, N.Y., U.S.	*n15	109
Seldovia, Ak., U.S.	D9	79
Selenge, stm., Asia	B5	31
Selenica, Alb.	B2	25
Selenter, l., F.R.Ger.	D4	15
Sélestat, Fr.	C7	16
Seletyleniz, Lake, l., Sov. Un.	C8	28
Selfridge, N.D., U.S.	C5	111
Sélibaby, Maur.	C2	45
Selidovo, Sov. Un.	q20	27
Seligenstadt, F.R.Ger.	E9	19
Seliger, Lake, l., Sov. Un.	C9	27
Seligman, Az., U.S.	B3	80
Seligman, Mo., U.S.	E4	102
Selinsgrove, Pa., U.S.	E8	115
Selinunte, hist., Italy	F4	23
Selizharovo, Sov. Un.	D9	27
Selkirk, Mb., Can.	D3	70
Selkirk, On., Can.	E5	73
Selkirk, Scot., U.K.	C5	10
Selkirk Mountains, mts., N.A.	D9	69
Selle, Pic la, mtn., Haiti	C5	64
Selleck, Wa., U.S.	B4	124
Seller Lake, l., Mb., Can.	C3	70
Sellers, Al., U.S.	C3	78
Sellers, S.C., U.S.	C9	117
Sellersburg, In., U.S.	H6	91
Sellersville, Pa., U.S.	F11	115
Sells, Az., U.S.	F4	80
Selm, F.R.Ger.	B2	19
Selma, N.S., Can.	D6	71
Selma, Al., U.S.	C2	78
Selma, Ca., U.S.	D4	82
Selma, In., U.S.	D7	91
Selma, N.C., U.S.	B4	110
Selma, Or., U.S.	E3	114
Selman, Ok., U.S.	A2	113
Selmer, Tn., U.S.	B3	119
Selsey, Eng., U.K.	E7	13
Selsey Bill, c., Eng., U.K.	D7	12
Selva, Arg.	B4	54
Selvagens, Ilhas, is., Port.	m14	22
Selvas, for., Braz.	C3	56
Selvin, In., U.S.	H3	91
Selway, stm., Id., U.S.	C3	89
Selwyn Lake, l., Can.	A6	69
Selwyn Mountains, mts., Can.	D6	66
Selz, N.D., U.S.	B6	111
Seman, Al., U.S.	C3	78
Semani, stm., Alb.	B2	25
Semans, Sk., Can.	F3	75
Semara, W. Sah.	D2	44
Semarang, Indon.	G4	34
Semenovka, Sov. Un.	E9	27
Semeru, mtn., Indon.	G4	34
Seminary, Ms., U.S.	D4	101
Seminoe Dam, Wy., U.S.	D6	127
Seminoe Mountains, mts., Wy., U.S.	D6	127
Seminoe Reservoir, res., Wy., U.S.	D6	127
Seminole, Al., U.S.	E2	78
Seminole, Ok., U.S.	B5	113
Seminole, Tx., U.S.	C1	120
Seminole, co., Fl., U.S.	D5	86
Seminole, co., Ga., U.S.	F2	87
Seminole, co., Ok., U.S.	B5	113
Seminole, Lake, res., U.S.	F2	87
Seminole Park, Fl., U.S.	*p10	86
Semipalatinsk, Sov. Un.	D11	29
Semisopochnoi Island, i., Ak., U.S.	E3	79
Semitau, Indon.	E4	34
Semiyarskoye, Sov. Un.	C9	29
Semliki, stm., Afr.	A5	48
Semmes, Al., U.S.	E1	78
Semmens Lake, l., Ma., U.S.	B4	70
Semmering Pass, Aus.	E7	18
Semnān, Iran	B5	38
Semois, stm., Eur.	E5	17
Semora, N.C., U.S.	A3	110
Sempach, Switz.	B5	21
Sempacher See, l., Switz.	B5	21
Semur-en-Auxois, Fr.	D6	16
Sen, stm., Kam.	F6	35
Sena, N.M., U.S.	B4	108
Senachwine Lake, l., Il., U.S.	B4	90
Senador Pompeu, Braz.	C3	57
Sena Madureira, Braz.	C4	58
Senanga, Zam.	E3	48
Senate, Sk., Can.	H1	75
Senath, Mo., U.S.	E7	102
Senatobia, Ms., U.S.	A4	101
Sendai, Japan	D13	33
Sendai, Japan	K5	33
Sendai Bay, b., Japan	G10	33
Seneca, Il., U.S.	B5	90
Seneca, Ks., U.S.	C7	93
Seneca, Mo., U.S.	E3	102
Seneca, Ne., U.S.	B5	104
Seneca, N.M., U.S.	A6	108
Seneca, Or., U.S.	C8	114
Seneca, Pa., U.S.	D2	115
Seneca, S.C., U.S.	B2	117
Seneca, S.D., U.S.	B6	118
Seneca, Wi., U.S.	E3	126
Seneca, co., N.Y., U.S.	C4	109
Seneca, co., Oh., U.S.	A2	112
Seneca Falls, N.Y., U.S.	C4	109
Seneca Lake, l., N.Y., U.S.	C4	109
Senecaville, Oh., U.S.	C4	112
Senecaville Lake, res., Oh., U.S.	C4	112
Seneffe, Bel.	D4	17
Senegal, ctry., Afr.	C2	45
Sénégal, stm., Afr.	C2	45
Senetosa, Point, c., Italy	D2	23
Seney, Mi., U.S.	B5	99
Senftenberg, Ger.D.R.	C6	18
Senga Hill, Zam.	C5	48
Senguerr, stm., Arg.	D3	54
Senhor do Bonfim, Braz.	D2	57
Senigallia, Italy	C4	23
Senj, Yugo.	C2	24
Senja, i., Nor.	C7	14
Senlac, Sk., Can.	E1	75
Senlis, Fr.	C5	16
Senneterre, P.Q., Can.	k11	74
Senoia, Ga., U.S.	C2	87
Sens, Fr.	C5	16
Sense, stm., Switz.	C3	21
Senta, Yugo.	C5	24
Sentery, Zaire	C4	48
Sentinel, Ok., U.S.	B2	113
Sentinel Butte, N.D., U.S.	C2	111
Sentinel Butte, mtn., N.D., U.S.	C2	111
Sentinel Peak, mtn., B.C., Can.	B6	69
Sentinel Range, mts., Ant.	B4	7
Senzu, Japan	n17	33
Seo de Urgel, Spain	A6	22
Seoni, India	F7	37
Seoul (Sŏul), S. Kor.	D10	31
Sepik, stm., Pap. N. Gui.	h11	50
Sępólno [Krajeńskie], Pol.	B4	26
Sept-Îles (Seven Islands), P.Q., Can.	h13	74
Sepulga, stm., Al., U.S.	D3	78
Sequatchie, Tn., U.S.	D8	119
Sequatchie, co., Tn., U.S.	D8	119
Sequatchie, stm., Tn., U.S.	D8	119
Sequim, Wa., U.S.	A2	124
Sequoia National Park, Ca., U.S.	D4	82
Sequoia National Park, Ca., U.S.	D4	82
Sequoyah, co., Ok., U.S.	B7	113
Serafimovich, Sov. Un.	G14	27
Serafina, N.M., U.S.	B4	108
Seraing, Bel.	D5	17
Serang, Indon.	G3	34
Serasan, i., Indon.	k8	35
Serbia, hist., Yugo.	C5	24
Serdo, Eth.	C5	47
Serdobsk, Sov. Un.	E15	27
Sered', Czech.	D6	26
Şereflikoçhisar, Tur.	C9	40
Seremban, Malay.	E2	34
Serengeti Plain, pl., Tan.	B5	48
Serenje, Zam.	E5	48
Sergeant, Pa., U.S.	C4	115
Sergeant Bluff, Ia., U.S.	B1	92
Sergino, Sov. Un.	C22	8
Sergipe, state, Braz.	D3	57
Séria, Bru.	E4	34
Sérifos, Grc.	D5	25
Sérifos, i., Grc.	C5	40
Serina, Italy	E8	20
Seringapatam Reef, rf., Austl.	B3	50
Serinhaém, Braz.	k6	57
Serles, Tn., U.S.	B3	119
Sernyy Zavod, Sov. Un.	C10	29
Serón, Spain	D4	22
Serov, Sov. Un.	D9	29
Serowe, Bots.	B4	49
Serpa, Port.	D2	22
Serpentine Lakes, l., Austl.	E4	50
Serpents Mouth, strt.	K14	64
Serpukhov, Sov. Un.	D12	27
Serra dos Órgãos National Park, Braz.	h6	56
Sérrai, Grc.	B4	25
Serrana Bank, Col.	C7	62
Serra Negra, Braz.	*m8	56
Serranilla Bank, Col.	B8	62
Serra Talhada, Braz.	B2	56
Serres, Fr.	E1	20
Serrezuela, Arg.	A3	54
Serrinha, Braz.	D3	57
Sêrro, Braz.	B4	56
Sfax, Tun.	C7	44
Sertã, Port.	C1	22
Sertânia, Braz.	C3	57
Sertãozinho, Braz.	k8	56
Serua, i., Indon.	G8	34
Serui, Indon.	F9	34
Serule, Bots.	B4	49
Serutu, i., Indon.	E4	34
Sêrxü, China	E4	31
Sese Islands, is., Ug.	B5	48
Sesfontein, Nmb.	A1	49
Sesheke, Zam.	E3	48
Sesia, stm., Italy	B2	23
Sesser, Il., U.S.	E4	90
Sessums, Ms., U.S.	B5	101
Sesto [Fiorentino], Italy	C3	23
Sesto San Giovanni, Italy	D5	20
Sestri Levante, Italy	E2	20
Sestroretsk, Sov. Un.	A8	27
Setana, Japan	E9	33
Sète, Fr.	F5	16
Sete Guedas National Park, Braz.	C2	56
Sete Lagoas, Braz.	B4	56
Seth, W.V., U.S.	C3	125
Seto, Japan	I8	33
Seto Portage, B.C., Can.	D6	69
Seto Sea, Japan	I6	33
Settat, Mor.	C3	44
Settee Lake, l., Sk., Can.	B3	75
Setting Lake, l., Mb., Can.	B2	70
Settle, Eng., U.K.	F6	13
Setúbal, Port.	C1	22
Setúbal, Bay of, b., Port.	C1	22
Seul, Lac, l., On., Can.	o16	73
Seul Choix Point, c., Mi., U.S.	C5	99
Sevan, Lake, l., Sov. Un.	E3	28
Sevastopol, Sov. Un.	E6	29
Seven Devils Lake, res., Ar., U.S.	D4	81
Seven Devils Mountains, mts., Id., U.S.	D2	89
Seven Heads, c., Ire.	F3	11
Seven Hills, Oh., U.S.	h9	112
Seven Islands Bay, b., Nf., Can.	f9	72
Seven Mile Beach, N.J., U.S.	E3	107
Sevenoaks, Eng., U.K.	m13	10
Seven Persons, Ab., Can.	E5	68
Seven Sisters Peaks, mts., B.C., Can.	B3	69
Seven Springs, N.C., U.S.	B5	110
Seventy Mile House, B.C., Can.	D7	69
Severance, Co., U.S.	A6	83
Severance, Ks., U.S.	C8	93
Severance, N.H., U.S.	D4	106
Severn, Md., U.S.	B4	97
Severn, N.C., U.S.	A5	110
Severn, Va., U.S.	C6	123
Severn, stm., On., Can.	n17	73
Severn, stm., U.K.	D5	10
Severn, Mouth of the, mth., U.K.	C5	12
Severna Park, Md., U.S.	B4	97
Severnaya Zemlya, is., Sov. Un.	B11	29
Severn River, b., Md., U.S.	B4	97
Severochesky, prov., Czech.	C9	19
Severodonetsk, Sov. Un.	q21	27
Severodvinsk, Sov. Un.	C16	8
Severomorsk, Sov. Un.	C15	14
Severouralsk, Sov. Un.	C21	8
Severy, Ks., U.S.	E7	93
Sevier, Ut., U.S.	E3	121
Sevier, co., Ar., U.S.	D1	81
Sevier, co., Tn., U.S.	D10	119
Sevier, co., Ut., U.S.	E4	121
Sevier, stm., Ut., U.S.	D3	121
Sevier, East Fork, stm., Ut., U.S.	F3	121
Sevier Bridge Reservoir, res., Ut., U.S.	D4	121
Sevier Desert, des., Ut., U.S.	D3	121
Sevier Lake, l., Ut., U.S.	D2	121
Sevierville, Tn., U.S.	D10	119
Sevilla, Col.	C2	60
Sevilla, Spain	D3	22
Sevilla (Seville), Spain	D3	22
Seville see Sevilla, Spain	D3	22
Seville, Fl., U.S.	C5	86
Seville, Oh., U.S.	A4	112
Sevlievo, Bul.	D7	24
Sèvre, stm., Fr.	g11	16
Sèvre Niortaise, stm., Fr.	D3	16
Sèvres, Fr.	g9	16
Sewal, Ia., U.S.	D4	92
Sewanee, Tn., U.S.	D8	119
Seward, Ak., U.S.	C10	79
Seward, Ks., U.S.	D6	93
Seward, Ne., U.S.	D8	104
Seward, N.Y., U.S.	C6	109
Seward, Ok., U.S.	B4	113
Seward, Pa., U.S.	F3	115
Seward, co., Ks., U.S.	E3	93
Seward, co., Ne., U.S.	D8	104
Seward Peninsula, pen., Ak., U.S.	B7	79
Sewaren, N.J., U.S.	k7	107
Sewell, Chile	E3	54
Sewell, N.J., U.S.	D2	107
Sewell, stm., W.V., U.S.	D4	125
Sewickley, Pa., U.S.	E1	115
Sexsmith, Ab., Can.	B1	68
Sextonville, Wi., U.S.	E3	126
Seychelles, ctry., Afr.	G24	2
Seydişehir, Tur.	k6	57
Seydisfjördur, Ice.	n26	14
Seyhan (Sarus), stm., Tur.	C10	40
Seylac, Som.	F9	47
Seym, stm., Sov. Un.	F9	27
Seymchan, Sov. Un.	C18	29
Seymour, Austl.	H5	51
Seymour, Ct., U.S.	D3	84
Seymour, Ia., U.S.	D4	92
Seymour, Il., U.S.	C5	90
Seymour, In., U.S.	G6	91
Seymour, Mo., U.S.	D5	102
Seymour, Tn., U.S.	D10	119
Seymour, Tx., U.S.	C3	120
Seymour, Wi., U.S.	D5	126
Seymour Inlet, b., B.C., Can.	D4	69
Seymour Johnson Air Force Base, mil., N.C., U.S.	B5	110
Seymour Lake, l., Vt., U.S.	B4	122
Seymourville, Mb., U.S.	h9	95
Sézanne, Fr.	C5	16
Sezimbra, Port.	C1	22
Sezze, Italy	D4	23
Sfax, Tun.	C7	44
Shaanxi, prov., China	D6	31
Shabbona, Il., U.S.	B5	90
Shabeellaha Dhexe, prov., Som.	E6	47
Shabeellaha Hoose, prov., Som.	E5	47
Shabeelle (Shebele), stm., Afr.	E5	47
Shabogamo Lake, l., Nf., Can.	h8	72
Shabunda, Zaire	B4	48
Shabwa, P.D.R.Yem.	B6	47
Shache, China	F10	29
Shackelford, co., Tx., U.S.	C3	120
Shackleton, Sk., Can.	G1	75
Shackleton Glacier, Ant.	A31	7
Shackleton Ice Shelf, Ant.	C23	7
Shackleton Range, mts., Ant.	A10	7
Shadehill, S.D., U.S.	B3	118
Shadehill Dam, S.D., U.S.	B3	118
Shadehill Reservoir, res., S.D., U.S.	B3	118
Shades Creek, stm., Al., U.S.	g7	78
Shades Mountain, mtn., Al., U.S.	g7	78
Shadow Mountain National Recreation Area, Co., U.S.	A4	83
Shadrinsk, Sov. Un.	B6	28
Shady Cove, Or., U.S.	E4	114
Shady Dale, Ga., U.S.	C3	87
Shady Grove, Al., U.S.	D3	78
Shady Grove, Fl., U.S.	B3	86
Shady Grove, Ky., U.S.	e10	94
Shady Grove, Pa., U.S.	G6	115
Shady Point, Ok., U.S.	B7	113
Shady Rest, Ct., U.S.	D2	84
Shady Side, Md., U.S.	C4	97
Shady Spring, W.V., U.S.	D3	125
Shady Valley, Tn., U.S.	C12	119
Shafer, Lake, l., In., U.S.	C4	91
Shafer Butte, mtn., Id., U.S.	F2	89
Shafter, Ca., U.S.	E4	82
Shafter, Nv., U.S.	C7	105
Shafter, Tx., U.S.	p12	120
Shaftesbury, Eng., U.K.	C5	12
Shaftsbury, Vt., U.S.	E2	122
Shaftsbury Center, Vt., U.S.	E2	122
Shageluk, Ak., U.S.	C8	79
Shag Harbour, N.S., Can.	F4	71
Shaguotun, China	D9	32
Shahada, India	K4	35
Shahbā', Syria	F11	40
Shahbanou Farah Dam, Iran	C4	39
Shahdād (Khabīs), Iran	F8	39
Shāhdādkot, Pak.	D1	37
Shahdol, India	F8	37
Shāhganj, India	C4	36
Shahhāt, Libya	C4	43
Shāhjahānpur, India	C7	36
Shāh Jūy, Afg.	E13	39
Shāhpur, India	I6	37
Shāhpur, India	C4	36
Shāhpura, India	E5	37
Shahrak, Afg.	D12	39
Shahr-e Bābak, Iran	F8	39
Shahr Kord, Iran	C5	39
Shāhrūd see Emāmshahr, Iran	B5	38
Shāhrūd, stm., Iran	C5	39
Shakawe, Bots.	A3	49
Shakhrisyabz, Sov. Un.	B13	39
Shakhty, Sov. Un.	E7	29
Shakhunya, Sov. Un.	B3	28
Shaki, Nig.	E5	45
Shakopee, Mn., U.S.	F5	100
Shakotan, Cape, c., Japan	E10	33
Shaktoolik, Ak., U.S.	C7	79
Shala, Lake, l., Eth.	D4	47
Shalath, B.C., Can.	D6	69
Shaler Mountains, mts., N.T., Can.	B10	66
Shaler Township, Pa., U.S.	*E2	115
Shalkar, Lake, l., Sov. Un.	m12	97
Shallmar, Md., U.S.	m12	97
Shallotte, N.C., U.S.	D4	110
Shallotte Inlet, b., N.C., U.S.	D4	110
Shallowater, Tx., U.S.	C2	120
Shallow Lake, On., Can.	C3	73
Shallow Water, Ks., U.S.	D3	93
Shām, Jabal ash, mtn., Oman	D6	38
Shamattawa, Mb., Can.	B5	70
Shambaugh, Ia., U.S.	D2	92
Shambe, Sud.	G12	43
Shamīl, Iran	H8	39
Shamokin, Pa., U.S.	E8	115
Shamokin Dam, Pa., U.S.	E8	115
Shamrock, Sk., Can.	G2	75
Shamrock, Fl., U.S.	C3	86
Shamrock, Tx., U.S.	B2	120
Shamva, Zimb.	A5	49
Shandī, Sud.	F12	43
Shandon, Ca., U.S.	E3	82
Shandon, Oh., U.S.	n12	112
Shandong, prov., China	D5	31
Shandong Bandao (Shantung Peninsula), pen., China	D9	31
Shangdu, China	D5	31
Shanghai, China	E9	31
Shangqiu, China	H4	32
Shangrao, China	F8	31
Shangshui, China	E7	32
Shangsi, China	A7	36
Shangxian, China	H4	32
Shangzhi, China	B13	31
Shaniko, Or., U.S.	B6	114
Shannock, R.I., U.S.	F2	116
Shannon, Ga., U.S.	B1	87
Shannon, Il., U.S.	A4	90
Shannon, Ms., U.S.	A5	101
Shannon, co., Mo., U.S.	D6	102
Shannon, co., S.D., U.S.	D3	118
Shannon, stm., Ire.	E2	11
Shannon, Lake, l., Wa., U.S.	A4	124
Shannon, Mouth of the, mth., Ire.	E2	11
Shannon Airport, Ire.	E3	11
Shannon City, Ia., U.S.	D3	92
Shannontown, S.C., U.S.	D7	117
Shanshan, China	C3	31
Shantar Islands, is., Sov. Un.	D16	29
Shantou (Swatow), China	G8	31
Shantung, La., U.S.	h9	95
Shantung see Shandong, prov., China	D8	31

Name	Map Ref	Page
Shantung Peninsula see Shandong Bandao, pen., China	D9	31
Shanwa, Tan.	B5	48
Shanxi, prov., China	D7	31
Shaobo, China	H8	32
Shaoguan, China	G7	31
Shaowu, China	K7	32
Shaoxing, China	F9	31
Shaoyang, China	F7	31
Shap, Eng., U.K.	F6	13
Shapinsay, i., Scot., U.K.	A6	13
Shapio Lake, l., Nf., Can.	g9	72
Shapki, Sov. Un.	s32	14
Shapleigh, Me., U.S.	*E2	96
Shaqqah, Bi'r ash, well, Egypt	G5	40
Sharafkhāneh, Iran	B2	39
Sharangad, Mong.	B2	32
Sharbatāt, Ra's ash, c., Oman	D5	38
Sharbot Lake, On., Can.	C8	73
Shari, Japan	E12	33
Sharīṭah, Ra's, c., Oman	H8	39
Shark Bay, b., Austl.	E1	50
Sharkey, co., Ms., U.S.	C3	101
Shark Point, c., Fl., U.S.	H5	86
Sharktooth Mountain, mtn., B.C., Can.	E7	66
Sharm al Shaykh, Eg.	D6	43
Sharon, Ct., U.S.	B2	84
Sharon, Ga., U.S.	C4	87
Sharon, Ks., U.S.	E5	93
Sharon, Ma., U.S.	B5	98
Sharon, N.H., U.S.	E3	106
Sharon, N.D., U.S.	B8	111
Sharon, Ok., U.S.	A2	113
Sharon, Pa., U.S.	D1	115
Sharon, S.C., U.S.	B5	117
Sharon, Tn., U.S.	A3	119
Sharon, Vt., U.S.	D4	122
Sharon, W.V., U.S.	m13	125
Sharon, Wi., U.S.	F5	126
Sharon Grove, Ky., U.S.	D2	94
Sharon Hill, Oh., U.S.	p20	115
Sharon Park, Oh., U.S.	n12	112
Sharon Springs, Ks., U.S.	D2	93
Sharon Springs, N.Y., U.S.	C6	109
Sharon Valley, Ct., U.S.	B2	84
Sharonville, Oh., U.S.	n13	112
Sharp, co., Ar., U.S.	A4	81
Sharpe, Lake, res., S.D., U.S.	C6	118
Sharpe Lake, l., Mb., Can.	B5	70
Sharpes, Fl., U.S.	D6	86
Sharpley, De., U.S.	h7	85
Sharpley, In., U.S.	D3	92
Sharpsburg, Ky., U.S.	B6	94
Sharpsburg, Md., U.S.	B2	97
Sharpsburg, N.C., U.S.	B5	110
Sharpsburg, Pa., U.S.	k14	115
Sharps Chapel, Tn., U.S.	C10	119
Sharpsville, In., U.S.	D5	91
Sharpsville, Pa., U.S.	D1	115
Sharp Top Mountain, mtn., Ar., U.S.	C2	81
Sharptown, Md., U.S.	C6	97
Sharptown, N.J., U.S.	D2	107
Sharya, Sov. Un.	B3	28
Shashi, China	E7	31
Shashi, stm., Afr.	B4	49
Shashke, Sov. Un.	C7	28
Shasta, co., Ca., U.S.	B3	82
Shasta, Mount, vol., Ca., U.S.	B2	82
Shasta Lake, res., Ca., U.S.	B2	82
Shatney Mountain, mtn., N.H., U.S.	f7	106
Shatsk, Sov. Un.	D13	27
Shattuck, Ok., U.S.	A2	113
Shattuckville, Ma., U.S.	A2	98
Shatura, Sov. Un.	D12	27
Shauck, Oh., U.S.	B3	112
Shaunavon, Sk., Can.	H1	75
Shaw, Ms., U.S.	B3	101
Shaw, Or., U.S.	k12	114
Shaw Air Force Base, mil., S.C., U.S.	D7	117
Shawanaga, On., Can.	B4	73
Shawangunk Mountains, mts., N.Y., U.S.	D6	109
Shawano, Wi., U.S.	D5	126
Shawano, co., Wi., U.S.	D5	126
Shawano Lake, l., Wi., U.S.	D5	126
Shawboro, N.C., U.S.	A6	110
Shawbridge, P.Q., Can.	D3	74
Shawhan, Ky., U.S.	B5	94
Shawinigan, P.Q., Can.	C5	74
Shawinigan Lake, B.C., Can.	g12	69
Shawinigan-Sud, P.Q., Can.	C5	74
Shawmut, Al., U.S.	C4	78
Shawmut, Mt., U.S.	D7	103
Shawnee, Co., U.S.	B5	83
Shawnee, Ga., U.S.	D5	87
Shawnee, Ks., U.S.	k16	93
Shawnee, Oh., U.S.	C3	112
Shawnee, Ok., U.S.	B5	113
Shawnee, Wy., U.S.	D7	127
Shawnee, co., Ks., U.S.	D8	93
Shawnee Hills, Oh., U.S.	B2	112
Shawneetown, Il., U.S.	F5	90
Shawsheen, stm., Ma., U.S.	f11	98
Shawsville, Md., U.S.	A4	97
Shawsville, Va., U.S.	C2	123
Shawville, P.Q., Can.	D3	74
Shaxian, China	F8	31
Shayang, China	I5	32
Shay Gap, Austl.	D3	50
Shchekino, Sov. Un.	D11	27
Shchelkovo, Sov. Un.	n18	27
Shchetovo, Sov. Un.	q22	27
Shchigry, Sov. Un.	F11	27
Shchors, Sov. Un.	F9	27
Shchuchinsk, Sov. Un.	C8	32
Shchurovo, Sov. Un.	n18	27
Shebele (Shabeelle), stm., Afr.	D5	47
Sheberghān, Afg.	A4	36
Sheboygan, Wi., U.S.	E6	126
Sheboygan, co., Wi., U.S.	k10	126
Sheboygan, stm., Wi., U.S.	k10	126
Sheboygan Falls, Wi., U.S.	E6	126
Shedd, Or., U.S.	C3	114
Shedden, On., Can.	E3	73
Shediac, N.B., Can.	C5	71
Sheekh, Som.	D6	47
Sheelin, Lough, l., Ire.	D3	10
Sheenjek, stm., Ak., U.S.	B11	79
Sheep Creek, stm., Ab., Can.	C1	68
Sheep Haven, b., Ire.	B4	11
Sheep Mountain, mtn., Az., U.S.	E1	80
Sheep Mountain, mtn., Wy., U.S.	B5	127
Sheep Peak, mtn., Nv., U.S.	G6	105
Sheep Range, mts., Nv., U.S.	G6	105
Sheep's Head, c., Ire.	F2	11
Sheeps Heaven Mountain, mtn., Ma., U.S.	A1	98
Sheerness, Ab., Can.	D5	68
Sheerness, Eng., U.K.	C8	12
Sheet Harbour, N.S., Can.	E7	71
Shefar'am, Isr.	B7	41
Shefayim, Isr.	g10	41
Sheffield, N.Z.	O14	51
Sheffield, Eng., U.K.	D6	10
Sheffield, Al., U.S.	A2	78
Sheffield, Il., U.S.	B4	90
Sheffield, Ia., U.S.	B4	92
Sheffield, Ma., U.S.	B1	98
Sheffield, Pa., U.S.	C3	115
Sheffield, Tx., U.S.	D2	120
Sheffield, Vt., U.S.	B4	122
Sheffield Lake, Oh., U.S.	A3	112
Sheffield Lake, l., Nf., Can.	D3	72
Shefford, co., P.Q., Can.	D5	74
Sherbrooke, co., P.Q., Can.	D5	74
Sheguiandah, On., Can.	B3	73
Sheho, Sk., Can.	F4	75
Shehuen, stm., Arg.	D2	54
Sheila, N.B., Can.	B5	71
Shēkhābād, Afg.	D14	39
Shekhūpura, Pak.	B4	37
Shelagski, Cape, c., Sov. Un.	B33	128
Shelagyote Peak, mtn., B.C., Can.	B4	69
Shelbiana, Ky., U.S.	C7	94
Shelbina, Mo., U.S.	B5	102
Shelburn, In., U.S.	F3	91
Shelburn, Or., U.S.	C4	114
Shelburne, N.S., Can.	F4	71
Shelburne, On., Can.	C4	73
Shelburne, Ma., U.S.	A2	98
Shelburne, Vt., U.S.	C2	122
Shelburne, co., N.S., Can.	F4	71
Shelburne Falls, Ma., U.S.	A2	98
Shelburne Falls, Vt., U.S.	C2	122
Shelburne Pond, l., Vt., U.S.	C2	122
Shelby, Al., U.S.	B3	78
Shelby, In., U.S.	B3	91
Shelby, Mi., U.S.	E4	99
Shelby, Ms., U.S.	B3	101
Shelby, Mt., U.S.	B5	103
Shelby, Ne., U.S.	C8	104
Shelby, N.C., U.S.	B1	110
Shelby, Oh., U.S.	B3	112
Shelby, co., Al., U.S.	B3	78
Shelby, co., Il., U.S.	D5	90
Shelby, co., In., U.S.	E6	91
Shelby, co., Ia., U.S.	C2	92
Shelby, co., Ky., U.S.	B4	94
Shelby, co., Mo., U.S.	B5	102
Shelby, co., Oh., U.S.	B1	112
Shelby, co., Tn., U.S.	B2	119
Shelby, co., Tx., U.S.	D5	120
Shelby City, Ky., U.S.	C5	94
Shelbyville, In., U.S.	F6	91
Shelbyville, Ky., U.S.	B4	94
Shelbyville, Mo., U.S.	B5	102
Shelbyville, Tn., U.S.	B5	119
Shelbyville, Lake, res., Il., U.S.	D5	90
Sheldahl, Ia., U.S.	e8	92
Sheldon, Il., U.S.	C6	90
Sheldon, Ia., U.S.	A2	92
Sheldon, Mo., U.S.	D3	102
Sheldon, N.D., U.S.	C8	111
Sheldon, S.C., U.S.	F6	117
Sheldon, Tx., U.S.	r14	120
Sheldon, Vt., U.S.	B3	122
Sheldon, Wi., U.S.	C3	126
Sheldon Springs, Vt., U.S.	B3	122
Sheldonville, Ma., U.S.	B5	98
Shelekhov, Gulf of, b., Sov. Un.	C18	29
Shelikof Strait, strt., Ak., U.S.	D9	79
Shell, Wy., U.S.	B5	127
Shell, stm., Mb., Can.	D1	70
Shell, Loch, b., Scot., U.K.	C2	13
Shellbrook, Sk., Can.	D2	75
Shell Creek, Tn., U.S.	C11	119
Shell Creek, stm., U.S.	A2	83
Shell Creek, stm., Wy., U.S.	B5	127
Shelley, B.C., Can.	C6	69
Shelley, Id., U.S.	F6	89
Shellharbour, Austl.	G8	51
Shell Lake, Sk., Can.	D2	75
Shell Lake, Wi., U.S.	C2	126
Shell Lake, l., Mn., U.S.	D3	100
Shell Lake, l., Wi., U.S.	C2	126
Shellman, Ga., U.S.	E2	87
Shellman Bluff, Ga., U.S.	E5	87
Shellmouth, Mb., Can.	D1	70
Shellpot Creek, stm., De., U.S.	h7	85
Shell Rock, Ia., U.S.	B5	92
Shell Rock, stm., Ia., U.S.	B5	92
Shell Rock, West Fork, stm., Ia., U.S.	B5	92
Shellsburg, Ia., U.S.	B5	92
Shelly, Mn., U.S.	C2	100
Shelly Mountain, mtn., Id., U.S.	F5	89
Shelter Harbor, R.I., U.S.	F2	116
Shelter Island, N.Y., U.S.	m16	109
Shelton, Ct., U.S.	D3	84
Shelton, Ne., U.S.	D7	104
Shelton, Wa., U.S.	B2	124
Shemogue, N.B., Can.	C5	71
Shemya Air Force Base, mil., Ak., U.S.	E2	79
Shenandoah, Ia., U.S.	D2	92
Shenandoah, Pa., U.S.	E9	115
Shenandoah, co., Va., U.S.	B4	123
Shenandoah, stm., U.S.	A5	123
Shenandoah, North Fork, stm., Va., U.S.	B4	123
Shenandoah, South Fork, stm., Va., U.S.	B4	123
Shenandoah Mountain, mtn., U.S.	B3	123
Shenandoah National Park, Va., U.S.	B4	123
Shenandoah Valley, val., U.S.	B4	123
Shenango River Lake, res., U.S.	D1	115
Shengxian, China	J9	32
Shenipsit Lake, l., Ct., U.S.	B6	84
Shenmu, China	D6	31
Shenqiu, China	H6	32
Shensi see Shaanxi, prov., China	D6	31
Shenyang, China	C9	31
Sheopur, India	E6	37
Shepard, Ab., Can.	D3	68
Shepard Island, i., Ant.	B35	7
Shepardsville, In., U.S.	E3	91
Shepaug, stm., Ct., U.S.	C2	84
Shepaug Dam, Ct., U.S.	D2	84
Shepaug Reservoir, res., Ct., U.S.	C2	84
Shepetovka, Sov. Un.	F6	27
Shepherd, Mi., U.S.	E6	99
Shepherd, Mt., U.S.	E8	103
Shepherd, Tx., U.S.	D5	120
Shepherdsville, Ky., U.S.	C4	94
Sheppard Air Force Base, mil., Tx., U.S.	C3	120
Shepparton, Austl.	G8	50
Sheppey, Isle of, i., Eng., U.K.	C8	12
Sheppton, Pa., U.S.	E9	115
Shepton Mallet, Eng., U.K.	C5	12
Sheqi, China	H5	32
Sherard, Ms., U.S.	A3	101
Sherborn, Ma., U.S.	h10	98
Sherborne, Eng., U.K.	D5	12
Sherbro Island, i., S.L.	E2	45
Sherbrooke, N.S., Can.	D8	71
Sherbrooke, P.Q., Can.	D6	74
Sherbrooke Lake, l., N.S., Can.	E5	71
Shereshevo, Sov. Un.	B8	26
Shergarh, India	D4	37
Sherghar, India	B4	37
Sheridan, Co., U.S.	*B6	83
Sheridan, Il., U.S.	B5	90
Sheridan, In., U.S.	D5	91
Sheridan, Ky., U.S.	e9	94
Sheridan, Me., U.S.	B4	96
Sheridan, Mi., U.S.	E5	99
Sheridan, Mt., U.S.	E4	103
Sheridan, Or., U.S.	B3	114
Sheridan, Wy., U.S.	B6	127
Sheridan, co., Ks., U.S.	C3	93
Sheridan, co., Mt., U.S.	B12	103
Sheridan, co., Ne., U.S.	B3	104
Sheridan, co., N.D., U.S.	B5	111
Sheridan, co., Wy., U.S.	B5	127
Sheridan, Mount, mtn., Wy., U.S.	B2	127
Sheridan Gardens, Wy., U.S.	*B6	127
Sheridan Lake, Co., U.S.	C8	83
Sheringham, Eng., U.K.	D7	10
Sherman, Ct., U.S.	C2	84
Sherman, Me., U.S.	C4	96
Sherman, Ms., U.S.	A5	101
Sherman, N.Y., U.S.	C1	109
Sherman, Tx., U.S.	C4	120
Sherman, co., Ks., U.S.	C2	93
Sherman, co., Ne., U.S.	C6	104
Sherman, co., Or., U.S.	B6	114
Sherman, co., Tx., U.S.	A2	120
Sherman Mills, Me., U.S.	C4	96
Sherman Mountain, mtn., Ar., U.S.	B2	81
Sherman Reservoir, res., Ne., U.S.	C7	104
Sherman Center, Ma., U.S.	A4	98
Sherman Station, Me., U.S.	C4	96
Sherpur, Bngl.	E12	37
Sherrard, Il., U.S.	B3	90
Sherrelwood, Co., U.S.	B6	83
Sherridon, Mb., Can.	B1	70
Sherrill, Ar., U.S.	C4	81
Sherrill, N.Y., U.S.	B5	109
Sherrodsville, Oh., U.S.	B4	112
's Hertogenbosch, Neth.	B6	16
Sherwood, P.E., Can.	C6	71
Sherwood, Ar., U.S.	C3	81
Sherwood, Md., U.S.	B5	101
Sherwood, Ms., U.S.	B4	101
Sherwood, N.D., U.S.	A4	111
Sherwood, Oh., U.S.	A1	112
Sherwood, Or., U.S.	h12	114
Sherwood, Tn., U.S.	D8	119
Sherwood, Wi., U.S.	h9	126
Sherwood Manor, Ct., U.S.	A5	84
Sherwood Park, Ab., Can.	C4	68
Sherwood Park, De., U.S.	i7	85
Shetek, Lake, l., Mn., U.S.	G3	100
Shetland Islands, is., Scot., U.K.	g10	10
Shetucket, stm., Ct., U.S.	C7	84
Shevchenko, Sov. Un.	E8	29
Shevlin, Mn., U.S.	C3	100
Shevut 'Am, Isr.	f10	41
Shewa, prov., Eth.	D4	47
Shewa Gimira, Eth.	D4	47
Shexian, China	J8	32
Sheyenne, N.D., U.S.	B6	111
Sheyenne, stm., N.D., U.S.	C8	111
Sheyenne Lake, res., N.D., U.S.	B5	111
Shiant Islands, is., Scot., U.K.	C2	13
Shiawassee, co., Mi., U.S.	F6	99
Shibām, P.D.R.Yem.	D4	38
Shibata, Japan	H9	33
Shibecha, Japan	E12	33
Shibetsu, Japan	E12	33
Shibetsu, Japan	D11	33
Shibin al Kawm, Eg.	D3	41
Shibīn al Qanāṭir, Eg.	D3	41
Shicheng, China	K7	32
Shickley, Ne., U.S.	D8	104
Shickshinny, Pa., U.S.	D9	115
Shidao, China	F10	32
Shideler, In., U.S.	D7	91
Shiderty, stm., Sov. Un.	C8	23
Shiel, Loch, l., Scot., U.K.	C3	13
Shieldaig, Scot., U.K.	C3	13
Shields, N.D., U.S.	C4	111
Shields, stm., Mt., U.S.	D7	103
Shihezi, China	C2	31
Shijiazhuang, China	D7	31
Shikārpur, Pak.	C4	36
Shikohābād, India	E8	37
Shikoku, i., Japan	E11	31
Shilka, Sov. Un.	A8	31
Shilka, stm., Sov. Un.	A8	31
Shillington, Pa., U.S.	F10	115
Shillong, India	C9	36
Shiloh, Ga., U.S.	D2	87
Shiloh, N.J., U.S.	E2	107
Shiloh, N.C., U.S.	A6	110
Shiloh, Oh., U.S.	B3	112
Shiloh, Tn., U.S.	B3	119
Shiloh National Military Park, Tn., U.S.	B3	119
Shimabara, Japan	J5	33
Shimanovsk, Sov. Un.	D15	29
Shimber Berris, mtn., Som.	C5	47
Shimen, China	F7	31
Shimizu, Japan	I9	33
Shimoda, Japan	o17	33
Shimodate, Japan	m19	33
Shimoga, India	F6	36
Shimo Island, i., Japan	J4	33
Shimonoseki, Japan	E11	31
Shimotsuma, Japan	m18	33
Shin, Loch, l., Scot., U.K.	A4	10
Shinall Mountain, mtn., Ar., U.S.	h10	81
Shinano, stm., Japan	H9	33
Shindand, Afg.	B3	36
Shiner, Tx., U.S.	E4	120
Shingbwiyang, Burma	C10	36
Shinglehouse, Pa., U.S.	C5	115
Shingleton, Mi., U.S.	B4	99
Shingū, Japan	J8	33
Shinjō, Japan	G10	33
Shinkolobwe, Zaire	D4	48
Shinnston, W.V., U.S.	B4	125
Shin Pond, Me., U.S.	B4	96
Shinshiro, Japan	o16	33
Shinyanga, Tan.	B5	48
Shinyanga, prov., Tan.	B5	48
Shiocton, Wi., U.S.	D5	126
Shiogama, Japan	G10	33
Shiojiri, Japan	m16	33
Shioya, Cape, c., Japan	H10	33
Ship Bottom, N.J., U.S.	D4	107
Ship Cove, Nf., Can.	E4	72
Ship Harbour, N.S., Can.	E7	71
Ship Island, i., Ms., U.S.	g7	101
Ship Island Pass, strt., Ms., U.S.	g7	101
Shipka Pass, Bul.	D7	24
Shipki Pass, India	B7	37
Shipley, Eng., U.K.	G7	13
Shipman, Il., U.S.	D3	90
Shipman, Va., U.S.	C4	123
Shippegan, N.B., Can.	B5	71
Shippensburg, Pa., U.S.	F6	115
Shippenville, Pa., U.S.	D2	115
Shiprock, N.M., U.S.	A1	108
Ship Rock, mtn., N.M., U.S.	A1	108
Shipshewana, In., U.S.	A6	91
Shipyard, Belize	D7	63
Shiquan, China	E6	31
Shiquan He, stm., China	B7	37
Shirabad, Sov. Un.	C13	39
Shīrāz, Iran	C5	38
Shirbīn, Eg.	C3	41
Shire, stm., Afr.	E5	48
Shiretoko, Cape, c., Japan	D12	33
Shiribetsu, Mount, mtn., Japan	E10	33
Shiriya, Cape, c., Japan	F10	33
Shīr Kūh, mtn., Iran	F7	39
Shirley, Ar., U.S.	B3	81
Shirley, Il., U.S.	C4	90
Shirley, In., U.S.	E6	91
Shirley, Ma., U.S.	A5	98
Shirley, N.Y., U.S.	*n16	109
Shirley Basin, Wy., U.S.	D6	127
Shirley Center, Ma., U.S.	A4	98
Shirley Mills, Me., U.S.	C3	96
Shirley Mountains, mts., Wy., U.S.	D6	127
Shīrvān, Iran	C8	39
Shishaldin Volcano, vol., Ak., U.S.	E7	79
Shishmaref, Ak., U.S.	B6	79
Shishou, China	J5	32
Shisou, Japan	n16	33
Shively, Ky., U.S.	B4	94
Shivpuri, India	E6	37
Shivwits, Ut., U.S.	F2	121
Shivwits Plateau, plat., Az., U.S.	A2	80
Shizuishan, China	D6	31
Shizuoka, Japan	E12	31
Shkhara, Mount, mtn., Sov. Un.	*E7	29
Shkodra (Scutari), Alb.	A2	40
Shkotovo, Sov. Un.	E6	33
Shoal, stm., Fl., U.S.	C1	70
Shoal Creek, stm., U.S.	B4	119
Shoal Harbour, Nf., Can.	D4	72
Shoal Lake, Mb., Can.	D1	70
Shoal Lake, l., Can.	E4	70
Shoals, In., U.S.	G4	91
Shoals, Isles of, is., Me., U.S.	E2	96
Shoalwater, Cape, c., Wa., U.S.	C1	124
Shobonier, Il., U.S.	E4	90
Shoe Cove, Nf., Can.	D4	72
Shoemakersville, Pa., U.S.	F10	115
Sholāpur, India	E6	36
Sholes, Ne., U.S.	B8	104
Shongaloo, La., U.S.	B2	95
Shongopovi, Az., U.S.	B5	80
Shonkin, Mt., U.S.	C6	103
Shonto, Az., U.S.	A5	80
Shooting Creek, N.C., U.S.	f9	110
Shope Spring, Tn., U.S.	C11	119
Shoreacres, B.C., Can.	E9	69
Shore Acres, Ma., U.S.	h13	98
Shore Acres, N.C., U.S.	C4	107
Shore Acres, R.I., U.S.	E4	116
Shoreham, Mi., U.S.	F4	99
Shoreham, Vt., U.S.	D2	122
Shoreview, Mn., U.S.	m12	100
Shorewood, Il., U.S.	k8	90
Shorewood, Mn., U.S.	n11	100
Shorewood, Wi., U.S.	E6	126
Shorewood Hills, Wi., U.S.	*E4	126
Short Beach, Ct., U.S.	D4	84
Shorter, Al., U.S.	C3	78
Shorterville, Al., U.S.	D4	78
Short Falls, N.H., U.S.	D4	106
Short Mountain, mtn., Tn., U.S.	D8	119
Shortsville, N.Y., U.S.	C3	109
Shoshone, Ca., U.S.	E5	82
Shoshone, Id., U.S.	G4	89
Shoshone, co., Id., U.S.	B2	89
Shoshone, stm., Wy., U.S.	B4	127
Shoshone, North Fork, stm., Wy., U.S.	B3	127
Shoshone, South Fork, stm., Wy., U.S.	B3	127
Shoshone Falls, wtfl, Id., U.S.	G4	89
Shoshone Lake, l., Wy., U.S.	B2	127
Shoshone Mountains, mts., Nv., U.S.	D4	105
Shoshone Peak, mtn., Nv., U.S.	G5	105
Shoshone Range, mts., Nv., U.S.	C5	105
Shoshoni, Wy., U.S.	C4	127
Shostka, Sov. Un.	F9	27
Shouldice, Ab., Can.	D4	68
Shouns, Tn., U.S.	C12	119
Shoup, Id., U.S.	D4	89
Showell, Md., U.S.	D7	97
Show Low, Az., U.S.	C5	80
Shpola, Sov. Un.	G8	27
Shreve, Oh., U.S.	B3	112
Shreveport, La., U.S.	B2	95
Shrewsbury, Eng., U.K.	D5	10
Shrewsbury, Ma., U.S.	B4	98
Shrewsbury, Mo., U.S.	*13	102
Shrewsbury, N.J., U.S.	C4	107
Shrewsbury, Pa., U.S.	G8	115
Shropshire (Salop), co., Eng., U.K.	B5	12
Shrule, Ire.	D2	11
Shuangcheng, China	B10	31
Shuangjiang, China	G4	31
Shuangliao, China	C9	31
Shuangyang, China	C10	32
Shuangyang, China	C11	32
Shuangyashan, China	B11	31
Shubenacadie, N.S., Can.	D6	71
Shubenacadie Lake, l., N.S., Can.	E6	71
Shucheng, China	I7	32
Shueib Dam, Jord.	h13	41
Shu'fāt, Isr. Occ.	h11	41
Shujāābād, Pak.	C5	36
Snuksan, Mount, mtn., Wa., U.S.	A4	124
Shulan, China	D3	33
Shulaps Peak, mtn., B.C., Can.	D6	69
Shule He, stm., China	C4	31
Shulerville, S.C., U.S.	E8	117
Shullsburg, Wi., U.S.	F3	126
Shumagin Islands, is., Ak., U.S.	E7	79
Shumen, Bul.	D8	24
Shumerlya, Sov. Un.	D16	27
Shumikha, Sov. Un.	B6	28
Shumway, Il., U.S.	D5	90
Shūnat Nimrīn, Jord.	h13	41
Shunchang, China	K7	32
Shungnak, Ak., U.S.	B8	79
Shuoxian, China	E5	32
Shuoxian, China	H7	32
Shuqrah, P.D.R.Yem.	D4	38
Shuqualak, Ms., U.S.	C5	101
Shūr, stm., Iran	F7	39
Shūr, stm., Iran	F5	39
Shūr, stm., Iran	D9	39
Shūrāb, Iran	C8	39
Shuri, Japan	O5	52
Shurugwi, Zimb.	A5	49
Shushan, N.Y., U.S.	B7	109
Shūshat al Maghārah, mtn., Eg.	D5	41
Shūshtar, Iran	C4	38
Shuswap, stm., B.C., Can.	D8	69
Shuswap Lake, l., B.C., Can.	D8	69
Shutesbury, Ma., U.S.	B3	98
Shuwak, Sud.	C4	47
Shuwaykah, Isr. Occ.	f11	41
Shuya, Sov. Un.	N6	52
Shuzenji, Japan	o17	33
Shwebo, Burma	D10	36
Shwegyin, Burma	B6	79
Si see Xi Jiang, stm., China	G7	31
Siam see Thailand, ctry., Asia	B2	34
Siam, Gulf of see Thailand, Gulf of, b., Asia	C2	34
Sian see Xi'an, China	E6	31
Siantan, i., Indon.	K7	35
Siargao, i., Phil.	D8	34
Siátista, Grc.	B3	25
Siau, i., Indon.	E7	34
Siauliai, Sov. Un.	D4	27
Sibay, Sov. Un.	C8	28
Sibbald, Ab., Can.	D5	68
Šibenik, Yugo.	D2	24
Siberia, In., U.S.	H4	91
Siberia, reg., Sov. Un.	C13	29
Sibert, Ky., U.S.	C6	94
Sibi, Pak.	C4	36
Sibigo, Indon.	F1	34
Sibiryakov, i., Sov. Un.	B7	128
Sibiti, Congo	B1	48
Sibiu, Rom.	C7	24
Sibley, Il., U.S.	C5	90
Sibley, Ia., U.S.	A2	92
Sibley, La., U.S.	B2	95
Sibley, Ms., U.S.	D2	101
Sibley, Mo., U.S.	h11	102
Sibley, co., Mn., U.S.	F4	100
Sibolga, Indon.	E1	34
Sibsāgar, India	C9	36
Sibu, Malay.	E5	34
Sibuatan, mtn., Indon.	K3	35
Sibutu, Island, i., Phil.	D1	78
Sibutu Passage, strt., Asia	E5	34
Sibuyan Sea, Phil.	C7	34
Sicamous, B.C., Can.	D8	69
Si Chang, i., Thai.	F4	35
Sichomovi, Az., U.S.	B5	80
Sichuan, prov., China	E5	31
Sicily, i., Italy	F4	22
Sicily Island, La., U.S.	C4	95
Sicklerville, N.J., U.S.	D3	107
Sicuani, Peru	C3	56
Sidamo, prov., Eth.	E4	47
Sideling Hill Creek, stm., Md., U.S.	A1	97
Sidell, Il., U.S.	D6	90
Siderno Marina, Italy	E6	40
Sidheros, Akra, c., Grc.	E6	40
Sidhirókastron, Grc.	B4	40
Sidi Barrānī, Eg.	C5	43
Sidi Ifni, Mor.	B3	44
Sidikalang, Indon.	m11	34
Sīdī Muḥammad, 'Ayn, well, Libya	H3	43
Sidi Bennour, Mor.	C3	44
Sidi bel Abbès, Alg.	A5	44
Sidlaw Hills, hills, Scot., U.K.	D5	13
Sidley, Mount, mtn., Ant.	B36	7
Sidmouth, Eng., U.K.	D4	12
Sidney, Me., U.S.	D3	96
Sidney, Mt., U.S.	C12	103
Sidney, Ne., U.S.	C3	104
Sidney, N.J., U.S.	B3	107
Sidney, N.Y., U.S.	C5	109
Sidney, Oh., U.S.	B1	112
Sidney Center, N.Y., U.S.	C5	109
Sidney Lanier, Lake, res., Ga., U.S.	B2	87
Sidon see Ṣaydā, Leb.	B3	38
Sidon, Ms., U.S.	B3	101
Sidonia, Tn., U.S.	A3	119
Sidorovka, Sov. Un.	D25	8
Sidra, Gulf of (Khalīj Surt), b., Libya	C3	43
Sidrolândia, Braz.	C2	56
Siedlce, Pol.	B7	26
Sieg, stm., F.R.Ger.	C3	18
Siegburg, F.R.Ger.	C3	18
Siegen, F.R.Ger.	C4	18
Sieglar, F.R.Ger.	C2	19
Siegle, La., U.S.	*B3	95
Siemianowice Śląskie, Pol.	g10	27
Siemiatycze, Pol.	B7	26
Siemreab, Kam.	C2	34
Siena, Italy	C3	23
Sieper, La., U.S.	C3	95
Sieradz, Pol.	C5	26
Sierentz, Fr.	A3	21
Siero, Spain	A3	22
Sierpc, Pol.	B5	26
Sierra, co., Ca., U.S.	C3	82
Sierra, co., N.M., U.S.	D2	108
Sierra Blanca, Tx., U.S.	o12	120
Sierra Blanca Peak, mtn., N.M., U.S.	D4	108
Sierra City, Ca., U.S.	C3	82
Sierra Colorada, Arg.	C3	54
Sierra Estrella, mts., Az., U.S.	m8	80
Sierra Gorda, Chile	D2	55
Sierra Leone, ctry., Afr.	E2	45
Sierra Madre, Ca., U.S.	m12	82
Sierra Mojada, Mex.	B4	63
Sierra Nevada (Simón Bolívar), National Park, Ven.	B3	60
Sierraville, Ca., U.S.	C3	82
Sierra Vista, Az., U.S.	F5	80
Sierre, Switz.	C3	20
Sierrita Mountains, mts., Az., U.S.	F4	80
Siesta Key, i., Fl., U.S.	E4	86
Siewierz, Pol.	g10	26
Sifnos, i., Grc.	D5	40
Sifton, Mb., Can.	D1	70
Sigean, Fr.	F5	16
Sigel, Il., U.S.	D5	90
Sigel, Pa., U.S.	D3	115
Sighetu Marmaţiei, Rom.	B6	24
Sighişoara, Rom.	B7	24
Sighty Crag, mtn., Eng., U.K.	E6	13
Sigli, Indon.	k11	34
Siglufjörður, Ice.	m23	14
Sigmaringen, F.R.Ger.	A5	20
Signachi, Sov. Un.	B15	40
Signal Hill, Ca., U.S.	*n12	82
Signal Mountain, Tn., U.S.	D8	119
Signal Mountain, mtn., Tn., U.S.	C9	119
Signal Mountain, mtn., Vt., U.S.	C4	122
Signal Mountain, mtn., Va., U.S.	g11	123
Signal Peak, mtn., Az., U.S.	D1	80
Signal Peak, mtn., Ut., U.S.	F2	121
Signau, Switz.	C4	21
Signy-l'Abbaye, Fr.	E4	17
Sigourney, Ia., U.S.	C5	92
Sigsbee, Ga., U.S.	E3	87
Sigsig, Ec.	B2	58
Sigtuna, Swe.	t35	14
Siguatepeque, Hond.	C4	62
Sigüenza, Spain	D3	45
Siguiri, Gui.	D3	45
Sigurd, Ut., U.S.	E4	121
Sihabuhabu, mtn., Indon.	K3	35
Sihanoukville see Kampong Saom, Kam.	C2	34
Sihl Lake, l., Switz.	B6	21
Sihua, Peru	C2	58
Si'īr, Isr. Occ.	C7	41
Siirt, Tur.	D13	40
Siis, i., Micron.	Q18	52
Sijiri, Bi'r, well, Syria	C7	41
Sikar, India	E6	37
Sikasso, Mali	D3	45
Sikes, La., U.S.	B3	95
Sikeston, Mo., U.S.	E8	102
Sikhote-Alin Mountains, mts., Sov. Un.	E16	29
Sikiá, Grc.	C5	40
Sikinos, i., Grc.	D5	40
Sikkim, state, India	C8	36
Siklós, Hung.	C4	24
Sil, stm., Spain	A2	22
Silandro, Italy	A3	23
Silang, Phil.	o13	34
Silao, Mex.	m13	63
Silchar, India	D1	78
Silcox, Mb., Can.	B7	70
Siler, Tur.	B7	40
Siler City, N.C., U.S.	B3	110
Silerton, Tn., U.S.	B3	119
Silesia, hist reg., Pol.	C4	26
Siletz, Or., U.S.	C3	114
Silex, Mo., U.S.	B6	102
Silgarhi-Doti, Nepal	C8	37
Silica, Oh., U.S.	e6	112
Siliguri, India	C8	36
Silili, Mount, mtn., W. Sam.	F11	52
Silistra, Bul.	B7	24
Silivri, Tur.	B7	40
Siljan, l., Swe.	G6	14
Silkeborg, Den.	B3	15
Sillery, P.Q., Can.	n17	74
Silloth, Eng., U.K.	F5	13
Sils Nakaya, Az., U.S.	E4	80
Silsbee, Tx., U.S.	D5	120
Silsby Lake, l., Mb., Can.	B4	70
Sils im Domleschg, Switz.	D8	21
Sils, Co., U.S.	B3	83
Silva, N.D., U.S.	A6	111
Silva Jardim, Braz.	h6	56
Silvânia, Braz.	B5	56
Silver, S.C., U.S.	D7	117

Name	Map Ref	Page
Silver Bay, Mn., U.S.	C7	100
Silver Bay, N.Y., U.S.	B7	109
Silver Bell, Az., U.S.	E4	80
Silver Bow, co., Mt., U.S.	E4	103
Silver City, Ia., U.S.	C2	92
Silver City, Ms., U.S.	B3	101
Silver City, Nv., U.S.	D2	105
Silver City, N.M., U.S.	E1	108
Silver City, S.D., U.S.	C2	118
Silver Cliff, Co., U.S.	C5	83
Silver Creek, Ga., U.S.	B1	87
Silver Creek, Ms., U.S.	D3	101
Silver Creek, Ne., U.S.	C8	104
Silver Creek, N.Y., U.S.	C1	109
Silver Creek, Wy., U.S.	E5	127
Silver Creek, stm., In., U.S.	H6	91
Silver Creek, stm., Ne., U.S.	g11	104
Silver Creek, stm., Or., U.S.	D7	114
Silverdale, Ks., U.S.	E7	93
Silverdale, Wa., U.S.	B3	124
Silver Fork, Ut., U.S.	*C4	121
Silver Grove, Ky., U.S.	h14	94
Silverhill, Al., U.S.	E2	78
Silver Hill, Md., U.S.	f9	97
Silver Island Mountains, mts., Ut., U.S.	C2	121
Silver Lake, In., U.S.	B6	91
Silver Lake, Ks., U.S.	C8	93
Silver Lake, Ma., U.S.	f11	98
Silver Lake, Mn., U.S.	F4	100
Silver Lake, N.H., U.S.	C4	106
Silver Lake, Or., U.S.	D5	114
Silverlake, Wa., U.S.	C3	124
Silver Lake, Wi., U.S.	F5	126
Silver Lake, l., On., Can.	E4	70
Silver Lake, l., De., U.S.	D3	85
Silver Lake, l., Ma., U.S.	A3	92
Silver Lake, l., Me., U.S.	C3	96
Silver Lake, l., Nv., U.S.	B5	105
Silver Lake, l., N.H., U.S.	E2	106
Silver Lake, l., N.H., U.S.	C4	106
Silver Lake, l., Or., U.S.	D7	114
Silver Lake, l., Wa., U.S.	g13	124
Silvermines, Ire.	E3	11
Silverpeak, Nv., U.S.	F4	105
Silver Peak Range, mts., Nv., U.S.	F4	105
Silver Plume, Co., U.S.	*B5	83
Silver Point, Tn., U.S.	C8	119
Silver Run, Md., U.S.	A3	97
Silver Spring, Md., U.S.	C3	97
Silver Spring, Fl., U.S.	C4	86
Silver Springs, Nv., U.S.	D2	105
Silver Springs, N.Y., U.S.	C2	109
Silver Star, Mt., U.S.	E4	
Silver Star Mountain, mtn., Wa., U.S.	A5	124
Silverthrone Mountain, mtn., B.C., Can.	D4	69
Silvertip Mountain, mtn., Mt., U.S.	C3	103
Silverton, B.C., Can.	E9	69
Silverton, Co., U.S.	D3	83
Silverton, Id., U.S.	B3	89
Silverton, N.J., U.S.	C4	107
Silverton, Oh., U.S.	o13	112
Silverton, Or., U.S.	C4	114
Silverton, Tx., U.S.	B2	120
Silverville, In., U.S.	G4	91
Silves, Port.	D1	22
Silvia, Col.	C2	60
Silvies, stm., Or., U.S.	D7	114
Silview, De., U.S.	B3	85
Silvis, Il., U.S.	B3	90
Silwān (part of Jerusalem), Isr. Occ.	h11	41
Simanggang, Malay.	E4	34
Simao, China	G5	31
Simav, Tur.	C7	40
Simav, stm., Tur.	B7	25
Simcoe, On., Can.	E4	73
Simcoe, co., On., Can.	C5	73
Simcoe, Lake, l., On., Can.	C5	73
Simdega, India	F10	37
Simeulue, i., Indon.	m11	34
Simferopol, Sov. Un.	E6	29
Simi, i., Grc.	D6	40
Similan Islands, is., Thai.	H2	35
Similkameen, stm., N.A.	E7	69
Simití, Col.	B3	60
Simi Valley, Ca., U.S.	E4	82
Simla, India	B6	36
Simla, Co., U.S.	B6	83
Şimleu Silvaniei, Rom.	B6	24
Simme, stm., Switz.	C3	21
Simmern, F.R.Ger.	D2	19
Simmesport, La., U.S.	D4	95
Simmie, Sk., Can.	H1	75
Simmons, Mo., U.S.	D5	102
Simms, Mt., U.S.	C5	103
Simms Point, c., Bah.	m16	64
Simms Stream, stm., N.H., U.S.	g7	106
Simonette, stm., Ab., Can.	B1	68
Simonhouse Lake, l., Mb., Can.	B1	70
Simonstorp (part of Norrköping), Swe.	u34	14
Simonstown (Simonstad), S. Afr.	D2	49
Simonsville, Vt., U.S.	E3	122
Simoom Sound, B.C., Can.	D4	69
Simpang-kiri, stm., Indon.	K2	35
Simplício Mendes, Braz.	C2	57
Simplon Pass, Switz.	C4	20
Simplon Tunnel, Eur.	A2	23
Simpson, Sk., Can.	F3	75
Simpson, Il., U.S.	F5	90
Simpson, Ks., U.S.	C6	93
Simpson, La., U.S.	C3	95
Simpson, Mn., U.S.	G6	100
Simpson, N.C., U.S.	B5	110
Simpson, W.V., U.S.	k10	125
Simpson, co., Ky., U.S.	D3	94
Simpson, co., Ms., U.S.	D4	101
Simpson Creek, stm., W.V., U.S.	k10	125
Simpson Desert, des., Austl.	E6	50
Simpson Peninsula, pen., N.T., Can.	C15	66
Simpsonville, Ky., U.S.	B4	94
Simpsonville, S.C., U.S.	B3	117
Simrishamn, Swe.	J6	14
Sims, Ca., U.S.	C2	81
Sims, Il., U.S.	E5	90
Sims, N.C., U.S.	B4	110
Simsboro, La., U.S.	B3	95
Simsbury, Ct., U.S.	B4	84
Sims Chapel, Al., U.S.	D1	78
Simunul, Malay.	E4	34
Sinabang, Indon.	K2	35
Sinai, S.D., U.S.	C8	118
Sinaia, Rom.	C7	24
Sinai Peninsula, pen., Eg.	C3	38
Sinajana, Guam	L10	52
Sinaloa, state, Mex.	B3	63
Sinaloa [de Leyva], Mex.	B3	63
Sinan, China	F6	31
Sinanju, N. Kor.	G2	33
Sinarū, Eg.	E2	41
Sīnāwan, Libya	C2	43
Sincé, Col.	B2	60
Sincelejo, Col.	B2	60
Sinclair, Mb., Can.	E1	70
Sinclair, Wy., U.S.	A4	96
Sinclair, Lake, res., Ga., U.S.	C3	87
Sinclairville, N.Y., U.S.	C1	109
Sind, prov., Pak.	C4	36
Sind, stm., India	D7	37
Sindal, Den.	A4	15
Sindara, Gabon	F2	46
Sindelfingen, F.R.Ger.	E3	19
Sindirgi, Tur.	C7	40
Sind Sāgar Doāb, plat., Pak.	B3	37
Sinelnikovo, Sov. Un.	G10	27
Sines, Port.	D1	22
Sinfra, I.C.	E3	45
Singapore, Sing.	E2	34
Singapore, ctry., Asia	E2	34
Singapore Strait, strt., Asia	L5	35
Singaraja, Indon.	G5	34
Singen (Hohentwiel), F.R.Ger.	B4	20
Singer, La., U.S.	D2	95
Singhampton, On., Can.	C4	73
Singida, Tan.	C6	48
Singida, prov., Tan.	C5	48
Singitic Gulf, b., Grc.	B4	25
Singkawang, Indon.	E3	34
Singkep, i., Indon.	F2	34
Singkil, Indon.	E1	34
Singleton, Austl.	F8	51
Sinhŭng, N. Kor.	F3	33
Siniscola, Italy	D2	23
Sinj, Yugo.	D3	24
Sinjah, Sud.	C3	47
Sinjār, Isr. Occ.	g12	41
Sinkāt, Sud.	B4	47
Sinkiang see Xinjiang Uygur, prov., China	C2	31
Sinking Creek, stm., Ky., U.S.	C5	94
Sinking Spring, Oh., U.S.	C2	112
Sinks Grove, W.V., U.S.	D4	125
Sinnamahoning, Pa., U.S.	D5	115
Sinnamary, Fr. Gu.	A4	59
Sinnemahoning Creek, stm., Pa., U.S.	D5	115
Sinnemahoning Creek, First Fork, stm., Pa., U.S.	D5	115
Sînnicolau Mare, Rom.	B5	24
Sinnūris, Eg.	E2	41
Sinop, Tur.	A10	40
Sinpo, N. Kor.	F4	33
Sinton, Tx., U.S.	E4	120
Sintra, Port.	f9	22
Sint-Truiden, Bel.	D5	17
Sinú, stm., Col.	B2	60
Sinuiju, N. Kor.	D9	31
Sinyavino, Sov. Un.	s32	14
Sinzig, F.R.Ger.	C2	19
Sion, Switz.	E3	18
Sioux, co., Ia., U.S.	A1	92
Sioux, co., Ne., U.S.	B2	104
Sioux, co., N.D., U.S.	C4	111
Sioux Center, Ia., U.S.	A1	92
Sioux City, Ia., U.S.	B1	92
Sioux Falls, S.D., U.S.	D9	118
Sioux Lookout, On., Can.	o17	73
Sioux Rapids, Ia., U.S.	B2	92
Sipanok Channel, mth., Sk., Can.	D4	75
Siparia, Trin.	O22	65
Siping, China	C9	31
Sipiwesk Lake, l., Mb., Can.	B3	70
Siple, sci., Ant.	B4	7
Siple, Mount, mtn., Ant.	B36	7
Sipsey, Al., U.S.	B2	78
Sipsey, stm., Al., U.S.	B2	78
Sipsey Fork, stm., Al., U.S.	A2	78
Sipura, i., Indon.	F1	34
Siquirres, C.R.	I6	62
Siquisique, Ven.	A4	60
Şir Abū Nu'Ayr, i., U.A.E.	I7	39
Siracusa (Syracuse), Italy	F5	23
Sirājganj, Bngl.	D8	36
Sir Alexander, Mount, mtn., B.C., Can.	C7	69
Sirdar, B.C., Can.	E9	69
Sir Douglas, Mount, mtn., B.C., Can.	D3	68
Sir Edward Pellew Group, is., Austl.	C6	50
Siren, Wi., U.S.	C1	126
Siret, Rom.	B8	24
Siret, stm., Eur.	B8	24
Şirhān, Wādī as, val., Asia	C7	43
Sirik, Cape, c., Malay.	E4	34
Sir James MacBrien, Mount, mtn., N.T., Can.	D7	66
Sīrjān, Iran	*G7	39
Sirmans, Fl., U.S.	B3	86
Sirmione, Italy	D6	20
Sironj, India	E6	37
Síros, i., Grc.	D5	25
Sirpur, India	E7	37
Sirrī, i., Iran	I7	39
Sirsa, India	C6	36
Sir Sandford, Mount, mtn., B.C., Can.	D9	69
Sirvintos, Sov. Un.	A8	26
Sir-Wilfrid, Mont, mtn., P.Q., Can.	B2	74
Sir Wilfrid Laurier, Mount, mtn., B.C., Can.	C8	69
Sisak, Yugo.	C3	24
Sisaket, Thai.	B2	34
Sishui, China	G7	32
Sisib Lake, l., Mb., Can.	C2	70
Sisipuk Lake, l., Can.	B1	70
Siskiyou, co., Ca., U.S.	B2	82
Siskiyou Mountains, mts., U.S.	F3	114
Siskiyou Pass, Or., U.S.	E4	114
Sisquoc, Ca., U.S.	E3	82
Sissach, Switz.	B4	21
Sisseton, S.D., U.S.	B8	118
Sisseton Indian Reservation, U.S.	B8	118
Sissiboo, stm., N.S., Can.	E4	71
Sisson Branch Reservoir, res., N.B., Can.	B2	71
Sissonville, W.V., U.S.	C3	125
Sīstān, reg., Afg.	F10	39
Sīstān, Daryācheh-ye, l., Asia	B6	38
Sister Bay, Wi., U.S.	C6	126
Sisterdale, Tx., U.S.	E3	120
Sisteron, Fr.	E6	16
Sisters, Or., U.S.	C5	114
Sistersville, W.V., U.S.	B4	125
Sītāpur, India	C7	36
Sitia, Grc.	E6	40
Sítio da Abadia, Braz.	A3	56
Sitionuevo, Col.	A3	60
Sitka, Ak., U.S.	D12	79
Sitka National Historical Park, Ak., U.S.	m22	79
Sitka Sound, strt., Ak., U.S.	m22	79
Sittang, stm., Burma	E10	36
Sittard, Neth.	D5	17
Sittwe (Akyab), Burma	D5	62
Siuna, Nic.	C11	40
Siverek, Tur.	D12	40
Sivrihisar, Tur.	C8	40
Sīwah, Eg.	C2	38
Siwalik Range, mts., India	B6	36
Six-Fours-la-Plage, Fr.	F6	16
Sixian, China	H7	32
Six Mile, S.C., U.S.	B2	117
Sixmile Creek, stm., Fl., U.S.	n8	86
Sixmilecross, N. Ire., U.K.	C4	11
Sixt, Fr.	D21	15
Sizhan, China	B2	33
Sjælland, i., Den.	J4	14
Sjællands Odde, pen., Den.	B5	15
Sjenica, Yugo.	D5	24
Sjöbo, Swe.	C7	15
Skælskør, Den.	C5	15
Skærbæk, Den.	C2	15
Skagen, Den.	A4	15
Skagerrak, strt., Eur.	I3	14
Skagit, co., Wa., U.S.	A4	124
Skagit, stm., N.A.	A3	69
Skagway, Ak., U.S.	D12	79
Skälderviken, b., Swe.	B6	15
Skalka Reservoir, res., Czech.	D3	124
Skamania, Wa., U.S.	D3	124
Skamania, co., Wa., U.S.	C2	124
Skamokawa, Wa., U.S.	C2	124
Skanderborg, Den.	B3	15
Skaneateles, N.Y., U.S.	C4	109
Skaneateles Lake, l., N.Y., U.S.	C4	109
Skanee, Mi., U.S.	B2	99
Skånes-Fagerhult, Swe.	B7	15
Skanör, Swe.	C6	15
Skántzoura, i., Grc.	C5	25
Skara, Swe.	H5	14
Skarven, l., Swe.	t35	14
Skarzysko-Kamienna, Pol.	C6	26
Skawa, stm., Pol.	h11	26
Skawina, Pol.	D5	26
Skäzer, Afg.	C15	39
Skedee, Ok., U.S.	A5	113
Skeena, stm., B.C., Can.	F7	66
Skeena Mountains, mts., B.C., Can.	E7	66
Skegness, Eng., U.K.	D7	10
Skeldon, Guy.	A3	59
Skeleton Lake, l., On., Can.	B5	73
Skellefteå, Swe.	E9	14
Skellefteälven, stm., Swe.	E8	14
Skellytown, Tx., U.S.	B2	120
Skelton, W.V., U.S.	n13	125
Skelton Glacier, Ant.	f40	7
Skene, Ms., U.S.	B3	101
Skerries, Ire.	D5	11
Skhimatárion, Grc.	g11	25
Skhíza, i., Grc.	C4	25
Skíathos, i., Grc.	C4	25
Skiatook, Ok., U.S.	A5	113
Skiatook Reservoir, res., Ok., U.S.	A5	113
Skibbereen, Ire.	E2	10
Skibby, Den.	C5	15
Skiddaw, mtn., Eng., U.K.	F5	13
Skidegate, B.C., Can.	C2	69
Skidegate Inlet, b., B.C., Can.	C2	69
Skidmore, Mo., U.S.	A2	102
Skidmore, Tx., U.S.	E4	120
Skien, Nor.	H3	14
Skierniewice, Pol.	C6	26
Skiff, Ab., Can.	E5	68
Skihist Mountain, mtn., B.C., Can.	D7	69
Skikda (Philippeville), Alg.	B6	44
Skillet Fork, stm., Il., U.S.	E5	90
Skillman, N.J., U.S.	C3	107
Skipperville, Al., U.S.	D4	78
Skipton, Eng., U.K.	G7	13
Skíros, Grc.	C5	40
Skíros (Scyros), i., Grc.	C5	40
Skive, Den.	B3	15
Skjern, Den.	C2	15
Skjern Å, stm., Den.	C2	15
Skoczów, Pol.	h9	26
Skofja Loka, Yugo.	B2	24
Skokie, Il., U.S.	A6	90
Skokomish Indian Reservation, Wa., U.S.	B2	124
Skole, Sov. Un.	D7	26
Skópelos, i., Grc.	C5	25
Skopin, Sov. Un.	E12	27
Skopje, Yugo.	D5	24
Skørping, Den.	B3	15
Skotselv, Nor.	p27	14
Skövde, Swe.	H5	14
Skovorodino, Sov. Un.	D15	29
Skowhegan, Me., U.S.	D3	96
Skownan, Mb., Can.	D2	70
Skradin, Yugo.	D2	24
Skreen, Ire.	C3	11
Skull Valley, Az., U.S.	C3	80
Skull Valley, val., Ut., U.S.	C3	121
Skull Valley Indian Reservation, Ut., U.S.	C3	121
Skunk, stm., Ia., U.S.	D6	92
Skurup, Swe.	C5	15
Skvira, Sov. Un.	G7	27
Skwentna, Ak., U.S.	g16	79
Skwentna, stm., Ak., U.S.	g15	79
Skwierzyna, Pol.	B3	26
Skye, i., Scot., U.K.	B3	10
Skykomish, Wa., U.S.	B4	124
Skykomish, stm., Wa., U.S.	B4	124
Skyland, Nv., U.S.	D2	105
Skyland, N.C., U.S.	f10	110
Skylight, Ky., U.S.	g11	94
Skylight Mountain, mtn., Ar., U.S.	B1	81
Skyline, Al., U.S.	A3	78
Skyring, Seno, strt., Chile	h11	54
Skyway, Co., U.S.	C6	83
Skyway, Wa., U.S.	*f11	124
Slackwood, N.J., U.S.	*C3	107
Slade, Ky., U.S.	C6	94
Slagelse, Den.	C5	15
Slagle, La., U.S.	C2	95
Slamet, mtn., Indon.	G3	34
Slane, Ire.	D5	11
Slaney, stm., Ire.	E5	11
Slangerup, Den.	C6	15
Slănic, Rom.	C7	24
Slaný, Czech.	n17	26
Slapout, Ok., U.S.	A1	113
Slapy, Czech.	o17	26
Slapy Reservoir, res., Czech.	D9	19
Slater, Co., U.S.	A3	83
Slater, Ia., U.S.	C4	92
Slater, Mo., U.S.	B4	102
Slater, S.C., U.S.	A3	117
Slatersville, R.I., U.S.	A3	116
Slatersville Reservoir, res., R.I., U.S.	B3	116
Slate Spring, Ms., U.S.	B4	101
Slatina, Rom.	C7	24
Slatington, Pa., U.S.	E10	115
Slaton, Tx., U.S.	C2	120
Slaughter, La., U.S.	D4	95
Slaughter Beach, De., U.S.	E4	85
Slaughters, Ky., U.S.	C2	94
Slave, stm., Can.	D10	66
Slave Lake, Ab., Can.	B3	68
Slavgorod, Sov. Un.	D10	29
Slavonia, hist reg., Yugo.	C3	24
Slavonska Požega, Yugo.	C3	24
Slavonski Brod, Yugo.	C4	24
Slavsk, Sov. Un.	A6	26
Slavyanoserbsk, Sov. Un.	q21	27
Slavyansk, Sov. Un.	G11	27
Slavyansk-na-Kubani, Sov. Un.	I12	27
Stawków, Pol.	g10	26
Stawno, Pol.	A4	26
Slayden, Ms., U.S.	A4	101
Slayton, Mn., U.S.	G3	100
Slaytonville, De., U.S.	E3	85
Sleaford, Eng., U.K.	A7	12
Slea Head, c., Ire.	E1	11
Sleat, Point of, c., Scot., U.K.	C2	13
Sleat, Sound of, strt., Scot., U.K.	C2	13
Sledge, Ms., U.S.	A3	101
Sled Lake, l., Sk., Can.	C2	75
Sleeper, Mo., U.S.	D5	102
Sleeping Bear Dunes National Lakeshore, Mi., U.S.	D4	99
Sleeping Bear Point, c., Mi., U.S.	D4	99
Sleepy Creek, W.V., U.S.	B6	125
Sleepy Eye, Mn., U.S.	F4	100
Sleepy Point, c., Fiji	H15	52
Sleetmute, Ak., U.S.	C8	79
Slemp, Ky., U.S.	C6	94
Slick, Ok., U.S.	B5	113
Slick Rock, Co., U.S.	C2	83
Slickville, Pa., U.S.	F2	115
Slidell, La., U.S.	D6	95
Slide Mountain, mtn., N.Y., U.S.	D6	109
Sliderock Mountain, mtn., Mt., U.S.	D3	103
Slieve Mish Mountains, mts., Ire.	E2	11
Slieve Miskish Mountains, mts., Ire.	F2	11
Slievenamon, mtn., Ire.	E4	11
Sligo, Ire.	C3	11
Sligo, Pa., U.S.	D3	115
Sligo, co., Ire.	C3	11
Sligo Bay, b., Ire.	C3	10
Slim Buttes, mtn., S.D., U.S.	B2	118
Slinger, Wi., U.S.	E5	126
Slippery Rock, Pa., U.S.	D1	115
Sliven, Bul.	D8	24
Slivenec, Czech.	n17	26
Sloan, Ia., U.S.	B1	92
Sloan, Nv., U.S.	H6	105
Sloan, N.Y., U.S.	C2	109
Sloans Valley, Ky., U.S.	D5	94
Sloat, Ca., U.S.	C3	82
Sloatsburg, N.Y., U.S.	*D6	109
Slobodskoy, Sov. Un.	C7	28
Slobozia, Rom.	D8	24
Slocan, B.C., Can.	E9	69
Slocan Lake, l., B.C., Can.	E9	69
Slocomb, Al., U.S.	D4	78
Slocum, R.I., U.S.	E3	116
Slonim, Sov. Un.	E5	27
Slope, co., N.D., U.S.	C2	111
Slough, Eng., U.K.	k11	13
Slovak, Ar., U.S.	B5	81
Slovakia, hist reg., Czech.	D5	19
Slovan, Pa., U.S.	F1	115
Slovenia, hist reg., Yugo.	C2	24
Sluch, stm., Sov. Un.	F6	27
Slunj, Yugo.	C2	24
Slupca, Pol.	B4	26
Slupsk, Pol.	A4	26
Slutsk, Sov. Un.	E6	27
Slyne Head, c., Ire.	D1	10
Slyudyanka, Sov. Un.	D13	29
Smackover, Ar., U.S.	D3	81
Smackover Creek, stm., Ar., U.S.	D3	81
Smålandsfarvandet, strt., Den.	C5	15
Small Point, Me., U.S.	g8	96
Smallwood Reservoir, res., Nf., Can.	D3	66
Smarr, Ga., U.S.	D3	87
Smarts Mountain, mtn., N.H., U.S.	C2	106
Smartt, Tn., U.S.	D8	119
Smeaton, Sk., Can.	D3	75
Smečno, Czech.	n17	26
Smederevo, Yugo.	C5	24
Smela, Sov. Un.	G8	27
Smelterville, Id., U.S.	B2	89
Smethport, Pa., U.S.	C5	115
Smethwick (Warley), Eng., U.K.	D1	10
Smicksburg, Pa., U.S.	E3	115
Smidovich, Sov. Un.	B6	33
Smiley, Sk., Can.	F1	75
Smiley, Tx., U.S.	E4	120
Smirnovo, Sov. Un.	H11	27
Smith, Ab., Can.	B3	68
Smith, Nv., U.S.	E2	105
Smith, co., Ks., U.S.	C5	93
Smith, co., Ms., U.S.	C4	101
Smith, co., Tn., U.S.	A5	119
Smith, co., Tx., U.S.	C5	120
Smith, stm., U.S.	D3	123
Smith, stm., Mt., U.S.	D5	103
Smith, Cape, c., On., Can.	B3	73
Smith and Sayles Reservoir, res., R.I., U.S.	B2	116
Smith Bay, b., Ak., U.S.	A9	79
Smith Center, Ks., U.S.	C5	93
Smith Island, i., B.A.T.	C6	7
Smith Island, i., U.S.	D5	97
Smith Island, i., Va., U.S.	C7	123
Smithdale, Ms., U.S.	D3	101
Smithers, B.C., Can.	B4	69
Smithers, W.V., U.S.	C3	125
Smithfield, Il., U.S.	C3	90
Smithfield, Me., U.S.	D3	96
Smithfield, Mo., U.S.	D3	102
Smithfield, Ne., U.S.	D6	104
Smithfield, N.C., U.S.	B4	110
Smithfield, Oh., U.S.	B5	112
Smithfield, Pa., U.S.	G2	115
Smithfield, Ut., U.S.	B4	121
Smithfield, Va., U.S.	D6	123
Smithfield, W.V., U.S.	k9	125
Smithland, Ia., U.S.	B1	92
Smithland, Ky., U.S.	e9	94
Smithmill, Pa., U.S.	E5	115
Smith Mills, Ky., U.S.	C2	94
Smith Mountain Lake, res., Va., U.S.	C3	123
Smith Peak, mtn., Id., U.S.	A2	89
Smith Peninsula, pen., Ant.	B6	7
Smith Point, c., N.S., Can.	D6	71
Smith Point, c., Ma., U.S.	D7	98
Smith River, Ca., U.S.	B1	82
Smiths, Al., U.S.	C4	78
Smithsburg, Md., U.S.	A2	97
Smiths Cove, N.S., Can.	E3	71
Smiths Falls, On., Can.	C8	73
Smiths Ferry, Id., U.S.	E2	89
Smiths Grove, Ky., U.S.	C3	94
Smithton, Austl.	o15	50
Smithton, Il., U.S.	E4	90
Smithton, Mo., U.S.	C4	102
Smith Town, Ky., U.S.	D5	94
Smithtown, N.Y., U.S.	n15	109
Smithville, Ga., U.S.	E2	87
Smithville, Ms., U.S.	A5	101
Smithville, Mo., U.S.	B3	102
Smithville, N.H., U.S.	E4	106
Smithville, N.J., U.S.	D3	107
Smithville, Oh., U.S.	B4	112
Smithville, Tn., U.S.	C7	119
Smithville, Tx., U.S.	D4	120
Smithville, W.V., U.S.	B3	125
Smithville Flats, N.Y., U.S.	C5	109
Smithville Lake, res., Mo., U.S.	B3	102
Smithwick, S.D., U.S.	D2	118
Smoaks, S.C., U.S.	E6	117
Smoke Creek Desert, des., Nv., U.S.	C2	105
Smokerun, Pa., U.S.	E5	115
Smokey Dome, mtn., Id., U.S.	F4	89
Smoky, stm., Ab., Can.	B2	68
Smoky, Cape, c., N.S., Can.	C9	71
Smoky Cape, c., Austl.	F9	51
Smoky Hill, North Fork, stm., U.S.	B6	93
Smoky Hill, stm., U.S.	C5	93
Smoky Junction, Tn., U.S.	C9	119
Smoky Lake, Ab., Can.	B4	68
Smoky Mountains, mts., Id., U.S.	F4	89
Smøla, i., Nor.	F2	14
Smolan, Ks., U.S.	D6	93
Smolensk, Sov. Un.	D8	29
Smoot, Wy., U.S.	D2	127
Smooth Rock Falls, On., Can.	o19	73
Smoothstone Lake, l., Sk., Can.	C2	75
Smyadovo, Bul.	g11	93
Smygehamn, Swe.	C6	15
Smyrna see İzmir, Tur.	C6	40
Smyrna, De., U.S.	C3	85
Smyrna, Ga., U.S.	C2	87
Smyrna, N.Y., U.S.	C5	109
Smyrna, S.C., U.S.	A5	117
Smyrna, Tn., U.S.	B5	119
Smyrna, stm., De., U.S.	C3	85
Smyrna Mills, Me., U.S.	B4	96
Smyth, co., Va., U.S.	f10	123
Smythe, Mount, mtn., B.C., Can.	E8	66
Snaefell, mtn., I. of Man	F4	13
Snag, Ab., Can.	A4	76
Snake, stm., N.A.	D5	100
Snake, stm., Ne., U.S.	B4	104
Snake Creek, stm., Ne., U.S.	B4	104
Snake Falls, wtfl, Ne., U.S.	B5	104
Snake Indian, stm., Ab., Can.	C1	68
Snake Mountain, mtn., U.S.	A10	119
Snake Mountain, mtn., Vt.	C2	122
Snake Range, mts., Nv., U.S.	E7	105
Snake River Plain, pl., Id., U.S.	F5	89
Snake River Range, mts., U.S.	C2	127
Snake Valley, val., U.S.	D7	121
Snares Islands, is., N.Z.	R11	51
Sneads, Fl., U.S.	B2	86
Sneads Ferry, N.C., U.S.	C5	110
Sneedville, Tn., U.S.	C10	119
Sneek, Neth.	A6	16
Sneem, Ire.	F2	11
Snelling, S.C., U.S.	E5	117
Snezhnoye, Sov. Un.	q21	27
Śniardwy Lake, l., Pol.	B6	26
Snipe Keys, is., Fl., U.S.	H5	86
Snipe Lake, l., Ab., Can.	B2	68
Snizort, Loch, b., Scot., U.K.	C2	13
Snøhetta, mtn., Nor.	F3	14
Snohomish, Wa., U.S.	B3	124
Snohomish, co., Wa., U.S.	A4	124
Snohomish, stm., Wa., U.S.	B4	124
Snoqualmie, Wa., U.S.	B4	124
Snoqualmie, stm., Wa., U.S.	B4	124
Snoqualmie Pass, Wa., U.S.	B4	124
Snøtinden, mtn., Nor.	D5	14
Snov, stm., Sov. Un.	F8	27
Snover, Mi., U.S.	E8	99
Snow, Ok., U.S.	C6	113
Snowbank Lake, l., Mn., U.S.	B7	100
Snow Camp, N.C., U.S.	B3	110
Snowden, Sk., Can.	D3	75
Snowdon, mtn., Wales, U.K.	D4	10
Snowdoun, Al., U.S.	C3	78
Snowflake, Az., U.S.	C5	80
Snowflake, Mb., Can.	E2	70
Snow Hill, Ar., U.S.	D3	81
Snow Hill, Md., U.S.	D7	97
Snow Hill, N.C., U.S.	B5	110
Snowking Mountain, mtn., Wa., U.S.	A4	124
Snow Lake, Mb., Can.	B1	70
Snow Lake, Ar., U.S.	C4	81
Snowmass, Co., U.S.	B4	83
Snowmass Mountain, mtn., Co., U.S.	B3	83
Snow Mountain, mtn., Me., U.S.	C2	96
Snow Peak, mtn., Wa., U.S.	A7	124
Snow Road Station, On., Can.	B8	73
Snow Shoe, Pa., U.S.	D6	115
Snowshoe Lake, l., Me., U.S.	B4	96
Snowshoe Peak, mtn., Mt., U.S.	B1	103
Snowville, N.H., U.S.	C4	106
Snowville, Ut., U.S.	B3	121
Snowville, Va., U.S.	*C2	123
Snow Water Lake, l., Nv., U.S.	C7	105
Snowy, stm., Austl.	H7	51
Snowy Mountain, mtn., N.Y., U.S.	B6	109
Snowy Mountains, mts., Austl.	G8	50
Snowyside Peak, mtn., Id., U.S.	F4	89
Snyatyn, Sov. Un.	D4	31
Snyder, Ar., U.S.	D4	81
Snyder, Ne., U.S.	C9	104
Snyder, Ok., U.S.	C3	113
Snyder, Tx., U.S.	C2	120
Snyder, co., Pa., U.S.	E7	115
Snyder Knob, mtn., W.V., U.S.	C5	125
Soacha, Col.	*C3	60
Soalala, Madag.	g9	49
Soap Lake, Wa., U.S.	B6	124
Soar, stm., Eng., U.K.	B6	12
Soatá, Col.	B3	60
Sobat, stm., Sud.	D3	47
Sobėšlav, Czech.	D9	19
Sobieski, Mn., U.S.	E4	100
Sobieski, Wi., U.S.	D5	126
Sobinka, Sov. Un.	D13	27
Sobral, Braz.	B2	57
Sobti, well, Mali	B4	45
Søby, Den.	D4	15
Socastee, S.C., U.S.	D9	117
Sochaczew, Pol.	B6	26
Sochaux, Fr.	A2	21
Sochi, Sov. Un.	E6	29
Social Circle, Ga., U.S.	C3	87
Society Hill, S.C., U.S.	C8	117
Society Islands, is., Fr. Poly.	H12	6
Socompa, Paso de, A.	D2	55
Socorro, Braz.	m8	56
Socorro, Col.	B3	60
Socorro, N.M., U.S.	C3	108
Socorro, co., N.M., U.S.	D2	108
Socotra (Suquţrā), i., P.D.R.Yem.	D5	38
Socuéllamos, Spain	C4	22
Soda Creek, B.C., Can.	C6	69
Sodankylä, Fin.	D12	14
Soda Springs, Id., U.S.	G7	89
Sodaville, Or., U.S.	C4	114
Soddy-Daisy, Tn., U.S.	D8	119
Söderala, Swe.	G7	14
Söderhamn, Swe.	G7	14
Söderköping, Swe.	H7	14
Södertälje, Swe.	t35	14
Sodo, Eth.	D4	47
Sodus, N.Y., U.S.	B3	109
Sodus Point, N.Y., U.S.	B3	109
Soest, F.R.Ger.	C4	18
Sofádhes, Grc.	C4	25
Sofala, dept., Moz.	A5	49
Sofia (Sofiya), Bul.	D6	24
Sofia, stm., Madag.	g9	49
Sofiyevka, Sov. Un.	G9	27
Sogamoso, Col.	B3	60
Sögel, F.R.Ger.	B3	18
Sognafjorden, Nor.	G1	14
Sögüt, Tur.	C8	25
Soham, N.M., U.S.	B4	108
Sointula, B.C., Can.	D4	69
Soissons, Fr.	C5	16
Sokal, Sov. Un.	F5	27
Sökcho, S. Kor.	G4	33
Söke, Tur.	D6	40
Sokehs Passage, strt., Micron.	Q17	52
Sokhondo, Mount, mtn., Sov. Un.	E14	29
Sokodé, Togo	E5	45
Sokol, Sov. Un.	B13	27
Sokółka, Pol.	B7	26
Sokolo, Mali	D3	45
Sokolov, Czech.	*C2	19
Sokołów [Podlaski], Pol.	D6	45
Sokoto, Nig.	D6	45
Soła, stm., Pol.	h10	26
Sol, Pico do, mtn., Braz.	m7	56
Solana Beach, Ca., U.S.	*F5	82
Solander Island, i., N.Z.	Q11	51
Solano, co., Ca., U.S.	C2	82
Solano, N.M., U.S.	B5	108
Soldatovo, Sov. Un.	F26	8
Soldier, Ia., U.S.	C2	92
Soldier, Ks., U.S.	C8	93
Soldier, stm., Ia., U.S.	C2	92
Soldier Creek, S.D., U.S.	*D5	118
Soldier Creek, stm., Ks., U.S.	C8	93
Soldier Key, i., Fl., U.S.	s3	86
Soldier Pond, Me., U.S.	A4	96
Soldiers Grove, Wi., U.S.	E3	126
Soldier Summit, Ut., U.S.	D4	121
Soldotna, Ak., U.S.	g16	79
Soledad, Col.	A3	60
Soledad, Ca., U.S.	D3	82
Soledad, Ven.	B5	60

Name	Map Ref	Page
Soledad Díez Gutiérrez, Mex.	*C4	63
Soleduck, stm., Wa., U.S.	B1	124
Solen, N.D., U.S.	C5	111
Solesmes, Fr.	D3	17
Solihull, Eng., U.K.	B6	12
Solikamsk, Sov. Un.	D8	29
Sol-Iletsk, Sov. Un.	C5	28
Soliman, Tun.	F3	23
Solingen, F.R.Ger.	C3	18
Sollas, Scot., U.K.	C1	13
Sollefteå, Swe.	F7	14
Sollentuna, Swe.	*I35	14
Söller, Spain	C7	22
Sollihögda, Nor.	p28	15
Solna, Swe.	H7	14
Solomon, Az., U.S.	E6	80
Solomon, Ks., U.S.	D6	93
Solomon, stm., Ks., U.S.	C6	93
Solomon, North Fork, stm., Ks., U.S.	C4	93
Solomon, South Fork, stm., Ks., U.S.	C4	93
Solomon Islands, ctry., Oc.	G9	52
Solomons, Md., U.S.	D5	97
Solon, China	B9	31
Solon, Ia., U.S.	C6	92
Solon, Me., U.S.	D3	96
Solon, Oh., U.S.	A4	112
Solon Mills, Il., U.S.	h8	90
Solon Springs, Wi., U.S.	B2	126
Solothurn, Switz.	E3	18
Solothurn, state, Switz.	B3	20
Solovyevsk, Sov. Un.	D15	29
Solsberry, In., U.S.	F4	91
Solsgirth, Mb., Can.	D1	70
Šolta, i., Yugo.	D3	24
Soltau, F.R.Ger.	B4	18
Solvay, N.Y., U.S.	B4	109
Sölvesborg, Swe.	B8	15
Solway, Mn., U.S.	C3	100
Solway Firth, est., U.K.	C5	10
Solwezi, Zam.	D4	48
Soma, Tur.	C6	25
Somalia, ctry., Afr.	D6	47
Sombor, Yugo.	C4	24
Sombra, On., Can.	E2	73
Sombrerete, Mex.		
Sombrero Channel, strt., India	G9	36
Sombrio, Braz.	D3	56
Somerdale, N.J., U.S.	D2	107
Somers, Ct., U.S.	B6	84
Somers, Ia., U.S.	B3	92
Somers, Mt., U.S.	B2	103
Somers, Wi., U.S.	F6	126
Somerset, Ber.	p19	64
Somerset, Mb., Can.	E2	70
Somerset, Co., U.S.	C3	83
Somerset, In., U.S.	C6	91
Somerset, Ky., U.S.	C5	94
Somerset, Ma., U.S.	C5	98
Somerset, N.J., U.S.	B3	107
Somerset, Oh., U.S.	C3	112
Somerset, Pa., U.S.	F3	115
Somerset, Tx., U.S.	k7	120
Somerset, Wi., U.S.	C1	126
Somerset, co., Eng., U.K.		
Somerset, co., Me., U.S.	C2	96
Somerset, co., N.J., U.S.	B3	107
Somerset, co., Pa., U.S.	G3	115
Somerset East, S. Afr.	D4	49
Somerset Island, i., Ber.	p19	64
Somerset Island, i., N.T., Can.	B14	66
Somerset Reservoir, res., Vt., U.S.	E3	122
Somers Point, N.J., U.S.	E3	107
Somersville, Ct., U.S.	B6	84
Somersworth, N.H., U.S.	D5	106
Somerton, Az., U.S.	E1	80
Somervell, co., Tx., U.S.	C4	120
Somerville, Al., U.S.	A3	78
Somerville, In., U.S.	H3	91
Somerville, Ma., U.S.	B5	98
Somerville, N.J., U.S.	B3	107
Somerville, Oh., U.S.	C1	112
Somerville, Tn., U.S.	B2	119
Somerville, Tx., U.S.	D4	120
Somerville Lake, res., Tx., U.S.	D4	120
Somes (Szamos), stm., Eur.	B6	24
Somme, dept., Fr.	E2	17
Somme, stm., Fr.	B4	16
Sommepy-[Tahure], Fr.	E4	17
Sömmerda, Ger.D.R.	B6	19
Sommesous, Fr.	F4	17
Somonauk, Il., U.S.	B5	90
Somosomo, Fiji	H16	52
Somosomo Strait, strt., Fiji	H15	52
Somoto, Nic.	E7	63
Sompeta, India	H10	37
Somuncurá, Meseta de, plat., Arg.	C3	54
Somvix, Switz.	C6	21
Son, stm., India	D7	36
Soná, Pan.	F7	62
Sŏnchŏn, N. Kor.	G2	33
Soncino, Italy	D5	20
Sonda, India	D3	15
Sønderborg, Den.	D3	15
Sønderho, Den.	C3	15
Sønder Omme, Den.	C3	15
Sondershausen, Ger.D.R.	C5	18
Sønderup, Den.	B2	15
Sondheimer, La., U.S.	B4	95
Sondrio, Italy	C4	20
Sonepur, India	D7	36
Sonestown, Pa., U.S.	D8	115
Song, India	G4	37
Songarh, India		
Song Cau, Viet.	F8	35
Songea, Tan.	D6	48
Songhua Jiang, stm., China	B10	31
Songjiang, China	E9	31
Sŏngjin see Kimchaek, N. Kor.	C10	31
Songkan, China	J2	32
Songkhla, Thai.	D6	34
Songnim (Kyŏmipo), N. Kor.	G2	33
Songololo, Zaire	C1	48
Songtao, China	J3	32
Sonhāt, India		
Sonid Youqi, China	C5	32
Sonid Zuoqi, China	C5	32
Son La, Viet.	B5	35
Sonmiāni, Pak.	D2	36
Sonmiāni Bay, b., Pak.	I13	39
Sonneberg, Ger.D.R.	C5	18
Sonnette, Mt., U.S.	E11	103
Sonning, Sk., Can.	E2	75
Sono, Rio do, stm., Braz.	E2	57
Sonobe, Japan	n14	33
Sonoita, Mex.	A2	63
Sonoita, Az., U.S.	F5	80
Sonoma, Ca., U.S.	C2	82
Sonoma, co., Ca., U.S.	C2	82
Sonoma Peak, mtn., Nv., U.S.	C4	105
Sonoma Range, mts., Nv., U.S.	C4	105
Sonora, Ca., U.S.	D3	82
Sonora, Ky., U.S.	C4	94
Sonora, Oh., U.S.	C4	112
Sonora, Tx., U.S.	D2	120
Sonora, state, Mex.	B2	63
Sonqor, Iran	D3	39
Sonsón, Col.	B2	60
Sonsonate, El Sal.	E7	63
Sontag, Ms., U.S.	D3	101
Son Tay, Viet.	A3	34
Sonthofen, F.R.Ger.	A9	21
Sonyea, N.Y., U.S.	C3	109
Sooke, B.C., Can.	E6	69
Soo Locks, N.A.:	B6	99
Sopchoppy, Fl., U.S.	B2	86
Soper, Ok., U.S.	C6	113
Soperton, Ga., U.S.	D4	87
Sophia, N.C., U.S.	B3	110
Sophia, W.V., U.S.	D3	125
Sopot, Pol.	A5	26
Sopron, Hung.	B3	24
Soquel, Ca., U.S.	*D3	82
Sor, stm., Port.	C1	22
Sora, Italy	D4	23
Sörak, Mount, mtn., S. Kor.	G4	33
Sorata, Bol.	C2	55
Sorbas, Spain	D4	22
Sorel, P.Q., Can.	C5	71
Sorell, Cape, Austl.	o15	50
Sorento, Il., U.S.	D4	90
Soresina, Italy	B2	23
Soreq, stm., Isr.	h10	41
Soria, Spain	B4	22
Soriano, Ur.	f7	54
Soriano, dept., Ur.	f8	54
Sorocaba, Braz.		
Sorochinsk, Sov. Un.	C4	28
Soroki, Sov. Un.	G7	27
Sorong, Indon.	F8	34
Soroti, Ug.	A5	48
Sørøya, i., Nor.	B10	14
Sorraia, stm., Port.	C1	22
Sorrento, Italy	D5	23
Sorrento, Fl., U.S.	D5	86
Sorrento, La., U.S.	D5	95
Sør Rondane Mountains, mts., Ant.	B15	7
Sorsogon, Phil.	C6	34
Sortavala, Sov. Un.	A8	27
Sorum, S.D., U.S.	B3	118
Sörumsand, Nor.	p29	14
Sösan, S. Kor.	H3	33
Sosnogorsk, Sov. Un.	C19	8
Sosnovka, Sov. Un.	E13	27
Sosnowiec, Pol.	C5	26
Soso, Ms., U.S.	D4	101
Sosva, Sov. Un.	C21	8
Sottern, l., Swe.	t33	14
Sotteville-lès-Rouen, Fr.	C4	16
Souanké, Congo	A1	48
Soubré, I.C.	E3	45
Soucook, stm., N.H., U.S.	D4	106
Soudan, Mn., U.S.	C6	100
Souderton, Pa., U.S.	F11	115
Souflion, Grc.	B6	25
Soufrière, St. Luc.	J14	64
Soufrière, mtn., Guad.	Q8	65
Soufrière, mtn., St. Vin.	U26	65
Sougehan, stm., N.H., U.S.	E3	106
Soulac, Fr.	E3	16
Soulanges, co., P.Q., Can.		
Sounding Creek, stm., Ab., Can.	D5	68
Sounding Lake, l., Ab., Can.	C5	68
Sound View, Ct., U.S.	D6	84
Sources, Mount aux, mtn., Afr.	C4	49
Soure, Braz.	C5	59
Soure, Port.		
Souris, Mb., Can.	E1	70
Souris, P.E.I., Can.	C7	71
Souris, N.D., U.S.	A5	111
Souris, stm., N.A.	A7	76
Souris, stm., Ia., U.S.	C2	92
Sourlake, Tx., U.S.	D5	120
Sourland Mountain, hill, N.J., U.S.	C3	107
Sous, Oued, val., Mor.	C3	44
Sousa, Braz.		
Sousse, Tun.	B7	44
Soustons, Fr.	F3	16
South, stm., On., Can.	B5	73
South, stm., Ia., U.S.	C4	92
South, stm., N.C., U.S.	C4	110
South Acton, Ma., U.S.	g10	98
South Acworth, N.H., U.S.	D2	106
South Addison, Me., U.S.	D5	96
South Africa, ctry., Afr.	C4	49
South America		E53
South Amboy, N.J., U.S.	C4	107
South Amherst, Ma., U.S.	B2	98
South Amherst, Oh., U.S.	A3	112
Southampton, On., Can.	D2	73
Southampton, N.B., Can.	D2	71
Southampton, Eng., U.K.	E6	10
Southampton, Ma., U.S.	B2	98
Southampton, N.Y., U.S.	n16	109
Southampton, Pa., U.S.	*F11	115
Southampton, co., Va., U.S.	D5	123
Southampton, Cape, c., N.T., Can.	D16	66
Southampton Island, i., N.T., Can.	D16	66
South Andaman, i., India	F9	36
South Anna, stm., Va., U.S.	C5	123
South Ashburnham, Ma., U.S.	A3	98
South Aulatsivik Island, i., Nf., Can.	g9	72
South Australia, state, Austl.	E5	50
South Bald Mountain, mtn., U.S.	A5	83
South Baldy, mtn., N.M., U.S.	D2	108
Southbank, B.C., Can.	C5	69
South Barnstead, N.H., U.S.	D4	106
South Barre, Ma., U.S.	B3	98
South Barre, Vt., U.S.	C3	122
South Barrule, hill, I. of Man	F4	13
South Bay, Fl., U.S.	F6	86
South Bay, b., On., Can.	n14	99
South Beloit, Il., U.S.	A4	90
South Bend, In., U.S.	A5	91
South Bend, Ne., U.S.	h12	104
South Bend, Tx., U.S.	C3	120
South Bend, Wa., U.S.	C2	124
South Bentinck Arm, b., B.C., Can.	C4	69
South Berwick, Me., U.S.	E2	96
South Bethany, De., U.S.	F5	85
South Bethlehem, N.Y., U.S.	C7	109
South Bloomfield, Oh., U.S.	C3	112
South Boardman, Mi., U.S.	D5	99
South Bolton, P.Q., Can.	D5	74
Southborough, Ma., U.S.	B4	98
South Boston, Va., U.S.	D4	123
South Bound Brook, N.J., U.S.	B3	107
South Branch, Mi., U.S.	E2	72
South Branch, Nf., Can.	D7	99
South Branch Lake, l., Me., U.S.	C4	96
South Branch Mountain, mtn., W.V., U.S.	B6	125
Southbridge, Ma., U.S.	B3	98
South Bristol, Me., U.S.	E3	96
South Britain, Ct., U.S.	D3	84
South Broadway, Wa., U.S.	C5	124
South Brookfield, N.S., Can.	E5	71
South Bruny, i., Austl.	o15	50
South Burlington, Vt., U.S.	C2	122
Southbury, Ct., U.S.	D3	84
South Byfield, Ma., U.S.	A6	98
South Byron, N.Y., U.S.	B2	109
South Canaan, Pa., U.S.	D11	115
South Cape, c., Nor.	B13	128
South Carolina, state, U.S.	D6	117
South Carver, Ma., U.S.	C6	98
South Channel, strt., Marsh Is.	S18	52
South Chaplin, Ct., U.S.	B7	84
South Charleston, Oh., U.S.	C2	112
South Charleston, W.V., U.S.	C3	125
South Charlestown, N.H., U.S.	D2	106
South Chatham, Ma., U.S.	C7	98
South Chatham, N.H., U.S.	B4	106
South Chicago Heights, Il., U.S.	m9	90
South China, Me., U.S.	D3	96
South China Sea, Asia	H14	30
South Cle Elum, Wa., U.S.	B5	124
South Coffeyville, Ok., U.S.	A6	113
South Colby, Wa., U.S.	e10	124
South Colton, N.Y., U.S.	f10	109
South Congaree, S.C., U.S.	D5	117
South Connellsville, Pa., U.S.	G2	115
South Corning, N.Y., U.S.	C3	109
South Dakota, state, U.S.	C5	118
South Danville, N.H., U.S.	E4	106
South Dartmouth, Ma., U.S.	C6	98
South Dayton, N.Y., U.S.	C1	109
South Daytona, Fl., U.S.	C5	86
South Decatur, Ga., U.S.	*h8	87
South Deerfield, Ma., U.S.	B2	98
South Deerfield, N.H., U.S.	D4	106
South Deer Isle, Me., U.S.	D4	96
South Dennis, Ma., U.S.	C7	98
South Dennis, N.J., U.S.	E3	107
South Dorset, Vt., U.S.	E2	122
South Dos Palos, Ca., U.S.	D3	82
South Downs, plat., Eng., U.K.	E6	10
South Dum-Dum, India	F12	37
South Duxbury, Ma., U.S.	B6	98
Southeast Cape, c., Ak., U.S.	C6	79
Southeast Easton, Ma., U.S.	B5	98
Southeast Pass, strt., La., U.S.	E7	95
Southeast Point, c., R.I., U.S.	h7	116
South Effingham, N.H., U.S.	C5	106
South Elgin, Il., U.S.	B5	90
South El Monte, Ca., U.S.	*m12	82
South English, Ia., U.S.	C5	92
Southern, prov., Mwi.	E6	48
Southern, prov., Zam.	E4	48
Southern Alps, mts., N.Z.	O13	51
Southern Bug, stm., Sov. Un.	H8	27
Southern Cross, Austl.	F2	50
Southern Indian Lake, l., Mb., Can.	f8	70
Southern Pines, N.C., U.S.	B3	110
Southern Uplands, plat., Scot., U.K.	C5	10
Southern Ute Indian Reservation, Nv., U.S.	D2	83
South Euclid, Oh., U.S.	g9	112
Southey, Sk., Can.	G3	75
South Fabius, stm., Mo., U.S.	A5	102
South Fallsburg, N.Y., U.S.	D6	109
South Farmingdale, N.Y., U.S.	*n15	109
Southfield, Ma., U.S.	B1	98
Southfield, Mi., U.S.	o15	99
South Flevoland, reg., Neth.	B5	17
South Fork, Pa., U.S.	F4	115
South Fork Indian Reservation, Nv., U.S.	C6	105
South Fort George, B.C., Can.	C6	69
South Foster, R.I., U.S.	C2	116
South Fox Island, i., Mi., U.S.	C5	99
South Freeport, Me., U.S.	g7	96
South Fulton, Tn., U.S.	A3	119
South Gastonia, N.C., U.S.	B1	110
South Gate, Ca., U.S.	n12	82
Southgate, Ky., U.S.	h14	94
Southgate, Mi., U.S.	p15	99
South Georgia, i., Falk. Is.	I7	53
South Gifford, Mo., U.S.	A5	102
South Glamorgan, co., Wales, U.K.	C4	12
South Glastonbury, Ct., U.S.	C5	84
Southglenn, Co., U.S.	*B6	83
South Glens Falls, N.Y., U.S.	B7	109
South Grafton, Ma., U.S.	B4	98
South Grand, stm., Mo., U.S.	C3	102
South Greenfield, Mo., U.S.	D4	102
South Gulf of Évvoia, b., Grc.	g11	25
South Hackensack, N.J., U.S.	*B4	107
South Hadley, Ma., U.S.	B2	98
South Hadley Falls, Ma., U.S.	B2	98
South Hamilton, Ma., U.S.	A6	98
South Hampton, N.H., U.S.	E5	106
South Hanover, Ma., U.S.	h12	98
Southhaven, Ms., U.S.	A3	101
South Harpswell, Me., U.S.	g7	96
South Harwich, Ma., U.S.	C7	98
South Haven, In., U.S.	A3	91
South Haven, Ks., U.S.	E6	93
South Haven, Mi., U.S.	F4	99
South Heart, N.D., U.S.	C3	111
South Heart, stm., Ab., Can.	B2	68
South Hero, Vt., U.S.	B2	122
South Hero Island, i., Vt., U.S.	B2	122
South Hill, Va., U.S.	D4	123
South Hingham, Ma., U.S.	h12	98
South Holland, Il., U.S.	k9	90
South Holland, prov., Neth.	B4	17
South Holston Lake, res., U.S.	A9	119
South Hooksett, N.H., U.S.	D4	106
South Hopkinton, R.I., U.S.	F1	116
South Houston, Tx., U.S.	r14	120
South Huntington, N.Y., U.S.	*n15	109
South Hutchinson, Ks., U.S.	f11	93
South Indian Lake, Mb., Can.	A2	70
Southington, Ct., U.S.	C4	84
South International Falls, Mn., U.S.	B5	100
South Island, i., Micron.	Q18	52
South Island, i., N.Z.	O13	51
South Island, i., S.C., U.S.	E9	117
South Jacksonville, Il., U.S.	D3	90
South Jordan, Ut., U.S.	C3	121
South Junction, Mb., Can.	E4	70
South Kenosha, Wi., U.S.	F6	126
South Kent, Ct., U.S.	C2	84
South Killingly, Ct., U.S.	B8	84
South Komelik, Az., U.S.	F4	80
South Lake Tahoe, Ca., U.S.	C4	82
South Lancaster, Ma., U.S.	B4	98
Southland, Tx., U.S.	C2	120
South Laramie, Wy., U.S.	*E7	127
South Laurel, Md., U.S.	B4	97
South Lebanon, Me., U.S.	E2	96
South Lebanon, Oh., U.S.	C1	112
South Lee, Ma., U.S.	B1	98
South Lincoln, Vt., U.S.	C3	122
South Londonderry, Vt., U.S.	E3	122
South Loup, stm., Ne., U.S.	C6	104
South Lunenburg, Vt., U.S.	C5	122
South Lyme, Ct., U.S.	D6	84
South Lyndeborough, N.H., U.S.	E3	106
South Lyon, Mi., U.S.	F7	99
South Magnetawan, On., Can.	B4	73
South Magnetic Pole, Ant.	C26	7
South Manitou Island, i., Mi., U.S.	C4	99
South Mansfield, La., U.S.	B2	95
South Marsh Island, i., Md., U.S.	D5	97
South Medford, Ma., U.S.	g11	98
South Merrimack, N.H., U.S.	E3	106
South Miami, Fl., U.S.	G6	86
South Miami Heights, Fl., U.S.	s13	86
South Middleboro, Ma., U.S.	C6	98
South Milford, In., U.S.	A7	91
South Mills, N.C., U.S.	A6	110
South Milwaukee, Wi., U.S.	F6	126
Southminster, Eng., U.K.	C8	12
South Modesto, Ca., U.S.	D3	82
South Molton, Eng., U.K.	C4	12
South Montrose, Pa., U.S.	C10	115
South Moose Lake, l., Mb., Can.	C1	70
South Mountain, Pa., U.S.	G7	115
South Mountain, mtn., Pa., U.S.	B2	97
South Mountain, mtn., Id., U.S.	G2	89
South Mountain, mtn., N.M., U.S.	k8	108
South Mountains, mts., Az., U.S.	m8	80
South Mountains, mts., Va., U.S.	B4	123
South Naknek, Ak., U.S.	D8	79
South Negril Point, c., Jam.	E4	64
South New Berlin, N.Y., U.S.	C5	109
South New River Canal, Fl., U.S.	r3	86
South Newbury, Ma., U.S.	A6	98
South Newbury, Vt., U.S.	C4	122
South Newfane, Vt., U.S.	F3	122
South Northfield, Vt., U.S.	C3	122
South Nyack, N.Y., U.S.	*D7	109
South Ogden, Ut., U.S.	B4	121
South Orange, N.J., U.S.	B4	107
South Orkney Islands, is., B.A.T.	C8	7
South Orrington, Me., U.S.	D4	96
South Otselic, N.Y., U.S.	C5	109
South Paris, Me., U.S.	D2	96
South Park, val., Co., U.S.	B5	83
South Pasadena, Ca., U.S.	*m12	82
South Pass, Wy., U.S.	D4	127
South Pass, strt., Marsh Is.	S17	52
South Pass, La., U.S.	F6	95
South Pass City, Wy., U.S.	D4	127
South Patrick Shores, Fl., U.S.	D6	86
South Peacham, Vt., U.S.	C4	122
South Pekin, Il., U.S.	C4	90
South Pittsburg, Tn., U.S.	D8	119
South Platte, stm., U.S.	I6	76
South Point, c., Austl.	H1	50
South Point, c., Barb.	K20	65
South Point, c., Nf., Can.	D7	99
South Point, c., Mi., U.S.	D7	99
South Pole, Ant.	A7	7
South Pomfret, Vt., U.S.	D3	122
Southport (Gold Coast), Austl.	E9	50
Southport, Fl., U.S.	u16	86
Southport, In., U.S.	E5	91
Southport, N.Y., U.S.	C4	109
Southport, N.C., U.S.	D4	110
South Portland, Me., U.S.	E2	96
South Portsmouth, Ky., U.S.	B6	94
South Poultney, Vt., U.S.	E2	122
South Prairie, Wa., U.S.	k8	124
South Queensferry (Queensferry), Scot., U.K.	E5	13
South Range, Mi., U.S.	A2	99
South Range, Wi., U.S.	B2	126
South Reading, Vt., U.S.	E3	122
South Renovo, Pa., U.S.	D6	115
South Revelstoke, B.C., Can.	D8	69
South River, On., Can.	B5	73
South River, N.J., U.S.	C4	107
South River, b., Md., U.S.	C4	97
South Ronaldsay, i., Scot., U.K.	A5	10
South Royalston, Ma., U.S.	A3	98
South Royalton, Vt., U.S.	D3	122
South Rustico, P.E.I., Can.	C6	71
South Ryegate, Vt., U.S.	C4	122
South Salem, Oh., U.S.	C2	112
South Salt Lake, Ut., U.S.	*C4	121
South Sandwich Islands, is., Falk. Is.	D10	7
South San Francisco, Ca., U.S.	h8	82
South San Gabriel, Ca., U.S.	*m12	82
South Saskatchewan, stm., Can.	F11	66
South Seaville, N.J., U.S.	E3	107
South Shetland Islands, is., B.A.T.	C7	7
South Shields, Eng., U.K.	C6	10
South Shore, Ky., U.S.	B6	94
South Shore, Mo., U.S.	f12	102
South Shore, S.D., U.S.	B9	118
Southside, Al., U.S.	B3	78
Southside, N.C., U.S.	B1	110
Southside, Tn., U.S.	A4	119
Southside Place, Tx., U.S.	r14	120
South Sioux City, Ne., U.S.	B9	104
South Skunk, stm., Ia., U.S.	C4	92
South Slocan, B.C., Can.	E9	69
South Solon, Oh., U.S.	C2	112
South Sound, strt., Ire.	D2	11
South Spicer Island, i., N.T., Can.	C17	66
South Sterling, Pa., U.S.	D11	115
South Stony Brook, N.Y., U.S.	n15	109
South St. Paul, Mn., U.S.	n12	100
South Strafford, Vt., U.S.	D4	122
South Streator, Il., U.S.	B5	90
South Superior, Wy., U.S.	E4	127
South Sutton, N.H., U.S.	D3	106
South Swansea, Ma., U.S.	C5	98
South Taranaki Bight, N.Z.	M15	51
South Toms River, N.J., U.S.	D4	107
South Torrington, Wy., U.S.	D8	127
South Tucson, Az., U.S.	E5	80
South Tunnel, Tn., U.S.	A5	119
South Twin Lake, l., Nf., Can.	D4	72
South Twin Mountain, mtn., N.H., U.S.	B4	106
South Tyne, stm., Eng., U.K.	F6	13
South Uist, i., Scot., U.K.	B3	10
South Valley Stream, N.Y., U.S.	n15	109
South Van Buren, Mo., U.S.	E6	102
South Venice, Fl., U.S.	E4	86
South Ventana Cone, vol., Ca., U.S.	D3	82
South Vienna, Oh., U.S.	C2	112
South Wabasca Lake, l., Ab., Can.	B4	68
South Wadesboro, N.C., U.S.	C2	110
South Wallingford, Vt., U.S.	E3	122
South Walpole, Ma., U.S.	h10	98
South Waterford, Me., U.S.	D2	96
South Waverly, Pa., U.S.	C8	115
South Wayne, Wi., U.S.	F4	126
South Weare, N.H., U.S.	E3	106
South Webster, Oh., U.S.	D3	112
South Wellfleet, Ma., U.S.	C8	98
South Wellington, B.C., Can.	f12	69
South West Africa see Namibia, dep., Afr.	B2	49
South West Bay, b., Bah.	n16	64
South West Cape, c., Austl.	o15	50
Southwest Cape, c., N.Z.	Q11	51
Southwest Channel, Fl., U.S.		
Southwest City, Mo., U.S.	E3	102
Southwest Harbor, Me., U.S.	D4	96
Southwest Head, c., N.B., Can.	E3	71
Southwest Miramichi, stm., N.B., Can.	C3	71
Southwest Mountains, mts., Va., U.S.	B4	123
Southwest Pass, strt., La., U.S.	F6	95
Southwest Pass, strt., La., U.S.	E3	95
Southwest Passage, strt., Marsh Is.	S18	52
Southwest Point, c., R.I., U.S.	h7	116
South Weymouth Naval Air Station, mil., Ma., U.S.	h12	98
Scuth Whitley, In., U.S.	B6	91
South Whittier, Ca., U.S.	*n13	82
Scuthwick, Ct., U.S.	B2	98
South Williamson, Ky., U.S.	C7	94
South Williamsport, Pa., U.S.	D7	115
South Wilmington, Il., U.S.	B5	90
South Windham, Ct., U.S.	C7	84
South Windham, Me., U.S.	E2	96
South Windsor, Ct., U.S.	B5	84
Southwold, Eng., U.K.	B9	12
South Wolfeboro, N.H., U.S.	C4	106
South Wolf Island, i., Nf., Can.	B4	72
Southwood Acres, Ct., U.S.	A5	84
Southwood, Vt., U.S.	C4	122
South Woodbury, Vt., U.S.	C4	122
South Woodstock, Ct., U.S.	B8	84
South Woodstock, Vt., U.S.	D3	122
South Yarmouth, Ma., U.S.	C7	98
South Yorkshire, co., Eng., U.K.	A6	12
South Zanesville, Oh., U.S.	C3	112
Soverato, Italy	F6	23
Sovereign, Sk., Can.	F2	75
Sovetsk (Tilsit), Sov. Un.	G4	27
Sovetskaya Gavan, Sov. Un.	E16	29
Soviet Union, ctry., Asia	D11	29
Söweto, S. Afr.	C4	49
Söya, Cape, c., Japan	A10	33
Soyo, Ang.	C1	48
Sozh, stm., Sov. Un.	D8	27
Sozopol, Bul.	B6	25
Spa, Bel.	E5	17
Spadra, Ar., U.S.	B2	81
Spain, ctry., Eur.	C6	22
Spalding, Austl.	F2	51
Spalding, Sk., Can.	E3	75
Spalding, Eng., U.K.	D6	10
Spalding, Id., U.S.	C2	89
Spalding, Ne., U.S.	C7	104
Spalding, co., Ga., U.S.	C2	87
Spanaway, Wa., U.S.	B3	124
Spangle, Wa., U.S.	B8	124
Spangler, Pa., U.S.	E4	115
Spaniard's Bay, Nf., Can.	E5	72
Spanish, On., Can.	A2	73
Spanish, stm., On., Can.	A3	73
Spanishburg, W.V., U.S.	D3	125
Spanish Fork, Ut., U.S.	C4	121
Spanish Fort, Al., U.S.	E2	78
Spanish North Africa, dep., Afr.	*B4	44
Spanish Peak, mtn., Or., U.S.	C7	114
Spanish Ranch, Ca., U.S.	D3	82
Spanish Town, Jam.	F5	64
Sparkman, Ar., U.S.	D3	81
Sparks, Ga., U.S.	E3	87
Sparks, Nv., U.S.	D2	105
Sparland, Il., U.S.	B4	90
Sparr, Fl., U.S.	C4	86
Sparreholm, Swe.	t34	14
Sparrows Point, Md., U.S.	B5	97
Sparta see Spárti, Grc.		
Sparta, Ga., U.S.	C4	87
Sparta, Il., U.S.	E4	90
Sparta, Ky., U.S.	B5	94
Sparta, Mi., U.S.	E5	99
Sparta, Mo., U.S.	D4	102
Sparta, N.J., U.S.	A3	107
Sparta, N.C., U.S.	A1	110
Sparta, Oh., U.S.	B3	112
Sparta, Tn., U.S.	D8	119
Sparta, Wi., U.S.	E3	126
Sparta Mountains, mts., N.J., U.S.	B3	107
Spartanburg, In., U.S.	D8	91
Spartanburg, S.C., U.S.	B4	117
Spartanburg, co., S.C., U.S.	B3	117
Spartansburg, Pa., U.S.	C2	115
Spárti (Sparta), Grc.	D4	25
Spartivento, Cape, c., Italy	E2	23
Spartivento, Cape, c., Italy		
Spas-Demensk, Sov. Un.	D10	27
Spassk-Dalniy, Sov. Un.	E16	29
Spassk-Ryazanskiy, Sov. Un.	D13	27
Spáta, Grc.	h11	25
Spátha, Ákra, c., Grc.	E4	40
Spaulding, Ok., U.S.	B5	113
Spavinaw, Ok., U.S.	A6	113
Spavinaw Creek, stm., Ok., U.S.	A7	113
Spear, Cape, c., Nf., Can.	E5	72
Spearfish, S.D., U.S.	C2	118
Spearhill, Mb., Can.	D2	70
Spearman, Tx., U.S.	A2	120
Spearsville, La., U.S.	B3	95
Spearville, Ks., U.S.	E4	93
Spectacle Pond, l., Me., U.S.	E4	86
Speculator, N.Y., U.S.	B6	109
Spedden, Ab., Can.	B5	68
Spednic Lake, l., N.A.	C5	96
Speed, In., U.S.	H6	91
Speed, Ks., U.S.	C4	93
Speed, N.C., U.S.	B5	110
Speed, W.V., U.S.	C3	125
Speedway, In., U.S.	E5	91
Speedwell, Tn., U.S.	C10	119
Speedwell, Va., U.S.	D1	123
Speers, Sk., Can.	E2	75
Speigner, Al., U.S.	C3	78
Speight, Ky., U.S.	C7	94
Spelter, W.V., U.S.	k10	125
Spenard (part of Anchorage), Ak., U.S.	g17	79
Spencer, Id., U.S.	E6	89
Spencer, In., U.S.	F4	91
Spencer, Ia., U.S.	A2	92
Spencer, Ma., U.S.	B4	98
Spencer, Ne., U.S.	B7	104
Spencer, N.Y., U.S.	C4	109
Spencer, N.C., U.S.	B2	110
Spencer, Oh., U.S.	A3	112
Spencer, S.D., U.S.	D8	118
Spencer, Tn., U.S.	D8	119
Spencer, W.V., U.S.	C3	125
Spencer, co., In., U.S.	H4	91
Spencer, co., Ky., U.S.	B4	94
Spencer, Cape, c., Ak., U.S.	k21	79
Spencer Gulf, b., Austl.	F6	50
Spencer Lake, l., Me., U.S.	C2	96
Spencerport, N.Y., U.S.	B3	109
Spencers Island, N.S., Can.	D5	71
Spencerville, Md., U.S.	B4	97
Spencerville, Oh., U.S.	B1	112
Spencerville, Ok., U.S.	C6	113
Spences Bridge, B.C., Can.	D7	69
Spennymoor, Eng., U.K.	F7	13
Sperkhiós, stm., Grc.	E4	25
Sperling, Mb., Can.	E3	70
Sperrin Mountains, mts., N. Ire., U.K.	C3	10
Sperry, Ok., U.S.	A6	113
Sperryville, Va., U.S.	B4	123
Spesutie Island, i., Md., U.S.	B5	97
Spey, stm., Scot., U.K.	D5	10
Speyer, F.R.Ger.	D4	18
Sphinx, hist., Eg.	E3	41
Spiceland, In., U.S.	E7	91
Spicer, Mn., U.S.	E4	100
Spickard, Mo., U.S.	A4	102
Spider Lake, l., Wi., U.S.	B2	126
Spiekeroog, F.R.Ger.	A7	17
Spiekeroog, i., F.R.Ger.	B3	18
Spiez, Switz.	C4	21
Spigno Monferrato, Italy	A6	20
Spilsby, Eng., U.K.	D7	10
Spinazzola, Italy	E6	23
Spindale, N.C., U.S.	B1	110
Spink, co., S.D., U.S.	C7	118
Spink Colony, S.D., U.S.	C7	118
Spirit Lake, Id., U.S.	B2	89
Spirit Lake, Ia., U.S.	A2	92
Spirit Lake, l., Wa., U.S.	C3	124
Spirit River, Ab., Can.	B1	68
Spirit River Flowage, res., Wi., U.S.	C4	126
Spiritwood, Sk., Can.	D2	75
Spiritwood, N.D., U.S.	C7	111
Spiro, Ok., U.S.	B7	113
Spišská Nová Ves, Czech.	B6	26
Spit Island, i., Mid. Is.	K3	52
Spitsbergen, i., Nor.	B13	128
Spivey, Ks., U.S.	E5	93
Split, Yugo.	D3	24
Split, Cape, c., N.S., Can.	D5	71
Split Lake, l., Mb., Can.	A4	70
Split Rock Creek, stm., U.S.	G2	100
Splügen, Switz.	C5	21
Splügen Pass, Eur.	C5	20
Spofford, Tx., U.S.	E2	120
Spofford Lake, l., N.H., U.S.	E2	106
Spokane, La., U.S.	B5	95
Spokane, Wa., U.S.	B8	124
Spokane, co., Wa., U.S.	B8	124
Spokane, stm., U.S.	B8	124
Spokane, Mount, mtn., Wa., U.S.	B8	124
Spokane Indian Reservation, Wa., U.S.	B8	124
Spöl, stm., Eur.	C9	21
Spoleto, Italy	D5	23
Spondin, Ab., Can.	D5	68
Spoon, stm., Il., U.S.	C3	90
Spooner, Wi., U.S.	C2	126
Spooner Lake, l., Wi., U.S.	C2	126
Spotswood, N.J., U.S.	C4	107
Spotsylvania, Va., U.S.	B5	123
Spotsylvania, co., Va., U.S.	B5	123
Spotted Island, i., Nf., Can.	A4	72
Spottsville, Ky., U.S.	C2	94
Spragge, On., Can.	A2	73

Name	Map Ref	Page

Sprague, Mb., Can. — E4 70
Sprague, Al., U.S. — C3 78
Sprague, Ne., U.S. — D9 104
Sprague, Wa., U.S. — B8 124
Sprague, W.V., U.S. — n13 125
Sprague, stm., Or., U.S. — E5 114
Sprague Lake, l., Wa., U.S. — B7 124
Sprague River, Or., U.S. — E5 114
Spragueville, Ia., U.S. — B7 92
Spragueville, N.Y., U.S. — A5 109
Spragueville, R.I., U.S. — B3 116
Sprakensehl, F.R.Ger. — F4 15
Spratly Island, i., Asia — D4 34
Spray, Or., U.S. — C7 114
Spread Eagle, Wi., U.S. — C5 126
Spreckelsville, Hi., U.S. — *C5 88
Spree, stm., Eur. — B7 18
Spremberg, Ger.D.R. — C7 18
Sprigg, W.V., U.S. — D2 125
Spring, Tx., U.S. — q14 120
Spring, stm., U.S. — A4 81
Spring, South Fork, stm., U.S. — A4 81
Spring, South Fork, stm., U.S. — E6 102
Spring Arbor, Mi., U.S. — F6 99
Spring Bay, b., Ut., U.S. — B3 121
Springbok, S. Afr. — C2 49
Springboro, Oh., U.S. — C1 112
Springboro, Pa., U.S. — C1 115
Springbrook, On., Can. — C7 73
Springbrook, Ia., U.S. — B7 92
Spring Brook, N.D., U.S. — A2 111
Springbrook, Wi., U.S. — C2 126
Spring Brook, stm., Pa., U.S. — n18 115
Spring City, Pa., U.S. — F10 115
Spring City, Tn., U.S. — D9 119
Spring City, Ut., U.S. — D4 121
Spring Coulee, Ab., Can. — E4 68
Spring Creek, Pa., U.S. — C2 115
Spring Creek, Tn., U.S. — B3 119
Spring Creek, stm., U.S. — D4 104
Spring Creek, stm., Co., U.S. — B8 83
Spring Creek, stm., Ga., U.S. — F2 87
Spring Creek, stm., Nv., U.S. — C4 105
Spring Creek, stm., N.D., U.S. — B3 111
Spring Creek Colony, S.D., U.S. — *B7 118
Springdale, Nf., Can. — D3 72
Springdale, Ar., U.S. — A1 81
Springdale, Mt., U.S. — E6 103
Springdale, Oh., U.S. — n13 112
Springdale, Or., U.S. — B4 114
Springdale, Pa., U.S. — E2 115
Springdale, S.C., U.S. — D5 117
Springdale, Ut., U.S. — F3 121
Springdale, Wa., U.S. — A8 124
Spring Dale, W.V., U.S. — D4 125
Springdell, Ut., U.S. — *C4 121
Springe, F.R.Ger. — A4 19
Springer, N.M., U.S. — A5 108
Springer, Ok., U.S. — C4 113
Springerton, Il., U.S. — E5 90
Springerville, Az., U.S. — C6 80
Springfield, N.B., Can. — D4 71
Springfield, N.S., Can. — E5 71
Springfield, On., Can. — E4 73
Springfield, Ar., U.S. — B3 81
Springfield, Co., U.S. — D8 83
Springfield, Fl., U.S. — u16 86
Springfield, Ga., U.S. — D5 87
Springfield, Id., U.S. — F6 89
Springfield, Il., U.S. — D4 90
Springfield, Ky., U.S. — C4 94
Springfield, La., U.S. — D5 95
Springfield, Me., U.S. — C4 96
Springfield, Ma., U.S. — B2 98
Springfield, Mi., U.S. — *F5 99
Springfield, Mn., U.S. — F4 100
Springfield, Mo., U.S. — D4 102
Springfield, Ne., U.S. — C9 104
Springfield, N.H., U.S. — D2 106
Springfield, N.J., U.S. — B4 107
Springfield, Oh., U.S. — C2 112
Springfield, Or., U.S. — C4 114
Springfield, S.C., U.S. — E5 117
Springfield, S.D., U.S. — E8 118
Springfield, Tn., U.S. — A5 119
Springfield, Vt., U.S. — E4 122
Springfield, W.V., U.S. — B6 125
Springfield, Lake, res., Il., U.S. — D4 90
Springfontein, S. Afr. — D4 49
Spring Garden, Al., U.S. — B4 78
Spring Glen, Ut., U.S. — D5 121
Spring Green, Il., U.S. — E3 126
Spring Green, Wi., U.S. — h8 90
Spring Grove, Il., U.S. — E8 91
Spring Grove, Mn., U.S. — G7 100
Spring Grove, Pa., U.S. — G8 115
Springhill, N.S., Can. — D5 71
Springhill, Al., U.S. — D4 78
Spring Hill, Ar., U.S. — D2 81
Spring Hill, Fl., U.S. — D4 86
Spring Hill, Fl., U.S. — k10 91
Spring Hill, In., U.S. — f8 92
Spring Hill, Ks., U.S. — D9 93
Springhill, La., U.S. — A2 95
Spring Hill, Tn., U.S. — B5 119
Springhill Junction, N.S., Can. — D5 71
Spring Hope, N.C., U.S. — B4 110
Springhouse, B.C., Can. — D6 69
Spring Island, i., S.C., U.S. — G6 117
Spring Lake, Fl., U.S. — D4 86
Spring Lake, Mi., U.S. — E4 99
Spring Lake, N.J., U.S. — C4 107
Spring Lake, N.C., U.S. — B4 110
Spring Lake, Ut., U.S. — C4 121
Spring Lake, l., Me., U.S. — C2 96
Spring Lake, res., U.S. — B3 90
Spring Lake Heights, N.J., U.S. — C4 107
Spring Lick, Ky., U.S. — C3 94
Spring Mills, Pa., U.S. — E6 115
Spring Mountains, mtn., Nv., U.S. — G6 105
Spring Place, Ga., U.S. — B2 87
Springport, In., U.S. — D7 91
Springport, Mi., U.S. — F6 99
Springs, S. Afr. — C4 49
Springside, Sk., Can. — F4 75
Springvale, Austl. — D8 50
Springvale, Me., U.S. — E2 96
Springvale, Mo., U.S. — A3 102
Spring Valley, Sk., Can. — H3 75
Spring Valley, Ca., U.S. — o16 82
Spring Valley, Il., U.S. — B4 90
Spring Valley, Mn., U.S. — G6 100
Spring Valley, N.Y., U.S. — g12 109
Spring Valley, Oh., U.S. — C1 112
Spring Valley, Wi., U.S. — D1 126
Springview, Ne., U.S. — B6 104
Springville, Al., U.S. — B3 78

Springville, In., U.S. — G4 91
Springville, Ia., U.S. — B6 92
Springville, Ms., U.S. — A4 101
Springville, N.Y., U.S. — C2 109
Springville, Pa., U.S. — C10 115
Springville, Tn., U.S. — A3 119
Springville, Ut., U.S. — C4 121
Springwater, Sk., Can. — F1 75
Springwater, N.Y., U.S. — C3 109
Spruce, stm., Wi., U.S. — D7 99
Spruce Brook, Nf., Can. — D2 72
Spruce Creek, Pa., U.S. — E5 115
Sprucedale, On., Can. — B5 73
Spruce Fork, stm., W.V., U.S. — m12 125
Spruce Grove, Ab., Can. — C4 68
Spruce Knob, mtn., W.V., U.S. — C6 125
Spruce Knob-Seneca Rocks National Recreation Area, W.V., U.S. — C5 125
Spruce Lake, Sk., Can. — D1 75
Spruce Mountain, mtn., Az., U.S. — C3 80
Spruce Mountain, mtn., Nv., U.S. — C7 105
Spruce Pine, Al., U.S. — A2 78
Spruce Pine, N.C., U.S. — f10 110
Spruce Run Reservoir, res., N.J., U.S. — B3 107
Spruga, Switz. — D6 21
Spur, Tx., U.S. — C2 120
Spurfield, Ab., Can. — B3 68
Spurgeon, In., U.S. — H3 91
Spurn Head, c., Eng., U.K. — A8 12
Spurr, Mount, mtn., Ak., U.S. — g15 79
Spy Hill, Sk., Can. — G5 75
Squamish, B.C., Can. — E6 69
Squam Lake, l., N.H., U.S. — C4 106
Squam Mountains, mts., N.H., U.S. — C3 106
Squantum, N.H., U.S. — E3 106
Squa Pan, Me., U.S. — B4 96
Square Islands, Nf., Can. — B4 72
Square Lake, l., Me., U.S. — A4 96
Squatteck, P.Q., Can. — B9 74
Squaw Cap Mountain, mtn., N.B., Can. — B3 71
Squaw Harbor, Ak., U.S. — D7 79
Squaw Hill, mtn., Wy., U.S. — E7 127
Squaw Lake, Mn., U.S. — C4 100
Squaw Peak, mtn., Mt., U.S. — C2 103
Squaw Rapids, Sk., Can. — D4 75
Squibnocket Point, c., Ma., U.S. — D6 98
Squire, W.V., U.S. — D3 125
Squires, Mo., U.S. — E5 102
Squirrel, Il., U.S. — E7 89
Srbobran, Yugo. — C4 24
Srednekolymsk, Sov. Un. — C18 29
Sredniy Vasyugan, Sov. Un. — D24 8
Śrem, Pol. — B4 26
Sremska Mitrovica, Yugo. — C4 24
Sremski Karlovci, Yugo. — C4 24
Srepok, stm., Asia — C3 34
Sretensk, Sov. Un. — D14 29
Sri Lanka, ctry., Asia — G7 36
Srinagar, India — B5 36
Środa Śląska, Pol. — C4 26
Środa [Wielkopolsk], Pol. — B4 26
Staatsburg, N.Y., U.S. — D7 109
Stab, Ky., U.S. — C5 94
Stachanov, Sov. Un. — A4 13
Stack Reservoir, res., R.I., U.S. — C3 116
Stack Skerry, rock, Scot., U.K. — A4 13
Stack's Mountains, mts., Ire. — E2 11
Stacy, Ar., U.S. — B5 81
Stacy, Mn., U.S. — E6 100
Stacyville, Ia., U.S. — A5 92
Stacyville, Me., U.S. — C4 96
Stade, F.R.Ger. — B4 18
Stadskanaal, Neth. — B6 17
Stadthagen, F.R.Ger. — A4 19
Stadtkyll, F.R.Ger. — D6 17
Stadtlohn, F.R.Ger. — B1 19
Stadtroda, Ger.D.R. — C6 19
Stäfa, Switz. — B6 21
Staffa, i., Scot., U.K. — D2 13
Stafford, Eng., U.K. — D5 10
Stafford, Ks., U.S. — E5 93
Stafford, N.H., U.S. — B6 84
Stafford, N.Y., U.S. — C2 109
Stafford, Oh., U.S. — C4 112
Stafford, Ok., U.S. — B2 113
Stafford, Va., U.S. — B5 123
Stafford, co., Ks., U.S. — D5 93
Stafford, co., Va., U.S. — B5 123
Stafford Pond, l., R.I., U.S. — D6 116
Staffordshire, co., Eng., U.K. — B5 12
Stafford Springs, Ct., U.S. — B6 84
Staffordsville, Ky., U.S. — C7 94
Staffordville, N.J., U.S. — D4 107
Staines, Eng., U.K. — m11 10
Stairs Mountain, mtn., N.H., U.S. — B4 106
Stakhanov, Sov. Un. — G12 27
Stålboga, Swe. — t34 14
Stalden, Switz. — D4 21
Staley, N.C., U.S. — B3 110
Stalin (Kuçovë), Alb. — D4 24
Stalingrád see Katowice, Pol. — C5 26
Stalin Lake, Mb., Can. — F13 66
Stallworthy, Cape, c., N.T., Can. — k33 66
Stalowa Wola, Pol. — C7 26
Stalwart, Sk., Can. — F3 75
Stalwart, Mi., U.S. — B6 99
Stambaugh, Mi., U.S. — B2 99
Stamford, Eng., U.K. — B7 12
Stamford, Ct., U.S. — E1 84
Stamford, Ne., U.S. — D6 104
Stamford, N.Y., U.S. — C6 109
Stamford, Tx., U.S. — C3 120
Stamford, Lake, res., Tx., U.S. — C3 120
Stamping Ground, Ky., U.S. — B5 94
Stampriet, Nmb. — B2 49
Stamps, Ar., U.S. — D2 81
Stanaford, W.V., U.S. — D3 125
Stanardsville, Va., U.S. — B4 123
Stanberry, Mo., U.S. — A3 102
Stanchfield, Mn., U.S. — E5 100
Standard, Ab., Can. — D4 68
Standard, Il., U.S. — B4 90
Standerton, S. Afr. — C4 49
Standing Rock, Al., U.S. — B4 78
Standing Rock, N.M., U.S. — B1 108
Standing Rock Indian Reservation, U.S. — B4 118
Standish, Me., U.S. — E2 96
Standish, Mi., U.S. — E7 99

Standish, N.Y., U.S. — f11 109
Stanfield, Az., U.S. — E3 80
Stanfield, Or., U.S. — B7 114
Stanford, Ca., U.S. — *k8 82
Stanford, Il., U.S. — C4 90
Stanford, In., U.S. — F4 91
Stanford, Ky., U.S. — C5 94
Stanford, Mt., U.S. — C6 103
Stangeville, Wi., U.S. — D6 126
Stanger, S. Afr. — C5 49
Stanhope, P.Q., Can. — D6 74
Stanhope, Eng., U.K. — F6 13
Stanhope, Ia., U.S. — B4 92
Stanhope, N.J., U.S. — B3 107
Staniard Creek, Bah. — B5 64
Stanislaus, co., Ca., U.S. — D3 82
Stanisławów, Pol. — k15 26
Stanke Dimitrov, Bul. — D6 24
Stanley, N.B., Can. — C3 71
Stanley, Falk. Is. — I5 53
Stanley, Id., U.S. — E4 89
Stanley, Ks., U.S. — D9 93
Stanley, Ky., U.S. — C2 94
Stanley, La., U.S. — C2 95
Stanley, N.M., U.S. — B4 108
Stanley, N.C., U.S. — B1 110
Stanley, N.D., U.S. — A3 111
Stanley, Va., U.S. — B4 123
Stanley, Wi., U.S. — D3 126
Stanley, co., S.D., U.S. — C5 118
Stanley Falls see Boyoma Falls, wtfl, Zaire — A4 48
Stanleytown, Va., U.S. — D3 123
Stanleyville, N.C., U.S. — A2 110
Stanleyville see Kisangani, Zaire — A4 48
Stanly, co., N.C., U.S. — B2 110
Stanmore, Ab., Can. — D5 68
Stann Creek, Belize — D7 63
Stans, Switz. — C4 20
Stansbury Mountains, mts., Ut., U.S. — C3 121
Stansbury Park, Ut., U.S. — *C3 121
Stanstead, P.Q., Can. — D5 74
Stanstead, co., P.Q., Can. — D6 74
Stanthorpe, Austl. — E9 50
Stanton, Al., U.S. — C3 78
Stanton, Ca., U.S. — *n13 82
Stanton, Ia., U.S. — D2 92
Stanton, Ky., U.S. — C6 94
Stanton, Mi., U.S. — E5 99
Stanton, Mo., U.S. — C6 102
Stanton, Ne., U.S. — C8 104
Stanton, N.J., U.S. — B3 107
Stanton, N.D., U.S. — B4 111
Stanton, Tn., U.S. — B2 119
Stanton, Tx., U.S. — C2 120
Stanton, co., Ks., U.S. — E2 93
Stanton, co., Ne., U.S. — C8 104
Stantonsburg, N.C., U.S. — B5 110
Stantonville, Tn., U.S. — B3 119
Stanwood, Ia., U.S. — C6 92
Stanwood, Mi., U.S. — E5 99
Stanwood, Wa., U.S. — A3 124
Staples, Mn., U.S. — D4 100
Staples, Tx., U.S. — H8 120
Stapleton, Al., U.S. — E2 78
Stapleton, Ga., U.S. — C4 87
Stapleton, Ne., U.S. — C5 104
Star, Id., U.S. — F2 89
Star, Ms., U.S. — C3 101
Star, N.C., U.S. — B3 110
Star, Tx., U.S. — D3 120
Starachowice, Pol. — C6 26
Staraya Russa, Sov. Un. — C8 27
Stara Zagora, Bul. — D7 24
Starbuck, Mb., Can. — E3 70
Starbuck, Mn., U.S. — E3 100
Starbuck, Wa., U.S. — C7 124
Starbuck Island, i., Kir. — G12 6
Star City, Sk., Can. — E3 75
Star City, Ar., U.S. — D4 81
Star City, In., U.S. — C4 91
Star City, W.V., U.S. — B5 125
Starford, Pa., U.S. — E4 115
Stargard [Szczeciński], Pol. — B6 26
Stargo, Az., U.S. — D6 80
Staritsa, Sov. Un. — C10 27
Stark, Ks., U.S. — E8 93
Stark, N.H., U.S. — A4 106
Stark, co., Il., U.S. — B4 90
Stark, co., N.D., U.S. — C3 111
Stark, co., Oh., U.S. — B4 112
Starke, Fl., U.S. — C4 86
Starke, co., In., U.S. — B4 91
Starkey, Va., U.S. — C3 123
Starks, La., U.S. — D2 95
Starksboro, Vt., U.S. — C2 122
Starkville, Co., U.S. — D6 83
Starkville, Ms., U.S. — B5 101
Starkville, N.Y., U.S. — C6 109
Starkweather, N.D., U.S. — A7 111
Star Lake, l., Mn., U.S. — D3 100
Starlight, Pa., U.S. — C11 115
Starnberg, F.R.Ger. — E5 18
Starnberg Lake, l., F.R.Ger. — E5 18
Starobelsk, Sov. Un. — G12 27
Starodub, Sov. Un. — E9 27
Starogard [Gdański], Pol. — B5 26
Starokonstantinov, Sov. Un. — G6 27
Staroshcherbinovskaya, Sov. Un. — H12 27
Star Peak, mtn., Nv., U.S. — C3 105
Star Prairie, Wi., U.S. — C1 126
Starr, S.C., U.S. — C2 117
Starr, co., Tx., U.S. — F3 120
Star Mountain, mtn., Tn., U.S. — D9 119
Starrucca, Pa., U.S. — C11 115
Start Bay, b., Eng., U.K. — D4 12
Startex, S.C., U.S. — B3 117
Start Point, c., Eng., U.K. — E5 10
Starý Plzenec, Czech. — D8 19
Staryy Oskol, Sov. Un. — F11 27
Stassfurt, Ger.D.R. — C5 18
Staszów, Pol. — C6 26
State Center, Ia., U.S. — B4 92
State College, Pa., U.S. — E6 115
State Line, In., U.S. — D2 91
State Line, Ms., U.S. — D5 101
Stateline, Nv., U.S. — E2 105
State Line, Pa., U.S. — G6 115
Staten Island, i., N.Y., U.S. — *k12 109
Statenville, Ga., U.S. — F4 87
State Road, N.C., U.S. — A2 110
Statesboro, Ga., U.S. — D5 87
Statesville, N.C., U.S. — B2 110
Statham, Ga., U.S. — C3 87
Statue of Liberty National Monument, N.J., U.S. — k8 107
Staufen, F.R.Ger. — B3 20
Staunton, Il., U.S. — D4 90

Staunton, In., U.S. — F3 91
Staunton, Va., U.S. — B3 123
Stavanger, Nor. — H1 14
Stave Lake, l., B.C., Can. — f13 69
Staveley, Eng., U.K. — A6 12
Stavelot, Bel. — D5 17
Stavely, Ab., Can. — D4 68
Stavenisse, Neth. — C4 17
Staveren, Neth. — B5 17
Stavropol, Sov. Un. — E7 29
Stawell, Austl. — H4 51
Stayner, On., Can. — C4 73
Stayton, Or., U.S. — C4 114
Stead, N.M., U.S. — A6 108
Steamboat, Nv., U.S. — D2 105
Steamboat Canyon, Az., U.S. — B6 80
Steamboat Mountain, mtn., Mt., U.S. — C4 103
Steamboat Mountain, mtn., Wy., U.S. — E4 127
Steamboat Rock, Ia., U.S. — B4 92
Steamboat Springs, Co., U.S. — A4 83
Stearns, Ky., U.S. — D5 94
Stearns, co., Mn., U.S. — E4 100
Stearns Brook, stm., N.H., U.S. — A4 106
Stebbins, Ak., U.S. — C7 79
Steblev, Sov. Un. — G8 27
Štěchovice, Czech. — o17 26
Štěchovice, Czech. — o17 26
Stecker, Ok., U.S. — C3 113
Stecoah, N.C., U.S. — f9 110
Steele, Al., U.S. — B3 78
Steele, Mo., U.S. — E8 102
Steele, N.D., U.S. — C6 111
Steele, co., Mn., U.S. — F5 100
Steele, co., N.D., U.S. — B8 111
Steele, Mount, mtn., Wy., U.S. — E6 127
Steele City, Ne., U.S. — D8 104
Steelton, Pa., U.S. — F8 115
Steelville, Mo., U.S. — D6 102
Steelville, Il., U.S. — E4 90
Steen, Mn., U.S. — G2 100
Steenbergen, Neth. — C4 17
Steens, Ms., U.S. — B5 101
Steens Mountain, mts., Or., U.S. — E8 114
Steenwijk, Neth. — B6 17
Steep Falls, Me., U.S. — E2 96
Steephill Lake, l., Sk., Can. — B4 75
Steep Point, c., Austl. — E1 50
Steep Rock Lake, On., Can. — o17 73
Ştefănești, Rom. — B8 24
Ştefanie, Lake, l., Afr. — E4 47
Stefansson Island, i., N.T., Can. — B11 66
Steffisburg, Switz. — C4 21
Stege, Den. — D6 15
Steger, Il., U.S. — B6 90
Stehekin, Wa., U.S. — A5 124
Steilacoom, Wa., U.S. — f10 124
Stein, F.R.Ger. — D5 19
Stein [am Rhein], Switz. — E4 18
Steinauer, Ne., U.S. — D9 104
Steinbach, Mb., Can. — E3 70
Steinbach-Hallenberg, Ger.D.R. — C5 19
Steinfort, Lux. — E5 17
Steinhatchee, Fl., U.S. — C3 86
Steinhatchee, stm., Fl., U.S. — C3 86
Steinhausen, Nmb. — B2 49
Steinhuder, l., F.R.Ger. — F3 15
Steinkjer, Nor. — E4 14
Stella, On., Can. — C8 73
Stella, Ky., U.S. — f9 94
Stella, Mo., U.S. — E3 102
Stella, Ne., U.S. — D10 104
Stella, mtn., Italy — C5 20
Stellarton, N.S., Can. — D7 71
Stem, N.C., U.S. — A4 110
Stenay, Fr. — E5 17
Stendal, Ger.D.R. — B5 18
Stendal, In., U.S. — H3 91
Stenen, Sk., Can. — F4 75
Stenness, Loch of, l., Scot., U.K. — A5 13
Stepanakert, Sov. Un. — F3 28
Stepenitz, stm., Ger.D.R. — E6 15
Stephan, S.D., U.S. — C6 118
Stephen, Mn., U.S. — B2 100
Stephens, Ar., U.S. — D2 81
Stephens, Ga., U.S. — C3 87
Stephens, co., Ga., U.S. — B3 87
Stephens, co., Ok., U.S. — C4 113
Stephens, Port, b., Austl. — F9 51
Stephens City, Va., U.S. — A4 123
Stephens Knob, hill, Ky., U.S. — D5 94
Stephens Lake, l., Mb., Can. — A4 70
Stephenson, Mi., U.S. — C3 99
Stephenson, co., Il., U.S. — A4 90
Stephenson, Mount, mtn., Ant. — C6 7
Stephens Passage, strt., Ak., U.S. — m23 79
Stephenville, Nf., Can. — D2 72
Stephenville, Tx., U.S. — C3 120
Stephenville Crossing, Nf., Can. — D2 72
Stepnica, Pol. — E8 15
Stepnyak, Sov. Un. — C8 28
Steppes, plat., Sov. Un. — C8 28
Step Pyramid, hist., Egypt — C3 41
Steps Point, c., Am. Sam. — G13 52
Steptoe, Wa., U.S. — B8 124
Steptoe Valley, val., Nv., U.S. — C7 105
Sterkstroom, S. Afr. — D4 49
Sterling, Ak., U.S. — g16 79
Sterling, Co., U.S. — A7 83
Sterling, Ct., U.S. — C9 84
Sterling, Il., U.S. — B4 90
Sterling, Ks., U.S. — D5 93
Sterling, Ma., U.S. — B4 98
Sterling, Ne., U.S. — D9 104
Sterling, N.D., U.S. — C5 111
Sterling, Ut., U.S. — D4 121
Sterling, Va., U.S. — A5 123
Sterling, co., Tx., U.S. — D2 120
Sterling City, Tx., U.S. — D2 120
Sterling Heights, Mi., U.S. — o15 99
Sterling Reservoir, res., Co., U.S. — A6 83
Sterling Run, Pa., U.S. — D5 115
Sterlington, La., U.S. — B3 95
Sterlitamak, Sov. Un. — D8 29
Sternberg, Ger.D.R. — E5 15
Šternberk, Czech. — D4 26

Sterrett, Al., U.S. — B3 78
Štětí, Czech. — C9 19
Stettin see Szczecin, Pol. — B3 26
Stetsonville, Wi., U.S. — C3 126
Stettin Lagoon, b., Eur. — B7 18
Stettler, Ab., Can. — C4 68
Steuben, Mi., U.S. — B4 99
Steuben, Wi., U.S. — E3 126
Steuben, co., In., U.S. — A7 91
Steuben, co., N.Y., U.S. — C3 109
Steubenville, Oh., U.S. — B5 112
Stevenage, Eng., U.K. — C7 12
Stevens, N.J., U.S. — C3 107
Stevens, co., Ks., U.S. — E2 93
Stevens, co., Mn., U.S. — E3 100
Stevens, co., Wa., U.S. — A7 124
Stevens Creek Dam, Ca., U.S. — C4 — D1 120
Stevenson, Al., U.S. — A4 78
Stevenson, Ct., U.S. — D3 84
Stevenson, Wa., U.S. — D4 124
Stevenson Lake, l., Mb., Can. — C4 70
Stevenson Mountain, mtn., Ar., U.S. — B1 81
Stevens Pass, Wa., U.S. — B4 124
Stevens Peak, mtn., Id., U.S. — B3 89
Stevens Point, Wi., U.S. — D4 126
Stevens Pottery, Ga., U.S. — D3 87
Stevens Village, Ak., U.S. — B10 79
Stevensville, Mi., U.S. — F4 99
Stevensville, Mt., U.S. — D2 103
Stevensville, Pa., U.S. — C9 115
Steward, Il., U.S. — B5 90
Stewardson, Il., U.S. — D5 90
Stewart, B.C., Can. — B3 69
Stewart, Al., U.S. — C2 78
Stewart, Mn., U.S. — F4 100
Stewart, Ms., U.S. — B4 101
Stewart, Oh., U.S. — C4 112
Stewart, Tn., U.S. — A4 119
Stewart, co., Ga., U.S. — D2 87
Stewart, co., Tn., U.S. — A4 119
Stewart, Yk., Can. — D5 66
Stewart Island, i., N.Z. — Q11 51
Stewart Mountain, mtn., Az., U.S. — k9 80
Stewarton, Scot., U.K. — E4 13
Stewarts Point, Nv., U.S. — G7 105
Stewartstown, N. Ire., U.K. — C5 11
Stewartstown, N.H., U.S. — f6 106
Stewartstown, Pa., U.S. — G8 115
Stewartstown Hollow, N.H., U.S. — g7 106
Stewartsville, Al., U.S. — B3 78
Stewartsville, In., U.S. — H2 91
Stewartsville, Mo., U.S. — B3 102
Stewart Valley, Sk., Can. — G2 75
Stewartville, Mn., U.S. — G6 100
Stewiacke, N.S., Can. — D6 71
Steynsburg, S. Afr. — D4 49
Steyr, Aus. — C7 18
Stickney, Il., U.S. — *k9 90
Stickney, S.D., U.S. — D7 118
Stif, Alg. — B6 44
Stigler, Ok., U.S. — B6 113
Stikine, stm., N.A. — E6 66
Stikine, stm., Ak., U.S. — D13 79
Stilesville, In., U.S. — E4 91
Stilís, Grc. — C4 25
Still, stm., Ct., U.S. — B3 84
Stillaguamish, North Fork, stm., Wa., U.S. — A4 124
Stillaguamish, South Fork, stm., Wa., U.S. — A4 124
Stillhouse Hollow Lake, res., Tx., U.S. — D4 120
Stillman Valley, Il., U.S. — A4 90
Stillmore, Ga., U.S. — D4 87
Still Pond, Md., U.S. — B5 97
Still River, stm., Ct., U.S. — B4 84
Stillwater, Mn., U.S. — E6 100
Stillwater, N.Y., U.S. — C7 109
Stillwater, Ok., U.S. — A4 113
Stillwater, co., Mt., U.S. — E7 103
Stillwater Range, mts., Nv., U.S. — D3 105
Stillwater Reservoir, res., N.Y., U.S. — B5 109
Stillwater Reservoir, res., R.I., U.S. — B3 116
Stillwell, Ga., U.S. — D5 87
Stilson, Ga., U.S. — D5 87
Stilwell, Ks., U.S. — D9 93
Stilwell, Ok., U.S. — B7 113
Stimson, Mount, mtn., Mt., U.S. — C3 103
Stinesville, In., U.S. — F4 91
Stinking Lake, l., N.M., U.S. — A3 108
Stinnett, Tx., U.S. — B2 120
Stinson Lake, N.H., U.S. — C3 106
Ştip, Yugo. — E6 24
Stirling, Austl. — F2 50
Stirling, Ab., Can. — E4 68
Stirling, On., Can. — C7 73
Stirling, Scot., U.K. — B5 10
Stirling, N.J., U.S. — B4 107
Stirling City, Ca., U.S. — C3 82
Stirrat, W.V., U.S. — D2 125
Stites, Id., U.S. — C3 89
Stittsville, On., Can. — B9 73
Stjördalshalsen, Nor. — F4 14
Stockach, F.R.Ger. — A7 21
Stockbridge, Ga., U.S. — C2 87
Stockbridge, Ma., U.S. — B1 98
Stockbridge, Mi., U.S. — F6 99
Stockbridge, Vt., U.S. — D5 126
Stockbridge-Munsee Indian Reservation, Wi., U.S. — D5 126
Stockdale, Oh., U.S. — D3 112
Stockdale, Tx., U.S. — E4 120
Stockerau, Aus. — G16 18
Stockertown, Pa., U.S. — E11 115
Stockett, Mt., U.S. — C5 103
Stockham, Ne., U.S. — D8 104
Stockholm, Swe. — H8 14
Stockholm, Me., U.S. — A4 96
Stockholm, S.D., U.S. — B9 118
Stockholm, Wi., U.S. — D1 126
Stockhorn, mtn., Switz. — C3 20

Stockland, Il., U.S. — C6 90
Stockley, De., U.S. — F4 85
Stockport, Eng., U.K. — D5 10
Stockport, Ia., U.S. — D6 92
Stockport, Oh., U.S. — C4 112
Stockton, Al., U.S. — E2 78
Stockton, Ca., U.S. — D3 82
Stockton, Ga., U.S. — F4 87
Stockton, Il., U.S. — A3 90
Stockton, Ks., U.S. — C4 93
Stockton, Md., U.S. — D7 97
Stockton, Mo., U.S. — D4 102
Stockton, N.Y., U.S. — C1 109
Stockton, N.J., U.S. — C3 107
Stockton Island, i., Wi., U.S. — B3 126
Stockton Lake, res., Mo., U.S. — D4 102
Stockton Plateau, plat., Tx., U.S. — D1 120
Stockton Springs, Me., U.S. — D4 96
Stockville, Ne., U.S. — D5 104
Stockwell, In., U.S. — D4 91
Stod, Czech. — D8 19
Stoddard, N.H., U.S. — D2 106
Stoddard, Wi., U.S. — E2 126
Stoddard, co., Mo., U.S. — E8 102
Stoeckl, Mount, mtn., N.A. — A2 69
Stœng Treng, Kam. — C3 34
Stoke-Centre, P.Q., Can. — D6 74
Stoke-on-Trent, Eng., U.K. — D5 10
Stokes, N.C., U.S. — B5 110
Stokes, co., N.C., U.S. — A2 110
Stokes, Mount, mtn., N.Z. — N15 51
Stokesdale, N.C., U.S. — A3 110
Stokesley, Eng., U.K. — F7 13
Stokke, Nor. — p28 14
Stolac, Yugo. — D3 24
Stolberg, F.R.Ger. — C3 18
Stolbovaya, Sov. Un. — n17 27
Stolbovoy, i., Sov. Un. — C18 29
Stollberg, Ger.D.R. — C7 19
Stolzenau, F.R.Ger. — F3 15
Stone, Eng., U.K. — B5 12
Stone, Id., U.S. — G6 89
Stone, Ky., U.S. — C7 94
Stone, co., Ar., U.S. — B3 81
Stone, co., Ms., U.S. — E4 101
Stone, co., Mo., U.S. — E4 102
Stoneboro, Pa., U.S. — D1 115
Stone City, Ia., U.S. — B6 92
Stone Corral Lake, l., Or., U.S. — E7 114
Stonefort, Il., U.S. — F5 90
Stonega, Va., U.S. — f9 123
Stoneham, Co., U.S. — A7 83
Stoneham, Ma., U.S. — g11 98
Stone Harbor, N.J., U.S. — E3 107
Stonehaven, N.B., Can. — B4 71
Stonehaven, Scot., U.K. — B5 10
Stonehenge, Austl. — B4 51
Stone Mountain, Ga., U.S. — C2 87
Stone Mountain, mtn., Ga., U.S. — C2 87
Stone Mountain, mtn., Vt., U.S. — B5 122
Stone Mountains, mts., U.S. — A1 110
Stoner, B.C., Can. — C6 69
Stones River National Battlefield, hist., Tn., U.S. — B4 119
Stoneville, Ms., U.S. — B3 101
Stoneville, N.C., U.S. — A3 110
Stoneville, S.D., U.S. — C3 118
Stonewall, Mb., Can. — D3 70
Stonewall, La., U.S. — B2 95
Stonewall, Ms., U.S. — C5 101
Stonewall, Ok., U.S. — C5 113
Stonewall, co., Tx., U.S. — C2 120
Stonewood, W.V., U.S. — k10 125
Stoney Creek, stm., Va., U.S. — C5 123
Stonington, Ct., U.S. — D8 84
Stonington, Il., U.S. — D4 90
Stonington, Me., U.S. — D4 96
Stono, stm., S.C., U.S. — F8 117
Stono Inlet, b., S.C., U.S. — F8 117
Stony Beach, Sk., Can. — G3 75
Stony Brook, N.Y., U.S. — n15 109
Stony Brook, stm., N.J., U.S. — C3 107
Stony Creek, Ct., U.S. — D5 84
Stony Creek, Va., U.S. — D5 123
Stony Creek, stm., Va., U.S. — C5 123
Stonyford, Ca., U.S. — C2 82
Stony Island, i., Nf., Can. — B4 72
Stony Island, i., N.Y., U.S. — B4 109
Stony Mountain, Mb., Can. — D3 70
Stony Plain, Ab., Can. — C3 68
Stony Point, N.Y., U.S. — *D7 109
Stony Point, N.C., U.S. — B1 110
Stony Rapids, Sk., Can. — m7 75
Stony Ridge, Oh., U.S. — e6 112
Stör, stm., F.R.Ger. — B2 18
Stora Lulevatten, l., Swe. — D8 14
Stora Sundby, Swe. — t34 14
Storden, Mn., U.S. — F3 100
Store Bælt, strt., Den. — J5 14
Store Heddinge, Den. — J5 14
Storey, co., Nv., U.S. — D2 105
Storkow, Ger.D.R. — A8 19
Storla, S.D., U.S. — D7 118
Storm Lake, Ia., U.S. — B2 92
Storm Lake, l., Ia., U.S. — B2 92
Storm Mountain, mtn., Ak., U.S. — h16 79
Stormont, co., On., Can. — B10 73
Stornoway, Scot., U.K. — A3 10
Storozhinets, Sov. Un. — G5 27
Storuman, Swe. — D6 14
Storuman, l., Swe. — E7 14
Story, Ar., U.S. — C2 81
Story, Wy., U.S. — B6 127
Story, co., Ia., U.S. — B4 92
Story City, Ia., U.S. — B4 92
Stotesbury, Mo., U.S. — D3 102
Stotts City, Mo., U.S. — D4 102
Stottville, N.Y., U.S. — C7 109
Stoughton, Sk., Can. — H4 75
Stoughton, Ma., U.S. — B5 98
Stoughton, Wi., U.S. — F4 126

Name	Map Ref	Page
Stour, stm., Eng., U.K.	E6	10
Stour, stm., Eng., U.K.	E7	10
Stourbridge, Eng., U.K.	B5	12
Stourport-on-Severn, Eng., U.K.	B5	12
Stout, Oh., U.S.	D2	112
Stoutland, Mo., U.S.	D5	102
Stoutsville, Mo., U.S.	B6	102
Stoutsville, Oh., U.S.	C3	112
Stovall, Ga., U.S.	D2	87
Stovall, Ms., U.S.	A3	101
Stovall, N.C., U.S.	A4	110
Stove Creek, Sk., Can.	E4	75
Stover, Mo., U.S.	C5	102
Støvring, Den.	B3	15
Stow, Me., U.S.	D2	96
Stow, Ma., U.S.	B4	98
Stow, Oh., U.S.	A4	112
Stow Creek, stm., N.J., U.S.	E2	107
Stowe, Pa., U.S.	F10	115
Stowe, Vt., U.S.	C3	122
Stowe Township, Pa., U.S.	*k13	115
Stowmarket, Eng., U.K.	B8	12
Stoy, Il., U.S.	E6	90
Stoyoma Mountain, mtn., B.C., Can.	E7	69
Stoystown, Pa., U.S.	F4	115
Strabane, N. Ire., U.K.	C3	10
Strabane, Pa., U.S.	F1	115
Strachur, Scot., U.K.	D3	13
Stradbally, Ire.	D4	11
Stradone, Ire.	D4	11
Strafford, Mo., U.S.	D4	102
Strafford, N.H., U.S.	D4	106
Strafford, Vt., U.S.	D4	122
Strafford, co., N.H., U.S.	D4	106
Straffordville, On., Can.	E4	73
Straight, Oh., U.S.	e9	113
Strakonice, Czech.	D2	26
Straldzha, Bul.	D8	24
Stralsund, Ger.D.R.	A6	18
Strand, S. Afr.	D2	49
Strandburg, S.D., U.S.	B9	118
Strandby, Den.	A4	15
Strandhill, Ire.	C3	11
Strandquist, Mn., U.S.	B2	100
Strang, Ne., U.S.	D8	104
Strang, Ok., U.S.	A4	113
Stranger Creek, stm., Ks., U.S.	k15	93
Strangford, N. Ire., U.K.	C6	11
Strangford Lough, l., N. Ire., U.K.	C4	10
Strängnäs, Swe.	t35	14
Stranraer, Sk., Can.	F1	75
Stranraer, Scot., U.K.	C4	10
Strasbourg, Sk., Can.	F3	75
Strasbourg, Fr.	C7	16
Strasburg, Ger.D.R.	E7	15
Strasburg, Co., U.S.	B6	83
Strasburg, Il., U.S.	D5	90
Strasburg, Mo., U.S.	C3	102
Strasburg, N.D., U.S.	C5	111
Strasburg, Oh., U.S.	B4	112
Strasburg, Pa., U.S.	G9	115
Strasburg, Va., U.S.	B4	123
Strasswalchen, Aus.	B9	20
Stratford, On., Can.	D3	73
Stratford, N.Z.	M15	51
Stratford, Ca., U.S.	D4	82
Stratford, Ct., U.S.	E3	84
Stratford, De., U.S.	*B3	85
Stratford, Ia., U.S.	B4	92
Stratford, N.H., U.S.	A3	106
Stratford, N.J., U.S.	D2	107
Stratford, N.Y., U.S.	B6	109
Stratford, Ok., U.S.	C5	113
Stratford, S.D., U.S.	B7	118
Stratford, Tx., U.S.	A1	120
Stratford, Wi., U.S.	D3	126
Stratford Centre, P.Q., Can.	D6	74
Stratford Landing, Va., U.S.	*B5	123
Stratford-on-Avon, Eng., U.K.	D6	10
Stratford Point, c., Ct., U.S.	E3	84
Stratham, N.H., U.S.	D5	106
Strathaven, Scot., U.K.	E4	13
Strathclair, Mb., Can.	D1	70
Strathclyde, prov., Scot., U.K.	E4	13
Strathcona, On., Can.	C8	73
Strathcona, Mn., U.S.	B2	100
Strathcona Provincial Park, B.C., Can.	E5	69
Strathlorne, N.S., Can.	C8	71
Strathmere, N.J., U.S.	E3	107
Strathmore, Ab., Can.	D4	68
Strathmore, Ca., U.S.	D4	82
Strathmore, co., Ab., Can.	C4	107
Strathroy, On., Can.	E3	73
Strathy Point, c., Scot., U.K.	B4	13
Strattanville, Pa., U.S.	D3	115
Stratton, Co., U.S.	B8	83
Stratton, Me., U.S.	C2	96
Stratton, Ne., U.S.	D4	104
Stratton, Oh., U.S.	B5	112
Stratton Meadows, Co., U.S.	C6	83
Stratton Mountain, mtn., Vt., U.S.	E3	122
Straubing, F.R.Ger.	D6	18
Straubville, N.D., U.S.	C8	111
Straughn, In., U.S.	E7	91
Strausberg, Ger.D.R.	E7	15
Strausstown, Pa., U.S.	F9	115
Strawberry, Ar., U.S.	B4	81
Strawberry, stm., Ar., U.S.	A4	81
Strawberry, stm., Ut., U.S.	C5	121
Strawberry Mountain, mtn., Or., U.S.	C8	114
Strawberry Plains, Tn., U.S.	C10	119
Strawberry Point, Ia., U.S.	B6	92
Strawberry Point, c., Ma., U.S.	B6	98
Strawberry Range, mts., Or., U.S.	C8	114
Strawberry Reservoir, res., Ut., U.S.	C4	121
Strawn, Il., U.S.	C5	90
Strawn, Ks., U.S.	D8	93
Strawn, Tx., U.S.	C3	120
Strážnice, Czech.	D4	26
Streamstown, Ab., Can.	C5	68
Streamwood, Il., U.S.	*h8	90
Streator, Il., U.S.	B5	90
Středočeský, prov., Czech.	D9	19
Streeter, N.D., U.S.	C6	111
Streetman, Tx., U.S.	D4	120
Streetsboro, Oh., U.S.	*A4	112
Streetsville, On., Can.	m14	73
Strehaia, Rom.	C6	24
Strelka, Sov. Un.	D27	8
Strelka-Chunya, Sov. Un.	C13	29
Stresa, Italy	D4	20
Stříbro, Czech.	D8	19
Strichen, Scot., U.K.	C6	13
Strimón (Struma), stm., Eur.	B4	25
Strimón, Gulf of, b., Grc.	B4	25
Stringer, Ms., U.S.	D4	101
Stringtown, Co., U.S.	B4	83
Stringtown, Ky., U.S.	B5	94
Stringtown, Ms., U.S.	B3	101
Stringtown, Ok., U.S.	C5	113
Strofádhes, is., Grc.	D3	25
Stroh, In., U.S.	A7	91
Strokestown, Ire.	D3	11
Stromboli, i., Italy	E5	23
Strome, Ab., Can.	C4	68
Strome Ferry, Scot., U.K.	C3	13
Stromness, Scot., U.K.	B5	13
Stromsburg, Ne., U.S.	C8	104
Strömsund, Swe.	D4	99
Strong, Ar., U.S.	D3	81
Strong, Me., U.S.	D2	96
Strong, stm., Ms., U.S.	C4	101
Strong City, Ks., U.S.	D7	93
Strong City, Ok., U.S.	B2	113
Strongfield, Sk., Can.	F2	75
Stronghurst, Il., U.S.	C3	90
Strongs, Mi., U.S.	B6	99
Strongsville, Oh., U.S.	A4	112
Stronsay, i., Scot., U.K.	A5	10
Stronsay Firth, strt., Scot., U.K.	A6	13
Strontian, Scot., U.K.	D3	13
Stroud, Eng., U.K.	C5	12
Stroud, Ok., U.S.	B5	113
Stroudsburg, Pa., U.S.	E11	115
Struble, Ia., U.S.	B1	92
Struer, Den.	I3	14
Struga, Yugo.	E5	24
Strule, stm., N. Ire., U.K.	C4	11
Strum, Wi., U.S.	D2	126
Struma (Strimón), stm., Eur.	B4	25
Strumble Head, c., Wales, U.K.	B2	12
Strumica, Yugo.	E6	24
Strunk, Ky., U.S.	D5	94
Struthers, Oh., U.S.	A5	112
Stryama, stm., Bul.	D7	24
Stryker, Mt., U.S.	B2	103
Stryker, Oh., U.S.	A1	112
Strykersville, N.Y., U.S.	C2	109
Stryy, Sov. Un.	G4	27
Stryy, stm., Sov. Un.	D7	26
Strzegom, Pol.	C4	26
Strzelce Krajeńskie, Pol.	B3	26
Strzelce [Opolskie], Pol.	C5	26
Strzelecki Creek, stm., Austl.	E7	50
Strzelin, Pol.	C4	26
Strzelno, Pol.	B4	26
Strzemieszyce, Pol.	g10	26
Stuart, Fl., U.S.	E6	86
Stuart, Ia., U.S.	C3	92
Stuart, Ne., U.S.	B6	104
Stuart, Ok., U.S.	C5	113
Stuart, Va., U.S.	D2	123
Stuart, stm., B.C., Can.	B5	69
Stuart, Mount, mtn., Wa., U.S.	B5	124
Stuart Lake, l., B.C., Can.	B5	69
Stuarts Draft, Va., U.S.	B3	123
Stubbekøbing, Den.	D6	15
Stub Hill, mtn., N.H., U.S.	f7	106
Studley, Ks., U.S.	C3	93
Stühlingen, F.R.Ger.	A5	21
Stull, Wi., U.S.	B5	70
Stull Lake, l., Can.	B5	70
Stump Creek, Pa., U.S.	D4	115
Stump Lake, l., N.D., U.S.	B7	111
Stump Pond, res., R.I., U.S.	D3	116
Stumptown, W.V., U.S.	C4	125
Stumpy Point, N.C., U.S.	B7	110
Stupart, stm., Mb., Can.	B4	70
Stupino, Sov. Un.	D11	27
Sturbridge, Ma., U.S.	B3	98
Sturgeon, Mo., U.S.	B5	102
Sturgeon, stm., Mi., U.S.	D2	75
Sturgeon, stm., Mi., U.S.	B3	99
Sturgeon Bay, Wi., U.S.	D6	126
Sturgeon Bay, b., Mb., Can.	C3	70
Sturgeon Falls, On., Can.	A5	73
Sturgeon Lake, l., On., Can.	D6	100
Sturgeon Lake, l., Ab., Can.	B2	68
Sturgeon Lake, l., On., Can.	C6	73
Sturgeon Lake, l., Sk., Can.	D2	75
Sturgeon Landing, Sk., Can.	C5	75
Sturgeon-weir, stm., Sk., Can.	C4	75
Sturgis, Sk., Can.	F4	75
Sturgis, Ky., U.S.	C2	94
Sturgis, Mi., U.S.	G5	99
Sturgis, Ms., U.S.	B4	101
Sturgis, S.D., U.S.	C2	118
Sturt Creek, stm., Austl.	C4	50
Sturt Desert, des., Austl.	D3	51
Sturtevant, Wi., U.S.	F6	126
Stutsman, co., N.D., U.S.	B6	111
Stutterheim, S. Afr.	D4	49
Stuttgart, F.R.Ger.	D4	18
Stuttgart, Ar., U.S.	C4	81
Stuttgart, Ks., U.S.	C4	93
Styr, stm., Sov. Un.	F5	27
Styria, hist reg., Aus.	E7	18
Su, Canal do, strt., Braz.	F11	37
Suanpan, stm., India	B2	81
Subiaco, Ar., U.S.	B2	81
Subi Besar, i., Indon.	K8	35
Subiaco, It.	D7	22
Straubing, F.R.Ger.	D6	18
Subic, Phil.	o13	34
Subic Bay, b., Phil.	o13	34
Sublette, Il., U.S.	B4	90
Sublette, Ks., U.S.	E3	93
Sublette, co., Wy., U.S.	D2	127
Sublett Range, mts., Id., U.S.	G6	89
Sublimity, Or., U.S.	C4	114
Sublime, Tx., U.S.	*A4	120
Subotica, Yugo.	B4	24
Sucarnoochee, stm., Al., U.S.	C1	78
Succasunna, N.J., U.S.	B3	107
Success, Sk., Can.	G1	75
Success, Ar., U.S.	A5	81
Success, Mo., U.S.	D5	102
Success, Mount, mtn., N.H., U.S.	B4	106
Suceava, Rom.	B8	24
Suceava, stm., Rom.	B8	24
Sucha [Beskidzka], Pol.	F5	26
Suchdol, Czech.	n17	26
Suches, Guat.	B2	87
Süchow see Xuzhou, China	E8	31
Suck, stm., Ire.	D2	10
Sucre, Bol.	D2	59
Sucre, state, Ven.	A5	60
Sucre, dept., Col.	B2	60
Sucuaro, Col.	C4	60
Sucurú, stm., Braz.	C3	61
Sucy-en-Brie, Fr.	g11	16
Sudan, Tx., U.S.	B1	120
Sudan, reg., Afr.	C2	41
Sudan, ctry., Afr.	E7	42
Sudbury, On., Can.	A4	73
Sudbury, Eng., U.K.	B8	12
Sudbury, Ma., U.S.	B5	98
Sudbury, Vt., U.S.	D2	122
Sudbury, co., On., Can.	p19	73
Sudbury, stm., Ma., U.S.	B5	98
Sudbury Center, Ma., U.S.	g10	98
Sudbury Reservoir, res., Ma., U.S.	g10	98
Suddie, Guy.	A3	59
Süderbrarup, F.R.Ger.	D3	15
Süderbrarup, F.R.Ger.	B5	18
Sudetes, mts., Eur.	C4	26
Sudlersville, Md., U.S.	B6	97
Sudogda, Sov. Un.	D13	27
Sudr, 'Ayn, well, Eg.	E5	41
Sudzha, Sov. Un.	F10	27
Sue, stm., Sud.	D2	47
Sueca, Spain	C5	22
Suez (As Suways), Eg.	C3	38
Suez, Gulf of, b., Eg.	C3	38
Suez Canal, Eg.	B3	38
Suffern, N.Y., U.S.	D6	109
Suffield, Ab., Can.	D5	68
Suffield, Ct., U.S.	B5	84
Suffolk, Va., U.S.	D6	123
Suffolk, co., Eng., U.K.	B8	12
Suffolk, co., Ma., U.S.	B5	98
Suffolk, co., N.Y., U.S.	n15	109
Sugar, stm., U.S.	F4	126
Sugar, stm., N.H., U.S.	D2	106
Sugar, North Branch, stm., N.H., U.S.	D2	106
Sugar City, Co., U.S.	C7	83
Sugar City, Id., U.S.	F7	89
Sugar Creek, Mo., U.S.	h11	102
Sugarcreek, Pa., U.S.	D2	115
Sugar Creek, stm., In., U.S.	E3	91
Sugar Creek, stm., In., U.S.	F6	91
Sugar Creek, stm., Oh., U.S.	C2	112
Sugar Creek, stm., Pa., U.S.	C8	115
Sugar Grove, N.C., U.S.	A1	110
Sugar Grove, Oh., U.S.	C3	112
Sugargrove, Pa., U.S.	C3	115
Sugar Grove, Va., U.S.	D1	123
Sugar Grove, W.V., U.S.	C5	125
Sugar Hill, Ga., U.S.	B2	87
Sugar Hill, N.H., U.S.	B3	106
Sugar Island, i., Mi., U.S.	B6	99
Sugarland Run, Va., U.S.	A5	123
Sugar Loaf, Va., U.S.	C3	123
Sugarloaf, mtn., N.H., U.S.	A4	106
Sugarloaf Mountain, mtn., Me., U.S.	C2	96
Sugar Loaf Mountain, mtn., Md., U.S.	B3	97
Sugarloaf Mountain, mtn., Mt., U.S.	C4	103
Sugar Loaf Mountain, mtn., Ok., U.S.	B7	113
Sugarloaf Point, c., Austl.	F9	51
Sugar Mountain, mtn., Mi., U.S.	k9	99
Sugar Notch, Pa., U.S.	n17	115
Sugartown, La., U.S.	D2	95
Sugar Valley, Ga., U.S.	B1	87
Sugden, Ok., U.S.	C4	113
Suggi Lake, l., Sk., Can.	C4	75
Suggsville, Al., U.S.	D2	78
Suhār, Oman	C5	38
Sühbaatar, Mong.	A6	31
Suhl, Ger.D.R.	C5	18
Suiattle, stm., Wa., U.S.	A4	124
Suibin, China	C5	33
Suichuan, China	F7	31
Suide, China	D7	31
Suifenhe, China	C11	31
Suihua, China	B10	31
Suijiang, China	F5	31
Suileng, China	C3	33
Suining, China	E6	31
Suipacha, Arg.	g7	54
Suipacha, Bol.	D2	55
Suippes, Fr.	E4	17
Suir, stm., Ire.	D3	10
Suisun City, Ca., U.S.	*C2	82
Suit, N.C., U.S.	f8	110
Suita, Japan	*I7	33
Suitland, Md., U.S.	C4	97
Suixian, China	E7	31
Suixian, China	G6	32
Suizhong, China	D9	32
Sukabumi, Indon.	G3	34
Sukadana, Indon.	F3	34
Sukaraja, Indon.	F4	34
Sukarnapura see Jayapura, Indon.	F10	34
Sukhobuzimskoye, Sov. Un.	D27	8
Sukhona, stm., Sov. Un.	C7	29
Sukhothai, Thai.	B1	34
Sukhumi, Sov. Un.	G17	8
Sukkur, Pak.	C4	36
Sukumo, Japan	J6	33
Sukunka, stm., B.C., Can.	B7	69
Sula, Cal., U.S.	E3	103
Sulaimān Range, mts., Pak.	C4	36
Sula Islands, is., Indon.	F7	34
Sula Sgeir, i., Scot., U.K.	A2	13
Sulęcin, Pol.	B3	26
Sulaco, stm., Hond.	C4	62
Sulawesi see Celebes, i., Indon.	F6	34
Sule Skerry, rock, Scot., U.K.	A4	13
Sulejówek, Pol.	B5	26
Sulina, Rom.	C9	24
Sulingen, F.R.Ger.	F2	15
Sulitelma, mtn., Eur.	D7	14
Sulligent, Al., U.S.	B1	78
Sullivan, Il., U.S.	D5	90
Sullivan, In., U.S.	F3	91
Sullivan, Ky., U.S.	C2	94
Sullivan, Mo., U.S.	C6	102
Sullivan, N.H., U.S.	D2	106
Sullivan, Wi., U.S.	E5	126
Sullivan, co., In., U.S.	F3	91
Sullivan, co., Mo., U.S.	A4	102
Sullivan, co., N.H., U.S.	D2	106
Sullivan, co., N.Y., U.S.	D6	109
Sullivan, co., Pa., U.S.	D8	115
Sullivan, co., Tn., U.S.	C11	119
Sullivan Lake, l., Ab., Can.	A4	54
Sullivans Island, S.C., U.S.	k12	117
Sully, Ia., U.S.	C5	92
Sully, co., S.D., U.S.	C5	118
Sully, Italy	C4	23
Sulphur, La., U.S.	D2	95
Sulphur, Ok., U.S.	C5	113
Sulphur, stm., Ab., Can.	C1	68
Sulphur, stm., U.S.	D5	120
Sulphur, stm., Ar., U.S.	D1	81
Sulphur Rock, Ar., U.S.	B4	81
Sulphur Spring Range, mts., Nv., U.S.	C5	105
Sulphur Springs, Ar., U.S.	A1	81
Sulphur Springs, In., U.S.	D7	91
Sulphur Springs, Mo., U.S.	g13	102
Sulphur Springs, Oh., U.S.	B3	112
Sulphur Springs, Tx., U.S.	C5	120
Sulphur Springs Valley, val., Az., U.S.	E6	80
Sultan, Wa., U.S.	B4	124
Sultānpur, India	D9	37
Sulu Archipelago, is., Phil.	D6	34
Sulūq, Libya	C4	43
Sulu Sea, Asia	D5	34
Sulzbach, F.R.Ger.	B4	21
Sulzbach-Rosenberg, F.R.Ger.	D6	19
Sulzberger Bay, b., Ant.	B33	7
Sumas, Wa., U.S.	A3	124
Sumatra, Fl., U.S.	B2	86
Sumatra, Mt., U.S.	D9	103
Sumatra (Sumatera), i., Indon.	F2	34
Sumava Resorts, In., U.S.	B3	91
Sumba, i., Indon.	G6	34
Sumbar, stm., Sov. Un.	B7	39
Sumbawa, i., Indon.	G5	34
Sumbawa Besar, Indon.	G5	34
Sumbawanga, Tan.	C5	48
Sumbay, Peru	E3	58
Sumbe (Ngunza), Ang.	D1	48
Sumburgh Point, c., Scot., U.K.	h10	10
Sümeg, Hung.	B3	24
Sumenep, Indon.	G4	34
Sumgait, Sov. Un.	A4	39
Sumiswald, Switz.	B4	21
Sumiton, Al., U.S.	B2	78
Summerberry, Sk., Can.	G4	75
Summerdale, Al., U.S.	E2	78
Summerfield, Fl., U.S.	C4	86
Summerfield, Ks., U.S.	C7	93
Summerfield, La., U.S.	B3	95
Summerfield, Mo., U.S.	C6	102
Summerfield, N.C., U.S.	A3	110
Summerfield, Oh., U.S.	C4	112
Summerford, Nf., Can.	D4	72
Summerhill, Ire.	D5	11
Summer Hill, Il., U.S.	D3	90
Summer Lake, Or., U.S.	E6	114
Summer Lake, l., Or., U.S.	E6	114
Summerland, B.C., Can.	E8	69
Summerland Key, Fl., U.S.	H5	86
Summers, co., W.V., U.S.	D4	125
Summersville, Mo., U.S.	D6	102
Summersville, W.V., U.S.	C4	125
Summersville Lake, res., W.V., U.S.	C4	125
Summerton, S.C., U.S.	D7	117
Summertown, Ga., U.S.	D4	87
Summertown, Tn., U.S.	B4	119
Summerville, Ga., U.S.	B1	87
Summerville, Or., U.S.	B8	114
Summerville, Pa., U.S.	D3	115
Summerville, S.C., U.S.	E7	117
Summit, Il., U.S.	k9	90
Summit, Ms., U.S.	D3	101
Summit, N.J., U.S.	B4	107
Summit, Ok., U.S.	B6	113
Summit, R.I., U.S.	D2	116
Summit, S.D., U.S.	B8	118
Summit, Tn., U.S.	h11	119
Summit, co., Co., U.S.	B4	83
Summit, co., Oh., U.S.	A4	112
Summit, co., Ut., U.S.	C5	121
Summit Grove, In., U.S.	E3	91
Summit Hill, Pa., U.S.	E10	115
Summit Lake, B.C., Can.	B6	69
Summit Lake, l., Ia., U.S.	A3	92
Summit Lake Indian Reservation, Nv., U.S.	B2	105
Summit Mountain, mtn., Nv., U.S.	D5	105
Summit Peak, mtn., Co., U.S.	D4	83
Summit Point, W.V., U.S.	B7	125
Summit Station, Oh., U.S.	k11	112
Summitville, Co., U.S.	D4	83
Summitville, In., U.S.	D6	91
Summitville, Tn., U.S.	D8	119
Summum, Il., U.S.	C3	90
Sumner, Il., U.S.	E6	90
Sumner, Ia., U.S.	B5	92
Sumner, Ms., U.S.	B3	101
Sumner, Mo., U.S.	B4	102
Sumner, Ne., U.S.	D6	104
Sumner, Wa., U.S.	A4	113
Sumner, Wa., U.S.	B3	124
Sumner, co., Ks., U.S.	E6	93
Sumner, co., Tn., U.S.	A5	119
Sumner Strait, strt., Ak., U.S.	m23	79
Sumoto, Japan	I7	33
Šumperk, Czech.	D4	26
Sumpter, Or., U.S.	C8	114
Sumrall, Ms., U.S.	D4	101
Sumter, S.C., U.S.	D7	117
Sumter, co., Al., U.S.	C1	78
Sumter, co., Fl., U.S.	D4	86
Sumter, co., Ga., U.S.	D2	87
Sumter, co., S.C., U.S.	D7	117
Sumterville, Al., U.S.	C1	78
Sumy, Sov. Un.	D6	29
Sun, stm., Mt., U.S.	C4	103
Sunapee Lake, l., N.H., U.S.	D2	106
Sunart, Loch, l., Scot., U.K.	D3	13
Sunbright, Tn., U.S.	C9	119
Sunburg, Mn., U.S.	E3	100
Sunburst, Mt., U.S.	B5	103
Sunbury, Oh., U.S.	B3	112
Sunbury, co., N.B., Can.	D3	71
Sunchales, Arg.	A4	54
Suncho Corral, Arg.	E3	55
Sunchón, N. Kor.	G12	33
Sunchón, S. Kor.	I3	33
Sun City, Az., U.S.	*k8	80
Sun City, Ca., U.S.	*F5	82
Sun City, Fl., U.S.	p10	86
Sun City, Ks., U.S.	E5	93
Suncook, N.H., U.S.	D4	106
Suncook, stm., N.H., U.S.	D4	106
Suncook Lakes, l., N.H., U.S.	D4	106
Sundance, Wy., U.S.	B8	127
Sundance Mountain, mtn., Wy., U.S.	B8	127
Sundarbans, reg., Asia	D6	36
Sunda Strait, strt., Indon.	G3	34
Sunday Strait, strt., Austl.	C3	50
Sundbyberg, Swe.	t35	14
Sunderland, On., Can.	C5	73
Sunderland, Eng., U.K.	C6	10
Sunderland, Md., U.S.	C4	97
Sunderland, Ma., U.S.	B2	98
Sunderland, Vt., U.S.	E2	122
Sundown, Mb., Can.	E3	70
Sundown, Tx., U.S.	C1	120
Sundre, Ab., Can.	D3	68
Sundridge, On., Can.	B5	73
Sunds, Den.	B3	15
Sundsvall, Swe.	F7	14
Sunfield, Mi., U.S.	F5	99
Sunflower, Ms., U.S.	B3	101
Sunflower, co., Ms., U.S.	B3	101
Sunflower, Mount, mtn., Ks., U.S.	C2	93
Sungaiguntung, Indon.	E2	34
Sungaipenuh, Indon.	F2	34
Sungai Petani, Malay.	J4	35
Sungari see Songhua Jiang, stm., China	B10	31
Sungari Reservoir, res., China	E3	33
Sungurlu, Tur.	B10	40
Sunland Park, N.M., U.S.	F3	108
Sunlight Creek, stm., Wy., U.S.	B3	127
Sunman, In., U.S.	F7	91
Sunne, Swe.	H5	14
Sunnybrae, N.S., Can.	D7	71
Sunnybrook, Ab., Can.	C3	68
Sunnyland, Fl., U.S.	q11	86
Sunnymead, Ca., U.S.	*F5	82
Sunnynook, Ab., Can.	D5	68
Sunnyside, Nf., Can.	E5	72
Sunnyside, Ut., U.S.	u16	86
Sunnyside, Ut., U.S.	D5	121
Sunnyside, Wa., U.S.	C5	124
Sunnyslope, Ab., Can.	D4	68
Sunny South, Al., U.S.	D2	78
Sunnyvale, Ca., U.S.	k8	82
Sunnyview, S.D., U.S.	C9	118
Sunol, Ca., U.S.	h9	82
Sunol, Ne., U.S.	C3	104
Sun Prairie, Wi., U.S.	E4	126
Sunray, Or., U.S.	C4	113
Sunray, Tx., U.S.	A2	120
Sunrise, Fl., U.S.	*r13	86
Sunrise, Wy., U.S.	D8	127
Sunrise Manor, Nv., U.S.	G6	105
Sunrise Mountain, mtn., N.J., U.S.	A3	107
Sun River, Mt., U.S.	C5	103
Sunset, Fl., U.S.	D3	95
Sunset, Me., U.S.	D4	96
Sunset, Tx., U.S.	C4	120
Sunset, Ut., U.S.	B3	121
Sunset Beach, Hi., U.S.	f9	88
Sunset Crater National Monument, Az., U.S.	B4	80
Sunset Lake, l., Vt., U.S.	D2	122
Sunset Park, Ks., U.S.	g12	93
Sunshine, Austl.	*G7	50
Sunshine, Ak., U.S.	f16	79
Sunshine, Ak., U.S.	D4	96
Sunspot, N.M., U.S.	E4	108
Suntar, Sov. Un.	C14	29
Suntrana, Ak., U.S.	C10	79
Sun Valley, Id., U.S.	F4	89
Sun Valley, Nv., U.S.	D2	105
Sunyani, Ghana	E4	45
Suoyarvi, Sov. Un.	F15	14
Superb, Sk., Can.	F1	75
Superior, Az., U.S.	D4	80
Superior, Ia., U.S.	A3	92
Superior, Mt., U.S.	C2	103
Superior, Ne., U.S.	B1	126
Superior, Wy., U.S.	E4	127
Superior, Lake, l., N.A.	A10	76
Superstition Mountains, mts., Az., U.S.	m10	80
Suphan Buri, Thai.	C8	15
Süphan Daǧı, mtn., Tur.	C14	40
Supi Oidak, Az., U.S.	E3	80
Supply, N.C., U.S.	C4	110
Supreme, La., U.S.	k9	95
Supung Reservoir, res., Asia	F2	33
Sūq ash Shuyūkh, Iraq	B3	38
Suquamish, Wa., U.S.	B3	124
Sur, Point, c., Ca., U.S.	D3	82
Sura, stm., Sov. Un.	D16	27
Surabaya, Indon.	G4	34
Surakarta, Indon.	G4	34
Surany, Czech.	D5	26
Surat, Austl.	C7	51
Surat, India	D5	36
Sūratgarh, India	D5	36
Surat Thani, Thai.	D1	34
Sumter, co., S.C., U.S.	E2	87
Sur Bāhir, Isr. Occ.	k11	41
Surco, Peru	*D2	58
Surendranagar (Wadhwān), India	D4	37
Suresnes, Fr.	g9	16
Suretka, C.R.	F6	62
Surettes Island, N.S., Can.	F4	71
Surf City, N.J., U.S.	D4	107
Surfside, Fl., U.S.	*s13	86
Surfside Beach, S.C., U.S.	D10	117
Surgères, Fr.	D3	16
Surgoinsville, Tn., U.S.	C11	119
Surgut, Sov. Un.	C4	28
Sūri, India	D8	36
Suriápet, India	I7	37
Surigao, Phil.	D6	34
Suriname, dept., Sur.	A3	59
Suriname, ctry., S.A.	C6	56
Suring, Wi., U.S.	D5	126
Surkhan Darya, stm., Sov. Un.	D3	39
Surprise, Ne., U.S.	C8	104
Surquillo, Peru	*D2	58
Surrency, Ga., U.S.	E4	87
Surrey, N.D., U.S.	A4	111
Surrey, co., Eng., U.K.	B6	12
Surry, Me., U.S.	D4	96
Surry, Va., U.S.	C6	123
Surry, co., N.C., U.S.	A2	110
Surry, co., Va., U.S.	C6	123
Surry Mountain Lake, res., N.H., U.S.	D2	106
Sursee, Switz.	B5	21
Surt, Libya	C3	43
Sürüç, Tur.	D12	40
Suruga Bay, b., Japan	o17	33
Surveyor, W.V., U.S.	n13	125
Suryānī, Dayr as, hist., Eg.	D2	41
Susa, Italy	B1	23
Sušac, i., Yugo.	D3	24
Sušak (part of Rijeka), Yugo.	C2	24
Susak, i., Yugo.	C2	24
Susanino, Sov. Un.	s31	14
Susank, Ks., U.S.	D5	93
Susanville, Ca., U.S.	B3	82
Sušice, Czech.	D2	26
Susitna, stm., Ak., U.S.	C10	79
Susoh, Indon.	K2	35
Susong, China	l7	32
Susquehanna, Pa., U.S.	C10	115
Susquehanna, co., Pa., U.S.	C10	115
Susquehanna, stm., U.S.	A5	97
Susquehanna, West Branch, stm., Pa., U.S.	D5	115
Susques, Arg.	D2	55
Sussex, N.B., Can.	D4	71
Sussex, N.J., U.S.	A3	107
Sussex, Va., U.S.	D5	123
Sussex, Wi., U.S.	m11	126
Sussex, co., De., U.S.	F4	85
Sussex, co., N.J., U.S.	A3	107
Sussex, co., Va., U.S.	D5	123
Sussex Shores, De., U.S.	F5	85
Sustut, stm., B.C., Can.	A4	69
Susurluk, Tur.	C7	40
Sutcliffe, Nv., U.S.	D2	105
Sutherland, S. Afr.	D3	49
Sutherland, Ia., U.S.	B2	92
Sutherland, Ne., U.S.	C4	104
Sutherland, Ut., U.S.	D3	121
Sutherland, co., Scot., U.K.	C5	123
Sutherland Springs, Tx., U.S.	k7	120
Sutherlin, Or., U.S.	D3	114
Sutlej (Xiangquan He), stm., Asia	B6	36
Sutlej, Abohar Branch, stm., India	B5	37
Sutlej, Hākra Branch, stm., Pak.	C4	37
Sutter, co., Ca., U.S.	C3	82
Sutter Creek, Ca., U.S.	C3	82
Sutton, P.Q., Can.	D5	74
Sutton, Ak., U.S.	g17	79
Sutton, Ma., U.S.	*B4	98
Sutton, Ne., U.S.	D8	104
Sutton, N.H., U.S.	D3	106
Sutton, N.D., U.S.	B7	111
Sutton, Vt., U.S.	B4	122
Sutton, W.V., U.S.	C4	125
Sutton, co., Tx., U.S.	D2	120
Sutton Coldfield, Eng., U.K.	B6	12
Sutton-in-Ashfield, Eng., U.K.	D6	10
Sutton Lake, res., W.V., U.S.	C4	125
Sutton Park, N.J., U.S.	B3	107
Suttons Bay, Mi., U.S.	D5	99
Sutton West, On., Can.	C5	73
Suttsu, Japan	E10	33
Sutwik Island, i., Ak., U.S.	D8	79
Suva, Fiji	I15	52
Suva Harbour, b., Fiji	I15	52
Suwa, Japan	m17	33
Suwałki, Pol.	A7	26
Suwanee, Ga., U.S.	B2	87
Suwannee, Fl., U.S.	C3	86
Suwannee, co., Fl., U.S.	B3	86
Suwannee, stm., U.S.	C4	86
Suwannee Lake, l., Mb., Can.	A1	70
Suwannee Sound, strt., Fl., U.S.	C3	86
Suwanose Island, i., Japan	L4	33
Suwaylih, Jord.	B7	41
Suwaymah, Jord.	h13	41
Suwŏn, S. Kor.	H3	33
Suxian, China	H7	32
Suyo, Peru	B1	58
Suzhou, China	E9	31
Suzu, Japan	B11	33
Suzu, Cape, c., Japan	H8	33
Suzuka, Japan	o15	33
Suzzara, Italy	C5	24
Svalbard, ter., Nor.	B13	128
Svaneke, Den.	C8	15
Svärtagård, Swe.	u35	14
Svartån, stm., Swe.	t34	14
Svatovo, Sov. Un.	G12	27
Svay Rieng, Kam.	k9	95
Svedala, Swe.	C7	15
Svedrup, i., Sov. Un.	B7	128
Sveg, Swe.	F6	14
Svendborg, Den.	C4	15
Svene, Nor.	p27	14
Svenljunga, Swe.	A7	15
Svensen, Or., U.S.	A3	114
Svenstrup, Den.	B3	15
Sverdlovsk, Sov. Un.	q22	27
Sverdlovsk, Sov. Un.	D9	29
Sverdrup Islands, is., N.T., Can.	m32	66
Svetlaya, Sov. Un.	C9	33
Svetlograd, Sov. Un.	I14	27
Svicha, stm., Sov. Un.	D8	26
Svilajnac, Yugo.	C5	24
Svilengrad, Bul.	E8	24
Svindal, Nor.	p29	14
Svinninge, Den.	C5	15
Svir, stm., Sov. Un.	A10	27
Svirstroy, Sov. Un.	A9	27
Svishtov, Czech.	D4	26
Svitavy, Czech.	D4	26
Svobodnyy, Sov. Un.	G19	8
Svobodnyy, Cape, c., Sov. Un.	C11	33
Svyatoy Nos, Cape, c., Sov. Un.	B16	29
Swadlincote, Eng., U.K.	B5	12
Swaffham, Eng., U.K.	B8	12
Swain, co., N.C., U.S.	f9	110
Swain Mountain, mtn., Ca., U.S.	A3	82
Swain Reefs, rf., Austl.	D9	50
Swainsboro, Ga., U.S.	D4	87
Swakopmund, Nmb.	B1	49
Swale, stm., Eng., U.K.	B4	92
Swalwell, Ab., Can.	D4	68
Swampscott, Ma., U.S.	B6	98
Swan, i., Braz.	A2	81
Swan, stm., Ab., Can.	B3	68
Swan, stm., Mb., Can.	C1	70
Swanage, Eng., U.K.	D6	12
Swan Creek, Il., U.S.	C3	90
Swan Creek, stm., Oh., U.S.	e6	112
Swandale, W.V., U.S.	m14	125
Swan Falls, wtfl, Id., U.S.	F2	89
Swan Hill, Austl.	G7	50

211

Name	Map Ref	Page
Swan Hills, Ab., Can.	B3	68
Swan Hills, hills, Ab., Can.	B3	68
Swanington, In., U.S.	C3	91
Swan Lake, Mb., Can.	E2	70
Swanlake, Id., U.S.	G6	89
Swan Lake, Ms., U.S.	B3	101
Swan Lake, Mt., U.S.	C3	103
Swan Lake, l., Mb., Can.	C1	70
Swan Lake, l., Ne., U.S.	D4	96
Swan Lake, l., Ne., U.S.	C3	104
Swanlinbar, Ire.	C4	11
Swannanoa, N.C., U.S.	f10	110
Swan Peak, mtn., Mt., U.S.	C3	103
Swanquarter, N.C., U.S.	B6	110
Swan Range, mts., Mt., U.S.	C3	103
Swan River, Mb., Can.	C1	70
Swan River, Mn., U.S.	C5	100
Swansboro, N.C., U.S.	C5	110
Swansea, Wales, U.K.	E4	10
Swansea, Il., U.S.	E4	90
Swansea, Ma., U.S.	C5	98
Swansea, S.C., U.S.	D5	117
Swansea Bay, b., Wales, U.K.	C4	12
Swansea Center, Ma., U.S.	C5	98
Swans Island, Me., U.S.	D4	96
Swanson, Sk., Can.	F2	75
Swanson Lake, res., Ne., U.S.	D4	104
Swanton, Md., U.S.	m12	97
Swanton, Ne., U.S.	D8	104
Swanton, Oh., U.S.	A2	112
Swanton, Vt., U.S.	B2	122
Swan Valley, Id., U.S.	F7	89
Swanville, Mn., U.S.	E4	100
Swanwick, Il., U.S.	E4	90
Swanwyck Estates, De., U.S.	*B3	85
Swanzey Center, N.H., U.S.	E2	106
Swarthmore, Pa., U.S.	p20	115
Swartswood, N.J., U.S.	A3	107
Swartswood Lake, l., N.J., U.S.	A3	107
Swartz, La., U.S.	B4	95
Swartz Creek, Mi., U.S.	F7	99
Swatara, Mn., U.S.	D5	100
Swatow see Shantou, China	C6	91
Swayzee, In., U.S.	C5	49
Swaziland, ctry., Afr.	A3	92
Sweatman, Ms., U.S.	D5	102
Swedeborg, Mo., U.S.	D5	102
Swedeburg, Ne., U.S.	g11	104
Sweden, ctry., Eur.	F6	14
Swedesboro, N.J., U.S.	D2	107
Sweeny, Tx., U.S.	r14	120
Sweet, Id., U.S.	F2	89
Sweet Briar, Va., U.S.	C3	123
Sweetgrass, Mt., U.S.	B5	103
Sweet Grass, co., Mt., U.S.	E7	103
Sweet Home, In., U.S.	C3	81
Sweet Home, Or., U.S.	C4	114
Sweet Home, Tx., U.S.	E4	120
Sweetser, In., U.S.	C6	91
Sweet Springs, Mo., U.S.	C4	102
Sweet Springs, W.V., U.S.	D4	125
Sweet Valley, Pa., U.S.	D9	115
Sweetwater, Al., U.S.	C2	78
Sweetwater, Id., U.S.	*C2	89
Sweetwater, Ok., U.S.	B2	113
Sweetwater, Tn., U.S.	D9	119
Sweetwater, Tx., U.S.	C2	120
Sweetwater, co., Wy., U.S.	E3	127
Sweetwater, stm., Wy., U.S.	D4	127
Sweetwater Creek, Fl., U.S.	p10	86
Sweetwater Creek, stm., Ok., U.S.	B1	113
Sweetwater Station, Wy., U.S.	D4	127
Swellendam, S. Afr.	D3	49
Swenson, Tx., U.S.	C2	120
Swepsonville, N.C., U.S.	A3	110
Świder, stm., Pol.	m14	26
Świdnica, Pol.	C4	26
Świdwin, Pol.	B3	26
Świebodzice, Pol.	C4	26
Świebodzin, Pol.	B3	26
Świecie, Pol.	B5	26
Świętochłowice, Pol.	g9	26
Świętokrzyskie, Góry, mts., Pol.	C6	26
Swift, In., U.S.	B3	100
Swift, co., Mn., U.S.	E3	100
Swift, N.H., U.S.	B4	106
Swift Creek, stm., N.C., U.S.	B5	110
Swift Creek Reservoir, res., Wa., U.S.	n17	123
Swift Current, Sk., Can.	G2	75
Swiftcurrent Creek, stm., Sk., Can.	H1	75
Swift Diamond, stm., N.H., U.S.	g7	106
Swifton, Ar., U.S.	B4	81
Swiftown, Ms., U.S.	B3	101
Swiftwater, N.H., U.S.	B3	106
Swilly, Lough, b., Ire.	B4	11
Swinburne, Cape, c., N.T., Can.	B13	66
Swindle Island, i., B.C., Can.	C3	69
Swindon, Eng., U.K.	E6	10
Swinford, Ire.	D3	11
Swink, Co., U.S.	C7	83
Swink, Ok., U.S.	C6	113
Swinomish Indian Reservation, Wa., U.S.	A3	124
Świnoujście, Pol.	B3	26
Swisher, Ia., U.S.	C6	92
Swisher, co., Tx., U.S.	B2	120
Swiss, W.V., U.S.	C3	125
Swisshome, Or., U.S.	C3	114
Swissvale, Pa., U.S.	k14	115
Switz City, In., U.S.	F3	91
Switzer, W.V., U.S.	D3	125
Switzerland, Fl., U.S.	m8	86
Switzerland, co., In., U.S.	G7	91
Switzerland, ctry., Eur.	E4	18
Swords, Ire.	D5	11
Swords, Ga., U.S.	C3	87
Swoyerville, Pa., U.S.	D10	115
Sycamore, Al., U.S.	B3	78
Sycamore, Ga., U.S.	E3	87
Sycamore, Il., U.S.	B5	90
Sycamore, Ks., U.S.	E8	93
Sycamore, Mo., U.S.	E5	102
Sycamore, Oh., U.S.	B2	112
Sycamore, S.C., U.S.	E5	117
Sycamore Creek, stm., Tn., U.S.	A4	119
Sycamore Creek, stm., W.V., U.S.	m13	125
Sychevka, Sov. Un.	D10	27
Syców, Pol.	C4	26
Sydenham, On., Can.	C8	73
Sydney, Austl.	F9	50
Sydney, N.S., Can.	C9	71
Sydney Mines, N.S., Can.	C9	71
Sykeston, N.D., U.S.	B6	111

Name	Map Ref	Page
Sykesville, Md., U.S.	B4	97
Sykesville, N.J., U.S.	C3	107
Sykesville, Pa., U.S.	D4	115
Syktyvkar, Sov. Un.	C8	29
Sylacauga, Al., U.S.	B3	78
Sylamore, Ar., U.S.	B3	81
Sylhet, Bngl.	D9	36
Sylling, Nor.	p28	14
Sylt, i., F.R.Ger.	A4	18
Sylva, N.C., U.S.	f9	110
Sylvan, Pa., U.S.	G5	115
Sylvan Beach, N.Y., U.S.	B5	109
Sylvan Grove, Ks., U.S.	C5	93
Sylvan Hills, Ar., U.S.	h10	81
Sylvania, Al., U.S.	A4	78
Sylvania, Ga., U.S.	D5	87
Sylvania, Oh., U.S.	A2	112
Sylvania, Pa., U.S.	C8	115
Sylvan Lake, Ab., Can.	C3	68
Sylvan Lake, Mi., U.S.	o15	99
Sylvan Lake, l., In., U.S.	B7	91
Sylvan Pass, Wy., U.S.	B2	127
Sylvarena, Ms., U.S.	C4	101
Sylvester, Ga., U.S.	E3	87
Sylvester, Tx., U.S.	C2	120
Sylvester, Mount, hill, Nf., Can.	D4	72
Sylvia, Ks., U.S.	E5	93
Sylvia, Tn., U.S.	A4	119
Sym, stm., Sov. Un.	C26	8
Symmes Creek, stm., Oh., U.S.	D3	112
Symsonia, Ky., U.S.	f9	94
Syosset, N.Y., U.S.	*E7	109
Syracuse see Siracusa, Italy	F5	23
Syracuse, In., U.S.	B6	91
Syracuse, Ks., U.S.	E2	93
Syracuse, Mo., U.S.	C5	102
Syracuse, N.Y., U.S.	B4	109
Syracuse, Oh., U.S.	D4	112
Syracuse, Ut., U.S.	B3	121
Syr Darya, stm., Sov. Un.	E9	29
Syria, ctry., Asia	B3	38
Syriam, Burma	D2	35
Syrian Desert, des., Asia	B3	38
Syros see Ermoúpolis, Grc.	D5	40
Sysladobsis Lake, l., Me., U.S.	C4	96
Sysola, stm., Sov. Un.	C19	8
Syurkum, Cape, c., Sov. Un.	A10	33
Syzran, Sov. Un.	D7	29
Szabadszállás, Hung.	B4	24
Szamos (Someş), stm., Eur.	B6	24
Szamotuły, Pol.	B4	26
Szarvas, Hung.	B5	24
Szczakowa (part of Jaworzno), Pol.	g10	26
Szczebrzeszyn, Pol.	C7	26
Szczecin (Stettin), Pol.	B3	26
Szczecinek, Pol.	B4	26
Szczuczyn, Pol.	B7	26
Szczytno, Pol.	B6	26
Szechwan see Sichuan, prov., China	E5	31
Szeged, Hung.	B5	24
Székesfehérvár, Hung.	B4	24
Szekszárd, Hung.	B4	24
Szentendre, Hung.	B4	24
Szentes, Hung.	B5	24
Szigetvár, Hung.	B3	24
Szolnok, Hung.	B5	24
Szombathely, Hung.	B3	24
Szprotawa, Pol.	C3	26
Sztum, Pol.	B5	26
Szubin, Pol.	B4	26
Szydłowiec, Pol.	C6	26
Szymanów, Pol.	m12	26

T

Name	Map Ref	Page
Taal, Phil.	p13	34
Taal, Lake, l., Phil.	p13	34
Tab, In., U.S.	D3	91
Ţābah, Sau. Ar.	E4	40
Tabar Islands, is., Pap. N. Gui.	h13	50
Tabarka, Tun.	F2	23
Ţabas, Iran	E8	39
Ţabas, Iran	E10	39
Tabasco, state, Mex.	D6	63
Tabatinga, Braz.	k7	56
Tabayin, Burma	A1	35
Tabbys Peak, mtn., Ut., U.S.	C3	121
Tablas, Cabo, c., Chile	A2	54
Tablas, i., Phil.	C6	34
Table Bay, b., Nf., Can.	B3	72
Table Bay, b., S. Afr.	D2	49
Table Grove, Il., U.S.	C3	90
Table Head, c., Nf., Can.	B4	72
Table Mountain, mtn., Nf., Can.	E2	72
Table Mountain, mtn., Az., U.S.	E5	80
Table Rock, Ne., U.S.	D9	104
Table Rock Lake, res., U.S.	E4	102
Table Top, mtn., Az., U.S.	E3	80
Taboada, Spain	A2	22
Tábor, Czech.	D3	26
Tabor, Ia., U.S.	D2	92
Tabor, Mn., U.S.	B2	100
Tabor, S.D., U.S.	E8	118
Tabor, Mount, mtn., Isr.	B7	41
Tabora, Tan.	C5	48
Tabora, prov., Tan.	C5	48
Tabor City, N.C., U.S.	C4	110
Tabou, I.C.	E3	45
Tabuaeran Island (Fanning Island), atoll, Kir.	F12	6
Tabūk, Sau. Ar.	C3	38
Tabuk, Phil.	B4	71
Täby, Swe.	*H8	14
Tacámbaro de Codallos, Mex.	n13	63
Tacheng, China	B1	31
Tachichi Point, c., Japan	P17	52
Tachikawa, Japan	n18	33
Táchira, state, Ven.	B3	60
Tachov, Czech.	D2	26
Tacloban, Phil.	C7	34
Tacna, Peru	E3	58
Tacna, Az., U.S.	E1	80
Tacna, dept., Peru	E3	58
Tacoma, Co., U.S.	D3	83

Name	Map Ref	Page
Tacoma, Wa., U.S.	B3	124
Taconic, Ct., U.S.	A2	84
Taconic Range, mts., U.S.	A1	98
Taconite, Mn., U.S.	C5	100
Tacoronte, Spain	m13	22
Tacuarembo, Ur.	E1	56
Tacuatí, Para.	D4	55
Tad, W.V., U.S.	m13	125
Tademaît, Plateau du, plat., Alg.	D5	44
Tadjoura, Dji.	C5	47
Tadoule Lake, l., Mb., Can.	f8	70
Tadoussac, P.Q., Can.	A8	74
T'aebaek-Sanmaek, mts., Asia	H4	33
Taegu, S. Kor.	D10	31
Taejŏn, S. Kor.	D10	31
Taeyu-dong, N. Kor.	F2	33
Tafalla, Spain	A5	22
Tafí Viejo, Arg.	E2	55
Tafresh, Kūh-e, mtn., Iran	D5	39
Taft, Ca., U.S.	E4	82
Taft, La., U.S.	k11	95
Taft, Ok., U.S.	B6	113
Taft, Tn., U.S.	B5	119
Taft, Tx., U.S.	F4	120
Taftān, Kūh-e, mtn., Iran	G10	39
Taftsville, Vt., U.S.	D4	122
Tafuna International Airport, Am. Sam.	G13	52
Tagaytay, Phil.	o13	34
Tagbilaran, Phil.	D6	34
Taghmon, Ire.	E5	11
Taghrīfat, Libya	D3	43
Tagliamento, stm., Italy	C8	20
Tagolo Point, c., Phil.	D6	34
Taguan Point, c., Guam	L10	52
Taguatinga, Braz.	D1	57
Tagus, N.D., U.S.	A4	111
Tagus (Tejo) (Tajo), stm., Eur.	C1	22
Tahan, mtn., Malay.	E2	34
Tahat, mtn., Alg.	E6	44
Tahgong, Puntan, c., N. Mar. Is.	D7	52
Tahiti, i., Fr. Poly.	H13	6
Tahlequah, Ok., U.S.	B7	113
Ţahmā wa Minshāt 'Abd as Sayyid, Eg.	E3	41
Tahoe, Lake, l., U.S.	E1	105
Tahoe City, Ca., U.S.	C3	82
Tahoka, Tx., U.S.	C2	120
Taholah, Wa., U.S.	B1	124
Tahoma, Ca., U.S.	C3	82
Tahoua, Niger	D6	45
Tahquamenon, stm., Mi., U.S.	B5	99
Tahsis, B.C., Can.	E4	69
Tahtā, Eg.	C3	38
Tahtsa Lake, l., B.C., Can.	C4	69
Tahtsa Peak, mtn., B.C., Can.	C4	69
Tahuya, Wa., U.S.	B2	124
Taï, I.C.	E3	45
Tai'an, China	F7	32
Tai'an, China	D10	32
Taibus Qi, China	D6	32
T'aichung, Tai.	G9	31
Taigu, China	F5	32
Taihape, N.Z.	M15	51
Taiho, Japan	N6	52
Taihu, China	A10	32
Tai Lake, l., China	E8	31
Tailem Bend, Austl.	G6	50
Tailevu Point, c., Fiji	H15	52
Taim, Scot., U.K.	B4	10
T'ainan, Tai.	G9	31
T'ainaron, Akra, c., Grc.	D4	40
Taining, China	K7	32
Taioibeiras, Braz.	B4	56
Taipei, Tai.	G9	31
Taiping, Malay.	E2	34
Taipu, Braz.	g6	57
Taira see Iwaki, Japan	H10	33
Taishun, China	K8	32
Taitao, Península de, pen., Chile	D2	54
T'aitung, Tai.	G9	31
Taivalkoski, Fin.	E13	14
Taiwan, ctry., Asia	G9	31
Taiwan Strait, strt., Asia	G8	31
Taiyuan, China	D7	31
Taizhao, China	E3	31
Taizhou, China	H8	32
Ta'izz, Yemen	D4	38
Tajarhī, Libya	E2	43
Tajik S.S.R., state, Sov. Un.	F9	29
Tajimi, Japan	I8	33
Tajique, N.M., U.S.	C3	108
Tajo (Tejo) (Tagus), stm., Spain	C3	22
Tajumulco, Volcán, vol., Guat.	C2	62
Tajuña, stm., Spain	B4	22
Tajūrā', Libya	C2	43
Tak, Thai.	B1	34
Takabanare Island, i., Japan	O6	52
Takahe, Mount, mtn., Ant.	B17	7
Takaka, N.Z.	N14	51
Takamatsu, Japan	E11	31
Takaoka, Japan	H8	33
Takapuna, N.Z.	L15	51
Takara Island, i., Japan	L4	52
Takasaki, Japan	H9	33
Takashippu, Japan	O5	52
Takatō, Japan	n17	33
Takatsuki, Japan	o14	33
Takaw, Burma	B3	35
Takayama, Japan	H8	33
Take Islands see Tok Islands, is., Asia	H5	52
Takeo, Camb.	J2	35
Takeshiri Island, i., Japan	D10	33
Takestān, Iran	C4	39
Takev, Kam.	G6	35
Takhta-Bazar, Sov. Un.	D11	29
Takhtakupyr, Sov. Un.	E6	28
Takigawa, Japan	E10	33
Takikawa, Japan	C10	66
Takilma, Or., U.S.	E3	114
Takingeun, Indon.	J2	35
Takishiri Island, i., Japan	D10	33
Takla Lake, l., B.C., Can.	B5	69
Takla Makan, des., China	F11	29
Takoma Park, Md., U.S.	f8	97
Takotna, Ak., U.S.	C8	79
Takpocha, Okso, mtn., N. Mar. Is.	D7	52
Taku, stm., Ak., U.S.	k23	79
Taku Pa, Thai.	H3	35
Taku Glacier, Ak., U.S.	k22	79
Takut, Burma	A3	35
Tala, Mex.	G8	62
Tala, Ur.	m12	56
Tala, Hill of, hist., Ire.	E1	56
Talaga, Phil.	p13	34
Talagante, Chile	A2	54
Talakan, Sov. Un.	B6	33

Name	Map Ref	Page
Talakmau, mtn., Indon.	E1	34
Talala, Ok., U.S.	A6	113
Talanga, Hond.	C4	62
Talara, Peru	B1	58
Talas, Sov. Un.	E8	28
Talasea, Pap. N. Gui.	k13	50
Talata Mafara, Nig.	D6	45
Talaud Islands, is., Indon.	E7	34
Talavera de la Reina, Spain	C3	22
Talawdī, Sud.	C3	47
Talbert, Ky., U.S.	C6	94
Talbot, In., U.S.	D3	91
Talbot, co., Ga., U.S.	D2	87
Talbot, co., Md., U.S.	C5	97
Talbot Island, i., Fl., U.S.	B5	86
Talbotton, Ga., U.S.	D2	87
Talca, Chile	B2	54
Talcahuano, Chile	B2	54
Talco, Tx., U.S.	C5	120
Talcott, W.V., U.S.	D4	125
Talcottville, N.Y., U.S.	B5	109
Taldy-Kurgan, Sov. Un.	D9	28
Talent, Or., U.S.	E4	114
Taliabu, i., Indon.	F6	34
Taliaferro, co., Ga., U.S.	C4	87
Talica, Sov. Un.	B6	28
Talihina, Ok., U.S.	C6	113
Talim Island, i., Phil.	o13	34
Tali Post, Sud.	D3	47
Talisay, Phil.	o14	34
Talisheek, La., U.S.	D6	95
Talish Mountains, mts., Asia	B4	39
Talkeetna, Ak., U.S.	C10	79
Talkeetna Mountains, mts., Ak., U.S.	f17	79
Ţalkhā, Eg.	C3	41
Talking Rock, Ga., U.S.	B2	87
Tall 'Afar, Iraq	D14	40
Talla Bena, La., U.S.	B4	95
Talladega, Al., U.S.	B3	78
Talladega, co., Al., U.S.	B3	78
Talladega Mountain, mtn., Al., U.S.	B3	78
Talladega Springs, Al., U.S.	B3	78
Tallahala Creek, stm., Ms., U.S.	D4	101
Tallahassee, Fl., U.S.	B2	86
Tallahatchie, co., Ms., U.S.	B3	101
Tallahatchie, stm., Ms., U.S.	B3	101
Tall al Abyaḍ, Syria	B3	38
Tallangatta, Austl.	A5	113
Tallant, Ok., U.S.	A5	113
Tallapoosa, Ga., U.S.	C1	87
Tallapoosa, Mo., U.S.	E8	102
Tallapoosa, co., Al., U.S.	C4	78
Tallapoosa, stm., Al., U.S.	C3	78
Tallard, Fr.	E2	20
Tallassee, Al., U.S.	C4	78
Talleyville, De., U.S.	A3	85
Tallinn, Sov. Un.	D5	29
Tall Kalakh, Syria	E11	40
Tallmadge, Oh., U.S.	A4	112
Tallow, Ire.	E3	11
Tallula, Il., U.S.	D4	90
Tallulah, La., U.S.	B4	95
Tallūzā, Isr. Occ.	f12	41
Talmage, Sk., Can.	H4	75
Talmage, Ks., U.S.	C6	93
Talmage, Ne., U.S.	D9	104
Talmage, Ut., U.S.	C5	121
Talo, mtn., Eth.	C4	47
Talofofo, Guam	M10	52
Talofofo Bay, b., Guam	M10	52
Taloga, Ok., U.S.	A3	113
Talon, Lake, l., On., Can.	A5	73
Talowah, Ms., U.S.	D4	101
Talpa, Tx., U.S.	D3	120
Talpa de Allende, Mex.	m11	63
Talquin, Lake, res., Fl., U.S.	B2	86
Talsi, Sov. Un.	C4	27
Taltal, Chile	E1	55
Tama, co., Ia., U.S.	B5	92
Tama, Ia., U.S.	B5	92
Tamacuarí, Pico, mtn., S.A.	B7	113
Tamaha, Ok., U.S.	B3	60
Tamalameque, Col.	B3	60
Tamale, Ghana	E4	45
Tamalpais, Mount, mtn., Ca., U.S.	h7	82
Taman, Sov. Un.	I11	27
Tamana, Mount, hill, Trin.	O23	65
Tamanar, Mor.	C3	44
Tamano, Japan	I6	33
Tamaqua, Pa., U.S.	E10	115
Tamar, stm., Eng., U.K.	D3	12
Tamarac, Fl., U.S.	*r13	86
Tamarack, Mn., U.S.	D5	100
Tamarite [de Litera], Spain	B6	22
Tamaroa, Il., U.S.	E4	90
Tamassee, S.C., U.S.	B1	117
Tamaulipas, state, Mex.	C5	63
Tamazula de Gordiano, Mex.	n12	63
Tamazulapan [del Progreso], Mex.	o15	63
Tamazunchale, Mex.	A6	48
Tambach, Kenya	B6	48
Tambacounda, Sen.	D2	45
Tambaú, Braz.	k8	56
També, Braz.	n17	57
Tambelan Besar, i., Indon.	L7	35
Tambelan Islands, is., Indon.	E3	34
Tambo, Austl.	E4	50
Tambo, stm., Peru	E3	58
Tambo, stm., Peru	B1	58
Tambo Grande, Peru	B1	58
Tambohorano, Madag.	g8	49
Tambov, Sov. Un.	D7	29
Tambre, stm., Spain	A2	22
Tambura, Sud.	D2	47
Tamchaket, Maur.	C2	45
Tamdybulak, Sov. Un.	E6	28
Tame, Col.	C4	60
Tâmega, stm., Port.	B2	22
Tamenghest, Alg.	E6	44
Tamenghest, Oued, val., Alg.	E5	44
Tamgué, Massif du, mts., Gui.	D2	45
Tamiahua, Mex.	C5	63
Tamiahua, Laguna de, b., Mex.	C5	63
Tamiami Canal, Fl., U.S.	G6	86
Tamil Nadu (Madras), state, India	F5	36
Tamina, Switz.	C7	21
Tamiš, stm., Yugo.	C5	24
Tam Ky, Viet.	G9	35
Tamms, Il., U.S.	F4	90
Ţammūn, Isr. Occ.	B7	41
Tamney, Ire.	B4	11
Tamo, Ar., U.S.	C4	81

Name	Map Ref	Page
Tamora, Ne., U.S.	D8	104
Tampa, Fl., U.S.	E4	86
Tampa, Ks., U.S.	D6	93
Tampa Bay, b., Fl., U.S.	E4	86
Tampere, Fin.	G10	14
Tampico, Mex.	C5	63
Tampico, Il., U.S.	B4	90
Tampico, In., U.S.	G6	91
Tampico, Mt., U.S.	B10	103
Tams, W.V., U.S.	D3	125
Tamsagbulag, Mong.	B7	31
Tamshiyacu, Peru	B3	58
Tamuning, Guam	J5	52
Tamworth, Austl.	F9	50
Tamworth, Eng., U.K.	B6	12
Tamworth, N.H., U.S.	C4	106
Tana, Chile	C2	55
Tana, stm., Eur.	B12	14
Tana, stm., Kenya	B7	48
Tana, Lake, l., Eth.	C4	47
Tanabe, Japan	J7	33
Tanabi, Braz.	C3	56
Tanacross, Ak., U.S.	C11	79
Tanafjorden, Nor.	B13	14
Tanaga Island, i., Ak., U.S.	E4	79
Tanah, mtn., Indon.	F1	34
Tanahbala, i., Indon.	F1	34
Tanahgrogot, Indon.	F5	34
Tanahmasa, i., Indon.	F1	34
Tanakpur, India	C8	37
Tanami, Austl.	C4	50
Tan An, Viet.	G7	35
Tanana, Ak., U.S.	B9	79
Tanana, stm., Ak., U.S.	C10	79
Tananarive see Antananarivo, Madag.	g9	49
Tanap, N. Mar. Is.	D8	52
Tanapag, Lagunan, b., N. Mar. Is.	D7	52
Tanaro, stm., Italy	B2	23
Tanauan, Phil.	o13	34
Tanauella, Italy	D2	23
Tanavuso Point, c., Fiji	H15	52
Tancheng, China	G8	32
Tanchŏn, N. Kor.	F4	33
Tancook Island, N.S., Can.	E5	71
Tānda, India	D9	37
Tandalī, Sud.	C3	47
Tăndărei, Rom.	C8	24
Tandil, Arg.	B5	54
Tando Ādam, Pak.	E2	37
Tandou Lake, l., Austl.	F3	51
Tanega Island, i., Japan	E11	31
Tanegashima Strait, strt., Japan	K5	33
Taney, co., Mo., U.S.	E4	102
Taneycomo, Lake, res., Mo., U.S.	E4	102
Taneytown, Md., U.S.	A3	97
Taneyville, Mo., U.S.	E4	102
Tanezrouft, des., Afr.	E4	44
Tanga, Tan.	C6	48
Tanga, prov., Tan.	B6	48
Tanganicuaro [de Arista], Mex.	n12	63
Tanganyika, Lake, l., Afr.	C5	48
Tangent, Or., U.S.	C3	114
Tangerhütte, Ger.D.R.	A6	19
Tangermünde, Ger.D.R.	B5	18
Tanggula Mountains, mts., China	E3	31
Tanghe, China	E7	31
Tangier, N.S., Can.	E7	71
Tangier (Tanger), Mor.	B3	44
Tangier, In., U.S.	E3	91
Tangier, Va., U.S.	C7	123
Tangier Island, i., Va., U.S.	C6	123
Tangier Sound, strt., Md., U.S.	D6	97
Tangipahoa, La., U.S.	D5	95
Tangipahoa, co., La., U.S.	D5	95
Tangipahoa, stm., La., U.S.	D5	95
Tangra Lake, l., China	B8	36
Tangshan, China	D5	45
Tanguiéta, Benin	E6	45
Tanguisson Point, c., Guam	L10	52
Tangwang He, stm., China	B10	31
Tangyuan, China	C4	33
Tanimbar Islands, is., Indon.	G8	34
Tanjore see Thanjāvūr, India	F6	36
Tanjung, Indon.	F5	34
Tanjungbalai, Indon.	E1	34
Tanjungkarang-Telukbetung, Indon.	G3	34
Tanjungpandan, Indon.	F3	34
Tanjungselor, Indon.	E5	34
Tānk, Pak.	B5	36
Tännäs, Swe.	F5	14
Tanner, Al., U.S.	A3	78
Tanner, W.V., U.S.	C4	125
Tanner, Mount, mtn., B.C., Can.	E8	69
Tannersville, N.Y., U.S.	C6	109
Tannis Bugt, b., Den.	A4	15
Tannu-Ola Mountains, mts., Asia	A3	31
Tannūrah, Ra's at, c., Sau. Ar.	H5	39
Tanout, Niger	C6	45
Tanque, stm., Fr. Gu.	B4	59
Tanque Verde, Az., U.S.	E5	80
Ţanţā, Eg.	B3	38
Tantallon, Sk., Can.	G5	75
Tantani, mtn., Peru	m14	63
Tantoyuca, Mex.	C5	63
Tanum (Tanumshede), Swe.	H4	14
Tanza, Phil.	o13	34
Tanzania, ctry., Afr.	C5	48
Tao, i., Thai.	H4	35
Tao'an, China	B9	31
Tao'er He, stm., China	B9	31
Taopi, Mn., U.S.	G6	100
Taormina, Italy	F5	23
Taos, Mo., U.S.	C5	102
Taos, N.M., U.S.	A4	108
Taos, co., N.M., U.S.	A4	108
Taos Pueblo, N.M., U.S.	A4	108
Taoudenni, Maur.	B4	45
Taoyuan, China	J4	32
Tapachula, Mex.	E6	63
Tapaga, Cape, c., W. Sam.	G12	52
Tapajós, stm., Braz.	C3	59
Tapaktuan, Indon.	m11	34
Tapanahony, stm., Sur.	C6	59
Tapanui, N.Z.	P12	51
Tapauá, Braz.	D2	59
Tapauá, stm., Braz.	D2	59
Tapejara, Braz.	B2	56
Tapeta, Lib.	E3	45
Tāpi, stm., India	D5	36
Tapirapé, stm., Braz.	E3	59
Tapoco, N.C., U.S.	f9	110
Tappahannock, Va., U.S.	C6	123

Name	Map Ref	Page
Tappan, N.Y., U.S.	g13	109
Tappan, Lake, res., N.J., U.S.	g9	107
Tappan Lake, res., Oh., U.S.	C6	111
Tappen, N.D., U.S.	N14	51
Tapuaenuku, mtn., N.Z.	G13	52
Taputapu, Cape, c., Am. Sam.	B4	47
Taqāţu'Ḥayyā, Sud.	D2	56
Taquara, Braz.	D2	56
Taquara, Braz.	B1	56
Taquari, stm., Braz.	D2	56
Taquari, stm., Braz.	h5	57
Taquaritinga do Norte, Braz.	B5	111
Tar, stm., N.C., U.S.	C3	73
Tara, On., Can.	D10	29
Tara, Sov. Un.	B9	28
Tara, stm., Sov. Un.	D4	24
Tara, stm., Yugo.	D5	13
Tara, Hill of, hist., Ire.	C2	56
Tarabai, Braz.	h8	57
Tara Hills, Ca., U.S.	E5	34
Tarakan, Indon.	C9	24
Tarakliya, Sov. Un.	B4	22
Tarancón, Spain	D2	56
Taranto, Italy	E6	23
Taranto, Gulf of, b., Italy	C1	13
Tarapacá, Col.	D2	55
Tarapacá, prov., Chile	C2	55
Tarapoto, Peru	C3	58
Tarare, Fr.	E6	16
Tarascon-sur-Ariège, Fr.	F4	16
Tarascon-sur-Rhône, Fr.	F6	16
Tarata, Bol.	C2	55
Tarata, Peru	E3	58
Tarawa, atoll, Kir.	F10	6
Tarawera, N.Z.	M16	51
Tarazit, Massif de, mts., Niger	C6	45
Tarazona, Spain	B5	22
Tarbagatay Range, mts., Asia	D10	28
Tarbat Ness, c., Scot., U.K.	B5	10
Tarbellville, Vt., U.S.	E3	122
Tärbes, Fr.	F4	16
Tarbert, Scot., U.K.	D4	13
Tarbert, Scot., U.K.	C2	13
Tarboro, N.C., U.S.	B5	110
Tarbū, Libya	D3	43
Tarcenay, Fr.	B1	21
Tarcento, Italy	C9	20
Tarcoola, Austl.	F5	50
Tardoki-Yani, Mount, mtn., Sov. Un.	B9	33
Taree, Austl.	F9	50
Tarentum, Pa., U.S.	E2	115
Tarfawi, Bi'r, well, Sud.	A3	47
Tarfaya, Mor.	D2	44
Targhee Pass, U.S.	E7	89
Tarifa, Spain	D3	22
Tarifa, Point, c., Spain	D3	22
Tariffville, Ct., U.S.	B4	84
Tarigtig Point, c., Phil.	n14	34
Tarija, Bol.	D3	55
Tarija, dept., Bol.	D3	55
Tarim He, stm., China	E11	29
Tarim Pendi, des., China	E11	30
Tarkastad, S. Afr.	D4	49
Tarkio, Mo., U.S.	A2	102
Tarko-Sale, Sov. Un.	C24	8
Tarkwa, Ghana	E4	45
Tarlac, Phil.	B6	34
Tarland, Scot., U.K.	C3	112
Tarlton, Oh., U.S.	C3	112
Tarm, Den.	C3	15
Tarm, stm., Fr.	B5	24
Tarnobrzeg, Pol.	C6	26
Tarnopol, Sk., Can.	E3	75
Tarnov, Ne., U.S.	C8	104
Tarnów, Pol.	C6	26
Tarnowskie Góry, Pol.	C5	26
Taro, stm., Italy	B2	23
Taroom, Austl.	B7	51
Taroudant, Mor.	C3	44
Taro, F.R.Ger.	D4	82
Tarpey, Ca., U.S.	D4	82
Tarpon, Lake, l., Fl., U.S.	o10	86
Tarpon Springs, Fl., U.S.	D4	86
Tarqui, Peru	B2	58
Tarquinia, Italy	C4	23
Tarragona, Spain	B6	22
Tarrant, co., Tx., U.S.	C4	120
Tarrant City, Al., U.S.	B3	78
Tarrega, Spain	B6	22
Tarry, Ar., U.S.	C3	81
Tarryall Creek, stm., Co., U.S.	B5	83
Tarryall Mountains, mts., Co., U.S.	B5	83
Tarrytown, Fl., U.S.	D4	86
Tarrytown, Ga., U.S.	D4	87
Tarrytown, N.Y., U.S.	D7	109
Tårs, Den.	A4	15
Tartagal, Arg.	A3	54
Tartāsh, Libya	D5	29
Tartas, stm., Sov. Un.	B5	111
Tartu, Sov. Un.	D6	27
Tartuguan Point, c., Guam	M10	52
Ţarţūs, Syria	H5	39
Tārūt, i., Sau. Ar.	H5	39
Tarutung, Indon.	L3	35
Tarver, Ga., U.S.	F3	87
Tasāral, Sov. Un.	D8	28
Tasāwah, Libya	D2	43
Taseko, stm., B.C., Can.	D6	69
Taseko Lakes, l., B.C., Can.	D6	69
Taseko Mountain, mtn., B.C., Can.	D6	69
Tashauz, Sov. Un.	E5	28
Tash-Kumyr, Sov. Un.	E8	28
Tashkent, Sov. Un.	E7	28
Tasikmalaya, Indon.	G3	34
Tăšinge, i., Den.	D4	15
Taskan, Sov. Un.	C18	9
Taşköprü, Tur.	B10	40
Tasman Bay, b., N.Z.	N14	51
Tasmania, state, Austl.	o15	50
Tasman Peninsula, pen., Austl.	o15	50
Tasman Sea, Oc.	I9	6
Tasso, Tn., U.S.	D9	119
Taswell, In., U.S.	H4	91
Tata, Hung.	B4	24
Tatabánya, Hung.	B4	24

Name	Map Ref	Page
Tatamagouche, N.S., Can.	D6	71
Tatarbunary, Sov. Un.	C9	24
Tatarsk, Sov. Un.	B9	28
Tatar Strait, strt., Sov. Un.	D17	29
Tate, Sk., Can.	F3	75
Tate, Ga., U.S.	B2	87
Tate, co., Ms., U.S.	A4	101
Tateville, Ky., U.S.	D5	94
Tateyama, Japan	I9	33
Tathlina Lake, l., N.T., Can.	D9	66
Tatitlek, Ak., U.S.	C10	79
Tatla Lake, l., B.C., Can.	C5	69
Tatlayoko Lake, B.C., Can.	D5	69
Tatnam, Cape, c., Mb., Can.	f9	70
Tatta, Pak.	D4	36
Tattershall, Eng., U.K.	A7	12
Tattnall, co., Ga., U.S	D4	87
Tatui, Braz.	C3	56
Tatum, N.M., U.S.	D6	108
Tatum, S.C., U.S.	B8	117
Tatumville, Tn., U.S.	A2	119
Tatvan, Tur.	C14	40
Tauá, Braz.	C2	57
Taubaté, Braz.	C3	56
Tauber, stm., F.R.Ger.	D4	19
Tauberbischofsheim, F.R.Ger.	D4	19
Taucha, Ger.D.R.	B7	19
Tauern Tunnel, Aus.	C9	20
Taughmaconnell, Ire.	D3	11
Taumarunui, N.Z.	L15	51
Taum Sauk Mountain, mtn., Mo., U.S.	D6	102
Taung, Boph.	C3	49
Taungdwingyi, Burma	D10	36
Taunggyi, Burma	D10	36
Taunton, Eng., U.K.	E5	10
Taunton, Ma., U.S.	C5	98
Taunton, Mn., U.S.	F2	100
Taunton, stm., Ma., U.S.	C5	98
Taunton Lakes, N.J., U.S.	D3	107
Taunus, mts., F.R.Ger	C3	19
Taupo, Lake, l., N.Z.	M15	51
Tauragė, Sov. Un.	D4	27
Tauranga, N.Z.	L16	51
Taureau, Réservoir, res., P.Q., Can.	C4	74
Taurianova, Italy	E6	23
Tauroa Point, c., N.Z.	K14	51
Taurus Mountains, mts., Tur.	D8	40
Tauste, Spain	B5	22
Tavannes, Switz.	B3	21
Tavares, Tur.	D5	86
Tavas, Tur.	D7	25
Tavda, Sov. Un.	C4	28
Tavda, stm., Sov. Un.	C6	29
Tavernier, Fl., U.S.	G6	86
Taveuni, i., Fiji	H16	52
Tavira, Port.	D2	22
Tavistock, On., Can.	D4	73
Tavistock, Eng., U.K.	D3	12
Tavolzhan, Sov. Un.	C9	28
Tavoy, Burma	F10	36
Tavoy Point, c., Burma	F2	35
Tavşanlı, Tur.	C7	25
Taw, stm., Eng., U.K.	D4	12
Tawakoni, Lake, res., Tx., U.S.	C4	120
Tawas City, Mi., U.S.	D7	99
Tawas Lake, l., Mi., U.S.	D7	99
Tawatinaw, Ab., Can.	B4	68
Tawau, Malay.	E5	34
Tawe, stm., Wales, U.K.	C4	12
Tawitawi Group, is., Phil.	D6	34
Tawitawi Island, i., Phil.	D5	34
Ţawkar, Sud.	B4	47
Tāwurghā', Libya	C3	43
Taxco de Alarcón, Mex.	n14	63
Tay, stm., Scot., U.K.	B5	10
Tay, Firth of, est., Scot., U.K.	B5	10
Tay, Loch, l., Scot., U.K.	B4	10
Tayabamba, Peru	C2	58
Ṭayāsīr, Isr. Occ.	f12	41
Taycheedah, Wi., U.S.	k9	126
Tayga, Sov. Un.	B11	28
Taylor, B.C., Can.	A7	69
Taylor, Az., U.S.	C5	80
Taylor, Ar., U.S.	D2	81
Taylor, Mi., U.S.	p15	99
Taylor, Ms., U.S.	A4	101
Taylor, Ne., U.S.	C6	104
Taylor, N.D., U.S.	C3	111
Taylor, Pa., U.S.	D10	115
Taylor, Wi., U.S.	D2	126
Taylor, co., Fl., U.S.	B3	86
Taylor, co., Ga., U.S.	D2	87
Taylor, co., Ia., U.S.	D3	92
Taylor, co., Ky., U.S.	C4	94
Taylor, co., Tx., U.S.	C3	120
Taylor, co., W.V., U.S.	B4	125
Taylor, stm., Co., U.S.	C4	83
Taylor, Mount, mtn., N.M., U.S.	B2	108
Taylor Knob, hill, Tn., U.S.	G10	119
Taylor Mill, Ky., U.S.	k14	94
Taylor Mountain, mtn., Id., U.S.	E4	89
Taylor Park Reservoir, res., Co., U.S.	D5	82
Taylor Ridge, mtn., Ga., U.S.	B1	87
Taylors, S.C., U.S.	B3	117
Taylors Falls, Mn., U.S.	E6	100
Taylors Island, Md., U.S.	D5	97
Taylors Island, i., Md., U.S.	D5	97
Taylorsport, Ky., U.S.	h13	94
Taylor Springs, Il., U.S.	D4	90
Taylorsville, Ga., U.S.	B2	87
Taylorsville, Ky., U.S.	B4	94
Taylorsville, Ms., U.S.	D4	101
Taylorsville, N.C., U.S.	B1	110
Taylorsville, Ut., U.S.	*C4	121
Taylorville, Il., U.S.	D4	90
Taymā', Sau. Ar.	D7	43
Taymouth, N.B., Can.	C3	71
Taymyr Lake, l., Sov. Un.	B13	29
Taymyr Peninsula, pen., Sov. Un.	B12	29
Tay Ninh, Viet.	G7	35
Tayport, Scot., U.K.	B6	13
Tayshet, Sov. Un.	D12	29
Tayside, prov., Scot., U.K.	D5	13
Taytay, Phil.	C5	34
Taytsy, Sov. Un.	s31	14
Tayug, Phil.	n13	34
Taz, stm., Sov. Un.	C11	29
Taza, Mor.	C4	44
Taz Bay, b., Sov. Un.	C7	28
Tazerbo, well, Libya	D4	43
Tazewell, Tn., U.S.	C10	119
Tazewell, Va., U.S.	e10	123
Tazewell, co., Il., U.S.	C4	90
Tazewell, co., Va., U.S.	e10	123
Tazrouk, Alg.	E6	44
Tbessa, Alg.	B6	44
Tbilisi, Sov. Un.	E7	29
Tchibanga, Gabon	F2	46
Tchien, Lib.	E3	45
Tchula, Ms., U.S.	B3	101
Tczew, Pol.	A5	26
Tea, S.D., U.S.	D9	118
Tea, stm., Braz.	D4	60
Teachey, N.C., U.S.	C4	110
Tea Creek, stm., Sk., Can.	C2	75
Teapa, Mex.	D6	63
Teaneck, N.J., U.S.	h8	107
Teangue, Scot., U.K.	C3	13
Tearaght, i., Ire.	E1	11
Tearinibai, Kir.	R18	52
Teasdale, Ut., U.S.	E4	121
Teaticket, Ma., U.S.	C6	98
Tea Tree Gully, Austl.	*F6	50
Te Awamutu, N.Z.	M15	51
Tebbetts, Mo., U.S.	C6	102
Tebicuary, stm., Para.	E4	55
Tebingtinggi, Indon.	E1	34
Tecalitlán, Mex.	m12	63
Teche, Bayou, stm., La., U.S.	D4	95
Tecirghiol, Rom.	C9	24
Tecka, Arg.	C2	54
Tecolotito, Mex.	B4	108
Tecomán, Mex.	D4	63
Tecolutla, stm., Mex.	m15	63
Tecomán, Ca., U.S.	E5	82
Tecopa de Galeana, Mex.	D4	63
Tecuala, Mex.	C3	63
Tecuci, Rom.	C8	24
Tecumseh, On., Can.	E2	73
Tecumseh, Ks., U.S.	k14	93
Tecumseh, Mi., U.S.	G7	99
Tecumseh, Ne., U.S.	D9	104
Tecumseh, Ok., U.S.	B5	113
Tecumseh, Mount, mtn., N.H., U.S.	C3	106
Ted Ceidaor Dabole, Som.	E5	47
Tedrow, Oh., U.S.	A1	112
Tedzhen, Sov. Un.	C10	39
Teec Nos Pos, Az., U.S.	A6	80
Teegarden, In., U.S.	B5	91
Tees, Ab., Can.	C4	68
Tees, stm., Eng., U.K.	C6	10
Teesside see Middlesbrough, Eng., U.K.	C6	10
Teeswater, On., Can.	C3	73
Tefé, Braz.	C2	59
Tefé, stm., Braz.	B4	58
Tefé, Lago de, l., Braz.	C2	59
Tefenni, Tur.	D7	25
Tefft, In., U.S.	B4	91
Tegal, Indon.	G3	34
Tegelen, Neth.	C6	17
Tegern Lake, l., F.R.Ger.	B7	20
Teglio, Italy	D9	21
Tegucigalpa, Hond.	E7	63
Teguise, Spain	m15	22
Tehachapi, Ca., U.S.	E4	82
Tehachapi Mountains, mts., Ca., U.S.	E4	82
Tehama, co., Ca., U.S.	B2	82
Tehek Lake, l., N.T., Can.	C13	66
Tehran, Iran	B5	38
Tehri, India	B7	37
Tehuacán, Mex.	D5	63
Tehuantepec, Mex.	D5	63
Tehuantepec, Golfo de, b., Mex.	D6	63
Tehuantepec, Istmo de, Mex.	D6	63
Tehuitzingo, Mex.	n14	63
Teide, Pico de, mtn., Spain	m13	22
Teifi, stm., Wales, U.K.	B3	12
Teigen, Mt., U.S.	C8	103
Teignmouth, Eng., U.K.	D4	12
Teiteiripucchi, i., Marsh Is.	S18	52
Tekamah, Ne., U.S.	C9	104
Tekax de Álvaro Obregón, Mex.	C7	63
Tekeli, Sov. Un.	E9	28
Tekeze, stm., Afr.	C4	47
Tekirdağ, Tur.	B6	40
Tekkali, India	H10	37
Tekoa, Wa., U.S.	B8	124
Tekonsha, Mi., U.S.	F5	99
Tekro, well, Chad	B4	46
Te Kuiti, N.Z.	M15	51
Tel, stm., India	D7	36
Tela, Hond.	D7	63
Telavi, Sov. Un.	E3	28
Telde, Spain	m14	22
Telegraph Creek, B.C., Can.	m16	69
Telén, Arg.	B3	54
Teleneshty, Sov. Un.	B9	24
Teleorman, stm., Rom.	C7	24
Telephone, Tx., U.S.	C4	120
Télérthéba, Djebel, mtn., Alg.	E6	44
Telescope Peak, mtn., Ca., U.S.	D5	82
Telfair, co., Ga., U.S.	E4	87
Telford, Pa., U.S.	F11	115
Telford, Tn., U.S.	C11	119
Telfs, Aus.	B7	20
Télimélé, Gui.	D2	45
Telkwa, B.C., Can.	B4	69
Tell, Tx., U.S.	B2	120
Tell City, In., U.S.	I4	91
Teller, Ak., U.S.	B6	79
Teller, co., Co., U.S.	C5	83
Tellico Plains, Tn., U.S.	D9	119
Tel Mond, Isr.	D3	83
Telogia, Fl., U.S.	B1	86
Telok Anson, Malay.	E2	34
Teloloapan, Mex.	D5	63
Telos Lake, l., Me., U.S.	B3	96
Tema, Ghana	E5	45
Temax, Mex.	C7	63
Tembo, Zaire	C2	48
Temecula, Ca., U.S.	F5	82
Temerloh, Malay.	K5	35
Temirtau, Sov. Un.	D10	29
Témiscaming, P.Q., Can.	G17	66
Témiscouata, co., P.Q., Can.	B9	74
Témiscouata, Lac, l., P.Q., Can.	B9	74
Temora, Austl.	G6	51
Temósachic, Mex.	B3	63
Tempe, Az., U.S.	D4	80
Tempe Downs, Austl.	D5	50
Temperance, Mi., U.S.	G7	99
Temperance, stm., Mn., U.S.	C8	100
Temperanceville, Va., U.S.	C7	123
Tempio Pausania, Italy	D2	23
Temple, Ga., U.S.	C1	87
Temple, Mi., U.S.	D5	99
Temple, N.H., U.S.	E3	106
Temple, Ok., U.S.	C3	113
Temple, Pa., U.S.	F10	115
Temple, Tx., U.S.	D4	120
Temple City, Ca., U.S.	*m12	82
Templemore, Ire.	E4	11
Temple Hill, Ky., U.S.	D4	94
Templeton, Ca., U.S.	E3	82
Templeton, In., U.S.	C3	91
Templeton, Ma., U.S.	A3	98
Templeton, Pa., U.S.	E3	115
Templeville, Md., U.S.	B6	97
Templin, Ger.D.R.	B6	18
Temuco, Chile	B2	54
Temuka, N.Z.	P13	51
Temwen, i., Micron.	Q17	52
Tena, Ec.	B2	58
Tenafly, N.J., U.S.	B5	107
Tenaha, Tx., U.S.	D5	120
Tenakee Springs, Ak., U.S.	D12	79
Tenāli, India	*E7	36
Tenancingo [de Degollado], Mex.	D5	63
Tenancingo del Valle, Mex.	n14	63
Tenant Mountain, mtn., N.Y., U.S.	B6	109
Tenants Harbor, Me., U.S.	E3	96
Tenasserim, Burma	F10	36
Tenay, Fr.	E6	16
Tenby, Wales, U.K.	C3	12
Tendaho, Eth.	C5	47
Tende, Fr.	E7	16
Ten Degree Channel, strt., India	G9	36
Tendoy, Id., U.S.	E5	89
Tendre, Mont, mtn., Switz.	C2	21
Ténéré, des., Niger	C7	45
Tenerife, i., Spain	m13	22
Ténés, Alg.	B5	44
Teng, stm., Burma	B2	35
Tengah Islands, is., Indon.	G5	34
Tengchong, China	F4	31
Tengiz, Lake, l., Sov. Un.	D9	29
Tengxian, China	G7	32
Tenino, Wa., U.S.	C3	124
Tenke, Zaire	D4	48
Tenkiller Ferry Lake, res., Ok., U.S.	B6	113
Tenkodogo, Burkina	D4	45
Ten Mile, Tn., U.S.	D9	119
Ten Mile Lake, l., Mn., U.S.	D4	100
Tenmile Creek, stm., W.V., U.S.	k10	125
Ten Mile Lake, l., Nf., Can.	C3	72
Tennant, Ia., U.S.	C2	92
Tennant Creek, Austl.	C5	50
Tennent, N.J., U.S.	C4	107
Tennessee, Il., U.S.	C3	90
Tennessee, state, U.S.	B5	119
Tennessee, stm., U.S.	D10	76
Tennessee City, Tn., U.S.	A4	119
Tennessee Pass, Co., U.S.	B4	83
Tennessee Ridge, Tn., U.S.	A4	119
Tennga, Ga., U.S.	B2	87
Tennille, Ga., U.S.	D4	87
Tennyson, In., U.S.	H3	91
Tenosique [de Pino Suárez], Mex.	D6	63
Tenryū, stm., Japan	n16	33
Tensas, co., La., U.S.	B4	95
Tensas, stm., La., U.S.	B4	95
Tensaw, stm., Al., U.S.	E2	78
Tensed, Id., U.S.	B2	89
Ten Sleep, Wy., U.S.	B5	127
Tenstrike, Mn., U.S.	C4	100
Ten Thousand Islands, is., Fl., U.S.	G5	86
Teocaltiche, Mex.	C4	63
Teófilo Otoni, Braz.	B4	56
Tepa, Indon.	G7	34
Tepalcatepec, Mex.	m12	63
Tepalcatepec, stm., Mex.	m12	63
Tepatitlán [de Morelos], Mex.	C4	63
Tepeji del Río, Mex.	n14	63
Tepic, Mex.	C4	63
Teplice, Czech.	C2	26
Tepoca, Cabo, c., Mex.	A2	63
Tequila, Mex.	m12	63
Ter, stm., Spain	A7	22
Téra, Niger	D5	45
Teraina Island (Washington Island), i., Kir.	F12	6
Teramo, Italy	C4	23
Ter Apel, Neth.	B7	17
Tercan, Tur.	C13	40
Terceira, i., Port.	g9	44
Tercero, stm., Arg.	A4	54
Terebovlya, Sov. Un.	G5	27
Terek, stm., Sov. Un.	G18	28
Terek pass, Sov. Un.	G23	28
Terekty, Sov. Un.	D7	28
Terence Bay, N.S., Can.	E6	71
Terengganu, state, Malay.	J5	35
Terenos, Braz.	C2	56
Teresina, Braz.	C2	57
Teresinha, Braz.	B4	59
Teresópolis, Braz.	C4	56
Terespol, Pol.	E3	17
Terhune, In., U.S.	D5	91
Teriberka, Sov. Un.	C16	14
Terlingua, Tx., U.S.	D1	120
Terlton, Ok., U.S.	A5	113
Termez, Sov. Un.	F9	29
Termini Imerese, Italy	F4	23
Térmoli, Italy	C5	23
Ternate, Indon.	E7	34
Terneuzen, Neth.	B5	16
Terney, Sov. Un.	D18	33
Terni, Italy	C4	23
Ternopol, Sov. Un.	G5	27
Terpeniya Bay, b., Sov. Un.	B11	33
Terpeniya, Cape, c., Sov. Un.	B12	33
Terra Alta, W.V., U.S.	B5	125
Terrace, B.C., Can.	B3	69
Terrace, Mn., U.S.	E3	100
Terrace Bay, On., Can.	G15	66
Terracina, Italy	D4	23
Terral, Ok., U.S.	D4	113
Terra Nova, Nf., Can.	D4	72
Terra Nova National Park, Nf., Can.	D4	72
Terra Rica, Braz.	C2	56
Thāno Bula Khān, Pak.	E1	37
Terrasson, Fr.	E4	16
Terraville, S.D., U.S.	C2	118
Terrebone, Bayou, stm., La., U.S.	k10	95
Terrebonne, P.Q., Can.	D4	74
Terrebonne, Or., U.S.	C5	114
Terrebonne, co., P.Q., Can.	D4	74
Terrebonne Bay, b., La., U.S.	E5	95
Terre Haute, Il., U.S.	C3	90
Terre Haute, In., U.S.	F3	91
Terre Hill, Pa., U.S.	F9	115
Terrell, N.C., U.S.	B2	110
Terrell, Tx., U.S.	C4	120
Terrell, co., Ga., U.S.	E2	87
Terrell, co., Tx., U.S.	D1	120
Terrell Hills, Tx., U.S.	k7	120
Terrenceville, Nf., Can.	E4	72
Terri, Mont, mtn., Switz.	B3	20
Terril, Ia., U.S.	A3	92
Terror, Mount, mtn., Ant.	e38	7
Terry, La., U.S.	B4	95
Terry, Ms., U.S.	C3	101
Terry, Mt., U.S.	D11	103
Terry, co., Tx., U.S.	C1	120
Terry Peak, mtn., S.D., U.S.	C2	118
Terrytown, Ne., U.S.	C2	104
Terryville, Ct., U.S.	C3	84
Terryville, N.Y., U.S.	*n15	109
Tersakkan, stm., Sov. Un.	C7	28
Terschelling, i., Neth.	A6	16
Terskey-Alatau Range, mts., Sov. Un.	E9	28
Teruel, Col.	C2	60
Teruel, Spain	B5	22
Terutao, i., Thai.	I3	35
Terwagne, Bel.	C3	24
Tešanj, Yugo.	C3	24
Tescott, Ks., U.S.	C6	93
Teseney, Eth.	B4	47
Teshekpuk Lake, l., Ak., U.S.	A9	79
Teshio, Japan	D10	33
Tesiyn, stm., Asia	B4	31
Teslin, Yk., Can.	D6	66
Teslin Lake, l., Can.	D6	66
Tessalit, Mali	B5	45
Tessaoua, Niger	D6	45
Tessier, Sk., Can.	F2	75
Tessin, Ger.D.R.	D6	15
Test, stm., Eng., U.K.	E6	10
Tesuque, N.M., U.S.	B4	108
Tesuque Pueblo, N.M., U.S.	B4	108
Tetachuck Lake, l., B.C., Can.	C5	69
Tetagouche, stm., N.B., Can.	B3	71
Tetas, Punta, c., Chile	D1	55
Tetbury, Eng., U.K.	C5	12
Tete, Moz.	A5	49
Tete, dept., Moz.	E5	48
Tête-à-la-Baleine, P.Q., Can.	C2	72
Tête-Jaune-Cache, B.C., Can.	C8	69
Teterow, Ger.D.R.	B6	18
Teteven, Bul.	D7	24
Tetlin, Ak., U.S.	C11	79
Teton, Id., U.S.	F7	89
Teton, co., Id., U.S.	F7	89
Teton, co., Mt., U.S.	C4	103
Teton, co., Wy., U.S.	C2	127
Teton, stm., Mt., U.S.	C5	103
Teton Pass, Wy., U.S.	C2	127
Tetonia, Id., U.S.	F7	89
Teton Range, mts., Wy., U.S.	C2	127
Teton Village, Wy., U.S.	C2	127
Tétouan, Mor.	B3	44
Tetovo, Yugo.	E5	24
Tetrino, Sov. Un.	D18	14
Tettnang, F.R.Ger.	A8	21
Teuchern, Ger.D.R.	B7	19
Teuco, stm., Arg.	D3	55
Teufen, Switz.	B7	21
Teuini, Braz.	C4	58
Teulada, Italy	E2	23
Teúl de González Ortega, Mex.	m12	63
Teulon, Mb., Can.	D3	70
Teuri Island, i., Japan	D10	33
Teutopolis, Il., U.S.	D5	90
Teviot, stm., Scot., U.K.	E6	13
Tevriz, Sov. Un.	B8	28
Te Waewae Bay, b., N.Z.	Q11	51
Tewantin-Noosa, Austl.	E9	50
Tewksbury, Ma., U.S.	A5	98
Texada Island, i., B.C., Can.	E5	69
Texarkana, Ar., U.S.	D1	81
Texarkana, Tx., U.S.	C5	120
Texas, co., Mo., U.S.	D5	102
Texas, co., Ok., U.S.	e9	113
Texas, state, U.S.	D3	120
Texas City, Tx., U.S.	E5	120
Texcaltitlán, Mex.	n14	63
Texcoco, Lago de, l., Mex.	g10	63
Texcoco [de Mora], Mex.	n14	63
Texel, i., Neth.	A6	16
Texhoma, Ok., U.S.	e9	113
Texhoma, Tx., U.S.	A2	120
Texico, N.M., U.S.	C6	108
Texline, Tx., U.S.	A1	120
Texoma, Lake, res., U.S.	D5	113
Teyvareh, Afg.	E12	39
Teziutlán, Mex.	m12	63
Tezpur, India	C9	36
Tezzeron Lake, l., B.C., Can.	B6	69
Thabana Ntlenyana, mtn., Leso.	C4	49
Thacker, W.V., U.S.	D2	125
Thackeray, Il., U.S.	C4	90
Thackerville, Ok., U.S.	D4	113
Thai Binh, Viet.	B7	35
Thailand, ctry., Asia	B2	34
Thailand, Gulf of, b., Asia	C3	34
Thai Nguyen, Viet.	B6	35
Thal, Pak.	C4	37
Thale, Ger.D.R.	B6	19
Thale Luang, b., Thai.	I4	35
Thalia, Tx., U.S.	C3	120
Thame, Eng., U.K.	C6	12
Thames, N.Z.	L15	51
Thames, co., On., Can.	E3	73
Thames, stm., Eng., U.K.	E6	10
Thames, stm., Ct., U.S.	D7	84
Thames, Firth of, b., N.Z.	L15	51
Thames, Mouth of the, stm., Eng., U.K.	E7	10
Thamesville, On., Can.	E3	73
Thāna, India	*E5	36
Thanh Hoa, Viet.	B6	35
Thanjāvūr (Tanjore), India	F6	36
Thann, Fr.	D7	16
Thannhausen, F.R.Ger.	A6	20
Thãno Bula Khān, Pak.	E1	37
Thaon[-les-Vosges], Fr.	C7	16
Tharad, India	E3	37
Thar Desert (Great Indian Desert), des., Asia	D2	37
Tharrawaddy, Burma	E10	36
Thásos, Grc.	B5	25
Thásos, i., Grc.	B5	40
Thatcher, Az., U.S.	E6	80
Thatcher, Id., U.S.	G7	89
Thaton, Burma	E10	36
Thawville, Il., U.S.	C5	90
Thaxton, Ms., U.S.	A4	101
Thayer, Il., U.S.	D4	90
Thayer, In., U.S.	B3	91
Thayer, Ia., U.S.	C3	92
Thayer, Ks., U.S.	E8	93
Thayer, Mo., U.S.	E6	102
Thayer, Ne., U.S.	D8	104
Thayer, W.V., U.S.	n13	125
Thayer, co., Ne., U.S.	D8	104
Thayetmyo, Burma	C1	35
Thayne, Wy., U.S.	D1	127
Thazi, Burma	B2	35
Thealka, Ky., U.S.	C7	94
Theba, Az., U.S.	E3	80
Thebes, Il., U.S.	F4	90
Thebes, hist., Eg.	C3	38
Thebes see Thívai, Grc.		
The Backway, b., Nf., Can.	A2	72
The Barrens, plat., Tn., U.S.	B5	119
The Bight, Bah.	B6	64
The Cheviot, mtn., Eng., U.K.	E6	13
The Colony, Tx., U.S.	C4	120
The Coteau, hills, Sk., Can.	F2	75
The Dalles, Or., U.S.	B5	114
The Dells, val., Wi., U.S.	E4	126
Thedford, On., Can.	D3	73
Thedford, Ne., U.S.	C6	104
The Dome, mtn., Yk., Can.	F2	104
The Entrance, Austl.	F8	51
The Everglades, sw., Fl., U.S.	G6	86
The Father, mtn., Pap. N. Gui.	k13	50
The Fens, sw., Eng., U.K.	B8	12
The Fishing Lakes, l., Sk., Can.	G3	75
The Flat Tops, mts., Co., U.S.	B3	83
The Flume, wtfl, N.H., U.S.	B3	106
The Graves, is., Ma., U.S.	g12	98
The Hague ('s Gravenhage), Neth.	A6	16
The Heads, c., Or., U.S.	E2	114
The Hummocks, R.I., U.S.	D6	116
The Landes, reg., Fr.	E5	16
Thelma, Ky., U.S.	C7	94
Thelon, stm., N.T., Can.	D12	66
The Minch, strt., Scot., U.K.	A4	10
The Narrows, strt., Wa., U.S.	f10	124
The Naze, c., Nor.	I2	14
The Naze, c., Eng., U.K.	C9	12
The Oa, reg., Scot., U.K.	E2	13
Theodore, Austl.	D9	50
Theodore, Al., U.S.	E1	78
Theodore Roosevelt Lake, res., Az., U.S.	D4	80
Theodore Roosevelt National Park (South Unit), N.D., U.S.	C2	111
Theodore Roosevelt National Park (North Unit), N.D., U.S.	B2	111
Theodosia, Mo., U.S.	E5	102
Theológos, Grc.	B5	25
The Palisades, clf, N.J., U.S.	h9	107
The Pas, Mb., Can.	C1	70
The Peak, mtn., N.C., U.S.	A1	110
The Pinnacle, hill, Ct., U.S.	B4	84
The Pinnacle, hill, Mo., U.S.	B7	102
The Plains, Oh., U.S.	C3	112
The Plains, Va., U.S.	B5	123
Thérain, stm., Fr.	C4	16
The Range, N.B., Can.	C4	71
The Raven Point, c., Ire.	E5	11
Theresa, N.Y., U.S.	A5	109
Theresa, Wi., U.S.	E5	126
Therien, Ab., Can.	B5	68
Thermaïkós Kólpos (Gulf of Salonika), b., Grc.	B4	40
Thérmon, Grc.	C3	25
Thermopolis, Wy., U.S.	C4	127
The Rock, Ga., U.S.	C2	87
The Rockies,mts., Wa., U.S.	C3	124
Theron mountains, mts., Ant.	B5	7
The Solent, strt., Eng., U.K.	D6	12
The Sound see Øresund, strt., Eur.	J5	14
Thessalon, On., Can.	p19	73
Thessaloniki (Salonika), Grc.	B4	40
Thessaly, hist reg., Grc.	C4	25
The Storr, mtn., Scot., U.K.	C2	13
Theta, Tn., U.S.	B5	119
Thetford, Eng., U.K.	D7	10
Thetford, Vt., U.S.	D4	122
Thetford Center, Vt., U.S.	D4	122
Thetford Mines, P.Q., Can.	C6	74
The Thimbles, is., Ct., U.S.	E5	84
The Village, Ok., U.S.	B4	113
The Wash, b., Eng., U.K.	D7	10
Thibar, Tun.	F2	23
Thibaudeau, Mb., Can.	A4	70
Thibodaux, La., U.S.	E5	95
Thicket Portage, Mb., Can.	B3	70
Thickwood Hills, hills, Sk., Can.	D2	75
Thida, Ar., U.S.	B3	81
Thief, Mn., U.S.	B2	100
Thief, stm., Mn., U.S.	B2	100
Thief Lake, l., Mn., U.S.	B2	100
Thief River Falls, Mn., U.S.	B2	100
Thiel Mountains, mts., Ant.	A2	7
Thielsen, Mount, mtn., Or.	D4	114
Thiene, Italy	D7	20
Thiensville, Wi., U.S.	E6	126
Thiers, Fr.	E5	16
Thiès, Sen.	D2	45
Thika, Kenya	B6	48
Thimbu, Bhu.	D7	37
Thingangyun, Burma	*E10	36
Thionville, Fr.	C7	16
Thíra, i., Grc.	D5	40
Third Lake, l., N.H., U.S.	f7	106
Thirsk, Eng., U.K.	F7	13
Thisted, Den.	H2	15
Thistle, Ut., U.S.	D4	121
Thívai (Thebes), Grc.	C5	25
Tho Chu, i., Viet.	H5	35
Tholen, Neth.	B4	17
Thomas, Ok., U.S.	B3	113
Thomas, W.V., U.S.	B5	125
Thomas, co., Ga., U.S.	F3	87
Thomas, co., Ks., U.S.	C2	93
Thomas, co., Ne., U.S.	C4	104
Thomasboro, Il., U.S.	C5	90
Thomas Creek, stm., Fl., U.S.	k8	86
Thomas Mountains, mts., Ant.	B5	7
Thomaston, Al., U.S.	C2	78
Thomaston, Ct., U.S.	C3	84
Thomaston, Ga., U.S.	D2	87
Thomaston, Me., U.S.	D3	96
Thomaston, Tx., U.S.	E4	120
Thomaston Reservoir, res., Ct., U.S.	C3	84
Thomastown, Ire.	E4	11
Thomastown, Ms., U.S.	C4	101
Thomasville, Al., U.S.	D2	78
Thomasville, Ga., U.S.	F3	87
Thomasville, Mo., U.S.	E6	102
Thomasville, N.C., U.S.	B2	110
Thomasville, Tn., U.S.	A4	119
Thomlinson, Mount, mtn., B.C., Can.	B4	69
Thompson, Mb., Can.	B3	70
Thompson, Ct., U.S.	B8	84
Thompson, Ia., U.S.	A4	92
Thompson, Mi., U.S.	C4	99
Thompson, Mo., U.S.	B5	102
Thompson, N.D., U.S.	B8	111
Thompson, Oh., U.S.	A4	112
Thompson, Pa., U.S.	C10	115
Thompson, Ut., U.S.	E6	121
Thompson, stm., B.C., Can.	D7	69
Thompson, stm., U.S.	A4	102
Thompson Creek, stm., U.S.	D5	101
Thompson Falls, Mt., U.S.	C1	103
Thompson Island, i., Ma., U.S.	g11	98
Thompson Lake, l., U.S.	D2	96
Thompson Peak, mtn., Ca., U.S.	B2	82
Thompson Peak, mtn., N.M., U.S.	h9	108
Thompson Reservoir, res., Or., U.S.	E5	114
Thompsons Station, Tn., U.S.	B5	119
Thompsontown, Pa., U.S.	E7	115
Thompsonville, Il., U.S.	F5	90
Thompsonville, Mi., U.S.	D5	99
Thomson, Ga., U.S.	C4	87
Thomson, Il., U.S.	B3	90
Thomson, Mn., U.S.	D6	100
Thomson, stm., Austl.	D7	50
Thomson's Falls, Kenya	A6	48
Thônes, Fr.	E1	21
Thonon-les-Bains, Fr.	C2	20
Thonotosassa, Fl., U.S.	D4	86
Thor, ia., U.S.	B3	92
Thorburn, N.S., Can.	D7	71
Thoreau, N.M., U.S.	B1	108
Thorhild, Ab., Can.	B4	68
Thornaby, Ar., U.S.	C3	81
Thornbury, On., Can.	C4	73
Thorndale, On., Can.	D3	73
Thorndale, Tx., U.S.	D4	120
Thorndike, Me., U.S.	D3	96
Thornfield, Mo., U.S.	E5	102
Thornhill, Mb., Can.	E2	70
Thornhill, On., Can.	k15	73
Thornhill, Scot., U.K.	E5	13
Thornton, On., Can.	C5	73
Thornton, Ar., U.S.	D3	81
Thornton, Co., U.S.	*B6	83
Thornton, Id., U.S.	F7	89
Thornton, Ia., U.S.	B4	92
Thornton, Ms., U.S.	C3	101
Thornton, N.H., U.S.	C3	106
Thornton, Tx., U.S.	D4	120
Thornton, Wa., U.S.	B8	124
Thornton, W.V., U.S.	k11	125
Thorntown, In., U.S.	D4	91
Thornville, Oh., U.S.	C3	112
Thornwood, N.Y., U.S.	*m15	109
Thornwood, W.V., U.S.	C5	125
Thorny Mountain, mtn., Mo., U.S.	D6	102
Thorofare, N.J., U.S.	D2	107
Thorold, On., Can.	D5	73
Thorp, Wa., U.S.	B5	124
Thorp, Wi., U.S.	D3	126
Thorsby, Ab., Can.	C3	68
Thorsby, Al., U.S.	C3	78
Thouars, Fr.	D3	16
Thousand Islands, is., N.Y., U.S.	A4	109
Thousand Lake Mountain, mtn., Ut., U.S.	E4	121
Thousand Oaks, Ca., U.S.	*E4	82
Thousand Springs Creek, stm., U.S.	B7	105
Thrace, hist reg., Eur.	B7	25
Thrapston, Eng., U.K.	B7	12
Thrashers, Ms., U.S.	A5	101
Three Bridges, N.J., U.S.	B3	107
Three Fingered Jack, mtn., Or., U.S.	C5	114
Three Forks, Mt., U.S.	E5	103
Three Hills, Ab., Can.	D4	68
Three Kings Islands, is., N.Z.	K14	51
Three Lakes, Wi., U.S.	C4	126
Three Mile Bay, N.Y., U.S.	A4	109
Three Mile Plains, N.S., Can.	E5	71
Three Nunataks, mtn., Ant.	g41	7
Three Oaks, Mi., U.S.	G4	99
Three Points, Cape, c., Ghana	F4	45
Three Rivers, Ca., U.S.	D4	82
Three Rivers, Mi., U.S.	G5	99
Three Rivers, N.M., U.S.	D3	108
Three Rivers, Tx., U.S.	E3	120
Three Rock Cove, Nf., Can.	D2	72
Three Sisters, mtn., Or., U.S.	C5	114
Three Springs, Pa., U.S.	F6	115
Throckmorton, Tx., U.S.	C3	120
Throckmorton, co., Tx., U.S.	C3	120
Thu, i., Viet.	G8	35
Thule (Qaanaaq), Grnld.	B14	61
Thun, Switz.	E3	18
Thun, Lake, l., Switz.	E3	18
Thunder Bay, co., On., Can.	o17	73
Thunder Bay, On., Can.	o17	73
Thunder Bay, stm., Mi., U.S.	D6	99
Thunder Bay, North Branch, stm., Mi., U.S.	C6	99
Thunderbird, Lake, res., Ok., U.S.	B4	113
Thunder Butte, S.D., U.S.	B4	118
Thunder Butte, mtn., S.D.	B4	118
Thunder Butte Creek, stm., S.D., U.S.	B3	118
Thunder Hawk, S.D., U.S.	B4	118
Thunder Hills, hills, Sk., Can.	C2	75

Name	Map Ref	Page
Thung Song, Thai.	H3	35
Thur, stm., Switz.	A6	21
Thurgau, state, Switz.	B5	20
Thüringer Wald, mts., Ger.D.R.	C5	19
Thuringia, hist reg., Ger.D.R.	C5	18
Thurles, Ire.	D3	10
Thurlow Dam, Al., U.S.	C4	78
Thurman, Ia., U.S.	D2	92
Thurman, Oh., U.S.	D3	112
Thurmont, Md., U.S.	A3	97
Thurø, i., Den.	C4	15
Thursday Island, Austl.	B7	50
Thurso, P.Q., Can.	D2	74
Thurso, Scot., U.K.	A5	10
Thurso, stm., Scot., U.K.	B5	13
Thurston, Ne., U.S.	B9	104
Thurston, On., U.S.	C3	112
Thurston, co., Ne., U.S.	B9	104
Thurston, co., Wa., U.S.	C3	124
Thurston Island, i., Ant.	B3	7
Thusis, Switz.	E4	18
Thuvu, Fiji	I14	52
Thwaites Iceburg Tongue, Ant.	B2	7
Thyborøn, Den.	B2	15
Thyborøn Kanal, strt., Den.	B2	15
Tiahuanaco, Bol.	C2	55
Tiancang, China	C5	31
Tianjin (Tientsin), China	D8	31
Tianjun, China	D4	31
Tianmen, China	I5	32
Tianshui, China	E6	31
Tianzhen, China	D6	32
Tiaong, Phil.	p13	34
Tiawah, Ok., U.S.	A6	113
Tibagi, Braz.	C2	56
Tibaji, stm., Braz.	C2	56
Tibasti, Sarīr, des., Libya	E3	43
Tibati, Cam.	D2	46
Tibbie, Al., U.S.	D1	78
Tibé, Pic de, mtn., Gui.	E3	45
Tiber (Tevere), stm., Italy	C4	23
Tiberias (Teverya), Isr.	F10	40
Tibesti, mts., Chad	A3	46
Tibet (Xizang), prov., China	E3	31
Tibet, Plateau of, plat., China	G11	30
Tibiri, Niger	D6	45
Tibooburra, Austl.	E7	50
Tiburon, Ca., U.S.	*h8	82
Tiburón, Isla, i., Mex.	B2	63
Tice, Fl., U.S.	F5	86
Tichborne, On., U.S.	C8	73
Tichfield, Sk., Can.	F2	75
Tichît, Maur.	C3	45
Tichnor, Ar., U.S.	C4	81
Ticino, state, Switz.	C4	20
Ticino, stm., Eur.	B2	23
Tickfaw, La., U.S.	D5	95
Tickfaw, stm., La., U.S.	C5	95
Ticomán (part of Mexico City), Mex.	g9	63
Ticonderoga, N.Y., U.S.	B7	109
Ticul, Mex.	C7	63
Tidehead, N.B., Can.	B3	71
Tidikelt, pl., Alg.	D5	44
Tidioute, Pa., U.S.	C3	115
Tidjikdja, Maur.	C2	45
Tidra, Île, i., Maur.	C1	45
Tiel, Neth.	C5	17
Tièl, Sen.	D1	45
Tieling, China	C9	31
Tielmes de Tajuña, Spain	p18	22
Tielt, Bel.	C3	17
Tienen, Bel.	B6	16
Tien Shan, mts., Asia	E10	30
Tientsin see Tianjin, China	D8	31
Tien Yen, Viet.	B7	35
Tie Plant, Ms., U.S.	B4	101
Tierp, Swe.	G7	14
Tierra Amarilla, Chile	E1	55
Tierra Amarilla, N.M., U.S.	A3	108
Tierra Blanca, Mex.	D5	63
Tierra del Fuego, Antártida e Islas del Atlántico Sur, ter., Arg.	h12	54
Tierra del Fuego, Isla Grande de, i., S.A.	h12	54
Tie Siding, Wy., U.S.	E7	127
Tietar, stm., Spain	C3	22
Tietê, Braz.	C3	56
Tietê, stm., Braz.	C2	56
Tieton, Wa., U.S.	C5	124
Tieton, stm., Wa., U.S.	C4	124
Tiffany Mountain, mtn., Wa., U.S.	A6	124
Tiffin, Oh., U.S.	E3	102
Tiffin, Ia., U.S.	C6	92
Tiffin, Oh., U.S.	A2	112
Tiffin, co., Oh., U.S.	A1	112
Tiflis see Tbilisi, Sov. Un.	E7	27
Tift, co., Ga., U.S.	E3	87
Tifton, Ga., U.S.	E3	87
Tigard, Or., U.S.	h12	114
Tiger, Ga., U.S.	B3	87
Tigerton, Wi., U.S.	D4	126
Tigerville, S.C., U.S.	A3	117
Tighnabruaich, Scot., U.K.	E3	13
Tigil, Sov. Un.	D18	29
Tignall, Ga., U.S.	C4	87
Tignère, Cam.	D2	46
Tignish, P.E., Can.	C5	71
Tigray (Tigre), prov., Eth.	C4	47
Tigre, Arg.	g7	54
Tigre, stm., Peru	B2	58
Tigre, stm., Ven.	B5	60
Tigrett, Tn., U.S.	B2	119
Tigris (Dicle), stm., Asia	B4	38
Tiguabos, Cuba	D6	64
Tiguentourine, Alg.	D6	44
Tih, Jabal at, plat., Eg.	E5	41
Tihuatlán, Mex.	m15	63
Tiji, Libya	B3	108
Tijuana, Mex.	A1	63
Tijucas, Braz.	D3	56
Tikal, hist., Guat.	D7	63
Tikamgarh, India	E7	37
Tikhoretsk, Sov. Un.	I13	27
Tikhvin, Sov. Un.	B9	27
Tiko, Cam.	E1	46
Tikrīt, Iraq	E14	40
Tiksi, Sov. Un.	B15	29
Tilamuta, Indon.	E6	34
Tilarán, C.R.	E5	62
Tilburg, Neth.	B6	16
Tilbury, On., Can.	E2	73
Tilbury, Eng., U.K.	m13	10
Tilcara, Arg.	D2	55
Tilden, Il., U.S.	E4	90
Tilden, Ne., U.S.	B8	104
Tilden, Tx., U.S.	E3	120
Tilemsès, Vallée du, val., Mali	C5	45
Tilford, Ky., U.S.	C6	94
Tilford, S.D., U.S.	C2	118
Tilghman, Md., U.S.	C5	97
Tilghman Island, i., Md., U.S.	C5	97
Tilimsen, Alg.	C4	44
Tiline, Ky., U.S.	e9	94
Till, stm., Eng., U.K.	E6	13
Tillabéry, Niger	D5	45
Tillamook, Or., U.S.	B3	114
Tillamook, co., Or., U.S.	B3	114
Tillar, Ar., U.S.	D4	81
Tillatoba, Ms., U.S.	B4	101
Tiller, Or., U.S.	E4	114
Tillery, Lake, res., N.C., U.S.	B2	110
Tilley, Ab., Can.	D5	68
Tillman, S.C., U.S.	G5	117
Tillman, co., Ok., U.S.	C2	113
Tillmans Corner, Al., U.S.	E1	78
Tillson, N.Y., U.S.	D6	109
Tillsonburg, On., Can.	E4	73
Tilly, Ar., U.S.	B3	81
Tillyfourie, Scot., U.K.	C6	13
Tílos, i., Grc.	D6	40
Tilpa, Austl.	E5	51
Tilrhemt, Alg.	C5	44
Tilston, Mb., Can.	E1	70
Tilting, Nf., Can.	D4	72
Tilton, Il., U.S.	C6	90
Tilton, N.H., U.S.	D3	106
Tiltonsville, Oh., U.S.	B5	112
Tim, Sov. Un.	F11	27
Timaná, Col.	C2	60
Timaru, N.Z.	P13	51
Timashevsk, Sov. Un.	I12	27
Timbalier Bay, b., La., U.S.	E5	95
Timbalier Island, i., La., U.S.	E5	95
Timbaúba, Braz.	h6	57
Timbédra, Maur.	C3	45
Timber, Or., U.S.	B3	114
Timbered Knob, mtn., Mo., U.S.	E5	102
Timberlake, N.C., U.S.	A4	110
Timber Lake, S.D., U.S.	B4	118
Timberlake, Va., U.S.	C3	123
Timberville, Va., U.S.	B4	123
Timblin, Pa., U.S.	E3	115
Timbo, Ar., U.S.	B3	81
Timbuktu see Tombouctou, Mali	C4	45
Timerzit, Mor.	C4	44
Timewell, Il., U.S.	C3	90
Timimoun, Alg.	D5	44
Timiris, Cap, c., Maur.	C1	45
Timiskaming, co., On., Can.	p19	73
Timișoara, Rom.	C5	24
Timken, Ks., U.S.	D4	93
Timmendorfer Strand, F.R.Ger.	E4	15
Timmins, On., Can.	o19	73
Timmonsville, S.C., U.S.	C8	117
Timms Hill, hill, Wi., U.S.	C3	126
Timnath, Co., U.S.	A5	83
Timok, stm., Eur.	D6	24
Timor, i., Indon.	G6	34
Timor, Sea	B4	50
Timpanogos Cave National Monument, U.S.	C4	121
Timpas Creek, stm., Co., U.S.	D7	83
Timpson, Tx., U.S.	D5	120
Timrå, Swe.	F7	14
Tims Ford Lake, res., Tn., U.S.	B5	119
Tin, Ra's at, c., Libya	C4	43
Tina, Mo., U.S.	B4	102
Tinaca Point, c., Phil.	D7	34
Tinahely, Ire.	E5	11
Tinaquillo, Ven.	B4	60
Tindouf, Alg.	D3	44
Tineo, Spain	A2	22
Tingha, Austl.	E8	51
Tinghert, Plateau du (Hammâdat Tinghert), plat., Afr.	D6	44
Tingjegaon, Nepal	C9	37
Tinglev, Den.	D3	15
Tingley, Ia., U.S.	D3	92
Tingmerkpuk Mountain, mtn., Ak., U.S.	B7	79
Tingo Maria, Peru	C2	58
Tingréla, I.C.	D3	45
Tingri, China	C11	37
Tingsryd, Swe.	B8	15
Tinguipaya, Bol.	C2	55
Tinguiwick, P.Q., Can.	D6	74
Tinian, i., N. Mar. Is.	F8	6
Tinian Harbor, b., N. Mar. Is.	E7	52
Tinizong, Switz.	C8	21
Tinker Air Force Base, mil., Ok., U.S.	B4	113
Tinkerville, N.H., U.S.	B3	106
Tinkisso, stm., Gui.	D2	45
Tinnie Park, Il., U.S.	k9	90
Tinnie, N.M., U.S.	D4	108
Tinniswood, Mount, mtn., B.C., Can.	D6	69
Tinogasta, Arg.	D2	55
Tínos, Grc.	D5	40
Tínos, i., Grc.	D5	40
Tinqueux, Fr.	E3	17
Tinsley, Ms., U.S.	C3	101
Tinsman, Ar., U.S.	D3	81
Tinsukia, India	C10	36
Tintah, Mn., U.S.	D2	100
Tintigny, Bel.	E5	17
Tintina, Arg.	G3	53
Tintinara, Austl.	G3	51
Tinton Falls, N.J., U.S.	C4	107
Tio, Eth.	C5	47
Tioga, Il., U.S.	C6	90
Tioga, La., U.S.	C3	95
Tioga, N.D., U.S.	A3	111
Tioga, Pa., U.S.	C7	115
Tioga, W.V., U.S.	C4	125
Tioga, co., N.Y., U.S.	C4	109
Tioga, co., Pa., U.S.	C7	115
Tioga, stm., Pa., U.S.	B7	115
Tiogue Lake, res., R.I., U.S.	D3	116
Tioughnioga, stm., N.Y., U.S.	C5	109
Tioman, i., Malay.	K6	35
Tionesta, Pa., U.S.	C3	115
Tionesta Creek, stm., Pa., U.S.	C3	115
Tionesta Lake, res., Pa., U.S.	D3	115
Tipler, Wi., U.S.	C5	126
Tiplersville, Ms., U.S.	A5	101
Tippah, stm., Ms., U.S.	A4	101
Tipp City, Oh., U.S.	C1	112
Tippecanoe, In., U.S.	B5	91
Tippecanoe, co., In., U.S.	D4	91
Tippecanoe, stm., In., U.S.	C4	91
Tipperary, Ire.	D2	10
Tipperary, co., Ire.	E4	11
Tippo, Ms., U.S.	B3	101
Tipton, Ca., U.S.	D4	82
Tipton, In., U.S.	D5	91
Tipton, Ia., U.S.	C6	92
Tipton, Ks., U.S.	C5	93
Tipton, Mo., U.S.	C5	102
Tipton, Ok., U.S.	C2	113
Tipton, Tn., U.S.	B2	119
Tipton, co., In., U.S.	D5	91
Tipton, co., Tn., U.S.	B2	119
Tipton, Mount, mtn., Az., U.S.	B1	80
Tiptonville, Tn., U.S.	A2	119
Tip Top, Ky., U.S.	C6	94
Tip Top Mountain, mtn., On., Can.	o18	73
Tiquisate, Guat.	C2	62
Tīrān, Jazīrat, i., Sau. Ar.	I10	40
Tirana (Tiranë), Alb.	B2	40
Tiranë see Tirana, Alb.	B2	40
Tirano, Italy	A3	23
Tiraque, Bol.	C2	55
Tiraspol, Sov. Un.	H7	27
Tirat Karmel, Isr.	B6	41
Tirat Zevi, Isr.	B7	41
Tire, Tur.	C6	40
Tire Hill, Pa., U.S.	F4	115
Tírgoviște, Rom.	C7	24
Tîrgu-Frumos, Rom.	B8	24
Tîrgu-Jiu, Rom.	C6	24
Tîrgu-Neamţ, Rom.	B8	24
Tîrgu-Ocna, Rom.	B8	24
Tîrgu-Secuiesc, Rom.	B8	24
Tirich Mīr, mtn., Pak.	A5	36
Tirlyanskiy, Sov. Un.	E20	8
Tîrnava Mică, stm., Rom.	B7	24
Tîrnăveni, Rom.	B7	24
Tírnavos, Grc.	C4	40
Tiro, Oh., U.S.	B3	112
Tirol (Tyrol), state, Aus.	B7	20
Tiros, Braz.	B3	56
Tirschenreuth, F.R.Ger.	D7	19
Tirso, stm., Italy	D2	23
Tirstrup, Den.	B4	15
Tiruchchirāppalli (Trichinopoly), India	F6	36
Tirunelveli (Tinnevelly), India	G6	36
Tiruppur, India	*F6	36
Tisa (Tisza), stm., Eur.	C5	24
Tisaren, l., Swe.	t33	14
Tisch Mills, Wi., U.S.	h10	126
Tisdale, Sk., Can.	E3	75
Tishomingo, Ms., U.S.	A5	101
Tishomingo, Ok., U.S.	C5	113
Tishomingo, co., Ms., U.S.	A5	101
Tiskilwa, Il., U.S.	B4	90
Tisnaren, l., Swe.	u33	14
Tissemsilt, Alg.	B5	44
Tista, stm., Asia	D12	37
Tisvildeleje, Den.	B6	15
Tiszafüred, Hung.	B5	24
Tiszakécske, Hung.	B5	24
Titicaca, Lago, l., S.A.	E4	58
Titonka, Ia., U.S.	A3	92
Titovo Užice, Yugo.	D4	24
Titov Veles, Yugo.	A4	48
Titus, co., Tx., U.S.	C5	120
Titusville, Fl., U.S.	D6	86
Titusville, N.J., U.S.	C3	107
Titusville, Pa., U.S.	C2	115
Tivaouane, Sen.	C1	45
Tiverton, N.S., Can.	E3	71
Tiverton, On., Can.	C3	73
Tiverton, Eng., U.K.	E5	10
Tiverton, R.I., U.S.	D6	116
Tiverton Four Corners, R.I., U.S.	E6	116
Tivoli, Italy	D4	23
Tivoli, N.Y., U.S.	C7	109
Tivoli, Tx., U.S.	E4	120
Tixtla [de Guerrero], Mex.	o14	63
Tizapán (part of Mexico City), Mex.	h9	63
Tizard Bank, atoll, Asia	C4	34
Tizimin, Mex.	C7	63
Tizi-Ouzou, Alg.	B5	44
Tiznit, Mor.	D3	44
Tjeukemeer, l., Neth.	B5	17
Tlacolula [de Matamoros], Mex.	D5	63
Tlacotalpan, Mex.	D5	63
Tlacotepec, Mex.	o13	63
Tláhuac (part of Mexico City), Mex.	h9	63
Tlahualilo de Zaragoza, Mex.	g9	63
Tlalnepantla, stm., Mex.	g9	63
Tlalnepantla [de Comonfort], Mex.	g9	63
Tlalpan (part of Mexico City), Mex.	h9	63
Tlalpujahua, Mex.	n13	63
Tlaltenango [de Sánchez Román], Mex.	C4	63
Tlaltenco (part of Mexico City), Mex.	h9	63
Tlapa, Mex.	o14	63
Tlapacoyan, Mex.	n15	63
Tlapaneco, stm., Mex.	o14	63
Tlaquepaque (San Pedro Tlaquepaque), Mex.	m12	63
Tlaxcala, state, Mex.	D5	63
Tlaxcala [de Xicohténcatl], Mex.	D5	63
Tlaxco [de Morelos], Mex.	n14	63
Tlaxiaco, Mex.	D5	63
Tłuszcz, Pol.	k14	26
Tmassah, Libya	D3	43
Toadlena, N.M., U.S.	A1	108
Toamasina, Madag.	g9	49
Toamasina, prov., Madag.	g9	49
Toano, Va., U.S.	C6	123
Toano Range, mts., Nv., U.S.	A2	105
Toast, N.C., U.S.	A2	110
Toay, Arg.	B4	54
Toba, Japan	o15	33
Toba, i., Indon.	E1	34
Toba, stm., B.C., Can.	D5	69
Tobacco Root Mountains, mts., Mt., U.S.	E5	103
Tobago, i., Trin.	K14	64
Tobago Cays, is., St. Vin.	V26	65
Toba Inlet, b., B.C., Can.	D5	69
Tobarra, Spain	C5	22
Tobaru, Japan	O5	52
Tobermory, On., Can.	B3	73
Tobermory, Scot., U.K.	D2	13
Tobias, Ne., U.S.	D8	104
Tobiishi Point, c., Japan	P17	33
Tobi-shima, i., Japan	G9	33
Tobin, Mount, mtn., Nv., U.S.	C4	105
Tobin Lake, l., Austl.	D4	50
Tobin Lake, l., Sk., Can.	D4	75
Tobin Range, mts., Nv., U.S.	C4	105
Tobins Harbor, Mi., U.S.	h10	99
Tobique, stm., N.B., Can.	B2	71
Tobol, Sov. Un.	C6	28
Tobol, stm., Sov. Un.	D9	29
Tobolsk, Sov. Un.	D9	29
Tobruk see Ţubruq, Libya	C4	43
Toby, Mount, mtn., Ma., U.S.	B2	98
Tobyhanna, Pa., U.S.	D11	115
Tocantinópolis, Braz.	C1	57
Tocantins, stm., Braz.	D6	53
Tocantins National Park, Braz.	A3	56
Toccoa, Ga., U.S.	B3	87
Toccoa, stm., Ga., U.S.	B2	87
Toccoa Falls, Ga., U.S.	B3	87
Toccopola, Ms., U.S.	A4	101
Toce, stm., Italy	C4	20
Tochcha Lake, l., B.C., Can.	B5	69
Tochigi, Japan	H9	33
Toco, Chile	D2	55
Toco, Trin.	N24	65
Tocoa, Hond.	C4	62
Tocopilla, Chile	D1	55
Tocsin, In., U.S.	C7	91
Tocúmen, Pan.	F8	62
Tocumwal, Austl.	G5	51
Tocuyo, stm., Ven.	A4	60
Todd, N.C., U.S.	A1	110
Todd, co., Ky., U.S.	D2	94
Todd, co., Mn., U.S.	D4	100
Todd, co., S.D., U.S.	D5	118
Todd Estates, De., U.S.	*B3	85
Toddville, Md., U.S.	D5	97
Toddy Pond, l., Me., U.S.	D4	96
Todi, Gui.	D3	45
Tōdi, mtn., Switz.	C4	20
Todoga, Cape, c., Japan	G11	33
Todos os Santos, Baía de, b., Braz.	C5	57
Todos Santos, Bol.	C2	55
Todos Santos, Mex.	D3	63
Todtnau, F.R.Ger.	B3	20
Toe Head, c., Ire.	F2	11
Toe Head, c., Scot., U.K.	C1	13
Tofield, Ab., Can.	C4	68
Tofino, B.C., Can.	E5	69
Tofte, Mn., U.S.	C8	100
Toftlund, Den.	D3	15
Togdheer, prov., Som.	D6	47
Togiak, Ak., U.S.	D7	79
Togian Islands, is., Indon.	F6	34
Togo, Sk., Can.	F5	75
Togo, ctry., Afr.	E5	45
Togtoh, China	D4	32
Togwotee Pass, Wy., U.S.	C2	127
Tohakum Peak, mtn., Nv., U.S.	C2	105
Tohatchi, N.M., U.S.	B1	108
Tohopekaliga, Lake, l., Fl., U.S.	D5	86
Toi, Cape, c., Japan	K5	33
To Island, i., Japan	I9	33
Toivola, Mi., U.S.	B2	99
Toivola, Mn., U.S.	C6	100
Toiyabe Range, mts., Nv., U.S.	D4	105
Tok, Ak., U.S.	C11	79
Tokachi, Mount, mtn., Japan	E11	33
Tokaj, Hung.	A5	24
Tokara Islands, is., Japan	F10	31
Tokara Strait, strt., Japan	D6	86
Tokat, Tur.	B11	40
Tōkchŏn, N. Kor.	C2	124
Tokeland, Wa., U.S.	C2	124
Tokelau, dep., Oc.	G11	6
Tokio, Ar., U.S.	C2	81
Tokio, N.D., U.S.	B7	111
Tokio, Tx., U.S.	C1	120
Toki Point, c., Wake I.	A1	52
Tok Islands (Take Islands), is., Asia	H5	33
Tokmak, Sov. Un.	H10	27
Tokmak, Sov. Un.	E9	28
Tokoroa, N.Z.	M15	51
Tokunoshima Island, i., Japan	F10	31
Tokushima, Japan	E11	31
Tokuyama, Japan	J5	33
Tōkyō, Japan	D12	31
Tōkyō Bay, b., Japan	n18	33
Tokzār, Afg.	D13	39
Tol, i., Micron.	Q18	52
Tolar, N.M., U.S.	C6	108
Tolbukhin (Dobrich), Bul.	D8	24
Toleak Point, c., Wa., U.S.	B1	124
Toledo, Braz.	C2	56
Toledo, Spain	C3	22
Toledo, Il., U.S.	D5	90
Toledo, Oh., U.S.	A2	112
Toledo, Wa., U.S.	C3	124
Toledo, Montes de, mts., Spain	C3	22
Toledo Bend Reservoir, res., U.S.	C2	95
Toler, Ky., U.S.	C7	94
Tolga, Alg.	C6	44
Toliara, Madag.	h8	49
Toliara, prov., Madag.	h8	49
Tolima, dept., Col.	C2	60
Tolima, Nevado del, mtn., Col.	C2	60
Toliman, Mex.	m14	63
Tolitoli, Indon.	E6	34
Tolken, l., Swe.	B1	15
Tolland, Ct., U.S.	B6	84
Tolland, co., Ct., U.S.	B6	84
Tollense, l., Ger.D.R.	E7	15
Tollesboro, Ky., U.S.	B6	94
Tolleson, Az., U.S.	m8	80
Tollette, Ar., U.S.	C2	81
Tolley, N.D., U.S.	A4	111
Tollhouse, Ca., U.S.	D4	82
Tolloche, Arg.	G3	53
Tolmachevo, Sov. Un.	B8	27
Tolmezzo, Italy	A4	23
Tolmin, Yugo.	B1	24
Tolna, Hung.	B4	24
Tolna, N.D., U.S.	B7	111
Tolo, Gulf of, b., Indon.	F7	34
Tolono, Il., U.S.	C5	90
Tolosa, Spain	A4	22
Tolovana Park, stm., Ak., U.S.	B3	114
Tolsta Head, c., Scot., U.K.	C3	13
Tolstoi, Mb., Can.	E3	70
Tolstoy, S.D., U.S.	B6	118
Toltén, Chile	B2	54
Tolt Reservoir, res., Wa., U.S.	B4	124
Tolú, Col.	B2	60
Toluca, Il., U.S.	C4	90
Toluca, Nevado de, vol., Mex.	n14	63
Toluca [de Lerdo], Mex.	D5	63
Tolyatti, Sov. Un.	C3	28
Tom, Ok., U.S.	D7	113
Tom, Mount, hill, Ct., U.S.	C2	84
Tomah, Wi., U.S.	E3	126
Tomahawk, Wi., U.S.	C4	126
Tomahawk Lake, l., Wi., U.S.	C4	126
Tomakomai, Japan	E10	33
Tomakovka, Sov. Un.	H10	27
Tomanivi, mtn., Fiji	H15	52
Tomar, Port.	C1	22
Tomaszów Lubelski, Pol.	C7	26
Tomaszów Mazowiecki, Pol.	C6	26
Tomatlán, Mex.	D3	63
Tomball, Tx., U.S.	D5	120
Tomave, Bol.	C2	55
Tombador, Serra do, plat., Braz.	B4	58
Tombigbee, stm., U.S.	D1	78
Tomboco, Ang.	C1	48
Tombouctou (Timbuktu), Mali	C4	45
Tombstone, Az., U.S.	F5	80
Tombstone Mountain, mtn., Yk., Can.	D5	66
Tombua (Porto Alexandre), Ang.	E1	48
Tomé, Chile	B2	54
Tomelilla, Swe.	C7	15
Tomelloso, Spain	C4	22
Tomichi Creek, stm., Co., U.S.	C4	83
Tomini, Gulf of, b., Indon.	E6	34
Tomini, Mali	D4	45
Tomintoul, Scot., U.K.	C5	13
Tomkins Cove, N.Y., U.S.	D6	109
Tommot, Sov. Un.	D15	29
Tom Nevers Head, c., Ma., U.S.	D8	98
Tomnolen, Ms., U.S.	B4	101
Tomo, stm., Col.	A4	60
Tomobe, Japan	m19	33
Tomori, Japan	O5	52
Tompkins, Sk., Can.	G1	75
Tompkins, co., N.Y., U.S.	C4	109
Tompkinsville, Ky., U.S.	D4	94
Tompkinsville, Md., U.S.	D4	97
Tom Price, Austl.	D2	50
Toms, Ridgeway Branch, stm., N.J., U.S.	C4	107
Toms Creek, Va., U.S.	f9	123
Toms, Sov. Un.	D11	29
Toms River, N.J., U.S.	D4	107
Tonalá, Mex.	D6	63
Tonalea, Az., U.S.	A5	80
Tonantins, Braz.	D4	60
Tonasket, Wa., U.S.	A6	124
Tonate, Fr. Gu.	B4	59
Tonawanda, N.Y., U.S.	B2	109
Tonawanda Indian Reservation, N.Y., U.S.	B2	109
Tonbridge, Eng., U.K.	C8	12
Tønder, Den.	E6	34
Tone, Japan	m19	33
Tonekābon, Iran	B5	38
Toney, Al., U.S.	A3	78
Tonga, ctry., Oc.	H11	6
Tonganoxie, Ks., U.S.	C8	93
Tongbei, China	B3	33
Tongcheng, China	I7	32
Tongchuan, China	G3	32
Tongeren, Bel.	D5	17
Tonghai, China	C4	33
Tonghua, China	C10	31
Tongjiang, China	C6	33
Tongliao, China	C9	31
Tongling, China	E8	31
Tongoy, Chile	F1	55
Tongren, China	K3	32
Tongue, Scot., U.K.	B4	13
Tongue, stm., Mt., U.S.	E10	103
Tongue, stm., Tx., U.S.	p13	120
Tongue, Kyle of, b., Scot., U.K.	A1	97
Tongue River Reservoir, res., Mt., U.S.	D3	103
Tonica, Il., U.S.	B4	90
Tonj, Sud.	D2	47
Tonk, India	C6	36
Tonkawa, Ok., U.S.	A4	113
Tonkin, hist reg., Viet.	B6	35
Tonkin, Gulf of, b., Asia	B3	34
Tonle Sap, l., Kam.	C2	34
Tonneins, Fr.	E4	16
Tonnerre, Fr.	D5	16
Tönning, F.R.Ger.	D5	15
Tonopah, Az., U.S.	D3	80
Tonopah, Nv., U.S.	E4	105
Tonosí, Pan.	G7	62
Tönsberg, Nor.	H4	14
Tontitown, Ar., U.S.	A1	81
Tonto, stm., Mex.	n15	63
Tonto Basin, Az., U.S.	D4	80
Tontogany, Oh., U.S.	f6	112
Tonton, Phil.	n13	34
Tonto National Monument, Az., U.S.	D4	80
Tonto Natural Bridge, Az., U.S.	C4	80
Tooele, Ut., U.S.	C3	121
Tooele, co., Ut., U.S.	D2	121
Toole, co., Mt., U.S.	B5	103
Toomsboro, Ga., U.S.	D3	87
Toomsuba, Ms., U.S.	C5	101
Toone, Tn., U.S.	B3	119
Toowoomba, Austl.	E9	51
Topawa, Az., U.S.	F4	80
Topaz, Ca., U.S.	C4	82
Topeka, In., U.S.	A6	91
Topeka, Ks., U.S.	C8	93
Topinabee, Mi., U.S.	C6	99
Topki, Sov. Un.	D11	29
Topley, B.C., Can.	B4	69
Toplica, stm., Yugo.	D5	24
Topocalma, Punta, c., Chile	A2	54
Topock, Az., U.S.	C1	80
Topol'čany, Czech.	D5	26
Topolnitsa, stm., Bul.	D7	24
Topolobampo, Mex.	B3	63
Topolovgrad, Bul.	D8	24
Toponas, Co., U.S.	A4	83
Topozero, l., Sov. Un.	E14	14
Toppenish, Wa., U.S.	C5	124
Toppenish Ridge, mtn., Wa., U.S.	C5	124
Top Pond, l., Nf., Can.	E3	72
Topsfield, Me., U.S.	C5	96
Topsfield, Ma., U.S.	A6	98
Topsham, Me., U.S.	E3	96
Topsham, Vt., U.S.	C4	122
Topton, N.C., U.S.	f9	110
Topton, Pa., U.S.	F10	115
Toquerville, Ut., U.S.	F2	121
Toquima Range, mts., Nv., U.S.	E5	105
Torbalı, Tur.	C6	25
Torbat-e Ḥeydarīyeh, Iran	D9	39
Torbat-e Jām, Iran	D10	39
Torbay, Nf., Can.	E5	72
Tor Bay, b., Eng., U.K.	D4	12
Torbert, Mount, mtn., Ak., U.S.	g15	79
Torbrook, N.S., Can.	E5	71
Torcello, Italy	D8	20
Torch, stm., Sk., Can.	D3	75
Torch Lake, l., Mi., U.S.	D5	99
Torekov, Swe.	B6	15
Torez, Sov. Un.	q21	27
Torgau, Ger.D.R.	C6	18
Torhout, Bel.	B5	16
Toride, Japan	n19	33
Tori Island, i., Japan	J4	33
Torit, Sud.	E3	47
Tormes, stm., Spain	B3	22
Tornado Mountain, mtn., Can.	E3	68
Torneträsk, l., Swe.	C9	14
Torngat Mountains, mts., Can.	f8	72
Tornillo, Tx., U.S.	o11	120
Tornio, Fin.	E11	14
Tornquist, Arg.	B4	54
Toro, Spain	B3	22
Torö, Swe.	u35	14
Törökszentmiklós, Hung.	B5	24
Toronto, On., Can.	D5	73
Toronto, Ks., U.S.	E8	93
Toronto, Oh., U.S.	B5	112
Toronto Lake, res., Ks., U.S.	E7	93
Toro Peak, mtn., Ca., U.S.	F5	82
Toropets, Sov. Un.	C8	27
Toro Rumi, mtn., Peru	D3	58
Toro, Ug.	A5	48
Torpoint, Eng., U.K.	A8	15
Torquay, Sk., Can.	H4	75
Torquay (Torbay), Eng., U.K.	E5	10
Torrance, Ca., U.S.	n12	82
Torrance, co., N.M., U.S.	C3	108
Torre Annunziata, Italy	I9	23
Torre de Cerredo, mtn., Spain	A3	22
Torre del Greco, Italy	D5	23
Torredonjimeno, Spain	D4	22
Torrejón de Ardoz, Spain	p18	22
Torrejoncillo, Spain	C2	22
Torrelavega, Spain	A3	22
Torremaggiore, Italy	D5	23
Torrens, Lake, l., Austl.	F6	50
Torrente, Spain	C5	22
Torreón, Mex.	B4	63
Torreon, N.M., U.S.	C3	108
Torre-Pacheco, Spain	C5	22
Torres, Braz.	D3	56
Torres Novas, Port.	C1	22
Torres Strait, strt., Austl.	A7	50
Torres Vedras, Port.	C1	22
Torrevieja, Spain	C5	22
Torrey, Ut., U.S.	E4	121
Torridge, stm., Eng., U.K.	D3	12
Torridon, Loch, b., Scot., U.K.	C3	13
Torriglia, Italy	E5	20
Torrington, Ct., U.S.	B3	84
Torrington, Eng., U.K.	D3	12
Torrington, Ct., U.S.	B3	84
Torrington, Wy., U.S.	D8	127
Torrinha, Braz.	m7	56
Torrox, Spain	D4	22
Tors Cove, Nf., Can.	E5	72
Torshälla (part of Eskilstuna), Swe.	t34	14
Tórshavn, Faer. Is.	C7	8
Tortilla Flat, Az., U.S.	D4	80
Tortola, i., V.I., Br.	G12	64
Tortosa, Spain	B6	22
Tortosa, Cape, c., Spain	B6	22
Tortue, Île de la, i., Haiti	D7	64
Tortuga, Golfo, b., Col.	C2	60
Torugart Pass, Asia	E9	28
Torun, Pol.	B5	26
Torup, Swe.	B7	15
Tory Hill, On., Can.	C6	73
Tory Island, i., Ire.	C2	10
Torysa, stm., Czech.	D6	26
Tory Sound, strt., Ire.	B3	11
Torzhok, Sov. Un.	C10	27
Torzym, Pol.	A10	19
Tosa-shimizu, Japan	J6	33
Tosno, Sov. Un.	B8	27
Tostado, Arg.	G3	53
Tosya, Tur.	B10	40
Toszek, Pol.	g9	26
Totagatic, stm., Wi., U.S.	B2	126
Totana, Spain	C5	22
Tótkomlós, Hung.	B5	24
Totma, Sov. Un.	B2	28
Totnes, Eng., U.K.	D4	12
Totness, Sur.	A3	59
Totolapan (part of Mexico City), Mex.	h9	63
Totonicapán, Guat.	C2	62
Totora Palca, Bol.	C2	55
Totowa, N.J., U.S.	B4	107
Totoya Island, i., Fiji	I16	52
Totson Mountain, mtn., Ak., U.S.	C8	79
Totten Glacier, Ant.	C24	7
Tottenham, Austl.	F6	51
Tottenham, On., Can.	C5	73
Tottenham (part of London), Eng., U.K.	k12	10
Tottori, Japan	D11	33

Name	Map Ref	Page

Totz, Ky., U.S. — D6 94
Touba, I.C. — E3 45
Touba, Sen. — D1 45
Toubkal, Jbel, mtn., Mor. — C3 44
Touchet, Wa., U.S. — C7 124
Touchet, stm., Wa., U.S. — C7 124
Touchwood Lake, l., Mb., Can. — B4 70
Tougan, Burkina — D4 45
Touggourt, Alg. — C6 44
Tougué, Gui. — D2 45
Touhy, Ne., U.S. — C9 104
Touisset, Ma., U.S. — C5 98
Toul, Fr. — C6 16
Toulépleu, I.C. — E3 45
Toulon, Fr. — F6 16
Toulon, Il., U.S. — B4 90
Toulouse, Fr. — F4 16
Toungo, Nig. — E7 45
Toungoo, Burma — E10 36
Touraine, hist reg., Fr. — D4 16
Tourcoing, Fr. — B5 16
Tourlaville, Fr. — C3 16
Tourmakeady, Ire. — D2 11
Tournai (Doornik), Bel. — D3 17
Tournon, Fr. — E6 16
Tournus, Fr. — D6 16
Touros, Braz. — C3 57
Tours, Fr. — D4 16
Touside, Pic, mtn., Chad — A3 46
Toussaint Creek, stm., Oh., U.S. — f7 112
Toutle, North Fork, stm., Wa., U.S. — C3 124
Tovar, Ven. — B3 60
Tovarkovskiy, Sov. Un. — E12 27
Tovey, Il., U.S. — D4 90
Tow, Tx., U.S. — D3 120
Towaco, N.J., U.S. — B4 107
Towada, I., Japan — F10 33
Towanda, Il., U.S. — C5 90
Towanda, Ks., U.S. — E7 93
Towanda, Pa., U.S. — C9 115
Towanda Creek, stm., Pa., U.S. — C8 115
Towaoc, Co., U.S. — D2 83
Tower, Mi., U.S. — C6 99
Tower, Mn., U.S. — C6 100
Tower City, N.D., U.S. — C8 111
Tower City, Pa., U.S. — E8 115
Tower Hill, Il., U.S. — D5 90
Town and Country, Mo., U.S. — B8 124
Town Creek, Al., U.S. — A2 78
Town Creek Manor, Md., U.S. — D5 97
Towner, Co., U.S. — C8 83
Towner, N.D., U.S. — A5 111
Towner, co., N.D., U.S. — A6 111
Town Hill, Ct., U.S. — B3 84
Town Hill, mtn., U.S. — A1 97
Town Hill, hill, Ber. — p20 64
Townley, Al., U.S. — B2 78
Town of Tonawanda, N.Y., U.S. — C2 109
Towns, Ga., U.S. — D4 87
Towns, co., Ga., U.S. — B3 87
Townsend, De., U.S. — C3 85
Townsend, Ga., U.S. — E5 87
Townsend, Ma., U.S. — A4 98
Townsend, Mt., U.S. — D5 103
Townsend, Tn., U.S. — D10 119
Townsend, Va., U.S. — C7 123
Townshend, Vt., U.S. — E3 122
Townshend Reservoir, res., Vt., U.S. — E3 122
Townsville, Austl. — C8 50
Townsville, N.C., U.S. — A4 110
Townville, Pa., U.S. — C2 115
Townville, S.C., U.S. — B2 117
Towrzī, Afg. — B4 36
Towson, Md., U.S. — B4 97
Towuti, Lake, l., Indon. — F6 34
Toxey, Al., U.S. — D1 78
Toyah, Tx., U.S. — o13 120
Toyahvale, Tx., U.S. — o13 120
Toyama, Japan — D12 31
Toyama Bay, b., Japan — H8 33
Toyohashi, Japan — I8 33
Toyokawa, Japan — *I8 33
Toyonaka, Japan — o14 33
Toyota, Japan — n16 33
Tozeur, Tun. — C6 44
Tozghi, mtn., Pak. — G11 39
Trabancos, stm., Spain — D3 22
Traben-Trarbach, F.R.Ger. — D2 19
Trabzon, Tur. — B12 40
Tracadie, N.B., Can. — B5 71
Tracadie, N.S., Can. — D8 71
Tracy, N.B., Can. — D3 71
Tracy, P.Q., Can. — C4 74
Tracy, Ca., U.S. — D3 82
Tracy, Ia., U.S. — C5 92
Tracy, Mn., U.S. — F3 100
Tracy, Mo., U.S. — B3 102
Tracy City, Tn., U.S. — D8 119
Tracys Creek, stm., Md., U.S. — A5 97
Tracyton, Wa., U.S. — e10 124
Tradate, Italy — E6 21
Trade, Tn., U.S. — C12 119
Trade Lake, l., Wi., U.S. — B4 75
Tradewater, stm., Ky., U.S. — C2 94
Trading Post, Ks., U.S. — D9 93
Traer, Ia., U.S. — B5 92
Traer, Ks., U.S. — C3 93
Trafalgar, In., U.S. — F5 91
Trafalgar, Cape, c., Spain — I4 22
Trafford, Pa., U.S. — k14 115
Trafford, Lake, l., Fl., U.S. — F5 86
Traiguén, Chile — B2 54
Trail, B.C., Can. — E9 69
Trail, Mn., U.S. — C3 100
Trail, Or., U.S. — E4 114
Trail City, S.D., U.S. — B5 118
Trail Creek, In., U.S. — A4 91
Traill, co., N.D., U.S. — B8 111
Traill, i., Grnld. — B16 128
Trail Ridge, mtn., U.S. — F4 87
Traipu, Braz. — E11 57
Trairi, stm., Braz. — h6 57
Tralee, Ire. — D2 10
Tramelan, Switz. — B3 21
Trammel, Va., U.S. — e9 123
Tramore, Ire. — E4 11
Trampas, N.M., U.S. — A4 108
Tramping Lake, Sk., Can. — E1 75
Tramping Lake, l., Sk., Can. — E1 75
Tranås, Swe. — H6 14
Trancão, stm., Port. — I9 22
Trancas, Arg. — E2 55
Trancoso, Port. — B2 22
Tranebjerg, Den. — C4 15
Tranemo, Swe. — A7 15
Trang, Thai. — D1 34
Trangan, i., Indon. — G8 34
Trani, Italy — D6 23

Tranninh, Plateau du, plat., Laos — C5 35
Tranquility, N.J., U.S. — B3 107
Tranquillity, Ca., U.S. — D3 82
Transfer, Pa., U.S. — D1 115
Transkei, ctry., Afr. — D4 49
Transvaal, prov., S. Afr. — B4 49
Transylvania, La., U.S. — B4 95
Transylvania, co., N.C., U.S. — f10 110
Transylvania, hist reg., Rom. — B6 24
Transylvanian Alps, mts., Rom. — C7 24
Trapani, Italy — E4 23
Trapco, Md., U.S. — C5 97
Trappe, Md., U.S. — C5 97
Trappe Creek, stm., Md., U.S. — D7 97
Trhové Sviny, Czech. — E9 19
Triadelphia, W.V., U.S. — A4 125
Triadelphia Reservoir, res., Md., U.S. — B3 97
Trianda, Grc. — D7 25
Trapper Peak, mtn., Mt., U.S. — E2 103
Traralgon, Austl. — G8 50
Traryd, Swe. — B7 15
Trasimeno, Lake, l., Italy — C4 23
Trask, Mo., U.S. — E6 102
Traskwood, Ar., U.S. — C3 81
Tras-os-Montes, hist reg., Port. — B2 22
Trat, Thai. — C2 34
Traun, stm., Aus. — D7 18
Traunik, Mi., U.S. — B4 99
Traunstein, F.R.Ger. — E6 18
Traun Lake, l., Aus. — E6 18
Trave, stm., Eur. — E4 15
Travelers Rest, S.C., U.S. — B3 117
Travers, Ab., Can. — D4 68
Travers, Switz. — C2 21
Traverse, co., Mn., U.S. — E2 100
Traverse City, Mi., U.S. — D5 99
Traverspine, stm., Nf., Can. — B1 72
Travers Reservoir, res., Ab., Can. — D4 68
Travis, co., Tx., U.S. — D4 120
Travis Air Force Base, mil., Ca., U.S. — C2 82
Travnik, Yugo. — C3 24
Tray Mountain, mtn., Ga., U.S. — B3 87
Treadway, Tn., U.S. — C10 119
Treasure, co., Mt., U.S. — D9 103
Treasure Island, Fl., U.S. — *p10 86
Treasure Island Naval Station, mil., Ca., U.S. — h8 82
Trebbia, stm., Italy — E5 20
Trebbin, stm., Ger.D.R. — E6 15
Trebinje, Yugo. — D4 24
Trebišov, Czech. — D6 26
Treble Mountain, mtn., B.C., Can. — B3 69
Trebloc, Ms., U.S. — B5 101
Třeboň, Czech. — D3 26
Trece Martires, Phil. — o13 34
Třinec, Czech. — *D5 26
Trees, La., U.S. — B1 95
Tregaron, Wales, U.K. — D5 10
Tregarva, Sk., Can. — G3 75
Trego, Mt., U.S. — B2 103
Trego, Wi., U.S. — C2 126
Trego, co., Ks., U.S. — D4 93
Tréguier, Fr. — C2 16
Treherne, Mb., Can. — E2 70
Treig, Loch, res., Scot., U.K. — D4 13
Treinta y Tres, Ur. — E2 56
Treis, F.R.Ger. — C2 19
Trélazé, Fr. — D3 16
Trelew, Arg. — C3 54
Trelleborg, Swe. — J5 14
Tremadoc Bay, b., Wales, U.K. — D4 10
Tremblant, Mont, mtn., P.Q., Can. — C3 74
Tremblay, Fr. — g11 16
Trembleur Lake, l., B.C., Can. — B5 69
Trementina, N.M., U.S. — B5 108
Tremiti Islands, is., Italy — C5 23
Tremont, Il., U.S. — C4 90
Tremont, Ms., U.S. — A5 101
Tremont, Pa., U.S. — E9 115
Tremont City, Oh., U.S. — B2 112
Tremonton, Ut., U.S. — B3 121
Tremošna, Czech. — D8 19
Tremp, Spain — A6 22
Trempealeau, Wi., U.S. — D2 126
Trempealeau, co., Wi., U.S. — D2 126
Trempealeau, stm., Wi., U.S. — D2 126
Trenary, Mi., U.S. — B4 99
Trenche, stm., P.Q., Can. — B5 74
Trenčín, Czech. — D5 26
Trenque Lauquen, Arg. — B4 54
Trent, Ger.D.R. — D7 15
Trent, S.D., U.S. — D9 118
Trent, Tx., U.S. — C2 120
Trent, stm., Eng., U.K. — D6 10
Trent, stm., N.C., U.S. — B5 110
Trente et un Milles, Lac des, l., P.Q., Can. — C2 74
Trentino-Alto Adige, prov., Italy — C7 20
Trento (Trent), Italy — A3 23
Trenton, N.S., Can. — D7 71
Trenton, On., Can. — C7 73
Trenton, Al., U.S. — A3 78
Trenton, Fl., U.S. — C4 86
Trenton, Ga., U.S. — B1 87
Trenton, Il., U.S. — E4 90
Trenton, Ky., U.S. — D2 94
Trenton, Mi., U.S. — F7 99
Trenton, Mo., U.S. — A4 102
Trenton, Ne., U.S. — D4 104
Trenton, N.J., U.S. — C3 107
Trenton, N.C., U.S. — B5 110
Trenton, N.D., U.S. — A2 111
Trenton, Oh., U.S. — C1 112
Trenton, S.C., U.S. — D4 117
Trenton, Tn., U.S. — B3 119
Trenton, Tx., U.S. — C4 120
Trepassey, Nf., Can. — E5 72
Trepassey Bay, b., Nf., Can. — E5 72
Tres Algarrobos, Arg. — B4 54
Tres Arboles, Ur. — E1 56
Tres Arroyos, Arg. — C4 54
Tresckow, Pa., U.S. — E10 115
Três Corações, Braz. — C3 56
Tres Esquinas, Col. — C2 60
Treshnish Point, c., Scot., U.K. — D2 13
Tres Irmãos, Serra das, hills, Braz. — E3 57
Treska, stm., Yugo. — E5 24
Três Lagoas, Braz. — C2 56
Três Marias, Represa, res., Braz. — B3 56
Tres Piedras, N.M., U.S. — A4 108
Tres Puntas, Cabo, c., Arg. — D3 54
Três Rios, Braz. — h6 56
Três Ritos, N.M., U.S. — A4 108
Trestle Creek, Id., U.S. — A2 89

Treuchtlingen, F.R.Ger. — E5 19
Treuenbrietzen, Ger.D.R. — A7 19
Treutlen, co., Ga., U.S. — D4 87
Treviglio, Italy — B2 23
Trévillers, Fr. — B2 21
Treviño, Spain — A4 22
Treviso, Italy — B4 23
Trevlac, In., U.S. — F5 91
Trevor, Wi., U.S. — n11 126
Trevorton, Pa., U.S. — E8 115
Trevose, Pa., U.S. — o22 115
Treynor, Ia., U.S. — C2 92
Trevose Head, c., Eng., U.K. — D2 12
Trezevant, Tn., U.S. — A3 119
Triaucourt [-en-Argonne], Fr. — F5 17
Tribbett, Ms., U.S. — B3 101
Tribbey, Ok., U.S. — B4 113
Tribune, Sk., Can. — H4 75
Tribune, Ks., U.S. — D2 93
Trichinopoly see Tiruchchiräppalli, India — F6 36
Trichūr, India — F6 36
Tri City, Or., U.S. — E3 114
Tridell, Ut., U.S. — C6 121
Trident, Mt., U.S. — E5 103
Trident Peak, mtn., Nv., U.S. — B3 105
Trier, F.R.Ger. — D3 18
Trieste, Italy — B4 23
Trieste, Gulf of, b., Eur. — B4 23
Trigg, co., Ky., U.S. — D2 94
Triglav, mtn., Yugo. — B1 24
Trigo Mountains, mts., Az., U.S. — D1 80
Triguéros, Spain — D2 22
Trikala, Grc. — C3 40
Trikhonis, Lake, l., Grc. — C3 25
Trikora Peak, mtn., Indon. — F9 34
Tri Lakes, In., U.S. — B7 91
Trilby, Fl., U.S. — D4 86
Trilla, Il., U.S. — D5 90
Trillick, N. Ire., U.K. — C4 11
Trim, Ire. — D5 11
Trimble, Mo., U.S. — B3 102
Trimble, Tn., U.S. — A2 119
Trimble, co., Ky., U.S. — B4 94
Trimont, Mn., U.S. — G4 100
Trimountain, Mi., U.S. — A2 99
Trinchera, Co., U.S. — D6 83
Trinchera Creek, stm., Co., U.S. — D5 83
Trincomalee, Sri L. — G7 36
Trindade, i., Braz. — H8 5
Tring-Jonction, P.Q., Can. — C6 74
Trinidad, Bol. — B3 55
Trinidad, Col. — B3 60
Trinidad, Cuba — D4 64
Trinidad, Ur. — E1 56
Trinidad, i., Trin. — K14 64
Trinidad, Bahía, b., Pan. — k11 62
Trinidad, Isla, i., Arg. — B4 54
Trinidad and Tobago, ctry., N.A. — K14 64
Trinidad Head, c., Ca., U.S. — B1 82
Trinity, Nf., Can. — D5 72
Trinity, Al., U.S. — A2 78
Trinity, Tx., U.S. — D5 120
Trinity, co., Ca., U.S. — B2 82
Trinity, co., Tx., U.S. — D5 120
Trinity, stm., Ca., U.S. — B2 82
Trinity, stm., Tx., U.S. — D5 120
Trinity, East Fork, stm., Tx., U.S. — n10 120
Trinity, Elm Fork, stm., Tx., U.S. — m10 120
Trinity, South Fork, stm., Ca., U.S. — B2 82
Trinity, West Fork, stm., Tx., U.S. — n9 120
Trinity Bay, b., Nf., Can. — D5 72
Trinity Center, Ca., U.S. — B2 82
Trinity Islands, is., Ak., U.S. — D9 79
Trinity Mountain, mtn., Id., U.S. — F3 89
Trinity Mountains, mts., Ca., U.S. — B2 82
Trinity Peak, mtn., Nv., U.S. — C3 105
Trinity Range, mts., Nv., U.S. — C3 105
Trinity Springs, In., U.S. — G4 91
Trino, Italy — B2 23
Trinway, Oh., U.S. — B3 112
Trion, Ga., U.S. — B1 87
Tripoli (Ṭarābulus), Leb. — B3 38
Tripoli (Ṭarābulus), Libya — C2 43
Tripoli, Ia., U.S. — B5 92
Tripolis, Grc. — D4 40
Tripolitania (Ṭarābulus), nist reg., Libya — C3 43
Tripp, S.D., U.S. — D8 118
Tripp, co., S.D., U.S. — D6 118
Trisanna, stm., Aus. — B9 21
Triste, Golfo, b., Ven. — A4 60
Triumph, La., U.S. — E6 95
Triune, Tn., U.S. — B5 119
Triunfo, Braz. — C3 57
Trivandrum, India — G6 36
Trnava, Czech. — D4 26
Trobriand Islands, is., Pap. N. Gui. — k13 50
Trochu, Ab., Can. — D4 68
Trögstad, Nor. — p29 14
Troisdorf, F.R.Ger. — C2 19
Trois-Pistoles, P.Q., Can. — A8 74
Trois-Rivières, P.Q., Can. — C5 74
Trois-Saumons, P.Q., Can. — B7 74
Troisvierges, Lux. — D6 17
Troitsk, Sov. Un. — D9 29
Troitskoye, Sov. Un. — B8 33
Trolldalen, Nor. — p28 14
Trollhättan, Swe. — H5 14
Trombetas, stm., Braz. — C3 59
Trombly, Mi., U.S. — B3 99
Tromper Wiek, b., Ger.D.R. — D7 15
Tromsö, Nor. — C8 14
Trona, Ca., U.S. — E5 82
Tronador, Monte, mtn., S.A. — C2 54
Trondheim, Nor. — F4 14
Trondheimsfjorden, Nor. — F3 14

Troon, Scot., U.K. — E4 13
Tropea, Italy — E5 23
Tropic, Ut., U.S. — F3 121
Trophy Mountain, mtn., B.C., Can. — D8 69
Trosa, Swe. — u35 14
Trosky, Mn., U.S. — G2 100
Trossachs, Sk., Can. — H3 75
Trostan, mtn., N. Ire., U.K. — B5 11
Trotters, N.D., U.S. — B2 111
Trotwood, Oh., U.S. — C1 112
Troup, Tx., U.S. — C5 120
Troup, co., Ga., U.S. — C1 87
Trousdale, Ks., U.S. — E4 93
Trousdale, co., Tn., U.S. — A5 119
Trousers Lake, l., N.B., Can. — B3 71
Trout, La., U.S. — C3 95
Trout, stm., Ab., Can. — A3 68
Trout, stm., Fl., U.S. — m8 86
Trout, stm., Vt., U.S. — B3 122
Trout Creek, On., Can. — B5 73
Trout Creek, Mi., U.S. — n12 99
Trout Creek, Mt., U.S. — C1 103
Trout Creek, Ut., U.S. — D2 121
Trout Creek Pass, Co., U.S. — C5 83
Troutdale, Or., U.S. — *B4 114
Troutdale, Va., U.S. — D1 123
Trout Lake, Mi., U.S. — B6 99
Trout Lake, Wa., U.S. — D4 124
Trout Lake, l., N.T., Can. — D8 66
Trout Lake, l., On., Can. — o16 73
Trout Lake, l., On., Can. — A5 73
Trout Lake, l., Mn., U.S. — B6 100
Trout Lake, l., Wi., U.S. — B4 126
Troutman, N.C., U.S. — B2 110
Trout Peak, mtn., Wy., U.S. — B3 127
Trout River, Nf., Can. — D2 72
Trout Run, Pa., U.S. — D7 115
Troutville, Va., U.S. — C3 123
Trouville [-sur-Mer], Fr. — C4 16
Trowbridge, Eng., U.K. — E5 10
Troy, Al., U.S. — D4 78
Troy, Id., U.S. — C2 89
Troy, Il., U.S. — E4 90
Troy, In., U.S. — H4 91
Troy, Ia., U.S. — D5 92
Troy, Ks., U.S. — C8 93
Troy, Mi., U.S. — o15 99
Troy, Ms., U.S. — A5 101
Troy, Mo., U.S. — C7 102
Troy, Mt., U.S. — B1 103
Troy, N.H., U.S. — E2 106
Troy, N.Y., U.S. — C7 109
Troy, N.C., U.S. — B3 110
Troy, Oh., U.S. — B1 112
Troy, Ok., U.S. — C5 113
Troy, Or., U.S. — B9 114
Troy, Pa., U.S. — C8 115
Troy, S.C., U.S. — D3 117
Troy, S.D., U.S. — B9 118
Troy, Tn., U.S. — A2 119
Troy, Vt., U.S. — B4 122
Troy, W.V., U.S. — B4 125
Troy (Ilion), hist., Tur. — C6 25
Troyes, Fr. — C6 16
Troy Grove, Il., U.S. — B4 90
Troy Mills, Ia., U.S. — B6 92
Troy Peak, mtn., Nv., U.S. — E6 105
Trstenik, Yugo. — D5 24
Truax, Sk., Can. — H3 75
Trubchevsk, Sov. Un. — E9 27
Trubschachen, Switz. — C4 21
Truc Giang, Viet. — G7 35
Truchas, N.M., U.S. — A4 108
Truchas Peak, mtn., N.M., U.S. — B4 108
Truckee, Ca., U.S. — C3 82
Truckee, stm., U.S. — D2 105
Trujillo, Hond. — D7 63
Trujillo, Peru — C2 58
Trujillo, Spain — C3 22
Trujillo, Ven. — B3 60
Trujillo, state, Ven. — B3 60
Truk, is., Micron. — F9 6
Truk International Airport, Micron. — Q18 52
Truk Lagoon, b., Micron. — Q18 52
Truman, Mn., U.S. — G4 100
Trumann, Ar., U.S. — B5 81
Trumansburg, N.Y., U.S. — C4 109
Trumbull, Ct., U.S. — E3 84
Trumbull, Ne., U.S. — D7 104
Trumbull, co., Oh., U.S. — A5 112
Trumbull, Mount, mtn., Az., U.S. — A2 80
Trün, Bul. — D6 24
Truro, N.S., Can. — D6 71
Truro, Eng., U.K. — E4 10
Truro, Ia., U.S. — C4 92
Truro, Ma., U.S. — C7 98
Truscott, Tx., U.S. — C3 120
Truskmore, mtn., Ire. — C3 11
Trussville, Al., U.S. — *B3 78
Trustom Pond, l., R.I., U.S. — G3 116
Trust Territory of the Pacific Islands see Pacific Islands, Trust Territory of the, dep., Oc. — F9 6
Truth or Consequences (Hot Springs), N.M., U.S. — D2 108
Trutnov, Czech. — C3 26
Truxton, Az., U.S. — B2 80
Truxton, Mo., U.S. — B6 102
Truxton, N.Y., U.S. — C4 109
Tryon, N.C., U.S. — f10 110
Tryon, Ne., U.S. — C5 104
Trysil, Nor. — G5 14
Trzcianka, Pol. — B4 26
Trzebiatów, Pol. — A3 26
Trzebnica, Pol. — C4 26
Tržič, Yugo. — D3 24
Tsagaan-Tologoy Hiid, Mong. — D9 32
Tsaidam Basin see Qaidam Pendi, depr., China — C2 31
Tsakir, Sov. Un. — A5 31
Tsala Apopka Lake, l., Fl., U.S. — D4 86
Tsaratanana, Madag. — g9 49
Tsast Bogd Mountain, mtn., Mong. — B3 31
Tsau, Bots. — B3 49
Tsavo, Kenya — B7 48
Tschetter Colony, S.D., U.S. — D7 118
Tschida, Lake, res., N.D., U.S. — C4 111
Tselinograd, Sov. Un. — D10 29
Tsentral'nyy, Sov. Un. — D26 27
Tsetserleg, Mong. — B5 31
Tshabong, Bots. — C3 49
Tshane, Bots. — B3 49
Tshela, Zaire — B1 48
Tshikapa, Zaire — C3 48

Tshilongo, Zaire — D4 48
Tshimbo, Zaire — C4 48
Tshofa, Zaire — C4 48
Tshuapa, stm., Zaire — B3 48
Tshukudu, Bots. — B3 49
Tshwaane, Bots. — B3 49
Tsiafajavona, mtn., Madag. — g9 49
Tsihombe, Madag. — i9 49
Tsimlyansk Reservoir, res., Sov. Un. — E7 29
Tsinan see Jinan, China — D8 31
Tsinghai see Qinghai, prov., China
Tsingtao see Qingdao, China — D9 31
Tsining Shan see Qin Ling, mts., China — E6 31
Tsintsabis, Nmb. — A2 49
Tsiroanomandidy, Madag. — g9 49
Tsitsihar see Qiqihar, China — B9 31
Tsitsutl Peak, mtn., B.C., Can. — C5 69
Tsivory, Madag. — h9 49
Tskhinvali, Sov. Un. — E2 29
Tsna, stm., Sov. Un. — E13 27
Tsodilo Hill, hill, Bots. — A3 49
Tsogttsetsiy, Mong. — C1 32
Tsu, Japan — I8 33
Tsuchiura, Japan — H10 33
Tsugaru Strait, strt., Japan — F10 33
Tsuken Island, i., Japan — O5 52
Tsulukidze, Sov. Un. — A14 40
Tsumeb, Nmb. — A2 49
Tsumis Park, Nmb. — B2 49
Tsuruga, Japan — I8 33
Tsurugi, Mount, mtn., Japan — J7 33
Tsuruoka, Japan — G9 33
Tsushima, Japan — n15 33
Tsu Shima, is., Japan — E10 31
Tsuyama, Japan — I6 33
Tua, stm., Port. — B2 22
Tual, Indon. — G8 34
Tualatin, Or., U.S. — *h12 114
Tualatin, stm., Or., U.S. — h11 114
Tuam, Ire. — D2 10
Tuamotu Archipelago, is., Fr. Poly. — H13 6
Tuangku, i., Indon. — K2 35
Tuapse, Sov. Un. — G16 8
Tuasivi, W. Sam. — F11 52
Tuasivi, Cape, c., W. Sam. — F11 52
Tuatapere, N.Z. — Q11 51
Tubac, Az., U.S. — F4 80
Tuba City, Az., U.S. — A4 80
Tubarão, Braz. — D3 56
Tubás, Isr. Occ. — B7 41
Tubbercurry, Ire. — C3 11
Tübingen, F.R.Ger. — D4 18
Tubre, Italy — C6 20
Tubruq (Tobruk), Libya — C4 43
Tubuai Islands, is., Fr. Poly. — H3 6
Tucacas, Ven. — A4 60
Tucannon, stm., Wa., U.S. — C8 124
Tucano, Braz. — D3 57
Tuchola, Pol. — B4 26
Tuckahoe, N.J., U.S. — E3 107
Tuckahoe, N.Y., U.S. — h13 109
Tuckahoe, stm., N.J., U.S. — E3 107
Tuckahoe Creek, stm., Md., U.S. — C6 97
Tuckerman, Ar., U.S. — B4 81
Tuckernuck Island, i., Ma., U.S. — D7 98
Tuckers Crossing, Ms., U.S. — D4 101
Tuckerton, N.J., U.S. — D4 107
Tucson, Az., U.S. — E5 80
Tucumán, prov., Arg. — E2 55
Tucumcari, N.M., U.S. — B6 108
Tucumcari Mountain, mtn., N.M., U.S. — B6 108
Tucupita, Ven. — B5 60
Tucuruí, Braz. — C5 59
Tucznawa, Pol. — g10 26
Tudela, Spain — A5 22
Tudmur (Palmyra), Syria — E12 40
Tufi, Pap. N. Gui. — k12 50
Tuftonboro, N.H., U.S. — C4 106
Tugaloo Lake, res., U.S. — B1 87
Tugaske, Sk., Can. — G2 75
Tug Fork, stm., U.S. — C2 125
Tuguegarao, Phil. — B6 34
Tukangbesi Islands, is., Indon. — G6 34
Tükrah, Libya — k12 40
Tuktoyaktuk, N.T., Can. — C6 66
Tukums, Sov. Un. — D4 27
Tukuyu, Tan. — C5 48
Tukwila, Wa., U.S. — f11 124
Tula, Mex. — C5 62
Tula, Sov. Un. — D11 27
Tula, Ms., U.S. — A4 101
Tula de Allende, Mex. — m14 63
Tulalip Indian Reservation, Wa., U.S. — A3 124
Tulancingo, Mex. — C5 62
Tulare, S.D., U.S. — C7 118
Tulare, Ca., U.S. — D4 82
Tulare, co., Ca., U.S. — D4 82
Tulare Lake, l., Ca., U.S. — D4 82
Tularosa, N.M., U.S. — D3 108
Tularosa Mountains, mts., N.M., U.S. — D1 108
Tularosa Valley, val., N.M., U.S. — E3 108
Tulbagh, S. Afr. — D2 49
Tulcán, Ec. — B2 58
Tulcea, Rom. — C9 24
Tulchin, Sov. Un. — C5 27
Tulelake, Ca., U.S. — B3 82
Tule Lake Sump, sw., Ca., U.S. — B3 82
Tule River Indian Reservation, Ca., U.S. — E4 82
Tulia, Tx., U.S. — B2 120
Tuli, Zimb. — B4 49
Tülkarm, Isr. Occ. — B7 41
Tulla, Ire. — D3 11
Tullahassee, Ok., U.S. — B6 113
Tullahoma, Tn., U.S. — B5 119
Tullamore, Ire. — D4 11
Tulle, Fr. — E4 16
Tullins, Fr. — D8 16
Tulln, Aus. — D8 18
Tullos, La., U.S. — C3 95
Tullow, Ire. — E5 11
Tully, Austl. — C4 50
Tully, N.Y., U.S. — C4 109

Tulmaythah, Libya — F3 40
Tuloma, stm., Sov. Un. — B15 8
Tulot, Sov. Un. — B5 8
Tulsa, Ok., U.S. — A6 113
Tulsa, co., Ok., U.S. — B6 113
Tulsequah, B.C., Can. — E6 66
Tulsk, Ire. — D3 11
Tuluá, Col. — C2 60
Tulun, Sov. Un. — D13 29
Tulungagung, Indon. — G4 34
Tulu Welel, mtn., Eth. — D3 47
Tuma, stm., Nic. — D5 62
Tumacacori, Az., U.S. — F4 80
Tumacacori National Monument, Az., U.S. — F4 80
Tumaco, Col. — C2 60
Tumaco, Ensenada de, b., Col. — C2 60
Tumalo, Or., U.S. — C5 114
Tumatumari, Guy. — A3 59
Tumba, Swe. — I35 14
Tumba, Lac, l., Zaire — B2 48
Tumbarumba, Austl. — G7 51
Tumbaya, Arg. — D2 55
Tumbes, Peru — B1 58
Tumbes, dept., Peru — B1 58
Tumble Mountain, mtn., Mt., U.S. — E7 103
Tumbling Shoals, Ar., U.S. — B3 81
Tumen, China — C10 31
Tumen Jiang, stm., Asia — E4 33
Tumeremo, Ven. — B5 60
Tumkür, India — F6 36
Tumnin, stm., Sov. Un. — A10 33
Tumon Bay, b., Guam — L10 52
Tumtum, Wa., U.S. — B8 124
Tumu, Ghana — D4 45
Tumuc-Humac Mountains, mts., S.A. — B3 59
Tumut, Austl. — G7 51
Tumwater, Wa., U.S. — B3 124
Tunapuna, Trin. — N23 65
Tunas de Zaza, Cuba — D4 64
Tunaycha, l., Sov. Un. — C11 33
Tunbridge, Vt., U.S. — D4 122
Tunbridge Wells, Eng., U.K. — E7 10
Tunduru, Tan. — D6 48
Tundzha, stm., Eur. — D8 24
Tunga, stm., India — F6 36
Tungla, Nic. — D5 62
Tungurahua, prov., Ec. — B2 58
Tuni, India — I9 37
Tunica, La., U.S. — D4 95
Tunica, Ms., U.S. — A3 101
Tunica, co., Ms., U.S. — A3 101
Tunis, Tun. — F3 44
Tunis, Gulf of, b., Tun. — F3 23
Tunisia, ctry., Afr. — C6 44
Tunis Mills, Md., U.S. — C5 97
Tunja, Col. — B3 60
Tunkhannock, Pa., U.S. — C10 115
Tunk Lake, l., Me., U.S. — D4 96
Tunnel Hill, Ga., U.S. — B1 87
Tunnel Springs, Al., U.S. — D2 78
Tunnelton, In., U.S. — G5 91
Tunnelton, W.V., U.S. — B5 125
Tunø, i., Den. — C4 15
Tunp Range, mts., Wy., U.S. — D2 127
Tuntutuliak, Ak., U.S. — C7 79
Tununak, Ak., U.S. — C6 79
Tunungayualok Island, i., Nf., Can. — g9 72
Tunuyán, Arg. — A3 54
Tunuyán, stm., Arg. — A3 54
Tunxi, China — F8 31
Tuolumne, Ca., U.S. — D3 82
Tuolumne, co., Ca., U.S. — C4 82
Tuolumne, stm., Ca., U.S. — D3 82
Tupã, Braz. — C2 56
Tupanciretã, Braz. — B6 56
Tupelo, Ar., U.S. — B4 81
Tupelo, Ms., U.S. — A5 101
Tupelo, Ok., U.S. — C5 113
Tupiza, Bol. — D2 55
Tupman, Ca., U.S. — E4 82
Tupper, B.C., Can. — B7 69
Tupper Lake, N.Y., U.S. — A6 109
Tupper Lake, l., N.Y., U.S. — A6 109
Tuppers Plains, Oh., U.S. — C4 112
Tupperville, On., Can. — E2 73
Tupungato, Arg. — A3 54
Tupungato, Cerro, mtn., S.A. — A3 54
Tuquan, China — B9 32
Túquerres, Col. — C2 60
Tura, India — E13 37
Tura, stm., Sov. Un. — C13 29
Turan Lowland, pl., Sov. Un. — A2 28
Turbaco, Col. — A3 60
Turbat, Pak. — D1 36
Turbenthal, Switz. — B6 21
Turbeville, S.C., U.S. — D7 117
Turbo, Col. — B2 60
Turbotville, Pa., U.S. — D8 115
Turda, Rom. — B7 24
Turek, Pol. — B5 26
Turgay, Sov. Un. — D8 28
Turgay, stm., Sov. Un. — D8 28
Türgovishte, Bul. — D8 24
Turgutlu, Tur. — C6 40
Turi, Sov. Un. — B5 27
Turia, stm., Spain — C5 22
Turiaçu, stm., Braz. — B1 57
Turimiquire, Cerro, mtn., Ven. — A5 60
Turin, Ab., Can. — E4 68
Turin (Torino), Italy — B1 23
Turin, Ga., U.S. — C2 87
Turin, Ia., U.S. — B1 92
Turin, N.Y., U.S. — B5 109
Turinsk, Sov. Un. — C9 29
Turiy Rog, Sov. Un. — D5 33
Turka, Sov. Un. — G4 27
Turkestan, Sov. Un. — E9 29
Túrkeve, Hung. — C8 24
Turkey, N.C., U.S. — C4 110
Turkey, Tx., U.S. — B2 120
Turkey, ctry., Asia — C10 40
Turkey, stm., Ia., U.S. — B6 92
Turkey Creek, La., U.S. — D3 95
Turkey Creek, stm., Ne., U.S. — D3 104
Turkey Point, c., Md., U.S. — B5 97
Turkmen S.S.R., state, Sov. Un. — A4 40
Turk Mine, Zimb. — A4 49
Turks and Caicos Islands, dep., N.A. — D8 64
Turks Island Passage, strt., T./C. Is. — D8 64
Turks Islands, is., T./C. Is. — D8 64
Turku (Åbo), Fin. — G10 14

Name	Map Ref	Page
Turkwel, stm., Kenya	A6	48
Turley, Ok., U.S.	A6	113
Turlock, Ca., U.S.	D3	82
Turmalina, Braz.	B4	56
Turmus 'Ayyā, Isr. Occ.	B7	41
Turnbull, Mount, mtn., Az., U.S.	D5	80
Turneffe Islands, is., Belize	D7	63
Turner, Ar., U.S.	C4	81
Turner, Me., U.S.	D2	96
Turner, Mi., U.S.	D7	99
Turner, Mt., U.S.	B8	103
Turner, Or., U.S.	C4	114
Turner, co., Ga., U.S.	E3	87
Turner, co., S.D., U.S.	D8	118
Turner Mountain, hill, Ct., U.S.	C1	84
Turners Falls, Ma., U.S.	A2	98
Turney, Mo., U.S.	B3	102
Turnhout, Bel.	B6	16
Turnor Lake, l., Sk., Can.	m7	75
Turnov, Czech.	C3	26
Turnu-Măgurele, Rom.	D7	24
Turochak, Sov. Un.	E26	8
Turon, Ks., U.S.	E5	93
Turpan, China	C2	31
Turpin, Ok., U.S.	e10	113
Turquino, Pico, mtn., Cuba	E5	64
Turrell, Ar., U.S.	B5	81
Turret Peak, mtn., Az., U.S.	C4	80
Turriff, Scot., U.K.	C6	13
Turshiz see Kāshmar, Iran	B5	38
Turtkul, Sov. Un.	E9	29
Turtle, stm., On., Can.	E5	70
Turtle Creek, N.B., Can.	D5	71
Turtle Creek, Pa., U.S.	k14	115
Turtle Flambeau Flowage, res., Wi., U.S.	B3	126
Turtleford, Sk., Can.	D1	75
Turtle Lake, N.D., U.S.	B5	111
Turtle Lake, Wi., U.S.	C1	126
Turtle Lake, l., Sk., Can.	D1	75
Turtle Mountain Indian Reservation, N.D., U.S.	A6	111
Turtle Mountains, hills, N.A.	A5	111
Turtle River, Mn., U.S.	C3	100
Turton, S.D., U.S.	B7	118
Turukhansk, Sov. Un.	C11	29
Turya, stm., Sov. Un.	F5	27
Tuscaloosa, Al., U.S.	B2	78
Tuscaloosa, co., Al., U.S.	B2	78
Tuscany, hist reg., Italy	C3	23
Tuscarawas, stm., Oh., U.S.	B4	112
Tuscarawas, co., Oh., U.S.	B4	112
Tuscarora, Nv., U.S.	B5	105
Tuscarora Indian Reservation, N.Y., U.S.	B2	109
Tuscarora Mountain, mtn., Pa., U.S.	F6	115
Tuscarora Mountains, mts., Nv., U.S.	B5	105
Tuscola, Il., U.S.	D5	90
Tuscola, Ms., U.S.	C4	101
Tuscola, Tx., U.S.	C3	120
Tuscola, co., Mi., U.S.	E7	99
Tusculum, hist., Italy	h9	23
Tuscumbia, Al., U.S.	A2	78
Tuscumbia, Mo., U.S.	C5	102
Tushka, Ok., U.S.	C5	113
Tuskahoma, Ok., U.S.	C6	113
Tuskegee, Al., U.S.	C4	78
Tusket, N.S., Can.	F4	71
Tusket, stm., N.S., Can.	E4	71
Tustin, Ca., U.S.	*n13	82
Tustin, Mi., U.S.	D5	99
Tustumena Lake, l., Ak., U.S.	g16	79
Tutayev, Sov. Un.	C12	27
Tuthill, S.D., U.S.	D4	118
Tuticorin, India	G6	36
Tutrakan, Bul.	C8	24
Tuttle, N.D., U.S.	B6	111
Tuttle, Ok., U.S.	B4	113
Tuttle Creek Dam, Ks., U.S.	C7	93
Tuttle Creek Lake, res., Ks., U.S.	C7	93
Tuttlingen, F.R.Ger.	E4	18
Tutubu, Tan.	C5	48
Tutuila, i., Am. Sam.	G13	52
Tutupaca, Volcán, vol., Peru	E3	58
Tututalak Mountain, mtn., Ak., U.S.	B7	79
Tutwiler, Ms., U.S.	A3	101
Tuvalu, ctry., Oc.	G10	6
Tuve, Swe.	A5	15
Tuvuca, i., Fiji	H16	52
Tuwayq, Jabal, mts., Sau. Ar.	C4	38
Tuxedo, N.C., U.S.	f10	110
Tuxedo Park, De., U.S.	i7	85
Tuxford, Sk., Can.	G3	75
Tuxpan, Mex.	n12	63
Tuxpan, Mex.	C3	63
Tuxpan, stm., Mex.	m15	63
Tuxpan de Rodríguez Cano, Mex.	C5	63
Tuxtepec, Mex.	n15	63
Tuxtla Gutiérrez, Mex.	D6	63
Túy, Spain	A1	22
Tuyen Quang, Viet.	B6	35
Tuy Hoa, Viet.	F8	35
Tuymazy, Sov. Un.	C4	28
Tüysärkān, Iran	D4	39
Tuz Gölü, l., Tur.	C9	40
Tuzigoot National Monument, Az., U.S.	C4	80
Tūz Khurmātū, Iraq	E15	40
Tuzla, Yugo.	C4	24
Tweed, On., Can.	C7	73
Tweed, stm., U.K.	C5	10
Tweedsmuir Provincial Park, B.C., Can.	C4	69
Tweedy Mountain, mtn., Mt., U.S.	E4	103
Twelve Mile, In., U.S.	C5	91
Twelve Mile Lake, l., Sk., Can.	H2	75
Twelve Pins, mts., Ire.	D2	11
Twelvepole Creek, stm., W.V., U.S.	C2	125
Twelvepole Creek, East Fork, stm., W.V., U.S.	D2	125
Twelvepole Creek, West Fork, stm., W.V., U.S.	D2	125
Twentymile Creek, stm., W.V., U.S.	C3	125
Twentynine Palms, Ca., U.S.	E5	82
Twentynine Palms Marine Corps Base, mil., Ca., U.S.	E5	82
Twig, Mn., U.S.	D6	100
Twiggs, co., Ga., U.S.	D3	87
Twillingate, Nf., Can.	D4	72
Twillingate Island, i., Nf., Can.	D4	72
Twin Bridges, Mt., U.S.	E4	103
Twin Brooks, S.D., U.S.	B9	118
Twin Buttes, Or., U.S.	C4	114
Twin Buttes Reservoir, res., Tx., U.S.	D2	120
Twin City, Ga., U.S.	D4	87
Twin Creek, stm., Oh., U.S.	C1	112
Twin Falls, Id., U.S.	G4	89
Twin Falls, co., Id., U.S.	G4	89
Twining, Mi., U.S.	D7	99
Twin Knolls, Az., U.S.	m9	80
Twin Lakes, Co., U.S.	B4	83
Twin Lakes, Ga., U.S.	F3	87
Twin Lakes, In., U.S.	B5	91
Twin Lakes, Wi., U.S.	F5	126
Twin Lakes, l., Ct., U.S.	A2	84
Twin Lakes, l., Ia., U.S.	B3	92
Twin Lakes, l., Me., U.S.	C4	96
Twin Lakes Mountain, mtn., N.Y., U.S.	B6	109
Twin Mountain, N.H., U.S.	B3	106
Twin Mountains, mts., Wy., U.S.	E7	127
Twin Peaks, mts., Id., U.S.	E4	89
Twin Rivers, N.J., U.S.	C4	107
Twin Rocks, Pa., U.S.	F4	115
Twinsburg, Oh., U.S.	A4	112
Twinton, Tn., U.S.	C8	119
Twin Valley, Mn., U.S.	C2	100
Twisp, Wa., U.S.	A5	124
Twist, Ar., U.S.	B5	81
Two Butte Creek, stm., Co., U.S.	D8	83
Two Buttes, Co., U.S.	D8	83
Two Creeks, Mb., Can.	D1	70
Twodot, Mt., U.S.	D6	103
Twoforks, stm., Sk., Can.	C2	75
Two Harbors, Mn., U.S.	C7	100
Two Hills, Ab., Can.	C5	68
Two Mile Beach, N.J., U.S.	F3	107
Two Prairie, Bayou, stm., Ar., U.S.	h11	81
Two Rivers, Wi., U.S.	D6	126
Two Rivers, North Branch, stm., Mn., U.S.	B2	100
Two Rivers, South Branch, stm., Mn., U.S.	B2	100
Tyachev, Sov. Un.	D7	26
Tyaskin, Md., U.S.	D6	97
Tybee Island, Ga., U.S.	D6	87
Tychy, Pol.	g9	26
Tye River, Va., U.S.	C4	123
Tygart Lake, res., W.V., U.S.	B5	125
Tygart River, Falls of the, wtfl, W.V., U.S.	k10	125
Tygarts Creek, stm., Ky., U.S.	B7	94
Tygart Valley, stm., W.V., U.S.	B4	125
Tyger, stm., S.C., U.S.	B4	117
Tygh Valley, Or., U.S.	B5	114
Tyler, Al., U.S.	C3	78
Tyler, Mn., U.S.	F2	100
Tyler, Pa., U.S.	D4	115
Tyler, Tx., U.S.	C5	120
Tyler, co., Tx., U.S.	D5	120
Tyler, co., W.V., U.S.	B4	125
Tyler, Lake, res., Tx., U.S.	C5	120
Tyler Branch, stm., Vt., U.S.	B3	122
Tyler Heights, W.V., U.S.	C3	125
Tylersburg, Pa., U.S.	E11	115
Tylersville, Pa., U.S.	E7	115
Tylerton, Md., U.S.	E5	97
Tylertown, Ms., U.S.	D3	101
Tymochtee Creek, stm., Oh., U.S.	B2	112
Tynagh, Ire.	D3	11
Tyndall, Mb., Can.	D3	70
Tyndall, S.D., U.S.	E8	118
Tyndall Air Force Base, mil., Fl., U.S.	u16	86
Tyndinskiy, Sov. Un.	D15	29
Tyndrum, Scot., U.K.	D4	13
Tyne, stm., Eng., U.K.	C5	10
Tyne, stm., Scot., U.K.	E6	13
Tyne and Wear, co., Eng., U.K.	E7	13
Týnec, Czech.	o18	26
Tynemouth, Eng., U.K.	F5	13
Tyner, Ky., U.S.	C6	94
Tyner, N.C., U.S.	A6	110
Tyner, Valley, P.E., Can.	C6	71
Tyngsboro, Ma., U.S.	A5	98
Týn nad Vltavou, Czech.	D9	19
Tynset, Nor.	F4	14
Tyonek, Ak., U.S.	C9	79
Tyre (Şūr), Leb.	B3	38
Tyringham, Ma., U.S.	B1	98
Tyrma, Sov. Un.	A6	33
Tyro, Ks., U.S.	E8	93
Tyrone, Ky., U.S.	B5	94
Tyrone, N.M., U.S.	E10	108
Tyrone, Ok., U.S.	e9	113
Tyrone, Pa., U.S.	E5	115
Tyronza, Ar., U.S.	B5	81
Tyrrell, co., N.C., U.S.	B6	110
Tyrrell, Lake, l., Austl.	G4	51
Tyrrhenian Sea, Eur.	D3	23
Ty Ty, Ga., U.S.	E3	87
Ty Ty Creek, stm., Ga., U.S.	E3	87
Tyub-Karagan Peninsula, pen., Sov. Un.	E4	28
Tyukalinsk, Sov. Un.	B8	29
Tyuleniy Island, i., Sov. Un.	B12	39
Tyumen, Sov. Un.	D6	28
Tyuratam, Sov. Un.	G4	75
Tyvan, Sk., Can.	B3	12
Tywyn, Wales, U.K.	E3	13
Tzaneen, S. Afr.	B5	49

U

Name	Map Ref	Page
Uatumã, stm., Braz.	C3	59
Uaupés (Vaupés), stm., S.A.	C4	60
Ubá, Braz.	C4	56
Ubaira, Braz.	D3	57
Ubaitaba, Braz.	D3	57
Ubangi (Oubangui), stm., Afr.	A2	48
Ubaye, stm., Fr.	B4	20
Ubayyiḍ, Wādī al, val., Asia	B4	38
Ube, Japan	E11	33
Úbeda, Spain	C4	22
Uberaba, Braz.	B5	56
Uberlândia, Braz.	B5	56
Überlingen, F.R.Ger.	E4	18
Ubiaja, Nig.	E6	45
Ubly, Mi., U.S.	E8	99
Ubombo, S. Afr.	C5	49
Ubon Ratchathani, Thai.	B2	34
Uborka, Sov. Un.	D7	33
Ubrique, Spain	D3	22
Ubundu (Ponthierville), Zaire	B4	48
Ucayali, dept., Peru	*C3	58
Ucayali, stm., Peru	C3	58
Uccle, Bel.	B6	16
Ucharal, Sov. Un.	D10	28
Uchiura Bay, b., Japan	E10	33
Uchiza, Peru	C2	58
Uchoa, Braz.	C3	56
Uckange, Fr.	E6	17
Ucluelet, B.C., Can.	E5	69
Ucon, Id., U.S.	F7	89
Udaipur, India	D5	36
Udall, Ks., U.S.	E6	93
Udall, Mo., U.S.	E5	102
Udaquiola, Arg.	B5	54
Uddevalla, Swe.	H4	14
Uden, Neth.	C5	17
Udgīr, India	H6	37
Udhampur, India	C6	36
Udine, Italy	A4	23
Udon Thani, Thai.	B2	34
Udot, i., Micron.	Q18	52
Udu Point, c., Fiji	H16	52
Uecker, stm., Ger.D.R.	B6	18
Ueckermünde, Ger.D.R.	B6	18
Ueda, Japan	H9	33
Uehling, Ne., U.S.	C9	104
Uele, stm., Zaire	A3	48
Uelen, Sov. Un.	C21	29
Uelkal, Sov. Un.	C21	29
Uelsen, F.R.Ger.	B6	17
Uelzen, F.R.Ger.	B5	18
Ueno, Japan	o15	33
Uere, stm., Zaire	A4	48
Uetersen, F.R.Ger.	A6	21
Uetendorf, Switz.	C4	21
Uetersen, F.R.Ger.	E3	15
Ufa, Sov. Un.	D8	29
Uffenheim, F.R.Ger.	D5	19
Uffing, F.R.Ger.	h12	104
Ugab, stm., Nmb.	B2	49
Ugalla, stm., Tan.	C5	48
Uganda, ctry., Afr.	A5	48
Ugashik, Ak., U.S.	D8	79
Ugashik Lakes, l., Ak., U.S.	D8	79
Ugep, Nig.	E6	45
Ugine, Fr.	D2	20
Uglegorsk, Sov. Un.	B13	31
Uglich, Sov. Un.	C12	27
Ugra, stm., Sov. Un.	D10	27
Ugürchin, Bul.	D7	24
Uh, stm., Eur.	D7	26
Uherské Hradiště, Czech.	D4	26
Úhlava, stm., Czech.	D8	19
Úhlingen, F.R.Ger.	A5	21
Uhlman Lake, l., Mb., Can.	A2	70
Uhrichsville, Oh., U.S.	B4	112
Uhříněves, Czech.	n18	26
Uig, Scot., U.K.	C2	13
Uige, Ang.	C2	48
Uige, dept., Ang.	C2	48
Uijŏngbu, S. Kor.	H3	33
Uiju, N. Kor.	C9	31
Uil, Sov. Un.	D4	28
Uil, stm., Sov. Un.	D4	28
Uinkaret Plateau, plat., Az., U.S.	A2	80
Uinta, co., Wy., U.S.	E2	127
Uinta, stm., Ut., U.S.	C5	121
Uintah, Ut., U.S.	*B4	121
Uintah, co., Ut., U.S.	D6	121
Uintah and Ouray Indian Reservation, Ut., U.S.	C5	121
Uinta Mountains, mts., Ut., U.S.	C5	121
Uitenhage, S. Afr.	A6	49
Uithuizen, Neth.	A6	17
Uivak, Cape, c., Nf., Can.	f9	72
Uji, Japan	o15	33
Uji Islands, is., Japan	K4	33
Uji, Tan.	B4	48
Uji-yamada see Ise, Japan	I8	33
Ujjain, India	D6	36
Ujung Pandang (Makasar), Indon.	G5	34
Uka, Japan	N6	52
Uka, Sov. Un.	D19	29
Ukerewe, i., Tan.	B5	48
Ukhta, Sov. Un.	C8	29
Ukiah, Ca., U.S.	C2	82
Ukiah, Or., U.S.	B8	114
Ukmerge, Sov. Un.	D5	27
Ukraine, state, Sov. Un.	D1	48
Uku, Ang.	B3	31
Ulaangom, Mong.	E4	79
Ulak Island, i., Ak., U.S.		
Ulan Bator (Ulaanbaatar), Mong.	B6	31
Ulan-Ude, Sov. Un.	D13	29
Ulanów, Pol.	E25	8
Ulchin, S. Kor.	H4	33
Ulcinj, Yugo.	E4	24
Uldza, stm., Asia	B7	31
Ulen, Mn., U.S.	C5	91
Ulen, Mn., U.S.	C2	100
Uleta, Fl., U.S.	*s13	86
Ulfborg, Den.	B2	15
Ulhāsnagar, India	*E5	36
Uliastay, Mong.	B4	31
Ulindi, stm., Zaire	B4	48
Ulla, stm., Spain	A1	22
Ulladulla, Austl.	G8	51
Ullapool, Scot., U.K.	B4	10
Ullared, Swe.	A6	15
Ullin, Il., U.S.	F4	90
Ullswater, l., Eng., U.K.	F6	13
Ulŭng Island, i., S. Kor.	H5	33
Ulm, F.R.Ger.	E4	18
Ulm, Ar., U.S.	C4	81
Ulm, Mt., U.S.	C5	103
Ulman, Mo., U.S.	C5	102
Ulongué, Moz.	I5	14
Ulricehamn, Swe.	I4	31
Ulsan, S. Kor.		
Ulster, co., N.Y., U.S.	D6	109
Ulster, hist reg., Eur.	C4	11
Ulúa, stm., Hond.	C3	62
Ulubat Lake, l., Tur.	B7	25
Uluborlu, Tur.	B8	40
Uludağ, mtn., Tur.	B7	40
Ulukışla, Tur.	D10	40
Ulungur He, stm., China	B2	31
Ulva, i., Scot., U.K.	D2	13
Ulverston, Eng., U.K.	o15	99
Ulverstone, Austl.	h8	82
Ulyanovsk, Sov. Un.	D7	29
Ulysses, Ks., U.S.	E2	93
Ulysses, Ne., U.S.	C8	104
Ulysses, Pa., U.S.	C6	115
Umala, Bol.	C5	55
Uman, Sov. Un.	D5	27
Umán, i., Micron.	Q18	52
Umarkot, Pak.	C4	36
Umatac, Guam	M9	52
Umatac Bay, b., Guam	M9	52
Umatilla, Fl., U.S.	D5	86
Umatilla, Or., U.S.	B7	114
Umatilla, co., Or., U.S.	B8	114
Umatilla, stm., Or., U.S.	B7	114
Umatilla Indian Reservation, Or., U.S.	B8	114
Umba, Sov. Un.	D16	14
Umbagog Lake, l., U.S.	A4	106
Umboi, i., Pap. N. Gui.	k12	50
Umbrail Pass, Eur.	C9	21
Umbria, hist reg., Italy	C4	23
Umbuzeiro, Braz.	C3	57
Umcolcus Lake, l., Me., U.S.	B4	96
Umeå, Swe.	F9	14
Umeälven, stm., Swe.	E8	14
Umhausen, Aus.	B6	20
Umlazi, S. Afr.	*C5	49
Umm al Marādim, i., Kuw.	G4	39
Umm el Faḥm, Isr.	B7	41
Umm Lajj, Sau. Ar.	C3	38
Umm Qaddādah, Sud.	C2	47
Umm Ruwābah, Sud.	C3	47
Umnak Island, i., Ak., U.S.	E6	79
Umniati, stm., Zimb.	A4	49
'Umrān, Yemen	B5	47
Umsaskis Lake, l., Me., U.S.	B3	96
Umtanum Ridge, mtn., Wa., U.S.	C5	124
Umtata, Transkei	D4	49
Umuahia, Nig.	E6	45
Umzinto, S. Afr.	D5	49
Una, stm., Braz.	k6	57
Una, stm., Yugo.	C2	24
Unadilla, Ga., U.S.	D3	87
Unadilla, Ne., U.S.	h12	104
Unadilla, stm., N.Y., U.S.	C5	109
Unaí, Braz.	B5	56
Unaka, N.C., U.S.	f8	110
Unaka Mountains, mts., U.S.	C11	119
Unalakleet, Ak., U.S.	C7	79
Unalaska Island, i., Ak., U.S.	E6	79
Unayzah, Sau. Ar.	C4	38
Uncasville, Ct., U.S.	D7	84
Uncia, Bol.	C2	55
Uncompahgre, stm., Co., U.S.	C3	83
Uncompahgre Butte, mtn., Co., U.S.	C2	83
Uncompahgre Mountains, mts., Co., U.S.	C3	83
Uncompahgre Peak, mtn., Co., U.S.	C3	83
Uncompahgre Plateau, plat., Co., U.S.	C2	83
Underhill, Vt., U.S.	B3	122
Underhill Center, Vt., U.S.	B3	122
Underwood, Al., U.S.	B3	78
Underwood, Ia., U.S.	C2	92
Underwood, Mn., U.S.	D3	100
Underwood, N.D., U.S.	B4	111
Underwood, Wa., U.S.	D4	124
Unecha, Sov. Un.	E9	27
Uneiuxi, stm., Braz.	D4	60
Unezhma, Sov. Un.	F17	14
Ungarie, Austl.	F6	51
Ungava, Péninsule d', pen., P.Q., Can.	g12	74
Ungava Bay, b., Can.	E19	66
Unggi, N. Kor.	C11	31
Unhošt', Czech.	n17	26
União, Braz.	B2	57
União da Victória, Braz.	D2	56
União dos Palmares, Braz.	C3	57
Unicoi, Tn., U.S.	C11	119
Unicoi, co., Tn., U.S.	C11	119
Unicoi Mountains, mts., U.S.	D9	119
Unije, i., Yugo.	C2	24
Unimak Island, i., Ak., U.S.	D7	79
Unimak Pass, strt., Ak., U.S.	E6	79
Unini, stm., Braz.	C2	59
Union, Arg.	A4	81
Union, Ar., U.S.	C3	78
Union, Il., U.S.	A5	90
Union, Ia., U.S.	B4	92
Union, Ky., U.S.	k13	94
Union, La., U.S.	h10	95
Union, Ms., U.S.	C4	101
Union, Mo., U.S.	C6	102
Union, Ne., U.S.	D10	104
Union, N.H., U.S.	D4	106
Union, N.J., U.S.	*B4	107
Union, N.C., U.S.	A5	110
Union, N.D., U.S.	A8	111
Union, Oh., U.S.	*C1	112
Union, Or., U.S.	B9	114
Union, S.C., U.S.	B4	117
Union, Wa., U.S.	B2	124
Union, W.V., U.S.	D4	125
Union, co., Ar., U.S.	D3	81
Union, co., Fl., U.S.	B4	86
Union, co., Ga., U.S.	B2	87
Union, co., Il., U.S.	F4	90
Union, co., In., U.S.	E8	91
Union, co., Ia., U.S.	C3	92
Union, co., Ky., U.S.	C2	94
Union, co., Ms., U.S.	A4	101
Union, co., N.J., U.S.	B4	107
Union, co., N.M., U.S.	A6	108
Union, co., N.C., U.S.	B2	110
Union, co., Oh., U.S.	B2	112
Union, co., Or., U.S.	B8	114
Union, co., Pa., U.S.	E7	115
Union, co., S.C., U.S.	B4	117
Union, co., S.D., U.S.	E9	118
Union, co., Tn., U.S.	C10	119
Union, West Branch, stm., Me., U.S.	D4	96
Union Bay, B.C., Can.	E5	69
Union Beach, N.J., U.S.	C4	107
Union Bridge, Md., U.S.	A3	97
Union Center, S.D., U.S.	C3	118
Union Center, Wi., U.S.	E3	126
Union Church, Ms., U.S.	D3	101
Union City, Ca., U.S.	h8	82
Union City, Ga., U.S.	C2	87
Union City, In., U.S.	D8	91
Union City, Mi., U.S.	F5	99
Union City, N.J., U.S.	h8	107
Union City, Oh., U.S.	B1	112
Union City, Ok., U.S.	B4	113
Union City, Pa., U.S.	C2	115
Union City, Tn., U.S.	A2	119
Union Creek, Or., U.S.	E4	114
Unión de Reyes, Cuba	C3	64
Unión de Tula, Mex.	n11	63
Union Flat Creek, stm., Wa., U.S.	C8	124
Union Furnace, Oh., U.S.	C3	112
Union Gap, Wa., U.S.	C5	124
Union Grove, Wi., U.S.	F5	126
Union Hall, Va., U.S.	C3	123
Union Lake, Mi., U.S.	*o15	99
Union Lake, l., N.J., U.S.	E2	107
Union Mill, Hi., U.S.	C6	88
Union Mills, In., U.S.	B4	91
Union Mills, Md., U.S.	A3	97
Union Pier, Mi., U.S.	G4	99
Union Point, Ga., U.S.	C3	87
Union Springs, Al., U.S.	C4	78
Union Springs, N.Y., U.S.	C4	109
Union Star, Mo., U.S.	B3	102
Uniontown, Ks., U.S.	E9	93
Uniontown, Ky., U.S.	C2	94
Uniontown, Oh., U.S.	B4	112
Uniontown, Pa., U.S.	G2	115
Uniontown, Oh., U.S.	C8	124
Union Village, R.I., U.S.	B3	116
Union Village, Vt., U.S.	D4	122
Union Village Reservoir, res., Vt., U.S.	D4	122
Unionville, Ct., U.S.	B4	84
Unionville, Ga., U.S.	D3	87
Unionville, Il., U.S.	F5	90
Unionville, In., U.S.	F5	91
Unionville, Ia., U.S.	D5	92
Unionville, Me., U.S.	D5	96
Unionville, Mi., U.S.	E7	99
Unionville, Mo., U.S.	A4	102
Unionville, Nv., U.S.	C3	105
Unionville, N.C., U.S.	A5	112
Unionville, Oh., U.S.	A5	112
Unionville, Tn., U.S.	B5	119
Unionville, Va., U.S.	B5	123
Unionville Center, Oh., U.S.	B2	112
Unisan, Phil.	p13	34
United, Pa., U.S.	F3	115
United Arab Emirates, ctry., Asia	C5	38
United Kingdom, ctry., Eur.	C5	10
United Nations Headquarters, N.Y., U.S.	h12	109
United Pueblos Indian Reservations, N.M., U.S.	A3	108
United States, ctry., N.A.	C4	76
United States Air Force Academy, mil., Co., U.S.	B6	83
United States Military Academy, mil., N.Y., U.S.	C6	109
United States Naval Academy, mil., Md., U.S.	C4	97
Unity, Sk., Can.	E1	75
Unity, Il., U.S.	F4	90
Unity, Me., U.S.	D3	96
Unity, N.H., U.S.	D2	106
Unity, Or., U.S.	C8	114
Unity, cn. state, Switz.	C4	20
Unity Pond, l., Me., U.S.	D3	96
Unity Reservoir, res., Or., U.S.	C8	114
Unityville, S.D., U.S.	D8	118
Universal, In., U.S.	E3	91
Universal City, Tx., U.S.	*E3	120
Universales, Montes, mts., Spain	B5	22
University City, Mo., U.S.	C7	102
University Gardens, N.Y., U.S.	*n15	109
University Heights, Ia., U.S.	C6	92
University Heights, Oh., U.S.	h9	112
University Park, Ia., U.S.	C5	92
University Park, N.M., U.S.	E3	108
University Park, Tx., U.S.	n10	120
University Place, Wa., U.S.	f10	124
Unlingen, F.R.Ger.	A5	20
Unna, F.R.Ger.	B2	19
Unnen, l., Swe.	B7	15
Unst, i., Scot., U.K.	g10	10
Unstrut, stm., Ger.D.R.	B6	19
Unterwasser, Switz.	B7	21
Unuk, stm., N.A.	m24	69
Unuwhao, hill, N.Z.	K14	51
Unwin, Sk., Can.	D1	75
Ünye, Tur.	B11	40
Unzha, stm., Sov. Un.	B6	31
Uozu, Japan	H8	33
Upata, Ven.	B5	60
Upatoi Creek, stm., Ga., U.S.	D2	87
Upemba, Lac, l., Zaire	C4	48
Upernavik, Grnld.	B15	61
Upernivik, Grnld.		
Upi, stm., Col.	C3	60
Upia, stm., Col.	C3	60
Upington, S. Afr.	C3	49
Upland, Ca., U.S.	E5	82
Upland, In., U.S.	D7	91
Upland, Ne., U.S.	D7	104
Upolu, i., W. Sam.	G11	6
Upolu Point, c., Hi., U.S.	C6	88
Upper, prov., Ghana	D4	45
Upper Ammonoosuc, stm., N.H., U.S.	A4	106
Upper Arlington, Oh., U.S.	B2	112
Upper Arrow Lake, l., B.C., Can.	D9	69
Upper Black Eddy, Pa., U.S.	E11	115
Upper Blackville, N.B., Can.	C4	71
Upperco, Md., U.S.	A4	97
Upper Darby, Pa., U.S.	G11	115
Upper Fairmount, Md., U.S.	D6	97
Upper Fraser, B.C., Can.	B7	69
Upper Frenchville, Me., U.S.	A4	96
Upper Gagetown, N.B., Can.	D3	71
Upper Ganges Canal, India	C6	37
Upper Gloucester, Me., U.S.	E2	96
Upper Greenwood Lake, N.J., U.S.	A4	107
Upper Humber, stm., Nf., Can.	D3	72
Upper Indian Pond, l., Nf., Can.	D3	72
Upper Iowa, stm., Ia., U.S.	A5	92
Upper Island Cove, Nf., Can.	E5	72
Upper Jay, N.Y., U.S.	f11	109
Upper Kapuas Mountains, mts., Asia	E4	34
Upper Kent, N.B., Can.	C2	71
Upper Klamath Lake, l., Or., U.S.	E4	114
Upper Manitou Lake, l., On., Can.	E5	70
Upper Marlboro, Md., U.S.	C4	97
Upper Merion Township, Pa., U.S.	*F7	115
Upper Moreland Township, Pa., U.S.	*F11	115
Upper Musquodoboit, N.S., Can.	D7	71
Upper New York Bay, b., U.S.	k8	107
Upper Red Lake, l., Mn., U.S.	B4	100
Upper Saddle River, N.J., U.S.	A4	107
Upper Saint Clair, Pa., U.S.	*F1	115
Upper Sandusky, Oh., U.S.	B2	112
Upper Sheila, N.B., Can.	B5	71
Upper Silesia, hist reg., Pol.	g9	26
Upper Strasburg, Pa., U.S.	F6	115
Upper Tract, W.V., U.S.	C5	125
Upperville, Va., U.S.	B5	123
Upper Volta see Burkina Faso, ctry., Afr.	D4	45
Upper Wilson Pond, l., Me., U.S.	C3	96
Upper Woods Harbour, N.S., Can.	F4	71
Uppsala, Swe.	H7	14
Upright, Cape, c., Ak., U.S.	C5	79
Upsala, Mn., U.S.	E4	100
Upshi, India		
Upshur, co., Tx., U.S.	C5	120
Upshur, co., W.V., U.S.	C4	125
Upson, Wi., U.S.	B3	126
Upson, co., Ga., U.S.	D2	87
Upton, P.Q., Can.	D5	74
Upton, Ky., U.S.	C4	94
Upton, Me., U.S.	D1	96
Upton, Ma., U.S.	B4	98
Upton, Wy., U.S.	B8	127
Upton, co., Tx., U.S.	D2	120
Urabá, Golfo de, b., Col.	B2	60
Uracoa, Ven.	B5	60
Urad Qianqi, China	D3	32
Ural Mountains, mts., Sov. Un.	D8	29
Uralsk, Sov. Un.	D8	29
Urandi, Braz.	A4	56
Urania, La., U.S.	C3	95
Uranium City, Sk., Can.	m7	75
Uraricoera, Braz.	B2	59
Uraricoera, stm., Braz.	B2	59
Urasoe, Japan	O5	52
Urawa, Japan	I9	33
Urbana, Ar., U.S.	D3	81
Urbana, Il., U.S.	C5	90
Urbana, In., U.S.	C6	91
Urbana, Md., U.S.	B3	97
Urbana, Mo., U.S.	D4	102
Urbana, Oh., U.S.	B2	112
Urbancrest, Oh., U.S.	m10	112
Urbandale, Ia., U.S.	C4	92
Urbank, Mn., U.S.	D3	100
Urbania, Italy	C4	23
Urbino, Italy	C4	23
Urcos, Peru	C2	58
Urdaneta, Phil.	o13	34
Urdoma, Sov. Un.	D10	28
Ure, stm., Eng., U.K.	F7	13
Ures, Mex.	D3	63
Urfa, Tur.	D12	40
Urgench, Sov. Un.	E6	29
Uri, cn. state, Switz.	C4	20
Uriah, Al., U.S.	D2	78
Uribia, Col.	A3	60
Urich, Mo., U.S.	C4	102
Urique, Braz.	B3	63
Uritsk (part of Leningrad), Sov. Un.	s31	14
Urk, Neth.	C5	17
Urla, Tur.	C6	25
Urlingford, Ire.	E4	11
Urmi, stm., Sov. Un.	B6	33
Urmia see Orūmīyeh, Iran		
Uroa, Lake, l., Iran	B4	38
Uroyán, Montañas de, mts., P.R.	B2	65
Urr, stm., Scot., U.K.	F5	13
Urrao, Col.	B2	60
Ursa, Il., U.S.	C2	90
Ursina, Pa., U.S.	G3	115
Ursine, Nv., U.S.	*F7	105
Urstey (part of Warsaw), Pol.	m13	26
Uruaçu, Braz.	A3	56
Uruapan, Braz.	B3	56
Uruapan [del Progreso], Mex.	D4	63
Urubamba, Peru	D3	58
Urubamba, stm., Peru	C3	59
Urubu, stm., Braz.	C3	59
Urucará, Braz.	C3	59
Uruçuca, Braz.	D3	57
Urucuí, Braz.	C2	57
Urucurituba, Braz.	C3	59
Uruguaiana, Braz.	D1	56
Uruguay, ctry., S.A.	E1	56
Uruguay (Uruguai), stm., S.A.	C2	31
Ürümqi (Urumchi), China	C2	31
Urung, Point, c., Guam	L10	52
Urusha, Sov. Un.	D15	29
Uruti, Braz.	B3	56
Uryu, stm., Japan	D11	33
Uryupinsk, Sov. Un.	F14	27
Urzhum, Sov. Un.	B7	28
Urziceni, Rom.	C8	24
Usa, stm., Sov. Un.	B20	7
Uşak, Tur.	C7	40
Usakos, Nmb.	B2	49
Usedom, Ger.D.R.	B7	15
Usedom, i., Eur.	E8	15
Usemo, l., Sov. Un.	s32	14
Ushibuka, Japan	J4	33
Ushtobe, Sov. Un.	E9	29
Ushuaia, Arg.	h12	54
Usk, B.C., Can.	B3	69
Usk, Wa., U.S.	A8	124
Üsküdar (Scutari) (part of Istanbul), Tur.	B7	40
Uslar, F.R.Ger.	B4	19
Úslava, stm., Czech.	D8	19
Usman, Sov. Un.	E12	27
Usolye-Sibirskoye, Sov. Un.	D13	29
Uspenskiy, Sov. Un.	D8	28
Usquepaug, R.I., U.S.	F3	116
Ussel, Fr.	E5	16
Ussuri (Wusuli), stm., Asia	B11	31
Ussuriysk, Sov. Un.	E16	29
Ust-Bolsheretsk, Sov. Un.	D18	29
Uster, Switz.	B4	20
Ustica, i., Italy	E4	23
Ústí nad Labem, Czech.	C3	26
Ustinov (Izhevsk), Sov. Un.	D8	29
Ust-Ishim, Sov. Un.	B8	29
Ustka, Pol.	A4	26
Ust-Kamchatsk, Sov. Un.	D19	29
Ust-Kamenogorsk, Sov. Un.	E11	29
Ust-Kut, Sov. Un.	D13	29
Ust-Maya, Sov. Un.	C16	29
Ust-Olenek, Sov. Un.	B14	29
Ust-Shchugor, Sov. Un.	C9	28

Name	Map Ref	Page
Ust-Srednekan, Sov. Un.	C18	29
Ust-Tsilma, Sov. Un.	C8	29
Ust-Tym, Sov. Un.	B9	28
Ust-Urt Plateau, plat., Sov. Un.	E8	29
Ust-Usa, Sov. Un.	C8	29
Ustyuzhna, Sov. Un.	B11	27
Usu, China	C1	31
Usulután, El Sal.	E7	63
Usumacinta, stm., N.A.	D6	63
Utah, co., Ut., U.S.	C4	121
Utah, state, U.S.	D4	121
Utah Lake, l., Ut., U.S.	C4	121
Utajärvi, Fin.	E12	14
Ute, Ia., U.S.	B2	92
Ute Creek, stm., N.M., U.S.	A6	108
Ute Mountain Indian Reservation, U.S.	D2	83
Ute, Ia., U.S.	A4	108
Ute Reservoir, res., N.M., U.S.	B6	108
Utete, Tan.	C6	48
Uthai Thani, Thai.	B1	34
Utica, Il., U.S.	B5	90
Utica, In., U.S.	H6	91
Utica, Ks., U.S.	D3	93
Utica, Ky., U.S.	C2	94
Utica, Mi., U.S.	F7	99
Utica, Ms., U.S.	C3	101
Utica, Mo., U.S.	B4	102
Utica, Mt., U.S.	D6	103
Utica, Ne., U.S.	D8	104
Utica, N.Y., U.S.	B5	109
Utica, Oh., U.S.	B3	112
Utica, Oh., U.S.	D5	113
Utica, Pa., U.S.	D2	115
Utica, S.D., U.S.	E8	118
Utiel, Spain	C5	22
Utikuma Lake, l., Ab., Can.	B3	68
Utö, i., Swe.	u36	14
Utopia, Tx., U.S.	E3	120
Utopia, Lake, l., N.B., Can.	D3	71
Utrata, stm., Pol.	m13	26
Utrecht, Neth.	A6	16
Utrecht, prov., Neth.	B5	17
Utrera, Spain	D3	22
Utsjoki, Fin.	C12	14
Utsunomiya, Japan	D12	31
Uttaradit, Thai.	B2	34
Uttar Pradesh, state, India	C6	36
Uttoxeter, Eng., U.K.	B6	12
Utuado, P.R.	B2	65
Utulei, Am. Sam.	F13	52
Uusikaupunki, Fin.	G9	14
Uvá, Col.	C3	60
Uvalda, Ga., U.S.	D4	87
Uvalde, Tx., U.S.	E3	120
Uvalde, co., Tx., U.S.	E3	120
Úvaly, Czech.	n18	26
Uvarovo, Sov. Un.	E14	27
Uvat, Sov. Un.	B7	28
Uverite Point, c., Fiji	H14	52
Uvinza, Tan.	C5	48
Uvira, Zaire	B4	48
Uvs Lake, l., Asia	A3	31
Uwajima, Japan	J6	33
Uwayl, Sud.	D2	47
'Uwaynāt, Jabal al, mtn., Afr.	E4	43
Uwharrie, stm., N.C., U.S.	B3	110
Uxbridge, On., Can.	C5	73
Uxbridge (part of London), Eng., U.K.	k12	10
Uxbridge, Ma., U.S.	B4	98
Uxmal, hist., Mex.	C7	63
Uyar, Sov. Un.	D27	8
Uyuni, Bol.	D2	55
Uyuni, Salar de, pl., Bol.	D2	55
Uzbek S.S.R., state, Sov. Un.	E9	29
Uzès, Fr.	E6	16
Uzh, stm., Sov. Un.	F7	27
Uzhgorod, Sov. Un.	G6	27
Uzlovaya, Sov. Un.	E11	27
Uzunköprü, Tur.	B6	40
Uzwil, Switz.	B7	21

V

Vaal, stm., S. Afr.	C4	49
Vaals, Neth.	D5	17
Vaasa, Fin.	F9	14
Vác, Hung.	B4	24
Vaca Key, i., Fl., U.S.	H5	86
Vacaria, Braz.	D2	56
Vacaville, Ca., U.S.	C3	82
Vacha, Ger.D.R.	C5	19
Vacherie, La., U.S.	h10	95
Vader, Wa., U.S.	C3	124
Vadis, W.V., U.S.	B4	125
Vadito, N.M., U.S.	A4	108
Vadnais Heights, Mn., U.S.	*m12	100
Vado, N.M., U.S.	E3	108
Vadsö, Nor.	B13	14
Vaduz, Liech.	E4	18
Vagay, Sov. Un.	B7	28
Vaggeryd, Swe.	A8	15
Vagnhärad, Swe.	u35	14
Vagos, Port.	B1	22
Váh, stm., Czech.	D4	26
Vahsel Bay, b., Ant.	B9	7
Vaiden, Ms., U.S.	B4	101
Vaigai, stm., India	G6	36
Vaihingen, F.R.Ger.	E3	19
Vail, Az., U.S.	E5	80
Vail, Co., U.S.	B4	83
Vail, Ia., U.S.	B2	92
Vail Homes, N.J., U.S.	*C4	107
Vailoa see Palauli, W. Sam.	F11	52
Vails, N.J., U.S.	C4	107
Vaitele Bay, b., W. Sam.	F12	52
Vakfikebir (Büyükliman), Tur.	B12	40
Vakh, stm., Sov. Un.	C25	8
Vākhān, reg., Afg.	k17	39
Vakhrushev, Sov. Un.	B11	33
Valais, state, Switz.	C3	20
Valatie, N.Y., U.S.	C7	109
Val-Barrette, P.Q., Can.	C2	74
Val-Bélair, P.Q., Can.	n17	74
Valcartier-Village, P.Q., Can.	C3	54
Valcheta, Arg.	C3	54
Valcourt, P.Q., Can.	D5	74
Valdagno, Italy	D7	20
Valdai Hills, hills, Sov. Un.	C9	27
Val-David, P.Q., Can.	C3	74
Valday, Sov. Un.	C9	27
Valdemarsvik, Swe.	H7	14
Valdemorillo, Spain	o16	22
Valdepeñas, Spain	C4	22
Valderaduey, stm., Spain	A3	22
Valders, Wi., U.S.	D6	126
Valdés, Península, pen., Arg.	C4	54
Valdese, N.C., U.S.	B1	110
Valdes Island, i., B.C., Can.	f12	69
Valdez, Ak., U.S.	C10	79
Valdez, N.M., U.S.	A4	108
Valdilecha, Spain	p18	22
Valdivia, Chile	B2	54
Valdivia, Col.	B2	60
Valdobbiadene, Italy	D7	20
Val-d'Or, P.Q., Can.	k11	74
Valdosta, Ga., U.S.	F3	87
Vâle, Nor.	p28	14
Vale, Or., U.S.	D9	114
Vale, S.D., U.S.	C2	118
Vale, Tn., U.S.	A3	119
Valeene, In., U.S.	H5	91
Valemount, B.C., Can.	C8	69
Valença, Braz.	C4	56
Valença, Braz.	D3	57
Valença, Port.	A1	22
Valença do Piauí, Braz.	C2	57
Valençay, Fr.	E6	16
Valence, Fr.	E6	16
Valence, Spain	C5	22
Valencia, Az., U.S.	m7	80
Valencia, Pa., U.S.	E2	115
Valencia, Ven.	A4	60
Valencia, co., N.M., U.S.	C3	108
Valencia [de Alcántara], Spain	C2	22
Valencia Heights, S.C., U.S.	D6	117
Valencia Island, i., Ire.	E1	10
Valenciennes, Fr.	B5	16
Valentigney, Fr.	D7	16
Valentine, Ne., U.S.	B5	104
Valentine, Tx., U.S.	o12	120
Valera, Ven.	B3	60
Valhalla, N.Y., U.S.	D7	109
Valhermoso Springs, Al., U.S.	A3	78
Valier, Il., U.S.	E4	90
Valier, Mt., U.S.	B4	103
Valier, Pa., U.S.	E3	115
Valinda, Ca., U.S.	*m13	82
Valjevo, Yugo.	C4	24
Valka, Sov. Un.	C6	27
Valkeakoski, Fin.	G11	14
Valkenswaard, Neth.	C5	17
Valki, Sov. Un.	G10	27
Valladolid, Ec.	B2	58
Valladolid, Mex.	C7	63
Valladolid, Spain	B3	22
Vallåkra, Swe.	C6	15
Vallauris, Fr.	F7	16
Vall de Uxó, Spain	C5	22
Vallecas, Spain	B4	22
Vallecito, Co., U.S.	D3	83
Vallecito Reservoir, res., Co., U.S.	D3	83
Vallecitos, N.M., U.S.	A3	108
Valle de la Pascua, Ven.	B4	60
Valle del Cauca, dept., Col.	C2	60
Valle de Santiago, Mex.	m13	63
Valledupar, Col.	A3	60
Vallée-Jonction, P.Q., Can.	C7	74
Vallegrande, Bol.	C3	55
Vallejo, Ca., U.S.	C2	82
Vallenar, Chile	B1	55
Valles Mines, Mo., U.S.	C7	102
Valletta, Malta	H11	8
Valley, Ne., U.S.	C9	104
Valley, Wa., U.S.	A8	124
Valley, co., Id., U.S.	E3	89
Valley, co., Mt., U.S.	B10	103
Valley, co., Ne., U.S.	C6	104
Valley Bend, W.V., U.S.	C5	125
Valley Center, Ks., U.S.	E6	93
Valley Centre, Sk., Can.	F2	75
Valley City, Il., U.S.	D3	90
Valley City, N.D., U.S.	C8	111
Valley City, Oh., U.S.	A4	112
Valley Cottage, N.Y., U.S.	g13	109
Valley Creek, stm., Al., U.S.	g6	78
Valley Falls, Ks., U.S.	C8	93
Valley Falls, Or., U.S.	E6	114
Valley Falls, R.I., U.S.	B4	116
Valley Farms, Az., U.S.	E4	80
Valleyfield, Nf., Can.	D5	72
Valleyford, Wa., U.S.	B8	124
Valley Forge, Pa., U.S.	o20	115
Valley Grove, W.V., U.S.	A4	125
Valley Head, Al., U.S.	A4	78
Valley Head, W.V., U.S.	C4	125
Valley Lee, Md., U.S.	D4	97
Valley Mills, Tx., U.S.	D4	120
Valley Park, Mo., U.S.	f12	102
Valley Spring, Tx., U.S.	D3	120
Valley Springs, Ar., U.S.	A3	81
Valley Springs, S.D., U.S.	D9	118
Valley Station, Ky., U.S.	g11	94
Valley Stream, N.Y., U.S.	n15	109
Valleyview, Ab., Can.	B2	68
Valley View, Pa., U.S.	E8	115
Valley View, Tx., U.S.	C4	120
Valley View, Tx., U.S.	C4	120
Valliant, Ok., U.S.	D6	113
Vallo della Lucania, Italy	D5	23
Vallonia, In., U.S.	G5	91
Vallorbe, Switz.	E3	18
Valls, Spain	B6	22
Vallscreek, W.V., U.S.	D3	125
Val Marie, Sk., Can.	H2	75
Valmeyer, Il., U.S.	E3	90
Valmiera, Sov. Un.	C5	27
Valmont, P.Q., Can.	C5	74
Valmontone, Italy	h9	23
Valognes, Fr.	C3	16
Valona see Vlora, Alb.	B2	40
Valparaiso, Chile	A2	54
Valparaiso, Mex.	m13	63
Valparaiso, Fl., U.S.	u15	86
Valparaiso, In., U.S.	B3	91
Valparaiso, Ne., U.S.	C9	104
Valparaíso, prov., Chile	A2	54
Val-Racine, P.Q., Can.	D6	74
Valréas, Fr.	E6	16
Vals, Cape, c., Indon.	G9	34
Val-Saint-Michel, P.Q., Can.	n17	74
Valsetz, Or., U.S.	C3	114
Vals Platz, Switz.	D7	21
Valtournanche, Italy	E4	21
Valuyki, Sov. Un.	F12	27
Val Verda, Ut., U.S.	C4	121
Val Verde, co., Tx., U.S.	E2	120
Valverde del Camino, Spain	D2	22
Vamdrup, Den.	C3	15
Vamori, Az., U.S.	F4	80
Vamos, Tur.	C14	40
Van, Tur.	C5	40
Van, Tx., U.S.	C5	120
Van, W.V., U.S.	n12	125
Vanadium, N.M., U.S.	E1	108
Van Alstyne, Tx., U.S.	C4	120
Vananda, B.C., Can.	E5	69
Van-Bruyssel, P.Q., Can.	B5	74
Van Buren, Ar., U.S.	B1	81
Van Buren, In., U.S.	C6	91
Van Buren, Ky., U.S.	C4	94
Van Buren, Me., U.S.	A5	96
Van Buren, Mo., U.S.	E6	102
Van Buren, Oh., U.S.	A2	112
Van Buren, co., Ar., U.S.	B3	81
Van Buren, co., Ia., U.S.	D6	92
Van Buren, co., Mi., U.S.	F4	99
Van Buren, co., Tn., U.S.	D8	119
Vance, Ms., U.S.	A3	101
Vance, S.C., U.S.	E7	117
Vance, co., N.C., U.S.	A4	110
Vance Air Force Base, mil., Ok., U.S.	A3	113
Vanceboro, Me., U.S.	C5	96
Vanceboro, N.C., U.S.	B5	110
Vanceburg, Ky., U.S.	B6	94
Vancleave, Ms., U.S.	E5	101
Vancleve, Ky., U.S.	C6	94
Vancorum, Co., U.S.	C2	83
Vancouver, B.C., Can.	E6	69
Vancouver, Wa., U.S.	D3	124
Vancouver Island, i., B.C., Can.	E4	69
Vancouver Island Ranges, mts., B.C., Can.	D4	69
Vandalia, Il., U.S.	E4	90
Vandalia, Mo., U.S.	B6	102
Vandalia, Mt., U.S.	B10	103
Vandalia, Oh., U.S.	*C1	112
Vandemere, N.C., U.S.	B6	110
Vandenberg Air Force Base, mil., Ca., U.S.	E3	82
Vander, N.C., U.S.	B4	110
Vanderbilt, Mi., U.S.	C6	99
Vanderbilt, Pa., U.S.	F2	115
Vanderbilt, Tx., U.S.	E4	120
Vanderbilt Peak, mtn., N.M., U.S.	E1	108
Vanderburgh, co., In., U.S.	H2	91
Vandercook Lake, Mi., U.S.	*F6	99
Vandergrift, Pa., U.S.	E2	115
Vanderhoof, B.C., Can.	C5	69
Vanderpool, Tx., U.S.	E3	120
Vandervoort, Ar., U.S.	C1	81
Vanderwagen, N.M., U.S.	B1	108
Van Diemen, Cape, c., Austl.	B5	50
Van Diemen Gulf, b., Austl.	B5	50
Vandiver, Al., U.S.	B3	78
Vandling, Pa., U.S.	C11	115
Vanduser, Mo., U.S.	E8	102
Vandyne, Wi., U.S.	k9	126
Vanegas, Mex.	C4	63
Vänern, l., Swe.	H5	14
Vänersborg, Swe.	H5	14
Van Etten, N.Y., U.S.	C4	109
Vang, Mount, mtn., Ant.	B6	7
Vanga, Kenya	B6	48
Vangaindrano, Madag.	h9	49
Van Gölü, l., Tur.	C14	40
Vanguard, Sk., Can.	H2	75
Van Horn, Tx., U.S.	o12	120
Van Horne, Ia., U.S.	B5	92
Vanier, On., Can.	h12	73
Vanimo, Pap. N. Gui.	h11	50
Vankleek Hill, On., Can.	B10	73
Van Lear, Ky., U.S.	C7	94
Vanleer, Tn., U.S.	A4	119
Vanlue, Oh., U.S.	B2	112
Van Meter, Ia., U.S.	C4	92
Vanna, Ga., U.S.	B3	87
Vanndale, Ar., U.S.	B5	81
Vannes, Fr.	D2	16
Vanrhynsdorp, S. Afr.	D2	49
Vansant, Va., U.S.	e9	123
Vanscoy, Sk., Can.	F2	75
Vantaa (Vanda), Fin.	*G11	14
Vantage, Sk., Can.	H2	75
Van Tassell, Wy., U.S.	D8	127
Vanua Balavu, i., Fiji	H16	52
Vanua Levu, i., Fiji	H15	52
Vanuatu, ctry., Oc.	H10	6
Vanua Vatu, i., Fiji	I16	52
Vanves, Fr.	g10	16
Van Vleck, Tx., U.S.	r14	120
Van Vleet, Ms., U.S.	B5	101
Van Wert, Ga., U.S.	C1	87
Van Wert, Ia., U.S.	D4	92
Van Wert, Oh., U.S.	B1	112
Van Wert, co., Oh., U.S.	B1	112
Van Wyck, S.C., U.S.	B6	117
Vanwykswlei, S. Afr.	D3	49
Van Zandt, co., Tx., U.S.	C5	120
Vanzant, Mo., U.S.	E5	102
Värähi, India	F3	37
Varallo, Italy	D3	20
Varāmīn, Iran	D5	39
Varanasi (Benares), India	C7	36
Varangerfjorden, Nor.	B14	14
Varano, Lake, b., Italy	D5	23
Varaždin, Yugo.	B3	24
Varazze, Italy	B2	23
Varberg, Swe.	I5	14
Vardar (Axiós), stm., Eur.	B4	40
Varde, Den.	C2	15
Varde Å, stm., Den.	C2	15
Vardenis, Sov. Un.	B15	40
Vardö, Nor.	B14	14
Varel, F.R.Ger.	B4	18
Varena, Sov. Un.	A8	26
Varennes, P.Q., Can.	D3	74
Varennes, Pa., U.S.	C1	115
Vareš, Yugo.	C4	24
Varese, Italy	B2	23
Varese, Lake, l., Italy	B2	23
Varginha, Braz.	C3	56
Vári, Grc.	h11	25
Varina, Or., U.S.	B3	92
Varina, Va., U.S.	C5	123
Varjão, Braz.	B3	56
Varkana, Fin.	F12	14
Varkhán, stm., Afg.	E12	39
Varna, Bul.	D8	24
Varna, On., Can.	D3	73
Varna, Il., U.S.	B4	90
Várnamo, Swe.	I6	14
Varnsdorf, Czech.	C3	26
Varnville, S.C., U.S.	F5	117
Varön, i., Swe.	A6	15
Vars, On., Can.	h13	73
Varysburg, N.Y., U.S.	C2	109
Várzea, stm., Braz.	D2	56
Várzea da Palma, Braz.	B4	57
Várzea Grande, Braz.	B1	56
Varzi, Italy	E5	20
Varzuga, stm., Sov. Un.	D17	14
Vashon, Wa., U.S.	B3	124
Vashon, Point, c., Wa., U.S.	f11	124
Vashon Island, i., Wa., U.S.	f11	124
Vasilkov, Sov. Un.	F8	27
Vaslui, Rom.	B8	24
Vass, N.C., U.S.	B3	110
Vassalboro, Me., U.S.	*D3	96
Vassar, Ks., U.S.	D8	93
Vassar, Mi., U.S.	E7	99
Vassouras, Braz.	h6	56
Västerhaninge, Swe.	t36	14
Västervik, Swe.	I7	14
Vasto, Italy	C5	23
Vasyugan, stm., Sov. Un.	C9	28
Vatican City, ctry., Eur.	D4	23
Vaticano, Cape, c., Italy	E5	23
Vatnajökull, Ice.	n24	14
Vatomandry, Madag.	g9	49
Vatra Dornei, Rom.	B7	24
Vättern, l., Swe.	H6	14
Vatulele, i., Fiji	I14	52
Vatu Vara, i., Fiji	H16	52
Vaucluse, S.C., U.S.	D4	117
Vaucouleurs, Fr.	F5	17
Vaud, state, Switz.	C2	20
Vaudreuil (Saint-Michel-de-Vaudreuil), P.Q., Can.	D3	74
Vaudreuil, co., P.Q., Can.	D3	74
Vaughan, On., Can.	D5	73
Vaughan, Ms., U.S.	C3	101
Vaughan, N.C., U.S.	A4	110
Vaughan, W.V., U.S.	m13	125
Vaughn, Mt., U.S.	C4	103
Vaughn, N.M., U.S.	C4	108
Vaughn, Or., U.S.	C3	114
Vaughnsville, Oh., U.S.	B1	112
Vaupés, dept., Col.	C3	60
Vaupés (Uaupés), stm., S.A.	B2	60
Vauvilliers, Fr.	D7	16
Vauxhall, Ab., Can.	D4	68
Vavoua, I.C.	B3	45
Vawn, Sk., Can.	D1	75
Vaxholm, Swe.	t36	14
Växjö, Swe.	I6	14
Vãytorp, Swe.	B7	15
Vaygach Island, i., Sov. Un.	C8	28
Váyia, Grc.	g10	25
Vazante, Braz.	B5	56
Vealmoor, Tx., U.S.	C2	120
Veazie, Me., U.S.	D4	96
Veblen, S.D., U.S.	B8	118
Vechta, F.R.Ger.	F2	15
Vechte, stm., Eur.	A7	16
Veckholm, Swe.	t35	14
Vecsés, Hung.	B4	24
Veddige, Swe.	A6	15
Vedea, stm., Rom.	C7	24
Vedia, Arg.	A4	54
Veedersburg, In., U.S.	D3	91
Veendam, Neth.	A6	17
Veenendaal, Neth.	C5	17
Vega, i., Nor.	E4	14
Vega Alta, P.R.	B3	65
Vegreville, Ab., Can.	C4	68
Veguita, N.M., U.S.	C3	108
Vejer [de la Frontera], Spain	D2	22
Vejle, Den.	C3	15
Vejle, co., Den.	C3	15
Vela, Cabo de la, c., Col.	A3	60
Velarde, N.M., U.S.	A4	108
Velas, Cabo, c., C.R.	E5	62
Velbert, F.R.Ger.	D6	15
Velda Rose Estates, Az., U.S.	D4	80
Velden, F.R.Ger.	A8	20
Velebit Mountains, mts., Yugo.	C4	24
Velestínon, Grc.	C4	25
Vélez, Col.	B3	60
Vélez Blanco, Spain	D4	22
Vélez-Málaga, Spain	D3	22
Vélez Rubio, Spain	D4	22
Velhas, Rio das, stm., Braz.	B5	56
Velika Morava, stm., Yugo.	C5	24
Velikaya, stm., Sov. Un.	D7	27
Velikaya Lepetikha, Sov. Un.	*H10	27
Veliki Luki, Sov. Un.	C9	27
Velikiy Ustyug, Sov. Un.	C7	29
Veliko Túrnovo, Bul.	D7	24
Vélingara, Sen.	D2	45
Vélingara, Sen.	E3	45
Velingrad, Bul.	D6	24
Velizh, Sov. Un.	D8	27
Velké Meziříčí, Czech.	D4	26
Velletri, Italy	D4	23
Vellinge, Swe.	C7	15
Vellore, India	F6	36
Velma, Ok., U.S.	C4	113
Velpen, In., U.S.	H3	91
Velsen (part of IJmuiden), Neth.	B4	17
Velsk, Sov. Un.	C7	29
Veltrusy, Czech.	n17	26
Velva, N.D., U.S.	A5	111
Velvary, Czech.	n17	26
Vemb, Den.	C2	15
Ven, i., Swe.	C6	15
Venado, Mex.	C4	63
Venado Tuerto, Arg.	A4	54
Venango, Ne., U.S.	D3	104
Venango, Pa., U.S.	C1	115
Venango, co., Pa., U.S.	D2	115
Venceslau Brás, Braz.	C3	56
Venda, ctry., Afr.	C5	49
Vendôme, Fr.	D4	16
Venedocia, Oh., U.S.	B1	112
Venedy, Il., U.S.	E4	90
Veneta, Or., U.S.	C3	114
Venetia, hist reg., Italy	A3	23
Venetie, Ak., U.S.	B10	79
Veneto, prov., Italy	D7	20
Venev, Sov. Un.	D12	27
Venezuela, ctry., S.A.	B4	60
Venezuela, Golfo de, b., S.A.	A3	60
Veniaminof, Mount, mtn., Ak., U.S.	D8	79
Venice, Ab., Can.	B4	68
Venice (Venezia), Italy	*D3	20
Venice, Fl., U.S.	E4	86
Venice, Il., U.S.	E3	90
Venice, La., U.S.	E6	95
Venice, co., La., U.S.	g12	104
Venice, Gulf of, b., Eur.	B4	23
Vénissieux, Fr.	E6	16
Venlo, Neth.	B7	16
Venn, Sk., Can.	F3	75
Vennachar, On., Can.	B7	73
Vene, i., Den.	B2	15
Vent, Aus.	C6	20
Venta, stm., Sov. Un.	C3	27
Ventana, Az., U.S.	B3	110
Ventimiglia, Italy	C1	23
Ventnor, On., Can.	C9	73
Ventnor, Eng., U.K.	D6	12
Ventnor City, N.J., U.S.	E4	107
Venton, Md., U.S.	D6	97
Ventoux, Mont, mtn., Fr.	E6	16
Ventry, Ire.	E1	11
Ventspils, Sov. Un.	C3	27
Venturi, stm., Ven.	C4	60
Ventura (San Buenaventura), Ca., U.S.	E4	82
Ventura, Ia., U.S.	A4	92
Ventura, co., Ca., U.S.	E4	82
Venturia, N.D., U.S.	C6	111
Venus, Fl., U.S.	E5	86
Venus, Pa., U.S.	D2	115
Venus, Tx., U.S.	n9	120
Venustiano Carranza, Mex.	D6	63
Vera, Arg.	E3	55
Vera, Spain	D5	22
Vera, Ok., U.S.	A6	113
Vera, Tx., U.S.	C3	120
Vera Cruz, In., U.S.	C7	91
Veracruz, state, Mex.	C5	63
Veracruz [Llave], Mex.	D5	63
Veranópolis, Braz.	D3	57
Verával, India	D5	36
Verbania, Italy	D3	20
Verbena, Al., U.S.	C3	78
Vercel, Fr.	B1	21
Vercelli, Italy	D3	20
Verchères, P.Q., Can.	D4	74
Verchères, co., P.Q., Can.	D4	74
Verda, Ky., U.S.	D6	94
Verde, stm., Braz.	B5	56
Verde, stm., Braz.	B2	56
Verde, co., Mex.	C2	56
Verde, stm., Mex.	m12	63
Verde, stm., Mex.	m14	63
Verde, stm., Para.	D4	55
Verde, stm., N., Mex.	C4	80
Verde, Point, c., Nf., Can.	E4	72
Verde Island, i., Phil.	p13	34
Verde Island Passage, strt., Phil.	p13	34
Verdel, Ne., U.S.	B7	104
Verden, F.R.Ger.	B4	18
Verden, Ok., U.S.	B3	113
Verdi, Mn., U.S.	F2	100
Verdi, Nv., U.S.	D2	105
Verdigre, Ne., U.S.	B7	104
Verdigris, Ok., U.S.	A6	113
Verdigris, stm., U.S.	A6	113
Verdi Peak, mtn., Nv., U.S.	C6	105
Verdon, Ne., U.S.	D10	104
Verdon, S.D., U.S.	B7	118
Verdun, Fr.	C6	16
Verdun, P.Q., Can.	q19	74
Verdunville, W.V., U.S.	*D2	125
Vereeniging, S. Afr.	C4	49
Vereshchagino, Sov. Un.	D19	8
Vergara, Spain	A4	22
Vergara, Ur.	C3	108
Vergas, Mn., U.S.	D3	100
Vergennes, Il., U.S.	F4	90
Vergennes, Vt., U.S.	C2	122
Vergin, Sk., Can.	F4	75
Verín, Spain	B2	22
Veríssimo Sarmento see Camissombo, Ang.	C3	48
Veríssimo, Braz.	B3	56
Verkhnedvinsk, Sov. Un.	D7	27
Verkhneimbatsk, Sov. Un.	C26	8
Verkhnekolymsk, Sov. Un.	C18	29
Verkhneuralsk, Sov. Un.	E20	8
Verkhneusinskoye, Sov. Un.	E27	8
Verkhniy Baskunchak, Sov. Un.	D3	28
Verkhniy Ufaley, Sov. Un.	D6	29
Verkhnyaya Tura, Sov. Un.	D21	8
Verkhoyansk, Sov. Un.	C16	29
Verkhoyansk Mountains, mts., Sov. Un.	C15	29
Verlo, Sk., Can.	G2	75
Vermilion, Ab., Can.	C5	68
Vermilion, Il., U.S.	D6	90
Vermilion, Oh., U.S.	A3	112
Vermilion, co., Il., U.S.	C6	90
Vermilion, co., La., U.S.	E3	95
Vermilion, stm., Ab., Can.	C5	68
Vermilion, stm., Il., U.S.	B5	90
Vermilion, stm., Il., U.S.	C5	90
Vermilion, stm., La., U.S.	D3	95
Vermilion, stm., Oh., U.S.	A3	112
Vermilion Bay, On., Can.	o16	73
Vermilion Bay, b., La., U.S.	E3	95
Vermilion Hills, hills, Sk., Can.	G2	75
Vermilion Lake, l., Mn., U.S.	C6	100
Vermilion Pass, Can.	D2	68
Vermilion Range, hills, Mn., U.S.	C7	100
Vermillion, Ks., U.S.	C7	93
Vermillion, co., In., U.S.	E2	91
Vermillion, East Fork, stm., S.D., U.S.	D8	118
Vermillion, stm., S.D., U.S.	D8	118
Vermillion Bluffs, clf, Co., U.S.	A2	83
Vermillion, stm., P.Q., Can.	B4	74
Vermont, Il., U.S.	C3	90
Vermont, state, U.S.	D3	122
Vermontville, Mi., U.S.	F5	99
Vernal, Ut., U.S.	C6	121
Vernalis, Ca., U.S.	h10	82
Verndale, Mn., U.S.	D3	100
Verneuil, Fr.	C4	16
Verneukpan, pl., S. Afr.	D3	49
Vernon, Al., U.S.	B1	78
Vernon, B.C., Can.	D8	69
Vernon, Co., U.S.	B8	83
Vernon, Ct., U.S.	B6	84
Vernon, Fl., U.S.	u16	86
Vernon, In., U.S.	G6	91
Vernon, N.Y., U.S.	B5	109
Vernon, Tx., U.S.	B3	120
Vernon, Ut., U.S.	C3	121
Vernon, Vt., U.S.	F3	122
Vernon, co., La., U.S.	C2	95
Vernon, co., Mo., U.S.	D3	102
Vernon, co., Wi., U.S.	E3	126
Vernon, Lake, l., On., Can.	B5	73
Vernon Bridge, P.E., Can.	C7	71
Vernon Center, Mn., U.S.	G4	100
Vernon Hill, Va., U.S.	D3	123
Vernon Hills, Il., U.S.	h9	90
Vernonia, Or., U.S.	B3	114
Vernon River, P.E., Can.	C7	71
Vero Beach, Fl., U.S.	E6	86
Véroia, Grc.	B4	40
Verona, On., Can.	C8	73
Verona, Italy	B3	23
Verona, Il., U.S.	B5	90
Verona, Ky., U.S.	k13	94
Verona, Ms., U.S.	A5	101
Verona, Mo., U.S.	E4	102
Verona, N.J., U.S.	B4	107
Verona, N.D., U.S.	C5	111
Verona, Pa., U.S.	k14	115
Verona, Tn., U.S.	B5	119
Verona, Wi., U.S.	F4	126
Verónica, Arg.	g8	54
Verret, N.B., Can.	B1	71
Verret, Lake, l., La., U.S.	E4	95
Verrières-le-Buisson, Fr.	h10	16
Versailles, Fr.	C5	16
Versailles, Ct., U.S.	C7	84
Versailles, Il., U.S.	D3	90
Versailles, In., U.S.	F7	91
Versailles, Ky., U.S.	B5	94
Versailles, Mo., U.S.	C5	102
Versailles, Oh., U.S.	B1	112
Vershire, Vt., U.S.	D4	122
Versmold, F.R.Ger.	A3	19
Versoix, Switz.	C2	20
Vert, Cap, c., Sen.	E4	42
Verte, stm., P.Q., Can.	B8	74
Verte, Île, i., P.Q., Can.	A8	74
Verton, Fr.	D9	12
Vertou, Fr.	D3	16
Vertus, Fr.	F4	17
Verviers, Bel.	B6	16
Vervins, Fr.	C5	16
Verwall Group, mts., Aus.	B9	21
Verwood, Sk., Can.	H3	75
Verzasca, stm., Switz.	D6	21
Verzenay, Fr.	C6	16
Veseleyville, N.D., U.S.	A8	111
Veselí nad Lužnicí, Czech.	D4	26
Veseloye, Sov. Un.	H10	27
Vesoul, Fr.	A1	21
Vesper, Ks., U.S.	D4	93
Vesper, Wi., U.S.	D4	126
Vesta, C.R.	F6	62
Vesta, Mn., U.S.	F3	100
Vestaburg, Mi., U.S.	E6	99
Vestal, N.Y., U.S.	C4	109
Vestal Center, N.Y., U.S.	C4	109
Vestavia Hills, Al., U.S.	g7	78
Vestby, Nor.	p28	14
Vesterålen, is., Nor.	C6	14
Vesterø Havn, Den.	A4	15
Vesterøya, i., Nor.	p28	14
Vestfjorden, Nor.	D5	14
Vestmannaeyjar, Ice.	o22	14
Vestsjælland, co., Den.	C5	15
Vesuvius, Va., U.S.	C3	123
Vesuvius, vol., Italy	D5	23
Vesyegonsk, Sov. Un.	B11	27
Veszprém, Hung.	B3	24
Vésztő, Hung.	B5	24
Vetal, S.D., U.S.	D4	118
Veteran, Ab., Can.	C5	68
Veteran, Wy., U.S.	E8	127
Vetlanda, Swe.	I6	14
Vetluga, Sov. Un.	B3	28
Vetluzhskiy, Sov. Un.	B3	28
Vetovo, Bul.	D8	24
Vetren, Bul.	D7	24
Veurne, Bel.	C2	17
Vevay, In., U.S.	G7	91
Vevey, Switz.	E3	18
Veynes, Fr.	E6	16
Veyo, Ut., U.S.	F2	121
Veyrier-du-Lac, Fr.	E1	21
Vézère, stm., Fr.	E4	16
Vezirköprü, Tur.	B10	40
Viacha, Bol.	C2	55
Viadana, Italy	B3	23
Viamonte, Arg.	A4	54
Vian, Ok., U.S.	B7	113
Viana, Braz.	B2	57
Viana do Alentejo, Port.	C1	22
Viana do Castelo, Port.	B1	22
Viangchan (Vientiane), Laos	B2	34
Vianópolis, Braz.	B3	56
Viar, stm., Spain	C3	22
Viareggio, Italy	C3	23
Vibank, Sk., Can.	G4	75
Viborg, Den.	B3	15
Viborg, S.D., U.S.	D8	118
Viborg, co., Den.	B3	15
Vibo Valentia, Italy	E6	23
Viburnum, Mo., U.S.	D6	102
Vic, Fr.	C7	16
Vicálvaro, Spain	p17	22
Vicco, Ky., U.S.	C6	94
Vicente, Point, c., Ca., U.S.	n12	82
Vicenza, Italy	D7	20
Viceroy, Sk., Can.	H3	75
Vich, Spain	B7	22
Vichada, dept., Col.	C4	60
Vichada, stm., Col.	C4	60
Vichuga, Sov. Un.	C13	27
Vichuquén, Chile	D5	16
Vichy, Fr.	D5	16
Vici, Ok., U.S.	A2	113
Vick, La., U.S.	C3	95
Vicksburg, Mi., U.S.	F5	99
Vicksburg, Ms., U.S.	C3	101
Vicksburg National Military Park, Ms., U.S.	C3	101
Viçosa, Braz.	C4	57
Viçosa, Braz.	D7	57
Viçosa do Ceará, Braz.	D8	57
Vicosoprano, Switz.	D8	21
Victor, Ia., U.S.	C5	92
Victor, Mt., U.S.	D3	103
Victor, N.Y., U.S.	C3	109
Victor, S.D., U.S.	B9	118
Victor Harbor, Austl.	G7	51
Victoria, Arg.	A4	54

Name	Map Ref	Page
Victoria, B.C., Can.	E6	69
Victoria, Nf., Can.	E5	72
Victoria, P.E., Can.	C6	71
Victoria, Chile	B2	54
Victoria, Gren.	W25	65
Victoria (Hong Kong), H.K.	G7	31
Victoria, Malay.	D5	34
Victoria, Phil.	o13	34
Victoria, Il., U.S.	B3	90
Victoria, Ks., U.S.	D4	93
Victoria, Ms., U.S.	A4	101
Victoria, Mo., U.S.	C7	102
Victoria, Tn., U.S.	D8	119
Victoria, Tx., U.S.	E4	120
Victoria, Va., U.S.	D4	123
Victoria, state, Austl.	G7	50
Victoria, co., N.B., Can.	B2	71
Victoria, co., N.S., Can.	C9	71
Victoria, co., Tx., U.S.	C6	73
Victoria, co., Tx., U.S.	E4	120
Victoria, stm., Austl.	C5	50
Victoria, stm., Nf., Can.	D3	72
Victoria, Lake, l., Afr.	B5	48
Victoria, Lake, l., Austl.	F3	51
Victoria, Mount, mtn., Burma	D9	36
Victoria, Mount, mtn., Pap. N. Gui.	k12	50
Victoria Beach, Mb., Can.	D3	70
Victoria de Durango see Durango, Mex.	C4	63
Victoria de las Tunas, Cuba	C3	64
Victoria Falls, Zimb.	A4	49
Victoria Falls, wtfl, Afr.	A4	49
Victoria Harbour, On., Can.	C5	73
Victoria Island, i., N.T., Can.	B10	66
Victoria Lake, res., Nf., Can.	D3	72
Victoria Land, reg., Ant.	B28	7
Victoria Peak, mtn., Belize	B3	62
Victoria Road, On., Can.	C5	73
Victoria Strait, strt., N.T., Can.	C12	66
Victoriaville, P.Q., Can.	C6	74
Victoria West, S. Afr.	D3	49
Victorica, Arg.	B3	54
Victorino, Ven.	C4	60
Victorino de la Plaza, Arg.	A4	54
Victorville, Ca., U.S.	E5	82
Victory, Ok., U.S.	C2	113
Victory, Wi., U.S.	E2	126
Vicuña, Chile	F1	55
Vicuña Mackenna, Arg.	A4	54
Vida, Mt., U.S.	C11	103
Vidal, Ca., U.S.	E6	82
Vidalia, Ga., U.S.	D4	87
Vidalia, La., U.S.	C4	95
Vidette, Ga., U.S.	C4	87
Vidin, Bul.	D6	24
Vidisha, India	F6	37
Vidor, Tx., U.S.	D5	120
Vidor, Tx., U.S.	D5	120
Vidora, Sk., Can.	H1	75
Viechtach, F.R.Ger.	D7	19
Viedma, Arg.	C4	54
Viedma, Lago, l., Arg.	D2	54
Vieja, Sierra, mts., Tx., U.S.	o12	120
Vielsalm, Bel.	D5	17
Vienenburg, F.R.Ger.	B5	19
Vienna (Wien), Aus.	D8	18
Vienna, On., Can.	E4	73
Vienna, Ga., U.S.	D3	87
Vienna, Il., U.S.	F5	90
Vienna, In., U.S.	G6	91
Vienna, La., U.S.	B3	95
Vienna, Md., U.S.	D6	97
Vienna, Mo., U.S.	C6	102
Vienna, S.D., U.S.	C8	118
Vienna, Va., U.S.	B5	123
Vienna, W.V., U.S.	B3	125
Vienne, Fr.	E6	16
Vienne, stm., Fr.	D4	16
Vientiane see Viangchan, Laos	B2	34
Vieques, P.R.	B5	65
Vieques, Isla de, i., P.R.	G12	64
Vieques, Pasaje de, strt., P.R.	B4	65
Vieques, Sonda de, strt., P.R.	B4	65
Viernheim, F.R.Ger.	D3	19
Viersen, F.R.Ger.	C6	17
Vierzon, Fr.	D5	16
Viesca, Mex.	B4	63
Vieste, Italy	D6	23
Vietnam, ctry., Asia	B3	34
Vieux Desert, Lac, l., Wi., U.S.	B4	126
Vieux Fort, St. Luc.	J14	64
Vieux-Fort, Pointe du, c., Guad.	R8	65
View Park, Ca., U.S.	*m12	82
Vigan, Phil.	B6	34
Vigevano, Italy	B2	23
Vignola, Italy	E6	20
Vigo, Spain	A1	22
Vigo, co., In., U.S.	F3	91
Vigsø Bugt, b., Den.	A2	15
Vihowa, Pak.	B5	36
Vijayapuri, India	I7	37
Vijayawāda (Bezwada), India.	E7	36
Vik, Ice.	o23	14
Vikersund, Nor.	p27	14
Viking, Ab., Can.	C5	68
Viking, Mn., U.S.	B2	100
Vila Alferes Chamusca, Moz.	B5	49
Vila Bela de Santíssima Trindade, Braz.	F7	57
Vila da Maganja, Moz.	A6	49
Vila de Manica, Moz.	A5	49
Vila de Rei, Port.	C1	22
Vila de Sena, Moz.	A6	49
Vila do Conde, Port.	B1	22
Vila Fontes, Moz.	A6	49
Vilafranca del Penedés, Spain	B6	22
Vila Franca de Xira, Port.	C1	22
Vilaine, stm., Fr.	D2	16
Vilanculos, Moz.	B6	49
Vila Nova de Foz Côa, Port.	B2	22
Vila Nova de Gaia, Port.	B1	22
Vila Nova de Milfontes, Port.	D1	22
Vila Real, Port.	B2	22
Vila Real de Santo António, Port.	D2	22
Vilas, Co., U.S.	D8	83
Vilas, S.D., U.S.	C8	118
Vilas, co., Wi., U.S.	B4	126
Vila São Luís, Braz.	B3	57
Vila Vasco da Gama, Moz.	D5	48
Vila Velha, Braz.	C4	56
Vila Viçosa, Port.	C2	22
Vildbjerg, Den.	C2	15
Vildo, Tn., U.S.	B2	119
Vileyka, Sov. Un.	D6	27
Vilhelmina, Swe.	E7	14
Vilhena, Braz.	o13	35
Viliya, stm., Sov. Un.	A8	26
Viljandi, Sov. Un.	B5	27
Vilkaviškis, Sov. Un.	A7	26
Vil'kitskiy, i., Sov. Un.	B7	128
Vilkovo, Sov. Un.	I7	27
Villa Abecia, Bol.	D2	55
Villa Adriana, hist., Italy	h9	23
Villa Ahumada, Mex.	A3	63
Villa Ángela, Arg.	E3	55
Villa Aroma, Bol.	C2	55
Villa Bella, Bol.	B2	55
Villacañas, Spain	C4	22
Villacarrillo, Spain	C4	22
Villach, Aus.	E6	18
Villacidro, Italy	E2	23
Villa Clara, prov., Cuba	C3	64
Villa Constitución, Arg.	A4	54
Villa Cuauhtémoc, Mex.	k15	63
Villa de Arriaga, Mex.	m13	63
Villa de Cura, Ven.	A4	60
Villa del Rosario, Arg.	A4	54
Villa de Méndez, Mex.	B5	63
Villa Dolores, Arg.	A3	54
Villadossola, Italy	D5	21
Villa Eufronio Viscarra, Bol.	C2	55
Villafamés, Spain	B5	22
Villafranca del Bierzo, Spain	A2	22
Villafranca de los Barros, Spain	C2	22
Villafranca [di Verona], Italy	B3	23
Villa Frontera, Mex.	B4	63
Villa García, Mex.	k13	63
Villagarcía, Spain	A1	22
Village, Ar., U.S.	D2	81
Village, Va., U.S.	C6	123
Village Creek, stm., Al., U.S.	f7	78
Village Springs, Al., U.S.	B3	78
Villa González, Mex.	C5	63
Villa Grove, Co., U.S.	C5	83
Villa Grove, Il., U.S.	D5	90
Villaguay, Arg.	A5	54
Villa Hayes, Para.	E4	55
Villahermosa, Mex.	D6	63
Villa Huidobro, Arg.	A4	54
Villa Iris, Arg.	B4	55
Villajoyosa, Spain	C5	22
Villalba, Spain	A2	22
Villalonga, Arg.	B4	54
Villalpando, Spain	B3	22
Villa María, Arg.	A4	54
Villa María Grande, Arg.	A5	54
Villamartín, Spain	D3	22
Villa Mazán, Arg.	E2	55
Villamil, Ec.	g5	58
Villa Montes, Bol.	D3	55
Villanova, Pa., U.S.	*o20	115
Villanueva, Col.	A3	60
Villanueva, N.M., U.S.	B4	108
Villanueva del Arzobispo, Spain	C4	22
Villanueva de la Serana, Spain	C3	22
Villanueva de los Infantes, Spain	C4	22
Villanueva [del Río y Minas], Spain	D3	22
Villanueva de Córdoba, Spain	C3	22
Villa Obregón (part of Mexico City), Mex.	h9	63
Villa Ocampo, Arg.	E4	55
Villa Ojo de Agua, Arg.	E3	55
Villa Oliva, Para.	E4	55
Villa Park, Ca., U.S.	*n13	82
Villa Park, Il., U.S.	k8	90
Villaputzu, Italy	E2	23
Villard, Mn., U.S.	E3	100
Villard-Bonnot, Fr.	E6	16
Villa Rica, Ga., U.S.	C2	87
Villa Ridge, Il., U.S.	F4	90
Villa Ridge, Mo., U.S.	C7	102
Villarreal, Spain	C5	22
Villarrica, Chile	B2	54
Villarrica, Para.	E4	55
Villarrobledo, Spain	C4	22
Villarrubia [de los Ojos], Spain	C4	22
Villars-le-Terrior, Switz.	D3	21
Villas, N.J., U.S.	E3	107
Villa San Martín (Loreto), Arg.	E3	55
Villa Unión, Arg.	E2	55
Villa Unión, Mex.	C3	63
Villa Unión, Mex.	B4	63
Villa Valeria, Arg.	A4	54
Villaverde, Spain	p17	22
Villavicencio, Col.	C3	60
Villaviciosa, Spain	A3	22
Villazón, Bol.	D3	55
Villefranche, Fr.	E5	16
Villefranche [-sur-Saône], Fr.	D6	16
Villegreen, Co., U.S.	D7	83
Villejuif, Fr.	g10	16
Ville Marie, P.Q., Can.	G17	66
Villemomble, Fr.	g11	16
Villena, Spain	C5	22
Villenauxe-la-Grande, Fr.	C5	16
Villeneuve-d'Ascq, Fr.	*B5	16
Villeneuve-le-Roi, Fr.	h10	16
Villeneuve [-lès-Avignon], Fr.	F6	16
Villeneuve-Saint-Georges, Fr.	h10	16
Villeneuve-sur-Lot, Fr.	E4	16
Villeneuve-sur-Yonne, Fr.	C5	16
Villepinte, Fr.	g11	16
Ville Platte, La., U.S.	D3	95
Villeroy, P.Q., Can.	C6	74
Villers-Bretonneux, Fr.	E2	17
Villers-Cotterêts, Fr.	C5	16
Villersexel, Fr.	A1	21
Villers-Outréaux, Fr.	D3	17
Villers-Semeuse, Fr.	E4	17
Villerupt, Fr.	C6	16
Ville Saint-Georges, P.Q., Can.	C7	74
Villeta, Para.	F5	55
Villeurbanne, Fr.	E6	16
Villingen-Schwenningen, F.R.Ger.	D4	18
Villisca, Ia., U.S.	D3	92
Vilna, Ab., Can.	B5	68
Vilnius, Sov. Un.	D5	29
Vilppula, Fin.	F11	14
Vils, stm., F.R.Ger.	D6	19
Vils, stm., F.R.Ger.	E7	19
Vilsbiburg, F.R.Ger.	E7	19
Vilseck, F.R.Ger.	D6	19
Vilshofen, F.R.Ger.	E7	19
Vilvoorde, Bel.	B6	16
Vilui, Levu, stm., Fiji	H14	52
Vilyuysk, Sov. Un.	C15	29
Vimianzo, Spain	A1	22
Vimmerby, Swe.	I6	14
Vimperk, Czech.	E8	19
Vimy Ridge, Ar., U.S.	k10	81
Vina, Ca., U.S.	C2	82
Viña del Mar, Chile	A2	54
Vinalhaven, Me., U.S.	D4	96
Vinalhaven Island, i., Me., U.S.	D4	96
Vinaroz, Spain	B6	22
Vincennes, Fr.	g10	16
Vincennes, In., U.S.	G2	91
Vincennes Bay, b., Ant.	C23	7
Vincent, Al., U.S.	B3	78
Vincent, Ia., U.S.	B3	92
Vincent, Oh., U.S.	C4	112
Vincent, Tx., U.S.	C2	120
Vincentown, N.J., U.S.	D3	107
Vinces, Ec.	B2	58
Vinchina, Arg.	E2	55
Vinchina, stm., Arg.	E2	55
Vinco, Ok., U.S.	B4	113
Vindelälven, stm., Swe.	E8	14
Vindeln, Swe.	E8	14
Vinderup, Den.	B2	15
Vindhya Range, mts., India	D6	36
Vine Brook, stm., Ma., U.S.	g11	98
Vine Grove, Ky., U.S.	C4	94
Vineland, N.J., U.S.	E2	107
Vinemont, Al., U.S.	A3	78
Vineyard Haven, Ma., U.S.	D6	98
Vineyard Sound, strt., Ma., U.S.	D6	98
Vingåker, Swe.	t33	14
Vinh, Viet.	B3	34
Vinhais, Port.	B2	22
Vinh Long, Viet.	C3	34
Vinh Yen, Viet.	B6	35
Vining, Ks., U.S.	C6	93
Vining, Mn., U.S.	D3	100
Vinita, Ok., U.S.	A6	113
Vinkovci, Yugo.	C4	24
Vinland, Ks., U.S.	m15	93
Vinnitsa, Sov. Un.	E5	29
Vinson Massif, mtn., Ant.	B4	7
Vinton, Ia., U.S.	B5	92
Vinton, La., U.S.	D2	95
Vinton, Oh., U.S.	D3	112
Vinton, Va., U.S.	C3	123
Vinton, co., Oh., U.S.	C3	112
Vintondale, Pa., U.S.	F4	115
Viola, Ar., U.S.	A4	81
Viola, De., U.S.	D3	85
Viola, Id., U.S.	C1	89
Viola, Il., U.S.	B3	90
Viola, Ks., U.S.	E6	93
Viola, Tn., U.S.	D8	119
Viola, Wi., U.S.	E3	126
Violet, La., U.S.	k12	95
Vipiteno, Italy	C7	20
Virac, Phil.	n13	34
Virden, Mb., Can.	E1	70
Virden, Il., U.S.	D4	90
Virden, N.M., U.S.	E1	108
Vire, Fr.	C3	16
Vire, stm., Fr.	C3	16
Viren, i., Swe.	t34	14
Virgem da Lapa, Braz.	B4	56
Vírgenes, Cabo, c., S.A.	E3	54
Virgil, Ks., U.S.	E7	93
Virgil, N.Y., U.S.	C4	109
Virgil, S.D., U.S.	C7	118
Virgilina, Va., U.S.	D4	123
Virgin, Ut., U.S.	F2	121
Virgin, stm., U.S.	G8	105
Virgin Gorda, i., V.I., Br.	G12	64
Virginia, Ire.	D4	11
Virginia, S. Afr.	C4	49
Virginia, Al., U.S.	g6	78
Virginia, Il., U.S.	D3	90
Virginia, Mn., U.S.	C6	100
Virginia, Ne., U.S.	D9	104
Virginia, state, U.S.	C4	123
Virginia Beach, Va., U.S.	D7	123
Virginia City, Mt., U.S.	E5	103
Virginia City, Nv., U.S.	D2	105
Virginia Peak, mtn., Nv., U.S.	D2	105
Virgin Islands, dep., N.A.	G12	64
Virgin Islands, is., N.A.	B6	65
Virgin Mountains, mts., U.S.	A1	80
Virginópolis, Braz.	B4	56
Virgin Passage, strt., N.A.	B5	65
Virgolândia, Braz.	B4	56
Virochey, Kam.	C3	34
Viroflay, Fr.	g9	16
Viroqua, Wi., U.S.	E3	126
Virovitica, Yugo.	C3	24
Virpazar, Yugo.	D4	24
Virserum, Swe.	I6	14
Virton, Bel.	E5	17
Virú, Peru	C2	58
Vis, i., Yugo.	D3	24
Visalia, Ca., U.S.	D4	82
Visalia, Ky., U.S.	k14	94
Visayan Sea, Phil.	C6	34
Visby, Swe.	I8	14
Visconde do Rio Branco, Braz.	C4	56
Viscount, Sk., Can.	F3	75
Viscount Melville Sound, strt., N.T., Can.	B11	66
Visé, Bel.	D5	17
Višegrad, Yugo.	D4	24
Viseu, Braz.	B1	57
Viseu, Port.	B2	22
Vishākhapatnam (Vizagapatam), India	E7	36
Vishera, stm., Sov. Un.	A5	28
Viskan, stm., Swe.	A6	15
Vislanda, Swe.	B8	15
Viso, Mount, mtn., Italy	B1	23
Visoko, Yugo.	D4	24
Visp, Switz.	E3	18
Vista, Mb., Can.	D1	70
Vista, Ca., U.S.	F5	82
Vista, Mo., U.S.	C3	102
Vista, Nv., U.S.	*D2	105
Vista Alegre, Braz.	C4	60
Vistonís, Lake, l., Grc.	B5	25
Vistula, Ia., U.S.	A6	91
Vistula see Wisła, stm., Pol.	B5	26
Vistula Lagoon, b., Eur.	A5	26
Vit, stm., Bul.	D7	24
Vita, Mb., Can.	E3	70
Vitanovac, Yugo.	D5	24
Vitarte, Peru	C2	58
Vitebsk, Sov. Un.	D6	29
Vitichi, Bol.	D3	55
Viti Levu, i., Fiji	H14	52
Viti Levu Bay, b., Fiji	H15	52
Vitim, stm., Sov. Un.	D14	29
Vitor, Peru	E3	58
Vitória, Braz.	C4	56
Vitória, Spain	A4	22
Vitória da Conquista, Braz.	B4	56
Vitória [de Santo Antão], Braz.	C3	57
Vitória do Mearim, Braz.	A5	57
Vitória Quebrangulo, Braz.	k5	57
Vittel, Fr.	C6	16
Vittoria, On., Can.	E4	73
Vittoria, Italy	F5	23
Vittorio Veneto, Italy	B4	23
Vivero, Spain	A2	22
Vivian, La., U.S.	B2	95
Vivian, S.D., U.S.	D5	118
Viviana Park, Ut., U.S.	C4	121
Vivoratá, Arg.	B5	54
Viwa, i., Fiji	H14	52
Vize, Tur.	B6	40
Vizianagaram, India	E7	36
Vizille, Fr.	E6	16
Viziru, Rom.	C8	24
Vizzini, Italy	F5	23
Vjosa, stm., Eur.	B3	25
Vladimir, Sov. Un.	D7	29
Vladimir-Aleksandrovskoye, Sov. Un.	C11	31
Vladimirovo, Sov. Un.	B12	33
Vladimir-Volynskiy, Sov. Un.	F5	27
Vladivostok, Sov. Un.	E16	29
Vlasenica, Yugo.	C4	24
Vlašim, Czech.	D9	19
Vlasotince, Yugo.	D6	24
Vlieland, i., Neth.	A6	16
Vlissingen, Neth.	B5	16
Vlorë (Valona), Alb.	B2	40
Vlotho, F.R.Ger.	A3	19
Vltava, stm., Czech.	D3	26
Voca, Tx., U.S.	D3	120
Vodlozero, l., Sov. Un.	F17	14
Vodňany, Czech.	D9	19
Voghera, Italy	B2	23
Vohenstrauss, F.R.Ger.	D7	19
Vohibinany, Madag.	g9	49
Vohimarina, Madag.	f9	49
Vohipeno, Madag.	h9	49
Voi, Kenya	B6	48
Void, Fr.	F5	17
Voil, Loch, l., Scot., U.K.	D4	13
Voinjama, Lib.	E3	45
Voiron, Fr.	E6	16
Voisin, Lac, l., Sk., Can.	C2	75
Voitsberg, Aus.	E7	18
Vojens, Den.	C3	15
Vokhma, Sov. Un.	B3	28
Vokhma, stm., Sov. Un.	B3	28
Volary, Czech.	E8	19
Volborg, Mt., U.S.	D11	103
Volcano, Hi., U.S.	D6	88
Volcano Island, i., Phil.	o13	34
Volcano Islands, is., Japan	E8	6
Volchansk, Sov. Un.	F11	27
Volga, S.D., U.S.	C9	118
Volga, W.V., U.S.	B4	125
Volga, stm., Sov. Un.	E7	29
Volga Plateau, plat., Sov. Un.	C3	28
Volgodonsk, Sov. Un.	H13	27
Volgograd (Stalingrad), Sov. Un.	E7	29
Volgograd Reservoir, res., Sov. Un.	D7	29
Volin, S.D., U.S.	E8	118
Volkach, F.R.Ger.	D5	19
Volkhov, Sov. Un.	B9	27
Volkhov, stm., Sov. Un.	B8	27
Völklingen, F.R.Ger.	D1	19
Volkovysk, Sov. Un.	E5	27
Vollenhove, Neth.	B5	17
Volney, Va., U.S.	D1	123
Volnovakha, Sov. Un.	H11	27
Volochayevka Vtoraya, Sov. Un.	B7	33
Volochisk, Sov. Un.	G6	27
Volodarskiy (part of Leningrad), Sov. Un.	s31	14
Volodarskoye, Sov. Un.	C7	28
Vologda, Sov. Un.	D7	29
Vólos, Gulf of see Pagasitikós Kólpos, b., Grc.		
Volsk, Sov. Un.	C4	40
Volta, prov., Ghana	E5	45
Volta, Lake, res., Ghana	E5	45
Volta Noire (Black Volta), stm., Afr.	D4	45
Volta Redonda, Braz.	C4	56
Volterra, Italy	C3	23
Voltri, Italy	B2	23
Volturno, stm., Italy	D5	23
Voluntown, Ct., U.S.	C8	84
Volusia, co., Fl., U.S.	C5	86
Vólvi, Lake, l., Grc.	B4	25
Volzhsky, Sov. Un.	G15	27
Vombsjön, l., Swe.	C7	15
Vona, Co., U.S.	B8	83
Vonda, Sk., Can.	E2	75
Von Frank Mountain, mtn., Ak., U.S.	C9	79
Vónitsa, Grc.	C3	25
Vorona, Tn., U.S.	D9	119
Von Ormy, Tx., U.S.	k7	120
Vopnafjördur, Ice.	n25	14
Vorarlberg, state, Aus.	B5	20
Vorderrhein, stm., Switz.	C7	21
Vorderthal, Switz.	B6	21
Vordingborg, Den.	C5	15
Vorkuta, Sov. Un.	C9	29
Vorona, stm., Sov. Un.	E14	27
Voronezh, Sov. Un.	D6	29
Voronezh, stm., Sov. Un.	E12	27
Voronya, stm., Sov. Un.	C16	14
Voroshilovgrad, Sov. Un.	H9	27
Vørterkaka Nunatak, mtn., Ant.	B15	7
Vosges, dept., Fr.	A2	21
Vosges, mts., Fr.	C7	16
Voskresensk, Sov. Un.	n18	27
Voss, Nor.	G2	14
Voss, N.D., U.S.	A8	111
Vostochnyy, Sov. Un.	B11	33
Vostok, isl., Ant.	B23	7
Vostok Island, i., Kir.	G12	6
Votaw, Tx., U.S.	D5	120
Votice, Czech.	D9	19
Vouga, stm., Port.	B1	22
Vouliagméni, Grc.	h11	25
Vouvray, Fr.	D4	16
Vouziers, Fr.	C6	16
Voyageurs National Park, Mn., U.S.	B5	100
Voyeykov Ice Shelf, Ant.	C25	7
Vozhega, Sov. Un.	A13	27
Voznesensk, Sov. Un.	H8	27
Voznesenskoye, Sov. Un.	A8	33
Voznesenye, Sov. Un.	A10	27
Vrå, Den.	A3	15
Vranje, Yugo.	D5	24
Vratsa, Bul.	D6	24
Vrbas, Yugo.	C4	24
Vrbas, stm., Yugo.	C3	24
Vrchlabí, Czech.	C3	26
Vrede, S. Afr.	D5	49
Vreden, F.R.Ger.	A1	19
Vredenburgh, Al., U.S.	D2	78
Vreed en Hoop, Guy.	A3	59
Vrena, Swe.	u34	14
Vriezenveen, Neth.	B6	17
Vrigstad, Swe.	A8	15
Vrin, Switz.	C7	21
Vršac, Yugo.	C5	24
Vršovice (part of Prague), Czech.	n17	26
Vrútky, Czech.	D5	26
Vryburg, S. Afr.	C3	49
Vryheid, S. Afr.	C5	49
Všetaty, Czech.	n18	26
Vsetín, Czech.	D5	26
Vsevidof, Mount, mtn., Ak., U.S.	E6	79
Vsevolozhsk, Sov. Un.	r31	14
Vuaqava, i., Fiji	I16	52
Vúcha, stm., Bul.	E7	24
Vuda Point, c., Fiji	H14	52
Vukovar, Yugo.	C4	24
Vulcan, Ab., Can.	C4	68
Vulcan, Mi., U.S.	C3	99
Vulcan, Mo., U.S.	D7	102
Vulcano, i., Italy	E5	23
Vúlchedrúma, Bul.	D6	24
Vung Tau, Viet.	G7	35
Vung Tau, Cape, c., Viet.	G7	35
Vunidawa, Fiji	H15	52
Vuoloyarvi, Sov. Un.	r31	14
Vuya Point, c., Fiji	H15	52
Vyartsilya, Sov. Un.	F14	14
Vyatka, stm., Sov. Un.	D7	29
Vyatskiye Polyany, Sov. Un.	B4	28
Vyazemskiy, Sov. Un.	C7	33
Vyazma, Sov. Un.	D10	27
Vyazniki, Sov. Un.	C14	27
Vyborg, Sov. Un.	C5	29
Vychegda, stm., Sov. Un.	C18	8
Vygozero, l., Sov. Un.	F16	14
Vyksa, Sov. Un.	D14	27
Vyritsa, Sov. Un.	s31	14
Výrovka, stm., Czech.	n19	26
Vyshniy Volochek, Sov. Un.	C10	27
Vyškov, Czech.	D4	26
Vysočany (part of Prague), Czech.	n17	26
Vysoká, Czech.	n18	26
Vysoké Mýto, Czech.	D4	26
Vyšší Brod, Czech.	E9	19
Vytegra, Sov. Un.	C6	29

W

Name	Map Ref	Page
Wa, Ghana	D4	45
Waal, stm., Neth.	B6	16
Waalwijk, Neth.	C5	17
Waawaa, Puu, mtn., Hi., U.S.	D6	88
Wabamun, Ab., Can.	C3	68
Wabamun Lake, l., Ab., Can.	C3	68
Wabana (Bell Island), Nf., Can.	E5	72
Wabasca, Ab., Can.	f1	68
Wabasca, stm., Ab., Can.	f1	68
Wabash, Ar., U.S.	C5	81
Wabash, In., U.S.	C6	91
Wabash, co., In., U.S.	C6	91
Wabash, co., Il., U.S.	E6	90
Wabash, Ne., U.S.	h12	104
Wabasha, Mn., U.S.	F6	100
Wabasha, co., Mn., U.S.	F6	100
Wabasso, Fl., U.S.	E6	86
Wabasso, Mn., U.S.	F3	100
Wabaunsee, Ks., U.S.	C7	93
Wabaunsee, co., Ks., U.S.	D7	93
Wabeno, Wi., U.S.	C5	126
Wabigoon, On., Can.	E5	70
Wabigoon Lake, l., On., Can.	E5	70
Wabowden, Mb., Can.	B2	70
Wabrzezno, Pol.	B5	26
Wabuska, Nv., U.S.	D2	105
Waccamaw, stm., U.S.	D9	117
Waccamaw, Lake, l., N.C., U.S.	C4	110
Waccasassa Bay, b., Fl., U.S.	C4	86
Wachapreague, Va., U.S.	C7	123
Wachusett Mountain, mtn., Ma., U.S.	B4	98
Wachusett Reservoir, res., Ma., U.S.	B4	98
Wacissa, Fl., U.S.	B2	86
Wacker, Il., U.S.	A3	90
Waco, Ga., U.S.	C1	87
Waco, Ks., U.S.	g12	93
Waco, Ne., U.S.	D8	104
Waco, Tx., U.S.	D4	120
Waco, N.C., U.S.	B1	110
Waco Lake, res., Tx., U.S.	D4	120
Waconda Lake, res., Ks., U.S.	C5	93
Waconia, Mn., U.S.	F5	100
Waddán, Libya	D3	43
Waddán, Jabal, mtn., Libya	D3	43
Waddell, Az., U.S.	m8	80
Wadden Zee, Neth.	A6	16
Waddington, Mount, mtn., B.C., Can.	D5	69
Waddy, Ky., U.S.	B4	94
Wade, Ok., U.S.	D5	113
Wade, Mount, mtn., Ant.	A32	7
Wadena, Mn., U.S.	D4	100
Wadena, Sk., Can.	F4	75
Wadena, co., Mn., U.S.	D4	100
Wadena, Ia., U.S.	B6	92
Wädenswil, Switz.	B6	21
Wadesboro, N.C., U.S.	C2	110
Wadesville, In., U.S.	H2	91
Wadham Islands, is., Nf., Can.	D5	72
Wadhwän see Surendranagar, India	F3	37
Wādī al Jayb (Ha Arava), val., Asia	G10	40
Wadley, Al., U.S.	B4	78
Wadley, Ga., U.S.	C4	87
Wad Madanī, Sud.	C3	47
Wadmalaw Island, i., S.C., U.S.	F7	117
Wadowice, Pol.	D5	26
Wadsworth, Al., U.S.	C3	78
Wadsworth, Il., U.S.	h9	90
Wadsworth, Nv., U.S.	D2	105
Wadsworth, Oh., U.S.	A4	112
Waelder, Tx., U.S.	E4	120
Wagener, S.C., U.S.	D5	117
Wageningen, Sur.	A3	59
Wager Bay, b., N.T., Can.	C15	66
Wagga, Sud.	A3	47
Wagga Wagga, Austl.	G8	50
Waggoner, Il., U.S.	D4	90
Waging [am See], F.R.Ger.	E6	18
Waginger Lake, l., F.R.Ger.	E6	18
Wägital Lake, l., Switz.	B6	21
Wagner, Mt., U.S.	B8	103
Wagner, S.D., U.S.	D7	118
Wagners Lake, Ne., U.S.	*C8	104
Wagon, Ok., U.S.	B6	113
Wagoner, Ok., U.S.	B6	113
Wagoner, co., Ok., U.S.	B6	113
Wagon Mound, N.M., U.S.	A5	108
Wagontire Mountain, mtn., Or., U.S.	D7	114
Wagram, N.C., U.S.	C3	110
Wagrowiec, Pol.	B4	26
Waha, Libya	D3	43
Wahai, Indon.	F7	34
Wah Cantonment, Pak.	*B5	36
Wahiawa, Hi., U.S.	B3	88
Wahiawa Reservoir, res., Hi., U.S.	g9	88
Wahkiakum, co., Wa., U.S.	C2	124
Wahkon, Mn., U.S.	D5	100
Wahlern, Switz.	C3	21
Wahoo, Ne., U.S.	C9	104
Wahoo Creek, stm., Ne., U.S.	g11	104
Wahpeton, N.D., U.S.	C9	111
Wah Wah Mountains, mts., Ut., U.S.	E2	121
Wahweap Creek, stm., Ut., U.S.	F4	121
Waialua, Hi., U.S.	B3	88
Waialua Bay, b., Hi., U.S.	B3	88
Waianae, Hi., U.S.	B3	88
Waianae Range, mts., Hi., U.S.	f9	88
Waiau, stm., N.Z.	O14	51
Waiawa Stream, stm., Hi., U.S.	g10	88
Waiblingen, F.R.Ger.	E4	19
Waidhofen [an der Thaya], Aus.	D7	18
Waidhofen [an der Ybbs], Aus.	E7	18
Waigeo, i., Indon.	F8	34
Waihee, Hi., U.S.	C5	88
Wai Islands, is., Kam.	H5	35
Waikabubak, Indon.	G5	34
Waikapu, Hi., U.S.	C5	88
Waikari, N.Z.	O14	51
Waikato, stm., N.Z.	L15	51
Waikawa, N.Z.	Q12	51
Waikelo, Indon.	G5	34
Waikerie, Austl.	G2	51
Waikiki Beach, Hi., U.S.	g10	88
Wailagi Lala, i., Fiji	H16	52
Wailea, Hi., U.S.	D6	88
Wailua, Hi., U.S.	A2	88
Wailuku, Hi., U.S.	C5	88
Wailuku, stm., Hi., U.S.	D6	88
Waimanalo, Hi., U.S.	g11	88
Waimanalo Bay, b., Hi., U.S.	g11	88
Waimate, N.Z.	P13	51
Waimea, Hi., U.S.	B2	88
Waimea, stm., Hi., U.S.	A2	88
Wainganga, stm., India	D7	36
Waingapu, Indon.	G6	34
Waini Point, c., Guy.	A3	59
Wainunu Bay, b., Fiji	H15	52
Wainwright, Ab., Can.	C5	68
Wainwright, Ak., U.S.	A8	79
Wainwright, Oh., U.S.	B4	112
Waiohinu, Hi., U.S.	D6	88
Waipahu, Hi., U.S.	B3	88
Waipara, N.Z.	O14	51
Waipawa, N.Z.	M16	51
Waipio Acres, Hi., U.S.	g9	88
Waipio Peninsula, pen., Hi., U.S.	g10	88
Waipukurau, N.Z.	N16	51
Wairau, stm., N.Z.	N14	51
Wairoa, N.Z.	M15	51
Waitaki, stm., N.Z.	P13	51
Waitara, N.Z.	M15	51
Waite, Me., U.S.	C5	96
Waite Park, Mn., U.S.	E4	100
Waitsburg, Wa., U.S.	C7	124
Waits River, Vt., U.S.	C4	122
Waitsfield, Vt., U.S.	C3	122
Waitville, Sk., Can.	E3	75
Waiwo, Indon.	F8	34
Wajima, Japan	A8	32
Wajir, Kenya	A7	48
Waka, Tx., U.S.	A2	120
Waka, Zaire	A5	48
Wakami Lake, l., On., Can.	A2	73
Wakarusa, In., U.S.	A5	91
Wakarusa, stm., Ks., U.S.	D8	93
Wakasa Bay, b., Japan	I3	33
Wakatipu, Lake, l., N.Z.	P12	51
Wakatomika Creek, stm., Oh., U.S.	B3	112
Wakaya, i., Fiji	H15	52
Wakayama, Japan	E12	31
Wake, co., N.C., U.S.	B4	110
Wa Keeney, Ks., U.S.	C4	93
Wakefield, P.Q., Can.	C6	74
Wakefield, Eng., U.K.	C6	12
Wakefield, Ks., U.S.	C6	93
Wakefield, Ma., U.S.	B5	98
Wakefield, Mi., U.S.	n12	99
Wakefield, Ne., U.S.	B9	104
Wakefield, R.I., U.S.	F3	116
Wakefield, Va., U.S.	D6	123
Wake Forest, N.C., U.S.	B4	110
Wake Island, dep., Oc.	E10	6
Wake Island Air Force Base, mil., Wake I.	B2	52
Wake Lagoon, b., Wake I.	B2	52
Wakeman, Oh., U.S.	A3	112

Name	Map Ref	Page
Wakenda, Mo., U.S.	B4	102
Wakita, Ok., U.S.	A4	113
Wakkanai, Japan	B13	31
Wakkerstroom, S. Afr.	C5	49
Wakonda, S.D., U.S.	D8	118
Wakpala, S.D., U.S.	B5	118
Wakopa, Mb., Can.	E2	70
Wakuach, Lac, l., P.Q., Can.	g8	72
Waku Kungo, Ang.	D2	48
Wakulla, Fl., U.S.	B2	86
Wakulla, co., Fl., U.S.	B2	86
Walachia, hist reg., Rom.	C7	24
Walbourg, Fr.	F7	17
Walbridge, Oh., U.S.	e6	112
Wałbrzych (Waldenburg), Pol.	C4	26
Walchen Lake, l., F.R.Ger.	B7	20
Walcott, Ar., U.S.	A5	81
Walcott, Ia., U.S.	C7	92
Walcott, N.D., U.S.	C9	111
Walcott, Wy., U.S.	E6	127
Walcott, Lake, res., Id., U.S.	G5	89
Wałcz, Pol.	B4	26
Wald, Switz.	B6	21
Waldbröl, F.R.Ger.	C2	19
Waldeck, Sk., Can.	G2	75
Walden, Co., U.S.	A4	83
Walden, N.Y., U.S.	D6	109
Walden, Vt., U.S.	C4	122
Waldenburg see Wałbrzych, Pol.	C4	26
Waldenburg, Ar., U.S.	B5	81
Walden Heights, Vt., U.S.	C4	122
Walden Pond, l., Ma., U.S.	g10	98
Walden Ridge, mtn., Tn., U.S.	D8	119
Waldheim, Sk., Can.	E2	75
Waldheim, Ger.D.R.	B8	19
Waldkappel, F.R.Ger.	B4	19
Waldkirchen, F.R.Ger.	E8	19
Waldmünchen, F.R.Ger.	D7	19
Waldnaab, stm., F.R.Ger.	D6	18
Waldo, B.C., Can.	E10	69
Waldo, Ar., U.S.	D2	81
Waldo, Fl., U.S.	C4	86
Waldo, Ks., U.S.	C5	93
Waldo, Oh., U.S.	B2	112
Waldo, co., Me., U.S.	D3	96
Waldoboro, Me., U.S.	D3	96
Waldo Lake, l., Ma., U.S.	h11	98
Waldo Lake, l., Or., U.S.	D4	114
Waldorf, Md., U.S.	C4	97
Waldorf, Mn., U.S.	G5	100
Waldport, Or., U.S.	C2	114
Waldron, Sk., Can.	G4	75
Waldron, Ar., U.S.	C1	81
Waldron, In., U.S.	F6	91
Waldron, Ks., U.S.	E5	93
Waldron, Mi., U.S.	G6	99
Waldron, Mo., U.S.	h10	102
Waldsassen, F.R.Ger.	C7	19
Waldshut, F.R.Ger.	E4	18
Waldwick, N.J., U.S.	A4	107
Walen, Lake, l., Switz.	B5	20
Walenstadt, Switz.	B7	21
Wales, Ak., U.S.	B6	79
Wales, Ma., U.S.	B3	98
Wales, N.D., U.S.	A7	111
Wales, Ut., U.S.	D4	121
Wales, ter., U.K.	D5	10
Waleska, Ga., U.S.	B2	87
Walford Station, On., Can.	A2	73
Walgett, Austl.	E8	50
Walgreen Coast, Ant.		7
Walhachin, B.C., Can.	D7	69
Walhalla, Mi., U.S.	E4	99
Walhalla, N.D., U.S.	A8	111
Walhalla, S.C., U.S.	B1	117
Walhonding, stm., Oh., U.S.	B3	112
Walikale, Zaire	B4	48
Walker, Ia., U.S.	B6	92
Walker, Ks., U.S.	D4	93
Walker, La., U.S.	g10	95
Walker, Mi., U.S.	E5	99
Walker, Mo., U.S.	C4	100
Walker, S.D., U.S.	B4	118
Walker, co., Al., U.S.	B2	78
Walker, co., Ga., U.S.	B1	87
Walker, co., Tx., U.S.	D5	120
Walker Lake, l., Mb., Can.	B3	70
Walker Lake, l., Nv., U.S.	E4	105
Walker Mountain, mtn., Ga., U.S.	B3	87
Walker Mountain, mtn., Va., U.S.	C1	123
Walker River Indian Reservation, Nv., U.S.	D3	105
Walker Springs, Al., U.S.	D2	78
Walkersville, Md., U.S.	B3	97
Walkersville, W.V., U.S.	C4	125
Walkerton, On., Can.	C3	73
Walkerton, In., U.S.	B5	91
Walkertown, N.C., U.S.	A2	110
Walkerville, Mi., U.S.	E4	99
Walkerville, Mt., U.S.	D4	103
Wall, S.D., U.S.	D3	118
Wallace, N.S., Can.	D7	71
Wallace, On., Can.	B6	73
Wallace, Id., U.S.	B3	89
Wallace, In., U.S.	E3	91
Wallace, Ks., U.S.	D2	93
Wallace, Mi., U.S.	C3	99
Wallace, Ne., U.S.	D4	104
Wallace, N.Y., U.S.	C3	109
Wallace, N.C., U.S.	C5	110
Wallace, S.D., U.S.	B8	118
Wallace, Va., U.S.	f9	123
Wallace, W.V., U.S.	B4	125
Wallace, co., Ks., U.S.	D2	93
Wallaceburg, On., Can.	E2	73
Wallace Lakes, res., La., U.S.	B2	95
Wallacetown, On., Can.	E3	73
Wallagrass, Me., U.S.	A4	96
Walland, Tn., U.S.	D10	119
Wallaroo, Austl.	F6	50
Walla Walla, Wa., U.S.	C7	124
Walla Walla, co., Wa., U.S.	C7	124
Walla Walla, stm., U.S.	C7	124
Walldürn, F.R.Ger.	D4	19
Walled Lake, Mi., U.S.	o15	99
Wallen, In., U.S.	B7	91
Wallenpaupack, Lake, l., Pa., U.S.	D11	115
Wallen Ridge, mtn., Tn., U.S.	C10	119
Waller, Tx., U.S.	q14	120
Waller, co., Tx., U.S.	E4	120
Wallingford, Eng., U.K.	C6	12
Wallingford, Ct., U.S.	D4	84
Wallingford, Ia., U.S.	A3	92
Wallingford, Vt., U.S.	E3	122
Walling Mountain, mtn., Ma., U.S.	B1	98
Wallington, N.J., U.S.	h8	107
Wallis, Tx., U.S.	E4	120
Wallis and Futuna, dep., Oc.	G11	6
Wallis Sands, N.H., U.S.	D5	106
Wallkill, N.Y., U.S.	D6	109
Wallkill, stm., N.Y., U.S.	D6	109
Wall Lake, Ia., U.S.	B2	92
Wall Lake, l., Ia., U.S.	A4	92
Walloomsac, stm., U.S.	F2	122
Walloon Lake, l., Mi., U.S.	C6	99
Wallowa, Or., U.S.	B9	114
Wallowa, co., Or., U.S.	B9	114
Wallowa Mountains, mts., Or., U.S.	B9	114
Wallpack Center, N.J., U.S.	A3	107
Walls, Ms., U.S.	A3	101
Wallsburg, Ut., U.S.	C4	121
Wallsend, Eng., U.K.	C6	10
Wallula, Wa., U.S.	C7	124
Wallula, Lake, res., U.S.	C7	124
Wallum Lake, l., U.S.	A1	116
Walney Island, i., Eng., U.K.	C5	10
Walnut, Ca., U.S.	*m13	82
Walnut, Il., U.S.	B4	90
Walnut, Ia., U.S.	C2	92
Walnut, Ks., U.S.	E8	93
Walnut, Ms., U.S.	A5	101
Walnut, N.C., U.S.	f10	110
Walnut, stm., Ks., U.S.	E6	93
Walnut Bottom, Pa., U.S.	F7	115
Walnut Canyon National Monument, Az., U.S.	B4	80
Walnut Cove, N.C., U.S.	A2	110
Walnut Creek, Ca., U.S.	h8	82
Walnut Creek, stm., Ks., U.S.	D4	93
Walnut Grove, Al., U.S.	A3	78
Walnut Grove, Mn., U.S.	F3	100
Walnut Grove, Ms., U.S.	C4	101
Walnut Grove, Mo., U.S.	D4	102
Walnut Hill, Fl., U.S.	u14	86
Walnut Hill, Me., U.S.	g7	96
Walnut Hill, hill, Ma., U.S.		
Walnut Mountain, hill, Ct., U.S.	B3	84
Walnut Park, Ca., U.S.	*n12	82
Walnutport, Pa., U.S.	E10	115
Walnut Ridge, Ar., U.S.	A5	81
Walpole, Ma., U.S.	B5	98
Walpole, N.H., U.S.	D2	106
Walsall, Eng., U.K.	D6	10
Walsenburg, Co., U.S.	D6	83
Walsh, Ab., Can.	E5	68
Walsh, Co., U.S.	D8	83
Walsh, co., N.D., U.S.	A8	111
Walsingham, Cape, c., N.T., Can.	C20	66
Walsrode, F.R.Ger.	F3	15
Walston, Pa., U.S.	E4	115
Walter Bathurst, Cape, c., N.T., Can.	B17	66
Walterhill, Tn., U.S.	B5	119
Walters, La., U.S.	C4	95
Walters, Mn., U.S.	G5	100
Walters, Ok., U.S.	C3	113
Walters Falls, On., Can.	C4	73
Waltershausen, Ger.D.R.	C5	19
Waltersville, Ms., U.S.	C3	101
Waltham, Or., U.S.	C4	114
Waltham, Ma., U.S.	B5	98
Waltham, Mn., U.S.	G6	100
Waltham Station, P.Q., Can.	B8	73
Walthill, Ne., U.S.	B9	104
Walthourville, Ga., U.S.	E5	87
Walton, N.S., Can.	D6	71
Walton, On., Can.	D3	73
Walton, Fl., U.S.	E6	86
Walton, In., U.S.	C5	91
Walton, Ks., U.S.	D6	93
Walton, Ky., U.S.	B5	94
Walton, Ne., U.S.	h11	104
Walton, N.Y., U.S.	C5	109
Walton, W.V., U.S.	C3	125
Walton, co., Fl., U.S.	u15	86
Walton, co., Ga., U.S.	C3	87
Walvisbaai (Walvis Bay), S. Afr.	B1	49
Walvis Bay see Walvisbaai, S. Afr.	B1	49
Wāmā, Afg.	D15	39
Wamac, Il., U.S.	E4	90
Wamba, Nig.	E6	45
Wamba, Zaire	A4	48
Wamba, stm., Afr.	C2	48
Wamego, Ks., U.S.	C7	93
Wamesit, Ma., U.S.	A5	98
Wamic, Or., U.S.	B5	114
Wampsville, N.Y., U.S.	B5	109
Wampum, Pa., U.S.	E1	115
Wamsutter, Wy., U.S.	E5	127
Wāna, Pak.	B4	36
Wanaka, N.Z.	P12	51
Wanaka, Lake, l., N.Z.	P12	51
Wanakena, N.Y., U.S.	A6	109
Wanamingo, Mn., U.S.	F6	100
Wan'an, China	K6	32
Wanapitei, stm., On., Can.	A4	73
Wanapum Dam, U.S.	C6	124
Wanapum Lake, res., Wa., U.S.	B6	124
Wanaque, N.J., U.S.	A4	107
Wanaque Reservoir, res., N.J., U.S.	A4	107
Wanatah, In., U.S.	A4	91
Wanblee, S.D., U.S.	D4	118
Wanchese, N.C., U.S.	B7	110
Wandering River, Ab., Can.	B4	68
Wando, S. Kor.	I3	33
Wando, S.C., U.S.	F8	117
Wandoan, Austl.	C7	51
Wandoo Woods, S.C., U.S.	k11	117
Wandsworth (part of London), Eng., U.K.	m12	10
Wanette, Ok., U.S.	C4	113
Wanganui, N.Z.	M15	51
Wangaratta, Austl.	G8	50
Wangen [im Allgäu], F.R.Ger.	B5	20
Wangeroge, i., F.R.Ger.	B2	15
Wangkui, China	A12	32
Wangqing, China	C10	31
Wanham, Ab., Can.	B1	68
Wanilla, Ms., U.S.	D3	101
Wanipigow, stm., Can.	D4	70
Wankie National Park, Zimb.	A4	49
Wann, Ne., U.S.	g12	104
Wann, Ok., U.S.	A6	113
Wannaska, Mn., U.S.	B3	100
Wanship, Ut., U.S.	C4	121
Wantage, Eng., U.K.	C6	12
Wantagh, N.Y., U.S.	*E7	109
Wanup, On., Can.	A4	73
Wanxian, China	E6	31
Wanzai, China	J6	32
Wapakoneta, Oh., U.S.	B1	112
Wapanucka, Ok., U.S.	C5	113
Wapato, Wa., U.S.	C5	124
Wapawekka Hills, hills, Sk., Can.	C3	75
Wapawekka Lake, l., Sk., Can.	C3	75
Wapella, Sk., Can.	G5	75
Wapella, Il., U.S.	C5	90
Wapello, Ia., U.S.	C6	92
Wapello, co., Ia., U.S.	C5	92
Wapisu Lake, l., Mb., Can.	B2	70
Wapiti, Wy., U.S.	B3	127
Wapiti, stm., Can.	B1	68
Wapiti Ridge, mtn., Wy., U.S.	B3	127
Wappapello, Mo., U.S.	E7	102
Wappapello, Lake, res., Mo., U.S.	D7	102
Wappingers Falls, N.Y., U.S.	D7	109
Wapsipinicon, stm., Ia., U.S.	B6	92
Wapske, N.B., Can.	C2	71
Wapske Lake, l., Sk., Can.	A4	75
Wapwallopen, Pa., U.S.	D9	115
Wāqid, Eg.	D2	41
Waqqāş, Jord.	B7	41
Waquoit, Ma., U.S.	C6	98
War, W.V., U.S.	D3	125
Waramaug, Lake, l., Ct., U.S.	C2	84
Warangal, India	E6	36
Warba, Mn., U.S.	C5	100
Warburg, Ab., Can.	C3	68
Warburg, F.R.Ger.	B4	19
Warburton, Austl.	H5	51
Warburton Creek, stm., Austl.	C1	78
Ward, Ar., U.S.	*B4	81
Ward, Co., U.S.	*A5	83
Ward, S.C., U.S.	D4	117
Ward, S.D., U.S.	C9	118
Ward, co., N.D., U.S.	A4	111
Ward, co., Tx., U.S.	D1	120
Ward, Mount, mtn., Ant.	B6	7
Wardell, Mo., U.S.	E8	102
Warden, Ab., Can.	C4	68
Warden, P.Q., Can.	D5	74
Warden, Wa., U.S.	C6	124
Wardensville, W.V., U.S.	B6	125
Warder, l., F.R.Ger.	E4	15
Wardha, India	D6	36
Wardha, stm., India	D6	36
Ward Hill, hill, Scot., U.K.	B5	13
Wardlow, Ab., Can.	D5	68
Ward Mountain, mtn., Mt., U.S.	D2	103
Wardner, B.C., Can.	E10	69
Wardner, Id., U.S.	B2	89
Wardsboro, Vt., U.S.	E3	122
Wardsville, On., Can.	E3	73
Wardville, Ok., U.S.	C5	113
Ware, Ma., U.S.	B3	98
Ware, co., Ga., U.S.	E4	87
Ware, stm., Ma., U.S.	B3	98
Wareham, Eng., U.K.	D5	12
Wareham, Ma., U.S.	C6	98
Warehouse Point, Ct., U.S.	B5	84
Waren, Ger.D.R.	B2	19
Warendorf, F.R.Ger.	B2	19
Waresboro, Ga., U.S.	E4	87
Ware Shoals, S.C., U.S.	C3	117
Waretown, N.J., U.S.	D4	107
Warfield, B.C., Can.	E9	69
Warfield, Ky., U.S.	C7	94
Warfield, Va., U.S.	D5	123
Warfordsburg, Pa., U.S.	G5	115
Wargla, Alg.	C6	44
Warick, R.I., U.S.	D4	116
Warin, Ger.D.R.	E5	15
Waring, Tx., U.S.	E3	120
Wark, Eng., U.K.	E6	13
Warkworth, On., Can.	C7	73
Warkworth, N.Z.	L15	51
Warley see Smethwick, Eng., U.K.	D5	10
Warman, Sk., Can.	E2	75
Warman, Mn., U.S.	D5	100
Warmbad, Nmb.	C2	49
Warmbad, S. Afr.	B4	49
Warm Beach, Wa., U.S.	A3	124
Warminster, Eng., U.K.	C5	12
Warminster, Pa., U.S.	F11	115
Warm Lake, Id., U.S.	D1	75
Warm River, Id., U.S.	E7	89
Warm Springs, Ar., U.S.	A4	81
Warm Springs, Ga., U.S.	D2	87
Warm Springs, Nv., U.S.	C5	105
Warm Springs, Or., U.S.	C5	114
Warm Springs, Va., U.S.	B3	123
Warm Springs Indian Reservation, Or., U.S.	C5	114
Warm Springs Reservoir, res., Or., U.S.	D8	114
Warnemünde (part of Rostock), Ger.D.R.	A6	18
Warner, Ab., Can.	E4	68
Warner, N.H., U.S.	D3	106
Warner, Ok., U.S.	B6	113
Warner, S.D., U.S.	B7	118
Warner, stm., N.H., U.S.	F3	106
Warner Mountain, mtn., Ma., U.S.	B1	98
Warner Mountains, mts., Ca., U.S.	B3	82
Warner Peak, mtn., Or., U.S.	E7	114
Warner Robins, Ga., U.S.	D3	87
Warner Springs, Ca., U.S.	F5	82
Warnes, Bol.	C3	55
Warnow, stm., Ger.D.R.	B5	18
Warpath, stm., Mb., Can.	C2	70
Warracknabeal, Austl.	H4	51
Warr Acres, Ok., U.S.	*B4	113
Warragul, Austl.	I5	51
Warrego, stm., Austl.	E8	50
Warren, Austl.	E8	51
Warren, On., Can.	A4	73
Warren, Ar., U.S.	D3	81
Warren, Ct., U.S.	C2	84
Warren, Id., U.S.	D3	89
Warren, Il., U.S.	A4	90
Warren, In., U.S.	C7	91
Warren, Me., U.S.	D3	96
Warren, Mi., U.S.	B3	98
Warren, Mn., U.S.	F7	99
Warren, Mi., U.S.	B2	100
Warren, N.H., U.S.	C3	106
Warren, N.Y., U.S.	C6	109
Warren, Oh., U.S.	A5	112
Warren, Or., U.S.	B4	114
Warren, Pa., U.S.	C3	115
Warren, R.I., U.S.	D5	116
Warren, Tx., U.S.	D5	120
Warren, Vt., U.S.	C3	122
Warren, co., Ga., U.S.	C4	87
Warren, co., Il., U.S.	C3	90
Warren, co., In., U.S.	D3	91
Warren, co., Ia., U.S.	C4	92
Warren, co., Ky., U.S.	C3	94
Warren, co., Ms., U.S.	C3	101
Warren, co., Mo., U.S.	C6	102
Warren, co., N.J., U.S.	B3	107
Warren, co., N.Y., U.S.	B7	109
Warren, co., N.C., U.S.	A4	110
Warren, co., Oh., U.S.	C1	112
Warren, co., Pa., U.S.	C3	115
Warren, co., Tn., U.S.	D8	119
Warren, co., Va., U.S.	B4	123
Warren Center, Pa., U.S.	C9	115
Warrendale, Pa., U.S.	h13	115
Warren Park, In., U.S.	k10	91
Warren Peaks, mts., Wy., U.S.	B8	127
Warrenpoint, N. Ire., U.K.	C5	11
Warren Point, R.I., U.S.	F6	116
Warrens, Wi., U.S.	D3	126
Warrensburg, Il., U.S.	D4	90
Warrensburg, Mo., U.S.	C4	102
Warrensburg, N.Y., U.S.	B7	109
Warrensburg, Tn., U.S.	C10	119
Warrensville, Pa., U.S.	D8	115
Warrensville Heights, Oh., U.S.	h9	112
Warrenton, S. Afr.	C3	49
Warrenton, Ga., U.S.	C4	87
Warrenton, Mo., U.S.	C6	102
Warrenton, N.C., U.S.	A4	110
Warrenton, Or., U.S.	A3	114
Warrenton, Va., U.S.	B5	123
Warrenville, Il., U.S.	k8	90
Warrenville, S.C., U.S.	D4	117
Warri, Nig.	E6	45
Warrick, co., In., U.S.	H3	91
Warrington, Eng., U.K.	D5	10
Warrington, Fl., U.S.	u14	86
Warrior, Al., U.S.	B3	78
Warrior Mountain, mtn., Md., U.S.	k13	97
Warrior Reservoir, res., Al., U.S.	C2	78
Warriors Mark, Pa., U.S.	E5	115
Warrnambool, Austl.	G7	50
Warroad, Mn., U.S.	B3	100
Warsaw, On., Can.	C6	73
Warsaw (Warszawa), Pol.	B6	26
Warsaw, Il., U.S.	C2	90
Warsaw, In., U.S.	B6	91
Warsaw, Ky., U.S.	B5	94
Warsaw, Mo., U.S.	C4	102
Warsaw, N.Y., U.S.	C2	109
Warsaw, N.C., U.S.	C4	110
Warsaw, Oh., U.S.	B3	112
Warsaw, Va., U.S.	C6	123
Warspite, Ab., Can.	B4	68
Warstein, F.R.Ger.	B3	19
Warta, Pol.	C5	26
Warta, stm., Pol.	B3	26
Wartburg, Tn., U.S.	C9	119
Warth, Aus.	B6	20
Warthen, Ga., U.S.	C4	87
Wartime, Sk., Can.	F1	75
Wartrace, Tn., U.S.	B5	119
Warwick, Austl.	D8	51
Warwick, On., Can.	D3	73
Warwick, P.Q., Can.	D6	74
Warwick, Eng., U.K.	D6	10
Warwick, Ga., U.S.	E3	87
Warwick, Ma., U.S.	A3	98
Warwick, N.Y., U.S.	D6	109
Warwick, N.D., U.S.	B7	111
Warwick, R.I., U.S.	D4	116
Warwick, Ok., U.S.	B4	113
Warwickshire, co., Eng., U.K.	B6	12
Wasaga Beach, On., Can.	C4	73
Wasatch, co., Ut., U.S.	C4	121
Wasatch Plateau, plat., Ut., U.S.	D4	121
Wasatch Range, mts., U.S.	B5	76
Wascana Creek, stm., Sk., Can.	G3	75
Wasco, Ca., U.S.	E4	82
Wasco, co., Or., U.S.	B6	114
Wasco, co., Or., U.S.	B5	114
Waseca, Mn., U.S.	F5	100
Waseca, co., Mn., U.S.	F5	100
Washademoak Lake, l., N.B., Can.	D4	71
Washago, On., Can.	C5	73
Washakie, co., Wy., U.S.	C4	127
Washakie Needles, mts., Wy., U.S.	B4	127
Washburn, Il., U.S.	C4	90
Washburn, Ia., U.S.	B5	92
Washburn, Me., U.S.	B4	96
Washburn, N.D., U.S.	B5	111
Washburn, Wi., U.S.	B3	126
Washburn, co., Wi., U.S.	C2	126
Washburn, Mount, mtn., Wy., U.S.	B2	127
Wāshim, India	G6	37
Washington, Ar., U.S.	D2	81
Washington, Ct., U.S.	C2	84
Washington, D.C., U.S.	C3	97
Washington, Ga., U.S.	C4	87
Washington, Il., U.S.	C4	90
Washington, In., U.S.	G3	91
Washington, Ia., U.S.	C6	92
Washington, Ks., U.S.	C6	93
Washington, Ky., U.S.	B6	94
Washington, La., U.S.	D3	95
Washington, Me., U.S.	D3	96
Washington, Mo., U.S.	C6	102
Washington, N.C., U.S.	B5	110
Washington, Ok., U.S.	B4	113
Washington, Pa., U.S.	F1	115
Washington, Tn., U.S.	D9	119
Washington, Ut., U.S.	F2	121
Washington, Vt., U.S.	C4	122
Washington, Va., U.S.	B4	123
Washington, W.V., U.S.	B3	125
Washington, co., Al., U.S.	D1	78
Washington, co., Ar., U.S.	A1	81
Washington, co., Co., U.S.	A7	83
Washington, co., Fl., U.S.	u16	86
Washington, co., Ga., U.S.	C4	87
Washington, co., Id., U.S.	E2	89
Washington, co., Il., U.S.	E4	90
Washington, co., In., U.S.	G5	91
Washington, co., Ia., U.S.	C6	92
Washington, co., Ks., U.S.	C6	93
Washington, co., Ky., U.S.	C4	94
Washington, co., La., U.S.	D5	95
Washington, co., Me., U.S.	D5	96
Washington, co., Md., U.S.	A2	97
Washington, co., Mn., U.S.	E6	100
Washington, co., Mo., U.S.	D7	102
Washington, co., Ne., U.S.	C9	104
Washington, co., N.Y., U.S.	B7	109
Washington, co., N.C., U.S.	B6	110
Washington, co., Oh., U.S.	C4	112
Washington, co., Ok., U.S.	A6	113
Washington, co., Or., U.S.	B3	114
Washington, co., Pa., U.S.	F1	115
Washington, co., R.I., U.S.	E2	116
Washington, co., Tn., U.S.	C11	119
Washington, co., Ut., U.S.	F2	121
Washington, co., Vt., U.S.	C3	122
Washington, co., Va., U.S.	f9	123
Washington, co., Wi., U.S.	E5	126
Washington, state, U.S.	B5	124
Washington, Cape, c., Fiji	I14	52
Washington, Lake, l., Fl., U.S.	D6	86
Washington, Lake, l., Mn., U.S.	E4	100
Washington, Lake, l., Ms., U.S.	B3	101
Washington, Lake, l., Wa., U.S.	e11	124
Washington, Mount, mtn., N.H., U.S.	B4	106
Washington Court House, Oh., U.S.	C2	112
Washington Crossing, N.J., U.S.	C3	107
Washington Depot, Ct., U.S.	C2	84
Washington Island see Teraina Island, i., Kir.	F12	6
Washington Island, i., Wi., U.S.	C7	126
Washington Park, Il., U.S.	E3	90
Washington Terrace, Ut., U.S.	B4	121
Washington Township, N.J., U.S.	*B4	107
Washingtonville, Pa., U.S.	D8	115
Washita, Ok., U.S.	B3	113
Washita, co., Ok., U.S.	B2	113
Washita, stm., Ok., U.S.	C4	113
Washoe, co., Nv., U.S.	C2	105
Washoe City, Nv., U.S.	D2	105
Washougal, Wa., U.S.	D3	124
Washow Bay, b., Mb., Can.	D3	70
Washta, Ia., U.S.	B2	92
Washtenaw, co., Mi., U.S.	F7	99
Washtucna, Wa., U.S.	C7	124
Washuków, Pol.	B7	26
Wasilla, Ak., U.S.	C10	79
Wasioja, Mn., U.S.	F6	100
Waskada, Mb., Can.	E1	70
Waskaiowaka Lake, l., Mb., Can.	A3	70
Waskatenau, Ab., Can.	B4	68
Waskesiu Lake, l., Sk., Can.	D2	75
Waskish, Mn., U.S.	B4	100
Waskom, Tx., U.S.	C5	120
Waspam, Nic.	C5	62
Wasque Point, c., Ma., U.S.	D7	98
Wassaw Sound, strt., Ga., U.S.	E6	87
Wassenaar, Neth.	B4	17
Wasseralfingen, F.R.Ger.	E5	19
Wasserburg [am Inn], F.R.Ger.	D6	18
Wasserkuppe, mtn., F.R.Ger.	C4	19
Wass Lake, l., Mb., Can.	C4	70
Wasson, Il., U.S.	F5	90
Wassookeag, Lake, l., Me., U.S.	C3	96
Wassuk Range, mts., Nv., U.S.	E3	105
Wassy-sur-Blaise, Fr.	F4	17
Wasta, S.D., U.S.	C3	118
Waswanipi, P.Q., Can.	o20	73
Wataga, Il., U.S.	B3	90
Watampone, Indon.	F6	34
Watapi Lake, l., Sk., Can.	B6	68
Watatic, Mount, mtn., Ma., U.S.	A4	98
Watauga, S.D., U.S.	B4	118
Watauga, Tx., U.S.	*n9	120
Watauga, co., N.C., U.S.	A1	110
Watauga, stm., Tn., U.S.	C12	119
Watauga, Lake, res., Tn., U.S.	C12	119
Watchaug Pond, l., R.I., U.S.	F2	116
Watchet, Eng., U.K.	C4	12
Watch Hill, R.I., U.S.	G1	116
Watch Hill Point, c., R.I., U.S.	C4	127
Watchung, N.J., U.S.	B4	107
Waterboro, Me., U.S.	E2	96
Waterbury, Ct., U.S.	C3	84
Waterbury, Vt., U.S.	C3	122
Waterbury Center, Vt., U.S.	C3	122
Waterbury Reservoir, res., Vt., U.S.	C3	122
Waterdown, On., Can.	D5	73
Wateree, stm., S.C., U.S.	C6	117
Wateree Lake, res., S.C., U.S.	C6	117
Waterfall, U.S.	n23	79
Waterflow, N.M., U.S.	A1	108
Waterford, P.E.I., Can.	C5	71
Waterford, Ire.	I5	11
Waterford, Ct., U.S.	D7	84
Waterford, Ca., U.S.	D3	82
Waterford, Mi., U.S.	o15	99
Waterford, Ms., U.S.	A4	101
Waterford, N.Y., U.S.	C7	109
Waterford, Pa., U.S.	C2	115
Waterford, Va., U.S.	A5	123
Waterford, Wi., U.S.	F5	126
Waterford, co., Ire.	I5	11
Waterford Harbour, b., Ire.	I6	11
Waterford Mills, In., U.S.	A6	91
Waterford Works, N.J., U.S.	D3	107
Watergrasshill, Ire.	E3	11
Waterhen Lake, l., Mb., Can.	C2	70
Waterloo, Bel.	D4	17
Waterloo, On., Can.	D4	73
Waterloo, P.Q., Can.	D5	74
Waterloo, S.L.	E2	45
Waterloo, Al., U.S.	A1	78
Waterloo, Ar., U.S.	D2	81
Waterloo, Il., U.S.	E3	90
Waterloo, In., U.S.	B7	91
Waterloo, Ia., U.S.	B5	92
Waterloo, Ks., U.S.	g11	93
Waterloo, Mt., U.S.	E4	103
Waterloo, Ne., U.S.	g12	104
Waterloo, N.Y., U.S.	C4	109
Waterloo, Or., U.S.	C4	114
Waterloo, S.C., U.S.	C3	117
Waterloo, Wi., U.S.	E5	126
Waterloo, co., On., Can.	D4	73
Waterman Four Corners, R.I., U.S.	C3	116
Waterman Reservoir, res., R.I., U.S.	B3	116
Waterport, N.Y., U.S.	B2	109
Waterproof, La., U.S.	C4	95
Waters, Mi., U.S.	D6	99
Watersmeet, Mi., U.S.	n12	99
Waterton, stm., N.A.	E4	68
Waterton-Glacier International Peace Park, N.A.	B3	103
Waterton Lakes National Park, Ab., Can.	E3	68
Waterton Park, Ab., Can.	E4	68
Watertown, Ct., U.S.	C3	84
Watertown, Ma., U.S.	g11	98
Watertown, N.Y., U.S.	B5	109
Watertown, S.D., U.S.	C8	118
Watertown, Tn., U.S.	A5	119
Watertown, Wi., U.S.	E5	126
Water Valley, Ky., U.S.	f9	94
Water Valley, Ms., U.S.	A4	101
Water Valley, Tx., U.S.	D2	120
Water View, Va., U.S.	C6	123
Water Village, N.H., U.S.	C4	106
Waterville, N.S., Can.	D5	71
Waterville, Ire.	F1	11
Waterville, Ia., U.S.	A6	92
Waterville, Ks., U.S.	C7	93
Waterville, Me., U.S.	D3	96
Waterville, Mn., U.S.	F5	100
Waterville, N.Y., U.S.	C5	109
Waterville, Oh., U.S.	A2	112
Waterville, Pa., U.S.	D7	115
Waterville, Vt., U.S.	B3	122
Waterville, Wa., U.S.	B5	124
Waterville Valley, N.H., U.S.	C3	106
Watervliet, Mi., U.S.	F4	99
Watervliet, N.Y., U.S.	C7	109
Watford, On., Can.	E3	73
Watford, Eng., U.K.	k12	10
Watford City, N.D., U.S.	B2	111
Watha, N.C., U.S.	C5	110
Wathena, Ks., U.S.	C9	93
Watkins, Co., U.S.	*B6	83
Watkins, Ia., U.S.	C6	92
Watkins Glen, N.Y., U.S.	C4	109
Watkinsville, Ga., U.S.	C3	87
Watonga, Ok., U.S.	B3	113
Watonwan, co., Mn., U.S.	F4	100
Watonwan, stm., Mn., U.S.	G4	100
Watou, Bel.	D2	17
Watova, Ok., U.S.	A6	113
Watrous, Sk., Can.	F3	75
Watrous, N.M., U.S.	B5	108
Watsa, Zaire	A4	48
Watseka, Il., U.S.	C6	90
Watson, Sk., Can.	E3	75
Watson, Ar., U.S.	D4	81
Watson, Il., U.S.	D5	90
Watson, In., U.S.	H6	91
Watson, Mn., U.S.	E3	100
Watson, Mo., U.S.	A2	102
Watson, Ok., U.S.	C7	113
Watson Chapel, Ar., U.S.	C3	81
Watson Lake, Yk., Can.	D7	66
Watsontown, Pa., U.S.	D8	115
Watsonville, Ca., U.S.	D3	82
Watten, Fr.	D2	17
Watten, Loch, l., Scot., U.K.	B5	13
Wattenberg, Co., U.S.	A6	83
Wattensaw Bayou, stm., Ar., U.S.	C4	81
Watts, Ok., U.S.	A7	113
Watts (part of Los Angeles), Ca., U.S.	n12	82
Watts Bar Dam, Tn., U.S.	D9	119
Watts Bar Lake, res., Tn., U.S.	D9	119
Wattsburg, Pa., U.S.	B2	115
Wattsville, Al., U.S.	B3	78
Wattsville, S.C., U.S.	B4	117
Wattwil, Switz.	B5	20
Watu, Zaire	B3	48
Watubela Islands, is., Indon.	F8	34
Watuppa Pond, l., Ma., U.S.	C5	98
Waubamik, On., Can.	B4	73
Waubaushene, On., Can.	C5	73
Waubay, S.D., U.S.	B8	118
Waubay Lake, l., S.D., U.S.	B8	118
Waubun, Mn., U.S.	C3	100
Wauchope, Austl.	E9	51
Wauchula, Fl., U.S.	E5	86
Waucoma, Ia., U.S.	A5	92
Wauconda, Il., U.S.	h8	90
Waugh Mountain, mtn., Id., U.S.	D4	89
Waukau, Wi., U.S.	E5	126
Waukee, Ia., U.S.	C4	92
Waukeenah, Fl., U.S.	B3	86
Waukegan, Il., U.S.	A6	90
Waukesha, Wi., U.S.	*F7	126
Waukesha, co., Wi., U.S.	E5	126
Waukewan, Lake, l., N.H., U.S.	C3	106
Waukomis, Ok., U.S.	A4	113
Waukon, Ia., U.S.	A6	92
Wauna, Wa., U.S.	f10	123
Waunakee, Wi., U.S.	E4	126
Wauneta, Ne., U.S.	D4	104
Waungumbaug Lake, l., Ct., U.S.	B6	84

Waupaca, Wi., U.S. — D4 126
Waupaca, co., Wi., U.S. — D5 126
Waupun, Wi., U.S. — E5 126
Wauregan, Ct., U.S. — C8 84
Waurika, Ok., U.S. — C4 113
Waurika Lake, res., Ok., U.S. — C3 113
Wausa, Ne., U.S. — B8 104
Wausau, Fl., U.S. — u16 86
Wausau, Wi., U.S. — D4 126
Wausau, Lake, res., Wi., U.S. — D4 126
Wausaukee, Wi., U.S. — C6 126
Wauseon, Oh., U.S. — A1 112
Waushara, co., Wi., U.S. — D4 126
Wautoma, Wi., U.S. — D4 126
Wauwatosa, Wi., U.S. — m12 126
Wauzeka, Wi., U.S. — E3 126
Waveland, In., U.S. — E3 91
Waveland, Ms., U.S. — E4 101
Waveney, stm., Eng., U.K. — D7 10
Waverley, Austl. — *G8 50
Waverley, Austl. — *F9 50
Waverley, N.S., Can. — E6 71
Waverly, Al., U.S. — C4 78
Waverly, Ga., U.S. — E5 87
Waverly, Il., U.S. — D4 90
Waverly, In., U.S. — E5 91
Waverly, Ia., U.S. — B5 92
Waverly, Ks., U.S. — D8 93
Waverly, Ky., U.S. — C2 94
Waverly, Mn., U.S. — E5 100
Waverly, Mo., U.S. — B4 102
Waverly, Ne., U.S. — D9 104
Waverly, N.Y., U.S. — C4 109
Waverly, Oh., U.S. — C3 112
Waverly, Tn., U.S. — A4 119
Waverly, Va., U.S. — C5 123
Waverly, W.V., U.S. — B3 125
Waverly Hall, Ga., U.S. — D2 87
Wavre, Bel. — D4 17
Wāw, Sud. — D2 47
Wawa, On., Can. — p18 73
Wawa, Nig. — E5 45
Wawa, stm., Nic. — C6 62
Wawaka, In., U.S. — B7 91
Wāw al Kabīr, Libya — D3 43
Wawanesa, Mb., Can. — E2 70
Wawasee, Lake, l., In., U.S. — B6 91
Wawayanda Lake, l., N.J., U.S. — A4 107
Wawayanda Mountain, mtn., U.S. — A4 107
Waweig, N.B., Can. — D2 71
Wawota, Sk., Can. — H4 75
Waxahachie, Tx., U.S. — C4 120
Waxhaw, N.C., U.S. — C2 110
Waxweiler, F.R.Ger. — D6 17
Waya, i., Fiji — H14 51
Wayagamac, Lac, l., P.Q., Can. — B5 74
Wayan, Id., U.S. — G7 89
Waycross, Ga., U.S. — E4 87
Wayland, Ia., U.S. — C6 92
Wayland, Ky., U.S. — C7 94
Wayland, Ma., U.S. — g10 98
Wayland, Mi., U.S. — F5 99
Wayland, Mo., U.S. — A6 102
Wayland, N.Y., U.S. — C3 109
Wayland Springs, Tn., U.S. — B4 119
Waylyn, S.C., U.S. — k12 117
Waymart, Pa., U.S. — C11 115
Wayne, Ab., Can. — D4 68
Wayne, Mi., U.S. — p15 99
Wayne, Ne., U.S. — B8 104
Wayne, N.J., U.S. — B4 107
Wayne, N.Y., U.S. — C3 109
Wayne, Oh., U.S. — A2 112
Wayne, Ok., U.S. — C4 113
Wayne, Pa., U.S. — F11 115
Wayne, W.V., U.S. — C2 125
Wayne, co., Ga., U.S. — E5 87
Wayne, co., Il., U.S. — E5 90
Wayne, co., In., U.S. — E7 91
Wayne, co., Ia., U.S. — D4 92
Wayne, co., Ky., U.S. — D5 94
Wayne, co., Mi., U.S. — F7 99
Wayne, co., Ms., U.S. — D5 101
Wayne, co., Mo., U.S. — D7 102
Wayne, co., Ne., U.S. — B8 104
Wayne, co., N.Y., U.S. — B3 109
Wayne, co., N.C., U.S. — B4 110
Wayne, co., Oh., U.S. — B4 112
Wayne, co., Pa., U.S. — C11 115
Wayne, co., Tn., U.S. — B4 119
Wayne, co., Ut., U.S. — E4 121
Wayne, co., W.V., U.S. — C2 125
Wayne City, Il., U.S. — E5 90
Waynesboro, Ga., U.S. — C4 87
Waynesboro, Ms., U.S. — D5 101
Waynesboro, Pa., U.S. — G6 115
Waynesboro, Tn., U.S. — B4 119
Waynesboro, Va., U.S. — B4 123
Waynesburg, Ky., U.S. — C5 94
Waynesburg, Oh., U.S. — B4 112
Waynesburg, Pa., U.S. — G1 115
Waynesville, Ga., U.S. — E5 87
Waynesville, Mo., U.S. — C4 90
Waynesville, N.C., U.S. — f10 110
Waynesville, Oh., U.S. — C1 112
Waynetown, In., U.S. — D3 91
Waynewood, Va., U.S. — g12 123
Waynoka, Ok., U.S. — A3 113
Wayside, Ms., U.S. — B2 101
Wayside, Tx., U.S. — B2 120
Wayside, Wi., U.S. — h10 126
Wayzata, Mn., U.S. — n11 100
Wazi Khwa, Afg. — B4 36
We, i., Indon. — J1 35
Weakley, co., Tn., U.S. — A3 119
Weare, N.H., U.S. — D3 106
Weatherby, Mo., U.S. — B3 102
Weatherford, Ok., U.S. — B3 113
Weatherford, Tx., U.S. — C4 120
Weatherly, Pa., U.S. — E10 115
Weatogue, Ct., U.S. — B4 84
Weaubleau, Mo., U.S. — D4 102
Weaver, Al., U.S. — B4 78
Weaver Lake, l., Mb., Can. — C3 70
Weaver Mountains, mts., Az., U.S. — C3 80
Weaverville, Ca., U.S. — B2 82
Weaverville, N.C., U.S. — f10 110
Webb, Sk., Can. — G1 75
Webb, Al., U.S. — D4 78
Webb, Ia., U.S. — B2 92
Webb, Ms., U.S. — B3 101
Webb, co., Tx., U.S. — F3 120
Webb Air Force Base, mil., Tx., U.S. — C2 120
Webb City, Mo., U.S. — D3 102
Webb City, Ok., U.S. — A5 113
Webber Lake, l., Mb., Can. — B5 70

Webbers Falls, Ok., U.S. — B6 113
Webberville, Mi., U.S. — F6 99
Webb Hill, hill, Ma., U.S. — B3 98
Webb Lake, l., Me., U.S. — D2 96
Webbwood, On., Can. — A3 73
Webbwood Spring, Mo., U.S. — f12 102
Weber, co., Ut., U.S. — B4 121
Weber, Mount, mtn., B.C., Can. — B3 69
Weber City, Va., U.S. — f9 123
Webster, Ab., Can. — B1 68
Webster, Fl., U.S. — D4 86
Webster, In., U.S. — E8 91
Webster, Ma., U.S. — B4 98
Webster, Mn., U.S. — F5 100
Webster, N.H., U.S. — D3 106
Webster, N.Y., U.S. — B3 109
Webster, N.D., U.S. — A7 111
Webster, Oh., U.S. — B1 112
Webster, Pa., U.S. — F2 115
Webster, S.D., U.S. — B8 118
Webster, Tx., U.S. — r14 120
Webster, Wi., U.S. — C1 126
Webster, co., Ga., U.S. — D2 87
Webster, co., Ia., U.S. — B3 92
Webster, co., Ky., U.S. — C2 94
Webster, co., La., U.S. — B2 95
Webster, co., Ms., U.S. — B4 101
Webster, co., Mo., U.S. — D5 102
Webster, co., Ne., U.S. — D7 104
Webster, co., W.V., U.S. — C4 125
Webster City, Ia., U.S. — B4 92
Webster Groves, Mo., U.S. — f13 102
Webster Mills, Pa., U.S. — G5 115
Webster Reservoir, res., Ks., U.S. — C4 93
Webster Springs, W.V., U.S. — C4 125
Websterville, Vt., U.S. — C4 122
Wecota, S.D., U.S. — B6 118
Weda, Indon. — E7 34
Weddell Sea, Ant. — C9 7
Wedderburn, Or., U.S. — E2 114
Wedgefield, S.C., U.S. — D6 117
Wedgeport, N.S., Can. — F4 71
Wedgewood, Mo., U.S. — f13 102
Wedowee, Al., U.S. — B4 78
Wedron, Il., U.S. — B5 90
Weed, Ca., U.S. — B2 82
Weed, N.M., U.S. — E4 108
Weed Heights, Nv., U.S. — E2 105
Weedon, P.Q., Can. — D6 74
Weed Patch Hill, hill, In., U.S. — F5 91
Weedsport, N.Y., U.S. — B4 109
Weedville, Pa., U.S. — D5 115
Weehawken, N.J., U.S. — h8 107
Weekapaug, R.I., U.S. — G1 116
Weekes, Sk., Can. — E4 75
Weeksbury, Ky., U.S. — C7 94
Weekstown, N.J., U.S. — D3 107
Weeksville, N.C., U.S. — A6 110
Weems, Va., U.S. — C6 123
Weener, F.R.Ger. — A7 17
Weeping Water, Ne., U.S. — D9 104
Weeping Water Creek, stm., Ne., U.S. — h12 104
Weert, Neth. — B6 16
Weesen, Switz. — B7 21
Weesp, Neth. — B5 17
Weferlingen, Ger.D.R. — A6 19
Wegdahl, Mn., U.S. — F3 100
Weggis, Switz. — B5 21
Wegorzewo, Pol. — A6 26
Wegrów, Pol. — B7 26
Wegscheid, F.R.Ger. — A4 21
Wehr, F.R.Ger. — A4 21
Weichang, China — C8 31
Weida, Ger.D.R. — C7 19
Weiden, F.R.Ger. — D6 18
Weidman, Mi., U.S. — E6 99
Weifang, China — D8 31
Weihai, China — D9 31
Wei He, stm., China — E6 31
Weilburg, F.R.Ger. — C3 19
Weiler, F.R.Ger. — A8 21
Weilheim, F.R.Ger. — E5 18
Weimar, Ger.D.R. — C5 18
Weimar, Tx., U.S. — E4 120
Weinan, China — E6 31
Weinböhla, Ger.D.R. — B8 19
Weiner, Ar., U.S. — B5 81
Weinert, Tx., U.S. — C3 120
Weinfelden, Switz. — A7 21
Weingarten, F.R.Ger. — D3 19
Weingarten, F.R.Ger. — A8 21
Weinheim, F.R.Ger. — D4 18
Weining, China — F5 31
Weinsberg, F.R.Ger. — D4 19
Weipa, Austl. — B7 50
Weippe, Id., U.S. — C3 89
Weir, P.Q., Can. — D3 74
Weir, Ks., U.S. — E9 93
Weir, Ky., U.S. — C2 94
Weir, Ms., U.S. — B4 101
Weir, stm., Mb., Can. — A4 70
Weirdale, Sk., Can. — D3 75
Weir River, Mb., Can. — A4 70
Weirsdale, Fl., U.S. — D5 86
Weirton, W.V., U.S. — A4 125
Weiser, Id., U.S. — E2 89
Weiser, stm., Id., U.S. — E2 89
Weishan Lake, l., China — G7 32
Weishi, China — G6 32
Weisner Mountain, hill, Al., U.S. — A4 78
Weisse Elster, stm., Ger.D.R. — B7 19
Weissenburg, F.R.Ger. — D5 18
Weissenburg, Switz. — C3 21
Weissenfels, Ger.D.R. — B6 19
Weissenhorn, F.R.Ger. — A6 20
Weissen Lake, l., Aus. — C9 20
Weisshorn, mtn., Switz. — C3 21
Weisswasser, Ger.D.R. — B9 19
Weitra, Aus. — E9 19
Weixi, China — F4 31
Weizhou Dao, i., China — B8 35
Wejherowo, Pol. — A5 26
Wekusko Lake, l., Mb., Can. — B2 70
Welaka, Fl., U.S. — C5 86
Welch, Ok., U.S. — A6 113
Welch, Tx., U.S. — C1 120
Welch, W.V., U.S. — D3 125
Welches, Or., U.S. — B5 114
Welcome, Mn., U.S. — G4 100
Welcome, S.C., U.S. — B3 117
Weld, Me., U.S. — D2 96
Weld, co., Co., U.S. — A6 83
Welda, Ks., U.S. — D8 93
Weldon, Sk., Can. — D3 75
Weldon, Ar., U.S. — B4 81

Weldon, Il., U.S. — C5 90
Weldon, Ia., U.S. — D4 92
Weldon, N.C., U.S. — A5 110
Weldon, Tx., U.S. — D5 120
Weldona, Co., U.S. — A7 83
Weleetka, Ok., U.S. — B5 113
Welega, prov., Eth. — D4 47
Welkom, S. Afr. — C4 49
Welland, On., Can. — E5 73
Welland, stm., Eng., U.K. — D6 10
Wellandport, On., Can. — D5 73
Wellborn, Fl., U.S. — B4 86
Wellborn, Tx., U.S. — D4 120
Wellersburg, Pa., U.S. — G4 115
Welles Harbor, b., Mid. Is. — K3 52
Wellesley, On., Can. — D4 73
Wellesley, Ma., U.S. — B5 98
Wellesley Islands, is., Austl. — C6 50
Wellfleet, Ma., U.S. — C7 98
Wellfleet, Ne., U.S. — D5 104
Wellford, S.C., U.S. — B3 117
Wellin, Bel. — D5 17
Welling, Ok., U.S. — B7 113
Wellingborough, Eng., U.K. — B7 12
Wellington, Austl. — F7 51
Wellington, B.C., Can. — f11 69
Wellington, On., Can. — D7 73
Wellington, N.Z. — N15 51
Wellington, S. Afr. — D2 49
Wellington, Eng., U.K. — B5 12
Wellington, Eng., U.K. — C4 12
Wellington, Al., U.S. — B4 78
Wellington, Co., U.S. — A5 83
Wellington, Il., U.S. — C6 90
Wellington, Ks., U.S. — E6 93
Wellington, Me., U.S. — C3 96
Wellington, Mo., U.S. — B4 102
Wellington, Nv., U.S. — E2 105
Wellington, Oh., U.S. — A3 112
Wellington, Tx., U.S. — B2 120
Wellington, Ut., U.S. — D5 121
Wellington, Co., U.S. — A5 83
Wellington, Isla, i., Chile — D2 54
Wellington Channel, strt., N.T., Can. — m33 66
Wellington Station, N.S., Can. — E6 71
Wellington Station, P.E.I., Can. — C5 71
Wellman, Ia., U.S. — C6 92
Wellman, Tx., U.S. — C1 120
Wellpinit, Wa., U.S. — B8 124
Wells, B.C., Can. — C7 69
Wells, Eng., U.K. — C5 12
Wells, Ks., U.S. — C6 93
Wells, Me., U.S. — E2 96
Wells, Mi., U.S. — C3 99
Wells, Mn., U.S. — G5 100
Wells, Nv., U.S. — B7 105
Wells, N.Y., U.S. — B6 109
Wells, Tx., U.S. — D5 120
Wells, Vt., U.S. — E2 122
Wells, co., In., U.S. — C7 91
Wells, co., N.D., U.S. — B6 111
Wells, stm., Vt., U.S. — C4 122
Wells Lake, l., Austl. — E3 50
Wells Beach, Me., U.S. — E2 96
Wellsboro, In., U.S. — B4 91
Wellsboro, Pa., U.S. — C7 115
Wellsburg, Ia., U.S. — B5 92
Wellsburg, N.Y., U.S. — C4 109
Wellsburg, W.V., U.S. — A4 125
Wellsford, Ks., U.S. — E4 93
Wells Gray Provincial Park, B.C., Can. — C8 69
Wells River, Vt., U.S. — C4 122
Wells Tannery, Pa., U.S. — F5 115
Wellston, Mi., U.S. — D5 99
Wellston, Oh., U.S. — C3 112
Wellston, Ok., U.S. — B4 113
Wellsville, Ks., U.S. — D8 93
Wellsville, Mo., U.S. — B6 102
Wellsville, N.Y., U.S. — C3 109
Wellsville, Oh., U.S. — B5 112
Wellsville, Ut., U.S. — B4 121
Wellton, Az., U.S. — E1 80
Wellwood, Mb., Can. — D2 70
Wellmlingen, F.R.Ger. — A4 21
Welo, prov., Eth. — C5 47
Wels, Aus. — D7 18
Welsford, N.B., Can. — D3 71
Welsh, La., U.S. — D3 95
Welshpool, Wales, U.K. — D5 10
Welton, Ia., U.S. — C7 92
Welty, Ok., U.S. — B5 113
Welwitschia, Nmb. — B1 49
Welwyn, Sk., Can. — G5 75
Welwyn Garden City, Eng., U.K. — k12 10
Welzow, Ger.D.R. — B9 19
Wem, Eng., U.K. — B5 12
Wema, Zaire — B3 48
Wembere, stm., Tan. — B5 48
Wembley, Ab., Can. — B1 68
Wemding, F.R.Ger. — E5 19
Wemme, Or., U.S. — B5 114
Wenasoga, Ms., U.S. — A5 101
Wenatchee, Wa., U.S. — B5 124
Wenatchee, stm., Wa., U.S. — B5 124
Wenatchee Lake, l., Wa., U.S. — B5 124
Wenatchee Mountains, mts., Wa., U.S. — B5 124
Wenchang, China — C9 35
Wenchi, Ghana — E4 45
Wenchou see Wenzhou, China — F9 31
Wendel, Ca., U.S. — B3 82
Wendell, W.V., U.S. — k10 125
Wendell, Id., U.S. — G4 89
Wendell, Ma., U.S. — A3 98
Wendell, N.H., U.S. — D2 106
Wendell, N.C., U.S. — B4 110
Wenden, Az., U.S. — D2 80
Wendeng, China — F10 32
Wendo, Eth. — D4 47
Wendover, Nv., U.S. — C7 105
Wendover, Ut., U.S. — C1 121
Wenham Lake, l., Ma., U.S. — f12 98
Wenham Swamp, sw., Ma., U.S. — f12 98
Wenlock, stm., Austl. — B7 50
Wenona, Il., U.S. — B4 90
Wenona, Md., U.S. — D5 97
Wenonah, N.J., U.S. — D2 107
Wenshan, China — G5 31
Wentworth, Austl. — F7 50
Wentworth, N.S., Can. — D6 71
Wentworth, N.H., U.S. — C3 106
Wentworth, N.C., U.S. — A3 110
Wentworth, S.D., U.S. — C8 118
Wentworth, Wi., U.S. — B2 126

Wentworth, co., On., Can. — D4 73
Wentworth, Lake, l., N.H., U.S. — C4 106
Wentzville, Mo., U.S. — C7 102
Wenzhou (Wenchou), China — F9 31
Weohyakapka, Lake, l., Fl., U.S. — E5 86
Weott, Ca., U.S. — B2 82
Wepener, S. Afr. — C4 49
Wequetequock, Ct., U.S. — D8 84
Werbomont, Bel. — D5 17
Werdau, Ger.D.R. — C6 18
Werder, Ger.D.R. — A7 19
Werdohl, F.R.Ger. — B2 19
Werfen, Aus. — E6 18
Werl, F.R.Ger. — B2 19
Wernberg, F.R.Ger. — D6 19
Werne, F.R.Ger. — B2 19
Werneuchen, Ger.D.R. — A7 19
Wernigerode, Ger.D.R. — C5 18
Werra, stm., Eur. — C4 18
Wertach, stm., F.R.Ger. — D5 18
Wertheim, F.R.Ger. — D4 19
Wertingen, F.R.Ger. — E5 19
Wervik, Bel. — D3 17
Wesco, Mo., U.S. — D6 102
Wesel, F.R.Ger. — C3 18
Weser, stm., F.R.Ger. — B4 18
Weskan, Ks., U.S. — D2 93
Weslaco, Tx., U.S. — F4 120
Weslemkoon Lake, l., On., Can. — C7 73
Wesley, Me., U.S. — D5 96
Wesley, Ga., U.S. — D4 87
Wesley, Ia., U.S. — A4 92
Wesley, Me., U.S. — D5 96
Wesleyville, Nf., Can. — D5 72
Wesleyville, Pa., U.S. — B2 115
Wesselburen, F.R.Ger. — D5 18
Wessel Islands, is., Austl. — B6 50
Wesserunsett Lake, l., Me., U.S. — D3 96
Wessington, S.D., U.S. — C7 118
Wessington Springs, S.D., U.S. — C7 118
Wesson, Ar., U.S. — D3 81
Wesson, Ms., U.S. — D3 101
West, Ms., U.S. — B4 101
West, Tx., U.S. — D4 120
West, stm., P.E., Can. — C6 71
West, stm., Ct., U.S. — D5 84
West, stm., Ma., U.S. — h9 98
West, stm., Vt., U.S. — E3 122
West Abington, Ma., U.S. — h12 98
West Acton, Ma., U.S. — g10 98
West Alexander, Pa., U.S. — F1 115
West Alexandria, Oh., U.S. — C1 112
West Allis, Wi., U.S. — m11 126
West Alton, Mo., U.S. — f13 102
West Amityville, N.Y., U.S. — n15 109
West Andover, Ma., U.S. — A5 98
West Arichat, N.S., Can. — D8 71
West Athens, Ca., U.S. — n12 82
West Athens, Me., U.S. — D3 96
West Augusta, Va., U.S. — B3 123
West Babylon, N.Y., U.S. — *E7 109
West Baden Springs, In., U.S. — G4 91
West Baldwin, Me., U.S. — D2 96
Westbank, B.C., Can. — E8 69
West Bank, ter., Isr. Occ. — B7 41
West Barnet, Vt., U.S. — C4 122
West Barnstable, Ma., U.S. — C7 98
West Barrington, R.I., U.S. — C5 116
West Baton Rouge, co., La., U.S. — D4 95
West Bay, N.S., Can. — D8 71
West Bay, Fl., U.S. — u16 86
West Bay, b., Fl., U.S. — u16 86
West Bay, b., N.C., U.S. — B6 110
West Bay, b., Tx., U.S. — r15 120
West Bay Shore, N.Y., U.S. — *n15 109
West Bend, Sk., Can. — F4 75
West Bend, Ia., U.S. — B3 92
West Bend, Wi., U.S. — E5 126
West Bengal, state, India — F11 37
West Berkshire, Vt., U.S. — B3 122
West Berlin see Berlin (West), F.R.Ger. — B6 18
West Berlin, N.J., U.S. — D3 107
West Bethel, Me., U.S. — D2 96
West Billerica, Ma., U.S. — f10 98
West Blocton, Al., U.S. — B2 78
West Bloomfield, N.Y., U.S. — C3 109
Westboro, Mo., U.S. — A2 102
Westboro, Wi., U.S. — C3 126
Westborough, Ma., U.S. — B4 98
West Bountiful, Ut., U.S. — C4 121
Westbourne, Mb., Can. — D2 70
West Bowdoin, Me., U.S. — f7 96
West Boylston, Ma., U.S. — B4 98
West Branch, Ia., U.S. — C6 92
West Branch, Mi., U.S. — D6 99
West Branch Reservoir, res., Ct., U.S. — B5 84
West Brentwood, N.H., U.S. — E4 106
West Bridgewater, Ma., U.S. — B5 98
West Bridgewater, Vt., U.S. — D3 122
West Bromwich, Eng., U.K. — B6 12
West Brookfield, Ma., U.S. — B3 98
West Brooklyn, Il., U.S. — B4 90
Westbrookville, N.Y., U.S. — D6 109
West Burke, Vt., U.S. — B5 122
West Burlington, Ia., U.S. — D6 92
Westbury, N.Y., U.S. — *n15 109
West Butte, mtn., Mt., U.S. — B5 103
West Buxton, Me., U.S. — E2 96
Westby, Wi., U.S. — E3 126
Westby, Mt., U.S. — B12 103
West Cache Creek, stm., Ok., U.S. — C3 113
West Caldwell, N.J., U.S. — B4 107
West Campton, N.H., U.S. — C3 106
West Canaan, N.H., U.S. — C2 106
West Canada Creek, stm., N.Y., U.S. — B6 109
West Cape Howe, c., Austl. — G3 50
West Cape May, N.J., U.S. — F3 107
West Carroll, co., La., U.S. — B4 95
West Carrollton, Oh., U.S. — C1 112
West Carry Pond, l., Me., U.S. — C2 96
West Carson, Ca., U.S. — *n12 82
West Carthage, N.Y., U.S. — B5 109
West Castleton, Vt., U.S. — D2 122
West Charleston, Vt., U.S. — B4 122
West Chatham, Ma., U.S. — C8 98
West Chazy, N.Y., U.S. — f11 109
Westchester, Fl., U.S. — *s13 86
Westchester, Il., U.S. — k9 90
Westchester, co., N.Y., U.S. — D7 109
West Chester, Oh., U.S. — n13 112

West Chester, Pa., U.S. — G10 115
Westchester, co., N.Y., U.S. — D7 109
West Chesterfield, N.H., U.S. — E1 106
Westchester Station, N.S., Can. — D6 71
West Chicago, Il., U.S. — k8 90
West Chop, c., Ma., U.S. — D6 98
West City, Il., U.S. — F5 90
Westcliffe, Co., U.S. — C5 83
West Coffeyville, Ks., U.S. — E8 93
West College Corner, In., U.S. — E8 91
West Columbia, S.C., U.S. — D5 117
West Columbia, Tx., U.S. — E5 120
West Concord, Ma., U.S. — B5 98
West Concord, Mn., U.S. — F6 100
West Concord, N.C., U.S. — B2 110
Westconnaug Reservoir, res., R.I., U.S. — C2 116
West Cornwall, Ct., U.S. — B2 84
West Cote Blanche Bay, b., La., U.S. — E4 95
West Covina, Ca., U.S. — m13 82
West Creek, N.J., U.S. — D4 107
West Crossett, Ar., U.S. — D4 81
West Cumberland, Me., U.S. — E2 96
West Cummington, Ma., U.S. — B2 98
West Danby, N.Y., U.S. — C4 109
West Danville, Vt., U.S. — C4 122
West Decatur, Pa., U.S. — E5 115
West Demerara-Essequibo Coast, dept., Guy. — A3 59
West Dennis, Ma., U.S. — C7 98
West Des Moines, Ia., U.S. — C4 92
West Dover, Vt., U.S. — F3 122
West Dudley, Ma., U.S. — B4 98
West Dummerston, Vt., U.S. — F3 122
West Elk Mountains, mts., Co., U.S. — C3 83
West Elk Peak, mtn., Co., U.S. — C3 83
West Elkton, Oh., U.S. — C1 112
West Elmira, N.Y., U.S. — *C4 109
West Elwood, In., U.S. — D6 91
West Eminence, Mo., U.S. — D6 102
West Emma Creek, stm., Ks., U.S. — D6 93
West End, Bah. — A4 64
West End, N.C., U.S. — B3 110
West Enfield, Me., U.S. — C4 96
West Enosburg, Vt., U.S. — B3 122
West Epping, N.H., U.S. — D4 106
Westerkappeln, F.R.Ger. — A2 19
Westerland, F.R.Ger. — A4 18
Westerly, R.I., U.S. — F1 116
Western, Ne., U.S. — D8 104
Western, prov., Ghana — E4 45
Western, prov., Kenya — A5 48
Western, prov., Zam. — E3 48
Western Australia, state, Austl. — D3 50
Western Channel, strt., Asia — I4 33
Western Desert, des., Eg. — C2 38
Western Dvina (Daugava), stm., Sov. Un. — D7 27
Western Ghāts, mts., India — E5 36
Western Grove, Ar., U.S. — A3 81
Western Head, c., Nf., Can. — D2 72
Western Head, c., N.S., Can. — F5 71
Western Hills, Co., U.S. — *B6 83
Western Island, i., Me., U.S. — C4 72
Western Isles, prov., Scot., U.K. — B2 13
Westernport, Md., U.S. — m12 97
Western Reservoir, res., Md., U.S. — k12 97
Western Sahara, dep., Afr. — D2 44
Western Samoa, ctry., Oc. — G11 6
Western Shore, N.S., Can. — E5 71
Western Springs, Il., U.S. — k9 90
Westerschelde, est., Neth. — B5 16
Westerstede, F.R.Ger. — A7 17
Westervelt, Il., U.S. — D5 90
Westerville, Ne., U.S. — C6 104
Westerville, Oh., U.S. — B3 112
Westerwald, mts., F.R.Ger. — C4 18
West Fairlee, Vt., U.S. — D4 122
West Fairview, Pa., U.S. — *F8 115
Westfall, Ks., U.S. — C5 93
West Falmouth, Ma., U.S. — C6 98
West Fargo, N.D., U.S. — C9 111
West Farmington, Me., U.S. — D2 96
West Farmington, Oh., U.S. — A5 112
West Feliciana, co., La., U.S. — D4 95
Westfield, N.B., Can. — D3 71
Westfield, Il., U.S. — D6 90
Westfield, In., U.S. — D5 91
Westfield, Ia., U.S. — B1 92
Westfield, Ma., U.S. — B2 98
Westfield, N.J., U.S. — B4 107
Westfield, N.Y., U.S. — C1 109
Westfield, N.D., U.S. — A2 110
Westfield, Pa., U.S. — C6 115
Westfield, Vt., U.S. — B4 122
Westfield, Wi., U.S. — E4 126
Westfield, stm., Ma., U.S. — B2 98
Westfield Center, Oh., U.S. — A4 112
Westfir, Or., U.S. — D4 114
West Flanders, prov., Bel. — C3 17
Westford, Ct., U.S. — B7 84
Westford, Ma., U.S. — f10 98
Westford, Vt., U.S. — B2 122
West Fork, Ar., U.S. — B1 81
West Fork, stm., W.V., U.S. — B4 125
West Frankfort, Il., U.S. — F5 90
West Freehold, N.J., U.S. — C4 107
West Friendship, Md., U.S. — B4 97
West Frisian Islands, is., Neth. — A6 16
Westgate, Fl., U.S. — F6 86
Westgate, Ia., U.S. — B6 92
West Germany see Germany, Federal Republic of, ctry., Eur. — C5 96
West Glacier, Mt., U.S. — B3 103
West Glamorgan, co., Wales, U.K. — C4 12
West Glocester, R.I., U.S. — B1 116
West Glover, Vt., U.S. — B4 122
West Goshen, Ct., U.S. — B3 84
West Gouldsboro, Me., U.S. — D4 96
West Granby, Ct., U.S. — B4 84
West Grand Lake, l., Me., U.S. — C5 96
West Granville, Ma., U.S. — B2 98
West Green, Ga., U.S. — E4 87
West Greene, Al., U.S. — B1 78
West Greenville, R.I., U.S. — B3 116
West Groton, Ma., U.S. — A4 98
West Grove, Ia., U.S. — D5 92
West Grove, Pa., U.S. — G10 115
West Halifax, Vt., U.S. — F3 122
West Ham, Va., U.S. — *C5 123
West Hamlin, W.V., U.S. — C2 125

West Hampstead, N.H., U.S. — E4 106
Westhampton, Ma., U.S. — B2 98
West Hanover, Ma., U.S. — h12 98
West Harrison, In., U.S. — F8 91
West Hartford, Ct., U.S. — B4 84
West Hartford, Vt., U.S. — D4 122
West Hartland, Ct., U.S. — A4 84
West Hatfield, Ma., U.S. — B2 98
West Haven, Ct., U.S. — D4 84
West Haven, N.Y., U.S. — *B4 114
West Haverstraw, N.Y., U.S. — *D7 109
West Hazleton, Pa., U.S. — E9 115
West Helena, Ar., U.S. — C5 81
West Hempstead, N.Y., U.S. — *k13 109
West Hickory, Pa., U.S. — C3 115
West Hill Reservoir, res., Ma., U.S. — B4 98
Westhoff, Tx., U.S. — E4 120
West Hollywood, Ca., U.S. — *m12 82
Westhope, N.D., U.S. — A4 111
West Hopkinton, N.H., U.S. — D3 106
West Huntington, W.V., U.S. — *n15 109
West Hyannisport, Ma., U.S. — C7 98
West Ice Shelf, Ant. — C21 7
West Indies, is. — A3 53
West Island, i., Ma., U.S. — C6 98
West Jefferson, N.C., U.S. — *E7 109
West Jefferson, Oh., U.S. — C2 112
West Jersey, Il., U.S. — B4 90
West Jordan, Ut., U.S. — C4 121
West Kennebunk, Me., U.S. — E2 96
West Kingston, R.I., U.S. — F3 116
West Lafayette, In., U.S. — D4 91
West Lafayette, Oh., U.S. — B4 112
Westlake, Oh., U.S. — h9 112
Westlake, Or., U.S. — D2 114
West Lake, l., Me., U.S. — C4 96
Westland, Mi., U.S. — F7 99
West Laramie, Wy., U.S. — E7 127
West Lawn, Pa., U.S. — F10 115
West Lebanon, In., U.S. — D3 91
West Lebanon, Me., U.S. — E2 96
West Leisenring, Pa., U.S. — G2 115
West Leyden, N.Y., U.S. — B5 109
West Liberty, Il., U.S. — E5 90
West Liberty, Ia., U.S. — C6 92
West Liberty, Ky., U.S. — C6 94
West Liberty, Oh., U.S. — B2 112
West Liberty, W.V., U.S. — f8 125
West Lima, Wi., U.S. — E3 126
West Lincoln, Vt., U.S. — C2 122
Westline, Pa., U.S. — C4 115
West Linn, Or., U.S. — B4 114
West Loch Roag, b., Scot., U.K. — B1 13
West Loch Tarbert, b., Scot., U.K. — C1 13
West Loch Tarbert, b., Scot., U.K. — E3 13
Westlock, Ab., Can. — B4 68
West Long Branch, N.J., U.S. — C4 107
West Lorne, On., Can. — E3 73
West Louisville, Ky., U.S. — C2 94
West Manchester, Oh., U.S. — C1 112
West Mansfield, Ma., U.S. — B5 98
West Mansfield, Oh., U.S. — B2 112
West Marion, N.C., U.S. — f10 110
Westmeath, On., Can. — B8 73
Westmeath, co., Ire. — D4 11
West Medway, Ma., U.S. — B5 98
West Melbourne, Fl., U.S. — *D6 86
West Memphis, Ar., U.S. — B5 81
Westmere, N.Y., U.S. — *C7 109
West Miami, Fl., U.S. — s13 86
West Middlesex, Pa., U.S. — D1 115
West Middleton, In., U.S. — D5 91
West Midlands, co., Eng., U.K. — *B8 12
West Mifflin, Pa., U.S. — F2 115
West Milan, N.H., U.S. — A4 106
West Milford, N.J., U.S. — A4 107
West Milton, Oh., U.S. — C1 112
West Milton, Pa., U.S. — D8 115
West Milwaukee, Wi., U.S. — m12 126
Westminster (part of London), Eng., U.K. — k12 10
Westminster, Ca., U.S. — n12 82
Westminster, Co., U.S. — B5 83
Westminster, Md., U.S. — A4 97
Westminster, Ma., U.S. — A4 98
Westminster, S.C., U.S. — B1 117
Westminster, Vt., U.S. — E4 122
Westminster West, Vt., U.S. — E3 122
West Modesto, Ca., U.S. — D3 82
West Monroe, La., U.S. — B3 95
Westmont, Ca., U.S. — n12 82
Westmont, Il., U.S. — k9 90
Westmont, N.J., U.S. — D2 107
Westmont, Pa., U.S. — F4 115
West Monterey, Pa., U.S. — D2 115
Westmoreland, Ks., U.S. — C7 93
Westmoreland, N.H., U.S. — E2 106
Westmoreland, Tn., U.S. — A5 119
Westmoreland, co., Pa., U.S. — F2 115
Westmoreland, co., Va., U.S. — B6 123
Westmoreland, Ca., U.S. — F6 82
Westmorland, co., N.B., Can. — C5 71
West Mountain, mtn., N.Y., U.S. — B6 109
West Mountain, mtn., Vt., U.S. — B5 122
West Muncie, In., U.S. — D7 91
West Musquash Lake, l., Me., U.S. — C5 96
West Mystic, Ct., U.S. — D8 84
West Newbury, Ma., U.S. — A6 98
West Newbury, Vt., U.S. — C4 122
West Newfield, Me., U.S. — E2 96
West Newton, Pa., U.S. — F2 115
West Nicholson, Zimb. — h8 107
West Nishnabotna, stm., Ia., U.S. — C2 92
West Norriton, Pa., U.S. — o20 115
West Nottingham, N.H., U.S. — D4 106
West Olive, Mi., U.S. — F7 99
Weston (part of York), On., Can. — m14 73
Weston, Co., U.S. — D6 83
Weston, Ct., U.S. — E2 84
Weston, Id., U.S. — G7 89
Weston, Il., U.S. — C5 90
Weston, Ma., U.S. — g10 98
Weston, Mo., U.S. — B3 102
Weston, Ne., U.S. — C9 104
Weston, Oh., U.S. — A2 112
Weston, Or., U.S. — B8 114
Weston, Vt., U.S. — E3 122

Name	Map Ref	Page
Weston, W.V., U.S.	B4	125
Weston, Wi., U.S.	D4	126
Weston, Wy., U.S.	B7	127
Weston, co., Wy., U.S.	C8	127
Weston-super-Mare, Eng., U.K.	E5	10
West Orange, N.J., U.S.	B4	107
West Ossipee, N.H., U.S.	C4	106
Westover, Al., U.S.	B3	78
Westover, Md., U.S.	D6	97
Westover, Pa., U.S.	E4	115
Westover, Tn., U.S.	B3	119
Westover, W.V., U.S.	B5	125
Westover Air Force Base, mil., Ma., U.S.	B2	98
West Palm Beach, Fl., U.S.	F6	86
West Paris, Me., U.S.	D2	96
West Park, N.Y., U.S.	D7	109
West Paterson, N.J., U.S.	*B4	107
West Pawlet, Vt., U.S.	E2	122
West Pearl, stm., La., U.S.	D6	95
West Pelham, Ma., U.S.	*B2	98
West Pelzer, S.C., U.S.	B3	117
West Pembroke, Me., U.S.	D5	96
West Pensacola, Fl., U.S.	u14	86
West Peoria, Il., U.S.	C4	90
West Peru, Me., U.S.	D2	96
West Peterborough, N.H., U.S.	E3	106
Westphalia, In., U.S.	G3	91
Westphalia, Ks., U.S.	D8	93
Westphalia, Mi., U.S.	F6	99
Westphalia, Mo., U.S.	C5	102
Westphalia, hist reg., F.R.Ger.	C3	18
West Pittsburg, Ca., U.S.	*g9	82
West Pittsburg, Pa., U.S.	E1	115
West Pittston, Pa., U.S.	m17	115
West Plains, Mo., U.S.	E6	102
West Plymouth, N.H., U.S.	E3	106
West Point, Al., U.S.	A3	78
West Point, Ar., U.S.	B4	81
West Point, Ca., U.S.	C3	82
West Point, Ga., U.S.	D1	87
West Point, Il., U.S.	C2	90
Westpoint, In., U.S.	D3	91
West Point, Ia., U.S.	D6	92
West Point, Ky., U.S.	C4	94
West Point, Ms., U.S.	B5	101
West Point, Ne., U.S.	C9	104
West Point, N.Y., U.S.	D7	109
Westpoint, Tn., U.S.	B4	119
West Point, Ut., U.S.	*B3	121
West Point, Va., U.S.	C6	123
West Point, mtn., Ak., U.S.	C11	79
West Point Lake, res., U.S.	C1	87
Westport, Nf., Can.	D3	72
Westport, N.S., Can.	E3	71
Westport, On., Can.	C8	73
Westport, Ire.	D2	10
Westport, N.Z.	N13	51
Westport, Ct., U.S.	E2	84
Westport, In., U.S.	F6	91
Westport, Ky., U.S.	B4	94
Westport, Ma., U.S.	C5	98
Westport, Mn., U.S.	E3	100
Westport, N.H., U.S.	E2	106
Westport, N.Y., U.S.	A7	109
Westport, Or., U.S.	A3	114
Westport, S.D., U.S.	B7	118
Westport, Tn., U.S.	B3	119
Westport, Wa., U.S.	C1	124
Westport Point, Ma., U.S.	C5	98
West Portsmouth, Oh., U.S.	D2	112
West Prairie, stm., Ab., Can.	B2	68
West Pubnico, N.S., Can.	F4	71
West Puente Valley, Ca., U.S.	m13	82
West Quoddy Head, c., Me., U.S.	D6	96
Westray, i., Scot., U.K.	A5	10
Westray Firth, strt., Scot., U.K.	A5	13
West Reading, Pa., U.S.	F10	115
West Redding, Ct., U.S.	D2	84
Westrhauderfehn, F.R.Ger.	A7	17
West Ridge, Ar., U.S.	B5	81
West Rindge, N.H., U.S.	E2	106
West River, Md., U.S.	C4	97
West Road, stm., B.C., Can.	C5	69
West Rumney, N.H., U.S.	C3	106
West Rupert, Vt., U.S.	E2	122
West Rutland, Vt., U.S.	D2	122
West Rye, N.H., U.S.	D5	106
West Sacramento, Ca., U.S.	*C3	82
West Saint Modeste, Nf., Can.	C3	72
West Saint Paul, Mn., U.S.	n12	100
West Salem, Il., U.S.	E5	90
West Salem, Oh., U.S.	B3	112
West Salem, Wi., U.S.	E2	126
West Salt Creek, stm., Co., U.S.	B2	83
West Sayville, N.Y., U.S.	*n15	109
West Scarborough, Me., U.S.	E2	96
West Seneca, N.Y., U.S.	C2	109
West Siberian Lowland, pl., Sov. Un.	C10	29
Westside, Ia., U.S.	B2	92
West Simsbury, Ct., U.S.	B4	84
West Slope, Or., U.S.	g12	114
West Spanish Peak, mtn., Co., U.S.	D6	83
West Spit, spit, Marsh Is.	S18	52
West Springfield, Ma., U.S.	B2	98
West Springfield, N.H., U.S.	E2	106
West Springfield, Va., U.S.	g12	123
West Stafford, Ct., U.S.	B6	84
West Stockbridge, Ma., U.S.	B1	98
West Suffield, Ct., U.S.	B5	84
West Sullivan, Me., U.S.	D4	96
West Sumner, Me., U.S.	D2	96
West Sunbury, Pa., U.S.	D2	115
West Sussex, co., Eng., U.K.	D7	12
West Swanzey, N.H., U.S.	E2	106
West Terre Haute, In., U.S.	F3	91
West-Terschelling, Neth.	A5	17
West Thompson Lake, res., Ct., U.S.	B8	84
West Thornton, N.H., U.S.	C3	106
West Tisbury, Ma., U.S.	D6	98
West Topsham, Vt., U.S.	C4	122
West Townsend, Ma., U.S.	A4	98
West Townshend, Vt., U.S.	E3	122
West Union, Il., U.S.	D6	90
West Union, Ia., U.S.	B5	92
West Union, Oh., U.S.	D2	112
West Union, S.C., U.S.	B1	117
West Union, W.V., U.S.	B4	125
West Unity, Oh., U.S.	A1	112
West University Place, Tx., U.S.	r14	120
West Upton, Ma., U.S.	B4	98
Westvale, N.Y., U.S.	*B4	109
West Valley City, Ut., U.S.	C4	121
West Valley, N.Y., U.S.	C2	109
West Vancouver, B.C., Can.	f12	69
West Van Lear, Ky., U.S.	C7	94
West View, Pa., U.S.	h13	115
Westville, N.S., Can.	D7	71
Westville, Fl., U.S.	u16	86
Westville, Il., U.S.	C6	90
Westville, In., U.S.	A4	91
Westville, N.H., U.S.	E4	106
Westville, N.J., U.S.	D2	107
Westville, Ok., U.S.	A7	113
Westville, Pa., U.S.	D4	115
Westville, S.C., U.S.	C6	117
Westville Lake, res., Ma., U.S.	B3	98
West Walker, stm., U.S.	E2	105
West Wardsboro, Vt., U.S.	E3	122
West Wareham, Ma., U.S.	C6	98
West Warren, Ma., U.S.	B3	98
West Warwick, R.I., U.S.	C4	116
West Webster, N.Y., U.S.	*B3	109
Westwego, La., U.S.	k11	95
West Whittier, Ca., U.S.	*n12	82
West Willington, Ct., U.S.	B6	84
West Wilton, N.H., U.S.	E3	106
West Winfield, N.Y., U.S.	C5	109
West Winfield, Pa., U.S.	E2	115
Westwood, B.C., Can.	D8	69
Westwood, Ca., U.S.	B3	82
Westwood, Ks., U.S.	k16	93
Westwood, Ky., U.S.	B7	94
Westwood, Ma., U.S.	B5	98
Westwood, Mi., U.S.	*F5	99
Westwood, N.J., U.S.	B4	107
West Woodstock, Vt., U.S.	D3	122
West Wyalong, Austl.	F8	50
West Wyoming, Austl.	n17	115
West Yarmouth, Ma., U.S.	C7	98
West York, Il., U.S.	D6	90
West York, Pa., U.S.	G8	115
West Yorkshire, co., Eng., U.K.	*G7	13
Wetar, i., Indon.	G7	34
Wetaskiwin, Ab., Can.	C4	68
Wete, Tan.	C6	48
Wethersfield, Ct., U.S.	C5	84
Wetmore, Co., U.S.	C5	83
Wetmore, Ks., U.S.	C8	93
Wetmore, Mi., U.S.	B4	99
Wetmore, Or., U.S.	C7	114
Wet Mountains, mts., Co., U.S.	C5	83
Wetonka, S.D., U.S.	B7	118
Wettingen, Switz.	B4	20
Wetumka, Ok., U.S.	B5	113
Wetumpka, Al., U.S.	C3	78
Wetzel, co., W.V., U.S.	B4	125
Wetzlar, F.R.Ger.	C4	18
Wevelgem, Bel.	D3	17
Wever, Ia., U.S.	D6	92
Wewak, Pap. N. Gui.	h11	50
Wewahitchka, Fl., U.S.	B1	86
Wewela, S.D., U.S.	D6	118
Wewoka, Ok., U.S.	B5	113
Wexford, Ire.	D3	10
Wexford, co., Ire.	E5	11
Wexford, co., Mi., U.S.	D5	99
Wexford Bay, b., Ire.	E5	11
Weyakwin Lake, l., Sk., Can.	C3	75
Weyanoke, La., U.S.	D4	95
Weyauwega, Wi., U.S.	D5	126
Weybridge, Eng., U.K.	m12	10
Weyburn, Sk., Can.	H4	75
Weyerhaeuser, Wi., U.S.	C2	126
Weyers Cave, Va., U.S.	B4	123
Weymouth, N.S., Can.	E4	71
Weymouth, Ma., U.S.	B6	98
Weymouth, Eng., U.K.	E5	10
Weymouth [and Melcombe Regis], Eng., U.K.	E5	10
Weymouth Bay, b., Eng., U.K.	D5	12
Whakatane, N.Z.	L16	51
Whalan, Mn., U.S.	G7	100
Whales, Bay of, b., Ant.	B32	7
Whaleysville, Md., U.S.	D7	97
Whalom, Ma., U.S.	A4	98
Whangarei, N.Z.	K15	51
Wharfe, stm., Eng., U.K.	D6	10
Wharton, N.J., U.S.	B3	107
Wharton, Oh., U.S.	B2	112
Wharton, Tx., U.S.	E4	120
Wharton, W.V., U.S.	n12	125
Wharton, co., Tx., U.S.	E4	120
Wharton, N.Z.	O13	51
What Cheer, Ia., U.S.	C5	92
Whatcom, co., Wa., U.S.	A4	124
Whatcom, Lake, l., Wa., U.S.	A3	124
Whately, Al., U.S.	D2	78
Whatcroft, Ky., U.S.	C2	94
Wheatfield, In., U.S.	B3	91
Wheatland, Ca., U.S.	C3	82
Wheatland, In., U.S.	G3	91
Wheatland, Ia., U.S.	C7	92
Wheatland, Mo., U.S.	D4	102
Wheatland, N.D., U.S.	C8	111
Wheatland, Pa., U.S.	D1	115
Wheatland, Wy., U.S.	D7	127
Wheatland, co., Mt., U.S.	D7	103
Wheatland Reservoir, res., Wy., U.S.	E7	127
Wheatley, On., Can.	E2	73
Wheatley, Ar., U.S.	C4	81
Wheaton, Il., U.S.	B5	90
Wheaton, Md., U.S.	C7	97
Wheaton, Mn., U.S.	E2	100
Wheaton, Mo., U.S.	E3	102
Wheat Ridge, Co., U.S.	B5	83
Wheelbarrow Peak, mtn., Nv., U.S.	F5	105
Wheeler, Ar., U.S.	A1	81
Wheeler, In., U.S.	B3	91
Wheeler, Ks., U.S.	C2	93
Wheeler, Ms., U.S.	A5	101
Wheeler, Or., U.S.	B3	114
Wheeler, Tx., U.S.	B2	120
Wheeler, Wi., U.S.	D2	126
Wheeler, co., Ga., U.S.	D4	87
Wheeler, co., Ne., U.S.	C7	104
Wheeler, co., Or., U.S.	C6	114
Wheeler, co., Tx., U.S.	B2	120
Wheeler Air Force Base, mil., Hi., U.S.	g9	88
Wheeler Dam, Al., U.S.	A2	78
Wheeler Lake, res., Al., U.S.	A2	78
Wheeler Peak, mtn., Nv., U.S.	E7	105
Wheeler Peak, mtn., N.M., U.S.	A4	108
Wheelersburg, Oh., U.S.	D3	112
Wheeling, Il., U.S.	h9	90
Wheeling, Mo., U.S.	B4	102
Wheeling, W.V., U.S.	A4	125
Wheeling Creek, stm., W.V., U.S.	f8	125
Wheelock, N.D., U.S.	A2	111
Wheelock, Tx., U.S.	D4	120
Wheelock Mountain, mtn., Vt., U.S.	B4	122
Wheelockville, Ma., U.S.	*B4	98
Wheelon, Ut., U.S.	*B3	121
Wheelwright, Ky., U.S.	C7	94
Wheelwright, Ma., U.S.	B3	98
Whelen Springs, Ar., U.S.	D2	81
Whernside, mtn., Eng., U.K.	F6	13
Whetstone, stm., U.S.	E2	100
Whickham, Eng., U.K.	F7	13
Whidbey Island, i., Wa., U.S.	A3	124
Whidbey Island Naval Air Station, mil., Wa., U.S.	A3	124
Whigham, Ga., U.S.	F2	87
Whigville, Ct., U.S.	C4	84
Whipholt, Mn., U.S.	C4	100
Whipple, W.V., U.S.	n13	125
Whiskey Gap, Ab., Can.	E4	68
Whiskey Peak, mtn., Wy., U.S.	D5	127
Whiskeytown-Shasta-Trinity National Recreation Area, Ca., U.S.	B2	82
Whisky Chitto Creek, stm., La., U.S.	C2	95
Whitacres, Ct., U.S.	A5	84
Whitakers, N.C., U.S.	A5	110
Whitbourne, Nf., Can.	E5	72
Whitby, On., Can.	D6	73
Whitby, Eng., U.K.	C6	10
Whitchurch, Eng., U.K.	B5	12
Whitchurch-Stouffville, On., Can.	D5	73
Whitcombe, Mount, mtn., N.Z.	O13	51
Whitcomb Mountain, mtn., U.S.	A4	106
White, Ga., U.S.	B2	87
White, S.D., U.S.	C9	118
White, co., Ar., U.S.	B4	81
White, co., Ga., U.S.	B3	87
White, co., Il., U.S.	E5	90
White, co., In., U.S.	C4	91
White, co., Tn., U.S.	D8	119
White, stm., B.C., Can.	D3	68
White, stm., U.S.	C4	81
White, stm., U.S.	D5	118
White, stm., U.S.	C7	121
White, stm., Az., U.S.	D5	80
White, stm., In., U.S.	H2	91
White, stm., Mi., U.S.	E4	99
White, stm., Nv., U.S.	E6	105
White, stm., Vt., U.S.	D4	122
White, stm., Wa., U.S.	B5	124
White, East Fork, stm., In., U.S.	G5	91
White, Lake, l., Austl.	D4	50
White Bay, b., Nf., Can.	D3	72
White Bear, Sk., Can.	G1	75
White Bear, stm., Nf., Can.	B3	72
White Bear Islands, is., Nf., Can.	A3	72
White Bear Lake, Mn., U.S.	E5	100
White Bear Lake, l., Nf., Can.	A2	72
White Bear Lake, l., Sk., Can.	H4	75
White Bird, Id., U.S.	D2	89
White Bluff, Tn., U.S.	A4	119
White Breast Creek, stm., Ia., U.S.	C4	92
White Butte, mtn., N.D., U.S.	C2	111
White Cap Mountain, mtn., Me., U.S.	C3	96
White Carpathians, mts., Czech.	D4	26
White Castle, La., U.S.	D4	95
White Center, Wa., U.S.	e11	124
White City, Fl., U.S.	C1	86
White City, Ks., U.S.	D7	93
White City, Or., U.S.	E4	114
White City, Ut., U.S.	C4	121
Whiteclay, Ne., U.S.	B3	104
White Clay Creek, stm., U.S.	A3	104
White Clay Creek, stm., De., U.S.	B3	85
White Cliffs, Austl.	E4	51
White Cloud, Ks., U.S.	C8	93
White Cloud, Mi., U.S.	E5	99
White Coomb, mtn., Scot., U.K.	C5	10
Whitecourt, Ab., Can.	B3	68
White Creek, stm., Vt., U.S.	E2	122
Whiteday, stm., W.V., U.S.	h10	125
White Deer, Pa., U.S.	D8	115
White Deer, Tx., U.S.	B2	120
White Earth, Mn., U.S.	C3	100
White Earth, N.D., U.S.	A3	111
White Earth Indian Reservation, Mn., U.S.	C3	100
White Earth Lake, l., Mn., U.S.	C3	100
Whiteface, Tx., U.S.	C1	120
Whiteface, stm., Mn., U.S.	C6	100
Whiteface Mountain, mtn., N.Y., U.S.	f10	109
White Face Mountain, mtn., Vt., U.S.	B3	122
Whitefield, Me., U.S.	*D3	96
Whitefield, N.H., U.S.	B3	106
Whitefield, Ok., U.S.	B6	113
Whitefish, Mt., U.S.	B2	103
Whitefish Bay, Wi., U.S.	m12	126
Whitefish Bay, b., Mi., U.S.	B6	99
Whitefish Falls, On., Can.	A3	73
Whitefish Lake, l., Ab., Can.	B4	68
Whitefish Lake, l., Mn., U.S.	D4	100
Whitefish Point, Mi., U.S.	B6	99
Whitefish Range, mts., Mt., U.S.	B2	103
Whiteford, Md., U.S.	A5	97
White Fox, Sk., Can.	D3	75
White Fox, stm., Sk., Can.	D3	75
White Gull Creek, stm., Sk., Can.	D3	75
White Hall, Ar., U.S.	C3	81
White Hall, Ga., U.S.	*C3	87
Whitehall, Il., U.S.	D3	90
White Hall, Md., U.S.	A4	97
Whitehall, Mi., U.S.	E4	99
Whitehall, Mt., U.S.	D4	103
Whitehall, N.Y., U.S.	B7	109
Whitehall, Oh., U.S.	m11	112
Whitehall, Pa., U.S.	*k14	115
Whitehall, S.C., U.S.	F6	117
Whitehall, Wi., U.S.	D2	126
Whitehall Reservoir, res., Ma., U.S.	h9	98
Whitehaven, Md., U.S.	D6	97
White Haven, Pa., U.S.	D10	115
Whitehead, N. Ire., U.K.	C6	11
Whitehorn, Point, c., Wa., U.S.	A3	124
White Horse, N.J., U.S.	C3	107
Whitehorse, S.D., U.S.	B5	118
Whitehorse, Yk., Can.	D5	66
White Horse Beach, Ma., U.S.	C6	98
Whitehouse, Scot., U.K.	C6	13
Whitehouse, Oh., U.S.	A2	112
White House, Tn., U.S.	A5	119
White House Station, N.J., U.S.	B3	107
White Island, i., Ant.	f38	7
White Island, i., Ant.	C17	7
White Island Shores, Ma., U.S.	C6	98
White Knob Mountains, mts., Id., U.S.	F5	89
White Lake, On., Can.	B8	73
White Lake, S.D., U.S.	D7	118
White Lake, Wi., U.S.	C5	126
White Lake, l., On., Can.	B8	73
White Lake, l., La., U.S.	E3	95
Whitelaw, Can.	A1	68
Whitelaw, Wi., U.S.	h10	126
Whiteman Air Force Base, mil., Mo., U.S.	C4	102
White Meadow Lake, N.J., U.S.	B3	107
White Mesa Natural Bridge, Az., U.S.	A4	80
White Mills, Pa., U.S.	C11	115
White Mountain, Ak., U.S.	C7	79
White Mountain Peak, mtn., Ca., U.S.	D4	82
White Mountains, mts., Ca., U.S.	D4	82
White Mountains, mts., N.H., U.S.	B3	106
White Oak, Ga., U.S.	E5	87
White Oak, N.C., U.S.	C4	110
White Oak, Oh., U.S.	o12	112
White Oak, Ok., U.S.	A6	113
White Oak, Pa., U.S.	*k14	115
White Oak, S.C., U.S.	C5	117
White Oak Creek, stm., Oh., U.S.	D2	112
Whiteoak Creek, stm., Tn., U.S.	A4	119
White Oak Lake, res., Ar., U.S.	D2	81
White Oak Mountain, mtn., Ar., U.S.	C2	81
White Owl, S.D., U.S.	C3	118
White Pass, N.A.	D12	79
White Pigeon, Mi., U.S.	G5	99
White Pine, Mi., U.S.	m12	99
White Pine, Tn., U.S.	C10	119
White Pine, co., Nv., U.S.	D6	105
White Plains, Al., U.S.	B4	78
White Plains, Ga., U.S.	C3	87
White Plains, Ky., U.S.	C2	94
White Plains, Md., U.S.	C4	97
White Plains, N.Y., U.S.	D7	109
White Plains, N.C., U.S.	A2	110
White Pond, S.C., U.S.	E5	117
Whiteriver, Az., U.S.	D6	80
White River, S.D., U.S.	D5	118
White River Plateau, plat., Co., U.S.	B3	83
White Rock, B.C., Can.	E6	69
White Rock, R.I., U.S.	F1	116
White Rock, S.C., U.S.	C5	117
White Rock Creek, stm., Ks., U.S.	C5	93
Whiterocks, Ut., U.S.	C6	121
White Rocks, mtn., Ky., U.S.	C6	94
Whites, Ms., U.S.	B5	101
Whitesail Lake, l., B.C., Can.	C4	69
White Salmon, Wa., U.S.	D4	124
White Salmon, stm., Wa., U.S.	D4	124
Whitesand, stm., Sk., Can.	F4	75
Whitesand Bay, b., Eng., U.K.	D3	12
White Sands Missile Range, mil., N.M., U.S.	E3	108
White Sands National Monument, N.M., U.S.	E3	108
Whitesboro, N.J., U.S.	E3	107
Whitesboro, N.Y., U.S.	B5	109
Whitesboro, Tx., U.S.	C4	120
Whites Brook, N.B., Can.	B2	71
Whitesburg, Ga., U.S.	C2	87
Whitesburg, Ky., U.S.	C7	94
Whites City, N.M., U.S.	E5	108
Whites Creek, stm., Tn., U.S.	g10	119
White Sea, Sov. Un.	C5	91
White Settlement, Tx., U.S.	*n9	120
Whiteshell Provincial Park, Mb., Can.	D4	70
Whiteside, Mo., U.S.	C6	102
Whiteside, co., Il., U.S.	B3	90
Whiteson, Or., U.S.	B3	114
Whitestone, Va., U.S.	C6	123
White Stone, Va., U.S.	C6	123
White Stone Lake, l., Mb., Can.	A3	70
Whitestown, In., U.S.	E5	91
White Sulphur Springs, Mt., U.S.	D6	103
White Sulphur Springs, W.V., U.S.	D4	125
Whitesville, De., U.S.	G4	85
Whitesville, Ky., U.S.	C3	94
Whitesville, N.Y., U.S.	C3	109
Whitetail, Mt., U.S.	B11	103
White Tank Mountains, mts., Az., U.S.	k7	80
White Volta, stm., Afr.	D4	45
Whitewater, Mb., Can.	E1	70
Whitewater, Ks., U.S.	E6	93
Whitewater, Mo., U.S.	D8	102
Whitewater, Wi., U.S.	F5	126
Whitewater, stm., U.S.	F7	91
Whitewater, stm., Ks., U.S.	E6	93
Whitewater, East Fork, stm., U.S.	E8	91
Whitewater Baldy, mtn., N.M., U.S.	D1	108
Whitewater Bay, b., Fl., U.S.	G6	86
White Woman Creek, stm., Ks., U.S.	D2	93
Whitewood, Sk., Can.	G4	75
Whitewood, S.D., U.S.	C2	118
Whitewright, Tx., U.S.	C4	120
Whitfield, Al., U.S.	C1	78
Whitfield, co., Ga., U.S.	B2	87
Whitfield Estates, Fl., U.S.	q10	86
Whithorn, Scot., U.K.	B4	10
Whiting, In., U.S.	A3	91
Whiting, Ia., U.S.	B1	92
Whiting, Ks., U.S.	C8	93
Whiting, Me., U.S.	D5	96
Whiting, N.J., U.S.	D4	107
Whiting, Vt., U.S.	D2	122
Whiting, Wi., U.S.	D4	126
Whiting Bay, Scot., U.K.	E3	13
Whiting Field Naval Air Station, mil., Fl., U.S.	u14	86
Whitingham, Vt., U.S.	F3	122
Whitinsville, Ma., U.S.	B4	98
Whitkow, Sk., Can.	E2	75
Whitla, Ab., Can.	E5	68
Whitlash, Mt., U.S.	B5	103
Whitley, co., In., U.S.	B6	91
Whitley, co., Ky., U.S.	D5	94
Whitley City, Ky., U.S.	D5	94
Whitlock, Ky., U.S.	D4	82
Whitman, Ma., U.S.	B6	98
Whitman, Ne., U.S.	B4	104
Whitman, N.D., U.S.	A7	111
Whitman, W.V., U.S.	D2	125
Whitman, co., Wa., U.S.	B8	124
Whitmans Pond, l., Ma., U.S.	h12	98
Whitmell, Va., U.S.	D3	123
Whitmer, W.V., U.S.	C5	125
Whitmire, S.C., U.S.	B4	117
Whitmore Lake, Mi., U.S.	p14	99
Whitmore Mountains, mts., Ant.	A2	7
Whitmore Village, Hi., U.S.	f9	88
Whitney, On., Can.	B6	73
Whitney, Id., U.S.	G7	89
Whitney, Pa., U.S.	F3	115
Whitney, S.C., U.S.	B4	117
Whitney, Tx., U.S.	D4	120
Whitney, Lake, res., Tx., U.S.	D4	120
Whitney, Mount, mtn., Ca., U.S.	D4	82
Whitney Point, N.Y., U.S.	C5	109
Whitney Point Lake, res., N.Y., U.S.	C5	109
Whitneyville, Me., U.S.	D5	96
Whitsett, N.C., U.S.	A3	110
Whitstable, Eng., U.K.	C9	12
Whitt, Tx., U.S.	C3	120
Whittemore, Ia., U.S.	A3	92
Whittemore, Mi., U.S.	D7	99
Whitten, Ia., U.S.	B4	92
Whittier, Ak., U.S.	C10	79
Whittier, Ca., U.S.	F4	82
Whittier, N.H., U.S.	C4	106
Whittier, N.C., U.S.	f9	110
Whittlesey, Eng., U.K.	B7	12
Whittlesey, Mount, hill, Wi., U.S.	B3	126
Whitwell, Tn., U.S.	D8	119
Wholdaia Lake, l., N.T., Can.	D12	66
Whonnock, B.C., Can.	f13	69
Whyalla, Austl.	F6	50
Whycocomagh, N.S., Can.	D8	71
Wiau Lake, l., Ab., Can.	B5	68
Wiawso, Ghana	E4	45
Wiay, i., Scot., U.K.	C1	13
Wibaux, Mt., U.S.	D12	103
Wibaux, co., Mt., U.S.	D12	103
Wiborg, Sk., Can.	G3	75
Wichita, Ks., U.S.	E6	93
Wichita, co., Ks., U.S.	D2	93
Wichita, co., Tx., U.S.	B3	120
Wichita Falls, Tx., U.S.	C3	120
Wichita Mountains, mts., Ok., U.S.	C3	113
Wick, Scot., U.K.	A5	10
Wickatunk, N.J., U.S.	C4	107
Wickenburg, Az., U.S.	C3	80
Wickes, Ar., U.S.	C1	81
Wickett, Tx., U.S.	D1	120
Wickham, P.Q., Can.	D5	74
Wickiup Reservoir, res., Or., U.S.	D5	114
Wickliffe, Ky., U.S.	f8	94
Wickliffe, Oh., U.S.	*A5	112
Wicklow, Ire.	E6	11
Wicklow, co., Ire.	E5	11
Wicklow Head, c., Ire.	E6	11
Wicklow Mountains, mts., Ire.	D5	10
Wicomico, co., Md., U.S.	D6	97
Wicomico, stm., Md., U.S.	D6	97
Wiconisco, Pa., U.S.	E8	115
Widefield, Co., U.S.	C6	83
Widen, W.V., U.S.	C4	125
Widener, Ar., U.S.	B5	81
Widerøe, Mount, mtn., Ant.	B15	7
Wide Ruins, Az., U.S.	B6	80
Widnes, Eng., U.K.	A5	12
Widuchowa, Pol.	B4	26
Wiebelskirchen, F.R.Ger.	D2	19
Wieliczka, Pol.	C5	26
Wieluń, Pol.	C5	26
Wiener Neustadt, Aus.	C8	18
Wieprz, stm., Pol.	C7	26
Wieprza, stm., Pol.	h10	26
Wiergate, Tx., U.S.	D6	120
Wiesau, F.R.Ger.	E8	19
Wiesbaden, F.R.Ger.	C4	18
Wiese, stm., F.R.Ger.	A4	21
Wiesenburg, Ger.D.R.	A7	19
Wiesental, F.R.Ger.	D3	19
Wiesloch, F.R.Ger.	D3	19
Wiggins, Co., U.S.	A6	83
Wiggins, Ms., U.S.	E4	101
Wiggins Peak, mtn., Wy., U.S.	C3	127
Wight, Isle of, i., Eng., U.K.	E6	10
Wigston, Eng., U.K.	I11	13
Wigtown, Scot., U.K.	G4	13
Wigtown Bay, b., Scot., U.K.	G4	13
Wijhe, Neth.	B6	17
Wikieup, Az., U.S.	C2	80
Wikwemikong, On., Can.	B3	73
Wil, Switz.	B5	20
Wilbar, N.C., U.S.	A1	110
Wilbarger, co., Tx., U.S.	B3	120
Wilber, Ne., U.S.	D9	104
Wilberforce, On., Can.	B6	73
Wilberforce, Oh., U.S.	C2	112
Wilbraham, Ma., U.S.	B3	98
Wilbur, Or., U.S.	D3	114
Wilbur, Wa., U.S.	B7	124
Wilburn, Ar., U.S.	B4	81
Wilburton, Ok., U.S.	C6	113
Wilcannia, Austl.	F7	50
Wilcox, Sk., Can.	G3	75
Wilcox, Ne., U.S.	D6	104
Wilcox, Pa., U.S.	C4	115
Wilcox, co., Al., U.S.	D2	78
Wilcox, co., Ga., U.S.	E3	87
Wilcox, Mount, mtn., Ma., U.S.	B1	98
Wilczek, i., Sov. Un.	A8	128
Wild, stm., U.S.	B4	106
Wild Ammonoosuc, stm., N.H., U.S.	B3	106
Wildbad [im Schwarzwald], F.R.Ger.	E3	19
Wild Branch, stm., Vt., U.S.	B4	122
Wildcat Creek, stm., In., U.S.	D4	91
Wildcat Creek, South Fork, stm., In., U.S.	D4	91
Wildcat Hill, hill, Can.	D4	75
Wildcat Top, mtn., Tn., U.S.	D10	119
Wilder, Id., U.S.	F2	89
Wilder, Vt., U.S.	D4	122
Wilder Dam, U.S.	C2	106
Wildersville, Tn., U.S.	B3	119
Wildervank (part of Veendam), Neth.	A7	16
Wildeshausen, F.R.Ger.	F2	15
Wildhaus, Switz.	B7	21
Wildhay, stm., Ab., Can.	C2	68
Wildhorn, mtn., Switz.	D3	21
Wild Horse, Co., U.S.	C7	83
Wildhorse Creek, stm., Ok., U.S.	C4	113
Wild Horse Reservoir, res., Nv., U.S.	B6	105
Wildest Lake, l., Sk., Can.	C4	75
Wildorado, Tx., U.S.	B1	120
Wild Rice, stm., N.D., U.S.	C8	111
Wild Rice, South Branch, stm., Mn., U.S.	C2	100
Wildrose, N.D., U.S.	A2	111
Wild Rose, Wi., U.S.	D4	126
Wildspitze, mtn., Aus.	C6	20
Wildsville, La., U.S.	C4	95
Wildwood, Ab., Can.	C3	68
Wildwood, Fl., U.S.	D4	86
Wildwood, Il., U.S.	h9	90
Wildwood, N.J., U.S.	F3	107
Wildwood, Ut., U.S.	*C4	121
Wildwood Crest, N.J., U.S.	F3	107
Wiley, Co., U.S.	C8	83
Wiley, Wa., U.S.	C5	124
Wilhelm, Mount, mtn., Pap. N. Gui.	k12	50
Wilhelmina Gebergte, mts., Sur.	B3	59
Wilhelm-Pieck-Stadt Guben, Ger.D.R.	C7	18
Wilhelmshaven, F.R.Ger.	B4	18
Wilhoit, Az., U.S.	C3	80
Wilkau [-Hasslau], Ger.D.R.	C7	19
Wilkes, co., Ga., U.S.	C4	87
Wilkes, co., N.C., U.S.	A1	110
Wilkes-Barre, Pa., U.S.	D10	115
Wilkesboro, N.C., U.S.	A1	110
Wilkes Island, i., Wake I.	A1	52
Wilkes Land, reg., Ant.	B25	7
Wilkeson, Wa., U.S.	B3	124
Wilkesville, Oh., U.S.	C3	112
Wilkie, Sk., Can.	E1	75
Wilkin, co., Mn., U.S.	D2	100
Wilkinsburg, Pa., U.S.	F2	115
Wilkinson, In., U.S.	E6	91
Wilkinson, Ms., U.S.	D2	101
Wilkinson, W.V., U.S.	D3	125
Wilkinson, co., Ga., U.S.	D3	87
Wilkinson, co., Ms., U.S.	D2	101
Wilkins Sound, strt., Ant.	B5	7
Will, co., Il., U.S.	B6	90
Willacoochee, Ga., U.S.	E3	87
Willacy, co., Tx., U.S.	F4	120
Willamette, stm., Or., U.S.	C3	114
Willamette, Middle Fork, stm., Or., U.S.	D4	114
Willamette Pass, Or., U.S.	D4	114
Willamina, Or., U.S.	B3	114
Willangee, Austl.	E3	51
Willapa, Wa., U.S.	C2	124
Willapa Bay, b., Wa., U.S.	C1	124
Willard, Ks., U.S.	C8	93
Willard, Mo., U.S.	D4	102
Willard, N.M., U.S.	C3	108
Willard, N.Y., U.S.	C4	109
Willard, N.C., U.S.	C5	110
Willard, Oh., U.S.	A3	112
Willard, Ut., U.S.	B3	121
Willard Bay, b., Ut., U.S.	B3	121
Willards, Md., U.S.	D7	97
Willard Stream, stm., Vt., U.S.	B4	122
Willcox, Az., U.S.	E6	80
Willcox Playa, l., Az., U.S.	E5	80
Willemstad, Neth. Ant.	H19	57
Willet, N.Y., U.S.	C5	109
Willette, Tn., U.S.	C8	119
William "Bill" Dannelly Reservoir, res., Al., U.S.	C2	78
William P. Lane, Jr. Memorial Bridge, Md., U.S.	C5	97
Williams, Az., U.S.	B3	80
Williams, In., U.S.	G4	91
Williams, Mn., U.S.	B4	100
Williams, co., N.D., U.S.	A2	111
Williams, co., Oh., U.S.	A1	112
Williams, stm., Vt., U.S.	E3	122
Williams, stm., W.V., U.S.	C4	125
Williams, Cape, c., Ant.	B29	7
Williams Air Force Base, mil., Az., U.S.	D4	80
Williams Bay, Wi., U.S.	F5	126
Williamsburg, In., U.S.	E8	91
Williamsburg, Co.,	*C5	83
Williamsburg, Ia., U.S.	C5	92
Williamsburg, Ks., U.S.	D8	93
Williamsburg, Ky., U.S.	D5	94
Williamsburg, Md., U.S.	C6	97

Index

Name	Map Ref	Page
Williamsburg, Ma., U.S.	B2	98
Williamsburg, Mi., U.S.	D5	99
Williamsburg, N.M., U.S.	D2	108
Williamsburg, Oh., U.S.	C1	112
Williamsburg, Va., U.S.	F5	115
Williamsburg, Va., U.S.	C6	123
Williamsburg, W.V., U.S.	D4	125
Williamsburg, co., S.C., U.S.	D8	117
Williamsfield, Il., U.S.	C3	90
Williams Fork, stm., Co., U.S.	A3	83
Williams Lake, B.C., Can.	C6	69
Williams Mountain, mtn., Ok., U.S.	C7	113
Williamson, Ga., U.S.	C2	87
Williamson, Ia., U.S.	C4	92
Williamson, N.Y., U.S.	B3	109
Williamson, W.V., U.S.	D2	125
Williamson, co., Il., U.S.	F4	90
Williamson, co., Tn., U.S.	B5	119
Williamson, co., Tx., U.S.	D4	120
Williamson, Mount, mtn., Ca., U.S.	*D4	82
Williamson Head, c., Ant.	C28	7
Williamsport, Nf., Can.	C3	72
Williamsport, In., U.S.	D3	91
Williamsport, Md., U.S.	A2	97
Williamsport, Oh., U.S.	C2	112
Williamsport, Pa., U.S.	D7	115
Williamsport, Tn., U.S.	B4	119
Williamston, Mi., U.S.	F6	99
Williamston, N.C., U.S.	B5	110
Williamston, S.C., U.S.	B3	117
Williamstown, On., Can.	B10	73
Williamstown, Ks., U.S.	k15	93
Williamstown, Ky., U.S.	B5	94
Williamstown, Ma., U.S.	A1	98
Williamstown, Mo., U.S.	A6	102
Williamstown, N.J., U.S.	D3	107
Williamstown, N.Y., U.S.	B5	109
Williamstown, Oh., U.S.	B2	112
Williamstown, Pa., U.S.	E8	115
Williamstown, Vt., U.S.	C3	122
Williamstown, W.V., U.S.	B3	125
Williamsville, De., U.S.	G5	85
Williamsville, Il., U.S.	D4	90
Williamsville, Ms., U.S.	B4	101
Williamsville, Mo., U.S.	E7	102
Williamsville, N.Y., U.S.	C2	109
Williamsville, Vt., U.S.	F3	122
Williford, Ar., U.S.	A4	81
Willimantic, Ct., U.S.	C7	84
Willimantic, stm., Ct., U.S.	B6	84
Willimantic Reservoir, res., Ct., U.S.	C7	84
Willingboro, N.J., U.S.	C3	107
Willingdon, Ab., Can.	C4	68
Willis, Ks., U.S.	C8	93
Willis, Mi., U.S.	p14	99
Willis, Tx., U.S.	D5	120
Willis, Va., U.S.	D2	123
Willisburg, Ky., U.S.	C4	94
Willis Island, i., Nf., Can.	D3	49
Williston, S. Afr.	E4	44
Williston, Fl., U.S.	C4	86
Williston, N.C., U.S.	C6	110
Williston, N.D., U.S.	A2	111
Williston, S.C., U.S.	E5	117
Williston, Tn., U.S.	B2	119
Williston, Vt., U.S.	C2	122
Williston Basin, U.S.	B2	111
Williston Lake, res., B.C., Can.	B6	69
Williston Park, N.Y., U.S.	*E7	109
Willisville, Ar., U.S.	D2	81
Willisville, Il., U.S.	F4	90
Willis Wharf, Va., U.S.	C7	123
Willits, Ca., U.S.	C2	82
Willmar, Sk., Can.	H4	75
Willmar, Mn., U.S.	E3	100
Willmore Wilderness Provincial Park, Ab., Can.	C1	68
Willoughby, Austl.	*F9	50
Willoughby, Oh., U.S.	A4	112
Willoughby, Lake, l., Vt., U.S.	B4	122
Willoughby Hills, Oh., U.S.	A4	112
Willow, Ak., U.S.	g17	79
Willow, Ar., U.S.	C3	81
Willow, Ok., U.S.	B2	113
Willow, stm., B.C., Can.	C6	69
Willow Branch, In., U.S.	E6	91
Willowbrook, Sk., Can.	F4	75
Willow Brook, Ca., U.S.	*n12	82
Willow Bunch, Sk., Can.	H3	75
Willow Bunch Lake, l., Sk., Can.	H3	75
Willow City, N.D., U.S.	A5	111
Willow City, Tx., U.S.	D3	120
Willow Creek, Mt., U.S.	E5	103
Willow Creek, stm., Ab., Can.	D4	68
Willow Creek, stm., Nv., U.S.	E5	105
Willow Creek, stm., Ut., U.S.	D6	121
Willow Creek, stm., Wy., U.S.	C6	127
Willow Glen, La., U.S.	C3	95
Willow Grove, De., U.S.	D3	85
Willow Grove, Pa., U.S.	F11	115
Willow Grove Naval Air Station, mil., Pa., U.S.	F11	115
Willow Hill, Il., U.S.	E5	90
Willow Hill, Pa., U.S.	F6	115
Willowick, Oh., U.S.	A4	112
Willow Island, Ne., U.S.	D5	104
Willow Lake, S.D., U.S.	C8	118
Willowmore, S. Afr.	D3	49
Willow Reservoir, res., Wi., U.S.	C3	126
Willow River, B.C., Can.	B6	69
Willow River, Mn., U.S.	D6	100
Willow Run, De., U.S.	i7	85
Willow Run, Mi., U.S.	p14	99
Willows, Sk., Can.	H3	75
Willows, Ca., U.S.	C2	82
Willow Springs, Il., U.S.	k9	90
Willow Springs, Mo., U.S.	E6	102
Willsboro, N.Y., U.S.	f11	109
Wills Hill, hill, Ma., U.S.	f11	98
Willshire, Oh., U.S.	B1	112
Wills Mountain, mtn., U.S.	k13	97
Wilston, Va., U.S.	B5	123
Wilmar, Ar., U.S.	D4	81
Wilmer, Al., U.S.	E1	78
Wilmer, Tx., U.S.	n10	120
Wilmerding, Pa., U.S.	k14	115
Wilmersdorf, Ger.D.R.	E7	15
Wilmette, Il., U.S.	A6	90
Wilmington, Austl.	F2	51
Wilmington, De., U.S.	B3	85
Wilmington, Il., U.S.	B5	90
Wilmington, Ma., U.S.	A5	98
Wilmington, N.Y., U.S.	f11	109
Wilmington, N.C., U.S.	C5	110
Wilmington, Oh., U.S.	C2	112
Wilmington, Vt., U.S.	F3	122
Wilmington Manor, De., U.S.	i7	85
Wilmington Manor Gardens, De., U.S.	*B3	85
Wilmont, Mn., U.S.	G3	100
Wilmore, Ks., U.S.	E4	93
Wilmore, Ky., U.S.	C5	94
Wilmot, N.S., Can.	E4	71
Wilmot, Ar., U.S.	D4	81
Wilmot, In., U.S.	B6	91
Wilmot, Ks., U.S.	E7	93
Wilmot, Oh., U.S.	B4	112
Wilmot, S.D., U.S.	B9	118
Wilmot Flat, N.H., U.S.	D3	106
Wilno, On., Can.	B7	73
Wilsall, Mt., U.S.	E6	103
Wilsey, Ks., U.S.	D7	93
Wilson, Ar., U.S.	B5	81
Wilson, Ks., U.S.	D5	93
Wilson, La., U.S.	D4	95
Wilson, Mi., U.S.	C3	99
Wilson, N.Y., U.S.	B2	109
Wilson, N.C., U.S.	B5	110
Wilson, Ok., U.S.	C4	113
Wilson, Pa., U.S.	E11	115
Wilson, Tx., U.S.	C2	120
Wilson, Ut., U.S.	B3	121
Wilson, Wy., U.S.	C2	127
Wilson, co., Ks., U.S.	E8	93
Wilson, co., N.C., U.S.	C2	110
Wilson, co., Tn., U.S.	A5	119
Wilson, co., Tx., U.S.	E3	120
Wilson, stm., Austl.	C4	51
Wilson, Mount, mtn., Az., U.S.	B1	80
Wilson, Mount, mtn., Ca., U.S.	m12	82
Wilson, Mount, mtn., Co., U.S.	D2	83
Wilson, Mount, mtn., Nv., U.S.	E7	105
Wilson, Mount, mtn., Or., U.S.	B5	114
Wilson Creek, Wa., U.S.	B6	124
Wilson Creek, stm., Wa., U.S.	B5	124
Wilson Creek, stm., Wa., U.S.	B6	124
Wilson Dam, Al., U.S.	A2	78
Wilson Lake, res., Al., U.S.	A2	78
Wilson Lake, res., Ks., U.S.	D5	93
Wilson Piedmont Glacier, Ant.	e39	7
Wilsons, Va., U.S.	C5	123
Wilsons Beach, N.B., Can.	E3	71
Wilsons Mills, Me., U.S.	D1	96
Wilsons Mills, N.C., U.S.	B4	110
Wilsons Promontory, c., Austl.	G8	50
Wilsonville, Al., U.S.	B3	78
Wilsonville, Ct., U.S.	A8	84
Wilsonville, Il., U.S.	D4	90
Wilsonville, Ne., U.S.	D5	104
Wilsonville, Or., U.S.	h12	114
Wilstedt, F.R.Ger.	E3	15
Wilster, F.R.Ger.	E3	15
Wilton, Al., U.S.	B3	78
Wilton, Ar., U.S.	D1	81
Wilton, Ct., U.S.	E2	84
Wilton, Ia., U.S.	C6	92
Wilton, Me., U.S.	D2	96
Wilton, Mn., U.S.	C3	100
Wilton, N.H., U.S.	E3	106
Wilton, N.Y., U.S.	B7	109
Wilton, N.D., U.S.	B5	111
Wilton, Wi., U.S.	E3	126
Wilton Center, N.H., U.S.	E3	106
Wilton Manors, Fl., U.S.	*r13	86
Wiltshire, co., Eng., U.K.	C6	12
Wiltz, Lux.	C6	16
Wiluna, Austl.	E3	50
Wimauma, Fl., U.S.	E4	86
Wimapedi, stm., Mb., Can.	B2	70
Wimbledon [part of London], Eng., U.K.	m12	10
Wimbledon, N.D., U.S.	B7	111
Wimborne, Ab., Can.	D4	68
Wimborne [Minster], Eng., U.K.	D6	12
Wimico, Lake, l., Fl., U.S.	C1	86
Winagami Lake, l., Ab., Can.	B2	68
Winamac, In., U.S.	B4	91
Winburg, S. Afr.	C4	49
Winburne, Pa., U.S.	E5	115
Wincheck Pond, l., R.I., U.S.	E1	116
Winchell Mountain, mtn., Ma., U.S.	B2	98
Winchendon, Ma., U.S.	A3	98
Winchendon Springs, Ma., U.S.	A3	98
Winchester, On., Can.	B9	73
Winchester, Eng., U.K.	E6	10
Winchester, Ar., U.S.	D4	81
Winchester, Id., U.S.	C2	89
Winchester, Il., U.S.	D3	90
Winchester, In., U.S.	D8	91
Winchester, Ks., U.S.	k15	93
Winchester, Ky., U.S.	C5	94
Winchester, Ma., U.S.	g11	98
Winchester, Ms., U.S.	D5	101
Winchester, Mo., U.S.	A6	102
Winchester, Nv., U.S.	G6	105
Winchester, N.H., U.S.	E2	106
Winchester, Oh., U.S.	D2	112
Winchester, Tn., U.S.	B5	119
Winchester, Va., U.S.	A4	123
Winchester Bay, Or., U.S.	D2	114
Winchester Center, Ct., U.S.	B3	84
Wind, stm., Wa., U.S.	D4	124
Wind, stm., Wy., U.S.	C4	127
Windber, Pa., U.S.	F4	115
Wind Cave National Park, S.D., U.S.	D2	118
Windcrest, Tx., U.S.	*E3	120
Winder, Ga., U.S.	C3	87
Windermere, B.C., Can.	D10	69
Windermere, On., Can.	B5	73
Windermere, Eng., U.K.	C5	10
Windermere, l., Eng., U.K.	F6	13
Windfall, Ab., Can.	B2	68
Windfall, In., U.S.	D6	91
Windgap, Pa., U.S.	E11	115
Windham, Ct., U.S.	C7	84
Windham, Mt., U.S.	C6	103
Windham, N.Y., U.S.	C6	109
Windham, co., Ct., U.S.	B7	84
Windham, co., Vt., U.S.	F3	122
Windham Center, Me., U.S.	*E2	96
Windhoek, Nmb.	B2	49
Windigo, stm., P.Q., Can.	B4	74
Winding Stair Mountain, mts., Ok., U.S.	C6	113
Wind Lake, Wi., U.S.	F5	126
Wind Lake, l., Wi., U.S.	n11	126
Windom, Mn., U.S.	G3	100
Windom Peak, mtn., Co., U.S.	D3	83
Window Rock, Az., U.S.	B6	80
Wind Point, Wi., U.S.	n12	126
Wind River Indian Reservation, Wy., U.S.	C4	127
Wind River Peak, mtn., Wy., U.S.	D3	127
Wind River Range, mts., Wy., U.S.	C3	127
Windsbach, F.R.Ger.	D5	19
Windsor, Nf., Can.	D4	72
Windsor, On., Can.	E1	73
Windsor, P.Q., Can.	D5	74
Windsor (New Windsor), Eng., U.K.	E6	10
Windsor, Co., U.S.	A6	83
Windsor, Ct., U.S.	B5	84
Windsor, Il., U.S.	D5	90
Windsor, Ma., U.S.	A1	98
Windsor, Mo., U.S.	C4	102
Windsor, N.J., U.S.	C3	107
Windsor, N.C., U.S.	B6	110
Windsor, N.D., U.S.	C6	111
Windsor, Pa., U.S.	G8	115
Windsor, S.C., U.S.	E4	117
Windsor, Vt., U.S.	E4	122
Windsor, Va., U.S.	D6	123
Windsor, co., Vt., U.S.	D3	122
Windsor Forest, Ga., U.S.	*E5	87
Windsor Heights, Ia., U.S.	e8	92
Windsor Hills, Ca., U.S.	*n12	82
Windsor Locks, Ct., U.S.	B5	84
Windthorst, Sk., Can.	G4	75
Windthorst, Tx., U.S.	C3	120
Windward Islands, is., N.A.	I14	64
Windward Passage, strt., N.A.	E7	64
Windygates, Mb., Can.	E2	70
Windy Hill, S.C., U.S.	C8	117
Windy Hills, De., U.S.	*B3	85
Windy Hills, l., Sk., Can.	C4	75
Windy Peak, mtn., Wa., U.S.	A6	124
Windy Point, c., Nf., Can.	C4	72
Winefred, stm., Ab., Can.	B5	68
Winefred Lake, l., Ab., Can.	B5	68
Winfall, N.C., U.S.	A6	110
Winfield, Ab., Can.	C3	68
Winfield, Al., U.S.	B2	78
Winfield, Ia., U.S.	C6	92
Winfield, Ks., U.S.	E7	93
Winfield, Md., U.S.	B3	97
Winfield, Mo., U.S.	C7	102
Winfield, Pa., U.S.	E8	115
Winfield, Tn., U.S.	C9	119
Winfield, W.V., U.S.	C3	125
Winfred, S.D., U.S.	D8	118
Wing, Al., U.S.	D3	78
Wing, Ar., U.S.	C2	81
Wing, N.D., U.S.	B5	111
Wing, stm., Mn., U.S.	D3	100
Wingate, In., U.S.	D3	91
Wingate, Md., U.S.	D5	97
Wingate, N.C., U.S.	C2	110
Winger, Mn., U.S.	C3	100
Wingham, On., Can.	D3	73
Wingo, Ky., U.S.	f9	94
Winifred, Mt., U.S.	C7	103
Winifreda, Arg.	D4	54
Winifrede, W.V., U.S.	m12	125
Winigan, Mo., U.S.	A5	102
Winisk, On., Can.	n18	73
Winisk, stm., On., Can.	n18	73
Winisk Lake, l., On., Can.	n18	73
Wink, Tx., U.S.	D1	120
Winkelman, Az., U.S.	E5	80
Winkler, Mb., Can.	E3	70
Winkler, co., Tx., U.S.	D1	120
Winlaw, B.C., Can.	E9	69
Winlock, Wa., U.S.	C3	124
Winn, Me., U.S.	C4	96
Winn, co., La., U.S.	C3	95
Winnabow, N.C., U.S.	C4	110
Winneba, Ghana	E4	45
Winnebago, Il., U.S.	A4	90
Winnebago, Mn., U.S.	G4	100
Winnebago, Ne., U.S.	B9	104
Winnebago, Wi., U.S.	h8	126
Winnebago, co., Il., U.S.	A4	90
Winnebago, co., Ia., U.S.	A4	92
Winnebago, co., Wi., U.S.	D5	126
Winnebago, stm., Ia., U.S.	A4	92
Winnebago, Lake, l., Wi., U.S.	E5	126
Winnebago Indian Reservation, Ne., U.S.	B9	104
Winneconne, Wi., U.S.	D5	126
Winnemucca, Nv., U.S.	C4	105
Winnemucca Lake, l., Nv., U.S.	C2	105
Winner, S.D., U.S.	D6	118
Winneshiek, co., Ia., U.S.	A6	92
Winnetka, Il., U.S.	A6	90
Winnetoon, Ne., U.S.	B8	104
Winnett, Mt., U.S.	C8	103
Winnfield, La., U.S.	C3	95
Winnibigoshish, Lake, l., Mn., U.S.	C4	100
Winnie, Tx., U.S.	E5	120
Winnipeg, Mb., Can.	E3	70
Winnipeg, stm., Can.	D4	70
Winnipeg, Lake, l., Mb., Can.	C3	70
Winnipeg Beach, Mb., Can.	D3	70
Winnipegosis, Mb., Can.	D2	70
Winnipegosis, Lake, l., Mb., Can.	C2	70
Winnipesaukee, N.H., U.S.	C4	106
Winnipesaukee, Lake, l., N.H., U.S.	C4	106
Winnisquam, N.H., U.S.	C3	106
Winnisquam Lake, l., N.H., U.S.	C3	106
Winnsboro, La., U.S.	B4	95
Winnsboro, S.C., U.S.	C5	117
Winnsboro, Tx., U.S.	C5	120
Winnsboro Mills, S.C., U.S.	C5	117
Winona, Ks., U.S.	C2	93
Winona, Mi., U.S.	B2	99
Winona, Mn., U.S.	F7	100
Winona, Ms., U.S.	B4	101
Winona, Mo., U.S.	D6	102
Winona, N.H., U.S.	C3	106
Winona, W.V., U.S.	C4	125
Winona, co., Mn., U.S.	F7	100
Winona Lake, In., U.S.	B6	91
Winooski, Vt., U.S.	C2	122
Winooski, stm., Vt., U.S.	C2	122
Winooski, North Branch, stm., Vt., U.S.	C3	122
Winschoten, Neth.	A7	16
Winsen, F.R.Ger.	E4	15
Winsford, Eng., U.K.	A5	12
Winside, Ne., U.S.	B8	104
Winslow, Az., U.S.	C5	80
Winslow, Il., U.S.	A4	90
Winslow, In., U.S.	H3	91
Winslow, Me., U.S.	D3	96
Winslow, Ne., U.S.	C9	104
Winslow, N.J., U.S.	D3	107
Winslow, Wa., U.S.	e10	124
Winsted, Ct., U.S.	B3	84
Winsted, Mn., U.S.	F4	100
Winston, Fl., U.S.	D4	86
Winston, Mo., U.S.	B3	102
Winston, N.M., U.S.	D2	108
Winston, Or., U.S.	D3	114
Winston, co., Al., U.S.	A2	78
Winston, co., Ms., U.S.	B4	101
Winston-Salem, N.C., U.S.	A2	110
Winstonville, Ms., U.S.	B3	101
Winsum, Neth.	A6	17
Winter, Wi., U.S.	C2	126
Winter Beach, Fl., U.S.	E6	86
Winterberg, F.R.Ger.	B3	19
Winter Garden, Fl., U.S.	D5	86
Winter Harbor, Me., U.S.	D4	96
Winter Harbour, B.C., Can.	D3	69
Winter Haven, Fl., U.S.	D5	86
Winterport, Me., U.S.	D4	96
Winter Park, Co., U.S.	B5	83
Winter Park, Fl., U.S.	D5	86
Winter Park, N.C., U.S.	C5	110
Winterpock, Va., U.S.	C5	123
Winters, Ca., U.S.	C2	82
Winters, Tx., U.S.	D3	120
Winterset, Ia., U.S.	C4	92
Winter Springs, Fl., U.S.	*D5	86
Wintersville, Oh., U.S.	B5	112
Winterswijk, Neth.	C6	17
Winterthur, Switz.	E4	18
Winterthur, Switz.	h7	85
Winterton, Nf., Can.	E5	72
Winterville, Me., U.S.	B4	96
Winterville, Ms., U.S.	B2	101
Winterville, N.C., U.S.	B5	110
Winthrop, Ar., U.S.	D1	81
Winthrop, Ct., U.S.	D5	84
Winthrop, Ia., U.S.	B6	92
Winthrop, Me., U.S.	D3	96
Winthrop, Ma., U.S.	g11	98
Winthrop, Mn., U.S.	F4	100
Winthrop, N.Y., U.S.	f10	109
Winthrop, Wa., U.S.	A5	124
Winthrop, Lake, l., Ma., U.S.	h10	98
Winthrop Harbor, Il., U.S.	A6	90
Winton, Austl.	D7	50
Winton, Bah.	m18	64
Winton, Mn., U.S.	C7	100
Winton, N.C., U.S.	A6	110
Winton Lake, res., Oh., U.S.	o12	113
Winyah Bay, b., S.C., U.S.	E9	117
Wiota, Ia., U.S.	C3	92
Wirral, N.B., Can.	D3	71
Wirt, Mn., U.S.	C5	100
Wirt, co., W.V., U.S.	B3	125
Wirtz, Va., U.S.	C3	123
Wisbech, Eng., U.K.	D7	10
Wiscasset, Me., U.S.	D3	96
Wisconsin, state, U.S.	D4	126
Wisconsin, stm., Wi., U.S.	E3	126
Wisconsin, Lake, res., Wi., U.S.	E4	126
Wisconsin Dells, Wi., U.S.	E4	126
Wisconsin Rapids, Wi., U.S.	D4	126
Wisdom, Mt., U.S.	E3	103
Wise, N.C., U.S.	A4	110
Wise, Va., U.S.	f9	123
Wise, co., Tx., U.S.	C4	120
Wise, co., Va., U.S.	e9	123
Wiseman, Ak., U.S.	B9	79
Wise River, Mt., U.S.	E4	103
Wiseton, Sk., Can.	F2	75
Wishart, Sk., Can.	F3	75
Wishart, Mo., U.S.	D4	102
Wishaw, Scot., U.K.	E5	13
Wishek, N.D., U.S.	C6	111
Wishram, Wa., U.S.	D5	124
Wisła (Vistula), stm., Pol.	C7	26
Wisłok, stm., Pol.	C7	26
Wisłoka, stm., Pol.	D6	26
Wismar, Ger.D.R.	B5	18
Wismar Bucht, b., Ger.D.R.	D5	15
Wisner, La., U.S.	C4	95
Wisner, Ne., U.S.	C8	104
Wissant, Fr.	D9	12
Wissembourg, Fr.	C7	16
Wissota, Lake, res., Wi., U.S.	D2	126
Wister, Ok., U.S.	C7	113
Wister Lake, res., Ok., U.S.	C7	113
Witbank, S. Afr.	C4	49
Witchekan Lake, l., Sk., Can.	D2	75
Witch Lake, Mi., U.S.	B3	99
Witham, Eng., U.K.	C8	12
Witham, stm., Eng., U.K.	A7	12
Withamsville, Oh., U.S.	C1	112
Withee, Wi., U.S.	D4	126
Witherbee, N.Y., U.S.	A7	109
Withernsea, Eng., U.K.	D7	10
Witherspoon, Mount, mtn., Ak., U.S.	g18	79
Withlacoochee, stm., U.S.	B3	86
Withlacoochee, stm., Fl., U.S.	C4	86
Withrow, Wa., U.S.	B6	124
Witless Bay, Nf., Can.	E5	72
Witney, Eng., U.K.	C6	12
Witry-lès-Reims, Fr.	D4	17
Witt, Il., U.S.	D4	90
Witten, F.R.Ger.	C10	119
Witten, S.D., U.S.	D5	118
Witten, i., F.R.Ger.	D3	15
Wittenberg, Ger.D.R.	D6	18
Wittenberg, Wi., U.S.	D4	126
Wittenberge, Ger.D.R.	B6	18
Wittenheim, Fr.	B2	20
Wittlich, F.R.Ger.	D3	18
Wittmann, Az., U.S.	D3	80
Wittstock, Ger.D.R.	B6	18
Witu Islands, is., Pap. N. Gui.	h12	50
Witvlei, Nmb.	B2	49
Witzenhausen, F.R.Ger.	B4	19
Wiveliscombe, Eng., U.K.	C4	12
Wiwoń [-ŭp], N. Kor.	F3	33
Wixom, Mi., U.S.	o14	99
Wixom Lake, res., Mi., U.S.	E6	99
Wkra, stm., Pol.	A5	26
Władysławowo, Pol.	A5	26
Włocławek, Pol.	B5	26
Włodawa, Pol.	C7	26
Włoszczowa, Pol.	C5	26
Woburn, P.Q., Can.	D7	74
Woburn, Ma., U.S.	B5	98
Woden, Ia., U.S.	A4	92
Woerden, Neth.	B4	17
Wohlen, Switz.	B5	21
Wohlthat Mountains, mts., Ant.	B14	7
Woito, On., Can.	B7	73
Wokam, i., Indon.	G8	34
Woking, B.C., Can.	B1	68
Woking, Eng., U.K.	m11	10
Wokingham, Eng., U.K.	C7	12
Wolbach, Ne., U.S.	C7	104
Wolcott, In., U.S.	C3	91
Wolcott, N.Y., U.S.	B4	109
Wolcott, Vt., U.S.	B4	122
Wolcottville, In., U.S.	A7	91
Woldegk, Ger.D.R.	B7	15
Wolf, Ok., U.S.	B5	113
Wolf, Wy., U.S.	B5	127
Wolf, stm., Ms., U.S.	E4	101
Wolf, stm., Tn., U.S.	e9	119
Wolf, stm., Wi., U.S.	C5	126
Wolf, Isla, i., Ec.	f5	58
Wolf, North Fork, stm., Tn., U.S.		119
Wolf, Volcán, vol., Ec.	f5	58
Wolf Creek, Mt., U.S.	C4	103
Wolf Creek, Or., U.S.	E3	114
Wolf Creek, stm., U.S.	A2	113
Wolf Creek, stm., Ia., U.S.	B5	92
Wolf Creek, stm., Mt., U.S.	D7	99
Wolf Creek, stm., Mt., U.S.	C7	103
Wolf Creek, stm., W.V., U.S.	m13	125
Wolf Creek Pass, Co., U.S.	D3	83
Wolfe, co., Ky., U.S.	C6	94
Wolfeboro, N.H., U.S.	C4	106
Wolfeboro Falls, N.H., U.S.	C4	106
Wolfe City, Tx., U.S.	C4	120
Wolfegg, F.R.Ger.	A8	21
Wolfen, Ger.D.R.	B7	19
Wolfenbüttel, F.R.Ger.	B5	18
Wolfenschiessen, Switz.	C5	21
Wolfhagen, F.R.Ger.	B4	19
Wolf Island, Mo., U.S.	E8	102
Wolf Lake, Il., U.S.	F4	90
Wolflake, In., U.S.	B7	91
Wolf Lake, Mi., U.S.	E4	99
Wolf Lake, l., Ab., Can.	B5	68
Wolf Lake, l., Il., U.S.	k9	90
Wolford, N.D., U.S.	A5	111
Wolf Point, Mt., U.S.	B11	103
Wolfratshausen, F.R.Ger.	B7	20
Wolfsberg, Aus.	E7	18
Wolfsburg, F.R.Ger.	B5	18
Wolfsville, Md., U.S.	A2	97
Wolf Swamp, sw., N.C., U.S.	C5	110
Wolfville, N.S., Can.	D5	71
Wolgast, Ger.D.R.	A6	18
Wolhusen, Switz.	B4	20
Wolin, Pol.	B5	18
Wolin, i., Pol.	E8	15
Wollaston, Cape, c., N.T., Can.	B9	66
Wollaston, Islas, is., Chile	k12	54
Wollaston Lake, l., Sk., Can.	m8	75
Wollongong, Austl.	F9	50
Wolmaransstad, S. Afr.	C4	49
Wolmirstedt, Ger.D.R.	A6	19
Wotomin, Pol.	k14	26
Wotów, Pol.	C4	26
Wolseley, Sk., Can.	G4	75
Wolsey, S.D., U.S.	C7	118
Wolsztyn, Pol.	B4	26
Wolverhampton, Eng., U.K.	D5	10
Wolverine, Mi., U.S.	C6	99
Wolverton, Eng., U.K.	D6	10
Wolverton, Mn., U.S.	D2	100
Womack Hill, Al., U.S.	D1	78
Woman Lake, l., Mn., U.S.	D4	100
Womelsdorf, Pa., U.S.	F9	115
Wonalancet, N.H., U.S.	C4	106
Wonder Lake, Il., U.S.	A5	90
Wonderland, Ca., U.S.	B3	82
Wonewoc, Wi., U.S.	E3	126
Wŏnju, S. Kor.	H3	33
Wonotobo Vallen, wtfl, Sur.	B3	59
Wonowon, B.C., Can.	A7	69
Wŏnsan, N. Kor.	D10	31
Wonthaggi, Austl.	G8	50
Wood, N.C., U.S.	A4	110
Wood, Pa., U.S.	F5	115
Wood, S.D., U.S.	D5	118
Wood, co., Oh., U.S.	A2	112
Wood, co., Tx., U.S.	C5	120
Wood, co., W.V., U.S.	B3	125
Wood, co., Wi., U.S.	D3	126
Wood, stm., B.C., Can.	C8	69
Wood, stm., Sk., Can.	H2	75
Wood, stm., R.I., U.S.	F2	116
Wood, stm., Wy., U.S.	C3	127
Wood, Mount, mtn., Mt., U.S.	E7	103
Woodall Mountain, mtn., Ms., U.S.	A5	101
Woodberry, Ar., U.S.	D3	81
Woodbine, Ga., U.S.	F5	87
Woodbine, Ia., U.S.	C2	92
Woodbine, Ks., U.S.	D7	93
Woodbine, Ky., U.S.	D5	94
Woodbine, Md., U.S.	B3	97
Woodbine, N.J., U.S.	E3	107
Woodbourne, N.Y., U.S.	D6	109
Woodbridge, Eng., U.K.	B9	12
Woodbridge, Ct., U.S.	D3	84
Woodbridge, N.J., U.S.	B4	107
Woodbridge [Township], N.J., U.S.	B4	107
Wood Buffalo National Park, Can.	E10	66
Woodburn, In., U.S.	B8	91
Woodburn, Ky., U.S.	D3	94
Woodburn, Or., U.S.	B4	114
Woodbury, Ct., U.S.	C3	84
Woodbury, Ga., U.S.	D2	87
Woodbury, N.J., U.S.	D2	107
Woodbury, N.Y., U.S.	E7	109
Woodbury, Tn., U.S.	B5	119
Woodbury, co., Ia., U.S.	B1	92
Woodbury Mountain, mtn., Vt., U.S.	C4	122
Woodfield, S.C., U.S.	C6	117
Woodford, Ire.	D3	11
Woodford, S.C., U.S.	D5	117
Woodford, co., Il., U.S.	C4	90
Woodford, co., Ky., U.S.	B5	94
Woodfords, Ca., U.S.	C4	82
Woodhaven, Mi., U.S.	*F7	99
Woodhull, Il., U.S.	B3	90
Woodhull, N.Y., U.S.	C3	109
Woodlake, Ca., U.S.	D4	82
Wood Lake, Mn., U.S.	F3	100
Wood Lake, Ne., U.S.	B5	104
Wood Lake, l., Sk., Can.	B4	75
Woodland, Al., U.S.	B4	78
Woodland, Ca., U.S.	C3	82
Woodland, Ga., U.S.	D2	87
Woodland, Il., U.S.	C6	90
Woodland, Me., U.S.	C5	96
Woodland, Mi., U.S.	F5	99
Woodland, Ms., U.S.	B4	101
Woodland, N.C., U.S.	A5	110
Woodland, Pa., U.S.	E5	115
Woodland, Wa., U.S.	D3	124
Woodland Acres, Co., U.S.	D6	83
Woodland Beach, De., U.S.	C4	85
Woodland Mills, Tn., U.S.	A2	119
Woodland Park, Co., U.S.	C5	83
Woodland, On., Can.	h11	73
Woodlawn, Il., U.S.	E4	90
Woodlawn, Ky., U.S.	e9	94
Woodlawn, Md., U.S.	g10	97
Woodlawn, Md., U.S.	n13	112
Woodlawn, Tn., U.S.	A4	119
Woodlawn, Va., U.S.	D2	123
Woodleaf, N.C., U.S.	B2	110
Woodlyn, Pa., U.S.	*p20	115
Woodlynne, N.J., U.S.	*D2	107
Woodman, N.H., U.S.	C5	106
Woodmere, N.Y., U.S.	*k13	109
Woodmont, Ct., U.S.	E4	84
Wood Mountain, Sk., Can.	H2	75
Wood Mountain, mtn., Sk., Can.	H2	75
Woodport, N.J., U.S.	B3	107
Woodridge, Mb., Can.	E3	70
Woodridge, Il., U.S.	k8	90
Wood-Ridge, N.J., U.S.	h8	107
Wood River, Il., U.S.	E3	90
Wood River, Ne., U.S.	D7	104
Wood River Junction, R.I., U.S.	F2	116
Woodroffe, Mount, mtn., Austl.	E5	50
Woodrow, Sk., Can.	H2	75
Woodruff, Az., U.S.	C5	80
Woodruff, Ks., U.S.	C4	93
Woodruff, S.C., U.S.	B3	117
Woodruff, Ut., U.S.	B4	121
Woodruff, Wi., U.S.	C4	126
Woodruff, co., Ar., U.S.	B4	81
Woods, co., Ok., U.S.	A3	113
Woods, Lake, l., Austl.	C5	50
Woods, Lake, res., Tn., U.S.	B5	119
Woods, Lake of the, l., N.A.	E4	70
Woodsboro, Md., U.S.	A3	97
Woodsboro, Tx., U.S.	E4	120
Woods Cross, Ut., U.S.	C4	121
Woodsdale, N.C., U.S.	A4	110
Woodsfield, Oh., U.S.	C4	112
Woods Hole, Ma., U.S.	C6	98
Woodside, Austl.	l6	51
Woodside, Ca., U.S.	*k8	82
Woodside, De., U.S.	D3	85
Wood's Island, Nf., Can.	D2	72
Woodson, Ar., U.S.	C3	81
Woodson, Tx., U.S.	C3	120
Woodson, co., Ks., U.S.	E8	93
Woodstock, N.B., Can.	C2	71
Woodstock, On., Can.	D4	73
Woodstock, Al., U.S.	B2	78
Woodstock, Ct., U.S.	B8	84
Woodstock, Ga., U.S.	B2	87
Woodstock, Il., U.S.	A5	90
Woodstock, Md., U.S.	B4	97
Woodstock, N.H., U.S.	C3	106
Woodstock, Va., U.S.	B4	123
Woodstock Valley, Ct., U.S.	B7	84
Woodston, Ks., U.S.	C4	93
Woodstown, N.J., U.S.	D2	107
Woodsville, N.H., U.S.	B2	106
Woodville, Austl.	*F6	50
Woodville, On., Can.	C5	73
Woodville, N.Z.	N15	51
Woodville, Fl., U.S.	B2	86
Woodville, Ga., U.S.	C3	87
Woodville, Id., U.S.	F6	89
Woodville, Ky., U.S.	e9	94
Woodville, Ms., U.S.	D2	101
Woodville, Oh., U.S.	A2	112
Woodville, Tx., U.S.	D5	120
Woodville, Wi., U.S.	D1	126
Woodward, Al., U.S.	B3	78
Woodward, Ia., U.S.	C4	92
Woodward, Ok., U.S.	A2	113
Woodward, co., Ok., U.S.	A2	113
Woodwards Cove, N.B., Can.	E3	71
Woodway, Tx., U.S.	*D4	120
Woodway, Wa., U.S.	*f9	124
Woodworth, La., U.S.	C3	95
Woodworth, N.D., U.S.	B6	111
Woody, stm., Can.	C1	70
Wooldridge, Mo., U.S.	C5	102
Wooler, Eng., U.K.	E6	13
Woolford, Md., U.S.	C5	97
Woollahra, Austl.	*F9	50
Woolmarket, Ms., U.S.	E5	101
Wooler Creek, stm., Ky., U.S.	h13	94
Woolsey Peak, mtn., Az., U.S.	D3	80
Woolstock, Ia., U.S.	B4	92
Woolwich, Eng., U.K.	g8	96
Woomera, Austl.	F6	50
Woonsocket, R.I., U.S.	A3	116
Woonsocket, S.D., U.S.	C7	118
Woonsocket Reservoir Number Three, res., R.I., U.S.	B3	116
Wooster, Oh., U.S.	B4	112
Woosung, Il., U.S.	B4	90
Woqooyi Galbeed, prov., Som.	C5	47
Worb, Switz.	C4	21

Name	Map Ref	Page
Worbis, Ger.D.R.	B5	19
Worcester, S. Afr.	D2	49
Worcester, Eng., U.K.	D5	10
Worcester, Ma., U.S.	B4	98
Worcester, N.Y., U.S.	C6	109
Worcester, Vt., U.S.	C3	122
Worcester, co., Md., U.S.	D7	97
Worcester, co., Ma., U.S.	A3	98
Worcester Mountains, mts., Vt., U.S.	C3	122
Worden, Il., U.S.	E4	90
Worden, Mt., U.S.	E8	103
Worden, Or., U.S.	E5	114
Worden Pond, l., R.I., U.S.	F3	116
Wordsworth, Sk., Can.	H4	75
Workington, Eng., U.K.	C5	10
Worksop, Eng., U.K.	A6	12
Workum, Neth.	B5	17
Worland, Mo., U.S.	C3	102
Worland, Wy., U.S.	B5	127
Worley, Id., U.S.	B2	89
Wormerveer, Neth.	B4	17
Worms, F.R.Ger.	D4	18
Worms, Ne., U.S.	C7	104
Worms Head, c., Wales, U.K.	C3	12
Woronoco, Ma., U.S.	B2	98
Worth, Il., U.S.	k9	90
Worth, Mo., U.S.	A3	102
Worth, co., Ga., U.S.	E3	87
Worth, co., Ia., U.S.	A4	92
Worth, co., Mo., U.S.	A3	102
Wortham, Tx., U.S.	D4	120
Worthing, Eng., U.K.	E6	10
Worthing, S.D., U.S.	D9	118
Worthington, In., U.S.	F4	91
Worthington, Ia., U.S.	B6	92
Worthington, Ky., U.S.	B7	94
Worthington, Mn., U.S.	G3	100
Worthington, Mo., U.S.	A5	102
Worthington, Oh., U.S.	B2	112
Worthington, Pa., U.S.	E2	115
Worthington, W.V., U.S.	k10	125
Worthington Knob, mtn., Tn., U.S.	D8	119
Worthington Peak, mtn., Nv., U.S.	F6	105
Worthington Springs, Fl., U.S.	C4	86
Worthville, Ky., U.S.	B4	94
Worthville, N.C., U.S.	B3	110
Worton, Md., U.S.	B5	97
Wostok, Ab., Can.	C4	68
Wotton, P.Q., Can.	D6	74
Wounded Knee, S.D., U.S.	D3	118
Wounta, Nic.	E8	63
Wowoni, i., Indon.	F6	34
Woy Woy, Austl.	F9	50
Woźniki, Pol.	f10	26
Wrangel Island, i., Sov. Un.	B21	29
Wrangell, Ak., U.S.	D13	79
Wrangell, Mount, mtn., Ak., U.S.	f19	79
Wrangell Island, i., Ak., U.S.	m24	79
Wrangell Mountains, mts., N.A.	D4	66
Wrangell Mountains, mts., Ak., U.S.	C11	79
Wrangell-Saint Elias National Park, Ak., U.S.	C11	79
Wrath, Cape, c., Scot., U.K.	A8	10
Wray, Co., U.S.	A8	83
Wray, Ga., U.S.	E3	87
Wren, Oh., U.S.	B1	112
Wrens, Ga., U.S.	C4	87
Wrenshall, Mn., U.S.	D6	100
Wrentham, In., U.S.	E4	68
Wrentham, Ma., U.S.	B5	98
Wrexham, Wales, U.K.	D5	10
Wriezen, Ger.D.R.	B7	18
Wright, Al., U.S.	A2	78
Wright, Ar., U.S.	C3	81
Wright, Ia., U.S.	C5	92
Wright, Ks., U.S.	E4	93
Wright, Mn., U.S.	D5	100
Wright, co., Ia., U.S.	B4	92
Wright, co., Mn., U.S.	E5	100
Wright, co., Mo., U.S.	D5	102
Wright, mount, mtn., Mt., U.S.	C4	103
Wright Brothers National Memorial, hist., N.C., U.S.	A7	110
Wright City, Mo., U.S.	C6	102
Wright City, Ok., U.S.	C6	113
Wright-Patterson Air Force Base, mil., Oh., U.S.	C1	112
Wrightson, Mount, mtn., Az., U.S.	F5	80
Wrightstown, N.J., U.S.	C3	107
Wrightstown, Wi., U.S.	D5	126
Wrightsville, Ar., U.S.	C3	81
Wrightsville, Ga., U.S.	D4	87
Wrightsville, Pa., U.S.	F8	115
Wrightsville Beach, N.C., U.S.	C5	110
Wrightsville Reservoir, res., Vt., U.S.	C3	122
Wrightwood, Ca., U.S.	E5	82
Wrigley, N.T., Can.	D8	66
Wrigley, Tn., U.S.	B4	119
Wrigley Gulf, b., Ant.	B36	7
Wrocław (Breslau), Pol.	C4	26
Wrong Lake, l., Mb., Can.	C3	70
Wroxeter, On., Can.	D3	73
Wroxham, Eng., U.K.	D7	12
Wroxton, Sk., Can.	F5	75
Września, Pol.	B4	26
Wschowa, Pol.	C4	26
Wuchang, China	J3	32
Wuchuan, China	D4	32
Wuchuan, China	B9	35
Wuda, China	D6	31
Wudaoliang, China	D3	31
Wudu, China	E6	31
Wufeng, China	I4	32
Wugang, China	F7	31
Wuhai, China	E2	32
Wuhan, China	E7	31
Wuhu, China	H7	32
Wu Jiang, stm., China	F6	31
Wukari, Nig.	E6	45
Wum, Cam.	D2	46
Wümme, stm., F.R.Ger.	E3	15
Wunsiedel, F.R.Ger.	C6	19
Wunstorf, F.R.Ger.	A4	19
Wuntho, Burma	D10	36
Wupatki National Monument, Az., U.S.	B4	80
Wuppertal, F.R.Ger.	C3	18
Wurtsboro, N.Y., U.S.	D6	109
Wurtsmith Air Force Base, mil., Mi., U.S.	D7	99
Württemberg, hist. reg., F.R.Ger.	D4	18
Würzburg, F.R.Ger.	D4	18
Wurzen, Ger.D.R.	C6	18
Wuskwatim Lake, l., Mb., Can.	B2	70
Wusong, China	I9	32
Wusuli (Ussuri), stm., Asia	B11	31
Wutongqiao, China	F5	31
Wuwei, China	D5	31
Wuwei, China	I7	32
Wuxi, China	E9	31
Wuxing, China	E9	31
Wuyi, China	F6	32
Wuyiling, China	B10	31
Wuyuan, China	C6	31
Wuzhan, China	A2	33
Wuzhi Peak, mtn., China	B3	34
Wuzhong, China	F2	32
Wuzhou (Wuchou), China	G7	31
Wyaconda, Mo., U.S.	A6	102
Wyaconda, stm., Mo., U.S.	A6	102
Wyalusing, Pa., U.S.	C9	115
Wyandanch, N.Y., U.S.	*n15	109
Wyandot, co., Oh., U.S.	B2	112
Wyandotte, Mi., U.S.	F7	99
Wyandotte, Ok., U.S.	A7	113
Wyandotte, co., Ks., U.S.	C9	93
Wyandra, Austl.	C6	51
Wyanet, Il., U.S.	B4	90
Wyarno, Wy., U.S.	B6	127
Wyatt, In., U.S.	A5	91
Wyatt, Mo., U.S.	E8	102
Wyckoff, N.J., U.S.	*A4	107
Wyco, W.V., U.S.	D3	125
Wye, stm., U.K.	C5	12
Wyebridge, On., Can.	C5	73
Wye Mills, Md., U.S.	C5	97
Wyeville, Wi., U.S.	D3	126
Wykoff, Mn., U.S.	G6	100
Wylie, Lake, res., U.S.	A5	117
Wylliesburg, Va., U.S.	D4	123
Wyman, Ia., U.S.	C6	92
Wyman Lake, res., Me., U.S.	C3	96
Wymondham, Eng., U.K.	B9	12
Wymore, Ne., U.S.	D9	104
Wyncote, Pa., U.S.	*o21	115
Wyndham, Austl.	C4	50
Wyndmere, N.D., U.S.	C8	111
Wyndmoor, Pa., U.S.	*F11	115
Wynnburg, Tn., U.S.	A2	119
Wynndel, B.C., Can.	E9	69
Wynne, Ar., U.S.	B5	81
Wynnewood, Ok., U.S.	C4	113
Wynnewood, Pa., U.S.	*o20	115
Wynona, Ok., U.S.	A5	113
Wynoochee, stm., Wa., U.S.	B2	124
Wynot, Ne., U.S.	B8	104
Wynyard, Austl.	o15	50
Wynyard, Sk., Can.	F3	75
Wyocena, Wi., U.S.	E4	126
Wyodak, Wy., U.S.	B7	127
Wyola, Mt., U.S.	E9	103
Wyoming, On., Can.	E2	73
Wyoming, De., U.S.	D3	85
Wyoming, Il., U.S.	B4	90
Wyoming, Ia., U.S.	B6	92
Wyoming, Mi., U.S.	F5	99
Wyoming, Mn., U.S.	E6	100
Wyoming, N.Y., U.S.	C2	109
Wyoming, Oh., U.S.	o13	112
Wyoming, Pa., U.S.	n17	115
Wyoming, R.I., U.S.	E2	116
Wyoming, co., N.Y., U.S.	C2	109
Wyoming, co., Pa., U.S.	D9	115
Wyoming, co., W.V., U.S.	D3	125
Wyoming, state, U.S.	C5	127
Wyoming Peak, mtn., Wy., U.S.	D2	127
Wyoming Range, mts., Wy., U.S.	D2	127
Wyomissing, Pa., U.S.	F10	115
Wyrzysk, Pol.	B4	26
Wysocking Bay, b., N.C., U.S.	B7	110
Wysokie Mazowieckie, Pol.	B7	26
Wyszków, Pol.	B6	26
Wythe, co., Va., U.S.	D1	123
Wytheville, Va., U.S.	D1	123
Wytopitlock, Me., U.S.	C4	96
Wyvis, Ben, mtn., Scot., U.K.	C4	13

X

Name	Map Ref	Page
Xaafuun, Som.	C7	47
Xainza, China	B8	36
Xai-Xai (João Belo), Moz.	C5	49
Xalin, Som.	D6	47
Xambioá, Braz.	D5	59
Xam Nua, Laos	A2	34
Xangongo, Ang.	E1	49
Xánthi, Grc.	B5	40
Xapecó, stm., Braz.	B2	56
Xapuri, Braz.	B2	55
Xarardheere, Som.	B3	49
Xau, l., Bots.	B3	49
Xboril, Mex.	D6	63
Xcalak, Mex.	D7	63
Xenia, Il., U.S.	E5	90
Xenia, Oh., U.S.	C2	112
Xiaguan, China	F5	31
Xiajiang, China	F8	31
Xiajin, China	F6	32
Xiamen (Amoy), China	G8	31
Xi'an (Sian), China	E7	31
Xiangfan, China	E7	31
Xiang Jiang, stm., China	J5	32
Xiangkhoang, Laos	B2	34
Xiangtan, China	F7	31
Xiangxiang, China	K5	32
Xianning, China	J6	32
Xianyang, China	E6	31
Xianyou, China	F8	31
Xiapu, China	F9	31
Xichang, China	B4	34
Xifeng, China	C11	32
Xigazê, China	C8	36
Xilitla, Mex.	m14	63
Xin Barag Zuoqi, China	B8	31
Xinbin, China	D11	32
Xincai, China	H6	32
Xingcheng, China	D9	32
Xinghua, China	H8	32
Xingtai, China	D7	32
Xingu, stm., Braz.	C4	59
Xinhua, China	K4	32
Xining, China	D5	31
Xinjiang, China	H6	32
Xinjiang Uygur, prov., China	C2	31
Xinjin, China	C9	31
Xinmin, China	C9	31
Xinning, China	K4	32
Xinwen, China	G7	32
Xinxian, China	D7	31
Xinxiang, China	D7	31
Xinyang, China	E7	31
Xinye, China	H5	32
Xinyi He, stm., China	G8	32
Xinzhou, China	C8	35
Xique-Xique, Braz.	D2	57
Xishui, China	I6	32
Xi Ujimqin Qi, China	B7	32
Xiushui, China	J6	32
Xixabangma Mountain, mtn., Asia	C8	36
Xixian, China	F4	32
Xizang see Tibet, prov., China	E3	31
Xochimilco (part of Mexico City), Mex.	h9	63
Xuancheng, China	I8	32
Xuanhua, China	C8	31
Xuanwei, China	E7	31
Xuddun, Som.	D6	47
Xuddur, Som.	E5	47
Xunhe, China	B4	33
Xunke, China	B4	33
Xupu, China	K4	32
Xuwen, China	B9	35
Xuyi, China	H8	32
Xuy Nong Chao, is., Viet.	B7	35
Xuyong, China	F6	31
Xuzhou (Süchow), China	E8	31

Y

Name	Map Ref	Page
Ya'an, China	F5	31
Ya'bad, Isr. Occ.	B7	41
Yabassi, Cam.	E2	46
Yabbenohr Island, i., Marsh Is.	S17	52
Yablis, Nic.	C6	62
Yablonovy Mountains, mts., Sov. Un.	D14	29
Yabu, Japan	N5	52
Yabucoa, P.R.	B4	65
Yacata, i., Fiji	H16	52
Yachats, Or., U.S.	C2	114
Yacheng, China	B3	34
Yaco (Iaco), stm., S.A.	B3	58
Yacolt, Wa., U.S.	D3	124
Yacuiba, Bol.	D5	55
Yad Eli'ezer, Isr.	h10	41
Yadkin, co., N.C., U.S.	A2	110
Yadkin, stm., N.C., U.S.	B2	110
Yadkinville, N.C., U.S.	A2	110
Yad Mordekhay, Isr.	C6	41
Yadong, China	D12	31
Yadua, i., Fiji	H15	52
Yagasa Cluster, is., Fiji	I16	52
Yagoua, Cam.	C3	46
Yaguajay, Cuba	C4	64
Yaguas, stm., Peru	B3	58
Yahk, B.C., Can.	E9	69
Yahuma, Zaire	A3	48
Yainax Butte, mtn., Or., U.S.	E5	114
Yaizu, Japan	o17	33
Yakima, Wa., U.S.	C5	124
Yakima, co., Wa., U.S.	C5	124
Yakima, stm., Wa., U.S.	C6	124
Yakima Indian Reservation, Wa., U.S.	C5	124
Yakima Ridge, mtn., Wa., U.S.	C5	124
Yakima Valley, val., Wa., U.S.	C5	124
Yako, Burkina	D4	45
Yakobi Island, i., Ak., U.S.	m21	79
Yakoma, Zaire	A3	48
Yaku Island, i., Japan	E11	31
Yakutat, Ak., U.S.	D12	79
Yakutat Bay, b., Ak., U.S.	D11	79
Yakutsk, Sov. Un.	C15	29
Yala, Thai.	D2	34
Yalaha, Fl., U.S.	D5	86
Yale, B.C., Can.	E7	69
Yale, Il., U.S.	D5	90
Yale, Ia., U.S.	C3	92
Yale, Mi., U.S.	E8	99
Yale, Ok., U.S.	A5	113
Yale, S.D., U.S.	C8	118
Yale, Va., U.S.	D5	123
Yale, Mount, mtn., Co., U.S.	C5	83
Yale Lake, res., Wa., U.S.	D3	124
Yalinga, Cen. Afr. Rep.	D4	46
Yallahs Hill, hill, Jam.	F15	65
Yalobusha, co., Ms., U.S.	A4	101
Yalobusha, stm., Ms., U.S.	B4	101
Yalong Jiang, stm., China	E5	31
Yalova, Tur.	B7	40
Yalta, Sov. Un.	I10	27
Yalu Jiang, stm., Asia	C9	31
Yalutorovsk, Sov. Un.	B7	28
Yalvaç, Tur.	C8	40
Yamachiche, P.Q., Can.	C5	74
Yamagata, Japan	D13	31
Yamaguchi, Japan	I5	33
Yamal Peninsula, pen., Sov. Un.	B9	29
Yamantau, Mount, mtn., Sov. Un.	D8	29
Yamaska (Saint-Michel), P.Q., Can.	C5	74
Yamaska, co., P.Q., Can.	C5	74
Yambio, Sud.	E2	47
Yambol, Bul.	D8	24
Yamdena, i., Indon.	G8	34
Yamethin, Burma	D10	36
Yamhill, Or., U.S.	h11	114
Yamhill, co., Or., U.S.	B3	114
Yamkino, Sov. Un.	n18	27
Yamma Yamma, Lake, l., Austl.	E7	50
Yamoussoukro, I.C.	E3	45
Yampa, Co., U.S.	A4	83
Yampa, stm., Co., U.S.	A2	83
Yampa Plateau, plat., U.S.	A1	83
Yamparáez, Bol.		
Yamsay Mountain, mtn., Or., U.S.	E5	114
Yamsk, Sov. Un.	D18	29
Yamuna, stm., India	C7	36
Yamzho Lake, l., China	C9	36
Yana, stm., Sov. Un.	C16	29
Yanac, Austl.	H3	51
Yanam, India	E7	36
Yan'an, China	D6	31
Yanaoca, Peru	D3	58
Yanaul, Sov. Un.	D20	8
Yanbu', Sau. Ar.	E7	43
Yancey, co., N.C., U.S.	f10	110
Yanceyville, N.C., U.S.	A3	110
Yancheng, China	H5	32
Yancheng, China	H9	32
Yanfolila, Mali	D3	45
Yangambi, Zaire	A3	48
Yangbajain, China	B13	37
Yangchou see Yangzhou, China	E8	31
Yangchun, China	G7	31
Yangdŏk, N. Kor.	G3	33
Yangiyul, Sov. Un.	G22	8
Yangjiang, China	G7	31
Yangquan, China	D7	31
Yang Sin, mtn., Viet.	F8	35
Yangtze (Chang Jiang), stm., China	E8	31
Yangxian, China	H2	32
Yangyang, S. Kor.	G4	33
Yangzhou (Yangchou), China	E8	31
Yanji, China	C10	31
Yankeetown, Fl., U.S.	C4	86
Yankeetown, In., U.S.	I3	91
Yankton, S.D., U.S.	E8	118
Yankton, co., S.D., U.S.	D8	118
Yanonge, Zaire	A3	48
Yanqi, China	C2	31
Yanshan, China	E7	32
Yanshi, China	G5	32
Yanshou, China	D4	33
Yantai, China	D9	31
Yantic, stm., Ct., U.S.	C7	84
Yantley, Al., U.S.	C1	78
Yantra, stm., Bul.	D7	24
Yanush, Ok., U.S.	C6	113
Yanzhou, China	D8	31
Yao, Chad	C3	46
Yao, Japan	*I7	33
Yaosca, Nic.	D5	62
Yaoundé, Cam.	E2	46
Yap, i., Micron.	F8	6
Yapen, i., Indon.	F9	34
Yapeyú, Arg.	H14	52
Yaque del Norte, stm., Dom. Rep.	E8	64
Yaqui, stm., Mex.	B3	63
Yar, Sov. Un.	B4	28
Yaracuy, state, Ven.	A4	60
Yaraka, Austl.	D7	50
Yardley, Pa., U.S.	F12	115
Yardville, N.J., U.S.	C3	107
Yarensk, Sov. Un.	C18	8
Yarim, Yemen	C5	47
Yaritagua, Ven.	A4	60
Yarker, On., U.S.	C8	73
Yarkovo, Sov. Un.	B7	28
Yarmouth, N.S., Can.	F3	71
Yarmouth, Ia., U.S.	C6	92
Yarmouth, Me., U.S.	E2	96
Yarmouth, Ma., U.S.	C7	98
Yarmouth, co., N.S., Can.	F4	71
Yarmuk, stm., Asia	B7	41
Yarnell, Az., U.S.	C3	80
Yarnema, Sov. Un.	F18	14
Yaroslavl, Sov. Un.	D6	29
Yarovskoye Marsh, sw., Sov. Un.	B8	28
Yarqah, Mayyat, well, Eg.	E5	41
Yarqon, stm., Isr.	B6	41
Yarram, Austl.	I6	51
Yarrow, B.C., Can.	f13	69
Yarrowsburg, Md., U.S.	B2	97
Yartsevo, Sov. Un.	C27	8
Yartsevo, Sov. Un.	D9	27
Yarumal, Col.	B2	60
Yarshov, Sov. Un.	C5	28
Yasawa Group, is., Fiji	H14	52
Yasinovataya, Sov. Un.	q20	27
Yasinya, Sov. Un.	A7	24
Yasothon, Thai.	E6	35
Yass, Austl.	F8	50
Yata, Bol.	B2	55
Yates, co., N.Y., U.S.	C3	109
Yatesboro, Pa., U.S.	E3	115
Yates Center, Ks., U.S.	E8	93
Yates City, Il., U.S.	C3	90
Yatesville, Ga., U.S.	D2	87
Yathkyed Lake, l., N.T., Can.	D13	66
Yatsuga, Mount, mtn., Japan	n17	33
Yatsushiro, Japan	J5	33
Yatsushiro Sea, Japan	J4	33
Yattah, Isr. Occ.	C7	41
Yauca, Peru	E3	58
Yauco, P.R.	B2	65
Yauco, Embalse de, res., P.R.	B2	65
Yauli, Peru	D2	58
Yaupi, Ec.	B2	58
Yauri, Peru	D3	58
Yautepec, Mex.	n14	63
Yauyos, Peru	D2	58
Yavapai, co., Az., U.S.	C3	80
Yavari (Javari), stm., S.A.	B3	58
Yavatmāl (Yeotmal), India	G7	37
Yavi, Cerro, mtn., Ven.	B4	60
Yaviza, Pan.	F9	62
Yavne, Isr.	C6	41
Yavorov, Sov. Un.	G4	27
Yawatahama, Japan	J6	33
Yawgoog Pond, l., R.I., U.S.	E1	116
Yaxian, China	B3	34
Yazd (Yezd), Iran	B5	38
Yazoo, co., Ms., U.S.	C3	101
Yazoo, stm., Ms., U.S.	C3	101
Yazoo City, Ms., U.S.	C3	101
Yding Skovhej, hill, Den.	I3	15
Ye, Burma	E10	36
Yeadon, Pa., U.S.	p21	115
Yeagertown, Pa., U.S.	E6	115
Yeibji Bou, Chad	A3	46
Yecla, Spain	C5	22
Yedintsy, Sov. Un.	D3	91
Yefremov, Sov. Un.	E12	27
Yegindybulak, Sov. Un.	D9	28
Yegoryevsk, Sov. Un.	D12	27
Yeguas, Punta, c., P.R.	B4	65
Yehud, Isr.	g10	41
Yekaterinoslavka, Sov. Un.	A4	33
Yelabuga, Sov. Un.	D19	8
Yelabuga, Sov. Un.	B7	33
Yelan, stm., Sov. Un.	C16	29
Yelets, Sov. Un.	D6	29
Yélimané, Mali	C2	45
Yell, co., Ar., U.S.	B2	81
Yell, i., Scot., U.K.	g10	10
Yellandu, India	I8	37
Yellow see Huang He, stm., China	D8	31
Yellow, stm., U.S.	u15	86
Yellow, stm., Fl., U.S.	h8	87
Yellow, stm., Ga., U.S.	C3	87
Yellow, stm., In., U.S.	B4	91
Yellow, stm., Wi., U.S.	D3	126
Yellow Creek, Sk., Can.	E3	75
Yellow Creek, stm., Tn., U.S.	A4	119
Yellow Grass, Sk., Can.	H3	75
Yellowhead Pass, Can.	C1	68
Yellow Jacket, Co., U.S.	D2	83
Yellowjacket Mountains, mts., Id., U.S.	D4	89
Yellowknife, N.T., Can.	D10	66
Yeilow Lake, l., Wi., U.S.	C1	126
Yeilow Medicine, co., Mn., U.S.	F2	100
Yellow Pine, Al., U.S.	D1	78
Yellow Pine, Id., U.S.	E3	89
Yellow Sea, Asia	D9	31
Yellow Springs, Md., U.S.	B3	97
Yellow Springs, Oh., U.S.	C2	112
Yellowstone, co., Mt., U.S.	D8	103
Yellowstone, stm., U.S.	D10	103
Yellowstone, Clarks Fork, stm., U.S.	F7	103
Yellowstone Lake, l., Wy., U.S.	B2	127
Yellowstone National Park, Wy., U.S.	B2	127
Yellowstone National Park, co., Mt., U.S.	E6	103
Yelliville, Ar., U.S.	A3	81
Yelm, Wa., U.S.	C3	124
Yelnya, Sov. Un.	D9	27
Yeltes, stm., Spain	B2	22
Yelverton Bay, b., N.T., Can.	k35	66
Yelvington, Ky., U.S.	C3	94
Yelwa, Nig.	D5	45
Yemanzhelinsk, Sov. Un.	C6	28
Yemassee, S.C., U.S.	F6	117
Yemen, ctry., Asia	D4	38
Yemen, People's Democratic Republic of, ctry., Asia	D4	38
Yena, Sov. Un.	D14	14
Yenakiyevo, Sov. Un.	G12	27
Yenangyat, Burma	B1	35
Yenangyaung, Burma	B1	35
Yenashimskiy Polkan, Mount, mtn., Sov. Un.	D12	29
Yen Bai, Viet.	B6	35
Yendéré, Burkina	D4	45
Yendi, Ghana	E4	45
Yenice, stm., Tur.	B9	40
Yenisey, stm., Sov. Un.	C11	29
Yenisey Ridge, mts., Sov. Un.	D27	8
Yeniseysk, Sov. Un.	D12	29
Yentna, stm., Ak., U.S.	f16	79
Yeo Lake, l., Austl.	E3	50
Yeoman, In., U.S.	C4	91
Yeotmal see Yavatmāl, India	G7	37
Yeovil, Eng., U.K.	E5	10
Yeppoon, Austl.	D10	50
Yeránia Óri, mts., Grc.	g10	25
Yerba Buena, Chile	E1	55
Yerington, Nv., U.S.	E2	105
Yerington Indian Reservation, Nv., U.S.	D2	105
Yermakovskoye, Sov. Un.	E27	8
Yermentau, Sov. Un.	C8	28
Yermo, Ca., U.S.	E5	82
Yermolayevo, Sov. Un.	C5	28
Yerres, Fr.	h10	16
Yerres, stm., Fr.	F2	17
Yerseke, Neth.	C4	17
Yershov, Sov. Un.	I9	27
Yerupaja, Nevado, mtn., Peru	D2	58
Yeso, N.M., U.S.	C5	108
Yesomite, Ky., U.S.	C5	94
Yessentuki, Sov. Un.	G17	8
Yessey, Sov. Un.	C13	29
Yeste, Spain	C4	22
Yetter, Ia., U.S.	B3	92
Yeu, Île d', i., Fr.	D2	16
Yevlach, Sov. Un.	E3	28
Yevpatoriya, Sov. Un.	I9	27
Yexian, China	F8	32
Yeysk, Sov. Un.	H12	27
Yezd see Yazd, Iran	B5	38
Yi, stm., Ur.	E1	56
Yiannitsá, Grc.	B4	25
Yiáros, i., Grc.	D5	25
Yibin, China	F5	31
Yichang, China	I5	32
Yichuan, China	B10	31
Yichun, China	B10	31
Yidu, China	I4	32
Yidu, China	F8	32
Yigo, Guam	L10	52
Yilan, China	B10	31
Yiliang, China	G5	31
Yimianpo, China	D4	33
Yinchuan, China	D6	31
Yindu, China	G7	31
Ying He, stm., China	E8	31
Yingkou, China	C9	31
Yingshan, China	H7	32
Yingxian, China	F7	31
Yining, China	E11	29
Yin Mountains, mts., China	C5	25
Yioúra, i., Grc.	C5	25
Yirga Alem, Eth.	D4	47
Yirol, Sud.	D3	47
Yishan, China	G6	31
Yithion, Grc.	D4	40
Yitong, China	C11	32
Yixian, China	D9	32
Yixing, China	I8	32
Yiyang, China	F7	31
Yiyang, China	J3	32
Yizheng, China	H7	32
Yogyakarta, Indon.	m14	34
Yoho National Park, B.C., Can.	D9	69
Yoichi, Japan	E10	33
Yojoa, Lago de, l., Hond.	C5	62
Yokadouma, Cam.	E2	46
Yokkaichi, Japan	I7	33
Yoko, Cam.	D2	46
Yokoate Island, i., Japan	L4	33
Yokohama, Japan	D12	31
Yokoshiba, Japan	n19	33
Yokosuka, Japan	D12	31
Yokum Seat, mtn., Ma., U.S.	B1	98
Yola, Nig.	E7	46
Yolo, co., Ca., U.S.	C2	82
Yom, stm., Thai.	B1	34
Yomba Indian Reservation, Nv., U.S.	D4	105
Yona, Guam	M10	52
Yonabaru, Japan	O5	52
Yonago, Japan	I6	33
Yonaha Mountain, hill, Japan	N6	52
Yoncalla, Or., U.S.	D3	114
Yonezawa, Japan	H10	33
Yong'an, China	F8	31
Yongdeng, China	D5	31
Yŏngdŏk, S. Kor.	H4	33
Yonges Island, S.C., U.S.	F7	117
Yŏngan, N. Kor.	F4	33
Yonghŭng, N. Kor.	G3	33
Yŏngil Bay, b., S. Kor.	H4	33
Yongji, China	G4	32
Yongnian, China	F6	32
Yongshou, China	G2	32
Yongxiu, China	J6	32
Yonkers, N.Y., U.S.	E7	109
Yonne, stm., Fr.	D5	16
Yopal, Col.	B3	60
Yorba Linda, Ca., U.S.	*n13	82
York, Austl.	F2	50
York, On., Can.	D5	73
York, Eng., U.K.	D6	10
York, Al., U.S.	C1	78
York, Il., U.S.	D6	90
York, In., U.S.	A8	91
York, Me., U.S.	E2	96
York, Ne., U.S.	D8	104
York, N.D., U.S.	A6	111
York, Pa., U.S.	G8	115
York, S.C., U.S.	B5	117
York, co., N.B., Can.	C3	71
York, co., On., Can.	D5	73
York, co., Me., U.S.	E2	96
York, co., Ne., U.S.	D8	104
York, co., Pa., U.S.	G8	115
York, co., S.C., U.S.	A5	117
York, stm., On., Can.	B7	73
York, stm., Va., U.S.	C6	123
York, Cape, c., Austl.	B7	50
York, Kap, c., Grnld.	B14	61
York Beach, Me., U.S.	E2	96
Yorke Peninsula, pen., Austl.	F7	50
York Factory, Mb., Can.	A5	70
York Harbor, Me., U.S.	E2	96
York Haven, Pa., U.S.	F8	115
Yorklyn, De., U.S.	A3	85
York Point, c., Nf., Can.	C4	72
Yorkshire, N.Y., U.S.	C2	109
York Springs, Pa., U.S.	F7	115
Yorkton, Sk., Can.	F4	75
Yorktown, Ar., U.S.	C4	81
Yorktown, In., U.S.	D7	91
Yorktown, Ia., U.S.	D2	92
Yorktown, N.J., U.S.	C2	107
Yorktown, N.Y., U.S.	*D7	109
Yorktown, Tx., U.S.	E4	120
Yorktown, Va., U.S.	C6	123
Yorktown Heights, N.Y., U.S.	*D7	109
Yorktown Manor, R.I., U.S.	C3	116
Yorkville, Il., U.S.	B5	90
Yorkville, N.Y., U.S.	B5	109
Yorkville, Oh., U.S.	B5	112
Yorkville, Tn., U.S.	A2	119
York Wolds, hills, Eng., U.K.	C6	10
Yoro, Hond.	C4	62
Yorosso, Mali	D4	45
Yoseki, Zaire	A3	48
Yosemite National Park, Ca., U.S.	D4	82
Yosemite National Park, Ca., U.S.	D4	82
Yoshkar-Ola, Sov. Un.	B3	28
Yos Sudarsa, i., Indon.	G9	34
Yost, Ut., U.S.	B2	121
Yost Lake, res., U.S.	A5	113
Yŏsu, S. Kor.	I3	33
Yotala, Bol.	C2	55
Yotvata, Isr.	E7	41
Youbou, B.C., Can.	g11	69
Youghal, Ire.	D2	10
Youghal Bay, b., Ire.	D2	10
Youghiogheny, stm., U.S.	F2	115
Youghiogheny River Lake, res., U.S.	G3	115
You Jiang, stm., China	G6	31
Youkounkoun, Gui.	D2	45
Young, Austl.	G7	51
Young, Sk., Can.	F3	75
Young, Az., U.S.	C5	80
Young, Ur.	E1	56
Young, co., Tx., U.S.	C3	120
Young America, In., U.S.	C5	91
Young Harris, Ga., U.S.	B3	87
Youngs, Lake, l., Wa., U.S.	f11	124
Youngs Creek, In., U.S.	H4	91
Youngs Point, On., Can.	C6	73
Youngstown, Ab., Can.	D5	68
Youngstown, Fl., U.S.	B1	86
Youngstown, N.Y., U.S.	B1	109
Youngstown, Oh., U.S.	A5	112
Youngsville, La., U.S.	D3	95
Youngsville, N.M., U.S.	A3	108
Youngsville, N.C., U.S.	A4	110
Youngtown, Az., U.S.	k8	80
Youngwood, Pa., U.S.	F2	115
Youssoufia, Mor.	C3	44
Youxi, China	K8	32
Youyang, China	J3	32
Youyu, China	C7	31
Yozgat, Tur.	C10	40
Ypacaraí, Para.	E4	55
Ypané, stm., Para.	D4	55
Ypres see Ieper, Bel.	B5	16
Ypsilanti, Mi., U.S.	F7	99
Ypsilanti, N.D., U.S.	C7	111
Yreka, Ca., U.S.	B2	82
Yssingeaux, Fr.	E6	16
Ystad, Swe.	J5	14
Yü, Mount, mtn., Tai.	G9	31
Yuan, stm., India	D7	37
Yuan'an, China	I4	32
Yuanjiang, China	G5	31
Yuan Jiang, stm., China	F7	31
Yuanling, China	F7	31
Yuanping, China	E5	32
Yuanshi, China	F6	32
Yuba, co., Ca., U.S.	C3	82
Yuba, stm., Ca., U.S.	C3	82
Yuba City, Ca., U.S.	C3	82
Yūbari, Japan	E10	33
Yucaipa, Ca., U.S.	*E5	82
Yucatán, state, Mex.	C7	63
Yucatan Channel, strt., N.A.	C7	63
Yucca, Az., U.S.	C1	80
Yucca Lake, l., Nv., U.S.	F5	105
Yucca Mountain, mtn., Nv., U.S.	G5	105
Yucheng, China	F7	32

Name	Map Ref	Page

Yuci, China — F5 32
Yudu, China — F8 31
Yueqing, China — F9 31
Yueyang, China — F7 31
Yug, stm., Sov. Un. — A3 28
Yugoslavia, ctry., Eur. — C4 24
Yuhuan, China — J9 32
Yukhnov, Sov. Un. — D10 27
Yukon, Ok., U.S. — B4 113
Yukon, W.V., U.S. — D3 125
Yukon, prov., Can. — D5 66
Yukon, stm., N.A. — C9 79
Yule Bay, b., Ant. — B29 7
Yulee, Fl., U.S. — B5 86
Yuli, Nig. — E7 45
Yulin, China — D6 31
Yulin, China — G7 31
Yulin, China — G7 31
Yulin, China — B3 34
Yuma, Az., U.S. — E1 80
Yuma, Co., U.S. — A8 83
Yuma, Mi., U.S. — D5 99
Yuma, co., Az., U.S. — E1 80
Yuma, co., Co., U.S. — A8 83
Yuma Desert, des., N.A. — E1 80
Yuma Marine Corps Air Station, mil., Az., U.S. — E1 80
Yumbi, Zaire — B4 48
Yumen, China — D4 31
Yumenzhen, China — C4 31
Yuna, Japan — N6 52
Yuna, stm., Dom. Rep. — E8 64
Yuncheng, China — D7 31
Yungas, reg., Bol. — C2 55
Yungay, Chile — B2 54
Yungay, Peru — C2 58
Yungui Plateau, plat., China — F5 31
Yunhe, China — J8 32
Yunnan, prov., China — G5 31
Yunnan Plateau see Yungui Plateau, plat., China — F5 31
Yunta, Austl. — F2 51
Yunxian, China — G5 31
Yunxian, China — E7 31
Yurécuaro, Mex. — m12 63
Yurga, Sov. Un. — D25 1
Yurimaguas, Peru — C2 58
Yurino, Sov. Un. — C16 27
Yuriria, Mex. — m13 63
Yurochi Island, i., Marsh Is. — P18 52
Yuryevets, Sov. Un. — C14 27
Yuryev-Polskiy, Sov. Un. — C12 27
Yuscarán, Hond. — E7 63
Yushan, China — J8 32
Yushkozero, Sov. Un. — E15 14
Yushu, China — E4 31
Yutan, Ne., U.S. — C9 104
Yutian, China — E7 32
Yuty, Para. — E4 55
Yuwang, China — F2 32
Yuxian, China — E6 32
Yuyao, China — I9 32
Yuzha, Sov. Un. — C13 27
Yuzhno-Sakhalinsk, Sov. Un. — E17 29
Yuzhnoye, Sov. Un. — C11 33
Yverdon, Switz. — E3 18
Yvetot, Fr. — C4 16
Yvonand, Switz. — C2 21
Yzeure, Fr. — D5 16

Z

Zaandam, Neth. — B4 17
Zaanstad, Neth. — A6 16
Zabīd, Yemen — D4 38
Ząbki, Pol. — k14 26
Ząbkowice, Pol. — g10 26
Ząbkowice [Śląskie], Pol. — C4 26
Zābol, Iran — B6 38
Zābolī, Iran — H10 39
Zabré, Burkina — D4 45
Zabrze, Pol. — C5 26
Zacapa, Guat. — E7 63
Zacapu, Mex. — n13 63

Zacatecas, Mex. — C4 63
Zacatecas, state, Mex. — C4 63
Zacatecoluca, El Sal. — D3 62
Zachary, La., U.S. — D4 95
Zacoalco [de Torres], Mex. — C4 63
Zacualpan, Mex. — m14 63
Zacualtipán, Mex. — m14 63
Zadar, Yugo. — C2 24
Zadetkale, i., Burma — G3 35
Zadetkyi, i., Burma — H3 35
Zadonsk, Sov. Un. — E12 27
Zafra, Spain — C2 22
Zafra, Ok., U.S. — C7 113
Zagań, Pol. — C3 26
Zaghouan, Tun. — B7 44
Zagorá, Grc. — C4 25
Zagora, Mor. — C3 44
Zagorsk, Sov. Un. — C12 27
Zagreb, Yugo. — C2 24
Zagros Mountains, mts., Iran — E3 39
Zagyva, stm., Hung. — B5 24
Zähedän, Iran — C6 38
Zahl, N.D., U.S. — A2 111
Zahlah, Leb. — F10 40
Zahna, Ger.D.R. — B7 19
Zaïliyskiy Alatau Range, mts., Sov. Un. — E9 28
Zaire, dept., Ang. — C1 48
Zaire, ctry., Afr. — B3 48
Zaire Basin (Congo Basin), Afr. — B3 48
Zaječar, Yugo. — D6 24
Zaka, Zimb. — B5 49
Zakataly, Sov. Un. — B16 41
Zākhū, Iraq — D14 40
Zakopane, Pol. — D5 26
Zakroczym, Pol. — B6 26
Zala, stm., Hung. — B3 24
Zalaegerszeg, Hung. — B3 24
Zalamea de la Serana, Spain — C3 22
Zalamea la Real, Spain — D2 22
Zalău, Rom. — B6 24
Zaleski, Oh., U.S. — C3 112
Zalewo, Pol. — B5 26
Zalingei, Sud. — C1 47
Zalma, Mo., U.S. — D7 102
Zaltbommel, Neth. — C5 17
Zama, Ms., U.S. — C4 101
Zambales Mountains, mts., Phil. — o13 34
Zambezi (Balovale), Zam. — D3 48
Zambezi, stm., Afr. — H8 42
Zambézia, dept., Moz. — A6 49
Zambia, ctry., Afr. — D4 48
Zamboanga, Phil. — D6 34
Zambrano, Col. — B3 60
Zambrów, Pol. — B7 26
Zamora, stm., Ec. — B2 58
Zamora, Spain — B3 22
Zamora-Chinchipe, prov., Ec. — B2 58
Zamora de Hidalgo, Mex. — D4 63
Zamość, Pol. — C7 26
Zamzam, Wâdî, val., Libya — C2 43
Zanaga, Congo — B1 48
Zanesville, In., U.S. — C7 91
Zanesville, Oh., U.S. — C4 112
Zanjän, Iran — B4 38
Zanpa Cape, c., Japan — O5 52
Zante see Zákinthos, i., Grc. — D3 40
Zanzibar, Tan. — C6 48
Zanzibar, i., Tan. — C6 48
Zaozhuang, China — G7 32
Zap, N.D., U.S. — B4 111
Zapadna Morava, stm., Yugo. — D5 24
Západočeský, prov., Czech. — D8 19
Zapala, Arg. — B2 54
Zapata, Tx., U.S. — F3 120
Zapata, co., Tx., U.S. — F3 120
Zapata, Península de, pen., Cuba — C3 64

Zapatoca, Col. — B3 60
Zapopan, Mex. — m12 63
Zaporozhye, Sov. Un. — E6 29
Zapotillo, Ec. — B1 58
Zara, Tur. — C11 40
Zaragoza, Col. — B3 60
Zaragoza, Mex. — k13 63
Zaragoza, Mex. — B4 63
Zaragoza, Spain — B5 22
Zarand, Iran — F8 39
Zárate, Arg. — A5 54
Zaraysk, Sov. Un. — D12 27
Zaraza, Ven. — B4 60
Zard Küh, mtn., Iran — E5 39
Zarembo Island, i., Ak., U.S. — m23 79
Zarephath, N.J., U.S. — B3 107
Zaria, Nig. — D6 45
Zarnekow, Ger.D.R. — E7 15
Zarqā', Nahr az, stm., Jord. — B7 41
Zarrentin, Ger.D.R. — B4 15
Zarrīn Shahr, Iran — *E5 39
Zaruma, Ec. — B2 58
Zarumilla, Peru — B1 58
Żary, Pol. — C3 26
Zarzal, Col. — C2 60
Zarzis, Tun. — C7 44
Zasenbeck, F.R.Ger. — F4 15
Zasieki, Pol. — C3 26
Zásmuky, Czech. — o19 26
Zastavna, Sov. Un. — A7 24
Zastron, S. Afr. — D4 49
Žatec, Czech. — C2 26
Zator, Pol. — h10 26
Zavala, co., Tx., U.S. — E3 120
Zavalla, Tx., U.S. — D5 120
Zavitinsk, Sov. Un. — D15 29
Zavodo-Petrovskiy, Sov. Un. — B7 28
Zawiercie, Pol. — C5 26
Zāwiyat Masūs, Libya — C4 43
Zawr, Ra's az, c., Sau. Ar. — H4 39
Zāyandeh, stm., Iran — E6 39
Zaysan, Sov. Un. — E11 29
Zaysan, Lake, l., Sov. Un. — E11 29
Zaza, stm., Cuba — C4 64
Zbraslav, Czech. — o17 26
Žd'ár [nad Sazavou], Czech. — D3 26
Zdice, Czech. — o16 26
Zdolbunov, Sov. Un. — F6 27
Zduńska Wola, Pol. — C5 26
Zealandia, Sk., Can. — F2 75
Zearing, Ia., U.S. — B4 92
Zeballos, B.C., Can. — D4 69
Zebla, mtn., Tun. — F2 23
Zebrzydowice, Pol. — h9 26
Zebulon, Ga., U.S. — C2 87
Zebulon, Ky., U.S. — C7 94
Zebulon, N.C., U.S. — B4 110
Zeebrugge (part of Brugge), Bel. — B5 16
Zeeland, Mi., U.S. — F5 99
Zeeland, N.D., U.S. — D6 111
Zeeland, prov., Neth. — C3 17
Zeerust, S. Afr. — C4 49
Zefat (Safad), Isr. — F10 40
Zegrze, Pol. — k14 26
Zehdenick, Ger.D.R. — B6 18
Zeigler, Il., U.S. — F4 90
Zeil, Mount, mtn., Austl. — D5 50
Zeist, Neth. — A6 16
Zeitz, Ger.D.R. — C6 18
Zekiah Swamp Run, stm., Md., U.S. — D4 97
Żelechów, Pol. — C6 26
Zelenodolsk, Sov. Un. — B3 28
Zelenogorsk, Sov. Un. — A7 27
Zelenograd, Sov. Un. — C11 27
Železná Ruda, Czech. — D8 19
Zelienople, Pa., U.S. — E1 115
Zell, S.D., U.S. — C7 118
Zella-Mehlis, Ger.D.R. — C5 18
Zell am Ziller, Aus. — B7 20
Zeller Lake, l., Aus. — B8 20
Zelma, Sk., Can. — F3 75

Zelzate, Bel. — C3 17
Zembra, i., Tun. — F3 23
Zemetchino, Sov. Un. — E14 27
Zemio, Cen. Afr. Rep. — D5 46
Zenda, Ks., U.S. — E5 93
Zendeh Jān, Afg. — D10 39
Zenica, Yugo. — C3 24
Zenith, Wa., U.S. — f11 124
Zenith, Ks., U.S. — E5 93
Zenobia Peak, mtn., Co., U.S. — A2 83
Zenon Park, Sk., Can. — D4 75
Zeona, S.D., U.S. — B3 118
Žepče, Yugo. — C4 24
Zephyr, Tx., U.S. — D3 120
Zephyr Cove, Nv., U.S. — E2 105
Zephyrhills, Fl., U.S. — D4 86
Zerbst, Ger.D.R. — C6 18
Zermatt, Switz. — C6 20
Zernez, Switz. — C6 20
Zeta, stm., Yugo. — D4 24
Zeulenroda, Ger.D.R. — C6 19
Zeven, F.R.Ger. — E3 15
Zevenaar, Neth. — C6 17
Zevgolation, Grc. — D3 25
Zeya, Sov. Un. — D15 29
Zeya, stm., Sov. Un. — D15 29
Zeya Reservoir, res., Sov. Un. — D15 29
Zgierz, Pol. — C5 26
Zgorzelec, Pol. — C3 26
Zhanatas, Sov. Un. — E7 28
Zhangbei, China — D6 32
Zhangjiakou, China — C7 31
Zhangye, China — D5 31
Zhangzhou (Changchou), China — G8 31
Zhanjiang, China — G7 31
Zhanyu, China — B10 32
Zhao'an, China — G8 31
Zhaodong, China — A11 32
Zhaoqing, China — G7 31
Zhaotong, China — F5 31
Zhaoxing, China — C5 33
Zhaoyuan, China — B11 32
Zhaozhou, China — D2 33
Zhari Namco, l., China — B8 36
Zharkamys, Sov. Un. — D5 28
Zhashui, China — H3 32
Zhaxigang, China — A7 37
Zhdanov, Sov. Un. — E6 29
Zhejiang, prov., China — F9 31
Zheleniya, Cape, c., Sov. Un. — B9 29
Zhen'an, China — H3 32
Zheng'an, China — J2 32
Zhenglan Qi, China — C6 32
Zhengyangguan, China — H7 32
Zhengzhou (Chengchou), China — E7 31
Zhenjiang, China — E8 31
Zhenlai, China — B10 32
Zhenping, China — I3 32
Zhidachov, Sov. Un. — D8 26
Zhigansk, Sov. Un. — C15 29
Zhijiang, China — F2 32
Zhilaya Kosa, Sov. Un. — D4 28
Zhitomir, Sov. Un. — D5 29
Zhmerinka, Sov. Un. — G7 27
Zhob, stm., Pak. — B2 37
Zhongba, China — C7 36
Zhongdian, China — F5 31
Zhongwei, China — D6 31
Zhongxian, China — E6 31
Zhongxiang, China — I5 32
Zhoushan Islands (Chousan Islands), China — E9 31
Zhuanghe, China — E10 32

Zhucheng, China — F8 32
Zhuji, China — J9 32
Zhukovskiy, Sov. Un. — n18 27
Zhumadian, China — H6 32
Zhuoxian, China — E6 32
Zhushan, China — E7 31
Zhuzhou, China — F7 31
Zia Indian Reservation, N.M., U.S. — h7 108
Zia Pueblo, N.M., U.S. — *B3 108
Zibā', Sau. Ar. — C3 38
Zibo, China — D8 31
Ziebach, co., S.D., U.S. — C4 118
Ziegenhain, F.R.Ger. — C5 24
Zielona Góra, Pol. — C3 26
Zierikzee, Neth. — C3 17
Ziesar, Ger.D.R. — A7 19
Ziftā, Eg. — D3 41
Zigey, Chad — C3 46
Zigong, China — F5 31
Zigui, China — E7 31
Ziguinchor, Sen. — D1 45
Zikhron Ya'aqov, Isr. — B6 41
Zile, Tur. — B10 40
Žilina, Czech. — D5 26
Zillah, Libya — D3 43
Zillah, Wa., U.S. — C5 124
Ziller, stm., Aus. — B7 20
Zilwaukee, Mi., U.S. — E7 99
Zima, Sov. Un. — D13 29
Zimapán, Mex. — C5 63
Zimba, Zam. — E4 48
Zimbabwe, ctry., Afr. — A5 49
Zimmerman, Mn., U.S. — E5 100
Zimnicea, Rom. — D7 24
Zin, Nahal, val., Isr. — D7 41
Zinal, Switz. — D4 21
Zinc, Ar., U.S. — A3 81
Zincville, Ok., U.S. — A7 113
Zinder, Niger — D6 45
Zingst, Ger.D.R. — D6 15
Zion, Il., U.S. — A6 90
Zion, N.J., U.S. — C3 107
Zion, S.C., U.S. — C9 117
Zion Gate, hist., Isr. Occ. — m14 41
Zion National Park, Ut., U.S. — F3 121
Zion Reservoir, res., Az., U.S. — C6 80
Zionsville, In., U.S. — E5 91
Zionville, N.C., U.S. — A1 110
Zipaquirá, Col. — B3 60
Zirándaro, Mex. — n13 63
Zirkel, Mount, mtn., Co., U.S. — A4 83
Zirndorf, F.R.Ger. — D5 19
Zirreh, Gaud-i-, l., Afg. — C3 36
Zistersdorf, Aus. — D8 18
Zitácuaro, Mex. — n13 63
Zittau, Ger.D.R. — C7 18
Ziwa Magharibi, prov., Tan. — B5 48
Ziway, Lake, l., Eth. — D4 47
Ziyang, China — J2 32
Ziyuan, China — K4 32
Žižkov (part of Prague), Czech. — n17 26
Zlatograd, Bul. — E7 24
Zlatoust, Sov. Un. — D9 29
Zlín, Czech. — C5 26
Zlonice, Czech. — n17 26
Złotoryja, Pol. — C3 26
Złotów, Pol. — B4 26
Zlynka, Sov. Un. — E8 27
Zmeinogorsk, Sov. Un. — C10 28
Znamenka, Sov. Un. — G9 27
Žnin, Pol. — B4 26
Znojmo, Czech. — D4 26
Zofingen, Switz. — B4 21
Zogno, Italy — C4 21
Zográfos, Grc. — *D4 25
Zohreh, stm., Iran — F5 39
Zolfo Springs, Fl., U.S. — E5 86
Zollikofen, Switz. — B3 21
Zollikon, Switz. — B6 21
Zolochev, Sov. Un. — G5 27
Zolotonosha, Sov. Un. — G9 27
Zolotoy, Cape, c., Sov. Un. — B12 31

Zomba, Mwi. — E6 48
Zomergem, Bel. — C3 17
Zongo, Zaire — A2 48
Zonguldak, Tur. — B8 40
Zörbig, Ger.D.R. — B7 19
Zorita, Spain — C3 22
Zorritos, Peru — B1 58
Zortman, Mt., U.S. — C8 103
Żory, Pol. — g9 26
Zossen, Ger.D.R. — B6 18
Zottegem, Bel. — D3 17
Zouar, Chad — A3 46
Zoutkamp, Neth. — A6 17
Zreïgat, Bir, well, Maur. — B3 45
Zrenjanin (Petrovgrad), Yugo. — C5 24
Zrmanja, stm., Yugo. — C2 24
Zschopau, Ger.D.R. — C8 19
Zuata, stm., Ven. — B4 60
Zubtsov, Sov. Un. — C10 27
Zuénoula, I.C. — E3 45
Zuera, Spain — B5 22
Zug, Switz. — E4 18
Zug, W. Sah. — E2 44
Zug, state, Switz. — B4 20
Zug, Lake, l., Switz. — E4 18
Zugdidi, Sov. Un. — A13 40
Zugspitze, mtn., Eur. — B6 20
Zuider Zee see IJsselmeer, l., Neth. — A6 16
Zulia, state, Ven. — B3 60
Zülpich, F.R.Ger. — C1 19
Zumbi, Ponta do, c., Braz. — B2 57
Zumbo, Moz. — A5 49
Zumbro, stm., Mn., U.S. — F6 100
Zumbro Falls, Mn., U.S. — F6 100
Zumbrota, Mn., U.S. — F6 100
Zumpango, Mex. — n14 63
Zungeru, Nig. — E6 45
Zunhua, China — C8 31
Zuni, N.M., U.S. — B1 108
Zuni, Va., U.S. — k14 123
Zuni, stm., U.S. — C6 80
Zuni Indian Reservation, N.M., U.S. — B1 108
Zuni Mountains, mts., N.M., U.S. — B1 108
Zunyi, China — F6 31
Zuoquan, China — F5 32
Zuqar, i., Yemen — C5 47
Zürich, On., Can. — D3 73
Zürich, Switz. — E4 18
Zürich, Ks., U.S. — C4 93
Zürich, Mt., U.S. — B7 103
Zürich, state, Switz. — B4 20
Zürich, Lake, l., Switz. — E4 18
Zuru, Nig. — D6 45
Zusam, stm., F.R.Ger. — E5 19
Zussdorf, F.R.Ger. — A7 21
Zutphen, Neth. — A7 16
Zuwārah, Libya — C2 43
Zuwayzā, Jord. — C7 41
Zvenigorodka, Sov. Un. — G8 27
Zvishavane, Zimb. — B5 49
Zvolen, Czech. — D5 26
Zvornik, Yugo. — C4 24
Zweibrücken, F.R.Ger. — D3 18
Zweisimmen, Switz. — C3 20
Zwenkau, Ger.D.R. — B7 19
Zwettl, Aus. — D7 18
Zwickau, Ger.D.R. — C6 18
Zwickauer Mulde, stm., Ger.D.R. — C7 19
Zwiesel, F.R.Ger. — D8 19
Zwingle, Ia., U.S. — B7 92
Zwischenahn, F.R.Ger. — A7 16
Zwolle, Neth. — A7 16
Zwolle, La., U.S. — C2 95
Zylks, La., U.S. — A1 95
Żyrardów, Pol. — B6 26
Zyryanovsk, Sov. Un. — D10 28
Żywiec, Pol. — D5 26